THE ZONDERVAN ENCYCLOPEDIA OF THE BIBLE

THE ZONDERVAN ENCYCLOPEDIA OF THE BIBLE

Volume 5
Q–Z

Merrill C. Tenney, General Editor / Moisés Silva, Revision Editor

Revised, Full-Color Edition

ZONDERVAN.com/
AUTHORTRACKER
follow your favorite authors

ZONDERVAN

The Zondervan Encyclopedia of the Bible
Copyright © 2009 by Zondervan
First edition copyright © 1975, 1976 by Zondervan

Requests for information should be addressed to:
Zondervan, *Grand Rapids, Michigan 49530*

Library of Congress Cataloging-in-Publication Data

    The Zondervan encyclopedia of the Bible / Moisés Silva, revision editor ; Merrill C. Tenney, general editor. — Rev. full-color ed.
        p. cm.
    Rev. ed. of: The Zondervan pictorial encyclopedia of the Bible.
    Includes bibliographical references.
    ISBN 978-0-310-24135-5 (hardcover, printed)
    ISBN 978-0-310-24136-2 (set)
    1. Bible — Encyclopedias. I. Silva, Moisés. II. Tenney, Merrill Chapin, 1904-1985.
III. Zondervan pictorial encyclopedia of the Bible. IV. Title: Encyclopedia of the Bible.
BS440.Z63 2009
220.3 — dc22   2009004956

All Scripture quotations, unless otherwise indicated, are taken from the *Holy Bible, New International Version*®. NIV®. Copyright © 1973, 1978, 1984 by International Bible Society. Used by permission of Zondervan. All rights reserved.

Any Internet addresses (websites, blogs, etc.) and telephone numbers printed in this book are offered as a resource. They are not intended in any way to be or imply an endorsement by Zondervan, nor does Zondervan vouch for the content of these sites and numbers for the life of this book.

All rights reserved. No part of this publication may be reproduced, stored in a retrieval system, or transmitted in any form or by any means — electronic, mechanical, photocopy, recording, or any other — except for brief quotations in printed reviews, without the prior permission of the publisher.

Interior design by Tracey Walker

Printed in China

09 10 11 12 13 14 15 • 23 22 21 20 19 18 17 16 15 14 13 12 11 10 9 8 7 6 5 4 3 2 1

IMAGE SOURCES

The Amman Archaeological Museum. Amman, Jordan.
Todd Bolen/www.BiblePlaces.com
The British Museum. London, England.
The Cairo Museum. Cairo, Egypt.
The Church of Annunciation Museum. Nazareth, Israel.
Direct Design. Amarillo, Texas.
The Egyptian Ministry of Antiquities.
The Ephesus Archaeological Museum. Selchok, Turkey.
The Eretz Israel Museum. Tel Aviv, Israel.
The House of Anchors. Kibbutz Ein Gev. Sea of Galilee, Israel.
International Mapping.
The Isma-iliya Museum. Isma-iliya, Egypt.
The Israel Museum, Jerusalem, courtesy of the Israel Antiquities Authority.
The Istanbul Archaeological Museum. Istanbul, Turkey.
Dr. James C. Martin.
The Jordanian Ministry of Antiquities. Amman, Jordan.
Ministero per I Beni e le Attivita Culturali—Soprintendenza Archaeologica di Roma. Rome, Italy.
Mosaic Graphics.
Musée du Louvre. Paris, France.
Phoenix Data Systems
Z. Radovan/www.BibleLandPictures.com
Reproduction of the City of Jerusalem at the time of the Second Temple—located on the grounds of the Holy Land Hotel, Jerusalem.
Sola Scriptura. The Van Kampen Collection on display at the Holy Land Experience. Orlando, Florida.
The Turkish Ministry of Antiquities. Ankara, Turkey.
The Yigal Allon Center. Kibbutz Ginosar, on the western shore of the Sea of Galilee, Israel.

ABBREVIATIONS

I. General

ℵ	(Aleph) Codex Sinaiticus
A	Codex Alexandrinus
AASOR	Annual of the American Schools of Oriental Research
AB	Anchor Bible
ABD	*Anchor Bible Dictionary*
ABR	*Australian Biblical Review*
ad loc.	*ad locum*, at the place
AHR	*American Historical Review*
AJA	*American Journal of Archaeology*
AJP	*American Journal of Philology*
AJSL	*American Journal of Semitic Languages and Literature*
AJT	*American Journal of Theology*
Akk.	Akkadian
ANE	Ancient Near East(ern)
ANEP	*The Ancient Near East in Pictures Relating to the Old Testament*, ed. J. B. Pritchard (1954)
ANET	*Ancient Near East Texts Relating to the Old Testament*, ed. J. B. Pritchard, 3rd ed. (1969)
ANF	Ante-Nicene Fathers
ANRW	*Aufstieg und Niedergang der römischen Welt* (1972–)
aor.	aorist
APOT	*Apocrypha and Pseudepigrapha of the Old Testament*, ed. R. H. Charles, 2 vols. (1913)
Apoc.	Apocrypha
approx.	approximate(ly)
Aq.	Aquila
ARAB	*Ancient Records of Assyria and Babylonia*, ed. D. D. Luckenbill, 2 vols. (1926–27)
Arab.	Arabic
Aram.	Aramaic
Arch	Archaeology
ARM	*Archives royales de Mari*
Assyr.	Assyrian
ASV	American Standard Version
AThR	*Anglican Theological Review*
AUSS	*Andrews University Seminary Studies*
B	Codex Vaticanus
b.	born
BA	*Biblical Archaeologist*
BAR	*Biblical Archaeology Review*
BASOR	*Bulletin of the American Schools of Oriental Research*
BASORSup	*Bulletin of the American Schools of Oriental Research Supplemental Studies*
BBR	*Bulletin for Biblical Research*
BC	F. J. Foakes-Jackson and K. Lake, eds., *The Beginnings of Christianity*, 5 vols. (1920–33)
BDAG	W. Bauer, *A Greek-English Lexicon of the New Testament and Other Early Christian Literature*, 3rd ed., rev. F. W. Danker (2000)
BDB	F. Brown, S. R. Driver, and C. A. Briggs, *A Hebrew and English Lexicon of the Old Testament* (1907)
BDF	F. Blass, A. Debrunner, and R. W. Funk, *A Greek Grammar of the New Testament and Other Early Christian Literature* (1961)
BDT	*Baker's Dictionary of Theology*, ed. E. F. Harrison (1960)
BECNT	Baker Exegetical Commentary on the New Testament
BETS	*Bulletin of the Evangelical Theological Society*
BHK	*Biblia Hebraica*, ed. R. Kittel, 3rd ed. (1937)
BHS	*Biblia Hebraica Stuttgartensia*, ed. K. Elliger and W. Rudolph (1983)
Bib.	*Biblica*
BJRL	*Bulletin of the John Rylands Library*
BKAT	Biblischer Kommentar, Altes Testament
BNTC	Black's New Testament Commentaries
BRev	*Bible Review*
BSac	*Bibliotheca Sacra*
BWL	*Babylonian Wisdom Literature*, ed. W. G. Lambert (1960)
BZ	*Biblische Zeitschrift*
C	Codex Ephraemi Syri
c.	*circa*, about

CAH	*Cambridge Ancient History*
CANE	*Civilizations of the Ancient Near East*, ed. J. M. Sasson, 4 vols. (1995)
CBQ	*Catholic Biblical Quarterly*
CBSC	Cambridge Bible for Schools and Colleges
CD	Cairo: Damascus (i.e., *Damascus Document*)
cent.	century
CEV	Contemporary English Version
cf.	*confer*, compare
CGTC	Cambridge Greek Testament Commentary
ch(s).	chapter(s)
CT	*Christianity Today*
CIG	*Corpus inscriptionum graecarum*
CIL	*Corpus inscriptionum latinarum*
CIS	*Corpus inscriptionum semiticarum*
col(s).	column(s)
COS	*The Context of Scripture*, ed. W. W. Hallo, 3 vols. (1997–2002)
CRINT	Compendia rerum iudaicarum ad Novum Testamentum
D	Codex Bezae
d.	died, date of death
DAC	*Dictionary of the Apostolic Church*, ed. J. Hastings, 2 vols. (1915–18)
DBI	*Dictionary of Biblical Interpretation*, ed. J. H. Hayes, 2 vols. (1999)
DBSup	*Dictionnaire de la Bible: Supplément*, ed. L. Pirot and A. Robert (1928–)
DCG	*Dictionary of Christ and the Gospels*, ed. J. Hastings, 2 vols. (1906–08)
DDD	*Dictionary of Deities and Demons in the Bible*, ed. K. van der Toorn et al., 2nd ed. (1999)
DJD	Discoveries in the Judaean Desert
DJG	*Dictionary of Jesus and the Gospels*, ed. J. B. Green et al. (1992)
DLNT	*Dictionary of the Later New Testament and Its Developments*, ed. R. P. Martin and P. H. Davids (1997)
DNTB	*Dictionary of New Testament Background*, ed. C. A. Evans and S. E. Porter (2000)
DOTHB	*Dictionary of the Old Testament: Historical Books*, ed. B. T. Arnold and H. G. M. Williamson (2005)
DOTP	*Dictionary of the Old Testament: Pentateuch*, ed. T. D. Alexander and D. W. Baker (2003)
DOTT	*Documents from Old Testament Times*, ed. D. W. Thomas (1958)
DPL	*Dictionary of Paul and his Letters*, ed. G. F. Hawthorne et al. (1993)
DSS	Dead Sea Scrolls
E	east
EA	El-Amarna Tablets. See *Die el-Amarna-Tafeln, mit Einleitung und Erläuterung*, ed. J. A. Knudtzon, 2 vols. (1908–15; suppl. by A. F. Rainey, 2nd ed., 1978)
EBC	*The Expositor's Bible Commentary*, ed. F. E. Gaebelein et al., 12 vols. (1979–92)
EBr	*Encyclopedia Britannica*
ed(s).	editor(s), edited, edition
e.g.	*exempli gratia*, for example
EGT	*Expositor's Greek Testament*, ed. W. R. Nicoll, 5 vols. (1897–1910)
Egyp.	Egyptian
EKKNT	Evangelisch-katholischer Kommentar zum Neuen Testament
EncBib	*Encyclopaedia Biblica*, ed. T. K. Cheyne and J. S. Black, 4 vols. (1899–1903)
EncJud	*Encyclopedia Judaica*, 16 vols. (1972)
Eng.	English
ERE	*Encyclopedia of Religion and Ethics*, ed. J. Hastings, 13 vols. (1908–27)
ERV	English Revised Version
esp.	especially
ESV	English Standard Version
et al.	*et alii*, and others
ETR	*Etudes théologiques et religieuses*
ETSB	*Evangelical Theological Society Bulletin*
Euseb.	Eusebius
EvQ	*Evangelical Quarterly*
EvT	*Evangelische Theologie*
Exp	*The Expositor*
ExpTim	*Expository Times*
ff.	following (verses, pages, etc.)
FCI	*Foundations of Contemporary Interpretation*, ed. M. Silva, 6 vols. in 1 (1996)
fem.	feminine
FFB	*Fauna and Flora of the Bible*, UBS Handbook Series, 2nd ed. (1980)
fig.	figure, figurative(ly)
fl.	*floruit*, flourished
FOTL	Forms of the Old Testament Literature
ft.	foot, feet
GCS	Die griechische christliche Schriftsteller

Ger.	German
GKC	Gesenius-Kautzsch-Cowley, *Gesenius' Hebrew Grammar*, 2nd ed. (1910)
Gk.	Greek
GNB	Good News Bible
HAL	*Hebräisches und aramäisches Lexikon zum Alten Testament*, by L. Koehler et al., 5 fascicles (1967–95)
HALOT	*Hebrew and Aramaic Lexicon of the Old Testament*, by L. Koehler et al., 5 vols. (1994–2000)
HAT	Handbuch zum Alten Testament
HDB	Hastings' *Dictionary of the Bible*, 5 vols. (1898–1904); rev. ed. in 1 vol. by F. C. Grant and H. H. Rowley (1963)
Heb.	Hebrew
HGHL	*Historical Geography of the Holy Land*, by G. A. Smith, 25th ed. (1931)
Hitt.	Hittite
HibJ	*Hibbert Journal*
HJP	*A History of the Jewish People in the Time of Jesus Christ*, by E. Schürer, 5 vols., 2nd ed. (1885–90); rev. ed., *The History of the Jewish People in the Age of Jesus Christ (175 B.C.–A.D. 135)*, by G. Vermès and F. Millar, 4 vols. (1973–87)
HNT	Handbuch zum Neuen Testament
HNTC	Harper's New Testament Commentaries
HTKAT	Herders theologischer Kommentar zum Alten Testament
HTKNT	Herders theologischer Kommentar zum Neuen Testament
HTR	*Harvard Theological Review*
HUCA	*Hebrew Union College Annual*
IB	*Interpreter's Bible*, ed. G. A. Buttrick et al., 12 vols. (1951–57)
ibid.	*ibidem*, in the same place
ICC	International Critical Commentary
id.	*idem*, the same (as previously mentioned)
IDB	*Interpreter's Dictionary of the Bible*, ed. G. A. Buttrick, 4 vols. (1962); supplementary vol., ed K. Crim (1976)
i.e.	*id est*, that is
IEJ	*Israel Exploration Journal*
Ign.	Ignatius
illus.	illustration
impf.	imperfect
impv.	imperative
inscr.	inscription
Int	*Interpretation*
IPN	*Die israelitischen Personennamen*, by M. Noth (1928)
Iren.	Irenaeus
ISBE	*International Standard Bible Encyclopedia*, ed. M. G. Kyle, 4 vols. (1929); rev. ed., G. W. Bromiley, 4 vols. (1979–88)
JANESCU	*Journal of the Ancient Near Eastern Society of Columbia University*
JAOS	*Journal of American Oriental Society*
JASA	*Journal of the American Scientific Affiliation*
JB	Jerusalem Bible
JBL	*Journal of Biblical Literature*
JBR	*Journal of Bible and Religion*
JCS	*Journal of Cuneiform Studies*
JE	*The Jewish Encyclopedia*, ed. I. Singer, 12 vols. (1925)
JEA	*Journal of Egyptian Archaeology*
JETS	*Journal of the Evangelical Theological Society*
JJS	*Journal of Jewish Studies*
JNES	*Journal of Near Eastern Studies*
JNSL	*Journal of North Semitic Languages*
Jos.	Josephus
JPOS	*Journal of the Palestine Oriental Society*
JPS	Jewish Publication Society, *The Holy Scriptures according to the Masoretic Text: A New Translation . . .* (1945)
JQR	*Jewish Quarterly Review*
JR	*Journal of Religion*
JRS	*Journal of Roman Studies*
JSJ	*Journal for the Study of Judaism in the Persian, Hellenistic, and Roman Periods*
JSNT	*Journal for the Study of the New Testament*
JSOT	*Journal for the Study of the Old Testament*
JSP	*Journal for the Study of the Pseudepigrapha*
JSS	*Journal of Semitic Studies*
JTS	*Journal of Theological Studies*
KAI	*Kanaanäishce und aramäische Inschriften*, by H. Donner and W. Röllig, 2nd ed., 3 vols. (1966–69)
KAT	Kommentar zum Alten Testament
KB	L. Koehler and W. Baumgartner, *Lexicon in Veteris Testamenti libros*, 2nd ed. (1958; for 3rd ed., see *HAL*)

KD	C. F. Keil and F. Delitzsch, *Biblical Commentary on the Old Testament*, 25 vols. (1857–78)
KEK	Kritisch-exegetischer Kommentar über das Neue Testament (= Meyer-Kommentar)
KJV	King James Version
Lat.	Latin
LCL	Loeb Classical Library
lit.	literal(ly), literature
LN	J. P. Louw and E. A. Nida, *Greek-English Lexicon of the New Testament Based on Semantic Domains*, 2 vols., 2nd ed. (1989)
LSJ	H. G. Liddell, R. Scott, and H. S. Jones, *A Greek-English Lexicon*, 9th ed., with rev. supplement (1996)
LXX	The Seventy = Septuagint
Maj. Text	Majority Text
masc.	masculine
mg.	margin
mi.	mile(s)
MM	J. H. Mouton and G. Milligan, *The Vocabulary of the Greek Testament* (1930)
MNTC	Moffatt New Testament Commentary
MS(S)	manuscript(s)
McClintock and Strong	J. McClintock and J. Strong, *Cyclopedia of Biblical, Theological, and Ecclesiastical Literature*, 12 vols. (1867–87)
MT	Masoretic text
N	north
n.	note
NA	Nestle-Aland, *Novum Testamentum Graecum*
NAB	New American Bible
NAC	New American Commentary
NASB	New American Standard Bible
NBD	*New Bible Dictionary*, ed. J. D. Douglas et al.; unless otherwise noted, references are to the 3rd ed. (1996)
NCB	New Century Bible
NCBC	New Century Bible Commentary
NCE	*New Catholic Encyclopedia*, ed. W. J. McDonald et al., 15 vols. (1967)
NCV	New Century Version
n.d.	no date
NE	northeast
NEAEHL	*The New Encyclopedia of Archaeological Excavations in the Holy Land*, ed. E. Stern et al., 4 vols. (1993)
NEB	New English Bible
neut.	neuter
NewDocs	*New Documents Illustrating Early Christianity*, ed. G. H. R. Horsley and S. Llewelyn (1981–)
NHC	Nag Hammadi Codex
NHL	*Nag Hammadi Library in English*, ed. J. M. Robinson, 4th ed. (1996)
NIBCNT	New International Bible Commentary on the New Testament
NIBCOT	New International Bible Commentary on the Old Testament
NICNT	New International Commentary on the New Testament
NICOT	New International Commentary on the Old Testament
NIDNTT	*New International Dictionary of New Testament Theology*
NIDOTTE	*New International Dictionary of Old Testament Theology and Exegesis*
NIGTC	New International Greek Testament Commentary
NIV	New International Version
NIVAC	New International Version Application Commentary
NJB	New Jerusalem Bible
NJPS	*Tanakh: The Holy Scriptures. The New JPS translation according to the Traditional Hebrew Text*
NKJV	New King James Version
NLT	New Living Translation
NovT	*Novum Testamentum*
NPNF	Nicene and Post-Nicene Fathers
NRSV	New Revised Standard Version
NT	New Testament
NTAp	*New Testament Apocrypha*, ed. E. Hennecke, 2 vols., trans. R. McL. Wilson (1963–65); unless otherwise indicated, references are to the rev. ed. by W. Schneemelcher, trans. R. McL. Wilson (1991–92)
NTD	Das Neue Testament Deutsch
NTS	*New Testament Studies*
NW	northwest
OCD	*Oxford Classical Dictionary* (1949)
ODCC	*Oxford Dictionary of the Christian Church*, ed. F. L. Cross and E. A. Livingstone, 3rd ed. (1997)
Onom.	Eusebius's *Onomasticon*, according to E. Klostermann, ed., *Das Onomastikon der biblischen Ortsnamen* (1904)

op. cit.	*opere citato*, in the work previously cited	SHERK	*The New Schaff-Herzog Encyclopedia of Religious Knowledge*, 13 vols. (1908–14)
orig.	original(ly)		
OT	Old Testament	SIG	*Sylloge inscriptionum graecarum*, ed. W. Dittenberger, 4 vols., 3rd ed. (1915–24)
OTL	Old Testament Library		
OTP	*Old Testament Pseudepigrapha*, ed. J. H. Charlesworth, 2 vols. (1983–85)	sing.	singular
		SJT	*Scottish Journal of Theology*
p., pp.	page, pages	SP	Sacra Pagina
pass.	passive	*ST*	*Studia theologica*
PEQ	*Palestine Exploration Quarterly*	Str-B	H. L. Strack and P. Billerbeck, *Kommentar zum Neuen Testament aus Talmud und Midrash*, 6 vols. (1922–61)
Pers.	Persian		
pf.	perfect		
PG	*Patrologia graeca*, ed. J.-P. Migne, 162 vols. (1857–96)	Sumer.	Sumerian
		s.v.	*sub verbo*, under the word
PJ	*Palästina-Jahrbuch*	SW	southwest
pl.	plural	Syr.	Syriac
PL	*Patrologia latina*, ed. J.-P. Migne, 217 vols. (1844–64)	Symm.	Symmachus
		Tac.	Tacitus
POxy	Oxyrhynchus Papyri	TDNT	*Theological Dictionary of the New Testament*, ed. G. Kittel and G. Friedrich, 10 vols. (1964–76)
prob.	probably		
Pseudep.	Pseudepigrapha		
ptc.	participle	TDOT	*Theological Dictionary of the Old Testament*, ed. G. J. Botterweck and H. Ringgren (1974–)
PTR	*Princeton Theological Review*		
RA	*Revue d'assyriologie et d'archéologie orientale*		
		TEV	Today's English Version
Rahlfs	A. Rahlfs, *Septuaginta, id est, Vetus Testamentum graece iuxta LXX interpretes*, 3rd ed. (1949)	Tg.	Targum
		Theod.	Theodotion
		THKNT	Theologischer Handkommentar zum Neuen Testament
RB	*Revue biblique*		
RE	*Realencyclopädie für protestantische Theologie und Kirche*, ed. J. J. Herzog and A. Hauck, 24 vols. (1896–1913)	*ThTo*	*Theology Today*
		TNIV	Today's New International Version
		TNTC	Tyndale New Testament Commentaries
REB	Revised English Bible	TOTC	Tyndale Old Testament Commentaries
repr.	reprint(ed)	TR	Textus Receptus
rev.	revised	trans.	translation, translator, translated
RevExp	*Review and Expositor*	TWNT	*Theologisches Wörterbuch zum Neuen Testament*, ed. ed. G. Kittel and G. Friedrich, 10 vols. (1932–79)
RevQ	*Revue de Qumran*		
RGG	*Die Religion in Geschichte und Gegenwart*, ed. K. Galling, 7 vols., 3rd ed. (1857–65)		
		TynBul	*Tyndale Bulletin*
		TZ	*Theologische Zeitschrift*
Rom.	Roman	UBS	United Bible Society, *The Greek New Testament*
RSPT	*Révue des sciences philosophiques et théologiques*		
		UF	*Ugarit-Forschungen*
RSV	Revised Standard Version	Ugar.	Ugaritic
RV	Revised Version	*UM*	*Ugaritic Manual*, by C. H. Gordon, 3 parts (1955)
S	south		
SacBr	A. F. Rainey and R. S. Notley, *The Sacred Bridge: Carta's Atlas of the Biblical World* (2005)	*UT*	*Ugaritic Textbook*, by C. H. Gordon, 3 parts (1965)
		v., vv.	verse, verses
Sansk.	Sanskrit	*VT*	*Vetus Testamentum*
SE	southeast	viz.	*videlicet*, namely
sec.	section	v.l.	*varia lectio*, variant reading

vol(s).	volume(s)
vs.	versus
Vulg.	Vulgate
W	west
WBC	Word Biblical Commentary
WEB	World English Bible
WH	B. F. Westcott and F. J. A. Hort, *The New Testament in the Original Greek*, 2 vols. (1881)
WTJ	*Westminster Theological Journal*
ZAW	*Zeitschrift für die alttestamentliche Wissenschaft*
ZDMG	*Zeitschrift der deutschen morgenländischen Gesellschaft*
ZDPV	*Zeitschrift der deutschen Palästina-Vereins*
ZNW	*Zeitschrift für die neutestamentliche Wissenschaft*
ZRGG	*Zeitschrift für Religions und Geistesgeschichte*

II. Books of the Bible
Old Testament

Gen.	Genesis
Exod.	Exodus
Lev.	Leviticus
Num.	Numbers
Deut.	Deuteronomy
Josh.	Joshua
Jdg.	Judges
Ruth	Ruth
1 Sam.	1 Samuel
2 Sam.	2 Samuel
1 Ki.	1 Kings
2 Ki.	2 Kings
1 Chr.	1 Chronicles
2 Chr.	2 Chronicles
Ezra	Ezra
Neh.	Nehemiah
Esth.	Esther
Job	Job
Ps.	Psalm(s)
Prov.	Proverbs
Eccl.	Ecclesiastes
Cant.	Canticles (Song of Songs)
Isa.	Isaiah
Jer.	Jeremiah
Lam.	Lamentations
Ezek.	Ezekiel
Dan.	Daniel
Hos.	Hosea
Joel	Joel
Amos	Amos
Obad.	Obadiah
Jon.	Jonah
Mic.	Micah
Nah.	Nahum
Hab.	Habakkuk
Zeph.	Zephaniah
Hag.	Haggai
Zech.	Zechariah
Mal.	Malachi

New Testament

Matt.	Matthew
Mk.	Mark
Lk.	Luke
Jn.	John
Acts	Acts
Rom.	Romans
1 Cor.	1 Corinthians
2 Cor.	2 Corinthians
Gal.	Galatians
Eph.	Ephesians
Phil.	Philippians
Col.	Colossians
1 Thess.	1 Thessalonians
2 Thess.	2 Thessalonians
1 Tim.	1 Timothy
2 Tim.	2 Timothy
Tit.	Titus
Phlm.	Philemon
Heb.	Hebrews
Jas.	James
1 Pet.	1 Peter
2 Pet.	2 Peter
1 Jn.	1 John
2 Jn.	2 John
3 Jn.	3 John
Jude	Jude
Rev.	Revelation

Apocrypha

1 Esd.	1 Esdras
2 Esd.	2 Esdras (= *4 Ezra*)
Tob.	Tobit
Jdt.	Judith
Add. Esth.	Additions to Esther
Wisd.	Wisdom of Solomon

Sir.	Ecclesiasticus (Wisdom of Jesus the Son of Sirach)	*2 En.*	*2 Enoch*
Bar.	Baruch	*4 Ezra*	*4 Ezra* (= 2 Esdras)
Ep. Jer.	Epistle of Jeremy	*Jub.*	*Book of Jubilees*
Pr. Azar.	Prayer of Azariah	*Let. Aris.*	*Letter of Aristeas*
Sg. Three	Song of the Three Children (or Young Men)	*Life Adam*	*Life of Adam and Eve*
		3 Macc.	*3 Maccabees*
		4 Macc.	*4 Maccabees*
Sus.	Susanna	*Mart. Isa.*	*Martyrdom of Isaiah*
Bel	Bel and the Dragon	*Pss. Sol.*	*Psalms of Solomon*
Pr. Man.	Prayer of Manasseh	*Sib. Or.*	*Sibylline Oracles*
1 Macc.	1 Maccabees	*T. Benj.*	*Testament of Benjamin* (etc.)
2 Macc.	2 Maccabees	*T. 12 Patr.*	*Testaments of the Twelve Patriarchs*
		Zad. Frag.	*Zadokite Fragments*

III. Pseudepigrapha

As. Moses	*Assumption of Moses*
2 Bar.	*2 Baruch*
3 Bar.	*3 Baruch*
1 En.	*1 Enoch*

Other Christian, Jewish, and Greco-Roman texts are referred to by their standard abbreviations. See, e.g., *The SBL Handbook of Style* (1999), ch. 8, appendix F, and appendix H.

THE ZONDERVAN
ENCYCLOPEDIA
OF THE BIBLE

A late tradition regards this mountain, called Quarantania, as the site of Jesus' temptation.

Q. The symbol used to designate a hypothetical source of sayings of Jesus and other discursive materials found in Matthew and Luke but not in Mark (or John). This abbreviation is thought to be derived from the German word for "source," *Quelle*. According to the Two-Source Theory of gospel origins, both Matthew and Luke used the Gospel of Mark for their basic narrative framework, and both also had access to a collection of dominical sayings (Q) that apparently was unknown to Mark. For many scholars, Q was a written document (possibly composed in Aramaic originally), and some have spent considerable effort trying to reconstruct it (see J. M. Robinson et al., eds., *The Critical Edition of Q* [2000]; R. Valantasis, *The New Q: A Fresh Translation with Commentary* [2005]). For others, Q refers to a body of oral tradition. Still others use the abbreviation simply as a convenient way of referring to the material that is shared by Matthew and Luke but missing in Mark. Finally, some writers strongly deny the validity of this concept (e.g., M. Goodacre, *The Case against Q: Studies in Markan Priority and the Synoptic Problem* [2002]). See GOSPELS III.B.

Qadesh. See KADESH ON THE ORONTES.

Qere kuh-ray′ (קְרֵי, either impv. ["read!"] or, more prob., pass. ptc. ["what is read"] of Aram. קְרָא H10637 "to call, read"). This term is applied to Hebrew or Aramaic readings preferred by the Masoretes over the written, consonantal text of the OT. They are either corrections or variant changes placed in the margin by the SCRIBES. Rules prohibited changing the authoritative, consonantal text; but the Masoretes sometimes attached the vowels of a preferred reading to the unchanged consonants (called the KETIB, "what is written") and then indicated the appropriate consonants of the amended word in the margin. More than 1,300 such marginal notes are said to be found in the MT. See TEXT AND MANUSCRIPTS (OT) VI.   L. J. WOOD

qesitah kes′i-tah See WEIGHTS AND MEASURES IV.I.

Qoheleth koh-hel′ith. See ECCLESIASTES, BOOK OF.

qoph kohf (קוֹף H7761, "monkey"). The nineteenth letter of the Hebrew ALPHABET (ק), with a numerical value of 100. It was one of several "emphatic" consonants, the exact pronunciation of which is uncertain. The sound may have been similar to that of the consonant *k*, but articulated toward the back of the mouth, near the soft palate (as in Arabic).

Quadratus, Apology of kwahd′ruh-tuhs (*Kodratos*). One of the earliest Christian apologies. It was presented to Emperor HADRIAN at a time when Christians were being persecuted, possibly in ASIA MINOR in A.D. 123–124 or 129 (or in ATHENS in 125 or 128–129). The only part of the text preserved is a brief quotation of about fifty words in EUSEBIUS (*Eccl. Hist.* 4.3.2), which states that some persons whom Christ had healed or raised from the dead survived to Quadratus's own time.

P. WOOLLEY

quail. Although the origin of the Hebrew term *šĕlāw* H8513 is uncertain, there is full agreement that it refers to the quail, and no other bird fits the biblical texts (Exod. 16:13; Num. 11:31–32; Ps. 105:40). These require (a) a clean bird and

(b) one that passed in great numbers. This miraculous supply to the traveling Israelites is mentioned on two specific occasions; first in the Desert of Sin, in the SW of the SINAI Peninsula, some six weeks after leaving Egypt (see SIN, WILDERNESS OF); second at KIBROTH HATTAAVAH, not far away, a year later. This is another example of natural resources being used by God, the miraculous element being in the precise timing of the supply. Although such concentrated flocks may have been exceptional, the quail must have passed across the Sinai area twice a year, and it is reasonable to assume that they were taken and eaten more or less regularly.

Quail are almost the smallest game birds and the only ones that truly migrate. The best known is the common quail (*Coturnix coturnix* or *C. communis*) of Europe and Asia. It is only seven inches long, mottled brown and much like a miniature partridge. Like many of its relatives, it is more often heard than seen, the call being made as much by night as by day. These birds breed over most of Europe and in W Asia. In autumn they migrate toward N Africa, many of them crossing the route of the exodus, and do so again on their return journey in spring. There is some difficulty about the translation of Num. 11:31. The KJV renders, "two cubits high upon the face of the earth," implying that they were piled to that height (similarly NRSV and other versions); the NIV says that the wind brought the quail down "to about three feet above the ground," which is preferable (suggesting that they were flying close to the ground).

Although strong fliers over short distances, quail need help from the wind for long migration flights, and the narrative says that they came in with the wind. An unfavorable change of wind can bring them to the ground and make them easy prey for humans. Various estimates have been made about the numbers taken in these incidents, and one researcher has suggested that the Israelites killed some nine million. This could be a gross overestimate, but there is recent evidence that such a figure is not entirely fanciful. Heavy exploitation of migratory quail took place throughout the 19th cent. and well into the 20th. For many years, Egypt exported over two million a year; in 1920, a peak of three million was reached. This was far more than the quail population could stand, and mass migration soon ceased. (See A. Parmelee, *All the Birds of the Bible* [1959], 76; O. L. Austin, *Birds of the World* [1961], 95; *FFB*, 66–67.) G. S. CANSDALE

Quarantania kwah´ruhn-tay´nee-uh. Also Quarantana. The name given by Christians to a high mountain near JERICHO where, according to a late tradition, Jesus was tempted by Satan (Matt.

A late tradition regards this mountain as the site of Jesus' temptation.

4:8–10). The name alludes to the forty days of the TEMPTATION OF CHRIST; in Arabic it is known as Jebel Kuruntul. (See McClintock-Strong, *Cyclopedia*, 8:835.)

quarry. An excavation made by removing stone for building purposes. This term is used by the KJV twice to render *pĕsîlîm* (pl. of *pāsîl* H7178) in a difficult passage (Jdg. 3:19, 26). The Hebrew word elsewhere refers to an image carved for religious purposes (Deut. 7:5 et al.), thus the NIV here translates "idols," but some think such a reference makes little sense in the context. The NRSV renders it "sculptured stones," whereas the NJPS treats it as a place name, "Pesilim" (for other interpretations, see *HALOT*, 3:948–49). Modern versions use *quarry* occasionally to render other Hebrew terms, such as the phrase *maqqebet bôr* (lit., "the excavation of the pit," Isa. 51:1). See also SHEBARIM.

Stone quarries abound in Palestine (see STONE). Suitable ROCK is plentiful. The limestone used is easily worked and hardens when exposed to air. Stones yet in their quarries, only partially extracted, illustrate methods used in biblical days. A narrow-bladed pick was used to cut around the sides of the projected stone. The cut was wide enough only for the workman's arm and pick. Sometimes wedges, inserted in pre-cut holes in a line, were driven deep with a heavy hammer to split the rock. Other times wooden strips were inserted in pre-cut cracks and then made to swell with water. Once loose, the stone was moved with crowbars and then transported by sledges or rollers. The largest stones, weighing several hundred tons each, have been found at BAALBEK. They were moved from a quarry nearly one mile distant. (See G. A. Reisner et al., *Harvard Excavations at Samaria*, 2 vols. [1924], 1:37–38, 96ff.; J. Simons, *The Geographical and Topographical Texts of the Old Testament* [1959], 271, 287.) L. J. WOOD

quart. See WEIGHTS AND MEASURES III.C.

Quarter, Second (New). See SECOND DISTRICT.

quartermaster. This term, referring to an army officer responsible for the subsistence of a group of soldiers, is used by the NRSV and other versions to render the expression *śar mĕnûḥâ* (lit., "chief of resting"; cf. KJV, "a quiet prince"), which occurs only once (Jer. 51:59; NIV, "staff officer").

Quartus kwor´tuhs (Κούαρτος G3181, from Latin *Quartus*, "fourth"). An early Christian who sent greetings to the Christians in Rome (Rom. 16:23). PAUL refers to him as "our [*lit.*, the] brother," and some have speculated that Quartus was the physical brother of a previously mentioned individual in the list. Most scholars believe that the expression is simply equivalent to "Brother Quartus," indicating spiritual kinship, though it is possible that he was an associate of the apostle.

Ancient Jerusalem quarry.

quaternion kwah-tuhr´nee-uhn. See SQUAD.

queen. Of the several Hebrew words that can be translated "queen," *malkâ* H4893 (fem. of *melek* H4889, "king") is the most common. It is the term used for the QUEEN OF SHEBA (1 Ki. 10:1 et al.), for VASHTI and ESTHER (Esth. 1:9; 2:22; et al.), and for the wife of the Babylonian monarch BELSHAZZAR (Dan. 5:10). The plural form occurs in one passage (Cant. 6:8–9; with regard to the form *mĕleket* H4906, see QUEEN OF HEAVEN). The second most common word for "queen," *gĕbîrâ* H1485 (lit., "mighty woman, mistress," fem. of *gĕbîr* H1484, "lord, master"), is used of TAHPENES, Pharaoh's wife (1 Ki. 11:19); of MAACAH, the queen mother of King Asa (1 Ki. 15:13; 2 Chr. 15:16); of JEZEBEL (2 Ki. 10:13); and of NEHUSHTA, the mother of

Jehoiachin (Jer. 29:2; cf. 2 Ki. 24:8). The rare form šēgal *H8712* ("royal consort") occurs twice (Neh. 2:6; Ps. 45:9 [NIV, "royal bride"]). Finally, the term śārâ *H8576* ("woman of nobility, princess") is appropriately rendered "queen" in at least one passage (Isa. 49:23; cf. also Lam. 1:1 NIV). In the NT, the Greek word *basilissa G999* is applied to the Queen of the South (i.e., of Sheba, Matt. 12:42; Lk. 11:31) and to the Ethiopian queen, CANDACE (Acts 8:27); the title is also assumed by the prostitute Babylon (Rev. 18:7).

The only ruling queen the Hebrews ever had was ATHALIAH, who had been queen mother until her son AHAZIAH died; she reigned for seven years, until JEHOIADA the priest overthrew her (2 Ki. 11:1–20). The wives of the Hebrew kings were understood to be queens. Two of them are noted for the rights they assumed: MICHAL, daughter of SAUL, mocked and defied her husband, King DAVID (2 Sam. 6:20–23); JEZEBEL, wife of AHAB, has been memorialized as ELIJAH's persecutor (1 Ki. 19:1–3).

The queen mother was generally the widow of the former king and mother of the reigning one. Certain obligations devolved upon her and she received appropriate respect. SOLOMON bowed to his mother, BATHSHEBA (1 Ki. 2:19). Asa, however, removed his heretical mother, MAACAH, for unbecoming religious behavior (1 Ki. 15:13). It is also worthy of note that in Judah at least the name of the king's mother always received mention in the record of his coming to the throne (e.g., 2 Ki. 12:1). (See N.-E. A. Andreasen, "The Role of the Queen Mother in Israelite Society," *CBQ* 45 [1983]: 179–94.)

R. L. ALDEN

Queen of Heaven. An object of Jewish worship in the time of JEREMIAH. Most of the information regarding this cult comes from outside the Bible. The only biblical clues available are in Jer. 7:18 and 44:17–19, 25. The former passage states, "The children gather wood, the fathers light the fire, and the women knead the dough and make cakes of bread for the Queen of Heaven." It is generally agreed that the cakes were made in the shape of a human being. Many such fragments have been found in clay, usually with accented female features. In Jer. 44:17 it is recorded that the people intended to "burn incense to the Queen of Heaven and … pour out drink offerings to her … in the towns of Judah and in the streets of Jerusalem."

The problem is compounded by the use of the unusual MT form of the word "queen," *mĕleket H4906*. Some consider this an erroneous writing of the normal *malkâ H4893*. Others have understood it to be *mĕleʾket*, construct form of *mĕlāʾkâ H4856*,

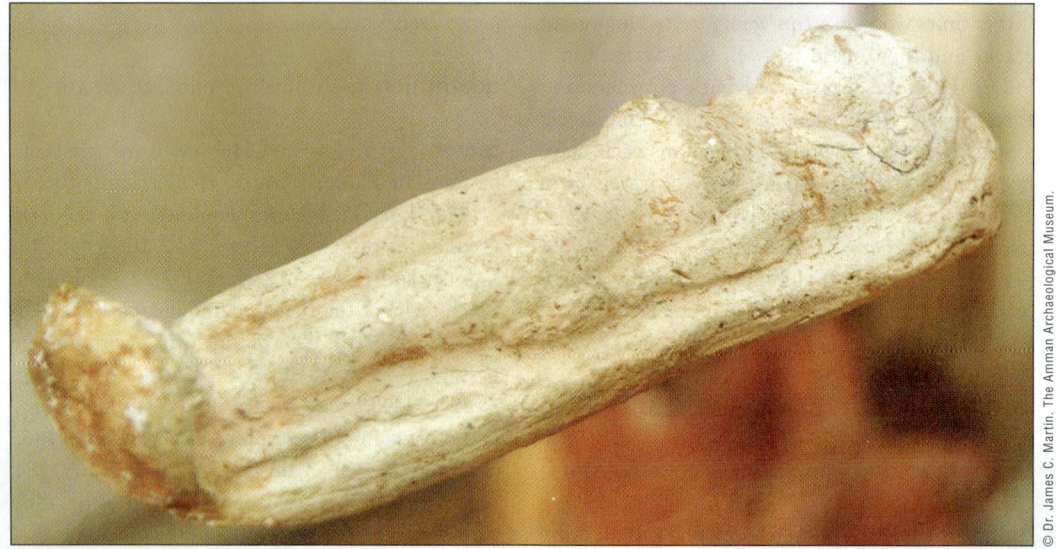

Some consider Ashtoreth, a well-known Canaanite fertility deity, to be the "Queen of Heaven" who according to Jeremiah was worshiped on rooftops.

"work, handiwork" (cf. Jer. 7:18 LXX, *tē stratia tou ouranou*, "to the army of heaven"; the Aram. Tg. reads here "to the stars of heaven").

It is well accepted that this was a borrowed deity. Several of Israel's neighbors had consorts for their male deities—goddesses and a queen of heaven. In Assyria, the goddess Ishtar was called the "lady of heaven," whereas in the literature from Ugarit she is "queen of heaven." The Canaanite Astarte, or Ashtoreth, was a well-known fertility goddess. This seems to be the domain of the Queen of Heaven mentioned in Jer. 44, since the people were rejoicing in her for their general welfare and freedom from famine. The people of Ugarit also had Anath, a kind of mother goddess. This name appears in the texts from Elephantine, Egypt, where Anat-Yaho is represented as the consort of Yaho (Yahweh). Perhaps this was a recurrence of the Queen of Heaven cult against which Jeremiah preached. (See E. O. James, *The Cult of the Mother Goddess* [1959]; *The Ancient Gods* [1960], 77–106; S. M. Olyan in *UF* 19 [1987]: 161–74; S. Ackerman in *Gender and Difference in Ancient Israel*, ed. P. L. Day [1989], 109–24; *ABD*, 5:586–88; *DDD*, 678–79.)

R. L. Alden

queen of Sheba. A ruler from the old Arab state of Sheba who visited King Solomon ostensibly "to test him with hard questions" only to discover that his wisdom surpassed all that she had heard (1 Ki. 10:1–13; 2 Chr. 9:1–12). There may have been trade motives in the visit as well. Her camels brought spices, gold, and precious stones (1 Ki. 10:2, 10). What Solomon gave in return is not specified, although it seems clear that he gave her some commodities (v. 13). Trading was an important facet of Solomon's activities, and the Red Sea and Arabian peninsula came within the ambit of his interest. Indeed, he had a port on the Red Sea at Ezion Geber (1 Ki. 9:26–28; 10:11–12, 22–29). Specific reference is made in 10:15 to the gold which he obtained "from merchants and traders and from all the Arabian kings and the governors of the land." Hence a visit from an Arab queen would not be inconceivable.

The ancient kingdom of Saba, the S Arabic name of the old Sabean state, lay in the SW corner of the Arabian peninsula, roughly the area of modern Yemen. The state and its people, the Sabeans, are referred to often in the OT (Job 6:19; Ps. 72:10, 15; Isa. 60:6; Jer. 6:20; Ezek. 27:22–23; 38:13). Important excavations conducted during 1951–52 in Marib, the old capital, have given a remarkable insight into the Sabean civilization. Its origins are unknown, but there is some evidence that it may have been occupied by Semites who migrated S in the middle of the 2nd millennium. By the 10th cent. B.C. there was a flourishing kingdom in the region, and a diplomatic and trade mission led by a queen to the kingdom of Solomon some 1,500 mi. to the N was possibly part of a total policy of commercial expansion. Assyrian inscriptions from the 8th and 7th centuries B.C. mention several queens and this suggests a matrilineal system of succession.

The tradition that the Abyssinian royal line is descended from Solomon and the queen of Sheba is difficult to prove (or disprove!). Ethiopia was probably colonized from S Arabia by the Sabeans. Arabic legends give many details about the queen who married Solomon, and Josephus linked the queen of Sheba with Ethiopia (*Ant.* 2.10.2; 7.6.5–6). (See W. Phillips, *Sheba's Buried*

The land of Sheba.

City [1955]; G. W. Van Beek in *The Bible and the Ancient Near East: Essays in Honor of W. F. Albright*, ed. G. E. Wright [1961], 229–48; K. A. Kitchen in *The Age of Solomon: Scholarship at the Turn of the Millennium*, ed. L. K. Hardy [1997], 126–53.)

J. ARTHUR THOMPSON

Questions of Bartholomew. See BARTHOLOMEW, GOSPEL (QUESTIONS) OF.

quest of the historical Jesus. See BIBLICAL CRITICISM V.E; JESUS CHRIST III.G.

quick, quicken. The adjective *quick* in modern usage refers most often to speed, but the KJV translators used it in its older sense, "alive": "… and they go down quick into the pit" (Num. 16:30); "Then they had swallowed us up quick" (Ps. 124:3); "… who shall judge the quick and the dead" (2 Tim. 4:1); "For the word of God is quick, and powerful" (Heb. 4:12). Similarly, the verb *quicken* is used in the KJV with the meaning "revive, make alive"; although this sense is still found in modern usage, current English versions prefer different renderings (e.g., in Ps. 119:50 the KJV has "thy word hath quickened me," but the NRSV, "your promise gives me life," and the NIV, "Your promise preserves my life"). The verb is found in contexts that speak of REGENERATION (e.g., Eph. 2:1) and RESURRECTION (e.g., Rom. 4:17). Note, however, that the KJV often uses the adverb *quickly* in the sense "with speed" (Gen. 18:6 et al.).

quicksands. This term is used by the KJV to render Greek *Syrtis G5358*, which refers to an area of the Libyan coast known for its shifting sandbars (Acts 27:17). See SYRTIS.

Quintus Memmius. See MEMMIUS, QUINTUS.

Quirinius kwi-rin´ee-uhs (Κυρήνιος *G3256*, some MSS Κυρίνιος, a more precise representation of the Latin *Quirinius*). KJV Cyrenius (a transliteration of the Greek without reference to the Latin form). Publius Sulpicius Quirinius was what the Romans called a "new man": like Cicero, he came to office and held a consulship (12 B.C.) and provincial governorships without the aid and advantage of a family tradition in politics or administration. TACITUS (*Annals* 3.48) devoted a brief chapter to Quirinius when he recorded his death in A.D. 21. He wrote:

> About the same time he [Tiberius] desired of the senate that "the decease of Sulpicius Quirinius might be celebrated by a public funeral." Quirinius was born at Lanuvium, a municipal town, and was nowise related to the ancient patrician family of the Sulpicii; but being a brave soldier, was for his active services rewarded with the consulship under Augustus, and soon after with a triumph, for driving the Homonadenses out of their strongholds in Cilicia; next, when the young Caius Caesar was sent to settle the affairs of Armenia, Quirinius was appointed his principal adviser, and at the same time had paid court to Tiberius, then in his retirement at Rhodes. This the emperor represented now to the senate; he extolled the kind offices of Quirinius, and branded Marcus Lollius as the author of the perverse behavior of Caius Caesar to himself, and of all the tensions between them. But the memory of Quirinius was not agreeable to the rest of the senate, by reason of the danger he brought upon Lepida, as I have before related, and his sordid meanness and overbearing conduct in the latter part of his life.

Quirinius was a notable soldier, with a desert campaign to his credit in CYRENE, which along with CRETE he ruled as PROCONSUL about 15 B.C. Between 12 and 2 B.C. he was engaged on a pacification project in PISIDIA against the mountaineers, whom Tacitus, in the passage quoted above, described inaccurately as Cilician. Dates are vague, and for biblical scholars these are tangled with the problem of the date of the nativity. A fair statement might run as follows: The "first census," which took place "while Quirinius was governor [*i.e.*, imperial legate] of Syria" (Lk. 2:2), could not have been the one to which GAMALIEL referred, as reported in Acts 5:37. That registration was in A.D. 6 or 7. It therefore follows, given the customary fourteen-year census cycle, that the previous enrollment was in 8 or 7 B.C.; hence the problem. LUKE is clearly claiming that Quirinius conducted an earlier census in Palestine distinct from the one to which he makes reference in his second book.

Consideration of this problem can begin with the assumption that Luke was a competent historian, careful of his facts, and not prone to unverified statements. His work generally supports such a reputation. Reference, therefore, to an earlier census taken by Quirinius in Palestine must be taken seriously. To assume such a census, while complete proof is lacking, requires no distortion of known historical facts. Luke's claim is consistent with an extraordinary command for Quirinius in the E, between one and two decades prior to his regular governorship of SYRIA. It was established Roman practice, going far back into Republican history, to appoint able officers to posts of special authority to deal with a local situation beyond the power or ability of the official within whose proper sphere it lay. AUGUSTUS was notably wary of placing too much power in the hands of the governors of those provinces that called for large military forces, and he often demonstrated a preference for special commissioners directly responsible to himself for the resolution of problems of extraordinary complexity.

According to Ronald Syme (*Roman Revolution* [1939], 755), Quirinius was busy on the frontier problems of the Pisidian highlands between 12 and 2 B.C., though this is not to say that the subjugation of the Homonadenses, mentioned by Tacitus, required ten years of continuous campaigning. It does appear, however, that Quirinius was strategically placed for a piece of special work in the E in the middle years of this decade. It does no violence to Luke's language, or to the known facts of history, if Quirinius was especially commissioned at this time to supervise the Palestine census. Luke could not know that so much evidence would disappear with the lapse of time—that historians would wonder why he spoke of Quirinius as governor of Syria, when it was common knowledge that Quintilius Varus occupied that important post.

Quintilius Varus, who was governor of Syria from 7 to 4 B.C., was a man for whom Augustus may justifiably have entertained no great regard. Augustus, above all, was an able judge of men, and it was Quintilius Varus who, in A.D. 9, reprehensibly lost three legions in the Teutoburger forest in Germany, one of the most shocking disasters to Roman arms in the century. Assuming that Augustus had some misgivings over the ability of Varus to handle an explosive situation, it is easy to see a reason for a special intrusion, under other direction, in the affairs of Varus's province.

A reasonable reconstruction might assume that Varus came to Syria in 7 B.C., an untried man. The census was due in Palestine in 8 or 7 B.C., and it could well be that Augustus ordered Quirinius, who had just successfully dealt with the problem of the Pisidian highlanders, to undertake the delicate task. HEROD had recently lost the favor of the emperor and may have been temporizing about the taking of the census, a process that always enraged the difficult Jews. Quirinius's intervention, the requisite organization, and the preparation for the census, could easily have postponed the actual date of registration to the end of 5 B.C., a reasonable date. (The matter is argued at length in E. M. Blaiklock, *The Century of the New Testament* [1962], appendix 4. For the view that the reference to a census under Quirinius is not historical, see R. E. Brown, *The Birth of the Messiah: A Commentary on the Infancy Narratives in Matthew and Luke* [1977], 547–56. For a discussion of several other proposed solutions, see D. L. Bock, *Luke*, 2 vols, BECNT [1994–96], 1:903–9.)

The picture emerges of a notable Roman, distinguished for his career of faithful service to Augustus, and perhaps for that reason earning the unpopularity at which Tacitus twice glanced. It is possible to observe his rise. Quirinius's first wife was Appia Claudia, no undistinguished name. His second wife was Aemilia Lepida, a descendant of Sulla and Pompey, and destined bride of the young L. Caesar, untimely dead. He grew old, says Syme, "in envied opulence, the prey of designing society ladies" (*Roman Revolution*, 381). He was shrewd enough to pay discreet court to TIBERIUS, in exile at Rhodes, and lost nothing by such wisdom when Tiberius, in default of other heirs, succeeded Augustus. He left no heirs himself.

E. M. BLAIKLOCK

quiver. A case for holding and carrying arrows (Heb. *tĕlî H9437*). It was generally made of LEATHER and slung over the shoulder of the hunter or soldier. ESAU the hunter carried one (Gen. 27:3); two passages use the same Hebrew word in connection

This Assyrian relief (c. 700 B.C.) depicts a quiver case held by a soldier.

with WAR equipment (e.g., Job 39:23; Isa. 22:6). The other four occurrences of the word are metaphorical. One of them speaks of a man's family as the quiver and his children as the arrows (Ps. 127:5). The prophet, pictured as an arrow, is said to be concealed in God's quiver (Isa. 49:2). Because a killer uses his arrows, Jeremiah likens the empty quiver to an open tomb (Jer. 5:16); he also says of God's afflictions, "He pierced my heart with arrows [*lit.*, sons] from his quiver" (Lam. 3:13). A different Hebrew word, *šeleṭ H8949*, should perhaps be rendered "quiver" in some passages (e.g., Jer. 51:1; cf. NRSV and NJPS), but this term is of uncertain meaning and probably means "shield" (KJV and NIV; see the discussion in *HALOT*, 4:1522–23).

R. L. ALDEN

Qumran koom´rahn. Khirbet Qumran is a site near the NW shore of the DEAD SEA where the Wadi Qumran flows from the Judean hills into the Dead Sea. Though long known to travelers, the site was not excavated until the discovery of the DEAD SEA SCROLLS in neighboring caves from 1947 onward drew attention to it. The excavations were carried out in 1951 and 1953–56 under the direction of R. de Vaux and G. L. Harding. The site, which stands on a plateau about half a mile from the shore, consists of a complex of buildings and an associated cemetery. The earliest building there dates from the 8th–7th cent. B.C. and is probably to be connected with King UZZIAH (2 Chr. 26:10); the area possibly should be identified with the "City of Salt" (Josh. 15:62; but see SALT, CITY OF).

The site was deserted for some centuries after this settlement and there was no sign of activity until the 2nd cent. B.C., when the ancient building was modified and used by a small group of settlers (Level Ia), but the most flourishing period (Ib) followed in about 110 B.C. when, with an enlarged population, the complex was provided with an elaborate water system, a pottery, smithy, laundry, bakery, mill, kitchens, refectory, and assembly halls.

The site of Qumran with the Dead Sea and the mountains of Moab in the background. (View to the E.)

This phase ended about 30 B.C. following a fire; a few years later there was an earthquake, and the site remained virtually uninhabited until 4 B.C., when it was reconstructed by new settlers (Level II) much on the lines of Ib; it remained in occupation until its destruction by the Romans in A.D. 68 during the First Jewish Revolt. It was fortified (III) and continued as a Roman post until the end of the century. The site again was used as a center by the rebels during the Second Jewish Revolt (A.D. 132–135), but no serious rebuilding was again undertaken. See WARS, JEWISH.

The surrounding caves in which were found the DSS contained pottery contemporary with Levels Ib and II. Many of the scrolls had been copied at Khirbet Qumran (a scriptorium was found in Level II), and probably were deposited in the caves in A.D. 68 when the Roman conquest was imminent. The identity of the community is uncertain, but most scholars would now connect them with the ESSENES. (See J. T. Milik, *Ten Years of Discovery in the Wilderness of Judaea* [1959], 45–56; J. Finegan, *Light from the Ancient Past: The Archaeological Background of Judaism and Christianity*, 2nd ed. [1959], 273–76; R. de Vaux, *Archaeology and the Dead Sea Scrolls* [1973]; P. R. Davies, *Qumran* [1982]; J. Magness, *The Archaeology of Qumran and the Dead Sea Scrolls* [2002]; K. Galor et al., eds., *Qumran: The Site of the Dead Sea Scrolls* [2006]; *ABD*, 5:590–94; *NEAEHL*, 4:1235–41.)

T. C. MITCHELL

quotations in the New Testament. The form and content of citations in the NT will be treated under the following headings:

  I. Numbers and kinds
  II. Textual affinities
  III. The style of OT quotations
  IV. The purposes for which the OT is quoted
  V. Quotations from sources other than the OT

I. Numbers and kinds. Most of the quotations in the NT are drawn from the OT. The bulk of these occur in the Synoptic Gospels, the epistles of Paul, Hebrews, and Revelation. How many there are depends largely on the number of allusive OT quotations counted—and that is a delicate matter. The number of explicit OT quotations has been variously estimated in the range of 150–300, allusive quotations over 1,000. Revelation contains numerous allusive quotations, but none which are explicit.

The explicit quotations of the OT are easy to identify; quotation formulas often introduce them. Allusive quotations are clauses, phrases, and sometimes single words that may easily escape notice. For example, the unattentive reader might well miss that the words from the cloud at Jesus' TRANSFIGURATION (Matt. 17:5) came from three separate passages in the OT: "This is my Son [Ps. 2:7] …; with him I am well pleased [Isa. 42:1]. Listen to him [Deut. 18:15]!" More easily overlooked is Matthew's changing the description of Joseph of Arimathea (see JOSEPH #13) as "a prominent member of the Council" in Mk. 15:43 to "a rich man" (Matt. 27:57) to conform with a prediction by Isaiah that the Suffering Servant would have "his grave … with *a rich man* in his death" (Isa. 53:9 RSV).

There is the possibility that some coincidences of wording between the OT and the NT are fortuitous, as is probable in the narratives of the flights to Egypt by JEROBOAM I (1 Ki. 11:40) and the Holy Family (Matt. 2:13–15). In most instances, however, there is justification in seeing conscious allusions, for Jewish education was steeped in OT lore. Because of rote memory, many of the

A page from the book of Leviticus in the Septuagint (Tischendorf's ed., 1875). The authors of the NT frequently used a form of this Greek version when quoting the OT.

rabbis were "living concordances." The DEAD SEA SCROLLS have shown that an author's weaving OT phraseology into his own words was a common literary practice in NT times.

II. Textual affinities. In quoting the OT, the NT writers occasionally transliterate the original Hebrew (or Aramaic); cf. "Immanuel" (Matt. 1:23), and "Eloi, Eloi, lama sabachthani" (Mk. 15:34). Usually they follow the text of the LXX, frequently even when it differs from the MT. The NT may disagree, however, with the LXX throughout an entire quotation or only in parts of a quotation. Sometimes the disagreement with the LXX will show agreement with the MT, the TARGUMS, the Syriac version (Peshitta; see VERSIONS OF THE BIBLE, ANCIENT III.C), the Greek version attributed to Theodotion (see SEPTUAGINT IV.C), and variant readings in Hebrew MSS, the DSS, rabbinical tradition, and JOSEPHUS—and sometimes complete independence from any known OT textual tradition. Often combinations of different textual traditions occur within a single OT quotation. It is especially well known that this phenomenon characterizes the so-called "formula-citations" in Matthew, introduced by a statement such as "this took place to fulfill what the Lord had said through the prophet" (Matt. 1:21 et al.).

The mixed text probably should not be attributed to inaccurate citation by memory (as is often stated). That is made unlikely by the numerous agreements with various textual traditions and by agreement among different NT writers against all others (Matt. 11:10; Mk. 1:2; Lk. 7:27 [these three citing Mal. 3:1]; Rom. 9:33 and 1 Pet. 2:6 [citing Isa. 28:16]; see J. Scott, *Principles of New Testament Quotation* [1877], 93).

Scholars have put forward a number of hypotheses to account for the aberrant text of numerous OT quotations in the NT. J. R. Harris argued that the NT writers used a "Testimony Book," that is, a catena or series of OT proof texts (*Testimonies*, 2 vols. [1916–20]). Many of the textual variants are then traceable to such a book, as are also recurring combinations of OT passages, supposed misascriptions, and the known "Testimony Book" of Cyprian, an early church father. Support for the hypothesis comes from the catena of messianic texts discovered in Qumran Cave 4 (See J. M. Allegro in *JBL* 75 [1956]: 186; 77 [1958]: 350). Doubtless, early Christian evangelists and teachers drew on a common stock (oral and/or written) of favorite OT proof texts for tenets of the Christian faith. But there is little reason to think that a "Testimony Book" par excellence or any number of them are the reason for the frequent failure of NT writers to follow the LXX. One reason for not thinking so is that a number of the aberrant quotations do not convey the idea of messianic FULFILLMENT, and probably did not, therefore, stem from a catena of Christian proof texts.

According to Paul Kahle, the non-LXX elements in NT quotations of the OT reflect written Greek targums widely used before the church adopted the LXX as its standard version of the OT (*The Cairo Geniza*, 2nd ed. [1959], 209–64). The mass of variant readings in MSS of the LXX—variants that Kahle uses along with the aberrant text of OT quotations in the NT to prove the existence of Greek targums—present a discernible pattern of development from an archetype, not a hodgepodge of unrelated variants from independent Greek targums. Furthermore, the DSS have shown that many of the variants in the Septuagintal MSS were the result of progressive assimilation to the Hebrew text of the OT, not the result of amalgamation of differing Greek targums utilized by NT writers.

Krister Stendahl proposes that Matthew emanates from a Qumran-like "school" that practiced PESHER (interpretative) selection and adaptation of known variant readings in the quoted OT texts (*The School of St. Matthew and Its Use of the Old Testament* [1954]; cf. the treatment of the OT text in the DSS, especially the Habakkuk Commentary). This hypothesis, however, labors under two basic weaknesses: (1) the DSS have shown that in NT times the OT text contained mixed readings that later became isolated in separate streams of textual tradition, so that the variants in OT quotations may be due to the mixed OT text used by NT and Qumran writers rather than to deliberate selection and adaptation by them; (2) an aberrant text is frequently an OT quotation where no hermeneutical motive for changing the LXX (or MT) is apparent. The same objections militate against the view of Barnabas Lindars that the aberrant text of many

OT quotations in the NT stems from reworking of the texts according to apologetic needs as the church confronted Judaism (*New Testament Apologetic: The Doctrinal Significance of the Old Testament Quotations* [1961]).

In the synoptics, only the explicit quotations of the OT in the Markan tradition are purely Septuagintal (or nearly so). On the other hand, some of Matthew's formula citations are wholly or partly Septuagintal as well as non-Septuagintal, showing affinities with the MT, the Aramaic targums, etc. This same sort of willy-nilly mixture occurs in the other OT quotations, including those that are allusive. It would appear, then, that the explicit quotations in the Markan tradition were conformed to the LXX because they stood out and because their grammatical independence in context subjected them to easy assimilation, and that the mixed text in other OT quotations stems partially from the mixed state of the OT text in NT times and partially from the Jewish practice of free translation in "targumizing." Agreeing to the mixture of Hebrew, Aramaic, and Greek textual traditions in many NT quotations of the OT is the archaeological evidence that these three languages were commonly used in 1st-cent. Palestine (see R. H. Gundry, *The Use of the Old Testament in St. Matthew's Gospel* [1967], 172–78; id. in *JBL* 83 [1964], 404ff.). Divergences from the LXX in OT quotations outside the synoptics (as in John and the Pauline epistles) are likewise best explained as the result of loose, ad hoc renderings in the targumic style (cf. E. D. Freed, *Old Testament Quotations in the Gospel of John* [1965]; E. E. Ellis, *Paul's Use of the Old Testament* [1957]—although both of these writers find more interpretative changes of the OT text than the present writer is inclined to see; and Ellis hypothesizes that Christian prophets engaged in oracular adaptations).

III. The style of OT quotations.

The formulas by which explicit quotations are introduced are varied. "It is [or stands] written" emphasizes the permanent validity of the OT REVELATION. "That it might be fulfilled" points up the consummation of the OT revelation in NT events. The OT passage may be attributed to the human author ("Isaiah says") or to God himself ("God/the Lord says," "the Holy Spirit says"). Other formulas are "the Scripture says," "the law says," "the prophet says," "it says," and numerous variations. These introductory formulas exhibit the highest possible concept of OT INSPIRATION on the part of Jesus and the NT writers. Not only does God often appear as the author of Scripture; the identification is so close that sometimes the Scripture is personified. At the same time the references to Moses, David, Isaiah, and others show recognition of the human element.

Notice should be made of the *ḥaraz* method, that is, quoting from two or three sections of the Hebrew OT canon (e.g., Rom. 11:8–10 from Isa. 29:10; Deut. 29:4 [MT v. 3]; and Ps. 69:22–23 [LXX 68:23–24]) or, less formally, chain-quoting different passages from the same section (e.g., Rom. 9:25–29 from Hos. 2:23 [MT v. 25]; 1:10 [MT 2:1]; and Isa. 10:22–23). Some combinations of quotations seem also to rest on key words. Outstanding are the quotations about the "stone" in Rom. 9:33 (Isa. 8:14; 28:16) and 1 Pet. 2:6–8 (Isa. 28:16; Ps. 118:22; Isa. 8:14).

Problems of ascription arise. For example, the quotation in Matt. 27:9 concerning the thirty pieces of silver comes from Zech. 11:13, but it is ascribed to Jeremiah. All sorts of explanations are offered; but probably it is taken for granted that the reader will see the relationship to Zechariah, so that attention is called to easily missed parallels in Jer. 19, such as the allusions to a potter and field (cf. the analogy of 2 Chr. 36:21 in relation to Lev. 26:34–35 and Jer. 25:12; 29:10). In other instances a quotation lacks ascription in the NT and it may be difficult to determine its source; notorious examples include Matt. 2:23 ("He will be called a Nazarene"); Jn. 7:38 ("... streams of living water will flow from within him"); and Eph. 5:14 ("Wake up, O sleeper ...").

The NT writers often quoted an OT text without indicating the source. The ancients had no feelings about plagiarism in such a practice. Nor did they sharply distinguish between direct and indirect quotations. To weave interpretative phraseology into a quotation (making it inexact) was not to disregard its sacredness, but to honor that sacredness by treating the text as supremely important for interpretation and application. By the same token, it does not really matter that the text of the quotation differed somewhat from that of the Hebrew OT. It is the meaning that counts. Only if the point of the quotation may rest on a change of text does a serious problem arise. That is a matter of judgment in each claimed instance. For an example, see the commentaries on Heb. 10:5 ("a body you prepared for me" versus "my ears you have pierced," Ps. 40:6).

It frequently is charged that the NT writers misinterpreted the OT text. Many times, however, they point to TYPOLOGY in the OT passage without meaning to deny the original meaning in its historical setting. Beyond that, scholars are dealing with matters of judgment—and each place where it is claimed that misinterpretation has occurred has to be considered separately. For example, does PAUL's argument that the singular "seed [or offspring]" in God's promise to ABRAHAM ("and to thy seed," Gen. 13:15 KJV) must refer to one person, Christ, wrongly overlook the use of "seed, offspring" as a collective singular? Hardly, for the context of the quotation shows that Paul is thinking of Christ as a collective singular—the corporate Christ, or Jesus Christ plus all those united to him by faith (note the conclusion of the argument, Gal. 3:29). Or does Paul's use of Hab. 2:4 ("The righteous shall live [have eternal life] by faith [trust in Christ]"—Rom. 1:17 ASV) violate an original meaning, "The righteous shall physically survive by virtue of their fidelity to Yahweh"? Again, one must answer negatively, for the verb "to live" in Hab. 2:4 carries the full meaning, "to enjoy divine favor," and fidelity to God is rooted in trust. Indeed, the OT passage seems to contrast the arrogant self-confidence of the wicked with the patient trust of the righteous, so that trust is the primary connotation rather than (or at least arising out of) fidelity.

Concerning the OT quotations in the Gospels, it is also charged that Christian desire to find fulfilled prophecies has resulted in the warping and creation of tradition about Jesus to fit OT texts. Against such a view are the facts that Christians failed to exploit many OT passages easily susceptible to the motif of fulfillment and that many of those they did exploit were not, so far as one can tell, messianically interpreted in Judaism at that time. Some of the quotations are so out of the way that it is doubtful a Christian writer would have thought to create a corresponding tradition about Jesus. Or the tradition is so realistic that derivation from the OT is unlikely. Not even among the DSS, where the desire to find fulfillment was so strong that the OT text is tortuously treated, does one meet creation of tradition to fit prophecy. For these and other reasons, one is to accept the priority and trustworthiness of the tradition concerning Jesus, and view the attached OT texts as later accretions rather than sources.

IV. The purposes for which the OT is quoted.
The motif of fulfillment in OT quotations is very strong. Quotations that fall under the category of fulfillment have to do with both direct predictions of future events and typological significance beyond the intention of the OT writers. The main motifs of these quotations in the NT are as follows: Jesus acts as Yahweh himself. He is the foretold Messianic King, the Isaianic Servant of Yahweh, and the Danielic Son of man. He culminates the prophetic line, the succession of OT righteous sufferers, and the Davidic dynasty. He reverses the work of ADAM, fulfills the divine promise to ABRAHAM, and recapitulates the history of Israel.

The priesthood of MELCHIZEDEK and AARON both prefigure (the latter sometimes contrastingly) the priesthood of Christ. The paschal lamb and other sacrifices represented the sacrificial, redemptive death of Jesus, and also Christian service. Jesus is life-giving bread like the manna, the rock source of living water, the serpent lifted up in the wilderness, and the tabernacle-temple abode of God among his people.

JOHN THE BAPTIST was the predicted prophetic forerunner. Jesus inaugurated the foretold eschatological period of salvation and the new covenant. JUDAS ISCARIOT fulfilled the role of the wicked opponents of OT righteous sufferers. The church is (or individual Christians are) the new creation, the spiritual seed of Abraham by incorporation into Christ, the new Israel, and the new temple. The Mosaic law prefigured grace both positively and negatively. Noah's flood stands for the last judgment and for Christian baptism. The passage through the Reed (Red) Sea and circumcision also picture baptism. Jerusalem stands for the celestial city. Entrance into Canaan prefigures the entrance of Christians into spiritual rest. Proclamation of the gospel to all men fulfills the promise to Abraham and prophetic predictions of universal salvation. That OT quotations fall under a limited set of recognizable themes sharply contrasts with the piecemeal treatment of the OT text in the DSS and rabbinical writings. The early Christians must have learned their OT hermeneutics from Jesus himself (cf. Lk. 24:27, 32).

Underlying the fulfillment quotations is the concept of *Heilsgeschichte* (salvation-history). God directs history according to his redemptive purpose. He reveals what he will do through his prophets. Their predictive word has a potency to bring about its own fulfillment, for it comes from the Lord of history. Thus, when the fulfillment takes place, confirmation results. Confirmation also comes when, looking back, one sees predictive symbolism in the pattern of OT events, persons, and institutions—that is, typology—not within the purview of the OT writers, but divinely intended.

One must not think that the early Christians searched haphazardly through the OT for any proof text for fulfillment that they could find. In his book *According to the Scriptures* (1952), C. H. Dodd showed that most of the NT quotation material relating to Jesus and the church comes from fairly restricted text plots in the OT. These he outlined as follows:

(1) *Apocalyptic-Eschatological Scriptures*—Joel 2–3; Zech. 9–14; Dan. 7 (primary); Mal. 3:1–6; Dan. 12 (supplementary).

(2) *Scriptures of the New Israel*—Hos. 1–14; Isa. 6:1—9:7; 11:1–10; 28:16; 40:1–11; Jer. 31:10–34 (primary); Isa. 29:9–14; Jer. 7:1–15; Hab. 1–2 (supplementary).

QUOTATIONS FROM AND REFERENCES TO ISAIAH 53 IN THE NEW TESTAMENT

ISAIAH 53	NEW TESTAMENT
53:1–12	Lk. 24:27, 46; 1 Pet. 1:11
53:1	Jn. 12:38; Rom. 10:16
53:2	Matt. 2:23
53:3	Mk. 9:12
53:4	Matt. 8:17; 1 Pet. 2:24
53:4–5	Rom. 4:25
53:5	Matt. 26:67; 1 Pet. 2:24
53:5–6	Acts 10:43
53:6	1 Pet. 2:25
53:6–7	Jn. 1:29
53:7	Matt. 26:63; 27:12, 14; Mk. 14:60–61; 15:4–5; 1 Cor. 5:7; 1 Pet. 2:23; Rev. 5:6, 12; 13:8
53:7–8 LXX	Acts 8:32–33
53:8–9	1 Cor. 15:3
53:9	Matt. 26:24; 1 Pet. 2:22; 1 Jn. 3:5; Rev. 14:5
53:11	Rom. 5:19
53:12	Matt. 27:38; Lk. 22:37; 23:33–34; Heb. 9:28; 1 Pet. 2:24

(3) *Scriptures of the Servant of the Lord and the Righteous Sufferer*—Isa. 42:1—44:5; 49:1–13; 50:4–11; 52:13—53:12; 61; Pss. 69; 22; 31; 38; 88; 34; 118; 41; 42–43; 80 (primary); Isa. 58:6–10 (supplementary).

(4) *Unclassified Scriptures*—Pss. 8; 110; 2; Gen. 12:3; 22:18; Deut. 18:15, 19 (primary); Pss. 132; 16; 2 Sam. 7:13, 14; Isa. 55:3; Amos 9:11–12 (supplementary).

To the above may be added Exod. 1–4; 24; 34; Num. 23–24; 2 Ki. 1; Ps. 78; Dan. 2; the last part of Dan. 11 (to go with ch. 12, which Dodd cites); Isa. 13; 34–35; and the last chapters of Isaiah generally beyond the limits of Dodd's text-plots; Mic. 4–5; 7; Zech. 1–6; and the rest of Malachi (beyond Mal. 3:6). Since the church recognized these OT passages as specially relevant to the new dispensation, an individual quotation became a pointer to the text-plot as a whole.

Sometimes the OT may be quoted only for the purpose of literary allusion; but usually, if not always, closer examination will discover a deeper rationale, such as fulfillment. In other usages, the OT quotation becomes the basis of comment (as in Jesus' teaching on marriage and divorce—Mk. 10:2–9 and parallels), sometimes in an argumentative setting (as in Jesus' debate with the Sadducees over resurrection—12:18–27 and parallels). Or the OT may be quoted prescriptively (cf. the repetition of nine out of the TEN COMMANDMENTS in scattered passages throughout the NT).

V. Quotations from sources other than the OT. Apart from OT quotations in the NT, Matthew and Luke quote Mark and perhaps Q and other sources (cf. Lk. 1:1–4 and see GOSPELS III.B). Quotations of Jesus' sayings appear (usually very allusively) in the epistles. Paul quoted an otherwise unrecorded saying (*agraphon*) of Jesus in Acts 20:35: "It is more blessed to give than to receive." See AGRAPHA. In Acts, Luke quotes a number of early Christian sermons and speeches. Of course, the evangelists quote large amounts of the teaching of Jesus—not always verbatim. The difference in the style of Jesus' speech in John and in the synoptics is to be explained by at least three considerations: (1) in the process of translation from Aramaic and Hebrew into Greek, John's own Greek style imposed itself more heavily than that of the synoptists; (2) John paraphrased more than the synoptists; (3) John deliberately preserved a strand of tradition not prominent in the synoptics—but that Jesus did speak in the Johannine style is proved by Matt. 11:25–27 and Lk. 10:21, 22.

Prayers are quoted in the NT: Matt. 6:9–13; Lk. 11:2–4 (the Lord's Prayer); Acts 4:24–30 (a persecution prayer in the early church); and 1 Cor. 16:22 (if MARANATHA is to be understood as an imperative form, "Our Lord, Come!"; cf. Rev. 22:20). So also are early Christian hymns, confessional creeds, and other traditional material: Lk. 1:46–55, 68–79; 2:14, 29–32; Jn. 1:1–14; Rom. 1:3–4; 4:24, 25; 10:9; 1 Cor. 11:23–26; 12:3; 15:3–5; Eph. 5:14; Phil. 2:5–11; Col. 1:15–20; 1 Tim. 3:16; 1 Pet. 3:18–22; Rev. 4:8, 11; 5:9–10. The above references are only representative. Some are less certain than others because of the difficulty in distinguishing quotations from the authors' own compositions. In particular, E. G. Selwyn proposes heavy quotation in 1 Peter and other epistles of such sources as liturgical hymns and creedal forms, a persecution fragment containing exhortations, catechetical documents, and *verba Christi*, thus accounting for the many similarities among the NT epistles (*The First Epistle of St. Peter* [1958]; see further R. P. Martin, *Worship in the Early Church* [1964], chs. 3–5 and literature there cited). There remains the possibility that Paul quoted his own earlier writings and that other epistolary writers quoted Paul. Jude extensively quoted 2 Peter, or vice versa (see the commentaries and introductions).

Lists of household duties and catalogues of virtues and vices in the epistles may be adaptive quotations of similar material in Jewish and/or Hellenistic ethical codes. There are possible quotations from or allusions to apocryphal books, as in Matt. 11:28–30 (Sir. 51:23–27); Rom. 2:4 (Wisd. 11:23); Heb. 1:1–3 (Wisd. 7:25–27); Heb. 11:35–37 (2 Macc. 6–7). Jude quotes from the pseudepigraphal *1 En.* 1:9 (Jude 14–15) and apparently from a now lost part of the *Assumption of Moses* (Jude 9). Many of the phrases in Revelation have been attributed to extracanonical Jewish apocryphal literature (see, e.g., R. H. Charles, *The Book of Enoch* [1912], xcviff.). Material that appears in the pagan writers Epimenides, Aratus, Cleanthes, Callimachus, and

Menander is quoted in Acts 17:28; 1 Cor. 15:33; and Tit. 1:12. Finally, Paul appears to quote slogans of his opponents in passages such as 1 Cor. 6:12; 8:1; and 2 Cor. 10:10.

(In addition to the titles mentioned in the body of this article, see D. M. Turpie, *The Old Testament in the New* [1868]; C. Taylor, *The Gospel in the Law* [1869]; D. M. Turpie, *The New Testament View of the Old* [1872]; C. H. Toy, *Quotations in the New Testament* [1884]; F. Johnson, *The Quotations of the New Testament from the Old* [1896]; O. Michel, *Paulus und seine Bibel* [1929]; C. H. Dodd, *The Old Testament in the New* [1952]; J. Doeve, *Jewish Hermeneutics in the Synoptic Gospels and Acts* [1954]; R. V. G. Tasker, *The Old Testament in the New Testament*, 2nd ed. [1954]; E. E. Ellis, *Paul's Use of the Old Testament* [1957]; S. Kistemaker, *The Psalm Citations in the Epistle to the Hebrews* [1961]; D.-A. Koch, *Die Schrift als Zeuge des Evangeliums: Untersuchungen zur Verwendung und zum Verständnis der Schrift bei Paulus* [1986]; D. A. Carson and H. G. M. Williamson, eds., *It Is Written: Scripture Citing Scripture: Essays in Honour of Barnabas Lindars, SSF* [1988]; R. B. Hays, *Echoes of Scripture in the Letters of Paul* [1989]; C. D. Stanley, *Paul and the Language of Scripture: Citation Technique in the Pauline Epistles and Contemporary Literature* [1992]; A. Obermann, *Die christologische Erfüllung der Schrift im Johannesevangelium: Eine Untersuchung zur johanneischen Hermeneutik anhand der Schriftzitate* [1996]; R. E. Ciampa, *The Presence and Function of Scripture in Galatians 1 and 2* [1998]; F. Wilk, *Die Bedeutung des Jesajabuches für Paulus* [1998]; S. Moyise, *The Old Testament in the New: An Introduction* [2001]; J. R. Wagner, *Heralds of the Good News: Isaiah and Paul in Concert in the Letter to the Romans* [2003]; C. D. Stanley, *Arguing with Scripture: The Rhetoric of Quotations in the Letters of Paul* [2004]; J. P. Heil, *The Rhetorical Role of Scripture in 1 Corinthians* [2005]; G. K. Beale and D. A. Carson, eds., *Commentary on the Old Testament in the New Testament* [2007].)   R. H. Gundry

© Dr. James C. Martin

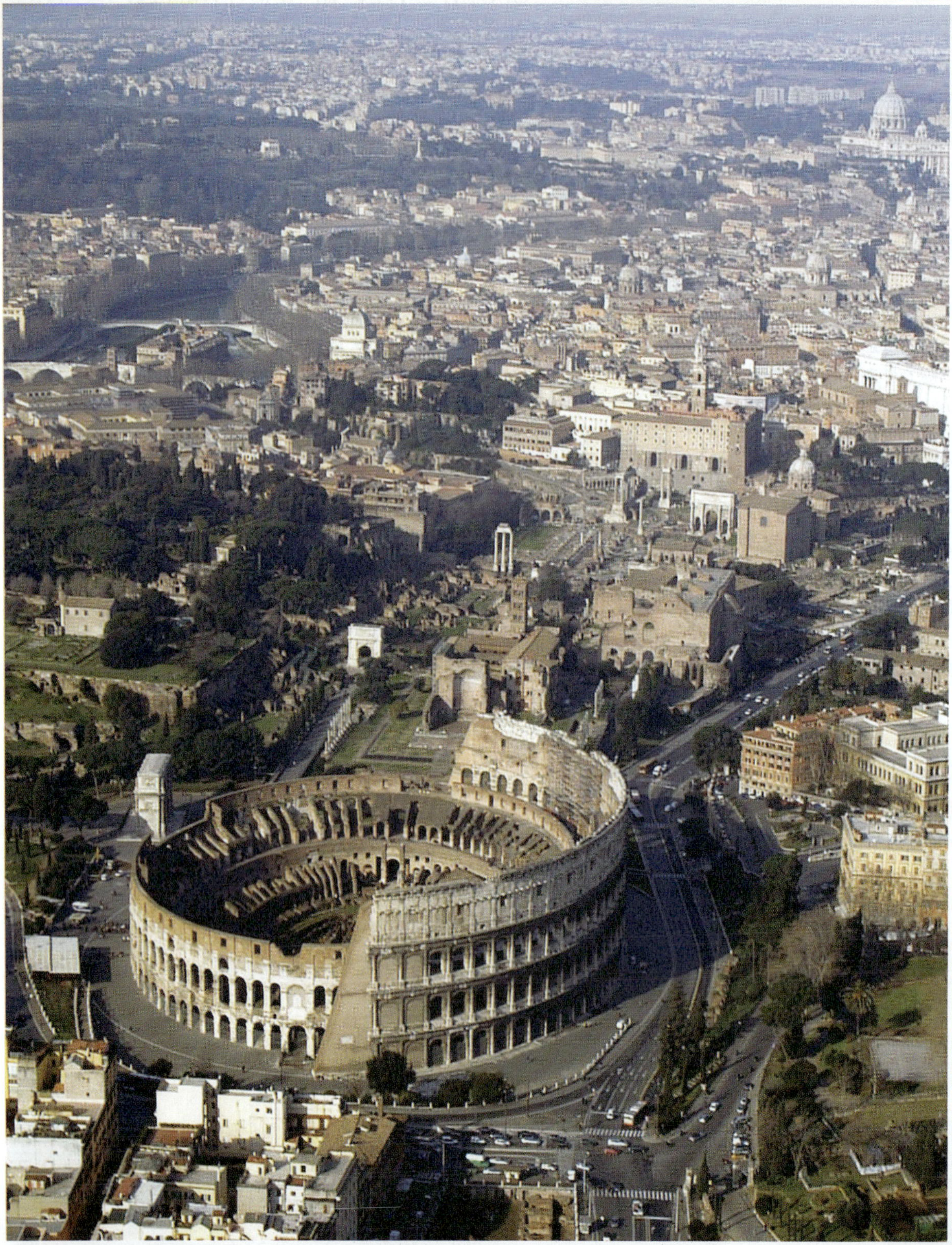

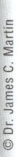

Aerial view of the city of Rome (looking W).

Ra rah. See RE.

Raamah ray′uh-mah (רַעְמָה H8311 and רַעְמָא H8309 [1 Chr. 1:9], derivation uncertain). Son of CUSH, grandson of HAM, and father of SHEBA and DEDAN (Gen. 10:7; 1 Chr. 1:9). Raamah thus appears as the eponymous ancestor of a tribe in ARABIA. The traders of both Raamah and Sheba brought to the markets of TYRE their best of all kinds of spices, precious stones, and gold (Ezek. 27:22). Its location has not yet been fixed. On the basis of the SEPTUAGINT rendering, *Regma* (*Ragma* in Ezekiel), many have identified it with a city of that name mentioned by Ptolemy (*Geogr.* 6.7.14) and located in E Arabia on the Persian Gulf, but this location is problematic. Others believe that Raamah is the same as Ragmat(um), an ancient city in the oasis of Najran mentioned in S Arabian inscriptions (cf. *HALOT,* 3:1268; *ABD,* 5:597), though it is objected that Old South Arabic *g* does not correspond to Hebrew ʿ*ayin* (cf. *ISBE* rev. [1979–88], 4:27). The suggested equivalence between biblical Raamah and the *Rhammanitōn* mentioned by Strabo (*Geogr.* 16.4.24) is rejected by some. (Note further W. F. Albright, "Dedan," in *Geschichte und Altes Testament* [1953], 1–12.) See also NATION II.A.3.   B. K. WALTKE

Raamiah ray′uh-mi′uh (רַעַמְיָה H8313, perhaps "Yahweh has thundered" or "[born during] a thunderstorm"). An Israelite mentioned among leading individuals who returned from Babylon with ZERUBBABEL (Neh. 7:7; called "Reelaiah" in Ezra 2:2 and "Resaiah" in 1 Esd. 5:8 [KJV, "Reesaias"]).

Raamses ray-am′seez. See RAMESES.

Rabbah (Ammon) rab′uh (רַבָּה H8051, "great [city]"). The capital city of AMMON, also known as Rabbath-Ammon (cf. Heb. *rabbat bĕnê* ʿ*ammôn*, lit., "Rabbath of the sons of Ammon," i.e., "Rabbah of the Ammonites," Deut. 3:11; Ezek. 21:20). Its modern name is Amman, the capital of the Hashemite Kingdom of Jordan. Rabbah seems to be the only Ammonite city that is mentioned by name in the Bible. It is located about 23 mi. E of the JORDAN River and lies at the headwaters of the Wadi Amman, which soon becomes the JABBOK River. This very strong spring on the edge of the desert was the reason for the city's existence. Ammon, or a fortified sector within it, was called "the city of waters" (2 Sam. 12:27 KJV; NIV, "its water supply"; see P. K. McCarter, Jr., *II Samuel,* AB 9 [1984], 312).

I. Bible History. In the first reference to Rabbah (Deut. 3:11), the city is cited as the permanent location of the famous iron bed of OG, king of BASHAN. This "bed," possibly a sarcophagus, has been an enigma to scholars, since Og ruled at the beginning of the Iron Age, when this metal was uniquely valuable (see IRON). Within the territory of GAD, the city of AROER is located to the E of Rabbah (Josh. 13:25). The next reference to the capital of the Ammonites details the siege of that city by the Israelites under the direction of JOAB, along with the interwoven episode of DAVID and BATHSHEBA (2 Sam. 11:1—12:31). Joab captured the section of the city located around the springs, but he waited for King David himself to capture the citadel section on the steep hill above the springs (12:27–31; 1 Chr. 20:1–3). The city was a rich prize and its captured population was put to the corvée or public works battalion. This demonstrates that David anticipated his son SOLOMON when the latter rebuilt JERUSALEM.

David, like Solomon, needed many laborers whom he secured from his prisoners of war. Later, when David was fleeing from his son ABSALOM, he came to MAHANAIM and was aided by some friends, among whom was the son of NAHASH, the king of Rabbah (2 Sam. 17:27–29). Apparently David had established a new dynasty on the Ammonite throne after he captured the capital.

By the time of the prophet AMOS, the city was again an independent capital of the Ammonite kingdom, which was expanding its boundaries up into GILEAD. Because of the unusually brutal ruthlessness of this military conquest, Amos predicted the destruction of Rabbah (Amos 1:13–14). In JEREMIAH's day the Ammonites were again conquering the same territory of Gilead, and the prophet predicted the city's destruction (Jer. 49:1–3). EZEKIEL made two prophecies against the Ammonites. He predicted that the king of BABYLON would capture Rabbah in the same campaign that would see the destruction of Jerusalem (Ezek. 21:20). The capital of the Ammonites, however, was not to meet its annihilation on this occasion; it would come later at the hands of the Arabs of the desert (25:1–7). It was Rabbah's control over these desert tribes of the Wadi Sirhan, who traded also with the Arabs, that had made Rabbah wealthy throughout many years. Ezekiel predicted that the Ammonite kingdom would return to desert pasture land through military conquest by the same desert tribes.

II. Intertestamental history. The first reference to Rabbah after the close of the OT is its capture by PTOLEMY Philadelphus. The city was renamed Philadelphia in his honor and it continued to bear that name through the Roman period, although occasionally the older name Rabbath Ammon appeared in historical writings. ANTIOCHUS the Great captured the city in 218 B.C. after a long siege. In 199 B.C. it returned to the Ptolemaic sphere of influence. The city became Roman when POMPEY took over Palestine in 63 B.C. The NABATEANS, who were its normal occupants in the 1st cent. B.C., were conquered by HEROD the Great c. 30 B.C. Under the Romans Philadelphia became one of the cities of the DECAPOLIS, the southernmost city of that confederation.

III. Archaeological history. Rabbah's abundant water supply was the secret of the city's continuing life. Archaeological artifacts show occupation from the Palaeolithic through the Neolithic and Chalcolithic times (excavations in 1994 uncovered homes and towers thought to date to c. 7000 B.C.). The same is true of its occupation in all the Bronze and Iron Ages (except Iron III), as well as the Hellenistic and Roman periods. A tomb from the HYKSOS period shows the wealth of the city at that time. Still more interesting is a Late Bronze Age temple in open country c. 2.5 mi. from the city. The richness of the finds seems to show that commerce from the Mediterranean of significant volume and great wealth was passing through Rabbah in addition to the normal N-S commerce of the KING'S HIGHWAY shortly before the Israelites under MOSES came through TRANSJORDAN. The main commercial route was always this one between ARABIA and DAMASCUS.

Rabbah of Ammon.

Typical pottery from the Ammonite culture in Transjordan dating to the Late Bronze Age (c. 1550–1200 B.C.).

The great Roman and Byzantine buildings on the citadel hill are too valuable to be removed in order to uncover earlier history. The cost of land purchase in the modern city around the citadel also makes it too expensive for archaeological digging. The only biblical phase found to date is a part of the city's Iron Age wall.

The archaeological remains above ground are almost all from the Roman period (esp. 2nd and early 3rd cent. A.D.), Byzantine, or Umayyad. From Roman times there can be seen today the great theater (cut in part out of the solid rock of the hill) seating c. 6,000 people. It is still used on special occasions. Nearby is an odeum (i.e., a small theater) for various types of performances. There are also two temples, a nymphaeum (i.e., a monument consecrated to the nymphs of the springs), a bath, an aqueduct, and remains of various colonnaded streets. These great buildings of the Roman period are valuable for NT parallels since the basic architectural forms changed little, and one can have a good idea of what Jerusalem, Jericho, and Samaria looked like when Jesus visited these cities. Still finer examples of a Palestinian Roman city can be found at Jerash (GERASA). It is one of the spectacular ruins of the Near East.

(See further F.-M. Abel, *Géographie de la Palestine* [1933], 2:424–25; G. L. Harding, *The Antiquities of Jordan* [1959], 45–54; L. G. Herr, *The Amman Airport Excavations 1976*, AASOR 48 [1983]; R. Dornemann, *The Archaeology of the Transjordan in the Bronze and Iron Ages* [1983], passim; B. MacDonald et al., eds., *The Archaeology of Jordan* [2001], index s.v. "Amman"; *NEAEHL*, 4:1243–52.)

J. L. KELSO

Rabbah (Judah) rab´uh (רַבָּה H8051, with the definite article attached, "the great [city]"). A town in the hill country of the tribe of JUDAH (Josh. 15:60). Rabbah and KIRIATH JEARIM are the only towns included in the last district listed in this passage; apparently, they were intended to guard the western approach to JERUSALEM. It is generally agreed that Rabbah is the same as *Rbt* (vocalized Rubute or Robbotu), a town mentioned in Egyptian sources (cf. Y. Aharoni, *The Land of the Bible: A Historical Geography*, rev. ed. [1979], 163, #105). Aharoni identified it with modern Khirbet Ḥamideh, but this site is in the SHEPHELAH (c. 2 mi. WSW of AIJALON and 5 mi. ESE of GEZER) rather than in the hill country, and he himself acknowledged that such a location "would violate the geographic principle upon which the entire list is founded" (ibid., 355). The identification of Rabbah is thus uncertain. (For fuller discussion, see A. F. Rainey in *ISBE* rev. [1979–88], 4:29–30.)

Rabbath rab´uhth. See RABBAH (AMMON).

rabbi rab´i (ῥαββί G4806, from Heb. רַב H8042 [Aram. רַב H10647], with 1st person pronominal suffix, "my master, my teacher"). A term used by the Jews after the OT period in designation of their religious teachers. First employed as a term of respect, particularly in reference to SCRIBES trained in the law (Matt. 23:2–7), it came to be used during the 1st cent. as a title, the pronominal suffix losing its significance. It was translated into the Greek by the word *didaskalos* G1437, meaning TEACHER (Matt. 23:8; Jn. 1:38). Due to its significance (the adjective *rab* H8041 means "great"), Jesus forbade his disciples to accept it in self-designation (Matt. 23:8). Christ was so addressed (Matt. 26:25, 49; Mk. 9:5; et al.), as was JOHN THE BAPTIST (Jn. 3:26). In some of these passages, the use of the term appears to be a form of address corresponding roughly with English *sir*. The title "Rabboni" (Gk. *rhabbouni* G4808, Mk. 10:51; Jn. 20:16) derives from a heightened form of the word in ARAMAIC (*rabbān* or *rabbôn*). (See further *ABD*, 5:600–602.)

L. J. WOOD

rabbinic literature. See MISHNAH; TALMUD.

rabbit. See HARE.

Rabbith rab′ith (רַבִּית H8056, with the definite article attached, meaning possibly "the great [city]"). A town within the tribal territory of ISSACHAR (Josh. 19:20). Rabbith is listed between ANAHARATH (prob. a site some 7 mi. SE of Mount TABOR) and KISHION (prob. near the S slope of the mountain), and many think it is the same town as *dobrat H1829* (DABERATH, on the N side of the mountain; cf. Z. Kallai, *Historical Geography of the Bible* [1986], 424–25). Indeed, CODEX VATICANUS has *Dabirōn* for the MT's *rabbit*, but some scholars do not accept this identification.

rabboni ra-boh′ni. See RABBI.

Rabmag rab′mag (רַב H8041, "great, chief," and מָג H4454, possibly from Akk. *maḫḫu*, "soothsayer" [BDB, 550], but the whole phrase is prob. a loan from Akk. *rab-mu[n]gi*, a title applied to high military officials). Also Rab-mag. The Babylonian title borne by NERGAL-SHAREZER (Jer. 39:3). Most English versions simply transliterate the term, but the NIV renders it as "a high official." The title was apparently given to special royal envoys. See also RABSARIS; RABSHAKEH.

Rabsaris rab′suh-ris (רַב H8041, "great, chief," and סָרִיס H6247, "eunuch, official"; the phrase corresponds to Akk. *rab-ša-rēši*, lit., "chief of the one at the head"). Also Rab-saris. Title applied to one of three officials sent by SENNACHERIB, king of Assyria, to HEZEKIAH (2 Ki. 18:17 NRSV and most versions); the other two were the TARTAN and the RABSHAKEH. The title is applied also to Nebo-Sarsekim (Jer. 39:3; see SARSECHIM) and to NEBUSHAZBAN (v. 13), both of whom were Babylonian senior officials. In every instance, the NIV renders this phrase "chief officer." See also RABMAG. L. L. WALKER

Rabshakeh rab′shuh-kuh (רַב־שָׁקֵה H8072, from Akk. *rab-šāqê*, "chief cupbearer" [cf. Heb. רַב H8041, "great, chief," and שָׁקֵה H9197 hiphil, "to give to drink"]). Title applied to high-ranking Assyrian officials. When SENNACHERIB attacked LACHISH, he sent the Rabshakeh, along with the TARTAN and the RABSARIS, to deliver an ultimatum to HEZEKIAH (2 Ki. 18:17 et al.; cf. Isa. 36:2 et al.). The Rabshakeh, however, acted as the chief spokesman. The NIV, instead of transliterating the term, renders it "field commander." See also CUPBEARER; RABMAG. L. L. WALKER

raca rah′kah (ῥακά G4819 [some MSS have ῥαχά], prob. from Aram. רֵיקָא [also רֵיקָה], "empty"). A term of reproach or insult. In the Bible the word occurs only in Matt. 5:22, where Jesus warns that "anyone who says to his brother, 'Raca,' is answerable to the Sanhedrin" (NRSV, "if you insult a brother or sister, you will be liable to the council"). The Aramaic word *rêqāʾ* is used figuratively in rabbinic literature as a term of contempt, meaning "worthless, good for nothing, stupid." For example, the MIDRASH on Eccl. 9:15 states that NOAH said to his contemporaries, "Woe, ye foolish ones [*rqyyʾ*]! Tomorrow a flood will come, so repent" (*Qoh. Rab.* 9.17). The TALMUD relates that "once when a certain pious man was praying by the roadside, an officer came by and greeted him and he did not return his greeting. So he waited for him till he had finished his prayer. When he had finished his prayer he said to him: Fool [*ryqʾ*]!" (*b. Ber.* 32b). Note also that a Greek papyrus letter dating from the 3rd cent. B.C. already uses the form *rhacha* as an insult (cf. BDAG, 903, which includes a summary of patristic interpretations; for further discussion, see J. Jeremias in *TDNT*, 6:973–76). G. H. WATERMAN

Racal ray′kuhl (רָכָל H8218, perhaps from a root meaning "to trade"). KJV Rachal; TNIV Rakal. A place in S Judah to which DAVID sent some of the plunder he took from ZIKLAG (1 Sam. 30:29). The SEPTUAGINT (CODEX VATICANUS) reads *en Karmēlō*, and on that basis many scholars emend the MT to read *bĕkarmel* (see CARMEL), referring to a town not far from ESHTEMOA, the previous place mentioned on the list (v. 28).

race. A population distinguishable from others; a tribe or nation composed of people that derive from the same stock. (For the meaning "a contest of speed," see ATHLETE.) There are two primary considerations to be made when discussing the human races. One is biological, dealing with the processes of differentiation among populations as well as the classification of the results of these processes. The second one is sociological, which deals rather with the mechanisms within SOCIETY that influence the processes of differentiation as well as the reaction of a given social group to the end results of the various processes of differentiation. During the last decades of the 20th cent., scientific discussions of race underwent significant changes.

    I. The biological problem of race
        A. Definition of race
        B. Means of classifying races
        C. A classification of races
        D. How races differentiate
        E. Modern races versus prehistoric races
    II. The sociological problems of race
        A. Deriving from the religious community
        B. Deriving from the whole of society

I. The biological problem of race. No two human beings are alike. Two may look very much alike, but upon closer examination details of the physical features will reveal distinctions. Even when the outward physical features appear almost identical, there will still remain distinction of blood type. At the same time, it is commonly agreed in scientific circles today that all living human beings belong to a single species. A species is composed of all those organisms that interbreed to produce viable fertile offspring.

Anthropologists generally agree that humans form a single, continuously varying species that is *polymorphic* (i.e., showing marked variability in many structural characteristics), *polytypic* (i.e., within any given population a number of types of individuals will occur), and *polygenic* (i.e., at a great number of "gene loci," two or more alleles [alternative forms of a gene] are found in relatively stable proportions, which vary from one population to another depending upon selective pressures). They also agree that most phenotypical characteristics are the product of multiple gene effects. The human species is composed of a large number of breeding populations, differing from one another because of local adaptive pressures, geographic impediments, and, in some cases, social impediments to free gene flow between populations. This means that in all their major biological characteristics, they have more features in common than they have distinguishing differences.

Somewhere between considering only two humans and considering all humans within one species, it becomes apparent that certain distinctive traits tend to cluster in populations that have lived predominantly in one part of the world or other. The clustering of such traits becomes the basis for classification of populations. There is no question but that such traits tend to cluster in specific populations; populations native in central Africa have much higher frequencies of genes that produce dark skin than do European populations. The frequency of the gene for blue eye color progressively diminishes southward from Scandinavia through central Europe to the Mediterranean and Africa. The problem arises in attempting to classify the subdivisions of populations on the basis of such traits. Prior to modern-day attempts to classify races on genetically based biological studies, *taxonomy* (lit., "arrangement of names") formed the basis of classification. It is generally conceded that Linnaeus's system is the most complete. Before Darwin's time, such name schemes became an end in themselves. In more recent times there has been a shift in the use of classifications: from one that presents a picture of the ordained and eternal to one that represents distances and relationships.

Many schemes that attempt to group or classify populations have been presented. Some of these schemes have been based on physical traits alone, such as the color of the skin, the color and form of the hair, the eye color, and other characteristic physical features. One such approach divides all

Man blowing shofar during Elul at Western Wall.

the people of the world into three major stocks: the *Caucasoid* (Caucasian) or white; the *Negroid* or black; and the *Mongoloid* or yellow. Each in turn is divided further into subgroups. This was the dominant scheme of classification when the children's chorus was composed: "Jesus loves the little children, / All the children of the world, / Red and yellow, black and white, / All are precious in his sight, / Jesus loves the little children of the world." The expression of the love of Jesus is quite biblical. The "racial classification" is neither biblical nor adequate.

Another scheme is based on geography alone. This classification coincides basically with the ethnic divisions within a geographically defined land mass, such as the Asiatic. Other approaches are based on blood types such as A, B, or O. Still other schemes are based on the differences of language and/or custom.

Since the term *race* has been applied to all of these classifications, confusion has resulted, and some noted anthropologists such as Ashley Montague have urged the elimination of the term. The idea has strong support in theory. In the selection of a trait to utilize in classification, if one character is used, it is possible to divide a species into subspecies according to the variation in this character. If two characters are used, it is still possible, but there will be some problems arising from the mixture. As the number of characters increases it becomes nearly impossible to determine actual races. Further, the selection of the racially determining traits becomes a wholly arbitrary choice. It is felt by some that, because of the complexity of the problem, the concept of race becomes meaningless.

There is the further problem that all populations have a history. What can be done in classifying the United States population in light of extensive immigration? Again, with the observed fact that most of today's differentiations are the result of culture, some feel that the new conditions are so different that it is better not to use the term at all. In the words of Washburn, "races are products of the past, relics of times and conditions which have long ceased to exist."

It becomes quite obvious that if the term or the concept is used at all, it must be done with the greatest caution. If used meaningfully to classify populations, the classification must grow out of the purpose of the classification. As J. Buettner-Janusch (*Origins of Man: Physical Anthropology* [1966]) has suggested, "Classifications are not immutable, and the ones that we use must be appropriate for the occasion."

A. Definition of race. A scientific biological classification based on established genetic criteria permits the breaking of the human species into smaller, biologically determined units. "A race is a human population that is sufficiently inbred to reveal a distinctive genetic composition manifest in a distinctive combination of physical traits." This definition is a biological one based on *genotype* or genetic makeup rather than on a *phenotype* distinction of persons who have a fairly definite combination of distinguishing physical traits. It does not ignore the physical characteristics; rather, it recognizes them to be part of the picture as contributing to classification but not the sole criterion of classification.

B. Means of classifying races. According to E. Adamson Hoebel (*Anthropology: The Study of Man* [1966]), four basic ideas are emphasized in the above definition: population, inbreeding, genetic composition, and distinctive physical traits.

A *population* may be defined as "a group of possible observations or of individuals united by some common principle." Generally speaking, a geographical distinction is made focusing on people who have inhabited a given continent or a section of continent in the past and who still do inhabit it to a great extent (e.g., Caucasians). They are more likely to share common ancestry. Within each geographical area or the race that results might be found *local races*, again based on a geographic consideration. These are localized over broad areas within a continent or island chain (e.g., Nordics). S. M. Garn and C. S. Coon, who originally formulated this approach to racial analysis, suggest that the number of such races might be thirty. Finally, within each of these categories of local races might be found what have been called *microgeographic races*. These are extremely isolated, tightly inbreeding, small populations set off from other such populations (e.g., the Kentucky mountaineers of the southern Appalachians).

Inbreeding is the result of isolation and limited mobility and itself results in a random distribution of genes among a population of humans. Such distribution assures that a given population has specific genes not shared by other populations. They would have these to a greater or lesser extent. The more outside contact a population might have, the greater the distribution of the genes. The more restricted the contact, the more limited the distribution of the genes and the more highly specialized the genetic make-up of the population. Both geographic and social factors enter into the isolation of a group or population. Oceans may keep two populations from interbreeding on the international scene, whereas exogamy/endogamy (required marriage outside/within a specific group) may restrict marriage opportunities and thus reduce interbreeding on the local scene.

Genetic composition suggests that the hereditary materials in the sex cells are arrays of more or less discrete units. These were called *genes* in 1909 by W. Johannsen. The laws of inheritance produced by G. Mendel suggest four areas in which genetic theory clarifies the problem of heredity. The parental heredities do not mix in the progeny: when the descendants mature and proceed to form their own sex cells, the components of the parental heredities segregate, mutually uninfluenced and uncontaminated by their generation-long sojourn in the same body. Further, heredity is particulate and not continuous: the hereditary materials in the sex cells are arrays of more or less discrete units. Also, although a child gets half his genes from his mother and the other half from his father, he or she receives only half the total genes (never all) each parent possesses. Finally, even though the gene theory seems notoriously capricious to a casual observer, there is system in this apparent caprice.

Following Mendel's discoveries, specialists began to unfold the wonder of the gene and its influence in the life processes. It was discovered in 1902 that genes were contained in chromosomes. The chromosomes were later found to contain DNA (deoxyribonucleic acid) and protein. In 1961, Marshall Nirenberg of the National Institute of Health found that all of life is not only built from the same basic DNA units, but is also assembled by one kind of code. All life was shown to be controlled by its own specific genetic code.

A whole concatenation of *physical traits* marks a given race. Yet it is clear that one individual never possesses all the traits that characterize his race. Such traits may be physical or they can also involve blood

This photo from the beginning of the 20th cent. shows a nomadic Arab guide on a horse.

types. Physical traits are the obvious characteristics of height, skin color, and kind of hair, for example. Blood is classified according to its agglutinative reactions, that is, according to whether the hemoglobin (red blood corpuscles) clump together when mixed with alien blood. Such blood types as O, A, B, and AB form the basis for blood type classifications.

C. A classification of races. Modern anthropologists usually resist racial classifications. In the past, perhaps the most complete and extensive classification (based on the preceding definition of race) was the one suggested by E. Adamson Hoebel. It consists of nine major categories, subdivided according to local races as follows:

(1) EUROPEAN (population of Europe, North Africa, and the Middle East, and their worldwide descendants)
    (a) Northwest European: Scandinavia, northern France and Germany, the Low Countries, the United Kingdom, and Ireland
    (b) Northeast European: Eastern Baltic, Russia, and modern Siberia
    (c) Alpine: central France, southern Germany, Switzerland, and northern Italy, to the Black Sea
    (d) Mediterranean: population surrounding the Mediterranean, eastward through Asia Minor

(2) INDIAN (population of the Indian subcontinent)
    (a) Indic: India, Pakistan, and Ceylon
    (b) Dravidian: aboriginal population of southern India

(3) ASIAN (population of Siberia, Mongolia, China, Japan, SE Asia, and Indonesia)
  (a) Classic Mongoloid: Siberia, Mongolia, Korea, and Japan
  (b) North Chinese: northern China and Manchuria
  (c) Turkic: western China and Turkestan
  (d) Tibetan: population of Tibet
  (e) Southeast Asian: southern China through Thailand, Burma, Malaya, the Philippines, and Indonesia
  (f) Ainu: aboriginal population of Japan
  (g) Eskimo: northern maritime fringe of N America and ice-free fringes of Greenland
  (h) Lapp: arctic Scandinavia and Finland
(4) MICRONESIAN (population of the western Pacific Islands from Guam to the Marshalls—no local races distinguished)
(5) MELANESIAN (population of the western Pacific Islands S of Micronesia, extending from New Guinea to Fiji)
  (a) Papuan: mountain highlands of New Guinea
  (b) Melanesian: coastal area of New Guinea and most of the other islands in the Melanesian archipelago
(6) POLYNESIAN (population of the eastern Pacific Islands from Hawaii to New Zealand and Easter Island)
  (a) Polynesian: aboriginal population
  (b) Neo-Hawaiian: 19th to 20th cent. blend of Polynesian, European, and Asiatic
(7) AMERICAN (i.e., Native Americans, earlier called "Indians")
  (a) North American: Canada and the Continental United States
  (b) Central American: southwestern United States, Mexico, and Central America to Brazil
  (c) South American: all South America, except Tierra del Fuego
  (d) Fuegian: population around the Straits of Magellan
  (e) Ladino: new Latin-American population resulting from blending of Mediterranean, Central and South American ("Indians"), Forest Negroes, and Bantu
  (f) North American Colored: 18th to 20th cent. population blended of northwestern Europeans and Africans
(8) AFRICAN (population of Africa S of the Sahara)
  (a) East African: E African Horn, Ethiopia, and Nilotic Sudan
  (b) Sudanese: the Sudan, except for Nilotics
  (c) Forest Negro: W Africa and most of the Congo
  (d) Bantu: S Africa and adjacent parts of E Africa
  (e) Bushman-Hottentot: surviving post Pleistocene population in S Africa
  (f) Pygmy: small-statured population living in the equatorial rain forest
  (g) South African Colored: population of S Africa produced by a blend of NW European and Bantu, plus some Bushman-Hottentot
(9) AUSTRALIAN
  (a) Murrayian: aboriginal population of southeastern Australia
  (b) Carpentarian: aboriginal population of central and northern Australia

The Negrito populations are sporadically scattered throughout SE Asia, Indonesia, and New Guinea. They thus straddle several normal geographic areas and cannot be placed in any one of the major categories.

The attempts to identify racial differences by describing physiological traits have become highly controversial. What follows is a traditional but problematic description.

European (formerly Caucasoid). The European race is not actually white. It belongs to the group possessing varying pigmentation. Eye color varies from light blue to dark brown. Hair is blond to black and of fine to medium texture; it may be straight, wavy, or curly, but is rarely kinky and never woolly. The males tend to grow hair on their chests, arms, legs, and faces as well as on the tops of their heads. The nose is narrow and high, rarely broad or flat. Although the forehead is usually sloping, the face is not prognathous. Chins tend to jut, and lips are thin. Stature is medium to tall.

Indian. The fact that India is a subcontinent isolated from the rest of Asia by vast mountain ramparts qualifies its population for consideration as a geographical race. The population is, in fact, made up of hundreds of local races and microgeographic races. Tribal and caste endogamy has split the population into numerous intrabreeding groups separated by great social distances that are more inhibiting than geographical distances. In the N of India, skin color is variably light. In the S, it may be very dark. Stature is short, except in the extreme NW, where there has been much European (mostly Middle Eastern) intermixture. Most Indians are brunettes, and the hair is usually wavy. Body hair on males is moderately frequent. The head is almost always dolichocephalic. Eyes are dark brown and large. Body build is gracile.

Asian (formerly Mongoloid). The most outstanding Asian physical trait is the slant eye, more elegantly known to anthropologists as the internal epicanthic fold. The infants also have a unique feature, the "Mongolian patch," which is a purplish, triangular area of skin at the base of the spine. Skin color is brown or yellowish-tan. Eyes are brown or dark-brown, and the hair is black. It is very coarse and straight, growing long on the head and scarcely at all on the face or body. Most Asian populations are brachycephalic. The cheekbones are broad and high, while the nose is squat and low-bridged, thus giving a flat-faced appearance. While their body trunks are fairly long, heavy, and broad, they are usually short and squat in stature, because their legs are short.

Micronesian. This population resulted from a blending of SE Asians and Melanesians. It is medium-statured, brown-eyed, and dark-skinned. Hair is black and frequently frizzy. The head is brachycephalic to mesocephalic.

Melanesian (formerly Oceanic Negro). The peoples of the Black Islands are black in skin color (some are brown) and hair color. The hair is long and frizzy; hence the nickname "Fuzzy-Wuzzies" given them by American soldiers in World War II. The head is usually dolichocephalic, and the nose is high and broad (sometimes called Semitic). Eyes are dark and set in a very prognathous face, which has notably thick lips. Body hair is scanty. Stature is medium and the body well-formed.

Polynesian. Predominantly they are of Indic mixed with Melanesian and S Asian stocks. The race is very similar to the Malayo-Indonesians except that the stronger Mediterranean heredity gives a wavy form to the hair, elongates the face and body, lightens the skin, and produces a high nose. African traits show up in a tendency to fullness of lips. The dominant roundheadedness of the Asian characterizes most Polynesians. Hair grows luxuriantly on the head, but, as is to be expected in an Indic-Asian-Melanesian mixture, it is scanty on the face and body. As well-fed islanders, they have developed large and powerful bodies.

American (formerly Amerind). The "Indians" of the Americas are highly variable in stature, head form, and details of facial features. In general, however, they reveal their Asian ancestry in a predominance of brachycephaly; brown eyes; black, usually straight hair; thin lips; broad, high cheekbones; occasional internal epicanthic fold; and yellow or reddish-brown skin covering a broad and heavy body. Blood-type frequencies, as already noted, differ markedly from those of the Asian, however.

African (formerly Negro). Africans are the possessors of the darkest pigmentation of all mankind; nevertheless, few Africans are actually black. Most are dark-brown or brownish-black in skin color. Hair is prevailingly black, coarse, wiry, and tightly curled, kinky, or woolly. With few exceptions, heads are long and narrow. The occipital region juts out, as does the lower portion of the face, which in appearance is accentuated by the thick, everted mucous membrane that forms the lips. The African nose is broad, with flaring wings and a broad, deeply depressed bridge. The hair on the head, though thick, is short in length, while the male beard is sparse; body hair is rare. Stature is medium tall. The forearm is long, and the legs are thin (i.e., the calves do not ordinarily develop thick musculature).

Australian. The Australian aborigine is physically a "lowbrow." His forehead slopes back from the heaviest supraorbital ridges to be found in any surviving race. His skull is narrow and houses a brain that is notably smaller in volume than that of any other living race. His face juts forward, and his dental arches even more so. His dark-brown eyes are set beside a deeply depressed nasal root, below which the broad thick tip of the nose flares up in a great bulb. The whole face is compressed from symphysis to nasion. The Australian is neither very short nor very tall. He grows a slender, short body on a pair of pipestem legs.

It needs to be stressed again, however, that since the 1970s there has been increasing opposition to the task of classifying races. The measurement of human variation on the basis of genetic analysis makes clear that individual (rather than population) differences account for most of the variation, and many believe that such data refutes the concept of biologically distinct races. By 1998, the American Anthropological Association had gone on record as opposing racial classification.

D. How races differentiate. "The differences between human races are, after all, rather small, since the geographic separation between them is nowhere very marked. The races gradually diverge. There is, of course, nothing fatal about this divergence, and under some circumstances the divergence may stop or even be turned into convergence. This is particularly true of the human species. The human races were somewhat more sharply separated in the past than they are today. Although the species inhabits almost every variety of environment on earth, the development of communications and the increase of mobility, especially in modern times, has led to much intermarriage and to some genetic convergence of the human races" (T. Dobzhansky, *Mankind Evolving: The Evolution of the Human Species* [1962]).

Races differentiate within the human species as a result of four factors. (1) *Selection* is the operation of environment at various levels to prevent or encourage the reproduction of genes of the individuals carrying them. If forces of any kind favor individuals of one genetic complexion over others, in the sense that they live and reproduce more successfully, the favored individuals will necessarily increase their bequest of genes to the next generation relative to the rest of the population. (2) *Genetic drift* refers to the loss of genes through sampling accidents in the process of segregation and recombination of genes. In a large population the relative amount of any given individual's contribution to the next generation is much less than would be the case where the population size is small, though a given mutation stands a better chance of being transmitted in the larger population than in the smaller. Whereas selection is directional, genetic drift is nondirectional, due primarily to its being the result of chance. (3) *Mutation* is the molecular reorganization of the genetic code. The gene fails

Wall painting from the tomb of Ptah-Hotep in Saqqara, depicting ancient Egyptians.

to copy itself exactly in the process of replication. It has been estimated that this happens in only one in 50,000 to 100,000 replications. According to some, the vast majority of mutations result in physiological inactivation, as for example, the depigmented and eyeless fishes that inhabit underground rivers and pools in caves. Mutation, however, has been proven only to produce variation within a species. There has never been proof of the development of a new species by this mechanism. The resultant change is thus likely to be regression rather than progression. *Genetic flow* is the transmission of genes from one population to another.

Three very significant factors—geography, environment, and sociology—enter into the problem of the differentiation of the races to encourage or impede the processes of differentiation indicated above. (1) *Geography* becomes a factor in differentiating races in terms of space and physiographic features. Each serves to result in geographical proximity or isolation. Because thousands of miles of ocean separate the Iroquois from the Australian, it is not likely that they will interbreed. A mountain range may effectively separate two populations simply because of the time and effort necessary to cross the mountain to effect interaction. On the other hand, in many primitive groups it is likely that every person is genetically related to the other.

(2) Ectogenetic theories of human development suggest that the *environment* plays a major role in human change, determining in certain instances just what kind of change takes place. These theories suggest that alterations induced in the inhab-

itants of warm climates will differ from those in cold climates and that different races, species, etc., will eventually appear. Such theories have generally been discredited, since the environment itself is not recognized to impose changes on the organism, but there is recognition that environment does have some effect on the differentiation of races. The human organism is known to adapt to a specific environment in two ways: either an organism can possess a morphology suitably generalized so that it can get along adequately in a variety of environments, or it can preserve the genetic potential for producing variants capable of getting along under specifically differing conditions.

(3) Finally, *social isolation* may produce differentiation. This may be due to social, religious, political, or economic factors. If one society is Catholic and another Buddhist, there is limited expectation of interbreeding.

E. Modern races versus prehistoric races.

It is relatively simple to conceive of races in the present day. We accept them as part of our everyday involvement in living. However, scientists have not always been able clearly to differentiate racial groups in the past. In studying the human fossil record and reconstructing the line of human development, a unilinear approach is likely to be presented. *Homo sapiens* is thus pictured as being in a line of descent from *Australopithecus* through such developments as *Homo erectus* and/or *Neanderthals* (although there is debate concerning where the direct relationships lie). We may never know for sure, but any of the fossil humans could have easily been separate races rather than part of a unilinear development of distinct human types.

Carleton Coon elaborated a theory of race originally proposed by Franz Weidenreich. Based on a concept of parallel lines of development, Coon suggested that whereas the contemporary Asian population traces its lineage back to *Homo erectus pekinensis*, the contemporary European population traces its lineage to *Homo sapiens steinheimensis*. In all, he posits five racial lines in this way, "each as old as man himself," back to *Homo erectus*. More recent work, however, has led most scientists to the view that the human species cannot be subdivided into biologically distinct races.

II. The sociological problems of race

A. Deriving from the religious community

1. The Bible and race. The Bible does not have a specific term for "race"; nor is there a concept of race developed in Scripture. Yet, the Bible has been made the center of very deep-rooted feelings regarding this subject. Such feelings, as well as the theories that have sustained them, have derived from sociological rather than biblical sources. Within specific societies, the rise of racial distinctions has developed into racist attitudes. They derive mainly from ethnocentric orientations to the universe that make one kind of people the center of the universe, so to speak, and all other peoples inferior to them. Once such racial distinctions are made, a variety of authorities are naturally called upon to substantiate the point of view selected. It is at this time, and for this purpose, that the Bible is utilized, since it has been an authoritative source for a large portion of the civilized world since its writing.

The early chapters of Genesis are susceptible to the interpretation that the races were separate species created by God as they are today. The range of interpretation is quite broad. There are those who have taken the ADAM and EVE account to apply only to Caucasians. It has even been argued that the Negroes appearing in Egyptian monuments, as well as the skulls of the Indian mound builders of Ohio, differed in no way from their living descendants. This would imply that there was no important change in living creatures in the only slightly longer time since the creation itself, established time-wise by Archbishop Ussher at 4004 B.C. Some others have argued that Cain was black and thus founded the Negro race, an idea very attractive to racists, since they can then associate Cain's behavior with the Negro type. Other extreme theories have focused on intelligence, but the Negro, by all measures that are scientific, covers the full range of intelligence of any living human with lighter pigmentation of skin.

Additional points of view centered on the family of NOAH. Some firmly believed that the Negro differentiated slowly from the racial type of the family of Noah. Others considered the Negro a direct descendant of HAM, who supposedly (according to an unfounded tradition) was born black. One variation on the "Hamite" theme is that SHEM and his descendants moved eastward into Asia; JAPHETH moved westward into Europe; and Ham moved southward into Africa. Since people who lived in Asia are reddish brown, apparently Shem was of that color; since those who come from Europe are of lighter skin color, therefore Japheth must have been of that color; and since Africans are dark-skinned people, therefore Ham was a dark-skinned person. None of these arguments takes into consideration the possibility that all three of the brothers were of a darker skin pigmentation, one that characterizes the peoples of the Near East. The differentiation of color likely came many hundreds of years after the time of the sons of Noah.

Another variation on the Hamite theme is that Ham was turned into a dark-skinned individual through the curse placed upon him. The curse of Noah was really on CANAAN, one of four children of Ham, not on Ham himself. Apparently the curse had no lasting import, since history tells us that Canaan's descendants dominated the whole land of Palestine until long after the death of MOSES. There is further no indication that the curse had any "spiritual" import; that it had any sanction of God that would make it an enduring curse; that it had any relation to skin pigmentation; and that Canaan was in any way connected with the Negro population. W. F. Albright even went so far as to indicate that all known races in the region of the OT world belonged to the so-called "white" or "Caucasian" race, with the exception of the Cushites (Ethiopians), who were strongly Negroid in type.

The tower of BABEL account has become the focus for other theories of the origin of race. Some have considered that God miraculously produced the races in the same instant that he confounded the languages. A man by the name of Ariel even suggested that the tower of Babel was built by Negroes who had no connection with the family of Noah.

Such theories or fancies have been utilized to establish racial distinctions as they relate to racists' arguments. At any one point in the history of civilization it has been difficult to distinguish the true from the false interpretations of Scripture. Present-day scientific schemes, on the other hand, do not serve to negate the Scriptures; rather they negate the untruth that has grown up around the truth of Scripture, as people have "seen in part" and dogmatically asserted that they have seen the whole.

With such a background, it is possible to suggest what the Bible does say about the question of human races. Scripture does talk about *ethnic* groups by name, going so far as to describe specific customs characteristic of these groups, such as in the book of Ruth. Elsewhere the Bible refers to geographical locations and the language problems that arise. Thus Acts 2 states that the HOLY SPIRIT came upon the disciples of Christ after his death, and that they "began to speak in other tongues" (v. 4) so that the people from the different geographical areas were bewildered "because each one heard them [the disciples] speaking in his own language" (v. 6). PAUL too recognized legitimate distinctions of language (1 Cor. 14:10). In some instances, the Bible refers to black or dark skin color, but only in terms of illness (Job 30:30) or beauty (Cant 1:5); in no case is there a derogatory reference or any indication of inferior status assigned to those of black skin.

Prior to the building of the tower of Babel, "the whole world had one language" (Gen. 11:1). It appears that the people preferred to live in a nondivided geographical zone and had opportunity to interrelate rather continuously. Following the construction of the tower of Babel, the larger group was divided into a number of groups, as could be assumed from the concept "scattered" (v. 8). They apparently proceeded to migrate in a broader, divided geographical zone. They thus became a number of separate or geographically isolated inbreeding populations rather than one inbreeding population. Whether the confounding of the language was instantaneous or not does not appear to be the point of the story. It appears rather that there was a causal effect, that in order to confound their language, they were scattered.

Such scattering was certain to produce two effects, effects that are known today from the genetic and linguistic sciences: the separation of inbreeding populations produces distinct phenotypic characteristics within each separate population; and through the process of language change, isolated populations develop distinct languages. Just when this scattering took place is not clear from the biblical account. The narration possibly is not in the proper temporal sequence. It appears rather that the incident may have been interjected here by the author to clarify a point in the genealogical listing, which point is lost to us due to the writing-translation process. Either way, we have a very clear insight into the scientific process of genetic and linguistic differentiation. The best scientific minds today tend to agree that *Homo sapiens* appeared and began to differentiate into races at the same time. The Bible does not need to be contradictory at this point.

Finally, two concepts become clear in the biblical record. The first is that when dealing with people of distinct ethnic and linguistic backgrounds, one must deal with them in keeping with their backgrounds, as for example in Acts 2, when the disciples spoke in tongues. A second concept is that of Christian love manifested by Jesus in all his dealings with the people of diverse backgrounds, such as the woman of Samaria. There appeared to be no place for racism or racial distinctions based on superiority-inferiority in his experience.

2. Racial supremacy. Racial prejudice may arise from a variety of causes, including economic and political as well as social; from a concept of superiority-inferiority; from biological differences or from combinations of these. It thus implies that "the differentiation of races is not a matter of science; it is by immediate perception that we recognize emotionally the differences we call racial." Racial prejudice lies at the base of white-negro relations, which appears to have reached its climax in the United States; conflicts between Jews and non-Jews reached their climax during Hitler's regime in Germany and still lie behind much of the trouble in the Middle East.

The questions that arise from the problem of prejudice are: Do some races have a superior capacity for cultural attainment? Are they inherently more intelligent? Do they have an inherently greater capacity for leadership and domination that justifies their control and exploitation of allegedly less fortunately endowed races?

When one examines the comparative anatomy of races, there is no clear indication of superiority of any given race. When races are compared with subhuman primates, Africans come out most "ape-like" in five characteristics and Europeans in three; but Africans are least "apelike" in six of the selected traits, while the Europeans are least so in only three. Such a comparison becomes somewhat absurd.

In comparisons of the brain size as correlated with intelligence, O. H. Klienberg concludes: "In general there appears to be an exceedingly small, though positive correlation between head size and intelligence." But this can be due as much to good nutrition as to inheritance.

Intelligence tests do tend to indicate something about intelligence level when they are composed and applied to members of the same society. They produce somewhat absurd results when they are applied cross-culturally, since many of the basic factors upon which the specific intelligence test is prepared are changed. How can an intelligence test designed to test Americans who learn individually and make decisions individually be used with any success among Australian aborigines or even Maya-related Indians of Central America who learn and make decisions in the group, not individually? S. D. Porteus attempted such an application among the Australians and they were disturbed when he did not help them solve the tests, especially since he had even been made a tribal member.

Such testing produces very little evidence for racial superiority. So-called "intelligence tests" measure innate skill plus cultural experience. Any results must be critically evaluated in light of the knowledge of the culture. Aptitude tests do reveal racial differentials in visual, motor, and vocal skills, but these too are influenced by culture, and no test can fully control this variable. Finally, many skills of intelligence and aptitude definitely change when the cultural environment changes.

B. Deriving from the whole of society

1. Sociological controls in a breeding population. Society interacts with the environment to control the breeding population. The reaction of one society with the environment may very well determine with what other society it will make contact, for example, in economic exchange, thus enlarging or restricting the interbreeding potential of each society.

The social structure of a given society also controls the breeding population. The paired principle of exogamy/endogamy, for example, which establishes marriage relationships between societies as well as within societies, regulates, most effectively, interbreeding between groups. Rules of exogamy/endogamy indicate the group outside of which one must go to find a suitable marriage partner, and also indicate the larger group within which one must find a suitable marriage partner. Any group not a part of the intermarriage potential of a given group will be sociologically isolated from that group, and thus differentiation will likely result. Such arrangements between societies as economic trade commitments, political liaisons, or religious affiliations will limit or increase contact between these societies.

2. Sociological reactions to distinct populations. We do know certain things about all races. All humans, as T. Dobzhansky has pointed out, are adapted to learn language—any language; to perform skillful tasks—a fabulous array of tasks; to cooperate; to enjoy art; to practice religion, philosophy, and science. The study of cultures should give a profound respect for the biology of human capacity to learn.

Unfortunately, however unfounded the basis for racial prejudice may be, the importance of the attitudes and behavior proceeding from it in many countries is indisputable. It is here that the most profound damage to society and the individual is sensed. Denial of equality of opportunity stultifies the genetic diversity with which men and women became equipped during their development. Inequality conceals and stifles some peoples' abilities and disguises the lack of ability in others. In 1900 the life expectancy of white males in the United States was forty-eight years and in that same year the life expectancy of the African American males was thirty-two years. As the life expectancy of the whites increased from forty-eight to about seventy-five years, that of the African Americans increased from thirty-two to sixty-nine years. It was evident that although there was progress, this progress lagged many years behind the whites who obviously had better economic and social opportunities.

As long ago as 1950, the *Statement on Race* of the United Nations Educational, Scientific, and Cultural Organization (UNESCO) affirmed: "Available scientific knowledge provides no basis for believing that the groups of mankind differ in their innate capacity for intellectual and emotional development.... Some biological differences between human beings within a single race may be as great or greater than the same biological differences between races.... Vast social changes have occurred that have not been connected in any way with changes in racial type. Historical and sociological studies thus support the view that genetic differences are of little significance in determining the social and cultural differences between different groups of men.... There is no evidence that race mixture produces disadvantageous results from a biological point of view. The social results of race mixture, whether for good or ill, can generally be traced to social factors."

(In addition to the titles mentioned in the body of the article, see E. Tilson, *Segregation and the Bible* [1958]; S. M. Garn, *Human Races* [1965]; J. Marks, *Human Biodiversity: Genes, Race, and History* [1995]; A. Barnard and J. D. Spencer, eds., *Encyclopedia of Social and Cultural Anthropology* [1996]; S. Molnar, *Human Variation: Races, Types and Ethnic Groups*, 4th ed. [1998]; T. C. Holt, *The Problem of Race in the Twenty-first Century* [2000]; J. L. Graves, Jr., *The Emperor's New Clothes: Biological Theories of Race at the Millennium* [2001]; R. D. Coates, ed., *Race and Ethnicity: Across Time, Space, and Discipline* [2004]; C. L. Brace, *"Race" is a Four-Letter Word: The Genesis of the Concept* [2005]; S. Cornell and D. Hartmann, *Ethnicity and Race: Making Identities in a Changing World* [2007].) M. K. MAYERS

Rachab ray′kab. KJV NT form of RAHAB.

Rachal ray′kuhl. KJV form of RACAL.

Rachel ray′chuhl (רָחֵל *H8162*, "ewe"; Ῥαχήλ *G4830*). Daughter of LABAN, wife of JACOB, and mother of JOSEPH and BENJAMIN (Gen. 29:6 et al.). Jacob, obeying the instructions of his father ISAAC (28:1–2), traveled to the region of PADDAN ARAM in search of a wife from the family of his mother REBEKAH (Laban's sister). When he came to a well near HARAN (29:2), he met his cousin Rachel, "a shepherdess" who had brought her father's sheep to water them (29:9). Jacob fell in love with Rachel, who is described as "lovely in form, and beautiful," so he offered to work seven years for Laban in return for marrying her (29:17–18). Laban agreed, but deceitfully gave to Jacob his older daughter LEAH and then proposed that Jacob work an additional seven years for Rachel (29:21–27). Jacob was willing to accept these terms: the years he had already worked "seemed like only a few days to him because of his love for" Rachel (29:20). Thus after concluding the week-long wedding festivities with Leah, he was given Rachel and then proceeded to work the additional seven years (29:28–30).

Because Jacob did not really love Leah, and thus presumably treated her as a second-class wife, God made her fertile and she gave birth to four sons (Gen. 29:31–35). Rachel, on the other hand, was barren, and her jealousy toward Leah made her cry out to Jacob, "Give me children, or I'll die!" (30:1). Jacob responded in anger that it was God who had kept her from having children (30:2). Rachel then proceeded to give her maidservant BILHAH to Jacob as a CONCUBINE, hoping that the latter would bear children who would be counted as Rachel's own. Bilhah gave birth to two sons, DAN and NAPHTALI, and Rachel felt vindicated, exclaiming that in her struggle with Leah she had prevailed (30:3–8). Leah, not to be outdone, gave to Jacob her maidservant ZILPAH, who proceeded to bear two more sons (30:9–12).

Leah, evidently, continued to hold a subordinate position, for when Rachel asked for some of the MANDRAKES (a fruit thought to promote fertility) that Leah's oldest son REUBEN had gathered, Leah retorted, "Wasn't it enough that you took away my husband? Will you take my son's mandrakes too?" (Gen. 30:14–15). In return for the mandrakes, Rachel allowed Leah to sleep with Jacob. Then "God listened to Leah," and she gave birth to two more sons and a daughter (30:17–21). Then finally, after all these years, "God remembered Rachel; he listened to her and opened her womb. She became pregnant and gave birth to a son and said, 'God has taken away my disgrace.' She named him Joseph, and said, 'May the LORD add to me another son'" (30:22–24).

Some time later, when Jacob decided to leave Haran, Rachel stole her father's household gods, the possession of which was apparently indicative of family honor or leadership (Gen. 31:30–35; see TERAPHIM). It may be that, since both Rachel and Leah felt they had been defrauded by Laban when he kept their dowries (vv. 14–16), her taking the household gods was thought to secure a blessing for Jacob's family (perhaps a parallel to Jacob's stealing his father's blessing, which should have gone to the eldest child, ESAU ch. 27).

Young women still function as shepherdesses as did Rachel.

After Jacob and his family arrived in Palestine, they first settled near SHECHEM (Gen. 33:18), where DINAH, Leah's daughter, was violated, an act that led to the slaughter of the city's male inhabitants at the hands of SIMEON and LEVI (ch. 34). Under God's direction, Jacob moved to BETHEL, where he built an altar to God (35:1–7). Later, on the way from Bethel to EPHRATH (BETHLEHEM), Rachel went into hard labor. "As she breathed her last—for she was dying—she named her son Ben-Oni [*i.e.*, son of my sorrow]. But his father named him Benjamin [*i.e.*, son of the right hand]" (35:18). Rachel was buried there, and Jacob set up a pillar that marked RACHEL'S TOMB for centuries (35:19; cf. 48:7). (For a brief discussion of the literary qualities of this narrative, see *ABD*, 5:605–8.)

It is important to note that, as the mother of Joseph (whose sons EPHRAIM and MANASSEH became ancestors of two large Israelite tribes) and of Benjamin, Rachel was the ancestress of three of the most prominent tribes in the Hebrew nation.

Not surprisingly, she is alluded to elsewhere in the Bible. When BOAZ announced his intention to marry RUTH, the elders of Bethlehem congratulated him with these words, "May the LORD make the woman who is coming into your home like Rachel and Leah, who together built up the house of Israel" (Ruth 4:11).

In the 8th cent. B.C., the Assyrians advanced toward Ramah, a town in Benjamin a few miles N of Jerusalem (see RAMAH #3), and more than a century later "the weeping prophet," anticipating further destruction and EXILE, announced this word from the Lord: "A voice is heard in Ramah, / mourning and great weeping, / Rachel weeping for her children / and refusing to be comforted, / because her children are no more" (Jer. 31:15). The woman who had so desperately longed for children now finds herself bereaved of them. Matthew quotes these words in connection with the slaughter of the infants in Bethlehem by HEROD (Matt. 2:18). The significance of this quotation is debated, but it may express an eschatological hope: "The tears of the Exile are now being 'fulfilled'—i.e., the tears begun in Jeremiah's day are climaxed and ended by the tears of the mothers of Bethlehem. The heir to David's throne has come, the Exile is over, the true Son of God has arrived, and he will introduce the new covenant ... promised by Jeremiah [cf. Jer. 31:31–34; Matt. 26:28]" (D. A. Carson in *EBC*, 8:95).

Rachel's tomb. According to Gen. 35:19–20, JACOB set up a pillar over RACHEL's grave, a landmark still existing at the time of SAMUEL (1 Sam. 10:2). E. P. Eddrupp noted: "As Rachel is the first related instance of death in childbearing, so this pillar over her grave is the first recorded example of the setting-up of a sepulchral monument" (*A Dictionary of the Bible*, ed. W. Smith [1863], 2:989).

Many scholars think that the Bible presents two divergent traditions with regard to the site of the grave. S. H. Hooke argued that (a) according to several passages (Gen. 35:16; 1 Sam. 10:2; Jer. 31:15), EPHRATH, the stated site (Gen. 35:19), lay on the N border of the tribe of BENJAMIN, c. 10 mi. N of JERUSALEM; but (b) according to two passages (Gen. 35:19 and 48:7), it was near BETHLEHEM, presumably S of Jerusalem (*HDB* rev., 830). Moreover, the traditional site is just N of Bethlehem, some 4 mi. S of Jerusalem. S. V. Fawcett added that Matthew's quotation of Jer. 31:15 with reference to the slaughter of the infants around Bethlehem (Matt. 2:16–18) would indicate that Matthew accepted the traditional view (*IDB*, 4:5). Regarding the identification of Ephrath with Bethlehem as a late, erroneous gloss, both of these scholars rejected the traditional site and preferred an unidentified Ephrah in the N of Benjamin.

However, the three verses cited supporting a location N of Jerusalem do not contradict the clear statements in Gen. 35:19 and 48:7. (1) Gen. 35:16 reads literally, "there was still a stretch of land to go to Ephrath," a statement that implies a site S of Jerusalem. (2) 1 Sam. 10:2 says that it was located on the border (Heb. *gĕbûl H1473*) of Benjamin. This could refer to Benjamin's S border just S of Jerusalem (Josh. 15:8; 18:15–17), because the city mentioned in 1 Sam. 9, presumably close to the border, is not identified. Furthermore, the expression "by Rachel's tomb" (1 Sam. 10:2) need not be pressed, since otherwise the further definition "at Zelzah" (unidentified) would be superfluous. On the other hand, the traditional site may not be authentic: it appears to be too far S of Benjamin's border. (3) Finally, the statement in Jer. 31:15 furnishes no evidence that Rachel's tomb was in RAMAH, 5 mi. N of Jerusalem. The prophet may have evoked in sublime prosopopoeia Rachel bewailing her children at Ramah either because he foresaw that the captives of Judah and Benjamin would be brought to Ramah after the fall of Jerusalem before being led into exile (Jer. 40:1), or because Ramah was a height in the territory of Benjamin where the desolation of the land was visible.

JOSEPHUS and the TALMUD agree in placing her tomb near Bethlehem. ORIGEN, EUSEBIUS, and JEROME accepted this site. Later the pilgrims described it as a pyramid formed of twelve stones. The Crusaders rebuilt it, erecting a building 23 ft. square formed by four columns bound by pointed arches 12 ft. wide and 21 ft. high, the whole crowned by a cupola. In 1788 the arches were walled up, giving it the appearance of a *weli*. In 1841 Sir Moses Montefiore obtained for the Jews the key of *Qubbet Rahil*, and added a poor square vestibule with a *mihrab* for Muslims (E. Hoade, *Guide to the Holy Land* [1946], 347). B. K. WALTKE

Raddai rad´i (רַדַּי H8099, "[Yahweh] rules"). Fifth son of JESSE and brother of DAVID (1 Chr. 2:14).

raft. See SHIPS.

Ragau ray´gaw. See RAGES; REU.

Rages rah´guhs (Ῥάγοι [some MSS Ῥάγα], from Old Pers. *Rāgâ*). A strategic road-center and strongly fortified city in NE MEDIA of the Persian empire. Rages is generally identified with the modern ruins of Ray (Rai, Rhay, Rhey), c. 5 mi. SE of modern Teheran. It was located just S of the high mountain range of Alborz bordering the Caspian Sea and controlled the Caspian Gates. The city was eleven days' journey from ECBATANA and was one of the oldest centers of civilization in Iran. Because of its location, Rages played an important part in the wars of Media and of ALEXANDER THE GREAT and his successors.

Rages is mentioned seven times in TOBIT, where it is usually called "Rages of Media." Tobit had left ten talents of silver at Rages (Tob. 1:14; 4:1, 20). His son Tobias, accompanied by the angel Raphael, started for Rages in quest of the money; it was finally recovered by the angel (5:5[6]; 6:9, 13; 9:2). The "Ragau" mentioned in JUDITH refers to the nearby territory around the Elburz mountain range (Jdt. 1:5, 15; Gk. *Ragau*; RSV, "Ragae"). (See A. V. Jackson, "A Historical Sketch of Ragha, the Supposed Home of Zoroaster's Mother," in *Spiegel Memorial Volume* [1908], 237–45; *University of Pennsylvania Bulletin*, 5/5 [1935]: 41–49; 6/3 [1936]: 79–87; 6/4 [1936]: 133–36; A. T. Olmstead, *History of the Persian Empire* [1948], 30, 111, 114–15.) D. E. HIEBERT

Raguel ruh-gyoo´uhl (רְעוּאֵל H8294, "friend of God"; Ῥαγουηλ). **(1)** KJV alternate form of REUEL (Num. 10:29).

(2) Ancestor of TOBIT and descendant of NAPHTALI (Tob. 1:1 NRSV, following CODEX SINAITICUS).

(3) Father of Sarah; the latter was given in marriage to Tobit's son, Tobias (Tob. 3:7, 17). Raguel features throughout the narrative (6:11–13; 7:1–15; 8:9–15; 10:7–13; 14:12–13).

(4) One of several archangels mentioned in the book of *1 Enoch* (20.4 et al.). J. C. MOYER

Rahab ray´hab (רָחָב H8147, meaning uncertain; Ῥαχάβ G4829 [Matt. 1:5] and Ῥααβ G4805 [LXX; Heb. 11:31; Jas. 2:25]). A prostitute of JERICHO, at whose house two spies stayed just prior to the conquest of Palestine by JOSHUA (Josh. 2:1–21).

A partially reconstructed house built over a wall of ancient Jericho (c. 2200–1500 B.C.). Rahab lived in a house that was part of the city walls.

Terrified by the approach of the Israelites, she made an agreement with the spies to protect them if they would guarantee the safety of her family and herself. She concealed them from the agents of the king of Jericho, and helped them to escape through her window on the city wall. At the fall of Jericho, Joshua spared Rahab and her relatives (6:17, 22, 25). According to Matthew's GENEALOGY OF JESUS CHRIST, Rahab became the wife of Salmon (see SALMA) and the mother of BOAZ (Matt. 1:5). The author of Hebrews cites her as an example of FAITH (Heb. 11:31), and James refers to her demonstration of faith by good works (Jas. 2:25). (See M. L. Newman in *Understanding the Word: Essays in Honor of Bernhard W. Anderson*, ed. J. T. Butler et al. [1985], 167–81; *ISBE* rev. [1979–88], 4:33–34; *ABD*, 5:611–12.) M. C. TENNEY

Rahab (monster) ray´hab (רַהַב H8105, "assault, violence"). In the poetical books of the OT the name is applied to a monster or demonic power.

The allusions occur in the context of God's power in nature: he overcomes Rahab in a contest of force (Job 9:13; 26:12 [in parallel with "serpent," v. 13]; Ps. 89:10 [in parallel with "enemies"]; Isa. 51:9 [in parallel with DRAGON]). Each of these passages is connected with the providential act of God in restraining the sea, and as a demonstration of his supreme power. (See also LEVIATHAN; MYTH.) The concept was applied to the deliverance of Israel from Egypt, when God opened the waters of the sea to provide a safe passage for his people (Isa. 51:10). Possibly because of this association with the exodus, Rahab became a symbolic name for EGYPT. It is included in the list of hostile nations cited in Ps. 87:4, and it is specifically identified with Egypt in Isa. 30:7. (See *ABD*, 5:610–11; *DDD*, 684–87.)

M. C. TENNEY

Raham ray´hum (רַחַם H8165, possibly "[God has] shown] mercy," but this derivation is uncertain [for a meaning such as "girl-like," see BDB, 933]). Son of Shema and descendant of CALEB (1 Chr. 2:44). Some believe that Raham was the name of a town (understanding "father" in the sense of "founder").

Rahel ray´hel. KJV alternate form of RACHEL (only Jer. 31:15).

raiment. See DRESS; CLOTH.

rain. The limited rainfall in Palestine was of great importance to its inhabitants (note the various Hebrew terms used in Deut. 32:2). The annual amounts received in various parts of the country are described in the article PALESTINE (section V, "Climate"). The average figures, however, are liable to mislead, since totals vary greatly from year to year. In Jerusalem, for example, the long-term average is 26.1 in., but the maximum recorded in any one year is 40 in. and the minimum 12 in. With fluctuations of this magnitude in the total, the impact upon a society dependent for its livelihood on the land can well be imagined.

Most important to the farmer is the distribution of rainfall throughout the year. This distribution is very uneven indeed. No rain falls at all during the four hottest months of the year. The hot, dry summer is a common feature of most of the lands surrounding the Mediterranean; it is balanced by a cool wet winter, but, from the farmer's point of view, the two critical periods are the beginning and end of the wet season, when temperatures are high enough to promote growth and the soil is moist enough to work.

The farmer's year is therefore linked closely to the coming of the rains. In October these begin, generally with a series of thunderstorms, and plowing and sowing can then be started on the hard-baked soil. If the start of the rainy season is delayed, crop yields suffer; if the delay is a long one, crop failure may result. Hence, these "early rains" are of the utmost importance. At the other end of the winter, rains continuing into late April and May, when temperatures are high, are of much more value than in January or February, when they are low; they increase yields for every day that the rains are prolonged. The farmer therefore hopes for the "latter rains."

This combination of early and late rains is referred to several times in the Bible. For example,

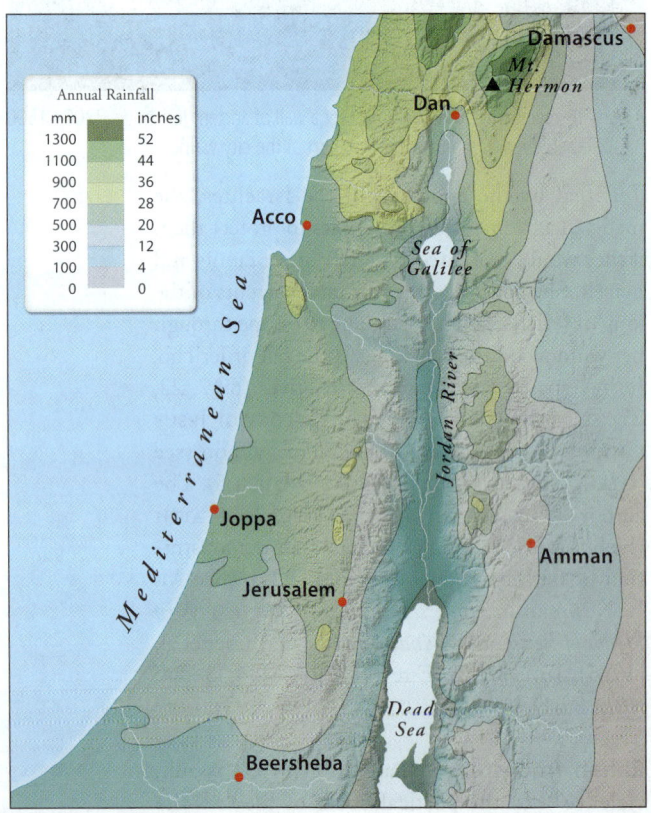

Average rainfall in ancient Palestine.

the Lord promised the Israelites that if they obeyed his commands he would send "rain [*māṭār H4764*] … in its season, the early rain [*yôreh H3453*] and the later rain [*malqôš H4919*]" so that they might have a full harvest (Deut. 11:13–14 NRSV [NIV, "both autumn and spring rains"]; cf. also Jer. 5:24; Hos. 6:3; Joel 2:23; Jas. 5:7). Also mentioned is the failure of the rains, as seen in the reference to FAMINE, an event never far from the thoughts of the inhabitants of Palestine, from the time of Abraham onward.

(See further N. Rosenau, "One Hundred Years of Rainfall in Jerusalem," *Israel Meteorological Service, Series A*, No. 13 [1955]; D. Baly, *The Geography of the Bible* [1957], chs. 4–6; G. Adam Smith, *The Historical Geography of the Holy Land*, 25th ed. [1931], 62–70; D. Elbashan, "Monthly Rainfall Isomers in Israel, 1931–1960," *Israel Journal of Earth Sciences* 15 [1966]: 1–7; J. Ben-Yoseph, "The Climate in Eretz Israel during Biblical Times," *Hebrew Studies* 26 [1985]: 225–39.)

J. H. PATERSON

rainbow. A colorful arc formed by the prismatic refraction and reflection of sunlight in raindrops or mist. Such reflections are seen as concentric circles from an aircraft but as bows or arcs from the ground. The Hebrew word *qešet H8008* (lit., "bow") in Gen. 9:1–16 has been traditionally interpreted to mean the rainbow. The rabbis added the comment that the natural phenomenon was already in evidence, but that after the flood it was denoted the sign of the COVENANT (see FLOOD, GENESIS). There is some evidence that the Akkadian term *qaštu* with the determinative *kakkab* ("star") means "bow star" and is applied in the literature to the bright star Sirius, but the terms of the covenant (Gen. 9:8–17) lend weight to the traditional meaning "rainbow." This rainbow is a characteristic of heavenly scenes (Ezek. 1:28), and the notion is repeated in Revelation, which uses the standard Greek term for "rainbow," *iris G2692* (Rev. 4:3; 10:1). W. WHITE, JR.

raisin cake. The Hebrew term *ʾăšîšâ H862* (mistakenly rendered "flagon" by the KJV) refers to cakes that were formed after the grapes had completely dried; when coated, they were imperishable. More often than not such desiccated plant stuffs were soaked in water or broth and mixed with gruel made from some cereal grain for consumption. They often were compounded with other fruits, such as FIGS and DATES, and seasoned with salts or spices. Raisin cakes were used as cultic offerings by many ancient peoples (cf. Hos. 3:1) and appear in lists of commodities from various sea ports. They are mentioned as part of an offering meal for travelers and soldiers (2 Sam. 6:19; 1 Chr. 16:3). One passage (Isa. 16:7) prophesies that the Moabites will lament for the "raisin cakes" of KIR HARESETH; it is unclear whether the verse speaks of the destruction of the town's vineyards (perhaps more specifically of the loss of an important cultic food; cf. H. Wildberger, *Isaiah 13–27* [1997], 146), or whether the prophet is playing on the word's similarity to the term for "man" (*ʾîš H408*; cf. NIV and note the parallel in Jer. 48:31, 36). Although frequently thought to be an aphrodisiac, there is only a remote allusion to this usage in the OT (Cant. 2:5).

Another Hebrew word, *ṣimmûqîm H7540*, which occurs four times (1 Sam. 25:18; 30:12; 2 Sam. 16:1; 1 Chr. 12:40), is translated as "clusters of raisins" by the KJV and other versions, but it too probably refers to raisin cakes (so NIV, NJPS; cf. *HALOT*, 3:1033). W. WHITE, JR.

Rakal ray′kuhl. TNIV form of RACAL.

Rakem ray′kim. See REKEM (PERSON) #3.

Rakkath rak′uhth (רַקַּת *H8395*, possibly "marshy bank"; cf. RAKKON). A fortified city within the tribal territory of NAPHTALI (Josh. 19:35). According to Jewish tradition, it was the place where later TIBERIAS was built, but modern scholars usually locate Rakkath a short distance NNW of Tiberias, identifying it with Khirbet el-Quneiṭireh (Tell Eqlaṭiyeh), a small ancient site on the W shore of the Sea of Galilee. Some believe that Rakkath and KARTAN are the same place. B. K. WALTKE

Rakkon rak′on (רַקּוֹן *H8378*, with definite article attached, meaning possibly "the narrow place" or "the shore" or "the marshy bank"; cf. RAKKATH). Apparently a town near JOPPA within the territory allotted to the tribe of DAN (Josh. 19:46). The location of such a town is unknown, although one proposal is Tell er-Reqqeit, c. 6 mi. N of Joppa.

According to Z. Kallai (*Historical Geography of the Bible* [1986], 370), "the Rakkon" is actually a river, to be identified with modern Nahar el-Barideh. Some scholars, however, believe the text should be emended. Instead of the words "and Me [= waters] Jarkon and Rakkon" (MT, *ûmê hayyarqôn wĕhāraqqôn*), the SEPTUAGINT reads simply "and on the west [*lit.*, from the sea] Jarkon" (*kai apo thalassēs Ierakōn*), thus omitting Rakkon altogether. It is uncertain whether the original reading is preserved by the MT (in which case the Gk. translator [or the scribe of his Hebrew scroll] omitted the word by homoeoteleuton when his eye skipped from the end of *hayyarqôn* to the end of *wĕhāraqqôn*) or by the LXX (in which case the MT's Rakkon should be interpreted as a scribal dittography or doublet of Jarkon). See also ME JARKON.

ram (animal). See SHEEP.

Ram (person) ram (רָם *H8226*, prob. "[God] is exalted"; Ἀράμ *G730*). **(1)** Son of HEZRON, descendant of JUDAH through PEREZ, and ancestor of King DAVID (Ruth 4:19; 1 Chr. 2:9–10). Ram is included in the GENEALOGY OF JESUS CHRIST (Matt. 1:3–4 [KJV and other versions, "Aram"]; Lk. 3:33 [NRSV, "Arni," following ℵ B and other MSS]).

(2) Firstborn son of JERAHMEEL and descendant of Judah (1 Chr. 2:25, 27). This Ram is apparently the nephew of #1, above (i.e., Jerahmeel's brother, 2:9).

(3) Apparently the head of a clan; ELIHU, the last speaker in the book of JOB, is described as belonging to "the family of Ram" (Job 32:2).

J. C. MOYER

ram, battering. See ARMOR, ARMS.

Rama ray'muh. KJV NT form of RAMAH.

Ramah ray'muh (רָמָה *H8230*, with the definite article attached [except Neh. 11:33, Jer. 31:15], meaning "the height" or "the hill"). A fairly common geographical name given to several towns in ancient Israel; these were usually situated on some lofty perch.

(1) In NAPHTALI. This city is mentioned once (Josh. 19:36). E. Robinson (*Biblical Researches in Palestine, Mount Sinai and Arabia Petraea*, 3 vols. [1841], 3:79) was apparently the first modern scholar to note that the name is preserved in that of the village er-Rameh, about 8 mi. WSW of Safad (present-day Zefat) and 9 mi. E of Acco. The situation of this Arab town (Christian and Druze) is topographically remarkable; it sits on the lower slope of Jebel Heider (today Har Ha'ari) near the pass that separates that mountain from the other hills in the high ridge that rises sharply from the Wadi esh-Shaghur (the Beth Kerem mentioned in rabbinic literature, e.g., *m. Middot* 3:4) to form a massive wall between Lower GALILEE on the S and Upper Galilee on the N. Thus er-Rameh stands on the natural dividing line between those two regions; it is also near the junction of the Acco-Safad road with the route leading S to NAZARETH.

The biblical context in which Ramah appears conforms to the geographical location of er-Rameh; the towns listed before Ramah are in Lower Galilee, and those that follow it are in Upper Galilee (even HAZOR, which was bound to have been more closely attached to the latter though it was in the Huleh Valley). The terms Upper and Lower Galilee are not recorded in the Bible, but the distinction is obvious in the topography; furthermore, the order of Naphtali's cities in this list certainly reflects a knowledge of the two regions. JOSEPHUS (*War* 3.3.1 §39) was well aware of that division and placed the demarcation line at the northern Beersheba, today Khirbet Abu esh-Shiba, which stands on a high hill just 3 mi. E of er-Rameh. Such a strong position would naturally be cited by the military commander of Galilee who was concerned with fortifying the strategic points. On the other hand, the rabbis, who were interested in matters of everyday life, gave as the boundary point between the two Galilees a rural center known for its market and its religious leaders, namely, Kefar Hananiah (Kefr ʿInan, a village in the valley below Beersheba, *m. Šebīʿit* 9:2).

In the village of er-Rameh, the ancient remains (including an Aram. inscription "In memory of Rabbi Eleazer son of Tedeor, who built this guest house") date to the Roman and Hellenistic periods. As for the biblical Ramah, its actual site was at Khirbet Zeitun er-Rameh, also known as Khirbet Jul, an ancient mound about 2 mi. E of er-Rameh on the S side of the Safad road. It is a typical tell

Cities named Ramah in the Promised Land.

of Iron Ages I and II, located on a rocky outcrop in the valley. The exact limits of the ancient settlement are hard to determine today since the whole area is covered by the famous olive orchards of this region. (On the inscription, cf. J. Ben-Zvi in *JPOS* 13 [1933]: 94–96; A. Marmorstein in *PEQ* no vol. [1933]: 100–101. See further Y. Aharoni, *The Settlement of the Israelite Tribes in Upper Galilee* [1957], 2, 76, 78, 81, 86; M. Avi-Yonah, *The Holy Land* [1966], 133–35.)

(2) In ASHER. The boundary description of the Asher tribe, the exact line of which is difficult to follow, apparently places the town of Ramah somewhere between Great SIDON and "the fortified city of Tyre" (Josh. 19:29). This latter place is known in nonbiblical sources by the name *Usū* (Assyrian spelling, *Ushū*) and was located at Tell Rashidiyeh, the classical *Palaityros* (Strabo, *Geogr.* 16.2.24). Therefore, this Ramah should most likely be sought in the area NW of modern TYRE, but the precise location is unknown. The oft-proposed identification with the small village of er-Ramiyeh seems out of the question because it is too far S. (See further Robinson, *Biblical Researches*, 3:64; A. Alt in *ZAW* 4 [1927]: 59–81; R. Dussaud, *Topographie historique de la Syrie antique et medievale* [1927], 11; M. Noth in *ZDPV* 58 [1935]: 185–255, esp. 222–23; Aharoni, *The Settlement of the Israelite Tribes in Upper Galilee*, 88.)

(3) In BENJAMIN (Josh. 18:25). The evidence for the identification of this town is some of the most conclusive for any site in Israel. It is clearly to be located close to BETHEL (Jdg. 4:5), the modern Beitin, on the ancient trunk road leading N from BETHLEHEM and passing to the W of JERUSALEM (19:13). Josephus (*Ant.* 8.12.3 §303–6), in discussing the events of 1 Ki. 15:16–17, places the town, which he calls *Ar[a]mathōn*), forty stades (c. 5 Rom. mi., or 4.6 Eng. mi.) from Jerusalem; whereas EUSEBIUS and JEROME put it at 6 Rom. mi. N of the Holy City (*Onomasticon*, 144.15–16; 145.13–14). Robinson noted that the name is preserved at the modern village of er-Ram, which is 5.5 mi. N of Jerusalem.

The prophetess DEBORAH exercised her authority as a judge in Israel at a place between Bethel and Ramah (Jdg. 4:5). Instead of turning in to spend the night at GIBEAH, the Levite from the hill country of Ephraim could have gone on a little way farther to Ramah (19:13). In addition to standing on the N–S highway, er-Ram is also within striking distance of the E–W road from Jerusalem via GIBEON and the descent of BETH HORON to GEZER. During the monarchy, the hostile act of BAASHA consisted in the establishment of a strong point at Ramah that could effectively block traffic to and from Jerusalem along this vital route (1 Ki. 15:17; 2 Chr. 16:1). In retaliation, ASA persuaded the Syrians to attack Israel from the N; by thus relieving pressure on the front with Judah, he was able to dismantle the fortification at Ramah and to use the building blocks for constructing two new forts of his own at GEBA and MIZPAH.

Thus the boundary between Judah and Israel was fixed at a line dissecting the former tribal inheritance of Benjamin in half (1 Ki. 15:17–22; 2 Chr. 16:2–6). The partition of Benjamin in this manner is reminiscent of the division reflected in Josh. 18:21–28, where Ramah belongs to the southernmost district. A brief oracle by Hosea against Gibeah, Ramah, and

BETH AVEN is apparently directed at Benjamin, perhaps with particular reference to this "Judahite" half of the tribe (Hos. 5:8). When one column of SENNACHERIB's army was evidently storming southward from Samaria toward Jerusalem, Ramah stood in the direct line of the Assyrian advance (Isa. 10:29). Jeremiah describes Ramah as the scene of RACHEL's weeping for her children (Jer. 31:15; cf. Matt. 2:18 [KJV, "Rama"]).

Some of Ramah's former residents were among the postexilic returnees (Ezra 2:26; Neh. 7:30; called "Kirama" [KJV, "Cirama"] in 1 Esd. 2:26). The town is also mentioned in the list of settlements (11:33), which largely pertained to places outside of the Yehud province; therefore, it might be supposed that Ramah was one of those towns in which some portion of the population had maintained a foothold during the time when the main body of Judeans were in exile. (See further Robinson, *Biblical Researches*, 1:576; H. Vincent in *RB* 16 [1907]: 410–12; W. F. Albright in AASOR 4 [1924]: 134–40; Z. Kallai-Kleimann in *VT* 8 [1958]: 134–60.)

It is most likely that Ramah of Benjamin was the birthplace of SAMUEL the prophet. The home of ELKANAH and HANNAH is called *hārāmātayim ṣôpîm* (1 Sam. 1:1), but the Hebrew construction is somewhat awkward. Since Elkanah was a descendant of ZUPH, a Levite of the Kohathites (1 Chr. 6:35) who had settled in N Benjamin (1 Sam. 9:5; cf. Josh. 21:5; 1 Chr. 6:22–26, 35, 66–70), it would appear that the correct understanding of the name in 1 Sam. 1:1 is "Ramathaim of the Zuphite(s)." The -*aim* sufformative is probably to be understood as a locative rather than a simple dual suffix (cf. GITTAIM et al.). All of the other references to Samuel's home town (except 25:1 and 28:3) happen to have the locative sufformative -*â* resulting in the form *hārāmātâ*; the SEPTUAGINT renders this name *Armathaim*, or *Armathem*, even inserting it in 1 Sam. 1:3 after "his city."

The identity of Ramathaim Zophim with Ramah is confirmed by a comparison of 1 Sam. 1:1 with 1:19 and 2:11. Although Samuel was born there, he grew up at SHILOH but returned to his home when the latter was abandoned as the religious center of Israel. At Ramah he made his headquarters, and from there he went on his annual circuit to Bethel, Gilgal, and Mizpah (1 Sam. 7:15–17). The elders of Israel came to him at Ramah when making their request for a king (8:4). It was doubtless at Ramah in "the land of Zuph" that SAUL first encountered Samuel and was secretly anointed king (9:5 — 10:10). The probable association of Rachel's tomb with Ramah in Benjamin (Jer. 31:15; Matt. 2:18; cf. Gen. 35:16–20) suits the description of Saul's homeward journey (1 Sam. 10:2–5, 10). Samuel continued to dwell at Ramah even after he had severed his relations with Saul (15:34; 16:13). Here DAVID sought refuge from Saul, whose attempts to have the renegade prince arrested were brought to naught (19:18–24). This passage also confirms the existence of a place called NAIOTH at Ramah (19:19, 22–23; 20:1), which probably represented a quarter or settlement, in this case inhabited by a band of prophets. Finally, Ramah became the last resting place of the prophet Samuel (25:1; 28:3).

Noteworthy for the identification with Ramah of Benjamin is the fact that Josephus refers to Samuel's home as *Armatha* (*Ant*. 6.3.3 §35 et al., with minor spelling variations), whereas he uses *Armathōn* in the only other context where he refers to Ramah (*Ant*. 8.12.3 §303–6; cf. above). These forms have led to the identification by Eusebius (*Onom*. 32.21–23) of Ramathaim with the NT ARIMATHEA, which he located at *Remphis* (modern Rentis in the district of Diospolis-Lod; cf. *Onom*. 144.27–29). Eusebius did not make the connection between Ramah of Benjamin and Ramathaim-Arimathea; instead he equated the latter with the Arumah (*Rouma*, ibid.) of Jdg. 9:41 (LXX *Arima* [CODEX ALEXANDRINUS], *Arēma*). Whether Arimathea is to be placed at Rentis or not, Arumah is most likely Khirbet el-ʿOrmah (5 mi. SE of SHECHEM).

Nevertheless, Eusebius's association of Ramathaim and Arimathea with Rentis is strengthened by the fact that a municipal district lying between Lydda (LOD) and APHAIREMA had the name *Ramathain* (Jos. *Ant*. 13.4.9 §127, where the MSS have such variants as *Ramatha* and *Armathaim*; 1 Macc. 11:34 reads *Rathamin*, but with the important variants *Ramathaim* and *Ramathem*). Thus it seems certain that a town called Haramatha(im) did exist at Rentis; the NT Arimathea may have been here (the late Medieval Christian tradition

This minaret tower in the modern village of er-Ram identifies the ancient site of Ramah of Benjamin, the prophet Samuel's hometown.

placing it at Ramleh is, of course, quite absurd, since the latter was only founded in A.D. 716 by Khaliph Suleiman; the name is derived from Arab. *raml*, "sand"), but the OT references to Samuel's home point rather to a site in the hill country N of Jerusalem, that is, to an identification with Ramah of Benjamin. (See further S. R. Driver, *Notes on the Hebrew Text and the Topography of the Books of Samuel* [1913], 1–4; H. W. Wiener in *JPOS* 7 [1927]: 109–11; F. M. Abel, *Géographie de la Palestine* [1938], 2:428–29.)

(4) In the NEGEV. A town mentioned in the description of SIMEON's tribal inheritance (Josh. 19:8). The MT states that the towns of Simeon and their respective villages extended "as far as Baalath Beer, Ramath Negev" (*rāʾmat negeb*; KJV, "Ramath of the south"; NIV, "Ramah in the Negev" within parentheses). The Greek MSS show some confusion in the text: CODEX ALEXANDRINUS reads, "as far as Baalath Beer Ramoth, going to Bameth towards the south," whereas CODEX VATICANUS has, "as far as Barek, going to Bameth towards the south." The SEPTUAGINT translation of the geographical term "Negev" by a directional one ("south") must be disregarded; it is more likely that the Hebrew "Ramath Negev" stands as an adverbial accusative of direction.

The verse may thus be rendered: "as far as Baalath Beer (in the direction of) Ramath Negev."

Such an interpretation obviates two conjectures previously proposed, namely, that the reference is to the S boundary of Simeon's settlement (W. F. Albright in *JPOS* 4 [1924]: 161), or that Ramath Negev should be equated with Baalath Beer (F.-M. Abel, *Géographie de la Palestine* [1938], 2:258; cf. NIV). In the parallel passage (1 Chr. 4:33), the MT has simply "as far as Baal" (some LXX MSS read *Balat* or *Balaad*); and Ramath Negev is also missing from the roster of settlements in the Negev of JUDAH (Josh. 15:21–32), which included Simeon. On the other hand, it seems likely that this town appears as Ramoth Negev (1 Sam. 30:27), one of the places to whose elders DAVID sent some of his spoil from the Amalekites. There is no indication of its locale.

One of the OSTRACA discovered in Tell ʿArad (see ARAD) raises anew the whole question of the identification and location of Ramath/Ramoth Negev. The legible portion of the text (on the reverse) reads as follows: "[…] from Arad … and from […], and you [pl.] shall send them to Ramoth [or Ramath] Negev under the command of Malchiah son of Qerabʾur and he will commit them into the charge of Jeremiah the son of Elisha in Ramoth Negev lest something should happen to the city. And the king's word is stringently incumbent upon you. Behold, I have sent to admonish you. Get the men to Elisha! Lest Edom should come there." (See Y. Aharoni in *BASOR* 197 [Feb. 1971]: 16–42.)

The epistle is obviously a memorandum from a higher authority demanding confirmation of a previous order by the king that troops be sent from Arad and some other place to Ramoth Negev. The transfer of these forces was for the purpose of warding off an impending Edomite attack (another ostracon found earlier at Tell ʿArad referred to a certain Malchiah in conjunction with Edom, the king of Judah [unnamed] and some evil that was coming upon the land; perhaps the two letters relate to the same event, but this is far from certain). The script of the Ramoth Negev ostracon dates it to the end of the Judean monarchy (i.e., it is contemporary with the LACHISH letters and the seventeen texts in the Eliashib archive found at Arad in 1964). The Edomite threat to Ramoth Negev probably corresponds to the situation depicted in Ps. 137:7 and Obad. 10–14, according to which Edom took advantage of Judah's downfall in 586 B.C. to pillage the hapless settlements in Cisjordan. Obadiah's prophetic retribution called for a reversal of this deed: "People from the Negev will occupy the mountains of Esau" (v. 19).

Current speculation about the identification of Ramoth Negev centers on Khirbet Ghazzeh (Ḥorvat ʿUza) at the eastern edge of the Negev of Judah, some 20 ESE of Beersheba, guarding a major route from Edom (Y. Aharoni, *The Land of the Bible: A Historical Geography*, rev. ed. [1979], 441; however, see Kinah); besides the casemate fortress there from Iron Age II, a certain quantity of Iron I sherds has also been found in the general vicinity (cf. I. Beit-Arieh, *Horvat ʿUza and Horvat Radum: Two Fortresses in the Biblical Negev* [2007]). On the other hand, the lofty commanding position of Khirbet Gharreh (Tel ʿIra) and its location in the center of the Negev of Judah (i.e., on the fringe of Simeon's inheritance) are strong arguments in favor of the latter's candidacy (see now Y. Aharoni et al., *The Carta Bible Atlas*, 4th ed. [2002], 216).

(5) In Gilead. The name Ramah occurs as the short form of Ramoth Gilead in one context (2 Ki. 8:29 = 2 Chr. 22:6; the NIV reads "Ramoth").

A. F. Rainey

Ramath ray′muhth. See Ramah #4; Ramath Lehi; Ramath Mizpah.

Ramathaim-zophim ram′uh-thay′im-zoh′fim. See Ramah #3.

Ramathem ram′uh-thim. KJV Apoc. variant of Rathamin (1 Macc. 11:34).

Ramathite ray′muh-thit (רָמָתִי H8258, gentilic of רָמָה H8230). A native of Ramah. David's vinedresser was known as "Shimei the Ramathite" (1 Chr. 27:27), but which of the several towns that bore this name is meant cannot be determined.

Ramath Lehi ray′muhth-lee′hi (רָמַת לֶחִי H8257, "jawbone hill"). The scene of Samson's rout of the Philistines with the jawbone of a donkey for a weapon (Jdg. 15:17). See Lehi.

Ramath Mizpeh ray′muhth-miz′puh (רָמַת הַמִּצְפֶּה H8256, "hill of the watchtower"). A town assigned to the tribe of Gad in the division of Palestine (Josh. 13:26). It is mentioned between Heshbon and Betonim when delineating the Gadite territory E of the Jordan and perhaps should be identified with Mizpah #2 (for a summary of proposals, see *ABD*, 5:617).

Rameses ram′uh-seez (רַעְמְסֵס H8314 [רַעַמְסֵס in Exod. 1:11], from Egyp. *Rʿmśś*, short form of *Pr-Rʿmśśw*, "[house of] Ramses"). KJV and other versions have Raamses once (Exod. 1:11; cf. also NJPS at 12:37). The usual orthographic distinction in English between the name of the city (Rameses or Raamses) and the name of some pharaohs (Ramesses or Ramses) has no basis in the Egyptian language. According to Gen 47:11, Jacob and his sons were given "property in the best part of the land, the district of Rameses," apparently a term equivalent to "the region of Goshen" (45:10 et al.; see Goshen), where the city of Rameses was located. Rameses and Pithom are named as the store cities that the Hebrews built (Exod. 11:1), and it was from Rameses that they began their journey out of Egypt (12:37; Num. 33:3, 5).

Rameses (Pi-Ramessē or Per-Ramesses) was the residence city of the 19th and 20th Egyptian dynasties in the NE Nile delta. Its location has been much debated: some place it at Tanis (Zoan, S of Lake Menzaleh) and others c. 17 mi. farther S near Qantir (Tell el-Dabʿa, site of the earlier Hyksos capital, Avaris). Tanis was advocated by its

A portion of the granary excavation at Tell el-Dabʿa. This site should probably be identified with Rameses (Pi-Ramessē), the city built by the Israelites during their captivity in Egypt.

excavator P. Montet (in *RB* 39 [1930]: 5–28) and by A. H. Gardiner (in *JEA* 19 [1933]: 122–28), mainly on the sheer quantity of monuments of Ramses II found there (blocks, columns, statues, stelae, obelisks); if this was not Pi-Ramessē, what was it called in that period?

The case for Qantir was proposed by M. Hamza on the basis of vineyard OSTRACA found there that include the name Pi-Ramessē (*Annales du Service des Antiquités de l'Égypte* 30 [1930]: 31–68). Subsequently, L. Habachi assembled from the Qantir district a whole series of doorways from houses of officials of Ramses II and III, and showed that the "Horbeit stelae" actually originated from Qantir, where it witnessed to a garrison and cult of Ramses II (ibid., 52 [1954]: 443–47, 500, 510–14, 545–59). Then S. Adam excavated the remains of a colossus of Ramses II, appropriate to a major temple there (ibid., 55 [1958]: 318–24). Thus, like Tanis, Qantir has Ramesside remains of considerable importance, but (unlike Tanis) it has never been fully excavated.

Several factors clearly favor Qantir as the probable site of Rameses. First, nothing of Ramesside (or earlier) date at Tanis was found *in situ*—all was reused by later kings (L. Habachi, private communication; J. van Seters, *The Hyksos* [1966], 129–31). Neither palaces nor tombs were found, in contrast to Qantir, whence came a tiled palace-doorway of Sethos I (now in the Louvre), and similar tiles of Ramses II. Second, Pi-Ramessē was situated on the Waters of Ra, that is, the Bubastite-Pelusiac (old eastern) arm of the Nile, navigable from the sea—true of Qantir in antiquity, but not of Tanis. Third, the fertility of the Rameses region indicated in contemporary papyri (e.g., *ANET*, 471) agrees well with Qantir but not with the salt flats of Tanis. Fourth, Pi-Ramessē and Tanis occur as separate entities (##410 and 417) in the Onomasticon list (A. H. Gardiner, *Ancient Egyptian Onomastica*, 2 [1947], 171*ff., 199*ff.), which does not favor identifying them. Fifth, Rameses was at the head of the main route to Palestine via Sile (near modern Qantara), fitting Qantir but not Tanis. Sixth, Qantir as Rameses agrees better with other requirements of the route of the exodus, such as SUCCOTH (see EXODUS, THE). This identification is now generally accepted (cf. E. P. Uphill, *The Temples of Per Ramesses* [1984]; M. Bietak, *Avaris, the Capital of the Hyksos: Recent Excavations at Tell el-Dabʿa* [1996]). K. A. KITCHEN

Ramesses ram´uh-seez. See RAMSES.

Ramiah ruh-mi´uh (רְמִיָה *H8243*, "Yahweh is exalted"). One of the descendants of PAROSH who agreed to put away their foreign wives (Ezra 10:25).

Ramoth (person) ray´moth (רָמוֹת *H8238* [not in NIV], possibly "heights"). One of the descendants of BANI who agreed to put away their foreign wives (Ezra 10:29 KJV, following the *Qere*; NIV and other versions follow the *Ketib*, JERAMOTH).

Ramoth (place) ray´moth (רָאמוֹת *H8030*, "heights"). (1) Short form of RAMOTH GILEAD (Deut. 4:43; Josh. 20:8; 21:38; 1 Chr. 6:80 [Heb. 6:65]).

(2) A city in the NEGEV to which DAVID sent gifts after his devastating attack upon the camp of the Amalekites (1 Sam. 30:27).

(3) A town within the tribal territory of ISSACHAR that was designated a Levitical city for the

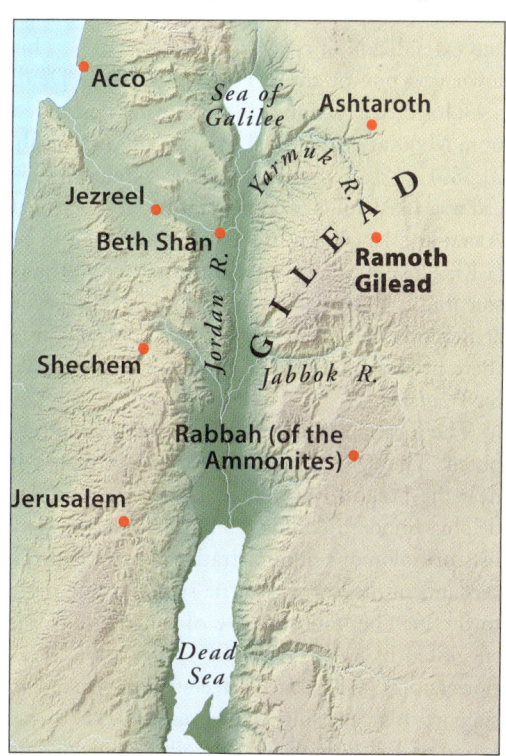

Ramoth Gilead.

descendants of GERSHON (Gershom, 1 Chr. 6:73). It is doubtless the same as JARMUTH (Josh. 21:29) because it occupies the same position in the list of Levitical cities and there are many other discrepancies between the two rosters (cf. Y. Aharoni, *The Land of the Bible: A Historical Geography*, rev. ed. [1979], 301–5). Moreover, Ramoth is probably the same as REMETH (Josh. 19:21). A stela of Seti I (1309–1290) states that the ʿApiru (see HABIRU) from Mount Yarmuta had attacked the Asiatics (*ANET*, 255). Mount Yarmuta is doubtless to be associated with Jarmuth-Remeth-Ramoth of Issachar, that is, in the elevated region NW of BETH SHAN. Thus the form Jarmuth is probably more original than Ramoth. W. F. Albright (in *ZAW* 44 [1926]: 231) suggested as the site Kaukab el-Hawa, the Crusading Belvoir, located some 6 mi. NNE of Beth Shan on a plateau 999 ft. above sea level in a region of springs. B. K. WALTKE

Ramoth Gilead rayʹmuhth-gilʹee-uhd (רָמוֹת גִּלְעָד H8240, "heights of GILEAD"). Under Solomon's administration Ramoth Gilead was designated as the center of the district that was E of the Jordan and extended N of the Yarmuk (1 Ki. 4:13). This town was one of the CITIES OF REFUGE (Deut. 4:43; Josh. 20:8) assigned to the Levites descended from MERARI in the tribal territory of GAD (Josh. 21:38; 1 Chr. 6:80). A frontier town, Ramoth Gilead was a key military outpost in the wars between ARAM and Israel; AHAB was killed in battle there (1 Ki. 22:3–40; 2 Chr. 18). Some time later, Ahab's son Joram (JEHORAM) was wounded in a battle at Ramoth Gilead, then JEHU was anointed king there by one of ELISHA's young prophets (2 Ki. 8:28—9:14).

The location of Ramoth Gilead has been disputed. The *Onomasticon* of EUSEBIUS places it near the JABBOK River some 15 mi. W of Philadelphia (modern Amman, biblical RABBAH). The lists of Solomon's administrative centers and the accounts of the war with Syria suggest a site more to the N. The imposing site of Ḥuṣn Ajlun was suggested by W. F. Albright as a possible location, and N. Glueck's surface studies seemed to support this possibility. However, the 1967 excavation of Tell Ramith (er-Rumeith) conducted by P. Lapp uncovered evidence that provides a strong case for the identification of this site with Ramoth Gilead. Ramith is c. 17 mi. NE of JABESH GILEAD, 8 mi. SE of BETH ARBEL, and 3 mi. S of modern Ramtha. The continuity of the name and the geographic location have been noted as significant. The parallels between the literary record and the occupational history (as determined by excavated architectural evidence and artifacts) support the view that Ramith corresponds with Ramoth Gilead. This identification is now generally accepted. (See *NEAEHL*, 4:1291–93.) H. JAMIESON

rampart. This English term is used occasionally in Bible versions, primarily to render Hebrew ḥêl H2658 (from a root meaning "to go around"). It is used of the bulwarks surrounding Zion (Ps. 48:13), and figuratively of the sea as a physical barrier protecting Thebes (Nah. 3:8 NRSV; NIV, "defense"). It is used also of a moat referring to both the walls and the water-filled ditch at Beth Maacah (2 Sam. 20:15 NRSV; NIV, "fortifications"). The northern side of ancient Jerusalem above the Valley of HINNON was protected by such a wall (Lam. 2:8). Most of these walls, as at Jericho, were built up of tamped earth and in later periods faced with stone blocks.

W. WHITE, JR.

Ramses ramʹseez (Egyptian *Rʿ-ms-sw*, meaning "Re is the one who created him"; cf. RAMESES). Also Ramesses. The name of eleven PHARAOHS of EGYPT; it was also the epithet of two others.

I. Nineteenth dynasty

A. Ramses I. Founder of the 19th dynasty, from N Egypt and from a military family. Elderly at accession, he reigned only sixteen months and was notable as the father of the redoubtable Sethos I.

B. Ramses II. Reigned sixty-six years (either 1304–1238 or 1290–1224 B.C.). Son of Sethos I and Queen Mut-tuy, both of military background (cf. G. A. Gaballa and K. A. Kitchen, *Chronique d'Égypte* 43/85 [1968]); and like Queen Hatshepsut and Amenophis III, he used the myth of the divine birth of Pharaoh to emphasize the legitimacy of his kingship (cf. G. A. Gaballa, *Orientalia* 36 [1967]: 299–304, plates 63–65).

Ramses II battled long against the HITTITES in SYRIA. In his fourth year, he probably weaned the kingdom of Amurru from their sway. In year 5, he marched against KADESH ON THE ORONTES straight into a Hittite trap, but extricated himself by remarkable personal valor and the timely arrival of auxiliaries. The famous battle received epic treatment in scenes and texts on temple walls; politically, it was a setback, but it was redeemed by Ramses' personal heroism and by his subsequent campaigns (years 8, 10, etc.). His conquests also extended into SEIR and MOAB, including Dibon and (Raba)-Batora(?). The Hittites faced threats from Assyria and elsewhere, and both powers tired of the conflict. So, in his year 21, Ramses II sagely made peace with Hattusil III by a treaty of alliance faithfully honored thereafter (cf. *ANET*, 199–203). The peace was cemented by Ramses' marrying in year 34 a daughter of Hattusil, and still later a second Hittite princess. (See further J. A. Breasted, *Ancient Records of Egypt: Historical Documents from the Earliest Times to the Persian Conquest*, 5 vols. [1906–7], 3, §§410, 415–24, 427–28; K. A. Kitchen in *JEA* 50 [1964]: 68–69, and 52 [1966]: 47–70.)

In sheer quantity, the buildings of Ramses II surpass those of all other pharaohs. Suffice it to recall his ambitious capital on the NILE delta, Pi-Ramessē (biblical RAMESES), his completing the vast Hypostyle Hall (134 columns, nave 80 ft. high) at THEBES in the Karnak temple of the god Amun (see AMON #4), the erection of the Ramesseum, his funerary temple containing a 1,000-ton colossus (Shelley's Ozymandias), on the Theban W bank, and finally in Nubia the two spectacular rock temples at Abu Simbel (in modern times moved piecemeal to safety because of the new Nile high dam; see M. Peters-Destéract, *Abou Simbel, à la gloire de Ramsès* [2003]). Internally, Ramses' reign was an era of peace and considerable prosperity; the impact of his image on later Egypt may be judged from the adoption of his name by almost a dozen later kings. On the intellectual plane, literature flourished; besides stories, love lyrics, and the Kadesh battle poem, one may note the Satirical Letter (Papyrus Anastasi I) showing its author's knowledge of Canaan (*ANET*, 475–79). Ramses II may have been the pharaoh of the exodus; his proud self-confidence would fit the king of Exod. 5–12 (see EXODUS, THE). (See further K. A. Kitchen, *Pharaoh Triumphant: The Life and Times of Ramesses II, King of Egypt* [1983]; C. Lalouette, *L'empire des Ramsès* [1985]; C. Jacq, *Ramsès*, 2 vols. [1998]; J. A. Tyldesley, *Ramesses: Egypt's Greatest Pharaoh* [2000]; C. Lalouette, *Le monde des Ramsès* [2002]; M. Van de Mieroop, *The Eastern Mediterranean in the Age of Ramesses II* [2007].)

C. Ramses-Siptah. This pharaoh, who changed his name to Merenptah-Siptah, reigned six years at the end of the dynasty and died young. Powers behind his throne were the dowager queen Tewosret and the chancellor Bay (of Syrian origin, with the powers of a Joseph; see A. H. Gardiner in *JEA* 44 [1958]: 12–22).

II. Twentieth dynasty

A. Ramses III. Son of Setnakht, who founded the dynasty. Ramses III reigned thirty-one years and fought three epic battles to deliver Egypt from threats of invasion. In year 5, he fended off the Libyans, but indecisively. In year 8, he fought a remarkable amphibious action in S Palestine and the E delta mouths against the SEA PEOPLES including the PHILISTINES, repulsing their army and destroying their fleet. In year 11, he finally defeated the Libyans more effectively. He also found occasion to fight in EDOM (Seir, cf. *ANET*, 262a). At first, as the last great pharaoh of the empire, he outwardly maintained its façade. The end of his reign saw the onset of internal administrative decay that grew

This limestone colossus of Ramses II at the Memphis museum in Egypt is over 40 ft. long.

apace under his successors, and his closing years were marred by an attempted assassination. This king consciously modeled himself on Ramses II, for example, in style of titulary, and even in the names of his sons. The most important building of this reign was his great funerary temple in W Thebes (Medinet Habu, superbly published by the Oriental Institute in Chicago as *Medinet Habu*, 8 vols. [1930–70], and *The Excavation of Medinet Habu*,

Inside the entry hall of the tomb of Ramses III, in the Valley of the Kings.

5 vols. [1934–54]; outline reports in *Oriental Institute Communications*, nos. 5, 7, 10, 15, 18; historical texts are translated by W. F. Edgerton and J. A. Wilson, *Historical Records of Ramses III* [1936]).

B. Ramses IV. This pharaoh reigned only six years, though according to a famous stela from Abydos he had prayed for a reign of sixty-seven years like Ramses II. He compiled a list of his father Ramses III's benefactions to Egypt's temples to support his succession; the Papyrus Harris is the longest Egyptian papyrus known (135 ft. long; translated in Breasted, *Ancient Records*, 4, §§151ff.).

C. Ramses V. Son of Ramses IV; he reigned only four years, dying of smallpox while still but a youth. His reign is famed for the vast Papyrus Wilbour, part of a land-survey of Middle Egypt, a document of immense value for study of administration and institutions (A. H. Gardiner, *The Wilbour Papyrus*, 4 vols. [1941–52]).

D. Ramses VI. Reigned at least seven years; he took over and completed his nephew Ramses V's tomb in the Theban Valley of Kings with important funerary texts.

E. Ramses VII. Reigned seven years; whether he preceded or succeeded the next king is uncertain.

F. Ramses VIII. An ephemeral ruler who reigned only three years.

G. Ramses IX. Reigned eighteen years. The high-priesthood of Amun at Thebes was ruled by one powerful family; administration was now so lax that even the tombs of the pharaohs themselves were being robbed. Jealousy between the mayors of E and W Thebes brought the scandal to light, leading to a royal commission reported on in a remarkable series of tomb-robbery papyri (see T. E. Peet, *The Great Tomb-Robberies of the Twentieth Dynasty*, 2 vols. [1930]; J. Capart et al. in *JEA* 22 [1936]: 169–93).

H. Ramses X. Of this reign of nine years, hardly anything is known.

I. Ramses XI. Last of his line, Ramses XI reigned at least twenty-seven years. The state was troubled by Libyan marauders and by civil war involving the viceroy of Nubia and perhaps the death or exile of a high priest of Amun of Thebes. The acute weakness of the state was outwardly resolved by appointing two high officials under the king, one each for Upper and Lower Egypt. This was marked by a new era and year count from year 19, the so-called "Renaissance." In the S, one Herihor was army commander, high priest of Amun and vizier; he aspired to royal rank but achieved it only in name. His descendants became hereditary high priests of Amun, a state within the state, during the 21st dynasty, which partly explains Egypt's quiescence in foreign affairs early in the Hebrew monarchy. In the N, one Smendes was ruler and succeeded Ramses XI as king, to found the 21st dynasty, having (it seems) married a Ramesside princess.

III. Twenty-first dynasty and after. Psusennes I, c. 1040 B.C., occasionally adopted the double name Ramses-Psusennes, to stress his link (through Smendes) with the Ramessides, and so his legitimacy of rule. His successors were the contemporaries of DAVID and SOLOMON. The title "King's Son of Ramses" was a high honorific title in this and the two following dynasties. (For this period, cf. K. A. Kitchen, *The Third Intermediate Period in Egypt, 1100–650 B.C.*, 2nd ed. [1986]. For general works on the Ramessides, see W. C. Hayes, *Scepter of Egypt*, 2 [1959]; W. Helck, *Beziehungen Aegyptens zu Vorderasien* [1962]; K. A. Kitchen, *Ramesside Inscriptions Translated and Annotated: Notes and Comments* [1994–]; *SacBr*, 91–99.)   K. A. KITCHEN

ram's horn. See MUSIC, MUSICAL INSTRUMENTS IV.C.

rams' skins. The tanned skins of rams (Heb. ʿōrōt ʾēlim *H6425* + *H380*), dyed red, were used as the third of four coverings over the TABERNACLE proper (Exod. 25:5; 26:14; 35:7, 23; 36:19; 39:34). Sheep skin, tanned with oil, is used today by Middle Eastern shepherds. It gives good protection against wind and rain. Syrians still dye rams' skins red, rubbing the tanned skin with a red dye solution. From it colorful shoes and saddles are made.   L. J. WOOD

ransom. As a verb, this English term means "to free someone by paying a price," and it is used in modern Bible versions primarily to render Hebrew *pādâ H7009*, "to buy out, deliver" (Lev. 19:20 et al.; KJV, "redeem"). As a noun, *ransom* refers to "that which is paid for someone's release," and it translates both Hebrew *kōper H4111* (Exod. 30:12 et al.; cf. the cognate verb *kāpar H4105* piel, "to cover") and Greek *lytron G3389* (Matt. 20:2; Mk. 10:4; cf. cognates in 1 Tim. 2:6; Heb. 9:15). See ATONEMENT; DELIVER; EXPIATION; REDEMPTION.

rape. See CRIMES AND PUNISHMENTS I.B.4.

Rapha ray′fuh (רָפָא *H8325*, prob. "[God] has healed"; cf. REPHAEL). **(1)** Fifth son of BENJAMIN and grandson of JACOB (1 Chr. 8:2). However, the parallel lists of Benjamin's sons (Gen. 46:21; Num. 26:38–40; 1 Chr. 7:6) omit mention of Rapha altogether. See discussion under NOHAH #1.

(2) See BETH RAPHA.

(3) A different form of the Hebrew word (*rāpâ H8335*, always with the definite article attached, 2 Sam. 21:16–22; 1 Chr. 20:6, 8) is rendered "Rapha" in the NIV (NJPS, "the Rapha"), but "giants" in the NRSV and other versions. See REPHAITES.

Raphael raf′ay-uhl (Ραφαηλ, from Heb. רְפָאֵל *H8330*, "God has healed"; see REPHAEL). **(1)** Son of Raguel and ancestor of TOBIT (Tob. 1:1 NRSV, following CODEX SINAITICUS).

(2) The name of an ANGEL that figures prominently in the book of Tobit (Tob. 3:17 et al.). Near the end of the book, Raphael identifies himself as "one of the seven angels who stand ready and enter before the glory of the Lord" (Tob. 12:15 NRSV; the RSV, following other MSS, reads, "who present the prayers of the saints and enter into the presence of the glory of the Holy One"). In the same passage, he says to Tobit, "… when you and Sarah prayed, it was I who brought and read the record of your prayer before the glory of the Lord.… I was sent to you to test you. And at the same time God sent me to heal you and Sarah your daughter-in-law" (vv. 12, 14). Raphael thus served as a guardian angel for Tobit, protecting him from death for burying Jews who had been massacred in Nineveh, and acting as his traveling companion in his journey from Nineveh to Ecbatana. Raphael's chief function, however, was as a healer (note the meaning of his name). He cured the blindness of Tobit and expelled the demon from Sarah, the woman who later married Tobit's son Tobias.

In *1 Enoch* 20, there is a description of seven angels (six, according to the Ethiopic MSS). Earlier in that book, Raphael and MICHAEL are commissioned to punish the fallen angels who had married human wives in the time of Noah. Raphael was told to bind Azazal hand and foot and throw him into a pit (*1 En.* 10.4; cf. 2 Pet. 2:4). Even in this mission, however, Raphael is acting as a healer, for the purpose of this action was that he might heal the earth that had been defiled by these evil angels. According to the *Book of Noah*, a treatise on medicine mentioned in the Jewish midrashim, men were afflicted with various diseases after the flood, and God sent Raphael to disclose to Noah the use of curative plants and roots to heal them. Another Jewish tradition names Raphael as the third of the angels who appeared to Abraham (Gen. 18:2–22). Raphael imparted to Sarah the strength to conceive even though she was past the age of childbearing.

He is not mentioned in the canonical books of the Bible. (See *DDD*, 688.) G. H. WATERMAN

Raphah ray´fuh (רָפָה *H8334*, prob. "[Yahweh] has healed"). Son of Binea and descendant of SAUL through JONATHAN (1 Chr. 8:37); called REPHAIAH in the parallel genealogy (9:43; see *ABD*, 5:621–22). J. C. MOYER

Raphaim raf´ay-im. See RAPHAIN.

Raphain raf´ay-in (Ραφαιν). KJV Raphaim. Son of Ahitub and ancestor of JUDITH (Jdt. 8:1).

Raphia ruh-fi´uh (Ραφία). A city on the frontier between Egypt and Palestine, about 20 mi. SW of GAZA. It was in this area that PTOLEMY IV clashed with ANTIOCHUS III (3 Macc. 1:1). Because of its strategic location, Raphia is mentioned frequently in extrabiblical documents (cf. *ABD*, 5:622).

Raphon ray´fon (Ραφων). A city in GILEAD near which the Gentile leader Timothy gathered a new army after being routed by Judas MACCABEE (1 Macc. 5:37). By crossing the ravine to encounter the enemy on the bank opposite the city, however, the Jews again routed the Gentiles. Raphon is apparently included in THUTMOSE III's list of conquered cities (#29; see Y. Aharoni, *The Land of the Bible: A Historical Geography*, rev. ed. [1979], 160). It is identified with modern er-Rafeh, on the right bank of the Nahr el-Ehreir, c. 8 mi. NE of KARNAIM. B. K. WALTKE

Raphu ray´fyoo (רָפוּא *H8336*, "healed"). Father of PALTI; the latter was one of the spies sent out by Moses (Num. 13:9).

rapture. See SECOND COMING VIII; TRIBULATION.

Rasses ras´eez. KJV Apoc. form of RASSIS (Jdt. 2:23).

Ras Shamra rahs shahm´ruh. The name of a Syrian mound, about 7 mi. N of Laodicea ad Mare on the Syrian coast. At this mound, beginning in 1929, archaeological finds were made that have been of enormous value for the study of Phoenician and Canaanite religion, inaugurating a new era in OT research. See UGARIT.

Rassis ras´is (Ρασσις). KJV Rasses. A place whose people were destroyed by the army of HOLOFERNES (Jdt. 2:23; instead of "the people of Rassis," the NRSV translates, "the Rassisites"). Its location is unknown, but the context in Judith would indicate the region of CILICIA. The Latin VULGATE reads Tharsis, which (if not a textual corruption of Rassis) may be the Cilician city of TARSUS. Some scholars think that Rassis is the same as Rossos, a place mentioned by Strabo (*Geogr.* 14.5.19; 16.2.8) and Ptolemy (*Geogr.* 5.14); if so, the reference may be to the modern Mount Arsus in Cilicia, near the site of Issus, where ALEXANDER THE GREAT defeated Darius III. J. C. MOYER

Rassisite ras´i-sit. See RASSIS.

rat. See MOUSE.

Rathamin rath´uh-min (Ραθαμιν). KJV Ramathem. A governmental district that, along with Lydda (LOD) and APHAIREMA, was transferred by DEMETRIUS II of Syria from SAMARIA to JUDAH (1 Macc. 11:34). The name is generally considered to have suffered metathesis in the SEPTUAGINT to a form more natural in Greek (Jos. *Ant.* 13.4.9 §127 spells it *Rhamatēain* [the MSS have orthographic variants]). Most scholars equate Rathamin with Ramathaim, SAMUEL's birthplace. See RAMAH #3. J. LILLEY

Rathumus ruh-thyoo´muhs. KJV Apoc. form of REHUM (1 Esd. 2:16–17 et al.).

raven. The rendering "raven" (family *Corvidae*) for Hebrew *ʿōrēb H6854* (Gen. 8:7 et al.) and Greek *korax G3165* (only Lk. 12:24) is not in doubt and it is amply confirmed by several contexts (e.g., the black color, Cant. 5:11; the reference to eyes being "pecked out by the ravens," Prov. 30:17). Palestine has six members of the crow family—raven, fantailed raven, hooded crow, and jay, which are all resident; and rook and jackdaw, which are winter visitors, though a colony of the latter stays to nest in a partly man-made cave in the S Judean hills. The

English practice is to use *crow* as a general word for the family, but in particular for the (carrion) crow. This principle seems to apply also to these Hebrew and Greek words, though the brightly colored jay is so different that this is probably excepted.

The true raven is found in suitable places over the northern half of the northern hemisphere. It is a heavy, powerful bird about 25 in. long with a massive 3-in. beak that could easily knock an eye out. The large, untidy nest is usually placed on a rock ledge but sometimes in a tree. The fan-tailed raven, of the rocky gorges, has a shorter tail and is about 18 in. long (i.e., about the same as the hooded crow). Almost any animal food, dead, dying, or weak, is acceptable, which explains why the raven that Noah released had no need to return to the ark (Gen. 8:7). The raven family is logically included in the lists of unclean food (G. R. Driver in *PEQ* no vol. [1955]: 5–20). Yet God used some of them, perhaps hooded crows that are fond of storing food, to bring supplies to Elijah (1 Ki. 17:4, 6). The raven is often seen and its deep "pruk pruk" heard, but the commonest of the crows today is the hooded, which haunts roadsides, waiting to pick any small animals knocked down or run over by cars. (See *FFB*, 69–70.) G. S. Cansdale

Razis ray′zis (Ραζίς). An elder of Jerusalem, highly regarded by the Jews for his exemplary life, who was accused before the Syrian general Nicanor as an opponent of Hellenism, and committed suicide in a gory manner rather than allow himself to be arrested (2 Macc. 14:37–46). (See discussion in *ABD*, 5:623–24.)

razor. A sharp-edged cutting instrument for cutting and shaving the hair or beard; referred to in the OT especially in connection with the Nazirite vow (Heb. *taʿar* H9509 in Num. 6:5; 8:7; Isa. 7:20; Ezek. 5:1; *môrâ* H4623 in Jdg. 13:5; 16:17; 1 Sam. 1:11). The word is also used metaphorically of the tongue (Ps. 52:2). Razors were made of metal, and were simply or elaborately made. Many specimens have survived from antiquity. See also knife. S. Barabas

Re ray (Egyp. *Reʿ*, meaning "sun"). Also *Ra*. The principal sun god of ancient Egypt, shown as a man with falcon's head, wearing the sun's disc. In very early times, Re was identified with the creator

This bronze statue of Sekhmet, Egyptian goddess of war, depicts her with the head of a lioness; the sun disk on top symbolizes the god Re.

god Atum of Heliopolis (see *DDD*, 119–19) and became chief deity there. He is commonly referred to as Re-Harakhte, "Re-Horus of the Horizon," as the morning sun in the eastern horizon.

Re first had royal patronage in the 2nd dynasty, and reached greatest prominence with the pyramid builders of the 4th and 5th dynasties (c. 2600–2400 B.C.), when the kings first called themselves "Son of Re"; thereafter, the funerary god Osiris grew in prominence. The universal claims of Re and influence of Heliopolitan theology led to combinations with other deities: Amen-Re, Sobk-Re, etc. In the 18th dynasty, Akhenaten made the sun god—manifest in the solar disc as Aten—sole god of Egypt, but thereafter (19th and 20th dynasties) Amun of Thebes (see Amon #4), Re, and Ptah of Memphis formed a trio and could be conceived of as three aspects of a single deity. Re appears in the OT only in the name of Joseph's father-in-law, Potiphera the priest of On (Heliopolis). (See *DDD*, 689–92.) K. A. Kitchen

reader-response criticism. See interpretation II.G.

Reaiah ree-ay´yuh (רְאָיָה H8025, "Yahweh has seen"). **(1)** Son of Shobal and descendant of Judah (1 Chr. 4:2).

(2) Son of Micah and descendant of Reuben (1 Chr. 5:5; KJV, "Reaia").

(3) Ancestor of a family of temple servants (Nethinim) who returned with Zerubbabel from exile in Babylon (Ezra 2:47; Neh. 7:50; apparently called "Jairus" in 1 Esd. 5:31 [KJV, "Airus"]). J. C. Moyer

reaping. The act of cutting or gathering the produce of the fields, usually in the late summer. In Bible times, as in primitive areas today, reapers cut the grain with a sickle or pulled it up by the roots. In Leviticus, there is legislation regarding reaping. The people were to leave the corners of the field for the poor to reap (Lev. 19:9; 23:22). In the seventh and fiftieth years, they were to reap none at all.

Sowing and reaping served to illustrate investment and reward. As an example, Prov. 22:8 has, "He who sows wickedness reaps trouble." Somewhat the opposite is in Ps. 126:5, "Those who sow

Reaping by hand in the fields near Bethlehem, a task still being performed in modern times.

in tears reap with songs of joy." A different figure is used in the book of Revelation, "So the one who was seated on the cloud swung his sickle over the earth, and the earth was reaped" (Rev. 14:16). See agriculture; harvest. R. L. Alden

reason. The concept of reason has taken on a life of its own in the history of ideas, particularly in the West. In some cases it has come to mean proper use of the laws of logic. In others it means the primacy of the head over the heart or other faculties—"Please be reasonable," as the saying goes. In still others it has come to refer to an area of human competency beyond which one must have faith. However, none of these notions is quite compatible with the Bible's emphasis. Admittedly, there is no single, all-inclusive biblical definition of reason. This is partly because the writers of Scripture do not distinguish between the different human faculties with the same kind of precision as modern anthropology might do. Various Hebrew and Greek words interface with our term *reason*. Still, there is a field of purported subject matter which characteristically belongs to the biblical concept of reason.

That field can best be broken down into the source and the function. The ultimate source for reason is God. Taking reason to refer to knowledge and wisdom, it can be considered an attribute of God, one which he graciously reveals to human beings. Job 12:13 puts it succinctly: "To God belong wisdom and power; / counsel and understanding are his." It is God himself, through his Spirit, who gives true wisdom to human beings (Job 32:8; Jas.

3:17). By contrast, Job "darkens my counsel with words without knowledge" (Job 38:2). Or, taking reason to refer to well articulated words, then again God is the source. The second person of the TRINITY is identified as the LOGOS by John (Jn. 1:1; Rev. 19:13). Christ, come in the flesh, is the embodiment of the WORD. What is it he was personifying? In the OT the "word of the Lord" was often the speech uttered by prophets (Hos. 1:1; Joel 1:1). That word was powerful. Isaiah 55:11 compares the word to the rain and snow from heaven: they will not return without accomplishing their purposes.

Christ also personifies wisdom. True wisdom, incarnate in him who is greater than SOLOMON, is here in the world. To delight in it is the way of salvation, but to refuse it is to bask in folly (Lk. 7:35; 12:42; cf. Prov. 8:22–23, 31–36 with Jn. 1:3–13). It was Christ himself who opened the minds of the disciples so they could understand the Scriptures (Lk. 24:45). The wisdom of the mature can be obtained only from the source of the gospel, the God who sent his Son and now makes his REVELATION known through his HOLY SPIRIT. It is given freely, by grace, and none of the "rulers of this age" can generate it (1 Cor. 2:6–14; cf. Eph 1:17). What does this wisdom enable persons with the Holy Spirit to do? To have the mind of Christ, and thus make judgments about all things, without being the slaves of false wisdom (vv. 15–16). PAUL writes to TIMOTHY that the Lord will give him insight into all that he is saying in the inspired text (2 Tim. 2:7).

The function of reason involves several overlapping concepts. Reason can simply refer to the cause or the explanation for a state of affairs. For example, the *reason* the years of abundance would be forgotten is that the famine was so severe during Joseph's time (Gen. 41:31; cf. 47:13). Or, again, the *reason* the PHARISEES did not hear what Jesus was saying is that they did not belong to God (Jn. 9:47). Similarly, it can refer to the grounds for an action. Paul tells the Romans the *reason* God gave sinners over to their shameful lusts is that they exchanged the truth of God for a lie (Rom. 1:26).

But *reason* more especially refers to the capacity to make judgments and connections. At the divine level, it means that God is a thinking God, and that his arguments are sound. As a result, his word is truth (Jn. 17:17). Human beings are meant to live in conformity to that truth. For example, JAMES asks, rhetorically, "do you suppose it is to no purpose [*lit.*, in vain; NIV, without reason] that the Scripture says, 'He yearns jealously …?'" (Jas. 4:5 ESV). And he answers that we should submit ourselves to God (v. 7), adding that God alone is the judge and lawgiver. "When you judge the law, you are not keeping it, but sitting in judgment on it" (4:11). Another way of putting this is, we should think God's thoughts after him (as the astronomer Johannes Kepler is said to have expressed it). Our thinking is not original but derivative.

At one level, reasoning means simply to be in possession of one's rational faculties. For example, after a period of insanity, NEBUCHADNEZZAR's ability to think rationally was restored (Dan. 4:34, 36). The demon-possessed man, once healed, was at Jesus' feet, "dressed and in his right mind" (Lk. 8:35). And yet, at another level, reasoning in the Bible is almost never simply descriptive, but is also prescriptive. It almost always implies an ability to make sound judgments. To reason means to judge correctly, according to God's standards. One way of describing those norms is in terms of maturity. For example, Paul compares his present rational process to that of his childhood. He used to reason (*logizomai G3357*) like a child, but now he is an adult, and so has put away childish ways (1 Cor. 13:11). Another way of describing rational norms is in terms of coherence. To the Romans Paul describes the sacrificial service of believers to the Lord as "spiritual [reasonable] worship" (Rom. 12:1). The idea seems to be a systematic or whole-souled dedication. There is always a moral character in human reasoning, which is the reflection of God's standards. Rationality is never a neutral mechanism. It comes in a context, which means it can be faithful or sinful. Thus it is proper to refer to what theologians have called the "noetic effects of sin" (cf. Rom. 1:21, 28; Eph. 2:3).

Several words derived from *logos G3364* have a legal or contentious connotation. For example, PETER tells his readers to be ready to present a defense (*apologia G665*) when someone asks what is the reason (*logos*) for the hope they possess (1 Pet. 3:15). We derive our term APOLOGETICS from this. Presenting a reasonable case for our faith means arguing properly, giving sound reasons for belief.

The OT background for this concept is in the many occasions where terms like *hôkiaḥ* (hiph. of *yākaḥ* H3519, "argue, rebuke," etc.) are used for a prosecution. Job wishes he could "argue his case" with God (Job 13:3, 6). One of the most celebrated texts about the mercy of God in the prophetic literature begins, "'Come now, let us reason together,' says the Lord" (Isa. 1:18; in this verse the niphal of the verb is used). The idea here is of turning a legal dispute against Israel, which God would surely win, into a message of acquittal. Here, again, reasoning properly is making judgments according to God's standards.

In all these cases human reasoning is limited. Paul praises God as the one "who is able to do immeasurably more than all we ask or imagine" (Eph. 3:20). The contrast here is not between reason and FAITH, a dubious distinction and one that has troubled the church for many centuries. Faith is not a human power that rises above the rational. The contrast is between our limited power to imagine or predict and the far greater power of God to accomplish his great purposes. Similarly, when the apostle promises the Philippians that "the peace of God, which transcends all understanding, will guard your hearts and your minds in Christ Jesus" (Phil. 4:7), he is not comparing a heavenly feeling of peace to an earthly rationality. Rather, he is saying that human understanding could not have imagined a way to be kept in the PEACE of Christ. Indeed, our hearts and minds are being kept in that reconciled relationship.

It is unlikely that the Bible assigns any sort of primacy to reason, at least in the way traditional theology and philosophy has often done. It is no doubt true that our whole being, which includes emotions, will, imagination, intuitions, and so on, should conform to reason. If we understand reason to be correct judgment, according to God's standards, then all of our faculties ought to be able to conform to that norm, not just the mind. Indeed, it is not certain that the Bible separates something called the mind from the other faculties in any clear-cut manner. The greatest commandment is to "Love the Lord your God with all your heart and with all your soul and with all your mind" (Matt. 22:37). This is a way of piling up the terms and saying that our whole being should love the one God. See also APOLOGETICS. W. EDGAR

Reba ree´buh (רֶבַע H8064, perhaps "fourth one"). One of five kings of MIDIAN killed by the Israelites in a battle on the plains of MOAB (Num. 31:8). Moses was commanded by God to exact vengeance on the Midianites because they had enticed Israel with their gods. In another passage (Josh. 13:21) the kings are said to be princes of (NIV, "allied with") SIHON, the AMORITE ruler, possibly indicating that they were his vassals. Apparently Sihon had taken possession of the area of Moab and made the Midianite tribes residing there subject to him. The form *rbʿ* is attested in Arabic both as a personal and as a place name; perhaps Reba should be linked with Naqb Rubaʿi, near PETRA (see *ABD*, 5:628–29). J. C. MOYER

Rebecca ri-bek´uh. See REBEKAH.

Rebekah ri-bek´uh (רִבְקָה H8071, possibly "cow" [*HALOT*, 3:1182; if so, an affectionate term, comparable to RACHEL, "ewe"]; Ῥεβέκκα G4831). KJV NT Rebecca (a spelling followed by other versions). Daughter of BETHUEL, who was nephew to ABRAHAM (Gen. 22:23) and lived in the Aramean country near the EUPHRATES. Rebekah was LABAN's sister. She became the wife of ISAAC and the mother of ESAU and JACOB.

Rebekah's encounter with Abraham's steward (prob. ELIEZER) is remembered as a classic example of divine PROVIDENCE and guidance (Gen. 24). She met this aged traveler with his camels outside her city as she returned one evening from the well. When he asked her for a drink, she readily gave it, but she also offered to draw for his camels, and did so with good will, little knowing that the man had just prayed for this very sign. Finding that she was a relative of his master, and realizing that she was also beautiful, he recognized the abundant answer to his prayer. When Rebekah's father and brother heard what the steward had to say, they could only acknowledge the Lord's leading. They wanted her, however, to delay for a few days of leave-taking; asked to decide, she preferred to go immediately. So Rebekah was brought to Isaac, "and he loved her; and Isaac was comforted after his mother's death" (v. 67). (On the narrative qualities of the story, see *ABD*, 5:629–30.)

For twenty years of her marriage Rebekah had no children (see BARRENNESS); then in answer to

Isaac's prayer, God gave her twins (Gen. 25:20–26). Her experience while carrying them foreshadowed conflict between her descendants, and she was told that God had chosen the younger twin for his blessing. Malachi cites the evidence of it in Israel's experience (Mal. 1:2–3), and Paul shows that God was establishing and typifying the principle of electing grace (Rom. 9:10–13).

Jacob, the younger son, unadventurous, always in camp, became Rebekah's favorite (Gen. 25:28); and she plotted the deception by which he gained his father's formal blessing (ch. 27). Esau then would have murdered Jacob, but God overruled in this also. Esau had married HITTITE women to the disappointment of his parents; Rebekah induced Isaac to send Jacob back to HARAN to find a wife.

According to Gen. 49:31, Rebekah was buried in the family tomb at MACHPELAH near HEBRON.

J. LILLEY

Recab ree´kab (רָכָב *H8209*, from a root meaning "chariot" or possibly "rider"). Also Rechab, Rekab. **(1)** Son of RIMMON, from the tribe of BENJAMIN; he and his brother treacherously murdered ISH-BOSHETH, their king, and met with the due reward of their deed at DAVID's hands (2 Sam. 4:2–12). See discussion under BAANAH #1.

(2) Father (or ancestor) of Jehonadab/JONADAB (2 Ki. 10:15, 23; 1 Chr. 2:55; Jer. 35:6–8, 14–19). See RECABITE.

(3) Father of MALKIJAH; the latter was a postexilic ruler of BETH HAKKEREM who repaired the DUNG GATE in Jerusalem (Neh. 3:14). Some speculate that he may have been a descendant of #2 above.

Recabite rek´uh-b*i*t (רֵכָבִי *H8211* [always in the phrase בֵּית הָרֵכָבִים, "house of the Recabites"], gentilic of רָכָב *H8209*). Also Rechabite, Rekabite. Name applied to a nomadic family that descended from RECAB (#2) and JONADAB; they were famous for their rules to abstain from WINE, build no houses, sow no seed, and plant no vineyard (Jer. 35; cf. also 1 Chr. 4:12, where some MSS of the LXX read, "the men of Recab" [see RECAH]).

I. Relationship to the Kenites. According to 1 Chr. 2:55 certain KENITES "came from Hammath, the father of the house of Recab." HAMMATH, like various other names in this genealogy, may refer to a place as well as to a person, and the preposition "from" seems to imply that the Kenites in view came from a place Hammath. Moreover, we are told elsewhere that a Kenite named HEBER separated from the rest of the Kenites (who descended from HOBAB) and settled in KEDESH of NAPHTALI (Jdg. 4:11, 17), in the same general region as Hammath (cf. Josh. 19:35–37). As for the term "father" in 1 Chr. 2:55, it may indicate either that the Recabites had a blood relationship with the Kenites or that Hammath was the founder of the Recabites as a professional guild (cf. BDB, 3, s.v. *ʾāb H3*, meaning 5). In either case the text is of interest because some of the Kenites gained their livelihood in metallurgy (R. J. Forbes, *Studies in Ancient Technology*, 8 vols. [1955–64], 8:91–92), possibly the trade of the Recabites.

II. Jonadab's social and religious status. The founder of the Recabite discipline was Jehonadab/Jonadab (2 Ki. 10:15, 23; Jer. 35:6, 14). Scholars differ in their view of his social standing. M. Ben-Gavriel described him as "a naive man of the wilderness" ("Das nomadische Ideal in der Bibel," *Stimmen der Zeit* 171 [1962–63]: 253–63), and M. H. Pope envisioned him as one of the "proto-Rechabites … a nomad clan who pastured their flocks in marginal areas of the N Kingdom" (*IDB*, 4:15).

However, F. S. Frick saw Jehonadab as a member of a guild with high social standing. He argued thus: first, the name Jehonadab combines the theophoric element (*yh*) with the root *ndb*, and the cognate noun *nādib H5618* is used to denote a member of the ruling class of the monarchical period. Moreover, "all of the personal names in the Bible which contain the root *n-d-b*, belong to members of this class, and there is no apparent reason why Jehonadab should be considered an exception" ("The Rechabites Reconsidered," *JBL* 90 [1971]: 282). Second, the designation "the son of Recab" (2 Ki. 10:15) possibly does not indicate a true father-son relationship or even a descendant of one Recab. Rather "son" (Heb. *bēn H1201*; see BEN-), like the Akkadian terms *maru* and *aplu*, could indicate that he was a member of a guild named *rekab*; that is, an occupational group associated in some way with chariotry (Heb. *rekeb H8207*, "chariot"), a specialty group well attested in the ANE.

"Son of Recab" could also indicate that Jehonadab was a native of a place named Recab, possibly so-called because of its association with chariotry. According to either of these last interpretations, it may not be coincidental that JEHU took Jehonadab into his chariot for the trip to SAMARIA. Third, the dialogue between Jehu and Jehonadab serves to confirm a military alliance (cf. 2 Ki. 10:16

Modern-day bedouin tent in Jordan. The Recabites used similar dwellings and refused to build houses (Jer. 35:7–10).

with 1 Ki. 22:4; 2 Ki. 3:7). JOSEPHUS (*Ant.* 9.6.6) assumed that these men may have had a prior association, which may have come about in the king's chariotry (Frick, "Rechabites," 283–84). One thing is clear: because of the prominent place which the new ruler gave him (2 Ki. 10:16, 23), his influence was a matter of some importance.

Regarding his religious position there is no ambiguity. Like ELIJAH and ELISHA, he was a radical supporter of Yahwism in the face of the increasing threat of Baalism under the Omrides. The statement that Jehonadab "was on his way to meet" Jehu (2 Ki. 10:15) shows that Jehonadab took the initiative.

III. The purpose of Jehonadab's rules. Scholars have differed also in their understanding of the object of the rules formulated by Jehonadab for his descendants. K. Budde, followed by most moderns, held that the object of the regulations was the preservation of primitive simplicity, that is, the maintenance of nomadism because civilization and settled life inevitably leads to apostasy from Yahweh. Pope states, "The Rechabites struck at the root of the evil, the tendency to assimilate, by making the nomad mode of life a religious obligation and by rejecting virtually everything Canaanite except the language" (*IDB*, 4:15). This understanding rests on the assumption that (1) abstention from intoxicants, (2) tent-dwelling, and (3) the disdaining of AGRICULTURE are clear signs of a nomadic society (see NOMAD). This understanding is further supported by a parallel group among the NABATEANS mentioned by Diodorus of Sicily (cf. S. Cohen in *IDB*, 3:491).

Frick, on the other hand, contended that this group of Nabateans is not a valid parallel sample because it ignores the significant difference in time, the disparate purpose of the discipline in Nabatean society (to avoid conquest), and the caution urged by Cohen in the use of classical sources vis-à-vis the Nabateans ("Rechabites," 281). Moreover, he cited Albright to question whether teetotalism is a trait of nomadism at all (ibid., 285). Finally, he suggested that the Rechabites' rules can be interpreted as belonging to a guild of metal-workers involved in the making of chariots and other weaponry. His arguments were as follows: (1) Metallurgists in antiquity formed proud endogamous lines of families that could account for the staying power of the Recabites. (2) In a preindustrial society, the smith had to dispose of the formidable body of technical lore that was handed down and guarded jealously from generation to generation. He noted that "like other measures designed to guard the secrets of the trade, so too might the abstention from intoxicants be another attempt to prevent 'loose lips' from 'sinking ships.'" (3) The smith's social status among agriculturalists was an honored one. (4) Because a smith remained in one locality until the supply of ore and/or fuel was exhausted, he was prevented from establishing a permanent domicile or engaging in agriculture. (5) Whereas other craftsmen were not hindered from engaging in part-time agricultural work, the smith's work required such skill that agriculture was excluded (ibid.). See METALS AND METALLURGY.

IV. Yahweh's use of the Recabites. This much is sure: the Recabites are not commended by Yahweh for their rules as such but rather for their faithfulness to the rules. K. Budde acknowledged: "An independent value in the precepts of Jonadab is not asserted" ("The Nomadic Ideal in the Old Testament," *The New World* 4 [1895]: 727); and S. Talmon wrote: "By way of a simile the prophet had set the Rechabites before the nation as an example of steadfastness. But the *tertium comparatonis* lies in their relation to a command not in the contents of the command" ("The 'Desert Motif' in the Bible and the Qumran Literature," in *Biblical Motifs: Origins and Transformations*, ed. A. Altmann [1966], 37).

V. The survival of the Recabites. For their steadfastness, these few Recabites—who were able to fit into one chamber of the TEMPLE and all of whose names mentioned in the text contain Yahweh as a theophoric element (Jer. 35:3)—are promised that they will never fail to have a descendant to represent them (v. 19). The fulfillment of this promise is possibly reflected in several details: (1) the title of Ps. 71 in the SEPTUAGINT (= Ps. 70) reads: "... of the sons of Jehonadab and of the earliest captives"; (2) a certain MALKIJAH son of Recab who repaired the DUNG GATE in NEHEMIAH's restoration of Jerusalem (Neh. 3:14) may have been a Recabite; (3) there is a Jewish tradition that the Recabites enter the temple service by the marriage of their daughters to priests; (4) the church father Hegesippus makes the dubious assertion that a Recabite priest protested the martyrdom of JAMES (Eusebius, *Eccl. Hist.* 2.23); (5) the TALMUD states that the Recabites had a special day, the seventh of Ab, for participation in the wood festival of priests and people (*b. Taʿan.* 26a); (6) a Christian work known as *History of the Rechabites*, produced in the 6th cent., but probably based on earlier Jewish traditions, provides an expanded retelling of the biblical material (see *OTP*, 2:443–61); and (7) professed descendants of the sect still exist in Iraq and Yemen. (See further L. Gautier, *A propos des Récabites: Un chapitre de l'histoire religieuse d'Israel avant l'exil* [1927]; S. Talmon in *IEJ* 10 [1960]: 174–80; S. Abramsky in *Eretz-Israel* 8 [1967]: 255–64 [Heb. with an Eng. summary, 76*]; F. S. Frick in *ABD*, 5:630–32.) B. K. WALTKE

Recah ree'kuh (רֵכָה *H8212*, meaning uncertain). TNIV Rekah. Apparently a town inhabited by some descendants of JUDAH (1 Chr. 4:12). Nothing is known about such a place, and some scholars, following a variant SEPTUAGINT reading (*Rēchab* in CODEX VATICANUS and the Lucianic recension), emend the text to RECAB.

receipt of custom. See CUSTOM, RECEIPT OF.

Rechab, Rechabite ree'kab, rek'uh-bit. See RECAB; RECABITE.

Rechabites, History of the rek'uh-bit. See RECABITE V.

Rechah ree'kuh. KJV form of RECAH.

recompense. See RETRIBUTION; REWARD.

reconciliation. The act of restoring harmony, bringing again into unity or agreement what has been alienated. According to biblical teaching, there is need for reconciliation between God and human beings because of the alienation between them, which has its source in SIN and the righteous aversion to it on the part of God. The Bible teaches that God himself has provided the means of reconciliation through the death of his Son Jesus Christ.

I. The biblical data. The Greek noun meaning "reconciliation" (*katallagē G2903*) and the cognate verb (*katallassō G2904*) occur nine times in four Pauline passages (Rom. 5:10–11; 11:15; 2 Cor. 5:18–19; in 1 Cor. 7:11 reconciliation between human beings is in view). A compound form of the verb (*apokatallassō G639*, possibly intensive in meaning) is found in two other passages (Eph. 2:16; Col. 1:20–22).

When reconciliation has its full biblical meaning of SALVATION, the alienation it removes is clearly the result of sin (Isa. 59:12). This is apparent from 2 Cor. 5:18–19, where reconciliation is brought into connection with God's not imputing trespasses; thus for PAUL reconciliation is the parallel or equivalent of JUSTIFICATION (Rom. 5:9–10; cf. 2 Cor. 3:9). This is not strange, because the means of reconciliation is the death of God's Son (Rom. 5:10). The purpose of sacrificial death is EXPIATION.

The DEATH OF CHRIST and the IMPUTATION of his RIGHTEOUSNESS to the sinner is ground for removing the cause of alienation between God and human beings, namely, the guilt of sin. See ATONEMENT.

But reconciliation has a broader meaning than justification. The concept derives from the socio-economic sphere (cf. 1 Cor. 7:11). It speaks in general of the restoration of a proper relationship between two parties. It refers broadly to overcoming an enmity, without specifying how this enmity is removed. In Paul's writings reconciliation is contrasted with "enmity" and "alienation" (Rom. 5:10; Eph. 2:14–15; Col. 1:22). In the positive sense it has the meaning of PEACE (Rom. 5:1, 10; Eph. 2:15–16; Col. 1:20–21). The removal of the reason for alienation brings about a condition of peace between the warring parties.

In its biblical sense, *peace* is the inclusive term referring to the restoration of fellowship between God and sinners. The inclusive sense of *reconciliation*, as it is used regarding salvation, that is, overcoming of enmity and alienation, is reflected in what it has in view, namely, the restoration of peace between God and the sinner. Thus Paul can exult, "Therefore, since we have been justified through faith, we have peace with God through our Lord Jesus Christ" (Rom. 5:1).

The concept of reconciliation comes up also in connection with the uniting of the GENTILES with the COVENANT line (Rom. 11:15). In this passage the characteristic traits of reconciliation are present. Paul says of the Gentiles that they were without Christ, aliens from Israel, and strangers to the covenant of promise. They were far off and foreign. Christ is the One who brings peace, who preached peace, who is our peace. He is said to have removed and abolished enmity, to have brought the Gentile near, and to have made of Gentile and Jew one. Gentile and Jew have been brought into a single commonwealth. What is in mind is not directly the removal of enmity between God and the sinner but the abolishing of the distinction in Christ of Jew and Gentile. Nevertheless, what separated them is identified as the law. It is by the cross of Christ that what separated them, the enmity, has been broken down. Thus they could be brought together and united in one body. Christ "has made the two one," thus making peace (Eph. 2:14–16).

This and the other elements of reconciliation must be seen against the background of the all-embracing purpose of God to reconcile all things to himself through Jesus Christ (Col. 1:20–21). This indicates the scope of the idea of reconciliation. Having made peace through the blood of Christ's cross, God has the great purpose of reconciling to himself all things in heaven and in earth. Thus it is possible to speak of the GOSPEL of salvation in its broadest scope as the "ministry of reconciliation," and the appeal of the gospel to the sinner as the call to be reconciled to God (2 Cor. 5:20).

II. Doctrinal formulation. The doctrine of reconciliation brings into focus our alienation from God because of sin and his provision for restoring us to his favor. In its most embracive meaning, reconciliation has to do with the removal of that which stands in the way of the proper relationship between God and the world in the most inclusive sense of the word. Thus it must have in its purview all the facets of the restoration of the world, including the final reconciliation of all things in Christ to the Father at the last day.

The Scripture passages that refer explicitly to reconciliation invariably speak of the sinner's being reconciled to God and not of God's being reconciled to the sinner. At first sight, it might be thought that there are scriptural grounds for concluding, with classic theological liberalism, that the alienation was altogether on the human side. Liberalism would not admit that God was estranged. God remained always the same, always favorably inclined toward mankind, in spite of its weakness and sin.

That the Scriptures speak explicitly only of God's reconciling the sinner to himself does not mean, however, that it is only the sinner who has been alienated from God and not God from the sinner. Because of sin, we have come under the righteous judgment and curse of God. God is too holy to look upon sin; he recoils from it. This righteous judgment of God must be satisfied, and this satisfaction is accomplished, the Scriptures teach, by the perfect sacrifice of Jesus Christ. The idea of sacrifice involves the idea of expiation for sin, which is necessary if God is to be reconciled. Although the Bible does not refer explicitly to God's being reconciled, the scriptural teaching will not allow that reconciliation to be only on the human side. Reconciliation is of God to sinners as well as of sinners to God.

Furthermore, the alienation involves more than a sense of estrangement on our part. This can be seen from Christ's teaching in Matt. 5:23–24. Christ commanded one who brings his gift to the altar and there remembers that his brother has a grievance against him to postpone making his offering until he has been reconciled to his brother. This command cannot be taken to mean simply that the one offering his gift should replace an attitude of animosity toward his brother with one of good will; for this he would not have to leave the altar. It means that he should remove whatever is the ground for his brother's complaint against him. He should bring a change into the situation that occasioned alienation between them, so that he and his brother can again be in harmony. Christ teaches, therefore, that whatever is behind the alienation should be removed before the worshiper presents his sacrifice. Likewise in the relationship between God and sinners, it is not simply a question of an attitude on our part that must be changed. What must be changed is the condition of alienation that has arisen because of sin. If this alienation is to be removed, the ground of the alienation, namely, the guilt of sin, which deserves the divine wrath, condemnation, and curse, must be removed. (See J. Murray, *Redemption: Accomplished and Applied* [1955], 33–42.)

Since this is the case, it is not at all surprising that the scriptural teaching concerning reconciliation is brought into the most intimate connection with those of justification and the expiatory death of Jesus Christ. What effects reconciliation is the sacrifice of Christ, whereby the sinner is relieved of the guilt and the condemnation of sin and receives the righteousness of Christ imputed to him. Since release from condemnation involves also being freed from bondage by the payment of a ransom, reconciliation also has an intimate connection with REDEMPTION.

The new relationship between God and human beings, resulting from their reconciliation, is that of sonship. It is the result of ADOPTION (cf. Gal. 4:4–5). Adoption is the goal of the great divine purpose of reconciliation. It is a direct result of redemption, justification (Rom. 3:25–26; 4:25), and reconciliation (2 Cor. 5:18–19).

Contrary to liberalism, subsequent modern theology has had more place for the idea of divine WRATH. It has had a greater place, therefore, for the idea that reconciliation involves God as well as the sinner. Some theologians have come to assert that the divine *yes* is at the foundation of every divine *no*. Karl Barth (*Church Dogmatics* 4/1/2 [1956]) taught that all people are elected and are reconciled. They must only be brought to realize it.

Especially because of the influence of Sören Kierkegaard and Karl Marx, the idea of alienation and estrangement has become a major theme of contemporary philosophy, theology, and literature. This accounts in great measure for the importance that the doctrine of reconciliation has assumed in current theological thought. The notion is often secularized, however, referring only to a reconciliation of one with his own deeper nature. Even in contemporary theology this secularizing tendency is present. Its peculiar tendencies do not allow contemporary theology to view reconciliation in its proper relationship to the sacrificial death of Christ, expiation, and the imputation of righteousness, all of which are essential to the biblical doctrine. (See further *HDB*, 4:204–7; G. C. Workman, *At Onement or Reconciliation with God* [1911]; F. W. Dillistone, *The Significance of the Cross* [1944]; H. Ridderbos, *Paul: An Outline of His Theology* [1975], ch. 5.) R. D. KNUDSEN

recorder. An important official in Israel who functioned as a herald (Heb. *mazkir* H4654, lit., "one who causes to remember"). Although the Hebrew term occurs nine times, the precise duties of this official are never mentioned. If the term is descriptive of the office, then the recorder might have been connected with the chronicling of state events. Yet this task seems to have been the function of the royal SCRIBE or secretary.

Another possibility is that it was a vocal office parallel to the Egyptian *whm.w*, "he who repeats, calls, announces" (i.e., the pharaoh's herald). Among his tasks was that of official spokesman. This seems to be the case with JOAH son of Asaph, a recorder during the reign of HEZEKIAH; along with two other officials, Joah represented the king in negotiations that nation come from the "red" man ESAU, but also the color of much of its landscape is red (cf. PETRA, "the red Rose City"). When the reference is to the color of human skin, English prefers the term *ruddy* (1 Sam. 16:12; 17:42; Cant. 5:10; Lam. 4:7).

Red was a natural color for some cereal (Gen. 25:30), wine (Prov. 23:31), a heifer (Num. 19:2), some horses (Zech. 1:8; 6:2; Rev. 6:4 [Gk. *pyrros G4794*, from *pyr G4786*, "fire"]), and the sky before fair weather (Matt. 16:2–3 [Gk. verb *pyrrazō G4793*]). Red spots may indicate leprosy on a person (Lev. 13:19) or in a garment (v. 49). Red or PURPLE was used on expensive things such as the ram skins for the TABERNACLE (Exod. 25:5 et al.), or war shields (Nah. 2:3). The well-known verse Isa. 1:18 uses three parallel words for "red" to describe SIN (in addition to the verb ʾādēm, it includes the nouns *šānî H9106*, usually rendered "scarlet," and *tôlāʿ H9355*, "crimson"). R. L. ALDEN

redaction criticism. See BIBLICAL CRITICISM V.E.

Redeemer myth. See GNOSTICISM.

redemption. Redemption is deliverance from the power of an alien dominion and enjoyment of the resulting freedom (see LIBERTY). In its original sense and in its biblical usage redemption is intimately associated with the ideas of RANSOM and substitution. It often involves the concept of restoration to one who possesses a more fundamental right or interest. The heart of the biblical message of redemption is the deliverance of the people of God from the bondage of sin by the perfect substitutionary sacrifice of Jesus Christ (see ATONEMENT) and their consequent restoration to God and his heavenly kingdom. A redeemer is one who possesses the right or who exercises the right of redemption. The Bible presents Christ as the redeemer of God's elect.

I. The biblical data. The English verb *redeem* in the OT generally corresponds to two Hebrew terms. One of them, *pādâ H7009*, was used for the money payments required by law in Israel for the redemption of the FIRSTBORN (Exod. 13:12–13), thus releasing the Israelites from the obligation imposed after the exodus that every firstborn son

A cross-legged scribe writing under the inspiration of Thot, god of science and literature; the little shell on the left thigh was used for mixing the paint. This statue, made of black schist on a limestone base, was found in a house at Tell el-Amarna, Egypt. (© Dr. James C. Martin. The Cairo Museum. Photographed by permission.)

with the RABSHAKEH, who in turn represented the Assyrian king, SENNACHERIB (2 Ki. 18:18, 37; Isa. 36:3, 22). Another Joah, the son of Joahaz, was recorder during the reign of JOSIAH (2 Chr. 34:8); along with Shaphan and Maaseiah, he was delegated to pay the laborers who repaired the temple during Josiah's reform. Earlier, a certain JEHOSHAPHAT was recorder during the reigns of both DAVID and SOLOMON, but the nature of his office is not indicated (2 Sam. 8:16; 20:24; 1 Ki. 4:3; 1 Chr. 18:15). The mention of recorders from David to Josiah indicates that the office continued until the end of the monarchy. (See further R. de Vaux, *Ancient Israel* [1965], 127–32.) J. C. MOYER

red. Out of several Hebrew words that may be translated "red," the most common root is *ʾdm* (e.g., verb *ʾādēm H131*, "to be red"; adjectives *ʾādōm H137*, *ʾadmônî H145*). This root is related to the noun *ʾădāmâ H141*, "earth, land," indicating a connection with the color of the soil in the Middle East. The root appears also in the name of the first man, ADAM, who was formed "from the dust of the [red] ground" (again, *ʾădāmâ*, Gen. 2:7). The name of the nation EDOM has the same origin: not only does and male animal be dedicated to the service of God (Exod. 21:8; Lev. 25:47–49; 27:27; Num. 3:46–49; 18:15–16). This verb was used also of the release of persons from SLAVERY (Exod. 21:8; Lev. 25:47–49). The second term, *gāʾal H1457*, was used of the recovery of property that had passed into other hands (Lev. 25:26; Ruth 4:4–8) and also of the commutation of a vow (Lev. 27:13, 15, 19–20) or a TITHE (27:31). God is spoken of as the GOEL or Redeemer especially in Isaiah (Isa. 41:14; 43:14; et al.), but in several other books as well (Job 19:25; Pss. 19:14; 78:35; Prov. 23:11 [NIV, "Defender"]; Jer. 50:34). (See further *NIDOTTE*, 1:789–94; 3:578–82.)

In the OT the idea of redemption is closely associated with the laws and customs of the Israelite people. If a life was taken, a kinsman had the right of avenging or redeeming the blood of the victim (Num. 5:8; 1 Ki. 16:11). According to the theocratic arrangement in Israel, the land belonged to God and the Israelite families only possessed the right to use the fruit of the land (*usufruct*). If a family forfeited this use because its parcel of land had to be sold or because there was no heir, the parcel was returned to the family at the JUBILEE YEAR, which came every fifty years (Lev. 25:8–17). Prior to this year, the nearest kinsman had the right and the responsibility to redeem the property, that is, to liquidate the debt so that the property might be restored to its original owner (25:23–28).

Closely related to this custom was that of LEVIRATE marriage. The brother-in-law or other near kinsman of someone who had died without leaving a male heir was obliged to marry the widow of the deceased in order to preserve the family name and property rights. In the marriage of BOAZ and RUTH, both of the above customs were involved. The idea of redemption also appears when a person has been deprived of something that is part of his or her personal integrity. Thus NAOMI called the son born to Boaz and Ruth a kinsman-redeemer because he delivered her from the reproach she had incurred for lack of a surviving male heir (Ruth 4:14; cf. J. M. Sasson, *Ruth*, 2nd ed. [1989], 163–64). The birth of an heir now delivered her honor, as it were, from an alien dominion and restored it to her.

Because God spared the Israelites from the final plague in Egypt, he established a claim on the firstborn Israelite male children and cattle, which were henceforth supposed to be dedicated to God's service (Exod. 13:2). In their stead God placed the tribe of LEVI and its cattle (Num. 3:12–13, 41, 45). Since there was not enough of them to provide a substitute for all the firstborn, God required the Israelites to "redeem" the remaining firstborn by paying a sum of money (3:46–51). In this fashion the firstborn were released from the divine claim upon them and were restored to their families. From this time the firstborn male children were redeemed by the payment of a sum of money, a firstborn donkey by the substitution of a lamb, etc. (Exod. 13:12–13; 34:19–20).

In the NT the relevant words are the verbs *agorazō G60* and *lytroō G3390*. The former, a common term meaning "to buy, purchase," is used several times with reference to the redemption of believers (1 Cor. 6:20; 7:23; 2 Pet. 2:1; Rev. 5:9; *exagorazō G1973* in Gal. 3:13; 4:5). The second verb is related to the noun *lytron G3389*, which means "ransom." The noun form appears in the NT only twice (Mk. 10:45; Matt. 20:28; the synonym *antilytron G519* in 1 Tim. 2:6), and it literally refers to a means of loosing, for instance, the payment of a ransom price. It was used by ancient writers almost universally to refer to a ransom paid for prisoners. The verbal form does not always include the idea of ransom in the NT (Lk. 24:21; Tit. 2:14; the same is true of the nouns *lytrōsis G3391* and *apolytrōsis G667*, Lk. 1:68; 21:28; Rom. 3:24; 8:23; et al.), but this concept is most closely associated with them (see esp. 1 Pet. 1:18). The term "redeemer," *lytrōtēs G3392*, occurs in the NT only in Acts 7:35, where it is used of MOSES. (See further B. B. Warfield, *Biblical Doctrines* [1929], 327–98; *TDNT*, 4:340–56; *NIDNTT*, 3:177–223.)

II. Doctrinal formulation. Redemption is deliverance from a bondage, a release of someone or something from an alien power that has a claim upon it. The outstanding example of redemption in the OT was the deliverance of the children of Israel from bondage, from the dominion of the alien power of Egypt. See EXODUS, THE.

The biblical idea of redemption also involves the deliverer and what he performs to effect the deliverance. Release must be effected by someone who, for whatever reason, has a prior or more fundamental claim to what is to be delivered. According to Israelite custom, it was possible for someone to deliver himself or something for himself (Lev. 25:49); however, more characteristically, the redeemer was someone else, such as a near relative, who because of his position in the family possessed the right and the obligation of redemption. One who had the right to redeem, whether he exercised it as a matter of fact or not, was called a redeemer ($gō'ēl$). In its central reference to salvation, the Bible teaches that redemption is always by another party. In the story of the great deliverance from Egypt attention falls not only upon the act of redemption itself but upon the redeemer as well, upon God working through his prophet Moses. God had the prior claim upon Israel because he had obtained them as his people. His act of redemption liberated Israel from the alien dominion of Egypt and restored them to him who was their rightful Lord. See SALVATION.

What the redeemer does in order to accomplish redemption is not always the same. Moses was called a redeemer (Acts 7:35) because as God's prophet he was instrumental in leading the children of Israel out of Egypt. Naomi called Boaz "one of our redeemers" because his position in the family gave him the right to effect the restoration of the family property. She called the son born of Boaz and Ruth "a redeemer" because he delivered her from her reproach.

The earliest usage of the words for redemption, as we have seen, associates them with the payment of a price, a ransom. This is also true of the biblical teaching concerning redemption as it bears on salvation. The people of God are redeemed by the payment of the debt of their sin by the perfect satisfaction accomplished by Jesus Christ.

In the early church redemption was correctly associated with the idea of ransom. The notion arose, however, that Christ had redeemed his people by paying a ransom to the devil. This theory was attacked and refuted by Anselm in his *Cur Deus Homo* (*Why God Became Man*). The Scriptures are virtually silent about one to whom ransom is paid. If it is anyone, it is God himself. The focus of attention, in any case, is not the one to whom ransom is paid but the sufficiency of the payment made by Christ. This was nothing less than the substitution of his own life for that of the redeemed (Matt. 20:28).

Modern liberal theology altogether dissociated redemption from the ideas of ransom and satisfaction, and thought of redemption simply as deliverance from the alien dominion of the world. Deliverance from the world certainly expresses an important facet of redemption. However, liberal theology erred in rejecting the scriptural teaching that the price of redemption was the satisfaction of the demands of the law and release from its guilt by Christ's substitution of his own life for that of the sinner. Liberalism maintained that the idea of substitution was unworthy of high religion, according to which everyone must stand before God in his or her own freedom and responsibility as an ethical personality.

In understanding the meaning of redemption, one should not forget that it is a deliverance or a release from a claim. The claim can be lifted only by one who has the right to do so, and he performs something to effect this release. Although it is not always present, the idea is never remote that this claim is satisfied by the payment of a price. This meaning was present in the ancient usage of the vocabulary of redemption, and it is part and parcel of the biblical message concerning redemption from SIN. Those who are under the alien dominion of sin, who are unable to deliver themselves, are delivered by the Savior Jesus Christ, who perfectly satisfied the demands of the law, thereby establishing his right to release from its claims those who are enthralled by it; who effected their release by the substitution of his own life (Gal. 3:13); and who restored them to the kingdom of their heavenly Father. The means of redemption and what it accomplishes are clearly set forth in Eph. 1:7–8: "In him we have redemption through his blood, the forgiveness of sins, in accordance with the riches of God's grace that he lavished on us with all wisdom and understanding" (cf. Col. 1:14).

Since redemption is a release from the bondage of sin, its meaning is as broad as the scope of sin and the evil attending it. The release falls, broadly speaking, under two heads: (1) redemption from the CURSE of the law (Gal. 3:10, 13), from the legal prescriptions of the OT dispensation (4:1–5), and from the requirement of obedience to the law as a way of life (3:10; 2:16, 19; Phil. 3:9); (2) redemption from the guilt and the power of sin (Tit. 2:14).

The inclusiveness of redemption from sin and from its attending evils is shown by the fact that the final consummation of the entire redemptive process is called "the redemption" (Lk. 21:28; Rom. 8:23; Eph. 1:14; 4:30 ["the day of redemption"]). The exposition of this consummation (Eph. 1:14) clearly sets forth the elements of redemption. Those who have believed in Jesus Christ have been sealed by his HOLY SPIRIT. God has placed his stamp on them as a sign that they are his and as an assurance against loss.

PAUL regards the children of God as already having been purchased and as awaiting the final redemption when they shall receive their INHERITANCE. This event is called "the redemption of the purchased possession" (Eph. 1:14 KJV). The redeemed will be freed from the sinful world under whose dominion they still remain and they will be restored to the One who has the prior claim upon them by virtue of the fact that he has obtained them for his own possession. At their redemption the entire creation will be restored to him who is its rightful Lord.

(See further T. J. Crawford, *The Doctrine of the Holy Scripture Respecting the Atonement*, 4th ed. [1954]; L. Morris, *The Apostolic Preaching of the Cross* [1955]; J. Murray, *Redemption: Accomplished and Applied* [1955]; A. J. Hultgren, *Christ and His Benefits: Christology and Redemption in the New Testament* [1987].)   R. D. KNUDSEN

red heifer. See HEIFER, RED.

Red Sea. In modern usage, this name refers to the NW arm of the Indian Ocean, separating Africa from the Arabian Peninsula; at the end it splits into the Gulf of Suez on the W and the Gulf of Aqabah on the E. In the OT, the name is a translation of the Hebrew phrase *yam-sûp* (H3542 + H6068), meaning literally "Sea of Reeds." The SEPTUAGINT renders it with *erythra thalassa* (G2261 + G2498), "Red Sea," a term that had earlier been used by HERODOTUS (though he applied it more generally to include even the Indian Ocean). As used in the Bible, the name appears to refer to three distinct places.

I. The waters of the exodus. From comparison of Exod. 14 with 15:22, and by noting the poetic parallelism within 15:4, it is clear that the "sea" crossed by the Hebrews in ch. 14 was the *yam-sûp*. At first sight, Hebrew *sûp* resembles Arabic *ṣuf*, "weeds" (including seaweed), but the difference in sibilants (*s* and the emphatic *ṣ*) makes any connection unlikely. Rather, the word *sûp* corresponds precisely to Egyptian *ṭwf(y)*, "papyrus," and *yam-sûp* to Egyptian *pʾ-ṭwf*, "papyrus-marshes," particularly in the NE delta of the NILE (see PAPYRUS). In an ancient Egyptian document, the products of *pʾ-ṭwf* are said to come to Pi-Ramessē (or Per-Ramesses; see RAMESES), and the phrase is set in parallel with SHIHOR (Papyrus Anastasi III, 2.11–12, trans. in *ANET*, 471b; see also R. A. Caminos, *Late-Egyptian Miscellanies* [1954], 74; A. H. Gardiner, *Ancient Egyptian Onomastica* 2 [1947], 201*, 202*:418; id. in *JEA* 5 [1918]: 251–52; A. Erman and H. Grapow, *Wörterbuch der Aegyptischen Sprache*, 5 [1931, *Belegstellen* 1953], 359:6–10). Shihor is indubitably the northeasternmost stretch of the Pelusiac (easternmost) arm of the Nile, running from just W of the present Suez Canal (roughly the latitude of Tineh) to the Mediterranean coast in antiquity, but not extant today. Thus, *pʾ-ṭwf* would be associated with the ancient lakes and marshes corresponding approximately to the SE corner of present Lake Menzaleh

The Red Sea.

and to the region S of it, such as Lake Ballaḥ and its environs southward to the Bitter Lakes. (For a different view of the relationship between the Hebrew and Egyptian terms, see J. R. Huddleston in *ABD*, 5:633–42, esp. 636–37.)

This general location on a N-S line due E of the probable site of Rameses near Qantir (and even E of Tanis, its main rival for that distinction) agrees well with Exod. 10:13, 19. A strong E wind was the means of bringing locusts into Egypt and troubling the PHARAOH at his residence; conversely, after his appeal to MOSES, a strong W wind bore them back eastward into the Sea of Reeds, implying that the latter was E from Rameses. This geographical factor thus supports an identification of the Sea of Reeds of the exodus with the area of lakes and marsh already mentioned, and not with the present-day Gulf of Suez. The very name "Sea of Reeds" would suggest waters that bordered on fresh-water marshes, etc., where papyrus and reeds might grow, again not true of the Gulf of Suez and the modern Red Sea. The foregoing philological evidence on *sûp* and the geographical factors here noted were not seriously considered by N. H. Snaith (in *VT* 15 [1965]: 395ff.); yet his views have been taken up by B. F. Batto (in *JBL* 102 [1983]: 27–35), who argues that *yam-sûp* has nothing to do with a reedy body of water but rather refers to a mythological "sea at the end [of the world]" (cf. Heb. *sôp* H6067, "end").

A former theory that the present Gulf of Suez may have extended much farther N in antiquity to include, for example, the Bitter Lakes, seemed to be firmly excluded by the siting of the ancient Egyptian port at Merkhah on the W coast of Sinai in the 15th cent. B.C. at levels unchanged into modern times (see W. F. Albright in *BASOR* 109 [Feb. 1948]: 14–15). However, J. K. Hoffmeier (*Israel in Egypt: The Evidence for the Authenticity of the Exodus Tradition* [1997], 207–10) has revived this theory and used it to answer Batto's objections.

In any case, the wilderness through which the Hebrews were to go near the *yam-sûp* (Exod. 13:18) was that of SHUR (15:22), this being roughly the N Sinai desert E of the Suez Canal and between the Mediterranean coast and about the latitude of Lake Timsah. This agrees with a Sea of Reeds in the Lake Ballaḥ area, and both locations are, in turn, readily compatible with a possible route of the exodus from Rameses (at Qantir) to SUCCOTH (prob. Tell el-Maskhuta) and then to the wilderness edge, turning back up to Lake Ballaḥ and so across a Sea of Reeds somewhere there (alternatively, the crossing may have been farther S, such as at the junction of the Great and Little Bitter Lakes; cf. C. G. Rasmussen, *Zondervan NIV Atlas of the Bible* [1989], 89). Thence, the Hebrews went S through Shur/Etham toward the W coast of the Sinai peninsula. See EXODUS, THE.

The phenomenon of E and W winds respectively flooding and uncovering routes in these lakes and fens of the Nile delta persists even in modern times (cf. Ali Shafei, *Bulletin de la Société Royale de Géographie d'Égypte* 16 [1946]: 278 and figs. 10, 11). The deliverance of the Hebrews through their crossing of the sea was remembered forever after, under Moses (Deut. 11:4), Joshua (2:10 and 4:23, even among aliens; 24:6), among the psalmists (e.g., Pss. 78:13; 106:7, 9, 22; 136:13), and after the EXILE (Neh. 9:9) into the NT (Acts 7:36; 1 Cor. 10:1–2; Heb. 11:29).

In Ps. 78:12 and 43, the term "fields of Zoan" (NRSV) has long been identified with the corresponding Egyptian *sḫt-dꜥ (nt)*, "Field of Djaꜥ" or "Field of Djaꜥnet" (i.e., of Tanis, biblical ZOAN). This region was the hinterland of the 14th Lower Egyptian province in the terminology of later times (Gardiner in *JEA* 5 [1918]: 248–49), and this probably adjoined the lower course of the Pelusiac arm of the Nile between Qantir and near Qantara,

Some identify the Bitter Lakes, pictured here, with the Red (or Reed) Sea which the Israelites crossed during the exodus out of Egypt.

in line with the suggested route of the exodus and location of the Sea of Reeds.

II. Gulf of Suez. After reaching the wilderness of Shur/Etham (Exod. 15:22; Num. 33:8), the Hebrews in three days (prob. on the third day, our mode of reckoning) reached MARAH, went on to ELIM, and thereafter encamped by the *yam-sûp* (Num. 33:10–11) before proceeding into the Desert of Sin (Exod. 16:1; Num. 33:11) en route to SINAI, which they reached after three more stops (Exod. 17; 19:1–2; cf. Num. 33:12–15). On this reckoning, the *yam-sûp* (of Num. 33:10–11) would be somewhere on the Gulf of Suez coast of Sinai, if Mount Sinai/Horeb is located in the S of that peninsula. (There seems no warrant for identifying this *yam-sûp* with the Mediterranean Sea, as this would bring the Hebrews along the forbidden way of the land of the PHILISTINES. To identify it with the Gulf of Aqabah would probably require a Mount Sinai located in MIDIAN to the E of that Gulf, possible but perhaps improbable because it would take the Hebrews across the howling wilderness of et-Tih instead of the wadis of south-central Sinai.) An application of the name *yam-sûp* to the Gulf of Suez may perhaps be considered as simply an extended use of terminology to include the gulf adjoining the lakes region to the S.

III. Gulf of Aqabah. From periods in Hebrew history subsequent to the exodus, it is clear that the term *yam-sûp* could also be applied to the present-day Gulf of AQABAH, along the E coast of the Sinai peninsula. First Kings explicitly locates EZION GEBER—SOLOMON's seaport settlement—beside Eloth (ELATH) on the shore of the *yam-sûp* in the land of EDOM (1 Ki. 9:26), a location which fits the Gulf of Aqabah but neither that of Suez nor of Lake Ballaḥ. Jeremiah 49:21 alludes to the *yam-sûp* in an oracle on Edom, again probably the Gulf of Aqabah. From this basis, one may work back to occasional references in the Pentateuch. Deuteronomy 1:1 locates the words of Moses "in the desert east of the Jordan—that is, in the Arabah—opposite Suph, between Paran and Tophel, Laban, Hazeroth and Dizahab." PARAN is the wilderness in the vicinity of KADESH BARNEA (Num. 10:12; 13:26; et al.), and the ARABAH is the S end of the JORDAN Rift Valley, between the Dead Sea and the Gulf of Aqabah. Hence, SUPH is some place in this vicinity, if it is not merely an abbreviation for *yam-sûp*, the Gulf of Aqabah itself. (Such a place-name Suph might even be reflected also as Suphah in the poetic fragment in Num. 21:14, but this is, of course, by no means certain.)

After dwelling by Kadesh Barnea (Num. 13:26) in the wilderness of Paran (12:16), the Hebrews were commanded to go to the wilderness by the way to the *yam-sûp* (14:25; Deut. 1:40). Thereafter occurred the incident of KORAH, DATHAN, and ABIRAM, who were swallowed up by the earth with their tents (Num. 16), an incident that may have occurred among the mudflats or *kewirs* of the Arabah (on the phenomenon, cf. Greta Hort, *Australian Biblical Review* 7 [1959]: 2–26, esp. 19–26), not so far from the Gulf of Aqabah. Similarly, after the burial of AARON at Mount HOR consequent upon a further sojourn around Kadesh Barnea (20:22—21:3), Israel again went by the way of the *yam-sûp* "to go around Edom" (21:4; cf. Deut. 2:1; Jdg. 11:16), a route that would appear to take them S from Kadesh Barnea to the head of the Gulf of Aqabah as if to go past the southern extremity of Edom and then to by-pass that land northward along its eastern border, and on past MOAB (both nations refusing Israel entry, Num. 20:14–21; Jdg. 11:17).

In the case of Exod. 23:31, one may possibly have a SW borderline of the promised land, running from the head of the Gulf of Aqabah (*yam-sûp*) up to the Mediterranean (sea of the Philistines), that is, roughly along the course of the Wadi el-ʿArish as elsewhere attested (see EGYPT, BROOK OF). The contemporary narrow and wide uses of a term like *yam-sûp* are not so unusual (cf. Egyptian parallels for seas and eastern lands cited in *NBD*, 1004b).

K. A. KITCHEN

reed. This English term is applied to various tall grasses that grow primarily in wet areas (see also BULRUSH). Hebrew words that can be translated "reed" include *ʾagmôn H109* (Job 41:20 et al.; cf. *ʾăgam H106*, "[reed] pond," Exod. 7:19 et al.), *ʾāḥû H286* (Gen. 41:2 et al.), *sûp H6068* (Exod. 2:3 et al., but used primarily in the combination *yam-sûp*, "Sea of Reeds"; see RED SEA), and especially *qāneh H7866* (prob. *Arundo donax*, 1 Ki. 14:15 et al.). This

Papyrus reeds growing in wetlands.

last term has a broad semantic range and can refer to a cane or even a beam. This can be said also for the Greek word *kalamos* G2812; the crowds smote the Lord Jesus on the head with a reed (Mk. 15:19), and someone put a soaked sponge on a reed so as to get him to drink when he was on the cross (15:36). Also, an angel is said to measure the new Jerusalem with a *kalamos* (Rev. 21:16). See MEASURING REED.

The *Arundo donax*, also known as the "giant reed" and the "Persian reed" (used for the manufacture of woodwind instruments) is found in the JORDAN Valley and around the DEAD SEA. Sometimes confused with bamboo, it can grow to the height of 18 ft., carrying at its tip a white plume. Its unusually hard stem may have a diameter of 3 in. These thick, strong stems were used as canes or walking sticks, hence the reference in Ezek. 29:6 and 2 Ki. 18:21, where King SENNACHERIB referred to Egypt as the staff of a bruised reed. In the latter passage, the reference to the piercing of a hand refers to the fact that the hard stem of the reed can break up into sharp, thin slivers with points that can easily make holes in the flesh. (See *FFB*, 171–72.)

Whether the cane or rod used to convey the sponge to our Lord's mouth was the *Arundo donax* is not important. There are experts who consider that the necessarily long stem used was that of the durra (or dhura), sometimes called the Jerusalem corn. The true durra is the Egyptian rice corn, which can grow to a height of 16 ft. Its stout stems are filled with a thick, dry pith which is never sweet. The plant grows well without irrigation.

Pens in biblical days were made from reeds; thus 3 Jn. 13—"I have much to write you, but I do not want to do so with pen and ink"—refers to a reed pen, as do the pens mentioned in 3 Macc. 4:20. These pens would normally be used to write on papyrus, while the INK might be lamp black stirred into gall juice. A special KNIFE obviously was used for making the nib of the reed pen (cf. "penknife" in Jer. 36:23 NRSV). Reed pens can be made from the tall grass, *Phragmites communis* (a perennial allied to the *Arundo*). This common reed, found in the Holy Land, has stems that can grow 12 ft. in height. The stems are much valued for thatching in Britain.

The PAPYRUS reed (*Cyperus papyrus*) grew down the NILE in the shallower parts and produced huge main, thick horizontal roots, often 20 ft. long, out of which grew shorter roots for anchorage purposes. Whole plants were dug up, the roots being used for tool handles, and the stems being made into sandals, ropes, mats, and baskets. The pith of the stems could be eaten, either cooked or raw (cf. Ezek. 3:1–3; Rev. 10:9–10), and it could be extracted to make writing material.

Sometimes the English word *rush* is used in Bible versions as roughly synonymous with *reed* (e.g., Job 8:11 KJV; Isa. 19:6 NRSV and NIV). The problem is increased because a large number of different species of rush grow in Palestine. There are some fifteen different types of club rush, such as *Scirpus maritimus* and *Scirpus lacustris,* and some twenty types of the common rush, *Juncus maritimus,* which are found at the seaside. There is also *Juncus effusus,* found in the bogs and wet places.

W. E. SHEWELL-COOPER

Reeds, Sea of. See RED SEA.

Reelaiah ree´uh-lay´uh (רְעֵלָיָה H8305, derivation uncertain). An Israelite mentioned among leading individuals who returned from Babylon with Zerubbabel (Ezra 2:2; called "Raamiah" in Neh. 7:7 and "Resaiah" in 1 Esd. 5:8 [KJV, "Reesaias"]). See also Reeliah.

Reeliah ree´uh-li´uh (Ρεελιου [the reading of most mss]; Rahlfs and the Göttingen *Septuaginta* have Βορολιου, following Codex Vaticanus). An Israelite mentioned among leading individuals who returned from Babylon with Zerubbabel (1 Esd. 5:8 [KJV, "Reelius"]). It corresponds in position to Bigvai in Ezra 2:2 and Neh. 7:7, but in form it seems to be the equivalent of Reelaiah.

Reelius ree´uh-li´uhs. KJV Apoc. form of Reeliah (1 Esd. 5:8).

Reesaias ree´uh-say´yuhs. KJV Apoc. form of Raamaiah (1 Esd. 5:8).

refine. This English term, referring to the process of eliminating impurities, is used to render the Hebrew verbs *zāqaq* H2423, "to filter, distill, purify" (1 Chr. 28:18 et al.), and *ṣārap* H7671, "to smelt, refine" (Ps. 12:6 et al.). In the NT, it translates Greek *pyroō* G4792 (lit., "to burn with fire," Rev. 1:15 [NIV, "glowing"]; 3:18; the NIV also uses it once to render *dokimazō* G1507 ("to test," 1 Pet. 1:7). The process of eliminating impurities, especially from metals.

The process of refining was quite simple. It involved heating the ore to the melting point and then extracting the metal. The metal was refined by heating it to the liquid state and then skimming or blowing off the impurities, or dross. Naturally, such refined gold or silver was more precious and expensive. The altar of incense was made of refined gold (1 Chr. 28:18) and the Laodicean church was urged to buy such refined gold (Rev. 3:18). The Bible provides some indication of the process: there is mention of the furnace (Ps. 12:6), the chemical lye (Isa. 1:25), and the bellows used to create a draft (Jer. 6:29).

The process of refining illustrates God's dealing with his people; he is the refiner, they are the metal. So Isaiah can say figuratively, "See, I have refined you, though not as silver, / I have tested you in the furnace of affliction" (Isa. 48:10; cf. 1:25). Malachi uses both Hebrew words together: "He will sit as a refiner [*měṣārēp*] and purifier of silver; he will purify the Levites and refine [*ziqqaq*] them like gold and silver" (Mal. 3:3). The psalmist prayed for such a process when he said, "Test me, O Lord, and try me, / examine [*ṣrp*] my heart and my mind" (Ps. 26:2b). R. L. Alden

refuge. This English term, which is especially common in the book of Psalms, is used to render a variety of Hebrew words, in particular the noun *maḥseh* H4726 (Ps. 14:6 et al.); the expression "to take refuge" translates the Hebrew verb *ḥāsâ* H2879 (2:12 et al.). Such terms express security from danger, such as is found in a shelter during a storm. God is the shelter of the pious (Ps. 104:18; Isa. 4:6). Because a refuge is often a place to which one flees (cf. Heb. *nûs* H5674), the concept can also be expressed with the term *mānôs* H4960 (e.g., Ps. 59:16). Moreover, some nouns that mean "tower," "stronghold," and so on are used figuratively for "refuge" (e.g., *miśgāb* H5369 in 9:9). In the case of the expression cities of refuge, the term is *miqlāṭ* H5236 (Num. 35:6 et al.).

Regem ree´guhm (רֶגֶם H8084, perhaps "friend" [BDB, 920] or "voice" [i.e., of God; cf. *HALOT*, 3:1187]). Son of Jahdai and apparently a descendant of Judah in the line of Caleb (1 Chr. 2:47). See discussion under Jahdai.

Regem-Melech ree´guhm-mee´lik (רֶגֶם מֶלֶךְ H8085, perhaps "friend of the king" or "[the god] Milk has spoken"; see Regem). TNIV Regem-Melek. An Israelite leader who, with Sharezer, was sent by the people of Bethel to the temple priests to inquire regarding the propriety of continuing to fast in commemoration of the destruction of the temple (Zech. 7:2). There is uncertainty as to whether a personal name or a title ("the king's friend" applied to Sharezer?) is intended. Some emend the text to read *rabmag melek*, thus, "The people of Bethel had sent Sharezer, Rabmag of the king." See Rabmag. S. Barabas

regeneration. The biblical doctrine of the new birth.

I. The biblical witness.

Jesus' nocturnal conversation with NICODEMUS, a member of the SANHEDRIN, is the most important scriptural witness to the doctrine of regeneration. Representing some faction of the important religious sect of the PHARISEES, Nicodemus came to Jesus to inquire about the KINGDOM OF GOD. In addressing Jesus he recognizes him as a teacher and acknowledges the divine origin of his message. No one, he says, could have performed the MIRACLES that Jesus did unless God were with him. Himself a teacher of the Jews, he comes to Jesus, whom he believes will be able to instruct him.

In making his reply Jesus does not deny the truth of what Nicodemus has said about him. Nevertheless, he shows his dissatisfaction with the assumptions that prompted Nicodemus's visit by abruptly changing the course of the discussion. Instead of simply giving him information, Jesus says, "I tell you the truth, no one can see the kingdom of God unless he is born again" (Jn. 3:3). Surprised, Nicodemus turns in his mind to what is familiar to him, namely, natural childbirth. "How can a man be born when he is old?... Surely he cannot enter a second time into his mother's womb to be born!" (v. 4). In answering Jesus reinforces what he has previously said, "You should not be surprised at my saying, 'You must be born again'" (v. 7).

Undoubtedly Jesus refers here to the necessity of a new birth. The very abruptness with which he breaks off the thread of the conversation shows that he wanted Nicodemus to realize that his query could not be answered properly by simply adding to his store of information or simply correcting him in one or another respect. It was not sufficient for him to carry on with the life that he already had; it was necessary for him to be born again.

That the newness of this birth is in mind here cannot be questioned; nevertheless, the Greek word *anōthen G540*, "again," should probably be translated "from above" (cf. NRSV and see Jn. 3:31). This rendering is supported by the fact that Jesus proceeds immediately to contrast the natural birth and the new birth as to their origins. "Flesh gives birth to flesh, but the Spirit gives birth to spirit" (v. 6). What is required for entering the kingdom of God is that one be born "of water and the Spirit" (v. 5). When he refers to regeneration, John always describes it as a birth from God (cf. 1:13). Thus what is in mind is not only the newness of the birth, but also its origin in the supernatural activity of the Spirit.

The source of the new birth, as Jesus' reference to the inscrutable activity of the wind shows, lies beyond the range of our earthly experience (Jn. 3:8). It is not enough, therefore, to call this a "new birth"; it is a birth "from above," by the agency of the creative activity of the Spirit of God. The ideas of newness, regeneration, and a supernatural origin in the activity of the HOLY SPIRIT are all joined together in Tit. 3:5. Here SALVATION is said to occur by means of "the washing of rebirth [*palingenesia G4098*] and renewal [*anakainōsis G364*] by the Holy Spirit."

In salvation, therefore, there is a washing and a renewing, a change in the innermost attitudes and inclinations of the HEART. And the change is of such a nature that it can be compared only with the generation and birth of life. Unlike natural birth, however, this birth does not have its origin in the human WILL but in the sovereign power of God. It is a birth that is not of the flesh nor of blood but of the Spirit (Jn. 1:13). The analogy of birth shows that regeneration is a radical change, which brings one from an earlier condition of SIN and DEATH to a renewed state of HOLINESS and LIFE.

In the same vein the Bible speaks of one who has been regenerated as a "new creation" in Christ (2 Cor. 5:17). According to PAUL (Gal. 6:15), what really matters is a new creation. Thus the Christian is exhorted "to put on the new self, created to be like God in true righteousness and holiness" (Eph. 4:24). So also the new birth is described as an act of being brought forth (Jas. 1:18 RSV) or being given life (Jn. 5:21; Eph. 2:5). Believers are said to have been made alive from the dead (Rom. 6:13). They are also called God's "workmanship" (Eph. 2:10).

Having been dead in trespasses and sins (Eph. 2:1, 5), blind and unresponsive to the things that pertain to the Spirit of God (1 Cor. 2:14), unable to do any work that merits salvation (2 Tim. 1:9; Tit. 3:5), the person who has been corrupted in all of his powers is re-created in Christ Jesus. Even as a newborn child has had nothing to do with his or her conception and birth, the transformation of the new birth is one that cannot be accounted for by any powers resident within the person but only by the power of the Spirit that is from above.

II. The biblical theological perspective. The Greek word for "regeneration" (*palingenesia G4098*) is found only in Matt. 19:28 and Tit. 3:5. In the first instance it refers to the restoration of the entire universe at the end time (see ESCHATOLOGY). Only in the latter case does it refer to the initiation of a new life in the believer. More commonly this new beginning is expressed by the Greek verb *gennaō G1164*, "to beget," which in the passive means, "to be born" (cf. Jn. 1:13; 3:3–8; 1 Pet. 1:3 and 23 [*anagennaō G335*, "to beget anew"]; 1 Jn. 2:29; 3:9; 4:7; 5:1, 4, 18). Other passages use the verb *zōopoieō G2443*, "to make alive" (e.g., Jn. 6:63; 2 Cor. 3:6; *syzōopoieō G5188* in Eph. 2:4; Col. 2:13). In one passage the Greek verb *apokyeō G652* is used, which means "to bear" or "to bring forth" (Jas. 1:18). The idea of the production of a new life is also expressed by the word *ktizō G3231*, "to create" (Eph. 2:10). The resulting work is then called a *kainē ktisis*, a "new creation" (2 Cor. 5:17; Gal. 6:15), or a *kainos anthrōpos*, a "new man" (Eph. 4:24 KJV; see MAN, NEW).

The more specific doctrine of the new birth occurs, however, in the context of the broader biblical teaching concerning *renewal*. In the NT, the verb *anakainoō G363* and its cognate noun *anakainōsis G364* appear a few times only in the Epistles (Rom. 12:2; 2 Cor. 4:16; Col. 3:10; Tit. 3:5; Heb. 6:6; in Eph. 4:23 the verb is *ananeoomai G391*). That the words themselves do not often appear does not mean, however, that the doctrine is unimportant. The biblical idea of renewal is taught at all stages of the revelation of God.

In the OT the ideas of cleansing (see CLEAN) and PURIFICATION are very prominent. In a great number of cases this cleansing is ceremonial or ritual. That is to say, it is part of a rite whose performance qualified one for something, such as participation in a religious ceremony or being publicly accepted in the tribe. Examples are the ceremonial purification of the high priest before his entering the holy place (Lev. 16:1–4) and the ritual cleansing of a woman after childbirth (ch. 12). These ceremonial cleansings, although they were symbolic and did not necessarily correspond with an inward holiness on the part of the one who performed them, were not purely external and devoid of ethical significance, as liberal theology has claimed. They were symbolic of the righteousness and holiness of heart that was demanded of the people of God. Thus the prophets denounced the people when these ceremonies became external and were no longer understood in their deeper significance. There was the prophecy of a new day in which the law of God would be inscribed on the heart, when there would be a people who were truly separated to God (Jer. 31:33; see COVENANT, THE NEW).

Although the element of renewal that is the new birth is not so clearly taught in the OT as it is in the NT, the OT idea of the relationship between God and his people requires a perfect standard of righteousness and holiness, and its promise of renewal is that of a renewal of the heart. The central meaning of God's COVENANT with his people was that he would be a God to them and that they would be his people (Gen. 17:1, 7–8). This meant that they were separated to him. It was symbolized in their being called out of the nations and their being circumcised. CIRCUMCISION signified the covenant with God in its deepest intent (17:10). It meant that they were set apart for him and for the holiness which was fitting to this union with him. Union with God was symbolized also in terms of the MARRIAGE bond, and breaking his covenant was compared with whoredom (Jer. 2:2; 3:1; Hos. 1:2; et al.).

It is to this inner relationship and to its realization that the OT symbolism refers. Indeed, this relationship had not yet been fully realized. God's people were still under age. They had to be governed by a LAW that was greatly detailed and burdensome (Acts 15:10; Gal. 3:19, 23–26; 4:1–7; 5:1), a law that often could be observed externally without any corresponding change of heart. Furthermore, access to God was through a human priesthood (see PRIESTS AND LEVITES), and God's word was received through a special group, the PROPHETS.

Nevertheless, the OT itself recognizes the temporary nature of these arrangements. It promises that a time will come when the Spirit will be poured out upon all flesh (Joel 2:28). It also recognizes the inner meaning of the law, using its provisions to refer to the deepest meaning of the covenant. "The LORD your God will circumcise your hearts and the hearts of your descendants, so that you may love him with all your heart and with all your soul, and live" (Deut. 30:6). It also calls the people out of their indifference and rebellion to the true service of God. "I will give them an undivided heart and put a new spirit in them; I will remove from them their heart of stone and give them a heart of flesh"

This *mikveh*, uncovered at the S end of the temple mount, was used for purification rites in Jewish ceremonies. Ceremonial cleansing or washing, a key symbolic act in the ritual of the OT, formed part of the background for the theological idea of regeneration in the NT.

(Ezek. 11:19; cf. 36:26; 37:1–14; Jer. 31:33). In response one finds the beautiful expressions of piety of the OT saints, "Cleanse me with hyssop, and I will be clean; / wash me, and I will be whiter than snow.... Create in me a pure heart, O God, / and renew a steadfast spirit within me" (Ps. 51:7, 10).

In a few passages, as we have observed, the NT speaks of renewal specifically in terms of a new birth by the power of the Holy Spirit. Even in the NT, however, the doctrine of the new birth occurs in the context of the more general teaching of renewal, which includes not only this birth itself but everything that flows out of it, namely the new life in Christ in its entirety. Regeneration in the narrow sense of the new birth may indeed be distinguished from this broader idea of renewal; but it should not be isolated from it.

III. Doctrinal development. Considering the fact that there is no elaborate body of teaching about the new birth in the Scriptures and that this teaching is set in the context of a broader teaching concerning renewal, it is not surprising that the term *regeneration* did not immediately have in the church the more precise significance it later acquired in theology.

In the early church the term was used to denote a change intimately connected with the remission of sins. No clear distinction was made between regeneration, the act of God in which a person is made holy (see also SANCTIFICATION), and JUSTIFICATION, the act of God in which a person is declared to be righteous. In his controversy with Pelagius, who taught that the human will is free to choose the good, the church father Augustine maintained that regeneration is a work of God alone that changes the heart and that makes it possible for one to understand the gospel and to be converted. There was, however, still no clear distinction made between regeneration and other doctrines pertaining to renewal.

The failure to distinguish between regeneration and justification had adverse effects in scholastic theology. Justification came to be regarded as the more inclusive notion; it was supposed to include regeneration and to be an act in which God and the sinner cooperated. According to the dominant view, that of Thomas Aquinas, justification was first an infusion of grace, that is, the birth of a new creation (regeneration) and, based upon it, the FORGIVENESS of sins and the removal of guilt. In the Roman Catholic Church there is still a certain confusion of regeneration and justification. The declarative nature of justification is lost to sight and justification is regarded to be an act or a process of renewal in which a person's subjective life is changed. The sinner, in the opinion of the Roman church, is not *declared* to be just but is *made* just.

Like the church fathers, the Reformers, including both Luther and Calvin, employed the term *regeneration* in a broad sense. Calvin used it to designate the entire process by which the believer is renewed, including not only the divine act by which the new life comes into being in the Christian, but also the conversion and sanctification that flow from it. This broad use of the word continued on even in the followers of the Reformers. It led, however, to confusion. Gradually, therefore, there arose a stricter use of the term, which came to be distinguished from, but included under, *conversion*.

Francis Turretin distinguished two types of conversion, namely, "habitual" or "passive" conversion, which is the production of a habit or disposition of the soul, and "actual" or "active" conversion, in which this inner disposition comes to expression in REPENTANCE and FAITH. The first, he said, might more aptly be called *regeneration*. Thus the meaning of this term became restricted and was distinguished from the broader conception of renewal. The word *regeneration* is presently often used to denote only the implantation of a new life, not to its manifestations.

In the theology that arose in the wake of the rationalism of the Enlightenment, there was a denial that regeneration was an act of God renewing the heart unto salvation. Rationalism, to be exact, secularized the Christian view of regeneration. That is to say, the idea that the Holy Spirit re-creates the innermost life was transformed into the notion that there is in everyone an unspoiled creative source of REASON. The need for an inner renewal of human life was eliminated. Human beings were supposed to have a pure spring of truth and goodness already within themselves. It was only necessary to let this reason come to expression. Indeed, reason had to disentangle each individual from the web of irrational circumstances surrounding his life; but reason itself, at the very heart of the personality, had no need of regeneration. Of itself, reason was supposed to be able to change people, to redirect their will and their emotions.

In reaction to the intellectualism of rationalism, theological liberalism found a place again for the idea of regeneration. Friedrich Schleiermacher, who has been called the father of modern theology, is supposed to have reintroduced the idea of regeneration into theology. In Schleiermacher's thought, individual understanding is no longer at the center. What is now central is the divine life as it is manifested in Jesus Christ. Through a personal encounter with Christ, there is within the individual the birth of a new religious personality. His weak and suppressed God-consciousness is strengthened and made dominant, there is a break with his old situation, and there is the beginning of a new life of personal communion with God. Schleiermacher thought of regeneration as being this critical point, where the old life breaks off and a new life begins.

Although Schleiermacher broke with the rationalism and intellectualism of modernism, regeneration is for him still nothing more than strengthening and making dominant something that is already present in man. The encounter with Jesus Christ simply awakens the slumbering consciousness of the divine.

The theology of neoorthodoxy, which developed between the two world wars, protested that liberal theology had been man-centered and had allowed no real place for regeneration as truly a work of God. A point was sought from which regeneration could be viewed as a new creation, from a source which transcended anything in the human being. It had to be something more than a projection of a person's own possibilities.

Karl Barth's theology of the Word maintains that whenever the Word of God is present, in distinction from the mere words of human beings, there is revelation and a radical change from death to life. The person is transformed by the word, which uses the words of human beings breaking in as grace onto the level of human life.

Barth believed that he had corrected the man-centeredness of liberal theology and had developed a position that allowed for the radical change from death to life of the new birth. The focus is supposed to have shifted from the individual and his possibilities to God's electing love in Christ. God's grace is triumphant, making all things new.

Barth, however, has always insisted that when the saving Word of God enters history it invades a realm that is foreign to it. It must transform human words into the Word of God. As soon as it has entered history, it has already taken a form that is at the disposal of human beings. It is no longer the Word of God; it has become the words of men. God's saving revelation can be only from moment to moment. Nothing can simply be said *to be* the Word of God; the Word of God must always *become* the Word of God.

Similarly the new birth is supposed to have a transcendent source. As soon, however, as it is thought to impart a new disposition or qualities that would serve to distinguish one individual or group from another, it has become self-sufficient, Barth thinks, and is in conflict with the living confrontation with God and his revelation. To think that regeneration effects such a change is to deny the freedom of God and his revelation and to place them at our disposal.

This view brings Barth into sharp opposition to orthodox theology. The latter saw no difficulty in holding at one and the same time to the sovereignty of God in his revelation and to the idea that regeneration implants new dispositions, principles, tastes, etc., that underlie and determine the character of a person and all of his acts. To accept the traditional position means for Barth to have reverted to the notion that human beings can be something in and of themselves, apart from their relationship to God and from their dependence upon him. For Barth the traditional position involves a denial of the biblical teaching of justification by faith. Insofar as believers are thought to live by virtue of something they possess as a quality of their life, they live by sight and no longer by grace through faith. There is an observable, describable principle within them that is supposed to result in a nearly mechanical fashion in their sanctification.

More recently Barth has emphasized the positive relation that pertains through grace between God and humanity. By the inner logic of his own position Barth has come to the view that all people are already elected in Christ. They are already in Christ; they must simply come to recognize that fact. As the more positive side of Barth's theology has gotten the upper hand—as the theme of divine judgment has been consciously subordinated to the theme of the triumph of grace—the radical change from death to life of the new birth has become indistinct. It has faded into the difference between those who do and those who do not yet acknowledge the fact that they already have been elected in Christ.

Barth believes that he has truly interpreted the scriptural teaching concerning the grace of God which is new every morning. However, this has been impossible for Barth because of his unwillingness to accept the true authority of Scripture. Instead, he has established a sanctuary for human autonomy, which can dictate how the saving revelation of God and the work of the Spirit are to appear in history.

In spite of Barth's intentions he cannot obtain, therefore, a view of regeneration that affects the very heart of human existence. In their autonomous critical powers and in their historical cultural activity, human beings are neutral. They have no need of regeneration. Indeed, here regeneration is not allowed to touch. Human autonomy is allowed to establish a realm into which the saving revelation of God cannot penetrate directly.

In contrast, the scriptural position is that human beings were created in the IMAGE OF GOD and that in their pristine goodness were given the task of subduing the world to the glory of God; that they sinned, becoming corrupted in all of their powers; and that they are in need of a regeneration that affects the very heart of their existence, a renewal that will reestablish them in the service of the Creator with all of their heart, soul, and mind.

IV. Doctrinal formulation. A survey of the idea of regeneration in the Scriptures shows that it is not sharply defined. It warrants, however, making a distinction between (a) regeneration in the sense of the initial act by which God through the power of his Holy Spirit re-creates one into the new life in Christ and (b) regeneration in a broader sense that includes conversion, sanctification, and the final restoration of all things. Regeneration in the narrower sense it has assumed in theology should not be considered in isolation from this broader context. It is, indeed, first of all a new birth; but it also has to do with the entire process of renewal both in its personal and in its cosmic dimensions.

The reason for this double meaning is likely that regeneration in the narrow sense of the new birth is not simply an act that can be set off rigidly from other acts. Instead, it is a renewal at the very root of human existence whose significance must extend to everything that falls within the scope of divine salvation. This radical change, at the very heart of the creation, must manifest itself, therefore, throughout its entire extent. The purpose of God is the salvation of the whole person and thus of the entire cosmos over which he was made the vicegerent.

This insight was grasped and elaborated clearly by the Dutch theologian Abraham Kuyper. For him regeneration was more than one link among others in the chain of salvation. It became a universal theological principle of *palingenesis* (*palingenesia*). Kuyper grasped the radical nature of SIN. He understood that it affected the cosmos at its root and that from this center corruption spread into all of its parts. Kuyper, therefore, was able to give an equally central and decisive place to the re-creation of the cosmos in Christ Jesus. It became necessary for the Christian to be concerned not only with the question of personal holiness but also with the principles that should guide the regenerated mind in all of its activities, in society as well as in the church.

When it is viewed in this fashion, regeneration is not thought to add any new part to the person. It does not endow individuals with any new function. Regeneration is a renewal of human beings in the heart, a renovation in the deepest center of their existence. As such it differs from justification. The latter is a judicial declaration that the sinner is righteous on the basis of the righteousness of Christ, which has been imputed to him. One must, however, take into consideration not only the guilt but also the pollution of sin. It is necessary for one not only to be declared righteous, but also to be made holy. This is effected by regeneration. A principle of holiness is injected into the center of one's being. This holiness, to be sure, is not complete; nevertheless, it introduces into one's life the renewing power whose principle is nothing less than the perfect righteousness and holiness of God. The apostle John can say of the one who has been regenerated, "No one who is born of God will continue to sin, because God's seed remains in him; he cannot go on sinning, because he has been born of God" (1 Jn. 3:9).

Because regeneration affects the very heart of human existence, neither its place nor its effects can be localized. One cannot ask where it takes place, if one means one part of the human being in distinction from another. As the Scriptures teach, the work of the Spirit is inscrutable. It can be observed only in its effects. Jesus himself taught this, employing the wind as an analogy. The wind blows where it will. One observes its effects; but he cannot tell where it comes from or where it is going. So, Jesus says, is everyone who is born of the Spirit (Jn. 3:8). Likewise the scope of regeneration may not be limited. The entire person, in his or her intellectual, volitional, and emotive nature, has been corrupted by sin; therefore the entire person must be renewed according to the image of Christ.

If one understands the central meaning of regeneration, recognizing that it cannot be localized either as to its place or its effects, it will be clear that the difference between the regenerate and the unregenerate appears in an antithesis that runs through all of life. On the one hand, there will be a regenerated consciousness that seeks to subject everything to the Lordship of Christ; on the other hand, there will be a consciousness which, in the spirit of apostasy, will attempt to place creatures in their supposed independence from God at the center. One will then be obliged to bring this regenerated consciousness to bear upon all of life and its activities, not only on the study of the Bible and of theology but also on science, education, politics, and so forth.

This position, set forth by Abraham Kuyper and developed by others, provides a theological foundation for understanding the biblical doctrine that the entire creation participates in REDEMPTION. The entire creation also eagerly awaits the redemption of the children of God (Rom. 8:19–23). Both the human and subhuman creations are to be renewed in a new heaven and a new earth (see HEAVENS, NEW). That does not mean that every individual will be saved; nor does it mean that the works of darkness will not be judged. Nevertheless, all things—that is, every aspect of the creation—will participate in salvation. All things will be renewed in the new heaven and the new earth.

(See further B. B. Warfield, *Biblical Doctrines* [1929], 439–63; A. Kuyper, *The Work of the Holy Spirit* [1941], 293–332; L. Berkhof, *Systematic Theology* [1941], 465–79; J. Murray, *Redemption: Accomplished and Applied* [1955], 119–29; R. D. Knudsen in *Christian Faith and Modern Theology*, ed. C. F. H. Henry [1964], 307–21; P. Toon, *Born Again: A Biblical and Theological Study of Regeneration* [1987]; W. Grudem, *Systematic Theology: An Introduction to Christian Doctrine* [1994], ch. 34.)

R. D. KNUDSEN

Rehabiah ree´huh-bi´uh (רְחַבְיָה H8152 and רְחַבְיָהוּ H8153, "Yahweh has made wide" [i.e., has been generous]). Son of ELIEZER, grandson of MOSES, and ancestor of a leading Levite family (1 Chr. 23:17; 24:21; 26:25).

Rehob (person) ree´hob (רְחֹב H8150, possibly related to a root meaning "to be wide"). **(1)** Father of HADADEZER king of ZOBAH, whom DAVID defeated at the EUPHRATES (2 Sam. 8:3, 12). Some have taken the expression "son of Rehob" to indicate that Hadadezer was from BETH REHOB (cf. 10:6), suggesting that he united this town and Zobah under his rule (cf. the discussion in P. K. McCarter, Jr., *II Samuel*, AB 9 [1984], 248). See also REHOB (PLACE) #1.

(2) One of the Levites who signed the covenant of NEHEMIAH (Neh. 10:11).

Rehob (place) ree´hob (רְחֹב *H8149*, "broad place, open plaza"). **(1)** A town or district at the N end of the JORDAN Valley marking the limit of the journey of the Israelite spies (Num. 13:21). During the reign of DAVID it was one of the Aramean strongholds (see ARAM) that sent forces to the aid of AMMON (2 Sam. 10:8; called BETH REHOB in v. 6; cf. Jdg. 18:28). Its exact location is unknown.

(2) A town on the N border of ASHER, listed between ABDON and HAMMON (Josh. 19:28). In the topographical list of THUTMOSE III, this Rehob may be included (no. 87, *rḥb*). Its location is uncertain, but some identify it with Tell el-Balaṭ, some 12 mi. SE of TYRE (cf. Y. Aharoni, *The Land of the Bible: A Historical Geography*, rev. ed. [1979], 162); another possibility is Tell el-Raḥb, 4 mi. farther to the SE (S. Aḥituv, *Canaanite Toponyms in Ancient Egyptian Documents* [1984], 164). Other scholars believe that this Rehob is the same as #3 below (see discussion in *ABD*, 5:660–61).

(3) A town on the S border of Asher, listed after APHEK (Josh. 19:30); it was a Levitical city assigned to the descendants of GERSHON (21:31; 1 Chr. 6:75 [Heb. 6:60]). However, the people of Asher were unable to drive the Canaanite inhabitants out of the city (Jdg. 1:31). A town by the name of Rahabu is mentioned beside DOR in a list of RAMSES II (from Amara West in Nubia), and therefore many believe this Rehob should be located in the southern plain of Acco (cf. B. Mazar, *Yedioth* 27 [1963]: 139–44 [in Heb.]). It is probably to be identified with Tell el-Bir el-Gharbi (also T. Berweh and T. Bira), some 6 mi. ESE of Acco (see *NEAEHL*, "Bira, Tel," 1:262–63). Another proposal is Khirbet Daʿuk, about a mile closer to Acco (Z. Kallai, *Historical Geography of the Bible* [1986], 428).

B. K. WALTKE

Rehoboam ree´huh-boh´uhm (רְחַבְעָם *H8154*, possibly "the people have become extended" or "the [divine] kinsman has been generous" [cf. REHABIAH]; Ῥοβοάμ *G4850*). KJV NT Roboam. Son of SOLOMON and first king of JUDAH after the division of the kingdom (1 Ki. 11:43—12:27; 14:21—15:6; 2 Chr. 9:31—12:16).

I. Family. Rehoboam was probably born before Solomon's accession to the throne; his mother was NAAMAH, an Ammonite princess (1 Ki. 11:42; 14:21). Following his father's example, Rehoboam maintained a large HAREM. Among his wives, MAHALATH belonged to DAVID's family by both parents; but he subsequently preferred MAACAH, daughter of Abishalom (ABSALOM), and nominated her eldest son ABIJAH as his successor. Several of his other sons he placed in command of fortified towns (2 Chr. 11:18–23).

II. Chronology. Rehoboam succeeded his father at the age of forty-one and reigned for seventeen years until his death. E. R. Thiele (*The Mysterious Numbers of the Hebrew Kings*, 3rd ed. [1983], 79–80) gives the dates as 931/930 to 914/913 B.C., on the basis of his analysis of the data in Kings, and working back from the battle of Qarqar in 853 (fixed by Assyrian records). Some check on this is afforded by SHISHAK's invasion in the fifth year of Rehoboam; the Egyptian evidence consists of an inscription and reliefs on the Bubastite gate of the temple of Amun at Karnak, built in Shishak's twenty-first year (*ANET*, 242–43). The unfinished state of these reliefs, and the apparent failure of Egypt to follow up her advantage politically, indicate that the campaign took place toward the end of Shishak's reign; and it is not mentioned in any earlier monument (W. F. Albright in *BASOR* 130 [April 1953]: 4–8).

Interest accordingly centers on Shishak's dates; Albright accepts a possible range from 937 to 930 for his accession, and arrives at a date for the invasion around 918, with a tolerance of five years either way. This agrees with his conclusion in an earlier article (*BASOR* 100 [Dec. 1945]: 16–20), relying on the synchronism in 2 Chr. 16:1 (see ASA), and on a theory that some of the figures and synchronisms given for ZIMRI, OMRI, and AHAB are secondary; he places Rehoboam's accession in 922. A. H. Gardiner, however, gives Shishak's reign as about 945–925 (*Egypt of the Pharaohs: An Introduction* [1961], 448), which tends to justify Thiele's conclusions.

M. Rowton (in *BASOR* 119 [Oct. 1950]: 20–22) supports a later date from Phoenician evidence, linking the foundation of Carthage in the seventh year of Pygmalion (for which the classical writer Timaeus gives a date equivalent to 814 B.C.) with the twelfth year of HIRAM, which would then be 959; according to JOSEPHUS, this was Solomon's fourth year, in which the temple was founded. His fortieth would thus be 923. The basic evidence is not substantial, and Rowton concedes that this is only a cross-check. Others place Rehoboam's reign in the period 926 to 910 (J. H. Hayes and P. K. Hooker, *A New Chronology for the Kings of Israel and Judah* [1988], 16–20). See also CHRONOLOGY (OT).

III. Revolt of Israel

A. Situation. Rehoboam came to the throne at a time of stress, due to several factors. (1) Heavy state expenditure, particularly on the court and standing army, was financed partly by taxation, which probably fell most severely on the agricultural north. This conclusion may be drawn on a priori grounds, and from the data in 1 Ki. 4 on Solomon's organization of districts (Y. Aharoni, *The Land of the Bible: A Historical Geography*, rev. ed. [1979], 315–17). (2) Forced labor was a standing complaint; notwithstanding a disclaimer in 1 Ki. 9:22, which may be taken to mean that there was no permanent loss of status for Israelites, it is clear from ADONIRAM's position and unpopularity (4:6; 12:18) that the precedent of the corvée for building the temple (5:13–17) was too regularly followed. (3) Despite Solomon's large standing army, he had lost control of the DAMASCUS area, and the Arameans were raiding N of Israel (11:25). (4) The lax attitude to foreign religions was inviting divine judgment, expressed in AHIJAH's words to JEROBOAM (11:29–39). Jeroboam's position, and doubtless the prophecy itself, were known to Solomon and to Israel generally (12:3).

B. Confrontation. A national assembly was called at SHECHEM to confirm Rehoboam's accession. This apparently was not done for Solomon (the only exact precedent, since David's coronation began a fresh dynasty); such was the difference in the political atmosphere. It was not yet established that there was a hereditary right of accession apart from the wishes of the people, though there was a natural tendency to de facto hereditary succession, which might be called a presumptive right, even with the sons of GIDEON and SAUL. J. M. Myers (*II Chronicles*, AB 13 [1965], 65) notes that no question was ever made of Rehoboam's succession in Judah, and the cry of revolt was, "We have no inheritance in the son of Jesse" (1 Ki. 12:16 NRSV), that is, an assertion of tribal separatism. However, the assembly was not in itself mutinous, as R. Kittel seems to imply (*Geschichte des Volkes Israels*, 3rd ed. [1912–17], 2:347–54); otherwise the king would surely have taken military precautions.

The "assembly"—that is, the elders representing the people—demanded relief from the burdens imposed by Solomon, intimating that this would be a condition of allegiance. Rehoboam was faced

The Promised Land becomes the Divided Kingdom during the rule of Rehoboam.

with a choice: in principle, should his authority be constitutional or absolute? His older advisers (Solomon's council of state) recommended that he make concessions and win the people; but he took the advice of his contemporaries to make it clear that he would tolerate no challenge to his authority. The identity of these two groups was considered in a discussion of a paper by A. Malamat (in *BA* 28 [1965]: 34–65), who sees the young men as mainly of the royal family and of military rank; G. Evans (in *JNES* 25 [1966]: 273–79) is less sure of their official status.

Rehoboam accordingly answered the assembly with the famous phrase: "My father scourged you with whips; I will scourge you with scorpions" (1 Ki. 12:14; the term "scorpions" is prob. a reference to loaded scourges, a particularly painful whip). The assembly thereupon repudiated the Davidic dynasty, raising the now traditional cry of dissolution: "To your tents, Israel!" (v. 16). It was not seriously proposed to restore the premonarchic order; the state needed a king, and Jeroboam was apparently consecrated at the same convention. The point was that Israel still claimed a freedom to which her king owed respect.

C. Aftermath. Adoniram, who controlled the labor force and was therefore directly concerned with public order, was sent to quell the riot; but he was stoned to death, and Rehoboam himself escaped to Jerusalem. There he summoned the militia of Judah and Benjamin to try to reduce Israel by force, but the prophet SHEMAIAH forbade the expedition publicly in the name of the Lord; so the assembly dispersed, and a state of hostilities ensued (1 Ki. 14:30; 2 Chr. 12:15). This is not incompatible with the avoidance of a pitched battle; indeed, it helps to explain the major clash under ABIJAH, who clearly invaded Israel (perhaps under provocation) and cherished some hope of restoring the Davidic kingdom there.

IV. Shishak's expedition. The attempt of Shishak (Sheshonq I) to reassert Egyptian authority in Palestine is described (so far as it affected Judah) in 1 Ki. 14:25–28 and 2 Chr. 12:1–12, and represented on the wall of the temple of Amun at Karnak; it occurred in Rehoboam's fifth year (see

This wall in the temple at Karnak lists the cities conquered by King Shishak of Egypt during the reign of Rehoboam.

II above). A number of correlations have been obtained between the Karnak inscription and place names occurring in the Bible, but the inscription was not properly understood until B. Mazar (in *Volume du congrès: Strasbourg 1956* [1957], 57–66) suggested reading alternate lines in opposite directions (*boustrophedon*). This put the recognizable names in a sequence which indicated that Shishak, after detaching a force to invade the NEGEV, came into the hills by Gibeon (N of Jerusalem), crossed into the Jordan Valley, and went through the Vale of JEZREEL and back by the coast road. Archaeological evidence illustrates his trail of devastation at GEZER, BETH SHEMESH (if this was the Egyptian *rbt*), and MEGIDDO (K. M. Kenyon, *Archaeology in the Holy Land* [1960], 273ff.).

Doubtless Shishak's main concern was to assert suzerainty over Jeroboam, who had been a refugee at his court; also, Solomon had been Egypt's ally by marriage. The inscriptions speak of "northern rebels and aggressors of the Mitanni." Although Shishak was not so concerned with the hill state of Judah, Jerusalem might well have expected to suffer the same fate as the cities of the plain. B. Mazar (in *IEJ* 2 [1952]: 82–88) observes that while the account in Kings relates primarily to the replacement of the gold shields by bronze, and to the origin of the custom of carrying them in procession, Chronicles (typically) deals with the episode in the context of Shemaiah's prophecy. The king and his people, having left the service of the Lord, would now know what it was to be at the mercy of a tyrant (2 Chr. 12:8). It was a case of "the king's heart is in the hand of the LORD" (Prov. 21:1). The common source of Kings and Chronicles gives the impression that Shishak actually entered or sent officers into the city; Aharoni (*The Land of the Bible*, 326) thinks that an embassy met him at Gibeon, since the next place mentioned in his inscription is Zemaraim, to the N. These suggestions are not incompatible.

V. Defense. Two lines of evidence suggest that Shishak's force in the Negev established a buffer state under Egyptian control in the valley of GERAR: (1) the character of the forces attacking Judah about thirty years later (see ASA); and (2) the list of hill towns fortified by Rehoboam against Philistine, Egyptian, and perhaps Edomite threats (Myers, *II Chronicles*, 69–70). E. Junge's view, that they were fortified by Josiah (*Der Wiederaufbau des Heerwesens des Reiches Juda unter Josia* [1937]), is controlled by his theory that the Chronicler continually projects the Josianic situation into the more remote past. A. Alt inclines to accept the Chronicler's account, and also sees in the Levitical towns of Judah a line of frontier forts (*Kleine Schriften*, 3 vols. [1953–59], 2:306–15). Even on this basis, the southern border was now withdrawn to the hills. On his northern frontier, Rehoboam did not consider himself to be on the defensive.

VI. Religious policy. Rehoboam claimed to be loyal to the Lord and to his temple; this is attested by his replacing the shields given to Shishak with replicas for the traditional ceremonies, by Abijah's speech (2 Chr. 13), and, indirectly, by Jeroboam's need to set up counter attractions to the Jerusalem temple. Many Levites moved into Judah as a result (11:13–17).

The Chronicler records, however, that after three years, when he felt established, Rehoboam abandoned the teaching of the Lord; and Shemaiah declared Shishak's invasion to be God's answering judgment (2 Chr. 11:17; 12:1). The king and court accepted the rebuke, but with half-hearted repentance. The episode of the invasion is introduced in Kings by a description of the backsliding, not of the king specifically, but of the people as a whole. It may be that Rehoboam was not strong-minded enough to stem the popular tide; and it should not be forgotten that Solomon had opened the door wide to foreign practices. (For the view that the Chronicler portrays Rehoboam primarily as a villain, see G. N. Knoppers in *JBL* 109 [1990]: 423–40.)

J. LILLEY

Rehoboth ri-hoh′both (רְחֹבוֹת *H8151*, "broad places"). (1) A well dug by ISAAC after his troubles with ABIMELECH and the herdsmen of GERAR (Gen. 26:22, where the LXX translates the name as *Eurychōria*, "open space, room"). The PHILISTINES had filled in the old well so that Isaac's servants had to dig new ones. But the herdsmen of Gerar claimed the first two for themselves (vv. 20–21). When a third one was uncontested, Isaac named it "Rehoboth," saying, "Now the LORD has given us room and we will flourish in the land" (v. 22). This Rehoboth has often been identified with modern Ruḥaibeh, c. 22 mi. SW of BEERSHEBA, though the narrative suggests a site farther N, between Gerar and Beersheba (cf. *NEAEHL*, 4:1274–77).

(2) The hometown of SHAUL, an early Edomite king (Gen. 36:37; 1 Chr. 1:48). The text names it *rěḥōbôt hannāhār*, "Rehoboth of the river," and since EUPHRATES is sometimes referred to as "the River" (e.g., Deut. 11:24; Josh. 24:3), the phrase can be translated "Rehoboth on the Euphrates" (cf. NRSV). If this is correct, the place in view may be modern Raḥba, S of the mouth of the Khabur (HABOR), a tributary of the EUPHRATES in N SYRIA. More likely, however, the site should be looked for in EDOM, in which case the river in question may be Wadi er-Riḥab (just S of the Edom-Moab border), leading to a possible identification of Rehoboth with modern Khirbet ʿAin Riḥab. (See further *ISBE* rev. [1979–88], 4:73; *ABD*, 5:664.)

Rehoboth Ir ri-hoh′both-ihr′ (רְחֹבֹת עִיר *H8155*, "broad places of the city," i.e., city squares or plazas). A city built by NIMROD in ASSYRIA (Gen. 10:11). Alternatively, it may have been built by ASSHUR, as indicated by the KJV rendering, "Out of that land went forth Asshur, and builded Nineveh, and the city Rehoboth" (cf. also NJPS). Because no such place is known from Assyrian sources, most interpreters believe the reference is to an area within (or in the environs of) NINEVEH. Thus, instead of "Nineveh and Rehoboth Ir," the words should probably be translated, "Nineveh with its city squares" (NIV mg.) or the like. It is uncertain, however, whether the Hebrew phrase should be paralleled with the Assyrian term *rēbīt Ninua*, which in later times supposedly referred to a NE suburb of Nineveh. It has also been suggested that *rĕḥōbōt ʿîr* is an epithet, so that the words should possibly be rendered, "Nineveh, the broad [*or* broadest] city," or "Nineveh, the city of open streets." (See further J. M. Sasson in *RB* 90 [1983]: 94–96; *ABD*, 5:664.)

Rehum ree´huhm (רְחוּם H8156, possibly "[God has been] compassionate"). **(1)** An Israelite mentioned among leading individuals who returned from Babylon with ZERUBBABEL (Ezra 2:2; 1 Esd. 5:8 [KJV, "Roimus"]; called NEHUM in Neh. 7:7). See also #4 below.

(2) A Persian officer who coauthored a letter to King ARTAXERXES opposing the rebuilding of the Jerusalem TEMPLE (Ezra 4:7–16). When a favorable reply came (vv. 17–22), Rehum, Shimshai, and their associates "went immediately to the Jews in Jerusalem and compelled them by force to stop" (v. 23; cf. 1 Esd. 2:16–30 [where KJV has "Rathumus"]). The NIV refers to him as "commanding officer," but the Aramaic phrase *bĕʿēl-ṭĕʿēm* (H10116 + H10302, lit. "lord of command") probably indicates a civil rather than military position; some think he may have been the governor of SAMARIA (however, see H. G. M. Williamson, *Ezra, Nehemiah*, WBC 16 [1985], 61–62).

(3) Son of Bani; he was in charge of some of the Levites who helped NEHEMIAH repair the wall of Jerusalem (Neh. 3:17).

(4) One of the leaders of the people who sealed the covenant of Nehemiah (Neh. 10:25). Some connect this Rehum with #1 above.

(5) One of the priestly leaders who returned with Zerubbabel (Neh. 12:3). Some scholars believe that here the name should be emended to HARIM (cf. v. 15).

Rei ree´i (רֵעִי H8298, possibly "friendly"). One of the supporters of SOLOMON at the time ADONIJAH attempted to secure the throne of DAVID (1 Ki. 1:8). He may have been an officer in the royal guard. However, the Lucianic recension of the SEPTUAGINT, evidently reading the Hebrew as *rʿwy*, translates "Shimei and his friends," and some scholars emend the MT accordingly (cf. also Jos. *Ant.* 7.14.4 §346, "Shimei, David's friend").

reins. See KIDNEYS.

Rekab, Rekabite. TNIV forms of RECAB, RECABITE.

Rekah. TNIV form of RECAH.

Rekem (person) ree´kuhm (רֶקֶם H8390, pausal form רָקֶם H8388 [1 Chr. 7:16], meaning uncertain). **(1)** One of five kings of MIDIAN killed by the Israelites in a battle on the plains of MOAB (Num. 31:8; Josh. 13:21). See REBA. Some scholars think that the name Rekem may indicate a place rather than (or in addition to) a person, and JOSEPHUS says that it was in fact the ancient name of PETRA in Edomite territory (*Ant.* 4.7.1 §161; see also *ABD*, 5:665).

(2) Son of HEBRON and descendant of JUDAH in the line of CALEB (1 Chr. 2:43–44).

(3) Son of Peresh (or of Sheresh), grandson of MAKIR, and great-grandson of MANASSEH (1 Chr. 7:16 NRSV, NJPS). The KJV, NIV, and other translations, without good reason, render this name according to its pausal form, "Rakem."

Rekem (place) ree´kuhm (רֶקֶם H8389, meaning uncertain). A town within the tribal territory of BENJAMIN (Josh. 18:27). It was probably a few miles NW of JERUSALEM, but its location is unknown. This town is to be distinguished from Rekem in EDOM; see REKEM (PERSON) #1.

religions, ancient. See ASSYRIA AND BABYLONIA IV; CANAAN IX; EGYPT VII; FERTILITY CULTS; GREEK RELIGION AND PHILOSOPHY; MYSTERY RELIGIONS; ROMAN RELIGION.

remain. See ABIDE.

Romaliah rem´uh-li´uh (רְמַלְיָהוּ H8255, perhaps "Yahweh has adorned" or "Yahweh, be exalted!"; cf. J. D. Fowler, *Theophoric Personal Names in Ancient Hebrew* [1988], 135–36). Father of PEKAH, one of the last kings of Israel (2 Ki. 15:25 et al.).

remember. The concept of remembering plays a much more important role in the OT than it does in the NT. Though the appeal to remembrance is present in the latter, it is much more prevalent in the Hebrew Bible, particularly in the Psalter. As such, there can be no doubt that the action of remembering is quite significant for various contexts in Scripture. To remember is part and parcel of the experience of Israel as well as of the God of Israel.

It has been recognized that in the Hebrew Bible "to remember" (Heb. *zākar H2349*) is both a thought process and a way of initiating action. This means that remembering is not merely what one might term a psychological recall, or bringing something to mind. To remember also suggests activity that is quite concrete. This is particularly the case when God remembers, as we shall see below. One can suggest that in many cases in the Bible the thought of remembering is hardly ever separated from activity.

In order to better understand the verb we will look first of all at how it is used in the context of human beings, and secondly at how it is used with God as subject. In the book of Deuteronomy we find that the memory motif is present with significant force. The command is not only to remember, but also more emphatically not to forget. This emphasis is there so that the new generation of Israel will have a link to the past. The people are challenged to remember the mighty acts of God on behalf of their forefathers. It is in this way that the past can be actualized into the present. By remembering, the people of God can participate in the wonder of the exodus that was experienced by previous generations (Deut. 9:7; see EXODUS, THE). In this same book, the people are encouraged to observe the SABBATH in order to remember the past slavery and liberation from Egypt (5:12–15). The concern once again is to insure that the past in a very real sense becomes part of the present, for this will have an effect on the conduct and the activity of the people in the future. In this manner, remembering is a creative activity by which they create and re-create history with the hopes of creating a community that does not suffer from historical amnesia.

In the book of PSALMS, the verb *remember* appears most often in the lament or complaint psalms. Here the poet often asks God to remember the evil action of the enemies. On the other hand he may ask that God not remember his sins. In this sense, the act of not remembering is tantamount to FORGIVENESS. Finally, the poet often asks God to remember his faithfulness, steadfast love, and commitment to the individual Israelite or to the community as a whole.

God's remembering carries with it definite action or consequences. The statement that "God remembered Noah" (Gen. 8:1) does not mean that the Lord had forgotten NOAH or that he was merely bringing Noah to mind. It means that God would take action to rescue him from the terrible flood. A similar situation is described when God "remembered" HANNAH, changing her reality of BARRENNESS and giving her a son (1 Sam. 1:19–20). One can argue that the remembering of God is often synonymous with his salvific activity. On the other hand, if God forgets someone, that someone for all practical purposes no longer exists. In summary, God remembers his covenant, his word, his promises, and his love for his people. In this sense, God's remembering most often implies movement towards a person. See also MEMORIAL.

S. VOTH

remembrance, book of. See BOOK OF REMEMBRANCE.

Remeth ree´mith (רֶמֶת *H8255*, possibly variant of רָאמוֹת *H8030*, "heights"). A border town in the tribal territory of ISSACHAR (Josh. 19:21). It is probably identical with Ramoth (1 Chr. 6:73) and Jarmuth (Josh. 21:29). See RAMOTH (PLACE) #3.

remission (of sins). See FORGIVENESS.

Remmon rem´uhn. KJV alternate form of Rimmon (only Josh. 19:7). See RIMMON (PLACE) #1.

Remmon-methoar rem´uhn-meth´oh-ahr. See RIMMON (PLACE) #2.

remnant. The special theological sense of this term derives from its secular use. The common notion of "something left over" occurs in the Bible with some frequency. For example, reference is made to the remainder of the cereal offering (Lev. 2:3), or of the holy oil (14:18), or of the male prostitutes that were exterminated (1 Ki. 22:46). It is in describing political divisions of various sorts that the word *remnant* is found frequently. The remainder of the pagans in Palestine after the conquest under JOSHUA is spoken of (Josh. 23:12), and OG is described as the remnant of the REPHAITES (Deut. 3:11). Reference is made also to the remnants of various other people groups (2 Sam. 21:2; Isa. 14:22, 30; 16:14).

Many times the word *remnant* is applied to political divisions and social groupings within Israel. We read about "the rest of the populace" who were left in the city of Jerusalem after the capture of the city by NEBUCHADNEZZAR (2 Ki. 25:11); about the evil "survivors" within Judah (Ezek. 14:22); and the residue of the people in the N who were invited by HEZEKIAH to participate in the PASSOVER (2 Chr. 30:6). Later on in Jewish history the companies of ZERUBBABEL and EZRA are described as "remnants" (Ezra 9:8 et al.).

The shift from these uses to the theological meaning is easy to understand. Such a concept is of prime interest. The judgment of God upon a remnant, or, contrariwise, the manifestation of grace to them, shows how history and theology are intertwined. An example of a pertinent text is Mic. 5:3, which states: "Therefore Israel will be abandoned / until the time when she who is in labor gives birth / and the rest [*yeter H3856*] of his brothers return / to join the Israelites." In other words, God intended to give up his people into the hands of their enemies (including the Romans?) until Christ should be born of Israel (or Mary); then all his scattered brothers would return and be joined in one body.

Jews worshiping in a synagogue at the Western Wall. Some view such a scene as a sign that a remnant would return.

G. Hutcheson understands the remnant here to be elect Gentiles, then unconverted, who are brethren in respect to his eternal love in election, God's purpose being to make them brethren by conversion (*Exposition of the Minor Prophets* [1655, repr. 1962], 136–38). These are conjoined with Jews in one spiritual body. E. B. Pusey believes that the withdrawal of God's protection spoken of here refers to the time of the EXILE (*The Minor Prophets* [1860], 72). The context, however, would seem to require what was then a future event.

That there is a great emphasis placed upon the significance of a true spiritual relationship in the NT cannot be denied. He who does the will of God is brother and sister and mother to Christ (Matt. 12:50), and Christ is not ashamed to call them brethren (Heb. 2:11). The promise is to those who are called of God (Acts 2:39). Pusey believes that both Jews and Gentiles who respond to the gospel are in the remnant.

C. L. F. Feinberg (*The Minor Prophets* [1976], 174) sees in Mic. 5:3 a reference to the literal return of the Jews who have been scattered by the judgment of God, but F. Delitzsch feels that the returning spoken of is of a spiritual kind, that is, returning to God in conversion (*Biblical Commentary on the Prophecies of Isaiah* [1877], 1:272–74). That the Bible teaches a literal return to Palestine (not necessarily to be identified with the contemporary Zionist movement) seems clearly taught by such passages as Jer. 31:7–9 and Mic. 5:7–8.

Romans 9:27–29 is a crucial passage in the theology of the remnant (Gk. *hypoleimma G5698*, citing Isa. 10:22–23, where Heb. *šĕʾār H8637* is used). It states that though the number of the sons of Israel is vast, yet only a remnant of them will be saved. This is an obvious reference to the Abrahamic promise of numerous descendants. Yet from this vast number only a portion would be redeemed. In this passage PAUL is discussing the ELECTION of persons to SALVATION, persons who were chosen of God to be his spiritual children. The attempt is being made to discourage the Jews from relying upon a carnal interpretation of the promise to ABRAHAM. Natural descent from the great patriarch guaranteed nothing in terms of a spiritual INHERITANCE. God never said that being a Jew according to the flesh was enough. It was wrong for Israel to equate herself with the remnant. It is noteworthy that the remnant will include GENTILES (Rom. 9:24–25). God's promises are to the people of faith.

Romans 11:5 speaks of "a remnant [*leimma G3307*] chosen by grace." The passage refers to the experience of the prophet ELIJAH, who was reminded in the time of discouragement that there were many in Israel who had not bowed the knee to BAAL. The point is that these faithful ones are parallel to a remnant of grace in the present time. Paul stresses not only the number of the faithful, but even more the fact that God has chosen them for himself (cf. J. Murray, *The Epistle to the Romans* [1960–65], 2:69–70). Sovereign election is clearly involved. While Israel was in an apostate condition, yet this remnant remained faithful, and so must all.

The principal idea in all of this is to establish clearly the fact that God has not cast away his people. God's election is not based on moral attainment but on the good pleasure of God. R. Haldane says: "It was an unconditional choice, resulting from the sovereign free favor of God" (*Exposition of the Epistle to the Romans* [1958, orig. 1859], 526). The great emphasis upon the mercy of God must be maintained in all discussions of the remnant. (See further G. F. Hasel, *The Remnant: The History and Theology of the Remnant Idea from Genesis to Isaiah*, 3rd ed. [1980]; *ISBE* rev. [1979–88], 4:130–34; *ABD*, 5:669–71.)   B. C. STARK

Remphan rem´fuhn. KJV form of REPHAN.

rending of garments. See MOURNING.

repentance. This concept is encountered repeatedly in both OT and NT. It is expressed in Hebrew primarily by the verbs *nāḥam H5714* (niphal), "to regret, be sorry," and *šûb H8740*, "to return." In Greek it is represented almost always by the verb *metanoeō G3566*, "to change one's mind," and its cognate noun *metanoia G3567*.

I. Repentance on the part of God. Most occurrences of this concept in the OT have to do with God's repentance. This is seen, for example, where God repented that he had made man (Gen. 6:6; NIV, "was grieved") and again repented of the judgments by which he had condemned Israel (Exod. 32:14; NIV, "relented"). Several times the Lord repented of the chastisements he had planned, that is, judgments that he had threatened to execute on his people (Jer. 18:8, 10; 26:3, 19; 42:10; cf. Amos 7:3, 6; Jon. 3:10). These are a few of many instances when the Lord is represented as having changed his mind.

Elsewhere, however, the Lord is said to be "weary with repenting" (Jer. 15:6 KJV; NIV, "I can no longer show compassion"). The consistency of the Lord in carrying out his purposes is reflected in Ps. 110:4: "The LORD has sworn and will not change his mind" (cf. Jer. 4:28). He is said to be more consistent than man for he is less likely to be changeable or vacillating (1 Sam. 15:29). Indeed there is a paradox in some of these passages. In one instance God is presented as regretting or repenting that he had set up SAUL as king (15:11, 35). In the same context, however, he is presented as unchanging and as not given to repentance (15:29—"he is not a man, that he should change his mind"; cf. Ezek. 24:14). In many instances God's change of mind or repentance is attributed to a person's intercession (Exod. 32:12, 14; Amos 7:3, 6; Jon. 3:9–10). In these texts the meaning obviously is that repentance means a change of plan or reconsideration of an earlier plan. It can be interpreted as a change of mind: it is a turning about and going in the opposite direction, a change of attitude.

II. Human repentance. Some instances of repentance involve human relationships, such as the change of attitude toward the tribe of BENJAMIN on the part of the rest of the Israelites (Jdg. 21:6). With this may be compared occurrences of the Greek word *metamelomai G3564* in the NT, as in Matt. 21:29, which speaks of a disobedient son who changed his mind and obeyed. Such examples have the connotation of regret, as when PAUL said he did not repent concerning his sanctions toward the Corinthians (2 Cor. 7:8).

More important, however, is the specifically theological concept, namely, a basic change in one's attitude toward God. In many OT incidents, there is apparently no provision made for a person to turn from his sin and to seek pardon. For example, the numerous plagues reported in Exodus and Numbers were the result of sin against God, for which there was no alternative but to take the punishment meted out. One exception is the last of the fourteen murmurings in the wilderness as reported in Num. 21. In this case a bronze serpent was erected by which, if people looked, they could be cured of the bite of the fiery serpents. Perhaps for the first time in biblical history the sinner's punishment could be averted simply by looking, with no suffering involved. No opportunity, however, appears to have been provided for the sinful actions of the sons of ELI or of SAMUEL; they were simply punished for their sin. When ACHAN sinned, nothing is said about his being given an opportunity to repent.

One of the earliest examples of repentance is seen in King DAVID's reaction to NATHAN's parable. Because David said, "I have sinned," FORGIVENESS was granted: "You are not going to die" (2 Sam. 12:13). The noblest language of the repentant sinner is to be found in Ps. 51. There was something akin to repentance on the part of AHAB, when, after hearing the sentence against him, he began to go around "meekly," with the result that the Lord lessened his punishment (1 Ki. 21:27–29). When AMOS preached to the surrounding nations, there was again no measure of hope for the sinner, only the sentence of doom. However, it is in the later chapters of his book that one finds the earliest emphasis on repentance as a means by which the sinner could avert the WRATH of God. The concept often occurs in a context where the term does not.

The 8th-cent. prophets often expressed the idea by means of terms translated "seek" or "return." One of the keynotes of the prophecy of Amos is expressed in essentially two words—"seek" and "live" (Amos 5:4, 6, 14). The doctrine comes to its full flower in HOSEA, whose central message was an anguished cry to Israel to repent before catastrophe fell. The people of NINEVEH were accredited with having enough theology and good sense to expect that the Lord would change his mind if they changed their practices, so when they repented the Lord repented (Jon. 3:9–10).

The classic expression for this doctrine and the place where it is most clearly articulated is in the book of EZEKIEL, where it is contrasted with the older group morality. The prophet makes it clear that the innocent suffering with the guilty (as with Achan's family) will no longer be in effect, but each person will be judged on the basis of his own conduct. This means that the sinner who changes his ways, ceases to sin, and does what is right shall escape the penalty of his sin and live (Ezek. 18; 33:10–20). Even MANASSEH, one of the most wicked kings of Judah, is pictured as being shown mercy because he repented (2 Chr. 33:12–13). This so impressed a later writer that he composed the apocryphal *Prayer of Manasseh*, found in intertestamental literature (see MANASSEH, PRAYER OF). It was a common rabbinic teaching that if a nation repented sincerely enough, the MESSIAH would then come.

It is into this background that JOHN THE BAPTIST came preaching, "Repent, for the kingdom of heaven is near." The same emphasis was followed by Jesus and still later by his disciples (Matt. 3:2; 4:17; Mk. 6:12). Indeed, repentance became the main theme of John the Baptist, and in his preaching the emphasis changed from national repentance (which EZRA and DANIEL had called upon the people to render) to individual repentance. He insisted that repentance be accompanied by the fruits of repentance in a changed life.

The Synoptic Gospels indicate that unless one repents and becomes like a child, he has no hope of heaven (Matt. 18:1–10). Conversely, Jesus' severest strictures were directed to the impenitent (Matt. 9:13; Lk. 18:14). The term *repentance* is absent from the fourth gospel. The Synoptic Gospels and the Acts stress repentance, often in an eschatological setting. The Epistles are addressed to believers, and repentance receives less emphasis. The doctrine seems to be minimized in the letter to the Hebrews in order to underscore the danger of apostasy. The last book in the Bible again stresses the importance of repentance in the letters to the seven churches. No hope is held out for the proud person who thinks it is beneath his dignity to express regret for his sins and mistakes, but assurance is given to the humble in heart that FORGIVENESS and cleansing are given through the blood of Jesus Christ to the sincerely penitent (1 Jn. 1:7–10). G. A. TURNER

Rephael rē'ay-uhl (רְפָאֵל H8330, "God has healed"; cf. also RAPHAEL; REPHAIAH). Son of Shemaiah, grandson of OBED-EDOM, and a gatekeeper from the Korahites (1 Chr. 26:7; cf. v. 1). See

Korah. Rephael and his brothers are described as "leaders in their father's family because they were very capable men" (v. 6).

Rephah ree´fuh (רֶפַח H8338, perhaps "abundance" [cf. *HALOT*, 3:1278]). Son (or descendant) of Ephraim (1 Chr. 7:25). His precise place in the genealogy is not clear, and the name Rephah does not occur in the parallel list (Num. 26:35–36).

Rephaiah ri-fay´yuh (רְפָיָה H8341, "Yahweh has healed"; cf. Rephael). **(1)** A descendant of David through Jehoiachin and Zerubbabel (1 Chr. 3:21). The Hebrew text is difficult. Some believe that Rephaiah was the son of Hananiah (cf. J. M. Myers, *I Chronicles*, AB 12 [1965], 22); others, the son of Jeshaiah (cf. NRSV and NJPS, following the LXX). C. F. Keil argued that the MT "is clearly corrupt" and that the connection of Rephaiah (and others in v. 21b) "with Zerubbabel is for us unascertainable" (KD, *Chronicles*, 84; for a fuller discussion that supports the originality of the LXX reading, see G. N. Knoppers, *I Chronicles 1–9*, AB 12 [2004], 322–23) .

(2) Son of Ishi and descendant of Simeon during the reign of Hezekiah; Rephaiah and his brothers led 500 Simeonites in an invasion of "the hill country of Seir" (1 Chr. 4:42). Because of overpopulation and the need for pasture and flocks, these Simeonites expanded in two directions: westward toward Gedor (vv. 38–40; LXX, "Gerar") and eastward toward Seir, where they displaced the Amalekite element residing among the Edomites since their dispersal in the time of Saul and David (1 Sam. 15:7–8; 30:18).

(3) Son of Tola and grandson of Issachar, described as head of family (1 Chr. 7:2).

(4) Son of Binea and descendant of King Saul through Jonathan (1 Chr. 9:43); the shorter form Raphah is used in the parallel genealogy (9:43).

(5) Son of Hur; he ruled "a half-district of Jerusalem" and was in charge of repairing a section of the city wall near the Broad Wall (Neh. 3:9). The Judean province of the Persian period was divided into five districts: Jerusalem, Keilah, Beth Zur, Beth Hakkerem, and Mizpah (see vv. 12–18).

B. K. Waltke

Rephaim ref´ay-im. See Rephaites.

Rephaim, Valley of ref´ay-im (רְפָאִים H8329; for meaning, see Rephaite). A basin SW of Jerusalem whose N end marked the N boundary of the tribe of Judah and the S boundary of the tribe of Benjamin (Josh. 15:8; 18:16). This area is today called simply the *Baq‘a* or "valley" and constitutes a

General view of the Valley of Rephaim (looking SW). David defended his kingship against the Philistines who came up this valley twice after the death of King Saul.

suburb of Jerusalem. On the N it touches the Valley of Hinnom and the Valley of Deir el-Musallabeh (the Monastery of the Holy Cross).

After David captured Jerusalem and the Philistines heard about his being anointed king, they camped in the Valley of Rephaim anticipating an attack on the new capital of Israel (2 Sam. 5:17–21). David took up the challenge and defeated the Philistines at Baal Perazim. The Philistines prepared a second attack, but this time David routed them with an attack from the E on their rear guard (2 Sam. 5:22–25; the account of these two episodes is expanded in 1 Chr. 11:15–19 and 14:10–17). The seventh and last mention of the Valley of Rephaim is in Isa. 17:5, where, to illustrate the survival of the idol-hating remnant, the prophet says, "It will be … as when a man gleans heads of grain in the Valley of Rephaim."

The Bible records no reason that this valley should be named after the early inhabitants of Canaan whom the Israelites thought to be giants (cf. Gen. 14:5; 15:20; Josh. 17:15). One can only guess that the people called "Rephaim" (Rephaites) lived in the vicinity of this valley.

R. L. Alden

Rephaites ref′ay-its (רְפָאִים *H8328*, often with the definite article, meaning possibly "the healers" or "the weak" [see *HALOT*, 3:1274–75]). The Hebrew form *rĕpā'im*, evidently the plural of *rāpā'* or perhaps *rāpâ* (see Rapha #3), is transliterated by the KJV as "Rephaim" when it refers to the valley of that name (see Rephaim, Valley of) but as the superfluous plural "Rephaims" on two occasions (Gen. 14:5; 15:20); elsewhere, the KJV translates "giants." The NRSV and other versions transliterate "Rephaim" throughout. The NIV uses the more natural English form "Rephaites" when the term designates a people group, but preserves "Rephaim" when the reference is to the valley.

There is a term that has the same form (*rĕpā'im H8327*, possibly "shades") but that probably should be regarded as a distinct word (these terms may be related, though the etymology is disputed; see *NIDOTTE*, 3:1174–76). This second word denotes the inhabitants of the netherworld in the OT (esp. in poetic and wisdom literature), in Phoenician funerary inscriptions (Tabnith and Eshmunazar, c. 300 B.C.; cf. G. A. Cooke, *North Semitic Inscriptions* [1903], 26ff., 30ff.), and probably in a group of fragmentary and obscure Ugaritic mythological texts (*rpum, rpim*). The most that can be said with certainty about this use of *Rephaim* is that the Israelites applied the term to people who were dead and gone. The word is used in parallel with *mētim*, "dead ones" (Ps. 88:10; Prov. 2:18; Isa. 26:14), who are in Sheol (Prov. 9:18; Isa. 14:9): they cannot praise God now (Ps. 88:10) and their case is now hopeless (Isa. 26:14). Some texts may suggest that they are conscious in their insubstantial afterlife: they tremble (Job 26:5); they welcome the newly dead to Sheol (Isa. 14:9) and constitute a united assembly (Prov. 9:18; Isa. 14:9). These texts are best interpreted by understanding the poets to be using the figure of speech called *prosopopoeia*, whereby an imaginary or absent person is represented as speaking or acting (cf. E. W. Bullinger, *Figures of Speech Used in the Bible* [1898], 861, 866). According to Isa. 26:19, these will at some future day be raised into light. There is a suggestion in the Bible (14:9; 26:14), in the Phoenician inscriptions, and in the Ugaritic texts that they are the aristocracy of the dead. See also dead.

Whatever the connection between these terms, the people group known as Rephaites were inhabitants of Transjordan in pre-Israelite times. The Moabites called them Emites, while the Ammonites referred to them as Zamzummites (Deut. 2:11, 20). They were subdued by Kedorlaomer c. 2000 B.C. in Ashteroth Karnaim (Gen. 14:5). Ashtaroth, capital of ancient Bashan, sits on the famous king's highway and is near Karnaim, which inherited its place as the regional capital under Aramean and Assyrian rule. The Rephaites were one of ten ethnic groups whose lands God promised to Abraham (Gen. 15:20). This promise, apparently, was later qualified to exclude that portion of their land that had been taken over by Moab and Ammon (Deut. 2:9–12, 19–21), and thus it came to designate specifically the Rephaite holdings in Gilead and the whole of Bashan (Deut. 3:13), but also the forest of Ephraim (Josh. 17:15). Og, king of Bashan, who reigned in Ashtaroth and Edrei and who was defeated by Moses, was the last survivor of the remnant of the Rephaites (Josh. 12:4; 13:12).

According to Deut. 2:10–11, the Rephaites were "strong and numerous, and as tall as the Anakites" (see ANAK). Og, for example, possessed a king-size iron bed (or sarcophagus?), 13 ft. long and 6 ft. wide (3:11). Probably this information, combined with statements about the descendants of Rapha, who were giants associated with the PHILISTINES in the time of DAVID (see below), caused the occasional translation of "giants" in the SEPTUAGINT and *Targum Onkelos* (see TARGUM). G. E. Wright reasoned that "the Israelite tradition of giant Rephaim undoubtedly arose in part from the contemplation of megalithic structures especially in Transjordan." In a note he added, "comparatively few of these structures have been found in Western Palestine" ("Troglodytes and Giants in Palestine," *JBL* 57 [1938]: 37). But here Wright is inconsistent with his normal and preferred method of interpreting artifacts. Instead of regarding such artifacts as occasioning an Israelite etiology, they should be regarded as circumstantial evidence supporting the biblical narrative.

The name Rephaites is also applied to GIANTS among the Philistines who fought against David and his mighty warriors along their disputed border at both GEZER (1 Chr. 20:4) and GATH (vv. 6, 8). In the latter two verses (as in 2 Sam. 21:16–22), they are described as descendants of "the Raphah" (so NJPS; the NIV has "Rapha"; KJV, "the giant"; NRSV, "the giants"). The relationship between the ethnic Rephaites and these Philistine warriors is debated; perhaps the latter were not precisely "descendants" but rather "devotees" of a deity named Rapha (so P. K. McCarter, Jr., *II Samuel*, AB 9 [1984], 449–50; but see R. F. Youngblood, *EBC*, 3:862–65 and 1058–61). (For further discussion and bibliography, see *ABD*, 5:674–76; *DDD*, 692–700.)   B. K. WALTKE

Rephan ref´uhn (Ῥαιφάν G4818, variants Ῥεμφάν, Ῥομφάμ, etc., meaning uncertain). KJV Remphan; NASB Rompha. The name of an astral deity mentioned in Acts 7:43, which cites the SEPTUAGINT translation of Amos 5:26. In the latter, the MT has *kiyyûn* H3962, which may represent the Akkadian word *kayamānu*, a term applied to Saturn (see KAIWAN). Some have speculated that the Hebrew scribes substituted the vowels of *šiqqûṣ* H9199 ("a detested thing") for those of the Akkadian word to reflect the detestability of the pagan god (but see S. Gevirtz in *JBL* 87 [1968]:267–76). How the LXX came to have the unexpected *Rhaiphan* is uncertain. It may be the result of a mistaken transliteration (Heb. *k* and *r* are sometimes confused) or it may be a form of Repa, a late Egyptian name for the god of the planet Saturn, substituted by the Alexandrian translators for the less intelligible *kiyyûn* (cf. F. F. Bruce, *The Acts of the Apostles: Greek Text with Introduction and Commentary*, 3rd ed. [1990], 204).   J. C. MOYER

Rephidim ref´i-dim (רְפִידִים H8340, prob. "camping [places]"). A stop in the wilderness wanderings of the Israelites (Exod. 17:1, 8; 19:2; Num. 33:14–15). The passage in Numbers locates Rephidim on the journey from ALUSH to the Desert of SINAI, but the location of these places is uncertain. On the basis of the traditional Mount Sinai, near the S end of the peninsula formed by the gulfs of Suez and Aqabah, Rephidim might be the Wadi Feiran (cf. PARAN) or the Wadi Rufaid.

At Rephidim the Israelites rebelled against MOSES because there was no water to drink. The

Rephidim.

This area in Sinai, Wadi Feiran, may be the location of Rephidim.

people complained: "Why did you bring us up out of Egypt to make us and our children and livestock die of thirst?" (Exod. 17:3). God instructed Moses to strike the rock. He did, and water came forth (v. 6). Because of the attitude of the people, Moses named the place MASSAH and MERIBAH, meaning "testing" and "contention" (17:7). Moses repeatedly referred to this incident to remind the people of God's faithfulness and their faithlessness (Num. 20:13, 24; 27:14; Deut. 6:16; 9:22; 32:51; 33:8). The author of Ps. 81 also recalled this ancient site and its significance (v. 7).

It was also at Rephidim that AMALEK fought with Israel (Exod. 17:8–13). Here it was that Israel was victorious as long as Moses' hands were held up. After JOSHUA mowed down the enemy, Moses, obedient to God's command, built an altar and called it, "The LORD is my Banner" (v. 15; KJV, "Jehovah-nissi"). There is reason to believe that the visit of JETHRO, Moses' father-in-law, recorded in Exod. 18, also took place at Rephidim. The next chapter (19:2) records the nation's leaving Rephidim. It is never again mentioned in the Bible. (See E. Kraeling, *Bible Atlas* [1956], 107–9.)

R. L. ALDEN

reprobate. This adjective, meaning "corrupt" or "depraved," is seldom if ever used in modern Bible versions. The KJV uses it once in the OT (but in the archaic sense "rejected," with reference to silver, Jer. 6:30), and three times in the NT (Rom. 1:28; 2 Tim. 3:8; Tit. 1:16); the noun "reprobates" occurs three times in one passage (2 Cor. 13:5–7). In all the NT passages, the Greek word is *adokimos* G99 (which also appears in 1 Cor. 9:27 and Heb. 6:8, the latter passage referring to "worthless" land). Its basic meaning seems to be "not standing the test, and so rejected."

PAUL says of the ungodly world, "Furthermore, since they did not think it worthwhile [*ouk edokimasen*] to retain the knowledge of God, he gave them over to a depraved [*adokimon*] mind, to do what ought not to be done" (Rom. 1:28). J. Murray paraphrases it, "To a mind that is rejected because deemed worthless" (*The Epistle to the Romans* [1960–65], 1:49). Paul uses athletic metaphors (1 Cor. 9:27) in calling for self-control and concludes by saying that he himself is not exempt from this need, for it is always possible that having preached to others, and not having heeded his own preaching, he might be "disqualified." On the other hand, to those at Corinth who were suggesting that Paul was a counterfeit apostle who did not measure up to the standards of an apostle, he suggested that they examine themselves to see whether Christ is in them, otherwise *they* will fail to meet the test

(2 Cor. 13:5–7). Paul refers to some men who "as far as the faith is concerned, are rejected" (2 Tim. 3:8; NRSV, "counterfeit faith") and to others who are "unfit for doing anything good" (Tit. 1:16).

R. E. DAVIES

reptiles. See FAUNA.

Resaiah ri-say′yuh. See RAAMIAH.

Resen ree′suhn (רֶסֶן H8271, possibly from Assyrian *rēš ēni*, "head of spring"). A city in ASSYRIA said to have been "between Nineveh and Calah" and to have been built by NIMROD (Gen. 10:11–12; the Hebrew text can be understood to mean that the builder was ASSHUR [cf. KJV and NJPS]). It is unclear whether the description "that is the great city" (v. 12b) refers to Resen, or to NINEVEH, or (most likely) to CALAH.

No city of suitable prominence has been identified in this area, and some scholars have thought Resen corresponds to one of several Assyrian places referred to as Resh-eni ("fountain head"). One such place is mentioned by SENNACHERIB in connection with his work to supply Nineveh with water, but this village was situated NE of Nineveh, whereas Calah (modern Nimrud) is to the SE. Others have identified Resen with modern Selamiyeh, less than 3 mi. NW of Nimrud, which seems more plausible (but see *ISBE* rev. [1979–88], 4:141). Still others consider Resen not a place name as such, but rather a parenthetical description of some impressive water installation or military construction (cf. E. Speiser, *Genesis*, AB 1, 2nd ed. [1978], 68).

B. K. WALTKE

reservoir. A place for the storage of WATER. This English term is used by the NIV and the NRSV to render Hebrew *miqwâ* H5225, a form that occurs only once (Isa. 22:11). However, the NIV uses it also to translate the phrase *miqwēh mêmêhem*, literally, "the gathering of their waters" (Exod. 7:19) and *bĕrēkôt māyim*, "pools of water" (Eccl. 2:6). The general climate of PALESTINE made it necessary to devise ways of preserving the water supply through the dry months from May through September. The rocky terrain provided convenient opportunity for water storage with minimal effort. The rain or spring

Reservoir located at the NW corner of the temple mount in Jerusalem.

water was channeled into these storage facilities (see CISTERN), and with care it could be kept palatable for a considerable time. An adequate supply of water was vital at all times, especially during siege (cf. 2 Chr. 32:3, 4). See also POOL.

B. C. STARK

resh raysh (from late Heb. רֵישׁ, "head"). The twentieth letter of the Hebrew ALPHABET (ר), with a numerical value of 200. It is named for the shape of the letter, which in its older form resembled a human head. Its sound corresponds roughly to that of English *r*, although in some traditions it has a uvular pronunciation.

Resheph (deity) ree′shif. Also Rashaph, Rasaph. A deity worshiped through most of the ANE and associated with pestilence, death, and the underworld. According to W. F. Albright, Resheph was closely related to the Babylonian NERGAL and was identified by the Greeks with APOLLO (*Archaeology and the Religion of Israel* [1942], 79). The very ancient documents discovered in EBLA show that Resheph was a prominent deity as early as the 3rd millennium B.C., for one of the city gates was given his name. Much pertinent information comes from Egypt, where Rephesh was a minor deity related to war and healing. In UGARIT, Resheph was more prominent and was represented both as a god of plague and as a benevolent deity. The Hebrew word *rešep* H8404, meaning "flame" or the like (Job 5:7; Pss. 76:3; 78:48; Cant. 8:6), and possibly by extension "pestilence" (Deut. 32:24; Hab. 3:5), may derive from the name of this god (although it is possible that the semantic development moved in the opposite direction). Some scholars think that the Habakkuk reference in particular ("pestilence followed his steps") ironically alludes to Resheph, the plague-god, as a servant of the true God. (See further *HALOT*, 3:1297–98; *ISBE* rev. [1979–88], 4:141–42; *ABD*, 5:678–79; *DDD*, 700–703.)

B. K. WALTKE

Resheph (person) ree′shif (רֶשֶׁף H8405, possibly "flame"). Son of Rephah and descendant of EPHRAIM (1 Chr. 7:25). The MT (lit., "and Rephah his son and Resheph and Telah his son") could be interpreted to mean that both Rephah and Resheph were sons of BERIAH, the son of Ephraim (vv. 23–24), but most modern versions insert "his son" after "Resheph" (following a few Heb. MSS and the Lucianic recension of the LXX). In any case, the specific connection of the names in v. 25 to the Ephraimite genealogy is unclear. Moreover, some scholars believe that the words in the MT, *wĕrešep wĕtelaḥ bĕnô* ("and Resheph and Telah his son"), are a scribal error for *wĕšûtelaḥ bĕnô* ("and Shuthelah his son"; see SHUTHELAH #2).

resin. See GUM.

rest. Freedom from LABOR; repose. Rest is frequently referred to in the Bible. God first set the example, and then offered it as a blessing to humans. When he finished his work of CREATION, "on the seventh day he rested from all his work. And God blessed the seventh day and made it holy, because on it he rested from all the work of creating that he had done" (Gen. 2:2–3). As with God, rest is a reward to human beings for their work. It is a tonic for the tired, and a release from labor. Rest restores and relieves body, mind, and soul overwrought from various burdens.

I. Physical rest. Rest is a divine institution, a natural law, and a human necessity. As God ordained work for ADAM (Gen. 2:15), he also ordained rest, patterned after the creation-sabbath. He created the day cycle for work during the day and rest during the night. Moreover, he commanded his people to rest one day in seven. "Six days you shall do your work, but on the seventh day you shall rest" (Exod. 23:12 NRSV); "the seventh day is a Sabbath of rest, holy to the LORD" (31:15). This rest included the beasts of burden, bondservants, and aliens so that all might be refreshed. This idea was extended to include the seventh or sabbatical year, in which the land also was to have rest. Both field and vineyard were to lie fallow, and their voluntary crops were to feed the poor and the wild beasts (23:10–11; Lev. 25:1–7).

Rest is nature's means of building body tissues and restoring energies. It is usually acquired in sleep, which consumes about one-third of a person's time. When JACOB fled from ESAU and night overtook him, he rested at BETHEL with his head on a stone (Gen. 28:11). ISSACHAR would see "how good is his resting place" (49:15). MOSES sought rest for the Hebrew children from their burdens of slavery in Egypt (Exod. 5:5). God's prophets and apostles needed rest from their religious services, some of which were strenuous. ELIJAH rested under a broom tree from fatigue in fleeing from JEZEBEL (1 Ki. 19:4). The wealthy Shunammite friends built a special guest room for the prophet ELISHA to rest in when passing that way on his preaching circuit (2 Ki. 4:11).

When the disciples returned from their preaching mission, Jesus said to them, "Come with me by yourselves to a quiet place and get some rest" (Mk. 6:31). In Jesus' busy ministry it was necessary for him to grasp rare moments for rest, as at Jacob's well (Jn. 4:6), and to sleep, as in a boat in a storm on Galilee (Mk. 4:38). PAUL, in his urgent mission, said, "For when we came into Macedonia, this body of ours had no rest" (2 Cor. 7:5). Contrarily, there are times to forego rest: to work (Prov. 6:9), and to watch (Matt. 26:45).

II. Social rest. A community, tribe, or nation sometimes needs rest from a common pursuit, internal turmoil, or an enemy. The Israelites anticipated rest in the Promised Land after long years of wandering and conflict with enemies (Deut. 12:9–10). Rest from enemies meant PEACE, freedom from war. At times in the period of the judges, "the land had rest for forty years" or "for eighty years" (Jdg. 3:11, 30 NRSV). Though DAVID was a man of war, he attained peace, that is, rest from his enemies, before his death, and received promise from God that his son would reign in peace (1 Chr. 22:8–9,

18). Solomon later was able to say, "But now the Lord my God has given me rest on every side" (1 Ki. 5:4). During the reign of Asa, "the land had rest for ten years" (2 Chr. 14:1 NRSV).

III. Spiritual rest. Natural rest is a shadow of the ultimate state of blessedness, a taste of which is experienced here. It begins with Jesus' offer, "Come to me, all you who are weary and burdened, and I will give you rest. Take my yoke upon you and learn from me, for I am gentle and humble in heart, and you will find rest for your souls" (Matt. 11:28–29). Long ago God had said, "In repentance and rest is your salvation" (Isa. 30:15). Rest is the tonic most sought after when sin, sickness, or separation causes frustration of the mind and anguish of the soul.

Paul said, "When I came to Troas … my mind could not rest because I did not find my brother Titus there" (2 Cor. 2:12–13 NRSV). Out of mortal illness David cried, "O my God, I cry by day, but you do not answer; / and by night, but find no rest" (Ps. 22:2 NRSV). But healing and rest evoke thanksgiving: "Be at rest once more, O my soul, / for the Lord has been good to you" (Ps. 116:7). Similarly, Job cried out of his misery, "I have no peace, no quietness; / I have no rest, but only turmoil" (Job 3:26). Certainly alienation from God deprives one of rest, as with the Gerasene demoniac (Mk. 5:1–5) and the unclean spirit (Lk. 11:24).

Heaven holds the fondest dreams of rest. It is the place of God's rest (Acts 7:49). John records, "Then I heard a voice from heaven say, 'Write: Blessed are the dead who die in the Lord from now on.' 'Yes,' says the Spirit, 'they will rest from their labor, for their deeds will follow them'" (Rev. 14:13). When Job was on the brink of despair from the loss of children, health, wealth, and sympathy of friends, he visualized a state of spiritual rest. He regretted that he had been born: "For now I would be lying down in peace; / I would be asleep and at rest" (Job 3:13; cf. v. 17). Canaan, the land of promised rest (Deut. 3:20), was an earthly symbol of paradise rest, not acquired in Joshua's conquest (Heb. 4:8). Obviously then, "There remains … a Sabbath-rest for the people of God; for anyone who enters God's rest also rests from his own work, just as God did from his. Let us, therefore, make every effort to enter that rest" (4:9–11). So, for believers, "the promise of entering his rest still stands" (4:1). See also Sabbath.   G. B. Funderburk

restitution. See crimes and punishments.

restoration. The act of bringing back to a former state. This term is especially applied to the period of Hebrew history following the exile. The time covered by the restoration of the Israelites will be regarded here as beginning about 515 B.C. and terminating with the time of Malachi, about 450 B.C. Once the edict of Cyrus, proclaimed in 538, had given official permission for expatriate groups in Babylonia to return to their homelands and renew the pattern of their former ways of life, those members of the captive Jewish population who had caught the vision of a new existence in Judea along theocratic lines, as indicated by Ezekiel, were not slow to begin the arduous journey back to the desolated homeland. As the prophecies of Haggai and Zechariah make plain, the initial enthusiasm which the returned exiles had manifested for the rebuilding of the ruined temple became dissipated at a comparatively early period. The most that the inhabitants of Jerusalem were apparently willing or able to do was the reconstruction of their own houses in the city. However, the situation was remedied by the timely intervention of Haggai and Zechariah in the year 520, and five years later the successor to the temple of Solomon was dedicated amid scenes of great rejoicing.

The policy of the Persian rulers was remarkable for the amount of political freedom that was given to the constituent elements of the empire. This enlightened attitude of the government presented certain difficulties for the Persians initially, for after the suicide of Cambyses II, son of Cyrus, in 522 B.C., some of the provinces Cyrus had conquered tried to break away from imperial rule. However, order was finally restored by the Achaemenid prince Darius the Great (522–486), but while he was regaining control of the situation, the people of Judea managed to establish some degree of independence. When Darius finally imposed imperial rule, he followed a policy of benevolence toward the returned exiles in Judea.

According to Ezra 6:13, a military governor named Tattenai was in charge of the Persian province of Judah, and the state was encouraged to function as a religious rather than a political entity, with JESHUA appointed as high priest in the time of Haggai. Precisely what happened to ZERUBBABEL after 515 B.C. is unknown, but it has been suggested that he either died or was removed from office by the Persian government as a precautionary measure against the establishing of a Judean state independent of Persian control. From that time onward the political situation in Judah seems to have been stabilized by the formulation of a theocratic system supported by the central Persian administration.

Of the fifty-seven years that followed the dedication of the second temple, the book of EZRA has nothing to report. This situation is unfortunate, for this particular period of biblical history is lacking in extensive documentation. As far as the Persian empire was concerned, the death of Darius I in 486 B.C. was followed by the accession of his son XERXES I, who ruled for twenty years from 485. This man, to whom there is a probable reference under the name of AHASUERUS in Ezra 4:6, maintained the administration of the empire at a high level of efficiency, and crushed the political aspirations of some of his more restless subjects. An inscription from his reign, which was found in 1939 at PERSEPOLIS, demonstrated the vigor of his rule and made clear his zeal for the Persian god Ahuramazda: "When I became king there were among those lands ... which rebelled. Then Ahuramazda helped me. By Ahuramazda's will such lands I conquered ... this which I did I achieved it all by the will of Ahuramazda ...." When Xerxes died in 465, he was succeeded by his second son Artaxerxes I Longimanus (464–424), who is evidently the Artaxerxes mentioned in Ezra 4:7–23.

For the inhabitants of Judea the period of the restoration was marked by a valiant struggle to overcome the poverty that was evident on every hand. The city of Jerusalem was far from being rebuilt, and though the temple had been completed, there were still no walls to protect the city dwellers from their enemies in the locality. Consequently Samaritans and Arabs could enter the city and plunder the crops whenever they chose. This dispiriting fact, along with the waning of enthusiasm for further building activity after the temple had been restored, compelled the Jews to eke out a precarious existence in and around Jerusalem.

In the midst of this forbidding situation help arrived rather unexpectedly from Jews who were scattered throughout the Persian empire and who were concerned about the welfare of the struggling repatriates in Judea. These people brought their influence to bear upon the central administration, with the result that in 458 B.C. Artaxerxes appointed Ezra the scribe, a member of a Jewish priestly family, as a royal commissioner for Jewish affairs in Judea. Ezra arrived in Jerusalem armed with a decree that required the Jews to obey his instructions regarding the regulating of religious life. He proposed drastic measures for dissolving marriages contracted with heathen women. When he attempted to erect some kind of defensive wall around Jerusalem, his enemies both inside and outside the city allied against him and he returned to Persia in 457, doubtless to report to the central authority.

The prophecy of Malachi, dated about 450, shows the conditions of contemporary society in Jerusalem. The people were dispirited by the apparent failure of God to meet even the most pressing needs of his people (cf. Zech. 8:4–13), and many were openly skeptical about the value of a life lived in obedience to God. With clear contempt for the traditions of the Torah, many irreligious Jews were committing adultery, indulging in perjury, and oppressing the poor (Mal. 3:5). The priests also had become lax in their duties, manifesting boredom with their religious functions (1:13) and treating sacrificial regulations so lightly that they offered inferior animals in the service of God (1:7–8). Because the prophetic word was no longer taken seriously, Malachi found that he had to argue his case in a manner unknown to earlier prophets. Drastic action was clearly necessary to remedy the deterioration, and it fell to NEHEMIAH, who was appointed civil governor of Judea in 445 B.C., to furnish the leadership which restored the confidence of the community in the divine purpose, and made feasible the religious reforms of Ezra. See ISRAEL, HISTORY OF, XII.   R. K. HARRISON

resurrection. The divine miracle of restoring a deceased person to life in BODY and SOUL, either to temporal life, as was the case with LAZARUS (Jn. 11), or more properly to eternal, glorified life, to which Christ was raised and those who are his will be raised at his return. Scripture also teaches a resurrection to eternal punishment in body and soul of those who lived and died without Christ (Matt. 10:28; Jn. 5:28–29; Acts 24:15; see PUNISHMENT, ETERNAL). When the word *resurrection* is qualified, as a rule the expression "the resurrection of [*or* from] the dead" is used (Matt. 22:31; Lk. 20:37; Acts 4:2; 17:32; 23:6; 24:21; 26:23; 1 Cor. 15:12–13). The resurrection of believers is sometimes called "the resurrection of the righteous" (Lk. 14:14; Acts 24:15) or "the resurrection of life" (Jn. 5:29 NRSV); that of the unbelievers, "the resurrection of condemnation" (Jn. 5:29 NRSV) or "of the unrighteous" (Acts 24:15 NRSV). The expression "resurrection of the body," frequently used in the church CREEDS, is based on Scripture (cf. Matt. 27:52; Rom. 8:11; 1 Cor. 15:35, 42–44; Phil. 3:21). The early fathers introduced the phrase "resurrection of the flesh," which is still found in various creeds. The church adopted this expression because many heretics, denying an eternal future for the body, understood the word *dead* as meaning "dead souls." By confessing that the flesh will be raised, the church emphasized the biblical truth that the dead will be raised in their physical bodies. Though the expression is not found in Scripture itself, there is good reason to retain it, for many explain the word *body* in the phrase "resurrection of the body" as denoting the "self" or "person," to the exclusion of the physical body (see below).

I. Known from the infallible Scriptures. Paganism was and is without the resurrection hope (Eph. 2:12; 1 Thess. 4:13). Greek philosophy taught the IMMORTALITY of the soul, the soul being considered divine; whereas for the body, being matter and therefore considered evil, there was no hope. Paul's proclamation of the resurrection was ridiculed in Greece (Acts 17:32). Liberal theology, denying the infallibility of the Bible, generally reduces the resurrection hope to a modern version of the immortality of the soul; that is, man's true "self" continues to exist in an immaterial, ghost-like spirit body. To Karl Barth, who also rejects the infallibility of the Bible in the traditional sense of the word, the end means "eternalization"; that is, after this life men and women will eternally exist in the mind of God, not in reality (*Church Dogmatics* [1964–82], 3/2:698ff.; 3/3:99ff.; 257ff.). According to Scripture the soul is not divine or as such immortal, nor is the body evil. Created in the IMAGE OF GOD, the man and the woman were "very good" in every aspect of their being (Gen. 1:27, 31; 2:21) and were destined to ETERNAL life in body and soul (3:22). Even after the FALL, we do not need deliverance from the body; we rather need that our body and soul be delivered from the power of SIN and DEATH, which Christ grants to believers (Jn. 6:40; 11:24–26; 1 Cor. 15:54–56).

II. The work of God and Christ. It is God who by an almighty creative act raised the dead (Matt. 22:29; 1 Cor. 6:14; 15:38; 2 Cor. 1:9; 4:14). This work, however, is mainly accomplished through agents, namely, prophets and apostles (1 Ki. 17:17–24; 2 Ki. 4:32–37; Acts 20:10), and particularly through God's Son, Jesus Christ, who is the Father's unique agent (Jn. 6:39–40). He himself is the resurrection and the LIFE (Jn. 11:25). He brought life and immortality to light (2 Tim. 1:10), and his own resurrection in glory guarantees the resurrection of those who are his (1 Cor. 15:20–23, 47–49; 1 Thess. 4:14–18). Though Christ as God's agent will also raise those who lived and died without him, their resurrection is not the result of his

This wall painting at the Russian Church of the Ascension on the Mount of Olives depicts the raising of Lazarus, the setting for Jesus' words: "I am the resurrection and the life" (Jn. 11:25).

redemptive work, nor is it redemptive in nature. He raises them as the divinely appointed Judge (Jn. 5:26–30), from whose hand each person will receive "what is due him for the things done while in the body, whether good or bad" (2 Cor. 5:10).

III. Resurrection and resurrection hope in the OT. In the OT account three persons were raised from the dead: the widow's son at Zarephath (1 Ki. 17:17–24), the son of the Shunammite (2 Ki. 4:32–37), and the man whose dead body was cast into Elisha's grave (2 Ki. 13:21). The claim that the widow's son had not died cannot be sufficiently substantiated. Although these resurrections meant only a temporal restoration to earthly life, they undoubtedly strengthened Israel's faith in the almighty power of Yahweh as the God who was able even to raise the dead.

A. Lack of early and frequent evidences of the resurrection hope. The OT contains only a few and rather late statements that give clear evidence of an eschatological resurrection HOPE. This by no means implies that such a hope was unknown in Israel. To God's people the emphasis was upon a long life on earth (Exod. 20:12) with but a dim view of an eternal future for the whole man. This is because God's redemptive work in Christ was only gradually revealed. The full resurrection hope could therefore not be known nor enjoyed until Christ had conquered death.

The true believers in Israel must have known that their mighty God—who proclaims, "I put to death and I bring to life" (Deut. 32:39)—had more in store for them than this life and not only for their souls but also for their bodies, for the two are inseparable according to OT teachings. According to Heb. 11:19, "Abraham reasoned that God could raise the dead," and the preceding verses state that the PATRIARCHS were looking forward to "the city with foundations," desiring "a better country" than Canaan (vv. 10, 16). To these passages full justice is done only if one regards them as implying the resurrection hope, however vague in that early stage. This hope must have grown when in later days God's resurrection power was clearly shown. The fact that ENOCH (Gen. 5:24, Heb. 11:5) and ELIJAH (2 Ki. 2:11–12) were taken to be with God before they died must also have strengthened the hope of an eternal future for human beings in their completeness, that is, body and soul. It is, therefore, unwarranted and unnecessary to look for the source of Israel's resurrection hope in some ancient "world folktales," or to Iranian and other teachings concerning "a common eschatological event" (*IDB*, 1:41).

B. The resurrection hope expressed. The main OT passages that call for consideration are the following: HANNAH sang, "The LORD brings death and makes alive; / he brings down to the grave and raises up" (1 Sam. 2:6). Though some scholars claim that Hannah referred to a real resurrection, the context seems to exclude this interpretation, for her psalm refers to what the Lord regularly is doing on earth. This verse therefore is to be understood as stating that the Lord is able to take away human life as well as to preserve it, even before the gates of death. (For elaborate interpretations of this and other Scripture passages briefly dealt with in this article, see J. A. Schep, *The Nature of the Resurrection Body* [1964].)

JOB exclaimed, "I know that my Redeemer lives, / and that in the end he will stand upon the earth. / And after my skin has been destroyed, / yet in my flesh I will see God; / I myself will see him / with my own eyes—I, and not another. / How my heart yearns within me!" (Job 19:25–27). Though most modern commentators deny that Job is speaking of an eschatological resurrection and judgment, the logical line of thought seems to favor the so-called post-mortem interpretation: Job was sure that after his death God would stand up as his GOEL and vindicate him. In accordance with the RSV, the Hebrew expression *mibbĕśārî* (v. 26) is best rendered, "from my flesh." With his own eyes, out of his restored flesh, having been raised from the dead, Job will see his divine judge vindicating him. Claiming that such a resurrection hope is unthinkable at such an early stage is begging the question.

DAVID expresses this hope: "Therefore my heart is glad and my tongue rejoices; / my body also will rest secure, / because you will not abandon me to the grave, / nor will you let your Holy One see decay. / You have made known to me the path of life; / you will fill me with joy in your presence, / with eternal pleasures at your right hand" (Ps. 16:9–11). The *parallelismus membrorum* in v. 9 makes it necessary to understand the second line ("my body [*lit.*, flesh] will rest secure") as speaking of safety in this life. Consequently v. 10, starting with "because," cannot be understood as referring to a future resurrection. The statements in this passage, however, speak in such general and absolute terms of the complete victory of life, that David, under the inspiration of the Holy Spirit, must have had a prophetic glimpse of the everlasting, glorious life which his descendant, Jesus Christ, was to bring to light in his resurrection (Acts 2:26–32; 13:35–37).

Isaiah assures us that the Sovereign Lord "will swallow up death forever" and "wipe away the tears from all faces" (Isa. 25:8a). This verse is not a gloss but quite a natural sequel to v. 7, where it is stated that the shroud (of mourning and grief, cf. 2 Sam. 15:30; Esth. 6:12; Jer. 14:3) that is spread over all nations will be destroyed. Thus Isa. 25:8a explains *why* this symbol can be destroyed: death itself will be completely destroyed by Yahweh. Within the framework of a moving description of the eschatological feast to be made "for all peoples" (v. 6), v. 8 speaks clearly of the absolute destruction of death in the great Day of the Lord (cf. 1 Cor. 15:54; Rev. 21:4). In the following chapter Isaiah exclaims, "But your dead will live; / their bodies will rise. / You who dwell in the dust, / wake up and shout for joy" (26:19). In contrast to v. 14 (which does not imply that there is no future resurrection, but that Israel's oppressors are dead and therefore unable to harm God's people), v. 19 prophesies the eschatological, physical resurrection of the righteous dead, namely, those faithful Israelites who had died under the "other lords" of v. 13. That the prophet does not speak of a "general" resurrection does by no means imply that at the time such a resurrection was unknown. The comfort given to the true Israelites would rather presuppose the belief in it.

Ezekiel portrays the vision of the valley of dry bones, lying disconnected and lifeless but revived by the almighty power of God's Spirit, this revival implying resurrection (Ezek. 37:1–10). According to some, this vision, which is a prophecy of Israel's restoration as a nation (vv. 11–14), presupposes the common belief in a bodily, future resurrection of the dead. This may be so, but it cannot be conclusively substantiated.

Daniel clearly predicted a resurrection: "Multitudes who sleep in the dust of the earth will awake: some to everlasting life, others to shame and everlasting contempt" (Dan. 12:2). The prophet comforted the faithful Israelites for whom an unprecedented tribulation was looming in the near future (v. 1). Many of them would have to lay down their lives for Yahweh's sake. These martyrs were comforted by the assurance of a bodily resurrection in glory, whereas those who denied the Lord would be raised to "shame and everlasting contempt." A general resurrection of the dead is obviously not intended here—which is not to say that he did not believe in it, but rather that he wanted to comfort his brethren who would have to endure suffering and death for righteousness' sake. Even so, his prophecy gives unmistakable evidence of faith in an eschatological, bodily resurrection.

God promises through Hoseah, "I will ransom them from the power of the grave; / I will redeem them from death. / Where, O death, are your plagues? / Where, O grave, is your destruction?" (Hos. 13:14). Alluding to this promise, Paul speaks of the complete victory over death and the grave (1 Cor. 15:55). This does not imply that Hos. 13:14 predicted the resurrection of the dead. The whole context speaks of judgment on God's unfaithful people, and so the natural interpretation of v. 14 is that no one will be able to save Ephraim from destruction so that death and Sheol could be defied. On the contrary, the Lord will have no mercy.

In conclusion it may be said that the OT teaches with varying degrees of explicitness the resurrection of the dead, a doctrine which is divinely inspired and not derived from pagan sources. It should also be noted that in Jewish noncanonical literature many references to the resurrection may be found, though conceptions and interpretations of the various passages differ widely. (Space does not permit the discussion of these passages. Cf. T. H. Gaster in *IDB*, 4:41–43; G. W. E. Nickelsburg in *ABD*, 5:684–91.)

IV. Resurrection in the NT. The primary Greek noun meaning "resurrection" is *anastasis G414* (lit., "a raising up, a rising up," Matt. 22:23 et al.), derived from the verb *anistēmi G482* ("to raise up," Jn. 6:39–40 et al.; intransitive, "to rise up," Mk.

9:10 et al.). Another noun, *egersis* G1587 (lit., "a waking"), is used only once, with reference to Jesus' resurrection (Matt. 27:53), but the cognate verb *egeirō* G1586 (lit., "to awaken") occurs frequently with the emphasis on God's initiative and activity (Acts 2:24 et al.); the passive form can have an intransitive meaning, "to wake up, rise," but when used of the resurrection it is more likely a true passive (cf. Rom. 6:4). For further discussion of these terms, see RESURRECTION OF JESUS CHRIST IV.

A. The historical record. Some of the raisings from the dead recorded in the NT were performed by Jesus himself: JAIRUS's daughter (Mk. 5:35–43 and parallels), the widow's son (Lk. 7:11–17), and Lazarus (Jn. 11). When Jesus died, many deceased saints were raised (Matt. 27:52–53), whereas PETER was the agent in the raising of DORCAS (Acts 9:36–42), and PAUL in that of EUTYCHUS (20:9–12). The raisings by Jesus were signs of his messiahship. Through him the new age, bringing victory over sin and death, had come (Matt. 11:5; Lk. 7:22; Jn. 11:25). The mysterious resurrection of the "many saints" pointed in the same direction, since it coincided with Jesus' death; and also the raisings of Dorcas and Eutychus, for the apostles always acted as Jesus' agents in various acts of healing (Acts 3:6; 16:18; 2 Cor. 12:12; cf. Matt. 10:8). Since all these raisings were only signs of Jesus' resurrection power, they meant only a return to this mortal life; the final victory over death waits until the end.

Jesus' own resurrection, taking place on Sunday morning after his death and burial on Friday evening (Matt. 28:1 and parallels), differs from all other raisings as Jesus himself differs from other human beings. He is God incarnate (Jn. 1:14), the last ADAM, representing sinful and lost mankind (Rom. 5:12–19; 1 Cor. 15:45–49), the only MEDIATOR between God and man (1 Tim. 2:5); he came to destroy the works of the devil (who has the power of death, Heb. 2:14; 1 Jn. 3:8) and to save sinners (1 Tim. 1:15). In that capacity he died "for our trespasses" (Rom. 4:25 NRSV), "a ransom for all" (1 Tim. 2:6), and was "raised to life for our justification" (Rom. 4:25). Jesus "through the Spirit of holiness was appointed the Son of God in power by his resurrection from the dead" (Rom. 1:4 TNIV), raised in a "glorious body" (Phil. 3:21) never to die again (Rom. 6:9). He is the great High Priest by "the power of an indestructible life" (Heb. 7:16), the source of true, glorious, and everlasting life spiritually and physically for all who are in him (Jn. 3:16; 6:56–58; 11:25–26; 14:19; 2 Cor. 13:4; 2 Tim. 1:10; Rev. 1:18).

The earliest record of Jesus' resurrection and of some appearances of the risen Lord is given by Paul through divine revelation (1 Cor. 15:3–8; cf. 11:23). According to Paul the preaching of the gospel as well as faith in Christ are futile without Christ's resurrection (15:17). Further detailed descriptions of the empty tomb and the appearances, on which the church's faith in Jesus' resurrection is based (Acts 1:3), are to be found in the Gospels (Matt. 28; Mk. 16; Lk. 24; Jn. 20–21). For a full discussion see RESURRECTION OF JESUS CHRIST.

B. The future resurrection. Christ is to raise and judge everyone. Unequivocally the NT teaches the raising of all the dead—those in Christ as well as those without him—by Jesus Christ himself, who will judge them according to their works (Jn. 5:28–29; Acts 17:31; Rom. 14:10; 2 Cor. 5:10; Rev. 11:18; 20:11–15). The end of God's ways cannot be the INTERMEDIATE STATE, in which people exist without their bodies (Heb. 12:23; Rev. 20:4). Each human being in his or her totality was created for eternity, whereas the judgment will be concerned about what everyone has done in the body (2 Cor. 5:10); hence the necessity of a bodily resurrection, either to eternal life or to eternal judgment under the wrath of God (Matt. 10:28; 25:34; Jn. 3:36; 5:29; Rev. 20:15). Though Christ as the divinely appointed judge (Acts 17:31) will raise all the dead, only the resurrection of his believers, to life eternal, is guaranteed by Christ's resurrection (1 Cor. 15:20–24; 1 Thess. 4:14). From 1 Cor. 15:23 it seems clear that "all" in v. 22 denotes all who belong to Christ. Since the essence of Scripture is the gospel of salvation, little is said in the NT about the resurrection of those without Christ. All the emphasis, especially in the great chapter of the resurrection (1 Cor. 15), is on that of the believers.

When will the dead be raised? According to the general teachings of the NT and particularly according to those of Paul (1 Cor. 15:51–52; 1 Thess. 4:16), the resurrection of the deceased believers will take place at the SECOND COMING of the Lord when also those in Christ who at that moment are alive will be changed. All believers of all the ages constitute one company of glorified saints, who are privileged to meet their Redeemer in the air. After having first been acquitted before Christ's glorious throne and welcomed into his Father's kingdom (Matt. 25:31–40), they will participate in pronouncing judgment on the unbelievers and fallen angels (Matt. 25:41–46; 1 Cor. 6:2–3). Whether the unbelievers will be raised at the same time as the believers or, as some suggest, somewhat later, cannot be determined with certainty.

A controversial subject among evangelicals is the question whether there will be only one physical, general resurrection, or at first a partial one and after that a final general resurrection. Those favoring the latter opinion appeal to Rev. 20:4–6, which states that those who were faithful during the reign of Antichrist "came to life and reigned with Christ a thousand years. (The rest of the dead did not come to life until the thousand years were ended.) This is the first resurrection." Others, who are of the opinion that there will be only one bodily resurrection, point to the fact that apart from this controversial text, nowhere in Scripture is a first resurrection to be distinguished from a second. They therefore understand the "first resurrection" (v. 5) to be the promotion of the faithful saints to glorious life with Christ immediately after death in the intermediate state (cf. Phil. 1:23; Heb. 12:22). Space does not permit further discussion of this exegetical problem. See MILLENNIUM.

V. The resurrection body. Most present-day theologians reject the idea of a resurrection in a body of flesh, either on so-called scientific grounds, which implies a denial of God's power (cf. Mk. 12:24), or because they regard the flesh as the source or seat of sin. According to this viewpoint, people will be raised as spirits, or in an "angelic," immaterial body. Though in Scripture and particularly in Paul's writings the word *flesh* sometimes denotes the evil human nature, nowhere is the flesh-body as such proclaimed evil and the source of sin. It is the heart, the religious center of one's personality, which is evil (Gen. 8:21; Mk. 7:14–23; Rom. 2:5). The flesh-body is an ethically neutral

The resurrected Christ ascending into heaven. Painting on the ceiling of the Church of the Ascension on the Mount of Olives.

medium which, as far as believers are concerned, belongs to Christ (1 Cor. 6:15); it is a temple of the HOLY SPIRIT (1 Cor. 6:19) and a means to serve God (Rom. 6:12–13).

That in Scripture the word *body* would denote the "self" or the "spiritual personality," as some aver, cannot be substantiated (see the detailed critique of this view by R. H. Gundry, *Sōma in Biblical Theology: With Emphasis on Pauline Anthropology* [1976]). The resurrection of the dead in a body of flesh is guaranteed by Jesus' resurrection in a body of "flesh and bones," with scars of his wounds visible, and capable of being touched and of eating food (Lk. 24:38–43; Acts 10:41). At his ascension Jesus did not discard this flesh-body, as is clear from Acts 1:11; Phil. 3:21; Rev. 1:17. Since the resurrected believers will be like the risen Christ (1 Cor. 15:49; Phil. 3:21; 1 Jn. 3:2), they too will be raised in their bodies of flesh (cf. 1 Cor. 15:35–42). Only in this way is a person saved in his totality, and able to live on a new earth (Isa. 65:17–19; 66:22; Matt. 5:5; Rev. 21:1–3).

Some passages are thought to deny a physical resurrection. For example, Jesus told the SADDUCEES (Matt. 22:30; Mk. 12:25) that the resurrected saints will be like angels. The context, however, makes it clear that the resemblance will lie in the fact that after the resurrection there will be no marriage. Luke recorded the reason for this change: "they can no longer die" (Lk. 20:36); in other words, reproduction is no longer needed to fill the places that have become vacant because of death. There is no reference here to the nature of the resurrection body, and the passages quoted do not even imply that the distinction between male and female will be abolished.

Again, the resurrection body is called a "spiritual" body (1 Cor. 15:44). This, however, does not mean

Tombs (*kokhim*) at the Church of the Holy Sepulchre in Jerusalem. The resurrection of Jesus occurred in the newly hewn tomb of Joseph of Arimathea.

that it will be a body consisting of spirit. Rather, the statement characterizes the resurrection body as one completely filled and governed by the Holy Spirit. Another statement by Paul, namely, that "flesh and blood cannot inherit the kingdom of God" (15:50), is often considered to exclude the idea of a resurrection body of flesh. The apostle, however, teaches something entirely different. The expression "flesh and blood" never denotes the "substance" of the body, but man in his totality as a frail and perishable creature (Matt. 16:17; Gal. 1:16; Eph. 6:12; Heb. 2:14). It has the same meaning in 1 Cor. 15:50a, shown by the fact that in the parallel clause (v. 50b) the word "perishable" is used, which obviously denotes the whole person in his corruptibility and not the substance of his body. The entire context shows that human beings, as frail, perishable creatures, cannot enter God's glorious, eschatological kingdom. They first must be made immortal, imperishable, powerful, and glorious. There is no denial of a resurrection in a body of flesh.

Though the resurrection body will be essentially identical to the present body in that it is a body of flesh, there will be a tremendous change regarding the conditions of its existence. Paul emphasized the necessity of such a change for the dead as well as for those who are living when Jesus returns (note the word "must" in 1 Cor. 15:53). This change is necessary because the resurrected believer enters upon a new world of impeccable perfection and heavenly glory (1 Cor. 15:47–49) like that of Christ (2 Cor. 3:18), a glory that will differ in accordance with the individual believer's dedication to the Lord in this life (Dan. 12:3; 1 Cor. 3:14–15; 2 Cor. 9:6). In these wonderful resurrection bodies the believers will be able to ascend to heaven and meet their returning Lord in the air (1 Thess. 4:16–17). The change will be so miraculous and spectacular that no one is able to form any adequate conception of it on this side of the grave, or give a trustworthy detailed description.

(See further R. S. Candlish, *Life in the Risen Saviour* [1858]; W. Milligan, *The Resurrection of the Dead* [1894]; B. F. Westcott, *The Gospel of the Resurrection* [1906]; J. F. Darragh, *The Resurrection of the Flesh* [1921]; E. Käsemann, *Leib und Leib Christi: Eine Untersuchung zur paulinischen Begrifflichkeit* [1933]; K. Barth, *Die Auferstehung der Toten* [1935]; J. A. T. Robinson, *The Body* [1952]; J. Murray, *Redemption Accomplished and Applied* [1955], 174–81; O. Cullmann, *Immortality of the Soul or Resurrection of the Dead* [1958]; R. Martin-Achard, *From Death to Life: A Study of the Development of the Doctrine of the Resurrection in the Old Testament* [1960]; M. E. Dahl, *The Resurrection of the Body* [1962]; M. C. Tenney, *The Reality of the Resurrection* [1963]; J. A. Schep, *The Nature of the Resurrection Body* [1964]; R. H. Gundry, *Sōma in Biblical Theology: With Emphasis on Pauline Anthropology* [1976]; Richard B. Gaffin, Jr., *Resurrection and Redemption: A Study in Paul's Soteriology*, 2nd ed. [1987]; M. J. Harris, *From Grave to Glory: Resurrection in the New Testament* [1990]; J. Holleman, *Resurrection and Parousia: A Traditio-Historical Study of Paul's Eschatology in I Corinthians 15* [1996]; S. Bacchiocchi, *Immortality or Resurrection? A Biblical Study on Human Nature and Destiny* [1997]; G. R. Habermas, *The Risen Jesus and Future Hope* [2003]; J. H. Charlesworth et al., *Resurrection: The Origin and Future of a Biblical Doctrine* [2006]. In addition, see relevant sections in dogmatic works and in books on eschatology.)   J. A. SCHEP

Resurrection, Treatise on the. The title of a brief document preserved in Coptic in the NAG HAMMADI LIBRARY (NHC I, 4). Written in the form of a letter probably in the late 2nd cent., it purports to be a response to a certain Rheginos, who is said to have inquired into "what is proper concerning the resurrection" (44.5). The author asserts that "the Savior swallowed up death" (45.14–15) and that therefore "we are drawn to heaven by him, like beams by the sun, not being restrained by anything. This is the spiritual resurrection which swallows up the psychic in the same way as the fleshly" (45.36–46.2). Toward the end of the document, he exhorts the reader not to live in conformity with the flesh, for "already you have the resurrection" (49.11–16). This last statement appears to provide a striking parallel to Paul's warning against the teaching of HYMENAEUS and PHILETUS (2 Tim. 2:18). The language of the treatise (e.g., "the emanation of Truth and Spirit," 45.12) reflects Valentinian influence (see GNOSTICISM), and the author also appears to have been influenced by Middle Platonism. (English trans. in *NHL*, 52–57.)

resurrection of Jesus Christ. After JESUS CHRIST died and was buried on Good Friday, he was raised from the dead in body and soul on the first day of the week. His resurrection was not a mere resuscitation, as was the case with LAZARUS and others whose resurrections are recorded in Scripture (see the general article on RESURRECTION). They returned to temporal life only to die again. Jesus Christ, however, was raised to life eternal and everlasting glory (Rom. 6:9–10; Heb. 7:16; 1 Pet. 1:21; Rev. 1:18).

    I. The place of the resurrection in the NT kerygma
    II. The resurrection a historical fact to be accepted by faith
    III. Christ's resurrection and history
    IV. Raised and risen
    V. The empty tomb as evidence of Jesus' resurrection
    VI. The postresurrection appearances
        A. The record
        B. The appearance narratives under attack
        C. Various theories
        D. The truth
    VII. Jesus' resurrection body
        A. Spiritualizing views
        B. A real body of flesh
        C. The same body, but in a glorified condition
    VIII. The significance of Jesus' resurrection

I. Place of the resurrection in the NT kerygma. In the KERYGMA—the NT proclamation of the good news—Jesus' resurrection occupies the central and all-important place. The GOSPELS find their climax in the description of Jesus' resurrection (Matt. 28; Mk. 16; Lk. 24; Jn. 20–21). In the first kerygma of the early church the resurrection is the focal point (Acts 2:24–32; 3:14–16, 26; 4:10; 5:30; 7:55–56; 10:39–43). It also has this central place in PAUL's letters. In 1 Cor. 15:17–19 the apostle states that the whole Christian faith and the salvation it brings stands or falls with the resurrection of our Lord. (See also Acts 17:31; Rom. 8:11; 1 Cor. 6:14; Gal. 1:1; Eph. 1:20; Col. 2:12.) Everywhere in the NT the resurrection is proclaimed as the decisive turning point in the life of Jesus and in the history of the world's redemption. This is due to the uniqueness of Christ's person, as being both God incarnate (Jn. 1:14), and the promised MESSIAH (4:25–26), and to the uniqueness of the work he had come to do, namely, to reconcile sinful mankind to God by dying an atoning death on a cross (Matt. 20:28; Rom. 5:10; 2 Cor. 5:18–19; Col. 1:21–22; 1 Tim. 2:5–6); while as the risen Lord he imparts to sinners the redeeming fruit of his death: JUSTIFICATION (Rom. 4:25; 5:9–10), SANCTIFICATION (8:1–2; 1 Cor. 1:30), and glorification (Rom. 8:30; 2 Cor. 3:18; 4:17).

II. The resurrection a historical fact to be accepted by faith. The sources for the knowledge of Christ's resurrection are the Scriptures, especially the Gospels, which contain the records of the experiences of eyewitnesses to whom the Lord appeared, giving "many convincing proofs that he was alive" (Acts 1:3), but also the special revelation given to Paul (Acts 9:1–6; 1 Cor. 15:3–8). These sources proclaim the resurrection as a historical fact of supernatural character.

Since the Scriptures are given by INSPIRATION and therefore can be trusted as the infallible revelation of God, the resurrection is an object of FAITH and of faith alone. Liberal theologians of older and recent schools, rejecting the infallibility of the Bible, have been trying to find out precisely what happened in connection with Jesus' resurrection by applying the historical method of higher criticism as a tool of human research and reasoning in the field of revelation. The result invariably was—and is—a denial of the resurrection as Scripture speaks of it, that is, Jesus Christ's real and literal rising from the tomb in his own body of flesh and bones (Lk. 24:39–40; Jn. 20:27). According to the critics, many statements in the Gospels and the rest of the NT are without proof and must be rejected as "later embellishment of the primitive tradition" (R. Bultmann in *Kerygma and Myth: A Theological Debate*, ed. H. W. Bartsch, 2 vols. [1953–62], 1:38).

A physical resurrection is also considered inconsistent in the 20th cent. with the findings of "the natural sciences, especially biology" (Paul M. Van Buren, *The Secular Meaning of the Gospel, Based on an Analysis of Its Language* [1963], 17). These sciences are declared to leave no place for anything supernatural. Liberal theology cannot deny, of course, that the faith in a bodily resurrection as recorded in the Gospels must be explained. According to some, it originated from the loving esteem of the early believers for their dead Master and their longing for his return from death, which led them to believe that they had seen him. Others presume that after his death Jesus actually "appeared" to his disciples, but only in a "spiritual" way. In a later paragraph these and other theories will be discussed.

At this stage it may suffice to emphasize that the resurrection of Jesus Christ, though a historical fact, cannot possibly be established by historical verification if "historical" means according to modern methods of historical research to the exclusion of faith in the trustworthiness of Scripture. Even if modern historians could prove that a certain man, Jesus of Nazareth, after his death became alive again, it would not mean a historical verification of Christ's resurrection. As has been stated, this was not merely the resuscitation of some dead person called Jesus of Nazareth, but the resurrection to eternal life and glory of God's Son in the flesh, the Messiah of Israel and the Savior of a lost world,

by whose resurrection the reconciliation, which he brought about by his cross, was made effective unto eternal life for all who believe in him as he is revealed in the Scriptures.

Where this faith controls the investigations into "what happened," the Gospels provide ample "proof" that Jesus really and literally arose from the tomb in his own physical, though glorified, body. Where such faith in the Scriptures is lacking, any attempt to "historically verify" Jesus' resurrection must of necessity fail. God does not permit man to find out his secrets by way of human research and reasoning, but only by faith in him as the revealer of truth through his word and Spirit (Matt. 11:25; 16:17; 1 Cor. 1:20–25).

III. Christ's resurrection and history. Claiming that the resurrection is a historical fact does not exclude that it also transcends history and may be rightly called "the beginning of a new history, which is no longer part of this our history" (K. Runia in *Reformed Theological Review* 25 [1966]: 47). By this new history is to be understood the history of human life in its immortal, glorified condition regarding body and soul. That new history is the end of God's ways for the believers. For them it will begin when Jesus returns from heaven, creating a new heaven and a new earth, which will be the suitable dwelling place for God's children in their glorified condition (Rev. 21:1–4; see HEAVENS, NEW). Then the river of present history, full of sin, misery, and death, will flow into the ocean of the never-ending new history of human existence in immortal glory, a history without sin, misery, or death.

It was upon that new history that Jesus entered as the "forerunner" of all believers, when he rose from the dead. From that moment on, history was affected, guided, and fully controlled by him (Matt. 28:18), but he has transcended it. That is why during the subsequent forty days Jesus, though several times appearing to his disciples, did not live with them in constant physical fellowship as before. The only reason he stayed on earth these forty days was to give convincing proof of the reality of his resurrection to the disciples, and through them to all believers (Acts 1:3). Except for that reason, he could have ascended into heaven immediately after his resurrection, as one who no longer belonged to current history but who had reached the goal of the new, eternal history of the end.

This truth Mary had to learn when she laid hold on Jesus in a way that suggested, "Master, now we shall never let you go again." Jesus' reply that she should not hold him fast because he was in the process of ascending to the Father (Jn. 20:17) makes it clear that in the resurrection he had crossed the dividing line between mankind's history and the new eternal history in IMMORTALITY and GLORY. This is also the reason he did not appear to the unbelieving Jews but only to his followers, through whose witness the unbelievers of that day and those of all ages had to be brought to faith.

IV. Raised and risen. In the Greek NT *anastasis G414* is almost always the noun employed to denote Jesus' resurrection; in one instance *egersis G1587* is used. Since both nouns can mean "rising" as well as "raising," their use is not decisive for the question whether Jesus was raised up or actively rose from the dead.

The situation is different with the related verb *anistēmi G482*: when it is transitively used, as is often the case in the Epistles (e.g., Rom. 4:24; 6:4; 8:11; 1 Cor. 15:15; Gal. 1:1), the resurrection is clearly proclaimed to be the work of the Father. Many times, however, this verb is used intransitively ("rise") especially in the Gospels but also now and then in the Epistles (e.g., Mk. 8:31; 9:9–10, 31; 10:31, 34; Lk. 18:33; 24:7, 46; Jn. 20:9; Acts 17:3; 1 Thess. 4:14). In such cases it is debatable whether the focus is on Jesus' actively rising from the dead. This intransitive use of the verb in itself is not sufficient proof of Jesus' rising from the dead by his own power, since the intransitive meaning is sometimes also employed to denote the resurrection of the dead (e.g., Mk. 12:25; 1 Thess. 4:16), of whom it certainly cannot be said that they will arise by their own power. Nevertheless, against the background of Jesus' own words in Jn. 10:17–18 that he has power to lay down his life and to take it again, the frequent use of the intransitive verb "rise" for Jesus' resurrection may be significant.

Similarly, the verb *egeirō G1586* (lit., "to awaken"), which in the active voice frequently describes God's activity (e.g., Acts 2:24), can have an intransitive meaning in the passive voice, though when used of the resurrection it is more likely that a true passive is intended, with God (the Father) as the agent, explicit or implied (Rom. 6:4 et al.). There is no inconsistency, however, between Jesus' "being raised" by the Father and his "rising" by his own power. As the obedient Servant of the Lord, who took the sinner's sins and curse upon himself, he had to wait for the Father to raise him up, thereby proving that Jesus' atoning work was indeed finished (Jn. 19:30). On the other hand, as God incarnate he had also the authority and power to take again the life he had voluntarily laid down, thus actively abolishing death, bringing life and immortality to light (2 Tim. 1:10), being "appointed the Son of God in power" (Rom. 1:4 TNIV).

V. The empty tomb as evidence of Jesus' resurrection. The fact that on Sunday morning the sepulchre was found empty is recorded in all the Gospels. According to the synoptics there were heavenly messengers in the tomb who adduced as convincing proof of Jesus' resurrection the fact that his body was not there (Matt. 28:6; Mk. 16:5–6; Lk. 24:1–5, 23). John describes how "the other disciple," obviously John himself, believed that Jesus was risen, for upon entering the sepulchre he not only found it empty, but also noticed how carefully Jesus' grave clothes had been folded and laid aside (Jn. 20:1–8). This detail excluded Mary's theory that Jesus' body had been taken away and buried somewhere else. John must have realized that if this had been the case, those who removed the body would certainly not have undressed it first and left the clothes lying in such an orderly condition. In the light of this, the empty tomb must certainly be reckoned among the convincing evidences of Jesus' resurrection.

Ancient and modern unbelief has tried to explain away the evidence of the empty tomb. This process began immediately after the resurrection. When the guard had informed the Jewish leaders of what had happened, the latter bribed the soldiers to spread the rumor that the disciples had stolen Jesus' body while they were asleep (Matt. 28:11–15). That this was an obvious lie is clear for the following reasons: (1) While the soldiers were asleep they could not possibly have seen the disciples doing their work! (2) It is unthinkable that a number of disciples could have approached the tomb through the midst of the sleeping soldiers, removed the heavy sealed stone, carried away the corpse, and so on, all without even one of the soldiers waking.

Other "explanations" are equally unacceptable and unreasonable. To mention a few of them: (1) The suggestion has been made that the women, misled by the darkness, went to the wrong sepulchre, where a young man told them that they were mistaken. In this case one must reject the words the "young man" spoke: "he is risen." Without any textual evidence these words are simply discarded as not belonging to the original text. This theory is to be rejected for the following reasons: (a) According to Mk. 16:2 the sun had risen and the women who had seen where Jesus' body was laid (Mk. 15:47; Lk. 23:55) knew the place. (b) If the theory were correct Mary Magdalene must have made the same mistake twice. (c) Not only the women but also Peter and John found the tomb empty.

(2) The so-called Swoon Theory: Jesus allegedly had not died on the cross but fainted, and in the tomb he revived. This suggestion is unacceptable on the following grounds: (a) Jesus' death was officially verified and ascertained (Mk. 15:44–45). (b) His side was pierced with a spear, which would have killed him had he not been dead already. (c) A cruelly wounded, crucified man would not have been able to "disentangle himself from the long windings of the grave clothes" (W. Barclay, *Crucified and Crowned* [1961], 145) nor to remove the heavy stone before the entrance of the tomb. (d) Even if he had been physically able to do all these things, the guard would have prevented his escape.

(3) Either the disciples removed and hid Jesus' body in order to create "evidence" for an alleged resurrection, or thieves stole it. Regarding the latter suggestion, one can imagine thieves stealing the costly spices and expensive linen grave clothes (Jn. 19:39–40), but not a corpse which they first undressed, leaving the spices and clothing behind in the tomb, nicely folded at that. Moreover, as already indicated, the guard would have noticed and prevented all this. For these reasons alone this suggestion is simply ridiculous. Concerning the disciples' stealing the body, this theory implies that they were the most impudent deceivers. Even a Jewish scholar declares this to be impossible: "The nineteen hundred years' faith of millions is not founded on deception" (J. Klausner, *Jesus of Nazareth: His Life, Times, and Teaching* [1925], 35).

(4) Jewish or Roman authorities may have removed the body from the tomb and taken it into their own safe keeping. The main objection is that in this case it would have been very easy for the authorities to prove that the disciples were deceivers when they publicly proclaimed that Jesus was risen (Acts 2:24–25); the authorities could then have produced the body.

(5) The empty tomb is not explicitly mentioned in 1 Cor. 15:1–8, a passage that is thought to represent the earliest tradition of the resurrection. Some critics infer from this omission that the gospel stories of the empty tomb must have been created by the early church some time later in order to make the case for the resurrection stronger. Against this theory the following objections can be raised: (a) It intimates that the early church was capable of such deception that it created fancy stories and then passed them on as records of historical facts. (b) The empty tomb is clearly implied, for to the words "Christ died" Paul adds "he was buried" (vv. 3–4). There is a special reference to the fact that Jesus' dead body was laid in the tomb. Against this background Paul's statement, "he was raised on the third day," can only mean that Jesus came out of the tomb alive. This is confirmed by Paul's speech recorded in Acts 13:29–30, where the tomb is emphatically mentioned.

(6) Often the sign of the empty tomb is rejected on the ground of alleged contradictions in the stories concerned. Matthew and Mark, for example, mention only one angel, whereas Luke speaks of "two men." However, there is no reason to speak of a contradiction in this respect. Why, for instance, is it not possible that there were two angels, as Luke says, but that the one who spoke was in the foreground and made the deepest, unforgettable impression on the women? Could this not be the reason Matthew and Luke put all the emphasis on that spokesman, without thereby denying that there was another angel in the background? In general, if all the details of what happened in and around the empty tomb were known—which is by no means

the case — many so-called contradictions would certainly vanish. The evangelists were not fools who contradicted each other while proclaiming the truth of Jesus' resurrection in days when eyewitnesses of the empty tomb were still alive. Such contradictions are particularly unlikely if, as most scholars claim, Matthew and Luke consulted Mark's gospel and inserted parts of it into their own.

Concluding our discussion of the empty tomb, one can say that the fact that so many different and obviously unconvincing explanations are offered by those who try to overthrow the evidence of the empty tomb strongly confirms the biblical truth that the tomb was empty solely because the Lord had actually and physically risen from the dead.

VI. The postresurrection appearances

A. The record. During the forty days after the resurrection, Jesus appeared some eleven times to his followers in order to give them "many convincing proofs" of the reality of his resurrection (Acts 1:3). Some of these appearances took place in or near the holy city and are the so-called "Jerusalem appearances": (1) MARY in the garden (Jn. 20:10–17); (2) the women by the wayside (Matt. 28:9–10); (3) Simon PETER (Lk. 24:34); (4) the disciples on the road to EMMAUS (Lk. 24:13–27); (5) the company of apostles and disciples gathered in the evening of the resurrection day (Lk. 24:33–34; Jn. 20:19–25); (6) THOMAS a week later (Jn. 20:26–29); (7) the disciples, who saw Jesus ascend into heaven from the MOUNT OF OLIVES (Lk. 24:50–51; Acts 1:9).

Other appearances occurred in GALILEE and are the so-called "Galilean appearances": (1) The seven disciples on the seashore (Jn. 21); (2) Jesus' followers gathered on the mountain (Matt. 28:16), which appearance in all probability was the same as that to the 500 brethren, recorded by Paul (1 Cor. 15:6). In addition to these Jerusalem and Galilean appearances, the risen Lord showed himself to JAMES (1 Cor. 15:7) and finally to Paul on the road to Damascus (Acts 9), an event that Paul puts on a par with all the other appearances (1 Cor. 15:8).

B. The appearance narratives under attack. The reliability of the appearance narratives has been denied mainly on the following grounds: (1) In the earliest record (1 Cor. 15:5–8), Paul mentions only five appearances. One of these is not even found in the Gospels. The critics conclude that at a later stage the church must have "created" some extra "stories" for apologetic purposes. This suggestion is unacceptable for two reasons: (a) without any ground, it accuses the early church of committing "pious fraud"; (b) the alleged incongruity between the two records can easily be explained. Paul apparently related only "those incidents that were of special force, appearances to leaders of the community or to a number of witnesses" (E. L. Allen in *NTS* 35 [1956–57]: 350). The evangelists strengthened this early evidence by adding other material gathered from eyewitnesses and therefore equally true.

(2) The critics assume an irreconcilable conflict between Matthew's record of a Galilean appearance and Luke's tradition of Jerusalem appearances. Here, however, there is no conflict but only a difference that can easily be explained. A comparative study of the Gospels shows clearly that each evangelist made his own selection from the material he collected from his sources, in accordance with the special aim he had in view. Luke restricted himself to the appearances in Jerusalem because it was the main center (Lk. 24:47), without thereby denying that Jesus also appeared elsewhere, as Matthew and John record.

The Church of the Primacy of Peter (Tabgha, SW of Capernaum) is the traditional site where Jesus met with Peter after his resurrection.

(3) The narratives allegedly contradict each other. Mary, for instance, is not permitted to touch Jesus (Jn. 20:17), whereas Thomas is invited to do so (20:27). Here again there is no conflict. The situations were different. Mary, as has been discussed already, wanted to keep Jesus on earth, in continuous physical fellowship with the disciples as before. She was not forbidden to touch but only to hold him. Doubting Thomas, however, was a future apostle on whose witness depended so much for the spread of the gospel. He had to be able to convince himself fully of the reality of Jesus' resurrection.

C. Various theories. Most theologians who reject a physical resurrection admit that "something happened" that created the Easter faith of the church. Regarding the question, "What happened?" they suggest various theories. The most important are the following:

(1) The Subjective Vision Theory, which suggests that the disciples, as a result of their extremely strong longing for their dead Master, imagined that they saw him and heard him speak to them. Some writers speak of hallucinations, others of illusions or visions, but they agree that the experience was completely subjective, taking place not in reality but in the excited minds of the disciples. This theory is unacceptable for the following reasons: (a) Hallucinations of this kind always "happen as the climax to a period of exaggerated wishful thinking" (John R. W. Stott, *Basic Christianity* [1958], 55). The disciples, however, instead of being "on the lookout" for Jesus' resurrection, disbelieved or doubted when they were told about it — and even when they saw the risen Lord himself (Matt. 28:17; Mk. 16:8, 11, 14; Lk. 24:11, 37; Jn. 20:24–25). (b) The sober, detailed, matter-of-fact appearance narratives exclude the idea of hallucinations as the source of the Easter faith.

(2) The Objective Vision Theory, suggesting that Jesus' immortal soul or the spiritual Christ who was the continuation of Jesus of Nazareth (P. Tillich, *Systematic Theology*, 3 vols. [1951–63], 2:156–57) granted the disciples some objective but immaterial vision, showing that the Lord was still spiritually alive. This theory founders on the fact that the appearance narratives place special emphasis on the reality of Jesus' resurrection body and its identity with the body that was buried; an identity of which Jesus himself gave ample proof (Lk. 24:39, 41; Jn. 20:17, 18; 21:9–14). The Gospels offer no ground whatever for discarding these parts of the records as pious frauds, created by the early church.

D. The truth. There can be no doubt then that the appearances were real and that Jesus showed himself to the disciples in a risen, physical body of "flesh and bones" (Lk. 24:39), the same body in which he had died, with even the scars of the wounds still visible (Jn. 20:25–27). On the ground of these appearances the church may have absolute certainty that her Saviour really conquered death in all its horrible aspects, including its disastrous effect on our physical body.

VII. Jesus' resurrection body

A. Spiritualizing views. All through history there have been opponents of the idea of a real physical resurrection, either of Christ or of the dead in general. Many of them were, and are guided by the ancient Greek conception of the BODY as intrinsically evil, the soul being by nature divine and therefore immortal (see DUALISM). Recent liberal theologians reject the Greek concept as far as the terms are concerned. They speak of the resurrection of the body. However, to them the latter is not the physical body, for which they say there can be no hope in the light of our modern world view: "A resurrection which consists of a dead man being raised to physical life is crudely mythical" (E. Brunner, *Das Ewige als Zukunft und Gegenwart* [1953], 26, 122).

To such theologians the term *body* denotes "the person," "I," or "Self" (e.g., J. A. T. Robinson, *The Body* [1952], passim). This "body" exists after death in an immaterial state, and its continued existence is called its "resurrection." It is obvious that there is hardly any essential difference between this widespread theory and the Greek concept. "While its advocates speak of Jerusalem, one suspects that the accent is Athenian" (E. E. Ellis, *Paul and his Recent Interpreters* [1961], 48). Little wonder that some of them declare that the only physical resurrection body of Christ is the church. Jesus' personal resurrection body is considered completely nonmaterial or consisting of some ghost-like "spirit-matter." (For a full discussion and critique of this understanding of "body," see R. H. Gundry, *Sōma in Biblical Theology: With Emphasis on Pauline Anthropology* [1976].)

B. A real body of flesh. All spiritualizing concepts of Jesus' resurrection body are contrary to the clear teaching of Scripture. There is first the fact that often his followers recognized him by his face and voice (Matt. 28:9; Lk. 24:31; Jn. 20:16, 19–20; 21:12). Furthermore several of them touched his body or were invited to do so (Matt. 28:9; Lk. 24:39; Jn. 20:17, 27), whereas he also ate before their eyes and had a meal with them (Lk. 24:30, 42–43; Jn. 21:12–13; Acts 10:40–41). In addition, Jesus himself declared emphatically: "A ghost does not have flesh and bones, as you see that I have" (Lk. 24:39). There can be no doubt that Scripture teaches the physical reality of Jesus' resurrection body.

C. The same body, but in a glorified condition. That Jesus' resurrection body was the same in which he had been buried is proved by the fact that he showed the disciples his hands, feet, and side, in which the scars of the cross were still visible (Lk. 24:39; Jn. 20:20). Thomas was even summoned to touch these very scars for the purpose of identification. It is obvious that "those marks were the infallible proof that his body risen was identical with his body buried" (M. L. Loane, *It is the Lord* [1965], 17).

All this does not exclude the tremendous change brought about in the condition of Jesus' body at the moment he was raised from the dead. There are mysterious elements in the appearance narratives, as, for instance, that the risen Lord could appear and disappear at will in a surprising way. He "disappeared" out of the sight of the men at Emmaus (Lk. 24:31), clearly a supernatural act. The statement that "Jesus himself stood among them" (v. 36) also suggests a sudden and miraculous appearance, which perhaps was the reason the disciples supposed they saw a spirit (v. 37). Recording the same event, John states that Jesus came and stood among them "with the doors locked" (Jn. 20:19).

Since Scripture does not tell how Jesus overcame the obstacle of the closed doors, one cannot be dogmatic about it. To conclude from such mysterious and miraculous features that from the time of the resurrection the Lord's human nature partakes of the divine omnipresence (cf. R. C. H. Lenski, *The Interpretation of St. John's Gospel* [1931], 1340–41) seems unwarranted. This interpretation contradicts the continuous teaching of Scripture that Christ, though true God, was also true man, and that he still is man (1 Tim. 2:5). In his human body as man, Jesus was not divinely omnipresent, nor could he ever become that. It would cast serious doubts on his true humanity and render the ASCENSION meaningless.

Another mysterious element is the fact that Jesus was often not recognized at first sight. "Some doubted" (Matt. 28:17), a statement that is best understood to mean that they doubted Jesus' identity. Mary Magdalene mistook Jesus for the gardener and did not even recognize his voice (Jn. 20:14–15). While this may have been caused by Jesus himself, as was the case with the disciples at Emmaus (Lk. 24:16), it is equally possible that the change which the resurrection had brought about in Jesus' body also played a role. "None of the disciples dared ask him, 'Who are you?'" (Jn. 21:12). They knew it was the Lord. One may conclude that Jesus' appearance was more or less unusual and made some disciples uncertain as to his identity.

All these mysterious and miraculous elements, together with the miraculous ascension, show that Jesus' body, though consisting of flesh and bones, was now in a glorified condition and capable of acting independently of the laws of time and space. This does not imply that he himself was beyond time and space, for this again would mean a denial of his true humanity. His body was what Paul called a SPIRITUAL BODY, the pattern for the believers' resurrection body (1 Cor. 15:44; Phil. 3:20). The word *spiritual* in this connection does not mean "immaterial," as those who adhere to spiritualizing views understand it. In Paul's vocabulary the word *spiritual* invariably means Spirit-controlled, that is, controlled by the HOLY SPIRIT. A spiritual body is thus a body that is able to do all that the Spirit of God wants it to do, with unlimited possibilities. Such was and is the resurrection body of the Lord, imperishable, glorious, powerful, incorruptible, immortal, and victorious, as Paul describes the spiritual body

(1 Cor. 15:42–50). It is impossible to explain such a glorified, mysterious body of flesh and bones in scientific terms. We must believe the Word and leave to God the things we cannot understand.

VIII. The significance of Jesus' resurrection.
Because Jesus' person and work are unique, his resurrection is therefore of unique and paramount significance. Jesus' resurrection in glory is a most wonderful manifestation of the power of God, who raised him from the dead. The believer may rest assured that this same power is also working in him unto salvation (2 Cor. 13:4; Eph. 1:19–20; 1 Pet. 1:5–7). By his resurrection Jesus was "appointed the Son of God in power" (Rom. 1:4 TNIV). The Jewish leaders had condemned him to death because he claimed to be the Son of God and equal to God (Matt. 26:63–65; Mk. 14:61–64; Lk. 22:70–71). By raising him from the dead the Father gave undeniable evidence that Jesus is indeed the Son of God.

Jesus' resurrection was the beginning of his EXALTATION as Lord and Christ, God's anointed King, Prophet, and Priest on the heavenly throne (Acts 2:29–36; Phil. 2:9–11), in accordance with Jesus' own proclamation: "All authority in heaven and on earth has been given to me" (Matt. 28:18). By the power and in the name of the risen Savior the apostles performed miracles as a sign of his lordship (Acts 4:17–18). There is no salvation but for those who confess with their mouth that he is Lord and believe with their heart that God raised him from the dead (Rom. 10:9). By raising Jesus from the dead, God proclaimed him to be the divinely appointed judge of the world (Acts 17:31), according to our Lord's own words (Jn. 5:22, 27). Since the salvation of the world depends solely and completely on Christ's death and resurrection, our attitude to him is decisive for our eternal condition (Jn. 3:16, 19, 35–36).

In Jesus' resurrection, the believer has the divine guarantee of his justification and reconciliation. The ground for these fundamental blessings is to be found in Christ's atoning death (Rom. 5:10, 17–19), but without the resurrection that death would have had no atoning power. The CROSS without the resurrection would mean that God had not been satisfied by Jesus' death. The resurrection is God's "Amen" to Jesus' loud cry: "It is finished," and therefore the guarantee that by Jesus' death the believer has indeed been reconciled to God and made righteous. For this reason Paul can suggest that the fact that Christ has been raised is of greater importance than his death (8:34).

When Christ was raised, the believers whom he represented in his death and resurrection were raised with him (Col. 3:1). His death meant the end of the burden of sin that was upon him, and when he arose he entered upon a life without that burden. From now on he lives to God in freedom and glory (Rom. 6:9–11). Because of their UNION WITH CHRIST, believers must reckon themselves dead to sin, and putting to death all sin, they must live the new resurrection life in fellowship with their risen Lord (Rom. 6:5–6, 12–14; Col. 3:5). Moreover, Jesus' resurrection in a glorious, immortal, powerful, spiritual body of flesh guarantees to believers their future resurrection in a similar body (Rom. 6:5; 1 Cor. 15:47–48; Phil. 3:21; 1 Jn. 3:2).

(In addition to the works already referred to in this article, the following selection from the numerous books dealing with Christ's resurrection is presented: R. S. Candlish, *Life in a Risen Saviour* [1858]; W. Milligan, *The Resurrection of our Lord* [1890]; E. McCheyne, *The Gospel of a Risen Saviour* [1892]; H. Latham, *The Risen Master* [1901]; B. F. Westcott, *The Gospel of the Resurrection* [1906]; K. Lake, *The Historical Evidence for the Resurrection of Jesus Christ* [1907]; J. Orr, *The Resurrection of Jesus* [1909]; C. H. Robinson, *Studies in the Resurrection of Christ* [1911]; F. Morrison, *Who Moved the Stone?* [1930]; K. Barth, *Die Auferstehung der Toten* [1935]; P. Althaus, *Die Wahrheit des kirchlichen Osterglauben* [1940]; J. Knox, *Christ the Lord* [1941]; S. Zwemer, *The Glory of the Empty Tomb* [1947]; F. V. Filson, *Jesus Christ, the Risen Lord* [1956]; R. R. Niebuhr, *Resurrection and Historical Reason* [1957]; E. Sauer, *The Triumph of the Crucified* [1957]; F. X. Durwell, *The Resurrection* [1960]; A. M. Ramsey, *The Resurrection of Christ* [1961]; M. C. Tenney, *The Reality of the Resurrection* [1963]; D. P. Fuller, *Easter Faith and History* [1964]; J. A. Schep, *The Nature of the Resurrection Body* [1965], 107–81; W. Künneth, *The Theology of the Resurrection* [1965]; U. Wilckens, *Resurrection: Biblical Testimony to the Resurrection* [1977]; G. R. Osborne, *The Resurrection Narratives: A Redactional Study* [1984]; G. O'Collins, *Jesus Risen: An Historical, Fundamen-*

tal, and Systematic Examination of Christ's Resurrection [1987]; S. Evans et al., eds., *The Resurrection: An Interdisciplinary Symposium on the Resurrection of Jesus* [1997]; P. Beasley-Murray, *The Message of the Resurrection: Christ Is Risen!* [2001]; R. Swinburne, *The Resurrection of God Incarnate* [2003]; N. T. Wright, *Christian Origins and the Question of God, Vol. 3: The Resurrection of the Son of God* [2003]; G. Lüdemann, *The Resurrection of Christ: A Historical Inquiry* [2004]; R. B. Stewart, ed., *The Resurrection of Jesus: John Dominic Crossan and N. T. Wright in Dialogue* [2006].) J. A. SCHEP

retribution. The act of paying back to someone according to that person's just deserts. Retribution is usually, although not exclusively, considered in terms of punishment for wrongdoing. In systematic theology, the distinction is sometimes made between God's *remunerative justice*, in which he distributes REWARDS, and his *retributive justice*, in which he expresses his hatred of sin by inflicting penalties.

I. Biblical words used. The English term *retribution* is not used in the KJV, but it is found occasionally in modern versions. For example, the NIV uses it to render Hebrew *gĕmûl* H1691 (as in Isa. 35:4; NRSV, "recompense," following KJV) and other words. In the NRSV it appears several times in the book of Jeremiah as the rendering of Hebrew *nĕqāmâ* H5935 (Jer. 11:20 et al.; NIV, "vengeance," following KJV). Both the NIV and the NRSV use it once to render Greek *antapodoma* G501 (Rom. 11:9). In addition, there are several verbs—*render, repay, requite, reward*—used by the KJV and other versions to represent the same idea, particularly when God is said to deal with someone according to that person's actions (e.g., Ps. 62:12b; Jer. 51:56; 2 Tim. 4:14; Rev. 22:12).

The idea of retribution certainly has a prominent place in the Bible, as is indicated by the frequent use of additional words, such as WRATH (Ps. 2:12 et al.) and VENGEANCE (Isa. 34:8 et al.). In Eden one sees the retribution of God against ADAM, EVE, and the serpent (Gen. 3:14–19). The punishment of CAIN (4:11, 12), the flood (6:5–8; see FLOOD, GENESIS), and the destruction of SODOM and GOMORRAH (18:20–21; 19:15, 24–29) are examples of retribution. When Israel entered the Promised Land by divine instruction, the nation was clearly confronted with promises of blessings that would result from obedience and threats of retributive punishment that would result from disobedience (Deut. 27:14–26; Josh. 8:34). The many promises and warnings of the prophets and of Christ are also indicative of the fact of retribution.

II. Biblical principles

A. The nature of God. As can be seen from the above discussion, the doctrine of retribution flows from the very nature of God. The God of Scripture is a God clearly characterized by righteousness, justice, and omnipotence. Therefore, he desires to, and is able to, punish evil and reward righteousness. Because he is such a God, people receive exactly what they deserve, except when his justice is tempered by his MERCY, in which case he treats people better than they deserve. The retributive nature of God is revealed in Scripture. Mercy is not simply a matter of ignoring evil; rather, God in Christ crucified takes the just deserts of sin upon himself rather than letting sin go unpunished (cf. 2 Cor. 5:21).

B. The inevitability of retribution. Because retribution is founded on the very nature of God, the Bible pictures it as inescapable: "Do not be deceived: God cannot be mocked. A man reaps what he sows. The one who sows to please his sinful nature, from that nature will reap destruction; the one who sows to please the Spirit, from the Spirit will reap eternal life" (Gal. 6:7–8). This is only a reflection of the teaching already found in the OT: "But you have planted wickedness, / you have reaped evil, / you have eaten the fruit of deception" (Hos. 10:13). The use of this parallel to sowing seed indicates that punishment is an inner necessity and a natural consequence and yet is also a result of the action of God. Not only special REVELATION but also human CONSCIENCE is deeply imbued with the conviction that people will be punished according to their deeds. The whole order of the natural world is one in which the violation of physical laws produces inescapable disaster. Every action produces exact and inescapable reaction.

C. The suitability of punishment. The Bible stresses the idea that there is a "poetic justice," a punishment that exactly fits the crime. As Jesus taught, "For in the same way you judge others, you will be judged, and with the measure you use, it will be measured to you" (Matt. 7:2). The writer of Proverbs states: "If a man digs a pit, he will fall into it; / if a man rolls a stone, it will roll back on him" (Prov. 26:27). The last book of the Bible asserts, "because they shed the blood of saints and prophets, you have given them blood to drink. It is what they deserve!" (Rev. 16:6 NRSV; see also Rom. 1:27; Rev. 18:6–7).

D. Apparent contradictions. The OT deals with the problem of the apparent contradictions to the principle of retribution. The book of JOB especially considers the fact that the superficial application of this idea is false. Job seems to be suffering out of all proportion to his sin, and in spite of his outstanding godliness, while many ungodly men prosper. Other sections of the OT also deal with this problem. "This is what the wicked are like— / always carefree, they increase in wealth. / Surely in vain have I kept my heart pure; / in vain have I washed my hands in innocence. / All day long I have been plagued; / I have been punished every morning" (Ps. 73:12–14). "Like cages full of birds, / their houses are full of deceit; / they have become rich and powerful / and have grown fat and sleek. / Their evil deeds have no limit" (Jer. 5:27–28a).

The book of Job indicates that the problem is more complex than it had been thought to be, and that God has other purposes for suffering besides punishment. The book of PSALMS sometimes expresses the conviction that although there seems to be a contradiction, this condition is only temporary and the ungodly who are prospering will surely yet be punished. Note especially Ps. 37:1–2, "Do not fret because of evil men / or be envious of those who do wrong; / for like the grass they will soon wither, / like green plants they will soon die away." The final answer to this apparent contradiction to the doctrine of retribution, however, comes in the NT, which places its stress on retribution in the world to come.

III. Retribution in this life. The OT emphasizes the fact of retribution in this life. For example, this is the basic theme of Ps. 1 and is also mentioned

Statue on Mount Carmel depicting Elijah's retribution on the prophets of Baal.

in many other passages such as Prov. 11:31, "If the righteous receive their due on earth, / how much more the ungodly and the sinner!"

In Scripture as a whole, there is considerable emphasis on retribution being administered to the collective group. Paul shows that the sin of ADAM had its effects on all human beings (Rom. 5:12–19). The obedience of ABRAHAM had an obvious effect on his seed as well as upon himself. The entire family of ACHAN was punished for his sin (Josh. 7:10–26). When, however, the people of Judah used the sins of their forefathers as the excuse for their troubles, the prophets Jeremiah and Ezekiel stressed the fact that the individual will be punished for his own sins; "whoever eats sour grapes—his own teeth will be set on edge" (Jer. 31:30; cf. Ezek. 18:4–20).

Sometimes God uses human instruments to carry out his retribution. For example, Babylon was the instrument of God to punish wicked Judah.

When Habakkuk complained of the fact that the sins of Judah went unpunished, God said, "I am raising up the Babylonians, / that ruthless and impetuous people, / who sweep across the whole earth / to seize dwelling places not their own" (Hab. 1:6). But, in turn, God used other nations to punish wicked Babylon, for when Habakkuk complained that Babylon was even more ungodly than Judah, God's answer concerning Babylon's fate was: "Because you have plundered many nations, / the peoples who are left will plunder you" (2:8).

Individual Christians, however, are not to take the administration of retribution into their own hands. They are not to operate on the OT principle of "Eye for eye, and tooth for tooth" (Matt. 5:38–39). In fact, believers can dare to live on a higher plane because they are assured of the just administration of retribution on the part of God. "Do not take revenge, my friends, but leave room for God's wrath, for it is written: 'It is mine to avenge; I will repay,' says the Lord" (Rom. 12:19).

IV. Retribution in the world to come. God used the tribulations of his people to cause them to realize that retribution only begins to operate in this life and that its perfect fulfillment is to be looked for in the world to come. Seeing great injustice in the world, but convinced of the justice of God, the HOLY SPIRIT convinced them that God would vindicate his cause in the eternal future. The many passages of Scripture about the judgment day (2 Cor. 5:10; 2 Pet. 2:9; 3:7), about a RESURRECTION to condemnation or to blessing (Dan. 12:2–3; Jn. 5:29), and about the anguish of HELL (Matt. 8:12; 10:28; 13:42) all demonstrate this fact. While some writers unwisely use the term retribution as almost exclusively dealing with the world to come, it is true that this is the main focus of the NT. In accordance with Scripture, orthodox theology teaches that retribution in the world to come is not confined to a limited time but is unending (see PUNISHMENT, ETERNAL).

God's people are not to be surprised when in spite of their righteousness they suffer a great deal in this life, for the promise is not that godliness will result in ease in this life: "Dear friends, do not be surprised at the painful trial you are suffering, as though something strange were happening to you" (1 Pet. 4:12). All of this will be taken into account by God in distributing the eternal reward. "For our light and momentary troubles are achieving for us an eternal glory that far outweighs them all" (2 Cor. 4:17). Conversely, although the wicked seem to prosper, the Bible teaches that they will be fittingly punished by God for all eternity. It is then that the ungodly will suffer the full effects of God's retributive justice.

(See further W. Jackson, *The Doctrine of Retribution* [1875]; E. Beecher, *History of Opinions on the Scriptural Doctrine of Retribution* [1878]; G. W. King, *Future Retribution* [1891]; H. Buis, *The Doctrine of Eternal Punishment* [1957]; B. E. Kelly, *Retribution and Eschatology in Chronicles* [1996]; O. W. Allen, *The Death of Herod: The Narrative and Theological Function of Retribution in Luke-Acts* [1997]; K. L. Wong, *The Idea of Retribution in the Book of Ezekiel* [2001]; K. Cooper and J. Gregory, eds., *Retribution, Repentance, and Reconciliation* [2004]; *NIDOTTE*, 4:1140–49.)

H. BUIS

Reu ree'yoo (רְעוּ H8293, possibly short form of רְעוּאֵל H8294, "friend of God" [see REUEL]; Ῥαγαύ G4814). Son of PELEG and descendant of SHEM (Gen. 11:18–21; 1 Chr. 1:25); included in Luke's GENEALOGY OF JESUS CHRIST (Lk. 3:35; KJV, "Ragau"). Attempts to identify the name Reu with a geographical area in MESOPOTAMIA have not been successful.

Reuben roo'bin (רְאוּבֵן H8017, "See! A son!"; gentilic רְאוּבֵנִי H8018 [always with def. article], "Reubenite"; Ῥουβήν G4857). Firstborn son of JACOB and LEAH; the name is also applied to the Israelite tribe that descended from him. According to the biblical text, Jacob loved RACHEL more than Leah, but "the LORD saw that Leah was not loved," and thus "he opened her womb" (Gen. 29:30–31). When her son was born, she named him Reuben "because the LORD has looked [*rāʾâ*] on my affliction [*bĕʿonyî*]" (v. 32 RSV). The etymology of the name has caused considerable debate (cf. J. Skinner, *A Critical and Exegetical Commentary on Genesis*, ICC, 2nd ed. [1930], 386), but it is now generally recognized to be made up of the imperative of the verb *rāʾâ* H8011 ("See!" or "Behold!") and the noun *bēn* H1201 ("A son!"). The name thus welcomes the

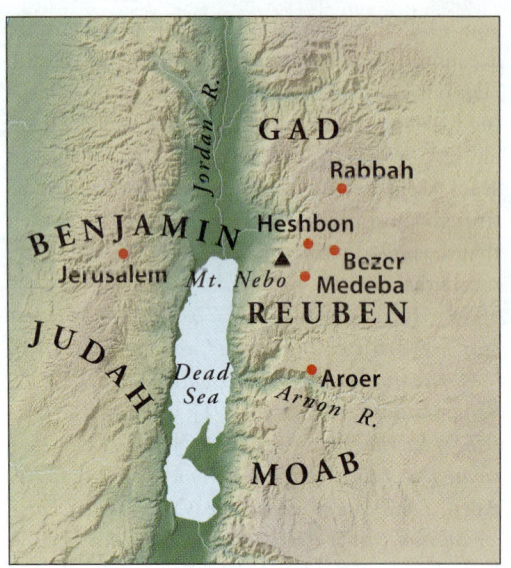

The tribal territory of Reuben.

arrival of a male child. If so, Leah's explanation (NIV, "the LORD has seen my misery") involves a wordplay; also playful — but no less serious for that reason — is her further comment, "my husband will love me [*yeʾĕhābanî*] now" (cf. G. G. Nicol in *JTS* 31 [1980]: 536–39).

As a child (but evidently old enough to be around the field workers), Reuben on one occasion brought some MANDRAKES to his mother. The fruit apparently was thought to be an aphrodisiac or to aid in conception, so when Rachel asked Leah for some of the mandrakes, the latter used the occasion to regain her conjugal rights (Gen. 30:14–16). As the FIRSTBORN, Reuben would rightly have become the leader of the sons of Jacob, but he lost his ascendancy by an illicit affair with his father's concubine, BILHAH (35:22; 49:4). Subsequently, the narrative places him in a more favorable light. When the other sons of Jacob plotted against JOSEPH, Reuben interceded with them and prevented his murder by suggesting that they imprison him in an empty cistern instead (37:21–22). Years later, when Joseph incognito confronted his brothers in Egypt, Reuben reminded them that he had urged them not to harm Joseph (42:22). Upon their return to Canaan, he offered his sons to Jacob as surety to guarantee the safety of BENJAMIN, whom he needed to take to Egypt on a second trip for grain. When the family finally migrated to Egypt with Jacob, Reuben had four sons of his own (46:8–9). (See further F. M. Cross in *ZAW* 100 [1988 Suppl.]: 46–65.)

The tribe of Reuben is mentioned first in some lists (Exod. 1:1–4; Num. 1:5, 20–21), but not always (cf. Num. 2:10); the leadership now belonged to JUDAH (2:3). In the line of march through the wilderness, the tribe of Reuben led the second division that followed the Levites, who transported the TABERNACLE (Num. 10:17–18). When KORAH rebelled against MOSES, he was joined by three Reubenites (DATHAN, ABIRAM, and ON, Num. 16:1), and some scholars believe that this action reflects an attempt to bring the tribe of Reuben back into a position of greater prominence.

At the time of the conquest the tribe of Reuben, along with the tribe of GAD and the half-tribe of MANASSEH, petitioned for the right to remain on the high plateau E of the Jordan where there was ample room for grazing cattle. The permission was granted on condition that they would give military support to the tribes on the W bank of the river until the latter had completed the subjugation of the land (Num. 32:1–32; Josh. 4:12–13). In Moses' final partition of the land this agreement was confirmed, and the E bank of the Jordan became the heritage of the tribes of Reuben, Gad, and Manasseh (Josh. 13:8–23; 18:7). See TRIBES, LOCATION OF, I.A.

Severed from the other tribes by the valley of the Jordan, the tribes of Reuben, Gad, and the half-tribe of Manasseh felt alienated from the others and wanted to have a center of worship for themselves. They eventually established an altar of their own, which the western tribes interpreted as a move toward religious secession. The latter threatened war, but the eastern tribes disavowed any desire to desert the worship of Yahweh. On the contrary, they did not wish to be excluded from the united worship of the nation. A war was averted, and the issue was closed (Josh. 22:10–34).

The tribe of Reuben was not involved in the struggles with the Canaanite kings subsequent to the days of JOSHUA (Jdg. 5:15, 16), though it may have participated in the civil war with the Benjamites (Jdg. 20:10; 21:5), since "all the tribes" are mentioned. Reubenites served in the army of

David (1 Chr. 11:42; 12:37), and the tribal group was incorporated into the political structure of David's realm (26:32; 27:16). In the period of the divided kingdom it seems to have been less active in the affairs of the nation, and finally its territory passed under the domination of Syria (2 Ki. 10:32, 33). Some vestiges of the tribe must have persisted until the Assyrian captivity, since it is mentioned in conjunction with the tribe of Gad and the half-tribe of Manasseh when the latter were deported to Assyria by TIGLATH-PILESER (1 Chr. 5:26).

The name of Reuben occurs only once in the NT in the enumeration of the tribes comprised in the sealing of the 144,000 (Rev. 7:5).

M. C. TENNEY

Reuel roo´uhl (רְעוּאֵל *H8294*, "friend of God"). KJV also Raguel (only Num. 10:29). **(1)** Son of ESAU by BASEMATH daughter of ISHMAEL (Gen. 36:3–4, 10; 1 Chr. 1:35). His four sons became clan chiefs in EDOM (Gen. 36:13, 17; 1 Chr. 1:37).

(2) Priest of MIDIAN and father-in-law of MOSES (Exod. 2:18; Num. 10:29), usually referred to as "Jethro." Some scholars connect the use of the name Reuel with the Edomite tribe (above, #1; cf. *ABD*, 5:693–94). See discussion under JETHRO.

(3) Father of ELIASAPH; at the time of the census in Sinai, Eliasaph was appointed leader of the tribe of GAD (Num. 2:14 KJV and most versions, following MT). Instead of Reuel, the NIV reads DEUEL because that is the form used in every other reference to this individual (Heb. *děʿûʾēl H1979*, Num. 1:14; 7:42, 47; 10:20). The difference no doubt resulted from the common scribal error of confusing the Hebrew consonants ד and ר. The SEPTUAGINT reads *Ragouēl* in all five passages, and on that basis some scholars argue that Reuel is the original form.

(4) Son of Ibnijah, descendant of BENJAMIN, and ancestor of Meshullam; the latter is listed among the Benjamites who resettled in Jerusalem (1 Chr. 9:8).

B. K. WALTKE

Reumah roo´muh (רְאוּמָה *H8020*, derivation uncertain). The concubine of NAHOR, brother of ABRAHAM (Gen. 22:24). Her four sons probably became ancestors of Aramean tribes who lived in the environs of DAMASCUS. See ARAM (COUNTRY).

revelation. God's disclosure of himself through CREATION, HISTORY, the human CONSCIENCE, and SCRIPTURE. Revelation is given both in event and word. There is no technical term for the concept in Scripture, although the NIV uses "revelation" to render two Hebrew words meaning VISION (2 Sam. 7:17; 1 Chr. 17:15; Prov. 29:18; Hab. 2:2–3); moreover, most versions use it to translate the Greek noun *apokalypsis G637* ("unveiling, disclosure"), which seems to have a specialized theological meaning in PAUL (Rom. 16:25 et al.; cf. also Rev. 1:1 and see REVELATION, BOOK OF). It should also be noted that the common Hebrew verb *gālâ H1655* ("to uncover") is frequently used of God's self-disclosure (Gen. 35:7 et al.). Similarly, the Greek verbs *apokalyptō G636* and *phaneroō G5746* are often employed in a strong theological sense (e.g., Matt. 11:25; Jn. 1:31; Rom. 1:17; 16:26).

I. The twofold aspect. Theologians generally distinguish between *general* (natural) and *special* revelation. General revelation is God's witness to himself toward all through creation, history, and the conscience (e.g., Ps. 19; Acts 14:8–18; 17:16–34; Rom. 1:18–32; 2:12–16). Certain basic views on general revelation may be noted. First to be stated is that of Roman Catholicism, with which many Protestants agree. Those who adopt this view argue that general revelation provides the basis for the construction of a natural theology. (Natural theology refers to the effort to construct a doctrine of God in which his existence is established without appeal to faith or special revelation but solely through reason and experience.)

This view holds that theology is two-storied. On the first level a natural theology is built from the building blocks of general revelation cemented into place by REASON. This natural theology includes proofs for the existence of God and the IMMORTALITY of the soul. It is insufficient for a saving knowledge of God, but it is essential for one who would rise to that level. Admittedly, most people do not arrive at even this first level through reason but by FAITH; nevertheless it is thought imperative that the theoretical possibility of such a rationalistic approach be held. On the second level a revealed theology is built from the building blocks of special revelation cemented into place by faith. This revealed theology includes all the distinctive beliefs of the Christian faith, such as the DEITY OF CHRIST, substitutionary ATONEMENT, the TRINITY, etc. Only on this level is one brought to a redemptive encounter with God in Christ. This approach has led to a rationalistic apologetic and is built upon a largely Arminian theology.

Second to be outlined is the position of Karl Barth, who denies both natural theology and general revelation. According to Barth, revelation is given exclusively in the Christ-event. The Bible is the fallible but authoritative pointer to him. From a Scriptural perspective it would appear that Barth overreacted to the exponents of a natural theology and threw out the baby with the bath water. This forced him to interpret in a contrived fashion those Scripture passages which speak of general revelation and brought him to a falling out with his friend Emil Brunner (see their interchange in *Natural Theology: Comprising "Nature and Grace" by Emil Brunner and the Reply "No!" by Karl Barth* [1946]).

Third, we note the position of John Calvin, who maintained that general revelation may be correctly understood only through the lenses of special revelation. Following the lead of PAUL in Rom. 1, those who adopt this position contend that while one could find a natural theology in v. 20, the apostle goes on to show that fallen men and women engage in a suppression of and substitution for the truth. Even in regard to the so-called "Nature Psalms" it must be remembered that these were the expressions of godly people who therefore viewed nature through the perspective of special revelation. This approach has led to a revelational apologetic and is built upon a largely Reformed theology.

Special revelation is God's disclosure of himself in salvation history (revelation in reality) and in the interpretive word of Scripture (revelation in Word). Quantitatively this encompasses more than we have in Scripture. In contrast, neoorthodox theology maintains that revelation is never propositional; that is, it does not consist of words but only of events. The Bible is therefore viewed as only a record of revelation; it represents merely a human attempt to understand and bear witness to the revelatory works of God. For Barth, revelation occurs when God's disclosure of himself in the Christ-event is responded to by faith. According to this viewpoint, the Bible may be the authoritative pointer to this experience but not revelation itself.

II. Features of a biblical concept of revelation.
The *ultimate* object of all God's revelation is to bring us to himself. It is not creedal formulations or doctrinal statements but personal encounter with God that marks the ultimate goal of his revelation. The biblical concept of TRUTH is not merely that of detached critical reflection but also of subjective, even passionate involvement with the God of truth himself. Revelation provides the answer to the sinner's twofold predicament: (1) ignorance of God and therefore of himself, and (2) guilt before God. God has revealed himself in Christ not only to make us knowledgeable but also to make us holy.

Biblical revelation is by divine acts of history. God accomplishes his plan for mankind in connection with specific, temporal events. The historical skepticism of Rudolf Bultmann can never gain acceptance by those who maintain a consistently biblical view of faith. There is no Christ of faith without the Jesus of history. The whole course of biblical history is the story of what God has done for his people; it is a record of "the saving acts of the LORD" (Mic. 6:5 NRSV). Christ is the mid-point of this saving history; it is in him that the decisive word was spoken.

Biblical revelation culminates in JESUS CHRIST. The INCARNATION is the supreme act by which God reveals himself. Christ is the center of the GOSPEL (Rom. 1:3, 16; 1 Cor. 15:1–4; Gal. 4:4; Heb. 1:1–2; et al.). The OT is revelation in anticipation of the Christ; the NT is revelation in reflection on the Christ. Barth wrongly asserts that God reveals himself solely in Christ (Christomonism). We cannot argue from the fact of exclusive salvation in Christ to that of an exclusive revelation in Christ. Scripture will not permit this. In Heb. 1:1–2 it is stated that God has spoken not only in his Son but also in the PROPHETS. This passage would seem to teach that although God's special revelation of himself has come most *fully* in his Son, it was not given only in him. In addition to this passage, there is the fact of God's having revealed himself in creation, history, and the conscience (general revelation).

Biblical revelation is also divine interpretation of meaning (revelation in word). The biblical narration of the divine saving events includes the divine communication of the meaning of those events. Specifically, the basis of the NT message is the narration of interpreted events. In the NT the events are mainly recorded in the Gospels; the interpretation of these events is found mainly in the Epistles. (As an illustration of these two elements, historical event and interpretive word, see 1 Cor. 15:3–4.)

The NT account of saving events is integrally connected with the OT by the first Christians. In 1 Cor. 15:3–4, Paul ties in the death, burial, and resurrection with OT Scriptures — "according to the Scriptures." Note that this phrase is used twice. Paul was keenly conscious of the *continuity* of the two covenants. He viewed the NT salvation-historical KERYGMA as the completion of a process begun in the OT.

All revelatory events — past, present, and future — are summed up in the CRUCIFIXION and RESURRECTION OF CHRIST, which are to be viewed together as one event. The God of the future has revealed himself climactically in his Son; according to Heb. 1:2, the incarnation ushered in the last days, the eschaton. Past and present can be properly understood only in terms of the future as already revealed in the incarnate Christ. See ESCHATOLOGY.

This revelation is brought to human beings by the Bible. The redemptive acts of God together with their divine interpretation were recorded by the inspired apostles and prophets. The Bible thus becomes the means in conjunction with the inner witness of the Spirit whereby revelation given directly to prophets and apostles becomes revelation to needy sinners of every succeeding generation. The Bible is not only a pointer to revelation but is itself also revelation.

Revelation must be understood in terms of three factors: (1) *The revealer* — in this case God. (2) *The instruments of revelation* — the Scripture speaks of various modalities such as vision, dream, deep sleep, URIM AND THUMMIM, the lot, theophanies, angels, divine speaking, historical event, and the incarnation, resulting in *a product*, namely, the Word of God (the BIBLE). Up to this point we have revelation only objectively conceived. (3) Finally, we have *the receiver* — people who respond in faith to the One of whom the message testifies. This is revelation subjectively conceived.

The Bible as the product of God's revealing activity is the means whereby the redemptive work of Christ is communicated to sinners, though communication is ultimately achieved only when there is a response of FAITH on the part of the receiver. Thus, revelation must be subjectively appropriated. The objective side of the divine work of revelation (terminating in a record) needs to be supplemented by an internal subjective work of the HOLY SPIRIT. This inner work of the Spirit has classically been spoken of as illumination. The point here is well illustrated by the experience of young SAMUEL, of whom it is said at one point: "Now Samuel did not yet know the LORD: The word of the LORD had not yet been revealed to him" (1 Sam. 3:7). From the context we learn that God spoke to Samuel four times, but only in the last instance did that which was objectively the word of the Lord become the word of the Lord to Samuel (v. 10). PAUL speaks of this distinction when describing the result of his ministry among the Thessalonians: "And we also thank God continually because, when you received the word of God, which you heard from us, you accepted it not as the word of men, but as it actually is, the word of God, which is at work in you who believe" (1 Thess. 2:13). The word translated "received" (*paralambanō G4161*) may indicate outward hearing, for it is contrasted with "accepted" (*dechomai G1312*), which here clearly refers to a response from the heart. Truth known must become truth accepted.

The authority of the Bible is derived from its divine INSPIRATION. The Bible is profitable for teaching, reproof, correction, and training in righteousness because it is God-breathed (2 Tim. 3:16–17); that is, it is divine in origin. Though God employed the personalities of the human authors, the message is ultimately from God himself. A proper view of inspiration can be obtained only in the context of a correct view of revelation.

An adequate view of revelation will also recognize that the Bible must be rightly interpreted. There must be a proper methodology employed in an effort to understand the Scriptures. Hermeneutics is a crucial area of concern today. See INTERPRETATION. Traditionally a conservative hermeneutic maintained that the proper approach to the study of the Bible is a historical-grammatical one. The movement known as the "New Hermeneutic" argued that the primary task of the interpreter is that of translating the biblical message into contemporary terms, often, it seems, at the expense of the original message itself. A consistently biblical view of revelation cannot condone any hermeneutic which in the name of relevancy relieves the interpreter from a responsible handling of the text.

Whenever one approaches the Scripture to ascertain its message, the first aim must be to understand what the author is intending to say to his readers. In other words, one must first *listen*. One must be very cautious so as not to read his own existentially laden views into the text of Scripture. If this danger is not continually guarded against, one may hear a false address. In other words, individual understanding and experience must be seen not only as possible exegetical aids but also as possible sources of error. After carefully ascertaining what the original message was, one must then go on to ask how that message may relate to the reader and contemporary culture. The *ultimate* goal of exegesis is only fully achieved when the NT faith is appropriated, but this is the second step, not the first.

Revelation must be carefully differentiated from two other concepts: inspiration and illumination. Whereas revelation has to do with the communication of information as regards what God has done for and said to sinners, inspiration has to do with that act whereby God through his Spirit employed his servants to record authoritatively this information. Revelation has sometimes been defined in such a way as to suggest that although all of Scripture is inspired not all is revelation. It would seem preferable, however, to view all of Scripture as revelation, that is, as giving us that information which is deemed divinely essential for our good and God's glory. Illumination, on the other hand, has to do with the work of the Spirit whereby the reader is enabled to understand the record (1 Cor. 2:13, 14). Whereas revelation is *objective* disclosure, illumination has to do with *subjective* apprehension. In revelation God uncovers the truth; in illumination the believer comes to understand it.

These three concepts form essential steps in God's communicating to his creatures. Revelation has to do with *what* is communicated; inspiration with *how* it is communicated; illumination with *why* it is communicated.

(See further G. C. Berkouwer, *General Revelation* [1955]; J. Baillie, *The Idea of Revelation in Recent Thought* [1956]; C. F. H. Henry, ed., *Revelation and the Bible* [1958]; J. G. S. S. Thomson, *The Old Testament View of Revelation* [1960]; B. Ramm, *Special Revelation and the Word of God* [1961]; F. G. Downing, *Has Christianity a Revelation?* [1964]; J. I. Packer, *God Speaks to Man* [1965]; W. Pannenberg., ed., *Revelation as History* [1968]; M. C. Tenney, ed., *The Bible: The Living Word of Revelation* [1968]; C. H. Pinnock, *Biblical Revelation* [1971]; B. A. Demarest, *General Revelation: Historical Views and Contemporary Issues* [1982]; M. N. A. Bockmuehl, *Revelation and Mystery in Ancient Judaism and Pauline Christianity* [1990]; C. E. Gunton, *A Brief Theology of Revelation* [1995]; N. M. Samuelson, *Revelation and the God of Israel* [2002].) C. M. HORNE

Revelation, Book of the. The last book of the NT, frequently called *The Apocalypse of John* from the use of the Greek word *apokalypsis G637* ("unveiling") in Rev. 1:1. This book is unique as the sole totally apocalyptic work in the NT. In its literary genre it resembles strongly portions of the OT books of EZEKIEL, DANIEL, and ZECHARIAH; and, like them, it is the product of a writer belonging to a minority group that was either threatened with PERSECUTION or actually suffering under it. Revelation belongs to the latter part of the 1st Christian century, when the Christian church had withdrawn from JUDAISM and was initially recognized as a separate movement by the Roman state.

  I. Background
     A. Historical
     B. Social
     C. Religious
  II. Unity
  III. Authorship
  IV. Date
  V. Place of origin
  VI. Destination
  VII. Occasion
  VIII. Purpose
  IX. Canonicity
     A. Early recognition
     B. The Western church
     C. The Eastern church
     D. Full acceptance

X. Text
XI. Content
XII. Interpretation
XIII. History of Interpretation
XIV. Theology

I. Background

A. Historical. The milieu of the book of Revelation seems to be largely the cities of the Ionian coast belonging to the Roman province of ASIA. There numerous cults flourished, all of which would have been hostile to the ethics and theology of the Christian church. Its denunciation of their IDOLATRY and its insistence on MONOTHEISM, together with the strict moral code it advocated, would have created antagonism instantly. Its rapid growth jeopardized economic prosperity, since it emptied the temples of their worshipers and so deprived the image-makers and vendors of sacrificial animals of their living. During this period also the emperors, particularly NERO (A.D. 54–68) and DOMITIAN (A.D. 81–96), had expected a degree of popular adulation that was little short of worship (see EMPEROR WORSHIP). The Christians refused to accord that sort of homage to the emperors, and thus exposed themselves to the charge of being unpatriotic, if not actually subversive.

B. Social. The pressures which these religious, social, and political differences exerted on the Christian church produced a definite reaction. In order to maintain their identity they were compelled to take a stand. The author of Revelation himself was apparently exiled for his faith, and it is no surprise that his writing reveals the hostility to the prevailing corruption of the Roman state. Its character is stigmatized as a prostitute clothed in scarlet and purple, "drunk with the blood of the saints, the blood of those who bore testimony to Jesus" (Rev. 17:6). While the prophecies of the book may not be confined in their application to events contemporaneous with the author, they certainly relate to them and draw their imagery from the circumstances of the church of that day.

C. Religious. The severance of the church from Judaism probably was completed after the fall of Jerusalem in A.D. 70. By that time the church and synagogue had developed in two different directions. The doctrine of JUSTIFICATION by faith apart from the works of the law had driven a wedge between the advocates of orthodox Judaism and the community of Christian believers. The destruction of the TEMPLE had broken whatever slight connection might have remained between the church and the center of the Jewish faith in which it had been cradled. The antagonism to the church from some in Philadelphia "who claim to be Jews though they are not" finally brought the accusation that they were "the synagogue of Satan" (Rev. 3:9) and resulted in a complete breach between the two.

Within the church itself there were signs of declension that are reflected in the letters to the seven churches of Asia. Initial fervor had cooled, immoralities and heresies had infiltrated the ranks of teachers and communicants alike, and an increasing laxity prevailed. Revelation represents an attempt to revive zeal by portraying the tensions of the time and by summoning its readers to a preparation for the return of Christ in judgment.

II. Unity. R. H. Charles, whose voluminous commentary deals with the composition of the Apocalypse in detail, proposed that this author died after he had finished writing Rev. 1:1—20:3, "and that the materials for its completion, which were for the most part ready in a series of independent documents, were put together by a faithful but unintelligent disciple in the order which he thought right" (*A Critical and Exegetical Commentary on the Revelation of St. John*, ICC, 2 vols. [1920], 1:l). Charles asserted that the Apocalypse exhibited a general unity of style, diction, and dramatic progress that marked it as one production, though he insisted that the author used "sources" that were not his own creation.

The structure of the Apocalypse indicates the work of one mind rather than of several, and such apparent incongruities as Charles cites for evidence of "sources" (*Revelation*, 1:lxxxixff.) may be explained at least partially by the circumstances of its production. The character of the visions and the exile of the author would account for minor digressions, repetitions, and lack of polish in the language. Furthermore, every writer uses "sources" to some degree in composing an extensive work, whether those "sources" are drawn from memory, from personal contacts, or from documents. The unity consists in one's original integration and interpretation of the material. If the writer weaves it into a new fabric of ideas, it can have a real unity; any connection with its former usage becomes a secondary consideration.

If the consecutive heptads of Revelation indicate anything, they imply a central organization emanating from one mind. The parentheses and apparent irregularities of construction can be attributed to the author's exile and to the character of the visions which he recorded.

Furthermore, the internal structure of Revelation argues for unity. The introduction of each of the letters to the seven churches contains an allusion to the initial portrait of Christ; the final promises to the overcomers anticipate the coming of the City of God. Throughout the narrative beginning with Rev. 4, the centrality of the throne of God is marked, so that it becomes the focus of all the visions. A definite progress appears in the development of the successive judgments, so that they may be regarded as a continuous sequence from the opening of the seals in ch. 5 to the consummation of judgment in ch. 20. There are some digressions and parenthetical episodes, but these do not disrupt the fundamental unity of the book.

III. Authorship. According to the statements of the author, his name was John. He professed to be a "servant [*lit.*, slave]" of Jesus Christ, a "brother" of the people to whom he wrote, and a sharer in their trials and spiritual privileges (Rev. 1:1, 9). The visions comprised in the book had been received while he was on the island of PATMOS, presumably exiled for his Christian faith. He was well known among the churches of Asia, and was classed as a "prophet" (22:6, 9, 19) to whom revelatory visions had been imparted.

External tradition identifies him with JOHN THE APOSTLE, the son of ZEBEDEE, to whom the fourth gospel and the Johannine epistles were likewise ascribed. JUSTIN MARTYR (c. A.D. 150) stated that the Apocalypse was written by "a certain man with us, whose name was John, one of the apostles of Christ" (*Dialogue with Trypho* 81). IRENAEUS, Bishop of Lyons, on various occasions refers to the Apocalypse as the work of "John," by which he means Jesus' disciple (*Against Heresies* 4.20.11; cf. also 4.14.2; 4.17.6; et al.). TERTULLIAN (c. A.D. 200) ascribed the Revelation to John (*Against Praxeas* 17; *On the Soul* 55.8.1; *Answer to the Jews* 9; *Against Marcion* 2.5; 3.14–15; *Against Heretics* 23; *Scorpiace* 13), and specifically identified John as the apostle. ORIGEN (c. A.D. 225) also attributed the Apocalypse to John (*De principiis* 1.3.10; *Against Celsus* 6.6.; 6.32; 8.17). From the middle

The island of Patmos as it looks today. It was here that John received his visions and wrote the book of Revelation.

of the 2nd cent. to the middle of the 3rd cent. the Johannine origin of Revelation seems to have been generally accepted by the churches of the W and also in ALEXANDRIA.

Definite objections to the Johannine authorship were first raised by Dionysius of Alexandria, who contested the traditional opinion on the following grounds: (1) the Apocalypse claims John as its author, whereas the Johannine gospel and epistles were written anonymously; (2) the vocabulary of the Apocalypse differs radically from the acknowledged Johannine writings; (3) the grammar of those writings is generally good Greek whereas the Apocalypse abounds in solecisms.

Dionysius's arguments were reproduced by EUSEBIUS, who followed his lead in questioning the authority of the book (*Eccl. Hist.* 7.24–25). In essence they are identical with those advanced against the Johannine authorship of Revelation, and they are not conclusive. The statement that the gospel and epistles are anonymous while the Apocalypse names its author is somewhat misleading. It is true that the gospel and the epistles do not *name* their author, but he was evidently well known to the readers and was presumably one of the Twelve. He certainly claimed to be an eyewitness of Christ. The writer of the Apocalypse calls himself John, and claims that he bore witness to "the word of God and to the testimony of Jesus Christ" (Rev. 1:2), phraseology that recalls distinctly the language of the fourth gospel (Jn. 1:14; 21:24). While identity of authorship cannot be proved on this basis, it is not impossible. There is no compelling reason to conclude that the author of the gospel could not have written the Apocalypse simply because he named himself in the latter work and not in the former.

The difference in vocabulary may be explained by the difference in subject matter. The gospel is a quiet and meditative account of the life of Jesus, drawn from the memories of many years and viewed from the perspective of Christian experience. The Apocalypse is the record of visions received under stress while in exile, and probably transcribed without the aid of an AMANUENSIS. The gospel deals with familiar sights and sounds connected with a normal human life in Palestine; the Apocalypse is filled with symbolic visions, peopled with strange beings, and placed in a totally supernatural panorama. Notwithstanding these disparities, there are some resemblances. In both writings Jesus is called by similar titles: "the Word of God" (Jn. 1:1; Rev. 19:13), "the Lamb" (Jn. 1:29 [*amnos G303*]; Rev. 5:6 [*arnion G768*]), the "Shepherd" (Jn. 10:11; Rev. 7:17). In both the activity of Satan is prominent (Jn. 8:44; 13:2, 27; 14:30; Rev. 2:10; 12:9; 20:2, 7, 10); and the climactic quality of the death of Christ is emphasized (Jn. 12:32; Rev. 1:5; 5:6). The parallels are not always exact, but they are sufficient to warrant the conclusion that between the acknowledged Johannine writings and the Apocalypse there is a noticeable verbal accord.

The so-called grammatical anomalies can be explained on the basis of the apocalyptic quality of the writing or upon the attempt of the writer to render into Greek Semitic idioms foreign to its structure. The well-known example, "from him who is, and who was, and who is to come," involving the substantival use of a finite verb and the use of a preposition with a nominative case (Rev. 1:4), is simply an attempt to express in Greek a title that could only be translated literally from a Semitic language. Beneath the Greek of both John and Revelation is an undercurrent of Aramaic or Hebrew. Perhaps the Gospel of John was smoothed out somewhat by an assistant or an amanuensis who added the final comment (Jn. 21:25).

While the evidence for the Johannine authorship of Revelation may not be absolutely complete, the evidence to the contrary is by no means conclusive. The weight of early testimony favors the view that the Apocalypse was written by John son of Zebedee, and there is no proof that he could not have done so. Obviously the writer was highly respected by the churches of Asia and was regarded as an authority whose writings deserved the status of Scripture.

IV. Date. Three possible dates have been suggested for the Apocalypse. EPIPHANIUS (*Pan.* 51.12, 32), writing in the 3rd cent., stated that John wrote the Apocalypse upon his return from Patmos, which took place in the reign of CLAUDIUS (A.D. 41–54). The date is too early, for the churches of Asia probably had not been founded at that time, and the tension between Christians and the Roman state had not developed to the point reflected in this book. It is possible that Epiphanius was referring to Nero, who also was named Claudius.

An argument for a date during the administration of Nero (A.D. 54–68) has been constructed from the statement in Revelation that the number of the beast is 666 (Rev. 13:18). That sum is realized by adding together the numerical values of the

A fresco in the Greek Orthodox monastery on the island of Patmos depicting one of the visions of the apostle John.

Hebrew letters that correspond to Caesar Nero (*qsr nrwn*, with the following values: $q = 100$, $s = 60$, $r = 200$, $n = 50$, $r = 200$, $w = 6$, $n = 50$). Two major objections can be raised against this view. There are several other combinations of letters that will yield the same result, and furthermore it is very unlikely that Hellenic provincials of Asia would have reckoned ciphers in Hebrew equivalents.

The declaration concerning the "mountains" that support the woman of Rev. 17 has been adduced to support a date in the time of Nero: "The seven heads are seven hills on which the woman sits. They are also seven kings. Five have fallen, one is, the other has not yet come; but when he does come, he must remain for a little while. The beast who once was, and now is not, is an eighth king. He belongs to the seven and is going to his destruction" (vv. 9–11). If this passage be interpreted to mean the successive rulers of the Roman state, the first five could be Julius Caesar, Augustus, Tiberius, Caligula, and Claudius. On this reckoning, if the first five had "already fallen," then the sixth who "is" would be Nero, thus placing the writing of Revelation in his reign.

This interpretation is too uncertain to warrant any final conclusion. One cannot be sure that the five "heads" begin with Julius Caesar. If they refer to the emperors, they probably commence with Augustus. Nero would then be the fifth; Vespasian would be the sixth, since the three emperors following Nero did not reign long enough to be important to the provinces. Titus would be the seventh, and Domitian the eighth. Since the eighth is said to be "of the seven," the allusion may pertain to Domitian, for he seemed to reincarnate the tyranny and brutality of Nero. Furthermore, the Asian churches had not reached their full development in Nero's time.

The traditional view ascribes the Revelation to the reign of Domitian on the testimony of Irenaeus (*Against Heresies* 5.30.3; see also Euseb. *Eccl. Hist.* 3.18; 4.8). Clement of Alexandria agreed (*Quis Dives* 42), and Victorinus, in his *Commentary on the Apocalypse* (17.10), confirmed the statement.

This traditional date is probably the best of the options. It allows for the growth and incipient decline of the churches of Asia. E. Stauffer (*Christ and the Caesars* [1955], 179) has pointed out that the mysterious cipher of 666 will apply to the standard abbreviation of Domitian's imperial title: A[utokrator] KAI[sar] DOMET[ianos] SEB[astos] GER[manikos]. By adding the numerical values of the abbreviated Greek letters of which the English transliteration is given above, the sum of 666 is obtained. While the sole applicability of this cipher to Domitian cannot be proved, it fits his name as well as that of Nero. In addition, some have pointed to ancient reports that Domitian demanded to be worshiped as *dominus et deus*, which would accord with the description of the "beast" that wielded political power and exacted universal worship (Rev. 13:15); more recent research, however, has cast doubts on the reliability of that evidence.

V. Place of origin. The visions were received in Patmos, a small rocky island in the Aegean Sea off the coast of Asia Minor, on which a penal colony was located. Political prisoners were sent there for exile or for forced labor in the mines. John states that he was in Patmos for "the word of God and the testimony of Jesus" (Rev. 1:9). Whether these visions were recorded at Patmos (or perhaps later in Ephesus) is uncertain, though probably no long time elapsed between receiving them and reducing them to writing. In any case they reflect the language and atmosphere of the Roman province of Asia from which the writer had come and to which he belonged. Stauffer (*Christ and the Caesars*, 166–91) suggests that the Apocalypse expresses the apprehensiveness prevailing among the Asian churches during the last years of Domitian's reign, when the emperor's fear of revolt and invasion from the E exposed the Christian church to suspicion.

VI. Destination. The churches to whose leaders the book of Revelation was addressed were situated on a roadway that ran N along the coast from Ephesus to Pergamum via Smyrna. From Pergamum another road ran southward farther inland, touching Thyatira, Sardis, Philadelphia, and Laodicea, and thence back to Ephesus. A messenger carrying this document could make a complete circuit, passing through all of these cities. Ephesus was the seat of the magnificent temple of Artemis; Smyrna was the chief seaport of Asia; at Pergamum were located the colossal altar of Zeus, the temple of Aesculapius (Asclepius), and the seat of provincial government. Thyatira was a center of agriculture and of a textile industry. Sardis, a city of declining fortunes, was one of the most ancient settlements and had been the capital of Lydia. Philadelphia was the gateway to the fertile plains of the inner plateau. Laodicea was a prosperous center of banking, wool growing, and the manufacture of medication for eyes. Paul wrote to Ephesus and Laodicea; Ignatius was familiar with several of these cities. They included most of the leading centers of the Asian province and probably represented the strongest churches with which the writer was acquainted.

VII. Occasion. Domitian's reign had begun in troubled times. The destruction of Pompeii and Herculaneum by the eruption of Vesuvius in A.D. 79 was followed by a disastrous fire that devastated Rome and by a plague of disease that ravaged the city until 81, the year of Domitian's accession.

Domitian was an egomaniac who demanded abject worship from the Roman people. He claimed the title of *Dominus et Deus* (Lord and God) and was the first of the emperors to assume the status of deity, though others had received worship unwillingly during their lifetime and had been deified by the senate after death. When his small son died in the year 83, Domitian had him proclaimed to be a god, and his mother Domitia a goddess. A coin issued in memory of the child represented him as sitting on the orb of the world, with the moon and planets around him. The apotheosis of the mother and child, the deification of the emperor and, in his person, of the state, the acclamation which ascribed to him extravagant titles and impossible powers—all this may be mirrored in the imagery of Revelation. The arrogant and blasphemous claims of Domitian are countered by the apocalyptic honors given to Christ as Sovereign and Saviour.

Roman historians do not chronicle a widespread persecution of the church under Domitian. He executed his cousin, Titus Flavius Clemens, and banished his wife, Domatilla, on grounds of "atheism," that is, the adoption of Jewish customs and treason. Possibly these charges reflect Christian faith, since Clemens, if he were a Christian, would worship no visible god, would accept the Hebrew Scriptures,

The seven churches of Revelation 2 and 3.

and would refuse to worship the emperor. Eusebius (*Eccl. Hist.* 3.17) says that Domitian "established himself as the successor of Nero, in his hatred and hostility to God. He was the second that raised a persecution against us." Eusebius also quotes Hegesippus's testimony that John returned to Ephesus upon being released from exile after the accession of NERVA in A.D. 96 (*Eccl. Hist.* 3.20).

VIII. Purpose. Revelation, then, was written for churches that were under the shadow of imperial persecution, whether or not it was a general policy. The imminent danger of official repression was a continued threat to their existence. Because of the prevailing uncertainty, they needed both encouragement and warning: encouragement to keep them from despair and consequent abandonment of faith, and warning to make them alert to the dangers of external attack and of internal apostasy. Both of these elements, together with a general reflection of prevalent conditions in the empire, appear in the Apocalypse.

The encouragement of the churches was focused on the coming of Christ to judge his enemies, to deliver the church from peril, and to establish the City of God. In almost every one of the letters to the churches occurs some phrase relating to Christ's expected appearance (Rev. 2:5, 16, 25; 3:3, 11, 20), and the phrase "I am coming soon" (3:11) is reiterated three times in the epilogue (22:7, 12, 20). Preparation for the second advent is the dominant theme of Revelation.

IX. Canonicity

A. Early recognition. According to available patristic testimony, Revelation was not at first universally accepted as authoritative by the church. There are possible allusions to the Apocalypse in the *Shepherd of Hermas* (c. 140), but no extended quotations. According to JEROME, Melito of Sardis (c. 160–190) wrote a commentary on it. Justin Martyr (c. 135) stated categorically that it was written by John, one of the apostles of Christ (*Dial. Trypho* 81), and Irenaeus, Bishop of Lyons, was equally emphatic concerning its apostolic origin and genuineness (*Against Heresies* 4.20.11). The early testimony of Asia Minor as given above was supported by the opinion of the Gallic churches, probably because of the influence of Irenaeus, who had come to Gaul from Ephesus. Phrases in the *Epistle of the Churches of Vienne and Lyons* indicate that their author(s) must have known and used Revelation. See CANON (NT).

B. The Western church. The Alexandrian church was also acquainted with the Apocalypse. Clement regarded it as Scripture (*Paidagogus* 11.119), and his pupil Origen accepted it (*In Joannem* 5.33; Euseb. *Eccl. Hist.* 6.25.9). Though Dionysius of Alexandria rejected it as non-Johannine, he was aware that it had been received by the church.

The Roman church, represented by the MURATORIAN CANON (c. 170) included it, and Hippolytus (fl. 190–235) quoted it frequently. The church of Carthage, which owed its origin to Rome, also accepted it, for Tertullian (fl. 190–220) quoted from eighteen of its twenty-two chapters.

The Western church of the 2nd cent. almost unanimously accepted Revelation. The only two dissident voices were those of MARCION, who was biased against any writing that he thought was Jewish, and the Alogi (mentioned by Epiphanius, *Pan.* 51, and by Irenaeus, *Ag. Her.* 3.11.9), who repudiated any work that gave support to the idea of the perpetuation of the gift of prophecy. By the 3rd cent. its place in the Western canon was fully established.

C. The Eastern church. The Eastern churches were almost unanimously committed to the rejection of the Apocalypse. Dionysius, the bishop of Alexandria, had repudiated its canonicity, and Eusebius (260–340) followed his lead. The latter, in his classification of the canonical books, was uncertain whether to list it with the disputed works (*antilegomena*) or with those termed spurious (*notha*; cf. *Eccl. Hist.* 3.25). Possibly he was influenced by his reaction to PAPIAS's interpretation of the MILLENNIUM. Eusebius's influence was powerful. Cyril of Jerusalem (315–386) later forbade churchmen to read it in public from the pulpit, and even deprecated it for private devotions. The later churches of Asia Minor did not utilize it, for it is not mentioned in the Canon of the Synod of Laodicea (c. 360) nor in the *Apostolic Constitutions*, nor in the list of Gregory Nazianzus (d. 389).

Theodore of Mopsuestia (c. 340–428) rejected the Apocalypse in company with the CATHOLIC EPISTLES. His lead was followed by the Nestorian church, as well as by the Antiochian school of the 4th cent. By the 6th cent., however, the Apocalypse was accepted into the Eastern church. Andrew of Caesarea in Cappadocia wrote a commentary on it, and Leontius, a scholar in Jerusalem, said that it was the last canonical book in the NT.

D. Full acceptance. Full acceptance in the canon was recognized in the Festal Letter of Athanasius, written from Alexandria in 367. The Damasine Council of 382 and the Council of Carthage (397), which certified the officially recognized list of NT Scriptures for the W, both included it. In the Western church its position was firmly established from the 2nd cent.; in the Eastern church its authority was acknowledged much later.

X. Text. The Apocalypse is contained wholly or in part in CODEX SINAITICUS (ℵ, 4th cent.), CODEX ALEXANDRINUS (A, 5th cent.), CODEX EPHRAEMI RESCRIPTUS (C, 5th cent.), and several other uncials (e.g., P 046 051 052 0207 0229). Two papyrus MSS, P^{18} (Oxyrhynchus 1079, 3rd/4th cent.) and P^{47} (Chester Beatty, 3rd cent.), also contain sizable fragments. Numerous cursive MSS contain significant readings that vary from the TR, but since none of these is earlier than the 11th cent., the chief weight of textual evidence lies with the uncial and papyrus MSS. As might be expected, the bulk of the cursives contain the Byzantine type of text. The two papyrus MSS mentioned agree strongly with ℵ A C P 0207, while 046 together with 1 and some other cursives constitute a third group.

There are a few important variants: in Rev. 1:5, the TR reads *lousanti*, "washed," and the Alexandrian text reads *lysanti*, "loosed"; in 5:9, *hēmas*, "us," is omitted by A; 15:3, *ho basileus tōn ethnōn*, "the king of the nations," is supported by ℵ^1 A P 046 051 1 and numerous other cursives against *ho basileus tōn aiōnōn*, "the king of the ages," supported by P^{47} ℵ* C 94 and other cursives; in 19:13, *bebammenon*, "dipped," is found in A and the Byzantine text, while *errantismenon*, "sprinkled," in P and 2329. A large number of small but relatively unimportant variants occur, most of which are probably alterations for the purpose of interpreting seemingly awkward expressions or clarifying grammatical difficulties. There are no major omissions or gaps in the text.

XI. Content. Although the Revelation seems to be a medley of weird imagery, it does evince an orderly structure. It can be divided into six main sections by the repeated phrase, "I was in the spirit." Each recurrence of this phrase introduces a section of the book that deals with some particular aspect of the apocalyptic manifestation of Christ. The key to Revelation lies in its CHRISTOLOGY rather than in its chronology, though there is a progressive development of action that pervades it from beginning to end. It may be outlined as follows:

 I. Prologue: Christ communicating (Rev. 1:1–8)
   A. The title (1:1)
   B. The agent (1:1–2)
   C. The blessing (1:3)
   D. The destination (1:4)
   E. The greeting (1:4–5)
   F. The motto (1:5–7)
   G. The authorization (1:8)
 II. Vision I: Christ and the churches (1:9—3:22)
   A. The portrait (1:9–20)
   B. The letters (2:1—3:22)
     1. To Ephesus (2:1–7)
     2. To Smyrna (2:8–11)
     3. To Pergamum (2:12–17)
     4. To Thyatira (2:18–29)
     5. To Sardis (3:1–6)
     6. To Philadelphia (3:7–13)
     7. To Laodicea (3:14–22)
 III. Vision II: Christ and the cosmos (4:1—16:21)
   A. The scene in heaven (4:1—11:19)
     1. The worship before the throne (4:1–11)
     2. The commission of the Lamb (5:1–14)
     3. The opening of the seals (6:1—8:5)
       a. Seal 1: conquest (6:1–2)
       b. Seal 2: war (6:3–4)
       c. Seal 3: famine (6:5–6)
       d. Seal 4: death (6:7–8)

118   REVELATION, BOOK OF THE

       e. Seal 5: martyrdom (6:9–11)
       f. Seal 6: cosmic calamity (6:12—7:17)
       g. Seal 7: silence (8:1–5)
    4. The seven trumpets (8:6—11:19)
       a. Judgment on earth (8:6–7)
       b. Judgment on sea (8:8–9)
       c. Judgment on rivers (8:10–11)
       d. Judgment on heavens and announcement of woe (8:12–13)
       e. Judgment on people and announcement of woe (9:1–12)
       f. Demoniacal horsemen (9:13–21)
       g. Parenthesis: The angel and the seer (10:1—11:14)
         (1) The little book (10:1–11)
         (2) Measuring the temple and announcement of woe (11:1–14)
       h. The seventh trumpet (11:15–19)
   B. The signs (12:1—14:20)
     1. The woman, the man-child, and the dragon (12:1–17)
     2. The beast from the sea (13:1–10)
     3. The beast from the earth (13:11–18)
     4. The Lamb on Mount Zion (14:1–5)
     5. The angelic messengers (14:6–13)
     6. The reaper on the cloud (14:14–16)
     7. The vine of the earth (14:17–20)
   C. The bowls (15:1—16:21)
     1. The song of triumph (15:1–4)
     2. The presentation (15:5—16:1)
     3. The first bowl: sores (16:2)
     4. The second bowl: sea turned to blood (16:3)
     5. The third bowl: rivers turned to blood (16:4–7)
     6. The fourth bowl: heat of sun (16:8–9)
     7. The fifth bowl: darkness (16:10–11)
     8. The sixth bowl: Armageddon (16:12–16)
     9. The seventh bowl: earthquake (16:17–21)
IV. Vision III: Christ in conquest (17:1—21:8)
   A. The judgment of Babylon (17:1—18:24)
     1. The judgment of the culture (17:1–18)
     2. The judgment of the city (18:1–24)
   B. The response of heaven (19:1–10)
   C. The conquest of evil (19:11—20:14)
     1. The conquering Christ (19:11–16)
     2. The destruction of Antichrist (19:17–21)
     3. The binding of Satan (20:1–3)
     4. The millennial reign (20:4–6)
     5. The destruction of Satan (20:7–10)
     6. The final judgment (20:11–14)
   D. The new Jerusalem (21:1–8)
V. Vision IV: Christ in the city of God (21:9—22:5)
   A. The appearance of the city (21:9–21)
   B. The illumination of the city (21:22–23)
   C. The inhabitants of the city (21:24–27)
   D. The delights of the city (22:1–5)
VI. Epilogue: Christ challenging (22:6–21)
   A. To obedience (22:6–9)
   B. To labor (22:10–15)
   C. To vigilance (22:16–21)

XII. Interpretation. The interpretation of Revelation is difficult and uncertain, and no two interpreters agree fully on all details. The symbolic character of the language and the obscurity of many of its allusions render dogmatic finality on all points impossible to attain. In general there are four main types of interpretation that appear in the historic attempts to explain this book.

The first of these is the *preterist* interpretation, which regards the Apocalypse as descriptive of the historic conditions of the Asian churches at the end of the 1st cent. Virtually all of the symbolism is therefore to be understood in terms of conditions contemporaneous with the writing of the book and in no way predictive of the future. Babylon and the beasts refer to the Roman state; the woman of Rev. 12 represents the persecuted church; the various judgments are highly colored representations of natural calamities that occurred within the lifetime of the seer. This interpretation, which is held by many recent commentators, has the advantage of viewing the Apocalypse in the light of the times in which it was written, and of reproducing the probable initial reaction of its readers to its teachings. It does not, however, do justice to the predictive element which it contains.

The second type of interpretation is the *historicist* position, which assumes that the book of

Revelation depicts the entire course of Christian history from the time of the writer until the consummation of the ages. The various seals, trumpets, and bowls are regarded as chronologically successive, marking significant stages in the development of the Christian church, particularly in the west. Since the Revelation begins with the status of the churches of Asia, which were obviously contemporaneous with the date of writing, and ends with the final conflict with evil and the establishment of the City of God in the indefinite future, it seemed only reasonable to conclude that the material between these two termini should deal with the intervening historical process. The chief difficulty with this view is that the intervening period is of undefined length, and that the identification of any one of the symbols with a particular historical event must necessarily be uncertain. It might be possible to establish a connection between each symbol and certain known events only to have subsequent years prove that the identification was erroneous.

Furthermore, the *historicist* view, by attempting to interpret the Apocalypse through the development of the church in the last nineteen centuries, seldom if ever takes cognizance of the church outside of Europe. It is concerned mainly with the period of the Middle Ages and the Reformation and has relatively little to say of developments after A.D. 1500. If the Revelation really purports to provide a symbolic picture of the development of the church between the end of the 1st cent. and the PAROUSIA of Christ, one would expect a full representation of that period.

A third interpretation, called the *futurist*, assigns all of the Revelation following the third chapter to the end of the church age. The letters to the churches of Asia thus become representative either of seven distinct types of churches persistent throughout the period preceding Christ's coming or else seven successive periods of church history during that same interval. According to this scheme, none of the action depicted in Rev. 4–22 is applicable to the present; it is really a preview of the end. The seals, trumpets, and bowls are a literal description of the final tribulation that will seize the wicked inhabitants of earth prior to Christ's return, and the vision of the City of God refers to the eternal state of the righteous.

The fourth interpretation is the *idealist*, which assumes that the visions of the Apocalypse are in no sense literal. They represent only the general conflict of good and evil under the apocalyptic figures that were familiar to Jews and Christians in the 1st cent. For this reason the Apocalypse is equally applicable to all ages of the church, since it belongs exclusively to none.

Each of these views, divergent as they are, contains some element of truth. The preterist view asserts rightly that Revelation must have some bearing on events contemporary with its production, else its imagery would be foreign to its readers and its teachings would seem irrelevant. Undoubtedly they could see the persecuting Roman state and the seductive prevailing paganism portrayed in the figures of the beasts and the harlot (Rev. 13 and 17). On the other hand, the City of God was not established in the world, nor was paganism abolished in the 1st cent.

The historicist can argue with some plausibility that if the first chapter of Revelation begins with the lifetime of the writer, "what is now" (Rev. 1:19), and ends with the eternal state, the intervening symbols must be concerned with the historical development that lies between the two termini. The question then arises whether these symbols deal with *events* or *principles*. If they deal with events, by what rule can the important events typified be distinguished from those of lesser significance, and how can we

Remains of a Byzantine church at Philadelphia. The 1st-cent. Christian congregation in this city was one of the churches addressed by Jesus in the book of Revelation (Rev. 3:7–13).

be sure of the individual correspondence so that we can determine which have already been fulfilled in the series and which are yet to be realized? No two historicists agree exactly in equating the symbols with history, and some of their interpretations seem forced to the point of being ludicrous.

The futurist position has the advantage of consistency in connecting the major events of the Revelation with Christ's return. Since his second advent has not yet occurred, there can be little controversy over fulfillment, for none of the book has taken place except for the existence of the seven churches. Undoubtedly a large segment of Revelation was intended to describe the future, for the voice from heaven speaking to the Seer said, "Come up here, and I will show you what must take place after this" (Rev. 4:1). On the other hand, "after this" is ambiguous, for "this" could refer to the church age if the first three chapters were so interpreted; or it might mean simply "this present moment." Moreover, "after" could refer to the future of the Seer, which would include our "present," or it could mean the eschatological events which accompany the second coming of Christ.

The idealist interpretation emphasizes the spiritual conflict that underlies the Apocalypse and renders the book immediately relevant to all periods of the Christian church. Unquestionably, Revelation is not simply a map of history written in advance; it is rather a philosophy of history written from the standpoint of heaven. Nevertheless, if the idealist position be carried to its extreme conclusion, one might argue that the Revelation is only a collection of myths that embody spiritual teaching but that have no relation to any actual happenings in heaven or on earth. The book thus becomes a flexible symbolism that can be adjusted to the circumstances and whims of the latest reader.

Perhaps the fairest solution to the problem would be to say that all elements may be incorporated in a final exegesis of Revelation. Undoubtedly its thought is often couched in symbolic terms that originated in the OT Scriptures and in the current imagery of the late 1st century. The intent of the book was to cultivate spiritual life and to lay down principles for conduct rather than to predict particular historical occurrences. It does, however, mark the trends of history as God's redemptive purpose moves on to its future climax and consummation. The predictive aspect of Revelation cannot be denied without destroying the real thrust of its message.

XIII. History of interpretation. Although Melito of Sardis (c. 170), Irenaeus (c. 180), and Hippolytus (c. 220) are credited with writing on the Revelation, the earliest extant commentary was composed by Victorinus (d. 303). It is homiletical rather than technical, and somewhat fanciful in its interpretations. Victorinus's exposition was not systematic, but it indicated that the Revelation must have been used extensively in the Western church during the 3rd cent. It is possible that the work attributed to Victorinus was heavily corrected by some disciple of AUGUSTINE, who edited it in accordance with his master's views. In that case the *Commentary* is not a reliable witness of the actual teaching of Victorinus. The text follows a symbolical and amillennial pattern similar to that of Augustine, but Jerome (*De viribus illustris* 19) classed Victorinus as a chiliast, along with Tertullian and Lactantius.

Tyconius, a leader of the African church (c. 390), wrote a commentary on the Apocalypse that followed the "spiritualizing" tradition. His work is no longer available except as quoted by others, but the wide range of authors who cited him—including Augustine of Africa, Primasius of Spain, and Bede of England—shows that it was influential. The methodology of Tyconius was followed by numerous subsequent expositors, chief among whom was Augustine. His treatise, *De civitate Dei*, identified the kingdom of God and the City of God with the church visible and invisible, and fostered an allegorical interpretation of the Apocalypse. In the Western church Augustine's teaching strengthened the growth of the papacy, which assumed political sovereignty on the ground that the kingdom of God should rule the world.

Primasius (c. 550) adopted the allegorical method of Tyconius. He was followed by Autpertus (c. 775), a Benedictine monk of southern France, who made a digest of Victorinus, Tyconius, and Primasius. Alcuin (735–800), the great teacher of Charlemagne's court and an Englishman by birth, perpetuated the allegorical method of his predecessors.

Rabanus Maurus (775–836), the pupil of Alcuin, and his disciple, Walafrid Strabo (807–849), maintained the same tradition. Walafrid introduced a *Glossa ordinaria*, a set of marginal or interlinear notes, which were frequently incorporated in Bibles of the Middle Ages.

No great change from the method or content of Tyconius and his successors took place during the Middle Ages. In the writings of Anselm of Havelberg (1129–1155) the broad allegorical interpretation was changed to a more concrete historicism. Rupert of Deutz (fl. 1111–1129) attempted to interpret Revelation on the basis of biblical history. Although much of his explanation seems strained, he tried to establish a connection between prophecy and secular history so that some sort of continuity might be preserved.

Rupert's procedure was later used significantly by Joachim of Floris (1130–1201), who introduced a new concept into the interpretation of the Apocalypse. In place of the predominantly mystical and allegorical approach, he emphasized a chronological division of the book. He drew a parallel between the seven seals and seven divisions of the Christian era, ending with a consummation that should follow immediately his own times. He broke from the system of Tyconius and became the protagonist of a new trend in interpretation. He proposed that history should be divided into three ages: the age of the Father, extending from the creation to Christ; the age of the Son, from Christ to his own day; and the age of the Spirit, of indefinite length terminating with the day of judgment. He thus introduced a type of dispensationalism which indicated that the age of the Son, in which the medieval church flourished, was not final. This concept contributed to the rise of the Reformation.

Renewed interest in the Apocalypse was stimulated by the controversial atmosphere of the Reformation. The concepts of the antichrist beast (Rev. 13) and of the harlot on the beast (chs. 17–18) were applied to the papacy and to Rome. Although neither Luther nor Calvin wrote commentaries on Revelation, their polemic literature employed the apocalyptic denunciations of evil in conflict with papal power. By so doing they conveyed the impression that the antichrist or beast denoted the papacy, and that with the overthrow of the papacy the consummation of the kingdom of God would be achieved.

The Roman Church responded by counterinterpretation. Francisco Ribera (1537–1591), a Jesuit scholar of Salamanca, published a 500-page commentary on the Apocalypse in 1591 which was later reproduced in several revised editions. He argued that the Antichrist was not the Roman papacy but an individual ruler whose appearance lay still in the future. Bellarmin, the most learned apologist for Catholicism in the Reformation (1542–1621), held essentially the same position, as did numerous other apologists. Luis de Alcázar (1554–1613), a Spanish Jesuit of Seville, advocated the preterist position, and asserted that the Apocalypse applied chiefly to the events preceding the fall of Rome in 476.

The controversies of the Reformation crystallized these three chief systems of interpretation. In subsequent Protestant theology the futuristic system was widely developed by the Fifth Monarchy men in the 17th cent. Their excesses brought it into disrepute, but it was renewed in the 19th cent. by the early teachings of the Plymouth Brethren and by the Bible Conference movement in the 19th–20th cent. The Roman Church in general followed Augustine in identifying the church with the kingdom of God, and by asserting that the millennium is the interval between the ascension of Christ and his future advent.

Commentaries on Revelation written within the Protestant church in modern times have been divided between a few preterists like Moses Stuart of the 19th cent. and James Snowden of the 20th, the historicists represented by E. B. Elliott and by A. J. Gordon, and the futurists such as J. A. Seiss, whose work on the Apocalypse (first published in 1865) was one of the first popular presentations of this view and one of the most influential. For a fuller list of more recent authors, see the subjoined bibliography, which represents differing periods and schools of thought in the modern era.

XIV. Theology. Although the Apocalypse is not intended to be a treatise on theology, it contains a very definite scheme of doctrine, more often reflected in its assumptions than expressed by its declarations. Its obvious emphasis is ESCHATOLOGY. Confronted by a hostile world and by threats of repression if not

Relief on the altar of Domitian.

extermination, the seer deals with the future of the church in the divine plan for the ages.

His first assumption is the personality and sovereignty of God. The centrality of the throne in the book of Revelation is a continual reminder of the superiority of God to all circumstances and persons. He is greater than the menace of imperial Rome; his power transcends that of the persecuting state. His will determines when and how judgment will be inflicted, and his plan must triumph irrespective of human wickedness and rebellion. He is called "Almighty" (Rev. 4:8; 11:17; 15:3; 16:7, 14; 19:6, 15; 21:22) and is depicted as creator of all things (4:11; 14:7) and judge of every human being (20:11–15).

The triunity of God is hinted at in Rev. 1:4–5, which speaks of the one "who is, and who was, and who is to come, and … the seven spirits before his throne, and … Jesus Christ." Reference to the three persons of the Trinity persists through the rest of the book, though they are not always mentioned in the same context. Revelation is strongly Christological. The historical character of Jesus is asserted unequivocally. He is a member of the Jewish people (5:5); has twelve apostles (21:14); was crucified in Jerusalem (11:8); and rose from the dead (1:5, 18). His present exaltation (3:21) is depicted by the portrait of ch. 1.

His authority over the progress of history (Rev. 5:6–12) is one of the keys to the action of the entire book. He is depicted as the Lamb, slaughtered as a sacrifice (5:6); as the Lion of Judah, heir to the throne of David (5:5), and as the conquering Son of Man, who appears in the clouds to complete the harvest of earth (14:15). He is called the "Word of God" (19:13), a title elsewhere applied to him only in the Gospel of John. He is the guardian and critic of the churches (1:12–20), and the final judge of earth (22:12). The main theme of the Apocalypse is the return of Christ and the establishment of his kingdom (11:15), and he is portrayed as the light of the final City of God (21:23).

The work of the Holy Spirit is mentioned, though its place in individual spiritual experience is not stressed. The Spirit is represented by "the seven spirits before his [God's] throne" (Rev. 1:4). He provided the atmosphere in which the seer received his visions (1:10; 4:2; 17:3; 21:10), although the use of the expression "in the Spirit" (*en tō pneumati*) possibly may be interpreted to refer to a mystical experience rather than to a person. The Spirit with the bride of Christ issues the command to come and partake of the water of life (22:17).

The status of the sinner before God is clearly defined. Those who are apart from God are afraid of him (Rev. 6:16–17); they are the easy prey of demonic forces (9:4; 13:3, 14; 17:8) and are destined to be judged for their deeds (20:12–13). Salvation is guaranteed to believers (7:3). The destinies of both believers and unbelievers are clearly defined; the rebellious and unbelieving are doomed to the lake of fire (21:8), while the redeemed become the inhabitants of the eternal City of God (22:14).

The theological aspect of personal spiritual experience is stressed mainly in the first three chapters, which deal with the seven churches of Asia. Personal love for Christ, loyalty under suffering, tenacity of faith, are the major qualities stressed by this book.

The demonic world of evil under the domination of Satan is clearly recognized (Rev. 9:4–11). The entire conflict of which Revelation speaks is spiritual, and the warfare on earth is preceded by warfare in heaven, in which Satan is vanquished by the angelic hosts of righteousness (12:7). The antagonist of God will finally be overcome (12:9), will be bound for an interval (20:1–3), and will finally be remanded to the lake of fire (20:10). The oppressive and persecuting politico-religious complex, represented by the "beasts" of Rev. 13, will likewise be destroyed.

In similar fashion angelology plays a larger part in Revelation than in the other books of the NT. To each of the seven churches is assigned an angel to whom the message for the church is addressed.

Throughout the book angels appear as messengers, or as executors of the divine will (Rev. 5:2; 7:2, 3; 8:2; 10:1; 12:7; 14:6–9, 17; 15:1; 17:1; 18:1, 21; 19:17; 20:1; 21:9; 22:8). The "living creatures" of Rev. 4:6–8 parallel the seraphim of Isa. 6 and presumably constitute an angelic order of beings. Both angels and demons belong to a realm of conscious spiritual beings, divided between good and evil (Rev. 12:7).

Obviously the emphasis of Revelation is eschatological. All other aspects of doctrine are related to the divine program of history. The letters to the seven churches focus on the future; the final promise to each of the churches begins with "I will" and alludes to some reward or retribution yet to come (Rev. 2:7, 10, 17, 28; 3:5, 12, 20).

The main section of the book professes to deal with "what is to take place after this." The character of God is disclosed in the light of his plan for the future and for the new creation; the work of Christ is related to judgment more than to his present soteriological function. His ultimate triumph over the forces of evil and the establishment of the City of God, the eternal state of God's redeemed people (Rev. 19–22), constitute the goal of the eschatological process.

(Significant commentaries include M. Stuart, *Commentary on the Apocalypse* [1845]; E. B. Elliott, *Horae Apocalypticae*, 3rd ed. [1847]; R. C. Trench, *Commentary on the Epistles to the Seven Churches in Asia: Revelation II. III*, 3rd ed. [1867]; J. A. Seiss, *The Apocalypse: A Series of Special Lectures on the Revelation of Jesus Christ*, 3 vols., 10th ed. [1909]; H. B. Swete, *The Apocalypse of St. John* [1911]; R. H. Charles, *A Critical and Exegetical Commentary of the Revelation of St. John*, ICC, 2 vols. [1920]; G. H. Lang, *The Revelation of Jesus Christ* [1945]; C. C. Torrey, *The Apocalypse of John* [1958]; A. B. Caird, *The Revelation of St. John the Divine*, BNTC [1966]; J. F. Walvoord, *The Revelation of Jesus Christ* [1966]; L. Morris, *The Book of Revelation*, TNTC [1987]; P. E. Hughes, *The Book of Revelation: A Commentary* [1990]; R. L. Thomas, *Revelation: An Exegetical Commentary*, 2 vols. [1992–95]; D. E. Aune, *Revelation*, WBC 52, 3 vols. [1997–98]; R. H. Mounce, *The Book of Revelation*, NICNT, rev. ed. [1998]; G. K. Beale, *The Book of Revelation: A Commentary on the Greek Text*, NIGTC [1999]; G. L. A. Brighton, *Revelation* [1999]; D. E. Johnson, *The Triumph of the Lamb: A Commentary on Revelation* [2001]; P. Prigent, *Commentary on the Apocalypse of St. John* [2001]; R. Osborne, *Revelation*, BECNT [2002]; J. Kovacs and C. Rowland, *Revelation: The Apocalypse of Jesus Christ* [2004]; S. S. Smalley, *The Revelation to John: A Commentary on the Greek Text of the Apocalypse* [2005]; I. Boxall, *The Revelation of Saint John*, BNTC [2006]; E. F. Lupieri, *A Commentary on the Apocalypse of Saint John* [2006].

(See also W. M. Ramsay, *The Letters to the Seven Churches of Asia* [1904]; R. H. Charles, *Studies in the Apocalypse*, 2nd ed. [1922]; N. B. Stonehouse, *The Apocalypse in the Ancient Church* [1929]; H. C. Hoskier, *Concerning the Text of the Apocalypse* [1929]; L. E. Froom, *The Prophetic Faith of Our Fathers* [1950]; E. Stauffer, *Christ and the Caesars* [1955]; J. W. Bowman, *The Drama of the Book of Revelation* [1955]; M. C. Tenney, *Interpreting Revelation* [1957]; A. Yarbro Collins, *Crisis and Catharsis: The Power of the Apocalypse* [1984]; C. J. Hemer, *The Letters to the Seven Churches of Asia in Their Local Setting* [1986]; L. L. Thompson, *The Book of Revelation: Apocalypse and Empire* [1990]; R. Bauckham, *The Climax of Prophecy: Studies on the Book of Revelation* [1993]; S. S. Smalley, *Thunder and Love: John's Revelation and John's Community* [1994]; E. Schüssler Fiorenza, *The Book of Revelation: Justice and Judgment*, 2nd ed. [1998]; J. M. Court, *The Book of Revelation and the Johannine Apocalyptic Tradition* [2000]; S. Pattermore, *The People of God in the Apocalypse: Discourse, Structure, and Exegesis* [2004]; J. Hernández, *Scribal Habits and Theological Influences in the Apocalypse* [2006]; L. R. Huber, *Like a Bride Adorned: Reading Metaphor in John's Apocalypse* [2007]; and the bibliographies compiled by R. L. Muse, *The Book of Revelation: An Annotated Bibliography* [1996], and W. E. Mills, *Revelation* [2002].)   M. C. TENNEY

revenge. See AVENGER OF BLOOD; VENGEANCE.

reverence. Profound respect felt and shown to someone, especially God. The English term is used a number of times in Bible versions to render several Hebrew and Greek terms. Reverence consists of fear, awe, and deference in worshipful tribute paid to God (or some other deity) and to things sacred. Various OT references are related to contrasts between the WORSHIP of Yahweh with that of other gods. Among a series of prohibitions in LEVITICUS against the religious practices of magic and witchcraft of other peoples are also commands for the Israelites to worship the true God. One of them appears twice: "Observe my Sabbaths and have reverence for my sanctuary. I am the LORD" (Lev. 19:30; 26:2). These texts use the Hebrew verb *yārēʾ H3707*, "to fear," which can also be used with reference to pagan gods (e.g., those of the Amorites, Jdg. 6:10 [NIV, "do not worship"]; cf. the cognate nouns *yirʾâ H3711*, Ps. 5:7, and *môrāʾ H4616*, Mal. 2:5). The corresponding Greek noun, *phobos G5832* ("fear"), is sometimes used in the NT in a similar way (e.g., "reverence for Christ," Eph. 5:21). A different term, *eulabeia G2325* ("circumspection, piety"), can also be translated "reverence" (cf. Heb. 5:7; 12:28). See FEAR. G. B. FUNDERBURK

reward. Something given in return for an action, whether good or evil; recompense, requital. In the preponderance of biblical citations, it is the reward of good for good deeds that is in evidence. In the OT the obedience of the people of God to their COVENANT obligations resulted in both spiritual and physical benefits. The OT threefold blessing of (1) the continuance of the descendants of ABRAHAM, (2) the settlement in Canaan, and (3) the final culmination of the covenant in the MESSIAH—all were included as aspects of the reward for the faithfulness of Israel. Spiritual blessings were uppermost, while, as in all God's providential dealings with his people, obedience to the law and its structure of the spheres of life brought about material well-being.

The glory of the OT conception was that God in his mercy substituted another vicarious offering for the sins of his people in the ritual of the SACRIFICE, and finally in the accomplishment of redemption in his servant: "But he was pierced for our transgressions, / he was crushed for our iniquities; / the punishment that brought us peace was upon him, / and by his wounds we are healed" (Isa. 53:5). This same concept is reaffirmed in the NT, although by the end of the 1st cent. B.C. much of JUDAISM had already fallen prey to the "legalism" that is demonstrated in the notion of "reward" in the APOCRYPHA and PSEUDEPIGRAPHA as well as the DEAD SEA SCROLLS. The NT presents two separate levels of reward: the spiritual, which results only from faith in Christ, and the physical, which accrues to all who follow God's creation ordinances (e.g., the laws of hygiene).

The classic theological distinction that grew out of this insight was between "special grace" and "common grace." The liberal and existential theological constructions rejecting the biblical concept of CREATION and FALL have become involved in the inscrutable problem of human responsibility. Paul makes this clear in regard to all rewards: "It does not, therefore, depend on human desire or effort, but on God's mercy" (Rom. 9:16 TNIV). The Scripture teaches degrees of rewards dependent upon the individual's faithfulness to God's commands. Such rewards are like all others in Scripture, promised both for the present life and for the glorification of the believer in the world to come. "As the outcome of your faith you obtain the salvation of your souls" (1 Pet. 1:9 RSV). The ultimate reward of the Christian is to be in the presence of Christ. W. WHITE, JR.

Rezeph ree´zif (רֶצֶף *H8364*, meaning uncertain). A city in MESOPOTAMIA conquered by the Assyrians (2 Ki. 19:12=Isa. 37:12). When SENNACHERIB was threatening to crush Jerusalem, he sent a message to HEZEKIAH in which he asked, "Did the gods of the nations that were destroyed by my forefathers deliver them: the gods of Gozan, Haran, Rezeph and the people of Eden who were in Tel Assar?" The identification of Rezeph is uncertain because several places in the general area bear a similar name. One likely candidate is the Raṣappa of Assyrian records, identified with modern Reṣafeh (several variant spellings), some 80 mi. NNE of Palmyra (TADMOR) and 15 mi. S of the EUPHRATES. How or when the city of Rezeph fell is unknown, but in 701 B.C., when mentioned in this passage, it had been in Assyria's possession for at least a century. CUNEIFORM texts mention several governors during the period between 839 and 673, so it probably first came under Assyrian domination during the reign of SHALMANESER III. (See further *ISBE* rev. [1979–88], 4:180; *ABD*, 5:708.) J. C. MOYER

Rezia ri-zi´uh. KJV form of RIZIA.

Rezin ree´zin (רְצִין *H8360*, possibly "delight" or "[God] is pleased"; the Akk. form, *Raḫ(q)ianu*, may indicate that the name was written in Old Aram. as רקין, representing the pronunciation *radyān* [cf. *ABD*, 5:708; but *HALOT*, 3:1284, suggests *raʿyān*]).

(1) King of ARAM (SYRIA) who supported PEKAH king of Israel in his fight against Judah (2 Ki. 5:37; 16:5; Isa. 7:1). Rezin is also credited with recovering ELATH (2 Ki. 16:6, but see below). He was the last Aramean king to rule DAMASCUS, for in 732 B.C. TIGLATH-PILESER III conquered the city and put him to death (16:9). Tiglath-Pileser's *Annals* refer to Rezin's "father's house" as being at Ḥadara, 30 mi. SW of Damascus; and M. Unger infers that Rezin's father was a local prince (*Israel and the Aramaeans* [1957], 172 n. 31).

At one point JEROBOAM II of Israel had reconquered Damascus (2 Ki. 14:28), so Rezin may have taken the throne by force. The first clear knowledge of his position is that he, along with MENAHEM, paid tribute to Tiglath-Pileser in 740, after the fall of ARPAD, and at some time between 743 and 739 (*ANET*, 282–83). During the Assyrian campaign against Urartu (737–735), Rezin and Pekah—the latter having usurped the throne of Israel—made an alliance, seeking to organize a coalition against ASSYRIA. When AHAZ of Judah refused to be drawn in, these "two smoldering stubs of firewood" (Isa. 7:4) tried to bring Judah into line by military pressure and to set up a puppet king identified as "the son of Tabeel." E. Kraeling's view (*Aram and Israel, or, The Aramaeans in Syria and Mesopotamia* [1918], 117) that Rezin himself is meant is unlikely (see B. Mazar in *IEJ* 7 [1957]: 237). Rezin drove S to the Red Sea, always a direction of Syrian interest, and captured the port Elath, which he handed over to the Edomites (2 Ki. 16:6, emending MT *ʾrn* to *ʾdm*). J. A. Montgomery (*A Critical and Exegetical Commentary on the Book of Kings*, ICC [1951], 458) emends the verse so as to avoid mentioning Rezin (cf. also NRSV), but his involvement is not improbable. Seals found at Tell Kheleifeh bear witness to alternate Israelite and Edomite occupation.

The northern allies had to be content with the knowledge that Judah, beaten into her defenses and beset by Edomites and Philistines (2 Chr. 28:18), was powerless to interfere. In 734 the Assyrian answered his vassal's call for help. He struck through GALILEE at PHILISTIA, returned to mop up N Israel, and extracted tribute from TYRE. Rezin was thus isolated in Damascus and was killed when the city fell after a two-year siege; so the Aramean empire of Damascus came to an end. (See further W. F. Albright, *BASOR* 87 [Oct. 1942]: 22–23; A. Alt, *Kleine Schriften zur Geschichte des Volkes Israel* 2 [1953], 150–62; D. W. Thomas, ed., *Documents of Old Testament Times* [1958], 54, 57; W. Hallo in *BA* 23 [1960]: 47ff.; B. Mazar in *BA* 25 [1962]: 98–116; H. Tadmor in *IEJ* 12 [1962]: 114–22; H. Donner, *Israel unter der Völkern* [1964], 59–63; E. Vogt in *Bib* 45 [1964]: 348–54; Y. Aharoni, *The Land of the Bible: A Historical Geography*, rev. ed. [1979], 370–76; W. T. Pitard, *Ancient Damascus* [1987], 181–89; E. Lipiński, *The Aramaeans: Their Ancient History, Culture, Religion* [2000].)

(2) Ancestor of a family of temple servants (NETHINIM) who returned from the EXILE (Ezra 2:48; Neh. 7:50).

J. LILLEY

Rezon ree′zuhn (רְזוֹן H8139, "dignitary, ruler"). Son of Eliadah and king of ARAM (1 Ki. 11:23–25). Rezon began his career in the service of HADADEZER, Aramean king of ZOBAH. Probably at the time when DAVID defeated Hadadezer (2 Sam. 8:3), Rezon forsook his master, gathered men about him, and became a captain of freebooters. It was possibly years later, during the reign of SOLOMON, that he occupied DAMASCUS and founded there the dynasty which created the most powerful of the Aramean kingdoms. This ordering of events is necessary to allow time for David's establishment of garrisons among the Arameans from Damascus and his putting them under tribute after his victory over Hadadezer c. 984 B.C. (2 Sam. 8:5–6). After Rezon's seizure of Damascus he became an adversary against Solomon (1 Ki. 11:23). Many scholars identify him with HEZION, grandfather of BEN-HADAD I (1 Ki. 15:18), and suggest that "Rezon" was a title (cf. *HALOT*, 3:1210; but see W. T. Pitard, *Ancient Damascus* [1987], 96–106).

B. K. WALTKE

Rhegium ree′jee-uhm (Ῥήγιον G4836). A town on the toe of the Italian peninsula opposite Messana; modern Reggio di Calabria. The spelling of the name is disrupted and complicated by naive ancient ideas of etymology. The Greeks, thinking of Sicily as "broken" from Italy by the 7-mi.-wide Messina strait, derived the word from *rhēgnymi G4838*, "to break," whereas Italians favored the Latin root *reg-* meaning "royal"—hence the *h* or the absence of it. The name is probably pre-Greek, and if one derivation is to be preferred to the other, the Latin or Italian origin of the word is the more likely.

Rhegium was a Greek colony founded in 720 B.C. by Chalcis with a strong infusion of citizens from Messenia, which itself was a colony only a few years older. Rhegium was originally an oligarchy, but little is known of the first two centuries of its history. It was the birthplace of the poet Ibycus (mid-5th cent. B.C.). Anaxilas is named as its "tyrant" (in the Greek sense of that word) in the generation of 494 to 476 B.C., and he led the city into an era of imperialism. Thus involved in Sicilian politics, Rhegium met destruction at Syracuse's hands in 387. Rebuilt, it is found later in control of Campanian mercenaries (280 to 270), and successfully resisted the two conquerors Pyrrhus and Hannibal in the same century. As the occupant of a strategic watch-point opposite the Sicilian bridgehead into Italy, Rhegium was especially cultivated by Rome, and proved a loyal ally, receiving municipal status in 90 B.C.

Rhegium was a safe haven in a strait notoriously difficult for ancient ships to navigate (see the legends of Scylla and Charybdis). PAUL's ship, having tacked widely to make Rhegium (Acts 28:13), waited under the lee of the Italian shore for a funneling S wind to drive her through the strait with its complex currents, en route to PUTEOLI. Rhegium remained a Greek-speaking city throughout imperial times, taking the name Rhegium Julium under AUGUSTUS. (See further Strabo, *Geogr.* 6.257–58; Herodotus, *Hist.* 6.23; 7.165, 170; Thucydides, *Hist.* 4.24–25 et al.; Polybius, *Hist.* 1.7 et al.; Livy, *Hist.* 23.30; 36.42.)

E. M. BLAIKLOCK

Rheims Version. See VERSIONS OF THE BIBLE, ENGLISH, IV

Rhesa ree'suh ('Ρησά *G4810*). Son of ZERUBBABEL, included in Luke's genealogy of Jesus CHRIST (Lk 3:27). Because this person is otherwise unknown, some have proposed that the name reflects the Aramaic word for "the prince" (*rē'šā'* or *rēšā'*) and that in an earlier form of the genealogy it was intended as the title of Zerubbabel (cf. J. Jeremias, *Jerusalem in the Time of Jesus* [1969], 296; but see D. L. Bock, *Luke*, BECNT, 2 vols. [1994–96], 1:354).

rhetorical criticism. Also *rhetorical analysis*. Although this label can be used broadly of any interpretation based on literary theory, it is specifically applied to the study of texts from the perspective of classical oratory and rhetoric (the art of effective and persuasive communication). The development of rhetorical techniques can be traced back to the 5th cent. B.C., and their analysis is associated especially with later Roman writers, such as Cicero (106–43 B.C.) and Quintilian (c. A.D. 35–100). The term *rhetorical criticism* is sometimes applied to the literary study of the OT (cf. *ABD*, 5:712–15; *DBI*, 2:396–99), but it is in connection with NT scholarship, and particularly the Epistles, that this discipline has flourished in recent decades.

Notable early exponents include the classicist George A. Kennedy (*New Testament Interpretation Through Rhetorical Criticism* [1984]) and the NT scholar H. D. Betz (*Galatians: A Commentary on Paul's Letter to the Churches in Galatia*, Hermeneia [1979]). This approach focuses on methods of argumentation and figures of speech. Subsequent writers have sought to ground their work on modern rhetoric, which pays greater attention to the audience and thus the broad social context of the speech. (See D. F. Watson and A. J. Hauser, *Rhetorical Criticism of the Bible: A Comprehensive Bibliography with Notes on History and Method* [1994]; R. D. Anderson, *Ancient Rhetorical Theory and Paul*, rev. ed. [1999]; C. J. Classen, *Rhetorical Criticism of the New Testament* [2000]; S. E. Porter and D. L. Stamps, eds., *Rhetorical Criticism and the Bible* [2002]; D. E. Aune, *The Westminster Dictionary of New Testament and Early Christian Literature and Rhetoric* [2003]; D. F. Watson, *The Rhetoric of the New Testament: A Bibliographic Survey* [2006].)

Rhoda roh'duh ('Ρόδη *G4851*, "rose"). The name of a slave girl in the house of MARY, the mother of John Mark, who came to answer the door when PETER arrived there after his miraculous deliverance from prison (Acts 12:13). She recognized Peter's voice and joyfully announced to the company gathered there for prayer that Peter was at the door; she was accused of being mad but persisted in her claim (vv. 14–15). Nothing more is known of her. The name was common, especially among slave girls.   G. H. WATERMAN

Rhodes rohdz′ (Ῥόδος *G4852*, "rose"). Modern Ródhos, a large island of the Dodecanese group, over 500 square mi. in area, 12 mi. off the coast of ancient CARIA in SW ASIA MINOR (modern Turkey). Rhodes is hilly, but cut by fertile and productive valleys. Its name may be an assimilated formation, for roses are not—and, to the best of modern knowledge never were—a characteristic flower of the island. The name is also applied to its capital city.

The island was originally settled by Dorian Greeks, and three city states emerged originally from the occupation. In the 5th cent. B.C. these states were members of the Athenian Confederacy with, presumably, democratic constitutions. Strife with ATHENS broke out in 411 and lasted for five years. The result was the federation of the three states into one unit with a new capital, Rhodes. The three constituent city-states appear to have retained a large measure of autonomy, and kept democratic institutions—a situation interrupted, in the second half of the 4th cent., by a period of Persian domination.

After the conquests of ALEXANDER THE GREAT, Rhodes, aided by her advantageous position and her maritime skill, captured and held a considerable carrying trade with the E end of the Mediterranean, which had been opened by Alexander to the commerce and penetration of the western world. Rich, powerful, and naturally garrisoned by the sea, she maintained her independence under the "successors" of Alexander, policed the seas against the perennial piracy of the Asiatic coast, and functioned, as Athens had once done, as a center of exchange and capital. Generally in the Hellenistic period, Rhodes sided with Egypt rather than with Syria.

Shrewdly appraising the rise of Roman power, Rhodes assisted the Republic in the wars against Philip V of Macedon and ANTIOCHUS of Syria (201–197 B.C.), and was rewarded with territory in Caria and LYCIA. In the third war with Macedon (see MACEDONIA), Rhodes angered ROME by an attempt at neutrality, and in spite of a vigorous oration by Cato, the famous censor—an oration that survives in part as the earliest sample of Latin oratory—Rhodes was punished by the institution of Delos as a rival port (166 B.C.). It was a shrewd economic blow, and this, with the amputation of the mainland territories in Caria and Lycia, went far to destroy Rhodes' commercial prosperity.

Rhodes regained some of her standing as a Roman ally by withstanding a siege by Mithridates when that dynamic king of PONTUS all but

Aerial view of the harbor in Rhodes.

destroyed Rome's position E of the AEGEAN in 88 B.C. Rhodes assisted POMPEY with a fleet when he cleared the E end of the Mediterranean of pirates in 67 B.C., and later when he fought against CAESAR. After Caesar's victory in the Civil War, Rhodian ships assisted him in the siege of ALEXANDRIA. Later it became the place of self-exile of TIBERIUS when AUGUSTUS rejected him as his successor.

It is generally thought that the inhabitants of Rhodes are meant by the term RODANIM (Gen. 10:4; 1 Chr. 1:7). The island is probably mentioned by EZEKIEL as one of the places that had commercial dealings with TYRE (Ezek. 27:15; here the MT has DEDAN, but LXX reads *Rhodiōn*). When PAUL passed that way, traveling from TROAS to CAESAREA (Acts 21:1), Rhodes was little more than a port of call with a degree of prosperity and distinction as a beautiful city, but no more than that. It is still a beautiful city, full of ancient and Crusader remains, on a lovely island. (See further *ABD*, 5:719–20; *OCD*, 1315–16.) E. M. BLAIKLOCK

Rhodocus rod′uh-kuhs (Ροδοκος). A Jewish traitor who disclosed to the Syrians the plans of Judas MACCABEE concerning the fortress of BETH ZUR, which Judas had strengthened. When discovered, Rhodocus was found guilty and imprisoned (2 Macc. 13:21).

Ribai ri′bī (רִיבַי H8192, possibly short form of יְרִיבַי H3744, "[Yahweh] contends [for me]"; see JERIBAI). Father of ITHAI, one of David's mighty warriors (2 Sam. 23:29 [MT "Ittai"]; 1 Chr. 11:31).

Riblah rib′luh (רִבְלָה H8058, meaning uncertain). (1) A town said to be "in the land of Hamath" (2 Ki. 23:33 et al.). It is possibly the same as Shabtuna, included in the topographical list of THUTMOSE III (Y. Aharoni, *The Land of the Bible: A Historical Geography*, rev. ed. [1979], 161 [#73], 441; however, see *SacBr*, 97a). The town was some 50 mi. SSW of HAMATH and less than 7 mi. S of KADESH ON THE ORONTES; its ruins are just ENE of the modern village of Ribleh (near the border between Syria and Lebanon).

When Pharaoh NECO made a campaign through Palestine, JOSIAH king of Judah lost his life (2 Ki. 23:29). In his stead, the people made Josiah's younger son, JEHOAHAZ, king. This popular choice did not please Neco, who put Jehoahaz in bonds at Riblah "so that he might not reign in Jerusalem"; he then made Jehoahaz's older brother, Eliakim, king, but changed his name to JEHOIAKIM (vv. 30–34). Neco had apparently reached the ORONTES River by that time and was making Riblah his headquarters. Topographically and geographically, it is well situated, and one can understand why a military monarch would have chosen it for a base of operations.

In 605 B.C., about five years after Neco's campaign, Nebuchadnezzar and the Babylonians gained the upper hand and made Riblah their staging ground for operations against Palestine. ZEDEKIAH, the new king whom Nebuchadnezzar had put on the throne in Jerusalem, resisted

Riblah.

such vassalhood and rebelled against the king of Babylon. When Jerusalem was besieged, Zedekiah fled. Nebuchadnezzar's army captured him near JERICHO, took him to Riblah, and put out his eyes just after making him witness his sons' execution (2 Ki. 25:1–7; cf. Jer. 39:1–7; 52:1–11). Later, other rebellious Israelite leaders lost their lives at the same town (2 Ki. 25:18–21; Jer. 52:24–27). The town is probably mentioned also in a prophetic oracle where God says he will make the land desolate "from the wilderness to Riblah" (Ezek. 6:14 NRSV; the NIV, following the MT, has DIBLAH).

(2) An unidentified place somewhere E. or NE of the Sea of Galilee, included in a description of the boundaries of the Promised Land (Num. 34:11, here used with the definite article, "the Riblah"). The view that this Riblah is the same as #1 above creates confusion in the text. The town was evidently a short distance E of AIN, which also is unidentified, though some think it is the modern Khirbet 'Ayyun, c. 5 mi. E of the S tip of the Sea of Galilee. (The LXX reads *Arbēla*, but ARBELA was prob. W of the Sea of Galilee.) R. L. ALDEN

riches. See WEALTH.

riddle. Throughout the biblical world the use of riddles was common. One may somewhat arbitrarily distinguish a riddle from a fable or enigma, the primary point in a riddle being its intention to puzzle the hearer. Enigmas may be conceived of as utterances which, though difficult to understand, are not difficult by design; it may be only a lack of information on the part of the interpreter that makes it a puzzle. A FABLE is simply a fictitious story (often involving members of the plant and animal kingdoms), told to convey a certain spiritual idea; it is not necessarily difficult of understanding though it may be so. The principal word to be treated is Hebrew *ḥîdâ H2648*, which occurs seventeen times in the OT (eight of these in one passage, Jdg. 14:12–19). It is usually translated "riddle" (in several instances with the cognate verb *ḥûd H2554*), though occasionally one finds such renderings as "dark sayings" (Ps. 78:2 KJV, NRSV; "hidden things," NIV) and "hard questions" (1 Ki. 10:1=2 Chr. 9:1).

MOSES is stated to have communed with God "face to face," and this is contrasted with "dark speech" (Num. 12:8 KJV). The word is used of a fable in one passage (Ezek. 17:2; NIV, "allegory"); here and in another verse (Ps. 49:4) it is parallel to *māšāl H5442* (meaning PARABLE or PROVERB). SAMSON's riddle (Jdg. 14:12–19) is the most notable example of a riddle in the OT. In alluding to experiences of killing a lion and later finding honey in its carcass, Samson said, "Out of the eater, something to eat; / out of the strong, something sweet" (Jdg. 14:14; see P. Nel in *Bib.* 66 [1985]: 534–45; O. Margalith in *VT* 36 [1986]: 225–34). The QUEEN OF SHEBA came to SOLOMON "to test him with hard questions" (1 Ki. 10:1), and according to JOSEPHUS (*Ant.* 8.5.3 §§148–49), Solomon and HIRAM engaged in a contest of riddles, the latter with some help coming out victor (cf. also Sir. 47:15). In view of this it is surprising that the Hebrew word for "riddle" is found only once in the book of Proverbs (Prov. 1:6), but there are sections of the book that might well qualify for that designation. (On the cryptograms in Jer. 25:26 and 51:1, see ATBASH.)

A true riddle is found in Rev. 13:18, where the number 666 is apparently an obscure reference to some individual. The attempts to interpret it are legion and no consensus reigns. We know from the SIBYLLINE ORACLES that such numerical references were common. The Greek word *ainigma G141* (used in the LXX sometimes to render *ḥîdâ*, e.g., Num. 12:8) appears in the NT only once in the phrase "now we see through a glass, darkly" (1 Cor. 13:12 KJV]); it has been suggested that the translation "through a mirror, by means of an enigmatic word," might be better (cf. M. S. Terry, *Biblical Hermeneutics* [1890], 183). Some of Jesus' sayings qualify as enigmas (Lk. 22:36; Jn. 3:1–3; 4:10–15; 6:53–59). Great caution needs to be exercised in interpreting the "dark sayings" of the Scripture. Special care should be given to understand exactly what the words in the original language meant. Due regard to context, always important, is especially called for in such instances. (See further A. B. Mickelsen, *Interpreting the Bible* [1963], 199–211; *ABD*, 5:721–23.)

B. C. STARK

ridge of Judea. See JUDEA, RIDGE OF.

rie. KJV spelling of "rye"; see SPELT.

righteousness. Morally right behavior or character. In the Bible and theology, this term has broad and profound significance. The Hebrew word translated "righteousness" is *ṣĕdāqâ H7407* (Gen. 15:6 et al.), which can also be rendered "justice, honesty, loyalty" (verb *ṣādaq H7405*, "to be right" [hiphil, "to declare as in the right"]; adj. *ṣaddîq H7404*, "righteous, just"). The NT uses Greek *dikaiosynē G1466* (Matt. 3:15 et al.), sometimes rendered "justification" (verb *dikaioō G1467*, "to do justice, vindicate, deem or declare righteous"; adj. *dikaios G1465*). In its general use, *righteousness* represents any conformity to a standard, whether that standard has to do with the inner character of a person or the objective standard of accepted law. J. H. Thayer (*Greek-English Lexicon of the New Testament* [1889], 149a) suggests the definition, "the state of him who is such as he ought to be." In the wide sense, it refers to that which is upright or virtuous, displaying integrity, purity of life, and correctness in feeling and action. In negative terms, it means faultlessness or guiltlessness; with reference to a person, it has to do with his conformity to God's HOLINESS. In a false sense, it may refer to those who pride themselves on their own virtues—sometimes real, sometimes imaginary—and such "righteous" ones are really under the condemnation of a righteous God (cf. Matt. 9:13; Mk. 2:17; Lk. 5:32; 15:7).

- I. Righteousness in the OT
  - A. As related to the nature of God
  - B. As related to the covenant
- II. Righteousness in the NT
  - A. The idea in the Gospels
  - B. The crucial treatment in Paul
- III. Righteousness in the modern world
  - A. The existential emphasis
  - B. The abiding nature of law
- IV. Righteousness in world religions

I. Righteousness in the OT. The biblical approach preeminently concerns itself with the person whose way of thinking, feeling, and acting is wholly conformed to the righteousness of God. (In this sense, only Christ can be called "righteous" [cf. Acts 7:52; 22:14; 1 Pet. 3:18; 1 Jn. 2:1], which raises the theological question that is the burden of the NT: if God requires righteousness and if no one is righteous [Rom. 3:10, 26], how may a person be "justified," i.e., "declared righteous"?) Righteousness is also closely associated with the theme of God's COVENANT with his people.

A. As related to the nature of God. The center of reference in biblical theology is first of all the righteousness of God. The fundamental idea, a starting place for any biblical view of righteousness, is very simply this: there is no law *above* God, but there is a law *in* God. Holiness is of his essence, and righteousness is a mode of this holiness. L. Berkhof speaks of righteousness as "transitive" holiness (*Systematic Theology* [1941], 74–75; cf. also A. H. Strong, *Systematic Theology*, 3 vols. [1907], 1:290). What is being clearly said is that God is, in his essence, by his very nature, holiness itself; and righteousness is the mode or way by which his essence is expressed toward his created world or toward anything apart from himself. See GOD, BIBLICAL DOCTRINE OF.

To take a clue from Paul Tillich and his discussion of "Being" or his very useful expression, "Ground of Being," then what God *is* (his aseity) is the basis or ground upon which existence and creation rest. Everything apart from God's essence is dependent and contingent upon what he is himself; he is what holiness and righteousness must be. Righteousness is "rectitude of the divine nature by virtue of which God is infinitely righteous in himself ..., that perfection of God by which he maintains himself over against every violation of his holiness." In other words, there is a sense in which God cannot help himself when he resists anything in the universe contrary to his own nature. Evil can no more survive in the presence of God than a microbe can survive in the light of the sun. However one might wish it otherwise, this is something which is of the nature of ultimate reality. It cannot be swayed or tampered with any more than the nature of God can be changed. When this has been said, not everything has been said; for no mention has yet been made of the LOVE of God nor of his GRACE (which are also of his essence). Theological discussion insofar as it is biblical and Christian may be reduced to superficial sentimentalism unless the absolute holiness of God and the perfect coincidence which exists between his nature and his action are made clear and strong at the outset.

At this point there can be no caprice or passion, no shiftiness in absolute standards. In the infinite depths of reality there is the automatic, essential revolt against moral evil. It is not a matter of arbitrary will; it is a necessary moral requirement of the essence of God. God being God, he is what he is, and he is bound by his nature to do what his nature requires. If God is big enough, that is, infinite and eternal, there is no other source of righteousness, justice, law, or integrity.

On the face of it, this looks narrow and harsh, and the religion of the Jews, reflected in the OT, is criticized as being legalistic; moreover, any phase of the Christian religion that appears to rest on the OT, such as Calvinism or Puritanism, is also condemned as legalism or harsh moralism. Apparently the Jews believed not only that they were a people chosen of God, but also that they were directed by REVELATION from God. Perfectly clear in this revelation is God's absolute righteousness. By means of revelation, the righteousness of God was made known through such prophets as MOSES, was codified basically in the Decalogue (see TEN COMMANDMENTS), became relevant to the complexities

A representation of what the Decalogue might have looked like in paleo-Hebrew script. The righteousness required by God was codified in the laws given to Moses.

It needs to be said very strongly, therefore, in this day when the law of God is made subservient to the love of God (and such love can be sentimentalism apart from law), that the Hebrews saw no conflict between the two concepts. How else could God love his people more than by being always and forever himself? How could a universe possibly hang together without absolute rectitude at its core? How could a nation survive without some dependence on absolute righteousness? How could a people be happy where the lines of truth were anything less than perfectly clear? What physics means to the scientist in the 20th cent., moral law meant to the ancient Jew. What is "fit-for-man" is "well-for-man." What the Hebrews discovered — or better, what they knew had been revealed to them providentially — was that it is only in conformity to God's righteousness that human beings can possibly experience the highest felicity for which their nature has been created. To bring one's self into conformity with God's righteousness is to righten one's self, and so discover harmony and peace. The laws of God are the directions on the package of life. To disobey means confusion; to obey means fulfillment.

Perhaps some light on this — for it does seem a strange doctrine in the 20th cent. — will be shed if one glances at another world religion, Taoism, the religion of the Way. Significantly, Christians were first called "those of the Way." Jesus said of himself, "I am the way" (Jn. 14:6). Taoists sought what was called "The Way of the Universe" and attempted to harmonize their lives with the law of the heavens. The STOICS, with all their Greek sophistication, were speaking of the same kind of harmony through self-control and endurance in accord with the order of the universe. Any approach to life that demands conformity to nature recognizes this theme. The Roman Catholics historically have emphasized natural law — a built-in truth in the universe that is equally built into human nature; and human beings simply destroy themselves and lose any hope of fulfillment when they go against natural law.

The decisive factor in the OT is that Tao, Way, Truth, Law are superseded by Person. God is a living God who created and sustains everything in his own universe according to his own need and will. His own need and will are absolute holiness reflected in

of living in the Levitical code and the Deuteronomic code, and is also basic to the proper WORSHIP of God as seen in the symbols and activities of the TABERNACLE and the TEMPLE. The basis of operation for both the nation and the individual is clearly set before them in the Holy Writings. Thus the whole system is rightly criticized as legalistic if one may assume that things having a legal character ought to be criticized.

What shall be done, then, with the strange gladness with which the whole LAW is treated in the OT? If one may generalize, the law of God, as it reflects the righteousness of God, is the gift of God. It is not a series of harsh demands, but a joyous reality which not only makes his people different from the other nations, but somehow makes them better; and by this he means that somehow it makes them happier. The law is something to share with one's children, to talk about with one's friends, to carry when walking abroad, to meditate on "day and night." "Oh, how love I thy law!" is a frequent theme of the psalmist. It is something to sing about, and the singing in the great temple choirs were frequently shouts of joy.

righteousness and codified, finally, in human laws. It is the benevolence in his holiness that leads to his condescension in revealing his holy will.

It is easy to be repelled by certain expressions such as appear in the Ten Commandments, such as, "I, the LORD your God, am a jealous God" (Exod. 20:5). At first glance this seems small-minded in anyone who could be thought about as God almighty. But JEALOUSY goes hand and hand with love and need not be small-minded. One who really loves, for that very love's sake simply cannot suffer the presence of anyone or anything that will harm or destroy or even so much as mar the beloved. This is the jealous concern for a child by a parent who keeps putting the best before him or her and who is constantly fearful of even the smallest thing that can undermine the child. Even in Camelot, Arthur's love for Guinevere was not great enough to exclude Lancelot, and so his wife, his family, his kingdom, and the hope of humanity in that generation were destroyed. When God said, "You shall have no other gods before me" ("in my presence"—Exod. 20:3), it was not because the almighty God was afraid of the competition. He feared what any perfect lover would fear, that anything less than God which could become a god would be a destroyer. The danger of false gods is finally a false life. When the *summum bonum*, the highest good, is not perfection, then the lesser values become less than they should be.

Even in retributive justice, the Jews saw the healing of discipline. Sometimes an arm has to be broken to be reset. Sometimes an athlete has to unlearn to learn correctly. Only thus is he set free. How many times must humanity go through the fires of judgment before there is found freedom in the righteousness of God?

Basically, and in summary, OT biblical thought is completely dominated by its theocentric norm. It rests on the fact that God is absolute holiness in essence, a fact established by special revelation. The demands on human beings for their righteous living, therefore, are never relativistic. The demands are absolute. One may count on God's being fair in his dealings, but the frightful thing is that he must be, by his nature, absolutely fair. Since he is the center of all reality and existence, then everything in his universe is related to him in these same absolute demands. The conclusion of the matter is, as Paul underscores in Romans, "There is no one righteous, not even one" (Rom. 3:10). In the presence of God, "who can stand"? The answer is perfectly plain: no one! There are no rewards for obedience, no claims for recognition, and finally, no excuses, because unholiness cannot exist in the presence of holiness. Absolute cleanliness has no spots.

The Roman Catholics have found some relief in the idea of "original righteousness" (*justitia originalis*). According to this view, God graciously imparted to human beings a perfect rectitude in their original condition before the FALL. This was supposed to have included freedom from concupiscence, bodily immortality, and impassibility. Also, happiness seems to have been a guarantee. It is difficult to see on what authority this position rests. But even if it be true, it is irrelevant and incomplete—irrelevant because people no longer live before the fall, and incomplete because one of the greatest problems in righteousness, as will appear upon examining the NT, is the problem of *positive* righteousness. For someone to be free from overt sin is one problem; to fulfill the demands of love is a much greater problem.

As one follows the efforts of the ancient Israelites to live up to the demands of absolute righteousness, one is struck with the hopelessness, not only of their attainments, but also of the direction of their efforts. Immediately after the Ten Commandments (Exod. 20), there is a section known as the Little Book of the Covenant (21:1—23:19). This is a first effort to translate the Decalogue into rules and regulations. Some of it seems of extremely minor importance, and some of it is simply quaint. The same efforts are reflected in the books of Leviticus, Numbers, and Deuteronomy. Much of what is recorded there no longer speaks to the human condition, since it is culturally restricted. The whole Jewish effort of obedience degenerated into what became true legalism under the PHARISEES. Although one must be careful not to paint all Pharisees with the same brush, nor to suggest that they had no positive qualities, the group as a whole was severely criticized by Jesus. They were the experts in the law—people who spent full time on righteousness, and yet Jesus insisted that the righteousness of his followers must exceed that of the scribes and Pharisees. Their demands on their fellow-Jews became, as Paul recognized, "a yoke of slavery" (Gal. 5:1). Something had gone dead wrong in their approach to righteousness.

B. As related to the covenant. It is clear from what has been said that righteousness has to do with the fulfillment of the demands of relationships, whether with other people or with God. It is also clear that we fail in these relationships. This being so, what approach does OT religion have in the face of the absolute demands and the insufficient responses? The burden of the OT message, and this fits exactly into the NT development, is that righteousness must be considered in ways other than absolute obedience. Though human righteousness fails, God's endures. This is the meaning of mercy, steadfast love, or the "grace" of the Christian message. In spite of the sinner's failures, the righteous God is as Isaiah described him, "a righteous God and a Savior" (Isa. 45:21). God intervenes on behalf of his own to save them from the disintegrating effects of SIN, forgiving their sin and justifying them before himself and before all the world.

The connection of all this with the NT message is quite obvious: "While we were still sinners, Christ died for us" (Rom. 5:8). The movement of the Scriptures is all the way from the revelation of a God who stands for the right, through the OT where he battles for the right, to the climactic revelation of a God who receives in himself the heaviest shocks of the battle against evil. *Christus Victor* (the great title of G. Aulén's book on the atonement) means that God himself entered into the lists until the victory was won. "God was reconciling the world to himself in Christ" (2 Cor. 5:19). The NT problem for Paul in the crucial verses in Romans (Rom. 3:25–26) is how God may be "just and the one who justifies." One must recognize that this process already begins by way of OT COVENANTS.

The OT may well be looked upon as a series of fresh starts. A righteous God does not give up on his wayward people. There was a covenant with ADAM having to do with absolute obedience. The turning point is reached with ABRAHAM, for in Gen. 12:1–3 there begins a series of covenants by the God and Father of the faithful. God drew near also to ISAAC, and he set up agreements with a man called JACOB, whom normally one would not have thought of as even the object of God's concern. Yet Jacob became Israel, the father of the Jewish nation, prince of God. Under MOSES, God came with the law; he came to DAVID; and gloriously he spoke to the Hebrews, and through them to the world, in the great prophets of the 8th cent. B.C. and following.

Grace is rightly defined as the "unmerited favor of God." There would be no OT story apart from the initiative of God's unmerited favor. Even after Adam's first sin, God came seeking when Adam was hiding. This is the plot of the Scriptures. The "Hound of Heaven" never leaves off his pursuit; "in these last days he has spoken to us by his Son" (Heb. 1:2).

What is clearly evident is that in spite of what must be said about God's absolute holiness and righteousness, both in essence and in his inability even to look upon sin or to touch the untouchable, the OT is already insisting that the righteousness of God, however pure, moves constantly in love toward the sinner. Note the NT development: "God made him who had no sin to be sin for us." God's righteousness in the OT is his own fulfillment of the demands of a relationship which, if one may speak in human terms, he himself simply cannot drop. Out of this idea there is evident throughout the whole of the OT that what appears in God as a responsibility because of a relationship may also become the mark of a person's righteousness. Our sin may despoil our relationship to God, but we may also sin in our irresponsibility toward other relationships. If one could read this background, it would be clear that, for the Jew, God's righteousness is not so much a matter of purity, although this is never minimized, as it is his refusal ever to let go of his responsibility. "O Love that wilt not let me go." We are to practice the same kind of righteousness.

Each person is set within a multitude of relationships: king with people, judge with complainant, priests with worshipers, common people with their families, tribesman with community, community with resident alien and poor, and all with God. Righteousness is the fulfillment of the specific demands of the specific relationships. An excellent illustration of all this appears in the life

David's righteousness is illustrated by his refusal to kill King Saul when he had the opportunity to do so near the oasis of En Gedi. (View looking W from the shores of the Dead Sea.)

of DAVID, a "man after [God's] own heart," who was "righteous" because he refused to slay SAUL, with whom he stood in a covenant relation (1 Sam. 13:14; 24:17; 26:23), and he condemned those who murdered ISH-BOSHETH (2 Sam. 4:11). After the downfall of Saul's house, MEPHIBOSHETH had no right to expect kindness from King David (19:28). The demands of righteousness change with the relationship.

As in Jewish literature, the "Wise Man" was the one who could best see life from God's viewpoint (cf. Spinoza: *sub specie aeternitatis*), so the righteous person was the one who best understood and preserved God's relationships. The book of JOB is usually considered to be WISDOM LITERATURE. It is also, if one may use the term, "righteous" literature. In defending himself, Job defended the OT view of the righteous in their relationships with God: "I was eyes to the blind / and feet to the lame. / I was a father to the needy; / I took up the case of the stranger. / I broke the fangs of the wicked / and snatched the victims from their teeth" (Job 29:15–17; cf. also 31:13–23). The book of Proverbs also reflects the righteous in their communal relationships (Prov. 10:7; 11:10; 12:10; 14:34; 16:8; 21:26; 23:24; 29:7; 31:9; et al.).

In the wider contexts, what is demanded of the private citizen is the requirement of king and judge. In Western law, the emphasis is on forensic justice in which there is an impartial decision for the two parties based on some legal standard. For the judge in Israel, righteousness is more the fulfillment of the demands of the community for balance and harmony. The judge wishes to restore the righteousness of the community, and in some cases may therefore give one of the parties not his due, but his overdue. Righteous judgments are protective and restoring. This helps to give an understanding of the outcries of the prophets, especially in behalf of the disinherited and the downtrodden. An illustration in modern society would be the "righteousness" of programs in which the disinherited are given schooling according to their need, not according to their "right." The principle of "separate but equal" in this approach to righteousness cannot restore equality until something has been done about centuries of inequality.

One of the most interesting creations of the OT economy is the SABBATICAL YEAR, coupled with the JUBILEE YEAR. The sabbatical year may be interpreted as a means of conservation for the land similar to the modern ideas of rotation of crops. Nevertheless, as the land lay fallow during the sabbatical year, the poor had certain rights on the land. The Year of Jubilee, however, was more to the point. After seven sabbaticals, for a total of forty-nine years, the fiftieth year was then declared a Year of Jubilee, in which all lands returned to their original family holdings, and everyone had a fresh start.

One could hear it argued vociferously in contemporary America that this is unjust, unfair, and that people and their descendants ought to "get what's coming to them." According to OT concepts of justice, "what's coming to them" is a fresh opportunity, in spite of the mistakes, bad investments, and poor judgment of their parents in the use of the family inheritance. Even those sold into slavery for indebtedness were set free. No family (and this is the communal emphasis again) can be totally and finally disinherited. That this system did not work very well in ancient Israel is an illustration of human selfishness and covetousness, but the prophets cried constantly for restoration of the inheritance, making it plain what was considered righteousness in OT law. The social sensitivity of the OT prophets (esp. Amos and Isaiah) is as plain as any emphasis on personal salvation in relation to God's holy demands. How far this idea of righteousness can be removed from what is generally thought of as being "religious" is illustrated by the unhappy story of JUDAH and TAMAR, where the whole concept of righteousness is plainly related to the use and misuse of proper family relationships (Gen. 38).

What is true of the judge is true also of the king. It was his responsibility to establish a kingdom of righteousness, and the emphasis is not on forensic righteousness but on communal cohesion and stability. Psalm 72 is a picture of peace and prosperity established by a king who judges righteously. The appeal of Jeremiah is that Jehoiakim is king for justice and righteousness (cf. Jer. 22:3, 15). Significantly, prophetic passages concerning the MESSIAH speak of a kingdom in which there shall be righteousness and peace, and where the king shall establish the kingdom against all enemies. (Cf. Isa. 9:7; 11:3; 16:5; 32:1–8; Jer. 23:5, 6; 33:14–16.)

What is true of citizens, judges, and kings reflects what must be true of the righteousness of God. The covenant relationship is prior to law. Much is made by Paul in the NT of the fact that the faith of Abraham preceded the law of Moses. Abraham was chosen of God, not because of his righteousness—surely he was a sinner like any other person—but because God chose to establish a people through him by which he could bring his saving power to bear upon all. Abraham "believed the LORD, and he credited it to him as righteousness" (Gen. 15:6). By the same token, Habakkuk established the commanding principle of Pauline and Reformation theology with his dictum, "the righteous will live by his faith" (Hab. 2:4).

Thus the righteous God, with no one to deal with except sinners, draws near with his covenant promises, initiates the process by which sinners may be brought into a saving relationship, sustains them in this relationship by his power and not theirs, and forgives and restores those who by faith accept these promises and return in repentance when they have broken the covenant. It is not what people are, but what they may become as God holds them and as they respond, which makes the covenant possible. It is not a question of their attainments or perfections, it is a question of a saving relationship provided for by a merciful, infinitely patient God.

What began with Abraham in Mesopotamia was established again in Egypt, and the psalmists never tired of telling what God did "with a mighty hand," with a people lost in helplessness and even ignorant of their own religious inheritance. "You yourselves have seen what I did to Egypt, and how I carried you on eagles' wings and brought you to myself. Now if you obey me fully and keep my covenant, then out of all nations you will be my treasured possession. Although the whole earth is mine, you will be for me a kingdom of priests and a holy nation" (Exod. 19:4–6). Notice God's initiatory act, even against all human expectancies; and notice, too, the future reference, not to what they are but to what they are to become. Israel could suffer the wrath of God, but they could not fall out of his hands. As H. H. Farmer once put it, "We may sin ourselves into the wrath of God, but we cannot sin ourselves out of the love of God" (cf. Ps. 89:28–37, esp. vv. 32–33).

What, then, is the function of the law in a covenant relationship of grace? It is to set the norm, establish the right, speak a word of judgment on anything less than the best, and lead one to the almighty God who can enable one increasingly to fulfill the requirements of holiness. The law has no power in itself to make a good life. It establishes what the good life ought to be and may be by the power of God. One further truth: the law (which Paul says "was put in charge to lead us to Christ," Gal. 3:24) is the guide for those within the covenant. Only inside the covenant do individuals really care what response they shall make to the God who has called them to be his children.

To the OT Jew, then, the law is a part of the whole gift of grace. Hear the psalmist sing: "The law of the LORD is perfect, / reviving the soul.... The commands of the LORD are radiant, / giving light to the eyes.... The ordinances of the LORD are sure / and altogether righteous. / They are more precious than gold, / than much pure gold; / they are sweeter than honey, / than honey from the comb" (Ps. 19:7–10). Apparently, for the Jew, although the law was binding, it was far from oppressive. On the contrary, how happy he was that his God had made plain to him how to live a life of stability and satisfaction.

One other help in the understanding of this whole covenant relationship is to see how God acted in behalf of his people against their enemies. From the vantage point of the Christian era it is hard to discern the viewpoint of the chosen people as against "the other nations," the GENTILES. It looks narrow and provincial now, but from the OT viewpoint it makes good sense. How else could God who has entered into his covenant act expect to protect his own from "the others"? This would be expected of the father of a family, of a king, and surely of a person's God. Perhaps the Hebrews missed some points that one can see now from a perspective they did not have. For one thing, they were chosen of God, not because they were something special, but in order that they might become the channel of something special. God said to Abraham, "I will bless you ... so that you will be a blessing" (Gen. 12:2 NRSV). The Jews lost their way when they thought the blessing ended with them.

There was not one iota of selfishness in one's being chosen of God. The NT concept of ELECTION has in it the same danger unless it is seen that one is "elected" as an agent of God toward others. For another thing, the channel of blessing was to be universal, not narrow. Perhaps God's great protection of the Jew, which seems to be narrow and provincial, is offensive because of the fact that people do not understand the problem and so they make the same mistake that the Jew made—they consider election an end in itself. God had to start somewhere, he had to choose someone; he had at all costs to protect his investment in his plan of salvation. That only a REMNANT remained as a channel for his blessing is indicative of the high cost of this whole process, even in the OT. The Gentiles had to be left out at the onset, but most of the Jews had to be left out, too, before some of them were fit channels for a salvation that has to come to all. The servant of God in the covenant eventually had to become the suffering servant, and yet, in the whole process, the absolutely holy God, for love's sake, was working out a way by which sinners would become "heirs of God." What is difficult to see in the OT is not necessarily easier to see in the NT. Israel, the suffering servant, is replaced by *the* Suffering Servant, who in perfect obedience "fulfilled all righteousness." It is the burden of Paul's approach to Christianity to reveal how this was done. See SERVANT OF THE LORD.

II. Righteousness in the NT. It is an assumption of all NT studies that the epistles of PAUL chronologically preceded the records of the four GOSPELS. As the CANON OF THE NT appears in our hands, however, the Gospels precede the other writings, and this of course makes its own good sense, because the life and teachings of Christ preceded the explanations and commentaries of the other documents in the treatment of righteousness.

A. The idea in the Gospels. Our understanding of righteousness in the NT comes primarily out of the writings of Paul rather than from the Gospels. As R. W. Dale so nicely put it, "Christ did not come to preach the gospel; he came that there might be a gospel to preach." It is true that he came "to fulfill all righteousness" (Matt. 3:15), but what he had to say on the subject specifically does not begin to touch the full explication which appears in the Pauline letters. He was not a theology, he was a person. The theology followed the exhibition of righteousness in his person. With this in mind, therefore, the expectancy regarding righteousness in the Gospels, at least insofar as Jesus taught on the subject, is not great.

The term *righteous* is used in the Gospels to mean a "pious" person, or a "religious" person, or one regarding whom, in a popular sense, it might be said that he lived a "good" life. JOSEPH was called a "righteous" man, and this was the reason he would not turn Mary over to the authorities when she was found to be pregnant. Strict construction of Jewish law would have demanded that Mary be stoned to death, but Joseph, being "righteous," planned to put her away out of sight (Matt. 1:19). He was evading the demands of the law and refused to make out of his betrothed a public spectacle. As a just man, he would be, in the terminology of our day, a kind or sensitive man.

In a stricter sense the Pharisees made an appearance of "righteousness" (Matt. 23:28), and surely in such passages the idea is that of formal righteousness in keeping the meticulous requirements of the Jewish law. ABEL was regarded as righteous (23:35); the heroes of the past were righteous (23:29); and the promise of the messianic kingdom was that the righteous would in due time enter it (13:43–49; 25:37–46). Popular usage makes it impossible to draw out any sharp distinction or definition. The situation is akin to Jesus' strange answer to the rich young ruler: "Why do you call me good?... No one is good—except God alone" (Lk. 18:19). This was not Jesus' denial of his own goodness, but a concern that the rich young ruler should use the term in a strict rather than in a popular sense. The whole burden of their exchange had to do with real goodness, and Jesus was insisting that the word *good* applied to God alone and that he and the young ruler, if they were to talk about goodness at all, should talk about it in the absolute sense. Thus the Gospels reflect the popular use of the word *righteous* even though in careful conversation one could insist that only God is righteous.

Much the same sort of popular usage is reflected in the other Gospels. Neither Mark nor Luke records any new statement of Christ containing the term *righteousness*. Mark's use of the term (Mk. 2:17) is parallel to Matthew's usage (Matt. 9:13) and adds nothing to one's understanding of it (cf. also Lk. 5:32 with Matt. 9:13). The description of Christ by the centurion as "a righteous man" (Lk. 23:47), and the statement that Joseph of Arimathea was "a good and righteous man" (23:50 NRSV) add nothing to the clarification of this term, for these are all popular usages.

Such data as appear in the teachings of Jesus occur seven times in the first gospel, twice in the fourth gospel, and no more (Matt. 3:15; 5:6, 10, 20; 6:1 [piety], 33; 21:32; Jn. 16:8, 10). The passages in Matthew give some variety to the interpretations of righteousness, although those in the SERMON ON THE MOUNT show a basic similarity. The two references to JOHN THE BAPTIST (Matt. 3:15; 21:32) raise the general question of the practice of righteousness under the impetus of Levitical law. In the first instance occurs the rather puzzling answer of Jesus when JOHN THE BAPTIST hesitated to baptize him. John recognized in every way his inferiority to Jesus; he never went beyond the bounds of the forerunner. He saw the difference between his BAPTISM and that of the Lord, and indeed, part of his message was the infinite distance that separated him and his ministry from that of Christ. He said to Jesus, "I need to be baptized by you" (3:14), thinking surely of baptism as a sign of REPENTANCE. John needed the baptism of repentance as all sinners do, and the difference was that Jesus did not. In answer to John's demurrer Jesus answered, "Let it be so now; it is proper for us to do this to fulfill all righteousness" (3:15).

Assuming then that Jesus did not need the baptism of repentance, the question before all commentators, therefore, is what righteousness, or what kind of righteousness, was to be fulfilled in this act? It is well to remember, as Paul expressed it, that Jesus was "born of a woman, born under the law" (Gal. 4:4). He was circumcised the eighth day; an offering was made for him in the temple according to Jewish custom; and at the age of twelve, on his trip to Jerusalem, he became "a son of the law" (*bar mitzvah*). He grew up in a normal Jewish home, obedient to his parents. According to Levitical customs, any man going into the service of God was subjected to baptismal rites. It seems the best interpretation, therefore, that righteousness refers simply to a continuance of Jesus' obedience to the laws of his people, both civil and canonical. The meaning generally given is that John's baptism of Jesus was "to fulfill every righteous ordinance."

This interpretation is supported by the other reference to John the Baptist in Matthew, where Jesus was engaged in conflict with his enemies, and as he sometimes did, he was forcing his opponents to consider their reaction to him in terms of their reaction to John, "For John came to you to show you the way of righteousness, and you did not believe him, but the tax collectors and the prostitutes did" (Matt. 21:32). He is here concluding the thrust of his parable of the two sons, the better of whom said he would not do the will of his father, but nevertheless did it. For the purposes of interpretation one need not dwell on the parable, but what does "the way of righteousness" here mean? Again it is to be interpreted as a continuity from OT law and custom. John was, in some sense, the last of the OT prophets, and his "way of righteousness" concluding the OT dispensation was at the threshold of the new righteousness, which was to come in Christ in the new dispensation.

Remains of the Byzantine Church of John the Baptist in Samaria (Sebaste) where, according to tradition, John's body was buried. Jesus said that John had come "to show … the way of righteousness" (Matt. 21:32).

Turn to the passages in the SERMON ON THE MOUNT. Three of these may be construed as having to do with the righteousness of God—absolute, essential righteousness, ideal and perfect righteousness (Matt. 5:6, 10; 6:33). There are those who hunger and thirst for righteousness (5:6) and are persecuted for their righteousness (5:10) but who are, nevertheless, to continue to seek the Father's kingdom and his righteousness (6:33). The first of these, "Blessed are those who hunger and thirst for righteousness, for they will be filled" (5:6), is paralleled by another BEATITUDE: "Blessed are the pure in heart, for they will see God" (5:8). Kierkegaard's insight is helpful when he suggests that to be "pure in heart" is to will *one thing*—namely the will of God. A person's eye is to be "single" and not "evil." Jesus described his own "meat and drink" as doing the will of his Father. When, therefore, he said that there is satisfaction for those who "hunger and thirst for righteousness," he was not speaking of attainment or victory, but of the set of the life.

True satisfaction comes in the constant vision and in the direction in which a person is moving. The whole inclination of one's life is described as a hunger and a thirst; and yet, strangely, this very constancy of hunger and thirst is its own satisfaction. Literature is replete with illustrations of some variation of the search for the Holy Grail. Apparently there is no greater description of a worthy and satisfying venture than that of a continuing searching-and-finding. How interesting it is that the Promised Land for the Israelites was set before them as a land "flowing with milk and honey." Honey by itself cloys and satiates. Milk clears the taste. A promised land is one in which the endless delights are constantly opened up again to greater delights. The hungering and the thirsting continues even while one is being filled. "A man's reach should exceed his grasp, or what's a heaven for?" (R. Browning, *Andrea del Sarto*, line 97).

As is truly the case, the seekers after righteousness are the objects of PERSECUTION in every generation. Consequently, Jesus' word is pertinent: "Blessed are those who are persecuted because of righteousness" (Matt. 5:10). Indeed, "great is your reward in heaven, for in the same way they persecuted the prophets who were before you" (5:12). Those who hunger and thirst for righteousness may be persecuted for this strange difference in their lives; yet they find themselves in the great company of those who constantly held out for a better day— "the prophets who were before you."

In the great passages on anxiety (Matt. 6:25–34), Jesus draws the line between those who are anxious about many things ("What shall we eat?… What shall we drink?… What shall we wear?" [v. 31]) and those who accept the necessity of such things, but are concerned for greater needs. "Seek first," he says, "his kingdom and his righteousness, and all these things will be given to you as well" (6:33). Jesus is not denying the necessity of "these things." What he knows is that unless the foundations are established in righteousness, the "things" also will disappear. All materialistic societies fall away to the dust heaps of history when they play fast and loose with the foundations of righteousness. In this verse (6:33) righteousness means the will of God brought to bear on the affairs of life. This was the ideal of the OT theocracy, which never quite matured. Jesus again was speaking of the righteousness of God. Throughout these three passages, therefore (5:6, 10; 6:33), the absolute righteousness of God, with which the OT begins, is confirmed.

In two other passages in Matthew the old question of formal righteousness is again raised. Significantly, Jesus not only speaks of this righteousness but also illustrates it; and in his illustration he makes out of the whole subject of righteousness an "open-ended" possibility. "For I tell you that unless your righteousness surpasses that of the Pharisees and the teachers of the law, you will certainly not enter the kingdom of heaven" (Matt. 5:20). As is well known, the SCRIBES, and especially the PHARISEES, were experts in religious disciplines. The scribal movement arose after the return of the Jews from EXILE. By that time in their history the Jews had nothing to recommend them except their religion. They had no political power, no military might, no economic significance. Caught in the midst of tremendous world powers, and existing only as a remnant, their contribution to history was to be a religion through which salvation would come to all people. But this religion had to be hedged about, and the scribes arose as a class to protect in the strictest possible ways the *differentia* of their faith. At this stage they were a necessary disciplinary force, but by the time of Jesus their concern for the minutiae of JUDAISM had almost made a mockery out of their religion. The "burden" of the law (Acts 15:28) could not possibly be borne by the ordinary man in his daily walk. These experts, therefore, not only satisfied what they considered to be all the demands of the law, but by such exercises they often satisfied themselves, and some finally took cold hard pride in their attainments.

Jesus' contribution at this point on the subject of righteousness was to move from the form of the law to its spiritual content. The question now became not so much a matter of action as of motive, the one great commandment being to LOVE God and to love one's neighbor as oneself. Only thus could the righteousness of Jesus' followers exceed "that of the Pharisees and the teachers of the law." In the Sermon on the Mount Jesus illustrated how this should be so. It is not a question of murder so much as a question of anger in the heart. It is not so much adultery as the eye of lust. The framework of the law must abide insofar as it is God's law, but one is not "righteous" in Jesus' way of thinking unless his motives rest in love.

A turn on this same approach is illustrated in the next chapter of Matthew. "Be careful not to do your 'acts of righteousness' in front of others, to be seen by them" (Matt. 6:1 TNIV). Jesus accepted the so-called "exercises" of religion—almsgiving, prayer, fasting. He assumed that a religious person will engage in such practices. But T. S. Elliott says it well in *Murder in the Cathedral* when he writes, "a Pharisee is a man who does the right thing for the wrong reason." Again it is a question of motive, and Jesus criticized harshly those who perform their religious exercises to be seen of others.

When the move is made to John's gospel the theological climate changes. Matthew's gospel was aimed at the Jew with all the background assumptions of centuries of Judaism. The "most theological of the Gospels," namely John's, includes only two verses—actually only one record—of Jesus speaking of righteousness. In his farewell discourses Jesus was speaking of the deepest things of the Christian faith, and in the sixteenth chapter there is a very different and a very involved discussion of the person and the action of the HOLY SPIRIT. It is impossible to treat the subject of the Holy Spirit with any completeness at all in this context, so it must be limited to straight-forward statements without support or commentary.

From the best available evidence, therefore, one may conclude that when Jesus says that the Holy Spirit "will convict the world of guilt in regard to sin and righteousness and judgment: ... in regard to righteousness, because I go to the Father ..." (Jn. 16:8, 10), he is looking forward from this quiet meeting to what surely must appear later in the instructive writings of the apostles as they are recorded in the remainder of the NT. It is surely evident that what Jesus was and what he did, and what is yet to transpire because of the living Christ, were nothing but questions and doubts to the disciples on the eve of the crucifixion. The function of the Holy Spirit was to inspire truthfully what the apostles must say regarding the fact and the meaning of Christ. Righteousness, therefore, in these two verses, is the complete righteousness of God, completely portrayed in the life and teachings of

Jesus, which the apostles came to understand and which they shared with mankind.

The word *righteous* is used elsewhere in John's gospel three times but not as Jesus' own teaching: as a description of Christ's righteous judgment (Jn. 5:30), as a description of human judgment (7:24), and as a description of God the Father (17:25). These usages do not concern the argument at this point because in one form or another they have already come under discussion. The next crucial question, in regard to the whole subject of righteousness is what the apostles, especially Paul, would do with the absolute righteousness of God, the portrayal of that righteousness in Christ, the failure of the righteousness of human beings, and the whole question of how unrighteous people may stand in the presence of the righteous God.

B. The crucial treatment in Paul. The key to Paul's view of righteousness, as it is basic to an understanding of the whole gospel of Christ, is found in his major treatise, the letter to the ROMANS. There is no question but that Paul studied closely the structure and content of this masterpiece. It is here, if anywhere, that we have his "theology," and with the possible exception of EPHESIANS, it is the finest creation of this first mind of the first century.

The theme of Romans is "Righteousness." After his usual formal introduction, and in Romans this is well structured and quite extensive, he announces his thesis: "I am not ashamed of the gospel, because it is the power of God for the salvation of everyone who believes: first for the Jew, then for the Gentile. For in the gospel a righteousness from God is revealed, a righteousness that is by faith from first to last, just as it is written: 'The righteous will live by faith'" (Rom. 1:16–17, citing Hab. 2:4). The fundamental problem in this thesis is what Paul called "a righteousness of God" (*dikaiosynē theou*). The question of interpretation is concerned with the genitive *theou*, for the form allows three possible interpretations.

First, it may be taken as a simple possessive, a common use of the genitive. In this usage it would refer to an attribute of God's own character. This reverts to the beginning of this discussion, which concerned the very essence of God. The righteousness of God is a part of him, an essential of his nature. There is no question that the Greek form used allows for this interpretation, and whatever other meaning one brings to bear on it, this view cannot be ruled out. The whole discussion of righteousness in the OT and in the Gospels has either emphasized or assumed this approach as the ground of any understanding of the word.

Second, the "righteousness of God" may carry the secondary meaning discussed above (I.B). It is that righteousness of God which shows itself in his relationships to his covenant people, in which righteousness is self-imparting rather than distributive. By this is meant throughout the discussion that whereas righteousness might require some bill of rights and wrongs in judgment, some expression of LEX TALIONIS (the law of retaliation), or even some display of the wrath of God in punishment, the enthusiasm of the Jew for the righteousness of God rested in the covenant relationship God had initiated. In this they thought of his righteousness as supporting his own people—what a king would be expected to do. In the OT, generally, it is understood that when a king judged, he did so to preserve and enhance the life of the whole community, and thereby make possible a better life for the individual. He is conceived of as helping people to their rights. His righteousness was an overflow rather than a balance, just as one would expect to do something extra for a person with a broken leg on a safari.

In the Psalms and Isaiah, the people of God are vindicated by God, who shows his righteousness by delivering them from their enemies. Inside the community of Israel, the righteousness of God is on the side of the poor rather than the rich, the weak rather than the strong. His righteousness is thus manifested not only to his own people but to the nations, and one of the great appeals of the prophets was that God's glory is known to the nations because in righteousness he established his own people (Pss. 35:24, 28; 51:14; 71:2–6, 24; Isa. 51:5; 54:17; 56:1).

It is quite evident that this kind of righteousness is communal rather than individual. The OT, while insisting that the "people of God" are supported by God's righteousness, also makes very clear that individuals within the community may very well experience a sense of sin and the threat of the righteous judgment of God. An interesting example of this combination of national righteousness and individual sin appears in Ps. 143:1–2. It is evident in this communal use of the idea of righteousness that God's nation can be justified, but if the sinful individual who cannot face God's judgment is to be justified, the process must be different. National and individual sins and successes seem to be sorted out in the OT.

Third, Paul's understanding of "righteousness" is crucial. Paul's preaching of the gospel in the context of the primitive church cannot possibly be a message to a national group such as that seen in the nation of Israel. God is not rescuing his oppressed people in any communal sense; he is preaching to individual sinners, Jews and Gentiles alike, whose only community is their common need of salvation. His message, therefore, must make clear that the altogether righteous God, who cannot act against his own nature, must somehow remain righteous while at the same time accepting the unrighteous. As Paul classically expresses it, the purpose of the gospel was "to demonstrate his justice at the present time, so as to be just and the one who justifies [declares to be righteous] those who have faith in Jesus" (Rom. 3:26).

After announcing the theme of the righteousness of God (Rom. 1:17), Paul took great pains to show that no human righteousness has worked nor will work. He illustrated this truth first from the pagan world, where he allowed for "natural theology." He put it this way: "For since the creation of the world God's invisible qualities—his eternal power and divine nature—have been clearly seen, being understood from what has been made" (1:20). The pagan world, therefore, is "without excuse," because the natural world, the created world, is a revelation of the power and deity of God. People everywhere, however, have stopped short with the created world and have worshiped the creation rather than the Creator, and this, in whatever form it takes, is IDOLATRY. It follows, therefore, that men and women practicing idolatry have in the worship of things constantly demeaned themselves by worshiping what is lower even than a human being. It is the sort of thing that can happen now when a person stops with the symbols of his faith—bread, wine, beauty, a holy place—and forgets the reality which is symbolized. An observer may stop with the technique of a painting, or even its beauty, whereas the height of the esthetic experience should be to have spirit meet spirit with the artist himself. The remainder of Paul's declaration of pagan disintegration vividly portrays in the background of Roman culture how idolatry eventually goes through perversion to decay.

Paul then took up the failure of the Jews who have had the gift of greater light. "What advantage, then, is there in being a Jew, or what value is there in circumcision? Much in every way! First of all, they have been entrusted with the very words of God" (Rom. 3:1–2; cf. 2:17–29). The Jews' highest claim has been that they have received a revelation of God, especially through the Torah. Knowing the law, however, they have failed to keep the law. Paul quoted their own psalmists against them. "There is no one righteous, not even one; / there is no one who understands, / no one who seeks God. / All have turned away, / they have together become worthless; / there is no one who does good, / not even one" (3:10–12; cf. Pss. 14:1–2; 53:1–2). Paul's summation is clear enough; he is referring to both pagan and Jew (from the Jewish viewpoint: the "outsider" and the "insider") and says that "no one will be declared righteous in [God's] sight by observing the law" (Rom. 3:20). Or again, "There is no difference, for all have sinned and fall short of the glory of God" (vv. 22–23). And since he has already said in the announcement of his theme that "the wrath of God is being revealed from heaven against all the godlessness and wickedness of men" (1:18), the human condition in the presence of a holy, righteous God is hopeless. It is only with this hopelessness established that Paul was ready to present the good news.

If one may assume then that whatever righteousness a person has is a gift of God, then one is forced to face the question of how God's righteousness becomes a person's righteousness; in addition, it is necessary to portray how such righteousness shows itself in the life of individuals, and perhaps also in their society. Paul, in writing of righteousness in Romans, says first of all that a righteousness of God has been revealed through faith for faith (Rom. 1:17); he then goes on to say that this righteousness of God is the righteousness of Christ, who has been set forth as a PROPITIATION for sin, and that the right attainment of the righteousness of Christ is dependent upon faith (3:26). What, therefore, actually transpires?

From God's standpoint the simple, yet profound problem is how God may be "just and the justifier," or in other words, how his holiness may be kept inviolate while he is engaged in accepting a person who is unholy. By the very essence of his nature, his WRATH is against all unrighteousness (Rom. 1:18). He cannot "look upon," let alone participate, in sin (cf. Hab. 1:13 NRSV). His solution, then, is to set forth Christ who in human flesh "fulfills all righteousness." It is awkward for modern theology to accept the language and sometimes the crude mechanisms of medieval theories of ATONEMENT; yet, whatever the language, the truths involved must not be lost—vicarious ATONEMENT, RANSOM, and the like must be preserved.

Christ took on humanity, human nature. In human flesh he lived without sin, so that it can be said that if one human being was ever sinless, then at one point in history human nature was sinless. In perfect obedience a life was lived in which human nature was untainted. What is difficult is to understand the nature of *humanity* as against individual human beings. Perhaps a simple illustration will help. When fifty people are in a room there are fifty human beings, and there surely is humanity. If fifty more people are brought into the room there are more human beings, but not necessarily more humanity. This becomes clear when everyone is put out of the room except one person. Although there is now only one human being, there is nevertheless complete "humanity" in that one person. This is the kind of concept that is recognized in a word like *love*. It represents the kind of reality that can neither be divided nor multiplied. A woman who has twelve children does not love each child one-twelfth; nor does a woman with twelve children necessarily have more love than a woman with six. Such ideas as humanity and love will not subject themselves to multiplication and division. We repeat, therefore, that "humanity," as it appears in Jesus, is pure, sinless, and an example of perfect obedience.

Following the thinking of Anselm, there is set forth in the sacrifice of Christ on the cross the death of the God-man. Because of his identity as God, this sacrifice is of infinite value; because of his identity as man, it is the death of an innocent person. The perfect humanity of Christ thus blocks off the necessary judgment of God against the humanity of other men and women, and at the same time an infinite price is being paid for what Anselm considered an infinite sin, that is, sin against God. The limitations of human language are inescapable, but several things are said very clearly: Christ did for human beings what they could not do for themselves. With his perfections he offered up a perfect humanity. He died in our stead. Whatever was accomplished satisfied the infinite demands of the holiness of God. There are those for whom this description satisfies; as Paul says in Romans, "Christ was a propitiation" for sin. In other words, the death of Christ "satisfied" God. A ransom was paid, or as Denney so nicely suggests, the satisfaction of God's holiness released his love.

But there is more. "God was reconciling the world to himself in Christ" (2 Cor. 5:19). This carries thought into the structure of the TRINITY, which happily is not the problem here. It is not likely that anyone will completely unravel what transpired in the Godhead; but this much must be maintained: whatever price Jesus was paying on the cross was paid by God himself. One cannot contrast a loving Jesus with a wrathful Father. Even if this were the solution, any father worthy of the name would necessarily suffer in the suffering of his son. But this split in the Godhead is not at all necessary. "God *was in* Christ." The agonies of the cross are a revelation of the heart of God, and they reveal that God, who makes the demands of holiness, in the last analysis pays those demands for those incapable of making the payment themselves. Therefore, the law of God is established, and the love of God finds its fullest expression in the one offering. Thus the cross becomes the symbol of the Christian faith in exhibiting what sin really is from God's viewpoint, and what God is willing to do about it for his lost creation. In this one event God is surely "just and the justifier." He maintains the demands of his law and justifies the sinner because he himself has paid the price to maintain the law. See further JUSTIFICATION.

Now comes the question of the application of this righteousness. God has dealt with sin for its complete removal, and this is all of grace. The

RIGHTEOUSNESS

Lamb "was slain from the creation of the world" (Rev. 13:8). God in his almighty holiness and everlasting love has made provision for opening up the way of salvation. It is a way in which God gets the sinner right with God himself; he justifies him. From the human viewpoint, we lay hold on this offered salvation by faith. The word FAITH is maligned, misunderstood, limited, and yet Paul offers no other way except through the attainments of God's free gift through faith.

It is sometimes claimed that it is sufficient to think of the cross as the setting of a standard which we can imitate. The death of Christ is an "example" and those who would follow Christ (because they call themselves Christians) ought to follow his example. The climax of his exemplary life is complete self-giving all the way to death. As is said in three of the four Gospels reflecting the words of Jesus, "If anyone would come after me, he must deny himself and take up his cross and follow me" (Matt. 16:24 et al.). Such devotional literature as Thomas a Kempis's *Imitation of Christ* follows this idea. It must be maintained that such an idea is solid and true and has a certain saving force in a person's life. This is not to say, however, that this interpretation is sufficient. The righteousness of God, which is to be our righteousness, does not come by imitation. More significantly, we are moved to imitate Christ because in some sense "the righteousness of God" has already been given to us.

One other very widespread interpretation of the cross is that which describes the crucifixion as an exhibition of God's amazing love. How can anyone, therefore, once he sees such love expressed in his behalf, fail to respond in newness of life? This sounds reasonable, but as George Adam Smith reflects in speaking of Hosea, "love stands defeated on some of the greatest battlefields of life." The candle that stays burning in the window gives no assurance that the prodigal will ever come home. A love that "will not let me go" will not necessarily save me. What is needed, therefore, is the gift of FAITH (and the NT surely says that even faith is a gift) which will enable a sinner to respond to the example and answer to the love. Just how does one go about this?

Faith means that one accepts Christ, and this in turn means accepting the fact that what he has done for mankind needed to be done. We are not simply repeating statements of faith; we are being totally converted in the happening of three things: (1) We accept God's view as our own on the true nature of our need. (2) We accept his solution to the problem. (3) We accept the fact (and this is where pride, the deadliest of the sins, is broken) that there is no hope at all in any of our own righteousness which we might wish to bring forward—and so

Jewish man praying at the Western Wall in Jerusalem. Prayer may be viewed as an "act of righteousness," but one that can be misused (Matt. 6:1, 5–6).

we rest, or trust entirely, on the finished work of Christ. We have no negotiations to carry on, nothing to offer to the whole transaction except our sin; we do not argue our worthiness, and in the last analysis a Christian is one who accepts Christ as the Word (Logos) on all things. This is what had to be done; this is what was done; where do I will to stand in relationship to it? Thus a person believes and accepts. Whereas JUSTIFICATION is the act, SANCTIFICATION becomes the process as Jesus' pure humanity becomes a part of ours, increasingly. As John says, "the blood of Jesus, his Son, purifies us from all sin" (1 Jn. 1:7).

What, then, is righteousness in the Christian interpretation of the word? It is primarily and basically a relationship, never an attainment. It may be said of Jesus, but never of any other human being, "in him all righteousness dwelt." The condition of any and every person is always the same—one of total dependence. Faith really means that sinners have no security except as they hold on, or better, are held on to. As John Oman expresses it, "It is not so much a question of the rung of the ladder which we occupy, but whether we are climbing or falling." Christian righteousness is never an attainment; it is a direction, a loyalty, a commitment, a hope—and only someday an arrival.

How beautifully this dismisses all pride, all Pharisaism, all judgmental accusations toward one's brothers. How beautifully this creates humanity, understanding, and in the right sense, meekness. How beautifully this says that righteousness is through faith for faith, or that the righteous shall live by faith.

III. Righteousness in the modern world. It is evident that throughout the Bible there is development in the concept of righteousness. This is not to say that one concept of righteousness was replaced by another or a better one; the growth is not of that sort. It is a matter of addition rather than correction.

In the beginning the idea of righteousness was rooted and grounded in the very nature of God. His essence, consciously or unconsciously, became the touchstone of every righteous act by human beings. At the same time it was clearly understood that the righteousness of God, with such corollaries as holiness and justice, constituted not only the proper ground of human action, but the very integrity of the physical universe and the material world.

It is easy to criticize, as many noted scholars do, the unusual ways in which the Hebrew Scriptures (e.g., the laws in the Pentateuch) seek to express the righteousness of God. The modern temptation is to make a claim that the expression of righteousness in the Bible is simply a reflection of cultural pressures. As must be said so many times in such a superficial analysis, there is no question that there was a cultural milieu out of which certain social practices did arise. But the point is missed if we do not understand that there was a fixed element at the basis of the variety of expression. For the Hebrews there was no doubt that the righteousness of God had been revealed in the Torah, that the righteousness of God was even revealed in the minutiae of the Levitical codes. It is impossible to understand both the OT and the NT apart from this deep concern to honor the righteousness of God by expressing it in daily living. It is this concern which is the fixed element in all the rich variety of expression that has followed in the Bible, in the life of the church, and, one may hope, in the unsettled ethical expressions of the present.

What came next in the growth of the Hebrew concept was the belief that God's righteousness included a certain covenant demand that could be made on God's people. The Hebrews belonged to Yahweh because he had chosen them and had initiated a covenant to "carry them through." For this reason he would protect them from their enemies, he would lead them into the good life, he would restore them after sin and repentance. If necessary (and it became necessary), he would save them, even if only through a remnant. The righteousness of God thus not only became the source of unchangeable holiness, but also gave rise to the need of a Savior and Redeemer.

By the time of Hosea and Isaiah, God the Savior and Redeemer is a Suffering Servant. Such a concept is a study in itself, but in this context it is an inescapable fact that the cross is already necessitated in the visions of the great prophets. Thus, in brief, the OT idea of righteousness has moved from a standard of conduct to a King who cares for his subjects, to a Savior who finally gave himself for their salvation.

In the NT it is Christ who is set forth as "the righteousness of God." What was once law has become a person. What was foreseen as a way of redemption is now illustrated in a redemptive life. The cross of Christ became the climax of a life that was always the way of the cross.

Paul then formally asserted what was latent in the OT and patent in the NT, that the righteousness of God is now poured out through the life and death of Christ; first for the redemption of sinners and second as a source of newness of life in them. What started as a code of ethics based on the nature of God ultimately became a source of life and the power to grow into the very nature of God. Another code of ethics or another standard of righteousness could simply break the human heart in its constant failure; Christian righteousness is (and how often this is missed) a power more than a standard, a life more than a rule, a loyalty and a saving relationship for everyday living.

A. The existential emphasis. The modern emphasis in the treatment of righteousness has been dominated by the rise of existentialism in philosophy. This approach focuses on the "moment of existence" in which a decision is made, emphasizing that any decision is determined by the stance of the person making the decision and the total situation in time in which the decision is made. In moral decision, for example, it is possible for two different people in what looks like the same situation to come up with what look like diametrically opposed decisions, and it is possible at the same time that each can be right. It is also possible for the same person to make a correct moral decision on one day and on the next day do just the opposite and still be morally right. This approach has sometimes been referred to as "situational ethics."

The classic example of this viewpoint grows out of the commandment "Thou shalt not kill" (more correctly translated "Thou shalt do no murder"). It is highly probable that an individual citizen would find no occasion where he could kill another citizen as a righteous act. The issue becomes a different kind of problem in warfare or in judicial action, especially when a servant of the state serves as the hangman or the man who pulls the lever for the electric chair. These questions are highly debatable, of course, but they are illustrative. With regard to the private citizen himself, he might justify as a righteous act the killing of someone for the defense of one of his children. What is conceivable, and what must be understood, is that general circumstances would never allow a person to kill for righteousness' sake, whereas particular occasions could arise where killing is the only righteous act.

Recalling now the absolute righteousness of the OT, which became colored in time by the social righteousness of the OT prophets, where the absolute demands of the law became a definite series of adjustments within the demands of a person's social relationships, one sees that such an existential approach can be biblical. Even more so the NT emphasis on a person's relationship to God as determinative of his righteousness brings one to this same approach. When there is added to this the idea of obedience in the daily walk; supreme loyalty to a living, dynamic, and personal Master; a recognition that no one completely fulfills the law; and that "all our righteous acts are like filthy rags" (Isa. 64:6), there is justification for those who find an existential approach a satisfactory one in their Christianity. Modern theology, as defined by Karl Barth and illustrated by Reinhold Niebuhr, has touched every facet of ethical decision. Barth's insistence that one should "walk by faith," and always in a "crisis" situation, and always with incompleteness in the positive righteous acts, is biblical, and certainly basic as far as it goes. Niebuhr's insistence that all are sinful and in a sinful society and therefore are never capable of absolute righteous judgments can also be easily established.

B. The abiding nature of law. The question therefore naturally arises whether or not the ethics that grow out of modern theology have destroyed any absolutes in righteousness. When it is remembered that the whole idea of righteousness in the Hebrew background grew out of the recognition of necessary obedience to an absolutely righteous God, it looks as if all that kind of righteousness has been badly clouded. Moral decisions are made, apparently, without any fixed point of reference, and with an easy acceptance of the theory that any perfection in righteousness is impossible and therefore irrelevant. "Situational ethics" can lead, and often does lead, to ethical relativism. With such fears the critics of the "new theology" must deal.

The answer of modern theology is that there is one absolute—namely love. It follows, therefore, that in any existential situation where the issues are bound to be ambiguous, the fixed point is the absolute of love, and the apologists for this position are quick to point out that when love is spoken of as an absolute, it is defined by the love of God, which is revealed in Jesus Christ. This becomes the control, and it is argued that basically and finally, in such love, there is no relativism. The "righteousness of God" of which Paul wrote is revealed "through faith for faith," and the righteous do indeed "live by faith." In this relationship of faith, a person's first concern should be for the love of God, and a "righteous" decision is made on that basis alone.

The first thing that must be said is that, properly construed, it cannot be faulted. Anyone living under the direction of the power of the love of God will be "righteous" because of a right relationship to God showing itself in obedience—faith will be shown by works. Since the love of God, of which the Scripture speaks, is *agape* love, it will not run off into sentimentalism or emotionalism.

The other thing that must immediately be said, however, is that in spite of a simple absolute, there still remains the necessity for laws for control. Such laws relate to the law of Scripture and eventually, and certainly, to the Decalogue, and beyond that to the righteous essence of God. After all that has been said for existentialism, why is this true? Primarily for one reason: if moral action is based on the absolute of love, it is not yet evident that anyone knows enough or is morally equipped enough, free of prejudice and pressure, to recognize the answer of love in a decision and then to follow specifically the right that he or she sees. It can be assumed that an altogether righteous person would do nothing less than what absolute love would dictate, but how is a person to act short of such attainment in his moral life?

Paul wrote, "the law was put in charge to lead us to Christ" (Gal. 3:24). To follow his thinking, and to allow to situational ethics everything possible, there must be agreement that in Christ there is no longer the necessity for law, but that no one is in that perfect relationship and that, therefore, the law is his control until such time as he reaches perfection. The idealists, or the perfectionists, are right when they argue that traffic in cities would be no problem if people were only more thoughtful, more unselfish, kinder, in other words, if people were more nearly perfect or more "Christian." People being as they are, the only possible freedom in heavy traffic grows out of the control of the law. "The counsel of perfection" will not do in a sinful society, and the law takes God's people on the way toward a perfection and a maturity where the "schoolmaster" (KJV) has worked his way out of a job. The road to freedom is always by way of discipline. "If you hold to my teaching,… you will know the truth, and the truth will set you free" (Jn. 8:31–32).

IV. Righteousness in world religions. Not much is gained by a study of righteousness beyond the biblical presentation. All that can be said is that a survey of world religions brings to the fore the same emphases as the Bible does. Such general agreement points toward the Roman Catholic emphasis on natural theology and, of course, raises pressing questions for students of comparative religions. It is instructive that every facet of the subject of righteousness appears somewhere in some other religion. Perhaps the remark of Herbert H. Farmer of Cambridge University is germane: "The Christian religion brings to definition what is found in other religions, and it contains the totality of the best they have to offer." Those who support the Christian faith find fulfillment in Christ.

Judaism. Fundamentally, the Jews related righteousness to the TORAH. A person was righteous in proportion to his obedience and conformity. In the intertestamental period the Pharisees were in the ascendancy, and their meticulous obedience is reflected in the Gospels, where they are the objects of Jesus' fiercest invective. Unfortunately, Jesus' attack on the Pharisees is thought to apply equally to JUDAISM in its subsequent history. The popular Christian position condemns Judaism for its legalism. This is to be blind to the great development of Judaism following the beginning of the Christian era. Such an attitude is superficial when one takes seriously the great spirits who arose and even now appear in Judaism. Righteousness, according to the Jews, never lost its OT interpretation of righteousness in relationships. Righteousness always meant and still does mean for the Jew, not merely the following of the rigid letter of the law nor a ritual holiness tied down to a sacred scroll; more than most, the Jews were concerned with efforts toward self-sanctification. They were concerned with character and good living, but they never lost sight of equity as well as law, or of the mercy and longsuffering reflected in the Psalms that have given heart to Judaism in every generation. Righteousness in Judaism, from the Christian viewpoint, lacks only one thing; namely, the necessity of the righteousness of God imparted to us through faith in Christ.

Buddhism. Buddha is the "Savior" for Hinduism, and as such, offers the best way of salvation possible to that subtle and confused faith. If one begins with the wheel of life, in which a person is caught eternally; and if one believes in the transmigration of souls, by which the unfortunate human being keeps returning to life over and over again;

and if one accepts life as miserable, as it is easy for a Hindu to do; and if one is never sure whether acts in this life are sufficient or proper enough to raise or lower one's entrance into life the next time around—what can be done to rescue such a person? Strange to Western ears is the salvation offered by Buddha, namely a careful discipline in this life, not to improve one's condition in the next life, but to assure his complete escape from the wheel of existence. Salvation means to be blotted out or to lose oneself in the vast ocean of being. Buddhism is basically a life-denying religion. The solution to life is to escape it, either by exercises in mysticism now or through a break from existence at death. Whereas Christianity says, "This is the victory that has overcome the world" (1 Jn. 5:4), Buddha would say, "This is the victory that *escapes* the world." Where, then, is the place for righteousness? Theoretically, at least, there is no place. Actually, and practically, Buddhism teaches that one must align himself with the order of the universe—that wrongdoing leads to punishment and right conduct leads to reward. Such teachings, however, are merely for the tyro in the faith or the unconverted person. For the mature Buddhist, works of righteousness have no meaning in the final renunciation of life.

Egyptian religion. It is not surprising that the Egyptian concept of righteousness is at least akin to that of the ancient Hebrews. Moses was educated in all the arts of the Egyptians at the time when they were a world power. There was in ancient Egyptian religion a keen appreciation of the final judgment based on righteousness, truth, and justice. The righteous person was one who lived according to truth and justice. More surprising was their great emphasis on generosity, kindness, deference to superiors, and hospitality. Perhaps the odd emphasis, although characteristic of Egyptian theology, was a whole series of demands with reference to the care of the dead. This is a striking difference in the Egyptian viewpoint which does not find its way into other religions, with the possible exception of Confucianism, which, however, is concerned more with ancestor worship than with the eternal felicity of the dead.

Islam. Righteousness is looked upon in the usual way: concern for one's character, honesty in human relationships, and a serious approach to one's own rights and the rights of others. These things are highly regarded in the lands dominated by the religion of Islam, but find very little place in their writings. Righteousness is tested out primarily in justice, and this justice is directed toward social action. Two things characterize the Islamic approach: (1) Righteousness expressed in justice is a concern primarily toward those who are of the same tribe or religion; this reflects something of the early OT approach. (2) Questions of righteousness and justice have a way among the Muslims of becoming vaguely discolored by primary considerations for good manners, "white lies," or any action governed by the belief that the end justifies the means. At first glance, Islamic righteousness looks like the same rigorism of righteousness reflected by the Jew and his Torah, or the Christian Puritan and his Decalogue, but such considerations as hospitality can well work havoc with awkward and austere demands of the law. Generosity, chivalry, and heroism seem more important to the Muslim, especially where family and tribe cloud the issues, than the absolute demands of the law.

(See further J. Denney, *Studies in Theology* [1902], 109–24; A. H. Strong, *Systematic Theology*, 3 vols. [1907–09], 1:290–95; A. R. Gordon et al., *ERE*, 9:780–92; N. H. Snaith, *The Distinctive Ideas of the Old Testament* [1946], 111–12; A. Nygren, *Commentary on Romans* [1949], 9ff.; W. M. Ramsay, *Basic Christian Ethics* [1950], 2–24; J. Ziesler, *The Meaning of Righteousness in Paul: A Linguistic and Theological Enquiry* [1972]; B. Przybylski, *Righteousness in Matthew and His World of Thought* [1980]; H. G. Reventlow and Y. Hoffman, eds., *Justice and Righteousness: Biblical Themes and Their Influence* [1992]; H. Gossai, *Justice, Righteousness, and the Social Critique of the Eighth-Century Prophets* [1993]; A. K. Grieb, *The Story of Romans: A Narrative Defense of God's Righteousness* [2002]; *ABD*, 5:724–73; *NIDOTTE*, 3:744–69; *NIDNTT*, 3:352–77.) A. H. LEITCH

Righteousness, Teacher of. See DEAD SEA SCROLLS VI.

Rimmon (deity) rim′uhn (רִמּוֹן *H8235*, "pomegranate," possibly an alteration of Akk. *Rammānu*, "the thunderer"). An Aramean representation of HADAD, the god of storm, rain, and thunder. In SYRIA (ARAM) this god is called BAAL that is, the lord par excellence, and to the Assyrians he was known as Rammānu, "the thunderer." J. Gray noted: "The identity of Rimmon with Hadad … is confirmed by the fact that 'Hadad' occurs as an element in the theophoric name Ben-hadad borne by several kings of Syria, and Tabrimmon, the father of Ben-hadad, the contemporary of Asa of Judah" (*IDB*, 4:99). NAAMAN, the commander of the Aramean army, worshiped in the temple of this deity at DAMASCUS (2 Ki. 5:17–19). D. J. Wiseman concluded: "The temple [of Rimmon] was probably on the site in Damascus [subsequently] occupied by the Roman temple of Zeus, whose emblem, like Rimmon's, was a thunderbolt. The famous Umayyad mosque now stands there" (*NBD*, 1021). See also HADAD RIMMON.　　　　B. H. WALTKE

Rimmon (person) rim´uhn רִמּוֹן *H8233*, "pomegranate"). A Benjamite of BEEROTH whose two sons, BAANAH and RECAB, guerrilla captains, assassinated SAUL's son, ISH-BOSHETH (2 Sam. 4:2–9).
　　　　B. H. WALTKE

Rimmon (place) rim´uhn רִמּוֹן *H8234*, "pomegranate"). A common place name that presumably reflects the existence of pomegranate trees in the respective locations. The name is also used as a compound (see EN RIMMON; GATH RIMMON; RIMMON PEREZ).

(1) A town in the NEGEV by the border of EDOM at first assigned to the tribe of JUDAH (Josh. 15:32) and later assigned to SIMEON (Josh. 19:7 [KJV, "Remmon"]; 1 Chr. 4:32). In these texts Rimmon is preceded by AIN, and some believe these two names should be read as one; the reference is probably to EN RIMMON, a village resettled after the EXILE (Neh. 11:29). According to Zech. 14:10, Rimmon marked the S extremity of the land, to be turned into a plain with Jerusalem towering over it when Yahweh comes. Its location is uncertain, but some scholars identify it with modern Tell Khuweilifeh (Tel Ḥalif), some 9.5 mi. NNE of BEERSHEBA; the nearby site of Khirbet Umm er-Rammamin may preserve the name. (See *NEAEHL*, 4:1284–85, s.v. "Rimmon, Ḥorvat ")

(2) A town along the NE border of the tribe of ZEBULUN (Josh. 19:13; KJV, "Remmon-methoar," taking the difficult word *hammĕtō'ār* ["which curved"?] as part of the name). This city was assigned to the Levites descended from MERARI (1 Chr. 6:77, where it is called "Rimono" [*rimmônô H8237*]; the parallel passage, Josh. 21:35, reads *dimnâ*, probably a scribal error for *rimmōnâ* [see DIMNAH]). This Rimmon is located on the S edge of the Sahl el-Baṭṭof (Valley of Bet Netofa), at modern Rummaneh, a village 6 mi. NNE of NAZARETH.

The area around "the rock of Rimmon," usually identified with the modern-day village of Rammun.

(3) Six hundred survivors of the Benjamites took refuge for four months at "the rock of Rimmon" when pursued after the slaughter at GIBEAH (Jdg. 20:45, 47; 21:13); this Gibeah is thought by some to be the same as GEBA (modern Jebaʿ, which is c. 3 mi. NE of the site usually thought to be Gibeah of Benjamin/Saul, namely, Tell el-Ful). Ever since E. Robinson identified the rock of Rimmon with modern Rammun (*Biblical Researches in Palestine, Mount Sinai and Arabia Petraea*, 3 vols. [1841], 1:440), most scholars have followed his lead. Rammun is located on a lofty, conical chalk hill c. 6 mi. NNE of Jebaʿ and 3 mi. E of BETHEL. This hill is visible in all directions, protected by ravines on most sides, and contains many caves. Some have argued, however, that the narrative suggests a location in a wilderness area closer to Gibeah and that the hill where Rammun sits would probably not be described as a "rock" (cf. *ISBE* rev. [1979–88], 4:196; *ABD*, 5:773–74). Alternate proposals include a cave in Wadi es-Suweiniṭ (c. 1 mi. E of Jebaʿ and 1 mi. S of MICMASH) and a rocky plateau 4 mi. E of Rammun. (A few scholars have thought that the word for "pomegranate tree" in 1 Sam. 14:2 is in fact a reference to the rock of Rimmon. In addition, the NRSV, following an old conjecture, reads "He has gone up from Rimmon" in Isa. 10:27; see discussion in H. Wildberger, *Isaiah 1–12: A Commentary* [1991], 447.)   B. H. WALTKE

Rimmon, rock of. See RIMMON (PLACE) #3.

Rimmono ri-moh′nuh (רִמּוֹנוֹ *H8237*, "pomegranate"). A city within the tribal territory of ZEBULUN that was assigned to the Levites descended from MERARI (1 Chr. 6:77). See RIMMON (PLACE) #2.

Rimmon Perez rim′uhn-pee′riz (רִמֹּן פֶּרֶץ *H8236*, "pomegranate breach," probably referring to a pass where POMEGRANATE trees were found). KJV Rimmon-parez. One of the stopping places of the Israelites in their wilderness journey (Num. 33:19–20). It was located between Rithmah and Libnah, but the precise location of all these places (prob. somewhere in the general area of PARAN) is unknown.

ring. A circular ornament worn mainly on the finger. Rings were used in great antiquity, as archaeolo-

Gold ring of Tutankhamen of Egypt found at Tell el-ʿAjjul (enlarged impression on the right).

gists have discovered among Assyrian, Babylonian, and Egyptian artifacts. The PATRIARCHS probably wore them. Rings for costume were usually of SILVER or GOLD, but BRONZE rings were added to these in furniture. The SIGNET ring, probably the earliest form, may have been used first to replace the neck cord in bearing the SEAL (Gen. 38:18; the Heb. for "seal" here, *ḥōtām H2597*, is used later with reference to the signet ring worn on a finger on the right hand, Jer. 22:24). The Egyptians, who used rings in profusion, wore them on the finger. PHARAOH gave his signet ring to JOSEPH as a symbol of authority (*ṭabbaʿat H3192*, Gen. 41:42). Ahasuerus (XERXES) gave his to HAMAN to seal a royal decree (Esth. 3:10, 12; later it was taken from him and given to MORDECAI, 8:2, 8, 10). Seals were of a variety of emblems, such as lion, bull, scarab, alligator, and royal designs. (Cf. also Aram. *ʿizqâ H10536*, Dan. 6:17.)

A costly ring was of special importance to royalty, nobility, and social station (Jas. 2:2; Gk. *chrysodaktylios G5993*, "gold ring"). The returning prodigal received a ring from his father as a symbol of dignity (Lk. 15:22; *daktylion G1234*). Besides finger rings, EARRINGS also were worn by women and children (Gen. 35:4; Exod. 32:2), as discovered at GEZER, MEGIDDO, and TAANACH. Nose rings (Heb. *nezem H5690*) were also quite popular among feminine paraphernalia (Gen. 24:22, 30, 47; Isa. 3:21; see NOSE JEWELS).

The Hebrew term *ṭabbaʿat* also occurs numerous times with reference to the ornaments made for the TABERNACLE (Exod. 25:12 et al.): MOSES gave instructions for their use on the ARK OF THE COVENANT, the CURTAINS, the BREASTPIECE and EPHOD of the high priest, and the ALTARS of incense and burnt offerings. In addition, rings could be used as a medium of exchange. See further JEWELS AND PRECIOUS STONES. G. B. FUNDERBURK

ringstraked. An archaic English term meaning "marked with circular stripes." It is used by the KJV to describe the marks on the livestock that became JACOB's while working for his uncle LABAN (Gen. 30:35, 39, 40; 31:8, 10, 12). Modern versions have "streaked" or "striped."

Rinnah rin´uh (רִנָּה *H8263*, prob. "jubilation"). Son of Shimon and descendant of JUDAH (1 Chr. 4:20).

Riphath ri´fath (רִיפַת *H8196*, meaning unknown). Son of GOMER and grandson of JAPHETH (Gen. 10:3; in 1 Chr. 1:6 the MT has "Diphath," evidently a scribal error due to the similarity between the Heb. consonants ד and ר). His name, like those of his brothers ASHKENAZ and TOGARMAH, appears to be non-Semitic and probably Anatolian. Riphath has been identified with the Riphaean mountains (Knobel, who identified the latter with the Carpathian range in the NE of Dacia), the river Rhebas in Bithynia (Bochart), the Rhibii, a people living eastward of the Caspian Sea (Schulthess), and the Ripheans or Riphasians, the ancient name of the Paphlagonians (Jos. *Ant.* 1.6.1 §126). This last view is favored by their contiguity with Ashkenaz, that is, the SCYTHIANS. (See *A Dictionary of the Bible*, ed. W. Smith [1863], 1045.) B. K. WALTKE

Rissah ris´uh (רִסָּה *H8267*, derivation uncertain). A stopping place in the wilderness wanderings of the Israelites (Num. 33:21–22). It was between Libnah and Kehelathah, but the location of these places is unknown.

Rithmah rith´muh (רִתְמָה *H8414*, possibly "[place of the] broom trees"). A stopping place in the wilderness wanderings of the Israelites (Num. 33:18–19). It was located between HAZEROTH (possibly ʿAin Khadra, c. 30 mi. NE of Jebel Musa) and RIMMON PEREZ (unknown). Proposals for the identification of Rithmah include a valley E of AQABAH named er-Retame and a wadi S of KADESH BARNEA named Abu Retemat (see NUMBERS, BOOK OF VII.C).

river. The lands of the Bible include the two great areas of riverine civilization of the ancient world—those of the NILE and the EUPHRATES. In these regions, where the river was the life-giver and was worshiped as such, it formed the main geographical feature in the consciousness of the people. It is not surprising that the Bible sometimes refers to the Euphrates simply as "the River" (Josh. 24:3; Ps. 72:8; et al.). Hence the basic image of the river as a source of LIFE, and consequently of comfort and PEACE, which is so frequently encountered in Scripture (e.g., Isa. 48:18; 66:12).

PALESTINE never possessed a riverine civilization comparable to those of the great valleys to the N and S of it. The JORDAN is too small in volume, and too entrenched in its deep valley, to provide the kind of irrigation AGRICULTURE that supported EGYPT or MESOPOTAMIA. Indeed, in biblical times

Key rivers in the Promised Land.

the valley of the Jordan was sparsely inhabited, filled with dense vegetation, and the home of wild animals. Only in Ezekiel's vision does there appear a river large enough to flow down into the Jordan rift and support widespread cultivation (Ezek. 47): a river of life entering the DEAD SEA at the precise point where the Jordan—so often the Bible's symbolic river of death—enters it in reality, at a point due E of the temple in Jerusalem. The same visionary image reappears in the NT (Rev. 22).

Once the Israelites left Egypt and its stable civilization by the Nile, rivers appear more often as boundaries or as milestones in their career than as a source of satisfaction or supply. In an age when there were no bridges, the crossing of even so relatively minor a river as the Jordan was a major hazard, in the case of the Israelites requiring divine intervention (Josh. 3). Once the people were across the river, they were in a sense cut off from their past: even to return briefly to the E bank of Jordan they would most probably have had to wait for the low water season. In the same way, Joshua reminded them of the step their ancestor ABRAHAM had taken when he crossed "the River" (24:3, 14–15, meaning the Euphrates) on his way to the land of promise; it was a symbolic step, cutting him off from a past to which he would never return.

The Jordan, with its E-bank tributaries, forms the only major river system of Palestine, although the mountains of LEBANON to the N feed numerous streams from their snowfields. Many of the smaller rivers of the land flow only seasonally. See BROOK; VALLEY. J. H. PATERSON

river of Egypt. See EGYPT, RIVER OF.

Rizia ri-zi′uh (רִצְיָא H8359, possibly "pleasing"). Son of Ulla and descendant of ASHER, included among the "heads of families, choice men, brave warriors and outstanding leaders" (1 Chr. 7:39–40).

Rizpah riz′puh (רִצְפָּה H8366, "glowing coal"). Daughter of Aiah and a concubine of SAUL (2 Sam. 3:7). After the death of Saul, his son ISH-BOSHETH, now king in name only, accused ABNER of sleeping with Rizpah. If true, this act would have amounted to a claim to the throne (cf. 2 Sam. 16:20–22; 1 Ki. 2:22). In response to this probably false accusation, Abner promptly proffered the northern kingdom to DAVID (c. 997 B.C.).

Later (c. 970) a three years' famine was divined to the displeasure of Yahweh at the slaughter of the Gibeonites by Saul in violation of the covenant Israel had made with them (2 Sam. 21:1; cf. Josh. 9:3, 15–20). When David inquired of the Gibeonites what atonement he should make, they refused monetary compensation in accordance with the Mosaic law (Num. 35:33), but demanded seven sons of Saul to expose before Yahweh. The king gave them two of Rizpah's sons and five of MERAB's (2 Sam. 21:7–8; the MT has MICHAL instead of Merab). Then Rizpah spread sackcloth on the rock—a sign that the land repented—and began her heroic vigil by the bodies, keeping off the birds and beasts of prey (cf. Ps. 79:2) from the beginning of barley harvest (c. April) until the anger of Yahweh relented and "the rain poured down from the heavens" (2 Sam. 21:10; it is unclear whether the reference is to an unusual late spring RAIN or to the "early rains" of the fall). For her devotion David had their bones with the bones of Saul and Jonathan buried in the tomb of Saul's father, Kish (vv. 11–14). B. K. WALTKE

roads.
  I. Roads in antiquity
    A. Archaeological remains of roads
    B. Trade and commerce on ancient roads
    C. Defense and extension of roads
    D. Religious and political uses of roads
  II. Roads in OT times
    A. Terms
    B. International roads
    C. Internal roads
  III. Roads in NT times
    A. Terms
    B. Persian and Hellenistic roads
    C. Roman roads
    D. Herodian roads
    E. Internal roads
    F. International roads

I. Roads in antiquity. The oldest trails ever found are the tracks of ancient hunters following

ROADS

and pursuing migrating game. The earliest domestication of sheep had certainly occurred by 9000 B.C., and the ground beaten down by continual moving of the flocks from fold to pasture has left primitive road beds in the oldest village sites. The establishment of townships, which marks the Neolithic era in the ANE, also brought about the purposeful improvement of road surfaces, even though this may have been nothing more than the leveling of natural faults and the removal of large stones. There is no doubt that ancient prehistoric peoples did trade goods and materials over long distances. These routes followed the natural courses of travel, rivers, streams, valleys, and plains. There can be no doubt, however, that ideas and artifacts were handled over long distances by nomadic groups for many millennia. By the time writing and record-keeping spread across the ANE, the notions and habits of road building were already well developed. The nation-building process that arose soon after the Neolithic era was extended throughout the Eurasian land mass by an international system of roads. With the centralization of authority and economic power, which produced the archaic religious state, road technology became basic to survival. In time the building and upkeep of roads became a central task of government and passed into the realm of juridics, philosophy, and literature.

A. Archaeological remains of roads. Artifactual evidence of roads falls into four classes: (1) road beds; (2) fill; (3) piles of materials for building beds and fill; (4) markers and distance posts. Roadbeds were originally compacted by the continual passage of feet either human or animal, the single innovation being the driving of domestic flocks over a path or precinct. The "threshing floors" of the patriarchal period (cf. Gen. 50:10; Heb. *gōren* H1755) were compacted in this fashion. Fills were composed of transports of material from former buildings of clay or stone. The erection of wayside markers to indicate lines and distances is a complex subject. There is no doubt that they must have had a cultic significance. Roadside shrines are known from almost all ancient cultures. The PILLARS or stone cairns erected by the PATRIARCHS were no doubt similar in nature (Gen. 28:18 et al.; Heb. *maṣṣēbâ* H5167). Elaborate road markers with extensive inscriptions came into use after the beginning of the 2nd millennium B.C. Greek and Roman sources frequently mention such constructions. It is exceedingly difficult to trace a mere dirt track by archaeological means unless it alters the speciation or condition of the plants growing over it. In such cases it may be detected by aerial photography. A few ancient tracks were built over repeatedly through the centuries and may be detected by the course of modern roadways.

B. Trade and commerce on ancient roads. It is now supposed that the making and use of TOOLS is one of the surest signs of human civilization. This was the main impetus to the TRADE in basic materials and simple manufactures that sprung up in antiq-

Three key roadways in the Promised Land.

A section of the famous silk road in Turkey, a route used in ancient times for trade and commerce.

uity. Lapis lazuli, gold, silver, electrum, iron, amber, and tin were probably the earliest trade goods. There is clear evidence that some of these items were traded from group to group across Europe and the Middle E by the time of the last glaciation. It may be safely assumed that the germinal collections of human groups were in the sheltered areas below the mountains and around the shores of the great fresh-water lakes of the Eurasian continent. From Switzerland through Palestine and Turkey and on across Russia a number of these bodies of water are located. Certainly Neanderthals and their predecessors foraged and hunted from one such locus to another, virtually following the same track with each season. The similarity of Paleolithic art and tool-making industries across this region demonstrates the degree of trade. With the rise of the Proto-Euphratean townships, barter turned to commerce. The rivers were not sufficient to carry trade across the deserts and the hills of N Iraq, and so ancient caravan trails were developed. Generally the northern tribes traded animals, asses, horses, and mules to the southerners for the products of the River Valley civilizations.

C. Defense and extension of roads. The lack of natural boundaries and defenses for overland TRAVEL rendered the CARAVANS vulnerable to attacks from bands of marauding tribes people. The earliest political unions of Sumerians and Semites had to deal with defense and extension of the roads. To defend a road and the terrain adjacent meant to set up garrisons along its length. To punish and discourage raiders necessitated extending military expeditions ever farther from the homeland.

The earliest evidence for prepared roadbeds and construction over them has been found in S Mesopotamia and in two of the Minoan centers of culture. In both cases there was no planning of the town, only the paving over of the crisscrossing streets around the market plaza that stood in front of the palace or temple complex. The ever-needed task of widening and repairing the processional and market streets is frequently recorded in CUNEIFORM tablets of all ages. There is substantial extrabiblical textual evidence of transport and travel in the ANE. Sumerian, Babylonian, Egyptian, and Hittite myths and legends all involve characters who go wayfaring, in fact this is the common literary device, as in the GILGAMESH cycle, to connect discrete legends into a literary framework. Texts from Egypt tell of trips to Syria-Palestine (e.g., Sinuhe, c. 1960 B.C.), and tablets from Assyria speak of road-building corvées sent in advance of the army (e.g., Tiglath-Pileser I, c. 1115 B.C.).

Although ridgeways, trackways, and fords were continually improved after the horse and cavalry were introduced about 2000 B.C., paved roads and streets were still confined to towns. The processional streets of ASSYRIA were set on roadbeds of gravel that were overlaid with burnt brick. A mastic or bitumen substance was employed as a binder. Carefully dressed and sized slabs of flagstone or gypsum were fitted between heavy curbing to form a street surface. In many towns cart tracks were cut into the street surface to act as guides, almost like rails, which guided the heavily loaded ox carts through the narrow streets. These grooves are normally 4–5 ft. in width, providing a two-ox gauge standard. Log or plank roads were suitable in areas where there was sufficient timber and a cold enough winter to retard rotting, but only in the most northern areas of Palestine were such roadways possible. STONE, the ever-present material of ancient humans, was the most widely utilized.

Across the great deserts of SINAI and ARABIA there were no roads at all, only well-worn caravan tracks. Bridges and causeways of compacted stones were widely built around towns; and the foundations of such in and near Jerusalem, Jericho, Hazor, and elsewhere are no doubt from the 2nd millennium B.C. Since water travel was limited to the rivers and coastal navigation until the time of Rome and Carthage, no open quays fed by networks of roads, a common Roman plan, have been unearthed. No doubt the coming of the CART and afterward the CHARIOT and the mounted horseman impelled the improvement of roads. The exceedingly rough terrain of the Palestinian hill country retarded this technical development, just as the lack of natural harbors never allowed Palestine to be a natural theater for Greek colonization or trade.

D. Religious and political uses of roads. The religious texts of the Sumerians, Akkadians, Babylonians, Elamites, Persians, Egyptians, and Hittites all include details of religious processions and festivals in which the idol of the city-cult was manifest to the populace. Since the precincts of the various gods were clearly defined in the archaic religious states, the traveler was at a grave disadvantage. This was the more perilous because of the frequent attacks by raiders and highwaymen common to all the thinly populated areas of the ANE. It is for this reason that the patriarchs traveled in small squads of armed men (Gen. 14:14–15).

In the early dynastic inscriptions from Mesopotamia, the maintenance and safety of the roads was a boon from the tutelary deity; it was also a sign of the king's prowess and a surety of his legitimacy to rule (e.g., SENNACHERIB's boasting of the roads he built in NINEVEH). However, the excavations at NIMRUD and elsewhere demonstrate that these paved and arched roads did not proceed far beyond the city walls. The W Semitic ruler Azitawadda speaks in terms of security on the roads: "In my times there were in all the borders of the Plain of Adana, from the rising of the sun to the setting, peaceful pursuits [*lit.*, work of spinning] even in places where previously a man was fearful to walk, but in my days even a woman could go, through the favor of Ba'al and the gods" (Phoen. and Hitt. bilingual from Karatepe, c. 9th cent. B.C.).

Although the Assyrians and their allies certainly improved and employed roads for military transport, the principal motivation for land travel beyond the narrow confines of the TIGRIS and EUPHRATES toward the W was the Old Babylonian *tamkārum* or merchant, whose trading posts were spread across the ANE no later than the early 2nd millennium. However, it was the HURRIANS and the HITTITES who seemed to have held their confederacies together by the use of Babylonian cuneiform writing and military roads. It was the Greek cities of the coast of ASIA MINOR where town planning and access roads were first tried; and it was the Persian royal house which instituted road and postal systems as necessities for administration. In the closing centuries of the ancient world, Rome was to embrace both innovations and weld from the ancient states a world empire. Ultimately the processional street of the capital served not only to disseminate the state cult, but also to draw pilgrims from across the empire into it. This simple situation did as much as anything to erode the archaic religious states and bring about the rise of individualism in the Hellenistic age.

II. Roads in OT times. Roads play an important part in the narrative and instruction of the OT. The water courses of Palestine are in no case suitable for the purposes of trade or conquest, and its position between Anatolia to the N and Egypt to the S determined the central highland route and the coastal route to be the most heavily traveled in the country.

A. Terms. In keeping with the Semitic custom of using relatively few adjectives and a great many specific nouns, the OT references to roads contain many terms usually derived from the topographic features through which the road or track passed. Hebrew *ʾōraḥ* H784 appears over fifty times in the OT, almost exclusively in poetic passages (e.g., Gen. 49:17). Since at no point is it used in any passage involving the construction of roads or the preparation of roadbuilding materials, the meaning must be limited to "path" and "pathway." The verbal form *ʾāraḥ* H782, meaning "to be on the road, to wander," is found in a few passages (e.g., Job 34:8); its participle occurs in the OT exclusively in the sense of "wanderer" or "wayfarer" (Jdg. 19:17 et al.).

The most frequent term, *derek* H2006, appears over 700 times in the OT, most often in the simple sense of "way" (Gen. 3:24 et al.). By extension the term means "direction" (1 Ki. 8:44 et al.) and "distance" (Gen. 30:36 et al.). The verbal development of the same root means variously "to tread down," "to march to some place," and is extended to mean "press down, bend down" (Jdg. 9:27 et al.). The noun is important in the biblical theology of the OT because of its use in the sense of "conduct" (Gen. 6:12) and "custom" (19:31). In ANE literature the idea of "road of life, philosophical and moral course of action" does occur. The most striking example of this type of usage is in the poem *Ludlul bēl nēmeqi*, "Who has learned the plan of the heavenly gods? Who knows the scheme of the Nether World? Where have mortals comprehended the road of the gods?" (W. White, *A Babylonian Anthology* [1966], 32ff.).

However, the fact that such language in the OT is an inherent part of the concept of SIN and RIGHTEOUSNESS demonstrates the vast difference between the biblical notion and those common in the cultures round about Israel. To wend one's way wickedly was a totally foreign notion to the ancient world. This is the reason for its being used in the introduction to the Psalms as the second degree of wickedness in which the ungodly delight (Ps. 1:1). The forsaking of the wicked way is at the center of the OT concept of REPENTANCE (Isa. 55:7–9 et al.). In the OT, the idea of turning down a road is used specifically of one's willful decision: "Leave this way, / get off this path, / and stop confronting us / with the Holy One of Israel" (30:11). In similar fashion, to follow the commands of the covenant God is to be taught in "his ways" and to "walk in his paths" (2:3). Moreover, the doctrines of dispersed people, wayfaring prophets, and a messenger-Messiah are found in the OT alone. The "way of the LORD" is of prime importance because it encompasses the route of MESSIAH (40:3–4 et al.).

The noun *môrād* H4618, "slope, precipice" (from the common verb *yārad* H3718, "to go down"), can be used of a "descent" taken by travelers: "on the road down from Beth Horon to Azekah" (Josh. 10:11; similarly Jer. 48:5; contrast *maʿăleh* H5090, "ascent" [from *ʿālā* H6590, "to go up"], 2 Sam. 15:30 NRSV et al.). The reference is possibly to wadis or dry valleys left on Palestinian hillsides by quick, seasonal floods; when these natural declinations were used as paths the term was generated. More common is the noun *mĕsillâ* H5019, "track, highway" (Num. 20:19 et al.; from *sālal* H6148, "to pile up," as in building a road [cf. Jer. 18:15]); it can also be used figuratively with reference to the course of the stars (Jdg. 5:20) and to the conduct of life (Prov. 16:17 et al.). Several other terms meaning "road" or "path" are used occasionally (cf. the lexical variety in Jer. 18:15).

B. International roads. Most of the road network from the E coast of the Mediterranean to the N TIGRIS Valley ran far to the N of Israel. Even the Assyrian invaders headed across the hinterlands of Syria before turning S just E of the springs of the Jordan and falling on the borders of Samaria. No doubt an early road ran through the Judean desert from the Jebusite fortress of Jerusalem down to the oasis of JERICHO. From there it probably ran over the desert to the cities of inner Jordan.

However, the three major international trade routes ran from N to S through the three zones of Palestine: the coastal plain, the central mountain range, and the Jordan Rift Valley. The first of these is referred to once as "the way of the sea" (Isa. 9:1). This road ran the length of the country from TYRE southward through Acco and MEGIDDO, APHEK to

The key international road in ancient times known as the Via Maris (Way of the Sea) came along the NW shore of the Sea of Galilee through the plain N of Magdala. (View to the N, with Mount Hermon at the top left; Magdala is off the bottom right.)

Joppa and Gaza, and finally across the salt water marshes to the borders of Egypt. A main trunk ran off this route to the NE through the wide plain of Jezreel and on up to Damascus and then to the Euphrates. It is thought that the term "the way of the sea" meant not that the route followed the seacoast but that it was the way "to the sea." Two Egyptian sources list the towns along this route: the earlier one is the series of bas-reliefs of Seti I (c. 1381 B.C.), while the later is the 19th-dynasty papyrus of Hori (Papyrus Anastasi I), both of which give reliable details of the roadway. They follow the lead of the much earlier *Tale of Sinuhe*, which describes it as "the way of Horus." The towns of the more northern sector of the sea road were listed in the inscriptions of Thutmose III (c. 1490) and often were copied or rewritten in the annals of later Pharaohs. Assyrian sources from Sennacherib (c. 704) list the cities of the road, and Megiddo its hub. In later times it became known as the Via Maris.

The second great road, the king's highway (*derek hammelek*, Num. 20:17, 21:22), ran the length of the Transjordan highlands. It was used for caravan travel from S Arabia to Damascus. It is alluded to as the route of the invading Elamite princes (Gen. 14:5–7), and the southern section is mentioned on the Israelite march to Moab from Kadesh Barnea (Num. 20). Most of the highland towns were strung out along its length, but the terrain crisscrossed by deep wadis and high hills was not easily invaded and so few campaigns were fought along its length. Two periods of flourishing towns were marked along this route, at the end of the 3rd and early 2nd millennium and again from the 18th cent. to the beginning of the Israelite Bronze Age.

The innermost series of roads along and across the Jordan is marked only by the remains of settlements mostly on the W side of the river. Unlike either of the other two great roads, this network was used primarily for internal travel. Its course from Hazor through Jerusalem and then to Beersheba marked it as the path of pilgrimage to Jerusalem and the chief highway of Jewish trade. The section near Bethlehem is called "the way to Ephrath" (Gen. 35:19; 48:7).

C. Internal roads. Some roads that linked the various regions of Palestine crossed longitudinally through natural valleys or gaps in the mountains between the two great international routes. Specific routes in the N and S had been avenues of commerce in the most ancient times for the Canaanites in the N and the Midianites in the S. These were the routes leading out of the central hilly country into the plains and desert. Needless to say, many routes must have tied together the small towns of the NEGEV but are simply omitted from the written records extant. The following list is based on the work of Y. Aharoni (and summarized in his book, *The Land of the Bible: A Historical Geography*, rev. ed. [1979], 57–62, and map 3 on p. 44).

(1) "The road to Beth Haggan" (2 Ki. 9:27), a segment of a road that goes from SHECHEM to the Plain of JEZREEL via the ascent to GUR.

(2) "The road toward Bashan" (Num. 21:33; Deut. 3:1), actually a northern section of the king's highway, from HESHBON to ASHTAROTH.

(3) "The way [NIV, from the direction] of the soothsayers' tree" (Jdg. 9:37; the NRSV and NJPS have, "from the direction of Elon-meonenim"), a minor local route near Shechem.

(4) "The way of the plain" (2 Sam. 18:23), a Transjordanian road that ran parallel to the Jordan River, going through such towns as Adam (see ADAM (PLACE)) and SUCCOTH.

(5) "The way to the Jordan" (Josh. 2:7 NRSV), a road that went from Jericho to Transjordan.

(6) "The Ophrah road" (1 Sam. 13:17 NJPS), a local route from MICMASH through OPHRAH and on to BAAL HAZOR.

(7) "The way of the wilderness" (Josh. 8:15; Jdg. 20:42 KJV), leading from BETHEL to the vicinity of Jericho; probably the same as "the way of the wilderness of Gibeon" (2 Sam. 2:24 KJV).

(8) "The way to Beth Horon" (1 Sam. 13:18; cf. KJV), a steep road leading to GIBEON and JERUSALEM; it was the northernmost road ascending into the Judean hill country, thus referred to also as "the ascent/descent of Beth Horon" (Josh. 10:10–11).

(9) "The way of the Arabah" (2 Sam. 4:7; 2 Ki. 25:4; Jer. 39:4; 52:7), that is, the familiar road from Jerusalem to Jericho of the NT. It crossed through the narrow valley of dunes to the Pass of ADUMMIM (Josh. 15:7; 18:17), and on into Transjordan.

(10) "The way of Beth Shemesh" (1 Sam. 6:12 KJV; cf. v. 9), the western sector of a road going up to Jerusalem via the Valley of SOREK and the Valley of Rephaim (see REPHAIM, VALLEY OF); possibly the same as "the road to Timnah" (Gen. 38:14).

(11) "The way to Beth Jeshimoth" (Josh. 12:3 KJV), a Transjordanian road that connected BETH JESHIMOTH and HESHBON; it joined the road from Jericho.

(12) "The route of the nomads" (Jdg. 8:11; KJV, "the way of them that dwelt in tents"; NRSV, "the caravan route"), probably referring to the Wadi Sirḥan, a bedouin route going E from the king's highway.

(13) "The desert road of Moab" (Deut. 2:8), evidently a route E of the king's highway and parallel to it, but joining it at RABBAH (AMMON).

(14) "The way of Edom" (2 Ki. 3:20 KJV), taken by some authors to be a mistake in the MT for the longer form of the name, "the way of the desert of Edom" (v. 8 Heb.). The question asked by JEHORAM, however, indicates that a choice of routes was open to the allied kings; parallel longitudinal routes are in evidence in these and similar passages.

(15) "The road to Horonaim" (Isa. 15:5; cf. Jer. 48:5), which extended from ZOAR to KIR HARESETH.

(16) "The road to Atharim" (Num. 21:1), extending from KADESH BARNEA N through AROER to ARAD, and continuing on to HEBRON (see ATHARIM).

(17) "The road to Shur" (Gen. 16:7), taken by HAGAR on the way to Egypt (see SHUR).

(18) "The way to the hill country of the Amorites" (Deut. 1:19 NRSV), a caravan route connecting Kadesh Barnea with the ARABAH.

(19) "The Mount Seir road" (Deut. 1:2), possibly part of one of the great international highways, connecting the Sinai desert to Edom through ELATH.

III. Roads in NT times

A. Terms. Unlike the OT, the Greek NT has a very restricted vocabulary for "road" and the like (possibly reflecting the fact that the Greeks of classical antiquity were a seafaring rather than a caravaning people). Virtually the only noun used, common since Homeric times in all dialects, is *hodos* G3847, which appears nearly a hundred times in the NT, both literally (e.g., Mk. 11:8) and figuratively (e.g., Matt. 21:32). The term *trochia* G5579, meaning literally "wheel-track," occurs only once, and then in an OT citation that uses it in a figurative sense, "Make level paths for your feet" (in Heb. 12:13, quoting Prov. 12:13). The NT does use a variety of verbs to express such meanings as "go," "walk," "travel," and so forth. Special note should be taken of the common term *anabainō G326*, "to go up, ascend," used in particular of the ascent to Jerusalem, sometimes with a theological nuance (e.g., Lk. 19:28; cf. the "songs of ascents," Pss. 120–134, and see MUSIC VI.D).

B. Persian and Hellenistic roads. The fine road system inherited by the Herodian rulers was built by the Hellenistic rulers under Persian influence. Herodotus, Xenophon, and other Greek writers of the classical period found the efficiency of the Persian posts and their elaborate system of desert tracks to be a source of admiration. However, there is no evidence that the Persians of the Achaemenid regime ever actually built a "high" or paved road between towns. The archaeological evidence points to the fact that they paved only the royal and ceremonial avenues around the capital cities.

No Persian roads actually entered Palestine, but they went due W from Khorsabad to the northeasternmost tip of the Mediterranean and then on to Ephesus. The Hellenistic rulers utilized this main highway across the desert and added to it trunks connecting the Via Maris. The Persians continued the Babylonian practice of building roadways with burnt bricks and bituminous mortar. The inherent efficiency of the satrapical system, with its semi-autonomous governors, kept the transportation system in operation long after the central royal authority had been swept away. The Hellenists thus inherited a system after 322 B.C. which functioned well and which needed little attention if allowed to repair itself through tax levies. In Egypt the postal system was maintained up to Roman times. A road was built from ALEXANDRIA to the RED SEA. Even after the harbors on the coast of Turkey were abandoned, the roads still bore their share of traffic well into Byzantine times.

C. Roman roads. The origin of the Roman road technology lies in the mists of Etruscan antiquity. It is basic to Roman engineering that the rudiments of drainage, embanking, and paving were all well-developed before the Romans built their roads. The essence of the roads was the fact that

Roman milestone located along a road passing through the Shephelah of Judah.

they were designed and built with all three of these other aspects in consideration. Town planning, hilly terrain, and a sense of communal organization all combined to motivate the building of firm road beds with carefully graded paving. The web of Roman roads began in the 3rd cent. B.C. and spread out a little more each decade until it encompassed Europe, Britain, North Africa, Greece, and the Middle East. It was under AUGUSTUS that the roads of Syria-Palestine were paved for the usual Roman reasons: to drain the economic riches of the area by taxation and franchise, and to protect Roman interest against robbers and independent hill people. The executors of this Roman policy were the Herodians.

D. Herodian roads. Both the NT and JOSEPHUS bear witness to the building enterprises of HEROD the Great and his successors. The great TEMPLE in Jerusalem, the palaces in Galilee, and the many fortifications (e.g., MASADA) were built with Roman engineering and Jewish craftsmen. The magnificent royal causeway across the valley from the palace to the temple has been unearthed at its foundations by Israeli archaeologists. The plazas and palaces of the sea coast and the fortifications inland, all ordered by Herod, lend evidence to his fame and ability as a builder. However, it is implicit in the gospel narratives that Jesus and his disciples stuck to the footpaths and country tracks on foot, rather than travel the main roads. This can be deduced from the names of the hamlets and villages through which they passed. The towns in most cases have disappeared, and the actual courses of the paths can only be surmised.

E. Internal roads. The NT contains no road names but only general references, such as "the road—the desert road—that goes down from Jerusalem to Gaza" (Acts 8:26). Surely the roads mentioned in the OT were as a rule those traveled in NT times. The severity of the terrain is such that in many places no other ascent, descent, or passage is possible. The chief postcommonwealth development in Palestinian roads was in the area of GALILEE; none of the common places of Jesus' northern ministry are mentioned in the OT, and all the trackways and pathways are new. It was not until TRAJAN (A.D. 98–117) that the Jordanian road system was built and the bedouins employed as police. The Judea of Jesus' time was an underdeveloped rural area pressured by a mighty external empire that renovated, rebuilt, and exploited with relentless precision, holding materialism as its highest good. The OT economy and community perished from Palestine by being rendered obsolete.

F. International roads. The roads that brought Rome's imperial designs to Palestine were destined to carry the gospel out. The Roman army built in excess of 50,000 miles of roads in the area of Syria-Palestine and banished by the sword the robbers who had troubled Israel from patriarchal times. The Christians were not blind to this fact and many gave Roman statecraft its due: "The Romans have given the world peace, and we travel without fear along the roads and cross the seas wherever we wish" (Irenaeus, *Adv. Haer.* 4.30.3).

(See further G. A. Smith, *The Historical Geography of the Holy Land* [1894]; C. Skeel, *Travel in the First Century after Christ, with Special Reference to Asia Minor* [1901]; W. H. Burr, *Ancient and Modern Engineering* [1903]; W. M. Ramsay in *HDB*, 5:375–402; W. W. Mooney, *Travel Among the Ancient Romans* [1920]; M. P. Charlesworth, *Trade Routes and Commerce of the Roman Empire* [1924]; G. K. Chesterton, *The End of the Roman Road* [1924]; R. J. Forbes, *Notes on the History of Ancient Roads and Their Construction* [1934]; W. Andrae, *Alte Festrassen im Nahen Orient* [1941]; A. Salonen, *Die Landfahrzeuge des alten Mesopotamiens* [1951]; R. J. Forbes, *Studies in Ancient Technology*, 8 vols. [1955–64], 2:126–76; K. Miller, *Itineraria romana* [1964]; V. W. van Hagen, *The Roads That Led to Rome* [1967]; B. Isaac et al., *Roman Roads in Judaea*, 2 vols [1982–96]; D. A. French, *Roman Roads and Milestones of Asia Minor*, 2 vols. [1981–88]; D. A. Dorsey, *The Roads and Highways of Ancient Israel* [1991]; R. A. Staccioli, *The Roads of the Romans* [2003, valuable for its numerous photographs]; *ABD*, 5:776–77.) W. WHITE, JR.

robbery. See CRIMES AND PUNISHMENTS.

robe. A long loose outer garment, usually elegant and rich in texture, color, and style. A robe is therefore the dress of royalty and stately rank, ecclesiastical eminence, and social distinction. The primary term in Hebrew is *mĕʿîl H5077*, used for example of the robes worn by King SAUL (1 Sam. 24:11) and his son JONATHAN (18:4). The robe for religious rank was prescribed by MOSES, particularly for the PRIESTS (Exod. 28:4, 31, 34), a precedent that was followed by SAMUEL (1 Sam. 28:14). Other terms are used with reference to the "richly ornamented" robes worn by JOSEPH and by DAVID's daughter, TAMAR (Gen. 37:3; 2 Sam. 13:18; see SLEEVE), the royal robes of AHAB and JEHOSHAPHAT (1 Ki. 22:10), and those worn in the royal court of PERSIA (Esth. 5:1; 6:8–11; 8:15).

In the NT, the Greek term *stolē G5124* is used with reference to the garments worn by the SCRIBES and priests in Jesus' time (Mk. 12:38; Lk. 20:46). It was also the apparel of the angel at the empty tomb (Mk. 16:5) and of the angels at the ascension (Acts 1:10). In John's vision a robe is worn by the exalted Jesus (Rev. 1:13), and a white robe was given to each of the martyrs (6:11). A more general term, *himation G2668*, is used of the purple or scarlet robe put on Jesus, probably a cape or cloak such as worn by a king or general (Jn. 19:2; Matt. 27:31 [in v. 28, *chlamys G5948*, a military mantel]); the same word is used with reference to his "robe dipped in blood" (Rev. 19:13). See also DRESS.

G. B. FUNDERBURK

Robinson's Arch. Name given to a structural feature of the W wall of the Jerusalem TEMPLE. This arch, which is over 50 ft. wide and projects W out over the Tyropoeon Valley, is located 39 ft. N of the SW corner of the temple area; it spanned a paved road running along the foot of the Western Wall (see diagram under TEMPLE, JERUSALEM). "Four layers of large blocks have remained in the arch, which originally came to rest on a tremendous pier built parallel to the Western Wall and at a distance of about forty-two feet from it" (B. Mazar, *The Mountain of the Lord* [1975], 132). The earlier view that the arch was only the first of a series "has now been disproved completely"; rather, the arches graded downward in height and formed "part of a monumental stairway system" (ibid.; see reconstruction on p. 112 and photo opposite p. 128; cf. also J. Wilkinson, *Jerusalem as Jesus Knew It* [1978], 61, with illustrations 37, 61, 62; and the drawings in M. Ben-Dov, *Historical Atlas of Jerusalem* [2002], 109–10).

Coronel Charles Warren estimated the width of the span, then sank a shaft looking for the pier that would mark the other end of the arch. He located it c. 50 ft. from the temple wall. Between the pier and the wall he also located some of the voussoirs of the arch where they had fallen upon a contemporary paved street some 40 ft. below the bridge. After breaking through that street, Warren found a second paved street some 18 ft. still farther down, and upon it a voussoir from an earlier bridge (C. Warren and C. R. Conder, *Survey of Western Palestine*, 9 vols. [1881–88], 5.176–83). JOSEPHUS wrote that this earlier bridge was built by the HASMONEANS. They later destroyed it lest it be of assistance to POMPEY in his attack on the temple area in 63 B.C.

HEROD the Great erected a new bridge in connection with his rebuilding of the entire temple area. This bridge was destroyed with the temple itself in A.D. 70. The spring of the arch of that Herodian bridge in the temple wall is called Robinson's Arch. It is named after the great Palestine geographer Edward Robinson, who discovered it in 1838.

J. L. KELSO

This protrusion jutting out from the W wall of Herod's temple is known as Robinson's Arch; it is all that remains of a monumental stairway that led into the temple.

Roboam roh-boh´uhm. KJV NT form of REHOBOAM.

rock. The two Hebrew terms for "rock" are not easy to distinguish, but *selaʿ* H6152 often refers to a high, cliff-like feature, while *ṣûr* H7446 seems to indicate a crag or slab of rock. Both types of features abound in the Bible lands, where centuries of forest destruction and soil erosion have removed the vegetation cover even from those areas that originally possessed any. In particular, Israel in the desert wanderings for forty years must have spent much of their lives among the bare outcrops of the Wilderness of SINAI and southern PALESTINE. Within the land itself, the "bare bones" of rock are almost constantly visible in the landscape as the scarps and projections of the underlying limestones and sandstones, while the world-famous city of PETRA in EDOM was carved out of the rock—in this case the red Nubian sandstone.

As a result, the rocks of Palestine repeatedly play a part in the Bible story, and the book is also rich in metaphors that follow from the first biblical reference to God as "the Rock" (Deut. 32:4). At least three reasons may be adduced: (1) In the unsettled state of this region in OT times, it was a sensible precaution to use the natural defensive quality of rocky sites to build fortress cities. So great were the natural advantages of such sites for defense that many of these fortresses were to all intents impregnable, given the military techniques of the period; siege or treachery offered the only hopes of capture. (2) The rock offered shelter from the storm (whether actual or figurative). The limestones of Palestine are full of CAVES, and thus we find DAVID hiding from SAUL in the cave of ADULLAM (1 Sam. 22:1) or the rocks around EN GEDI (24:1–3). (3) The rock served as a source of water to Israel in the wilderness (Exod. 17:6; Num. 20:11). It is a well-known feature of limestone terrain that water seeps down through crevices to break out at unexpected points in the form of springs; God evidently guided Moses to points where this could take place.

The NT transfers the symbolic image of the OT to make Christ "the spiritual rock" from which his people drank (1 Cor. 10:4). Various rabbinic sources refer to a movable well in the form of a rock that followed the Israelites in the wilderness, although interpreters are divided regarding the relevance of this tradition for Paul's statement (see discussion by P. E. Enns in *BBR* 6 [1996]: 23–38). Some commentators have also suggested that when John reports the piercing of "Jesus' side with a spear, bringing a sudden flow of blood and water" (Jn. 19:34), he is alluding to MOSES' act of striking the rock on which God stood (Exod. 17:6; see G. M. Burge, *The Anointed Community: The Holy Spirit in the Johannine Tradition* [1987], 93–95). Just as in the wilderness that act caused physical water to flow and thus met the needs of God's people, so at the CRUCIFIXION the striking of God who had come in the flesh made possible the granting of living water—that is, the HOLY SPIRIT—to believers (cf. Jn. 1:1, 14; 4:10–14; 7:38–39).

J. H. PATERSON

rock badger. See CONEY.

Rock of Escape (of Separation). See SELA HAMMAHLEKOTH.

rocks. See STONES.

rod. A length of tree limb or bush stock, employed at first for support or weapon. It was fashioned distinctively for individual use, straight with a thick end or with the shepherd's crook. Little distinction is drawn between the Hebrew words used for "rod" or "staff." The term *maqqēl H5234* apparently meant

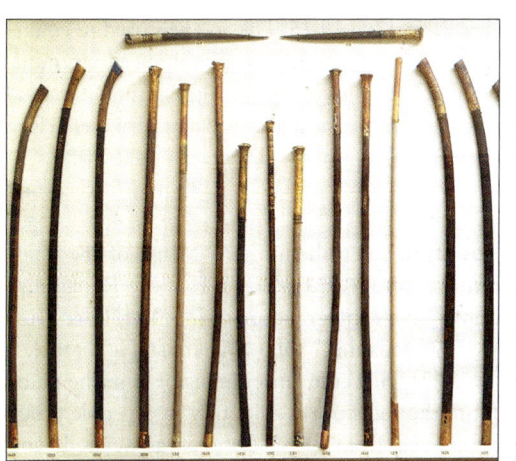

An assortment of rods found in Egyptian tombs.

"twig" or "branch" or "sucker," as that of the poplar which JACOB stripped in breeding cattle (Gen. 30:37–41) or of the almond which God used as an object lesson (Jer. 1:11). A more common word, *maṭṭeh H4751* (apparently from a root meaning "to stretch out, lengthen"), is most frequently used of a rod in the hand, as the staffs of MOSES and AARON (Exod. 4:2; 7:9; et al.). The noun *šēbeṭ H8657* refers to any kind of rod (e.g., Exod. 21:20), but since a stick can be used as a weapon or as an instrument of punishment, this term came to mean "[authoritative] scepter" (e.g., Amos 1:5). Finally, *mišʿenet H5475* (from a root meaning "support") can refer to a cane used by someone that has been injured or by someone elderly (Exod. 21:19; Zech. 8:4), but it has a general meaning as well (e.g., 2 Ki. 18:21). The NT term is Greek *rhabdos G4811*.

For DAVID, the staff was a symbol of divine guidance and care: "your rod [*šēbeṭ*] and your staff [*mišʿenet*], / they comfort me" (Ps. 23:4). The rod also became the symbol of authority and rule prevalent in Bible use: Moses "took the staff of God in his hand" (Exod. 4:20); and he and Aaron wrought numerous miracles with rods (Exod. 8:5–6; 14:16; Num. 20:11). See AARON'S ROD, STAFF. "The rod of discipline" was for a child (Prov. 22:15) or a fool (14:3) or a slave (Exod. 21:20). The rod as a symbol of God's anger and chastisement occurs in numerous passages (2 Sam. 7:14; Job 9:34; 21:9; Isa. 9:4; 10:5; 30:31; Lam. 3:1; 1 Cor. 4:21). That Jesus would rule all nations "with a rod of iron" was foretold in Ps. 2:9 (NIV, "iron scepter") and seen in

Rev. 2:27; 12:5; 19:15. The rod was used in counting sheep (Lev. 27:32), and symbolically in numbering God's chosen (Ezek. 20:37). Finally, the rod was used for measuring, as the new Jerusalem (Rev. 11:1; 21:15–16 [here Gk. *kalamos* G2812]).

G. B. FUNDERBURK

Rodanim roh´duh-nim (רוֹדָנִים, pl. of the unattested form רֹדָן H8102). TNIV, "the Rodanites." Son of JAVAN and grandson of JAPHETH (Gen. 10:4 [KJV, "Dodanim," following most Heb. MSS]; 1 Chr. 1:7). However, since the name is in the plural form, the reference is evidently to a people group descended from Javan (who is associated with GREECE and surrounding areas). The SEPTUAGINT reads *Rhodioi* ("Rhodians"), and most scholars believe that indeed the Rodanim were thought to be inhabitants of the island of RHODES. On the other hand, some have argued that the spelling "Dodanim" is original (cf. *ABD*, 5:788).

H. A. HOFFNER, JR.

Rodanites roh´duh-nits. TNIV form of RODANIM.

roe, roebuck. The smallest deer native to Europe and SW Asia (*Capreolus capreolus*). Modern versions use "roe deer" or "roebuck" to render Hebrew *yaḥmûr* H3502 (which occurs only in Deut. 15:5 and 1 Ki. 4:23), though some scholars believe this word refers to the fallow deer (see DEER for general discussion; cf. also *FFB*, 26). The KJV uses both "roe" and "roebuck" to translate other terms that probably refer to the GAZELLE (Deut. 12:15 et al.).

Rogelim roh´guh-lim (רֹגְלִים H8082, prob. "[place of] those who tread," referring to fullers who cleaned textiles). A town in TRANSJORDAN identified as the home of BARZILLAI (2 Sam. 17:27; 19:31), who along with others befriended DAVID when the latter arrived in MAHANAIM in his flight from ABSALOM; he later escorted David back over the Jordan. The location of Rogelim is unknown. The description of Barzillai as "the Gileadite from Rogelim" may suggest a place in GILEAD, but even this is uncertain. F.-M. Abel (*Géographie de la Palestine* [1933], 2:437–38) suggested the identification of Rogelim with a site near Wadi er-Rujeileh

called Tell Barsina (or Bersinya, c. 16 mi. SE of the Sea of Galilee and 25 mi. N of Mahanaim), based on the similarity of these names to Rogelim and Barzillai. This proposal was questioned by N. Glueck (*Explorations in Eastern Palestine*, 4 vols, in 5, AASOR 25–28 [1934–51], 4/1:176–77), who found no evidence of settlement there before the Roman period; Glueck proposed instead Zaharet (Dhaharat) Soqʿah, which is just to the SE of Bersinya.

B. K. WALTKE

Rohgah roh´guh (רָהְגָּה H8108 [*Ketib* הָגָה רוֹ], meaning unknown). Son of Shomer (KJV, "Shamer"; NRSV, "Shemer") and descendant of ASHER (1 Chr. 7:34).

Roimus roh´i-muhs. KJV Apoc. form of REHUM (1 Esd. 5:8).

roll. See SCROLL.

rolling thing. See TUMBLEWEED.

Romamti-Ezer roh-mam´ti-ee´zuhr (רֹמַמְתִּי עֶזֶר H8251, "I have lifted help" or "I have exalted [my] helper"). Son of HEMAN, the king's seer (1 Chr. 25:4). The fourteen sons of Heman, along with the sons of ASAPH and JEDUTHUN, were set apart "for the ministry of prophesying, accompanied by harps, lyres and cymbals" (v. 1). The assignment of duty was done by lot, and the twenty-fourth lot fell to Romamti-Ezer, his sons, and his relatives (25:29).

Roman empire. The word *empire* requires definition, for it is used in two distinct senses, geographical and political, and both are applicable to the Roman empire. Geographically, an empire is an aggregation of territories under a single absolute command. Until comparatively recently, Great Britain held a world empire, and one of Disraeli's dramatic political coups was to dub Queen Victoria the Empress of India. Similarly, Rome ruled a ring of territories around the Mediterranean, a widening area of command and authority acquired by a long historical evolution that began when the Latin tribes by the Tiber broke the encirclement of the hinterland hill tribes and continued to expand until Rome's frontiers rested on Hadrian's Wall in far Northumberland, on the long riverline of the Rhine and the Danube, on the Black Sea Coast of Asia Minor, on the Sahara, and on indeterminate eastern and northeastern lines which wavered with Roman policy toward Parthia, and which, apart from the Arabian desert, found no clear-cut southeastern definition on the Red Sea coasts and in the valley of the Nile.

All this area had fallen under the Roman *imperium* or command by the long process by which first the republic, and then the principate, probed for a stable frontier, a quest that was never ended and that paused only when out-reaching power touched its limits. Those limits were on the longest river line in Europe, and were without sharp and secure finality around the whole arc of the eastern provinces. The empire was a hard won and not readily defensible mass of territory, destined to divide down its middle line and succumb, first in the W, and then in the E, to the pressures engendered in the more remote land masses of Europe and Asia, from whose tribal incursions Rome had sought for long and significant centuries to protect the culture and civilization of the Mediterranean. With the Roman empire went the "Roman Peace," coterminous and coextensive. Within these frontiers the church first found root and growth, and when the vast mass disintegrated, it proved to be the historical link that tied a crumbling world to its successor, the new Europe which arose when the torpor and confusion of the Dark Ages passed.

The term *empire* is used most commonly in a political sense to distinguish between the republic and the principate, between the rule of the senate and the rule of the constitutional autocrats who were called, in view of their exercise of supreme military command, by the term *imperator* (whence *emperor*). The Roman empire, in this sense of the word, is that period of Roman history that begins with the final victory of Octavian in the republic's last civil war and ends with the collapse of all Roman authority, first in the W and then in the E — the final termination of the great historical movement that began with the coherence of the tribes of the Latin enclave around the fortified hills of the Lower Tiber River valley. The term *imperator* was not originally prominent among the various titles available to the ruler. AUGUSTUS (as the senate, conferring an honorific title, called the victorious Octavian) preferred to be called *princeps*, or first

The Roman Empire.

citizen; hence, the preferable term *principate* for the empire politically considered. See also ROME.

I. The transition. It must not be supposed that the Roman people at large saw in the Battle of Actium (31 B.C.) that decisive watershed in their history which historians find it convenient to mark today. The accumulation of power in the hands of one man, power constitutionally conferred, was no new phenomenon over the half century of tense and troubled politics that preceded the emergence of Augustus as the giver of peace and order. Inevitable strains and stresses—which the possession of provincial responsibility and the inexorable extension of territory that was regarded as necessary to security brought to bear upon Rome's ruling class—were partial causes behind faction, division, and civil strife. Again and again, distracted and confused within, under the continual threat of revolt and a military coup, the ruling oligarchy had resorted to autocracy in their endeavor to retain control of the city, Italy, and the menaced provinces.

The great POMPEY, for example, enjoyed two periods of extraordinary command in the sixties of the 1st cent. B.C. During the first he cleared the E Mediterranean of the Cilician pirate fleets which, in the midst of Rome's civil troubles, had gained control of the seaways and had interrupted the food supplies on which the urban proletariat, a sinister force in Rome's confused political situation, depended. During the second period, Pompey pacified and organized the whole provincial complex of the E, a contribution to the future Roman Peace that it would be difficult to overestimate. Both of Pompey's commands involved overriding authority and an adaptation of republican forms to monarchical rule—the very pattern of the coming autocracy, which was Augustus's clever solution to the problem of Rome's anarchy.

Had Pompey not been a loyal and responsible servant of the senate, he might easily have retained the powers conferred constitutionally upon him. Using a devoted army, backed and financed by the immense resources of the E, which he had organized, might have dictated his own terms to the helpless senate. He might thus have arranged his own succession and have been marked by historians as the first of the "emperors." As it was, Pompey duly surrendered his military and legislative power, and the senate, now visibly unable to manage the resurgent problems of power, blundered on toward civil war.

Julius CAESAR was not as honorable a man as Pompey was. His rise to power followed directly that of Pompey. Twelve years after 62 B.C., when Pompey dutifully resigned his great power, Julius Caesar had become the problem to the senate which they had long helplessly foreseen. He had beaten Gaul into submission, demonstrated Roman power across the channel, and presented a challenge to the divided oligarchy which they could meet in their political bankruptcy only by resorting to their old champion Pompey, the one man around whom some show of strength might rally, the one soldier able to meet the military genius of Caesar—hence the Civil War, described in a self-justifying book by Caesar himself. The decade is, thanks to Cicero's speeches, letters, and the abundance of other material of historical worth, a well-documented period, and it is possible to follow week by week the events of portent and significance that saw the death throes of republican Rome.

The Civil War, with Caesar and Pompey as the great opponents, was the senate's last attempt to control the military command. From the duel of the two dynasts, Caesar emerged as victor. The decisive battle was fought at Pharsalus on the Thessalian plain on 9 August 48 B.C. Pompey was murdered in Egypt before the year ended. By March of the year 45, Caesar's swift decisive strength had broken up and subdued the remaining pockets of senatorial resistance. In Egypt, Queen CLEOPATRA, last of the great line of the Ptolemies, secured her personal fortunes by snaring Julius Caesar, the conqueror.

Caesar then turned his undoubted genius to the restoration of law and order in Rome, and of peace throughout the Roman world. His power was absolute and unchallenged, and he exercised it with firmness, clemency, and contempt for opposition, qualities that might have marked him as the first "emperor," had he also possessed political subtlety, some measure of patience, and even a simulated show of respect for the discredited republican regime. It is unwise to despise an enemy, however discredited, and the famous Ides of March in 44 B.C. saw Caesar fall under the daggers of a die-

Remains of the house of Julius Caesar located in the Roman forum.

hard group of senatorial conspirators who had no alternative policy or program with which to replace his firm, efficient dictatorship. The republic was dead, and no act of violence could bring the corpse to life, for all the magnificence of the eloquence with which Cicero, the great orator and political archaist, sought to stir it to movement and activity.

Nor had anyone remembered Caesar's adoptive son and heir—a member of the *gens Octavia*, and after Caesar's adoption called Octavianus Caesar—a lad of nineteen years who was studying in Greece. With sublime audacity young Octavian came to Italy and claimed his heritage. The young man had a flair for diplomacy, a genius for picking and choosing men to help him, and a sense of timing in political affairs that matched both qualities. Octavian, however, for all these personal advantages that were conspicuously lacking in the great and independent Julius, could hardly have achieved the astounding success which crowned his audacious venture, had not vast moral forces awaited his clever manipulation. Rome was not spared a second civil war, and in 42 B.C. Philippi followed Pharsalus of six years before as another decisive place and date in Roman history. Allied with Antony, Caesar's one-time lieutenant, Octavian broke the remaining forces of reaction.

The Mediterranean world, nonetheless, amid Rome's preoccupation with civil strife, approached close to disaster. The Parthians, whose perennially hostile presence was the problem of Rome's eastern frontier, were menacing Palestine and Egypt. Antony proceeded E to gain control of the threatened provinces, but proved to be no Caesar. The E was in turmoil when Cleopatra, one of the most dynamic women of that age, gained control of Antony, and with her schemes for an eastern Roman empire almost anticipated history by four centuries.

Octavian had chosen with his usual unerring deliberation to remain in Italy. He held there Rome's true strength, and the challenge from Alexandria was one that Rome could not ignore. War came again, but was concluded at Actium in 31 B.C. when Octavian and his able commanders broke the power of those who challenged peace. Peace was all that a sadly tormented world asked, and Italy and all the provinces were ready to confer divine honors on the man whose genius had brought the boon it so desired. In 27 B.C., after a semblance of "restoring the republic," celebrated in coinage and inscription, Octavian received the title of Augustus. He succeeded where Julius had failed because he paid lip service to the forms of constitutional and republican government. He called himself *princeps*, or "first citizen," a popular-sounding title that claimed little. He was *imperator* by virtue of the fact that, like the President of the United States, he was in supreme command of all the troops. It was a title used only in rare military contexts.

Concentrated in Augustus's hands were also the old powers of the republic. There were still CONSULS, but he was one of the two. He also held the "tribunician power," that is, all the rights, privileges, and functions of the old plebeian magistrates, the "tribunes," which had been once a bulwark of the dispossessed, but had found strange and potent misuse in the century of constitutional strife which had destroyed the republic. When he would, he also assumed the power of the censors, those old custodians of honor and piety.

But all these powers Augustus held, just as others had at times held them, by the senate's or the people's gift. Elections of a sort were held. The senate still functioned, and provincial administration was shared by the prince (i.e., the *princeps*) and the senate, the former retaining command of all those frontier regions that required the presence of an army. Augustus could read history too well not to have marked the role which a century of commanders had played in Roman revolution through the use of the military forces they had bound to themselves by advantages conferred or by personal magnetism.

II. Augustus (emperor from 27 B.C to A.D. 14). So it was that the first Roman emperor—who ordered "that a census should be taken of the entire Roman world" (Lk. 2:1)—entered history. Those who blessed the peace he gave to a weary world were not aware that a sharp change had taken place. A leader, to be sure, had appeared, and he was indeed one of the great men of all time, but his powers, autocratic in sum and total, bore ancient and familiar names. Only the farseeing knew that the old regime was dead, and, if they knew, grieved little for it.

The new regime sought to revive the virtues of the old, just as it had remedied its vices. Augustus promoted religious revival. As far as legislation could effect that end, he sought to restore the old standards and old moralities. A great outburst of literary activity, some of it promoted effectively by Augustus's "Minister without Portfolio," Maecenas, gave Latin letters their golden age. Augustus knew how to use the ability of great poets to establish his peace and add power and persuasion to his rehabilitation of law and order. The world at large, scarcely believing that an evil age of breakdown and war was ending, was willing to barter liberty for peace. No wonder that a highly sensitive spirit like Vergil the poet, looking back over the history of Rome, saw a mighty destiny working to a beneficent end that found final expression in the work and person of one man. He wove the thought into his epic poem, the *Aeneid*.

Augustus did much to establish the geographical boundaries of the empire. His work is not well documented, but twenty years of planning and petty warfare were devoted to the security of the frontiers. He had no zest for conquest. Consolidation was his aim. Ambitious plans for the subjugation of Parthia, Julius's unfinished project, were abandoned, and until the age of TRAJAN, who effected brief conquest, diplomacy was the attempted Roman solution of the intractable problems of that troubled frontier. GALATIA was made a province in 25 B.C., and Judea in A.D. 6. Spain was pacified, Gaul reorganized. The hill tribes of the northern Alpine areas, like those of Asia Minor, were brought laboriously under subjection. Rhaetia, Noricum, Pannonia, and Moesia were established along the Danube and Balkan frontiers, essential buffers against the tribal hinterlands of Europe. Disastrous defeat, and Varus's loss of three legions in A.D. 9, caused Augustus to abandon what might have been the salutary establishment of a frontier on the Elbe, instead of along the nearer and longer line of the Rhine. All was a vast contribution to the peace of the Mediterranean. It is small wonder that, in the newly prosperous provinces, the imperial cult grew apace (see EMPEROR WORSHIP).

III. Tiberius (A.D. 14–37). By good fortune, the canny choice of loyal men, and perhaps the immense weight of popular desire for peace, Augustus had no trouble from one of Rome's two unsolved or insoluble problems. One was the effective and permanent control of the army commanders, men whose abilities and eminence were necessary for the defense of long and menaced frontiers, but whose ambitions and independence were destined to play a disastrous part in four centuries of history.

The other problem was the succession. Augustus is a prime illustration of the decisive role of personality in the processes of history, and as the revered person of the man who founded the Roman Peace moved toward old age and death, people wondered who would replace him. TACITUS captures the atmosphere of the occasion well in the opening chapters of his *Annals*. No one was better aware of the problem than Augustus himself, who, by misfortune, had no male offspring of his own. His efforts to secure the succession in the direct line of the Julian house were cruelly thwarted by the premature deaths of promising young men on whom he had pinned his hopes: Marcellus, his nephew, subject of Vergil's moving tribute (*Aeneid* 6.882–86); Gaius and Lucius, his grandsons; and Drusus, his favorite stepson.

TIBERIUS, his other stepson, was eventually left as the sole successor, but not until he had become an embittered man by the spectacle of Augustus's visible attempts to find an alternative. Tiberius was fifty-six years of age when Augustus died in A.D. 14. He was a tried and able commander, but, as a Claudian on his mother Livia's side, possessed of all the notorious pride of that ancient and distinguished family, and rendered the more dour by the rejection from which he had suffered. Perhaps Augustus, so able a judge of human nature, had marked his innate sourness and suspicion and foreseen those defects that brought so much unpopularity to Tiberius during and after the twenty-three years of his principate.

It was no doubt Tiberius's defects of character that led him to place such misguided trust in Aelius Sejanus, the prefect of the PRAETORIAN GUARD, the emperor's Household Corps, and to whose influence and ascendancy during Tiberius's absence from Rome some of the tyrannous acts of the reign may be ascribed. It was Tiberius's suspicious nature which betrayed him into the too common use of "delation"—treason trials, reminiscent of those of some modern autocracies, and based on the evidence of common informers (*delatores*). This became a practice loathed by its perennial victims, the old senatorial aristocracy, and later resorted to by every weak or suspicious emperor, notably DOMITIAN. It was Tiberius's misfortune that Tacitus, one of the most powerful writers of Rome, was a chronicler for his reign. Modern historians, emancipating themselves from the long influence of the mordant Tacitus, have done more justice to Tiberius's real abilities.

Tacitus wrote in Rome as a Roman senator, and it is a little difficult when reading him to remember that, over Tiberius's considerable reign, the frontiers still endured as Augustus had fixed them, and that even the Parthians were held in check. The organization of CAPPADOCIA into a province was the only innovation Tiberius made to the Augustan system. Portents, however, were gathering. Senatorial administration was clearly more subject to the will of the *princeps*; Sejanus showed what a local military commander could do, and the possibilities of personal tyranny were obvious.

IV. Caligula (A.D. 37–41). The young madman who followed Tiberius underlined the latter lesson. Hereditary succession invariably produces sooner or later the incompetent, the foolish, or the bad. It produced all these qualities in the person of Gaius, nicknamed CALIGULA, or "Little Boots," by the troops on the Rhine who had known him as the son of the popular Germanicus. Mercifully, he was assassinated before he provoked a Jewish revolt.

V. Claudius (A.D. 41–54). It was a sinister fact that, when Gaius fell under the sword of an officer of the praetorian guard, the same military group drew from obscurity Gaius's uncle, CLAUDIUS, a man of fifty years, who, even more than Tiberius, had suffered a lifetime of rejection and humiliation. He suffered from some form of cerebral palsy, which at times made him physically repulsive, but like many victims of a spastic condition was none the less an able man, certainly the most learned ever to hold the principate. Enforced withdrawal from society had driven Claudius to low companions and to study. The influences of both were apparent in his reign.

Claudius sensibly developed the imperial civil service, using the abilities of the freedman class. Pallas and Narcissus, and Pallas's brother Felix, were his appointments, and the personal faults and vices of these men were not an indictment of the fundamental good sense of Claudius's governmental innovations. He sought also salutarily to extend the Roman franchise. He embarked on a vigorous frontier policy, and the two Mauretanias in A.D. 42, Britain and Lycia in 43, and Thrace in 46, were added to the empire. Claudius died by poison, on the threshold of premature dotage, at the hands of his evil wife Agrippina, who was anxious to secure the succession for Nero, her son by an earlier marriage. Claudius's death was concealed until the praetorian guard, firm in the hands of Afranius Burrus, Agrippina's nominee, and conciliated by the now customary donation, brought Nero to power at the immature age of seventeen.

VI. Nero (A.D. 54–68). It was Nero's youth and his artistic and hedonistic preoccupations that left the bluff Burrus, and the famous philosopher Seneca, Nero's tutor, free to manage the world's affairs for five years. The *quinquennium Neronis*, as this period was known, became a proverb for happy conditions in the provinces. The young prince deserved no credit. Agrippina had cleared the way for Nero with murder and intrigue. Her plotting continued. Unpitied victims were Pallas and Narcissus, but Seneca and Burrus became frightened when the ambitions of Agrippina took a wider reach. How far they sanctioned Nero's turning on the woman who had helped him to power can never be known, but the end was matricide.

Nero was clearly beyond control, and the tool of the unscrupulous. Burrus died, and Seneca was ultimately driven to suicide, but the details of a lamentable reign, which included the first PERSECUTION of the Christians, need not be followed. There was deterioration around the frontiers. Only the able Corbulo held the security of the Parthian frontier, while the equally able Suetonius subdued Britain aflame with Boudicca's revolt, in which London and Colchester were burned and the new province all but lost. In A.D. 66 the long threat of the Jewish rebellion became a reality (see WARS, JEWISH). Vindex rebelled in Gaul, and Galba in Spain, grim portents of the tragic year 69. Universal hatred surrounded Nero in Rome. The Julio-Claudian house, in short, came to an end amid turmoil on the frontiers, disaffection in the armed forces, and the first major threat to the Roman Peace. The wonder is that so much of Augustus's work, and Claudius's wise innovations, survived.

VII. The year of the four emperors (A.D. 69). The Christians who had survived Nero's purge, and who now labored under legal proscription, could have seen in the horrors of this year of anarchy a divine judgment. The wonder was that Rome again survived. The "beast" appeared wounded to death, "but the fatal wound [was] healed" so that the "whole world was astonished and followed the beast" (Rev. 13:3). Vindex had demonstrated the disaffection in Gaul, and when Galba, the aristocratic governor of Spain, made common cause with the Gallic rebel, the legions on the Rhine became aware of their insecurity, crushed Vindex, and tried to set up their commander Verginius Rufus as emperor. The "secret of empire," as Tacitus put it, was out. It was that "an emperor can be made elsewhere than in Rome." It was never to be forgotten. The praetorian guard declared for Galba. Nero fled, and died a suicide in a Roman suburb.

A year of complex civil war followed. By January 15 Galba was dead, killed by the praetorians who had declared for him. Otho, another Spanish governor, and first husband of Poppaea, Nero's wife, knew how to court the household troops and was set up as emperor. The Rhine legions set up Vitellius and marched on Italy. It was the opportunity of the German tribes, but was never taken. The "beast" was to survive. By April 17, Otho

A Roman coin minted with the image of Emperor Galba.

was dead and Vitellius supreme, but the eastern provinces proclaimed Vespasian, the able general who was in the midst of fighting down the ghastly and expensive Jewish rebellion. Vespasian sent his able deputy, Mucianus, to Italy at the head of a legionary force, retaining enough strength in Palestine to hold the turbulent forces loose there. In a battle near Cremona, where Otho had been beaten by Vitellius and driven to Nero's resort of suicide, the Syrian legions triumphed. Before the year's end, Vitellius was destroyed, and by right of survival Vespasian became the ruler of Rome. The Flavian dynasty was born and endured for a generation. The continuing strength or good fortune of Rome was demonstrated by the fact that, through such civil turmoil, the frontiers held and the Jewish war continued. The Apocalypse quoted popular amazement. People were saying: "Who is like the beast? Who can make war against it?" (Rev. 13:4).

VIII. Vespasian (A.D. 69–79). Vespasian was a rough and able soldier. It was the achievement of his decade of rule that peace and prosperity were restored to the troubled frontiers, the finances of the realm brought to order, and the essential character of the principate retained. Like many a soldier, Vespasian was a born organizer, and his careful restoration on the frontiers, especially in Britain, were to stand Rome in good stead for many years. It is to Vespasian's credit, and later to Trajan's, that the first serious barbarian challenge was postponed for a century. When Vespasian died, Agricola was feeling his way toward a frontier on the Tyne, Parthia was screened by new defenses, and Palestine left devastated by atrocious war. In Rome there was something like an Augustan Age in new building. Vespasian's decade is not a well-documented age.

IX. Titus (A.D. 79–81). Vespasian's popular son Titus, the able young soldier who had finished the Jewish war when his father was called to the duties of the principate in Rome, ruled for less than three years after Vespasian's death and left the high office, because of his premature death at the age of forty years, to the execrable Domitian, his younger brother. Pompeii, buried by Vesuvius in August 79, is a tremendous document of Titus's Italy.

X. Domitian (A.D. 81–96). Domitian was thirty years of age when he unexpectedly succeeded to the principate. His personal history bore some resemblance to that of Tiberius, a fact which he recognized, for Tiberius's memoirs were Domitian's favorite reading. Vespasian and Titus, both capable soldiers, had held the younger brother of their house in some contempt. His awareness of that fact did not improve his personality or enhance his fitness to rule. Suspicious, cruel, and by nature tyrannical, Domitian filled his reign with treason trials, political murder, and persecution. Senators suffered along with Christians. Tacitus, enraged and embittered by the decimation of his class in this unhappy fifteen years, turned with hatred on Tiberius, whose concept of princely power provided the hated Domitian with so many precedents. The gentle Pliny the Younger, as well as the bitter Juvenal, agreed with Tacitus in this estimate of Domitian's evil principate and of the Reign of Terror which finally brought him down. With Domitian's death in A.D. 96, which must have nearly coincided with that of John the apostle, last survivor of the original disciples, the NT century, which began with Augustus's census (perhaps 5 B.C.), ended. This article need not follow its history much further.

XI. Five good emperors. Nerva (A.D. 96–98), Trajan (98–117), Hadrian (117–138), Antoninus Pius (138–161), and Marcus Aurelius (161–180) cover almost a century, the "Indian Summer," as Arnold Toynbee has called it, of Roman greatness. Edward Gibbon regarded this era as the happiest known to mankind. The famous passage in his *Decline and Fall of the Roman Empire* (vol. 5, ch. 1, par. 1) runs: "In the second century of the Christian era the empire of Rome comprehended the fairest part of the earth, and the most civilised portion of mankind. The frontiers of that extensive monarchy were guarded by ancient renown and disciplined valour. The gentle but powerful influence of laws and manners, had gradually cemented the union of the provinces.… The image of a free constitution was preserved with decent reverence.… During a happy period of more than fourscore years the public administration was conducted by the virtue and abilities of Nerva, Trajan, Hadrian, and the two Antonines. It is the design of this and the two succeeding chapters to describe the prosperous condition of their empire; and afterwards, from the death of Marcus Antoninus to deduce the most important circumstances of its decline and fall, a revolution which will ever be remembered and still is felt by the nations of the earth."

Over this period urbanization proceeded apace; the warrior prince Trajan extended the frontiers to their widest yet; Hadrian, most traveled of all the emperors, consolidated them; the great wall across Britain is the lasting monument to his work. Portents, however, gathered, and the philosopher ruler Marcus Aurelius was hard pressed to beat back a Teutonic incursion into the Danubian provinces.

Hadrian's principate saw the second rebellion of the Jews and the virtual destruction of the Jews as a nation. Those who seek information on the collapse and recovery of Rome's power, which covered the years 180 to 330, the final eclipse of the W, the transfer of power to Byzantium or Constantinople, and the 1,000 years of the Eastern empire should seek the information in the comprehensive works listed below.

(J. B. Bury, *A History of the Roman Empire from Its Foundation to the Death of Marcus Aurelius* [1896]; S. Dill, *Roman Society from Nero to Marcus Aurelius* [1905]; H. S. Jones, *Companion to Roman History* [1912]; G. H. Stevenson, *Roman Provincial Administration to the Age of the Antonines* [1939]; M. Cary, *A History of Rome Down to the Reign of Constantine* [1954]; J. B. Bury, *The History of the Later Roman Empire* [1958]; J. Wells and R. H. Barrow, *A Short History of the Roman Empire to the Death of Marcus Aurelius* [1958]; E. M. Blaiklock, *The Century of the New Testament* [1962]; A. H. M. Jones, *The Cities of the Eastern Roman Provinces*, 2nd ed. [1971]; A. Garzetti, *From Tiberius to the Antonines: A History of the Roman Empire AD 14–192* [1974]; F. Millar, *The Roman Empire and Its Neighbors*, 2nd ed. [1981]; C. M. Wells, *The Roman Empire*, 2nd ed. [1992]; D. C. A. Shotter, *Rome and Her Empire* [2003]; F. Millar, *Rome, the Greek Word, and the East*, 2 vols. [2002–04]; D. S. Potter, ed., *A Companion to the Roman Empire* [2006].)   E. M. BLAIKLOCK

Roman law. The legal system of ROME throughout the whole range of its 1,000 years of development, from the *Duodecim Tabulae*, "Twelve Tables," until the *Codex Iustinianeus*, "Code of Justinian," and the subsequent fall of the Eastern empire; and connoting, in addition to this primary meaning, the actual Code of Justinian itself.

Evolved by the decemvirate about 451–449 B.C., the Twelve Tables formed a code of rules to meet the exigencies of regulating the day-to-day affairs of ordinary citizens following the successful ascendancy of the plebs over the populus. Consisting of equal representation by patricians and plebeians alike, the decemvirs codified and published those parts of the old customary law essential for administration of justice in the reorganized condition of the civil law and government. The extant fragments of the Twelve Tables scarcely justify Cicero's eulogistic reference to their being almost the perfection of human wisdom. Indeed, the Tables were anything but a *corpus juris* of the law previous to the irruption of the Gauls, being merely short statements of points of law which, however, provided the substratum on which the whole future complex of Roman law was structured.

The nascency of the formulary system is perceptible in the recognition by the Tables of the important early forms of action: *sacramentum*, a protean procedure for the enforcement of practically every right; *manus injectio*, symbolizing self-help; *judicis postulatio*, a process for settling boundary disputes; and *pignoris capio*, dealing with the satisfaction of debt by hypothecation or pledge. (See Livy, *Hist.* 3.31–37; Cicero, *Leg.* 11; *Rep.* 2.37, 63; Gaius, *Dig.* 10.1; 47.22; H. J. S. Maine, *Ancient Laws* [1861]; W. A. Hunter, *Introduction to Roman Law*, new ed. rev. A. F. Murison [1994]; E. A. Meyer, *Legitimacy and Law in the Roman World: Tabulae in Roman Belief and Practice* [2004].)

Outlined in Justinian's *Digest* (1.2, de origine iuris, etc.), the germination and growth of Roman law as a system found its first written expression in the Twelve Tables, and owed its initial development to the exertions of private *jurisconsults* whose writings and views were not infrequently adopted by the *praetors* in their annual edicts. The earlier law, or *ius civile*, had hardened into a rigid and rigorous formalism, and it was to this praetorian law, which in the early empire was formulated in a perpetual edict, that the *ius honorarium* owed its softening application of principles of equity and natural justice. It was at this stage that legal rights emerged out of legal remedies, because the *ius honorarium* mainly operated as a rule regulating civil actions. The Twelve Tables operated for over 1,000 years down to the Theodosian Codex (A.D. 438) and the *Corpus iuris civilis* of Justinian, during which time the laws of Rome were never codified. (See T. Mommsen and P. M. Meyer, *Theodosiani libri 16* [1904–05].)

The Institutes of Justinian finally cast the laws of Rome into a shape convenient to the practitioner as well as the student of law. Even when the barbarians ruled the W, Roman law was the personal law for Romans, and, in the E, under Justinian. They were largely superseded by imperial constitutions, and while obscured by Greek commentaries, the principles of Roman law were to some extent restored by a restatement known as *The Basilica* in 887, and were revised by order of Constantine VII about 945. The Basilica does not contain the whole of the Justinian Code, but includes some materials not in the Code. It comprises the Institutes, the Digest or Pandect, Code, Novellae, and the Imperial Constitutions made after Justinian's reign. (See E. Gibbon, *Decline and Fall of the Roman Empire*, ch. 44.)

A recognition of the doctrines of the old system, which was swept away in the later days of the empire, is essential to an appreciation of Roman law as it applies to the NT background. The chief of the elementary doctrines of the *ius civile* were the peculiar principles determining the situation of the *pater familias* or the head of the family. The agnatic rule of descent (i.e., through males) regulated kinship in the fundamental social unit that was the patriarchal family, outside of which was the *gens* or class with which the family unit was linked by common ancestry. The law of the Twelve Tables recognized testamentary disposition, namely by will, as already in existence. Intestate succession by agnation was *per capita*, not *per stirpes*, all agnates of equal degree taking equally.

At the other end of the historical spectrum, it is noteworthy that the most important accretion to Roman law was the concept of *lex naturae*, borrowed from the STOICS, by which was meant the principle that the actions of human beings were to

Bronze vessel from the 1st cent. used as a dry measure. It may have been used by Roman tax collectors to extract 5 percent tax from a commodity producer.

be guided by the same law which directed the universe. The *ius gentium* emerged from this, so that, with the *ius naturae*, these two agencies ameliorated and enlarged the *ius civile*, a process analogous to the modifying influence of equity on the common law of England centuries later, although, in fact, the development of common law owed little to Roman influences, which, however, have permeated most other legal systems of the civilized world.

It is appropriate at this point to comment on the *ius gentium*, or law of nations, administered by the praetors and applied to nations under Roman dominion. The *ius gentium* was the common law for all people, the word *ius* expressing legal rights as well as rules of law. Roman jurists regarded the *ius gentium* as based on consent, because of its inherent reasonableness and appeal to the conscience.

The supremacy of Rome in the affairs of JUDEA is marked by the rule of HEROD, who was confirmed by AUGUSTUS in the possession of the entire HASMONEAN kingdom. His salutary exertions on behalf of the people were climaxed by reconstruction of their temple, but personal blemishes of ambition and cruelty stamped Herod as a despot and a tyrant whose efforts failed to "romanize" the Jews.

Interesting aspects of Roman law reflected in the NT include references to ADOPTION in Paul's epistles (Rom. 8:15, 23; 9:4; Gal. 4:5; Eph. 1:5). In Roman law, adoption was a very ancient institution rooted in ancestor worship, the maintenance of the family *sacra* being such that an old man dying without issue was permitted to arrogate some citizen as *pater familias* and so make him a son. Similarly, another mode of adoption by which *filii familias* could be adopted was devised. The *adoptatus* was absorbed into the family where he was equated to a natural child.

Paul speaks of "heirs of God and co-heirs with Christ" (Rom. 8:17; Eph. 3:6), and it is noteworthy that these references to the Roman system draw upon the feature that the main function of the will was not the disposition of property, but the appointment of a successor, the *heres*, who was not simply an heir, but the actual representative of the deceased. Even where the *heres* or *heredes* were appointed *heredes* only to a half, their appointment would be construed as covering the whole estate. The common law knows no concept such as that of the *hereditas*, an entity coming into being by the death of the *de cuis* (predecessor) and then merging into the personality of the *heres* or actual successor. Whether the ancestor and *heres* had one *persona*, or whether the *hereditas* was the *ius*, or legal situation, of the deceased, does not really affect the aptness of the Pauline allusion.

Under the Roman law of persons, all people were either free or SLAVES. A slave was legally both a thing and a person, and he could be freed by manumission, a process whereby the slave was touched with a wand (*vindicta*) by the plaintiff (*adsertor liberatis*) in the course of a fictitious lawsuit and thereupon became a freedman in contradistinction to his former condition of bondsman. A freedman owed his patron *obsequium* (complaisance).

Roman law, like any other legal system, could not and did not remain unaffected by social, cultural, political, and economic influences. However, Roman law was neither orientalized nor hellenized, but retained its essentially national character. Some institutions of later Roman law, such as the family and slavery, were influenced by Christian principles of humanity and benignity, thus enlarging the Roman concept of equity as the realization of plain natural justice in accord with everyone's conscience. Christianity did not greatly alter the framework of Roman law. This was accomplished by Justinian, whose great codification will be discussed in some detail shortly.

The civil law and procedure against their historical setting having been outlined, some comment on *Interpretatio* is appropriate. From the outset, the interpretation of the law and of the actions founded upon it were the responsibility of the college of pontiffs. About the 3rd cent. B.C. the administration of the law became secularized, and plebeians were admitted to the college. The early jurists were termed *veteres* who advised both clients and judges. Another class, referred to as advocates, undertook forensic argument. About 242 B.C. the *praetor urbanus* and the *praetor peregrinus* came into being as magistrates who at the commencement of their term issued edicts stating the procedural rules they intended to follow, hence the *edictum perpetuum* in contrast to edicts of an occasional nature. A body of precedent, or *edictum tralaticium*, was built up, any new matter being called *edictum novum*. The *praetor* was not necessarily a skilled lawyer, but would consult his *considium*, or body of expert advisers. He was also amenable to public and professional opinion.

The *praetors* enjoyed a limited sphere of power. Their office was elective. They were subject to consular *intercessio*, or veto. On the other hand, the two consuls, elected by the *comitia centuriata*, exercised unlimited *imperium* derived from the monarchy. In fact, in a time of grave crisis, either consul might appoint a dictator to exercise supreme authority for up to six months.

The *aediles* were magistrates of the Roman people charged with the police of the city and control of the markets.

The censorship office was for roll-taking and tax-gathering and had great dignity. The censors (two in number) also administered governmental business. Later in their history, they determined the composition of the senate, and exercised a general control over public morals.

Quaestors (two annually) were nominated by the consuls to assist them in fiscal matters.

Tribunes (up to ten) enjoyed enormous power. The tribunate was a plebeian office, the person of the tribune being sacrosanct. They had power of veto over the acts of other magistrates and could even hold the state to ransom in the furtherance of partisan interests.

Mention must be made of the *responsa prudentium*, or opinions of professional jurists, which by the time of Augustus were issued by the emperor's authority under seal. Such weight was attached to the *responsa*, or answers, of eminent jurists, that Gaius enumerated the *responsa* among the sources of written law.

As a result, the law had to be extracted from a mass of legal literature which served as a foundation of Justinian's *Digest*.

The Institutes of Justinian form the principal source of the knowledge of Roman law. Beginning with a definition borrowed from Ulpian, the first book begins, "Iustitia est constans et perpetua voluntas ius suum cuique tribuens" ("Justice is a set and constant purpose giving to everyone his due"). This is justice in the sense of a moral virtue, or attribute of human character, not a legal standard. According to Justinian, legal study comprised two branches: public law, dealing with the constitution of the state, and private law, concerned with individuals. The Institutes are preoccupied with private law, there being only a closing title on criminal law (*ius publicum*).

The *ius privatum* is subdivided into the *ius naturale* (natural precepts), *ius gentium* (precepts of universal law), and *ius civile* (civil law).

The law of nature is described as "the law which nature has taught all animals…. This is the source of the union of male and female, which we call matrimony, as well as of the procreation and rearing of children." The civil law is defined as the rules of law, "which each people makes for itself." The universal law is defined as "the law which natural reason has prescribed for all mankind held in equal observance amongst all people."

Justinian distinguishes between *ius scriptum* (written law) and *ius non scriptum* (unwritten law). The sources of the written law, according to Justinian, are *lex plebiscitum, senatu consultum, magistratuum edicta, responsa prudentium, principum placita*. Repeating the language of Gaius, Justinian says, "The whole of our law relates either to persons, or to things or to actions."

Summarizing, the Institutes deal with free men and slaves, persons of independent and dependent status, juristic persons, the modes of acquisition of property, gifts, servitudes, leases, real securities, possession, succession, wills, contractual obligation, sale, hire, partnership, pacts, agency, quasi-contract, theft, delicts, debt, assignments, the law of actions, the formulary procedure, summons, trial, execution, and interdicts. The Institutes were published on November 21, A.D. 533, with statutory force, along with the Digest, from December 30 of that year. Justinian also fixed, at the same time, the course in legal education at five years. (See J. B. Moyle, *Imperatoris Iustiniani Institutiones libri quattuor*, 5th ed. [1912]; R. W. Lee, *The Elements of Roman Law, with a Translation of the Institutes of Justinian*, 4th ed. [1956].)

From the Twelve Tables to the Institutes the Romans did not establish a systematic body of criminal law, the Roman jurists being not so much interested in the distinction between the violation of public and private interests, as with *iudica publica* and private *actiones poenales*. The state did not concern itself with robbery (*rapina*), theft (*furtum*), property damage, and assault (*iniuria*), the procedure being by way of private suit. Certain crimes were, however, prosecuted by public organs in *iudicia publica*, namely, treason (*perduellio*), desertion to the enemy, certain types of murder (*parricidium*). Special criminal courts were later set up to deal with the more grave offenses against life and personal fame, adultery, and falsification of documents. Juries were introduced by Augustus, but they had no jurisdiction over Roman citizens. The state of the delinquent's will (*dolus*) was taken into account in criminal trials. Roman penology was concerned with the vindictive and deterrent aspects of penalties rather than the reformatory aspects.

What of the trial and death of Jesus? There is no dispute that the trial was before Pilate, and thus, at that stage, a Roman trial. Jesus was brought before Pilate by the Jewish authorities. Pilate asked him if he was King of the Jews, to which Jesus replied, "You say so" (Matt. 27:11 NRSV; NIV, "Yes, it is as you say"), which was tantamount to a plea of guilt of revolt against the Roman emperor and the king recognized by him. Such a confession would have been sufficient in Roman law for conviction of the defendant. Against this view, the Jewish trial theory is historically and theologically more widespread, and the whole complex question is exhaustively discussed by Haim H. Cohen, Justice of the Supreme Court of Israel, in an article in *Israel Law Review* [1967], 332.

What is the comparison between the common law of England with its adaptation to the United States of America and the law of the Romans? The method of both systems is casuistic. Generalizations and definitions are avoided. Both systems proceed from case to case in quest of a utilitarian set of rules, even at the price of some logical incoherence. There are noticeable differences, for example, in the notion of the family. The common law looks upon the family as a natural conception based upon marriage and consanguinity. The Romanist sees the family as a purely civil entity, into which, from antiquity, strangers could be admitted by adoption. Again, the sharp Roman distinction between possession and ownership is unknown to the common law. We have already noted that the concept of *hereditas* had the connotation almost of a person. The *heres* as a universal successor finds but faint resemblance to the common law executor or administrator. The Romans had no general theory of contract, but a law of contracts. Delictal liability is closer to the idea of vengeance than our criminal and tortious liability. But in both systems a developing trend toward equitable principles is discernible.

(See further A. Borkowski and P. du Plessis, *Textbook on Roman Law* [2005]; C. Ando and J. Rüpke, eds., *Religion and Law in Classical and Christian Rome* [2006].) J. A. B. O'Keefe

Roman religion

I. Italic foundations. The basic indigenous religion of Rome first took shape in the primitive and patriarchal agricultural community from which the nation emerged. Its form and nature were similar to those of the religions of neighboring Italic peoples, the Oscan and Umbrian tribes, which hemmed in the enclave around the Tiber occupied by the Latin people. The primitive Roman religion may be glimpsed in Ovid's monumental *Fasti* and in parts of Varro, Livy, Macrobius, and Aulus Gellius. It was animistic, recognizing deity in spiritual presences rather than in the persons of anthropomorphic gods. Such spirits dwelt in and about natural features, rivers, woods, springs. Prospero's "elves of hills, woods, standing lakes and groves" (*Tempest* 5.1) touches the thought. They had power to aid or harm, and their presence was felt in the sense of awe that pervades the human spirit before nature's strength, beauty, power, or beneficence. As one stepped into the woods (*silva*), the heart might be lifted in prayer to Silvanus. Neptunus derives his name in like fashion from a primitive Italic word for water. Portunus was the tutelary spirit of harbors (*portus*). Augustine, in a satiric passage (*The City of God* 4.8), makes fun of this Roman faculty for coining names of deity, and no doubt in the strict sense of the word it was polytheistic; but it is a little less than just to the religious sense of the early Italian, who thought thus to address a power of which he was aware, and with which he sought contact, but which he could not envisage or wholly understand.

There was some concept of a supreme deity. Jupiter, or Diespiter, as he was primitively called, was the spirit of the sky (*diei pater,* father of day or of daylight) and was adapted to this role, but the early Italic farmer was more preoccupied with the spirits of his environment. These concerns account for such periodic festivals as the Saturnalia at the time of sowing (*sero satum*) and the Robigalia, which sought to avert blight (*robigo*) from the crop. The house was full of such spirit presences. Ianus was the spirit of the door (*ianua*), Vesta of the hearth (the primitive root means "to burn"), and the Penates the guardians of the stored food (*penus*). The *Lar familiaris* probably protected the slaves.

"In its sphere," wrote Cyril Bailey, "the functional will is powerful. It must be approached with a sense of awe — for this is what *religio* appears first to mean — but its normal relation to men is kindly, and its goodwill may be kept by the offering of appropriate gifts at the appropriate time" ("Religion and Philosophy," in *The Legacy of Rome* [1923], 240). Moreover these cults of the countryside persisted long after Roman religion was overlaid and transformed by importation from Greece and the E, even after the coming of Christianity. Augustine's attack was delivered not on the Greco-Roman pantheon, but on the little gods of the ancient litanies. In cults of local saints and rural rituals and feasts, it is possible to this day in country districts of Italy to find traces of the ancient religions absorbed into the practices of Christianity.

II. The religion of the city. The rural festivals, when Rome became the absorbing and central scene of Latin life, were maintained with appropriate new significance. Cyril Bailey, in the essay already quoted, summarizes well (pp. 243–44):

> The old rustic spirits took on new functions in their new surroundings: Iuppiter, the sky-spirit, and therefore the god of oaths sworn under the vault of heaven, becomes the deity of internal justice; Mars, in the main at any rate an agricultural deity in the earlier stage, becomes now the god of war. In this stage there are from our present point of view two features of special note. In the first place we have the gradual but unmistakable establishment of a state religion. The old cults had been in the hands of individual households: the state now takes them over and consecrates them to its own uses. A great temple is built on the Capitoline Hill—the centre of the new Rome—and in it is established the worship of a divine triad symbolizing the religious majesty of the state, at first Iuppiter, Quirinus, and Mars, symbol no doubt of the union of the two old settlements on the Palatine and Quirinal hills, and then, after Etruscan influence had made itself felt, Iuppiter, Iuno, and Minerva. A priestly hierarchy too was created, *flamines* for the principal deities, and the college of *pontifices*, associated with many of the minor rites presided over by the *pontifex maximus*, who becomes the repository of sacred law and keeps the secret of the festival calendar, which he only reveals to the people month by month. The vague contract-notion in the earlier relation between god and man is embodied now in the juristic system of the state: the *ius divinum* becomes a department of the *ius civile*.

Just as the cults of the country permeated daily life, so the same beliefs and practices penetrated and infused the life of the larger household, the state. Augury and auspices, adopted from those experts in ritual and divination, the Etruscans of central Italy, dominated all the affairs of state. A real institutional religion with colleges of pontiffs and priests grew around such practice and provided model and framework for the church.

It was at this time that Rome also developed her practice of absorption. It was part of the spirit of the old Italian religion that it saw and recognized divine life everywhere—hence, the readiness to assimilate the cults and deities of subjected peoples. Minerva appears to have come from Falerii to be the patroness of trade guilds, Castor and Pollux from Tusculum, and Hercules, the Italian form of Heracles, from the southern Greek communities. It was a trait of Roman character, visible in the infinite adaptations of local government to serve the ends of her imperial control, that she found herself able so to assimilate. Hence, the clash of state and church when Christianity, which refused all compromise, demanded full commitment and an unchallenged monopoly over life.

III. The Greek invasion. "Captive Greece," wrote Horace, "led captive her fierce conqueror" (*Epistle* 2.1.156). This was true of religion as well as of literature and art. Rome's willingness to accept and receive met its most transforming challenge when the republic, becoming a Mediterranean and imperial power after the Punic wars that filled the second half of the 3rd cent. B.C., made wider contacts with the Greeks in Sicily and their own Hellenic homeland. Roman belief ran strongly in the direction of Greek ANTHROPOMORPHISM. Her native deities fused with the gods of the Greek pantheon. Jupiter was ZEUS; Hera, Zeus's consort, was therefore Juno. Neptune was Poseidon; Mars, Ares; Minerva, Athena; Diana, ARTEMIS; Mercury, HERMES; while Bacchus or DIONYSUS found his counterpart in the old nature spirit Liber.

The lesser deities were not omitted. Faunus, the old patron of agriculture and shepherding, became Pan. Curiously, APOLLO found no parallel. He was an early introduction from Etruria, in fact, and was accepted as a god of healing as early as 433 B.C. Games for Apollo, the *ludi Apollinares*, were established in 212 B.C. In Augustus's day his cult, thanks to the enthusiasm of the prince for the god whose aid he had evoked at the decisive climax of Actium, was widely extended. The young bright god was, in the mind of Augustus, a symbol of hope for the new Rome he sought to create, and a central figure in the revival of old worship sponsored by the prince.

In Ennius (239–169 B.C.) and Plautus (251–184 B.C.), two of the earliest extant writers of Rome, one sees the process of identification almost complete. Perhaps the need to translate aided the process, a curious convention that extended its influence as far as the translators of the KJV, who, in the story of Paul and Barnabas at Lystra (Acts 14:12), render the Zeus and Hermes of the original as Jupiter and Mercury. Ennius (*Ann.* 1. frag.) gives the full list of the Greek deities under their Latin titles. This list falls into two hexameters: "Iuno Vesta Minerva Ceres Diana Venus Mars / Mercurius Iovis Neptunus Volcanus Apollo." Plautus does the same, adding Latona, Spes, Ops, Castor, Pollux, Virtus, Hercules, Summanus (identified with Pluto), Sol, and Saturnus, all of whom, except Latona and Summanus, had temples in Rome.

In the midst of this wholesale identification of Roman cults and deities with those of Greece, Italian cults of primitive antiquity were maintained in Rome itself and served by aristocratic priesthoods.

There is, for example, the priestly college of the Arval Brethren, an ancient agricultural cult that was restored by Augustus as part of his great religious revival in 21 B.C. A hymn of this primitive ritual dating back to the 5th cent. has been preserved, almost unintelligible in its ancient Latin, but significantly addressed to Mars, still an agricultural deity.

It is possible therefore to picture the religion of Rome in the 2nd and 3rd centuries B.C. as a composite and intermingled phenomenon, with ancient country cults in city dress, old deities—transformed and hellenized—worshiped in temples like those of the Greek world, Italian rituals of divination tangled with obscure Etruscan practice and attached to the worship of various deities in the service of the state, in all an astonishing syncretism of past and present, race and race. It was without doubt a vast confusion that contributed heavily to the prevailing skepticism in urban society in matters of religious belief—that skepticism which marked Roman society at the end of the republican era.

The result was that the gods of the pantheon became little more than the devices and ornaments of literature. The practice of official cults continued with little meaning, and under the protection of Roman conservatism was fed by a measure of superstition. In the countryside the old cults continued almost in their ancient forms. In the private practice of individuals religion took what form it could. Cyril Bailey concludes: "So beneath the surface of the Graeco-Roman religion the old faith survived: in the houses at Pompeii we find small shrines peopled with statues not of the Graeco-Roman hierarchy but of little Lares and Penates, and the real religious affection of Virgil—the most truly Roman of the poets for all his Greek culture—lies not with the gods of Olympus, but with the *di agrestes* of the Roman countryside. And if the common people thus possessed their souls in the old faith, salvation came also to the cultivated from the source which at first sight seemed the most destructive influence of all—Greek philosophy" (p. 247).

There is no doubt that, with the collapse of religious belief, philosophy provided a religion and a way of life for more thoughtful Romans (see Greek religion and philosophy II.C). Stoicism

The Romans absorbed Greek deities like Nike, goddess of victory, pictured here on one of the buildings at Ephesus.

ROMAN RELIGION

Roman group statue representing the deities Ariadne, Bacchus, and Pan. (Terra-cotta, made in Tunisia, 2nd cent. A.D.)

religious lore and experience into Rome. The situation indicates a vacuum in the Roman spirit that some sought to fill with philosophy, others with the exotic religions of the alien.

The state itself, in fact, once gave a lead. In one of those moods of collective self-condemnation that occasionally mark her history, as early as 204 B.C. at the end of the second war with Carthage, Rome had introduced from PHRYGIA in ASIA MINOR the cult of the Great Mother or Cybele. It was an orgiastic cult, served by dancing drum-beating eunuch priests, with strange and horrible rites of mutilation and ecstatic experience. Such emotional refuge has been sought by certain types of mind in all ages in revolt against formalism and frigidity in accepted religion. The worship of Cybele in Rome became so popular that the senate was constrained to regulate it. It inspired the most weird of Catullus's poems (63).

Later, in the Mithridatic wars of the first half of the last pre-Christian century (88–63 B.C.), legionaries found the Cappadocian goddess Ma with its ritual of the *taurobolium*, or baptism in bull's blood, a path to "eternal rebirth." Later the conquest of Egypt brought the cult of Isis to Rome with its fastings and resurrection-drama (see OSIRIS). Such cults were entrenched before the end of the republic, and Augustus, endeavoring to restore the earlier Greco-Roman and more primitive Italian cults, found it impossible to suppress them. With similar urgency, and no doubt with no greater real success, the senate had sought, as early as 186 B.C., to crush the orgiastic rites of Dionysus in southern Italy where, through the influence of worshipers in the Greek communities, they had gained a foothold (Livy, *Hist.* 39.8–18; the senatorial decree, put out on this occasion, is a precious example of early Latin, *CIL*, 1.196). Habitually, such cults meet suppression by going underground.

By the 3rd cent. many other eastern cults, those of the Syrian ATARGATIS, the Phrygian Sebazios, and the Persian Mithras, were widely established. MITHRAISM may, indeed, be traced back to Sulla's day, but the 2nd and 3rd cent. A.D. were its heyday, chiefly in the Roman army. Mithraea are found in London and on Hadrian's Wall, and the cult of the god, not an ignoble one, was a serious rival of Christianity.

was undoubtedly such a force for many Romans in the last century of the republic and the opening century of the empire. Epicureanism, in the minds of characters as varied as Cicero's friend Atticus and the poet Lucretius, also became a way of life and a system of belief. Cicero, Horace, Seneca, all in their different ways and to different depths of personal experience eclectics, found in philosophy the comfort and the steadying strength which an outmoded paganism denied them. But there was another outcome, for the starved Roman spirit sought satisfaction (see below).

IV. Eastern cults. The Roman faculty for adaptation and absorption of alien religions has already been noted. As the expansion of the geographical empire continued, more and more foreign deities confronted the Romans, and more and more of them found acceptance in her hospitable pantheon. The Greek gods moved in on the strength of Greek culture. They were part of the expanding empire of HELLENISM. Beyond Greece lay Asia with its vast complex of MYSTERY RELIGIONS and FERTILITY CULTS, and from Asia came the next great inflow of

V. Caesar-worship. The worship of the spirit of Rome and the emperor has been dealt with under a separate heading (see EMPEROR WORSHIP). Suffice it to point out in conclusion that its concept, though finding origin in the deification of the rulers of the E, had roots in the old Italian concept of deified abstractions. If the mystery cults met the challenge of Christianity on the emotional level, and the monotheistic speculations of such writers as Cicero, Seneca, Epictetus, and Marcus Aurelius on the philosophical level, Caesarism met it on the social and political level. The Christian faith came to a world hungry, insecure, and unsatisfied, to a morally disintegrating society, and to utter religious confusion.

(See further S. Dill, *Roman Society in the Last Century of the Western Empire* [1898]; R. D. Hicks, *Stoic and Epicurean* [1910]; F. Cumont, *The Mysteries of Mithra* [1910]; W. W. Fowler, *The Religious Experience of the Roman People* [1911]; E. V. Arnold, *Roman Stoicism* [1911]; E. Bevan, *Stoics and Sceptics* [1913]; W. W. Fowler, *Roman Ideas of Deity* [1914]; S. Dill, *Roman Society from Nero to Marcus Aurelius* [1919]; T. R. Glover, *The Conflict of Religions in the Early Roman Empire* [1919]; H. J. Rose, *Religion in Greece and Rome* [1959]; J. Ferguson, *The Religions of the Roman Empire* [1970]; G. Dumézil, *Archaic Roman Religion*, 2 vols. [1970]; J. H. W. G. Liebeschuetz, *Continuity and Change in Roman Religion* [1979]; R. MacMullen, *Paganism in the Roman Empire* [1981]; R. Turcan, *The Cults of the Roman Empire* [1996]; M. Beard et al., *Religions of Rome*, 2 vols. [1998]; H.-J. Klauck, *The Religious Context of Early Christianity: A Guide to Graeco-Roman Religions* [2000]; R. Turcan, *The Gods of Ancient Rome: Religion in Everyday Life from Archaic to Imperial Times* [2000]; J. Scheid, *An Introduction to Roman Religion* [2003]; J. B. Rives, *Religion in the Roman Empire* [2006]; C. Ando, *The Matter of the Gods: Religion and the Roman Empire* [2008].)

E. M. BLAIKLOCK

Romans, Epistle to the. The longest of the thirteen NT letters bearing the name of PAUL, and the first letter in the long-established order of the *corpus Paulinum*.

  I. Authorship
  II. Destination
  III. Christianity in Rome
  IV. Occasion, purpose, and date
   V. Outline
  VI. Contents
    A. Prologue
    B. The foundation of Christian doctrine
    C. The righteousness of God in history
    D. The Christian way of life
    E. Epilogue
  VII. Text
  VIII. Canonicity and authority

I. Authorship. If one disregards certain erratic schools of thought (such as the Dutch school of W. C. van Manen at the beginning of the 20th cent.) that have denied apostolic authorship to any of the documents in the *corpus Paulinum*, the Pauline authorship of Romans is uncontested. With GALATIANS and the two letters to the CORINTHIANS, Romans belongs to the four "capital epistles" (*Hauptbriefe*) that are basic material for determining the main lines of Paul's teaching. In one sense it is otiose to speak of the Pauline authorship of Romans and its three companion letters, since for most theological purposes "Paul" and "the author of Romans, Galatians, and 1 and 2 Corinthians" are synonymous terms.

II. Destination. In the opening salutation the addressees are denoted as "all in Rome who are loved by God and called to be saints" (Rom. 1:7; for the textual problem of the phrase "in Rome" see section VII below). The fact that Paul did not speak of the "church" in ROME may be significant; perhaps at this time there was no city-wide church in the city with a community consciousness of its own, as there was, for example, in CORINTH, where Paul himself had planted and tended the church. On the other hand, the fact that Paul can address a letter to all the Christians in Rome implies some assurance on his part that they would all have access to it. Even if the only church life in Rome was found in decentralized groups or household churches, the fact of their common faith in Christ would tend to give them a sense of fellowship one with another

III. Christianity in Rome. There is no record of the planting of Christianity in Rome. The position of the city as the center of communications throughout the Roman empire would insure that Christianity, once it was securely established in the eastern provinces, would reach the capital sooner rather than later. The mention of "visitors from Rome (both Jews and converts to Judaism)" (Acts 2:10–11) as the only European contingent in the list of those present in Jerusalem at the first Christian PENTECOST may suggest that some of these, impressed by what they heard, carried the message back to Rome. In the 4th cent. the Latin writer conventionally called "Ambrosiaster," in the preamble to his commentary on this epistle, says that the Romans "had embraced the faith of Christ, albeit according to the Jewish rite, without seeing any sign of mighty works or any of the apostles." These words probably preserve a sound tradition. What he wrote about the "Jewish rite" reflects the probable truth of the matter, that it was Jewish Christians who first carried the gospel to Rome. As late as the time of Hippolytus, early in the 3rd cent., Christian worship at Rome retained some elements derived from JUDAISM, and from "nonconformist" rather than normative Judaism (e.g., the preliminary bath of purification that converts were required to undergo on the Thursday preceding Easter, by way of preparation for their baptism on Easter Day itself, according to the Hippolytan APOSTOLIC TRADITION). That the base of Roman Christianity was Jewish—although when Paul wrote it comprised more Gentile than Jewish believers—is a natural inference from Rom. 11:13–24.

The Jewish colony that existed in Rome as early as the 2nd cent. B.C. was greatly augmented from 63 B.C. onward, after JUDEA was incorporated into the Roman empire; Cicero in 59 B.C. represented it as large, clannish, powerful, and influential. The city authorities from time to time tried to evict masses of undesirable immigrants, and occasionally the Jewish colony attracted their unfriendly attention in this regard. In A.D. 19, when TIBERIUS was emperor, there was a large-scale expulsion of Jews from Rome because of a financial scandal (Jos. *Ant*. 18.3.5ff.), but in a decade or two they were back in larger numbers than ever. CLAUDIUS, at the beginning of his principate (A.D. 41), took some steps to restrict them (Dio Cassius, *Hist*. 60.6), but about eight years later he resorted to the more drastic course of expulsion. This expulsion, mentioned in Acts 18:2, is ascribed by SUETONIUS (*Claudius* 25) to the Roman Jews' "constant indulgence in riots at the instigation of Chrestus." These last words are enigmatic; it is conceivable that at this time there was in Rome a Jewish agitator named Chrestus of whom nothing else is known. It is more likely that Suetonius reproduced a garbled version of the rioting which repeatedly broke out within the Jewish colony as a result of the introduction of Christianity. That on this occasion the expelled Jews included some who acknowledged Jesus as the Messiah is evident from the fact that Aquila and his wife Priscilla were among them; they appear to have been Christians before they met Paul in Corinth, for Paul never refers to them as though they were converts of his (see PRISCILLA AND AQUILA).

The expulsion under Claudius was no more durable than that under Tiberius. The edict may have been allowed to lapse with Claudius's death (A.D. 54), if not earlier; a few years later the Jewish colony in Rome was as flourishing as ever, and as before it included Jewish believers in Jesus. By the time Paul wrote the letter to the Romans, not more than eight years after the edict of expulsion, the Christian community in the capital comprised a considerable Gentile element which probably by that time outnumbered the Jewish membership. At any rate, Paul could assure his readers that their faith was "being reported all over the world" (Rom. 1:8).

The letter to the Romans was sent from Corinth to Rome.

Some idea of the composition of the Roman church at this time may be gathered from the greetings in Rom. 16, if one regards this chapter as destined for Rome (on this question see section VII below). Many people whom Paul had met at various places in the eastern provinces from time to time were then resident in Rome, so that he had many friends there, although thus far he had never visited the city. They included members of the households of certain scions of the HEROD family, and also two of Paul's kinsmen and fellow prisoners who, he says, "are outstanding among the apostles" (v. 7) and were Christians before he himself was, with one or two others like RUFUS (prob.), whose association with the Christian movement went back to the earliest days. The presence of such men and women in the Roman church, even if they were a handful in proportion to the total membership, must have contributed greatly to its strength.

It may be that by the time this letter was written Christianity was beginning to make its way into the upper strata of Roman society. In A.D. 57 the wife of Aulus Plautius (who had added Britain to the Roman empire fourteen years before) was accused before a domestic court of having embraced a "foreign superstition" which, from the description of her way of life, might have been Christianity (Tacitus, *Annals* 13.32). She was acquitted, and continued for the rest of her life to enjoy the esteem of her friends in spite of her retiring ways, which presented a sharp contrast to the social frivolity of many of her contemporaries. Some color is given to the view that her "foreign superstition" was Christianity by archaeological evidence for the prevalence of Christianity in her family in the following century.

By the time of the first great persecution of Roman Christians, which broke out as the sequel to the fire of A.D. 64, they were so numerous that a pagan historian (Tacitus, *Annals* 15.44) and a Christian father (*1 Clement* 6.1) both described the martyrs on that occasion as "a huge multitude." The Roman church survived the ordeal and continued to increase and enjoy the esteem of Christians throughout the world as a church "worthy of God, worthy of honour, worthy of praise, worthy of success, worthy in purity, pre-eminent in love, walking in the law of Christ and bearing the Father's name" (Ignatius, *To the Romans*, preface). See further ROME, CHURCH AT.

IV. Occasion, purpose, and date. The writing of this letter is a milestone in the course of Paul's ministry as apostle to the GENTILES. In Acts 19:21 LUKE says that toward the close of his three years' evangelization of EPHESUS and the province of ASIA, Paul planned to visit MACEDONIA and ACHAIA, the theater of an earlier phase of his ministry, and then go to JERUSALEM, adding, "After I have been there … I must visit Rome also." Luke puts the matter from his own perspective: Rome is the goal of his narrative, and when he has brought Paul there some years later and portrayed him preaching the gospel unhindered at the heart of the empire, under the eyes of the highest authorities, he has achieved his purpose. Paul's perspective was different; to him, Rome was not a goal but a place he must visit in transit, or at best a base from which he could set out on a further phase of his ministry, with a view to repeating in the western Mediterranean the program which (at the time indicated in Acts 19:21) he had almost completed in the eastern regions. That Paul's plan for this westward advance was conceived around the time indicated by Luke may be gathered from this letter.

With the evangelization of the province of Asia, Paul had completed his program of missionary pioneering in ASIA MINOR and the AEGEAN world. The gospel had been preached and churches had been planted in the principal cities and along the principal roads of Galatia, Asia, Macedonia, and Achaia. During the brief visit to the Balkan peninsula which followed his Ephesian ministry, Paul carried the gospel farther W than he had previously done, at least as far as the border of ILLYRICUM (Rom. 15:19), the province on the eastern shore of the Adriatic. In his own words, "there is no more place for me to work in these regions" (15:23). His missionary zeal had not weakened through the arduous experiences of the past years; there were other non-Jewish lands to be won for the gospel, and the responsibility of evangelizing them rested peculiarly on Paul as the Gentiles' apostle par excellence. Some lands along the Mediterranean seaboard had, however, been evangelized already

Aerial view of the remains of ancient Rome. (View to the NNE.)

by others than Paul; he looked for virgin soil, for territory where the name of Christ had never been heard. SPAIN, the oldest Roman province in the W and an important bastion of Roman civilization, was such a place; to Spain, then, Paul decided to go and continue his apostolic service there.

First, however, he determined to go to Jerusalem and give an account of his stewardship thus far — not his stewardship to the church of Jerusalem or its leaders, for he denied that he had in any sense been commissioned by them, but to the risen Christ. One may ask why he should have thought it necessary to go to Jerusalem for this purpose; could he not have accomplished it in Ephesus or Corinth? Perhaps he could have done so; but a consideration of his reason may help to understand the place which Jerusalem held in Paul's thinking. Although it was in DAMASCUS that he first began to preach the gospel, he describes the first stage of his mission as having been fulfilled "from Jerusalem all the way around to Illyricum" (Rom. 15:19), as though Jerusalem were his point of departure. It was in Jerusalem many years before that Paul had a vision of the Lord in the temple and heard his command: "Go; I will send you far away to the Gentiles" (Acts 22:21). To that same spot he would return and present to his Master as a spiritual sacrifice the fruit of his "priestly duty of proclaiming the gospel of God" (Rom. 15:16).

He planned also to take with him to Jerusalem delegates of the Gentile churches he had founded in the Aegean provinces, bearing gifts from their churches as a contribution to relieve the poverty of the mother church in Jerusalem; thus, he hoped, the bonds of fellowship would be more securely forged between those churches and the headquarters of Jewish Christianity, where the Gentile mission in general, and Paul's activity in particular, tended to be viewed with misgivings and suspicion. When this service had been completed, and not before, he would be free to turn his steps in the direction of Spain. On the route to Spain he would have an opportunity of realizing an ambition cherished for many years — the ambition of seeing Rome. Roman citizen though he was from birth, he had never visited the city. It was, therefore, in large measure to prepare the Christians of Rome for his projected visit that he sent them this letter.

The date of the letter is probably to be fixed at some point in the winter of A.D. 56–57. The chronology of this phase of Paul's career can be determined to some degree by the inscriptional evidence from Delphi dating GALLIO's entry on the proconsulship of Achaia (cf. Acts 18:12) in the summer of the year 51 (or, less prob., 52), and by the numismatic evidence pointing to 59 as the year of Felix's supersession by Festus in the procuratorship of Judea (cf. 24:27). In terms of the narrative of Acts, the writing of the letter may be placed during Paul's three months in Greece (20:3). The reference to his host Gaius (Rom. 16:23, valid evidence whatever the destination of this chapter may have been) points to Corinth as the city where Paul was resident at the time (cf. 1 Cor. 1:14); so does the reference to "Erastus, the city treasurer" (Rom. 16:23 NRSV)—if, as seems likely, this Erastus is to be identified with the man of that name mentioned as curator of public buildings in a Corinthian inscription uncovered in 1929 (cf. NIV, "the city's director of public works").

In addition to paving the way for his visit to Rome, Paul hoped to secure the good will of the Roman Christians to such an extent that they would provide him with a forward base for his Spanish mission—in the way, for example, that Antioch of Syria had served as a base for Barnabas and himself when they evangelized Cyprus and the cities of S Galatia. (This element is perhaps taken too far by R. Jewett, *Romans: A Commentary* [2007], who argues vigorously that the primary purpose of the letter is "to gain support for a mission to the barbarians in Spain, which requires that the gospel of impartial, divine righteousness revealed in Christ be clarified to rid it of prejudicial elements that are currently dividing the congregations in Rome" [p. 1].)

Paul knew that outside his own mission field (and even to some degree inside it) his reputation suffered from the criticisms of his opponents. Therefore he availed himself of the opportunity to place before the Roman Christians a systematic statement of the gospel as he understood and proclaimed it, and of his policy as apostle to the Gentiles. He does not impose his authority on these readers as he does when he writes to his own converts; yet he makes it plain that the authority by which he carries on his ministry is imparted to him by the risen Christ, who called him to be his apostle.

The gospel expounded in this letter is recognizably "the gospel according to Paul" as known from his other letters, and especially from Galatians. Whereas Galatians was an urgent response to a critical situation in Paul's mission field, Romans is a more dispassionate and orderly unfolding of the same theme to which Galatians is related "as the rough model to the finished statue" (J. B. Lightfoot, *St. Paul's Epistle to the Galatians*, 10th ed. [1890], 49; for current debate on the purpose of Romans see the bibliography at the end of the article). A great deal of the present letter was therefore of general interest, and it is probable that from the first, at Paul's own instance, copies of it were circulated to other churches as well as to that in Rome (see section VII below).

How well the letter accomplished its immediate purpose is uncertain; not for three years was Paul able to visit Rome, and when he came it was not as a free agent but as a prisoner under armed guard to stand trial before Caesar, to whose supreme court he had appealed from the jurisdiction of the procurator of Judea. The reception of the letter may have had something to do with the welcome he received from some Roman Christians as he approached their city along the Appian Way, when he was still some 40 mi. distant. "The brothers there," says his companion Luke, "had heard that we were coming, and they traveled as far as the Forum of Appius and the Three Taverns to meet us. At the sight of these men Paul thanked God and was encouraged" (Acts 28:15).

V. Outline

A. Prologue (Rom. 1:1–15)
  1. Salutation (1:1–7)
  2. Introduction (1:8–15)
B. The foundation of Christian doctrine (1:16—8:39)
  1. The theme of the gospel: the righteousness of God revealed (1:16–17)
  2. Sin and retribution: the universal need diagnosed (1:18—3:20)
    a. The pagan world (1:18–32)
    b. The moralist (2:1–16)
    c. The Jew (2:17—3:8)
    d. All mankind under condemnation (3:9–20)
  3. The way of righteousness: the universal need met (3:21—5:21)
    a. God's provision (3:21–31)
    b. An OT precedent (4:1–25)
    c. The blessings that accompany justification: peace, joy, hope (5:1–11)

     d. The old and the new humanity
        (5:12–21)
  4. The way of holiness (6:1—8:39)
     a. Freedom from sin (6:1–23)
        (1) A supposed objection (6:1–2)
        (2) The meaning of baptism (6:3–14)
        (3) The slave market analogy
            (6:15–23)
     b. Freedom from the law (7:1–25)
        (1) The marriage analogy (7:1–6)
        (2) The dawn of conscience (7:7–13)
        (3) The conflict within (7:14–25)
     c. Freedom from death (8:1–39)
        (1) Life in the Spirit (8:1–17)
        (2) The glory to come (8:18–30)
        (3) The triumph of faith (8:31–39)
C. The righteousness of God in history
   (9:1—11:36)
  1. The problem of Israel's unbelief (9:1–5)
  2. God's sovereign choice (9:6–29)
  3. Human responsibility (9:30—10:21)
     a. The stumbling stone (9:30–33)
     b. The two ways of righteousness
        (10:1–13)
     c. The worldwide proclamation
        (10:14–21)
  4. God's purpose for Israel (11:1–29)
     a. Israel's alienation not final (11:1–16)
     b. The parable of the olive tree
        (11:17–24)
     c. The restoration of Israel (11:25–29)
  5. God's purpose for mankind (11:30–36)
D. The Christian way of life (12:1—15:13)
  1. The living sacrifice (12:1–2)
  2. The common life of Christians (12:3–8)
  3. The law of Christ (12:9–21)
  4. The Christian and the state (13:1–7)
  5. Love and duty (13:8–10)
  6. Christian life in days of crisis (13:11–14)
  7. Christian liberty and Christian charity
     (14:1—15:6)
     a. Christian liberty (14:1–12)
     b. Christian charity (14:13–23)
     c. The example of Christ (15:1–6)
  8. Christ and the Gentiles (15:7–13)
E. Epilogue (15:14—16:27)
  1. Personal narrative (15:14–33)
  2. Commendation of Phoebe (16:1–2)
  3. Greetings to various friends (16:3–16)
  4. Final exhortation and blessing
     (16:17–20)
  5. Greetings from Paul's companions
     (16:21–23)
  6. Doxology (16:24–27)

VI. Contents

A. Prologue (Rom. 1:1–15). Paul expands the opening salutation (Rom. 1:1–7) to emphasize his special calling and the nature of the gospel which he has been commissioned to proclaim. The gospel has God as its author and his Son Jesus Christ as its subject matter; it is no innovation, but was promised of old by the prophets. Jesus Christ traced his human lineage from King David (this is part of the early Jewish KERYGMA, calculated to show that Jesus possessed the genealogical credentials for the Davidic messiahship); but his RESURRECTION, accomplished by the power of the HOLY SPIRIT, set him forth "with power" as "Son of God." To bring the nations under the Son's obedience Paul, his servant, had been chosen by him and endowed with apostolic grace. Since Rome belongs to the Gentile world it falls within the sphere of Paul's apostleship, and to the Christians of Rome he addressed himself with his customary greeting of "grace and peace."

The introduction to his argument (Rom. 1:8–15) assures his readers that he regularly prays for them and thanks God for them, since he is well acquainted with their good reputation, and explains that his reason for not having visited them was lack of opportunity, since he has often planned to see them, in order to preach the gospel at Rome as elsewhere in the Gentile world and enjoy mutual fellowship and refreshment in their company. The preaching of the gospel is for him an obligation he will never have fully discharged as long as he lives.

B. The foundation of Christian doctrine (Rom. 1:16—8:39). The main section of the letter begins with a brief statement of the nature and theme of the GOSPEL: it is God's mighty means for the salvation of all believers, Jew and Gentile alike, and it displays the RIGHTEOUSNESS of God—not merely God's righteous character but his gracious bestowal of a righteous status on believers, in accordance with Hab. 2:4, which Paul possibly construes to mean, "he who through faith is righteous shall live" (Rom. 1:16–17).

The necessity for sinners to receive God's righteousness by faith if they are to receive it at all is then unfolded (Rom. 1:18—3:20). Stage by stage the moral bankruptcy of humanity is demonstrated. A somber backdrop to the GRACE of God in the gospel is the WRATH of God manifesting itself in human history: wrong ideas of God lead to wrong ways of life. The indictment of the pagan world (1:18–32) was not only common form in Jewish literature of the time; it could also be corroborated in the judgment of many Gentile writers. The repeated "God gave them over" (vv. 24, 26, 28) bespeaks the working of divine RETRIBUTION in history. The statement that people had the knowledge of God at their disposal in his works of creation (vv. 19–20) is paralleled by Paul's speech to the Athenian AREOPAGUS (Acts 17:24–31); the differences of perspective between the two passages are due to the different audiences addressed. The moral argument of these verses had already been summarized in Jewish literature: "For the idea of making idols was the beginning of fornication, and the invention of them was the corruption of life" (Wisd. 14:12).

Paul then envisages a bystander applauding this denunciation of pagan immorality and turns on him to assure him that he is in no better case (Rom. 2:1–16). Such denunciations can be paralleled among pagan moralists as well as among Jews of that period, and although Paul had a Jewish critic in mind from the outset of ch. 2, his language through v. 16 would be largely applicable to such a pagan as SENECA. It is not enough to avoid the grosser forms of immorality if one is involved in the society which fosters them or practices essentially the same vices in a more refined way. The JUDGMENT of God is completely impartial; it is proportioned to the works of each person, whether Jew or Gentile, moralizer or libertine. If some people presume that since divine retribution has not manifested itself in their lives in the manner detailed in ch. 1, they are exempt from that judgment, let them thank God for his goodness, and reflect that this goodness is a sign of God's patience, giving them opportunity to repent. If Jews break the LAW of Moses, they must repent of their transgression,

A marble statue of Emperor Claudius, who ordered the expulsion of Jews from Rome in the early 50s.

but the fact that Gentiles have not received that law does not exempt the latter from the necessity of REPENTANCE: they have a divine law written in the conscience; when they break it they know that they are doing wrong, and will be judged in the light of it at the last judgment.

Turning more directly to the Jews (Rom. 2:17–29), Paul writes that they have no cause to suppose that they enjoy a position of special favor before God because of the privileges God has lavished on the nation. It is not the knowledge but the doing of the law that is important. The Jew who knows the will of God by REVELATION is more guilty if he disobeys it than the Gentile who has no such knowledge. There are many ways of breaking the divine commandments, and when Paul applied to the reputation of Jews in the Roman empire the words of Isa. 52:5—"God's name is blasphemed among the Gentiles because of you" (Rom. 2:24)—he said something that found corroboration in both Jewish and Gentile writers of the period. What is of primary importance is that a person's heart must be right with God; apart from that, the knowledge of the law and the covenant of CIRCUMCISION are valueless. God will accept an uncircumcised Gentile who does his will rather than a circumcised Jew who does not. It is the circumcision of the heart that matters (cf. Deut. 10:16); by etymology the true Jew is the person whose life wins "praise" from God (Rom. 2:28–29; cf. Gen. 29:35; 49:8), and such praise is not confined to people of any one race.

If this is so, someone may ask, is there any advantage in being a Jew? This quotation of a question or objection by someone breaking into Paul's argument is a feature of the DIATRIBE style of Greek rhetoric, repeatedly used by the apostle in this letter. Paul's reply is that there is great advantage in belonging to the people to whom the oracles of God were committed, in order that they might be the instrument for the accomplishment of his purpose in the world. It is true that some of them proved unfaithful to their trust, but since God is God, no imperfection in the instrument can thwart his purpose. Nor can he be blamed for not foreseeing such imperfection: no lawsuit against God can ever succeed. Nor can those who have been unfaithful to their trust claim indulgence because their unfaithfulness has been overruled by God for his glory: the doing of evil that good may come is always to be condemned (Rom. 3:1–8).

Despite the advantages inherited by Jews, their failure to treat these advantages responsibly means that before God they have no claim to favor over Gentiles. A CATENA of OT passages, establishing the sinfulness of all mankind, applies to Gentiles but in the first instance to Jews, since they were the people with whom the sacred writers were primarily concerned. The whole world is bound to plead guilty at God's tribunal; no one can expect to be justified there on the ground of his works or his obedience to God's law; the law which sets forth God's will reveals in the event the sinner's inability to do that will (Rom. 3:9–20).

Every attempt of human beings to establish their own righteousness before God being ruled out of court, the way is open for the introduction of God's way of righteousness, and to this Paul devotes the crucially important passage which follows (Rom. 3:21–23). The first part may be paraphrased thus:

But now a way to get right with God has been revealed, apart from the righteousness prescribed in the law. This way, which is attested by the law and the prophets, is provided by God through faith in Jesus Christ, for all who believe in him. There is no difference: Jew and Gentile alike have sinned, and all fall short of God's glory; but Jew and Gentile alike can be brought into a right relationship with God and secure his pardon. This they receive freely, by his pure grace, because of the redemptive work accomplished by Christ Jesus. He has been set before mankind by God as the One whose sacrificial death has made atonement for sin, and what he has procured becomes effective in a person through faith. God's righteousness has been demonstrated; in his forbearance he passed over sins committed before Christ came, instead of exacting their proper penalty, and he did so in prospect of the demonstration of his righteousness in this present epoch. While remaining perfectly righteous, he pardons those who believe in Jesus and brings them into a right relationship with himself.

The "sacrifice of atonement" (Rom. 3:25) provided in Christ averts the wrath mentioned earlier (1:18) and wipes out the sinner's guilt. It is not an act by which the sinner attempts to placate God (as if such a thing were possible) but an act in which God graciously takes the initiative. The phrase "sacrifice of atonement" renders one Greek word, *hilastērion* G2663, used elsewhere in the Greek Bible for the MERCY SEAT where God assured his people, when they confessed their sin through their sacerdotal representative, of his forgiveness and acceptance. What was done by a ritual object lesson has now been accomplished effectively in Christ "by his blood"; and all may share in its benefits by resting their faith in him. See also ATONEMENT; EXPIATION; PROPITIATION.

If this is God's way of justifying men and women, it affords them no opportunity of taking any credit to themselves; it springs from his grace, not their merit. It is a way open on equal terms to Jew and Gentile, since God is the God of both; therefore neither has now any advantage over the other. Moreover, far from setting the law aside, it vindicates the law (Rom. 3:27–31). (Since the publication of E. P. Sanders, *Paul and Palestinian Judaism: A Comparison of Patterns of Religion* [1977], there has been considerable debate regarding Paul's view of "works of law" and related topics. See the essays in D. A. Carson et al., eds., *Justification and Variegated Nomism*, 2 vols. [2001–04].)

To show how the principle of JUSTIFICATION by FAITH vindicates the law, Paul returns to the account of ABRAHAM in Genesis (Rom. 4:1–25). If obedience to God's will were the ground of justification, Abraham could make a good case for himself (cf. Gen. 26:5). According to the record, the ground of Abraham's justification was his simply taking God at his word: "Abraham believed God, and it was credited to him as righteousness" (Rom. 4:3, quoting Gen. 15:6). The place which this OT text already occupied in Paul's thinking may be seen from his use of it in Gal. 3:6. When he proceeds to speak of God as he "who justifies the wicked" (Rom. 4:5), the apostle boldly declares that God in the gospel does the very thing which in the law he says he will not do (cf. Exod. 23:7, "I will not acquit the wicked," where LXX has the same verb and noun as Paul uses).

Before developing the argument about Abraham, Paul looks at another OT use of the Hebrew verb *ḥāšab* H3108 ("credit, reckon, count"): "Blessed is the man / whose sin the LORD does not count against him" (Ps. 32:2; cf. Rom. 4:6–8). The nonreckoning of sin to the sinner is equivalent to his being reckoned righteous. Abraham's case was not isolated; DAVID's testimony was similar.

Reverting to Abraham, Paul asks whether his faith was reckoned to him as righteousness before or after he was circumcised (Rom. 4:9–10), but the apostle has no need to labor the point: Abraham was justified by faith while he was uncircumcised, years before he received the covenant of circumcision (Gen. 17:24). In this fact Paul finds a charter admitting Gentile believers, equally with Jewish believers, to the status of Abraham's heirs. It is faith, not circumcision, that is relevant. Abraham's spiritual fatherhood of Gentile as well as Jewish believers was adumbrated when God gave him a new name and said, "I have made you the father of many nations" (Rom. 4:17, quoting Gen. 17:5). His faith was no easy faith: it was faith exercised in the face of an overwhelming weight of circumstances that for most people would have made such faith seem ridiculous. But in Abraham's eyes the promise of God absolutely outweighed all those circumstances, making them of no account; he believed the bare promise before there was any external sign or likelihood of its coming to pass, and this was counted to him for righteousness. In the same way, God confers a righteous status on all who believe the Word he has spoken through the crucified and risen Jesus.

Having thus demonstrated the biblical foundation of the good news of justification by faith, Paul proceeds to describe the blessings that accompany it in the believer's life (Rom. 5:1–11). A textual problem arises in v. 1 because of the common confusion between the vowels *omicron* (Gk. ο) and *omega* (ω or "long" *o*) in the copying of MSS: the first variant (*echomen*) yields the rendering "we have peace" and suits the context better than the somewhat more strongly attested "let us have peace" (*echōmen*). PEACE, JOY, and HOPE are the boons which the justified enjoy, no matter what afflictions they have to endure. Their endurance produces strength of character, but best of all, the Holy Spirit whom they have received, and who conveys these boons to them, has poured the love of God into their hearts. The saving work that has been so effectually inaugurated in their lives will continue until its consummation at the end time; when the eschatological wrath is poured out, they will be delivered from it by the Savior who has already procured their justification by the shedding of his blood. This is their hope, both sure and joyful; meanwhile they "rejoice in God through our Lord Jesus Christ, through whom we have now received reconciliation" (v. 11).

Paul's account of God's way of righteousness concludes with a parallel drawn between the old humanity and the new (Rom. 5:12–21). ADAM, head of the old CREATION, who involved his posterity in SIN and DEATH through his disobedience, is set over against Christ, Head of the new creation, who brings his people into righteousness and life through his obedience. This is one of the two classic passages where Paul develops the concept of Christ as the second Adam (the other is 1 Cor. 15:20–23, 45–49). This concept can be traced elsewhere in his letters and may be linked with teaching associated in other parts of the Bible with the figure of the SON OF MAN. By the redemptive work which the gospel proclaims, the old "Adam-solidarity" of guilt and despair is shattered, to be replaced by the new "Christ-solidarity" of pardon and hope. For the saving effects of Christ's obedience (his lifelong obedience culminating in the crowning obedience of his submission to death) are much more comprehensive and far-reaching than the ruinous effects of Adam's disobedience.

If it be asked what place the law has in this concept, the answer is that it does not affect the great issue of death in Adam versus life in Christ; the law was introduced to bring to light the sin that was already latent. This it did, and at the same time it stimulated an increase in acts of sin. "But where sin increased, grace increased all the more" (Rom. 5:20).

From his exposition of the way of righteousness (Rom. 3:21—5:21), Paul continues in chs. 6–8 to speak of the way of HOLINESS, and he introduces this subject by supposing a questioner who, having heard him say that "where sin increased, grace increased all the more," asks why one should not go on sinning in order that grace may continue to abound (6:1). The question was probably not an imaginary one; Paul knew some members of the Gentile churches whose conduct seemed to be based on just such an argument. He replies that there can be no peaceful coexistence between death to sin and life in sin and shows what he means by two arguments: (1) he brings out the practical implication of BAPTISM (vv. 3–14), and (2) he draws an analogy from the institution of SLAVERY (vv. 15–23).

Baptism "into Christ Jesus" betokens incorporation into him, so that henceforth baptized believers are "in Christ Jesus"; sharing Christ's death they have died to the old way, and sharing his resurrection they live in the new way (see UNION WITH CHRIST). To live in sin would be, for such persons, a contradiction of their life in Christ; it would be repudiating their BAPTISM, severing themselves from Christ. As it is, the persons they once were (the "old self" of Rom. 6:6) are no more; the life they now live is the life which the risen Christ lives out in them. Christ died once in relation to sin (as the sin-bearer) but death has no more power over him; similarly, those in Christ are "dead to sin but alive to God" (v. 11) and are no more compelled, as they once were, to let their limbs and faculties be used for sin. They should therefore dedicate them to God as instruments to do his will, and they will find themselves liberated from the dominion of sin. The phrase "not under law, but under grace" (v. 14) in this context underscores the close association in Paul's mind between law and sin (cf. 7:4–13).

Sin, in other words, can be personified as a slave owner. The slave is forced to do his master's bidding. If the slave dies, his master has no further power over him. Similarly, those who are in Christ have died as far as their relation to sin, their former slave-owner, is concerned. Or, to change the figure somewhat, if the slave becomes the property of another master, he is henceforth bound to obey the new master, not the old one. So believers, formerly slaves of sin, have now been liberated into the free service of God. Their former master paid them the wages of death; their new Master gives them life in Christ—not as a reward for service rendered, but as a free gift.

Law, which is good, nevertheless stimulates sin, which is bad. Law reveals and denounces sin but cannot bring deliverance from it. To be liberated from sin to righteousness is one side of a coin, the other is liberation from law to grace. From the subject of freedom from sin (Rom. 6) Paul turns to its cognate: freedom from law (ch. 7). To illustrate this aspect of Christian freedom he has recourse to another legal relation: that between husband and wife. By law a wife is bound to her husband so long as he lives; only if he dies is she free to marry another man. (Whether Paul is thinking of Roman or Jewish law makes little difference.)

In the application of the analogy the husband is the law and the wife is the believer, but it is not the law that dies, but the believer who has died with Christ. The point, however, is that, as death breaks the marriage bond, so the believer's death with Christ breaks the bond that bound him to the law and sets him free to be united "to him who was raised from the dead" (v. 4). Union with the law stimulated sinful passions and produced fruit for death; union with Christ enables one to deny those passions and bring forth fruit for God. One may surmise that Paul's Jewish-Christian readers understood his argument better than the Gentile Christians, whether they approved of it or not. Admittedly, Paul's language about the law runs counter to the traditional testimony of Jewish piety, but he spoke out of the experience of one who had exchanged the bondage of the old "written code" for "the new way of the Spirit" (v. 6).

Romans 7:7–25 is written in the first person singular, but the first part of the passage uses the past tense, giving way in v. 14 to a section written in the present tense. Ostensibly both sections are autobiographical, and although the view that they are truly autobiographical has been relegated by some "to the museum of exegetical absurdities" (P. Demann, cited in F. J. Leenhardt, *The Epistle to the Romans* [1961], 181), the poignancy of much of the language still compels some readers to discern no "abstract argument but the echo of the personal experience of an anguished soul" (M. Goguel, *The Birth of Christianity* [1953], 213–14). Perhaps one can say that "here Paul's autobiography is the biography of Everyman" (T. W. Manson in *Peake's Commentary on the Bible*, ed. M. Black [1962], 945). At one level Paul describes his innocent boyhood and the growing sense of bondage after he assumed personal responsibility to keep the law, finding that it tempted him to do the very thing it forbade. At another level he probably was describing Adam before and after the prohibition to eat of the forbidden tree; at still another he recapitulates the history of the human family—before the giving of the law ("from Adam to Moses," 5:14), after the giving of the law (cf. 5:20), and then freed from the law in Christ (7:25a; cf. 5:21).

After this portrayal of the dawn of conscience, Paul continues in the present tense to describe the inner conflict experienced by one who approves the divine law and desires to keep it, but is prevented from doing so by "another law" which forces him against his will to do the evil that he loathes. "I myself in my mind am a slave to God's law, but in the sinful nature a slave to the law of sin" (Rom. 7:25b); a person's own resources, for all the excellence of his intentions, are inadequate for doing the will of God and defying the power of evil. Only "through Jesus Christ our Lord" (v. 25a) comes the strength for this.

Such strength is available for all "who are in Christ Jesus" (Rom. 8:1); there is no reason why they should go on in a state of penal servitude (which may be the meaning of "condemnation" in 8:1). A new principle has begun to live within them, "the law of the Spirit of life" (8:2), and liberates them not only from the thraldom of sin and the bondage of the law, but from death itself. This is the theme of ch. 8, where the mainspring of the way of holiness—the presence of the life-giving Spirit in the believer—is fully unfolded.

Life in the Spirit (Rom. 8:1–17) enables the believer to fulfill "the righteous requirements of the law" (v. 4) as life under the law could not, because of the unsatisfactory human material with which the law had to operate. The Son of God, bearing our humanity, presented himself as a sin offering (v. 3), and carried that humanity into death and out of it into resurrection: now "the Spirit of him who raised Jesus from the dead" dwells in his people (v. 11) and imparts new life and resurrection power to them. Christian holiness is not a matter of painstaking conformity to an external code; it is rather a matter of the Spirit's producing in the believer's life those graces which were seen in perfection in the life of his Lord. The possession of the Spirit of Christ is the Christian's indispensable hallmark (v. 9). It is the Spirit who enables us to realize our heritage as sons of God and to acknowledge this by calling God ABBA ("father") as Jesus himself did (vv. 15–16). The Spirit, moreover, conveys the assurance of the future quickening of this mortal body and of the glory to be shared with Christ by those who suffer for him now (vv. 11, 17).

This coming glory (Rom. 18–30) will not only compensate the believer for the trials endured in the present age; it is something to which all creation eagerly looks forward, for when the sons of God are revealed in glory, all creation will be released from the frustration under which it has labored since the fall (vv. 19–22). This investiture with glory will coincide with the day of resurrection, "the redemption of our bodies" (v. 23), when the saving effect of the PASSION of Christ will be consummated and believers will be manifested as sons of God. Till that day dawns, the Spirit helps them in their weakness, intercedes on their behalf, and cooperates with them in everything for good (vv. 26–28). When it dawns, it will be recognized as the fulfillment of God's eternal purpose, conceived when he foreknew and foreordained his people in Christ before the world's foundation (vv. 29–30).

The verb "glorified" in v. 30 is in the past tense because, although it refers to a future experience, its accomplishment is settled already in the counsel of God.

With such a hope, the believer may well exult in God (Rom. 8:31–39). Though all things seem to be against him, God is for him; though men condemn him, Christ at God's right hand is his all-prevailing advocate and intercessor. Neither earth's privations nor hell's hostility can separate believers from the love of God, manifest and active in Christ.

C. The righteousness of God in history

(Rom. 9:1–11:36). This section may seem to be a parenthesis in the argument of the letter, but in Paul's mind they were crucially necessary. The fact that the people who had been specially prepared for the gospel declined for the most part to believe it, although it was from their midst that the Christ himself came "according to the flesh" (9:5 NRSV), presented Paul and no doubt many of his contemporaries with a problem in THEODICY. Had God's purpose gone awry? Was he lacking in foresight? Surely, if Paul's claims were valid, his own kith and kin would have been the first to acknowledge them. Paul appreciated the problem all the more because in his earlier days he himself had been involved in Israel's unbelief. As he faces the problem, he begins with the particular issue of Jewish resistance to the gospel and ends with an exposition of the divine purpose in history.

The first two answers he gives to the problem are these: (1) The Jewish resistance to the Gospel has come about in the unchallengeable ordering of God's electing purpose (Rom. 9:6–29). (2) In resisting the gospel Israel is following a precedent repeatedly shown throughout her history (9:30–10:21). To these Paul adds two more, much more hopeful in tone: (3) The fact that a REMNANT of Israel has believed the gospel is the token that Israel as a whole will yet do so (11:1–16). (4) If Israel's present rejection of the gospel has meant so much blessing for Gentiles, Israel's future acceptance of the gospel will mean even greater blessing for the world (11:17–32).

(1) God's sovereign choice (Rom. 9:6–29). Throughout sacred history God has chosen one and set aside another. Of the sons of ABRAHAM, God chose ISAAC and not ISHMAEL; in the next generation, of the two sons of Isaac, he chose JACOB and not ESAU, giving notice of his choice before either Jacob or Esau was born, in order to establish his sovereignty in ELECTION (9:6–13). Even those who have been set aside promote his purpose, whether willingly or not: PHARAOH, so stubborn of heart, was a signal instrument in God's hand for the display of his power and the exaltation of his name: "Therefore God has mercy on whom he wants to have mercy, and he hardens whom he wants to harden" (9:14–18).

To the complaint that God is unjust in acting thus, since no one can resist his decree, the uncompromising answer is given, following the precedent of OT prophets (cf. Isa. 29:16; 45:9), that the pot has no right to complain of the potter's workmanship. What if God chose to make some "vessels," from Gentiles as well as from Jews, to be recipients of his mercy, and others to be destroyed, object lessons of his judgment? Paul did not say that God has in fact done this latter thing, but argued that, if he chose to do so, no one is competent to call him to account (Rom. 9:19–24).

What God in fact has done, says Paul, is to display his mercy in uncovenanted fashion, by calling as his people those who had no claim to be so designated (in accordance with a principle revealed in Hosea) and preserving only a remnant of his former people Israel (in accordance with a principle emphasized in Isaiah). So the apostle concludes his first exposition of God's way of election (Rom. 9:6–29), but he will revert to this subject before the end of his present argument.

(2) Israel's responsibility (Rom. 9:30–10:21). If on the one hand Israel's unbelief exemplifies divine election, it has to be seen on the other hand in terms of human responsibility. The stone of stumbling described in Isa. 28:16, realized in Christ and the gospel, had tripped them up, because they did not entrust themselves to it and so avoid being put to shame (9:30–33).

With a further confession of his heartfelt longing and prayer for his kinsmen's salvation, Paul ascribes their present unbelief and unenlightened zeal to their ignorance of God's way of righteousness (Rom. 10:1–3). They pursued the righteousness based on the law, in terms of Lev. 18:5 (living by doing), not knowing that with the coming of Christ an end has been put to the age of law, so that now it is every believer who is justified. This way of righteousness by faith was foreshadowed in Deut. 30:11–14, here interpreted as teaching that righteousness and salvation come to those who confess Jesus aloud as Lord and believe in him inwardly as the risen One (Rom. 10:4–8). To the same effect is the assurance of the passage about the stone of stumbling already quoted: "Anyone who trusts in him will never be put to shame" (10:11; cf. 9:33). This assurance applies equally to Jew and Gentile: "There is no difference" between them because all have sinned (3:22–23), but also "there is no difference" (10:12) because all receive God's abundant mercy on an equal footing: "every one who calls upon the name of the Lord will be saved" (10:13).

They had to hear his saving name proclaimed before they could believe in him, but there was ample opportunity for this: the preachers had sped far and wide with the joyful news, and in every part of the world where there were Jewish communities it had now been made known (cf. Ps. 19:4). If Israel did not believe, it was not for lack of hearing; their refusal to pay heed to what they heard gave substance to the prophet's complaint: "Lord, who has believed our message?" (Rom. 10:16, citing Isa. 53:1). In the gospel God's hand had been stretched out "to a disobedient and obstinate people" (Rom. 10:21, citing Isa. 65:2), whereas the Gentiles, who previously had had no relationship with the God of Israel, seized eagerly on the gospel blessings when they first heard of them, thus for their part fulfilling other OT prophecies. Among these is the passage in the Song of Moses where God tried to make Israel jealous by means of "those who are not a nation" (Deut. 32:21, interpreted of the Gentiles in Rom. 10:19). The nature and effect of this jealousy will appear in ch. 11; meanwhile, Paul has made his point that Israel refused the gospel in spite of every opportunity to accept it (10:14–21).

(3) Israel's alienation not final (Rom. 11:1—16). It must not, however, be thought that Israel's present unbelief and setting aside are permanent. As in OT days the preservation of a remnant carried with it hope for the future, so now the existence of "a remnant chosen by grace" (to which Paul himself belongs, 11:5) contains promise of the ultimate salvation of all Israel. For the present, Israel has stumbled, but has not fallen irrevocably. Their temporary "transgression" has meant blessing for the world; their restoration will mean far greater blessing (11:1–16).

(4) The parable of the OLIVE tree (Rom. 11:17–24). Paul, as apostle to the Gentiles, thinks highly of his ministry, not only because of the blessing it brings to Gentile believers but also because, in the purpose of God, the conversion of the Gentiles will, in fulfillment of Deut. 32:21 (quoted in Rom. 10:19), provoke Israel to jealousy and stimulate them to demand a share in those blessings that are their natural heritage. The history of the people of God is portrayed in terms of an olive tree from which some of the original branches have been lopped off to make way for the grafting in of branches from a wild olive (a process which in 11:24 Paul rightly says is "contrary to nature"). The lopped-off branches are Jews, separated from the stock of the people of God because of unbelief; the ingrafted branches are Gentiles, incorporated into the people of God through faith. But—and here one may detect a warning to the Gentile Christians in Rome and elsewhere—the ingrafted branches may in their turn be lopped off through unbelief and the severed branches may through faith be reunited with the parent stock. By faith Jew and Gentile alike stand; by unbelief they fall (11:13–24).

God's purpose for blessing mankind far exceeds anything that human beings could have hoped. If he has found all people, Jew and Gentile alike, guilty of disobedience and has pronounced this verdict on them, it is not that he may sentence them to the appropriate penalty, but "that he may have mercy upon all" (Rom. 11:32). When the Deliverer comes from Zion (cf. Ps. 14:7) and banishes ungodliness from Jacob, mankind will enjoy undreamed-of bliss. Who could have supposed that Israel's unbelief was to become God's instrument for good to such an overwhelming degree? God's wisdom cannot be compared with the human mind; he is the source, guide and goal of all (11:25–36).

D. The Christian way of life (Rom. 12:1—15:13). The proper response to the gospel of grace that has been unfolded in the foregoing chapters is the yielding of the believer's life to God as a "living sacrifice," presented in the course of one's "spiritual act of worship," so that the mind henceforth may be transfigured to conform with the will of God (12:1–2). This change will manifest itself, among other things, in the common life of the Christian fellowship. The figure of the body and its limbs, already used in this way (1 Cor. 12:12–27) and destined to be developed further in COLOSSIANS and EPHESIANS, is introduced here to illustrate the interdependence and cooperation of all for the good of the whole; and whatever service each one does should be done with a ready heart (Rom. 12:3–8).

The life of the Spirit will manifest itself outwardly in acts of love to fellow members of the Christian brotherhood and to all people. The SERMON ON THE MOUNT may not have been written down at this early date in the form in which we know it, but its contents were familiar in the church and formed the basis of the "law of Christ" (cf. Gal. 6:2), which Paul here applied. Revenge must never occur to a believer's mind. Paul quoted in this regard the passage from Prov. 25:21–22, beginning, "If your enemy is hungry, give him food …"; but he omitted the clause "and the Lord will reward you" and added the injunction, "Do not be overcome by evil, but overcome evil with good" (12:19–21).

The passage about the Christian and the state (Rom. 13:1–7) has given rise to long debate (see GOVERNMENT). Its spirit and tone can no doubt be linked with Paul's happy experience of Roman law and order, as reflected in the narrative of Acts; but the permanent teaching is plain. So long as the civil authorities remain within their divinely given commission, they can command the believer's obedience and cooperation; only when Caesar demands the things that are God's must the believer say "No" (cf. Acts 4:19; 5:29). Such a demand on the part of the state is not contemplated here; there is a great difference between Rom. 13 and Rev. 13, although the Roman empire is the supreme worldly authority in both places. It is very unlikely that the "governing authorities" (Rom. 13:1) are angelic principalities and powers; the latter do not receive taxes, and the Bible, far from counseling believers to submit to them, portrays them as servants to the people of God.

Apart from his special duty to the powers that be, the Christian has the general duty of love to all people. Believers may be dead to the law in the sense of Rom. 7:4, but the whole OT law is summed up in the commandment of LOVE (as Jesus had affirmed in Mk. 12:29–31); from this law the Christian is never set free (Rom. 13:8–10).

Opening of Paul's letter to the Romans in a parallel Greek/Latin edition published in 1835.

The days are critical; Christians must be vigilant. Already coming events were casting their shadows; with hindsight one can think of the persecution of A.D. 64 and the revolt of A.D. 66. However, Paul looked beyond intervening woes to the fullness of salvation that would attend the advent of Christ. In language reminiscent of the idiom of Qumran (see DEAD SEA SCROLLS), he enjoins his readers to put on the "armor of light" in readiness for spiritual conflict and to live lives worthy of Christ. It is striking that, when the apostle commends the cultivation of those virtues that grace the character of Christ in the Gospels, he does so in the words, "clothe yourselves with the Lord Jesus Christ." One recalls how Augustine's conversion followed immediately upon his reading Rom. 13:13–14.

In Rom. 14:1—15:6 Paul deals with the apparently conflicting demands of Christian liberty and Christian charity. He had to deal with this issue in the churches he had founded, such as CORINTH (cf. 1 Cor. 8:1–13; 10:23–33); he expounds the general principles for the benefit of the Roman Christians. In most Christian communities there would be some people whose CONSCIENCES, like the apostle's, were completely emancipated in neutral matters such as food and sacred seasons, but they had to live alongside others who religiously avoided eating certain things and doing ordinary work on special days. "Each one should be fully convinced in his own mind," says Paul (14:5). The emancipated Christian must not despise brothers or sisters who are more scrupulous than he in such matters; the scrupulous Christian must not condemn believers who cheerfully do things of which his own conscience disapproves. Each believer is the Lord's servant, whether in life or in death; it is to the Lord that he must render account at the last.

So far so good; but Paul knew from his experience elsewhere that Christians with tender consciences were easily upset and likely to be tripped up in their spiritual progress. Those who had robust consciences like himself had a duty to consider their weaker fellow Christians. Paul would have refused to listen to any attempt to place limitations on his freedom, and warned his converts, as in Galatia and at Colosse, against listening to any such attempts directed toward themselves. But it was possible, while refusing legal restrictions, to accept voluntary limitations on one's freedom of action in the interests of a brother "for whom Christ died" (Rom. 14:15). Such a spontaneous gesture of Christian charity would be in fact one way of exercising Christian liberty. Truly emancipated believers are not in bondage to their emancipation: they can choose to indulge and they can choose to refrain. Their choice will be determined by the Lord's glory and the spiritual welfare of others. If scrupulous Christians are encouraged by the example of one with a more robust conscience to do something of which their own conscience disapproves, their conscience is damaged by their doing so, and the damage will be debited by the Lord to their insufficiently considerate fellow Christian.

It is the privilege of the strong to help the weak and be patient with them; the example of Christ is sufficient argument. Instead of living for his own interests, he lived for others and endured reproach for his Father's sake, as OT Scripture had foretold (Rom. 15.3, quoting Ps. 69:9). This quotation of OT Scripture reminds Paul that all Scripture was given for the instruction and encouragement of the people of God, and he prays for such harmony among his readers so that their lives would redound to the glory of God.

Continuing the theme of the example of Christ (Rom. 15:7–13), Paul states that Christ became a servant to Jews and Gentiles alike — to the former, to fulfill the promises made to the patriarchs, and to the latter, that they too might "glorify God for his mercy" (v. 9). There follows a catena of OT Scriptures, drawn from all three divisions of the Hebrew Bible (Law, Prophets, and Psalms), showing that the Gentile mission was foretold in them. (The means by which the Gentiles' ingathering would be accomplished, by their incorporation as fellow members of the body of Christ on an equal footing with Jewish believers, was a MYSTERY first revealed in NT times, but the fact of their ingathering had been predicted.) With a benediction echoing the wording of the final quotation, Paul closes this division of the letter.

E. Epilogue (Rom. 15:14—16:27). In 15:14–33 Paul tells his readers about the present position of his apostolic program. His work in the eastern Mediterranean area is finished, and he looks forward to visiting Rome on his way to Spain (see section IV above), once he has presented the fruit of this work in Jerusalem and handed over the Gentile churches' CONTRIBUTION for the relief of the believers there. Meanwhile, he requests their prayers; he is well aware of the hazards that the immediate future might have in store for him.

PHOEBE, a "deaconess" of the church at CENCHREA (the eastern seaport of Corinth), will carry the letter to its destination; Paul commends her to his readers' fellowship (Rom. 16:1–2). He then sends greetings to a number of his friends. Although Paul had not previously visited Rome, it was not surprising that there were many people there whom he had met elsewhere during his journeys; indeed, precedent suggests that he was more apt to send individual greetings of this kind in a letter to a church with which he was not acquainted at first hand, than to one where he knew practically everybody (in the latter case, if he singled out a few for special mention, others might ask, "Why leave me out?"). The mention of EPENETUS, his first convert in the province of Asia (v. 5), and of PRISCILLA and AQUILA (v. 3), who were last mentioned as being in Ephesus (Acts 18:26; 1 Cor. 16:19), has suggested to many commentators that this list of greetings may have been appended to a copy of the letter sent to the Ephesians; most of the names however, have Roman rather than Ephesian affinities (Rom. 16:3–16).

The exhortation of Rom. 16:17–20 is more urgent and personal than anything appearing earlier in the letter; Paul was afraid that the Roman Christians might be visited by troublemakers such as those who had upset churches of his own planting, and he warns against them. Satan, the author of discord, will be crushed under their feet if they remain true worshipers of the God of peace. Paul has already sent greetings from the Gentile churches (v. 16); he then sends greetings from some of his personal friends who are with him at the time of writing (vv. 21–23). Paul regularly dictated his letters to amanuenses, but TERTIUS is the only one of these whose name is known (v. 22). The doxology of 16:25–27 recapitulates the main themes of the letter, as they have been introduced in the opening salutation (1:1–7).

VII. Text. There are two sets of textual problems in Romans that require special attention, one at the beginning and the other at the end. Apart from these, the text of the letter is reasonably straightforward, although F. G. Kenyon concluded—from the pattern of agreement and disagreement in the various Pauline epistles between P^{46} and the other early witnesses to the text—that the textual tradition of Romans might go back to a time before the publication of the *corpus Paulinum*, when the letters circulated separately. (If copies were in fact sent to various churches to begin with, the history of textual variation could have started as early as A.D. 57.)

The words "in Rome" are omitted from Rom. 1:7 in the Greco-Latin Codex G and also in the texts on which the commentaries on Romans by Origen and Ambrosiaster were based; moreover, G omits them in 1:15 as well. This textual form, together with adjustments of such an abridged text in companions of G, can best be accounted for in terms of their absence from the archetype of the "Western" text of the Pauline letters. (Their absence from a text used by Origen indicates that this shorter reading was not exclusively Western.)

At the end of the letter, indications of three distinct editions are provided by the varying position of the final doxology in the authorities for the text. In P^{46}, the oldest Pauline manuscript (end of 2nd cent.), it is placed at the end of Rom. 15. Although the doxology is then followed by 16:1–23, the implication is that there was in antiquity one form of the text that ended with 15:33 and the doxology (and that to this shorter text 16:1–23 was subsequently added from a copy of the longer text). The simplest explanation of this phenomenon is that copies of the letter were sent not only to Rome but also to other places—the personal greetings being omitted from copies sent to churches other than that in which the persons named were present. Whether the copy including the personal greetings was intended for Rome (so C. H. Dodd, *The Epistle to the Romans*, MNTC [1932], xviiff.) or Ephesus (T. W. Manson, *Studies in the Gospels and Epistles* [1962], 234ff.) cannot be decided by textual criticism (to the present writer the Roman destination of the greetings seems more probable).

There is, however, much more abundant evidence for an even shorter edition of the letter which terminated at the end of Rom. 14. The Byzantine text type has the doxology there instead of at the end of ch. 16; a few witnesses (A P 5 33 et al.) have it at the end of ch. 14 and also at the end of ch. 16; the original "Western" text of Paul appears to have lacked the doxology altogether. The origin of this shortest edition is hardly in doubt; Origen states what is antecedently probable in any case when he deals with the final doxology in his commentary on Romans: "Marcion, who introduced interpolations into the evangelic and apostolic scriptures, removed this section completely from this epistle, and not only so, but he cut out everything from that place where it is written 'whatsoever is not of faith, is sin' [14:23] right to the end" (English trans. from Rufinus's Latin version of Origen). The ancient chapter summaries in Codex Amiatinus and some other VULGATE MSS, which were taken over from a pre-Vulgate Latin version, indicate a text in which 14:23 was followed immediately by the doxology; Tertullian and Cyprian of Carthage also seem to have known this short edition.

In this respect, as in several others, MARCION's text of the Pauline letters appears to have influenced the transmission of their text in circles that were far from subscribing to Marcionite views. Why Marcion should have brought the text of Romans to an end with 14:23 is plain if one looks at the OT quotations in 15:3–12, or the statement in 15:4 that "everything that was written in the past was written to teach us," or the description of Christ in 15:8 as "a servant of the Jews … to confirm the promises made to the patriarchs." These passages were contrary to Marcion's view that the OT was irrelevant to Christ and the gospel, and were probably regarded by him as Judaizing intrusions into the pure apostolic text.

The omission of "in Rome" in Rom. 1:7 and 15 belongs not (as might have been expected) to the textual tradition which omits only the personal greetings of ch. 16 and thus generalizes the letter, but to the textual tradition which brought the letter to a close at 14:23—that is, to the tradition stemming from Marcion's text. Why Marcion should have omitted these two references to Rome is uncertain; perhaps, since the Roman church repudiated his teaching as unacceptable, he judged that church to be unworthy to be named as a recipient of a letter from Christ's one true apostle. (Although Marcion's text did not include the doxology at the end, it was added to his text later, possibly from the long edition.)

There remain some unresolved problems, but the conclusion in general is that there were in antiquity three recensions of the letter: (1) the long recension, including the personal greetings and the doxology, which was probably the recension found in the first edition of the *corpus Paulinum*; (2) a shorter recension, lacking the personal greetings, derived from an early copy sent to another church than that primarily addressed (P[46] would in this case preserve a textual tradition antedating the publication of the first *corpus Paulinum*); and (3) a still shorter recension, lacking ch. 15 as well as ch. 16 (and also in some of its forms lacking the references to Rome in 1:7, 15); this recension, while widely attested in orthodox circles, can be ascribed to Marcion's dogmatic interference with the apostolic text.

VIII. Canonicity and authority. The canonicity of Romans was never an issue in the church. From the earliest beginnings of the formation of the CANON its place within it has been secure, both among heretical groups like the Valentinians and Marcionites, and in the Catholic Church.

Behind canonicity lies intrinsic authority, and in this regard the record of Romans is impressive. Time and again in the course of Christian history it has liberated the human mind, brought people back to an understanding of the essential gospel of Christ, and started spiritual revolutions. One has only to think of the part played by the letter in the careers of leaders like Augustine, Luther, John Wesley, and Karl Barth, and in the movements associated with their names, to appreciate its enduring evangelical dynamism.

(Significant commentaries include R. Haldane, *Exposition of Romans* [1835–39]; C. Hodge, *Commentary on Romans* [1835]; C. J. Vaughan, *St. Paul's Epistle to the Romans* [1874]; F. Godet, *The Epistle to the Romans* [1880]; H. C. G. Moule, *The Epistle of St. Paul to the Romans* [1894]; H. P. Liddon, *Explanatory Analysis of St. Paul's Epistle to the Romans* [1893]; F. J. A. Hort, *Prolegomena to Romans and Ephesians* [1895]; J. Denney in *The Expositor's Greek Testament*, ed. W. R. Nicoll [1897–1910], 2:555–725; W. Sanday and A. C. Headlam, *A Critical and Exegetical Commentary on the Epistle to the Romans*, ICC [1902]; C. H. Dodd, *The Epistle of Paul to the Romans*, MNTC [1932]; K. Barth, *The Epistle to the Romans* [1933]; A. Nygren, *Commentary on Romans* [1952]; A. M. Hunter, *The Epistle to the Romans* [1955]; C. K. Barrett, *The Epistle to the Romans* [1957]; J. Murray, *The Epistle to the Romans*, NICNT, 2 vols. [1959–1965]; E. Brunner, *The Epistle to the Romans* [1959]; M. Luther, *Lectures on Romans*, trans. W. Pauck [1961]; F. J. Leenhardt, *The Epistle to the Romans* [1961]; J. Calvin, *The Epistles of Paul to the Romans and Thessalonians*, trans. R. Mackenzie [1961]; F. F. Bruce, *The Epistle to the Romans*, TNTC [1963]; C. E. B. Cranfield, *A Critical and Exegetical Commentary on the Epistle to the Romans*, ICC, 2 vols. [1973–75]; O. Michel, *Der Brief an die Römer*, KEK 4, 14th ed. [1978]; U. Wilckens, *Der Brief an die Römer*, EKKNT, 3 vols. [1978–82]; E. Käsemann, *Commentary on Romans* [1980]; J. D. G. Dunn, *Romans*, WBC 38A and 38B [1988]; J. A. Fitzmyer, *Romans*, AB 33 [1993]; B. Byrne, *Romans* [1996]; D. J. Moo, *The Epistle to the Romans*, NICNT [1996]; T. R. Schreiner, *Romans*, BECNT

[1998]; E. Lohse, *Der Brief an die Römer*, KEK 4, 15th ed. [2003]; G. R. Osborne, *Romans* [2004]; B. Witherington III and D. Hyatt, *Paul's Letter to the Romans: A Socio-Rhetorical Commentary* [2004]; R. Penna, *Lettera ai Romani*, 3 vols. [2004–]; R. Jewett, *Romans: A Commentary*, Hermeneia [2007].

(See also T. W. Manson, *Studies in the Gospels and Epistles* [1962], 225–241; H. Gamble, Jr., *The Textual History of the Letter to the Romans: A Study in Textual and Literary Criticism* [1977]; S. K. Stowers, *The Diatribe and Paul's Letter to the Romans* [1981]; A. J. M. Wedderburn, *The Reasons for Romans* [1988]; G. N. Davies, *Faith and Obedience in Romans: A Study of Romans 1–4* [1990]; K. P. Donfried, *The Romans Debate*, rev. ed. [1991]; D. B. Garlington, *Faith, Obedience, and Perseverance: Aspects of Paul's Letter to the Romans* [1994]; M. D. Nanos, *The Mystery of Romans: The Jewish Context of Paul's Letter* [1996]; R. H. Bell, *No One Seeks for God: An Exegetical and Theological Study of Romans 1.18–3.20* [1998]; M. Reasoner, *The Strong and the Weak: Romans 14.1–15:13 in Context* [1999]; C. Bryan, *A Preface to Romans: Notes on the Epistle in Its Literary and Cultural Setting* [2000]; J. Ross Wagner, *Heralds of the Good News: Isaiah and Paul in Concert in the Letter to the Romans* [2002]; P. F. Esler, *Conflict and Identity in Romans: The Social Setting of Paul's Letter* [2003]; K. Haacker, *The Theology of Paul's Letter to the Romans* [2003]; T. H. Tobin, *Paul's Rhetoric in Its Contexts: The Argument of Romans* [2004]; A. A. Das, *Solving the Romans Debate* [2007]; and the history of research by M. Theobald, *Der Römerbrief* [2000].)   F. F. BRUCE

Rome (Ῥώμη *G4873*; Ῥωμαῖος *G4871*, "Roman"; cf. Ῥωμαϊστί *G4872*, "Roman [*i.e.*, Latin] language" [Jn. 19:20]). A city-state in the Italian peninsula (see ITALY). Located on the Tiber River some 15 mi. from the W Mediterranean, it became the capital of the ROMAN EMPIRE.

The origins of the Roman people can be traced back to the 2nd millennium B.C., often regarded as a time of "folk-wandering." The Indo-European tribes who were to form the ethnic pattern of Europe until modern times were on the move, and a strong drift in the tribal movement was toward the warmer lands of the Mediterranean basin. The Iberian, Italian, and Greek peninsulas were infiltrated in successive waves, and the language map of Italy reveals something of the process of occupation. It would appear that one tribal group moved down the W coast, left a group of its nationals around the mouth of the Tiber, and proceeded to found settlements in Sicily. Linguistic correspondences between Latin and Sicilian dialects prompt this conjecture.

Tribes speaking a distinct but allied dialect, either following the same invasion routes or crossing the Adriatic, enfolded the enclave by the Tiber mouth. These were the Umbrian- and Oscan-speaking peoples. In the middle of Italy lay the cities of an alien race from ASIA MINOR, the Etruscans, whose name survives in modern Tuscany. These non-Europeans, still imperfectly known to history, had a higher culture than the incoming nomads, and during the first half of the 1st millennium B.C. they held an empire which extended to the northern Lombardy plains. They dominated Rome itself in its early years. Add the Greek settlements all around the coast of the southern half of the land mass, and the picture of the Italian peninsula about the 8th and 7th centuries, the traditional period of Rome's first appearance, begins to emerge. It was an enclave of Latin-speaking tribesmen around the lower Tiber valley, a dominant Etruscan empire in the Upper Tiber and Arno valleys and in the north. Indo European tribesmen established themselves throughout the mountain spine of the long peninsula, and in the Campanian plain and Greek cities in an irregular chain around the southern coastline from Cumae to Tarentum.

Alien occupation of the arc of hill country that fenced off the area of the Tiber mouth, the effective barrier of Etruscan occupation to the N, and the Oscan possession of Campania to the S, imposed a certain unity on the Latin-speaking agriculturalists who held the narrow enclave by the river. Their scattered groups cohered into various leagues and communities. There was also the need for common defense against the mountaineers, those traditional raiders of adjacent lowlands in all historical contexts. It was the fashion to build stockaded retreats, preferably on an outcrop of rock like the ACROPOLIS of ATHENS or some similar eminence to which the plainsmen could retreat with flocks and families, while a fighting task force dealt with the raiding hillmen.

In such fashion Rome came into existence. The Palatine hill was probably the first "acropolis" of the shepherds and peasants of the fertile plain. Where the Tiber pursues its lower westward course to the sea, the river valley forms a deep trough, averaging a mile in width, and cuts into the soft volcanic tufa which at this point floors the river basin, the same geological material that made it so easy to cut the hundreds of miles of catacomb galleries running beneath the city. The edges of this wide depression were eroded in prehistoric times by tributary waterways to shape the famous group of eight hills on which Rome stood: the Capitol, the Palatine, the Aventine, the Caelian, the Oppian, the Esquiline, the Viminal, and the Quirinal. The Vatican might be added, making nine, rather than the traditional seven, but some of them were no more than flat-topped spurs.

In modern Rome it is difficult to distinguish the group. Twenty-seven centuries of continuous human occupation have filled valley bottoms, cut away edge, escarpment, and eminence, and leveled down what once must have been a striking group of strongholds, each the fort and stockaded retreat of some family group of the peasant community which occupied the adjacent territory.

Through this irregular terrain the Tiber makes an "S" curve, shallows, and divides to form an island. At this point is found the only practicable fording place between the river mouth and the upper reaches of its waterway. Thus it was that geography played its eternal role in history, because, as the population of Italy matured and grew, the occupants of the hills by the ford found themselves in natural control of the trade and communications between the higher civilizations of the Etruscans to the N of them, and the Greek cities to the S. Another road, perhaps a "salt route," ran from the sea up the valley to serve the highland tribes.

Cities set on a crossroads of trade are inevitably cast for a role of greatness. They attract immigration and form strong outward looking communities with some interest in a larger world. Archaeological evidence, the sole source of the knowledge of primitive Rome, suggests that the hill forts by the Tiber coalesced to form a federation by the 6th cent. B.C. Burials from the Capitoline and Palatine hills on the edge of the marshy valley bottom which was to be the Forum cease about this time, and the Cloaca Maxima, the Great Sewer, the first of the vast engineering works that were to be a major Roman contribution to the world, seems to have been started about the same time to drain the now common territory of the united community.

It would therefore appear that Rome found her name and unity in the half-legendary period of her kings, whose rule, encrusted though it became with Roman folklore, is established fact. The famous foundation legends, such as the tales of Aeneas coming from far Troy to father a new race, and of Romulus and Remus suckled by the wolf, are inventions on the model of Greek foundation myths, perhaps actually the inventions of canny Greeks of the S Italian Greek cities that marked the rising power on the Tiber.

The later kings were certainly Etruscans, and Tarquin is an Etruscan name. The story of "false Sextus" and "Tarquin the Proud," and their expulsion from Rome, with Horatius Cocles holding the bridge against their counterattack, are parts of a saga of the Latin city's struggle for liberation from alien rule. There is fact in the stories; the battle for Latin independence was an experience that hardened and consolidated the young city, and left a horror of royal rule so strong that Julius CAESAR was forced at the height of his power to refuse the title of king. Fragments of the Servian Wall reveal that Rome at this time was a fortified city, able to close its gates against the stranger and resist alien domination.

The traditional date for the founding of the republic is 510 B.C., and at that point in time the tremendous story of Rome's move to world empire began. A. J. Toynbee (in his famous *Study of History*, 10 vols. [1947–57], 1:271–355) develops the thesis of "Challenge and Response." All human progress, the historian avers, is the result of a successful reaction to some confrontation with difficulty, danger, or hardship. The story of Rome's expansion provides a striking illustration. The population that now filled the hills and valley floors was a composite community, gravely divided, as the old stories of patricians and plebeians indicate, over questions of status and privilege. She was also an upstart among Italy's peoples, holding coveted advantages, and still hemmed in by the powerful empire of the

Remains of the ancient Forum in Rome.

Etruscans to the N, whose powerful stronghold, Veii, was only 12 mi. distant, by the more remote but rich Greek colonies to the S, and by the tough Oscan and Umbrian tribes of the hinterland and central Italy.

Perhaps it was the military menace from without which imposed unity within and prompted that resourcefulness which traditionally, in early Rome, solved political problems without bloodshed. It is part of the wonder of Roman history that, until the onset of the intractable constitutional problems of the two centuries B.C. which finally brought the republic to ruin, Rome resolved the vast tensions of her class struggle by debate, wise compromise, and a legal inventiveness that laid the foundations for another tremendous contribution of Rome to human history—ROMAN LAW. By the middle of the 4th cent. B.C., the republic had solved the problems of internal schism, economic, ethnic, or whatever tension it was which divided "the orders," and was reacting to that long quest for a stable frontier which took her first to the Alps and the surrounding seas and finally to the Tyne, the Euphrates, and the Red Sea.

By this time, too, Rome was large and populous. The valleys and levels between the ancient hills afforded a natural road-building pattern that remained recognizable through all the history of Rome, even to the present day, vast though the accumulation of human debris is on the site. The story of building, rebuilding, destruction, and reconstruction is one which, on a site so securely occupied, archaeology will never have the opportunity fully to investigate. When the city began to build her brief stretch of underground railway a generation ago, construction proceeded at a snail's pace as the tunnelers passed through the rubble and ruin of centuries of republican Rome.

The adjective *republican* must be used with some reserve. Theoretically, a species of democracy and popular voting existed, and there was wide privilege of office. In practice, however, the ancient families, not all of whom the Romans called *patrician*, dominated the senate and provided the sort of leadership which Britain knew in the days of her ruling aristocracy. It was, in fact, an oligarchy of blood, wealth, and experience that functioned well and guided Rome through two vital centuries. It is probably true to say that the common people had in practice no great power or influence, but their sovereignty was legally recognized. To rest on the letter of the law was a Roman instinct which bypassed and modified much social stress.

Those two vital centuries saw the dynamic republic break the encirclement of the hill tribes, reduce the Etruscans to impotence, dominate S

Italy with its Greek cities and tribal hinterland, and become a world power. Egypt, under the Ptolemies of Alexandria, signed a treaty with Rome in 273 B.C., and it was not long after this that Rome discovered that the central Mediterranean itself was too small for one power based in Italy, and another, of alien breed, based in Africa across the narrow waist of the Inland Sea, especially since Sicily lay as a bridgehead of contention between the two. The Carthaginian wars filled half a century and left Rome established in Spain, S Gaul, and Africa, and led to a confrontation with the Hellenistic monarchies of the E Mediterranean, an encounter which, little by little, with the decline of Greek power, took Rome to the destiny of Middle Eastern empire.

As empire in the geographical sense of that word grew, so the city by the Tiber expanded. A city is a magnet, and it draws in a varied population. The second clash with Carthage had seen Hannibal's invasion of Italy, and the peninsula did not really recover from the burning and devastation of that decade of disaster. The small peasantry suffered, and with the simultaneous flowing into Rome of tribute and loot from abroad, as history moved on through the 2nd cent. B.C., a change came over the land utilization of Italy. The rich landholders bought out the independent farmers, who had once been the backbone of the land; and the dole-fed urban mob—that tool and weapon of the demagogue through the century of constitutional strife and city disorder which destroyed republican Rome—was daily swollen by new accretions from the countryside. Add to these the drifters who always congregate where wealth, vice, opportunity, and entertainment are plentiful, and the pattern of Rome's urban growth may be guessed from the analogy of many a modern city.

As early as the 3rd cent. there is evidence of the great *insulae*, the "islands," or huge tenement houses, which were a feature of later Rome, and suggest the overcrowding, the squalor, and the slums that were creeping around and amid the mansions of senator, aristocrat, and "knight," the term applied to the new class of business men and tax farmers, the hated *publicani*, whose exploitation of the provinces was another factor in the decay of republican Rome.

Amid squalor there was also magnificence, and it is possible from the records to piece together the story of varied building activity. At the end of the 2nd cent. B.C., when Rome was penetrating the Hellenistic lands of the E Mediterranean, there was a tremendous influx of wealth and capital from the newly constituted provinces, and the opportunities for exploitation their government afforded the new ruling class. Much of this new wealth found expression in architecture. POMPEY, the great soldier who organized the eastern provinces into ordered and coherent form in the sixties of the 1st cent. B.C., also did much to adorn and beautify Rome.

AUGUSTUS, the first of the emperors, whose leadership and diplomatic genius gave peace to Rome after the ordeal of her two civil wars and century of strife, also gave attention to the restoration of the damaged city and to its further adornment. In an inscription discovered on the wall of a temple built in his honor at Ancyra, Augustus boasts that he "found Rome built of brick, and left it built of marble." Augustus also made a bold and farsighted attempt to give life again to Rome's old religion, and to establish above all the worship of APOLLO, whose youthful godhead was a symbol to him of the restoration he sought for the sorely damaged state. See ROMAN RELIGION. The architectural consequence was a great upsurge in temple building, and most notably a magnificent library and shrine dedicated to the ruler's favorite god, a building of which remnants still stand.

Augustus thus set the fashion for the emperors who came after him, and it is, in fact, from the early centuries of the Christian era that most of Rome's surviving ruins date: the great baths of Caracalla and Diocletian, for example, and those of Constantine; columns and triumphal arches; and the most striking of all the city's surviving memorials, the Flavian Amphitheater, still called by its medieval name of Colosseum.

A vivid picture of life in Rome at the end of the 1st cent. is found in the third satire of the embittered poet Juvenal, a mordant description imitated for Paris by Boileau, and for London by Samuel Johnson. Juvenal knew Rome from the slum pavement, from the viewpoint of the poor and the underprivileged, and he wrote savagely of the poverty and the inhumanity of the great metropolis with its cruel inequalities between the absurdly rich and the shockingly poor.

Aerial view of Rome (looking W), with St. Peter's Church (background, center top) and the Colosseum (left foreground).

The population probably passed the million mark about this time, and the city was as cosmopolitan as New York and London. "The Syrian Orontes is now a tributary of the Tiber," shouted Juvenal in the satire quoted, and in his list of the pains and misfortunes of his small world he included the foreign rabble with the perils of fire, traffic, assault, and battery, and the collapse of jerry-built slum hovels.

PAUL found a Christian church already active in Rome when he arrived under escort, probably in March, A.D. 59. See ROME, CHURCH AT. Perhaps CLAUDIUS's expulsion of the Jews a decade earlier marked some of the tensions in the ghetto associated with the first Christian intrusion into the synagogue. It is a fair guess that the Christian gospel was preached there first in the latter half of the fifth decade of the century. The strength of the Christian population may be calculated from the burials in the catacombs. Reliable calculations suggest that the vast tangle of the catacombs contains up to 600 mi. of galleries. The lowest estimate of the graves they contain is 1,750,000; an admissible probability is something like 4,000,000. This is obviously a question that could be settled quite conclusively. At any rate, some ten generations of Christians are buried in the catacombs, so that, on the second figure, there was a Christian population in and about Rome of 400,000 for one generation. On the smaller computation the number would be 175,000.

Such averaging, of course, is not good statistical method, for the number of Christians was smaller in the earlier and larger in the later generations of the period concerned. If the figure of 175,000 is taken as representing a middle point in that period, perhaps about the middle of the 3rd cent. A.D., those who remember E. Gibbon's estimate of the Christian population of Rome will immediately mark a huge discrepancy.

Gibbon's guess, recorded in his *Decline and Fall of the Roman Empire*, was that the Christians at the end of the 3rd cent. numbered something like one-twentieth of the population of Rome. That population is reliably estimated at something like one million. The most conservative interpretation of the catacomb burial figures would, therefore, suggest that not one-twentieth but one-fifth of Rome's people in the middle empire were Christians, and it is possible that the proportion was at times much greater. To quote in conclusion the present writer's *Cities of the New Testament* (p. 87):

> Rome, like Babylon, became an image of carnal, organized paganism. In the lurid

poetry of the document of protest which closes the canon of the New Testament, empire and city are mingled as symbols of sin. Chapters 17 and 18 of the Apocalypse look grimly forward to just such a fate for Rome as Rome had wreaked on Jerusalem, on Corinth, on Carthage, and many another city of her foes, just such a fate as Rome did in fact suffer under the fire and sword of Alaric the Goth. The former oracle, passionate in its imagery, pictures Rome sitting like a woman of sin on her famous seven hills, polluting the world with her vice. The second of the two chapters, cast in the form of a Hebrew "taunt-song," and imitating Ezekiel's chapter on Tyre, pictures the galleys loading cargo for Rome in some eastern port. There was "merchandise of gold, and silver, and precious stones, and of pearls, and of fine linen, and purple, and silk, and scarlet, vessels of ivory, and precious wood, and of brass, and iron, and marble, cinnamon, and frankincense, beasts, and sheep, and horses, and chariots, and slaves, and the souls of men."

The climax is shocking, as the writer pictures Ostia, the Tiber port of Rome, in the stark ruin which, indeed, it may be seen today, its great warehouses empty shells revealed by the archaeologist's spade, its streets empty, and its courtyards desolate. Amid all the voices of praise from the first century one alone cried protest against Rome's domination of the souls of men. That voice was a Christian voice, and history took heed of it.

(See further W. W. Fowler, *Social Life at Rome in the Age of Cicero* [1908]; W. E. Heitland, *The Roman Republic*, 3 vols. [1909]; T. Rice Holmes, *The Roman Republic* [1909]; D. Randall-MacIver, *Italy Before the Romans* [1928]; F. B. Marsh, *A History of the Roman World, 146–30 B.C.* [1939]; R. Syme, *The Roman Revolution* [1939]; R. W. Moore, *The Roman Commonwealth* [1942]; T. Frank, *Rome and Italy of the Republic* [1933]; E. M. Blaiklock, *The Century of the New Testament* [1962]; id., *The Cities of the New Testament* [1965]; A. H. McDonald, *Republican Rome* [1966]; G. Alfoldy, *The Social History of Rome* [1985]; F. Millar, *The Roman Republic and the Augustan Revolution* [2002]; H. H. Scullard, *A History of the Roman World, 753 to 146 B.C.*, 5th ed. [2003]; H. I. Flower, ed., *The Cambridge Companion to the Roman Republic* [2004]; M. Le Glay et al., *A History of Rome*, 3rd ed. [2005]; C. S. Mackay, *Ancient Rome: A Military and Political History* [2005].)
E. M. BLAIKLOCK

Rome, church at. The Christian community in the capital city of the ROMAN EMPIRE. See also ROME; ROMANS, EPISTLE TO THE.

I. Origin. When and by whom Christianity was first introduced at the imperial city is, as P. Schaff states, an "impenetrable mystery" (*History of the Christian Church*, vol. 1, 3rd ed. [1890], 366). A significant Christian community had already existed in Rome for a considerable time before PAUL wrote his epistle to this church (c. A.D. 58), as evidenced by Rom. 1:8–13; 16:19. The biblical account, however, does not record any apostolic visits until c. A.D. 62 (Acts 28:15). At the time Paul wrote the epistle he had not been to Rome (cf. Rom. 1:13; 15:22). Therefore it is very improbable that Paul had any *direct* role in founding the church there. Several other sources have been suggested, as follows.

A. "Visitors from Rome." Present in JERUSALEM on the Day of PENTECOST were Jews and converts to JUDAISM from many parts of the ancient world, including "visitors from Rome" (Acts 2:9–11). The latter are thought to have been numbered among the 3,000 converted that day (v. 41) and to have established the church in Rome when they returned home. Although this possibility cannot be eliminated, many consider it improbable. If accepted, it would not provide an adequate explanation for the Gentile nature of the church nor for evident organization separate from the synagogue.

B. Peter. The traditional Roman Catholic position is that the church was first founded by the apostle PETER, its first bishop. Frequently based upon the tradition of an early visit (A.D. 42) and either twenty or twenty-five years of continued ministry ("a long exploded fable," Schaff, *History*, 1:366–67), or a return just prior to Paul's first visit, appears to have little basis in fact. There is no scriptural evidence for direct Petrine origin.

It is well argued that Paul would not have interfered with a church begun by Peter because of his stated position of not actively ministering in another's field of labor (Rom. 15:20). At the time of the Roman epistle Paul declares his intention of ministering at Rome (1:10–13; 15:22–24), a desire which evidently was well known (Acts 19:21). Furthermore, if there had been the slightest possibility of Peter's being connected with the Roman church, Paul would have either greeted his fellow apostle by name or referred to his esteemed ministry, neither of which he does — a curious oversight in light of the fact that he makes a special point of mentioning ANDRONICUS and JUNIAS as "outstanding among the apostles, and they were in Christ before I was" (16:7). Certainly if the praiseworthy reputation of the Roman Christians (1:8) was the result of Peter's influence, Paul could not possibly have been ignorant of the fact.

It ought to be noted that even the sources upon which the tradition is based make *both* Peter and Paul responsible for the establishment of the Roman church. IRENAEUS says, "That tradition derived from the apostles of the very great, the very ancient and universally known church founded and organized at Rome by the two most glorious apostles Peter and Paul, as also (by pointing out) the faith preached to men, which comes down to our time by means of successions of the bishops … committed into hands of Linus the office of the Episcopate" (*Haer.* 3.3.2–3).

To deny Peter the role of founding the church in Rome does not preclude his later visit and martyrdom in that city. Peter probably came to Rome late in Paul's second imprisonment and was later martyred at "about the same time" as Paul, according to EUSEBIUS (*Eccl. Hist.* 2.25, citing an address to the Romans by Dionysius, Bishop of Corinth: "Flourishing seed that had been planted by Peter and Paul at Rome and Corinth … they suffered martyrdom about the same time"). Eusebius also cites Tertullian, Gaius, Irenaeus, Origen, and others attesting Peter's martyrdom in Rome.

Schaff (*History*, 1:370–72) surmises that, if Peter came to Rome c. A.D. 63, the two apostles would have ministered to different spheres, Peter to the Jew and Paul to the Gentile, and would have mutually promoted harmony. It is in this sense that they may have been "joint founders." It is further surmised that their martyrdom would have drawn the two communities together. The final "consolidation" of the Jewish and Gentile sections, Schaff suggests, was the work of Clement of Rome after the fall of Jerusalem (see CLEMENT, EPISTLES OF).

C. Pauline converts. A more probable explanation of the origin of the church in Rome is to be found in the Christian converts who carried the gospel to the capital of the empire. The members of the Roman congregation(s) were well known to the apostle. He makes specific reference to twenty-six individuals and no less than five groups by name (Rom. 16.3–16). Not only did Paul know them by name, but he also comments on their faith and activity for the gospel. Apparently some were converted through his ministry (cf. v. 5).

It is suggested that since the gospel was carried as far as "Phoenicia and Cyprus and Antioch" during the persecution following STEPHEN's death (Acts 11:19), it is reasonable to suppose that some would have found their way to Rome also. Although possible, no historical evidence exists to support this conclusion. While not entirely free from problems, the more probable origin of the organized church in Rome was the converts and contacts Paul made with those who were exiled from Rome during the reign of CLAUDIUS, c. A.D. 50 (18:2–3).

The pagan historian SUETONIUS (*Claudius* 25) reports that "since the Jews were continually making disturbances at the instigation of Chrestus, he [Claudius] expelled them from Rome." Writing seventy years after the event, Suetonius apparently used a variant or incorrect spelling for *Christus* to describe a controversy between Jewish and Christian leaders. Christians would have been included in the edict as a "Jewish" sect and have thus been exiled, providing Paul's first contact with PRISCILLA AND AQUILA in CORINTH. Luke's identification of Aquila as a "Jew … a native of Pontus, who had recently come from Italy" (Acts 18:2–3; cf. 2:9) is no proof that he was not a Christian, but rather classifies him as one of "all Jews" who were expelled. The fact that Paul took up residence with him, with no indication that Aquila was converted

Aerial view of St. Peter's Church at Rome. (View to the NW.)

at Corinth, suggests the strong probability that he was already a Christian from Rome.

That Priscilla and Aquila became trusted colaborers is evidenced by their accompanying Paul to EPHESUS. They ministered to APOLLOS and were residents there when Paul wrote 1 Corinthians (Acts 18:18, 26; 1 Cor. 16:19). At the time of the Roman epistle, the apostle refers to them prominently as "fellow workers" at Rome (Rom. 16:3). It is likely that others among Paul's converts migrated or returned to Rome and that these contacts explain the origin of the organized church in the imperial city.

II. Composition. The composition of the church at Rome has been the subject of much speculation and debate (for a helpful summary of recent views, see T. R. Schreiner, *Romans*, BECNT [1998], 10–15). Paul addresses the believers there as Gentiles (Rom. 1:5, 6, 13; 11:13; 15:16), though it is unlikely that it was a *totally* Gentile church. Schaff (*History*, 1:372) suggests the possibility that there were two groups, Jewish and Gentile, and that they "may have formed distinct communities, or rather two sections of one Christian community."

It is estimated that the Jewish population at Rome during the apostolic period was between 20,000 to 30,000. They worshiped in seven well-established synagogues and owned three cemeteries. Most of these Roman Jews were the descendants of slaves captured during the campaigns of Pompey, Cassius, and Antony. That many of these freedmen Jews were wealthy is evident from the large sums annually sent to Jerusalem. The influence this community exerted upon Roman population was significant: "The very passages [and they are numerous] which express hatred of the Jews imply a sense of their influence" (W. J. Conybeare and J. S. Howson, *The Life and Epistles of St. Paul*, 2 vols. [1869], 2:369 n. 5; see further H. J. Leon, *The Jews of Ancient Rome*, updated ed. [1995]). During the early years before they were distinguished from the Jews, the Christians shared in the complete toleration which the Jews enjoyed in Rome. Just when Christianity became officially a *religio illicita* is treated below.

The mere presence of Jews in Rome, however, does not argue for a Roman church that was primarily Jewish (as argued by some scholars). When Paul ministered to the Jewish leaders (Acts 28:21–22), they appeared to be ignorant of any firsthand information about Christian beliefs. It would appear from the Romans epistle that the church Paul addressed was primarily though not entirely Gentile in composition. It seems unlikely the "apostle to the Gentiles" would have addressed any other than Gentiles as he does, for that would have violated the supposed apostolic division of labor (cf. Gal. 2:7–10). In addition, history has not preserved any Pauline epistle to a non-Pauline church.

It is sometimes argued that Paul's frequent appeal to the law (cf. Rom. 7:1) is evidence for a significantly large group of Jewish believers in the church. To this, many scholars rightly respond that the OT was the channel through which the church understood Christian truth.

III. Reputation and growth. Paul states in his letter that the Roman church had established a reputation for: (1) faith "reported all over the world" (Rom. 1:8); (2) individuals whose spiritual influence went beyond the local setting (16:3–7); (3) obedience that was widely known and thus sufficient maturity to be the source of the apostle's rejoicing (16:19). That there were some problems and dissensions is also evident (16:17). The Roman believers' loyalty and affection for the apostle is attested by their journeying some distance to meet him when they heard he was approaching the city (Acts 28:14–16).

Paul's reference to "Caesar's household" (Phil. 4:22), probably during his Roman imprisonment, is often thought to have included some of the people mentioned in Rom. 16 and to be an indication that high-ranking individuals had become converts. Although possible, Lightfoot states that the term used comprised "all persons in the emperor's service, whether slaves or freemen, in Italy and even in the provinces" (*St. Paul's Epistle to the Philippians* [1868], 171). Just how many adherents the early Roman church had is unknown and no statistical sources are available. Apparently the church was not a large one at the time of the Roman epistle (c. A.D. 57), but by the year 64, during the persecution under Nero, the Christians had grown sufficiently to be known, arrested, and martyred in sufficient numbers to have occasioned public sympathy (cf. *1 Clement* 6.1; Tacitus, *Annals* 15.44).

E. M. Blaiklock surmises that on the average one-fifth of the Roman population were Christians over the period of the ten generations the church was underground (from Nero to the early 4th cent.). Numerically this would mean that each generation numbered between 175,000 and 400,000 believers buried in the catacombs. The great variation allows for the lowest to the highest estimates of burials in the more than 350 mi. of catacombs beneath the city (*Cities of the New Testament* [1965], 86). Once the church went underground, the growth and size of the Roman congregation are impossible to ascertain.

IV. Persecutions. Just when Christianity became a *religio illicita* is unknown. At the time Paul was acquitted by Nero it was no crime to be a Christian. Even during the first recorded state PERSECUTION, Nero's charge against the Christians was not their faith but their alleged plot to burn the city (Tacitus, *Annals* 15.44). By then Christians were a recognizable group. Tradition places the martyrdom of Peter and Paul at Rome under Nero, c. A.D. 67 (Euseb. *Eccl. Hist.* 2.25.5–8). The next persecution occurred during the reign of DOMITIAN, c. A.D. 95, when the Christians received the same treatment as the Jews who refused to pay a tax levied for the temple dedicated to Jupiter. Tradition identifies this as the occasion for the exile of JOHN THE APOSTLE to the Isle of PATMOS (Rev. 1:9).

The first discernible policy of persecution took place in BITHYNIA under the governorship of PLINY the Younger, c. A.D. 112, during the reign of TRAJAN. Correspondence between Pliny and Trajan evidences a governmental policy that made being a Christian a crime punishable by death except for recantation (Pliny, *Ep.* 10.96–97). IGNATIUS was martyred during this persecution. Although the official edict defining the state position is lost, it is evident that by the early 2nd cent. the imperial policy regarded it a crime to be a Christian.

The subject of persecution beyond the apostolic period is outside the scope of this article but it is necessary to point out that persecution to the time of Decius (c. 250) was generally local and sporadic. After that the imperial policy sought to eliminate Christianity empire wide. The most intense period came under Emperor Diocletian in 303 and 304, during which believers suffered extensively and so crowded the prisons that "there was no room left for those condemned for crime" (Euseb. *Eccl. Hist.* 8.6.9). In 311 Emperor Galerius issued an Edict of Toleration from his deathbed which permitted Christians to exist providing they did not violate the peace of the empire. Persecution did not universally cease until Constantine issued the Edict of Milan in 313.

V. Place in history. That the church at Rome should gain a prominence very early is to be expected since it was located in the imperial city, the capital of the whole Mediterranean basin. That it should retain and increase in prestige and power after Constantine moved the capital to Byzantium/Constantinople is explained by: (1) a firmly established episcopacy in the Western church concerned about apostolic succession; (2) long-standing tradition of privilege associated with the names of Peter and Paul; (3) relative freedom from the doctrinal errors that generally plagued the Eastern church; (4) declaration of the doctrinal supremacy of the Bishop of Rome by the First Ecumenical Council of Constantinople in 381 and by Emperor Valentinian III in 445; (5) ever-growing acceptance of the Petrine theory of apostolic succession; (6) an organizational structure that, built by capable leaders, expanded to assume increasing temporal authority in a declining empire. It is thus that by the end of the 6th cent. the old Roman church had become the Roman Catholic Church and the Bishop of Rome had become the pope.

(See further W. Ramsay, *The Church in the Roman Empire before A.D. 170* [1893]; G. Edmundson, *The Church in Rome in the First Century* [1913]; A. G. Mackinnon, *The Rome of Saint Paul* [1930]; E. M. Blaiklock, *Rome in the New Testament* [1959]; R. E. Brown and J. P. Meier, *Antioch and Rome: New Testament Cradles of Catholic Christianity* [1983]; J. S. Jeffers, *Conflict at Rome: Social Order and Hierarchy in Early Christianity* [1991]; K. P. Donfried and P. Richardson, eds., *Judaism and Christianity in First-Century Rome* [1998]; P. Oakes, ed., *Rome in the Bible and the Early Church* [2002]; P. Lampe, *From Paul to Valentinus: Christians at Rome in the First Two Centuries* [2003]; S. Cappelletti, *The Jewish Community of Rome: From the Second Century B.C. to the Third Century C.E.* [2006].) H. A. WHALEY

Rompha rohm′fuh. Variant form of REPHAN.

roof. The top of a HOUSE or other building, accessible by outside stairs. Occasionally pitched roofs were used, but most were flat, usually formed of clay packed with stone rollers, supported by mats of rushes or branches across wood beams or palm tree trunks. In Babylonia and Egypt mudbrick arches or

A basalt roof roller used to pack on mud thatched roofs of buildings.

vaults sometimes formed the substructure, and the top surface was leveled off with clay or brick fill. The roof (Heb. *gāg* H1511) was commonly occupied (Deut. 22:8), used for storage (Josh. 2:6), for rest in the evening (2 Sam. 11:2), and was even used in idolatrous worship (Jer. 19:13). An uncommon Hebrew word for "beam" or the like (*qôrâ* H7771) is used in Gen. 19:8 with reference to a roof structure, describing the latter in terms of one supporting member. In this passage the term is idiomatic for "house" or "home," a use reflected also in the phrase "under my roof" (Gk. *stegē* G5094, Matt. 8:8). The roof was not a hindrance to securing healing for the paralytic (Mk. 2:4). H. G. STIGERS

room. See ARCHITECTURE.

rooster. The adult male of the common domestic CHICKEN. It may be the bird mentioned in 1 Ki. 4:23 (Heb. *barbur* H1350) as part of SOLOMON'S daily fare. It is not unlikely that Solomon, who had extensive commerce with the E, should have imported poultry from that region. Proverbs 30:31 includes the "strutting rooster" among "things that are stately in their stride" (v. 29), although the meaning of the Hebrew (*zarzir H2435* + *motnayim H5516*) is uncertain.

Domestic poultry originated in Asia, although the precise location is unknown. One breed came from Malacca and one from Java. The rooster or cock was known in India, but not in Egypt, during ancient times. Pisthetaerus called it the Persian bird, and it is probable that the Greeks obtained these domestic birds from Persia. They were perhaps introduced into Palestine by the Romans, who prized them both for food and for cock fighting. The MISHNAH says that the people did not rear roosters at Jerusalem because of the holy things. This restraint could not have applied to foreigners, and many Jews must also have kept them.

Except for one reference to the rooster's crowing (Gk. *alektorophōnias G231*) as a designation for early morning (Mk. 13:35), all the NT occurrences of the Greek word for "rooster" (*alektōr G232*) are in connection with PETER's denial of Christ (Matt. 26:34, 74–75; Mk. 14:30, 68 [lacking in some important textual witnesses], 72; Lk. 22:34, 60–61; Jn. 13:38; 18:27). In each of the gospel accounts, Jesus predicted at the Last Supper that Peter would disown him three times "before the rooster crows"; and in all four accounts it is recorded that the cock crowed immediately after Peter had denied Christ. Luke says that the cock-crowing reminded Peter of Jesus' words and prompted him to go out and weep bitterly (Lk. 22:61–62). In Mark's account a second crowing is mentioned (Mk. 14:30, 72). This no doubt refers to the same general time as the crowing of the other Gospels, that is, just before dawn. The first crowing, usually unnoticed, may have occurred shortly after midnight.

Tradition has grown up around this incident, leading to the belief that there was one particular rooster that God used to awaken Peter's conscience. There is even a church in Jerusalem named the Church of St. Peter in Gallicantu built in memory of Peter's repentance on this occasion. It is probable that there was a whole chorus of roosters crowing and that the reference is not to a specific bird but only to the time when cocks crowed.

G. H. WATERMAN

root. That part of the plant which penetrates the soil and draws up sap and nourishment for the plant. The numerous references to roots in the Bible (Heb. *šōreš H9247*; Gk. *rhiza G4844*) are mostly figurative, drawn from the important relation which the root bears to the plant. Roots near water symbolize prosperity (Job 29:19; Ezek. 31:7); the opposite is a "withered" root (Hos. 9:16). A root growing old in the ground (Job 14:8) signifies loss of vitality, while "to take root" or "be rooted" denotes becoming or being firmly established (2 Ki. 19:30; Eph. 3:17). Judgment upon sinners is pictured as rottenness of root (Isa. 5:24), roots drying up (Job 18:16; Isa. 14:30), or being uprooted in destruction (Ezek. 17:9; Lk. 17:6; Jude 12). The ax lying at the root of the tree indicates impending judgment (Matt. 3:10).

The root is the source of a moral or spiritual condition. Thus the love of money is pictured as "a root of all kinds of evil" (1 Tim. 6:10), while a "bitter root" causes the defilement of apostasy (Heb. 12:15; cf. Deut. 29:18).

The root of a family or nation is its progenitor (Rom. 11:16). MESSIAH as "the Root of Jesse" (Isa. 11:10) is not a mere shoot from the root but himself the origin and strength of the messianic line; "the Root and the Offspring of David" (Rev. 22:16; cf. 5:5) denotes Christ's divine-human nature as the source and descendant of DAVID. The messianic Servant's appearance as a "root out of dry ground" (Isa. 53:2) depicts his lowly surroundings in contrast to his inner vigor.

D. E. HIEBERT

rope. See CORD, ROPE.

rose. This term is used by the KJV to render Hebrew *ḥăbaṣṣelet H2483*, which occurs twice: in Cant. 2:1 ("the rose of Sharon") and in Isa. 35:1 ("the desert shall rejoice and blossom as the rose"). The identification of the plant is disputed, however. Although it cannot be what we normally mean by "rose," the NIV and other modern versions follow this traditional rendering in the former passage; they use a different term, CROCUS, in the latter.

The plant should not be confused with what is today called the "rose of Sharon" (*Hibiscus syriacus*, an Asian shrub that produces bell-shaped flowers of different colors). The reference in Cant. 2:1 could be to *Hypericum calycinum* (sometimes called "Aaron's beard"), which is not sweet-smelling; known to grow in W Asia Minor and in the Sharon Valley, it is more or less evergreen, and its golden, powder-puff flowers are seen for four long months. This plant will grow almost anywhere, even under trees. It could therefore have succeeded in the Plain of Sharon, even if it had to grow among different vegetation. Other suggestions include the following: *Tulipa montana*, which, as its name suggests, is a tulip that grows happily in the mountains; *Tulipa sharonensis*, a red flower found growing abundantly around Sharon; *Narcissus tazetta*, a scented plant of the lily family that grows plentifully in Palestine, bearing on one stem clusters of cream-colored flowers with a yellow cup; and *Asphodelus*, also a kind of lily (*HALOT*, 1:287). It is uncertain whether Isa. 35:1 refers to the same plant.

In the Apocrypha, roses are mentioned several times. The Greek term for "rose," *rhodon*, occurs in the book of Ecclesiasticus (Sir. 24:14; 39:13; 50:8; the latter text is preserved in Heb., which has *nēs* H5890, "blossom"). It is unlikely that these refer to the wild rose (*Rosa canina*), for this plant would not flourish by wadis and brooks. More probably the reference is to *Nerium oleander*, a shrub 4–12 ft. tall that does very well by water, and especially in the Jordan Valley; the flowers may be pink or white, and when these are double they do look like the rose. See flora (under *Apocynaceae*). The Latin *rosa* in 2 Esd. 2:19 is thought to be the Phoenician rose, which grows 8–9 ft. high, and produces sweet-smelling white single flowers, plus many golden stamens; it will grow at elevations as high as 5,000 ft. and therefore fits into the picture of the "seven mighty mountains" mentioned in the context.

W. E. Shewell-Cooper

Rosetta stone. A bilingual stela of basalt inscribed in Egyptian and Greek, with Egyptian written in both the hieroglyphic and demotic scripts (see languages of the ANE I.B; writing). The text is a decree promulgated by the Egyptian priesthoods in honor of Ptolemy V Epiphanes in his 9th year, 196 B.C. The monument was unearthed in 1799 by Lieutenant Bouchard of Napoleon's army, when consolidating a fort near Rosetta (hence the name); after the British defeat of Napoleon's forces, the stone reached the British Museum in 1802. Along with an obelisk and its plinth from Philae (inscribed in Egyptian and Greek respectively), the stone's bilingual text played a vital role in the initial decipherment of the ancient Egyptian writing systems attempted by Thomas Young (Britain) and achieved by Jean François Champollion. The latter's brilliant success was confirmed by the German scholar Lepsius, and the way was opened into the entire written patrimony of ancient Egypt, covering 3,000 years of history and civilization of the utmost value for the humanities in general, and for biblical backgrounds in particular. (See J. D. Ray, *The Rosetta Stone and the Rebirth of Ancient Egypt* [2007].)

K. A. Kitchen

Rosh rosh (רֹאשׁ H8033, "head, chief"). Son of Benjamin and grandson of Jacob (Gen. 46:21). The name does not appear in the parallel lists (Num. 26:38–39; 1 Chr. 8:1–5; see Beker #1), and the Septuagint of Genesis lists Rosh as son of Bela and grandson of Benjamin. It has also been conjectured that the names "Ehi and Rosh, Muppim and Huppim" (ʾḥy wrʾš mpym whpym) in the Genesis passage are a textual corruption of "Ahiram and Shupham and Hupham" (ʾḥyrm wšwpm whwpm; cf. Num. 26:38–39).

(2) According to some scholars, the Hebrew words describing Gog as "chief prince of Meshech and Tubal" (Ezek. 38:2–3; 39:1) should rather be translated "prince of Rosh [*nĕśîʾ rōʾš*], Meshech, and Tubal" (cf. ASV; also NIV mg.). A people or country named *Rosh* is impossible to identify, although Russia and Rasu (in Assyria) have been suggested. Russians, however, are mentioned for the first time in the 10th cen. A.D. by Byzantine writers under the name of *Rhōs*, and by Ibn Fosslan under the name of *Rus*, a people dwelling on the river Volga. It is therefore unlikely that the prophet could be referring to them.

S. Barabas

row, rower. See ships.

ruby. A relatively rare and costly precious stone, generally red to deep crimson in color, but sometimes with pale rose or purple tints. Like sapphire, it is a variety of corundum (aluminum oxide), which next to diamond is the hardest known naturally occurring mineral. The red color of ruby is thought to be due to the presence of traces of chromium. Rubies occur in crystalline limestones and in gem-bearing gravels derived from these rocks, the best gems coming from Burma. Several Hebrew words possibly refer to this precious stone: *kadkōd* H3905 (Isa. 54:12; Ezek. 27:16), *pĕnînîm* H7165 (Job 28:18 et al., where the reference may be to [pearls of] CORAL), and *ʾōdem* H138 (Exod. 28:17 et al., where NRSV and NJPS have CARNELIAN).   D. R. BOWES

rudder. See SHIPS.

ruddy. See RED.

rude. This English term, in the sense "untrained, unskilled," is used by the KJV in 2 Cor. 11:6, where PAUL concedes that he was inexpert and lacking in technical training. The NIV and other versions use the same term, but in the sense "discourteous," in 1 Cor. 13:5, where the apostle states that LOVE "is not rude" (KJV, "doth not behave itself unseemly").

rue. A strong-scented woody herb. The term correctly translates Greek *pēganon* G4379, which occurs only once (Lk. 11:42, "you give God a tenth of your mint, rue and all other kinds of garden herbs"; the parallel passage, Matt. 23:23, mentions MINT, DILL, and CUMMIN). The ordinary rue grown today in herb gardens is *Ruta graveolens*, the leaves of which are gray-green and produce a pungent odor. The biblical passage could refer to this species, for it did grow in Palestine. It could, however, equally be *Ruta chalepensis latifolia*, which has less deeply divided foliage. This species is also found in Palestine, growing naturally. In addition to being used as a condiment, rue has some medicinal value.
W. E. SHEWELL-COOPER

Rufus roo´fuhs (Ῥοῦφος G4859, hellenized form of the common Latin name *Rufus*, "red"). **(1)** Son of SIMON of Cyrene (who was forced to carry Jesus' cross) and brother of ALEXANDER (Mk. 15:21). Mark's mention of Alexander and Rufus suggests that these brothers may have been known to his readers; and since his gospel is usually thought to have a Roman origin, it is possible that this Rufus is the same as #2 below.

(2) A Christian in ROME to whom PAUL sent greetings (Rom. 16:13). The apostle refers to him as "chosen in the Lord" (prob. suggesting, "a genuine believer" or the like) and states that his mother "has been a mother to me, too." We may infer that this family was originally from the eastern part of the empire and had there hosted or otherwise helped Paul. In the 2nd cent., POLYCARP (*Phil.* 9.1) refers to a certain Rufus who, along with IGNATIUS and Zosimus, was a model of spiritual endurance (presumably an allusion to martyrdom), but there is no reason to think this Rufus is the same individual mentioned by Paul.

rug. See CARPET.

Ruhamah roo-hay´muh (רֻחָמָה [from רחם H8163], "pitied, loved"). A symbolic name given to Israel to indicate the return of God's mercy (Hos. 2:1; NIV, "My loved one"). There is a play on words involved, for the second child of GOMER, Hosea's wife, was called LO-RUHAMAH, "not pitied" (Hos. 1:6, 8), to indicate that God had turned his back on Israel because of her apostasy. See also AMMI; LO-AMMI.

Rule of the Community. See DEAD SEA SCROLLS IV.

ruler. This English term, referring to someone who governs, but without clear indication of the specific office involved, can be used to render a variety of Hebrew words, such as the noun *nāśîʾ* H5954 (Gen. 17:20 et al.), the participle of the verb *māšal* H5440 (45:8 et al.), and others. The common Greek term used in the NT is *archōn* G807 (Matt. 9:18 et al.), but *hēgemōn* G2450 appears frequently as well (Matt. 2:6). The various terms may refer to a king (1 Ki. 1:35; 11:34; Ps. 105:20, 21; Ezek. 19:14; Mic. 5:1, 2; Matt. 2:6), a prince (Jer. 30:21), a prime minister (Gen. 45:8, 26; Dan. 2:48; 5:7, 16; 11:43), a head of a tribe (1 Chr. 9:20), a deputy (Jdg. 9:30), a judge (Jn. 7:27, 35), a member of the SANHEDRIN (Jn. 3:1), the high priest (Acts 23:5), SATAN (Jn. 12:31; 16:11; Eph. 6:12), Jesus Christ the king (Rev. 1:5). See also RULER OF THE SYNAGOGUE.   S. BARABAS

ruler of the synagogue. This phrase, or the simpler "synagogue ruler," is used to render Greek

This 1st-cent. inscription describes the building of a synagogue in Jerusalem by Theodotus, "synagogue ruler." His name occurs at the beginning of the first line; the Greek word for "synagogue ruler," ΑΡΧΙΣΥΝΑΓΩΓΟΣ, occurs at the beginning of the second line (except for the first two letters, which come at the end of the first line).

archisynagōgos G801, referring to the person chosen to care for the physical arrangements of the SYNAGOGUE services ("president of the synagogue" would be the equivalent designation today). Several men serving in this capacity are named or mentioned in the NT. They include JAIRUS, the father of a twelve-year-old girl whom Jesus raised from death (Mk. 5:22–43; cf. Matt. 9:18–26; Lk. 8:40–56); an unnamed man who became indignant because Jesus healed a crippled woman on the SABBATH (Lk. 13:10–17); those who permitted PAUL and BARNABAS to speak in the synagogue at ANTIOCH OF PISIDIA (Acts 13:15); CRISPUS, the ruler of the synagogue at CORINTH, who believed in Christ as a result of Paul's preaching there (18:8); and SOSTHENES, also a synagogue ruler at Corinth, who was seized and beaten when GALLIO refused to hear charges brought against Paul (Acts 18:7; cf. 1 Cor. 1:1). (For a discussion of synagogue officers in NT times, see *HJP*, rev. ed. [1973–87], 2:433–39.) See also ELDER (NT).   G. H. WATERMAN

Rumah roo′muh (רוּמָה *H8126*, "height"). A town that was the home of a certain Pedaiah and/or his daughter Zebidah, who was the wife of JOSIAH and the mother of JEHOIAKIM (2 Ki. 23:36). The site has been variously located. Some suggest that it is identical with DUMAH (#1), one of the towns in the mountains of Judah, near HEBRON (Josh. 15:52), not far from LIBNAH, the native town of another of Josiah's wives (2 Ki. 23:31). Although the consonants ר and ד are easily confused in all stages of the Hebrew text, the suggestion is unlikely because the SEPTUAGINT, though deriving from a historically distinct text type, reads *Rouma*. Others suggest that it is to be identified with ARUMAH, a place mentioned in the vicinity of SHECHEM (Jdg. 9:41). This suggestion finds support in JOSEPHUS, who says that Zebidah's hometown was *Ahoumas*, no doubt a scribal error for Arumah (*Ant.* 10.5.2 §87). But elsewhere Josephus refers to a *Rouma* that was apparently in GALILEE (*War* 2.7.21 §233). Probably this town, modern Khirbet er-Rameh in the Sahl el-Baṭṭof (Valley of Bet Netofa), near RIMMON in Galilee, is in view. In the *Annals* of TIGLATH-PILESER III it is called Arumah (*ANET*, 283). If this location in Galilee is correct, the notice that one of Josiah's wives came from here is of interest because it shows that the dense Israelite population was not removed completely by Tiglath-Pileser when he conquered this area and deported its occupants (cf. Y. Aharoni, *The Land of the Bible: A Historical Geography*, rev. ed. [1979], 371–74).   B. K. WALTKE

rush. See REED.

rust. A brittle coating that tarnishes the surface of metals, especially iron, due to oxidation or corrosion. The few biblical references to rust are all figurative. In one of Ezekiel's parables, the thick rust or deposit in a cooking pot of bronze became symbolic of the unpurged wickedness of the inhabitants of Jerusalem (Ezek. 24:6–13 [Heb. *ḥelʾâ H2689*]). In two NT passages a similar type of indictment, using the symbolism of the rusting of silver and gold, is pronounced against those who accumulate WEALTH (Matt. 6:19–20 [Gk. *brōsis G1111*]; Jas. 5:3 [NIV, "corroded" and "corrosion," translating *katioō G2995* and *ios G2675*]). In both cases the question arises whether the rust testifies to the impermanence of the wealth or whether it witnesses against the rich who prefer to hoard the wealth and let it rot rather than use it for benefiting others. The latter may better suit the context, for in the apocalyptic imagery rust is almost a living avenging force (cf. *TDNT*, 3:335). A. JOHNSON

Ruth, Book of (רוּת H8134, possibly "refreshment" or, less likely, "[female] companion"). One of the historical books of the OT in the English Bible. In the Hebrew Bible, it is found among the Writings (HAGIOGRAPHA or KETUBIM) and grouped with the Five MEGILLOTH (Scrolls). Each of the Megilloth was associated with one of Israel's principal feasts, and Ruth was read at the Feast of Weeks (PENTECOST).

  I. Background
  II. Authorship
  III. Purpose
  IV. Date
  V. Literary value
  VI. Contents

I. Background. The setting of the book of Ruth, "the loveliest complete work on a small scale" (Goethe), is the period of the judges, c. 1200–1020 B.C. (see JUDGES, BOOK OF; JUDGES, PERIOD OF). In contrast to the international background of the book of Judges, which traces the moral, religious, and political decline of Israel on a broad scale, Ruth throws light upon a domestic scene where the standards of loyalty and integrity were still high.

II. Authorship. Jewish tradition maintained that SAMUEL wrote the books of Ruth, Judges, and 1–2 Samuel. Since the death of this leader is noted in 1 Sam. 25:1, he could not be the author of 1–2 Samuel (regarded as one book in the Hebrew Bible). Similarly, the genealogy of Ruth 4:17–22 implies that DAVID had already been crowned king, so it is unlikely that Samuel was the author of Ruth, at least in its present form. The book itself contains no clue concerning its authorship.

III. Purpose. Since an understanding of the book's purpose and character is determinative of the date, it must be considered first. There is no other short book in Scripture to which so many widely divergent motives have been attributed. The chief of these are the following:

(1) A postexilic tract produced to combat the narrow exclusivism said to have been introduced by EZRA and NEHEMIAH, in particular their legislation on mixed marriages (e.g., Neh. 10:30; 13:23–27). But apart from a stress on Ruth's foreign origin (Ruth 1:22; 2:2, 6, 10, 21; 4:5, 10), such a purpose is far from obvious. The canonicity of the book of Ruth was dependent, humanly speaking, on Jews who were the spiritual heirs of Ezra. Moreover, in the TALMUD the first place in the Writings was given to Ruth, which indicates an absence of tension between the attitude of the book and that of traditional JUDAISM. The possibility of a literary warfare on ideological issues at this early date is questionable.

(2) A document designed to show how a Moabite woman was included in the ancestry of David. The tracing of NAOMI's line through OBED and JESSE to David (Ruth 4:17) provides a climax to the story, and the connection with Israel's greatest king may account in measure for its preservation. But this falls short of providing an adequate motive.

(3) A plea for an extension of the practice of LEVIRATE marriage, thus averting the tragedy of a family line being extinguished. The purpose then would be one of encouraging humanity toward the childless widow.

(4) A moral fiction. The idyllic nature of the story and the seemingly metaphorical names of its characters—Naomi ("pleasant"), Ruth ("companion"?), MAHLON ("sickly"), KILION ("frailty"?), ORPAH ("stiff-necked"?)—have led to its being described as a "*Novelle*" (Gunkel) or "an interesting tale of long ago" (R. H. Pfeiffer, *Introduction to the Old Testament* [1941], 719). These names, however, conform to common Hebrew patterns, and the name of Naomi's husband, ELIMELECH ("my God is king"), already attested in the TELL EL-AMARNA tablets of the 14th cent. B.C., is typical of early compounds (e.g., ABIMELECH, AHIMELECH). In any case, the narrative itself purports to be historical (Ruth 1:1), and there is no evidence of anachronisms.

(5) A book intended to present Ruth as the perfect PROSELYTE. According to the later rabbis, the point of the story was that she made a clean break

with her own people and was completely loyal to the nation and religion of her adopted family.

(6) Perhaps one should not look for a single, all-embracing motive for the book. Surely its preservation is due to the fact that it enshrines so much of what is basic in human relationships and in true Israelite religion. It is the story of a loyal, disinterested relationship that secured its just reward. The upright, considerate, and industrious BOAZ was a model Israelite. It demonstrates an overruling PROVIDENCE and the all-embracing LOVE of God, illustrating the fact made explicit in Acts 10:34–35. Its simplicity and domesticity—it is a story of ordinary people—make their appeal to the heart. It speaks a word of hope to the hopeless, the desolate, and the bereaved.

IV. Date. It is evident that the book of Ruth may be dated on a priori grounds, in relation to the ideological views of the preceding section. Here one considers the more objective evidence. The inclusion of Ruth among the Hagiographa, the third section of the Hebrew Scriptures, is not necessarily determinative of a late date (see CANON OF THE OT). It may have been placed there because of its association with the other books of the Megilloth.

Certain Aramaisms and late forms have led some scholars to accept a postexilic date, but the issue is contested by others who maintain that "Aramaisms" (whether real or apparent) occur in Hebrew from the Mosaic period onward. There is also the possibility of minor modifications of language to make the text intelligible to successive generations. Those who accept a 7th-cent. B.C. date for DEUTERONOMY maintain that the book of Ruth must predate the law of Deut. 23:3. The dating of the laws in relation to their observance or nonobservance is hazardous. Accepting a Mosaic origin for the PENTATEUCH, it is evident that many of its provisions were inoperative in the period of the judges.

The purity of style and the classical Hebrew text argue strongly for a preexilic date, but certain features show a gap between the events themselves and the story in its present form. The mention of David in Ruth 4:17, the genealogy of 4:18–22, and the explanation of an ancient custom in 4:7 all point to a period after the accession of David. The lack of hostility toward MOAB is compatible with the early years of David (1 Sam. 22:3–4; contrast 2 Sam. 8:2, 12) but not with the later period of the monarchy, when Moab frequently fell under the prophetic condemnation (e.g., Isa. 15–16; 25:10; Jer. 9:26; 25:21; 27:3; Ezek. 25:8–11). No certain date can be given, but a provisional date for the final composition of Ruth during the early monarchy seems not unreasonable.

V. Literary value. Universal assent would be given to the statement that Ruth is a veritable masterpiece of the storyteller's art. The briefest of introductions sets a scene of hopeless desolation (Ruth 1:1–5). Naomi's consideration for her daughters-in-law and Ruth's absolute loyalty, even to the point of accepting a strange and possibly hostile environment, are made clear (1:6–22). An apparently fortuitous encounter with Boaz (2:1–19) leads Naomi to plan for Ruth's future (2:20—3:5). The story unfolds with a rare delicacy, suspense being maintained until the last—for one breathtaking moment it seems that Boaz was destined not to be Ruth's husband (4:4). All worked out happily and the line of Elimelech was not extinguished. A simple climax, without any embellishment, came when David was named as a descendant of this union (4:17). Naomi, Ruth, and Boaz, the main characters, are skillfully portrayed, and the scene throughout is a simple one, easily comprehended, with two main locations, namely, a roadside in Moab, and Bethlehem during the barley and wheat harvests. The fact that this short story is true makes for an even greater impact.

From Bethlehem to Moab and back.

The fields E of Bethlehem to which Naomi returned with her daughter-in-law, Ruth. (View to the N.)

VI. Contents

A. A Disastrous expedition (Ruth 1:1–5). An approximate date for these events, working back from the genealogy of 4:17 (which may be selective), is 1100 B.C. A famine in Judah drove Elimelech and his family to Moab as sojourners, and as such they had no legal rights there. No direct judgment is given on their departure from their own land (which God had given them) or on the foreign marriages contracted by Mahlon and Kilion, but this may be implicit in the triple disaster that struck the family. Moreover, the lament of 1:21 suggests the loss of considerable material possessions brought from BETHLEHEM, possibly before the full effect of the famine was felt.

B. Return to Bethlehem-Judah (Ruth 1:6–22). Clearly there was a deep affection between Naomi and her daughters-in-law. But their future prospects of marriage would be remote if they journeyed, as aliens, to Judah. Nor was there any hope through the custom of levirate marriage (Ruth 1:11–13; cf. Deut. 25:5–6), for Naomi had little chance of bearing further children. Orpah accepted the wisdom of Naomi's advice and returned. There may be an evidence of territorial henotheism in Ruth 1:15, with the gods being limited to the territory of their worshipers, but this is not certain. Ruth's love and loyalty, however, were such that she was prepared to leave her parents (2:11), her people, and their god. Possibly, as her vow seems to indicate (1:17), she was a worshiper of Yahweh before this decision was made. Her magnificent utterance (vv. 16–17) may be compared with the blunter, soldierly protestation of loyalty by ITTAI the Gittite, another foreigner (2 Sam. 15:21). So Naomi and Ruth traveled the 50 mi. to Bethlehem, where the stir among the women folk suggests that the family of Elimelech had enjoyed considerable standing in the community. Now Naomi had been brought low, a fact which she attributed to the Almighty.

C. A chance encounter (Ruth 2:1–19). The measures Boaz took for Ruth's protection (v. 8; cf. v. 22) show the danger that she, an alien young woman, faced in such a situation. In addition, there was the prospect of hard toil in the heat of the sun for scant reward, in spite of the provisions of Lev. 19:9–10 (cf. Deut. 24:19–21). Ruth was prepared to accept this, toiling indefatigably (Ruth 2:7) to support Naomi in her penury. Boaz, whose introduction as a man of substance (v. 1) gives point to the whole narrative, was aware of the details of the return from Moab (vv. 11–12), but appears to be moved by nothing more than charitable and humane considerations. So a day of drudgery was transformed into a pleasant and fruitful experience.

Naomi was quick to realize that such a harvest was an indication of extraordinary events (v. 19).

D. The plan of Naomi (Ruth 2:20—3:18). The reference to the dead (2.20) shows that a plan was already in process of formulation, although Naomi took time to work out the details. Meanwhile Ruth

Gleaning in the fields in modern-day Israel, depicting what this task was like during the time of Ruth.

enjoyed security and relative prosperity among the harvesters of Boaz. There are seasonal variations in Palestine but, in general, the barley HARVEST began in mid-April and the wheat harvest ended in the first weeks of June. The suggested course of action (3:1–5), springing from Naomi's desire to provide for her daughter-in-law, constituted a direct appeal to Boaz to accept the obligation of the next of kin. It may be assumed that it was the customary course of action in such a situation. Sleeping by the gathered grain (3:7) would be a normal precaution against marauders. Events proceeded with reserve and no hint of any impropriety, and Boaz, who appears as an older man (cf. his address in 2:8–9) and a bachelor, was obviously delighted at the prospect of marriage to such an attractive person as Ruth. But before the marriage could be realized a practical difficulty had to be overcome: there was a relative who had a prior claim. Two problems in the narrative were easily resolved: (1) Naomi herself had a greater claim than Ruth upon any near kinsman; this she voluntarily relinquished in favor of her daughter-in-law; (2) Naomi must have known that Boaz was not the next of kin, but in all probability he was the one she preferred and so she placed the responsibility for making the necessary arrangements upon him (3:18).

E. Events in the gate (Ruth 4:1–12). The gate, together with the open space immediately inside the city, was the traditional place of justice, commerce, and everyday encounter. There the elders, whose influence in local matters was paramount, were to be found. See ELDER (OT). There Boaz contrived a meeting between himself, the next of kin, and the requisite number of elders. There would be no lack of witnesses among the bystanders. The procedure followed combined elements from the law of levirate marriage (Deut. 25:5–6) and the law governing REDEMPTION of property (Lev. 25:25–34). When a man died, his brother was required to marry the widow, and the first son born would then perpetuate the name and the line of the deceased. Boaz and the unnamed next of kin were not, however, the brothers of Mahlon, but as the proceedings were regarded as legal, this incident may be an evidence of a pre-Mosaic custom which extended the scope of levirate marriage to include the nearest relative.

As well as having the duty of marrying the widow of the deceased and redeeming the family property, the redeemer-kinsman (see GOEL) was also the AVENGER OF BLOOD (Deut. 19:6, 12). Boaz had first to ascertain the willingness, or otherwise, of the next of kin to fulfill his obligations. The initial willingness of the next of kin (Ruth 4:4) was modified when he was informed that a necessary condition was marriage to Ruth, possibly because the redeemed land would be lost to him if a son, reckoned legally as the son of the dead, should be born (or perhaps he was already married). The ancient custom of drawing off the shoe (vv. 7–8) signified an abandonment of the obligation of the next of kin, probably by the acceptance of the shoe as a token payment from the next in succession. The good wishes of the witnesses reflect the prevalent view that prosperity in marriage was measured in terms of children, who would guarantee the permanence of the family line. An incidental difficulty is that the son born was reckoned to Mahlon (v. 10), Elimelech (v. 17, by implication), and Boaz (v. 21). An answer to this problem is not immediately apparent, but it probably lies in the type of levirate marriage contracted, the details of which are lost in the mists of antiquity. The concern of the author is to demonstrate the successful conclusion, and to trace the connection with David.

(See further W. Rudolph, *Das Buch Ruth, das Hohe Lied, die Klagelieder*, KAT 17 [1962]; A. E. Cundall and L. Morris, *Judges and Ruth*, TOTC [1967]; E. F. Campbell, Jr., *Ruth*, AB 7 [1975]; R. L. Hubbard Jr., *The Book of Ruth*, NICOT [1988]; J. M. Sasson, *Ruth: A New Translation with a Philological Commentary and a Formalist-Folklorist Interpretation*, 2nd ed. [1989]; E. Zenger, *Das Buch Ruth*, 2nd ed. [1992]; F. W. Bush, *Ruth, Esther*, WBC 9 [1996]; K. Nielsen, *Ruth: A Commentary*, OTL [1997]; D. I. Block, *Judges, Ruth*, NAC 6 [1999]; Y. Zakovitch, *Das Buch Rut: Ein jüdischer Kommentar* [1999]; A. Lacocque, *Le livre de Ruth* [2004]; V. H. Matthews, *Judges and Ruth* [2004]. See also H. H. Rowley, *The Servant of the Lord* [1952], 171–94; J. M. Myers, *The Linguistic and Literary Form of Ruth* [1955]; É. Levine, *The Aramaic Version of Ruth* [1973]; A. Berlin, *Poetics and Interpretation of Biblical Narrative* [1983], 83–110; M. D. Gow, *The Book of Ruth: Its Structure, Theme and Purpose* [1992]; M. C. A. Korpel, *The Structure of the Book of Ruth* [2001]; and the bibliography compiled by W. E. Mills, *Ruth and Esther* [2002].)

A. E. CUNDALL

rye. See SPELT.

Temple of Artemis at Sardis. (View to the E.)

S. In SEPTUAGINT studies, a symbol used to designate CODEX SINAITICUS. See also TEXT AND MANUSCRIPTS (NT).

Saba, Sabaite say´buh, say´buh-it. See SABEAN; SHEBA.

sabachthani. See ELI, ELI, LAMA SABACHTHANI.

Sabaoth sab´ay-oth. See LORD OF HOSTS.

Sabat, Sabateas, Sabatus sab´uht, sab´uh-tee´uhs, sab´uh-tuhs. KJV Apoc. forms of (1) SHEBAT and SHAPHAT, (2) SHABBETHAI, and (3) ZABAD (respectively: 1 Macc. 16:14; 1 Esd. 5:34; 9:48; 9:28).

Sabbaias suh-bay´uhs (Σαββαιας). One of the descendants of Annan who had married foreign women (1 Esd. 9.32, KJV, "Sabbeus"). The name apparently corresponds to SHEMAIAH in the parallel passage (Ezra 9:32).

Sabban sab´an. KJV Apoc. form of BINNUI (1 Esd. 8:62).

Sabbath sab´uhth (שַׁבָּת H8701, possibly "cessation, rest" [but see *HALOT*, 4:1409–10; *NIDOTTE*, 4:1157]; σάββατον G4879 [loanword from Heb., often used in the pl., even with sing. meaning]). The Hebrew weekly day of rest and worship, which was observed on the seventh day of the week, beginning at sundown on Friday and ending at sundown on Saturday.

  I. Origin of the Sabbath
    A. Theories of origin
    B. Teaching of the Bible
  II. History of the Sabbath
    A. Mosaic legislation
    B. Historical and prophetical books of the OT
    C. Intertestamental period
    D. NT period
    E. Post-NT period
  III. Views of the Christian's obligation to keep the Sabbath
    A. The "Christian Sabbath" view
    B. The seventh-day Sabbath view

I. Origin of the Sabbath

A. Theories of origin

1. Planetary theory. It is generally agreed that the origin of the Sabbath is closely related to the origin of the week. In the 19th cent. it was commonly believed that the use of a seven-day week arose out of the ancient veneration of the seven planets. In ancient Babylonian ASTROLOGY these included the sun and the moon, and five of the heavenly bodies known as planets today—Mars, Mercury, Jupiter, Venus, and Saturn. The days of the week then were named after the planets or the gods associated with the planets.

The names of the days of the week used today reflect this ancient regard for the planets. Sunday is named for the Sun; Monday for the Moon; Tuesday for Mars (Old Eng. *Tiw*, god of war, like Roman Mars; cf. French *mardi*); Wednesday for Mercury (Old Eng. *Woden*, i.e., Odin, supreme god; cf. French *mercredi*); Thursday for Jupiter (Thor, Norse god of thunder; cf. French *jeudi*); Friday for Venus (Frigga, Norse goddess of love; cf. French *vendredi*); and Saturday for Saturn.

215

There is no proof, however, that the names of the planets were applied to the days of the week prior to the beginning of the Christian era (Willy Rordorf, *Sunday: The History of the Day of Rest and Worship in the Earliest Centuries of the Christian Church* [1968], 24–27). Besides, there is no certain knowledge that the recognition of these seven "planets" led to the formation of a seven-day week. Consequently, this theory has long been abandoned.

2. Pan-Babylonian theory. The most popular theory at the close of the 19th cent., especially among the more liberal historical critics, was that the Hebrew institution of the Sabbath was directly traceable to Babylonia. During that century there were discovered a large number of Babylonian CUNEIFORM tablets, in several of which the word *šabattu(m)* appears. The word was used to designate the fifteenth day of the month, or the time of the full moon in the Babylonian lunar month. In one tablet it is described as the *um nuḫ libbi*, which has been interpreted to mean "a day of appeasement of the heart," or a day of pacification of the god.

Other Babylonian tablets indicate that the seventh, fourteenth, twenty-first, and twenty-eighth days of certain months were observed as unlucky or evil days. On these days the king was forbidden to eat meat roasted on coals or any food touched by fire. He was also forbidden to ride in his chariot, to change his clothes, or to discuss affairs of state. On these days the priests were not to consult the oracles, and the physicians were not to treat the sick. On these days, according to another series of Babylonian clay tablets, special sacrifices were offered to the gods (John R. Sampey in *ISBE* [1929], 4:2630; A. E. Millgram, *Sabbath: The Day of Delight* [1944], 340–41).

While there are remote resemblances between the dietary and travel restrictions imposed on the Babylonian king on these days and some of the biblical laws regarding the Sabbath, the differences between them far outweigh any resemblances. The Babylonian days were reckoned from the beginning of the month; the Hebrew Sabbath was observed every seventh day. The Babylonian restrictions applied to only certain classes of the population; the Hebrew Sabbath was a day of rest for all the people. There was no cessation of business

Sabbath days were part of a larger calendrical system. This Babylonian astronomical text, written in cuneiform, provides information on how the movements of the sun and the moon were calculated so as to determine the length of days, months, and years.

transactions on the Babylonian days, but they were considered more favorable for such activity; no work of any kind was permitted on the Hebrew Sabbath. Furthermore, the term *šabattum* was not applied to these days, but was restricted to the fifteenth day of the month.

The Pan-Babylonian theory of the origin of the Sabbath was based not only on the alleged resemblances between the Babylonian evil days and the Sabbath, but also on alleged similarities between the Babylonian creation tablets and the biblical account of creation. Alexander Heidel has shown that the Babylonian epic ENUMA ELISH, while presenting a number of analogies to the first two chapters of Genesis, is essentially different from the biblical story of CREATION, and concludes that no incontrovertible evidence can be produced for any Babylonian borrowings in the biblical record (*The Babylonian Genesis* [1942], 117). Walter Maier is more positive and emphatic: "If there is any connection between the Babylonian epic and the first chapter of Genesis, then the cuneiform poem must be a demoralized, degenerate, vague, and mythological reëchoing of the revealed truth of the Bible" ("Mimeographed Notes on Genesis," 14).

3. Lunar festival theory. The ingenious theory (closely related to the Pan-Babylonian) that the Hebrew Sabbath is a survival of an ancient lunar festival, which may or may not have been derived from Babylonia, seems to have some support in the Bible. The Bible frequently associates together the Sabbath and the NEW MOON, in each case mentioning the latter first (2 Ki. 4:23; Isa. 1:13; Amos 8:5). A passage from the Pentateuch seems to lend support to this theory. In Lev. 23:11, 15 the Hebrews are commanded to begin the counting of the wave offering from "the morrow after the Sabbath" (KJV), and Jewish tradition interpreted this phrase to mean the morrow after the first day of the PASSOVER, which always fell on a day of the full moon. If this tradition is correct, the word "Sabbath" here refers, not to the weekly Sabbath, but to the day of the full moon. (The Qumran community, however, had a different understanding of Lev. 23:10–11; see 11QTemple [= 11Q19] XVIII, 11–12.)

Each of the four phases of the MOON occurs approximately seven days after the previous phase. It was thought that the days on which the new moon, the full moon, the half moon, and the waning moon appeared were observed by sacrifices to the lunar god, and later by rest from work (R. J. Floody, *Scientific Basis of Sabbath and Sunday* [1906], 44–45). Several considerations support the idea that there was some kind of relation between the observance of the moon phases and the observance of the weekly Sabbath. (1) Ancient CALENDARS were based on the movements of the moon. (2) The Jews celebrated the day of the new moon by sacrifice and feasting and probably by the suspension of everyday occupations (1 Sam. 20:18–34; 2 Ki. 4:23). (3) The Jews had certain fixed Sabbaths which fell on the day of the full moon, namely the Passover, the feast of Tabernacles, and the feast of Purim. (4) The Babylonian *šabattum*, which was used to designate the fifteenth day of the month, or the time of the full moon in the Babylonian lunar month, is equivalent etymologically to the Hebrew *šabbāt*.

The Hebrew Sabbath, however, was not connected with the phases of the moon. It occurred at the end of a seven-day periodic week that was independent of both the lunar month and the solar year. Millgram (*Sabbath*, 342) concludes: "The question still remains — how could or how did the ancient Semitic observance of the new moon and the full moon, or the observance of the four phases of the moon as evil days, become the *periodic* week with its *humanitarian* Sabbath? This question cannot be answered satisfactorily. The only conclusion that may be drawn is that the seven-day Hebrew week, with its humanitarian rest day as we have it now, is a unique creation of the Hebrew religious genius, and is one of the most valuable Hebrew contributions to the civilization of mankind."

B. Teaching of the Bible

1. Sanctification of the seventh day at creation. The Hebrews did not claim to be the creators of this unique institution. They affirmed that God himself was its creator. The record of its origin which they preserved for us is in the opening chapters of Genesis. These chapters describe God's creative activity during six days and his sanctification of the seventh day by his cessation from his creative work (Gen. 1:1—2:3). The word *šabbāt* is not employed, but it is certain that the author meant to assert that God blessed and hallowed the seventh day as the Sabbath.

The grouping of the creation narrative into six periods called days, followed by a seventh day of rest, seems to have been done purposefully to establish a weekly sacred day. Later scriptural teaching on the Sabbath seems to corroborate this. The fourth commandment of the Decalogue, as recorded in Exodus, gives as the reason for the Israelites' observance of the Sabbath the fact that God "made the heavens and the earth, the sea, and all that is in them, but he rested on the seventh day. Therefore the LORD blessed the Sabbath day and made it holy" (Exod. 20:11). The words of Jesus, "The Sabbath was made for man, not man for the Sabbath" (Mk. 2:27), point back beyond the Mosaic command to the original purpose and will of God.

It seems clear, therefore, that the divine origin and institution of the Sabbath took place at the beginning of human history. At that time God not only provided a divine example for keeping the seventh day as a day of rest, but also blessed and set apart the seventh day for the use and benefit of human beings. There is no mention of the observance of the Sabbath by the PATRIARCHS, although a period of seven days is mentioned several times in the account of NOAH and the flood (Gen. 7:4, 10; 8:10, 12), and a week is mentioned in the story of JACOB and RACHEL (29:27). Whether the patriarchs had knowledge of or observed the Sabbath does not matter; the revelation of God to Moses was that he had instituted the Sabbath at the close of creation.

2. The ordinance concerning the manna. The first mention of the word *šabbāt* is in Exod. 16:23, which gives certain regulations concerning the gathering and preparation of the MANNA, when the Israelites were in the Desert of Sin. At the command of the Lord, Moses told the people to gather and prepare twice as much manna on the sixth day as on other days (Exod. 16:5). When the leaders of the congregation reported to Moses that the people had done so, Moses replied, "This is what the LORD commanded: 'Tomorrow is to be a day of rest, a holy Sabbath to the LORD'" (16:23). The next day Moses commanded the people to eat what had been kept over, and added, "… today is a Sabbath to the LORD. You will not find any of it on the ground today. Six days you are to gather it, but on the seventh day, the Sabbath, there will not be any" (16:25–26). Some of the people, notwithstanding this explicit command, went out to gather manna on the seventh day (16:27). At this point the LORD said to Moses, "How long will you refuse to keep my commands and my instructions? Bear in mind that the LORD has given you the Sabbath; that is why on the sixth day he gives you bread for two days. Everyone is to stay where he is on the seventh day; no one is to go out" (16:28–29).

This passage shows that the Sabbath was certainly made known to Israel before the giving of the law at Sinai. The Israelites did not arrive at Sinai until the following month (Exod. 16:1; 19:1). The passage also shows that this was not the first institution of the Sabbath. The incidental manner in which the matter is introduced and the remonstrance of the Lord for the disobedience of the people both imply that the Sabbath had previously been known. The Lord's inquiry, "How long will you refuse to keep my commands and my instructions?" (16:28), sounds as if it had long been in existence. In fact, the equation of the Sabbath with the seventh day, the statement that the Lord gave the Israelites the Sabbath, and the record that the people, at God's command, rested on the seventh day, all point unmistakably to the primeval institution of the Sabbath.

3. The fourth commandment of the Decalogue. The fourth commandment itself does not purport to be the first promulgation of the Sabbath. Its introductory words, "Remember the Sabbath day" (Exod. 20:8), suggest that the Sabbath had been previously known but either forgotten or neglected. The reason given in the commandment for the sanctification of the Sabbath day was the example of God at the close of creation (20:9–11). The commandment pointed back to the original institution of the Sabbath.

The fourth commandment made the Sabbath a distinctive Hebrew institution. It formed an integral part of the COVENANT God made with Israel at Sinai. The covenant consisted of the TEN COMMANDMENTS uttered by the Lord himself from the mount (Deut. 4:13; 5:2–21). The fourth commandment has a central place in that covenant, serving as the connecting link between those instructions having to do with duties toward God and those having to do with duties toward others.

The Ten Commandments are prefixed by a declaration that God had brought Israel out of the land of Egypt (Exod. 20:2; Deut. 5:6). These words can apply in their literal sense only to the children of Israel. The wording of the commandments themselves also indicates that they were given specifically to the Israelites. The fifth commandment contains a promise of long life in the land which the Lord was about to give to Israel (Exod. 20:12; Deut. 5:16). Similarly, the Deuteronomic version of the fourth commandment gives the deliverance of Israel from bondage in Egypt as the primary reason for the observance of the Sabbath (Deut. 5:15). The keeping of the Sabbath is elsewhere declared to be the sign of Israel's allegiance to God (Exod. 31:13; cf. Neh. 9.14). It served to distinguish Israel from the other nations. There can be no doubt that in its original setting and application the fourth commandment was a law intended specifically for the people of Israel.

At the same time it is evident that the fourth commandment contains principles that are applicable to all people. It recognizes the moral duty of human beings to WORSHIP their Creator, for which stated times and places are needed as well as surcease from the ordinary employments of life. It recognizes also the basic human need for a weekly day of rest. History has demonstrated the need of human beings for the recuperation of physical and mental energies once in every seven days as well as the need for a day of the week set apart for spiritual devotion and instruction. The Sabbath command provided for these needs of the ancient Israelites. Moreover, the appeal to God's own rest indicates that observance of the Sabbath mirrors God's behavior and character. In this sense, the fourth commandment is a specific instance of the broader command, "Be holy because I, the LORD your God, am holy" (Lev. 19:2).

II. History of the Sabbath

A. Mosaic legislation. The regulations for the observance of the Sabbath in the Mosaic legislation are relatively simple. The Sabbath was to be observed on every seventh day; it was to be observed by all: the servants, the humble beasts of burden, the members of the Hebrew household, and the guests who were staying within their gates were all commanded to cease from labor on that day (Exod. 20:8–11; Deut. 5:12–15).

The humanitarian aspect of this freedom from toil on the Sabbath is especially emphasized in DEUTERONOMY, where the deliverance of Israel from the oppressive bondage of Egypt is given as the reason for the keeping of the Sabbath (Deut. 5:14, 15). The gathering of manna on the seventh day had been expressly forbidden (Exod. 16:27–29). Likewise, the kindling of a fire on the Sabbath was banned (35:3). The penalty for profaning the Sabbath by doing any work on it was death (31:14). In one specific case, a man who was found gathering sticks on the Sabbath day was stoned to death (Num. 15:32–36).

The Sabbath, however, was not a day of total inactivity. The priests carried on their duties about the TABERNACLE. The bread of the Presence (see SHOWBREAD) was to be set on the table in the holy place on the Sabbath day (Lev. 24:8). A special sacrifice, in addition to the ordinary daily sacrifice, was to be offered on the Sabbath day (Num. 28:9–10). The rite of CIRCUMCISION was performed on the Sabbath if that was the eighth day after the child's birth (Lev. 12:3; cf. Jn. 7:22). The Sabbath is listed among the sacred festivals, that is, "the appointed feasts of the LORD" (Lev. 23:2–3). It, like them, was proclaimed to be "a holy convocation" (23:3). This can only mean that it was regarded as a day for the calling together of the congregation of Israel to worship. In the early history of the Israelites, the Sabbath was a day of welcome rest from labor and of solemn worship at the sanctuary of God.

B. Historical and prophetical books of the OT. The first mention of the Sabbath in the historical books is found in a question uttered by the husband of the Shunammite woman at whose home ELISHA had been entertained. She had asked for one of the servants and one of the donkeys that she might go to see the prophet (2 Ki. 4:22). Her husband expressed surprise at her request and said, "Why go to him today?... It's not the New Moon or Sabbath" (v. 23). His mention of the Sabbath was incidental, but his remark plainly infers that it was customary to suspend work and to visit the prophet on the Sabbath.

Visiting a prophet on the Sabbath would necessarily be limited to the few. There is evidence that visiting the TEMPLE on the Sabbath was a more widespread custom. There are a number of references in Chronicles to the ritual performed in the temple on that day (1 Chr. 9:32; 23:31; 2 Chr. 2:4; 8:13; 23:4; 31:3). The prophet Isaiah, in his condemnation of the hypocrisy of the worshipers, seems to indicate that assemblies took place in the temple on that day (Isa. 1:13).

Isaiah denounced the formalistic Sabbath observance of his time (Isa. 1:12–13), and defined true Sabbath-keeping as turning from one's own ways and from one's own pleasures, and taking delight in the Lord (58:13–14). Other prophets raised their voices in protest against the abuse of the Sabbath (Jer. 17:21–22; Ezek. 22:8; Amos 8:4). They regarded the destruction of Jerusalem and the captivity of the Jews as due, at least in part, to the desecration of the Sabbath (Jer. 17:27; Ezek. 20:23, 24).

Hosea predicted that God would make Israel's Sabbaths to cease because of her unfaithfulness (Hos. 2:11); but that this cessation of Sabbath observance was not meant to be permanent is made clear by Isaiah and Ezekiel (Isa. 66:23; Ezek. 44:24).

During the period of the EXILE, the Sabbath rose in prominence as compared to the other religious festivals of the Jews, since it was independent of the temple in Jerusalem, whereas the other festivals were in part dependent on that religious center. In the period of the return from exile, Sabbath observance was revived in Palestine, in large measure through the reforms of NEHEMIAH. On his return to Palestine, he was shocked to see the widespread desecration of the holy day. People labored in the fields, gathered the harvests, and bought and sold publicly on the Sabbath day. Nehemiah rebuked the nobles of Judah and ordered the gates of Jerusalem closed during the Sabbath (Neh. 13:15–22). His vigorous efforts were largely responsible for the establishment of the Sabbath as a day of universal rest among the Jews of Palestine.

C. Intertestamental period. In the years following the reforms of Nehemiah and Ezra, their successors, the SCRIBES, developed an elaborate code of regulations and restrictions governing Sabbath observance. These were intended to safeguard and preserve the spirit of the Sabbath, just as the shell protects the kernel. They were an attempt to "make a fence around the Torah" (cf. *m. ʾAbot* 1:1) so that its proper observance would be guaranteed. The discussion of actual or hypothetical cases led to the formulation of thirty-nine articles that prohibited all kinds of ordinary agricultural, industrial, and domestic work, unless it was by its nature, or in the circumstances of the case, necessary (G. F. Moore, *Judaism in the First Centuries of the Christian Era: The Age of the Tannaim*, 3 vols. [1927–30], 2:27–30).

The efforts of the scribes to promote a regard for the Hebrew Sabbath were successful. The Sabbath became so deeply rooted in Jewish consciousness and so treasured by individual Jews, that in the days of the Maccabees many chose to die rather than desecrate it. The Jews refused to engage in battle, even in self-defense, on their holy day. Later, however, MATTATHIAS, the leader of the revolt against the tyranny of ANTIOCHUS IV, ruled that it was permissible to take up arms in self-defense on the Sabbath (1 Macc. 2:41; see MACCABEE).

The ruling of Mattathias is significant because it was the first of many such rulings designed to liberalize the restrictions of Sabbath observance. Many ways were found to get around the letter of the law. The motive for the extended casuistry on the Sabbath was undoubtedly to make the law more practicable, but it led to many fanciful and far-fetched interpretations. For example, from the rabbinical interpretation of the command in Exod. 16:29 ("Everyone is to stay where he is on the seventh day"), it was determined that a SABBATH DAY'S JOURNEY might not exceed 2,000 cubits beyond one's dwelling. However, if a person had deposited at that distance on the day preceding the Sabbath enough food for two meals, he thereby constituted it his dwelling, and hence might go on for another 2,000 cubits. Similarly, if families living in private houses that opened into a common court deposited food in the court before the Sabbath, thereby establishing a "connection" between the houses and making them one dwelling, they were permitted to carry things from one house to another without breaking the law (A. Edersheim, *The Life and Times of Jesus the Messiah*, 2 vols. [1889], 2:777).

One of the outstanding features of this period was the rise of the SYNAGOGUE. This institution became the center of the religious life of JUDAISM, not only in those places that were far removed from Jerusalem, but also alongside the temple in Jerusalem. Attendance at the synagogue became customary on the Sabbath day (cf. Lk. 4:16). The Hebrew Sabbath became distinctively a day of worship, a worship connected largely with the synagogue.

D. NT period

1. Jesus and the Sabbath. At the beginning of the NT period, the true meaning of the Sabbath had been obscured by the multitudinous restrictions laid upon its observance. Sabbath observance had largely become external and formal. Many people had become more concerned for the punctilious observance of a day than for the poignant needs of human beings. It was inevitable that Jesus should come into conflict with the Jewish leaders over this issue. It was Jesus' custom to attend the synagogue on the Sabbath (Lk. 4:16; cf. Mk. 1:21; 3:1; Lk. 13:10). In his teaching he upheld the authority and validity of the OT law (Matt. 5:17–20; 15:1–6; 19:16–19; 22:35–40; Lk. 16:17). His emphasis, however, was not on an external observance of the law, but on a spontaneous performance of the will of God that underlay the law (Matt. 5:21–48; 19.3–9). Jesus sought to clarify the true meaning of the Sabbath by showing the original purpose for its institution: "The Sabbath was made for man, not man for the Sabbath" (Mk. 2:27).

On six different occasions Jesus came into direct conflict with Jewish prejudices in regard to the Sabbath. He defended his disciples for plucking grain on the Sabbath by alluding to the time when DAVID and his men ate the bread of the Presence (Matt. 12:1–4; Mk. 2:23–26; Lk. 6:1–4). By so doing, Jesus placed the Sabbath commandment in the same class as the ceremonial law that prohibited the eating of this sacred bread by others than the priests, and taught that human need had precedence over the legal requirements of the Sabbath. He also reminded his critics that the priests in the temple desecrated the Sabbath and were guiltless (Matt. 12:5). He may have been referring to the weekly performance of worship rituals or more specifically to the practice prescribed by the law of circumcising a male child on the Sabbath if that were the eighth day after his birth (Lev. 12:3; Jn. 7:22–23). It was on this same occasion that Jesus said that the Sabbath was made for man, and not man for the Sabbath (Mk. 2:27), indicating that he regarded the Sabbath as a provision for human need and welfare and not as a burdensome legal requirement. It was also on this occasion that Jesus asserted his lordship over the Sabbath (Matt. 12:8, Mk. 2:28; Lk. 6:5).

Jesus expressed anger over those Jews at the synagogue in CAPERNAUM who showed more concern for the punctilious observance of the Sabbath than for a human being who was deprived of the use of a hand; he then proceeded to heal the man before them all (Mk. 3:1–5). On another occasion, when the ruler of the synagogue became indignant because Jesus healed a woman who had been crippled by an evil spirit for eighteen years, he defended his action by appealing to the common practice of untying one's domestic animals to lead them to water on the Sabbath (Lk. 13:10–17). Again, when Jesus, under the critical eye of the PHARISEES, healed a man on the Sabbath who had dropsy, he defended his action by asking if his critics would not rescue an ox or a donkey that had fallen into a well on that day (14:1–6).

The remaining two occasions when Jesus' action on the Sabbath brought him into conflict with the Jewish leaders are recorded by John. One was the healing of the impotent man at the pool of BETHESDA (Jn. 5:1–18); the other was the healing of the man born blind (9:1–41). On the first of these occasions Jesus defended his right to heal on the Sabbath on the grounds that his Father did not suspend his beneficent activity on that day (5:17), and on the second occasion he condemned the spiritual blindness of the Pharisees (9:40, 41).

In all of these instances, Jesus showed that he placed human need above the mere external observance of the Sabbath. Jesus never did or said anything to suggest that he intended to take away the privileges afforded by such a day of rest. On the other hand, it cannot be said that Jesus intended to perpetuate the Hebrew Sabbath or extend its application to all people. As far as the record of the Gospels is concerned, he never made explicit mention of the fourth commandment. By emphasizing the principles that lay back of the law, the spirit and purpose of the law instead of its formal and external regulations, he prepared the way for the

Reconstruction of an ancient synagogue in Capernaum. This may have been the site where Jesus was criticized for healing on the Sabbath (Mk. 3:1–6).

abolishing of all the external laws and ordinances of the OT.

2. Paul and the Sabbath. The early Christians were loyal Jews. They worshiped daily in the temple at Jerusalem (Acts 2:46; 5:42). They attended services in the synagogue (9:20; 13:14; 14:1; 17:1–2, 10; 18:4). They revered the law of Moses (21:20). The Jewish Christians undoubtedly continued to observe the Sabbath. When Gentiles were brought into the Christian community, a problem arose with regard to their relation to the Jewish law. There were those who insisted that it was necessary for them to submit to the rite of circumcision and keep the law of Moses, which would, of course, include the Sabbath command (Acts 15:1, 5; Gal. 2:3–5). Others, of whom Paul became the leader, affirmed that it was not necessary for the Gentile converts to accept the religion of Judaism. Paul argued that, since they had received the Spirit without observing Jewish law, they were not obligated to adopt Jewish ceremonial in order to live righteously (Gal. 3:2–3; cf. Acts 15:7–10).

The apostle Paul regarded the law as a yoke of bondage from which the Christian had been set free (Gal. 5:1). In his "revolt against external law" (P. Cotton, *From Sabbath to Sunday* [1933], 11), Paul made no distinction between moral and ceremonial law (although many believe that some such distinction is reflected in 1 Cor. 7:19 and elsewhere). It was all a part of that old covenant which was done away in Christ (2 Cor. 3:14). It was a set of regulations "that was against us and that stood opposed to us," but God canceled it and "took it away, nailing it to the cross" (Col. 2:14). In this context, Paul mentions the Sabbath along with festivals and New Moon celebrations, all of which are declared to be "a shadow of the things that were to come" (2:16–17). To observe "special days and months and seasons and years" is to be slaves to "the weak and miserable principles" (Gal. 4:9–10; cf. Col. 2:20). The observance of days, along with the avoidance of certain foods, is a characteristic of someone "whose faith is weak" (Rom. 14:1–6).

Paul provides no grounds for imposing the Hebrew Sabbath on the Christian. The Christian is free from the burden of the law. The Spirit of Christ enables him to fulfill God's will apart from external observance of the law's demands. The author of Hebrews likewise speaks of the Hebrew Sabbath only as a type of "God's rest," which is the inheritance of all the people of God (Heb. 4:1–10). He does not tell his readers to keep the Sabbath, but rather urges them to "make every effort to enter that rest" (4:11).

E. Post-NT period. The early church fathers of the 2nd and 3rd Christian centuries were practically unanimous in their view of the Hebrew Sabbath. Some insisted that it was completely abrogated, while others emphasized its typical character, but all agreed that it was not binding on the Christian.

Ignatius, disciple of the apostle John and bishop in Antioch of Syria, wrote to the Magnesians in the early years of the 2nd cent.: "Be not deceived with strange doctrines, nor with old fables. For if we still live according to the Jewish law, we acknowledge that we have not received grace"; and then goes on to categorize his readers as "those who were brought up in the ancient order of things" but who "have come to the possession of a new hope, no longer observing the Sabbath" (*Magn.* 8.1; 9.1; see *ANF*, 1:62, 63).

Justin Martyr, the first great Christian apologist around the middle of the 2nd cent., explains in his *Dialogue with Trypho* why the Christians do not keep the law of Moses, submit to circumcision, or observe the Sabbath. He asserts that (1) true Sabbath observance under the new covenant is the keeping of a perpetual Sabbath which consists of turning from sin; (2) the righteous men of old, Adam, Abel, Enoch, Noah, and the like, pleased God without keeping Sabbath; and (3) God imposed the Sabbath upon the Israelites because of unrighteousness and hardness of heart (*ANF*, 1:199–200, 204, 207).

Irenaeus, Bishop of Lyons during the latter part of the 2nd cent., viewed the Sabbath as symbolical of the future kingdom of God, "in which the man who shall have persevered in serving God shall, in a state of rest, partake of God's table" (*Against Heresies* 4.16, see *ANF*, 1.481). He cites Abraham as an example of one who believed God "without circumcision and without observance of Sabbaths" (ibid.).

Clement of Alexandria, writing around the close of the 2nd cent., says: "The Sabbath, by abstinence from evil, seems to indicate self-restraint" (*Stromata* 7.12; see *ANF*, 2:545).

Tertullian, at the beginning of the 3rd cent., says: "We have nothing to do with Sabbaths or the other Jewish festivals, much less with those of the heathen" (*On Idolatry* 14; see *ANF*, 3:70). In another work he says that those who would contend for the continued obligation of Sabbath-keeping and circumcision must show that Adam and Abel, Noah and Enoch, and Melchizedek and Lot also observed these things. He goes on to say that the Sabbath was figurative of rest from sin and typical of man's final rest in God. It, together with the other ceremonial regulations of the law, was intended to last only until a new Lawgiver should arise who would introduce the realities of which these were shadows (*An Answer to the Jews* 2; see *ANF*, 3:153, 155–56).

The Hebrew Sabbath has, of course, continued to be observed by non-Christian Jews to the present time. During the first centuries some Jewish Christians also continued the practice of observing the seventh day of the week as well as the assembly for worship on the first day of the week. But their influence on Christianity, though discernible for several centuries, especially in the E, dwindled rapidly after the destruction of Jerusalem in A.D. 70 (Cotton, *From Sabbath to Sunday*, 58–63). The testimony of the ante-Nicene fathers is that for the vast majority of Christians, the Sabbath was a Jewish institution that was not binding on Christian believers.

III. Views of the Christian's obligation to keep the Sabbath

A. The "Christian Sabbath" view.

This view holds that Sunday is the Christian Sabbath, the observance of which is a moral obligation based on the fourth commandment of the Decalogue. Church historian Philip Schaff calls it the "Anglo-American theory" because it has been so widely held in Great Britain and the United States. He traces its origin to the Puritans at the close of the 16th cent. (*History of the Christian Church*, vol. 7, 4th ed. [1903], 493–94).

This view emphasizes the divine institution of the Sabbath at the close of creation. God's blessing and sanctification of the seventh day is taken to mean that he intended one day in seven to be observed by all people in all ages as a sacred day of rest and worship. The fourth commandment of the Decalogue, which alludes to the primeval institution of the Sabbath, is regarded as a moral command, and therefore of universal and perpetual obligation. It is argued that the day of the week on which the Sabbath is to be kept was not of the essence of the law, but rather the observance of one day in every seven. Jesus affirmed that he was "Lord

A modern synagogue in Cairo, Egypt, where Jews today still worship on the Sabbath.

even of the Sabbath" (Mk. 2:28) and therefore had the authority to change the day of its observance. It usually is held that this change took place during the forty days between Christ's resurrection and ascension, when he spoke to them concerning the kingdom of God (Acts 1:3).

Sabbatarians insist that Jesus intended to perpetuate the Sabbath and extend its application to all people. Much stress is laid on the statement of Jesus, "The Sabbath was made for man, not man for the Sabbath" (Mk. 2:27), as evidence that Jesus regarded the Sabbath as an institution that is grounded in the very constitution of man, and which was instituted by God from the very beginning not only for Israel but for the whole human race (W. F. Crafts, *The Sabbath for Man* [1885], 366). The teachings of Paul regarding the Sabbath are taken to refer only to the Jewish Sabbath and not to the "Christian Sabbath."

This view has appealed to many Christians because it seeks to establish a firm scriptural basis for the observance of Sunday. The Bible does teach that God instituted the Sabbath at the close of creation, but it is identified as "the seventh day" (Gen. 2:3; Exod. 16:29; 20:10; Deut. 5:14), not as one day in seven. There is a moral element in the fourth commandment, for it provides for the worship of God. There are, however, also ceremonial elements in the commandment which applied only to the Israelites. While this command is included among the moral laws of the Decalogue, it is also included among those civil and religious observances that were obviously temporal and provisional. It can be argued that Jesus himself treated the Sabbath law as ceremonial when he defended his disciples for plucking grain on the Sabbath, for a moral law could never be suspended by circumstances of hunger or by the requirements of a merely ceremonial regulation. Paul made no distinction between ceremonial and moral requirements when he declared that Christians are freed from the law.

The basic weakness of this theory is the teaching that a change was made in the day of the week to be observed as the Sabbath. There is no indication in the NT that Jesus transferred the Sabbath to another day of the week, nor that anyone else did so (although it is argued that the change is suggested by Jesus' meeting the disciples on the first day of the week [Jn. 20:19, 26], by the significance of that day in the life of the early church [Acts 20:7; 1 Cor. 16:2], and by the expression "the Lord's Day" [Rev. 1:10]). Furthermore, if one insists on the perpetual and universal obligation of the fourth commandment, and at the same time recognizes that there is no NT ground for a change in the day of its observance, the only logical position to which he is forced is to maintain that the seventh day of the week, and not the first day, should be observed as the Sabbath, as the fourth commandment stipulates. This is precisely the position taken by the seventh-day sabbatarians. See also LORD'S DAY.

B. The seventh-day Sabbath view. This view, held by the Seventh-day Baptists who originated in England in the 17th cent., and by the Seventh-day Adventists who originated in America in the 19th cent., insists that Christians are obligated to keep the seventh day of the week as the Sabbath. In support of this position, they appeal largely to the OT, especially to the language of the fourth commandment, which, they point out, clearly states that the seventh day is the Sabbath, appointed by God to commemorate his work of creation. The Ten Commandments are referred to as "the law of God," to be distinguished from the ceremonial and civil laws which are called "the law of Moses" (A. L. Baker, *Belief and Work of Seventh-Day Adventists* [1942], 74).

The seventh-day sabbatarians also find evidence for the observance of the seventh day in the NT. They appeal to the practice of Jesus and the apostles of attending the synagogue on the Sabbath (Lk. 4:16; Acts 13:14, 42; 16:13; 17:1–2; 18:4). They appeal to Jesus' prophecy regarding the destruction of Jerusalem and his exhortation that his disciples pray that their flight should not be on the Sabbath (Matt. 24:20). They even contend that the reference in Rev. 1:10 to "the Lord's Day" is a reference to the seventh-day Sabbath (Baker, *Belief and Work*, 73–74).

Since, according to Seventh-day Adventists, it is useless to search for the change from seventh-day observance to first-day observance in the NT, they assert that this change was made by the Roman Catholic Church. They teach that, during the early centuries of the church, a great apostasy set in, in which the pagan festival of Sunday was gradually substituted for the ancient Sabbath by "unconsecrated leaders of the Church" and by the half-pagan emperor Constantine (E. G. White, *The Great Controversy* [1926], 58–59).

The insistence of seventh-day sabbatarians on the wholly moral character of the fourth commandment and on its perpetual and universal obligation is based upon statements that find no support in the Bible. They ignore the clear statements that the fourth commandment was addressed to the Israelites whom the Lord had delivered from Egypt. Moreover, the distinction they make between "the law of God" and "the law of Moses" is not supported by Scripture. Likewise, their interpretation of the words of Christ and of Paul that are quoted in defense of the perpetuity of the Sabbath command, if pressed to its logical conclusion, proves too much. The word *law* as used by Jesus and Paul refers to more than just the Ten Commandments. Seventh-day sabbatarians do not insist that all the laws of the Mosaic legislation are meant to be observed by Christians in this age, but they fail to see that Paul definitely included the Sabbath command among those ordinances which were done away in Christ. Their claim that the Roman Catholic Church changed the Sabbath from the seventh day to the first day of the week is without foundation. In spite of some Roman Catholic writers that claim that such a change was made by "the Catholic Church," the evidence from the early church fathers is conclusive that these early church leaders did not regard Sunday as a continuation of the Hebrew Sabbath.

While later writers came to think of Sunday as bearing some analogy to the Hebrew Sabbath, and others called the Christian holy day a Sabbath (Eusebius, *Commentary on the Ninety-first Psalm*, quoted by J. A. Hessey, *Sunday: Its Origin, History and Present Obligation* [1889], 299–300; Alcuin, *Homily* 18, *post Pentecost*, quoted by A. E. J. Rawlinson, *The World's Question and the Christian Answer* [1944], 78; P. Alphonsus quoted by Hessey, *Sunday*, 903), they grounded its observance more on the authority of the church than on the fourth commandment. The Reformers, although they advocated the Christian observance of Sunday, did not base its observance on the Sabbath command.

(In addition to the titles mentioned in the body of the article, see R. L. Dabney, *The Christian Sabbath: Its Nature, Design and Proper Observance* [1882]; W. W. Everts, *The Sabbath: Its Permanence, Promise and Defense* [1885]; A. E. Waffle, *The Lord's Day: Its Universal and Perpetual Obligation* [1885]; W. D. Love, *Sabbath and Sunday* [1896]; H. R. Gamble, *Sunday and the Sabbath* [1901]; A. A. Hodge, *The Day Changed and the Sabbath Preserved* [1916]; J. P. Hutchison, *Our Obligations to the Day of Rest and Worship* [1942]; G. H. Waterman, "The Origin and History of the Christian Sunday" [unpublished thesis, Wheaton College, 1948]; S. Bacchiocchi, *From Sabbath to Sunday: A Historical Investigation of the Rise of Sunday Observance in Early Christianity* [1977]; R. T. Beckwith and W. Stott, *This Is the Day: The Biblical Doctrine of the Christian Sunday in its Jewish and Early Church Setting* [1978]; D. A. Carson, ed., *From Sabbath to Lord's Day: A Biblical, Historical, and Theological Investigation* [1982]; K. A. Strand, ed., *The Sabbath in Scripture and History* [1982]; G. Robinson, *The Origin and Development of the Old Testament Sabbath: A Comprehensive Exegetical Approach* [1988]; M. J. Dawn, *Keeping the Sabbath Wholly: Ceasing, Resting, Embracing, Feasting* [1989]; T. C. Eskenazi et al., eds., *The Sabbath in Jewish and Christian Traditions* [1991]; H. A. McKay, *Sabbath and Synagogue: The Question of Sabbath Worship in Ancient Judaism* [1994]; S. Bacchiocchi, *The Sabbath under Crossfire: A Biblical Analysis of Recent Sabbath/Sunday Developments* [1998]; B. A. Ray, *Celebrating the Sabbath: Finding Rest in a Restless World* [2000]; M. J. Dawn, *The Sense of the Call: A Sabbath Way of Life for Those Who Serve God, the Church, the World* [2006]).

G. H. WATERMAN

Sabbath canopy. According to 2 Ki 16:17–18, King AHAZ removed certain items from the TEMPLE, apparently in fear of, or to be sent as tribute to, TIGLATH-PILESER III. One of these items is described as *mûsak haššabbāt*, an architectural term of uncertain meaning. The noun *mûsāk* H4590 is usually derived from the verb *sākak* H6114 ("to block, cover"), leading to such renderings as "covert for the sabbath" (KJV), "covered portal for use on the sabbath" (NRSV), and "Sabbath canopy" (NIV). The same verb, however, can mean (in the hiphil) "to hedge in, shut off" (cf. Job 3:23; 38:8), and since Ezek. 46:1 speaks of a gate in the temple that was to be kept closed except on the Sabbath and on the day of the New Moon, some think the item in question may have been a barrier or grille (cf. NJPS, "sabbath passage"). Another proposal is to derive the noun from the verb *nāsak* H5818 ("to pour") and to read the second noun as *šebet* H8699 ("seat"), which might yield the translation, "cast-metal seat" (see M. J. Mulder in *Von Kanaan bis Kerala*, ed. W. D. Delsman et al. [1982], 161–72; note that the LXX has *ton themelion tēs kathedras*, "the foundation of the throne," apparently understanding the Heb. as *mûsad haššebet*).

F. G. CARVER

Sabbath day's journey. The Greek expression *sabbatou echon hodos* occurs in the NT only once (Acts 1:12; NIV, "Sabbath day's walk") referring to the distance from the MOUNT OF OLIVES to JERUSALEM. This unit of measure (somewhat similar to the Egyptian unit of 1,000 double steps) evidently served to indicate the limit of travel on the Sabbath, but the phrase became a common expression for a relatively short distance. From the Eastern Gate of Jerusalem to the present site of the Church of the Ascension on Mount Olivet, the distance is slightly over half a mile, and indeed a Sabbath day's journey was reckoned by the rabbis as 2,000 cubits (c. 3,000 ft.; see C. K. Barrett, *A Critical and Exegetical Commentary on the Acts of the Apostles*, ICC, 2 vols. [1994–98], 1:85).

It is assumed that the regulation had its origin in the Mosaic period in the injunction to the Israelite not to leave camp to collect manna on the Sabbath (Exod. 16:29). In the Jerusalem Targum this command reads: "Let no man go walking from the place beyond 2,000 cubits on the seventh day." There are other regulations to which appeal is made in an effort to locate the origin of this practice or precept. One is the provision that the area belonging to the Levitical cities included land that extended from the wall 2,000 cubits on every side (Num. 35:5). Another is the supposed distance that separated the ark of the covenant and the people both on the march and at camp (Josh. 3:4). As far as this specific regulation is concerned, it applied only to leaving the city, the prescribed distance being measured from the city gate. Within the city proper, no matter how large it might be, there was no such limitation.

The original intent of the provision was to insure a quiet, leisurely Sabbath and to keep it from becoming a harried and busy day (Exod. 16:29). It was also designed to keep the Israelite worshiper in the area of the center of his worship. The motive was noble but, unfortunately, it resulted in a barren legalism. As a consequence, there were casuistic schemes to circumvent it. It did, however, permit a legitimate exception. If one were caught at a distance on a journey, he might travel to the nearest shelter for safety. But there were deliberate schemes to by-pass the rule. One such method was to go out on Friday and establish a residence somewhere by depositing at least two meals there; from that site, the person was allowed to travel an additional 2,000 cubits on the Sabbath (m. *ʿErubin* 8.1–2, several chapters in this tractate deal with other ways of combining Sabbath-limits). The Qumran community had stricter limits: according to the *Damascus Covenant* (CD X, 21), a person "is not to walk more than 1,000 cubits outside his city." J. H. Bratt

Sabbatheus sab´uh-thee´uhs. KJV Apoc. form of Shabbethai (1 Esd. 9:14).

sabbatical year. The final year in a cycle of seven years within the Hebrew calendar, set aside as a year of rest for the soil, care for the poor and for animals, remission of debts, and manumission of Israelite slaves. The year following seven such sabbatical years was known as the Jubilee Year, during which the soil was given another year of rest, and during which there was also the manumission of Israelite slaves and the reversion of landed property to the original owner or his heirs.

The Book of the Covenant, which refers to the sabbatical year merely as "the seventh year," provided for the automatic release of Hebrew slaves in the seventh year (Exod. 21:2). It should be pointed out, however, that this may simply mean that an Israelite could serve as a slave to a fellow Israelite only for six years, and was freed after that time, whether or not the seventh year fell on a sabbatical year. The Book of the Covenant did provide for the land to remain uncultivated during the sabbatical year, so that the poor people and the wild animals might eat from it (Exod. 23:10–11; cf. Neh. 10:31).

In the Holiness or Priestly Code (Lev. 17–26), the seventh year is designated as "a sabbath of rest [*šabbat šabbātôn*]" for the land (25:4). During that year, the Israelites were not to sow their fields or prune their vineyards (25:4). Moreover, they were not to reap any harvest that grew of itself, nor gather any grapes from the undressed vine, but such spontaneous fruitage was to be for the poor people and the animals, both domestic and wild (25:5–7). A close parallel should be noted between the regulations with regard to the sabbatical year and those with regard to the weekly Sabbath (25:2–7; Exod. 20:8–11; Deut. 5:12–15).

The Holiness Code also provided special observance of the seventh year in a series of seven sabbatical years (Lev. 25:8–9) and the observance of the fiftieth year as the year of Jubilee, during which the land was also to remain untilled and the vines undressed, and during which everyone should return to his family estate and all Hebrew slaves serving other Hebrews should be set free (25:10–55). The only properties exempt from this law were (a) houses within walled cities that were not redeemed within one year (25:29–31), and (b) the houses of the Levites (25:32–34).

In the Deuteronomic Code, the sabbatical year is called "the year for canceling debts" (Deut. 15:9; NRSV, "the year of remission" [Heb. šěnat haššěmiṭâ, lit., "the year of dropping"]). This code provided for the cancellation of all debts owed by one Israelite to another at the end of the sabbatical year (15:1–3), adding a warning against unwillingness to lend to a poor neighbor in view of the nearness of the sabbatical year (15:7–11). This code also provided for the manumission of Israelite slaves held by fellow-Israelites during the sabbatical year (15:12–15). A further provision was made in the Deuteronomic covenant for the reading of the law at the Feast of Booths during that year (31:10–13).

It is not known how well the Israelites observed the sabbatical years, but 2 Chr. 36:21 implies that they failed to do so, hence were taken into captivity "until the land had made up for its sabbaths" (NRSV; cf. also Lev. 26:34). The gathering of the returned exiles to hear Ezra read the law was undoubtedly in fulfillment of the Deuteronomic covenant (Neh. 8:1–8) and must, therefore, have been in the sabbatical year. One of the reforms instituted by Nehemiah was the enforcement of the observance of the sabbatical year (10:31).

There is evidence from extrabiblical literature that the Jews observed the sabbatical year after the exile. According to the first book of Maccabees, Beth-Zur fell to Antiochus IV because the food supply of the garrison was quickly exhausted, since the siege took place during a sabbatical year (1 Macc. 6:49–54). Josephus relates that during the reign of John Hyrcanus (see Hasmonean II.A) the Jewish nation refrained from aggressive warfare during the sabbatical year (Jos. *Ant.* 13.8.1; *War* 1.2.4). He also relates that Julius Caesar remitted the annual tribute from the Jewish people in the sabbatical year, since in it the people did not till their fields or gather their fruit (*Ant.* 14.10.6). In the book of Jubilees, Enoch is said to have "recounted the sabbaths of the years" (*Jub.* 4.18).

The Qumran community seems to have observed the sabbatical year by noncultivation of the soil and cancellation of debts. Rabbinical writers refer to a similar observance, but the absence of detailed discussion of such observance in the Talmud bears witness to its gradual discontinuance. There is no evidence that it was ever observed outside of Palestine. Even in Palestine, it became meaningless, impractical, and eventually obsolete. (See further *ABD*, 5:857–61.)

G. H. Waterman

Sabbeus sa-bee′uhs. KJV Apoc. form of Sabbaias (1 Esd. 9:32).

Sabean suh-bee′uhn (סְבָא H6014 [Isa. 45:14; cf. Ezek. 23:42]; שְׁבָא H8644 [Job 1:15]; שְׁבָאִים H8645 [Joel 3:8]). Also Sabaean. This name occurs three (possibly four) times in the Bible as the rendering of three Hebrew forms. In Isa. 45:14, the term sěbā'îm is used with reference to a tall people in a context that also speaks of Egypt and Cush, suggesting that these Sabeans were from SE Africa. It is possible that the same form occurs in Ezek.

The Sabeans lived in the land of Seba (Sheba).

23:42 (*Ketib* = *sôbāʾîm*, *Qere* = *sābāʾîm*, "drunkards"?) with reference to certain people "from the desert," but the meaning of this text is very uncertain. In Job 1:15, we read that Job's oxen and donkeys were carried off by the Sabeans; here the name *šĕbāʾ* is used, and the context of the story appears to be N Arabia. Finally, in Joel 3:8 the Phoenicians and Philistines are told: "I will sell your sons and daughters to the people of Judah, and they will sell them to the Sabeans, a nation far away"; in this ambiguous reference, the form used is *šĕbāʾîm* (a gentilic from *šĕbāʾ*).

The matter is further complicated by the fact that the Bible distinguishes between a son of Cush named Seba and a grandson of Cush named Sheba (Gen. 10:7; 1 Chr. 1:9; the names Cush and Seba occur together in Isa. 43:3, while Seba and Sheba are associated in Ps. 72:10). Moreover, there were two additional people by the name of Sheba who were descended not from Ham (father of Cush) but from Shem, namely, Sheba son of Joktan (Gen. 10:28) and Sheba son of Jokshan (25:3); the latter was a grandson of Abraham and brother of Dedan.

According to some scholars, a genetic distinction should be made between northern Sabeans (descended from a Semitic Sheba) and southern Sabeans (descended from a Hamitic Sheba or Seba; see W. S. LaSor in *ISBE* rev. [1979–88], 4:255). Others argue for a common progenitor, partly on the (questionable) grounds that the discrepancy between the Hebrew consonants *samek* (ס) and *śin* (שׂ) can be explained from phonetic correspondences between Epigraphic South Arabian and Hebrew. And the possibility must be left open either (a) that at some point the southern Sabeans colonized some regions of N Arabia or (b) that the Sabean state began in N Arabia, with a movement toward, and settlement of, the southern part of the country during the middle of the 2nd millennium B.C. (Cf. I. Ephʿal, *The Ancient Arabs: Nomads on the Borders of the Fertile Crescent, 9th-5th Centuries B.C.* [1982], 88–89, 227–29; K. A. Kitchen in *The Age of Solomon: Scholarship at the Turn of the Millennium*, ed. L. K. Handy [1997], 126–53.) See also Nations II.A.2.

Be that as it may, the name Sabeans normally refers to the people of Saba (Sheba), a kingdom in S Arabia in the area presently known as Yemen and Ḥadramaut; its capital was Marib. Their position at the end of the Arabian peninsula was of twofold advantage: (1) they were remote from the powers to the N, and so relatively secure; and (2) they were centrally located with respect to merchandising goods from nearby Africa and India. These included gold, incense, gem stones, probably ivory, etc. (Ps. 72:15; Isa. 60:6; Jer. 6:20; Ezek. 27:22; 38:13), giving rise to a great caravan industry (cf. Job 6:19). Evidently trading in slaves was also carried on (Joel 3:8; cf. Job 1:15). Fertile land and an extensive irrigation system, illustrated by the dam and sluices seen at Marib, made the country fairly self-sustaining.

The history of Saba is extensive, including not only the biblical references, but also a strong pre-Islamic tradition. The biblical narrative suggests that the Sabeans were established prior to the 10th cent., for their queen journeyed to Jerusalem to visit Solomon (1 Ki. 10:1–13; 2 Chr. 9:1–12), probably to confer with him concerning his probable infringement of the Sabean trading hegemony. See Queen of Sheba. Assyrian cuneiform inscriptions mention Sabean kings as givers of tribute (these date as early as 715 B.C.), and the ostraca from Samaria list contributions of oil and wine sent by the Sabeans to Jeroboam in the first part of the 8th cent. From the 3rd cent. B.C. there appear references to these people in the works of historians and geographers, and in some Syriac and Ethiopic religious texts. By the 3rd cent. A.D., S Arabia had been consolidated into a strong state which continued until the rise of Islam. (See further G. Van Beek, "Recovering the Ancient Civilization of Arabia," *BA* 15 [1952]: 1–18; A. V. Korotaev, *Ancient Yemen: Some General Trends of Evolution of the Sabaic Language and Sabaean Culture* [1995]; K. Schippmann, *Ancient South Arabia: From the Queen of Sheba to the Advent of Islam* [2001].)

There is strong evidence to suggest that the Sabeans of Marib were closely related to some people groups in SE Africa (the linguistic connection between Ethiopian and Epigraphic South Arabian is well established). Some scholars believe that the initial migration was from the horn of Africa to Arabia (cf. LaSor in *ISBE*, 4:254); others suggest that the Sabeans from Arabia established a trade colony in Nubia (cf. G. A. Herion in *ABD*, 5:861). Either theory would account for Josephus's reference to Saba as "a royal city of Ethiopia," later named Meroë (*Ant.* 2.10.2 §249; cf. also Strabo, *Geogr.* 16.4.10) and for the apparent association of the Sabeans with Cush/Ethiopia in Isa. 45:14. (The name *Sabean* or *Sabaean*, as used in the present article, is to be distinguished from the use of the same name with reference to the *Sabians*, a religious group mentioned in the Koran; the term is sometimes also applied to the Mandeans.)

M. H. Heicksen

Sabi say′bi (Σαβει, Σαβιη). **(1)** Variant form of Shobai (1 Esd. 5:28; cf. ASV and see the LXX at Neh. 7:45).

(2) According to Codex Alexandrinus, Sabi was a servant of Solomon whose descendants returned from Babylon with Zerubbabel (1 Esd. 5:34; cf. KJV). Most mss, however, join this name with the preceding one; see Pokereth-Hazzebaim.

Sabta, Sabtah sab′tuh (סַבְתָּא *H6029* [1 Chr. 1:9], סַבְתָּה *H6030* [Gen. 10:7], derivation unknown). Son of Cush and grandson of Ham, included in the Table of Nations (Gen. 10:7; 1 Chr. 1:9). The view that the text should be emended so that the name corresponds with that of Shabako, an Egyptian pharaoh who ruled in the 8th cent. B.C. (see M. Astour in *JBL* 84 [1965]: 422–25), has not been widely accepted (see also Sabteca). Presumably, Sabta(h) is also a place name. If the Cushites settled in the area occupied by Ethiopia, the name may correspond to one of several places mentioned by Greek authors (e.g., Strabo, *Geogr.* 16.4.8, refers to a lake named *Saba*). It is possible, however, that the Cushites extended across the Red Sea from Nubia northeastward over the Arabian peninsula, and some scholars prefer a location in S Arabia, in particular Ḥadramaut (Hazarmaveth), which Strabo refers to as *Sabata* (*Geogr.* 16.4.2; see further *ABD*, 5:861–62).

Sabteca sab′tuh-kuh (סַבְתְּכָא *H6031*, derivation unknown). KJV Sabtecha; TNIV Sabteka. Son of Cush and grandson of Ham, included in the Table of Nations (Gen. 10:7; 1 Chr. 1:9). Sabteca is also very likely the name of a place in Arabia, although its identification is uncertain (for possibilities, see *ABD*, 5:862). Some scholars identify Sabteca with Shabataka, an Egyptian pharaoh from Ethiopia at the beginning of the 7th cent. B.C. (see Sabta).

Sabtecha sab′tuh-kuh. KJV form of Sabteca.

Sabteka sab′tuh-kuh. TNIV form of Sabteca.

Sacar say′kahr (שָׂכָר *H8511*, "reward"). NRSV Sachar; TNIV Sakar. **(1)** A Hararite who was the father of Ahiam, one of David's mighty warriors (1 Chr. 11:35; called Sharar in the parallel, 2 Sam. 23:33).

(2) Fourth son of Obed-Edom, included in the list of divisions of the Korahite doorkeepers (see Korah) in the reign of David (1 Chr. 26:4).

Sachar say′kahr. See Sacar.

Sachia suh-ki′uh. See Sakia.

sackbut. See music, musical instruments IV.D.

sackcloth. Strong, rough cloth woven from the long, dark hair of the oriental goat or the camel. The Hebrew word *śaq H8566* (as well as the loanword in Greek, *sakkos G4884*) can refer both to the cloth itself and to a bag (sack) made from it. When large, such a bag was used at times as a container for grain (Gen. 42:25). On some occasions it was utilized for saddlebags (Josh. 9:4) and provided a common bedding material (2 Sam. 21:10). Its main use, however, was as an article of clothing and as such it was somewhat similar to the *cilicium* of the Romans.

It appears that since it was made of cheap and durable material, sackcloth served the purpose of an ordinary item of garb. Palestinian shepherds wore it in the exercise of their pastoral task. At times it seems to have served as the distinctive garb of the prophets (Isa. 20:2; Zech. 13:4), but gradually it came to bear a primarily symbolical meaning. On some occasions it took the form of a loincloth and served as an undergarment (2 Ki. 6:30). In most cases, however, it was the chief article of clothing. See dress. Women as well as men wore it (Jdt.

9:1), and in exceptional instances it was even placed on animals (Jon. 3:8).

The wearing of sackcloth was regarded as proper garb for serious and sober occasions. Since it was dark in texture, it was deemed fitting in times of grief and sadness. Jacob clothed himself in it at the report of the death of his favorite son Joseph (Gen. 37:34), and David commanded Joab and the other mourners to wear it upon the death of Abner (2 Sam. 3:31).

Sackcloth was also a mark of abject penitence. When Jeremiah called Judah to repent of her sins, he urged them to put on sackcloth (Jer. 6:26). The penitent Jews wore it in the great reformation of Nehemiah (Neh. 9:1), and Jesus told the citizens of Capernaum and Bethsaida that if the mighty works done in their environs had been done in Tyre and Sidon, the latter would have repented in sackcloth and ashes (Matt. 11:21). The rough and itchy texture served as an aid to self-chastisement, and tossing ashes over the sackcloth ensemble was the sign of the accentuation of their distress (Isa. 58:5; Dan. 9:3). Its use as an indicator of penitence was not restricted to Israel. It also found place in the cultures of Moab (Isa. 15:3), Ammon (Jer. 49:3), Tyre (Ezek. 27:31), and as has been noted, Nineveh (Jon. 3:5).

There was reference to sackcloth in times of national calamity and danger, as when King Hezekiah heard the Assyrian threat (Isa. 37:1). Similarly, when the servants of Ben-Hadad asked for mercy from the king of Israel after the Arameans had been disastrously defeated, they made their plea with sackcloth around their wastes (1 Ki. 20:32). In summary, it was deemed the most suitable garb for times of distress, danger, grief, crisis, and national emergency. (See H. F. Lutz, *Textiles and Costumes among the People of the Ancient Near East* [1933], 25–26, 176–77.)

J. H. Bratt

sacrament. A term applied primarily to the Christian rites of baptism and the Lord's Supper.

I. The meaning of the term. The Latin noun *sacramentum* (from the verb *sacro*, "to set apart as sacred") was originally used in a variety of secular contexts with such meanings as "guarantee" and "oath." In a religious context, however, the term would refer to something sacred or consecrated, and in the Vulgate it translates the Greek word *mystērion* G3696, "mystery" (cf. Eph. 1:9; 3:2–3, 9; Col. 1:26–27; 1 Tim. 3:16; Rev. 1:20; 17:7). In a wide sense it came to designate any sign which possessed a hidden meaning. Religious rites and ceremonies such as the sign of the cross, anointing with oil, preaching, confirmation, prayer, aid to the sick, etc., were equally called sacraments. Adolph Harnack indicates that Tertullian "already used the word to denote sacred facts, mysterious and salutary signs and vehicles, and also holy acts. Everything in any way connected with the Deity and his revelation, and therefore, for example, the content of revelation as doctrine, is designated 'sacrament'; and the word is also applied to the symbolical which is always something mysterious and holy" (*History of Dogma*, 7 vols. [1897–99], 2.138–39).

It became increasingly evident that the religious significance of the term was too free and broad for careful biblical precision, although the word itself is not used in the Bible. For this reason theologians early endeavored to assign definitions to the word that would reflect a more scriptural exactness. As might be expected, however, such efforts brought agreement neither on the essence nor on the number of the sacraments.

In modern times Gerardus van der Leeuw and Edward Schillebeeckx have argued that the Christian sacraments receive their meaning from the background of a general sacramentology. Such a general sacramentology is said to be a providential precursor of the Christian sacraments, a tutor to bring us to Christ. One of the difficulties with this view is that it raises the problem of "pansacramentalism" with its anthropologically rather than biblically anchored general sacramentology.

Conservatives maintain that sacraments exist because of a divine signifying. Not every sign is a sacrament, and therefore it is impossible to base the Christian sacrament on a phenomenological analysis. The sacraments of the church are those appointed by Christ in the NT. They are signs and seals of the covenant between God and his people. They are visible and outward attestations of the covenant entered into between them. As signs they represent the blessings of the covenant of redemption; as seals they ratify and confirm its validity.

II. The relation between the Word and sacrament. Priority is to be given to the Word, written and preached. The Word can exist in completeness without the sacraments, but the sacraments cannot exist in any meaningful way without the Word. The interpretive Word of God is of decisive significance for the power and the understanding of these visible signs of his redemptive work.

There are certain points of similarity between the Word and sacraments. (1) Their author is the same, and God has decreed that they should both be means of grace. (2) Christ is their focal point of meaning; he is their center. (3) They both must be accepted in faith, as Calvin rightly stated, "They avail and profit nothing unless received in faith." (4) Both are instruments used by the HOLY SPIRIT, who alone makes both real to the Christian.

There are also certain points of dissimilarity between the Word and sacraments. (1) They differ in their necessity. The Word is indispensable to salvation; the sacraments are not. Some have been redeemed without the use of sacraments (e.g., believers before the time of Abraham, the penitent thief on the cross). The Christian is under a compelling moral obligation to obey his Master's commands respecting the sacraments unless external circumstances make it impossible, but this necessity of precept is not to be confused with a necessity of means. The sacraments are nothing less but nothing more than a *visible* sign of the Word. Faith alone (*sola fide*) is the instrumental cause of salvation (Jn. 5:24; 6:29; Acts 16:31 et al.).

(2) They differ in their application. The Word is to be preached to everyone (Matt. 28:18–20), whereas the sacraments are to be administered only to those who profess faith and, as held by a large segment of Protestants, to those within the covenant relationship, as infants in the case of baptism. The sacraments are meaningless to those who are not within the CHURCH. In the case of the Lord's Supper, PAUL even indicates that professing Christians should be warned lest they partake unworthily (1 Cor. 11:27–32).

(3) They differ in their object. The Word is designed to initiate and strengthen faith, whereas in the Protestant tradition the sacraments are understood to contribute either solely or principally to its strengthening. There is some difference between the Lutheran and Reformed perspective on this point.

Baptismal font in the Church of the Nativity (Bethlehem, c. 5th cent.).

(4) They differ in their medium of expression. The Word expresses itself most powerfully through the medium of sound (preaching), whereas the sacraments do so through the medium of sight, in association with taste and touch. The sacraments are a *visible* Word; a sacrament is "a visible form of an invisible grace."

III. The number of the sacraments. The question concerning the number of sacraments is integrally bound to the matter of their essential nature. The Roman Catholic Church maintains that their essential nature is that of an infusion of supernatural grace into all of life from beginning to end. With appeal to the selective principle of divine appointment and tradition, to the harmony and beauty which they display, and to the doctrinal authority of the church, the number of sacraments was inviolably fixed at seven: (1) baptism (Matt. 28:19; Jn. 3:5); (2) confirmation (Acts 8:14; 19:6); (3) Eucharist (Matt. 26:26–29; Mk. 14:22–25; Lk. 22:15–20; Jn. 6:1–71; 1 Cor. 11:23–25); (4) penance (Jn. 20:21–23); (5) extreme unction (Jas. 5:13–15); (6) orders (Lk. 22:19; 1 Cor. 11:26); (7) matrimony (Matt. 19:4–9; Eph. 5:21–32).

In sharp contrast to this multiplicity of sacraments stands the Protestant doctrine with but two: (1) baptism and (2) the Lord's Supper (Eucharist). It should be noted that such diverse ceremonies as orders, matrimony, and extreme unction may all be biblical in their own way, but they were clearly not directly instituted by the Lord himself as uniquely signifying the saving work of Jesus Christ and therefore they do not qualify as sacraments. Jesus calls his death a baptism and a cup (Matt. 20:22), and unlike the other observances these actions themselves directly reflect the redemptive work which Jesus Christ accomplished. By their very nature, therefore, these two sacraments stand in a class by themselves and cannot simply be included with other ecclesiastical ceremonies; they are unique.

IV. The efficacy of the sacraments. The question as to the efficacy of the sacraments has been argued around the concept of symbolism (Reformation) versus realism (Rome). It should be clearly understood however, that symbolical does not mean without real efficacy. Symbol is not opposed to reality (see SYMBOLISM). The real question concerns the manner in which this reality is represented.

According to Roman Catholic theology, the sacraments work *ex opere operato*; that is, the working is *objective* and does not depend in any way upon the recipient. The sacrament is an instrument of God and the cause of redemptive grace. This idea has led some to see in Roman Catholic sacramentality a certain magical quality. This *ex opere operato* was understood as a matter-of-fact working from above in which there was no element of human subjectivity. To view the Roman Catholic sacramental doctrine as *magical* would be too simplistic. In addition to her appeal to the objectivity of the sacraments, Rome has maintained that a certain subjective disposition is necessary for the working of the sacraments—a disposition that simply presents no opposing obstacle. The problem then becomes one of understanding how this necessary disposition may be harmoniously connected with the *ex opere operato*, that absolutely objective structure of the sacrament which works independently of the recipient.

Representative of the Reformed Protestant position on the efficacy of the sacraments is the statement of the *Westminster Shorter Catechism* (answer to question 91), "The sacraments become effectual means of salvation, not from any virtue in them, or in him that doth administer them; but only by the blessing of Christ and the working of his Spirit in them that by faith receive them." The efficacy thus is not found in the sacraments themselves as outward acts but rather in the blessing of Christ and his Spirit conditioned upon faith in the recipient.

Reformed theology maintains that the efficacy of the sacraments is seen in three ways: (1) as *representative* of the benefits of the new covenant; (2) as *seals* of the same; and (3) as the *application* of the same. As *seals* the sacraments constitute outward signs of an already established inner spiritual relationship with Christ through faith. They are presumptive evidence for the validity of the divine redemptive covenant; that is, they are applied subsequent to the time when the individual is presumed to be regenerate. The sacraments in no way accomplish that of which they are a sign. As seals they are applied in obedience to the command of Christ, as an outward *sign* of the inward grace that is confidently expected in the case of infant baptism, or believed to have been actually received in the case of adults.

When the sacraments are viewed as applying grace, what is meant is that they are a means of actually bringing us grace. They do not simply portray something in order to bring to remembrance but they also do something in order to bring spiritual strength. This is not to contend for a special sacramental grace but rather for the idea that the working of the sacraments rests essentially on saving grace.

Representative of the Lutheran Protestant position on the efficacy of the sacraments is the statement of the *Augsburg Confession* (article 5), "For the obtaining of this faith, the ministry of teaching the Gospel and administering the Sacraments was instituted." According to the conservative Lutheran theologian Francis Pieper (*Christian Dogmatics*, 3 [1953], 111), the Lutheran symbols stress the fact that the sacraments and the Word of the gospel have the same purpose; namely, that of the attestation and conferring of the forgiveness of sins and the strengthening of faith in this forgiveness. Lutherans agree with Reformed Protestants in affirming the necessity of faith, but they tend to ascribe the efficacy of the sacraments to a real objective virtue of grace resident in the elements.

(See further G. C. Berkouwer, *The Sacraments* [1969]; C. K. Barrett, *Church, Ministry, and Sacraments in the New Testament* [1985]; L. D. Bierma,

The Doctrine of the Sacraments in the Heidelberg Catechism: Melanchthonian, Calvinist, or Zwinglian? [1999]; J. F. White, *Sacraments as God's Self Giving* [2001].)

C. M. HORNE

sacrifice and offerings. Religious ritual was a major expression of ancient Israel, especially the rites of animal sacrifice with their accompanying libations, effusions, sacred meals, etc. Such liturgical acts have their parallels in the contemporary cultures of the ANE, but this is not to say that biblical sacrifice was merely an imitation of neighboring cultures. It is the ideology expressed in the ritual complex as a whole that makes the Israelite religion unique. The presentation of sacrificial rituals in OT passages furnishes a counterpart to the more hortatory proclamations of the prophets. The concepts and ideology of OT ritual underlies NT theology regarding the problem of SIN and the sinner's RECONCILIATION to God by means of ATONEMENT.

   I. Introduction
  II. The ancient world
      A. Mesopotamia
      B. North Syria and Anatolia
      C. Ugarit and Phoenicia
      D. The Hellenic world
 III. Biblical data
      A. Vocabulary
      B. Materials
      C. Sources
  IV. Types of sacrifices
      A. Expiatory offerings
      B. Consecratory offerings
      C. Communal offerings
   V. Redemptive history
      A. Pre-Mosaic
      B. From Moses to Samuel
      C. During the monarchy
      D. Postexilic period
      E. Prophets, sages, and poets
      F. The NT

I. Introduction. The older approach to the study of sacrifice as a religious phenomenon was usually based on some 19th-cent. concepts of cultural progress. The source of rituals was sought among primitive societies; the rites of the BEDOUIN were taken as normative for explaining the development of OT sacrifice. Today, the comparative study of tribal customs in underdeveloped areas is the domain of the anthropologist; its main contribution is the interpretation of the preliterary cultures of Palestine (e.g., the Chalcolithic).

Even though the Bible also affirms that sacrificial practices go back to the dawn of civilization (Gen. 4:3–4), the terminology used in the PENTATEUCH for describing the earliest rituals is that of LEVITICUS. In other words, even the most ancient examples of sacrifice are depicted by means of a nomenclature rooted in a highly developed, well-organized sacerdotal framework. Certain schools of biblical criticism have asserted that the ritual system embodied in the Pentateuch cannot be earlier than the postexilic period. However, archaeological discoveries pertaining to the sacrificial systems of Mesopotamia and the Levant in the 3rd and 2nd millennia B.C. have shown that very complex rituals were practiced all across the FERTILE CRESCENT long before the entry of the Israelites into Canaan. Since the biblical claim is quite explicit to the effect that the patriarchal culture, especially in the sphere of religion, sprang from the great centers of civilization, Mesopotamia and Egypt (cf. Joshua's unequivocal statement, Josh. 24:2, 14), there is no reason to doubt that even the Israelites could have known and also practiced a sophisticated order of ritual.

For the study of sacrifice in the ancient world, modern investigators may avail themselves of both the material remains of TEMPLES and other cultic centers, including the bones of sacrificial animals found in association with them. Many such installations have been found in MESOPOTAMIA, N SYRIA, and even in PALESTINE, as well as EGYPT, Anatolia (ASIA MINOR), and the AEGEAN region. Some date to the prehistoric era, that is, before the use of writing, whereas many are from the richly documented 2nd and 1st millennia B.C. The only real temple found thus far in a true context of a fortified center from Israelite times is that at ARAD, though Iron Age "high places" and "cultic centers" of various types have been discovered elsewhere (e.g., HAZOR, LACHISH, MEGIDDO).

On the other hand, the main source for the elucidation of ancient sacrificial ritual consists of collections of written documents now at our disposal.

Today it is customary to classify these texts of a ritual nature according to the manner in which the rite is depicted (cf. B. A. Levine's articles in *JAOS* 85 [1965]: 309–18; *Lešonenu* 30 [1966]: 3–11 [in Heb.]). A definite set of instructions for the conduct of rituals, including the implements, materials, actions, prayers, and incantations to be performed, is called a *prescriptive* ritual. Such contexts were composed and preserved for the guidance of the PRIESTS or other functionaries in the conduct of their duties.

A written source that tells how and when a certain rite or series of rites was performed is referred to as a *descriptive* ritual. Under this latter category are two subclasses. Narratives, whether historical, mythological, or legendary, may include the description of a sacrifice made by the leading personage in the story; quite often they go into considerable detail to stress that the rite was performed according to regulations. This was a literary means of teaching the reader or hearer about the necessity and propriety of fulfilling one's sacrificial obligations. The "narrative *descriptive* rituals" form this class. The second is comprised of a much more prosaic, often boring type of documents, namely, the laconic temple records of expenditures and income in terms of the required ingredients for rituals performed. In some cases they represent a sort of accountant's journal of the sacrifices made during a specific period of time. Mesopotamia and Ugarit (cf. below) have produced many such records, but their analysis for the purpose of defining ancient sacrificial ritual is only beginning. The usefulness of this terminological classification of the sources will be obvious in the ensuing discussion.

II. The ancient world. The following is not meant to be definitive for any of the cultures dealt with; only salient features that by comparison or contrast shed light on the sacrifices of the OT will be pointed out.

A. Mesopotamia. The dominant idea of sacrifice in the "Land of the Two Rivers" was that of provision for the gods. In the Creation Epic (see ENUMA ELISH), Marduk is said to have created mankind (the black-headed ones) for this purpose: "Verily, savage-man will I create. / He shall be charged with the service of the gods / That they might be at ease" (*ANET*, 68a). The other deities of the pantheon, grateful for Marduk's deliverance from chaos and provision for their needs, expressed their devotion and adoration: "May he shepherd the black-headed ones, his creatures. / May he establish for his fathers the great food-offerings. / Their support they shall furnish, shall tend their sanctuaries. / May he cause incense to be smelled … / May food-offerings be borne for their gods and goddesses. / Without fail let them support their gods! Their lands let them improve, build their shrines, / Let the black-headed wait on their gods (ibid., 69a-b).

The dependence of the deities upon the food provided by man is further illustrated by a narrative description of the sacrifice offered by the flood hero, Utnapishtim, after his escape from the deluge: "I poured out a libation on the top of the mountain. / Seven and seven cult vessels I set up, / Upon their pot stands I heaped cane, cedarwood, and myrtle. / The gods smelled the savor, / The gods smelled the sweet savor, / The gods crowded like flies about the sacrificer" (ibid., 95a). This picture of the gods famished by hunger because mankind had been destroyed and was no longer providing their meals, swarming around the offerer like flies, may reveal a touch of humor but it also brings home the pathos of Mesopotamian religion. The gods were subject to the same appetites as mortals; therefore they had enslaved the human race and required of them that they furnish their meals as the fruit of human toil on the earth. The parallel with Gen. 8:20–22 is quite striking, but the difference is even more so. (For the significance of the "pleasing odor" [KJV "sweet savor"] in Israelite ritual, see below.)

This central idea is also reflected in the social organization of ancient Sumerian society (see SUMER). Each deity in the pantheon had his own estate, consisting of a city and its adjacent territory. He was the lord of his manor, and the priest-king, the *ensi*, was the manager of his estate. The temple was the central institution to which all products due to the deity were brought. By the Old Babylonian period (19th–18th centuries B.C.), the monarchy and the palace had come to overshadow even the temple as a social, economic, and political institution, but the kings were always concerned with providing the gods their due.

The role of sacrifice was inextricably bound up with prayer and supplication in the attempt of the individual to obtain health, prosperity, and well-being from his deity. Copies of prayers to be offered were concluded by a special section addressed either to the supplicant or to the priest—the expert who must perform the rites with precision if the prayer was to be effective. The so-called Babylonian "Righteous Sufferer" described his miserable state as that of one who had failed to carry out his ritual obligations to his god and goddess; such neglect consisted of not praying (with the lack of accompanying rituals), of neglecting the holy days, of failing to teach his people reverence and obedience, of eating without the proper blessings, of neglecting to bring cereal offerings to his goddess, of forgetting his lord and of taking his oath frivolously (*BWL*, 39, lines 12–22). On the contrary, he claimed: "For myself, I gave attention to supplication and prayer. To me prayer was discretion, sacrifice my rule" (ibid., lines 23–24). After his restoration to health, he resumes his worship: "I persisted in supplication and prayer before them [the gods]. Fragrant incense I placed before them. I presented an offering, a gift, accumulated donations. I slaughtered fat oxen and butchered *fattened sheep* (?). I repeatedly libated honey-sweet beer and pure wine" (ibid., 60, lines 91–95).

Although animals were habitually slaughtered, no evidence has been produced for any special attention being paid to the blood as an element of ritual. The beast itself was food for the deity, but its blood was evidently allowed to return to the earth. The ancient hero Etana, who earnestly besought the sun god (Shamash) to grant him an heir, said: "Thou hast consumed, O Shamash, my fattest sheep, / The earth drinking the blood of my lambs. / I have honored the gods and revered the spirits; / The oracle priestesses have done the needful to my offerings. / The lambs, by their slaughter, have done the needful to the gods" (*ANET*, 117a-b). The earth's drinking of the blood is a natural expression for death by slaughter, and is also applied to warriors (cf. Code of Hammurabi, reverse xxviii.10; *ANET*, 179b).

Of special significance, however, was the use made of the entrails. The lungs, intestines, and, above all, the liver were utilized in the determination of oracles. There was even a special set of oracular conditions that could be determined by the behavior of the sacrificed lamb in its death throes. A vast literature grew up in the form of collections of events, historical or theoretical, that were indicated by markings, indentations, holes, and other features of the organ being examined. The offerer frequently made his sacrifice with the express purpose of gaining supernatural insight into the future. Thus the king of Babylon resorted to just such a practice in the course of his campaign in the Levant that resulted in the attack on Jerusalem (Ezek. 21:21).

The most widely known prescriptive ritual text from Mesopotamia is that for the New Year Festival at Babylon (*ANET*, 331–34). It gives the order of events, including sacrifices and the recital of prayers and other texts, as required for each day of the celebration. One of the most relevant for comparison with OT ritual is the act of purification performed on the fifth day. The officiating priest "shall call a slaughterer to decapitate a ram, the body of which the *mašmašu*-priest shall use in performing the *kuppuru*-ritual for the temple." After the necessary incantations and purifications have been performed, the *mašmašu*-priest takes the lamb's carcass and the slaughterer takes its head; both of them proceed to the river and throw their gory burdens into it. Then they remain in the open country for seven days from the fifth to the twelfth of Nisan. The parallel with the "scapegoat" ritual of the OT is only general and not in details. There was no act of confession for sin; instead, the

Megiddo temple complex with a large round altar used for blood sacrifices by ancient Canaanites (c. 2200–1500 B.C.).

expulsion of demons was the goal of this rite, as is clearly seen in the incantation that follows it (ibid., 333b–334a).

Presenting the food prepared from sacrificial cereals, animals, spices, and liquids before the deities was a central feature of the Mesopotamian cultus. After the god, in the form of an idol, had viewed the foodstuffs, they were taken away to be eaten by the king (contrast the well-known passage in the APOCRYPHA, Bel 3–22). The principle seems to have been that the god had obtained the necessary nourishment by gazing upon the food or having it passed before his eyes. In turn, his doing so imparted a special blessing to it that was passed on to the king.

B. North Syria and Anatolia. One of the most striking allusions to sacrifice from the AMORITE kingdom of MARI is the description of the ritual for making peace by slaying a donkey foal. An official reported: "I went to GN to kill a donkey foal between the Khaneans and Idamaras. They brought forth a puppy and a goat and, my lord, I was afraid. A puppy and a goat I would not give. I caused to be slain a donkey foal the offspring of a she-ass; I made peace between the Khaneans and Idamaras" (*ARM*, 2, no. 37, 11.5–14). Apparently two rituals were known to them, and the official insisted on the donkey sacrifice (the word rendered "goat" was formerly misunderstood as "lettuce").

A text from ALALAKH (Level VII) records the sacrifices to be offered in connection with an oath in the name of Adad and Ishtar by the king and his brother. The W Semitic emphasis upon burning the animals (instead of cooking them as food for the deity) is expressed by the prescription: "The fire will consume the lambs and the birds" (Alalakh Text no. 126.15, 19).

The HITTITE rituals with their detailed prescriptive texts (e.g., *ANET*, 346ff.) have many suggestive parallels to OT passages. Most interesting is the ceremony in which one of the sacrificial animals, such as a dog, is cut into pieces and placed on either side of an improvised gate through which the participants have to pass. A similar rite using the bodies of prisoners of war is also attested. Whether there is any connection between the Hittite practice and the ritual acts of ABRAHAM (Gen. 15:10–11,

17) or of the leaders of Judah (Jer. 34:18–20) is impossible to say (cf. Ezek. 16:3, 45).

C. Ugarit and Phoenicia. The tablets from UGARIT furnish some important ritual texts of both prescriptive and descriptive types. The literary pieces give special attention to the enactment of sacrificial rites at crucial points in the narrative. The legendary King Keret conducted a special sacrifice to invoke blessing upon an impending military expedition: "He washed and rouged himself.... He entered the shade of the tent. He took a sacrificial lamb in his hands … its commensurate loaves as food offering, he took the … of sacrificial bird(s); he poured wine in a silver cup, honey in a golden bowl; he went up to the top of the tower.... He lifted his hands heavenward; he sacrificed to the Bull, his father El; he invoked Baal with his sacrifice, the son of Dagon with his victuals" (*Krt* 11.156–71). A mythological selection contains the enigmatic statement: "Two sacrifices does Baal hate, three the rider of the clouds, the sacrifice of shame, and the sacrifice of fornication, and the sacrifice of abuse of handmaidens" (*UT*, 51: III, 17–21).

The word rendered "sacrifice" (*dbḥ*) may also be "festival," as proven by a syllabary tablet where Akkadian *isinnu*, "festival," is equated with Ugaritic *dabḥu*. The translation of entries in accounting records such as *ḫmšy. bd/bḥ mlkt / mdrʿ*, "five (jars) of wine for the *sacrifice* of the queen in the sown land" (*UT*, 1090:14–16) may have to be altered to "the *festival* of the queen, etc." Nevertheless, the prosaic ledgers of the palace and temple library at Ugarit contain both descriptive (accounts of supplies issued) and prescriptive ritual texts.

The sacrificial terminology applied to animals designated for the various gods include *ʾatm*, "guilt offering," and *šrp*, "peace offering." The animals offered were the sheep, male (*š*) and female (*dqt*), the cow (*gdlt*), the bull (*ʾalp*), and also fowl (*ʿsr*); incense (*qṭr*), and libations of wine (*yn, ḥmr, trt-*) and honey (*nbt*) were also utilized. The occasions recorded are usually calendrical, for example, *ym ḥdt*, "day of the new (moon)," and the magic, mythological, or ethical significance is generally impossible to determine (except for narrative passages). One broken tablet listing sacrifices begins by an allusion to *slḥ . npš*, "forgiveness of soul" (*UT*, 9:1).

These Ugaritic texts, dating from at least as early as the 14th–13th centuries B.C., show how the technical terminology of the OT was already in wide use during the 2nd millennium. For the Canaanite practices of Israel's contemporaries in PHOENICIA, we are dependent upon OT allusions. ELIJAH and the prophets of BAAL evidently prepared their sacrifices in the same manner (1 Ki. 18); common sacrificial terms were applied to the customs at the temple of Baal in SAMARIA (2 Ki. 10:24), as well as to the Aramean rites of NAAMAN (5:7). Two Punic (i.e., late Phoenician) lists of prices for sacrificial animals, one found at Carthage and the other at Marseilles (whence it had been carried), reveal a nomenclature very much like that of the OT, though scholars are in disagreement about the exact comparisons. The main terms in those lists are *šwʿt* ("sin offering"?), *kll* ("whole [burnt] offering"), and *šlm* ("peace offering"). The distribution of the meat varies according to the type of sacrifice; even from the *kll*, a small portion was given to the priest (contrast the "whole burnt offering" in Israel, below). There are differences between the two lists; therefore, one need not be surprised that the regulations do not match exactly those of the OT.

D. The Hellenic world. The common Mediterranean practice of burning the offering (unlike Mesopotamia) is also reflected in Greek sources. The Homeric epics describe in some detail the typical sacrifice to an Olympian god (e.g., *Iliad* 1.446–74). After the washing of hands, grain was scattered about; then the animal's head was drawn back so as to face upward, its throat was slit and afterward it was flayed. Slices from the thighs wrapped in fat were burned on the altar amid libations of red wine. Next the offerers tasted the inner parts (*splanchna*, pl. of *splanchnon G5073*), contrary to Israelite practice (see below), and carved the rest of the meat into small pieces, which they roasted for themselves on skewers. Thus, a sacred meal was even part of the sacrifice meant to appease an angry god.

Sacrifices to the Olympians of heaven bore some sharp contrasts to those made for the underworld deities of the earth. The animal was usually a white ox for the former, a black ram (or pig) for the latter; the throat was turned upward to the Olympian, downward to the earth deity for whom pains were taken to see that the blood soaked into the earth. The heavenly gods were worshiped in their splendid classical temples and the sacrifice made on the raised altar (*bōmos G1117*; cf. Heb. *bāmâ H1195*, "high place"); the chthonian deities received their homage in caves of underground shrines, and the offering was laid either on a low "hearth" altar or in a pit. The proper time for sacrificing to the Olympians was morning, but to the underworld gods it was at evening or late at night. A good example of the rites for an earth deity is that for the dreaded Hecate, goddess of demons and phantoms, who normally received sacrifices of dogs, black female lambs, and honey (Apollonius Rhodius, *Argonautica* 3.1029–39).

Descriptive ritual texts of the nonnarrative class include not only inscriptions from the classical period, such as the sacrificial calendar (4th cent. B.C.) from Cos, but also some of the clay tablets

This monument from Ephesus shows a worshiper taking a ram for sacrifice.

in the Linear B script from 14th–13th cent. B.C. Pylos and Knossos. The classical graphic representations can also be supplemented by the sacrificial rite portrayed on the sarcophagus from the Late Bronze Age Cretan town of Agia Triada. The underworld nature of the ritual (funerary) is the reason for the collection of the victim's blood as it flows from its slashed throat.

III. Biblical data

A. Vocabulary. The act of sacrificing is expressed by a special group of Hebrew verbs that had doubtless obtained their technical meanings through centuries of usage. The most common is *zābaḥ H2284*, "to slaughter for sacrifice." Its general meaning was probably "to slaughter an animal for food" (cf. Deut. 12:15 et al.; the Arab. cognate *dabaḥa* is widely used for acts of slaughtering, besides those explicitly pertaining to sacrifice). The semantic relationship to the act of slaughtering is illustrated by Isa. 34:6, "For the LORD has a sacrifice [noun *zebaḥ H2285*] in Bozrah / and a great slaughter [*ṭebaḥ H3181*] in Edom." In spite of the superficial resemblance of the two nouns used here, they are not etymologically related (their Semitic roots were *dbḥ* and *ṭbḥ* respectively). The Hebrew verb often takes a cognate accusative (e.g., *wayyizbĕḥû zĕbāḥîm*, lit., "and they sacrificed sacrifices," 1 Sam. 6:15).

The slaying of the sacrificial animal can be portrayed by the use of a more common verb for slaughtering, *šāḥaṭ H8821* (Exod. 29:16; Ezek. 44:11 et al.). One could also speak simply of "making" a sacrifice (Heb. *ʿāśâ H6913*, Exod. 10:25; 1 Ki. 12:27; Jer. 33:18). Other aspects of the sacrificial act could be highlighted by the use of different verbs; for example, one might "bring" the offering (*bôʾ H995* hiphil, Amos 4:4) or "present" it (*nāgaš H5602* hiphil, 5:25).

The idea of "presenting" or "offering" the sacrifice to God is most often expressed by the verb "to bring near" (*qārab H7928* hiphil), which appears profusely in ritual contexts (Lev. 7:16; 22:26; cf. also Exod. 29:3 et al.). The cognate noun from the same root is *qorbān H7933*, meaning literally "that which is brought near" (the verb and noun are used as a phrase twenty-five times in the ritual passages from Lev. 1:2 to Num. 31:50). It is this term that appears as CORBAN (*korban G3167*) in Mk. 7:11, where it is explained as *ho estin dōron*, "which is a gift [for God]" (the LXX also renders the Heb. term by *dōron G1565*, Lev. 1:2 et al.; cf. Jos. *Ag. Apion* 1.22; *Ant.* 4.4.4). An inscription on the fragment of a stone vessel discovered in the excavations of NT Jerusalem consists of the word *qorbān*. Just above the word appears a symbol (like a trident) that occurs on small offering plates from the preexilic temple at Arad; the symbol is preceded by the letter *qoph* (ק), evidently an abbreviation for the noun.

Other aspects of the process are reflected in such verbs as "to prepare" (Zeph. 1:7), "to cook" (Ezek. 46:24), and "to bless" (1 Sam. 9:13). The standard verbs for the incineration of sacrificial materials on the altar are the hiphil of *ʿālâ H6590* ("to offer up [*lit.*, cause to go up]," Lev. 17:8 et al.; cf. the term for "burnt offering," *ʿōlâ H6592*) and the hiphil of *qāṭar H7787* ("to vaporize, to cause to go up in smoke," Lev. 1:9 et al.). This latter verb, in the hiphil or causative stem, is the normal form from that root for reference to Israelite offerings; the piel or factitive stem is almost always used for non-Israelite forms of worship (e.g., 2 Ki. 17:11; the only exception is Amos 4:5). The common verb for "to burn" (*śārap H8596*) is never used of burning on the altar but only of incinerating those parts of the sacrifice that had to be disposed of "outside the camp" (e.g., Lev. 4:12; contrast from the same root the Ugar. noun *šrp*, "burnt offering," mentioned above).

The concept that the offering was in effect a gift from the offerer to God is also made explicit in the phrase *mattĕnōt qodšêhem*, literally, "the gifts of their holy things" (Exod. 28:38; NIV, "sacred gifts"). Furthermore, the special feature of being "set apart, made holy" is closely tied in with the view that the sacrifice is a gift. For discussion of such terms as the verb *qādaš H7727* and its cognates, which often pertain specifically to sacrifices or parts thereof (e.g., Lev. 27:9), see the article HOLINESS.

B. Materials. The various materials and elements that comprised the sacrifices and the offerings of ancient Israel will be reiterated in detail below. Certain general observations are necessary, however, in anticipation of the discussion regarding specific offerings. For example, the thing offered had to be the property of the offerer (Lev. 1:2); he might purchase it or bring it from his home. The agricultural nature of all the elements is obvious; except perhaps for the INCENSE, all of the items were edible. Unlike the Mesopotamian view (discussed above) that the sacrifices were necessary to the gods as essential food (cf. Deut. 32:37–38), the God of Israel is only said to enjoy the "pleasant aroma" of specific kinds of offering (see below). Even so, the sacrifices are called by the Lord, "my offering [*qorbānî*], my food [*laḥmî*] for my offerings by fire, my pleasing odor" (Num. 28:2, lit. trans.), and "my food, the fat and the blood" (Ezek. 44:7 NRSV). However, these were consumed or effused on the altar and not arrayed before him in the manner of the Mesopotamian divine meal.

On the other hand, the PRIESTS received certain portions that they were required to eat in a sacred place (Lev. 6:26 et al.), and sometimes the offerer was allowed to take part of the animal home for a meal of communal nature (see below, IV.C). The acceptable animals were of domesticated varieties raised for the purpose of providing food (and other products); work animals such as the donkey, which were not eaten, were not used for sacrifice (contrast the allusions to slaying an ass at Mari, above). Throughout the Levitical regulations it is stressed that the sacrificial animal had to be without physical "blemish" or "defect" (*mûm* H4583; LXX *mōmos* G3700, "blame"). Such disqualifying blemishes are defined and summarized in Lev. 22:17–25. The minimum age for any animal offered was eight days (vv. 26–30).

Although libations of wine and cereal offerings played a prominent role in the rituals, the most important sacrifices were those of animals. The surrender of a living victim was a major factor in nearly every kind of sacrificial ritual; that the life was being forfeited was signified by the extraction of the animal's BLOOD: "For the life of a creature is in the blood, and I have given it to you to make atonement for yourselves on the altar; it is the blood that makes atonement for one's life" (Lev. 17:11). The people were therefore forbidden to eat the blood (Lev. 17:10; also Gen. 9:4; Lev. 3:17; 7:26; Deut. 12:16, 23; 15:23; 1 Sam. 14:31–34), since LIFE belongs only to God.

The very careful attention paid to the use and disposal of the blood in the various kinds of sacrifices indicates that, even with nonexpiatory offerings, the principle of blood atonement was not entirely absent. In fact, the role of the blood in the different rituals is one of the unifying features in all of Israelite sacrifice. The ancient meaning of "to make atonement" in this context (*kāpar* H4105 piel, Lev. 17:11 et al.) was apparently that the sin of the offerer was "wiped away," not in the literal sense of being ritually purified only, but in the ethical sense that it no longer interfered with the offerer's relationship to God. See ATONEMENT; EXPIATION.

Certain other parts of the animal, in particular the inner organs and the fat attached to them (see below), were always burned on the altar; they were considered to belong exclusively to God. By contrast, some of these very parts were eaten by the sacrificer(s) in Greek epic literature, as mentioned above. The skins were most often given to the priest (Lev. 7:8).

C. Sources. The OT passages pertaining to sacrifice can also be classified according to the categories utilized for other ancient texts.

1. Prescriptive. The principal source for specific instructions concerning the correct performance

Altar found in Megiddo, most likely used for burning incense or as a stand for grain or meal offerings.

of Israelite sacrificial ritual is the opening section of Leviticus (Lev. 1–7). It consists of two separate treatises. The first (1:1–6:7) is didactic in nature and discusses the sacrifices under two categories: (a) those of a "pleasing aroma" (*rêaḥ-nîḥōaḥ* H8194 + H5767; LXX, *osmē euōdias* G4011 + G2380 [cf. Eph. 5:2; Phil. 4:18], KJV, "sweet savor"), namely, the *burnt* offering (Lev. 1:3–17), the *grain* offering (2:1–16; KJV, "meat"; RSV, "cereal"; NJPS, "meal"), and the *peace* offering (3:1–17; NIV, "fellowship"; NRSV and NJPS, "well-being"); and (b) those pertaining to expiation, namely, the *sin* offering (4:1–5:13) and the *guilt* (KJV, "trespass") offering (5:14–6:7 [Heb. 5:14–26]).

The order in which the various sacrifices are treated reflects a pedagogical classification for the training of the sacerdotal specialists. Great attention is paid to the minute details of each ritual; the different offerings are grouped according to their logical, or conceptual, associations. The grain offering appears immediately after the burnt offering because it was always presented with the latter in actual practice (not stated in this context, but cf. Num. 15:1–21; chs. 28–29 passim); it also accompanied the peace offering (Lev. 7:12–14; Num. 15:3–4). In all three of these sacrifices, special attention is paid to the incineration of the inward parts on the altar to produce an "aroma pleasing to the LORD" (Lev. 1:9, 17; 2:2, 9, 12; 3:5, 11, 16); therefore they represent an expression of right relationship with him. The divine favor was bestowed when "the LORD smelled the pleasing aroma" (Gen. 8:21); displeasure was followed by refusal to smell the offerings (Lev. 26:31). There must have been some observation or sign by which the officiating priest announced to the offerer that his sacrifice had been accepted (1 Sam. 26:19; cf. Amos 5:21–23).

The other category was comprised of two sacrifices, both of which were for making atonement to gain forgiveness for the offerer (Lev. 4:20 et al.). The occasions demanding such offerings are defined (viz., sin on the part of individuals of various ranks or of the whole congregation), and special attention is paid to the ritual handling of the blood. The sin and guilt offerings are thus in the same class and bear a close relationship to one another (for the unique features of the latter as a specialized sin offering, see below).

The second treatise (Lev. 6:8–7:38 [Heb. 6:1–7:38]) concentrates mainly on certain administrative details pertaining to each offering. It consists of a series of paragraphs, each giving the instructions for one type of sacrifice; these latter have to do with the disposal of the materials presented, some parts being allocated to the priest(s), some to the offerer, whereas others were either consumed on the altar or disposed of outside the camp. The designation "most holy" (*qōdeš qādāšîm*, with the second word traditionally pronounced *qodāšîm*) in reference to sacrifices had a practical, administrative significance; it pertained to those offerings, or portions thereof, that were to be eaten only by qualified members of the priesthood (Lev. 2:3, 10; 10:12–17; 14:13; Num. 18:9). Therefore, in the administrative treatment of the sacrifices, the offering that was wholly consumed (and thus not eaten by priests) came first, followed by those allotted to the functionaries (Lev. 6:17, 25, 29 [Heb. MS vv. 10, 18, 22]; 7:1, 6) and concluded by the peace offerings, large parts of which were returned to the offerer.

The order also corresponds to their relative frequency in the rituals of the sacred calendar (Num. 28–29; 2 Chr. 31:3; Ezek. 45:17a): burnt offering (Lev. 6:9–13), grain offering (6:14–23), sin offering (6:24–30), and finally the guilt offering (7:1–6); the latter, though it was not prescribed for holy days, is included here because it had the same set of instructions as the sin offering (v. 7; the term used here and in the other paragraphs is *tôrâ* H9368, lit., "law"). Each paragraph concludes with a statement about the logistic or administrative detail peculiar to the offering discussed; next comes a brief summary of the items treated thus far (7:7–10), followed by an additional section giving the instructions of the peace offerings (7:11–36). These latter had no special function in the sacred calendar except at the Feast of Weeks (23:19–20); otherwise their offering was purely voluntary and therefore not subject to any fixed reckoning (other sacrifices could also be made by individuals and groups as the occasion demanded). The difference between the fixed "income" from the calendrical offerings and the sporadic presentation of others is clearly reflected in the closing verse of the roster prescribing the daily and periodic sacrifices (Num. 29:39).

The same general order is followed, namely, burnt, cereal (and drink), sin (or guilt), and sometimes peace offerings in other "bookkeeping" contexts. The most illuminating study is that by Levine (in *JAOS* 85 [1965]: 309–18, esp. 314–18) on the list of donations made by the tribal leaders for the dedication of the altar (Num. 7). He has shown that this narrative is structured like an everyday ledger from a sanctuary; the summary lists the animals as burnt, grain, sin, and peace offerings (7:87–88), following the pattern of the respective entries for each donor (7:15–17). The "two-dimensional" nature of this record, as defined by Levine, is also quite understandable. The Levitical scribe had to use such a record for two purposes: (1) to credit the offerers and (2) to keep track of the treasures and food supplies coming in, the latter being especially important logistically, since they were the rations for the officiating priests and Levites (Num. 18:8–11; 2 Chr. 31:4–19).

The same administrative sequence is almost invariably used whenever prescriptions are made concerning the type and number of offerings *to be brought* (e.g., Num. 15:24). Such was the case with each of the festivals and holy days (the daily sacrifice was only a burnt offering of two lambs with their grain and drink offerings, one in the morning and the other in the evening 28:1–8); on the SABBATH, two additional male lambs with their grain and drink offerings were added (28:9–10). Burnt offerings with their associated grain offerings and libations were listed, followed by an additional notation prescribing a sin offering for each of the following: NEW MOON (28:11–15), each day of PASSOVER (28:19–22), Weeks (28:26–30; Lev. 23:15–19; see PENTECOST), Trumpets (Num. 29:1–5), Day of Atonement (29:8–11a; see ATONEMENT, DAY OF), and each day of the Feast of Booths (29:12–16 et passim; see FEASTS).

For specific acts of ritual sacrifice, such as the purification of a woman after giving birth (Lev. 12:6, 8), the same order appears in the instructions as to what offerings to bring. The best case in point is the list of required sacrifices for the successful termination of a NAZIRITE vow; the Nazirite was to furnish a burnt, sin, and peace offering (with some special grain offerings, Num. 6:14–15). However, a striking point emerges from the actual conduct of the ritual.

The priest carried out the sacrifices in a different order, namely, the sin offering and then burnt offering followed by the peace offering (6:16–17). In the case of a broken vow, the first step was also the sacrificing of a sin offering and then a burnt offering (6:11) to renew the vow; the reconsecration of the votary's head was accomplished by a separate guilt offering, which was already a second and distinct ritual act (6:12). The Nazirite passage thus points up the difference between (a) the "bookkeeping" order in which offerings were prescribed and later entered into the sanctuary records, and (b) the "procedural" order in which the rites were actually conducted.

The contrast between the two orders is most striking in the prophetic prescriptive text concerning the prince in the apocalyptic restoration. We first read that his duty involved "the burnt ... grain ... and drink offerings" at the calendrical holidays; but then the text states that he was to "provide" (lit., "he will make," $hû$-ya‘$ăśeh$) "the sin ... grain ... burnt ... and fellowship [peace] offerings" (Ezek. 45:17). That there was a fixed order for carrying out the sacrifices different from that in which they were furnished and audited is obvious.

A strikingly similar picture is reflected in another prescription, namely, Ezekiel's vision of the liturgy by which the altar was to be reinstituted (Ezek. 43:18–27). A sin offering was to be made on the first (vv. 18–21) and second days (v. 22) of the ceremony. The latter was immediately followed by a burnt offering (vv. 23–24); the sin and burnt offerings of the second day were repeated for seven days (vv. 25–27). From the eighth day on, the way was clear for burnt and peace offerings (v. 27).

Further examples of the "procedural" sequence include the ritual purification of a leper (guilt and sin offering, which belong to the expiatory category, followed by the burnt offering [Lev. 14:12, 19–20]), of the man with a discharge (sin, burnt [15:15]), and of the woman with a hemorrhage (also sin, burnt; 15:30). The same order prevails in the various sacrifices for the Day of Atonement (16:3, 6, 11, 15, 24). Thus the prescriptive ritual texts cited above are seen to reflect three methods of recording the sacrifices: (1) didactically/conceptually, (2) administratively, and (3) procedurally.

The instructions for ordaining AARON and his sons preserve the procedural order of sacrifices in the prescriptive text (Exod. 29), and the same order is confirmed in the narrative descriptive text (Lev. 8). First, the sin offering was made (Exod. 29:10–14; Lev. 8:14–17) and then the burnt offering (Exod. 29:15–18; Lev. 8:18–21); the climax of the altar rites was the sacrifice of ordination (*millu'im* H4854, lit., "setting in, installation," Exod. 29:19–34; Lev. 8:22–29), which was in fact a specialized form of communal or peace offering.

2. Descriptive. Numbers 7 (discussed below) shows that a descriptive text, that is, one that tells what was offered, need not always reflect the "procedural" order of the sacrifices. If the descriptive text is in the form of a temple ledger, as Levine has shown, then it is more likely to be composed according to the administrative order. Such is the case with this chapter.

On the other hand, the narrative descriptions normally follow the procedural sequence. Leviticus 8, which describes the installation ceremony for Aaron and his sons, has been discussed above. This was followed by the formal inauguration of the whole Israelite sacrificial system as portrayed in ch. 9. The initial offerings for Aaron followed the order: sin offering, burnt offering (9:7–14). The sequence of the people's offering that followed was: sin, burnt, grain, and peace offerings (9:15–22). Even the narrative prescription, the command from the Lord, is given in the same functional order (9:2–4).

The great cleansing and restoration of the temple and its ritual in Jerusalem was conducted in the reign of King HEZEKIAH according to the same pattern (2 Chr. 29:20–36). An extensive sin offering was made first (vv. 20–24); next followed the burnt offering, the ritual of which was accompanied by elaborate acts of worship in music and song (vv. 25–30). At this stage the king announced that the people had consecrated themselves "to [a state of holiness vis-à-vis] the LORD" (v. 31); they were therefore in a state of purity that qualified them to engage in further sacrifices (vv. 31–35) of devotion (burnt offerings) and thanksgiving (peace offerings).

In view of the preceding passages, it seems most likely that the same ritual sequence was followed at the dedication of Solomon's temple. Unfortunately, 1 Ki. 8:5 (cf. 2 Chr. 5:6) is ambiguous; it only states that the king and the people were "sacrificing." Later, the burnt, grain, and peace offering sequence is maintained (1 Ki. 8:64; 2 Chr. 7:7). These latter probably correspond to the voluntary sacrifices offered after the conclusion of the atonement ritual proper (cf. 2 Chr. 29:31–35; Ezek. 43:27). By analogy, one may assume that 1 Ki. 8:5 refers to the atonement ritual of sin, burnt, and grain offerings (cf. 2 Chr. 29:20, 31; Ezek. 43:18–27).

The "procedural" sequence of the offerings, that is, the actual order in which they were offered on any occasion that demanded more than one type, provides the key to understanding the religious (spiritual) significance of the sacrificial system. First of all, sin had to be dealt with; the appropriate offering (sin or guilt) had to be made. This was closely linked with a burnt offering that followed it immediately (with its accompanying grain offering in many cases) and thus completed the self-committal (2 Chr. 29:31) that qualified the supplicant(s) for the last stage of the liturgy. The crowning phase was the presentation of burnt and peace offerings, the former including both the voluntary gifts of individuals and the calendrical offerings symbolizing the constant devotion of the people as a whole, the latter representing the communal experience in which the Lord, the priest, and the worshiper (along with his friends and the indigent in his community, Deut. 12:17–19) all had a share.

IV. Types of sacrifices. By describing the various types of offering in their "procedural" order, the significance of their respective ritual acts as expressions of OT ethical MONOTHEISM can be placed in its proper perspective.

A. Expiatory offerings. Two offerings fall in this category. The particular aspect of conduct for which they were required will be discussed after the liturgical details have been summarized for both of them.

1. Sin offering (*ḥaṭṭā't* H2633, LXX *hamartia* G281; Lev. 4:1–35; 6:24–30 [Heb. 16:17–23]). The type of animal required was suited to the rank of the offerer. The high priest brought a young bull (Lev. 4:3), as did the congregation (v. 14) except, apparently, when a ritual infraction was involved

This altar found in Miletus would have been used for various kinds of sacrifices.

(Num. 15:24). A ruler brought a male goat (Lev. 4:25), but a commoner could furnish a female goat (v. 28; Num. 15:27) or a lamb (Lev. 4:32). A poor person could bring two doves or two young pigeons (one of the pair served as a burnt offering, Lev. 5:7), or in extreme cases he might even substitute a tenth of an ephah of fine flour (vv. 11–13; cf. Heb. 9:22).

The offerer brought the animal and executed the symbolic act of laying his hand on it (Lev. 4:4 et al.). In this way he identified the offering with himself. He did not confess his sin in this act because the animal was not being sent away (cf. the goat for AZAZEL, 16:21). It was also his duty to slay the animal (on the N side of the altar, 4:24, 29; cf. 1:11).

The priest collected the blood; when the sacrifice was a bull for himself or for the congregation, he took some of it into the shrine to sprinkle before the veil (Lev. 4:5–7) and put some on the horns of the incense altar there (vv. 16–18). On the Day of Atonement, he took his and the people's sacrificial blood into the Holy of Holies (16:14–15). From all the other animals the blood was applied to the horns of the altar of burnt offering (4:7, 18); that of the birds was effused on the side of the altar (5:9). Finally, the remaining blood from every type of offering was poured or drained out at the base of the altar (4:7).

The choice parts of the viscera—the fatty tissue over and on the entrails, the two kidneys and their fat, and the appendage to the liver—were all consumed on the altar (Lev. 4:8–10). The carcass and the remaining entrails were disposed of as refuse by burning outside the camp in the case of a bull for the priest or the people (vv. 11–12, 21). This rule prevailed for the bull in the ordination rites of Aaron and his sons (Exod. 29:10–14; Lev. 8:14–17). Otherwise, the priest received the edible flesh for food; it was to be eaten within the sacred precincts and very strict rules of ritual purity governed its handling (6:25–30; cf. 10:16–20).

A sin offering of one male goat was required at each of the sacred festivals: the New Moon (Num. 28:15), each day of Passover (vv. 22–24), Weeks (v. 30), Trumpets (29:5), Day of Atonement (v. 11; besides the special sin offerings for that day), each day of Booths (v. 16, 19). The high priest brought a bull for himself and then offered one of the two goats on the Day of Atonement.

Rites of PURIFICATION called for lesser sin offerings, namely, lambs or birds after childbirth (Lev. 12:6–8), leprosy (14:12–14, 19, 22, 31), abscesses and hemorrhages (15:15, 30), or defilement during the period of a vow (Num. 6:10–11). (The strictly individual cases requiring sin offerings are discussed following the guilt offering below.)

2. Guilt offering (*ʾāšām* H871; LXX *plēmmeleia* ["fault, offense"]; Lev. 5:14—6:7 [Heb. 5:14–26]; 7:1–7). The guilt (KJV, "trespass") offering was a specialized kind of sin offering (cf. 5:7) required in cases when someone had been denied his rightful due; reparation of the valued amount defrauded was required plus a fine of 20 percent (Lev. 5:16; 6:5 [Heb. 5:24]). The animal prescribed was usually a ram (Lev. 5:15, 18; 6:6 [Heb. 5:25]; 19:20); the cleansed leper and the defiled Nazirite were to bring a male lamb (14:12, 21; Num. 6:12). The offerer's part in the ritual was probably identical to that of the sin offering; however, the priest was to sprinkle the blood around the altar (Lev. 7:2). The choice viscera were consumed on the altar as usual (7:3–5). In the case of the cleansed leper, some of the blood was then applied to the tip of his right ear and to his right thumb and his right big toe (14:14). As with the sin offering, the animal went to the priest as food (7:6–7; 14:13).

The guilt offering was commanded in instances when another party had suffered some deprivation. Ritual infractions, such as eating unlawfully of the testify (Lev. 6:1–5 [Heb. 5:20–25]). Seduction of a betrothed slave girl (19:20–22) was also a violation of property rights.

In every case, the guilty party must confess his sin, make full restoration plus the fine of one fifth, and offer the guilt offering. If the offended party was no longer alive and there were no surviving relatives, the payment went to the priests (Num. 5:5–10).

3. Efficacy. The obligatory sin and guilt offerings for ritual infractions (Lev. 4:14; 5:2–3; 22:14; Num. 15:22–29) illustrate that in antiquity the morals and ethics of every society were closely integrated into a framework of ritual observance. The OT ideal saw the ritual acts as expressions of faith and devotion; the universal human inclination (not confined to Israel) is to substitute the outward act for the concomitant inward attitude (Hos. 6:6).

Both ritual and ethical sins committed inadvertently (*bišgāgâ*) could be atoned for by sacrifice (Lev. 4:2, 13, 22, 27; 5:14), but only after the offender had come to the realization of his fault (4:13–14; cf. 5:17; 14:23, 28; Num. 15:24). Other offenses that were committed consciously and with real intent included acts of dishonest dealing (Lev. 6:1–5; cf. Exod. 22:7–15 [Heb. 22:6–14]) and failure to comply with rules of testimony, etc. (Lev. 5:1, 4).

However, sins committed "with an upraised hand" (*běyād rāmâ*; NIV, "defiantly") could not be atoned for by sacrificial ritual (Num. 15:30–31). To this latter category belong all offenses requiring the death penalty. In general, these can be classified as violations of the TEN COMMANDMENTS: the second commandment forbids IDOLATRY (Lev. 20:2; Deut. 13:6; 17:2–7), offering children to MOLECH (Lev. 20:3), witchcraft, and false prophesying (Exod. 22:18; Lev. 20:6, 27; Deut. 13:5; 18:20; 1 Sam. 28:9); the third consists of BLASPHEMY (Lev. 24:14, 16, 23; 1 Ki. 21:10); the fourth involves violation of the Sabbath (Exod. 31:14; 35:2; Num. 15:32–36) and probably also the ritual infractions discussed below; the fifth, striking or reviling a parent (Exod. 21:15, 17); the sixth, murder (Lev. 24:17, 21) and kidnapping (Exod. 21:16); the seventh, adultery (Lev. 20:10; Deut. 22:22), incestuous and unnatural sexual relations (Exod. 22:19; Lev. 18:29; 20:11,

Altar dedicated to Zeus and used in sacrificial ritual; found in Hierapolis.

"holy things" (Lev. 5:4–19; 22:14), required payment of the sum (or commodity) that had rightfully belonged to God plus another one fifth of the amount concerned; the fine was given to the priest (5:16; 2 Ki. 12:16). The case of the leper can be assigned to this category in that the Lord was deprived of the service due from the infected person so long as his disease kept him outside the pale of the ritually clean society (Lev. 14:12–18). Likewise, the Nazirite who became defiled during the course of his period of separation to God had to bring a guilt offering as reparation for what he had pledged and not fulfilled (Num. 6.12).

On the social plane, violation of property rights through defraudation could be atoned for only by the guilt offering and its 20 percent fine. Such acts included cheating in matters of deposit or security, robbery or oppression, failing to report the finding of lost property, or false swearing or failing to

14), unchastity (Lev. 21:9; Deut. 22:21, 23), and rape (22:25); and the ninth, false witness in capital cases (19:16, 19).

The precedent case concerning violation of the Sabbath (Num. 15:32–36) required an explicit oracle before the penalty could be imposed. The offense incurred the supreme penalty whenever it constituted rejection of the COVENANT as embodied in its principal sign (Exod. 20:8–11; Deut. 5:12–15; and esp. Exod. 31:12–17). The various laws against violation of the ritual calendar and related statues can probably be seen as extensions of this concept—disregard for the sacrificial system could be tantamount to rejection of the covenant, which was itself instituted by a sacrifice (24:3–8) Such infractions included the following: nonobservance of the Passover or eating leavened bread during this feast (Exod. 12:15, 19; Num. 9:13); nonobservance of the Day of Atonement (Lev. 23:29–30); eating blood or the choice viscera of the sacrifices (7:25–27; 17:14); failure to slaughter burnt or peace offerings at the proper sanctuary (17:4, 9); eating sacrifices while in an unclean state (7:20–21; 22:3–4); eating the remainder of a peace offering too late (19:8); touching holy things illegally (Num. 4:15, 18, 20); defiling the sanctuary by personal uncleanness (19:13, 20); misuse of the holy ointment (Exod. 30:32–33) or perfume (30:38).

The second illustration of "high-handed sin" was KORAH's rebellion and the subsequent bitterness on the part of the people (Num. 16). In this case, the offense was so great that atonement could not be obtained by a sin offering; nevertheless, by intercession and the symbolic burning of incense, atonement for the people was achieved (16:46–47). Likewise, Moses had interceded for them and gained at least partial atonement in the incident of the golden calf (Exod. 32:11–13, 30–35). Forgiveness could be granted to one of "a broken and contrite heart" even when the offenses (adultery and murder) were too great for atonement by sacrifice (Ps. 51:16–17 [cf. the superscription to this psalm and 2 Sam. 12:13]). When the prophet ISAIAH and his people were defiled by moral uncleanness beyond the limits of restoration by ritual (Isa. 6:5; cf. 1:10–17), guilt could still be taken away and sin forgiven by application of a coal from the incense altar, symbol of prayer and intercession (6:6–7).

In short, the sin and guilt offerings were efficacious for less serious violations against the eighth and ninth commandments and for certain ritual infractions, but in every case the offender had to be fully aware of his responsibility and to make reparation when necessary. For greater sins, ritual was to no avail, but the forgiveness and atonement could be granted on condition of true REPENTANCE.

D. Consecratory offerings. The sacrifices in this category reflect the more universal idea of *offering*. The emphasis is on surrender of the gift to God (though only a handful of the grain offering was consumed on the altar). They represented the act of committal that should accompany the repentance expressed by the sin and guilt offerings. They also opened the way to the fellowship of communal sacrifices that could follow.

1. Burnt offering (*ʿōlâ H6592* [lit., "that which goes up"]; LXX *holokautōma G3906* and other terms; Lev. 1:3–17; 6:8–13 [Heb. 6:1–6]; note also the apparent synonym *kālîl H4003*, Ps. 51:19 [Heb. 51:21], and Phoen. *kll*, mentioned above). The ritual of the burnt offering called for a bull (Lev. 1:3–5), a sheep or a goat (v. 10), or a bird (v. 14). The offerer brought the animal, laid his hand on it and slew it on the N side of the altar (vv. 3–5, 11); the bird was simply handed over to the priest (v. 15). The priest collected the blood, presented it before the Lord, and sprinkled it around the altar (vv. 5, 11); in the case of a bird, he wrung off its head and drained the blood out on the side of the altar (v. 15). Thus, the burnt offering was linked to the blood atonement concept by the attention paid to the blood, but that was not the central feature of the rite. The stress was placed instead on the flaying and dissection of the animal, the washing of its unclean parts, and the careful arrangement of all the pieces (except the crop and feathers of the bird) on the altar (vv. 6–9, 12–13). The consumption of the whole was meant to be "a pleasing aroma" to the Lord. Only the animal skin was left for the priest (7:8); the main administrative concern was for constant maintenance of the fire (thus the need for an uninterrupted supply of fuel) and the proper attire of the officiating priest during the ritual of renewing the fire each morning (6:8–13 [Heb. 6:1–6]).

As mentioned above, the burnt offerings were by far the most frequent sacrifices at the Israelite sanctuary and were therefore listed first in administrative prescriptions and descriptions. This is due to their central role in the rites for holy days. The "continual" or "regular" (*tāmîd* H9458) burnt offering was made twice daily, a male lamb morning and evening (Exod. 29:38–42; Num. 28:1–8). The entire procedure for the morning sacrifice is vividly described in the MISHNAH (tractate *Tamid*). Two additional lambs were offered each Sabbath (28:9–10). No sin offerings accompanied these sacrifices.

On the other hand, a sin offering of one goat was required along with the burnt offerings on the other holy days. At the beginning of each month (the New Moon), a set of two young bulls, one ram, and seven male lambs were sacrificed (Num. 28:11–14). The same number of animals was required for each day of the Passover and Unleavened Bread Festival (vv. 19–24) and again on the Feast of Weeks (vv. 26–29). For the Festival of Trumpets and the Day of Atonement the standard was one bull, one ram, and seven lambs (29:2–4, 8), besides the special burnt offerings for the atonement ritual itself, which consisted of one ram for the high priest and one for the people (Lev. 16:3, 5, 24).

The climax of the annual festivals, the Feast of Booths, was marked by a series of elaborate burnt offerings (plus one goat per day as a sin offering). On the first day, the regulations called for thirteen young bulls, two rams, and fourteen male lambs (Num. 29:12–16). Each day thereafter, the increment of bulls was decreased by one until on the seventh day there were only seven (the number of rams and lambs remained the same, vv. 17–35). The eighth day saw a return to the amounts designated for Trumpets and the Day of Atonement, namely, one bull, one ram, and seven lambs (vv. 35–38; for the associated grain and drink offerings, see below).

Various purification rituals also called for burnt offerings as well as sin offerings: after childbirth (Lev. 12:6–8), abscesses (15:14–15), and hemorrhages (15:29–30), or after defilement during a Nazirite vow (Num. 6:10–11). Though not specified in these cases, there were grain offerings for the cleansing from leprosy (Lev. 14:10, 19–20, 22,

31) and the completion of a Nazirite vow (Num. 6:14, 16).

The burnt offering, signifying complete surrender to God, was therefore associated with the sin offering in the process of atonement (as in the purification rites above; cf. also 2 Chr. 29:27). They were also coupled with the peace offerings as an expression of devotion and committal (29:31–35; 1 Ki. 8:64; 2 Chr. 7:7). This latter aspect typifies the function of the burnt offerings in Genesis (e.g., Gen. 8:20); it is also the key to its requirement as a continual, daily sacrifice.

2. Grain offering (*minḥâ* H4966 ["gift, offering"]; LXX *thysia* G2602 ["sacrifice"]; Lev. 2:1–14; 6:14–23 [Heb. 6:7–11]). A regular concomitant to the animal sacrifices was an offering of food (KJV, "meat"; RSV, "cereal"; NJPS, "meal"; NIV and NRSV, "grain"). Outside the ritual codes, the term *minḥâ* could refer to any kind of gift, including animals (Gen. 4:3–5; Jdg. 6:18; 1 Sam. 2:17); but in prescriptive texts it signifies a concoction of fine flour (see BREAD II), olive OIL, and FRANKINCENSE. Its form could be baked cakes, wafers, or morsels (Lev. 2:4–6). The offering of FIRSTFRUITS was to be "heads of new grain roasted in the fire" (v. 14). No leaven or honey was permitted on the cakes being offered (v. 11), though these commodities were acceptable as a firstfruits offering (v. 12), in which case they went to the clergy but not on the altar.

The offerer was responsible for bringing the prepared loaves or wafers to the sanctuary. The priest burned one handful on the altar as its "memorial portion" (Lev. 2:2), and the rest was his to eat (6:16 [Heb. 6:9]; 7:9). When the priest made a grain offering for himself, the whole was burnt on the altar (6:22–23 [Heb. 6:15–16]).

The grain offering normally accompanied every burnt offering, especially those in the sacred calendar (Num. 28–29). The quantities of fine flour and oil were fixed according to the animal being sacrificed; for example, a ram offering required twice as much flour as a lamb, and a bull required three times as much (15:2–10). Other joyous occasions included the cleansing of a leper (Lev. 14:10, 20–21, 31; unspecified quality for a bird) and the successful consummation of a Nazirite vow (Num. 6:15, 19).

Perhaps a grain offering was understood, though not mentioned, in the rites for cleansing after childbirth (Lev. 12:6–8), abscesses (15:14–15) or hemorrhages (15:29–30). One has the impression, however, that the omission was intentional; note that no grain offering went with the burnt offerings for the high priest and the people in the special ritual for the Day of Atonement (16:3, 5, 24). Perhaps sacrifices of a more somber nature were intentionally made without a grain offering.

Conversely, peace offerings were always accompanied by grain offerings (Lev. 7:12–14; Num. 15:4): one of each from the cakes and wafers went to the priest, while the rest was to be eaten with the flesh of the sacrificial animal. A special use of the grain offering was the one-tenth of an ephah of barley meal required in the jealousy ritual; it was to have no oil or frankincense (5:15, 18, 25, 26). A very poor person could bring one-tenth of an ephah of fine flour, also without oil or frankincense, as a sin offering (Lev. 5:11–13).

3. Drink offering (*nesek* H5821; LXX *spondē*). A libation normally accompanied burnt and peace offerings (Num. 15:5, 7, 10); the standard was one-fourth of a hin of wine for lamb, one-third for a ram, and one-half for a bull. The expression "fermented drink," used with reference to the drink offering (28:7; Heb. *šēkār* H8911 [NRSV, "strong drink"]), is apparently only a synonym for WINE (*yayin* H3516, Exod. 29:40). The use of wine was probably a conscious substitute for the blood used by the heathen (Ps. 16:4). The libation was considered as an additional "pleasing aroma" offering (Num. 15:7). Like the burnt offering, all was expended, nothing was given to the priest; the entire libation was poured out in the sanctuary (28:7).

Drink offerings are specifically mentioned with the daily offering (Exod. 29:40–41; Num. 28:7), and with that for the Sabbath (28:9) and for the New Moon (28:14). Likewise, reference is made to them in connection with the second and following days of the Feast of Booths (29:18, 21 et al.); for the first day (vv. 12–16) their absence is probably unintentional. The same may hold true for the Passover, First Fruits, and Feast of Trumpets rituals (28:16—29:11; cf. Ezek. 45:17). A libation was specified for the Nazirite's concluding rites (Num. 6:17), but not for the cleansing of the leper (Lev. 14:10–20). Perhaps the drink offering was such an integral part of the burnt offering ceremony that it could be taken for granted; still, it is not impossible that it was purposely excluded from certain rites. It never accompanied a sin or guilt offering alone.

C. Communal offerings. This latter category consists of those offerings that expressed a voluntary desire on the part of the offerers. They were not required (except in the case of the Nazirite and the Feast of Booths [Num. 6:17; Lev. 23:19–20]) by explicit regulations, but were permitted on condition that the offerer had met the requirements of expiation and consecration. Burnt offerings could accompany these sacrifices as an additional expression of devotion (see above).

1. Peace offering (*šelem* H8968, usually in the phrase *zebaḥ šĕlāmîm* [NIV, "fellowship offering"; NRSV and NJPS, "sacrifice of well-being"]; LXX *thysia sōtēriou* ["sacrifice of salvation," but in 1 Sam. 10:8 et al. the term *eirēnikos*, "peaceful," is used]; Lev. 3:1–16; 7:11–36). This is the basic sacrifice of all communal offerings; the others are simply different types of the peace offering. In terms of "holiness" (i.e., restrictedness), they were not so strictly defined as those discussed above. Animals from the herd or flock, male or female (3:1, 6, 12), were permissible. The usual rules of physical perfection were in force except for one relaxation in the case of the *freewill* offering, which could have one member longer than the other (22:23). Unleavened cakes were also stipulated, at least for the *thank* (7:12–13) and *votive* (Num. 6:15, 17, 19) offerings. These three types are discussed below with regard to their special features.

The presentation and laying on of the hand were the same as for other offerings; but instead of slaughtering the animal on the N side of the altar, it was done at the door of the sanctuary, that is, at the entrance to the outer court (Lev. 3:1–2, 7–8, 12–13; 7:29–30). The priest collected the blood and threw it against the altar as with the burnt offering (3:2, 8, 13). The choice viscera were burnt for a "pleasing aroma" (3:3–5, 6–11 [including the fat tail of the sheep], 14–16 [cf. 7:22–25]; 7:30–31).

Certain portions of the offering were also allotted to the priest; he was permitted to eat it in any ritually clean place and to share it with his family (Lev. 7:14, 30–36; Num. 6:20). He received one of the cakes and the breast as a *wave offering* (see below), and the right thigh as the offerer's "contribution" (*těrûmâ* H9556, Exod. 28:27–28; Lev. 7:32 [KJV, "heave offering"]; the term literally means "a lifting," but it did not refer to a special type of presentation ceremony).

The culmination of every peace offering was the communal meal. Except for the portions burned on the altar or assigned to the priest, the body of the sacrificial animal was given to the offerer. He used it as food for a communal meal that would include himself, his family, and also the Levite in his community (Deut. 12:12, 18–19). This had to be at the divinely appointed sanctuary (12.6–7, 11, 12, 15–19, 26; cf. 1 Sam. 1:3–4), and very strict rules of purity were observed by the participants (Lev. 7:19–21; 19:5–8). One may contrast the ritual slaughtering of animals for a banquet, which was permitted at any local altar (Deut. 12:16, 20–22).

The meat of a *thank offering* had to be eaten on the same day as the sacrifice (Lev. 7:15), whereas that of the *votive* or *freewill offering* could be finished on the next day (7:16–18). Whatever was left over from either kind had to be burned before the time limit on its consumption had expired.

The peace offering was only specified in three instances, namely, in the celebration of the Feast of Weeks (Lev. 23:19–20), in the ritual for completion of a Nazirite vow (Num. 6:17–20), and at the installation of the priesthood (cf. the *ordination offering*, below). Other public ritual occasions included the inauguration of the Tent of Meeting (Lev. 9:1–21) and of the temple (1 Ki. 8:63; 2 Chr. 7:5). National events that called forth the peace offering included the following: successful conclusion of a military campaign (1 Sam. 11:15), cessation of famine or pestilence (2 Sam. 24:25), acclamation of a candidate for kingship (1 Ki. 1:9, 19), and a time of national spiritual renewal (2 Chr. 29:31–36). At the local level they were sacrificed for the annual family reunion (1 Sam. 20:6) or other festive events, such as the harvesting of the firstfruits (Exod. 22:29–31; 1 Sam. 9:11–13, 22–24; 16:4–5).

2. Wave offering (*těnûpâ* H9485 [NRSV and NJPS, "elevation offering"]; the LXX translates with a variety of terms; Lev. 7:30 et al.). The priest's portion of the peace offering was "waved" before the Lord as a special act signifying that it was his (the motion may have resembled the wielding of a saw or a staff, Isa. 10.15; according to a different understanding, the motion was simply one of "raising" the item, thus the rendering "elevation offering" [see discussion in *HALOT*, 4:1762–63]). Then it went to the officiant as his personal share. The presentation of the ceremonial food to the Mesopotamian deity, after which it was given to the king, immediately comes to mind. The basic difference seems to be that the deity there was considered to have partaken of the food and to have added his "radiance" to it, whereas in Israel the priest ate the divine portion as God's representative, thus showing that the food was being shared by him.

The same technical term was applied to offerings other than the communal sacrifices: the precious metals given for the construction of the sacred artifacts (Exod. 35:22; 38:29), the guilt offering of the cleansed leper (Lev. 14:12, 21, 24), the sheaf of firstfruits (23:15), the two loaves at the Feast of Weeks (vv. 17, 20), and the Levites themselves (Num. 8:11, 13, 15, 21). In the latter case, it is evident that no physical waving or lifting was involved, so the term probably could refer to a particular type of offering even if the original gesture was not used. (See further J. Milgrom, "The Alleged Wave-Offering in Israel and in the Ancient Near East," *IEJ* 22 [1972]: 33–38.)

3. Thank offering (*zebaḥ hattôdâ* H2285 + H9343; LXX *thysia tēs aineseōs* ["sacrifice of praise"]; Lev. 7:12–15; 22:29). This is the most frequently mentioned type of peace offering. It represented an act of thanksgiving for blessings already bestowed (Pss. 56:12–13; 107:22; 116:17; Jer. 33:11). In many contexts, the term *thank offering* is the virtual synonym of *peace offering* (e.g., 2 Chr. 29:31; Jer. 17:26; cf. 2 Chr. 33:16).

4. Votive offering (*nēder* H5624; LXX *euchē* G2376; Lev. 7:16–17 et al.). This kind of sacrifice was a ritual expression of the vow, which covered a wider range of practices. It was usually a peace offering, and the flesh could be eaten on the second day but not on the third (Lev. 7:16–17). However, it could also be a burnt offering (22:17–20). A specific example was the vow of a Nazirite that was consummated by a peace offering (Num. 6:17–20). In the broadest sense, the vow included any kind of offering or gift promised to the Lord (e.g., Num. 30).

5. Freewill offering (*nĕdābâ* H5607; LXX *hekousios* G1730; Lev. 7:16; 22:18, 21, 23; 23:28; Num. 15:3; 29:39; Deut. 12:6, 17). This was the minimum offering that one could bring to the holy convocations, which took place thrice a year (Exod. 23:16; 34:20; Deut. 16:10, 16–17; 2 Chr. 35:8; Ezra 3:5). Like the votive offering, it could consist of burnt as well as peace offerings (Lev. 22:17–24; Ezek. 46:12), and if it were the latter, the flesh could be consumed on the second day but had to be burned before the third (Lev. 7:16–17). Unlike the other peace offerings, the animal for a freewill sacrifice could have one limb longer than the other (22:23).

6. Ordination offering (*millu'îm* H4854 [lit., "setting in, installation"; KJV, "consecration"]; LXX *teleiōsis* G5459 ["perfection"]; Exod. 29:19–34; Lev. 8:22–29). This offering was intimately related to the concept of "filling the hand" (*millē' yād*, Exod. 29:9 et al.), which meant consecrating someone to divine service (cf. 32:29 et al.) and required a state of ritual purity and spiritual devotion (2 Chr. 29:31).

The details of the ritual are in a prescriptive text (Exod. 29:19–34) and in a narrative descriptive passage (Lev. 8:22–32). Moses appears in the role of the officiant, since Aaron and his sons were obviously not qualified to serve in their own ordination. He brought the ram of consecration and the priests laid their hands on it. Then Moses slew it and handled the blood in a special manner. It was applied by him to the tip of the right ear, thumb, and big toe of Aaron and of each of his sons; then the rest was thrown about the altar. The wave offering was also unique in its execution; the choice viscera, three of the accompanying cakes, and the right thigh were all placed in the hands of the candidates for priesthood and waved before the Lord; then they were all consumed together on the altar as a "pleasing aroma." Though Moses did not receive the thigh, he was granted the breast, which he waved himself and took as his portion. Finally, the anointing oil, mixed with blood from the altar, was sprinkled upon the candidates and their garments. They were thus prepared to eat the remaining flesh of the ordination offering, which they had to boil at the entrance to the court of the sanctuary. Like the votive offering, none was allowed to remain until the following day.

V. Redemptive history

A. Pre-Mosaic. The terminology used with regard to the patriarchal age is that of the Torah as a whole; it is unlikely that the same words in Genesis mean something different from the other books of Moses. Thus, CAIN and ABEL each brought a "gift" (Gen. 4:1–7), which was usually of a grain nature as brought by Cain (Lev. 2 et al.) but could also refer to an animal offering (1 Sam. 2:17; 26:19). NOAH offered up "burnt offerings," and the pleasing odor of the sacrifice is stressed (Gen. 8:20–21). JOB is also depicted as making "burnt offerings" periodically (Job 1:5) and for specific purposes (42:7–9).

The PATRIARCHS normally are said to have "called on the name of the LORD" (e.g., Gen. 12:8; 13:4; 21:33; 26:25). The association of this phrase with the building of an altar shows that it refers to the approach to God through sacrifice. With JACOB, the naming of the specific altar is also stressed (33:20; 35:7). ABRAHAM is said to have offered a "burnt offering" (ch. 22) but Jacob offered "sacrifices" (31:54; 46:1). The most unusual sacrifices in Genesis are the covenant ritual with the divided carcasses (15:9–11; cf. Jer. 34:18–20), and the almost consummated sacrifice of ISAAC (Gen. 22).

B. From Moses to Samuel. The covenant sacrifice inaugurating the relationship between the Lord and his people (Exod. 24:3–8) is not paralleled by specific rituals in the Mosaic liturgy. Burnt and peace offerings were first offered and then the blood from them (not from a sin offering) was thrown, half against the altar and half upon the people.

In the land of Canaan, the Israelites made sacrifices at various places, such as BOKIM (Jdg. 2:1–5) and OPHRAH (6:24–26). The human sacrifice of JEPHTHAH's daughter (11:30–40) was hardly normative; instead it is pointed out as evidence of Israel's low spiritual state at that time.

The main center for sacrificial ritual was at SHILOH (1 Sam. 1:3), where faithful Israelites came for an annual festive offering. That the ritual there was highly developed and complex in detail is proven by the explicit description of malpractice on the part of ELI's sons (2.13–17) in taking their portion of the meat before the viscera were burned. Shiloh was not, however, the only legitimate place of sacrifice; others included BETH SHEMESH (6:14–15), MIZPAH (7:9), RAMAH (7:17; 9:11–24), GIBEAH (10:5), and GILGAL (10:8; 11:15; 13:9). Family and clan sacrifices were commonplace (16:2–5).

C. During the monarchy. Under SAUL, the main center of worship was evidently NOB (1 Sam. 21:1), though private offerings were made at Shiloh (2 Sam. 15:12). Saul's and DAVID's families made peace offerings and held family feasts at the time of the New Moon (1 Sam. 20:5, 24–25).

David inaugurated a new cult center in Jerusalem at the threshing floor at Ornan (ARAUNAH, 1 Chr. 21:23–26), to which he moved the ARK OF THE COVENANT (2 Sam. 6:17–18; 1 Chr. 16:2, 40). The horned altar had been located at GIBEON (1 Chr. 21:29; 2 Chr. 1:6) but was soon moved to JERUSALEM (1 Chr. 22:1). David is credited with a complete reorganization of the ritual and the attendant personnel (23:28–31).

With the construction and dedication of the TEMPLE under SOLOMON, Jerusalem became the main focus of sacrificial ritual (1 Ki. 8:5, 62–65; 2 Chr. 5:6; 7:4–8; cf. discussion above). Nevertheless, HIGH PLACES continued in use locally (1 Ki. 3:2; 13:1–5; 18:30–32; 19:10; 2 Ki. 14:4; 15:4, 35 et al.). JEROBOAM I of the northern kingdom established shrines at DAN (PLACE) and BETHEL (1 Ki. 12:27, 28); besides these famous sites in Israel, BEERSHEBA may have enjoyed a similar status in Judah (Amos 5:5). Various references show that sacrifices were offered regularly at Jerusalem (2 Chr. 13:10–11; 23:18; 24:14; 2 Ki. 12:4–16, 16.13–15). Sacrificing on the high places was also tolerated in Judah (2 Chr. 15:17; 20:33); HEZEKIAH abolished many of them (2 Ki. 18:4) and seems to have reconstituted the temple as the sacrificial center (2 Chr. 29:21–35; 32:12). The high places returned under MANASSEH (33:3–4) and were again removed by JOSIAH (35:6–14).

D. Postexilic period. Offerings were reconstituted soon after the return (Ezra 3:2–7), and when DARIUS authorized building the temple he ordered that provisions be furnished for the cultus (6:9–10). Henceforth, the second temple remained the center for Judean sacrificial ritual (6:17; 7:17; 8:35; 10:19; Neh. 10:33–37; 13:5, 9).

At ELEPHANTINE in Egypt, a colony of Jewish mercenaries had maintained their own temple, replete with meal offering, incense, and burnt offering. It had been standing since before 525 B.C. when CAMBYSES invaded Egypt and was destroyed by jealous opponents in 410. In 407, the priest of this temple and his colleagues wrote to Bigvai/Bagohi (see BAGOAS), governor of Judah, as well as to Delaiah and Shelemiah, sons of SANBALLAT, asking them to exert their influence toward having the ruined temple rebuilt. Though they pointedly yearned for restoration of the entire sacrificial cultus, the reply suggests that they apply to Arsames, their governor, for resumption of the meal offering and the incense—which they did (*ANET*, 492). This tendency to permit worship at local shrines but without animal sacrifice may be reflected in the fact that the Jewish temple at LACHISH (so-called Solar Shrine) had no altar for burnt offering whereas its preexilic counterpart at Arad did. The Lachish temple was evidently built in the Hellenistic period (prob. under John Hyrcanus, late 2nd cent. B.C.; see Y. Aharoni in *IEJ* 18 [1968]: 157–69).

E. Prophets, sages, and poets. The prophets of the first temple period often spoke out against sacrificial ritual (Amos 5:21–27; Hos. 6:6; Mic. 6:6–8; Isa. 1:11–31; Jer. 6:20; 7:21–22). Righteous and just behavior, along with obedience to the Lord, are contrasted with the conduct of rituals unaccompanied by proper ethical and moral attitudes (Amos 5:24; Mic. 6:8; Isa. 1:16–17; Jer. 7:23). It has thus been assumed by many scholars that the prophets condemned all sacrificial rituals. Roland de Vaux (*Ancient Israel* [1961], 454) has shown the absurdity of such a conclusion, for Isa. 1:15 also condemns prayer. No one holds that

Sacrifices are still preformed today by the Samaritans here on Mount Gerizim.

the prophets rejected prayer as such; it was prayer offered without the proper moral commitment that was being denounced, and the same holds true for the oracles against formal rituals.

Certain other statements (e.g., Amos 5:25; Jer. 7:22) have been taken to mean that the prophets knew nothing of a ritual practice followed in the wilderness experience of Israel. De Vaux (*Ancient Israel*, 428) has noted that Jeremiah clearly knew Deut. 12:6–14 and regarded it as the law of Moses. The prophetic oracles against sacrifice in the desert are really saying that the original Israelite sacrificial system was not meant to be the empty, hypocritical formalism practiced by their contemporaries. The demand by Hosea for "mercy, not sacrifice, and acknowledgment of God rather than burnt offerings" (Hos. 6:6; cf. Matt. 9:13; 12:7) is surely to be taken as a relative statement of priorities (cf. also 1 Sam. 15:22). The inner attitude was prerequisite to any valid ritual expression (Isa. 29:13).

Foreign elements that had penetrated the Israelite sacrificial system were, of course, roundly condemned by the prophets. Such was especially the case in Israel (Amos 4:4–5; Hos. 2:13–15; 4:11–13; 13:2) but also in Judah (Jer. 7:17–18; Ezek. 8 et al.).

The wisdom literature sometimes reflects the same concern for moral and ethical values over empty sacerdotal acts (Prov. 15:8; 21:3, 27). A similar attitude is expressed in the Psalms; some passages might be taken as a complete rejection of sacrifice (e.g., Pss. 40:7–8; 50:8–15), but they actually express the same demand for a correct inner attitude as the prophets do (for the special significance of 51:18–19, see above).

F. The NT. Jesus took for granted the sacrificial system in effect in his own time and did not call for its abolition (Matt. 5:24). He even enjoined cleansed lepers to fulfill their ritual obligations (8.4; Lk. 17:14). He also spoke at least twice of his own impending death as a sacrifice (Mk. 10:45 and Matt. 20:28; Lk. 22:20 and Mk. 14:24; Matt. 26:28). In the fourth gospel, JOHN THE BAPTIST refers to him as the "Lamb of God" (Jn. 1:29, 36; cf. Rev. 13:8).

Even PAUL, the apostle to the Gentiles, took part in the sacrificial ritual pertaining to some Jewish Christians who had taken a vow (Acts 21:26). He thus acted in harmony with accepted Christian practice of that day. In his epistles he expressed a highly developed and sophisticated interpretation of Christ's crucifixion as an expiatory sacrifice (Rom. 3:25; 5:9; also 1 Cor. 10:16; Eph. 1:7; 2:13; Col. 1:20). He identified the Messiah with the sin offering (Rom. 8:3; 2 Cor. 5:21) and the Passover Lamb (1 Cor. 5:7). He obviously expected his readers to be knowledgeable with regard to the OT ritual system. The "pleasing aroma" sacrifices, especially the whole burnt offering, provided the basis for his plea "to offer your bodies as living sacrifices, holy and pleasing to God" (Rom. 12:1).

PETER states that the believers are redeemed by the blood of Christ (1 Pet. 1:18–19; cf. 1:2; 3:18). First John also ascribes to it propitiation for and cleansing from sin (1 Jn. 1:7; 2:2; 5:6, 8; cf. also Rev. 1:5). The epistle to the Hebrews deals in great detail with various aspects of sacrificial ritual, especially that for the Day of Atonement. All are viewed as earthly "shadows" of spiritual realities (Heb. 8:5; 10:1). The Messiah's sacrifice of himself is efficacious because it was made in the "eternal Spirit" (9:14) and thus he has entered eternally into the presence of the Father.

(In addition to the titles mentioned in the body of the article, see J. H. Kurtz, *Sacrificial Worship of the Old Testament* [1863]; H. C. Trumbull, *The Blood Covenant* [1885]; C. F. Keil, *Manual of Biblical Archaeology*, 2 vols. [1887–88], 1:246–482 and 2:1–101; A. Cave, *The Scriptural Doctrine of Sacrifice* [1890]; G. F. Oehler, *Theology of the Old Testament* [1892], 261–351; P. Fairbairn, *The Typology of Scripture* [1900], 201–23, 377, 405; G. B. Gray, *Sacrifice in the Old Testament* [1925]; W. R. Smith, *The Religion of the Semites*, 3rd ed. [1927]; E. O. James, *The Origins of Sacrifice* [1933]; W. O. E. Oesterley, *Sacrifices in Ancient Israel* [1938]; R. K. Yerkes, *Sacrifice in Greek and Roman Religion and in Early Judaism* [1952]; A. L. Oppenheim, *Ancient Mesopotamia* [1964], 183–98, 206–27; A. F. Rainey, "The Order of Sacrifices in Old Testament Ritual Texts," *Bib* 51 [1970]: 485–98; B. Levine, *In the Presence of the Lord: A Study of Cult and Some Cultic Terms in Ancient Israel* [1974]; F. M. Young, *The Use of Sacrificial Ideas in Greek Christian Writers from the New Testament to John Chrysostom* [1979]; J. Milgrom, *Studies in Cultic Theology and Terminology* [1983]; G. A. Anderson, *Sacrifices and Offerings in Ancient Israel: Studies in Their Social and Political Importance* [1987]; F. H. Gorman, Jr., *The Ideology of Ritual: Space, Time, and Status in the Priestly Theology* [1990]; J. Quaegebeur, ed., *Ritual and Sacrifice in the Ancient Near East* [1993]; R. T. Beckwith and M. J. Selman, *Sacrifice in the Bible* [1995]; D. M. Clemens, *Sources for Ugaritic Ritual and Sacrifice, Vol. 1: Ugaritic and Ugarit Akkadian Texts* [2001]; W. K. Gilders, *Blood Ritual in the Hebrew Bible: Meaning and Power* [2004]; J. Klawans, *Purity, Sacrifice, and the Temple* [2006]; G. A. Anderson in *ABD*, 5:870–86; D. G. Reid in *DNTB*, 1036–50; R. E. Averbeck in *DOTP*, 706–33.)   A. F. RAINEY

sacrilege. The KJV uses the expression "commit sacrilege" once to render the Greek verb *hierosyleō* G2644, which more probably means "to rob temples" (Rom. 2:22; cf. the noun *hierosylos* G2645 in Acts 19:37, and cognate terms in 2 Macc. 4:39; 13:6). In Roman law the term *sacrilegium* was applied to the removal of a sacred object from a sacred place, and carried severe penalties. Cicero wrote: "Let him be treated as a parricide who steals or carries off ought sacred or what is entrusted to a sacred person" (*Leg.* 2.9). The NRSV uses "sacrilege" to render *bdelygma* G1007 ("detestable thing"), but only in the expression "desolating sacrilege" (Matt. 24:15; Mk. 13:14); see ABOMINATION OF DESOLATION.

J. H. BRATT

Sadamias sad´uh-mi´uhs. KJV Apoc. variant of SHALLUM (2 Esd. 1:1).

Sadas say´duhs. KJV Apoc. variant of AZGAD (1 Esd. 5:13).

Saddeus sad´ee-uhs. KJV Apoc. variant of IDDO (1 Esd. 8:45).

saddle. A seat for riding an animal. Perhaps an early invention of the Persians, the saddle served both as a carriage for riders and as a covering to prevent the animal's back from chafing. The Hebrew noun *merkāb* H5323 is used in the former sense in Lev. 15:9, where the rule on uncleanness extends also to the "saddle" (KJV, NRSV), though the precise meaning of this term is uncertain. Ordinarily, as is indicated in the record of ABRAHAM's going up to Mount Moriah with ISAAC (Gen. 22:3) and of BALAAM's setting out to curse Israel (Num. 22:21), it was the donkey that was saddled (in both of these passages the verb *ḥābaš* H2502 is used). In one instance (Gen. 31:34), reference is made to the saddle (*kar* H4121) of a camel, probably a basket-like seat.

J. H. BRATT

Sadducee sad'joo-see (Σαδδουκαῖος G4881, derivation uncertain). A member of an important Jewish sect, more political than religious, which arose among the priestly aristocracy of the HASMONEAN period, but which ceased to exist with the demise of the aristocracy after the destruction of Jerusalem (A.D. 70). The Sadducees are perhaps today best known for their opposition to the popular party of the PHARISEES, with whom they differed on various doctrinal and political questions.

I. Name. The derivation of the name *Sadducee* has been the subject of considerable discussion but has not been established with any certainty. If one may bypass some of the more ingenious guesses (e.g., that it derives from the STOICS, or from the Persian word for "infidel," or from the hypothetical name of a now unknown person), there are left three significant possibilities.

(1) Since in Hebrew the name consists of the same three radicals (*ṣdq*) as the word for "righteousness," it has been argued that *Sadducees* means "righteous ones." This account, however, leaves unexplained the necessary vowel shift from the *i* of *ṣaddîq* H7404 ("righteous") to the *u* of *ṣĕdûqî* ("Sadducee"). Moreover, although this explanation of the name was accepted by certain of the early fathers of the church (cf. Epiphanius, *Panarion* 14.2.1), it is not at all clear in what sense "righteousness" could be attributed to, or even claimed by, the Sadducees as their distinguishing characteristic.

(2) An explanation that has gained popularity in modern times and is held by the majority of contemporary scholars, traces the word back to the proper noun *ṣādôq* H7401 (Gk. *Sadōk* G4882, sometimes spelled *Saddouk* in the LXX). *Sadducee* thereby becomes the equivalent of *Zadokite* ("descendant of Zadok"), the ZADOK in question being the descendant of AARON who became a leading priest under DAVID (2 Sam. 8:17; 15:24–29), and chief priest under SOLOMON (1 Ki. 1:32; 2:35). The priestly line begun by Zadok continued to the Babylonian EXILE and was reinstituted after the exile in the person of Joshua ben Jehozadak (Hag. 1:1; see JESHUA), coming to an end only when the unscrupulous ANTIOCHUS IV installed MENELAUS as high priest in 171 B.C. The line of authentic Zadokite priests nevertheless continued until around A.D. 70 at the rival sanctuary at Leontopolis in Egypt (cf. Jos. *Ant.* 13.3.1 §§65–73). The Zadok priesthood itself remained highly honored in Israel (cf. Ezek. 40:45–46; 44:15–16), as is evident from ECCLESIASTICUS (Sir. 51:12, Heb. [missing in the LXX]), and the writings of the QUMRAN Community (e.g., 1QS V).

Since in JOSEPHUS and the NT the Sadducees are closely associated with the high priesthood, it has been argued that the use of the name *Sadducee* was an attempt to legitimatize the Jerusalem priesthood by associating it with the line of Zadok. But, in point of fact, the Jerusalem priesthood of the Hasmonean period was manifestly not of Zadokite lineage, so that on the other hand it has been suggested that the use of *Sadducee* or *Zadokite* in referring to that priesthood could be derogatory—that is, an ironical reference to the disreputable (although legitimate) priesthood of the pre-Hasmonean era.

(It is, of course, not impossible that the name may trace back to a Zadok other than the high priestly Zadok. There is actually a late 9th-cent. rabbinic tradition, the *ʾAbot de Rabbi Nathan*, which derives *Sadducee* from an obscure Zadok of the 2nd cent. B.C. who was a disciple of Antigonus of Socoh. However, since a second disciple of Antigonus, a certain Boethus, is said by R. Nathan to have originated the sect known as the Boethusians, it is generally held that with respect to *Sadducee* the tradition is merely a late etymological guess. If the word is derived from the name Zadok, almost certainly it would go back to Zadok the high priest.)

(3) In light of the difficulty of using *Zadokite* to refer to a non-Zadokite priesthood, T. W. Manson (in *BJRL* 22 [1938]: 144–59) rejected the previous explanation and suggested in its place that the Aramaic/Hebrew word is a transliteration of the Greek word *syndikoi*, meaning "syndics, judges, fiscal controllers." The use of this term can be traced back to 4th cent. B.C. Athens. It came during the Roman period to refer to individuals having responsibilities and authority quite similar to that held by the Sadducees in Jerusalem (i.e., serving in somewhat of a mediatorial role between the Roman authorities and the local or national community). Thus the word was used also to refer to members of the Jewish senate, the SANHEDRIN. Besides avoiding the

major problem intrinsic to the previous explanation, Manson notes that his theory is more consistent with the fact that among the Sadducees were many laymen, for whom a priestly designation (such as *Zadokite*) would be meaningless. Thus the word is said by Manson to have originally denoted the "syndics" or Jewish officials of the Hasmonean era; the Sadducees themselves, however, may well have preferred the etymology which designated them as "righteous."

Looked at objectively, Manson's explanation seems to possess more plausibility than the first two proposals. Etymology, however, is often notoriously unpredictable, and it is thus easily possible that, even with their respective difficulties, one of the other explanations is really the correct one. It would seem safe to say that soon after the word achieved currency and its referent was established, its real etymology became unimportant (and may even have been forgotten), and that alternative etymological possibilities sprang readily to mind.

II. Origin and history. We are limited in our knowledge of the Sadducees to the indirect information Josephus provides, supplemented by what can be learned from the NT and the MISHNAH. Unfortunately, the precise origin of the Sadducees cannot be determined from these sources. The first mention of the Sadducees by Josephus (*Ant.* 3.5.9 §§171–73) refers to the period of Jonathan MACCABEE, successor to his brother Judas. He states, "At this time there were three sects among the Jews, who had different opinions concerning human actions: the one was called the sect of the Pharisees, another the sect of the Sadducees, and the other the sect of the Essenes." Something of the respective tenets of these three schools is given, but Josephus provides no account of their origin. Quite probably, however, the Sadducees or their precursors are to be identified with the aristocratic members of the early senate or Sanhedrin of Israel, which began prior to the Maccabean revolt and continued through the Hasmonean period.

Josephus next relates how the high priest John Hyrcanus (135–104 B.C.) was cajoled into transferring his allegiance and favor from the Pharisees to the Sadducees (*Ant.* 13.10.5–6 §§288–98). This is the apparent beginning of the close connection between the Sadducees and the high priesthood that continues into the NT period. A natural alliance between the two existed on the basis of the political interests of the aristocratic Sadducees and the eminent position of the Hasmonean princes. However, the privileged status which the Sadducees began now to enjoy was abruptly lost when Salome Alexandra, succeeding her husband Jannaeus as monarch (76 B.C.), acted upon his advice and granted considerable power to the Pharisees, who were so influential among the masses. See HASMONEAN II.

When Alexandra died (67 B.C.), her two sons quarreled over the succession. Aristobulus II, backed by the Sadducees, eventually won out over Hyrcanus II, the contender supported by the Pharisees. But Hyrcanus, at the instigation of Antipater, continued in a struggle for the crown that was brought to an end only by an appeal to Rome. POMPEY eventually invaded Jerusalem (63 B.C.) and installed Hyrcanus II as high priest by way of reward for his assistance. Much later (40 B.C.), the Sadducees were probably supporters of Antigonus, son of Aristobulus II, who succeeded in wresting the high priesthood from Hyrcanus II. When HEROD the Great captured Jerusalem three years later, he took vengeance on the "partisans of Antigonus" (Jos. *War* 1.18.4 §358; cf. *Ant.* 15.1.1 §2) who had opposed Hyrcanus II, among whom were doubtless a large number of Sadducees.

With Herod the standing of the Sadducees declined appreciably (cf. Jos. *Ant.* 14.9.4 §§171ff.). He diminished the power of the Sanhedrin and hereditary high priesthood with a disconnected succession of high priests of his own choosing. (Josephus counts, in the period of 107 years from Herod to the fall of Jerusalem, no less than 28 high priests, *Ant.* 20.10.5 §250.) Not only was the high priesthood as an institution degraded under Herod, but the Sadducees (who remained closely associated with the high priests) themselves suffered an increasing decline in the public opinion. The frequent linking of the Sadducees with the Boethusians—the high-priestly house of Boethus, appointed by Herod (cf. Jos. *Ant.* 15.9.3 §§320–22; 19.6.2 §§297–98)—attests to this low esteem of the Sadducees. (On the basis of ascriptions of legal rulings in the rabbinic literature, a recent analysis

Stone weight inscribed in Aramaic, found in the so-called Burnt House of Jerusalem, and bearing the name Bar Kathros. The Babylonian Talmud refers to "the house of Kathros" as a priestly family who probably belonged to the Sadducean party (b. Pesaḥim 57a).

has given fresh support to the view that the Sadducees and the Boethusians constituted one group. See E. Regev, *Ha-ṣeduqim ve-hilḥatam: ʿal dat ve-ḥevrah bi-yeme bayit sheni* [The Sadducees and Their Halakah: Religion and Society in the Second Temple Period, 2005].)

When in A.D. 6 JUDEA became a Roman province, the Sanhedrin, and with it the Sadducees and the high priest, were able to exercise more control in governing the country, but always of course under the watchful eye of the Roman governor. From this time onward the high priests were aristocratic Sadduceans, and the majority of the members of the Sanhedrin were Sadducees (cf. Acts 4:1; 5:17; Jos. *Ant*. 20.9.1 §199). Yet the Pharisees, though a minority in the Sanhedrin, were highly influential in that body because of their popularity with the masses. As Josephus puts it, "they accomplished nothing," having to go along with the Pharisees, "since otherwise the masses would not tolerate them" (*Ant*. 18.1.4 §17). With the fall of Jerusalem and the end of the second temple in A.D. 70, the Sadducees disappear from history. Their existence was inextricably tied to their political and priestly power, and when that came to an end they, unlike the Pharisees, were unable to survive.

III. Composition and character. The determinative trait of the Sadducean party seems not to have been its priestly associations, as is commonly believed, but rather its aristocratic character. While it is true that the high priesthood and the chief priests consisted almost exclusively of Sadducees, there were many Pharisees among the priests, and probably even among the upper priestly classes. More important, however, many Sadducees were to be found among the lay nobility who exercised important authority as members or "elders" of the Sanhedrin. Accordingly, that which was common to the Sadducees was not clerical status, but aristocratic eminence. It is natural then that the Sadducean circle was a very exclusive one, remaining closed to the populace as a whole. Josephus states that only a small number of people knew the doctrine of the Sadducees, that these were "men of the highest standing" (*Ant*. 18.1.5 §§16–17), and that the Sadducees had "the confidence of the wealthy alone" (13.10.6 §298).

It is unfortunate that the Sadducees have usually been understood only by way of their contrast to the Pharisees, for this has led to oversimplification and misunderstanding. Thus facile dichotomies have become popular, such as the view that the Sadducees represented the clergy and temple, but the Pharisees the laity and synagogue; that the Sadducees were the proponents and the Pharisees the resisters of hellenization; that the Pharisees were the urban bourgeoisie, the Sadducees the rural landowners; that the Pharisees were concerned with religion and the Sadducees with politics. It is undeniable that there is some truth in these various assertions, but none of these contrasts should be absolutized and made alone to account for the peculiar character of the Sadducees. The latter were what they were due to a subtle combination of many factors, in varying degree. The Pharisees and the Sadducees were clearly opposed on certain issues, yet the difference between them is usually not absolute.

The aristocratic makeup of the Sadducees, together with their power in the Sanhedrin and their control of the high priesthood, made it inevitable that their dominating interests should be political in nature. Their wealth and position on the one hand, and on the other hand the fact that their power was delegated to them by the Roman occupation, combine to account for the most outstanding trait of the Sadducees, their rigid conservatism. This conservatism, of course, was inevitably tempered by the dictates of the Romans. Since their political involvements were conditioned by their vested interests in the preservation of the status quo, it follows that they pursued policies designed to appease the governing authorities of Rome.

A sample of 1st-cent. ceremonial or priestly stone vessels unearthed in Jerusalem at the Burnt House.

Thus, paradoxically, the Sadducees were seen to be in line with the hellenizing tendencies of their predecessors, and the populace hated them for their accommodation to the Romans, based as it was on private expediency.

The primary concern of the Sadducees in all of this was to keep the nation peaceable and thereby to avoid trouble for the Romans and, in turn, themselves. In their administration of the internal justice of the country, the Sadducees were exceptionally strict in matters of law and order. Josephus refers to the party of the Sadducees as being "more heartless [*or* fierce; Gk. *ōmos*] than any of the other Jews when they sit in judgment" (*Ant.* 20.9.1 §199; in 13.10.6 §294 he refers to the Pharisees as being "naturally lenient in the matter of punishments" compared to the Sadducees). Similarly, any popular movement was a potential threat to the Sadducees, especially any that could be regarded as in any sense an "uprising." This accounts for their diligence in attempting to suppress the Christian movement by disposing of Jesus. The chief priests undoubtedly express the Sadducean viewpoint (which here coincided with that of the Pharisees) when they warn, "If we let him go on like this, everyone will believe in him, and then the Romans will come and take away both our place [*i.e.*, the temple] and our nation," to which CAIAPHAS the high priest, unwittingly prophetic, adds, "it is better for you that one man die for the people than that the whole nation perish" (Jn. 11:48–50).

As to their behavior in interpersonal relationships, Josephus says that they were far inferior to the Pharisees. While the latter were affectionate one to another and lived harmoniously, the Sadducees, he says, are "boorish," and with their "peers" (*tous homoiousi*) they are "as rude as to aliens" (*War* 2.8.14 §166). This has been seen by some as consonant with the sociological explanation of the Sadducees as crude, unpolished, provincial landowners (in contrast to the urbane Pharisees). To be sure, Josephus has a decidedly negative view of the Sadducees (whom he left to become a Pharisee), yet there are also some indications in the NT that the Sadducees were less than refined (cf. Matt. 26:67–68; Acts 23:2). Josephus also represents the Sadducees as inclined toward argumentation to the extent that they "reckon it a virtue to dispute" with their teachers (*Ant.* 18.1.4 §16), and probably Josephus means this in a derogatory sense. Thus the Sadducees, with all the advantages of higher culture that wealth brings, nonetheless were apparently lacking in the elements of refinement and decency that one usually tends to associate with the aristocracy.

The Sadducees, then, by virtue of their peculiar position, were preeminently concerned with politics and the stability of the state. But while these secular concerns were dominant, it cannot be denied that there was also a clearly religious aspect to the Sadducean viewpoint, and it especially is in the realm of their religious teaching that the conservatism of the Sadducees is apparent.

IV. Teaching. For the most part what we know of the religious teaching of the Sadducees we know only indirectly, that is, only in its negation of certain Pharisaic doctrines. The Sadducees, having rejected a great amount of the Pharisaic teaching as innovative, are properly seen as the conservative religious party; they appear to have regarded themselves as the stalwart guardians of the "pure faith" of the past. (Of course, from the point of view of modern "conservative" thought, the Sadducees appear "liberal," as in their rejection of the resurrection.)

Unquestionably the most important denial on the part of the Sadducees was that of the Pharisees' oral law, "the tradition of the elders" (see discussion under MISHNAH). Some scholars argue that this only states the obvious, namely, that the Sadducees were not Pharisees. However, understanding how the oral law functioned and why the Sadducees opposed it throws considerable light on the conflicts between these two groups. In particular, the Sadducees denied that the oral law of the Pharisees traced back to Moses and that it was authoritative and binding. Josephus gives explicit information on this point, informing us not only of the fact that the Sadducees abrogated the regulations of the Pharisees, but also giving the reason for this as the absence of these regulations from the "laws of Moses" (*Ant.* 13.10.6 §297). Josephus, indeed, seems to attribute the controversies and differences between the Pharisees and Sadducees to this fundamental disagreement. The Sadducees were probably in agreement with some parts of the oral law, but nonetheless rejected any suggestion that observance of the oral law was obligatory. With regard to matters not specified in the written law, the Sadducees seemed concerned to protect the right of private opinion. It may well be that behind this Sadducean viewpoint lay the vital concern of preserving the traditional priestly prerogative of interpreting the law, to which the Pharisaic structure of oral law posed no small threat.

To the Sadducean mind, the Pharisaic attempt to "build a hedge" around the Torah — i.e., to protect against transgression by detailed regulations — was mistaken and unnecessary. Indeed, the Sadducees seemed to perceive that such legal stipulation could have the effect of annulling the Mosaic law itself. Paradoxically, however, the Sadducees too had a tradition of "decrees" or interpretation of the law of Moses that was, in principle at least, indistinguishable from the HALAKAH, or legal tradition, of the Pharisees (cf. Matt. 16:12; *m. Makkot* 1:6). On the whole, the Sadducees appear to have interpreted the Mosaic law more literally than did the Pharisees. While they tended to scoff at the scrupulousness of the Pharisees, they themselves were very exacting in matters of Levitical PURITY, doubtless in keeping with their concern for the prestige of the priesthood and the temple ritual. Needless to say, however, the Pharisees regarded the Sadducees as sinners of the worst kind who by their immoral conduct prostituted the sacred ritual of the temple (cf. the Pharisaic PSALMS OF SOLOMON, where the "sinners" spoken of are to be identified with the Sadducees).

Turning to specific doctrinal beliefs of the Sadducees, one may begin by looking at what Josephus tells us of their view of free will and predestination (or Fate, as he calls it, using the Greek concept). Whereas the Pharisees apparently tried to synthesize the two, the ESSENES leaned to the one extreme of attributing all to Fate, while the Sadducees were at the other extreme of attributing all to free will. "They do away with Fate altogether" and throw everything back upon the free will and responsibility of man (*Ant.* 13.5.9 §173; *War* 2.8.14 §164). For the Sadducees a person's own decision accounted for his well-being or misfortune. This belief of the Sadducees has rightly been taken as implying a certain feeling of self-sufficiency on their part and a repudiation of any dependence upon divine PROVIDENCE.

A second negation further removed from God any effective relevance by arguing that there is no RESURRECTION of the dead, nor any future life whether of bliss or sorrow. For the Sadducean denial of the resurrection of the body, NT evidence is plentiful (cf. Mk. 12:18–27 and parallels; Acts 23:8; cf. 4:2). From Josephus we learn that the Sadducees believed that the SOUL perishes with the BODY (*Ant.* 18.1.4 §16) and therefore can receive neither penalties nor rewards in an afterlife (*War* 2.8.14 §165). It is immediately obvious how this denial intensified an already this-worldly perspective which the Sadducees had by virtue of their position. If a person must be content with the present life alone, he is bound to capitalize on any present advantages he may enjoy. And this appears, in fact, to have been the practical philosophy of the Sadducees. It may be added that the messianic hope appears to have played no role in the Sadducean perspective.

Along with the resurrection and the IMMORTALITY of the soul, the Sadducees appear to have rejected the belief in angels and demons. In contrast to the Pharisees, who held to these doctrines, the Sadducees, we are told, "say that there is no resurrection, and that there are neither angels nor spirits" (Acts 23:8). The idea of a spiritual world containing elaborate hierarchies of angels and demons flourished particularly in the intertestamental period. This probably gave the Sadducees a basis for rejecting such notions as innovative, although it must be admitted that angels and thus the spiritual world are encountered in the OT—even in the Pentateuch, which for the Sadducees was finally authoritative. See ANGEL; DEMON.

The doctrinal stance of the Sadducees as we have outlined it raises questions concerning their view of the Bible. Are not most of the doctrines the Sadducees rejected to be found within the OT? How then can we explain that the Sadducees rejected them? Confronted with this question, some of the early church fathers (e.g., Hippolytus, Origen, Jerome) concluded that for the Sadducees only the books of Moses were canonical Scripture. At the same period of time the SAMARITAN community held to a canon consisting exclusively of the Pentateuch. However, the Samaritans were only half-Jews, and it is difficult to believe that evidence of the Sadducees' rejection of the non-Mosaic writings would not have been noted either by Josephus or in the NT. Moreover, the church fathers may well have been speculating concerning the answer to the above questions.

A more probable solution would seem to lie along the following lines. The Sadducees accepted the CANON OF THE OT commonly received by the Jews, with the one reservation that the authority of the later writings was necessarily subordinate to that of the books of Moses. It was probably the allegedly immoderate development of specific doctrines in the intertestamental period that caused the Sadducees to overreact as they did in denying these doctrines altogether. Their final appeal was doubtless to the Pentateuch, but even here, as we have noted, they were inconsistent. Nor can we deny that their doctrinal views were tempered by the "common sense" of contemporary secular thought, such as it was, in the realms of REVELATION and ESCHATOLOGY. In their reactionary conservatism the Sadducees attempted to capitalize on their self-made image of themselves as the protectors of the pure and true religious tradition which alone went back to Moses.

V. Sadducees in the NT. The Sadducees are referred to by name only in the Synoptic Gospels and Acts, and then not very often. To these references may be added those places where the "chief priests" are mentioned, for these were surely of the Sadducean stripe. It must be admitted, however, that by comparison with the Pharisees, the Sadducees seem insignificant in the Gospels. This may be plausibly explained by considering several factors. In the first place, unlike the Sadducees, the Pharisees enjoyed the esteem of the masses and professed a special concern for righteousness as manifested in their careful allegiance to the oral law. This made them natural targets of Jesus. The Sadducees, on the other hand, had influence only among the aristocracy, a segment of society with which Jesus had little to do, and were mainly concerned with their political interests. The Sadducees were, moreover, restricted for the most part to Jerusalem, whereas the Gospels center on the Galilean ministry of Jesus.

Early in the gospel narratives, the Sadducees have almost no role to play. They do make an appearance along with the Pharisees at the Jordan, where John castigates them as a "brood of vipers" (Matt. 3:7), but they do not seem to have been particularly interested in the early ministry of Jesus. The next reference to the Sadducees in the chronology of the synoptics occurs when they, again accompanied by the Pharisees, ask Jesus for a "sign from heaven" (16:1). Just after this, Matthew records Jesus' warning concerning the "yeast of the Pharisees and Sadducees" (vv. 6, 11) which is "the teaching of the Pharisees and Sadducees" (v. 12). The word "Sadducees" does not occur in the parallels to this passage, although Mark does refer to "the yeast of the Pharisees and that of Herod" (Mk. 8:15), the latter quite probably referring to the Herodians, who would certainly appear analogous to the Sadducees in many ways. The Matthean passage should not be interpreted to mean that the teaching of the Pharisees was identical to that of the Sadducees. The warning concerns the teaching of each group, which was in its own peculiar way corrupt and contrary to the message of Jesus.

The most significant mention of Sadducees in the Gospels concerns an interview with Jesus in Jerusalem, at the end of his ministry, in which they tried to trap Jesus with a crafty question concerning the resurrection (Matt. 22:23–33; Mk. 12:18–27; Lk. 20:27–38). In his answer, Jesus accused them of knowing neither the Scriptures nor the power of God, and he then proceeded to cite the Pentateuch (Exod. 3.6) in support of the doctrine of the resurrection.

The Sadducees appear to have been unconcerned about Jesus early in his career. Only as it became clear that he posed a threat to their security and position (as in his cleansing of the temple; cf. Mk. 11:18) did they begin to become alarmed and decide to take action (cf. Jn. 11:47–53). Indeed, confronted with Jesus and his claims, the Sadducees were able to unite with the Pharisees, their traditional enemies, for the purpose of disposing of Jesus. Both parties collaborated in his arrest and "trial" by the Sanhedrin (Mk. 14:53–65).

The Sadducees were agitated by the preaching of the apostles in the early church. The book of Acts records that they arrested Peter and John for "proclaiming in Jesus the resurrection of the dead" (Acts 4:2). Some time later, the Sadducees were "filled with jealousy" at the abundance of signs and wonders wrought by the apostles and arrested them again (5:17). This action of the Sadducees is consistent with both their character and special interests. Josephus, indeed, implicates the Sadducees in the death of James, the half-brother of Jesus (*Ant.* 20.9.1 §§199–200; cf. Acts 12:1–2). The final reference to the Sadducees in Acts (and in the NT) occurs in the trial of Paul before the Sanhedrin, where in almost humorous fashion Paul is able to get the Pharisees and Sadducees into an intramural battle on the question of the resurrection, which brings the meeting to an end in a great clamor (Acts 23:6–10).

The NT evidence, while not of considerable extent, is nonetheless valuable in itself and consistent with the picture of the Sadducees that can be gleaned from the writings of Josephus. It may finally be remarked that the evidence of Jewish oral tradition as codified in the Mishnah and other rabbinic compilations tends on the whole to support that same picture, whether on the Saducean aversion to Pharisaic scruples (e.g., *m. Parah* 3:3; *Yadayim* 4:6–7) or concerning the question of life after death (e.g., *m. Berakot* 9:4). At the same time, the rabbinic literature must be used somewhat judiciously; produced from the later standpoint, it views the Sadducees as heretics and virtual enemies of Israel (cf. *m. ʿEruhin* 6:2; *m. Niddah* 4:2), and thus its references to the Sadducees often are highly polemical.

(See further W. O. E. Oesterley, *The Jews and Judaism During the Greek Period* [1941]; J. Z. Lauterbach, *Rabbinic Essays* [1951]; T. W. Manson, *The Servant-Messiah* [1953]; L. Finkelstein, *The Pharisees*, 2 vols. [1962]; B. Reicke, *The New Testament Era* [1968]; J. Jeremias, *Jerusalem in the Time of Jesus* [1969]; R. Meyer in *TDNT*, 7:35–54; J. Le Moyne, *Les sadducéens* [1972]; *HJP*, rev. ed. [1973–87], 2:404–14; G. G. Porton in *The Solomon Goldman Lectures*, 4 [1985]: 119–34; J. Neusner, ed., *The Pharisees and Other Sects*, 2 vols. [1990]; G. Stemberger, *Jewish Contemporaries of Jesus: Pharisees, Sadducees, Essenes* [1995]; A. J. Saldarini, *Pharisees, Scribes, and Sadducees in Palestinian Society: A Sociological Approach*, new ed. [2001]; H. Newman, *Proximity to Power and Jewish Sectarian Groups of the Ancient Period* [2006].) D. A. Hagner

sadhe sah´day. See TSADHE.

Sadoc say´dok. KJV NT form of ZADOK.

saffron. An aromatic plant used for producing condiment and perfume, and for other purposes. The Hebrew term *karkōm* H4137, used in the SONG OF SOLOMON to describe the bride (Cant. 4:14), could be Indian saffron (*Curcuma longa*) or crocus saffron (*Crocus sativus*), the latter name indicating the plant from which the flavoring powder is derived. Saffron comes from the upper end of the style of the flower. Over 4,000 crocus flowers are needed to produce 1 oz. of saffron. The flowers must be picked early, just as they start to open, and the pistils are then carefully removed. These are then dried in a portable kiln, so as to evaporate the moisture. In hot countries, the stigmas can be dried in the sun. The powder is used for flavoring cakes, stews, and curries. The plant is a native of Palestine and would have been known to SOLOMON. (See *FFB*, 174–75.) W. E. Shewell-Cooper

Sahidic version suh-hid′ik. See VERSIONS OF THE BIBLE, ANCIENT, IV.A.

sail. See SHIPS.

sailor. The Hebrew expression "men of ships" (*ʾanšê ʾŏniyyôt H408 + H641*) occurs once with reference to HIRAM's sailors who served in SOLOMON's fleet (1 Ki. 9:27). Otherwise, Hebrew uses the noun *mallāḥ H4876* to express the meaning "sailor, mariner" (Ezek. 27:9, 27, 29; Jon. 1:5; additional terms variously translated "oarsman, pilot, seaman, shipwright" are used in Ezek. 27:26–29). The NT uses the Greek noun *nautēs G3731* (Acts 27:27, 30; Rev. 18:17; the latter verse includes other related terms). The Acts passage contains the most graphic maritime account in Scripture: a record of PAUL's voyage to Rome when the sailors conspired to desert the ship and were forcibly dissuaded by Paul and the centurion. See also PILOT; SHIPS.

saint. A person sacred to God; the term is applied to members of the Jewish and Christian congregations. This English word is used to render several terms. One of them is the Hebrew adjective *qādôš H7705* (Aram. *qaddîš H10620*), which means "set apart, consecrated, holy." When the plural is used substantivally, it is translated "holy ones" or "saints" (Ps. 16:3 et al.; Aram., Dan. 7:18 et al.). The focus of this term is on the CONSECRATION of the subject involved rather than upon moral purity. Of course, all things and people consecrated to God are ideally to be free from moral and ceremonial defilement. God himself is the thrice-holy One (Isa. 6:3). See further HOLINESS.

Another Hebrew word, *ḥāsîd H2883*, has stronger moral overtones ("faithful, pious, godly, kind"). Related to *ḥesed H2876* (see LOVINGKINDNESS; MERCY), it is never applied to objects used in worship, but only to people (twice to God). The Psalms use the term with special frequency (e.g., Ps. 30:4). In the intertestamental period it was applied to a strictly orthodox party that may have become the precursors of the PHARISEES (see HASIDEAN; MACCABEE).

In the NT the adjective *hagios G41*, when used as a noun, usually refers to members of the Christian church. It is used once in the Gospels (Matt. 27:52) of the saints of the former age. The other references are in Acts, the Epistles, and Revelation. *All* believers are called "saints," even when their character is dubiously holy. The term is applied usually to the group of Christians constituting a church, rather than to one individual Christian (e.g., Acts 9:13; Rom. 8:27; Rev. 5:8). The reference is to those who belong to God as his own. In some instances, however, their saintly character becomes prominent (e.g., Rom. 16:2; Eph. 5:3).

It is easy to see how the term *saints* would inevitably take on an ethical and moral meaning. If a person belonged to Christ, showed Christian character by an exemplary life, and made notable progress in sanctification, so that his or her reputation as a good, moral, and spiritual Christian became widely spread among the churches, people would begin to speak of that person's exceptional "saintly" character. In that way the term would gradually be used only of such persons who were outstanding in spirituality.

That is probably the origin of the Roman Catholic custom of restricting the usage of the term to notable persons like the apostles and those whom the church selected and honored officially as "saints." The fact that most Christians still have sinful characteristics, even though they are genuine Christians, would cause the church gradually to withhold the term from ordinary Christians and apply it only to such especially spiritual individuals. Even the restriction of the use of the term to those whom the church hierarchy selected can be explained by the difficulty of selecting the best individuals to whom it could be applied. There would have to be a final authority to decide such a selection, and during the lifetime of those who knew the saint personally, it would be difficult to cover up minor defects of character. That is probably the reason why people must be dead many years before they can even be considered by the Roman Catholic Church as suitable saintly material.

According to Roman Catholic theology, individuals can store up a reservoir of merit by good deeds and blameless lives. That reservoir becomes available to other humble Christians in answer to prayers offered to the saint. Those who feel themselves particularly in need of merit would then pray to the saint for help and merit.

The worship of the saints would easily develop from such a doctrine. If a saint could really give his or her merit to any person, would not that saint be likely to give special favor to those who burned candles and brought special offerings to the saint? Would not the saint be more likely to give greater favors to those who brought better offerings? Gradually prayers and petitions would be offered almost exclusively to the saint, and the honor and worship which belongs to God alone would be transferred almost exclusively to the alleged saint. Because of the danger of such a situation arising, one can readily understand why God forbade all PRAYERS and WORSHIP to anyone but to God himself. All so-called "aids to worship" have that danger intrinsic in them.

Among Protestants today, the word *saints* has almost totally lost its original denotation, that is, of being set aside for the exclusive ownership and use of the Triune God. Very few people in the Christian church would consider themselves to be "saints," for the original meaning of the word, unfortunately, has largely fallen into disuse.

F. E. HAMILTON; R. L. HARRIS

Sakar say′kahr. TNIV form of SACAR.

Sakia suh-ki′uh (שְׂכְיָה H8499, possibly "Yahweh has fenced in"). KJV Shachiah; NRSV Sachia; NJPS Sachiah. Son of SHAHARAIM and descendant of BENJAMIN; a family head (1 Chr. 8:10; many Heb. mss have Sibya, reflected in LXX Sabia). Sakiah was one of seven children that were born to Shaharaim in MOAB by his wife HODESH after he had divorced Hushim and Baara (vv. 8–9).

Sakkuth sak′uhth. Also Sikkuth. This name is used by some versions to represent the Hebrew word *sikkût* in Amos 5:26: "You shall take up Sakkuth your king, and Kaiwan your star-god" (NRSV). Such a rendering assumes that the Hebrew term is a loanword from Akkadian *sakkud*, and it is often thought that both this name and Kaiwan are references to the planet Saturn as a deity. The evidence for this interpretation, however, is not strong (see bibliographical refs. under KAIWAN and cf. *DDD*, 722–23). Accordingly, the NIV understands the word as a form of *sukkâ* H6109, "tent, tabernacle"

(cf. also *skēnē* G5008 in LXX, quoted in Acts 7:43; and among the DSS see CD VII, 14–16), yielding the translation, "You have lifted up the shrine of your king, the pedestal of your idols." See also REPHAN.

Sala say′luh. (1) KJV NT form of SHELAH.

(2) NT variant of Salmon; see SALMA, SALMON.

Salah say′luh. KJV form of SHELAH.

Salamiel suh-lay′mee-uhl (Σαλαμιήλ). Son of Sarasadai and ancestor of JUDITH (Jdt. 8:1; KJV, "Samael"). The reference is probably to SHELUMIEL (Num. 1:6 et al.).

Salamis sal′uh-mis (Σαλαμίς G4887). A harbor on the E coast of the island of CYPRUS. The ancient site, N of modern Famagusta, has been completely silted in by the River Pedias. According to Greek mythology it was founded after the Trojan war by Teucer (son of Telamon), who was from the island of Salamis near ATHENS. However, there is archaeological evidence of an earlier Mycenean settlement. It traded actively with Phoenicia, Egypt, and other countries of the ANE. The sources of commerce were grain, wine, olive oil, and salt.

The city is mentioned as a tributary of ASHURBANIPAL of Assyria in 668 B.C. Assyrian influence

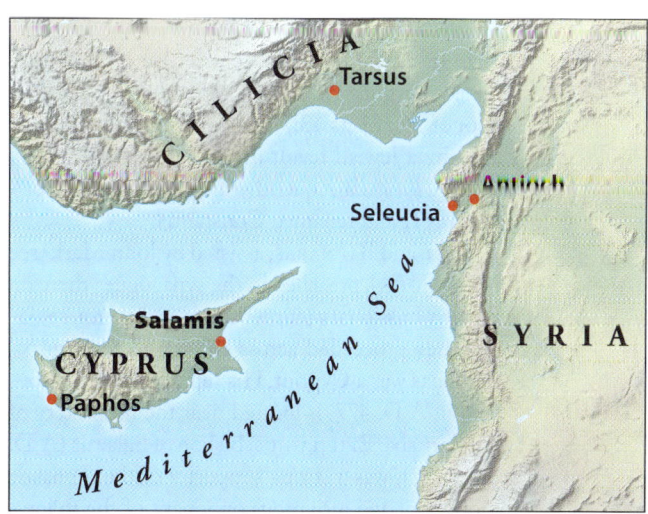

Salamis.

The civic center of the Roman city of Salamis. On the left is the wrestling ground of the gymnasium, with the theater on the right.

is evident from terra-cotta figures found on the site. Salamis took part in the revolt of the Ionian Greeks against Persia in the 5th and 4th centuries. Demetrius I Poliorcetes, in quest of all of Alexander's empire, defeated Menelaus, the brother of Ptolemy I, off Salamis in 306 B.C. The Egyptians recovered the island in 295, and a large number of Jews were encouraged by the Ptolemies to settle in the city.

The Romans annexed the island in 58 B.C. in repayment for loans made to Ptolemy Auletes. At first, Cyprus was part of the province of CILICIA, but in 31 B.C. it became a separate imperial province. In 22 B.C. it became a senatorial province; hence, Sergius PAULUS is correctly identified as PROCONSUL (Acts 13:7). Salamis was greatly damaged by a Jewish revolt in A.D. 116–117 and by earthquakes; subsequently, it was rebuilt by Constantius II and renamed Constantia.

PAUL and BARNABAS, assisted by John Mark (see MARK, JOHN), preached in the synagogues there on the first missionary journey (Acts 13:5). From Salamis they proceeded across the island to PAPHOS. Barnabas was a Cypriot. His reputed tomb, discovered in A.D. 477, is located near the monastery of Ail Barnaba. EPIPHANIUS, bishop of Salamis (A.D. 367–402), was a strong supporter of the monastic movement and a rigorous opponent of the followers of ORIGEN.   A. RUPPRECHT

Salasadai sal´uh-sad´i. KJV Apoc. form of SARASADAI (Jdt. 8:1).

Salathiel, Salatiel suh-lay´thee-uhl, -tee-uhl. See SHEALTIEL.

Salcah, Salchah sal´kuh. KJV forms of SALECAH.

Salecah sal´kuh (סַלְכָה H6146, derivation unknown). KJV Salcah and Salchah; TNIV Salekah. A town that defined the eastward extent of BASHAN (Deut. 3:10; Josh. 12:5; 13:11; 1 Chr. 5:11). Taken from King OG, Salecah was apparently assigned to the eastern part of MANASSEH (Josh. 13:29–31), but was later inhabited by Gadites (1 Chr. 5:11) see GAD, TRIBE OF. Its identification is not certain. A suitable site with a similar name is modern Salkhad (the name is not etymologically equivalent, however; cf. Nabatean ṣlḥd, Arabic Ṣalḥad). Located on an extinct volcanic cone 8 mi. S of Jebel ed-Druze, this site controls the SE approach to the fertile HAURAN Valley (biblical Bashan), the southern approaches to DAMASCUS, and the western end of the desert route to the Persian Gulf. The old E-W Roman road is still visible. Its location and importance make it the proper eastern extremity of Bashan. The chief remains are those of the citadel, the present form of which is Ayyubid although some elements are Roman. Coins of ARETAS, king of the NABATEANS (9 B.C. TO A.D. 40), also have been found there. A. BOWLING

Salem say′luhm (שָׁלֵם *H8970*, "complete, safe"). An abbreviated form of JERUSALEM. Though occurring only four times in Scripture, Salem is the city's first designation (Gen. 14:18) and, along with ZION, identifies the place of God's dwelling (Ps. 76:2). The title given to MELCHIZEDEK, king of Salem (Heb. 7:1), is understood by the writer of Hebrews as "king of peace" (v. 2), in its sense of security, prosperity, and well-being (see PEACE). The name Salem/Shalem may also have connoted to Jerusalem's original Jebusite inhabitants (see JEBUS) a "prospering" Canaanite deity of that name (see *ABD*, 5:1152–53; *DDD*, 755–57).

In Gen. 33:18 the LXX renders Hebrew *šālēm H8969* (prob. meaning "safely") as a proper name (*Salēm*; cf. also Vulg. and Syr., as well as KJV's SHALEM). On that basis, some have associated Salem with SHECHEM (see SALIM; the reference to the "valley of Salem" in Jdt. 4:4 is unclear). In addition, a few scholars have either emended Gen. 14:18 or interpreted the name there as a common noun, yielding such translations as "a king allied with him" or "a submissive king" (see discussion in H. Vincent, *Jérusalem de l'Ancien Testament* [1956], 2:612–13; *HALOT*, 4:1539). J. B. PAYNE

Salim say′lim (Σαλίμ *G4890*, also Σαλείμ, prob. from Heb. שָׁלֵם *H8970* [see SALEM]). A place used to specify the location of AENEON, where JOHN THE BAPTIST was baptizing (Jn. 3:23). Salim must have been a well-known site, but it has not been identified with certainty. Three suggestions merit discussion: (1) EUSEBIUS (*Onom.* 40, followed by JEROME) located it at Salumias c. 7.5 mi. SSE of Scythopolis (BETH SHAN). Salumias is probably modern Tell er-Radghah (Tell Sheikh es-Selim), and there are several springs nearby, next to the ruins of Umm el-ʿAmdan. This territory could well have been part of the DECAPOLIS rather than part of SAMARIA. (2) W. F. Albright (*The Archaeology of Palestine*, rev. ed. [1960], 247) suggests the well-known site of Salim that is a few miles E of Nablus (ancient SHECHEM). This is the town nearest to the springs of Wadi Farʿa (Farah), though some have argued that John was unlikely to minister in Samaria. (3) Another proposal is Wadi Saleim, only about 6 mi. NE of Jerusalem (cf. *IDB*, 4:166), but this identification has not gained favor. A. BOWLING

Sallai sal′*i* (סַלַּי *H6144*, meaning uncertain). (1) One of the leaders from Benjamin who volunteered to settle in Jerusalem after the return from the Exile (Neh. 11:8). The Hebrew text is difficult; see discussion under GABBAI.

(2) See SALLU #2.

Sallu sal′oo (סַלּוּא *H6132* [Neh. 11:7], סַלּוּ *H6139* [Neh. 12:7], סָלוּא [1 Chr. 9:7]; possibly "[God] has returned [*or* restored]"; see SALU). (1) Son of MESHULLAM, mentioned in a list of Benjamites who resettled in Jerusalem after the EXILE (1 Chr. 9:7; Neh. 11:7). It is possible that Sallu was a family name rather than the name of an individual.

(2) A priest who returned with ZERUBBABEL from the exile (Neh. 12:7). Later, in the days of the high priest JOIAKIM, the head of Sallu's family was Kallai (v. 20, where most versions, following the MT, read "Sallai," an alternate form or a textual corruption).

Sallumus sal′uh-muhs. KJV Apoc. form of SHALLUM (1 Esd. 9:25).

Salma, Salmon sal′muh, sal′muhn (שַׂלְמָא *H8514* [1 Chr. 2:11, 51, 54], שַׂלְמָה [Ruth 4:20], שַׂלְמוֹן *H8517* [Ruth 4:21], all of these alternate spellings possibly meaning "mantle" or "spark", Σαλμών *G4891* [Matt. 1:4–5], Σαλά [Lk. 3:32]). (1) Son of HUR, grandson of CALEB, and descendant of JUDAH; he is described as the "father" (i.e., founder) of BETHLEHEM and as the ancestor of several important clans (1 Chr. 2:51, 54).

(2) Son of Nahshon and father of BOAZ (Ruth 4:20–21); included in the GENEALOGY OF JESUS CHRIST (Matt. 1:4–5; Lk. 3:32 [NRSV, "Sala"]). S. BARABAS

Salmai sal′mi. See SHALMAI.

Salmon. See SALMA, SALMON.

Salmone sal-moh′nee (Σαλμώνη *G4892*; outside the NT spelled variously, Σαλμώνιον, Σαμμώνιον, etc.). A promontory, now called Cape Sidero, constituting the most easterly portion of CRETE. When PAUL and company boarded ship at MYRA in LYCIA, they had to cope with strong northwesterly winds. Hugging the shore, they reached CNIDUS in SW ASIA MINOR with some difficulty. There the land protection ceased. It would have been possible to lie at anchor in their harbor awaiting a fair wind, but because of their urgent desire to reach ROME the only course was to tack to the S and sail "to the lee of Crete, opposite Salmone" (Acts 27:7). Luke added, "We moved along the coast with difficulty and came to a place called Fair Havens, near the town of Lasea" (v. 8).   J. H. BRATT

Salom say′luhm. KJV Apoc. form of SHALLUM (Bar. 1:7) and SALU (1 Macc. 2:26).

Salome suh-loh′mee (Σαλώμη G4897, possibly "peaceful"). **(1)** One of the women who followed and ministered to Jesus in GALILEE, were witnesses to the CRUCIFIXION, and afterwards went to the tomb to anoint his body (Mk. 15:40–41; 16:1). A comparison between these passages and Matt. 27:56 identifies her as the wife of ZEBEDEE, and therefore mother of James and John (see JAMES I; JOHN THE APOSTLE). Her request for prominence for her sons in the kingdom was rebuked by the Lord and drew the indignation of the other disciples (Matt. 20:20–24; Mk. 10:35–41). Many infer from Jn. 19:25 that she was the sister of MARY, MOTHER OF JESUS, but others take the phrase "his mother's sister" as a reference to "Mary the wife of Clopas" which follows.

(2) The daughter of HERODIAS and Herod Philip (Jos. *Ant.* 18.5.4 §§136–37); her name is not given in the Gospels. Because her dancing before Herod Antipas, her father's half-brother, pleased him so much, he promised to grant her whatever request she might make. Prompted by her mother, she asked for the head of JOHN THE BAPTIST, who had rebuked the marriage of Herodias and Antipas (Matt. 14:3–11; Mk. 6:16–28). See discussion under HEROD V.B.2. Salome became wife first to her uncle Philip, tetrarch of Traconitis (Lk. 3:1, not to be confused with Herod Philip), and then to her cousin Aristobulus, son of Herod king of Chalcis.   A. M. ROSS

salt. A white, crystalline compound known chemically as sodium chloride. Found in great quantity in the DEAD SEA area and purchased by the Jews from traders in the N, salt served various purposes. It was used as a condiment to season food for humans (Job 6:6) and beasts (Isa. 30:24), and to preserve it from putrefaction (Exod. 30:35). It was the mandatory accompaniment of some of the SACRIFICES, notably the grain (Lev. 2:13) and burnt offerings (Ezek. 43:24). Because of its medicinal values, newborn babies were bathed in it and rubbed with it (16:4). That it was regarded as of great value is indicated by its inclusion with WINE and OIL as the basic staples of life (cf. Jos. *Ant.* 12.3.3 §140). It may also have served a destructive purpose: when ABIMELECH captured SHECHEM, he sowed the ground with salt as punishment on them (Jdg. 9:45; cf. the Romans' treatment of Carthage). It is possible, however, that this simply indicated the placement of a ban upon them or that it symbolized desolation.

The figurative usage is indeed common. On the one hand, heaps and pits of salt conveyed the picture of barrenness and sterility (Deut. 29:23; Ps. 107:34; Zeph. 2:9). On the other hand, salt symbolized the valuable and the virtuous. A pact of friendship was sealed with the gift of salt (still observed by Arabs today), and the agreement between God and his people was termed a COVENANT OF SALT (Num. 18:19; 2 Chr. 13:5), salt being emblematic of loyalty and perpetuity. In the SERMON ON THE MOUNT the Lord implies the wholesomeness and vitality of Christians when he calls them "the salt of the earth" (Matt. 5:13). The idea of purification is prominent in Mk. 9:49, where the Lord says that in the final judgment "everyone will be salted with fire." The apostle PAUL urges wisdom, prudence, and wholesomeness in the Christian's conversation when he says, "Let your conversation be always full of grace, seasoned with salt, so that you may know how to answer everyone" (Col. 4:6).   J. H. BRATT

Salt, City of (עִיר־הַמֶּלַח H6551 + H4875). One of six cities allotted to JUDAH in the desert (Josh. 15:62). Four of these—MIDDIN, SECACAH, NIBSHAN, and the City of Salt—are often identified with four Iron II settlements in el-Buqeʿah, a valley SW of JERICHO (see ACHOR), and many have thought that the City of Salt in particular is the same as Khirbet QUMRAN (though some recent writers believe that Qumran should rather be identified with Secacah; cf. Z. Kallai, *Historical Geography of the Bible* [1986], 396 n. 143). Alternate proposals include ʿAin el-Ghuweir (c. 9 mi. S of Qumran) and even Tell el-Milḥ (much farther away, c. 14 mi. SE of BEERSHEBA; but see MOLADAH). It should be noted that the LXX (according to CODEX VATICANUS) identified the City of Salt with SODOM, and that a variant reading (in CODEX ALEXANDRINUS, prob. a secondary adjustment of the Greek to the MT) renders "the cities of salt(s)," which may also be a reference to the CITIES OF THE PLAIN. (For further discussion, see F. M. Cross, Jr., and J. T. Malik in *BASOR* 142 [April 1956]: 5–17; P. Bar-Adon in *BASOR* 227 [Oct. 1977]: 1–25; H. Eshel in *IEJ* 45 [1995]: 37–40.)   A. BOWLING

salt, covenant of. See COVENANT OF SALT.

Salt, Valley of (גֵּיא־מֶלַח H1628 + H4875). The scene of two important victories of the Israelite armies over EDOM. The first was when DAVID's army, led by ABISHAI, slew 18,000 Edomites (1 Chr. 18:12; in the parallel passage, 2 Sam. 8:13, which does not mention Abishai, the KJV says "Syrians" [i.e., Arameans], following the MT reading, ʾărām; the title of Ps. 60, probably a late addition to the text, speaks of 12,000 men and attributes the victory to JOAB). The other victory occurred two centuries later when AMAZIAH, king of Judah, slew 10,000 Edomites in the Valley of Salt, captured and slew another 10,000, and then took their capital SELA (2 Ki. 14:7; 2 Chr. 25:11), thus reversing the independence the Edomites had won earlier upon the death of JEHOSHAPHAT.

The exact location of the Valley of Salt is disputed. Wadi el-Milḥ (salt), to the S of BEERSHEBA, which flows by the foot of Tell el-Milḥ, has been suggested because of the similarity of names. Because that area lay outside Edomite territory, others have proposed es-Sebkha, S of the Dead Sea, a barren saline area. Still another proposal is GE HARASHIM, but the location of this valley is also uncertain.   F. B. HUEY, JR.

Salthas sal´thuhs (Σαλθας). One of the descendants of Pashhur who agreed to put away their foreign wives (1 Esd. 9:22 [KJV, "Talsas"; RSV, "Elasah"]; the parallel in Ezra 10:22 reads "Elasah").

Salt Sea. See DEAD SEA.

Salu say´loo (סָלוּא H6140, possibly "[God] has returned [or restored]"; see SALLU). Father of ZIMRI; the latter was a leader in the tribe of SIMEON who took a Midianite woman and was killed by PHINEHAS (Num. 25:14; 1 Macc. 2:26 [KJV, "Salom"]).

Salum say´luhm. KJV Apoc. form of SHALLUM (1 Esd. 5:28; 8:1).

salutation. This English term is used by the KJV seven times to render the Greek noun *aspasmos* (G833), "greeting" (Mk. 12:38 et al.; in the three other passages where this Gk. word occurs [Matt. 23:7, Lk. 11:43; 20:46], the KJV has "greetings"). See GREET. In biblical studies, the English word is used primarily to designate the opening greeting in an EPISTLE.

salvation. Deliverance from the power and consequences of sin; a central doctrine in the Bible and in Christian theology.

    I. The need for salvation
        A. Sin
        B. Guilt
        C. Estrangement
   II. The nature of salvation
        A. Biblical terms
        B. Biblical categories
        C. The necessity of the atonement
        D. Theories of the atonement
        E. The extent of the atonement
  III. The accomplishment of salvation
        A. The divine elective purpose
        B. Christ's redemptive work
  IV. The application of salvation
        A. *Ordo salutis*
        B. Calling
        C. Regeneration
        D. Conversion
        E. Justification
        F. Adoption
        G. Sanctification
        H. Perseverance
        I. Glorification

SALVATION

I. The need for salvation

A. Sin. According to the Genesis account, God at the CREATION entered into a COVENANT in which ADAM and EVE, by following the pathway of OBEDIENCE, might rise to a confirmed state of HOLINESS; whereas, should they choose to disobey, they would then fall to enslavement under SIN. Obedience would lead to eternal LIFE in communion with God; disobedience would bring DEATH and SLAVERY. The positive dimension of this covenant is to be inferred from the Scripture, whereas the negative side is explicit.

As Gen. 3 makes clear, the creatures chose to disobey the Creator. When confronted with the serpent, Eve succumbed to the challenge to assert her independence from God. She endeavored to deify herself and dethrone God. PRIDE is the essence of sin! Sin is not only "any want of conformity unto, or transgression of, the law of God" (*Westminster Shorter Catechism*, Q. 14); it is also, and perhaps even more fundamentally, the breakdown of our personal relationship with our Creator. When we disobey a command of God we offend the loving and holy One who as the absolute Spirit Person sustains all life.

In Adam all sinned (Rom. 5:12). The apostle PAUL establishes the universal condemnation of all human beings because of their sinning. All, whether Gentile or Jew, have sinned and are failing to reflect the glory of that original impress of the IMAGE OF GOD (3:23).

War, as depicted on this large Greek podium frieze (5th–4th cent. B.C.), attests to the reality of sin and death in the world and thus the need for spiritual deliverance.

© James C. Martin. The British Museum. Photographed by permission.

B. Guilt. Because of sin, human beings are deserving of God's judgment. After establishing from Ps. 14 that Jews and Gentiles are alike under the power of sin, Paul states, "Now we know that whatever the law says, it says to those who are under the law, so that every mouth may be silenced and the whole world held accountable to God" (Rom. 3:19). In theological language GUILT means liability to punishment on account of sin; it means to be answerable to God for contradicting his holiness. Guilt must not be confused with moral pollution nor with mere demerit. For various reasons one may feel guilty when there is neither pollution nor personal demerit. Likewise one may not feel guilty where both exist.

The sense of guilt for disobeying God is immediately evident in the account of the FALL. After Adam and Eve had taken of the forbidden fruit, we learn of their vain effort to hide from God. A sense of SHAME compelled them to flee from their Creator. Men and women in their fallen condition have been doing this down through the entire course of human history. But all people exist in a responsible relationship to their Creator, and if they do not fulfill this responsibility in loving obedience to him through faith in Jesus Christ, then only judgment and the second death await them.

C. Estrangement. Because of sin, the human predicament may be described as one in which sinners find themselves the victims of anxiety, dread, despair, frustration, alienation, absurdity, meaninglessness, and estrangement. They have cut themselves off from God, their fellow human beings, and themselves. In this situation people either seek to make meaning by deifying themselves (humanism) or they abandon any hope of discovering meaning (nihilism). Evidences of estrangement from God, others, and even oneself scream at us in contemporary art forms—literature, music, painting, sculpture, architecture, drama, motion pictures.

II. The nature of salvation

A. Biblical terms. The primary Hebrew word for "salvation" is *yĕšûʿâ* H3802 (Exod. 15:2 et al.), from the verb *yāšaʿ* H3828, which in the hiphil stem means "to help, save" (Exod. 14:30 et al.). Other cognates are the nouns *yēšaʿ* H3829, *môšāʿâ* H4636 (only Ps. 68:20), *môšiaʿ* H4635 ("savior"), and *tĕšûʿâ* H9591 ("deliverance, victory"). An understanding of this OT word group is imperative to appreciate what is implied in Matthew's statement concerning the meaning of the name Jesus (Matt. 1:21; from *yĕhôšuaʿ* H3397, "Yahweh is salvation"). The usage of these terms discloses the following important concepts as integral to the overall meaning of salvation (see further *NIDOTTE*, 2:556–62).

(1) In the majority of OT references salvation is seen to be the work of a sovereign God (Isa. 43:11). It is Yahweh who saves his people from Egypt (Ps. 106:7–10); from Babylon (Jer. 30:10); from trouble (Jer. 14:8). See also 2 Sam. 22:3; Isa. 43:3; Ezek. 34:22; Hos. 1:7; 13:10–14 et al.

(2) Salvation is accomplished in history. The first occurrence of the verb with reference to God is found in Exod. 14:30, which summarizes Israel's deliverance from Egyptian bondage: "That day the Lord saved Israel from the hands of the Egyptians." This national deliverance made the deepest impression on the Hebrew mind, an impression which was to be maintained by the annual Passover feast (Deut. 16:1). This deliverance of Israel from Egypt is the supreme OT sign of Yahweh's saving grace. It pointed beyond itself to that central saving event of history, the coming of Jesus Christ. It is most significant that Luke describes the decisive victory of Christ over Satan in terms of a new exodus (Lk. 9:31, where the word "departure" translates Gk. *exodos* G2016).

(3) Salvation is deliverance from enemies. Among these enemies were death and its fear (Pss. 6:4–5; 107:13–14); the lion's mouth (Ps. 22:21); the battlefield (Deut. 20:4); the wicked (Ps. 59:2); sickness (Isa. 38:21); trouble (Jer. 30:7); and sins (Ps. 51:14; 130:8; Ezek. 36:29). In OT times God was conceived to be the Savior from all foes, both spiritual and physical.

(4) Salvation is deliverance to the Lord. Yahweh not only delivered his people from that which would destroy them but he also brought them to himself. His salvation was not merely a rescue from a dangerous situation but it was also a rescue for a special purpose: that those rescued should worship, praise, and glorify him through lives dedicated to obeying him in all of life (1 Chr. 16:23; Isa. 43:11–12; 49:6–7; Zech. 8:13). A unique feature of the OT concept of salvation, as compared to the pagan religions of that time, is the fact that it was understood as the prerequisite, rather than simply the goal, of obedience. The order is well expressed by the psalmist, "I cry to you; save me, / that I may observe your decrees" (Ps. 119:146 NRSV). The entire Bible makes it very clear that the imperative of *do* for sinners is based upon the indicative of *done* by God.

(5) Salvation is appropriated solely by faith in God apart from any reliance upon supposed merit or human effort. This was true salvation both on a national and individual scale (Pss. 44:3; 55:16; 86:2; 138:7 et al.).

The Greek noun *sōtēria* G5401 is used frequently in the LXX as the equivalent of *yēšaʿ*, denoting the saving power of God in the crises of history nationally and in the people of God individually. This saving grace is further seen not to be confined to this age but also to anticipate the future, and it causes those who have experienced it to rejoice and glorify their Creator. In the NT this Greek word can be used of deliverance from enemies (Lk. 1:69, 71; Acts 7:25; Jude 25) and of bodily health and safety (Acts 27:20, 34; Heb. 11:7), but the

Michelangelo's famous *Pietà*; this marble sculpture at St. Peter's Church in Rome depicts Mary holding Jesus after the crucifixion.

distinctive use is in respect to spiritual deliverance. Several important ideas emerge in this sphere (see further *NIDNTT*, 3:205–23).

(1) The whole initiative of salvation is with God. "For God did not appoint us to suffer wrath but to receive salvation through our Lord Jesus Christ" (1 Thess. 5:9; see also Jn. 3:16–17; 2 Thess. 2:13; 1 Tim. 1:15; 2 Tim. 1:9; Tit. 3:5; Rev. 7:10, 19.1).

(2) Jesus is the center of God's saving work; in no one else is there salvation (Acts 4:12; Heb. 2:10; 5:9). Without him and his work there is no *sōtēria*.

(3) Salvation in the NT sense of spiritual deliverance means a total salvation. God saves the sinner body and soul. Specifically, it includes salvation from physical illness (Matt. 9:21; Lk. 8:36), from lostness (Matt. 18:11; Lk. 19:10), from sin (Matt. 1:21), from wrath (Rom. 5:9).

(4) Salvation is eschatological. Although Christians begin to enjoy their salvation here and now, there is yet a time coming when they will realize it in all its fullness. That time will be at the SECOND COMING of Christ, a day when he will be enthroned as King of all the world (Rom. 13:11; 1 Cor. 5:5; 2 Tim. 4:18; Heb. 9:28; 1 Pet. 1:5; Rev. 12:10).

In summary, *sōtēria* is the rescue of fallen men and women through Christ from all that would ruin their soul in this life and in the life to come.

B. Biblical categories

1. General obedience. The concept of obedience is used of Christ with sufficient impact in the NT to be taken as a comprehensive characterization of his redeeming work (see OBEDIENCE OF CHRIST). Paul writes, "For just as through the disobedience of the one man the many were made sinners, so also through the obedience of the one man the many will be made righteous" (Rom. 5:19). Again, writing of Christ, he states, "And being found in appearance as a man, / he humbled himself / and became obedient to death — / even death on a cross!" (Phil. 2:8). The writer of the epistle to the Hebrews states, "Although he was a son, he learned obedience from what he suffered" (Heb. 5:8). Christ redeemed us by rendering a perfect obedience to the will of his Father. This he did by obeying all the demands of the law (moral, ceremonial, and civil) and by suffering its penal sanctions.

2. Specific. The NT employs four terms which when taken together give a most comprehensive portrayal of the saving work of the Triune God: SACRIFICE views salvation as the answer to the sinner's guilt; PROPITIATION views it as the answer to God's righteous wrath; RECONCILIATION refers to the removal of the ground of God's alienation from fallen human beings; and REDEMPTION speaks of a release from bondage to sin.

(1) *Sacrifice.* The Greek word *thysia* G2602, used almost thirty times in the NT, is squarely rooted in the OT. The most frequent single occurrence of the term in the NT is found in the book of Hebrews. The primary though not exclusive meaning of the term in Scripture is that of an expiation of guilt, that is, ATONEMENT. (See esp. Heb. 5:1; 7:27; 8:3; 9:9, 23, 26; 10:1, 5, 8, 11, 12, 26; 11:4; 13:15–16.)

(2) *Propitiation.* This English term is used three times by the KJV: in one instance it renders Greek *hilastērion* G2663 (Rom. 3:25 [NIV and NRSV, "sacrifice of atonement"]; the Gk. word also occurs in Heb. 9:5 with reference to the MERCY SEAT), and in the other two it translates *hilasmos* G2662 (1 Jn. 2:2; 4:10 [NIV and NRSV, "atoning sacrifice"]). The RSV has rendered all three texts with the word EXPIATION, which has a more restrictive meaning. It would appear that behind the use of the Greek terms there is the twofold sense of propitiation and expiation. The particular stress of the word is probably best taken as indicating God's diverting of his righteous WRATH from the sinner through the atoning work of his Son. Propitiation does not imply that the Son had to win over an incensed Father to an expression of love toward us; rather, it was precisely because of his eternal love that the Father sent his Son to be the propitiation for our sins.

(3) *Reconciliation.* The Greek verb *katallassō* G2904 and its cognates (noun *katallagē* G2903 and compound verb *apokatallassō* G639) are used in several Pauline passages (Rom. 5:10–11; 11:15; 1 Cor. 7:11 [of marriage]; 2 Cor. 5:18–20; Eph. 2:16; Col. 1:20–22). Reconciliation was a work of God in Christ whereby he removed the ground of his holy alienation toward sinners and thus did not impute their sins against them. The subjective change of the sinner's attitude toward God is a result of the historical event of the cross, the objective work of reconciliation accomplished by Christ.

(4) *Redemption.* This term (Gk. verb *lytroō* G3390 and various cognates; also *agorazō* G60) speaks the language of purchase and ransom. Redemption is the securing of a release by the payment of a price. In the theological sense, redemption means the release from sin through the shed blood of Christ. Redemption from sin embraces the several aspects from which sin is to be viewed scripturally: (1) redemption from its guilt (Rom. 3:24); (2) redemption from its power (Tit. 2:14); (3) redemption from its presence (Rom. 8:23).

C. The necessity of the atonement. There are two major views reflected in the historical development of theological thought. The hypothetical view maintains that God could have saved sinners without atonement. Other means were open to an all-powerful God, but he chose this means as the best for the accomplishment of his purpose. Two outstanding exponents of this view were Augustine and Aquinas. The second view holds to "consequent absolute necessity": God did not have to save anyone, but consequent upon the fact that he determined to do so, he had to do it by means of atonement. Prominent theologians holding this position include G. Smeaton, A. A. Hodges, and L. Berkhof.

D. Theories of the atonement

1. The ransom theory. This view goes back to the 3rd-cent. theologian ORIGEN. Sometimes termed the military theory, it argues that Christ paid a ransom to Satan for the deliverance of those who were his rightful captives. This position has been called the patristic theory inasmuch as it was held in one form or another by a number of the early church fathers.

2. The satisfaction theory. First formulated by Anselm (1033–1109), this view maintains that Christ's death provided full satisfaction for our sins and that his merit was more than equal to any obligation the sinner could possibly incur toward God. Christ's death was centrally conceived of as his voluntary discharge of the sinner's obligation to God.

3. The moral influence theory. Abelard (1079–1142) argued that the life and death of Christ was the supreme revelation of God's love calculated to awaken in the sinner a reciprocal love and gratitude. The response of love is then taken to be the basis of both justification and the forgiveness of sin.

4. The example theory. According to Socinus (1539–1604), Christ's death effected reconciliation by affording motives and encouragement to

Agora (market place) at Perga. One of the Greek words used for "redeem" is *agorazō*, based on the imagery of purchase at the market place.

the sinner to repent and believe. Christ's power to save is based on the import of his teaching and the influence of his example. Christ's death was simply that of a noble martyr.

5. The governmental theory. Grotius (1583–1645) proposed that Christ's death is an exhibition of divine regard for the law, though he did not suffer its precise penalty; God graciously accepted his suffering as a substitute for the penalty. The atonement is viewed as a satisfaction, not to any internal principle of the divine nature, but to the necessities of government.

6. The dramatic theory. Gustaf Aulén (1879–1977) maintained that the essence of Christ's work is to be seen in terms of liberation from the tyrants of sin, death, wrath, and the devil. Aulén argued that this was the view of the early fathers, subsequently lost by Anselm and medieval scholasticism but recaptured by Martin Luther.

7. The penal substitution theory. This view, represented for example by John Calvin (1509–64), maintains that Christ's death must be seen centrally in forensic terms: Christ suffered the penalty of sin as a substitute for the sinner. Penal substitution is central to the biblical teaching of atonement (Isa. 53:5–6; Rom. 5:6).

All the theories defined above have elements of truth, but none of them taken by itself provides a totally adequate explanation of the atonement. Christ by his death did make full satisfaction for our sins; he did by his death seek to evoke the love and gratitude of the believer, but not as a basis of acceptance before God. He did provide an example for believers to follow (Matt. 16:24; 1 Pet. 2:21–23). Most significantly however, he provided a substitute for us.

E. The extent of the atonement. The extent of the atonement is a matter about which there has been much controversy. There are three major views within what may be loosely called Protestantism.

1. Unrestricted universalism. This is the view that God purposed to save all (including angels, according to some who hold this view) by means of the death of Christ, and that in consequence all will be saved eventually, whether in this life or the afterlife. This position is reflected in ecumenical theology, but there is also an evangelical type of universalism.

2. Qualified universalism. According to this view, God planned to save all by the atonement, but all will not be saved because ultimately many fail to believe. This view is held mainly by Arminians.

3. Particularism. This view maintains that God purposed by the atonement to save only the elect and that in consequence only they are saved. Held by consistent Calvinists, this doctrine is often referred to as "limited atonement," but it is more correctly termed "particular redemption."

The specific issue of extent revolves around the question of the design or intent of the redeeming work of Christ, not that of its value. In *The Canons of the Synod of Dort* we read with respect to value: "The death of the Son of God is the only and most perfect sacrifice and satisfaction for sin; is of infinite worth and value, abundantly sufficient to expiate the sins of the whole world." With respect to intent the *Canons* state: "For this was the sovereign counsel and most gracious will and purpose of God the Father, that the quickening and saving efficacy of the most precious death of his Son should extend to all the elect."

III. The accomplishment of salvation

A. The divine elective purpose. Its basis of salvation is seen in God's eternal counsel—his elective purpose. There are three major views to be noted in respect to the doctrine of ELECTION.

1. The Arminian view. This view maintains that God elects on the basis of foreseen faith. According to Arminius (1560–1609), "This decree has its foundation in the foreknowledge of God, by which he knew from all eternity those individuals who *would*, through his preventing grace, *believe*, and, through his subsequent grace *would persevere*, according to the before described administration of those means which are suitable and proper for conversion and faith; and by which foreknowledge, he likewise knew those who *would not believe and persevere*" (*The Works of James Arminius*, 3 vols. [1872–75], 1:247).

Appeal for this position is made to such passages as Rom. 8:29–30 and 1 Pet. 1:1–2. It is further understood that God graciously grants to all people sufficient ability to accept Christ. In Arminian theology this is known as the doctrine of prevenient grace.

2. The Barthian view. According to this view election is, primarily, the election of Jesus Christ; secondly, the election of the community; and thirdly, the election of the individual. The first of these ideas is most important in Barth's development of the doctrine. Reconciliation in Christ can be understood only in terms of the mystery of God's decisive word of election in Christ, a word that respects *all* people. The miracle of God's electing grace is discovered in the fact that Jesus Christ is *at the same time* the electing God and the elect man. While it is necessary to speak of a double predestination, this may be done only in terms of the cross. All people of God whereby he chooses a certain number of people to be the recipients of saving grace according to his sovereign good pleasure, apart from any merit in the creature actual or foreseen.

Those who adopt this position appeal to such passages as Eph. 1:4–5 and Rom. 8:28–30. In the former passage the phrase "according to the kind intention of his will" (NASB) is said to establish the unconditional character of election. In the latter passage the verb *foreknow* is taken to mean "set regard upon beforehand," implying, "know from eternity with sovereign distinguishing affection and delight," hence, "whom he foreloved."

In summary, it may be fairly stated that whatever view one may adopt concerning election, the fact of it must be seen as the biblical basis upon which God's redemptive work was accomplished. What God determined in his eternal counsel he then had to accomplish in history.

B. Christ's redemptive work. The execution of salvation is seen in Christ's redemptive work in history. This is an area of major dispute in present theological discussion. Two major views seem to emerge from all the controversy.

1. The existential school. According to Rudolf Bultmann, the essence of the Christian message as set forth in the NT is that of *a call to decision*—a response that brings with it a new understanding of oneself, a sense of authentic existence. Bultmann almost entirely divorces the question of existence in the NT from that of salvation history. Regarding the historical Jesus, Bultmann states, "I do indeed think that we can now know almost nothing concerning the life and personality of Christ" (*Jesus and the Word* [1834], 8). Bultmann maintains that we can preach the Christ of faith without the Jesus of history. His view can be called an existentialistic approach to the biblical message developed in the context of a historical skepticism.

Bultmann belongs to the radical-critical school of German biblical criticism. Following a "form historical" method (see FORM CRITICISM), he views Jesus as only a man whom the later faith of the church deified. He acknowledges that the Gospels relate to the history of Jesus from a supernatural perspective which at the same time bears

According to Karl Barth's doctrine of salvation, election is primarily the election of Jesus Christ.

are both reprobate and elect in Christ. There is no question here of a distribution of election and reprobation over such and such individuals, as in the historic Reformed position, but only of double predestination in and concerning Christ.

Barth's radical revision of the Reformation view of election inevitably raises the question of whether his position requires as a logical corollary the acceptance of universalism. Although Barth replies with an emphatic negative, many of his critics cannot accept such an answer. G. C. Berkouwer states, "There is no alternative to concluding that Barth's refusal to accept the apokatastasis (universalism) cannot be harmonized with the fundamental structure of his doctrine of election" (*The Triumph of Grace in the Theology of Karl Barth* [1956], 116).

3. The Calvinistic view. Calvinism maintains that God elects unconditionally; that is, there is nothing in the creature which conditions his choice of some and passing over of others. The moving cause is in the sovereign will of God alone (Eph. 1:4–5). According to this view, election is that eternal act the character of preaching, but he argues that this preaching does not give us a trustworthy account of what occurred; it represents only the faith of the later church. Herman Ridderbos states, "The gospels, according to Bultmann, are not concerned with Jesus but with the faith and the preaching of the church with respect to Jesus. And what interests him as an historian is the question: How did this preaching acquire this form? or in other words: Along what way or in what manner has this preaching grown up or developed into our gospel accounts?" (*Bultmann* [1960], 12).

2. The historical school. According to Oscar Cullmann, the essence of the Christian message is both salvation history (*Heilsgeschichte*) and Christian existence. The essential feature of Christianity which distinguishes it from other religions is the fact of the central divine act in history of the death and resurrection of Jesus Christ. Only in Judaism is the historical of equally fundamental importance. The focal point of Christianity is not metaphysics but history. Redemption is something accomplished by God through Christ in time.

Cullmann states, "Redemptive history is the heart of all theology which is based upon the Bible. It represents an essential aspect of all theology. It is the perspective from which the very objects of all Christian theology, God and Christ, are seen. Obviously the objects of theology are God and Christ, but the perspective from which they are viewed is not that of metaphysical or existentialist speculation, but rather that of redemptive history" (*Soli Deo Gloria: New Testament Studies in Honor of William Childs Robinson*, ed. J. McDowell Richards [1968], 13).

In ancient times redemptive history was challenged in the name of a metaphysical philosophy (GNOSTICISM); more recently it is being challenged in the name of an existential position (modern philosophy). But now as then, Christianity proves to be invulnerable to all such attempts to destroy it. As Scripture makes clear, the very *essence* of Christianity is redemptive *history*. Bultmann's dehistorization of the NT in terms of the extended approach of Heidegger spells a tragic departure from historic Christianity. Theology is thereby reduced to anthropology and another gospel is preached.

One further word should be given to differentiate between those of the *Heilsgeschichte* position and those of a more traditionally conservative position. While both schools would agree as to the historical objectivity and divine meaning of God's redemptive work, they would not agree as to the basis on which these biblical events are to be interpreted. Those of the *Heilsgeschichte* school would tend to look to some suprarational existential experience to discern it, whereas those of the more conservative school would tend to look to the divinely inspired record of Scripture as ultimately definitive of its meaning.

IV. The application of salvation

A. Ordo salutis. The Latin phrase *ordo salutis* (lit., "the way of salvation") refers to the process whereby the work of salvation, accomplished in Christ, is subjectively realized in the hearts of sinners. The emphasis is not on what a person does in appropriating the grace of God, but on what God does in applying it. Though this is a unitary process, when one examines the biblical data it becomes evident that various movements can be distinguished in the process, movements that are to be understood in terms of logical order rather than temporal sequence.

One important question that arises in a discussion of an *ordo salutis* is, Does the Bible supply information sufficient for the construction of a single fixed order? A study of Scripture appears to lead to a negative answer. It would seem, however, to allow for the legitimacy of constructing a flexible *ordo salutis* for dogmatic or systematic reasons. In fact, more positively, it may be stated that we gain definite guidance for our arrangement of topics from the Scripture themselves, though we must use great caution.

Paul in Rom. 8:28–30 gives us a strong indication for a broad *ordo salutis*. In this passage certain intimations of a logical sequence are readily discovered: (1) God's purpose is prior to his calling, v. 28; (2) the progression of thought in v. 29 is foreknowledge, then predestination; (3) vv. 29–30 make clear that we cannot reverse foreknowledge and glorification—foreknowledge is the ultimate cause and glorification the ultimate end; (4) similarly, foreknowledge and predestination are prior to calling, justification, and glorification—the reverse is inconceivable; (5) finally, glorification cannot be prior to calling and justification. But even in this passage the order is far from complete. There is no mention of regeneration, conversion, adoption, perseverance, sanctification, etc.

B. Calling. According to Rom. 8:30, *calling* would seem to be the initial saving act of God. The scriptural doctrine of redemptive calling is twofold in aspect.

1. The general call. This is a CALL that comes through the preaching of the gospel, inviting sinners to salvation in Christ. It is a call that issues forth from the KERYGMA (the apostolic message concerning Christ). This message is not to be optionally related but authoritatively proclaimed. It contains three essential elements that respectively answer the questions "what?" "why?" and "so what?": (1) historical fact—the death, burial, and resurrection of Christ; (2) theological interpretation—"for our sins"; (3) ethical demand—believe and repent!

This general call given by the prophets under the OT, by John the Baptist, Christ himself, and the apostles, and by all succeeding ministers in all ages, is a call that is frequently rejected (Matt. 22:14; 23:37). Indeed, it is always insufficient of itself to lead to real conversion. It must be accompanied by the powerful grace of God. Unless through the Spirit the arm of the Lord is revealed, the proclamation of the gospel will not be believed, nor the call of it responded to in faith.

2. The effectual call. This is a *creative* call that accompanies the external proclamation of the gospel, bringing the hearer to the divinely intended response of faith and repentance. The effectual call is efficacious; that is, it always results in salvation. In the NT the terms for calling, when used soteriologically, are almost always applied not to the general call of the gospel, but to the call that actually brings sinners into a state of salvation, that is, the effectual call (cf. Rom. 8:30; 1 Cor. 1:9, 26; 2 Pet. 1:10 et al.).

The NT reveals a number of things about this call. It is immutable (2 Tim. 1:9); it is issued by the Father (Rom. 8:30; 1 Cor. 1:9; Gal. 1:15; Eph. 1:17–18; 2 Tim. 1:9 et al.); it is based on the eternal purpose of God (2 Tim. 1:9); it is accomplished through the communication of the Word (2 Thess. 2:14); it brings us into fellowship with Christ (1 Cor. 1:9); it brings us into freedom (Gal. 5:13); it brings us into peace (1 Cor. 7:15).

As the gospel is proclaimed, the general call goes forth like sheet lightning, but God in accordance with his sovereign purpose causes it to strike like a forked flash in the lives of some. Such are those who have been effectually called out of the gross darkness of their sins into the glorious light of the Son of righteousness (1 Pet. 2:9). Indeed, salvation is of Yahweh.

C. Regeneration. It is God the Father who calls his own out of the kingdom of darkness into the kingdom of light, but the sinners must do the coming. And yet, how can they? Are they not dead in trespasses and sin? The spiritual dilemma of the minister is analogous to the utter futility of a doctor's efforts to revive the lifeless body of a patient. Whether we preach the terrors of hell or the blessings of heaven, whether we proclaim the law or the gospel, there can be no response apart from a miracle of grace. But it is the glory of God's sovereign grace that it overcomes this dilemma. God's call, when it is effectual, carries with it the operative grace necessary to secure a response of faith in Christ. This grace is the grace of REGENERATION or quickening. In the Calvinistic tradition this grace of regeneration is bestowed only on the elect, but in the Arminian tradition all people are given ability to respond either in faith or disbelief to the call of the gospel. The Arminian position is based on the doctrine of prevenient grace.

The Greek noun *palingenesia* G4098 is found only twice in Scripture. In Matt. 19:28 it is used eschatologically to denote the renewal of the world prior to the coming of the kingdom; and in Tit. 3:5 it is used soteriologically, perhaps denoting BAPTISM as the sign and seal of regeneration. The reality of the latter, however, is referred to in a number of words and images. Perhaps the best known figure is that of new birth. Jesus said to NICODEMUS, "I tell you the truth, no one can see the kingdom of God unless he is born again" (Jn. 3:3). The Greek word for "again" (*anōthen G540*) can also mean "from above" (cf. 3:31; 19:11 et al.). In either case the language presupposes a first birth to which regeneration is the second. Note the following contrasts between the two. The first birth is of sinful parents, the second of God; the first is of corruptible seed, the second of incorruptible seed; the first is of the flesh or carnal, the second of the Spirit or spiritual; the first marks one as Satan's slave, the second as Christ's free person; in the first, the sinner is viewed as an object of divine wrath, in the second as an object of divine love.

In Jn. 3 one reads of the meeting of Nicodemus with Jesus. Nicodemus was a leader in the orthodox religious party of his day, undoubtedly a member of the SANHEDRIN, but he was unregenerate. On this occasion he desired to see Jesus in order to discover the secret of entry into the KINGDOM OF GOD (the redemptive rule of God through Christ). But even before he had opportunity to express what was in his mind, Jesus provided the answer to his question: a person may not so much as see the kingdom unless he is born again. It is divinely necessary that one be sovereignly regenerated by the Spirit of God.

A difficult problem emerges from Jn. 3:5 respecting the meaning of the word *water*. There are four major views usually set forth. First, some maintain that the water is that of John's baptism and that it is therefore symbolic of repentance. From the standpoint of historical context, this view would seem to commend itself. Second, some maintain that since water according to Jewish usage could denote the male semen, it might be symbolic of birth. If one adopts this view, it would seem more likely to suggest spiritual than natural birth. It seems unlikely that Jesus would have insulted the intelligence of Nicodemus by telling him that unless he was born physically he could not be born spiritually. Third, some maintain that the water is that of Christian baptism. The meaning would then be that a person must be baptized and also be born of the Spirit if he is to enter the kingdom. But this view seems most untenable, for Nicodemus would have understood this figure against the OT background rather than in terms of Christian baptism. Fourth, some maintain that water is a symbol for the Word of God (cf. Eph. 5:26). The weakness in this view is that it involves an interpolation of Paul's usage of this figure into Christ's conversation with one who is filled with OT concepts, not Pauline ones.

In connection with this problem, it seems more profitable to consider the OT parallel in Ezek. 36:25–26. This passage would suggest that *water is symbolic of purification and Spirit of renovation.* Other phrases descriptive of the concept of regeneration include: "renewal by the Holy Spirit" (Tit. 3:5), "a new creation" (2 Cor. 5:17), "the new self" (Eph. 4:24). Those who are regenerated are referred to as "newborn babies" (1 Pet. 2:2). Regeneration is also indicated by the phrase "make alive" (Eph. 2:5; cf. Jn. 6:63; Rom. 8:1–10).

In the most definitive sense, regeneration denotes that act of God whereby spiritually dead sinners are made alive through the HOLY SPIRIT. By this act God plants a new spiritual life in the soul; one is born again from above. Regeneration in this restricted sense is solely a work of God. Hence when Christ says to Nicodemus, "You must be born again" (Jn. 3:7), these words speak not of a moral obligation (we cannot beget ourselves) but of a divine necessity. Regeneration is a passive work; a sinner can no more contribute to his spiritual conception than an infant can to his natural conception. The very nature of the work clearly shows that it is not in the power of human beings to do it; it is represented in Scripture as a *creation*, a *new* creation, and only God can truly create (1:13).

Regeneration is an instantaneous work of the Spirit; it is not like progressive sanctification. As an infant is generated at once and not by degrees, so it is in spiritual generation. One does not gradually become alive. No person can be said to be more regenerated than another, though of course once regenerated one may be said to be more sanctified than another. This work of regeneration is a mysterious work as Christ indicates in his words to Nicodemus. This work of the Spirit is like the wind: "you cannot tell where it comes from or where it is going" (Jn. 3:8).

D. Conversion. It may be noted that both the Hebrew and Greek terms for CONVERSION mean basically "to turn" and, in the religious sense, denote a change of outlook and a new direction in life and action. Conversion involves a turn both toward and away from something or someone. Positively, the turn toward something or someone is what may be appropriately called FAITH. In the religious sphere it is a turn *toward* God (Acts 26:20; cf. 9:35; 11:21; 15:19; 1 Pet. 2:25).

This turn, or act of faith, may be defined as an understanding of and mental assent to certain basic facts concerning the person and work of Christ (1 Cor. 3:14–15) culminating in a committal of one's entire being to the person of whom those facts testify. Three important elements are to be noted in this definition.

(1) *Knowledge*. The first indispensable element in saving faith is information. We must know who Christ is, what he has done, and what he is able to do. We are not called to put faith in someone of whom we have no knowledge. In order to exercise faith we must know about the death, burial, and resurrection of Jesus Christ. Without such knowledge, faith would be but a foolish leap in the dark.

(2) *Assent*. The second element is that of conviction concerning the truthfulness of that which is known. It is possible, of course, to understand the import of certain propositions of truth and yet not believe these propositions. In saving faith, truths known are also accepted as true.

(3) *Trust*. The third element is that of commitment. Knowledge of the truth of the gospel and assent to it do not constitute saving faith. These must be accompanied by trust in the person of Jesus Christ himself. Christian faith is not merely intellectual assent to the divinely revealed truths of Scripture; it must include personal encounter with Christ, the One in whom all truth is summed up.

Negatively, turning away from something or someone is what may be called REPENTANCE. The biblical term for repentance indicates a change of mind and conduct. It properly denotes a change for the better, a change of mind that is productive of good works. Repentance is the gift of God, the purchase of Christ, and the work of the Holy Spirit (Acts 11:18). It is produced by the Spirit at regeneration or quickening. Moreover, the Scriptures teach that there is not only a necessity for an initial conversion of the sinner, but also subsequent conversions of erring saints (it is the latter which is prob. stressed in Ps. 119:59–60). Repentance is a turning from idols (1 Thess. 1:9), from vain things (Acts 14:15), from darkness (26:18a), and from the power of Satan (26:18b). It is a turn from transgression (Isa. 59:20).

As for the means of conversion, Scripture clearly teaches that the *efficient* cause is God, not the sinner. The drastic change wrought by conversion is not in our power to effect. An Ethiopian might just as well try to change his skin or a leopard his spots (Jer. 13:23; cf. Jn. 1:13; Rom. 9:16).

The *instrumental* cause of conversion is the ministry of the Word: "faith comes from hearing the message, and the message is heard through the word of Christ" (Rom. 10:17). And yet, even the preaching of the Word is not sufficient of itself to produce the response of conversion. It is obvious that sinners may hear and yet not turn. To be effective, the proclamation must be accompanied by the power and demonstration of the Spirit (1 Cor. 2:1–5). Certain cases of conversion in the NT should be carefully studied: the Philippian jailer (Acts 16:19–34); the dying malefactor (Lk. 23:32–43); Paul (Acts 9:1–22); the Ethiopian treasurer (8:26–40); Cornelius (ch. 10); Lydia (16:13–15); Timothy (2 Tim. 3:14–15); conversions at Pentecost (Acts 2).

E. Justification. In a fundamental sense, JUSTIFICATION is concerned not with our spiritual *condition* but with our spiritual *relation*; it is not a matter of our actual *state* but of our judicial *position*. Justification is the answer to the disrupted relationship between creatures and their God brought about through sin. As the result of sin all people stand before God as guilty, condemned and separated from their Creator. Justification is the restoration of mankind to its original relation to God through the work of Christ. Significantly it includes, according to Paul, removal of guilt by the IMPUTATION of Christ's righteousness (Rom. 8:33), removal of condemnation by the gift of forgiveness (v. 34), and removal of separation by the restoration to fellowship (v. 35).

Justification must be seen from a twofold perspective, actual and declarative. Actual justification means that sinners are *constituted* righteous by having Christ's RIGHTEOUSNESS imputed to them. Only in this way may a just God justify the ungodly. Declarative justification means that the one who has been *constituted* righteous in Christ is also judged righteous before him. Justification is a forensic or legal term, and it should be carefully distinguished in meaning from sanctification, which is experiential and progressive. The distinction between the two concepts may be stated as follows: Justification has to do with Christ *for* us, sanctification with Christ *in* us. Justification has to do with our position; sanctification, with fellowship. Justification has to do with our acceptance; sanctification with our attainment.

The foundation of justification is God's grace, not human works. Paul emphasizes that a person is justified by faith apart from the works of the law (Rom. 3:28). The apostle is concerned to make unmistakably clear that God has accomplished in Christ what sinners are completely unable to do for themselves. What God has done for the sinner in Christ is totally unmerited, unprompted, and unsought. This is the essence of grace (3:24). Our justification depends wholly on God and not on anything in us.

Long ago Job asked, "How can a mortal be righteous before God?" (Job 9:2). This most important question raises the matter of method. The only satisfactory answer is found in the Word of God. The justification of the sinner is pronounced in the word of the gospel. As near as the word of faith is to us, just so near is the word of God's acquittal. The merit of our Lord becomes ours "through faith" (Eph. 2:18; cf. Rom. 3:21–22).

It is imperative to understand that faith is never the ground of justification, but only its means or channel; it is the hand which simply reaches out to accept the gift. The NT consistently uses the phrase "through [*or* by] faith." No Greek preposition is ever employed with such grammatical case of the noun *faith* as to require a translation like "because of" or "by reason of" faith. Faith is never portrayed as meritorious; it is always and only instrumental. Faith is our positive answer to God's justifying grace; it is the correlative of promise.

When we consider the value of justification, certain things become immediately clear from the NT. Justification provides the ground of PEACE with God (Rom. 5:1). When we stand before God as righteous in Christ, we may experience the peace of God in our lives and share this with others. It is also the basis for LIBERTY in Christ. This means freedom from bondage to sin and freedom to serve others. When we are released from anxiety about ourselves, we are able to use our lives for others. It also means freedom to enjoy all the good things of life within the context of genuine love for others (Rom. 14).

F. Adoption. The sonship referred to under this category is not to be confused with that which Christ sustains to the Father as the only Son. Nor is it to be equated with the relationship which all human beings sustain to God as his children by creation (Acts 17:25–29; Heb. 12:9; Jas. 1:18; Mal. 2:10; see FATHERHOOD OF GOD).

The doctrine of ADOPTION is exclusively Pauline. The Greek word *huiothesia* G5625 occurs only five times in Paul's letters. Once it is applied to Israel as a nation (Rom. 9:4); once to its full realization at the PAROUSIA (8:23); and three times as a present reality in the life of the Christian (Rom. 8:15–16; Gal. 4:5; Eph. 1:5).

In Rom. 8:15 it is probably best to understand the Spirit of adoption as the Holy Spirit (note the parallelism with Gal. 4:6 as an argument for this view). The Holy Spirit is not the one who adopts; this is more especially said to be the work of the Father—but the Spirit is the one through whom the child of God is able to cry ABBA ("Father") and exercise the rights and privileges of God's child. In Gal. 4:5 Paul indicates that God's purpose is twofold: redemption and adoption. God purposed not simply to release slaves but to make sons. In Eph. 1:5 Paul states that God "predestined us" (marked us out in advance) as those who were to receive the honored status of sons.

There has been much discussion as to whether the root of Paul's use of the term *adoption* is Jewish, Greek, Roman, or some other tradition. Many recent scholars favor a Greco-Roman background (but see *DPL*, 15–18). In the act of adoption a child was taken by a man from a family not his own, introduced into a new family, and regarded as a true son, entitled to all the privileges and responsibilities belonging to this relation.

The reality of spiritual adoption may be outlined as follows: (1) Fallen sinners are strangers to the family of God; as enemies of God their father is the devil (Jn. 8:44). (2) Yet despite this fact they are invited to enter God's family; to take his name upon them; to share in his fatherly care and discipline. (3) Such as accept this invitation are received into his family and protection. From this point they are called the children of God and are privileged to address him as Father. God as the heavenly Father of believers provides care (Lk. 11:11–13), sustenance (Ps. 23:1), protection (Ps. 114:1–2), instruction (through his word and by his providence), correction (Heb. 12:7; cf. 5–11), and an inheritance (Rom. 8:17).

G. Sanctification. When we are converted to God, we must ask how our new life is to be lived out here on earth. When such a question is faced, the subject of biblical ETHICS becomes an important aspect of the doctrine of SANCTIFICATION; the one cannot be properly considered without the other. Sanctification has to do with the progressive outworking of the new life implanted by the Spirit in regeneration. Christian ethics has to do with the study of the basis upon which, the power whereby, and the goal toward which the believer's life is lived.

The indicative of justification leads to the imperative of sanctification; justification is the theological base of an evangelical ethic. The gift of God in Christ impels to a recognition of our task for him. In the Pauline writings, expositions of the doctrine of justification are generally followed by exhortations to duty. It is not good works that make a good person; rather, it is a good person who does good works.

The distinctive feature of a Christian ethic is found in the matter of motivation. As our Lord made clear in the SERMON ON THE MOUNT (Matt. 5:7), more important than *what* one does is *why* one does it. Goodness is not merely a matter of outward action, but more fundamentally of inward attitude. Jesus interiorizes the moral law. Note for example Matt. 5:21–22, "You have heard that it was said to the people long ago, 'Do not murder, and anyone who murders will be subject to judgment.' But I tell you that anyone who is angry with his brother will be subject to judgment." Sanctification and ethics have to do fundamentally with what we are and only secondarily with what we do.

The basic meaning of *holy* is usually thought to be "separated, set apart" (see HOLINESS). God is holy as separate from his creatures, but also as separate from sin. It is this latter ethical aspect of God's holiness that provides the basis for our understanding of the doctrine of sanctification; and yet, sanctification is not only a separation *from* that which is sinful but also a separation *unto* a reflection of the IMAGE OF GOD. Sanctification is the progressive refashioning of our natures by the Holy Spirit, into the image of God, through Jesus Christ (see 2 Cor. 5:17).

The sanctified are the elect of God. All whom the Father chose in eternity, he sanctifies in time in Christ. The subjects of election, redemption, and sanctification are the same persons (Rom. 8:28–30). Sanctification involves the totality of the believer's being—BODY, SOUL, SPIRIT (1 Thess. 5:23). In respect to the soul and/or spirit, Paul indicates that (1) the understanding is enlightened (Eph. 4:23), (2) the will is subservient to the will of God (Phil. 2:13), (3) the affections are made holy (Rom. 12:10). In respect to the body and all its members, the apostle exhorts believers to offer themselves "to God as those who have been brought from death to life; and offer the parts of your body to him as instruments of righteousness" (Rom. 6:13).

Sanctification involves the believer's being *positionally* set apart unto God by virtue of his new life in Christ. This is not a matter of the degree of one's spirituality. Concerning the carnal Christians at CORINTH, Paul wrote, "But you were washed, you were sanctified, you were justified in the name of the Lord Jesus Christ and by the Spirit of our God" (1 Cor. 6:11; the past tense of the Greek verbs points to these acts as already accomplished). This aspect of sanctification coincides with justification.

Sanctification includes the believer being *experientially* set apart to God by reason of the ministry of the indwelling Spirit. This aspect of sanctification is progressive; it admits of degrees. Although no one can be more or less regenerate than another, for one is either dead or alive, one may be more sanctified than another. Scripture frequently exhorts believers to grow in holiness. "But grow in the grace and knowledge of our Lord and Savior Jesus Christ" (2 Pet. 3:18; see 2 Thess. 1:3). The Bible speaks of *growing* in grace, *abounding* in hope and love, and *increasing* in the knowledge of divine things. There would be no reason for such speaking if experiential sanctification were perfected at the moment of regeneration.

Sanctification also involves the believer's being *completely* set apart to God. Ultimately his practice and position will be brought into perfect accord (see Eph. 5:26–27; Jude 24, 25). This aspect of sanctification coincides with glorification.

Sanctification is required of every Christian (1 Thess. 4:3). It is not the responsibility of an elite group within the church. There is no scriptural basis for the adoption of a twofold standard of Christian commitment, one for "full-time Christian workers" and another for "Christian laymen." Scripture speaks of *all* believers as SAINTS ("holy ones," 1 Cor. 1:1–2).

The ethical standards (principles) for the development of a holy life, a life that increasingly reflects the *imago Dei*, are set forth in Scripture on both a personal and a social level. In Paul's epistle to the Colossians, for example, he deals with personal ethics under the rubrics of "putting off" and "putting on." In chapter 3, the apostle first describes what are the things to be put to death (Col. 3:5, 8–9), namely, "sexual immorality, impurity, lust, evil desires and greed, which is idolatry," as well as "anger, rage, malice, slander, and filthy language from your lips." Next he speaks of what is to be put on (vv. 12–14), namely, "compassion, kindness, humility, gentleness and patience," being forgiving and above all loving. Then the apostle deals with ethics on a social level, giving instruction concerning wives and husbands (vv. 18–19), parents and children (v. 21), and slaves and masters (3:22—4:1). This latter area may find its functional equivalent today in the relationship of employee to employer.

In all the relationships of life, personal and social, Christians are to seek the kingdom of God and his righteousness. The dynamic for the realization of this goal is the Holy Spirit. The motivation is God-given agape LOVE. The guidance is provided by the moral law, to be appropriately applied under the leading of the Holy Spirit in each situation. Since God is holy we are to be also.

H. Perseverance. This is the doctrine that all believers will be preserved by God's grace to the end through a faith that works. PERSEVERANCE does not mean that everyone who professes faith in Christ, is baptized, and made a member of a church is thereby secure for eternity. Many who profess to have salvation do not possess it. Nor does it mean that it is impossible for a Christian to backslide, that is, to follow a path of disobedience to God for a time (cf. Lk. 2:31–34).

The NT would seem to suggest a synthesis between God's preserving grace and the believer's persevering. This is well expressed, for example, by Peter when he says that "through faith [Christians] are shielded by God's power until the coming of the salvation that is ready to be revealed in the last time" (1 Pet. 1:5). There are basically three ideas in this text. First, believers are "shielded." The Greek verb here (*phroureō* G5864, "to guard") is often used in military contexts; it suggests that our life is garrisoned by God, who stands over us as a sentinel all our days. Second, believers are kept "through faith." The final preservation of believers is never divorced from the use of means; believers are preserved through a faith that works. Third, believers are kept "until the coming of … salvation." This undoubtedly refers to the final consummation or ultimate realization of our salvation, which will be revealed in the last time (Rom. 13:11).

In the history of theological thought, there have developed three major views regarding perseverance: the Remonstrant, the Lutheran, and the Calvinist views. The followers of Jacob Arminius, led by Bischop and Grotius, presented to Holland and Friesland in 1610 a series of articles known as the Remonstrance. Among these articles was one which taught that true believers could and often did fall away, completely and finally, from saving faith. Some Lutherans, among whom was Gerhard, maintained that one must differentiate between *total* and *final* falling (cf. Ezek. 18:24). He exegetes 1 Jn. 2:19 as teaching that the elect can fall totally for a time, but does not agree with the Reformed confession of perseverance. Finally, the Reformed view maintains that all true believers are preserved unto the end through a persevering faith. Some of the texts cited in support of this view include Jn. 6:39, 40; 10:27–30; 17:11; cf. 11:42; Phil. 1:6; 1 Pet. 5:10; 1 Jn. 3:9; 5:18 et al.

Those who would adopt a Reformed view on this matter must face the problem of biblical warnings. Are we not to take seriously those passages that warn against APOSTASY? Must we not acknowledge the possibility of a real and final falling away from faith? What of all those "if" passages that cannot simply be answered by translating "since"? There are not a few of these (e.g., Jn. 15:6, 10, 14; Col. 1:23; Heb. 3:14; 6:4–8). In addition to those passages that speak conditionally, there are a number that warn against apostasy as a real threat (e.g., Heb. 3:12–13; 12:25; 1 Tim. 1:19; 2 Tim. 2:18; 2 Pet. 2:1). Actual cases of apostasy include DAVID, SOLOMON, HYMENAEUS, ALEXANDER, PHILETUS, and DEMAS. These and other passages might suggest that the doctrine of perseverance is hopelessly indefensible. Reformed theologians would argue, however, that such conditional warning passages must be related to the *total context of Scripture*. Even if this is done, who is to establish whether the unconditional texts are to be interpreted in terms of the conditional or vice versa? If God's grace, according to Scripture, does not stop short at the limits of human freedom, then faith and grace cannot be viewed synergistically as is done in the Arminian view.

According to Reformed theology, if we properly understand the biblical relationship of faith to grace, then we will realize that our persevering cannot be a factor independent of God's preserving us. God's grace insures our persevering but this does not make it any less *our* persevering (Jude 21, 24). The warning passages are then properly seen as *means* which God uses in our life to accomplish his purpose in grace. G. Berkouwer has well stated, "The profundity of the doctrine of perseverance must be sought precisely in the fact that admonition is included in it and that at the same time, through faith, perseverance is confessed as a gift" (*Faith and Perseverance* [1958], 111).

One of the most difficult passages in a consideration of perseverance is Heb. 6:4–8. There are three major views that may be noted. First, there is the *saved-lost theory*, which maintains that a true believer may be lost through deliberate apostasy. It should be noted, however, that this passage also indicates the impossibility of repentance following such apostasy. Second, there is the *hypothetical theory*, which maintains that the writer is dealing with suppositions and not with fact, in order that he may correct wrong ideas. This view would seem to minimize the impact of the warning. Third, there is the *non-Christian theory*, which holds that there is no genuine faith in the hearts of the persons being described. This view argues that the experiences mentioned describe how exceedingly close it is possible for one to come to being a Christian without actually becoming one. SIMON MAGUS is appealed to as an illustration of this position.

Another problem passage is Jn. 15:1–6. The central question here is, What is the nature of the barren branches (vv. 2, 6)? Some would contend that these represent genuine believers who lose their spiritual life by failing to abide in Christ. Others, of a Calvinistic persuasion, would maintain that these branches are such as merely profess to belong to Christ. When it is said that they will be *taken away*, this is understood to mean that they will be finally expelled from all connection with Jesus Christ and his church. (In this reference to barren branches Jesus is undoubtedly thinking of JUDAS ISCARIOT, who although connected with Christ outwardly was never truly one of his.) This *taking away* and *burning* may happen in various stages. Such mere professing Christians may gradually wither and drop off at their own accord or they may have to be excised by the knife of EXCOMMUNICATION. Still others may continue in this world. But ultimately every such branch is taken away at death.

One of the strongest supports of the doctrine of perseverance is found in the significance of Christ's intercessory PRAYER. During the closing days of Jesus' earthly life he encountered PETER in a mood of intense self-confidence. On that occasion Peter boasted to his Master that he would follow him wherever it might lead and at whatever cost. Jesus, knowing Peter better than Peter himself, revealed that Satan desired to sift him as wheat, but he added, "I have prayed for you, Simon, that your faith may not fail" (Lk. 22:32). Now even though Peter denied his Lord three times, as the Master had predicted, yet his faith did not utterly fail; for no sooner had he sinned than he wept bitter tears of repentance. But not only did Jesus pray for Peter, he also prays for all who are his. His intercession includes those who are still unbelievers but who are nonetheless among the elect (Jn. 17:20–21; cf. Rom. 8:31–35; Heb. 7:25). See INTERCESSION OF CHRIST.

I. Glorification. GLORIFICATION is the final climactic act in God's redeeming work (Rom. 8:30), to be realized at the PAROUSIA. It will involve the perfecting of the soul and/or spirit as well as the body. Although the NT represents glorification as a complete juridical exoneration, it also views it as a moral perfecting. A number of Scriptures make this clear (Eph. 5:27; Phil. 1:10; Col. 1:30; 1 Cor. 1:8; 1 Thess. 3:13; 5:23 et al.).

Glorification also means *full* participation in eternal LIFE. By God's grace believers even now have eternal life (Jn. 5:24); but the *fullness* of this life is yet to be realized (vv. 25–28). John states, "Dear friends, now we are children of God, and what we will be has not yet been made known. But we know that when he appears, we shall be like him, for we shall see him as he is" (1 Jn. 3:2). ETERNAL life includes two ideas: a new quality of life and a never-ending life. When the sinner is restored to his proper relationship with God through Christ he enters a new quality of life—a life in harmony with the life of God himself. This is a kind of life drastically different from that previously possessed; it is indeed an abundant life. Glorification then means the full bestowal of eternal life upon believers—the final realization of a perfect relationship with God as we are with him forever.

Glorification will bring a full realization of freedom from sin and death (Jn. 8:33–36; Rom. 6–8; Gal. 5:1, 13). Then we shall be what we truly are. While in this life, we strive through the Spirit to be like our Lord; then our souls shall be perfectly conformed to his image (Rom. 8:28–29). Glorification is our transformation into "the whole measure of the fullness of Christ" (Eph. 4:13).

Glorification also includes the perfecting of the BODY. Scripture attributes a dignity to the human body. Genesis teaches that a person is not a soul merely inhabiting a physical entity. It is the *total* person who is said to have been created in the image of God (Gen. 1:26–30; 2:4–8, 15–18). It is the total person who is affected by sin. The focal point of divine judgment is DEATH, and although the death of the body does not exhaust the biblical concept of death, it is nevertheless central to it. Physical death (separation of the soul and/or spirit from the body) is the outward sign of spiritual death (separation of the person from God).

Christ's RESURRECTION guarantees ours. According to the NT, Christ rose from the dead bodily (Matt. 28:9; Lk. 24:31, 43, 50; Jn. 20:17, 22, 27 et al.), and this glorious body in which he arose is the pattern after which ours will be fashioned (Phil. 3:20–21; cf. 2 Cor. 5:1–5). In the KJV of Phil. 3:21 we read that Christ will change "our vile body." The word for "vile" is better rendered "lowly," as in several modern versions. Although many Greek pagans viewed the body as the prison of the SOUL, Paul viewed the body as designed by God for the abode of the Spirit (1 Cor. 6:19). In our present state, because of the influence of sin, our body is in a state of humiliation, but at Christ's return it will be refashioned after the glorious body of our Lord (1 Jn. 3:2). The details regarding the nature of this change are outlined in 1 Cor. 15.

Glorification, then, is the climax of God's saving work, a work that extends from eternity to eternity. Glorification involves the *total* person—soul and/or spirit together with the body. In that day all will be complete; death will be swallowed up in victory, and God will be everything to everyone.

(In addition to the titles mentioned in the body of the article, see B. B. Warfield, *The Plan of Salvation* [1915]; J. Murray, *Redemption: Accomplished and Applied* [1955]; K. Barth, *Church Dogmatics*, vol. 4, parts 1–4 [1956–62]; C. M. Horne, *Salvation* [1971]; B. Demarest, *The Cross and Salvation: The Doctrine of Salvation* [1997]; D. F. Ford, *Self and Salvation: Being Transformed* [1999]; J. M. Frame, *Salvation Belongs to the Lord: An Introduction to Systematic Theology* [2006]. See also the bibliographies under the articles that deal with various aspects of salvation, such as ATONEMENT, JUSTIFICATION, REDEMPTION, and so forth.)   C. M. HORNE

salve. See EYESALVE.

Samael sam´ay-uhl. KJV Apoc. form of SALAMIEL (Jdt. 8:1).

Samaias suh-may´yuhs. KJV Apoc. form of SHEMAIAH (1 Esd. 1:9; 8:39; Tob. 5:13 [NRSV 5:14, "Shemeliah"]).

Samaria (city) suh-mair´ee-uh (שֹׁמְרוֹן H9076, possibly "guarding [place], observation [point]," derived from the personal name שֶׁמֶר H9070, "guardian" [1 Ki. 6:24]; Aram. שָׁמְרָיִן H10726; Σαμάρεια G4899). The capital of the northern kingdom of Israel. See also SAMARIA (TERRITORY) and SAMARITAN.

I. The site. Samaria had an excellent hilltop location c. 40 mi. N of JERUSALEM and c. 25 mi. from the Mediterranean (see GREAT SEA). In the spring, when the wild flowers are in blossom, the setting is exquisite. The king could see the Mediterranean Sea from his palace windows as he looked W down the fertile "valley of barley," leading to the Plain of SHARON and the sea. Samaria was located on the main N-S ridge ROAD of PALESTINE, and almost directly W across the mountain ridge from the preceding capital, TIRZAH. It was c. 6.5 mi. NW of SHECHEM, the kingdom's first capital.

The city was on an oval hilltop c. 300 ft. high and isolated from the hills around it except to the E, where a saddle joined it to the N-S ridge. Although lower than some surrounding hills, it was beyond artillery (catapult) range from them. The city withstood several sieges by the Arameans, and one of three years' duration by the Assyrians, before it fell (2 Ki. 17:5). This is especially interesting in view of the fact that the city's spring was a mile away and the inhabitants had to rely on CISTERNS. When HEROD the Great rebuilt the city, he named it Sebaste in honor of his patron AUGUSTUS (Gk. *sebastos* G4935, "revered," corresponds to Lat. *augustus*; cf. Acts 25:25). The present Arab village at the E end of the site still carries the Herodian name, Sebastiyeh. The OT population of the city can only be conjectured, but SARGON deported 27,290 of its population. Its maximum population even in NT times was probably not more than 40,000. The size of the hilltop, of course, determined the city's size, c. 20 acres.

II. Israelite history. The city of Samaria is referred to over a hundred times in the OT, although it was not built until some fifty years after the death of SOLOMON. It was founded c. 875 B.C. by OMRI. "He bought the hill of Samaria from Shemer for two talents of silver and built a city on the hill, calling it Samaria, after Shemer, the name of the former owner of the hill" (1 Ki. 16:24; see SHEMER). Omri died before completing the new city and it was finished by his son, AHAB. The new capital was in every way an improvement on the former one, Tirzah.

The site was excavated by Harvard University in 1908 under the direction of G. Schumacher and in 1909–10 under G. A. Reisner. A second expedition in 1931–33 was sponsored by a multiple group: Harvard University, Hebrew University of Jerusalem, the Palestine Exploration Fund, the British Academy, and the British School of Archaeology in Jerusalem (in 1935 the British institutions listed above carried on another dig). The expedition was under the direction of J. W. Crowfoot, and K. M. Kenyon was in charge of the work in the royal quarter. The most important findings of all these digs will be incorporated into the historical sections of this article, although more recent work by R. E. Tappy has led to a revision of the architectural and stratigraphic history in the 11th–7th cent. B.C.

There had been occupation on the hilltop in the Early Bronze Age, and the archaeological evidence from a later period could be interpreted as the remains of Shemer's estate. The city built by Omri and Ahab was largely replaced by later constructions; the portions of the original city found by the archaeologists show that it was well designed and excellently constructed. The work was apparently done by skilled Phoenician craftsmen, as similar work has been found at TYRE. Israel and PHOENICIA were allies, and Ahab had married the daughter of the king of the Phoenicians. The palace was probably similar to others in the ANE, for it followed

The tell of ancient Samaria.

their pattern in that it was a two-story building; Ahab's son AHAZIAH was fatally injured in a fall from a second-story window (2 Ki. 1:2–17). The palace buildings probably also followed the usual design of being built around open courtyards. In one of the courtyards a rectangular shallow pool was found, which measured 33.5 x 17 ft. Perhaps this was the place where the blood was washed from Ahab's chariot (1 Ki. 22:38). The total palace area seems to have been c. 178 x 89 meters.

The palace was called an ivory house (1 Ki. 22:39; Amos 3:15). There are three theories of interpretation. One considers the polished white limestone of the buildings as "ivory colored." Another thinks the reference is to wooden wall panels inlaid with ivory. The third, and most likely, is to apply it to the ivory inlay furniture used. Since the inlays are small, they fit the pattern of furniture better than large wall panels.

Over 500 of the ivory plaques or fragments of them have been found. They were at times touched up with glass, enamel, and lapis lazuli inlays, and some were covered with gold leaf. There were figures from nature: plants, flowers, trees, and wild animals. There were also plaques portraying Egyptian gods. The ivories were probably carved in Phoenicia; at least some of the designs were taken from Egyptian models. Work similar to that at Samaria has been found in Syria.

Other interesting palace finds were numerous clay sealings with imprints showing. These were the seals with which papyrus rolls were closed and made official by the seal imprint of a government official. The area where they were found would be the place where the government's official documents, both foreign and local, were kept. The inside of the seals showed the impression of the strings that bound the papyrus.

The entire city of Samaria probably occupied about 20 acres. The palace area was at the higher W end of the hill. The common people lived in the lower city, that is, the E end of the city. Less than one-third of the palace area has been excavated and only a small segment of the lower city.

Samaria was well fortified with both an outer and an inner city wall. The former averaged c. 20 ft., with the greatest width 32 ft. It was the casemate type and was provided with towers and bastions. The casemates were narrow rectangular rooms with the length of the casemate being the width of the wall. They were filled with earth. The inner wall was solid stone c. 5 ft. in thickness. There also seems to have been a third defensive wall on the hillside just below the outer wall, but the evidence is not conclusive.

The city's main gate was naturally at the E end of the city, where the hill joined the main mountain mass. This may be the gate where Ahab and JEHOSHAPHAT sat on their royal thrones and listened to the prophets predicting the outcome of a battle with the Arameans at RAMOTH GILEAD (2 Chr. 18:9). It may also have been the gate where the lepers were conversing with one another as to what death they would choose under the city's siege by BEN-HADAD. It would also be the place where the mob trampled to death the king's captain of the gate as they rushed out of the city for food when the siege was lifted (2 Ki. 7:1–20).

Near the gateway a fragment of a large stone stela was found, but only three letters remained and they gave no clue to the inscription The script would date it about the time of JEROBOAM II, who was Samaria's greatest king. Such memorial stelae were common at the gates of capital cities. Limestone pilasters with proto-Ionic capitals were found nearby, showing that an important public building had stood there. These are similar to those used by Solomon's architects.

Omri's place in the history of ASSYRIA is more significant than it is in Bible history. Although several dynasties replaced one another in the kingdom of Israel, Assyria always referred to each of them as "the house [or dynasty] of Omri." Ahab has much more prominence in Scripture; even so, he was a minor figure in comparison with his wife JEZEBEL, and especially with the prophet ELIJAH. Ahab built a temple for BAAL to please his wife, who was a worshiper of Melqart, the Baal of the city of Tyre, where her father had been high priest before becoming king (1 Ki. 16:32–33). Ahab's acquiescence to his wife's religion occasioned Elijah's dramatic appearance at Mount Carmel and his demonstration there that Jezebel's Baal and ASHERAH were powerless gods. Ahab's Baal sanctuary in Samaria has not yet been identified by archaeologists. The multiple rebuildings at Samaria have made it very difficult for archaeologists to identify in detail any of the portions of major buildings found after the time of Omri and Ahab. The objects found in the buildings, the architectural fragments of walls, arches, etc., are the best clue to the use of these structures.

Samaria was besieged by Ben-Hadad of SYRIA (ARAM), but Israel made a massive sortie from the city and defeated the Arameans, whose king was drunk at the time of battle (1 Ki. 20:1–22). Ahab defeated Ben-Hadad a second time the following spring; the Aramean king surrendered to Ahab. The Israelites were attacked by Ben-Hadad a third time, but Ahab was critically wounded at Ramoth Gilead and died before he could reach Samaria. His bloody chariot was washed in one of the palace pools, as mentioned earlier (22:1–38).

Ahab's son Ahaziah reigned only two years. He died as the result of an accident when he fell out of a second-story window in the palace at Samaria (2 Ki. 1:2–17). He was succeeded by his brother JEHORAM (Joram). Ben-Hadad again besieged Samaria, and the situation was so desperate that some of its citizens resorted to cannibalism. The prophet ELISHA predicted that the siege would be lifted within twenty-four hours, and so it was, for the Arameans thought that the Hittites and the Egyptians had become allies of the Israelites and were on the march ready to attack them (6:24—7:20). Like his father Ahab, Jehoram was wounded in battle at Ramoth Gilead (8:28), but escaped with his life, only to be murdered shortly afterward by JEHU, one of his military leaders in that battle (9:24).

The dynasty of Omri ended and was succeeded by the dynasty of Jehu. The descendants of Omri were exterminated by Jehoram's court officials, who beheaded all the male relatives of Ahab at Jehu's orders (2 Ki. 10:1–11). In antiquity a royal coronation normally took place in the presence of the nation's chief deity; so Jehu called for the service to be held in the great Baal temple that Ahab had built for Jezebel. When the temple was jammed with Baal worshipers, Jehu ordered his army to kill them all. He burned the wooden pillar of Baal and demolished the sanctuary. The site was then made a latrine. Although Jehu did everything possible to annihilate Phoenician Baalism, he still continued the synthetic Yahweh-Baal cult of Jeroboam I as the nation's official cult (10:18–31).

The kingdom of Israel suffered heavy defeats under Jehu. HAZAEL, king of DAMASCUS, incorporated all TRANSJORDAN into his kingdom (2 Ki. 10:32–33). Jehu became a vassal of SHALMANESER III, king of Assyria, according to the records of that monarch. Jehu's son, JEHOAHAZ, suffered still more at the hands of the Arameans; but the tables were turned under his son Jehoash (JOASH), for the Assyrian pressure on Damascus enabled that Israelite king to recover his Transjordanian territory; Jehoash even captured Jerusalem and made Samaria rich with its booty (14:8–14). Then Jeroboam II came to the throne at Samaria and the northern kingdom reached its greatest territorial expansion (from the DEAD SEA to LEBO HAMATH) and its greatest prosperity. The prophets Hosea and Amos often concentrated their remarks on life in Samaria, the capital city, although the historical books said little of that city in this period of her history.

Samaria has been rebuilt so often in the areas excavated by archaeologists that only fragments of buildings are left. The first major reconstructions seem to have come about the time of Jehu. The reason for this work is unknown. Perhaps destruction by an earthquake made rebuilding necessary, as earthquakes were frequent in the history of Palestine. At any rate the new work was very inferior to that of Omri and Ahab. Jehu, by his destruction of the Phoenician Baalism of the Omri-Ahab dynasty, would not likely be able to secure skilled Phoenician craftsmen; and apparently he had to rely on Israelite labor.

The next building phases came about the time of Joash and Jeroboam II, when wealth flowed into Samaria from all directions. Although there were several building phases, they were inferior to the earliest work. The excellent masonry has been replaced and the newer more crude work has its deficiencies concealed under heavy coats of plaster.

The most important objects found in this period were sixty-five OSTRACA from the time of Jeroboam II. These were business documents written on pieces of broken pottery (one of the most common writing materials used in ordinary business). Scholars differ concerning their exact nature, but they seem to be receipts for produce (wine and oil) given to the government at Samaria as taxes. They list the name and city of the taxpayer and also the name of the tax collector. They seem to show that the federal departments set up by Solomon were still intact at this time in the northern kingdom. Twenty-two cities or towns are mentioned.

Although Samaria was at the peak of her glory under Jeroboam II, the city was to be destroyed within twenty-five years; the whole of its last period was chaotic. Jeroboam's son, Zachariah, was assassinated within six months by Shallum, who in turn was assassinated a month later (2 Ki. 15:8–14). The latter killing was in the city of Samaria, and Menahem, the killer, was from Israel's former capital city of Tirzah just E across the mountains from Samaria. The Assyrians, however, were again in the W, and Menahem paid tribute to Tiglath-Pileser III (called Pul, 15:19). Pekahiah, the son of Menahem, was soon killed by Pekah, one of his generals, in the palace at Samaria (15:23–25). Pekah along with other western monarchs rebelled against Assyria. Tiglath-Pileser III then captured most of the kingdom of Israel and made it into three Assyrian provinces: Gilead, Megiddo, and Dor (15:29).

During this fighting, Hoshea killed Pekah, probably with the help of the Assyrians, for he was accepted as king over the last remnant of the northern kingdom, that is, the land adjacent to the city of Samaria itself (2 Ki. 15:30). Hoshea was loyal to Assyria for a time, but when Shalmaneser found him planning to revolt, he imprisoned him and attacked Samaria (17:1–6). The city withstood a siege of three years but fell to the new Assyrian king, Sargon II, in 721 B.C. Sargon's records reveal that he deported 27,290 persons from Samaria.

Sargon specifically stated that he rebuilt Samaria and made it greater than it had been under the Israelite monarchs. The land was resettled with refugees from other Assyrian conquests (2 Ki. 17:24), but it is uncertain whether Samaria in this text refers to the territory of Samaria or to the capital city itself. More deportees came in under Esarhaddon (Ezra 4:2) and Ashurbanipal (Osnappar, 4:9–10). Loyal Yahweh worshipers continued to come to Jerusalem from the city of Samaria even after Nebuchadnezzar's conquest of the city and temple (Jer. 41:5). Archaeological data give the names of two of the Assyrian governors of Samaria in the 7th cent. A fragment of a cuneiform tablet addressed to a Babylonian governor was found in the city's debris. Archaeologists have not found much evidence for this period in the palace area, since the Hellenistic and Roman city builders removed much of earlier building and sank deep foundations in other places.

When the Babylonians seized world power from the Assyrians, they continued to have Samaria as the capital of the province of Samaria, now called Samerina; but they also added to it the territory around Jerusalem. When the Persians took over world empire, Samaria was continued as the capital of the province of Samerina. Although Sanballat, the governor of that province, plays a large part in the postexilic period, his capital city Samaria is mentioned only in Ezra 4:17. See further Israel, history of.

III. Intertestamental history. With the coming of Alexander the Great to Palestine, the city of Samaria assumed a new character. It became the most important Greek city in central Palestine; and the Samaritan influence in what was the old province of Samaria was now only religious. Shechem from this time became the important Samaritan city. Its importance was climaxed by the building of a temple on nearby Mount Gerizim (see Samaritan).

When Alexander the Great moved S from Tyre to attack Egypt, he appointed Andromachus as governor of Samaria, but Andromachus was killed by some of the Samaritan leaders, who then fled to the Jordan valley. Their hideout has been excavated by the American School of Oriental Research and much valuable data on this episode has been found. Alexander punished the city by deporting a part of its population, and by making the city a Macedonian colony in 331 B.C.

The city's defenses were greatly improved, probably by Perdiccas, as soon as the Macedonians occupied it. Some scholars date these defenses later to the Ptolemaic-Seleucid fighting, but this is unlikely. Although the old Israelite defenses were used, the walls on the middle terrace were strengthened with massive circular towers of excellent craftsmanship. They averaged 40–48 ft. in diameter. A new defense wall with a battered face was found in one area and dated c. the 2nd cent. B.C. This wall,

Remains of the theater built at Hellenistic Samaria (Sebaste).

although some 13 ft. thick, was breached by the troops of John Hyrcanus (see HASMONEAN II.A) when they captured Samaria in 107 B.C.

The objects found in the houses of this period show that Samaria was a typical Hellenistic city. The general cultural level seems to have been as high as that of any Israelite or Roman city on the site. The city was economically prosperous and seems to have done much commercial trading of its grains for wine with the island of RHODES, for Rhodian jar handles are found in great quantity (over 2,000) everywhere on the site. Greek and Egyptian deities were worshiped. After the death of Alexander, the city belonged to the Ptolemies (see PTOLEMY) most of the time up to 198 B.C., when it became the permanent property of the Seleucids (see SELEUCUS).

John Hyrcanus moved against Samaria after his capture of Shechem and his destruction of the Samaritan temple on Mount Gerizim. The Samaritans had asked both the Seleucids and the Ptolemies for troops, but John Hyrcanus defeated both these units sent against him. He then besieged Samaria and captured it within a year, c. 107 B.C. JOSEPHUS (*Ant*. 13.10.3 §281) states that the city was so thoroughly destroyed that no sign of it remained. However, archaeologists found this statement to be a great exaggeration of the facts. The city was occupied at least in part by the time POMPEY conquered Palestine, and he added it to the Roman empire in 63 B.C. The city, however, had not been refortified after its capture by Hyrcanus. Samaria was annexed to the province of Syria by the Romans.

The Roman proconsul Gabinius (57–55 B.C.) ordered the restoration of Samaria; the breaches in the fortifications made by John Hyrcanus were repaired. New straight streets were also laid out and the houses were built in regular block patterns as today. Five different streets were found, but they were very narrow, only c. 8–10 ft. wide. Each block averaged four houses and a row of shops. The best house occupied half a block and had three shops at one end and fifteen rooms built around two open courts. The houses were plastered and painted in panelings of red, purple, white, and yellow. This is a good picture of much of city life wherever Romans built their towns in NT times. The general layout of the city's forum may belong to this period although it was certainly completed by HEROD the Great.

The greatest builder in the history of Palestine was not Solomon, but Herod the Great. Samaria was a city he loved, and he embellished it in every way. He began the reconstruction of the city in 30 B.C. and spent at least ten years at the task. As mentioned above, he renamed it Sebaste in honor of his patron, Emperor Augustus. On the site of

Omri's palace, the highest point in the city, he erected a large beautiful temple for the worship of Augustus as a god! This is the same Herod who built the temple of Yahweh at Jerusalem in which Christ himself worshiped. Incidentally, the Roman Emperor Augustus was not appreciative of this temple which Herod dedicated to his worship.

Josephus gives only a brief description of Herod's Samaria (*Ant.* 15.8.5 §§296–98), but archaeologists have brought the city to life. Herod built a new city wall, strengthened with towers. The wall was more than 2 mi. in length. The lower sections of the circular towers which constituted the W gate of the city are still intact. It is the only one of the city's gates excavated to date. The construction work was probably done by local craftsmen, as it is inferior to the work on the walls of Jerusalem, where Herod did his finest building.

Only small portions of Herod's temple to the Divine Augustus have survived for the archaeologist to study. This temple was rebuilt and radically modified in pattern at a later date, perhaps in the reign of Septimius Severus. Herod's temple had a great forecourt which was approximately square, c. 240 ft. on a side. It was enclosed by several walls.

At the S end of the forecourt a staircase 90 ft. wide that led to the temple proper was in two units, broken by a landing about halfway up. At the foot of the staircase and on the floor of the courtyard was a massive altar. In the debris just E of the altar a large fragment of a statue of a Roman emperor was found. Some scholars believe this was a statue of the Emperor Augustus, to whom the temple was dedicated. The temple itself seems to have had a wide portico in front of the cella. The latter was 45 ft. wide. On either side of it were narrow corridors that made the temple proper the same width as the portico. The columns used in the temple were probably of the Corinthian order, as this order was used in his other major projects. Close to the temple were some major buildings that may have been used by the temple priests.

The dates of two of the city's monuments are uncertain. Some scholars date them to Gabinius and others to Herod the Great. One is the stadium in the valley below the city. As its columns are of the Doric order, they may be the work of Gabinius, since Herod preferred the Corinthian order. The first phase of the forum is also uncertain, although most of it that is seen today is much later. Herod was a great lover of the theater and he must have had one in this city he loved so well. The colonnaded street seen in the olive orchard above the ruins today is late Roman in date, but Herod probably constructed at least one major street of this same type.

Herod the Great willed Samaria to his son Archelaus (see HEROD IV), but he was such a poor ruler that Rome removed him. Samaria was then placed under the jurisdiction of the Roman governor, whose headquarters were at CAESAREA.

IV. NT history. This Herodian city was the Samaria of the NT. It is not specifically mentioned in the Gospels. In Acts, Samaria is mentioned as a place where PHILIP went to preach and as the center for the work of SIMON MAGUS (Acts 8:5, 9), but it is uncertain whether the city or the territory is meant (in v. 5 the earliest MSS have "the city of Samaria," but most witnesses omit the definite article, thus, "a city of Samaria"). In v. 14, a reference to the city seems likely, as the apostles did their crucial doctrinal work in urban areas. There is a strong tradition that JOHN THE BAPTIST was buried at Samaria, but there is no proof. Two early churches here honor him.

When the Jews revolted against Rome, Samaria was one of the first cities to suffer. The Jews captured and sacked it in A.D. 66 in the first months of the revolt. The city, however, must have made a good comeback, for there is a fragmentary inscription of VESPASIAN that would favor such a view. Neither written records nor archaeological data throw much light on Samaria in the closing days of the NT. The peak period of Samaria's greatness was c. A.D. 180–230. Most of the city's Roman ruins visible today belong to that period.

(See further G. A. Reisner et al., *Harvard Excavations at Samaria* [1924]; J. W. Crowfoot et al., *The Buildings at Samaria* [1942]; J. W. and G. M. Crowfoot and K. M. Kenyon, *The Objects from Samaria* [1957]; A. Parrot, *Samaria: The Capital of the Kingdom of Israel* [1958]; B. Becking, *The Fall of Samaria: An Historical and Archaeological Study* [1992]; *ABD*, 5:914–21; *NEAEHL*, 4:1300–1310; R. E. Tappy, *The Archaeology of Israelite Samaria*, 2 vols. [1992–2001]; id. in *The Oxford Encyclopedia of Archaeology in the Near East*, ed. E. M. Meyers [1997], 4:463–67; id. in *DOTHB*, 854–62.)

J. KELSO

Samaria (territory). A name applied to the general region in which the city of Samaria was located; see SAMARIA (CITY). This use of the term, however, is attested only after the fall of the city.

I. Geography. There is very little definite data on the boundaries of the territory of Samaria. Usually it is considered as the land occupied by the tribes of EPHRAIM and W MANASSEH. Geographically, the S boundary is the road that goes from JERICHO to BETHEL and then descends via the valley of AIJALON to the Mediterranean. The N boundary consists of Mount Carmel (see CARMEL, MOUNT) and Mount GILBOA and the hills that connect these two bastions. The Mediterranean is the W boundary with the Jordan on the E. Both SHECHEM and the city of Samaria are near the center of the area, with Samaria more to the N and W. The area made its wealth from its productive farm lands and its international trade routes.

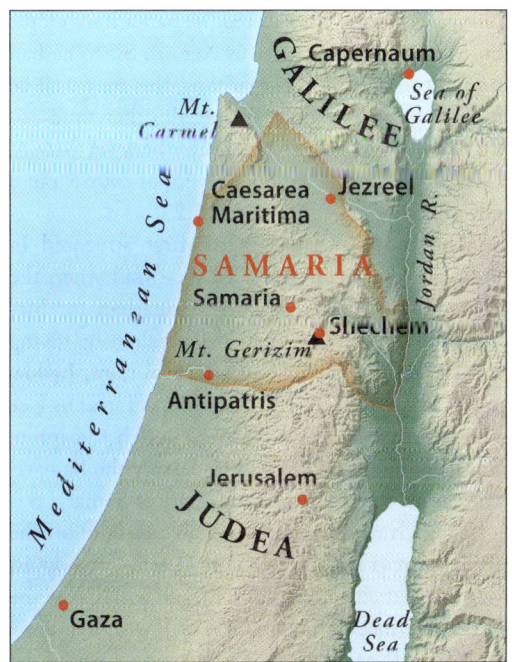

The region of Samaria.

The natural produce included grains and olives and the fruit of vineyards and orchards, plus flocks and herds. Samaria always had a good produce market in nearby commercial PHOENICIA. Note the economic-political marriage between AHAB and JEZEBEL. It was to the benefit of commerce that both the N-S ROADS, one along the coast and one along the high ridge, went through the territory of Samaria. There were three roads running E and W. The S road, as mentioned above, went from Jericho to Bethel to the Mediterranean. The center highway had a much better grade through a natural pass at Shechem between Mounts GERIZIM and EBAL. The N road was a continuation of the coastal road, where it cut across the plain of DOTHAN to modern Jenin and down through the vale of JEZREEL to the JORDAN River at BETH SHAN (later called Scythopolis). Most of the land commerce between Egypt and Syria went through the district of Samaria.

II. Political history. The use of SAMARITAN as a political term came only after the conquest of Samaria by the Assyrian SARGON II in 721 B.C. (see 2 Ki. 17:29, which has the only OT occurrence of Heb. *šōmĕrōnî* H9085, "Samaritan"). Sargon made it into the province of Samerena. His records specifically speak of 27,290 persons being deported from the capital city of Samaria. He apparently took prisoners from other cities, since he settled large numbers of deportees in the province of Samaria, taking them from Babylon, Cuthah, Avva, Hamath, and Sepharvaim (2 Ki. 17:24). Later deportees were also settled in the province by ESARHADDON and his son ASHURBANIPAL (Osnappar, Ezra 4:2, 10). The basic population of the land, however, remained essentially Israelite, for not a single permanent feature of any of the religions practiced by the colonists influenced the Samaritan faith.

When the Assyrian empire weakened, JOSIAH tried to annex the Samaritan territory but he lost it to his military rival Pharaoh NECO. The latter, however, soon lost it in turn to NEBUCHADNEZZAR, who seems to have incorporated this old Assyrian province into his own Babylonian empire in 612 B.C. At that time the province reached as far S as Bethel, for that city was spared when Nebuchadnezzar destroyed Jerusalem in 586. Apparently he

SAMARIA (TERRITORY)

Topography of the hill country of Samaria. (View to the NE.)

then added this new area around Jerusalem to the old Samaritan province. The Persians seemed to have continued the same provincial policy as the Babylonians, for SANBALLAT was politically in charge of this area until NEHEMIAH reduced its size slightly by making the Jerusalem section into a semi-independent political unit under the high priests.

Historical evidence concerning the province of Samaria between the RESTORATION under NEHEMIAH and the era of ALEXANDER THE GREAT is scanty. JOSEPHUS recorded a number of interesting stories relating to Alexander in Palestine, but most historians reject them as fiction. It is known, however, that Alexander pensioned off some of his soldiers from the TYRE campaign at the city of Samaria. The Greek general whom he left in charge of the district of Samaria was murdered by the local people. After that the city was severely punished, and apparently the Samaritan population was uprooted, for afterward the city seemed to be essentially Greek. The details have been confirmed by modern archaeological findings. Shechem became the only major Samaritan city. The southern half of the province of Samaria seems always to have continued in the Samaritan faith. Paganism apparently prevailed in the northern half of the province around the capital city itself.

The Ptolemies (see PTOLEMY) carried prisoners to ALEXANDRIA from both the Jews and the Samaritans. Both of these religious groups continued to be important in that city, even through NT times. ANTIOCHUS Epiphanes seems not to have bothered the Samaritans, unless 2 Macc. 6:2 is correct where it implies that he rededicated the Samaritan temple on Mount Gerizim to Zeus Xenios. Since he had no fighting with the Samaritans, this may well be incorrect, as the Samaritans at all other times, so far as is known, were fanatical whenever Mount Gerizim was profaned. He would, of course, put a governor at Gerizim (2 Macc. 5:23).

The province of Samaria first appeared in the Maccabean story (see MACCABEE) when the Seleucid Demetrius rewarded Jonathan for lifting the siege of the Acra in Jerusalem by giving him three districts of Samaria: Ephraim, Lydda, and Ramathaim. By 128 B.C. John Hyrcanus (see HASMONEAN II.A) was strong enough to capture Shechem and Gerizim and to destroy the Samaritan temple there. As the capital city of Samaria was a strong Greek fortress, it was able to hold off the Jewish forces for a year before it fell. Scythopolis was the next city to be captured, and with its fall the entire province of Samaria was in Jewish hands.

When POMPEY captured Palestine, he annexed the city of Samaria to the province of SYRIA, and the Samaritans again became the local power in the district. In NT times Samaria extended from the free cities of Scythopolis and Jenin on the N to a line c. 15 mi. S of Shechem. The history of Samaria in NT times is treated under the article SAMARITAN. (See further S. Dar and S. Applebaum, *Landscape and Pattern: An Archaeological Survey of Samaria 800 B.C.E.–636 C.E.*, 2 vols [1986]; E. Stern, *Archaeology of the Land of the Bible. Volume II: The Assyrian, Babylonian, and Persian Periods, 732–332 BCE* [2001]; A. Zertal, *The Manasseh Hill Country Survey* [2004–7]; *ABD*, 5:926–31; *NEAEHL*, 4:1310–18.)   J. L. KELSO

Samaritan suh-mair′uh-tuhn (שֹׁמְרֹנִי *H9085*, gentilic of שֹׁמְרוֹן *H9076*; Σαμαρίτης *G4901*). An inhabitant of SAMARIA (TERRITORY).

I. History. Samaritans were Israelites who lived in the northern kingdom, but there is only one mention of them in the OT (2 Ki. 17:29). The word *Samaritan* as used in the NT refers to an ethnic-religious group whose central sanctuary was on Mount GERIZIM during intertestamental times. These Samaritans are best known through the mention of them in the gospel narratives. The Samaritan sect continues to this day; its members interpret their name as derived from the word *šōmĕrim* (a participial form of *šāmar H9068*, "to keep"), that is, "guardians [of the law]."

It is impossible to write an accurate history of the Samaritans because their records are so scanty; the references to them are also highly contradictory. Their history began after the Assyrian capture of the city of Samaria in 721 B.C., and the deportation of 27,290 of Israel's population (these figures are taken from Sargon's record of the conquest). Their major historic break with the Israelite tradition came at the time of this Assyrian conquest of Palestine. Their present-day traditions (which are not authenticated by documents from biblical times) are said to go back to Adam.

Samaritans believed that JOSHUA built a sanctuary on Mount Gerizim, which was the center for early Israelite worship. They dated the religious break with the Jews to the time of ELI, whom they accused of erecting a rival sanctuary at SHILOH. For a brief time, they claimed, there were two sanctuaries and two priesthoods. The PHILISTINES soon destroyed the Shiloh sanctuary, and SAUL persecuted the JOSEPH tribes (EPHRAIM and MANASSEH), depriving them of their sanctuary at Gerizim. Their tradition says that for a time they fled to BASHAN. The Samaritans recorded little about the decline of the city of Samaria except to imply that this was a political rather than a religious loss. See SAMARIA (CITY). SHECHEM, not Samaria, had always been and would continue to be their holy city. They modified the story of the lion plague (2 Ki. 17:24–33) by adding that the Assyrian king also permitted them to reinstitute their worship on Mount Gerizim.

As recorded by Jewish sources, however, the Samaritans are descendants of the colonists whom the Assyrians planted in the northern kingdom and who intermarried with the Israelite population that the Assyrians had left in the land. More likely they were the pure descendants of the Israelites left in the land, for Samaritan theology shows no sign of the influence of paganism among the colonists sent by the Assyrians. If there was intermarriage, the children became true Israelites.

Furthermore, shortly after the Assyrian conquest of Samaria, some people from Manasseh, Zebulun, and Asher went to King HEZEKIAH's great Passover in Jerusalem (2 Chr. 30:11). The city of Samaria was located in the tribe of Manasseh. As late as the time of JOSIAH, Manasseh and Ephraim contributed to the repairs on the Jerusalem TEMPLE (34:9). These two tribes became the core of the later Samaritan population. Both JEREMIAH and EZEKIEL treated the northern tribes as an integral part of covenant Israel. Ezekiel insisted on blending them with Judah as a common restored covenant people.

When ZERUBBABEL was building a new temple, the descendants of the foreigners brought in by ESARHADDON asked to take part, claiming that they were true Yahweh worshipers (Ezra 4:2), but they were refused. Later, foreigners from many places (4:9–10) joined in a petition to ARTAXERXES against Jerusalem, but DARIUS gave the Jews permission to continue to rebuild the temple. Nothing was said regarding the Samaritans, for they were not involved in this episode. The objection was raised by foreigners working together as a political block against Jerusalem.

When NEHEMIAH came to Jerusalem as a special representative of the Persian crown, he was opposed by SANBALLAT, the governor of the Persian subprovince of Samaria (Neh. 2:10—6:14; 13:28). Earlier, when Jerusalem was captured by the Babylonians, NEBUCHADNEZZAR had apparently added it to the province of Samaria. Sanballat recognized that Nehemiah was creating a new political unit around the city of Jerusalem, and this territory would, of course, be taken from Sanballat. Both Sanballat and his partner TOBIAH the Ammonite were Yahweh worshipers. This, therefore, was primarily a political struggle, not a religious issue. It may, however, have ended as a religious schism, if one follows the reasoning of the historians who date the Samaritan break to this feud.

The actual split between the descendants of the religious groups that had constituted the kingdoms of Israel and Judah came when the "Samaritans" built their own temple on Mount Gerizim. There is no exact date for this event. JOSEPHUS (*Ant.* 11.8.1–4) tells of the building of this temple, but the account is so confused that different scholars, on the basis of the evidence, date the building of this temple anywhere from the time of Nehemiah to the time of Alexander the Great. J. A. Montgomery (*The Samaritans, the Earliest Jewish Sect: Their History, Theology and Literature* [1907], 66–70) suggested that Josephus was expanding the Neh. 13:28–29 episode and so favored that date for the temple. It was destroyed by John Hyrcanus in 128 B.C. Some scholars believe that this Samaritan temple can be found beneath the temple built by the Roman emperor HADRIAN on Mount Gerizim.

The Samaritans were in general rejected by the Jews in the intertestamental period. The book of ECCLESIASTICUS speaks of them as "not even a people" and as "the foolish people that live in Shechem" (Sir. 50:25–26). The *Testament of Levi* (7.2) also calls Shechem "a city of fools." This derogation is relevant to Jn. 8:48, which records that the Jews called Jesus a Samaritan.

The Samaritans are mentioned by the gospel writers in connection with the ministry of Christ. He passed through Samaria and dealt with a Samaritan woman at the well of SYCHAR. He remained at Sychar for two days' ministry (Jn. 4:1–42). His interview with the Samaritan woman reflects both the antipathy between Jews and Samaritans and the dispute concerning the rightful place for the worship of God.

At another Samaritan village, Jesus was rejected (Lk. 9:52–53). Luke's gospel indicates that good qualities could be found in Samaritans, for a Samaritan leper returned to thank Christ for healing (17:11–19), and one of his best-known parables immortalized "a good Samaritan" (10:29–37).

On the key essentials of the doctrine of worship, however, Christ was completely Jewish in his talk with the Samaritan woman. The difference also shows that when Christ sent out the twelve disciples to work among the Jews, he gave them strict orders to stay away from Gentile and Samaritan cities (Matt. 10:5–7). At his ascension he commanded that world evangelism begin at Jerusalem, then reach out into Judea, then to Samaria, and finally to the uttermost parts of the earth. Thus, Samaria was regarded as a special unit. Acts 8:1–25 records the story of the mission work among the Samaritans. J. A. Montgomery writes as follows: "To sum up the witness of the New Testament: the Samaritan appears as an Israelite, but one whose religion is in the condition of ignorance and whose institutions are irregular" (*The Samaritans*, 164). The Samaritans, however, were not actually excommunicated by the Jews until about A.D. 300.

Politically the Samaritans prospered under POMPEY's conquest of Palestine and the administration of HEROD the Great. Herod made Samaria one of

Remains of a Byzantine church built over the Samaritan temple on Mount Gerizim.

the magnificent cities of Palestine. Here he erected one of his great pagan temples, which he dedicated to his patron, Emperor AUGUSTUS. One of his wives was a Samaritan, and she was the mother of Herod Antipas.

Herod willed the Samaritan district to his son Archelaus, who proved such a poor ruler that Augustus deposed him in A.D. 6. Samaria then fell under the Roman governor, who ruled from CAESAREA. Josephus (*Ant.* 18.3.4. §§85–87) wrote that it was PILATE's bloody handling of a fanatical assembly at Mount Gerizim that led to his removal as governor in A.D. 36. The Samaritan faith was a legal religion (*religio licita*) in the Roman empire. The Samaritans had synagogues in Egypt, Rome, and other key cities of the empire. Like the Jews, they had been taken to Egypt by the Ptolemies; from there, like the Jews, they had expanded into the key commercial cities of the Mediterranean, especially those that did business with Alexandria. Two Samaritan scholars of high repute are known. Theodotus, c. 200 B.C., wrote an epic on Shechem, of which forty-seven hexameters are presented in EUSEBIUS. Thallus, c. 40 B.C., wrote a history of the world.

The Samaritans, with all of Palestine, suffered greatly in the first Jewish revolt. Although VESPASIAN took action against the more fanatical Samaritans at Gerizim, the countryside was spared. He founded a new city to replace the old Shechem and called it Flavia Neapolis (modern Nablus); by the 4th cent. it was one of the great cities of Palestine. The Samaritans considered Emperor Hadrian as their first great persecutor. He destroyed most of their sacred writings and desecrated their sacred Mount Gerizim by building his own Roman temple to Jupiter, perhaps on the site of the old Samaritan temple.

Although the Samaritans suffered under later Roman emperors, their worst persecutions came from the Christians. Emperor Constantine granted them religious freedom, but it was not long afterward that persecution came to them. It was so severe that they revolted in 484, massacred the Christians nearby, and even attacked Caesarea. Bethel was suddenly refortified lest its population be massacred. The final great revolt, extending from Scythopolis to Caesarea, came in 529. Emperor Justinian outlawed the Samaritan sect and destroyed their synagogues, which were not rebuilt. In self-defense many of the Samaritans at least nominally accepted Christianity. Later, the emperor's edict was softened, but the plight of the faithful Samaritan from then on was most difficult. Nevertheless, of the many religions practiced under the Roman empire, it is one of the few remaining today.

A few hundred Samaritans still live in Nablus and in Jaffa (now Holon, a suburb of Tell Aviv). Mount Gerizim is still their holy mountain, and they hold their PASSOVER services on the traditional site of sacrifice. The Day of Atonement, however, is the holiest day of their year. The Sabbath is rigidly observed. They are distinctly a religious community. Their high priest acts also as their political official in relationship to whatever Palestinian government may be in power.

II. Theology. One can only conjecture concerning the total theology of the Samaritans in OT and NT times. What is known of their own writings is based primarily upon the work of their theologians who wrote in the 4th cent. A.D. during the revival under Baba Rabba.

Although the Jews and Samaritans had no dealings ordinarily with one another, the Jewish rabbinical records are in general not anti-Samaritan. It was about A.D. 300 before the Jews excommunicated the Samaritans. As late as the 2nd cent. A.D., some of the rabbis spoke highly of them. They were sometimes compared to the SADDUCEES, since both denied the RESURRECTION of the body and both objected to the PHARISEES' emphasis upon the traditions of the elders. The Jews' major theological indictment against the Samaritans was their insistence upon Mount Gerizim as the true place of worship instead of Jerusalem.

The Samaritan theology of NT times (as nearly as can be traced from scanty records) seems to be similar to that of the Jews. Both considered themselves to be true Yahweh worshipers. Both placed the supreme emphasis on the PENTATEUCH not only as Scripture but also as a detailed way of life. The Samaritans rejected the remainder of the Jewish canon; according to the records available, however, the Jews never specifically indicted them for this heresy. One might conjecture that the Samaritans did not include the other OT books in the canon because of the emphasis on the major importance of Jerusalem as a central sanctuary, and the relation of that city to the MESSIAH. The Samaritans, as did the Jews, looked for a Messiah, as is seen in the Samaritan woman's reference to him (Jn. 4:25).

As noted above, the major point of difference was the Samaritans' insistence that Mount Gerizim was the only true central sanctuary for all Israel. The text of the SAMARITAN PENTATEUCH in Deut. 27:4 reads Gerizim, not Ebal as in the Hebrew MT. The Genesis passages that could be interpreted as emphasizing Jerusalem, such as the reference to MELCHIZEDEK as king of SALEM and ABRAHAM's offering of Isaac on Mount MORIAH, were no problem to the Samaritans, who located these events at sites of similar name near Gerizim. Their interpretation may date from NT times, or even later. Following the TEN COMMANDMENTS in Exodus and Deuteronomy, the Samaritan text adds another commandment requiring the building of an altar on Mount Gerizim and the celebration of a sacrificial service there.

Samaritans of OT times probably held the same views of MOSES as did the Jews, but when the Samaritans developed their own theology after A.D. 400, they exalted Moses excessively and gave him titles that Christians reserve uniquely for Christ.

Like the Jews, the Samaritans looked for a final judgment with rewards and punishments in charge of the Messiah. Both Jews and Samaritans emphasized CIRCUMCISION, the SABBATH, and the kosher laws. Thus Jesus could stay in a Samaritan home for two days, eating their food and drinking water from JACOB'S WELL (Jn. 4:1–42).

GNOSTICISM plays a part in later Samaritan theology. Some scholars attribute a strong influence to the work of SIMON MAGUS of Samaria (Acts 8:9–24) in the early days of that heresy. Similarities have been noted between Samaritan beliefs and the DEAD SEA SCROLLS, although it is difficult to establish a connection between them. The 4th cent. A.D. is the most important century in the post biblical period, for the basic work on Samaritan religion and the canon for their social customs was written under Baba the Great. Their TARGUM of the Pentateuch (an Aramaic translation to be distinguished from the Samaritan Pentateuch) was written in the 5th or 6th cent. A.D.

(See further M. Gaster, *The Samaritans: Their History, Doctrines and Literature* [1925]; J. Macdonald, *The Theology of the Samaritans* [1964]; R. J. Coggins, *Samaritans and Jews: The Origins of Samaritanism Reconsidered* [1975]; J. Bowman, ed., *Samaritan Documents Relating to their History, Religion, and Life* [1977]; S. Lowy, *The Principles of Samaritan Bible Exegesis* [1977]; B. W. Hall, *Samaritan Religion from John Hyrcanus to Baba Rabba: A Critical Examination of the Relevant Material in Contemporary Christian Literature, the Writings of Josephus, and the Mishnah* [1987]; A. D. Crown, ed., *The Samaritans* [1989]; N. Schur, *History of the Samaritans* [1989]; A. D. Crown, *A Bibliography of the Samaritans*, 2nd ed. [1993]; A. D. Crown et al., *A Companion to Samaritan Studies* [1993]; I. Hjelm, *The Samaritans and Early Judaism: A Literary Analysis* [2000]; R. T. Anderson and T. Giles, *The Keepers: An Introduction to the History and Culture of the Samaritans* [2002]; R. Plummer, *Early Christian Authors on Samaritans and Samaritanism: Texts, Translations and Commentary* [2002]; I. Hjelm, *Jerusalem's Rise to Sovereignty* [2004]; R. T. Anderson and T. Giles, *Tradition Kept: The Literature of the Samaritans* [2005].)   J. L. KELSO

Samaritan Pentateuch. The form of the Hebrew text of the PENTATEUCH preserved and accepted by the SAMARITAN sect (it is to be distinguished from the Samaritan TARGUM, which is a translation of the Pentateuch into ARAMAIC). The Samaritan Pentateuch has been transmitted in the early type of rounded Hebrew letters (formerly called Phoenician) that largely ceased to be used by the Jews after they adopted the "square" Aramaic characters at the time of EXILE. In the course of copying and recopying, the forms of some of these letters have so changed that the Samaritan writing differs in a number of regards from the earlier form.

The first copy of the Samaritan Pentateuch to reach Europe came early in the 17th cent. when Pietro della Valle purchased a copy of it, and also a copy of an ARAMAIC translation of it (the Samaritan TARGUM), from a Samaritan whom he met in Damascus. Since that time dozens of other copies have reached Europe. Early in the 19th cent.,

H. F. W. Gesenius, the noted Hebraist, examined the Samaritan text very closely and declared that it was so full of minor errors as to be of no use for textual study of the Bible. In more recent years certain other scholars have gone to the opposite extreme, declaring that it represents a popular text widely circulated among the Jews as late as the 1st cent. B.C. See TEXT AND MANUSCRIPTS (OT).

There has been considerable discussion as to the time when the Pentateuch came into the hands of the Samaritans. There is no reason why copies of the TORAH might not have been available in northern Israel when the Assyrians led a great many of its people into exile in 721 B.C. Similarly, the priest whom the king of Assyria sent at a slightly later date to teach the law of the God of the land to those he had transported to this area from other regions (2 Ki. 17:27) probably brought with him a copy of the Pentateuch. In either case the book would likely not have been an exact copy of the official Torah that was preserved in the temple in Jerusalem (cf. Deut. 17:18; 31:25–26), but one of the copies belonging to private individuals or groups, or one that had been copied and recopied in one of the local centers.

In spite of these facts, so clearly attested in the Bible, it often has been asserted that the Samaritans had no copy of the law until the time when NEHEMIAH drove away from the temple a grandson of the high priest who had married a daughter of the Samaritan SANBALLAT (Neh. 13:28). There is, however, no scriptural statement that this renegade took a copy of the Torah from Jerusalem with him.

Some scholars insist that the peculiarities of the Samaritan Pentateuch point to an early Jewish textual tradition distinct from that of the MT, and that most of its similarities to the MT result from its having been influenced by it during the centuries between 300 B.C. and A.D. 100. However, there is no evidence of a close enough relationship between the Samaritans and the Jews during this period to suggest that such an alteration of the Samaritan Pentateuch might have occurred at this time. In fact, all the evidence that exists points in the opposite direction. There is a long history of opposition between the people at Samaria and those whose worship centered in Jerusalem. Hard feelings from the time of the divided kingdom were probably never entirely healed. When the Jews returned from exile the Samaritans offered to help in building the temple, but ZERUBBABEL and JESHUA vigorously repulsed them (Ezra 4:3, 10, 17). At about 300 B.C., Ben Sira closed his book of ECCLESIASTICUS with sharp words of criticism for "the foolish people that live in Shechem" (Sir. 50:26). In Maccabean times Jewish tradition represents the Samaritans as joining with the Seleucid oppressors. A few years later John Hyrcanus destroyed the Samaritan temple on Mount GERIZIM. In the time of Christ it was declared that the Jews and the Samaritans had no dealings with one another (Jn 4:9)

The great similarity between the Samaritan Pentateuch and the MT despite the long period of independent development, argues for the general accuracy of the Torah. During the long time when the kingdoms of Israel and Judah were separate there would have been abundant opportunity for small textual changes in popular MSS that were not copied with the extreme care devoted to the official copies at Jerusalem. The people of northern Israel, cut off from access to Jerusalem, would be likely to write explanatory glosses on the margins of their private copies of the law. These glosses largely included phrases taken from other parts of the Torah. On a number of occasions where the

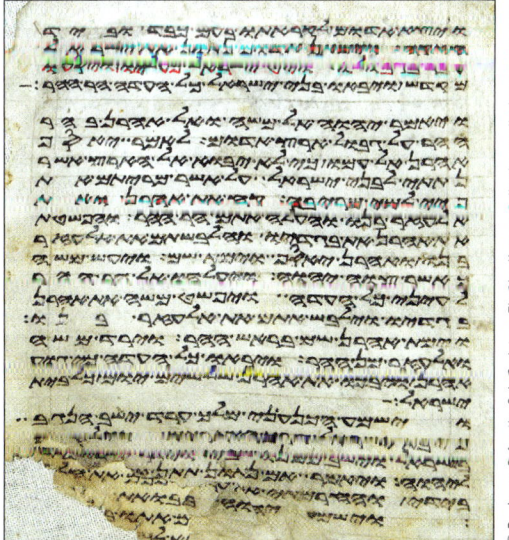

A 13th-cent. MS of the Samaritan Pentateuch.

Samaritan Pentateuch reports that Moses said or did something, it prefaces this statement by an explicit declaration that it was a divine command that he should do so. When the Lord orders Moses to deliver a message, and the MT merely says that he did so, the Samaritan Pentateuch is apt to repeat in detail the words of the message. Sometimes, but not usually, it agrees with the LXX. In a few places there is evidence of intentional alteration for doctrinal reasons, such as the substitution of Mount Gerizim for Mount EBAL as the place where the law was to be written on the stones of the altar (Deut. 27:4), but these are comparatively few.

The orthography of the Samaritan Pentateuch is much fuller than that of the Pentateuch in the MT. This is most readily explained as a natural development in styles of spelling. The Masoretes (see MASORAH) preserved the Pentateuch, as far as possible, as it had originally been written. The books of Chronicles, written after the exile, use the orthography of the later period. In the course of copying, points of orthography in the Samaritan Pentateuch were gradually changed in line with later developments.

In the fourth cave at QUMRAN there have been found many fragments of an early copy of Exodus (4QpaleoExod^m), written in the paleo-Hebrew script, an earlier form of the type of writing used in the present copies of the Samaritan Pentateuch. These fragments seem to possess the same textual peculiarities as the Samaritan Pentateuch. It was probably one of the unofficial texts that were circulated among private individuals and groups in Palestine during the 1st cent. B.C.

(See further H. F. W. Gesenius, *De Pentateuchi Samaritani* [1815]; A. von Gall, *Der hebräische Pentateuch der Samaritaner* [1914–18]; J. D. Purvis, *The Samaritan Pentateuch and the Origin of the Samaritan Sect* [1968]; E. Tov, *Textual Criticism of the Hebrew Bible* [1992], 80–100; B. K. Waltke in *ABD*, 5:932–40.) A. A. MACRAE

Samaritan Targum. See TARGUM II.

Samatus suh-may´tuhs (Σαματος). One of the sons of Ezora who agreed to put away their foreign wives (1 Esd. 9:34; the RSV identifies him with SHEMAIAH [cf. Ezra 10:42]).

samech sah´mek (סָמֶךְ, "support," from סָמַךְ H6164, "to support, help"). The fifteenth letter of the Hebrew ALPHABET (ס), with a numerical value of 60 (the reason for its name is uncertain). Its sound corresponds to that of English *s*.

Sameius suh-mee´yuhs. KJV Apoc. form of SHEMAIAH (1 Esd. 9:21).

Samgar sam´gahr (סַמְגַּר H6161, meaning uncertain). According to some scholars, Samgar (Jer. 39:3) is a place name corresponding to Babylonian *Sinmagir*, a province N of BABYLON ruled by NERGAL-SHAREZER (Neriglissar), one of NEBUCHADNEZZAR's officials who participated in the siege of Jerusalem (cf. W. McKane, *A Critical and Exegetical Commentary on Jeremiah*, ICC, 2 vols. [1986–96], 2:974–76). This view is adopted by the NIV, which identifies three officials in the text: (1) Nergal-Sharezer of Samgar, (2) a chief officer (RABSARIS) by the name of Nebo-Sarsekim, and (3) a high official (RABMAG) who was also called Nergal-Sharezer, but who may be the same as (1). The NRSV and other versions, following the MT more closely, identify four individuals: (1) "Nergal-sharezer," (2) "Samgar-nebo," (3) "Sarsechim the Rabsaris," and (4) "Nergal-sharezer the Rabmag" (the KJV, failing to understand that "Rabsaris" and "Rabmag" are titles, identifies six officials; see also SARSECHIM). It has also been suggested that the Babylonian term *sinmagir* or *simmagir* "denotes a duty carried out by Neriglissar" (*HALOT*, 2:759; cf. *Assyrian Dictionary*, 15:272).

Samgar-nebo sam´gahr-nee´boh (סַמְגַּר־נְבוּ). A Babylonian army officer who participated in the siege of Jerusalem (Jer. 39:3 KJV and other versions). See SAMGAR.

Sami say´mi. KJV Apoc. variant of SHOBAI (1 Esd. 5:28).

Samis say´mis. KJV Apoc. form of SHIMEI (1 Esd. 9:34).

Samlah sam´luh (שַׂמְלָה H8528, possibly an alternate form of שַׂלְמָה [see SALMA], but note *ABD*, 5:948). An early king of EDOM who ruled in Mas-

REKAH (Gen. 36:36–37; 1 Chr. 1:47–48). Nothing else is known about him.

Sammus sam´uhs. KJV Apoc. form of SHEMA (1 Esd. 9:43).

Samos say´mos (Σάμος G4904, "height" [cf. Strabo, *Geogr.* 8.3.19]). An island in the AEGEAN SEA off the W coast of ASIA MINOR, opposite the headlands of Mycale and the city of EPHESUS. Samos is 27 mi. long and 14 mi. wide, and it is separated from the mainland by a strait of one mile. The entire island is mountainous, but the terraced land is remarkably fertile. It produced olives, unusually fine wine, and abundant timber for native shipbuilders in antiquity. Settled by Ionian immigrants from Epidaurus, the island enjoyed great prosperity throughout antiquity, but particularly in the 6th cent. Allied with ATHENS during the 5th cent., it later passed into the hands of PERSIA, EGYPT, and then PERGAMUM. It was bequeathed to ROME by Pergamum in 133 B.C. and became part of the province of ASIA. In the 1st cent. A.D. it became an autonomous city-state. (See G. Shipley, *A History of Samos, 800–188 BC* [1987].)

Samos is mentioned in the APOCRYPHA as one of the places to which the Romans sent a letter indicating that the Jews should not be harmed (1 Macc. 15:19). It is also mentioned in the NT in connection with PAUL's sea voyage from TROAS to MILETUS as he returned to JERUSALEM at the end of his third missionary journey (Acts 20:15). The verb used in this text (*paraballō* G4125) leaves unclear whether the ship only passed by the island or actually stopped there. C. K. Barrett (*A Critical and Exegetical Commentary on the Acts of the Apostles*, ICC, 2 vols. [1994–98], 2:958) suggests that the "Western" editor of Acts, understanding the verb to mean that the traveling party did not reach Samos, thought an alternate port of call was needed and added the clause "and tarried to Trogyllium" (KJV, following most MSS). See TROGYLLIUM.

A. RUPPRECHT

Samothrace sam´uh-thrays (Σαμοθρᾴκη G4903, "Thracian height"). An island in the NE AEGEAN SEA, about 20 mi. off the coast of THRACE. The apostle PAUL and his companions, on their way from TROAS to NEAPOLIS, anchored on this island for a night (Acts 16:11).

Samothrace is very mountainous, and its central peak, Mount Fengari (5,577 ft.), is the most conspicuous landmark of the N Aegean. From it Poseidon was said to have surveyed the plains of TROY (Homer called it Poseidon's island, *Iliad* 13.12). Samothrace was virtually uninhabited until the 7th cent. B.C. because of its hostile coast. PLINY the Elder (*Nat.* 4.23) says that it became an anchorage for ships plying the N Aegean because they had to anchor somewhere due to the hazards of sailing at night.

The FERTILITY CULT of the great mother Cybele, as well as the MYSTERY RELIGION associated with the Cabeiri (or Cabiri), flourished on the island. During Hellenistic times the cult of the Cabeiri rivaled that of Demeter and Persephone at ELEUSIS. Philip of Macedon and his wife Olympias were initiates, as were many prominent Romans later. The Cabeiri were twin gods of unknown origin. HERODOTUS (*Hist.* 2.49) assigned them to the Pelasgians, the traditional settlers of Greece. Others consider them of Phrygian or Phoenician origin.

The island was excavated by French and Austrian teams in the 19th cent. and more recently by New York University. The sanctuary of the great gods, a rotunda dedicated to Queen Arsinoë II of Egypt, and a propylon of Ptolemy II have been uncovered. The most famous find was the "Winged Victory [or Nike] of Samothrace," currently in the Louvre, which was erected in a fountain to commemorate a naval victory of the Rhodians, in c. 190 B.C. (See further K. Lehmann, *Samothrace: A Guide to the Excavations and the Museum*, 6th ed. [1998]).

A. RUPPRECHT

Sampsames samp´suh-meez (Σαμψάμης, but the MSS have several spelling variations). One of the places to which the Roman consul Lucius wrote a letter in favor of the Jews (1 Macc. 15:23). The name Sampsames is not otherwise attested, but some scholars believe it may be the same as ancient Amisos (modern Samsun in Turkey), a trading port in PONTUS on the Black Sea (see J. A. Goldstein, *I Maccabees*, AB 41 [1976], 498). Another suggestion is Samosata, the capital of COMMAGENE, in what is now SE Turkey.

Samson sam´suhn (שִׁמְשׁוֹן H9088, possibly "sunny"; Σαμψών G4907). Son of MANOAH; a leader and hero of Israel, famous for his prodigious strength displayed against the PHILISTINES (Jdg. 13–16).

I. Name. The biblical account gives no etymology or other explanation for the name *Samson*. Nevertheless, most scholars have thought that the name derives from *šemeš* H9087, "sun" (for other possibilities, see *HALOT*, 4:1592–93). The ending *-ōn* is probably a diminutive or affectionate suffix, yielding a meaning such as "little sun," "sunny," or "sun's child." It is perhaps relevant that Samson was born only a few miles from BETH SHEMESH, a city whose name means "house of the sun." The city was presumably once the site of a shrine of the sun-god, so probably both names are survivals from pre-Israelite Canaan, where the worship of the SUN was evidently practiced. This has led some to understand the Samson story as a solar myth, but such an interpretation has been refuted (see T. H. Gaster, *Myth, Legend and Custom in the Old Testament* [1969], 434ff.).

II. Historical background. Samson was born during the period of the judges, probably around the beginning of the 11th cent. B.C. (see JUDGES, PERIOD OF). During this time God raised up national heroes to deliver his people from their enemies. These deliverers were termed *šōpĕṭîm*, literally meaning "judges," but in this context the Hebrew term (ptc. of *šāpaṭ* H9149) can be translated "rulers, chieftains, leaders." Samson is the last "judge" mentioned before the transitional period of ELI and SAMUEL to the monarchy. Israel's most formidable enemies at this time were the Philistines, whom God had used to oppress Israel because of their evil deeds (Jdg. 13:1). Into this situation Samson was born in order to begin to deliver Israel from the hand of the Philistines (13:5).

III. Birth. The four chapters of Judges devoted to Samson were built on the theme of a broken vow—a time-honored motif in the history of literature. Even before he was born, Samson was designated as a NAZIRITE, and the writer took a full chapter to emphasize that element (Jdg. 13).

Samson was born into a family from the tribe of DAN. His parents had formerly been childless because of the wife's BARRENNESS (Jdg. 13:2). In the ancient world, childlessness was considered one of the worst things that could happen to a couple, and particularly to the woman, whom the husband could divorce for this reason. Male children were more desirable for three reasons. (1) they carried on the family name (note the frequent mention of "X son of Y" throughout the Bible); (2) their labor was more valuable in an agricultural society; (3) they were not as expensive as girls, because a girl of marriageable age had to have a dowry from her father. It is not surprising then that the Bible makes emphasis on several barren women whom God empowered to have a son: SARAH (Gen. 16:1; 18:1–15; 21:1–3); REBEKAH (25:21–26); RACHEL (30:1–2, 22–24); HANNAH (1 Sam. 1); and ELIZABETH (Lk. 1:5–25).

Because of the unusual character of such births, they were sometimes divinely announced ahead of time. Both ABRAHAM, the husband of Sarah, and ZECHARIAH, the husband of Elizabeth, were told that their barren wives would conceive. However, the annunciation of Samson did not come to his father, Manoah, but to his mother, who remains unnamed. Manoah prayed for an additional visit of the man of God, and when the request was granted he asked for instructions regarding the nurture of the promised son. Eventually Manoah presented a sacrifice to the angel and asked his name (Jdg. 13:15–17). He received no answer, since names were considered the essence of a person, and to know the name would have carried with it the ability to control the person (cf. Gen. 32:29). Only after the angel disappeared in the flame of the sacrifice did Manoah and his wife realize that they had been talking to an ANGEL (Jdg. 13:21–23).

Central to the promise of a son were the instructions the angel gave. The boy to be born was to be consecrated to God as a Nazirite from birth. The Nazirite vow involved three prohibitions: (1) against eating or drinking the fruit of the vine; (2) against contamination by any unclean thing; (3) against cutting the hair. Three times the injunction was repeated, each time addressed to his mother (Jdg. 13:4–5, 7, 14). The implication is that the boy was to be so completely consecrated to God that his mother had to refrain from these things while he was still in the womb. The repetitions were clearly purposeful, and leave the reader with no uncertainty regarding the theme of the story.

The regulations for a Nazirite are given in Num. 6:2–21, but in the book of Judges the order was changed so that the prohibition against the cutting of the hair came last. This again was purposeful, since the climax of the story came when Samson broke his vow and allowed his hair to be cut.

IV. Life. Samson's life was the story of his breaking the Nazirite vow. Hebrew storytelling is at its best in describing how he violated the prohibitions, climaxing with the cutting of his hair by DELILAH.

Samson's first adventure, or misadventure, involved a trip down to TIMNAH (Jdg. 14:1–4), a town in Philistine territory but not more than a few miles from Samson's house in ZORAH. Passage between Israel and Philistia was easy because the Philistines controlled SW Israel (15:11). In Timnah, Samson fell in love with a Philistine woman. This was to be the first of three women who were to prove his undoing. Samson came home to his parents with the request that they acquire her as his wife. Although his parents objected, preferring instead an Israelite for a daughter-in-law, God "was seeking an occasion to confront the Philistines" (14:4).

Two additional trips to Timnah to see his girlfriend brought the first violation of his Nazirite vow (Jdg. 14:5–9). On one occasion he met a lion on his way and killed it with his bare hands (14:6). He stopped to see the carcass of the lion on his next trip, and found it full of honey. So he took some, ate it, and brought some home to his parents. Numbers 6:6 specifically indicates that a Nazirite was not to go near a dead body. Since the text says that Samson did not tell his parents what he had done (Jdg. 14:6, 9), the implication is that he knew he was breaking his vow.

Samson's fourth trip to Timnah was to marry the Philistine woman (Jdg. 14:10–20). He gave a feast to celebrate the occasion. The Hebrew word for "feast" (*mišteh* H4492) implies a drinking bout, which the Philistines would have enjoyed. Though the text does not specifically say that Samson drank, the clear implication is that he did, and thereby broke the second regulation of his Nazirite vow.

Also at the wedding festivities Samson proposed a RIDDLE that turned on a play of words (Jdg. 14:14, 18; cf. J. R. Porter in *JTS* 13 [1962]: 106–9). His friends answered the riddle, apparently waiting until the last moment before the marriage was to be consummated (14:18). Enraged, Samson went to ASHKELON, killed thirty men, and used their garments to pay off the wager he had made with his friends. He then returned home without consummating his marriage. Some have argued that the intended marriage was a type of matriarchal marriage known as *sadîqâ*, where the husband either lives with his wife's family or makes periodic visits to her. However, since Samson left in a rage (14:19) we do not know whether he intended to bring his bride home after the ceremonies were over or live at her house.

When he returned to Timnah to visit his wife, he was prevented by her father; she had been given in marriage to Samson's best man (Jdg. 15:1–2). According to Canaanite custom, influenced by Sumerian and Babylonian law, the father could give his daughter away to someone else when the first bridegroom left before the consummation of the marriage. But it was expressly forbidden to give her to the best man, who was to protect the groom's interests. Samson's revenge was to burn the corn fields of the Philistines in heroic fashion by attaching torches to the tails of 150 pairs of foxes (15:3–5). Ovid tells that it was customary to send foxes into the fields with firebrands tied to their tails at the annual festival of Ceres (*Fasti* 4.680ff.).

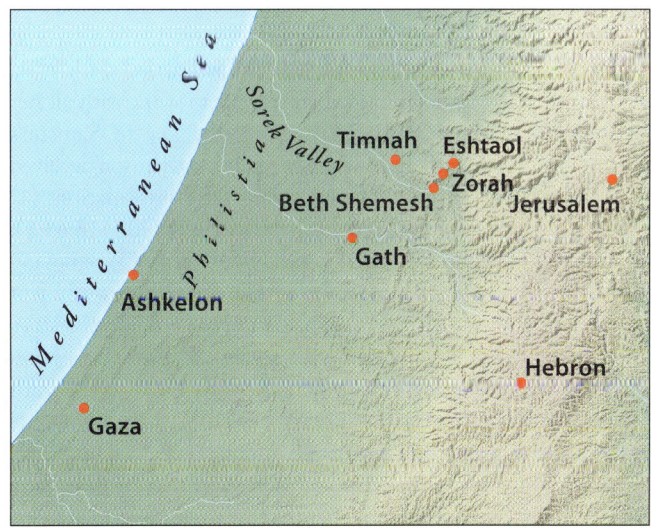

The story of Samson is closely connected to the Sorek Valley and the Philistine Plain.

A similar tactic was employed by Hannibal when he scared the Roman troops by sending oxen into their fields with firebrands tied to their horns (Livy, *Hist.* 22.16ff.). The Philistines, knowing that the law was on Samson's side, took revenge on the bride and her father by burning them—the common treatment of an adulterer (15.6). So Samson responded by killing many Philistines (15:8). Later, on another occasion, he killed a thousand Philistines with only the jawbone of a donkey (15:15–16).

Samson's second woman was a harlot he found in Gaza (Jdg. 16:1–3). While Samson was having sexual relations with her, the Philistines plotted his death. But despite their well-laid plans, he escaped by carrying the city gates to a hill near Hebron, some 40 mi. away. This was the worst humiliation, because city gates symbolized national strength.

Samson's breaking of his third vow brought his downfall. The Philistines were desperate and plotted his end continuously. Their opportunity came when Samson fell in love with Delilah, the third woman in his life (Jdg. 16:4–22). She lived in the valley of Sorek, only a few miles from his home. The Philistine lords, who were five in number (cf. 3:3) and ruled the Philistine pentapolis, now came to Delilah with a fantastic bribe. Each offered her 1,100 pieces of silver, a sum with purchasing power well into five figures. She is nowhere named as a Philistine and perhaps she was not, since the bribe was so high. Yet her collaboration seems to indicate she was a Philistine; the size of the bribe would then show how valuable Samson was.

Delilah immediately went to work with all her womanly charms, seeking the key to Samson's strength. For a while she failed, as Samson deceived her three times by giving false information: (1) snapping seven fresh bowstrings (Jdg. 16:6–9); (2) breaking new ropes (16:10–12); (3) removing a whole loom woven into his seven locks of uncut hair (16:13–14). This last event brought the story to the point of climax because Samson's deception regarding his hair came close to revealing the truth (note also the literary device of three items climaxed by a fourth one, Amos 1:3 et al.). The climax itself came when Samson succumbed to Delilah's coaxing and told her that his strength resided in his hair. She lulled him to sleep and cut off his seven locks, depriving Samson of his strength. In addi-

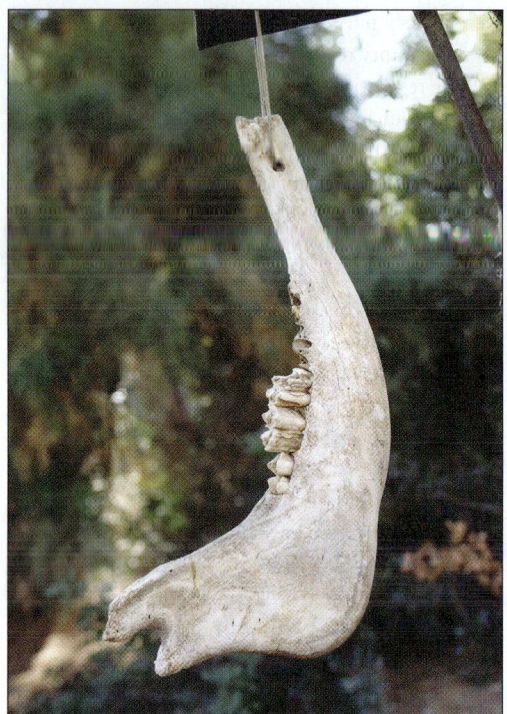

On one occasion, Samson killed 1,000 Philistines with the jawbone of a donkey (Jdg. 15:15).

tion, Samson was made a captive of the Philistines. His eyes were put out (a customary penalty, cf. 1 Sam. 11:2 and 2 Ki. 25:7), and he was set to grinding in a prison at Gaza (Jdg. 16:21). Here his hair began to grow again (16:22).

Samson was not the only one whose long hair was associated with heroic strength. Achaean warriors often were called the "long-haired" (Homer, *Iliad* 2.323, 443 et al.). The fighting strength of the god Phoebus was associated with his unshorn hair (ibid., 20.39). Finally, the Gilgamesh Epic states that the mighty Enkidu had long hair like a woman; and the glyptic art bears this out.

V. Death. Samson's death came with his final heroic deed. To celebrate Samson's capture and give glory to Dagon, their god, the Philistines assembled at a temple in Gaza. Samson was called out of prison to make sport before the assembled body. Led by a little lad to a position between two pillars, Samson asked to feel the pillars. He then prayed to God for strength to avenge himself. God answered, and Samson pulled down the supporting pillars of the temple.

Though it resulted in his own death, he killed more Philistines with this act than during all of his life. He had judged Israel for twenty years (Jdg. 16:28–31).

VI. Character. Samson was a somewhat enigmatic figure, with very little similarity to other judges. He resembled them only by being possessed of the Spirit, who seized him suddenly and drove him to violent action, exhibiting itself in extraordinary strength. But his exploits were always individual. He called no one else to his aid, led no troops to battle, and was in no sense a national leader. In fact, all he did was to avenge his own personal wrongs on the Philistines. Yet the key to the understanding of Samson is to be found in these individual exploits. They are of such extraordinary proportions that Samson must be understood as a heroic figure, living in a heroic age, and recorded in heroic literature. (For evidence, see the writings of C. H. Gordon, esp. *The Common Background of Greek and Hebrew Civilizations* [1965], and the unpublished dissertation of C. E. Armerding, *The Heroic Ages of Greece and Israel: A Literary-Historical Comparison* [1968]). Comparisons with other heroic figures, such as Hercules and Gilgamesh, are very illuminating. But comparisons do not mean point-for-point parallels. It is stretching the evidence, for example, to find twelve labors of Samson to parallel the twelve labors of Hercules, as some have done. (See G. G. Cohen in *EvQ* 42 [1970]: 131–41.)

VII. Historical significance. The setting of Samson's exploits was along the border between the Philistines and the tribe of Dan. Thus the primary historical significance of the story is the insight it gives us into life along the border. This information is largely sociological — marriage customs and wedding festivities, relationships with women, riddles, bribes, etc. There is also information about the Philistine domination of Israel. The tribe of Dan at one time had expanded out to the Mediterranean coast (Jdg. 5:17), but in Samson's day both Dan and Judah were controlled by the Philistines (15:11). The pressure was so great that at least part of the tribe of Dan migrated N (chs. 17–18). The weapons of Samson — a jawbone, his bare hands, and physical strength — clearly indicate that Israel was without the weapons of war and explain the Philistine success. The Philistines had a superior material culture that included the smelting of IRON. They specifically guarded this knowledge and prevented the Israelites from learning it and using it to make iron weapons (1 Sam. 13:19–23). Thus Israel was no match for the Philistines, unless they had a man of extraordinary strength like Samson fighting for them.

VIII. Religious significance. Since Samson is a heroic figure living in a heroic age, one must be careful in drawing religious significance from his life. His exploits resulted from the circumstances of a rough-and-ready life. Thus his virtues and vices were those of the heroic age in which he lived and should not be imitated or avoided, as the case may be. Samson broke his Nazirite vow and disobeyed God, and therein is his religious significance. His life is a negative example of a charismatic leader who came to a tragic, yet heroic, end. Nevertheless, his partial victory over the enemy was reason to be named with the heroes of the faith (Heb. 11:32).

(In addition to the standard commentaries on Judges, see P. Carus, *The Story of Samson and Its Place in the Religious Development of Mankind* [1907]; A. S. Palmer, *The Samson-Saga and Its Place in Comparative Religion* [1913]; A. G. Van Daalen, *Samson* [1966]; J. L. Crenshaw, *Samson: A Secret Betrayed, a Vow Ignored* [1978]; id., "Samson," in *ABD*, 5:950–54; P. Galpaz-Feller, *Samson: The Hero and the Man* [2006]; G. Mobley, *Samson and the Liminal Heroes in the Ancient Near East* [2006].)

J. C. MOYER

Samuel sam′yoo-uhl (שְׁמוּאֵל H9017, derivation uncertain [see also SHEMUEL, rendered "Samuel" by NIV in 2 Chr. 7:2]; Σαμουήλ G4905). The last Israelite leader prior to the monarchy (see JUDGES, PERIOD OF). In his ministry Samuel served as judge, priest, and prophet. The first nineteen chapters of 1 Samuel provide the basic source material for his life. The Hebrew form *šĕmû'ēl* possibly means "his name is God" (see *HALOT*, 4:1554–55; J. D. Fowler, *Theophoric Personal Names in Ancient Hebrew* [1988], 119, 124), but by a wordplay on the verb *šāmaʿ* H9048 (note the consonant *ʿayin* rather than *ʾaleph*) it can be understood as "heard by God" (1 Sam. 1:20; the explanation here also evokes the name שָׁאוּל H8620, "one asked for"; see SAUL).

The parents of Samuel were ELKANAH and HANNAH. By lineage Elkanah was a Levite, a descendant of KOHATH but not of the Aaronic line (1 Chr. 6:26, 33 [KJV, "Shemuel"]). Geographically Elkanah was identified as an Ephraimite, since he lived in the mountainous territory of EPHRAIM in the city of Ramah, more specifically identified as Ramathaim (1 Sam. 1:1; see RAMAH #3).

Samuel's parents were God-fearing Israelites who annually went to SHILOH to worship at the TABERNACLE. Hannah, who was not blessed with children as was Elkanah's other wife PENINNAH, made it a matter of earnest prayer that she might have a son (1 Sam. 1:10–11). In due time when God granted her request she named her son Samuel and kept her vow by dedicating him to a life of service (vv. 20–38). Whereas Samuel as a Levite might have started priestly service at the age of twenty-five, he was, through this act of dedication by Hannah, brought to the tabernacle as a child. Elkanah and Hannah returned annually to supply Samuel with clothes while he was reared in Shiloh under the supervision of ELI the priest. Hannah's song of praise is recorded in 2:1–10.

Although Samuel came from a godly home, the tabernacle environment was not godly. Eli, the high priest in Israel, had failed to teach his sons the fear of God according to his paternal responsibility prescribed in the book of Deuteronomy. Consequently, his sons HOPHNI and PHINEHAS had neither respect for their father nor reverence for God in their duties as priests. Through their violation of the laws of sacrifice and their immoral acts with women, the sons of Eli precipitated God's judgment upon Eli's family as announced by a prophet identified as a man of God (1 Sam. 2:27–36). In this environment at the central sanctuary in Shiloh, the child Samuel grew to young manhood.

While these conditions prevailed and Eli was aging, the divine call came to Samuel (1 Sam. 3:1–18). Fortunately Eli had enough spiritual perception to advise Samuel that God was speaking to him. When Samuel responded in an attitude of obedience, saying, "Speak, for your servant is listening," he became the recipient of God's message of judgment upon the house of Eli. Pressed by Eli, the young man Samuel as a spokesman for God shared with Eli the solemn divine verdict that the iniquity of Eli's priestly family could be purged with neither sacrifice nor offering.

Subsequent to his call, Samuel was established as a prophet in the land of Israel from the southern border of BEERSHEBA to the northern extremity of DAN. Although details concerning Samuel himself are briefly given in the record, the general conditions are vividly portrayed.

The low ebb of Israel's religion is apparent in the crucial battle with the PHILISTINES in the APHEK area, c. 35 mi. NW of JERUSALEM. Losing the battle, the Israelites prevailed upon Hophni and Phinehas to bring the ARK OF THE COVENANT, which was considered the holiest object in Israel, to the battlefield (1 Sam. 4:1–3). Religion among the Israelites had declined to such a low perspective spiritually that they believed God's presence was materially associated with the ark. Believing that God would not let himself be captured, they anticipated a divine intervention that would bring them victory. The nation of Israel, however, was shockingly defeated, and the ark was captured by the Philistines. The sons of Eli were killed in battle; Eli himself died when news reached him that the ark was stolen and that in all probability the city of Shiloh was destroyed by the Philistines. Although the biblical narrative does not mention the destruction of Shiloh, there are references in Jeremiah (Jer. 7:12, 14; 26:6, 9) and in Psalms (Ps. 78:60) that imply that it had been destroyed. Shiloh ceases to be mentioned as a religious center after 1 Sam. 4. (See W. F. Albright in *BASOR* 9 [Feb. 1923]: 10–11, for archaeological information; cf. also H. Kjaer in *JPOS* 10 [1930]: 87–114.)

Years later, possibly twenty, the ark was returned and stored in the home of ABINADAB in KIRIATH JEARIM. During these years Samuel must have been very active in his teaching ministry throughout Israel, challenging the people to turn from IDOLATRY (1 Sam. 7:1–3). When the Israelites responded favorably, Samuel called a national public assembly at MIZPAH in BENJAMIN where they fasted and prayed. Learning of this gathering, the Philistines organized a military attack on Mizpah. As a prophet-statesman Samuel prayed for Israel and officiated as a priest in offering sacrifice. Through a divinely sent thunderstorm, the Philistines were confused and subsequently routed. In memory of this miraculous intervention and victory Samuel erected a stone, naming it EBENEZER ("stone of help"), acknowledging, "Thus far has the LORD helped us" (v. 12). In this way Samuel's ministry as a prophet led the Israelites into a wholehearted love relationship with God, resulting in Israel's victory over the Philistines, and brought temporary peace to the Israelites.

Samuel resided in Ramah, where he built an altar to God (1 Sam. 7:17). As judge, Samuel held courts annually in BETHEL, GILGAL, MIZPAH (vv. 15–16), and probably in numerous cities throughout the land that are not mentioned in the biblical record. Samuel had gained the respect of the Israelites as a judge and as a prophet throughout the entire nation. However, Joel and Abijah, the sons of Samuel, were apparently known as judges who accepted bribes, twisted justice, and consequently did not reflect the dimensions of a prophetic ministry.

When the Israelites confronted Samuel with the request for a king they gave two reasons for their petition. Negatively, they were disappointed in Samuel's delegation of authority to his sons, and, positively, they wanted to be like other nations by having a king. Samuel was greatly disturbed by this request, but he was divinely assured that this was God's permissive will and that he should outline the responsibilities the Israelites would assume under a king (1 Sam. 8:1–22). Reluctantly, Samuel consented to their plea for a king.

As prophet in Israel, Samuel was divinely commissioned to anoint SAUL as king. Searching for his father's donkeys, Saul came into the Ephraim highlands in the Zuph district. At his servants' suggestion, Saul went to Ramah to inquire of the prophet Samuel. The latter detained him until the next day and privately anointed him as king of Israel. He later anointed Saul publicly (1 Sam. 9:1—10:27).

Samuel's commission to anoint Saul as king made it very plain that a king in Israel was leader over God's people Israel (1 Sam. 9:16) or "over his inheritance" (10:1). Saul was anointed by a prophet who had been divinely confirmed through miracles and was recognized in his ministry as a spokesman for God. The people over whom the king was to rule were God's people and God's possession. The "leader" or king had stewardship responsibility, being accountable to God for the power he exercised as a ruler over the Israelites. As Samuel outlined the ways of the kingdom (10:25), he provided a written copy that was deposited "before the LORD," and in all likelihood was kept with the other written documents which Moses (Deut. 31:9) and Joshua (Josh. 24:25–26) and possibly others had provided previously. The position of a king as indicated by Samuel was in accord with what Moses had prescribed in Deut. 17, that the king as well as his people were to be subject to the written terms of God's revelation given through Moses.

Samuel publicly reaffirmed his support of Saul after his initial victory over the Ammonites. He assured all Israel of his intercessory prayers and warned them about the dangers of diminishing their attitude of wholehearted devotion to God (1 Sam. 11–12). Serving in his capacity as priest and prophet, Samuel warned Saul about his failures and reminded him of his responsibilities. Becoming impatient in waiting for Samuel in Gilgal, Saul assumed the priestly responsibility of officiating at the offering of a burnt sacrifice (13:8–15). When Samuel arrived, he reprimanded Saul that as prince over God's people he had failed, then warned him that his kingship would not last.

When Samuel was divinely instructed to commission Saul to execute God's judgment upon the Amalekites, Saul failed in this assignment, and the relationship between prophet and king was crucially strained. On this occasion Samuel distinctly enunciated the basic principle that obedience is

Nebi Samwil, traditional burial place of the prophet Samuel marked by a modern-day minaret.

better than sacrifice (1 Sam. 15:22). With the solemn warning that Saul had forfeited the kingdom, the prophet Samuel and King Saul parted. Samuel returned to Ramah to grieve over Saul and his failures as king of Israel.

Subsequently Samuel was divinely commissioned to offer sacrifice in BETHLEHEM and anoint DAVID as king of Israel (1 Sam. 16). Fleeing from Saul, David was temporarily sheltered in Samuel's home in NAIOTH of Ramah (19:18). When Saul attempted to arrest David, the Spirit of God came upon Saul's police officers as well as upon Saul himself as soon as they met Samuel and the prophets associated with him. When Samuel died, all Israel mourned his death (25:1; 28:3). He was buried at Ramah.

The final message of Samuel came to Saul after Samuel's death. Facing defeat by the Philistines on Mount GILBOA, Saul in desperation conferred with a woman in ENDOR who was a spirit-medium. Beyond this woman's control, Samuel spoke directly to Saul, informing him that death awaited Saul and his sons the next day (1 Sam. 28:4–19).

Although Samuel served as judge and priest, he made the most significant impact upon Israel's religious life as a prophet. Whereas the greatest revelation to Israel as a nation came through MOSES, it was Samuel who represented God in the anointing of the first two kings of Israel. After Moses' death the written revelation provided guidance for JOSHUA, who was confirmed by miracles in divine leadership. During the reign of the judges, DEBORAH and an unnamed prophet (Jdg. 4:4; 6:8) are the only ones specifically identified as speaking for God. Samuel responded to God's call, and through his prophetic ministry not only revived his generation but also influenced others to respond to the prophetic ministry. Numerous prophets seem to have arisen during this era. NATHAN, GAD, and others during Davidic times may have been influenced by Samuel as he taught throughout the cities of Israel.

In his religious leadership responsibilities, Samuel as well as David appointed gatekeepers for the tent of meeting (1 Chr. 9:17–26). Samuel also observed the PASSOVER in such a memorable manner that it was unsurpassed until the time of JOSIAH (2 Chr. 35:18). Gifts for the house of God were also dedicated under Samuel's leadership. In addition to the book deposited "before the LORD" (1 Sam. 10:25), Samuel is also credited with writing a volume identified as "the records of Samuel the seer" (1 Chr. 29:29). The account of Samuel's life and ministry and the national developments up to the time of his death may reasonably be credited to Samuel as they are given in the book bearing his name. See SAMUEL, BOOKS OF.

Samuel is known as a great man of prayer and intercession (1 Sam. 15:11; Ps. 99:6) through whom God's blessing came to Israel. He ranks high among the prophets and outstanding leaders through whom God's favor was evident among his people (Acts 3:24; 13:20; Heb. 11:32). (See further J. P. Free, *Archaeology and Bible History* [1956], 146–53; M. Noth, *The History of Israel* [1958], 164–78; H. Snell, *Ancient Israel* [1963], 49–70; S. J. Schultz, *The Old Testament Speaks*, 4th ed. [1990], 115–25; J. Bright, *A History of Israel*, 4th ed. [2000], 184–92; J. Hutzli, *Samuel und Saul: Ein Beitrag zur narrativen Poetik des Samuelbuches* [2005].) S. J. SCHULTZ

Samuel, Books of. Two historical books of the OT that cover a period of more than one hundred years, from the birth of SAMUEL to shortly before the death of DAVID. In the Hebrew Bible, they are regarded as one book and are ranked among the Former Prophets. See CANON (OT).

   I. Title
  II. Contents
     A. Samuel and the reign of Saul
     B. The rise of David to the throne
     C. Problems in the reign of David
     D. Conclusion
 III. Composition
     A. Critical theories
     B. Samuel in the realm of political literature
     C. Authorship
     D. Date
 IV. Purpose
  V. Text
 VI. Special problems
     A. Doublets
     B. Who killed Goliath?
     C. The witch of Endor
VII. Theology
     A. The will of God
     B. The doctrine of sin
     C. The Davidic covenant

I. Title. As in the case of the books of KINGS, 1 and 2 Samuel were originally one book in the Hebrew Bible. The Greek version (see SEPTUAGINT) apparently first made the division into two books by calling them *bibloi basileiōn a* and *b*, that is, 1–2 Kingdoms (or Reigns). In similar fashion, Kings became 3–4 Kingdoms, since the content continued the historical sketch begun in Samuel. (Toward the end of the 4th cent. A.D., JEROME affixed the title *Libri Regum*, Books of Kings, to these four books. His modification of "Kingdoms" to "Kings" was intended to reflect the Hebrew title, *mĕlākim*, for the books we now call 1–2 Kings. Eventually the Latin VULGATE reverted to the name "Samuel" for the first two books.) In the Hebrew Bible, the division into 1 and 2 Samuel first appears in a 1448 MS. Daniel Bomberg's printed edition of 1516 acknowledged the division of Samuel and Kings into four books, but it preserved the Hebrew title for each pair. This practice has been continued in subsequent editions.

Samuel's name was attached to these books because of his prominence in the first sixteen chapters of 1 Samuel with regard to the establishment of the monarchy. It was he who, as the last judge (see JUDGES, PERIOD OF), anointed the two kings who hold the spotlight in 1 and 2 Samuel. Talmudic tradition also ascribes the authorship of part of 1 Samuel to the prophet (*b. Baba Batra* 14b).

II. Content. The unity of 1 and 2 Samuel is evident from the close links which tie the books together. The major divisions in the outline do not include a break at the end of 1 Samuel. Instead, the summary passages in 1 Sam. 14 and 2 Sam. 8 provide the keys to understanding the structure of the books.

A. Samuel and the reign of Saul (1 Sam. 1–14)

1. The ministry of Samuel (1 Sam. 1–7)

Samuel's birth and Hannah's song (1 Sam. 1:1—2:10). The book begins by relating God's gracious answer to the faithful prayers of childless HANNAH. Samuel, the son for whom she prayed, was dedicated to the Lord as a child and made a servant to the high priest ELI. Hannah's song of thanksgiving for the goodness of the sovereign God is recorded in ch. 2.

Samuel's ministry under Eli (1 Sam. 2:11—3:21). In contrast to the faithfulness of the boy Samuel, Eli's sons were godless men who even stole the sacrifices of the people. One night, God revealed to Samuel that Eli's family would be cut off from the priesthood because of the blasphemy of the sons Eli had failed to discipline.

Philistine victory destroys Eli's family (1 Sam. 4:1–22). God's prediction came true when the PHILISTINES routed the Israelite army, killing Eli's two sons and capturing the coveted ARK OF THE COVENANT. At the news of this catastrophe, the aged Eli fell heavily, mortally injuring himself.

The captivity and return of the ark (1 Sam. 5:1—7:17). The Philistines soon discovered that their battle prize, deposited near the idol of

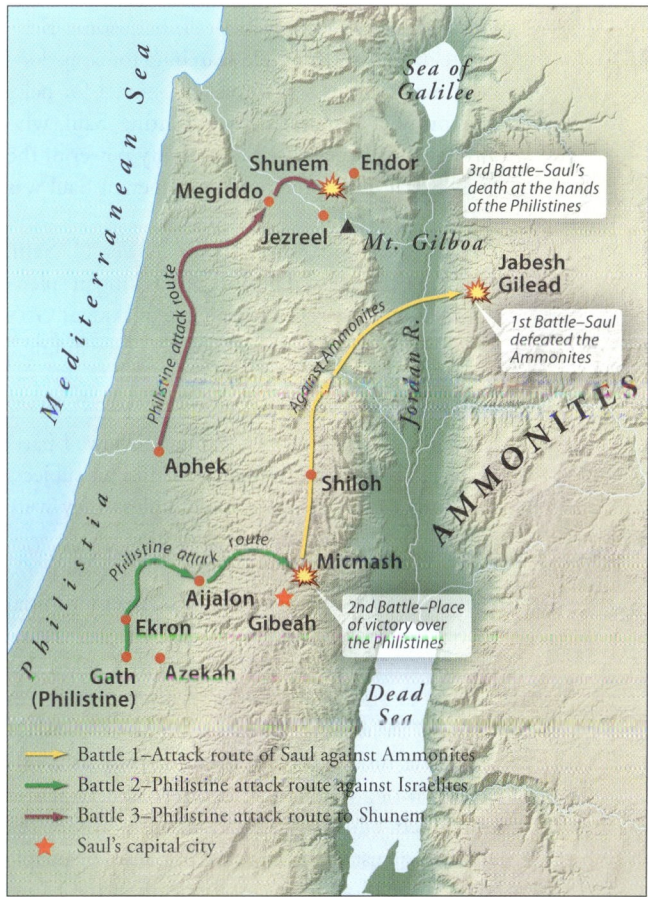

The battles of Saul.

DAGON, resulted in the smashing of that idol and in outbreaks of TUMORS. After circulating the ark unsuccessfully from city to city, the Philistines sent it back to Israel accompanied by an appropriate guilt-offering. Samuel used the occasion of the ark's return to recall all the people to the true worship of God. Another battle with the Philistines ensued, and God overthrew them decisively.

2. The initial years of Saul's reign (1 Sam. 8—14)

The request for a king (1 Sam. 8:1–22). In Samuel's old age, the people insisted that he appoint for them a king, so that Israel could be like all the other nations. Samuel resisted their demand by showing that a king would draft their children into his service and would tax their goods. Nevertheless, the people persisted and God instructed Samuel to comply with their request.

Saul anointed as king (1 Sam. 9:1—10:27). God's choice as king was a tall, handsome Benjamite named SAUL. While searching for stray donkeys, Saul and his servant asked Samuel for help. The prophet responded by anointing Saul, who subsequently experienced the mighty power of the Holy Spirit. Later, the humble, reluctant Saul was presented to the jubilant people.

Saul victorious over the Ammonites (1 Sam. 11:1–15). Saul passed his first test as king in splendid fashion. He rescued the people of JABESH GILEAD from a serious Ammonite threat by winning a solid victory.

Samuel's charge to Israel (1 Sam. 12:1–25). In his last address to the people, Samuel reviewed parts of Israel's history and warned Saul and his subjects that they would be swept away unless they were faithful to the commandments of God.

Saul and Jonathan war successfully against the Philistines (1 Sam. 13:1—14:52). After an initial successful skirmish, Saul and his son JONATHAN had to face the entire Philistine army. Saul, in his anxiety to ask for God's favor, offered sacrifices himself. Samuel informed him that God would terminate his reign on account of this disobedience. Through Jonathan's bravery the Israelites triumphed; but Jonathan had unwittingly violated an oath against eating imposed by Saul. The people rescued Jonathan from certain death at the hands of his father.

B. The rise of David to the throne (1 Sam. 15—2 Sam. 8)

1. David's struggle with King Saul (1 Sam. 15–31)

Saul's disqualification after Amalekites defeated (1 Sam. 15:1–35). Coupled with Saul's intrusion into the priesthood in ch. 13 was his failure to devote to complete destruction all the goods of the defeated Amalekites (see AMALEK), including animals and the king, AGAG. Samuel denounced Saul for this and revealed clearly that he was being rejected as king.

David is anointed and plays for Saul (1 Sam. 16:1–23). Saul's successor was a talented young shepherd from BETHLEHEM named DAVID. Samuel anointed David, upon whom the Spirit of God then came. Ironically, David was soon invited to Saul's court as a musician to soothe the king, from whom the Lord's Spirit had recently departed.

David's victory over Goliath (1 Sam. 17:1–58). David displayed his great faith in God by defeating in single combat the nine-foot Philistine menace, GOLIATH. This was the first of several military victories by David which displayed his ability as a leader and endeared him to the people.

David's flight from Saul and friendship with Jonathan (1 Sam. 18:1—20:42). The jealousy of the deteriorating king was soon aroused against his successful young rival. David became a target for Saul's spear and was sent into battle by Saul in the hope that he would be killed. JONATHAN, however, made a covenant with David, insuring their friendship, and helped him escape from Saul.

David's plight occasions priests' disaster (1 Sam. 21:1—22:23). In his desperation, the fleeing David persuaded AHIMELECH and the priests at NOB into giving him supplies and arms. A leading servant of Saul overheard the discussion and related it to Saul. The enraged king then commanded the death of all the priests for allegedly conspiring with David against the crown.

David's mercy to the pursuing Saul (1 Sam. 23:1—24:23). Relentlessly, Saul now tried to capture David, who was hiding in the Judean wilderness. David had the opportunity of slaying his tormentor in a cave, but he refused to strike down the Lord's anointed. By revealing his mercy to Saul, David secured a temporary repentance from the pursuing king.

David and Abigail (1 Sam. 25:1–44). This chapter partly explains how a fugitive like David could survive in the desert. The protection that he and his men afforded NABAL's possessions should have been rewarded with supplies. When Nabal refused to pay, David decided to attack, but the wise intercession of Nabal's wife restrained him. After Nabal died, Abigail became one of David's wives.

Saul's repentance and David's despair (1 Sam. 26:1–27:12). Forgetting his earlier promises, Saul resumed his pursuit of David. Once more, David passed up an opportunity to kill the sleeping king, and the king responded by begging David's forgiveness. But David doubted Saul's sincerity with good reason and fled to the Philistines, allying himself temporarily with ACHISH, king of GATH.

Saul and the witch of Endor (1 Sam. 28:1–25). When the Philistines with David on their side prepared to attack Israel, Saul rightly trembled and sought a message from God. Unable to contact him through legitimate means, he resorted to divination, inducing a medium to produce the departed Samuel for him. Samuel announced that disaster lay ahead for Saul and Israel.

David rejected by Philistines and victorious over Amalekites (1 Sam. 29:1–30:31). As the armies prepared for battle, the suspicious Philistine commanders voted to dismiss David from their ranks, lest he decide to fight for Israel. Returning to ZIKLAG, David discovered that the Amalekites had burned the city and carried off the women and children. After inquiring of the Lord, David and his men recovered all the people and goods.

Death of Saul and Jonathan (1 Sam. 31:1–13). First Samuel ends with the short account of the great Philistine victory. Saul and his sons were killed on Mount GILBOA, and the Philistines celebrated.

2. David's unification of Judah and Israel (2 Sam. 1–8)

David's lament over Saul and Jonathan (2 Sam. 1:1–27). Instead of gloating over the fall of his enemy, David lamented the death of these men. He eulogized their courage and strength and particularly mourned for his dear friend Jonathan.

David is made king of Judah, and Ish-Bosheth succeeds Saul (2 Sam. 2:1–32). The people of Judah were the first to crown their tribesman and good friend (cf. 1 Sam. 30:26–30), the heir apparent to Saul's throne. Meanwhile, general ABNER had installed a surviving son of Saul, ISH-BOSHETH, as king over the rest of Israel. Serious fighting soon broke out between the two factions.

Abner and Ish-Bosheth assassinated (2 Sam. 3:1–4:12). When Ish-Bosheth accused Abner of disloyalty, the powerful commander decided to support David and unify Israel under his rule. These plans were thwarted by JOAB, who quickly killed his potential rival general to avenge his brother's death, much to the disgust of David.

David is made king over all Israel (2 Sam. 5:1–25). Finding themselves without leadership, the rest of the tribes now acknowledged David's right to rule the entire nation. David responded by storming the stronghold of ZION, which was still under Jebusite control. The Philistines then failed in an attempt to defeat David before he could consolidate the forces of a united Israel.

David brings the ark to Jerusalem (2 Sam. 6:1–23). Unlike Saul, David was intensely interested in the worship of the Lord, including the role of the ark of the covenant, which had lain neglected during his predecessor's reign. Thus it was with great joy that the king led the procession bringing the ark to the new capital.

The Davidic covenant (2 Sam. 7:1–29). David's zeal for God moved him to consider the need for a TEMPLE to house the ark. Although God postponed the fulfillment of David's wish, he promised that David's dynasty would possess the throne of Israel eternally.

Summary of David's rule (2 Sam. 8:1–18). This chapter outlines the expansion of David's kingdom under the prospering hand of God. Israel's major enemies were all defeated as the empire and fame of David were extended.

C. Problems in the reign of David (2 Sam. 9–20)

1. David's kindness to Mephibosheth (2 Sam. 9:1–13).
In relating to the descendants of Saul, David displayed covenant kindness toward the crippled son of Jonathan. He restored property to MEPHIBOSHETH and provided for his material needs.

2. Victory over Syrians and Ammonites (2 Sam. 10:1–19). In battles perhaps already referred to (ch. 8), David defeated a coalition of Arameans and Ammonites after the latter had badly insulted David's messengers.

3. David's sins involving Bathsheba (2 Sam. 11:1–12:31). The problems of David increased quickly after he committed adultery with BATHSHEBA. This led to the murder of URIAH and the sharp displeasure of God. NATHAN delivered a pointed parable that brought the king to repentance. After the death of Bathsheba's first child, SOLOMON was born.

4. The sins of Amnon and Absalom (2 Sam. 13:1–14:33). When AMNON, David's son, raped his half-sister TAMAR, ABSALOM retaliated by murdering Amnon two years later. Absalom fled from David not to be recalled to Jerusalem for three years. Relations between the king and Absalom remained strained.

5. Absalom's rebellion and death (2 Sam. 15:1–18:33). Absalom's bitterness toward David erupted into a full-fledged rebellion that forced the king to flee from the capital. By leaving a few faithful followers in Jerusalem, David was able to nullify the wise advice AHITHOPHEL gave to Absalom. The forces of David and Absalom finally clashed, with Joab gaining the victory for David. Contrary to the king's express orders, Joab killed Absalom, deeply grieving David.

6. David's recovery of power (2 Sam. 19:1–20:26). Gradually, Judah and Israel united again behind David, conducting him back to Jerusalem. A Benjamite named SHEBA, however, led a short-lived rebellion against the king.

D. Conclusion (2 Sam. 21–24)

1. Gibeonites avenged; victory over Philistines (2 Sam. 21:1–22). The last four chapters of 2 Samuel appear to be appended to the book without reference to chronological order. First, the cause for a famine was found in Saul's killing of certain Gibeonites, whom the Israelites were bound by treaty to protect. Several of Saul's descendants were hung by the Gibeonites to avenge Saul's folly. Later David again waged war with the Philistines, and his men killed relatives of Goliath.

2. David's hymn of thanksgiving and last words (2 Sam. 22:1–23:7). In a hymn that also appears as

From David's vantage point of his palace on the ridge of the City of David, he could look down on the roof of Bathsheba's house where he saw her bathing. (View to the S.)

Ps. 18, David praises his mighty God for deliverance from all his enemies. Then David reviews the everlasting covenant God made with him.

3. David's mighty men (2 Sam. 23:8–39). The thirty-seven bravest warriors of David are listed, along with a description of the achievements of the five greatest.

4. The plague because of David's census (2 Sam. 24:1–25). When David self-confidently insisted on numbering the nation in spite of God's prohibition, the Lord struck dead 70,000 men. The plague was finally stopped at the site of the future temple.

III. Composition

A. Critical theories. Higher critics have offered several diverse explanations as to the origin of 1 and 2 Samuel. All of them accept the composite nature of these books and seek to account for many "obvious" contradictions, duplicate accounts, and other evidences of multiple authorship over a long period of time. Many hold to the view that the Deuteronomic editors, who supposedly wrote or rewrote much of Deuteronomy–Kings somewhere between 621 and 550 B.C., were responsible for the final composition of Samuel. See DEUTERONOMISTIC HISTORY. This is asserted in spite of the different character and organization of Judges, compared, for example, with either Joshua or Samuel.

The majority of critics feel that 1 and 2 Samuel were formed by the interweaving of several sources, usually two or three. Otto Eissfeldt (*The Old Testament: An Introduction* [1965], 271–80) links Samuel with sources J (Yahwist), E (Elohist), and L (Lay) of the documentary hypothesis. These sources, supposedly extending from Genesis to Samuel or even Kings, form the basis for these books, with E almost disappearing in Samuel. Source L, an invention of Eissfeldt, reports folk tales in colorful fashion, but has little reference to theological concerns. It does, however, evidence an interest in the ark of the covenant.

Other critics have expressed doubt as to whether or not J and E really continue in Samuel. William F. Albright (*Archaeology, Historical Analogy, and Early Biblical Tradition* [1966], 44–45) explicitly denies the validity of J and E for dividing Samuel: he argues that, although useful in the Pentateuch, neither they nor other criteria of form can be employed to identify the sources behind Samuel. M. Segal (in *JQR* 55 [1965]: 318–39; 56 [1965]: 32–50, 137–57), who rejects the documentary hypothesis, posits a combination of two stories of David, the first being a splendid biography by a contemporary, whereas the second is of later date and legendary in origin. Added to this were independent stories of the ark, Saul, and Samuel.

The tradition-historical school emphasizes saga-cycles like the ark narratives, which circulated orally until they were written down in a loosely connected form. Some postpone the written phase until after the exile. Most critics believe that the material in Samuel includes both legendary "hearsay" and highly accurate historical writing. Hence, its reliability is extremely uneven. Many feel that the fragmented stories about David in 1 Sam. 16 to 2 Sam. 8 are a sort of historical novel glorifying David. They have a basis in history, but are embellished with the fanciful additions common to saga.

On the other hand, the material in 2 Sam. 9–20, often linked with 1 Ki. 1–2 under the title of the "Succession Narrative" or "Court History" of David, is regarded as a superb example of historiography. The author of these chapters is said to have been a master at character portrayal and apparently an astute eyewitness who scarcely ever deviated from the facts. The critics are willing to accept the essential unity of these chapters, in contrast with the rest of 1–2 Samuel.

B. Samuel in the realm of political literature. A rather close connection has been observed between 1 Sam. 15 — 2 Sam. 8 and a 13th-cent.-B.C. HITTITE document known as the "Apology of Hattusilis." It appeared likely that the central section of Samuel belongs to a genre of literature which could be termed a "dynastic defense" or "apology." (See the present author's dissertation, *The Apology of Hattusilis Compared with Other Political Self-Justifications of the Ancient Near East* [1967].)

In recent years the study of different genres, types, or forms of literature has been summed up under the label of FORM CRITICISM. This broad designation includes features that, from a conservative standpoint, are both positive and negative. Some aspects of form criticism are very helpful for a proper understanding of biblical literature. In the "form" or "genre" of "dynastic defense," a king or his supporters outlines those reasons that make his rule legitimate. This is particularly necessary in the case of kings like Hattusilis and David, who founded dynasties and could have been charged with usurpation. With regard to David, Saul's tribe of Benjamin might have made this accusation (cf. 2 Sam. 20). The Hittites also did not have an absolute monarch, for the nobles exercised some control over the king.

These texts have been compared to the more common annalistic writing, but several features distinguish them from that category. Ordinarily, annals follow a strict year-by-year chronological arrangement, discussing important events in a monarch's reign. Developments leading up to the enthronement of a ruler are mentioned very briefly if at all. Mursilis, the most important annalist among the Hittite kings, devotes only a few lines to the years prior to his accession. In both the central portion of Samuel and in the "Apology of Hattusilis," however, great stress is placed on events which occurred before the men became kings. There is a climactic arrangement that builds until the heroes are placed on the throne. The circumstances surrounding their success are clearly spelled out.

A further divergence from the annals relates to the summary method used. Sometimes events are treated as blocks of time, and there is no effort to move systematically from year to year. The summaries in 2 Sam. 7–8 tie together the activities of several years. In the Bible, a more annalistic style of writing can be found in Kings and Chronicles, where the discussion is restricted to individual reigns and does not deal with events preceding the accession of the various kings.

There are numerous parallels between the Hittite and Hebrew texts which may indicate that parts of Samuel have been patterned after the Hittite document. Both "dynastic defenses" describe in detail the disqualification of their predecessors (1 Sam. 15). Their own ability to lead and to rule is evident from repeated military success against national enemies. This is why David's slaying of Goliath and his frequent victories over the Philistines are so clearly reported.

The growing popularity of the men is also important. David was respected by the servants of Saul (1 Sam. 18:5, 30), the people in general, and the prince he was replacing, Jonathan. Even Saul, in his calmer moments, acknowledged that David would succeed him (24:20). By virtue of his marriage to Saul's daughter MICHAL, David increased his claim to the throne. King Hattusilis also contracted an important marriage in this regard.

A prominent characteristic of both kings was leniency toward political foes. Neither allowed his over-zealous followers to assassinate the ruling king, thus contrasting their methods to those of usurpers. Instead, both appealed to deity to plead their case as a "court battle" in heaven (1 Sam. 24:15).

After coming to power, the kings displayed great energy in religious matters. They were concerned about the worship of the nation and the blessing of one's deity (Yahweh, for David; Ishtar, for Hattusilis) upon the king (2 Sam. 6–7). Even ch. 7, in which the critics have seen copious Deuteronomic revision, contains a covenant relating to David and his successors, a covenant that can be paralleled in certain respects in the "Apology of Hattusilis."

Finally, both texts contain a summary of their reigns, demonstrating divine blessing upon their rule through expansion and the establishment of peace with surrounding nations (2 Sam. 8).

Within the sphere of ANE political literature there are no texts that exhibit the genre of "apology" as well as these two examples. Since there is wide evidence of the impact of foreign cultures upon Israel at this time, it is possible that this Hittite document had an important bearing upon Samuel. This would help to explain the purpose and arrangement of this section of the biblical narrative.

As mentioned earlier, the corresponding summary passages (1 Sam. 14; 2 Sam. 8) furnished the clue to the outline. Although Saul does not die until 1 Sam. 31, the listing of his family, officials, and accomplishments in 14:47–52 makes the transition from Saul to David. From that point on, David's rise to the throne is primary.

R. Whybray (*The Succession Narrative* [1968]) has defended the view that this narrative also has a political purpose. He compares it to the

Saul's reign and life came to a close on the heights of Mount Gilboa (1 Sam. 31), pictured here looking E from the Jezreel Valley.

propagandist motives of political novels in Egypt. The purpose of the narrative is to justify Solomon's claim to the throne by revealing how David's other sons, such as Amnon and Absalom, were unfit to rule. To support this theory, however, 1 Ki. 1 and 2 are needed as the climax to 2 Sam. 9–20. This questionable view treats 2 Sam. 21–24 as a later insertion interrupting a continuous narrative. It would appear rather that the central section of Samuel has a much closer connection with dynastic justification.

C. Authorship. The theory of "dynastic defense" directly affects the matter of authorship. Tradition has attributed the writing of part of 1 Samuel to the prophet himself, but there is no indisputable evidence as to authorship. R. H. Pfeiffer (*Old Testament Introduction* [1941], 356–57) suggests that AHIMAAZ the priest wrote part of it, while Segal offers JEHOSHAPHAT the recorder as David's trustworthy biographer.

The perplexing reference in 1 Chr. 29:29 to the acts of David written in the books of Samuel, Nathan, and Gad offers a tempting solution. For some reason, Chronicles does not otherwise refer to 2 Samuel, with which it has many parallel passages. Either the works of these three were independent books used as sources by the writers of both Samuel and Chronicles, or else they refer to 1–2 Samuel.

If the three-part outline of Samuel can be substantiated, the correspondence with these men is very close. Samuel could easily have written the first half of the book. The prophet Nathan already has been suggested as the author of 2 Sam. 9–20, because of his close association with David's court. This would leave the other prophet, Gad, as author of the "apology." While impossible to prove, Gad's authorship is a reasonable assumption, since he did accompany David during part of this hectic period (1 Sam. 22:5) and would have been in a position to know the events described.

Perhaps an author-editor combined the works of these three at a later time, also using the Book of JASHAR (2 Sam. 1:18) as a source. This would account for the smooth transition from section to section and the overall unity of the books. The parts are clearly interrelated and the language is basically the same.

D. Date. The answers to the questions raised in the previous section are vitally related to the date of Samuel. If Samuel, Nathan, and Gad are the real authors, the books were written essentially during David's day or shortly thereafter. Parts of Samuel, particularly from 2 Sam. 9–20, are acknowledged by many critics as being of 10th-cent.-B.C. origin. The same critics, however, will relegate other portions of the books to various later periods extending to the exile.

Yet, since the form and content of the "apology" resemble political literature that is solidly dated earlier than David, one can argue for an early date for these chapters also. The need for a dynastic defense could have arisen not only under David's rule but during Solomon's reign as opposition to his policies mounted, or during the early divided kingdom when David's throne was seriously threatened. In 1 Sam. 27:6 there is reference to Ziklag as belonging "to the kings of Judah to this day" (NRSV). This would imply that the kingdom already had been divided, unless it is a later addition. Perhaps this verse demonstrated that an author-editor used as sources an independently existing "apology" and "court history" of David, and that Samuel was written sometime during the divided monarchy.

Conservatives have varied in dating the composition of the books anywhere from 970 to 722 B.C. Lack of reference to the fall of SAMARIA provides a solid *terminus ad quem* (latest possible date). Based on the eyewitness accounts and on the general antiquity of linguistic features, the earlier date appears far closer to the truth.

IV. Purpose. The books of Samuel were written to present a connected history of the events surrounding the establishment of the monarchy. They deal with the last judges and introduce the first two kings during this vital transition period. Samuel's ministry as a prophet is also of importance for understanding the development of the prophetic office as well as the later work of leading prophets.

Originally, the "apology of David" underlying 1 Sam. 15—2 Sam. 8 was probably aimed at the contemporary Jews who were doubting the legitimacy of David's dynasty, perhaps during the reign of Solomon. By defending his actions and revealing God's clear choice of David, the author attempted to convince the nation that the right to rule did indeed belong to David and his offspring.

The moral and spiritual lessons inherent in the experience of Samuel, Saul, David, and others are of timeless value. By describing the catastrophe which nearly befell David and the nation, the author warns the people about the effects of personal and national sin. The emphasis upon David is intended to acquaint all believers with this man after God's own heart, who, in spite of serious sin, was chosen to deliver his people and to head an eternal dynasty culminating in Christ.

The books provide an illuminating historical background to some of the psalms, and important facts about the beloved Jerusalem are also presented.

V. Text. The traditional Hebrew text represented by the Masoretic recension is strangely defective in 1 and 2 Samuel. There are cases where emendations are mandatory because of the poorly preserved text. For example, 1 Sam. 13:1 omits the number before "years" while describing Saul's age.

Why the MT of Samuel presents more difficulties than the text of other OT book is not clear. Gleason L. Archer (*A Survey of Old Testament Introduction*, rev. ed [1994], 314) suggests that the official text formulated during the intertestamental period depended upon an ancient *Vorlage* that may have been worm-eaten, or frayed through overuse. The Masoretes then faithfully reproduced this defective "official" text. Segal feels that Samuel was neglected because of competition from the more popular book of Chronicles. Being read less, the text of Samuel somehow became corrupt.

Fragments of Samuel among the DEAD SEA SCROLLS appear to indicate that the Hebrew underlying the LXX was probably superior to the Masoretic tradition (cf. P. K. McCarter, Jr., *I Samuel*, AB 8 [1980], 9–11). The Greek translators seem to have handled their Hebrew texts with overall faithfulness, and should be trusted more than they have been in the past. In Samuel at least, the LXX is of great value for determining the true reading in many difficult passages. The oldest Hebrew copy of Samuel at Qumran bears some readings that are superior to either the Greek or Hebrew texts.

VI. Special problems

A. Doublets. Critics often attempt to prove that Samuel is full of discrepancies and contradictions by referring to the many "doublets" in the text. The descriptions of the same event in two different ways "betrays" the use of different sources or parallel accounts. Examples include the following: twice Saul is made king; twice David is introduced to Saul; twice the Ziphites inform Saul of David's hiding place. There are supposedly many others also, but in each case there is a satisfactory explanation.

The events surrounding Saul's two "coronations" are quite different. On the first occasion, Saul was chosen by lot and presented to the people. Some of the "troublemakers" (1 Sam. 10:27) were dubious of his ability to produce, however, and refused to acknowledge him. In ch. 11, Saul vigorously led Israel to victory over the Ammonites, and Samuel brought the people to Gilgal to "reaffirm the kingdom" (11:14). There they "made Saul king" (v. 15 NRSV) amid great rejoicing and unity. The words "made Saul king" do not occur in ch. 10, and the reference to renewing or confirming the kingdom implies that Saul had been designated previously as king (thus NIV, "confirmed Saul as king").

David was introduced to King Saul in 1 Sam. 16:21. At that time, Saul welcomed him as a musician and armor-bearer, hired to soothe the disturbed king. After David returned from the slaughter of Goliath, Saul asked him, "Whose son are you?" (17:58). There is no need to infer that Saul had forgotten his first name, but only that of his father. One of the benefits of David's victory was freedom for his father's house, as the men of Israel had told him before the battle (17:25, 27). Apparently this included exemption from taxation or other services ordinarily rendered to the king. Hence, knowing the name of David's father became important.

Under the stress and excitement of facing such a formidable foe as Goliath, Saul could also have been excused for a lapse of memory. David was only a court musician and an armor-bearer, so his name may not have been indelibly impressed upon the erratic king's mind. Moreover, 1 Sam. 18:2 states that Saul would not allow David to return home, suggesting a difference from his earlier policy (17:15).

The two episodes involving the Ziphites (1 Sam. 23 and 26) are also superficially similar. In both they betray David's location to Saul, but the succeeding events are quite different. Whenever a jealous king pursues his handsome, popular rival in headlong flight, it would be a captivating story and likely to be reported. In extrabiblical ANE literature there are abundant examples of the repetition of similar events. Within the Hittite annals of Mursilis, for instance, there are several references to the ill health and recovery of an old king. Scholars have concluded that these were separate events rather than different descriptions of the same illness. Abraham's twofold representation of Sarah as his sister (Gen. 12 and 20) is of a similar nature.

B. Who killed Goliath? Another apparent contradiction that could also be classed as a doublet concerns the two slayers of Goliath. The more popular version credits David for this deed, but 2 Sam. 21:19 says that ELHANAN slew Goliath. Most critics believe that Elhanan actually killed the giant, and only later was the hero's role transferred to the better-known David. This supposition, however, finds no support in the rest of Scripture. If David did not kill Goliath, it becomes difficult to account for Saul's intense jealousy and for the song crediting David with slaying "tens of thousands" (1 Sam. 18:7). His conquering of the Philistine giant was his greatest triumph and paved the way for his leadership of Israel.

According to 1 Sam. 21:9, David was forced to take Goliath's sword from the priest Ahimelech. David had evidently dedicated the weapon to the Lord after his victory. His action parallels that of King Hattusilis III, the Hittite whose "Apology" was earlier compared with Samuel. There is a strong possibility that Hattusilis was also involved in a battle of champions. H. A. Hoffner, Jr. (in *CBQ* 30 [1968]: 220–25) has discussed the evidence based on the "Apology of Hattusilis" (2.31–47). After leading his men to an unexpectedly overwhelming victory perhaps by individual combat, the Hittite warrior dedicated his weapon to the goddess ISHTAR. A battle of champions on Hittite soil would provide an interesting analogy to the phenomenon already well-known in Greek and Hebrew literature.

The context in 2 Sam. 21 also supports David's right to the victory. Four of David's mighty men are said to have killed descendants of the giant (v. 22). It is unlikely that David's warriors would have accomplished what their king himself could not do. The struggles of Goliath's relatives were an attempt to avenge the giant's death. A blood-feud of this type was a natural sequel to David's victory.

The parallel in 1 Chr. 20:5 supplies the needed solution, since it refers to Elhanan's triumph over LAHMI, the brother of Goliath. Apparently the MT of Samuel was defective at this point, changing "Lahmi the brother of" (*'et laḥmî 'aḥî*) into "the Bethlehemite" (*bêt hallaḥmî*). For other proposals, see ELHANAN.

C. The witch of Endor. Saul's experience with the medium or witch of ENDOR in 1 Sam. 28 is a difficult passage to interpret. This woman was one of many wizards or spiritists who operated in Israel in spite of laws banning them. Isaiah condemned those who consulted "mediums and wizards" rather than listen to the word of God (Isa. 8:19–20). In Saul's case, he was desperate to know the future and sought some message from the departed Samuel, whose advice he had usually taken too lightly while he was alive.

Several explanations have been given regarding this event and the powers of mediums in general. Some feel that Samuel did not appear in any form; it was only a psychological phenomenon in which Saul thought he saw Samuel owing to his confused state of mind and the mysterious effects of darkness. This interpretation is hard to derive from the scriptural account.

Within a more conservative framework, it has been proposed that God allowed Saul to see a form which resembled Samuel, but which was not actually the body or spirit of the prophet himself. The more obvious explanation, however, recognizes that Samuel did actually appear to Saul in visible form and that the deceased prophet communicated with Saul. Samuel looked like "a god" (1 Sam. 28:13 RSV), implying an unusual appearance for this spirit in visible form.

While not denying the powers of mediums and spiritists within the demonic sphere, one need not conclude that calling up the dead normally lay within their ability. In this instance, God intervened and sent Samuel to his disobedient king. The woman revealed her surprise at the unusual success of this venture by crying out loudly when she saw Samuel (1 Sam. 28:12). This implies that she and her colleagues could not ordinarily bring up the dead. The episode does demonstrate the conscious existence of departed spirits and supports the doctrine of the IMMORTALITY of the soul.

VII. Theology. Although the main emphasis of Samuel is historical and not theological, there are several chapters that touch directly upon important doctrines.

A. The will of God. Scholars have puzzled over the attitude of God toward the establishment of the monarchy. There is sufficient evidence to indicate that God was displeased with the rejection of the THEOCRACY (1 Sam. 8:7). Samuel tried to dissuade the people from desiring a king, but the majority were adamant in their demand. Yet, even before Saul was anointed, God promised to bless him and to use him in delivering his people (9:16). Apparently some distinction can be made between the directive and permissive will of God in this case. The wish for a king was sinful, but God allowed this wish to become reality and blessed the kingdom greatly in subsequent years.

Another aspect of the will of God relates to predestination and human responsibility, both of which find support in Samuel. After Saul had been king for some time, he disobeyed the commandment of God by performing sacrifices. Samuel severely reprimanded him for this behavior and announced that Saul had forfeited his right to a lasting dynasty. God "would have established your kingdom over Israel for all time" (1 Sam. 13:13). Instead, Saul's sin led the Lord to transfer the leadership to David.

It is clear that Saul's sin is pinpointed as the cause for his loss of dynastic rights. Yet, as early as patriarchal times JACOB prophesied, "The scepter will not depart from Judah" (Gen. 49:10). The ruling tribe would be JUDAH, to which David belonged, and not BENJAMIN, the tribe of Saul. Hence, would not the scriptural fulfillment have necessitated the disqualification of Saul? Interestingly, Samuel did not console Saul by saying, "It was not your fault, it had to happen." Saul was not excused for his sin but was judged for it. God, of course, foreknew this event making it certain long before, but human responsibility remained very much in the picture.

B. The doctrine of sin. Both 1 and 2 Samuel illustrate all too vividly the sinfulness of the human heart and the inevitable results of SIN. Godly leaders like Eli, David, and even Samuel are singled out for their failures before the Lord. Strangely enough, all three men reared children who rebelled against God. As fathers, they experienced great difficulty in bringing their sons into the deep relationship with God they enjoyed. Eli's sons robbed the sacrifices, blasphemed God, and committed fornication, all in the role of priests (1 Sam. 2:13–17, 22; 3:13). It is no wonder that God destroyed them before the Philistines. Because of the wickedness of Samuel's sons, the people were further motivated to ask for a king (8:5).

Saul began his monarchy as a humble, Spirit-controlled man. As his reign progressed, however, he disobeyed the Lord, came under the influence of an evil spirit, and was consumed with murderous jealousy. He was finally reduced to dealing with a spiritist in an effort to contact the dead.

The experience of David provides the greatest instruction, both positively and negatively. This great king, a man after God's own heart, nevertheless became secretly involved in adultery and murder after exhibiting great faith and devoutness for years. When David acknowledged his sin and was restored spiritually (2 Sam. 12:13), the Lord forgave him, thus showing his great mercy. Although David's confession was deep and sincere, he had to suffer the inevitable consequences of sin, even of forgiven sin. Bathsheba's first child died, and David's first son Amnon imitated his father by committing fornication with Tamar. This precipitated Absalom's avenging murder, which led directly to the major rebellion under Absalom. God still blessed the reign of David, however, and he even exalted Solomon, Bathsheba's second son, to the throne.

C. The Davidic covenant. One of the most important OT COVENANTS was made with David (2 Sam. 7). This covenant amplifies the provisions of the Abrahamic covenant of Genesis by promising to David an eternal throne and kingdom. The right to rule over Israel will always belong to one of his descendants, a promise anticipating the everlasting reign of Christ. God's great faithfulness and steadfast love for his servant were clearly seen in his gracious forgiveness of David's sin. In view of God's sure word, David rejoiced in the promise given to his household. His "last words" of 2 Sam. 23:1, 5 refer to this "everlasting covenant."

On the human level, the relationship between David and Jonathan provides an excellent illustration of covenant responsibility. They exhibited intense love and loyalty for each other even though Jonathan had reason to share Saul's jealousy of David. As a result of their covenant, David kindly cared for Jonathan's crippled son after he was established as king.

(Important commentaries include C. F. Keil and F. Delitzsch, *Biblical Commentary on the Books of Samuel* [1868]; H. P. Smith, *A Critical and Exegetical Commentary on the Books of Samuel*, ICC [1899]; S. R. Driver, *Notes on the Hebrew Text and the Topography of the Books of Samuel*, 2nd ed. [1913]; H. W. Hertzberg, *I and II Samuel: A Commentary*, OTL [1964]; P. R. Ackroyd, *The First Book of Samuel* [1971]; id., *The Second Book of Samuel* [1977]; P. K. McCarter, Jr., *I Samuel*, AB 8 [1980]; R. W. Klein, *1 Samuel*, WBC 10 [1983]; P. K. McCarter, Jr., *II Samuel*, AB 9 [1984]; J. G. Baldwin, *1 and 2 Samuel: An Introduction and Commentary*, TOTC [1988]; A. A. Anderson, *2 Samuel*, WBC 11 [1989]; R. D. Bergen, *1, 2 Samuel*, NAC 7 [1996]; R. Alter, *The David Story: A Translation with Commentary of 1 and 2 Samuel* [1999]; M. J. Evans, *1 and 2 Samuel*, NIBCOT 6 [2000]; T. W. Cartledge, *1 and 2 Samuel* [2001]; B. T. Arnold, *1 and 2 Samuel*, NIVAC [2003]; D. T. Tsumura, *The First Book of Samuel*, NICOT [2007].

(See also B. C. Birch, *The Rise of the Israelite Monarchy: The Growth and Development of I Samuel 7–15* [1976]; C. Conroy, *Absalom, Absalom! Narrative and Language in 2 Sam. 13–20* [1978]; J. P. Fokkelman, *Narrative Art and Poetry in the Books of Samuel: A Full Interpretation Based on Stylistic and Structural Analyses*, 4 vols. [1981–93]; V. P. Long, *The Reign and Rejection of King Saul: A Case for Literary and Theological Coherence* [1989]; G. Keys, *The Wages of Sin: A Reappraisal of the 'Succession Narrative'* [1996]; H. H. Klement, *II Samuel 21–24: Context, Structure, and Meaning in the Samuel Conclusion* [2000]; A. Fincke, *The Samuel Scroll from Qumran: 4QSam^a Restored and Compared to the Septuagint and 4QSam^c* [2001]; A. F. Campbell, *1 Samuel*, FOTL 7 [2003]; S. Frolov, *The Turn of the Cycle: 1 Samuel 1–8 in Synchronic and Diachronic

Perspectives [2004]; K.-P. Adam, *Saul und David in der judäischen Geschichtsschreibung: Studien zu 1 Samuel 16–2 Samuel 5* [2007]; and the bibliographies compiled by W. E. Mills, *1 Samuel* [2001] and *2 Samuel* [2001].)　　　　　　H. WOLF

Sanabassar, Sanabassarus san´uh-bas´uhr, san´uh-bas´uh ruhs. KJV Apoc. forms of SHESHBAZZAR (1 Esd. 2:12, 15; 6:18, 20).

Sanasib san´uh-sib. KJV Apoc. variant of ANASIB (1 Esd. 5:24).

Sanballat san-bal´at (סַנְבַלַּט *H6172*, from Akk. *Sin-uballiṭ*, "Sin [the moon god] has saved" or "may Sin give life"). A man identified as a HORONITE (prob. a native of BETH-HORON) who, along with TOBIAH and GESHEM, opposed NEHEMIAH's efforts to rebuild JERUSALEM (Neh. 2:10, 19; 4:1–9; 6:1–14). A grandson of ELIASHIB the high priest married Sanballat's daughter (13:28).

Among the ELEPHANTINE papyri of 407 B.C., a letter to Bagoas, governor of Judah, refers to another letter sent to "Delaiah and Shelemiah, the sons of Sanballat the governor of Samaria" (*ANET*, 492b). See SAMARIA (TERRITORY). This wording suggests that Sanballat was then very old and that the effective control was in the hands of his sons. In the time of Nehemiah he may already have been governor of Samaria. This would account for his influence, and he had probably hoped to become joint governor of Samaria and Judah if Nehemiah had not come. (For other possible motives that may explain Sanballat's opposition, see H. G. M. Williamson in *ABD*, 5:973–75.)

In spite of his foreign name, Sanballat gave his sons names with a Yahweh ending, but he may well have been descended from the mixed races who had been brought into the northern kingdom and who had a syncretistic worship with a preference for Yahweh (2 Ki. 18:23). JOSEPHUS makes Sanballat the founder of the SAMARITAN temple on Mount GERIZIM, with his son-in-law Manasseh as high priest, Manasseh being brother to the Jewish high priest, Jaddua (*Ant.* 11.8.2). The situation Josephus describes is not unlike that of Neh. 13:28–29, but he dates it in the time of ALEXANDER THE GREAT about a century later. He may have mistaken the name (or the period), but it is possible that he is referring to a different man of the same name. On the basis of Josephus and of the "Samaria papyri" discovered at Wadi ed-Daliyeh in 1962, F. M. Cross (in *HTR* 59 [1966]: 201–11) has argued that a grandson and a great-great-grandson of Sanballat bore the same name and were also governors of Samaria. (See further C. C. Torrey in *JBL* 47 [1928]: 380–89; H. H. Rowley, *Men of God: Studies in Old Testament History and Prophecy* [1963], 211–45.)　　　　J. S. WRIGHT

sanctification. The act or process of acquiring sanctity or HOLINESS as a result of association with deity. It is one of the most important concepts in biblical and historical theology. See also CONSECRATION.

　I. In the OT
　　A. Vocabulary
　　B. Concern for inward righteousness
　II. In the NT
　　A. Vocabulary
　　B. Facets of sanctification
　　C. Crisis or process?
　　D. Actual or potential?

I. In the OT

A. Vocabulary. The basic Hebrew word lying behind such terms as "sanctification" and "holiness" is *qōdeš H7731*, which has various cognate terms. Its etymology is uncertain (for discussion, see HOLINESS I.A). Numerous passages speak of holiness or sanctification as linked with God's presence, as at the BURNING BUSH (Exod. 3:5), at Mount SINAI (19:16–25; 24:17), in the desert (14:24), and in the TABERNACLE and TEMPLE (40:34–38; 1 Ki. 8:11). In these passages God's presence is marked by radiance and light; significantly, the concepts of holiness and glory are often conjoined (e.g., Exod. 29:43; 1 Chr. 16:29; Ps. 29:2).

The most basic meaning of *sanctification*, however, is generally believed to be "separation." In each of the thousand places where this term and its cognates appear in the canonical Scriptures, the meaning of separation is either explicit or implicit, and in no instance is this meaning excluded. Mount Sinai (Exod. 19:23), the FIRSTBORN (13:2), the SABBATH (20:11), and even a pagan army (Isa. 13:3) were "sanctified" by being set apart.

The objective of sanctification is PURITY, whether ritual or moral. The former is that normally required of priests and other officials in divine service (Exod. 22:31); it is ritual correctness. In the moral and ethical sense, purity is conveyed in such texts as these: "I have sworn by my holiness—and I will not lie" (Ps. 89:35; cf. Amos 4:2); "Be holy because I, the LORD your God, am holy" (Lev. 19:2; cf. Deut. 7:6; Ps. 51:7, 10; Isa. 4:3; 6:3; Hab. 1:12). It should be noted that the idea of moral purity or goodness is not inherent in the relevant terms; this connotation comes rather from the God with whom the term is linked. In eleven OT usages the concept of sanctification is linked with amoral deities and shrines and has no moral content (e.g., Gen. 38:21–22; Deut. 23:17; 1 Ki. 14:24; Job 36:14; Hos. 4:14). Since Yahweh is righteous, the sanctification he effects is ethical and moral as well as cultic in character.

B. Concern for inward righteousness. From an emphasis on ceremonial purity in priestly contexts, the moral meaning comes to be predominant in the later prophets and wise men. An analysis of the moral meaning of sanctification brings one to the vision recorded in Isa. 6, which shows that the "concept of holiness is central to the whole theology of Isaiah" (O. Procksch in *TDNT*, 1:93). The two important declarations in this passage are (1) removal of guilt and (2) atoning for sin (v. 7), reflecting an awareness of SIN that is deeper than specific acts for which the removal of guilt is needed. It is rather the corrupt source from which sinful acts arise. The prophet therefore experiences not only pardon and the removal of guilt, but purging of the inner defilement at its source.

In several passages the notion of spiritual cleansing is explicit (e.g., Job 14:4; 17:9; Pss. 15; 19:13; 24:4; 101:2; 139:23–24; Hab. 1:13). Passages such as these show that the OT is cognizant not only of outward sins but of inward defilement as well, and they give hope for inner renewal of the spirit. The statements reflect a concern, not only with the formal or forensic removal of guilt, but also with the residual, inward pollution or sinfulness. The most explicit and detailed description of sanctification is to be found in Ps. 51. The psalmist (prob. DAVID) prays for pardon of actual offenses. But he is concerned with more than a rectification of the past; he also pleads for cleansing and renewal of his disposition.

Influenced by a study of comparative religions, scholarship of an earlier day tended to give an exaggerated emphasis to the amoral, cultic aspect of the Hebraic concept. There is now an increasing recognition that the moral content is present throughout,

The wall (*temenos*) surrounding this temple found at Timna in N Sinai was meant to separate the sanctuary from its surroundings—an illustration of the "setting apart" that is involved in the concept of sanctification.

and to an increasing degree from the early prophets onward (Pss. 15:1–5; 24:3–6; 51:1–17; Hos. 4:1–10; Amos 2:6–11). See RIGHTEOUSNESS.

In the Jewish literature produced after the close of the OT, the WISDOM OF SOLOMON reflects a deep appreciation of the spiritual life. A much deeper awareness of the pervasiveness and subtlety of sin is seen in the thoughtful lines of *2 Baruch* and *4 Ezra* (these may well be contemporary with the writings of the NT; see BARUCH, APOCALYPSE OF (SYRIAC) and ESDRAS, SECOND). An even more profound concern with sanctification and holy living is discernible in the scrolls produced by the residents of QUMRAN in the decades prior to John and Jesus. In several of their hymns, and especially in the *Manual of Discipline*, the conviction is expressed that the Spirit of Truth will purge the believer's heart from all impurity and make perfect his relationship with his God (1QS IV). The Qumran literature is more optimistic with reference to sanctification than were the authors of *2 Baruch* and *4 Ezra*. The holy life envisioned therein is ascetic and legalistic in contrast to the assurance, freedom, and joyousness of the NT. See DEAD SEA SCROLLS.

II. In the NT

A. Vocabulary. Perhaps the most important Greek term for sanctification is *hagiasmos* G40, which connotes the state of grace or sanctity not inherent in its subject, but the result of outside action. The term occurs ten times in the NT (Rom. 6:19, 22; 1 Cor. 1:30; 1 Thess. 4:3–4, 7; 2 Thess. 2:13; 1 Tim. 2:15; Heb. 12:14; 1 Pet. 1:2). The act of sanctifying is expressed by the verb *hagiazō* G39, which occurs almost thirty times and in several cases means moral purification (Jn. 17:17, 19; Acts 20:32; Eph. 5:26; 1 Thess. 5:23; 2 Tim. 2:21; Heb. 13:12; 1 Pet. 3:15). The noun *hagios* G41 is found over 220 times, and in more than sixty passages the plural form is translated SAINTS, the common NT designation of believers. It means that Christians are now separated from the world and joined to Christ (1 Cor. 1:2; cf. Num. 16:3–10; 2 Chr. 23:6). In Ephesians this term is joined with *amōmos* G320 in two passages that describe the church as being "holy and blameless" (Eph. 1:4; 5:27), the latter term referring to the unblemished sacrificial victim, and twice used of Christ (Heb. 9:14; 1 Pet. 1:19; cf. Lev. 22:21). The noun *hagiōsynē* G43 is used of the moral purity that the gospel requires and imparts (2 Cor. 7:1; 1 Thess. 3:13; cf. Rom. 1:4).

B. Facets of sanctification. Clearly definable distinctions emerge in the NT. There is, for example, the sanctification of God the Father: when Jesus prayed, he acknowledged the holiness or sanctity of his Father (Jn. 17:11), and in his model prayer he taught believers to ask for the hallowing of the Father's name (Matt. 6:9; Lk. 11:2; cf. 1 Pet. 3:15; Moses' failure in this regard led to his exclusion from the Promised Land, Num. 20:12; Deut. 3:26). There is also the sanctification of the Son: we read that he was "sanctified" by the Father (Jn. 10:36) at the INCARNATION, and the Son "sanctified" or dedicated himself for the sake of his disciples (17:19). In these instances the meaning clearly is "separation"; it designates a relationship rather than inner moral renewal.

Most frequently, however, the NT speaks of the sanctification of the believer. (1) *Positional* sanctification is also properly called *status* or *cultic* sanctification. What was the predominant meaning in the OT is retained, but to a lesser degree in several NT passages. The meaning of separation is clear with reference to gifts offered to God (Matt. 23:19; cf. Rom. 15:16; 1 Tim. 4:5) and with reference to believers (1 Cor. 1:2; cf. Rom. 1:7). The Corinthian believers were "sanctified" in the sense of being set apart and yet remained "carnal" or unsanctified spiritually. Sanctification in this sense is attributive or imputational; it designates one's status, position, or relationship, and not necessarily one's nature or spiritual condition. Some regard it as imputed righteousness or JUSTIFICATION, but others distinguish justification from the initial sanctifying act referred to in these and other passages (see esp. J. Murray, "Definitive Sanctification" [orig. 1967], in *Collected Works of John Murray* [1976–82], 2:277–84).

(2) *Progressive* sanctification begins in the believer from the moment of his becoming "in Christ." Actual sanctification is the most common usage of the term; it designates *imparted* righteousness. Progressive sanctification occurs when one becomes a "partaker of the divine nature" (2 Pet. 1:4 KJV), a "new creation" in Christ (2 Cor. 5:17), or is "born anew" (Jn. 3:5, 8). It involves not only a changed relationship to God but also a changed nature, a real as well as a relative change. Among the passages that stress this aspect of sanctification are Acts 26:18; 1 Cor. 1:30; 6:11; and Heb. 9:14 (cf. Rom. 5:1–4; 2 Cor. 5:17; Jas. 1:21; 1 Pet. 1:3, 22–23; 2:1). The epistle to the Hebrews, in particular, speaks of initial sanctification in this manner, thus linking the OT and the NT concept and nomenclature (Heb. 2:11; 8:10; 9:14; 10:10, 14; 13:12) and making it the equivalent of regeneration.

(3) *Entire* sanctification is the most debatable aspect of the subject. All major theological traditions agree with reference to sanctification up to this point. The Reformed traditions, Orthodox, and Catholic do not, however, find in Scripture or in experience provision for full deliverance from sin while "in the flesh." Those who find in Scripture and in grace provision for complete victory over sin

prior to death are many in the Arminian, Pietist, Quaker, and Wesleyan traditions. Caspar Schwenkfeld, a contemporary of Luther, was among the earliest of the reformers to call for a "reformation of the Reformation" and to protest against a tendency to an accommodation of sin in some Catholic and Reformation theology. (Some have attributed the latter, in part, to the influence of oriental DUALISM imported into Christian theology via AUGUSTINE, who was influenced by a MANICHEAN philosophy before he became a Christian.)

Basic to the concept of entire sanctification is one's concept of sin. If our definition of sin is influenced by the term *hamartia* G281, indicating any want of full conformity to the will of God, then sanctification can hardly be "entire" or complete. If, however, like Wesley, we stress sin as *anomia* G490, "lawlessness" (1 Jn. 3:4), that is, a conscious and deliberate departure from the known will of God, then we may embrace promises that offer entire sanctification as a gift of grace (Rom. 6:1–23; 1 Thess. 5:23; 1 Jn. 3:3). Such readers gather from Scripture (e.g., Matt. 5:8; Jn. 17:17; Rom. 6:6–19; 2 Cor. 7:1; Eph. 4:24; 5:26; Phil. 2:15; Col. 1:22; 1 Thess. 3:13; 5:23; 1 Pet. 1:16) that the call to salvation is nothing less than a call to full deliverance from indwelling sins of attitude and motive as well as deeds.

The position of the Scriptures that can be cited in support of entire sanctification is both negative and positive. The negative aspect may be seen when PAUL, after reminding his readers that as "holy ones" they are temples of God (2 Cor. 1:2; 6:16), exhorts them: "let us purify ourselves from everything that contaminates body and spirit, perfecting holiness out of reverence for God" (7:1). The apostle here refers to a pollution that is both religious (disloyalty to God) and ethical (association with iniquity, 6:14), and yet that to which the "saints" are subject. The positive aspect is seen in the command to "perfect" or bring to completion the quality of holiness, which is now only potential. That this is a present option is apparent from the tense of the verb.

C. Crisis or process? The evidence from Scripture, reason, and experience leads to the conclusion that sanctification is both process and crisis. The process begins when one is "risen with Christ" in the new birth. Paul's emphasis on faith blends well with this emphasis upon a stage in the Christian life when believers recognize their inner defilement, deliberately renounce self-centeredness, and embrace by faith God's provision in Christ for full deliverance and perfection in love (Col. 1:22; 1 Thess. 5:23; Eph. 3:19; Rom. 6:11–14; Gal. 2:20). "This conscious self-consecration to the indwelling Spirit ... is uniformly represented as a single act ... (2 Cor. 7.11) ... Such an awakening and real consecration ... was rather a thing of definite decision (expressed by the aorist, Rom. 13:14; Col. 1:9f.; Eph. 6:11, 13–16) than of vaguely protracted process (expressed by presents)" (J. B. Bartlet in *HDB*, 4:393). Many scholars, however, question whether the aorist and present forms convey such meanings.

The call to sanctification is nowhere sounded more urgently than in Romans, where Paul, after explaining justification and its results (Rom. 3:21—5:21), makes it emphatically clear that the Christian is to make no provision for residual sin (6:1–23). In the light of its context the struggle with indwelling sin in ch. 7 is not the description of the normal "saint" but rather the futility of justification by law, apart from Christ (7:24—8:2). The same call to holy living is sounded in several other epistles (cf. Gal. 5:1, 13; Col. 1:22, 28; 3:1–15; 1 Thess. 3:13; 5:23). In the latter the call is sometimes interpreted as an eschatological event in the future. In several passages (Col. 1:23; 1 Thess. 5:23; 1 Jn. 3:3) the future is the climax, but there is little if any exegetical ground for concluding that full deliverance from sin must wait until the soul is separated from the body.

D. Actual or potential? Sanctification, defined broadly as the work of God's grace whereby a person reaches perfection in righteousness, begins when one becomes a believer and hence is "in Christ." It continues progressively until death brings the believer into Christ's presence unless he "does despite to the Spirit of grace." It is only as one by dedication and faith realizes in actuality what is provided in the atonement that this grace is experienced; it does not follow as a matter of course, as the exhortations in the NT imply. Parallel to the work of sanctification is the infilling of the HOLY SPIRIT in the believer, perfection in love, having the "mind of Christ," and "walking as he walked."

(See further W. Marshall, *The Gospel Mystery of Sanctification* [1692]; J. Wesley, *A Plain Account of Christian Perfection* [1777]; R. C. Ryle, *Holiness: Its Nature, Hindrances, Difficulties, and Roots*, 2nd ed. [1883]; R. S. Taylor, *A Right Conception of Sin* [1939]; C. W. Brown, *The Meaning of Sanctification* [1945]; G. C. Berkouwer, *Faith and Sanctification* [1952]; J. Murray, *Redemption Accomplished and Applied* [1955], 141–50; S. Neill, *Christian Holiness* [1960]; K. Keiger, ed., *Insights into Holiness* [1962]; G. A. Turner, *The Vision which Transforms* [1964]; J. I. Packer, *Keep in Step with the Spirit* [1984]; M. E. Dieter et al., *Five Views on Sanctification* [1987]; W. Grudem, *Systematic Theology: An Introduction to Christian Doctrine* [1994], ch. 38; D. Peterson, *Possessed by God: A New Testament Theology of Sanctification and Holiness* [1995]; S. Hauerwas, *Sanctify Them in Truth: Holiness Exemplified* [1998]; J. M. Howard, *Paul, the Community, and Progressive Sanctification* [2007].) G. A. Turner

sanctuary. A holy place set apart from profane use for the purpose of worship of, or communion with, a deity. The forerunners to Israel's sanctuaries were the patriarchal worship places, usually designated by a theophany or some other special revelation of God (e.g., Gen. 12:7; 26:24–25; 28:16–17). The Hebrew term *miqdāš H5219* is most frequently used of the TABERNACLE, but also of the TEMPLE and of pagan holy places (Isa. 16:12 [NIV, "shrine"]; Ezek. 28:18). The first reference to a sanctuary (Exod. 15:17) speaks of the abode of God to which he brings his redeemed people to reign over them as King. This eschatological sanctuary (cf. Heb. 8:2; Gk. *hagios G41* used in the pl.) forms the reality of which the earthly sanctuaries of God are but the foreshadowing. The sanctuary is a place for the Lord to dwell in the midst of his people (Exod. 25:8), and since the presence of God is the important factor, the establishment of the right relationship with God ultimately renders the special holy place unnecessary (Ezek. 11:16; Rev. 21:22; see also Jn. 4:21, 23). (See N. H. Snaith, *The Distinctive Ideas of the Old Testament* [1944], 24–32; R. de Vaux, *Ancient Israel* [1961], 274–311.) G. Goldsworthy

sand. Although biblical references to sand (Heb. *ḥôl H2567*; Gk. *ammos G302*) are numerous, on only one occasion does physical sand figure in the record, namely, when Moses buried an Egyptian whom he had killed, in the hope of keeping the affair secret (Exod. 2:12). All other references are figurative, the most common being to speak of sand grains as an indication of large numbers or amounts.

The regions in which the Bible narrative unfolds contain many areas of sand and sand-hills. From Egypt, through the wilderness of Sinai, the Israelites would have been marching over sand for a good part of their journey. Although the desert of Sinai is rocky rather than sandy, patches of loose sand are encountered very frequently. Within the Promised Land, there was and is a wide belt of coastal sand dunes bordering the Mediterranean along the shores of S Palestine. This belt has tended to spread inland unless stopped by forest planting or marram grass. It is the true "sand of the seashore."

Apart from this coastal sand, it should also be borne in mind that in a dry climate every river and torrent eroding the barren surface of the land quickly becomes charged with a load of sand and debris, which it spreads along its banks where it debouches into the plain. This gives point to the Lord's parable of the house built on the sand (Matt. 7:26); presumably it was built on these valley deposits, beside the river, where it was within reach of the flood level of the storm water.

References to sand as symbolizing very large numbers occur from Gen. 22:17 onward; not only Abraham's descendants are so described, but also the corn gathered by Joseph in Egypt (41:49) and, rather curiously, the wisdom of Solomon and his breadth of knowledge (1 Ki. 4:29). In Matt. 7:26, of course, sand serves as a symbol of instability or lack of foundation. J. H. Paterson

sandal. A covering for the foot consisting of a sole fastened to the instep or ankle by straps. Both the Hebrew *naʿal H5837* (Gen. 14:23 et al.) and the Greek *hypodēma G5687* (Matt. 3:1 et al.) are rendered "shoe" by the KJV, but modern versions have "sandal" because the latter term more accurately portrays to the modern mind a picture of the ANE shoe. The KJV does use "sandal" in the two instances where the NT has the Greek synonym *sandalion G4908* (Mk. 6:9; Acts 12:8; this latter term is a diminutive of *sandalon*, which originally referred to a wooden sole with straps).

Sandals or shoes of some kind were worn in the ANE from very early times to protect the feet. However, the poor frequently walked barefoot when no great distance was to be covered. The form of ancient footwear can be known chiefly from monuments of Assyria, Egypt, and Persia. Some kind of covering on the feet can be distinguished in a painting on wood, dating as far back as the 4th millennium B.C., but the exact shape is not clear. The Beni Hasan panel (c. 1900 B.C.) shows a group of Asiatics in Egypt, the men wearing soles fastened to the foot by crossing straps with a strap running round the ankle, and the women having boots reaching above the ankle with a white band at the top. A black obelisk of Shalmaneser III (9th cent. B.C.) portrays Jehu and the Israelites having shoes with upturned toes, while the Assyrians to whom they were paying tribute were wearing sandals with heel caps. In a painting of Sargon II (8th cent. B.C.) the method of fastening is seen more distinctly. The sandals have sides coming above the arch of the foot and are held in position by a double strap over the toes. These are probably the sandals of the wealthier class. A simpler type consisted of soles of wood, leather, or some fibrous material kept in position by leather thongs. Ezekiel described women's sandals made of "leather" [Heb. *taḥaš* H9391], possibly a reference to seal skin, or the skin of a dolphin-like animal (Ezek. 16:10). See sea cow.

The wearing of shoes often spoke of travel or readiness to travel. Thus the Israelites were to eat the Passover with shoes on, that is, in readiness to depart immediately (Exod. 12:11). They also experienced a miraculous preservation of their sandals while wandering (Deut. 29:5). Similarly, the Lord's disciples did not need the customary extra pair of sandals for their journey (Matt. 10:10; Lk. 10:4; 22:35). Because having one's shoes on indicates that a person is ready for travel or work, Paul instructs believers to have their "feet fitted [*hypodeō* G5686] with the readiness that comes from the gospel of peace" (Eph. 6:15).

Shoes were commonly taken off on entering a house, and water was provided for guests to bathe their feet. The washing of feet was necessary, especially because the sandals afforded only partial protection from dust or insects (Lk. 7:44). To unloose the shoe was often the work of a slave, who might also carry the shoes to an appropriate place (Matt. 3:11; Lk. 3:16). The latter practice may lie behind Pss. 60:8 and 108:9; as shoes might sometimes be thrown to a slave to carry away, the figure suggests power exercised over Edom to make its people serve God's purpose.

Being the least expensive of personal items, the sandal-thong sometimes signified cheapness. Hence, Abraham would not agree to take even the most insignificant possession of the king of Sodom (Gen. 14:23). A similar use of the shoe itself is found: to sell "the needy for a pair of sandals" (Amos 2:6; 8:6) meant to sell them for a very low price. It appears that a poor man's shoes were the most trifling pledge that could be accepted. Where these were lacking, the debtor was likely to be enslaved by the unrelenting creditor. The absence of shoes is a mark of poverty (Lk. 15:22); it also points to the plight of the captive (Isa. 20:2–4). Growing out of the concept of cheapness is the idea that shoes depict the most humble part of a person. Accordingly, John the Baptist disclaimed any worthiness to touch the sandals of Christ (Matt. 3:11; Mk. 1:7; Lk. 3:16; Jn. 1:27; Acts 13:25); even the lowliest part of the Messiah was too exalted for comparison with the forerunner.

If the Septuagint of 1 Sam. 12:3 reflects accurately the original Hebrew text, shoes might be offered as a bribe to a judge (see P. K. McCarter, Jr., *I Samuel*, AB 8 [1980], 209–10). In 2 Sam. 15:30 being barefoot is a sign of mourning, but the wearing of shoes (Ezek. 24:17, 23) during a period of mourning is an attempt to conceal grief. Twice in the OT the command was given to remove shoes in the presence of God or his supernatural representative (Exod. 3:5; Josh. 5:15), possibly because of the defilement contracted by the shoes in traveling. It is in keeping with this symbolism denoting reverence that no mention is made of shoes in the descriptions of priestly dress. The service of the tabernacle and temple was performed barefoot. Muslims observe a similar custom in modern times, either removing or covering the shoes when about to enter a mosque. To have a shoe removed on refusal to undertake a levirate marriage was to be shown contempt (Deut. 25:9–10), but in the arrangement between Boaz and Elimelech's nearer relative, the former confirmed the bargain by giving his sandal (Ruth 4:7–8). (Cf. E. A. Speiser in *BASOR* 77 [Feb. 1940]: 15–20; R. de Vaux, *Ancient Israel* [1961], 22, 37, 59, 86, 169.) See also DRESS IV.

W. J. CAMERON
R. L. THOMAS

Sanhedrin san-hee′druhn (συνέδριον *G5284*, "a sitting together, a council-board"; transliterated into Mishnaic Heb. as סַנְהֶדְרִין [the occasionally encountered spelling *Sanhedrim* is the result of a mistaken assumption that the Heb. word was in reality a masc. pl. noun]). The council or governing body that met in JERUSALEM in NT times and that constituted the highest Jewish authority in Palestine prior to A.D. 70. It must be distinguished from lesser, local courts of law to which the name *sanhedrin* was also regularly applied.

I. Sources for the study of the Sanhedrin. The three primary sources of information for our knowledge of the Sanhedrin are (1) the NT documents, (2) the writings of the Jewish historian JOSEPHUS, and (3) rabbinic tradition, particularly as codified in the MISHNAH (in the tractate *Sanhedrin*), but also in the TALMUD (and its supplement, the TOSEFTA). The information that can be gleaned from the NT and Josephus is, of course, indirect, whereas the rabbinic materials often intend specifically to provide details about the Sanhedrin. This fact is counterbalanced, however, by the comparatively late date (about A.D. 200) at which the rabbinic materials that had been handed down orally were finally written down.

It is, unfortunately, impossible to reconcile the description of the Sanhedrin in the rabbinic materials with that found in the NT and Josephus. An attempt has been made to do just this, however, by alleging that there were two major Sanhedrins in Jerusalem: (1) a political Sanhedrin composed of a priestly aristocracy headed by the high priest, concerned with civil affairs and the administration of criminal justice (of which we read in the NT and Josephus) and (2) a religious Sanhedrin composed of a laity of PHARISEES headed by a RABBI, concerned with matters of religious life and the interpretation of the TORAH (of which we read in the rabbinic materials). While this ingenious and attractive theory has been accepted by a number of Jewish scholars (e.g., Lauterbach, Hoenig, Zeitlin, Mantel), it has not found general consent and is here rejected as a conjecture that is too facile and goes too far beyond what the concrete evidence warrants. The reliability of the NT and Josephus far exceeds that of the rabbinic writings, which often reflect the state of affairs after, rather than before, the destruction of Jerusalem in A.D. 70. Consequently the traditions of the rabbis, while they may sometimes convey trustworthy information concerning the Sanhedrin, must be used with special caution. Where there is conflicting testimony between the NT and Josephus on the one hand and the rabbinic materials on the other hand, historically speaking, one is on safer ground to accept the former as trustworthy and to reject the latter as anachronistic.

II. Terminology. The Greek word *synedrion* is frequently encountered in Classical and Hellenistic Greek, where it commonly means "place of gathering," but also comes to connote the gathering itself and in some instances even its authority. The word occurs also in the SEPTUAGINT, where it refers to an assembly or court (but not to the Sanhedrin as commonly understood). While *synedrion* is common in the NT (over twenty occurrences) and in Josephus, it is not the only term or phrase used in referring to the great council of Jerusalem. The term *gerousia G1172*, "council of elders, senate," is found occasionally in the OT APOCRYPHA and Josephus, and occurs once also in the NT (Acts 5:21). Another word used to refer to the Sanhedrin is *presbyterion G4564*, "council of elders," which is used twice in the NT (Lk. 22:66; Acts 22:5).

A term used often by Josephus in referring to the Sanhedrin is *boulē G1087*. While this particular word is used by NT writers only in such senses as "purpose" and "will," the cognate noun *bouleutēs G1085*, "councillor," is used by Luke in referring to JOSEPH of Arimathea in his capacity as member of the Sanhedrin (Lk. 23:50; the noun *bouleutērion*, "council," also is used by Josephus. The council is often referred to in the NT by speaking of its members as chief priests, elders, and scribes. The rabbinic sources use, in addition to *sanhedrîn*, words and phrases such as *bêt dîn gādôl* ("great house of justice") and Aramaic *kĕnîštāʾ* ("assembly").

III. History.

The rabbinic tradition as recorded in the Mishnah (*m. Sanh.* 1:6) traces the origin of the Sanhedrin back to the command of God to Moses to gather together seventy men chosen from among the elders of Israel (Num. 11:16). After the EXILE it was said to have been reorganized by EZRA. While the precise origins of the Sanhedrin remain obscure, it is commonly argued that historically one cannot speak of the Sanhedrin proper until Hellenistic times, that is, the period of Israel's domination by the Ptolemies and Seleucids (see ANTIOCHUS; PTOLEMY; SELEUCUS).

There are, to be sure, certain anticipations or foreshadowings of the Sanhedrin in the period immediately following the exile (see RESTORATION). The place of the elders in Israel was, of course, ever an important one. Early in the history of Israel priests and judges administered justice in specific cases (e.g., Deut. 19:15–21). Long before the exile, JEHOSHAPHAT king of Judah (872–848 B.C.) is reported to have appointed a law court in Jerusalem consisting of "priests and heads of Israelite families to administer the law of the LORD and to settle disputes" (2 Chr. 19:8). Just after the exile, the importance of the elders (e.g., Ezra 5:5; 6:7–8, 10:8) as well as of the priests and nobles (e.g., Neh. 2:16; 5:7; 7:5) in leadership and adjudication is readily evident. See ELDER (OT). Despite the acknowledged similarity, however, it is still not the Sanhedrin of the NT period.

The first explicit mention of the body known as the Sanhedrin in historical sources is found in Josephus, who in his account of a decree of Antiochus III (223–187 B.C.) refers to the *gerousia* or "senate" of the Jews (*Ant.* 12.3.3 §§138ff.). This "senate" was composed of priests and elders under the direction of the high priest, being constituted as an organized body concerned not merely with judicial matters, but having the broader responsibility of acting as the governing body for the whole of Palestine. It was the practice of the Hellenistic kings to give a large degree of freedom to subject nations in the governing of their internal affairs. This seems to have been true of the Jewish nation under the Ptolemies and Seleucids. The senate of this period is also referred to in the books of the Maccabees (e.g., 1 Macc. 12:6; 2 Macc. 1:10; 4:44; cf. "the elders of the people," 1 Macc. 7:33). During

Interior of the Huldah Gates, located at the S end of the temple mount. The members of the Sanhedrin would have frequently used this entrance to the temple.

the period of independence under the HASMONEAN Dynasty, the power of the council was somewhat curtailed, but it continued to exist as a body. The monarchical rulers of this period needed the support of the nobility who composed its members. It was the queen Salome ALEXANDRA (76–67 B.C.) who, at the advice of her dying husband Alexander Jannaeus, first installed large numbers of Pharisees in the Sanhedrin, making this group dominant in a council that had hitherto consisted wholly of SADDUCEES (Jos. *War* 1.5.2 §110).

After the Roman occupation of 63 B.C., the council continued to exist under the leadership of the high priest Hyrcanus (II). Within a few years, however, Gabinius, the Roman governor of Syria (57–55 B.C.), greatly reduced the power of the Jerusalem council by dividing the land into five "sanhedrins" (*synedria*, Jos. *Ant.* 14.5.4 §91, *synodoi*, *War* 1.8.5 §170) or administrative councils. The high council thereby became merely one among the five, and its regional jurisdiction diminished considerably.

This limitation was only temporary, however, for under the direction of Caesar, Hyrcanus was reappointed "ethnarch," and the Jerusalem council regained its status, appearing again to have had authority over the whole of the land. Indeed, in 47 B.C. there was the remarkable occurrence that

HEROD was summoned from Galilee to appear before the Sanhedrin for having executed a certain Hezekiah without the permission of the high court (Jos. *Ant.* 14.9.3 §§166–68, a passage where the actual word *synedrion* occurs for the first time in historical sources with specific reference to the Jerusalem council, after which however this use of the word becomes common). For the sake of Hyrcanus, Herod was absolved of this crime, but after he was made king of the Jews he took bloody revenge by killing the members of this Sanhedrin (ibid., §175; it is doubtful whether "all" the members are to be taken literally; cf. 15.1.2 §6).

The Sanhedrin continued to exist under Herod, but it was filled with tractable men and its power was severely limited. Herod used the court to carry out his will, but did not allow it or the high priest (Herod was unqualified for this office) to interfere with his reign. At the death of Herod in 4 B.C., his kingdom was divided among his three sons, the most important part (including Judea and Samaria) going to Archelaus who ruled as "ethnarch." Despite the plea of the people to AUGUSTUS for more self-government (cf. Jos. *Ant.* 17.11.2 §§304ff.), the status and power of the Sanhedrin underwent no particular change.

In A.D. 6, however, when JUDEA was made a Roman PROVINCE, the Sanhedrin and its president, the high priest, were granted almost exclusive control of the internal affairs of the nation, similar to that which it had under the Hellenistic kings. The sacred status of Jerusalem and its environs was recognized by the Romans and, so long as public order was maintained and tax revenues were forthcoming, they were content for national matters to be under the control of the Jerusalem Sanhedrin. It is during the period of the Roman governors (A.D. 6–66) that the Sanhedrin came to possess the greatest power and jurisdiction of its history, although the Jewish authority was always ultimately answerable to the Roman governor. Josephus can speak of the dominion of the nation as having been entrusted to the high priests of this period (*Ant.* 20.10.1–5 §§224–51).

This is the Sanhedrin which we encounter in the NT documents. It is a body composed largely of members of the aristocracy (the chief priests and Sadducees), which under the leadership of the high priest exercises considerable judicial authority in handling Jesus of Nazareth according to the Gospels, and his disciples according to the book of Acts. Its area of jurisdiction also appears to include the DIASPORA to some degree (witness PAUL's request for letters to the synagogue at DAMASCUS from the high priest, Acts 9:1–2).

With the Jewish rebellion, which began in A.D. 66, martial law came into effect, and when Jerusalem finally fell in the year 70, the Sanhedrin was permanently dissolved. From this point onward Palestine was governed solely by strict Roman provincial administration. Almost immediately, it appears, a new "Sanhedrin" was constituted at Jamnia (see JABNEEL). This institution, however, was markedly different from its predecessor in that, needless to say, it had no political or governing power whatsoever, and was limited exclusively to the judgment of religious questions. Despite the rabbinic claims that this body stood in continuity with the Sanhedrin of earlier periods, it is evident that by comparison the new Sanhedrin was powerless. Whereas the Jerusalem Sanhedrin of the period of the Roman governors consisted largely of aristocratic men led by the high priest, the decrees of which were binding under penalty of severe punishment, the new Sanhedrin or *Beth Din* (court of Justice), as it was called, consisted exclusively of rabbinic scholars under a scholar-president whose decrees were theoretical and bore only the authority warranted by voluntary respect for scholarly wisdom.

IV. Composition. Although the rabbinic tradition knows only of a "Sanhedrin" composed entirely of scholarly scribes and Pharisees, we know that throughout its history the Sanhedrin was dominated by a priestly aristocracy. And, to speak in terms of the parties that developed during Hasmonean times, the nobility almost without exception consisted of Sadducees. Pharisees were admitted into the Sanhedrin in considerable numbers at two particular junctures in its history: once under Salome Alexandra (as noted above) and subsequently under Herod the Great, who took this measure to limit more effectively the power of the older nobility who opposed him.

According to the Mishnah (*m. Sanh.* 1:6), the membership of the Great Sanhedrin numbered seventy-one. This statement seems to reflect accurately the situation before the fall of Jerusalem. (Mention is made also of smaller, local sanhedrins composed of twenty-three members.) Tribunals were quite probably modeled in number after the tribunal of seventy instituted by Moses according to Num. 11:16–17, and there are some indications that, among the Jews, councils of seventy were favored. The extra man was apparently the leader or president of the Sanhedrin, who according to the evidence of Josephus and the NT, was the high priest. The rabbinic tradition, however, does not associate the Great Sanhedrin with the high priest. Instead, it attributes the leadership of the council to a president (*nāśîʾ* 115954, "prince, ruler") who was simply one of the scribes of the council. He was assisted by a vice-president (*ʾab bêt dîn*, "father of the house of justice") who was also a scribe. This almost certainly reflects the situation after A.D. 70 and is sometimes wrongly taken as accurately describing the Sanhedrin of the time of Christ.

The office of high priest was, of course, hereditary, although on occasion this was altered for political expediency. Exactly how other members of the Sanhedrin came to hold office remains obscure. A likely conjecture is that the body was self-perpetuating in the sense of electing its own members. The office was probably given for life, but again this is uncertain. The criteria for membership were probably age and wealth, although the Mishnah mentions only one necessity — that the candidate be learned in rabbinic doctrine.

Particularly in the NT, one encounters repeated references to "chief priests"; this term renders Greek *archiereis*, which is the plural of *archiereus* G797, normally translated "high priest." The group of chief priests, which formed the leading component of the Sanhedrin, consisted of former high priests, including members of the most important of the priestly families. Probably next to this group in prestige was the lay nobility, who like the priestly aristocracy were also of Sadducean sympathies, and who are probably referred to under the title "elders." Another important group, an element of increasing importance in the Sanhedrin of the 1st cent., is that of the "scribes," the professional scholars who were experts in matters of Mosaic law. The scribes, by way of contrast with the other groups, were usually Pharisees. Although they were a minority in the Sanhedrin, they apparently enjoyed considerable popular support. So much so, that not only could nothing be accomplished without the Pharisees, but as Josephus indicated, the Sadducees often went along with them in order merely to be tolerated by the masses (*Ant.* 18.1.4 §§16–17).

Remains of a priestly estate located in Jerusalem's upper city.

V. Session. The Sanhedrin, like other local courts according to the Mishnah, almost certainly was prohibited from meeting on the SABBATH or on feast days. Whether it could in extreme circumstances legally meet on a feast day as it did in the TRIAL OF JESUS cannot be known, but seems improbable. In cases involving capital punishment, the sentence could not lawfully be delivered until the day following the trial, and therefore such trials were also prohibited on the eve of either a Sabbath or a feast day (*m. Sanh.* 4:1). Cases involving potential capital punishment were similarly barred from taking place at night (ibid.). According to the Tosefta, the hours of meeting on regular days were from the time of the morning sacrifice to the evening sacrifice (*t. Sanh.* 7:1).

There is some disagreement concerning where the Sanhedrin held its meetings. According to the Mishnah it met in the temple precincts to the S of the temple court, in what was called "The Chamber of Hewn Stone" (*m. Mid.* 5:4). Josephus, however, appears to locate the meeting place of the Sanhedrin in two different spots (cf. *War* 5.4.2; 6.6.3). The NT has the Sanhedrin gathered at the palace of the high priest for the trial of Jesus, but the circumstances are exceedingly irregular (the meeting at night was illegal, and it could not have taken place in the temple precincts, which would have been locked) and cannot be taken as normative in any sense.

The Mishnah provides us with further information concerning the meetings of the Sanhedrin. The members are said to have sat in a semicircle in order that all might see one another, while in front of them on the right and left were positioned two scribes who kept a written record of the testimony for acquittal or conviction (*m. Sanh.* 4:3). Also present were three rows of "disciples of the Sages" from which additional judges could be appointed, while a member of the congregation would be chosen to fill the gap caused among the disciples of the Sages (ibid., 4:4). A great amount of additional information of the actual process of justice is available in the Mishnah; for example, capital cases had to begin with reasons for acquittal, and whereas testimony in such cases could be unanimous for acquittal, it could not be unanimous for condemnation—someone had to argue on behalf of the accused (ibid., 4:1). However, the question of whether or not such information can be accepted as at all accurate for the period of our concern remains crucial.

VI. Competence. The Sanhedrin certainly had complete control of the religious affairs of the nation as the Mishnah indicates. The high court was the supreme authority in the interpretation of Mosaic law and, when it mediated in questions disputed in the lower courts, its verdict was final. Beyond this, the Sanhedrin also governed civil affairs and tried certain criminal cases under the authority of the Roman governor. The Romans were quite content to let subject nations regulate internal affairs, but there were, of course, always limits. They, for example, would have reserved the right to intervene at will, and while it is probable that they usually went along with the high court's decisions, they were under no compulsion to do so.

One of the most vexing questions concerning the Sanhedrin was whether or not the Romans had granted it the power of capital punishment. There is a fair amount of evidence that seems to indicate that the Sanhedrin did have the right to try capital cases and to execute capital punishment. In the Mishnah regulations are given for different types of execution. (Four kinds of capital punishment which could be inflicted by the court are enumerated in *m. Sanh.* 7:1.) There is, moreover, reference to the burning of a priest's daughter for adultery, which probably occurred before the fall of Jerusalem. Further records of actual executions are found in Josephus, who provides an account of the Sanhedrin's trial and stoning of JAMES, the brother of Jesus, as well as some other Christians (*Ant.* 20.9.1 §200). Documentary evidence has been discovered by archaeologists which proves that GENTILES (even Roman citizens) could be put to death by the Jewish authorities for trespassing the restricted areas of the temple precinct. In the NT itself there is the account of the trial and stoning of STEPHEN by the Sanhedrin (Acts 6:9—8:1).

While this evidence is weighty, it is not necessarily conclusive. The regulations in the Mishnah quite probably describe the situation after the "reconstitution" of the Sanhedrin at Jamnia. The execution of the priest's daughter referred to in the Mishnah may be readily explained if it occurred during the reign of Herod Agrippa I (who ruled as king over the whole of Palestine) in the years A.D. 41–44, when there was a temporary interruption in the procuratorial system of government in Palestine (see HEROD VII). It is also during this interval between Roman PROCURATORS that the execution of James son of Zebedee took place, this by the hand of Agrippa himself (Acts 12:1–2). Years later, when James brother of Jesus was executed, Agrippa II quickly had the high priest responsible (Annas II, or Ananus) removed from office (Jos. *Ant.* 20.9.1 §§201–3).

Thus the right of capital punishment over those trespassing the holy places of the temple is surely to be regarded as an extraordinary privilege granted by the Romans merely for the sake of expediency. It would be rash to extrapolate from this instance and allege that therefore the Sanhedrin would also possess the right of capital punishment in other matters, at least over its own people, the Jews. The stoning of Stephen took place after a trial before the Sanhedrin on the charge of blasphemy. (Herein lies another problem in that technically Stephen was not guilty of blasphemy since he did not pronounce the ineffable Name, and thus at most he should have received forty stripes less one.) However, the execution bears the marks of precipitate action on the part of an enraged mob. On the other hand, if it was the carefully deliberate action of the Sanhedrin, it is not difficult to believe that occasionally the Jewish authority perpetrated an illegality which to the Romans was not very significant, and which was thus conveniently overlooked.

The NT data clearly point to the conclusion that the Sanhedrin did *not* possess the power of capital punishment. Jesus appears to have been turned over to the Romans because the crime of which he was alleged to be guilty was regarded as deserving of capital punishment. At any rate, the assertion of Jn. 18:31 made by the Jews to PILATE is beyond question: "we have no right to execute anyone." Remarkably, there is a piece of Talmudic evidence that supports this assertion. In the Jerusalem Talmud, it is said that the right of capital punishment was taken from Israel forty years prior to the destruction of the temple (*y. Sanh.* 1:1 [18a]; 7:2 [24b]). The round number forty quite probably means to convey the period of Roman procuratorship (precisely, A.D. 6–66). All of this fits with what is known of the Roman custom in the government of the provinces. Capital punishment was almost always held by the governor as his own personal prerogative. It was on occasion granted to free cities in the empire, but that it would be granted to a city such as Jerusalem, or to a nation so infamously unruly as Judea, is hardly to be expected.

VII. The Sanhedrin in the NT. The action of the Sanhedrin in the NT bears out the picture here presented. The Sanhedrin is perhaps most conspicuous in its role in the trial of Jesus in the Gospels. Without getting into the intricacies of the trial itself, the following may be said. The Sanhedrin had every right to prosecute Jesus for alleged crimes whether religious or civil. From what can be pieced together from the gospel narratives (Matt. 26; Mk. 14; Lk. 22; Jn. 19), the Sanhedrin rather than being a vehicle for the accomplishment of justice—for which the rabbinic model in the Mishnah is exemplary—here became guilty of a gross travesty of justice. The time and nature of its meetings, the manner in which the "trial" was conducted, its strange outcome—all point to the intent desire of the Jewish authorities to do away with Jesus. Here we have a group of desperate men who, while trying to keep a show of propriety and at least a semblance of "legality," take what can only be regarded as very desperate measures. Long before his arrest and trial they had determined to have Jesus put to death (Matt. 12.14, Mk. 3.6, Jn. 11:53). It was only a question of how to do this, and under what charges to hand him over to the Romans for the capital punishment they themselves could not legally administer. Ultimately they found this in the political charge of sedition.

In the Acts of the Apostles, the Sanhedrin on occasion behaves more as one should expect this council to act. The apostles are brought before the court and admonished not to continue stirring up the people with their message (Acts 4.5–22, 5:17–42). At one point when some members of the council wanted to kill them (5:33), a Pharisee of the council, the famous rabbi GAMALIEL, made an eloquent plea for justice (5:35–39). Similarly, when Paul was arraigned before the Sanhedrin, he was able (with some skill and knowledge) to elicit support from the Pharisees of the council, who declared, "We find nothing wrong with this man" (23:9). In the stoning of Stephen, however, the court appeared in a bad light, being guilty of an illegal as well as impetuous act.

There can be little question that the Sanhedrin in its full complement included some outstanding men. In addition to Gamaliel, already mentioned, the council included Joseph of Arimathea, who was a disciple of Jesus secretly (Jn. 19:38; see JOSEPH #14), and NICODEMUS, who was also drawn to Jesus. The latter showed a genuine concern for justice in the high council's intentions concerning Jesus when he said to his fellow members, "Does our law condemn anyone without first hearing him to find out what he is doing?" (Jn. 7:50). One may only suppose that in the fiasco which served as Jesus' trial, these more honorable members of the Sanhedrin were not present at the clandestine meetings, or that they did object even though we have no record of their protestations. It has occasionally been suggested that Saul of Tarsus was a member of the Sanhedrin prior to his conversion. Acts 8:1

and 26:10 do not necessarily mean that Saul voted as a member of the council. What is meant is probably only that he gave his assent unofficially, for it is improbable that Saul, who is described as "a young man" (7:58), could have been a member of the august council of elders.

(See further H. Danby in *JTS* 21 [1919]: 51–76; S. Zeitlin in *JQR* 36 [1945–46]: 109–40, and 37 [1946–47]: 189–98; J. Jeremias in *ZNW* 43 [1950–51]: 145–50; S. B. Hoenig, *The Great Sanhedrin* [1953]; T. A. Burkill in *Vigiliae Christianae* 10 [1956]: 80–96; J. Blinzler, *The Trial of Jesus* [1959]; H. Mantel, *Studies in the History of the Sanhedrin* [1961]; J. Jeremias, *Jerusalem in the Time of Jesus* [1967], 222–32; E. Bammel, *The Trial of Jesus: Cambridge Studies in Honour of C. F. D. Moule* [1970]; P. Winter, *On the Trial of Jesus*, 2nd ed. [1974]; *HJP*, rev. ed. [1973–87], 2:199–226; P. J. Tomson, *Presumed Guilty: How the Jews Were Blamed for the Death of Jesus* [2005]; E. Lohse in *TDNT*, 7:860–71; A. J. Saldarini in *ABD*, 5:975–80.)

D. A. HAGNER

Sansannah san-san'uh (סַנְסַנָּה *H6179*, prob. "stalk of the date palm"). One of the "southernmost towns of the tribe of Judah in the Negev toward the boundary of Edom" (Josh. 15:31; cf. v. 21). It is probably the same as modern Khirbet esh-Shamsaniyat, some 8 mi. NE of BEERSHEBA. A comparison with the parallel lists (Josh. 19:5; 1 Chr. 4:31) has led some to equate Sansannah with HAZAR SUSAH (Hazar Susim), but this identification remains uncertain.

A. BOWLING

Saph saf (סַף *H6198*, meaning unknown). A descendant of Rapha (see REPHAITES) who was killed by SIBBECAI the Hushathite in a fight with the PHILISTINES at Gob (2 Sam. 21:18). In the parallel passage, he is called "Sippai" (evidently an alternate form of the name), and the battle is said to have taken place in GEZER (1 Chr. 20:4). See discussion under GOB.

Saphat, Saphatias. Sapheth say'fat, saf'uh-ti'uhs, say'fith. KJV Apoc. variants of SHEPHATIAH (respectively 1 Esd. 5:9; 8:34; 5:33).

Saphir say'fuhr. KJV form of SHAPHIR.

Sapphira suh-fi'ruh (Σάπφιρα *G4912*, from Aram. שַׁפִּירָא [determined state of שַׁפִּיר *H10736*], "beautiful"). Wife of ANANIAS. The couple sold a piece of property and pretended to bring the money to the apostles. For their hypocrisy in pretending not to have kept any of the money for themselves, and lying to the HOLY SPIRIT, they both died suddenly within three hours of each other, much to the fear of the early church and of all who heard about it (Acts 5:1–11). (For a discussion of the literary qualities of this narrative, see Robert F. O'Toole in *ABD*, 5:980–81.)

A. M. ROSS

sapphire. A blue precious stone (Heb. *sappir H6209*; Gk. *sapphiros G4913*); like RUBY, it is a variety of corundum (aluminum oxide), which next to DIAMOND is the hardest known naturally occurring mineral. The blue color of sapphire, "clear as the sky itself" (Exod. 24:10), is thought to be due to titanium. Many think, however, that ancient writers used the term to refer to the blue colored mineral LAPIS LAZULI, which is easier to cut.

Sapphire possesses a fibrous structure that is generally very faint. Where this structure is well developed, an optical effect of six rays of light emanating from a center is shown and the precious stone is called a "star sapphire." The term *sapphire* has also been used to refer to all gem varieties of corundum except those that are red (rubies); these include oriental TOPAZ (yellow), oriental EMERALD (green), and oriental AMETHYST (purple). The transparent colorless variety is called "white sapphire"; it has been referred to by some writers as ADAMANT. Sapphire, together with ruby and many other gem stones, has come from Ceylon for 2,500 years. They mainly occur in detrital gravels derived from the denudation of metamorphic rocks, including crystalline limestones. They are also obtained from the basement crystalline rocks. (See E. S. Dana and W. E. Ford, *A Text-book of Mineralogy*, 4th ed. [1932], 481–83; A. M. Bateman, *Economic Mineral Deposits*, 2nd ed. [1950], 847–48.)

D. R. BOWES

Sara sair'uh. KJV NT form of SARAH.

Sarabias sair'uh-bi'uhs. KJV Apoc. form of SHEREBIAH (1 Esd. 9:48).

Sarah, Sarai sair′uh, say′ri (שָׂרָה H8577 [from Gen. 17:15 on], alternate form שָׂרַי H8584 [Gen. 11:29—17:5], "princess"; Σάρρα G4925). **(1)** The wife of ABRAHAM (Gen. 11:29-30), and also his half-sister on his father TERAH's side (20:12). She is highly esteemed by the Jews as a kind of mother-figure and example of piety. She seems also to be admired as an epitome of feminine pulchritude. Legendary accounts of this appear in postbiblical Jewish writing (cf. *DOTP*, 735), and there is a flowery description of her in the GENESIS APOCRYPHON (1QapGen XX, 2-8).

Sarai journeyed with Abram from UR to HARAN (Gen. 11:31), and after a time there to CANAAN (12:5). Sojourns at SHECHEM and between the towns of BETHEL and AI followed, but because of a famine in the land they fled to EGYPT. Even at the age of sixty-five (cf. 12:4 and 17:17) she had so retained her beauty that Abram feared that he might be killed for his wife when they were in Egypt. To minimize this possibility he let it be known that she was his sister (12:10-13). PHARAOH took Sarai into his HAREM or palace and gave generously to Abram. Because of plagues on his household, however, Pharaoh suspected the truth and she and her husband were sent away.

A second incident in which a similar pretense was used occurred at the court of ABIMELECH, king of GERAR, when again Sarai posed as Abram's sister (Gen. 20; cf. the parallel in ch. 26, concerning Isaac and Rebekah). Abimelech was warned in a dream, and following a prayer by Abram, the plague that had fallen on his house was lifted, but again Sarai and Abram had to leave.

The first mention of Sarai stated that "she had no children" (Gen. 11:30). Her BARRENNESS was a continual reproach, and after ten years in Canaan she gave her Egyptian handmaiden, HAGAR, to Abram for a concubine (16:1-3). When Hagar conceived she despised Sarai, who in her jealousy mistreated Hagar to the extent that the latter had to escape into the wilderness for a time; but after seeing a vision, she returned to the house of Abram (16:4-9). Hagar gave birth to a son named ISHMAEL, who is regarded as ancestral to the ARABIAN peoples, in fulfillment of a prediction made to Hagar in the wilderness: "I will so increase your descendants that they will be too numerous to count" (16:10, cf. 17:20). (On the conflict between the two women as a literary pattern, see A. Brenner in *VT* 36 [1986]: 257-73. This story has been a focus of much modern feminist hermeneutics.)

Sarai's name was changed to Sarah as a mark of something new: God's promise that she would bear a son (Gen. 17:15-16; "Sarai" is thought to be an older form of the name, but there appears to be no significant difference between the two forms). This son was to be the ancestor of a great posterity, from whom prominent leaders should come. Sarah laughed at the announcement because she was already ninety, and her husband, Abraham, was one hundred years of age. But the promise came to pass, and some fourteen years after Ishmael, Isaac was born (21:1-3). All was joyous until the feast held for Isaac's weaning, when Sarah's jealousy lest Ishmael should receive the inheritance resulted in the now permanent casting out of Hagar and Ishmael, who went and lived in the wilderness of PARAN (21:8-21). Sarah is thus shown as a very human person who, because of her jealousy and hasty judgment, falls something short of the ideal character. Nevertheless, her FAITH (Rom. 4:19; cf. Isa. 51:2; Heb. 11:11) and proper familial regard (1 Pet. 3:6) are noted in these NT passages. Her name is not mentioned in the allegorical treatment of the covenants in Gal. 4:21-31, but it is obvious that she is specifically referred to in this passage as well.

Sarah died at the age of one hundred twenty-seven years, at KIRIATH ARBA (i.e., HEBRON, Gen. 23:2). To provide a place of burial, Abraham purchased land at Hebron which included a cave known as MACHPELAH, which was destined to become the family burying place (23:3-20, cf. 25:10; 49:31), and which today is surmounted by a well known building used as a mosque. Hebron is indelibly associated with the family of Abraham, and its early name, Kiriath Arba ("fourfold city") comes from the leader of the Anakites, whose name was ARBA (Josh. 14:15). It was the center of the community of giants during the exodus and conquest, and was captured by CALEB during a late conquest military action. However, during the earlier times of Abraham the area was settled by the HITTITES (KJV, "sons of Heth," Gen. 23:3), and the land was purchased from a man named EPHRON for a price of 400 shekels of silver (23:16). (For a full-scale feminist literary interpretation, see T. J. Schneider, *Sarah: Mother of Nations* [2004].)

(2) Daughter of Raguel and wife of TOBIAS (Tob. 3:7 et passim). She is the heroine of a somewhat fanciful and engaging narrative set at the time of the Assyrian captivity. Sarah had previously been married to seven husbands who were killed by a demon, and she suffered reproach from her maids. On the very day that TOBIT, father of Tobias, implored God to end his sufferings, Sarah offered a similar prayer. God heard them both and sent the angel RAPHAEL, who released Sarah from the demon and made possible her marriage to Tobias (3:16–17). The story abounds with details of family life, conveying a sense of verisimilitude to the reader.

(3) KJV alternate form of SERAH (Num. 26:46).

M. H. HEICKSEN

Saraias suh-ray´uhs. KJV form of SERAIAH (1 Esd. 5:5; 8:1; 2 Esd. 1:1).

Saramel sair´uh-mel. KJV Apoc. form of ASARAMEL (1 Macc. 14:28).

Saraph sair´uhf (שָׂרָף H8598, "burning one"). Son of SHELA and grandson of JUDAH; he and one (or more) of his brothers are said to have ruled in MOAB and JASHUBI LEHEM (1 Chr. 4:22; the NRSV emends the text and renders, "who married into Moab but returned to Lehem").

Sarapis. See SERAPIS.

Sarasadai sair´uh-sad´i (Σαρασαδαι). Son of Israel and ancestor of JUDITH (Jdt. 8:1; KJV, "Salasadai"). The reference is probably to ZURISHADDAI (Num. 1:6 et al.).

Sarchedonus sahr´kuh-doh´nuhs. KJV Apoc. form of ESARHADDON (Tob. 1:21–22).

Sardeus sahr-dee´uhs. KJV Apoc. form of Zerdaiah (1 Esd. 9:28). See AZIZA.

sardine. An archaic term used by the KJV to render Greek *sardion* G4917, which refers to the mineral CARNELIAN (Rev. 4:3; the KJV translates "sardius" in 21:20).

D. R. BOWES

Sardis sahr´dis (Σάρδεις G4915; see also SEPHARAD). A city of W ASIA MINOR. Sardis lay on the junction of the principal highways linking EPHESUS, SMYRNA, and PERGAMUM with the high country of inner Asia Minor. The kingdom of LYDIA, of which Sardis was the ancient capital and royal seat, straddled the communications route between the AEGEAN coast and the hinterland and was in consequence an area where the Greek and native culture met and creatively mingled. Under the 6th-cent.-B.C. Lydian king Croesus—whose name became a legend for wealth, prosperity, and the doom which sometimes falls shockingly upon the rich and fortunate—Sardis was famed for its affluence. Gold and silver minted coinage had its origin there, and the Pactolus River, which flowed nearby, was a proverb for its easily won alluvial gold.

The site itself was marked by geography for greatness. The broad ridge of Mount Tmolus thrusts seaward from the central plateau, and a cluster of sharp-sided promontories of highland dominate the Hermus valley plain, where Tmolus ends. On one of these easily defended ridges stood the stronghold of Sardis, 1,500 ft. above the alluvial plain onto which, in days of peace, her population and habitations flowed. Like Troy, Sardis was a citadel and place of refuge, the residence of king and courtier. It must have been inhabited from the first arrival of humans in the Hermus valley, and a place of importance from the first days of the Lydian kingdom in the 13th cent. B.C.

Under Croesus, in the Golden Age of Sardis, Lydian power extended to the Aegean coast and the cities of the Ionian Greeks: Smyrna, Ephesus, and the rest. It was the doctrine of the historian HERODOTUS that power and wealth breed arrogance, and arrogance ends in ruin; in Sardis and its greatest king the historian found a somber and striking illustration. PERSIA was rising to power in the E in the middle of the 6th cent., and Croesus marked the fact with anxious eye. "Croesus," says Herodotus, "learned that Cyrus had destroyed the empire of Astyages, and that the Persians were becoming daily more powerful. This led him to consider with himself whether it were possible to check the growing power of that people before it came to a head" (*Hist.* 1.46). One thought haunted Croesus as he weighed the chances of preventive war. Solon the lawgiver had once visited him in Sardis, and warned him to beware of self-satisfaction, and to count no one happy until the end of life had set him free at last from all danger of a sudden change of fortune. Said Solon: "Sire, he who unites the greatest number of advantages, and, retaining them to the day of his death, then dies in peace, that man alone is, in my judgment, entitled to bear the name of 'happy.' In every matter it behooves us to mark well the end, for often God gives men a gleam of happiness, and then plunges them into ruin" (1.32).

Among his precautions, Croesus consulted the Delphic oracle, who with customary ambiguity answered that "If Croesus attacked the Persians, he would destroy a great empire" (*Hist.* 1.53). This is what the king did. He crossed the river frontier and destroyed a great empire — his own. Croesus retreated to his stronghold and the armies of Cyrus closed in. How disaster befell is best told in Herodotus's own words (1.84):

> On the fourteenth day of the siege, Cyrus made proclamation that he would give a reward to the man who should first mount the wall. After this he made an assault but without success. His troops retired, but one Hyroeades resolved to approach the citadel and attempt it at a place where no guards were ever set. On this side the rock was so precipitous, and the citadel so impregnable, that no fear was entertained of its being carried in this place.... Hyroeades, however, had observed a Lydian soldier descend the rock to retrieve a helmet which had rolled down from the top, and having seen the man pick it up and carry it back, thought over what he had witnessed, and formed his plan. He climbed the rock himself, and other Persians followed in his track, until a large number had mounted to the top. Thus Sardis was taken.

The real reason, of course, was decay of the structure of the conglomerate rock which formed the ridge. Its erosion had undermined the defenses. Little is left today of the substantial plateau on which the royal stronghold had stood and the connecting neck of land which joined it to the major mountain mass. (For information on the Persian period, see E. R. M. Dusinberre, *Aspects of Empire in Achaemenid Sardis* [2003].)

More than two centuries later, after ALEXANDER THE GREAT had destroyed the Persian empire, Sardis passed from hand to hand under the successive regimes. It fell first to Antigonus, then to the SELEUCIDS of SYRIA, and then to PERGAMUM when the Attalid dynasty broke free from Seleucid power, which was perennially overstretched in W Asia Minor. It was during an attempt by ANTIOCHUS the Great in 214 B.C. to bring Sardis back under Syrian rule that the lone feat of Hyroeades of 549 B.C. was precisely repeated.

ROME succeeded Pergamum in 133 B.C. when Attalus III, aware of emerging history, bequeathed his kingdom to the republic. Sardis became an administrative center of Roman Asia, and when in A.D. 26 the cities of the province contended for the honor of building a second temple for emperor worship, the envoys spoke long and eloquently about the past glory of the place. Sardis, as the apocalyptic letter put it, had a name but was dead (Rev. 3:1). Ramsay writes: "It was the city whose history conspicuously and pre-eminently blazoned forth the uncertainty of human fortunes, the weakness of human strength, and the shortness of the step that separates over-confident might from sudden and irreparable disaster. It was the city whose name was almost synonymous with pretentions unjustified, promise unfulfilled, appearance without reality, confidence that heralded ruin" (W. M. Ramsay, *The Letters to the Seven Churches* [1904], 376).

Temple of Artemis at Sardis. (View to the E.)

All the imagery of the letter is vivid in the history of the place, the works undone, the climbing "thief in the night," the sudden surprise. The Christian community was infected by the complacency of the place. All but a few had not "soiled their clothes"; that is, they had not compromised with the worship of Cybele—the horrible cult of hysteria and mutilation reflected in Catullus's grim poem *Attis*—or with the more subtle Caesar-cult that had become strong in Sardis after A.D. 17 when the beneficence of Rome and TIBERIUS, after the mighty Asian earthquake of that year, put the city heavily in debt.

Some Christian inscriptions have been found in Sardis, but nothing is known of the origins or end of the Christian community, unless Ramsay is right in finding their sad relics in a strange Muslim splinter sect. The temple of ARTEMIS, whose worship enveloped that of Cybele in the city, has been uncovered together with evidence of its transformation into a church.

(See further E. M. Blaiklock, *The Cities of the New Testament* [1965], 112–19; E. Yamauchi, *The Archaeology of New Testament Cities in Western Asia Minor* [1980], ch. 5; G. M. A. Hanfmann et al., *Sardis from Prehistoric to Roman Times: Results of the Archaeological Exploration of Sardis 1958–1975* [1983]; C. J. Hemer, *The Letters to the Seven Churches of Asia in Their Local Setting* [1986], ch. 7.; D. G. Mitten et al., *Sardis: Twenty-seven Years of Discovery* [1987]; J. H. Kroll, *The Greek Inscriptions of the Sardis Synagogue* [2001]; R. S. Ascough, ed., *Religious Rivalries and the Struggle for Success in Sardis and Smyrna* [2005].)   E. M. BLAIKLOCK

Sardite sahr´dit. KJV form of "Seredite." See SERED.

sardius. This term (now usually spelled *sard*) is used by the KJV to render Greek *sardion* G4917, which refers to the mineral CARNELIAN (Rev. 21:20; the KJV translates "sardine" in 21:20).

sardonyx. A semiprecious variety of CHALCEDONY, which is very fine-grained silica (silicon dioxide). Like AGATE, it consists of layers of different colors, in this case white or bluish-white and red, or brownish-red, but the layers are in even planes and the banding straight. It is mentioned as the material used for one of the foundations of the wall of the future Jerusalem (Rev. 21:20; NRSV, "onyx"). See also ONYX.   D. R. BOWES

Sarea sah´ree-uh. One of five writers employed by EZRA to transcribe the law (2 Esd. 14:24).

Sarepta suh-rep´tuh. KJV NT form of ZAREPHATH.

Sargon sahr´gon (סַרְגוֹן H6236, from Ass. *Šarrukēn*, "the king is legitimate"). The name of three Mesopotamian kings: Sargon of AKKAD (c. 2300 B.C.; cf. B. Lewis, *The Sargon Legend: A Study of the Akkadian Text and the Tale of the Hero Who Was Exposed at Birth* [1980]) and the Assyrians Sargon I (c. 1900) and Sargon II (721–705). The name is found only once in the Bible, where it refers to Sargon II of ASSYRIA (Isa. 20:1). This Sargon was the son of TIGLATH-PILESER III, successor to his brother SHALMANESER V, and father of SENNACHERIB. His reign is amply known from his inscriptions at Khorsabad and from letters and historical texts found at NINEVEH and Nimrud (CALAH). Although he is named only once in the OT, his campaigns are of importance for understanding the historical background of the prophecies of ISAIAH.

Sargon II claimed the fall of SAMARIA (721 B.C.), which had been besieged by Shalmaneser V for three years (2 Ki. 17:5–6) until his death in 722. According to Sargon's own records, he deported 27,290 people from the area of Samaria to Mesopotamia. During the first part of his reign he faced serious domestic problems, which were settled only by grant of privileges to the citizens of ASSHUR. The next year (720) Ilu-bihdi of HAMATH led ARPAD, DAMASCUS, and PALESTINE into revolt. Sargon defeated this anti-Assyrian coalition near Qarqar in N SYRIA. Also in 720 the kingdom of JUDAH, under AHAZ, together with PHILISTIA, EDOM, and MOAB, submitted to vassalage and paid tribute. In the following years, people deported from Babylonia, Hamath, and elsewhere were resettled in SAMARIA; these, with others brought in later, mingled with the surviving Israelite population, and their descendants were eventually known as the SAMARITANS.

This relief of Sargon II from the palace of Khorsabad (c. 710 B.C.) pictures the king wearing the royal tiara and holding a staff as he faces a high official or crowned prince.

Sargon had scarcely completed the reduction of Samaria when he was greeted by a rebellion in Babylonia in 720 B.C. led by the Chaldean prince Marduk-apal-iddina (biblical MERODACH-BALADAN), who ruled 721–711 in Babylonia not simply as a barbarian chieftain but as a great Mesopotamian monarch who left behind traces of his building activities in various cities. Although backed by Humbanigash, king of ELAM, an indecisive battle was fought at Der, between the Tigris and the Zagros, making it expedient for Sargon to leave Merodach-Baladan as king in Babylonia. Thus Sargon lost control of Babylonia and did not regain it for about twelve years.

Meanwhile, other campaigns claimed his attention. In ASIA MINOR, Mita (Midas), king of the Phrygian Mushki, proved a troublesome foe. A rebellion by the vassal state of CARCHEMISH in Syria (717 B.C.) provoked Sargon to destroy that ancient center of HITTITE culture and deport its population, and subsequently to make various campaigns into Asia Minor. Sargon also turned on Urartu (ARARAT), already weakened by Tiglath-Pileser III and now gravely threatened by the incursions of an Indo-Aryan barbarian people called the CIMMERIANS, who were moving down from the Caucasus. Seizing the opportunity, Sargon broke the power of Urartu completely, thus removing an ancient rival — and Assyria's strongest dike against the barbarian tide at the same time.

After 720 B.C. Sargon conducted no major campaign in Palestine. This may have encouraged the restless vassals to imagine that he was a man who could be trifled with. By 713 ASHDOD rebelled; other Philistine towns were then drawn into the revolt and, as Sargon told it, Judah, Edom, and Moab were invited to join. That Egyptian aid had been promised is clear both from the Assyrian texts and the Bible (Isa. 20:5). In fact, according to Isa. 18:1–2, ambassadors of the Cushite (Ethiopian) pharaoh himself waited on HEZEKIAH, hoping to enlist his cooperation. Opinions were divided in Judah; Isaiah was bitterly opposed to such an alliance, both calling on his king to give the Ethiopian envoys a negative answer, and symbolically illustrating the folly of trusting in Egypt by walking about Jerusalem barefoot and clad only in a loincloth (20:2–4).

Sargon at this time was at the peak of power and preparing to reconquer Babylon. Ashdod, the center of revolt, was quickly taken by storm, and Judah, Moab, and Edom paid homage to the conqueror. The expected Egyptian aid failed completely to materialize and Judah was held in subjection. Later Hezekiah revolted against Sargon's son, Sennacherib.

At the start of 710 B.C., Sargon was everywhere victorious. The whole of Syria-Palestine and most of the Zagros range were firmly in Assyrian hands; Urartu was dressing its wounds; the Egyptians were friendly; the Elamites and Phrygians were hostile but peaceful. Babylon, under Merodach-Baladan, remained a thorn in the side of Assyria, and in 710 Sargon attacked it for the second time in his reign. It was a smashing victory, with Merodach-Baladan fleeing to Elam for refuge, and the fame of Sargon continued to grow. The repeated efforts made by its enemies to undermine the Assyrian empire had been of no avail; at the end of Sargon's reign it was larger and apparently stronger than ever.

As a war chief, Sargon liked to live in Nimrud, the military capital of the empire, where he occupied, restored, and modified ASHURNASIRPAL's palace. Moved by great pride, he soon decided to have his own palace in his own city. In 717 B.C. he laid the foundations of "Sargon's fortress," *Dur-Sharrukin*, a hitherto virgin site 12 mi. NE of Nineveh, near the modern village of Khorsabad.

Ten years later the workmen completed a town that was square in plan, each side measuring about one mile. The palace itself stood on a 60-ft. high platform overriding the city wall and comprised more than 200 rooms and thirty courtyards. The royal abode was richly decorated and the gates of the town were guarded by colossal bull-men. Evidence, however, indicates that the city was scarcely inhabited and almost immediately abandoned at the king's death. One year after Dur-Sharrukin was officially inaugurated, Sargon was killed (705 B.C.). His successors preferred Nineveh, and Khorsabad, deserted, fell slowly to ruins.

(See further H. W. F. Saggs in *Iraq* 17 [1955]: 146–49; H. Tadmor in *JCS* 12 [1958]: 22–40; 77–100; W. W. Hallo in *BA* 23 [1960]: 50–56; G. Roux, *Ancient Iraq*, 2nd ed. [1980], 257–62; P. Albenda, *The Palace of Sargon King of Assyria* [1986]; S. Parpola and A. Fuchs, *The Correspondence of Sargon II*, 3 vols. [1987–2001]; A. K. Grayson in *CAH*, 3/2, 2nd ed. [1991], 86–102; A. Fuchs, *Die Inschriften Sargons II. aus Khorsabad* [1994]; M. Dietrich, *The Babylonian Correspondence of Sargon and Sennacherib* [2003].) L. L. WALKER

Sarid sair′id (שָׂרִיד *H8587*, possibly "survivor"; often emended to שָׂדוּד, possibly "barrier"). A border town within the tribal territory of ZEBULUN (Josh. 19:10, 12). If the MT is correct, perhaps the name of the town is related to SERED, one of the sons of Zebulun, but the site is unknown. However, on the basis of some Greek MSS and other versional evidence, many scholars believe that the original Hebrew reading was *šādûd* and that the site should be identified with modern Tell Shadud on the northern edge of the Plain of ESDRAELON c. 5 mi. SW of NAZARETH and 6 mi. NE of MEGIDDO. A. BOWLING

Saron sair′uhn. KJV NT form of SHARON.

Sarothie suh-roh′thee (Σαρωθιε). Ancestor of a group of SOLOMON's servants who returned from the Babylonian captivity with ZERUBBABEL (1 Esd. 5:34). The name is not found in the parallel lists (Ezra 2:57; Neh. 7:59).

Sarsechim sahr′suh-kim (שַׂר־סְכִים). A Babylonian army officer who held the title of RABSARIS and who participated in the siege of Jerusalem (Jer. 39:3 NRSV and other versions). Some scholars analyze the text differently and, joining this name with the previous one, read NEBO-SARSEKIM (cf. NIV); in 2007, M. Jursa discovered, in a British Museum tablet, what may be the corresponding Akk. name, *Nabu-šarrussu-ukin*, identified as "chief eunuch [official]" during the reign of NEBUCHADNEZZAR. Others, on the basis of v. 13, emend the text to read NEBUSHAZBAN (cf. J. Bright, *Jeremiah*, AB 21 [1965], 243). See also SAMGAR. S. BARABAS

Saruch sair′uhk. KJV NT form of SERUG.

Satan say′tuhn (שָׂטָן *H8477*, "adversary" or "accuser"; σατανᾶς *G4928* [from Aram. סָטְנָא], usually with the definite article [σατάν in 1 Ki. 11:14 LXX]). The grand adversary of God and human beings, identified with the DEVIL (Rev. 12:9; 20:2).

    I. References to Satan
       A. In the OT
       B. In the NT
    II. Scriptural picture of Satan
       A. Names
       B. Position
       C. Activities
       D. Limitations
       E. Origin
       F. Motive
       G. Judgment
       H. Doom
    III. Believers and Satan
    IV. Objections to the doctrine

I. References to Satan

A. In the OT. Without the definite article, the Hebrew term *śāṭān* means "an adversary, an opponent." Thus in 1 Sam. 29:4 it is used of DAVID as a possible enemy in battle; in 1 Ki. 11:14, 23, 25, it designates political adversaries to SOLOMON; in Num. 22:22 it is applied to the angel of the Lord who opposed BALAAM. In Ps. 109:6 it is used of

Terra-cotta mask of a demon (from Ur, 2000–1700 B.C.). Monstrous faces like this one, appearing repeatedly in Mesopotamian art, had magical significance.

a human accuser. With the article, *haśśāṭān*, "the adversary," it becomes a proper name and denotes the personal Satan. It is so used in Job 1–2 and in Zech. 3:1–2, where it clearly designates a celestial being (both passages in the LXX have *ho diabolos* G1333, "the slanderer, the devil"). In 1 Chr. 21:1 the word does not have the article and may be rendered "an adversary," but it is generally conceded that here, even without the article, the term is a proper name (cf. 2 Sam. 24:1).

It is sometimes said that in the OT the figure of Satan is not essentially an evil being, and that he appears simply as an angelic personage who has the task of testing human beings. Admittedly the full picture of Satan's evil character is not given in the few OT references to him, but clearly the recorded glimpses of his activities reveal that he acts in opposition to the best interests of humanity. The first two chapters of JOB unmistakably reveal his malicious nature; he also moved David to number Israel to his own hurt; and his accusations against Joshua (JESHUA) the high priest drew down on him the Lord's rebuke. It is a remarkable feature of the theology of the OT that so little mention is made of Satan as the great Adversary of God and his people. (In the APOCRYPHA, the term *satanas* occurs only in Sir. 21:27, where it probably means simply "adversary.")

B. In the NT. It is in the NT that the picture of Satan receives its full unfolding. The Greek term *satanas* occurs thirty-six times (the TR has the indeclinable form *satan* in 2 Cor. 12:7 and an additional occurrence of *Satanas* in Lk. 4:8). Without the definite article, the name is twice used in addressing PETER (Matt. 16:23; Mk. 8:33). The remaining occurrences, generally with the definite article, refer to the personal devil. (The article is missing in Matt. 4:10; Mk. 3:23 twice; Lk. 22:3; 2 Cor. 12:7.) Satan is also referred to more than thirty times as *diabolos*, which means "slanderer" or "calumniator," but no material distinction between the two terms is discernible in their usage. ("Devils" in the KJV is properly DEMONS.)

II. Scriptural picture of Satan

A. Names. Beside the two principal names already mentioned, various other names and descriptive designations are applied to Satan. They serve to reveal the dignity and character of this mighty celestial being. He is called ABADDON and APOLLYON (Rev. 9:11), both meaning "destroyer"; "the accuser of our brothers" (12:10); "your enemy" (*antidikos* G508, 1 Pet. 5:8); BEELZEBUL (Matt. 12:24); BELIAL (*Beliar* G1016, 2 Cor. 6:15); "the great dragon … that ancient serpent … the deceiver of the whole world" (Rev. 12:9 NRSV); "enemy" (*echthros* G2398, Matt. 13:28, 39); "the evil one" (13:19, 38); "a murderer … a liar and the father of lies" (Jn. 8:44); "the god of this age" (2 Cor. 4:4); "the ruler of the kingdom of the air" (Eph. 2:2); "the prince of this world" (Jn. 12:31; 14:30; 16:11); "the tempter" (Matt. 4:3; 1 Thess. 3:5).

B. Position. Satan holds a position of great power and dignity in the spiritual world. In Job 1:6 he is numbered among "the sons of God" (NIV mg.), although by his moral nature he is not one of them. He has personal access to the presence of God, a privilege that will be taken from him in a future day (Rev. 12:9). So exalted is his position that MICHAEL the archangel found him a formidable foe and "did not dare to bring a slanderous accusation against him" (Jude 9).

The NT reveals that Satan is the ruler over a powerful kingdom of evil which he rules with intelligent consistency. In refuting the charge that he was casting out demons by the power of Beelzebul, Jesus pointed out the absurdity of the charge, since it would mean that Satan "is divided against himself. How then can his kingdom stand?" (Matt. 12:26). Satan does not operate in isolation but is the head of a well-organized kingdom in which his subjects exercise delegated responsibility under his direction. He is the leader of a vast, compact organization of spirit-beings, "his angels" (Matt. 25:41; Rev. 12:7). As "the ruler of the kingdom of the air" (Eph. 2:2), he skillfully directs an organized host of wicked spirits in the HEAVENLY realms who do his bidding (6:12). The fallen angels who gave their allegiance to Satan (Rev. 12:4, 7, 9) apparently retain the ranks, dignities, and titles that were divinely given them.

Whatever the origin of the demons, it is clear that they render willing and wholehearted obedience to the rule of Satan (Matt. 12:28–29). Acts 10:38 makes it clear that the outburst of demonic activities during the ministry of Jesus was Satan-inspired. Satan, who is not omnipresent, exerts his influence practically everywhere through the work of his numerous subordinates. The book of Revelation reveals that at the close of this age and in the great tribulation there will be another fearful outburst of demonic activity (Rev. 9:1–11; 18:2).

Satan is also described as "the prince of this world" (Jn. 12:31 et al.). The WORLD he rules is the *kosmos* G3180, the present world system organized according to his own principles, methods, and aims (2 Cor. 4:3–4; Eph. 2:2; Col. 1:13; 1 Jn. 2:15–17). The greed and self-centered ambitions of the nations, the deceptive diplomacy of the political world, the bitter hatred and rivalry in the sphere of commerce, the godless ideologies of the masses of humanity—all spring out of and are fostered by satanic influence. Satan exercises his domination over "the children of disobedience" (Eph. 2:2 KJV). And the statement that "the whole world is under the control of the evil one" (1 Jn. 5:19) indicates that the world of unregenerated humanity lies in the grip of Satan and supinely yields to his power.

Satan has gained his power over mankind by trickery and usurpation. As the instigator of human SIN, whose punishment is DEATH, Satan gained "the power of death" and uses "the fear of death" as a means to keep people under his domination (Heb. 2:14–15). The statement that he is "a murderer from the beginning" (Jn. 8:44) does not mean that he can inflict death at will but that through the FALL of ADAM and EVE he brought about the death of the human race. In his death Christ broke the power of Satan over death and took the prey from under his control (cf. Rev. 1:18).

During the TEMPTATION OF CHRIST, Satan displayed all the kingdoms of the world, asserted that all had been delivered to him, and claimed that he could give them to whom he wished (Lk. 4:5–6). Significantly, Jesus did not dispute Satan's claim to sovereignty over this world. Christ categorically rejected the satanic offer to invest him with sovereignty over this world, but that offer will be accepted in the end-time by "the man of lawlessness" (2 Thess. 2:3–9; Rev. 13:4).

C. Activities. According to Job 1:7 and 2:2, Satan himself described his restless activity as consisting in "roaming through the earth and going back and forth in it." He is engaged in a worldwide and unremitting conflict against God and his people. This stamps him as "the enemy" of God and truth (Matt. 13:28, 39; 2 Thess. 2:9–12). His activities are associated with the realm of moral darkness (Acts 26:18).

The description "the tempter" (Matt. 4:3; 1 Thess. 3:5) designates Satan by his characteristic activity (the Greek is *ho peirazōn*; the present participle used substantivally is a common way of indicating a person's profession or line of work). His intention is ever to lead those tempted to fall into sin. The people of God are always the objects of his fierce hatred. The church of SMYRNA was informed that they would be the subjects of Satan's special onslaughts (Rev. 2:10). The Lord informed PETER, "Satan has asked to sift you as wheat" (Lk. 22:31).

Satan uses the weaknesses and limitations of human beings to entice them to sin (1 Cor. 7:5). He also employs the allurements of the world (1 Jn. 2:15–17; 4:4). He commonly tempts people to evil by the falsehood that they can attain a desired goal through the doing of wrong. His mode of operation is vividly demonstrated in the account of the fall in Gen. 3. Deception is a universal feature of his activities, justifying his description as "the deceiver of the whole world" (Rev. 12:9 NRSV). He constantly lays "snares" for sinners to make them his captives (1 Tim. 3:7; 2 Tim. 2:26). A fundamental temptation employed is PRIDE (1 Tim. 3:6).

Satan opposes the work of God through his counterfeiting activities. He oversows the wheat with weeds, placing counterfeit believers among "the sons of the kingdom" (Matt. 13:25, 38–39). These counterfeit believers form "a synagogue of Satan" (Rev. 2:9; 3:9). Satan often disguises himself as "an angel of light" by presenting his messengers of falsehood as messengers of truth (2 Cor. 11:13–15). Those who thus give themselves over to evil and become the agents of Satan to persuade others to do evil are the children and servants of the devil (Jn. 6:70; 8:44; Acts 13:10). Apostate workers may engage in great religious activity without accepting the power of God's truth (2 Tim. 3:1–9). Satan blinds human minds to the light of the gospel (2 Cor. 4:3–4) and induces people to accept his lie (2 Thess. 2:9–10). He induces them to give heed to "deceiving spirits and things taught by demons" through the pretentions of religious liars who have their conscience seared (1 Tim. 4:1–2). He hates the Word of God and eagerly acts to snatch it out of the hearts of the unsaved (Matt. 13:19). He actively hinders workers concerned to further the welfare of the saints (1 Thess. 2:17–18).

Satan also opposes the work of God through open and fierce opposition. The act of betrayal by JUDAS ISCARIOT was instigated by the devil (Lk. 22:3; Jn. 13:2, 27). Peter pictures Satan's ferocious activity when he warns believers that "the devil prowls around like a roaring lion looking for someone to devour" (1 Pet. 5:8). His violent attacks manifest themselves in the persecutions experienced by God's people (2 Tim. 3:11–13; Rev. 12:13–17).

D. Limitations. The Scriptures make it clear that Satan, although a mighty and determined enemy of God, is a limited being. He is a superhuman being, but not coequal with God. The power of Satan is derived (Lk. 4:6) and he is free to act only within the limits laid upon him by God. Satan was able to inflict loss and suffering upon Job only to the extent that God permitted (Job 1:12; 2:6). The members of the church at Smyrna were assured that their tribulation would last only "ten days" (Rev. 2:10). The length of their period of testing was set by the Lord, and Satan would not be able to go beyond it. At present the efforts of Satan on earth are restrained and frustrated by the operation of the divine Restrainer; with the removal of the restraint, Satan will be able to achieve the full outburst of evil in the end-time in the manifestation of the man of lawlessness (2 Thess. 2:7–8; some scholars interpret differently the phrase *ho katechon*, "the one restraining").

Believers are assured that God is greater than the forces of satanic evil and that they will never be able to defeat God and separate them from the love of God (Jn. 10:28; Rom. 8:38–39; 1 Jn. 4:4). Satan is permitted to afflict God's people, but they are assured he will never experience complete victory over them (Jn. 14:30–31; 16:33). God at times even uses Satan as his instrument to chasten and correct erring saints (Lk. 22:31–32; 1 Cor. 5:5; 1 Tim. 1:20).

Satan is not divine; thus he is not omnipotent, nor omniscient, nor omnipresent. He has vast power, but that power is definitely limited. He does not know all things, as is evident from his blunders during the course of history (e.g., his futile efforts to destroy the child Jesus). Satan cannot be personally present everywhere, though he makes his power felt worldwide through the operations of his many minions. Satan acknowledged his limitations in his conversation with God concerning Job (Job 1:7–11).

E. Origin. Satan is not eternal or self-existent. Scriptural MONOTHEISM leaves no room for any view of an eternal DUALISM of good and evil. His limitations are consistent with his nature as a created being. The words of Jesus in Jn. 8:44 indicate that Satan is a fallen being. The assertion that he "does not stand in the truth" (NRSV) indicates not only his past fall but also his resultant apostate character. Satan fell under God's condemnation through ambitious pride (1 Tim. 3:6). While numerous interpreters refuse to apply Ezek. 28:11–19 to Satan, and admittedly he is not named there, yet many scholars hold that the passage goes beyond the human king of TYRE to Satan, the unseen ruler and true source of all such pomp and pride as that of Tyre. Thus viewed, the passage would set forth the origin of Satan as a created being, his original position of power and dignity over the created universe, at least over this earth, and his fall through pride.

A similar passage, Isa. 14:12–14, is addressed to the MORNING STAR (KJV, "Lucifer") and likewise is held by many to go beyond the king of BABYLON and to refer to Satan, the prince of the godless world system of which Babylon was the type. Thus viewed, the fivefold "I will" (vv. 13–14) portrays Satan's rebellious self-exaltation, marking the beginning of the conflict between the will of God and Satan's own will. This interpretation of Ezek. 28:12–15 and Isa. 14:12–14 throws much light on the question of Satan's origin and is in harmony with the scriptural picture of Satan's close relations with world governments (Dan. 10:13; Jn. 12:31; Eph. 6:12). (For the view that the Isaianic passage cannot refer to Satan, see E. J. Young, *The Book of Isaiah: A Commentary*, 3 vols. [1965–72], 1:441.)

F. Motive. Satan's substitution of his own will for that of his Maker marked the beginning of the protracted conflict between good and evil which has extended through the ages. God has permitted the effort of Satan to establish his own will in opposition to the divine will to be thoroughly tested. The unrelenting conflict between the KINGDOM OF GOD and the kingdom of evil is the direct result of Satan's determination to establish his claim. The presence of sin, suffering, and death reveal the inevitable consequences of the satanic claim. Through his seduction of Adam and Eve (Gen. 3:1–7; 2 Cor. 11:3) Satan succeeded in establishing his domination over mankind. Through the work of the incarnate Christ that power was broken (Heb. 2:14–15).

In his efforts to establish his own will, Satan relentlessly works to thwart the purpose and work of God (Acts 13:10). And in his ambition to assume the place of God, Satan is mastered by a consuming passion to receive worship as God. That master passion was revealed in Satan's bald offer to invest Jesus with authority over the kingdoms of this world on condition that Jesus would worship him. This passion for worship will be gratified through his empowerment of the man of lawlessness in the end-time (2 Thess. 2:9–11; Rev. 13:4). IDOLATRY, with its diversion of worship from the true God, is motivated by demonic forces (1 Cor. 10:20; Ps. 106:34–38).

G. Judgment. The crucial battle between the kingdom of God and the kingdom of evil took place in the conflict between Christ and Satan. The explicit purpose of the coming of Christ into the world was "to destroy [render inoperative] the devil's work" (1 Jn. 3:8). Satan's initial defeat came in the wilderness temptation at the beginning of Jesus' messianic ministry (Matt. 4:1–11; Lk. 4:1–12). Because of that victory Jesus was able during his ministry to enter "a strong man's house and carry off his possessions" (Mk. 3:27). The decisive defeat of Satan came in the cross of Christ (Jn. 12:31; 16:11). There Satan was judged as a usurper and cast out as the legitimate ruler of this world. In the cross and the resurrection Christ broke the power of Satan over mankind (Col. 2:14–15; Heb. 2:14–15) and potentially delivered every soul from Satan's power. Those who in faith accept that deliverance are rescued from the dominion of darkness and transplanted into the kingdom of God's beloved Son (Col. 1:13).

While judgment has already been pronounced upon him, Satan is still permitted to operate as a usurper until the time of his final imprisonment. As a dethroned monarch he is still allowed to rule over those who accept his authority while he persecutes those who have declared their allegiance to Christ.

H. Doom. Scripture reveals the certain outcome of the conflict between good and evil and the inevitable doom of Satan and his hosts. Jesus saw a picture of that final defeat of Satan in the victory of the seventy disciples over the forces of evil (Lk. 10:18). Jesus asserted that "the eternal fire" had been "prepared for the devil and his angels" (Matt. 25:41).

The book of Revelation portrays the final judgment carried out on the devil. At the return of Christ in glory, Satan will be confined to the sealed bottomless pit for 1,000 years, during which time the earth will be free from his deceptive and seductive influences (Rev. 20:1–3). At the end of the 1,000 years, Satan will again be loosed from his prison and will again resume his deception of the inhabitants of the earth with great success. This final rebellion will be summarily crushed by divine action, and the devil will be thrown into "the lake of burning sulfur," where with the beast and the false prophet he "will be tormented day and night for ever and ever"

(20:7–10). His doom will be to share the eternal punishment of those whom he deceived (20:12–14). See LAKE OF FIRE; PUNISHMENT, ETERNAL.

III. Believers and Satan. Having been rescued from the kingdom of darkness, believers are assured of victory over the malicious activities of the devil. They are promised that "the God of peace will soon crush Satan under your feet" (Rom. 16:20). They find their security in the keeping power of Christ (Rom. 8:31–39; 1 Jn. 5:18).

For effective victory over Satan, believers must recognize that, on the basis of the work of Christ, Satan is a defeated foe. They are called upon to take a firm stand against the devil, "Resist the devil, and he will flee from you" (Jas. 4:7). Any attempt to flee from the devil would be useless, but in claiming the victory of Christ, a person can put the devil to flight. In order to experience victory over Satan believers cannot remain "unaware of his schemes" (2 Cor. 2:11). Recognizing that he is a powerful and crafty foe, they must "not give the devil a foothold" by allowing sin in their lives (Eph. 4:25–27). Instead, they must be "self-controlled" as well as "alert" to the danger from the devil, and firmly resist him in faith (1 Pet. 5:8–9). Paul repeatedly stresses the need to take a firm stand against the satanic enemy (Eph. 6:10–17).

God has made ample provision for the believer's victory over Satan. Victory over all satanic attack is possible to those who put on "the full armor of God" (Eph. 6:13–17). They also have the anointing of the HOLY SPIRIT, which enables them to discern truth and error (1 Jn. 2:20–21, 26–27). The intercessory work of Christ on the basis of his ATONEMENT is the divine provision for cleansing and restoration whenever they sin (Rom. 8:33–34; Heb. 7:25; 1 Jn. 2:1–2). The way of victory over "the accuser of our brothers" is given in Rev. 12:11: "They overcame him / by the blood of the Lamb / and by the word of their testimony; / they did not love their lives so much / as to shrink from death."

It is the commission of Christ's people to turn the lost "from darkness to light, and from the power of Satan to God" (Acts 26:18).

IV. Objections to the doctrine. The NT clearly pictures Satan as a malignant, superhuman personality. But the concept of a personal devil is unacceptable to many minds today. The objection is raised that the existence of a personal devil is incapable of scientific proof. Admittedly, spiritual realities cannot be proved by means of naturalistic scientific criteria, but consistency would require that the biblical revelation of a personal God also be rejected.

It is claimed that the devil is in reality a human invention to account for our sinfulness. This view seems laudable in its attempt to make people responsible for their own sins. In effect, however, it leads to a shallow view of the reality of sin in the world, and it cannot adequately account for the depths of iniquity in the world. An objective evaluation of the reality of sin reveals that it is "too masterly marshalled, too subtly planned, too skillfully directed, too logically remorseless, for any such facile explanation. There is design; there is diplomacy, there is cunning; there are stratagems and campaigns. There must be a master mind behind these activities" (quoted in F. A. Tatford, *The Prince of Darkness* [1967], 14).

The biblical view of a personal devil who is a limited being under the control of divine sovereignty best explains the awful realities of sin and fits a monistic worldview. The sane and restrained scriptural references to the devil are wholly consistent with the worldview presented in the Bible as a whole. These references are woven into the very warp and woof of the biblical revelation, and cannot be consistently demythologized without serious damage to the fabric as a whole. The recorded utterances of Jesus in the Gospels clearly assert the existence of a personal devil. In this he agreed with the views of the Jewish leaders of his day. His acceptance of the view cannot be explained simply on the basis of accommodation to prevailing views, since Jesus did not hesitate to expose the erroneous views of the Jewish leaders wherever he found them.

The view that the NT picture of a personal devil was derived from Persian dualism is answered by the nature of the NT picture of Satan. That picture is not dualistic: good and evil are not presented as distinct and coeternal principles. While Satan is seen as a mighty evil being, his kingdom is viewed as having a definite beginning and will have a definite end. The operation of evil is always viewed as being under the sovereign permission of the eternal God. God allows Satan to continue his work in order to give a cosmic demonstration of the bankruptcy of the satanic lie.

(See further F. C. Jennings, *Satan. His Person, Work, Place and Destiny* [n.d.]; D. L. Cooper, *What Men Must Believe* [1943], 234–79; E. Langton, *Satan, a Portrait: A Study of the Character of Satan Through All the Ages* [1945]; L. S. Chafer, *Systematic Theology*, 8 vols. [1947–48], 2:33–112; C. T. Schwarze, *The Program of Satan: A Study of the Purpose and Method of the Adversary* [1947]; D. G. Barnhouse, *The Invisible War* [1965]; J. Kallas, *The Satanward View* [1966]; F. A. Tatford, *The Prince of Darkness* [1967]; F. J. Huegel, *The Mystery of Iniquity* [1968]; J. D. Pentecost, *Your Adversary, the Devil* [1969]; J. B. Russell, *Satan: The Early Christian Tradition* [1981]; P. L. Day, *An Adversary in Heaven: śāṭān in the Hebrew Bible* [1988]; S. H. T. Page, *Powers of Evil: A Biblical Study of Satan and Demons* [1995]; R. H. Bell, *Deliver Us from Evil: Interpreting the Redemption from the Power of Satan in New Testament Theology* [2007]; *DDD*, 726–32.)

D. E. Hiebert

Sathrabuzanes sath′ruh-by*oo*′zuh-neez. See Shethar-Bozenai.

satrap say′trap. A ruling official in the far-flung Persian empire (Ezra 8:36; Esth. 3:12 et al.; Dan. 3:2–3 et al.; both the Heb. *ʾăḥašdarpān* H346 [Aram. H10026] and the Gk. *satrapēs* derive from a Persian word meaning "protector of the realm"). The satrap's jurisdiction extended over several provinces. Herodotus (*Hist.* 3.89–94) has given the standard list of the twenty Persian satrapies. In Latin literature the term *satrapes* occurs as early as Terence (159 B.C.).

The office was virtually that of a vassal king. The satrap held extensive power but was checked by the presence of a royal scribe who had regularly to render a report to the sovereign of the realm; moreover, the military forces were under the command of a general who held independent status. In Ezra 8:36 ("They also delivered the king's orders to the royal satraps and to the governors of Trans-Euphrates") the term seems to be used loosely, since the only satrap whom Ezra's commission would really concern was the one ruling in Trans-Euphrates itself (cf. 5:3). See also Persia III.C. (For an extensive treatment, see H. Klinkott, *Der Satrap* [2005].)

J. H. Bratt

satyr The Greek term *satyros* referred to a mythological god, half human and half beast (with pointed ears and goats' tail and legs), which inhabited the woods and engaged in the revelries of Dionysus. For lack of a better term, the KJV chose *satyr* to render Hebrew *śāʿîr* in Isa. 13:21 and 34:14, understanding the word to refer to demonic creatures that gambol in desolate areas. This rendering was followed by the RSV and other versions not only here, but also in Lev. 17:7 and 2 Chr. 11:15 (where the KJV has "devils"). The NRSV, while accepting the same interpretation, translates "goat-demon." The NIV interprets the term in Isaiah as the usual noun for "goat" or "wild goat" (*śāʿîr* II H8538), but acknowledges the sense "goat idol" or "goat demon" (*śāʿîr* III H8539) in the other two references. (Some scholars emend 2 Ki. 23:8, "the shrines at the gates" [*bāmôt haśśĕʿārîm*] to "the shrine of the goat-demons" [*bĕmat haśśĕʿîrim*].) It does seem likely that in some or all of these passages there is a reference to one of the demonically inspired pagan gods of Canaan, in the image of a goat, having a brutal and lustful nature, which was an object of worship for Israel and became a snare to them (cf. Deut. 32:17; Ps. 106:37). (See also *DDD*, 732–33.)

J. H. Bratt

Saul sawl (שָׁאוּל H8620, "one who has been begged for" [cf. Shaul]; LXX Σαούλ G4910 [also Acts 9:4; 13:21; 22:7, 13; 26:14], NT usually in the hellenized form Σαῦλος G4930). Son of Kish and first king of Israel. (In the NT, the name is applied only once to the Israelite king [Acts 13:21], elsewhere to Saul of Tarsus; see Paul. The KJV uses the form *Saul* also in reference to the Edomite king Shaul [Gen. 36:37–38; but not in 1 Chr. 1:48–49].)

I. Family. According to 1 Sam. 9:1, Saul's father was "a man of standing, whose name was Kish son of Abiel, the son of Zeror, the son of Becorath, the son of Aphiah of Benjamin." In 1 Chr. 8:33 and 9:39, however, Ner is listed as the father of Kish (cf. also 8:30 [LXX] and 9:36). Some argue that 1 Chronicles is incorrect, but, as is common in Hebrew genealogies, there are probably gaps between generations in these lists. (The Ner in 1 Sam. 14:50, identified as Saul's paternal uncle, must be a different person.) The place mostly associated with Saul was GIBEAH, but ZELA seemed to be the location of the family burial plot (2 Sam. 21:14).

There is no record that Saul had brothers or sisters. His first wife was AHINOAM, daughter of Ahimaaz. By her he had four sons: JONATHAN, MALKI-SHUA, ABINADAB, and ESH-BAAL (1 Chr. 8:33; 9:39). Esh-Baal became better known as ISH-BOSHETH (2 Sam. 2:8) and apparently was also called ISHVI (1 Sam. 14:49). Saul also had a concubine named RIZPAH, daughter of Aiah, by whom he fathered two sons, ARMONI and MEPHI-BOSHETH (2 Sam. 21:8, 11). Two daughters are mentioned: MERAB and MICHAL (1 Sam. 18:19–20).

II. Youth. The opening of 1 Sam. 9 gives the limited data available about young Saul. He came from a family of influence and some wealth, and he himself was handsome and tall (vv. 1–2). The text goes on to relate that Saul and a servant set out to look for some lost donkeys. They covered the territory of BENJAMIN and did not find them, so the servant suggested to Saul that they obtain information from SAMUEL, who was at RAMAH. God revealed to Samuel that Saul was the man chosen to be the king of Israel (vv. 15–17), so after a festive meal and a night's rest (vv. 22–27), the prophet called Saul aside and anointed him (10:1). A series of predictions followed (10:2–7), all of which came true as Saul returned home. The most important was an encounter with a band of prophets and an outpouring of the Spirit on Saul (vv. 9–11).

III. Proclaimed king. There are parallel accounts of Saul's rise to kingship (1 Sam. 10:1–24 and 11:1–15; some scholars assign early and late dates to these stories, but that conclusion is not necessary). Behind both accounts lies the initial discussion about the need of a king (8:1–22). The first story (ch. 10) gives the religious aspect of the authentication of Saul's qualifications to serve as ruler in Israel, and the other (ch. 11) gives the military perspective. The religious aspect included God's word to Samuel (9:15–16), Samuel's private anointing of Saul (10:1), the Spirit's infilling (10:9–13), and the public selection by lot at MIZPAH (10:20–24). The military aspect centered in the appeal of the men of JABESH GILEAD for help against the Ammonites, who were quickly defeated by Saul's army (11:1–11). This feat brought instant popularity. Samuel led the people to GILGAL and confirmed again the new status of Saul as king of Israel. (For a summary of critical discussion concerning this and other topics, see *ABD*, 5:989–99.)

IV. The general situation. Saul lived in troubled times. For a relatively long period Israel had been simply a loose confederation of twelve tribes with no single leader. Judges had arisen under the call of God to serve in various regions of the land in times of crisis (see JUDGES, PERIOD OF). There had been a common sanctuary at SHILOH, but it was now destroyed (1 Sam. 4:12–22; Jer. 7:14; 26:6, 9). New invaders from the islands of the sea, the PHILISTINES, had settled along the Mediterranean coast and had pushed up into the highlands. Israel had no military organization capable of stopping the invaders. Nor did they have weapons, for the Philistines had established a monopoly in the making and the maintenance of IRON tools (1 Sam. 13:19–22). The Philistines had made Saul's home town, Gibeah, into an outpost (10:5; 13:3). For some time Samuel, the prophet, had been the figure on whom the Israelites could center their hopes. Israel had no governing institutions, no economic institutions, no effective religious institutions

V. Initial acts to establish a nation. Saul's first major move was against the local Philistine garrison. He formed a small army of 3,000 men who were divided between himself and his son Jonathan, and the latter soon destroyed the garrison at GEBA. The enemy immediately reacted by bringing in a large force of chariots, cavalry, and troops, stationing them at MICMASH. They were dramatically defeated almost singlehandedly by Jonathan (1 Sam. 14:1–15), though the rest of Israel's force soon joined the fray and routed the enemy. From this victory Saul moved effectively against Israel's enemies to the E and to the S. Seemingly, Saul's army had a simple organization. There was a core group made up of three units that could operate separately (13:2) and a militia called "the people" (13:7 NRSV [NIV, "troops"]). Saul set up his headquarters at his family home at Gibeah (14:2; 15:34). Here (modern Tell el-Ful, some 3.5 mi. N of Jerusalem) a small but strong walled fortress has been found, which some have assumed to belong to Saul (see GIBEAH #4).

VI. Saul's relationship with Samuel. Saul owed everything to Samuel the prophet, but they soon came into conflict. At the time there was no clear distinction between civil and religious activities. In the early part of Saul's reign, there seemed to be a cooperative attitude, for in calling the people to war against the Ammonites, Saul linked his name with the name of Samuel (1 Sam. 11:7). The incident in 13:8–15 implies that the two men had agreed on the necessity of resisting the Philistines. Samuel was to be in charge of the religious ceremonies of the called meeting, and Saul in charge of the military aspects. On the pretext that Samuel's delay in coming to do his duty was unbearable, Saul performed the religious ceremony and brought upon himself a sharp rebuke from Samuel. On the surface Saul's excuses seem valid enough, but he had overstepped the bounds of his authority and thus revealed that he lacked the wisdom of a good leader. The possibility of an enduring dynasty was removed by his rash act (13:8–14).

A similar situation took place during the war against the Amalekites (1 Sam. 15:6–33; see AMALEK). At the beginning Samuel and Saul were united in their understanding of the reasons for and the goals of the war, as well as the procedures in dealing with an implacable foe after the victory had been won. However, at the moment when orders must be given to carry out the objectives, he yielded to other pressures and reneged on the agreement. He did his best to rationalize his actions to Samuel, but to no avail. The judgment was that a man who could not carry through on agreed objectives was not worthy and therefore rejected of God. In order not to humiliate Saul too drastically before the people, Samuel did agree to worship with him publicly. But Samuel refused to have anything to do with Saul throughout the remainder of the prophet's life.

Saul's last encounter with Samuel was an unpleasant event (1 Sam. 28:7–20). Saul had gone to the medium of ENDOR to gain occult information from Samuel, who had long been dead. To the amazement of all, Samuel appeared without occult incitement and severely condemned the king. A relationship that had originally been so fruitful was totally shattered beyond repair.

VII. Saul's relationship with David. Samuel's act of anointing David as a future ruler in Israel was, seemingly, a secret of which Saul knew nothing for many years. David's entrance on the national scene, his encounter with GOLIATH (1 Sam. 17:20–58), was dramatic and greatly impressed Saul; moreover, it won the admiration and affection of Jonathan, Saul's son.

David soon became a skilled soldier. His popularity soared to such heights that Saul was eclipsed. The effects of this turn of events were devastating, for Saul, under the influence of "an evil spirit from God," tried to kill David (1 Sam. 18:5–11). Then thwarted hate became fear as the new rival became more famous and acclaimed as a hero. Fear begat cunning and so, under the disguise of flattery, Saul sent David against the Philistines, with the lure of his daughter Merab as a prize, but also the hope that the enemy would kill the young man. When David returned successful, Saul partially reneged on his promise by substituting his second daughter, Michal, for Merab. To Saul's dismay the union blossomed into mutual love (18:12–30).

Saul's relationship with David became complicated by Jonathan's refusal to go along with his father's efforts to destroy David; in fact, Jonathan actively aided his friend to escape after temporarily persuading Saul to spare David's life (1 Sam. 19:1–7; 20:1–42). Even Michal took a stand against her father by aiding David (19:11–17). The intensity of Saul's hatred toward David increased to the extent that he soon recklessly slaughtered any group which gave him aid and comfort (21:1–9; 22:9–19), and wasted time and strength chasing David through the wilderness of Judah (23:24–26).

David was an elusive prey. He fled from Saul in the wilderness of ZIPH, because the local people were loyal to Saul and betrayed David's presence there. Saul gave chase and followed David to the wilderness of MAON, but had to cease because word came that the Philistines had invaded Israel (1 Sam. 23:19–29). Spies kept Saul informed and soon he pursued David to the wilderness of ENGEDI, among the barren hills just W of the DEAD SEA. It so happened that Saul made camp in the cave in which David and his men were hiding. While Saul slept, David cut off part of the king's robe, but refused to harm the king. Later, after all had left the cave, David called to Saul from a safe distance and informed him how near the king had been to death. This act of mercy so shamed Saul that he begged for mercy on his posterity. Saul confessed that he knew that David would be the next king. With this statement completed, Saul called off his chase and returned home (24:1–22).

VIII. Saul's last years. The threat from the Philistines became more severe, for they seemed determined to take advantage of Saul, whose government had suffered much from his quarrels with David. Saul could scarcely build a strong organization while pursuing David in the desert. Samuel was dead, so the religious life of the people was practically nil. Saul had outlawed Canaanite occult practices (1 Sam. 28:3), but he had never provided positive religious values or practices in their stead. Commercial activity had never been encouraged, so the economic condition of the tribes was at a low ebb. Effective social, cultural, and educational institutions had never been built in order to bind the tribes together as a unit. There was a small core army but, evidently, the training of the popular militia had been neglected.

Saul's kingdom seemed ripe for the picking; the Philistines were eager to be the pickers. The center of attack focused on the northern approaches to the highlands from the valley of JEZREEL (much like the Israeli-Jordan tactics of 1967).

Saul was not prepared for the battle, either militarily or spiritually. His unfortunate encounter with the medium of Endor and with the spirit of Samuel had unnerved him. The battle was a disaster from the beginning. Saul's army was quickly routed, then slaughtered by the Philistines as they sought to escape. Among the fallen were three of Saul's sons: Jonathan, Abinadab, and Malki-Shua. The king himself was wounded by an arrow. In agony, Saul begged his armor-bearer to thrust him through with a sword; he refused. Desperately, Saul fell on his own sword and thus ended his life in ignominy. When Saul's body was found by the Philistines, they dishonored it by cutting off the head, stripping off the armor and hanging the naked body on the outside wall of BETH SHAN (1 Sam. 31:1–10; 1 Chr. 10:1–10). The armor was put on public display in a temple.

The disgrace that had befallen Saul stirred a people whom he had helped early in his reign, the inhabitants of Jabesh Gilead. At great risk to

Aerial view of ancient Beth Shan (looking SE), where the bodies of Saul and Jonathan were hung after they were killed by the Philistines.

themselves, men from this city removed the bodies of Saul and his sons from the wall of Beth Shan and gave them proper burial.

IX. The spiritual odyssey of Saul. Saul is one of the most tragic figures of the OT. He entered his life's work with great promise, but ended it with shame and dishonor.

When first meeting Saul in the Scripture, the reader does not gain the impression that he was an unusual person, except that he was much taller than others. The fact that he assumes that a fee would have to be paid Samuel for a prediction of where the donkeys were located may reflect a lack of understanding of how true Hebrew prophecy differed from that practiced among his pagan neighbors. His lack of knowledge of who Samuel really was reveals his ignorance of the name of the great men of his people and his lack of interest in them. Saul's servant knew, but he did not.

Yet, Saul was a modest fellow, ready to admit his unimportance because his tribe, Benjamin, was insignificant. He did not protest the favors Samuel showered on him, but he did not revel in them either. Saul was attentive to Samuel's predictions and readily responded to the influence of the Spirit of God on his heart and the workings of the Spirit among the joyful band of prophets. Here is the first instance in Scripture in which the Spirit of God and a heart change are linked together.

Saul's spiritual experience, with resultant success in aiding the people of Jabesh Gilead against the Ammonites and defending his own people from the Philistines did not engender pride in his heart. He did not seek the leadership of Israel; he tried to evade it. But both Samuel and the Israelites saw Saul as God's choice.

The success God gave Saul in political and military affairs did give him trouble. For a time he shared leadership and decision making with Samuel, but soon chafed under the restraints of sharing power and popularity. And this became the watershed of his life. Tradition and custom in the ANE held that kings should be sole rulers, though Israel had never accepted this dictum. Saul was lured by it, and using Samuel's seemingly unnecessary delay as an excuse, Saul violated established shared leadership by taking on the functions of a priest as well as a king, on the basis of pious motive. It was a serious mistake, and he suffered the humiliation of a severe rebuke.

Saul possessed a serious personality flaw. He was given to rash decisions while under pressure. In a battle with the Philistines, Saul's son Jonathan ate honey, not knowing that his father had put a curse on anyone eating food during the battle. Saul faced a painful dilemma. If he ignored his son's act he would be guilty of negating his own command on the basis of favoritism. If he rigidly carried out his curse, he would have to kill his own son. It was a crisis of authority, and on the face of it Saul seemed heroic in his willingness to put Jonathan to death. But the army objected and openly forced the king to back down from his position. The crisis of authority became a crisis of confidence and Saul lost.

Saul became less sure of himself, and in the victory over Agag, the Amalekite, he quickly yielded to the people's greed for loot. He backed off from his judicial role as executioner of the criminal renegade, Agag. He had been willing to kill Jonathan but shrank from killing the bloody Amalekite. Saul's fumbling excuses before Samuel brought down the clap of doom upon his kingly future. Samuel and God parted company with Saul. The king never recovered from the shock of rejection, though he sought reinstatement carefully with tears.

Instead of the good Spirit of God, an evil spirit took over in Saul's life. His heart changed for the worse and a fearful depression repeatedly seized him. He fluctuated between positive and negative feelings toward those near him. He both loved and hated David (1 Sam. 16:21; 18:8, 11). Saul could brook no rival. The inner circle of government became charged with suspicion, fear, jealousy, and hate. Not only was David in danger of his life, but the king's children, Jonathan and Michal, became involved. In the holocaust of terror, kindly priests, who had helped David grudgingly with food, were slaughtered at Saul's orders by the evil informer, DOEG (21:7; 22:9, 18, 22).

In the series of events leading up to this tragic moment, one incident is most revealing. David had been located as under the protection of Samuel's prophetic band. Saul's police, repeatedly, were overawed by the presence of God's Spirit among the prophets and could not arrest David. Saul went personally, but the jealousy, hate, and fear which indwelt his soul reacted negatively in the presence of God's servants. Saul prophesied, but not as before; he lost his self-control and stripped himself of clothing. He lost self-consciousness, falling helplessly to the ground. For a king, it was a most humiliating experience, and Saul came out of it more venomous than before. Death and terror marked his associations with others from that time on.

David was Saul's special target and Saul almost trapped him. The king's dismay was devastating when he discovered that, unwittingly, he had slept in the same cave as David, who daringly had cut off a portion of Saul's robe. When, from a safe distance, David confronted Saul, the king reacted characteristically. His anger dissolved into groveling confession that David was in the right and ended with an entreaty for mercy. Saul tried to capture David again but was outsmarted and publicly ridiculed for leaving his person so poorly guarded. Saul confessed he was a sinner and a fool. The chase was over, but Saul's spirit was broken.

Faced with an impending attack by the Philistines, Saul violated his own prohibitions on DIVINATION and sought help from the medium of Endor. Through no skill of the old woman, Saul was met by the spirit of dead Samuel and heard the fatal words of doom.

Saul had no heart for the battle that ensued, nor for the captivity which seemed inevitable. His suicide was an act of utter hopelessness and fear, an act rare in the annals of Israel. The young man of great promise had become an old man of utter disgrace. See also SAMUEL, BOOKS OF.

(See further R. Kittel, *Great Men and Movements in Israel* [1929], 86–112; T. H. Robinson, *A History of Israel* [1932], 178–96; J. Fleming, *Personalities of the Old Testament* [1948], 96–116; M. F. Unger, *Archaeology and the Old Testament* [1954], 197–203; S. T. Frost, *Patriarchs and Prophets* [1963], 99–108; D. M. Gunn, *The Fate of King Saul: An Interpretation of a Biblical Story* [1980]; V. P. Long, *The Reign and Rejection of King Saul: A Case for Literary and Theological Coherence* [1989]; D. V. Edelman, *King Saul in the Historiography of Judah* [1991]; J. Bright, *A History of Israel*, 4th ed. [2000], 184–95; S. Nicholson, *Three Faces of Saul: An Intertextual Approach to Biblical Tragedy* [2002]; B. Green, *How Are the Mighty Fallen? A Dialogical Study of King Saul in 1 Samuel* [2003]; C. S. Ehrlich and M. C. White, eds., *Saul in Story and Tradition* [2006].)   G. H. LIVINGSTON

Savaran sav´uh-ruhn. KJV Apoc. variant of AVARAN (1 Macc. 6:43).

Savias suh-vi´uhs (Σαουια). Son of Boccas (Bukki) and ancestor of EZRA (1 Esd. 8:2 KJV). This name occurs in CODEX ALEXANDRINUS but not in CODEX VATICANUS (nor in the parallel passage, Ezra 7:4), and on this basis it is omitted by the NRSV.

savior. A term applied to mighty warriors, rulers, and ancient gods, but supremely in the Bible to Jesus Christ (Jn 4:42; Eph. 5:23). Basic to the OT is the concept that God is the deliverer of his people. No human being could save himself; only God was Savior (Ps. 44:3, 7; Isa. 43:11; 45:21; 60:16; Jer. 14:8; Hos. 13:4). In Hebrew "savior" is a participle (*môšiaʿ* H4635, from the verb *yāšaʿ* H3828), which may indicate that in the thought of the OT this term is not so much a title as it is a description of God's activity in behalf of his people. Although the word is not a messianic term in the OT, the MESSIAH is described in the OT as one coming to offer salvation to all nations (Isa. 49:6, 8; Zech. 9:9). Mighty leaders whom God used as instruments of deliverance for his people were also in the OT referred to as "saviors" (Jdg. 3:9, 15; 2 Ki. 13:5; Neh. 9:27; Obad. 21).

In many OT passages, the SEPTUAGINT translation employs the noun *sōtēr* G5400, which was commonly used among the Greeks as a divine appellation. They, as did the Hebrews, used the term with reference to mighty warriors and rulers, and it is even applied to philosophers such as Epicurus. But in the Greek NT, in contradistinction to other usage, the term is never applied to a mere human being, but only to God the Father and his Son, JESUS CHRIST. God is described as "savior" in the NT because he authored the salvation that Jesus accomplished (Lk. 1:47; 1 Tim. 1:1; 2:3; 4:10; Tit. 1:3; 2:10; 3:4; Jude 25). "Savior" is in the NT preeminently the title of Jesus. From the beginning he was announced to the world as Savior (Lk. 2:11). Although the term is not used by Matthew, Jesus' mission is described in that gospel as the One to save his people from their sins (Matt. 1:21). The distribution of the twenty-four uses of the term in the NT would indicate that, although the term was employed from the beginning in Christianity, it became especially important toward the close of the NT period. Two thirds of the usage occurs in the later books: ten in the Pastoral Epistles; five in 2 Peter; and one each in John, 1 John, and Jude. The Gospel of Mark and the earlier Pauline epistles do not use the term.

The contexts of the term *sōtēr* in the NT give insight into its significance in early Christianity. Jesus was described by John as "Savior of the world" in his record of the encounter with the Samaritan woman (Jn. 4:42). Jesus' significance was such as could not be confined to any single race or people. In the Pastoral Epistles, the phrase "the appearing of our Savior" is used (2 Tim. 1:10; Tit. 2:13), which testifies both to his supernatural origin and glory. The term is also associated with "kindness" and "love" (Tit. 3:4).

Jesus himself interpreted his mission as one of salvation, saying, "For the Son of man came to seek and to save what was lost" (Lk. 19:10). The term presupposes a danger, a disaster, from which the rescuer snatched the one whom he helped. The term in both the OT (Isa. 53) and the NT suggests deliverance from the worst affliction and trouble known to humanity — deliverance from SIN. There is an emphasis also in Jesus' ministry regarding the recipients of his deliverance; he was the Savior not only of the mighty and the rich or of the learned, but also of shepherds and outcasts such as ZACCHAEUS. See full discussion under SALVATION.

H. L. DRUMWRIGHT, JR.

savour. See ODOR.

saw. A tool with notched blade or teeth used for cutting hard material (Heb. *měgērâ* H4490 and *maśśôr* H5373). The saw was in common use in the ANE world. An Egyptian relief from the 5th dynasty (2560–2420 B.C.) shows two carpenters with long saws making planks. It was also one of the familiar implements of the Israelite carpenter or woodcutter (Isa. 10:15). Metal and stone as well as wood were sawn. Archaeological evidences show 12th-dynasty Egyptians (1989–1776 B.C.) using bronze saws with emery for cutting granite. In the construction of Solomon's TEMPLE, some of the costly stones were "trimmed with a saw" (1 Ki. 7:9). Sawing was hard work and captives taken in warfare were frequently assigned to it (2 Sam. 12:31; 1 Chr. 20:3). Because of its difficulty, many ancients preferred to use large stone blocks for building operations. The saw could also be an instrument of terrible death: the prophet ISAIAH is reputed to have suffered martyrdom by being sawn in two (cf. Heb. 11:37; verb *prizō* G4569).   J. H. BRATT

sayings of Jesus. See LOGIA; OXYRHYNCHUS SAYINGS OF JESUS.

scab. A crust on a sore. The KJV uses this English word to render the related Hebrew nouns *sappaḥat* H6204 (Lev. 13:2; 14:56) and *mispaḥat* H5030 (Lev. 13:6–8), which modern translations understand as references to skin rash or eruption, probably psoriasis (cf. the verb *sāpaḥ* H8558, Isa. 3:17). It also uses the term "scab" (or "scabbed") to render *gārāb* H1734, which may refer to scabies (Lev. 21:20; 22:22; Deut. 28:27). See DISEASE.

scale. See BALANCE; WEIGHTS AND MEASURES.

scales, fish. The rough exterior surface of a fish, removable by scraping. Only those aquatic animals that had scales and dorsal fins were permissible for

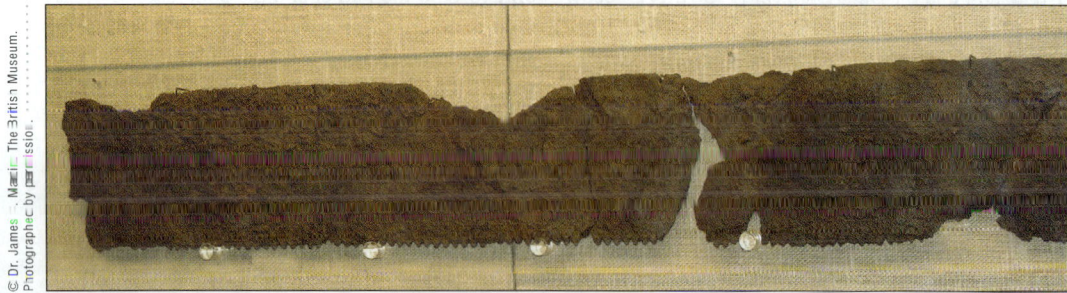

Iron saw used by the Assyrians for cutting stone (from Nimrud, 9th–7th cent. B.C.).

the Israelites to eat (Lev. 11:9–12; Deut. 14:9–10). In a figurative use, Ezekiel predicts that even as fish that cling to the hoary scales of a crocodile share its fate when it is caught, so also would the followers of the arrogant Egyptian pharaoh share the calamity that would overtake their leader (Ezek. 29:4). The Hebrew term (*qaśqeśet H7989*), like the English, can be used with reference to a military coat of mail (scale armor, 1 Sam. 17:5) because its small overlapping pieces resemble fish scales.   J. H. Bratt

scall. This archaic term, meaning "scurf" or the like, is used by the KJV to render Hebrew *neteq H5999*, which refers to a disease of the skin (Lev. 13:30–37; 14:54). Modern versions usually translate it as "itch."

scapegoat. See Azazel.

scarlet. A term applied to various bright red colors. This English word is used by the KJV and NIV to render Hebrew *šānî H9106* (Gen. 38:28 and frequently), though the NRSV and NJPS prefer to translate with crimson (a deeper, purplish red). In the NT, "scarlet" is the standard rendering of the Greek term *kokkinos G3132* (Matt. 27:28 et al.).

The dye used for coloring the wool and thread a scarlet color undoubtedly came from the insect *Coccus ilicis*. This is an insect pest that attacks the species of oak called *Quercus coccifera*, commonly called the kermes oak. The insect has sometimes been called the kermes bug. The oak is evergreen, never grows taller than 20 ft., and is of a dense sturdy habit. The acorns are borne in ones or twos, about one inch long, and they are half enclosed in a spiny cup. The insect which produces the dye is a scale that soon covers the young branches, if not controlled. These scales produce a white fluff similar to cotton wool, similar to the American blight (wooly aphis) and to the insect which attacks the cacti known as prickly pear — the cochineal, from which the red culinary coloring comes.

The actual preparation of the dyes was probably done by the Phoenicians, though it is agreed that the Egyptians taught the Israelites the actual application. It is obvious that this scarlet dye was known as far back as the first half of the 2nd millennium B.C., for Tamar's midwife put a scarlet thread around the hand of Zerah in order to make sure that he was known as the firstborn (Gen. 38:27–30). Scarlet clothing suggested luxury (2 Sam. 1:24; Prov. 31:21; Rev. 17:4), and the color is used to describe the beauty of a woman's lips (Cant. 4:3). In an important figurative use, however, both scarlet and crimson represent sin in contrast to the white purity of snow and wool (Isa. 1:18).   W. E. Shewell-Cooper

scented wood. See citron.

scepter. A staff representing the authority of a king or other sovereign. The rendering "scepter" may be viewed as a specialized meaning of various biblical words that commonly denote an ordinary rod or may have some other meaning in particular contexts. Hebrew *šēbeṭ H8657*, for example, can be used of a shepherd's staff (Mic. 7:14), of instruments for administering discipline (Prov. 22:15), including clubs studded with iron (Ps. 2:9), and so on. Similarly, *maṭṭeh H4751* may refer simply to a stick used for support (Gen. 38:28) or to a branch (Ezek. 19:12). Both terms, however, can refer specifically to the scepters of rulers (cf. Jer. 48:17). In addition, the term *měḥōqēq* (participle of *ḥāqaq H2980*, "to cut, inscribe, prescribe") is a poetical word standing for "commander's staff" or "scepter" (Ps. 60:7). In the NT, Greek *rhabdos G4811* also has a variety of uses (e.g., traveler's staff, Matt. 10:10; discipline stick, 1 Cor. 4:21; measuring rod, Rev. 11:1), but it can be used in particular of the Son's kingly scepter (Heb. 1:8, citing Ps. 45:6).

Scepters were associated mainly with kings, but lesser officials sometimes carried a staff of office. In the OT, reference is made to the scepters of the rulers of Israel, Egypt, Moab, Damascus, Ashkelon, and Judah (Pss. 60:7; 108:8; Jer. 48:17; Ezek. 19:11; Amos 1:5, 8; Zech. 10:11). Two passages often regarded as messianic associate a scepter with Israel's future rulers (Gen. 49:10; Num. 24:17). The Roman soldiers had the royal scepter in mind when they mockingly placed a reed in the hand of Jesus to represent it (Matt. 27:29). Several passages in Esther illustrate a special use made of the scepter by the Persian kings (Esth. 4:11; 5:2; 8:4). In these passages it is described as golden, meaning either that it was of solid gold or that it was gold-studded, like the scepters of the Homeric kings. Representations of Eastern kings show them holding two different kinds of scepter. One is long, slender, and ornamented; the other, shorter and mace-like. The former is seen on a limestone relief of DARIUS, who appears holding his scepter near the top, while the lower part of it rests on the ground. The latter type appears on a relief of ESARHADDON. W. J. CAMERON

Sceva see´vuh (Σκευᾶς G5005, possibly the Greek form of Latin *Scaeva* [from *scaevus*, "left"]). A Jewish chief priest living in EPHESUS (Acts 19:14–17). Since he would not have been able to function as such in the synagogues of ASIA MINOR, he may have exercised the office at Jerusalem; alternatively, he was simply a member of a high-priestly family or he had been the chief of one of the twenty-four courses of priests for which he was still honored. (See further C. K. Barrett, *A Critical and Exegetical Commentary on the Acts of the Apostles*, ICC, 2 vols. [1994–98], 2:909.)

Sceva's seven sons traveled from place to place attempting to exorcise demons by using the name of Jesus, but on one occasion the evil spirit denied knowing them with these famous words: "Jesus I know, and I know about Paul, but who are you?" (Acts 19:15). Lacking the authority of PAUL and Jesus, they were attacked by the demon-possessed man and had to flee "naked and bleeding" (v. 16). The incident was widely reported, with the result that awe and reverence for the name of the Lord Jesus came upon all the Ephesians. There was also a revival and renewal in the church; many of the believers confessed that they had not given up the practices of the occult and voluntarily surrendered their books of magic to a public bonfire. The power of the gospel was signally demonstrated, and the word of the Lord prevailed over all the rival forces of evil. (See R. B. Rackham, *The Acts of the Apostles*, 14th ed. [1951], 355–56; *ABD*, 5:1004.) A. Ross

schin shin. See SHIN.

school. See EDUCATION.

schoolmaster. See CUSTODIAN.

schools of prophets. See PROPHETS AND PROPHECY II.D.

science in the Bible. The term *science* refers to systematized knowledge covering general truths (or "laws") that are discovered through the scientific method (i.e., a procedure that involves observation, experimentation, and the testing of hypotheses in order to solve a perceived problem). The term is specifically used with regard to *natural science*, that is, knowledge of structural and behavioral pattern in the physical world.

I. The Bible and scientific method. Scientific method in the modern sense arose in the 17th and 18th centuries. Prior to that, the nearest thing to scientific method was speculation and postulation with little if any reference to experiment and test. The Bible is singularly free from such conjectures about general truths and the operation of general laws, especially in the realm of nature. If science is found in the Bible, it therefore must have a special significance, since it was not obtained and tested through scientific method. The specific case of natural science will be considered first, after which the more general case of all experiential reality will be considered.

II. Natural science

A. Purpose, plan, and pattern. The Bible, in its references to nature, is concerned primarily with purpose. Pattern is related to purpose through plan. Scripture acknowledges the existence of the physical universe as created by God (Gen. 1:1). The CREATION, much debated by scientists and theologians in modern times, is the dominant theme of biblical references to NATURE. It is explicitly catalogued in the first chapter of Genesis, and is repeatedly invoked in OT and NT alike to identify the one true God, and to attest to his power and wisdom. Done as an act of God's will (Ps. 33:9), the creation was purposeful. God made all things for himself (Prov. 16:4; Col. 1:16; Rev. 4.11) and created human beings for his glory (Isa. 43:7). The crowning purpose is salvation through faith in Christ (2 Cor. 5.17; Eph. 3.12, 17; 2 Tim. 1:9–10). The purpose will be accomplished when the church of Christ is perfected and the enemies of God destroyed (1 Cor. 15:20–28). When the purpose is fulfilled, the physical universe will undergo a total transformation, for God "will create new heavens and a new earth" (Isa. 65:17; cf. 2 Pet. 3:10–13; Rev. 20:11; 21:1). See HEAVENS, NEW.

To fulfill its purpose, the creation had to be wisely planned (Prov. 8:22–31). The plan and the wisdom evidenced by it are revealed in nature itself (Job 38–41; Ps. 19). It is part of that plan that humans dominate nature (Gen. 1:26, 28; Ps. 8:6–8), use it for their benefit (Gen. 1:29, 30; 9:1–4; Deut. 12:15), study it as revealing God's glory (Ps. 19), power (Rom. 1:20), providence (Ps. 104), and constancy (Ps. 89:2; Jer. 31:35–37; 33:20–26), and thus derive wisdom (Prov. 14:8) and great reward (Ps. 19:7–11).

It is Bible teaching that the universe is intelligently constructed on a complex and divinely ingenious self-consistent pattern, that it operates according to divinely ordained ways or laws, that the basic pattern and laws do not change with time, that the pattern and laws are intelligible to us, and that our welfare depends on understanding them. These basic concepts of nature are in sharp contrast to the teachings of other ancient cultures, which depict physical origins as by-products of the clashes between warring deities, and natural phenomena as unpredictable activities of willful and capricious gods.

B. The foundations of modern science.

The origin of modern science rests on a few basic assumptions to which experience has ascribed self-evidence. Among them are the uniformity of nature in space and time and the inviolability of natural law. These assumptions appear to be self-evident only because the discoveries of science have given them credence. There is neither necessity nor proof that these assumptions are universally valid in nature. Except they be accepted on faith, there is no basis for scientific endeavor.

It cannot be said that scientists would never have made such assumptions apart from the monotheistic culture of the ancient Hebrews. It is a matter of record that these assumptions were matters of religious faith in the Hebrew-Christian culture, and modern science was spawned in the Christian culture of Western Europe. Most of the scholars who laid the foundations of modern science were also people of strong Christian faith. Among them were Copernicus, Galileo, Johannes Kepler, Isaac Newton, Francis Bacon, and René Descartes. The uniformity of nature and the inviolability of natural law were for them matters of religious faith. Even the concept of a mechanistic universe was put forward as showing the perfection of God's creation and the absence of the need for a "gap-filling" God to account for natural phenomena that science could not explain.

It is a reasonable conclusion that modern science is heavily indebted to the Bible. It has major conceptual origins in the Bible, its basic assumptions were matters of religious faith, and the pursuit of scientific research is scripturally admonished.

C. The creation.

The Bible devotes little space to the manner in which the creation of the universe took place. The simple affirmation that "he spoke, and it came to be" (Ps. 33:9) runs like a silver cord from beginning to end. A few broad concepts are given in the first chapter of Genesis. This account teaches that the creation took place in a succession of steps, each step building on what went before and preparing for what was to follow. The earth was prepared for life before life appeared. Vegetable life preceded animal life. Different forms of animal life were evidently created at different times, with the suggestion that animal life first appeared in the water. Humans were a special creation subsequent to the creation of all other living things. These teachings are all consistent with modern scientific observations, though not necessarily with the interpretations placed on these observations by some modern scientists.

D. Pattern.

The Bible contains many references to commonly observable patterns in nature, not so much as if to reveal the patterns as to call attention to their significance in testifying to the WISDOM and PROVIDENCE of God. The assured regularity of the seasons, seed and harvest, day and night, are declared (Gen. 8:22; Jer. 3:19; 5:24). The seas, mountains, and valleys are kept in place by God's decree (Job 38:8–11; Ps. 104:8–9; Prov. 8:29; Jer. 5:22). Nature was made orderly by God's wisdom (Prov. 8:1–14). God's wisdom is seen in the instincts of birds (Jer. 8:7). The lightning and the rain have their ways prescribed by God's law (Job 28:26). The interdependence of different parts of nature is seen in the feeding of wild life (Pss. 104:27; 145:15). Recognition of these phenomena in their easily observable aspects is now so commonplace that the wonders of natural pattern are taken for granted. The more subtle cause-and-effect relationships by which structural and behavioral patterns in nature are scientifically explained are more challenging to modern science. On this subject the Bible is silent. These relationships are left for human beings to discover, and they are indeed discernible and intelligible to the human mind.

In the creation account (Gen. 1) the Bible presents a broad outline of pattern that is more significant to modern science. Distinction is made between radiation (light), space (firmament or expanse), and matter (waters, earth, dry land, seas). Distinction is made also between living and nonliving matter. Living matter is divided into five great categories: plants (1:12–13), marine animals and birds (1:20–21), land animals (1:24–25), and humans (1:26–27; 1 Cor. 15:39). Within each of these five major divisions matter originated and persists in certain broad and inviolable classes. Inviolability is inferred from the endowment of each class with a hereditary mechanism that assures perpetuation of that class (Gen. 1; Matt. 7:16; 1 Cor. 15:37–38) and protects it from admixture with other classes and the consequent ultimate degeneration of all classes of living things into a single conglomerate potpourri. These broad characteristics of the pattern of nature are consistent with modern scientific observations.

Another generality of scientific significance is the concept of the universe as growing old and wearing out like a garment (Ps. 102:25–26; Isa. 34:4). This seems to correspond to the scientific principle of increasing entropy in a closed system, known as the second law of thermodynamics. However, the applicability of this principle to the universe as a system is a matter of debate among scientists.

E. Anticipations of modern science. Some writers have found scriptural passages in which they see anticipations of modern scientific discovery (see H. Rimmer, *The Harmony of Science and Scripture*, 3rd ed. [1936]; O. E. Sander, *Does Science Support Scripture?* [1951]). The undulatory theory of matter is seen in Gen. 1:2; wireless telegraphy in Job 38:35; the concept of parallax in Jas. 1:17; atomic theory of matter in Heb. 11:3; atomic binding forces in Heb. 1:3; light as the basis of all substance in Gen. 1:3; nuclear fission in Gen. 1:4, with a final chain reaction in Isa. 34:4 and Lk. 21:25–28; an expanding universe in Isa. 40:22; motor cars in Joel 2:3–4; airplanes in Isa. 31:5 and 60:8; submarines in Rev. 9:1–11; radio in Eccl. 10:20 and television in Rev. 11:3–12; the sphericity of the earth in Job 22:14 (also Prov. 8:27; Isa. 40:22; Mk. 13:35–37); suspension of the earth in space in Job 26:7; the concept of air as having weight in Job 28:25; the water cycle as known by modern science in Job 36:27–28 (also Ps. 104:10, 13; Prov. 8:28; Eccl. 1:6–7). Other writers, among whom Bernard Ramm (*The Christian View of Science and Scripture* [1954]) is a chief exponent, hold that in each of these cases the context precludes interpretation that reads modern scientific discovery into its meaning.

F. Plan versus chance. Pattern in nature may arise from plan or it may arise from the random processes of chance. The validity of interpretation of scientific observations sometimes rests on which of these alternatives is assumed. The area of theories on organic evolution provides many examples where the direction of investigation and the interpretation of data may be significantly dependent on whether random chance or purposeful creation is assumed to play the dominant role in the formation of basic patterns. The Bible does not rule the random processes of chance out of the chain of causality, but it does insist emphatically on the purposeful and knowing creation by God as the true origin of the universe and of the basic structural and behavioral patterns of nature, and on the continuing providence of God as the ultimate basis of the stability of natural law.

III. All experiential reality. In its broadest sense science may be described as systematized knowledge of truth wherever truth may be identified. The Bible is a prolific sourcebook of truth (Ps. 119:160; Jn. 17:17) and its identification (Matt. 7:15–20; Jn. 14:6; 1 Jn. 4:1–6).

A. The spiritual realm. The Bible teaches that the physical realm is not all of reality, but that it is coexistent with a spiritual realm (Jn. 4:24; Rev. 16:14). The Bible teaches that the physical realm is permeated by the spiritual realm (Gen. 2:7; Eph. 6:12; 1 Pet. 5:8), and that the two realms interact on each other (Matt. 17:19–20; Jn. 13:2; Acts 2:2–4). It teaches also that the spiritual realm is eternal while the physical realm is temporal (Matt. 24:35), and that the ultimate source of all knowledge and power is in the spiritual realm (Ps. 111:10; Matt. 28:18; Rom. 11:33–36).

B. Spiritual-physical interactions. Pagans, both ancient and modern, frequently ascribe natural phenomena to unpredictable spiritual activity. Bible writers ascribed natural phenomena to the activity of God. In both cases natural chains of causality included supernatural agents. As science brought about an ever-increasing understanding of the patterns of natural behavior, spiritual forces disappeared from science as recognized elements in natural chains of causality. If natural processes were to be modified temporarily by supernatural intervention, natural law would appear to be violated, and the event would be called a MIRACLE. The Bible contains many accounts of miracles.

In some cases, such as the long day when Israel battled the AMORITES (Josh. 10:12–14; see DAY, JOSHUA'S LONG) and the DIAL of AHAZ (2 Ki. 20:11; Isa. 38:8), a noncritical interpretation would imply the historical occurrence of a worldwide catastrophe for which historical evidence is lacking. However, according to Ramm, critical examination of the texts and interpretation in the light of the contexts raise uncertainty as to what natural perturbations actually occurred, and greatly diminish the consequence of search for scientific explanations. In other OT cases the miracles ascribed to God's witnesses are wrought by God as authentication of his witness, and appear to be clear cases of spiritual-physical interactions.

Miracles performed in the course of Christ's ministry clearly demonstrate spiritual power over natural phenomena (Mk. 4:39; 6:41–44, 48; Jn. 2:1–11; 11:44) and disclose the potency of faith to exercise control over that power (Matt. 9:22; Jas. 5:16). The miracles of the VIRGIN BIRTH (Matt. 1:18–25; Lk. 1:26—2:7) and the RESURRECTION (1 Cor. 15:12–23) are central to Christian belief.

IV. Science and theology. The pursuit of knowledge in the field of science and in the field of theology have long been considered as two separate and unrelated professions. However, if science deals with what God did and theology deals with why he did it, then it would seem that a combination of these two professions in an interdisciplinary search for truth might profoundly benefit humanity. As the joining of philosophy and technology in Newton's day produced the scientific revolution and gave humanity the understanding of natural forces that led to the industrial revolution, would not the joining of theology and science in our day produce a "knowledge of truth" revolution and give humanity the understanding of spiritual forces that would lead to a spiritual revolution? If so, then as the industrial revolution freed people from the bondage of drudgery and dependence on their own physical power, the spiritual revolution should free them from the bondage of fear and dependence on their own spiritual power. See also ASTRONOMY.

(See further D. M. Macay, *Christianity in a Mechanistic Universe* [1966]; P. Harrison, *The Bible, Protestantism, and the Rise of Natural Science* [1998]; S. L. Bonting, *Creation and Double Chaos: Science and Theology in Discussion* [2005]; V. S. Poythress, *Redeeming Science: A God-Centered Approach* [2006].)

R. M. PAGE

scoff. The Hebrew verb *lîṣ* H4329, "to scoff, brag, deride" (the participle *lēṣ* H4370 functions as a noun, "scoffer"), is used in the Bible specifically as the opposite of wise behavior. To scoff is to willfully refuse to learn the way of the Lord and to mock those who do.

I. In the OT. In Proverbs the scoffer is characterized by his refusal to learn the way of WISDOM, the basis of true happiness. Since wisdom is more than an intellectual achievement, but is also an ethical-religious attitude of commitment to God, scoffing is more than a matter of naive ignorance; it is sinful, foolish PRIDE (Prov. 9:7–10; 21:24; 24:9). (See *NIDOTTE*, 2:798–800.)

God punishes his disobedient people by sending *his* reproach upon them, which is echoed by the attitude of the nations (Ps. 79:12–14; Jer. 24:9; 42:18;

44:8, 12; 49:13; Zeph. 2:8-10). This reproach of God is borne by a mediator, the anointed of the Lord (Ps. 89:50-51), the one who bears reproach for God's sake so there will be no reproach on others (Ps. 69:6-12; cf. Jn. 2:17), whose words are the words of Jesus on the cross (Ps. 22:7; cf. Matt. 27:46).

II. The scorning and vindication of Christ. This predicted mocking of the MESSIAH is explicitly fulfilled in both the Jewish and Roman trials, culminating in the mock coronation (Lk. 22:63; 23:11; Gk. *empaizō G1850*). The CROSS itself is a mark of shame (Gal. 3:13) and its preaching was regarded as offense and foolishness (1 Cor. 1:23; Gal. 5:11); even the message of the resurrection was an occasion for scoffing (Acts 17:32). Also in this the followers of Christ were not to be above their Master, and were to share in this aspect of suffering and rejection (Matt. 10:17); the heroes of faith of all ages have cruel mockings as their lot (Heb. 11:36), with MOSES regarding abuse suffered for Christ as the greatest wealth (11:26). But Christ's humiliation leads to his exaltation, and his triumph over the powers enables him to scoff publicly at them (Col. 2:13). In his work is seen God's choice of the weak and foolish things of the world to put to shame the wise and the strong (1 Cor. 1:18-31): Christ's victory over SATAN humiliates his opponents (Lk. 13:17).

III. The believer's triumph over scoffing. The underlying motive for scoffing at Christ is the desire for self-justification (Lk. 16:11), the refusal to accept Christ as one's only righteousness. For those who have their honor in Christ it is inappropriate that they seek the dishonor of any (Jas. 2:6). For any to fall away from Christ would mean their exclusion from any future repentance, for they would have put Christ again to shame (1 Cor. 11:27; Heb. 6:6).

There will continue to be mockers, questioning the return of Christ (2 Pet. 3:3; Jude 18), but God will not be mocked and will indeed come in judgment (Gal. 6:7). The shame of the cross includes also its "foolishness," but Christ is made unto us wisdom (1 Cor. 1:17-31). The life of faith is not ashamed of the shame of Christ (Heb. 11:26, 36) and boasts in Christ and in fellow Christians (2 Cor. 7:14; 9:4). This boasting is based on Christ's victory over evil, his shaming and mocking of it in its total defeat (1 Cor. 1:27-29; Col. 2:15; cf. Lk. 13:17). If self-justification is a mocking of Christ (Lk. 16:14-15), then glorying in him must be identified with justification by faith in him alone. The life of faith is necessarily one that has counted the cost of forsaking all to follow him; anything else deserves proper scoffing (Lk. 14:29). (See *TDNT*, 5:630-36.) See also MOCKING. D. C. DAVIS

scorn. See MOCKING.

scorpion. An arachnid characterized by a venomous stinger at the tip of its tail (Heb. *'aqrāb H6832*; Gk. *skorpios G5026*). Of the world's many hundreds of species of scorpions, some twelve (in the large *Buthidae* family, e.g., *Buthus occitanus israelis*) are known from the various regions of Palestine, from the NEGEV desert to the moist woodlands of the N. One route up the great escarpment across the Negev is known as Scorpion Pass (Num. 34:4; Josh. 15:3; Jdg. 1:36; see AKRABBIM).

Even though scorpions vary in size, proportions, and color, the outline of this small animal, with its pair of heavy pincers and forward-curving sting-tipped tail, makes it immediately recognizable. Size itself is no indication of potency of venom; at least one Middle E species has a most serious sting, but none is likely to kill a healthy person. Scorpions are classified near the spiders and, like them, they are entirely carnivorous. The sting is used with precision to paralyze the prey, which is then consumed by pumping digestive juices into it and sucking out the broken-down tissues. Toward nightfall scorpions emerge from the holes and crevices where they have spent the day and wander in search of prey. They do not normally attack humans but react instinctively if trodden on. (See further *FFB*, 70-71.)

The desert through which God led the Israelites is described as "that thirsty and waterless land, with its venomous snakes and scorpions" (Deut. 8:15). Elsewhere in the Bible, scorpions are mentioned figuratively as symbols of unpleasantness and danger (Eze. 2:6; Rev. 9:3-10). When REHOBOAM said to the Israelites, "My father scourged you with whips; I will scourge you with scorpions" (1 Ki. 12:11, 14; 2 Chr. 10:11, 14), he was probably referring to a many-thonged whip armed with hooked metal knobs and known as the scorpion. Jesus gave his disciples "authority to trample on snakes and scorpions" (Lk. 10:19). The Lord's rhetorical questions, "Which of you fathers, if your son asks for a fish, will give him a snake instead? Or if he asks for an egg, will give him a scorpion?" (11:12), may express a striking contrast; the "body" segment in some species of scorpions is fat and almost egg-shaped (esp. if resting and contracted), but this saying could echo a proverb. G. S. CANSDALE

Scorpion Pass. See AKRABBIM.

scourge. A whip used for flogging, especially to inflict punishment (see CRIMES AND PUNISHMENTS). Scourging was common among ancient peoples, but most instances of the Hebrew noun šôṭ H8765 in the OT are metaphorical. The figure is used for the tongue (Job 5:21), for a disaster that slays suddenly (9:23), and for divine judgment (Isa. 28:15, 18). The Lord is said to lash his enemies with a scourge (10:26). Israel was warned that the Canaanites might become a scourge on the nation (Josh. 23:13; Heb. šōṭēṭ H8849, possibly a textual error for šôṭim, pl. of šôṭ).

The only references to the scourge as an instrument of punishment are in 1 Ki. 12:11, 14 (= 2 Chr. 10:11, 14). It is not certain whether the word SCORPIONS here (which occurs as parallel to šôṭim) is merely a vivid figure or implies a weighted scourge. Mosaic law permitted a person found guilty in court to be beaten. The sentence was executed upon the prostrate man in the presence of the judge. The number of strokes was no doubt proportioned to the offense but might not exceed forty (Deut. 25:1–3). Later the Jews used a three-thonged whip, but kept to the stated limit, indicating one stroke short for fear of miscounting (cf. 2 Cor. 11:24; *m. Makkot* 3:10). Local SYNAGOGUE authorities and the SANHEDRIN administered scourging for offenses against the law (Matt. 10:17). It appears from Deut. 22:18 and JOSEPHUS (*Ant.* 4.8.23) that defamation was one of the offenses so punishable, but there is no record of other charges on which a person might be scourged.

The MISHNAH describes the method employed (*m. Makkot* 3:11–12). When the physical fitness of the offender had been ascertained, his hands were bound to a pillar and his back and chest bared. Thirteen strokes were administered on the chest and thirteen on each shoulder. If the victim died, no blame was attached to those inflicting punishment. The Roman Porcian law forbade scourging a Roman citizen, but slaves and non-Romans might be examined by scourging (cf. Acts 22:24–25, where the noun *mastix* G3465 and the verb *mastizō* G3464 are used). The Romans commonly used a scourge weighted by pieces of bone or metal, but the Greek verb *rhabdizō* G4810 (Acts 16:22; 2 Cor. 11:25) implies that lictors' rods were employed on the occasions mentioned. Scourging usually preceded CRUCIFIXION (cf. Livy, *Hist.* 33.36, *phragelloō* G5849 in Matt. 27:26 and Mk. 15:15; *paideuō* G4084 [lit., "punish"] in Lk. 23:16, 22; *mastigoō* G3463 in Jn. 19:1). (See *TDNT*, 4:515–19.) W. J. CAMERON

screech owl. See OWL.

screen. This English term is used by the NRSV and other versions to render Hebrew *māsāk* H5009, referring to a linen hanging that served as a door in the TABERNACLE (Exod. 26:36–37 et al.; KJV, "hanging"; NIV, "curtain"). In the specifications of the tabernacle given to MOSES, there was provision for three such curtains. They were made of blue, purple, and scarlet yarn and fine twined linen. They were attached by hooks to poles of acacia wood, but whether they were detached or parted for access is not clear.

The first screen was at the E end of the court of the tabernacle (Exod. 27:16). It was 20 cubits long, and was supported by four pillars decorated with silver fillets and standing in bronze bases. The screen was similar to the hangings of linen from which the walls of the court were made, except that it was decorated. The specifications for the court hangings seem to mean that there was one pillar every 5 cubits, in which case a detachable screen of 20 cubits would require five pillars. If there was such an interval between pillars, which is not certain, the screen could have been nondetachable and would therefore require four more pillars not already accounted for in the walls.

The second screen was the door to the tent (Exod. 26:36–37), and was similar to the court gate except that it was supported by five pillars either overlaid with gold or, more probably, decorated with gold overlaid fillets and capitals.

The third screen formed the division between the two parts of the tent, veiling the innermost holy place (Exod. 35:12). This hanging is most frequently referred to as the *pārōket* H7267 (26:31 et al.; see VEIL), several times as the *pārōket hammāsāk* (lit., "veil of the screen," 35:12 et al.), and once only as the *māsāk* (Num. 3:31; this is clearly the veil described as in the care of the Kohathites, since the screen of the tent was assigned to the care of the Gershonites, v. 25).

G. GOLDSWORTHY

scribe. This English noun (derived from Latin *scriba*, "[official] writer, secretary") is used to translate Hebrew *sōpēr* H6221 (also rendered "secretary" and the like, 2 Sam. 8:17 et al.; Aram. *sāpar* H10516) and Greek *grammateus* G1208 (Matt. 2:4 and frequently). In the ancient world, relatively few people received the training necessary to gain skill in the art of writing, and those who followed the scribal profession were usually regarded as scholars (cf. the NIV translation of 1 Cor. 1:20) and could hold high civic offices. Especially after the EXILE, Jewish scribes were involved not only in clerical activities, such as the copying of biblical MSS, but also in religious instruction. Accordingly, the NIV sometimes uses the rendering "teacher" in the OT (e.g., Ezra 7:6), and in the NT it consistently uses "teacher of the law." See also AMANUENSIS.

I. In the OT. In ancient Israel the scribal craft was principally confined to certain clans who doubtless preserved the trade as a family guild profession, passing the knowledge of this essential skill from father to son. Among the KENITES were "clans of scribes" dwelling at JABEZ (1 Chr. 2:55). The connection between MOSES' father-in-law, JETHRO, who was a PRIEST (Exod. 3:1), and the Kenites (Jdg. 1:16; 4:11) is an indicator that the art of writing was never far removed from the priesthood.

During the united and later Judean monarchies a substantial number of scribes came from the Levites. The point of contact between the ritual and scribal functions derives from the demand for fiscal organization of temple operations (e.g., in MESOPOTAMIA and EGYPT most of the earliest writings are associated with temple records). A Levite recorded the priestly assignments (1 Chr. 24:6), and the royal scribe helped in counting the public funds collected for the repair of the temple (2 Ki. 12:10–11; 2 Chr. 14:11). Since the furnishing of written copies of the law was a (scribal) Levitical responsibility (Deut. 17:18), the reforms of JEHOSHAPHAT (cf. 2 Chr. 17) cannot be disassociated from the scribal function.

Although the extent of literacy within Israelite society is a complex question, at least one "writing prophet" found it convenient, if not necessary, to employ a scribe (Jer. 36:26, 32), which strongly suggests that others did the same. The scribal function of composing private legal documents is widely attested in Mesopotamia and Egypt before, during, and after the biblical period. Although it is not stated that the scribe composed the text of a deed of sale (32:10–12), this may be implied, since the document was entrusted to BARUCH before witnesses.

Most important of all were the scribes who served in the government. They may have served as counselors (e.g., 1 Chr. 27:32) or borne the responsibility for mustering the army (2 Ki. 25:19). The highest ranking government scribe was that of the king. His position in the cabinet is difficult to judge, since ministerial lists may not be given in sequence of rank. If, however, the members of David's cabinet are listed in sequence in 2 Sam. 8:16–18 (cf. 1 Chr. 18:15–17, but differences in 2 Sam. 20:23–26), the royal scribe ranked below the top military commander, the RECORDER (*mazkîr* H4654), and the two chief priests, but above the commander over special forces and the "royal advisers" (so NIV; lit., "priests").

The list of SOLOMON's officers may then be given in ascending order (1 Ki. 4:2–6; AZARIAH, described as being "in charge of district officers," may have been a "royal adviser," since he appears nowhere else). Next are listed two scribes who were sons of David's scribe Shisha (see SHAVSHA), and next the recorder and the new commander of the army, along with the two high priests serving jointly. A new official, the one "in charge of the palace," surely ranked above the scribe. During

Artistic rendition of scribes at work.

the united monarchy at least, therefore, the scribe ranked below the recorder.

The hierarchy may have been different during the divided monarchies, since the scribe is twice listed between the recorder and the palace administrator (2 Ki. 18:18, 37; cf. Isa. 36:3, 22); here he served as one of three ministers appointed to negotiate with SENNACHERIB, who demanded the surrender of Jerusalem. Moreover, by JOSIAH's reign, the scribe SHAPHAN preceded both the recorder and "the ruler of the city" (cf. 2 Ki. 22:3–13 with 2 Chr. 34:8–21), suggesting that the relationship between scribe and recorder had been reversed since David's era. The high status of Shaphan's family is evident from the careers of his son AHIKAM and his grandsons GEDALIAH (who became palace administrator and was later appointed governor of Judah under the Babylonians) and MICAIAH son of Gemariah, who served the chief ministers of state under JEHOIAKIM (Jer. 36:11).

Royal scribes had offices (Jer. 36:12) that were evidently located in the building complex of the royal Judean palace, serving to illustrate the high standing of the king's secretary in the government. The prophets were aware also of an Akkadian counterpart to the royal scribe, with equally high standing (cf. Nah. 3:17) and military functions (cf. Jer. 52:25). The multilingual, pluralistic character of the Persian period likewise demanded administrative specialists (Esth. 3:12; 8:9), and provincial commanders also had scribes as seconds in command (Ezra 4:8–9, 17, 23).

II. Ezra and the intertestamental period. EZRA marked the watershed for the later development of the understanding of the term *scribe*. Indeed, the transition is already suggested in the book of Ezra: the term is used in an administrative sense in Artaxerxes' royal decree (Ezra 7:12–26), but in the narrative (7:6, 11) the term already refers to Ezra as a scribe who, by reason of his learning, is capable of interpreting the law for the common people. Moreover, by his priestly lineage (7:6) he symbolized the close connection between the priesthood and this official interpretation of the law. This connection, which existed probably until the 2nd cent. B.C., appears to be the continuation of the association between scribal and cultic functions of an earlier day. By Persian royal decree, the law of Moses was made civilly binding on Jews living in Trans-Euphrates (i.e., W of the EUPHRATES, 7:25). The essential task of interpreting Moses' law so that it could function in this new civil capacity was given to the priesthood (Ezra) and the Levites (cf. Neh. 8:6–9).

The sources for the next several centuries are almost exclusively later rabbinic literature. However, the priestly hegemony over the correct legal interpretation of the law can hardly be doubted. During the Persian era and most of the Ptolemaic period, the high priest was the most important local official of the government and a ranking member of the local aristocracy. He was the logical choice to receive ALEXANDER THE GREAT (b. *Yoma* 69a; Jos. *Ant.* 11.8.4–5), being escorted by nobles, and clearly was expected to function as the highest local official under Ptolemaic rule (Jos. *Ant.* 12.4.1). As late as the reign of ANTIOCHUS III over Palestine, the high priest was clearly the chief local official (2 Macc. 3:1–4), and priests and Levites dominated the roles of the specially privileged in Antiochus's letter of tax exemptions (Jos. *Ant.* 12.3.3). Significantly, "scribes of the temple" were included among those exempted from certain taxes.

The precise role of the "scribe" is still somewhat difficult to assess, however, for lack of source material. According to one rabbinic tradition (*m. ʾAbot* 1:1), the oral law (which according to rabbinic theology was also given to Moses on Sinai) was mediated from the prophets to the generation of SIMEON "the Just" (the identification is disputed; either the high priest active c. 300 B.C. or his grandson, c. 210 B.C.) by "the Great Assembly." When this tradition is compared with the rules cited in rabbinic literature as given from "the scribes," it seems quite probable that the "scribes" of the Persian and Ptolemaic periods were identical with (or at least participant in) this body of formulators of the oral law.

The rules and practices established by the scribes acquired a binding authority, particularly with the specially orthodox of later (NT) times. One tradition ascribes greater stringency to their teachings than to the written law (*m. Sanh.* 11:3), and a proselyte was required to follow the scribal traditions as well as the simply interpreted written law (*Sipra* on Lev. 19:34). The scribes were essentially biblical interpreters, for occasional scribal rules not based on Scripture caused later rabbis considerable consternation (*m. Kelim* 13:7). This situation fits very well with the enactments of a body or class of interpreters functioning during the Persian and Ptolemaic periods.

From the 2nd cent. B.C. are two additional sources of information on the scribes. In the Wisdom of Ben Sira (ECCLESIASTICUS), whose author clearly considered himself to be in the scribal tradition, is an "ode" to the "perfect scribe" (Sir. 38:24—39:11). This ode confirms the picture of a scribe as one schooled in the law and religious wisdom, understanding the implications of both the written law and oral traditions. As a result of his learning, he enjoyed a prominence in public assemblies, and both understood and exercised justice among the people. Moreover, he was considered particularly pious by virtue of his knowledge of the revealed will of God, a feature of rabbinic understanding of piety. If Ecclesiasticus is Sadducean in origin (or more appropriately proto-Sadducean), then we are faced with one more point of connection between the established priesthood and the class of scribes (see SADDUCEE).

Moreover, during the Maccabean revolt a company of scribes "sought justice" from the Seleucid-appointed high priest, Alcimus, in the confidence that since he was "a priest of the line of Aaron" (1 Macc. 7:12–14) they had nothing to fear. Although their confidence was short-lived, the fact of it reflects an abiding cooperation between the scribes and the established priesthood. The cooperation between the "pious" (see HASIDEAN) and the scribes, however, hints at the later development, when the priestly Sadducees opposed those who descended from the scribes, namely, the RABBIS and PHARISEES. At the time of the Maccabean revolt, however, the "party lines" had in all probability not yet been drawn.

III. In the NT. In the Gospels, scribes are found in connection with both the priestly (Sadducean) party (e.g., Matt. 2:4; 21:15) and the Pharisaic party (cf. Matt. 23). The scholars of this latter group were the leaders of what was to become rabbinic JUDAISM, known subsequently, however, as "sages" (or, "wise") and still later as rabbis. But the scribes (scholars) of both parties challenged Jesus principally on his disobedience to traditional practice under the law (e.g., eating with those obviously unobservant of these traditions [Mk. 2:16], and eating without ritually cleansing the hands, referring to the disciples [Matt. 15:2; Mk. 7:5]).

Matthew 23 (which parallels Lk. 11) is a classic condemnation of the scribal approach to the will of God. The scholars of both parties in all probability took part in whatever Jewish legal proceedings were initiated against Jesus during the week of his passion, but the very complex questions of the legality of such proceedings (under Roman rule) makes further conclusions very tenuous. PAUL clearly understood the scribe as a dialectician (1 Cor. 1:20–25) who was a scholar on the written and oral law; in Paul's view such dialectics were foolishness in the face of God's saving work in Christ. However, at least in certain segments of the early church, the function of the scribe as a Christian scholar and instructor in legal responsibility was preserved (Matt. 8:19, esp. 13:52 and 23:34), so that the Mosaic law was not abolished, but reapplied for the needs of the Christian church. The only mention

SCRIPTURE 355

of "scribes" in John's gospel is in a passage judged unauthentic on both textual and linguistic grounds (Jn. 7:53—8:11). After the period of the NT, *scribe* came to describe a teacher of children and composer of legal documents, the terms *sage* and then *rabbi* being used for the scholar of the law.

(See further R. de Vaux, *Ancient Israel* [1961], 131–32; J. Jeremias, *Jerusalem in the Time of Jesus* [1969], 233–45; *HJP*, rev. ed. [1973–87], 2:322–36; A. J. Saldarini, *Pharisees, Scribes and Sadducees in Palestinian Society: A Sociological Approach*, new ed. [2001]. For the view that the scribal profession involved not just the preservation of texts but also "educational enculturation," see David M. Carr, *Writing on the Tablet of the Heart: Origins of Scripture and Literature* [2005].) A. RAINEY

scrip. This archaic term is used by the KJV once in the OT (1 Sam. 17:40) and several times in the NT (Matt. 10:10 et al.). Modern versions usually translate "bag."

Scripture. The term *scripture* (from Latin *scriptura*, "a writing") can be used in a general sense of anything written, but it more frequently refers to sacred writings. The expression *the Scripture(s)* applies specifically to the BIBLE. (The term can also be used with reference to a particular biblical text, in which case it is usually not capitalized.)

I. Terminology
   A. Descriptive terms
   B. Introductory formulae
   C. Summary
II. The inspiration of Scripture
   A. The term
   B. The relation of inspiration to revelation
   C. The inspiration of the OT
   D. The inspiration of the NT
   E. The character of biblical inspiration
III. The authority of Scripture
   A. Its relation to inspiration
   B. The authority of the OT
   C. The authority of the NT
IV. The use of Scripture
   A. The practical ends for which Scripture was given
   B. Scripture and spiritual illumination
   C. The interpretation of Scripture

I. Terminology

A. Descriptive terms

1. Focusing on the written form. The Greek word *graphē* G1210 occurs with some frequency in the NT, both in the singular and in the plural, usually with the definite article. B. B. Warfield (*The Inspiration and Authority of the Bible* [1948], 232) has pointed out that even where the article is absent some other feature indicates definiteness (e.g., the use of an adjective, as in Jn. 19:37 and Rom. 16:26). Although its extrabiblical use is wider, it is always employed in the NT with reference to sacred Scripture. The plural denotes the sacred Scriptures as a whole (Matt. 21:42; Jn. 5:39, 1 Cor. 15:3–4) and so is collective rather than distributive in force. There is no passage where it clearly means "the books" considered as a purely formal (though it approaches this sense in 2 Pet. 3:16; Warfield [*Inspiration*, 234–35] maintained that the phrase here means "the other passages").

The use of the singular has led to a certain amount of debate. Some hold that it always refers to a particular OT passage, while others hold that it sometimes has the same significance as the plural. A stronger case can be made out for the latter view. G. Schrenk (*TDNT*, 1:753) points, for example, to Gal. 3:8, 22, "where the personification of *graphē* makes it quite inconceivable that Paul should simply have in view an individual text." An expression like "this scripture" is clear evidence that a single passage is in view (e.g., Mk. 12:10; Lk. 4:21; Acts 8:35; cf. Jn. 19:37). It is also likely, though not certain, that *graphē* denotes an individual saying whenever followed by a quotation (e.g., Jn. 7:38; 13:18; 19:24, 36). Even in such cases there may well be a reference to Scripture as a whole. The use of the singular for the whole OT is certainly not frequent outside the NT, but it is difficult to eliminate it from the NT itself. The phrase "Holy Scriptures" (*graphai hagiai*) occurs only once (Rom. 1:2), but the authoritative use of the OT as divinely inspired literature makes the term an altogether appropriate description.

Another term, *gramma* G1207 ("letter [alphabet character], writing"), occurs rarely in the NT with reference to the Scriptures per se. The expression *hiera grammata*, "holy Scriptures" (2 Tim. 3:15), is the only clear case, although Jn. 5:47 also approaches this technical sense. When PAUL uses *gramma* he often does so in a somewhat depreciatory sense (Rom. 2:29; 7:6; 2 Cor. 3:6–7; cf. 3:14–16). As appears from Paul's general use of the OT, his intention is not to belittle the law as Scripture, but only when conceived as making salvation possible by the works of the flesh. Hence he can oppose it to the Spirit, although he sees the Spirit as the Author of Scripture (Acts 28:25).

The phrase *to gegrammenon*, "the thing written," is of frequent occurrence in the SEPTUAGINT in its plural form (e.g., 2 Chr. 35:26; Dan. 9:11). It occurs also in the NT both in the singular (e.g., Lk. 20:17; 2 Cor. 4:13; cf. 1 Cor. 15:54) and in the plural (Lk. 18:31; Gal. 3:10; cf. Jn. 12:16), and it refers to a passage or a group of passages in terms of their content. It is interesting to note that it occurs also in Rev. 1:3 and 22:18–19 in reference to a NT book; and this suggests an extension of the concept of Scripture beyond the OT into the NT. The impressive nature of the context confirms this.

Finally, there is the noun *biblos* G1047, "book," and its diminutive form, *biblion* G1046. The latter, which often has the specific meaning of "scroll," is used in the LXX of particular books of sacred Scripture (Deut. 17:18; Jer. 25:13; Nah. 1:1). In Dan. 9:2 its use in the plural could be a reference to the collection of prophetic literature. The NT use of the singular is similar (Lk. 4:17), and the plural in 2 Tim. 4:13 could refer to a number of scrolls of OT books. The word *biblos* is used in a similar way in the singular (Josh. 1:8; Acts 1:20) and does not occur in the plural in biblical Greek. Even though these two words had not established themselves as technical expressions for Scripture in the same way as some other terms, this is their most characteristic use both in the LXX and the NT. The most significant exception (Rev. 5:1–10) is only an apparent one, for the heavenly book mentioned in this passage is sacred as well (cf. also 17:8; 20:12; and, significantly, 22:7, 9–10, 18–19).

2. Focusing on some further quality of the literature. The phrase "the word of God" (*ho logos tou theou*) centers attention on divine origin and is used of Scripture in Mk. 7:13; Jn. 10:35; Rom. 9:6; Heb. 4:12. This expression or, more frequently, "the word of the LORD," is extremely common in the OT, and the plural also often occurs. It is significant that the GOSPEL as proclaimed first authoritatively by the Lord (Lk. 8:21; 11:28) and by his apostles (Acts 6:7; 11:1; 1 Thess. 2:13; 1 Pet. 1:23) is also called "the word of God." This suggests that it comes into the same category as the OT Scriptures. Also important is the great value set upon "words of the Lord" (i.e., of Jesus) in the NT (Lk. 22:61; cf. Acts 20:35; 1 Cor. 7:10, 12, 25). In 1 Tim. 5:18 Paul apparently quotes as Scripture not only Deut. 25:4 but also Lk. 10:7, whether from this gospel or from the oral tradition of the words of Jesus. Once again, one finds an extension of the concept of the "word of God" beyond the OT into the NT.

Another expression, *ta logia tou theou*, "the oracles/words of God," is usually understood to be a reference to the OT (Acts 7:38; Rom. 3:2; Heb. 5:12; in 1 Pet. 4:11 it may refer to the inspired utterances of the Christian prophet of NT days). Some have maintained that it concerns rather the salvation-history contained in the Bible, but others argue cogently for the traditional view. As used in the classical and Hellenistic literature, Warfield says that "it means, not 'words' barely, simple 'utterances,' but distinctively 'oracular utterances,' divinely authoritative communications, before which men stand in awe and to which they bow in humility: and this high meaning is not merely implicit, but is explicit in the term" (Warfield, *Inspiration*, 403, see also J. W. Doeve in *Studia Paulina: In honorem Johannis de Zwaan septuagenarii* [1953], 111–23).

A medieval scroll (14th cent.) containing parts of the Hebrew Scriptures.

The term for "law," *nomos G3795*, is used in a variety of ways (see LAW [NT]), but when applied to sacred literature it normally designates the PENTATEUCH and so is sometimes called "the law of Moses" (cf. Matt. 12:5; Lk. 2:22) or "the law of the Lord" (Lk. 2:23). There are, however, passages where it clearly means the OT as a whole, for they give quotations from the Psalms and Isaiah as from "the law" (Jn. 10:34; 15:25; 1 Cor. 14:21). The Hebrew equivalent is *tôrâ H9368*, which really means "instruction," and the whole OT is divine instruction for the people of God. Similarly, the expression "the prophets" in the NT usually refers to prophetic literature (Matt. 5:17 et al.; sing. "the prophet" in 2:5 et al.), but it seems probable that Matt. 26:56 and Rom. 16:26 are references to the whole OT and not just to the literature that was prophetic in the strict sense. The entire OT is prophetic, for it is God's speech to human beings through human channels and it points forward to Christ (Lk. 24:27).

3. Composite terms. The Jews employed the phrase "the Law and the Prophets" or "the Law, the Prophets, and the Writings" to designate the whole OT. The Writings (HAGIOGRAPHA) are the other Scriptures which are not sufficiently homogeneous for a single title; this third general term was sometimes omitted, so that the OT was known by its two major types of literature. In the NT there are frequent references to "the Law and the Prophets" (Matt. 5:17; 22:40; Lk. 16:16; Rom. 3:21) or to "Moses and the Prophets" (Lk. 16:29). In one passage the expression used is "the Law of Moses, the Prophets and the Psalms" (Lk. 24:44), the last word pointing to the first and largest of the Writings and, perhaps, the one that spoke most clearly of Christ. Just as we have seen that "the Law" and also "the Prophets" may bear a narrower or a broader sense, so the term for "Writings" (*graphai*, "Scriptures") in the NT usually refers to the whole OT (see esp. Lk. 24:27, where the broader sense is prob. intended, but where there is perhaps an allusive glance in the direction of the narrower).

B. Introductory formulae

1. Stressing the written form. The form *gegraptai* (pf. pass. of *graphō G1211*) may be translated "it is written" or "it stands written"; its use implies the existence of an authoritative written document beyond which there is no appeal. In classical Greek it was used of legal documents, while in the NT it is uniformly employed of OT Scripture. It occurs most frequently in the Synoptic Gospels, Acts, and the Pauline epistles. Sometimes a reference to the place of citation is added (e.g., "it is written in the Law of Moses," 1 Cor. 9:9; "it is written in Isaiah the prophet," Mk. 1:2). The Gospel of John more frequently employs the periphrastic equivalent (ptc. *gegrammenon* plus the verb *eimi*, an expression peculiar to this book, Jn. 2:17 et al.). Schrenk (*TDNT*, 1:745) points to the fact that John used this periphrasis in relation to his own book (20:30) and declares, "Yet there is no less solemn emphasis on the testimony of writing in 1 John" (cf. 1 Jn. 1:4; 2:1; 2:12–14; 5:13). He goes on to refer to the conviction of the revelatory significance of writing in the Apocalypse (Rev. 1:11, 19; 14:13; 22:19). Here then is further evidence pointing in the direction of an extension of the concept of Scripture to include writings of the new covenant.

2. In terms suggestive of a living voice. Scriptural citations are frequently introduced with the expression "[he/it/] says" (*legei* or *phēsi*; in some of the passages other tense forms of the verbs are used and occasionally other verbs). Sometimes the subject is expressed: Scripture (Jn. 7:38, 42; Rom. 4:3; Jas. 4:5), God (Matt. 19:4–5; Acts 4:24–25), the Holy Spirit (Acts 28:25; Heb. 3:7), perhaps even Christ (Heb. 10:5). E. E. Ellis (*Paul's Use of the Old Testament* [1957], 107–13) has drawn attention to the formula "the Lord says" in the NT and especially in Paul (Rom. 12:19; 1 Cor. 14:21; cf. Acts 7:49; Heb. 8:8–12). This formula is of extremely frequent occurrence in the OT prophets, but the NT writers sometimes include it even when it is not present in the OT text. Moreover, formulae like this are employed sometimes of the utterances (Acts 21:11) or writings (Rev. 14:13; 1:8) of NT prophets.

What of passages where no subject is expressed or clearly implied in the context (Rom. 9:15; Eph. 4:8; 5:14; Jas. 4:6)? Some would understand them to mean, "God says," others, "Scripture says," while still others maintain that they sometimes mean, "It is said," with the assumption that the source is not important. Warfield (*Inspiration*, ch. 7) has demonstrated in masterly fashion that this last is not a live option. He says at the conclusion of his survey of the evidence, "We may well be content in the NT as in Philo to translate the phrase wherever it occurs, 'It says'—with the implication that *this* 'It says' is the same as 'Scripture says,' and that this 'Scripture says' is the same as 'God says.' It is this implication that is really the fundamental fact in the case" (p. 348). In line with this conclusion, and despite his general difference of approach from that of Warfield, Alan Richardson (*IDB*, 4:249) points to the inaccuracy of the RSV rendering "it is said" in Eph. 4:8 and 5:14. The latter passage presents difficulties, for the matter quoted cannot be found in so many words in the OT. It may perhaps represent a grouping of passages, of course, but some modern writers have suggested that it is from a primitive Christian hymn. The introductory formula suggests strongly its inspiration and so, if no convincing OT equivalent is to be found, it is best to view it as a NT prophetic utterance.

3. In terms of fulfillment. The verb *fulfill* (usually Gk. *plēroō* G4444) in connection with OT passages occurs widely in the NT but most frequently in Matthew and in John (Matt. 1:22 et al.; Jn. 12:38 et al.). It shows the unity of the biblical REVELATION in terms of prophecy and FULFILLMENT, of type and antitype. See PROPHETS AND PROPHECY; TYPOLOGY. John also saw this same principle in operation in relation to the words of Jesus (Jn. 18:9; cf. 2:22).

C. Summary. The use of the terminology considered above is striking testimony to the belief of the NT writers in the OT as a divinely inspired and authoritative book. This belief can be indicated without the use of such terms, of course, and the book of the Revelation, which contains no quotations with formula, nevertheless shows the most complete dependence upon the OT at every point. It is noteworthy also that the NT writers show some tendency to extend their own technical language to the utterances and writings of inspired persons under the new covenant.

II. The inspiration of Scripture

A. The term. As applied to Scripture, INSPIRATION has been well defined as "a supernatural influence of the Holy Spirit upon divinely chosen men in consequence of which their writings become trustworthy and authoritative" (C. F. H. Henry in *BDT*, 286). The word *theopneustos* G2535, which the KJV renders "given by inspiration of God," is found only once and means "God-breathed," that is, "breathed out by God" (2 Tim. 3:16). The English word *inspiration* tends to be misunderstood sometimes because it seems to suggest breathing into or within rather than breathing out. (The KJV uses it also in Job 32:8, where the Hebrew means simply "breath"; the passage does not address the present subject.)

B. The relation of inspiration to revelation. These are closely related without being identical. REVELATION is concerned with God's disclosure of truth to human beings, while inspiration is its communication in verbal form. The term *inspiration* may be properly applied to the spoken as well as to the written Word, as in the Spirit-given utterances of the OT prophets before these were given written form, but spoken and written communication is alike verbal. For revelation to have permanent form it needs to be communicated in writing, and thus inspiration is its servant. This does not mean that Scripture is simply the record of revelation (although it is this) for it possesses revelation status in its own right, as one sees from NT quotations of OT passages as "the word of God" (e.g., Jn. 10:35; Rom. 3:2). Much modern theology denies the propositional element in revelation and so it is not surprising to find that the return of revelation to a central place in the theological vocabulary has not been followed by a renewal of interest in inspiration. The Bible itself is concerned with both, however.

C. The inspiration of the OT

1. The OT phenomenon of inspiration. Many of the OT channels of revelation exhibit a clear consciousness of their inspiration. Particularly is this true of the line of prophets from Moses onward. In the light of 2 Sam. 23:1-3 it is instructive to note that DAVID is described in the NT as a prophet (Acts 2:30). In general, it would seem that the true prophet was not only an inspired person but also one who was conscious of his inspiration.

The prophets, by their employment of expressions such as "Thus says the LORD" and "The word of the LORD came unto me, saying," show that they were conscious of inspiration in the oral communication of divine truth. Of course, only those prophecies that were later committed to writing have survived, but there can be no doubt that the inspiration of a communication does not depend on its being in oral, as opposed to written, form (Jer. 36). So long as it is preserved unchanged, it matters little how many channels are employed before the Word reaches the recipient. Moses, for example, received the Word of God, but it passed to the people through AARON (Exod. 4:15, 28, 30). Although the end product in this instance was an utterance of Aaron, it lost none of its character as divine Word by this process of mediation. Moses also wrote the words of the Lord (24:3–4, 7). The Book of the Covenant is therefore just as much the Word of the Lord as the two tablets which God wrote on the mount (31:18).

An important quality of the word of the inspired servant of God is its divine and objective character. This does not mean that the Word of God included nothing from the prophet's experience—in the case of men like David, Jeremiah, and Hosea, it is clear that it often did—but that it was never simply their own thought and word. It was always the thought and Word of God. The prophet NATHAN was able to distinguish between his own thought and the Word of God (2 Sam. 7:3–17).

It is especially the divine origin of the inspired word which distinguishes the true from the false prophet, although this is obviously not open to direct testing. The tests of prophecy are such criteria as fulfillment and conformity to the revelation given earlier, especially through Moses (Deut. 13:1–5; 18:15–22; Jer. 23:9–40; Ezek. 12:21—14:11). In an excellent discussion of true and false prophecy, J. A. Motyer (*NBD*, 969–70) shows helpfully that it was not so much the fulfillment of the word of the true prophet but the nonfulfillment of the word of the false which was the test. It is worth noting that although the prophets were normally godly persons and their word was always adapted to the divine purposes of holiness, it is not even their godliness and character which constituted them as true prophets, as the (admittedly unusual) case of BALAAM shows (Num. 22:1—24:25; 31:16; 2 Pet. 2:15–16; Rev. 2:14). What matters is whether the message is the Word of the living God or simply a product of the prophet's own mind (Ezek. 13:2–3) or of an evil spirit (1 Ki. 22:19–20).

This discussion of inspiration in the OT has been concerned chiefly with prophecy because in the prophets inspiration is conscious. Other writers, such as historians and poets, do not disclose such a consciousness explicitly. Inspiration is not, however, to be equated with the declaration of it nor even with the consciousness of it. There is other testimony to the inspiration of other OT writers.

2. Christ's testimony to OT inspiration. The Lord recognized that OT books had human authors (Matt. 15:7, 22:43, 24:15; Mk. 7:10; Jn. 5:46), but he saw these as instruments of the divine Spirit. Jesus asserted that the word came through the prophets (Matt. 21:4–5; Lk. 18:31), and this suggests that they were employed by Another who was the ultimate Author of their word. For Jesus, Scripture is "the word of God" (Jn. 10:35). It is clear from Mk. 7:1–13 (a passage that deserves much more detailed study than can be given to it here) that the Lord rejected the authority of the "tradition of the elders" but that for him what "Moses said" (v. 10) constituted "the word of God" (v. 13). In Mk. 12:35–37 he clinched an argument, already weighty without it, with an affirmation of the inspiration of David when he wrote Ps. 110: "While Jesus was teaching in the temple courts, he asked, 'How is it that the teachers of the law say that the Christ is the son of David? David himself, speaking by the Holy Spirit, declared: 'The Lord said to my Lord: / "Sit at my right hand / until I put your enemies / under your feet."' David himself calls him 'Lord.' How then can he be his son?"

3. The testimony of the NT writers. Wherever we look in the NT, we find exactly the same attitude toward the OT as that manifested by Jesus. Like him, the writers of the NT acknowledged the human authorship of the books. The epistle to the Hebrews, however, seems to avoid reference to human authors wherever possible in order to underline the divine authorship of Scripture (cf. Heb. 1:5–8, 13 with 2:6). This is simply an emphasis upon a fact that is a general characteristic of the NT writers, namely, their unqualified acceptance of the divine origin of OT Scripture. The prophets "spoke in the name of the Lord" (Jas. 5:10).

In the Gospel of Matthew, for example, there is a certain amount of variety in the formulae of quotation employed, but it is clear always that for Matthew the OT writer was an instrument of God, whose word came "through the prophet" (cf. also Acts 1:16; 2:16; 28:25; Rom. 9:25). The Scriptures are "the oracles of God" (Acts 7:28; Rom. 3:2; Heb. 5:12 NRSV). Warfield pointed out the great significance of the use of the word "Scripture" instead of "God" in certain passages (Rom. 9:17; Gal. 3:8, 22; cf. also Jas. 4:5–6). He said, "These acts could be attributed to Scripture only as the result of such a habitual identification in the mind of the writer, of the text of Scripture with God as speaking that it became natural to use the term 'Scripture says' when what was really intended was 'God, as recorded in Scripture said'" (*Inspiration*, 299–300, cf. 145–46).

The importance of this phenomenon is that it discloses a psychological fact of great significance for the estimate of Paul's concept of OT Scripture. A partial parallel from the lips of the Lord may be found in Matt. 19:4–5, where it is clear that for him Scripture and God, as speaking, are to be equated.

D. The inspiration of the NT. The Spirit of God did not cease his work of inspiration with the completion of the OT canon. After a period of silence, a new era of prophecy dawned just prior to, and in witness to, the advent of Christ, as we see especially clearly in Lk. 1–2. Prophesying is mentioned in the passage from Joel to which Peter referred on the Day of PENTECOST (Joel 2:28–29; Acts 2:17–18). Moreover, there are sundry references to prophets in the Acts of the Apostles and elsewhere in the NT (Acts 11:28; 13:1; 15:32; 21:10–11; 1 Cor. 12:28–29; Eph. 4:11 et al.).

Of even greater importance than the prophets, however, were the apostles. The Twelve were specially chosen by the Lord and instructed by him throughout his ministry. To them he gave special promises concerning the work of the Spirit in them as the Spirit of Truth (Jn. 14:16–17, 25–26; 15:26; 16:12–15). He would witness to Christ by declaring to them the things of Christ, by calling to their minds the teaching of their Master, and by showing them things to come. In this way the Spirit would complement and complete the instruction which Jesus had given to them. See APOSTLE.

There is moreover evidence of a *consciousness* of inspiration in the NT apostles, just as there is in the case of the OT prophets. In this connection 1 Jn. 4:1–6 is a passage of interest, as it is concerned with false prophecy. After prescribing a confessional test, John concludes, "They are from the world and therefore speak from the viewpoint of the world, and the world listens to them. We are from God, and whoever knows God listens to us; but whoever is not from God does not listen to us. This is how we recognize the Spirit of truth and the spirit of falsehood." On the assumption of the apostolic authorship of the epistle, the first person plural of the assertion "We are from God" will allude to the apostles and their witness to Christ (cf. 1:1–5). The words "Spirit of truth" (the capital letter is to be preferred to the NRSV's "spirit of truth") are reminiscent of the upper room discourse (Jn. 14–16). Here there is a clear indication of a consciousness of inspiration. Note also the same phenomenon discernible in the following passages: 1 Cor. 2:9–10, 13; 7:40; Eph. 3:5; 1 Tim. 4:1; Rev. 1:1–3, 10–20; 22:18.

Once again, one needs to remember that a writer's failure to refer to his being inspired is no indication that inspiration is lacking, just as the claim to inspiration does not furnish logical proof of it. Paul was conscious that his word was accepted as the Word of God by the Thessalonians through faith (1 Thess. 2:13) and that the Holy Spirit wrought a conviction of its truth in their hearts (1:5). It is important also to remember that the only form in which we have the inspired utterances of God's servants in the NT as well as in the OT period is the written form.

E. The character of biblical inspiration

1. The Spirit as the ultimate Author of all that is rightly called Scripture. The Bible is not merely human literature; all that is rightly called *Scripture* is God-breathed (2 Tim. 3:16). This verse in its context refers primarily to the OT, but its principle is equally applicable to other literature to which one may apply this term. The precise delimitation comes under a study of the CANON of Scripture, but we may note that the claim to inspiration occurs in the NT as well as in the OT, and that Peter regarded the epistles of Paul as Scripture (2 Pet. 3.15–16).

2. All Scripture of full and equal inspiration. The statement of 2 Tim. 3:16 concerns "all Scripture." It is not permissible to translate these words as "every scripture inspired of God" (ASV, cf. NRSV mg.) if this is understood to distinguish Scriptures which are inspired from those which are not. Whether the adjective *pasa* (fem. of *pas* G4246, "all" or "every") is attributive or predicative is a matter of little consequence. It is the *interpretation* of the statement that matters. The NT knows nothing of "Scripture" which is not divinely originated.

This passage also justifies the use of the term *plenary* ("full") in reference to Scripture and the rejection of the concept of degrees of inspiration. Revelation certainly admits of degree, for a disclosure of truth may be small or great; but a book either is God-breathed or it is not. Scripture passages may even differ in their value, but they do not differ in their inspiration, and so must all find a place in the Word of God.

3. The control of the writers by the Spirit. Peter affirms that "prophecy never had its origin in the human will, but prophets, though human, spoke from God as they were carried along by the Holy Spirit" (2 Pet. 1:21 TNIV). Commenting on this, Warfield says, "What is 'borne' [carried] is taken up by the 'bearer' and conveyed by the bearer's power, not its own, to the bearer's goal, not its own" (*Inspiration*, 137). Inspiration is not the mere heightening of the powers of the writers but their control by the divine Spirit.

4. The Spirit's use of the individuality of the writers. Inspiration did not override or suppress the individuality of any particular writer but employed it. The Word of God came into existence through many different human channels, and the evidence of stylistic variation bears testimony to the reality of the human factor. This is true even of the OT prophets where the form in which the word was often received—in a vision or dream—testifies most strongly to the objectivity of it. It is even more evident in writings like the Epistles. Paul's letters, for example, show signs of his own individuality. A great deal of research went into the production of a book like the Gospel of Luke (Lk. 1:1–4). Charles Hodge wrote concerning inspiration from

This 5th-cent. parchment codex, known as the Sinaitic Syriac, is a palimpsest. The upper writing is a work known as *Lives of the Saints*, but the barely visible script underneath preserves the Old Syriac text of the Gospels.

God: "When he ordains praise out of the mouths of babes, they must speak as babes or the whole power and beauty of the tribute will be lost" (*Systematic Theology*, 3 vols. [1871–73], 1:157). When the Reformers used the term *dictation* in relation to Scripture, as they occasionally did, they seem to have employed it simply to lay stress upon the divine origin of Scripture and not to define its invariable method.

5. The "verbal" character of inspiration. Inspiration refers to the verbal communication of truth. While recognizing the Spirit's superintendence of all the processes that lie behind the actual writing (or speech), it is to the end-product that the term *inspired* is properly applied. It is *Scripture* which is God-breathed (2 Tim. 3:16). In the nature of the case, then, inspiration must be verbal, since it is concerned with the communication of the truth in language. This does not mean that it consists of the dictation of words but that the various processes which lie behind it, involving the writer's individuality, environment, training, experience, and other factors, are so manipulated by God that the result is words that are not only those of the human agent, but fully God's. The commonly held notion that the ideas were divinely given but that the writers were left to themselves in the verbal expression of the thought will not fit the biblical evidence. Various passages (e.g., Exod. 4:30; Jer. 1:9; Ezek. 2:7–8; 1 Cor. 2:13; Rev. 22:18–19) center attention on the words as divinely imparted. Such an attempt to drive a wedge between ideas and words faces psychological difficulties also. Moreover, there are passages of Scripture where stress is laid upon the use of one word rather than another (e.g., Matt. 22:43–45; Jn. 10:34–35; Gal. 3:16).

On the other hand, one must not fall into the opposite error of imagining that the words of Scripture have importance apart from the meaning they convey. It is the sense which is all-important, and it is for this reason that the inspired writers of the NT sometimes employed a free rendering of some OT passages when it could bring out more forcibly the point they were making. The matter would be a problem only if the sense of the original passage were violated. This raises the whole question of the use of the OT by the NT writers, which belongs to the subject of interpretation. See QUOTATIONS IN THE NT.

6. Inspiration as a finished work. Inspiration, which is a completed work of the Spirit, is not to be confused with illumination, which is continuous. Between the original inspired MSS and ourselves lie one or two processes. If the original languages are known to the reader, the only process is the transmission of the text. The science of textual criticism of the Bible is a very refined and exact one, and the study of it shows that the text, although not isolated completely from the normal processes of corruption that affect all transmission, has been wonderfully protected so that the message disclosed in Scripture has been available to each successive generation. See TEXT AND MANUSCRIPTS (OT); TEXT AND MANUSCRIPTS (NT). Translators have a duty to reverence the wording of the original and to seek to convey in another language the thought of the Hebrew and Greek. The extensive use of the SEPTUAGINT (a Greek version of the OT) by the NT writers shows that translation is legitimate, and it may be laid down that a translation may be—indeed *must* be—treated as the Word of God insofar as it conveys faithfully the thought of the original.

7. Inspiration and the difficulties of Scripture. The Christian receives God's Word on his own testimony. This does not mean, of course, that the reverent reader of Scripture encounters no problems. Difficulties in Scripture are a spur to seek divine enlightenment and to pursue diligent study. They are not a call to abandon a high doctrine of Scripture. The scientist's conviction of the unity of the universe is not overturned when he encounters problems. Likewise, the Christian's conviction of the unity of Scripture is not surrendered in the face of biblical difficulties. It is sometimes maintained that the doctrine of Scripture should be based on all the phenomena of Scripture, including its difficulties. It is questionable whether this is practicable, for the evaluation and harmonization of all the phenomena is considerably more than a lifetime's work. Moreover, the Bible itself contains clear statements concerning its own inspiration. It is on these that the doctrine of inspiration should be based. The acceptance of Scripture as divinely given on this basis implants the conviction of its unity, and the problems can now be approached, and progressively solved, in the light of this.

III. The authority of Scripture

A. Its relation to inspiration. The inspiration and the AUTHORITY of Scripture are distinguishable but inseparable. Matters of religion are of such great importance that merely human authority is insufficient. It is not the human authors as such who give the Bible its authority, but rather its divine Author. It is because it originates from him that its message is to be received and trusted. Accordingly, inspiration is rightly discussed before authority, and there can be no stable doctrine of biblical authority where there is no stable doctrine of inspiration.

B. The authority of the OT

1. Its recognition within the OT period. An examination of the historical books of the OT discloses the fact that the law was treated as authoritative by those who read it. On the borders of the Promised Land, God directed JOSHUA to it: "Be strong and very courageous. Be careful to obey all the law my servant Moses gave you; do not turn from it to the right or to the left, that you may be successful wherever you go. Do not let this Book of the Law depart from your mouth; meditate on it day and night, so that you may be careful to do everything written in it. Then you will be prosperous and successful" (Josh. 1:7–8; cf. 8:30–35; 22:5; 23:6; 1 Ki. 2:3; 2 Ki. 14:6; 22:8–13).

In 2 Ki. 23:24–25 the wording is particularly significant: "Furthermore, Josiah got rid of the mediums and spiritists, the household gods, the idols and all the other detestable things seen in Judah and Jerusalem. This he did to fulfill the requirements of the law written in the book that Hilkiah the priest had discovered in the temple of the LORD. Neither before nor after Josiah was there a king like him who turned to the LORD as he did—with all his heart and with all his soul and with all his strength, in accordance with all the Law of Moses." There is a close relationship between turning to the Lord and obeying the precepts of the law. (For recognition of the authority of the law in other parts of the OT, see Ps. 119; Dan. 9:10–13; Amos 2:4; Mal. 4:4.)

The law was obviously intended for posterity and not just for the generation to which it was first given, and evidence is not wanting that this is true of the prophetic revelations also (Isa. 30:8; Jer. 30:1–3; 36:1–3; Hab. 2:2–3). Daniel states, "In the first year of Darius son of Xerxes (a Mede by descent), who was made ruler over the Babylonian kingdom—in the first year of his reign, I, Daniel, understood from the Scriptures, according to the word of the LORD given to Jeremiah the prophet, that the desolation of Jerusalem would last seventy years" (Dan. 9:1–2). Daniel's prayer, which immediately follows this, makes it clear that he regarded the Word of God through Jeremiah as completely authoritative. Psalm 89 also shows the psalmist pleading the promises of God given to David (2 Sam. 7) in such a way as to show his acceptance of their divine authority.

2. Its recognition by Christ. Jesus did not quote the rabbis as authoritative, but he was constantly quoting Scripture in this way. He contrasts scribal tradition with the Word of God in the OT (Matt. 15:1–6). His oft-repeated formula, "it is written," being in the perfect tense, might well be translated, "it stands written," for it implies the present relevance and not just the original writing of OT Scripture (e.g., Matt. 11:10; Lk. 22:37; Jn. 6:45). Note should also be taken of the present tense as used by Jesus in Matt. 13:14; Lk. 20:42; and Jn. 5:45. Consider the significance of the words "to you" in Matt. 22:31–32. Addressing the SADDUCEES, Jesus said, "But about the resurrection of the dead—have you not read what God said to you, 'I am the God of Abraham, the God of Isaac, and the God of Jacob'?"

For Jesus, then, the OT was a book that spoke with a living voice, having abiding authority. His teaching in Matt. 5:21–48 is sometimes thought to involve a belittling of the OT in comparison with his own instruction, but this is a misunderstanding of the passage. The strong statements that precede it (5:17–20) show that this could not be his intention. He is actually showing how profound are the implications of the law, disclosing even higher standards than those the law required, and correcting certain wrong inferences from the law. The parenthetical assertion in Jn. 10:35 sums up his attitude to OT Scripture: "and the Scripture cannot be broken." Jesus treated the OT as authoritative even for his own life. The whole point of the temptation narratives (Matt. 4:1–11; Lk. 4:1–13) is that it was the Lord's duty, as true Man, to listen to the voice of God through the OT and not to the voice of Satan.

The Lord assumed the reliability of even small details in the OT. He referred to a number of events the historicity of which is called into question by many today: the marriage of ADAM and EVE (Matt. 19:4–5) and the stories of ABRAHAM (Jn. 8:56), NOAH, and LOT and his wife (Lk. 17:26–32). It may be objected that fictitious stories may be employed to convey spiritual truth. Yet such an argument cannot be consistently applied to the Lord's use of the OT. He was speaking to people who believed in the literal truth of the OT stories. There is no hint that he took them in any other way, and there are some passages where the whole point would be destroyed if they were not historical. It is impossible to defend his language in Matt. 12:41 and Lk. 11:50–51 unless the OT events he refers to are absolutely historical and factual. How can people who are represented as repenting in a fictitious story rise at an actual judgment to condemn actual people? (See J. W. Wenham, *Our Lord's View of the Old Testament* [1953], 12–14.)

3. Its recognition by the NT writers. Jews and Christians were agreed on the authority of the OT Scriptures. Accordingly, a major factor in Christian witness to the Jew in NT days was the demonstration of the OT witness to Christ. This characterized Peter's preaching at Pentecost and all the sermons to Jews in the Acts of the Apostles (e.g., Acts 2:24–36; 17:2–3, 11; 18:28; 28:23). The witness of the prophets was not treated by the apostles as authoritative only for the contemporaries of the prophets; rather, their prophecies in written form were regarded as having continuing validity (Rom. 1:1–2; 16:26; Mk. 1:2; 2 Tim. 3:16; 1 Pet. 2:6; 2 Pet. 1:20). For the NT writers, as for Jesus, the OT has present authority. They, too, use the formula "it is written" extensively, and the use of the present tense in the following passages should be noted: Rom. 4:3; 9:25, 27; Gal. 4:30; Heb. 8:13; 2 Pet. 1:19.

The up-to-date character of the OT also emerges in certain important passages where it is expressly stated that it was written with believers of the NT era in mind and not simply for those of old. For example, Paul, writing about Abraham (Gen. 15:6), has this to say: "The words 'it was credited to him' were written not for him alone, but also for us, to whom God will credit righteousness—for us who believe in him who raised Jesus our Lord from the dead" (Rom. 4:23–24; cf. Acts 7:38; 13:47; Rom. 15:4–5; 1 Cor. 9:9–10; 10:6–11; 2 Cor. 7:1).

C. The authority of the NT

1. The nature of apostleship. It is of vital importance to grasp the fact that the apostles of Christ were appointed by him to a very special office, which was unique and unrepeatable. In retrospect, we can see that one of the major tasks of the apostles was to be the production of the body of the NT literature. J. B. Lightfoot points out that although the word *apostolos* G693 "in the first instance is an adjective signifying 'despatched' or 'sent forth,'" when applied "to a person, it denotes more than *angelos*. The 'Apostle' is not only the messenger, but the delegate of the person who sends him. He is entrusted with a mission, has powers conferred upon him" (*St. Paul's Epistle to the Galatians*, 10th ed. [1890], 92).

It is not completely clear how many persons were looked upon as apostles of Christ, but there can be no debate about the original twelve or Paul, who, like them, was specially appointed by the Lord (1 Cor. 9:1; Gal. 1:1; cf. Acts 1:8, 22). Some consider that the word was still being used in this special way when it was applied to ANDRONICUS and JUNIAS (Rom. 16:7). BARNABAS (Acts 14:14; cf. 13:1) and JAMES the Lord's brother (1 Cor. 15:7; Gal. 2:9) may also be included in the circle of apostles of Christ. There is evidence, however, of a somewhat wider use of the term to denote specially designated messengers who were given a commission by a particular church for a particular purpose (2 Cor. 8:23; Phil. 2:25). These are to be distinguished from those who were apostles of Christ.

The Lord evidently regarded the selection of the original apostolic band as a matter of great moment, for he prepared for it by an extended time of prayer (Mk. 3:13–19; Lk. 6:12–16). Matthew 10:1—11:1 gives the terms of their commission during the period of his earthly ministry. Jesus concentrated on these men, giving far more time to their instruction than to the instruction of others. Whether they were right in appointing MATTHIAS after the defection and death of JUDAS ISCARIOT has been the subject of some debate, but in any case they realized that it was the divine choice which mattered supremely (Acts 1:24–35).

The apostle Paul often associated one or more Christians with him in the writing of an epistle, but it is noteworthy that for such a person he never used the term *apostle* (1 Cor. 1:1; 2 Cor. 1:1; Col. 1:1; 1 Thess. 1:1). The words, "As apostles of Christ we could have been a burden to you" (1 Thess. 2:6), are probably not an exception to this but simply the literary employment of "we" in a singular sense (cf. 3:1).

2. The nature of apostolic tradition. The term TRADITION means "that which is handed over," and the

An 18th-cent. Ethiopic MS of the Bible.

Jews possessed a large vocabulary of terms connected with tradition. They spoke of receiving it, holding it, keeping it, standing in it, and handing it over to another. They used it of the oral traditions of earlier rabbis that were handed over to their followers. Jesus was opposed to these rabbinic traditions when they were given the same reverence as the Word of God (Mk. 7:1–13; cf. Gal. 1:14). The NT writers took over this vocabulary and applied it to the true traditions, the deposit of apostolic testimony (see, e.g., the phraseology of Lk. 1:2; Acts 2:42; Rom. 6:17; 1 Cor. 11:2, 23; 15:1–5; Gal. 1:9, 12; Phil. 4:9; 1 Thess. 2:13; 4:1; 2 Thess. 2:15; 3:6; Jude 3). What is it that makes this tradition valid and authoritative when that of the Jews was not? It is the fact that it was the deposit of teaching which was given to the apostles by Jesus himself, both before and after the resurrection (Acts 1:1–2). It was "received from the Lord" (1 Cor. 11:23) and bore the stamp of his own supreme authority upon it.

The apostles were completely at one as transmitters of authoritative teaching from Jesus himself (1 Cor. 15:9–11). Does Gal. 2:11–14 constitute an exception? It should be noted that this passage does not refer to Peter's teaching but to an event in his life in which, as Paul indicates, he acted against his own convictions (not just against Paul's!) and so presumably against what he would have taught others. The veracity of his teaching is not in question at all. The preceding passage (2:1–10) shows that Paul and the earlier apostles agreed completely on matters of doctrine.

Paul set his teaching about the LORD'S SUPPER, which, because of his apostleship, has the authority of the Lord Jesus behind it, against the unruly practice of the Corinthians, which was without authority. In the Greek of 1 Cor. 11:23, the first "I" is emphatic, and will signify, "I as an apostle." Of course, the apostles not only transmitted tradition from the Lord, but, because they were inspired by the Spirit as the Spirit of truth and the Spirit of Christ, they also gave judgments on matters on which the tradition was silent. On certain matters concerning marriage, Paul found nothing in the traditions of the teaching of Jesus, but he gave his judgment as an inspired apostle (7:25, 40 [where there is a touch of irony]; cf. 14:37).

It is this distinction between dominical tradition and Spirit-inspired judgment which lies behind the distinctions Paul is making in 1 Cor. 7:10, 12, 25. In v. 6 the KJV reads, "But I speak this by permission, and not of commandment," a rendering that has sometimes occasioned difficulty. Modern versions remove the ambiguity: "I say this as a concession, not as a command." Not only command but even permission needs to be authoritatively declared, and Paul does this in his apostolic capacity. In this chapter, then, one may see Paul transmitting tradition and giving judgments, but doing both as an apostle, specially commissioned by Christ and specially endowed by the Spirit for this purpose.

3. Apostolicity and the authority of the NT. Paul refers to the church as "built on the foundation of the apostles and prophets, with Christ Jesus as the chief cornerstone" (Eph. 2:20). An examination of the epistle to the Ephesians makes it seem highly probable that the prophets referred to are NT rather than OT prophets, and also that they are described as the foundation of the church because of the foundational character of their teaching (cf. 3:4–5; 4:11). The converts of the day of Pentecost are said to have "devoted themselves to the apostles' teaching" (Acts 2:42), which was, of course, completely Christ-centered and Christ-dominated. The NT recognizes the possible existence of false prophets, and so it is significant that apostolic truth is made the test of all that claims to be prophetic and emanating from the Spirit of God. "If anybody thinks he is a prophet or spiritually gifted, let him acknowledge that what I am writing to you is the Lord's command. If he ignores this, he himself will be ignored" (1 Cor. 14:37–38; cf. 1 Jn. 4:1–6). Jude, confronted by false teachers, exhorted his readers "to contend for the faith that was once for all entrusted to the saints," to "remember what the apostles of our Lord Jesus Christ foretold," and to build themselves up on the "most holy faith" that had been brought to them (Jude 3, 17, 20; note also the significance of 1 Thess. 5:19–22 and 2 Thess. 3:6, 11–14).

There is no suggestion in the NT that one is to look to successors of the apostles for authoritative teaching. The apostolic office would seem, in a personal sense, to have been a temporary one, although it is a permanent gift of Christ to the church because of the inscripturation of the apostolic testimony in the writings of the NT. It is only through the NT that their teaching is now available so that sinners may believe on him through their word (Jn. 17:8, 14, 20) and continue to devote themselves to their teaching. The common idea that the apostles did not realize that they were writing inspired and authoritative literature is not true to the facts, for they placed considerable emphasis upon the authority of their written words (1 Cor. 14:37; 1 Thess. 5:27; 2 Thess. 3:14; Rev. 22:18–19).

The CANON OF THE NT lies outside the scope of this article, but it should be noted that, according to the NT itself, there were other inspired persons in NT days besides the apostles, that is, the prophets. The test of prophetic utterance was apostolic truth. The harmony between the nonapostolic writings of the NT and those that are clearly apostolic can be shown. The NT as a whole presents a marvelous unity of teaching, which is the perfect complement to the earlier inspired books collected together in the OT.

IV. The use of Scripture

A. The practical ends for which Scripture was given. It is highly significant that one of the most important passages exhibiting the biblical doctrine of inspiration links this concept most intimately with the practical use of Scripture: "... from infancy you have known the holy Scriptures, which are able to make you wise for salvation through faith in Christ Jesus. All Scripture is God-breathed and is useful for teaching, rebuking, correcting and training in righteousness, so that the man of God may be thoroughly equipped for every good work" (2 Tim. 3:15–17). The function of Scripture is instructional ("able to make you wise," "useful for teaching") and its end salvation and sanctified service. The fourfold profit indicated shows Scripture's use to be both theological and ethical, for it instructs the mind in divine truth and directs the reader in the right way; and both positive and negative, for "rebuking" and "correcting" imply that errors in thought and in life are attacked by it.

The instructional function of Scripture is never merely intellectual but also practical. Its aim is to produce not merely knowledge but also wisdom and personal application. "The secret things belong to the LORD our God, but the things revealed belong to us and to our children for ever, that we may follow all the words of this law" (Deut. 29:29; cf. 32:46–47; Josh. 1:7–8; Jas. 1:25–27; Rev. 1:3).

B. Scripture and spiritual illumination. It is important to distinguish inspiration from illumination and to notice the relationship each sustains to the other. This is indicated clearly in 1 Cor. 2:1–16. Speaking of "the testimony about God" that Paul, as an apostle, had proclaimed to the Corinthians (v. 1), he asserts that it was divinely revealed, and that this revelation was communicated by the human channels of inspiration to those enabled to receive it. "This is what we speak, not in words taught us by human wisdom but in words taught by the Spirit, expressing spiritual truths in spiritual words. The man without the Spirit does not accept the things that come from the Spirit of God, for they are foolishness to him, and he cannot understand them, because they are spiritually discerned" (vv. 13–14). Spiritual truths are a foreign realm to those who are unregenerate, and it is the Word of God which the Spirit uses to bring one to the birth (Jas. 1:18; 1 Pet. 1:23–25).

REGENERATION is described in various ways in the NT, but a significant analogy in this connection is the shining of a great light, the dawn of a new day (2 Cor. 4:6; Eph. 5:14). Through the indwelling of the Spirit the norm for the Christian is a progressive growth of enlightenment and spiritual understanding (Eph. 1:17–19; cf. Ps. 119:18,

97–104, 144; Prov. 4:18). Strictly speaking, it is not so much the illumination of the Word itself which the Spirit accomplishes (this is the neoorthodox concept of the matter) as the illumination of the human heart so that it understands the Word. In other words, the Scriptures are clear in themselves (the technical term is the "perspicuity of Scripture") but each person's heart, darkened by sin, needs a supernatural work of the Spirit before it is capable of receiving and understanding the truth of God.

C. The interpretation of Scripture

1. The importance of interpretation. If the Bible is an inspired and authoritative revelation of God, then it is of great importance that it be properly understood. See INTERPRETATION. It is possible for a person to twist the Scriptures to his own destruction (2 Pet. 3:16; cf. 2 Cor. 4:2; 1 Tim. 1:3–11). When Satan was tempting the Lord, he applied Scripture in a way that violated the context (Matt. 4:6). Jesus and the Pharisees were united on the inspiration and authority of the OT, but at variance frequently concerning its interpretation. Matthew, in particular, often showed him rebuking the Jewish leaders for their failure to understand the significance of certain OT passages (9:13; 12:3–8; 21:42; 22:23–32).

2. The divine interpreter. During the Lord's ministry, the disciples were recipients of his teaching, much of which involved interpretation of the OT, and he continued to instruct them in this way after the resurrection (Lk. 24:25–27, 32, 44–47). His interpretation carried the authority of his own divine person. He promised that the Holy Spirit would continue to instruct the disciples in divine truth (Jn. 16:12–15). The Christian is given a spiritual "instinct" for truth through the Spirit's indwelling: "I am writing these things to you about those who are trying to lead you astray. As for you, the anointing you received from him remains in you, and you do not need anyone to teach you. But as his anointing teaches you about all things and as that anointing is real, not counterfeit—just as it has taught you, remain in him" (1 Jn. 2:26–27; cf. 2:20–21). The Christian is assured that he need not be led away by false teaching. False teaching is also referred to in 2 Pet. 1:20–21: "Above all, you must understand that no prophecy of Scripture came about by the prophet's own interpretation of things. For prophecy never had its origin in the human will, but prophets spoke from God as they were carried along by the Holy Spirit" (TNIV). If the translation "the prophet's own interpretation" is correct, the statement underlines the fact that the prophecy is of divine and not of human origin. On the other hand, the phrase may refer to the reader (the Gk. simply says, "own interpretation," and Peter's readers have been told to pay attention to the prophetic word, v. 19), and so it may imply that because the prophecy was given by the Spirit it can be interpreted only by the Spirit. The "right of private judgment" is not license to twist the Scriptures, nor to engage in wild and fanciful exegesis, but liberty to study and to follow the Spirit's own principles of interpretation as these are exposed to view in Scripture itself.

3. The purpose of Scripture. The interpretation of any book must, of course, be related to its purpose, and the purpose of Scripture is frankly practical. It is given so that the people of God may be perfected in the life of godliness. The classic evangelical position is that when the Bible touches matters of history, science, etc., it does so in conformity to truth. It does so, of course, in popular, nontechnical language. There is a considerable amount of history in the Bible, but matters of science are usually touched upon only incidentally. It is right to maintain the inerrancy of Scripture in such matters, for it is "God-breathed" and the product of the Spirit of truth, but it is wrong to lose sight of the fact that the great purpose of the Bible is to teach sinners the things of God. All else is incidental to, and ministers to, this end.

4. Scripture as self-interpreting. The multiple authorship of Scripture shows itself in great variety of style, vocabulary, and emphasis. Beneath this variety is a basic unity of doctrine. Modern studies of the KERYGMA ("the thing proclaimed") in the NT have tended to underline the oneness of the preachers and writers of the early church in the gospel they declare in their preaching and assume in their writing. Similar studies of the OT can show that it finds its unity in the revelation of an all-sovereign righteous God who has redeemed his people Israel from Egypt and brought them into the land of promise. Moreover, the oneness of the two Testaments is the constant presupposition of the writers of the NT. This unity is, of course, the product of the inspiring work of the Holy Spirit, the ultimate Author of Scripture.

Consequently, a true interpretation of Scripture will demonstrate the harmony of the Bible with itself, not in any artificial or strained manner, but by seeking to do justice both to the natural sense of each passage and the unity of the whole. This does not mean that the interpreter comes to the text with a ready-made system of dogmatics, but it does mean that he keeps always in mind the fact that behind all the human authors is the divine Spirit, for this is what the Bible itself claims. It is important to remember also that the Bible contains many examples of interpretation, for the NT writers themselves interpret the OT, and the principles they apply have the authority of their inspiration behind them. Here is the Holy Spirit's own guide in the understanding of Holy Writ.

5. The grammatico-historical principle. The Bible is wholly divine in its origin, for its inspiration is plenary. It is also completely human in its language and its modes of expression, for in no case did the inspiring Spirit bypass human instrumentation in communicating truth. For this reason, Scripture is to be viewed as literature in which the ordinary laws of language and human expression are seen. There must be patient attention to words, phrases, and sentences, and every particular statement is to be understood in relation to its context. The Bible contains examples of many generally recognized literary devices such as omission (Acts 2:40), compression (contrast Mk. 1:29–31 with 1:32–34), parenthesis (Eph. 4:9–10), and ellipsis (e.g., in Heb. 8:7 the word "covenant" does not occur in the Greek but can be inferred from the context).

A great many figures of speech occur. Some of the more important are the following: irony (1 Ki. 18:27); litotes (Acts 12:18); hyperbole (2 Sam. 1:23); synecdoche (Lk. 24:44, where "Psalms" prob. stands for "the Writings," since the Psalter was the first book of this third division of the Hebrew canon). Simile and metaphor occur times without number. It should also be remembered that the Bible contains a variety of literary forms, such as prose, poetry, parable, allegory, etc., and the characteristics of each needed to have been studied by the writer beforehand. The historical context is also important, and the Bible reader should always be concerned to discover what a passage of Scripture would have meant to its original readers in their particular situation and in terms of their own background. This means that a knowledge of the history of the biblical period and the geography of the biblical area and the customs of the Hebrews and other peoples referred to in the Bible is of considerable value.

6. The theological principle. The grammatico-historical approach is not the only level at which the interpreter does his work. We need to remember the unity of Scripture and so to understand any particular passage in the light of the whole of Scripture. This means that we seek to understand not only the human author in his context (the particular book in which the passage occurs) but also the divine Author (the Bible as a whole). For example, one needs to remember that there is a progress of doctrine in Scripture so that truth is more and more unfolded (without the necessity for "unlearning" anything previously revealed) and that Christ is the culmination and climax of this divinely controlled process (Heb. 1:1–2). Christ is not only the goal of the biblical revelation, but also its great theme throughout (Lk. 24:27; Jn. 5:45–47; Rom. 3:21–26; 1 Pet. 1:10–12 et al.).

The Christological character of Scripture emerges in a number of ways. Christ was predicted in the OT (Matt. 2:5–6; Rom. 9:33 et al.). He is also typified; that is, a correspondence exists between some OT event, person, or institution and Christ, so that the OT element is a divinely intended anticipation, more or less partial or imperfect, of the Person or work of Christ. Great caution must be exercised in the realm of TYPOLOGY, and the clear teaching of the NT is the only safe guide to the typological elements in the OT. The NT writers describe Christ as the last Adam (1 Cor. 15:45), our paschal lamb (5:7), and our great high priest (Heb. 4:14); such descriptions are based upon this typological principle. The NT writers appear also to refer occasionally to a real presence of Christ in the OT story (1 Cor. 10:4), although the attempt of A. T. Hanson (*Jesus Christ in the Old Testament* [1965]) to show that this idea occurs in the NT with very great frequency would appear to take the evidence further than is warranted.

Many evangelical interpreters stress the presence of different DISPENSATIONS (administrative periods involving somewhat different methods of the divine dealing with human beings), while others emphasize the importance of the COVENANT concept in Scripture as disclosing a unity in all the stages of God's redemptive activity. Each of these two schools tends to be critical of the other, but it is worth noting that the most important of their principles of biblical interpretation is identical, for they both make the important assumption that the Bible discloses "unity in diversity." The evangelical understanding of the interpretation of Scripture may be summed up in that phrase, for it is simply another way of saying that the Bible is fully human and yet fully divine in the thought it conveys. Evangelical interpreters also agree that no alien philosophical principles (such as the existentialism employed by the school of Bultmann) should constitute presuppositions of interpretation, for all human philosophy must itself come under the judgment of God's Word written.

(In addition to the titles mentioned in the body of this article, see the bibliographic information under BIBLE; INSPIRATION; INTERPRETATION; REVELATION. For a historical treatment of scriptural authority from various perspectives, see *ABD*, 5:1017–56.) G. W. GROGAN

scroll. Sheets of PAPYRUS, LEATHER, or PARCHMENT joined together in long rolls, usually 10–12 in. wide and up to 35 ft. long, and used for various kinds of documents in ancient times. Prior to the invention of the CODEX, BOOKS were commonly produced in the form of scrolls. The material could be rolled from left to right between two wooden rollers, with part of the roller projecting as a handle. Rarely were both sides written on (but see Ezek. 2:10; Rev. 5:1). The writing was in short vertical columns a few inches wide, side by side, separated by a narrow space. The scroll was read by uncovering one column, then rolling it up on the other roller as the reading continued.

The use of the standard-length papyrus scrolls necessitated the division of the Hebrew PENTATEUCH into five books. One scroll was sufficient for a book the length of Isaiah. The Egyptians used some scrolls of enormous lengths, such as the Papyrus Harris (133 ft. long by 17 in. wide) and a Book of the Dead (123 ft. long by 19 in. wide). The more convenient book form (codex) was popularized by the early Christians, though its origins are unclear. There is little evidence of its use by the Jews prior to the 3rd cent. A.D. Most of the DEAD SEA SCROLLS were of leather, and Talmudic law required that copies of the Torah intended for public reading be written on scrolls made of leather of clean animals, for papyrus was a great deal more perishable than leather. Scrolls were often stored in pottery jars, such as those found in the caves of QUMRAN.

The most familiar reference to a scroll is found in Jer. 36, where BARUCH wrote down at JEREMIAH's dictation all that God had spoken to the prophet over a twenty-three year period. In this passage, the LXX takes it for granted that the scroll was made of papyrus, for it renders Hebrew *mĕgillâ* H4479 with *chartion* ("papyrus sheet"). It was surely papyrus and not leather that JEHOIAKIM cut in strips and burned, for the odor of burning leather would have been unbearable (Jer. 36:22–23). In EZEKIEL's inaugural vision, he was ordered to eat the scroll on which God's words had been written (Ezek. 2:9—3:3; cf. Rev. 10:8–10 [Gk. *biblion* G1046 and *biblaridion* G1044]). There was a flying scroll in ZECHARIAH's

This Hebrew scroll of the book of Isaiah dates to c. A.D. 1350.

vision (Zech. 5:1–2). DAVID refers to a scroll in a statement that the NT interprets as messianic (Ps. 40:7, cited in Heb. 10:7 [Gk. *kephalis* G1046 plus *bibliou*]). Most of the NT references to books have a roll in view (cf. esp. Lk. 4:17, 20). See also TEXT AND MANUSCRIPTS (OT); TEXT AND MANUSCRIPTS (NT).
F. B. HUEY, JR.

Scrolls, Dead Sea. See DEAD SEA SCROLLS.

sculptured stones. See QUARRY.

scurvy. See DISEASE.

Scythian sith´ee-uhn (Σκύθης G5033). A name designating primarily a nomadic people that inhabited the Caucasus, E and NE of the Black Sea. The term came to be applied more generally to horse-riders who raised livestock in that region and farther N and who were viewed as uncivilized (Col. 3:11).

The Scythians were one of several Indo-Iranian groups that appeared in the ANE around the 8th cent. B.C. First came the CIMMERIANS. When the Scythians then appeared, they were opposed both by the Cimmerians and by the Assyrian King ESARHADDON. The Cimmerians eventually moved farther to the W into ASIA MINOR. Eventually the Scythians allied themselves with the Assyrians, and the Medes sided with Babylonia (see ASSYRIA AND BABYLONIA; MEDIA). It is not clear whether the Scythians attempted to help the Assyrians in their hour of final collapse (the fall of NINEVEH in 612 B.C.). It is clear, however, that a large group of them launched an expedition down the coast of PHOENICIA and PALESTINE and were responsible for the destruction of ASHKELON and ASHDOD before Pharaoh Psammetichus (663–609) bought them off with a bribe. Eventually they were defeated and destroyed by the Medes, who expelled the remnants of them to the N.

Many identify the Scythians with the name ASHKENAZ (*ʾaškĕnaz* H867, prob. a corruption of earlier *Ashkuzai* as found in Akk. inscriptions), who in Gen. 10:3 and 1 Chr. 1:6 is said to be one of the sons of GOMER (Cimmerians), along with RIPHATH and TOGARMAH. Gomer in turn was one of the sons of JAPHETH. In Jer. 51:27, in a prophecy against Babylon, God threatened to raise up against her the kingdoms of ARARAT (Urartu), MINNI (Manneans), and Ashkenaz (Scythians). The biblical writers viewed the Scythians as a savage and cruel people, and HERODOTUS devotes considerable attention to their history and culture (*Hist.* 4.1–12). The memory of them persisted in the Holy Land in the popular Greek name of the city of BETH SHAN, *Skythōn polis* (SCYTHOPOLIS), "city of the Scythians."

(See further T. T. Rice, *The Scythians* [1957]; E. Yamauchi, *Foes from the Northern Frontier: Invading Hordes from the Russian Steppes* [1982], ch. 4; L. Galanina and N. Grach, *Scythian Art: The Legacy of the Scythian World, Mid-7th to 3rd century B.C.* [1987]; R. Rolle, *The World of the Scythians* [1989]; V. Schiltz, *Les Scythes et les nomades des steppes* [1994]; D. Braund, ed., *Scythians and Greeks: Cultural Interactions in Scythia, Athens and the Early Roman Empire (Sixth Century BC - First Century AD)* [2005].)
H. A. HOFFNER, JR.

Scythopolis sith-op´uh-lis (Σκυθόπολις [Jos. *War* 1.3.7 §65 et al.], from Σκυθῶν πόλις, "city of the Scythians" [Polybius, *Hist.* 5.70.4; Jdg. 1:27 LXX; Jdt. 3:10; 1 Macc. 12:29], gentilic Σκυθοπολίτης [1 Macc. 12:30]). The Greek name given to biblical BETH SHAN. HOLOFERNES is said to have camped between GEBA and Scythopolis for a month (Jdt. 3:10). During Maccabean times, the Jews living there testified to the goodwill of its Gentile inhabitants (2 Macc. 12:29–30). At the time of Christ it was one of the cities of the DECAPOLIS. The origin of the name is uncertain: some think it may recall the SCYTHIAN invasions of the late 7th cent. B.C., while others attribute it to the presence of Scythian forces in Beth Shan in Hellenistic times.
A. BOWLING

sea. In the Hebrew Bible, the term for "sea," *yām* H3542 (Aram. *yam* H10322 only in Dan. 7:2–3), is used by extension in the sense WEST, for that was the direction in which the GREAT SEA (i.e., the Mediterranean) lay to an observer in PALESTINE. The NT writers frequently use the common Greek term *thalassa* G2498, with *pelagos* G4269 ("high sea, open sea") occurring once in reference to the Mediterranean (Acts 27:5).

Four "seas" form the background to biblical events, and each appears in the record under a variety of names. (1) The RED SEA, often referred to as "the sea" (Exod. 14:2 et al.; cf. "Egyptian Sea" in Isa. 11:15). This was the obstacle which the Israelites had to overcome on their march out of Egypt, and once they were safely across and had watched its waters close over the pursuing Egyptians, they never returned to it. It is mentioned also in 1 Ki. 9:26, which records that SOLOMON built a fleet and a base on the Gulf of AQABAH for trading purposes.

(2) The Mediterranean. This body is first mentioned in Exod. 23:31 as "the Sea of the Philistines," since its coastlands were held, then and for long afterward, by this people group. In Num. 34:6–7, it is called the Great Sea, and this is its designation all through the topographic descriptions concerned with Israel's settlement in the land (Josh. 1:4 et al.; Ezek. 47:10 et al.). In Joel 2:20 and Zech. 14:8 it is called the "western" sea (lit., "at the back"), contrasted with the "eastern" sea (lit., "former"), that is, the Dead Sea on the other flank of the mountains of Judea. Indeed, dissimilar as these two bodies of water might appear to be, the OT writers seem to have thought of Israel as somehow hemmed in between them. At times it is simply called "the sea" (Num. 13:29; Josh. 16:8; Jon. 1:4; cf. Acts 10:6 et al.).

(3) The DEAD SEA. This appears first as the "Salt Sea" (Num. 34:12 et al.), then as "the sea of the Arabah" (Deut. 3:17; KJV, "the sea of the plain"), and three times as "the eastern sea" (Ezek. 47:18; Joel 2:20; Zech. 14:8; see previous paragraph). As with the Sea of Galilee (discussed below), the name "sea" is here given to what is in reality only a lake (cf. also CASPIAN SEA); unlike that body of water, however, the Dead Sea has no outlet—its level is maintained by a very high rate of evaporation from its surface. This same phenomenon is responsible for its extremely salty waters, and it is contrasted frequently with the Mediterranean for the fact that no fish can live in it. One of the visions of the prophets Ezekiel and Zechariah was that its waters would one day become fresh enough to support life; hence the picture of fishermen spreading their nets at EN GEDI and neighboring places (Ezek. 47:10).

(4) The Sea of Galilee (see GALILEE, SEA OF). This appears in the OT as the Sea of KINNERETH (Num. 34:11 et al.), and in the NT occasionally as the Sea of TIBERIAS (after the town of that name built on its shore by HEROD Antipas), or the Lake of GENNESARET (Lk. 5:1; this name is thought by some to be derived from Kinnereth). "Sea of Galilee" is, however, its usual name in the NT.

In the OT there are really only three naval episodes, the first when HIRAM, king of TYRE, floated rafts of timber along the Mediterranean coast to supply Solomon with materials for the temple (1 Ki. 5:9), the second when Solomon built his Red Sea fleet (9:26–28), and the third when JONAH fled from the Lord (Jon. 1). The Israelites seem to have had little contact with the sea and no maritime tradition; with the Phoenicians as their near neighbors they would, in any case, probably have been outclassed.

This lack of maritime interest may have been due, at least in part, to geographical reasons. S of PHOENICIA, the coastline of Palestine offers no good

The "seas" of the Bible.

natural harbors and only a few unimportant ones; the straight, dune-fringed coast provides no shelter (cf. G. Adam Smith, *The Historical Geography of the Holy Land*, 25th ed. [1931], ch. 7). On the other hand, D. Baly (*Geographical Companion to the Bible* [1966], 74) points out that a more valid explanation of Israel's disinterest in the sea may be that they so seldom occupied the coastline politically. Without assured access to the sea along the Philistine coast, they had little opportunity to become seafarers. In support of this suggestion is the fact that the only two national episodes linking the nation with the sea (noted above) occurred during the reign of Solomon, when the Philistines had been suppressed and Israel's power was at its height.

The sea is a source of much symbolic imagery (cf. *DDD*, 737–42). Some of the references are positive: "If only you had paid attention to my commands, / your peace would have been like a river, / your righteousness like the waves of the sea" (Isa. 48:18). On the whole, however, the Bible views the sea as a hostile and dangerous element (e.g., Job 26:12; Ps. 89:9). It is a part of the anticipated glories of the new heaven and earth that the sea has been eliminated (Rev. 21:1; cf. 12:18—13:1). See DEEP (THE).   J. H. PATERSON

sea, bronze. See SEA, MOLTEN.

Sea, Great. See GREAT SEA.

sea, molten. This expression is used by the KJV and other versions to render the Hebrew phrase *hayyām mûṣāq*, which occurs in only one context (1 Ki. 7:23=2 Chr. 4:2). The second word in the phrase comes from a verb that means "to pour" and is used in a more technical sense of metal that was melted and poured into a mold for casting. Thus the NIV renders, "the Sea of cast metal," which elsewhere is called "the bronze Sea" (*yām hannĕḥōšet*, 1 Chr. 18:8 and 2 Ki. 25:13 [= Jer. 52:17]). The reference is to a large receptacle for water, cast from molten BRONZE, which stood in the court of Solomon's TEMPLE.

SOLOMON commissioned Huram (see HIRAM #2) of TYRE, a skilled worker of bronze, to make the various castings for the temple. The sea was made from metal which DAVID had captured from ZOBAH (1 Chr. 18:8), and was in turn broken up and carried off by the Babylonians (2 Ki. 25:13). It is described as round, having a diameter of 10 cubits (c. 15 ft.) at the brim, a circumference of 30 cubits (c. 45 ft.), and a height of 5 cubits (c. 7.5 ft.; 1 Ki. 7:23–26). The brim was decorated with castings of knobs or GOURDS placed in two rows around the circumference of the lip. It was mounted on a base consisting of twelve oxen, also cast from bronze, three facing toward each of the four cardinal points of the compass. The metal was cast a handbreadth in thickness, and the lip was curved over like the flower of a lily.

The sea was positioned "at the southeast corner of the temple" (1 Ki. 7:39). This suggests that it was beside the altar; in any case it was not in a direct line between the altar and the temple door. The reason for this apparent variation from the TABERNACLE layout is not clear. Nor is it clear why the extra ten basins were provided if the sea had the same function as the tabernacle laver. The identical function of both, namely for the priests' washings, can be seen from a comparison of Exod. 30:17–21 with 2 Chr. 4:6.

There has been no lack of modern explanations of the significance of the bronze Sea in terms of ancient mythology. The identification of the bulls with the twelve signs of the zodiac is almost certainly anachronistic, but they have been favored also as symbols of fertility and hence linked with the Babylonian *Apsu*, the water of life and fertility. Such attempts to link Hebrew concepts with Babylonian origins often ignore the distinctive meanings conveyed in the revealed religion of Israel. The fact that there was a similar sea in the temple at Babylon which was linked to the myth of Apsu says nothing about the significance of the sea in Solomon's temple, for Israel had no myth of Apsu, but on the contrary had a firm conviction of the historical basis of its faith.

The volume and shape of the sea are problematical because of the lack of specifications and because of uncertainty over the measurement of baths and cubits (see WEIGHTS AND MEASURES). The shape described seems most naturally to fit a hemisphere, except that 1 Ki. 7:26 describes a lip that could alter the ratio of volume to circumference. Other suggestions of the shape are that it was cylindrical or that it bulged with a diameter considerably larger than the 10 cubits at the brim. A further difficulty arises from the discrepancy between the volumes recorded in 1 Ki. 7:26 (2,000 baths) and in 2 Chr. 4:5 (3,000 baths). Some suggest that the Chronicler, writing after the destruction of the temple, may have misunderstood his sources with regard to the shape, and so have applied a different formula for volume. Others argue that he may have had a different standard of measurement for cubit or bath, or that the text may have been corrupted in the course of transmission.   G. GOLDSWORTHY

sea cow. An aquatic herbivorous mammal also known as *dugong*. The term is used by the NIV to render Hebrew *taḥaš* H9391, which is of uncertain meaning (TNIV, "durable leather"). In almost all of its occurrences (the exceptions are Num. 4:25; Ezek. 16:10 [in the latter, where the reference is to sandals, the NIV translates "leather"]), this Hebrew noun occurs in combination with *ʿôr* H6425, "skin," and the phrase designates a material used for covering the TABERNACLE and some of its furnishings (Exod. 25:5; 26:14 et al.; Num. 4:8–14). Translations of the phrase include "badgers' skin" (KJV), "goatskin" (RSV), "dolphin skin" (NJPS), and simply "fine leather" (NRSV, prob. on the basis of a similar-sounding Egyptian verb meaning "to stretch leather"; cf. *HALOT*, 4:1720–21).

In determining the meaning of the term, the following facts are relevant: (1) It is generally agreed that these instructions were given near the mouth of the Gulf of AQABAH, which is desert. (2) The skins were of large size. The net area of the larger cover was approximately 13 by 44 ft., or 572 sq. ft.; here the plural "skins" is used, but the singular occurs consistently in connection with the furnishings (Num. 4:6–14), such as the ARK OF THE COVENANT (4 x 2 x 0.5 ft.). Few wild animals easily obtainable in the desert would provide big enough skins. (3) The material was both valuable and strong; it is associated with embroidered cloth and fine linen, but was also used as leather for sandals, not only as ornament (Ezek. 16:10).

The third point above makes goatskin most unlikely, while no suitable desert mammal can be suggested, so the most probable solution is a marine species. Some authorities have proposed the seal, but the nearest is the monk seal of the Mediterranean. Several dolphins live in the RED SEA, and it is possible that the Hebrew term is related to the Arabic word for "porpoise," *duḫas*; however, their skin is unsuitable for making into leather, and they are usually caught only by chance. More likely is the dugong or sea cow, the only truly marine species of the order *Sirenia* alive today. It was once plentiful in the Gulf of Aqabah, and until early in the 19th cent. its skin was the standard material for making sandals in the E Sinai peninsula. An adult dugong is 10 ft. long and one skin would easily cover the ark. For the larger cover perhaps between twenty and thirty skins would be needed.

The dugong is entirely vegetarian, eating brown seaweeds, grasses, etc. The forelimbs have become paddles and the hind limbs have disappeared, so it is quite unable to leave the water. Dugongs are not truly sociable but go about in groups of up to six. Once found in warm coastal waters from the Red Sea to Australia, they are now much reduced in numbers because they have been hunted for food; in some areas they are in danger of extinction. (See F. S. Bodenheimer, *Animals and Man in Bible Lands*, 2 vols. [1960–72], 1:52; *FFB*, 22–23.)

G. S. CANSDALE

sea gull. See GULL.

seah *seeʾuh*. See WEIGHTS AND MEASURES III.B.5.

seal. A device, usually in the form of a signet RING or cylinder engraved with the owner's name or with some design, used to secure goods, show ownership, attest documents, or impress an early form of trademark.

    I. Terminology
    II. Types
        A. Stamp seals
        B. Cylinder seals
        C. Scarabs
        D. Jar handles
    III. Uses
        A. Protection
        B. Indication of ownership
        C. Authentication of documents
        D. Trademark
        E. Ritual

IV. Significant seal discoveries
V. Figurative usage

I. Terminology. The primary Hebrew term for "seal" or "signet" is *ḥōtām* H2597 (Gen. 38:18; Exod. 28:11 et al.), from the verb *ḥātam* H3159, "to close up, seal, confirm" (Deut. 32:34; Job 9:7; Isa. 8:16 et al.; Aram. *ḥătam* H10291, Dan. 6:17). In addition, the word for "ring," *ṭabbaʿat* H3192, can be used specifically of a signet ring (Gen. 41:42; Esth. 3:10 et al.; in Aram., the term used is *ʿizqâ* H10536, Dan. 6:17).

The NT uses the common Greek noun *sphragis* G5382 (Rom. 4:11; 1 Cor. 9:2; 2 Tim. 2:19), which occurs frequently in the book of Revelation (Rev. 5:1–2 et al.). The cognate verb is *sphragizō* G5381 (Matt. 27:66; Jn. 3:33; 2 Cor. 1:22; Rev. 7:3–5 et al.); the compound form *katasphragizō* G2958 occurs only once (Rev. 5:1).

II. Types. At least four different types of seal can be identified.

A. Stamp seals. Glyptic ART (engraving or carving of seals or gems) flourished in the ANE from the 4th millennium B.C. down to the end of the Persian period in the 4th cent. B.C. Through the medium of these seals, one knows a great deal about the people of those days, the way they dressed, and their religious ideas. Seals often supply an indispensable witness to the developing thought of the ancients when other evidence is lacking.

The first seal was probably a development from the AMULET, which was worn as a charm. The earliest type, called a stamp seal, was an engraved gem or bead that was flat and produced a copy of itself by being pressed to soft CLAY. In earliest times it was probably felt that some of the seal's protective power would be transferred to the impression. The stamp seal was virtually discarded in MESOPOTAMIA at the beginning of the 3rd millennium in favor of the cylinder seal and came into use again only at the end of the 8th cent. B.C., when it again gradually became more common, eventually replacing cylinder seals altogether by Hellenistic times.

B. Cylinder seals. The cylinder seal probably began as little more than tiny clay spools scratched by twigs in attempts to depict a god, an animal, or perhaps a flower. The design would leave its impression when rolled on wet clay. Cylinder seals first appeared in Mesopotamia during the Uruk period of the Protoliterate Period (before c. 3000 B.C.) and were of a high quality. In all periods good and bad craftsmanship are found; the Jemdet Nasr seals are decidedly inferior to the artistry of the preceding Uruk period. The cylinder seal remained the most popular type of seal until the middle of the 1st millennium B.C. The cylinder seal reached Egypt in the 3rd millennium, but since the most common writing material there was PAPYRUS, it was not so well adapted to the cylinder for sealing documents, so the Egyptians preferred the stamp seal in a scaraboid form (see below, section C).

Many materials were used as cylinder seals, from baked clay to lapis lazuli, gold, silver, carnelian, blue chalcedony, rock crystal, pink marble, jasper shell-core, ivory, glazed pottery, wood haematite (an iron ore, Babylonian *aban shadi*). Care was exercised in the choice of stone from which the seals were cut, as some stones were considered "unlucky." A list of lucky and unlucky stones was compiled. The seal cutter ordinarily used stones that were readily available, except for lapis lazuli (imported from Persia, Afghanistan, or India) and shells (brought from the Persian Gulf).

Seals of softer material could easily have been cut with flint. For the harder materials, such as agate or quartz, a harder tool was required. It is most likely that coarse corundum was used for this purpose. All the early seals were undoubtedly incised by hand. The earliest seals were incised with geometric patterns, probably representations of a totem or some magical object. Religious scenes, animals and flowers, epic scenes from myths, scenes from everyday life, boats, banquets, and ritual marriage also figured prominently in the designs. Most of the scenes or designs of Mesopotamian seal cylinders usually have a religious meaning.

When writing was invented, the seal often incorporated the owner's name; such inscriptions began to appear in the middle of the Early Dynastic period (3000–2340 B.C.). Soon afterward the owner's title or rank and his father's name began to appear, and by the Akkadian period (2340–2180 B.C.) a space was often left by the seal cutter for adding the purchaser's name. Sometimes a declaration of loyalty to a god or king was included in the inscription. Seals have been unearthed in such quantity at sites through SE Europe and the Near and Middle E—from Greece and Egypt through to Iran—that the general dating of seals is now undisputed (at least within two or three centuries), though sometimes it is difficult to decide the exact period or even country of origin, particularly those from regions bordering Mesopotamia. HERODOTUS (*Hist.* 1.195) recorded that every Babylonian gentleman "carries a seal and a walking-stick." More than 6,000 cylinder seals from the ANE have been published, from sites such as Ur, Eshnunna, and Khafajeh on the Diyala River, and from the ancient Assyrian military capital of Kalhu (biblical CALAH, modern Nimrud).

The cylinders were hollowed by using a copper tool with emery, revolving it by hand or with the aid of the string of a bow. The seal was worn suspended by a cord about the neck or on the wrist or attached by a pin to some part of the owner's garment. Graves with skeletons having cylinders tied to the wrist have been found.

C. Scarabs. The use of stones and earthenware in the form of a scarab or beetle was, along with the amulet, one of the most distinctive contributions of Egyptian glyptic art. The scarab is a type of the stamp seal and is better adapted to papyrus, the principal writing material used in Egypt, than the cylinder seal. The beetle was venerated in Egypt, the dung beetle (*Scarabaeus sacer*) being the emblem of resurrection and continual existence. The Egyptians saw the sun rolling like a great ball across the sky and compared it to the beetle carrying its food or sometimes laying its eggs in animal droppings which it rolled into a ball. The Egyptians believed that the sun god RE, who at dawn was Khepera, took the form of a beetle at noon, and from this belief evolved the symbol of the beetle as an emblem of eternal life. It was only natural that the scarab should develop as the most distinctive form of seal among the Egyptians.

Scarabs were usually made from stea-schist, fibrous steatite, or schist, sometimes from quartz, carnelian, jasper, black obsidian, or limestone. They bore cartouches (symbols or designs cut in

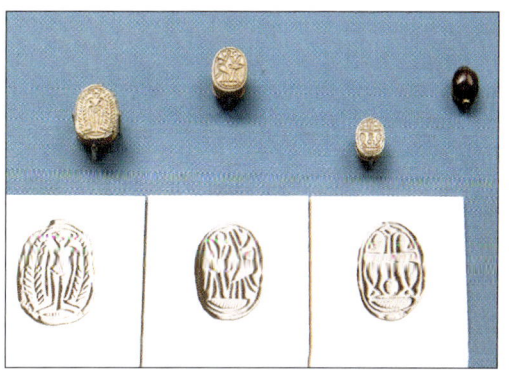

These scarabs (seals in the form of a beetle), made of amethyst, were discovered in Lachish and date to the middle of the 2nd millennium B.C.

the scarab) and were often coated with glaze. The scarab thus came to be used as a person's signature. Scarabs were set in seal rings with a swivel type of bezel rim or mounted in the Roman fixed fashion. Reference is made to PHARAOH's signet ring which he gave to JOSEPH (Gen. 41:42); undoubtedly this was a scarab and served as Joseph's authority for transacting the king's business. Scarabs were used to stud pectorals, crowns, and bracelets. Every pharaoh had his own scarab, often two. One gave his throne name and the other his name before ascending the throne. Cartouches of the principal pharaohs have been identified, and when they are found in diggings of ancient cities or in tombs, they are quite useful in establishing the dates of the material surrounding them. Egyptian scarabs were carried by traders and soldiers to the entire Mediterranean and Mesopotamian areas and have been invaluable in the dating of finds.

It became customary to bury scarabs with the dead; they were placed in the bandages of the mummy. Heart scarabs, 3 or 4 in. long, were placed where the human heart had been removed as part of the mummification process, or at the throat, engraved with the 64th chapter of the *Book of the Dead*, which contained a spell imploring the heart of the deceased not to betray him in the judgment before OSIRIS. Later a number of scarabs were placed about the body. Toward the end of the 18th dynasty, large heart scarabs were engraved in commemoration of significant secular events.

One of the most famous scarabs is the huge pectoral scarab of Amenhotep III (c. 1406–1370

B.C.), uncovered during the LACHISH excavations. It contains in eight parallel lines of hieroglyphics the record of a lion hunt in the tenth year of the reign of Amenhotep III (Amenophis) and Queen Tiye.

D. Jar handles. Though the principal use of seals was for signing documents, they were also used to make safe for shipment jars containing valuable papers or goods. A piece of cloth was placed over the neck of the bottle, soft clay was smeared on top of the binding cord, and the seal was then pressed into the wet clay. The unbroken seal was evidence that the merchandise was intact upon arrival. In Judea the seal was imprinted as a record of ownership on clay jar handles which were not yet hardened; this practice was not commonly used in Israel. There is also evidence that stamped jars were used for collecting taxes paid to the king, usually in wine or oil.

Four groups of impressions on jar handles of the 5th and 4th centuries have been found: (1) The three consonants of the word *Yehud* (JUDEA) in old Hebrew characters together with a monogram consisting of a cross with a circle around it; such seals probably had official significance. (2) A circle with a star incised within it, and the letters of Jerusalem in old Hebrew characters between the points of the star. (3) The letters of the name Yehud on a round or oval stamp-seal with no further decoration written in early Palestinian ARAMAIC, suggesting that in this period the older manner of writing was being replaced by the newer Aramaic characters. (4) Seals found at Tell en-Naṣbeh (MIZPAH) containing the letters *mṣh*, probably a reference to the Benjamite town of MOZAH (see E. Stern, *Archaeology of the Land of the Bible. Volume II: The Assyrian, Babylonian, and Persian Periods, 732–332 BCE* [2001], 335–36).

III. Uses. Seals served a variety of purposes.

A. Protection. The earliest seal developed from an amulet and therefore maintained some of the amulet's magical power. The seal would deter anyone from breaking open the sealed object for fear of the evil that might overtake him. Later the unbroken seal served as evidence that the object being protected had not been tampered with. When DANIEL was cast into the lion's den, the king sealed the den with his signet and those of his lords (Dan. 6:17). The tomb of Jesus was made secure by sealing the stone (Matt. 27:66).

B. Indication of ownership. The earliest method, as far as one knows, to distinguish a person's property was by use of the seal; this kind of seal has been found in Neolithic settlements in Mesopotamia. The seal was engraved with a design or mark distinctive to the owner.

C. Authentication of documents. The most common use of the seal was to authenticate written documents, letters, bills of sale, or receipts for goods or money. After incising the CUNEIFORM message in the soft clay, the scribe had the sender and witnesses remove from their necks their own cylinder seals and roll them over the still wet clay to make their signatures. JUDAH had to give his seal to TAMAR as a pledge (Gen. 38:18); he apparently wore it attached with a cord around his neck.

It was also common practice to wear the seal as a ring on the finger, as seen in Joseph's elevation by Pharaoh which included the giving of the signet ring (41:42). The giving of the ring was a sign that authority had been transferred to him; all important documents would receive his seal and all officials were under his orders; contracts were guaranteed by the seal. As vizier, Joseph governed in Pharaoh's name and acted for him in his absence.

JEREMIAH sealed a deed of purchase when he bought a piece of land (Jer. 32:10–14). JEZEBEL assumed her husband's authority by writing letters in his name and sealing them with his seal, and these letters resulted in the death of NABOTH (1 Ki. 21:8–13). When Jerusalem was restored and its walls rebuilt in the 5th cent., the leaders of the city set their seal to a written covenant agreeing to keep the law (Neh. 9.38; 10:1). The Persian king's edict sealed with his ring could not be revoked (Esth. 8:8). The use of the seal as a signature did not necessarily imply the inability of the person to write, but it did carry the authority of the owner. The signet came to be looked upon as a symbol of authority. Before he died, ANTIOCHUS IV Epiphanes entrusted his crown, robe, and signet to Philip as regent for his son (1 Macc. 6:15).

Seal of "Elishama son of Semahyah(u)" (bottom, with enlarged replica on top). Numerous bullae, or clay impressions made from seals, were found at the excavations in the City of David Area G, dating to the 7th–6th cent. B.C.

D. Trademark. Seals were used to impress an early form of trademark, as, for example, on pottery before firing. This was practiced in the Early Dynastic Period (c. 3000–2340 B.C.) at SUSA, and for many centuries in Syria and Palestine Judean jars bearing the stamp *lmlk*, "[belonging] to the king," may have been the identifying mark of the royal workshop that produced them (see A. Mazar, *Archaeology of the Land of the Bible, 10,000–586 B.C.E* [1990], 455–58; *SacBr*, 251–53).

E. Ritual. Seals seem to have been used in community rites, especially in the annual New Year Festival when the kings of ASSYRIA AND BABYLONIA sought the blessing of the gods and prosperity for the nation, and the gods in solemn assembly determined their destiny for the ensuing year. Large seals inscribed with the names of gods and kings have been found in the main temple of BABYLON. The impressions of divine and royal seals have been found affixed to religious covenants.

IV. Significant seal discoveries. A serious study of seals began in the 1880s with the work of J. Ménant. Pioneer work of cataloguing was done by William H. Ward and Louis Delaporte. More recent comprehensive work has been done by H. Frankfort and A. Moortgat. The most valuable seals are those that carry cuneiform inscriptions as well as designs. Of great interest is the lapis lazuli seal of Queen Shub-ad (c. 2500 B.C.), which was thrown into her tomb after all her other treasures and her court had been buried sacrificially with her.

Of more particular interest is the development of the seal in Israel and Judah. The first Israelite-inscribed seals that can be dated with certainty are from the dynasty of JEHU (842–815 B.C.). Israelite seals are probably adaptations of Canaanite or Phoenician work, the latter in turn being adaptations of the Egyptian scarab seal. They show a mixture of Egyptian and Syrian influence; seal designs include the lion, young bull, cherub (winged lion with human head), the griffin (a bird-headed, winged animal), and the four-winged cobra. Also included are the ram, fighting cock, gazelles, and a standing human figure, as well as more complex scenes, sometimes drawn from non-Israelite traditions. Seals have shed new light on the Israelite system of taxation and the ability of Israelite artists. Seals and other objects show that the artistic level of Judea was higher in the 6th cent. than that of Greece. Seals from Judah which became more common in the 8th cent. and are very numerous in the 7th and early 6th do not contain any combinations of names with BAAL as was quite common in Israel. A typical Palestinian seal was of the stamp type, round or oval, with a convex top. In the inscribed face a double line divided the surface. Above it was the name of the owner and below was the name of the owner's father.

Typical of the many seals unearthed by archaeologists is one found at MEGIDDO on the plain of ESDRAELON in 1904. Dating from the reign of JEROBOAM II (c. 775 B.C.), it is made of jasper and bears the image of a roaring lion with the words, "of Shema, the servant of Jeroboam," the words "the seal" or "the property" being understood at the beginning of the inscription. From the same period the personal seals of two of King UZZIAH's officials have been found, each calling himself "the servant of Uzziyau" (Uzziah); one of the men was named Abiyau (Abijah) and the other was Shebanyau (Shebaniah). There is also a seal that belonged to King JOTHAM of Judah (742–735).

Two jar handles found at DEBIR and one at BETH SHEMESH, dating from the end of the monarchy, were all made from the same original stamp seal bearing the inscription, "Belonging to Eliakim, steward of Yaukin." These seal impressions indicate that between 598 and 587 B.C. a person named Eliakim was steward or overseer (na'ar H5853) of the crown property of JEHOIACHIN while the latter was in captivity in Babylon and that this property was maintained intact and was not transferred to his successor, ZEDEKIAH.

A beautiful seal was found at Tell en-Naṣbeh, 8 mi. N of Jerusalem, with the inscription "To Jaazaniah, servant of the king." It probably refers to a Judean royal official of GEDALIAH mentioned in 2 Ki. 25:23, and would be dated after 587 B.C. during the governorship of Gedaliah, appointed by NEBUCHADNEZZAR over Judea after the fall of Jerusalem (Jer. 40:5, 8). The seal is incised with the figure of a fighting rooster, perhaps borrowed from Egypt.

A seal of DARIUS the Great (522–486) shows the king in a two-wheeled chariot between two date palms. The charioteer is driving over one lion; the king stands with bow in hand ready to shoot another lion standing on his hind legs. The winged disk is depicted at the top center of the seal, along with the letters of the god Ahura Mazda. At the left is a trilingual cuneiform inscription containing in Old Persian, Elamite, and Babylonian the words, "I am Darius the great king."

V. Figurative usage. Symbolic or figurative use of the seal is found in literature of all periods. An old Babylonian prayer says, "Like a seal may my sins be torn away." In the 8th cent., the prophet ISAIAH said, "Bind up the testimony / and seal up the law among my disciples" (Isa. 8:16). The bride is described as "a spring enclosed, a sealed fountain" (Cant. 4:12); and she says to her lover, "Place me like a seal over your heart, / like a seal on your arm; / for love is as strong as death, / its jealousy unyielding as the grave" (8:6). JEREMIAH makes effective use of the signet ring as a warning to JEHOIACHIN (Jer. 22:24–25). ZERUBBABEL is told that God will make him like a signet ring (Hag. 2:23). The earth, which was formless in the dark, "takes shape like the clay under a seal" (Job 38:14; cf. also 9:7; 33:6; 37:7; 41:15). The book of Daniel makes use of the figure in expressions such as "to seal up vision and prophecy" (Dan. 9:24) and "close up and seal the words of the scroll" (12:4).

The NT also employs the seal in a figurative sense. Jesus claimed that the Father had "placed his seal of approval" on the Son of Man (Jn. 6:27). PAUL described CIRCUMCISION both as a sign and as "a seal of the righteousness" that ABRAHAM obtained by faith (Rom. 4:11). Writing to the Corinthians he stated, "For you are the seal of my apostleship in the Lord" (1 Cor. 9:2). Most significant, the apostle spoke of the HOLY SPIRIT as the seal of ownership with which God has marked the believer (2 Cor. 1:22; Eph. 1:13; 4:30; cf. also 2 Tim. 2:19). In the book of Revelation, the seal is a recurring eschatological symbol (Rev. 5:1–2, 5, 9; 6:1–14; 7:2–8; 8:1; 9:4; 10:4; 20:3; 22:10).

(In addition to the titles mentioned in the body of the article, see W. H. Ward, *The Seal Cylinders of Western Asia* [1910]; W. M. F. Petrie, *Scarabs and Cylinders* [1917]; H. Frankfort, *Cylinder Seals* [1939]; W. F. Albright, *Archaeology and the Religion of Israel* [1942]; E. Porada, ed., *Corpus of Ancient Near Eastern Seals*, vol. 1 [1948]; H. Frankfort, *Stratified Cylinder Seals from the Diyala Region* [1955]; M. S. and J. L. Miller, *Encyclopedia of Bible Life* [1955], 133–36; D. J. Wiseman, *Cylinder Seals of Western Asia* [1959]; G. E. Wright, *Biblical Archaeology* [1957], 159–60, 197–98, 202–3; R. de Vaux, *Ancient Israel* [1961], 125–26; M. Gibson and R. Biggs, eds., *Seals and Sealing in the Ancient Near East* [1977]; E. Porada, ed., *Ancient Art in Seals* [1980]; B. Buchanan and P. R. S. Moorey, *Catalogue of Ancient Near Eastern Seals in the Ashmolean Museum*, 3 vols. [1966–88]; D. Collon, *Near Eastern Seals* [1990]; B. Sass and C. Uehlinger, eds., *Studies in the Iconography of Northwest Semitic Inscribed Seals* [1995]; J. G. Westenholz, ed., *Seals and Sealing in the Ancient Near East* [1995]; N. Avigad and B. Sass, *Corpus of West Semitic Stamp Seals* [1997]; J. Nijhowne, *Politics, Religion, and Cylinder Seals: A Study of Mesopotamian Symbolism in the Second Millennium B.C.* [1999]; J. A. Hill, *Cylinder Seal Glyptic in Predynastic Egypt and Neighboring Regions* [2004].)

F. B. HUEY, JR

sea monster. The NRSV and other versions use this phrase to render the Hebrew noun *tannin* H9490 in two passages (Gen. 1:21 [NIV, "creatures

This fresco of a sea monster (prob. one of a pair) was discovered in the house of Nero in Rome.

of the sea"]; Ps. 148:7 [NIV, "sea creatures"]; the RSV also uses it in Job 7.12, and the KJV in Lam. 4:3 [in the latter passage, the more likely reading is *tannim*, pl. of *tan* H9478, "jackal"]). For other uses of the Hebrew term, see DRAGON. The NRSV uses "sea monster" also to render Greek *kētos* G3063, which occurs only once (Matt. 12:40 [KJV, "whale"; NIV, "huge fish"]).

sea of glass. In his description of the heavenly council chamber, John says that "before the throne there was what looked like a sea of glass, clear as crystal" (Rev. 4:6). In a different vision he says, "I saw what looked like a sea of glass mixed with fire and, standing beside the sea, those who had been victorious over the beast and his image and over the number of his name" (15:2). These references have been interpreted in numerous ways. Some have considered this glassy sea to be the counterpart of the LAVERS or basins in Solomon's temple, which stood there as a symbol of the purity that was required of any person who would approach God (1 Ki. 7:38). Others point to the sea of bronze in the temple (7:23–26; see SEA, MOLTEN), which possibly alluded to the water above the skies (Gen. 1:7; Ps. 184:4; cf. Ezek. 1:22). The symbolism may have indicated the vastness and transcendence that separate God from his creation.

It is unclear what connection, if any, there is with the sea as a reservoir of evil out of which the "beast" arose (Rev. 13:1), and with John's statement that, when he saw the new heaven and earth, "there was no longer any sea" (21:1). It is likely that in John's cosmology, the sea—whether on earth or in heaven—indicated separation, and in the spiritual context all that separated human beings from God. The glassy sea stood in John's symbolism before the throne of God as a mute reminder that the entire universe was afflicted with rebellion against God. John's theology had a precise universal opposition between good and evil and between God and Satan that approached DUALISM. This is due to the seriousness with which he regarded the reality of evil. It was not, however, a true dualism because John regarded God as the creator of all things (4:11), even the sea of glass. (For other proposals, see the summary in G. R. Osborne, *Revelation*, BECNT [2002], 232.) H. L. DRUMWRIGHT, JR.

Sea of Kinnereth (Chinnereth). See GALILEE, SEA OF.

Sea of the Arabah. See ARABAH; DEAD SEA.

Sea of Tiberias. See GALILEE, SEA OF.

Sea Peoples. Documentary sources from Egypt and elsewhere attest to the existence of various people groups that began to reach the Syrian coast around 1300 B.C. (although there is sporadic evidence for an even earlier presence). These seafaring invaders caused considerable havoc in the ANE over an extended period of time. In the 12th cent., for example, RAMSES III claims to have defeated a confederation of "foreign countries" that had conspired "in their islands" and that consisted of "Philistines, Tjeker, Shekelesh, Denye(n), and Weshesh" (*ANET*, 262; for a fuller list with alternate spellings see *ABD*, 5:1059–61). Their precise origins cannot be established, but it seems likely that their migration was caused by disturbances in the AEGEAN related to the demise of the Mycenean civilization (see GREECE IV). For further details and bibliography, see PHILISTINES.

seasons. The periods of the year associated with certain phenomena or activities. The Hebrew noun *mô‘ēd* H4595, which has a broad range of meanings ("meeting place, assembly, appointed time"), can be appropriately rendered "season" in various contexts (e.g., Gen. 1:14; Ps. 103:19). The same is true of such words as *yôm* H3427 (lit., "day"; e.g., Num. 13:20) and *‘ēt* H6961 (lit., "time"; e.g., Lev. 26:4).

In the NT, the word "season" usually translates Greek *kairos* G2789 (lit., "time", e.g., Mk. 11.13; Acts 14:17; Gal. 4:10).

Specific words for "summer" are Hebrew *qayiṣ* H7811 (Gen. 8:22 et al.) and Greek *theros* G2550 (Matt. 24:32 et al.); for "winter," Hebrew *ḥōrep* H3074 (Ps. 74.17 et al., cf. also *sĕtāw* H6256 in Cant. 2:11) and Greek *cheimōn* G5930 (Matt. 24:20 et al.). The Greek word for "autumn," *phthinopōrinos* G5781, occurs once in the NT (Jude 12). In addition, the NIV uses the renderings "autumn/spring rains" for terms that mean literally "early/later rain" (e.g., Deut. 11:14; Jas. 5:7); see RAIN.

Like all other societies at a comparable cultural level, the Israelites had a strong awareness of the seasons and their importance in their lives. Basically, there are only two seasons in the Palestinian year, the dry season, which is hot, and the wet season, which is cool or cold. The incidence of these seasons would dominate the planning of any agricultural community, but Israel had a special consciousness of the seasons as a direct evidence of God's oversight, based on God's promise in Gen. 8:22 and the explicit warning of Lev. 26:3–4 (cf. Deut. 11:13–14). The unreliability of rainfall in PALESTINE gave them an awareness of dependence on God for the gift of a HARVEST.

At the time of the exodus, it was provided that Israel should measure time from the PASSOVER month, which became the first month of the year in the religious calendar (Exod. 12:2; the civil year began in the fall). This month became the starting point for measuring the other fixed occasions, such as the three times in the year when all the men of Israel were commanded to come together for the great religious festivals. However, once the people settled in the Promised Land and became cultivators rather than pastoralists, the rhythm of the farmer's year asserted itself, and the religious festivals came to acquire a new significance as marking the seasons. See AGRICULTURE.

Agriculturally, the year began with the "early" rains in October, when the sun-baked earth became sufficiently workable for plowing and sowing to take place. The crops grew through the wet season, and in April the harvest began, the first ripe crop being BARLEY. In June the main harvest occurred, followed by the gathering of grapes (see VINE) and OLIVES, and it was not until late September or early October that the cycle of the farm year was completed.

The FEASTS of Israel marked the progression of these seasons. The Passover occurred at the time of gathering the FIRSTFRUITS in April; the Feast of Weeks coincided with the main WHEAT harvest, and involved loaves of bread to underline the connection; the Feast of Tabernacles marked the "harvest home" and the start of the new crop year. D. Baly (*The Geography of The Bible* [1957], 99) sees in the water poured out at the Feast of Tabernacles a symbol of "the desperate need for rain," as the farmers began the labors of a new season. See also CALENDAR.

J. H. PATERSON

seat. In the OT, the Hebrew word *kissēʾ* H4058 often refers to any seat occupied by an important person, whether king, minister, or priest (Jdg. 3:20; 1 Sam. 1:9; 4:13, 18; 1 Ki. 2:19; Esth. 3:1). In NT times, special seats of importance were a part of the furniture of the SYNAGOGUE. Jesus rebuked the leaders of his day for seeking the "most important seats" there (Matt. 23:6; Mk. 12:39; Lk. 11:43; 20:46; the Gk. term here is *prōtokathedrias* G4751, parallel to *prōtoklisia* G4752, "place of honor" in a banquet). In the synagogues of Palestine, the back seats were occupied by children and unimportant people; the closer the seat was to the front, the greater the honor of the person who occupied it. The most honored seats of all were the seats of the ELDERS, which faced the congregation (cf. A. Edersheim, *The Life and Times of Jesus the Messiah*, 2 vols. [1899], 1:436). A man who sat in an elder's seat could be seen by all, and his importance could not be missed. In ALEXANDRIA, the principal synagogue had seventy-one such seats (a testimony to the size of the Jewish community), and they were held by the members of the "Council" of that community.

The Greek noun *kathedra* G2756 is applied to the seats or benches of the merchants who were selling doves in the temple (Matt. 21:12; Mk. 11:15). This word is also used in the expression "Moses' seat" (Matt. 23:2; see SEAT, MOSES'). In some instances in the NT, the word *bēma* G1037 is used to designate a JUDGMENT SEAT (Matt. 27:19; Jn. 19:13; Acts 18:12, 16–17; 25:6, 10, 17), referring to the place occupied by a governor or other official who was sitting in function as a judge. Twice it is used of Christ's sitting in judgment (Rom. 14:10; 2 Cor. 5:10), and some have thereby distinguished between the judgment of Christ and the judgment of God from his THRONE.   H. L. DRUMWRIGHT, JR.

seat, Moses'. Matthew reports Jesus as saying, "The teachers of the law and the Pharisees sit in Moses' seat. So you must obey them and do everything they tell you. But do not do what they do, for they do not practice what they preach" (Matt. 23:2). Archaeological evidence confirms that in the front of the SYNAGOGUES there was a stone seat where the authoritative SCRIBE (teacher of the law) sat and taught (see E. L. Sukenik, *Ancient Synagogues in Palestine and Greece* [1934], 57–61; M. Avi-Yonah, *Views of the Biblical World*, 5 [1961], 63). The phrase "sit in Moses' seat" may imply that the scribes viewed themselves as successors of MOSES (cf. D. A. Carson in *EBC*, 8:471–72, who also addresses the problem that the PHARISEES did not normally teach unless they also belonged to the scribal profession). In any case, the scribes did believe that they exercised the authority of Moses, in whom the written law and the main lines of the oral law were regarded as originating (see MISHNAH).

S. BARABAS

Seba see'buh (סְבָא H6013, meaning unknown). Son of CUSH and grandson of HAM (Gen. 10:7; 1 Chr. 1:9). The term is also applied to his descendants, a people group that inhabited the eastern part of ETHIOPIA or possibly a region in S ARABIA (Isa. 43:3). One passage associates Seba with SHEBA (Ps. 72:10). For discussion see SABEAN.

Sebam see'bam. Alternate form of SIBMAH.

Sebat see'bat. KJV form of SHEBAT.

Secacah si-kay'kuh (סְכָכָה H6117, prob. "covering" or "protection"). TNIV Sekakah. One of six towns allotted to the tribe of JUDAH in the desert (Josh. 15:61). Some settlements in el-Buqeʿah (i.e., ACHOR, a valley SW of JERICHO) dating to Iron II are thought to correspond with four of these towns, including Secacah. Assuming that the list of cities in this passage runs from N to S, Secacah would then be identified with Khirbet es-Samrah, about 4 mi. SW of QUMRAN. The remains feature the following: a large double-walled fortress with an enclosed cistern, nearby dam complexes for exploiting the scanty rainfall, and remains of several stone towers. The pottery fragments all come from a single period, Iron II. Some scholars, however, prefer to identify Secacah with Qumran. (For bibliography, see SALT, CITY OF.)   A. BOWLING

Sechenias sek'uh-ni'uhs. KJV Apoc. form of SHECANIAH (1 Esd. 8:29, 32).

Sechu see'kyoo. KJV form of SECU.

second Adam. This title, which does not occur in Scripture, results from a conflation of "the last Adam" (1 Cor. 15:45) and "the second man" (v. 47), and it incorporates a concept that is prominent in both 15:45–49 and Rom. 5:12–21. In his counter to a static Platonic anthropology that taught a heavenly real man and earthly copies, PAUL proclaimed a dynamic redemption for real people on earth and a fulfillment in history by the "spiritual" and "heavenly" man JESUS CHRIST (1 Cor. 15:46–49). In contradistinction to the first man's sin, which brought death and condemnation, the second man's "act of righteousness" and "obedience" results in an "abundant provision of grace" bringing JUSTIFICATION, RIGHTEOUSNESS, and eternal LIFE (Rom. 5:15–19). See ADAM II.D.

R. N. LONGENECKER

second coming. The future return of JESUS CHRIST to the earth. A prominent doctrine of CHRISTOLOGY, the predicted second advent of Christ is implied in hundreds of OT prophecies of future judgment on the world and a coming kingdom of righteousness on earth, and it is explicitly detailed in major NT passages. The last book of the Bible, the Revelation of Jesus Christ, refers specifically to his second coming (Rev. 19) and to the subsequent MILLENNIUM and future state (chs. 20–22). See also ESCHATOLOGY; PAROUSIA.

I. General OT references. The OT presents a mingled prophecy of the first and second advents of Christ (cf. 1 Pet. 1:10–12), often combining both comings in the same context (Isa. 61:1–3; Lk. 4:17–20). The first reference to the second coming may be found in Deut. 30:3, which the KJV renders, "Then the LORD thy God will turn thy captivity, and have compassion upon thee, and will return and gather thee from all the nations whither the LORD thy God hath scattered thee" (modern versions interpret the second occurrence of šûb H8740 not in the sense "return," but adverbially, "again," a common use when this term is followed by another verb). The "return" results in their regathering to their ancient land and their spiritual and physical restoration. This is typical of OT prophecies of the second advent. The OT seldom pictures the second coming *per se*, but often dwells upon the circumstances of the second coming, such as the preceding regathering of Israel to the land (Jer. 30:3; Amos 9:14–15), and the results of the second coming — the judgment of the nations (Isa. 2:4), deliverance of Israel (Jer. 31:28), and a kingdom of righteousness and peace on earth (Ps. 72:7).

II. The second coming in the Psalms.

The second coming of Christ is linked with the moral struggle between God and his creatures. Psalm 2, for instance, after picturing the world's rejection of the sovereignty of God, declares God's purpose, "I have installed my King / on Zion, my holy hill" (v. 6). In the verses that follow, the decree of God is stated concerning his purpose to place his Son over the nations: "You will rule them with an iron scepter; / you will dash them to pieces like pottery" (v. 9). On the basis of God's intention to make his Son the King of the earth, the exhortation to earthly kings is, "Serve the LORD with fear / and rejoice with trembling. / Kiss the Son, lest he be angry …" (vv. 11–12a). The conclusion is reached, "Blessed are all who take refuge in him." This psalm is typical of the OT passages relating to the second coming. The event itself is assumed, but the results are detailed.

Psalm 24 is another great passage dealing with Christ's coming as "the King of glory." The gates of Jerusalem are exhorted to open to this King when he comes. His rule on the earth is based on the promise that "The earth is the LORD's, and everything in it, / the world, and all who live in it" (v. 1). Another complete presentation of the second coming of Christ and its result is found in Ps. 72, presented in the form of a prayer, but describing the certain results of Christ's return. His dominion is described as "from sea to sea" (v. 8). Kings and nations are described as serving him (v. 11). This psalm ends with the prayer, "may the whole earth be filled with his glory" (v. 19).

Other psalms are similar in character. For example, Ps. 96 declares, "The LORD reigns" (v. 10), and affirms that "he comes to judge the earth" (v. 13). The present position of Christ seated at the right hand of the Father in Ps. 110:1 is considered temporary, for the day will come when "The LORD will extend your mighty scepter from Zion" (v. 2) and "will judge the nations" (v. 6).

III. The second coming in the Prophets.

The Major Prophets take up the same theme of the coming of the Lord to reign. A familiar text is Isa. 9:6–7, "For to us a child is born, / to us a son is given, / and the government will be on his shoulders. / … Of the increase of his government and peace / there will be no end. / He will reign on David's throne / and over his kingdom." The rule of the MESSIAH on earth is described in ch. 11 as one of complete righteousness and justice, of tranquility in nature, with universal knowledge of the Lord. Isaiah prays for the coming of the Lord, "O that you would rend the heavens and come down, / that the mountains would tremble before you!" (64:1). Isaiah's great prophecy concludes in chs. 65–66 with a description of the reign of Christ on earth and the judgments that relate to it.

Jeremiah speaks of the results of the Lord's coming when the Son of David "will reign wisely / and do what is just and right in the land" (Jer. 23:5). The judgments and tribulation that precede the second coming are followed by the deliverance of Israel according to chs. 30–31, and many other prophecies in Jeremiah deal with the ultimate triumph of God during the reign of Christ. The presentation of the right to rule over the earth following his second coming is described in the vision of Dan. 7:13–14, where "one like a son of man" is given dominion over the entire earth and an everlasting kingdom.

One of the most specific references to the second coming in the OT is in Zech. 14:3–5. Here the Lord is described as fighting in defense of Israel, and the statement is made, "On that day his feet will stand on the Mount of Olives, east of Jerusalem, and the Mount of Olives will be split in two from east to west, forming a great valley, with half of the mountain moving north and half moving south." The revelation goes on to picture that "the LORD will be king over the whole earth. On that day there will be one LORD, and his name the only name" (14:9).

IV. General NT references. The NT doctrine of the second coming of Christ tends to dwell more upon the event than the total circumstances, and it is more detailed than that of the OT. Constant references to the second coming make this a major theme of the NT (Matt. 12:30, 20, 22, 24:1–17:49; Mk. 13:24–37; Lk. 12:35–48; 17:22–37; 18:8; 21:25–28; Jn. 14:1–3; Acts 1:10–11; 15:16–18; Rom. 11:25–27; 1 Cor. 11:26; 15:51–58; 1 Thess. 4:13–18; 2 Thess. 1:7–10; 2 Pet. 3:3–4; Jude 14–15; Rev. 1:7–8; 2:25–28; 16:15; 19:11–21; 22:20). It is clear that the second coming is a dominant theme and one that colors the exposition of the entire NT.

V. The second coming in the Gospels. One of the most explicit passages relating to the second coming is found in the Olivet Discourse (Matt. 24–25; Mk. 13; Lk. 21:5–38). Matthew, which gives the most complete account, like OT prophecies relating to the second coming, describes the preceding great tribulation (Matt. 24:15–28). This will climax an age that includes war, famine, pestilence, earthquakes, and many persecutions.

Christ warned his disciples not to be deceived by premature, false reports that the Lord has returned. He describes the event in such language as to make the event unmistakable. The second advent is compared to lightning that comes from the E and shines to the W (Matt. 24:27). "Immediately after the distress of those days," he says, "the sun will be darkened, / and the moon will not give its light; / the stars will fall from the sky, / and the heavenly bodies will be shaken" (v. 29). The world will then see "the sign of the Son of Man … in the sky," that is, "They will see the Son of Man coming on the clouds of the sky, with power and great glory" (v. 30).

At this time there will be a loud trumpet call, and the angels will be commissioned to collect the elect of God in heaven and earth. The second coming is described as the time of the doom of the wicked in the earth. It is prophesied that "all the nations of the earth will mourn" (Matt. 24:30) as they see the second coming of Christ from heaven to the earth.

VI. The second coming in Jude. The epistle of JUDE presents the second coming as a time of judgment, quoting ENOCH, "See, the Lord is coming with thousands upon thousands of his holy ones to judge everyone, and to convict all the ungodly of all the ungodly acts they have done in the ungodly way, and of all the harsh words ungodly sinners have spoken against him" (Jude 14–15). As in Matt. 24, the second coming is declared in Jude to be a distinct event, one in which the holy angels will participate and culminating in dramatic judgment upon the wicked.

VII. The second coming in the Revelation. The book of Revelation, however, provides the most comprehensive prophecy of the second advent. The first 18 chapters of the book deal with that which precedes: the age of the churches (Rev. 2–3) and scenes in heaven and earth leading up to the second advent (chs. 4–18). Then follows a description of the second coming itself (ch. 19) and the epilogue (chs. 20–22, which deal with the millennium in ch. 20, and the new heaven and new earth in chs. 21–22). The obvious implication is that the second advent is the crowning event climaxing human history, paralleling in importance the first advent.

John opens his presentation of the second coming with the words, "I saw heaven standing open and there before me was a white horse, whose rider is called Faithful and True. With justice he judges and makes war" (Rev. 19:11). That he is none other than Christ himself is made clear from the titles, "The Word of God" (v. 13) and "King of kings and Lord of lords" (v. 16). His appearance is most awesome: "His eyes are like blazing fire, and on his head are many crowns" (v. 12). His robe is "dipped in blood" (v. 13), and he is followed by the "armies of heaven ... riding on white horses and dressed in fine linen, white and clean" (v. 14). Out of the mouth of Christ "comes a sharp sword with which to strike down the nations," and it is predicted, "He will rule them with an iron scepter" (v. 15). His coming signals his intention to tread "the winepress of the fury of the wrath of God Almighty" (v. 15).

This awe-inspiring scene is attended by the invitation of the angel to the birds of heaven to eat the flesh of men and beasts slain in the great battle which follows. The armies of the world gathered in the Holy Land at that time in the final great world conflict are destroyed. The beast or world political leader, and the false prophet, the world religious leader, who had dominated the preceding period, are thrown alive in the LAKE OF FIRE (Rev. 19:19–20). The armies themselves are slain by the sword issuing from the mouth of the rider (v. 21). In what would naturally be considered subsequent action in ch. 20, SATAN is bound, the martyred dead of the preceding period are resurrected, judgment is given, and the 1,000-year reign of Christ follows (20:1–4). If Scripture is taken in its normal sense, it yields a dramatic picture of this tremendous event that will judge wickedness and unbelief, deliver those trusting in the Lord, and inaugurate a kingdom of righteousness and peace on earth. The nonliteral view of the second advent as a present spiritual crisis, or as fulfilled for each individual at death, has never been considered an orthodox view. (However, for a different understanding of Rev. 20:1–4 and related events, see the articles on AMILLENNIALISM and POSTMILLENNIALISM. See also REVELATION, BOOK OF.)

VIII. The rapture of the church. In addition to major passages dealing with the second advent are prophecies of a rapture or catching up of believers in Christ to meet the Lord in the air. The coming of Christ for his own may have been mentioned by Christ in the upper room when he declared to his disciples, "In my Father's house are many rooms; if it were not so, I would have told you. I am going there to prepare a place for you. And if I go and prepare a place for you, I will come back and take you to be with me that you also may be where I am" (Jn. 14:2–3).

This simple revelation is later amplified by PAUL, who declares that, at the coming of Christ for his church, God will bring with him the souls of Christians who had died, in order that their bodies might be resurrected from the grave. The dramatic event is described with these words, "For the Lord himself will come down from heaven, with a loud command, with the voice of the archangel and with the trumpet call of God, and the dead in Christ will rise first. After that, we who are still alive and are left will be caught up together with them in the clouds to meet the Lord in the air. And so we will be with the Lord forever" (1 Thess. 4:16–17). In the passage that follows (5:1–11), this event is declared to be one that will come without warning to the unbelieving world, but one that believers in Christ should anticipate.

A parallel revelation of this event is given in 1 Cor. 15:51–58. Here it is plainly declared that all Christians will not die, but at the coming of the Lord all will be changed—the living given new bodies, and the dead in Christ resurrected (vv. 51–52). The new bodies that believers will receive are declared to be imperishable or immortal. According to 1 Jn. 3:2, they will be like the resurrection body of Christ and hence sinless. This hope of the coming of the Lord was held out as an imminent possibility to early Christians.

Because of certain similarities in describing the rapture and the second coming of Christ to the earth, probably the majority view, especially of amillennialists and postmillennialists, is that the rapture is a phase of the second coming of Christ and occurring at the same time. Many premillennialists, however, hold that the rapture occurs some years before the formal second advent to the earth. Usually a seven-year period, referred to in Dan. 9:27, in addition to certain other events, is placed between the rapture and the second coming itself. A compromise view held by relatively few interpreters is midtribulationism, which places the rapture forty-two months before the second advent, that is, before the great tribulation. Generally, interpreters distinguishing Israel and the church, and who interpret prophecy literally, tend toward pretribulationism. (For arguments "pro and con," see J. F. Walvoord, *The Rapture Question* [1957]; Alexander Reese, *The Approaching*

Advent of Christ: An Examination of the Teaching of J. N. Darby and His Followers [1937]; George E. Ladd, *The Blessed Hope* [1956]; G. Archer et al., *The Rapture: Pre-, Mid-, or Post-tribulational?* [1984]; Bob [R. H.] Gundry, *First the Antichrist* [1997]; C. M. Pate and D. W. Kennard, *Deliverance Now and Not Yet: The New Testament and the Great Tribulation* [2003].)

The early church fathers interpreted Scripture as teaching the rapture as possible any moment. Because they mistakenly identified their sufferings as those of the great tribulation, they did not distinguish the rapture itself from the second advent to the earth. Pretribulationists emphasize the imminency and deny that the rapture and the second advent are the same event. Modern posttribulationists usually deny imminency in the sense of daily expectation, and combine the rapture and the second advent to the earth as one event.

IX. Conclusion. Within orthodoxy, regardless of details of the time of prophetic fulfillment, a personal, visible, bodily, second coming of Jesus Christ has been considered the normal interpretation of prophecy from the 1st cent., and its denial has never been the orthodox interpretation. Generally speaking, those who affirm a literal first advent, a virgin birth of Christ, and a literal death and resurrection of Christ also hold to a literal second advent. (See further R. Anderson, *The Coming Prince* [1915]; W. E. Blackstone, *Jesus Is Coming* [1917]; L. Berkhof, *The Second Coming of Christ* [1953]; R. Pache, *The Return of Jesus Christ* [1955]; J. F. Walvoord, *The Millennial Kingdom* [1959], 263–75; J. D. Pentecost, *Things to Come* [1958], 370–426; G. C. Berkouwer, *The Return of Christ* [1972]; A. A. Hoekema, *The Bible and the Future* [1979], 109–238; W. Grudem, *Systematic Theology: An Introduction to Christian Doctrine* [1994], ch. 54.)   J. F. Walvoord

second death. See DEATH, SECOND.

Second District, Second Quarter. The district of JERUSALEM in which HULDAH the prophetess lived is referred to as the *mišneh* H5467 (2 Ki. 22:14 = 2 Chr. 34:22). This Hebrew term, which means "second," could simply be transliterated as "Mishneh" (cf. NJPS), but most versions prefer to translate it with such renderings as "Second Quarter" (NRSV), "Second District" (NIV), and "New Quarter" (TNIV). (The KJV understood it to mean "college," apparently following the TARGUM, which has *byt-ʾlpnʾ*, "house of instruction.") This area is mentioned also in a postexilic prophecy that speaks of a cry going up from the FISH GATE and wailing from the *mišneh* (Zeph. 1:10 [NIV and TNIV, "New Quarter"]; here the KJV has "second [gate]"). It is also possible that this part of Jerusalem is mentioned in Neh. 11:9, which the NIV translates, "Judah son of Hassenuah was over the Second District [TNIV, 'New Quarter'] of the city [*ʿal-hāʿîr mišneh*]" (most versions, however, understand the text to mean, "… was second over the city"). In addition, some scholars emend Neh. 3:6 to read "Mishneh" instead of "Jeshanah" (see discussion under OLD GATE).

The name evidently referred to an expansion of Jerusalem toward the W (opposite the Tyropoeon Valley) that probably took place during the reign of HEZEKIAH. Archaeological excavations during the 1970s uncovered a portion of the BROAD WALL that may have protected this new area, as well as evidence of Israelite occupation there c. 700 B.C. (cf. N. Avigad, *Discovering Jerusalem* [1983], 46–54). As a result of this expansion, the city grew from approximately 35 acres during the time of SOLOMON to at least 120 acres. See also JERUSALEM II.C.3.

Huldah the prophetess, who lived in the Second District of Jerusalem, was honored with a pyramid-shaped monument near the S steps of Herod's temple complex.

Second Temple Period. A label commonly employed (and preferred by many contemporary scholars) to designate the interval of time that has traditionally been called "intertestamental," that is, from the rebuilding of the Jerusalem temple after the EXILE (c. 520 B.C.) until its destruction by the Romans (A.D. 70). Thus this period begins near the end of the OT era and extends to NT times. See MACCABEE; HASMONEAN; RESTORATION; TEMPLE, JERUSALEM VI.

secret. See MESSIANIC SECRET; MYSTERY.

secretary. See AMANUENSIS; SCRIBE.

sect. This English term, referring to a dissenting religious group or faction, is used in Bible versions to render the Greek term *hairesis* G146, which literally means "a choosing," but by extension, "that which is taken or chosen" in a religious or political sense, thus a party or sect. Although the English term HERESY derives from this Greek word, the latter does not have that later and specialized ecclesiastical sense, but it simply refers to a body of people distinguishing themselves from others by choice (however, see 2 Pet. 2:1 NIV).

On three occasions in the NT, the term is used in reference to the Christian movement, and with a suggestion of reproach. In PAUL's trial before FELIX, TERTULLUS charged Paul with being "a ringleader of the Nazarene sect" (Acts 24:5). In reply, the apostle called Christianity "the Way, which they call a sect" (24:14). The Jews in Rome said to Paul, "we know that people everywhere are talking against this sect" (28:22). Elsewhere, the term is applied to the SADDUCEES (5:17) and to the PHARISEES (15:5; 26:5). In his epistles, Paul used it in the negative sense of "division, dissension" (1 Cor. 11:19; Gal. 5:20), while PETER possibly meant by it something like "[false] opinion" (2 Pet. 2:1). G. F. FUNDERBURK

Secu see′kyoo (שֶׂכוּ H8497, perhaps "lookout point"). KJV Sechu; TNIV Seku. A place known for its great cistern and apparently located between GIBEAH and RAMAH (#3); it was visited by SAUL when seeking information to search out DAVID and SAMUEL (1 Sam. 19:22). The proposed identification with Khirbet Shuweikeh, 3 mi. N of Ramah (cf. C. R. Conder and C. Warren, *The Survey of Western Palestine* [1884], 52), has not been accepted, so the location of Secu is unknown. Because the SEPTUAGINT (as represented by CODEX VATICANUS and other Greek MSS, though with orthographic variations) transliterates the name as *Sephi* (cf. also the Syr. Peshitta, *swpʾ*, "end"), some scholars emend the MT to read the noun שְׂפִי H8165, meaning probably "bare height" or "bare plain" (e.g., P. K. McCarter, Jr., *I Samuel*, AB 8 [1980], 328). A few Greek MSS (including CODEX ALEXANDRINUS) and the VULGATE have Socoh, but this reading is almost certainly secondary. A. K. HELMBOLD

Secundus si-koon′duhs (Σεκοῦνδος G4941 [or Σέκουνδος], from Lat. *Secundus*, "second"). A Thessalonian Christian who with others accompanied PAUL through GREECE on his return to ANTIOCH OF SYRIA from his third missionary journey. If he was one of the delegates entrusted with the offerings of the churches to the Jewish Christians, he may have accompanied Paul to Jerusalem (Acts 20:4; Rom. 15:25–26; 2 Cor. 8:23). See ARISTARCHUS.

A. M. ROSS

Sedecias sed′uh-ki′uhs. KJV Apoc. form of ZEDEKIAH (Bar. 1:1, 8).

Sedrach, Apocalypse of sed′rak. A pseudepigraphic Greek document that may have had a Jewish origin some time between the 2nd and 5th centuries A.D., though subsequently it was reworked by Christians. Its final form could be as late as the 11th cent., and it survives in only one 15th-cent. MS. Because the *Apocalypse* has clear points of contact with *4 Ezra* (see ESDRAS, SECOND), it is generally agreed that the name Sedrach is a corruption of Esdras. The work begins with these words, "A sermon by the holy and blessed Sedrach on love, repentance, orthodox Christians, and the second coming of our Lord Jesus Christ." After the sermon, Sedrach is taken to heaven and he discusses with God the problem of evil in the world. God then directs his Son to take Sedrach's soul to paradise, but not before Sedrach persuades God to reduce the time required for repentance. The document places much emphasis on divine love and compassion. (English trans. in *OTP*, 1:605–13.)

seduction. See CRIMES AND PUNISHMENTS I.B.4.

seed. The primary biblical words for "seed" (Heb. *zeraʿ* H2446 and Gk. *sperma* G5065) are used to indicate both agricultural and human seed, the latter both in a narrow physical sense and as a description of the descendants of a common ancestor. (Other Gk. terms for agricultural seed are *sporos* G5070 and *kokkos* G3133.)

Seedtime to the farmer in Palestine occurred in late October or November. After the dry, hot summer it was impossible to plow and plant until the early RAINS had softened the ground and made it workable. Sowing then took place; the Israelite was commanded not to mix his seed in any field or vineyard, but to plant only one crop (Lev. 19:19; Deut. 22:9), a stricture parallel to that regarding the mixture of human seed by intermarriage with other nations. See AGRICULTURE; CALENDAR; SEASON.

The main types of seed and crop grown by the Israelite farmer were WHEAT, BARLEY, and RYE, as well as a number of vegetables. Of these, the barley might be expected to mature first, roughly ten weeks after seedtime, or about the time of the PASSOVER. Maturing of the other crops occurred thereafter, the wheat approximately six weeks after the barley.

Our Lord gave the word *seed* a new dimension of meaning when he said "the seed is the word of God" (Lk. 8:11). Thereafter the NT combines the agricultural and physical concepts of the seed in its presentation of spiritual truth; the word of God is sown, taking root in the hearts of men and women, who are then born as children into the family of God (1 Pet. 1:23) and become a spiritual seed or nation.   J. H. PATERSON

seer. See PROPHETS AND PROPHECY.

Segub see′guhb (שְׂגוּב H8437, possibly "[God] is exalted"). **(1)** The youngest son of HIEL of BETHEL. During AHAB's reign, Hiel rebuilt JERICHO "at the cost of" his sons ABIRAM and Segub (1 Ki. 16:34). The TARGUM indicates that Hiel actually killed his sons, suggesting that he offered them as "foundation" or "threshold" sacrifices, a rite apparently practiced by the pagans of the area (cf. John Gray, *I and II Kings: A Commentary*, 2nd ed. [1970], 370). Such sacrifices are attested at GEZER, where three skeletons were found under a foundation from c. 1800 B.C. (cf. *BA* 30 [1967]: 56). Other scholars question this theory (cf. J. A. Montgomery, *A Critical and Exegetical Commentary on the Book of Kings*, ICC [1951], 287–88). R. de Vaux (*Ancient Israel* [1961], 441–42) says that if this incident was a foundation sacrifice, it was probably due to Phoenician influence. In any case, the writer of Kings considered the death of Hiel's sons as a fulfillment of JOSHUA's curse upon anyone who tried to rebuild Jericho (Josh. 6:26).

(2) Son of HEZRON and descendant of JUDAH (1 Chr. 2:21–22). Three of Hezron's sons had been mentioned earlier in the genealogy (v. 9). The reintroduction of Hezron in v. 21 is unusual, apparently motivated by the desire to note a connection between the tribes of Judah and MANASSEH: Segub was born when Hezron, at sixty years of age, married the daughter of MAKIR (son of GILEAD); and Segub's son, JAIR, became a powerful Manassite. It has been suggested that this portion of the genealogy reflects a Judahite claim on the twenty-three Gileadite towns mentioned in v. 22 (cf. *ABD*, 5:1068; for further discussion, see G. N. Knoppers, *I Chronicles 1–9*, AB 12 [2004], 305–8).

A. K. HELMBOLD

Seir see′uhr (שֵׂעִיר H8541, "hairy, shaggy," possibly indicating a thicket or wooded area). Aside from one reference to a Mount Seir in JUDAH N of KESALON (*śēʿîr* H8542, Josh. 15:10, prob. a ridge W of KIRIATH JEARIM) and two references to a HORITE whose descendants were chieftains in EDOM (*śēʿîr* H8543, Gen. 36:20–21; 1 Chr. 1:38), all other occurrences of the name Seir, including "Mount Seir" (Deut. 1:2; 2 Chr. 20:10, 22–23; Ezek. 35:2–3, 7, 15) and "land of Seir" (Gen. 32:3; 36:30), designate the mountain range of Edom lying E of the rift valley known as the ARABAH and roughly parallel to it.

The range extends from Wadi ARNON southward to the vicinity of modern AQABAH. PETRA and Mount HOR are among its chief features. The rugged cliffs of this range mark the W boundary of Edom while its eastern foothills extend as far as Edom's E boundary. Its height varies from roughly 600 to 6,000 ft. above sea level. The region was important to the Hebrews because of its command of the routes to Ezion Geber.

This area apparently derived its name from "Seir the Horite," founder of a line of rulers who lived there (Gen. 36:20–30). Subsequently, the descendants of Esau (Edom) dispossessed and destroyed the Horites in a manner comparable to the Hebrew conquest of Canaan (Deut. 2:12). The precise geographical distinction between Seir and Edom is a matter of some dispute (see *ABD*, 5:1072–73), but after the Edomite conquest the two names became virtual synonyms. At the time of Hezekiah, a group of Simeonites massacred a colony of Amalekites somewhere in the range and settled the site themselves (1 Chr. 4:42–43).

According to some scholars, various texts (Deut. 1:2, 44; 33:2; Josh. 11:17; 12:7; Jdg. 5:4) suggest that "Seir" also applied to a mountainous territory W of the Arabah. Most of these passages, however, either use geographical terms whose precise meaning is uncertain or are poetic (and poetry often capitalizes on ambiguity). N. Glueck (in *HUCA* 11 [1936]: 141–57) and others have nevertheless concluded that while the term originally denoted land E of the Arabah, subsequently, as the Edomites spread westward in the postexilic period, the name "Seir" was extended to their new holdings also. (See further L. E. Axelsson, *The Lord Rose up from Seir: Studies in the History and Traditions of the Negev and Southern Judah* [1987].)   A. Bowling

Seirah see´uh-ruh שְׂעִירָה *H8545*, "female goat" or "wooded" [see Seir]). KJV Seirath. A town or wooded region, apparently in the hill country of Ephraim W of Jericho, where Ehud sought refuge after killing Eglon (Jdg. 3:26; cf. v. 27). No suitable identification has been offered. Some have thought that the term simply designates a topographical feature in the Jordan Valley; if so, the sense of the text may be that Ehud escaped to "the woody hills" of Ephraim (cf. Josh. 17:15, 18; J. Simons, *The Geographical and Topographical Texts of the Old Testament* [1959], 288, §545). See Ephraim, forest of; Ephraim, hill country of.   A. Bowling

Seirath see´uh-rath. KJV form of Seirah.

Sekakah si-kay´kuh. TNIV form of Sekakah.

Seku see´kyoo. TNIV form of Secu.

Sela see´luh (סֶלַע *H6153*, "rock, cliff"). A fortified city that served as the capital of ancient Edom; early in the 8th cent. B.C., King Amaziah of Judah captured it and renamed it Joktheel (2 Ki. 14:7). At least one prophecy refers to this city (Isa. 42:11), but it is uncertain whether it is named elsewhere in the Bible. The name Sela is possibly applied once to a site in Amorite territory that is otherwise unidentified (Jdg. 1:36). In several passages, it is disputed whether the term should be interpreted as a place name or as the common word for "rock" (2 Chr. 25:12 [NIV, "a cliff"]; Isa. 16:1 [where the context is Moab rather than Edom]; and two texts that describe Edom as dwelling "in the clefts of the rock," Jer. 49:16; Obad. 3).

Ancient Sela has commonly been thought to be the same as Petra, the later capital of the Nabateans. There, on a rocky peak known as Umm el-Bayyara, excavations have uncovered Edomite remains dated to the 7th cent. B.C. (cf. W. A. Morton in *BA* 19 [1956]: 26–36). This site, however, lies about 50 mi. SSE of the Dead Sea, and some scholars prefer to identify Sela with modern es-Selaʿ (almost 30 mi. closer to the Dead Sea). In the latter location, archaeologists have found evidence of a fortified settlement dating as far back as the 9th cent. (See further S. Hart in *PEQ* 118 [1986]: 91–95.)

selah see´luh. See Hebrew poetry IV; Psalms, Book of, VII.A.2.

Sela Hammahlekoth see´luh-huh-mah´luh-koth (סֶלַע הַמַּחְלְקוֹת *H6154*, possibly "rock of divisions" or "slippery rock"). A well-known crag in the Desert of Maon where Saul almost captured David (1 Sam. 23:28; cf. v. 25). If the second element of the name is the noun *mahălōqet H4713* (from *ḥālaq H2745*, "to divide"), the rock may have been so named because it seemed to mark the parting of the ways between these two men (cf. NJPS, "Rock of Separation"). Others derive the noun from a different verb meaning "to be smooth, slippery" (*ḥālaq H2744*), perhaps suggesting that David was able to "slip away" from Saul (cf. NRSV, "Rock of Escape"). It is also possible that the crag was originally known as Slippery Rock simply because of its physical features (like hāhār hehālāq, "the Bare Mountain," Josh. 11:17), and that it took on additional significance after David took refuge there (cf. P. K. McCarter, Jr., *I Samuel*, AB 8 [1980], 379). The location of Sela Hammahlekoth is unknown, although some have proposed Wadi el-Malaqi, some 12 mi. ESE of HEBRON. The popular idea that it may be the rock later known as MASADA does not take into account that Masada is too distant from Maon to be identified with the biblical site.

Seled see'lid (סֶלֶד H6135, possibly from סלד H6134 "to jump [for joy]"). Son of Nadab and descendant of JUDAH through JERAHMEEL; the text notes that he had no children (1 Chr. 2:30).

Selemia sel'uh-mi'uh. One of five scribes trained to "write rapidly" and commissioned to record the apocalyptic vision of EZRA on "many writing tablets" (2 Esd. 14:24).

Selemias sel'uh-mi'uhs. KJV Apoc. form of SHELEMIAH (1 Esd. 9:34).

Seleucia si-loo'shuh (Σελεύκεια G4942). A city on the coast of SYRIA in the NE corner of the Mediterranean, some 5 mi. N of the mouth of the ORONTES River. Antioch, the capital of Syria (see ANTIOCH OF SYRIA), royal seat of the SELEUCID kings, was a few miles inland, near the point where the Orontes, after its northern course between the Lebanon ranges, turns sharply W to the sea.

The grave deforestation of the Lebanon ranges, which began thirteen centuries before Christ, when the Phoenician occupants of the coastal strip became aware that there was an international market for CEDAR timber, produced a problem of erosion that has not been adequately solved. Hence the heavy burden of eroded soil carried to the sea by the Orontes. Because of this erosion, the construction of Seleucia's artificial harbor somewhat N of the mouth of the Orontes proved to be wise. It was formed, according to the visible remains, of two stone jetties of which the southern one took a wider sweep and overlapped the northern, thus giving an entrance sheltered from the prevailing S wind and blocking the northward drift of the Orontes silt.

Even so, the silt deposited along the coast by the outflow of the river ultimately filled and choked Seleucia's outlet to the sea. The site of the harbor today is a damp flat, built of alluvial deposits, in which a few fragments of the harbor masonry can be distinguished. Seleucia, designed to serve as a port for ANTIOCH, was one of nine cities which bore the name of SELEUCUS, the first ruler of the dynasty which ruled Syria and adjacent territories from the beginning of the 3rd cent. B.C. until the Romans assumed control of the eastern Mediterranean two and a half centuries later.

One of the most astonishing phenomena of history was the transformation of the political pattern of the E Mediterranean by the rapid conquests of ALEXANDER THE GREAT and the partition of his subjugated territories by the Diadochi (Successors), as his generals who carved themselves kingdoms were called. One of them, Seleucus, boldly seized control of the northern central satrapies of Alexander's empire and took the title Nicator. He founded the Seleucid kingdom of Syria in 312 B.C., and in 301 he built the port which bore his name. Seleucus and ANTIOCHUS were both common Seleucid names. This accounts for the various Seleucias and Antiochs that are scattered over the map of the Hellenistic kingdom.

Seleucia.

SELEUCIA

The Syrian Seleucia was known as Seleucia Pieria, to distinguish it from the similarly named foundations in MESOPOTAMIA and in the neighboring region of CILICIA. The appended adjective Pieria preserves in all probability the name of an existing Phoenician port, overlaid by Seleucus's major foundation. The Syrian monarch intended his port to be a strong fortress guarding one of the chief approaches to his kingdom.

For all its strength, natural and engineered, Seleucia was captured about a half century later by PTOLEMY III Euergetes, who launched an attack on Syria, probably from CYPRUS as his base (1 Macc. 11:8). Lacking the compactness of Ptolemaic Egypt, Syria found it difficult to control the various territories and tortuous frontiers of her far-flung complex of heterogeneous peoples and provinces and lived in long rivalry with her fellow successor state of Egypt, but she suffered no setback more serious than this damaging inroad into the heart of her kingdom by the third Ptolemy. Seleucia remained in Egyptian hands, a nearby menace to the security of Antioch, for over thirty years. It was recaptured by Antiochus the Great in 219 B.C., but again fell briefly into the hands of the Ptolemies in 146 B.C. (For a lucid description of the port's military importance and of its topography, see the account of Antiochus's siege of Seleucia in Polybius, *Hist.* 5.59–60.)

Antiochus's recovery of Seleucia from Syria's Egyptian rival was part of the program of that military king to recapture and consolidate all the varied regions of the Seleucid kingdom, and it was obvious that he would restore Seleucia first of all. He regarded the port as a symbol of all his soldierly success, and the story is told that in 205 B.C. he entered Seleucia in triumph, like a second Alexander, with a train of elephants and masses of plunder. It was probably on this festive occasion that the monarch assumed the ancient royal title of the Achaemenid (Persian) rulers and called himself "the great king." His common appellation was "Antiochus the Great." Under his rule Seleucia was greatly beautified and its fortifications strengthened to enable the port more effectively to fulfill its major purpose and provide a bastion of defense for Antioch, the capital.

It was the far campaigning of Antiochus the Great, in his efforts to regain control of all areas once held by Seleucid Syria, that brought him into direct confrontation with the Romans. The latter, awakened to their international obligations by the Second Punic War, were realizing that their quest for a stable frontier must extend to the Hellenistic kingdoms of the E end of the Mediterranean. Antiochus's great political mistake was his failure to recognize the emerging power of ROME and her vital interest in these eastern regions. He thrust his conquests

The area of Syrian Seleucia with remains from its harbor.

too far to the W and was decisively defeated by the Romans. By a treaty signed at Apamea on the Orontes in 188 B.C., the Seleucid kingdom of Syria ceased to be a great power in the Mediterranean world, but retained her place as a continental power in the ANE. Seleucia was still a major fortress in Syrian hands. Rome, after all, was not seeking conquests so much as a stable eastern wall.

It was not till well over a century later that the Romans appeared in power in the heartlands of the Syrian empire. Mithridates of PONTUS and Tigranes of ARMENIA looked with hostility and suspicion on the consolidation of Roman power in ASIA MINOR. It was because of a general breakdown of order in the E Mediterranean and its associated territories that the Roman senate invested the great soldier POMPEY with special powers in 66 B.C. to deal with the growing chaos of the area and to restore peace.

Pompey's three years in the E were a remarkable feat of soldiering and administration. When he arrived, he found that an Armenian and Pontic invasion had reached as far as Jerusalem. Seleucia, thanks to the strengthened fortifications of a century before, was still intact in the rear of the invading armies. It was for this reason, after his rapid recovery of all territories W of the EUPHRATES, that Pompey bestowed on Seleucia the status of "free city." In his organization of the wide arc of eastern territories from Asia Minor to Egypt, Pompey eliminated what was left of the Seleucid kingdom. It had long been in decline, weakened by domestic and dynastic strife, and eroded along all its borders by progressive loss of control. Recognizing that fact, Pompey formed Syria into a Roman province. Seleucia remained a free town within the provincial borders, and an essential port of entry for the distant power that had assumed control. The port was further fortified to act as CAESAREA did on the same difficult coast—as a harbor, a base, and a bridgehead.

With the coming of Roman domination and the Roman peace to an area that had been rent and enfeebled by chaos, weak government, and chronic war, Seleucia began a century of significant development. The maritime activity of the port must have been great. It was not only a place of exit and entry for an important Roman province, but also a staging post for ships in an age when navigation favored coastal sailing. It was from Seleucia that PAUL and BARNABAS sailed for neighboring Cyprus (Acts 13:4) on the first Christian missionary journey. They undoubtedly returned that way, though no specific reference is made to the fact (14:26); readers would have taken for granted that Seleucia was the gateway to Antioch. It is unlikely that they sailed up the lower reach of the Orontes to Antioch itself, although for smaller ships this was navigationally possible.

It is also likely that it was from Seleucia, in Paul's second tour abroad, that he and SILAS set sail (Acts 15:40–41; it is an odd fact that, in the sea beyond the silt-covered remains of Seleucia's harbor works, there are two fragmentary of the old masonry which are known as Paul and Barnabas). Barnabas and Mark no doubt used the same departure point as well (15:39). Cyprus is visible on a clear day. The current on the coast sets in a northeasterly direction, but a good offshore wind would counteract its thrust and land the travelers in Cyprus in less than a day. Half a century later, IGNATIUS, bishop of Antioch, would likely have passed through Seleucia on his way to eventual martyrdom in Rome.

Seleucia retained its status as a free city, and this dignity was confirmed by VESPASIAN in A.D. 70. All through the 1st cent., Seleucia was the base of Rome's Syrian fleet. There were continual Roman attempts in imperial times to improve a not very satisfactory port, and there are traces of Roman engineering. Chief among these remains is a vast tunnel some 200 yards long, designed to direct some of the downflow from the hills away from Seleucia's harbor works. The problem of erosion and silting was evidently a serious concern. The tunnel bears the inscribed names of both Vespasian and his son TITUS. The inference might be that Seleucia had assumed large importance as a base and supply port during the Great Rebellion in Judea. It had a clear advantage over Caesarea for this purpose, because of its relative remoteness from the scene of war and guerrilla harassment.

Reverting to notable travelers moving through the port of Seleucia, mention must be made of the Neopythagorean sage, Apollonius of Tyana (a town in CAPPADOCIA). Born about the beginning of the Christian era, and surviving almost to the end of the century, this teacher and pagan missionary matched his contemporary Paul in the length of his journeys and in his zeal for a moral way of life. Philostratus wrote in his *Life of Apollonius* (3.58) that he "went down to the sea at Seleucia, and finding a ship sailed to Cyprus." The journey must have almost coincided with that of Paul and Barnabas. Like Paul, the sage wrote letters to various groups, and two of them are addressed to the councillors of Seleucia, who had asked him to visit them. He regarded the Syrian city as "hospitable to man and devoted to the gods" (*Epistles of Apollonius* 12–13).

The city at this time must have been a splendid place with a wealth of temples and an amphitheater cut out of a cliff, which may still be seen. The great road that linked Seleucia with Antioch may also be traced here and there, and the lofty ruin of the market gate through the city wall survives. On the steep lower slopes of Mousa Dagh, there are great man-made caverns which, it is suggested, were warehouses in the days of Seleucia's commercial prosperity and sea-borne trade.

Seleucia presents a strong challenge to modern archaeology. The University of Princeton has been interested in the whole area, and in 1932 began conducting extensive excavations at neighboring Antioch. For two years before the long interruption of the Second World War, digging was done at Seleucia. Some houses, the market gate, and a Doric temple were cleared, also a 5th-cent. memorial Christian church, the Martyrion, but excavation of the whole city calls for a major effort on the part of the Lebanese government that controls the site. (See further J. D. Grainger, *The Cities of Seleukid Syria* [1989].) E. M. BLAIKLOCK

Seleucid si-loo'sid. An adjective derived from the name SELEUCUS. As a noun, *Seleucid* refers to a member of the dynasty founded by Seleucus I. On the Seleucid empire, see also ANTIOCHUS; ISRAEL, HISTORY OF XIII–XIV; MACCABEE.

Seleucus si-loo'kuhs (Σέλευκος). The name of six kings of SYRIA, four of whom are of special significance.

(1) Seleucus I, Nicator (i.e., "Conqueror," c. 358–280 B.C.). The son of a Macedonian noble, he was a close associate of ALEXANDER THE GREAT in his eastern campaigns. He became the ruler of

Silver coin with the image of Seleucus I.

Syria and Babylonia after Alexander's death. In the wars of the Diadochi ("Successors"), he was Perdiccas's chief supporter in the early struggle, but later was a party to his demise. In 316 he lost his domains and was forced to flee to Egypt. With the help of PTOLEMY I he regained Babylon, Media, and Susiana. This marked the beginning of the Seleucid dynasty, which lasted until 65 B.C. The book of DANIEL apparently refers to Seleucus when it says that after the "king of the South" (Ptolemy) becomes strong, "one of his commanders will become even stronger than he and will rule his own kingdom with great power" (Dan. 11:5).

Seleucus was a separatist with Lysimachus, Ptolemy, and Cassander against Antigonus at Ipsus in 301. As a result of the victory, he gained control of Syria and CILICIA. In 281 he won ASIA MINOR from Lysimachus. He founded a number of famous cities, among them ANTIOCH OF SYRIA on the ORONTES, several towns by the name of SELEUCIA, and EDESSA. He settled many Jews in them and conferred upon them the rights of citizenship (Jos. *Ant.* 12.3.1). He founded his new capital at Antioch and married the daughter of Demetrius, but he did not repudiate his Bactrian wife Apama. Basically Western in outlook, he aspired to gain the throne of MACEDONIA and reestablish a unified empire, but he was murdered in the attempt by Ptolemy II.

(2) Seleucus II, Callinius (i.e., "Glorious Victor,"

265–226 B.C.). The eldest son of Antiochus II and father of Antiochus III. See ANTIOCHUS. Reference seems to be made in Dan. 11:6–9 to the way in which he gained the throne and to subsequent events. His mother was Laodice, whom his father put aside to marry Berenice, daughter of Ptolemy II and sister of Ptolemy III. After this marriage, Antiochus II returned to Laodice, only to be poisoned by her. In 247 she named her son Seleucus II king. Berenice then asked her brother to come to her aid and support her infant son's claim to the throne. The Third Syrian War followed, in which Syria and Babylonia were plundered. As a result of the weakness of the empire, Bactria and Parthia were also lost. Seleucus's younger brother Antiochus Hierax, supported by their mother, temporarily took command of Asia Minor. Seleucus then died as the result of a riding accident. It remained for his son Antiochus the Great to restore the kingdom.

(3) Seleucus III, Soter (i.e., "Savior," c. 245–223). He and his brother and successor Antiochus the Great are evidently referred to in Dan. 11:10 as the sons of Seleucus II. He reigned for only two years, and died mysteriously on a campaign against Attalus of Pergamum to regain Asia Minor.

(4) Seleucus IV, Philopator ("Father-loving," c. 218–175 B.C.). The son of Antiochus the Great and brother of Antiochus IV Epiphanes, he maintained a diminished empire by keeping scrupulously to the terms of the Peace of Apamea with Rome. This forbade further adventures in the W under penalty of heavy fine. He remained on friendly terms with the other two independent powers of the E, Egypt and Macedonia. He was assassinated by a plot of Heliodorus, his chief minister, and was succeeded by his brother. Seleucus IV is probably mentioned in Dan. 11:20 as the one who "will send out a tax collector to maintain the royal splendor." Although he undertook a large share of the expenses of the Jerusalem TEMPLE early in his reign (187–175), he later attempted to carry off its treasury through Heliodorus and Simon, a Jewish officer, perhaps because he owed a great sum of money to Rome (2 Macc. 3:4).

(See further E. Bevan, *The House of Seleucus: A History of the Hellenistic Near East under the Seleucid Dynasty*, 2 vols. [1902]; A. Bouché-Leclercq, *Histoire des Séleucides (323–64 avant J.-C.)*, 2 vols. [1913–14]; E. J. Bickerman, *Institutions des Séleucides* [1938]; M. Rostovtzeff, *The Social and Economic History of the Hellenistic World*, 3 vols. [1941]; E. Will, *Histoire politique du monde hellénistique: 323–30 av. J.-C.*, 2nd ed., 2 vols. [1979–82]; *CAH* 7/1, 2nd ed. [1984], chs. 6 and 11, and 8/1, 2nd ed. [1989], ch. 10; A. Kuhrt and S. Sherwin-White, eds., *Hellenism in the East: The Interaction of Greek and non-Greek Civilizations from Syria to Central Asia after Alexander* [1987]; J. D. Grainger, *Seleukos Nikator: Constructing a Hellenistic Kingdom* [1990]; S. Sherwin-White and A. Kuhrt, *From Samarkhand to Sardis: A New Approach to the Seleucid Empire* [1993]; J. Wolski, *Seleucid and Arsacid Studies: A Progress Report on Developments in Source Research* [2003]; G. G. Aperghis, *The Seleukid Royal Economy* [2004]; L. Capdetrey, *Le pouvoir séleucide: territoire, administration, finances d'un royaume hellénistique (312–129 avant J.-C.)* [2007].)

A. RUPPRECHT

self-control. One of the basic Christian virtues. It is the mastery of self, the exercise of restraint, especially in sensual pleasures. Self-control or temperance is insurance against self-indulgence in immorality, drunkenness, brawling, gossiping, conceit, and greed. In temperance one foregoes excesses in acceptable pursuits, such as eating, drinking, and conversation.

I. Lack of self-control. It is stated in an old proverb, "Like a city whose walls are broken through / is a person who lacks self-control" (Prov. 25:28 TNIV). Self-control fortifies the inner person. It builds a wall of defense against destructive forces of evil. The pathetic tragedy of the physically strong SAMSON was the result of his intemperance in sensual desires. His sexual love for ungodly women decreed his doom (Jdg. 14:1–2). Israel's beloved king, DAVID, reaped tragic results from lack of self-control in sexual pleasures (2 Sam. 11:1–5); and so did his son SOLOMON (1 Ki. 11:1–4). PAUL was keenly aware of the threat of sexual lust. Consequently, in writing to the church in the large, wicked city of CORINTH, he gave specific instructions on this subject, particularly as related to MARRIAGE. He urged self-control (Gk. *akrasia* G202) as a safeguard against immorality (1 Cor. 7:5).

II. Practice of self-control. Good examples and wise teachings are made available to Christians in the NT. Both JOHN THE BAPTIST and JESUS CHRIST practiced self-control, even though their enemies accused John of having a demon and Jesus of being "a glutton and a drunkard" (Lk. 7:33–34). John followed a strict course of self-control and abstinence, similar in some respects to that of the ESSENES. Though Jesus was sociable and enjoyed feasting with friends, he set the perfect example of self-control. He enjoyed the blessings of nature and humanity, but abstained from sensual pleasures.

Self-control, like other Christian virtues, is not easy to maintain. It requires exercise of will and the aid of the HOLY SPIRIT. Even the strong pagan may find himself lacking in self-control. Paul alarmed the Roman governor FELIX as he "discoursed on righteousness, self-control [*enkrateia G1602*] and the judgment to come" (Acts 24:25). And, as he wrote "to the unmarried and the widows" in the Corinthian church about SEX matters, he was quite aware of how difficult it was to exercise self-control (1 Cor. 7:8–9). Young churches planted in the midst of paganism throughout the Roman empire had a hard struggle against worldliness. CRETE was one of the worst localities for "liars, evil brutes, lazy gluttons" (Tit. 1:12), and other reprobates. With this kind of environment, Paul realized the demands that would be made on church leaders. Consequently, he charged TITUS to appoint bishops (overseers) with strong Christian qualities. Such an overseer "must be hospitable, one who loves what is good, who is self-controlled [*sōphrōn G5409*], upright, holy and disciplined" (v. 8).

Self-control is essential for success in the pursuit of any worthy goal. "Athletes exercise self-control [*enkrateuomai G1603*] in all things; they do it to receive a perishable wreath, but we an imperishable one" (1 Cor. 9:25 NRSV). Paul then asserted that he, like the athlete, constantly subdued his body for the Christian ministry. Self-control was constantly in Jesus' teaching, as with reference to murder, sexual lust, swearing, retaliation, hypocrisy, greed, and anxiety (Matt. 5:21—6:34). Paul, likewise, catalogued sources of temptation (Gal. 5:19–21) and advised how to combat them. "But the fruit of the Spirit is love, joy, peace, patience, kindness, goodness, faithfulness, gentleness and self-control. Against such things there is no law" (vv. 22–23; cf. 2 Pet. 1:5–7). With reference to the Christian ministry, Paul encouraged Timothy "to fan into flame the gift of God, which is in you through the laying on of my hands. For God did not give us a spirit of timidity, but a spirit of power, of love and of self-discipline [*sōphronismos G5406*]" (2 Tim. 1:6–7).

G. B. FUNDERBURK

self-righteousness. Confidence in one's own RIGHTEOUSNESS. In popular usage, a self-righteous person is one who views himself or herself as morally upright in contrast to others; it often implies adherence to the letter of legal requirements (legalism) without regard to their spirit. In a theological sense, the term *self-righteousness* is applied to the belief, attitude, or behavior of persons who seek God's acceptance by their own efforts, that is, by doing good works and keeping the divine statutes.

Although the term *self-righteousness* itself does not appear in the Bible, the concept is clearly indicated in various passages. For example, Luke informs us that Jesus related the parable of the PHARISEE and the TAX COLLECTOR to "some who were confident of their own righteousness and looked down on everybody else" (Lk. 18:8). Similarly, Paul says of the unsaved Israelites that "they did not know the righteousness that comes from God and sought to establish their own" (Rom. 10:1–3). The apostle further testifies that he wishes to gain Christ, "not having a righteousness of my own that comes from the law, but that which is through faith in Christ" (Phil. 3:9). In a more distant way this kind of "self-righteousness" is the burden of ELIHU's complaint against JOB (cf. Job 32:2; 33:8–12).

Often the concept has moral implications. Jesus refers to the Pharisees as "the righteous" in contrast to tax-collectors and sinners (Mk. 2:15–17 and parallels), but he clearly implies that "the righteous" were not really so: "unless your righteousness surpasses that of the Pharisees and the teachers of the law, you will certainly not enter the kingdom of heaven" (Matt. 5:20). Their "righteousness" was external, with an emphasis on conformity and quantity (cf. 23:1–36, esp. v. 28: "on the outside you appear to people as righteous but on the inside you are full of hypocrisy and wickedness"); the righteousness Jesus called for was internal, with an emphasis on quality (cf. 5:21–48), although it also involved action (cf. 7:21, 24; 25:31–40). (Of course, one must not infer that Jesus' condemnation of the Pharisees and scribes was universal in character, as though none of them relied on God for their true righteousness. See PHARISEE V.)

Thus the self-righteous person is righteous neither in the religious nor the moral sense. Those who trust in themselves do not have right standing with God through self-effort or adherence to the law; nor are they morally upright, since only their external conduct is affected and not their attitudes. See also JUSTIFICATION. G. D. FEE

selvedge. This English term, referring to the border of a fabric, is used by the KJV twice to render Hebrew קָצָה H7895, which literally means "end, edge" (Exod. 26:4; 36:11). Both passages have to do with the manufacture of curtains for the TABERNACLE.

Sem sem. KJV Apoc. and NT form of SHEM.

Semachiah sem´uh-ki´uh. See SEMAKIAH.

Semakiah sem´uh-ki´uh (סְמַכְיָהוּ H6165, "Yahweh has sustained" [cf. ISMAKIAH]). Son (or relative) of Shemaiah and grandson (or descendant) of OBED-EDOM (1 Chr. 26:7). This family of Korahites (see KORAH #3) belonged to one of the divisions of gatekeepers (v. 1).

semantics. The study of meaning. See INTERPRETATION.

Semei sem´ee-i. (1) KJV Apoc. form of SHIMEI (1 Esd. 9:33; Add. Esth. 11:2).
(2) KJV NT form of SEMEIN.

Semein sem´ee-uhn (Σεμεΐν G4946 [with various spellings in the MSS], from שִׁמְעִי H9059 [see SHIMEI]). KJV Semei. Son of Josech, included in Luke's GENEALOGY OF JESUS CHRIST (Lk. 3:26).

Semellius si-mel´ee-uhs. KJV Apoc. form of SHIMSHAI (1 Esd. 2:16–17, 25, 30).

Semis see´mis. KJV Apoc. form of SHIMEI (1 Esd. 9:23).

Semite. This term was apparently first used by A. L. Schlözer in 1781 to designate the descendants of SHEM (listed in Gen. 10:21–31). The descendants of Shem, however, do not correspond entirely to the Semitic-speaking peoples (see LANGUAGES OF THE ANE II). ELAM, for example (v. 22), was not a nation that spoke a Semitic language, while the Canaanites, who were certainly Semitic, are listed among the descendants of HAM (v. 15). To be sure, there is a clear connection between Egyptian (and other "Hamitic" languages) and Semitic, and modern scholars posit a large family called Afro-Asiatic. Perhaps there was a very primitive Semitic-Hamitic community in the vicinity of Arabia and Egypt. Such facts indicate that the Table of Nations in Gen. 10 was not entirely ethnological, but at least partly geographical. In any case, the term *Semite* was subsequently used by Johann Gottfried Eichhorn (*Einleitung ins Alte Testament*, 2nd ed. [1787], 1.15) with reference to the peoples whose habitat is ETHIOPIA, ARABIA, PALESTINE, PHOENICIA, SYRIA, and the countries of the EUPHRATES and TIGRIS Rivers.

The original home of the Semites is not known, although various theories have been suggested. At the dawn of civilization traces of Semitic languages are found throughout the FERTILE CRESCENT. Today the term *Semitic* is primarily applied to the various people associated with the Semitic languages. The Semitic family, therefore, includes most of the inhabitants of modern Syria, Iraq, Jordan, Israel, Arabia, and a high percentage of Turkey, Lebanon, and N Africa. The Semitic influence has reached England and the United States largely through Jews; the Arabs have greatly influenced Africa, and at one time, southern Europe. Although all Semites were at one time polytheistic, it was they who gave birth to the three great monotheistic religions of the world: Judaism, Christianity, and Islam. L. L. WALKER

Semitic. See LANGUAGES OF THE ANE II.

Semitism. Also *Semiticism*. A feature that is characteristic of one or more Semitic languages and that has been adopted by a non-Semitic language. In biblical studies, the term is applied specifically to the presence of Hebrew or Aramaic distinctives in the Greek of the SEPTUAGINT and the NT. Semitisms include various kinds of lexical borrowing (loanwords, loan translations, semantic loans), syntactical and stylistic features, and mistranslations. (See K. Beyer, *Semitische Syntax in Neuen Testament* [1961]; M. Wilcox, *The Semitisms of Acts* [1965]; M. Black, *An Aramaic Approach to the Gospels and Acts*, 3rd ed. [1967]; J. A. Fitzmyer, *Essays on the Semitic Background of the New Testament* [1971]; R. A. Martin, *Syntactical Evidence of Semitic Sources in Greek Documents* [1974]; E. C. Maloney, *Semitic Interference in Marcan Syntax* [1980]; S. Thompson, *The Apocalypse and Semitic Syntax* [1985]; M. Silva, *Biblical Words and Their Meaning: An Introduction to Lexical Semantics*, rev. ed. [1994], chs. 2–3; G. Walser, *The Greek of the Ancient Synagogue: An Investigation on the Greek of the Septuagint, Pseudepigrapha and the New Testament* [2001].) See also GREEK LANGUAGE III.B.

Senaah suh-nay'uh (סְנָאָה *H6171*, possibly "hated [woman]" [if from שָׂנֵא *H8533*], perhaps referring to people of lower classes). Either the ancestor of some Israelites who returned from EXILE or, more likely, a town in JUDAH resettled by them (Ezra 2:35; Neh. 7:38; 1 Esd. 5:23 [KJV, "Annaas," with some editions reading "Annas"]). Because the number of returnees seems rather large, some have interpreted the phrase *benê senāʾâ* ("sons of the rejected woman"?) as referring to the poorer classes of Jerusalem (cf. BDB, 702) or to some other group that was regarded with contempt. The matter is complicated by references to the son(s) of HASSENAAH and HASSENUAH (*hassenāʾâ H2189*, Neh. 3:3; *hassenûʾâ H2190*, 1 Chr. 9:7; Neh. 11:9), both of which could be understood as designating people from (the) Senaah. Some scholars suspect textual error (see H. G. M. Williamson, *Ezra, Nehemiah*, WBC 16 [1985], 34).   S. BARABAS

senate. An authoritative assembly possessing legislative powers. The English term derives from Latin *senatus*, meaning "an assembly of elders" (from *senex*, "old man"). The KJV uses "senator" once in the OT to render the Hebrew word for "elder" (Ps. 105:22), and "senate" once in the NT to render the Greek word for "council of elders," probably referring to the SANHEDRIN (Acts 5:21; "senate" also occurs several times in the KJV Apoc., Jdt. 11:14; 1 Macc. 8:15 et al.).

Among the Romans, the state council or senate was most ancient—from before the expulsion of the Tarquins. The Roman senate first consisted of 100 men, but later the number was increased to 300, and plebeians as well as patricians were made eligible. Under the ROMAN EMPIRE, the number was increased to 900 by Julius CAESAR but was reduced to 600 by AUGUSTUS, who added age and property requirements. Under the empire, the principal duties of the senate consisted of (1) the maintenance of state religion, (2) supervision of government property and finances, (3) control of the senatorial provinces, (4) legislative ratification of the emperor's decisions, (5) jurisdiction over breach of contract, cases of high treason, and offenses of senators, and (6) exercise of the right to nominate all magistrates except consuls.

H. L. DRUMWRIGHT, JR.

Seneca sen'uh-kuh. Latin orator, writer, philosopher, and statesman. Lucius Annaeus Seneca (the Younger) was born in southern Spain c. 4 B.C. (possibly as late as A.D. 1), but a relative took him to ROME while he was still a child. Trained in rhetoric, Seneca was attracted to STOIC philosophy and became a brilliant orator. In 49 he was appointed tutor to the young NERO, and when the latter became emperor five years later, Seneca (alongside Afranius Burrus) served as his minister and confidant. Seneca wielded considerable power for some years, but his reputation declined in the late 50s. He eventually retired from public life, and in the year 65, accused of conspiracy, was forced to commit suicide. (Much of our information comes from Tacitus, *Annals*, books 13–15. Among recent works, see also M. T. Griffin, *Seneca: Philosopher in Politics*, new ed. [1992]; G. Maurach, *Seneca: Leben und Werk*, 2nd ed. [1996]; P. Veyne, *Seneca: The Life of a Stoic* [2003]; B. Inwood, *Reading Seneca: Stoic Philosophy at Rome* [2005]; *OCD*, 96–98, s.v. "Annaeus Seneca (2).")

Seneca wrote a number of ethical treatises and other prose works that are a major source for our understanding of Stoicism. His poetic writings consist primarily of tragedies, and these proved influential during the Renaissance (cf. A. L. Motto and J. R. Clark, *Senecan Tragedy* [1988]). An apocryphal document known as *Epistles of Paul and Seneca*—composed in the 3rd cent. or later, and popular in the late Middle Ages—purports to preserve mutually admiring correspondence between these two figures (English trans. in *NTAp*, 2:46–53). These letters were no doubt composed with the purpose of commending Christianity to pagan society, which was strongly influenced by Stoicism; the unknown author(s) may also have wished to enhance Seneca's reputation among Christians. (For a comparison between Paul and Seneca, including a brief description of the apocryphal letters, see J. B. Lightfoot, *St. Paul's Epistle to the Philippians: A Revised Text with Introduction, Notes, and Dissertations* [1868], 270–333. See further J. N. Sevenster, *Paul and Seneca* [1961]; A. Fürst et al., *Der apokryphe Briefwechsel zwischen Seneca und Paulus* [2006].)

Seneh see´nuh (סְנֶה *H6175*, possibly "thorny" [BDB, 702, but see *HALOT*, 2:760]). A notable rock or crag which, together with Bozez, commanded the pass at Micmash (1 Sam. 14:4). This important access route to the Judean highlands follows the Wadi Qelt in its lower stages. In the vicinity of Micmash the route becomes narrower and passes through these two crags, thus forming one of the strategic locations for governing access to the Judean highlands. This accounts for its importance to the Philistines. Suitable rock formations are found along Wadi es-Suweinit in the immediate vicinity of ancient Micmash (c. 7 mi. NE of Jerusalem). A. Bowling

Senir see´nuh (שְׂנִיר *H8536*, meaning unknown; cf. Akk. *Saniru*). KJV also Shenir. The Amorite name for Mount Hermon (Deut. 3:9). At times the name has been used for larger portions of the Antilebanon range (as perhaps in Ezek. 27:5). However, Hebrew usage also distinguished between Hermon and Senir (Cant. 4:8), and between those and Baal Hermon as well (1 Chr. 5:23). It is tempting to suppose that such usage distinguishes the three individual peaks of Mount Hermon. A. Bowling

Sennacherib suh-nak´uh-rib (סַנְחֵרִיב *H6178*, from Akk. *Sin-aḫḫē-erība*, "Sin [the moon god] has replaced the [lost] brothers"). King of Assyria, 705–681 B.C. As his name implies, Sennacherib was not the eldest son of Sargon II, but he was chosen as crown prince and made military governor of the troublesome northern frontier. His boldness in difficult situations and firmness in dispensing justice was to stand him in good stead. When his father was assassinated in 705 B.C., Sennacherib acted quickly to take the throne before marching against dissidents.

I. Northern foes. Since Sargon's victories over the northern tribes, the latter had been subject to pressure from the Cimmerians (Assyr. *Gimirrai*) as the latter moved westward from the Caucasus toward Lydia. Sennacherib led expeditions to the central Zagros Mountains and to Tabal and Cilicia, where he captured Tarsus. His aim was to keep the trade routes open to friendly peoples outside the newly invaded areas. This action contained the borders and enabled him to devote his attention to the more restive parts of his empire.

II. Babylonia. In the same year as Sennacherib became king, the old enemy of his father, Marduk-apla-iddinna (Merodach-Baladan), sheikh of the Bit-Yakin, seized the throne of Babylon with the backing of Elamite troops (see Elam). Much of his time was spent in Borsippa, since this was closer to his tribal lands and more easily defensible by his fellow Arameans (see Aram). In 703 B.C. Sennacherib led an army against the rebel whom he defeated near Kish. After sacking Babylon he deported 208,000 prisoners and set a puppet king trained in Nineveh, one Bēl-ibni, on the throne.

Marduk-apla-iddinna retreated to the security of the southern marshes until the time, three years later, when he was able to elicit further Elamite assistance and rouse the Chaldean and Aramean tribes in collusion with Bēl-ibni. A swift Assyrian march broke up the attempt by this coalition to assert their independence. This time Marduk-apla-iddinna fled across the Persian Gulf to take refuge in S Elam, where he died. Sennacherib characteristically aimed to deal with the subversion at its source and thus he mounted a sea-borne invasion, using a fleet of ships, manned by sailors from Tyre, Sidon, and Cyprus, which floated down the Tigris and Euphrates Rivers. From a bridgehead on the coast, punitive raids were mounted against the villages that harbored the tribesmen from the marshes.

This punitive action had little lasting effect. Soon Elam retaliated by raiding across the Tigris to capture Ashur-nadin-shumi at Sippar. This was Sennacherib's youngest son, whom he had placed on the Babylonian throne under a special charter (699–694 B.C.). A pro-Elamite supporter, Nergal-ushēzib, replaced him. Then in 693 Assyrian troops redrawing from the S defeated Nergal-ushēzib at Nippur, but failed to recapture Babylon itself where another Aramean, Mushēzib-Marduk, had taken control.

Relief of Sennacherib on a magnificent throne watching prisoners being brought before him from the capture of the city of Lachish during the time of Hezekiah (from Nineveh, 7th cent. B.C.).

In the following year Sennacherib took drastic steps to reassert Assyrian authority in the S. He met and defeated the Elamites at Dēr, and local Assyrian officials ousted Mushēzib-Marduk, who had seized this moment to rouse the tribes. Fleeing to Elam he managed to bribe the Elamites and Arameans to waylay the Assyrians at Ḥalule, where an indeterminate but bloody battle was fought. Internal dissensions soon limited further Elamite help, so that an Assyrian force was able to besiege Mushēzib-Marduk in Babylon for nine months. When the city fell it was looted, its deity Marduk being taken off to Nineveh, and the city remained quiet through the rest of the reign.

III. Action against Judah. HEZEKIAH of Judah, perhaps incited by the Babylonian Marduk-apla-iddinna (Merodach Baladan) to join in the anti-Assyrian coalition (2 Ki. 20:12–13), seized Padi, the pro-Assyrian ruler of EKRON (18:8). When Sidon and Tyre refused tribute in 701 B.C., Sennacherib directed his third campaign to the W. Marching down the Phoenician coast, he captured Great and Little Sidon, Zarephath, Mahallib (Ahlab of Jdg. 1:31), Ushu, and Acco. Eluli (Elulaeus), who had fled, was replaced as king of Tyre with Ethbaal, but that seaport was bypassed. The kings of Sidon, Arvad, Byblos, Beth-Ammon, and Edom submitted, but Ashkelon, Beth Dagon, and Joppa, who refused, were sacked.

Hezekiah's resistance in these circumstances was outstandingly daring, especially as the Assyrians marching on ELTEKEH defeated the Egyptians on whom the anti-Assyrian forces doubtless relied for help. The elders of Ekron were flayed alive for handing over their king to Hezekiah. The Assyrians thereupon besieged LACHISH, which fell after a cruel siege, and sacked forty-six towns and villages in Judah, taking away 200,150 prisoners and much spoil. Despite the close siege works hemming in Jerusalem, Hezekiah refused a demand for surrender (2 Ki. 18:17; Isa. 36:1–21). According to Sennacherib, Hezekiah later paid tribute of "40 talents of gold and 800 talents of silver, precious stones," and other rare commodities. The Bible mentions only "300 [talents] of silver and 30 [talents] of gold" (2 Ki. 18:13–16), the difference being perhaps due to the remaining amount being given in other form, to variations in the standards of weights used, or to Assyrian exaggeration.

According to Sennacherib, Hezekiah freed Padi, who was given some former Judean territory as compensation for his ordeal on behalf of Assyria. Meanwhile, Sennacherib claims, "Hezekiah, the Judean, I shut up in Jerusalem, his royal city, like a bird in a cage. I put sentry-posts closely round the city, to turn back to his fate anyone who ventured out of the city-gate" (Taylor Prism; cf. *ANET*, 288a). The siege was unsuccessful due to the foresight of Hezekiah in protecting his water-supplies (2 Ki. 20:20; 2 Chr. 32:30) and his steadfast trust in God rather than in material support from allies (2 Ki. 19:32–34).

Sennacherib's own account makes no reference to the outcome of the siege—a sure acknowledgment of failure—or to the defeat of the Assyrian army, which the Bible describes as 185,000 dead "by the angel of the LORD" (2 Ki. 19:35). This latter event, says HERODOTUS (*Hist*. 2.141), was due to "a multitude of field mice which by night devoured all the quivers and bows of the enemy, and all the straps by which they held their shields.... Next morning they commenced their fight and great numbers fell as they had no arms with which to defend themselves."

There has long been debate whether all these events fall into one or two campaigns by Sennacherib. Those who argue for two campaigns see the reference to the approach of the Egyptian relief forces under TIRHAKAH (2 Ki. 19:9; Isa. 37:9) as indicative of later action, since this pharaoh did not come to the throne of Egypt until c. 690 B.C. This may be answered by the suggestion that he acted as commander-in-chief while "king of Ethiopia/Nubia (Cush)," for there is no confirmation that he was born c. 709 and that therefore he was too young to be in the field. The two-campaign theory assumes that it was in the first campaign of 701 that Hezekiah paid tribute and surrendered Padi and that he successfully withstood a later siege, c. 689–686, when Sennacherib struck against the Arabs S of DAMASCUS, of which there is no mention in the Assyrian records.

Those who hold this view believe that both campaigns have been conflated into one by the Hebrew historians. They, moreover, interpret 2 Ki. 19:37 as implying that Sennacherib's death took place immediately on his return from Palestine. The Hebrew text does not, however, state or imply the length of time between his return to Nineveh and his death in 681. The latter was some years after the Palestinian campaign on either view. There is no textual or historical evidence which precludes the now more generally accepted view of a single campaign in 701.

IV. Domestic policy. Sennacherib exercised a firm but tolerant rule at home. Encouraged by his W Semitic (Palestinian?) wife, Naqʾia-Zakutu, he spent much effort on rebuilding his capital, Nineveh. With prisoner-of-war labor he built his own "palace without a rival," with suites of rooms furnished in cedar, cypress, boxwood (walnut?), and ebony. Stone was extensively used, and the reception rooms were panelled with more than 9,000 sq. ft. of bas-reliefs depicting his victories, including the siege of Lachish (now in the British Museum). The city walls and gates were renovated and a New Year Temple and armory built to receive the spoils of war. Water for the city was brought via canals, an aqueduct (Jerwan), and a dam (Ajeila) to water the city and its surrounding parks between the Tigris and Khosr Rivers. Sennacherib introduced cotton growing to Assyria and claims to have used other new techniques in his architectural works, including open-cast bronze modeling "like the casting of half-shekels."

V. His death. According to 2 Ki. 19:37 (Isa. 37:38), Sennacherib was assassinated by his two sons while worshiping in the shrine of his god NISROCH. The sons escaped to Ararat, and Sennacherib's son Esarhaddon reigned in his stead. The Assyrian texts make no specific reference to this event and it has been thought that there are divergencies in the accounts. The Babylonian Chronicle states that he was murdered by "his son." Such variation in historical sources is not uncommon, since one son may well have been the ringleader or have actually done the deed.

Esarhaddon himself makes no reference to his father's death in his account of his own accession, though he does mention the hostility of his brothers, whom he had to defeat before gaining the throne. He claims to have defeated the rebels in Hanigalbat, from where two of them may have fled to Urartu. See ADRAMMELECH (PERSON) and SHAREZER. Thirty-two years later ASHURBANIPAL says that his grandfather Sennacherib had been "crushed between the figures of protecting deities," possibly the bull-colossi guarding the narrow temple doorway. Though the temple of Nisroch is not necessarily to be located in Assyria, it could be the temple of Ninurta (or Nusku?) in Nineveh.

(See further D. D. Luckenbill, *The Annals of Sennacherib* [1924]; L. L. Honor, *Sennacherib's Invasion of Palestine* [1926]; D. J. Wiseman in *Documents from Old Testament Times*, ed. D. W. Thomas [1958], 64–73; H. H. Rowley in *BJRL* 44 [1962]: 395–431; J. M. Russell, *Sennacherib's Palace without Rival at Nineveh* [1991]; A. K. Grayson in *CAH*, 3/2, 2nd ed. [1991], 103–22; M. Dietrich, *The Babylonian Correspondence of Sargon and Sennacherib* [2003]; L. L. Grabbe, ed., *"Like a Bird in a Cage": The Invasion of Sennacherib in 701 BCE* [2003].)

D. J. WISEMAN

sensual. The KJV uses this English adjective twice to render the Greek word *psychikos* G6035 (Jas. 3:15; Jude 19). This Greek term occurs in three other passages where the KJV uses the rendering "natural" (1 Cor. 2:14; 15:44, 46). In one of the references (Jas. 3:15), the term is applied to a wisdom that is "earthly" in contrast with "the wisdom that comes from heaven" (v. 17). In the other passages, the term is applied to people and contrasted with *pneumatikos* G4461 ("spiritual") and/or with (having the) *pneuma* G4460 ("Spirit"). Thus the person characterized as *psychikos* is one who does not have, or whose conduct is not controlled by, the HOLY SPIRIT (cf. the various renderings used by modern versions). (For the specific meaning, "preoccupied with bodily/sexual pleasures," see LUST; SEX.)

sensus plenior. See TYPOLOGY.

Senuah si-nyoo′uh. KJV alternate form of HASSENUAH.

Seorim see-or′im (שְׂעֹרִים H8556, possibly from שָׂעִיר H8537, "hairy"). A priest who received the fourth lot of the twenty-four divisions in DAVID's time (1 Chr. 24:8).

separation. See CONSECRATION; HOLINESS; SANCTIFICATION.

Sephar see′fuhr (סְפָר H6223, meaning uncertain). A place "in the east country" (prob. ARABIA) that, along with MESHA, served to delimit the territory occupied by the sons of JOKTAN, a descendant of SHEM through EBER (Gen. 10:30). The location of Sephar is unknown, although many scholars believe it was somewhere in S ARABIA (the names of several of Joktan's sons can be linked with geographical sites in this region; moreover, Mesha is usually thought to have been in N Arabia). Specific proposals include modern Zafar (a coastal city in Oman, though there is a place by the same name in Yemen) and Isfar (S of the valley of Ḥadramaut; see HAZARMAVETH). It has also been suggested that the word is a common noun meaning "border country" (*IDB*, 1:272). (Biblical Sephar is not to be confused with a place of the same name mentioned in the SAMARIA ostraca and identified with modern Sefarin, a few miles W of Samaria. See Y. Aharoni et al., *The Carta Bible Atlas*, 4th ed. [2002], map 139.)

Sepharad sef′uh-rad (סְפָרַד H6224, meaning unknown). A place mentioned by OBADIAH as the site of the exile of certain captives from Jerusalem (Obad. 20). A rabbinic tradition preserved in the TARGUM (which has *sepamya*ʾ, properly *ʾispamya*ʾ or *ʾispanyaʾ*, from Lat. *Hispania*) understood the name as a reference to SPAIN (cf. the term *Sefardi*, applied to Jews who first settled in Spain and Portugal). Some modern scholars identify Sepharad with Saparda, a country that appears in the Assyrian Annals of SARGON II as a district of SW MEDIA (though other documents suggest a location near ASIA MINOR).

Most probably, however, Sepharad should be identified with SARDIS, the capital of LYDIA. The difference in spelling is not linguistically objectionable, since an Aramaic-Lydian bilingual inscription, found at Sardis, refers to this city as *sprd*; moreover, Sardis appears as *Sparda* in Old Persian inscriptions, and as *Saparda* in Babylonian. If this view is correct, the biblical reference is of historical significance, for it attests to the existence of a Jewish colony in SW Asia Minor at a rather early date. The importance of Sardis as a center of trade between the sea routes of the AEGEAN and the interior land routes makes it not surprising that Jewish exiles should be found there.   T. E. MCCOMISKEY

Sepharvaim sef′uhr-vay′im (סְפַרְוַיִם H6226, meaning unknown; gentilic סְפַרְוִים H6227, "Sepharvites"). A city conquered in the 8th cent. B.C. by the Assyrians; SHALMANESER V resettled its inhabitants in SAMARIA (2 Ki. 17:24). The deities of the Sepharvites included ADRAMMELECH and ANAMMELECH (v. 31). Subsequently, SENNACHERIB's envoy mentioned Sepharvaim as a place whose gods were helpless against the Assyrians (2 Ki. 18:34; 19:13; Isa. 36:19; 37:13).

The location of Sepharvaim is uncertain. Among various proposed identifications, two deserve mention. (1) The less likely is Sippar (modern Abu Habba) in Mesopotamia, known as Sippar of Shamash and Sippar of Anunitum, thus accounting for the dual ending in the Hebrew form of the name. (2) Ezekiel refers to a town named SIBRAIM as lying between DAMASCUS and HAMATH (Ezek.

47:16; note that Hamath is included in all the passages where Sepharvaim is mentioned). This second possibility is attractive because it suits the Syrian context of Sepharvaim and the possible Syrian character of the god Adrammelech. (See *ABD*, 5:1090.)   A. Bowling

Sepharvite sef'uhr-vit. See Sepharvaim.

Sephela suh-fee'luh. KJV Apoc. form of Shephelah (1 Macc. 12:38).

Sepphoris sef'uh-ris (Σέπφωρις [Jos. *Ant.* 13.12.5 §338 et al.], with various spellings, cf. *HJP*, rev. ed., 1:179–871 2.172 78; apparently from נמצ H7600, "bird" [cf. צִפּוֹר and צִפֹּרָה]). A strongly fortified city c. 4 mi. NW of Nazareth. Although not mentioned in the Bible, Sepphoris was famous as a military, political, and cultural center and as one of the chief cities of Hellenistic Galilee. Herod Antipas (see Herod V) did much to rebuild and enhance the importance of the city (cf. Jos. *Ant.* 18.2.1 §27). Sepphoris figures prominently in the writings of Josephus and in rabbinic literature, and Jesus must have often visited it. (See *ABD*, 5:1090–93; *NEAEHL*, 4:1324–28.)   A. Bowling

Septuagint sep'too-uh-jint. This term, derived from Latin *Septuaginta* ("Seventy") and commonly abbreviated with the corresponding Roman numeral LXX, is the traditional (though imprecise) name given to the primary Greek version of the Hebrew Bible. The LXX appears to have been the first translation made of the OT or of any literary work of comparable size into another language, and it thus marks a milestone in human culture.

For biblical scholarship, the LXX is of great importance in several areas: (1) *OT textual criticism*—it attests to an ancient form of the Hebrew text that is often different from, and sometimes more reliable than, the standard Masoretic text (MT); (2) *OT hermeneutics*—it represents the earliest known interpretation of the Hebrew Bible (aside from interpretative features within the OT itself); (3) *NT language*—it is a major source for our understanding of Hellenistic Greek; (4) *NT hermeneutics*—it was used extensively by the NT writers and evidently influenced their formulation of Christian teaching. This article treats not only the LXX (in the stricter sense of the term) but also the other Greek versions of the Hebrew Bible produced in antiquity. (What follows is an abridgment of the initial chapters in K. H. Jobes and M. Silva, *Invitation to the Septuagint* [2000], to which the reader is referred for additional information.)

    I. Introduction
   II. Terminology
  III. Origin
  IV. Later Greek translations
      A. Aquila
      B. Symmachus
      C. Theodotion
      D. Other versions
   V. Recensions
      A. The Hexaplaric recension
      B. The Lucianic recension
  VI. Ancient witnesses
 VII. Modern editions

I. Introduction. The Bible contains ancient writings that have been continuously read from the time of its authors until our own. The first and oldest part of the Bible was written originally in Hebrew (except for the following passages written in Aramaic: Ezra 4:8—6:18; 7:12–26; Jer. 10:11; Dan. 2:4—7:28). The abiding importance of these sacred writings—first to the Jews and later to the Christians—demanded that throughout history they be translated into the languages of the peoples who received them as Scripture.

After the ANE was conquered by Alexander the Great (c. 333 B.C.), the Jewish people found themselves living in the Hellenistic culture. Their religious values and ancient ways collided with Greek practices, philosophies, and language. Just as today most Jewish people live outside of Israel, so it was during the Hellenistic period. Because as a rule the Jews of the Diaspora (Dispersion) who were scattered throughout the Mediterranean no longer spoke Hebrew, they needed to have the sacred writings in Greek, which had become the *lingua franca* of the Hellenistic world. Thus the Greek version of the Hebrew Bible became Scripture to the Greek-speaking Jewish communities in the Diaspora. Together with the Greek NT, it was later the Bible of most Christians during the first few centuries of the church. The Greek version remains even today the canonical text for the Orthodox Christian tradition, which traces its heritage to the Byzantine church of the eastern empire.

Because of its widespread importance, numerous copies of the Greek Bible were produced by scribes in many places throughout the centuries. There are more surviving MSS of the Greek OT than there are of any other ancient Greek text except the NT. Counting both complete and fragmentary MSS, nearly 2,000 handwritten copies of the Septuagint have survived. In comparison, there are only about 650 extant MSS of Homer's *Iliad*, the most popular work of antiquity, and fewer than 350 of the writings of the famous Greek tragedian, Euripides. For scholars interested in the complexities of textual criticism and the tendencies of scribes, the MSS of the Septuagint provide an enormous amount of material for study.

The LXX is written in the Koine, that is, the *common* Greek of the Hellenistic age, a form of the language that had developed from the classical Greek of 5th-century ATHENS. For students of the GREEK LANGUAGE during the Hellenistic period, the LXX is a major source of information. Moreover, because it is a translation of a Hebrew text into Greek, it provides a unique opportunity for those interested in comparing original Greek writings to "translation" Greek.

The Greek version also has great value for the study of the Hebrew text. The issues surrounding this use of the version are quite complex, but the fact remains that the LXX was translated from some Hebrew text that was not identical to the Hebrew text we use today. That original Greek translation, which was produced much earlier than any surviving copy of the Hebrew Bible, is an indirect witness to its *Vorlage*, that is, to the Hebrew parent text from which it was translated. In theory, the LXX should allow scholars to reconstruct that earlier Hebrew text, though in practice this attempt is fraught with difficult problems.

Translation between any two languages, however, always involves a degree of interpretation. The translators who produced the Greek version of the Hebrew Bible were also interpreters who came to the text with the theological and political prejudices of their time and thus had to deal with hermeneutical issues similar to those we face today. Their translations were no doubt influenced, whether deliberately or subconsciously, by what they believed the Hebrew meant in light of their contemporary situation, which may or may not have been what the author of the Hebrew intended. Clearly, this is bad news to the textual critic, who wants to use the Greek version to reconstruct its Hebrew parent text. On the other hand, precisely because the LXX reflects the theological, social, and political interests of the translator, it provides valuable information about how the Hebrew Bible was understood and interpreted at the time the translators were working.

Subsequently, the LXX played a significant role in the Christian church. The Greek version, not the Hebrew Bible, was the primary theological and literary context within which the writers of the NT and most early Christians worked. This does not mean that the NT writers were ignorant of the Hebrew Bible or that they did not use it. Since these authors were writing in Greek, however, they would naturally quote, allude to, and otherwise use the Greek version of the Hebrew Bible. This process is no different from that of a modern author writing, for instance, in Spanish, and quoting a widely used Spanish translation of the Bible.

Consequently, familiarity with the Greek OT cannot help but enlighten the student of the Greek NT. Biblical scholar Adolf Deissmann once wrote, "A single hour lovingly devoted to the text of the Septuagint will further our exegetical knowledge of the Pauline Epistles more than a whole day spent over a commentary" (*The Philology of the Greek Bible* [1908], 12). The connection can be illustrated at several levels. In the first place, the LXX provided some of the vocabulary that the NT writers drew upon. They often use terms or phrases that are found in the LXX and that were not in common usage in the first century (e.g., *pasa sarx*, "all flesh," Lk. 3:6). In such cases, they may be borrowing the terms from the Greek OT to affect a "biblical" style. The LXX certainly left its mark in Greek just as the KJV has in English.

Second, the NT writers sometimes use expressions found in the LXX to draw the reader's mind to specific passages of OT Scripture. Paul, for instance, uses the phrase "every knee shall bow" in Phil. 2:10 when he describes the ultimate exaltation of Christ. Clearly Paul is using vocabulary from the Greek of Isa. 45:23 not just to sound "biblical" but rather to bring that passage to mind in order to identify Jesus Christ with God.

Third, the NT writers frequently—perhaps as many as 300 times—quote the Greek OT directly (see QUOTATIONS IN THE NT). This fact accounts for some of the differences readers note when comparing these citations with the corresponding OT passages. For example, in Heb. 11:21 dying JACOB is said to have worshiped leaning on the top of his *staff*, a reference to the Greek text of Gen. 47:31. In almost all English Bibles, however, Genesis says that Jacob worshiped at the top of the *bed*, which is indeed what the Hebrew MSS say. The reason for the discrepancy is that the Hebrew text used by the Greek translator of Genesis consisted only of consonants; the correct vowels were to be inferred by the reader from the context. The Hebrew noun in Genesis could be read as either *maṭṭeh* H4751 ("staff") or *miṭṭâ* H4753 ("bed"), and the Greek translator inferred that the word "staff" was meant. Some centuries later, when vowel points were added to the Hebrew biblical texts, the noun in 47:31 was taken to mean "bed." (The NIV has translated 47:31 so as to agree with Heb. 11:21, presumably on the grounds that the traditional vowel-pointing of the Hebrew text is incorrect and that the Greek version preserves the correct sense. For a fuller treatment of this quotation, see M. Silva in *Scripture and Truth*, ed. D. A. Carson and J. W. Woodbridge [1983], 147–65.)

One must also appreciate that the continuity and development of thought between the OT and NT is of particular concern for BIBLICAL THEOLOGY. The LXX provides essential, but often overlooked, theological links that would have been familiar to Christians of the first century, but are not so obvious in the Hebrew version. No NT scholar can afford to ignore the LXX.

After NT times, the LXX, not the Hebrew text, was the Bible used by the early church fathers and councils for several centuries. As Christian doctrine on the nature of Christ and the TRINITY developed, discussion centered on the exegesis of key OT texts. Because most of the church fathers could not read Hebrew, exegetical debates were settled using the Greek OT. Some of the Greek words used to translate the OT had connotations associated with Greek culture and philosophy that were probably alien to the thought of the original Hebrew author. The simple fact that the Hebrew Scriptures existed in the Greek language and were read by people living in Greek culture led to exegesis by both Jewish and Christian interpreters (e.g., PHILO JUDAEUS and ARIUS, respectively) that was heavily influenced by Greek philosophy.

Of course, one must also consider that the Greek translator himself originally rendered the Hebrew in ways that were to some extent influenced by Greek culture and thought, making the text even more congenial to a later exegesis that would be similarly influenced. A good example is the LXX text of Prov. 8:22–31, which held a prominent place in the early discussions about the nature of Christ and his place in the Trinity. In this passage, wisdom is personified as the first of the Lord's works prior to the creation of the universe.

Primarily because of the opening verses of the Gospel of John, JESUS CHRIST became associated with this divine WISDOM (*sophia* G5053) or rationality (*logos* G3364; see LOGOS). In Greek philosophy, however, the Greek concept of an impersonal divine wisdom permeating the universe was very prominent, and so the nature of Jesus Christ and his relationship to God the Father had to be carefully delineated. Many early theologians, such as ORIGEN and TERTULLIAN, all used this passage from the Greek Proverbs in their discussions of the relationship between the Son and the Father. Subsequently Arius, a Christian presbyter of ALEXANDRIA (died 336), argued on the basis of the Greek of Prov. 8 that the Son was a created being, not coeternal with the Father. Subtle differences between the Greek and Hebrew worked in favor of Arius's argument, which led to years of intense debate. (The exegesis of this passage was settled by the Council of Nicaea in 325, when the Arian controversy was pronounced a heresy. For further details, see Jaroslav Pelikan, *The Christian Tradition: A History of the Development of Doctrine*, 5 vols. [1971–89], 1:191–210.)

This example is only one of many that show that the doctrines of orthodox Christianity were hammered out with exegetical appeals to an OT that was written in Greek, not Hebrew. While it is true that no point of orthodox Christian doctrine rests on the Greek text in contradiction to the Hebrew, it is also true that the LXX text was the Word of God for the church in its first few centuries. Moreover, the Eastern Orthodox churches, such as the Greek, Russian, and Syrian, inherited the Greek text as their Bible. Traditionally, the Orthodox churches have considered the Greek version to be divinely inspired (and even in some sense to have superseded the Hebrew text), although this is a matter of debate among Orthodox scholars today.

II. Terminology. Strictly speaking, there is really no such thing as "*the* Septuagint." Most translations of the Hebrew Bible are characterized by unity throughout. Not so with the LXX, which was produced by many people unknown to us, over two or three centuries, and almost certainly in more than one location. Consequently, the Greek OT does not have the unity that the term "the Septuagint" might imply.

Because the Greek translation of the Hebrew Bible has such a long and complicated history, the name Septuagint is used to refer to several quite different things. In its most general sense, the term is used to refer to any or all ancient Greek translations of the Hebrew Bible, just as one might now refer in general to the "English Bible," with no particular translation in mind. This is the sense in which the term is used in the title of this article, which deals with the ancient Greek version(s) of the Hebrew Bible. Often, the term is also used to refer to a particular printed edition of the Greek text, whether that edition reproduces the text of a MS or prints a reconstructed text.

Given these typical uses of the term "LXX," one might understandably, though mistakenly, infer that the Greek translation found in a given ancient MS or modern edition is a homogeneous text produced in its entirety at one point in time. In fact, no such homogeneity exists in any collection of the Greek books of the OT. Each edition—whether the ancient, hand-copied Codex Vaticanus or the modern, printed Rahlfs edition—is an amalgam, with each section of the Bible having a long and separate textual history.

The books of the Hebrew Bible were originally translated independently into Greek by different translators over several centuries. What we call *books* were at that time written on individual SCROLLS. A scroll, typically no longer than 35 ft., could not contain the Greek version of the Hebrew Bible in its entirety. Usually each book was written on a separate scroll. A different format, the CODEX, came into use in the second century of our era. This format made it possible to bind the texts from many separate scrolls into one volume, giving a false impression of homogeneity. Just because the texts were bound together did not mean they shared a common origin. In fact, there was no one uniform Greek version of the entire Hebrew Bible, just individual scrolls that had been copied from other scrolls through the ages. For instance, the Greek text of Genesis in some medieval codex may have been copied from a MS that was produced in the 1st cent. of our era and that contained the translation originally made in the 3rd cent. B.C. in Alexandria, while the Greek text of Esther *bound in the same codex* may have been copied from a MS produced in the 4th cent. of our era and containing a translation made in the 1st cent. B.C. in Jerusalem.

The particular collection of Greek texts of the biblical books that comprise the earliest one-volume Bibles, such as CODEX SINAITICUS or CODEX VATICANUS, occurred usually by the historical happenstance of whatever texts were at hand, irrespective of their origin and character. Therefore, whatever one may say about the history and characteristics of the Greek text of one biblical book may or may not be true of the others, even though they are found bound together in one codex. And because modern critical editions of the LXX are based on the ancient MSS, the same misleading appearance of homogeneity exists today.

When one enters the highly specialized world of textual criticism, the name Septuagint takes on a more precise and technical sense. It may be used specifically to distinguish the oldest Greek translation from subsequent translations and revisions of the Greek. If the term is used in this narrower sense, it refers only to the original Greek version of the PENTATEUCH, for that was the first part of the Hebrew Bible translated in the 3rd cent. B.C. The remaining books of the Hebrew canon were translated by different people in different places during the next two centuries. However, it has become customary, by extension, to use the term Septuagint with reference to the complete Greek canon of the Hebrew Bible.

It is probably better to refer to the original translation of books other than the Pentateuch as the *Old Greek* (OG) so as to distinguish it from the original translation of the Pentateuch as well as from the later revisions and new translations. (When referring to these initial Greek translations of the Hebrew Bible as a whole, some scholars prefer the combined abbreviation LXX/OG as a continual reminder of the diversity that characterizes the corpus.) However, when the Greek version of a biblical book survives in more than one form, it is not always possible to know with certainty which is the older. Nor is it possible to know for sure if the oldest surviving form was in fact the first Greek translation made of that book. Therefore, even the term *Old Greek* is not totally satisfactory. Unless the context requires a distinction, this article uses the abbreviation LXX in its general sense.

The scope of modern LXX studies extends beyond the CANON of the Hebrew Bible. It includes texts from the Hellenistic period that are not translations from the Hebrew at all, but rather Jewish writings composed in Greek, such as 3 and 4 MACCABEES and the WISDOM OF SOLOMON. Some other books, such as JUDITH, survive as complete copies only in Greek, even though they probably were translated from a Semitic source that is no longer extant. See APOCRYPHA. These texts may also be in mind when the name Septuagint is used.

The reader is cautioned, therefore, to pay particular care to the context in which the term is used, even by the same writer. Unfortunately, some writers use the term carelessly and equivocally, and the inevitable confusion that results from such ambiguity has led LXX scholars to call for standardizing the terminology. This may be easier said than done, however, for the ambiguities of the term go back to antiquity.

III. Origin.

The earliest extant account of the original Greek translation of the Hebrew Bible is found in the *Letter of Aristeas* (see ARISTEAS, LETTER OF). This document purports to be a lengthy, personal letter from a man named Aristeas to his "brother" (or friend) Philocrates. It describes, among other things, how the Jewish TORAH was first translated from Hebrew into Greek for the great library of the Egyptian king PTOLEMY Philadelphus (285–247 B.C.) in ALEXANDRIA. Copies of this "letter" survive in about two dozen medieval MSS, the earliest of which dates to the 11th cent. The length and character of the document, and the fact that it apparently was so widely copied and circulated, suggests that it was not personal correspondence from one person to another, but was intended as an "open" letter to a wider audience.

According to the author, the king's librarian requested the high priest of the temple in Jerusalem to send translators with the Hebrew Torah scrolls to Alexandria. The high priest complied, sending six men from each of the twelve tribes of Israel, that is, seventy-two translators, with a large escort carrying gifts for the king. (The twelve tribes of Israel had long ceased to exist, so if there is any truth to this unlikely story, the number of people sent would have been merely a symbolic gesture.) Aristeas was among the envoys.

The entourage from Jerusalem was welcomed to Alexandria with a royal banquet lasting several days, during which time the king and the envoys from the high priest discussed questions of theology and ethics. Finally, the translators were escorted to an island called Pharos, connected by a causeway to Alexandria. Working there for seventy-two days, they produced the first Greek translation of the Pentateuch. When the translation was complete, it was read to an assembly of the Jews of Alexandria, who enthusiastically received it and gave the translators a great ovation. The Jews asked the king's librarian to make a copy of the new translation for use in their community. To ensure that the original words of the translators would be preserved in perpetuity, the priests and elders pronounced a curse on anyone who should later change the text in any way.

Scholars today believe that this letter was written, not at a time contemporaneous with the events it describes, but in the 2nd cent. B.C., to defend JUDAISM in general and the Greek version in particular. During the conflict in Judaism over hellenization, some Jews embraced the Greek language and culture while others resisted such acculturation on religious principle. It is also very likely that the Greek translation of the Pentateuch did not enjoy universal favor among the Jews. A hundred years or more after the translation was produced, the *Letter of Aristeas* was probably written to address this situation. Claiming that the translation was made from the Jerusalem scrolls under circumstances that paralleled the giving of the law on Sinai, the author seeks to give the Greek version of the Scriptures used in Alexandria authority and veneration, such as the Hebrew texts in Jerusalem enjoyed.

Even though the authenticity of the letter should be rejected, some of its information is probably reliable. The first Greek translation of the Hebrew Torah would have been needed by Jews living in the Diaspora during the Hellenistic period (i.e., after Alexander's conquest in 333 B.C.). Even earlier, during the Persian period, significant communities of Aramaic-speaking Jews already lived in Egypt: papyri from ELEPHANTINE show an established Jewish community there as early as 495 B.C. After Alexander's conquest of the Persian empire, Alexandria became home to a large Greek-speaking Jewish population. It is therefore likely that the Pentateuch was first translated into Greek by or for the Alexandrian Jews during the reign of Ptolemy Philadelphus in the middle of the 3rd cent. (The historical and prophetic books of the Hebrew Bible were prob. translated into Greek during the following century, but we do not know where or by whom.)

The language of the translation bears the marks of the Greek spoken in Egypt, and it seems improbable that it would have been produced by a large group of Palestinian scholars. It is much more reasonable to believe that a handful of Greek-speaking Alexandrian Jews were responsible for it. As for the claim that the translation was based on Hebrew scrolls brought from Jerusalem, we have no clear evidence to refute it, but few scholars accept its validity. More difficult to assess is the role supposedly played by the king's librarian. Many scholars, thinking it unlikely that the Greeks themselves would have taken the initiative to produce a translation of the Hebrew Scriptures, reject this element of the story as pure embellishment. On the other hand, some specialists are hesitant to dismiss altogether the possibility that court officials may have had an active interest in gaining access to the formative documents of the large and significant Jewish population. The *Letter of Aristeas* may reflect some reliable information concerning the Ptolemaic court's support, if not sponsorship, of the translation.

But the questions do not end here. Even if the Greeks had some involvement in this project, surely the interests of the Jewish population itself must have been prominent. Was the translation then undertaken because of the needs of the Greek-speaking worshipers who no longer understood Hebrew? Or was it done rather for the academic purposes of Hebrew students and scholars who would be more likely to make sense of the translation's many difficult, literal renderings? It may well be that all of these concerns, and perhaps others as well, were motivating factors in the production of the LXX.

The very intensity with which the *Letter of Aristeas* defends the legitimacy of the translation raises an additional question. The great Hebraist of a previous generation, Paul Kahle (*The Cairo Geniza*, 2nd ed. [1959], chap. 3), argued forcefully that the author of this document was in fact defending the Alexandrian version *against competing Greek translations* (for a refutation of some of Kahle's arguments see the articles by D. W. Gooding and G. Zuntz reprinted in *Studies in the Septuagint: Origins, Recensions, and Interpretations*, ed. S. Jellicoe [1974], 158–80, 208–25). Most scholars, following the lead of Paul de Lagarde in the 19th cent., have generally believed that there was only one initial Greek translation of the Hebrew Bible, and that the recovery of that "Proto-Septuagint" (*Ur-Septuaginta*) is the great task at hand. Kahle insisted, however, that originally simultaneous Greek translations were produced over a period of time, in a manner not unlike that of the Aramaic TARGUMS, and that the *Letter of Aristeas* sought to impose the authority of one such translation over the other ones. Although Kahle's theories created a heated controversy during his lifetime, relatively few scholars were persuaded by them. Lagarde's position, with some modifications, has been confirmed by later investigation and functions as the working assumption for most specialists (see J. W. Wevers in *Bulletin of the International Organization for Septuagint and Cognate Studies* 21 [1988]: 23–34, esp. 24–26).

Writers subsequent to the *Letter of Aristeas* add little information of substance. PHILO JUDAEUS, a Jewish Alexandrian philosopher who lived in the 1st cent. of our era, embellished the story of the origin of the Greek version of the Bible. Probably relying on an earlier tradition, he writes that the translators worked independently of each other, yet produced the same translation word-for-word through divine dictation. Philo believed that the Greek translation had been divinely inspired just as the original Hebrew had been.

By the 2nd cent. there is evidence of an alternate Jewish tradition, found in rabbinical material, that gives the number of translators who went to Alexandria as seventy, not seventy-two (*Sepher Torah* 1:8; another tradition gives the number of translators as five). This detail is probably intended to justify the claim that the Greek version too, like the Hebrew, was divinely inspired. Seventy ELDERS of Israel accompanied MOSES to Mount Sinai and saw God (Exod. 24:1–2, 9–11); moreover, seventy elders received a share of the Spirit that was in Moses (Num. 11:10–25). By numbering the translators of the Torah as seventy, the tradition portrays them as assistants to Moses working centuries later to administer the Law. The name *Septuagint* reflects this tradition. It first appears in Greek (*hoi hebdomēkonta*, "the seventy") in the mid-second century and thereafter only in Christian writers, such as JUSTIN MARTYR, IRENAEUS, EUSEBIUS, and CHRYSOSTOM. The term was most often used by these writers to refer in general to the entire Greek OT, without distinguishing its various revisions and forms.

In the 3rd cent. the use of the term became even more confused. As will be noted below, ORIGEN took the various Greek texts in existence at his time and produced a recension that was "corrected" to the Hebrew text available to him. After his work, the name Septuagint began to be used to refer both to the Greek text he had used as his base *and* to the text that resulted from his revisions! The term is found in colophons in biblical MSS as early as the 4th cent. It is not known if such a notation was used to distinguish the text of these MSS from other Greek versions known to the scribes at that time, or was intended simply to identify the proper textual pedigree of the MS. In any case, the confusion resulting from the imprecise and ambiguous use of the name Septuagint today reflects the long and complicated history of the term and the texts to which it refers.

IV. Later Greek translations.

Early Christian writers sometimes referred to alternate Greek renderings found in translations other than that of "the Seventy." These references are often vague, but we can find many passages where they specifically identify translations attributed to three scholars: Aquila, Symmachus, and Theodotion. Sometimes they are referred to as a group, "the Three (Translators)." Today they are often called "the Later Versions" or (for reasons to be discussed below) "the Hexaplaric Versions." None of these works has survived, except for a few fragments, but we have valuable evidence in numerous patristic quotations, as well as in marginal notations in MSS. With regard to their origin, these later translations are to be clearly distinguished from "the Septuagint," but as we shall see, the textual transmission of all these documents eventually became closely intertwined.

The rise of Christianity from Judaism in the 1st cent. of our era is usually given as the reason non-Greek versions of the Hebrew Bible were needed. The Christian church first flourished in Jerusalem among Jews who recognized Jesus of Nazareth as the MESSIAH and who interpreted the death and resurrection of Jesus in light of the sacred Scriptures of the Judaism of their day. When Christianity spread outside the borders of Palestine, it was apparently the Greek version of the Jewish Scriptures from which the apostles, especially Paul, preached Christ. It is usually said that the resulting tension between Christians and Jews, both of whom used the Greek Bible but understood it so differently, was the primary reason for the synagogue to abandon the "Septuagint" to the church and to produce a new translation of the Hebrew texts.

While the early relationship between Christians and Jews no doubt played a major role in the history of the Greek versions, there was another factor that should not be overlooked. The DEAD SEA SCROLLS provide indisputable evidence that at the turn of the era, before the birth of Christianity, the text of the Hebrew Bible (for at least some of the books) circulated in more than one form. One of these, however, emerged as *the* standard text by the beginning of the 2nd cent., apparently supplanting all previous Hebrew texts. This situation alone would provide the need for a new Greek translation faithful to the newly standardized Hebrew text.

In addition, it is now clear that, even apart from Jewish-Christian polemics, there were different ideas about what a translation should look like. The discoveries in the Judean Desert have shed light on this issue as well. One of the more significant MSS found there is actually a Greek translation of the Minor Prophets. Dated no later than the 1st cent. of our era, it appears to be a revision of the "Septuagint" for those books of the Bible. This find provides clear evidence that prior to the 2nd-cent. debates among Jews and Christians, more than one Greek version of the Bible was in circulation.

A. Aquila. According to ancient testimony, Aquila was a Gentile who had been commissioned by his relative, the Roman emperor HADRIAN, to superintend the rebuilding of Jerusalem (renamed Aelia Capitolina) around the year 128. While there, he became a Christian, but later converted to Judaism and studied under prominent rabbis. Aquila eventually undertook a new Greek translation of the Hebrew Bible that (a) was based on the recently standardized Hebrew text; (b) sought to correct perceived deficiencies in the LXX, including those that affected Jewish-Christian disputes; and (c) adopted a very literalistic approach that possibly reflected certain rabbinic methods of interpretation. Aquila's work, completed perhaps around the year 140, was received enthusiastically by the Greek-speaking Jewish communities and remained the form trusted by the synagogue well into the 6th cent. and beyond.

The literal character of Aquila's translation has not always been adequately understood. Some scholars have given the impression that Aquila was either incompetent or eccentric, but the facts suggest otherwise. To begin with, we should note that Aquila allowed himself some flexibility in the area of syntax. Instead of representing Hebrew grammatical forms in one-to-one fashion, he would sometimes use the resources of the Greek language to provide stylistic variation.

In the area of vocabulary, undoubtedly, Aquila's policy was to represent every detail in the most consistent fashion, even at the cost of acceptable Greek. For example, Ps. 22:12b (MT 22:13b; LXX 21:13b) says, "strong [bulls] of Bashan *surrounded* me." The Hebrew verb here, *kittĕrûnî* (piel of *kātar* H1103), happens to be related to the noun *keter* H4195 ("turban"). Because this Hebrew noun is elsewhere rendered with the Greek *diadēma* G1343 ("band, diadem"), Aquila boldly makes up a new Greek verb, *diadēmatizō*, so that his translation would carry over into English as, "strong ones of Bashan diademized me." We must not think that Aquila misunderstood the meaning of the Hebrew verb or that he was simply being reckless. He was clearly guided by the principle of providing one-for-one lexical correspondences, and he did so even in the case of particles and certain word-endings.

Almost surely, Aquila's method was intended as an aid to biblical exegesis, perhaps for people who had a minimal knowledge of Hebrew. (Cf. the way that "literal" English translations of the Bible are sometimes advertised as the next best thing to knowing Greek and Hebrew.) There is also reason to believe that he may have been following a specific rabbinic approach to interpretation, although this point is disputed. In any case, we should remember that some distinguished writers, even today, argue that translations ought to preserve both the content *and the form* of the original. And for modern biblical scholars interested in reconstructing the Hebrew *Vorlage* or parent text of a Greek translation, Aquila's consistent method makes that task simpler.

B. Symmachus. Little is known about the origins of the Greek version attributed to Symmachus. He is said by some sources to have been an EBIONITE Christian who produced the translation around the year 170 of our era. A major recent study identifies Symmachus as a Jew (not an Ebionite) who undertook this task around the year 200 for the Jewish community in Caesarea of Palestine (A. Salvesen, *Symmachus in the Pentateuch* [1991], 296–97, building on the work of A. van der Kooij).

Scholars who have studied what remains of this translation agree that the work was carefully done. Alison Salvesen has examined the exegetical features of Symmachus's version of the Pentateuch and its syntax and vocabulary. She concludes that Symmachus produced a Greek translation of the Hebrew text of the Pentateuch that "combined the best Biblical Greek style, remarkable clarity, a high degree of accuracy regarding the Hebrew, and the rabbinic exegesis of his day: it might be described as a Greek Targum, or Tannaitic Septuagint" (ibid., 297; the term TANNAIM refers to rabbinic authorities during the first two centuries A.D.).

On the basis of syntactical and lexical characteristics found also in the other Greek versions,

Salvesen concludes that Symmachus "certainly knew Aquila," "probably knew Theodotion," and it seems "likely" to her that he also knew of the LXX as he produced his translation for the Jewish community of Caesarea in Palestine around the year 200. In short, Symmachus "aimed to produce a translation in clear Greek which accurately reflected the sense of the Hebrew original. His respect for the LXX is evident: he revised it in the spirit of the original translators of the Pentateuch, ironing out their lexical inconsistencies and inaccuracies, yet preserving smooth diction where he found it and extending it where it was absent" (ibid., 26; L. Greenspoon [in *ABD*, 6:251] believes that Symmachus's work is primarily a revision of Theodotion).

Another specialist, similarly, states that Symmachus's work on the Major Prophets is characterized by clarity (representing Hebrew idioms with natural Greek expressions), variety (one Hebrew term may be represented with several Greek terms), and coherence. Although the translator allowed himself the use of exegetical expansions, his approach was sober. In general, the translation stands mid-way between Aquila and the LXX. (See J. González Luis, *La versión de Símaco a los profetas mayores* [1981], 367–68. Note, however, that in OT books where the LXX is very literal, Symmachus renders more freely than either the LXX or Aquila.)

C. Theodotion. The Greek translation attributed to Theodotion is especially problematic. According to the traditional view, Theodotion was a convert to Judaism who lived in EPHESUS in the late 2nd cent. Taking the existing Greek version as his base, he revised it toward the standard Hebrew text. His work—which may fairly be characterized as "literal," but not excessively so—includes features reminiscent of Aquila. One peculiarity is his penchant for transliterating (i.e., using Greek letters to represent the sound of the Hebrew) rather than translating certain words, such as difficult terms for animals and plants. His translation of the book of Daniel supplanted that of the "Septuagint" (better, the Old Greek), which was widely regarded as defective.

One of the problems with this description is that certain renderings once thought distinctive to Theodotion are now known to have existed a century or two before he lived. Note, for example, the reference to Dan. 6:22 (MT and LXX, 6:23) in Heb. 11:33. Although the author of Hebrews is otherwise heavily dependent on the "Septuagint," this passage reflects Theodotion's rendering, "[God] shut the mouths of the lions" (*enephraxen ta stomata tōn leontōn*), rather than the Old Greek, which says, "God saved me from the lions" (*sesōke me ho theos apo tōn leontōn*). This phenomenon led to speculation about the existence of a "proto-Theodotion" (*Ur-Theodotion*) and recent discoveries have confirmed the view that, for at least parts of the Hebrew Bible, a translation very similar to Theodotion's was already in use in the 1st cent. B.C. For a variety of reasons, most scholars now prefer to speak of *kaige*-Theodotion, meaning by that term a well-defined, pre-Christian revision of the Old Greek. (One of its characteristics is the use of Gk. *kaige* to render Heb. *gam* H1685 [with or without the conjunction *w*]. It is also thought that this revision became the basis for the work of both Aquila and Symmachus.) The work of the historical Theodotion may then be viewed as a later updating of the revision.

Also under debate is the question of Daniel-Theodotion in particular. Some have argued that the characteristics of this translation do not fit those found in materials otherwise attributed to Theodotion. Moreover, doubts have been raised about the usual view that Daniel-Theodotion is a revision of the Old Greek. (See A. Schmitt in *BZ* 36 [1992]: 1–29; T. McLay, *The OG and Th Versions of Daniel* [1996].) These and other questions will continue to occupy scholars for years to come.

D. Other versions. In addition to "the Three," other attempts were made to translate parts of the Hebrew Bible into Greek. Some church fathers, for example, make reference to *ho Hebraios*, an ambiguous term that in some contexts appears to mean, "the Hebrew translator." One also finds quite a few references to "the Syrian" and nearly fifty to "the Samariticon." There is little that can be said with confidence about these versions. Moreover, as we shall see in the next section, Origen was familiar with three anonymous translations that have come to be known as Quinta, Sexta, and Septima. Of these, the Quinta is best attested, but not sufficiently to give us a complete picture.

V. Recensions. We have good reason to believe that by the middle of the 1st cent. B.C. or even earlier, the whole Hebrew Bible, with the possible exception of one or two books, had been translated into Greek. In the case of Judges, Daniel, and Esther (as well as Tobit, Susanna, and Judith, books not included in the Hebrew canon), two quite different Greek forms are found among surviving MSS. Most contemporary scholars believe that only one "original" Greek translation was made of each book prior to the Christian era, and that whatever differences are found between surviving texts of the same book reflect a revision of the Greek. In any case, by the turn of the era, at least one Greek translation of virtually every book of the Hebrew Bible was in circulation among Greek-speaking Jews.

In the past, scholars have made a fairly sharp distinction between two types of work produced subsequent to the "original" Septuagint: (a) new Greek translations of the Hebrew Bible, that is, primarily the three versions made by Aquila, Symmachus, and Theodotion; and (b) major recensions (systematic revisions) of the Septuagint itself. Following this traditional understanding, in the previous section we treated "the Three" as independent works to be distinguished from the LXX. Here, however, we focus again on the LXX as the original Greek version and ask questions about its transmission and revisions.

Unfortunately, the distinction between a revision and a new translation is very difficult to define clearly. After all, scholars today speak of *Kaige*-Theodotion as a revision, and even the work of Aquila is sometimes described this way. It remains true, however, that "the Three" were historically perceived, and probably intended, as new works more or less in competition with the LXX, whereas the "recensions" (Origen's in particular) were meant to provide reliable editions of the LXX itself.

The usual starting-point for a discussion of the recensions is a well-know comment by JEROME (c. 340–420), the most knowledgeable biblical scholar of his day. In his preface to Chronicles, Jerome complained that the Christian world was in conflict over three forms *(trifaria varietas)* of the LXX text: (a) one in Egypt, attributed to Hesychius; (b) a second dominant from Constantinople to Antioch and attributed to Lucian; and between them (c) Origen's (Hexaplaric) recension, used in Palestine. We know nothing about Hesychius, and scholars have been unsuccessful in identifying a Hesychian recension among the MSS (although for most biblical books there is such a thing as an Egyptian form of the text, which may be the basis for Jerome's comment). For all practical purposes, therefore, a description of the Christian recensions must be limited to those attributed to Origen and to Lucian of Antioch.

A. The Hexaplaric recension. The most important work on the text of the Greek OT was done by Origen, the Christian theologian of Alexandria (c. 185 to c. 254). After heading up the Christian catechetical school in Alexandria, Origen eventually settled in Palestine, in the city of CAESAREA. During this period he undertook the massive project of comparing the Greek versions known to him with the Hebrew text of his day, which apparently was close to what has come to us as the MT. Most of what is known about this work comes from two brief descriptions by Origen himself and from the writings of later church fathers who saw the work. Aware of the differences between the LXX and the Hebrew text, he set out to produce an edition that would take those variations into account. To accomplish his task he had the available texts written in parallel columns. For most of the OT he needed to use six columns, the feature from which the name of this work, the Hexapla, is taken. These columns contained the following: (1) the Hebrew text; (2) transliteration of the Hebrew text into Greek letters; (3) Aquila's translation; (4) Symmachus's translation; (5) the translation of the Seventy; (6) Theodotion's translation.

The purpose of the second column, containing a transliteration of the Hebrew into Greek letters, is somewhat puzzling. Some have suggested that it would have allowed a Greek speaker who did not know Hebrew to "read" (i.e., pronounce) the Hebrew Bible aloud, perhaps in the synagogue service. Others have thought that it enabled people who did know the Hebrew alphabet to vocalize a consonantal text. Before the early Middle Ages, the Hebrew text consisted of consonants only; the vowel sounds were to be inferred by the reader. Origen's second column may represent an earlier attempt to preserve the correct pronunciation of the Hebrew vowels for people whose native language was Greek and whose knowledge of Hebrew was not extensive.

The translations in columns 3 (Aquila), 4 (Symmachus), and 6 (Theodotion) of the Hexapla were described above. Column 5 contained the "Septuagint," apparently the standard Greek translation used by the Christian church at the time. It is usually thought that this column included the corrections that Origen believed needed to be made in light of the Hebrew text. For example, as he compared the texts of Isaiah, he found that several lines of the Hebrew in Isa. 40 (vv. 7b–8a) were missing from the LXX, so he inserted that material into the text of the fifth column. According to some scholars, however, the fifth column contained an *uncorrected* text, so that the revised translation was really a separate, subsequent project for which the Hexapla was the preparatory work.

With regard to the order of the columns, we do not know Origen's rationale for it. One interesting theory is that of Harry M. Orlinsky (in *JQR* 27 [1936–37]: 146–47), who argued that Origen wanted "to provide his [Christian] contemporaries with the much needed facilities to learn Hebrew, and thus to be able to make use of all six columns of his Hexapla." After supplying the Hebrew text and a second column to help the reader pronounce it, Origen next included Aquila's version because its word-for-word representation of the Hebrew provided a "crib" for the reader. Since Aquila is often unintelligible, however, Symmachus was needed to clarify it. "And equipped with the knowledge gained from the first four columns, the reader was ready to tackle the most important column of them all, the LXX."

For the book of Psalms and possibly a few other books, Origen was able to use three more Greek versions (but not more than two at a time), so for these books he expanded his work to eight columns — thus the term *Octapla*. Virtually nothing is known about the origin of these anonymous versions, referred to as the Quinta, the Sexta, and the Septima (that is, the fifth, sixth, and seventh versions). Since Origen included their text for only a few of the books, apparently none of these three versions contained the complete OT in the MSS available to Origen. The Quinta — the best attested of these three versions — is believed to have included 2 Kings, Job, Psalms, Song of Solomon, and the Minor Prophets.

Given the way modern scholars refer freely to the Hexaplaric texts, including the translations of Aquila, Theodotion, and Symmachus, readers may be left with the impression that fairly complete and reliable copies of these Greek texts exist. In fact, actual specimens are preserved only in (a) quotations by other ancient writers, (b) marginal notes in a handful of MSS, and (c) a very few fragments of copies of the Hexapla. The largest and most significant fragment of a copy of the Hexapla is the Mercati palimpsest in the Ambrosian Library of Milan. In 1896 Giovanni Mercati discovered that the underwriting of this MS contains five of the six columns of the Hexapla for about 150 verses of the Psalms. It apparently never did contain the first column, the Hebrew text. This copy was written in cursive letters around the 10th cent.

It is estimated that the Hexapla would have required about 6,000 pages bound in fifteen volumes. Such a massive work would probably never have been copied in its entirety. The only copy we know of was deposited in the library in Caesarea, Palestine, under the care of Pamphilus, the Christian martyr (c. 250–310). It was presumably destroyed with the library by Muslim Saracens in the 7th cent., if not earlier. The most comprehensive collection of Hexaplaric remains was published by F. Field over a century ago (*Origenis Hexaplorum quae supersunt sive veterum interpretum graecorum in totum Vetus Testamentum fragmenta*, 2 vols. [1875]). Since then, new fragments have been discovered and studied. In 1994, a new project was begun at Oxford University to produce a new, electronic database containing all the surviving evidence.

For students of the LXX, however, the most important issue surrounding Origen's work is the character of his revised Greek text, which presumably was to be found in the fifth column. (As mentioned earlier, however, some scholars believe that this column contained an unrevised text and that Origen's own recension was published separately.) Origen had set out to produce a restored Greek version of the Bible for the church, and his corrected text quickly became the standard OT for the eastern churches from Antioch to Alexandria. It was copied and promoted by church leaders for centuries. It, too, was called the "Septuagint," although it was no longer the same "Septuagint" text with which Origen had started out.

Origen himself states the purpose of this work in the *Letter to Africanus*, while the method he used is explained in his *Commentary on Matthew*. Apparently his purpose was to settle the dispute between Christians and Jews about the biblical texts. The Hexapla would show at a glance the Hebrew and all known Greek versions of it. Where the Greek Bible did disagree with the Hebrew Bible, Origen felt it important to "correct" the Greek version used *at that time* by the church to agree with the Hebrew version used *at that time* by the synagogue. In other words, Origen's purpose in constructing the Hexapla was quite different from the task of modern textual critics.

Origen may have been unaware that the Hebrew text available to him did not fully correspond with the Hebrew parent text from which the Greek translation had been produced. He could have easily been misled by the fact that in his day one standard Hebrew text already reigned supreme—the one that has survived today as the MT. We now know, however, that this text had undergone at least some development in the centuries before becoming standardized and that, for at least some books, the Hebrew Bible existed in more than one textual form. This means that the parent text from which any Greek translation had been made may or may not have had the same general form as the Hebrew text used by Origen. From the perspective of textual criticism, therefore, the basic assumption upon which he based his method was wrong. On the other hand, what looks like the work of a wrong-headed textual critic in the production of the Hexapla was actually the careful and valuable work of a well-intentioned Christian apologist.

As for his method, what Origen did was to compare the Greek of the LXX text, bit by bit, to the Hebrew text. The Greek sometimes had text that was not found in the Hebrew. Maybe these "pluses" had been in the Hebrew *Vorlage* from which the Greek was originally produced. Or maybe the pluses were introduced later as the Greek version developed independently of the Hebrew. In either case, out of respect for the sanctity of the LXX, Origen did not wish simply to delete Greek material not found in the Hebrew text. So he marked that material found in the LXX, but not in the Hebrew, with a special sign (an obelos). This and other signs used by Origen to mark his text are sometimes referred to as the Aristarchian symbols, because they had previously been used by an Alexandrian scholar named Aristarchus to do similar work on the various Greek texts of Homer.

Origen also found, however, that there was material in the Hebrew that was not in the LXX text. Perhaps the Hebrew *Vorlage* of the original translation did not contain the material, either because that Hebrew text was quite different from the one Origen had before him, or because the material was added to the Hebrew text after the Greek translation had been made. Or perhaps these minuses had originally been in the Greek translation, but were omitted, either intentionally or accidentally, at some later time. In any case, Origen felt compelled to insert Greek text to correspond to his Hebrew text. He did this by referring to the other existing Greek versions. If one of them contained a reading which corresponded well, in his opinion, to the Hebrew reading, he inserted that reading into the Greek text of the fifth column, placing it between special signs (an asterisk and a metobelos).

Through this process, Origen introduced isolated readings pulled from Aquila, Symmachus, and Theodotion (and possibly from Quinta, Sexta, and Septima) into the "Septuagint" text. Although he marked the original material, those markings were not always preserved. After Origen completed his work, the fifth column—that is, his recension of the LXX—was copied by itself and became the authorized Greek version of the Bible for the Christian church in Palestine. Because Origen's symbols were reproduced imperfectly or not at all, it became impossible to identify the origin of the various readings. It was this text that from that time forward was widely copied and circulated, which means that surviving MSS of the "Septuagint," with few exceptions, have a mixed text. Origen may have accomplished his goal successfully, but he greatly complicated the work of modern textual critics. In effect, the great task of LXX textual criticism is to reconstruct the pre-Hexaplaric text, which means *undoing* Origen's labors so as to rediscover the form of the "Septuagint" in the 2nd cent.

B. The Lucianic recension. Lucian of Antioch, born in Syria about the middle of the 3rd cent., died as a martyr in the year 312. He was a controversial theologian and a very influential biblical scholar. While the specific extent and nature of his textual work remain uncertain, he apparently updated an existing Greek text of both the OT and the NT. His revisions seem to have been primarily stylistic in nature. (Some scholars doubt that Lucian personally had anything to do with such revisions. For a survey of Lucian's life and work, see especially B. M. Metzger, *Chapters in the History of the New Testament* [1963], 1–41.)

The resulting Lucianic recension is also referred to as the Antiochene or Antiochian text, partly because Lucian may have used as his base the Greek text (perhaps Origen's fifth column?) that was then current in ANTIOCH OF SYRIA, partly because his revision was best known in that city. Lucian's recension is believed to be quoted in the writings of later Antiochene scholars such as Chrysostom and Theodoret. Moreover, isolated readings in the margins of several Greek and Syriac MSS are marked by the letter *l* (Gk. *lambda* and Syriac *lomadh*), and many of these readings should no doubt be recognized as Lucianic. With these clues, scholars have been able to identify, for most books, a large number of MSS as containing the Lucianic recension.

The revision commonly attributed to Lucian, or more vaguely to the Syrian church, is especially evident in the book of Psalms and in the NT. Indeed, most of the surviving MSS that include either of those two portions of the Greek Bible contain a revised text that is somewhat fuller—and stylistically more homogeneous—than other text forms. Whether or not Lucian was responsible for this work, it is generally agreed that the revision can be traced back to Antioch around the year 300. In addition to the Psalter, the Lucianic or Antiochene recension of the LXX is clearly attested in the Prophets and in some of the historical books (esp. Samuel-Kings-Chronicles). For the Pentateuch, however, scholars have been unable to identify a Lucianic text.

The most difficult and important problem related to this recension has to do with the presence of "Lucianic" readings attested long before Lucian lived. The Old Latin version (a translation from the Greek OT produced in the 2nd cent. of our era), as well as biblical quotations from such Latin fathers as Tertullian (who died early in the 3rd cent.) and Cyprian (d. 258), occasionally reflect a text that has some distinctives normally associated with the Antiochene text. Even earlier, Greek writers such as Justin Martyr (d. 165) and especially Josephus (c. 37–100) appear to have used a biblical text resembling that of the Antiochene recension. Most puzzling of all, one of the Hebrew fragments of Samuel discovered at QUMRAN (4QSam^a) also shows important points of contact with the Lucianic text.

Although some of the evidence has been disputed, many scholars speak of a proto-Lucianic text, meaning by that term an early revision of the LXX (better, OG) that brings it closer toward the Hebrew text. If so, the historical Lucian may have used such a revised text as the basis for his own revisions. This two-layer view helps to explain why the Lucianic or Antiochene text is characterized by two opposing tendencies: (a) on the one hand, the Lucianic MSS contain many readings that are closer to the Hebrew text than are those found in the other LXX MSS; (b) on the other hand, many of the stylistic changes in the Lucianic recension tend to move the Greek text away from the Hebrew. This problem is solved if "Lucian" made his stylistic alterations on a text that had earlier been adjusted toward the Hebrew.

VI. Ancient witnesses. While most of the surviving biblical texts have come to us through continuous transmission over the centuries, many other MSS have come to light only in modern times as a result of archaeological work. Indeed, ancient biblical texts dating as far back as the pre-Christian era have been found in archives of papyri excavated by archaeologists (see PAPYRUS). Manuscripts discovered in this way are extremely valuable, because they preserve the text as it existed when it was buried and have not been subjected to the vicissitudes of copying throughout subsequent centuries. The 4th-cent. CHESTER BEATTY Papyrus IV (= Rahlfs 961), one of the most significant finds, contains Gen. 9:1—44:22. Most papyrus fragments, however, contain small portions of biblical text—sometimes only a few letters or words. Therefore, while the papyri provide very ancient and important testimony of the text at the time they were buried, such little material makes it difficult to generalize about which form of the Greek Bible they represent.

Among important biblical papyri in Greek, the two earliest documents deserve special notice. Papyrus Fouad 266 (= Rahlfs 847 and 848), dated to c. 100 B.C., contains small portions of Deuteronomy that have great significance for the reconstruction of the text. Even earlier by perhaps half a century is PRyl. 458 (= Rahlfs 957), which contains about twenty scattered verses from Deut. 23–28. A few additional documents from the following two centuries have survived, and there are many other papyrus fragments of the Greek Bible that date from the 3rd cent. of our era and later.

One of the most dramatic papyrological finds began in 1947 when the first of the Judean Desert materials (popularly known as the DEAD SEA SCROLLS) came to light. Over the following decade, texts were found in eleven caves at Qumran, on the NW shore of the Dead Sea, and its environs. Most of these texts are in Hebrew and Aramaic, but Caves 4 and 7 preserved a small number of biblical texts in Greek. They are fragments of the Pentateuch, specifically Leviticus, Numbers, and Deuteronomy. A wider area of the Judean wilderness produced other significant finds, especially an entire scroll of the Minor Prophets in Greek (not to be confused with the Minor Prophets scroll in *Hebrew* discovered at Murabbaʿat). All of these documents are dated to the 1st cent. of our era or earlier.

In addition to the papyri, there are other early and important MSS written on PARCHMENT; they are referred to as *uncials* because they are written in the uncial or majuscule script (one should keep in mind, however, that the papyri are written in that same script). The three best-known biblical uncials contain the books of both the OT and the NT: CODEX VATICANUS (B), a 4th-cent. MS of exceptionally high quality that for most books of the OT has preserved a text relatively free from Hexaplaric influence; CODEX SINAITICUS (S or ℵ), produced about the same time, and usually having a text similar to that of B (unfortunately, very little of the Pentateuch and of the historical sections has been preserved); and CODEX ALEXANDRINUS (A), copied in the 5th cent., which in spite of showing many signs of Hexaplaric influence, is very valuable (in the book of Isaiah, for example, it is our best witness).

Among other important uncials, the following are worth special attention. Codex *Colberto-Sarravianus* (G), dated about the year 400, preserves portions of Genesis to Judges; its significance lies in the fact that it retains the Hexaplaric signs (although these are not always trustworthy). Codex *Coislinianus* (M), copied in the 7th cent., includes Genesis to 2 Samuel and the first chapters of 1 Kings (= 3 Reigns or 3 Kingdoms). Codex *Basiliano-Vaticanus* is an 8th or 9th cent. uncial with the double designation N-V; one portion (N) is in the Vatican Library and contains much of the Pentateuch (beginning with Lev. 13:59) and also the historical books; the other portion (V, also known as Codex Venetus) is in Venice and contains most of the poetic books, the Prophets, Tobit, Judith, and 1–4 Maccabees. Finally, Codex *Marchalianus* (Q) is a beautiful and very well preserved MS of the Prophets, dating from the 6th cent.; it contains an excellent text and includes the Hexaplaric signs.

Finally, well over 1,500 cursive or minuscule MSS of (parts of) the LXX have been preserved. Because they are later than the papyri and the uncials, they are relatively less important, but it would be a great mistake to ignore them. In the first place, a minuscule produced, say, in the 13th cent. may be a copy of an uncial dated many centuries earlier; if so, the text preserved in the minuscule is much more ancient than the MS itself. Moreover, the minuscules broaden our knowledge base significantly and thus help us to assess the value of the uncials in a more accurate way (a specific reading in a valuable uncial may be suspect if it is not broadly attested). Among interesting cursives, we may note especially the famous Chigi MS (88), which has two distinctions: it is one of the few MSS that include the Hexaplaric signs, and it is the only Greek MS that has preserved the Old Greek (rather than the Theodotionic) version of Daniel in its entirety. An important group of cursives that deserves attention is most frequently referred to by the lower-case letter designations boc_2e_2; these minuscules constitute our primary witnesses to the Lucianic or Antiochene text of Samuel-Kings.

In addition to Greek MSS, we have the evidence of "secondary versions" and of ancient citations. As the Christian church expanded, the translation of the Bible into other languages became necessary. Such translations, *when made from the Greek* (rather than from the Hebrew), have great value to scholars who try to identify and date distinctive features of the different Greek versions. If a translation of the Greek into another language was made before Origen produced the Hexapla, that translation offers, at least in theory, a witness to what the Greek text(s) looked like in the earliest centuries of the church. However, the secondary translation has also suffered the vicissitudes of time and transmission, which means that its original text must be established before we can use it to reconstruct its Greek *Vorlage*. It should also be kept in mind that these translations cannot always represent the Greek parent text precisely, and therefore their witness must be used with caution.

In the first few centuries of this era, Latin was the language not only of Italy but of other areas as well, including parts of N Africa. When the first translation of the Bible was made into Latin, it was made from a Greek text. This Latin version, referred to as the *Vetus Latina* or Old Latin (OL), was eventually replaced in the Latin-speaking church by Jerome's translation made in the early 5th cent. Jerome's work, known as the VULGATE, was a direct translation of the OT in Hebrew. In contrast, surviving MSS of the OL translation attest to a Greek *Vorlage*. Syriac (a member of the ARAMAIC family) was the language of a large and important section of the Christian church for many centuries. The *Syro-Hexaplar* (sometimes spelled Syro-Hexapla), an important secondary translation of Origen's Hexaplaric recension, was produced between the years 613 and 617. This work, translated from the Greek, is to be distinguished from the standard Syriac Bible, known as the Peshitta, which had been translated from the Hebrew about the 2nd cent. Translations of the LXX into Coptic (a late form of the Egyptian language) have been preserved in both the Sahidic and Bohairic dialects; they are an important witness to a valuable early Greek text used in Egypt. Other languages into which the LXX was translated include Arabic, Ethiopic, Armenian, Slavonic, and Georgian. Not many LXX scholars are competent in one or more of these languages, and relatively few MSS of these translations have survived.

Another secondary or indirect source for the Greek texts consists of quotations from the Bible surviving in ancient writings, especially the large corpus of the Christian fathers. In many ways, the value of these quotations for establishing the Greek text in use at that time is even more tenuous than consulting the secondary translations. This is because the writings of the fathers were themselves copied by scribes who may have edited the quotations to agree with the text known and used in their time and locale. Therefore, the textual critic must first establish how patristic writers originally quoted the passage. Moreover, one cannot be sure that they quoted a biblical verse word-for-word. They may have paraphrased it or omitted short phrases that were irrelevant to their point. These complications notwithstanding, it appears that the quotations of certain fathers agree more closely with the readings of some surviving MSS than with others. For instance, Chrysostom and Theodoret, both of Antioch, are considered to be primary witnesses to the Antiochene text as revised by Lucian.

VII. Modern editions. With the invention of the printing press in the 15th cent., it became possible to take a book and produce numerous copies that were exact replicas of one another. Mass duplication virtually eliminated the tedious work of scribes and prevented the inevitable errors and changes they introduced into the texts. When the first printed editions of the LXX were produced, however, the choice of a biblical text by the printers was sometimes based simply on which MSS were conveniently at hand rather than on deliberate selection, much less scholarly scrutiny. In a given codex the text of one biblical book may have been from Theodotion, for example, while another book in the same codex may have contained the Hexaplaric recension of the LXX. If a given codex was damaged, and therefore lacking all or part of a biblical book, the lacking text would be supplied from another codex near at hand, without thought to the pedigree of the texts contained therein. While the advent of modern printing technology stabilized the printed editions of the Bible, giving the appearance of homogeneity, the particular version it preserved and propagated was in fact an arbitrary amalgam of texts with various pedigrees and characteristics.

The first printed edition of the entire Greek OT was produced by Christian scholars in Spain between 1514 and 1517, then published a few years later as part of the *Complutensian Polyglot Bible*. The OT was presented in three columns: the Latin Vulgate with pride of place in the middle, the Hebrew text on its right, and the Greek text (with a Latin interlinear translation) on its left. In addition, the Aramaic Targum, accompanied by a Latin translation, was placed at the bottom of the page. This work was initiated and directed by Cardinal Francisco Ximenes de Cisneros, who claimed to have carefully selected his MSS, including some supplied by Pope Leo X from the Vatican library.

At about the same time, the so-called *Aldine* edition of the Greek Bible, based on a few, relatively late MSS, was published in Venice. Of greater importance is the *Sixtine* edition, published in 1587 under the auspices of Pope Sixtus V. This project was undertaken with care and thoroughness. After searching for MSS in various libraries, the editors, led by Cardinal Antonio Carafa, became convinced that what is now known as Codex Vaticanus or B (Vatican Library Gk. 1209) was the best MS upon which to base the new edition. Other MSS were used to fill the large gaps and correct errors in B, as well as to provide alternate readings from time to time. The Sixtine edition became the standard LXX text and was used by many subsequent editors.

In the 17th and 18th centuries, scholars began to collect and publish variant readings, that is, differences among the MSS for any given verse. This process gave birth to modern textual criticism and to the practice of publishing editions of ancient texts that include a critical apparatus (i.e., a section of notes indicating variant readings, usually found at the bottom of the page). The British scholars Robert Holmes and (after his death in 1805) James Parsons produced such an edition in five large volumes, which was published in Oxford between 1798 and 1827, under the title, *Vetus Testamentum Graecum cum variis lectionibus*. Using the Sixtine text as their base, this monumental work provides readings from about 300 MSS collated by a large number of British and Continental scholars. From our later vantage point, the methods used in this work can be easily criticized; and since the quality of the collations was not uniform, the edition must be used with care. Even today, however, specialists know that certain kinds of information can be found only in Holmes-Parsons.

Other editions were published during the 1800s, though none of them was truly satisfactory. Toward the end of that century, however, scholars in Cambridge, England, began to work on a diplomatic edition of Codex Vaticanus (i.e., an edition that reproduces as exactly as possible the text of the MS, although obvious scribal errors are corrected). This important document was collated against all the available uncials, many minuscules (thirty in Genesis, for example), the secondary versions, and quotations from Philo, Josephus, and the Christian fathers. A preliminary "portable" edition in three volumes, entitled *The Old Testament in Greek according to the Septuagint*, was produced by H. B. Swete in 1887–94 (3rd edition, 1901–07), and became the most widely used text during the first decades of the twentieth century. The more ambitious project, often referred to as the Larger Cambridge edition, was entrusted to A. E. Brooke and N. McLean, and in 1906 it began to be published in fascicles. Although never completed, this work is a great treasure; for the books of Joshua through Chronicles, it remains our primary source of information.

Given that every MS contains scribal errors and that no one existing MS preserves in its entirety the Greek text as it originally came from the translator or reviser, a different approach can be taken, namely, the production of a *critical text*. Instead of printing the entire text of one MS, an editor or editorial committee examines the textual variants and decides which reading is most likely original. This approach produces a reconstructed text, often referred to as *eclectic*, because the resulting printed text is not identical to *any* MS in its entirety. Although the text that appears on the printed page of such an edition is not found in any one surviving MS, it preserves the best readings selected from among all of them and is therefore closer to the text of the original documents.

The production of a critical text for the LXX has been the goal of many scholars. Above all, however, it was the vision of a brilliant and controversial scholar named Paul de Lagarde, whose work was taken up upon his death in 1891 by his student, Alfred Rahlfs. As a means to that end, a scholarly center known as the Septuaginta-Unternehmen was established in Göttingen in 1908. This organization soon became the world's primary center for LXX research. As its director, Rahlfs devoted his considerable talents and energies to searching for MSS, evaluating them, and designing a new system for their enumeration, as well as producing some of the most penetrating textual studies in the history of LXX scholarship.

Work on a full critical edition had to be postponed because of the First World War and its aftermath, but Rahlfs undertook the production of a provisional critical edition, which appeared just before his death in 1935. His text is based primarily on the three great uncials—Vaticanus, Sinaiticus, and Alexandrinus—but many other sources were used extensively. Rahlfs's edition, in spite of its provisional character, has since been regarded as the standard LXX text, even though for many books of the Bible it has now been superseded by individual volumes of the larger project, often referred to as "the Göttingen Septuagint."

For the fuller edition, Rahlfs himself published the volume on Psalms (and Odes) in 1931, though he emphasized the preliminary character of the work, since it was not based on fresh collations. Subsequently, Werner Kappler, Joseph Ziegler, Robert Hanhart, John W. Wevers, and Udo Quast have produced over twenty full and authoritative volumes. Entitled *Septuaginta: Vetus Testamentum Graecum*, this project combines a judiciously reconstructed critical text with a virtually exhaustive repository of information from all available sources.

Translations of the LXX into modern languages are not common. An English version was produced in the 18th cent. by Charles Thomson and published in 1808 (rev. ed. by C. A. Muse, *The Septuagint Bible: The Oldest Version of the Old Testament in the Translation of Charles Thomson* [1954]). More widely used has been the translation by Lancelot C. L. Brenton (*The Septuagint Version of the Old Testament* [1844], reprinted frequently under the title *The Septuagint with Apocrypha*). Because these English versions are based on unreliable texts and are otherwise problematic, the International Organization for Septuagint and Cognate Studies has sponsored a modern work entitled *A New English Translation of the Septuagint* (2007). Special mention should be made of *La Bible d'Alexandrie*, a multivolume French translation of the Septuagint with a philological and exegetical commentary that pays special attention to the patristic use of the Greek OT. In 1990, John W. Wevers published a very helpful commentary, *Notes on the Greek Text of Exodus*, which was followed by individual volumes on the other books of the Pentateuch. Other commentary projects are in preparation.

(The classic source for information on Septuagint studies is H. B. Swete, *An Introduction to the Old Testament in Greek*, 2d ed. [1914], which includes documentation for many of the details mentioned in this article. Much of Swete's material is updated in Sidney Jellicoe, *The Septuagint and Modern Study* [1968], and in N. Fernández Marcos, *The Septuagint in Context: An Introduction to the Greek Version of the Bible* [2000]. See also M. Harl et al., *La Bible Grecque des Septante: Du judaïsme hellénistique au christianisme ancien*, 2nd ed. [1994]; K. H. Jobes and M. Silva, *Invitation to the Septuagint* [2000]; F. Siegert, *Zwischen Hebräischen Bibel und Alten Testament: Eine Einführung in die Septuaginta* [2001]; M. Hengel, *The Septuagint as Christian Scripture: Its Prehistory and the Problem of Its Canon* [2002]; R. T. McLay, *The Use of the Septuagint in New Testament Research* [2003]; J. Dines, *The Septuagint* [2004]; A. Wasserstein and D. Wasserstein, *The Legend of the Septuagint* [2006].) K. H. JOBES; M. SILVA

sepulchre. See TOMB.

Sepulchre, Church of the Holy. An ancient church in Jerusalem, purportedly located over sites of Christ's crucifixion, burial, and resurrection, and hence regarded by many as the greatest "holy place" of Christendom. In locating the place of our Lord's passion, the NT states only that his death occurred "near the city" (Jn. 19:20), at "the place of the Skull (which in Aramaic is called Golgotha)" (v. 17), and that his burial was in a garden "where Jesus was crucified," in "a new tomb, in which no one had ever been laid" (v. 41). It was hewn out of the rock, and owned by JOSEPH of Arimathea (Matt. 27:60).

Tombs would naturally lie outside the walled areas of a city, but the site of the "holy sepulchre" remains otherwise unidentifiable. After the destruction of Jerusalem by the Romans in A.D. 70, but especially after the devastation in A.D. 135—which was followed by a leveling of the entire area, the banishment of all Jews (including Christian Jews), and the construction of the completely new Roman city of Aelia Capitolina on the site—any preserved memory of the exact spot of Jesus' tomb would seem unlikely.

The Church of the Holy Sepulchre occupies a spur of the NW hill of JERUSALEM. It lies within the present N wall of the Old City, which approximates that of Aelia Capitolina and of the N wall of HEROD Agrippa I (A.D. 41–44); whether it lay N, and hence outside, of the previous wall that is described by JOSEPHUS (*War* 5.4.2) has been a matter of debate (see JERUSALEM III.B). In any event, the site was used for a 2nd-cent. Roman forum, at the W end of which were erected temples to Jupiter, Juno, and Venus.

At Christianity's official recognition at the Council of Nicaea in 325, Bishop Macarius of Jerusalem was authorized by the emperor Constantine to tear down the temples. Beneath the temple erected to Venus, Macarius recovered a cavern, and this site has traditionally marked the "holy sepulchre." An argument, however, that favors this tradition lies in the unlikelihood that a spot *within* the then city of Jerusalem would have been selected by Macarius. Constantine immediately authorized the erection of a magnificent church, which was dedicated in 335.

The church was constituted of the *Anastasis* ("resurrection")—a rotunda resting on columns over the tomb, from which the surrounding rocks were cut away and to which the present rotunda corresponds—and a large basilica to the E, with courts both to its E and between it and the Anastasis. The church was badly damaged at the Persian conquest of Jerusalem in 614, and after the Arab occupation in 638 the Omariyeh Mosque took the place of its forecourt. In 1009 the Fatimid caliph Hakem did not simply demolish the church and its relics but had the very rocks of the supposed GOLGOTHA and sepulchre cut away and destroyed. The Anastasis alone was subsequently rebuilt in 1048 from funds supplied by the Byzantine emperor Constantine IX, Monomachus; it was honored by the Crusaders as the supreme object of their campaigns.

The church was inartistically restored and the formerly open dome closed in by the Greek community in 1809. Then in 1961 reconstruction was begun in order to restore more of its ancient form. Restoration of the dome was completed in 1997. Little remains to suggest the original sepulchre, which is more effectually visualized at the Garden Tomb and Gordon's Calvary, N of the Damascus Gate, but this is an unauthenticated site that has received notice only since 1867. (See W. Harvey, *Church of the Holy Sepulchre: Structural Survey* [1935]; A. Parrot, *Golgotha et Saint-Sepulcre* [1955]; K. Kenyon, *Jerusalem: Excavating 3000 Years of History* [1967], 147–54; J. Wilkinson, *Jerusalem as Jesus Knew It: Archaeology as Evidence* [1978], 190–94; D. Bahat in *BAR* 12/3 [Sept.-Oct. 1986]: 26–45; C. Morris, *The Sepulchre of Christ and the Medieval West* [2005].)

J. B. PAYNE

Aerial view of the domes of the Church of the Holy Sepulchre. (View to the S.)

Serah siluʿah (שֶׂרַח *H8580*, possibly "abundance, prospering"). Daughter of ASHER and granddaughter of JACOB (Gen. 46:17; Num. 26:46 [KJV, "Sarah"]; 1 Chr. 7:30). Aside from DINAH (Gen. 46:15), Serah is the only daughter mentioned in any of these lists, and Jewish tradition has attempted to explain this peculiarity in various ways. The biblical text itself gives no explanation, although one of the references (Num. 26:46) may hint that one of the Asherite clans was descended from her.

Seraiah si-ray′yuh (שְׂרָיָה H8588 and שְׂרָיָהוּ H8589 [only Jer. 36:26], "Yahweh has persevered" or "Yahweh has shown himself ruler"; cf. *HALOT*, 3:1356, and J. D. Fowler, *Theophoric Personal Names in Ancient Hebrew* [1988], 100). **(1)** A royal secretary (see SCRIBE) in DAVID's court (2 Sam. 8:17). For the variations on his name and further discussion, see SHAVSHA.

(2) Son of Azariah, descendant of ZADOK, and chief priest at the time of the fall of Jerusalem; he was seized and put to death at RIBLAH by NEBUCHADNEZZAR, probably not for anything he had done, but because he was a symbol of Hebrew autonomy (2 Ki. 25:18–21; Jer. 52:24–27; 1 Chr. 6:14). Seraiah was the father of JEHOZADAK, who was taken into exile by Nebuchadnezzar (1 Chr. 6:14–15); the grandfather of JESHUA, postexilic high priest (cf. Hag. 1:1 et al.); and an ancestor of EZRA (Ezra 7:1, where "son" means "descendant"; cf. 1 Esd. 5:5; 8:1; 2 Esd. 1:1 [KJV Apoc., "Saraias"]).

(3) Son of TANHUMETH from NETOPHAH and one of the military officers who supported GEDALIAH at MIZPAH (2 Ki. 25:23; in Jer. 40:8 the descriptive "Neophatite" is applied not to Tanhumeth but to EPHAI). Gedaliah, who had been made governor by Nebuchadnezzar, advised them to accept Babylonian rule and promised to treat them fairly (2 Ki. 25:24; Jer. 40:9–10).

(4) Son of KENAZ and brother of OTHNIEL, listed in the genealogy of JUDAH (1 Chr. 4:13–14).

(5) Son of Asiel and grandfather of Jehu; the latter is listed among the clan leaders in the tribe of SIMEON whose families increased greatly during the days of King HEZEKIAH and who dispossessed the Hamites and Meunites near Gedor (1 Chr 4:35; cf. vv. 38–41).

(6) An Israelite mentioned among leading individuals who returned from Babylon with ZERUBBABEL (Ezra 2:2; 1 Esd. 5:8 [KJV, "Zacharias"]; apparently called AZARIAH in Neh. 7:7). Perhaps he is the same Seraiah as a priest mentioned elsewhere (Neh. 12:1, 12).

(7) A priest who signed the covenant of Nehemiah (Neh. 10:2). Some identify him with #6 above.

(8) Son of Hilkiah; he is listed among the priests who settled in Jerusalem and is described as "supervisor in the house of God" (Neh. 11:11 [some scholars emend this text so that the description applies to Jedaiah]; apparently called Azariah in 1 Chr. 9:11).

(9) Son of Azriel; he was one of the officials of king JEHOIAKIM who were commanded to arrest JEREMIAH and his scribe BARUCH because of Jeremiah's prophecies that had been read to the king (Jer. 36:26).

(10) Son of Neriah (thus brother of Baruch, Jer. 32:12); he was a staff officer (see QUARTERMASTER) to whom Jeremiah gave a scroll so that he might read its prophecy to Zedekiah in Babylon (Jer. 51:59–64). The name "Seraiah [ben] Neriah" occurs in a seal impression dated to the 7th cent. B.C. and is thought to refer to the individual mentioned in Jeremiah (see N. Avigad in *IEJ* 28 [1978]: 56). A. K. HELMBOLD

seraph, seraphim ser′uf, ser′uh-fim (שָׂרָף H8597 [pl. שְׂרָפִים], possibly "glowing, burning," or "noble"). KJV "seraphims" (superfluous English pl. form). There are only two references in the Bible to the seraphs (Isa. 6:2, 6). The number of these creatures is not given. Each seraph is said to have six wings, a face, hands, and feet (the latter many scholars regard as a euphemism for the genitalia). Two wings covered the face, two covered the feet, displaying humility before God, and with two they flew. They expressed themselves in words that human ears comprehended (6:3, 7). The description seems to suggest a six-winged, humanoid figure (cf. *ANEP*, plate 655).

Seraphs are described by some scholars as winged demons or as guardian-griffins (called *šerref* in Egyp. [BDB, 977]). Others make a connection with the snake cults of the ANE, pointing both to the FIERY SERPENTS (KJV) that afflicted the Israelites in the wilderness and to the apotropaic bronze serpent (see NEHUSHTAN), which later was destroyed because it had become an object of worship (Num. 21:6–9; 2 Ki. 18:4). According to this view, the term for "fiery [serpent]" (*śārāp*; cf. also Deut. 8:15; Isa. 14:29; 30:6), which possibly alludes to the "burning" sting of the snakes' fatal bite or to their bright "glowing" color, is the same term used for "seraph." However, the seraphs as described by Isaiah are more like men than snakes. Moreover, although they handled hot coals from the altar (Isa. 6:6–7) or may have had fiery countenances, some scholars have thought that their name is derived, not from the verb meaning "to burn" (*śārap H8596*), but from a different Semitic root preserved in Arabic *šarafa*, "to be noble," suggesting that the seraphs were regarded as "princes" or "nobles" (*Gesenius' Hebrew and Chaldee Lexicon* [1859], 795–96; this and other etymologies are not widely accepted, however).

The seraphs or seraphim were probably an order of supernatural or angelic beings (see ANGEL) similar to the CHERUBS, possibly related to the living creatures of Rev. 4:6–8. They stood beside or hovered above the heavenly throne of God as functionaries and attendants. They acted as agents and spokesmen for God (Isa. 6:6–7). A chief duty was that of praising God (6:3). It has been suggested that this act was accomplished antiphonally with the seraphs on one side of the throne responding to those on the opposite side. They probably were not threshold guardians as some believe that Isa. 6:4 implies. (In addition to commentaries on Isaiah, see K. R. Joines in *JBL* 86 [1967]: 410–15, and J. de Savignac in *VT* 22 [1972]: 320–25; cf. also *NIDOTTE*, 3:1289–91; *DDD*, 742–44.)

D. E. ACOMB

Serapis si-rah′pis (Gk. Σέραπις [earlier Σάραπις], from Egyp. *Osir-Ḥapi*, i.e., *Osiris-Apis*, sacred bull at MEMPHIS). Also Sarapis. A Greco-Egyptian deity whose cult was instituted by PTOLEMY I (reigned 305–282 B.C.) at ALEXANDRIA, in a temple known as the Serapeum. Ptolemy perhaps intended to unite his Egyptian and Greek subjects in the worship of this god, but he attained only limited success. As a ZEUS-like figure, Serapis gained great popularity in the Greco-Roman world as a god of the afterlife, of fertility, of healing. He was a savior (e.g., of seafarers), giver of oracles and dreams, and linked with (or identified with) Helios, ASCLEPIUS, and other gods. To Egyptians, Serapis remained simply a form of OSIRIS, their god of the netherworld, fruitfulness, etc. (See H. I. Bell, *Cults and Creeds in Graeco-Roman Egypt* [1953]; J. E. Stambaugh, *Sarapis under the Early Ptolemies*

[1972]; S. A. Takács, *Isis and Sarapis in the Roman World* [1995]; R. Merkelbach, *Isis-regina, Zeus Sarapis: Die griechisch-ägyptische Religion nach den Quellen dargestellt* [1995]; *OCD*, 1355–56.)

K. A. KITCHEN

Sered sihr′id (סֶרֶד H6237, derivation uncertain; gentilic סַרְדִּי H6238, "Seredite" [KJV, "Sardite"]). Son of ZEBULUN, grandson of JACOB, and ancestral head of the Seredite clan (Gen. 46:14; Num. 26:26).

Sergius Paulus. See PAULUS, SERGIUS.

serjeant. KJV form of "sergeant," used to render Greek *rhabdouchos G4812*, which means literally "staff-bearer" but is used in a sense comparable to that of "[police] officer" (Acts 16:35, 38). The specific office in view is that of the Roman *lictor*, who functioned as a personal attendant or bodyguard, especially for MAGISTRATES (i.e., PRAETORS).

Sermon on the Mount. Traditional title given to Jesus' discourse recorded in Matt. 5–7. The term was apparently first used by AUGUSTINE (c. A.D. 400) in his Latin commentary on the Gospel of Matthew, and it was established in English usage by a notation in the Coverdale Bible (1535).

    I. Unity
        A. Arguments against unity
        B. Arguments for unity
    II. Manner
        A. Poetical
        B. Pictorial
        C. Proverbial
    III. Contents
        A. Beatitudes and supporting metaphors
        B. Christian life and Jewish ideal contrasted
        C. Christian worship
        D. The Christian's sympathy
        E. Metaphorical conclusion

I. Unity. Even though it is a moot question whether the material in Matt. 5–7 was ever preached as a sermon or not, many have found a lack of unity and a discontinuity in Matthew's account, pointing to a collection of disjointed sayings rather than to a homiletical development. Others have found a unifying theme and the development of thought toward a climax.

A. Arguments against unity. There are three basic arguments advanced against the unity of the sermon. These would tend to support the view that it was not delivered as a sermon, or that it is not a historical account of the single sermon in the setting ascribed to it (Matt. 5.1).

1. Nature of the material. Much of the material seems to be the epitome of what Jesus taught. A vast range of teaching is condensed and summarized in pithy statements that need to be reflected upon at length. These pointed gnomic sentences were characteristic of Jewish religious teaching, which sought to compress and distill important truths into easily remembered, graphic statements.

2. Disconnection of parts. Various parts of the sermon (e.g., Matt. 5:31–32 and 7:7–11) seem to have little, if any, connection with what goes before or follows in each instance. Some sections seem to be self-contained sermonettes (e.g., 6:1–6, 16–18). The sermon has been believed to contain a mosaic of some of the more striking fragments of as many as twenty of Jesus' discourses.

3. Parallels in Luke. The account in Lk. 6:17–49, commonly called the Sermon on the Plain, has been used against the unity and historicity of the Sermon on the Mount. Luke's material consists of only 30 verses, in comparison with 107 in Matthew. All but six of Luke's verses have more or less close parallels with Matthew's account of the sermon, while 47 verses in Matthew have no parallel at all in Luke. Moreover, 34 additional verses in Matthew have parallels elsewhere in Luke in various different settings. Because of these differences, from Augustine to the Reformation it was generally believed that Matthew's Sermon on the Mount was a different discourse from Luke's Sermon on the Plain.

Modern scholarship, however, has concluded that the differences between Matt. 5–7 and Lk. 6:17–49 are indications that Matthew received his material from two sayings-sources. The overlapping material between Matthew and Luke is assigned to a source they supposedly had in common, usually designated "Q." The material in Matthew that fails to overlap Luke is usually assigned to a second source called "M." There are also some minor differences in language in some of the parallel verses that are best explained by a multiple-source theory. See GOSPELS III.B.

B. Arguments for unity. Many able expositors have found a logical sequence in the sermon and a thematic development that they believe point to the essential coherence of Matt. 5–7 as a literary unit, although not necessarily to its exact historic setting.

1. Character of the audience. It is pointed out that the sermon was not delivered to a general audience nor to novices, but to selected disciples who had been for some time in association with Jesus. The reason given for Jesus' going up the mountain was to escape the crowds (Matt. 5:1). The sermon was thus addressed to the disciples and not the crowds, though the latter may have been sitting on the fringe of the disciple group. Matthew omits all indications of date, and it is incorrect to assume that it was at the beginning of Jesus' ministry. Jesus here is a teacher, not an evangelist.

2. Thematic development. Because of a central idea that is developed throughout the sermon progressing to a climax, many have held to the essential unity of Matt. 5–7. The theme, however, has been variously stated: "Christ's Idea of Righteousness," "The Goal of Life," "The Ideal Christian Life," and so on. Perhaps it is best to designate the theme as "the gospel of the kingdom" (4:23). The phrase "the kingdom of heaven" was Matthew's usual way of expressing the equivalent of "the kingdom of God," which is found in parallel passages in Luke. As would be immediately apparent, the understanding of what was meant by "kingdom" (whether literal or a reference to present reality) becomes determinative in the application. See KINGDOM OF GOD.

3. Editorial possibilities. It has been asserted that it is of no great importance to determine whether

Matthew and Luke give divergent reports of the same sermon or of two similar but distinctive sermons. It is a false assumption that the writer of each gospel told all that he knew and that what he did not tell was unknown to him. It is also false to assume that Jesus never repeated his teachings so that different reports of his words must be related to the same situation. It seems obvious also that Luke has edited out of his account the material that would have a special Palestinian-Jewish coloring. Matthew's account is characterized by such detail. If two sources lie ultimately behind Matt. 5–7, it is not impossible that Jesus himself combined the materials from two sermons that he had preached, and they came to Matthew in the form in which he presented them.

II. Manner. The manner, form, or style of the sermon reveals the literary characteristics of Semitic languages to a remarkable degree.

A. Poetical. Semitic poetry is characterized chiefly by a literary device called *parallelism*, which is a balancing of successive thoughts, phrases, or words. See HEBREW POETRY II. Synonymous parallelism finds the thought of the first literary member restated with different language—and thus usually intensified and/or expanded—in the second member (cf. Matt. 7:6–7). Antithetical parallelism finds the first literary member contrasted and opposed by an opposite (7:17). Synthetic parallelism has the second member completing the thought of the first (5:3). Another Semitic feature found in the sermon is *rhythm*, a term that refers not to some regular system of meter but to a pattern of beats of varying number separated by pauses (6:9b–13 is thought to be an example).

B. Pictorial. An abundance of illustration is taken from common life and nature. Solomon in all his glory, an enforced carrying of a Roman official's baggage for one mile, a burglar breaking in to steal, a builder of a house, trees in an orchard, gates to the road, pearls and hogs, salt and the sun, the hair of a person's head, anointing and fasting, birds and barns, logs and dogs, a serpent and bread, wolves and sheep—these do not exhaust the illustrative material of the sermon.

C. Proverbial. Proverbs have been defined as principles stated in pithy and ingenious words, often dealing with sharply phrased paradoxes. Such were used to penetrate the understanding and make the hearer aware. Crude literalism has always been a danger in the interpretation of the proverbial. It is the principle underlying the proverb that is important and not the literal meaning (Matt. 5:29–30). See PROVERB.

III. Contents

A. Beatitudes and supporting metaphors. The BEATITUDES (Matt. 5:3–12) were named from the Latin word *beatus* (pl. *beati*), used in the VULGATE to translate Greek *makarios* G3421. This Greek term is as old as Homer and Pindar, and was used of Greek gods as well as of human beings; it referred primarily to outward prosperity. Aristotle used it to mean "divine" blessedness in contrast to human happiness. It included the idea of not being subject to fate. Jesus apparently pointed with this word to the intention of God for human life, and thus the condition of being truly well-off. This divine intention for life was a portrait of Jesus himself in a sense. Jesus was the very embodiment of the Sermon on the Mount.

The first beatitude affirmed the blessedness of the "poor in spirit." Among the Hebrews, because the rich were often corrupt and the oppressors of the lowly and destitute, the term POOR was applied to the pious, religious people who were oppressed by the ungodly. Matthew apparently added "in spirit" (missing in Lk. 6:20) so that "poor" would not be misunderstood by Greek readers who were unacquainted with the Hebrew idiom. Isaiah 61:1 notes the interest of the coming MESSIAH in the poor (cf. Matt. 11:5–6; Lk. 4:17–18). The poor were the dependent, godly people, oppressed by the world, who had cast themselves upon God. To such people "the kingdom of heaven" belongs; or better, it is of such that the kingdom of heaven consists.

The second beatitude spoke of the blessedness of those who mourn, but just as "poor" did not refer to actual poverty, so "those who mourn" did not refer simply to those who were sad. The strongest word for MOURNING in the Greek language is used (*pentheō* G4291). In the SEPTUAGINT, it describes mourning for the dead and also the mourning for sins. Such people are desperately sorry and truly penitent for their sins. Their sorrow for sin may reach out to embrace the needy world. The passive voice of "comforted" suggests that God acted in their behalf to share with such people his own strength. God's COMFORT can come only when and where there has been REPENTANCE.

The third beatitude announced the blessedness of the meek. This statement clearly alludes to Ps. 37:11 (LXX 36:11). That psalm speaks of the need to cling to faith in the goodness of God and his care for the righteous in spite of adversity. Just as Israel followed God to the land of promise, so pilgrims in life who are "meek" will find the fullness of God's blessings at the end of the way.

The fourth blessing was on those "who hunger and thirst for righteousness." RIGHTEOUSNESS probably did not in this instance mean goodness as much as it meant right standing with God (in Isaiah, "righteousness" was used by the prophet to define "salvation"). The people in view are characterized by the most intense craving for the gift of God's grace, and God will feed or satisfy the seeking soul in the fullness of salvation.

The fifth through seventh beatitudes concern human relationships, whereas the first four look toward God. The fifth beatitude noted the blessedness of the merciful. MERCY deals with what was to be experienced of pain, misery, and distress. Mercy as active pity was revealed as an element in true righteousness (Mic. 6:8), an element lacking in Pharisaic righteousness (Matt. 23:23). The cry of distress, "Have mercy upon me," often found in Matthew addressed to Jesus, illustrates the meaning of this beatitude. God's mercy is both the cause and the effect for such action in the lives of his people. Because God has been merciful to them, the righteous know the meaning of mercy and are motivated to extend mercy to others; and because they have shown mercy, they are increasingly the object of God's mercy.

The sixth beatitude identified the "pure in heart" as those who would see God. The idea here is meant singleness of heart—an honest heart free from any hidden motive of self-interest. It was part of Jesus' "good news for the poor" that even if they could not attain to the ritual purity of the PHARISEES, they could see God. Jesus taught that the only defile-

Interior of the Church of the Beatitudes that overlooks the Sea of Galilee near Tabgha, Israel.

ment that really bars a person from God's presence comes from within. The believer whose heart is truly fixed on God will not lack God's presence.

The term "peacemakers" of the seventh beatitude refers to the true subjects of the Prince of Peace, who came to found a kingdom of peace. Such people exercise themselves in the extension of his sovereignty, the only source of peace in a world of alienation, strife, and passion. The passive voice "will be called" (i.e., by God) implies that God alone can bestow the title "sons."

The last (twofold) beatitude witnessed to the blessedness of those who suffered because of their loyalty to God. They have suffered because of their godly characters. It was not suggested by these words that the ideal Christian character could not be formed apart from PERSECUTION; rather it meant that where Christian character provoked persecution there would also be afforded an additional opportunity to prove one's relationship to God and to demonstrate the reality of citizenship in the heavenly kingdom.

The two metaphors that follow the Beatitudes were intended to show the effect of such ideal character in a world that needed such living. SALT was used in the Jewish sacrificial system (Lev. 2:13; Ezek. 43:24) and was also symbolical in establishing of covenants (Num. 18:19; 2 Chr. 13:5; see COVENANT OF SALT). Among the Jews, the Torah was compared with salt, and it was often stated that the world could not exist either without salt or without the Torah (Sir. 39:26). In practical experience, salt prevented putrefaction and insipidity. This, too, may have been in the mind of Jesus. Salt, however, must make contact with other substances to be able to work. It was a commodity of considerable value in Jesus' time, and whatever the particular application, the tremendous work of discipleship to a waiting world was underscored.

Whereas the action of salt is silent and unseen, the action of LIGHT is obvious and discernible. References to "light" or "lamp" were not infrequent in the rabbinic writings; in particular, Israel was referred to as God's lamp. Biblical material likewise made use of this symbol. It was God who lit Israel's lamp (Ps. 18:28). The nations would come to Israel's light (Isa. 60:3). The probable intent of Jesus' illustration was that through character as described in the Beatitudes, people may see God and glory in him.

B. Christian life and Jewish ideal contrasted. Jesus was not at war with the religion of the OT, and he was not the opponent of Mosaic law. He was, however, in strong opposition to the externalism of Pharisaism. He regarded the OT as having permanent validity (Matt. 5:17–19), but he attacked the interpretation and application of Scripture by the Pharisees, who were the popular religious authorities of that day. The examples chosen by Jesus against which to measure Pharisaic religion were not in contradiction to the law of Moses but, rather, intensified the meaning of the law. Jesus denounced the legalistic interpretation of the law, which militated against a realization of its spiritual significance.

1. Murder. In the first example (Matt. 5:21–26) Jesus interpreted the commandment against murder to prohibit also anger and hatred. The degrees of punishment suggested for those who violated this commandment—the "judgment" for anyone who has been angry with a brother, the "Sanhedrin" for anyone who has insulted his brother, and "hell of fire" for anyone who has said "you fool"—have puzzled interpreters. Some feel that Jesus argued as a skilled rabbi, and this type of argument looked for gradation of punishment. Others think that these references were meant as irony, holding up to ridicule such rabbinic distinctions. The central teaching is quite clear, however, in the concluding statement, which reveals that no act of worship is acceptable to God when the worshiper is wrongly related to other persons. Hostility toward others may not eventuate in the act of murder, but it is nonetheless a barrier to worship. A quarrel is never to be nurtured, but quickly resolved.

2. Adultery. The prohibition against ADULTERY was carried even further by Jesus to forbid also the desire to commit adultery (Matt. 5:27–30). The language used (lit., "so that he might lust after her") suggests deliberate intention. Beyond question, the teaching about the removal of the offending eye and the offending hand is figurative. The removal of offending organs could not actually remove sin from a person's heart. These were strong words that indicated the seriousness of the problem and the necessity of a remedy, whatever the cost.

3. Divorce. Next, in connection with the law against DIVORCE, Jesus stated the divine ideal of MARRIAGE as an indissoluble union—one man for one woman for life (Matt. 5:31–32). He identified the law of Moses that authorized limited divorce as a concession to the hardheartedness of human beings. The so-called "exceptive clause" that recognized divorce on the ground of "marital unfaithfulness" (the NIV rendering of *porneia* G4518) seems out of harmony with Mark and Luke, who do not have the clause. It seems best to emphasize that in the teaching of Jesus, marriage was a God-given institution, and divorce a violation of the divine will.

4. Oaths. The Jews were fond of oaths. The Pharisees considered themselves bound by an oath if it was stated in certain words. If it was not, the slightest verbal change relieved these formalists from all moral obligation. Intricate and complicated were the rules and regulations by which such a system operated. Jesus again expressed his interest in attitudes and inner motivation; he earnestly desired his followers to live and speak the truth because truth alone is right (Matt. 5:33–37).

5. Retaliation. The rabbis misinterpreted the law to mean that it commanded retaliation. Jesus said that the OT teaching was never intended to occasion violence; it was given to put a limit on such violence. Jesus taught a "Christian retaliation," by which actual good was given in return for evil (Matt. 5:38–42).

6. Love to others. "Love your neighbor" in the OT was understood to mean a fellow Israelite (Lev. 19:18). "Hate your enemy" does not occur explicitly in the OT (though the concept of hatred for the enemy is found in substance in the OT, e.g., Deut. 23:6 and Ps. 139:21–22). See HATE, HATRED. Because Christians are God's children and God so acted, they are to show LOVE even to their enemies and to pray for those who were unkind (Matt. 5:43–47).

7. Summary. Finally, Jesus called supremely for a likeness to God in the lives of his people (Matt. 5:48). This was not a command to sinlessness as such but was rather related especially to the love of God. Christians were to exercise complete love as did God, who sent sun and rain upon both the just and the unjust.

C. Christian worship. The Jews asserted three principal expressions of the religious life. They were the three great pillars on which the good life was based: almsgiving, prayer, and fasting (Matt. 6:1–18). In obvious ways, however, wrong motivation could rob those acts of their spiritual significance. In connection with those areas, Jesus underscored the necessity for right motivation in acts of WORSHIP. His disciples were to avoid religious parade when they gave alms (vv. 2–4), when they prayed (vv. 5–11), and when they fasted (vv. 16–18).

1. Almsgiving. To the Jews, the giving of ALMS was of great importance, and they counted it as a part of worship (Ps. 41:1). The rabbis themselves often taught that it should be done in secrecy, but there were many hypocrites who liked to publicize their charity to gain human credit. Jesus said that this was all such people would get. The only charity that could be a real act of worship was charity that sought to please God and avoided the attention of others for self-glory.

2. Praying. The disciples were warned about the wrong motivation in PRAYER; they were to pray to God and not to human beings. There was also a warning against vain repetitions. An additional warning was given in connection with praying with the idea that the individual must inform God. Real prayer must never be just for appearance. Jesus commended a spot free from distractions as the place of prayer and secrecy, which afforded opportunity for fellowship with the infinite God. The prayer given to the disciples as the example to guide them revealed these characteristics of real prayer: confidence ("our Father"), reverence ("hallowed be your name"), submission ("your will be done"), dependence ("give us today"), forgiveness ("forgive us ... as we have also forgiven"), and humility ("lead us not into temptation"). See LORD'S PRAYER.

3. Fasting. The practice of FASTING was counted by the Jews as a sign of special piety. The Pharisees fasted on Mondays and Thursdays in commemoration of Moses' ascending the mountain to receive the law and descending with the law. Some of the devout apparently smeared ashes on their faces as a token of their fast and thus gained the commendation of others for their piety. Jesus did not condemn fasting as such; once again, it was the wrong motivation that deserved the scathing denunciation.

4. Living. Jesus taught the meaning of genuine worship to be an exclusive devotion to God in this life. A person served God by living. His God consciousness was determinative in everything. This was the meaning of a heart that was "in heaven." Some people lived with this world dominating their lives—not so the Christian. The worldly wealth of the 1st cent. was frequently counted in garments and grain rather than in the coin of the realm, but it was foolish to let one's life be governed by avarice rather than by God. What a person garnered in the way of material substance could not by its very nature be permanent. His possession of it was uncertain, and it passed away quickly. Preoccupation with the goods of this world could draw, like a magnet, his heart away from God.

The metaphor of the eye in a moral sense was quite common among the Jews. A good eye signified a generous soul, and an evil eye a grasping and grudging one (Deut. 15:9; Prov. 23:6; 28:22). Even as people today speak of spiritual insight, so Jesus was insisting that people could lose their sense of true values in life and become possessed by their possessions. The word MAMMON (an Aramaic term) signified wealth and riches. In this passage it was personified, becoming the avaricious man's master. It is important to note that this did not apply to rich people only, for the greater temptation comes many times to the person who has not, but desires to have. Jesus made this truth apply to all when he said, "No one can serve two masters."

GREED and ANXIETY about life were next presented. Nothing was intended in these verses to forbid foresight, careful planning, or prudence: the remarks were rather directed against a care for this life that dishonors God because it fails to find its stability, confidence, and security in relationship to him. The heavenly Father has always been interested in and ready to meet the needs of human life at every level and in all experiences. God's kingdom must be placed first in life, and then there could be a foundation upon which to rest in confidence with reference to the material and temporal.

D. The Christian's sympathy. The connection of Matt. 7 with the rest of the sermon has been much disputed, with many scholars suggesting that it reveals lack of continuity. It seems, however, that these verses are bound together by a consideration of the sympathetic spirit.

1. Avoiding criticism. Jesus admonished his disciples not to be disparaging in their criticism (Matt. 7:1–5). He singled out and condemned the vice of lifting up oneself by pointing out the weaknesses and faults of others. The Christian was not to be unconcerned about a brother's fault, but it was impossible to help him when the helper's vision was poor.

2. Helping wisely. The disciples were warned against being overzealous in trying to help another (Matt. 7:6). Perhaps the "sacred" or "holy" thing referred to the use of the SHOWBREAD among the Jews. If it were not consumed, it must not be cast out to be eaten by the scavengers of the streets, the dogs. In the TALMUD (e.g., h Yebam. 94a), "pearl" was used to refer to the choice thoughts, sentiments, or tenderest experiences of a person. The "pigs" or "swine" were the unclean, those of vicious nature who did not have the character to appreciate such thoughts and sentiments. This passage calls for wisdom in dealing with the people of the world.

3. Praying earnestly. It was revealed that prayer was the best way to help; it was in prayer that the solution was to be found to the problems of life (Matt. 7:7–12). Two illustrations were given of the efficacy of genuine prayer. The first illustration underscored the truth that a father did not mock his child in the answer given to an earnest request. In the second illustration Jesus underscored the truth that a father does not give his child what would harm him, neither does God. The grand climax in the statement of the sympathetic approach to life is the "Golden Rule."

E. Metaphorical conclusion. With three metaphors, Jesus urged his hearers on to realize the intention of God for their lives: (1) "the two ways," which indicated that following Jesus was difficult, involving struggle, self-discipline, and effort; (2) "the two fruits," which warned against false guides whose real purpose was selfish and destructive — guides in life must be tested; and (3) "the two builders," which emphasized the importance of the right foundation for life, which is the teaching of Jesus — only those who obey him will be safe in the experience of testing.

(In addition to commentaries on the Gospel of Matthew, see R. C. Trench, *Exposition of the Sermon on the Mount* [1886]; E. S. Jones, *The Christ of the Mount* [1931]; W. Hendriksen, *The Sermon on the Mount* [1934]; E. T. Thompson, *The Sermon on the Mount and Its Meaning for Today* [1936]; E. Fox, *The Sermon on the Mount* [1938]; A. T. Ohrn, *The Gospel and the Sermon on the Mount* [1948]; R. W. Sockman, *The Higher Happiness* [1950]; A. M.

Hunter, *Design for Life* [1953]; J. W. Bowman and R. W. Tapp, *The Gospel from the Mount* [1957]; D. M. Lloyd-Jones, *Studies in the Sermon on the Mount*, 2 vols. [1959–60]; H. K. McArthur, *Understanding the Sermon on the Mount* [1960]; W. K. Pendleton, *The Pursuit of Happiness* [1963]. W. D. Davies, *The Setting of the Sermon on the Mount* [1964]; W. S. Kissinger, *The Sermon on the Mount: A History of Interpretation and Bibliography* [1975]; R. A. Guelich, *The Sermon on the Mount: A Foundation for Understanding* [1982]; G. Strecker, *The Sermon on the Mount: An Exegetical Commentary* [1988]; W. Carter, *What Are They Saying about Matthew's Sermon on the Mount?* [1994]; H. D. Betz, *The Sermon on the Mount*, Hermeneia [1995]; D. P. Scaer, *The Sermon on the Mount: The Church's First Statement of the Gospel* [2000]; C. G. Vaught, *The Sermon on the Mount: A Theological Investigation*, rev. ed. [2001]; R. K. Hughes, *The Sermon on the Mount: The Message of the Kingdom* [2001]; F. Zeilinger, *Zwischen Himmel und Erde: Ein Kommentar zur "Bergpredit" Matthäus 5–7* [2002]; D. Lioy, *The Decalogue in the Sermon on the Mount* [2004]; C. H. Talbert, *Reading the Sermon on the Mount: Character Formation and Decision Making in Matthew 5–7* [2004]; J. P. Greenman et al., eds., *The Sermon on the Mount through the Centuries: From the Early Church to John Paul II* [2008].) H. L. DRUMWRIGHT, JR.

Sermon on the Plain. Common title given to Jesus' discourse recorded in Lk. 6:17–49. See discussion under SERMON ON THE MOUNT.

Seron sihr´on (Σήρων). A military commander under ANTIOCHUS Epiphanes who was defeated at BETH HORON by Judas MACCABEE (1 Macc. 3:13–23). According to JOSEPHUS (*Ant.* 12.7.1 §§288–92), Seron was commander or governor (Gk. *stratēgos* G5130) of COELESYRIA, but this description is generally thought to reflect a misunderstanding (cf. J. A. Goldstein, *I Maccabees*, AB 41 [1976], 246; B. Bar-Kochva, *Judas Maccabaeus: The Jewish Struggle against the Seleucids* [1988], 133).

serpent. This English term is now less common than "snake," but *Serpentes* (= *Ophidia*) is the scientific name for the suborder of reptiles to which all snakes belong. The primary biblical terms for "serpent" or "snake" are Hebrew *nāḥāš* H5729 (Gen. 3:1 et al.) and Greek *ophis* G4058 (Matt. 7:20 et al.). There are, however, various other terms that can be so rendered (e.g., *tannîn* H9490, Exod. 7:9–10) or that can refer to particular species (e.g., *echidna* G2399, "viper," Matt. 3:7).

I. Problems of Identification. Except in the case of a few narratives, where the settings contain helpful clues, any attempt at precise identification would be pointless, especially since most occur in figurative passages. Snakes have long been the cause of superstition and irrational fear; many people of all countries, both civilized and primitive, still suffer from a serious snake phobia, usually acquired in early life. Snakes are mentioned some seventy times in the OT and NT, and in nearly two-thirds the use is figurative. Although the majority of Palestine species are harmless, their poisonous character is clearly implied some fifty times. The serpent is thus a frequent picture of evil and danger, whether personally (Matt. 3:7) or nationally (Isa. 14:29). The punishment given to the serpent in EDEN, "you will eat dust all the days of your life" (Gen. 3:14), is hard to interpret biologically, for all snakes are carnivorous and must swallow their prey whole, but this idea is repeated several times (e.g., Mic. 7:17, where a snake is assumed to feed by licking with its tongue, a belief that is still widely current). The subtlety of the serpent (Gen. 3:1) is also echoed in the NT, "be as shrewd as snakes" (Matt. 10:16), though this piece of wisdom is qualified by the following verses.

Serpent relief carved on basalt. (From the Pergamum excavations.)

II. Serpents in Palestine.

The Middle E has a wide range of snakes, from those reaching a maximum length of under one foot to several exceeding 6 feet and a girth of over 6 in. Most are quite harmless, but a few can give potentially lethal bites. Snakes are found in every region from desert to closed woodland, some widely and others confined to narrow habitats. Some are normally nocturnal and others diurnal, but their cold-blooded nature may make them vary their habits at certain seasons. All reptiles and amphibians are "cold-blooded," which means that they have no automatic temperature control but are dependent on external heat sources. They therefore regulate their exposure to sun, or protection from it, to keep their bodies within suitable limits, mostly about 60°–80° F. Doing so may entail (a) hibernation for short spells when the winter days are too cold; (b) estivation, under shelter, if the extreme summer temperature with low humidity makes life on the surface too difficult; or (c) staying on the higher ground at some seasons, being active for short periods early and late, between the heat of the day and the cold of the night.

III. Ignorance of snakes leads to myths.

In civilized lands the average citizen's knowledge of snakes is small and few species are known by name; this is in part because of the fear in which they are held. In less developed countries, many of them with a wealth of snakes, names are usually given to the more conspicuous or important species and these are known by hunters, shepherds, etc., while the common folk hardly know the names and certainly cannot apply them correctly. This attitude to snakes is not new, for ancient peoples did not know their snakes any more accurately; one would thus expect general names, rather than specific ones, to be used for the most part. Some myths still current were known to the ancient writers, such as the view that the pointed forked tongue is dangerous (cf. Ps. 140:3).

IV. Serpents in the Bible.

The first mention of a serpent is of course in Gen. 3:1, introducing the story of the FALL, and thus a theological rather than zoological matter. The mention of changing rods into snakes (Exod. 4 and 7) suggests that snake-charming and conjuring were already being practiced in Egypt before the exodus, for this was a trick in the repertoire of the court magicians. Clearly, the snake used was one of the larger species, possibly the harmless Montpelier snake, or more probably the Egyptian cobra (*Naja haje*), whose range also extends N toward Palestine and which is used by Egyptian snake-charmers today. Ancient Egyptian scarab-amulets depict cobras being held by the neck. This is, in fact, the correct and safe way to hold a venomous snake, but the significance of these pictures has been explained in modern times. Charmers have been filmed immobilizing cobras by holding them in this way until a state of rigid unconsciousness is induced (H. S. Noerdlinger, *Moses and Egypt* [1956], 26). See ASP.

The FIERY SERPENTS in the wilderness (Num. 21:6–9; Heb. *śārāp H8597*) merit fuller discussion. The location was the NEGEV desert on the borders of EDOM, probably to the SE of the DEAD SEA, while a basic fact of the narrative is that the snakes were highly venomous. These two facts reduce the possible species to four only: the two sand vipers (*Cerastes cerastes* and *C. vipera*); the false cerastes (*Pseudocerastes fieldi*); and one of the carpet or saw-scaled vipers (*Echis coloratus* or *E. carinatus*). See VIPER.

C. cerastes, which may reach a length of 30 in., is well adapted to desert life, being able to sink quickly and hide itself in the sand with a shuffling movement, leaving only the nostrils and eyes showing. Its venom is used mostly to kill small rodents such as jerboas, for which it waits, lying unseen on the surface of the sand, but its bite can be fatal to humans. *C. vipera* seldom reaches 15 in. and is less dangerous. The false cerastes is a highly specialized desert form, with a valve-like structure inside the nostril that enables it to exclude driven sand. Its venom is the least potent of the four species. In the wild it may take some dead prey in the form of migrant birds; this is unusual in snakes.

These three are of somewhat similar shape; they are typical vipers, with bodies rather fat for the length, with a very stubby tail ending in a sharp point (not poisonous) and with a large flat head, distinctly broader than the neck. As in all vipers, a pair of long curved fangs hinge in the front of the upper jaw and, normally, lie in folds of mucus lining the hard palate. The fangs are needle-sharp and hollow to the tip. To swing the fangs down and forward into position the mouth is opened wide, and the whole action, ending in the strike, is at great speed.

The serpents mentioned above are all found in the sandy deserts crossed after the exodus, but *Echis*, the carpet or saw-scaled viper, has perhaps the best claim to be the fiery serpent. It grows to over 2 ft., but is thinner than many vipers; it is darker than the sand vipers and its head is smaller. One or another form of the carpet viper is found from W Africa to E Africa and SW Asia to N India, and in some areas it is very common. For instance, in one part of Kenya some 7,000 were caught, marked, and released for research purposes; and in NW India 38,000 Zoological Survey killed artificially for nearly 100 six years.

Only a snake capable of being as numerous as this in one locality could do the damage described in Num. 21, and there is further confirmatory evidence. The venom of this genus is more powerful, weight for weight, than that of any other viper. This snake is well known for being easily provoked, while many of the large vipers are strangely placid. *Echis* also appears able to tolerate hotter conditions than most snakes and therefore would be more active by day. The saw-scaled viper's name comes from the rough nature of its scales, which produce a distinct rasping noise as its sides rub while it makes a characteristic figure-eight movement. When gliding over shingle or rock it moves normally but, like the sand viper and some desert rattlesnakes, it has developed a side-winding motion for traveling over loose sand.

Its venom is typical of the viper family in being hemolytic, that is, it affects the blood, breaking down the capillaries, rupturing the corpuscles, and finally causing death by massive and wide-spread internal hemorrhage. This can be a slow process, and death may occur after as long as four days, the progress depending on the site and severity of the bite. This fact is also relevant to the narrative, for it must have taken MOSES some time to cast the bronze serpent and publish news throughout the host of Israel, which amounted to many tens of thousands at even the lowest estimate. See NEHUSHTAN.

This incident is one of the clearest OT pictures of SALVATION (cf. Jn. 3:14–15), and there is a further point of interest. The injection of such venom is not always followed by intense pain, but the internal destruction goes on; it is possible that a victim may feel somewhat better after two or three days and assume that all is well, but after a severe bite the process continues until death. The timing of the incident shows divine overruling, and the results of looking in faith at the bronze serpent were wholly miraculous, but the setting needs no metaphysical explanation. (On the serpent as a religious symbol, see *ABD*, 5:113–16; cf. also *DDD*, 744–47.) G. S. CANSDALE

serpent, bronze (brasen). See NEHUSHTAN.

serpent charming. See SNAKE CHARMING.

Serpent's Stone. See ZOHELETH.

Serug sihr´uhg (שְׂרוּג *H8578*, meaning unknown; Σερούχ *G4952*). Son of Reu and descendant of SHEM (Gen. 11:20–23; 1 Chr. 1:26); included in Luke's GENEALOGY OF JESUS CHRIST (Lk. 3:35; KJV, "Saruch"). Some link Serug with a place in N SYRIA that apparently bears the Akkadian name *Sarugi* (cf. *HALOT*, 3:1355; *ABD*, 5:1117–18).

servant. The most common Hebrew word for servant in the OT is *ʿebed H6269*, usually translated in the SEPTUAGINT by the Greek words *doulos G1528* (which more properly means "slave"), *pais G4090* ("boy, youth"; cf. Heb. *naʿar H5853*), and less frequently *therapōn G2544* ("attendant," used esp. in cultic contexts; cf. Heb. *mĕšārēt*, piel ptc. of *šārat H9250*) and *oiketēs G3860* (usually "household slave"). The Hebrew term is used often in the OT to refer to SLAVES regarded as property, though possessing also certain rights (for laws pertaining to slaves see Exod. 21:1–11; Lev. 25:39–55; Deut. 15:1–18). In more instances, however, "servant" is a better translation than "slave" because the words have to do with service or obedience in a far more general sense than what is known today as slavery.

A servant can be anyone committed to someone more powerful; thus the term may be applied to a trusted steward (Gen. 24:2), a soldier in an army (Jer. 52:8), a court official (1 Sam. 8:14–15), or a vassal king (2 Ki. 17:3). The servant is dependent

Gilded shabti of the Egyptian priest of Amun (from Iwy, c. 1700 B.C.). Shabtis were small, mummy-shaped figurines that came to represent servants for the deceased in the afterlife.

on his master for protection (16:7), and in turn agrees to fight if need be to protect or further his master's interests (10:3). A servant-master relationship can be a kind of COVENANT (cf. Josh. 9:6–7), voluntarily undertaken with such words as "We are your servants" (Josh. 9:8; 2 Ki. 10:5) or "I will be your servant" (2 Sam. 15:34). A servant addressing the master can express humility and dependence by speaking of himself or herself as "your servant." This may remind the master of their agreement, especially if the servant is seeking help or protection, though in some instances it becomes little more than a formality, a polite substitute for "I."

This "covenantal" use of servant terminology is especially conspicuous in passages where the servant is a servant of God. ELIJAH proclaims his allegiance to God with the words, "I am your servant" (1 Ki. 18:36). Judges and kings address the Lord much as any servant would address an earthly master (Jdg. 15:18; 1 Sam. 3:9; 14:41; 23:10–11). Those who pray to God often refer to themselves as "your servant(s)" (2 Sam. 7:19–21, 27–29; Pss. 19:11, 13; 27:9; 31:16; 90:13, 16), and appeal to God's dealings in the past with his servants MOSES (1 Ki. 8:53; Neh. 9:14) or DAVID (1 Ki. 8:24–25; Ps. 132:10; cf. 89:39).

For his part, God acknowledges a person who gives allegiance to him as "my servant" (Moses, 2 Ki. 21:8; Mal. 4:4; Caleb, Num. 14:24; David, 2 Ki. 19:34; Ezek. 34:23; 37:24; Job, Job 1:8; Zerubbabel, Hag. 2:23; unnamed messianic figures, Isa. 52:13; Zech. 3:8). Prophets are called his servants both individually (1 Ki. 14:18; 2 Ki. 14:25; Isa. 20:3; 22:20) and as a group (2 Ki. 17:13, 23; Ezek. 38:17; Amos 3:7; Zech. 1:6). In the widest sense the servants of God are the people of God, all the faithful of Israel regarded either as his "servants" (Isa. 65:9) or collectively as "Israel my servant" (Isa. 41:8–9; cf. 44:1–2; Ps. 136:22).

If the servant-master relationship is based on a kind of covenant, it is natural that "people" of God and "servants" of God should often be parallel concepts (e.g., Deut. 32:36; Ps. 135:14; cf. Neh. 1:6; Ps. 105:25; Isa. 63:17). And since the covenant is mediated to the people of God through individual "servants" (such as the patriarchs, Moses, the kings of Israel, and the prophets), it is not surprising that sometimes the "people" are seen in close association with a single "servant" who is regarded as their representative before God (e.g., 1 Ki. 8:30, 52, 59, 66; cf. Neh. 1:11; Ps. 78:70–71). What is conspicuously lacking in the OT is the idea that a "servant of God" who exercises leadership over Israel is in some sense also a "servant of the people." Neither the modern notion of a "public servant" nor the Roman Catholic ideal of a "servant of the servants of God" has any explicit analogy in the OT. The closest approach to such a concept is perhaps the advice of the old men to REHOBOAM in 1 Ki. 12:7 ("If today you will be a servant to these people"), but it was advice that went unheeded.

The range of meaning in the servant idea in the OT is best illustrated in Lev. 25:42, where ʿebed is used in two senses: "Because the Israelites are my *servants*, whom I brought out of Egypt, they must not be sold as *slaves*." The covenant begins with redemption from slavery in Egypt, and to be servants in the covenant is not to be "slaves" of God but to be his people and his sons (cf. Exod. 4:22–23).

In the NT as in the OT, "servant" can refer to the people of God in general (Rev. 2:20; 19:5), to the prophets in particular (10:7; 11:18), or to a prophet and his people together (1:1). "Your servant(s)" can still be a self-designation of those who address God in prayer (Lk. 2:29; Acts 4:29; cf. Jesus' use of "your Son" in Jn. 17:1). Moses and David (Rev. 15:3; Lk. 1:69; Acts 4:25), as well as the community of Israel (Lk. 1:54), can still be called God's "servant," but more typically this title passes to Jesus (Matt. 12:18; Acts 3:13, 26; 4:27, 30; cf. Phil. 2:7). Decisive for this development is the identification of Jesus with the suffering servant of Isa. 52:13—53:12, because of his sacrificial death (cf. Mk. 10:45; 1 Pet. 2:24f.). See SERVANT OF THE LORD.

In terminology the NT differs from the LXX in distinguishing between *doulos* and *pais* often (though not always), using the former to mean "slave" while the latter moves in the direction of "child" or "son." NT writers can speak of slavery to sin (Jn. 8:34; Rom. 6:16), but also in a positive sense of slavery to Christ or to righteousness (Rom. 6:16–23; 1 Cor. 7:23). Paul himself indicates, however, that this language is a rather exceptional metaphor (Rom. 6:18). When he and other writers call themselves "servant of Jesus Christ" it is not the metaphor of slavery, but the OT covenantal use of "servant" which controls their thinking. To call oneself "servant" is simply the corollary of confessing Jesus Christ as "Lord." In contrast to the OT, a "servant of Jesus Christ" is also explicitly seen as a servant to the whole community of believers (Mk. 10:43–44; 2 Cor. 4:5). Again the decisive factor in the shift is Jesus, who reversed the customary patterns of authority (both pagan and Jewish) first by his teaching, and then by his own fulfillment of the servant role (Mk. 10:35–45; Matt. 23:8–12; Jn. 13:1–17).

J. R. MICHAELS

Servant of the Lord. The Hebrew expression ʿ*ebed yhwh*, "the servant of YAHWEH," occurs frequently in the OT, usually with reference to MOSES (e.g., Josh. 1:1 and often in this book). In biblical scholarship, however, the phrase "the Servant of the Lord" refers primarily to a messianic figure mentioned repeatedly in Isa. 42–53 whom God calls "my servant" (though the specific phrase ʿ*ebed yhwh* occurs only in Isa. 42:19). At the end of the 19th cent., Bernhard Duhm (*Das Buch Jesaia* [1892]) distinguished in this section four passages which modern criticism has generally agreed to treat as the "Servant Songs." They are 42:1–4; 49:1–6; 50:4–9; 52:13—53:12. The limits of the individual "Songs" are not clear; many would add 42:5–7; 49:7; 50:10–11; and others would see a fifth Servant Song in 61:1. Some scholars have carried this line of argument to the extent of postulating a separate author and period of origin for these passages. The general tendency, however, has been to interpret them in relation to their context in Isaiah and as an integral part of the prophet's message.

More recent scholars have sometimes questioned the view that there is a coherent line of thought linking the "Songs" together (cf. T. N. D. Mettinger, *A Farewell to the Servant Songs: A Critical Examination of an Exegetical Axiom* [1983]). Some even dispute that these passages are intended to portray a specific figure, since the term SERVANT is frequently used in the OT for those who are obedient to God and is therefore applied to Israel as she fulfills her vocation. Certainly other figures in the OT are described as "servants of God," especially the PROPHETS, the PATRIARCHS, and other individuals such as MOSES and DAVID (each of these frequently; e.g., Gen. 26:24; Exod. 14:31; Deut. 34:5; 2 Sam. 7:5; Isa. 20:3; Amos 3:7). To refer to someone as "servant of the Lord" was no novelty. In Isaiah itself, moreover, the term "servant" is used as frequently outside the Servant Songs as within (note these passages in the vicinity of the Songs: Isa. 41:8–9; 43:10; 44:1–2, 21; 45:4; 48:20). All of these are applied to Israel, sometimes in terms similar to the language of the Songs.

I. Identification of the Servant. Interpretations may be divided into three basic classes: the collective, the individual, and the cultic (cf. the discussions by C. R. North, *The Suffering Servant in Deutero-Isaiah: An Historical and Critical Study,* [1948], 6–116; and H. H. Rowley, *The Servant of the Lord, and Other Essays on the Old Testament* [1952], 4–48).

(1) *Collective interpretations.* The Servant is explicitly addressed as "Israel" in Isa. 49:3. This fact, and the close correspondence between the language of the Songs and that applied to Israel as God's Servant in surrounding chapters, have led many to see in the Servant-figure a projection of the prophet's ideal for the nation. It is the nation as a whole that is to undergo redemptive suffering. Others restrict the reference to a pious remnant within the nation, thus making allowance for the fact that the Servant has a mission *to* Israel (49:5–6; cf. 42:6) and suffers *for* the people (53:4–6, 8, 11–12). A further candidate for the title is the Davidic dynasty.

(2) *Individual interpretations.* The Songs refer to the Servant in the singular and describe the life and experience of an individual (his birth, obedience, suffering, death, and triumph). That this is not a mere poetical personification of the nation is shown by his mission *to* Israel, as mentioned above. Interpreters have therefore taken the Servant as either a specific historical figure known to the author (e.g., Moses, Jeremiah, Cyrus, Zerubbabel, the prophet himself, or some unknown contemporary), or an ideal figure of the future—the MESSIAH. The latter was the predominant Christian interpretation until the end of the last century.

(3) *Cultic interpretations.* Some Scandinavian scholars have seen the background to the Servant-figure in a cultic ceremony, involving the symbolic death and rising again of the king, deriving from the Babylonian myth of the dying and rising god, TAMMUZ, and its liturgy. The Servant would, in this view, be neither a historical figure, past, present, or future, nor a collective personification of the nation, but a mythological symbol. The existence of such a mythology and ritual within Israel is highly controversial, and such interpretations have received little support outside Scandinavia.

(4) *Synthetic interpretations.* Few scholars today hold to an exclusively collective or an exclusively individual interpretation. Some would see a progression of thought from the collective figure of the earlier Servant Songs to a more fully individualized figure in the fourth. The ideal for Israel was summed up in an ideal individual—the Messiah. Rowley (*Servant of the Lord*, 53) has suggested that "what began as a personification [has] become a person." Such an understanding of the Servant is best able to do justice to the apparently conflicting evidence of the text, as mentioned above. (See esp. the close juxtaposition of Isa. 49:3, where the Servant is addressed as "Israel," and 49:5–6, where he is described as having a mission *to* Israel.)

This view is reinforced by the growing recognition that the Israelite distinguished less sharply between the individual and the community than does the modern Western mind. The notion of CORPORATE PERSONALITY (associated particularly with the name of H. W. Robinson and not accepted by all) makes it possible for the Messiah not only to act *for* Israel, but also to sum up Israel in himself. The Servant, therefore, *is* Israel—the ideal Israel, who is capable of fulfilling the destiny of which the empirical Israel fell short. In that capacity he can suffer and die to redeem the people of God as their representative as well as their substitute.

The subtlety of the prophet's thought defies systematic analysis. It is in some such synthetic interpretation that the biblical data will be most fully satisfied. To describe the Servant as a messianic figure, in the sense of an individual who is central to the eschatological fulfillment of God's purposes for his people, is therefore a correct, though not an exhaustive, description; and a messianic application of the Servant passages, and especially of the passage where the individual terminology is clearest (Isa. 52:13—53:12), will be in accordance with the intention of the prophet.

II. The character and mission of the Servant.

Working from the traditionally delimited Servant Songs (though the limitations of this approach have been indicated above), the following picture of his character emerges. The Servant was chosen by the Lord (Isa. 42:1; 49:1) and endued with the Spirit (42:1); he was taught by the Lord (50:4), and found his strength in him (49:2, 5). It was the Lord's will that he should suffer (53:10); he was weak, unimpressive, and scorned by human beings (52:14; 53:1–3, 7–9), meek (42:2), gentle (42:3), and uncomplaining (50:6; 53:7). Despite his innocence (53:9), he was subjected to constant suffering (50:6; 53:3, 8–10), so as to be reduced to near despair (49:4). But his trust was in the Lord (49:4, 50:7–9); he obeyed him (50:4–5) and persevered (50:7) until he was victorious (42:4; 50:8–9).

The Servant's mission to Israel was to bring the rebellious nation back to God (Isa. 49:5), but his work extended further: he was a light to the nations, bringing judgment and salvation to the end of the earth (42:1, 3–4; 49:6). This mission was to be accomplished only through his suffering, in which he took the place of the people of the Lord, and bore the penalty that should be theirs (53:4–6, 8), interceding for them (53:12); his suffering ended in death (53:8–9; 53:12) as a sin offering on their behalf (53:10), thus accomplishing their acquittal (53:11). His mission accomplished, he was exalted to glory and worldwide influence (52:13, 15; 53:12).

III. The Servant in later Judaism.

Possible echoes of the Servant-figure have been detected in the OT itself, particularly in Zech. 9–14; a meek and suffering figure occurs in 9:9, 10; 11:4–17; 12:10–14; 13:7–9. It is the character of the figure portrayed, rather than any verbal echo, which might suggest the influence of the Servant in Isaiah. In later Hellenistic Judaism (see HELLENISM) there is little evidence of a messianic understanding of these passages, except what is implicit in the SEPTUAGINT translation of Isa. 52:13—53:12 (cf. W. Zimmerli and J. Jeremias, *The Servant of God*, rev. ed. [1965], 42–44, 53–55).

In Palestinian JUDAISM, on the other hand, a persistent messianic exegesis exists side by side with an embarrassment at the idea of a suffering Messiah. Thus *Targum Jonathan* on Isa. 52:13—53:12 (see TARGUM) explicitly identifies the Servant as the Messiah, but systematically manipulates the text to transfer every idea of suffering from the Servant to Israel, the Gentiles, or the wicked. Several other indications of a messianic exegesis in Palestinian Judaism are listed by Jeremias (in Zimmerli and Jeremias, *Servant of God*, 59–79). While some are disputed, their overall significance far outweighs the few isolated indications of an interpretation of the Servant as either the nation or a historical individual. This is the more surprising in view of the apologetic use made of these passages by Christians. The rabbis generally preferred rather to ignore the Servant idea than to interpret it as other than messianic. The evidence, therefore, suggests that in Palestinian Judaism of the time of Christ and afterward a messianic exegesis of the Servant was so firmly established that even the demands of the anti-Christian polemic could not unseat it.

IV. The Servant in the NT.

The NT writers are unanimous in stating both that the Servant is a messianic figure and that Jesus is the Servant. What is in dispute is the extent of the influence of this figure in the NT. Some writers (esp. M. D. Hooker, *Jesus and the Servant* [1959]) have argued that it was of minor importance, and that Jesus' predictions of his suffering were based not on the Servant-idea, but on the "one like a son of man" of Dan. 7:13. See SON OF MAN.

A. In the teaching of Jesus.

The only explicit quotation is Lk. 22:37. The Servant is also clearly alluded to in Mk. 10:45 and 14:24 (and possibly 9:12). In each of these cases the reference is to the suffering and death of Jesus as the fulfillment of that predicted for the Servant. In 10:45 and 14:24 stress is laid on the redemptive purpose of that suffering and its vicarious nature. There are also numerous predictions by Jesus that he *must* suffer, several of which base this necessity on Scripture (Matt. 26:54; Mk. 9:12; 14:21, 49; Lk. 18:31). The most probable source of these predictions is the Servant-idea in Isaiah—the clearest indication of a suffering Messiah in the OT, and an idea which Jesus elsewhere applied explicitly to his own suffering —rather than Dan. 7, for in the latter passage, which Jesus applied only to his exaltation and power, the idea of suffering is not clearly attributed to the central figure.

It is relevant, too, that the heavenly voice at the baptism of Jesus (Mk. 1:11), which is generally agreed to allude to Isa. 42:1, must have influenced his subsequent view of his mission. Therefore the Servant-idea appears as a major factor in Jesus' understanding of his own mission as one of redemption through a vicarious suffering and death.

B. In the rest of the NT. The Servant-idea, though not as prominent as one might expect, is attested in most of the major strata of the NT. That Jesus was at an early stage given the title of *pais theou* (a common rendering of ʿ*ebed yhwh* in the LXX) is seen by its use in Acts 3:13, 26 (Peter's speech) and 4:27, 30 (the prayer of the church). The title does not occur again, but explicit quotations from the Servant passages, with reference to Jesus and his gospel, occur in Matt. 8:17; 12:18–21; Jn. 12:38; Acts 8:32, 33; Rom. 10:16; 15:21. The emphasis in these quotations is not, however, as in Jesus' use of the passages, on the necessity of his redemptive suffering. This use of the Servant-idea is seen in some allusions in the theological writing especially of Peter and Paul. Its influence has been traced especially in 1 Pet. 2:21–25; 3:18; 1 Cor. 15:3; and Phil. 2:6–11. Further probable echoes are in Rom. 4:25; 5:19; 2 Cor. 5:21; and in John's use of the term "Lamb of God" (Jn. 1:29, 36; cf. Isa. 53:7).

This material is, however, not impressive in its bulk. It would appear that the view of Jesus as the Servant of the Lord, while prominent in Jesus' own teaching, and preserved in the earlier parts of the NT, especially in connection with the teaching of Peter, was later superseded by the titles LORD and SON OF GOD, though the fact of Christ's vicarious and atoning death, which the Servant passages explicitly teach, was firmly established as the basis of his redemptive work. See also CHRISTOLOGY V; ISAIAH, BOOK OF, VI.C.

(In addition to the titles mentioned in the body of the article, see H. W. Robinson, *The Cross of the Servant* [1926]; J. S. Van der Ploeg, *Les chants du Serviteur de Jahvé* [1936]; H. W. Wolff, *Jesaja 53 in Urchristentum* [1942]; I. Engnell in *BJRL* 31 [1948]: 54–93; J. Lindblom, *The Servant Songs in Deutero-Isaiah* [1951]; S. Mowinckel, *He That Cometh* [1956], 187–257; H. Ringgren, *The Messiah in the Old Testament* [1956], 39–53; O. Cullmann, *The Christology of the New Testament* [1959], 51–82; B. Lindars, *New Testament Apologetic* [1961], 77–88; R. T. France in *TynBul* 19 [1968]: 26–52; P. Grelot, *Les poèmes du Serviteur: De la lecture critique à l'herméneutique* [1981]; K. T. Kleinknecht, *Der leidende Gerechtfertigte: Die alttestamentlich-jüdische Tradition vom "leidenden Gerechten" und ihre Rezeption bei Paulus* [1984]; G. A. F. Knight, *Servant Theology: A Commentary on the Book of Isaiah 40–55*, rev. ed. [1984]; E. R. Ekblad, *Isaiah's Servant Poems according to the Septuagint: An Exegetical and Theological Study* [1999]; B. Janowski and P. Stuhlmacher, eds., *The Suffering Servant: Isaiah 53 in Jewish and Christian Sources* [2004].) R. T. FRANCE

service. The first biblical occurrences of the Hebrew noun ʿ*ăbōdâ* H6275 ("work, service") concern JACOB's service to LABAN (Gen. 29:27; 30:26). A different expression (lit., "to stand before") is used with reference to JOSEPH's entering "the service of Pharaoh" (41:46). After that is the well-known record of Egypt's oppression of the Israelites, making "their lives bitter with hard labor [ʿ*ăbōdâ*]" (Exod. 1:14). Reminiscent of this, MOSES provided laws prohibiting intra-Israelite SLAVERY and governing hired servants (Lev. 25:35–55). Various other types of secular service are mentioned throughout Scripture.

Religious service in the OT is closely associated with WORSHIP rituals in the TABERNACLE and the TEMPLE (Exod. 27:19 et al.). The PRIESTS AND LEVITES were responsible "for the service of the temple of the LORD" (1 Chr. 23:32; cf. Num. 8:11 et al.). As revelation progressed, service acquired a broader meaning. "The Son of Man did not come to be served, but to serve [Gk. *diakoneō* G1354]" (Matt. 20:28), and thereby Jesus set an example for his followers (cf. the FOOTWASHING incident, Jn. 13:3–17). He said, "Whoever serves me must follow me.... My Father will honor the one who serves me" (12:26). Early Christians soon grasped Jesus' concept of total religious service, including evangelism and missions. Paul said, "There are different kinds of service [*diakonia* G1355]" (1 Cor. 12:5), and he thanked Jesus Christ for "appointing me to his service" (1 Tim. 1:12). In a more general sense, all believers are to "serve [*douleuō* G1526] one another in love" (Gal. 6:13).   G. B. FUNDERBURK

Sesis see´sis. KJV Apoc. form of SHASHAI (1 Esd. 9:34).

Sesthel ses´thuhl (Σεσθηλ). One of the descendants of Addi that agreed to put away their foreign wives (1 Esd. 9:31; some think this name corresponds to BEZALEL in Ezra 10:30).

Seth seth´ (שֵׁת H9269, possibly "provision, restitution"; Σήθ G4953). KJV also Sheth (only 1 Chr. 1:1). Third son of ADAM and EVE, father of ENOSH, and ancestor of the godly messianic line that descends from him to NOAH (Gen. 4:25–26; 5:3–8; 1 Chr. 1:1; Sir. 49:16; included in Luke's GENEALOGY OF JESUS CHRIST, Lk. 3:38). He is reported to have lived 912 years (Gen. 5:8). When Eve named him Seth (*šēt*), she said, "God has granted [*šāt*, from *šît* H8883] me another child in place of Abel, since Cain killed him" (4:25). It is uncertain whether the name originally derives from the verb *šît* ("to place, set, appoint"); the statement may reflect a popular etymology or it may be simply a play on words. Some scholars believe that "the sons of Sheth" (Num. 24:17) should be related to Seth. See SHETH. In later tradition, Seth plays a prominent role (cf. A. F. J. Klijn, *Seth in Jewish, Christian and Gnostic Literature* [1977]). See SETH, THREE STELES OF.

Seth, Second Treatise of the Great. A polemical Gnostic document preserved in Coptic in the NAG HAMMADI LIBRARY (NHC VII, 2), and purporting to be a revelatory discourse from Jesus Christ. The name Seth occurs only in the title (found at the end), but presumably he is identified with Jesus (whoever added this title must have thought that one of several Gnostic documents in which the name Seth appears was the "first treatise" of Seth). The work was originally written in Greek, probably no earlier than the 3rd cent., and its purpose was evidently to set forth a docetic view of Christ and to oppose the claims of the orthodox church. See DOCETISM; GNOSTICISM. (English trans. in *NHL*, 362–71.)

Seth, Three Steles of. Earlier known as the *Apocalypse of Dositheus*, this Gnostic work is preserved in the NAG HAMMADI LIBRARY (NHC VII, 5). According to a Jewish tradition, the descendants of SETH inscribed their astrological knowledge on two steles or pillars for posterity (cf. Jos. *Ant.* 1.2.3 §§68–71); in Gnostic thought, Seth himself preserved in three steles the revelation given to ADAM (see ZOSTRIANUS, APOCALYPSE OF). In the present document, which claims to be "the revelation of Dositheus" (apparently a founder of GNOSTICISM), the three steles are in fact three hymns addressed to a divine triad and possibly formed part of a liturgy. The original Greek work may have been composed in the 3rd cent., but it is preserved only in a Coptic version. (English trans. in *NHL*, 396–401.)

Sethur see´thuhr (סְתוּר H6256, possibly "hidden [by God]"). Son of Michael, from the tribe of ASHER, and one of the twelve spies sent out by MOSES to reconnoiter the Promised Land (Num. 13:13).

settlement of Canaan. See TRIBES, LOCATION OF.

seven. See NUMBER. On the KJV rendering "seven stars" (Amos 5:8), see ASTRONOMY III. On the letters to the seven churches, see REVELATION, BOOK OF.

Seveneh suh-ven´uh. See SYENE.

seventy disciples. According to Lk. 10:1 and 17, Jesus sent out seventy disciples to minister as a part of his extended journey to Jerusalem (some important witnesses, including P[75] and CODEX VATICANUS, say "seventy-two"). The number seventy was symbolic to the Jews. It alluded to the group of elders that MOSES had chosen to help with the task of leading Israel in the wilderness (Num. 11:16–17, 24–25). See ELDER (OT). Apparently on the basis of that group (cf. *m. Sanh.* 1:6), the number of the members of the SANHEDRIN, the supreme council of the Jews, was set at seventy-one (i.e., seventy plus a leader). It was also the "number" of the NATIONS in the world (see Gen. 10, where LXX has seventy-two), and of the members of JACOB's family in Egypt (Gen. 46:27). Some have supposed that Jesus, by his choice of this number, was foreshadowing the preaching of the gospel to all nations. Others argue that the original number of disciples was seventy-two, and that later scribes altered it to seventy because the latter number had greater significance. (See discussion by J. A. Fitzmyer, *The Gospel according to Luke X–XIV*, AB 28A [1985], 845–46.)

H. L. Drumwright, Jr.

seventy weeks. According to Dan. 9:24, seventy weeks (lit., "seventy sevens") were decreed for Israel and Jerusalem "to finish transgression, to put an end to sin, to atone for wickedness, to bring in everlasting righteousness, to seal up vision and prophecy and to anoint the most holy." The period is said to begin with "the issuing of the decree to restore and rebuild Jerusalem" and ends with the time of "the Anointed One, the ruler" (v. 25). The seventy weeks are subdivided into seven weeks, sixty-two weeks, and one week. After the sixty-two weeks have been accomplished, the Anointed One is to be cut off, a period marked by desolation and war when the city and sanctuary are destroyed (v. 26). It is also stated that either the Anointed One or, more likely, the ruler or prince mentioned in v. 26b makes a firm covenant with many for one week, in the midst of which "he will put an end to sacrifice and offering. And on a wing of the temple he will set up an abomination that causes desolation, until the end that is decreed is poured out on him" (v. 27). This passage has received three basic interpretations, all of which agree that each week represents seven years so that in round figures the seventy weeks equal four hundred and ninety years.

I. The traditional view. This interpretation, with slight variations, has been held by most biblical scholars until relatively recent times. According to it, the end of the seventy weeks represents the time of the accomplished work of Christ on the cross. The four hundred and ninety years are thus the period of time from the edict to rebuild Jerusalem until the death of Christ on the cross. The question of when that edict was given is however greatly disputed. It is most often identified with the time of Artaxerxes' decree to send Ezra back to Jerusalem (c. 458 B.C.). This would put the seventieth week approximately in the time of Christ's earthly ministry. Usually the seventieth week is considered to have begun with Christ's baptism, and the "cutting off" is identified with his death about three and one-half years later. Others date the seventy weeks from the time of the decree issued by Cyrus (538 B.C.).

II. The critical view. Many modern scholars hold that the prophecy was written in the 2nd cent. B.C. In this view the writer of Daniel is not predicting but telling what has already happened. The seventy weeks began in 538 B.C. with Cyrus's decree and ended with the deposition of the high priest Onias III in 175 B.C. and his assassination in 172. The three and one-half years are the period from deposition to death. In this interpretation, Dan. 9:26–27 describes the attack on the city by Antiochus Epiphanes. While this view does not contain a full four hundred and ninety years, the problem is answered by appeal to the fact that we know little of how the years were actually reckoned in that period.

III. The dispensational view. This view basically considers the seventy weeks to have begun with Artaxerxes' decree and the sixty-ninth week to have ended with Christ's death. But the great "parenthesis" or unreckoned period from Christ's death until the SECOND COMING of Christ for his saints (more specifically, the "rapture") is the period of the Gentiles. Finally, the seventieth week is that period of the Antichrist in Jerusalem until Christ comes again to deliver his church, a period covering seven years.

This writer holds the traditional view and notes the obvious fulfillment by Jesus Christ of the goals listed in Dan. 9:24 . Note the great theological words contained in that one passage.

J. B. Scott

sewing. The origin of the skill of sewing is lost in the antiquity of the race. The book of Genesis, however, relates that Adam and Eve sewed fig leaves to make aprons for themselves (Gen. 3:7; the Heb. verb *tāpar* H9529 occurs also in Job 16:15; Eccl. 3:7; Ezek. 13:18). Sewing was done by both men and women in the Mediterranean world. The only explicit reference to sewing in the NT is Jesus' saying, "No one sews [*epiraptō* G2165] a patch of unshrunk cloth on an old garment" (Mk. 2:21; the more common verb

Bedouin woman sewing.

epiballō G2095, "to lay on," is used in the parallels, Matt. 9:16 and Lk. 5:36). It is very likely, however, that PAUL practiced the craft in tent-making, which was his trade. H. L. DRUMWRIGHT, JR.

sex. The Scriptures reflect the cautious attitude toward discussion of sexual matters that was prevalent in ancient times. The poetic and imaginative nature of the Hebrew language resulted in the use of euphemisms that tended to conceal linguistically such things as the male and female organs, sexual intercourse, and reproduction. In spite of such circumlocutions, however, the subject of sex and related topics are treated frequently and with frankness in the Bible.

  I. The teaching of the OT concerning sex
     A. Distinctions between the sexes
     B. The sex organs
     C. Sexual intercourse
     D. Sex education
  II. The teaching of the NT concerning sex
     A. Christ's teaching
     B. The teaching of the early church
  III. Summary

I. The teaching of the OT concerning sex. The OT contains the major portion of the biblical teaching concerning sex. Reference is made to distinctions between the sexes in the CREATION account in Genesis; and the PENTATEUCH contains numerous commandments related to sex and sexual acts. The narrative portions of the OT contain references to normal and abnormal sexual activities. Portions of the WISDOM Literature deal with sex in relation to such diverse themes as married love (SONG OF SOLOMON) and the dangers of promiscuity (PROVERBS). The Bible states that OT teachings were included in the Scriptures not only for the purpose of conveying redemptive truth but also for the "instruction" of believers through the centuries (1 Cor. 10:11). The OT references to sex seem to fall largely under the latter category.

A. Distinctions between the sexes. In Genesis mention is made of the creation of male and female (Gen. 1:27). The primary meaning of the word *sex* emphasizes the physical differences between the members of the human family.

1. The male role. According to the first chapter of Genesis, the first created human was a male called ADAM. The specific tasks assigned to him following his creation included the care of the garden of EDEN and the naming of the animals (Gen. 2:15–20). Other activities of early males included sheep herding and farming (4:1–2); ranching (4:20); and working with metals (4:22). The male in the OT was expected to be the head of the household and was to be the spiritual leader of the family (3:16; Exod. 12:1–6; 20:12; Deut. 6:20–25 et al.).

It seems that Jewish parents specially welcomed the birth of male children. This attitude was demonstrated in the desire for male progeny (1 Sam. 1:8–18). Also, a higher ransom was to be paid for males in contrast to females (Lev. 27:1–8). When the numbering of the Israelites was conducted, special attention was given to males (Num. 3:40–43). Jewish genealogies also gave special attention to males in their roles as progenitors of the families (Ezra 8:1–14); and the priesthood was reserved for males (Exod. 19:22; Lev. 1:11). The majority of the prophets were males, although female prophets, or prophetesses, were active in Israel at varied times (Exod. 15:20; Jdg. 4:4, 2 Ki. 22:14; 2 Chr. 34:22; Neh. 6:14; and Isa. 8:3).

Males were not allowed to put on women's garments (Deut. 22:5); and Jewish males were distinguished from other males in some of the surrounding nations by the rite of CIRCUMCISION (Gen. 34:14–17). Apparently Jewish males were to be distinguished in the wearing of their hair from females generally (1 Cor. 11:14) as well as from men in the surrounding nations (Lev. 19:27).

Ancient Israel was largely patriarchal and tended to give decided favor to the male role. Under this system, males apparently were afforded a number of privileges that were not available to females.

2. The female role. According to the creation account in Genesis, the first female, EVE, was created from the rib of Adam (Gen. 2:21–22). Prior to the creation of Eve, Adam was referred to as being without a "suitable helper" (2:20). According to Genesis, the creation of woman apparently served a utilitarian purpose as far as man was concerned. Adam called his wife "woman," a term that signified her being taken from man (2:23). Eve, the first female, was enticed to partake of the forbidden fruit and gave the same to her husband Adam (3:1–6). Following this act, the male and female apparently became aware in a sexual sense of the physical differences between them (3:7). The FALL is said to have resulted in a divine judgment on both the male and the female sexes. For the male, a different form of work would result; in the case of the female, an increased sense of pain in childbirth and a (heightened or dependent) desire for her husband was to be expected (3:14–16; the precise meaning of the passage is disputed).

The role of woman in the earliest days of recorded history generally was considered to be that of bearing and mothering children and of serving as a helper to the male (Gen. 4:1–2, 16–25). Gradually, the role of the female in the OT became more sophisticated, and over time women seemed to assume a greater share of the activities originally ascribed to males. The book of Proverbs describes a virtuous wife as one who engaged in spinning wool and making linen from flax, purchasing real estate, planting vineyards, selling linen garments (Prov. 31:10–31). At this point in Israel's history, such activities were considered desirable as far as women were concerned and were placed on a plane next to that of bearing and rearing children.

B. The sex organs. The Scriptures tend to avoid direct reference to the sex organs and to issues connected with sex. For example, when Gen. 17:11 refers to the rite of circumcision, the mention of the male sex organ is concealed by use of the expression *beśar ʿorlatkem*, literally, "the flesh of your foreskin." The injunction that a wife should not seize her husband's adversary by the male sex organs uses the term *mĕbušîm H4434* (Deut. 25:11), a word that occurs nowhere else in the Bible and that literally means "shame-provoking [things]" (cf. Latin *pudenda*). Again, reference is made to the desolation of Judah by the Assyrians as being as extensive as if one shaved "the hair of the feet" (Isa. 7:20; NIV, "the hair of your legs"); some believe that this usage of the word *feet* is an indirect reference to the lower parts of the body including the genitalia and pubic hair (cf. Ruth 3:1–4, 7–9; Deut. 28:57; perhaps Isa. 6:2). In a similar way, a circumlocution is used to refer to the testicles and the penis (Deut. 23:1). The word *seed* is used to refer to male semen, and a variety of injunctions are given in relation to this term (Gen. 3:15; Lev. 15:16–18; 22:4).

A similar approach was taken to the female genitalia. The female breast is referred to in several instances in the OT (e.g., Job 3:12; Cant. 1:13; 4:5; 8:10), and the womb is specifically mentioned in connection with birth and parentage (Gen. 25:23; 38:27; Prov. 31:2; Isa. 49:5). However, more precise terms such as are used today to identify the female genitalia were not used by the Hebrews in the Scriptures. Rather, generalities and euphemisms seem to be preferred. Also, it was considered shameful by the Hebrews to expose to public view either the male or the female genitalia (Gen. 9:21–23; Lev. 18:6–19; 20:17; 2 Sam. 6:20).

C. Sexual intercourse. Similarly, sexual intercourse is not referred to directly, but rather by expressions such as "becoming one flesh with" (Gen. 2:24), "knowing" (4:1, 17, 25; Jdg. 19:25), and "lying with" someone (Gen. 34:7; Num. 31:17, 18; Deut. 22:22). This language tends to emphasize the intimate nature of the sex act. The concept of "knowing" someone may have a relationship to the fall and the knowledge of good and evil with its possible sexual overtones (Gen. 2:17 and 3:7). The Scriptures manifest a clear awareness of the emotional and intimate nature of sexual intercourse along with the companionship involved between two lovers (Song of Solomon.). The primary purpose of sexual intercourse stressed in the Scriptures is procreation (Gen. 1:28). Sexual intercourse outside of marriage is condemned along with prostitution and other types of sexual activity that were not related to procreation (Exod. 20:14, 17; 22:16; Lev. 18:6–18; 19:20). Sexual intercourse with animals by either males or females is forbidden (Lev. 18:23; 20:15–16).

D. Sex education. Sex education according to present standards was largely unknown in ancient Israel. Apparently children learned about sex either through parental instruction or by personal experience. Sex instruction through the Scriptures or in public education was limited to statements regarding the expected role of the male and female in reproduction and warnings against the misuse or abuse of sex or the body. The OT specifically condemned a number of activities connected with the body and the sex organs: exposure of the sex organs (2 Sam. 6:20); adulterous interest in another man's wife (Lev. 18.20), the enticement of a virgin to commit sexual intercourse (Exod. 22:16); sexual intercourse with animals, mentioned earlier (Lev. 18:23); homosexuality (18:22 and 20:13); incest (Lev. 18:6–18; Deut. 27:20, 22); prostitution (Deut. 23:17–18); intercourse with an engaged slave (Lev. 19:20); and related subjects. It should be mentioned that polygamy was practiced in early Israel and men were allowed to have sex relations with their concubines. However, polygamy was replaced by monogamy in later Israel; and the Scriptures teach that while polygamy was permitted by God, it was never ordained by him (Matt. 19.3–8). Monogamy was the practice of the first humans, Adam and Eve (Gen. 1–5).

In contrast to the surrounding nations, the Israelites possessed a lofty moral code, even though they did not always live up to this ethic.

II. The teaching of the NT concerning sex.

The major emphasis of the NT was on teachings related to evangelization and the establishment of the church. For the most part, the early church seemed to rely upon the teachings of the OT with respect to sex and the sex role. However, the NT is not silent on the topic. When the topic is mentioned, it usually is dealt with in relation to the spiritual life of the church, and the total message of redemption as it related to the family and the individual.

A. Christ's teaching. The four Gospels emphasize the teachings and deeds of Christ that had a messianic and redemptive significance. As a result, only passing mention is made of subjects related to sex. During his earthly ministry, Christ referred to the topic primarily in its relation to redemptive truth and dealt with several problems of a sexual nature.

Christ condemned adultery, fornication, and lust, both outwardly (Matt. 15:19–20) and inwardly (5:27–32). He made reference to being a EUNUCH either by natural or human causes for the kingdom of heaven's sake (19:12). Christ forgave the woman taken in the act of adultery (Jn. 8:1–11) and frequently referred to virgins and marriage in his parabolic teachings. In general, however, his teachings concerning sex and related topics were subservient to his teachings concerning redemptive truth.

B. The teaching of the early church. The attitude toward sex prevalent among the early Christians reflected agreement with the highest moral ideals of the OT and the spiritual ideals of Christ. The Hebraic tendency to avoid direct reference to the sex organs and sexual intercourse persisted in the early church. For example, Paul referred to treating with greater modesty "the parts that are unpresentable" (1 Cor. 12:23); and the writer of Hebrews refers to the "bed" as undefiled when occupied by marriage partners (Heb. 13:4). While the subject of sex is not discussed specifically in the NT, topics related to the subject frequently are dealt with by the early church. It seems that the early Christians adopted generally the views and teachings of the OT concerning sex; and the OT teachings related to the subject seemed to provide adequately for their needs with respect to sex instruction.

The prevailing attitude toward women in the Jewish culture was adopted by the early Christians. In general this involved ascribing to men a major share of the leadership. The apostles were male and apparently the early elders were males according to existing records. However, women were not overlooked in the activities of the church. Paul placed restrictions upon the activities allowed to women but at the same time made mention of women occupying places of service and leadership in the churches (Rom. 16:1, 6, 12; Phil. 4:3; 1 Tim.

2:12–14; 3:11). The first convert in Europe was a business woman, LYDIA of THYATIRA (Acts 16:14); and women served as prophetesses and exercised charismatic gifts in the early worship services (Acts 21:8–9; 1 Cor. 11:5; note also 1 Cor. 11:6–15 and 14:34–40 concerning the role of women in the church).

While the early church relied largely on the OT with respect to specific instruction about sex, reference is made in the NT to a variety of related subjects. Sexual intercourse between marriage partners is considered appropriate and expected (Heb. 13:4); but married couples may forego, at times, natural sex relations in order to give themselves to prayer (1 Cor. 7:5). Refraining from sexual intercourse is referred to as "depriving each other," and uncontrolled sexual desire of the unmarried and widows is spoken of as "burning" (v. 9), in accordance with the Hebrew tendency to refer to sexual intercourse indirectly. Polygamy was condemned by the early church and monogamy was the expected practice (1 Cor. 7:1–2; 1 Tim. 3:2). Homosexuality (Rom. 1:26–28), prostitution, adultery, and fornication (Gal. 5:19; Jude 7) were condemned along with other vices prevalent in the early Christian era. It was stated that indulgence in such vices would keep a person from entering the kingdom of God (1 Cor. 6:9–10). No mention is made in the NT of formal sex education in the early church. It appears that such instruction was left largely to the home and family apart from the specific instructions cited above.

III. Summary.
The biblical teachings concerning sex manifest a high ethic, especially when contrasted with the prevailing views in the same period of history. The sex roles are distinguished and a division of labor commensurate with each role is apparent. However, women gained considerable status over time, and the Christian view of sex allowed for mutual respect among the sexes coupled with a monogamous view of marriage, which was based upon the original relationship of the first created beings.

Sexual activities during both the Christian and OT eras were discussed with caution and candor coupled with relative frankness. Apart from positive instruction regarding the responsibility for procreation, sexual instruction in the Bible was largely related to prohibitions that would discourage participation by the people of God in those sex practices exhibited in the surrounding nations. See also FAMILY; MARRIAGE.

(For further discussion, see W. G. Cole, *Sex and Love in the Bible* [1959]; R. Pattai, *Sex and Family in the Bible and the Middle East* [1959]; O. Piper, *The Biblical View of Sex and Marriage* [1960]; J. B. Hurley, *Man and Woman in Biblical Perspective* [1981]; M. R. Cosby, *Sex in the Bible: An Introduction to What the Scriptures Teach Us about Sexuality* [1984]; R. F. Collins, *Sexual Ethics and the New Testament: Behavior and Belief* [2000]; S. C. Barton, *Life Together: Family, Sexuality and Community in the New Testament and Today* [2001]; O. P. Robertson, *The Genesis of Sex: Sexual Relationships in the First Book of the Bible* [2002]; W. Loader, *The Septuagint, Sexuality, and the New Testament: Case Studies on the Impact of the LXX in Philo and the New Testament* [2004]; M. B. Skinner, *Sexuality in Greek and Roman Culture* [2005]; J. H. Ellens, *Sex in the Bible: A New Consideration* [2006]; R. M. Davidson, *Flame of Yahweh: Sexuality in the Old Testament* [2007].)

G. LAMBERT

Sextus, Sentences of. A document preserved in Coptic in the NAG HAMMADI LIBRARY (NHC XII, 1). The work is not Gnostic in character but is rather a Christian collection of ethical sayings that goes back to a Greek original composed probably in the 2nd cent. A.D. With an ascetic outlook, it emphasizes the need for mastering bodily passions; it proved to be a popular work and was translated into Latin, Syriac, and other languages (two Gk. MSS have also survived). The Coptic version, though fragmentary, is regarded as an important textual witness. (English trans. of the Coptic in *NHL*, 503–8. For a broad study, see H. Chadwick, *The Sentences of Sextus: A Contribution to the History of Early Christian Ethics* [1959].)

Shaalabbin, Shaalbim shay′uh-lab′uhn, shay-al′bim (שַׁעֲלַבִּין *H9125*, שַׁעַלְבִים *H9124*, prob. "[place of] foxes"; gentilic שַׁעַלְבֹנִי *H9126*, "Shaalbonite"). The form Shaalabbin occurs in a list of towns allotted to the tribe of DAN; it is included between Ir Shemesh (see BETH SHEMESH #3) and AIJALON

(Josh. 19:41–42). It must be the same as Shaalbim, which is associated with Mount Heres and Aijalon as places from which the Danites could not drive out the Amorites (Jdg. 1:34–35). Elsewhere, Shaalbim is listed as one of four towns, including Beth Shemesh, that were part of an administrative center under Solomon; governed by Ben-Deker, this center supplied provisions for the royal court (1 Ki. 4:9). The descriptive "Shaalbonite," used of Eliahba, one of David's mighty warriors (2 Sam. 23:32; 1 Chr. 11:33; NRSV renders, "Eliahba of Shaalbon"), very probably is a gentilic adjective of Shaalbim, and some argue that Shaalbon (which does not occur in the OT) may have been the original form of the place name. See also Shaalim. Shaalabbin/Shaalbim is generally identified with modern Selbit, c. 3 mi. NW of Aijalon, 8 mi. N of Beth Shemesh, and 16 mi. NW of Jerusalem. (See NBDPIL, 1.1330.) A. Bowling

Shaalbon, Shaalbonite shay-al′bon, shay-al′buh-nit. See Shaalbim.

Shaalim shay′uh-lim (שְׁעָלִים H9127, "hollows"). KJV Shalim. A region near Shalisha, between the hill country of Ephraim (see Ephraim, hill country of) and the tribal territory of Benjamin, where Saul went looking for his father's donkeys (1 Sam. 9:4; some think that "Benjamin" here is a textual error). Shaalim has often been identified with the Danite town of Shaalbim (see Shaalabbin), some 16 mi. W of Jerusalem. However, an area around Bethel, N of Jerusalem, would fit the context better. Accordingly, Shaalim is often thought to be the same as Shual, a region close to Ophrah (1 Sam. 13:17), a few miles N of Micmash.

A. Bowling

Shaaph shay′af (שַׁעַף H9131, prob. "balm," suggesting the comfort provided by a child). (1) Son of Jahdai (1 Chr. 2:47) and apparently a descendant of Judah in the line of Caleb (2:47). See discussion under Jahdai.

(2) Son of Caleb by his concubine Maacah; he is described as the "father" (i.e., founder) of Madmannah (1 Chr. 2:49). Some emend the text so that this Shaaph can be identified with #1 above (see *ABD*, 5:1147–48).

Shaaraim shay′uh-ray′im (שַׁעֲרַיִם H9139, "[pair of] gates"). (1) A town within the tribal territory of Judah located in the Shephelah (Josh. 15:36; KJV, "Sharaim"). The way from the Valley of Elah (some 18 mi. WSW of Jerusalem; see Elah, Valley of) to Gath and Ekron is identified as "the Shaaraim road" (1 Sam. 17:52). The site has not been positively identified, but an attractive proposal is modern Khirbet Sairah, very near Azekah (cf. A. F. Rainey in *BASOR* 251 [Summer 1983]: 6–7).

(2) One of the Simeonite towns where the clan of Shimei son of Zaccur lived (1 Chr. 4:31). Its location is uncertain, but some scholars regard Shaaraim here as a textual error for Sharuhen (Josh. 19:6). A. Bowling

Shaashgaz shay-ash′gaz (שַׁעַשְׁגַז H9140, meaning uncertain). A eunuch in the court of Ahasuerus (Xerxes), king of Persia (Esth. 2:14). He is described as being "in charge of the concubines," who resided in "the second house of the women" (KJV; NIV, "another part of the harem"). Initially, the young women who were candidates to become queen spent time in the part of the harem reserved for virgins, which was supervised by Hegai (v. 8); after spending a night with the king, they became concubines (lesser wives) under the custody of Shaashgaz. Esther, however, won the king's approval and was made queen rather than a lesser wife (v. 17).

Shabbethai shab′uh-thi (שַׁבְּתַי H8703, prob. "[born on] the Sabbath"). A Levite who apparently challenged Ezra's instruction that those who had married foreign women should divorce them (Ezra 10:15; cf. 1 Esd. 9:14 [KJV, "Sabbatheus"]). The Hebrew text, however, can be understood differently. See discussion under Jahzeiah. He is probably the same Shabbethai listed among the Levites who "instructed the people in the Law" (Neh. 8:7, 1 Esd. 9:48 [KJV, "Sabateas"]). Elsewhere, he and Jozabad are described as "two of the heads of the Levites, who had charge of the outside work of the house of God" (Neh. 11:16).

Shachia shuh-ki′uh. KJV form of Sakia.

Shaddai, Shadday. See El Shaddai.

shade, shadow. Most occurrences of the biblical words for "shadow" (Heb. *ṣēl* H7498 and Gk. *skia* G5014) are figurative. Only twice does an actual shadow play a significant part in the narrative: when HEZEKIAH asked that the shadow on the sundial might reverse its normal direction of movement, as a sign from God (2 Ki. 20:10; see DIAL), and when the sick were brought into the streets so that the shadow of PETER might fall on them as he passed (Acts 5:15). The many figurative references make use of an image which, like so much of the Bible's imagery, is drawn straight from the Middle Eastern environment. In a land of heat and violent storms, the need for shelter would be readily apparent, and since much of the land was treeless, protection was usually found in the shade of a rock or crag.

Figurative references to the shadow fall into three main groups. (1) Uses indicating the ephemeral nature of things, or their lack of substance (e.g., 1 Chr. 29:15; Job 8:9; Pss. 102:11; 144:4). By contrast, however, with the fleeting existence of human beings, God is eternal and unchanging. He does not alter his position or inclination as the hours or the years pass; he is not like the shadow on the sundial, but is always the same (Jas. 1:17).

(2) Uses indicating protection or defense, in the sense of shelter from the heat or the storm. Most of these references picture God as providing the shelter, and they are numerous in the Psalms (e.g., Pss. 17:8; 36:7; 57:1; 63:7; 91:1). On some occasions Israel was accused by God of seeking shelter elsewhere, and of hiding in the imaginary safety of other shadows—allies like Egypt whose help she enlisted in her wars (cf. Isa. 30:2, 3; Jer. 48:45).

(3) NT uses in which the sense is "foreshadow, adumbration, partial disclosure." PAUL, for example, states that the OT dietary regulations and special feasts "are a shadow of the things that were to come; the reality, however, is found in Christ" (Col. 2:5). Especially significant is the use of the term with reference to the TABERNACLE and its contents in the wilderness, implying that the realities of heaven cast a shadow on the earth—a shadow that will in most cases later be replaced by actuality—and that what God has ordained on earth is a representation of what is in heaven (Heb. 8:5, 10:1). The writer to the Hebrews explains that the physical structure in the desert, in which the Levitical offerings

Shadow cast on sundial.

took place, was only an illustration in visible form of spiritual reality, or spiritual truth. There exist in heaven, he suggests, spiritual facts of such character that, when they are translated onto the material plane, they take this particular form. The relationship of men and women to God can be concretized in this particular way. But, he adds, these material forms were never more than a foreshadowing of a new and more dramatic material expression of the spiritual reality—the coming and the sacrifice of Christ. Thus he seems to challenge the normal human pattern of thought, according to which material objects throw insubstantial shadows. In *this* case, it is the spiritual reality—insubstantial though it may appear—which casts its shadow in a material form, in advance of its own final establishment. See also TYPOLOGY. J. H. PATERSON

Shadrach, Meshach, Abednego shad′rak, mee′shak, uh-bed′ni-goh (שַׁדְרַךְ H8731 [Aram. H10701], perhaps from Akk. *šaduraku*, "I have been made to feel afraid"; מֵישַׁךְ H4794 [Aram. H10415], derivation unknown; עֲבֵד נְגוֹ H6284 [Aram. H10524], possibly "servant of [the god] NEBO"). The Babylonian names that ASHPENAZ, chief officer of NEBUCHADNEZZAR king of BABYLON, gave to three Israelite youths who were companions of DANIEL (Dan. 1:7). Their original Hebrew names were respectively HANANIAH ("Yahweh is gracious"), MISHAEL ("Who is like God?"), and AZARIAH ("Yahweh has helped"). These were changed presumably to honor the Babylonian religion, but the etymologies of the new names are obscure, and some believe that the biblical writer deliberately deformed them to satirize pagan culture.

Daniel and his three friends belonged to the Hebrew royal family and are described as "young men without any physical defect, handsome, showing aptitude for every kind of learning, well informed, quick to understand, and qualified to serve in the king's palace" (Dan. 1:3–4). They were to be educated for three years in the "language and literature of the Babylonians." They determined, however, not to defile themselves with the "royal food and wine"; instead, they ate vegetables and drank water for ten days (vv. 8–14). At the end of this trial period, it was obvious that "they looked healthier and better nourished than any of the young men who ate the royal food" (v. 15). Later, the three youths were appointed provincial administrators (2:49). They also proved to be of stalwart faith and piety, and withstood all pressures to worship the pagan image set up by Nebuchadnezzar. In consequence of this, all three were cast into a fiery furnace, but they were miraculously delivered (3:1–30). See Daniel, Book of.

Although not mentioned outside the book of Daniel, there are repeated allusions to the three Hebrew youths in the Apocrypha, and the martyrs of the Maccabean period seem to have been much encouraged by their example (1 Macc. 2:59–60; 3 Macc. 6:6; 4 Macc. 13:9; 16:3, 21; 18:12). The NT alludes to them when it mentions the heroes of faith who "quenched the fury of the flames" (Heb. 11:34). L. L. Walker

Shadud shay′duhd. See Sarid.

shaft. See water shaft.

Shage shay′geh. KJV form of Shagee.

Shagee shay′gee (שָׁגֵה H8707, derivation uncertain). KJV Shage. A Hararite and the father of Jonathan; the latter was one of David's mighty warriors (1 Chr. 11:34). In the parallel passage the MT reads "Jonathan, Shammah the Hararite (2 Sam. 23:32–33; the NIV and other versions emend to "Jonathan son of Shammah the Hararite"), and Shammah is also identified as "son of Agee [ʾāgēʾ] the Hararite" (23:11). Evidently there has been textual corruption in one or more of these passages. According to one view, the name Shagee in Chronicles is original, and 2 Sam. 23:32–33 should be emended accordingly (cf. KD, *Samuel*, 499: "שָׁמָה for בֶּן־שָׁגֵא probably arose from ver. 11"). Others believe Shagee is a false form, resulting from a confusion of the names Shammah and Agee (cf. *HALOT*, 4:1414). See also Hararite.

Shahar shay′hahr (שַׁחַר H8840, "dawn," referring prob. to the reddish morning twilight [cf. Ahishahar]). In English Bible versions, this name appears only in the title of Ps. 22 (KJV, "Aijeleth Shahar"; NIV, "The Doe of the Morning") and in the place name Zeret Shahar (Josh. 13:19). The Hebrew word, however, occurs over twenty times in the OT, and some scholars believe that at least in a few passages it alludes to the Amorite god Shahar (the Morning Star, referring to Venus at dawn). Ugaritic mythology describes the birth of Shahar and his twin Shalem (deity of the dusk or evening) to the Canaanite god El (cf. C. H. Gordon, *Ugaritic Literature* [1949], 60–62; *ABD*, "Shahar" and "Shalem," 5:1150–51 and 1152–53; *DDD*, 754–55).

Such expressions as "the eyelids of the morning" (Job 3:9 and 41:18 NRSV; NIV, "the rays of dawn") and "the wings of the dawn" (Ps. 139:9) are sometimes thought to reflect this Canaanite myth, without necessarily suggesting that the biblical writers themselves held to it. Similarly, the description of the king of Babylon as "morning star, son of the dawn" (Isa. 14:12; see morning star) has been interpreted as suggesting a divine being (cf. H. Wildberger, *Isaiah 13–27: A Continental Commentary* [1997], 63). H. M. Wolf

Shaharaim shay′huh-ray′im (שַׁחֲרַיִם H8844, "[two] dawns," possibly indicating time of birth between initial morning light and appearance of the sun's rays [cf. *HALOT*, 4:1469]). A descendant of Benjamin, although his place in the genealogy is unclear (1 Chr. 8:8). The passage contains some difficult textual problems and various emendations have been proposed. However, the MT appears to say that Shaharaim divorced two wives, Hushim (who had given birth to two sons, v. 11) and Baara, and that afterwards his third wife Hodesh gave birth to seven sons in Moab (vv. 9–10; it is not clear whether he had always lived in Moab or only after his divorces). Shaharaim had an extensive progeny, especially through Elpaal (born to Hushim). His grandson Shemed is said to have built the towns of Ono and Lod as well as surrounding villages (v. 12). Two other sons "were heads of families of those living in Aijalon and … drove out the inhabitants of Gath" (v. 13). (For further discussion, see G. N. Knoppers, *I Chronicles 1–9*, AB 12 [2004], 482–83.)

Shahazimah shay′huh-zi′muh. KJV form of Shahazumah.

Shahazumah shay′huh-zoo′muh (שַׁחֲצוּמָה H8833; the *Qere* is שַׁחֲצִימָה, but some scholars suggest vocalizing it שַׁחֲצֵימָה, supposedly the locative form of an otherwise unattested name, שַׁחֲצִים, meaning "double elevation" [see *HALOT*, 4:1463–64]). KJV Shahazimah. A site on the northern boundary of Issachar between Mount Tabor and Beth Shemesh (Josh. 19:22). Its location is unknown, though several proposals have been made, including modern el-Kerm (SE of Tabor), which appears to lie on the divide between the watersheds of Issachar and Naphtali (see discussion in Z. Kallai, *Historical Geography of the Bible* [1986], 195–96).

A. Bowling

Shalem shay′luhm (שָׁלֵם H8970, "complete"). A city of Shechem where Jacob went after he left Paddan Aram (Gen. 33:18 KJV; cf. also NIV mg.). Most scholars, however, believe that the Hebrew word here is the common adjective *šālēm* H8969 ("complete, whole, safe"), yielding the translation, "he arrived safely at the city of Shechem" (NIV). The Hebrew form is identical with the name usually rendered Salem (Gen. 14:18; Ps. 76:2).

Shalim shay′lim. KJV form of Shaalim.

Shalisha shuh-li′shuh (שָׁלִשָׁה H8995, possibly "third [part]"). Also Shalishah. A region near Shaalim, between the hill country of Ephraim (see Ephraim, hill country of) and the tribal territory of Benjamin, where Saul went looking for his father's donkeys (1 Sam. 9:4). Unfortunately, the topographical information in this text is difficult to sort out (cf. P. K. McCarter, Jr., *I Samuel*, AB 8 [1980], 174–75). Shalisha was probably in SE Ephraim, and it is usually thought that Baal Shalishah (2 Ki. 4:42) was found in that area, but the precise location is unknown.

Shallecheth shal′uh-kith. See Shalleketh.

Shalleketh shal′uh-kith (שַׁלֶּכֶת H8962, meaning uncertain [cf. שַׁלֶּכֶת H8961, "felling," Isa. 6:13]). Also Shallecheth. The name of a gate on the upper road in the W part of the temple enclosure in Jerusalem; the gatekeepers assigned to it were Shuppim and Hosah (1 Chr. 26:16; some scholars omit "Shuppim" as a textual error). Nothing else is known about this gate, although on the assumption that the name might mean "casting forth," the improbable suggestion has been made that the ashes and offal from the sacrifices were discarded there. Also doubtful is the view (*ABD*, 5:1153–54) that the name means "departing" and that therefore the reference is to the gate elsewhere called Sur (2 Ki. 11:5; the verb *sûr* H6073 means "turn aside, leave"). The Septuagint reads *pastophoriou*, "of [the] chamber," and on that basis some scholars emend the MT to *liškat* (construct of *liškâ* H4384, "hall") and translate, "the chamber gate" (cf. G. N. Knoppers, *I Chronicles 10–29*, AB 12A [2004], 864).

Shallum shal′uhm (שַׁלּוּם H8935 [also שָׁלֻם], possibly short form of שֶׁלֶמְיָהוּ H8983, "Yahweh has repaid [*or* replaced]"; see Shelemiah and cf. Meshelemiah and Meshullam). (**1**) Son of Jabesh and one of the last kings of Israel (2 Ki. 15:10–15). Shallum reigned over the ten tribes after having murdered Zechariah, who was the son of Jeroboam II and the last king of Jehu's dynasty. Within a month this usurper was himself assassinated by Menahem, c. 745 B.C.

(**2**) Son of Tikvah and husband of the prophetess Huldah; he had charge of the royal wardrobe (2 Ki. 22:14; 2 Chr. 34:22 ["son of Tokhath"]). Some identify him with #13 below.

(**3**) Son of Sismai and descendant of Judah in the line of Jerahmeel (1 Chr. 2:40). He descended from Jerahmeel's son, Sheshan, who gave his daughter in marriage to an Egyptian slave (vv. 34–35).

(**4**) Son of Josiah and king of Judah (1 Chr. 3:15; Jer. 22:11). See Jehoahaz #2.

(5) Son of SHAUL and grandson of SIMEON (1 Chr. 4:25).

(6) Son of the high priest ZADOK and ancestor of EZRA (1 Chr. 6:12–13; Ezra 7:2; 1 Esd. 8:2 [KJV, "Salum"]; 2 Esd. 1:1 [KJV, "Sadamias"]; Bar. 1:7 [KJV, "Salom"]); probably the same as MESHULLAM in the parallel lists (1 Chr. 9:11; Neh. 11:11).

(7) Son of NAPHTALI and grandson of JACOB (1 Chr. 7:13 MT, followed by most versions); the NIV, on the basis of some MSS and the parallel passages (Gen. 46:24; Num. 26:49), has SHILLEM.

(8) Son of KORE and descendant of KORAH; after the EXILE, he was the chief gatekeeper, "being stationed at the King's Gate on the east" (1 Chr. 9:17–19 [although some think that v. 19 refers to a different person], see also Ezra 2:42; Neh. 7:45; 1 Esd. 5:28 [KJV, "Salum"]). His firstborn, MATTITHIAH, "was entrusted with the responsibility for baking the offering bread" (1 Chr. 9:31). This Shallum is often identified with MESHELEMIAH (v. 21), SHELEMIAH (26:14), and MESHULLAM (Neh. 12:25). He is probably the same person listed among the gatekeepers who agreed to put away their foreign wives (Ezra 10:24; 1 Esd. 9:25 [KJV, "Sallumus"]).

(9) Father of JEHIZKIAH, an Ephraimite leader (2 Chr. 28:12).

(10) One of the descendants of Binnui who agreed to put away their foreign wives (Ezra 10:42).

(11) Son of Hallohesh; "ruler of a half-district of Jerusalem" who, with his daughters, repaired a section of the walls of Jerusalem (Neh. 3:12).

(12) Son of Col-Hozeh (Neh. 3:15 NRSV). See SHALLUN.

(13) Father of HANAMEL and uncle of JEREMIAH (Jer. 32:7). Some identify him with #2 above.

(14) Father of Maaseiah; the latter was a doorkeeper (NJPS, "guardian of the threshold") who had a room in the temple (Jer. 35:4). R. F. GRIBBLE

Shallun shal'uhn (שַׁלּוּן *H8937*, possibly "carefree" [cf. *HALOT*, 4:1511] or else a variant of שַׁלּוּם *H8935* [see SHALLUM]). Son of Col-Hozeh; he was a postexilic "ruler of the district of Mizpah" who rebuilt the FOUNTAIN GATE, "roofing it over and putting its doors and bolts and bars in place." Shallun was responsible also for repairing the wall of the Pool of SILOAM (see SHELAH, POOL OF), which was apparently used to irrigate the KING'S GARDEN (Neh. 3:15; NRSV, "Shallum"). What the line of this wall may have been is difficult to ascertain (see H. G. M. Williamson, *Ezra-Nehemiah*, WBC 16 [1985], 207–8).

Shalmai shal'mi (שַׁלְמַי *H8978* [Ezra 2:46 *Ketib*, שַׁמְלַי], but some MSS of Neh. 7.48 have שַׁלְמַי, which is thought to be the correct pointing; in either case, the derivation is uncertain [see *HALOT*, s.v. שׁלם, 3:1331–32]). Ancestor of a family of temple servants (NETHINIM) who returned after the EXILE with ZERUBBABEL (Ezra 2:46 [NRSV, "Shamlai"; NJPS, "Salmai"]; Neh. 7:48; 1 Esd. 5:30 RSV [KJV and NRSV, "Subai"]).

Shalman shal'muhn (שַׁלְמַן *H8986*, meaning uncertain). An otherwise unknown person who "devastated Beth Arbel on the day of battle, / when mothers were dashed to the ground with their children" (Hos. 10:14; see BETH ARBEL). Evidently this event was well known to the Israelites, but the identification of Shalman is difficult. Many think the reference is to SHALMANESER V, the Assyrian king who besieged SAMARIA in 725–723 B.C.; others have suggested that he should be equated with an 8th-cent. king of MOAB named Salamanu, mentioned by TIGLATH-PILESER III in a building inscription (text in *ANET*, 282a; for other possibilities and further discussion, see D. K. Stuart, *Hosea-Jonah*, WBC 31 [1987], 171–72). L. L. WALKER

Shalmaneser shal'muh-nee'zuhr (שַׁלְמַנְאֶסֶר *H8987*, from Ass. *Šulmānu-ašarēd*, "[the god] Shulman is chief"). (1) Shalmaneser I (1274–1245 B.C.), son of Adad-nirari I and the greatest warrior of the Middle Assyrian period, is known for having defeated the people of Urartu and Guti, and in the W, the Hurrians, Hittites, and Arameans. By his capture of CARCHEMISH he was the first to bring ASSYRIA into direct clash with the Egyptians in SW Asia.

(2) Little is known about Shalmaneser II (1030–1020 B.C.), who took action to strengthen Assyria after a period of domination by Aramean tribes.

(3) Shalmaneser III (859–824 B.C.), son of Ashurnasirpal II, was the first Assyrian king to

Basalt statue of Shalmaneser III (from Ashur, 9th cent. B.C.). On the robe is a cuneiform inscription in which Shalmaneser describes himself as "the great king, king of all the four regions, the powerful and the mighty rival of the princes of the whole universe."

come into direct contact with Israel. By a long series of raids he sought to contain the pressure of the hill-tribesmen in Urartu (see ARARAT) and the Medes and Persians in the Urmia region, but this did not prevent his main thrust to the W in thirty-one years of campaigning.

Three expeditions were needed to neutralize Bīt-Adini (Beth-Eden) and thus gain a hold of the EUPHRATES crossing. Its capital, Til-Barsip, was captured in 856 and renamed Kār-Shalmaneser. In 853 the main march was directed toward DAMASCUS via ALEPPO. After the capture of Argan, the army advanced to Qarqar on the ORONTES near Hama, where it was faced by a powerful alliance led by Irhuleni of HAMATH with 700 cavalry and 10,000 men backed by Adad-ʾidri (Hadadezer, the biblical BEN-HADAD II) with 1,200 chariots, 1,200 horsemen, and 20,000 infantry. AHAB the Israelite (Aḫabbu [māt]Sirʾilaia) supplied 2,000 chariots and 10,000 men. Contingents from twelve kings, including Cilicia, Arvad, Musru, Ammon, and Arabia brought the total muster to 62,900 men, 1,900 cavalry, and 3,900 chariots. Shalmaneser claimed the victory in a bloody contest in which 20,500 died. It is, however, significant that neither Hamath nor Damascus was taken, and that the Assyrians did not reappear in the W for three years (1 Ki. 16:29; 20:20; 22:1).

In 849 Shalmaneser again marched westward. CARCHEMISH, the last nominally independent state in the Upper EUPHRATES Valley, was incorporated into the growing provincial system under direct Assyrian control. The Assyrians claimed the defeat of Adad-ʾidri of Damascus, but this is unlikely to have been more than a temporary setback, since they had to take the field again the following year to meet the same king and his twelve allies near Ashtamaku. But again the Assyrians do not appear to have been able to follow up their claimed victory. In his fourteenth year (845) Shalmaneser massed a force of 120,000 men and claimed to have defeated Adad-ʾidri yet again.

By 841 the alliance had broken up and HAZAEL was ruling in Damascus in place of the murdered Adad-ʾidri (2 Ki. 8:15). He now had to face the Assyrians alone, and to do this he made a vigorous stand on Mount SENIR (HERMON, cf. Deut. 3:9), losing 16,000 men and some territory. However, the line of attack was diverted to the Mediterranean via the HAURAN. At Baʿal-rasi (N of Beirut) Shalmaneser received tribute from TYRE and SIDON brought in by ship, and from "Jehu, son of Omri"; according to the inscription and reliefs on the Black Obelisk set up in CALAH to commemorate the event, the tribute was carried by Israelite porters. Although this incident is not mentioned in the OT, it accords with the policy of the usurper JEHU, who may well have sought unsuccessfully for help against Hazael's raids on N Israel (2 Ki. 10:31–32). It explains the subsequent need for Assyrian intervention when SAMARIA made its bid for independence. After one further unsuccessful attempt to capture Damascus in 838, Sennacherib appears to have left the W alone, probably because of increasing internal disorders at home.

In Babylonia, Marduk-zakir-shumi was engaged in a struggle with his brother following the death of his father, Nabu-apla-iddinna, with whom Assyria had been in close treaty relationship (005–052). He now invoked the help of Shalmaneser, who in 851 moved to Babylon, defeated the rebels, and made a display of strength through Chaldean country (Kaldu) to the Persian Gulf.

Toward the end of his reign, Shalmaneser seems to have stayed at Calah, the city rebuilt by his father. Here he built himself a new palace and armory, an action perhaps necessitated by the revolt of one of his sons, Ashurdanin-apla, who had led Nineveh, Erbil, and Arrapha to revolt. Another son, Shamshi-Adad V, was taking action against the rebels when his aged father died and he claimed the throne.

(4) The reign of Shalmaneser IV (782–772 B.C.), son of Adad-nirari III who had taken tribute from Samaria (Rimah stela), was spent mostly in attempting to suppress local disturbances.

(5) Shalmaneser V (726–722 B.C.) continued his predecessor's practice of periodical marches through Syria to collect tribute. He made HOSHEA of Israel a vassal (2 Ki. 17:3), but when in his seventh regnal year Hoshea ceased to pay the annual tribute, Shalmaneser was quick to react. He besieged Samaria for three years, but it is not yet known why he was not in command when the city fell to SARGON II (723/2), unless he had retired to Nineveh where he died.

(For relevant texts, see *ANET*, 277–81. See also A. K. Grayson, *Assyrian Rulers of the Third and Second Millennia BC (to 1115)* [1987]; id., *Assyrian Rulers of the Early First Millennium BC*, 2 vols. [1991–96]; S. Yamada, *The Construction of the Assyrian Empire: A Historical Study of the Inscriptions of Shalmaneser III (859–824 B.C.) Relating to His Campaigns to the West* [2000]. For additional bibliography, see ASSYRIA AND BABYLONIA.)

D. J. WISEMAN

Shama shay´muh (שָׁמָע H9052, prob. "[God] has listened"). Son of Hotham the Aroerite (see AROER); he and his brother Jeiel were among DAVID's mighty warriors noted as the "Thirty" (1 Chr. 11:44).

Shamariah sham´uh-ri´uh. KJV alternate form of SHEMARIAH (only 2 Chr. 11:19).

shambles. This English term, in its archaic sense of "meat market," is used by the KJV once (1 Cor. 10:25). The Greek word it renders, *makellon* G3125, could refer to a food market more generally (cf. H. J. Cadbury, *JBL* 53 [1934]: 134–41). S. BARABAS

shame. The biblical words for "shame" occur over 150 times (Heb. noun *bōšet* H1425 and verb *bôš* H1017; Gk. noun *aischynē* G158 and verb *aischynomai* G159 and its compounds). They are associated with such concepts as defeat, reproach, nakedness, folly, contempt, poverty, unseemliness, cruelty, and nothingness. Shame is a debasing emotion arising from a consciousness of impropriety, offense, injured reputation, hurt pride, or guilt. In most biblical references it is associated with religion; only a few instances relate to social prestige. See HONOR; SOCIETY.

SIN is the primary source of all shame, expressing itself through various media. The first one mentioned in the Bible is nakedness, having a twofold meaning—physical and spiritual. In their primordial state "the man and his wife were both naked, and they felt no shame" (Gen. 2:25), but after they sinned they were ashamed of their nakedness in God's presence (3:10; cf. Rev. 3:18).

After expulsion from the Garden of Eden (see EDEN, GARDEN OF), righteousness precluded shame, while wickedness produced it. Those who deride and hate God's people invite their own shame (Job 8:22; Pss. 71:24; 129:5; 132:18; Isa. 66:5). Those who make idols and worship images are put to shame (Ps. 97:7; Isa. 42:17; Jer. 50:2; 51:17), as are diviners (Mic. 3:7). Heathen nations and their gods shall be put to shame (Jer. 46:24; 48:1, 20; 50:2). Israel's apostasy brought her shame through God's judgment (Ezra 9:7; Isa. 3:24; 30:3–5; Ezek. 16:36; Hos. 10:6; Nah. 3:5). Moreover, God's judgment put Israel to shame by other nations (Jer. 2:35–36).

Wicked and rude people may cause shame to those of nobler nature. DAVID's goodwill servants "were greatly ashamed" by the humiliating treatment given them by the Ammonite king, HANUN (2 Sam. 10:5 NRSV; the verb here is *kālam* H4007). David called on God because he was "scorned, disgraced and shamed" by his foes (Ps. 69:19). A man who mistreats his parents "is a son who brings shame and disgrace" (Prov. 19:26). Most of all, Jesus endured the shame of the cross at the hands of evil men (Heb. 12:2; cf. D. A. DeSilva, *Despising Shame: Honor Discourse and Community Maintenance in the Epistle to the Hebrews* [1995]).

In many passages, including some listed above, the idea moves from that of a subjective feeling of shame to the objective reality of judgment. DAVID said, "To you, O LORD, I lift up my soul; / in you I trust, O my God. / Do not let me be put to shame. / … No one whose hope is in you / will ever be put to shame, / but they will be put to shame / who are treacherous without excuse" (Ps. 25:1–3). This plea is often reiterated by psalmists and prophets (Pss. 25:20; 31:1, 17; 119:6, 31, 46; Isa. 49:23; Jer. 17:18; cf. Zeph. 3:11). PAUL, quoting from Isaiah's prophecy concerning Christ, says, "he who believes in him will not be put to shame" (Rom. 9:33b; cf. 1 Pet. 2:6).

The worst that a Hebrew could wish on his enemies was that they be put to shame (Ps. 31:17; 119:78). This malediction was often invoked, sometimes coupled with another curse, such as disgrace, confusion, and destruction (Pss. 35:4, 26; 71:13; cf. 40:14; 70:2; 109:28; Jer. 17:18). The final place of the wicked is accursed with shame. Elam and her accessories in crime will "bear their shame with those who go down to the pit" (Ezek. 32:24). In the resurrection, "Multitudes who sleep in the dust of the earth will awake: some to everlasting life, others to shame and everlasting contempt" (Dan. 12:2).

In the NT avoidance of shame was sought and taught. Joseph declined to put Mary to shame (Matt. 1:19 RSV). Jesus taught that humble decorum at feasts might avoid shame (Lk. 14:9). Paul taught that the worldly wise and strong were put to shame by God's choice of the weak and foolish (1 Cor. 1:27). Concerning bad conduct, he said, "It is shameful [*aischros* G156] even to mention what the disobedient do in secret" (Eph. 5:12). Some are so worldly that "their glory is in their shame" (Phil. 3:19). Paul was ashamed of the Corinthian church because it did not have believers wise enough to be peacemakers among the brotherhood (1 Cor. 6:5). To young TITUS he wrote that a Christian's deportment should be such "that those who oppose you may be ashamed because they have nothing bad to say about us" (Tit. 2:8; cf. 1 Pet. 3:16). Jesus had put his adversaries to shame (Lk. 13:17). Christians should be ready to meet Christ at his SECOND COMING without shame (1 Jn. 2:28). (See *NIDOTTE*, 1:621–27; *NIDNTT*, 3:561–64.)

G. B. FUNDERBURK

Shamed shay'mid. KJV alternate form of SHEMED.

Shamer shay'muhr. KJV alternate form of SHEMER.

Shamgar sham'gahr (שַׁמְגַּר H9011, apparently from Hurrian *Šimigari*, "[the god] Shimig has given" [cf. *HALOT*, 4:1552]). One of the Israelite leaders during the period of the judges (Jdg. 3:31; 5:6; see JUDGES, PERIOD OF). Shamgar is identified as "son of Anath," but some believe that here the Hebrew expression *ben-ʿănāt* may have originally meant something like "warrior of [the goddess] Anath" and that subsequently it came to be used as a military title (P. C. Craigie in *JBL* 91 [1972]: 239–40; see ANATH).

Shamgar is noted for having made a successful raid on the PHILISTINES with an oxgoad, a metal-tipped instrument which needed sharpening repeatedly (cf. W. F. Albright, *The Excavation of Tell Beit Mirsim*, 3 vols. [1932–43], 3:33). The suggestions that "the oxgoad" was the name of a ship (C. Marston, *The Bible Is True* [1934], 248) and that Shamgar was a Syrian sea captain allied with RAMSES II (J. Garstang, *Joshua-Judges* [1931], 63, 284ff.) are dubious. Although Shamgar may have been a Canaanite, he is listed among those who delivered the Israelites from oppression. Very likely this was the earliest oppression by the Philistines, who interfered with Israel's trade and restricted travel. Shamgar was successful in bringing relief to the Israelites before the

Canaanite oppression in the days of DEBORAH and BARAK. Because the biblical information regarding Shamgar is so limited, interpreters have made a variety of conjectures as to the origins of the story (cf. G. F. Moore in *JAOS* 9 [1898]; R. G. Boling in *ABD*, 5:1155–56). S. J. SCHULTZ

Shamhuth sham´huhth (שַׁמְהוּת *H9016*, thought by some to be a hybrid form of שַׁמָּה *H9015* and שָׁמוֹת *H9021*). An IZRAHITE who served as commander in charge of the division for the sixth month under DAVID (1 Chr. 27:8). Shamhuth is usually thought to be the same as SHAMMAH the Harodite, one of the Thirty (2 Sam. 23:25; called SHAMMOTH the Harorite in 1 Chr. 11:27).

Shamir (person) shay´muhr (שָׁמִיר *H9033*, "thorn" or "diamond"). Son of Micah and descendant of LEVI (1 Chr. 24:24).

Shamir (place) shay´muhr (שָׁמִיר *H9034*, "thorn" or "diamond"). (1) A town in the hill country of the tribe of JUDAH (Josh. 15:48). Shamir was part of a district that included such towns as JATTIR and SOCOH, but its precise location is unknown. Although some think that its name is preserved in modern Khirbet es-Sumara (c. 12 mi. SW of HEBRON), the identification cannot be confirmed.

(2) A town in the Ephraimite hill country (see EPHRAIM, HILL COUNTRY OF), and the home and burial place of TOLA, one of the judges (Jdg. 10:1–2). The site is unidentified (there is little to commend the suggestion that Shamir may be connected with SAMARIA). Why Tola, who came from the tribe of ISSACHAR, was living in Ephraim is a matter of speculation. A. C. SCHULTZ

Shamlai sham´li. See SHALMAI.

Shamma sham´uh (שַׁמָּא *H9007*, derivation uncertain). Son of Zophah and descendant of AHER (1 Chr. 7:37).

Shammah sham´uh (שַׁמָּה *H9015* and שַׁמָּא *H9007* [only 2 Sam. 23:11], derivation uncertain [cf. *HALOT*, 4:1554]). (1) Son of Reuel and grandson of Esau; a chief in EDOM (Gen. 36:13, 17; 1 Chr. 1:37).

(2) Third son of JESSE and older brother of DAVID. He was present when SAMUEL anointed David as future king of Israel (1 Sam. 16:9; cf. v. 13). He fought, with two older brothers, in the campaign against the PHILISTINES under SAUL and was with the Israelite forces in the Valley of ELAH when David killed GOLIATH (17:13, 19). Shammah apparently had two sons: the crafty JONADAB (2 Sam. 13:3, 32 [here he is called SHIMEAH]; 1 Chr. 2:13; 20:7 [SHIMEA]) and a warrior named JONATHAN (2 Sam. 21:21; here the *Ketib* has SHIMEI).

(3) A Harodite (see HAROD) who was one of David's mighty warriors (2 Sam. 23:25; called SHAMMOTH the Harorite in 1 Chr. 11:27). He is usually thought to be the same as SHAMHUTH the Izrahite (1 Chr. 27:8).

(4) Son of Agee the HARARITE (2 Sam. 23:11–12). This Shammah, regarded as one of David's three chief warriors (cf. v. 8), is said to have defended, successfully and alone, after the other troops had fled, "a field full of lentils" from a band of Philistines. (The parallel, 1 Chr. 11:12–14, appears to attribute this incident to ELEAZAR son of Dodo, but it is generally acknowledged that in this passage the reference to Shammah, with surrounding text, accidentally dropped out at some point in the textual transmission. See KD, *Samuel*, 494–95.) Shammah is apparently mentioned again in the list of the Thirty, but only as the father of the warrior Jonathan (2 Sam. 23:33, if the NIV's emendation is correct; however, see discussion of 1 Chr. 11:34 under SHAGEE). Some scholars also believe that this Shammah is the same as #3 above (with confusion of the descriptives Harodite and Hararite). A. C. SCHULTZ

Shammai sham´i (שַׁמַּי *H9025*, derivation uncertain). (1) Son of Onam and descendant of JUDAH in the line of JERAHMEEL (1 Chr. 2:28).

(2) Son of Rekem and descendant of Judah in the line of Jerahmeel's brother, CALEB (1 Chr. 2:44–45). The statement that Shammai's "son" was MAON may indicate that Shammai was the founder of the town by that name or that he was the ancestor of the people who settled there.

(3) Son of MERED (by BITHIA), included in the genealogy of Judah (1 Chr. 4:17).

(4) A Jewish scholar who lived at the end of the 1st cent. B.C. and the beginning of the 1st cent. A.D. See discussion under HILLEL.   S. BARABAS

Shammoth sham′oth (שַׁמּוֹת H9021, derivation uncertain). A Harorite (see HAROD), listed among DAVID's mighty warriors (1 Chr. 11:27); probably the same as SHAMMAH the Harodite (2 Sam. 23:25) and SHAMHUTH the Izrahite (1 Chr. 27:8).

Shammua sha-my*oo*′uh (שַׁמּוּעַ H9018, prob. "heard [by God]"). Also Shammuah (2 Sam. 5:14 some KJV editions). (1) Son of Zaccur and descendant of REUBEN; one of the twelve spies sent by MOSES to Canaan (Num. 13:4).

(2) Son of DAVID and BATHSHEBA, born after David moved from HEBRON to JERUSALEM (2 Sam. 5:14; 1 Chr. 14:4; called SHIMEA in 1 Chr. 3:5 MT).

(3) Son of Galal and descendant of the musician JEDUTHUN; one of the Levites who resettled in Jerusalem after the EXILE (Neh. 11:17; called SHEMAIAH in 1 Chr. 9:16).

(4) Head of the priestly family of BILGAH in the days of JOIAKIM the high priest (Neh. 12:18).
A. C. SCHULTZ

Shammuah sha-my*oo*′uh. KJV (some editions) alternate form of SHAMMUA (2 Sam. 5:14).

Shamsherai sham′shuh-ri (שַׁמְשְׁרַי H9091, derivation uncertain). Son of Jehoram and descendant of BENJAMIN; he is listed among the heads of families who lived in Jerusalem (1 Chr. 8:26).

Shapham shay′fuhm (שָׁפָם H9171, derivation unknown). A Gadite leader in BASHAN (see GAD, TRIBE OF), listed as second in importance (1 Chr. 5:12). He lived "during the reigns of Jotham king of Judah and Jeroboam king of Israel" (v. 17).

Shaphan shay′fuhn (שָׁפָן H9177, "coney, rock badger"). (1) Son of Azaliah and royal secretary (see SCRIBE) under JOSIAH, king of Judah (2 Ki. 22:3-20; 2 Chr. 34:8-20). It was Shaphan to whom HILKIAH the high priest gave the Book of the Law, which was discovered when the TEMPLE was being repaired in 621 B.C. Shaphan read from this law to Josiah, who then sent him with Hilkiah the priest and others to confer with HULDAH the prophetess. As a result, the king's reform movement gained impetus. Shaphan was an important leader in those reforms, and this must have brought him into close contact with the prophet JEREMIAH and his work. Shaphan's family for two generations participated as lay leaders in the religious life of Judah and supported the work of Jeremiah.

His influence upon his sons is clear, for he was the father of AHIKAM, also an official in the court and involved in the discovery of the Book of the Law (2 Ki. 22:12; 2 Chr. 34:20). According to Jer. 26:24, Ahikam saved the prophet from being lynched at the hands of a mob during some disturbances in the reign of King Jehoiakim. Another son of Shaphan, ELASAH (Jer. 29:3), was one of two messengers who took a letter of the prophet (ch. 29) to the exiles in Babylonia. Another son, GEMARIAH, was the owner of the house where BARUCH the scribe read the prophecy of Jeremiah to the people and later made a futile effort to prevent King JEHOIAKIM from destroying the scroll (36:10, 25). GEDALIAH, the governor of Judea after the Babylonian captivity, was his grandson (39:14).

(2) Father of JAAZANIAH; the latter was one of seventy idolaters that EZEKIEL saw in the temple (Ezek. 8:11).   A. C. SCHULTZ

Shaphat shay′fat (שָׁפָט H9151, prob. short form of שְׁפַטְיָהוּ H9153, "Yahweh has judged"; see SHEPHATIAH and cf. ELISHAPHAT). (1) Son of Hori and descendant of SIMEON; one of the twelve spies sent by MOSES to Canaan (Num. 13:5).

(2) Father of the prophet ELISHA (1 Ki. 19:16, 19; 2 Ki. 3:11; 6:31).

(3) Son of Shemaiah and postexilic descendant of DAVID through SOLOMON and ZERUBBABEL (1 Chr. 3:22). Some scholars believe he was the son of Shecaniah; see HATTUSH #1.

(4) A Gadite leader in BASHAN (1 Chr. 5:12; see GAD, TRIBE OF). Both the SEPTUAGINT and the TARGUM interpret the Hebrew *špṭ* as a common noun rather than a name. Some scholars, following the same approach and omitting the conjunction "and," translate the text, "Janai a judge in Bashan." G. N. Knoppers (*I Chronicles 1-9*, AB 12 [2004], 379) argues for the conjecture *haššōṭēr*, "Janai was the officer of Bashan."

(5) Son of Adlai; he was an official under King DAVID in charge of the herds in the valleys (1 Chr. 27:29).

(6) An ancestor of SOLOMON's servants (1 Esd. 5:34; KJV, "Sabat"). A. C. SCHULTZ

Shapher shay´fuhr. KJV form of SHEPHER.

Shaphir shay´fuhr (שָׁפִיר H9160, "beautiful, fair"). KJV Saphir. A geographic area, probably a town, against which Micah prophesied (Mic. 1:11). Past attempts at identification have been limited to looking for a site in PHILISTINE territory perhaps because of the association with GATH (v. 10). Tell es-Sawafir frequently has been suggested for several reasons, such as etymological similarity between the two names and suitability of location in Philistine territory some 4 mi. SE of ASHDOD. Others, pointing out that the context demands a Judean site, have suggested Khirbet el-Kom (el-Qom), c. 7 mi. W of HEBRON; this site is on Wadi es-Saffar, which possibly preserves the biblical name (cf. *IDB*, 4:308; but see *NEAEHL*, 4:1233). There is no solid evidence for either site, however, so the location of Shaphir remains unknown. A. BOWLING

Sharai shair´i (שָׂרַי H9232, perhaps "Yahweh has delivered" [cf. *HALOT*, 4:1654, proposal b]). One of the descendants of Binnui who agreed to put away their foreign wives (Ezra 10:40).

Sharaim shuh-ray´im. KJV alternate form of SHAARAIM.

Sharar shair´ahr (שָׁרָר H9243, possibly "firm, healthy"). A HARARITE who was the father of Ahiam, one of DAVID's mighty warriors (2 Sam. 23:33; called SHACAR in the parallel, 1 Chr. 11:35).

Sharezer shuh-ree´zuhr (שַׁרְאֶצֶר H8570, possibly short form of Akk. *Nabu šar uṣur*, "may [the god] Nebo protect the king" [cf. NERGAL-SHAREZER]). **(1)** Son of SENNACHERIB; he and his brother, Adrammelech, joined in murdering their father in the temple of NISROCH (2 Ki. 19:37; Isa. 37:38). See discussion under ADRAMMELECH. No extrabiblical sources attest to the name Sharezer for one of Sennacherib's sons. Since the Greek historian Abydenus (quoted by EUSEBIUS in the *Armenian Chronicle*) refers to the two brothers as Adramelus and Nergilus, some have thought that the full name of the latter was Nergal-šar-uṣur (Nergal-Sharezer). It could equally well be a rendering of Šar-eṭir-aššur, the name of a known son of Sennacherib.

(2) An Israelite leader sent by the inhabitants of BETHEL to inquire concerning the propriety of keeping the anniversary feast which commemorated the destruction of Jerusalem (Zech. 7:2; KJV, "Sherezer"). The text is difficult, however, and some argue that it should be rendered, "Bethel-Sharezer and Regem-Melech and his men sent to entreat the favor of the LORD" (cf. NJPS; if so, the name may be equivalent to Bel-šar-uṣur (i.e., Belshazzar, "may Bel protect the king"). Another possible rendering is, "Bethel—that is, Sharezer and Regem-Melech and his men—sent …" (cf. T. E. McComiskey in *The Minor Prophets: An Exegetical and Expository Commentary*, ed. T. McComiskey [1992–98], 3:1124). See also REGEM-MELECH. D. J. WISEMAN

Sharon shair´uhn (שָׁרוֹן H9227, "flat land" or "wet land"; gentilic שָׁרוֹנִי H9228, "Sharonite"; Σαρών G4926). KJV NT Saron. **(1)** When used with the definite article (*haššārôn*, prob. meaning "the plain"), this term refers to the largest of the coastal plains of northern Palestine, extending from the Crocodile River in the N to the Valley of AIJALON and JOPPA

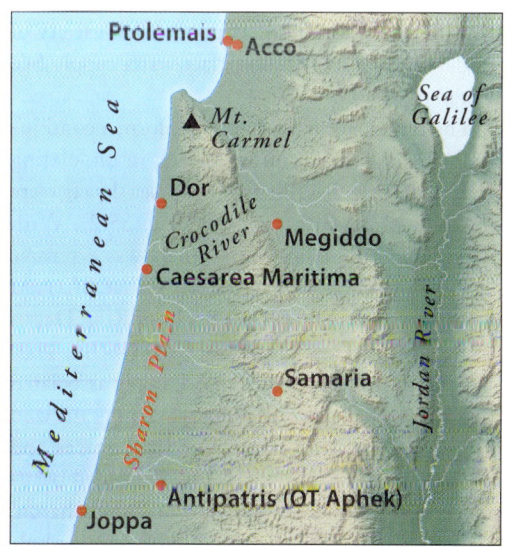

The Sharon Plain.

Aerial view of the Sharon Plain, SW of Mount Carmel, looking E.

in the S, a distance of about 50 mi., with a variable width of 9–10 mi. The relief is of Quaternary and Pleistocene origin, largely determined by ancient shorelines, sand-dune deposits, and the weathering of red sands that give a brilliant hue to much of its soil cover. The sand dunes, some of fossil character, tend to choke or divert the lower courses of the rivers, so that swampy conditions have tended to prevail in the past along the coast and valleys. The false bedded character of much of the surface geology and the encircling karstic nature of the hills to the interior explain the rich variety of aquifers and sources of subsurface water supply. See PALESTINE III.D.

The red Quaternary sands that form a continuous belt for some 20 mi. in the N, in undulating relief that rises to 180 ft. above sea level, were thickly covered with OAKS (cf. Isa. 35:2). With deforestation in biblical times, there was extensive pasturage (Isa. 65:10). It was here that SHITRAI the Sharonite supervised the flocks of King DAVID (1 Chr. 27:29). The "splendor" of Sharon (Isa. 35:2) suggests the dense vegetation originally associated with the whole plain. Its rich soil, now utilized extensively under irrigation for citrus groves and other commercial farming, formerly yielded beautiful covers of wild flowers. The "rose of Sharon" (Cant. 2:1) has been identified with various bulbous plants; see discussion under ROSE.

In Canaanite times, the chief town of Sharon was DOR (Josh. 11:2; 12:23; 1 Ki. 4:11). It was at first one of the unconquered Canaanite cities within the border of MANASSEH, impregnable because of its strong fortifications and use of chariots of iron (Josh. 17:18; Jdg. 1:19 et al.). Later, in SOLOMON's time, Dor was a fiscal district on the Carmel coast (see CARMEL, MOUNT). In Assyrian times, Dor was capital of an extended coastal province between Carmel and APHEK that reflected the strategic importance of the "way of the sea," the coast road between Egypt and Syria (Isa. 9:1). Later the district appears to have become subservient to an extended province of SAMARIA.

Joppa was also a walled town in Canaanite Sharon, fortified at least as early as the reign of Pharaoh THUTMOSE III (1490–1435 B.C.), who mentions it. At the division of the land it was allotted theoretically to the tribe of DAN (Josh. 19:46), but it did not come under Israelite control until David gained effective occupancy of the coast. Then HIRAM of TYRE floated his timber from the forests of LEBANON to the seaport of Joppa for the building of the temple at Jerusalem (2 Chr. 2:16); likewise at the rebuilding of the temple in the time of CYRUS, Joppa was the import center (Ezra 3:7).

In NT times the capital of the whole Roman province of JUDEA was built by AUGUSTUS at CAESAREA midway on the Sharon coast. Its port became a major Mediterranean harbor. The city was the Roman showpiece of its culture in the ANE. It figures prominently in the early contacts between the apostles and the Gentiles (Acts 10:1, 24; 11:11; 18:22; 21:8; 23:23–35; 25:13). See also LASHARON.

(2) Sharon was also the name of a pasture district E of the JORDAN (1 Chr. 5:16). It is referred to as among the possessions of GAD, along with GILEAD and BASHAN, but its precise location is unknown. Some think Sharon here may be a corruption of SIRION, the pasture lands of HERMON. Others believe it may be the "plateau" of Gilead between HESHBON and the ARNON Valley (Deut. 3:10). It is possible that the MOABITE STONE refers to this place (see *ANET*, 320). J. M. HOUSTON

Sharonite shar′uh-nit. See SHARON.

Sharuhen shah-roo′huhn (שָׁרוּחֶן *H8220*, from Egyp. *šʾ-ra-ḥu-na*). One of the cities within the territory of JUDAH that were allotted to the tribe of SIMEON (Josh. 19:6). A comparison of the Simeonite list (19:1–9) with the Judahite list (ch. 15) indicates that Sharuhen may be identical with SHILHIM (15:32; see also SHAARAIM). The city was located in the extreme SW corner of Canaan.

Sharuhen is mentioned in various Egyptian texts. It figured importantly in the successful attempts of the Egyptians to drive out the HYKSOS, although it resisted stoutly for three years before it fell. Its collapse marked the end of a century of Hyksos rule and the opening of the route to Asia, the prelude to the rise of the Egyptian empire and its extensive dominion of Syro-Palestine. The identification of Sharuhen is debated. Modern Tell el-Farʿah (c. 12 mi. SE of GAZA) has been a popular proposal in the past (still defended in *SacBr*, 75b), but many scholars prefer a site closer to the coast, such as Tell el-ʿAjjul (c. 4 mi. SW of Gaza). (See further details in *ABD*, 5:1163–65.) T. E. MCCOMISKEY

Shashai shay′shi (שָׁשַׁי *H8258*, derivation uncertain). One of the descendants of Binnui who agreed to put away their foreign wives (Ezra 10:40; 1 Esd. 9:34 [KJV, "Sesis"]).

Shashak shay′shak (שָׁשָׁק *H9265*, possibly an Egyp. name). Son of BERIAH (or of ELPAAL; cf. NRSV) and descendant of BENJAMIN, listed among the heads of families living in Jerusalem (1 Chr. 8:14, 25; cf. v. 28). See also AHIO.

Shaul shawl (שָׁאוּל *H8620*, "one who has been begged for" [cf. SAUL]; gentilic שָׁאוּלִי *H8621*, "Shaulite"). (1) Son of Samlah; he was an early king of EDOM who lived in "Rehoboth on the river" (Gen. 36:37–38 [KJV, "Saul"]; 1 Chr. 1:48–49). See REHOBOTH #2.

(2) Son of SIMEON (by a Canaanite woman), grandson of JACOB, and ancestor of the Shaulite clan (Gen. 46:10; Exod. 6:15; Num. 26:13; 1 Chr. 4:24).

(3) Son of Uzziah, descendant of LEVI through KOHATH, and ancestor of SAMUEL (1 Chr. 6:24).

Shaveh shay′vuh (שָׁוֵה *H8753*, possibly "level [place]" or "wasteland" [see TALU1, 4:1438]). A plain or valley near SALEM (Gen. 14:17). See discussion under KING'S VALLEY.

Shaveh Kiriathaim shay′vuh-kihr-ee-uh-thay′im (שָׁוֵה קִרְיָתַיִם *H8754*, prob. "plain of the [twin] cities"). The place where KEDORLAOMER defeated the EMITES (Gen. 14:5). Apparently it was a plain in the environs of KIRIATHAIM, a city in TRANSJORDAN.

shaving. Probably most Israelites, like ABSALOM, generally allowed their hair to grow for a considerable time before cutting it (2 Sam. 14:26). A BEARD was regarded as a natural accompaniment of manhood. The ceremonial law forbade priests

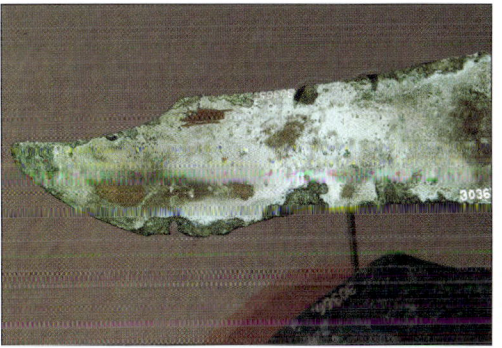

Egyptian bronze razor from the New Kingdom period (mid-to-late 2nd millennium B.C.).

to shave their heads on account of mourning (Lev. 21:5) or to adopt long flowing hair for the same reason (Ezek. 44:20). A NAZIRITE was not allowed to shave his head until the time covered by his vow expired (Num. 6:5) unless because of accidental defilement (6:9). In regard to the vows of SAMSON and SAMUEL, lifelong consecration was intended (Jdg. 13:5; 1 Sam. 1:11).

The main biblical implications of shaving were the following: (1) *Cleansing.* JOSEPH, when summoned to PHARAOH's presence, may have shaved his whole body to conform to Egyptian ideas of cleanliness (Gen. 41:14). The same concept appears in the ritual that marked the leper's recovery (Lev. 14:8–9) and the Levite's consecration to service (Num. 8:7), and it is indicated in Isaiah's figure (Isa. 7:20). (2) *Mourning.* Examples are found in Deut. 21:12; Job 1:20; and Jer. 7:29. (3) *Vows.* Shaving of the head followed the fulfillment of a vow (Num. 6:18; Acts 18:18; 21:24); but for Samson to submit to hair-cutting was to renounce the divine purpose for his life (Jdg. 16:19). (4) *Contempt.* This attitude was expressed by HANUN's ungracious action (2 Sam. 10:4; 1 Chr. 19:4). (5) *Humiliation.* PAUL says to the Corinthians that "it is a disgrace for a woman to have her hair cut or shaved off" (1 Cor. 11:5–6).   W. J. CAMERON

Shavsha shav′shuh (שַׁוְשָׁא *H8807*, meaning uncertain, but possibly an Egyp. word). A royal secretary (see SCRIBE) in DAVID's court (1 Chr. 18:16). The need for such an office reflects the development of governmental affairs both domestic and foreign. There are variations of this man's name: SHEVA (2 Sam. 20:25), SERAIAH (8:17), and SHISHA (1 Ki. 4:3). Many have thought that the spelling Shavsha is the original one. Others suggest that the man's true name was Seraiah and that the form Shisha (with its variants) reflects an Egyptian title (*šš š‘t*, "the writer of the king's letters"; see *HALOT*, s.v. שִׁישָׁא, 4:1483). In SOLOMON's reign, two of his sons occupied the same office (1 Ki. 4:3). Shavsha's own father is not named in the records, and this omission, together with the fact that the name Shavsha does not appear to be Hebrew, supports the idea that he was of foreign origin. It would be natural for such a man to be appointed to an office that handled foreign affairs and documents.   A. C. SCHULTZ

sheaf. A small quantity of GRAIN cut and gathered. The principal grains mentioned in the Bible are WHEAT and BARLEY: the former was grown on the lowland areas of PALESTINE and in the HAURAN region E of the Jordan, while the latter was the crop of the uplands. Both were harvested by the method which was standard in grain growing regions for centuries afterward, and can still be observed in the Middle E—the reaper with his sickle goes ahead, and cuts the grain; then it is gathered into bundles by workers (often women) who follow, and the bundles are tied, by using a few stalks, into sheaves. After the gatherers come the gleaners, who collect any loose stalks dropped in the REAPING. The best Bible description of the process occurs in the book of RUTH.

Such sheaves were used as a form of offering in the Levitical system of SACRIFICES (cf. Lev. 23:10–12). Probably they were sheaves of barley, the first crop to be harvested each year in Palestine. They represented the thank offering for the FIRSTFRUITS of the harvest.   J. H. PATERSON

Sheal shee′uhl (שְׁאָל *H8627*, often corrected to יִשְׁאָל, possibly "he has asked [*i.e.*, for a child]" [see *HALOT*, s.v. שְׁאוּל, 4:1370]). One of the descendants of Bani who agreed to put way their foreign wives in the time of EZRA (Ezra 10:29; 1 Esd. 9:30 [KJV, "Jasael"]).

Shealtiel shee-al′tee-uhl (שְׁאַלְתִּיאֵל *H8630* and שַׁלְתִּיאֵל *H9003* [Hag. 1:12, 14; 2:2], possibly "I have requested [a child] from God"; Σαλαθιήλ *G4886*). Also Salathiel (KJV in 1 Chr. 3:17, Apoc., and NT; NRSV in Matt. 1:12) and Salatiel (KJV in 1 Esd. 6:2). Eldest son of King JEHOIACHIN (Jeconiah) of Judah and father of ZERUBBABEL, the leader of the first group that returned from the Babylonian captivity (1 Chr. 3:17; Ezra 3:2 et al.; Neh. 12:1; Hag. 1:1 et al.). Included in the GENEALOGY OF JESUS CHRIST (Matt. 1:12; Lk. 3:27; on the latter passage, see NERI).

Sheariah shee′uh-ri′uh (שְׁעַרְיָה *H9138*, perhaps "Yahweh has acknowledged"). Son of Azel and descendant of BENJAMIN in the line of SAUL (1 Chr. 8:38; 9:44).

shearing house. See BETH EKED.

Shear-Jashub shee´uhr-jay´shuhb (שְׁאָר יָשׁוּב H8639, "a remnant will return"). Son of the prophet ISAIAH (Isa. 7:3; cf. 10:21–22). Shear-Jashub was present when Isaiah confronted King AHAZ, and his name is symbolical of the message the prophet delivered. Judgment in the form of the EXILE was an essential aspect of Isaiah's message, but there was also the promise of restoration for a purified REMNANT. The meeting took place c. 735 B.C., which means that Shear-Jashub must have been born near the start of the prophet's career; thus this doctrine of the remnant apparently was formed in the early period of Isaiah's ministry.   A. C. SCHULTZ

Sheba shee´buh (שְׁבָא H8644, meaning uncertain, for ##1–7 below; שֶׁבַע H8680 [2 Sam. 20:1–22; 1 Chr. 5:13; H8681 in Josh. 19:2], "seven," possibly suggesting "completeness" [*HALOT*, 4:1400]). **(1)** Son of Raamah, descendant of CUSH, and brother of DEDAN (Gen. 10:7; 1 Chr. 1:9).

(2) Son of JOKTAN and descendant of SHEM (Gen. 10:28; 1 Chr. 1:22).

(3) Son of JOKSHAN, descendant of ABRAHAM and KETURAH, and brother of Dedan (Gen. 25:3; 1 Chr. 1:32).

Many have argued that two or all three of the above are the same person because (a) all three are associated with names connected with ARABIA, (b) the first and third have Dedan as a brother, and (c) the second and third are in the line of Shem. The fact that the first one is in the line of Cush and HAM may indicate the close relationship between the S Arabians and Africans (Hamites). It is widely thought that the name Sheba is primarily a geographical term, as follows.

(4) A country in S Arabia, now Yemen, the most mountainous and fertile part of Arabia. The biblical writers probably regarded the person Sheba (#3?) as the source of this country's name and the progenitor of its people, the SABEANS. This country gained wealth through control of the trade in perfumes and incense, which were important in the life and religion of the ancient world. Camel caravans from Sheba (Job 6:19) carried northward to the Mediterranean countries the gold, precious stones, and frankincense of S Arabia (Isa. 60:6; Jer. 6:20; Ezek. 27:22). The capital of Sheba was first Sirwaḥ and then Marib. At the latter are the remains of a great dam and of the temple of the moon-god, Ilumquh. In the thousands of Sabean inscriptions are the names of many of their priest rulers.

In the 10th cent. B.C. the QUEEN OF SHEBA visited SOLOMON (1 Ki. 10:1–13; 2 Chr. 9:1–12). Her camel caravan brought typical products of Sheba: gold, precious stones, and spices, which she exchanged with Solomon. The country also played a role in Israel's expectations for the future. It was hoped that Sheba would give gifts to the king of Israel (Ps. 72:10, 15) and praise to the God of Israel (Isa. 60:6).

(5) A town within the tribal territory of SIMEON (Josh. 19:2). Sheba is missing in the parallel list (1 Chr. 4:28); moreover, if it is included in Joshua, the total comes to fourteen towns instead of thirteen (as stated in Josh. 19:6). Thus the NIV and other versions translate "or Sheba," indicating that this is an alternate name for BEERSHEBA. A few have thought that Sheba and Beersheba were parts of the same city. Still others emend Sheba to Shema (on the basis of the similar list in Josh. 15:26; the LXX at 19:2 [Codex B], as well as at 1 Chr. 4:28, reads *Samaa* or *Sama*). See SHEMA (PLACE).

(6) Son of BICRI; he is known for having revolted against DAVID (2 Sam. 20:1–22). Sheba's revolt appealed to followers of SAUL's family, since he was from the tribe of BENJAMIN and perhaps a relative of Saul. Also he appealed to all northern Israelites with his rallying cry, "We have no share in David, / no part in Jesse's son! / Every man to his tents, O Israel!" (20:1), a cry that was repeated later in JEROBOAM's rebellion (1 Ki. 12:16). JOAB and the royal bodyguard pursued Sheba until he took refuge in ABEL BETH MAACAH in the northernmost part of Israel. Joab besieged the city until the inhabitants decapitated Sheba and threw his head over the city wall to Joab.

(7) Son of Abihail; he was one of seven relatives from the Gadites who occupied the region E of GILEAD (1 Chr. 5:13, cf. vv. 10, 14). See GAD, TRIBE OF.   J. ALEXANDER THOMPSON

Shebah shee´buh. KJV form of SHIBAH.

Shebam shee´bam. KJV alternate form of SIBMAH.

Shebaniah sheb´uh-ni´uh שְׁבַנְיָהוּ H8677 [only 1 Chr. 15:24] and שְׁבַנְיָה H8676, perhaps "Yahweh has drawn near" [*HALOT*, 4:1396]; for other options, see J. D. Fowler, *Theophoric Personal Names in Ancient Hebrew* [1988], 130–31). **(1)** One of the priests appointed to blow the trumpet when DAVID transferred the ARK OF THE COVENANT to Jerusalem (1 Chr. 15:24).

(2) One of the postexilic Levites who led worship when the Feast of Tabernacles was celebrated (Neh. 9:4–5). He is probably the same as either #4 or #5 below.

(3) A priest who signed the covenant with NEHEMIAH (Neh. 10:4). In the days of the high priest JOIAKIM, the head of Shebaniah's family was a man named Joseph (12:14 KJV and most versions, following MT); here the NIV, following some Heb. MSS and ancient versions, has SHECANIAH (which harmonizes with v. 3), but it should be noted that in all the passages in Nehemiah where the MT has Shebaniah various witnesses read Shecaniah (the Heb. consonants ב and כ are easily confused).

(4–5) Two Levites who signed the covenant with Nehemiah (Neh. 10:10, 12). One of them should probably be identified with #2 above.

Shebarim sheb′uh-rim (שְׁבָרִים *H8696*, prob. pl. of שֶׁבֶר *H8691*, "fracture, crushing"). A place cited in connection with the retreat of the Israelites from AI (Josh. 7:5 KJV and other versions). It evidently lay somewhere between Ai and JERICHO, but the location is unknown. Some ancient versions understood *šĕbārîm* not as a name but as a common term, indicating that the men of Ai pursued the Israelites "until they broke [*i.e.*, vanquished] them" (cf. NAB, "until they broke ranks"). Similarly, modern scholars have suggested such renderings as "to the broken city walls" (cf. Z. Zevit in *BASOR* 251 [Summer 1983]: 31) and "as far as the stone quarries" (NIV). (For additional details and suggestions, see *ABD*, 5:1171–72.) T. E. MCCOMISKEY

Shebat shee′bat (שְׁבָט *H8658*, from Akk. *šabāṭu*). The eleventh month in the Hebrew CALENDAR, corresponding to January-February (Zech. 1:7 [KJV, "Sebat"]; 1 Macc. 16:14 [KJV, "Sabat"]).

Sheber shee′buhr (שֶׁבֶר *H8693*, meaning uncertain [for possibilities, see *HALOT*, 4:1406]). Son of CALEB (by his concubine MAACAH), included in the genealogy of JUDAH (1 Chr. 2:48).

Shebna, Shebnah sheb′nuh (שֶׁבְנָא *H8675*, also שֶׁבְנָא *H8674* [2 Ki. 18:26, 37], possibly short form of שְׁבַנְיָהוּ *H8677* [see SHEBANIAH]). In one passage (Isa. 22:15) Shebna is described as a "steward" (*sōkēn H6125*) and as being "in charge of the palace" (*ʿal-habbāyit*), evidently a very high and influential position that may have included authority over the standing army. Elsewhere, however, ELIAKIM son of Hilkiah is said to be the palace administrator, while Shebna appears as royal secretary (see SCRIBE); the two of them were part of the delegation sent by King HEZEKIAH to meet the emissaries of SENNACHERIB (2 Ki. 18:18, 26, 37; 19:2 = Isa. 36:3, 11, 22; 37:2). It appears that Shebna was demoted from his high position and that Eliakim replaced him. Given his unusual name, as well as the fact that his father's name is not mentioned, it is possible that Shebna was a foreigner.

The first passage as a whole (Isa. 22:15–25) is a denunciation of Shebna and the only instance in Isaiah of an oracle against a named individual. The specific charge against Shebna reveals his pretensions. He had taken it upon himself to have a grave chiseled in a high rock (something normally reserved for the nobility). Isaiah indicated that Shebna's tomb would not be used for the purpose intended, since he would be cast out of office (v. 19), replaced by Eliakim (vv. 20–21), and die in exile (v. 18). A further allusion to his vanity is in the reference to his splendid chariots (v. 18). Some critical scholars have alleged that vv. 19–23 are a later modification in the light of events, changing a prophecy of violent removal and death (vv. 17–18) into one of demotion only. Since nothing is known of Shebna subsequent to Sennacherib's invasion, the precise mode of fulfillment of the prophetic oracle is uncertain. (According to some interpreters, the Shebna of this passage is not the same person as the royal secretary, but it is most improbable that there were two officials of the same name, both without any "pedigree," holding one or other of the two most responsible state offices, in the same general period. On these matters, as well as the unlikely proposal that Shebna's grave has been discovered, see H. Wildberger, *Isaiah 13–27: A Continental Commentary* [1997], 384, 386.)

In 701 B.C. Sennacherib, having reduced most of the cities of Judah and having accepted an indemnity from Hezekiah for the latter's rebellion (2 Ki. 18:13–16), returned again to besiege Jerusalem. There must be some explanation for this unusual action, following Hezekiah's earlier submission. Possibly the danger of a major encounter with the main Egyptian army made the Assyrian king wary of leaving a humiliated but still powerful Jerusalem in his rear. Shebna appeared as one of three ambassadors who represented Hezekiah before the emissaries of Sennacherib (2 Ki. 18:18 = Isa. 36:3). Their request to the RABSHAKEH to conduct the negotiations in a language which the inhabitants of Jerusalem would not understand was rejected (2 Ki. 18:26–27 = Isa. 36:11–12). The arrogant, blasphemous words of the Assyrian, backed by the tangible evidence of military might, were reported to Hezekiah by Shebna and his companions, accompanied by appropriate signs of mourning (2 Ki. 18:37 = Isa. 36:22).

Then Eliakim and Shebna, as the two senior officials, and the leading priests were sent to the prophet Isaiah (2 Ki. 19:2 = Isa. 37:2), who had consistently opposed Hezekiah's anti-Assyrian, pro-Egyptian policies (e.g., Isa. 20; 30; 31) as inconsistent with a policy of dependence upon Yahweh alone (cf. Isa. 7:1–9). It may be that Isaiah's apparent antagonism toward Shebna is accounted for, in measure, by the leading part which the latter would have played in the national policy. Isaiah's oracle (37:22–29) reveals that the devastation wrought in the land by the Assyrians was determined by the Lord (v. 26), presumably as his chastisement for the false foreign policies of his people. He also promised that the arrogant Assyria would be forced out of the land like an unwilling beast (v. 29). (See further H. H. Rowley, *Men of God: Studies in Old Testament History and Prophecy* [1963], 98–132.)

A. E. CUNDALL

Shebuel shi-byoo′uhl. See SHUBAEL.

Shecaniah shek′uh-ni′uh (שְׁכַנְיָהוּ H8909 [only 2 Chr. 24:11; 31:15] and שְׁכַנְיָה H8908, "Yahweh dwells [or has taken up residence]"). TNIV Shekaniah. (1) Postexilic descendant of DAVID in the line of ZERUBBABEL (1 Chr. 3:21–22). The NRSV and other versions, following the SEPTUAGINT, understand Shecaniah to be the son of Obadiah (see REPHAIAH). This Shecaniah is to be identified with the father (or ancestor) of HATTUSH (Ezra 8:3) and of SHEMAIAH (Neh. 3:29).

(2) A descendant of AARON whose family in the time of DAVID made up the tenth division of priests (1 Chr. 24:11).

(3) A Levite who faithfully assisted KORE in distributing the contributions made to the temple during the reign of HEZEKIAH (2 Chr. 31:15).

(4) Son of Jahaziel; he and 300 members of his family returned with EZRA from Babylonia to Jerusalem in the reign of ARTAXERXES (Ezra 8:5; according to 1 Esd. 8:32 [KJV, "Sechenias"], the family descended from ZATTU, and this reading is adopted in Ezra 8:5 by the NIV and other versions).

(5) Son of Jehiel and descendant of Elam (Ezra 10:2). He acted as spokesman for the large congregation whose conscience on the subject of mixed marriages had been stirred by Ezra. Shecaniah confessed the national sin, expressed the nation's hope, suggested that a covenant be made before the Lord to eliminate the evil of intermarriage, and encouraged Ezra to take the lead in this reform. Since his name does not appear in the list of 10:18–44, it is possible that he was not personally guilty.

(6) Son of Arah and father-in-law of TOBIAH the Ammonite, NEHEMIAH's sworn adversary (Neh. 6:18).

(7) One of the priests and Levites who returned from exile with ZERUBBABEL (Neh. 12:3). Later, in the days of the high priest Joiakim, a certain Joseph was the head of his family (v. 14 NIV, following some ancient witnesses; see SHEBANIAH #3).

A. E. CUNDALL

Shechem (person) shek′uhm (שְׁכֶם H8902 and שֶׁכֶם H8903 [Num. 26:31; Josh. 17:2; 1 Chr. 7:19], probably from the corresponding place name meaning "shoulder, ridge"; gentilic שִׁכְמִי H8904, "Shechemite"). (1) Son of HAMOR the HIVITE; Shechem raped DINAH, the daughter of JACOB, and was killed by SIMEON and LEVI (Gen. 34:2–26; Josh. 24:32; Jdg. 9:28). See further SHECHEM (PLACE).

(2) Son of GILEAD, great-grandson of MANASSEH, and eponymous ancestor of the Shechemite clan (Num. 26:31). Elsewhere, however, "the sons of Shechem" (Josh. 17:2 Heb.) are listed with other Manassite clans as receiving an

inheritance W of the Jordan, in distinction from the Gileadites, who were granted territory in TRANSJORDAN. See also #3 below.

(3) Son of SHEMIDA and descendant of Manasseh (1 Chr. 7:19). Some argue that this Shechem is really Shemida's brother (cf. Num. 26:31–32) and therefore the same as #2 above.

Shechem (place) shek´uhm (שְׁכֶם H8901, "shoulder, ridge"; Συχέμ G5374). KJV also Sichem (Gen. 12:6; Sir. 50:26) and Sychem (Acts 7:16). An ancient Canaanite town in the hill country of Ephraim (Josh. 20:7; see EPHRAIM, HILL COUNTRY OF) in the neighborhood of Mount GERIZIM (Jdg. 9:7), being about 30 mi. N of JERUSALEM, just E of modern Nablus. It became an important Israelite political and religious center. The site is known today as Tell Balaṭah.

I. The name. It was once thought that the name derived from Shechem the son of Hamor (Gen. 33:18–19); see SHECHEM (PERSON) #1. It now seems more probable that the name referred to the geographical setting of the city, which is more or less on the "shoulder" or slope of Mount Gerizim. The name occurs in Egyptian texts dating from the 19th to the 17th centuries B.C. and in the TELL EL-AMARNA letters (see *ANET*, 230, 329, 477, 485–87, 489–90). It appears as Sakmemi, Sakmami, and Sekmem. The name also occurs in one of the early 8th-cent.-B.C. OSTRACA from SAMARIA.

Shechem's importance is closely linked to its position on the central Ridge Road in Palestine.

II. Excavations. Early archaeological expeditions were conducted at the site of Tell Balaṭah by Carl Watzinger from 1907 to 1909 and by Ernst Sellin and others between 1913 and 1934. In 1956 further excavations were begun by the Drew-McCormick Expedition in collaboration with the American School of Oriental Research, under the direction of G. E. Wright. The excavations, which continued until 1973, have uncovered the history of the site from the beginning of the 4th millennium B.C. down to c. 107 B.C., when the city evidently met its end.

The first signs of occupation were Chalcolithic campsites (c. 4000 B.C.) discovered immediately above bedrock in the lowest strata. Some pottery fragments were found for the following period, though it appears that the site was not actually occupied again till c. 1800. The city then quickly reached the height of its prosperity under the HYKSOS (1700–1550).

From the beginning of the Hyksos period, the story of the city is one of building and rebuilding. A massive wall was built around the city and a large palace built within it. In c. 1650 the palace area was covered over and the great temple of Shechem was erected in its place. Egyptian military expeditions may have destroyed the temple about a century later, after which it was rebuilt on a smaller scale. Recently, however, L. E. Stager (in *BAR* 29/4 [July–Aug. 2003]: 26–35, 66–69) has argued that the original structure was still standing when the Israelites invaded the land and that it may be the "tower of Shechem" mentioned in Jdg. 9:46–49. In any case, the destruction of the city by ABIMELECH (v. 45) is evident in the archaeological record. The site was then utilized for storage pits until the days of the monarchy, when a granary was built there. The city appears to have been reasonably prosperous again during the 9th and 8th centuries, though it could not compare with the status it had assumed under the Hyksos. There is ample evidence in the masses of brick and burned debris for the destruction of the city by the Assyrians when they invaded in 724–721.

For four centuries following this, the city reverted to village status until the SAMARITAN period. Around the year 325 B.C. the palace was again rebuilt and enjoyed some prosperity. There

Excavation remains of ancient Shechem (Tell Balaṭah) with Mount Gerizim in the background.

is a continuous coin record for this period of the town's existence. The abrupt end to this numismatic evidence suggests that the town may have been finally destroyed by John Hyrcanus (see HASMONEAN II.A) along with the city of Samaria in c. 107 B.C.

III. Physical features. Ancient Shechem lay in the pass that runs between Mount Ebal on the N and Mount Gerizim on the S. Part of the ancient road connecting the E bank of the Jordan with the Mediterranean coast ran through this valley and connected with a N–S route associated with "the soothsayers' tree" (Jdg. 9:37; see DIVINERS' OAK). The city enjoyed a good water supply and a fertile plain directly to the E. Shechem did not have the advantage of elevated terrain, thus necessitating its massive fortifications. Nevertheless, its location did mean control of some of the main roads through the mountainous regions of N Canaan, a feature of considerable military importance.

IV. Shechem in the Bible. Shechem first enters the biblical narrative in Gen. 12:6–7, when Abram (ABRAHAM) left HARAN and journeyed to Canaan with his family and possessions. Abram's first stopping place was the oak of MOREH near, or at, Shechem. The Canaanites were still in the land, but Yahweh appeared to Abram and renewed his covenant promise. Abram built an altar there.

In later years JACOB camped before the city of Shechem on his return from PADDAN ARAM. Here he bought a parcel of land from the sons of HAMOR, the HIVITE prince of the area, and built an altar to EL ELOHE ISRAEL ("God, the God of Israel," Gen. 33:18–19). Later, Shechem, Hamor's son, defiled Jacob's daughter DINAH, and this resulted in a formal agreement between the Shechemites and Israel to permit intermarriage between the two peoples. SIMEON and LEVI, however, took revenge, killing Hamor and Shechem and all the males, plundering the city, and taking captive all the women and children with their possessions (ch. 34).

It was near Shechem that Jacob hid the foreign gods of his family under the oak (Gen. 35:4). Interestingly, Jacob's sons later pastured their flocks near Shechem, where Joseph went to find them (37:12–13). It seems that Jacob wished to be friendly with the Shechemites (34:30; 49:5–7), and it appears that the pillaging of the town mentioned above did not permanently mar relations between the two peoples. Indeed, the body of JOSEPH, brought up from Egypt, is recorded to have been buried at Shechem (Josh. 24:32; cf. Acts 7:16).

According to the Amarna letters referred to above, Shechem fell to the HABIRU in the 15th cent. B.C. After the Israelite conquests in the land, JOSHUA called an assembly of the people at Shechem. Upon rehearsing the history of the people of Israel from their origin beyond the EUPHRATES to the conquest, Joshua summoned the people to unreserved service of Yahweh (Josh. 24). There he gave statutes and ordinances for Israel, and these were included in the Book of the Law of God. A great stone was set up under the oak in the sanctuary of Yahweh to serve as a witness to Israel's COVENANT with her God.

The fact that assemblies of the people were held at Shechem has suggested to many scholars that Shechem rather than SHILOH was the center of an amphictyonic league (see AMPHICTYONY). It has also been argued that Shechem served as the military and political center while Shiloh was the religious center. Both cities seem to have served as political and religious headquarters in some way or other, and it is impossible to determine the exact relationship between them.

Little is said of the town from Joshua until the time of Abimelech, GIDEON's son, except that the boundary between EPHRAIM and MANASSEH passed near it (Josh. 17:7), and that it served as one of the cities of refuge (20:7; 21:21) and was assigned to the descendants of KOHATH as a Levitical city (1 Chr. 6:66, 67). The mother of Abimelech was a Shechemite woman (Jdg. 8:31). On the death of Gideon, Abimelech went to Shechem and through his mother's family persuaded the Shechemites to make him king. Worthless men from BAAL BERITH, a Canaanite sanctuary that still existed in Shechem, were hired to help slay the seventy other sons of Gideon who would have had claim to the throne. It was there that the only other surviving son, JOTHAM, gave his famous parable which effected a curse upon Shechem. Abimelech ruled over Israel for three years, but he quickly lost favor with the people of Shechem. They warred against him but he finally took the city, destroying it and sowing it with salt. The house of EL-BERITH was also destroyed with its occupants, who had sought refuge from the destruction of the city (Jdg. 9).

Nothing is said of Shechem during the united kingdom period. It was at Shechem, however, that the northern tribes rejected REHOBOAM and made JEROBOAM their king, thus creating the divided monarchy (1 Ki. 12:1–19 = 2 Chr. 10:1–19). Shechem then became, for a time at least, Jeroboam's capital in the N and he began to rebuild it (1 Ki. 12:25). Within a short time, however, he moved the capital to PENUEL (PLACE) and then to TIRZAH, possibly in an effort to make the capital less vulnerable to Judean attack.

There is evidence that Shechem continued to exist with some degree of importance during the times of HOSEA and JEREMIAH (see Hos. 6:9; Jer. 41:5), though little is known of it in this period. Nothing is said, for example, of the fate of the town under Assyrian and Babylonian invasions. The OT itself gives no information concerning Shechem during the postexilic period. From other sources, however, we know that Shechem became the leading city of the SAMARITANS and was taken by John Hyrcanus (Jos. *Ant*. 11.8.6; 13.9.1). After the war of A.D. 70, the town was refounded and named Flavia Neapolis in honor of Flavius Vespasianus. The modern Nablus, W of Tell Balâṭah, derives its name from this rebuilt city. A small community of Samaritans has continued to live in the area in modern times.

(See further W. J. Harrelson, *The City of Shechem: Its History and Importance* [thesis, Union Theological Seminary, NY, 1953]; E. Nielsen, *Shechem: A Traditio-Historical Investigation* [1955]; G. E. Wright, *Shechem: The Biography of a Biblical City* [1965]; Dan P. Cole, *Shechem I: The Middle Bronze IIB Pottery* [1984]; E. F. Campbell, Jr., *Shechem II: Portrait of a Hill Country Vale* [1991]; id., *Shechem III: The Stratigraphy and Architecture of Shechem/Tell Balâṭah* [2002]; *ABD*, 5:1174–86; *NEAEHL*, 4:1345–59.) H. G. ANDERSEN

Shechinah shuh-ki´nuh. See SHEKINAH.

Shedeur shed´ee-uhr (שְׁדֵיאוּר *H8725*, prob. "SHADDAI is light"). Father of ELIZUR; the latter was a leader of the tribe of REUBEN at the time of MOSES (Num. 1:5; 2:10; 7:30, 35; 10:18).

sheep. The primary biblical words for "sheep" are Hebrew *ṣōʾn H7366* (which often has the collective sense of "flock") and Greek *probaton G4585*. The common Hebrew word for "ram" (male sheep) is *ʾayil H380*. There are, in addition, other Hebrew terms that may be rendered "sheep" in specific contexts (e.g., the more general term *śeh* H8445, Exod. 22:9 et al.). See also GOAT; LAMB; MOUNTAIN SHEEP.

I. Origin and early history. This topic is complex; many views have been published about possible wild ancestors and their period and place of origin. F. E. Zeuner's work (*A History of Domesticated Animals* [1963], ch. 7) is most complete and unlikely to be superseded unless some radically new material or method is found. The following paragraph owes much to his research, which includes a full review of the literature. (For a more recent study, see J. Clutton Brock, *A Natural History of Domesticated Mammals*, 2nd ed. [1999].)

Although several wild sheep have contributed to the stock, two species are the main ancestors. Urial (*Ovis orientalis*) is the more important; it is a central and western Asiatic species, living mostly in mountains, from W Tibet to Transcaspia. The adult sheep stands nearly 3 ft. at the shoulder, with strongly wrinkled horns curled in typical "Ammon" shape at the sides of the head; it is reddish in summer, with whitish underparts, and grayish brown in winter. The other is the mouflon, now found only in Corsica, Sardinia, and Asia Minor: it is the smallest wild sheep and is dark-reddish brown. In winter the adult rams have white or cream side patches. The Belt Cave in N Iran supplies the earliest known evidence of domesticated sheep, and this is near Urial country. By the Neolithic pottery age (c. 5000 B.C.) sheep were being herded, probably by dogs, and breeding under some control had started. They then spread rapidly, meeting with other groups domesticated independently, and finally few breeds could be regarded as purely from one source.

II. Characteristics of domestic sheep. Most breeds now differ widely from their wild forebears, and these differences began appearing early. The most obvious are the following:

(a) *Wool.* This is present in wild sheep but is most obvious only in winter, when it may cover the stiffer hairs. The felting and weaving properties of wool were soon recognized, and strains were bred to yield good wool in large amounts. Hair sheep are still found, especially in the tropics. See WOOL.

(b) *Tail.* Some breeds have tails with two or three times as many vertebrae as wild forms. In others the tail has become an organ for storing fat; this has been found with mummies of the twelfth dynasty (c. 2000 B.C.).

(c) *Color.* Westerners are so used to seeing white sheep that any other color seems odd. Early sheep were probably brown, but in Egypt there were white, brown, and black forms before 2000 B.C., perhaps much earlier. It is traditional to regard biblical sheep as white (cf. Isa. 1:18). While this is largely correct, Gen. 30:32–43 indicates that both sheep and goats were in various colors, presumably including white, but "spotted" is shown also to mean white spots on dark animals. It is often assumed that the sacrificial animals had to be white because of the requirement "without spot" (KJV in Num. 28:3, 9; 29:17, 26), but the Hebrew term (*tāmîm* H9459) refers to imperfections generally, not necessarily to color markings.

(d) *Habitat.* From a mountain origin the sheep developed into many breeds in a wide range of country from marsh to uplands and the desert edge. It became more demanding than the goat, needing better quality forage, largely grass (cf. 1 Chr. 4:39–40, "pasture for their flocks … rich, good pasture"). The erratic winter rains in parts of Palestine made the grass grow in patches, and shepherds, knowing where to find pasture, led their flocks there. It was from such an experience that DAVID wrote, "He makes me lie down in green pastures" (Ps. 23:2).

III. Uses. It is generally agreed that sheep were domesticated at first for their meat (see FOOD). Meat of the sheep, in contrast to that of the goat, is good from adult as well as young. Like CATTLE and goats, sheep are cloven-hoofed ruminants and therefore provide clean meat (Lev. 11:3), which became an important part of the Hebrew diet, as it still is in many Arab lands.

WEAVING had first begun with plant fibers; possibly also wool shed by wild animals had been used. With selective breeding, both quality and quantity of wool improved, and finally there was great trade in it. Part of the annual tribute paid by MESHA king of MOAB was the wool of 100,000 rams (2 Ki. 3:4). In some communities sheep were highly regarded for their milk, but there is only one clear biblical reference to this (Deut. 32:14). A modern breed (Awassi) derived from races long native to Palestine is now used there widely for milk and cheese production.

The use of SKINS was general long before domestication and thereafter increased greatly. "The priest who offers a burnt offering for anyone may keep its hide for himself" (Lev. 7:8); this was either sheep or goat. Persecuted refugees "went about in sheepskins and goatskins" (Heb. 11:37). See SHEEPSKIN. In addition, many peoples recognized the value of sheep for manuring pastures. In Egypt they were used for treading in seed as early as c. 2500 B.C. The wealth of Hebrew names indicates the importance of sheep to the Israelites, who were able shepherds and probably had several distinct breeds.

Genesis 30:32–43 is interesting in describing a false theory still widely believed—that things eaten or seen by the mother before or at birth can affect the color, shape, etc. of the young. JACOB put a striped white pattern in front of the lambing ewes in order to increase the proportion of marked animals. The text (vv. 41–42) indicates that he selected for vigor; the inference is that he unconsciously understood the flock genetics and mated accordingly, while wrongly attributing his success to his cleverness with the rods. However, it was God's providence in the breeding that brought success (cf. 31:11–12).

The sheep became preeminent in SACRIFICES, and very large numbers were used every year. Certain classes were wholly burnt, but in others most of the meat was used by offerer or priest. Some Hebrew names are seldom used except in this connection.

Above all, the sheep has deep metaphorical significance, especially in Ps. 23:1–4 and Isa. 53:6 ("We all like sheep have gone astray"). Significant occurrences in the NT include Jn. 1:29 ("Look, the Lamb of God, who takes away the sin of the world") and 10:14 ("I am the good shepherd"). Of seventy-four mentions in NT, only one is literal (sheep sold in the temple court, 2:14).

G. S. CANSDALE

sheepcote, sheepfold. An enclosure that served for the protection of sheep from the hazards of weather, robbers, and wild beasts. Located near the home of one of the owners or on the hills where the sheep grazed, it was roofless, walled by stone, and had only one door. It usually housed several flocks, each of which retained its own identity since each shepherd knew his sheep by name and was on intimate terms with them (Jn. 10:3–5).

J. H. BRATT

Sheepfold located in the hills near Nazareth.

Sheep Gate. The easternmost entrance into the N side of the ancient city of JERUSALEM (Neh. 12:39; Jn. 5:2). The Sheep Gate marked the terminus in the circuit of the walls, as rebuilt in 444 B.C. and as recorded by NEHEMIAH (Neh. 3:1, 32). Almost five centuries later Christ healed the man who had been lame for thirty-eight years at the neighboring pool of BETHESDA (or Beth-zatha, Jn. 5:2–9). This in turn confirms the location of the Sheep Gate. Pilgrim reports of the 4th Christian cent., the mosaic map from MEDEBA (5th cent.), and modern excavation of the large double pools by the Church of St. Anne unite to confirm the NE location of Bethesda and hence of the gate.   J. B. PAYNE

sheepskin. A simple garment made from the tanned pelt of sheep. It may well be that the sheepskin, still an ordinary article of dress in the E, was the initial covering of ADAM and EVE in the Garden of EDEN (Gen. 3:21). It was the common dress of the prophets of Israel, and this "hairy mantle" (Zech. 13:4 NRSV) was one of their distinctive marks. The Lord warned his followers against impostors who borrowed this dress when he said: "Watch out for false prophets. They come to you in sheep's clothing" (Matt. 7:15). The material was also used as covering for the TABERNACLE (Num. 4:25). See SKIN.   J. H. BRATT

Sheerah shee'uh-ruh (שֶׁאֱרָה H8641, perhaps "relative, descendant"). KJV Sherah. Daughter of EPHRAIM (according to some, of BERIAH); she is credited with having built Lower and Upper BETH HORON as well as an otherwise unknown town called UZZEN SHEERAH (1 Chr. 7:24). No other woman in the Bible is said to have founded a town.

Shehariah shee'huh-ri'uh (שְׁחַרְיָה H8843, possibly "Yahweh is dawning" [cf. Isa. 60.2 and see HAR]). Son of Jehoram and descendant of BENJAMIN; he is listed among the heads of families who lived in Jerusalem (1 Chr. 8:26).

Shekaniah shek'uh-ni'uh. TNIV form of SHECANIAH.

shekel. See WEIGHTS AND MEASURES IV.C.

Shekinah shuh-ki'nuh (שְׁכִינָה [from שָׁכַן H8905, "to dwell"], "dwelling, residence"; in Aram. the word appears also in the form שְׁכִינְתָּא). A postbiblical term applied especially to the divine presence.

I. Origin of the term. The word *Shekinah* arose among the Palestinian and Babylonian Jews, being based upon the OT doctrine of the divine presence in the world, which emphasized God's immanence and activity in the world order, and in contradiction to the Alexandrian teaching that God was supramundane in his being. The term was useful to the rabbis in that it afforded a reverent means of bringing the God who was "completely other" into contrast with the material universe, and especially into a visible or tangible relationship to his people Israel. No doubt the particular focus of the word upon "dwelling" grew out of the OT teaching that God chose to dwell among his people and put his name in a special place in the earth (Deut. 12:5–7). It was an interpretive effort to bridge the gap between HEAVEN as the place of God's eternal residence and the earth as the place of his real activity, especially his involvement in Israel's history.

The TARGUMS used the expressions "the Shekinah of God/Yahweh," "the glory of God," and "the word [*mêmrāʾ*] of God" as near synonyms; indeed, the terms became designations of God himself. For instance, the complaint of the Israelites, "Is the LORD among us or not" (Exod. 17:7) is translated by *Targum Onkelos*, "Is the Shekinah of the LORD among us or not?" (for similar circumlocutions, see the targumic renderings in Gen. 9:27; Exod. 25:8; 29:45; Num. 5:3; 6:25; 9:20; 14:14; 16:3; 35:34; Deut. 1:42; 32:40; Pss. 16:8; 44:10; 74:2; Hag. 1:8). Especially interesting is Lev. 26:11–12, which according to the Hebrew reads, "I will put my dwelling place [*miškān* H5438] among you, and I will not abhor you. I will walk among you and be your God, and you will be my people." *Targum Pseudo-Jonathan* paraphrases as follows: "I will set the Shekinah of my glory among you, and my word will not abhor you. The glory of my Shekinah will dwell among you, and my word will be for you as God redeemer, and you will be for my name as a holy people." In spite of such usage, however, it is abundantly clear that the Targums regarded the Shekinah as God himself and not as a mediator who stood between God and Israel. The term became a means of referring to God in less direct fashion (see esp. Exod. 33:14–16; 34:6, 9).

Many OT ideas fed the growth of the Shekinah concept. The ARK OF THE COVENANT was the place of God's habitation among his people in the early days (Num. 10:35–36). When the ark was captured by the PHILISTINES, it became their personal enemy so that they said, "Send the ark of the God of Israel away; let it return to its own place, or it will kill us and our people" (1 Sam. 5:11). The PILLAR OF FIRE AND CLOUD that guided Israel in the wilderness was understood to be a testimony of the divine presence. As the TABERNACLE and subsequent sanctuaries became the center of worship, so it was there that the Shekinah was found. Finally the TEMPLE in Jerusalem became the special sanctuary, and there the Shekinah was truly at home. The opinion of many scholars has been that the Babylonian idea of the enthronement of a deity in an innermost or secret sanctuary of a temple, where he remained if pleased with the worship of the people but from which he departed if angered, was the source of this trait assigned to the Shekinah.

II. Rabbinic use. The MISHNAH contains very few references to the Shekinah (only *m. Sanh.* 6:5 [omitted in some MSS]; *m. 'Abot* 3:2, 6), but in the TALMUD and the Midrashim (see MIDRASH) there was a much wider application of the teaching to the Scriptures. The presence of God in the world is described as being as pervasive as light (*Num. Rab.* 21:16). As the sun in the heavens reaches everywhere with its light, so God is inescapable in his world. The earth is said to shine with the glory of God, and thus to be the face or presence of the Shekinah (*'Abot de Rabbi Nathan* 2; see J. Goldin, *The Fathers according to Rabbi Nathan* [1955], 24).

In the HAGGADAH, the tabernacle was especially associated with the Shekinah; in fact, the day of the dedication of the tabernacle was said to have been the first day of the Shekinah's abiding in the universe, when it at last had found a home (*b. Šabb.* 85b). Solomon's temple was the successor to the tabernacle as the Shekinah's home. It was taught by some that at the time of the EXILE the Shekinah went with the captives into BABYLON, but others taught that it returned to heaven. Although the Shekinah was not to be found in the Jerusalem temple subsequent to the captivity, this did not mean that it ceased to be active in the world. Both Ishmael ben Elisha and Hoshaiah Rabbah taught that after the return to Jerusalem the Shekinah was in every place.

III. Symbolic representations. God spoke to MOSES out of the BURNING BUSH that was not consumed (Exod. 3:3–4). It was at the edge of the wilderness that God first went before his people as a pillar of cloud by day to lead them, and a pillar of fire by night (14:24). During the day the cloud was visible, and at night it was the fire. It was in this cloud that God was visibly present as the angel of the covenant (14:19). From the cloud God spoke to both Moses and Israel, and it was the cloud that rested upon Mount Sinai (24:15–18).

The ANGEL of the Lord was clearly God himself. According to Exod. 13:21, God himself "went ahead" of the Israelites, and later the statement was recorded that "the angel of God, who had been traveling in front of Israel's army, withdrew and went behind them. The pillar of cloud also moved from in front and stood behind them" (14:19). The Shekinah was represented as the angel of the Lord apparently when JACOB wrestled with God at Peniel. See PENUEL (PLACE). The angel of the Lord confronted HAGAR as she fled from SARAH (Gen. 16:7–14). Likewise the angel of the Lord appeared to ABRAHAM at the oaks of MAMRE (ch. 18).

Monastery and Chapel of the Transfiguration atop Mount Tabor. Jesus' transformation on the mount may be regarded as a manifestation of the Shekinah glory.

The lighting of the perpetual lamp symbolized the Shekinah, and there was the tradition that from his birth Moses was under the wings of the Shekinah. Since the Shekinah was felt to dwell between the wings of the CHERUBIM over the MERCY SEAT, which was the top of the ark of the covenant, it may be that the Shekinah was also identified with these angelic creatures. Worthy of note also is Isaiah's statement that "the angel of his presence saved them" (Isa. 63:9). The midrashic literature in the later period made the Shekinah almost an independent personality who stood between God and the world in a mediatorial role. Maimonides (1135–1204) taught that the Shekinah was a fiery created being who was the agent of divine activity in the world.

IV. NT parallels. As in the OT, so in the NT the term *Shekinah* was not used; but there is much indication of the idea of the immanence of God expressed in terminology that approximates the rabbinical usage. The Gospel of Luke among the synoptics especially reveals that trait. In the very beginning of that book, with the announcement of the birth of Jesus, Luke records concerning the shepherds, "An angel of the Lord appeared to them, and the glory of the Lord shone around them" (Lk. 2:9). The "glory of the Lord" is a reference, no doubt, to the supernatural LIGHT with which God appears, whether personally or by his messengers. The most notable instance of the influence of the Shekinah concept in Luke is in connection with the TRANSFIGURATION of Jesus: "As he was praying, the appearance of his face changed, and his clothes became as bright as a flash of lightning" (9:29). Outside the Gospels, the only allusion to this experience of Jesus elsewhere in the NT is 2 Pet. 1:16–18, in which the author by a shifting emphasis interpreted the transfiguration as heralding the PAROUSIA of Christ, perhaps because in the Synoptic Gospels the event follows a reference to the SECOND COMING of the Lord in glory and power.

It seems that the concepts of the Shekinah glory and the imminence of God in Jesus Christ have a happy union. In fact, in the Ethiopic text of the apocryphal *Apocalypse of Peter* the transfiguration was blended with the ASCENSION OF CHRIST, suggesting a correspondence between the cloud that received him and the glory that surrounded him. As the Shekinah in the thought of the Jews could depart this world and return to heaven, so Jesus was caught up in a cloud upon his departure (Acts 1:9). The second glimpse of Christ in the book of Acts was given in connection with PAUL's experience on the road to Damascus (9:3–6; 22:6–11; 26:12–16). Although the details of Paul's experience were given differently in the three accounts of it found in Acts, all three emphasized the blinding light from heaven, brighter than the sun, out of which the Christ communicated with him.

John's gospel is also noteworthy because of parallels to the Shekinah concept. That gospel begins with a passage that is most interesting because it says, "The Word became flesh and made his dwelling [*lit.*, tabernacled] among us" (Jn. 1:14; see LOGOS). The verb *eskēnōsen* (from *skenoo* G5012) recalls the Shekinah through which God appeared to his people in the tabernacle during the wilderness wanderings. The passage developed the idea further in that it seemed to regard the Shekinah as dwelling in the tabernacle of the flesh of Jesus, for it was said, "We have seen his glory," which was the manifestation of the Shekinah among human beings. The Johannine Word was the light which lighted everyone. (Note that the Aaronic blessing of Num. 6:25, "the LORD make his face shine upon you," was rendered by *Tg. Onk.*, "the LORD give you the light of his Shekinah.")

The term GLORY, very important as a representation of the Shekinah by the rabbis, was of special significance in John's gospel. Generally it referred to the action of God in the world through Jesus Christ. The true temple was not the edifice in Jerusalem, but the very body of Jesus. It was in him that the glory of God shone, and in his resurrection that God acted supremely in behalf of sinners (Jn. 2:21). His miracle of CANA, the first of the Johannine signs, was said to manifest his glory (2:11). There are eighteen occurrences of the term *glory* (Gk. *doxa* G1518) in John's gospel and only twenty-three in the synoptics combined; and among the synoptics Luke has thirteen. There is a noted predilection for the term that is shared by John and Luke.

In the Hebrew OT the *kabod* H3883 or "glory" of God was the visible manifestation of his majesty as he acted in power. John emphasized that Jesus' glory was visible throughout his ministry, and in spite of the fact that the transfiguration is not recounted in the fourth gospel, it was John who insisted that Jesus' glory was visible from the beginning and not just after his resurrection. Especially through the signs was this true (Jn. 2:11; 11:40; 17:4). The resurrection was regarded by all the Gospels as the supreme act of God that declared Christ's glory, but John thought of the passion, death, and resurrection of Jesus as one "hour." Throughout the entirety of that hour, John emphasized the glory of it all (12:23, 28; 13:32; 17:1). Jesus prayed, according to John, "Father, glorify me in your presence with the glory I had with you before the world began" (17:5). John wrote that Isaiah had seen Christ's glory (Jn. 12:41), but the *Targum Jonathan* expanded Isa. 6:5 to read, "my eyes have seen the glory of the Shekinah of the King of the Ages, LORD Sabaoth." Similarly, the epistle to the Hebrews declares Christ to be "the radiance of God's glory" (Heb. 1:3). PETER speaks of "the Spirit of glory" and describes God as "the Majestic Glory" (1 Pet. 4:14; 2 Pet. 1:17).

Another concept that was very significant to John is that of "abiding" (the Gk. verb *menō* G3531 occurs almost seventy times in his gospel and epistles), and of course the same notion is central to the understanding of Shekinah. According to *m. ʾAbot* 3:6, the Shekinah "rests" or "abides" among those who occupy themselves with God's law, and one of the passages quoted as proof is Exod. 20:24, "Wherever I cause my name to be honored, I will come to you and bless you." The NAME of God in Jewish thought constituted the essence of God himself. Interestingly, the DIDACHE (10.2) contains this prayer: "We give thanks to you, holy Father, for your holy name, which you made to tabernacle in our hearts." This echoes Jn. 17:4, 6, where the manifestation of the name of God was the same as the glorification of the Father, the bringing of the Shekinah to earth. In John, Jesus also prayed for his followers to be kept in the name that had been given to him, and in which he had kept them (Jn. 17:11–12).

Many passages in the writings of Paul are thought to have a parallel to the Shekinah. The Corinthian correspondence may be the earliest of his material to reveal the parallel, and this is especially to be seen in connection with the term *glory*. Paul used "Lord of glory" as a title for Christ (1 Cor. 2:8; cf. also Jas. 2:1). He also recalled the experience of Moses, who put a veil over his face that the Israelites might not see the end of the glory that had been upon him (2 Cor. 3:14)—no doubt an allusion to the Shekinah concept. Christ's people in contrast to Moses behold the "glory of the Lord" and are transformed from glory to glory (v. 18).

The GOSPEL was also related by Paul to this concept, speaking as he did of "the light of the gospel of the glory of Christ" (2 Cor. 4:4). Ephesians and Colossians employ similar terminology related to Christ (Eph. 1:17–18; 3:16; Col. 1:27). Romans likewise takes note of this with the observation that all have fallen short of the glory of God (Rom. 3:23). The sinner's hope in Christ is to share the glory of God (5:2; 8:18). (See further G. F. Moore, *Judaism in the First Centuries of the Christian Era: The Age of the Tannaim*, 3 vols. [1927–30], 1:434–38; E. E. Urbach, *The Sages: Their Concepts and Beliefs*, 2 vols. [1979], ch. 3; *ISBE* rev. [1979–88], 4:466–68.)

H. L. DRUMWRIGHT, JR.

Shelah (person) shee'luh (שֵׁלָה H8941, possibly "offshoot" [see *HALOT*, 4:15–17; cf. *ABD*, 5:1191]; gentilic שֵׁלָנִי H8989, "Shelanite"; Σαλά G4885). KJV also Salah, NT Sala. **(1)** Son (or descendant) of ARPHAXAD and more distant descendant of SHEM (Gen. 10:24; 11:12–15; 1 Chr. 1:18, 24); included in Luke's GENEALOGY OF JESUS CHRIST (Lk. 3:35, where Shelah is listed as son of CAINAN, following the LXX).

(2) Son of JUDAH (by his Canaanite wife), grandson of JACOB, and ancestor of the Shelanite clan (Gen. 38:5; 46:12; Num. 26:20; 1 Chr. 2:3; 4:21; the gentilic SHILONITE in 1 Chr. 9:5 [*šilônî*] and Neh. 11:5 [*šilônî*] is widely thought to be a textual corruption of "Shelanite" [*šēlānî*]). Shelah was promised in marriage to Judah's widowed daughter-in-law, TAMAR, but Judah failed to keep his promise (vv. 11, 14, 26).

Shelah, Pool of shee'luh (שֶׁלַח H8940, perhaps "canal"). A reservoir in JERUSALEM, near the FOUNTAIN GATE and the KING'S GARDEN; its wall was repaired by the ruler of the district of Mizpah, SHALLUN son of Col-Hozeh (Neh. 3:15 NRSV). It is thought by many to be identical with the King's Pool (2:14) and with the Lower Pool (Isa. 22:9).

While some identify it with the Pool of SILOAM (so NIV; similarly KJV ["Siloah"; cf. Isa. 8:6, "Shiloah"]), others regard it as a separate reservoir in the complex water system of JERUSALEM that was fed by the Spring of GIHON. The NJPS interprets the word not as a name but as a common noun and renders, "the irrigation pool." (On the distinction between the Pool of Shelah and "the artificial pool" [Neh. 3:16], see H. G. M. Williamson, *Ezra-Nehemiah*, WBC 16 [1985], 207.)   T. E. MCCOMISKEY

Shelanite shee′luh-n*i*t. See SHELAH.

Shelemiah shel′uh-mi′uh (שֶׁלֶמְיָהוּ H8983 and שֶׁלֶמְיָה H8982, "Yahweh has repaid [or replaced]"; cf. SHALLUM, SHILLEM). (1) A Levite who was responsible for the EAST GATE (1 Chr. 26:14). His full name was MESHELEMIAH (9:21; 26:1–2, 9).

(2–3) Two of the descendants of Binnui who agreed to put away their foreign wives (Ezra 10:39, 41). The parallel passage includes only one Shelemiah in this context (1 Esd. 9:34; KJV, "Selemias"), and it is possible that the second Shelemiah in the Ezra list was a descendant of Azzur (see MACNADEBAI).

(4) Father of Hananiah; the latter, along with Hanun son of Zalaph, was in charge of repairing the portion of the Jerusalem wall above the HORSE GATE (Neh. 3:30).

(5) A priest who, along with others, was appointed by NEHEMIAH to oversee the collection and distribution of tithes for the support of the Levites (Neh. 13:13).

(6) Son of CUSHI and grandfather of JEHUDI; the latter was the official sent to BARUCH, instructing him to bring to the court the scroll on which were written the prophecies of JEREMIAH (Jer. 36:14).

(7) Son of Abdeel; he was one of three men commanded by King JEHOIAKIM to seize Baruch and Jeremiah, a mission that proved unsuccessful (Jer. 36:26).

(8) Father of JEHUCAL; the latter and a priest were sent by King ZEDEKIAH to JEREMIAH to ask the prophet to pray for him and the people (Jer. 37:3; subsequently Jehucal [Jucal] joined others in recommending the death sentence for Jeremiah, 38:1–4).

(9) Father of Irijah; the latter was a sentry who seized Jeremiah on suspicion of deserting to the Babylonians during a temporary lifting of the siege (Jer. 37:13).   A. E. CUNDALL

Sheleph shee′lif (שֶׁלֶף H8991, meaning uncertain). Son of JOKTAN and grandson of EBER, listed in the Table of NATIONS (Gen. 10:26; 1 Chr. 1:20). Many think Sheleph is a tribal name, referring to a group in S ARABIA otherwise known by the name of as-Salif (or as-Sulaf; see *ABD*, 5:1192–93).

Shelesh shee′lish (שֶׁלֶשׁ H8994, possibly "gentle"). Son of Helem; listed among the brave warriors who were heads of families of the tribe of ASHER (1 Chr. 7:35; cf. v. 40).

Shelomi shi-loh′mi (שְׁלֹמִי H8979, possibly "my peace" [but see *ABD*, 5:1193]). Father of Ahihud, from the tribe of ASHER; the latter was among the leaders appointed to divide the land of Canaan among the tribes (Num. 34:27).

Shelomith shi-loh′mith (שְׁלֹמִית H8984 [male] and H8985 [female], possibly "at peace" or "complete"). Sometimes confused with SHELOMOTH, which according to some scholars is the original male form of the name. (1) Daughter of Dibri, from the tribe of DAN. Shelomith's unnamed son (by an Egyptian father), following a quarrel with another Israelite, blasphemed the divine name and was subsequently stoned to death (Lev. 24:11).

(2) Daughter of ZERUBBABEL and descendant of DAVID (1 Chr. 3:19); she is the only woman listed in this genealogy.

(3) Son of Shimei and descendant of LEVI through GERSHON (1 Chr. 23:9 KJV and NJPS, following the *Qere*; NIV and NRSV, "Shelomoth").

(4) Son of Izhar and also a Gershonite (1 Chr. 23:18; called "Shelomoth" in 24:22).

(5) Son of Zicri and descendant of MOSES; he was in charge of all the spoils of war and other gifts dedicated to the maintenance of the sanctuary (1 Chr. 26:25–28, following the *Qere*; NRSV, "Shelomoth").

(6) Son of REHOBOAM (by his favorite wife MAACAH) and descendant of DAVID (2 Chr. 11:20).

(7) Son of Josiphiah; he was family head of the descendants of BANI who returned with EZRA from EXILE (Ezra 8:10 NIV and NRSV, following LXX

and 1 Esd. 8:36 [where KJV reads "Assalimoth"]). The MT omits the name Bani, yielding the translation, "of the descendants of Shelomith: the son of Josiphiah, and with him 160 men" (cf. KJV and NJPS).

A. E. Cundall

Shelomoth shi-loh′moth (שְׁלֹמוֹת *H8977*, possibly "at peace" or "complete"). Sometimes confused with Shelomith. **(1)** Son of Shimei and descendant of Levi through Gershon (1 Chr. 23:9 NIV and NRSV, following the *Ketib*; KJV and NJPS, "Shelomith").

(2) Son of Izhar and also a Gershonite (1 Chr. 24:22; called "Shelomith" in 23:18).

(3) Son of Zicri and descendant of Moses; he was in charge of all the spoils of war and other gifts dedicated to the maintenance of the sanctuary (1 Chr. 26:25–28 NRSV, following the *Ketib*; KJV and NIV, "Shelomith").

A. E. Cundall

Shelumiel shi-loo′mee-uhl (שְׁלֻמִיאֵל *H8981*, "God is my peace [*i.e.*, salvation]"). Son of Zurishaddai; he was a leader from the tribe of Simeon, heading a division of 59,300 (Num. 2:12; 10:19). Shelumiel was among those who assisted Moses in taking a census of the Israelites (1:6) and who brought offerings to the Lord for the dedication of the tabernacle (7:36–41). See also Salamiel.

A. E. Cundall

Shem shem (שֵׁם *H9006*, possibly "name [*i.e.*, esteemed]" or, like Akk. *šummum*, "son, offspring"; perhaps short form of a theophoric name such as שְׁמוּאֵל *H9017* [see Shemuel]; Σήμ *G4954*). Son of Noah, possibly his firstborn (Gen. 5:32 et al.; 1 Chr. 1:4 et al.); included in Luke's genealogy of Jesus Christ (Lk. 3:36; KJV, "Sem"). Shem is considered the ancestor of the peoples known as the Semites and, in the classificatory sense, of those speaking Semitic languages. He and his wife were two of the eight persons who escaped from the flood in the ark (Gen. 7:13; see Flood, Genesis). Two years after leaving the ark, at the age of 100, he became the father of Arphaxad (Arpachshad); other sons and daughters were born during his 600-year life (11:10).

The Table of Nations gives additional details concerning Shem's descendants (Gen. 10:21–31; 1 Chr. 1:17–27). His sons Elam, Asshur, Arphaxad, Lud, and Aram are identified in the earlier Bible geographies as ancestral to the lands of Persia, Assyria, Chaldea (prob.), Lydia, and Syria, respectively. An uncertainty attached to Lud, as another person by the same name appears in connection with Egypt (10:13), but these later people are regarded as Hamitic. The Chronicler adds four additional sons of Shem (Uz, Hul, Gether, and Meshech, 1 Chr. 1:17 MT), but Genesis identifies these as sons of Aram (Gen. 10:23). If the Chronicles passage is not textually corrupt (cf. NIV, following some MSS of LXX), it may be that the author is simply referring to them in the general sense of descendants of Shem. In the development of the ethnic relationships of Shem's family, not all his descendants would necessarily have spoken Semitic languages and dialects. Hence the apparent discrepancies between the genealogical data of Gen. 10 and the historical affinities among the peoples of the Near E may be more imagined than real.

Historically, the earliest home of the Semites, or the families of the five sons of Shem, must have been in the foothills and valleys of Armenia. From this nuclear region, reconstruction of migrations indicates that their descendants moved outward in the various directions required by their settlement identifications. Arphaxad may have remained longest in the original settlement area, then worked his way southward along the eastern side of the Zagros range of mountains, finally to journey westward to the plain of Shinar (Gen. 11:2). G. Childe (*New Light on the Most Ancient East* [1953], 147, 155, 167–68) used archaeological data to show that the Semites probably had earlier contact with Egypt and carried cultural affinities from there into Sumer.

M. H. Heicksen

Shem, Paraphrase of. A gnostic document preserved in the Nag Hammadi Library (NHC VII, 1). Probably composed in Greek (c. A.D. 200), whence it was translated into Coptic, the work describes itself as a "paraphrase about the unbegotten Spirit" (though the meaning of the word *paraphrase* is ambiguous) and purports to be a revelation granted to Shem by Derdekeas (a redeemer figure; see Gnosticism). Shem relates that in his mind he was taken up to the top of the world. There he learned that Derdekeas, son of the Light, descended to the realm of Darkness to rescue the Spirit. The narrative makes allusion to a few OT events, but it gives little evidence of Christian influence. Some think that the *Paraphrase of Seth*, a heretical work mentioned by the Christian writer Hyppolitus, may have been a Christianized version of the *Paraphrase of Shem*. (English trans. in *NHL*, 339–61.)

Shem, Treatise of. A Jewish astrological work preserved only in a 15th-cent. Syriac MS, but probably composed in antiquity, maybe as early as the 1st cent. B.C. (the original language may have been Hebrew or Aramaic). Although attributed to SHEM, he is not actually mentioned in the work, which claims to predict the characteristics of the year, depending on which part of the zodiac the year begins. The emphasis it places on natural phenomena and on the movements of the heavenly bodies does not sit well with the biblical notion of divine PROVIDENCE. See ASTROLOGY. (English trans. in *OTP*, 1:473–86.)

Shema (person) shee′muh (שֶׁמַע H9050, prob. short form of שְׁמַעְיָהוּ H9062, "Yahweh has heard"; see SHEMAIAH). **(1)** Son of HEBRON and descendant of CALEB, included in the genealogy of JUDAH (1 Chr. 2:43–44). Many of the names in this passage refer to places, and Shema could be the name of a Judahite settlement; see SHEMA (PLACE).

(2) Son of Joel and descendant of REUBEN (1 Chr. 5:8); it is possible that Shema in this verse should be identified with Shemaiah, or perhaps with Shimei, both of whom are mentioned as descendants of Joel earlier in the passage (v. 4). See also JOEL #5.

(3) Son of ELPAAL and descendant of BENJAMIN; he and his brother BERIAH, heads of families in AIJALON, put to flight the inhabitants of GATH (1 Chr. 8:13). This Shema is apparently the same as the SHIMEI mentioned later in this genealogy (v. 21).

(4) One of the prominent men who stood near EZRA when the law was read at the great assembly (Neh. 8:4; 1 Esd. 9:43 [KJV, "Sammus"]).

A. E. CUNDALL

Shema (place) shee′muh (שֶׁמַע H9054, meaning uncertain). One of "the southernmost towns of the tribe of Judah in the Negev toward the boundary of Edom" (Josh. 15:26). Some scholars emend Shema to Sheba on the basis of a partially parallel passage that includes the latter name among Simeonite towns within Judahite territory (19:2); see SHEBA #5. Others identify Shema with the "son" of Hebron (1 Chr. 2:43); see SHEMA (PERSON) #1. In any case, the location of this town is not known (for proposals, cf. G. N. Knoppers, *I Chronicles 1–9*, AB 12 [2004], 312).

Shema, the shuh-mah′. Name give to the confession found in Deut. 6:4–9 (followed in SYNAGOGUE services by 11:13–21 and Num. 15:37–41). This designation derives from the first word of the passage, šĕmaʿ, "Hear!" (imperative form of the verb šāmaʿ H9048).

Shemaah shi-may′uh (שְׁמָעָה H9057, occurring with the definite article, הַשְּׁמָעָה, suggesting that the form should be emended to יְהוֹשָׁמָע, "Yahweh has heard"). A man from GIBEAH whose two sons, AHIEZER and JOASH, were among the ambidextrous relatives of SAUL who joined DAVID's forces at ZIKLAG (1 Chr. 12:3; cf. v. 1). On the basis of the primary SEPTUAGINT witnesses and a few Hebrew MSS, the plural "sons" is often emended to "son"; if the singular reading is original, then Shamaah was the father only of Joash.

Shemaiah shi-may′yuh (שְׁמַעְיָהוּ H9062 and שְׁמַעְיָה H9061, "Yahweh has heard"; cf. ELISHAMA). One of the most common biblical names, borne especially by priests and Levites; in some cases it is difficult to distinguish between them. **(1)** Son of Shecaniah and descendant of DAVID in the line of ZERUBBABEL (1 Chr. 3:22).

(2) Descendant of SIMEON and ancestor of Ziza; the latter was one of the clan leaders in the time of HEZEKIAH who invaded the land of the Hamites and the Meunites (1 Chr. 4:37; cf. vv. 38–41).

(3) Son of Joel and descendant of REUBEN (1 Chr. 5:4; possibly the same as SHEMA in v. 8).

(4) Son of Hasshub and descendant of LEVI through MERARI; listed among those who resettled in Jerusalem after the EXILE (1 Chr. 9:14) and among the heads of the Levites "who had charge of the outside work of the house of God" (Neh. 11:15).

(5) Son of Galal, also a Merarite, whose son Obadiah is included among those who resettled in Jerusalem (1 Chr. 9:16); he is evidently the same as SHAMMUA father of Abda (Neh. 11:17).

(6) Head of a Levitical family descended from ELIZAPHAN, listed among those who helped to bring the ARK OF THE COVENANT to Jerusalem in the reign of DAVID (1 Chr. 15:8, 11).

(7) Son of Nethanel; he was a Levitical scribe who recorded the results of King David's choice by lot of those who would serve in the twenty-four priestly divisions (1 Chr. 24:6).

(8) Firstborn son of OBED-EDOM; he and his brothers belonged to the division of the gatekeepers, and Shamaiah's sons "were leaders in their father's family because they were very capable men" (1 Chr. 26:4, 6–7).

(9) A "man of God" or prophet who advised REHOBOAM not to take military action against JEROBOAM and the ten northern tribes that seceded (1 Ki. 12:22–24 = 2 Chr. 11:2–4). Rehoboam was later the subject of another word from the Lord through Shemaiah, who predicted the king's defeat at the hand of SHISHAK, pharaoh of Egypt (2 Chr. 12:5–8). Along with IDDO the seer, Shemaiah was also a chronicler of the life of Rehoboam (12:15). There is some confusion in the SEPTUAGINT, which includes after 1 Ki. 12:24 a brief résumé of the account of AHIJAH the prophet and Jeroboam (reported in 11:29–40), but which assigns the prophet's role to Shemaiah.

(10) One of six Levites whom King JEHOSHAPHAT sent to teach the law in the cities of Judah (2 Chr. 17:8). Appointed to the same mission were a number of princes and priests.

(11) Descendant of JEDUTHUN the musician; he and his brother UZZIEL were among the Levites assigned to consecrate the temple in the days of HEZEKIAH (2 Chr. 29:14).

(12) A Levite who faithfully assisted KORE in distributing the contributions made to the temple during the reign of HEZEKIAH (2 Chr. 31:15).

(13) A leader of the Levites during the reign of King JOSIAH, along with his brothers CONANIAH and NETHANEL, Shemaiah provided 5,000 offerings (lambs) and five head of cattle for the renewed celebration of the Passover (2 Chr. 35:9; 1 Esd. 1:9 [KJV, "Samaias"]).

(14) Descendant of Adonikam and a family head who returned with EZRA from Babylon (Ezra 8:13; 1 Esd. 8:39 [KJV, "Samaias"]).

(15) One of a group of leaders sent by EZRA to Iddo to get attendants for the house of God (Ezra 8:16; 1 Esd. 8:44 [KJV, "Mamaias"]).

(16) One of the priests descended from Harim who agreed to put away their foreign wives (Ezra 10:21; 1 Esd. 9:21 [KJV, "Sameius"]).

(17) Another man in the line of Harim, evidently not the same as #16 above, but an ordinary Israelite, who had also married a foreign wife (Ezra 10:31).

(18) Son of Shecaniah; he was a priest who guarded the EAST GATE and who made repairs to the wall in front of his house (Neh. 3:29).

(19) Son of Delaiah; he was a hired prophet sent by TOBIAH and SANBALLAT to intimidate NEHEMIAH and so hinder progress on the rebuilding of the wall (Neh. 6:10). The fear of assassination was calculated to cause Nehemiah to flee into the temple, a forbidden act, and so bring reproach upon him in the eyes of the people, and perhaps divine wrath as well. Nehemiah wisely refused this ploy (vv. 11–13).

(20) One of the priests who participated with Nehemiah in the sealing of the covenant at the dedication of the wall (Neh. 10:8). He is probably the same Shemaiah mentioned in connection with the coming of Zerubbabel to Jerusalem (12:6). In the days of the high priest JOIAKIM, Jehonathan was the head of Shemaiah's priestly family (12:18).

(21) A priest who took part in one of the choirs at the dedication of the wall (Neh. 12:34).

(22) Descendant of ASAPH and grandfather of Zechariah; the latter was a musician who participated in the dedication of the wall (Neh. 12:35).

(23) Another musician who participated in the dedication of the wall (Neh. 12:36).

(24) A priest or Levite who participated in the choir at the dedication of the wall (Neh. 12:42).

(25) Father of a prophet named URIAH, from KIRIATH JEARIM. He prophesied against Jerusalem in the time of King JEHOIAKIM, who sought his life. Uriah, however, escaped to Egypt, but he was brought back and executed by Jehoiakim (Jer. 26:20–23).

(26) A NEHELAMITE who was a false prophet; JEREMIAH pronounced judgment upon him and predicted the extinction of his family (Jer. 29:24–32).

(27) Father of Delaiah; the latter was one of the officials who witnessed Jehoiakim's burning of the scroll containing the words of Jeremiah (Jer. 36:12).

(28) One of the descendants of Ezora who had married foreign wives (1 Esd. 9:34 RSV; KJV and NRSV, "Samatus").

(29) Father of Ananias (Hananiah) and Jathan (Nathan), acquaintances of TOBIT, who calls him "the great Shemaiah" (Tob. 5:13 RSV; KJV, "Samaias"; NRSV, "Shemeliah" [v. 14]).

M. H. HEICKSEN

Shemariah shem′uh-ri′uh (שְׁמַרְיָה H9080 [only 1 Chr. 12:5, MT 12:6] and שְׁמַרְיָהוּ H9079, "Yahweh has watched over"). (1) One of the ambidextrous Benjamite warriors who joined DAVID while he was in exile from SAUL at the Philistine city of ZIKLAG (1 Chr. 12:5; cf. v. 2).

(2) Son of King REHOBOAM by his first wife MAHALATH (2 Chr. 11:19; KJV, "Shamariah").

(3) One of the descendants of Harim who agreed to put away their foreign wives in the time of Ezra (Ezra 10:32).

(4) One of the descendants of Binnui who agreed to put away their foreign wives (Ezra 10:41). Regarding the textual problems in this verse, see discussion under MACNADEBAI. S. BARABAS

Shemeber shem-ee′buhr (שֶׁמְאֵבֶר H9008, meaning uncertain). The king of ZEBOIIM (Gen. 14:2); he and four other kings were defeated in the Valley of Siddim by KEDORLAOMER and his allies.

Shemed shee′mid (שֶׁמֶד H9013, derivation uncertain). Son of ELPAAL and descendant of BENJAMIN; he is credited with having built ONO and LOD (1 Chr. 8:12; KJV, "Shamed").

Shemeliah shem′uh-li′uh (Σεμελιας). Father of Hananiah and Nathan, acquaintances of TOBIT (Tob. 5:14; KJV, "Samaias" [v. 13]; RSV, "Shemaiah" [v. 13]).

Shemer shee′muhr (שֶׁמֶר H9070, possibly short form of שְׁמַרְיָהוּ H9080, "Yahweh has watched over"). (1) Owner of a hill purchased by King OMRI as the site for a city; the king called it SAMARIA (Heb. šōmĕrôn H9076) after Shemer (1 Ki. 16:24).

(2) Son of Mahli, descendant of LEVI through MERARI, and ancestor of the musician ETHAN (1 Chr. 6:46; KJV, "Shamer").

(3) An Asherite (1 Chr. 7:34 NRSV; KJV, "Shamer"; NIV, "Shomer"). See SHOMER.

Shemida shi-mi′duh (שְׁמִידָע H9026, possibly "the Name [*i.e.*, God] has understood"; gentilic שְׁמִידָעִי H9027, "Shemidaite"). Son of GILEAD, grandson of MANASSEH, and ancestor of the Shemidaite clan (Num. 26:32; Josh. 17:2; 1 Chr. 7:19 [some KJV editions, "Shemidah"]). S. BARABAS

sheminith shem′uh-nith. See MUSIC VI.C.

Shemiramoth shi-mihr′uh-moth (שְׁמִירָמוֹת H9035, meaning unknown). (1) A Levite and one of the gatekeepers assigned to be a musician when DAVID made preparation to transfer the ARK OF THE COVENANT to Jerusalem (1 Chr. 15:18). He is called one of the brothers of the "second order" (NRSV; NIV, "next in rank") who followed HEMAN, ASAPH, and ETHAN. Shemiramoth and some others "were to play the lyres according to *alamoth*" (v. 20; see MUSIC VI.C). Later, he was one of the Levites appointed "to minister before the ark of the LORD, to make petition, to give thanks, and to praise the LORD, the God of Israel" (16:4–5).

(2) One of six Levites whom King JEHOSHAPHAT sent to teach the law in the cities of Judah (2 Chr. 17:8). Appointed to the same mission were a number of princes and priests.

Shemuel shem′yoo-uhl (שְׁמוּאֵל H9017, possibly "his name is God"; see details under SAMUEL). (1) Son of Ammihud; he was a leader from the tribe of SIMEON, chosen to assist in the distribution of the land (Num. 34:20).

(2) Son of Tola and grandson of ISSACHAR, described as head of family (1 Chr. 7:2; NIV, "Samuel").

(3) KJV alternate form of Samuel (only 1 Chr. 6:33).

Shen shen (שֵׁן H9095, with the definite article, הַשֵּׁן, "the tooth" [possibly alluding to the shape of a topographical formation]). A place near which the stone named EBENEZER was set up by SAMUEL (1 Sam. 7:12). Shen was evidently not far from MIZPAH, but its location is unknown. On the basis of the SEPTUAGINT (which reads *tēs palaias*, "the old") and the Peshitta (*yšn*), many scholars emend the text to *yĕšānâ*, JESHANAH (cf. NRSV), a town some 5 mi. N of BETHEL.

Shenazar shi-naz´uhr. KJV form of SHENAZZAR.

Shenazzar shi-naz´uhr (שְׁנְאַצַּר H9100, prob. from Akk. *Sin-uṣur*, "may [the god] Sin protect"). KJV Shenazar. Son of the exiled King JEHOIACHIN (1 Chr. 3:18). See also SHESHBAZZAR.

Shenir shee´nuhr. KJV alternate form of SENIR.

Sheol shee´ohl (שְׁאוֹל H8619, derivation disputed; suggestions include "place of inquiry," alluding to necromancy [from שָׁאַל H8626, "to ask"; cf. BDB, 983], and "desolation, destruction" [from שָׁאָה H8615, "to be desolate"; cf. *HALOT*, 4:1368; fuller discussion in *ABD*, s.v. "Dead, Abode of the," 2:101–2, and *TDOT*, 14:240–41]). The place where the DEAD were believed to dwell. The Hebrew term is used sixty-five times in the OT, and more than half of its occurrences are found in the WISDOM Literature. The KJV translates it as "the grave" or "hell" ("the pit" three times). The NIV usually renders it "the grave" (Gen. 37:35 et al.; see R. L. Harris in *The NIV: The Making of a Contemporary Translation*, ed. K. L. Barker [1987], 75–92), but occasionally gives such contextual renderings as "the realm of death" (Deut. 32:22), "death" (Job 17:16 et al.), and "depths" (Ps. 139:8). The NRSV and other modern versions use the transliteration *Sheol*.

The Hebrews evidently shared with their contemporaries the belief that there was a region occupied by the dead as a shadowy underworld existence. A number of obvious parallels exist between the biblical descriptions and references in extrabiblical literature. According to the OT, the realm of the dead was a place of darkness: "… before I go to the place of no return, / to the land of gloom and deep shadow, / to the land of deepest night, / of deep shadow and disorder, / where even the light is like darkness" (Job 10:21–22; cf. Ps. 143:3). It was also viewed as a place of silence whose inhabitants cannot praise God (Ps. 6:5; 99:10–12; 94:17; 115:17). The book of Ecclesiastes states that "the dead know nothing" and that "in the grave, where you are going, there is neither working nor planning nor knowledge nor wisdom" (Eccl. 9:5, 10). The inhabitants of Sheol are but a shadow of their former selves; in fact, they are called by a term that may mean "shades" (*rĕpāʾîm* H8327; see REPHAITE).

Sheol is a place of continued existence rather than annihilation, and it does not lie beyond the reach of God. "If I ascend to heaven, you are there; / if I make my bed in Sheol, you are there" (Ps. 139:8 NRSV). "Sheol is naked before God, / and Abaddon has no covering" (Job 26:6 NRSV; see ABADDON). Thus there springs the hope mentioned several times in the OT that God will rescue his people from Sheol. The OT makes little distinction between the lot of the godly and the ungodly in this realm. The distinction developed later, during the intertestamental period.

Some ambiguity exists relative to the location of Sheol. In a large number of instances, Sheol is spoken of as a place "down to" which one goes. It is a question as to how closely the Hebrew identified Sheol with the grave itself. The place is depicted as being underground: "The earth opened its mouth and swallowed them up, along with their households—everyone who belonged to Korah and all their goods. So they with all that belonged to them went down alive into Sheol; the earth closed over them, and they perished from the midst of the assembly" (Num. 16:32–33). Elsewhere the dead are said to dwell "beneath the waters" (Job 26:5).

An important question regarding Sheol is this: At death, did the OT believers go to such a place of gloom or did they go to be with the Lord immediately? The former view was prevalent in the early church, which also held that Christ at his death descended into Sheol (HADES) to bring the OT believers to heaven with him. The latter view is held by those who believe that the Sheol concept was held by the Israelites in common with their pagan neighbors until God gradually revealed more and more information about the life after death, climaxing his revelation in Christ who brought life and immortality to light. Both views contain considerable difficulties.

(See further S. Zandstra in *PTR* 5 [1907]: 631–41; C. F. Burney, *Israel's Hope of Immortality* [1909]; E. F. Sutcliffe, *The Old Testament and the Future Life* [1947]; N. J. Tromp, *Primitive Conceptions of Death and the Nether World in the Old Testament* [1969]; K. Spronk, *Beatific Afterlife in Ancient Israel and in the Ancient Near East* [1986]; P. S. Johnston, *Shades of Sheol: Death and Afterlife in the Old Testament* [2002]; *DDD*, 768–70.) H. BUIS

Shepham shee′fuhm (שְׁפָם H9172, meaning uncertain). One of the sites in NE Canaan which served to delineate the E boundary of the Promised Land (Num. 34:10–11). It is mentioned between HAZAR ENAN (prob. modern Qaryatein, c. 70 mi. NE of DAMASCUS) and RIBLAH (an unknown location apparently not too far to the E or NE of the Sea of Galilee), but the site is unknown.

Shephatiah shef-uh-thi′uh (שְׁפַטְיָהוּ H9153 [only 1 Chr. 12:5; 27:16; 2 Chr. 21:2] and שְׁפַטְיָה H9152, "Yahweh has judged [i.e., obtained justice for the innocent]"). **(1)** Son of DAVID by his wife Abital; he was among David's children who were born in HEBRON (2 Sam. 3:4; 1 Chr. 3:3).

(2) Son of Reuel, descendant of BENJAMIN, and father of MESHULLAM; the latter was a family head who returned to Jerusalem from the Babylonian captivity (1 Chr. 9:8).

(3) A HARUPHITE from the tribe of Benjamin who joined David's band while the latter dwelt at ZIKLAG to escape SAUL's attempt to take him (1 Chr. 12:5).

(4) Son of Maacah and chief officer of the tribe of SIMEON while David was king (1 Chr. 27:16). He belonged to one of the divisions responsible for the affairs of the kingdom, serving a month at a time (v. 1).

(5) Son of JEHOSHAPHAT, king of Judah (1 Chr. 21:2). He and his brothers received a very generous inheritance (v. 3). Jehoshaphat's firstborn, JEHORAM, killed all his brothers when he became king (v. 4).

(6) Ancestor of an Israelite family, 372 of whom returned to Jerusalem from Babylon with ZERUBBABEL (Ezra 2:4; Neh. 7:9; the number is given as 472 in 1 Esd. 5:9 [KJV, "Saphat"]). Later, 80 more members of this family, plus their head Zebadiah, returned to Jerusalem with EZRA (Ezra 8:8; the number is given as 70 plus their head Zeraiah in 1 Esd. 8:34 [KJV, "Saphatias"]).

(7) Ancestor of a family of SOLOMON's servants who returned to Jerusalem with Zerubbabel (Ezra 2:57; Neh. 7:59; 1 Esd. 5:33 [KJV, "Shapheth"]).

(8) Son of Mahalalel, descendant of JUDAH, and ancestor of Athaiah; the latter was a postexilic provincial leader listed among those who lived in Jerusalem at the time of NEHEMIAH (Neh. 11:4).

(9) Son of Mattan; he was one of the officials who complained to ZEDEKIAH about the unfavorable predictions of Jeremiah (Jer. 38:1–4).

J. J. EDWARDS

Shephelah shi-fee′luh, shef′uh-luh (שְׁפֵלָה H9169, "lowland"; usually rendered as a common noun in the LXX, but Σεφηλα in 2 Chr. 26:10 et al.). This name occurs frequently in the NRSV, which however does

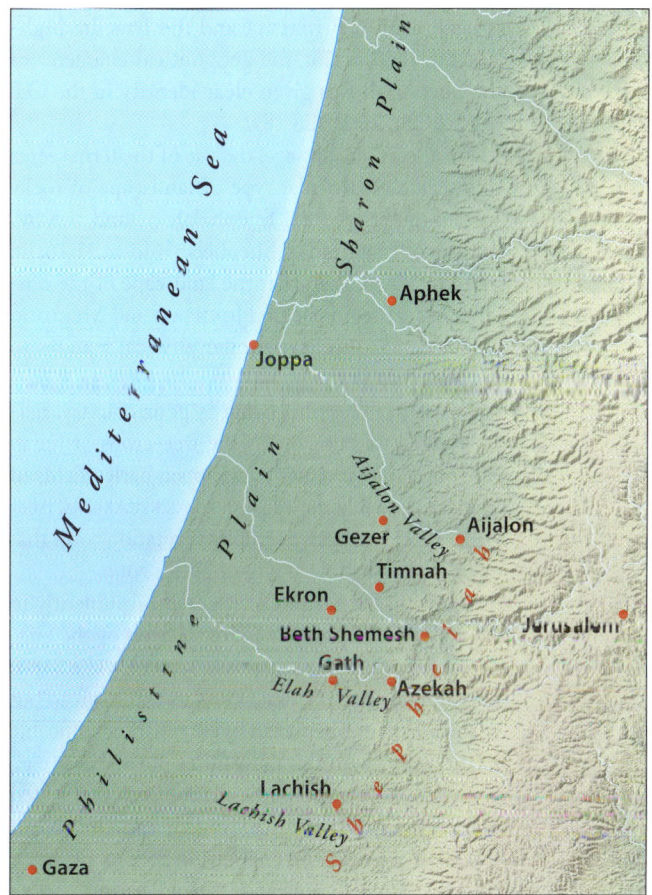

The Shephelah.

not use it consistently to translate the Hebrew term (it is rendered "lowland" in Joshua and Judges; similarly, the NJPS has "Shephelah" in most instances, but not all). The KJV uses a variety of renderings (e.g., "valley," "vale," "plain"), but has "Sephela" once in the APOCRYPHA (1 Macc. 12:28). The NIV renders the word as "western foothills" (Deut. 1:7 et al.) or simply as "foothills" (1 Ki. 10:27 et al.).

The term Shephelah refers to a well-known feature of the landforms of PALESTINE, namely, the low hill tract between the coastal plain and the high central hills of JUDEA and SAMARIA. It consists of hard Eocene limestones that form low, rocky plateaus and hilly swells that rise from the coastal plain to elevations of some 1,500 ft. above sea level. The word derives from *šāpēl* H9164, "to become low," and topographically it is accurate, suggesting the foothills below the main limestone dorsal of Judea-Samaria. As a buffer zone between the coastal plain of PHILISTIA and the Israelite highlands to the interior, the geopolitical character of the Shephelah was given clear identity in the OT (e.g., 2 Chr. 26:10; 28:18).

In at least one passage, the use of the term seems to indicate a particular type of landscape of rocky Eocene outcrops: "the Shephelah ... and the hill country of Israel and its Shephelah" (Josh. 11:16, lit. trans.). This suggests that the landscape of the central CARMEL region behind JOKNEAM and MEGIDDO was recognized to have similar physical features to the Shephelah proper, as its similar geological outcrops testify. The Shephelah is poor country, neither suited traditionally to the tree-crops of Judah (the olive and vine) nor to the open barley fields of Philistia. Possibly the allusion to its SYCAMORE trees (1 Ki. 10:27) suggests a scrubby vegetation cover that helps explain its role as a poor buffer zone.

As such, the Shephelah figured prominently in the conquest and settlement of the land by the Israelites. First, Judah took possession of the eastern hills around BETHLEHEM. Then its clans spread out to the northern Shephelah by establishing amicable relationships with the Canaanites in this area (e.g., Gen. 38). Meanwhile other Hebrew tribes seized the southern hill lands of Judea, and the fall of LACHISH marked the conclusion to this phase of conquest. Only GEZER and its neighboring AMORITE cities stood up to the pressures of the Israelites (Jdg. 1:29, 35). These decisive events occurred during the decline of the 19th Egyptian dynasty, when the central authority over Canaan ceased.

In the northern Shephelah, however, a group of Canaanite fortresses remained untaken: GEZER, Shaalbim (SHAALABBIN), and AIJALON. Several generations after the Israelites, waves of SEA PEOPLES, known as the PHILISTINES, invaded the coastal plain by land and sea. They became complete masters of the S Canaanite coast, from the Yarkon valley southward. Thrusting inland from their strongholds of EKRON and GATH — on the edge of the Shephelah and commanding strategic valley passes — the Philistines penetrated eventually into the eastern Shephelah. The narratives of SAMSON reflect the beginning of this conflict in the Shephelah when pressure was first exerted against the tribe of DAN (Jdg. 15:9–20). The boundary between the Philistines and the Israelites then lay between Ekron and BETH SHEMESH.

The struggle for the control of the Shephelah reached its climax when the house of ELI was defeated in battle (1 Sam. 4) and SHILOH, then the center of northern Israel, was destroyed (Ps. 78:60; Jer. 7:12, 16; 26:6, 9). By the beginning of SAUL's reign there were Philistine garrisons at GEBA of Benjamin (1 Sam. 10:5; 13:3). For some 150 years the Philistines dominated the Shephelah, with their superior monopoly of IRON smelting — perhaps inherited from the HITTITES (13:19–22). It was in this military crisis for Israel that the united Israelite monarchy was forged as a new political institution that transformed Palestine.

The struggle against the Philistines in the Shephelah continued throughout Saul's reign (1 Sam. 14:52). The duel between DAVID and GOLIATH took place in the Valley of Elah, between SOCOH and AZEKAH, where the frontier between Saul's territory and that of Gath was located (see ELAH, VALLEY OF). Border skirmishes are also alluded to, such as the raids of the Philistines to rob the threshing floors of KEILAH (23:1–6). Later, David gained a strategic advantage when he established JERUSALEM as a fortress capital. One does not have a clear picture of David's Shephelah campaigns, but one passage (2 Sam. 8:1) indicates he took from the Philistines those areas that were essential to forming a bridge between Jerusalem and the SHARON

The low hills of the Judean Shephelah, looking E through the Elah Valley.

plain, thus outflanking the Philistines and assuring supremacy of the region. Eventually Philistia was dominated by David by vassal treaty.

The transverse valleys of the Shephelah have been of critical significance in the history of the area, and help to explain the military importance of its major towns and fortresses. These valleys provided links between the coast and the Judean hill country. The most important of these, the Valley of Aijalon, was guarded by the fortress of Aijalon, referred to in the TELL EL-AMARNA tablets as Aialuna. It was fortified by REHOBOAM (2 Chr. 11:10), then subsequently retaken by the Philistines (28:18). The twin towns of Upper and Lower BETH HORON were also in the Aijalon Valley (Josh. 10:10–14), scene of the battle for which Joshua called upon the sun to stand still until the day's work was accomplished.

To the E, the Aijalon valley divides with approaches to both BETHEL and Jerusalem. South of it is the SOREK valley, where many of the exploits of Samson are recorded (Jdg. 16:4). Beth Shemesh, a border town, was in this valley. First set apart as a Levite town (Josh. 21:16) but later fortified, it was destroyed by Pharaoh SHISHAK (1 Ki. 14:25–28) and then rebuilt. There JOASH defeated AMAZIAH (2 Ki. 14:11–23), and then later the area was repossessed by the Philistines (2 Chr. 28:18). Further up the Sorek valley was KIRIATH JEARIM ("city of forests"), where the ARK OF THE COVENANT was kept for twenty years (1 Sam. 7:1–2).

A third valley is the Valley of Elah (the "terebinth valley") or Wadi es-Sant. A significant town here was Azekah (modern Tell Zakariyeh), where Joshua pursued the Amorites after their attack on GIBEON (Josh. 10:10–11), and where REHOBOAM later established a fortress (2 Chr. 11:9). The shortest route inland to Hebron is the Zephathah Valley or Wadi Zeita, with its town of Moresheth, home of the prophet MICAH (Mic. 1:1; see MORESHETH GATH). Here the armies of ASA gained a victory over "Zerah the Cushite" (2 Chr. 14:9). About 1.5 mi. to the N of it, the Romans built the town of Eleutheropolis.

Finally, in the Wadi Qubeiba to the S, Tell ed-Duweir is the site of the military stronghold of Lachish, of HYKSOS origin. It was destroyed by Joshua (Josh. 10:31–32), fortified by Rehoboam (2 Chr. 11:9), and besieged by SENNACHERIB (2 Ki. 18:13–17) and NEBUCHADNEZZAR (Jer. 34:1). In the light of events and the strategic significance of the Shephelah, it may be aptly termed "the buffer-zone of Palestine." (See further G. A. Smith, *Historical Geography of the Holy Land*, 25th ed. [1931], ch. 10; P. Pfeiffer and H. F. Vos, *The Wycliffe Historical Geography of Bible Lands* [1968],

110–16; A. F. Rainey in *BASOR* 251 [Summer 1983]: 1–22.) J. M. HOUSTON

Shepher shee´fuhr (שֶׁפֶר H9184, possibly "beauty"). KJV Shapher. The name of a mountain at which the Israelites camped in the period of the wilderness wandering (Num. 33:23–24). It is listed between Kehelathah and Haradah, but none of these sites can be identified. T. E. MCCOMISKEY

shepherd. One who cares for a flock of SHEEP (see also OCCUPATIONS I.B). The Hebrew term *rō‘ēh* (ptc. of *rā‘â* H8286, "to pasture, tend") is first found in Gen. 4:2 to describe the occupation of ABEL. Later ABRAHAM, ISAAC, JACOB, and Jacob's sons are identified as shepherds (13:7; 26:20; 30:36; 37:12–14). Because of their occupation the sons of Jacob, when they went to Egypt, were not allowed to dwell near the Egyptians, who considered shepherds unclean (46:34).

MOSES was tending sheep when God called him to lead Israel out of Egypt (Exod. 3:1). DAVID was also a shepherd when God called him to be king of Israel (1 Sam. 16:11). The life of the shepherd was excellent preparation for one who should lead God's people (cf. Amos 1:1). Shepherds were known for feeding and protecting the flock (Jer. 31:10; Ezek. 34:2), for seeking out the lost sheep (Ezek. 34:12), and for rescuing those which were attacked (Amos 3:12).

From the idea of the shepherd as a protector and leader of the flock came the concept of God as the Shepherd of Israel. Shepherds themselves first declared this likeness. Jacob so addressed God in the days just before his death (Gen. 48:15). David called God his shepherd in the well-known psalm Ps. 23, as did ASAPH in Ps. 80. ISAIAH expanded on this view of God, who is described by him as the shepherd who feeds Israel (Isa. 40:11). JEREMIAH speaks of God as one like a shepherd who protects his flock (Jer. 31:10). EZEKIEL completes this conception by describing the Lord as a God who seeks out his flock (Ezek. 34:12).

In keeping with this concept, one finds in the OT many passages that speak of the leaders of God's people as shepherds under God. In Num. 27:17 and 1 Ki. 22:17, the plight of Israel without leaders is likened to sheep without a shepherd. Later, the prophets, priests, and kings who had failed God and God's people were condemned as shepherds who deserted or misled the flock (Jer. 2:8; 10:21; 23:1–4; Ezek. 34:1–10 et al.).

It is not surprising then that in the NT we find our Lord described as a shepherd (*poimēn* G4478). He is the good shepherd who lays down his life for his sheep (Jn. 10:1–18). He knows how to separate his sheep from the goats (Matt. 25:32); and he suffers for the sake of the sheep as a good shepherd (26:31). The writer of Hebrews calls Jesus the "great Shepherd of the sheep" (Heb. 13:20). Peter also calls him "the Shepherd and Overseer of your souls" (1 Pet. 2:25). J. B. SCOTT

Shephi shee´fi. See SHEPHO.

Shepho shee´foh (שְׁפוֹ H9143, also שְׁפִי [1 Chr. 1:40], derivation uncertain). Son of SHOBAL and grandson of SEIR the HORITE (Gen. 36:23; in 1 Chr. 1:40 the KJV and other versions have "Shephi," following MT); he was a chieftain living in EDOM (Gen. 36:21).

Shephupham shi-fyoo´fuhm (שְׁפוּפָם H9145 [not in NIV], meaning unknown; prob. a textual corruption of שׁוּפָם H8792, gentilic שׁוּפָמִי H8793, "Shuphamite"). Son of BENJAMIN, grandson of JACOB, and eponymous ancestor of the Shuphamite clan (Num. 26:39 NRSV and other modern versions, following the MT). Both the KJV and the NIV have SHUPHAM, which is the reading of a few Hebrew MSS and several ancient versions. In the genealogical lists of Benjamin there seems to be the tendency toward the use of pairs of names of similar sound with some variations occurring. For example, in the present passage Shephupham/Shupham is paired with HUPHAM and Huphamites, whereas a parallel passage has SHUPPIM and HUPPIM (1 Chr. 7:12). Huppim occurs also in the initial list of Benjamin's sons, but instead of Shuppim that list has MUPPIM (Gen. 46:21). See also SHEPHUPHAN. There seems to have been a trend toward stylization and simplification of names. (See discussion in *ABD*, 5:1205.) H. E. FINLEY

Shephuphan shi-fyoo´fuhn (שְׁפוּפָן H9146, meaning unknown). Son of BELA and grandson of

BENJAMIN (1 Chr. 8:5). Some Hebrew MSS and the TARGUM read SHEPHUPHAM (cf. also *Sōphan* in a few MSS of the LXX).

Sherah shee′ruh KJV form of SHEERAH.

sherd. See POTSHERD.

Sherebiah sher′uh-bi′uh (שֵׁרֵבְיָה H9221, meaning uncertain [for suggestions, see *HALOT*, 4:1651, and *ABD*, 5:1205]). **(1)** A Levite who, with his extended family, joined EZRA at a river encampment in Babylon in preparation for journeying to Palestine (Ezra 8:18, 24; 1 Esd. 8:47 [KJV, "Asebebeiah"], 54 [KJV, "Esebrias"]). Mentioned alongside HASHABIAH, he is described as "a capable man" to whom were committed funds and vessels for the temple treasury at Jerusalem. This Sherebiah is probably the same Levite who assisted in Ezra's public reading and exposition of the law (Neh. 8:7; 1 Esd. 9:48 [KJV, "Sarabias"]), shared in leading worship (Neh. 9:4–5), and joined in sealing the covenant with Nehemiah (10:12). See also #2 below.

(2) A Levite who returned from exile in company with ZERUBBABEL and "who, together with his associates, was in charge of the songs of thanksgiving" (Neh. 12:8, 24). Some believe that he is the same as #1 above, but that presents chronological problems. It is also possible that "Sherebiah" was a family name. (For a discussion of the issues involved, see *ABD*, 5:1205–07.)   M. H. HEICKSEN

Sheresh shihr′ish (שֶׁרֶשׁ H9246, perhaps "offshoot" or "clever"). Son of MAKIR and grandson of MANASSEH (1 Chr. 7:16).

Sherezer shuh-ree′zuhr. KJV form of SHAREZER (only Zech. 7:2).

Sheshach shee′shak (שֵׁשַׁךְ H9263). TNIV Sheshak. This name, which occurs twice (Jer. 25:26; 51:41), is evidently a cryptogram for BABYLON. See ATBASH.

Sheshai shee′shi (שֵׁשַׁי H9259, derivation uncertain). One of three descendants of ANAK who lived in HEBRON when the Israelites spied out the land and who were defeated by the invading Israelites (Num. 13:22; Josh. 15:14; Jdg. 1:10). See AHIMAN.

Sheshak shee′shak. TNIV form of SHESHACH.

Sheshan shee′shan (שֵׁשָׁן H9264, meaning unknown). Son of Ishi and descendant of JUDAH through the line of JERAHMEEL (1 Chr. 2:31). He is said to have had a son named AHLAI, but subsequently the text states that he only had daughters, that he gave an unnamed daughter in marriage to his Egyptian servant JARHA, and that this daughter gave birth to a son named ATTAI (vv. 34–35). Some have argued that Ahlai was the name of Sheshan's daughter (in which case the introductory phrase in the Hebrew of v. 31, "the sons of Sheshan," is a general reference to progeny). Others have thought that Ahlai and Attai were one and the same person, or that Ahlai was the name given to Jarha when he was adopted, or that a distinction is being made between family relationships and genealogical pedigrees, or that the genealogy derives from two conflicting sources (cf. G. N. Knoppers, *I Chronicles 1–9*, AB 12 [2004], 310).

Sheshbazzar shesh-baz′uhr (שֵׁשְׁבַּצַּר H9256 [Aram. H10746], an Akk. theophoric name [cf. SHENAZZAR], though the precise derivation is disputed [see discussion in *HALOT*, 4:1664–65]). A postexilic Israelite referred to as the "prince" (Heb. *nāśîʾ* H5954) of Judah who brought the temple treasures from Babylon to Jerusalem (Ezra 1:8, 11; cf. 1 Esd. 2:12, 15 [LXX, vv. 8, 11; KJV, "Sanabassar"]). Elsewhere we are told that, having been appointed "governor" (Aram. *peḥâ* H10580) by CYRUS, Sheshbazzar "laid the foundations of the house of God in Jerusalem" (Ezra 5:14, 16; cf. 1 Esd. 6:18, 20 [LXX, vv. 17, 20; KJV, "Sanabassarus"]).

The identity of Sheshbazzar is disputed. If the designation "prince" indicates royalty, he may well have been the son of JEHOIACHIN (Jeconiah), king of Judah from 598 to 597 B.C., who was carried into captivity by NEBUCHADNEZZAR. Among the sons of Jehoiachin was one named SHENAZZAR (1 Chr. 3:18), which some scholars have considered a variant form of Sheshbazzar. The appointment of such a member of the Judean royal house as Persian governor or representative in Judah is totally in line with the rather magnanimous policy of Cyrus the Great toward his subject peoples. If the assumption is correct that the two names are the same essentially, then the decree of Cyrus (c. 538) recorded in Ezra 5:15–17 was directed to him and he was responsible for clearing the rubble and beginning the foundations of the walls. According to the historical record he was not able to finish his commission, but may possibly have died during the rebuilding (6:1–2 states that Darius, the next ruler of Persia, again ordered the renovation of the "house of God in Jerusalem"; this second decree must be set after 522). This approach would make Sheshbazzar the first governor of the Second Commonwealth and uncle of his successor Zerubbabel (5:1–2).

Some authorities, however, have proposed that Sheshbazzar and Zerubbabel were in fact the same person (1 Esd. 6:18 refers to Sheshbazzar and Zerubbabel as separate individuals, but this is probably a secondary reading). It is argued that if they are not the same person, then Ezra represents both Sheshbazzar and Zerubbabel as beginning the renovation and rebuilding of the TEMPLE (certainly Haggai and Zechariah credit Zerubbabel with this accomplishment). However, Ezra 3:2, which mentions Zerubbabel, refers to the state of the temple's reconstruction in the time closest to that of the author, while 5:16 refers to the previous decree of Cyrus. Insofar as Darius's decree was only a recommissioning of the previous edict, both leaders were carrying out Cyrus's original order. It is well known that the OT narratives of whatever era are not primarily concerned with chronological analysis.

A further argument has been raised that Sheshbazzar may have been the governor's Babylonian name while Zerubbabel was his Jewish name (on the analogy of Dan. 1:7). However, such a proposal does not take into account that Zerubbabel itself is a Babylonian name (Akk. *zēr-bābili*, "offspring of Babilu"; cf. J. J. Stamm in *Mitteilungen der vorderasiatischen Gesellschaft* 44 [1939]: 269–70). There is additional evidence that Zerubbabel's career is placed by the author of the Ezra chronicles in the reign of Darius.

Although Sheshbazzar is one of the minor characters of the OT narrative, he holds an important place in the continuation of the Davidic royal line, which, after the return and restoration of the city of David and the other covenant sites of his once glorious kingdom, should produce the MESSIAH. The hope of Cyrus, called God's "anointed" (Isa. 45:1), was that the divine temple of the Jews be rebuilt and that the core of Israel's heritage be preserved; both were accomplished through Sheshbazzar. (For the view that Sheshbazzar did not belong to the royal line and thus was not the same as Shenazzar, but that he should not be equated with Zerubbabel either, see T. C. Eskenazi in *ABD*, 5:1207–09.)

W. WHITE, JR.

Sheshonk. See SHISHAK.

Sheth sheth (שֵׁת H9269, possibly "provision, restitution"). **(1)** The expression "the sons of Sheth" is used in one of BALAAM's oracles with reference to the people of MOAB (Num. 24:17). The Hebrew form of the name is identical to that of SETH (Gen. 4:25–26 et al.), but since it is very unlikely that Seth could have been viewed as the ancestor of the Moabites—or of any other nation, for that matter—perhaps the Shethites were a people group living in or near Moab (possibly the Suteans mentioned in Egyptian and Babylonian texts; see *HALOT*, 4:1667). The Hebrew text is difficult, however, and many scholars emend *šēt* to *šāʾôn* H8623 ("roar, noise") on the basis of Jer. 48:45, which seems to be a quotation of Num. 21:28a plus 24:17b. This change results in a translation such as "the people of tumult" (NIV mg., "the noisy boasters").

(2) KJV alternate form of SETH (only 1 Chr. 1:1).

Shethar shee'thahr (שְׁתָר H9285, perhaps from Old Persian *cica*, "bright," as proposed by A. R. Millard in *JBL* 96 [1977]: 485, but see R. Zadok in *ZAW* 98 [1986]: 109). One of "the seven nobles of Persia and Media who had special access to the king and were highest in the kingdom" (Esth. 1:14). Queen VASHTI was banished by Ahasuerus (XERXES) on their advice.

Shethar-Bozenai shee'thahr-boz'uh-ni (שְׁתַר בּוֹזְנַי H10750, derivation uncertain [for proposals, cf. *EncBib*, 4:4462]). KJV Shethar-boznai. A Persian official who joined TATTENAI, the governor of the province of Trans-Euphrates, in complaining to King DARIUS about the Jewish rebuilding of the TEMPLE (Ezra 5:3, 6; 6:6, 13; called "Sathrabuzanes" in 1 Esd. 6:3, 7, 27; 7:1). Darius returned a decree requiring them to refrain from hindering the work and to assist completion of the building, and its continuing services, in every way possible.

M. H. HEICKSEN

Shethar-boznai shee´thahr-boz´ni. KJV form of SHETHAR-BOZENAI.

Sheva shee´vuh (שְׁוָא *H8737*, prob. an Aram. name meaning perhaps "similar [to his father]"). **(1)** A royal secretary (see SCRIBE) in DAVID's court (2 Sam. 8:17). For the variations on his name and further discussion, see SHAVSHA.

(2) Son of CALEB (by his concubine MAACAH) and descendant of JUDAH (1 Chr. 2:49). He is identified as "the father of Macbenah and Gibea," meaning probably that he was the founder of the two cities bearing those names.

shewbread. See SHOWBREAD.

Shibah shi´buh (שִׁבְעָה *H8683*, "oath" or "abundance"). KJV Shebah. The name that ISAAC gave to a well dug by his servants (Gen. 26:33). See discussion under BEERSHEBA.

shibboleth shib´uh-lith (שִׁבֹּלֶת *H8672*, "[head of] grain," or *H8673*, "flood"; contrasted in pronunciation with סִבֹּלֶת *H6027*). The password used by the Gileadites at the Jordan to detect the fleeing Ephraimites (Jdg. 12:6). The narrative describes how JEPHTHAH had just concluded a very successful campaign against the Ammonites without the aid of the Ephraimites. The latter were angered at being left out of such an opportunity to assert leadership among the tribes, and made very arrogant threats toward Jephthah (cf. the similar incident in 8:1–3). Jephthah replied that his call to the Ephraimites for help had gone unheeded. In the battle that followed, Jephthah's band of Gileadites gained the upper hand and held the fords of the Jordan. As the Ephraimites sought to escape across the river they were challenged to prove, by pronouncing the password, that they were not Ephraimites. Each of the fugitives in turn was unable to pass the test and, in mispronouncing the word, gave himself away and was killed.

Because the point to the story is not the meaning of the word but its pronunciation, the English versions transliterate (rather than translate) it as *shibboleth*; similarly, the Ephraimites' pronunciation is given as *sibboleth*. It is clear that the word was chosen because it would reveal one of the dialectal pronunciation differences between the two groups. What the difference was, however, has been a matter of considerable debate. There is no linguistic evidence to support the view that some Israelites pronounced *š* (*sh*) as *s* (even with the qualification "in certain cases," suggested in GKC §2w). The most likely explanation is that the Israelites in TRANSJORDAN (where GILEAD is located) preserved the earlier phoneme *t* (*th*), but that those W of the Jordan (Cisjordan) were unable to imitate it precisely and thus pronounced it in a way that resembled *s* (for the evidence, further discussion, and bibliography, see G. A. Rendsburg in *ABD*, 5:1210–12). If this view is correct, the Hebrew letter שׁ was used in this passage to represent the sound *t* (the latter should be distinguished from the spirant ת [as opposed to the plosive תּ], which arose in later times not as an independent phoneme, but as a contextual phonetic variation or allophone of the phoneme /t/).

G. GOLDSWORTHY

Shibmah shib´muh. KJV alternate form of SIBMAH (only Num. 32:38).

Shicron shik´ron. KJV form of SHIKKERON.

shield. See ARMOR, ARMS.

shiggaion shuh-gay´on. See MUSIC VI.A.

Shihon shi´hon. KJV form of SHION (some editions).

Shihor shi´hor (שִׁיחוֹר *H8065*, prob. from Egyp. *š(y)-ḥr*, "waters of [the god] Horus"). KJV also Sihor. A river described as lying "on the east of [*lit.*, before] Egypt" and cited as the southern extremity of the land that remained to be conquered in JOSHUA's old age (Josh. 13:3). It is mentioned in an Egyptian poetical work written in praise of the city of RAMESES; this document (Papyrus Anastasi III) cites the name in parallelism with *p̣-twf* ("reed-thicket, papyrus-marshes") and speaks of its production of salt and its use as a shipping way (trans. in *ANET*, 471; see also RED SEA I). The identification of Shihor depends on the location of the city of Rameses, which has been identified both with the modern San el-Ḥagar (Tanis or ZOAN) and with Qantir (c. 17 mi. S of San el-Ḥagar). At any rate, Shihor appears to have been an extremity of one of the arms of the NILE, perhaps the Pelusiac or the Bubastite.

This identification agrees with the occurrence of Shihor in Isa. 23:3, where it is in parallelism with "the River" (i.e., the Nile), and in Jer. 2:18, where it parallels the EUPHRATES, the chief river of ASSYRIA. Some have thought that the occurrence of Shihor in Josh. 13:3 and 1 Chr. 13:5 (where it is cited as the S extremity of the Davidic empire) would seem to warrant an identification of Shihor with the Wadi el-ʿArish, c. 100 mi. E of the Nile (see EGYPT, BROOK OF). Since, however, the area of the Sinai S of this wadi was for the most part uninhabited, it may be that these passages simply indicate the extreme limits of Israelite influence.

T. E. McCOMISKEY

Shihor Libnath shi′hor-lib′nath (שִׁיחוֹר לִבְנָת H8866, possibly "the waters of Libnath" [see SHIHOR]). Also Shihor-libnath. A town or stream that served to mark the SW boundary of the territory apportioned to the tribe of ASHER (Josh. 19:26). It was evidently in the area of Mount Carmel (see CARMEL, MOUNT), but its identification is uncertain (the LXX regards Shihor and Libnath as separate locations). Some scholars have suggested locations S of Carmel; for example, A. Alt identified Shihor Libnath with the swamps created by the outflow of Nahr ed-Difleh and Nahr ez-Zerqa, and others have followed him (cf. *HALOT*, 4:1478). Y. Aharoni, however, views that proposal as "impossible" and suggests instead the mouth of the River KISHON (*The Land of the Bible: A Historical Geography*, rev. ed. [1979], 258; cf. also Z. Kallai, *Historical Geography of the Bible* [1986], 176). He further thinks that Libnath in particular may be identified with the modern harbor town of Tell Abu Huwam (part of Haifa). If so, the town gave its name to the river ("the waters of Libnath").

T. E. McCOMISKEY

Shikkeron shik′uh-ron (שִׁכְּרוֹן H8914, meaning uncertain). KJV Shicron. A town on the NW border of the tribal territory of JUDAH, between the PHILISTINE city of EKRON and Mount BAALAH, toward the sea (Josh. 15:11). Shikkeron is probably to be identified with modern Tell el-Ful, some 4 mi. NW of Ekron and a little N of the Valley of SOREK.

Shilhi shil′hi (שִׁלְחִי H8944, meaning uncertain). The father of Azubah, who was King ASA's wife and mother of King JEHOSHAPHAT (1 Ki. 22:42; 2 Chr. 20:31). Because the name is otherwise unattested, some emend the text to read "Azubah from Shilhim" or understand the term as a gentilic, "Azubah daughter of a Shilhite" (see SHILHIM).

Shilhim shil′him (שִׁלְחִים H8946, meaning uncertain). A town in the NEGEV within the tribal territory of JUDAH (Josh. 15:32). It is probably to be identified with SHARUHEN, as suggested by the parallel list (19:6; however, see *ABD*, 5:1213).

Shillem shil′uhm (שִׁלֵּם H8973, prob. short form of שֶׁלֶמְיָהוּ H8983, "Yahweh has repaid" [see SHELEMIAH]; gentilic שִׁלֵּמִי H8980, "Shillemite"). Son of NAPHTALI, grandson of JACOB, and eponymous ancestor of the Shillemite clan (Gen. 46:24; Num. 26:49; in 1 Chr. 7:13 most versions, following the MT, have SHALLUM).

Shiloah shi-loh′uh (שִׁלֹחַ H8942, from שָׁלַח H8938, "to send"; possibly alternate form of שֶׁלַח H8940, which may mean "canal" [see SHELAH and cf. *HALOT*, 4:1518]). The prophet ISAIAH, in the days of King AHAZ, accused his people of rejecting "the gently flowing waters of Shiloah" (Isa. 8:6). The SEPTUAGINT renders this name as *Silōam* G4978, but one should not assume that the passage refers specifically to the Pool of Siloam mentioned in Jn. 9:7; more likely it has in view an aqueduct connecting the GIHON SPRING to the southern side of JERUSALEM (cf. H. Wildberger, *Isaiah 1–12: A Continental Commentary* [1991], 342). See discussion under SILOAM.

Shiloh shi′loh (usually שִׁלֹה H8926, but also שִׁלוֹ H8931 [Jdg. 21:19 et al.] and שִׁילוֹ H8870 [only

Jdg. 21:21; Jer. 7:12], meaning uncertain; the original form was probably שִׁלֹה, for the gentilic is שִׁילֹנִי H8872 [see SHILONITE]). A city in the territory of EPHRAIM, located by the biblical text as N of BETHEL, S of LEBONAH, and to the E of a road that connected Bethel to SHECHEM (Jdg. 21:19). It is identified with modern Khirbet Seilun, 20 mi. NNE of JERUSALEM. The ARK OF THE COVENANT and the TABERNACLE were there from the time of JOSHUA through that of SAMUEL. Shiloh was thus an important religious center for the Israelites. Its location was well suited to be a quiet place of worship. The town was surrounded by hills on all sides except the SW, and pasture lands and a water supply were nearby. The position is not strategic, however, and did not lend itself to defense nor to control of highways and land areas.

Shiloh.

I. Excavations. Shiloh was identified with Seilun by E. Robinson in 1838 on the basis of surface explorations and the similarity of names. Danish expeditions in 1926, 1929, and 1932 confirmed this identification. There were traces of occupation in the Middle Bronze period (c. 2100 to 1600 B.C.), but no evidence of Canaanite occupation was found for the Late Bronze period (c. 1600 to 1200). Evidence was found, however, for the occupation of the site again beginning about 1200 and continuing to about 1050, when Shiloh or parts of it were destroyed, probably by the PHILISTINES.

The Israelites were evidently the first to build extensively at the site. No sign of the shrine that played a central role in the life of SAMUEL was found (1 Sam. 1:9; 3:3). Evidence of a city wall, however, and also of a synagogue and a Christian church were discovered, and these suggest that the site was remembered for many centuries later.

II. Shiloh in the Bible. After the conquest, Joshua first dwelt at GILGAL and then at Shiloh (Josh. 14:6; 18:1). Why Shiloh was chosen is not known, though the fact that it was seemingly uninhabited in Canaanite times may have suggested it as an "uncontaminated" location for worship. The tent of meeting was set up in Shiloh and the Israelites assembled there. Three men from each tribe were selected to travel the length and breadth of the Promised Land and to write a description of it. They then returned to Shiloh, and Joshua cast lots to give the seven remaining tribes their inheritances (18:1; 19:51). Shiloh did assume some military importance for Israel when the Reubenites, the Gadites, and the half tribe of Manasseh built their own large altar by the Jordan (22:9, 12).

The importance of Shiloh as a center for Israelite worship continued into the time of the judges (see JUDGES, PERIOD OF), although the ark of the covenant was in Bethel at least for a time (Jdg. 20:26–27). The biblical writer remarks upon the length of time that the house of God was there (18:31). There was a yearly feast of Yahweh held at Shiloh in which hundreds of dancing girls took part (21:20–23). Some 400 virgin girls had been brought from JABESH GILEAD to Shiloh to serve this purpose, and they eventually became wives to the Benjamites who had suffered tragic defeat and who, through the loss of their wives, no longer had the means to perpetuate the tribe. This annual festival with dancing girls has suggested to some the existence of a kind of FERTILITY CULT at Shiloh.

Remains of ancient Shiloh in the hill country of Ephraim. (View to the E.)

Shiloh continues to figure largely in the religious life of Israel during Samuel's time. ELKANAH, Samuel's father, went to Shiloh year by year to sacrifice to Yahweh. ELI and his two sons, HOPHNI and PHINEHAS, were priests in Shiloh at the time. It was in the temple at Shiloh that HANNAH prayed for a child and there she brought him to be dedicated to Yahweh's service (1 Sam. 1:9–28). The two sons of Eli had largely corrupted the sacrificial system as it was meant to be practiced at Shiloh, and their conduct with the women who served at the entrance of the shrine was scandalous (2:12–17, 22–25). This account has again suggested to some the presence of a kind of Canaanite fertility cult at Shiloh. Yahweh's appearance to the boy Samuel at Shiloh and his establishment as a prophet there also emphasize the centrality of the place in the religious history of early Israel (3:21).

When the ark of God was captured and Israel was defeated at the hands of the Philistines, Shiloh lost its significance (1 Sam. 4:3–4, 12), and the priests evidently fled to NOB just N of Jerusalem (22:11). Shiloh, or at least its temple, was evidently destroyed in about 1050 B.C., but the visit of JEROBOAM's wife to the home of AHIJAH the prophet in Shiloh probably implies the existence of some kind of shrine there at least as late as 922 (1 Ki. 14:2, 4). It was generally recognized that God had "abandoned the tabernacle of Shiloh, / the tent he had set up among men. / He sent the ark of his might into captivity, / his splendor into the hands of the enemy" (Ps. 78:60–61). JEREMIAH implies that in his day the ruins of the shrine at Shiloh could still be seen, and this fact he used to give force to his declaration that the TEMPLE at Jerusalem would suffer a similar fate because of moral and religious corruption (Jer. 7:12, 14; 26:6, 9). The site of the city itself seems to have experienced some occupation as late as the time of GEDALIAH (41:5).

III. "Until Shiloh come." In Gen. 49:10, part of JACOB's blessing to his son JUDAH, we find the Hebrew phrase ʿad kî-yābōʾ šîlōh (Qere šîlô). Rendered "until Shiloh come" by the KJV, these words have been the occasion of a great deal of discussion and difficulty. It seems impossible to give a truly satisfactory explanation of the problem.

Shiloh in this passage has been taken traditionally as a name designating the MESSIAH. The name in this case might be derived from the verb šālâ H8922, "to be at ease," and would mean something like "the peace-giver." This derivation, however, is linguistically difficult. Shiloh is not found elsewhere in the Bible as a personal name, and the passage is not cited in the NT (as it likely would be if it had been regarded as a prediction of the Messiah).

Interestingly, the QUMRAN compilation known as *Patriarchal Blessings* understands the verse thus: "until the Messiah of righteousness [*or* righteous Messiah] comes, the branch of David" (*ʿd bwʾ mšyḥ hṣdq ṣmḥ dwyd*, 4Q252 V, 3–4). The Dead Sea community took the passage to mean that royal power belonged forever to the house of DAVID (who was of the tribe of Judah), in contrast to the HASMONEAN priest-kings who ruled over them. Thus Gen. 49:10 was interpreted messianically before the Christian era, though Shiloh was not taken as a personal name, as far as is known, until much later (cf. in the TALMUD, *b. Sanh.* 98b). Further support for a messianic understanding comes from the various TARGUMS to the Pentateuch; for example, *Targum Onkelos* paraphrases, "until the Messiah comes to whom the kingdom belongs" (*ʿd dyyty mšyḥʾ dlylyh hyʾ mlkwtʾ*).

A second interpretation suggests that Shiloh does refer to the city mentioned above, and the passage indicates that Judah or Judean rule was to continue until it extended as far as Shiloh (or until the Messiah came to Shiloh). If Shiloh is understood as being the center of Israelite worship and therefore as representative of Israel as a whole, the passage would find fulfillment in the prominence which the tribe of Judah gained and in the extension of her sovereignty by David. If in patriarchal times Shiloh was reckoned as a kind of foe to be conquered, this interpretation would be beset by perhaps the least difficulties.

Another suggestion, which involves a minor textual change, is based on the ancient versions, such as the Targumic paraphrase cited above as well as the SEPTUAGINT rendering (*heōs an elthē ta apokeimena autō*, "until the things stored up for him come"). According to this view, the word should be read as *šellō*, "what belongs to him" (i.e., the particle *ša-* H8611, "which," plus *lō*, "to him"). In support of this rendering, appeal can be made to Ezek. 21:27 (*ʿad-bōʾ ʾăšer-lô hammišpāṭ*, "until he comes to whom it rightfully belongs," probably an echo of Gen. 49:10). Thus the NIV renders, "until he comes to whom it belongs" (so also the Syriac version). Alternatively, some scholars understand the first element of the word to be *šay* H8856, "gift,"

and translate, "until tribute comes to him" (NRSV; similarly, NJPS).

Among various emendations proposed, a popular suggestion is *mōšĕlōh*, "his ruler." Interestingly, the Akkadian word for "prince" or "ruler" is *šēlu* (*šīlu*), and "his ruler" would appear as *šayyālô*. Other Assyrian technical terms are found in the OT (e.g., RABSHAKEH; TARTAN), and this may be a possible solution. It should be noted, however, that such terms occur in the OT only in the literature dating from the time that Assyria was in contact with the Hebrews, namely the 9th cent. B.C. and later.

(On the city and its excavations, see W. F. Albright in *BASOR* 9 [Feb. 1923]: 10–11; A. T. Richardson in *PEQ* no vol. [1927]: 85–88; H. Kjaer in *PEQ* no vol. [1927]: 202–13 and [1931]: 71–88; id. in *JPOS* 10 [1930]: 87–174; I. Finkelstein in *BAR* 12/1 [Jan.-Feb. 1986]: 22–41; *NEAEHL*, 4:1364–70. On the interpretation of Shiloh in Gen. 49:10, in addition to the commentaries on Genesis, see G. R. Driver in *JTS* 23 [1922]: 70; J. Lindblom in *Congress Volume: Copenhagen, 1953* [1953], 78–87; O. Eissfeldt in *Volume du congrès: Strasbourg, 1956* [1957], 138–47.)

H. G. ANDERSEN

Shiloni shi-loh´ni. KJV alternate form of SHILONITE (only Neh. 11:5).

Shilonite shi´luh-n*i*t (שִׁילֹנִי H8872 [in 1 Chr. 9:5, שִׁלֹנִי], gentilic of שִׁלֹה H8926; see SHILOH). (1) Descriptive term applied to AHIJAH the prophet, who tore the garment of JEROBOAM into twelve pieces and prophesied that ten tribes would be given him (1 Ki. 11:29 [NIV, "of Shiloh"]; 12:15; 15:29; 2 Chr. 9:29; 10:15).

(2) A clan descended from JUDAH, mentioned in two lists of those who returned from the Babylonian EXILE (1 Chr. 9:5 [TNIV, "Shelanites"]; Neh. 11:5 [NIV and TNIV, "of Shelah"; KJV, "Shiloni"]). If the Masoretic vocalization is correct, these may have been persons who traced their relationship and ancestry to the city of Shiloh and who after the exile resettled in Jerusalem. Many scholars, however, believe that both passages should read *šēlānî* H8989, "Shelanite," that is, descendants of SHELAH son of Judah (cf. Gen. 38:5; Num. 26:20). See also ASAIAH #4; MAASEIAH #16. M. H. HEICKSEN

Shilshah shil′shah (שִׁלְשָׁה H8996, perhaps "gentle" [cf. SHELESH]). Son of Zophah and descendant of ASHER (1 Chr. 7:37); some emend the text to "Shelesh" (v. 35).

Shimea shim′ee-uh (שִׁמְעָא H9055, prob. short form of a name such as שְׁמַעְיָהוּ H9062, "Yahweh has heard" [see SHEMAIAH]). **(1)** Son of JESSE (1 Chr. 2:13; KJV, "Shimma"; 20:7). See SHAMMAH #2.

(2) Son of DAVID (1 Chr. 3:5). See SHAMMUA #2.

(3) Son of Uzzah and descendant of LEVI through MERARI (1 Chr. 6:30 [Heb. text, v. 15]).

(4) Son of Michael, descendant of Levi through GERSHOM, and grandfather of ASAPH the musician (1 Chr. 6:39 [Heb. text, v. 24]).

Shimeah shim′ee-uh (שִׁמְאָה H9009 [1 Chr. 8:32], derivation uncertain; שִׁמְעָה H9056 [2 Sam. 13:3 et al.], prob. short form of a name such as שְׁמַעְיָהוּ H9062, "Yahweh has heard" [see SHEMAIAH]). **(1)** Son of JESSE (2 Sam. 13:3, 32; 21:21). See SHAMMAH #2.

(2) Son of Mikloth, descendant of BENJAMIN, and relative of King SAUL (1 Chr. 8:32; called "Shimeam" in 9:38).

Shimeam shim′ee-uhm (שִׁמְאָם H9010, derivation uncertain). See SHIMEAH #2.

Shimeath shim′ee-ath (שִׁמְעָת H9064, prob. short form of a name such as שְׁמַעְיָהוּ H9062, "Yahweh has heard" [see SHEMAIAH]). An "Ammonite woman" who was the mother of ZABAD, one of the murderers of King JOASH of Judah (2 Chr. 24:26). In the parallel passage (which has JOZABAD, 2 Ki. 12:21), Shimeath is not identified as a woman; the name could be masculine (in spite of the apparently feminine ending), and some scholars argue that Shimeath was in fact the father of Zabad/Jozabad. See also SHIMRITH.

Shimeathite shim′ee-uh-thīt (שִׁמְעָתִי H9065, prob. gentilic of a place name such as שִׁמְעָ H9054). Among the descendants of CALEB (through his son HUR and grandson SALMA) are listed three "clans of scribes who lived at Jabez: the Tirathites, Shimeathites and Sucathites. These are the Kenites who came from Hammath, the father of the house of Recab" (1 Chr. 2:55). Nothing else is known about these clans, and their names cannot be traced to a particular person or place. On the relationship between Calebites and KENITES, see discussion under JABEZ.

Shimei shim′ee-i (שִׁמְעִי H9059, "my listening" or short form of a name such as שְׁמַעְיָהוּ H9062, "Yahweh has heard" [see SHEMAIAH]). **(1)** Son of GERSHON, grandson of LEVI, and eponymous ancestor of the Shimeite clan; usually paired with his brother LIBNI (Exod. 6:17 [KJV, "Shimi"]; Num. 3:18, 21; 1 Chr. 6:17). In one passage (1 Chr. 6:42–43) Shimei is identified as son of Jahath and *grandson* of Gershon. Elsewhere (23:7–11) Shimei is paired with LADAN, while Jahath is listed as first son of Shimei. Some scholars posit two different descendants of Gershon named Shimei (cf. KD, *Chronicles*, 256); others believe that the genealogies have suffered textual corruption. The descendants of Shimei are mentioned unexpectedly in Zechariah's prophecy of future mourning, which focuses on the Levites in general and on the Shimeite clan in particular (Zech. 12:13). "Of two tribes he mentions one leading family and one subordinate branch, to show that not only are all the families of Israel in general seized with the same grief, but all the separate branches of those families" (KD, *Minor Prophets*, 2:392).

(2) Son of Gera, descendant of BENJAMIN, and relative of SAUL (2 Sam. 16:5). When DAVID was seeking to escape from his son ABSALOM, Shimei met the fleeing party at BAHURIM and began hurling stones as well as ugly words at the king (vv. 6–8). David's men offered to silence the insolent Benjamite but the king refused, believing that Yahweh would take note of the affliction he suffered under the tormenting tongue of Saul's house. A bit of the king's faith (or theology) showed itself in his response. God would reward such suffering with good, and he needed divine support right then more than he needed peace with Saul's house (16:11–12). With the turn of events that brought deliverance to David and his faithful followers, Shimei found it necessary to reverse his former behavior. As David returned to Jerusalem, Shimei met him again, but this time at the Jordan River with 1,000 Benjamites; in great humility and penance, he pleaded for mercy (19:16–23). The king restrained his men from seeking vengeance and assured the trembling Benjamite that he would not be executed. Later, however, as David saw his death approaching, he instructed SOLOMON to see to it that Shimei receive the punishment befitting his deeds (1 Ki. 2:8–9). Solomon brought Shimei to Jerusalem and warned him that he would be put to death if he ever left the city (vv. 36–37). Things went well for Shimei for three years, but when his slaves ran away he left the city to retrieve them. Upon his return, Solomon carried out the threatened penalty; Shimei was slain (vv. 38–46).

(3) Son of Jesse (2 Sam. 21:21 NRSV). See SHAMMAH #2.

(4) Son of Ela; he was appointed by Solomon from the tribe of BENJAMIN to provide food for the royal household (1 Ki. 4:18). Shimei was one of the twelve officers whose task it was to provide supplies one month of the year. If this appointment was a reward for faithful service under David, this Shimei may be the same man who with Rei remained faithful to David in ADONIJAH's attempt to usurp the throne (1:8).

(5) Son of Pedaiah, descendant of David, and brother of ZERUBBABEL (1 Chr. 3:19).

(6) Son of Zaccur and descendant of SIMEON; the text notes that he had twenty-two children (1 Chr. 4:26–27). Some interpret the Hebrew to mean that Shimei, Zaccur, and Hammuel were all sons of MISHMA.

(7) Son of Gog and descendant of REUBEN (1 Chr. 5:4).

(8) Son of LIBNI and descendant of Levi through MERARI (1 Chr. 6:29).

(9) A head of family in the tribe of BENJAMIN (1 Chr. 8:21; KJV, "Shimhi"). He is probably the same as Shema son of Elpaal (v. 13). See SHEMA #4.

(10) Son of the musician JEDUTHUN, he and his brothers, under their father's supervision, "prophesied, using the harp in thanking and praising the LORD" (1 Chr. 25:3 NIV and NRSV on the basis of one Heb. MS, the LXX [B et al.], and v. 17). He was also the head of the tenth company of temple musicians appointed by lot under DAVID (v. 17).

(11) A RAMATHITE whom David placed in charge of his vineyards (1 Chr. 27:27).

(12) Descendant of HEMAN the musician; he and his brother Jehiel were among the Levites assigned to consecrate the temple in the days of HEZEKIAH (2 Chr. 29:14). This may be the same Shimei who is later identified as brother of CONANIAH; the latter was in charge of the contributions brought to the temple, and Shimei assisted him (31:12–13).

(13) One of the Levites who agreed to put away their foreign wives in the time of EZRA (Ezra 10:23; 1 Esd. 9:23 [KJV, "Semis"]).

(14) One of the sons of Hashum who agreed to put away their foreign wives (Ezra 10:33; 1 Esd. 9:33 [KJV, Semei"]).

(15) One of the sons of Binnui who agreed to put away their foreign wives (Ezra 10:38; 1 Esd. 9:34 [KJV, "Samis"]).

(16) Son of Kish, descendant of Benjamin, and grandfather of MORDECAI (Esth. 2:5).

J. J. EDWARDS

Shimeon shim´ee-uhn (שִׁמְעוֹן H9058, possibly "[God] has heard"; see SIMEON). One of the sons of Harim who agreed to put away their foreign wives (Ezra 10:31; called "Simeon Chosamaeus" in 1 Esd. 9:32). The distinction in English between "Shimeon" and "Simeon" has no basis in the Hebrew.

Shimhi shim´hi. KJV alternate form of SHIMEI (only 1 Chr. 8:21).

Shimma shim´uh. KJV alternate form of SHIMEA (only 1 Chr. 2:13).

Shimon shi´muhn (שִׁימוֹן H8873, derivation uncertain). A descendant of JUDAH (1 Chr. 4:20); his place in the genealogy is unclear, but he was probably the head of a clan.

Shimrath shim´rath (שִׁמְרָת H8086, possibly short form of שְׁמַרְיָהוּ H9080, "Yahweh has watched over" [cf. SHEMER]). Son of SHIMEI (#9) and descendant of BENJAMIN (1 Chr. 8:21).

Shimri shim´ri (שִׁמְרִי H9078, "my protection" or short form of שְׁמַרְיָהוּ H9080, "Yahweh has watched over"). (1) Son of Shemaiah, descendant of SIMEON, and ancestor of Ziza; the latter was one of the clan leaders in the time of HEZEKIAH who invaded the land of the Hamites and the Meunites (1 Chr. 4:37; cf. vv. 38–41).

(2) Father of Jediael and of Joha the Tizite; both of his sons were among DAVID's mighty warriors (1 Chr. 11:45).

(3) Son of Hosah and descendant of LEVI through MERARI; listed among the gatekeepers appointed by David (1 Chr. 26:10; KJV, "Simri"). Although Shimri was not the firstborn, he was designated by Hosah as first in rank.

(4) Descendant of Levi through ELIZAPHAN; he was among the Levites who assisted in the temple reforms under Hezekiah (2 Chr. 29:13).

J. J. EDWARDS

Shimrith shim´rith (שִׁמְרִית H9083, possibly "guardian"). A "Moabite woman" who was the mother of JEHOZABAD, one of the murderers of King JOASH of Judah (2 Chr. 24:26). In the parallel passage (2 Ki. 12:21), the name is given as the masculine SHOMER, which is not likely to have been applied to a woman. Possibly the final consonant (Heb. *t*, transliterated *th*) dropped out by a scribal mistake. Some have argued that Shomer was the father of Shimrith (in which case the latter passage could be rendered "Jehozabad grandson of Shomer"), but others consider such a solution to be artificial and argue that, for theological reasons, the two Israelite fathers mentioned in 2 Kings were deliberately turned by the Chronicler into non-Israelite mothers. See also SHIMEATH.

Shimrom shim´rom. KJV alternate form of SHIMRON (only 1 Chr. 7:1 in some editions).

Shimron (person) shim´ron (שִׁמְרוֹן H9075, possibly "[God] has watched over"; gentilic שִׁמְרֹנִי H9084, "Shimronite"). Son of ISSACHAR, grandson of JACOB, and eponymous ancestor of the Shimronite clan (Gen. 46:13; Num. 26:24; 1 Chr. 7:1 [some editions of KJV, "Shimrom"]).

Shimron (place) shim´ron (שִׁמְרוֹן H9074, derivation disputed; the original form may have been מְעוֹן שׁ). A Canaanite city whose king was included in a military alliance initiated by JABIN of HAZOR, the purpose of which was to resist the Israelite invasion under JOSHUA (Josh. 11:1). It was later included in the territory assigned to the tribe of ZEBULUN (19:15). Shimron is usually thought to be the same as the "Shimron Meron" mentioned in 12:20; but the SEPTUAGINT may be correct in listing Shimron and Meron as two distinct towns, in which case the latter name corresponds to MADON (often emended to MEROM), found in the MT of the previous verse, but omitted by the LXX there.

Because the name appears as *Symoōn* in the LXX (Codex B), many scholars believe that the original name of the town was "Simeon" (*šimʿôn*) and that early in the transmission of the text the consonant ʿayin was inadvertently changed to *r* (possibly under the influence of the Hebrew name for Samaria, *šōmerôn*; cf. D. Barthélemy, *Critique textuelle de l'Ancien Testament*, 3 vols. [1982–92], 1:18–20). On that basis, the town is usually thought to be the same as the *Šmʿn* of Egyptian texts and the *Šamḫuna* of the TELL EL-AMARNA documents. Further evidence from JOSEPHUS and rabbinic literature leads to the same conclusion and supports the identification of Shimron/Simeon with modern Khirbet Sammuniyeh, some 5 mi. W of NAZARETH and 8 mi. NNE of MEGIDDO (see Y. Aharoni, *The Land of the Bible: A Historical Geography*, rev. ed. [1979], 118).

T. E. MCCOMISKEY

Shimron Meron shim´ron-mee´ron (מְרוֹן מִרְאוֹן שׁ H9077). Also Shimron-meron. See SHIMRON (PLACE).

Shimshai shim´shi (שִׁמְשַׁי H10729, possibly "child of the sun" or "my [little] sun"). A Persian secretary (see SCRIBE) who, with another official, REHUM, wrote a letter to ARTAXERXES asking him to prohibit the rebuilding of the TEMPLE by the Jews (Ezra 4:8–16; cf. 1 Esd. 2:16–24, where KJV has "Semellius"). They succeeded in their purpose; work on the temple was halted (Ezra 4:17–24; 1 Esd. 2:25–30).

S. BARABAS

shin shin (from שׁ H9094, "tooth"). The twenty-first letter of the Hebrew ALPHABET (שׁ), with a numerical value of 300. It is named for the shape of the letter, which in its older form (similar to English *w*) resembled the outline of sharp teeth. Its sound corresponds to that of English *sh*. Originally, the Hebrew alphabet made no distinction between *shin* (transliterated *š*) and *sin* (שׂ, transliterated *ś*); the pronunciation of the latter is uncertain, but it was probably an intermediate sound between *š* and *s* (see P. Joüon and T. Muraoka, *A Grammar of Biblical Hebrew*, 2 vols. [1991], 1:28–29).

Shinab shi´nab (שִׁנְאָב H9098, prob. from Akk. *Sin-abum*, "[the god] Sin is his father" [but see *ABD*, 5:1219–20]). The king of Admah, who joined four other S Palestinian rulers in a failed rebellion against Kedorlaomer (Gen. 14:2).

Shinar shi´nahr (שִׁנְעָר H9114, derivation debated, though possibly from Akk. *Šanḫar* [the name of a region in Syria, but also applied to Sumer] or *Samḫarū* [the name of a Kassite tribe]; see *HALOT*, 4:1607–08). A designation for the land of Babylonia. See Assyria and Babylonia.

In Genesis the name Shinar is used early to describe the land that included the cities of Babylon, Erech, and Akkad (possibly also Calneh) within the kingdom of Nimrod (Gen. 10:10). This was the place where migrants from the E settled and built the city and tower of Babel (11:2). A king of Shinar (Amraphel) took part in the coalition that raided Sodom and Gomorrah (14:1) and was defeated by Abraham. A fine garment looted by Achan near Jericho was described as a "fine Shinar mantle" (Josh. 7:21 NJPS; NIV, "beautiful robe from Babylonia"). It was to this land that Nebuchadnezzar took the captives from Jerusalem (Dan. 1:2), and from it the prophet foresaw that the faithful remnant would be gathered (Isa. 11:11). It was a distant and wicked place (Zech. 5:11).

The references to known Babylonian cities within Shinar (Gen. 10:10; 11:2) and the mention of Shinar as the place of exile (Dan. 1:2; cf. NIV mg.) makes the identification with Babylonia almost certain. In this way the Septuagint reads "Babylonia" in Isa. 11:11 and "land of Babylon" in Zech. 5:11. No undisputed equivalent of the Hebrew *šinʿār* has, however, yet been found in early texts from Babylonia itself. Egyptian lists of Asiatic countries known to Seti I and Amenhotep II include the name Shan(k)har (*ANET*, 243a, 247b), which has been taken to be the Babylonian Shinar (A. H. Gardiner, *Ancient Egyptian Onomastica*, 2 vols. [1947], 2:209).

An example of a Sumerian text, typical of the early cuneiform writing style of the region of Shinar.

Others, however, interpret this Egyptian name as a reference to an Upper Mesopotamian Singara (the modern Sinjar, W of Mosul); such a northern identification might suit Gen. 14:1 but is of itself not evidence for it. An etymology for the southern (Babylonian) Shinar has been proposed in the name *Šingi-uru*; moreover, in late Syriac (8th cent. A.D.) *Senʿar* denoted the land around Baghdad. (For a discussion of the origin of the name Shinar,

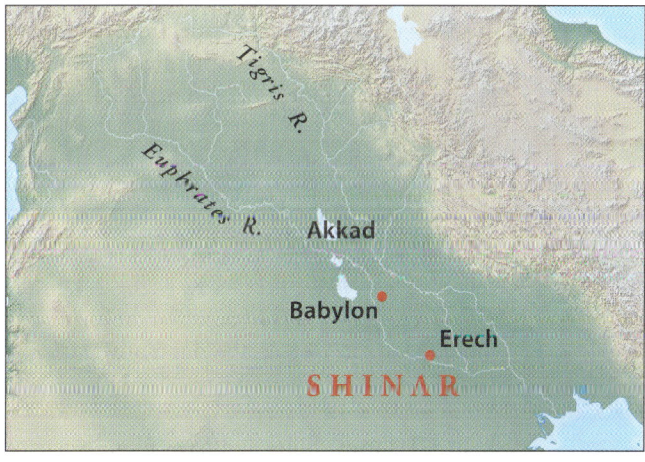

The region of Shinar is associated with the cities of Babylon, Akkad, and Erech.

see R. Zadok in *Zeitschrift für Assyriologie* 74 [1984]: 240–44.)   D. J. WISEMAN

Shion shi′uhn (שִׁיאֹן *H8858*, meaning unknown). KJV Shihon (some editions). A town within the tribal territory of ISSACHAR (Josh. 19:19). Its location is uncertain. Proposed identifications include ʿAyun esh-Shaʿin (c. 3 mi. E of NAZARETH), Khirbet Mugheir (c. 4 mi. SE of Nazareth), and Sirin (c. 14 mi. SE of Mount TABOR; cf. W. F. Albright in *ZAW* 44=N.F. 3 [1926]: 228–29, who suggested that an original *šʾwn* was corrupted to *šrwn*).

Shiphi shi′fi (שִׁפְעִי *H9181*, "my abundance" or "[Yahweh] is fullness"). Son of Allon, descendant of SIMEON, and father of Ziza; the latter was one of the clan leaders in the time of HEZEKIAH who invaded the land of the Hamites and the Meunites (1 Chr. 4:37; cf. vv. 38–41).

Shiphmite shif′mit (שִׁפְמִי *H9175*, possibly gentilic of שֶׁפָם *H9172*). Descriptive applied to ZABDI, an official under DAVID (1 Chr. 27:27). The reference of this term is uncertain, but some scholars have suggested that it designates a native of SHEPHAM.

Shiphrah shif′ruh (שִׁפְרָה *H9186*, "fair, beautiful"). One of the two Hebrew midwives who were ordered by the king of Egypt to kill all male children born to the Israelites (Exod. 1:15). See MIDWIFE.

Shiphtan shif′tan (שִׁפְטָן *H9154*, prob. from שָׁפַט *H9150*, "judgment," plus diminutive ending). Father of KENUEL; the latter was a leader from the tribe of EPHRAIM appointed to assist in dividing the land of Canaan among the tribes (Num. 34:24).

shipmaster. See SHIPS IV.

ships. The most common Hebrew term for "ship" or "boat" is *ʾŏniyyâ H641* (Gen. 49:13 et al.; cf. the collective *ʾŏnî H639*, "fleet," 1 Ki. 9:26–27). In the NT, Greek *ploion G4450* occurs more than sixty times (Matt. 4:21 et al.; the diminutive *ploiarion G4449* is used occasionally, e.g., Mk. 3:9).

I. In OT times. Ships and navigation in general find small place in the OT, save in metaphorical or poetic contexts (e.g., Pss. 98:7; 107:23–29; Prov. 23:34). The "ark" or "basket" in which MOSES was set adrift on the NILE (Exod. 2:3–6; see BULRUSHES, ARK OF) was probably a smaller version of the river and swamp boats that were built of bound fascines of PAPYRUS stems and were in common use on the inland waters of Egypt for hunting waterfowl, for fishing, and for transportation. Long before this time the Egyptians had built competent seagoing vessels, as is evidenced by the frescoes of Hatshepsut's expedition to open trade contacts with the Somali coast (mid-15th cent. B.C.).

The Hebrews generally, who were nomads turned agriculturalists, were not attracted by the SEA and had little experience of seafaring. They had the disadvantage of a harborless coastline, bereft of natural shelter for ships, except where the northern butt of Carmel provided a shelter from the sirocco and southerly weather in the shallow bay where modern Haifa stands (see CARMEL, MOUNT). Furthermore, over long periods of their history, the Hebrews were not in full control of the coastal plain. See PALESTINE III.D. Except for a cryptic reference in Jdg. 5:17, where some maritime activity on the part of the northern tribes of ASHER and DAN is envisaged, Hebrew seafaring was secondhand, and a fruit only of the partnership of the great SOLOMON with the Phoenicians of TYRE and SIDON.

The Phoenicians, on the other hand, racially and linguistically akin to the Hebrews, were the greatest seafaring folk of the ANE. In the dawn of history they had drifted, like other Semitic tribes, around the curve of the FERTILE CRESCENT and found themselves pinned by the presence of earlier occupying peoples to the narrow fringe of coastal

Relief from Corinth showing a sailing vessel with sailor.

territory between the LEBANON ranges and the sea. Accepting the challenge of their environment, they used the timber of the great forests behind them to conquer the sea in front and thus become the premier shipbuilders of the Mediterranean world. Until their maritime engineering revolutionized the building and navigation of ships, the vessels of the eastern Mediterranean had been little more than large canoes or barges. The caïque of the modern AEGEAN is probably the linear descendant of the ships of Homeric times, by which Agamemnon staged his seaborne assault on Troy. The *dhow* of Arab countries is probably, in the same fashion, the descendant of the ships of the Persian Gulf, the waterway where humans first taught themselves seafaring and shipbuilding.

The distinction between the naval vessel, built for speed and ready maneuver, and the merchant ship—slower, more seaworthy, and designed to hold a large cargo, a feature of all ancient maritime history—goes back to the days of Phoenician shipbuilding. The "ships of Tarshish," which find frequent reference in the OT (Ps. 48:7 et al.), were evidently a highly successful type of Phoenician merchantman designed for the ore trade. The word TARSHISH—often thought to refer to Tartessos in Spain, whither the fleets went to fetch silver ore, as they fetched tin from Cornwall—is, according to W. F. Albright, a term from the vocabulary of metallurgy and mining. Does the word mean "ore ship"?

Significantly, it was a Tarshish fleet that plied from the Gulf of AQABAH in the maritime partnership of Solomon and Tyre (1 Ki. 10:22 NRSV). Solomon's great smelting works were N of the head of the gulf. It was also a "ship going to Tarshish," harboring in the narrow roadstead behind the offshore reef at JOPPA, which JONAH boarded for his ill-starred attempt to escape the distasteful journey to NINEVEH (Jon. 1:3 NRSV). There seems little doubt that the term was applied after the fashion of "East Indiaman" and "China clipper" to describe vessels sturdy enough for the distant voyaging and the heavy cargoes implied.

Solomon's fleet on the Gulf of Aqabah was composed of Phoenician vessels, manned by Phoenician crews (1 Ki. 9:26–28; 10:11, 22). They plied to OPHIR (prob. in S Arabia) for gold or gold ore, and possibly to the Malabar coast. The ivory, apes, and baboons that came back with the returning merchantmen (10:22) suggest monsoon-riding voyages to India and Ceylon, and the traces of ancient Jewish communities on this distant coast may indicate that the Hebrew-Phoenician partnership extended to the establishment of commercial agents in the areas touched and served by the trade. For the purposes of this article, the significant point is the seaworthiness of the ships that undertook such navigation. JEHOSHAPHAT's later attempt to revive the RED SEA trade ended in considerable disaster, apparently in the homeport of the merchant fleet, EZION GEBER (22:48). In the divided kingdom, Judah was cut off by Israel from communications with the Phoenicians, and the enterprise of Jehoshaphat was in all probability brought to ruin by Jewish inexperience in shipbuilding and navigation.

II. Boats of Galilee. The boats of the Galilean fishermen were roomy, sturdy vessels, designed to carry a load of fish and also to withstand the squalls of the lake. See GALILEE, SEA OF. The lake lies at the upper end of the trench of the Rift Valley, which deepens to the DEAD SEA down the JORDAN Valley and then shallows to sea level down the ARABAH to the Gulf of Aqabah. Sudden fierce winds are contained and funneled by it, and the storms of Galilee are thus occasioned. It is not known how the boats

This mosaic of a Galilean sailboat was discovered at Magdala, on the NW shore of the Sea of Galilee.

were built, but they could hold a dozen men, and a man could sleep in their stern sheets. An unusually heavy load of fish could embarrass them.

III. Ancient Greek ships. The distinction noted above between warships and merchantmen, which emerged with the shipbuilding of the Phoenicians, was also observed in the ships of the AEGEAN. The earliest type of Greek ship was the *pentēkontoros*, named from its fifty oarsmen who sat twenty-five to a side. These were the vessels of early piracy and early trade—swift ships easy to handle and well adapted to the illegal trading ventures. They took the first Greek adventurers, like the later English intruders in the Spanish Main, into those areas of trade in the W Mediterranean where Carthage, Phoenicia's greatest colony, dominated commerce and forbade poaching on her preserves. The "fifty-oar" could easily escape the Carthaginian galleys.

With the emergence of Greek colonization and consequent commerce, the heavy merchantman appeared, a vessel designed to keep at sea day and night and face rough weather. For the warship, efficiency in swift and complicated maneuver were still given precedence over simple seaworthiness and carrying capacity in the determination of construction and design. The commonest type of Greek warship from the 6th cent. onward was the famous *trireme* (a Latin term meaning "three-oar" and corresponding to Gk. *triērēs*), so called because of its three "banks" of oars. It was light, undecked, and slim, measuring at the highest point of its development, in the 4th cent. B.C., some 120 ft. by 20 ft. The prow of the trireme rose into a lofty hooked post, and it was fitted commonly with a bronze-sheathed ram. On each side of the prow was painted an eye to ward off evil.

How the trireme was rowed is a matter of live controversy. There is a detailed description in a Victorian classic, *The Voyage and Shipwreck of St. Paul* (1848), by James Smith, a veritable mine of information. A more recent publication (L. Sprague De Camp, *The Ancient Engineers* [1963]) gives a useful summary of the controversial theories involved in the arrangement of the banks of oars in a trireme. It is probable that the term "banks" is quite misleading, and no certain theory has been worked out. Coins and vase paintings give no final solution. The ships raised from Lake Nemi, and destroyed by the retreating Germans in 1943, were moored pleasure barges dating from CALIGULA's era and give no help in the matter. Diagrams on p. 82 of the last work quoted above set out the four main possibilities as modern scholars envisage them. They related to the trireme only, and assume, as it appears must have been the case, that there was a rower to each oar. This can hardly have applied, however, to the *quinquereme* or "five-oar." There is a fifth possible arrangement mentioned, but not set out diagrammatically by the last-mentioned writer, which insures that each rower, however tiered, had an oar to pull of equal length with his fellows.

The trireme, at any rate, was the standard war vessel of Greek and Phoenician history. Its crew of about 200 men had cramped quarters, and the speed is variously estimated as four to seven knots. The proportion of length to beam was six or seven to one. The ships were built of larch, cypress, and fir, principally of the third. Hence the desperate attempts during the Peloponnesian War between Athens and Sparta, which filled the last generation of the 5th cent. B.C., to keep open the northeastern seaways, and to retain control of the coastline of the Thracian peninsulas from which Athens drew her vital shipbuilding timber (the British had similar problems of access to the Baltic pine during the wars with Napoleon). Steering was effected by rudder oars on both sides of the stern, a method that was retained until a comparatively late period. In a bas-relief over the doorway of the leaning tower of Pisa built in the 12th cent., ships are represented with the paddle rudders as those in the Bayeux tapestry representing the Norman invasion. They must have been in use until after the middle of the 13th cent., for the contracts to supply Louis IX with ships stipulated that the contractors were bound to furnish them with two rudders. This may, of course, mean a spare one; but we learn from Joinville (1224–1317) that the king's ship had rudders, expressed in the plural *gouvernaux*.

The merchant ship was propelled by sweeps or sails. At first it had one mast which bore a square sail made of hides, and, according to coin designs and vase decorations, a small forward mast was sometimes added to lift a smaller sail. De Camp discussed the question of sailing into the wind, and quoted Achilles Tatius's Greek novel of the 3rd cent. A.D. decisively. There is an account of a storm in which the narrator is wrecked on a voyage from Beirut to Alexandria, including what De Camp properly described as "a landlubber's account of an unsuccessful effort by the crew to keep from being blown ashore by tacking against the wind" (*Ancient Engineers*, 123). The passage is worth quoting at length, as it is germane to the problem faced by PAUL's pilot as he drove W before a "nor'easter," and feared the Syrtes sandbanks far to the S on her starboard beam:

> On the third day of our voyage, the perfect calm we had hitherto experienced was suddenly overcast by dark clouds and the daylight disappeared, a wind blew upwards from the sea full in the ship's face, and the helmsman bade the sailyard be slewed round. The sailors hastened to effect this, bunching up half the sail upon the yard by main force, for the increasing violence of the gusts obstructed their efforts; for the rest, they kept enough of the full spread to make the wind help them to tack. As a result of this, the ship lay on her side, one bulwark raised upward into the air and the deck a steep slope, so that most of us thought that she must heel over when the gale next struck us. We transferred ourselves therefore to that part of the boat which was highest out of water, in order to lighten that part which was down in the sea, and so if possible, by our own added weight depressing the former, to bring the whole again to a level; but all was of no avail: the high part of the deck, far from being weighed down by our presence, merely lifted us higher still away from the water. For some time we thus ineffectually struggled to bring to an equilibrium the vessel thus balanced on the waves: but the wind suddenly shifted to the other side so that the ship was almost sent under water, and instantly that part of the boat which had been down in the waves was now violently thrown up, and the part formerly raised on high was crushed down into the waters. Then arose a great wailing from the ship, and all changed their station, running, with shouts and cries, to the position in which they had been before they moved; and the same thing happening a third and a fourth, nay, many times, we thus imitated the motion of the ship; and even before we had finished one transmigration, the necessity for a second and contrary one was upon us. (Achilles Tatius, *Leucippe and Clitophon*, 3.1)

IV. Ships of Hellenistic and Roman times.

The Hellenistic Age came the closest of all eras of ancient Mediterranean culture to producing industrialization. SLAVERY, and consequent free labor in unlimited supply, put a brake on invention and labor-saving devices, but there was a great deal of basic mechanical knowledge and competent engineering, especially at ALEXANDRIA. This was evident at sea, especially in the growth of the large ship. There was a species of naval race between the Hellenistic kings in the 3rd cent. B.C. References to ships of vast oarage, propelled by great lead-weighted sweeps manned by forty and fifty men each, are encountered here and there. There is a reference in Athenaeus to something in the nature of a dry-dock designed to launch a 300-ft. pleasure barge.

For those primarily interested in the ships of the Mediterranean in the 1st cent., there are one or two sources of information that should be recorded. Wall paintings from Herculaneum and Pompeii, the two towns on the Bay of Naples overwhelmed by the eruption of Vesuvius in August A.D. 79, depict ships that are contemporary with the Alexandrian grain ship which brought Paul from Palestine to Rome. The general impression is that of a vessel that differed little in form of hull and lower portions from the common ship designs of the next eighteen centuries, except that both ends were similarly shaped. The contour of the top of the sides was almost straight along the middle section, but swept upward to some height at each end, sometimes terminating in ornaments like the backward bent neck of a goose; hence, the term *chēniskos* for the stern of a ship (Gk. *chēn*, "wild goose"). In the stern ornament of the ship depicted on the tomb of Naevoleia Tyche at Pompeii, the *chēniskos* terminates in a head of Minerva, a device like the later figurehead.

Isis (see OSIRIS) adorned the prow of the Alexandrian grain ship described in detail by Lucian, who wrote voluminously in the middle decades of the 2nd cent. His dialogue, *The Ship*, opens in Piraeus, whither a great Alexandrian grain ship had been driven by stress of storm. It was on its way to Italy in the days of Commodus. Three friends—Lycinus, Samippus, and Timolaus—are speaking. They had lost track of a fourth, Adimantus, who had slipped away, said Lycinus. "Then we stood a long time by the mast, looking up and counting the layers of hide and marveling at the sailor going up among the shrouds and then running quite safely along the yardarm up there holding on to the ropes." They discuss the elusive Adimantus, but Samippus is full of the size and sophistication of the great ship. He has been collecting statistics. He runs them off:

A hundred and twenty cubits long, the shipwright said, and well over a quarter as wide, and from deck to bottom, where it is deepest, in the bilge, twenty-nine. Then, what a tall mast, what a yard to carry! What a forestay to hold it up! How gently the poop curves up, with a little golden goose below! And correspondingly at the opposite end, the prow juts right out in front, with figures of the goddess, Isis, after whom the ship is named, on either side. And the other decorations, the paintings and the topsail blazing like fire, anchors in front of them, and capstans, and windlasses, and the cabins on the poop—all very wonderful to me. You could put the number of sailors at an army of soldiers. She was said to carry corn enough to feed all Attica for a year. And all this a little old man, a wee fellow, had kept from harm by turning the huge rudders with a tiny tiller.

The rule by which tonnage was calculated was to multiply the length of keel by the extreme breadth, and the product by half the breadth or depth, and divide the whole by ninety-four. Falconer has thus made the ship of Lucian to measure 1,938 tons. Her length, according to Lucian, was 120 cubits, which, at a foot and a half each, is 180 ft.; her breadth one-fourth, or 45 ft., and if one takes the extreme length of 180 ft. as the multiplier, the tonnage is exactly what he makes it: 180 x 45 x 22.5 divided by 94 = 1,938 tons. Timolaus had a conversation with the captain who described the storm which drove them into Piraeus. The passage, like other tales of storm in Ovid, Juvenal, and others, serves only to underline the reality and authenticity of the superbly told storm story in Acts 27, which is rich in illustrative detail.

V. The evidence of Paul's shipwreck. Acts 27 details a most illuminating story. The grain ship on which PAUL's party traveled was a vessel of considerable size. There were 276 people aboard. (Cf. JOSEPHUS, *Life* 3: "I reached Rome after being in great jeopardy at sea. For our ship foundered in the midst of the sea of Adria, and our company of some six hundred souls had to swim all that night. About daybreak, through God's good providence, we sighted a ship of Cyrene, and I and certain others, about eighty in all, outstripped the others and were taken on board.")

Paul's ship was following a northern route under the shelter of the ASIA MINOR coast, possibly because of the lateness of the season (Acts 27:9). W. M. Ramsay may be correct in his statement that this was the regular route from Egypt to Rome (*St. Paul the Traveller and Roman Citizen*, 14th ed. [1920], 319). According to Vegetius (*De re mil.* 4.39), the period from mid-September to mid-November was considered a particularly perilous time for navigation. No doubt the autumnal heat over the Sahara, combined with the continental chill in central Europe, provoked a heavy flow of southward moving air. The shipmaster used this strong wind to run rapidly S from CNIDUS, on the SW tip of the Asia Minor peninsula, to make for the S coast of CRETE. He hoped to sail along its 140-mi. barricade against the NE wind, and made FAIR HAVENS, or Good Harbors, halfway along the coast without mishap. The eastern half of the island is comparatively low, and was an effective windbreak.

Rejecting competent advice to spend the winter there, and no doubt anxious to deliver his cargo to OSTIA, the shipmaster took a risk and ran along the rest of the coast, which gathers itself suddenly and spectacularly into a solid mountain mass. The NE wind (see EUROCLYDON), piling hard against the northern coast of this elevated mass of high country, poured over the summits and through the passes down to the sea with that notorious frenzy which winds so funneled and channeled develop. They were unable to make the more suitable harbor of PHOENIX, which had been the shipmaster's pretext for sailing, and were forced to drive before the wind. The offshore island of CLAUDA gave them brief shelter, sensibly used to recover the ship's boat which, towing erratically and waterlogged behind, was disrupting steering and dragging on the ship. At all costs it was necessary to keep a westerly course and avoid a southward drift into the shallow SYRTIS bay, the oblong indentation in the N coast of Africa which was a veritable graveyard of ancient ships (a fact that promises much for underwater archaeology).

They were probably helped in this purpose as the wind veered when the center of the cyclone shifted and developed a more easterly thrust. At this point "they took measures to undergird the ship" (Acts 27:17 NRSV). Considerable misunderstanding and controversy has surrounded this phrase, and some have tried to prove that ropes designed to brace and contain the timbers were run lengthwise down the ship from stem to stem. If any such "helps" (KJV) were used they were not the "undergirding" of the passage in dispute, but tautened cables run from stem to stern and designed to hold and steady the mast whose straining and levering against the keel timbers might have been a real hazard in such a situation. The "undergirding" was surely ropes (cf. NIV), perhaps a loose network which could be lowered over the prow and slipped under the keel. These would be strengthened above the bulwarks by twisting the cables running at right angles to the line of the keel, until the whole became a taut and steadying net to aid the straining timbers. "See you not," says Horace, writing of the laboring ship of state in a metaphorical ode (1.14), "that your side is stripped of oars, the mast crippled by the rushing south wind and that without ropes the hull can scarcely bear the too peremptory sea?" This equipment was probably carried for such an emergency. The "tackle" cast overboard (v. 19) was the rigging, the sails perhaps waterlogged and weighty. Perhaps the long spar from which the mainsail hung, an overweight above, was likely to increase the rolling of the ship, or, if it could be lowered, was a clutter on the deck.

The ship in which the castaways continued from MALTA to PUTEOLI sailed under the sign of Castor and Pollux (see DIOSCURI), the Twin Brothers who were patrons of sailor men. The electrical discharge which Mediterranean sailors call "St. Elmo's fire" when they see it play around the mast was thought to indicate the presence of the Twins. Macaulay wrote: "Safe comes the ship to harbour, / Through tempest and through gale, / If once the Great Twin-Brethren / Sit shining on the sail" (see also Horace, *Odes* 1.12.27–32).

Other points of shipcraft and navigation mentioned in Luke's classic passage are soundings of depth, and the bracing of a ship against sea and wind by a system of compensatory anchors, a practice still followed. The writer has seen a Greek steamer thus braced and steadied under the shelter of Skyros in the Aegean, with a northeasterly wind blowing hard on the N coast of the island. (See further S. McGrail, *Boats of the World: From the Stone Age to Medieval Times* [2002]; C. M. Reed, *Maritime Traders in the Ancient Greek World* [2004]; C. Reynier, *Paul de Tarse en Méditerranée: Recherches autour de la navigation dans l'Antiquité (Ac 27–28, 16)* [2006].)

E. M. BLAIKLOCK

Shisha shi′shuh (שִׁישָׁא *H8881*, meaning uncertain, but possibly an Egyp. word). A royal secretary (see SCRIBE) in SOLOMON's court (1 Ki. 4:3). For the variations on his name and further discussion, see SHAVSHA.

Shishak shi′shak (שִׁישַׁק *H8882*, a Libyan name of unknown meaning; the form שׁוּשַׁק [1 Ki. 14:25, *Ketib*] is considered the more correct vocalization, for it appears in Akk. as *Susinqu* and *Šusanqu*). Also Sheshonk, Shishonk, Shoshenq. King of EGYPT (c. 945–924 B.C., but dated a decade later by some) who founded the 22nd (or Bubastite) dynasty. Several of his less important successors bore the same name.

I. Rise to power. Shishak's ancestors were among the Libyan lords of the Meshwesh who entered Egypt as mercenary soldiers (see LIBYA). In Egypt, the Meshwesh became the dominant members of a militaristic, land-holding aristocracy. At the same time, they attempted to become completely Egyptian, that is, to adopt the language and culture of Egypt.

Shishak's family settled in Heracleopolis in the NILE delta and, in several generations, succeeded in establishing a small feudal principality. His grandfather was important enough to have been given a royal princess of the 21st dynasty as a bride. (Though nominally rulers of all Egypt, the 21st dynasty effectively ruled only N Egypt, leaving the southern part of the country in the hands of the Theban priests of Amun.) When the last ruler of the previous dynasty died, Shishak's power was such that he was able to assume royal power in Bubastis (see PI BESETH). He gained legitimacy for his dynasty by marrying his son to a princess of the former dynasty. Within five years he had extended his power to include S Egypt also.

II. Relations with Palestine. Shishak's predecessors had maintained an interest in Asia. HADAD of EDOM took refuge in Egypt, probably with Siamun of the 21st dynasty (c. 978–959 B.C.; cf. 1 Ki. 11:14–22). The identity of the PHARAOH who conquered GEZER (9:16) is not clear. J. Breasted (*A History of Egypt*, 2nd ed. [1912], 529) argues that only Shishak of the Egyptian kings of that time was capable of such a venture. On the other hand, a bas-relief from Siamun shows this king striking at the Asiatics, and this has been taken by many as an indication that Siamun was the pharaoh who captured Gezer. Evidence does not permit a firm conclusion.

With JEROBOAM's flight to Egypt (1 Ki. 11:40) Shishak's personal role is clearly attested. He continued the policy of sheltering enemies of the Jewish kings while keeping an eye on Palestinian affairs. SOLOMON's death, the division of the state, and the weakening of Hebrew power are well known to Bible readers.

III. Shishak's raid into Palestine. In the fifth year of REHOBOAM, about Shishak's twentieth year, the latter raided Judah and Israel. The Bible reports only the plundering of Jerusalem (1 Ki. 14:25–26; 2 Chr. 12:2–12), but Egyptian records reveal the true scope of the raid. This record is found on a huge relief in the classical Egyptian stela at Karnak. The god Amun (see AMON #4) and a goddess are shown presenting ten lines of Asiatic captives to Shishak. Each of the 156 captives bore the name of a site captured by Shishak. From these names one learns that his raid extended N as far as the Sea of Galilee; thus he had plundered Israel as well. About half the names are legible and include the following: Taanach, Beth Shan, Gibeon, Beth Horon, Aijalon, and Socoh. There is little doubt that Jerusalem was originally included in the list. The name "Field of Abram" was the first extrabiblical occurrence of the patriarch's name known to scholars.

The raid was not a conquest; Egypt no longer had sufficient strength for permanent rule. However, Shishak still may have aimed at more than the plunder which helped to finance his building program. He also may have desired to intercept the profitable trade routes from the Red Sea to the Mediterranean, and to divert them from Hebrew territory to Egypt by destroying the cities located along the routes through Israel. (See further J. Breasted, *Ancient Records of Egypt*, 4 [1906], 344–61; B. Mazar in *Volume du congrès: Strasbourg, 1956* [1957], 57–66; Y. Aharoni, *The Land of the Bible: A Historical Geography*, rev. ed.

Karnak inscriptions describing Shishak's campaign in Palestine.

[1979], 323–30; K. A. Wilson, *The Campaign of Pharaoh Shoshenq I into Palestine* [2005]; *SacBr*, 158, 185–89.)   A. BOWLING

Shitrai shit′ri (שִׁטְרַי H8855, meaning uncertain [for possibilities, see *HALOT*, 4:1445]). A Sharonite who was DAVID's chief shepherd of the herds that pastured in SHARON (1 Chr. 27:29).

shittah tree. See ACACIA.

Shittim shi′tim (שִׁטִּים H8850, "acacia trees"; see ACACIA). A region in the plains of MOAB just NE of the DEAD SEA. It is probably the same as ABEL SHITTIM (Num. 33:49). Although some have questioned this identification, Abel Shittim is cited as the last encampment site in the record of the journey from Egypt to the Jordan River, while Shittim was the scene of the final events before the passage of the Jordan (25:1–3). If the two designations refer to the same place, Shittim would then be a commonly used abbreviation of the longer Abel Shittim ("meadow of the acacia trees"). While the modern Tell-el Kefrein (c. 5 mi. NNE of the Dead Sea) was previously regarded as the location of the site of ancient Shittim, most scholars today follow Nelson Glueck (*Explorations in Eastern Palestine IV*, AASOR 25–28 [1948], 371–82) in identifying the site with Tell el-Ḥammam (c. 5 mi. farther E). This site gives evidence of settlement in Iron Age I and II and probably Early Bronze Age I.

Shittim figures prominently in the history of the Hebrews. As mentioned above, it was the site of the last encampment of Israel before crossing the Jordan River into Canaan. Here the people fell into grave error, for many Israelites took wives from among the Moabites. This was apparently done at the instigation of BALAAM, who otherwise failed in his attempts to aid the Moabites in driving out the Hebrews (Num. 31:16). A plague in which 24,000 died was the punishment for their intermarriage and idolatry (25:9). It was here also that a census was taken of those twenty years of age and over. Apparently it was a military conscription, but it was done with a view toward the eventual settlement of the people in Canaan (26:2; cf. v. 53).

MOSES learned in Shittim that he would not see the Promised Land and that JOSHUA was to succeed him as the leader of the people (Num. 27:13–23). A successful military campaign against the Midianites was conducted by the Israelites during the encampment, which resulted in the gain of much booty. The tribes of Reuben and Gad and half of the tribe of Manasseh determined to remain on the E side

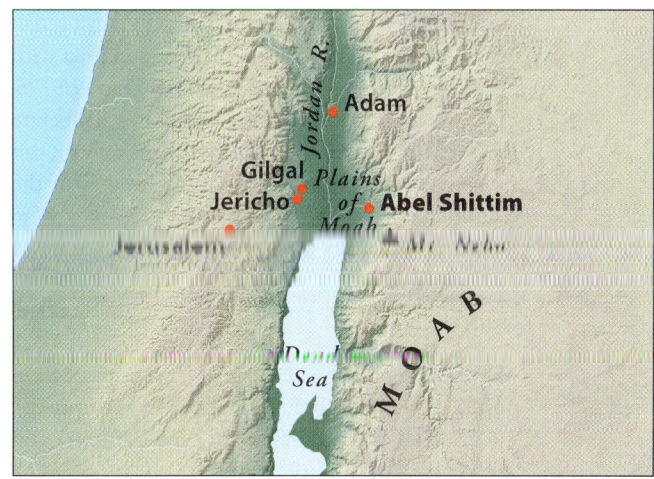

Shittim.

of the Jordan River, but only after Moses exacted a promise from them that they would aid the rest of the Israelites in their conquest of Canaan. Moses delivered his farewell address here, then viewed the Promised Land from Mount Nebo just before his death. Later, it was from Shittim that Joshua sent two spies to scout the city of Jericho (Josh. 2:1), and from here the Israelites departed for the passage of the Jordan (3:1).

MICAH refers to "what happened from Shittim to Gilgal" (Mic. 6:5), evidently reminding the Israelites of the grace of God revealed in the Jordan crossing. JOEL speaks of a fountain that will "water the valley of Shittim" (Joel 3:18 RSV; NIV, "the valley of acacias"), but this reference probably has in view a different location, such as the Wadi en-Nar, a section of the KIDRON as it runs toward the Dead Sea (see L. C. Allen, *Joel, Obadiah, Jonah, and Micah*, NICOT [1976], 124). It may be representative of the arid wilderness that Joel envisions as being transformed.   T. E. MCCOMISKEY

Shiza shi′zuh (שִׁיזָא H8862, derivation uncertain, although Noth [*IPN*, 31, 156] regarded it as a short form of מְשִׁיזַבְאֵל H5430, "God delivers"; see MESHEZABEL). Father of ADINA; the latter is described as "chief of the Reubenites" and included among DAVID's mighty warriors (1 Chr. 11:42).

Shoa shoh´uh (שׁוֹעַ H8778, derivation uncertain). A people group who, along with the Babylonians and others, would be brought by God against Judah (Ezek. 23:23). They have not been identified with certainty, but the name (cf. the verb *šāwaʿ* H8775, piel "to cry out for help") is probably a deliberate distortion of *Sutu*, an Akkadian word referring to a nomadic people who for a time lived E of the TIGRIS and also in the Syrian desert. They were often at war with the Assyrians, but were never completely conquered. See KOA; PEKOD.

S. BARABAS

Shobab shoh´bab (שׁוֹבָב H8744, prob. short form of מְשׁוֹבָב H5411, "brought back"; see MESHOBAB). (1) Son of CALEB (apparently by AZUBAH) and descendant of JUDAH (1 Chr. 2:18).

(2) Son of DAVID, listed among the children born to him in Jerusalem (2 Sam. 5:14; 1 Chr. 3:5; 14:4).

Shobach shoh´bak (שׁוֹבַךְ H8747 and שׁוֹפָךְ H8791 [in Chronicles], an Aram. name of uncertain meaning). TNIV Shobak. A general of the Aramean forces under HADADEZER who battled DAVID at HELAM (2 Sam. 10:16, 18; called "Shophach" [TNIV Shophak] in 1 Chr. 19:16, 18). The attack was an Aramean attempt to reverse two previous defeats at the hands of Israel. The army of Hadadezer had been defeated at ZOBAH (2 Sam. 8:3–8). Again when Israel was engaged in conflict with the Ammonites, the latter sought the Arameans as allies. JOAB sent his brother, ABISHAI, against the Ammonites while he met the Arameans, who fled (10:6–14). Bitter from defeat, the Arameans sent for their forces beyond the EUPHRATES and under Shobach attacked David at Helam. David's men were victorious again; Shobach was struck down and died.

J. J. EDWARDS

Shobai shoh´bi (שֹׁבָי H8662, meaning uncertain). Ancestor of a family of gatekeepers who returned with ZERUBBABEL from the EXILE (Ezra 2:42; Neh. 7:45; 1 Esd. 5:28 [KJV, "Sami"]).

Shobak shoh´bak. TNIV form of SHOBACH.

Shobal shoh´buhl (שׁוֹבָל H8748, perhaps "lion" [see discussion in *HALOT*, 4:1436]). (1) Son of SEIR the HORITE; he was a clan chief of EDOM (Gen. 36:20, 23, 29; 1 Chr. 1:38, 40).

(2) Son of HUR and descendant of CALEB, included in the genealogy of JUDAH as the "father" (i.e., founder) of KIRIATH JEARIM (1 Chr. 2:50, 52). This Shobal is evidently the same that is later called a "son" (i.e., descendant) of Judah (4:1–2; see G. N. Knoppers, *I Chronicles 1–9*, AB 12 [2004], 343–44). Some believe that the inclusion of Shobal in these genealogies reflects an immigration into Judahite territory by the Edomite clan referred to in #1 above. See discussion under MANAHATHITE.

Shobek shoh´bek (שׁוֹבֵק H8749, possibly "leader"). One of the leaders of the people who sealed the covenant with NEHEMIAH (Neh. 10:24).

Shobi shoh´bi (שֹׁבִי H8661, meaning uncertain). Son of NAHASH king of AMMON. Shobi and two companions, MAKIR son of Ammiel and BARZILLAI the Gileadite, brought provisions to DAVID and his men as they fled from ABSALOM and his supporters (2 Sam. 17:27–29). When Absalom's leaders rejected the counsel of AHITHOPHEL and followed that of HUSHAI, David and his followers succeeded in escaping an immediate conflict with Absalom and in making camp at MAHANAIM, where they received aid from Shobi. The provisions of food supplies brought by Shobi and his associates were sufficient to meet David's needs while he rested and prepared for his next move.

J. J. EDWARDS

Shocho, Shochoh, Shoco shoh´koh. See SOCO and SOCOH.

shoe. See DRESS IV; SANDAL.

Shoham shoh´ham (שֹׁהַם H8733, "jewel"). Son of Jaaziah and descendant of LEVI through MERARI (1 Chr. 24:27).

Shomer shoh´muhr (שֹׁמֵר H9071, "guardian"). (1) Father of JEHOZABAD, one of the murderers of

King JOASH of Judah (2 Ki. 12:21). In the parallel passage, however, Jehozabad is described as "son of Shimrith a Moabite woman" (2 Chr. 24:26). See discussion under SHIMRITH.

(2) Son of Hemer and descendant of ASHER (1 Chr. 7:32); two verses later he is called SHEMER (v. 34 NRSV, following MT, which has the pausal form *šamer*, thus KJV, "Shamer"). It is difficult to determine which form is original. Moreover, some scholars have suggested that Shomer and Shemer in this genealogy are two different individuals.

Shophach, Shophak shoh´fak. Alternate forms of SHOBACH.

Shophan shoh´fan. See ATROTH SHOPHAN.

shore. The meaning "shore" or "seashore" is usually represented in Hebrew by the noun *śāpâ H8557* (lit., "lip," Gen. 22:17 et al.), less frequently *ḥôp H2572* (Deut. 1:7 et al.) and *'î H362* ("coastland, island"; cf. Ps. 72:10 NIV). As in Hebrew, so also in Greek the word for "lip," *cheilos G5927*, can be used metaphorically of the shore (Heb. 11:12), but more frequent is *aigialos G129* (Matt. 13:2 et al.). The seashore plays little part in the Bible narrative, mainly because the Israelites were not a seafaring nation, nor was their grip upon the Mediterranean coastlands ever secure for long periods (see GREAT SEA; SEA; SHIPS). The frequent NT references to shores relate to the Sea of Galilee (see GALILEE, SEA OF). With these the Galileans were, of course, entirely familiar, since so much of their livelihood originated at the lake shore. In the almost continuous circle of shoreline towns that surrounded the lake in biblical times, not only lake fishing but all kinds of cross-lake transport (such as wheat from the rich arable lands E of the lake) formed the basis of employment. Consequently, Jesus might be said to have chosen the focal point of the region's life and activity for his pulpit when he went down to the lake shore to fulfill his ministry.

J. H. PATERSON

Shoshannim, Shoshannim-eduth shoh-shan´im, shoh-shan´im-ee´duhth. See MUSIC VI.B.

Shoshenq shoh´shenk. See SHISHAK.

shoulder. This word is used in the Bible both literally and figuratively. In both cases the shoulder is usually shown as the part of the body bearing a burden. This is natural since it is the only part of the body with an appreciable horizontal portion. The ancients carried heavy objects such as water jars on the shoulder (Gen. 21:14; Heb. *šĕkem H8900*). The shepherd who found his lost sheep is depicted as carrying it back upon his shoulders (Lk. 15:5; Gk. *ōmos G6049*). There is an echo here of Yahweh's dealings with his children: "the one the LORD loves rests between his shoulders" (Deut. 33:12; Heb. *kātēp H4190*). Both passages illustrate human helplessness and total dependence on God in dealing with personal sin.

Figuratively, the shoulder usually indicates submission, whether it be to an unwelcome burden or to an accepted responsibility. Matthew, in reference to the unnecessary laws imposed by the PHARISEES, quotes Jesus as saying, "They tie up heavy loads and put them on men's shoulders" (Matt. 23:4). Isaiah relates the Lord's promise to break the Assyrians' yoke upon his people and remove the burden from their shoulders (Isa. 14:25). The early priests were instructed to wear an EPHOD with a stone on the shoulder pieces in which were engraved the names of the tribes (Exod. 28:1–12). This meant that the priests bore the responsibility of the people's spiritual life. Finally, ISAIAH, speaking prophetically of Christ, referred to the responsibility of judgment when he said, "the government will be upon his shoulder" (Isa. 9:6).

D. A. BLAIKLOCK

shovel. This English term usually renders Hebrew *yāʿ H3582*, which refers to a ceremonial implement used in removing the debris from the altars of the TABERNACLE and TEMPLE (Exod. 27:3; 38:3; Num. 4:14; 1 Ki. 7:40, 45; 2 Ki. 25:14; 2 Chr. 4:11, 16; Jer. 52:18). In one other passage (Isa. 30:24) the uncommon words *raḥat H8181* (only here) and *mizreh H1665* (also in Jer. 15:7) are paired with reference to winnowing implements; the NIV translates "fork and shovel," whereas the NRSV has "shovel and fork" (KJV and NJPS, "shovel … fan").

W. WHITE, JR.

showbread. The consecrated unleavened bread ritually placed on a table in the TABERNACLE (and

TEMPLE) each SABBATH. This unusual English term (KJV, "shewbread") has traditionally been used to render the Hebrew phrase *leḥem happānîm* (*H4312* + pl. of *pāneh H7156*), meaning literally "bread of the face." References to the face of God allude to his special presence, as in the statement that "he brought you out of Egypt by his *pānîm* and his great strength" (Deut. 4:37). Therefore the NIV and NRSV use the rendering "the bread of the Presence" (NJPS, "the bread of display"; Exod. 35:13 et al.). The ritual bread in question is also referred to as a "memorial portion" (*ʾazkārâ H260*, Lev. 24:7), as bread of the "row" (*maʿăreket H5121*, Neh. 10:33), and as "continual" (*tāmîd H9458*, Num. 4:7; cf. *maʿăreket tāmîd*, "row of continuity," 2 Chr. 2:4 [Heb., v. 3]). Such language indicates the importance of this provision in the tabernacle. Just as the lampstand (see CANDLESTICK) was important for the OIL that was lit on it and the ALTAR of incense was significant for the INCENSE burned on it, so the third article of furniture in the holy place, the table of showbread, had meaning for Israel for the bread that was placed on it.

The showbread consisted of twelve loaves of unleavened bread (so JOSEPHUS, *Ant.* 3.6.6), each made of one-fifth of an ephah of fine flour. Such bread was usual for honored guests and especially for the king (Gen. 18:6; 1 Ki. 4:22). The loaves were placed on the table in the Holy Place, one above the other, in two columns. They remained on the table for a week, then were removed and eaten by the priests in the precincts of the sanctuary (Lev. 24:5–9). It was sacrilegious for anyone not a priest to eat the showbread (1 Sam. 21:2–3; Matt. 12:4), for the bread was referred to as "consecrated [holy] bread" (1 Sam. 21:6). The twelve loaves represented the twelve tribes of Israel (Lev. 24:8). The Kohathites had the charge over the showbread (1 Chr. 9:32; see KOHATH).

The "loaves" (KJV, "cakes"; Heb. *ḥallâ H2705*) were literally, according to some, "pierced" or "ring-shaped" because they were perforated, probably to permit quick and thorough baking. There is no indication that a cloth or covering was placed on the loaves. The dishes connected with the table of showbread may have been used to hold the showbread; the spoons were employed in placing the FRANKINCENSE on the bread; the bowls served for the wine of the drink offering. The saucers for the frankincense would permit a pleasant fragrance to permeate the holy place during the week. What remained in them was burned on the bronze altar every Sabbath (Lev. 24:7–9) along with what was not eaten of the stale loaves. The twelve loaves represented national unity (cf. 1 Ki. 18:31–32; Ezek. 37:16–22). When the tabernacle was moved in the wilderness journeys, the table of showbread was carried with the dishes, spoons, bowls, and cups that were connected with its use (Num. 4:7).

In the historical books of the OT the first reference to the showbread was in relation to DAVID at NOB. David and his men were permitted to satisfy their hunger with the hallowed bread since they were ceremonially clean (1 Sam. 21:6). All the synoptists mention this occasion (Matt. 12:4; Mk. 2:26; Lk. 6:4). In the temple of SOLOMON a special table overlaid with gold was made for the showbread (1 Ki. 7:48). Arrangement was made in the restoration temple for the showbread through a sacred tax (Neh. 10:32). It is known that ANTIOCHUS Epiphanes carried away the table of showbread when he stripped the temple of its treasures (1 Macc. 1:22). Judas MACCABEE replaced it with another (1 Macc. 4:49). When TITUS destroyed the temple in A.D. 70, he carried the table with other spoil to Rome. Its representation can be seen on the Arch of Titus at Rome, which depicts the triumphal procession.

H. F. Beck (in *IDB*, 1:464), speaking of similar practices among neighboring peoples, points to the component parts of a Babylonian sacrifice, one of which was the placing of unleavened loaves before the deity in multiples of twelve. External similarities cannot becloud the vast differences. For one thing, the bread in Israel was never technically a SACRIFICE. Furthermore, the bread symbolized in simple fashion the fact that God was the source in Israel's strength and nourishment. Similar sacred loaves are represented on Egyptian monuments, but care must be taken not to assume identity in content or purpose.

The showbread is said to have reminded the people of God's supply of daily need for bread and their continued dependence on God's provision for spiritual as well as physical needs. (Cf. the discourse in Jn. 6, esp. vv. 51–53.) Even later rabbinical authorities who added many minute details as to the number, size, position, and covering of the loaves could not obscure the original intention and thrust of the injunctions regarding the showbread. (See further J. Strong, *The Tabernacle of Israel in the Desert* [1952], 41–43.) C. L. FEINBERG

shrine. This English term (from Lat. *scrinium*), meaning originally "case, receptacle," refers in particular to a box where sacred relics or objects of worship are deposited, and by metonymy to a small building where such objects are kept or more generally to any place where devotion to a deity or saint is paid—thus a "sanctuary." The word is used by the KJV only once to render the common Greek term for "temple," *naos* G3724 (Acts 19:24), referring to certain small idol houses made by the silversmith DEMETRIUS. He sold these shrines to worshipers of Diana (ARTEMIS); it was a lucrative trade and one which he was not willing to lose. His opposition to the preaching of the gospel, which had hurt his business, instigated a riot in EPHESUS while PAUL was preaching there.

Modern versions also use "shrine" variously to translate other terms, such as Hebrew *bayit* H1074, "house" (e.g., Isa. 44:13; cf. *bayit ʾĕlōhîm*, lit., "house of God/gods," in Jdg. 17:5), and *bāmâ* H1195, "high place" (1 Sam. 9:12–14 et al., NRSV). In the NT, the adjective *esōteron* G2278, "inner," is used as a substantive with reference to the Holy of Holies once (Heb. 6:19) and here the NRSV renders "the inner shrine" (NIV, "the inner sanctuary"). See also TEMPLES I.A. J. B. SCOTT

shroud. This English noun is used once by the KJV in the archaic meaning, "shelter" (Ezek. 31:3). Modern versions use it occasionally either in the general sense of "a covering" (Isa. 25:7; Heb. *lôṭ* H4287, which occurs only here) or more specifically of the winding sheet with which the dead were covered (see RSV at Matt. 27:59; Mk. 15:46; Lk. 23:53; Gk. *sindōn* G4984, meaning "[fine *or* linen] cloth"). S. BARABAS

Shua shoo'uh (שׁוּעַ H8781, "salvation, prosperity" [cf. ABISHUA and MALKI-SHUA]; also שׁוּעָא H8783 [only 1 Chr. 7:32], but the derivation of the latter is less certain [cf. *HALOT*, 4:1445]). **(1)** A Canaanite man whose daughter married JUDAH (Gen. 38:2, 12 [KJV, "Shuah"]; 1 Chr. 2:3); she gave birth to three sons, ER, ONAN, and SHELAH. In Genesis the SEPTUAGINT, incorrectly, views Shua (*Saua*) as the name of the daughter (cf. J. W. Wevers, *Notes on the Greek Text of Genesis* [1993], 631, 636). In the Chronicles passage, the words *bat-šûaʿ* ("the daughter of Shua"; cf. KJV and NIV) are rendered as the name BATH-SHUA by the NRSV and other versions (but the same Hebrew expression occurs in Gen. 32:12).

(2) Daughter of Heber and descendant of ASHER (1 Chr. 7:32). The LXX reads *Sōla*, and some scholars suspect textual corruption (cf. *ABD*, 5:1225).

Shuah shoo'uh (שׁוּחַ H8756, meaning uncertain; gentilic שׁוּחִי H8760, "Shuhite"). **(1)** Son of ABRAHAM and KETURAH (Gen. 25:2; 1 Chr. 1:32). Some scholars link Shuah with the Akkadian place name *Šūḫu*, which refers to a region near the confluence of the rivers EUPHRATES and HABOR (cf. *ABD*, 5:1225–26). One of JOB's friends, BILDAD, is identified as "the Shuhite" (Job 2:11 et al.), but his connection with either Abraham's son or the Akkadian toponym is uncertain.

(2) KJV alternate form of SHUA (Gen. 38:2, 12).

(3) KJV form of SHUHAH (1 Chr. 4:11).

Shual (person) shoo'uhl (שׁוּעָל H8786, "fox, jackal"). Son of Zophah and descendant of ASHER (1 Chr. 7:36). Some scholars link him with SHUAL (PLACE) and infer that the Asherite clan of Shual had settled not within the tribal territory of Asher but rather in the southern hill country of EPHRAIM (cf. Y. Aharoni, *The Land of the Bible: A Historical Geography*, rev. ed. [1979], 244; *ABD*, 5:1226).

Shual (place) shoo'uhl (שׁוּעָל H8787, "fox, jackal"). A region in the vicinity of OPHRAH to which one of three detachments of PHILISTINES went while encamped at MICMASH (1 Sam. 13:17). The three-pronged maneuver was part of the retaliation of the Philistines for JONATHAN's attack on their outpost at GEBA. Two of the detachments went W and E, while the third headed N of Micmash in the direction of Ophrah. Shual is possibly an alternate form of SHAALIM, the country through which SAUL passed in seeking the lost donkeys of his father KISH

(1 Sam. 9:4). The precise location is uncertain. See also SHUAL (PERSON). T. E. MCCOMISKEY

Shubael shoo′bay-uhl (שׁוּבָאֵל *H8742* [1 Chr. 24:20; 25:20] and שְׁבוּאֵל *H8649* [23:16; 25:4; שְׁבָאֵל in 26:24], meaning possibly "Return, O God!"). Also Shebuel. **(1)** Descendant of LEVI through AMRAM, MOSES, and GERSHOM (1 Chr. 23:16 [KJV and other versions, "Shebuel"]; 24:20). On the basis of the first passage listed, Shubael is usually thought to be a son of Gershom, but if so, he must then be distinguished from the Shubael who was in charge of the temple treasuries at the time of DAVID (26:24 [KJV and other versions, "Shebuel"]).

(2) Son of HEMAN, the king's seer (1 Chr. 25:4 [KJV and other versions, "Shebuel"]). The fourteen sons of Heman, along with the sons of ASAPH and JEDUTHUN, were set apart "for the ministry of prophesying, accompanied by harps, lyres and cymbals" (v. 1). The assignment of duty was done by lot, and the thirteenth lot fell to Shubael, his sons, and his relatives (25:20). S. J. SCHULTZ

Shuhah shoo′huh (שׁוּחָה *H8758*, meaning unknown). KJV Shuah. Brother of Kelub and descendant of JUDAH (1 Chr. 4:11). His place in the genealogy is unclear.

Shuham shoo′ham (שׁוּחָם *H8761*, meaning unknown; gentilic שׁוּחָמִי *H8762*, "Shuhamite"). Son of DAN and eponymous ancestor of the Shuhamite clan (Num. 26:42); elsewhere called HUSHIM (Gen. 46:23).

Shuhite shoo′hit. See SHUAH.

Shulammite shoo′luh-mit (שׁוּלַמִּית *H8769*, derivation uncertain). The name of, or a designation given to, the bride in SONG OF SOLOMON (Cant. 6:13). The Hebrew form suggests that this term is the gentilic of an otherwise unknown place (or clan) named Shulam. Many scholars, however, suspect that the consonant *l* reflects an original *n* (the interchange between these two "liquid" consonants is attested in many languages, including Semitic). If so, the term would be *Shunammite*, referring to someone from the town of SHUNEM (cf. 2 Ki. 4:12 et al.). In this light it has been suggested that since ABISHAG was a "Shunammite" taken to minister to DAVID in his old age (1 Ki. 1:1–4, 15; 2:17–22), she was perhaps the "Shulammite" of SOLOMON's Song. It was common in ancient times for a conquering or succeeding king to take over the former king's HAREM, the background against which ABSALOM made it a point to go to David's harem (2 Sam. 16:22). Solomon, as David's successor, may have acquired Abishag along with other women of David's harem.

Several other interpretations of the term have been proposed (cf. *HALOT*, 4:1442; *ABD*, 5:1227). H. H. Rowley, for example, suggested that it might be a feminine formation of *šĕlōmōh H8976* and thus a title that served as a companion to Solomon (see *The Servant of the Lord* [1965], 228–29 n. 8). If so, the word would be vocalized *šĕlōmît* and might mean something like "Solomoness" or "queen."

H. E. FINLEY

Shumathite shoo′muh-thit (שֻׁמָתִי *H9092*, gentilic form of a presumed ancestor or place named שֻׁמָה). The Shumathites were a Judahite clan descended from CALEB through HUR and SHOBAL; they made up one of several families associated with KIRIATH JEARIM (1 Chr. 2:53).

Shunammite shoo′nuh-mit. See SHUNEM.

Shunem shoo′nuhm (שׁוּנֵם *H8773*, meaning unknown; gentilic שׁוּנַמִּי *H8774*, "Shunammite"). A town in the territory allotted to the tribe of ISSACHAR (Josh. 19:18). Shunem is identified with modern Solem, about 3 mi. N of JEZREEL and just S of Mount MOREH. The town appears as *šnm* in a list compiled by THUTMOSE III (1490–1436 B.C.), describing the extent of his dominion and conquests (Y. Aharoni, *The Land of the Bible: A Historical Geography*, rev. ed. [1979], 160). A number of Palestinian towns are included, indicating the extensive nature of Egyptian control of Syria-Palestine at this time. Shunem also appears as Shunama in the TELL EL-AMARNA letters, where its overthrow by Labʾaya early in the 14th cent. is cited. It must have been rebuilt shortly thereafter, however, for the presence of a working party there, under Biridiya, is mentioned in the Amarna material (*ANET*, 485b).

The village of Shunem, located on the SW side of Mount Moreh in the Jezreel Valley. (View to the E.)

The PHILISTINES encamped here in preparation for battle against the Israelites (1 Sam. 28:4); this maneuver led SAUL to occupy Mount GILBOA, about 8 mi. SSE of Shunem (the resultant conflict led to Saul's death on the slopes of the mountain). ABISHAG, DAVID's nurse who cared for him shortly before his death, was a Shunammite; ADONIJAH sought unsuccessfully to marry her, evidently in an attempt to strengthen his weak claim to the throne (1 Ki. 2:13–18, 22). The prophet ELISHA lodged frequently at Shunem in the home of a benefactress, the birth of whose son he accurately predicted; he later restored the child to life (cf. Jesus' raising of the widow's son at NAIN, which is on the N side of Mount Moreh and thus very close to Shunem). Elisha's use of Shunem as a stopping place on his way from SAMARIA indicates that the prophet ministered in an extensive circuit. (See further W. F. Albright, "The Topography of the Tribe of Issachar," ZAW 3 [1926]: 226–34.)

T. E. MCCOMISKEY

Shuni shoo´ni (שׁוּנִי H8771, meaning unknown; gentilic שׁוּנִי H8772, "Shunite"). Son of GAD, grandson of JACOB, and eponymous ancestor of the Shunite clan (Gen. 46:16; Num. 26:15).

Shupham shoo´fuhm (שׁוּפָם H8792, meaning unknown; gentilic שׁוּפָמִי H8793). Son of BENJAMIN, grandson of JACOB, and eponymous ancestor of the Shuphamite clan (Num. 26:39 KJV and NIV; other versions, "Shephupham," following MT). See discussion under SHEPHUPHAM.

Shuppim shuh´pim (שֻׁפִּם H9173 [not in NIV], meaning unknown). (1) Son of Ir and descendant of BENJAMIN (1 Chr. 7:12, 15 KJV and other versions; NIV, "Shuppites"). See HUPPIM; HUSHIM #2; SHEPHUPHAM.

(2) A doorkeeper who, along with HOSAH, was responsible for the SHALLECHETH Gate on the W side of Jerusalem (1 Chr. 26:16). Many scholars,

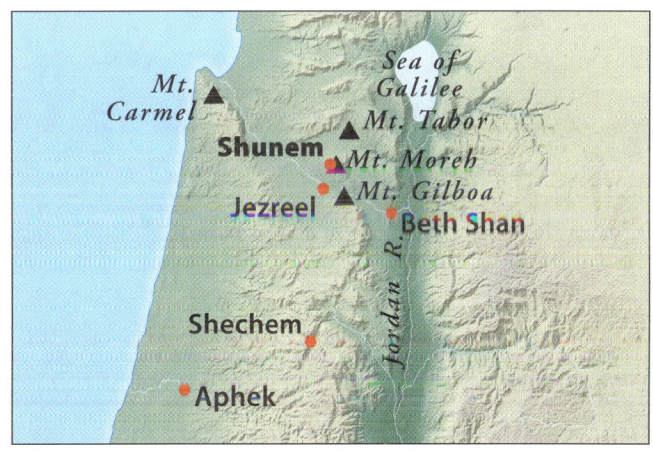

Shunem.

however, believe that Shuppim is the result of dittography (cf. *hāʾăsuppîm* at the end of v. 15) and delete the name.

Shuppites shuh′pīts (שֻׁפִּים H9157, meaning unknown). A clan descended from BENJAMIN through Ir (1 Chr. 7:12, 15 NIV; the KJV and other versions have "Shuppim"). See discussion under HUPPIM.

Shur shoor (שׁוּר H8804, "wall"). A desert region along the eastern border of EGYPT (Gen. 16:7). Because the name means "wall," some have argued that the reference is to a line of fortifications. Reference is first made to such a fortified wall on the eastern border of the NILE delta in the *Tale of Sinuhe*, where Sinuhe says he "came up to the Wall-of-the-Ruler, made to oppose the Asiatics and to crush the Sand-Crossers" (*ANET*, 19a; cf. p. 446a; see also Y. Aharoni, *The Land of the Bible: A Historical Geography*, rev. ed. [1979], 142, 197). This net of forts, set up to keep out the BEDOUIN tribes, is possibly referred to in the account of the ISHMAELITES who "settled in the area from Havilah to Shur, near the border of Egypt, as you go to Asshur" (Gen. 25:18). Similar descriptions occur elsewhere (1 Sam. 15:7; 27:8).

It is more likely, however, that the ancient fortifications gave their name to the region E of it, and it is to the latter that the above instances of Shur may refer. In Exod. 15:22 such is obviously the case, for Moses led "from the Red Sea and they went into the Desert of Shur" (this wilderness area, or possibly part of it, was also identified as the Desert of ETHAM, Num. 33:8). The same region is probably also intended when it is said that ABRAHAM "dwelt between Kadesh and Shur" (Gen. 20:1). The possibility must be left open, however, that Shur could refer to a more specific locality not yet identified.

In the account of HAGAR's flight from SARAH, mention is made of "the spring that is beside the road to Shur" (Gen. 16:7). Such a road was probably an ancient caravan route, the last segment of the northern route of the KING'S HIGHWAY, which came out of EDOM, passed through the wilderness of ZIN to KADESH BARNEA, and reached Egypt via "the Desert of Shur" (Exod. 15:22). (See further C. L. Woolley and T. E. Lawrence, *The Wilderness of Zin*, new ed. [1936], 57–62; *ABD*, 5:1230.) F. G. CARVER

Shushan shoo′shan. KJV form of SUSA.

Shushan-eduth shoo′shan-ee′duhth. See MUSIC VI.B.

Shuthalhite shoo′thuhl-hīt. KJV form of Shuthelahite; see SHUTHELAH.

Shuthelah shoo′thuh-luh (שׁוּתֶלַח H8811, meaning uncertain; gentilic שֻׁתַלְחִי H9279, "Shuthelahite"). **(1)** Son of EPHRAIM, grandson of JOSEPH, and eponymous ancestor of the Shuthelahite clan (Num. 26:35–36 [KJV, "Shuthalhites"]; 1 Chr. 7:20). There are some unexplained differences between the genealogies in these two passages (see G. N. Knoppers, *I Chronicles 1–9*, AB 12 [2004], 463–64).

(2) Son of Zaba and descendant of Ephraim (1 Chr. 7:21). Some suspect textual corruption and delete Shuthelah here as a repetition from the previous verse. Others insert Shuthelah in v. 25; see RESHEPH (PERSON).

shuttle. A device containing a reel or spool, it is used in WEAVING to carry the woof thread back and forth between the warp threads (Job 7:6). The Hebrew word (*ʾereg* H756) apparently refers to the LOOM in its only other occurrence (Jdg. 16:14). S. BARABAS

The Desert of Shur.

Sia, Siaha si´uh, si´uh-huh (סִיעָא H6103 [Neh. 7:47], an Aram. name possibly meaning "help"; the alternate spelling סִיעֲהָא H6104 [Ezra 2:44] appears to be a combination of the otherwise unattested Heb. form סִיעָה and an Aram. ending). A descendant of temple servants (NETHINIM) who returned from the EXILE with ZERUBBABEL (Ezra 2:44; Neh. 7:47; called "Sua" 1 Esd. 5:29 [KJV, "Sud"]).

Sibbecai sib´uh-ki (סִבְּכַי H6021, derivation uncertain, although one proposal is סָבַךְ H6018 ["to entangle"], perhaps yielding the sense, "Yahweh has intervened"). KJV Sibbechai; TNIV Sibbekai. A Hushathite (see HUSHAH) who was among DAVID's mighty warriors and who slew a GIANT named Saph or Sippai during a battle with the PHILISTINES at GOB (2 Sam. 21:18; 1 Chr. 11:29; 20:4; called MEBUNNAI in 2 Sam. 23:27). Sibeccai was the commander heading the eighth division (1 Chr. 27:11, where he is also referred to as a Zerahite; see ZERAH).   H. E. FINLEY

Sibbechai sib´uh-ki. KJV form of SIBBECAI.

Sibbekai sib´uh-ki. TNIV form of SIBBECAI.

sibboleth sib´uh-lith. See SHIBBOLETH.

Sibmah sib´muh (שִׂבְמָה H8424 and שְׂבָם H8423 [only Num. 32:3], possibly "cold" [referring to the water in that place; see *HALOT*, 3:1407]). A city in the territory allotted to the tribe of REUBEN (Num. 32:3 [where it is called "Sebam"; KJV, "Shebam"], 38 [KJV, "Shibmah"]; Josh. 13:19). Sibmah was apparently known for its vines and grapes: both Isaiah and Jeremiah predicted that its vines were to languish under the judgment of God (Isa. 16:8–9; Jer. 48:32). The town, usually mentioned in connection with such other places as HESHBON and KIRIATHAIM, was located in the pastoral plateau area of MOAB acquired by conquest from SIHON king of the AMORITES. The oracles of Isaiah and Jeremiah indicate that Sibmah must have fallen back into Moabite hands.

The precise location of the town is unknown. JEROME (*Commentary on Isaiah* at 16:8) reported that it was a mere half-mile (500 paces) from Heshbon. Modern scholars have often identified it with Qarn el-Qibsh, a ruin on a flat-topped hill some 3 mi. WSW of Heshbon overlooking Wadi Salmah (cf. N. Glueck, *Explorations in Eastern Palestine II*, AASOR 15 [1935], 110), though there is no archaeological evidence to support it (cf. Z. Kallai, *Historical Geography of the Bible* [1986], 441). Others think it should be located farther S.

H. E. FINLEY

Sibraim sib´ray-im (סִבְרַיִם H6028, derivation uncertain). A place between DAMASCUS and HAMATH, mentioned in EZEKIEL's prophecy as part of the N border of Israel (Ezek. 47:16). Some have suggested that that Sibraim is the same as SEPHARVAIM. In any case, its exact location is unknown.

Sibylline Oracles sib´uh-leen. A Jewish collection of prophecies, with many Christian additions, written in imitation of pagan oracles attributed to the sibyl (originally the term *sibyl* may have been a proper name, but it was applied to some ten prophetesses from various countries). The work consists of books that date as early as c. 150 B.C. (book 3, which focuses on the eschatological restoration of the Jewish kingdom) and as late as the 7th century A.D. (book 14, of uncertain origin). Some of the material is clearly Christian; for example, book 6 consists simply of a brief hymn to Christ, while book 7 includes oracles against various nations and may reflect Gnostic influence.

(For a discussion and trans. of the Christian material only, see *NTAp*, 2:652–85. A trans. of the whole work, including extensive introductions, may be found in *OTP*, 1:317–472. See also *HJP*, rev. ed. [1973–87], 3:618–54; J. J. Collins, *The Sibylline Oracles of Egyptian Judaism* [1974]; H. W. Parke, *Sibyls and Sibylline Prophecy in Classical Antiquity* [1988]; D. S. Potter, *Prophecy and History in the Crisis of the Roman Empire: A Historical Commentary on the Thirteenth Sibylline Oracle* [1990]; R. Buitenwerf, *Book III of the Sibylline Oracles and Its Social Setting: With an Introduction, Translation and Commentary* [2003]; J. L. Lightfoot, *The Sibylline Oracles. With an Introduction, Translation, and Commentary on the First and Second Books* [2008].)

Sicarii si-kahr´ee-i. See ASSASSINS.

Sichem sik′uhm. KJV alternate form of SHECHEM (only Gen. 12:6).

Sicily. This great three-cornered island off the toe of ITALY was first colonized by Italian or Indo-European stocks, whose language, not dissimilar from early Latin, suggests that the Sicani or Siculi were part of the folk-wandering of the 2nd millennium B.C. Phoenician settlement followed and produced a wide occupancy of the S and W of the island, especially after Phoenician Carthage became strong and expansive on the confronting African coast.

Toward the end of the 8th cent. B.C., the great influx of Greek urban colonists began. Syracuse was founded in 734 and became one of the major cities of the Mediterranean world. The Greek cities of the E and N grew into strong prosperous trading communities, and inevitably clashed with the rival colonizers of Sicily, the Carthaginians. The year 480 saw Greek victory at Himera, as well as a great upsurge and penetration of Greek culture through the island. It was at the end of this century that ATHENS attacked Syracuse and suffered naval and military disaster from which she never recovered completely. It was inevitable that Carthage and ROME should contend over Sicily, which lay an essential bridgehead between their expanding spheres of power. After Rome's victory in the Second Punic War (218–201 B.C.), the island became part of the Roman provincial system, and the main source of her wheat for over 150 years.

(See E. A. Freeman, *History of Sicily* [1891–94]; T. J. Dunbabin, *The Western Greeks* [1948]; M. I. Finley, *Ancient Sicily*, rev. ed. [1979]; R. J. A. Wilson, *Sicily under the Roman Empire: The Archaeology of a Roman Province, 36 BC–AD 535* [1990]; C. Smith and J. Serrati, eds., *Sicily from Aeneas to Augustus: New Approaches in Archaeology and History* [2000].)   E. M. BLAIKLOCK

sick, sickness. See DISEASE.

sickle. A curved cutting tool for harvesting grain. One Hebrew word for "sickle" (*ḥermēš H3058*) occurs in Deut. 16:9 and 23:25 (by emendation also in 1 Sam. 13:20, where the MT has *maḥărēšâ H4739*, "plowshare"). The other one (*maggāl H4478*) is found in Jer. 50:16 and Joel 3:13. The NT word (Gk. *drepanon G1535*) occurs in Mk. 4:29 and Rev. 14:14–19. In usage the NT follows the Joel passage in presenting the sickle as the instrument of divine WRATH and FULFILLMENT.   W. WHITE, JR.

Sicyon sish′ee-uhn (Σικυών [with orthographic variants], "cucumber [town]"). An ancient Greek city in the northern Peloponnesus, c. 11 mi. NW of CORINTH, located in a fertile plain c. 2 mi. from the sea. Sicyon was founded from Argos and was under its domination until it gained its independence by Orthagoras c. 660 B.C.; it was then ruled by tyrants for more than a century, reaching its greatest power under Cleisthenes. In the Peloponnesian War (431–404) it was an ally of Sparta, and in 251 it became a democracy under the leadership of Aratus and was given an important place in the Achaian Confederacy.

From the 6th to the 3rd cent. Sicyon was famous for its painting, sculpture, and pottery (Pliny the Elder, *Natural History* 35.151–52) as well as for its industrial skills in all kinds of manufacturing (Strabo, *Geogr.* 8.6.23). In 146 B.C., when the Romans destroyed Corinth, Sicyon inherited the Corinthian territory and the Isthmian Games. In 139 it was among the list of places to which the Roman consul LUCIUS wrote in behalf of the senate, begging them to be friendly to the Jews and to deliver all Jewish fugitives to SIMON MACCABEE (1 Macc. 15:23). That a considerable number of Jews resided in this area is confirmed by PHILO JUDAEUS (*Legatio ad Gaium* 281; *In Flaccum* 46). (See further C. H. Skalet, *Ancient Sicyon* [1928]; A. Andrewes, *The Greek Tyrants* [1956], 54–61; R. and K. Cook, *Southern Greece: An Archaeological Guide* [1968], 107–8; A. Griffin, *Sikyon* [1982].)

H. W. HOEHNER

Siddim, Valley of sid′im (שִׂדִּים *H8443*, derivation uncertain). A place identified with the "Salt Sea" where KEDORLAOMER and his allies defeated the kings of SODOM, GOMORRAH, and the other cities of the Jordan pentapolis (Gen. 14:3, 8, 10). The armies apparently followed the KING'S HIGHWAY in TRANSJORDAN to the field of battle somewhere in the locality of the DEAD SEA. J. P. Harland (in *BA* 5 [1942]: 17–32) suggested Siddim was the plain

S of el-Lisan, which has been down-faulted and submerged beneath the lake. Certainly, the lake terrain around the shores of the Dead Sea indicate that as a consequence of climatic oscillations, drainage evolution, and faulting, possibly twenty-five distinct lake levels have occurred in the trough since Pleistocene times. The exact locale of the Valley of Siddim remains speculative. J. M. Houston

Side si′dee (Σίδη). A city in Pamphylia to which a letter favoring the Jews and requesting the return of Jewish renegades who had fled there was sent by the Roman consul Lucius in 139 B.C. (1 Macc. 15:23). Side was located near the mouth of the river Eurymedon, at the site of the modern Eski Adalia. It was occupied by Alexander the Great and later was the site of the sea battle between the naval forces of Rhodes and the fleet of Antiochus the Great, in which Antiochus was defeated. Early in the 1st cent. it was the base for activity by Cilician pirates.

Side was particularly known for its harbor complex, which is still distinguishable. The ruins, extant today on the original promontory of the city, consist of a wall separating it from the mainland, several protective fortifications, and a theater of characteristically Roman construction. Evidence has been found of an extensive Jewish population in Byzantine times. (See G. E. Bean in *The Princeton Encyclopedia of Classical Sites*, ed. R. Stillwell et al. [1976]: 835–36; id. in *OCD*, 1404.) T. E. McComiskey

Sidon si′duhn (צִידוֹן H7477, possibly "fishing town"; gentilic צִידֹנִי H7479, "Sidonian"). KJV Zidon (Sidon in Gen. 10:15, 19, and NT). The first biblical occurrence of this name is in reference to the firstborn son of Canaan (Gen. 10:15 = 1 Chr. 1:13), but elsewhere it designates an important coastal city-state of Phoenicia. As a geographical term, it first occurs in Gen. 10:19 in a description of the territory of the Canaanites, which is said to have extended from Sidon to the S as far as Gaza. Jacob prophesied that the territory of Zebulun would reach all the way to Sidon (49:13; cf. Josh. 19:28). The city is mentioned at various points in the historical books of the OT (Josh. 11:8; Jdg. 1:31; 10:6; 18:28; 2 Sam. 24:6; 1 Ki. 17:9; Ezra 3:7) and figures in a number of prophetic oracles (Isa. 23:2–12; Ezek. 28:21–22 et al.).

Sometimes in the OT (Jer. 25:22 et al.), and often in the NT, Sidon is combined with Tyre, almost as a formula. One visit by Jesus to the region of Tyre and Sidon is recorded in the Gospels, at which time he had the encounter with the Syrophoenician woman (Matt. 15:21–28). This is the only recorded instance in the ministry of Jesus that he went outside the boundaries of Palestine. In his invectives upon the cities of Galilee, Jesus compared Korazin and Bethsaida to Tyre and Sidon and declared that the latter cities would have responded more quickly than the former (Matt. 11:21–22; Lk. 10:13–14). The people of Tyre and Sidon were involved in difficulties with Herod Agrippa at the time of his death (Acts 12:20). On Paul's shipwreck voyage to Rome a port call was made at Sidon (27:3).

The modern Lebanese city of Sidon is built over the ruins of the ancient city, also known as Saida. It is located about 28 mi. SSW of Beirut and about 25 mi. N of Tyre. On the N side of the city there was a good harbor, protected by a low line of rocks joining the promontory and the mainland. To the S of the city there was a large bay.

The ancient history of Sidon is closely related to that of the Phoenicians generally, an aggressive sea-faring people on the eastern Mediterranean coast. Sidon was one of the four most important towns of the Phoenicians—the other three being Aradus in the N (almost directly E of Cyprus), Byblos (Gebal, c. 28 mi. N of Beirut), and Tyre

Limestone foundation inscription from the Eshmun temple in Sidon (6th cent. B.C.). The Phoenician text reads: "Bodastarte, the son of Eshmunazar, the king of Sidon, has ordered this temple to be built for the god Eshmun."

in the S. Each of these cities was a more or less independent political unit, its immediate territory forming its kingdom. Occasionally some cities would have control over some neighboring territories, but they never fully united into a confederacy or nation.

During the 2nd millennium B.C. and the first half of the 1st millennium, Sidon was somewhat under the shadow of Tyre politically. Egyptian inscriptions of the 16th cent. mention Tyre and Sidon by name. In the TELL EL-AMARNA letters (1370–1348 B.C.) a king of Sidon named Zimreda is mentioned (no. 147; see *ANET*, 484). Under TIGLATH-PILESER I (1114–1076), the Assyrians made an expedition to the Mediterranean coast and received tribute from Byblos, Sidon, and Arvad (*ANET*, 275). HIRAM was king of Tyre at the time of DAVID and SOLOMON, and provided workmen and material to Solomon for the construction of the TEMPLE in Jerusalem (2 Chr. 2). He also assisted Solomon in the development of RED SEA trade (2 Chr. 8:17; cf. 1 Ki. 9:26–28; 10:11).

In the 9th cent. B.C., the Assyrians had control over a number of Phoenician cities. ASHURNASIRPAL II (883–859) received tribute from Tyre, Sidon, Byblos, and other cities consisting of gold, silver, tin, copper, linen garments, ebony, boxwood, ivory (*ANET*, 276). SHALMANESER III (858–824) also received tribute from the "countries of the inhabitants of Tyre, Sidon, and Byblos" in his twenty-first year (*ANET*, 280). A century later SENNACHERIB (704–681) in his third campaign marched against Luli, king of Sidon, and in his annals boasted about his complete rout of the Sidonian monarch, who fled to Cyprus where he died (*ANET*, 287–88). Sennacherib placed ETHBAAL on the Sidonian throne and exacted tribute from the land.

Later, Abdimilkutte became king of Sidon and refused to recognize the authority of the Assyrian king ESARHADDON (680–669), or to comply with his severe economic demands. Esarhaddon, however, in a battle in 677–676 destroyed Sidon, and the Sidonian king was killed at sea. The Assyrians took much booty—all the riches of the city and many subjects captive. With the help of neighboring peoples, Esarhaddon built a new city on a new location which he called Kar-Esarhaddon (*ANET*, 291). This Assyrian commercial colony was to replace the Phoenician merchant cities in handling Assyrian trade on the Mediterranean coast. Nevertheless, the Assyrians were never able to subjugate completely all the cities of the Phoenicians.

The first eastern king to gain complete control of the Phoenician territory was NEBUCHADNEZZAR II (605–562), in whose court the king of Sidon was a "subject" (*ANET*, 308). His destruction of the power of Tyre in 574 made Sidon the leading city of the area. Under the Persians, Sidon was a major city and the seat of a palace of the Persian king. Sidon gained a measure of independence in the 5th cent., as suggested by the inscription of the coffin of Eshmunazar (now in the Louvre), which reports that he added the Philistine cities of DOR and JOPPA to his kingdom. With the Greek conquest under ALEXANDER THE GREAT, epitomized in his spectacular siege of Tyre, the Phoenician cities became Greek and subsequently Roman in character and culture.

The skill of the artisans of Sidon is well attested in ancient times. The carving of IVORY to decorate furniture, architecture, and small objects was a flourishing industry in Sidon. The Assyrian documents record great quantities of ivory articles sent to the Assyrian kings as gifts and tribute. Homer lists one of the prizes at the funeral games of Patrocles as a beautiful Sidonian silver bowl (*Iliad* 23.741ff.). Such trade in ancient times reflects an extensive Sidonian influence in E and W.

The chief god of the Sidonians was Eshmun, and of the Tyrians, Melqart. These two were part of the familiar ANE FERTILITY CULT and harvest myth, represented in Babylonia as ISHTAR and TAMMUZ, in Egypt as Isis and Osiris. Eshmun also became the chief god of Carthage.

Unfortunately, the modern Sidon is built largely over the ruins of the ancient city, making any extensive and systematic excavation of the site very difficult. It is hoped that the increased archaeological investigation along the Phoenician coast may reveal more of the past history of Phoenicia, and of some of her major cities. (See further F. Eiselen, *Sidon: A Study in Oriental History* [1907]; N. Jidejian, *Sidon through the Ages* [1971]; R. Saïdah, *Sidon et la Phénicie Méridionale au Bronze Récent: à propos des tombes de Dakerman* [2004].)

B. VAN ELDEREN

siege. See WAR, WARFARE V.

sign. An unusual phenomenon interpreted as of supernatural origin and designed to provide instruction, give warning, or encourage faith. In this sense it is a rough synonym of MIRACLE.

    I. Vocabulary
        A. In the OT
        B. In the Septuagint
        C. In the NT
    II. Meanings
        A. Portents, prodigies
        B. Supernatural acts
        C. A basis for faith
    III. Significance

I. Vocabulary

A. In the OT. The term *sign* in contemporary English and in the English versions of the Scriptures has a great variety of meanings ("distinguishing mark, token, symbol," etc.—see also SYMBOLISM). The same is true of the biblical languages; in the OT there are five different terms with very similar meanings. The most common of these is *ʾôt* H253. In addition to its general sense (Gen. 1:14; 9:12; 17:22 et al.), it is used to designate the prodigies or wonders by which MOSES sought to convince PHARAOH that he was sent of God (Exod. 4:8–30). The great plagues which accompanied the exodus of the Israelites from Egypt are also described with this term (Exod. 7:3; 8:23; 10:1–2, 19:9). See EXODUS, THE; PLAGUES OF EGYPT. The same term is used in describing the means by which SAUL was certified to be the man of God's choice (1 Sam. 10:7, 9).

A term with which the foregoing is often linked is *môpēt* H4603, usually translated "wonder." The two words occur together, especially in the book of Deuteronomy, and are practically synonymous (Deut. 4:34; 6:22 et al.). A similar combination appears repeatedly in the NT (esp. the book of Acts, e.g., Acts 2:19, 22, 43); in general it is used to designate deeds by which God makes known his purpose and his power. Also translated "wonder(s)" or the like are *niplāʾôt* (niphal fem. pl. ptc. of *pālāʾ* H7098, Exod. 3:20 et al.) and its cognate noun *peleʾ* H7099 (15:11 et al.).

B. In the Septuagint. The Hebrew term *ʾôt* is rendered by the SEPTUAGINT with *sēmeion* G4956, a word that already in classical Greek could be used in the sense of "omen" (i.e., "sign from the gods"). And as the Hebrew term is often combined with *môpēt*, so is *sēmeion* linked with *teras* G5469, "signs and wonders." This combination occurs so frequently in both OT and NT that its use is idiomatic. The idiom is not limited to canonical literature. It is used, for example, in Jewish Hellenistic writings (e.g., Wisd. 8:8; 10:16; Philo, *Moses* 1.95; Jos. *Ant*. 20.8.6) and even by pagan authors (as early as Polybius, *Hist*. 3.112.8; more examples in BDAG, 920). Here as elsewhere, the LXX is the literary bridge between the OT and NT.

C. In the NT. In addition to the two Greek terms already mentioned, the NT often uses the common word for "power," *dynamis* G1539, with reference to miraculous deeds (esp. in the pl., Matt. 11:20–23 et al.; in combination with *sēmeion*, Acts 2:22 et al.). Similarly, the noun *ergon* G2240 ("work, deed") can be used of the miracles performed by God and Jesus (esp. in the Gospel of John, e.g., Jn. 7:3; 9:3).

II. Meanings

A. Portents, prodigies. Even the sophisticated Romans and Greeks were superstitious and were often awed by supernatural portents or prodigies that were believed to foretell coming events. Julius CAESAR is reported to have seen certain of these on the morning of his assassination. JOSEPHUS reports similar omens preceding the destruction of Jerusalem, A.D. 70. These people for the most part were God-fearers in the sense that they were afraid of the supernatural and looked eagerly for indications of the divine will and of future events in a prescientific age. Many natural phenomena were explained on the basis of supernatural agencies which priests, soothsayers, or ordinary citizens sought to interpret. PLUTARCH, for example, speaks of a monstrous birth as "a sign and a wonder" (*sēmeion esti kai teras, Sept. sap. con.* 3 [149.C]). It is applied to a freak of nature rather than to a supernatural event with religious significance.

In the OT certain messages indicate that one meaning of the term is in the nature of prodigies, portents, or omens (Ezek. 12:6; Dan. 4:2–3; 6:27). King AHAZ was offered a token of divine will (Isa. 7:10, 14; 8:18; 19:20; 20:3). HEZEKIAH asked and was granted similar tokens (Isa. 37:30; 38:7, 22). These were not miracles in the ordinary sense but were simply phenomena, supernatural in origin, which lent authenticity to the prophet's statement and served to strengthen the confidence of the skeptical and ignorant. The "sign" in such contexts is one means by which God communicates his thought to human beings and thus indicates his will. GIDEON, for example, obtained assurance and confirmation of God's directives through signs (Jdg. 6:17–22 et al.).

The same connotation of portent or omen is seen in NT usage, as when the Jews sought for a sign (Matt. 12:38) and the Master attributed their request to lack of real faith (12:39; cf. 16:1–4; 24:3). Sometimes it may indicate simply a means of identification (26:48). Repeatedly a demand for evidence of this kind is discouraged in the NT. It is regarded as an alibi to justify unbelief and was seldom, if ever, gratified. PAUL declared this desire for a "sign" to be characteristic of the Jews (1 Cor. 1:22; cf. 14:22). The story of LAZARUS AND DIVES teaches that more impressive "signs" are not a cure for unbelief; that even if one returned from the dead he could not effectively preach repentance (Lk. 16:31).

B. Supernatural acts. Both in the OT and NT the significance of miracles is that they indicate God's activity, and thus are a mode of divine REVELATION. Commonly a sign indicates God's power (Neh. 9:10; Ps. 78:43) and is often linked with the miracles attending the exodus (Jer. 32:21). At other times it represents something linked with a COVENANT (Gen. 1:14). These signs were regarded by the writers of the Bible as interventions by the Creator into the sphere of creation for the purposes of revelation and redemption. As such, they were an encouragement to faith and many times they provided a basis for faith. They were also the basis for hope. A supernatural act as a sign both from and for Yahweh would help remedy the existing situation with which the Israelites found themselves confronted (Isa. 55:13; 66:19). Often the "sign" or "signal" to the Israelites was for the benefit of the non-Israelites. The ensign or SIGNAL of the Lord, for example, could be a rallying point or marshaling ground for the armies being recruited to crush Babylon (13:2).

In a few incidents it is reported that phenomena similar to miracles were occasioned by sources other than Yahweh. The magicians were said to have done this in Egypt (Exod. 8:7). However, their success was only very limited as compared with that of Moses (v. 18). The magicians reported to Pharaoh, "This is the finger of God" (v. 19). SIMON MAGUS in Samaria was credited with the ability to perform what seemed to be miracles by his magic (Acts 8:9–11). For the most part, however, people in NT times had one explanation for miracles: they could be performed only with God's power (cf. Jn. 3:2). This conviction was shared by Jews and Gentiles, believers and unbelievers; this was what lent such cogency to the argument of the former blind man (Jn. 9:31) and left Jesus' enemies often speechless (Acts 4:14, 16) and frustrated (v. 21).

In addition, DEMONS are credited with the power to perform supernatural acts. Paul speaks of certain signs and wonders as originating in SATAN, but being permitted by God as punishment (2 Thess. 2:9). Even more pronounced is a picture of the future in which a profusion of so-called miracles is performed so that the majority of the people on earth are deceived. The healing of the beast is regarded as miraculous (Rev. 13:3) and results in worship of the beast. That apparent miracles can have demonic origin is implied also in 1 Jn. 2:26. Their purpose is deception. That deception can be a basis for divine punishment is also indicated in Rom. 1:28–32. Rejection of the true light may lead one to mistake evil for good. Jesus accused the PHARISEES of this when they were unwilling to regard his miracles as of divine origin but instead attributed them to Satan (Mk. 3:21–27). This spiritual blindness exposes one to the danger of an eternal sin (3:28–29). Thus the Scriptures warn, on one hand, against that nondiscrimination which fails to distinguish between the spurious and genuine miracles, and on the other hand, against spiritual blindness which refuses to acknowledge God as the source of supernatural acts.

C. A basis for faith. The OT writers accepted the reported miracles at face value. They attributed them to the activity of Yahweh. They used them as a basis for their own faith and as a means of convincing others that their God was the true God and was all-powerful. They sang of the mighty acts of God, and their creed consisted largely in reciting these divine deeds. This factor in their heritage stood them in good stead in times when they were hard-pressed and when evil seemed to overwhelm them. At such times they would look to God in faith and expect him to deliver them again. This was the germinal seed of their expectations for the future—a conviction that God would dramatically intervene for the redemption of his people (Pss. 85; 95; Hab. 3). The memory of such "mighty acts" was the basis of their optimism.

As for the NT, there is a paradoxical quality in the signs as reported in the Synoptic Gospels. On the one hand, the desire for signs was discouraged and rebuked because it indicated a lack of faith (Mk. 8; 11; 12). On the other hand, Jesus himself was a sign. In his message in the synagogue of NAZARETH it is obvious that Jesus regarded his previous acts of healing as a fulfillment of the messianic prophecy (Isa. 61:1–9) and thus as the basis of faith which recognized him as the MESSIAH. In a similar manner Paul appealed to the apostolic signs that accompanied his ministry as evidence of divine endorsement (2 Cor. 12:12). Repeatedly these signs or miracles were regarded as evidences of the authenticity of the gospel (Heb. 2:4). The miracle par excellence was the RESURRECTION OF JESUS CHRIST, again and again it was made the basis for belief in the veracity of the gospel. Apart from the divine intervention which resulted in Jesus' resurrection, Paul argues, faith is groundless (1 Cor. 15:14).

The relationship between miracle and unbelief is nowhere so clearly expressed as in the fourth gospel (see JOHN, GOSPEL OF). John does not use any word except *sēmeion*. The few miracles chosen for inclusion in this gospel are those in which the reaction of the people is the important thing. John is interested not only in the event but also in its meaning or significance. In this gospel, among the Pharisees and everyone else, a miracle or a work of God has only one explanation. It indicates God's power and approval. NICODEMUS accepted this as a basis for belief in Jesus (Jn. 3:2). The Pharisees' arguments with the restored blind man were powerless to resist his logic, the same logic Nicodemus used; namely, that such things as divine healing had no other explanation than the energy of God. Jesus used this argument repeatedly in his dialogues with the Jews as evidence that God favored his message and his person (ch. 5). At the same time a clamor for mere evidence received little encouragement (6:26; 20:29). In the Gospel of John the greatest miracle is the one incarnate in the man Jesus, as when he said, "I am the resurrection and the life" (11:25). (On the so-called "semeia source" of the Gospel of John, see G. van Belle, *The Signs Source in the Fourth Gospel: Historical Survey and Critical Evaluation of the Semeia Hypothesis* [1994].)

III. Significance. The relationship between MYTH, fact (HISTORY), and FAITH is always a live issue. There are those who argue that the validity of faith does not depend upon fact, a view popular since the days of A. Ritschl and never more so than now. Religious "myth" is often understood as a religious *interpretation* of an event. Sometimes it is assumed that the important thing is the interpretation, regarded as more significant than the event it interprets. This sophistication was quite unknown to the writers of the Bible. In both OT and NT the authors were sober historians endeavoring to provide a basis for faith by citing the facts; this is especially true of the Gospels. In the Epistles also the authors were confident that God's endorsement of the message is to be seen in the lives transformed as well as in the intrinsic merit of the proclamation. This is quite different from credulously accepting an alleged vision or apparition as a substitute for evidence verifiable by ordinary means of discerning truth. The biblical authors needed no vision.

It is often said that one can believe the miracles because of the miracle of Jesus Christ, rather than in Christ because of the miracles. Today, it is true, the miracle of Jesus' character makes other miracles seem inferior by contrast. In the biblical record itself the "signs and wonders" are either the basis for belief in Jesus' authenticity (Jn. 5:36) or an important source of confirmation of apostolic testimony (Heb. 2:4). (See further A. Richardson, *Miracle Stories of the Gospels* [1941], ch. 3; P. Minear, *Eyes of Faith* [1946], 143–45, 183–87; J. C. Exum, ed.,

Signs and Wonders: Biblical Texts in Literary Focus [1989]; F. J. Moloney, *Signs and Shadows: Reading John 5–12* [1996].)

G. A. TURNER

signal. The standard method for communicating in times of war and peace in antiquity was by signal fires. Such are mentioned in the OT (e.g., Jer. 6:1; Heb. *maś'ēt H5368*) and in the records from TELL EL-AMARNA and LACHISH. However, banners or flags are also mentioned (e.g., Isa. 5:26; Heb. *nēs H5812*); this latter term can be used specifically in the sense of "warning" (Num. 26:10). See also SIGN.

signature. This term is used by the NRSV once (Job 31:35) to render *tāw H9338*, the name of the last letter of the Hebrew ALPHABET, which in its earlier form resembled the English letter *X* (see TAU). The same Hebrew word is translated "mark" elsewhere (Ezek. 9:4, 6). In sealing documents, individuals would have used their own recognizable signs, thought to correspond with the fingernail impressions made on CLAY TABLETS (see discussion in *HALOT*, 4:1693–94).

signet. A seal used to indicate ownership or to give official authority to a document. In the NIV this English word occurs only in the phrase "signet ring" (Gen. 41:42). In the NRSV it also occurs by itself in a number of passages, usually as the rendering of Hebrew *ḥōtām H2597* (Exod. 28:11 et al.). For discussion, see SEAL.

Signet mold with the throne name of Tutankhamen (from Tell el-'Ajjul, c. 1330 B.C.).

signs of the heavens (sky). See ASTRONOMY, III.

Sihon si'hon (סִיחוֹן *H6095*, meaning unknown). A king of the AMORITES defeated by the Israelites on their way to Canaan (Num. 21:21–30). Moses had sent messengers to Sihon, hoping to obtain permission to lead the Israelites through his land. The king refused to grant this permission; rather he went out against Israel with his army, but was defeated and slain. Israel then claimed Sihon's land as its first conquered area. HESHBON had been his capital city; his S boundary was the river ARNON; and his N boundary was the river JABBOK (Num. 21:24). Further, his country was a land of many villages and cities (21:25); it became a part of the TRANSJORDAN claimed and settled by the tribes of REUBEN, GAD, and part of MANASSEH. See TRIBES, LOCATION OF, I.

Moses' defeat of Sihon was a great event remembered centuries later. Ballad singers made a poetic account of Sihon's downfall a part of their repertoire (Num. 21:27–30). Moses used it as a meaningful reference to the past when he "proclaimed to the Israelites all that the LORD had commanded him concerning them" (Deut. 1:3–4). He retold the great victory over Sihon (2:24–37) in order to recall how it had been a rallying point in going against OG of BASHAN (3:1–11), and to inspire confidence in God with respect to nations still before them across the Jordan (29:7; 31:4). It is of interest to observe that other peoples told about Sihon's defeat and spread the news, causing dread among the inhabitants on the W side of the Jordan (Josh. 2:10; 9:10).

JOSHUA used Sihon's defeat as a significant point of reference in Israel's past as he recounted great victories and apportioned the conquered land to certain tribes (Josh. 12:2, 5; 13:10, 21, 27). Historians included occasional references to it: JEPHTHAH, confronted by the belligerent Ammonites, related to them how Sihon dared to engage Israel in battle and how he had been defeated (Jdg. 11:12–28, esp. vv. 19–20); the territory assigned by SOLOMON to GEBER in Transjordan was known as GILEAD and also as "the country of Sihon king of the Amorites" (1 Ki. 4:19). EZRA, addressing his people in a public confession of sin, spoke about great events of

Israel's past, including the defeat of Sihon (Neh. 9:22). Psalmists reviewing and retelling past events wrote and sang about the way God gave victory over Sihon (Pss. 135:11; 136:19). JEREMIAH, in an oracle against MOAB, declared that destructive fire would come forth "from the house of Sihon" to bring about the collapse of Moab (Jer. 48:45 NRSV). H. E. FINLEY

Sihor si´hor. KJV alternate form of SHIHOR.

Sikkuth sik´uhth. See SAKKUTH.

Silas si´luhs (Σίλας G4976 [in Acts], apparently from Aram. אְיָלָא [= Heb. שָׁאוּל H8406, SAUL]; the form Σιλουανός G4977 [2 Cor. 1:19; 1 Thess. 1:1; 2 Thess. 1:1; 1 Pet. 5:12] is thought to be either a surname [cognomen from Lat. *silva*, "wood, forest"] or a latinized form of Σίλας, though some have suggested that the latter was rather a shortened form of his original name, *Silvanus*). A prominent member of the Jerusalem church and companion of the apostle PAUL on most of his second missionary journey. When the COUNCIL OF JERUSALEM decided that GENTILE believers were not obligated to be circumcised, Silas was one of two delegates appointed to accompany Paul and BARNABAS to ANTIOCH OF SYRIA with the letter announcing the council's decision (Acts 15:22–23). The sentiments of the council were orally expressed as well (v. 27), together with strengthening words of exhortation by Silas and Judas Barsabbas (see JUDAS #9), who are referred to as "prophets" (v. 32). After some time in Antioch, their mission accomplished, they returned to "those who had sent them" (v. 33; according to v. 34 in the KJV, Silas remained in Antioch, but this verse is omitted by most witnesses, including the earliest MSS).

Paul chose Silas as his companion for the second missionary journey after the apostle and Barnabas had a falling out over the John Mark incident (Acts 15:36–40; see MARK, JOHN). Not much is said directly of Silas until the incident at PHILIPPI when he and Paul were beaten and imprisoned, accused of causing a breach of the peace and preaching false doctrine (16:12–40). Undaunted, the two prisoners prayed and sang praises to God at midnight until an earthquake secured their miraculous release. After the conversion of the jailer and his family, and the realization by the magistrates that Paul and Silas were Roman citizens (see CITIZENSHIP), they took leave of Philippi and the brethren there for THESSALONICA (17:1–9). Later, in BEREA, Silas was left with TIMOTHY while Paul went to ATHENS to escape the riots (17:1–15). The apostle had asked his companions to join him when they could, but it was not until he had left Athens and arrived at CORINTH that they caught up with their leader (18:5).

Silas may be identified with Silvanus. As in the case of Paul, this man may have had both a Roman and a (hellenized) Semitic name. If the one who is invariably called Silas in Acts and the one who is invariably called Silvanus in the Epistles are one and the same, then the preaching mission of Silas in Corinth with Paul and Timothy is mentioned in 2 Cor. 1:19. This fits with the salutations of 1 and 2 Thessalonians (written from Corinth during the second missionary journey), where the same three send greetings to the saints at Thessalonica (1 Thess. 1:1; 2 Thess. 1:1).

The use of "we" throughout the main body of these epistles may mean that Silas and Timothy were actually coauthors with Paul, who adds his own personal postscript (1 Thess. 5:27; 2 Thess. 3:17; most scholars however consider that the companions are mentioned only in a supporting role). Such literary activity of Silvanus is alluded to by PETER: "With the help of Silas [Silvanus], whom I regard as a faithful brother, I have written to you briefly" (1 Pet. 5:12). While the full meaning of this remark is uncertain, it has been taken to mean that he was not simply bearer of the epistle, but also its AMANUENSIS, or he may have been only responsible for much of the style and arrangement of the letter. It is well known that ancient secretaries were allowed considerable freedom in writing down their master's ideas, even to the extent of filling in the contents of a bare outline. The master would check over and authenticate the finished product. Although the language would be that of the amanuensis, the fundamental ideas would be those of the master. In this case Peter would have regarded Silvanus as a trustworthy secretary ("a faithful brother"), "better fitted than anyone else to express in an intelligible and effective manner the thoughts and feelings which Peter entertained toward the Gentile Christians of

Asia Minor" (T. Zahn, *Introduction to the New Testament* [1909], 2:150–51).

If the Silvanus of 1 Peter can indeed be identified with the Silas of Acts, who was associated with Paul in the production of the Thessalonian letters (see the detailed discussion of L. Radermacher in *ZNW* 25 [1926]: 287–99; cf. also C. Bigg, *A Critical and Exegetical Commentary on the Epistles of St. Peter and St. Jude*, ICC [1903], 83–84), it is quite probable that a similar relationship with Peter existed in the writing of 1 Peter. E. G. Selwyn (*The First Epistle of Peter* [1952], 365–466) argues strongly for this probability on the grounds of a close connection of thought and language between 1 Peter, 1 and 2 Thessalonians, and the Apostolic Decree in Acts 15, of which Silas was one of the bearers. Also, it is not likely that a man of such stature should have been relegated by Peter to the office of a mere scribe or postman (ibid., 10–11). While similarities of thought and expression are capable of various explanations, the Silvanus hypothesis may be a reasonable alternative for those whose main objection to Petrine authorship is that an illiterate Galilean fisherman could not have written with such elegant diction and facility in Greek (but see PETER, FIRST EPISTLE OF, I).

However, this hypothesis has been challenged by F. W. Beare (*The First Epistle of Peter*, 3rd ed. [1970], 47–48, 212–16). His main objection—the meager references to the Holy Spirit—is a precarious criticism that has been adequately answered (see A. F. Walls's introduction to A. M. Stibbs, *The First Epistle General of Peter* [1959], 25–30). Another problem is the nonmention of Silvanus in the salutation of 1 Peter (as he appears in 1 Thess. 1:1 and 2 Thess. 1:1; cf. Rom. 16:22, where TERTIUS the scribe sends greetings). This suggests that Silvanus may have played a less important part than the amanuensis hypothesis implies.

Since *dia Siluanou* ("through Silvanus") is ambiguous, the amanuensis theory is inconclusive without stronger supporting evidence. The dynamic personal authority and tone of the whole letter (esp. 1 Pet. 5) makes it improbable that Peter's helper was allowed too much freedom in its basic message as we know it. When Peter says he has written "briefly" (v. 12), he is not minimizing his responsibility for the weight of the epistle, but suggesting that his words were shortened because he knew that Silvanus his delegate would enforce and supplement them in person.

On the basis of his association with the writings of Paul and Peter, as well as certain literary resemblances between 1 Peter and Hebrews, Silvanus (Silas) has been considered as a possible author of the epistle to the HEBREWS, but there is no corroborating evidence. (In addition to the commentaries, see F. F. Bruce, *The Pauline Circle* [1985], 23–28.)

A. M. ROSS

silk. This English term is used by the KJV in two passages (Prov. 31:22 [Heb. *šēš* H9254, "fine linen"] and Ezek. 16:10, 13 [*meši* H5429, only here, meaning possibly "rich fabric"]). It is doubtful that the woven thread of the Chinese silkworm (*Bombyx mori*) was known in the ANE in OT times. The Greek term for "silk" (*sirikos* G4986) appears only in Rev. 18:12. It is derived from a Hellenistic term (*Sēres*) that referred to people from China; certainly by the 1st cent. B.C. Chinese silk was known in ASIA MINOR.

W. WHITE, JR.

Silla sil´uh (סִלָּא H6133, meaning unknown). An unidentified place cited in connection with the murder of King JOASH, an event that is said to have taken place "at Beth Millo, on the road down to Silla" (2 Ki. 12:20). Its association with BETH MILLO (KJV and other versions, "the house of Millo") suggests that it may have been a sector of JERUSALEM or a place within its environs. See MILLO.

Siloam si-loh´uhm (Σιλωάμ G4978, from Heb. שִׁלֹחַ H8942; see SHILOAH). A pool and tower in biblical JERUSALEM; the term is also currently applied to the water tunnel that empties into the pool. As a defense against the attacks by ASSYRIA, which culminated in SENNACHERIB's campaign of 701 B.C. (cf. 2 Chr. 32:4), King HEZEKIAH of Judah constructed the Siloam water tunnel from the GIHON SPRING, southwestward through the rocky core of Mount ZION, and out into the central Tyropoeon Valley of Jerusalem (v. 30).

The tunnel is square cut, averaging 2 ft. wide and 6 ft. high. It follows an S-shaped course, so that the direct distance of 1,090 ft. involves 1,750 ft. of actual tunneling. This may reflect attempts to avoid harder rock formations or deeply cut structures at higher levels, such as tombs; certain of the turns were produced as the crews, working inward from both ends simultaneously, sought to contact each other. Considerable additional construction became necessary in the S portion, namely, a lowering of the tunnel floor in order to allow a gravity flow of the water.

An inscription just inside the SW portal was discovered in 1880, which has now been cut out from the rock and removed to the Istanbul Museum. Literally translated from the archaic Hebrew letters it reads: "The boring through [is completed]. And this is the story of the boring through: while yet [they plied] the drill, each toward his fellow, and while yet there were three cubits to be bored through, there was heard the voice of one calling unto another, for there was a crevice in the rock on the right hand. On the day of the boring through the stonecutters struck, each to meet his fellow, drill upon drill; and the water flowed from the source to the pool for a thousand and two hundred cubits, and a hundred cubits was the height of the rock above the head of the stone cutters" (GKC, frontispiece: photograph, tracing, and transcription into square character).

While the aforementioned pool may have remained outside the city walls as a covered cistern, with additional, concealed access tunnels and overflow channels (K. Kenyon, *Jerusalem: Excavating 3000 Years of History* [1967], 70–77), the water seems actually to have come "into the city" (2 Ki. 20:20), probably through an as yet undiscovered extension of the SW fortifications of Zion (cf. 2 Chr. 32:5, "another wall"). Isaiah appears to speak of Hezekiah's project when he mentions "a reservoir between the two walls for the water of the Old Pool" (Isa. 22:11). The "Old Pool" may refer to an original Upper Pool (7:3) near the Gihon Spring. The Lower Pool (22:9), possibly modern Birket el-Hamra, at the S tip of the pre-Hezekian city is known to have received water from it by a surface conduit called *haššilōaḥ* H8942 (LXX, *tou Silōam*), "the sending [one]" or "canal." The course of its upper 200 ft., with a minimal drop along the E side of Mount Zion—"gently flowing waters"—is still traceable. Thus it appears that the original Siloam Pool predated Hezekiah. However, by postexilic times, at least, the Lower Pool itself came to be called SHELAH (*šelaḥ* H8940), with the same meaning (Neh. 3:15), since it seems to have continued in use for overflow from Hezekiah's newer pool.

By Christian times the name Siloam had, understandably, become transferred to the newer pool, for JOSEPHUS (*War* 5.4.1–2) refers to the *pēgē* ("spring, fountain"), by which he meant the water at the outlet of Hezekiah's tunnel. The tower of Siloam, which collapsed at the cost of eighteen lives (Lk. 13:4), must have stood on the slope of Mount Zion to its E. The NT thus designates this pool, to which Jesus sent the man who had been born blind, as the Pool of Siloam and appropriately interprets it to signify "Sent" (Jn. 9:7). Traces remain of a Herodian reservoir and bath structure, c. 70 ft. square, with steps on the W side. Here the man would have washed, and he miraculously received his sight (vv. 8, 10).

A commemorative Byzantine church was constructed just NW of the reservoir in c. A.D. 440 by the Empress Eudocia, together with elaborate porticoes about the pool. Only fragments remain visible, and the pool itself now rests 18 ft. below the surrounding ground level. The surviving pool carries the title Birket Silwan, may be reached by a steep flight of stone steps, and measures 16 x 50 ft. A small mosque stands over the ruins of the church, and the name Silwan has become attached to the Arab village across the KIDRON Valley to the E.

(See further G. A. Smith, *Jerusalem: The Topography, Economics and History from the Earliest Times to A.D. 70*, 2 vols. [1907–08], 1:91–98; H. Vincent

Staircase leading to the depression that once functioned as the Pool of Siloam. The excavation remains here have been dated as early as the 1st cent. B.C.

and F.-M. Abel, *Jérusalem nouvelle*, 4 [1926], 860–64; J. Simons, *Jerusalem in the Old Testament* [1952], 175–94; H. Vincent, *Jérusalem de l'Ancien Testament*, 2 vols. [1954–56], 1.264–84, 289–97; J. Wilkinson, *Jerusalem as Jesus Knew It* [1978], 104–8; Y. Shiloh in *BAR* 7/4 [Jul.-Aug. 1981]: 24–39; V. Sasson in *PEQ* 114 [1982]: 111–17; W. H. Mare, *The Archaeology of the Jerusalem Area* [1987], 100–107; M. Ben-Dov, *Historical Atlas of Jerusalem* [2002], 59–64.)   J. B. PAYNE

Silvanus sil-vay′nuhs. See SILAS.

Silvanus, Teachings of. A loosely structured didactic work included in the NAG HAMMADI LIBRARY (NHC VII, 4). This 4th-cent. Coptic MS is a translation of an earlier Greek composition, possibly to be dated late in the 2nd cent. A.D. The name Silvanus, which appears only in the title, may be a pseudonymous attribution to SILAS, companion of the apostle PAUL, but perhaps it refers to an otherwise unknown author. The work may be regarded as WISDOM literature, few examples of which exist within the early Christian tradition. Among the Nag Hammadi treatises, this one is the least affected by GNOSTICISM. Although its contents are primarily ethical in character, it includes theological discussion, especially regarding the nature of God and Christ. (English trans. in *NHL*, 379–95; discussion in *ABD*, 6:341–43.)

silver. One of the precious METALS, white in color, ductile, and so malleable that it can be beaten into leaves as thin as 0.00025 mm. Silver has a density of 10.5 and melts at 961°C. It forms alloys with other metallic elements, including GOLD, COPPER, nickel, and zinc; 10–15 percent silver is commonly present in native gold. *Electrum*, which was used for many early coins, is the natural alloy of gold with 15–45 percent silver; it was called *asem* in ancient Egypt. The crystal structure of silver, like that of gold and copper, is a face-centered cubic lattice. The cell dimensions of the basic cubic units of four atoms of silver and of gold are almost identical, and therefore silver substitutes for gold, and vice versa, right up to 100 percent.

Because of its comparative scarcity, white color, high luster (silver is the most lustrous of all met-

Sumerian silver lyre from Ur (c. 2600 B.C.). Silver covers the lyre itself and the bull's head.

als), resistance to atmospheric oxidation, and malleability, silver has been used in the manufacture of articles of value such as ornaments (e.g., 1 Chr. 18:10; Acts 19:24), jewelry, and coinage (e.g., Lev. 5:15; Matt. 26:15). The oldest silver probably came from N SYRIA (the Aramean state of ZOBAH in 1 Sam. 14:47) and from parts of ASIA MINOR. Silver was known c. 4000 B.C. in Egypt, but was very rare. Menes, who founded the 1st dynasty c. 3100, set the value of silver at about one quarter that of gold. Chaldean silver ornaments are known from c. 2850, and silver formed part of ABRAHAM's wealth (Gen. 13:2). It is probable that by 800 B.C. all the countries between the Nile and the Indus used both silver and gold as money. Early Roman records indicate that before the term *argentum* was used, silver was referred to as *Luna* with a crescent moon symbol. The alchemists used the same symbol and termed silver either Luna or ARTEMIS (the great mother goddess of ASIA—cf. Acts 19:10, 22, 26–27).

Native silver occurs much more rarely than native gold, but it is widely distributed in small amounts and would have been the earliest source of the metal, as at Laurion, Greece (see MINES, MINING). It sometimes is of primary origin, but generally is secondary, occurring in a zone of secondary enrichment, in a silver lode or deposit. Together with other silver sulphides occurring in this zone, the silver developed by the action of hot water vapors or oxygen upon the primary silver sulphides, of which argentite is the most important ore mineral. The uppermost, weathered parts of silver lodes or deposits, above the zone of secondary enrichment, include cerargyrite (silver chloride), another important ore. These silver ores are mined primarily for their silver content. Much of the world production of silver comes from smelting ores of lead, such as galena, a lead sulphide, and sulphides of copper and zinc, all of which contain a small percentage of silver.

Silver can be extracted from its ores by a number of simple metallurgical processes, one being the process of cupellation with lead, thought to have been used by the Babylonians, and still used today. The silver ores are smelted with lead or lead ores in a simple furnace. The resultant lead-silver alloy is then melted on a porous hearth of bone-ash or marl. The lead is oxidized by the oxygen in the air to form a layer of molten lead oxide. Any other base metal impurities are also oxidized and dissolved in the molten lead oxide, which is skimmed away ("dross," Ezek. 22:18) or run off the top of the crucible or vessel. Only the silver, with any gold or platinum present, remains and is free of base metals (cf. Isa. 1.22).

The tarnish which forms on silver results from the action of sulphur or sulphur compounds in the air forming a film of silver sulphide on the surface. Such an effect is particularly marked in industrial cities, but in biblical times it would be a very rare occurrence and only adjacent to places where sulphide ores were being smelted. (See J. R. Partington, *A Textbook of Inorganic Chemistry*, 6th ed. [1950], 733–38; H. H. Read, *Rutley's Elements of Mineralogy*, 26th ed. [1970], 255–62.)

D. R. Bowes

silverling. This archaic term, meaning "small silver coin," is used once by the KJV (Isa. 7.23, where modern versions have "shekels").

silversmith. An artisan that crafts objects made of SILVER (see ARTIFICER). The English term is used to translate Hebrew *ṣôrēp* (Jdg. 17:4; Prov. 25:4), which is the participial form of the verb *ṣārap* H7671, meaning "to smelt, refine" (see REFINE). Thus the Hebrew word can also be used of goldsmiths (e.g., Isa. 40:19) and other refiners. In the NT, the Greek term used is *argyrokopos* G737, which does refer specifically to a silversmith; it is applied to DEMETRIUS, an artisan in EPHESUS "who made silver shrines of Artemis" (Acts 19:24).

Simalcue si-mal'kyoo-ee. KJV Apoc. form of IMALKUE (1 Macc. 11:39).

Simeon sim'ee-uhn (שִׁמְעוֹן H9058, possibly "[God] has heard" [but see *HALOT*, 4:1576–77, and cf. SHIMEON and SIMON]; gentilic שִׁמְעֹנִי H9063, "Simeonite", *Simeōnitēs*). Also Symeon (some versions in the NT). **(1)** Son of JACOB and ancestor of the Israelite tribe that bears his name. See discussion below.

(2) Grandfather of MATTATHIAS (#2) and thus great-grandfather of the Maccabean leaders (1 Macc. 2:1). See MACCABEE.

(3) Son of Judah, included in Luke's GENEALOGY OF JESUS CHRIST (Lk. 3:30). This Simeon had a son named Levi, but nothing else is known about him.

(4) A devout man of Jerusalem who had been promised by God that he would see the MESSIAH before he died (Lk. 2:25–26). When Jesus was taken by his parents to the temple for the performance of the purification rites, Simeon was prompted by the HOLY SPIRIT. Recognizing the baby Jesus as the MESSIAH, Simeon took him in his arms and uttered the famous prayer known by its first two Latin words, NUNC DIMITTIS (2:29–32). He further predicted the necessity of suffering involved in Jesus' redemptive work, especially as it would affect Mary. This incident is apparently related by Luke as a part of his program of locating independent witnesses to Christ's messiahship. (For the doubtful view that this Simeon was the supposed son of the rabbinic scholar HILLEL, see A. Cutler in *JBR* 34 [1966]: 29–35; contrast *HJP*, rev. ed. [1973–87], 2:367–68.)

(5) One of the prophets and teachers of the church at ANTIOCH OF SYRIA (Acts 13:1). See NIGER.

(6) The name used by JAMES with reference to Simon PETER (Acts 15:14 most versions; NIV, "Simon"). This use of Peter's Hebrew name may well have been intended to remind troubled Jews in the group that it was through a faithful Jew like Peter that God had inaugurated the Gentile mission.

The rest of this article is devoted to Simeon son of Jacob.

According to the book of Genesis, Jacob loved RACHEL more than he loved his other wife, LEAH (Gen. 29:30). Because of this, God opened Leah's womb and she bore first REUBEN and then Simeon; the latter received that name because God had "heard" Leah's grief (vv. 31–33). It was Simeon and his younger brother LEVI who used deception to avenge themselves upon SHECHEM the HIVITE after that prince violated their sister DINAH (34:25–31). The act made Jacob persona non grata in the area and aroused his anger upon the two brothers (34:30). Jacob's last testament indicates that his anger did not abate through the years, for he predicted that the descendants of the two would be scattered throughout the land because of their fathers' violent natures (49:5–7).

Some scholars, denying that the tribes ever had only one originator, hold that the Genesis accounts of Jacob's family are actually early history of the twelve tribes. From this point of view, the Simeon and Levi tribes attempted to settle in central Canaan, but because of their barbarian nature, they brought upon themselves concerted Canaanite attack. The result was that the two tribes were so completely shattered that they were never again cohesive entities (cf. A. de Pury in *RB* 76 [1969]: 5–49). This reconstruction, however, is at variance with the biblical data.

Simeon was the brother whom JOSEPH held hostage until BENJAMIN should be brought to him (Gen. 42:24). Some have suggested that this was in punishment for Simeon's violent nature, but it is much more likely that Joseph held him simply because he was the second oldest brother. Reuben, the eldest, was not held either because of his kindness to Joseph (37:21) or because the eldest brother had to be left in charge in order to prevent a perhaps violent struggle for leadership among the remaining brothers.

Simeon and his five sons (including SHAUL, the son of a Canaanite woman) settled in Egypt with the rest of Jacob's family and by the time of the exodus had developed into a tribe (Gen. 46:10; Exod. 1:2, 6:15). In those sections of Numbers that

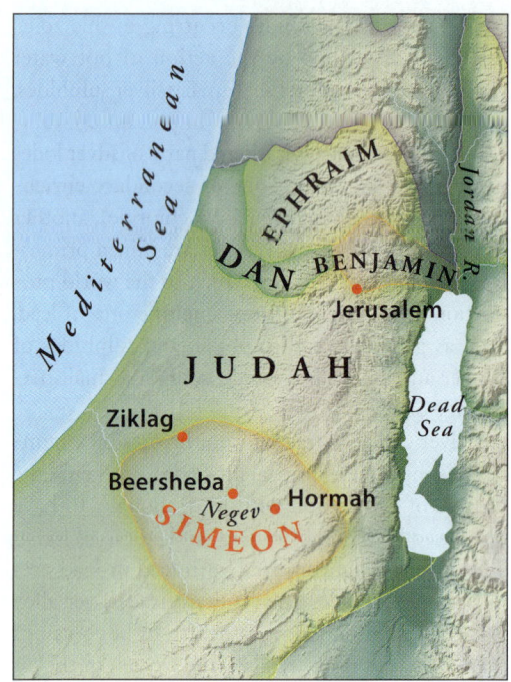

The tribal territory of Simeon.

deal with the organization of the Israelite camp, the tribe of Simeon is mentioned several times in its appropriate position, the second (Num. 1:6, 22, 23; 2:12; 7:36; 10:19). However, a comparison of the census figures in chs. 1 and 26 shows that while the nation as a whole lost only 2,000 during the wilderness sojourn (603,000 to 601,000), the tribe of Simeon lost more than 27,000. This represents a decline of more than 50 percent, from 59,300 to 22,100. The next larger tribe after the second census was EPHRAIM, which at 32,500 was nearly one-third larger. There were no smaller tribes than Simeon. Apparently, then, the tribe of Simeon was hard hit during the wandering. The man whom PHINEHAS killed at BAAL PEOR (25:14) was the head of a Simeonite clan. If the Simeonites were leaders in this apostasy, the resulting plague may have rested upon that tribe especially heavily and may partially account for the decline.

At any rate, it was perhaps because of the weakness of the Simeonite tribe that it seems to have lost its independent status at an early stage, for the Simeonites were not accorded a separate inheritance in the land (Josh. 19:1–9). Simeon alone, of all the tribes, was rather given certain villages within the boundaries of another tribe, JUDAH (19:2–9; cf. 15:20–63; for a recent discussion of the Simeonite town lists, see Z. Kallai in *VT* 53 [2003]: 81–96). These villages were located in the southern area of Judah, the NEGEV. (On the topography of Simeon's territory, see W. F. Albright in *JPOS* 4 [1924]: 149–61; more generally, K. H. Graf, *Der Stamm Simeon* [1866].)

It is not clear whether Simeon ever actually possessed these villages, for when DAVID became a vassal of ACHISH, this PHILISTINE king of GATH evidently controlled ZIKLAG, one of the Simeonite cities (1 Sam. 27:6). This suggests that Simeon, like several other tribes, had not been able to capture all its allotted territory. The tribe, nevertheless, must have remained important in the far southern area, for 1 Chr. 12:24–25 states that a greater number of men (7,100) came to David from Simeon in the early monarchy than did from Judah (6,800).

Simeon's special situation within Judah meant that the two groups were more and more melted into one, with Judah taking the lead (Josh. 21:9; Jdg. 1:3, 17–19). This is especially plain in that Simeon is not mentioned in the numerous tribal lists of Judges. Its absence from the books of Samuel and Kings is also noteworthy. According to 1 Chr. 4:29, Simeonites lived in their allotted cities until the reign of David. Whether this is meant to imply that they did not live there after that time is not clear. During the reign of HEZEKIAH, however, a group of them migrated to GEDOR (prob. modern Khirbet Judur, c. 8 mi. SW of BETHLEHEM), while another group migrated S into EDOM (1 Chr. 4:39–43). If the identification of Gedor is correct, this may indicate that the Simeonites, deposed from their cities, spread both northward and southward in the area of Judah during the monarchy.

The treatment of Simeon in 2 Chr. 15:9 and 34:6 is difficult to interpret. In both instances, the tribe appears to be grouped with Ephraim and Manasseh as typifying the northern kingdom versus Judah and Benjamin. This seems impossible unless one presumes that a majority of the Simeonites had migrated into the northern area, or unless one credits the Chronicler with a memory of the Simeonite tribe's ancient attempt to take Shechem. As noted above, the latter of these is contrary to the biblical witness, while the former, though possible, is without scriptural warrant. Perhaps the statements intend to say that peoples from both N (Ephraim and Manasseh) and S (Simeon) were drawn into Judah and Benjamin at this time. The fact that the second reference (1 Chr. 34:6) appends "as far as Naphtali" immediately after Simeon makes even this interpretation dubious, however.

Further complicating this question is the issue of the tribal make-up of the kingdoms of Judah and Israel. If Judah was composed of Judah and Benjamin (1 Ki. 12:21; 2 Chr. 15:9), then Simeon would have had to be counted as one of the ten tribes of Israel. Only in the unlikely circumstance that Levi was counted as one of the northern tribes would it then be possible to argue that Simeon was simply dropped from the enumeration. Some scholars have argued that SOLOMON so effectively broke the separate identities of the tribes that the idea of ten northern tribes was not literally carried out. See TRIBES, LOCATION OF.

The ideal disposition of the land (Ezek. 48) places Simeon in the S, but Issachar and Zebulun, both northern, are also placed there, thus removing the passage from the realm of historical evidence. The final reference to the tribe of Simeon occurs in Rev. 7:7, which states that 12,000 Simeonites, along with representatives of the other eleven tribes, were sealed against the coming doom.   J. OSWALT

similitude. This English term, meaning "corresponding likeness," is used a number of times in the KJV. In the OT it can render such terms as Hebrew *tĕmûnâ* H9454, "form, representation" (Num. 12:8 et al.). In the KJV NT it translates *homoiōma* G3930 (Rom. 5:14; cognate nouns in Heb. 7:15 and Jas. 3:9). The apostle PAUL can use this Greek term to express the reality of the INCARNATION. God has sent "his own Son in the likeness of sinful humanity" (Rom. 8:3 TNIV); Jesus was born "in human likeness" (Phil. 2:7; conversely, believers are united with Christ "in the likeness" [KJV] of his death and resurrection, Rom. 6:5). Using the cognate verb (*homoioō* G3929), the epistle to the Hebrews states that Jesus "had to be made like his brothers in every way" (Heb. 2:17; cf. 4:15). Though many have taken the "likeness" to point to some remaining "unlikeness," surely the intent of these passages is to teach the agreement of Christ's nature with true humanity. These passages underline the reality of Christ's work, including his continuing care and intercession for his people. On the concept that we have been made in God's likeness (Jas. 3:9), see IMAGE OF GOD.

D. C. DAVIS

Simon si′muhn (Σίμων G4981, from Heb. שִׁמְעוֹן H9058; see SIMEON). (1) One of the twelve disciples of Jesus. See PETER.

(2) Another of the twelve disciples of Jesus, called "the Zealot" (Matt. 10:4; Mk. 3:18; Lk. 6:15; Acts 1:13). See CANANAEAN.

(3) A brother of Jesus (Matt. 13:55; Mk. 6:3).

(4) A leper of BETHANY in whose house a woman anointed Jesus' head with expensive ointment (Mk. 14:3–9; cf. Jn. 12:1–8).

(5) A PHARISEE in whose house a sinful woman anointed the feet of Jesus with her tears and ointment. Simon's criticism of the act by an unclean woman of such low reputation drew forth from Jesus a parable which taught Simon the relation between forgiveness and appreciation (Lk. 7:36–50). Jesus commended the woman for her love and faith.

(6) A man from CYRENE in N Africa who was compelled to carry the cross of Christ (Matt. 27:32; Mk. 15:21; Lk. 23:26). Mark calls him "the father of Alexander and Rufus," who must have been well known to Mark's readers (prob. in the church at Rome, cf. Rom. 16:13 and see RUFUS). Simon was likely one of many Jews living in Cyrene, now visiting Jerusalem. (See S. B. Crowder, *Simon of Cyrene: A Case of Roman Conscription* [2002].)

(7) The father of JUDAS ISCARIOT (Jn. 6:71; 12:4 [KJV]; 13:2, 26).

(8) A magician of SAMARIA. See SIMON MAGUS.

(9) A tanner of JOPPA in whose house PETER stayed "for some time" (Acts 9:43; 10:6, 17, 32). His house was by the seaside outside the city wall, because the handling of dead bodies made tanning ceremonially unclean to a Jew.

(10–11) The name of two high priests during the intertestamental period. Simon I ("the Just"), who lived in the first half of the 3rd cent. B.C., was the son of ONIAS I and the father of Onias II. Toward the end of the century, Onias II was succeeded by his son Simon II. The ancient sources (e.g., Sir. 50:1–21; Jos. *Ant.* 12.2.5 §43) are sometimes ambiguous regarding which Simon is being referred to (cf. *HJP*, rev. ed. [1973–87], 2:359–60; J. C. VanderKam, *From Joshua to Caiaphas: High Priests after the Exile* [2004], 137–57, 181–88).

(12) A man from the tribe of BENJAMIN who was captain of the temple early in the 2nd cent. B.C. (2 Macc. 3:4 et al.).

(13) One of the Maccabean brothers. See SIMON MACCABEE.

(14) Simon ben Kosiba. See BAR KOKHBA.

A. M. ROSS

Simon Maccabee. Also Simon Maccabaeus. Son of Mattathias and ruler over JUDEA from 142 to 135 B.C.; surnamed Thassi (1 Macc. 2:3 et al.). Under his brother Judas MACCABEE, Judea had gained religious freedom after the persecutions of ANTIOCHUS IV Epiphanes. Judas and his party wished to achieve full political freedom, although he died before it was attained. When another brother, Jonathan, became ruler, the Hellenistic party was driven out and the Maccabees were in firm control. Under Simon, finally, the Jews became wholly independent of the SELEUCID or Syrian empire.

At the time, the Seleucid ruler DEMETRIUS II was being challenged by the general TRYPHO. Simon pledged loyalty to Demetrius on condition that he recognize the freedom of the Jews. Demetrius, who had already lost power in the S of his kingdom, granted remission of all outstanding taxes to the Jews and exempted them from paying tribute thereafter. This meant that Judea was now politically free. Documents were no longer dated according to the Seleucid era, but according to the year of Simon as "High Priest and Prince of the Jews."

Although Demetrius did not have power to bestow favors on Simon, since Trypho was still in power in Syria, Simon was able to take advantage of the Syrian civil war to enlarge his holdings. Gazara (GEZER), W of JERUSALEM, commanded a mountain path essential to commerce between Jerusalem and the port city of JOPPA, already in Jewish hands. Simon conquered Gazara and expelled its Gentile inhabitants, settling there "those who observed the law" (1 Macc. 13:43–48). As long as the Syrians controlled the citadel in Jerusalem, however, the capital city was not truly free. In the year 142 B.C., Simon was able to take the citadel from the Syrian garrison, which had to capitulate because of famine.

This event had great symbolic as well as strategic value. Enemy soldiers no longer had a foothold in Judea.

Simon is also noted for his administration of justice and the reestablishment of Jewish law in the land. Peace was finally achieved, and attention could be given to the beautifying of the temple and the establishment of a viable civil government. Mattathias and his sons had come to power in a popular uprising against the Syrian rulers. They had no legitimate right to civil rule, but under Simon legitimacy was granted. In the third year of his reign, in September 141 B.C., a great assembly declared Simon to be high priest, military commander, and civil governor "forever, until a trustworthy prophet should arise" (1 Macc. 14:41). Simon's priesthood and rule were declared legitimate and hereditary. The Hasmonean dynasty thus came into being. The terms of the decree were engraved on bronze tablets and set up in the court of the temple.

At about this time, Simon sent an embassy to Rome in order to gain recognition from the Roman senate. The embassy brought as a gift to Rome a golden shield weighing 1,000 minas. The Roman senate granted the Jews unrestricted possession of their territory and sent information on the contents of the senatorial decree to numerous independent states of Greece and Asia Minor. Evildoers who had fled from Judea were ordered delivered up to the Jewish high priest (1 Macc. 15:15–24).

Simon had renewed difficulties closer to home, however. Demetrius II was taken prisoner by the Parthian King Mithridates I in 138 B.C., and his brother Antiochus VII fought against the pretender Trypho. Antiochus sought the favor of the Jews, confirmed the privileges granted by his predecessors, and expressly gave them the right to coin money. Antiochus landed in Syria and gained the victory over Trypho, who fled, but was killed soon after during a siege at Apamea. With Trypho dead, Antiochus took a hard line toward the Jews. He repudiated his promises and demanded the surrender of Joppa, Gazara, the Jerusalem citadel, and other places Simon had taken. If Simon wished to keep the places occupied, he was to pay 1,000 talents. Simon refused to yield, offering only 100 talents. Antiochus sent an army against Simon, who dispatched his sons Judas and John to face the Syrian invaders. Judas was wounded, but John was successful in routing the enemy. John returned as victor to Jerusalem (1 Macc. 15:10–16:10).

Simon, like his brothers, died a violent death. His son-in-law Ptolemy, military commander of the Jericho area, wanted the supreme power for himself and planned to kill Simon and his sons. In February of 135 B.C. Simon visited the fortress of Dok, near Jericho, as Ptolemy's guest. During a great feast, Ptolemy had Simon, with two sons, Mattathias and Judas, slain. A third son who was not present, John Hyrcanus, survived to become the next ruling high priest (1 Macc. 16:11–24; on Hyrcanus, see Hasmonean II.A). (See further Jos. *Ant.* 13.6–7; 1JM, rev. ed. [1973–87], II 189–99; J. C. VanderKam, *From Joshua to Caiaphas: High Priests after the Exile* [2004], 270–85.)

C. F. Pfeiffer

Simon Magus may′guhs. Traditional name given to a man who practiced sorcery in Samaria (Acts. 8:9–24).

I. The biblical account. In recording the persecution that followed Stephen's death, Luke says that Christians "were scattered throughout Judea and Samaria" (Acts 8:1) and "preached the word wherever they went" (v. 4). He then particularizes with Philip's mission in Samaria. Philip's preaching commanded great attention and was attested by "miraculous signs" (v. 6), healings, and exorcisms (v. 7). The result was a wide acceptance of the gospel. Two significant incidents follow, the encounter with Simon Magus and (at the conclusion of the Samaritan tour) the encounter with the Ethiopian eunuch.

In the case of Simon, Luke has compressed much information, showing that firm handling of material which marks the whole of Acts. As to Luke's reason for its inclusion, J. E. Roberts describes it as an indication that "the Gospel, making its first essay on non-Jewish soil, was discovered to be mightier than the magic which exercised such a powerful influence over the contemporary world" (*DAC*, 2:498). Simon by his magical arts had gained a large following in Samaria and had assumed the title, "the divine power known as the Great Power" (Acts 8:10; there are examples from inscriptions of

Remains of the Roman forum at Samaria (Sebaste), city of Simon Magus. (View to the NE.)

the use of divine titles by other magicians). C. C. Torrey (*The Composition and Date of Acts* [1916], 18–20) suggested, on the basis of a presumed Aramaic original, the rendering, "the power of the God who is called Great," which would imply a combination of the Greek ZEUS and the Hebrew Yahweh ("the Power" was a rabbinical substitute for the divine name). Simon's reputation is emphasized in order to show the dramatic changes now brought about.

Philip encountered him in a town, probably Sebaste, the capital of the province, but it may have been Gitta, the traditional site of Simon's home. The magician himself became a convert (Acts 8:13, "believed," which is the normal term in Acts), was baptized with many others, and was amazed at the miracles of Philip, which apparently surpassed his own. How genuine was his conversion can only be judged by the sequel.

This remarkable response in Samaria caused the apostles to dispatch PETER and John (see JOHN THE APOSTLE), their most prominent members. Their special function was to lay hands on the converts so that they might receive the HOLY SPIRIT. It was these visible acts of the Jerusalem leaders which aroused Simon to an intense interest in their "craft." Perhaps the gift of tongues was evident, if one follows the analogies of Acts 10:44–46 and 19:6. The externality of Simon's faith seems indicated by his bold attempt to bribe the apostles into imparting their "power."

Peter's severe rebuke (Acts 8:20–23; the last verse echoes Deut. 29:18 and Isa. 58:6) implies Simon's basic misconception about the gifts of God, which are inward in their nature. Yet there remained the possibility of his seeking in penitence the forgiveness of God. His final plea (Acts 8:24) does not make it clear whether he had penetrated beyond the "signs" and the fear of retribution to any real faith, but his subsequent heretical reputation and the doubts raised by Luke himself make it safer to regard him as a nominal convert only. The story closes with a reference to a preaching tour that may have been partly designed to counter the cult of Simon.

II. Christianity and magic in Acts. A recurring motif in Acts is the conflict between Christianity and the magical practices that were so prevalent in the Graeco-Roman world of the 1st cent. (see MAGIC). It is here relevant only to note two parallels to the Simon Magus narrative, both involving Jewish magicians in a Gentile context.

At PAPHOS in CYPRUS, the proconsul SERGIUS PAULUS kept a Jewish magician ELYMAS Bar-Jesus, and Luke again describes the incident with accurate detail (Acts 13:6–12). This man, whose master was "an intelligent man," tried to nullify Paulus's response to the preaching of PAUL and BARNABAS. Paul's denunciation of Elymas recalls Peter's words to Simon in its directness and intensity: the magician is an enemy of the faith and an embodiment of Satan. Simon became temporarily blinded, so at the outset of the Gentile missionary outreach, an important Roman convert was preserved from the satanic assault.

Luke also describes the Jewish exorcists at EPHESUS (Acts 19:13–20) who encountered Paul's mission of healing and casting out of spirits. As Simon had tried to buy miraculous powers with money, so these sons of SCEVA tried to use "the name of the Lord Jesus" as a magic incantation. Their discomfiture resulted in a great turning to the faith in Ephesus and the repudiation of magic arts. The practice of DIVINATION is also illustrated by the story of the slave girl at PHILIPPI (16:16–18).

In all these incidents Luke shows an awareness of the "principalities and powers" that lay behind the magicians' actions. In the early Christian expansion were being further fulfilled the words of Jesus recorded in Luke's gospel: "But if I drive out demons by the finger of God, then the kingdom of God has come to you" (Lk. 11:20).

III. The relation between Simon Magus and Gnostic heresies.

The name of Simon Magus occurs frequently in the early history of "Christian" GNOSTICISM, and there has been much debate as to whether the Simoniani, a sect that lasted well into the 3rd cent., had its origins in the magician of Acts 8. The earliest postbiblical evidence is that of JUSTIN MARTYR (*1 Apol*. 1.26, 56), who says that a certain Simon from Gitta in Samaria during the reign of the Emperor CLAUDIUS practiced magic in both Samaria and Rome and was given divine honors (he mistakenly appeals to a Roman statue that bore the inscription *Simoni Deo Sancto*, "to Simon the Holy God," but which was actually erected in honor of a Sabine deity, Semo Sancus). Justin mentions that Simon was accompanied by Helena, a former prostitute whom Simon now called his "First Idea" (Ennoia), and says that a disciple of his, Menander, led many astray in Antioch by his sorcery. Justin attributes the movement to the efforts of evil spirits to overcome the spread of the Christian faith in the empire. IRENAEUS (*Adv. Haer*. 1.16) gives further details: Helena was in reality, Simon claimed, the mother of all the angelic orders, but when she came under the bondage of her own progeny he had become incarnate to free her and to bring all people to faith in himself.

These accounts show clearly that the people in view held to perversions of orthodox CHRISTOLOGY. Hippolytus and EPIPHANIUS also testify to these claims of Simon from their knowledge of Simonian writings, and JEROME quotes as Simon's the saying: "I am the Word of God, I am the Comforter, I am the Almighty, I am all there is of God." This is borne out by other traditions, perhaps deriving from Justin, that Simon evolved his own trinitarian formula. He was said to have revealed himself in Samaria as the Father, among the Jews as the Son, and among the Gentiles as the Holy Spirit. Simon is thus portrayed as the heretic par excellence of the subapostolic age. EUSEBIUS (*Eccl. Hist*. 2.13.1ff.) sums it up by declaring Simon to be the author of all heresy.

In another stream of literature, the CLEMENTINE "Homilies" and "Recognitions" (romances of the mid-2nd cent. about the search of Clement, a Roman, after the truth), Simon emerges as the antagonist of the apostle Peter. First he is linked with JOHN THE BAPTIST, together with another heretic named Dositheus, and is said to have learned his craft at ALEXANDRIA. Prolonged arguments between Peter and Simon are reported, and clashes between them at Caesarea and Antioch. In fact, the apostle is said to have devoted himself to undoing the havoc caused by Simon in numerous places. These encounters appear in other forms in such Gnostic writings as *Acts of Peter and Paul*, with Rome as the center of the conflict, and Peter finally conquering the heretic, who dies and fails to rise again.

To what extent can one link the Simon of Acts 8 with the central figure of these legends and with the Simonian sect? In the 19th cent. German scholars of the Tübingen school interpreted the postbiblical literature, particularly the Clementine romances, in such a way as to exaggerate greatly the cleavage between Peter and Paul (and between their followers) in the early church, and thus to cast serious doubt on the historicity of many incidents in Acts, the story of Simon Magus among them. However, it is now generally accepted that Luke's account is reliable. Simon's cult in Samaria may well have been the seed of the later aberrations of the Simoniani. How much actually stemmed from the historical Simon's travels and teachings will perhaps never be known. The cult became part of wider 2nd-cent. Gnosticism, and no doubt the church fathers tended to ascribe too much to Simon himself. He became the archsymbol of heresy.

The impression from the patristic evidence is that a real dread existed in the church at the repulsiveness of these deviations from the apostolic doctrine of Christ. This impression is closely akin to the spirit of Luke's account in the Acts of the early encounters with Satan and his instruments of evil. But, in the Acts, as in Luke's gospel, there is the certainty of a continuing victory for Christ and his church. ORIGEN was accordingly able to say in the 3rd cent. that the Simoniani had dwindled to insignificant numbers (*Cels.* 1.57).

(See further R. P. Casey in *BC*, 5 [1933], 151–63; A. D. Nock in ibid., 164–88; R. M. Grant, *Miracle and Natural Law in Graeco-Roman and Christian Thought* [1952], ch. 7; id., *Gnosticism and Early Christianity* [1960], ch. 3.; E. M. Yamauchi, *Pre-Christian Gnosticism: A Survey of the Proposed Evidence*, 2nd ed. [1983], 58–62, 201–3; J. Fossum in *The Samaritans*, ed. A. Crown [1989], 357–89.)   B. F. HARRIS

Simon the Canaanite. See CANANAEAN.

simple. This English term occurs in the Bible usually as the rendering of Hebrew *petî* H7343, "young, inexperienced, gullible" (Ps. 19:7 et al.; cf. the ptc. of the verb *pātâ* H7331 in Job 5:2). The OT usage is primarily in Proverbs. Those who are simple hate knowledge and the fear of the Lord (Prov. 1:29; cf. vv. 22, 32); they are fools (8:5) who shall inherit folly (14:18). While the prudent foresee, the simple just go on their way and are punished (21:11), as when they visit the harlot (7:7). While it is possible to place on one level the simple and the scorner (1:22), there is still more hope for the simple; when the scorner is punished, the simple learn from it (19:25; 21:11), which apparently could not be said of the scorner. Since the simple can still learn, they are invited to the dinner prepared for them by WISDOM (9:4), and the book of Proverbs itself is written to give wisdom to the simple and the young (1:4; cf. also Pss. 19:7; 119:130).

The NT usage is somewhat different. The KJV uses "simple" in one passage (Rom. 16:18–19) to render two Greek words that can mean "innocent" or "guileless" (*akakos* G179 and *akeraios* G193); the reference is to those who are unsuspecting and can be easily deceived. There is also a noun that can mean "simplicity" (*haplotēs* G605), but the nuance is positive, indicating sincerity and purity of attitude (e.g., 2 Cor. 11:3; Eph. 6:5).   D. C. DAVIS

Simri sim'ri. KJV alternate form of SHIMRI (only 1 Chr. 26:10).

sin. A transgression of God's commands or any failure to meet his standards; as a verb, the word means "to violate the divine law, to commit an offense against God or others." The primary Hebrew noun for "sin" is *ḥaṭṭāʾt* H2633 (Gen. 4:7 et al.; cf. the verb *ḥāṭāʾ* H3148, 39:9 et al.), but also used frequently are such terms as *ʿāwōn* H6411 ("misdeed, iniquity," 15:16 et al.) and *pešaʿ* H7322 ("transgression, crime," 31:36 et al.). In the NT, the standard term is Greek *hamartia* G281 (Matt. 12:31 et al.; cf. verb *hamartanō* G279, 18:15 et al.); other nouns include *adikia* G94 ("unrighteousness, wrongdoing," Acts 1:18 et al.), *paraptōma* G4183 ("violation, offense," Matt. 6:14 et al.), and so on. (For a fuller listing of the relevant Hebrew and Greek vocabularies, see *NIDOTTE*, 2:87–93; LN, §88.289–318.)

I. Origin. Sin "came into the world" (Rom. 5:12) when ADAM and EVE succumbed to TEMPTATION. The full responsibility for the presence and consequences of sin in the world fell full weight upon these human beings. DEATH itself silences every attempt to transfer even partially human guilt upon SATAN in whom sin arose and by whom Adam and Eve were tempted. Neither sin nor death itself, for all its finality, is the last word about the sinner, for if "death came through a man, the resurrection of the dead comes also through a man" (1 Cor. 15:21). If sin was projected through a demonic temptation as a possibility, and through Adam's transgression entered the world as an actuality, sin (and death) is also cosmically defeated and abolished in the world and history through the "second man" (1 Cor. 15:47), JESUS CHRIST. Through Christ sin is undone and forgiven, death ends in RESURRECTION, sinners become saints, and he "who holds the power of death" is destroyed (Heb. 2:14).

II. Sin and freedom. The concept of freedom does not account for sin. While sin is not unrelated to freedom, the latter does not explain the rise of the former (see LIBERTY). God has authentic freedom and cannot sin, and God created Adam with a freedom that was morally qualified and whose continuance depended on refraining from sin. Adam and Eve as created possessed the ability not to sin, and the person re-created in Christ, and begotten of God, "does not sin" (1 Jn. 5:18 RSV). The ability to sin is not of the essence of freedom. True freedom is constituted by ability to do the good, not by a morally unqualified faculty to do either the one or the other. Freedom belongs to the essence of human beings as created by God and as restored by Christ; in neither instance is it a morally neutral and unqualified aspect of humanity.

The effect of human sin upon freedom is defined in biblical thought, therefore, not as another form of freedom, but rather as SLAVERY and bondage (Rom. 6). Human beings as created were no more free to sin than, having sinned and fallen into moral bondage, they are free again to become what they once were. Sin constitutes a loss, not an exercise of freedom. Sin is a mystery, immoral and irrational, whose denouement is not found in the concept of human freedom. Freedom as an explanation of sin leads invariably into some form of Pelagianism (or Arminianism). If Adam was free to sin against his Maker, freedom by the same definition would contain the possibility of his self-propelled return to his Maker. If sin is a true exercise of freedom, such freedom, even after sin, remains also free both to act in Pelagian fashion to undo its sin and to return to God—or to refuse to return to God.

According to the Genesis account of the FALL into sin, Adam and Eve were not free to sin, but under divine command not to sin, on threat of death. They were under the restrictive divine command not to do what they in fact did. Freedom, as authority, is comprised of two components: might plus right. An authority that exercises a might without right is a totalitarian perversion of authority; a freedom that does what it has no right to do is an anarchistic perversion of true freedom.

The theological tenet that God created human beings free to sin (*posse peccāre*) is an explanation of sin in terms of sin. If God had endowed them with such freedom, he could not in justice allow them to suffer that bondage which sin inflicts upon freedom. In biblical thought, however, the fall into sin is regarded as a loss of freedom. According to the Genesis account, Adam and Eve lost their right to existence in the Garden of Eden, their right to life, and their right to be themselves—naked and not ashamed. In the continuing biblical account, sinners are exhibited as no longer free to be themselves. They are either slaves to sin and under the power of death—who in their devotion to idols become subhuman and like their idols (Ps. 115:8)—or they become captives to grace and through this captivity again receive their true freedom as a gift from God, a freedom permitting them to enjoy release from, and FORGIVENESS for, their sinful past and the gift of grace that justifies their right to live in an open and unending future.

III. Sin and divine sovereignty. Nor is the origin of sin accounted for in a biblically acceptable manner by the assertion that mankind is the secondary, and God the primary, ultimate cause of sin. Well-meaning but profoundly misguided defenders of the SOVEREIGNTY OF GOD have often declared that God himself is the source of sin. God is said to have willed sin, to be its primal cause, and even to have created sin. While such assertions are projected in defense of divine sovereignty, they are essentially blasphemous. It is deeply significant that none who make these bold assertions have been known to articulate them in their prayers and worship of God; confessing their sins, they cannot assert before God what they claim in their theology: that the One to whom they pray for forgiveness is the primary cause of their sin.

Rejecting both the notion that God willed sin and that sin is the product of chance, sober Christian thought has never dared say more than that God "permitted sin." The clearest expression of the relationship of the divine sovereign will to sin is not discoverable by a search in the area of the origin of sin, but is found at the cross where God at the cost of the death of his own Son overcomes and banishes sin.

Every rational analysis of sin reveals, as did Kierkegaard's psychological approach, that sin presupposes itself, and the history of Christian thought demonstrates that explanations of sin reduce sin into something that carries no guilt and requires no confession. Sin must be acknowledged and confessed, not explained. The Bible no more explains the rise of sin in the world of the angels and its connection with the origin of sin in our world, than it explains how human beings as God's creation could sin. There is neither a good moral reason nor a valid rational reason for the reality of sin. There can no more be a truly moral reason for EVIL than there can be a valid reason for irrationality. Sin is both immoral and irrational.

IV. History and fall. Sin is an essentially historical phenomenon. It has an event-character. To become real, it must happen. It is not an event within the trinitarian activity of the godhead, an activity both necessary and (therefore) eternal. The historical is neither necessary nor eternal; and sin, also being neither, is historical. Being real, sin happened once upon a time. The fall recorded in Genesis is a historical reality.

The Genesis sequence of creation-fall also clearly teaches that sin is neither an item of CREATION nor a quality of creation that in the process of time is progressively transformed into emerging good. Sin, on the contrary, is a contradiction to all created and uncreated reality. It is destructive of all good. The substitution of an evolutionary development of the good for the biblical historical fall is a misreading of the good that God in history accomplishes through Jesus Christ. The biblical account of the fall into sin is marked by the complex of contradictions between man and God, between husband and wife, and between man and nature, all of which immediately appeared as the consequence of sin.

No Christian can say *why* he or she sinned. If we could give a reason for, and thus an explanation of, our sin, sin would require neither forgiveness nor cancellation, being a justified act. It would have a right to exist. Both the origin of sin and its continuance in the life of every person is and remains an enigma for which there is no apology and no known theodicy. Sin has no defense, no right to existence. Every explanation of sin in terms of human freedom turns sin into something that carries neither guilt nor need of repentance; when explained in terms of the causality of the sovereign divine will, sin is naturalized within the being of God himself.

V. Original sin. The concept of original sin is theological, not temporal, and therefore throws no clear light on the *origin* of sin. Original sin refers neither to the first of all sins, nor to the first sin in human history, but to the first sin of Adam and only to that and not to the subsequent sins of Adam. In human history, Eve sinned first; nonetheless, it was by Adam's (later) sin that "sin entered into the world ... and death through sin" (Rom. 5:12). Original sin is the first sin of Adam, the source of all *other* sins, including Adam's subsequent sins, and is that power by which death passed upon all, even though they have not sinned in the manner of Adam's first sinful act (v. 14).

VI. Total depravity. Original sin provides a clue to the nature of sin and of death. According to the Genesis account, original sin is a proud, loveless, rebellious, thankless, destructive act of self-assertion, first against the God who gave human beings their reality and, simultaneously, against both the self and every other form of created reality. By his initial act of sin, Adam broke that relationship to God, to Eve, and to the natural world, on which in real though differing degrees his own life and well-being depended. Adam's sin is a declaration of self-sufficiency; he willed to go it alone. By that original, first sin of Adam everything is alienated; Adam and Eve each hide from the other by donning clothes, Adam hides from God, Adam blames God and Eve, Eve blames the serpent, and the self is alienated from itself.

To this deprivation of the self there is a corresponding total DEPRAVITY in which the self is deprived of all those moral and spiritual qualities that constitute the authentic self and its relation to all that is not-self. The self is totally depraved, for the self can do nothing worse or more destructive to God and to others than sin. Were it not so, death and hell would be an overkill that exceeded sin's guilt quality. Original sin—and all subsequent sins merely reemphasize it—so effectively breaks our relationship to all reality (the self, God, fellow human beings, nature) that we cannot reinstate original, authentic relationships. This is disclosed supremely at the cross, where sinners kill him in whom all reality, divine and created, is centered.

Thus original sin as that act which breaks all God-created relationships is neither merely moral, intellectual, nor affective, but something deeper than all of these. It is in essence religious. As David said, "Against you, you only, have I sinned / and done what is evil in your sight" (Ps. 51:4). It is this divine referent that constitutes the essence of original sin and via this reference becomes also our sin against ourselves, others, and nature. The nature of sin is wholly destructive; sin, therefore, elicits those full realities which the biblical concepts of death and the infinite divine wrath convey.

The truth that sin renders the sinner totally depraved cannot be read from human experience. Although history is saturated with manifold forms of sinful action, a true recognition of sin—as distinct from human error, ignorance, folly, or frailty—does not occur within the field of human observation or experience. No road leads from the experience of sin to the true knowledge of sin. The distinctively religious dimension of sin as an act which is in the first instance against God can be disclosed only by God himself. Human moral behavior is often better than total depravity can account for, an ambiguity that derives from God's gracious operations upon the sinner, and a truth that can be known only by REVELATION. That every sin against the neighbor, against the natural environment, is also a sin against God, is not a humanly attainable knowledge unless imparted by divine revelation. Similarly, the knowledge that the sinner's right relationship to God, neighbor, and natural environment cannot be reconstituted except by the grace of REGENERATION can also be known only by means of revelation.

VII. Sin and grace. Sin is transgression of the LAW, but it is never merely that. Since the purpose of law is GRACE as indicated by the fact that it was given to Israel within a COVENANT situation (Gal. 3:17) and by the law's own introductory preface (Exod. 20:2), sin is always an act against the goodness and grace of God.

This quality of sin as an act against the grace of God emphasizes that sin is never an individual issue, but always a social matter. Grace is an expression of God's will to be with and for his creatures in a community in which they are both for God and for their neighbors. This social character of grace corresponds to the demand of the law that we love both God and our neighbor. He who loves God cannot hate his neighbor; and he who hates his neighbor cannot love God (1 Jn. 2–3). Sin as the rejection of this gracious divine will to community is, therefore, not an individualistic act. It is rather a social act—even in its negative, antisocial form. Further, for the reason that sin is a social act, sin is committed not only by the single individual, but also by social groups, and thus it can be embodied in social structures. A nation can sin no less than an individual; there are national sins, and nations, no less than individuals, are called to repentance and amendment of life. Similarly, the church can sin and be called to confession and amendment of life, though it must be admitted that rarely do churches do what they require of their individual members.

This communal, social character of sin which reflects the communal, social character of divine grace, helps one to understand why justice is never an individual concept, but always and inherently, a social one. There is no individual, as distinct from a social, justice. All justice is social justice, because justice is the expression of God's HOLINESS as it maintains God's gracious purpose to be with and for sinners, but against their sinful assault on that purpose.

It must also be observed that because of the social character of sin, the distinction between a "personal" and a "social" ethic is grounded in a misunderstanding of the nature of sin. A "personal" ethic always turns out to be an ethic of the individual in contrast to a social ethic. All sin is, indeed, personal, whether that of the individual or of the corporate personality of the church or nation—as is also all love and right doing. But there is no individualistic personal ethic, as there is no individualistic grace or individualistic justice. The biblical ideas of grace, love, justice, as the biblical teaching that Adam's original sin is also our sin and Christ's one act of obedience can be our righteousness, are in theory surrendered when sin is individualistically defined by reference to a legalistic understanding of the law, without reference to the social character of God's grace.

This corporate quality of sin is also clearly seen in the NT teachings that we can be forgiven by God only as we forgive others (Matt. 6:14–15), can worship God at the altar only when in right relationship with our brothers (5:23–24), and can pray properly only when we address God as "our" Father and request daily bread, forgiveness of sins, and deliverance from evil as we pray in plural personal pronouns ("us" and "our").

VIII. Sin and punishment. Sin requires punishment. As an affront against the infinite majesty of God, sin calls for infinite punishment, and that without limit. The Bible, therefore, speaks of the wages of sin being death and of eternal punishment in HELL. Such punishment is the reflex of the holiness of God whereby he maintains himself against human sin. In responding to sin, God's holiness takes the form of justice expressing itself in infinite wrath and unlimited judgment. See PUNISHMENT, ETERNAL.

This divine response, however, takes place in history only at the CROSS, where the Son of God becomes the object of it—and dies. Elsewhere in human history God's WRATH and punishing justice is always corrective, a form of wrath for the sake of grace, a form of judgment that can be turned aside, averted, and repented of by God as men and women repent and respond to his grace. The only divine judgment and wrath God cannot withdraw or repent of in history is that which occurred at the cross. That all other manifestations of divine judgment upon sin are contingent rather than absolute, corrective rather than final, suggests that all justice which society administers to its criminals should be remedial and corrective, never merely punitive, and never final.

Original sin is the source of all other sins and these are so manifold as to defy number or name, yet each of them reflects something of the highly complex nature of sin. In view of this complexity it is not surprising that the Bible uses many words to denote sin. Sin is, moreover, in biblical thought many other things—unbelief, distrust, ingratitude, lovelessness, hatred. The greatest sin occurs in reaction to the cross where the nature of sin in all its aspects is revealed, and original sin and all its subsequent historical expressions is overcome and forgiven by God's gracious action in Christ. The greatest sin, therefore, is the rejection of Christ crucified, who shall judge everyone according to the gospel (Rom. 2:16), which is to say, in reference to God's gracious will and purpose.

(See further G. C. Berkouwer, *Sin* [1971]; B. Ramm, *Offense to Reason: A Theology of Sin* [1985]; W. Grudem, *Systematic Theology: An Introduction to Christian Doctrine* [1994], ch. 24; H. Blocher, *Original Sin: Illuminating the Riddle* [1999]; M. E. Biddle, *Missing the Mark: Sin and Its Consequences in Biblical Theology* [2005].) J. DAANE

Sin (city). See PELUSIUM.

sin (letter). See SHIN.

Sin, Wilderness of (סִין H6097, derivation uncertain). This desert region—not to be confused with the Wilderness of ZIN in the northern NEGEV—was on the route followed by the Hebrews when they left EGYPT, somewhere between ELIM and Mount SINAI (Exod. 16:1; 17:1; Num. 33:11–12 locates it more narrowly between the RED SEA and DOPHKAH). It was here that God provided both MANNA and QUAIL for the Israelites. Assuming that Mount Sinai should be identified with Jebel Musa or another mountain in its vicinity, some have suggested that the Wilderness of Sin is Debbet er-Ramleh, a sandy tract of desert at the foot of Jebel et-Tih, in the SW of the Sinai peninsula. Others believe it refers to the plain of el-Merkha on the W coast, half-way between the head of the Red Sea and the tip of the peninsula. Scholars who argue that the Israelites took a northerly route have proposed various other sites. The location remains unknown. See also EXODUS, THE. J. M. HOUSTON

Sinai, Mount sī'nī (סִינַי H10099, perhaps from Akk. *Sin*, name of the moon god; Σινά or Σινᾶ G4982 [the mountain is also called Horeb, חֹרֵב H2998, "dry, desolate"]). The name of the sacred mountain before which Israel encamped and upon which MOSES communicated with Yahweh. In the Bible, the name occurs almost exclusively in the PENTATEUCH. The Israelites reached Mount Sinai in the third month after their departure from Egypt and camped at its foot where they could view the summit (Exod. 19:1, 16, 18, 20). Yahweh revealed himself to Moses here and communicated the TEN COMMANDMENTS and other laws to the people through him. God established his COVENANT with the people through Moses as mediator, and this covenant has been remembered throughout Israel's history (e.g., Jdg. 5:5; Neh. 9:13; Ps. 68:8, 17; Mal. 4:4; Acts 7:30, 38). ELIJAH later visited Horeb in a time of particular discouragement and depression (1 Ki. 19:4–8). In the allegory of Gal. 4:24–25, Mount Sinai is representative of the bondage of the law in contrast to the Jerusalem above, which is free.

JOSEPHUS describes Mount Sinai in fearful terms as being "… the highest of all the mountains that are in that country, and is not only very difficult to be ascended by man, on account of its vast altitude, but because of the sharpness of its precipices also; nay, indeed, it cannot be looked at without pain of the eyes: and besides this, it was terrible and inaccessible, on account of the rumour that passed about, that God dwelt there" (*Ant.* 2.12.1; 3.5.1).

The location of Mount Sinai is uncertain. Some have proposed identifying it with one of a number of mountains in the vicinity of KADESH BARNEA. In a number of biblical references it is mentioned in connection with Edomite territory (including SEIR and TEMAN; see Deut. 33:2; Jdg. 5:4–5; Hab. 3:3), suggesting that Mount Sinai may have been N of the Sinai peninsula. The fact that Moses requested Pharaoh to allow Israel a three days' journey into the wilderness is somewhat more in keeping with Kadesh Barnea as an intended destination than is the location of Mount Sinai in the S of the Sinai peninsula (Exod. 3:18; 5:3; 8:27). There is also the fact that REPHIDIM is associated with MERIBAH and the two together are associated with Mount Horeb (17:1–7). Meribah is located in the area of Kadesh Barnea in Num. 20:2–13, and a number of springs are known to be there.

However, even the northern location for the mountain would hardly allow the journey from Egypt to be made in three days. The fact that Deut. 1:2 speaks of an eleven days' journey from Kadesh to Horeb would seem to militate against the identification of Mount Sinai with a mountain in the vicinity of Kadesh as well. The reconstruction of the route of the exodus is rendered well nigh impossible if this identification is assumed. See EXODUS, THE.

Some scholars have attempted to locate Sinai in NW ARABIA in the ancient land of MIDIAN (some recent claims specifically identify Sinai with Jebel al-Lawz in modern Saudi Arabia; see R. Cornuke and D. Halbrook, *In Search of the Mountain of God: The Discovery of the Real Mt. Sinai* [2000]). One reason given for this is that when Moses fled from Egypt he married into a Midianite family. That in itself, however, would not necessitate a return to Midianite territory following the exodus, though it might have made it more convenient. Besides that, however, is the fact that the tribe into which Moses married, the KENITES, were probably wandering smiths and they may well have been located at the traditional site of Sinai with its mines.

It is also argued that the description of the events on the mountain with its "thunder and lightning, with a thick cloud … and a very loud trumpet blast," as well as smoke and fire (Exod. 19:16–19), presupposes a mountain which experienced volcanic activity. The nearest mountains known to have been actively volcanic in ancient times are in Arabia, S of the head of the Gulf of AQABAH. The descriptive language may equally well have been drawn from weather phenomena, however. Alternatively, even if the language itself was drawn from volcanic phenomena, that does not necessitate actual volcanic activity at Mount Sinai.

Another suggestion made especially during the 19th cent. is that Mount Sinai was to be identified with Jebel Serbal (6,730 ft.), which is located by the Wadi Feiran (some distance to the W of the traditional Sinai). Significantly, the city of Pharan (Feiran) was the seat of a bishopric in the 4th and 5th centuries, and in the time of Justinian, orthodox monks moved from Jebel Serbal to the traditional site of Sinai. The *Pilgrimage of Sylvia*, edited in 1887 and describing the journey of Sylvia of Aquitaine between A.D. 385 and 388, seems to render this identification impossible, however. The account states that the "mount of God" was

35 Roman mi. from Pharan. This is the actual distance from the oasis at Feiran to the traditional Sinai. Also, there is no wilderness at the foot of Jebel Serbal that would fit the Pentateuch's description of the plain of encampment.

A more recent proposal identifies Sinai with Jebel Sin Bisher, a mountain that is much farther N than the traditional site and only about 15 mi. E of the Gulf of Suez (M. Har-El in *Geography in Israel*, ed. D. H. K. Amiran and Y. Ben-Arieh [1976]: 383–91, cited by C. G. Rasmussen, *Zondervan NIV Atlas of the Bible* [1989], 90, 210 nn. 9 and 14). The main argument in its favor is that it can be described—more accurately than is the case with competing sites—as being "a three-day journey" from Egypt (Exod. 3:18 et al.). Moreover, the character of the surrounding area (including various water sources) fits the biblical narrative.

Since the 4th cent., the more or less continuous Christian tradition has been that Mount Sinai is represented by what is now called Jebel Musa (mountain of Moses). This is located in the high mountains of the S tip of the Sinai peninsula. Various legends and traditions are associated with the site, and a number of chapels and shrines have been built in the area. Catherine of Alexandria is said to have been carried by angels after her martyrdom to the top of the mountain that now bears her name (8,536 ft.). This story dates from the 4th cent. The summit of Jebel Katarina is some 2.5 mi. SW of Jebel Musa.

By the 4th cent., communities of monks had retired to the region and were subjected to various massacres at the hands of the Saracens. One of them, Ammonius of Canopus (in Egypt) made a pilgrimage to Mount Sinai in c. A.D. 373, evidently reaching it in eighteen days from Jerusalem. In A.D. 536, Mount Sinai, Raithou (on the coast of the Red Sea), and the church at Pharan are noted as being under the presbyter Theonos. On the NW slope of Jebel Musa, Constantine's mother, Helena, built a small church in the 4th cent. The present Monastery of St. Catherine, famous for the fact that Tischendorf found CODEX SINAITICUS there in 1859, was built on the same site and is traced back to Justinian in A.D. 527.

Approaching the region from the N one may enter the valley of esh-Sheikh to the E or the Valley of er-Raha to the W. The latter is some 2 mi. long and at its SE end opens into a plain about 1 mi. wide at the foot of the steep cliffs of Ras es-Safsaf. Ras es-Safsaf is the NW peak (6,540 ft.) of a ridge that has Jebel Musa as its highest peak (7,363 ft.) 2.5 mi. to the SE. The plain of er-Raha may well have been the site of the encampment of Israel (Exod. 19:1–2; Num. 33:15). To the SE of Jebel Musa is the Wadi es-Sebayeh with its valley up to 1 mi. wide and 2.5 mi. long. This valley is sometimes identified as the place of the encampment though the former is generally preferred. Christian tradition generally claims Ras es-Safsaf as the biblical Horeb and Jebel Musa as Sinai.

From St. Catherine's monastery with its Chapel of the Burning Bush (cf. Exod. 3:2), the summit of Jebel Musa can be reached after a hard climb of one and a half hours. Part way up, a little spring is passed and said to have been the place where Moses tended Jethro's flock (3:1); at 6,900 ft. is the Chapel of Elijah (1 Ki. 19:8–9). Ras es-Safsaf takes its name from the Arabic word for "willow" and is a reference to Moses' staff (cf. Exod. 4:2). A large block of granite some 11 ft. high is said to be the rock from which Moses brought water (Num. 20:8). A hole in the rock is said to be the mold used for the golden calf (Exod. 32), and the place where the earth swallowed up KORAH and his followers is identified (Num. 16).

(See further E. Robinson, *Biblical Researches in Palestine, Mount Sinai and Arabia Petraea*, 3 vols. [1841], 1:90–144; McClintock-Strong, *Cyclopedia*, 9:767–72; E. H. Palmer, *The Desert of the*

Pinnacle of Jebel Musa, traditional site of Mount Sinai. (View to the S.)

Exodus [1871]; W. M. F. Petrie, *Researches in Sinai* [1906]; B. Rothenberg, *God's Wilderness* [1961]; G. E. Wright, *Biblical Archaeology*, rev. ed. [1962], 60–66 et passim; G. I. Davies, *The Way of the Wilderness: A Geographical Study of the Wilderness Itineraries in the Old Testament* [1979]; R. W. L. Moberly, *At the Mountain of God* [1983]; Z. Meshel, *Sinai: Excavations and Studies* [2000]; J. K. Hoffmeier, *Ancient Israel in Sinai: The Evidence for the Authenticity of the Wilderness Tradition* [2005]; *NEAEHL*, 4:1384–1403.) H. G. ANDERSEN

Sinaiticus sin′i-it′uh-kuhs. This term is applied primarily to two biblical MSS discovered in St. Catherine's Monastery (located at the foot of Jebel Musa, the traditional site of Mount SINAI). One of them is among the oldest copies of the entire Bible in Greek (see CODEX SINAITICUS); the other one, Syrus Sinaiticus, is a MS dated to c. A.D. 400 that contains the oldest known copy of the Old Syriac Gospels (see VERSIONS OF THE BIBLE, ANCIENT, III.B).

sincere. This term and its cognates *sincerity* and *sincerely* appear rarely in English versions of the OT, although certain Hebrew words, such as the noun *ṣĕdāqâ* H7407, "righteousness," approach this meaning (cf. Isa. 48:1 NJPS). In the NT, the Greek adjective *eilikrinēs* G1637 ("unmixed, pure, sincere") and its cognate noun *eilikrineia* G1636 occur a handful of times (also relevant are such terms as *hagnos* G56, Phil. 1:7, and *anypokritos* G537, 1 Tim. 1:5 et al.).

In the NT, sincerity is an all-embracing attitude, not just one virtue among many. In Phil. 1:9 (where *eilikrinēs* is often rendered "pure") it is a quality required at the judgment, and requires growth in both love and knowledge, fitting one to discern that which is truly excellent (v. 10). The eschatological perspective is in view also in 2 Pet. 3:11; the sincere mind believes God's promises of Christ's return, over against the attitude of the scoffers that covers up God's promises with proud self-evaluation of the future. In 1 Cor. 5:8, sincerity is the (unmixed, plain) unleavened bread that rejects immorality in the church and the pride that condones it.

Sincerity has also application in ministry to others. PAUL is not a peddler of the word of God, but one who has only LOVE as his motive (2 Cor. 2:17), and he preaches not with earthly wisdom, but "according to God's grace," that is, so he can be understood (1:12–14). Singleness of motive and message go together. D. C. DAVIS

sinew. A tough fibrous band connecting muscle to bone; synonymous with *tendon*. Sinews (Heb. *gîd* H1630) are depicted as holding the bones of the body together (Job 10:11; 40:17; Ezek. 37:6, 8). In the latter case the sinews were the first covering for the dry bones. JACOB's experience at PENUEL (Gen. 32:32; cf. v. 25) may have involved a mighty contraction of the muscle and tendon that tore muscle fibers and left Jacob limping at dawn. "Out of joint" would refer to any injury of the hip region; taken literally, it would imply a dislocation of the hip, a major injury making walking impossible (see THIGH). In the NT, PAUL uses the Greek noun *syndesmos* G5278 ("bond, ligament") figuratively when he compares the relationship between Christ and the CHURCH to the human body (Col. 2:19; see BODY OF CHRIST). D. A. BLAIKLOCK

singers, singing. See MUSIC II.B.

Sinim, land of si′nim. See SINITES; SYENE.

Sinites sin′its (סִינִים H6098, meaning unknown). A people group descended from CANAAN and mentioned in the Table of NATIONS (Gen. 10:17; 1 Chr. 1:15; it is possible, but unlikely, that the same people are referred to by the name *sînîm* in the MT of Isa. 49:12, for which see SYENE). Some scholars have suggested a connection between the Sinites and an ancient fortress on Mount Lebanon that Strabo (*Geogr.* 16.2.18) calls *Sinna*; similarly, JEROME, in his comments on this passage (*Liber quaestionum hebraicorum in Genesim*) refers to a "civitas Sini" in the same area. The discoveries in Ras Shamra have confirmed the existence of a coastal city-state named *syn*, located S of UGARIT (see C. H. Gordon, *UT*, 449 [ch. 19, #1750]), probably the same place that Akkadian sources refer to as *šiannu*; it may correspond to modern Siyano (c. 2 mi. E of Jeble-Gabala; see *HALOT*, 2:751).

sin offering. See SACRIFICE AND OFFERINGS IV.A.1.

Sion si′uhn. (1) KJV form of Siyon (Deut. 4:48).

(2) KJV alternate form of Zion (Ps. 65:1 and NT).

Siphmoth sif′moth (שִׁפְמוֹת H8560, meaning unknown). One of the cities of Judah with which David shared the spoils taken from Ziklag (1 Sam. 30:28). It was visited by David during the time in which he was a fugitive from King Saul. Siphmoth was evidently in the southern part of Judah's territory, but its location is unknown.

T. E. McComiskey

Sippai sip′i (סִפַּי H6205, meaning unknown). A descendant of the Rephaites who was killed by Sibbecai the Hushathite (1 Chr. 20:4). See Saph.

Sirach si′ruhk. See Ecclesiasticus.

Sirah si′ruh (סִרָה H6241, "thorn bush"). The name of a cistern or well from which Joab summoned Abner in order to put him to death (2 Sam. 3:26). Josephus (*Ant.* 7.1.5) states that Abner was in a place called Besira when he was recalled by Joab and locates the area at 20 stadia (c. 2.5 mi.) from Hebron; on that basis proposed identifications include a spring named ʿAin Sarah (1.5 mi. NW of Hebron) and a site called Ṣiret el-Bellaʿ (farther E).   T. E. McComiskey

Sirion sihr′ee-uhn (שִׂרְיוֹן H8590 [some mss שִׁרְיֹן], possibly "armor" [see *HALOT*, 3:1357]). The Phoenician name that the people of Sidon used for Mount Hermon (Deut. 3:9). This mountain served to indicate the northern limit of the territory held by Amorite kings (4:48 NRSV, following the Syriac version [but see Siyon]). The name occurs in poetic parallelism with Lebanon (Ps. 29:6); a similar connection is found in Ugaritic material (cf. *ANET*, 134a; L. R. Fisher, *Ras-Shamra Parallels: The Texts from Ugarit and the Hebrew Bible*, 3 vols. [1972–81], 1:248 [#328]; 2:333 [#105]).

Sisamai sis′uh-mi. KJV form of Sismai.

Sisera sis′uh-ruh (סִיסְרָא H6102, derivation uncertain; prob. not a Semitic name).

(1) Commander of the army under Jabin, the Canaanite king of Hazor (Jdg. 4:2–22).

Although the Israelites led by Joshua had defeated the northern coalition and destroyed the city of Hazor (Josh. 11:11), this city had been rebuilt and became the capital of the Canaanites. Jabin may have been the hereditary royal title among the Canaanite kings, even as Pharaoh was the title for Egyptian rulers. It is likely the Israelites were not so much concerned with the city of Hazor, which was the royal Canaanite residence—the real menace was the Canaanite power represented by the army under Sisera's command, apparently stationed near the slopes of Mount Carmel (see Carmel, Mount) in the city or region of Harosheth Haggoyim. The location of Harosheth Haggoyim is uncertain, but it was probably in the narrow valley, less than a mile wide, where the Kishon flows out of the Esdraelon Plain into the Plain of Acco and the Mediterranean Sea. It is possible that modern Tell ʾAmr, S of the Kishon, or Tell el-Harbaj, N of the river, represents this ancient Canaanite stronghold, c. 12 mi. NW of Megiddo. If so, this strategic site commanded the entrance to the Plain of Esdraelon at the E end of the Mount Carmel ridge.

During a twenty-year period of oppression, the Canaanites paralyzed Israelite commerce and subjected the Israelites to intolerable disruption of normal life. Armed resistance seemed almost impossible until Deborah arose as a prophetess to whom the people turned in hope. Apparently Sisera encountered no serious threats from the Israelites until Barak led a division of 10,000 against him. However, the military superiority of the Canaanites is clearly indicated in the fact that they had 900 chariots of iron while the Israelites apparently had none (Josephus [*Ant.* 5.5.1] credits the Canaanite army with 3,000 chariots, 10,000 horsemen, and 300,000 footmen). These chariots probably were two-wheeled, open behind, carrying a driver, a warrior, and a shield bearer. Thutmose III of Egypt had 924 chariots when he advanced Egyptian armies across Palestine during the 15th cent. B.C. (cf. *ANET*, 237).

When Sisera learned that an Israelite army had gathered on Mount Tabor, he advanced his chariot division into the plain. A sudden and probably unexpected rainstorm changed the Kishon Valley into a muddy terrain, benefiting the Israelites, who

The Kishon River, a wadi that flows through the Jezreel Valley, was the scene of Sisera's defeat at the hands of Deborah and Barak. (View to the E.)

were prepared to fight without the aid of chariots. Barak was advised by the prophetess Deborah that the Lord God of Israel would direct Sisera with his chariots and army down to the Kishon (Jdg. 4:7). It may have been the dry season, so that when a sudden rain made it impossible for the Canaanites to use their chariots, the Israelites had the real advantage. Probably all the charioteers abandoned their chariots in the conflict—at least, that is what Sisera did. The Canaanites were completely demoralized and were routed by the Israelites.

Sisera's course in fleeing from the battle with the Israelites took him to the home of HEBER the Kenite, who had settled near KEDESH (Jdg. 4:17; cf. v. 11). Whether this was by accident or deliberate planning is not indicated in the biblical account. Heber himself was apparently absent, but his wife, JAEL, invited Sisera into the tent. Accepting Jael's hospitality, Sisera felt quite secure and asked her to lie in his behalf to avoid detection by the enemy. After Jael provided him milk for nourishment and a rug for a covering, he fell asleep. Jael took advantage of this opportunity. With a mallet she drove a tent-peg through Sisera's temple. When Barak came by, Jael invited him into her tent to witness the fact that Israel's oppressor had been slain (vv. 18–22).

Similar to previous experiences in Israel's history where they were faced by a superior foe, the Israelites were at this time also keenly conscious of the fact that God had intervened in their behalf. Praise to God was appropriately expressed throughout Deborah's song (Jdg. 5, esp. vv. 20–31; cf. also 1 Sam. 12:9–11; Ps. 83:9–10). The accounts of Jael's heroic deed have been held to be contradictory by some scholars. It seems most reasonable that Jael killed Sisera while he was asleep (Jdg. 4:18–21). The poetic record (5:24–27) may well represent an embellishment of Jael's feat and was not intended to provide a concrete description of detailed developments. The following verses (5:28–30) portray in vivid language the disappointment of Sisera's mother in waiting for the return of her son.

The defeat of Sisera and his army undoubtedly broke the oppressive hold the Canaanites had on the Israelites. In the course of time the Israelites overcame the Canaanites even to the point of destroying King Jabin.

(2) The ancestor of a family of temple servants (NETHINIM) who returned from the EXILE with ZERUBBABEL (Ezra 2:53; Neh. 7:55; called "Serar" in 1 Esd. 5:32 [KJV, "Aserer"]). Because the temple servants were apparently non-Israelites (see

NETHINIM), some have speculated that this family descended from #1, above. S. J. SCHULTZ

Sisinnes si-sin´es. See TATTENAI.

Sismai sis´mi (סִסְמַי H6183, meaning unknown). KJV Sisamai. Son of Eleasah and descendant of JUDAH through the line of JERAHMEEL (1 Chr. 2:40).

sister. See FAMILY.

sistrum. See MUSIC, MUSICAL INSTRUMENTS IV.A.

Sithri sith´ri (סִתְרִי H6262, "[God is] my hiding place"). KJV Zithri. Son of Uzziel and descendant of LEVI through KOHATH (Exod. 6:22). One of Uzziel's brothers was AMRAM (father of MOSES, AARON, and MIRIAM), so Sithri was Moses' first cousin.

Sitnah sit´nuh (שִׂטְנָה H8479, possibly "enmity, contention"). The name of the second well dug by the servants of Isaac in the vicinity of GERAR (Gen. 26:21). The name reflects the conflict that ensued when the herdsmen of Gerar disputed with Isaac's herdsmen concerning the water rights. Although the exact location is uncertain, it was in the vicinity of REHOBOTH (26:22). T. E. MCCOMISKEY

Sivan si´van (סִיוָן H6094, meaning uncertain). The third month in the Jewish religious calendar (corresponding to May-June; Esth. 8:9).

six hundred sixty-six. See ANTICHRIST V.

sixty. See NUMBER I.B and I.D.

Siyon si´yuhn (שִׂיאֹן H8481, perhaps "small height"). Alternate name of Mount HERMON, possibly referring to a specific part of the range (Deut. 4:48; KJV and NJPS, "Sion"). However, some scholars suspect textual corruption and, following the Syriac Peshitta, emend to *śiryôn* H8590 (see SIRION), which was the Phoenician name for the mountain (cf. NRSV and see 3:9).

skin. Biblical references to animal skins used for clothing go back to the narrative of ADAM and EVE (Gen. 3:21). See DRESS; LEATHER. Rebekah put the skins of kids on JACOB's hands and neck so that he would feel rough, like ESAU, to his blind father (27:16). Animal skins were used also to manufacture leather bags for WINE (Josh. 9:4 et al.). Jesus, in response to complaints that his disciples were not fasting, commented that people do not "pour new wine into old wineskins. If they do, the skins will burst, the wine will run out and the wineskins will be ruined. No, they pour new wine into new wineskins, and both are preserved" (Matt. 9:17; cf. Mk. 2:22; Lk. 5:37–38). New wine was still fermenting, and the expansion caused by the resulting gases was easily accommodated by a new stretchable bottle. As skin bottles grew old, however, they lost their elasticity, becoming hard and brittle; new wine would cause them to burst.

There are some references to human diseases of the skin. That Job in his affliction suffered from smallpox is a good possibility. He was afflicted with sores from head to toe, to the extent that his friends could not recognize him (Job 2). The condition was very itchy, for he scraped himself with a piece of broken pottery. He commented, "my skin hardens, then breaks out again" (7:5 NRSV). All this fits smallpox, although there are other possibilities. Israelite law addressed the problem of skin disorders (e.g., Lev. 13); see DISEASE (sections on *boil, itch, leprosy, scurvy*).

There are well-known proverbs concerning skin that come from the Bible. Job declared, "I have escaped by the skin of my teeth" (Job 19:20 NRSV). Jeremiah asked, "Can the Ethiopian change his skin or the leopard its spots?" (Jer. 13:23).

D. A. BLAIKLOCK

skirt. This English term, which usually refers to an outer garment (or to part of such a garment) that hangs freely, is used almost twenty times by the KJV, mainly as the rendering of *kānāp* H4053 (e.g., Ruth 3:9, where the NIV has "the corner of your garment"). This common Hebrew term means "wing," but by extension it can be applied to the "edge," "hem," or "corner" of a garment (e.g., 1 Sam. 15:27). Less frequent is its near synonym *šûl* H1767, which can also mean "hem" (Exod. 28:33–34 et al.); this term is rendered "skirt" not only by the KJV but also by modern versions in several passages (Jer. 13:22 et al.). W. WHITE, JR.

Skull, Place of the. See GOLGOTHA.

sky. See HEAVEN.

slander. A false accusation that defames a person's reputation. The basic character of this sin is shown by its inclusion in the Decalogue (Exod. 20:16; see TEN COMMANDMENTS), and also in the immediate context from which Christ quotes the second and great commandment (Lev. 19:16 [Heb. *rākîl* H8215]; cf. v. 18 and see Matt. 19:19; 22:39; Jas. 2:8). There LOVE for one's neighbor is characterized by not slandering him.

That slander is against God's wisdom is stressed by Proverbs (e.g., Prov. 10:18 [*dibbâ* H1804]). When it is against God's messengers, it is against God himself and is so punished (Num. 14:36, where the reports of the Promised Land are spoken against; Rom. 3:8 [Gk. *blasphēmeō* G1059], where false doctrine is imputed to Paul). It is placing human standards over God's judgment, and is implicit BLASPHEMY (cf. Jas. 4:11–12). It belongs in the category of those ultimate sins to which God delivers men and women (Rom. 1:30 [*katalalos* G2897]; 2 Tim. 3:3 for its eschatological character).

The great slanderer is SATAN himself (*diabolos* G1333, "accuser, slanderer"). He attempts to alienate JOB from his God. The Apocalypse describes him as the one who continually accuses the brethren (Rev. 12:10). The deliberate false witness against Christ, particularly at his trial, must be seen in this context (Matt. 26:59; cf. the command to Christ's disciples to give *true* witness to him). It is on Christ's account that his followers are falsely accused (5:11), but when God has pronounced his judgment on the elect (justification), who dares bring any charge against them (Rom. 8:33)?

Slander is opposed to the whole character of the Christian life, the love for the brethren (1 Pet. 2:1). Instead of slandering, the believer must forgive, remembering how Christ has forgiven him (Eph. 4:31–32), and put on the new nature which is not characterized by lying, but which is renewed in knowledge after God's image (Col. 3:8–10). See also LIE; TRUTH.

D. C. DAVIS

slave, slavery. The term *slavery* refers to the ownership of one person by another so that the former is viewed in most respects as property rather than as a person. It was a deeply rooted part of the economy and social structure of the ANE of the Greco-Roman world. See also SERVANT.

    I. Slavery in the OT
       A. Literary sources
       B. Terminology
       C. Acquisition of slaves
       D. Legal status and rights of slaves
       E. Publicly owned slaves
       F. The importance of slavery
    II. Slavery in the NT
       A. Manumission
       B. Status of slaves

I. Slavery in the OT. Slavery was a widespread practice in the ANE during OT times. However, the number of slaves in Israel probably did not run as high as in classical times. In Israel it was cheaper to hire laborers for work than to keep slaves. The use of slaves seems to have been largely confined to household duties and to work in the field alongside the master and his family.

A. Literary sources. The OT legislation is recorded in several passages (Exod. 21; Lev. 25; Deut. 15). There are numerous references to slaves throughout the OT. Extrabiblical data on slavery among the Jews is limited to the papyri from ELEPHANTINE, an Egyptian colony of the 5th cent. B.C. The private and public documents of the ANE from the 3rd millennium B.C. to NT times are full of references to the practice of slavery in the parallel cultures.

B. Terminology. The primary Hebrew term for "slave" (or "servant") is ʿ*ebed* H6269; female slaves are referred to by the terms *šiphâ* H9148 and *ʾāmâ* H563. Some other words, such as *naʿar* H5853 ("young man") and *nepeš* H5883 ("soul, person") can be used to refer to servants or slaves (e.g., Gen. 18:7; Lev. 22:11; cf. also the expression *miqnat kesep*, "bought with silver [money]," Gen. 17:12–13 et al.).

C. Acquisition of slaves

1. War captives. The earliest means for the acquisition of slaves in the ANE was by military conquest.

Relief with gladiator scene (from Ephesus). Initially, all gladiators were either slaves or prisoners who could be freed if they survived at least three years of combat.

Thousands of men, women, and children were thus reduced to servitude. To the ancients this was considered a humanitarian improvement on the earlier practice of killing all of the enemy (Num. 31:7–35; Deut. 20:10–18; 1 Ki. 20:39; 2 Chr. 28:8–15). The ANE legal codes and the OT law sought to limit the excesses of brutal punishment that captives received. The Hebrew was told that if a soldier saw a beautiful woman among the captives and married her, he must treat her thereafter as a free person (Deut. 21:10–14). He was not permitted to sell her into slavery after he ceased to delight in her. The Hebrews were subject to enslavement after capture in war at the hands of countless adversaries. The Phoenicians, Philistines, Syrians, Egyptians, and Romans held them in bondage in great numbers.

2. Purchase. The OT provided that foreigners could be bought and sold as slaves and considered as property (Lev. 25:44–46). There are infrequent references to foreign slaves who were imported into Palestine (1 Chr. 2:34–35). Hebrews were also sold into slavery in other lands; hence the death penalty was prescribed for those who kidnapped and sold a freeborn person (Exod. 21:16; Deut. 24:7). The OT cites examples of a father selling his daughter (Exod. 21:7; Neh. 5:5); a widow selling her children to pay her husband's debt (2 Ki. 4:1); and men and women selling themselves (Lev. 25:39, 47; Deut. 15:12–17).

The price of slaves varied widely. Thirty shekels was the price according to Exod. 21:32. A scale of from three to fifty shekels is given in Lev. 27:3–7, according to the age and sex of the slave. An appeal could be made to a priest when there was disagreement on price (v. 8). Twenty shekels was the price for a young man (v. 5)—the price paid for Joseph (Gen. 37:28). The average price for a slave was forty shekels (2 Macc. 8:11). A ransom of one talent for a captive (1 Ki. 20:39) must indicate that he was an individual of great importance.

Children were sold into slavery under terms of a conditional contract. More frequently this was true of young, unmarried girls. Exodus 21 stipulates that if a man sells his daughter, she must become the wife or concubine of her master or of one of his sons when she reaches maturity. If no male member of the family takes her as a wife, she is to be set free without any payment of money from her (v. 11). This condition was put in the contract because young girls were frequently purchased with the intention of making prostitutes of them when they reached maturity. A forced sale of children into slavery is mentioned in Neh. 5:1–5. Presumably a father had pledged his children for loans during a time of economic hardship. As settlement for the debts the land was seized and the children were sold into slavery.

There is some evidence that the Hebrews did traffic in slaves, a common practice in the ANE. An Egyptian slave is mentioned in 1 Chr. 2:34. Two laws dealt with slave trade. Both Exod. 21:16 and Deut. 24:7 forbid the kidnapping and selling of freeborn individuals; the penalty for such was death. It is quite possible that some were being sold into foreign countries. In earlier times, Joseph certainly was handled in this fashion (Gen. 37:28). A second law (Deut. 23:15–16) prohibits the extradition of a runaway slave, presumably a Hebrew who had escaped from his master in a foreign country.

Self-sale into slavery seems to have been a common practice of the Israelites. The law made allowance for persons to sell themselves into slavery voluntarily (Exod. 21:5–6; Deut. 15:16–17). This provision refers to the person who refused to go free after some years of service. If he refused his freedom because he enjoyed the economic security of his new home, and because he wished to remain with the wife his master provided for him, and with his children, he would serve his master for life. Leviticus 25 describes the way in which an Israelite was to be treated who entered into the state of slavery voluntarily, or who sold himself to a fellow Israelite or resident foreigner. Provision was made for release after fifty years of bondage. The value of a slave was calculated on the basis of the number of years remaining for him to serve. Evidently the SABBATICAL YEAR release of the Book of the Covenant (Exod. 20–23, esp. 21:2) had been forgotten or more probably disregarded. The assumption on which the Leviticus code is based is that no Israelite, being a child of God, could fall into perpetual bondage.

3. Insolvency. One of the chief sources of slaves in Palestine was the citizen who was in default of payment for his DEBTS (Exod. 21:2–4; Deut. 15:12). The law sought to protect the slave by limiting his service to six years. The principle behind slavery for insolvency is clear in the terms of Exod. 22:2. The law provided that a thief should be sold into slavery, not because he had stolen goods, but rather because he was unable to recompense the owner for the loss of his property.

There are numerous references to Hebrews who were reduced to slavery to satisfy debts. A number of those who joined DAVID at the cave of ADULLAM were defaulting debtors (1 Sam. 22:2). Other passages mention instances of children who were seized to satisfy creditors (2 Ki. 4:1; Neh. 5:1–5). Isaiah referred to that practice when he wrote these words from God: "Or to which of my creditors did I sell you? / Because of your sins you were sold" (Isa. 50:1).

One of the reasons for insolvency was the high rates of INTEREST charged in the ancient world. The Israelites were protected, in theory at least, from this by legislation—recorded in Exodus and repeated in Leviticus and Deuteronomy—which forbade them to charge interest of their fellow men.

4. Other means. The non-Hebrew slave could be acquired as a gift; in this way LEAH received ZILPAH as her slave (Gen. 29:24). Non-Hebrew slaves could also be passed on from one generation to another; Lev. 25:46 provided for the perpetual servitude of the original inhabitants of Canaan in this manner. Finally, the children of slaves, born within the owner's house, became the property of the master, even if the father should later become a free man (Exod. 21:4; Lev. 25:54).

D. Legal status and rights of slaves

1. Manumission. The OT law regarding the release of slaves is stated in three passages (Exod. 21:1–11; Lev. 25:39–55; Deut. 15:12–18). The first of these provided that a male Hebrew slave should be freed after he had served six years. If he was married before he became a slave, his wife was to be released with him; if he was provided a wife by his master, the slave could go free, but his wife and children would remain the property of the owner. In such instances, if the slave chose to remain with his master and his wife and children, he was to appear before the judges, have his ear pierced, presumably for some tag to be affixed, and become a slave for life.

A female slave was treated quite differently. She was assumed in the sight of the law to be a CONCUBINE or wife of the owner or of one of his sons. Because it was in the best interest of the home for her to remain, a slave girl was released only under extraordinary conditions. If the owner was displeased with her, he could let her be redeemed, probably by her family. If he had promised her to one of his sons, she was to be treated as a daughter. If the owner took another wife, he was still responsible to provide for his slave concubine. If these three conditions were not met, the slave girl was set free.

The Book of the Covenant (Exod. 20–23) also provided for the release of slaves who had been maimed by their masters. Questions arise concerning the meaning of Exod. 21:26–27. Because in this passage the slave is not specifically described as being a Hebrew, some have suggested that the injunction applied only to non-Israelite slaves. However, it would be extraordinary to suggest that a man was accountable for beating a non-Hebrew slave, but not for beating a Hebrew slave. This, most likely, was a pronouncement that applied to the treatment of all slaves.

The law of release in Deuteronomy has one significant change. It stipulated that female slaves were to be treated in the same way as males. It was no longer assumed that a marriage commitment by the owner for himself, or one of his sons, was a condition of female servitude.

The third law of release is found in Lev. 25:39–55. It provided that a Hebrew could never be in perpetual bondage. An Israelite who sold himself into slavery was to be released in the JUBILEE YEAR. He was not to be considered a slave, but a bondservant or hireling. True slaves were acquired from the surrounding nations, and for them there was no release. They were inherited with other property (vv. 44–46). A third provision required that if a Hebrew sold himself because of poverty to a resident foreigner, one of his relatives would have the right to redeem him. The price was to be based on the amount for which he was originally acquired, prorated to the number of years left to Jubilee. He was to be released in the year of Jubilee if not redeemed before then.

It is difficult to say if the laws of release were observed by the Hebrews. No document of manumission has appeared. On the contrary, JEREMIAH rebuked the princes of Judah who followed the decree of ZEDEKIAH to release the slaves only to bring them into bondage again (Jer. 34:8–17). Some see in the Jubilee release an admission that the Israelites failed to observe the right of release after six years of servitude, according to the terms of the Book of the Covenant.

2. Religious rights. The slave was considered to be a part of his owner's family; hence he shared in their religious life. The laws guaranteed him a right to the SABBATH rest (Exod. 20:10; 23:12) and granted him a share in the religious feasts (Deut. 12:12; 16:11, 14). Thus the sojourner could not partake of the feast until he had been circumcised, but the slave, who as a member of the family had to be circumcised, always took part in the feasts (Exod. 12:43–45). Likewise, a slave in the house of a priest was allowed to eat of the offering of the holy things, but a sojourner in the household, or even the daughter of a priest, if she had married into a nonpriestly family, was forbidden to share in the offering (Lev. 22:10–12).

3. Civil rights. Slaves were protected in considerable measure from inhumane treatment. The murder of a slave was punishable by death (Exod. 21:12). If a master beat a slave, and he died as a result, the master was to be punished, but it is not clear what the punishment was (21:20–21). Again, if a master maimed his slave, the slave was to be set free (21:26). The terms of the prohibition on maiming were quite restrictive. A slave was to be set free if a beating resulted even in the loss of a tooth (21:27). Restrictions were also placed on the illegal sale of persons into slavery and on the return of runaway slaves.

4. Marriage. Hebrew slaves were allowed to marry. The code in Exodus stipulated that a Hebrew slave was to be set free in six years. As mentioned above, if he was married when he went into bondage, his wife and children were to be freed with him (Exod. 21:3), but if he was provided a wife by his master, then the wife and children were to remain the property of the owner. This last provision was evidently the cause of some perpetual servitude: if a man chose to remain with his wife and children, he was taken before the judge, his ear was pierced as a sign of perpetual servitude, and he was declared a slave for life (21:5–6).

The law in Exodus is somewhat perplexing in regard to female slaves. On the one hand, it allowed wives to be provided for Hebrew slaves (Exod. 21:2–4); on the other hand, it stated that women were to be treated differently (see above, D.1). Evidently a Hebrew woman could go into slavery only on the condition that she was to be a wife or concubine of her master or of one of his sons, and only foreign women were given to Hebrew slaves as their wives.

5. Peculium. From earliest times slaves were granted the right to accumulate *peculium*, that is, almost any form of personal property, including their own slaves (2 Sam. 9:10). The Code of Hammurabi recognized this right and even decreed the way in which the peculium would be distributed on the death of the slave owner. The OT (Lev. 25:47–55) provided that a man who sold himself into slavery might be redeemed by his nearest kin or by his own acquired wealth ("if he prospers, he may redeem himself," v. 49).

A unique provision for Hebrew slaves is to be found in Deut. 15:13–15. A slave who was freed in the sabbatical year was to be provided with goods from the increase of his master's prosperity as a reminder to all that the Hebrews were delivered from bondage in Egypt.

6. Asylum and extradition. The provision of the law of Deut. 23:15–16 in this regard is difficult to interpret: "If a slave has taken refuge with you, do not hand him over to his master. Let him live among you wherever he likes and in whatever town he chooses." This could hardly mean that every runaway slave in Israel was to be granted ASYLUM. It must refer, instead, to slaves from foreign countries who sought asylum among the Hebrews. There are parallels to this kind of provision in other ANE law codes.

7. Brandings. Since a slave was considered a piece of property, various means were used in the ANE to indicate his status. In Egypt slaves were stamped with the name of their owner and given a unique haircut. In Babylonia both these methods were used, as well as tattoos and small tablets that were worn around the wrist, ankle, or neck. There is no clear indication that the Israelites used any of these signs of servile status. The only provision in the law was that a slave who chose to remain in bondage after six years of servitude should have his ear pierced with an awl (Exod. 21:6; Deut. 15:17), presumably to fasten some sort of tag to him.

E. Publicly owned slaves. State slavery existed from earliest recorded time in the ANE. First mention of it is made in Josh. 16:10 and Jdg. 1:28 in reference to work performed for the state by the Canaanites after the conquest of the land. State slavery evidently became more widespread and more important economically when the Davidic kingdom was established. Under Solomon, slaves in large numbers were used by the state to work the copper mines and mills of the Arabah. Because of extremely harsh working conditions, they must have died in great numbers. Perhaps it was for this purpose that Solomon reduced to slavery all the descendants of "the Amorites, Hittites, Perizzites, Hivites and Jebusites" that the Israelites had not been able to exterminate (1 Ki. 9:20–21). After the exile they were combined in the census lists with the temple slaves, and their number is given as 392 (Ezra 2:55–58; Neh. 7:57–60).

Temple slaves or servants (see Nethinim) were common throughout the ANE in OT times. No mention of them was made in the OT until postexilic times. They were brought back by Zerubbabel and Ezra from Babylonia (Ezra 2:43–54; Neh. 7:46–56). Ezra states that there were 220 of them whom David and his officials had set apart to attend the Levites (Ezra 8:20). They apparently lived in separate quarters adjoining the temple, and worked under supervisors (Neh. 3:31; 11:21). Earlier in biblical history, mention is made of captives who served in the tabernacle: these included Midianites given to the priests and Levites before the Israelites entered the Promised Land (Num. 31:25–40), and later the Gibeonites who became woodcutters and water carriers "for the house of my God" (Josh. 9:23), but it is not clear that they functioned as temple slaves.

F. The importance of slavery. The legal codes define in considerable measure the limits of how slaves should be treated, but they tell little of what it was like to be a slave in the ANE. For that, one can only turn to OT narratives in which slaves were important figures. It should be noted first that slaves were members of the household and were grouped with the women and children (Exod. 20:17). The latter, like slaves, could be bought and sold. The wife and the slave-concubine were often hard to distinguish. As Paul suggests (Gal. 4:1), the child in Israel was "no different from a slave," for both were flogged (Exod. 21:20–27; Prov. 13:24).

Generally slaves were not owned in large numbers in Palestine except by the temple and the state. Slaves were usually domestics in the households of the well-to-do rather than agricultural or handicraft workers in large-scale operations. A warm affection frequently developed between master and slave. The codes in both Exodus and Deuteronomy specifically made provision for the slave who wished to remain in bondage because of his affection for his master. Such a relationship must have existed between ABRAHAM and ELIEZER of Damascus, for this servant was at one time designated the heir of his master (Gen. 15:1–4), and later he was sent to negotiate a marriage for the heir (ch. 24). A slave of SAUL was an adviser and confidant of his master (1 Sam. 9:5; 16:22), as was GEHAZI, the slave of ELISHA (2 Ki. 4:12; 8:4). Mention is also made of one JARHA, an Egyptian slave in the household who was given the daughter of his master in marriage (1 Chr. 2:35). Thus the frequent picture that is drawn is one of affection and trust on the part of both master and slave, very much within the confines of the family.

II. Slavery in the NT.

There is what some consider an awkward silence on the part of Christ in regard to the slave society of NT times. And the apostles Paul and Peter, far from condemning slavery, urged their converts who were slaves to obey their masters (Eph. 6:5–8; Col. 3:22–25; 1 Tim. 6:1–2; 1 Pet. 2:18–21). Paul further suggested that a runaway slave voluntarily return to his master (Phlm. 10–16). Nowhere did he suggest that Christians give up their slaves, but he did exhort masters to treat their slaves with kindness and consideration (Eph. 6:9; Col. 4:1). In short, the institution of slavery was not explicitly condemned, but its abuses were. The apostles' attitude is best explained by the unique way in which Romans of the 1st cent. A.D. treated their slaves and released them in great numbers.

Slavery had a long history in the Greco-Roman world by NT times. During the Roman conquest of the 3rd to 1st centuries B.C., slaves were introduced into Roman society by the hundreds of thousands. However, one must be exceedingly careful not to assign the barbaric treatment of slaves by the Romans in the pre-Christian centuries to the early Christian era. Sweeping humanitarian changes had been introduced into the Roman world by the 1st cent. A.D. which led to radically improved treatment of slaves.

As in OT times, people became slaves in the Greco-Roman world in a number of ways. Most were inherited or purchased. The latter were usually prisoners of war or persons illegally seized and sold by pirates to slave traders. Some few slave traders seem to have engaged in the ugly trade of breeding and selling slaves, a common business in earlier centuries. According to Cicero (*Parad.* 35) indebtedness was a cause of slavery in early Rome, but this practice was forbidden by law in 326 B.C.

A. Manumission. Slavery had become a well-traveled road to Roman CITIZENSHIP throughout the empire by the 1st cent. A.D. Captives were educated and trained in Roman ways before becoming citizens. The younger PLINY (*Ep.* 7.32.1) stated in justification of manumission that he freed his slaves because of a desire to see his native country increase in the number of its citizens. Dio Cassius (*Rom. Hist.* 46.7.6) put similar words in the mouth of AUGUSTUS Caesar, but the statement is less reliable than Pliny's. Behind these statements there is the fact that Rome was faced with a population decline of the freeborn citizenry. The freedman, therefore, under the name and patronage of his former master could fulfill obligations to the state, the most important of which was military service. Whatever the reasons, evidence of various kinds indicates that the Romans freed slaves in great numbers.

1. Frequency of manumission. There is considerable evidence of manumission. Tenney Frank (in *AJP* 53 [1932]: 360) made a study of the sacred treasury of the Romans for the years 81–49 B.C., and his conclusions are remarkable. One of the sources for the sacred treasury was a manumission tax of 5 percent of the value of the slave about to be freed. Using a value of 500 denarii per slave, a reasonable evaluation, he came to the conclusion that 500,000 slaves were freed during this period, for 12,000,000 sesterces were derived from the tax during this time. These figures are all the more startling when one learns that the total population of the city of Rome in 5 B.C. has been estimated at about 870,000.

Two other bits of evidence on the frequency of manumission during this period are significant. Julius CAESAR sent 80,000 poor people, mostly freedmen, out of the city of Rome to the provinces as colonists in the years 46–44 B.C. Earlier, in 57–56, when a dole of grain was established for needy citizens at Rome, many owners set their older slaves free. This indicates that it was not always humanitarianism which prompted some to free their slaves (Dio Cassius, *Rom. Hist.* 39.24).

Evidence from the early empire, since it was the time of the early church, is more significant and most unusual. In a study of 13,900 grave inscriptions from the *Corpus Inscriptionum Latinarum*, Frank has shown that of 4,485 persons born at Rome and who, with few exceptions, were poor citizens, 83 percent had foreign names and 70 percent had Greek names. This is a sure indication that the individual was a former slave or, perhaps, the son or daughter of a slave or freedman. There is further evidence that this percentage is probably too low. In instances where a record of succeeding generations appears, the percentage of Greek names shrinks from 64 percent to 38 percent. It appears that a freedman of ambition soon tried to shed a Greek name and presumably any other foreign name in favor of a Latin one (*AHR* 21 [1916]: 689–708). The reliability of one aspect of Frank's conclusions is borne out by other studies. At Minturnae 77 percent of all slaves and freedmen were Greek (University of Pennsylvania, *Excavations at Minturnae*, 1 [1935], 106–13). Likewise 76 percent of the freedmen and slaves of Cicero were Greeks and 73 percent of the slaves and freedmen of others, mentioned by Cicero, had Greek names.

The legislation of Augustus indicates that on the death of their masters slaves were being freed in wholesale numbers. To curb such activity, which Dionysius of Halicarnassus (*Rom. Ant.* 4.24) says was prompted by the owner's desire that his slaves should grace his funeral wearing the cap of freedom, the *lex Fufia Caninia* was passed in 2 B.C. The law stipulated that on their death owners might free a portion of their slaves on a sliding scale. If one owned two to ten slaves, one-half might be freed. If ten to thirty, one-third might be freed. If a master owned 100–500, only one-fifth might be freed (*Gai institutiones* 1.42–43). In all, the evidence supports the contention that slaves in ancient Rome were freed in great numbers. (For further discussion of manumission in Rome, see T. Wiedemann in *Classical Quarterly* 35 [1985]: 162–75.)

Slaves involved in various projects pictured on the walls of the tombs at Beni Hasan, Egypt.

2. Length of service. Information regarding the length of time a slave had to wait for his freedom is scanty. Cicero, however, made the point that a worthy slave could expect his freedom in about seven years (*Phil.* 8.32), a figure that coincides remarkably with the OT requirement (Exod. 21:2). It is not surprising, therefore, to find that in the works of Cicero a number of individuals, such as Tiro, Statius, Dionysius, and Eutychides, to name a few, were first mentioned in connection with some important duties they performed as slaves, and a few years later were called freedmen.

3. Economic status of freedmen. When a master freed his slave, he frequently established his freedman in a business and the master became a shareholder in it. Usually the slave had learned his trade as an apprentice in the master's household or handicraft shop. Then by extra labor he saved enough to buy his freedom, or it was granted gratuitously by his master.

Many examples of the prosperity of former slaves can be cited. Because OSTIA, the seaport of Rome, was a prosperous new community during the late republic and early empire, freedmen flocked there. Even a large proportion of the magistrates of the city were freedmen (Gordon in *JRS* 21 [1931]: 70). Many others became knights; this meant that they possessed property valued at more than 50,000 sesterces. Their names are interesting and indicate their former status and often their nationality: Antistius Agathangelus, Carminius Parthenopaeus, Combarisius Vitalis, Cornelius Epagathanius, Licinius Herodes, and Lutatius Charitonaenus. They amassed their wealth as grain dealers, carpenters, wine merchants, furniture makers, and surveyors. Two other prosperous freedmen at Ostia were a silversmith and a miller.

At Rome the situation was the same. There was a street of shops, the Sacra Via, which specialized in jewelry. All the owners of the shops who could be identified were freedmen. There were seven pearl merchants, two jewelers, two goldsmiths, one engraver, and one maker of silverplate. An inscription found at Rome illustrates the practice of the time. The patron of M. Canuleius Zosimus set up a memorial plaque to his freedman who died at twenty-eight years of age. He said of him, "he excelled in carving Clodian ware" (*CIL* 6.9222). There were two firms of bricklayers at Rome. These were headed by G. Domitius Trophimus and C. Calpetanus Favor, both of whom were freedmen with slaves working under them. One of the slaves, Hermes, was later freed by his master and became C. Calpetanus Hermes (*CIL* 15.319, 904, 1112–14).

4. Jewish freedmen. The Jews at Rome were an interesting group (see ROME, CHURCH AT). Many thousands of them came to the city as slaves in the periods of the late republic and early empire. H. J. Leon, in a study of the catacomb inscriptions (*The Jews of Ancient Rome* [1960], 237–38), discovered that there was not a single mention of a slave among them. This confirms the statement of PHILO JUDAEUS that many Jews came to Rome as slaves, but were soon set free (*Legatio* 23.155). Moreover, many Jews took lofty Roman names for themselves and, except for the fact that they were buried in the Jewish catacombs, would never have been recognized as Jews.

All of this evidence suggests that the Roman slave, far from living in perpetual servitude, could look forward to a day of opportunity. It became the common practice of the Romans to free their slaves and then establish them in a trade or profession. Many times the former slave became wealthier than his patron.

B. The status of slaves. While an individual was a slave, he was in most respects equal to his freeborn counterpart in the Greco-Roman world, and in some respects he had an advantage. By the 1st cent. A.D. the slave had most of the legal rights that were granted to the free man. Sepulchral inscriptions of the 1st and 2nd centuries indicate the prosperity and family solidarity of the imperial slave. Many had a considerable amount of money at their disposal and had rights to wife and family. In A.D. 20 a decree of the senate specified that slave criminals were to be tried in the same way as free men (Justinian, *Dig*. 48.2.12.3). Pliny the Younger treated the wills of his slaves as valid on the ground that the master's house was the substitute for the state (*Ep*. 8.16.2; 8.24.5). In A.D. 61 the family of a slave owner attempted to use an old prerogative: the execution of all of the slaves of the master, who had been killed by one of them. When the family of Pedanius Secundus ordered this, so great a riot broke out when the report reached Rome that troops had to be called in to quell it, and the slaves were not killed (Tacitus, *Annals* 14.42–45). There was also the interesting incident that took place during the reign of HADRIAN. The emperor was attacked by an insane slave, but, instead of being put to death, the slave was turned over to the care of a physician (*Scriptores historiae augustae: Hadriaus* 12.5).

The living conditions of many slaves were better than those of free men who often slept in the streets of the city or lived in very cheap rooms. There is considerable evidence to suggest that the slaves lived within the confines of their master's house. They usually lived on the top floor of their owner's city house or country villa (Columella, *De rustica* 1.63). In Pliny's Laurentian villa the quarters for the slaves and freedmen were in separate sections of the house, but were considered attractive enough to be used for the entertainment of overnight guests (Pliny the Younger, *Ep*. 2.17.22). At Pompeii in one villa, the Casa del Menandro, separate quarters for slaves were provided on one side of the building.

These rooms were on the second floor, included a kitchen and a latrine, and were connected to the rest of the house by a long corridor (A. Maiuri, *La casa del Menandro e il suo tesoro di argenteria*, 2 vols. [1933], 1:186–188).

The slave was not inferior to the free man of similar skills in regard to food and clothing. That most slaves at Rome were as well dressed as free persons is indicated in an unusual way. Seneca (*De clementia* 1.24.1) stated that legislation was introduced in the senate that slaves should be required to wear a type of clothing that would distinguish them from free men. It is presumed that the slave ate as well as the poor free man but there is no direct evidence on the subject. At least it is hard to believe that a master would provide well for his slaves in other ways and not feed them adequately.

The free laborer in NT times was seldom in better circumstances than his slave counterpart. The average free laborer at Rome and in the provinces could expect to earn about one DENARIUS a day. This was the pay of the workers in the vineyard of Jesus' parable (Matt. 20:2). Julius Caesar's troops received 225 denarii a year plus fringe benefits of food and booty (Libernam in *RE*, s.v. "Exercitus," 1672–74). One of Caesar's scribes, a skilled workman, received one denarius per day (H. Dessau, *Inscriptiones latinae selectae* [1892], 2/1:502 [#6087, LXII]). Augustus raised the pay by giving a bonus of 3,000 denarii for twenty years of service in addition to the salary of 225 denarii per year (Dio Cassius, *Rom. Hist.* 55.23).

Finally, in Diocletian's time, when food prices were approximately the same as those of the late republic and early empire, where they can be compared, the wages of the unskilled were set by imperial decree at one-half to one denarius a day (*Economic Survey of Ancient Rome*, ed. T. Frank, 6 vols. [1933–40], 1:404). At this point a comparison of the free man with the slave is worth noting (ibid., 2:266–83). The free man might receive one denarius a day in wages or c. 313 denarii a year, if he worked six days a week. He would spend half of that (2 or 2.5 sesterces per day) on food or 184 denarii a year. This would provide him with a diet of bread, vegetables, and fruit. Clothing of poor quality would cost 5–10 denarii a year. If the individual did not sleep in the streets as many did, housing would cost 30 sesterces a month or 90 denarii a year. Therefore, of the 313 denarii earned, 279 would be spent on basic necessities. However, the slave, in addition to receiving these basic necessities, was given 5 denarii a month as spending money (Seneca, *Ep.* 80.7). From these statistics one can only conclude that the average free man lived no better than the slave. In fact, in time of economic hardship it was the slave and not the free man who was guaranteed the necessities of life for himself and his family.

(See further I. Mendelsohn, *Slavery in the Ancient Near East* [1949]; W. L. Westermann, *The Slave Systems of the Greek and Roman Antiquity* [1955]; G. Kehnscherper, *Die Stellung der Bibel und der alten christlichen Kirche zur Sklaverei* [1957]; *Greek and Roman Slavery*, ed. T. Wiedemann [1981]; M. A. Dandamaev, *Slavery in Babylonia from Nabopolassar to Alexander the Great (626–331 BC)* [1984]; Y. Garlan, *Slavery in Ancient Greece* [1988]; N. R. E. Fisher, *Slavery in Classical Greece* [1993]; K. R. Bradley, *Slavery and Society at Rome* [1994]; J. A. Harrill, *The Manumission of Slaves in Early Christianity* [1995]; J. A. Glancy, *Slavery in Early Christianity* [2002]; R. Zelnick-Abramovitz, *Not Wholly Free: The Concept of Manumission and the Status of Manumitted Slaves in the Ancient Greek World* [2005]; J. A. Harrill, *Slaves in the New Testament: Literary, Social, and Moral Dimensions* [2006]; *OCD*, 1415–17.) A. RUPPRECHT

Slavonic versions. See VERSIONS OF THE BIBLE, ANCIENT V.E.

sleep. There is nothing unusual about most biblical uses of this word in its literal or physical sense. After JACOB dreamed about the ladder he simply woke from his sleep (Gen. 28:16); when EUTYCHUS fell down during PAUL's long sermon it was due to a typical human loss of concentration in weariness (Acts 20:9). In a few cases natural sleep was, for supernatural reasons, deepened. This is recorded in the account of the creation of EVE (Gen. 2:21–22). The men around SAUL were in a similar deepened sleep while DAVID and ABISHAI took the spear and jar of water from his head (1 Sam. 26:12).

The Bible refers to sleep also in a figurative sense. For example, the term is used to indicate spiritual indolence. SOLOMON was scathing when talking about those who were lazy: "A little sleep, a little slumber, / a little folding of the hands to rest— / and poverty will come on you like a bandit / and scarcity like an armed man" (Prov. 24:33–34; cf. 6:9). Similarly Christ, in talking to his followers about his SECOND COMING, exhorted them to be faithful and watchful: "If he comes suddenly, do not let him find you sleeping" (Mk. 13:36). PAUL, in exhorting Christians in everyday living and in warning them of the enormity of their task, stressed that "it is full time now for you to wake from sleep" (Rom. 13:11 RSV; cf. 1 Thess. 5:6–7). The same writer, in speaking of the light coming into the lives of believers, likened this process to an arousing from deep sleep (Eph. 5:14).

Where sleep is used to indicate physical DEATH, the picture is of a temporary state pending a final consummation. "We will not all sleep, but we will all be changed" (1 Cor. 15:51; cf. 1 Thess. 4:13–18). It is clear that this reference to death as sleep is figurative, and does not refer to sleep of the soul (cf. Lk. 16:24; 23:43; 2 Cor. 5:8; Rev. 6:9–10).

D. A. BLAIKLOCK

sleeves. The NRSV uses the phrase "a long robe with sleeves" as the rendering of Hebrew *kĕtōnet passim*, which occurs in the stories of JOSEPH and TAMAR (Gen. 37:3, 23, 32; 2 Sam. 13:18). The meaning of the term *pas H7168* is debated. In the Samuel passage, on the basis of the SEPTUAGINT (*ton chitōna ton karpōton* [from *karpos*, "wrist"]) and the VULGATE (*talari tunica* [from *talus*, "ankle"]), some scholars believe that the phrase indicates a garment reaching to the wrists and the ankles. In Genesis, however, both of these versions understand the garment as many-colored (*chitōna poikilon, tunicam polymitam*; cf. KJV, "a coat of *many* colours"). In garment inventories from Mesopotamia there is mention of a *kutinnū pišanu* (A. Oppenheim in *JNES* 8 [1949]: 177), apparently a valuable ceremonial vestment with gold work appliqué as its ornamentation (cf. NIV, "richly ornamented"; similarly NJPS). See ROBE.

slime. See BITUMEN.

sling. See ARMOR, ARMS IV.A.

slothfulness. See IDLENESS; SLUGGARD.

slow of anger. See LONGSUFFERING.

slug. See SNAIL.

sluggard. Proverbs describes the sluggard (Heb. *ʿāṣēl H6789*) as being so lazy and addicted to sleep that he does not keep his fields plowed and free from thorns; thus at harvest time he is bound to go hungry, while the diligent will prosper (Prov. 6:6, 9; 13:4; 15:9; 24:30; 26:13–16). Even if he had food, he is so lazy that he wouldn't lift it to his mouth (19:24). He refuses to go out to work by saying that there might be a lion outside (22:13); such private daydreams seem to him wiser than the counsel of seven (26:16). He prefers to desire (dream?) than to work (13:4; 21:25). He brings disaster to himself, and is also offensive to his employer (10:26).

On the other hand, the industry of the virtuous woman (Prov. 31:27) is blessed not only by wealth, but also by the opportunity to care for the poor (31:20), to see her husband become a leader (31:23), and most of all to receive the praise of the Lord (31:30). Sloth is not just one of many sins, but an attitude that harms one's entire duty to God and to neighbor.

Jesus' parable of the talents repeats the theme of foolish fear being the root of sloth (Matt. 25:25–26) and stresses the proper fear of the Lord as the source of diligence, making clear that it is at the return of Christ in judgment (cf. Proverbs' day of harvest) when diligent use of God's gifts will be rewarded and sloth punished. PAUL stresses the necessity of serving God up to the proportion of the gifts he has given us (Rom. 12:3–8) so that we are not slothful but aglow with the Spirit (12:11): sloth is against the Spirit! Likewise Hebrews emphasizes that after partaking of the Spirit (Heb. 6:4) we must go on to maturity (v. 1)—not becoming lazy, but showing diligence to the end (vv. 11–12).   D. C. DAVIS

smell. See ODOR.

smelt. See METALS AND METALLURGY.

smith, blacksmith. The Hebrew noun *ḥārāš H3093* commonly means "craftsman, artisan" and thus can be used of gem engravers, carpenters, stonemasons, and so on (e.g., Exod. 28:11; 2 Sam. 5:11). When the context indicates that an ARTIFICER works on IRON or some other METAL, the rendering "smith" or "blacksmith" is appropriate (1 Sam. 13:19; Isa. 44:12; 54:16). The originator of this craft was TUBAL-CAIN, who is said to have "forged all kinds of tools out of bronze and iron" (Gen. 4:22). The context of 1 Sam. 13:19 refers to the PHILISTINE blacksmiths who were the first to bring the craft of working iron into Palestine. The prophet ISAIAH describes how blacksmiths forged idols (Isa. 44:12; however, no iron idols have been found). Elsewhere (54:16) he refers to the making of an iron artifact of some kind, but it is not definitely specified (most versions understand it to be a "weapon"). The KJV and other versions use "smith" also to render *masgēr* H4994 (2 Ki. 24:14, 16; Jer. 24:1; 29:2), but the meaning of this term is uncertain (NIV, "artisan"). See CRAFTS; GOLDSMITH; OCCUPATIONS; SILVERSMITH. J. L. KELSO

smoke. Literal references to smoke in the Bible (Heb. *ʿāšān* H6940; Gk. *kapnos* G2837) are relatively few (e.g., Josh. 8:20–21; Jdg. 20:38–40). The offering of INCENSE produced a cloud of smoke that represented the prayers of God's people (Lev. 16:13; Ezek. 8:11 [in both of these passages the Heb. word is *ʿānān* H6727, "cloud"]; Rev. 8:4).

The most significant references to smoke indicate a visible concomitant of the presence of God in divine self-manifestations. In the instance of the Abrahamic covenant, while ABRAHAM slept "he saw a smoking fire pot with a flaming torch" passing between the pieces of the sacrifices he had divided (Gen. 15:17). When MOSES met with God on Mount SINAI, the mountain was "covered with smoke" (Exod. 19:18). The TEMPLE was filled with smoke when ISAIAH saw the Lord (Isa. 6:4); he also prophesied that God would "create over all of Mount Zion … a cloud of smoke by day and a glow of flaming fire by night" (4:5). In John's vision, the heavenly temple "was filled with smoke from the glory of God and from his power" (Rev. 15:8). Though not explicitly stated, one can assume that other references to the divine self-manifestation (e.g., Exod. 3:2; 13:21; Num. 10:34; 14:14) include also the presence of smoke. See PILLAR OF FIRE AND OF CLOUD.

There are other figurative uses. The fire of God's anger is accompanied by "smoke … from his nostrils" (Ps. 18:8; cf. Job 41:20). MOSES warned that the WRATH of God would "burn" (verb *ʿāšan* H6939) against idolaters (Deut. 29:20). The psalmist cried out, "Why does your anger smolder [*ʿāšan*] against the sheep of your pasture?" (Ps. 74:1). Smoke also symbolizes the transient: enemies (37:20; 68:2), idolaters (Hos. 13:3), the days of one's life (Ps. 102:3), and the heavens (Isa. 51:6). W. B. COKER

Smyrna smuhr´nuh (Σμύρνα G5044, "myrrh"). Smyrna is situated at the head of the gulf into which the Hermus flows, a well-protected harbor, and the natural outlet to the sea for the major trade route which runs inland along the Hermus valley. Aeolian Greeks may have been the first settlers here, a community overlaid and dominated by the later and more powerful Ionian Greeks, but facts are few from the shadowy years at the turn of the 1st millennium B.C., when these AEGEAN settlements were founded.

When history takes more certain shape at the end of the Dark Age, which fell on the Aegean world after the Dorian invasions—that last wave of infiltrating Hellenic tribes which ended the Mycenaean world (see GREECE IV)—Smyrna emerges as a sturdy community, ready to assert itself against the powerful neighboring kingdom of LYDIA. Mimnermus, poet of Smyrna in the 7th cent. B.C., some of whose poems have survived in single lines and fragments, mentions the tension in

Excavations at ancient Smyrna.

the Hermus valley between Smyrna and SARDIS. It seems to have brought catastrophe about 600, when Alyattes of Lydia destroyed Smyrna, and left its site devastated for three centuries. Lydian villages are traceable on the shore of the gulf, but the strong Ionian port lay dead.

The city rose from the dead—hence a phrase in the imagery of John's apocalyptic letter (Rev. 2:8). Lysimachus, who ruled Thrace (THRACIA) and the NW part of ASIA MINOR after the division of Alexander's empire, refounded Smyrna in 290 B.C. It became a Greek city again, with assembly and magistrates, and, thanks to the fine site, entered an era of vitality and prosperity that still continues (Izmir is one of the strongest urban communities in modern Turkey). Its progress was aided and promoted by a shrewd recognition of the coming dominance of ROME. ANTIOCHUS the Great of Syria (241–187) was pushing W in a determined attempt to consolidate his borderlands. Rome, aware of his encroaching ambitions, was thrusting firmly east. Smyrna was a superb bridgehead in a great peninsula, which Rome now was more and more clearly regarding as her buffer region and coming challenge. And Smyrna, too, in Rome's emerging eastern policy, was a useful counterpoise in the middle Mediterranean to the naval strength of RHODES.

It was to these significant services that the Smyrneans referred in A.D. 26 when they appealed for permission to build a temple to TIBERIUS. TACITUS (*Annals* 4.56) tells the story:

> The Smyrnaeans, having appealed to their ancient records to show whether Tantalus, the son of Jupiter, or Theseus, the son also of a god, or one of the Amazons was their founder, proceeded to the considerations in which they chiefly trusted, namely, their friendly services to the Roman people. They had aided Rome with a naval force, they said, not only in their wars abroad, but also in those they had fought in Italy. It was they, they said, who had first reared a temple in honor of Rome, when the power of the Roman people, though great, had not yet reached their highest glory, for the city of Carthage still stood, and powerful kings governed Asia. Sulla, too, they said, had experienced their generosity, when his army was in imminent peril from the bitter weather and scarcity of clothes. When the matter was made known in the citizens' assembly at Smyrna, all present stripped off their garments and sent them to the legions.

In consequence of the eleven applicants, Smyrna was preferred and became the site for the second Asian temple to the deity of Rome and the emperor, and the seat of the sinister Caesar-cult which was to cause so much suffering in the church (see EMPEROR WORSHIP). At Smyrna as elsewhere the imperial policy of suppression was carried out sporadically, and DOMITIAN, no doubt, was the cause of this outburst with the help of a hostile synagogue, against whose machinations John has a scornful word to say (Rev. 2:9). With legislation on the books against the church, as it had been since the middle sixties of the century, such situations as those which PAUL had found frustrating in an earlier decade, assumed a new possibility of danger. Smyrna had worshiped the spirit of Rome since 195 B.C. The temple to Tiberius increased the pride she held in this historic role.

Hence the exhortation to endure and win a "crown of life" (Rev. 2:10), a piece of imagery caught from a diadem of porticoes surrounding her hilltop, and described by Apollonius of Tyana (1st cent. A.D.): "For though their city is the most beautiful of all cities under the sun, and makes the sea its own, and holds the fountains of Zephyrus, yet it is a greater charm to wear a crown of men than a crown of porticoes, for buildings are seen only in their one place, but men are seen everywhere, and spoken about everywhere, and make their city as vast as the range of countries which they visit" (Philostratus, *Life of Apollonius* 4.7).

Aelius Aristides, who knew Smyrna well, spoke in similar terms (*Orations* 15.404 et al.). He compares the city to the crown of Ariadne, shining in the heavens, and to a statue with its feet in the sea, and rising to its crowned head at the hilltop. Apollonius was probably alive about the time the letter of Rev. 2 was written; he too may have been in peril under Domitian. Aristides wrote half a century or more later. Both writers show that "the crown of Smyrna" was a recognized image of rhetoric. It remains only to mention POLYCARP, the martyr bishop of Smyrna, who died in A.D. 155; as one of the last pupils of John, he made a link between the apostles and the middle 2nd cent.

The story of the actual coming of Christianity to Smyrna is not known. It was probably a result of Paul's activity in EPHESUS, followed up and extended by John. On the evidence of the apocalyptic letter, Smyrna's Christians stood well in the 1st cent. They continued to stand, and Smyrna was one of the Asian cities that withstood the Turks, and was among the last to fall to Islam. Such resistance played a part in history. The delaying action of surviving remnants of the empire in the E allowed Europe time to emerge from the Middle Ages, and receive with creative hands those gifts which brought the Renaissance and the modern world to birth.

(See further W. M. Ramsay, *Letters to the Seven Churches* [1904], chs. 19–20; C. J. Cadoux, *Ancient Smyrna* [1938]; E. M. Blaiklock, *Cities of the New Testament* [1965], ch. 18; E. Yamauchi, *The Archaeology of New Testament Cities in Western Asia Minor* [1980], ch. 4; C. J. Hemer, *The Letters to the Seven Churches of Asia in Their Local Setting* [1986], ch. 4; J. M. Cook, *Old Smyrna Excavations: The Temples of Athena* [1998]; R. S. Ascough, ed., *Religious Rivalries and the Struggle for Success in Sardis and Smyrna* [2005].) E. M. BLAIKLOCK

snail. This mollusk (of the class *Gastropoda*) is probably referred to by the Hebrew word *šabbĕlûl* H8671, which occurs only once: "Let them be like the snail that dissolves into slime" (Ps. 58:8, NIV, "a slug melting away as it moves along"). The visible trail formed by the snail's secretion was thought to show that the snail was melting away. Many snails, with a wide range of food habits, live in most regions of Palestine and some have become pests in the irrigated fields, where the added water allows them to be active for a longer part of the year. The KJV uses "snail" also as the rendering of Hebrew *ḥōmeṭ* H2793, a word of uncertain meaning that probably refers to a type of lizard (Lev. 11:30; NIV, "skink"; NRSV, "sand lizard"). G. S. CANSDALE

snake. See SERPENT.

snake charming. Various kinds of serpents were numerous in Palestine, and the art of snake charming was practiced in the country. Some snakes were susceptible to such influence (Eccl. 10:11) and others resisted the techniques of the charmer. In Jer. 8:17 serpent charming is used metaphorically to describe the enemies of Judah who are "vipers that cannot be charmed"; and in Ps. 58:4–5 it characterizes the wicked who are "a cobra that has stopped its ears, / that will not heed the tune of the charmer." F. G. CARVER

snare. A device used to entangle and capture animals. Several Hebrew nouns can be rendered "snare," especially *môqēš* H4613, which probably refers to a wooden contrivance for catching birds (cf. Amos 3:5). The near synonyms *paḥ* H7062 and *rešet* H8407 seem to indicate trapping nets (all three words are used together in Ps. 140:5). These and other words are almost always used in metaphorical contexts. For example, IDOLATRY is often described as a snare to God's people (Exod. 23:33). For further discussion see TRAP.

sneeze. The verb *sneeze* (rendering Heb. *zārar* H2453) occurs once to indicate that the SHUNAMITE's son had returned to life as a result of ELISHA's work (2 Ki. 4:35). The noun *sneeze* (or *sneezing*) is used by most versions in the description of the LEVIATHAN (Job 41:18; KJV, "neesings"); the Hebrew term in this passage (*ʿăṭîšâ* H6490) probably refers to the animal's snorting (cf. NIV).

snow. The Hebrew words for "snow" (noun *šeleg* H8920; verb *šālag* H8919 in Ps. 68:14) occur nearly twenty times in the Bible (the Aram. cognate *tĕlag* H10758 only in Dan. 7:9; Gk. *chiōn* G5946 only in Matt. 28:3; Rev. 1:14). Almost all the references, however, are figurative, indicating healing (Exod. 4:6 et al.), purity (Ps. 51:7; Isa. 1:18 et al.), refreshment (Prov. 25:13), and the like.

In the historical record, snow is mentioned only once, when it is said concerning BENAIAH son of Jehoiada: "He also went down into a pit on a snowy day and killed a lion" (2 Sam. 23:20; 1 Chr. 11:22). Mention in this context presumably indicates that the event was exceptional, not only as a feat of arms but also as a fact of climate, for the lion's home would be in the Jordan Valley, where snow is unknown. G. Adam Smith comments on Benaiah's exploits: "the beast had strayed up from Jordan, and been caught in a snowstorm. Where else could lions and snow come together?" (*Historical Geography of the Holy Land*, 25th ed. [1931], 63).

Although rare, snow is by no means unknown in the Judean hills. JERUSALEM has a mean January temperature of 48°F, with a daily range of some 13°. But there are two areas where snowfalls are both heavy and regular. (1) On the Lebanese mountains in the N, where Mount HERMON rises to 9,100 ft. and snow patches lie throughout the year (cf. Jer. 18:14). It was the distant view of these snows from the hot Galilean trench that prompted so much biblical imagery. (2) On the mountains of EDOM, E of the Jordan, where the land rises to over 5,000 ft. (Amman in Jordan has a January mean temperature of 40°F., and a daily range in that month of 7–8°). For many Israelites, therefore, snow was better known to them as a distant prospect than as a common experience. See PALESTINE V; RAIN.

J. H. PATERSON

snuffers. This English term, referring to a device used for cropping the snuff of a candle, occurs in the KJV and other versions as the rendering of two Hebrew words, both of which are applied to instruments made of gold used in tending fires and lamps in the TABERNACLE and the TEMPLE. One of the words, *mĕzammeret H4662*, was probably a type of knife used for shearing a wick (1 Ki. 7:50; 2 Ki. 12:13; 25:14; Jer. 52:18; 2 Chr. 4:22); the NIV renders it "wick trimmers." The precise meaning of the second term, *melqāḥayim H4920*, is less certain. According to Isa. 6:6, this tool could be used to handle live coals, and thus most versions render it "tongs" not only here but also in 1 Ki. 7:49 and 2 Chr. 4:21 (where *mĕzammeret* occurs in the same context). It is possible, however, that this instrument was also used as a wick trimmer (cf. Exod. 25:38; 37:23; Num. 4:9).

So soh (סוֹא *H6046*, derivation disputed). According to 2 Ki. 17:4, King HOSHEA of Judah betrayed the Assyrians by sending envoys to "So king of Egypt." There have been numerous attempts to identify this Egyptian king. An older proposal that the person in question was Sibʾe, an Egyptian general at the Battle of Raphia (c. 720 B.C.), has been discredited; subsequent studies have shown that the name in the Assyrian records should be read differently (namely, Reʾe; see R. Borger in *JNES* 19 [1960]: 49–53). Also unlikely is the view that the biblical text refers to Shabaka, who ruled Egypt at the very end of the 8th cent.; Hoshea's contemporary would have been an earlier pharaoh, Tefnakht I (727–720), whose capital was Sais. K. A. Kitchen has suggested that the name So is an abbreviated form of Osorkon IV (c. 730–715), a competing pharaoh at Tanis and Bubastis (*The Third Intermediate Period in Egypt* [1973], 182, 372–76). These and other identifications have not won wide acceptance (cf. *ABD*, 6:75–76).

Alternative interpretations of the text have been put forward. According to some scholars, *So* should be understood not as a proper name but rather as an Egyptian title (e.g., *ṱ*, "vizier," a high-ranking civil official with viceregal authority; see S. Yeivin in *VT* 2 [1952]: 164–68). More widely accepted, but not without problems, is the view that the reference is to the city of Sais (H. Goedicke in *BASOR* 171 [Oct. 1963]: 64–66; cf. M. Cogan and H. Tadmor, *II Kings*, AB 11 [1988], 196). In this case, the text should be rendered, "he had sent envoys to Sais, [to] the king of Egypt," and the king in question would be Tefnakht.

A. BOWLING

soap. This English term is used to render Hebrew *bōrît H1383*, which occurs twice in figurative passages (Jer. 2:22; Mal. 3:2), and *šeleg H8921*, which occurs once (Job 9:30, although many take this to be the common word for "snow," *šeleg H8920*). The reference is to alkaline salt (see LYE), extracted from the Asiatic soap plants such as *Mesembrianthemum cristallinum*, *Salicornia solacea*, *Salsala kali*, and the like (cf. I. Löw, *Die Flora der Juden* [1924–34], 1:637), which are reduced by burning to produce a pasty mass used as a bleach, especially in the presence of olive oil.

W. WHITE, JR.

Socho, Sochoh soh'koh. KJV forms of SOCO.

society. The Scriptures do not contain the word *society* nor do they articulate any systematic definition of the human social order. The terms employed in the Bible are concrete and empirical ones, such as *people* and *nation(s)*.

I. Human society in the OT. The relation of the individual to the society of which he was a part varied from one epoch of Israel's history to another. The institution of LEVIRATE marriage (Deut. 25:5–6; Lk. 20:28) suggests the solidarity of familial (or clan) life, while the parent-child relationship (e.g., Exod. 20:12) stresses the role of the home as the primary unit of society. See FAMILY. At the same time, the "congregation" of the LORD (cf. the use of the term in Deut. 23:1–3, 8) was regarded as possessing a unity of its own, so that exclusion from it amounted to virtual exile.

The solidarity of the human race is more than implied in the narrative describing the creation of ADAM and EVE. With the development, however, of the national self-consciousness within Israel, this resting upon the covenant of ABRAHAM and upon the events surrounding the exodus from Egypt and the giving of the law at Sinai, there developed a division of emphasis within the Hebrew tradition. On the one hand, there was a growing awareness of vocation—of chosenness—which tended toward separateness, both with respect to environing nations, and also at the point of interpersonal relations between Hebrews and non-Hebrews. On the other hand, there was a certain cosmopolitanism within the Levitical legislation, so that Israel's experiences in Egypt were to be regarded as a reminder that the people's treatment of the "stranger" was to be humane and even cordial. This is emphasized, for example, in Exod. 23:9 and Deut. 24:20.

There existed a type of national ambivalence with respect to those of other national stocks. The Levitical order prescribed a sort of prophylactic separation of Israel from her neighbors, this serving the purpose of maintaining a needed separatism. Such legislation was underlain by a positive humanitarianism. On the whole, it may be said that preexilic relations between Israel and neighboring people *as persons* was moderately cordial, so that URIAH the Hittite was a trusted officer under DAVID (2 Sam. 11:6–17), ITTAI the Gittite was captain of David's personal guard (18:2), the KENITES were treated as brethren (Jdg. 1:16; 5:24), and strangers in general had the right of ASYLUM in Israel's CITIES OF REFUGE (Num. 35.15).

Societal relations between the Jewish people and non-Jews deteriorated with the return of the exiles from the captivities. No doubt the ruthless treatment of Jews during the EXILE afforded a background for the growing antipathy of postexilic Jewish society for the Gentiles. Contributive to this polarity was also the strict reform that separated many mixed marriages under EZRA (Ezra 10:18–44). As necessary as these reform measures may have been, they could not have failed to generate much tension between Jews and the peoples from whom the "strange wives" came. Tensions during the intertestamental period were aggravated by the SAMARITAN division, and even more by the measures taken both to humiliate and to hellenize the Jews by ANTIOCHUS IV. The hardening of the Jewish institutional structure continued these tensions.

During OT times, the individual enjoyed a real but limited role as a unit within society, although gifted individuals, both men and women, did rise to positions of recognized leadership, outstandingly during the time of the judges (see JUDGES, PERIOD OF). Family life was central to Hebrew society; and within the family, both wifehood and childhood were protected by many safeguards. WIDOWS and ORPHANS, fair game for exploitation in many societies, were accorded special care and solicitude. DIVORCE was restricted, and the reciprocal rights of parents and children were established and safeguarded.

Although polygamy was tolerated during the patriarchal period, the overtones of the Mosaic literature seem clearly to indicate disapproval of the practice (see MARRIAGE). Without leveling any frontal assault upon the practice, the records give prominence to the negative and deleterious elements which derive from polygamy. There were drastic penalties prescribed upon adulterers and incorrigible sons (Lev. 20:9–10; Deut. 21:18–21). There is evidence, however, that common usage shored up and modified the infliction of these, so that the number of capital crimes was progressively reduced.

Property rights were protected in basic law (Exod. 20:15), and unlawful alienation of property was controlled and restitution carefully specified. Damage to life and limb was controlled early by the principle of equivalence ("an eye for an eye"), but it seems clear that this, along with the ancient practice of blood-revenge, was modified by the imposition of an alternate material restitution. Punishment for unintentional maiming and manslaughter was controlled by the institution of CITIES OF REFUGE. Special value was set upon female chastity, both premarital and within marriage, and rigid safeguards were set about the integrity of the female person.

While there was no overt distinction between public and private morality, it is clear that the ancient Hebrews, guided by divine inspiration, sought to apply principles to both interpersonal and interracial relationships reflective of their high providential origin as a people. There was a progressive elimination of purely tribal usages, a reduction of the number of capital crimes, and a concern for "widow, orphan, and stranger" which marked off Israel's societal life qualitatively from other social patterns of the times. Interracial relationships often were corrupted by the brutalities of invading peoples, and Israel's practices frequently reflected all too clearly the social evils of her environing peoples. At the same time, Israel made a good showing in her overall societal relationship when compared with other peoples of the ancient world.

II. Human society in the NT. As our Lord opened his ministry, he found the exaggerated nationalism that had grown up in the postexilic period to be a stubborn factor. Jews had, formally at least, no dealings with the SAMARITANS (Jn. 4:9), and those nationals of the adjoining nations who dealt with Jews were keenly aware that they were second-class persons (Mk. 7:26–28). The mandate to "love your neighbor" had been defiled by the wrongheaded inference, "hate your enemy" (Matt. 5:43).

Jesus, on the other hand, sought to extend the range covered by the term NEIGHBOR, and emphasized the sins of his own people rather than those committed by other nations. The parable of the Good Samaritan opened up to Judaism a whole new world of international concern. Again, our Lord did not hesitate to call attention to the Isaianic promise of mercy for the Gentiles (Matt. 12:18, 21) or to remind his hearers that the men of NINEVEH and the QUEEN OF SHEBA stood as a rebuke to their own hardness of heart (12:41–42).

The Scriptures indicate that Jesus Christ, while not ignoring either interpersonal or interracial relationships, sought to deal with society through the individual. The heart of men and women was regarded as a microcosm of the evil world; and the major thrust of the good news was in the direction of making clean the inside of the human heart.

The Pauline teaching stressed, in general, Christian compliance with the regulations of human society and did not elaborate a program for either the external remaking of society or Christian resistance to unjust societies. This does not mean that the Christian Scriptures do not contain elements and principles which when embodied did and do lead to profound modifications of human society, and as well, to monumental changes in the role of individuals with respect to their social groupings.

There is a futuristic thrust in biblical teaching with respect to human society in the endtime. There is an obvious difference between society as Rom. 13:1–7 treats it and that envisioned in Rev. 13. The former is to be recognized as God's instrument for our good. The latter is regarded as a final manifestation of the demonic in human life, and presumably should and will be resisted.

The NT makes few pronouncements that bear directly upon the specifics of society with respect to what one regards as modern social problems. At the same time the sacred writings do give expression to principles which, when embodied in significant numbers of individuals within a society, do implement public conscience and ultimately public policy. In the letter to PHILEMON, PAUL launches no direct or frontal attack upon the institution of human SLAVERY; at the same time, this inspired tract enunciates principles with respect to the structures of human relations and of forgiveness that would ultimately sound the death knell of slavery.

In general, however, the NT emphasizes a person's relation to God as primary, and interpersonal relations as being "under God," so that societal consequences should follow as a matter of course. That is to say, the individual in society is a responsible moral being, living in community by divine ordination and providential placement. The Christian faith is designed to cultivate a sensitivity to others, and to direct each person to accord to others the same dignity which one wishes to receive.

Finally, the Christian sustains a special relation to his society, as our Lord suggests in his words, "They are not of the world, even as I am not of the world," even as he prayed for their preservation following his death. Human life in society is always under the divine scrutiny; each person must on the one hand live creatively and redemptively within human institutions; and, on the other hand, maintain final citizenship in heaven. (See further H. W. Robinson, *The Christian Doctrine of Man* [1911]; R. Niebuhr, *The Nature and Destiny of Man*, 2 vols. [1943], 2:244–86; W. N. Pittenger, *The Christian Understanding of Human Nature* [1964], 126–78.)

H. Kuhn

III. Sociology and biblical studies. Since the publication of the first edition of this encyclopedia, biblical scholarship has been strongly affected by sociological (and anthropological) approaches to the study of the ancient world. Such a perspective has never been totally absent (cf. W. Robertson Smith, *Lectures on the Religion of the Semites*, rev. ed. [1907]; L. Wallis, *A Sociological Study of the Bible* [1912]; S. J. Case, *The Social Origins of Christianity* [1923]; W. C. Graham, *The Prophets and Israel's Culture* [1934]; E. A. Judge, *The Social Pattern of Christian Groups in the First Century* [1960]), but the last several decades have seen a much more vigorous and focused attempt to use social-scientific methods. Because of the wide diversity of assumptions and theoretical models employed, the value of this approach must be assessed with caution. There is no doubt, however, that sociological exegesis has a significant contribution to make (see the surveys and evaluations in *ABD*, 6:76–99).

When applied to the OT, this approach pays special attention to such questions as the origins of the nation of Israel (was it a seminomadic society? was it related to a kind of "peasant revolt"?), the development from a tribal confederacy to a monarchy, the social nature of biblical laws, the social setting of Israelite prophetic and wisdom literature, and the shift from prophecy to apocalypticism. (See J. W. Rogerson, *Anthropology and the Old Testament* [1978]; R. R. Wilson, *Prophecy and Society in Ancient Israel* [1980]; R. R. Wilson, ed., *Sociological Approaches to the Old Testament* [1984]; N. K. Gottwald, *The Hebrew Bible: A Socio-Literary Introduction* [1985]; R. E. Clements, ed., *The World of Ancient Israel: Sociological, Anthropological, and Political Perspectives* [1989]; V. H. Matthews and D. C. Benjamin, *Social World of Ancient Israel, 1250–587 BCE* [1993]; C. E. Carter and C. L. Meyers, eds., *Community, Identity, and Ideology: Social Science Approaches to the Hebrew Bible* [1996]; J. D. Pleins, *The Social Visions of the Hebrew Bible: A Theological Introduction* [2001]; P. F. Esler, ed., *Ancient Israel: The Old Testament in Its Social Context* [2006].)

In NT scholarship, various works have appeared that are best described as contributions to the *social history* of early Christianity. Others have sought to make specific use of social-scientific criticism. Also relevant are publications that use cultural anthropology to illuminate society in the 1st cent. (See M. Hengel, *Property and Riches in the Early Christian: Aspects of a Social History of Early Christianity* [1974]; G. Theissen, *Sociology of Early Palestinian Christianity* [1978]; A. Malherbe, *Social Aspects of Early Christianity*, 2nd ed. [1983]; B. Holmberg, *Sociology and the New Testament: An Appraisal* [1990]; J. H. Elliott, *What Is Social-Scientific Criticism?* [1993]; R. A. Horsley, *Sociology and the Jesus Movement*, 2nd ed. [1994]; R. L. Rohrbaugh, ed., *The Social Sciences and New Testament Interpretation* [1996]; B. J. Malina, *The New Testament World: Insights from Cultural Anthropology*, 3rd ed. [2001]; A. J. Blasi et al., eds., *Handbook of Early Christianity: Social Science Approaches* [2002]; W. A. Meeks, *The First Urban Christians: The Social World of the Apostle Paul*, 2nd ed. [2003].)

socket. The base into which the pintle of a DOOR was set to act as a pivot for swinging. Many inscribed door sockets have been found in excavations in MESOPOTAMIA. The socket in Solomon's TEMPLE was a recess cut in the stone sill (1 Ki. 7:50; Heb. *pōt* H7327, but see *HALOT*, 3:983). The KJV and NJPS use "socket" also to render Hebrew *ʾeden* H149, which refers to the base supporting the posts of the TABERNACLE curtains and walls (Exod. 26:19 et al.), some of silver, others of bronze, formed to mortise or tenon the elements supported.

H. G. Stigers

Soco, Socoh soh´koh (שׂוֹכוֹ H8450 [1 Chr. 4:18; 2 Chr. 11:7; 28:18] and שׂוֹכֹה H8458 [Josh. 15:35, 48; שֹׂכֹה in 1 Sam. 17:1, 1 Ki. 4:10], probably "thorny [place]"). KJV Socoh (Josh. 15:35, 48), Sochoh (1 Ki. 4:10), Socho (1 Chr. 4:18), Shochoh

The foreground mound of ancient Soco in the Shephelah.

(1 Sam. 17:1), Shoco (2 Chr. 11:7; 28:18); TNIV Soko, Sokoh. **(1)** A town in the SHEPHELAH of JUDAH, listed between ADULLAM and AZEKAH (Josh. 15:35). It was here that the PHILISTINES assembled prior to the confrontation between DAVID and GOLIATH (1 Sam. 17:1). Soco was one of the cities that REHOBOAM repossessed and fortified after the revolt of the northern tribes (2 Chr. 11:7; however, this passage may refer to #2 below). It was retaken by the Philistines in the reign of AHAZ (2 Chr. 28:18). The town is identified with modern Khirbet ʿAbbad, some 17 mi. WSW of JERUSALEM and 7 mi. SSE of Azekah (it is thought that the biblical name is preserved in nearby Khirbet Shuweikeh).

(2) A town in the southern hill country of Judah, listed between DANNAH and JATTIR (Josh. 15:48; perhaps mentioned in 2 Chr. 11:7, but see #1 above). This site is identified with another Khirbet Shuweikeh, E of modern Dahariyeh and about 10 mi. SW of HEBRON.

(3) A city in the SHARON Plain that was under the administration of Ben-Hesed in the time of Solomon (1 Ki. 4:10). This Socoh is probably no. 67 in the topographical list of THUTMOSE III and no. 38 in the list of SHISHAK. It has been identified with modern Khirbet Shuweiket er-Ras (a little N of modern Tul-Karem), some 11 mi. NW of SAMARIA and about the same distance from the Mediterranean coast.

(4) In 1 Chr. 4:18 it is difficult to know whether Soco is the name of a person or place. It occurs in a genealogy of the descendants of Judah, yet some of the other names listed are place names (cf. Josh. 15:48–58). Either the person took his name from the town (possibly #2 above), or "the sons of various clans are mentioned along with the names of their respective settlements in such a way that a clansman becomes the father of the place occupied" (Y. Aharoni, *The Land of the Bible: A Historical Geography*, rev. ed. [1979], 246). In this case HEBER was the founder or settler (not literally the "father") of Soco.

F. G. CARVER

soda. See LYE.

Sodi soh′dī (סוֹדִי H6052, possibly "[God is] my confidant"). Father of GADDIEL, from the tribe of ZEBULUN; the latter was one of the ten spies sent by MOSES into the Promised Land (Num. 13:10).

Sodom sod′uhm (סְדֹם H6042, meaning uncertain; Σόδομα G5047). One of the CITIES OF THE PLAIN destroyed by God because of their sin.

I. The biblical record. Sodom is first mentioned in the Table of NATIONS: "the borders of Canaan reached from Sidon toward Gerar as far as Gaza, and then toward Sodom, Gomorrah, Admah and Zeboiim, as far as Lasha" (Gen. 10:19). The next occurrence is in connection with the strife that arose between the herdsmen of LOT and those of his uncle ABRAHAM. To avoid further problems, Abraham offered Lot the choice of the land. Standing on the spine of Palestine at BETHEL, Lot looked eastward and, seeing that the JORDAN Valley was well watered, chose that part of the country (13:8–11).

The following chapter of Genesis records the battle of the "four kings against five" (Gen. 14:9). The record seems to indicate that the five cities of the plain, or valley, were vassals to KEDORLAOMER, the king of ELAM. After twelve years of such servitude they rebelled and hence invited the wrath of the suzerain (vv. 1–4). Apparently not merely these five cities but all the holdings in S Palestine were in rebellion, since the coalition from MESOPOTAMIA subdued other peoples to the S and W of the DEAD SEA before they joined forces in the Valley of SIDDIM against the kings of Sodom, GOMORRAH, ADMAH, ZEBOIIM, and Bela (see ZOAR). An interesting bit of information is inserted about the terrain on which the battle took place: "Now the Valley of Siddim was full of tar pits" (v. 10). The four eastern kings were successful, plundering Sodom and Gomorrah. "They also carried off Abram's nephew Lot and his possessions, since he was living in Sodom" (v. 12). Abraham with his men chased Kedorlaomer all the way to DAN (PLACE) and rescued Lot (vv. 14–16). The king of Sodom wanted to reward Abraham, but the patriarch refused everything except what his men had eaten (vv. 21–24).

The city of Sodom may lie beneath the waters of the Dead Sea, south of the Lisan.

The incidents that have given infamy to Sodom and Gomorrah are recorded in Gen. 18–19. In the course of the discussions between Abraham and his three heavenly visitors, the Lord mentioned the outcry against Sodom and Gomorrah (18:20–21). After some investigation Sodom was deemed worthy of destruction. Then ensued the dialogue between Abraham and God as to the number of righteous people in Sodom and how many should warrant its being spared (18:22–33). Since fewer than ten righteous persons could be counted, two angels went to Sodom to visit and warn Lot of the impending destruction. Lot was hospitable enough, but the men of the city wanted to "know" the visitors, evidently in a perverted sexual way (19:1–5; this passage has given rise to the English words SODOMITE, SODOMY).

The angelic visitors solemnly warned Lot to flee with his family (Gen. 19:12–15). Lot was reluctant to flee all the way to the hills, and asked for and was granted permission to escape to the nearby city of Zoar (vv. 17–22). With no time to spare, Lot fled with his wife and three daughters. "Then the LORD rained down burning sulfur on Sodom and Gomorrah—from the LORD out of the heavens. Thus he overthrew those cities and the entire plain, including all those living in the cities—and also the vegetation in the land. But Lot's wife looked back, and she became a pillar of salt" (vv. 24–26).

Sodom is never mentioned again in the Bible as a living city, but the memory of its sin and consequent destruction was kept alive by Moses, the prophets, Jesus, and the authors of the NT. Sodom and Gomorrah have become bywords and tokens of God's wrath on sin (e.g., Isa. 1:10; Ezek. 16:46; Zeph. 2:9; Matt. 11:23–24; Rev. 11:8 et al.).

II. Location. The most probable location of the five cities of the plain, including Sodom, is beneath the waters of the S end of the Dead Sea. South of the Lisan (*tongue*) peninsula the waters are very shallow, with an average depth of 10 ft. It is possible that at one time the S part was not only dry, but also fertile and occupied. The "tar pits" of Gen. 14:10 may be where the water was beginning to seep into that area. There is a mountain range about 5 mi. long W of the S end of the Dead Sea made up largely of crystalline salt. It is called Jebel Usdum (Mount Sodom); many free-standing pinnacles are there and one is appropriately named "Lot's wife." (There is a modern town called Sodom founded in 1953 on the W bank of the Dead Sea just N of Jebel Usdum.)

Another reason for believing that these cities now lie buried under the sea is the presence of a religious shrine at Bab edh-Dhraᶜ. This site is 5 mi. SE of the Lisan and is thought to have served worshipers from the valley cities. Its pottery evidence ranges from 2300 to 1900 B.C., which fits well with the date of Abraham. The strongest argument against this location is the use of the phrase "plain of the Jordan" (Gen. 13:10–12), which elsewhere refers to the broad plain just N of the Dead Sea (cf. 1 Ki. 7:46), but the term *kikkār* H3971 may well designate the whole rift in which are the Jordan and the Dead Sea.

(See further W. F. Albright in *BASOR* 14 [April 1924]: 5–7; M. G. Kyle, *Explorations in Sodom* [1928]; J. P. Harland in *BA* 5 [1942]: 17–32; 6 [1943]: 41–54; H. Shanks in *BAR* 6/5 [Sept.-Oct. 1980]: 26–36; W. C. van Hattem in *BA* 44 [1981]: 87–92; J. A. Loaer, *A Tale of Two Cities: Sodom and Gomorrah in the Old Testament: Early Jewish and Early Christian Traditions* [1990]; W. W. Fields, *Sodom and Gomorrah: History and Motif in Biblical Narrative* [1997]; M. J. Mulder in *ABD*, 6:99–103.)   R. L. ALDEN

Sodom, Sea of. See DEAD SEA.

Sodom, Vine of. See VINE.

sodomite, sodomy. Historically, the English term *sodomy* (derived from the story of SODOM and GOMORRAH in Gen. 18–19) has referred to any kind of nonprocreative sexual act, although it is usually applied specifically to homosexuality. The KJV uses the term *sodomite* to translate Hebrew *qādēš* H7728 ("set apart [for the use of the deity]"; Deut. 23:17; 1 Ki. 14:24; 15:12; 22:46; 2 Ki. 23:7), which evidently refers to a male shrine PROSTITUTE. In the NT the NRSV uses the same word to translate Greek *arsenokoitēs* G780 (1 Cor. 6:9; 1 Tim. 1:10), probably meaning "pederast," a man who assumes the dominant role in homosexual activity.

sojourner. See FOREIGNER.

Soko, Sokoh soh′koh. TNIV forms of SOCO, SOCOH.

soldier. See ARMY; WAR.

solemn assembly. This phrase is used by the KJV and other versions to render the Hebrew term ᶜ*ăṣārâ* H6809 (NIV simply "assembly"). It refers to the gathering and sanctifying of the community of Israel for a solemn occasion (in one passage it is used simply in a nonreligious sense, Jer 9:2). The term is used in a technical sense as the eighth day of the Feast of Booths (Lev. 23:36; Num. 29:35; Neh. 8:18; see FEASTS) and the seventh day of PASSOVER (Deut. 16:8). In both instances the people were instructed to do no work for they were in a state of ritual holiness. At the dedication of the TEMPLE, SOLOMON proclaimed a solemn assembly on the eighth day, "for they had celebrated the dedication of the altar for seven days and the festival for seven days more" (2 Chr. 7:9). For quite a different purpose, JEHU ordered the people, "Sanctify a solemn assembly for Baal" (2 Ki. 10:20 NRSV). He was then able to complete his purge of BAAL worshipers from the land of Israel through the massacre of those who gathered in that assembly.

In contrast to the feast days mentioned above, the solemn assembly also was convened for special days of fasting, as when a locust plague threatened the land (Joel 1:14; 2:15). Amos and Isaiah disparaged these solemn assemblies (among other things) as that which God could not endure (Isa. 1:13; Amos 5:21) because the people did not do justice in the land.   W. B. COKER

Solomon sol′uh-muhn (שְׁלֹמֹה H8976, prob. "peaceable" [but according to some, "replacement"; see also *HALOT*, 4:1540]; Σολομών G5048). Son of DAVID and third king of Israel (c. 970–930 B.C.). Shortly after his birth, the boy received the additional name JEDIDIAH, "beloved of Yahweh," from NATHAN the prophet, who had himself received the name from God (2 Sam. 12:24–25). In another passage, the name Solomon (which apparently derives from *šālôm* H8934, "peace") is connected with God's promise that he would "grant Israel peace and quiet during his [Solomon's] reign" (1 Chr. 22:9; for the view that the name derives from the verb *šālēm* H8966 [piel, "to recompense, restore"] and that BATHSHEBA regarded Solomon as compensation for the loss of her first child, see P. K. McCarter, Jr., *II Samuel*, AB 9 [1984], 303). It is probable that either Jedidiah or Solomon was a throne name.

I. Family. Solomon was the tenth son of King David and the second son of Bathsheba (her first child had died, 2 Sam. 12:15–19). Six of Solomon's half-brothers—Amnon, Kileab, Absalom, Adonijah, Shephatiah, and Ithream—had been born in HEBRON, each of a different mother (3:2–5).

Whereas SAUL and DAVID were born from the common people and grew up among them in village and countryside, Solomon was born in the palace at JERUSALEM and grew up among men of power. He had seen the heights of royal glory and the chaos of rebellion. He was well educated and never knew poverty or hunger. But he did know the consequences of intrigue, jealousy, and murderous hate. Before he grew to maturity several of his older half-brothers had met violent deaths and one half-sister had been raped.

II. The world situation at the end of David's death. Solomon never knew other than a unified Hebrew nation that was strong in a chaotic world. True, the rule of David had been shaken several times by internal rebellions, but it was still one nation at the end of David's life. David's personal strength and genius contributed greatly to Israel's unity, but just as important was the weakness of the other nations in the ANE.

EGYPT had suffered a serious international setback at the beginning of the 12th cent. from which she did not recover for two centuries. During this time, Egypt was unable to prevent, militarily, the rise of the kingdoms of Saul and David, or the extensive activities of Solomon. Yet she remained a formidable commercial power and was not above political maneuvers which could embarrass her neighbors. At the same time, the HITTITE empire of Anatolia (modern Turkey) was also eliminated by the same people, the displaced Phrygians and Philistines, who had moved E from W Anatolia, S Greece, Crete, and Cyprus. The same forces had severely crippled a newly rising power, ASSYRIA, with headquarters on the TIGRIS River. Assyria's eclipse continued for 300 years. BABYLON was equally impotent.

Solomon reigned over a vital portion of real estate, Palestine, which has been called the land bridge of the ANE. His country was strategically located for maximum political power and for tight control over trade routes that crisscrossed his realm. Solomon had troublesome neighbors, but no true rivals. It was a golden opportunity for Israel to make an optimum impact on her world; it was her "Golden Age."

III. Solomon's accession to the throne. Solomon was not the obvious heir apparent to the throne, for he was far from being David's oldest son. It is true that the firstborn, AMNON, and the third son, ABSALOM, had been eliminated by violence,

The kingdom of Solomon.

and it is possible that the second son, KILEAB, died young; but there were others who, theoretically, could qualify as David's successor. In fact, the right of succession by age had not been formally established in Israel as yet, and David was slow to make Solomon known as the next king.

According to 1 Chr. 22:7–10 (which evidently alludes to Nathan's message, recorded in ch. 17 and in 2 Sam. 7, i.e., before Solomon's birth), the Lord had revealed to David that Solomon would be the next to rule Israel. Moreover, David had sworn to Bathsheba that Solomon would succeed him (1 Ki. 1:13, 17). Then, toward the end of his reign, David assembled the Israelite leaders and informed them that Solomon was picked as the next king (1 Chr. 28:5; 29:1). Apparently, David did not personally move to make Solomon's future position formally legitimate because both he and Saul had been elevated to kingship by manifest acts of God. Surely, the same would happen in the case of Solomon—yet God did not so act.

A serious crisis developed. ADONIJAH (David's fourth son) was older than Solomon, so he could claim some rights to the throne. Accustomed to having his own way, and an easy prey to the intrigues of important men, Adonijah decided to force the issue by engineering a coup. Adonijah had powerful backing for his bid to claim the throne. JOAB, the general of the regular army, had always been a powerful leader and had control over strong forces to support Adonijah. ABIATHAR, a leading priest and, for long, David's close adviser, provided the appearance of religious blessing. There were other powerful public figures who were behind Adonijah hence, clever strategy demanded a surprise takeover under the guise of a normal religious festival at a sacred spring, EN ROGEL (a short distance below Jerusalem in the KIDRON Valley). Emphasis was placed on the Judean faction in the government (1 Ki. 1:5–10).

Word got out that the religious festival had an underlying political purpose. Nathan the prophet, a long-time personal confidant of the king, rushed to Bathsheba with the news. Together, they devised a means to rouse the dying king enough to obtain permission to launch a quick counter-move (1 Ki. 1:11–27). The plan succeeded. The king revived sufficiently to give orders that ZADOK, the other high-ranking priest at the GIBEON tabernacle (1 Chr. 16:39), anoint Solomon at the nearby GIHON SPRING. BENAIAH, the trusted commander of David's personal bodyguard, was to protect the procedures. All went as ordered. A trumpet blast signaled the climactic moment and the crowds lifted the cry, "Long live King Solomon!" (1 Ki. 1:34).

The move caught the backers of Adonijah by surprise. They understood immediately the ramifications of the event. The kind of game in which they were engaged was played for keeps, and the losers seldom survived. With Solomon, reprisal moved more slowly. Adonijah sought asylum at the horns of the high altar and was granted his life, provided he behaved himself. But Adonijah could not refrain from subtly maneuvering for power. With a show of innocence, he sought ABISHAG, the most recent member of David's harem, as a wife. He made his request through Bathsheba, assuming that Solomon could not refuse to grant the wishes of his own mother. Adonijah claimed that he had the right to be king and had the support of the people but God had worked against him. Surely, he should at least have one of the HAREM girls as his own (1 Ki. 2:13–17).

Bathsheba apparently did not comprehend the thrust of this clever ploy, so she innocently passed on the request to Solomon, who caught the implications of the tactic immediately. In the ANE, those who had possession of any part of a king's harem had a basis to make claims against the throne, especially if the king died. Solomon reacted drasti-

Remains of the northern palace at Megiddo, dated by some to the period of Solomon.

Solomon was anointed king at the Gihon Spring.

cally, too drastically no doubt, for he immediately ordered Adonijah's death (1 Ki. 2:24–25).

Abiathar was not killed; he was deposed from his high position in the priesthood and confined to his family's ancestral village, ANATHOTH (1 Ki. 2:26–27). JOAB was not so fortunate. He had been deeply involved in David's reign and loyal to him, but he had committed two bloody murders — of ABNER and of AMASA (v. 5) — in such a way that they appeared to be loyal acts. Hence, David could not punish Joab without losing army support. Yet, David knew they were vile murders and Joab must be punished, so he admonished Solomon to carry out the delayed justice (v. 6). Joab was now fatally vulnerable. He was openly in the wrong; he had lost public and army support. He fled to cling to the horns of the high altar, but to no avail. He was executed and his body sent home for burial (vv. 22–35). SHIMEI, who had reviled David, soon met a similar fate (vv. 36–46).

Solomon no longer had opposition from any high-ranking officer in David's government. He was free to reorganize the kingdom according to his own design. Humanly speaking, there were no power checks to his rule except the attitude of his people, the laws of God as summed up in an admonition given by David (1 Ki. 2:2–4), and Solomon's personal encounters with God.

IV. Solomon's spiritual life as a young king.

A significant spiritual experience occurred in Solomon's life while he was worshiping at Gibeon, an ancient HIGH PLACE where the Mosaic tabernacle and the bronze altar still stood a few miles NW of Jerusalem (2 Chr. 1:2–5). God appeared to Solomon by means of a dream, the structure of which was a dialogue between God and Solomon (1 Ki. 3:5–15).

The initial approach was made by God, with a simple request that Solomon ask what he wanted from God, for Solomon had been worshiping God by means of sacrifices. A wide range of possibilities lay before Solomon, but he made a single request based on what God had done for David and on his own sense of inadequacy. In spite of Solomon's quick and decisive treatment of his rivals, his initial diplomatic success with Egypt (1 Ki. 3:1), and popular response to his religious assemblies, he felt inferior to his task. In the presence of God, the young king saw his need clearly and confessed it. His request was for wisdom from God so he could rule his people properly and justly.

God's response was positive and generous. He granted Solomon wisdom but added to it other gifts: wealth and fame. There was a condition, however. Solomon must live according to God's commands, even as had David. Solomon's gratitude was expressed in a public religious service before the ARK OF THE COVENANT in Jerusalem. He began his reign with the blessing of God upon him, motivated by personal commitment to God.

V. Solomon's administrative organization.

Probably much of Solomon's organization had its roots in David's government, and back of that was an Egyptian model, but Solomon placed the stamp of genius upon its final form. There were two major aspects or divisions to his government: the princes or chief officials (1 Ki. 4:2–6; Heb. *śar* H8569) and the twelve provincial officers or district governors (vv. 7–19; Heb. *nāṣab* H5893).

The princes were headed by AZARIAH the priest, who was probably the king's closest adviser. Whereas David had one scribe, Solomon appointed two brothers, ELIHOREPH and AHIJAH (their father's name, Shisha, suggests Egyptian extraction; see SHAVSHA). These seemed to be in charge of private and foreign correspondence. JEHOSHAPHAT was in charge of national records and annals, and probably also the public relations aspects of court life. BENAIAH was promoted to Joab's position as commander of the standing army. Both ZADOK and ABIATHAR are listed as priests, but the latter had been retired from service due to his complicity with Adonijah's attempted coup. Another Azariah, Solomon's nephew, had responsibility over the administrative offices, and ZABUD, another nephew, was a close adviser to the king. AHISHAR was the prime minister of the court, having charge of immediate palace affairs and offices. ADONIRAM, apparently the Adoram of David's cabinet (2 Sam. 20:24) and later in REHOBOAM's group of officers (1 Ki. 12:18), was in charge of the labor force.

Twelve officers (1 Ki. 4:7–19) were royally appointed governors of artificially established provinces that largely ignored the old boundary lines of the tribes. They were primarily tax collectors and were responsible for supplying the court with a specified amount of food, each having one month of the year (vv. 7, 22–23). Each had soldiers and chariots under his control and seemed to provide men for labor or for the general army when needed. They had charge of building projects in their districts and constructed roads. Two of the officers, BEN-ABINADAB and AHIMAAZ, who had the provinces farthest to the N, were sons-in-law to Solomon. Only N Israelite territories are involved in this list, which suggests that Solomon was accepting the animosity between these areas and Judah and that the latter was administered separately (according to the LXX of v. 19, there was "one officer in the land of Judah"). If N Israel had to bear the main burden of taxation, it is not difficult to see how the tension between the N and S came to the explosion point at the end of Solomon's reign.

Some detail is given of the administration of the corvée (forced labor) gangs: 70,000 men were assigned as burden-bearers and 80,000 as stonecutters, all of whom were non-Israelites (1 Ki. 5:13–18; 2 Chr. 2:2, 17–18). The strain of the building projects seemed to have become so severe, however, that the king was forced to draft also 30,000 Israelites into the labor gangs. Later, JEROBOAM was to gain fame and power by protesting this violation of the freedom of the Israelites.

It has been assumed by some that the military organization set up by David was continued by Solomon with but few changes and additions. There were, first, a regular standing army with a main core of seasoned professionals and a body of mercenaries who served as the king's bodyguard. Joab had been the leader of the former, but, after his death, Benaiah, head of the mercenaries, became commander of both. Second, a militia was drawn from all the tribes for a minimum of one month's service each year (1 Chr. 27:1–15). Under Solomon these seemed to be under the twelve provincial governors (1 Ki. 4:7).

There were some chariots, horses, and mules in David's army, and these were greatly expanded under Solomon (1 Ki. 4:26; 10:26; 2 Chr. 9:25). The chariots and horses were mainly quartered in three major fortresses: HAZOR, MEGIDDO, and GEZER. For several decades it was assumed that the stables discovered at Megiddo belonged to Solomon, but subsequent work ties them to AHAB a century later, as are the extant stables at Hazor. Solomon, however, did have stables in the three cities, which served as strategic defensive points.

VI. Solomon's building operations. During Solomon's reign Israel experienced a sudden spurt of improvement in standard of living and in economic activity. The king was extravagant and spared no pains to turn his humble capital into a magnificent city. His first big project was one already started under his father, the construction of the TEMPLE.

Solomon determined that only the best was good enough for God's house. Already much material had been gathered, but the final size, style, and ornamentation was left largely to Solomon, who in turn procured the artisans of TYRE to insure high-quality work. Basic woods such as CEDAR and CYPRESS were purchased from Tyre, floated to a port on the coast, and hauled to Jerusalem. The fact that craftsmen from Tyre worked on the temple has led some to believe that the temple possessed many architectural features common to ancient PHOENICIA; all that remains to aid our knowledge of the temple, however, is limited largely to the detailed description of it in the Bible (1 Ki. 6:2–36; 7:13–50; 2 Chr. 3:1—4:22; cf. Ezek. 40:5–16).

The temple was modeled primarily after the Mosaic TABERNACLE, though its measurements were almost doubled. It was begun in Solomon's fourth year and was completed after seven years. It was located on the traditional Mount MORIAH, a rocky crest in the threshing floor of Ornan the Jebusite (2 Chr. 3:1; see ARAUNAH). The temple faced E and was surrounded by a spacious courtyard. Most of its brass work was cast at SUCCOTH, just E of the Jordan River, by a craftsman from Tyre named HIRAM. Lavish amounts of gold and silver decorated the interior. The temple was not for the people to worship in, but was a sanctuary for God. Some would call it a "royal chapel."

While the temple was being erected, Solomon built an elaborate palace, comprised of the Palace of the Forest of Lebanon, a colonnade (NRSV, "Hall of Pillars"), and "the throne hall, the Hall of Justice" (1 Ki. 7:1-12). Each was magnificent and costly. The king's private dwelling and that of his queen were part of another court in the rear (v. 8). Other major projects were the MILLO, perhaps a fortification built on an earth fill, and the wall surrounding the new buildings in Jerusalem itself. Three major fortress cities were built at Hazor, Megiddo, and Gezer, several of lesser importance elsewhere, plus a number of store-cities and cavalry forts (9:15-19).

Two prominent aspects of Solomon's buildings were the casemate wall and the six-chambered gates with two towers. The casemate wall had been developed several hundred years before Solomon's time and had been perfected by the HITTITE empire. It was made up of two parallel walls joined regularly by cross walls. The resulting rooms could be filled with rubble or earth. Sometimes they were reserved for storage. All cities in which archaeologists have found remains of Solomon's fortresses had this type of wall. For several decades, it was thought that Megiddo was different, but in 1960 a casemate wall found there was related to Solomon's time. Though discontinued as an outer wall, this type remained popular for inner citadels or isolated forts for many years.

Excellent examples of the Solomonic gate have been identified at Megiddo and at Hazor. Since Gezer is also mentioned in connection with these cities, it was suspected that one also existed there. When R. A. S. Macalister dug at Gezer at the beginning of the 20th cent. (see his book, *The Excavations at Gezer* [1912]), he did not recognize such a gate, but Yadin reexamined the documents and found one drawn on one map though dated much later than Solomon's reign. Subsequent work at Gezer has laid bare this gate much more clearly (see Y. Yadin in *IEJ* 8 [1958]: 80-86).

In Ezek. 40:5-16 the prophet gives a series of measurements of six gates in the temple compound. The description matches very well the actual size and shape of the three gates at Megiddo, Hazor, and Gezer, proving that Ezekiel was recording information about Solomonic gates that he would have known as a young boy in Jerusalem. The temple gates were completely destroyed by the Babylonians in 586 B.C. and never employed afterward as a pattern. This kind of gate was a hallmark of Solomon's major building projects.

VII. The extent of Solomon's empire. Solomon inherited from David a territory that touched the banks of the EUPHRATES to the N and the Brook of Egypt to the SW (see EGYPT, BROOK (WADI) OF). The Mediterranean Sea served as the western border, the Arabian desert the eastern border, and the southern anchor was the tip of the Gulf of AQABAH.

Direct control of some of this land soon slipped from Solomon's hands. A young Edomite, HADAD, had escaped to Egypt from David's conquest of EDOM, but now returned to wrest this country from Solomon (1 Ki. 11:14-22). Likewise to the N, REZON was able to make DAMASCUS his capital and a center of strong opposition to Israel (11:23-25).

The fact that Egypt was able to capture Gezer and then give it as a dowry with a daughter of the PHARAOH strongly suggests that Egypt had taken control of PHILISTIA. Since this area is not mentioned among the twelve districts, it is possible that Egypt had gained supremacy in the SW corner of Palestine. Still, what Solomon lacked in military occupation he made up by forging a series of treaties and dominating the economic traffic of the Levant.

VIII. Solomon's international relationships. One of Solomon's first treaties was with Egypt.

It was not altogether to his advantage, for he was required to take an Egyptian princess as a queen and to lose control of Philistia. The gain of Gezer was hardly full compensation, but future trade relations with Egypt proved valuable.

A treaty of special worth was forged with HIRAM of Tyre, who had been a close friend of David. Hiram was ruler of an extensive maritime domain, possessed rich natural resources, and had highly skilled artisans. Solomon drew heavily on all three for his building operations and his own shipping enterprise (1 Ki. 5:1–12; 9:10–14). In course of time, Solomon released to Hiram twenty cities in GALILEE, some think to pay a deficit in what Solomon had purchased, though others think that it was for a loan (2 Chr. 8:1–2 seems to say that Solomon got the cities back again). In addition, the biblical text (1 Ki. 10:24–25=2 Chr. 9:23–24) points to a network of treaties with countries of all sizes, and many of his wives seem to have been sureties for these treaties. One of these wives, an Ammonite, was the mother of Rehoboam, the next king (1 Ki. 14:21).

Trade considerations were closely tied to the political alliances that were forged. The king of Israel held a pivotal position because he controlled the main route along the sea and the main route E of Jordan, both of which connected the nations of the S with the nations to the N. Solomon was not only able to tax goods that passed along these routes; he was also able to act profitably as a middle man in the trade deals. Solomon particularly loved horse trading and set up an arrangement in which he procured chariots and horses from Egypt and KUE (in CILICIA) and sold them to other nations. Egypt had to get wood for the chariots from areas which Solomon controlled, so he had a virtual stranglehold on the industry (1 Ki. 10:28–29).

Solomon's relationship with Hiram of Tyre was not limited to buying lumber and skills for building projects; Solomon was able to exploit Hiram's maritime knowledge for his own advantage. SHIPS and sailors were obtained for a fleet that operated out of EZION GEBER (on the Gulf of AQABAH). This fleet made trade contacts with ARABIA and the eastern coast of Africa, bringing many strange and exotic goods and animals to Israel. Closely related to the shipping port was a mining and refinery project that exploited the rich copper deposits near Ezion Geber. Remains of the mining operations have been found there by archaeologists. The COPPER and BRONZE produced had ready buyers in other parts of the world. It would seem that Hiram's Mediterranean fleet could distribute widely these metals (1 Ki. 9:26, 28; 10:11–12, 22).

The celebrated visit of the QUEEN OF SHEBA was as much a trade mission as a trip motivated by a strong curiosity about the reputed wisest man in the world. Her elaborate gifts could serve as "samples" of what her country could offer to aggressive traders (1 Ki. 10:1–10, 13; 2 Chr. 9:1–9, 12). Thus the combination of fairly peaceful relations with other nations, dominance of the "land bridge" of the ANE, and the effective control of the major land trade routes poured wealth into Israel at a spectacular rate. Gold, silver, and cedar were no longer rarities in Jerusalem. But Solomon's extravagance strained the income to the limit; a fiscal deficit was not unknown even in the "Golden Age."

IX. Solomon's religious activities. After God's initial appearance by means of a dream to Solomon, the king plunged immediately into the task of constructing the temple. The dedication of this building was a high occasion in Solomon's life and in the life of the nation. The ceremony was elaborate and impressive. Everyone of any importance in Israel came to Jerusalem. The ark of the covenant was transferred from David's tabernacle to the temple by the priests and the Levites in an impressive procession. The time was the Feast of Tabernacles, soon after the autumnal equinox (2 Chr. 8:13).

While numerous sacrifices were being offered, the ark was placed in the Holy of Holies of the new sanctuary. God placed his blessing on the scene by symbolizing his presence by means of a cloud. The king himself gave public recognition to the divine presence and personally pronounced a blessing upon the assembled congregation. Solomon testified that he understood several important truths about the one true God. He is the Creator, who cannot be seen, but who would and did condescend to dwell among his people. God had also acted in the past by giving promises and fulfilling them by delivering the Israelites from Egypt, and by giving them David as king. To David he had granted a promise of a royal lineage which was fulfilled in

Solomon. The house of God was for the ark, the symbol of divine presence and deliverance.

Solomon then offered a remarkable prayer in which a clear monotheistic doctrine is dominant. God was not limited to the temple nor to the world itself. God's name was to be honored at the temple by means of worship and through the temple and the priests. God was to make his will known to his people, answering their prayers. God was to judge, but also to forgive his people, granting both spiritual and material blessings. Even the stranger and the exile were to have the same privilege of petition before God. Indeed, 1 Ki. 8:42 suggests that one reason for building the temple was to attract other people to pray to the one true God. After the prayer of dedication, Solomon participated with his leaders in an eight-day feast. On the last day he sent a joyful nation home. An event had occurred which was to linger long in national memory.

At the end of Solomon's building program, the Lord appeared to him again. God expressed his acceptance of the temple and the king's act of dedication. But a clear-cut condition was laid before the king that obedience to the laws of God was essential to fulfillment of the divine promise to David about the continuity of the throne. To be disobedient would mean God's abandonment of the temple, and the people to destruction and to captivity.

According to 2 Chr. 8:14–15, Solomon also reaffirmed the divisions of the priests in their duties, but oriented now to the temple itself. The pattern set by David was followed for both priests and Levites. Beyond this, little is said about other religious acts of Solomon in relation to the temple.

X. Solomon's cultural achievements.

There was a marked acceleration of interest in literature among the Israelites during Solomon's reign. Apart from the Scripture, little remains of the productions of the time; only a small inscription called the Gezer Calendar has been found (see AGRICULTURE V).

The Scripture has left record that Solomon's wisdom issued in an accumulation of oral and written evidence of his skills and insights. The king became regarded as the most erudite scholar of his day, surpassing the great wise men of Edom (1 Ki. 4:29–34). Three thousand proverbs and over a thousand songs are credited to him. He was known as a learned lecturer on botany and biology. He easily answered riddles put by the queen of Sheba.

A major portion of the WISDOM Literature in the OT is attributed to Solomon (including Ps. 72 and 127). The book of PROVERBS has three notations that ascribe most of its content to him (Prov.

This gate complex at Gezer may have been built by Solomon.

1:1; 10:1a; 25:1). Many have assumed that Eccl. 1:1, 12 refers to Solomon, though others doubt it (see ECCLESIASTES). The Song of Songs carries a superscription that connects the king with its composition (Cant. 1:1; see SONG OF SOLOMON).

Various scholars have attributed to the time of Solomon the final organization of several of the historical books, such as Joshua, Judges, Ruth, and the two books of Samuel. Some who reject Mosaic authorship of the Pentateuch have claimed that substantial parts of it were completed in Solomon's reign. These claims cannot be definitely proved. Other brief references to literary works in Solomon's time are "the book of the annals of Solomon" (1 Ki. 11:41), "the records of Nathan the prophet," "the prophecy of Ahijah the Shilonite," and "the visions of Iddo the seer" (2 Chr. 9:29). All of the literary works of Solomon's time are permeated with a consistently strong monotheistic doctrine.

XI. Summary of Solomon's contributions to Israel's national life.

Under Solomon, Israel for the first time experienced a relatively consistent period of peace and prosperity. The internal factions in the nation were balanced in a delicate and, for the most part, workable relationship. The recurrent tribal feudings and court-related revolts were a thing of the past. The standard of living in the nation climbed to unprecedented heights, and the availability of luxury items and materials was open to a large portion of at least the urban population. International relationships had their tense moments but no serious crises. For the time being, a network of treaties effectively kept diplomatic and commercial lines open and functioning. No known wars scarred the landscape or played havoc with the affairs of men.

For the first time the nation had a permanent national worship center in the capital city. The presence of the temple was to dominate the religious life and thinking of the Israelites until its destruction in 586 B.C. Even then it did not fade out; the structure was rebuilt and later thoroughly remodeled until again destroyed in A.D. 70. The influence of the priests became more powerful and the festivals became regularized. The presence of the temple enhanced the city of Jerusalem itself so that it became known as the city of God. The teaching function of the priests helped to disseminate the ancient truths revealed by God more widely in Israel. The temple became a powerful unifying force.

Also for the first time in Israel, its leadership had a successful example of passing of power from father to son. The reign of Solomon served to make actual and legitimate the covenant God made to David concerning the continuity of the Davidic family as a ruling power in Israel. The establishment of this principle of succession was to be the prime stable factor in the nation during the span of over three centuries. The length of time that David's dynasty ruled had scarcely a parallel in the history of the ANE during the 10th to the 6th centuries B.C.

Costly though it was, Solomon's building projects gave Israel a sense of national pride and of security that it had never known before. Finally they had constructed something which could stand in the world of the day as both artistic and magnificent. Pomp and ceremony augmented this new sense of nationhood effectively.

Solomon's contributions to Israel's culture were profound, but the greatest of these was in the realm of literature. Art in the form of sculpture and painting did not come within the scope of Israel's skills, but the art of human expression through the oral and written word was a different matter.

In comparison with other ANE languages, the Hebrew tongue was a newcomer. Its literary history was limited, but Solomon and those whom he influenced forged the HEBREW LANGUAGE into a highly honed tool of communication. In a very real way, Hebrew became one of the important languages of the world for the propagation of both divine truth and the deepest human insights prompted by that truth. Songs, witticisms, and riddles had been known in Israel before, but wisdom of the quality that Solomon brought forth was without parallel, even in the pagan literature of the day. Solomon had sparked a concern to put the truth of God and humanity into the medium of the written word that never died out in Israel.

XII. Summary of Solomon's shortcomings in administration. Solomon's reign was not without blemish, great though he was. His wisdom was profound, but it possessed serious flaws. Solomon's powers to judge were impressive; he could tell which of two women was the true mother of a baby (1 Ki. 3:16–28). He was unable to see, however, that due process of law is a needed check to arbitrary power. His executions of Joab, Adonijah, and Shimei could be outwardly justified, especially to that generation. Solomon showed that he was capable of decisive action. But these men needed their day in court even though they were guilty, for others later may not be manifestly in the wrong. Solomon had too much power over the lives of his subjects.

The administrative structure of Solomon's government lacked adequate checks and balances to guard against abuses of centralized power. The officials, both in Jerusalem and in the provinces, were so strong that it was exceedingly difficult for the voice of the people to be heard. It was too easy to whitewash mistakes and to smother dissent. The ease with which Jeroboam was forced out of the country is a case in point (1 Ki. 11:26–40).

Too much regimentation of the populace not only destroyed individual freedom but begat rank discrimination. Israel's minority group, composed of Canaanites, was reduced to a form of slavery, condemned to the labor gangs, but the Israelites were virtually untouched, except in emergency

This provided fertile soil for discontent and future revolt.

There were no proper checks on government spending, no review of taxation policies, of trade policies, or of foreign affairs policies by an independent branch of the government. It is little wonder that in each of these areas matters got out of control. Solomon had great skill in maintaining delicately balanced agreements among the tribes and among the surrounding nations, but could not, at least did not, cope seriously with the tensions necessitating the "balances of power." Hence, when he died, chaos broke out on every hand. During his reign the tendency was toward monopoly with no firm economic base in the country, no strong merchant class, and no real international bonds forged.

The religious branch was too firmly under the control of the government. True, Solomon had priests who were close advisers, but they had no truly independent voice. Too easily they could become a tool of the throne to control the people. Significantly, the prophet, so important a person in David's life, was practically nonexistent, as far as we know, in Solomon's time. The king had been urged by his father and by God to obey the commandments of God, but human voices to remind him of this charge were largely silent.

Solomon's government had no real sense of mission to the world. The king allowed foreign gods to be worshiped in and near Jerusalem, but made no apparent effort to spread Hebrew culture and religious viewpoints to the other nations. They could come to Jerusalem and be converted, but nothing is heard of Israelites going to them with a message of "One True God" who is the Creator, Judge, and Savior of all mankind.

The nation's financial resources were strictly limited to secular pursuits or to the rich ornamentation of the temple. Neither the king nor his subjects had any compulsion to use this wealth to uplift the common people in Israel, or in foreign lands, spiritually. The nation was broad-minded. They could tolerate polygamy and idolatry in the royal household; they could also tolerate poverty, with ignorance, in society both at home and abroad. Solomon and his nation had both the opportunity and the resources to spread the message of the living God throughout the ANE but let the golden moment slip through their fingers.

XIII. Summary of Solomon's personal life.

The young king began his reign with everything going for him. He was talented, well-trained, knowledgeable, and blessed by a fresh experience with God, who had granted him more than his heart desired. Solomon's major endeavor, the construction of the temple, was spiritually oriented. Its dedication was a high hour in his life. The words that he spoke on that occasion reveal spiritual understanding of great depth and breadth. God's second appearance to Solomon indicates that he maintained some keenness of spiritual life, but it was also a reminder that his obligations under the law of God still were binding on him.

The Scripture is quite clear that in his latter years Solomon began to move away from the strong ardor of his younger years. The reason is said to be centered in his oversized harem. Solomon had accumulated a total of 700 wives and 300 concubines (1 Ki. 11:3), many through political alliances. This procedure was in accord with the common customs of the day, but it was in conflict with the law of God, as noted in 11:2. The presence of the harem highlighted a general pagan view that the king was the prime sire of the nation and had an obligation to contribute as many children as possible. Implicitly, Solomon accepted this concept, with the result that wives and concubines played too dominant a role in his life and more and more blurred his perspective.

More significantly, he allowed many of these women to worship their pagan gods, in fact built pagan temples for them. Ironically, Solomon was not diligent in giving witness to the reality of his own God, but his pagan wives were evangelistic in their zeal and turned his heart from the true God (1 Ki. 11:4, 6). So serious was this breach of loyalty that God appeared to him the third time and rebuked him, saying that in his son's day the kingdom would be torn apart (vv. 9–13). The pagan shrines remained a snare to Israel until destroyed by Josiah (2 Ki. 23:13–14). Solomon's sin remained an example of evil in the days of Ezra's reforms (Neh. 13:26), and the place where they were erected has continued to be called the

Mount of Offense even to this day. See CORRUPTION, HILL (MOUNT) OF.

Granted that Ecclesiastes is the work of Solomon, it could be concluded that Solomon passed through periods of disillusionment, frustration, and despair, but that he was able to come through with a basic faith in the one true God. At least, it is true that all works of literature attributed to him contain a monotheistic stress that is unmistakable. However, his life served more as a spiritual warning to the Israelites in succeeding generations than as a witness of spiritual integrity comparable to that of his father.

(See F. James, *Personalities of the Old Testament* [1940], 149–65; W. F. Albright, *Archaeology and the Religion of Israel* [1942], 130–55; M. F. Unger, *Archeology and the Old Testament* [1954], 219–34; G. E. Wright, *Biblical Archaeology* [1957], 130–46; M. Noth, *The History of Israel* [1958], 203–23; Y. Yadin, *The Art of Warfare in Biblical Times* [1963], 275–90; Y. Aharoni, *The Land of the Bible: A Historical Geography*, rev. ed. [1979], 309–20; L. Rost, *The Succession to the Throne of David* [1982]; G. N. Knoppers, *Two Nations under God: The Deuteronomistic History of Solomon and the Dual Monarchies*, 2 vols. [1993–94]; L. K. Handy, ed., *The Age of Solomon: Scholarship at the Turn of the Millennium* [1997]; P. S. Ash, *David, Solomon and Egypt: A Reassessment* [1999]; J. Bright, *The History of Israel*, 4th ed. [2000], 211–28; J. J. Kang, *The Persuasive Portrayal of Solomon in 1 Kings 1–11* [2003]; W. Brueggemann, *Solomon: Israel's Ironic Icon of Human Achievement* [2005]; W. Dietrich, *The Early Monarchy in Israel: The Tenth Century B.C.E.* [2007]; *ABD*, 6:105–13.)   G. H. LIVINGSTON

Solomon, Odes of. See ODES OF SOLOMON.

Solomon, Pools of. See POOL.

Solomon, Psalms of. See PSALMS OF SOLOMON.

Solomon, Song of. See SONG OF SOLOMON.

Solomon, Testament of. A legendary tale dealing primarily with the interaction between SOLOMON and various demons. The tale is related in the first person, and twice Solomon refers to it as a "testament" written to warn others (Sect. 15.14 and at the very end, 26.8), but otherwise the work is unlike the TESTAMENTS OF THE TWELVE PATRIARCHS and other literature in this genre. It appears to have been composed in Greek by a Christian, possibly toward the end of the 2nd cent. or somewhat later. The *Testament of Solomon* has been preserved in sixteen Greek MSS, one of them an early fragment. (Critical ed. by C. C. McGown, *The Testament of Solomon* [1922]; English trans. with full introduction in *OTP*, 1:935.)

Solomon, Wisdom of. See WISDOM OF SOLOMON.

Solomon's Colonnade (Porch). What the KJV calls "Solomon's porch" (NRSV, "the portico of Solomon"; Gk. *stoa G5119*) was a roofed colonnade in the temple built by HEROD the Great. It bordered on the E side of the outer court of the temple, resting on a massive Herodian retaining wall (still largely visible as the lower courses of the present temple-area wall) built out over the KIDRON Valley. It may have been so named because of a tradition that SOLOMON had once constructed a similar E wall and cloister (Jos. *War* 5.5.1; cf. *Ant.* 8.3.9). It was here that Christ walked and talked during the Feast of Dedication (Jn. 10:23); here also his disciples seem later regularly to have gathered (Acts 5:12; cf. 3:11). See TEMPLE, JERUSALEM VII.C.7.

J. B. PAYNE

Solomon's servants. A class of state SLAVES in Israel instituted by King SOLOMON. Of course, all subordinates of a king might be considered his servants. For example, the feast Solomon gave for all his "servants" (1 Ki. 3:15) certainly included his officials, if not exclusively so (these officials are named in 4:1–19). But the specific Hebrew phrase translated "Solomon's servants" (ʿabdê šĕlōmōh, 1 Ki. 9:27; 2 Chr. 8:18; 9:10; Ezra 2:55, 58; Neh. 7:57, 50; 11:3) does not refer generally to all those who served Solomon in any capacity. Rather, it is a technical term designating a slave class.

State slaves were common in the ANE. Prisoners of war were made servants for big commercial or industrial enterprises carried out by the king. Not until the time of DAVID was Israel strong enough to have any state slaves. David began on a restricted scale with the Ammonites (2 Sam. 12:31). But the extensive building projects of Solomon called for state slavery on a vast scale. It was thus Solomon who reduced the native Canaanites to slavery (1 Ki. 9:20–21), and the new class of slaves was appropriately called ʿabdê šĕlōmōh (1 Ki. 9:27; 2 Chr. 8:18; 9:10; in these three passages, however, the NIV and other versions render "Solomon's men" or the like).

The class of state slaves continued throughout the monarchy, though varying in number and economic importance. The descendants of Solomon's servants after the EXILE are noted as having been merged with the NETHINIM or temple servants (Ezra 2:55–58; Neh. 7:57–60; 11:3; 1 Esd. 5:33–35). It is doubtful that in this case these two groups were regarded as slaves in the strict sense of the term. (See R. de Vaux, *Ancient Israel* [1965], 1:88–90, 141–42; I. Mendelsohn, *Slavery in the Ancient Near East* [1949], 92–106; A. F. Rainey in *IEJ* [1970]: 191–202; H. G. M. Williamson, *Ezra-Nehemiah*, WBC 16 [1985], 35–36.) J. C. MOYER

son. See CHILD; FAMILY.

song. See MUSIC, MUSICAL INSTRUMENTS VI.

Song of Solomon. One of the poetical books of the OT and the first of the five MEGILLOTH ("scrolls") that were read at Jewish FEASTS. It is generally known as the "Song of Songs" from the superlative form used in the title (šîr haššîrîm), which denotes the best or most excellent of songs. In Jewish religious tradition the Song was read at the feast of the PASSOVER. In the VULGATE the work was entitled *Canticum canticorum*, hence the alternative English title of *Canticles*.

    I. Background
   II. Authorship
  III. Date
  IV. Unity
   V. Place of origin
  VI. Destination
 VII. Occasion
VIII. Purpose
  IX. Canonicity
   X. Text
  XI. Content and outline
 XII. Interpretation
XIII. Theology

I. Background. Those who accept the traditional attribution of the book to King SOLOMON have seen the early monarchy as the background against which the work was composed. The pastoral qualities of the poetic imagery suggest a lengthy interlude of peace in the land during which the sedentary ideals of the Israelites were being realized, and this situation would accord with the "golden age" of DAVID and Solomon very well. The Song contains numerous references to animals and exotic plants, and in view of the tradition that associated botanical lore with Solomon it has been thought that if the work is a genuine Solomonic product it would again point to the early monarchy as the period from which it emerged.

The various geographical allusions in the book seem to indicate a phase of Hebrew history in which the kingdom had not yet been divided. Canticles speaks of such northern locations as LEBANON (Cant. 3:9; 4:8, 11, 15), HERMON (4:8), TIRZAH (6:4), DAMASCUS (7:4), and Mount Carmel (7:5; see CARMEL, MOUNT), as though, with JERUSALEM, they formed one united kingdom. This, however, need mean nothing more than that the poetic flights of the author transcended purely localized considerations. In any event, the book shows clearly that the author was familiar with the geography of the whole Syro-Palestine area from the mountains of Lebanon to En Gedi near the DEAD SEA (1:14). Although Canticles mentions some exotic commodities of the Far East, there is no internal evidence which would indicate that the material was written against any other than a strictly Palestinian background.

II. Authorship. Most modern scholars have rejected the Solomonic authorship of the book and instead have seen in Canticles a collection of songs celebrating premarital and marital love. These have generally been understood to have arisen against a pastoral background, with at least some of the lyrics being intended for use at Hebrew wedding ceremonies. It has been stated that the only evidence which can be cited as a specific indication of Solomonic authorship of the work is the title (or editorial introduction, as some scholars have described it, on the grounds that the relative pronoun ʾăšer *H889* is used only here; elsewhere šā- *H8611*, Cant. 1:6–7 et al.). In addition, the particle lĕ- *H4200* in the expression lišmōlōh (usually translated "Solomon's," indicating direct authorship by Solomon) is ambiguous and could also mean "to," "for," "concerning," or "after the fashion of."

The name of the celebrated Hebrew monarch appears six times in the text (Cant. 1:5; 3:7, 9, 11; 8:11, 12), of which the first and the last two actually comprise figurative allusions to the immense wealth of the king. In the third chapter Solomon is mentioned on three occasions in connection with an elaborate procession, where the reference is evidently to the historical personage of Solomon. The allusions to "the king" are also generally associated with Solomon (1:4, 12; 7:5). Although the great Hebrew king is the central figure in certain of the poems (notably 3:6–11), he is never actually represented as the speaker, and because of this certain scholars have assumed that at least some of the poems were written about him, rather than by him.

Despite this objection, there is nothing in the title of the book that would preclude the immediate circle of the Solomonic court as the place of origin of the various poetic elements. Since a great many of the Hebrew proverbs were formulated at this period under such auspices, there is no reason why certain exotic poems should not have issued from the same source at much the same time.

Arguments in favor of a non-Solomonic authorship have also entertained a comparatively late date for the book on linguistic grounds. For example, there are forty-nine terms in the work that do not occur elsewhere, some of these being botanical in nature. There are numerous words and phrases that are akin to the kind of ARAMAIC used in certain postexilic compositions, along with what appear to be loanwords from Persian and Greek sources. In answer to these objections it must be noted that the vocabulary of the book is naturally governed by the peculiar nature of the subject matter to a large extent. The fact that no other OT book is so full of technical terms for spices, plants, and shrubs will in itself require that at least some of the species would be referred to under the designation employed in the countries of their origin. The spice known in the orient as CINNAMON (Cant. 4:14) has simply been transliterated into Hebrew (qinnāmôn *H7872*, possibly from a Malayan word), and this practice has also been adopted in English.

Trade between N India and Mesopotamia was well-established in the 3rd millennium B.C., so that by the time of Solomon there was a long tradition of commercial contacts with the Far East. Some of the exotic substances mentioned in Canticles have obvious Sanskrit parallels, as with "nard" (Cant. 1:12; 4:13, 14; Heb. nērd *H5948*, from Sanskrit naladu; see SPIKENARD). Even the term ʾappiryôn *H712*, "carriage, litter" (3:9), supposedly a loanword from Greek *phoreion*, probably did not enter Palestine from the AEGEAN but was instead derived directly from Sanskrit *paryanka* (cf. English *palanquin*, from Malayan via Portuguese).

As far as the Aramaic forms in Canticles are concerned, their presence can throw no light at all upon questions of authorship. Aramaisms appear in numerous OT compositions, some of which are

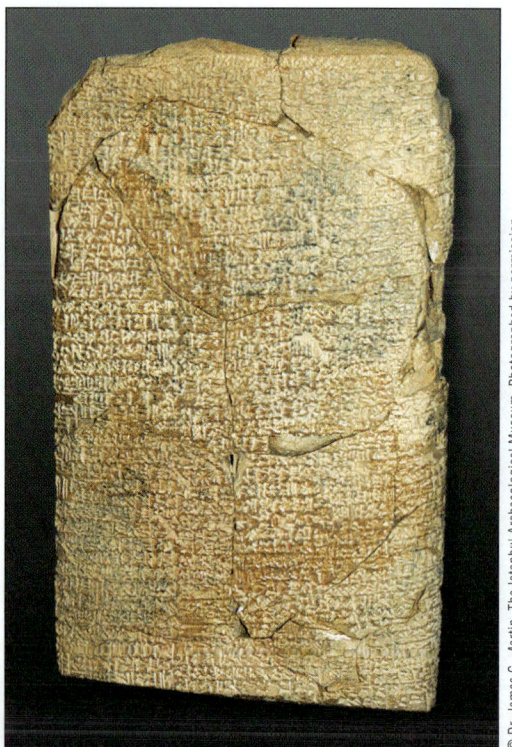

Terra-cotta cuneiform tablet inscribed with a Sumerian sacred marriage rite. From Nippur, 1st dynasty of Isin (c. 1974–1954 B.C.).

clearly of an early date, and this is hardly surprising in view of the fact that Aramaic is now known to have flourished in Assyria and elsewhere from at least the beginning of the 2nd millennium B.C. Already in the Tell el-Amarna period (15th to 14th centuries B.C.) the language was familiar to the Canaanites, and Aramaic elements have been demonstrated in various Ugaritic compositions. There appears to be nothing in the linguistic peculiarities of Canticles that would demand a late rather than an early date. Certainly there are no valid reasons for assigning the work to the Greek period (c. 300 B.C.), if only because of the prolonged history of cultural exchanges between the Aegean and the other nations of the ANE. Consequently there would seem to be little valid reason for objecting to the traditional attribution of authorship to Solomon or to someone associated in some way with him.

III. Date. Those critics who have assigned one or two of the poems in Canticles to Solomon have accordingly placed certain sections of the book within his reign (c. 970–930 B.C.). As far as the other sections are concerned, some have been assigned to a N Israelite origin prior to the fall of Samaria in 722, while others are thought to have originated in the 5th cent. As has been shown above, there is no single demonstrable element in Canticles which demands a date after the Solomonic period. The mention of Tirzah (Cant. 6:4) as though it was the northern counterpart of Jerusalem might point to the comparatively early date of composition of that portion of Canticles. Prior to the reign of Omri (c. 885–874), Tirzah had been the chief city of the northern kingdom, but when he came to the throne of Israel he established Samaria as his capital city, constructed numerous buildings in addition to erecting a splendid royal palace, and fortified the site strongly. If Tirzah was being suggested as the chief northern city (6:4) to match Jerusalem in the S, the poetic section concerned could well have dated from the 10th cent.

In general it can be said that the cultural background of the material as a whole points to a prolonged interval of sedentary life in the kingdom, and the ethos of Canticles is much more in accord with the conditions which obtained during the early monarchy than with the rigors of exilic or postexilic life. The presence of Aramaisms in the composition, as already suggested, has no bearing at all upon its date, and it may well be that the particular expressions were the result of nothing more than the influence of regional dialects. Unless it can be shown conclusively that the work could not have emanated from the period of Solomon, it seems best to assign the compilation of Canticles to the 10th cent. B.C.

IV. Unity. The extant work seems to have formed, or to have been based upon, a collection of rustic love poems of somewhat uncertain provenance. Although this is the most probable explanation of the general origin of Canticles, the book bears recognizable indications of a unity of style and general theme. The repetitions in the work would seem to point to the activities of a single compiler, since they serve to bring about a more marked sense of unity of theme than might be expected from an anthology of lyrics issuing from diverse authors over a fairly lengthy period of time. In view of what appears to be a genuine overall unity of emphasis, namely that of the richness of human love in its variant modes, it would seem that the attempts of those scholars who have fragmentized the book into something like thirty poems are hardly consonant with the emphasis and character of the finished product.

V. Place of origin. If the work is to be assigned to the general period of Solomon, as those who support the traditional view have maintained, the book was probably compiled in Jerusalem at the royal court. The prowess of Solomon as a lyricist is made plain in 1 Ki. 4:32, and as has been noted earlier, there are no particular elements which preclude a date in the early kingdom period for the composition of Canticles.

However, those writers who have rejected the Solomonic authorship of the book have thought that at least some of the poems may have arisen in the northern kingdom. This view has been maintained partly because the presence of Aramaisms in Canticles was thought to favor a N Israelite or Syrian place of origin, and also because Tirzah was mentioned in an apparently parallel position to Jerusalem (Cant. 6:4). If Tirzah was being suggested seriously in the poem as the northern equivalent of Jerusalem, it might indicate that the passage had been written at a time when Tirzah was the chief city in the N, and may even have comprised the place of origin of that section of Canticles. If the book is to be regarded as a unity it might then appear that Solomon pursued his bride into the northern part of his kingdom, a situation which, while unlikely, is by no means impossible. If those scholars who maintain that Canticles is an anthology of poetry independent of Solomonic authorship are correct, the passage in question could well have originated in or near Samaria.

Speculation of this kind concerning the place of origin of the various elements of Canticles is hazardous at the best, if only because there is absolutely no discernible provincialism in the book as a whole. Even if Canticles was compiled as an anthology of love lyrics that originated in widely separated areas of the kingdom, the manner in which they have been arranged makes it virtually impossible for them to be assigned to particular locales. If Canticles was composed at a given point in the Solomonic era, it is still possible for certain familiar poems to have been included as part of the larger work without, however, giving any significant hint as to where they originated. On any basis of compilation, therefore, the place of origin presents certain difficulties, though these are considerably less for those who support the traditional authorship than for those who postulate a non-Solomonic origin.

VI. Destination. Any estimate concerning the situation or persons for whom Canticles was written will depend largely on the way in which the material is to be interpreted. In overall terms the work does not seem to have been meant for any people other than the Israelites. If the poems were the work of Solomon they would certainly have been intended for a local audience, and the same would be true if the lyrics originated in connection with Israelite wedding ceremonies. If the poems are compositions that simply extol human love in its various facets, it seems unlikely that they were intended for use outside Israel.

In later Arabic times erotic poems known as *wasfs* were recited in the presence of the bride and groom just before the wedding ceremonies, and it has been supposed that at least some portions of Canticles fulfilled this function in Israel. While a local destination may have been intended in the composition of Canticles, the fact remains that many of the poems in the book do not lend themselves readily to recitation at wedding ceremonies. Although some might correspond to the type of *wasfs* used by the modern Arabs during the period of courtship, it is unwise to rely too heavily upon late Arabic practices as a means of arriving at conclusions concerning the literary genre or destination of the book.

VII. Occasion. Precisely what stimulated the composition of Canticles is unknown. If it is merely an anthology of love lyrics of general Solomonic provenance, it could well have arisen in connection with one or more of that monarch's numerous marriages. If the book represented a less purposeful collection of nuptial songs current in various parts of the kingdom, the occasion need only comprise the stimulus experienced by an unknown editor to preserve such love lyrics for posterity. The general unity of the theme and form which Canticles exhibits makes it appear probable that some specific occasion underlay the compilation of the work. Estimates as to the nature of this will naturally vary with the date assigned to the extant book, while those scholars who deny the basic unity of authorship of Canticles will be compelled increasingly to look for separate occasions for which the component parts might have been compiled. The very subjectivity of such a process will inevitably leave much to be desired in the conclusions.

VIII. Purpose. Many expositors have found some difficulty in justifying the inclusion of Canticles in the corpus of Hebrew Scripture, partly because of its general eroticism. However, the book could be described as an extended PROVERB (Heb. *mašal* H5442) which illustrates the richness and beauty of human love, and as such it stands firmly within the gnomic tradition of the Hebrew Wisdom Literature. Although some of the language and imagery may be unacceptable to Western tastes, it must be remembered that the material originated in the Orient, where very different attitudes frequently obtain.

The theme of the book is firmly rooted in the beauties of nature, from which it passes into a sym-

Considered the oldest love poem, this Sumerian inscription dates to c. 2030 B.C.

Hebrew Scriptures reminds one of a love which is purer than our own (so E. J. Young, *An Introduction to the Old Testament*, rev. ed. [1964], 337).

IX. Canonicity. From rabbinic sources it is evident that Canticles did not gain either an immediate or a ready acceptance into the Hebrew CANON of Scripture. The TALMUD (*b. Baba Bathra* 15a) went so far as to assign its composition to HEZEKIAH and his company of scribes, an opinion that may have been based on the activities of this group in connection with the editing of other apparently Solomonic material (cf. Prov. 25:1). The MISHNAH (*m. Yadayim* 3:5) indicates that the Song was accepted into the canon only after some dispute at or about the time of the supposed consultation at Jamnia (c. A.D. 95; but see JABNEEL #2). Following an affirmative verdict in the matter by Rabbi Judah and a negative vote by Rabbi Jose, the assembled scholars heard Rabbi AKIBA deliver his famous dictum: "In the whole world there is nothing to equal the day in which the Song of Songs was given to Israel: all the Writings are holy, but the Song of Songs is the holy of holies."

The fact that such a strongly worded statement should have been necessary at all indicates that in the days of Akiba there were some doubts about the origin and propriety of the book. Without question, the opposition to its inclusion in the Hebrew canon was prompted by the erotic nature of the contents. In the end this objection seems to have been outweighed by the traditions that associated its composition with Solomon, as well as by the allegorical interpretations current in both Christian and Jewish circles, which tended to elevate the poems above a purely erotic and physical level.

In order to preserve a modicum of propriety with respect to Canticles, Rabbi Akiba is also said to have pronounced a curse on those who sang portions of the Song of Solomon at banquets or similar festive occasions: "He who trills his voice in the chanting of the Song of Songs in the banquet halls, and treats it as a secular song, has no share in the world to come" (*t. Sanh.* 12.10). This prohibition may well have been directed at the bawdy or lewd allusions which might be expected to result from those singers who had been drinking copiously.

bolic representation of the object of desire. The traditions of love to which appeal is made are those of the upper classes, who alone would be able to afford the exotic, expensive substances mentioned in the poems. The outlook of author and reader alike was not inhibited by an attitude toward sexual relationships which regarded them as at best embarrassing, and at worst thoroughly evil; thus there was no difficulty in describing the various aspects of human love in a way that would meet with a sympathetic understanding. The book steers a course between sexual perversion or excess, on the one hand, and a rigid, ascetic denial of normal bodily and emotional needs on the other. It also provides an object lesson in close personal relationships that is needed in the Western world by showing that spirituality is not inconsistent with spontaneity and a lack of self-consciousness during moments of greatest physical intimacy. Not merely does the Song of Solomon speak of the purity that can characterize human love, but by its very inclusion in the

Certainly the best means of protecting the canonical status of the Song would be to assign to the work an esoteric religious meaning, and this doubtless gave impetus to the allegorizing of Canticles in rabbinic circles.

X. Text. Although there are occasions on which the Hebrew text is obscure, this factor seems due more to the presence of an unusual number of rare words (e.g., *rāhîṭ* H8112, Cant. 1:17; *talpiyyôt* H9444, 4:4) and other linguistic problems (e.g., the trans. of 6:12) than to transmissional errors. Since both the SEPTUAGINT and the Syriac Peshitta follow the MT fairly closely, they also are of limited help in clarifying the more difficult parts of the Hebrew. The complicated imagery of the book is an added obstacle to conjectural emendation.

XI. Content and outline. It is far from easy to present an analysis of Canticles in the conventional manner because of the closely interwoven nature of the speeches. These latter can be seen either as dialogue (e.g., Cant. 1:9–11) or soliloquy (e.g., 2:8—3:5), and tend to move from one participant in the conversation to another with a readiness which frequently defies precise identification. The "daughters of Jerusalem" are mentioned during the discourses (1:5; 2:7; 3:5 et al.) and have been credited with certain responses in the dialogue (1:8; 5:9; 6:1 et al.). A similar situation obtains for the inhabitants of Shulem (8:5) and Jerusalem (3:6–11). In broad terms the content of the Song of Solomon can be outlined as follows:

A. The bride expresses her longing for the bridegroom and sings his praises (1:1—2:7).

B. As their affection for one another deepens, the bride heaps further praise on her beloved, using exquisite figures from nature (2:8—3:5).

C. This passage contains the praises of King Solomon, the praise of the bride, and the espousal (3:6—5:1).

D. The bridegroom is absent for a time, during which the bride longs for his return and continues to praise him (5:2—6:9).

E. A series of descriptive passages narrate the beauty of the bride (6:10—8:4).

F. A concluding section deals with the durability of true love (8:5–14).

XII. Interpretation. It can be safely said that few if any OT books have experienced as wide a variety of INTERPRETATION as the Song of Solomon. Since there is no specifically religious theme in evidence in the book, and almost nothing in the sequence of the narratives that could be recognized as a plot, the erotic lyrics that comprise the book have provided almost limitless grounds for scholarly speculation as to their intrinsic meaning and significance. Aside from a straightforward erotic interpretation, five other approaches have been entertained in ancient and modern scholarship in differing ways and with significant degrees of variation. These are the allegorical, cultic, dramatic, lyrical, and typical.

(1) The *allegorical* approach (see ALLEGORY) was adopted by both the rabbis and the church fathers as a means of solving the problems associated with the acceptance of a group of love lyrics into the canon of Scripture, and is still favored by certain Roman Catholic and orthodox Jewish commentators. The MISHNAH and the TALMUD reflected this method of interpretation, while the TARGUM of Canticles thought of the work as demonstrating the graciousness of God to Israel in the mighty acts evident in her history. God is therefore the great lover of the poems and Israel is the recipient of his mercies. At the hands of Christian interpreters the allegory was modified so that the bride was the Christian church, a perspective already present in certain NT passages (e.g., Jn. 3:29; Eph. 5:22–23; Rev. 18:23; 22:17). This approach seems to have been first suggested by Hippolytus of Rome, but the classical allegorical form was developed by ORIGEN. He was followed by JEROME and many others; his interpretation was reflected in the chapter headings that were incorporated into the KJV. Most Christian expositors, however, avoided the problems associated with explaining Canticles in terms of a history of the church, although J. Cocceius saw in the book a history of Christendom culminating in the Reformation.

As a variation of the allegorical approach, some patristic writers thought of Canticles in terms of the relationship between God and the individual soul. This approach began with Origen and was adopted by some other fathers and certain medieval writers. Ambrose and a few Roman Catholic commentators identified the bride with the Virgin Mary, while

Martin Luther held that the maiden was nothing more than the Solomonic kingdom personified. Some interpreters have entertained a multiplicity of identities for the same bridal figure, representing her by turns as Israel, the Christian church, the Virgin Mary, and the individual believer. Unfortunately, as with all allegorical interpretations, the very subjectivity of the method tends to be self-defeating.

This situation has led to widely divergent interpretations of the same passage, a result that hardly inspires confidence in the particular form of interpretation. The reference to the beloved (Cant. 1:13) was seen by Rashi and Ibn Ezra as an allusion to the presence of God which rested on the sacred ARK OF THE COVENANT between the cherubim, while Cyril of Alexandria understood it to point to Christ and the two Testaments of Scripture. Bernard of Clairvaux, who preached eighty-six sermons on the first two chapters of Canticles alone, held that it indicated the crucifixion of Christ, which sustains the believer in times both of joy and sorrow. Quite aside from individual variations of interpretation, an important objection to the allegorical method, based on other OT writings, is that when the male-female relationship is described allegorically, there is always a clear indication of the method being employed (cf. Ezek. 16; 23; Hos. 1–3). In Canticles, however, there is not the slightest hint that allegory is being utilized anywhere in the lyrics. Be that as it may, the allegorical approach to Canticles was dominant in Protestant thought until recent times.

(2) The *cultic* interpretation has been favored by some scholars in the light of those ANE liturgies that commemorated the death and resurrection of a god. According to this view, the lover of Canticles was the dying and rising god, while the beloved was either his sister or his mother, who lamented his decease and went about searching frantically for his remains. Such mythical pairs familiar to the Israelites were the Canaanite BAAL and ANAT, the Babylonian TAMMUZ and ISHTAR, and the Egyptian Isis and OSIRIS. According to this interpretation the pagan liturgy was accommodated by the Israelites to the spring and autumn festivals as part of the New Year cultic observances. Adherents of this view adduced as external evidence the fact that Canticles was read liturgically at the Passover festival in the medieval period, and pointed to a reference in the Mishnah (*m. Taʿanit* 4:8) which spoke of the maidens of Jerusalem dancing and singing at a festival in the vineyards on the 15th day of Ab and following the Day of Atonement. Internal evidence for the theory was seen in the male and female figures which dominated the narrative, the vanishing lover and the bride searching in anguish, the exotic imagery, and the references to rare plants and spices, all of which were held to characterize the Tammuz liturgies.

Attractive as this theory may appear, it raises great difficulties in the way of acceptance. Four other canonical compositions, none of which has the slightest claim to a purely cultic origin, were also read at festive occasions. Furthermore, Canticles contains no specifically liturgical terms, and there can be no doubt that had it constituted a modified form of pagan mythology it would never have been admitted into the Hebrew canon. In addition, while there may well have been harvest festivals in Israel, as elsewhere in the ANE, there is absolutely no evidence to support the contention that rituals connected with the death and resurrection of a god were ever a part of such celebrations. It can only be concluded that the cultic approach to the meaning of Canticles places a forced interpretation upon the narratives as a whole.

(3) The *dramatic* understanding of the Song of Solomon arose when interest in the allegorical approach began to decline at the beginning of the 19th cent. In its earliest form, however, it went back to Origen, and it also found expression in the thought of John Milton. As developed from 1800, it assumed two principal forms. One of these, expounded by Franz Delitzsch (KD, *The Song of Songs and Ecclesiastes*, 4–5), saw in Canticles two main characters: Solomon and a country maiden described as the SHULAMMITE (Cant. 6:13), about whom Canticles wove a story. In essence, the book narrated the way in which King Solomon found this girl in her rustic surroundings and took her from her village to Jerusalem. There as his wife he learned to love her with a depth of affection that transcended purely physical attraction.

The other form of dramatic interpretation was advanced by G. H. A. Ewald (*Das Hohelied Salomo's* [1826]), who introduced a third principal figure into the narrative. According to Ewald, the story of Canticles revolved around King Solomon, the Shulammite maiden, and the newly designated figure of her lover, a shepherd from the countryside. Ewald suggested that the king, having become enamored of the physical attractions of the Shulammite, carried her off by force to his harem in Jerusalem. When she consistently resisted his advances, however, he reluctantly allowed her to return to the locale of her rustic lover. This theory, which became known as the "shepherd hypothesis," proved quite acceptable in some critical circles, though a few scholars added to the dramatic aspect of the theory by emphasizing the presence of a chorus of maidens somewhat after the fashion of classical Greek plays. The shepherd hypothesis was an advance in certain areas over the suggestions of Delitzsch in that it explained the reason for the lover being depicted as a shepherd (Cant. 1:7–8), and also accounted for the termination of the poem in a northern setting rather than in Jerusalem.

However, there are certain features of the view which might be extremely difficult to sustain for various reasons. In the first instance, the shepherd hypothesis introduces into the narrative a central figure for whose existence there is no real textual evidence at all. Furthermore, it assumes without warrant that the maiden resisted the advances of her lover, whereas in point of fact the narratives make it clear that she was possessed of a very different frame of mind. Again, whereas the views of Delitzsch propounded the joys of conjugal union as illustrated in the heroic King Solomon, those of Ewald depicted something closely approaching attempted seduction by the king. In this way Solomon became the villain of the drama, not the hero, an attitude that is foreign to other OT traditions concerning the renowned king. In addition, any dramatic interpretation of Canticles has to face the great difficulty raised by the scarcity of evidence for dramatic literature among the Semites, and not the least in Israel.

Another admission of the weakness of the evidence adduced in support of the dramatic interpretation is that some of those who held to this view thought that Canticles was more a dramatic reading than a "staged" production. It ought to be observed that for scholars to assume that the maiden mentioned in the poems can be identified with ABISHAG the Shunammite is entirely gratuitous. Again, the association of the "daughters of Jerusalem" with either the harem of Solomon or with some sort of professional chorus is purely conjectural. The fact is that the allegedly dramatic nature of the song is so little in evidence that it is impossible to delineate any concurring development of the plot. While it is true that the intensely personal speeches of Canticles fall into the two broad categories of dialogue and soliloquy, they defy analysis into such forms as scenes, acts, mimes, and the like, which are of the essence of a dramatic work.

(4) The fourth principal approach to the understanding of Canticles, the *lyrical*, was one which tended to take the narratives at something like face value and assign the simplest form of interpretation to them. Accordingly, those who hold to this view recognize in Canticles the presence of a collection of love lyrics or songs that had no necessary connection either with wedding festivities or other specific occasions. Nor were they to be regarded either as celebrating in terms of the male-female relationship the higher values of divine love, or as having emerged from a pagan cultic background in which the death and resurrection of some deity was being commemorated. Some adherents of this school of thought have associated the love poems in a rather general manner with the Solomonic tradition (cf. Cant. 3:6–11), but at the same time have denied unity of authorship to them, thinking of them principally as an anthology of native Israelite material issuing from diverse periods of history.

The description of Syrian marriage customs by J. G. Wetzstein in 1873 prompted K. Budde to advance a special form of the lyrical interpretation in 1893. His view understood Canticles as a collection of nuptial songs similar to those used in the seven-day marriage feast in which the bride and groom are crowned as king and queen, and at which the *wasfs* were offered also. Aside from the hazards involved in employing modern Syrian customs to illustrate ancient Palestinian practices, this view is weak, for the Shulammite is nowhere designated in Canticles as "queen." There would hardly be sufficient material in the extant composition for a week-long celebration, and there are certain other elements of modern Syrian practice that are lacking in the Song, such as the war chants honoring the prowess of the bridegroom. The chief virtue of the general lyrical interpretation is that it avoids the difficulties inherent in the allegorical, cultic, and dramatic understanding of Canticles.

(5) There is another approach to the interpretation of the Song of Songs that is closely related to the allegorical method and that has been favored by certain conservative scholars. This is known as the *typical* interpretation (see TYPOLOGY), and possesses the undoubted advantage of preserving the obvious sense of the poems while at the same time discerning a more elevated and spiritual meaning in contrast to the purely sensuous or erotic. The typical method manages to avoid the excesses that have so often arisen in the more detailed examples of interpretation as provided by the allegorical school, and in stressing the themes of love and devotion that are so evident in Canticles, it expounds the story in terms of the relationship of love existing between Christ and his faithful followers. This approach has been justified on the ground that many of the Arabic love poems have esoteric meanings, and also by an appeal to the biblical analogies of human marriage (Hos. 1–3; Ezek. 16:6–14; Eph. 5:22–33 et al.). The use Christ made of the narrative of JONAH (Matt. 12:40), as well as the reference to the serpent in the wilderness (Jn. 3:14), has also been adduced as compatible with this general method of interpretation.

The content of Canticles reveals an attitude toward nature that is seldom in evidence elsewhere in the OT. The normal estimate the Hebrews had of nature was that it comprised a contingent form of creation which revealed the splendor and majesty of God. Its essential forces were firmly under his control and could thus be employed to do his bidding, whether for good or ill. Although certain aspects of divine function were occasionally reflected in descriptions of the incidence of natural phenomena, these latter were always seen as subsidiary entities which in one way or another testified to the power and glory of God, the supreme Creator. For the Hebrews, therefore, nature was never entertained as being an end in itself, but invariably as the manifestation of a superior creative Power who alone demanded human reverence and obedience.

In Canticles, however, there is a distinct and uncharacteristic delight in nature for its own sake, an attitude that is projected with great skill by means of highly aesthetic imagery. The most obvious parallels to this situation can be found in Egyptian writings, where there are many frank appraisals of the beauties of nature and forceful descriptions of the appeal which oriental aromatic spices made to the senses. Furthermore, in comparable Egyptian sources, the lovers have been styled "my sister" and "my brother" and have also been compared with swift steeds and gazelles (cf. Cant. 1:9; 2:17 et al.). At the same time, the Egyptian parallels contain distinct traces of polytheism, of which there is no evidence at all in Canticles, and are also deficient in the voluptuous physical descriptions that are so conspicuous in the Song.

It would appear from ANE literature in general that the parallel between the cycles of nature and the mood of lovers was as well attested a part of the larger courtship and love experience as it is at the present time, if modern love lyrics can be adduced as evidence. In this event the material of Canticles could well comprise pure folk poetry that enshrined a projection of the human ideals of love into nature itself. While this attitude may be uncharacteristic of the way in which the Hebrews generally regarded the forces of nature, it is still a valid though perhaps intensely personal expression of an age-old constituent part of human nature. The very fact that the beloved one is urged to come into the fields at a time when the vital powers of the earth are once again asserting themselves (Cant. 2:8–17; 7:11–13) may be a further indication of the not uncommon direction taken by the fancy of the young and virile in the spring.

In the first instance the love poems seem to have been assigned to the genre of Wisdom Literature on the ground that the skills necessary to render them adequately to musical accompaniment called for *ḥokmâ* H2683 ("wisdom"). This tradition was based on the reputation Solomon gained for his ability to display his wisdom in songs (1 Ki. 4:32), as well as on the activities of native Canaanites such as ETHAN and HEMAN (4:31), who were named as heads of guilds of singers in the temple (1 Chr. 6:33, 44; 15:17–19). If these poems actually had some connection with wedding ceremonies, the skill of the performers at the feasts would be comparable to the professional abilities of female mourners who are described in Jer. 9:17 as "skilled women" (NRSV).

Since Canticles was associated with Solomonic authorship from its inception, the relationship between the composition and the epitome of wisdom in Israel seemed to confirm its status as Wisdom Literature still further. But with the rejection of Solomonic authorship, the collection of poems was assigned to other literary genres. Because the material is poetic in nature, it partakes of the general character of other OT poetic compositions (see HEBREW POETRY). These include such typical structural features as synonymous, synthetic, and antithetic forms of parallelism, along with a mixture of rhythmic accentuations or stresses in the lines of poetry. The forceful nature of the imagery which is entertained lends itself particularly well to poetic expression.

XIII. Theology. Canticles stands virtually alone in the Hebrew canon in that it contains no explicit theology. Those who argue for the origin of the material in terms of a number of folk lyrics see this feature as being entirely consistent with the absence of a settled situation in life. The theological position of the composition must therefore be ascertained inferentially, and on such a basis there can be no doubt that Canticles firmly enshrines the Hebrew religious tradition of MONOTHEISM. In this celebration of the joys of human love there are no traces whatever of the magical influences or the polytheistic beliefs that are to be found in parallel material from ancient Egypt. Although Canticles supplies very little actual information about Hebrew MARRIAGE institutions, it seems to be grounded in a basic ethos of monogamy, a situation that has not gone unnoticed by those who have argued against Solomonic authorship.

Although the poetic images are almost completely alien to modern tastes, the composition is never lewd or obscene, even by the standards of Western civilization. In fact, Canticles reflects the traditional canons of sexual morality contained in the Mosaic law, and never countenances anything that could be described on such a basis as immorality. It reflects the traditions of Gen. 2:24, which maintain that in marriage the male and female constitute a psychophysical unity, and its discussion of the whole range of the emotions of lovers is conducted at a high level of sensitivity and morality. The purity and beauty of human love as a divine gift is the dominant theme of the book. By contrast with the Greek lyricists and some modern authors, the work exhibits no self-consciousness regarding the natural relationship between male and female in marriage, and indicates that the richness of human love is a microcosm of the larger LOVE of God.

(Significant commentaries include C. D. Ginsburg, *The Song of Songs* [1857]; W. Pouget and J. Guitton, *The Canticle of Canticles* [1948]; R. Gordis, *The Song of Songs and Lamentations: A Study, Modern Translation and Commentary*, rev. ed. [1974]; M. H. Pope, *Song of Songs*, AB 7C [1977]; G. L. Carr, *Song of Songs*, TOTC [1984]; R. E. Murphy, *The Song of Songs*, Hermeneia [1990]; T. Longman III, *Song of Songs*, NICOT [2001]; G. Barbiero, *Cantico dei cantici: Nuova versione, introduzione e commento* [2004]; D. A. Garrett and P. R. House, *Song of Songs, Lamentations*, WBC 23B [2004]; Y. Zakovitch, *Das Hohelied*, HTKAT [2004]; J. C. Exum, *Song of Songs*, OTL [2005]; R. S. Hess, *Song of Songs* [2005].

(See also W. H. Schoff, ed., *The Song of Songs: A Symposium* [1924]; H. H. Rowley, *The Servant of the Lord and Other Essays* [1952], 189–234; R. K. Harrison, *Introduction to the Old Testament* [1969], 1049–58; J. M. Munro, *Spikenard and Saffron: A Study in the Poetic Language of the Song of Songs* [1995]; G. M. Schwab, *The Song of Songs: Cautionary Message concerning Human Love* [2002]; J. E. de Ena, *Sens et interprétation du Cantique des cantiques: Sens textuel, sens directionnels et cadre du texte* [2004]; A. C. Hagedorn, ed., *Perspectives on the Song of Songs* [2005]; D. P. Roberts, *Let Me See Your Form: Seeking Poetic Structure in the Song of Songs* [2007]; and the bibliography compiled by W. E. Mills, *Ecclesiastes; Song of Solomon* [2002].)

R. K. HARRISON

Song of Songs. See SONG OF SOLOMON.

Song of the Three Young Men (Children). See AZARIAH, PRAYER OF.

Son of God. One of the titles often applied to JESUS CHRIST in the NT. See also CHRISTOLOGY.

　I. OT origins of the term

SON OF GOD

II. Usage in the Synoptic Gospels
   A. Initial references
   B. Baptismal declaration
   C. The temptation
   D. Demonic confession
   E. Confession by the disciples
   F. Christ's self-confession
   G. The confession of Christ's enemies
III. Usage in Acts
IV. Meaning to the pagan world
V. Usage in Paul's epistles
   A. Early uses
   B. Late uses
VI. Johannine evidence
   A. Initial statements
   B. Confessional passages
   C. Personal claims
   D. Witness of Christ's enemies
   E. Conclusion
VII. Usage in Hebrews

I. OT origins of the term. The plural expression SONS OF GOD (Heb. *běnê hāʾĕlōhîm*) is used loosely to describe angelic beings who form a sort of "heavenly court" for Yahweh. See ANGEL. This is a possible explanation of the debated passage in Gen. 6:2–4. According to Job 1:6 and 2:1, even SATAN can be included in such a gathering. Job 38:7 seems to be an OT antecedent of the angels' song of Lk. 2:14. The expression "sons of the Most High" (Ps. 82:6, parallel to "gods") may also refer to angels. Such phrases, reflecting the common idiomatic use of "son" (see BEN-), are possibly applied to heavenly beings because they are sharers in the nature of God as spirit.

Whatever the origins of the term, however, it certainly carries no polytheistic associations in the OT. Oscar Cullmann (*The Christology of the New Testament*, 2nd ed. [1963], 272–75) and some other modern scholars prefer to see the "father and son" relationship of such beings to God as that of mission and obedience respectively. A better sense would be "sender and sent one," in view of the Hebrew and Greek words for "angel." This has the advantage of explaining other OT instances also. For example, Hos. 1:10 describes the Israelites as "sons of the living God"; perhaps loving obedience, rather than likeness, is the thought.

For the background of NT Christology, the use of the singular noun is more important. God refers to Israel, considered collectively, as "my son" (Hos. 11:1), and Matthew applies this passage directly to Christ (Matt. 2:15). Perhaps "covenant-love" constitutes the filial bond on both sides. Alternation of the plural and the singular (as a collective) is typical of OT theology; although the term is singular, it does not necessarily mean that an individual relationship of sonship has been established. Not until NT times will believers dare to cry, "Abba, Father," in this sense (Mk. 14:36; Rom. 8:15; see ABBA). Psalm 2:7 describes an individual relationship (see BEGOTTEN) that is applied to Christ in Acts 13:33 and Heb. 1:5. This is a royal psalm, and connects sonship of God with Davidic kingship. The Scandinavian school of scholars sees the passage as a relic of non-Israelite ideas of "divine kingship"; but of this there is no trace in the OT. Cullmann (*Christology*, 273) perhaps correctly thinks the reason is that the king represents Israel, already described as God's "Son."

In any case, this is sonship by ADOPTION and GRACE, as was that of Israel. It may be linked with the messianic nature of the king, for every king in Israel is "the anointed of the LORD" (1 Sam. 24:6); doubly so, those of DAVID's line. Naturally, when the type is fulfilled in Christ (see TYPOLOGY), the meaning goes far beyond that of the psalm to the sonship by nature and generation. (For a further example of "divine sonship," see Ps. 89:26–27.) Another preparatory use of the singular is the description of one of

Medieval mosaic in the church of Hagia Sophia (Istanbul) depicting Christ, the Son of God, on his throne.

the mysterious figures of Dan. 3:25 as *dāmēh lĕbar ʾĕlāhin* ("like a son of the gods"); v. 28 explains this as an "angel" sent by God, and later theology saw it as a Christophany, like other mentions of "the angel of the LORD" in the OT.

Further than this the OT cannot go without endangering its own foundational doctrine of the unity of God; but, as in the case of SON OF MAN, the linguistic framework has been prepared to receive the NT content.

II. Usage in the Synoptic Gospels

A. Initial references. Mark's gospel opens with the phrase "Jesus Christ the Son of God" (the textual evidence supporting the retention of "the Son of God" is strong, though not conclusive). This is all the more remarkable in view of Mark's limited use of the title (spoken only by demons and the centurion, Mk. 3:11; 5:7; 15:39). The first chapter of Luke records that Jesus was to be called "Son of the Most High" and "Son of God" (Lk. 1:32, 35). In Matt. 1:23 the IMMANUEL prophecy of Isa. 7:14 is cited as having been fulfilled in Jesus, and in Matt. 2:15 the phrase "my son" of Hos. 11:1 is applied directly to Christ.

Thus at the beginning of all three synoptics the divine sonship of Christ is postulated. As far as explanation goes, both Matthew and Luke attached great importance to the VIRGIN BIRTH. Matthew saw in it a fulfillment of the Immanuel prophecy and a token that in this child God would live among human beings. In Lk. 1:35 Christ's sonship is connected directly with his virgin birth through the power of the Spirit (although the fatherhood of God must not be understood in a crude sense). It cannot be said that the virgin birth is irrelevant to Christ's divine sonship; yet it was not merely because of his birth that Christ was hailed by this title in the early church. The story does not seem to have been widely told in NT days, perhaps because Jews and pagans alike would misunderstand it for totally different reasons. The material below will show what additional grounds the evangelists had for this assertion about Christ.

B. Baptismal declaration. Christ's sonship is reiterated in the account of his baptism (Mk. 1:11 with parallels). The words from heaven, "You are my Son, whom I love; with you I am well pleased," are a combination of Ps. 2:7 (messianic kingship) with Isa. 42:1 (the suffering SERVANT OF THE LORD). The context seems to associate sonship both with the possession of the HOLY SPIRIT and with the power to give the Spirit to others (Mk. 1:8). Some early Jewish-Christian groups misunderstood this event in an adoptionist sense, as though the man Jesus first received the Spirit at his baptism and was thereby transformed into a Son of God. But this is impossible in the light of such a verse as Lk. 1:35; and even Mark, who does not directly mention the virgin birth, accords Jesus the title of "Son of God" long before his baptism.

Nevertheless the connection between sonship and the Spirit is important (cf. Gal. 4:6). The baptism, whatever its other meanings, represents the public acceptance by Jesus of the path of sonship, which will, because it is the path of obedience, lead to suffering as surely as the path of messiahship ("I have a baptism to undergo," Lk. 12:50). It can be no accident that the testimony at the TRANSFIGURATION virtually repeated the wording of that at the baptism (Mk. 9:7). In view of the centrality of this baptismal declaration, it is not surprising that in the early church the baptism of the Christian was also associated with the confession of Jesus as "Lord" or as "Son of God" (Acts 8:37; 1 Cor. 12:3). In spite of some argument to the contrary, it does not seem that any distinction can be drawn between these confessions.

C. The temptation. In the accounts of the TEMPTATION OF CHRIST (Matt. 4:1–11; Lk. 4:1–13), the incident is directly related to Jesus' consciousness of divine sonship; without that, the temptations would not only lose their force as temptations, but would be meaningless. The temptation was apparently twofold: to doubt his own sonship or to misuse it by a spectacular and selfish display of divine power, which would be to fail to walk the path of obedience. To be a mere wonder-worker would qualify one to be a "son of God" in the pagan sense. Perhaps this partially explains Christ's reluctance to display his miraculous powers openly. Through Jesus' ministry (e.g., Mk. 8:31–33), and up to the eve of the crucifixion (Lk. 22:42), the temptation to avoid the Son's path of obedience was still present.

Since the Lord himself evidently told his disciples about the temptation, the concept of sonship must have lain at the heart of his own understanding of his person and ministry. The baptism is the witness of the Father to the Son, but the temptation is the witness of the Son's own self-knowledge.

D. Demonic confession. The testimony of DEMONS was not accepted by Christ (although he never denied its truth) probably because it was involuntary and did not spring from revelation and faith, in the Christian sense. But it was at least supernatural testimony and, as such, had importance. Mark 3:11–12 (taken with 1:23–25, where "Holy One of God" prob. has much the same meaning as "Son of God") makes plain that this kind of "rejected testimony" was commonplace during Christ's ministry (cf. Acts 19:15 and Jas. 2:19 for later days). That Christ had power to expel demons was never questioned, even by his enemies; the sole question of the scribes concerned the source of his undoubted powers (Mk. 3:22). There is therefore no valid reason for doubting the reality of such demonic testimony. Although rejected by Christ, it is recorded by the evangelists as yet another line of evidence for a truth which they already independently believed on other grounds.

E. Confession by the disciples. After the calming of the storm, the disciples "worshiped" Jesus, saying, "Truly you are the Son of God" (Matt. 14:33). Perhaps this was a momentary or shallow recognition by men awed by such a display of supernatural power; on other similar occasions, there was no such full theological confession (8:27). Whatever the force of their testimony, it is overshadowed by the declaration of PETER at CAESAREA PHILIPPI, which followed shortly afterward (16:16). This latter is not in the context of any miraculous exhibition of power; it may be Matthew's way of showing the inadequacy of the earlier confession. The saying, "You are the Christ, the Son of the living God," is the crisis point in Matthew's gospel. From this point onward Jesus would teach his followers the meaning of sonship, as well as messiahship, in terms of obedience to death (16:21). He accepted without question the title of Son and acknowledged it as proof of divine REVELATION (16:17). This revelation did not extend to the nature of messiahship (16:22), so it can hardly have extended to the nature of sonship. The same combination of sonship and messiahship probably appears in another confession by Peter (Jn. 6:69) and certainly in the high priest's question to Jesus (Mk. 14:61). The root of the combination certainly lies in the OT, where "Son" and "Messiah" are joined in the case of a Davidic king.

F. Christ's self-confession. This element already has been implied by the baptism and the temptation, but it is explicit in the so-called "Johannine thunderbolt" (Matt. 11:25–27; Lk. 10:21–22). This passage shows clearly that Jesus was conscious of a unique relationship to the Father, defined as sonship, which consisted of intimate knowledge and mediatorship between God and human beings. Such self-confession is also involved in the acceptance of the title on the lips of his followers (Matt. 14:33; 16:16). Similarly, when questioned by the high priest at his trial, Jesus admitted the title at once, although to do so was to court death for blasphemy. To deny would have been impossible, for it would have been to deny his own nature. There are also a few other synoptic passages in which Christ refers to himself, in Johannine style, as "the Son" in contrast to "the Father." Of these Mk. 13:32 is a striking example; no critic could discredit this statement as being fabricated by the church, since it poses the problem of the limitation of Jesus' OMNISCIENCE.

G. The confession of Christ's enemies. Like that of the demons, this is involuntary, in the sense that it does not spring from the perception of faith. Unlike that of the demons, it is not independent supernatural testimony to the truth of Jesus' claims; but it is the strongest possible proof of the existence of such claims. The question asked by the high priest at Christ's trial (Mk. 14:61) and the taunt of the crowd at the cross (Matt. 27:43) bear this out. Unless it were well known that Christ made or at least accepted such claims, both question and taunt would have been meaningless. That neither priest nor people believed the claims does not detract from the value of the evidence. Perhaps the testimony of the centurion at the cross (Mk. 15:39) also comes under this heading. Unless the centurion knew that such claims were made for Christ, the words would hardly have sprung unbidden to his lips; it is, however, possible that he had merely heard the taunt on the lips of the crowd.

III. Usage in Acts. In the book of Acts there is only one certain occurrence of the title Son of God, in connection with the early ministry of PAUL (Acts 9:20). This is surprising since Acts is a sequel to Luke, a gospel that contains a number of instances. It may be that such a title in evangelistic preaching to Jews would provoke a direct collision, which in early days before the rise of STEPHEN, the church, consciously or unconsciously, sought to avoid. The first generation can hardly have been ignorant of the term if it was in fact used by Christ of himself. Perhaps Cullmann (*Christology*, 303) is right in his view that they remembered the reticence with which Jesus himself used the title (cf. Mark throughout).

It should be noted, however, that the Greek word *pais* G4090 in Acts 3:13 and 26 perhaps should be translated "son" and not "servant." If the idea of "son" is inherent in the Servant Songs (as some scholars feel, with reference to "my chosen" in Isa. 42:1), then no such problem arises. Perhaps Acts is deliberately using an ambiguous word; the eye of faith will rightly see it as "Son of God" while the unbeliever will not be offended. The confession of the ETHIOPIAN EUNUCH, "I believe that Jesus Christ is the Son of God" (Acts 8:37), is not in the best MSS and therefore is not, in all probability, part of the original text.

In the second part of the book (Acts 13–28, focusing exclusively on Paul's missionary work), it is clear that the Jews fully understood the nature of the claim made by PAUL as meaning full divinity for Jesus. This had been indicated earlier by their plot to kill him (9:23). The apostle shows no anxiety to avoid such a collision; he was always an agitator by reputation (17:6; 21:21; 24:5). How he may have preached in the Damascus and Jerusalem synagogues is shown by his recorded preaching in the synagogue of ANTIOCH OF PISIDIA (13:16–41). He associated the divine sonship of Christ not primarily with his birth (as did Matthew and Luke), nor with his baptism (as did Mark), but with his resurrection, quoting the messianic statement in Ps. 2:7 as proof (Acts 13:33).

These three aspects are complementary, not mutually exclusive; and Paul did not understand Christ's resurrection in an "adoptionist" sense, as though the man Jesus became God's Son only when he was raised from the dead. The resurrection has, however, an evidential value, as God's seal to the truth of his Son's claims (cf. Rom. 1:4). The lack of further references to the title in Acts may be because Acts contains no further detailed account of Paul's "Jewish" preaching. The concept would not enter so naturally into evangelistic or apologetic preaching to Gentiles.

IV. Meaning to the pagan world. To the unbelieving Jew, the title Son of God, if it indeed conveyed equality with God, was a blasphemous title; but to the unconverted pagan, it was commonplace and thus not too meaningful. This fact may explain the apparent absence of the term in Paul's Gentile preaching as recorded in Acts, compared with its frequent occurrence in the epistles. In Hellenistic times, the title *theioi andres* ("divine men") was freely applied to various religious teachers and supposed miracle-workers (like the Neo-pythagorean Apollonius of Tyana, for instance). While in the minds of the educated the adjective may have been "faded," to the credulous multitude no doubt it had its full force.

In addition, Greco-Roman mythology was full of stories of heroes and demigods who had been born as a result of intercourse between gods and mortals. These beings were described as "sons of the gods" and were usually credited with miraculous powers. Such stories were utterly offensive to Jewish and Christian thought because of the physical understanding of divine generation, as well as the immoral behavior thereby attributed to the gods. Any borrowing from this source is thus unthinkable, in spite of the views of Rudolf Bultmann.

Another area of attribution of divinity to men was that of divine kingship. The Hellenistic *diadochoi* (successor kings) who followed ALEXANDER THE GREAT regularly proclaimed themselves as divine, or at least descended from the gods. Alexander himself had been saluted as "son of the god" by the priests of the desert oracle of Amun (see AMON #4) like any pharaoh before him. No doubt this was more for political than religious reasons, although temples and altars were dedicated to such kings. By the time of the NT, temples were rising to "Rome and Augustus"; an emperor was *divus* ("god") and *divi filius* ("god's son"). The concept had lost all true religious meaning to the pagan, but it still outraged Jewish-Christian theology; therefore, the Christian cannot have borrowed his doctrine from paganism. Conversely, the Gentile, accustomed to the faded metaphor, could hardly appreciate all that was meant by the Christian claim.

GNOSTICISM has also been suggested by Bultmann as a possible source; but Gnosticism was itself a parasitic growth upon Judaism and Christianity. Nevertheless, if the term had in fact already been in use among such speculative heretical sects, this is yet another reason why preachers should be slow to use it in Gentile evangelism. For Christians, when the term has been given its definition and theological content by the person and work of Christ, no such restraint is necessary; this would explain its wide use in John and the epistles. In view of the ambiguities mentioned above, it is hard to be certain of the exact force of the declaration by the centurion at the cross (Mk. 15:39); but certainly the Christian church saw in it a foreshadowing of its own beliefs.

V. Usage in Paul's epistles

A. Early uses. If the letter to the Galatians was written soon after Paul's first missionary journey (but see GALATIANS, EPISTLE TO THE, V and VI), then the earliest use of the title in his letters would be Gal. 2:20, where the apostle summarizes the Christian way as "faith in the Son of God" (cf. Acts 9:20). This is no mere description of Christ's person apart from his work; the Son of God is characterized as one "who loved me and gave himself for me." As always in the NT, sonship is linked with soteriology. Elsewhere Paul defines Christianity as the gospel "regarding his [God's] Son, who as to his earthly life was a descendant of David, and who through the Spirit of holiness was appointed the Son of God in power by his resurrection from the dead" (Rom. 1:3–4 TNIV). On these and other grounds, Bultmann would restrict the use of the title "Son" to the risen Christ; but this is to ignore the evidence of the Gospels; it is also to ignore Paul's own argument. Sonship entailed Christ's resurrection, and therefore resurrection by the Spirit's power is a proof of sonship.

The connection in thought between resurrection and sonship is thoroughly Pauline (cf. Acts 13:33), as is the connection between sonship and the Spirit. "Son of God" is stressed in the Romans context, for it is put alongside of "descendant of David," referring to the natural aspects of Christ's birth. It could be argued that Gal. 2:20 and Rom. 1:3–4 both spring from a background of controversy, in a Jewish milieu; but 2 Cor. 1:19 is certainly neutral and Gentile. The content of Christian preaching is defined as being "the Son of God." In view of the mention of "God" in the previous verse, the phrase must have its full force. The clue to its meaning for Paul lies in v. 20: "For no matter how many promises God has made, they are 'Yes' in Christ." The "Son of God," then, is a positive fulfillment and expression of all that God has promised and revealed himself to be; this is virtual equality with God.

B. Late uses. Ephesians 4:13 represents later Pauline theology. Spiritual maturity, which is the goal of all Christian ministry, is described as "knowledge of the Son of God." It is hard to divorce this statement from the "Johannine" idea expressed in Lk. 10:22, that knowledge of the Son is also knowledge of the Father. This in turn means that sonship is defined in terms of oneness with God. Colossians 1:15–20 contains the most advanced Christology of the NT, and all is predicated on God's "beloved Son," as v. 13 makes plain. He is not only the preexistent agent of CREATION, but also creation's goal; and sonship is given a new dimension in terms of headship of the new "people of God," the church. His chief claim to sonship is the "image of the invisible God" (v. 15), and "God was pleased to have all his fullness dwell in him" (v. 19).

VI. Johannine evidence

A. Initial statements. The fourth gospel nowhere goes beyond the theology expressed clearly in Matt. 11:25–27 and hinted at in numerous other places in the synoptic tradition. That John arranges his material differently, however, and that he brings out the full meaning of latent concepts, no thoughtful reader would deny. Thus John opens his gospel with a strong statement of Logos theology; Jesus Christ is the preexistent Word of God, active in creation, and this is firmly linked with his divine sonship (Jn. 1:14 is an explanation of 1:1–3). In John, sonship is always seen against this cosmic background, as in Hebrews and in the later Pauline epistles. The task of the Son is to show the Father's glory (1:14) and to make the Father known (1:18); the essence of sonship is the revelation of the Father. The uniqueness of Christ's sonship is brought out by the use of *monogenēs* G3666 ("only, unique") to describe him (1:14, 18; 3:16). See ONLY BEGOTTEN.

Another note of distinction is that Jesus alone is *huios* G5626 ("Son") of God; others who enter a relation of sonship by believing in his name, are but *tekna* ("children," from *teknon* G5451) of God (e.g., Jn. 1:12–13). This usage in John is too consistent to be accidental and must correspond to a difference of status. Nor is Christ's position merely established by an act of generation; it is the continual enjoyment of a unique relationship (1:18, "the One and Only, who is at the Father's side"). Like Mark, John does not directly refer to the virgin birth. However, that the Son comes directly from above, John knows (6:41); also that the Jews believe him to be the son of Joseph and Mary (6:42). In typically Johannine style, he does not explain the enigma, for it is no enigma to the believer.

B. Confessional passages. The sonship of Christ was revealed to human beings during his earthly ministry, and at an early stage. The testimony of JOHN THE BAPTIST ("this is the Son of God," Jn. 1:34) is based on Christ's possession and continual enjoyment of the Spirit. NATHANAEL's confession that follows, "Rabbi, you are the Son of God; you are the King of Israel" (1:49), is based on the perfect knowledge displayed by Jesus (cf. 4:29). Some critics reject these on the grounds that in the synoptics John the Baptist bears no such full testimony, though he clearly accorded messianic status to Jesus (Matt. 3:11–12). They also object that, in the synoptics, personal confessions such as Nathanael's must have occurred only at a much later date (Matt. 16:16). These objections are not valid. John also knew of a Petrine confession much later, although he words it somewhat differently (Jn. 6.69). Further, Nathanael's confession is couched in very Jewish terms, unacceptable to later Gentile Christianity ("Rabbi," "King of Israel"). MARTHA's confession in 11:27 is one of the fullest in the gospel, joining the three concepts of Christ, Son of God, and Coming One; otherwise, it follows the same lines. It is interesting, as a Pauline link, that Martha's witness is in a resurrection context.

C. Personal claims. John 10:36 is a clear instance of Christ's deliberately claiming the title for himself in the midst of controversy and close theological argument. It is also in the context of a claim to oneness with the Father (10:30), thus showing in what sense sonship is meant. Christ justifies his use of the title on the grounds that he is "the one whom the Father set apart and sent into the world." John 10:35 may be a veiled reference to Logos theology, but in any case, the words of Christ cannot be understood as less than a claim to full equality with God. There are also, as in the synoptics, numerous other passages in John where Jesus speaks of himself as "the Son" in distinction from "the Father," in a sense that leaves no doubt as to how he understood the uniqueness of the relationship.

D. Witness of Christ's enemies. John 19:7 is confirmation by the Jews that Jesus "claimed to be the Son of God"; again, they regarded it as a blasphemy worthy of death, so that they understood sonship in terms of equality with God. This occurs in a section of John rich in "King theology" (Jn. 18:33—19:22). It is likely therefore that John has in mind the Messianic King of Ps. 2, who is hailed as the Son of God.

E. Conclusion. Lastly the whole purpose of the gospel, as stated in Jn. 20:31, is to create faith "that Jesus is the Christ, the Son of God" (the primitive baptismal confession). From first to last, John associates sonship with messiahship. Sonship thus has a soteriological goal (3:16; 5:25). The Johannine epistles reiterate these truths even more strongly, but do not demand separate treatment.

VII. Usage in Hebrews. In the epistle to the Hebrews, the divine sonship of Christ is not only stated but also vindicated by the author. Thus

Hebrews, even more than the writings of John, comes very near to a full theological definition of sonship, all the more striking in that the book is a Jewish (even if Hellenistic-Jewish) production. Controversial definition is indeed demanded by the general plan of Hebrews, by which Jewish attacks are met directly. Point by point, it shows the superiority of Jesus to the "mediators" of the first covenant of Judaism. This inevitably leads to extended discussion of the nature of Christ's sonship, for it is as Son of God that he is superior to all others.

In the opening verses, Christ's superiority to the OT prophets is stressed, since he brought a full and final revelation of God, of whom he is spokesman. This is very close to the Johannine theology. Christ is also the Son because he is heir and inheritor of God's universe. So far, perhaps even Jewish "adoptionist" messianism could agree; but not when he is described as the One "through whom he made the universe" (Heb. 1:2). This is either the theology of preexistent WISDOM, familiar in ALEXANDRIA, or else straight Logos-theology of the Johannine type. In either case, the Son is identified as a "cosmic Christ," as in Col. 1:15–20. In Heb. 1:3, Christ is said to be "Son" because he "is the radiance of God's glory and the exact representation of his being." This is similar to the Christological definition of Phil. 2:6 (although there is no reference to sonship, obedience is stressed).

In developing the argument, the author states that Christ is superior to the angels because of his "name" (Heb. 1:4), referring clearly to his title as Son (v. 5). Moreover, his is sonship by generation (cf. 1:5, quoting Ps. 2:7). To safeguard against "adoptionist" thought, the author asserts Christ's preexistence; his birth is described as "when God brings the firstborn into the world" (Heb. 1:6). His immortality is further asserted in 1:8–12. Comparison with MOSES leads to the definition of 3:5–6. The status of Moses was only that of a servant; the position of Christ is that of a Son. True, the essence of both is seen as lying in "faithfulness." Hebrews 5:8 may be compared, where the essential nature of sonship is seen to consist in obedience (as in Phil. 2:8). The superiority of Christ to the Aaronic high priest is shown again by proclaiming him Son of God (4:14). Sonship is by generation; Ps. 2:7 is quoted, as well as Ps. 110:4, the latter because of the reference to the priest-king MELCHIZEDEK.

One other striking occurrence is Heb. 6:6: "they are crucifying the Son of God." This has a Pauline and soteriological ring, reminiscent of Gal. 2:20. It may well be a reference to the frequent use of the title "Son of God," by friend and foe alike, in the gospel accounts of the trial and crucifixion of Christ. It is also a final reminder that suffering and death are, to the NT, the path of the Son of God as much as the path of the Messiah, since the essence of sonship is obedience. (See M. Hengel, *The Son of God: The Origin of Christology and the History of Jewish-Hellenistic Religion* [1974]; *DDD*, 788–94; 795, 796–75. Note further the bibliographies under CHRISTOLOGY and NEW TESTAMENT THEOLOGY.) —R. A. COLE

Son of Man. The Greek expression *ho huios tou anthrōpou* occurs about eighty times in the Gospels (without the definite article in Jn. 5:27), always used by Jesus himself (in an apparent exception, 12:34, the crowd is quoting Jesus' statement). Elsewhere it occurs only four times: the full expression is used by STEPHEN in Acts 7:56 (the only genuine instance where someone other than Jesus refers to him by this title); without the definite article it occurs in an OT quotation (Heb. 2:6) and in the phrase "like a son of man" (Rev. 1:13; 14:14; alluding to Dan. 7:13). Traditionally the title Son of Man has been assumed to designate the lowly humanity of Christ in distinction from his divine nature. This meaning may be involved, but a much deeper significance emerges from a closer examination of its usage. See also CHRISTOLOGY.

I. OT and Jewish background. In Ezek. 2:1–3, the phrase "son of man" (Heb. *ben-ʾādām*) clearly designates "a child of Adam by descent" (R. B. Girdlestone, *Synonyms of the Old Testament* [1897], 46), as elsewhere in this prophecy, where it occurs fifty-seven times (the pl. *bĕnê ʾādām*, meaning simply "people, human beings," is common in the OT (e.g., Deut. 32:8; Ps. 11:4 et al.). The designation in Ps. 8:4 ("what is man that you are mindful of him, / the son of man that you care for him?"; cf. Ps. 144:3), from which the passage in Heb. 2:6 is quoted, appears to be applicable to both mortal

This mosaic from Hagia Sophia depicts the child Jesus and the Virgin Mary. The title Son of Man may refer to Jesus' humanity, but it also signifies several other important concepts.

man and Christ in his incarnate identification with human beings. The phrase also occurs in Ps. 80:17 ("Let your hand rest on the man at your right hand, / the son of man you have raised up for yourself"), which is an appeal, during the national decline, for a hero to appear and redeem Israel; this passage may well have influenced Jesus' messianic consciousness (J. Stalker in *ISBE* [1929], 5:2829).

But the most important OT occurrence of the phrase is found in Dan. 7:13, "In my vision at night I looked, and there before me was one like a son of man [Aram. *kĕbar ʾĕnāš*], coming with the clouds of heaven" (cf. also 10:16, 18). Here the expression is not a title; it means simply "human-like." The passage may allude to a personification of the ideal Israel or the saints of the Most High, but it also appears to suggest a messianic figure: "He was given authority, glory and sovereign power; all peoples, nations and men of every language worshiped him. His dominion is an everlasting dominion that will not pass away, and his kingdom is one that will never be destroyed" (v. 14).

The passage in Daniel influenced the pseudepigraphic literature, especially *1 Enoch* 45–71 (see ENOCH, BOOKS OF, I.A.), and some scholars would trace Jesus' use of the title Son of Man to this material, but the connection is doubtful. There has also been much discussion about the use of the phrase as an idiom in Jewish Palestinian ARAMAIC (esp. in the form *bar nāš* or *bar nāšāʾ*) meaning "a person, someone, anyone," and regularly used as some kind of vague self-designation (cf. the use of English "one" as a substitute for "I"). The precise nuance is debated, however, and even if the idiom provides part of the background for Jesus' usage (which seems likely), that hardly excludes the possibility that Dan. 7:13 played a role in his choice of this title.

II. NT use of the term Son of Man. Modern scholarship has devoted a great deal of attention to the claim of the Gospels that the Son of Man sayings go back to Jesus himself (see the influential article by C. Colpe in *TDNT*, 8:400–477). A few writers have argued that all of these sayings originated at a later stage of the tradition; others accept the authenticity of only one group of the sayings (e.g., those that may be classified as eschatological). Skeptical scholars, however, have failed to reach a consensus. Moreover, no persuasive evidence has been set forth to explain why the early Christians would have frequently put this title on Jesus' lips while virtually never using it themselves.

Scholars who do accept the authenticity of the sayings differ, for example, as to whether Jesus drew upon Ezekiel's use of the term Son of Man to emphasize his humanity and his dependence upon the Father for the execution of his earthly work (cf. Num. 23:19; Job 25:6; Heb. 2:11). As already noted, the designation in Ps. 8:4, from which Heb. 2:6 is quoted, appears to be applicable to both mortal man and Christ in his identity with human beings. There seems to be no room for reasonable doubt that Jesus' divine self-consciousness developed from his first visit to the temple at the age of twelve (Lk. 2:41–52), through his baptism and temptation (Matt. 3:13–17; 4:1–11) and other crises, to his climactic cry from the cross, "It is finished" (Jn. 19:30). From these experiences he emerged with an ever-increasing consciousness of his divine oneness with the Father (Jn. 8:16; 10:30–38).

The occurrence of the title Son of Man as used by Christ of himself points up certain important characteristics of his divine-human being and nature. (1) Son of Man signifies Christ's messiahship. Jesus consistently avoided the use of the term

MESSIAH because of the militaristic and political connotations which it had for the Jewish people of his time. Though some 1st-cent. Jews may have identified the term Messiah with Son of Man, this would have been exceptional. That the early Christians did so there can be no reasonable doubt (cf. E. Johnson in *IB*, 7:343–44).

(2) Christ's INCARNATION is linked early in his ministry with the title Son of Man. The uniqueness of Christ is suggested in his words to NICODEMUS: "No one has ever gone into heaven except the one who came from heaven—the Son of Man" (Jn. 3:13). Thus, the Son of Man is God *from heaven*, but in human form *on earth*. His incarnate divine-human nature reflects the purpose and character of his mission: God *in* and *with* human beings reconciling them *to* God (cf. Jn. 1:14; 12:13; see W. F. Howard and A. J. Gossip in *IB*, 8:507–8). Christ's redemptive cross makes explicit the meaning of the incarnation.

(3) Son of Man identifies Christ with dependent humanity (Matt. 8:20; Lk. 9:58). Whatever demands might be laid upon the scribe for discipleship (Matt. 8:19), he and all other followers would find a common human understanding and fellowship in the deepest deprivation and suffering with God as Son of Man.

(4) Son of Man signifies Christ's authoritative and redemptive mission (Matt. 9:6 and parallels; Lk. 19:10). However the authority of "the keys of the kingdom" (Matt. 16:19) may be understood, God retained exclusively for the Son of Man the authority to forgive sins on earth, though it may be permitted to his disciples to absolve sins in the sense of declaring forgiveness to others when they have met the divine requirements.

(5) Son of Man signifies Christ's total redemptive victory (Jn. 3:14). It is likely that the analogy Christ made between the serpent on the pole in the wilderness (Num. 21:9) and the Son of Man suggests much more than his death. In fact, Christ's death, as taught throughout the NT, is inseparable from his resurrection and ascension. Thus the lifting up of the Son of Man here would seem to prefigure the complete victory of Christ's redemptive work in his atoning death, glorious resurrection, and consummating ascension (cf. Dan. 7:13; Mk. 14:62; Acts 7:56).

(6) Son of Man signifies the universal lordship of Jesus Christ (Mk. 14:62). This lordship is asserted by Jesus in his preface to the Great Commission, where he claims "all authority in heaven and on earth" (Matt. 28:18, see COMMISSION, GREAT), and as expressed to his disciples in Acts 1:8. In fact, it is Christ's universal lordship that constitutes the burden of apostolic preaching in Acts. The word LORD in application to the risen Christ occurs 110 times in Acts—more often and more important than any other word in the book (cf. Matt. 3:3; Mk. 2:28; Lk. 6:5).

(7) Son of Man signifies preeminently the final judgment that Jesus Christ administers (Matt. 10:11–12; 19:30). Christ qualifies as judge of all because he, through his incarnation, became one with all human beings and still retained his deity. PAUL, in his Mars' Hill address at Athens, makes clear this climactic and final function of Christ (Acts 17:31), as he also did in his letter to the Romans (Rom. 2:16). And John vividly depicts this function of the Son of Man in the final great assize (Rev. 20:11–15).

(See further F. J. Foakes-Jackson and K. Lake in *BC*, 1:368–84; C. H. Kraeling, *Anthropos and the Son of Man* [1927]; H. B. Sharman, *Son of Man and Kingdom of God* [1943]; G. S. Duncan, *Jesus, Son of Man* [1947]; C. H. Dodd, *The Interpretation of the Fourth Gospel* [1953], 241–49; M. Casey, *Son of Man: The Interpretation and Influence of Daniel 7* [1979]; A. J. B. Higgins, *The Son of Man in the Teaching of Jesus* [1980]; S. Kim, *The "Son of Man" as the Son of God* [1983]; B. Lindars, *Jesus Son of Man: A Fresh Examination of the Son of Man Sayings in the Gospels in the Light of Recent Research* [1983]; C. C. Caragounis, *The Son of Man: Vision and Interpretation* [1986]; H. S. Kvanvig, *Roots of Apocalyptic: The Mesopotamian Background of the Enoch Figure and of the Son of Man* [1988]; D. R. A. Hare, *The Son of Man Tradition* [1990]; D. Burkett, *The Son of Man in the Gospel of John* [1991]; W. Kelber, *Christ the Son of Man* [1997]; *DDD*, 800–804, *DJG*, 775–81.)

C. W. CARTER

sonship. See ADOPTION; CHILDREN OF GOD

sons of God. The meaning of the Hebrew phrase *bĕnê hā'ĕlōhîm* in Gen. 6:1–4 is one of the difficult exegetical problems of the OT. To whom does this title refer: to pagan deities, pagan rulers, angels, descendants of the lineage of Seth, or people in general? Among pagans, mythological stories, some that go back to the HURRIANS (c. 1500 B.C.), tell of nature deities who engage in illicit relations among themselves and in some instances with humans. Is this passage a small remnant of such a story? Most OT scholars admit that erotic mythology is not a normal feature of the OT literature, yet claim that this is such a story (cf. C. Westermann, *Genesis 1–11: A Commentary* [1984], 363–83, esp. 371–72; *DDD*, 794–800). The OT writer allegedly altered an ancient MYTH and, with embarrassment, set it forth as a basis for God's judgment in the form of a flood (see FLOOD, GENESIS). If so, this method of analysis is contrary to procedure elsewhere in the OT.

According to an old Jewish interpretation, the "sons of God" were pagan royalty or members of the nobility who, out of lust, married women from the general population. A variation of this view is that the term refers to ANE kings who were honored as divine rulers and who were characterized by tyrannical and polygamous behavior. The main difficulty with this approach is that the Hebrew phrase is not used in this particular sense elsewhere in the OT.

The term does occur in several OT passages in reference to angels or "heavenly beings" (Job 1:6; 2:1; 38:7; Aram. *bar-ĕlāhin* in Dan. 3:25; cf. also Pss. 29:1; 89:6). See ANGEL. Thus a common interpretation is that fallen angels married women and begat children, and that this unnatural union explains the appearance of the NEPHILIM (Gen. 6:4; for a recent defense of this old interpretation, with a helpful summary of other views, see W. van Gemeren in *WTJ* 43 [1980–81]: 320–48). Many object to this approach on the basis of Jesus' comment that a married state does not apply to angels (Matt. 22:30).

Conservative interpreters have often identified the "sons of God" with the descendants of SETH. They argue, against the first two views above, that the form *hāʾĕlōhîm* elsewhere in the OT regularly refers to "the one true God" and rules out a pagan orientation for this phrase. Moreover, the concept of a father-child relation between God and his worshipers is not alien to the OT (Deut. 32:5; Ps. 73:15; Hos. 1:10; 11:1). Earlier in the Genesis narrative, in connection with the births of Seth and of his son ENOSH, the comment is made, "At that time men began to call on the name of the LORD" (Gen. 4:24). Thus the context, by identifying the Sethites as worshipers of God, seems to provide a referent for the otherwise ambiguous phrase, "sons of God." If so, the passage views the intermarriage of such worshipers with the ungodly as the immediate cause of the flood. The primary objection to this view is that the contrasting phrase in Gen. 6:2, "daughters of men [Heb. *hāʾādām H132*]," seems to be a general human designation rather than a way of describing a specific (ungodly) part of the population.

Still another approach argues that the passage should not be understood negatively as an explanation for the flood but simply as a conclusion to Gen. 5. According to this approach, the phrases "sons of God" and "daughters of man/Adam" simply refer to men and women in general, alluding respectively to Adam's divine origin and Eve's origin from Adam (see J. H. Sailhamer in *EBC*, 1:78). (For a wide-ranging collection of essays, see C. Auffarth and L. T. Stuckenbruck, eds., *The Fall of the Angels* [2004]; recent monographs include A. T. Wright, *The Origin of Evil Spirits: The Reception of Genesis 6.1–4 in Early Jewish Literature* [2005]; and A. Y. Reed, *Fallen Angels and the History of Judaism and Christianity* [2006].) G. H. LIVINGSTON

sons of the prophets. The Hebrew phrase *bĕnê-hannĕbîʾîm*, which the NIV renders as "company of the prophets," occurs almost always in connection with ELISHA (2 Ki. 2:3 et al., the only exception is 1 Ki. 20:35). The term is a technical one referring to the members of a prophetic order or guild, and has no reference to physical descent from a prophet. See PROPHETS AND PROPHECY II.D.

There were several different guilds or branches of the same guild located at various places: (1) BETHEL (2 Ki. 2:3), (2) JERICHO (2:5), (3) GILGAL (4:38), (4) the hill country of Ephraim (5:22; see EPHRAIM, HILL COUNTRY OF). Yet it appears that they were all under the authority of one prophet whom they called "master" (2:3, 5). When the master died or was taken, as Elijah was, one of the guild members took his place as the new master. The promotion had to be recognized by the guild members, and the test was whether the new master had the powers of the old master (2:8, 14) and whether the spirit of the old leader rested on the new one (2:15). The guild may have lived in a monastic community. They erected community buildings (6:1–2) and shared a common table (4:38–44). Yet some were married (4:1). Some of their work was done at the command of the master (4:38; 9:1), and often they sought his approval before doing something (2:16–18; 6:1–2). Yet they could act on their own (1 Ki. 20:35).

Though the technical term "sons of the prophets" does not occur elsewhere, there may be other indications of prophetic guilds. Such may be the case with the "band of prophets" in Saul's and Samuel's day (1 Sam. 10:5–12; 19:20). Likewise, where a large number of prophets is mentioned (1 Ki. 18:4, 19; 22:6) this is indicative of a guild. Groups acting in concert and designated only as "prophets" are probably also prophetic guilds (2 Ki. 23:2; Jer. 26:7–8, 11). Thus prophetic guilds continued throughout the monarchy. Finally, the singular form *ben-nābîʾ*, "son of a prophet" (Amos 7:14), should also probably be understood the same way; thus Amos affirms he is not a member of a prophetic guild. (See further R. B. Y. Scott, *The Relevance of the Prophets* [1942], 46–49; H. H. Rowley, *The Servant of the Lord* [1952], 97–34.)

J. C. Moyer

soothsayer. See DIVINATION.

sop. This English term is used by the KJV to render *psōmion* G6040, which occurs in only one passage (Jn. 13:26–27, 30). The Greek word is the diminutive of *psōmos*, "morsel," and refers to a small, wafer-like piece of bread dipped into the common dish as a kind of improvised spoon. Knives and forks were unknown at table; therefore the more liquid parts of a meal were secured by dipping a morsel of bread into them.

Sopater soh'puh-tuhr (Σώπατρος G5206, prob. short form of Σωσίπατρος G5399, "saving the father"). Son of Pyrrhus; a Christian from BEREA who, along with others, accompanied PAUL on his way back from GREECE (Acts 20:4). The group may have served as representatives when the apostle conveyed the offering from the Gentiles to the needy in Jerusalem (24:17). Sopater is usually thought to be the same as SOSIPATER (Rom. 16:21).

Sophereth sof'uh-rith. See HASSOPHERETH.

Sophia Jesu Christi. See EUGNOSTOS, LETTER OF.

Sophonias sof'uh-ni'uhs. KJV Apoc. form of ZEPHANIAH (2 Esd. 1:40).

sorcerer. See DIVINATION; MAGIC.

sore. Any lesion of the skin or mucous membranes. There is a specific kind of sore that probably was common in Israel. It is called "desert sore," a tropical ulcer found especially in the desert areas of N Africa and the Middle East. This sore resembles a varicose ulcer and is most commonly seen on the legs, dorsal side of hands, and on the face.

Sores must have been very common in biblical days, as they are so frequently mentioned. JOB's affliction is a typical example (Job 2:7). DAVID blames himself for his sores, "My wounds fester and are loathsome because of my sinful folly" (Ps. 38:5). There were rigid rules requiring diagnosis of sores and, in many cases, isolation of the patient. Some of these rules seem harsh, but they helped to retard the spread of contagious disease.

We do not know much about the medicines used to heal sores, except that BALM of Gilead is mentioned (Jer. 8:22; 46:11). This was a fragrant resin with the consistency of honey and was obtained from trees and shrubbery E of the Jordan. In my work with the Navajo Indians, I found that the medicine men were using a similar resin. It gave some relief from pain, was a stimulant to healthy tissue under the sore, and helped to destroy the infecting organism.

R. H. POUSMA

Sorek sor'ik (שֹׂרֵק H8604, "vine"). The valley where DELILAH, the lover of SAMSON, lived (Jdg. 16:4). This region was one of three parallel narrow E-W valleys that crossed the SHEPHELAH (rocky plateau stretching from AIJALON to GAZA).

The Sorek Valley. (View to the W.)

Eshtaol and Zorah were on the N of the valley, while Timnah, where Samson sought a wife (Jdg. 14:1), is located farther SW, near the mouth of the valley. The Valley of Sorek is known today as Wadi eṣ-Ṣarar, beginning about 13 mi. SW of Jerusalem and running in a NW direction for about 20 mi. toward the Mediterranean. Since Beth Shemesh was set apart in the days of Joshua as a Levitical city (Josh. 21:16), proximity to the SE mouth of the valley demanded that it be heavily fortified against Philistine harassments. Samson's betrayal by Delilah would no doubt have threatened this important Israelite stronghold.   A. Johnson

sorrel. This English term, referring to a brownish color, is used by the NRSV and other versions to render Hebrew *śārōq* H8601, which occurs only once (Zech. 1:8; NIV, "brown"). The Hebrew word may indicate a reddish color.

sorrow. The Bible speaks of sorrow in various contexts. For example, Christ's suffering and departure brings sorrow to his disciples' hearts (Jn. 16:6; cf. Matt. 9:15 — it is appropriate to mourn when the bridegroom leaves), but it was good that he go away, for then the Comforter (of the sorrowful) would come. As the woman in childbirth has sorrow but also joy at birth, so the disciples' sorrow will be turned into joy at his return (Jn. 16:21–22); when they ask and receive, their joy will then be made full.

If Christ brings joy, so sin should bring sorrow and mourning. Those who laugh now should mourn and weep (Lk. 6:25); sinners should be wretched and mourn (Jas. 4:9). Not only should there be mourning over one's own sins, but also over those of others in the church (1 Cor. 5:2 — the opposite of such mourning is arrogance; cf. 2 Cor. 12:21). Paul sorrows over the unbelief of Israel to

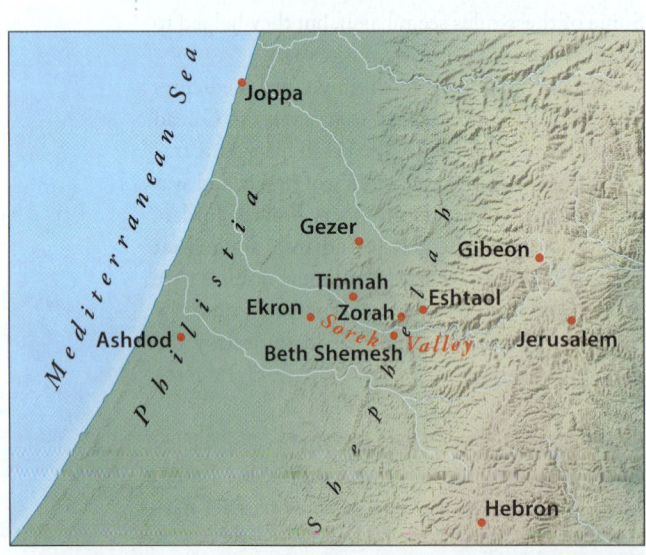

The Sorek Valley

the point of wishing himself accursed so that all Israel might be saved, the answer to his sorrow (Rom. 9:2; cf. 11:26). The mourning of the exploiters in sinful BABYLON is however not over its sin, but only over its downfall (Rev. 18:8, 11, 15, 19). Are the mourners of the BEATITUDES sorrowful for themselves alone or for the sin of the world? At any rate they shall be comforted (Matt. 5:4).

Second Corinthians is practically a treatise on the necessary sorrow that Christians must inflict on each other as they admonish and correct sin. PAUL did not desire to make another painful visit to CORINTH (2 Cor. 2:1), nor was his purpose ever just to bring sorrow (2:4). Instead his goal was godly grief, the sort that produces repentance, salvation, zeal, and finally Paul's own comfort and joy (7:8–13). Hebrews teaches that the Father's disciplining of his own sons indeed yields the fruit of repentance even though painful at the time (Heb. 12:11). PETER makes the similar statement that our rejoicing is in our imperishable inheritance, even though its genuineness is tested by various trials for a short time (1 Pet. 1:6). We shall be approved if we suffer unjustly (2:19–20). So the inheritance of comfort enables us to sorrow with hope. See also GRIEF. D. C. DAVIS

Sosipater soh·sip′uh-tuhr (Σωσίπατρος G5399, "saving the father"). **(1)** A captain under Judas MACCABEE (2 Macc. 12:19, 24).

(2) One of two or three "relatives" of Paul (the others being JASON and possibly LUCIUS) who sent greetings to the Christians in Rome (Rom. 16:21). For many scholars, however, the Greek term *syngenēs* G5150 here means "kinsman" (cf. RSV) and should be understood in the sense of "fellow-Jew" (cf. 9:3). Sosipater is usually identified with SOPATER (Acts 20:4).

Sosthenes sos′thuh-neez (Σωσθένης G6003). **(1)** Ruler of the synagogue at CORINTH during PAUL'S first visit there (Acts 18:17; see RULER OF THE SYNAGOGUE). It is possible that Sosthenes succeeded CRISPUS in this office when the latter became a Christian (v. 8). For some unclear reason, Sosthenes was seized and beaten by a crowd after GALLIO, proconsul of ACHAIA, had dismissed a Jewish prosecution of Paul. Possibly Sosthenes was the victim of an anti-Semitic demonstration by Greeks (cf. KJV following many MSS) or of Jewish spite against an unsuccessful spokesman.

(2) An early Christian whom Paul refers to as "our [*lit.*, the] brother" (1 Cor. 1:1). The fact that the apostle includes the name of Sosthenes with his own in the salutation suggests that this individual was well known to the Corinthians. Thus many have thought that this Sosthenes should be identified with #1 above. If so, he probably became a Christian during Paul's ministry in the city.

Sostratus sos′truh-tuhs (Σώστρατος). The governor of the citadel at Jerusalem under ANTIOCHUS IV (Epiphanes). He tried to obtain from the high priest, MENELAUS, the sum of money which the latter had promised to pay the king to be appointed high priest, but Menelaus refused. As a result, both Menelaus and Sostratus were summoned to appear before the king. Beyond this story, Sostratus is not known (2 Macc. 4:27–28). S. BARABAS

Sotai soh′ti (סוֹטַי H6055, derivation uncertain). Ancestor of a family of SOLOMON'S SERVANTS that returned from the Babylonian captivity with ZERUBBABEL (Ezra 2:55; Neh. 7:57; omitted in the parallel, 1 Esd. 5:33).

soul. This English term, which most often refers to the immaterial essence, or more specifically the moral and emotional nature, of human beings, is used to translate mainly Hebrew *nepeš* H5883 and Greek *psychē* G6034. Both of these words may indicate "breath," "life," and the like, but they have a wide range of connotations.

I. In the OT. The OT is not a textbook on psychology, yet its doctrine of HUMAN NATURE seems to involve a polarity: each person is a unified being but that being is profoundly creative and complex. This profoundness can be understood only by the use of a whole set of terms; hence, various dimensions of the human being are pictured by such terms as *soul*, *spirit*, *heart*, and *mind*. Of these terms, *soul* seems to be the most basic.

A. Etymology and definition. The term *nepeš* derives from *nāpaš* H5882 (niphal, "to breathe

[soul], be refreshed"). Although this verb occurs only a few times in the OT (Exod. 23:12; 31:17; 2 Sam. 16:14), it is common in other Semitic languages (Akk. *napāšu*; Arab. *nafasa*). The Hebrew noun, however, occurs hundreds of times in the OT with a variety of meanings, both concrete ("breath, throat, neck, person, corpse") and abstract ("life, soul, self, appetite").

B. Hebrew psychology. The English translation of *nepeš* by the term "soul" has too often been misunderstood as teaching a bipartite (soul and body—dichotomy) or tripartite (body, soul, and spirit—trichotomy) anthropology. Equally misleading is the interpretation that too radically separates soul from body as in the Greek view of human nature. See BODY; SPIRIT. N. Porteous (in *IDB*, 4:428) states it well when he says, "The Hebrew could not conceive of a disembodied *nepeš*, though he could use *nepeš* with or without the adjective 'dead,' for corpse (e.g., Lev. 19:28; Num. 6:6)." Or as R. B. Laurin has suggested, "To the Hebrew, man was not a 'body' and a 'soul,' but rather a 'body-soul,' a unit of vital power" (*BDT*, 492).

In this connection, the most significant text is Gen. 2:7, "the LORD God formed the man from the dust of the ground and breathed into his nostrils the breath of life [*nišmat ḥayyîm*], and the man became a living being [*nepeš ḥayyâ*]" (the KJV rendering "living soul" is misleading). Although the expression *nepeš ḥayyâ* can be applied to other forms of life (1:20–21, 24, 30), the intensive language of 2:7 still places human beings in a unique position from the rest of creation, even though OT terminology lacks technical precision. The point here is that Hebrew psychology recognizes the profoundness of life, which is the mysterious reality which gives being to both humans and animals, but OT thought still underlines the humans distinctiveness. As such, *nepeš* can mean simply "life" (e.g., Josh. 2:13; Jdg. 5:18; 2 Sam. 23:13–17; 1 Ki. 19:4). Similarly the term may refer to the "self" as an expression of personality: "my soul" (Gen. 49:6; Num. 23:10) may mean only "me"; "your soul" (Isa. 43:4; 51:23) probably means "you" (cf. Pss. 25:13; 121:7.)

The soul and its relationship to life are related to two other terms, *blood* and *spirit*. The *nepeš* resides in the BLOOD according to Gen. 9:4; Lev. 17:11, 14; Deut. 12:23. To describe the depths of a person's being as a feeling-thinking creature, the OT uses *spirit* and *heart* as synonyms for the soul in the sense of the seat of the appetites, emotions, desires, passions, and intelligence. It may be possible to conceive of the HEART (*lēb* H4213 and *lēbāb* H4222) as the cognitive, emotive faculty of the *nepeš*; whereas the SPIRIT (*rûaḥ* H8120) refers to the creative "life-principle" of the *nepeš*. Such distinctions are not consistently followed throughout the OT, and the generalized psychology of the OT should prevent the student of the Bible from identifying Hebrew thought with any particular modern school of psychology. Biblical realism is concerned to describe human life in relationship to Yahweh, not to provide esoteric speculation about the intrinsic nature of human beings and the world. (Cf. Gen. 6:5–6; 41:8; 42:21; 45:27; 49:6; Exod. 4:14, 21; 35:21; Lev. 19:17; 26:41; Num. 5:14, 30; Deut. 4:9, 29; 6:5; 10:12; 11:13, 18; 13:3, 6; 26:16; 30:2, 6, 10; 2 Sam. 3:21; Job 7:11; Ps. 77:3, 6; Prov. 4:23; Lam. 2:11; 3:20.)

C. Death and the soul. The most perplexing problem of OT anthropology and psychology is the relationship of the soul to DEATH and the afterlife. This problem centers not only on the nature of the soul, but also on the meaning and significance of SHEOL. The Bible speaks of the *nepeš* as departing and/or returning (Gen. 35:18; 1 Ki. 17:21–22). However, the crucial series of texts are those in which the OT writers indicate a fear of death and a fear of the loss of the self or soul through the experience of death (cf. Job 33:18–30; Pss. 16:10; 30:3; 116:8; Isa. 38:15–17).

What is essential to understanding the Hebrew mind is the recognition that the human being is a unit: body-soul! The soul is not, therefore, unaffected by the experience of death. OT ESCHATOLOGY does indeed contain seminal elements of hope implying the more positive teaching of the NT, as can be seen in the OT phrase, "rested with his fathers" (1 Ki. 2:10 et al.), in DAVID's confident attitude toward the death of his child (2 Sam. 12:12–23), and in JOB's hope for a RESURRECTION (Job 19:20–29). It is this essential soul-body oneness that provides the uniqueness of the biblical concept of the resurrection of the body as distinguished from the Greek idea of the immortality of the soul.

II. In the NT. The NT concept of the soul is predicated upon this OT teaching.

A. The soul as the self. Like the OT term, so also Greek *psychē* can signify the oneness of a person's total being or the self (Lk. 12:19; Acts 2:43; 3:23; Heb. 4:12). In this sense, soul may be simply the person in his or her totality; however, *psychē* does imply a transcendental reality that is in some cases independent of the body. This seems to be the force of Jesus' statement, "Do not be afraid of those who kill the body but cannot kill the soul" (Matt. 10:28). The most foolish mistake anyone can make is "to gain the whole world, yet forfeit his soul" (Mk. 8:34–38). Thus the *psychē* can be referred to as the object of redemption (e.g., Heb. 10:39; Jas. 1:21; 1 Pet. 1:9). While the frequency of this term is considerably less than that of *nepeš*, the key passages indicate a significant development upon the OT view of the soul.

B. The psychology of the soul. In the NT, terms and concepts relating to human nature are equally imprecise. The general emphasis, as in the OT, is upon one's relationship to God through JESUS CHRIST as Lord of life. A person's total being is redeemed by Christ (1 Thess. 5:23). It is "souls" as persons who respond to the apostolic KERYGMA (Acts 2:41; 14:22). It should be noted that the NT does not usually make a distinction between *psychē* G6034 and *pneuma* G4460 ("spirit"). The two apparent exceptions can best be understood not as affirming a trichotomous anthropology but as figures of speech pointing to the pervasive nature of SALVATION (1 Thess. 5:23) and to the penetrating power of the word of God (Heb. 4:12). To derive exact psychological descriptions from these two statements is pressing the nontechnical language of Scripture too far.

It is probably more accurate to view the terms *psychē* and *pneuma* as partial synonyms that are interchangeable in many contexts. For example, Jn. 10:15 speaks of Christ's giving up his *psychē* for the sheep, while 19:30 states that Jesus gave up his *pneuma* to the Father. Both Mk. 10:45 and Matt. 20:28 indicate that it is the *psychē* that Jesus gives as a ransom for the sinner's salvation. The emphasis in the NT turns more to the HEART (*kardia* G2840) than to the soul or spirit. If it is correct to identify the *psychē* as a person's transcendental self, the life of which is indicated by *pneuma*, then *kardia* may refer to that psychological center in which resides a person's powers of thought, volition, and emotion. Hence, it is the heart more than the soul to which the NT writers ascribe the functions of thinking, willing, and feeling (cf. Matt. 13:15–19; Mk. 7:19–22; Lk. 6:45; Jn. 12:40; Acts 2:37; 5:3–4; Rom. 10:6–10). These impressions are further supported by the use and meaning of such terms as "mind" (*nous* G3808) and "will" (*thelēma* G2525).

C. Eschatology and the soul. It is impossible to isolate the discussion of the *psychē* from the NT understanding of the INTERMEDIATE STATE and the final state of all Christians, which demands a resurrection of the body and a reunion of body and soul. The nature of the intermediate state is implied in Jesus' statement in Matt. 10:28, but more specific is 2 Cor. 5:1–10, in which PAUL describes the Christian's spiritual conflict over the possibility of remaining "clothed" but separate from Christ or being spiritually "naked" but in the presence of Christ. Both Christ and Paul imply that the soul or self can and sometimes does exist independently of the body although not in a normal manner. The intermediate state is, therefore, an abnormal condition in the relationship of soul and body. Consequently, what the Christian longs for is the resurrection of the body and transformation of the body at the SECOND COMING of Christ.

In 1 Cor. 15:35–58 Paul provides the clearest description of this issue. In this passage, the adjective *psychikos* G6035 is contrasted with *pneumatikos* G4461: the "soulish" body will be transformed into a "spiritual" body. The metaphysics of this passage is extremely difficult, but Paul's point seems to be that the essential nature of the resurrection body will be changed by the PAROUSIA (second coming). The book of Revelation refers to "souls" waiting for the final *eschaton*: resurrection and kingdom (Rev. 6:9; 20:4). According to 20:4–6 the righteous will experience "the first resurrection" and the unrighteous come to life subsequently. And in 1 Thess. 4:13–18 Paul presents an interesting insight into the nature of the intermediate state and the second coming. On the one hand, dead Christians are described as being "asleep," with their bodies in the grave and separated from Christ (v. 13); but the apostle goes on to say that "God will bring with Jesus those who have fallen asleep in him" (v. 14), that is, with Jesus in his state of exaltation. The passage implies as well the reunion of body and soul at the parousia: the body that is now in the grave will be reunited with the soul that is now with Christ.

(See further H. W. Robinson, *The Christian Doctrine of Man* [1926]; D. R. G. Owen, *Body and Soul* [1956]; A. B. Come, *Human Spirit and Holy Spirit* [1959]; G. C. Berkouwer, *Man: The Image of God* [1962]; W. N. Pittenger, *The Christian Understanding of Human Nature* [1964]; D. W. Mork, *The Biblical Meaning of Man* [1967]; L. Verduin, *Somewhat Less Than God* [1970]; J. W. Cooper, *Body, Soul, and Life Everlasting: Biblical Anthropology and the Monism-Dualism Debate* [1989]; D. E. Aune and J. McCarthy, eds., *The Whole and Divided Self* [1997]; W. G. Rollins, *Soul and Psyche: The Bible in Psychological Perspective* [1999]; J. B. Green, *Body, Soul, and the Human Life: The Nature of Humanity in the Bible* [2008].) D. M. LAKE

Soul, Exegesis on the. See EXEGESIS ON THE SOUL.

source criticism. See BIBLICAL CRITICISM; GOSPELS III; PENTATEUCH III.

south. The problem of defining directions in a community that did not possess the compass must always have been a difficult one. *East* and *west* could be related to sunrise and sunset, but the intermediate direction of *south* produced a number of different Hebrew concepts. For example, the term *yāmîn* H3545, "right [side]," could be used in the sense "south" because by convention a person was normally thought of as facing the sunrise (Josh. 17:7 et al. [cf. the place name Yemen]; similarly with the cognate *têmān* H9402, Isa. 43:6 et al. [cf. the place name TEMAN]). Most commonly, however, the Hebrew adopts *negeb* H5582, which probably means "parched," describing the region of semidesert and desert lying in a southerly direction, when viewed from the Israelite heartland. This term NEGEV has now become firmly attached, as a regional name, to the southern extension of the modern Israeli state. The NT uses the common Greek term *notos* G3803 (Lk. 13:29 et al.).

For Israel, "the south" must have had a significance not unlike that of "the Wild West" in American 19th-cent. thinking and its modern representations. This southern border of the kingdom was an uncertain and fluctuating affair, unmarked

General view of the Negev terrain in southern Israel.

by any clear topographic feature. Beyond it lurked the warlike desert tribes, such as the Amalekites (see AMALEK), and Israel learned to anticipate from this quarter unpleasant climatic effects (see STORM) as well as military attack (cf. 1 Sam. 30:1).

J. H. PATERSON

sovereignty of God. The English term *sovereignty* connotes a situation in which persons or political entities exercise supreme power over the whole area of their jurisdiction. A *sovereign* is one who enjoys full autonomy, allowing no rival immunities. As applied to God, these terms indicate his complete power over all of CREATION so that he exercises his will absolutely, without any necessary conditioning by a finite will or wills.

In the Bible no Hebrew or Greek term corresponds precisely to the abstract word *sovereignty*, although the idea is abundantly implied. The major metaphor employed is that of "ruler and subject." The doxologies and prophetic exclamations bear much of the weight of biblical statement of the divine sovereignty. To be noted are the following: "Now to the King eternal, immortal, invisible, the only God, be honor and glory for ever and ever" (1 Tim. 1:17); "the Most High is sovereign [Aram. *šallîṭ H10718*, 'ruler'] over the kingdoms of men and gives them to anyone he wishes" (Dan. 4:25); "But the LORD is the true God; / he is the living God, the eternal King. / When he is angry, the earth trembles; / the nations cannot endure his wrath" (Jer. 10:10).

God's sovereignty is his OMNIPOTENCE expressing itself in relation to the created world, with its inanimate structures and its empirical selves. He is declared to possess absolute authority, illustrated by the power held by the potter over the clay (Rom. 9:19–21). Nor is his intrinsic ability diminished by the qualities of HOLINESS and RIGHTEOUSNESS that are integral to his nature (cf. 11:22). As sovereign, he is the ETERNAL God. Within time, he commands the forces of nature (Matt. 5:45; 6:30). The exercise of sovereignty does not, of course, lead to the performance of the logically or the metaphysically absurd, nor of the morally contradictory.

The doctrine of divine sovereignty raises the problem of the relation of God's sovereign action to human activity. According to Gen. 1:28, the first man and woman received a conferred sovereignty over nature. Kings of the earth also rule by God's mandate (1 Sam. 15:11; 2 Chr. 1:9). Human sovereignties are delegated and revokable. At the same time, the capability of human beings for the exercise of choices, whether affirmative or negative, suggests that while the divine sovereignty is itself not limited, God may for wise reasons restrain its exercise.

In the history of Christian thought there has been theological perplexity at this point. In refuting the error of Pelagius, AUGUSTINE seemed at times to deny any valid human freedom. Martin Luther, in his conflict with Erasmus, seemed to do the same. John Calvin articulated a logical system of theology upon the basis of the doctrine of divine sovereignty; some Reformed writers feel that, with the best of intentions, Calvin carried the teaching to a point that seemed to do less than justice to human choice and human stewardship. In similar vein, Abraham Kuyper suggests, "This sovereignty is not a property of mankind. No mere man possesses any sovereignty; this belongs to God alone as the Almighty One" (*Dictaten dogmatiek* [1910], 1:417). Others, including Jacobus Arminius, sought to make place for the role of human choice within the context of the divine sovereignty, contending that God could foreknow genuinely contingent events, thus giving larger place to human free will than was implied by Reformed theologians. See also ELECTION; GOD, BIBLICAL DOCTRINE OF; PROVIDENCE.

(Reformed treatments include C. Hodge, *Systematic Theology*, 3 vols. [1871–73], 1:535–49 and 2:280–312; J. O. Buswell, *A Systematic Theology of the Christian Religion*, 2 vols. [1962–63], 1:163–76 and 2:134–48; W. Grudem, *Systematic Theology: An Introduction to Christian Doctrine* [1994], ch. 16. For Arminian discussions, see J. Miley, *Systematic Theology*, 2 vols. [1892–94], 1:211–13; H. O. Wiley, *Christian Theology*, 3 vols. [1940–43], 1:329–43, 357–60; T. Oden, *The Living God* [1987], 270–316. See also D. Basinger and R. Basinger, eds., *Predestination and Free Will: Four Views of Divine Sovereignty and Human Freedom* [1986].)

H. B. KUHN

SOW. See SWINE.

sower, sowing. See AGRICULTURE.

Spain spayn (Σπανία *G5056*). The westernmost of the European peninsulas was called variously, in reference to its primitive inhabitants, Iberia, Liguria, and Celtica. In historic times the name Hispania, the origin of which is unknown, prevailed. Unlike Italy and the Greek peninsula, Spain was invaded both by the westward wandering Indo-European tribes and by intruders over the Gibraltar Straits from Africa, a pattern of settlement that was to persist into medieval times.

Tartessus, a town and kingdom on the Baetis or Guadalquivir River, in the southern part of the peninsula, was probably visited by ships from Minoan CRETE in the middle of the 2nd millennium B.C. See TARSHISH (PLACE). But for the sake of its tin, Phoenician traders from TYRE brought the area into the orbit of their overseas commerce in 1100 B.C., founding Gades (Cádiz) as their headquarters nearby. Phoenician Carthage fell heir to this foothold, absorbed Tartessus, and penetrated the peninsula deeply. Greek colonization, in the process, was limited to the NE corner, where Massilia (Marseille) maintained two small footholds, Emporiae and Rhodae. After her first clash with ROME (264–241 B.C.), Carthage developed Spain as a base for her European power, a process Rome sought to check. The Second Punic War (218–201) broke out over Saguntum. Hannibal's disastrous invasion of Italy was staged from Spain, and Rome in her eternal quest for a stable frontier was forced first to fight and subdue Carthage in the Spanish peninsula, and then to undertake Spain's subjugation to eliminate the Carthaginian bridgehead (cf. 1 Macc. 8:1–4).

Such is the nature of the terrain, that Rome spent two centuries on this task. Some of her greatest soldiers fought to subdue the Spanish tribes, and on two notable occasions, the war against Sertorius (78–72 B.C.) and Julius CAESAR's subjugation of the legions of his rival POMPEY (49–45), Rome's own grim civil strife found a Spanish battleground. AUGUSTUS completed the pacification of the rugged hinterland in the course of his systematic organization of the frontiers and borderlands of the empire. From this point onward, Romanization, already established in the towns and coastal areas under a provincial organization almost two centuries old, began to penetrate. Roads, generosity over citizenship, and the other manifest advantages of the "Roman Peace" found an accelerating response, and Spain became notable for her contributions to imperial life and culture. Three emperors—TRAJAN, HADRIAN, and the first Theodosius—came from Spain. Men of letters from Spain included the two Senecas, Lucan, Pomponius Mela, Columella, Quintilian, Martial, Prudentius, and Orosius.

Spain's flair for Romanization may have been realized by PAUL, and that fact supports the contention that he worked on a strategic plan to bring the empire to Christ by planting Christian cells in the key points and areas of the great system. Whether he achieved his twice-expressed ambition of visiting Spain is not known for certain (Rom. 15:24, 28). According to Clement of Rome, writing some thirty years after Paul's death, the apostle went to "the limits of the West" (*1 Clem.* 1.5), but it would be dangerous to build too weighty an assumption on a phrase so vague.

(See further A. Schulten, *Tartessos: Ein Beitrag zur ältesten Geschichte des Westens* [1922]; R. Carpenter, *The Greeks in Spain* [1925]; C. H. V. Sutherland, *The Romans in Spain 217–117 B.C.* [1939]; S. J. Keay, *Roman Spain* [1988]; J. S. Richardson, *The Romans in Spain* [1996]; L. A. Curchin, *The Romanization of Central Spain: Complexity, Diversity, and Change in a Provincial Hinterland* [2004].)

E. M. BLAIKLOCK

span. See WEIGHTS AND MEASURES I.C.

sparrow. A small Old World songbird, usually brownish or grayish (family *Passeridae*; to be distinguished from similar New World species [i.e., finches such as the "tree sparrow"] of the family *Emberizidae*). It is generally agreed that Hebrew *ṣippôr H7606*, like various other terms, has both a general and a more specific meaning, but it is difficult to apportion the biblical uses precisely. The general sense "bird" is evident in Gen. 15:10 (where the word refers to the dove and pigeon of the previous verse), in Lev. 14:4–7, 49–53 (birds used in sacrifices), in Neh. 5:18 (edible fowls), and in several other contexts where it is implied that the birds would be eaten. Its general meaning could therefore be any fairly small clean bird.

However, where the word is in contrast with some other named bird, it probably has a specific meaning: "Even the sparrow has found a home, / and the swallow [*děrôr* H2000] a nest for herself, / where she may have her young— / a place near your altar" (Ps. 84:3; cf. Prov. 26:2); here the reference could well be to the house sparrow, a bird often associated with human habitations. In addition, the KJV renders Ps. 102:7, "a sparrow alone on the house top"; this is likely the blue rock thrush, a solitary bird of rocks and old buildings, and some authorities claim that this is indeed the "sparrow."

The Greek word for "sparrow" is *strouthion* G5141 (diminutive of *strouthos*, already in Homer). The Lord's words, "Are not two sparrows sold for a penny?" (Matt. 10:29–31; cf. Lk. 12:6–7), may have been spoken as he pointed to something that is still common in Arab countries, where small children trap and pluck small birds of all kinds, but especially larks and finches, and tie them in bundles for sale. (See G. R. Driver in *PEQ* no vol. [1955]: 130; *FFB*, 77.) G. S. CANSDALE

Sparta spahr´tuh (Σπάρτη). Also known as Lacedaemon (see LACEDAEMONIAN), Sparta was a powerful city-state in the S central Peloponnesus and chief antagonist of ATHENS. By Hellenistic times, however, its influence had declined. A number of references to Sparta are to be found in extrabiblical Jewish literature, though some of these have been questioned.

There seems to have been a colony of Jews in Sparta in the 2nd cent. B.C., and a warm relationship between the Spartans and the Jews had developed. JASON, the high priest, found asylum there in 168 B.C. (2 Macc. 5:9). Later Jonathan MACCABEE tried to strengthen his government by foreign alliances and appealed to the Spartans to renew a friendship that had begun with King Arios I of Sparta and ONIAS I, the high priest, on the basis of their common descent from Abraham (1 Macc. 7:5–23). The relationship was probably the result of an ethnological error (cf. S. Schüller in *JSS* 1 [1956]: 257–68). The Jews regarded the Pelasgi, the ancestors of the Spartans, as descendants of PELEG, the son of EBER (Gen. 11:16–19).

After the death of Jonathan, the Spartans wrote to SIMON MACCABEE to renew the friendship and league (1 Macc. 14:16–23). Finally, Sparta was included among the cities that received the declaration of friendship between the Roman senate and the Jews, written by the consul Lucius to the king of Egypt in 139 B.C. (1 Macc. 15:16–22). (See further L. F. Fitzhardinge, *The Spartans* [1980]; A. Powell, *Athens and Sparta: Constructing Greek Political and Social History from 478 BC*, 2nd ed. [2001]; P. Cartledge and A. Spawforth, *Hellenistic and Roman Sparta: A Tale of Two Cities*, 2nd ed. [2002].) A. RUPPRECHT

spear. See ARMOR, ARMS.

speckled bird. This phrase is used by the KJV and other versions to render Hebrew *ṣābûaʿ* H7380, which occurs only once (Jer. 12:9). The term literally means "colored [with stripes]," and some scholars (e.g., G. R. Driver in *PEQ* no vol. [1955]: 139) have argued that it refers to the striped HYENA, a view followed, for example, by the NRSV.

speech. See CONVERSATION; WORD.

spelt. This English term, referring to a coarse WHEAT, is used by the NIV and other versions to render Hebrew *kussemet* H4081, which occurs in three passages (Exod. 9:32; Isa. 28:25; Ezek. 4:9, the KJV has "rie" in the first two passages and "fitches" in the last [see FITCHES]). The Hebrew word may refer to the so-called one-grained wheat, *Triticum monococcum* (or *T. monoccum*, a diploid wheat also known as "einkorn" or "small spelt"), though most scholars believe it designates a hexaploid wheat that was introduced from Egypt, *T. spelta* (synonym *T. aestivum spelta*, also known as "big spelt"). This spelt is a very hard-grained wheat with loose ears. It is said to be a native of MESOPOTAMIA, but was also much grown in SYRIA and SINAI. A possible alternative is the tetraploid wheat, *T. dicoccum* ("medium spelt" or "farro," but better known as "emmer"; cf. NJPS). Less likely are the suggestions that the Hebrew word refers to the rye or the oat. (See *FFB*, 175–76.) W. E. SHEWELL-COOPER

spice. This English term is used primarily to render Hebrew *bōśem* H1411 (occurring almost twenty times in the pl. *bĕśāmîm*, Exod. 25:6 et al.; variant forms *beśem* [Exod. 30:23b] and apparently *bāśām* [Cant. 5:1]). This Hebrew word appears to refer to a type of balsam tree at least once (Cant. 8:14; possibly *Balsamodendron opobalsamum* [see FLORA under Burseraceae]), and elsewhere to the oil from that tree (note 4:16, where the *bōśem* of the garden is said to flow out or spread). It is possible that most of the occurrences of the term have to do with the aromatic balsam oil. Other relevant Hebrew words include *nĕkōʾt* H5780 (Gen. 37:25; 43:11), which may refer to the evergreen shrub *Astragalus tragacantha* (but see GUM), *sam* H6160 (esp. Exod. 30:34, though this word usually occurs in connection with INCENSE), and *reqaḥ* H8380 (only Cant. 8:2, but cf. cognates in Ezek. 24:10). In the NT the Greek term *arōma* G808 is used in connection with Jesus' burial (Mk. 16:1; Lk. 23:56; 23:1; Jn. 19:40); another word, *amōmon* G319, occurs only once (Rev. 18:13). See PERFUME.

The perfumed spices were used originally almost entirely at worship services. Long before the time of ABRAHAM, the Egyptians used scented spices. During excavations, these have been found in special containers. The priestly right of using scented spices was confirmed by MOSES (Exod. 30). The chief spices used were MYRRH, CINNAMON, calamus (see AROMATIC CANE), and CASSIA, and these powdered spices when mixed together were stirred into pure OLIVE oil to make what the Bible calls a holy ointment. It would seem that about fifty pounds of scented, powdered spices were stirred into one and one-half gallons of pure olive oil.

The spices were to be prepared by an "apothecary" (Exod. 30:25, 35 KJV; NIV and other versions, "perfumer"). These special spice perfumes were not to be made for any other purpose than worship. Later, the children of Israel disobeyed the instructions, for when they cried out for a king (1 Sam. 8), Samuel warned them that he would undoubtedly take their daughters to be makers of perfume, for this is what the word "confectionaries" means in that connection (see v. 13).

When King ASA died, he was laid "on a bier covered with spices and various blended perfumes, and they made a huge fire in his honor" (2 Chr. 16:14). They may have had to do this owing to the "disease in his feet" (v. 12), probably gangrene, which smelled unpleasant. This use of spices could presumably be termed religious, as it was used at a funeral. See also ALOE; BALM; DILL; FRANKINCENSE; HENNA; NARD; OINTMENT; SAFFRON; STACTE.

W. E. SHEWELL-COOPER

Sticks of cinnamon.

spider. Name given to a large and fairly well-defined class of the arthropods (joint-footed animals) differing from insects in having four pairs of legs and no wings. All spiders have special glands for producing silk; this is extruded in strands and used for making nests, egg cases, etc., as well as for web spinning by certain families, especially those known as the orb spinners, which make webs of some complexity. The Hebrew clearly refers to one of these, in figurative contexts, with the term *ʿakkābîš* H6571: "They hatch the eggs of vipers / and spin a spider's web [*qûr* H7770]" (Isa. 59:5; cf. v. 6); "What he [the godless] trusts in is fragile; / what he relies on is a spider's web" (Job 8:14). In the latter passage, the word translated "web" is *bayit* H1074, "house" (see NRSV and cf. v. 15); its use could change the metaphor somewhat, and it may refer to a different species, one that makes a more obvious nest.

Some scholars, on the basis of the SEPTUAGINT and the Syriac, emend the text of Job 27:18 (KJV, "He buildeth his house as a moth") from *kāʿāš*, "like a moth," to *kāʿakkābbîš*. Thus the RSV translates the whole verse, "The house which he builds is like a spider's web, like a booth which a watchman makes," a picture of the spider watching its trap from the vantage point alongside. Others suggest that the word here is not *ʿāš* H6931, "moth," but an otherwise unattested homonym meaning "[bird's] nest" (cf. NRSV and NJPS). The KJV uses "spider" also to translate *šĕmāmit* **H8532**, which occurs only once (Prov. 30:28); most modern scholars believe this word refers to a LIZARD. G. S. CANSDALE

spies. See SPYING.

spikenard. Most modern versions, *nard*. A fragrant ointment obtained from an E Indian plant, *Nardostachys jatamansi*. This member of the Valerian family has odorous fibrous roots. The Hebrew term *nērd* **H5948** occurs three times in Song of Solomon (Cant. 1:12 [NIV, "perfume"]; 4:13, 14). The corresponding Greek term, *nardos* **G3726**, is used of a PERFUME with which Jesus was anointed (Mk. 14:3; Jn. 12:3; both times with *pistikos* **G4410**, "genuine, pure"). This ointment is described as being very costly, probably because it had to be imported from INDIA (*Nardostachys* grows in the Himalayan mountains) in special, carefully sealed ALABASTER jars, to conserve the perfume. It was only when some wealthy house owner received special guests that he would break the seal of the jar, so as to be able to do the anointing. W. E. SHEWELL-COOPER

spindle. See DISTAFF; SPINNING.

spinning. The art of drawing out and twisting natural fibers into a continuous thread is mentioned in both OT and NT. Its origins are lost in deep antiquity. The remains of the Paleolithic age show signs of sewing and cobbling, and it is quite possible that spinning was known from the remote ages. The later bone needles are light and fine with finely drawn eyes, so they may have been used for spun fibers rather than for sinews or raw hide thongs. In the archaeological sites vegetable fibers are the earliest, particularly cotton and flax. It may well be that spinning was originated in the ancient river valley cultures where these fiber plants were domesticated and grown.

The earliest premechanical devices were the hooked stick used as a spindle and the receiving stick or DISTAFF. Such were usually made of wood and few have survived from antiquity except as illustrated on tombs. The other type of spinning device, the spindle whorl, a small torus of stone not much larger than a spool, is often found in Palestinian sites. It may be that the rare Hebrew term *kîšôr* **H3969**, which modern versions render "distaff" (Prov. 31:19), actually refers to the spindle whorl.

The Hebrew verb meaning "to spin" (*ṭāwâ* **H3211**) appears only in the context of the Israelite offerings of material and labor for the TABERNACLE (Exod. 35:25–26). In Israel it was the custom for women to do the spinning. The rabbinic tradition records the amazement of the Jews to find Babylonian men spinning. The legal literature of Judaism also records the types of threads spun, and their uses in the tabernacle and temple construction and coverings.

In the NT the Greek term *nēthō* **G3756** (earlier *neō*), "to spin," is used only in the illustration of the lilies of the field (Matt. 6:28; Lk. 12:27). The Greek art of spinning is depicted in a number of vase paintings, and is referred to both in prose and poetry by a large number of classical authors including Euripides and Aristophanes. As in the Jewish culture, it was a woman's responsibility. Its use in Jesus' sermon, where it is connected with the notion of "toil," was apt in any level of ANE society, where spinning was a necessary and constant task.

W. WHITE, JR.

spirit. This English term (from Latin *spiritus*, "breath") is usually the rendering of Hebrew *rûaḥ* **H8120** (prob. from *rîaḥ* **H8193**, "to smell," but attested in other Semitic languages in the sense "to breathe") and Greek *pneuma* **G4460** (from *pneō* **G4463**, "to blow, breathe"). Both of these nouns can also mean "air, blowing, breath, wind" (e.g., Job 41:16 [Heb. MS v. 8]; Ps. 18:15 [Heb. MS v. 16]; Jn. 3:8; 2 Thess. 2:8). This article deals with the use of these terms as applied to God, to other incorporeal beings, and to the immaterial part of human beings.

I. Spirit as incorporeal, intelligent being. E. de Witt Burton (*A Critical and Exegetical Commentary on the Epistle to the Galatians*, ICC [1921], 490) defines *pneuma* in the NT as "an incorporeal, sentient, intelligent being, or the element by virtue of which a being is sentient, intelligent, etc." Spirit involves LIFE but is not necessarily associated with material form, and thus the Bible often describes as "spirit" some incorporeal nature or being that has direction and purpose and power.

A. God as spirit. The NT makes the specific statement that "God is spirit, and his worshipers must worship in spirit and in truth" (Jn. 4:24). It is the NT which has the developed doctrine of the Holy Spirit; but the OT, in spite of its rich ANTHROPOMORPHISMS in speaking of God, implies frequently that God is spirit, and speaks of the Spirit of God as manifest in activity in nature and in the lives of human beings in a variety of ways. See discussion under HOLY SPIRIT I.

B. Other spiritual beings. The Bible also speaks of creatures that are "spirits," created by God and subject to him, but not having corporeal form. Their existence and their influence on human life is referred to in a number of places (e.g., 1 Ki. 22:21; Job 4:15; Lk. 24:39; Acts 23:8). They may be good spirits ministering to men and women (Heb. 1:14) or they may be evil (Jdg. 9:23; 1 Sam. 16:14–16; Matt. 10:1). Human beings may be indwelt by and subject to the Spirit of God, but they may also be subject to the one who is described as "the spirit who is now at work in those who are disobedient" (Eph. 2:2). False teachers are those who are led by "deceiving spirits" (1 Tim. 4:1), and because of the existence of such it is necessary for Christians to "test the spirits to see whether they are from God" (1 Jn. 4:1).

C. The disembodied human spirit. A few biblical passages speak of the human spirit as separate from the BODY at DEATH; for example, Heb. 12:23 refers to "the spirits of the righteous made perfect" (TNIV), and 1 Pet. 3:19 mentions "the spirits in prison." Such references are not contrary to the ultimate hope, expressed by PAUL in 2 Cor. 5:1–5, that beyond this life believers will not be naked spirit, but clothed with a heavenly body.

II. The life principle. Many uses of the term *spirit* in both OT and NT indicate that it is the life principle or life energy of human beings (occasionally of beasts, e.g., Eccl. 3:21). God gives this life spirit to them (Isa. 42:5; Zech. 12:1), and he sustains it (Job 10:12). In life, and at death when the spirit departs from the body, people can only commit their spirit into God's hands (Ps. 31:5; Eccl. 12:7; Lk. 23:46).

In a less absolute way, the human spirit is also the animation and vivacity that persons possess, physically or psychically; the notion of fainting, or losing heart and courage, can be described as the failing or the departing of the spirit within a person (e.g., Josh. 5:1; 1 Ki. 10:5; Pss. 142:3; 143:4, 7; Ezek. 21:7). Correspondingly, restoration from such a state is described in terms of the spirit returning or being revived in a person (e.g., Gen. 45:27; Jdg. 15:19; 1 Sam. 30:12). The physical raising of the daughter of JAIRUS is described as the returning of her spirit (Lk. 8:55). Moreover, renewal of life in its right relationship with God is cited as the giving of a new spirit (Ezek. 11:19; 36:26; Rom. 7:6; see REGENERATION), while God's continuing work of grace is the reviving of "the spirit of the lowly" (Isa. 57:15), and in Christian fellowship believers are refreshed in spirit by one another (1 Cor. 16:18; 2 Cor. 7:13).

These comments lead appropriately to the consideration of the contrast between FLESH (or BODY) and spirit found both in OT and NT. Flesh and spirit can be said to make up the whole person. Both body and spirit can be defiled (2 Cor. 7:1); both can be holy (1 Cor. 7:34). Spirit is the life principle, the essential person, the inner self; and the body is the outward personality. The body without the spirit is dead (Jas. 2:26). The flesh can be destroyed and the spirit saved (1 Cor. 5:5). A person can be absent in body but present in spirit (Col. 2:5). In some passages (e.g., Jn. 3:5–8; Rom. 8:3–14; Gal. 4:21—5:26) the distinction between flesh and spirit is between the will and power of a person doing what he chooses apart from God, and the life and will and power given by the Spirit of God enabling the believer to do what God chooses.

There is also the contrast in Scripture between "the letter" and "the spirit," that is, outward obedience to the written code of God's law over against its observance with understanding of its purpose and with love, from the heart (e.g., Rom. 2:27–28; 2 Cor. 3:6–11).

The distinction between SOUL (Heb. *nepeš* H5883) and spirit is more difficult. There are times in the OT when the two are mentioned in parallel (e.g., Isa. 26:9), just as there are also places where HEART (*lēb* H4213 or *lēbāb* H4222) and spirit appear to be equivalent (e.g., Isa. 57:15; Dan. 5:20 [Aram. *lĕbab*

H10381]). At other times, however, it can be argued that the spirit is regarded as the animating principle, while the soul is the living being produced.

In the NT there are passages where human beings seem to be regarded as bipartite, made up of body and spirit (e.g., Matt. 26:41), or where the terms "soul" (Gk. *psychē G6034*) and "spirit" are treated as synonyms (e.g., Lk. 1:46–47). In two passages persons seem to be spoken of as tripartite (1 Thess. 5:23; Heb. 4:12), though many argue that even these texts do not intend to make sharp or objective distinctions. Those who see a substantial difference often define it in terms of the higher and lower aspects of the human personality: the soul is said to be the manifestation of the immaterial part of a person toward the world, and the spirit its manifestation toward God. Appeal is made to 1 Cor. 2:14–15, which distinguishes between the person who is *psychikos G6035* ("soulish, natural") and the one who is *pneumatikos G4461* ("spiritual"), although the context indicates that the contrast has to do with whether or not someone has the Holy Spirit (cf. Jude 19, and note that the body too can be viewed as either natural or spiritual, 1 Cor. 15:44–46).

III. Essential being.
From being understood as the life principle, *spirit* came to denote also "the source and seat of insight, feeling, and will" (BDAG, 833, section 3b), that is, a person's essential being. This accounts for many uses of the word in OT and NT. The human spirit is "moved" (Ezra 1:1, 5) or "troubled" (Gen. 41:8); it "rejoices" (Lk. 1:47) or is "broken" (Exod. 6:9 NRSV); it is "willing" (Matt. 26:41) or "stubborn" (Deut. 2:30). A person may be patient or proud in spirit (Eccl. 7:8 NRSV), as well as poor in spirit (Matt. 5:3). The necessity of ruling one's spirit is stated (Prov. 25:28 KJV). It is the spirit (and soul) of a person that yearns and longs for God (Isa. 26:9), and it is to the believer's spirit that the indwelling Spirit of God bears witness (Rom. 8:16).

In this context mention may be made of passages that speak of a person having someone else's spirit, such as that of Moses (Num. 11:17, 25) or of Elijah (2 Ki. 2:9, 15; Lk. 1:17). Similarly also the influence of the spirit of the world (1 Cor. 2:12) or of false prophets (Ezek. 13:3) can be described.

IV. Dominant disposition.
As we have seen, many things can be said to describe the action of the spirit as the functioning of a person's essential being. From this kind of description it is a small step to the use of *spirit* to describe some dominant disposition or attitude. People may possess a lowly or haughty spirit (Prov. 16:18–19), a spirit of jealousy (Num. 5:14), a spirit of slavery (Rom. 8:15), a spirit of stupor (Rom. 11:8), or a spirit of wisdom (Deut. 34:9).

Under the influence of Semitic usage, a phrase such as "spirit of gentleness" (Gal. 6:1 NRSV) may mean "gentle spirit" (cf. 1 Pet. 3:4). As a result, there are times when it is difficult to be sure whether what is being described is a human disposition or instead the Spirit of God that makes that disposition possible. For example, the NRSV translates *pneuma huiothesias* (Rom. 8:15) as "a spirit of adoption," where the NIV has "the Spirit of sonship" (cf. also Eph. 1:17). The Holy Spirit comes to dwell in our spirit and gives us "a spirit of power, of love and of self-discipline" (2 Tim. 1:7).

(See further H. W. Robinson, *The Christian Doctrine of Man*, 3rd ed. [1926]; N. H. Snaith, *The Distinctive Ideas of the Old Testament* [1944], 143–53; E. Jacob, *Theology of the Old Testament* [1958], 161–66; A. Richardson, *An Introduction to the Theology of the New Testament* [1958]; G. A. F. Knight, *A Christian Theology of the Old Testament* [1959]; A. R. Johnson, *The Vitality of the Individual in the Thought of Ancient Israel*, 2nd ed. [1964]; J. W. Cooper, *Body, Soul, and Life Everlasting: Biblical Anthropology and the Monism-Dualism Debate* [1989]; W. G. Rollins, *Soul and Psyche: The Bible in Psychological Perspective* [1999]; K. Berger, *Identity and Experience in the New Testament* [2003].)

F. FOULKES

Spirit, Holy. See HOLY SPIRIT.

spirits in prison. This phrase occurs in only one passage: "For Christ died for sins once for all, the righteous for the unrighteous, to bring you to God. He was put to death in the body but made alive by the Spirit, through whom also he went and preached to the spirits in prison who disobeyed long ago when God waited patiently in the days of Noah while the ark was being built" (1 Pet. 3:18–20a;

it is uncertain whether the phrase *zōopoiētheis de pneumati* is a reference to the Holy Spirit or to Jesus' incorporeal being; if the latter, the rendering would be, "made alive in [his] spirit, in which [state] also he went …"). These verses have proven to be among the most difficult in the whole NT, and at least three major interpretations have been proposed.

(1) The traditional understanding has been that "the spirits in prison" were people from the time of Noah who had gone to Hades, and that Jesus, after his death but before his resurrection, went to this abode of the dead and preached to them (cf. 1 Pet. 4:6; for a fuller discussion, see DESCENT INTO HADES. Some who hold this view believe that these individuals were given another opportunity to be saved; others insist that Jesus was only proclaiming the victory of the gospel; still others suggest that Jesus was announcing the gospel to people who had already been saved.

(2) Another popular interpretation agrees that the phrase refers to people at the time of the flood, but argues that Peter has in view Noah's own witness to his contemporaries before they died. In other words, the preincarnate Jesus may be said to have preached in the spirit through Noah (for a recent and detailed defense of this view, see J. S. Feinberg in *WTJ* 48 [1986]: 303–36).

(3) Most modern scholars believe that Peter's words should be understood against the background of *1 Enoch* (esp. chs. 12–16), which speaks of fallen angels who intermarried with human beings in the period before the flood (Gen. 6:1–4; see discussion under SONS OF GOD) and whom God imprisoned inside the earth. While some scholars argue that Peter accepted the mythology itself, this is not a necessary inference; he may well have appealed to his reader's familiarity with the story to make a different point. According to this interpretation, Jesus (not necessarily before his resurrection, but possibly as he ascended to heaven) "delivered the final verdict of condemnation to the spirits … a condemnation previously predicted in the Enoch story. The practical value of Christ's victory over all spirits and all evil is that the forces of evil that opposed God and brought the unjust suffering of Peter's readers were also subjected to Christ's rule" (K. H. Jobes, *1 Peter*, BECNT [2005], 246 [pp. 235–51 offer a clear and up-to-date discussion of the various views]; for more extensive treatments, see the monographs by B. Reicke, *The Disobedient Spirits and Christian Baptism: A Study of 1 Pet. iii. 19 and Its Context* [1946], and W. J. Dalton, *Christ's Proclamation to the Spirits: A Study of 1 Peter 3:18–4:6* [1965]).

spiritual body. The phrase *sōma pneumatikon* is found only in 1 Cor. 15:44, where it characterizes the resurrection body in contrast to the "natural body" (*sōma psychikon*). According to some, "spiritual" here refers to substance, that is, the immaterial part of the person (see SPIRIT), thus a nonphysical entity. This view is unacceptable for several reasons. (1) The contrast between the adjectives *psychikos* G6035 and *pneumatikos* G4461 occurs in only one other passage (in this very epistle, 1 Cor. 2:14–15), where it cannot possibly refer to a physical/nonphysical distinction. (2) Other biblical passages make clear that the resurrection body will indeed be physical; see RESURRECTION V. (3) In the NT the term *spiritual*, when used of the things of God or of believers, invariably denotes a relation to the Holy Spirit, such as Spirit-given, Spirit-filled, etc. (Rom. 1:11; 7:14; 15:27; 1 Cor. 2:15; 3:1; 9:11; 10:3–4; 14:37; Gal. 6:1; Eph. 1:3; 5:19; Col. 1:9; 1 Pet. 2:5). Therefore the resurrection body will be spiritual because it belongs to the realm of the Holy Spirit in a distinctive way: it is his perfect instrument, Spirit-filled in the fullest sense, and endowed with Spirit-given power, holiness, and glory. (See J. A. Schep, *The Nature of the Resurrection Body: A Study of the Biblical Data* [1964], ch. 6; M. J. Harris, *From Grave to Glory: Resurrection in the New Testament* [1990].) J. A. SCHEP

spiritual gifts. The apostle Paul uses the noun *charisma* G5922 ("favor, something graciously bestowed, gift") in combination with *pneumatikos* G4461 ("spiritual") only once, when writing to the Romans: "I long to see you so that I may impart to you some spiritual gift to make you strong" (Rom. 1:11). Elsewhere he uses either of these terms by itself, almost always in the plural (*charismata*, Rom. 12:6 et al.; *pneumatika*, 1 Cor. 12:1 and 14:1), to designate the special endowments that the Holy Spirit bestows on believers for the benefit of the church as a whole (cf. 1 Cor. 12:4–11, esp. v. 7, where the word *phanerōsis* G5748, "manifestation," is used).

In one sense, God's "indescribable gift" is Christ (2 Cor. 9:15); in another sense the greatest gift is the Spirit himself, who is the source of all such gifts (1 Cor. 12:11). A ninefold list of the "gifts of the Spirit" is found in 1 Cor. 12:8–10; comparable lists are found in v. 28 of the same chapter as well as in Rom. 12:6–8 and Eph. 4:11–12. See also MINISTRY.

I. Spiritual gifts in the OT. The OT does not contain comprehensive lists of spiritual gifts as the NT does. The doctrine of the Spirit was only gradually revealed by God to Israel over her long history. In view of this, it is striking that what the NT would call "spiritual gifts" are so often specifically associated in the OT with the coming or presence of the Spirit of Yahweh. This applies equally to ecstatic manifestations (Num. 11:25) and to moral qualities (Gen. 41:38); for since the OT knew of no distinction between "sacred" and "secular," all human excellences are rightly attributed to God (cf. Jas. 1:17).

BEZALEL, for example, was "filled with the Spirit of God, with skill, ability and knowledge in all kinds of crafts" for the construction of the TABERNACLE and the glorifying of God (Exod. 31:3). Metal work, wood carving, embroidery—all were alike inspired by the Spirit and were his gifts. Similarly, we read that the Spirit of the LORD came upon OTHNIEL to "judge" Israel (Jdg. 3:10) and upon SAMSON to give him strength (14:6). JOSEPH's prudence is proof of the presence of the Spirit of God (Gen. 41:38), and prophetic activity of whatever kind, throughout the whole of the OT, is seen as the work of the Spirit (1 Sam. 10:6).

To sum up, then, in the OT all "gifts" are thought of as spiritual gifts. It is not that "spiritual gifts" are without moral significance; rather, the doctrine of spiritual gifts is all-comprehensive. Yet it is not unfair to say that, as God's revelation moves forward to its NT climax, there is more stress on those gifts of a moral and spiritual nature, and thus a closer approximation to the NT understanding. Prophecies, such as that of Joel 2:28–29, in addition, contain a clear looking forward to the coming "generalization" of spiritual gifts, no longer to be restricted to a few.

II. Spiritual gifts in the Gospels. In the books there is as yet no systematic treatment, perhaps impossible before PENTECOST. Yet there is an advance on the OT position, for such spiritual gifts as are mentioned are more closely associated with a "personalized" Spirit. This is more true of John, with his developed teaching about "the Counselor," than of the Synoptic Gospels; but in both alike, the Spirit and his gifts are associated directly with the MESSIAH. This is equally true from the beginning of the ministry of Christ to the teaching of the final week (cf. Matt. 3:11 with Jn. 16:14).

While there may be no systematic lists in the Gospels, various spiritual gifts are just as evident during the ministry of Jesus as after Pentecost, not only in the person of the Messiah, but also in the life of his disciples. The messianic age has dawned, and these are the signs and wonders associated with its coming, in which the humblest member of the kingdom may participate. Contrast Matt. 11:11 with Jn. 10:41—not even mighty JOHN THE BAPTIST could compare with these humble disciples (unless, as some modern scholars think, the contrast is between John the Baptist and Christ himself).

The picture drawn rests more upon the evidence of the spectacular spiritual gifts (HEALING, MIRACLES, EXORCISM, etc.) and not on the more prosaic gifts. This is not as serious a problem as it appears at first sight. First, both types of gifts come from one and the same Spirit, as Paul makes clear

In this model of Jerusalem, the building in the foreground is an artist's conception of the place where the disciples received the gift of the Holy Spirit on the Day of Pentecost.

(1 Cor. 12:4); therefore the presence of either should be proof of his presence and activity. Second, it is far easier, in the cursory narrative of the Gospels, to detect the former than it is to detect the latter, although doubtless both were equally present. The OT makes clear that the Spirit was at work long before Pentecost. To judge from passages like Joel 2:28–29 and Jn. 1:33, the real change to be expected at Pentecost was that the gifts of the Spirit would be generalized and permanent, not that the Spirit would only then commence his work.

In the Gospels, as later in the NT, the Spirit himself is the greatest "spiritual gift," whether in the synoptics (Lk. 11:13) or the fourth gospel (Jn. 20:22). Within this general framework, not only does the Messiah himself exhibit the gifts of the Spirit in his own life, but he also delegates these powers to his followers. The work of the seventy (or seventy-two) disciples sent out by Christ is a good instance of healing and exorcism done by the disciples (Lk. 10:9, 17). Luke 10:19 may be a further reference to outward signs, although perhaps in the context it should be interpreted only in the spiritual sense.

That sometimes the disciples failed in their attempt to exercise these powers does not show that they did not possess them, but simply that they were lacking in faith (Matt. 17:20). The Gospels, however, make clear that the ability to do such signs does not by itself conclusively prove a right relationship to God (Matt. 7:22). Compare the fact that orthodox Jewish rabbis exorcised demons just as much as the followers of Christ did (Lk. 11:19; cf. Acts 19:13–14).

The Lord's promise to his disciples was not only that they would receive the Spirit (Jn. 16:7), but also that, after the Spirit's coming, they would do even "greater works" than the Messiah himself (14:12). This is sufficiently clear anticipation of the post-Pentecostal period, when taken with other scattered references (even if Mk. 16:17–18 is rejected as not forming part of the original text of Mark).

III. Spiritual gifts in Acts. Pentecost is primarily an age of new spiritual experience, not an age of theological reflection and analysis. Therefore Acts contains an account of manifestations of spiritual gifts, rather than carefully constructed lists. Again it is easier to trace the presence of spiritual gifts by concentrating mainly on the more spectacular manifestations. However, not all these outward manifestations may find their source in the Holy Spirit, as the book itself makes clear (Acts 8:9; 19:13).

The Day of Pentecost (Acts 2) was particularly marked by the manifestation of glossolalia (see below). It is very well possible that the new gift of "interpretation" also appeared on that day, for PETER's sermon is an "interpretation" in general terms. In addition to tongues and interpretation, 3:1–10 shows the exercise of the power of healing. The gift of "discernment of spirits" was exercised by Peter (5:3). PHILIP expelled demons (8:7); Peter raised the dead (9:40). In addition to these specific instances, there are several "blanket" references to "signs and wonders" done by the apostles either individually (e.g., STEPHEN, 6:8) or collectively (e.g., 5:12–16).

Most of these spiritual manifestations can be matched in the life of PAUL, in the second half of Acts. Although he is not actually recorded as having spoken with tongues (a gift he certainly had; cf. 1 Cor. 14:18), Paul raised the dead (20:9–12), cast out demons (16:18), had the power of healing (14:10), and was bitten by a snake without suffering ill effects (28:5). Paul also showed discernment of spirits (13:9–10).

There is another spiritual gift mentioned in Acts: that of "prophecy" (see PROPHETS AND PROPHECY). Whatever is meant by this in the Pauline epistles, in Acts at least it certainly included a predictive element, like that in OT prophecy. It occurs in early and late chapters alike. One prophet mentioned by name is AGABUS, who predicted a famine (Acts 11:28) and Paul's imprisonment (21:11). Paul's statement to the elders of EPHESUS that the Holy Spirit had warned him about impending suffering (20:23) probably refers to many anonymous local prophets of the same type, among whom perhaps were the elders of ANTIOCH OF SYRIA (13:1) and Philip's daughters (21:9). No doubt, in the church described in the early chapters of Acts there also existed many other spiritual gifts of a less spectacular nature. Gifts of generosity are seen (4:34–37; cf. Rom. 12:8). Gifts of wisdom and utterance were obvious (Acts 4:13; 6:10). Gifts of ruling and administration were demonstrated in the appointment of the Seven (6:1–6); the gift of LOVE — to Paul, the greatest of all gifts — is seen everywhere in the Acts narrative, but perhaps 4:34–37 is the most clear example.

IV. Spiritual gifts in the Pauline epistles. In the epistles of Paul the reader at once feels on familiar ground; the world of Paul was like the world of today in many respects. Yet these epistles are not chronologically later than the latter half of Acts, which follows closely the Jewish-Christian world of the first twelve chapters. Even the various phenomena do not seem to have been very different in themselves: the difference is that they are now seen through the eyes of Paul rather than through the eyes of the Jerusalem church.

Luke seems here, as usual, to have consciously adopted the viewpoint of his Jerusalem sources and informants. In the Pauline epistles there is an analysis of the various phenomena by a keen, if sympathetic, theological observer. It is clear, for example, that a list of spiritual gifts — indeed a virtual classification and evaluation — like that of 1 Cor. 12:4–11 is not only the result of revelation, but also the fruit of long and careful reflection.

Paul began by emphasizing the essential unity of all spiritual gifts, in the will and purpose of the Triune God (1 Cor. 12:4–6). There is a unity of source and origin, but also a unity of goal; that is, although the gifts are individual, the purpose is collective (all are "for the common good," v. 7). Paul added a higher bond of unity, for all such gifts are to be used in love (ch. 13). This would at once remove all pride, all self-advertisement, all rivalry, and all selfishness, in the use of spiritual gifts.

Once the principle of basic unity of testimony and goal was established, Paul stressed the diversity of the gifts of the Spirit. The "message [NRSV, utterance] of wisdom," which he placed first (1 Cor. 12:8), quite clearly refers to some type of PREACHING or teaching, presumably within the church, if this gift is "for the common good." Perhaps the same charisma is mentioned in 14:19. If so, the gift would correspond to TEACHERS in the parallel list in 12:28 (cf. BARNABAS, "Son of Encouragement," Acts 4:36). The next gift is FAITH (1 Cor. 12:9), perhaps evidenced in answered PRAYER, or even by signs or wonders performed (Matt. 21:18–22).

Next come gifts of healing and working of miracles; Paul could not have appealed to them so confidently had such miracles not been common in CORINTH. See HEALING, GIFTS OF.

Prophecy (1 Cor. 12:10) is a gift that may well have two meanings in Paul; the predictive element undoubtedly existed in the primitive church (see above, section III), but there is no explicit reference to this aspect in the extant Pauline epistles. It seems, therefore, that Paul refers to prophecy as the ability to bring the "word of the Lord" in any given situation. Perhaps this corresponds with forceful Spirit-filled preaching, as distinct from teaching, a different gift of the same Spirit. "Prophets" are clearly distinct from "teachers" (12:29), but they are frequently associated in terms which suggest that the difference is not great (at Antioch, Acts 13:1, the same group seems to combine both functions). Prophecy builds up the church (1 Cor. 14:4). Unlike the gift of tongues, it is immediately understandable by all (14:24), even by the non-Christian. Perhaps this is why Paul gave "prophecy" such a high priority among spiritual gifts (14:1).

The ability to "distinguish between spirits" (1 Cor. 12:10) was doubtless all the more necessary in a charismatic age, when forms of worship and ministry were still fluid, and creeds or other tests of orthodoxy still embryonic. It was essential that believers should be able to tell whether the claimed "inspiration" was from God or from a Satanic source. Paul laid down the simple yardstick of the testimony born to Christ (12:1–3).

The final gifts mentioned in 1 Cor. 12:10 are "different kinds of tongues" and "interpretation of tongues" (see TONGUES, GIFT OF). Paul accepted these heartily as spiritual gifts; indeed he excelled in tongues himself, though he valued interpretation more highly (14:18). He placed them deliberately at the bottom of the list (12:28–30). Tongues are valueless if devoid of love (13:1). The gift of tongues is primarily directed to God, not to fellow believers (14:2); it edifies the individual, not the whole church (14:4). It may even be mistaken by the outsider for madness (14:23). None of these objections hold if it is exercised in love and humility, for the good of the whole, in an orderly way (14:29), to a limited extent (14:27), and with "interpretation" that gives a rational content to the message (14:5). Otherwise, Paul counsels the possessor of this gift (not a universal gift, 12:30, nor associated by Paul with any "higher level" of Christian experience) to remain silent in the church, though he may "speak to himself and to God" as much as he likes (14:28; cf. Rom. 14:22).

While there are some differences in the other lists of gifts (Rom. 12:6–8; Eph. 4:11–12), the general pattern is recognizably the same.

(See further H. A. Guy, *New Testament Prophecy* [1947]; G. S. Hendry, *The Holy Spirit in Christian Theology* [1957]; C. K. Barrett, *The Holy Spirit and the Gospel Tradition* [1958]; J. L. Sherrill, *They Speak with Other Tongues* [1964]; R. B. Gaffin, Jr., *Perspectives on Pentecost: Studies in New Testament Teaching on the Gifts of the Holy Spirit* [1977]; S. S. Schatzmann, *A Pauline Theology of Charismata* [1987]; K. S. Hemphill, *Spiritual Gifts: Empowering the New Testament Church* [1988]; W. A. Grudem, ed., *Are Miraculous Gifts for Today? Four Views* [1996]; M. Turner, *The Holy Spirit and Spiritual Gifts: In the New Testament Church and Today* [1998]; R. L. Thomas, *Understanding Spiritual Gifts: A Verse-by-Verse Study of 1 Corinthians 12–14*, rev. ed. [1999]; D. C. Bloesch, *The Holy Spirit: Works and Gifts* [2000]; C. Tibbs, *Religious Experience of the Pneuma: Communication with the Spirit World in 1 Corinthians 12 and 14* [2007].)   R. A. COLE

spiritual rock. See ROCK.

spiritual songs. See MUSIC, MUSICAL INSTRUMENTS III.B.

spit. In the OT the action of spitting (Heb. *yāraq* H3762 and *rāqaq* H8394) usually indicates a purposeful deed with an added notion of ritual defilement or legal rejection (Lev. 15:8; Num. 12:14; Deut. 25:9). The nominal form of this term (*rōq* H8371, "spittle") has a similar nuance (Job 30:10; Isa. 50:6; in Job 7:19, however, the idiom "until I swallow my spittle" indicates a period of very short duration). The notion of defilement or rejection occurs also in the accounts of Christ's PASSION (Matt. 26:67; 27:30; Mk. 10:34; 14:65; 15:19; Lk. 18:32); in these passages the compound form *emptyō* G1870 is used. The simple verb *ptyō* G4772 occurs in connection with several healing accounts (Mk. 7:33; 8:23; Jn. 9:6). In addition, modern English versions usually have "spit" as the rendering of *emeō* G1840 in Rev. 3:16, but this verb properly means "to vomit."

spoil(s). This noun is used very frequently by the KJV to render as many as nine different Hebrew nominal forms, the most common of which is *šālāl* H8965 (Gen. 49:27 et al.). The NIV, which uses "spoil" relatively few times (usually in the pl., e.g., Exod. 15:9), prefers the translation "plunder." Another important Hebrew word is *baz* H1020, which occurs a couple of dozen times, about half of them in Ezekiel (e.g., Ezek. 7:21; cf. *bizzâ* H1023, 2 Chr. 14:14 et al., and the verb *bāzaz* H1024, Gen. 34:27 et al.); less frequent are *malqôaḥ* H4917 (Num. 31:11–12 et al.) and *mešissâ* H5468 (2 Ki. 21:14 et al.; cf. the verbs *šāsâ* H9115, 1 Sam. 14:48 et al., and *šāsas* H9116, Jdg. 2:14 et al.). The NT uses Greek *akrothinion* G215 (Heb. 7:4), *harpagē* G771 (Heb. 10:34; cf. the verb *diarpazō* G1395, Matt. 12:29; Mk. 3:27), and *skylon* G5036 (Lk. 11:22).

In ancient times, the victor assumed the privilege to seize anything that could be carried away (Gen. 14:11; 2 Chr. 20:25), including women and children (Deut. 20:14). Also seized were cattle (Deut. 2:35; 1 Sam. 14:32; 2 Chr. 15:11; Jer. 49:32), clothing (Josh. 7:21; Jdg. 5:30; 2 Chr. 20:25; 28:15), and precious metals (Josh. 7:21; Jdg. 8:24, 25).

When Israel returned from the victory over the Midianites (see MIDIAN), they brought the spoils to MOSES and ELEAZAR for distribution (Num. 31). All the male children were killed, and of the women, only the virgins were kept alive. The spoil was then divided into two parts, one part to be equally distributed among the warriors and the other to the people at large. For the Lord's tribute the warriors were to give up one person or beast out of every five hundred; the people, one out of every fifty. In addition, they brought the Lord articles of gold, armlets, bracelets, signet rings, earrings, and beads.

The choice plunder was devoted to the deity; for example, GOLIATH's sword was housed at the sanctuary at NOB (1 Sam. 21:9), while the armor of defeated SAUL was placed by the PHILISTINES in their temple of ASHTAROTH (31:9–10). Later, some of the spoil won in battle was "dedicated for the repair of the temple of the LORD" (1 Chr. 26:27). Sometimes, prior to an assault, a city or tribe might be "devoted" to God (see BAN), which meant that everything animate was to be destroyed, all precious metals and objects given to God, and the remainder burned or rendered useless (Josh. 6:17–19). (See further J. Pedersen, *Israel: Its Life and Culture*, 2 vols. [1926–40], 2:1–32; R. de Vaux, *Ancient Israel* [1961], 255–57.)

L. L. WALKER

sponge. The only occurrences of this term (Gk. *spongos*, G5074) concern the drink of VINEGAR given to the Lord on the cross (Matt. 27:48; Mk. 15:36; Jn. 19:29). Sponges (phylum *Porifera*) are lowly marine animals whose horny skeletons have been used for a variety of domestic purposes since very early times.

G. S. CANSDALE

spouse. See MARRIAGE.

spring. See PALESTINE V; SEASONS. For the sense "source of water," see FOUNTAIN.

spring rain. See RAIN.

spying. The Hebrew verb *rāgal* H8078 in the piel stem has the meaning "to scout, explore, spy out" (Num. 21:32 et al.), and the participle of this verb is commonly used with reference to spies (Gen. 42:9 et al.). Two other verbs that have a similar meaning are *tûr* H9365 (e.g., Num. 13:2) and, less frequently, *ḥāpar* H2916 (Deut. 1:22; Josh. 2:2–3). The NT uses two Greek nouns, *enkathetos* G1588 (Lk. 20:20–21) and *kataskopos* G2946 (Heb. 11:31), as well as the verb *kataskopeō* G2945 (Gal. 2:4).

Spies and spying have always been necessary in WAR in order to discover the weakness of the enemy. In Gen. 42 JOSEPH accuses his brothers of being spies whose object was to discover the weaknesses of Egypt. MOSES sent twelve spies into the land of Canaan to determine its strengths and weaknesses and to see how productive the land was (Num. 13). When they returned with a divided report, Israel accepted the majority report and was forced to postpone conquest of the land for forty years. During this time Moses sent spies to JAZER, a fortified AMORITE city in GILEAD, and then captured the city (21:32).

Forty years later, during the conquest, whenever the capture of a town is related in detail, spies always precede the capture. In the case of JERICHO, JOSHUA sent two spies (Josh. 2–6). From Jericho an unspecified number of spies were sent to AI (chs. 7–8). Later the tribes of Joseph took BETHEL after spies had discovered from a traitor an entrance to the city (Jdg. 1:23–25). DAVID used spies to keep track of SAUL's movements (1 Sam. 26:4). Finally, the emissaries David sent to the Ammonites were assumed to be spies by the Ammonites and were treated accordingly (2 Sam. 10:3; 1 Chr. 19:3). (See R. de Vaux, *Ancient Israel* [1965], 213–40.)

In the NT, spies are alluded to twice. The scribes and chief priests sent spies to Jesus (Lk. 20:20–21; Gk. *enkathetos* G1588), and RAHAB is commended for welcoming the Israelite spies (Heb. 11:31, Gk. *kataskopos* G2946; cf. Jas. 2:25, which uses the word *angelos* G34, "messenger"). In addition, the apostle PAUL accuses the JUDAIZERS of spying out Christian freedom (Gal. 2:4; verb *kataskopeō* G2945).

J. C. MOYER

squad. This English term, referring to a small military group, is used in modern Bible versions to render Greek *tetradion* G5482, which occurs once with reference to the detachments assigned by Herod Agrippa to guard PETER as a prisoner (Acts 12:4; see HEROD VII). The Greek term, meaning "foursome," corresponds to Latin *quaterni* (thus KJV, "quaternions"), indicating a detachment of four soldiers; Peter was assigned four such groups, one for each watch of the night (thus NIV, "four squads of four soldiers each"). In the Acts account the disposition of the squad is given. Peter was sleeping chained to two soldiers (12:6) while the other two stood guard at the doors where Peter and the angel passed them on leaving (v. 10).

stable. See HORSE; MEGIDDO; STALL.

Stachys stay´kis (Στάχυς G5093, "head of grain"). A Christian in ROME to whom PAUL sent greetings, calling him "my beloved (Rom. 16:9; NIV, "my dear friend," Gk. *agapētos* G28). Because relatively few inscriptions in the city of Rome attest the name Stachys, some have inferred that he had been a close acquaintance of the apostle in the eastern parts of the empire and that subsequently he had migrated to the capital. (For a discussion of the names in

Rom. 16, see P. Lampe in *The Romans Debate*, ed. K. P. Donfried, rev. ed. [1991], 216–30.)

stacte stak´tee. This English term, found in the KJV and other versions at Exod. 30:34 (also in the NRSV at Sir. 24:15), is a transliteration of Greek *staktē* ("oil of myrrh," from *stazō*, "to drip"), used by the SEPTUAGINT to render Hebrew *nāṭāp H5753* in that verse. The SPICE in question was one of the fragrant ingredients used to produce INCENSE. The precise meaning of the Hebrew term is uncertain, but it evidently refers to "drops" (cf. the verb *nāṭap H5752*, "to secrete, drip") flowing from some aromatic plant, such as *Commiphora opobalsamum* or *Pistacia lentiscus* (cf. FFB, 147, 178; HALOT, 2:694–95). Another possibility is *Styrax officinalis*, a small tree found throughout Palestine that bears snowdrop-shaped, pendulous pure white flowers; if an incision is made in the bark, the fragrant resin is easily obtained. The NIV, appropriately, uses a generic rendering, "gum resin." See also FLORA (under *Burseraceae*, *Cistaceae*, and *Anacardiaceae*); GUM; MYRRH. W. E. SHEWELL-COOPER

stadion, stadia. See WEIGHTS AND MEASURES, I.G.

staff. See ROD.

stair. In the ANE, one-story houses might have a stair outside, usually of stone and without a railing. Two-story houses had the stair frequently inside, but with an exterior stair from balcony to roof. To provide access to deep wells, steps were cut into the sides, examples of which have been found in GIBEON, GEZER, MEGIDDO, and BETH ZUR.

A common Hebrew word that can be translated "stairs" or "steps" is *maʿălâ H5092* (more generally meaning "ascent"). It is used, for example, of the six steps that were part of the throne of King SOLOMON (1 Ki. 10:19–20), and of a stairway that went down from the City of David (Neh. 3:15; 12:37). The latter, which has been excavated, descended about 35 ft. to the end of the hill S of the temple area near the FOUNTAIN GATE (see *ABD*, 6:183–84). The term *lûl H4294* occurs only once (1 Ki. 6:8), where it probably refers to a winding stairway (so LXX, *heliktē anabasis*) connecting two levels of the TEMPLE; some suggest that the word indicates a "trapdoor" (see discussion in M. Cogan, *1 Kings*, AB 10 [2001], 240).

The "stairway" or "ladder" that JACOB saw in his dream (Gen. 28:12; Heb. *sullām H6150*) may have been a ramp of rising stones. (On 2 Ki. 20:11=Isa. 38:8, see DIAL.) In the NT, Greek *anabathmos G325* is used of the steps from which PAUL addressed the mob in Jerusalem (Acts 20:35, 40); the reference is to a stairway that led from the temple area to the ANTONIA fortress. H. G. STIGERS

stall. The Hebrew term *ʾurwâ H774* is used of the thousands of stalls that SOLOMON built for securing his CHARIOTS and HORSES (1 Ki. 4:26 = 2 Chr. 9:25; in the former passage the number "forty" instead of "four" is probably a textual corruption). Reference is made also to the "stalls for various kinds of cattle, and pens for the flocks" in the time of HEZEKIAH (2 Chr. 32:28). In two-story homes, CATTLE were usually housed in the ground level where there were stalls and MANGERS. The stables of MEGIDDO were arranged on either side of an aisle, each stall separated by posts and provided with a manger, paved with cobblestones. Tying holes occurred in the manger posts. The large number of stalls there (450 of them distributed in two separate buildings) indicates a large traffic in horse trading. Stables from approximately the same era are found at Tell el-Hesi (c. 16 mi. NE of GAZA), GEZER, TAANACH, and HAZOR.

Another Hebrew noun meaning "stall" is *repet H8348*, which occurs only once (Hab. 3:17). The term *marbēq H5272* is usually rendered "stall" in

Staircase leading up to a defensive tower at Beersheba.

two passages (Amos 6:4; Mal. 4:2), but the connotation is "stall-fed," that is, "fattened" (thus 1 Sam. 28:24; Jer. 46:21). Similarly, the KJV "stalled" in Prov. 15:17 should be rendered "fattened" (pass. ptc. of *ʾābas H80*; cf. 1 Ki. 4:23 [Heb. 5:3]). In the NT, "stall" or "manger" translates Greek *phatnē G5764* (Lk. 13:15). H. G. STIGERS

stallion. See HORSE.

standard. See BANNER.

star. See ASTRONOMY.

star, day (morning). See ASTRONOMY.

Star of Bethlehem. The narrative concerning the star that led the MAGI to the abode of the Christ child is found only in Matt. 2:1–12. The story is short and direct, the "wise men" being identified only as "from the east," and their sign as an *astēr G843* (four times, vv. 2, 7, 9, 10). The immediate reaction of HEROD and his courtiers to search the OT prophets for further information about the promised child-king indicates that it was from that source that the Magi had derived their information. However, the specific passages are not mentioned or cited (Matthew quotes Mic. 5:2 because it was that text the courtiers used in answering Herod).

The only plausible texts that could have been known are those dealing with a star and the birth of Israel's king (Num. 24:17 and Isa. 60:3). In the narrative in Numbers the strange character BALAAM son of Beor is cursing Israel at the invitation and under the employment of BALAK king of MOAB. This soothsayer performs the customary offices of the type of incantation priest known in the Mesopotamian literature as a *bārû(m)* (in fact, it has been suggested by some that the phrase "son of Beor" may actually mean, "member-of-*bārû*," that is, a title of identification with that group of soothsayers). One aspect of *bārû* practice, called *barûtu*, was to make up poems and imprecations involving the twisting of the names and titles of the enemy. The OT prophets do this frequently with the names of the pagan gods.

The central text in the curse-blessing of Balaam is Num. 24:17, which describes a future time, "the latter days" (v. 14; NIV, "days to come"), a phrase understood in the OT to mean the time of Israel's MESSIAH. At this time a person described as a "star" was to step forth from out of the people of Jacob. The parallel in the last half of v. 17 identifies the "star" as a "scepter," and so two standard symbols of the ANE world are brought to bear on the personage to appear. In CUNEIFORM literature, a sign that is read *dingir* and represents the simple configuration of a star is the determinative put before the name of a god to properly mark divinity. Some of the very ancient Akkadian kings who were later considered divine were so introduced.

The scene of this prophecy is most important as it accords well with ANE practice. The soothsayer was standing on a hill, PEOR (Num. 23:28), and looking out over the encampment of Israel. It was understood by all ancient ASTROLOGY that the events of the macrocosmic sky were predictive of subsequent events in the same quadrant of the microcosmic earth. Therefore Balaam was looking at the sky above Israel when he made his prediction on the basis of the astrological signs. In God's providence the nonsense of astrology was turned to a true prophetic vision. The elaborate poetic statements of Balaam, which preserve some of the oldest Hebrew in the OT, were undoubtedly literary efforts. It was on the basis of such texts that later predictions were made, as can be easily seen in the Jewish mystical and astrological works such as the Kabbalah.

The Neobabylonian records of the Persian period show a great deal of mystical and futuristic interest. In addition, it is known that such astrological data as the ephemerides (location tables) of the planets and the conditions of the moon's glow were studied. Reports of the findings were recorded and passed to the royal officers in charge. The collections of these texts have been invaluable in reconstructing the chronology and planetary configurations at the time they were inscribed. Although the goals of their efforts were speculative and superstitious, the methods employed were often amazingly accurate. It was probably the use of these various written materials that brought the wise men from the east.

The actual appearance of the star that guided the magicians is a difficult problem. In the rationalistic age of the 18th cent., the negative higher critical schools of the European universities attempted to find cause and effect for such inexplicable events in Scripture in some natural process. The result was that three common theories of the star arose. In the various books on the subject and many popular planetarium displays, one of the three reconstructions is presented. The most popular is that an unidentified comet passed by and was clearly visible both night and day, which would account for its apparent movement. The older theory is that a supernova occurred, and that its spectacular brilliance was seen by the astrologers. This thesis is often supported by some possible sightings of such phenomena from antiquity. The oldest reconstruction found in 17th-cent. rationalist commentators is that several planets converged with a bright star under optimum conditions of observation. (For further discussion see ASTRONOMY III.)

A more acceptable alternative seems to be that God provided a source of light that cannot now be determined, and that the wise men saw and interpreted it on the basis of the ancient texts at their disposal. The time of the Magi's visit is not given in the gospel narratives but is inferred in the fact that King Herod ordered the deaths of all children up to two years of age. This means that the age of Jesus was not known to Herod and that some time had elapsed since his birth. The casual assumption that the visit of the wise men was made on the night of our Lord's birth and that it was at the same time as the shepherds' adoration is unsupported by the text. There is also no support for the notion that the shepherds ever saw the star.

The classical commentators often tied in the passage in Isa. 60:3, "Nations will come to your light, / and kings to the brightness of your dawn." Although this statement could apply to Christ in a general sense, the additional reference to people coming "bearing gold and incense" (v. 6) suggests strongly that at least one aspect of the prophecy has to do with the presentation of the Magi.

The notion that the Magi were kings of oriental countries became very popular in the medieval period, and the adoration of the Magi was a popular theme in Renaissance art as far back as the Florentine school. Giotto (1267–1337) painted such a scene in the Arena Chapel showing the Magi in kingly garb. Many countries have made the Magi into an elaborate part of the popular mythology of Christmas by taking them out of the Bible chronicle and adding all manner of tales gathered from the folk legends of their people. The story is often glossed by unaccountable details. The common assumption in Western folklore that there were three is probably gathered from some non-Christian source, possibly the stories of the three pagan Norns of Norse Yule festivities, and/or from the fact that three gifts are mentioned by Matthew (Matt. 2:11). While the Roman churches of the W expanded the mass of the incarnation and further added the growing cult of Mary, the Eastern or Greek rite churches did little to elaborate the story of the wise men as given in the Scripture. The star plays little part in the Orthodox art and literature.

The question concerning the purpose of the star is directly answered in the text: "We saw his star in the east [NRSV, at its rising] and have come to worship him" (Matt. 2:2). The purpose of the star was to authenticate and publicize the INCARNATION, and to draw men and women to worship the celestial king. The many speculations about the aspects of the star and the frequent searches for a mechanistic explanation violate the very purpose of the gospel narrative. This is not to say that the gospel is not trustworthy in descriptions of phenomena. It does acknowledge that the evangelist sets forth the event in naive-theoretical language without intent to declare in any way a law of astronomy or erect a mathematical model. On the other hand, the tragic mistake so often made in dealing with such short and unique events in Scripture is to make them dramatic and colossal, to magnify them out of all proportion to the scale of the little agricultural populations of the ANE with their relatively humble worldviews. Although the Roman world of Palestine was so much smaller and so much simpler than later centuries, it was into that time and place that God was pleased to send his Son. In considering this momentous event it is necessary to keep the birth of the Messiah uppermost in consideration and to repress any intrusion of nonbiblical emphasis.

W. WHITE, JR.

state. See GOVERNMENT.

stature. This English term, usually referring to a person's height, occurs seventeen times in the KJV, but seldom in modern versions, which prefer "size" or other expressions (e.g., Num. 13:32, where the Heb. word is *middâ* H4500). In the NT the meaning "stature" is conveyed by Greek *hēlikia* G2461, and this meaning is clear in Lk. 19:3, where ZACCHAEUS is described as being a short person. The Greek word, however, often has the sense "age" (see esp. Jn. 9:21, 23; Heb. 11:11), which produces some ambiguity in several passages.

For example, when Luke describes the boy Jesus as having grown in wisdom and *hēlikia* (Lk. 2:52), is he referring to Jesus' physical size or to his age (cf. NRSV, "Jesus increased in wisdom and in years") or to his maturity? In the SERMON ON THE MOUNT Jesus asked the rhetorical question, "Which of you by taking thought can add one cubit unto his stature?" (Matt. 6:27 KJV; cf. Lk. 12:25). Some interpreters, understanding the word for "cubit" (Gk. *pēchys* G4388) figuratively of a small measure of time, translate, "Who of you by worrying can add a single hour to his life?" (so NIV; similarly, NRSV). The transition between these two senses of the word may be illustrated by Eph. 4:13, where PAUL speaks of believers attaining "the measure of the full stature of Christ" (NRSV). Even this literal rendering is understandable to an English reader, who naturally interprets *stature* (physical height) in the figurative sense of "maturity."

statute. See ORDINANCE.

staves. A form used by the KJV consistently as the plural of *staff*. See ROD.

steadfast. This adjective and its cognates (which the KJV spells *stedfast, stedfastly, stedfastness*) indicate firmness, determination, loyalty; they are used variously to render several Hebrew and Greek terms. The adverb is used a number of times in the KJV to translate verbs that have an intensive meaning, such as Greek *atenizō* G867 (as in Acts 1:10, "they looked stedfastly toward heaven"; NIV, "They were looking intently up into the sky"). In the NIV the adjective occurs relatively few times, especially to render Hebrew *nākôn* (niphal ptc. of *kûn* H3922, "to be firm," Ps. 51:10 et al.). The

Basalt stela from the late Hittite period (Maras, 9th cent. B.C.) depicting a banquet scene.

NRSV, however, uses the phrase "steadfast love" with great frequency as the translation of the noun *ḥesed* H2876 (Gen. 24:12 et al.); see discussion under LOVINGKINDNESS. See also FAITH, FAITHFULNESS; PATIENCE.

stealing. See CRIMES AND PUNISHMENTS.

stedfast. KJV form of STEADFAST.

steel. See METALS AND METALLURGY.

steer. See CATTLE III.

stela, stele. A stone slab (Lat. *stela*, Gk. *stēlē*), usually oblong, not forming part of a structure but set up in a vertical position, used for votive purposes or as a memorial to some person or event. Upon these slabs were carved INSCRIPTIONS often accompanied by ornamental designs or reliefs of particular significance. Such stelae have been found throughout Mesopotamia, Syria, Egypt, Asia Minor, and the

Greco-Roman world. Some of them have important connections with events narrated in the Bible. The stela was essentially of a secular character even though it may have been erected at a sanctuary and have had religious images carved on it. No Israelite stela has ever been discovered, although such a MONUMENT may be indicated by *yād H3338* in 1 Sam. 15:12 (cf. 2 Sam. 18:18). See also PILLAR.

L. L. WALKER

Stephanas stef'uh-nuhs (Στεφανᾶς *G5107*, "crown"). A Corinthian Christian who, with his household, was one of the few persons baptized personally by the apostle PAUL in CORINTH (1 Cor. 1:16). While he heartily endorsed baptism, PAUL is thankful that he did not baptize more than these lest a divisive and "superior" Pauline party develop in the church (vv. 10–15).

The household of Stephanas were the FIRSTFRUITS of the gospel in ACHAIA (1 Cor. 16:15–16; although individuals had earlier been converted in ATHENS [Acts 17:34], this family must have been the foundation for the first Christian community in the region). Paul commends them for devoted "service"—which probably included both Christian teaching and hospitality—to God's people and urges the Corinthian believers to be subject to such leaders. This instruction suggests that the Corinthians had failed to show proper esteem to Stephanas and his family.

Finally, Paul states that he rejoiced and that his spirit was lifted by the visit of Stephanas, FORTUNATUS, and ACHAICUS while he was in EPHESUS, and asked that recognition be given them (1 Cor. 16:17–18). These three men are said to "have supplied what was lacking from" the Corinthians. Most interpreters understand this comment to mean that the apostle missed the company of the Corinthian church as a whole and that the visit from these representatives served to relieve his sadness.

A. M. ROSS

Stephen stee'vuhn (Στέφανος *G5108*, "crown"). Hellenistic Christian apologist and first Christian MARTYR.

I. His background. All that is known of Stephen is recorded in Acts 6:5—8:2 (with incidental references in 11:19 and 22:20). His name and associations indicate that he was a Hellenistic (i.e., Greek-speaking) Jew. See HELLENISM. No account is given of his conversion or of his coming into the Christian fellowship. Though there is an obscure tradition that he was one of the SEVENTY DISCIPLES (Lk. 10:1; NIV, "seventy-two"), it is quite possible that he had not been a personal disciple of Jesus at all. He may likely have been reached by the early preaching of the apostles in Jerusalem.

The significance of the Hellenists is seen first in their numbers. It is remarkable that so soon after the resurrection of Jesus there should have been need for seven leaders to be in charge of the distribution of relief to the widows of the Greek-speaking Jews alone. This probably indicates the presence of hundreds or even thousands of Christians in Jerusalem whose native tongue was Greek. See GREEK LANGUAGE. Another surprise is the early transformation of the church from a Jewish movement to a fellowship composed almost exclusively of Gentiles. It goes almost without saying that the Hellenists had a crucial part in this transition. This development required a different leadership from that provided by the twelve apostles. Jews and Gentiles were separated by the major barriers of race, geography, and language. Hellenistic Jews, many of whom had lived outside of Palestine, had overcome part of the barriers and had learned to live with Gentiles. When converted, they readily adapted the message to a Greek context and held it in readiness when the Spirit of God moved the church to broaden its witness to the Gentiles. Stephen's insights were a significant contribution in this direction.

II. His work. Stephen's qualifications and leadership were of such a nature that some commentators find it hard to believe that he ever really "served tables." He is named first in the list of the Seven in Acts 6:5 (see DEACON III). He was "full of God's grace and power" (v. 8). He worked miracles (v. 8) and spoke with wisdom and spiritual power (v. 10). The Seven were appointed to the specific task of caring for the needs of the widows of the Hellenists in the daily distributions of food (vv. 1–3). Though no specific mention is made of their discharging this duty, it can be assumed that they did so with efficiency. At any rate, the church grew (v. 7).

It is quite possible that a more fundamental problem than a supposed discrimination in the handling of food caused the discontent. It may have been the lack of adequate Hellenistic representation on the administrative level of the church. With numbers approaching those of the Hebrew-speaking or Aramaic-speaking Jews, and with strong feelings of loyalty to their group, they likely wanted a commensurate voice. It does not follow that Stephen and the Seven were to devote all their time to "serving tables" for the Hellenists, any more than the apostles had served the others. They were administratively responsible to see that the work was done. Then they were freely to follow the ministry of the Word as the Holy Spirit motivated and enabled them. In this latter capacity, Stephen, at least, excelled.

III. His beliefs. According to the report in Acts 6:13–14, Stephen was understood to speak against the temple and the law. This serious charge reflects, at the least, that he held a viewpoint somewhat different from that of the thoroughly conservative Jews. The charge was brought by Hellenistic Jews who had probably moved back to Jerusalem because they considered their ancestral faith the one thing worth living for. They would be bitter in their opposition against anything that seemed to undermine their traditional faith.

It is not necessary to believe that Stephen had gone so far as PAUL in concluding that the law was no longer the final, binding code that he had formerly thought it to be. He had, no doubt, discovered the inadequacy of a mere formalism and ceremonialism in the temple worship. Perhaps Christ's own words regarding the TEMPLE (Jn. 4:20–24; Mk. 13:2) had shown him that true WORSHIP of God is not confined to the temple. He may also have seen in the words of Jesus the transitory nature of the law. Jesus had defended laxity in matters of tradition and had supported a freer attitude toward SABBATH observance (Mk. 2:15–16, 7:1–27, Lk. 15:1–2). He had granted consideration to Gentiles (Matt. 8:5–13; Mk. 7:24–30). He had even superseded the law on rare occasions (Matt. 5:33–37; Mk. 10:2–12). Jesus had recruited most of his followers from the common people who "listened to him with delight" (Mk. 12:37). It is clear that the observance of legal minutiae was not an absorbing concern with many of these people. Jesus was frequently criticized for allowing laxity.

The record of Jesus' freer tendency in these matters must have been preserved by the immediate followers of Jesus. As F. Filson suggests (*Pioneers of the Primitive Church* [1940], 66), many of the followers were so much in the grip of ancestral tradition that they gradually drew back into an attitude of 100 percent Jewishness and thus lost a basic feature of the attitude of Jesus. Stephen, with his broad background in the DIASPORA, maintained this important aspect of Jesus' message and held open the way for the future advance into Gentile evangelism. While he appears not to have evangelized Gentiles, his thought and his sources in the words of Jesus prepared the way for Paul. There is, indeed, also a remarkable parallel between the approach and method in Stephen's defense and that of certain of Paul's sermons (Acts 7:2–53 and 13:16–41).

IV. His arrest. The greater recognition of the Hellenists was followed by remarkable growth and success in the church. But progress also brought trouble. Stephen did not hesitate to preach his views in the Hellenistic synagogues. Naturally, others arose and disputed him. Stephen won the debate. They could not resist his superior understanding and convincing knowledge. Nor could they match the deep earnestness and spiritual insight with which he spoke (Acts 6:10). Worsted in debate, the synagogue Jews did not lose the upper hand. They circulated among the people between the public services, misrepresented Stephen's views, aroused suspicion and fears concerning his alleged "heresy" and "blasphemy," and set a trap for him. They seized Stephen and brought him before the assembled SANHEDRIN, introduced prearranged false witnesses, and charged him with BLASPHEMY (vv. 12–14).

The accusation included two charges: one against his person, a charge of blasphemous words against Moses that would make him a blasphemer against God, and another against his teaching, charging him with radical and revolutionary statements concerning the temple and the law. These charges are strikingly parallel to those leveled against Jesus (Matt. 26:65; Mk. 14:58; 13:2; 15:29). Stephen was accused of implied approval of the destruction of the temple and the change of the law. Christianity, so taught, was understood as threatening the overthrow of the Jews' religion and the very termination of their national existence.

V. His defense. The charge against Stephen's person was baseless except as one would pervert his words. But there was an element of truth in the charge against his teaching. The GOSPEL of Christ was sufficiently revolutionary to be a threat to the dead formalism and ceremonialism by which the temple worship was perpetuated. Having discovered reality, Stephen could never go back to the types and shadows. He was defending more than opinions or even convictions. He rested in a vital relationship with a Person. In the simplicity and confidence of that trust, he had no anxiety. The inner light broke out upon him until even his face was like that of an angel (Acts 6:15).

His response, then, was not primarily a self-defense but a defense of the gospel. He was more interested in effective witness to the truth than he was in living. If they accepted the truth of the gospel, he would, of course, survive. If not, his trust was still in Jesus.

The fundamental difference between Stephen and his opponents lay in that he judged the OT history from the prophetic viewpoint while they represented the legalistic view. To him, Jesus was the natural historical outcome of the OT revelation. The revelation of God and the development of the nation did not coincide. Stephen was not antinomian nor anti-Mosaic, but the Jewish nation was obstinate. From the early leaders down to the present council, they disobeyed God and his revelation. The new religion was only the divinely ordered development of the old. The real blasphemers were the disobedient Jews who rejected the revelation and killed Jesus.

Stephen made the point that God had never bound himself to one sanctuary or to one person, such as MOSES. God's self-manifestation began long before Moses or the temple. And Moses himself testified that it would not conclude with him. Another was to come. The Hebrews resisted Moses, killed the prophets, and continued in a largely unregenerate state to that very hour.

VI. His martyrdom. The council answered Stephen's countercharge with rage. Stephen gazed into heaven and uttered his memorable testimony in behalf of Christ. When he declared that through the opened heavens he saw Jesus on the right hand of God (Acts 7:56), the council broke loose, forgetting the formality of pronouncing sentence. They stoned him as a blasphemer uncondemned (Deut. 17:7; Lev. 24:14–16). Certain legal forms were observed to give the violence the appearance of legality, however.

The effect of Stephen's death was tremendous. The persecution that followed scattered the church and threatened loss, but the vigor of the believers' witness soon turned potential defeat into victory and growth. One cannot resist the impression that Stephen's noble witness and spirit lay behind the growth of the church and the eventual conversion of Saul. As Augustine said, "Si Stephanus non orasset, ecclesia Paulum non habuisset"—If Stephen had not prayed, the church would not have had Paul.

(See further C. Weizsäcker, *The Apostolic Age of the Christian Church* [1894], 62–75; G. Purves, *Christianity in the Apostolic Age* [1900], 51–55; B. Bacon in *Biblical and Semitic Studies: Critical and Historical Essays* [1901], 213–76; M. Simon, *St. Stephen and the Hellenists in the Primitive Church*

According to tradition, Stephen was stoned to death at a rocky outcrop N of the temple (depicted in this model of Jerusalem).

[1958]; R. Longenecker, *Paul, Apostle of Liberty* [1964], 34–35, 271–75; J. Kilgallen, *The Stephen Speech: A Literary and Redactional Study of Acts 7, 2–53* [1976]; F. F. Bruce, *Peter, Stephen, James, and John: Studies in Early Non-Pauline Christianity* [1979]; S. Légasse, *Stephanos: Histoire et discours d'Étienne dans les Actes des Apôtres* [1992]; D. L. Wiens, *Stephen's Sermon and the Structure of Luke-Acts* [1995]; A. Watson, *The Trial of Stephen: The First Christian Martyr* [1996]; T. Penner, *In Praise of Christian Origins: Stephen and the Hellenists in Lukan Apologetic History* [2004]; *DLNT*, 1123–26.)

W. T. DAYTON

Stephen, Revelation of. An apocryphal apocalypse mentioned by some of the post-Nicene apologetes as a text popular among the MANICHEAN heretics. No known text of the work is now extant; however, it has been often assumed that it was a recitation or narrative about the reappearance of STEPHEN, the first Christian martyr. A somewhat similar tale is known from several versions. The older is that related by a Christian priest, Lucian (c. A.D. 400), who lived in a town near Jerusalem. He is supposed to have had three visitations of Gamaliel that led to the discovery of the bodies of Stephen, Nicodemus, and Gamaliel. A number of translations have been made of the extant fragments of this work (*ANF*, 8:575–86; 9:141–74). A medieval romance of St. Stephen known only from an Old Church Slavonic version apparently is not related to the Manichean text. (See M. R. James, *The Apocryphal New Testament* [1924], 564–68.)

W. WHITE, JR.

steward. In the OT, this English term can be used to render a few individual Hebrew nouns, such as the rare word *sōkēn* H6125 (Isa. 22:15), but more commonly it translates a Hebrew phrase involving a relative pronoun, a preposition, and the noun *bayit* H1074, "house." For example, "Joseph's steward" (Gen. 43:19) represents Hebrew *ʾăšer ʿal-bêt yôsēp*, "the man who [was] upon the house of Joseph." In the NT, the KJV uses "steward" with some frequency as the rendering of two Greek nouns, *epitropos* G2208, "manager, foreman" (Matt. 20:8 et al.), and *oikonomos* G3874, "household manager, administrator" (Lk. 12:42 et al.).

stiff-necked. This expression is a literal rendering of the Hebrew phrase *qĕšēh-ʿōrep* (H7997 + H6902), "hard of neck," used especially to describe the intransigence and rebellious spirit of the Israelites in the period of their sojourn in the Sinai desert after the exodus from Egypt (Exod. 32:9 et al.). The SEPTUAGINT rendered the Hebrew literally into Greek with the compound *sklērotrachēlos* G5019, which is used only once in the NT (Acts 7:51, near the conclusion of STEPHEN's speech).

stoa. See PORCH; SOLOMON'S COLONNADE.

stocks. This English term, referring to an instrument of restraint and punishment, is used primarily to render Hebrew *mahpeket* H4551, which occurs only a few times (Jer. 20:2–3; 29:26; cf. also 2 Chr. 16:10, lit., "house of stocks," that is, "prison"). In Job 13:27 and 33:11 we find the term *sad* H6040, which probably refers to a restraining device like the stock (NIV, "shackles"), but the precise origin and meaning of the term is uncertain. It also occurs in the NT as the translation of Greek *xylon* G3833, which actually means "wood" (thus also the older meaning of English *stock*, cf. KJV at Jer. 2:27 et al.); in the narrative of Acts 16:24, it clearly refers to the posts to which prisoners' limbs were held fast by iron bolts. HERODOTUS (*Hist.* 9.37) relates how a soothsayer, Hegesistratus of Elis, cut off his own instep with a concealed weapon after the Spartans had fastened his foot in "iron-bound stocks" (*xylō sidērodetō*).

W. WHITE, JR.

Stoic stoh´ik (Στοϊκός G5121, from στοά G5119, "portico"). In the NT the Stoics are mentioned only once, in Acts 17:18, along with the EPICUREANS. In the same passage (v. 28) PAUL is said to have quoted the words of a Greek poet, "We are his offspring," a line that comes from the Stoic philosopher ARATUS. Beyond this quotation and the fact that the Stoics rejected the idea of a bodily RESURRECTION, Luke gives no information about their views. However, other portions of the NT, especially the epistles of Paul, use language to indirectly allude to concepts associated with Stoicism. (Because one of its tenets was that a person's essential being should not be affected by either pleasure or pain, the English word *stoic* has come to

Coin with the image of the Stoic philosopher/emperor, Marcus Aurelius (A.D. 161–180).

denote someone who is emotionally indifferent to suffering.)

The founder of Stoicism was a Phoenician thinker named Zeno (342–270 B.C.), who by a chance shipwreck arrived in ATHENS; while there, he was both attracted by the rigorous morality of the CYNICS and repelled by their crudities. His successor was CLEANTHES, a respectable old gentleman of little philosophic ability. Chrysippus assumed charge of the school from 232 to 206 B.C., reorganized it, and set it on its successful history of four centuries. Notable Stoic thinkers included SENECA (NERO's tutor), EPICTETUS (c. A.D. 50–130), and the emperor MARCUS AURELIUS (A.D. 121–180).

I. Logic. Under the subject of logic, the Stoics elaborated an empirical, sensory epistemology (a doctrine of KNOWLEDGE based on sensations). The SOUL at birth is without content, and sensations impress images upon it. Zeno insisted that the soul was a body, and Cleanthes crudely compared impressions on the soul with the elevations and depressions made by a signet in wax. When it became evident that this made memory difficult to explain, Chrysippus dropped the idea of elevations and depressions and spoke more vaguely of some sort of qualitative change.

Empiricism with its sensory epistemology is always embarrassed in the attempt to distinguish TRUTH from error. The Epicureans had tried to maintain truth by restricting it to sensory images. In their view, a person can never be deceived as to what his or her sensory image is; deception arises when people suppose, without evidence, that the image resembles an external object. Since this scheme effectively prevents knowledge of the external world, the Stoics made a different attempt. Of course, the criterion of truth in an empirical philosophy cannot be the logical consistency of a system. Somehow truth must be perceived immediately in the sensation itself. Many sensations do not accurately reproduce their objects, but the Stoics claimed that "comprehensive representations" do. This type of sensation carries the mark of its own validity; it has been stamped and sealed by an existing object, and it so clearly resembles the object that it forces one's assent—a person is just incapable of refusing to believe it.

The next important step in producing knowledge is to construct concepts. Many are elaborated by skill and method, but others, called common notions, arise naturally in all people. Human beings are rational because they have these common notions; and any proposition of physics or ethics is to be proved true by analyzing it into these common notions. Unfortunately, the sources for the teaching of Stoicism are extremely fragmentary at this point.

Though the Stoics wished to avoid skepticism, the process of learning had perhaps not yet arrived at knowledge. Zeno illustrated the scheme by a piece of action: he stretched out his fingers and showed the palm of his hand, saying, "Perception is like this"; then, when he had closed his fingers a little, "Assent is like this"; the closed fist he compared with "comprehension"; and finally, when he grasped the fist by the other hand, he said, "This is knowledge and only the wise man has it." Reference to the "wise man" anticipates Stoic ethics.

II. Physics. Stoic physics is essentially a return to the ancient philosopher Heraclitus: all reality is corporeal, composed not of discrete, inanimate atoms, but of living fire. As it appears, the world exhibits a dualism of agent and patient: some of the original fire has become inert and formless, while the remainder is the moving, molding principle, or

God, that permeates all things. Because the universal substance is fire, Stoic cosmology brings this world to an end in a great conflagration. Everything turns to fire.

The supposition has been made that 2 Pet. 3:10–12 borrowed this idea from Stoicism. The similarity, however, is unreal. First, the hylozoistic physics (= all matter has life) on which the Stoics based their conflagration is absent from the Bible. Stoic pantheism or immanentism is incompatible with CREATION, and the Bible proposes no analysis of things as being basically fire or any other element. In the second place, PETER predicted a sudden catastrophe that would be comparable to the flood (see FLOOD, GENESIS), but the Stoics described an ordinary, natural process that is already in progress. The completion is merely the end of the present process. Third, the destruction predicted by Peter is a judgment on sin; the Stoic conflagration is a sort of universal deification. Fourth, this biblical judgment against sin occurs just once; the Stoics, however, in conformity with the usual Greek emphasis on natural cycles, taught that the cosmic history repeats itself time and time again forever, not merely with respect to the conflagration at the end of each cycle, but also with respect to every detail in between. Against this theory of eternal recurrence, AUGUSTINE later laid the charge of deep pessimism. Clearly, therefore, Peter did not borrow from Stoicism.

To continue with other ideas Peter did not borrow, the Stoics held that every individual thing, such as a rock (and the world as a whole), is a composite of this form and matter. Form and matter are both bodies, interpenetrating each other, occupying the same space, forming a "complete mixture." The form or agent is the particular individuating quality, whose mode of action is designated by a term borrowed from morality—tone or tension. It is a spirit or fire or air, more often called a "seminal reason," a small edition of the Reason or Logos that controls the universe. Thus there is but one true cause, God, and also a multiplicity of causes. Their intimate relation ties in with the theory of fate.

III. Fate. Since Reason penetrates all things, every event is dependent on a universal law of Fate, Destiny, or Providence. Cleanthes excepted evil from divine determination, but the other Stoics rejected this inconsistency. Not only physics but logic as well implies divine determinism. Every proposition is either true or false; therefore a true proposition in the future tense states something inevitable. Human beings, in their ignorance, do not know whether a statement such as "Brutus will assassinate Caesar" is true or false. An omniscient mind knows. In any case, if it is true, the assassination is unavoidable; while, if the statement is false, the assassination is impossible. Since the statement must be either true or false, the future is determined.

The objections antiquity raised against determinism are the same ones that have been repeated ever since. The most popular of these is the so-called "lazy argument": if all events are foreordained, it is useless to exert oneself, for if a person's hope is not predestined, he cannot achieve it, while if it is predestined, it will occur anyhow. The Stoics had no trouble disposing of this objection. It was fated that Caesar should be assassinated; but it was fated that Caesar should be assassinated by Brutus, and not just anyhow. Therefore Brutus could not sit idly at home and depend on Fate to commit the assassination for him. The means to every end are as much determined as the end itself; so that to modernize the example, a given college student is foreordained to get an A in Greek philosophy—by studying, and not just anyhow. (See FOREORDAIN; PROVIDENCE.)

IV. Ethics. The Stoics answered all the other objections against Fate as well, but since a most important one concerns ETHICS, the others will be skipped. Opponents of determinism, from the Epicureans to the present day, have argued that moral responsibility depends on free will. The denial of free will, by Luther and Calvin as well as by the Stoics, is supposed to cut the nerve of moral endeavor.

It is interesting to note that the SADDUCEES held to free will, while the PHARISEES, who advocated a stricter lifestyle, were determinists, and so also were the still more demanding ESSENES. The free-will Epicureans, though not so licentious as their enemies have charged, were still no moral giants; but the Stoics strove for rigorous virtue. Luther and Calvin emphasized morality; free-will Romanists were sometimes scandalous.

The Stoics based responsibility on the will. People are responsible for their voluntary actions. The Epicureans and other opponents mistakenly supposed that anyone who says the will has a cause also says that there is no will. But obviously if one's character causes a volition, the volition surely occurs. How could its being cause conflict with its occurrence? Therefore, one is responsible for his own voluntary actions—these are "in our power"; but one is not responsible for involuntary actions or states, such as digestion, breathing, reputation (dependent on other people's opinions), or wealth (dependent on many circumstances beyond one's control).

The Stoics rejected the Epicurean ideal of pleasure and stressed virtue. Instead of persistently avoiding pain, they deemed it worthwhile to run risks in order, for example, to raise a family and discharge civic responsibilities—two activities the Epicureans condemned.

The actual achievement of virtue is difficult. Most people are vicious and foolish; only a few are wise. Just as one can drown in a foot of water as well as in an ocean, and just as a person a mile from Athens is as truly outside Athens as someone 10 mi. away, so he who violates virtue in one point is guilty of all. The change from vice to virtue, from foolishness to wisdom, like entrance into Athens, is a sudden, instantaneous conversion. Unfortunately, few people are converted, and these only late in life after a hard struggle. See further GREEK RELIGION AND PHILOSOPHY II.C.   G. H. CLARK

stomach. Although this English term refers strictly to the upper digestive tract, it can also be used more generally of the abdomen. Thus modern versions sometimes have "stomach" as the rendering of such terms as Hebrew *beṭen* H1061, "belly, womb" (Prov. 13:25 et al.), *ḥōmeš* H2824, "belly, abdomen" (2 Sam. 2:23 et al.), and *mēʿeh* H5055 (in the pl. or dual), usually "entrails, bowels, inner body" (Job 20:14–15), as well as Greek *koilia* G3120 (Matt. 15:17 et al.). The more precise term *stomachos* G5126 is used only by PAUL, who advised TIMOTHY to "use a little wine because of your stomach and your frequent illnesses" (1 Tim. 5:23). As the seat of physical satisfaction or lust, the stomach or belly is mentioned in a number of passages (Prov. 13:25; Jer. 51:34; Ezek. 3:3; Lk. 15:16; Rom. 16:18; Phil. 3:19). See also BELLY.   D. A. BLAIKLOCK

stomacher. This English term, referring to the front part of a bodice, is used by the KJV as the rendering of Hebrew *pĕtigîl* H7345, which occurs only once (Isa. 3:24). The etymology of the Hebrew word is unknown and its meaning is uncertain. Because it stands in contrast to *śaq* H8566 (see SACKCLOTH), it is usually rendered "rich robe" (NRSV) or "fine clothing" (NIV).

stone. A piece of rock of any shape, usually detached from bedrock and of no great size, such as may be found in stream beds (1 Sam. 17:40). Stones have been much used for various constructional purposes (e.g., Gen. 35:14). Stones are often separated from bedrock by human activity, such as quarrying (1 Chr. 22:15; see QUARRY), but they also become detached and shaped by the action of various processes of weathering, such as frost and running water. The term *stone* is commonly used as a synonym for *rock*, particularly where humans have put it to some practical purpose. It is also used with reference to ores in mineral deposits (Deut. 8:9), in relation to ground water bearing aquifers (Num. 20:11), and to gems (see JEWELS AND PRECIOUS STONES).

The importance of stones in the life of the people of the Holy Land, both practically and symbolically, is clear and understandable for dwellers in a generally stony type of environment. See PALESTINE IV. Heaps of stones were used to commemorate memorable events (Gen. 31:46; Josh. 4:5–8), the Mosaic law was inscribed on stone (Exod. 31:18), and the CORNERSTONE of a building had great significance (Ps. 118:22; Eph. 2:20). Stones were used for building altars (Josh. 22:10) as well as dwelling places. The difficulties of walking in stony regions were known to hill-dwelling Israelites (Ps. 91:12). Stones were used for killing people (Acts 7:59), including those being put to death for breaking the law (Deut. 22:24). A tomb hewn out of rock with a stone across the entrance was considered to be the final resting place of Jesus of Nazareth (Matt. 27:60; see BURIAL), but the stone rolled back from the door (28:2) is a representative of the RESURRECTION.

Ancient sling-stones found in the Lachish gate complex.

Both the nature and age of the bedrock of the ANE vary greatly. Over much of the southern part of the region, Precambrian rocks of the Arabo-Nubian Massif appear. These are more than 600 million years old and granite is common. Adjacent to this crystalline massif is a zone of flat-lying sedimentary strata in which sandstones, varying in age from 570–100 million years, predominate. Farther NW, N, and NE the strata are gently folded, with limestones common, and vary in age from 38 to 100 million years. In the region of N Syria, E Kurdistan and W Persia, the rocks are complexly folded and form part of the Alpine mountain belt. Younger sedimentary rocks occur in the Jordan Rift Valley and under the coastal plain of Palestine, while in Syria and down to the region of Lake Tiberias, volcanic activity (see BRIMSTONE) took place spasmodically over the past 38 million years. Thick piles of basalt lava flows developed, one of the youngest flows in Syria having been dated by radiocarbon analysis of carbonized organic matter as being only some 4,000 years old. This great variation in rock type and rock structure, combined with the extremes of climatic condition from desert in the S to snowcapped mountain peaks in the N, has resulted in great contrasts in the stones found in various parts of the region.

On either side of the RED SEA, the joint pattern of the granitic and related crystalline rocks exercised a strong control on the shapes of the exposed pieces of rock. The Red Sea mountains supplied Egypt, and later Imperial Rome, with monumental stones and some metals. There, as in the mountains of the SINAI Peninsula, frost wedging is active at high altitudes. The freezing of water that has seeped down through joints splits the granitic rocks into rough thin rectangular blocks (cf. tables of stone — Exod. 24:12), many of which are easily pried off (34:4). While much of the granite is coarse-grained and even-grained, graphic granite also occurs. In this, quartz intergrowths with FELSPAR resemble hieroglyphs (some have suggested that this could be a possible explanation of Deut. 9:13 and 5:22).

In the district from the Gulf of AQABAH to the DEAD SEA, which includes EDOM, wind played an important role in erosion, particularly in carving wide valleys between mountains of sandstone that often can be seen to rest on a plinth of the Aqabah Granite Complex. Narrow gorges, following faults or master joints, are also found in the district, including the vicinity of PETRA and the Wadi Yitan, where the KING'S HIGHWAY of biblical times ascended from Egypt to Jordan and on to Damascus and Mesopotamia (cf. Num. 20:14–18). However, there has been sufficient water, particularly during periodic floods, to carry off much of the products of weathering. This process has resulted in the exposure of very thick masses of sandstone with many spectacular cliffs. Deposits of both COPPER ore and IRON ore occur, the latter playing an important role in Israel's history in the times of DAVID and SOLOMON, while some of the sandstones are aquifers for ground water.

The plateau of Jordan, E of the River Jordan, is open and flat, with much of the higher ground covered by flint gravels, residuals after wind erosion of the chalk strata that once enclosed the FLINTS. Occasional flat topped hills break the monotony of the stony plateau, with the limestones of the Belqa Series that cap the hills used as building stone. Lightly incised wadis drain eastward to inland depressions that are filled with gravels, sands, salts, and muds. Toward the N there are some volcanic cones, and in Syria thick basalt lava flows form the Hauran Plain. They break down to yield good red soil. In the S, adjacent to the Dead Sea, canyons, such as the Wadi el-Ḥesa have cut down as much as 1,750 meters, generally along fault lines. In the canyon walls are exposed the whole sequence of geological formations, from the Aqabah Granite Complex upward.

The greater part of the hill country W of the River Jordan is hewn from hard well-bedded limestones and dolomites of the Judean Limestone. This rock formation contains aquifers feeding springs and wells, and in it many CAVES have been formed by the action of ground water. These caves have provided places of refuge (1 Sam. 13:6) as well as tombs for burial. The various strata of limestone and dolomite have been readily utilized for various constructional purposes, and with their strong vertical jointing, rockfalls would take place at times of earthquake (cf. Rev. 6:16). In both northern SAMARIA and in various parts of western GALILEE, white CHALK and chalky limestone of the Belqa Series are prominent rock types. The result is generally rounded or hummocky topography with white building stone readily available as rectangular blocks, which parted along joint and bedding planes, for example, in the district around NAZARETH.

A series of depressions, many of them fault bounded, cut through the hill country. They include the BEERSHEBA plain, with Beersheba the principal oasis of the NEGEV, and the ESDRAELON plain. These depressions, and the coastal plain with which they join, are underlain mainly by recently deposited alluvium, much of which is covered by blown sand and dunes. The few small stones that do occur are pieces of soft shale. Mount Carmel (see CARMEL, MOUNT) divides the coastal plain into two, N and S of Haifa. It is made up of a faulted block of Judean limestone, with various strata of well-jointed limestone and dolomite providing flat rectangular blocks easily erected into an edifice, such as an altar (1 Ki. 18:26).

The floor of the Jordan Rift Valley is barren and arid by contrast with the bordering mountain areas. The River Jordan meanders through its flood plain, incised to about 50 meters below the main plain of the valley and flanked on either side by badlands formed by the erosion of the very soft strata making up the main valley floor. South of the Dead Sea some of the rocks are white due to the presence of rock salt. This salt is interbedded with CLAYS, and the district is prone to landslides, particularly when EARTHQUAKES occur. This together with erosion channeling resulting from thunderstorm precipitation has meant the production of odd erosional forms, including some with the appearance of pillars of salt (cf. Gen. 19:26). Earthquake activity, which is common along the length of this rift valley, is probably also responsible for the rockfalls from limestone cliffs that have temporarily blocked the Jordan near Adam, about 24 mi. N of its entrance into the Dead Sea (Josh. 3:13–16); see ADAM (PLACE). D. R. BOWES

stones, precious. See JEWELS AND PRECIOUS STONES.

stoning. The act of throwing stones, usually for the purpose of killing a person. The most common form of capital punishment prescribed by biblical law was stoning. It usually took place outside the city (Lev. 24:23; Num. 15:35–36; 1 Ki. 21:13). The prosecution witnesses (the law required two or more, Deut. 17:6) placed their hands on the offender's head (Lev. 24:14) to transfer the guilt of the whole community to the offender. The witnesses then cast the first stones, and the rest of the people followed (Deut. 17:7). All this was done to purge out evil from the community (22:21).

The following ten offenses were punished by stoning: (1) IDOLATRY, that is, the worship of other gods or any heavenly bodies (Deut. 17:2–7); (2) enticement to idolatry (13:6–11); (3) BLASPHEMY (Lev. 24:14–23; 1 Ki. 21:10–15); (4) child sacrifice to MOLECH (Lev. 20:2–5); (5) spirit DIVINATION (20:27); (6) breaking the SABBATH (Num. 15:32–36); (7) ADULTERY (Deut. 22:21–24); (8) disobedience of a son (21:18–21); (9) violation of the BAN (Josh. 7:25, burning also occurs here); (10) homicide by an ox (Exod. 21:28–32). The last case is the only one concerning an animal, though 19:13 threatens both man and beast with stoning if either touches Mount SINAI. Finally, this punishment may be implied, though not expressly mentioned, when the death penalty is prescribed for the prophet who prophesies in the name of another god (Deut. 13:1–5). (See further R. de Vaux, *Ancient Israel* [1961], 143–63.)

The abundance of STONES in PALESTINE made stoning the most common death penalty. It was also a convenient way to express anger or hatred. It was often threatened (Exod. 17:4; Num. 14:10; 1 Sam. 30:6), especially against Jesus and Paul (Jn. 10:31–33; 11:8; Acts 14:5, 19). Actual cases of death by stoning are recorded several times: Adoram (1 Ki. 12:18; see ADONIRAM), ZECHARIAH (2 Chr. 24:21), and STEPHEN (Acts 7:58–59). See also CRIMES AND PUNISHMENTS.   J. C. MOYER

storax stor′aks. This English term, which can refer generally to any of the trees in the family *Styracaceae*, is used by the KJV Apoc. to render Greek *staktē* ("oil of myrrh"), referring to a PERFUME (Sir. 24:15; this Gk. word is used by the SEPTUAGINT to translate various Heb. terms, as in Gen. 37:25 et al.). The plant may be *Liquidambar orientale*, a tree (not found in the Holy Land) that yields a fragrant resin prepared from the inner bark. In addition, a few modern Bible versions (e.g., NJB) use *storax* to translate Hebrew *nāṭāp* H5753 (Exod. 30:34; see STACTE), and some scholars think that *libneh* H4242 (Gen. 30:37; Hos. 4:13; see POPLAR) refers to *Styrax officinalis* (*FFB*, 178–79). See further FLORA under *Styracaceae*.

store cities. Under the lashes of taskmasters the Israelites built PITHOM and RAMESES as "cities of stores [Heb. *miskĕnôt* H5016]" for PHARAOH (Exod. 1:11). SOLOMON built a number of such supply centers in HAMATH and in other unnamed places throughout his realm (1 Ki. 9:19; 2 Chr. 8:4, 6). During BAASHA's reign, BEN-HADAD concentrated upon and took the store cities of NAPHTALI along with other towns (2 Chr. 16:4). JEHOSHAPHAT, in a program of strengthening Judah, built both store cities and fortresses (17:12). HEZEKIAH too promoted the construction of storage facilities (32:28).

The "store city" apparently had its background in the practice of Egypt to provide storage for the excessive yield of a "fat" year as a reserve against the poor yield of a "lean" year, as was the case in JOSEPH's time. The storage facilities are perhaps illustrated in the long, rectangular, room-like structures found at BETH SHEMESH, LACHISH, and other places. Beginning with Solomon and throughout the reigns of the later kings, these cities were used for storing grains and oil to be sent later to the palace personnel in JERUSALEM (1 Ki. 4:7, 22, 23) or SAMARIA, or to be collected as an important part of government revenue, as is known from the OSTRACA of Samaria and other sources. (See J. Finegan, *Light from the Ancient Past: The Archaeological Background of Judaism and Christianity*, 2nd ed. [1959], 186–88; G. E. Wright, *Biblical Archaeology*, rev. ed. [1962], 131, 163–64.)   H. E. FINLEY

storehouse. MALACHI charged that the people of his day had robbed God because they had failed to bring their tithes into the *bēt hāʾôṣār*, literally

Partial reconstruction of the storehouses at Beersheba.

"house of the treasure," but usually rendered "storehouse" (Mal. 3:10); he evidently had reference to the TEMPLE treasury. See TREASURY OF THE TEMPLE. The same phrase is used in Neh. 10:38 (Heb. MS v. 39), which speaks about the Levites' taking a tenth of the tithes "to the chambers of the storehouse" (NRSV; the NIV here reads, "the storerooms of the treasury"). The NRSV uses "storehouse" also for the term *hāʾôṣār* by itself in Jer. 38:11, which states that EBED-MELECH took men with him to the palace ("the house of the king") in order to get rags and worn-out clothes with which to make a rope to lift JEREMIAH from his prison cistern; in this context the term apparently is an equivalent of "storeroom."   H. E. FINLEY

stork. Although the Hebrew word *ḥăsîdâ* H2884 (meaning "faithful" or "kind") is thought by some to refer to the HERON, the rendering "stork" is generally accepted. Three points in the contexts confirm this translation. (a) The bird in question is unclean (Lev. 11:19; Deut. 14:18); storks feed in muddy places and at some seasons take mainly frogs. (b) It is migratory (Jer. 8:7). (c) It is a large bird (able to lift a heavy basket, Zech. 5:9).

White storks (*Ciconia alba*) have black wings, while black storks (*C. nigra*) are entirely black. Both of them are regular birds of passage through Palestine, and the scavenging marabou stork (*Leptoptilos crumeniferus*) is a rare straggler. In spring white storks fly from their winter haunts in Africa and SW Arabia to their nesting grounds in Europe and Asia, and provide spectacular sights. Flocks of many hundreds come through from the end of February into May. (See BIRD MIGRATION.) They once nested in Palestine ("the stork has its home in the pine trees," Ps. 104:17), but those that stay for the summer now are probably yearlings.

Both on the ground, standing well over 3 ft. tall, and in the air, with neck outstretched and red legs trailing, this black-and-white bird is unmistakable. Dropping down to rest, it quickly spreads out over the fields and marshes to hunt for fish, frogs, and insects. The black stork is smaller; having wintered in S Africa, it comes through in very small groups, following a different path northward.

G. S. CANSDALE

storm. In the Palestinian environment, storms are frequent phenomena. Naturally, they figured prominently in the consciousness of some biblical writers such as the psalmists and the prophet ISAIAH, who saw them variously as a threat to security or a punishment inflicted upon wrongdoers. (Cf. Pss. 55:8; 83:15; Isa. 4:6; 25:4; 28:2.) Three kinds of storm are commonly experienced in PALESTINE. (1) Thunderstorms (see THUNDER) occur mainly at the start of the rainy season, in the autumn when the land is still hot; they are particularly frequent around the Sea of Galilee, where sea air flowing inland passes over the hot basin in which the lake lies. (2) WHIRLWINDS, such as the one by which ELIJAH was caught up (2 Ki. 2), are local vortices with more limited effects. (3) Most important are the desert storms, which occur when the wind blows out from the desert, bringing hot, parching air to the cultivated lands on the desert margins. Often referred to as *sirocco*, these winds blow from the S or E, that is, from the Arabian desert. They are experienced generally at the beginning and at the end of the summer season and frequently are accompanied by choking dust and very high temperatures. Blowing across the land of Palestine, they raise storms as far W as the Mediterranean (cf. Ps. 48:7). Jesus referred to the characteristics of the desert wind in Lk. 12:55.   J. H. PATERSON

storm god. See HADAD.

stove. See OVEN.

Straight Street. This street, the only one identified by name in the NT (Acts 9:11), was located in DAMASCUS, a city within the boundaries of SYRIA but belonging politically to the DECAPOLIS. The city obtained its freedom from Rome shortly after Christ's death and was under an Arabian ruler during the period covered by Acts 9 (see ARETAS). On this street was located the house of a certain JUDAS, where Saul of Tarsus was a guest (see PAUL). It was here that Saul was visited by ANANIAS, and here that he received his eyesight again, signaling his conversion and call.

By current standards, Straight Street (also referred to as *Via Recta*) would more properly be called a lane or alley, since the Greek word translated "street" (*rhymē* G4860) stands for a narrow road. Such a roadway stood in contrast to a broad, open place (*plateia* G4423) in the city. A narrow street bearing the same name exists in the modern city of Damascus. Covered with a Quonset-like structure in places, it begins at the eastern gate of the city and runs W into the center of the city. While this is the probable site of the 1st-cent. street, it is impossible to make a positive identification. Continuous occupation of the location has made excavation impossible, but several structures from Roman times are still preserved, indicating that there have been no major changes in the city's layout since early times.   R. L. THOMAS

stranger. See FOREIGNER.

strange vine. See VINE, VINEYARD II.

strange woman. This expression is used a number of times by the KJV in the book of Proverbs, usually as the translation of Hebrew *zārâ* (fem. of *zār* H2424, "foreign, unauthorized, illegitimate"), which refers either to a prostitute (see PROSTITUTION) or to a married Israelite woman involved in an illicit relationship (Prov. 5:3 et al.; NIV, "adulteress"; NRSV, "loose woman"; NJPS, "forbidden woman").

Strato's Tower. See CAESAREA.

straw. The dry residue of stalky plants. The common Hebrew term for "straw" is *teben* H9320 (Gen. 24:25 et al.; *matben* H5495 only in Isa. 25:10). In the NT, Greek *kalamē* G2811 is used only once in a figurative context (1 Cor. 3:12).

There would be more BARLEY straw available in Palestine than WHEAT straw, for barley was used for feeding horses, donkeys, and cattle, and most of the poor people ate barley BREAD. There was also undoubtedly SPELT straw available. It is uncertain, however, whether the straw mentioned in Exod. 5:7–18 was in fact barley or spelt straw, or whether it was merely the stalks of wild grasses, because the children of Israel were forced to gather what they needed for brick making. In instances where fodder is in view (e.g., Gen. 24:25; Isa. 11:7), perhaps *teben* refers to hay. W. E. SHEWELL-COOPER

street. In the cities of the ANE the streets were very narrow, often only wide enough to allow for the passage of a CHARIOT. They were also winding and without any plan, although very large cities sometimes had one or more avenues. Since refuse was thrown into streets, they were usually very dirty, and scavenger dogs ate a great deal of the garbage. Craftsmen and tradesmen who dealt with similar kinds of products carried on their business in the same streets or quarters. Streets were usually rutted and muddy, since they were not often paved. Herod Agrippa I, however, allowed JERUSALEM to be paved with white stones (Jos. *Ant.* 20.9.7 §222). Usually houses abutted directly onto the streets. Each of the houses had a door on the street side, but the windows were on the opposite side, facing courts. At the gates of the city walls there were large open places for the transaction of business. There justice was dispensed, punishment inflicted, proclamations read, and news spread. S. BARABAS

Strength of Israel. See GLORY.

stringed instruments. See MUSIC, MUSICAL INSTRUMENTS IV.D.

strong drink. See WINE AND STRONG DRINK.

stronghold. This English term, referring to a place that has been fortified or that otherwise provides security, is used to render various Hebrew nouns, especially *mēṣād* H5171 (Jdg. 6.2 et al. and see MASADA), *mĕṣûdâ* H5181 (1 Sam. 22:4), and *miśgāb* H5360, "high point [of refuge]" (2 Sam. 22:1 et al.). It occurs primarily in figurative contexts that speak of God as the protection of his people (Ps. 18:2 et al.). In the NT, Greek *ochyrōma* G4065 occurs once with reference to intellectual pretensions that oppose true knowledge and that must be demolished with spiritual weapons (2 Cor. 10:4). See also FORT; ROCK; TOWER.

structuralism. A term used variously in several academic disciplines to indicate a particular approach whereby the matter under study is regarded as a structure or system (in psychology, for example, *structuralism* refers to an older school that sought to understand the brain and its functions by analyzing the components or basic elements of the mind).

Of special significance for biblical studies was the development of *structural linguistics* in the first half of the 20th cent. Although many linguistic scholars do not refer to themselves as "structuralists" (a label that has a variety of connotations), virtually all of them recognize the basic tenet that language cannot be understood properly unless it is viewed as a system of structural relations or oppositions. For instance, a *phoneme* (a linguistically significant sound) must be defined not merely on the basis of its acoustic form, but also, and more importantly, in terms of how it contrasts to other similar phonemes. Similarly, the vocabulary of a language is best understood when each word is studied as part of a specific semantic field or domain, that is, a network of terms that sustain a meaning relationship (synonymy, antonymy, etc.) with one another.

(The seminal work on this principle was a set of class lectures by Ferdinand de Saussure, published posthumously by two of his students in 1916 as *Cours de linguistique générale*. For its relevance to the study of the Bible, see M. Silva, *Biblical Words and Their Meaning: An Introduction to Lexical Semantics*, rev. ed. [1994], chs. 4–6.)

The success of the structural approach in modern linguistics had a strong impact on other disciplines. Particularly well known is the work of the anthropologist C. Lévi-Strauss, who sought to understand various aspects of culture (such as kinship and myth) by appropriating the terminology of structuralism. In the process, however, the relevant principles were applied with less precision, a problem that became more evident subsequently when structural ideas were used in the study of literature and society (e.g., by R. Barthes; see the criticisms by Martin Krampen in *Classics of Semiotics*, ed. M. Krampen et al. [1987], 78–83). At this point, *structuralism* comes to mean a philosophical theory about the way human beings create intellectual systems. On this basis, some biblical scholars have developed an approach known as *structural exegesis*, which usually refers to the study of nonlinguistic relationships, such as those involving human self-expression and thought patterns. (See D. Jobling, *The Sense of Biblical Narrative: Structural Analyses in the Hebrew Bible*, 2 vols., 2nd ed. [1986]; D. Patte, *Structural Exegesis for New Testament Critics* [1990]; *ABD*, 6:214–16.)

stubble. The part of the plant stem left standing in the field after the crop has been harvested. The Hebrew term for "stubble" is *qaš H7990*, which in some instances may refer to CHAFF (e.g., Ps. 83:13), that is, the husks or fine particles that are separated from the grain during threshing and winnowing. The Israelites were forced to go to the fields to gather stubble because they were not permitted to use STRAW in their brickmaking (Exod. 5:12). God's consuming wrath is depicted in terms of a raging fire sweeping across a field of stubble (15:7). LEVIATHAN is portrayed as a monster strong and impregnable, unaffected by slingstones; his tough hide turns such stones into "stubble" (Job 41:28). Isaiah and other later prophets declared that evildoers were the object of God's judgment; they would face a demise like that of fire devouring stubble (Isa. 5:24; 47:14; Joel 2:5; Obad. 18; Nah. 1:10; Mal. 4:1).   H. E. FINLEY

stuff. This English term is used a number of times by the KJV, mainly as the rendering of Hebrew *kĕlî H3998* ("vessel, equipment," etc.), which in the plural can mean "goods, possessions" (Gen. 31:37 et al.). The RSV uses the phrase "scarlet stuff" frequently in Exodus to translate *tôlaʿat šānî* (*H9106* + *H9357*), which refers to the crimson-colored cloth employed for the curtains of the TABERNACLE (Exod. 26:1 et al.; cf. *šĕnî tôlaʿat* [in Lev. 14:4–6, 49–52; Num. 19:6], apparently a scarlet cord used for purification).

stumbling block. This English expression is used a number of times in Bible versions to render Hebrew *mikšôl H4842* ("hindrance") and Greek *skandalon G4998* ("trap"). In the OT the cause of stumbling may be literal, as an obstacle in the path of a blind man (Lev. 19:14), but most often it is used figuratively to picture the judgment of God against the rebellious (Jer. 6:21; Ezek. 3:20). Ethically, the stumbling block is that which causes iniquity, whether gold and silver (Ezek. 7:19) or idols (14:3–4, 7; 44:12).

In the NT the idea of "striking against" an object so as to stumble speaks figuratively of a weaker brother who stumbles in his Christian walk (Rom. 14:13; 1 Cor. 8:9). The cause of stumbling lies in the action of the stronger Christian who in taking advantage of his superior understanding of spiritual liberty fails to show consideration for one whose conscience is more easily offended. The stronger reference to a stumbling block in the NT is built on the figure of a trap that is baited for the unsuspecting prey. This term is used in connection with the failure of Israel to recognize her suffering Messiah (Rom. 11:9; 1 Cor. 1:23). In this case the CROSS is not viewed as a trap. Rather the preconceived ideas of Israel regarding the person and work of MESSIAH were the cause of their downfall, since these ideas excluded the possibility of his suffering. See OFFENCE.   R. L. THOMAS

Sua soo'uh. See SIA.

Suah soo'uh (סוּחָה *H6053*, meaning uncertain). Son of Zophah and descendant of ASHER (1 Chr. 7:36),

Suba soo′buh. KJV Apoc. form of SUBAS (1 Esd. 5:34).

Subai soo′bi (Συβαι). Ancestor of a family of temple servants (NETHINIM) who returned from the EXILE (1 Esd. 5:30; the RSV identifies him with SHALMAI).

Subas soo′buhs (Σουβας). KJV Suba. Ancestor of a family of SOLOMON's SERVANTS who returned from exile with ZERUBBABEL (1 Esd. 5:34; the name is not found in the parallel lists, Ezra 2:57 and Neh. 7:59).

suburbs. This English term—not in its modern meaning of built-up areas surrounding a city center, but in a more general sense—is used frequently by the KJV (esp. in Josh. 21 and 1 Chr. 6) to render Hebrew *migrāš* H4494, which evidently refers to demarcated open lands outside the walls of a CITY. These areas were built over only later as population increased or particular groups were forbidden to settle within the walls. Thus one finds a request for "suburbs … for our cattle" (Josh. 21:2 KJV) and a reference to "the fields of the suburbs" where some priests lived (2 Chr. 31:19 KJV). That such outskirts played an essential part in the life and economy of the urban community in Palestine is shown by their inclusion with each town apportioned to the tribes of Israel. The common rendering "pasturelands" (cf. NIV) seems to fit some contexts, but this meaning apparently arose as a result of a questionable etymology (as though from *gāraš* H1763, "to drive out [cattle]"; see J. Barr in *JSS* 29 [1989]: 15–31, esp. 21). J. H. PATERSON

Sucathite soo′kuh-thit (שׂוּכָתִי H8460, gentilic of the otherwise unattested place name שׂוֹכָה, meaning unknown). KJV Suchathite. Among the descendants of CALEB (through his son HUR and grandson SALMA) are listed three "clans of scribes who lived at Jabez: the Tirathites, Shimeathites and Sucathites. These are the Kenites who came from Hammath, the father of the house of Recab" (1 Chr. 2:55). Nothing else is known about these clans, and their names cannot be traced to a particular person or place. On the relationship between Calebites and Kenites, see discussion under JABEZ (PLACE).

Succession Narrative. See SAMUEL, BOOKS OF III.B.

Succoth suhk-uhth′ (סֻכּוֹת H6111, "booths"). TNIV Sukkoth. **(1)** A city within the tribal territory of GAD, generally identified with modern Tell Deir ʿAlla, a mound just N of the JABBOK River and about 3 mi. E of the JORDAN (H. J. Franken has suggested that Succoth should be identified with nearby Tell Ekhṣaṣ, but few have followed him). Succoth is first mentioned in connection with JACOB's travels after he wrestled with the angel of the Lord by the Jabbok River and was reconciled to his brother ESAU the next day (Gen. 33:17). The explanation this passage gives for the name Succoth (deriving it from Jacob's cattle booths or stalls) does not necessarily mean that Jacob founded the city. Later, in the days of JOSHUA, Succoth is mentioned along with ZAPHON as part of the inheritance of the tribe of Gad (Josh. 13:27).

GIDEON and his army, while pursuing the Midianites to victory, were ill-treated by the elders of Succoth and the neighboring city of Penuel, both of which refused to supply food (Jdg. 8:5–16). See PENUEL (PLACE). Gideon's punishment of the city of Succoth might well be identified with the destruction of a large sanctuary in Tell Deir ʿAlla, an event dated to the first half of the 12th cent. (Y. Aharoni, *The Land of the Bible: A Historical Geography*, rev. ed. [1979], 284 n. 224). SOLOMON found suitable clay ground to cast the large bronze vessels for the temple near Succoth (1 Ki. 7:46; 2 Chr.

Ruins of Tell el-Maskhutah, which some identify with the Egyptian town of Succoth.

4:17). In the Psalms, Succoth is referred to as the symbol of the victorious occupation of the country of Canaan E of the Jordan (Pss. 60:6; 108:7).

(2) A city in EGYPT between RAMESES and ETHAM; it was the first stop of the Israelites at the time of the exodus (Exod. 12:37; 13:20; Num. 33:5–6). The city is tentatively identified with modern Tell el-Maskhuta, a border fortress in the eastern portion of Wadi Tumilat, W of the bitter lakes. See discussion under PITHOM. A. JOHNSON

Succoth Benoth suhk´uhth-bee´noth (סֻכּוֹת בְּנוֹת H6112, "booths of daughters," but the form is prob. a corruption of an Akk. name). TNIV Sukkoth Benoth. A Babylonian deity. After defeating the northern kingdom of Israel and carrying away hostages, the Assyrians brought in peoples of various regions of Upper and Lower MESOPOTAMIA and settled them in SAMARIA. There were Babylonians among these peoples who had Succoth Benoth as their god or goddess (2 Ki. 17:30). In extrabiblical sources no such deity is attested, but many scholars hold that the name may derive from Ṣarpanitu ("shining," later Zēr-bānītu, "seed-creating"), who was MARDUK's consort; alternatively, the reference could be to ISHTAR, who was sometimes called Bānītu ("[female] creator"; see M. Cogan and H. Tadmor, *II Kings*, AB 11 [1988], 211).

Other possibilities have been considered. In its Hebrew form, Succoth Benoth may allude to the existence of booths or shrines where girls engaged in sacred PROSTITUTION. The first part of the name, however, is sometimes thought to reflect an Akkadian loanword, such as *sakkû* ("assign, dedicate") or *sakkud* (possibly referring to Saturn; see SAKKUTH); others derive it from a NW Semitic root, *skn*, "image" (E. Lipiński in *UF* 5 [1973], 202–4; see further *DDD*, 821–22). H. E. FINLEY

Sud suhd. KJV Apoc. form of SIA (1 Esd. 5:29).

Sudias soo´dee-uhs (Σουδιας). Ancestor of a family of Levites that returned from the EXILE (1 Esd. 5:26; possibly the same as HODAVIAH in the parallels, Ezra 2:40; 3:9; Neh. 7:43).

Suetonius swi-toh´nee-uhs. Gaius Suetonius Tranquillus was born in the tragic "year of the four emperors," A.D. 69, and died about 140. He was one of the few well-known Roman writers who was actually born in ROME. Suetonius was of equestrian rank, practiced law, and was for a time secretary to the Emperor HADRIAN (reigned 117–138). Among his many works, *Lives of the Caesars*, which survives almost intact from Julius CAESAR to DOMITIAN, had immense influence in giving a biographical turn to Roman historiography. Though no great historian, Suetonius endeavored to write objectively, and his collected material, if often biased and unfair, has immense value. Along with TACITUS, he is a primary source for the history of Imperial Rome during NT times. Of particular interest to biblical students is his apparent reference to Christ (wrongly written *Chrestus*): "Because the Jews at Rome caused continuous disturbances at the instigation of Chrestus, he [CLAUDIUS] expelled them from the city" (*Claudius* 25.4; cf. Acts 18:2). (See B. Baldwin, *Suetonius* [1983]; A. Wallace-Hadrill, *Suetonius: The Scholar and His Caesars* [1983].)
E. M. BLAIKLOCK

suffering. Numerous Hebrew and Greek terms convey such ideas as suffering, distress, anguish, pain, torment, and so on. The biblical contexts suggest some answers to the extremely difficult question as to why there is so much suffering in the world: (1) divine judgment for sin, (2) empathy for another's misery, (3) the vicarious bearing of another's penalty, (4) authentic repentance and faith in the Lord, (5) a warning to prevent a greater evil, or (6) discipline for training in Christlikeness. The appropriate response to each kind of suffering is as different as its raison d'être. Such significant differences make generalizations about the purpose of all suffering improper and misleading. In an attempt to avoid the error of generalization as far as possible, each type of suffering is considered separately below. More than one of these purposes may be operative in any given instance of suffering. When that is the case, however, the reasons may be more readily recognized if first clearly distinguished.

I. Judgmental suffering. How did human beings become subject to suffering? As created, both they and nature were "very good" (Gen. 1:31). What made life on earth a "vale of tears"? Neither a

SUFFERING

The sufferings of Christ are depicted in this painting of the Stations of the Cross from the Church of Emmaus.

capricious act of God nor fate. It was rather ADAM and EVE's pretentious and unbelieving violation of God's will. The pains of childbirth and of hard labor may be traced to divine JUDGMENT upon the first SIN (3:16–19). See FALL, THE.

In a fallen world we may bring suffering upon ourselves by failure to employ our God-given resources in accord with wisdom: "an idle person will suffer hunger" (Prov. 19:15 NRSV); "a companion of fools suffers harm" (13:20); "A prudent man sees danger and takes refuge, / but the simple keep going and suffer for it" (22:3; cf. 27:12). "Some give freely, yet grow all the richer; / others withhold what is due, and only suffer want" (11:24 NRSV). Apparently God sustains a providential order in which people are judged for laziness, lack of foresight, companionship of fools, and greed. Furthermore, distress may result from social pressures to condemn an innocent man. PILATE's wife sent word to him, "Don't have anything to do with that innocent man, for I have suffered a great deal today in a dream because of him" (Matt. 27:19).

Judgmental suffering also follows for sins against God's revelation through prophets and apostles. Israel's adults, so wonderfully delivered from Egypt, nevertheless continually murmured against MOSES and God. For their faithlessness they suffered and died in the wilderness; their children also suffered (Num. 14:31–33). Awareness of family and national solidarity was explicit in the culture. However, the children suffered only temporarily; they entered the Promised Land. In Dostoevsky's *The Brothers Karamazov*, Ivan cannot believe that children "share their fathers' responsibility for *all* their fathers' crimes" (emphasis added). Is it taught in the Bible that they do? As in the wilderness, judgment upon the head of a family or nation may have its temporal implications for those in the family or national unit. But EZEKIEL made it clear that a righteous father may have a wicked son, or a wicked father a righteous son. "The soul who sins is the one who will die. The son will not share the guilt of the father, nor will the father share the guilt of the son. The righteousness of the righteous man will be credited to him, and the wickedness of the wicked will be charged against him" (Ezek. 18:20).

Repeatedly Israel faced judgmental suffering for her iniquities (Ps. 107:17) and her guilt (Isa. 24:5–6). JEREMIAH cried out, "Oh, my anguish, my anguish! / I writhe in pain. / Oh, the agony of my heart! / My heart pounds within me, / I cannot keep silent. / For I have heard the sound of the trumpet; / I have heard the battle cry" (Jer. 4:19). Judah was destroyed because of the greatness of her iniquity (13:22). Jerusalem lay in ruins and Zion suffered bitterly for "the multitude of her transgressions" (Lam. 1:5 NRSV). Later NEHEMIAH confessed, "they were disobedient and rebelled against you and cast your law behind their back and killed your prophets, who had warned them in order to turn them back to you, and they committed great blasphemies. Therefore you gave them into the hands of their enemies, who made them suffer" (Neh. 9:26–27a NRSV).

The NT portrayal of judgmental suffering is equally severe. For premeditated lying to the apostles and the HOLY SPIRIT, ANANIAS and SAPPHIRA suddenly died (Acts 5:1–11). Those who profaned the Lord's body and blood at the communion table faced judgment. "For anyone who eats and drinks without recognizing the body of the Lord eats and drinks judgment on himself. That is why many among you are weak and sick, and a number of you have fallen asleep" (1 Cor. 11:29–30). As a result of sin the creation is subjected to futility and in bondage to decay until the revealing of the sons of God (Rom. 8:18–21).

In the judgment the believer's works of "wood, hay or straw" will be burned up and "he will suffer loss" (1 Cor. 3:12, 15). At death Lazarus went to ABRAHAM'S BOSOM, but the rich man in HADES called out, "I am in agony in this fire" (Lk. 16:24; see LAZARUS AND DIVES). When the Lord Jesus is revealed from heaven in flaming fire, taking vengeance on those who do not know God and do not obey the gospel, "They will be punished with everlasting destruction and shut out from the presence of the Lord" (2 Thess. 1:9).

II. Empathic suffering. In the face of intense suffering the prophets were appalled. Concerned for the church at CORINTH, PAUL wrote to them "out of great distress and anguish of heart and with many tears" (2 Cor. 2:4). All of us are to weep with those who weep (Rom. 12:15). Some suffering arises not from sin but from love. We may enter fully through imagination and concern into another's feelings. Empathy with others who suffer produces suffering.

Does God experience empathic suffering? In the days of NOAH, when the Lord saw that the thoughts of the human heart were constantly evil, he "was grieved that he had made man on the earth, and his heart was filled with pain" (Gen. 6:6). In sin God takes no pleasure; he permits it or, in the older English, suffers it. As H. Wheeler Robinson has said, "The only way in which moral evil can enter into the consciousness of the morally good, is as suffering" (*Suffering: Human and Divine* [1939]). God is not an impersonal principle, but the living Lord of Abraham, Isaac, and Jacob. With loving empathy he entered fully into the sufferings of Israel. "In all their distress he too was distressed, / and the angel of his presence saved them. / In his love and mercy he redeemed them; / he lifted them up and carried them / all the days of old" (Isa. 63:9).

Some misunderstanding of God's relation to suffering arises from a failure to do justice to his immanence and transcendence. Karl Barth's earliest writings had an extreme emphasis upon divine transcendence far beyond anything even analogous to human suffering. Recognizing this, Barth later stressed the humanity of God in the incarnate Christ. Barth held that, in Christ, God suffered all that man suffers. God in Christ suffered intensely during the PASSION week right up to the cross. At that point Barth, with the historic church, stopped. On the cross God the Father did not die. Some theologians, however, did not stop, for their God died never to rise. They stressed God's immanent involvement with humanity to the exclusion of his transcendent power over the deepest anguish of death itself.

Belief in a God who permits suffering, others think, destroys human freedom to alleviate it. One must remember, however, that permission is not pleasure. The God who suffers with the suffering encourages removal of the cause. "Why will you die, O house of Israel? For I take no pleasure in the death of anyone, says the Sovereign LORD. Repent and live!" (Ezek. 18:31b–32). Although God permits suffering, he has acted at inestimable cost to provide a just ground on which to justify the ungodly.

III. Vicarious suffering. Jesus Christ became incarnate "so that by his death he might destroy him who holds the power of death—that is, the devil—and free those who all their lives were held in slavery by their fear of death" (Heb. 2:14–15). The Lord did not simply permit sin; he came into the world to fight it. His decisive defeat of SATAN inspires sacrifice to remove the deepest causes of suffering.

To accomplish his purpose, Jesus had to "suffer many things and be rejected by the elders, chief priests and teachers of the law, and he must be killed and on the third day be raised to life" (Lk. 9:22; cf. 17:25; 24:26; Matt. 16:21; Mk. 8:31). The battle with evil necessitated suffering. Furthermore, the messianic predictions called for it. The risen Lord explained, "This is what is written: The Christ will suffer and rise from the dead on the third day" (Lk. 24:46). PETER declared that God had foretold by the mouth of all the prophets that his Christ should suffer. Some of Peter's hearers had, in ignorance, contributed to the fulfillment of that prophecy (Acts 3:18). The prophets themselves had been curious about the time and the Sufferer of whom they wrote (1 Pet. 1:11). Peter goes on record as a witness to the sufferings of Christ, as well as to the glory to be revealed (5:1).

Paul explained and proved from the Jewish Scriptures that it was necessary for Christ to suffer and to rise from the dead (Acts 17:3; 26:23). The writer of Hebrews stressed the vicarious nature of Christ's agony in that Jesus suffered death for (in behalf of) everyone (Heb. 2:9). Christ's substitutionary ATONEMENT is frequently mentioned in the NT. Furthermore, Jesus, as the author of salvation, was made perfect through suffering (2:10). He suffered temptation so that he could help the tempted (2:18). He did not suffer death repeatedly, but once for all (9:26). Just as sacrifices had been burned outside the camp, Jesus "suffered outside the city gate to make the people holy through his own blood" (13:12).

Through faith in the One who suffered in their place, sinners are delivered from eternal anguish. No stoic denial of suffering will change our sinfulness. Resentment does not help. To alleviate the suffering which is bound up with judgment on our sin, we must repent and trust Christ.

IV. Testimonial suffering. Inner distress, however, may result from genuine commitment to a Christlike life. Although believers receive a new nature, their old nature is not annihilated. Daily the Christian must combat temptations to serve the FLESH. Genuine Christian living is not merely for pleasure. It is not only an aesthetic existence, Søren Kierkegaard insisted. Neither is it a life of hypocritical law-keeping. A merely ethical existence is not a Christian existence. The genuinely religious life is one of continuous repentance and continuous commitment. Believers, aware constantly that they are not living up to the perfect ideal and that they are nothing apart from the grace of God, cast themselves upon divine grace. So, as Edward John Carnell explained in *The Burden of Søren Kierkegaard*, inner suffering is a doorway to all the blessings of the Christian life. The real satisfactions of life lie in the area of suffering, not indulgence and pleasure. So this type of suffering may testify, not to judgment on sin, but to an authentic Christian commitment.

People who choose to live for righteousness in an evil world must expect suffering also from external sources. Service for the Savior runs counter to the aspirations of this world's powers. Followers of Christ may suffer "for his sake" (Phil. 1:29 KJV), "for righteousness' sake" (1 Pet. 3:14 KJV), for the kingdom of God (2 Thess. 1:5), for the gospel (2 Tim. 2:9), "for the Name" (Acts 5:41), for the purpose of resisting SATAN (1 Pet. 2:19; 4:16; 5:9). Such PERSECUTION indicates that the believer shares or partakes of Christ's sufferings (2 Cor. 1:5; 1 Pet. 4:13).

Through intense suffering JOB gave testimony to the integrity of his trust in God. Satan charged that Job's faith depended upon temporal benefits received. Thereupon, God allowed the devil to test Job's allegiance by taking away all that he possessed (Job 1:9–12), and even his health (2:4–6). Calamity in Job's case was not judgmental for certain sins. To his "comforters" it seemed that Job must have been a hypocrite or a liar, but his plight was not penal. It was a test of his integrity as a testimony to others.

Jesus' disciples also fell into the error of thinking that all sickness was the result of some sin. Upon seeing the man born blind, they asked, "Rabbi, who sinned, this man or his parents, that he was born blind?" Jesus' response was, "Neither this man nor his parents sinned ... but this happened so that the work of God might be displayed in his life" (Jn. 9:2–3). The healing of the man born blind ended a life of suffering that was permitted so that he might become a key witness to the messiahship of Christ.

What response is appropriate when we experience suffering as a testimony to our unhypocritical trust in the Lord? Remembering Christ's example of endurance under stress, we shall follow in his steps (1 Pet. 2:21). One should not forget the heroes of faith who suffered "jeers and flogging, while still others were chained and put in prison. They were stoned; they were sawed in two; they were put to death by the sword. They went about in sheepskins and goatskins, destitute, persecuted and mistreated" (Heb. 11:36–37). Like Moses, one may consider suffering abuse for Christ greater wealth than the treasures of Egypt (11:26). So believers shall complete the suffering necessary for the building of the church (Col. 1:24), knowing that it assures future glory (1 Pet. 4:13). In comparison with that eternal glory, the present momentary affliction is slight (Rom. 8:18; 2 Cor. 4:17).

V. Preventative suffering. God may allow physical suffering to keep one from more serious spiritual problems. PAUL found it so. He said, "To keep me from becoming conceited because of these surpassingly great revelations, there was given me a thorn in my flesh, a messenger of Satan, to torment me" (2 Cor. 12:7). Because of this weakness, Paul had to rely more completely upon God's GRACE. In the midst of energetic service under most difficult conditions he found that grace sufficient. When weak in himself, he was strong in the Lord (vv. 8–10).

Pain may also be a warning signal of physical dangers. Without pain people would be subject to many calamities. A fourteen-year old girl in London who never felt any pain was covered with the scars of cuts, burns, and abrasions. According to the British Medical Research Council she was normal in other respects. She had bitten off the tip of her tongue, crushed her fingers, and fractured her thigh—all without pain. Previously a young playmate had yanked out handfuls of her hair. An attack of appendicitis would pass unnoticed until too late to operate.

Some suffering in a fallen world is a beneficial warning of the danger of more tragic possibilities. A medical doctor writing on psychosomatic illnesses says, "Pain is a sign that action should be taken; it implies that if action is not taken, the survival chances of the organism are going to decrease." For such signs one may indeed be thankful. Sometimes physical suffering becomes a sign of spiritual need. If a person flat on his back begins to look up to the Savior, there is also reason for gratitude.

VI. Educational suffering. The greatest good of the Christian life is not freedom from pain; it is Christlikeness. God works all things together for good by surrounding us with conditions that help us conform to the image of his Son (Rom. 8:28–29). Christ's life was one of total conflict with the forces of evil. As his followers, then, "We are hard pressed on every side, but not crushed; perplexed, but not in despair; persecuted, but not abandoned; struck down, but not destroyed. We always carry around in our body the death of Jesus, so that the life of Jesus may also be revealed in our body" (2 Cor. 4:8–10).

God is far less concerned with the comfort than with the character of his people. What produces character? Suffering produces endurance, and endurance produces character (Rom. 5:3–4). When we fail to endure, we may require DISCIPLINE as does any child: "God disciplines us for our good, that we may share in his holiness. No discipline seems pleasant at the time, but painful. Later on, however, it produces a harvest of righteousness and peace for those who have been trained by it" (Heb. 12:10–11). Anyone who does not experience the heavenly Father's discipline is an illegitimate child. "My son, do not make light of the Lord's discipline, / and do not lose heart when he rebukes you, / because the Lord disciplines those he loves, / and he punishes everyone he accepts as a son" (vv. 5–6, quoting Prov. 3:11–12).

The follower of the Lord not only passively accepts discipline, but actively disciplines himself. Like an athlete in training, Paul exercised self-control. To keep from being disqualified after preaching to others, he pommeled his body and subdued it (1 Cor. 9:25–27). The Bible does not support extreme ASCETICISM and self-flagellation as virtuous in themselves; neither does it underwrite self-indulgence as Christian liberty. There is freedom from the domination of sin in order to develop a Christlike character. Respecting that LIBERTY, many count all else refuse in order that they may "know Christ and the power of his resurrection and the fellowship of sharing in his sufferings, becoming like him in his death" (Phil. 3:10).

Christianity, Louis Bouyer explained, "does not encourage an unhealthy algolagnia; on the contrary, it offers us the possibility of making suffering, like death itself, fruitful." In one of his last *Letters to Malcolm*, C. S. Lewis observed that purification normally involves suffering. Looking back over his life he mused, "Most real good that has been done me in this life has involved it." To achieve the higher values in a fallen world requires disciplinary suffering. The immature may complain and cry; the mature will accept the fact and by God's grace discipline themselves.

VII. Conclusion. In summary, we need the wisdom of God to determine whether a given experience of suffering is judgmental, empathic, vicarious, testimonial, preventative, or educational. The very possibility of condemnation and eternal anguish for persistent pride, unbelief, and disobedience is a divine summons to repent. To wait until judgment begins to fall is sheer folly. Today is the day of salvation.

Whoever suffers a conviction of sin can count on divine empathy. God takes no delight in the necessity of judging the ungodly. He so desires their deliverance that he gave his Son to suffer their penalty at Calvary. For that vicarious suffering all believers give praise. Furthermore, they are grateful to be counted worthy of suffering with him in the battle against unrighteousness. With rejoicing we testify in the midst of suffering to the integrity of our commitment. We accept the warnings of physical pain and act to avoid the dangers signaled. We discipline ourselves and readily accept that of our heavenly Father.

Some experiences may not fit in any of these categories, alone or in combination. From the present limited perspective, no one can obtain all the answers. But the unknowns do not render meaningless that which we do know. As Albertus Pieters argued, "We may know little, but the little that we do know is more valid for our interpretation of the world than the much that we do not know."

(See further L. D. Weatherhead, *Why Do Men Suffer?* [1936]; C. S. Lewis, *The Problem of Pain* [1948]; E. F. Sutcliffe, *Providence and Suffering in the Old and New Testaments* [1953]; C. S. Lewis, *A Grief Observed* [1961]; M. Proudfoot, *Suffering: A Christian Understanding* [1964]; K. Kitamori, *Theology of the Pain of God* [1965]; E. S. Gerstenberger and W. Schrage, *Suffering* [1980]; C. H. Talbert, *Learning through Suffering: The Educational Value of Suffering in the New Testament and its Milieu* [1991]; F. Lindström, *Suffering and Sin: Interpretations of Illness in the Individual Complaint Psalms* [1994]; D. J. Harrington, *Why Do We Suffer? A Scriptural Approach to the Human Condition* [2000]; P. Hicks, *The Message of Evil and Suffering: Light into Darkness* [2006].)   G. R. LEWIS

Suffering Servant. See SERVANT OF THE LORD.

Sukkiim suhk′ee-im. See SUKKIITES.

Sukkiites suhk′ee-ites (סֻכִּיִּים H6113, derivation unknown). Also Sukkiim; KJV Sukkiims (superfluous English pl. form). A people group, evidently from Africa, who along with Libyans and Cushites assisted SHISHAK, king of Egypt, when he invaded Palestine (2 Chr. 12:3). The SEPTUAGINT renders the name as *Trōglodytai* ("cave dwellers"), apparently referring to an Ethiopian tribe mentioned by HERODOTUS (*Hist.* 4.183; this group is now identified with the Tibboos). The true identity of the Sukkiites is unknown.

Sukkoth suhk-uhth′. The Hebrew name of the Feast of Booths (Tabernacles). See FEASTS I.B.3. See also SUCCOTH and SUCCOTH BENOTH.

sulfur. See BRIMSTONE.

Sumer soo′muhr (from Akk. *šumeru*, although the Sumerians themselves used the term *kengir* [KI-EN-GI]). The ancient name of the land located in what is today the southern half of Iraq in the valleys of the TIGRIS and EUPHRATES Rivers. Other names used in antiquity to denote this area are Babylonia (see ASSYRIA AND BABYLONIA) and SHINAR. See also MESOPOTAMIA.

 I. Geography
 II. History
  A. The arrival of the Sumerians
  B. The early dynastic period
  C. The domination by the Akkadians and the Guti
  D. The Sumerian revival
 III. Social and economic institutions
 IV. Religion

I. Geography. The northernmost limit of the ancient land of Sumer was probably in the vicinity of modern Baghdad. Among the old cultural centers that fell within the borders of the land were the cities of Kish (Tell el-Oheimir), Kid Nun (Jemdet Nasr), Nippur (Niffer), Lagash (Telloh), Uruk (Warka), Ur (Tell Muqayyir), Eridu (Abu Shahrain), Shuruppak (Fara), Larsa (Senkere), and Umma (Jocha). Of these illustrious cities, two are mentioned in the OT, Uruk (see ERECH) and Ur.

Sumer.

Here also was located BABYLON, but the period of this city's first flourishing (c. 1800 B.C.) follows the end of the Sumerian periods in the history of Iraq.

II. History. The history of Sumer properly speaking is the history of her separate cities, since during the period under consideration they seldom acted in complete concert. Each city had its claims to fame: its local god, temples, monuments, or rulers. Among the more illustrious of rulers, Kish could claim Enmebaragesi, Akka, and Mesilim; Uruk could claim the famous GILGAMESH (around whose exploits the epic named after him was woven); Ur could boast Meskalamdug, Mesannepada, Urnammu, and Shulgi; Lagash could recount the deeds of Urnanshe, Urukagina, Gudea, and Eannatum. Each of the important cities had its own local deity or deities. Uruk had the goddess Inanna and the sky-god An. Ur venerated the moon-god Suen. Eridu was the cult center of the god of the sweet waters, Enki (also known as Ea). NIPPUR contained the temple of the air-god ENLIL. In Sippar was the seat of worship for the sun-god Utu.

A. The arrival of the Sumerians (c. 3300–3000 B.C.). The early peoples who migrated into the Tigris-Euphrates valley called themselves "the black-headed peoples." Their place of origin is unknown and has given rise to various theories. Since they employ the same ideogram for "mountain" and "land," their homeland is thought to have been in the NE (Caucasus). Their earliest settlements, however, were in the S, so another view is that they came from the E by sea, which may explain why, like the Semites who were also in the same area, they were not reinvigorated by periodic fresh immigration.

Archaeological excavations have demonstrated that the southern half of Iraq was inhabited before the coming of the Sumerians. Until relatively recent times the prehistory proper, the Stone Age of Iraq, was virtually unknown. The most ancient traces of human presence in Iraq were found in 1949 at Barda-Balka between Kirkuk and Suleimaniyah. They consisted of Paleolithic flint tools: heart-shaped hand axes and flake side-scrapers. They have been attributed to the beginning of the Middle Paleolithic period, about 120,000 years ago.

In southern Iraq the oldest known culture is that of a people somehow connected with the contemporary Halaf people in the N (c. 4500 B.C.). Traces of their presence have been found at Qalʿat Hajj Muhammed (near Uruk) and at ERIDU. They were followed by people whose culture is called Ubaidian from the name of the site (Tell al-ʿUbaid), where its remains were first identified. Around

4000 this people established the villages that grew into the cities of Eridu, Ur, Nippur, Kish, Adab, Kullab, Larsa, and Isin. Their language has been called "Proto-Euphratean," although all that is known of it is what has survived in certain pre-Sumerian nouns and the names of some Sumerian cities which may have been retained from earlier times. This culture, first imported into the southern delta, expanded northward along the two rivers and eventually spread through Upper Mesopotamia, N Syria, and Cilicia.

Farmers in the S followed a simple method of "basin irrigation," which, however, sufficed to support a growing population. The Ubaidians had already developed many skills and occupations, including those of the farmer, cattle breeder, fisherman, the potter, smith, stone mason, carpenter, reed-mat weaver, and worker in leather. The temple was always the largest and best-constructed building in the Ubaid village. Furthermore, the same traditions of religious architecture were followed on the same site from the Ubaid period to early historical times (c. 4000–3000). The temple, it would appear, was already the center of most economic, social, and governmental activities.

To the 500-year span of 3300 to 2800 B.C. have been assigned the Uruk and the Proto-Literate periods. To it one may assign also the coming of the Sumerians. There is no such thing as a Sumerian "race." The skulls from Sumerian graves are either dolichocephalic or brachycephalic. They suggest that the populace consisted of a mixture of Armenoid and Mediterranean races. The physical traits depicted on monuments—the big nose, the bulging eyes, the thick neck, and flat occiput—are conventional and do not indicate racial type. The same features have been observed on statues depicting Semites, while other statues representing Sumerians (e.g., Gudea) show a short, straight nose and a long head.

It should be admitted at the outset that only language can serve as a criterion for identification of Sumerians. Unfortunately, scholars have been unable to find any convincing example of a known language cognate to Sumerian, although many have been suggested. Sumerian is a non-Semitic, agglutinative, inflected, and partly tonal speech written in the cuneiform script, which would seem to have been their invention (see J-J. Glassner, *The Invention of Cuneiform: Writing in Sumer* [2003]). In various dialects it survives on several thousand CLAY TABLETS found during excavations in Babylonia. In the 4th millennium B.C. the writing was pictographic, the earliest examples being found at Warka (Uruk IV) and neighboring sites, but this soon gave way to a well-developed polysyllabic writing employing more than 400 different signs. A varied literature was influential, since the same script was taken over for use in the Semitic dialects of Akkadian (Assyrian and Babylonian) and for dialects in Syria and Palestine, as well as for such non-Semitic languages as Elamite, Kassite, Hittite, Hurrian, and Old Persian. Since many bilingual texts survive, there is much evidence for the language and through it of early Sumerian history. See LANGUAGES OF THE ANE I.A.

The geographical background of their oldest myths and stories seems to have been typical of S Iraq: rivers and marshes, reeds, tamarisks, palm trees. Archaeological evidence suggests no major break in pottery style sufficient to prove a large scale immigration of "Sumerians" during the Uruk period. Indeed, many scholars wonder if it is not quite beside the point even to pose the question of when and from where the Sumerians arrived. As one writer puts it, "They may … represent a branch of the population which occupied the greater part of the Near East in early Neolithic and Chalcolithic times. In other words, they may have 'always' been in Iraq" (G. Roux, *Ancient Iraq* [1964], 85). Nevertheless, other scholars insist that the Sumerians immigrated into S Iraq no earlier than c. 3500 and most likely from a home in the N to the W of the Caspian Sea.

B. The early dynastic period (c. 2700–2300 B.C.). A Sumerian king list written c. 2150 B.C. ascribes kingship first to the city of Eridu and then in turn to Badtibirra, Larak, Sippar, and Shuruppak. Eight kings reigned for 241,200 years in these five cities and then "the flood swept over the earth." Another text lists ten such rulers, but two of these may have been contemporaries; so, though there are superficial similarities between these lists and the ten ANTEDELUVIAN patriarchs (Gen. 5) and the preflood monarchs of the later Berossus account, no direct correlation is possible. (See T. Jacobsen, *The Sumerian King-List* [1939]; *ANET*, 265–66. In all lists it is the tenth who survives the flood and all display a longevity which, in the Babylonian accounts with ages of more than 20,000 years each, make the life-span of METHUSELAH [969 years; 5:27] look insignificant.) It is unfortunately impossible to authenticate most of the kings on this list. The earliest ruler who has been attested independently by historical evidence is En-me-barage-si, who ruled c. 2700 over the city of Kish. The second earliest ruler so attested is Mes-anne-padda, king of Ur (c. 2650).

The traditional history of Sumer, however, begins with a king named Etana, who may have ruled Kish c. 2800. It appears that Etana ruled over more than the city of Kish itself. Rather, he exercised control over all of Sumer and even surrounding lands. If Etana of Kish built an empire, it soon passed to the neighboring city of Uruk. For not long thereafter a king named Mes-kiagga-sher of Uruk (c. 2750) extended his rule from the Sea (Mediterranean?) to the Zagros Mountains. During the reigns of his son, En-mer-kar (c. 2730), and his successor, the warrior Lugal-banda (c. 2710), there were a series of military and political encounters with a city far to the NE named Aratta.

By the end of Lugal-banda's reign the power of the ruler of Kish began to reassert itself. En-me-barage-si of Kish (c. 2700) had defeated ELAM and founded Sumer's holiest shrine, the first temple of Enlil in Nippur, a center of pilgrimage for the Sumerians not unlike Jerusalem, Rome, or Mecca. Probably contemporary with En-me-barage-si of Kish were the kings of Ur (Mes-kalam-dug and A-kalam-dug), to whom pertained the famous royal cemetery excavated by Sir Leonard Woolley. Their successor, Mes-anne-padda (possibly also known by the name Me-silim), assumed the position of hegemony among the cities of Sumer during the reign of Agga of Kish, En-me-barage-si's son.

A third contemporary of Agga of Kish and Mes-anne-padda of Ur was the famous Gilgamesh of Uruk (c. 2650), about whose historical deeds was woven an elaborate fabric of legends. Precisely where historical truth ceases and poetic fancy begins in these tales is seldom possible to determine. That he was in fact the ruler under whom the city wall

This cuneiform tablet, discovered in Nineveh and dating to the end of the 2nd millennium B.C., contains a list of equivalent terms in Sumerian and Akkadian.

of Uruk was built, as is claimed in the Gilgamesh Epic, can be substantiated on the basis of the character of the brickwork in the walls (the so-called "plano-convex" bricks). Another legend recounts Gilgamesh's encounters with Agga of Kish, which likewise seems historical. The remainder of the epic, describing his noble quest for immortality, cannot be validated and probably is nothing more than a folk tale.

The generation of Agga, Gilgamesh, and Mes-anne-padda was followed by an interlude of foreign domination. The two foreign dynasties of Awan and Hamazi (coming from the mountains that border Iraq on the E) exercised control over a large part of Sumer. The foreigners were finally expelled by E-anna-tum, the ruler of LAGASH (c. 2550). He extended his control over the other Sumerian cities by defeating the armies of Ur and Uruk and Kish, and by settling a boundary dispute between his own city of Lagash and the neighboring city of Umma by force of arms. The last-named conflict was commemorated by a masterpiece of Sumerian sculpture, the Stela of the Vultures.

The century following E-anna-tum's death (c. 2500–2400) is somewhat confused. It appears that for short periods of time large portions of Sumer were controlled by Lugal-anne-mundu of Adab,

En-shakush-anna of Uruk, and a group of foreign kings from the city of MARI on the Middle Euphrates. Shortly before 2400 there arose in the city of Lagash a monarch named Urukagina, who is the earliest known ruler to have left in writing a record of sweeping social reforms designed to eliminate greed, oppression, and exploitation of the poor by the ruling classes. He reigned over Lagash for eight years, until Lagash was conquered by Lugal-zagge-si, king of Umma. Lugal-zagge-si of Umma then proceeded to capture Uruk, and claimed in his inscriptions to have conquered all of Mesopotamia and Syria. If this is not sheer boasting without substance, it may only indicate that Lugal-zagge-si secured the submission of the Semites of Mari, who in turn exercised some form of loose political control over the Syrian groups farther to the west. Lugal-zagge-si reigned for about twenty-nine years (c. 2400–2371).

C. The domination by the Akkadians and the Guti (c. 2300–2100 B.C.). Persons or groups of persons who spoke languages belonging to the Semitic family were not new to Sumer in the year 2300, but it was then that, for the first time, a ruler arose to exercise political control over all of Sumer, Mesopotamia in the N, and Syria in the W, whose name and native language were Semitic. His real name is not known. What is known is the royal name or title he employed: Sharru-kin (SARGON), which in his native language meant "legitimate king." In history books he is usually called Sargon of Agade (see AKKAD) or Sargon the Great to distinguish him from the other Sargons of later periods in the history of Babylonia and Assyria. So famous did he become and so popular his legend was in later times that it is difficult to separate his actual deeds from those falsely attributed to him. The former must certainly have been impressive, if they were able to stimulate the latter. There is no reason to doubt that his effective realm included all of Sumer in the S, Assyria in the N, Syria and the Euphrates Valley in the W. More extravagant claims of his expeditions to central Asia Minor (Burushanda), to Cyprus, Egypt, and possibly Ethiopia, are quite another matter.

It is understandable that around the career and origins of such a man of accomplishments should grow up legends. A text written in the 7th cent. B.C. describes Sargon's birth in terms similar to that of Moses: "My mother was a high priestess, my father I knew not. / … My city is Azupiranu, which is situated on the banks of the Euphrates. / My mother, the high priestess, conceived me, in secret she bore me. / She set me in a basket of rushes, with bitumen she sealed my lid. / She cast me into the river which rose not (over) me. / The river bore me up and carried me to Akki, the drawer of water. / … [Akki took me] as his son (and) reared me, / … appointed me as his gardener. / While I was a gardener, Ishtar granted me (her) love, / And for four and […] years I exercised kingship" (*ANET*, 119). The facts behind this romance are that Sargon was of humble origin and that, while serving as cup-bearer to Ur-Zababa, king of Kish, he managed to overthrow his lord and led an army against Uruk, where he met and defeated Lugal-zagge-si, whom he brought back to Kish in humiliation "in a dog collar" and exposed him at Enlil's gate. Sargon reigned for fifty-five years (c. 2371–2316), managing to hold together his far-flung possessions until the end.

Sargon's son, Rimush (reigned 2315–2307), was not so successful, and on more than one occasion had to quell rebellion in his own palace. Rimush was succeeded by Manishtusu (2306–2292), Naram-Sin (2291–2255), and Shar-kali-sharri (2254–2230), none of whom were able to equal the successes of their great ancestor Sargon. The later legends ignore all of these but Naram-Sin, whom they cast as the typical "bad-luck ruler." The legends portray him as impious and ill-fated and as the ruler during whose reign the empire collapsed. The truth of the matter is that Naram-Sin was far more capable than the other successors of Sargon. But toward the end of his reign he did meet a crushing defeat at the hands of the Guti, a semi-barbaric mountain folk. The kingdom of Akkad, however, survived until the end of the reign of his successor.

D. The Sumerian revival: the 3rd dynasty of Ur and the Isin-Larsa period (c. 2100–1800 B.C.). The deliverer of the Sumerian cities from the yoke of the Guti was an energetic warrior-ruler named Utu-hegal of Uruk (c. 2120–2114), who—followed by several other Sumerian princes defeated the Guti leader Tirigan and drove his followers out of the land. But Utu-hegal's own reign was short: in 2114 he was evicted by one of his own officials, Ur-Nammu, the governor of Ur. For the following 100 years the city of Ur maintained its hegemony over the other Sumerian cities. This is called the 3rd dynasty of Ur, or the Ur-III Period.

Contemporary with Utu-hegal of Uruk and Ur-Nammu of Ur was a prince of Lagash named Gudea. Although he was not a great conqueror, Gudea is famous for the works of literature and art that flourished at his court. Ur-Nammu of Ur has also left us several interesting pieces of literature, including the oldest known code of laws, three centuries older than the famous Code of HAMMURABI.

Equally impressive testimony to the advanced artistry and technical skill of the citizens of Ur at this time are the ZIGGURATS (stage towers, or pyramids), which appear in Sumerian cities from this time on and which may owe their inspiration to the ziggurat of Ur, constructed in the reign of Ur-Nammu. It had three stories and rose to over 100 ft. high. The impression of lightness which it conveys is due to its perfect proportions and to the fact that all its lines are slightly curved (convex), a technique employed nearly 2,000 years later by the Greek architects who built the Parthenon. The platforms were reached by flights of stairs leading up to the shrine which surmounted the entire structure. It stood on a large terrace in the midst of Ur's "sacred quarter," a walled precinct in the northern half of the city. While there is no agreement among scholars as to the precise purpose of these ziggurats, it is likely that they provided a meeting place for earth-bound man and the heavenly gods at a point halfway between the two spheres. The famous Tower of BABEL (Gen. 11:4), which apparently resembled the ziggurats, was meant to "reach unto heaven."

Ur-Nammu's son Shulgi reigned from 2095 to 2048, a total of forty-seven years. The temples and ziggurats begun by Ur-Nammu in Ur and other Sumerian cities were completed. The gods' images were installed in their shrines. The calendar was reformed. A new measure of grain, the royal *gur*, superseded the local measures formerly in use, thus facilitating intercity and international trade. No record indicates military expeditions before Shulgi's twenty-fourth year, when he embarked on a long series of annual campaigns in the NE (Kurdistan).

During the reigns of Amar-Suen, Shu-Sin, and Ibbi-Sin, groups of Semitic nomads, called Martu in Sumerian and Amurru in Akkadian (see AMORITE), began to assert themselves in the settled areas of southern Iraq, making themselves masters of the cities of Isin, Larsa, and Babylon. The rulers of Ur were well aware of this threat. During the reign of Amar-Suen a fortress named "That Which Keeps Away Tidnum [i.e., Amurru]" was built along the Euphrates between Sumer and Mari. The measure succeeded temporarily.

When Ibbi-Sin succeeded to the throne of Ur in 2029, the eastern provinces of Eshnunna and Susa declared themselves independent. In Ibbi-Sin's fifth year the Amorites (Amurru) penetrated deep into the heart of Sumer, cutting off Nippur and Isin in the N from Ur in the S. Soon thereafter (2017) Ibbin-Sin's deputy in Isin, Ishbi-Erra, proclaimed himself king in Isin. An Amorite sheikh called Nablanum had been made king in Larsa, only 25 mi. from Ur. Beset on all sides, Ibbi-Sin of Ur now succumbed to an Elamite attack on the capital city in 2006. During the 250 years following the destruction of Ur, the cities of Isin, Larsa, and Babylon struggled for control of S Iraq. In the N another Amorite named Shamshi-Adad of Assyria governed a large expanse.

In 1720 Hammurabi of Babylon defeated Rim-Sin of Larsa and emerged as the victor in this struggle for dominance in the S. The survey of the history of Sumer is concluded, because, although the Sumerian language continued to be taught in the schools and used in official documents, the common people, whatever their "racial" origins, were thoroughly semitized in language and customs.

III. Social and economic institutions. From as early as the Ubaid period the temple of the city god occupied a central and preeminent role in the life of the city. The high priest of that temple and representative of the god was called the *ensi*. Most of the arable land surrounding the city was owned by the city god (i.e., by his temple). Peasants tilled that land and were given a portion of the produce to live on. Although the *ensi* supervised the economy of the city, the crises arising from threat of attack called for a convening of the people in two assemblies. A temporary war leader was appointed for each crisis by the assemblies. This leader was called the *lugal* ("big man"). Like the OT judges, this *lugal* retired from his office after the threat had ceased. In time, kingship became a hereditary institution. Cities supported standing armies that were organized and well equipped. At first the "secular" *lugal* and the "cleric" *ensi* or *sanga* respected each other's separate domains, but eventually the *lugal* came to control the temple as well as the palace.

Most of the citizens were farmers, herdsmen, and fishermen, but many made their livelihood in the crafts as masons, carpenters, smiths, potters, jewelers, merchants, scribes, and physicians. Despite the large temple land holdings, many persons held private property: farms and gardens, houses and cattle. Slaves were few in number at first. Most slaves were prisoners taken in battle. But freemen might become the slaves of others as punishment for certain offenses. In time of need parents could sell their children as slaves. The slave wore the brand mark of his owner. He could be flogged as punishment. But slaves could engage in business, borrow money, and buy their freedom.

Law was formulated in writing as early as Urukagina of Lagash (c. 2420 B.C.) and Ur-Nammu of Ur (c. 2150; see *ANET*, 523–25). Private documents of law (contracts, deeds, wills, promissory notes, receipts) have been recovered. The supervision of the courts was in the hands of the city governor (*ensi*) or his representative (*mashkim*). Cases were heard by a panel of three or four judges (*di-kud*) who weighed evidence in the form of statements from witnesses and written documents. Conflicts in testimony were resolved by oath-taking. The decision of the judges was legally binding, but appeals could be made on the basis of new evidence.

IV. Religion. The prominence of the temple and its divine proprietor in the economy of the Sumerian city afford some indication of the nature of the pantheon so far as the ordinary layman was concerned. For him the complex and speculative cosmology and theology of the priest and scribe had little meaning. He was a member of an overgrown village family at the head of which was the *ensi*, who represented the city-god. He had little familiarity with the "functional" roles of the various gods venerated in his and other Sumerian cities. He did not choose to be born in this city, so he obviously did not choose his own god. Nor is there any evidence to show that persons transferred their residence and citizenship to a different town for religious reasons—at least not until ABRAHAM, the son of TERAH (Gen. 11–12). He was loyal to his city-god as he would be to his own father. Accomplishments of his city, whether in war or peace, were accomplishments of its god, and the god was thanked accordingly through dedications of statues, food offerings, or even the building of a new or larger temple.

"The Care and Feeding of the Gods" is what one scholar has called the process of the Sumerian cult. Each god was housed in a temple, clothed with finely woven garments, fed with the daily food offerings, and entertained by the singing of daily hymns by the priests and their staff. The cult image was the god. If an invading army carried off the image, they carried off the god. At regularly specified times of the year the staff of the temple threw a "party" (called a "festival" or *ezen*) for the god—a party to which his divine cronies from other cities were invited. Their statues were brought over land or in river barges to the "host" temple, and, of course, crowds of human attendants filled the city. Calendars of such regularly scheduled (*sag-ús*) festivals were drawn up.

The most glamorous of the yearly festivals was the *akiti* or New Year's Festival. The high point of

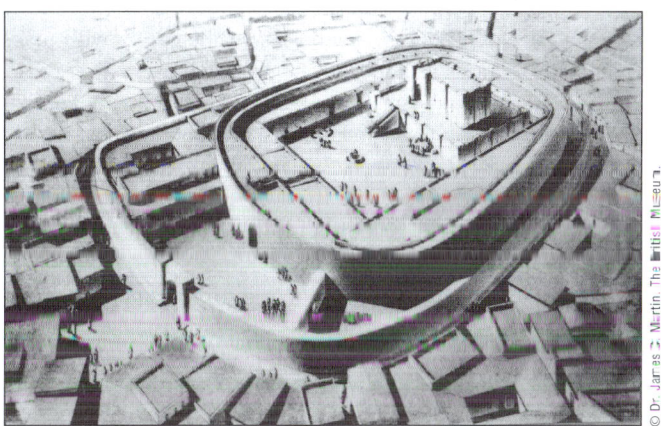

The Sumerian temple at Khafajeh (reconstruction by H. D. Darby).

the activities was the sacred marriage ceremony, in which the reigning king was united in marriage to Inanna, the goddess of love and reproduction. The role of Inanna in the *connubium* was played by the high priestess (*en*, Akk. *entu*), who was the bride of the king-god and kept herself for him. To the Sumerians it appeared that all vegetation died and all animal life languished during the hot summer months. Since it was the task of the god of vegetation to foster it, it was assumed that he had either died or been kidnapped and removed to the nether world, where he remained during the summer. He returned at the time of the autumnal equinox (the Sumerian New Year) and, when he had joined with his wife, produced that remarkable revival of plant and animal life so long awaited by the land's inhabitants. There were several such "dying gods" in Sumer, but the best known was *Dumu-zi(d)* ("true son"), whose name was pronounced by the Semites as TAMMUZ. Some scholars see as further representatives of this divine type the Ugaritic HADAD or BAAL, the Phoenician Adoni (ADONIS), the Egyptian OSIRIS, and the Hittite Telepinu.

Through literature and religion, the thought and manner of the Sumerians was transmitted to both contemporary and later civilizations and is of importance as the background of much in Gen. 1–11. The texts detail the range of its gods, rituals, and religious practices, as well as its incipient sciences (medicine, astronomy, mathematics, technology). The Sumerian mind concerned itself with nature, for it was largely an agricultural community with industry confined to a few city centers. It pondered the problems of death and the afterlife (Gilgamesh Epic), yet was abounding with practical wisdom (collections of proverbs, essays of advice, parables) as well as court and temple ritual in the desire to know the mind of the gods (omens, hymns, prayers). Sumerian myths discussed the role of deities ("The Birth of the Moon God"), vocation and creation of the world and of man, paradise, and evil.

Most texts were in poetic form; among them are long love poems and lamentations (see the selections in *ANET*, 37–39, 455–63, 582–92, 573–91, 611–19, 637–52). The longest historiographic text is the Curse of Agade (*ANET*, 646–51), which city was seen to have been destroyed by the Guti as punishment for its evil by the gods using international military forces. Wisdom literature includes essays, one of which, like JOB, discusses human suffering (*ANET*, 589–91). In language, thought, literary genre, and in other ways the influence of Sumer can be said to have been immense and lived on through the Babylonians to the Greeks and the W not without leaving its mark on the OT.

(See Fr. Thureau-Dangin, *Les inscriptions de Sumer et d'Akkad* [1905]; H. H. Frankfort, *The Birth of Civilisation in the Ancient Near East* [1951]; A. Falkenstein, *Das Sumerische* [1959]; A. Parrot, *Sumer* [1960]; M. A. Beek, *Bildatlas des assyrisch-babylonischen Kultur* [1961]; S. N. Kramer, *The Sumerians: Their History, Culture, and Character* [1963]; G. Roux, *Ancient Iraq* [1964]; H. Frankfort and C. J. Gadd in *CAH* 1/2, 3rd ed. [1971], chs. 12–13; S. N. Kramer, *History Begins at Sumer: Thirty-nine Firsts in Man's Recorded History*, 3rd ed. [1981]; J. N. Postgate, *Early Mesopotamia: Society and Economy at the Dawn of History* [1992]; J. Black et al., *The Literature of Ancient Sumer* [2004]; H. E. W. Crawford, *Sumer and the Sumerians*, 2nd ed. [2004]; *ABD*, 6:231–34; *CANE*, 2:807–17, 831–57.)

H. A. HOFFNER, JR.
D. J. WISEMAN

summer. The Hebrew word for "summer," *qayiṣ* H7811, can be used both for the season (Gen. 8:22 et al.) and for its produce (Jer. 40:10 et al.). In PALESTINE, the months between May and October are essentially rainless, so that summer is a season of drought (Ps. 32:4) and often oppressive heat, but also of field work (Prov. 10:5; Jer. 8:20). The main business of the season is the HARVEST, first that of the early crops (cf. Isa. 28:4), then the main crop. If the harvest is delayed, the produce will become overripe and spoil, as in the vision of summer fruit (Amos 8:1–2). In the NT, the Greek word *theros* G2550 occurs only in Jesus' comment about recognizing the signs of the end times (Matt. 13:28 and parallels). See also SEASONS.

J. H. PATERSON

sun. Under the titles of various deities, the sun was worshiped by many peoples of the ancient world. In the Bible, the sun is mentioned frequently, especially as part of the imagery of CREATION and in a number of common Semitic idiomatic expressions. The common Hebrew word for "sun" is *šemeš* H9087; rarely used are *ḥammâ* H2780 (Cant. 6:10 et al.) and *ḥeres* H3064 (Jdg. 14:18; Job 9:7; and some MSS at Isa. 19:18; cf. also the place names HERES and TIMNATH HERES). In the NT the Greek word is *hēlios* G2463.

I. The sun in the ANE and the OT. Simple ideographs of the sun date from the Paleolithic era onward, and every ancient language has a special term, usually with metaphysical or supranatural connotation, to describe the solar phenomenon. In SUMER, the sun was deified under the name *Utu* (accompanied by the determinative sign for deity, *dingir*). In the elaborate Sumerian pantheon, *Utu* was in charge of the moral order of things, boundaries, agreements, etc. He also was to judge the dead and determine their status in the netherworld. The Akkadian equivalent is the deity *Šamaš*, frequently mentioned in the historical and religious texts. In Sumerian and Akkadian pantheons the sun is a masculine deity, whereas in UGARIT and other W Semitic cultures it is feminine; the cult of the sun-goddess was widespread.

In EGYPT the sun-god RE was the high deity of the earliest predynastic cosmology, that of HELIOPOLIS. The deity of the Neolithic period seems to have been an ancient god, Atum, who later becomes syncretized with Re; thus Atum-Re is symbolized by the sacred post known as *ben-ben*, which stood in the center of the sacred precinct at Heliopolis. The incident of the removal of the capitol to TELL EL-AMARNA by the Pharaoh AKHENATEN (Amenhotep IV, 1370–1353 B.C.) marked a transition to the cult worship of Aten, the solar disc, and a loss of power and control by the former royal city of THEBES. After the death of Akhenaten and his successors Semenkhkara and Tutankhamen, the Amarna age ended.

Throughout the OT, the sun is stated to be the creation of God, fashioned with the intent of providing LIGHT on the fourth day of creation (Gen. 1:14–19). However, at the command of Yahweh it can be stayed (Josh. 10:12–13; see DAY, JOSHUA'S LONG); and in the day of judgment at the fulfillment of the "last days" it will be extinguished (Isa. 13:10 et al.; see ESCHATOLOGY III.I).

The worship or celebration of the sun was strictly forbidden (Deut. 4:19 et al.), and this cultic practice so common in the ANE was probably involved in the Tower of BABEL (Gen. 11:1–9). After the exodus and the conquest of Canaan, the Israelites came in contact with the cult of the sun, and many place names of the period of the judges and the first commonwealth reflect their ancient cultic status: BETH SHEMESH, "house of the sun" (Josh. 15:10 et al.); EN SHEMESH, "spring of the sun" (15:17 et al.); Shamash Edom, mentioned in Egyptian sources (*ANET*, 243a, 245b). A ritual involved with this solar deity was that of marking the sun's course with chariots and models of chariots left at the gate where the rising sun entered the city. This and other such practices were forbidden under JOSIAH (2 Ki. 23:5, esp. v. 11). See HOST OF HEAVEN IV; IDOLATRY; SUN WORSHIP.

The sun is used in certain idiomatic expressions as a symbol of ETERNITY (Ps. 72:5 et al.), a usage attested outside the Bible, as in the Phoenician inscription from Karatepe: "[may the name of] Azitawadda endure forever, like the name of the sun and the moon" (*KAI*, 1:6, sect. V, lines 6–7). Another use is the expression "under the sun" (Eccl. 1:3 et al.), referring to the sun's all-pervasive character, which is similar to a reference in Phoenician inscriptions (e.g., "among the living under the sun"; see *KAI*, 1:3, #14, line 12). Nowhere in the OT is the sun itself considered to be either divine or an attribute of God.

II. The sun in the NT. Aside from a number of literal occurrences of the term (e.g., Lk. 4:40; Acts 27:20), the sun is mentioned in the NT usually either in metaphorical contexts (e.g., "the righteous will shine like the sun," Matt. 13:43), or in passages dealing with the cosmic catastrophe to occur at the PAROUSIA (Matt. 24:29; Rev. 1:16 et al.). This last sense is derived from the OT prophetic usage. The sun in all cases is mentioned as the source of light and completely at the command of God. The darkening of the sun at the CRUCIFIXION is seen as a special effect of iniquity upon the cosmos.

III. The sun in postbiblical times. So strong was the reverence for the sun among the ancient pagans that notions and ideas from this cultus were soon syncretized with the gospel. Because the sun was worshiped in MITHRAISM and other cults of

Persian-Zoroastrian origin, this element was frequent in the various heresies. Nearly all the deities of the ancient classical world were portrayed in some sense illuminated by the sun, which became one of their divine attributes. In the earliest Christian art and literature this also occurred, so that Jesus is often shown on the sun-shield or *clipeus* and frequently in the solar chariot. The culmination of this movement was in the pantheistic hymnology of the high Middle Ages, in which Christ was ascribed all the attributions of the ancient solar disc. The Reformation discredited this vestige of paganism.

(See further W. T. Olcott, *Sun-Lore of All Ages* [1914]; F. Boll, *Die Sonne im Glauben und in der Weltanschauung der alten Völker* [1922]; J. Maier, "Die Sonne im religiösen Denken des antiken Judentum," in *ANRW* 2/19/1 [1979], 346–412; J. G. Taylor, *Yahweh and the Sun: Biblical and Archaeological Evidence for Sunworship in Ancient Israel* [1993]; J. Assmann, *Egyptian Solar Religion in the New Kingdom: Re, Amun and the Crisis of Polytheism* [1995]; D. Lorton, *Akhenaten and the Religion of Light* [1999]; M. Wallraff, *Christus verus sol: Sonnenverehrung und Christentum in der Spätantike* [2001].) W. WHITE, JR.

sun, chariots (horses) of the. See CHARIOTS OF THE SUN.

Sun, City of the. According to Isa. 19:18, five Egyptian cities will swear allegiance to Yahweh in the end times, and one of them will bear the name City of Destruction (see DESTRUCTION, CITY OF). The Hebrew word for "Destruction" is *heres* H2239, but the Great Isaiah Scroll from QUMRAN, along with a few Masoretic MSS, has *ḥeres* H3064, "Sun." This reading is also reflected in several ancient versions (e.g., Vulg. *civitas Solis*) and has been adopted by some modern translations (e.g., NRSV). It is possible that a pun is implied—what was then "City of the Sun" was to be called "City of Destruction." The prophecy that immediately follows speaks of God's revealing himself to the Egyptians and their serving him (v. 21), a blessing alongside Assyria and Israel (vv. 23–25).

Of Egyptian towns, one in particular was known as "City of the Sun," namely, HELIOPOLIS: the "destruction" could reflect the judgments expressed and the overthrow of Egyptian paganism (cf. Jer. 43:13 NRSV; Heb. *bêt-šemeš*, "house of the sun"). The scope in time of the prophecy cannot be fully delimited; Jewish settlements occurred in Egypt from before Persian through Hellenistic times, while Christianity has brought knowledge of God both in ancient and modern times. K. A. KITCHEN

Sunday. See LORD'S DAY.

sun worship. Evidences of sun worship are seen in many cultures, including India, Greece, the Maya of Central America, and so on. Of particular significance is this practice as seen in the ANE. In ASSYRIA AND BABYLONIA special sites such as Soppara and Larsa were set aside for sun worship. In PHOENICIA the solar BAAL was Baal-Hammon. Also, the god Shamash was a sun-god. In Egypt at On (HELIOPOLIS) in the NILE delta, the sun worship of Egyptians was centralized. From early times the Egyptians worshiped RE, the general name for

Egyptian sun worship is exemplified by this relief of the deities Harakhte (left) and Hathor, each with a solar disk.

the sun-god. More specifically, he was called Atum or Amun, and his priests dominated the religious world of Egypt. In the reign of Amenhotep IV (AKHENATEN), an attempt was made to establish the sun-disk, Aten, as the sole god of Egypt. This reform lasted only during his lifetime. He built his own city for the center of this worship.

In Scripture the practice was clearly forbidden. "And when you look up to the sky and see the sun, the moon and the stars—all the heavenly array—do not be enticed into bowing down to them and worshiping things the LORD your God has apportioned to all the nations under heaven" (Deut. 4:19). The penalty for sun worship was death by stoning if there were two or three witnesses (17:2–5). In the days after the divided kingdom such practices were followed by some kings of Judah and Israel. MANASSEH, the son of HEZEKIAH, built altars to the HOST OF HEAVEN and worshiped them, even in the house of the Lord (2 Ki. 21:3–5). Some kings of Judah dedicated horses and chariots to the worship of the sun and burned incense (23:5, 11; see CHARIOTS OF THE SUN).

The prophet JEREMIAH tells us that the kings of Judah loved and served the sun and worshiped it (Jer. 8:2). EZEKIEL provides a very graphic picture of sun worshipers facing E in the Lord's house (Ezek. 8:16). ASA (2 Chr. 14:5) and JOSIAH (34:4, 7) sought to destroy such worship by breaking down the altars to the sun in the cities in all Israel. However, it was still practiced at the time of the fall of Jerusalem (Jer. 19:13; Ezek. 6:4, 6). (For bibliography, see under SUN.) J. B. SCOTT

supernaturalism. See MIRACLE.

superscription. See MUSIC VI; PSALMS, BOOK OF, II.A.

superstition. Superstition may be defined as belief in the supernatural that is motivated by fear, proceeds from ignorance, and reflects an irrational view of reality. It may denote also the practices consequent upon such belief. Black magic, witchcraft, spirit-rapping, and the like, may be regarded as manifestations of a superstitious frame of mind. In the OT, the prohibition against DIVINATION by consulting a necromancer (one who has a "familiar spirit," Lev. 19:31; Deut. 18:11) and the record of the practice of soothsaying, augury, and the like (2 Ki. 21:6) show that the Israelites were often infected with the superstitious practices of those around them.

In NT times the Greek word *deisidaimonia* G1272 and the Latin *superstitio* are used in an imprecise way, which makes the exact meaning in a given instance sometimes difficult to determine. (See P. J. Koets, *Deisidaimonia: A Contribution to the Knowledge of the Religious Terminology In Greek* [1929]). For example, FESTUS reported to Agrippa (see HEROD VIII) that PAUL had been involved in disputes with the Jews "about their own superstition" (Acts 25:19 KJV). Considering Agrippa's Jewish connections, it seems unlikely that the newly arrived governor would have paid the king so ill a compliment as to have designated the Jewish faith a superstition in the modern sense of the term (thus the NIV and other versions here translate "religion").

Similarly, when Paul remarked before the Areopagus: "I perceive that in all things you are too superstitious" (Acts 17:22 KJV), he probably meant "most religious" (*deisidaimonesterous*, comparative form [used as superlative] of *deisidaimōn* G1273). Some believe, however, that in these passages there is the tacit implication of religion to excess, that which is subversive to true religion. Certainly Paul would have been thinking of misdirected religious feeling or action, the religious veneration of persons and objects that observe no such reverence, or the worship of God through improper rites and ceremonies. It is in this sense that Christian missionaries have opposed the practices of the heathen—and that Protestants rejected the intrusion of such ideas into the medieval church—as superstitious.

P. JEWETT

Suph סוּף (סוּף H6068, "reed[s]"). A place "in the desert east of the Jordan" near which MOSES expounded the law to Israel (Deut. 1:1). The Hebrew phrase *môl sûp* ("in front of Suph") is translated by the SEPTUAGINT with *plēsion tēs erythras*, "near the Red [Sea]," an understanding followed by the VULGATE, the TARGUMS, and the KJV (BDB, 693, suggests the possible conjecture *miyyam sûp*, "from the Red Sea" or, more literally, "from the Sea of Reeds"). If this interpretation is correct, the reference would be to the Gulf of AQABAH, and there is indeed some evidence for such a use of the term *yam-sûp* (see RED SEA III). Moreover, some argue that the association of Suph in this verse with PARAN, HAZEROTH, and the ARABAH gives support to this identification. Against it is the fact that nowhere else do we find the abbreviation *sûp* for *yam-sûp*; besides, it seems odd that a place in TRANSJORDAN should be described as being "in front of" or "near" Aqabah. (See also discussion in S. R. Driver, *A Critical and Exegetical Commentary on Deuteronomy*, ICC, 3rd ed. [1901], 3–5.)

Others have tried to identify Suph with specific places in MOAB. One possibility is SUPHAH (Num. 21:14), which might be modern Khirbet Sufa, not far from MEDEBA, but the Hebrew text in this verse is problematic. E. G. Kraeling (in *JNES* 7 [1948]: 201) suggested that Suph may be the same as Papyron, a site of unknown location mentioned by JOSEPHUS (*Ant.* 14.1.3 §33; *War* 1.6.3 §128); the only basis for this identification, however, is that the meaning of this place-name (from *papyros*, "papyrus," i.e., the Egyptian reed) is similar to that of Suph.

Suphah soo'fuh (סוּפָה *H6071*, "reed[s]"). Apparently a place within the territory of MOAB, mentioned in parallel with the ARNON River (Num. 21:14). Although some have identified it with modern Khirbet Sufa, a few miles SE of MEDEBA (cf. J. Simons, *The Geographical and Topographical Texts of the Old Testament* [1959], 261–62 n. 229), its location is unknown. Moreover, the meaning of this verse—a citation from the Book of the Wars of the Lord—is debated, for the Hebrew phrase begins with the direct object marker (*ʾet-wāhēb bĕsûpâ*) even though there is no verb. The KJV (following the TARGUM and the VULGATE) identifies *wāhēb* as a verb and renders, "What he did in the Red Sea" (see SUPH). Many scholars, assuming that the first part of the citation (which would have had a verb) is missing, translate with an ellipsis: "... Waheb in Suphah" (NIV [TNIV, "Zahab"]; cf. NJPS). Others emend the text, reading the particle *ʾet-* as a form of the verb *ʾātâ H910* ("to come"), taking *wāhēb* as a corruption of *yhwh*, and inter-

preting *sûpâ* as a common noun meaning "storm" (thus, "The LORD came in a whirlwind"; cf. D. L. Christensen in *CBQ* 36 [1974]: 359–60, followed by J. R. Huddleston in *ABD*, 6:241–42, but see B. A. Levine, *Numbers 21–36*, AB 4A [2000], 92–95). The TNIV offers an alternate rendering in the margin, "I have been given from Suphah" (cf. Aram. *yĕhab H10314*, "to give"). See WAHEB; WARS OF THE LORD, BOOK OF THE.

Supper, Lord's. See LORD'S SUPPER.

Sur soor (סוּר *H6075*, possibly from a verb meaning "to depart"; Σουρ [Jdt. 2:28]). **(1)** The name of a gate in the city of JERUSALEM that probably led from the palace to the environs of the TEMPLE (2 Ki. 11:6). See FOUNDATION GATE.

(2) A coastal town S of TYRE, mentioned in the account of the campaign of HOLOFERNES in Syria (Jdt. 2:28). Its site is uncertain. Some think the name is fictitious; others have suggested that Sur is a corruption of DOR.

surety. The KJV uses the expression "of a surety" several times as an emphatic expression meaning "surely, for certain" (Gen. 15:13 et al.). Elsewhere it refers to something or someone accepted as security (43:9 et al.). See PLEDGE.

surfeiting. This English term, in its archaic sense of "overindulgence," is used once by the KJV to translate Greek *kraipalē G3190*, which refers to uncontrolled drinking (Lk. 21:34). Modern versions usually employ "dissipation" as the rendering of this term. See DRUNKENNESS.

surname. This English word, as a noun or a verb, is used sixteen times by the KJV (esp. in the book of Acts) to translate various expressions, most often Greek *epikaleō G2126* (Acts 1:23 et al.). Modern versions prefer other renderings ("known as," "called," etc.) used in the sense of a name or title applied to someone, thus denoting that person's distinct and individual character. In the OT, the Hebrew verb *kānâ H4033* means "to bestow an honorable name/title" (Isa. 45:4; some scholars vocalize this verb as a pual in 44:5 and render "he will be called by the name of Israel").

Susa soo´suh (שׁוּשָׁן H8809, prob. from Egyp. *sšn*, the name of a plant; Aram. gentilic שׁוּשַׁנְכָי H10704 [KJV, "Susanchites"]; in Gk. sources, Σοῦσα and Σούσις). KJV Shushan. The ancient capital of ELAM and later of PERSIA, situated on the Karkheh River, in the plain of Iranian Khuzestan, near the Zagros mountains (modern Shūsh). The site has been excavated by the French since the late 19th cent. The earliest settlements date from the Neolithic era and show a separate development called "Susiana" by archaeologists. Documents in an unknown hieroglyphic script inscribed on CLAY TABLETS and called "Proto-Elamite" and marking an early stage in the production of WRITING have been discovered in the remains of Susa.

When the town emerges into the light of history it is the center of the Elamite civilization. In the Sumerian king list (see SUMER), which yields glimpses of dynasties from the 3rd millennium B.C., the name of Elam and its center of culture, Susa, is included. It appears that from this remote antiquity, Susa was a cult center and perhaps the city of the archaic religious state devoted to the high Elamite deity, In-Shushinak. During the third dynasty of UR, a period of Sumerian renaissance, the King Shulgi (c. 2095–2048 B.C.) conquered Susa and set a Sumerian governor (*ensi*) over the people. Under Sumerian and later Semitic domination, Susa was built and expanded in the manner of Mesopotamian cult centers with an astrological temple or stage-tower called a ZIGGURAT. Traders, priests, and other peaceful travelers often passed between Sumer and Elamite Susa. However, as Sumer again began to decline the Elamites took advantage of the situation and invaded and destroyed Ur in 2006 B.C. The Elamite success was short-lived, for Gungunum of Larsa overthrew Susa in 1924 B.C.

For approximately four centuries thereafter Susa is little noted in the CUNEIFORM records, but appears again to ally with ASSYRIA and threaten BABYLON in the S. The Elamite king Shutruk-Nahhunte wiped out the Kassite dynasty of Babylon in 1174 B.C. He carried back to Susa many famous art treasures from his Mesopotamian campaigns such as the Code of HAMMURABI, the Stela of Naram-Sin, and many inscribed texts. Shortly, however, the kings of Susa lost control of the W bank of the TIGRIS River, and slowly the once formidable empire ruled from Susa vanished.

The resurgence of Babylon in the Neo-Babylonian period led to the utter destruction of Susa by ASHURBANIPAL in 639 B.C. at the culmination of long-drawn hostilities. With the demise of Elamite sovereignty the way was open for the newly settled Indo-Europeans in Iran to assert themselves. With the rise of first the Medes and then the Persians, Susa became the regional capital of the Aryans. See MEDIA; PERSIA. Its location as the eastern terminus of the royal Achaemenid road from "Sardis to Susa" made it a center of trade and commerce.

Under the Persian Achaemenids, Susa was further embellished and extended after DARIUS chose it as his royal residence in 521 B.C. A building inscription of Darius has been excavated at Susa which states, "This palace that I built at Susa, its decorations were transported from distant places. The earth was excavated down until I reached the (bed)rock in the earth. When the excavation had been completed the depth of forty measures, rubble was packed down, in another place twenty

Calcite jar fragment from Susa, inscribed with the titles of Xerxes king of Persia (5th cent. B.C.).

measures in depth. On this fill the palace was erected" (R. Kent, *Old Persian Grammar, Texts, Lexicon* [1950], 144). The text goes on to list the commodities and the foreign areas from which they were brought; cedar wood from Lebanon, hard wood from Gandara, gold from Sardis, lapis lazuli and carnelian from Sogdiana, turquoise from Chorsmia, silver and ebony from Egypt, sculpture from the Ionian Greeks, ivory from Ethiopia and Sind. The king then adds, "Says Darius the king, At Susa a most magnificent construct was ordered, a most magnificent construct was completed, may Ahuramazda protect me and my father Hystaspes and my country."

Susa is mentioned frequently in the book of Esther as the scene of the affairs of the court of Darius's son and successor, XERXES. See ESTHER, BOOK OF. The opulence and magnificence of the palace is apparent in Esther and other ancient accounts. It became one of Alexander's most prized fortunes of war and the site of a mass marriage of Greek officers with the Persian royal women in 324 B.C. Its importance then declined and it was repeatedly overthrown and sacked during the medieval period.

(See further M. Dieulafoy, *L'acropole de Suse*, 4 vols. [1890–92]; R. de Mecquenem, *Archéologie susienne* [1943]; R. Ghirshman, *Cinq campagnes de fouilles à Suse 1946–1951* [1952]; P. Amiet, *Suse: 6,000 ans d'histoire* [1988]; E. M. Yamauchi, *Persia and the Bible* [1990], ch. 7; P. O. Harper et al., eds., *The Royal City of Susa: Ancient Near Eastern Treasures in the Louvre* [1992]; J. Perrot and D. Ladiray in *Royal Cities of the Biblical World*, ed. J. G. Westenholz [1996], 197–254.) W. WHITE, JR.

Susanchite soo'suhn-kit. See SUSA.

Susanna soo-zan'uh (Σουσάννα *G5052*, from שׁוֹשַׁן *H8808*, "lily"). **(1)** A pious Jewish woman who lived in Babylon during the EXILE. See SUSANNA, HISTORY OF.

(2) One of several women who had been healed by Jesus and who helped to support him and his disciples in their travels (Lk. 8:3). Nothing else is known about her, but she was probably among those who witnessed the CRUCIFIXION and then returned to the city to prepare spices and ointment for the anointing of the body (23:55–56). (For a discussion of Lk. 8:1–3, see B. Witherington in *ZNW* 70 [1979]: 242–48.)

Susanna, History of. One of the Greek additions to the text of Daniel (see DANIEL, BOOK OF). In the SEPTUAGINT this story originally was placed after Daniel as an appendix, but in some important surviving MSS it is found at the beginning of the book because of the story's reference to Daniel as a young boy (cf. Sus. 45). In the VULGATE the story of Susanna occurs at the end of Daniel as an integral part of the book (numbered as the 13th chapter); in the Protestant Bible it is found as a separate book in the APOCRYPHA.

I. Content. The narrative tells of Susanna, a pious woman of great beauty who lived with her wealthy husband Joakim in BABYLON. Adjacent to his house Joakim had a large garden in which Susanna loved to stroll at midday after the elders (judges) and litigants, who were in the practice of conducting their business in Joakim's house, had departed. Two of these elders, however, had for some time been secretly inflamed with desire for Susanna, and one sultry day they individually stole back to the garden where, having surprised each other, they were forced to confess their mutual designs on her. After she had sent away her servants in preparation to bathe, the elders confronted her with the alternative of either submitting to their desires or being exposed as having been caught with a young man. Susanna chose to be unjustly accused "rather than to sin in the sight of the Lord."

At the trial on the following day the men gave their false testimony. But as Susanna was being led away to her execution, the young Daniel was moved by the Lord (in answer to Susanna's prayer) to protest the precipitate action. At their invitation, Daniel sat with the judges in a renewed examination of the evidence. He shrewdly examined the men separately, inquiring under which tree in the garden Susanna and her alleged lover were seen. The contradictory answers to this question exposed the treachery of the two elders who in turn received the punishment that was to have been Susanna's. The innocence of Susanna had been vindicated, and the narrative concludes with a statement that from thence onward Daniel's reputation among the people was established.

II. Historicity. Although the narrative is given a *prima facie* historical setting (with references to Babylon during the youth of Daniel, and to Susanna as wife of Joakim and daughter of Hilkiah), it is doubtful that the story should be considered historical. It has been pointed out that a number of the circumstantial details of the story do not fit the situation one expects among members of a newly exiled population (e.g., Joakim's luxurious house and gardens, and his servants; synagogues; elected judges; the right of capital punishment). In addition, Susanna is of the same genre of mystery writing as BEL AND THE DRAGON, another addition to Daniel, and the story consists of motifs (the wrongly accused woman; the wise young judge) which are not unknown in ancient folk literature. It has been suggested by a number of scholars that the author infused some such ancient tale (or tales) with traditional Jewish piety and presented it in new form for his own purposes (cf. TOBIT). This explanation is, of course, conjectural but may be regarded as probably correct.

III. Author, language, and date. The author of this beautiful story remains anonymous. It is not even clear whether he wrote the original in Greek or Hebrew, although the play on words in connection with the name of the trees and the imminent punishments (Sus. 54–55, *schinoi* and *schisei*; vv. 58–59, *prinon* and *ataprisē* [*prisai* in Theodotion]) seems to suggest a Greek original (unless the Greek translator has endeavored to imitate the word play of a Semitic original). The date of the document is similarly difficult to determine, but the consensus of modern scholarship is that it dates from the 2nd cent. or the beginning of the 1st cent. B.C. Depending on whether one decides for a Hebrew or Greek original, Susanna is usually assigned a Palestinian or Alexandrian origin.

IV. Purpose. The question concerning the purpose of the author in writing the story is an interesting one. Several writers have conjectured that if the author wrote from a Palestinian milieu, he may well have written the story as a Pharisaic polemic (see PHARISEES) against the jurisprudence of the ruling SADDUCEES. An interesting piece of history could serve as the background to Susanna: the son of Simon ben Shetach, leader of the Pharisees in the time of Alexander Jannaeus (see HASMONEAN II.C), was condemned to death by testimony of a false witness who was duly exposed, but upon whom, by Sadducean interpretation of LEX TALIONIS, no punishment could be inflicted since the son of Simon had not yet been executed. (Thereupon, it is said, the son of Simon chose to die that his false accusers might also die.)

If this is the background of Susanna, the author could have intended the work as a satire on the "justice" of the Sadducean legal system as well as an apologetic for the careful cross-examination of witnesses and the punishment of perjurers. On the other hand, the story may well have originated in ALEXANDRIA, having been intended merely as an illustration of the justice of God in answering the prayer of the righteous. As an incentive to purity of life and trust in God, the story is of powerful significance.

V. Text and canonicity. The Greek text of Susanna is available in the standard editions of the LXX. As with the book of Daniel itself, there are two recensions, the Theodotionic and the Old Greek (see SEPTUAGINT IV.C). The story is substantially the same in the two versions, but there are numerous differences in detail, some of them significant; for example, Theodotion gives a much fuller account of the events leading to the elders' accusation (Sus. 14–27).

ORIGEN argued for the canonicity of the book; JEROME included it in the VULGATE. However, the Roman Catholic Church alone among Christian bodies has recognized the full canonicity and authority of Susanna (the decision was made at the Council of Trent, 1548). In the early Christian church Susanna was often understood as an ALLEGORY of the church.

(See D. M. Kay in *APOT*, 1:638–51; W. O. E. Oesterley, *The Books of the Apocrypha* [1915], 391–94; E. J. Goodspeed, *The Story of the Apocrypha* [1939], 65–70; R. H. Pfeiffer, *History of New Testament Times with an Introduction to the Apocrypha* [1949], 434–36, 448–54; B. M. Metzger, *An Introduction to the Apocrypha* [1957], 107–13; L. H. Brockington, *A Critical Introduction to the Apocrypha* [1961], 93–99; H. Engel, *Die Susanna-Erzählung: Einleitung, Übersetzung und Kommentar zum Septuaginta-Text und zur Theodotion-Bearbeitung* [1985]; M. J. Steussy, *Gardens in Babylon: Narrative and Faith in the Greek Legends of Daniel* [1993]; E. Spolsky, *The Judgment of Susanna: Authority and Witness* [1996]; D. J. Harrington, *Invitation to the Apocrypha* [1999], ch. 9; D. A. deSilva, *Introducing the Apocrypha: Message, Context, and Significance* [2002], ch. 10; L. DiTommaso, *The Book of Daniel and the Apocryphal Daniel Literature* [2005].) D. A. HAGNER

Susi soo´si (סוּסִי *H6064*, from a word meaning "horse"). Father of Gaddi; the latter, representing the tribe of MANASSEH, was one of the twelve spies sent out to reconnoiter the Promised Land (Num. 13:11).

suzerain. See TREATY.

swallow. A songbird (family *Hirundinidae*, suborder *Oscines*) characterized by a short bill and long pointed wings. Most English Bible versions use "swallow" as the rendering of Hebrew *děrôr H2000*, which occurs twice (Ps. 84:3; Prov. 26:2; both times in parallel with *ṣippôr H7606*, which probably refers to the SPARROW). This identification is plausible but cannot be confirmed. In addition, the KJV and other versions use "swallow" to translate ʿ*āgûr H6315*, which also occurs twice (Isa. 38:14; Jer. 8:7). This term, however, more likely refers to the short-footed thrush (*Pycnonotus Reichenovi*; see *HALOT*, 2:784, and NIV; others think it refers to the CRANE (cf. NRSV). In the same two verses, the NRSV uses "swallow" to render *sîs H6101*, also spelled *sûs* (NIV and NJPS have "swift").

G. R. Driver (in *PEQ* no vol. [1955]: 129–40) points out that Arab. *sis* is the same as Hebrew *sîs* (*sûs*) and means "swift," from its twittering call; he argues that the migratory habit of the swift confirms this identification (Jer. 8:7) rather than "swallow." This argument is not valid, for four of the six species of swallow and martins are migrants, and one of the three swifts is resident. Driver also sees a clear distinction between *děrôr* ("swallow") and *sîs* ("swift"), but the differentiation is not quite so simple. These birds belong to widely separated orders, yet they have developed on similar lines: they take all their food in the air, where they spend most of their daylight hours, and are almost helpless on the ground; many of them nest in man-made environments. Palestine has some six members of the swallow family: European swallows, red-rumped swallows, house martins, sand martins, and two crag martins. Two are resident and the others migratory. See BIRD MIGRATION.

Swallows and swifts (family *Apodidae*) are very similar in appearance, and ancient writers are unlikely to have distinguished precisely between them. It has been suggested that *děrôr* is a more general word including all insectivorous birds that feed on the wing. Either swallow or swift would fit the contexts of Ps. 84:3 and Prov. 26:2 equally well. (See *FFB*, 80.) G. S. CANSDALE

swan. See WATER HEN.

swearing. See OATH.

sweat. See BLOODY SWEAT.

sweet cane. See AROMATIC CANE.

swelling. See DISEASE (under *inflammation*).

swift. See SWALLOW.

swine. In modern English the word *swine* has largely been replaced by an equally old English term, *pig*. The (uncastrated) male is known as the *boar*, the female as the *sow*, and the litter is called a *farrow* of piglets. In agricultural areas a number of special words denote the sexes at various ages (e.g., a *gilt* is a young sow that has not farrowed). *Wild boar* is the general term for the wild ancestor of the domestic pig (see BOAR); most other wild species are called *hogs* (e.g., *Warthog*).

Pigs were brought into the service of human beings independently in several different parts of the world, those in Europe and W Asia from *Sus scrofa*, in its various subspecies, and those in China from the eastern species, *S. vittatus*. It is hard to determine exactly when this took place, and the position is complicated by human migrations, since people would take their livestock with them on their wanderings. It seems generally agreed that the pig first became domesticated in the Neolithic period, but after humans began living in permanent settlements. The settlements could be protected by fencing while the pigs roamed the forests finding their own food; grubbing for seeds and tubers allowed grass to replace up rooted thickets and so prepared the land for AGRICULTURE. There is clear evidence of pigs being kept about 2500 B.C. or earlier in Greece, Hungary, Egypt, and Mesopotamia.

To the early settlements the pig was of great value once it could be kept under control, for it not only helped break up land but also turned seeds almost or completely inedible to man — beechmast, acorns, etc. — into good fat and meat. In some lands, especially Egypt, pigs were made to tread the seed into the ground in flooded fields. Their bristles have always had some use, and their skins were sometimes made into a special type of leather, but their bones were useless for making into tools. Food production remains their sole use today, for modern breeds of pigs, permanently penned, convert vegetable food into animal food more quickly and efficiently than any other animal. (See the full discussion and detailed references in F. E. Zeuner, *A History of Domesticated Animals* [1963], ch. 10.)

Surprise has often been expressed that pork was so firmly forbidden as food to the Israelites, but modern discoveries about human disease have thrown new light on this. Thoroughly prepared and cooked pork is excellent meat, but the pig is the potential carrier of several dangerous diseases shared by humans and pigs. The most important of these is trichinosis, caused by a tape-worm which enters one stage in the muscles of a pig and progresses to its second stage only after being eaten. The development of this second stage involves invasion of various tissues, causing great pain and possibly death. Effective cooking in early days was not always possible and total prohibition was the safest policy. Further, the pig is by nature omnivorous and a scavenger; living around human habitations, it is always likely to pick up infected material, even that which has been buried, and transfer the infection elsewhere.

Of the seven OT occurrences of Hebrew *ḥăzîr* H2614, one refers to the boar (Ps. 80:13) and one is a proverb: "Like a gold ring in a pig's snout / is a beautiful woman who shows no discretion" (Prov. 11:22, referring no doubt to the custom of wearing a jewel in the nose; cf. Isa. 3:21). The other five refer directly to the pig's unclean nature (Lev. 11:7; Deut. 14:8; Isa. 65:4; 66:3, 17); it is clear that some of the people whom Isaiah was addressing were quite deliberately keeping pigs against the law. Pig-keeping was more widespread in NT times. In the incident of the swine in GADARA (Matt. 8:30–32 and parallels; Gk. *choiros* G5956) the owners were either Gentiles or nonpracticing Jews, but the pigs looked after by the prodigal son were certainly owned by a Gentile in some "distant country" (Lk. 15:13–16). The only other mention of pigs is in Jesus' proverb, "Give not that which is holy unto the dogs, neither cast ye your pearls before swine" (in Matt. 7:6 KJV). G. S. CANSDALE

sword. See ARMOR, ARMS.

sycamine sik´uh-meen. This term is used by the KJV to render Greek *sykaminos* G5189, which appears only once in Jesus' words, "ye might say unto this sycamine tree …" (Lk. 17:6). Modern versions properly render it as "mulberry tree." There is little doubt that the sycamine and the SYCAMORE are quite different trees, although both of them, along with the FIG, belong in the family *Moraceae* (see FLORA). Sycamine is probably the black MULBERRY (*Morus nigra*), which has been grown for its fruit in Palestine since earliest days. The tree may grow 35 ft. tall, producing a stiff-branched tree which gives dense shade. (The *Dictionary of the Royal Horticultural Society* [1951] identifies "Sycamine" as either *Morus nigra* or *Morus alba*; but the latter, a native of China grown for its leaves, which are the main food of silkworms, was introduced into Palestine only in modern times.) W. E. SHEWELL-COOPER

sycamore. This English term is derived from Greek *sykomoros* (in the NT, *sykomorea* G5191), which in turn is apparently composed of the nouns *sykon* G5192 (the fruit of the fig tree) and *moron* (mulberry tree), although some think that the word is a modification of a Semitic term. The plant in view is the sycamore-fig tree, often called the fig-mulberry (*Ficus sycomorus*), to be distinguished from both the FIG tree (*Ficus carica*) and what is today referred to as "sycamore" (either *Acer pseudoplatanus*, a Eurasian maple, or *Platanus occidentalis*, the buttonwood).

The corresponding Hebrew word is *šiqmâ* H9201, which appears seven times in the OT. DAVID had an official "in charge of the olive and sycamore-fig trees in the western foothills" (1 Chr. 27:28). SOLOMON is said to have made "cedar as plentiful as sycamore-fig trees in the foothills" (1 Ki. 10:27; cf. 2 Chr. 1:15; 9:27). Amos described himself as a shepherd who "also took care of sycamore-fig trees" (Amos 7:14). The destruction of such trees, along with vines, could be evidence of God's punishment (Ps. 78:47). The best-known reference, however, comes from the NT, which tells us that ZACCHAEUS, a short man, "ran ahead and climbed a sycamore-fig tree to see" Jesus (Lk. 19:4). Because the branches of the sycamore-fig are strong and wide-spreading, and because it produces many lateral branches, it was an easy evergreen tree for Zacchaeus to climb, and in which he could easily be hidden.

The fruits produced by the tree are in clusters and look like small figs; they are sweet, but by no means as good as the true fig. The fruit is produced several times during the year. It is a popular tree under which to pitch a tent, because of the ample shade it gives. It is necessary with sycamore-figs to puncture each fruit with the point of a knife at a certain stage so as to help insure that the little figs ripen properly. It was thus that Amos would have tended his trees (Heb. verb *bālas* H1179, *HALOT*, 1:134; cf. also *FFB*, 179–81). See also FLORA (under *Moraceae*); SYCAMINE.

W. E. SHEWELL-COOPER

Sychar si′kahr (Συχάρ G5373, either from ʿAskar [a site at the foot of Mount Ebal] or a corruption of Συχέμ G5374 [Shechem]). The one biblical reference to Sychar identifies it as a town in SAMARIA, near the parcel of ground that JACOB gave his son JOSEPH (Jn. 4:5; cf. Gen. 33:19). JEROME in his translation of EUSEBIUS's *Onomasticon* (165.1–4) distinguishes Sychar from SHECHEM (modern Tell Balaṭah, just E of Nablus), though elsewhere (e.g., *Quaestiones in Gen.* 66.6) he identifies them as the same place, arguing that the spelling Sychar is a

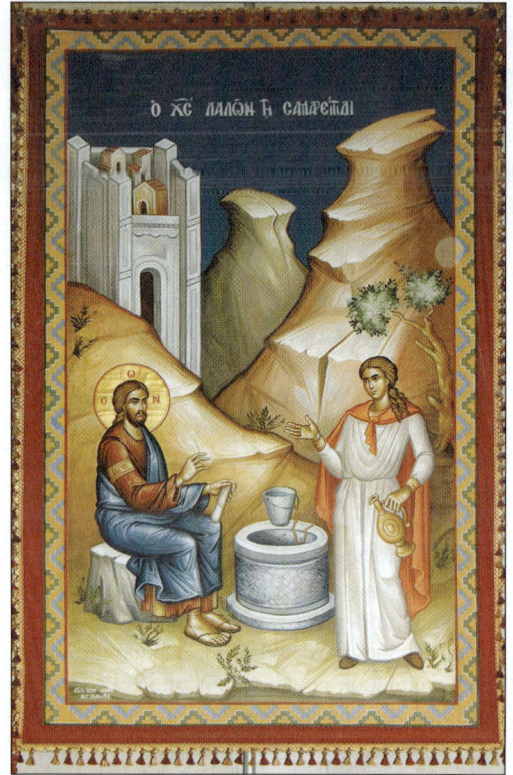

Painting inside of the Greek Orthodox Church of Jacob's Well at Sychar depicting the encounter between Jesus and the Samaritan woman at the well (Jn. 4).

scribal error for Shechem. The Old Syriac version also reads Shechem (F. C. Burkitt, *Evangelion da-Mepharreshe* [1904], 436). In the *Itinerary of Jerusalem* (dated A.D. 333) a Sechar is located one mile E of Nablus.

Recent debate still leaves the identity of Sychar open to question. Many modern scholars have identified it with an ancient site named ʿAskar, on the eastern slope of Mount EBAL, about half a mile N of JACOB's WELL and just E of Shechem. Several objections have been raised against this proposal. The narrative of Jn. 4:15 suggests the woman of Sychar was in the habit of going to Jacob's well for water. The village of el-ʿAskar, however, is not sufficiently close to Jacob's well. Moreover, at that village there is a copious spring more than adequate to supply the water needs of its inhabitants.

Others have argued that Sychar should be identified with Shechem, but the recent excavations of G. E. Wright (see his *Shechem: The Biography of a*

Biblical City [1965]) have revealed that the end of Shechem as a city occurred in 107 B.C. when Jews from Jerusalem under John Hyrcanus (134–104 B.C.) destroyed the Samaritan temple on Mount GERIZIM in 128 and finally destroyed the city of Shechem in 107. However, at the site of these ruins, Tell Balatah, there is evidence of occupation from the period of the Samaritans to Roman times. Jacob's well, according to an unbroken tradition, lies about half a mile to the E of the village of Balatah.

Historically, the well is one of the best-attested sites in Palestine, at least since NT times. It stands on the eastern edge of the valley, which forms the pass between Mounts Ebal and Gerizim. The water table that feeds the well rests upon an impermeable layer of basalt some 20 meters below the valley floor. With the accumulation of town debris and older sites since HYKSOS times, Shechem is 12–25 meters above the surrounding valley floor. The woman of Samaria was correct in asserting "the well is deep," possibly 32–55 meters in depth (cf. Jn. 4:11). The sacred associations of the well, and its quality of water, in contrast to the harder water from neighboring springs on the slopes of Mount Gerizim, would form attractions for the popularity of the well throughout its history.

J. M. HOUSTON

Sychem si'kuhm. KJV NT form of SHECHEM.

Syene si-ee'nee (סְוֵנֵה H6059, from Egyp. swn). NIV Aswan. An Egyptian city, located on the E bank of the NILE, on the site of modern Aswan, some 550 mi. S of Cairo, at the first cataract of the river and just opposite the island of ELEPHANTINE. In modern times much publicized because of the building of the new dam just to the S, the area of this cataract marked the effective southern boundary of EGYPT during much of the ancient history of that country. As a frontier town, Elephantine was the starting point for expeditions to Nubia, and during the Old Kingdom several of its residents served in official capacities as leaders of caravans or of military missions. The cataract served as a barrier to travel and transport, so the area was strategically and commercially important.

A number of rock tombs of notables are found on the W bank, opposite Aswan, at Qubbet el-Hawa. These date from the Old Kingdom (mostly 6th dynasty, e.g., Mekhu and Sabni, Hekaib, Khunes, Harkhuf, Pepynakht), the Middle Kingdom (Sirenput I and II), and the New Kingdom. To the S are the ruined Coptic monastery of St. Simeon and the modern mausoleum of Aga Khan.

Syene itself did not gain prominence until Saite times, but it gradually replaced the island town as the outstanding city of the district. Today its successor, Aswan, is still an important city of S Egypt. Remains of temples can be seen in the city, but excavation has been largely prevented by the presence of modern buildings. The area was sacred to Khnum, the ram-headed god to whom legend attributes the forming of mankind on his potter's wheel. Khnum, Satis, and Anukis composed the divine triad of the cataract region.

Southeast of Aswan are the old quarries which provided the fine granite for buildings and objects of art. Stone for temple and tomb structures, obelisks, colossi, and sarcophagi was cut here and transported by boat to determined sites throughout the length of Egypt. Still in the quarry is the huge unfinished obelisk 137 ft. long.

Syene appears in the Bible at least twice in prophetic utterances of EZEKIEL against Egypt that allude to the geographic extent of the country. One passage declares that God would make "the land of Egypt a ruin and a desolate waste from Migdol to Aswan, as far as the border of Cush" (Ezek. 29:10). The other one states that the allies of Egypt will be defeated: "From Migdol to Aswan / they will fall by the sword within her" (30:6). In addition, Syene is probably mentioned in Isa. 49:12; here the MT reads *sinim* (cf. KJV), but the Great Isaiah Scroll (1QIsa^a) has *swnyym*, which appears to be a gentilic form of *sĕwēnēh*. Thus the NIV translates, "See, they will come from afar— / some from the north, some from the west, / some from the region of Aswan." (See A. H. Gardiner, *Ancient Egyptian Onomastica*, 2 vols. [1947], II; H. Gauthier, *Dictionnaire de noms géographiques contenus dans les textes hiéroglyphiques*, 7 vols. [1925–31], 5:17–18, 1*–5*; P. Montet, *Géographie de l'Égypte ancienne*, 2 vols. [1957–61], 2:13–29.)

C. E. DEVRIES

syllabary. A system of written characters, each of which represents a syllable. See WRITING.

symbolism. The practice of using symbols (words or other signs that stand for something else) to communicate ideas or express intangible truths. The English word *symbol* derives (via Latin) from Greek *symbolon*, "token, sign" (cf. the cognate verb *symballō* G5202, lit., "to throw together," which in extrabiblical literature can mean "to compare"). Neither this Greek noun nor any term to express the abstract sense of "symbolism" occurs in the Bible, but the concept has an essential place in both the OT and NT. For a discussion of relevant Hebrew and Greek terms see SIGN.

  I. The nature of symbols and symbolism
     A. The problem of definition
     B. The antiquity of symbols
     C. The clue to symbolism
     D. A symbol defined
     E. The nature of symbolism and symbols illustrated
  II. Symbols in the Bible
     A. Their place and function in the biblical revelation
     B. Varieties of biblical symbols
  III. The cross
  IV. Postbiblical symbolism

I. The nature of symbols and symbolism

A. The problem of definition. The difficulties involved in constructing an adequate definition of a symbol stem in part from the overlapping usage of the words *sign*, *type*, and *symbol*. For example, *Webster's Third New International Dictionary* speaks of *symbol* as "something that stands for or suggests something else by reason of relationship, association, convention, or accidental but not intentional resemblance; especially a visible *sign* [italics added] of something [as a concept or institution] that is invisible." *The Concise Oxford Dictionary* (5th ed.) says under *sign*: "written mark conventionally used for word or phrase, *symbol* [italics added], thing used as representation of something." *Funk and Wagnalls New 'Standard' Dictionary* defines *type* as "something that is emblematic; that which represents or *symbolizes* [italics added] something else; *symbol* [italics added]."

Despite this overlapping, there are significant differences among the terms. In the first place, symbols are signs in the sense that they point to something else, but not all signs are symbols. A sign is a direct way of communicating, often for the practical purpose of leading to action. It is denotative and limited in the information it imparts. A symbol, however, is a connotative and often metaphorical way of communicating. It is far less limited and far more subtle in its scope than the sign (cf. F. W. Dillistone, *Christianity and Symbolism* [1955], 17). As Susanne K. Langer says, "Symbols are not proxy for their objects, but are *vehicles for the conception of objects*" (*Philosophy in a New Key* [1960], 60–61). Again the basic distinction between a type (a peculiarly biblical mode of communication) and a symbol is that a type always refers to an antitype that is future, whereas a symbol may have a past, present, or future reference. See TYPOLOGY.

Useful as these distinctions are, they must not be pressed rigidly. For the symbol is too flexible and subtle a mode of communication to be shut off entirely from the sign or type. A wall cannot be erected around the symbol; the door between it and the sign and the type is an open one. Sometimes what is for some only a sign or type becomes through individual response a symbol for others.

B. The antiquity of symbols. It is necessary, therefore, to probe more deeply into the nature of symbolism, looking back to beginnings. Symbolism is as old as humanity. Before the invention of the alphabet or the development of civilization, human beings had symbols. The ability to respond to symbols is a distinctive feature of humanity. Animals can respond to signs, but not to symbols. Anthropologists, regardless of their attitude toward religion, agree upon the great antiquity of symbolism.

The biblical evidence of this antiquity is plain; before the FALL God gave ADAM and EVE the first symbols—sun and moon (Gen. 1:14–16); the tree of life and the tree of the knowledge of good and evil with its forbidden fruit (2:9, 17; 3:1–7). After the fall the flaming sword guarded the tree of life (3:22–24). Likewise, after the flood God gave humans the RAINBOW, symbolizing the divine COVENANT not to destroy the earth again by water (9:12–17). As the French psychologist T. A. Ribot pointed out in 1915, "the symbol had appeared with the origin of humanity which was its golden age" ("La pensée symbolique," *Revue philosophique*, no vol. [1915], 385ff.).

C. The clue to symbolism. Acting upon this clue, E. Cailliet concluded, after four years of field work studying symbolism among the primitive people of Madagascar, that the essential mark of symbolism is a person's participation in the reality that the symbol suggests (*Symbolisme et âmes primitives* [1936]). For example, an ocean liner passes another ship flying the flag of a foreign nation; for a traveler that flag is only a sign or emblem. But suppose that the same traveler experiences isolation amid another culture with its strange language and customs and that suddenly, upon turning a street corner, he is confronted by the flag of his own nation. Then his heart will pound in his chest, stirred as old participations crowd into his mind. At that moment the flag is no longer a sign or emblem; it is a symbol, for the person is involved with his whole being in the reality to which it points. Or, moving the analogy to a higher level, consider the case of a Roman soldier in the 2nd cent. seeing the outline of a fish crudely drawn upon a wall. For him it is simply a sign that some of the despised sect of Christians have been there. But later a Christian woman passes by and sees the fish. Immediately she breathes more quickly, her mind is filled with rich associations, her heart is turned to Christ and his love. For her this simple design is emphatically not a sign but a true symbol.

D. A symbol defined. Therefore, what makes a symbol a symbol—what animates it and at bottom differentiates it from a sign, or sometimes even a type—is the sense of participation. It may be defined as follows: *A symbol is something that points to something else as the sign of a participation experienced or suggested* (Cailliet). The symbol not only "participates in the reality which is symbolized," as Paul Tillich says (*Systematic Theology* [1957], 2:9); it also engenders personal participation in that reality.

E. The nature of symbolism and symbols illustrated. The primitive character of the symbol persists in that people continue, even in modern times, to think with their whole body (Cailliet).

A person's space has three dimensions, because the body has three dimensions. We count as we do because we have ten fingers. The rhythm of our language relates to the life within us. Words, as well as nonverbal symbols, can cause our pulse to quicken, our face to flush, our body to tremble. Therefore, the recovery of wholeness implied in a genuine symbolism has its clear Christian implications. The believer's life is rooted in a deep sense of participation in Christ. The believer's witness is one of powerful suggestion, capable of being used by the Spirit to create in others this very sense of participation in the living Lord and Savior.

Because participation is the criterion of what makes a symbol a symbol, it follows that what may be for some only a sign intellectually grasped may for others become through believing participation a living symbol. For example, there are those who have regarded the plagues of Egypt and the overthrow of Pharaoh and his army in the Red Sea as signs of natural forces and nothing more, but for the children of Israel these events were, through participation, unforgettable symbols (typological symbols) of God's power manifest in judgment and deliverance. As Jews and, later on, Christians have looked back upon them even to this day, these things have continued to symbolize the experiential participation of God's people in his power exercised in their behalf. The same principle applies to the wealth of typology in the Pentateuchal account of the TABERNACLE and the priestly sacrifices and offerings. For some this is only an ancient priestly code. For others its typology comes to its climax and fulfillment in the antitype of Christ's redeeming work, recorded in the Gospels and expounded elsewhere in the NT (particularly in the epistle to the Hebrews). This typology ascends to the level of high symbolism through believing participation in the atoning work of Christ.

Another example—and one relating to words rather than to objects or actions—is that of the CREEDS. These are sometimes called *symbols*, and rightly so. Paul records in three words, "Jesus is Lord" (1 Cor. 12:3), the earliest Christian creed. Now to say those words and really to believe them implies the deepest kind of participation through acceptance of the sovereignty of Christ over one's whole life. So also with the classic affirmations of the faith, as in the APOSTLES' CREED and the Nicene Creed and their successors, the very words that begin them, "I believe," evidence their symbolic character.

The great antiquity of symbols must not obscure their contemporary importance. The development of modern mathematics and science (esp. physics) is closely tied to mental models or constructs. This kind of "symbolism" (cf. A. N. Whitehead and B. Russell, *Principia Mathematica*, 2nd ed. [1950]) is thoroughly objectified and thus wholly depersonalized. Therefore, it is far removed from the genuine participation-symbolism not only of the Bible but also of poetry, art, and the deeper levels of human life, on which people still depend for spiritual and emotional satisfaction even as they look to mental models for mathematical and scientific advance.

The roots of symbolism reach down to the core of modern man's being just as they are embedded in the being of primitive man. How deep these roots go, Louis Beinart shows in describing the crucial role played by Christianity in the revitalization of symbolism: "By its renewal of the great figures and symbolizations of natural religion, Christianity has also renewed their vitality and power in the depths of the psyche.... The adoption by Christ and the church of the great images of the sun and the moon, of wood, water, the sea, and so forth, amounts to an evangelization of the effective powers that they denote" (quoted by M. Eliade, *Images and Symbols: Studies in Religious Symbolism* [1961], 160–61).

II. Symbols in the Bible

A. Their place and function in the biblical revelation.
Symbols, which are universal among nations and are found in all literatures, are very numerous in Scripture. Moreover, it is in the biblical REVELATION that they attain their highest level. Since no book is closer to human life than the Bible, and since no book brings God and eternal things nearer to human beings, both the profusion of symbols in its pages and the loftiness of many of them are inevitable. Indeed, without symbols certain elements of the biblical revelation could not be communicated. When the Bible speaks about the nature of God and about eschatological subjects—e.g., the future kingdom, judgment, heaven and hell—only through symbolism can it convey to the finite mind ideas about eternal things.

B. Varieties of biblical symbols.
Symbols in the Bible are much too abundant for all of them to be listed here, but representative examples will show their basic character and abundance.

Among the many symbols drawn from *nature* are the sun, moon, stars, fire, thunder and lightning, rain, snow, sea, mountains, sands, deserts, rivers, springs, and valleys. *Nonhuman creatures* (lion, wolf, lamb, goat, ox, eagle, dove, vulture, serpent, locust, bee, scorpion, and spider), as well as various forms of *inanimate life* (trees, grass, flowers, grain) and *man-made objects* (yoke, crown, lamp, girdle, shoes, helmet, shield, sword, bread, wine, cross), are used symbolically. The same is true of *colors* (particularly red, blue, purple, and white), *metals* (gold, silver, iron), *precious stones* (ruby, emerald, sapphire, amethyst, pearl), and *numbers* (notably one, three, seven, eight, twelve, and forty).

Persons are sometimes symbolic in Scripture; for example, Adam, Abel, Cain, Abraham, Moses, Jonah, Ezekiel, Solomon. Christ, however, is not a symbol. The supreme Antitype of the richest biblical symbolic types, he *is* reality and truth in his unity with the Father and the Spirit. Closely related to persons are *names*. "In the OT, far from being a mere label, just an external description, a name expresses the profound reality of the being who carries it" (H. Michaud, "Name, O.T.," in *A Companion to the Bible*, ed. J. J. Von Allmen [1958], 278). So it is preeminently with the name Yahweh (Exod. 3:14) and its many compounds (e.g., Gen. 22:14; Exod. 17:15). Likewise in the NT with the names Jesus ("Yahweh is salvation") and Christ ("Anointed"). Among many other symbolic biblical names are Abram ("exalted father") and Abraham ("father of a multitude"); Jacob ("supplanter") and Israel ("he struggles with God"); Moses ("drawn out"); Solomon ("peaceable"). Among messianic names, especially significant is Immanuel, "God with us." Christ himself used names meaningfully: to Simon he gave the name Cephas/Peter ("rock"), and to James and John, Boanerges ("sons of thunder").

Offices held by persons, such as prophets, priests, kings, and judges, have symbolic meanings that ultimately relate to Christ and his divine offices.

itself was thought of as residing in the blood (Lev. 17:11). The great concentration of OT references to blood is in Leviticus, the book of sacrifices. Blood symbolizes life given up in death, and in the OT it has cleansing and expiatory meaning as it points to Christ's sacrifice. So in the NT, blood is a major symbol of the atoning death of Christ and its benefits. In instituting the EUCHARIST the Lord used the wine to point to the blood signifying his life given in vicarious sacrifice (Matt. 26:28; Mk. 14:24). Mention of the blood of Christ is frequent elsewhere in the NT (e.g., Rom. 5:9; 1 Pet. 1:18–19; 1 Jn. 1:7).

An important kind of biblical symbol is that relating to *actions*. Certain activities of some of the prophets come under this head. Jeremiah was ordered by the Lord to purchase a field at Anathoth in land occupied by Babylonians (Jer. 32:6–44); Ezekiel was told to perform a number of symbolic actions, including lying 390 days on his left side and 40 days on his right side (Ezek. 4:4–8), and shaving his head and beard (5:1–4); Hosea's experience with his wife Gomer and with her unfaithfulness is one of the great OT symbols (Hos. 1:2–3, 6–9; 3:1–3).

The *rite* of CIRCUMCISION was a continuing symbol for Israel. So also were her FEASTS: of primary importance were the SABBATH and the Day of Atonement (see ATONEMENT, DAY OF). In the NT, the SACRAMENTS of baptism and the Lord's Supper are profound action symbols of the believer's participation in Christ, while the Sabbath evidently becomes the Lord's Day in celebration of Christ's resurrection. That Christ's MIRACLES unquestionably have a symbolic aspect is evident from their place in the Gospel of John and John's designation of them by the word "sign" (*sēmeion* G4956).

By no means are all the multitudinous symbols in the Bible on the high level of participation that mark circumcision and the exodus in the OT and the Christological symbols in the NT. As suggested earlier, the boundaries between signs, types, and symbols are open ones. In some cases the nuances of participation are slight; in other cases the elevation of a sign or a type to the symbolic level is a subjective matter depending upon the believing insight of the person to whom the symbol communicates. Thus there are signs and types that have, as it were, symbolic potential.

This relief features a menorah, with *lulav* and date palm frond on either side — all symbols of the Jewish faith.

Parts of the human organism like the eye, the hand, the heart, the kidneys (reins), and bowels had for the ancient Hebrews symbolic significance. The BLOOD is in a class by itself, for this was considered the principal component of the body; indeed, life

III. The cross. The classic Christian symbol of the CROSS is historically, along with the empty tomb that is inextricably united to it (Heb. 13:20–21), an action symbol par excellence. As used by the NT writers, the cross is a terse verbal symbol of Christ's vicarious sacrifice at Calvary and of what God did through him (1 Cor. 1:18; Gal. 5:11; Col. 1:20 et al.). There is no mention in the NT of crosses being drawn or made as physical symbols of the cross on which Christ died and of his atoning work there. In the CATACOMBS, with their many symbols, the direct representation of the cross is strangely lacking except for two or three possible exceptions. (The manual sign of the cross was doubtless used in the early centuries.) In fact, there are in the catacombs few if any direct symbols of Christ's passion. This may be because of the great emphasis in apostolic Christianity on the resurrection and the future life. The faith to which the symbols in the catacombs point is that of hope in Christ.

Perhaps the meaning of the cross was so integral a part of their life in Christ that the members of the early church were restrained in representing it; or a fear of idolatry of the cross may have inhibited them. Also it took time for the object that was despised as a stumbling block (1 Cor. 1:23; Gal. 5:11) to become for all believers the triumphant symbol of glory and victory that it was for Paul (6:14). Indirectly the cross does appear in the catacombs of the first three centuries, veiled under the guise of symbols like the anchor or the trident. And at the close of this period the use of the monogram of the first two letters of the name "Christ" (Gk. X and P) suggests the cross when combined. As for the crucifix, it is not found in churches until after the 7th cent.

IV. Postbiblical symbolism. In the NT church, symbolism seems to have been centered in the sacraments (baptism and the Lord's Supper), the use of the Lord's Day (the first day of the week) for worship, and the practice of the laying on of hands. The profuse development of Christian symbolism began in subapostolic times with the use of symbols as seen in the catacombs. Christ is prominent as the Good Shepherd, as Judge of the dead, and so forth. There are also festal scenes pointing to future happiness and various symbols of the resurrection. But the cross as a directly represented symbol is, as has already been said, missing.

About the 3rd cent., when separate buildings for Christian worship began to be built, symbolism continued to flourish. As time passed, the cross (and later the crucifix) became prominent, extrabiblical tradition supplied symbols, and the extensive vocabulary of ecclesiastical symbolism manifest in church architecture and in religious art was developed. (Cf. G. Ferguson, *Signs and Symbols in Christian Art* [1961].)

The place of symbolism in Christian life and worship is assured. Biblically, it is an organic part of the written revelation; traditionally, it reflects cherished memories and customs of the church. Yet symbolism must always be interpreted and used with thoughtful discretion. For the reality is always greater than the symbol, and to confuse even the loftiest Christian symbols with the reality of the Lord, believing participation in whom they invite, may lead to the error of substituting the means for the end.

(In addition to the works mentioned in the body of this article, see H. S. Griffith, *The Sign Language of Our Faith: Learning to Read the Christian Symbols*, 2nd ed. [1944]; G. Cope, *Symbolism in the Bible and the Church* [1959]; O. Keel, *The Symbolism of the Biblical World: Ancient Near Eastern Iconography and the Book of Psalms* [1977]; P. Diel, *Symbolism in the Bible: The Universality of Symbolic Language and Its Psychological Significance* [1986]; P. Grelot, *Le langage symbolique dans la Bible: Enquête de sémantique et d'exégèse* [2001]; A. W. Steffler, *Symbols of the Christian Faith* [2002]; C. R. Koester, *Symbolism in the Fourth Gospel: Meaning, Mystery, Community*, 2nd ed. [2003]; P. Grelot, *The Language of Symbolism: Biblical Theology, Semantics, and Exegesis* [2006].)

F. E. GAEBELEIN

Symeon sim´ee-uhn. Alternate form of SIMEON in some English versions of the NT.

Symmachus sim´uh-kuhs. See SEPTUAGINT IV.B.

synagogue. A Jewish congregation and, by extension, the name of the building or structure where the congregation meets for worship. Like the word CHURCH, this term applies to the body of believers acting corporately and not to the physical constructs primarily. This is made clear by both the etymology and usage of the term in Jewish and non-Jewish literature. The word is universally understood as describing Jewish religious bodies and is applied to no other.

I. The name
II. History of the synagogue institution
    A. Origin: The OT period
    B. The intertestamental period
    C. The NT period
    D. The Diaspora
    E. The medieval and modern periods
III. Architecture and function
    A. Location
    B. Structure
    C. Furniture and decoration
    D. Religious and educational usage
IV. Organization and offices
    A. Elders and rulers
    B. Rabbis and laity
V. The service
    A. Shema
    B. Scripture and sermon
    C. Fasts and festivals
    D. Administration

I. The name. The Greek noun *synagōgē* G5252 (from the verb *synagō* G5251, "to gather, bring together") can be used generally of any gathering of people for either religious or secular purposes and can also be applied to any gathering place (for the latter, cf. Gen. 1:9 LXX). It is a widely distributed classical term and is used in inscriptions as well as literary texts. In the SEPTUAGINT it is used to render many different Hebrew words and expressions, but in a strong majority of the occurrences it is equivalent to *ʿēdâ* H6337, "assembly, community" (Exod. 12:3 et al.). The next most frequent equivalence is the close synonym *qāhāl* H7736, "company, convocation, assembly" (Gen. 28:3 et al.). The TARGUMS commonly render *ʿēdâ* with Aramaic *kĕništāʾ*, which was the standard rabbinic term for "synagogue" (cf. in postbiblical and modern Hebrew, *bēt-kĕneset*, from *kānas* H4043, "to gather").

II. History of the synagogue institution. The history of the synagogue as an institution among the Jews is exceedingly difficult to trace to its source. Its origins seem to lie outside of Palestine and apart from that sector of Jewish life that governed the country and produced the OT. The later traditions of the Aramaic period assume the antiquity of the synagogue. There is little documentary evidence before the Hellenistic age, the ELEPHANTINE papyri, and the NT for any synagogue. However, it must have come into being in the confused state of affairs between the fall of the first commonwealth and the establishment of the second.

A. Origin: The OT period. Certain of the historical aspects that led to the formation of the synagogue can be ascertained from the society which existed under Persian and later Hellenistic rule. The removal of the Levitical and other sacerdotal officers from Jerusalem deprived the TEMPLE of its necessary complement of attendants. The prohibition of journeys to Jerusalem and the loss of revenue must have rendered the unified cult center inoperative. The collapse of the old religious state meant a great increase in personal rather than official religious functions, a trend seen in the great prophetic voices, Isaiah and Jeremiah, even before the final collapse, and a theme renewed in Daniel. The necessity to preserve the TORAH, the five books of Moses, not merely as the central religious document but also as the only communication of Yahweh to his people motivated corporate Torah study. This trend was enforced by the pressure for syncretism with the Persian and Grecian paganism and the slow deterioration of the classical HEBREW LANGUAGE.

The result was a move to preserve not only the Torah but also its ancient speech. The first desire brought about the textual recension that became the Masoretic Text, the second gave rise to the Masoretes themselves (see MASORAH). However, both grew up not in Jerusalem but in the small DIASPORA communities and in the lands later won by force of Jewish arms under Judas MACCABEE and his followers. All that can be surely stated is that the synagogue arose as a corporate Torah study with all of the legal and binding relationships such a community would form among alien and displaced Jews.

The later literature always connects the origin of the synagogue with the period of Babylonian captivity and return under EZRA and NEHEMIAH. The terminology used for the great gathering and restatement of the Torah under Ezra is variant and uncertain, showing that new institutions were in formation. The scholarly treatment of the problem has tended to fall under the influence of two opposing schools of thought. The traditional one that Moses founded the synagogue is cited by JOSEPHUS (*Apion* 2.17 §75). It was popular at various times throughout the recent centuries. The second thesis that the synagogue was of societal origin and appeared during the EXILE was proposed by the Italian humanist Carlo Sigonio (1524–84). His views wreaked havoc among the more conservative Jews and Christians of the time but were finally dominant in the treatment by the Dutch theologian Campegius Vitringa (1659–1722).

Many other theories have been proposed, some locating the synagogue among the legal-political institutions of Israel rather than the religious. On the other hand, some very modern views would tend to see it as the focus of town life in what was really a nation of villages. This view is supported by the excavation of ancient synagogue sites. In a recent monograph, A. Runesson has proposed that the synagogue had a twofold development: in Palestine it arose from town assemblies (due to "the loosening of the control of the national authorities over torah teaching"), whereas in much of the Diaspora it derived from voluntary associations (*The Origins of the Synagogue: A Socio-Historical Study* [2002], 478–82).

The WORSHIP of the synagogue was very different from that of the temple in that it had no sacerdotal rituals and supported no sacrosanct priesthood. Instead a new order of religious leaders arose to serve the synagogue, the RABBI. The influence of the Persians and the Greeks over the spread of the synagogue cannot be denied, and there is every reason to assume that although it was Babylonian in origin it was to some degree Greek in spirit. The architecture of the early synagogues is similar to the Greco-Roman of the contemporary pagan constructs. Of special importance is the Jewish temple at Elephantine in upper Egypt. The papyri discovered there indicate that animal sacrifices took place and yet there is no evidence that this was true within the meeting houses in Palestine.

In fact the DEAD SEA SCROLLS indicate a strong preference for sacrifices and rituals only in the temple in Jerusalem. It may be that the synagogue was only one type of worship arrangement known at the time and that it was the one which survived the Roman destruction of the great temple. It is even highly probable that one or more synagogues existed within the temple compound in Jerusalem, and it may have been there that Jesus was found sitting among the lawyers at the age of twelve (Lk. 2:46). It is also clear from the later traditions that the basic unit of the synagogue was ten men who gathered for prayer. This would be similar to the OT congregations.

B. The intertestamental period. The vast growth of the synagogue and its appearance throughout the Diaspora is noted in many documents from the time between OT and NT. Both PHILO JUDAEUS and JOSEPHUS regularly mention the synagogue as do the earliest rabbinical sources. The dominant language of its services became ARAMAIC as the Persian empire waxed and waned and the central autonomy of Israelite kingship faded into the past. In the new religious rituals, the chanting of the prayers and the reading of the biblical text became the central function of the service. The officers of the new religious communities were given new titles, and in the Hellenistic period Greek terms for these were adopted. This was the formative period that saw the final supremacy of the synagogue. It was the customary center of the Jewish community and house of worship throughout the known world in Jesus' time. See JUDAISM.

C. The NT period. The term *synagōgē* is used in the Gospels and Acts over fifty times (elsewhere only Jas. 2:2; Rev. 2:9; 3:9). It is assumed in both the rabbinic literature and the NT that this was the valid leadership and executive of Judaism, no matter whether it was in Jerusalem or Corinth. A few inscriptions have been located from synagogues of this era, and they are distinctive in that they are in Greek uncials written in the Hellenistic style. The most extensive is the Theodotus Inscription, found on Mount Ophel not far from the ancient temple precinct. It specifically states that the purpose of the building upon which it was a marker was for "reading of the law," and that it was to serve as a hostel. Other inscriptions from the GALILEE area

Remains of the 1st-century B.C. Gamla synagogue (NE of the Sea of Galilee), one of the earliest synagogues discovered to date. (View to the SW.)

often list OT characters or indicate the donors, but again in epigraphic Greek. It is this cosmopolitanism and appeal to the common conscience which marks the synagogal success.

The gospel narratives mention a number of small towns in Galilee and the synagogues where Jesus taught (Matt. 4:23; 9:35; Lk. 4:16, 33). An additional group in this area has been excavated. They are small buildings with porches and columns (often *distyle-in-antis*, i.e., having the columns set between two antae), stone seats, and an outer portico. They must have served as law courts, schools, libraries, and market places, as well as for the Sabbath service. It is also clear that the Jewish males took part in the service. The most important legacy of the 1st-cent. synagogue was the form and organization of the apostolic church.

D. The Diaspora synagogues. The growth of popular religious organizations in Palestine was paralleled by similar establishments among the Jews of the dispersion. Large halls were built in DURA-EUROPOS and various parts of Egypt, and the worship of the Jews from the Diaspora mentioned in Acts 2:9–11 was presumably in synagogues in all those widely scattered places. Numerous ancient synagogues have been located within Palestine and in Syria, and some others in the neighboring lands of the E Mediterranean. There must have been hundreds of them by the end of the 2nd cent. A.D. By that time the original Greek term had come to mean exclusively a Jewish house of worship. These communities were displaced but in many cases had attained considerable wealth, and their synagogues are richly carved and well appointed with the crafts of their time. Like the church, the synagogue was becoming an institution of stature and capital and both were to produce a long and involved literary tradition.

E. The medieval and modern periods. As the Jews moved through the W Mediterranean and up into Spain and France they built and rebuilt synagogues. Where Christian states forbade public buildings, a new tradition of private and semiprivate chapels arose. Some of these have been found and many are well known from literature. The education of the young was more and more a function of the community through the synagogue, and its ancient tradition of a "Torah study" became very strong as the common speech became eroded and finally ceased to function in alien societies. From the 8th cent. the synagogues of Spain at Toledo were the centers of European Jewry. Later the same situation held true in Austria and E Germany, from which such travelers as Petahia of Ratisbon and others set out before the year 1000 to communicate with the great synagogue centers of the Orient.

The change of the millennium found Jewish synagogues stretching from England to the borders of China. However, the uneasy peace in which the Jews had lived between the Christian Holy Roman Empire and the Islamic E finally evaporated in the crusades. The reaction to the inability of Western Christian feudalism to regain Palestine led to pogrom after pogrom against the Jews. Thus they were driven into the newer lands of the Baltic coast and along the rivers of Orthodox Russia. There the great synagogues of Breslau, Leipzig, Vilna, Moscow, and the like held sway over world Jewry. In the 18th cent. Spanish and Portuguese Jews began to migrate to North America, the earliest American synagogue being the Congregation Touro of Newport, Rhode Island, founded in 1763. However, several congregations in Philadelphia were soon functioning thereafter and the Maimonides College became their first institution of higher learning. The modern synagogue can take many forms and be found in many places, but its primary functions still continue to be as house of worship, school for study, and social center for the Jewish people.

III. Architecture and function.

The architecture of the early Middle Eastern synagogues was similar to that which prevailed throughout the Hellenistic and later Roman age. The synagogue grounds were surrounded by a low wall within which the synagogue met. Documents from Turkey and other countries of the early medieval period show that often the congregation met out-of-doors although at other times in private rooms. Usually this room was divided in some fashion into a sector for men and a separate and lesser room for the women. In the magnificent Moorish and Italian synagogues this women's section took the form of a balcony running around three sides of the room and reached by outer stairs up through a sort of narthex. In the earliest Palestinian synagogues, such as those at MASADA, CAPERNAUM, KORAZIN, and Kefr Birʾim, stone seats in the form of a double tier ran the length of three walls. Such buildings had either a separate balcony for women or some separation down the center. In the Roman age many of these buildings were of a type of Corinthian Greek design with free standing columns in the front portico and arranged in rows within the sanctuary to support the vaulted ceilings.

A. Location. In accord with certain Talmudic instructions that must have been part of the oral lore of Judaism, all the synagogues were built in such a fashion that the congregations could face Jerusalem. The legal lore of the synagogue is found in the opening paragraphs of the tractate *Megillah*. The customs resolving the matter of synagogue construction are later. The common practice was to erect the building on a small hill or prominence, sometimes near water but always in such a fashion that the back wall which faced the door was toward Jerusalem. The temple in Jerusalem represented the sacerdotal element and ritual in Judaism and so the elaborate ceremonial architecture of the later synagogues was unnecessary until after the destruction of the temple in A.D. 70. Whether or not the local synagogues were built as models or miniatures of the great temple, or whether they were conceived as centers for the rituals is debated. By this time the style of construction was set and the synagogue was located in the center of the market square.

B. Structure. By the 1st Christian century the basilica type of building with its massive and ornamented façade became the standard synagogue form. However, the extent of symbolism and the expanse was limited by the economic ability of the congregation. There is no clear-cut evolution of synagogal architecture, and each community of the Diaspora seems to have built eclectic structures appropriate to their situation. The widespread use of the half square and round columns and the elaborate shell niches, both associated with Roman buildings, demonstrates how deeply the Greco-Roman civilization altered the Jewish mind. In or about the middle of the blank wall opposite the entrance doors was the location of the niche or chamber in which the sacred rolls of the Torah were kept. Such cabinets or chests (called in Heb. ʾărôn haqqôdeš), set in the E wall, were often ornamented and decorated with hangings and embellishments of considerable value.

One of the most interesting appointments of the early synagogues was the GENIZAH, a place either in a cellar or pit or in an old attic high in the wall where the worn and frayed parchment scrolls were placed. Since they bore the divine name of God, these scrolls could not be desecrated or destroyed and so they were interred. Ancient scrolls of inestimable value have been discovered in a number of genizahs from synagogues. In the center, later the front, of the hall was an upraised platform on which the scrolls were placed for reading; this platform was also used for the sermon, a sort of explanation of the text. Special coffers, cabinets, and closets for the ritual implements were later added through time-honored tradition and specific names became applied to them.

Certain differences have also developed between the Ashkenazi and Sephardic Jews because of their different cultural backgrounds. The German-Russian synagogues were more on the order of Gothic and Romanesque style churches, while the Spanish-Portuguese synagogues, some of the most magnificent ever built, were influenced by Mediterranean styles, with Arabesque vaults and other such features. In modern times the synagogues of the Western world have shown all the innovations of contemporary architecture; prestressed concrete, stainless steel, glass, and plastics have been used in these timeless expressions of Israel's faith. The magnificence of Frank Lloyd Wright's design for Beth Shalom, N of Philadelphia, Beth Am in suburban New York, and many recent synagogues in Europe and Israel are based upon ancient traditions and symbolisms but stated in the avant garde of the 20th cent.

C. Furniture and decoration. The furniture of the ancient and early medieval synagogue was utilitarian and connected with the service. The Torah ark was frequently carved or encrusted with some type of decoration, covered with magnificent hangings and covers (called *pārōket*) and often richly ornamented with silver and gold embroideries. The lecterns were carved and inlaid. The great seven-branched candelabra (*měnôrâ*) was often richly decorated, examples of the finest in the casting and etching arts were found in their manufacture for the wooden synagogues of Poland, Lithuania, and Russia. Many smaller articles, lamp stands, and the ritual implements for the high holy days (Rosh Hashanah and Yom Kippur, but also the lesser pilgrimages) were found in the synagogue. Special vestments and scroll tabernacles, usually in the form of elaborate miniatures, as well as the communal wedding rings, were also kept in the special cabinets provided.

Of special beauty are the Torah crowns, exquisite tiaras with precious and semiprecious stones hung or held over the Torah ark, or carried about in procession. Few people in history have held any book in such esteem and reverence that finery of such value was lavished upon the ornamentation of it. It is a sight of strange and reverential beauty.

The decoration of the synagogues was a subject of much debate and alteration of tastes. The earliest ones often show a strangely exotic degree of profusion in Hellenistic and Roman motifs. The ancient congregations at Capernaum and Korazin decorated their edifice with stone lions, elaborate bands of botanomorphic design and epigraphic inscriptions in uncial Greek. They carved many similar natural motifs on the furniture, and pomegranates, grapes, and similar fruit and vegetables are seen. This type of SYMBOLISM was developed from the OT as the temple was to have such ornamentation in the same fashion as the wilderness tabernacle. However, strict prohibition against the portrayal of the human form was also in evidence.

Under times of persecution the elaboration of the synagogue became simpler, and as various mystical movements caught the popular fancy of Christian and Jew alike in the high Middle Ages, the churches and the synagogues were often devoid of very much ostentation. There is no evidence that when the flavor of the arts was renewed in the Renaissance the Jewish synagogue builders followed suit. The types of murals and decorations which later played such a basic part in the humanist movement were never popular among the Jews. The strange mixture of classical themes and Christian symbolism seen in the art of the Renaissance was not adopted in the synagogue.

Even the scrolls themselves are free of miniature paintings, initial embossing, and the other church decorations of the time. However, an Arabic Muslim custom did become widespread, namely, the decoration of the upper parts of the synagogue with inscriptions that were later inlaid or leafed with gold, silver, or bronze. Such texts from the OT with the use of the unvaried Hebrew script made a pleasing decorative device. The words of the Scriptures were often carved into the wood work and paneled walls. The glass windows were painted but stained glass came to the synagogue long after it came to the church and then its designs and motifs are carried over from the glyptic arts, and often only Hebrew letters were placed in them. The innovative notions of the buttress and span which allowed the vast areas of glass in Chartres and Notre Dame are nowhere in evidence in the construction of the synagogues.

One decorative feature which survived the ages in the synagogue was the use of mosaic tiles. Numerous elaborate natural figures including the signs of the zodiac and small animals are found. The ancient synagogue at Beth Alpha is especially noted for these fine mosaics, and much of the furniture and ritual of the religious year are shown in these illustrations. Few synagogue frescos have survived from antiquity, but those from DURA-EUROPOS and elsewhere show artistic affinities, as does contemporary Christian art of the period to the sculpting of the mosaics. Again, the scenes are of the various festivals with some few architectural constructs and what may be patriarchal stories in smaller registers. The motif of the sun, the wheel, the candle, the plant, the fruit, and the various Greek running figures, arrow, and egg and dart are all found in the synagogue. Reverence for the creation has been a continuing theme in such art and pure color, and its blending and disjunction has become the theme of many modern synagogue treasures by Marc Chagal and other contemporary masters.

Since the purpose of the nonsacerdotal church buildings and that of the synagogues are functionally similar, their furniture with the exception of the ritual implements is practically indistinguishable. With the present pressure toward ever wider ecumenicity growing, it is conceivable that future synagogues and churches will be nearly identical.

D. Religious and educational usage. In the OT, it is impossible to separate religion from education. No ancient society subscribed to the modern notion of "secular." The community as a whole was responsible for the education of children and youths, and this took place in the synagogue. The later instruction of young people in the Bible and the Talmud was carried on in the *yeshivot*, the special schools for prerabbinical studies. In the earlier periods such usage of the sanctuary was frowned upon, but as the Hebrew language and learning began to fade from daily life the preservation of the ancient heritage became a sacred mission and the synagogue was used for the purpose. In this regard both lower schools and libraries of Hebraic and later Yiddish books were housed in the synagogue.

To the greater number of Jews the synagogue was a teaching organization and its house a school (Yiddish still refers to it as *schul*), but to the Gentiles of the Greco-Roman world it was a school of philosophy. Since the primary responsibility of the adult Jew in the corporate synagogue service was to read, reading the unpointed Hebrew text of the Torah was the goal of synagogue education. The earliest lessons were undoubtedly in the form of simple memorization of biblical passages followed by simple readings, such as the familiar Shema (Deut. 6:4–9, followed by 11:13–21 and Num. 15:37–41). The advanced students read the lessons from the great synagogue scrolls, guided by the commonplace synagogue official known as the *hazan*. It was in these simple schools that the elaborate oral tradition which grew up around the Torah began to take form. Unfortunately there is

Partial reconstruction of the synagogue at Korazin, dating to the 2nd or 3rd cent. A.D. (View to the SE.)

hardly any evidence derived from archaeology of the shape or substance of these studies except for some Egyptian papyri that may be fragments of school texts.

The early Jewish literature of the Haskalah movement in Eastern Europe grew out of the synagogue school. The personages and episodes that are vividly portrayed by such masters as Sholem Aleichem give the non-Jew a vital picture of life in the agricultural communities of Europe where the synagogue and its services were the center and crown of life. In such literature, the teacher is a man both respected and satirized in the community. The restrictions of modern life have rendered the majority of synagogue schools operable only on Sunday. However, they have survived and flourished as instructors in Jewish culture and art as well as Hebrew language and religion. The future of the synagogue in education appears to be leading in the direction of general community social service, and many newer synagogues have the phrase "Jewish Community Center" in their names. A parallel development has begun in the church as it seeks to secularize its appeal.

IV. Organization and offices. Over the centuries the roles of the synagogue officers have altered and the needs of the Jewish community have changed. The most important alteration has been the development of the rabbinate. In the OT, the authority of the Jewish community was vested in the convention or council of ELDERS. The ritual and ceremonial administration was under the direction of the Levitical priesthood assisted by a number of groups of professional aids such as singers, musicians, and the like. These officials represented a special and privileged class in the state. After the collapse of the monarchy and its attendant feudalism and the rise of an entrepreneurial class in the period of Hellenism, the offices of the synagogue were open to all. The increased democratization led to wider participation and a common religious interest. Without this change Judaism would never have survived the Hellenistic age and would have followed the other archaic religious states into oblivion. There were about five offices in number; however, some of them were probably simply voluntary and carried no stipend or salary.

A. Elders and rulers. The chief executive or president of the synagogue was called in Hebrew *rō'š hakkĕneset* (Gk. *archisynagōgos* G801; see RULER OF THE SYNAGOGUE). This official was known also among pagan associations, but by the 1st Christian cent. was more commonly applied to the Jewish officials and by the 5th cent. exclusively so. The title has also been found on epigraphic inscriptions. He was responsible not merely for the upkeep and operation of the house but also for the order and sanctity of the service (Lk. 13:14). Three individuals in the NT are so designated: JAIRUS (Mk. 5:22; Lk. 8:41); CRISPUS (Acts 18:8); and SOSTHENES (18:17). The interesting fact that two of these are Gentile names indicates the degree of syncretism Hellenistic Judaism had permitted.

This official had the responsibility of selecting the Torah reading and may have read it himself in the congregation. The evidence indicates that at first this was an elective office only, becoming hereditary and finally perfunctory after centuries of the synagogue's existence. The plural form that appears in Acts 13:15 has been the center of some debate, but a text from Apamea in Syria contains a listing of three such officials and uses the plural term. A similar difficulty has arisen concerning the phrase *archōn tēs synagōgēs*, "ruler/leader of the synagogue," which appears only in Lk. 8:41. This term is rare but has been located in contemporary inscriptions as an alternate and less proper form of *archisynagōgos*. Since the terms were still in a state of flux and as yet not fixed in the literary language, it is to be expected that such variants would be found.

The second functionary in the synagogue was the *ḥazzān hakkĕneset*, "servant of the synagogue" (cf. Gk. *hypēretēs* G5677, "servant, attendant" [Lk. 4:20], later used of ministers of the gospel [Lk. 1:2; Acts 26:16 et al.]). The duties of the hazan undoubtedly varied, but included at various times cleaning the premises, removing and replacing the scrolls, and perhaps overseeing the teaching of the children; but this has been debated. He also carried out the corporal punishments of the council (Matt. 10:17; 23:34; Mk. 13:9). Later the hazan became the chief singer of the service and the term is now used for "cantor." In modern times the hazan is also the director of religious education, and many Jewish institutions of higher learning offer curricula in the proper administration of the synagogue schools.

As with all offices of the ancient Israelite religious state, that of the hazan was functional. No doubt the functions varied from town to rural communities and from great to humble congregations, but the importance of the office grew with time. As the festivals and ceremonies developed along separate lines in Diaspora Judaism, so did the officers of the synagogue. The result is that a bewildering array of functions and honors are assigned to the hazan in the literature of the rabbis. One can only surmise the initial purpose of the office. It appears that the best translation in regard to the evidence is "second in authority." The modern responsibility of heading the synagogue school seems to have arisen after the Renaissance.

The third officer of the ancient synagogue was the *šăliaḥ ṣibbûr*, "leader of the prayers" (lit., "messenger of the congregation"). This individual was chosen as representative of the congregation, in whose place he responded to the liturgical prayers. Some scholars have assumed that he fulfilled the role of priest in this delegated responsibility, but it is clear that he was not sacrosanct and acted as a layman. In the NT period, the function could be assigned to any adult male in the congregation who was of good standing in the synagogue; and it may be in this capacity that Jesus read the passage from Isa. 61 in the synagogue at NAZARETH (Lk. 4:17–28). In later tradition this spontaneous quality was lost and the function was taken up by a regularly employed person of the congregation. There is an opinion that in the absence of any person willing to act in this capacity the chief officers might perform the function. Undoubtedly this practice led to the merging of this office with the permanent one of hazan so that the distinction between them was blurred (sometimes the two terms are interchanged). In the later synagogues of European Jewry, the liturgy became fixed with musical anthems, and both offices required cantorial training and musical talent.

A number of other officers are mentioned in records and discourses on the synagogue. Some of these must have existed in Roman times and have been absorbed into the later offices of the congregation. One of them was the *mĕtûrgĕmān* ("interpreter, translator"; cf. *targûm*, "interpretation"), a person who was apparently chosen from the congregation to render the text of the Scripture from Hebrew into Aramaic. This practice may be reflected in the phrase, *ho estin methermēneuomenon* "which being interpreted is," found seven times in the NT (Matt. 1:23; Mk. 5:41; 15:22, 34; Jn. 1:38 [with *legetai* instead of *estin*], 41; Acts 4:36). This custom may also be in view in Paul's exhortation in regard to speaking in tongues, "if there be no interpreter" (1 Cor. 14:28).

The *mĕtûrgĕmān* played a very important part in the synagogue service in areas such as Galilee where people were less familiar with Hebrew. A similar sort of personage must have functioned in lands of the Diaspora where Greek and Latin were spoken, because the inscriptions on such synagogue buildings are usually in those languages and rarely in Hebrew. It was such a custom of oral translation that led to the production of written Targums and that may lie also behind the Greek and the Latin versions of the OT. In the smaller synagogues where no yeshiva or rabbinic study was attached, the hazan undoubtedly fulfilled this function also. There is evidence that Hebrew teachers may have also interpreted orally the Scripture readings, possibly even commenting upon them.

The reading of Scripture and subsequent interpretation were preceded by the public proclamation of the Shema. This was stated by a special officer, the Herald of the Shema, after which the congregation answered "Amen." Such a public use of the prayer was always led by an officer and was referred to by a different terminology than that of private prayer. There is some evidence that the public praying of the Shema was read from a scroll and that other passages such as Exod. 20 may have been included. Some scholars have interpreted this action of the reading of the Decalogue as the promulgation of God's imperial decree, his law. This would accord well with the scriptural use of terms of royalty and the court to describe the reign of God. The literature of Judaism of all the ages makes clear that the kingly court of God was the synagogue in the Jewish mind and that the most sacred place and the utmost reverence was afforded the Torah. It was in light of this devotion that all the offices of the congregation took their place and authority. From the ruler of the synagogue to the "herald" all were servants of the Torah.

When in the medieval period the Decalogue was no longer used in the congregational worship and the scrolls were no longer read for the Shema prayers, then the character of the congregational offices changed also. Several administrative positions appear in the later history of the synagogue. The chief of these is the "collector" or "almoner," whose task it was to collect and distribute funds for the poor. The public giving of alms was a feature of the Jewish religious community. It is mentioned in the rabbinic literature and in the NT (e.g., Matt. 6:2–4). The Gospels and other contemporary sources indicate that while the temple in Jerusalem was supported by the royal establishment and received its revenue from special taxes, the synagogues were voluntary and free offerings were commonplace.

The collector of the synagogue who ministered to the poor was probably the model for the DEACON in the early church (1 Tim. 3:8 et al.). In later rabbinic times, when the sacerdotal rituals were replaced by the synagogue service, this usage was retained. It is this tradition which has become the base for the many Jewish philanthropic organizations that have brought aid to both Jews and non-Jews throughout the world. In the Christian church the model of the synagogue organization was retained in the ancient church and reclaimed in the Reformation. The Catholic churches from medieval times have followed the principle of sacerdotalism basic to the temple and the Levitical priesthood.

B. Rabbis and laity. The actual origin of the rabbinical office is lost in antiquity. The term RABBI (Heb. *rab* H8042 ["great"] with 1st person pronominal suffix) simply means "teacher" or "master," and was at no time a sacerdotal or ordained office. Any laymen learned in the Torah and Jewish law could be called "rabbi." After the destruction of the temple and its officialdom, some attempt appears to have been made to continue the sacerdotal offices, but as the majority of Jews moved in succeeding generations to the area of Galilee the rabbinical system arose. During the High Middle Ages it assumed the authority and primacy in the synagogue. When this time came, the rabbinate was supreme and no longer one of the laity. The ordination to the rabbinate was based on the individual's knowledge of Hebrew, Torah, Talmud, and Jewish law in general.

Although the modern rabbinate still inherits the background of Pharisaic Judaism, it is more concerned with learning than ritual. In fact, most Jewish rituals are performed in the home with the father or eldest son officiating. The synagogues in Catholic lands have tended to retain livery for the rabbis and certain laity, and rich vestments for certain services. On the other hand, those thriving in Protestant cultures have assumed many aspects of congregationalism and the dress of the bourgeoisie. This cultural syncretism has been the subject of both encouragement and scorn within Jewish circles for the whole of this century. The rise and progress of the State of Israel has tended to make the synagogues of the Diaspora emulate oriental Judaism in an ever increasing number of aspects. The contemporary rabbi is not only a Torah teacher but also a representative and instructor in Jewish custom.

V. The service

A. Shema. The recitation of the Shema and the accompanying blessings was the central portion of the simplest synagogue service, which as few as ten male members might enact. It was traditionally held that this prayer service stressing the monotheism of Yahweh was instituted by Moses himself. The eighteen short prayers that make up the general blessing are certainly earlier than the Christian era. The prayers in the service were always followed by the general "Amen" said by the congregation.

B. Scripture and sermon. The reading of the whole Torah in Hebrew was the central act of congregational worship and has been carried down in various forms to the present day. The Torah was divided into 154 or 155 sections and read through in its entirety in a three-year cycle. The selections were known as *sedarim*, and there is evidence in the writings of Philo Judaeus, Flavius Josephus, the NT, and the patristic authors that this system was in vogue in NT times. A reading from the prophets in the Jewish canon was also given in the form of the *haftarah*.

Both of these were followed by Aramaic interpretation. Then followed an extempore commentary given by a learned member of the congregation, a visiting rabbi, or possibly a visitor from another congregation. It is this custom that was apparently the means of Paul's frequent invitations to preach in the synagogues (Acts 13:14–41 et al.).

After the lectionary readings and on some occasions between them there were probably cantorial renditions of the Psalms, which were followed by set congregational responses. In the temple worship these passages were sung by antiphonal choirs but in the local synagogues they were congregational. There were undoubtedly some sung parts that terminated the service. Just what part a formal sermon played is uncertain. However, it is clear from the discourses of the prophets and kings of the OT that exhortations based upon the Torah were not unknown. The traditional material of the Targum and the involved rabbinic commentaries of the *Mikraoth Gedoloth* must have originated as running commentaries and organized sermons once delivered in the synagogue. Since Judaism had little evangelistic appeal during the early Diaspora the true sermonic type of presentation never developed. Later rabbis appear to have adopted the type of personal appeal in their homiletics that had already developed in Christian circles.

One important point concerning the synagogue service is that it was led by the members of the congregation. The sacerdotalism so often associated with later liturgical forms in Christian tradition was unknown in the synagogue. Undoubtedly this factor was obvious to the Reformers of the 16th cent. when they came into more frequent contact with the Jews as a result of the Renaissance. The high place accorded the Psalms in the Reformed congregations of France, Switzerland, and Holland may be traced to the synagogue service.

C. Fasts and festivals. The OT festivals of the Jewish religion follow the agricultural year. Since it was impossible after the Diaspora for all the Jews of the Mediterranean world to return to the temple in Jerusalem, many of the congregational feasts were held in the synagogues. These were held on the same date and at the same time as the temple ceremonies. Most of the feasts celebrated in the Jewish calendar are of later origin and appeared during the time of the synagogue. Only the faintest remnant of the great sacrifices of the atonement are still observed and these are wholly limited to the household observance of *Pesaḥ*, "Passover," which occurs in March-April. In the social gatherings of the synagogue it is more frequently the holidays of the State of Israel that are observed, and the celebrations are derived from the Jewish cultures of central Europe.

D. Administration. The addition of Hebrew schools has expanded the traditional role of the synagogues to seven days a week. The result has been a development of a professional corps of educators, teachers, and administrators to operate the system. Many synagogues in various parts of the world are large community centers and thus provide a wide array of social services as well as the formal religious services. The traditional oversight of the synagogue in the hands of a board of "elders" has not materially changed during the long history of the institution, although for efficiency's sake many synagogues also have a separate board of financial trustees. Unlike the variety of religious and structural variations in Christian church denominations, the rabbi is the executive of the synagogue in all cases.

(See further W. O. E. Oesterley and G. H. Box, *Synagogue* [1907]; M. Rosemann, *Der Ursprung*

Mosaic floor of the synagogue at Hammath Tiberias, dating to the late 3rd or early 4th cent.

der Synagoge [1907]; M. Friedländer, Synagoge und Kirche in ihren Anfängen [1908]; E. L. Sukenik, The Ancient Synagogues of Beth-Alpha [1932]; id., Ancient Synagogues in Palestine and Greece [1934]; id., The Ancient Synagogue of El Hammeh [1935]; L. Rost, Die Vorstufen von Kirche und Synagoge im Alten Testament [1938]; S. W. Baron, The Jewish Community [1942]; G. K. Lukomski, Jewish Art in European Synagogues [1947]; B. Kanael, Die Kunst der antiken Synagoge [1961]; I. Levy, The Synagogue [1963]; R. Wischnitzer, The Architecture of the European Synagogue [1964]; E. Goodenough, Jewish Symbols in the Greco-Roman Period, 13 vols. [1953–68]; J. Gutmann, ed., The Synagogue: Studies in Origins, Archaeology, and Architecture [1975], M. J. S. Chiat, Handbook of Synagogue Architecture [1982]; J. T. Burtchaell, From Synagogue to Church: Public Services and Offices in the Earliest Christian Communities [1992]; D. Urman and P. V. M. Flesher, eds., Ancient Synagogues: Historical Analysis and Archaeological Discovery, 2 vols. [1995]; D. Binder, Into the Temple Courts: The Place of the Synagogue in the Second Temple Period [1999]; L. I. Levine, The Ancient Synagogue: The First Thousand Years [2000]; A. Runesson, The Origins of the Synagogue: A Socio-Historical Study [2002]; B. Olsson and M. Zetterholm, eds., The Ancient Synagogue from Its Origins until 200 C.E. [2003]; S. T. Catto, Reconstructing the First-Century Synagogue [2007]; A. Runesson et al., The Ancient Synagogue from Its Origins to 200 C.E.: A Source Book [2008], JEWLIT XV, 4:1491–97.)

W. White, Jr.

Synagogue, Great. According to rabbinic tradition, the Great Synagogue or, more accurately, the Great Assembly (*kĕneset haggĕdôlâ, m. ʾAbot* 1:1–2 et al.) was an authoritative body of 120 elders established under Ezra and Nehemiah for the purpose of insuring greater obedience to the Mosaic laws. To this institution, which supposedly lasted about two centuries, were attributed various important accomplishments, including the composition of some biblical books, the creation of a liturgy, and the establishment of the canon. Modern scholarship in general regards this tradition as an unhistorical development of Neh. 8–10, which recounts Ezra's reading of the Torah before a national assembly as well as the positive response of the people.

(See *HJP*, rev. ed. [1973–87], 2:358–59.) There is no reference to such an institution prior to the 2nd cent. A.D. (the expression *epi megalēs synagōgēs* in 1 Macc. 14:28 is to be taken simply as a great gathering that included priests, rulers, elders, and others).

Synagogue of the Freedmen. See Freedmen, Synagogue of the.

Synoptic Gospels, synoptic problem. See biblical criticism IV.A.; Gospels III.B.1; Jesus Christ IV.A.

Syntyche sin´ti-kee (Συντύχη *G5516*, "fortunate"). A woman in the church at Philippi who, with Euodia, had labored together with Paul. There was a conflict between them, so Paul urged them to "agree with each other in the Lord" (Phil. 4:2–3). See discussion under Euodia.

Syracuse sihr´uh-kyooz (Συράκουσαι *G5352*). A city on the E coast of Sicily where Paul spent three days when the ship that carried his party put in en route for Puteoli from Malta (Acts 28:12).

Founded by Corinth in 734 B.C., Syracuse emerges into the full light of history with the rule of Gelon (540–478). Near the end of his reign, Gelon defeated the Carthaginians at Himera (in 480, the year of Salamis); and Syracuse, made thus the most important city of the western Mediterranean after Carthage, entered upon her century of imperial splendor and success. Hieron I succeeded Gelon, reigned for ten years, and extended Syracusan influence to adjacent Italy. The catastrophic defeat of Athens in its wanton attack on Syracuse (415–413) left the Sicilian city at the height of her military power and glory.

The reign of Dionysius I (430–367) saw the passing of this prestige and the evolution of Syracuse into an undisguised tyranny. Dionysius fell short of his ambition to drive the Carthaginians out of the island, suffered some defeats at their hands, and postponed a direct Carthaginian assault by treaties that must have revealed to the great Phoenician power the developing weakness of Syracuse under an inevitably debilitating tyranny. In art and in other spheres of culture, as in political and international influence, Syracuse was living through a deceptive Indian summer of greatness, seemingly powerful, but decayed internally by tyranny.

Decline was obvious and precipitous under Dionysius II, whom the great Plato had sought in vain to educate for authority. It was Timoleon (whose dates are uncertain) who restored a measure of constitutional rule, thrust the aggressive Carthaginians back, and introduced new citizens to strengthen the state. One Agathocles, a democratic leader, undid Timoleon's work and had himself made king. He died in 289 B.C., and his passing marked the beginning of the city's end. The Romans had become involved in Sicily after the middle of the 3rd cent. The island was too important a base for either side to neglect when Rome and Carthage became aware of their confrontation across the narrow waist of the Mediterranean. Struggle ensued between pro-Roman and pro-Carthaginian parties in the city, and Syracuse together with the whole island became an inevitable battleground. Syracuse, closed by the Carthaginian faction, was captured by the Roman general, Marcellus, after a fearful siege in which the Syracusan physicist, Archimedes, provided the defenders with sundry pieces of sophisticated artillery. Archimedes died in the grim aftermath of the capture of the city.

From 211 B.C. onward, therefore, Syracuse was Roman. It remained the most splendid city in the province and the seat of the governor's residence. AUGUSTUS sent settlers in 21 B.C. and made the city a colony. It was looted by the invading Franks in A.D. 280. No one knows how Christianity came to Syracuse, but extensive CATACOMBS bear witness to the solidity of its presence. E. M. BLAIKLOCK

Syria sihr´ee-uh (Συρία *G5353*, prob. a shortening and misapplication of Ἀσσυρία, ASSYRIA). In biblical scholarship, this name is usually applied to the territory N and NE of PALESTINE, covering roughly the area now occupied by the modern state of Syria (and a small part of SE Turkey); some scholars, however, use the term more broadly to include PHOENICIA (modern Lebanon), TRANSJORDAN (modern Jordan), and even Palestine (modern Israel).

Important ancient cities of Syria not mentioned in the Bible include EBLA and UGARIT. In the OT, the KJV and some other modern versions (following the LXX and Vulg.) use the name Syria to translate Hebrew ʾărām *H806*, which most frequently refers to the city-state of DAMASCUS and the neighboring territory. See discussion under ARAM (COUNTRY). (For an archaeological survey of Syria from prehistoric times through the Iron Age, see *ABD*, 6:270–81.)

In the intertestamental period, the term is usually applied to the SELEUCID empire, which had its capital in ANTIOCH OF SYRIA (see also COELE-SYRIA). In 64 B.C., the area became a Roman PROVINCE usually governed by an imperial legate (see GOVERNOR; QUIRINIUS). Its boundaries varied during the following centuries. References to Roman Syria are often paired with its neighboring province to the NW, CILICIA (Acts 15:23, 41; Gal. 1:21). Territories to the S, including ARABIA and JUDEA, were at times regarded to be part of the province of Syria. Under the emperor HADRIAN (ruled A.D. 117–138) it became a consular province named Syria Palaestina. (See A. H. M. Jones, *Cities of the Eastern Roman Provinces*, 2nd ed. [1971], ch. 10; E. Dabrowa, *The Governors of Roman Syria from Augustus to Septimius Severus* [1998]; K. Butcher, *Roman Syria and the Near East* [2003].)

Syriac, Syrian sihr´ee-ak, -uhn. The KJV uses the form *Syriack* to render ʾărāmî *H811* in Dan. 2:4 ("Then spake the Chaldeans to the king in Syriack"), but *Syrian* in the other occurrences of that Hebrew term (2 Ki. 18:26; Ezra 4:7; Isa. 36:11). In all of these passages the reference is to the ARAMAIC LANGUAGE, which served as the *lingua franca* of the ANE from about the 8th cent. B.C. until the Hellenistic period. Modern scholars apply the term *Syriac* to the particular dialect of Aramaic spoken in SYRIA beginning around the NT period. There is a very rich body of Christian literature written in the Syriac language, which is still spoken today (e.g., by a group known as Assyrian Christians).

Syriac versions. See VERSIONS OF THE BIBLE, ANCIENT III.

Syro-Hexapla si´roh-hek´suh-pluh. Also Syro-Hexaplar. Name given to a Syriac translation of ORIGEN's Hexaplaric recension of the Greek OT. See SEPTUAGINT VI.

Syrophoenician si′roh-fi-nish′uhn (Συροφοινίκισσα *G5355*, fem. of Συροφοίνιξ). This proper adjective describes a woman encountered by Christ when he journeyed to the region of TYRE in the territory of PHOENICIA (Mk. 7:24–26 KJV and most versions; NIV, "born in Syrian Phoenicia"). By means of this word her racial extraction is traced to that of the Phoenician stock which resided in the Roman province of SYRIA. Another group of Phoenicians, known as Carthaginians or Libophoenicians, resided in N Africa. The broader category of which she was a part is also given by Mark: she was a Greek or Gentile, that is, a non-Jew. Matthew refers to her as a Canaanite (Matt. 15:22), an earlier and more general term for residents of CANAAN — and one that would have had negative religious overtones for Jewish readers. Her difficulty in obtaining her request from Christ illustrates quite well the prior claim of the Jews on the ministry of Christ at his first advent. R. L. THOMAS

Syrtis suhr′tuhs (Σύρτις *G5358*). Name given to the shallow waters of the northern coast of Africa between Tunisia and Cyrenaica. Today the Gulf of Sidra forms the SE corner of this bay, which is known as the Greater Syrtis (the Gulf of Gabes, also called the Lesser Syrtis, lies more than 300 mi. to the W). Always a difficult place for navigation, legend exaggerated the dangers, perhaps to protect Phoenician trade by frightening off other ships. The sailors who were carrying PAUL to Rome, even though they were several hundred miles away from "the Syrtis" (i.e., the Greater Syrtis), did everything to avoid being driven into this dangerous shore (Acts 27:17; KJV, "the quicksands"; NIV, "the sandbars of Syrtis"). R. C. STONE

Various tools crafted by carpenters, including plow, threshing sledge, olive press, winnowing fork, and broom.

Taanach tay´uh-nak (תַּעֲנָךְ *H9505*, derivation uncertain). KJV also Tanach (only Josh. 21:25). One of the royal Canaanite cities defeated by Joshua (Josh. 12:21 et al.). It was situated on the S flank of the Valley of Jezreel (see Esdraelon), where the international coastal road or Via Maris struck inland from Sharon. The forested ravines of the northern Ephraim hill country were the most sensitive points of the route for ambush, and Taanach, Megiddo, and Jokneam guarded three important passes. These towns are first mentioned in the Egyptian chronicle of Thutmose III, in the 13th cent. B.C., possibly about the time the Israelites were threatening the Egyptian lines of communication from the hinterland of the interior hills (*ANET*, 235). Tablets excavated at Taanach in the reign of Thutmose III (or Amenhotep II) make clear that it was an important fortress city having juridical links with such towns as Rehob, Gurra, and Rubute. See Rehob (place) #2; Gur; Rabbah (Judah).

Taanach was assigned to the Levites descended from Kohath (Josh. 21:25), but the Manassites failed to expel the Canaanite inhabitants and instead made them tributary (Jdg. 1:27). There followed a period when the Canaanite cities tried to impose their authority over the Israelite tribes in Galilee, and the Song of Deborah refers to Taanach as the scene of a major battle (5:19). In Solomon's reign the town became an important center (1 Ki. 4:12). Later it was taken by Pharaoh Shishak, who makes allusion to it in his chronicles. In 1 Chr. 7:29 Taanach is included among the towns that were "along the borders of Manasseh."

Modern Tell Ti‘innik, the site of the ancient city, is situated on low hills, 5 mi. SE of Megiddo, with which it has been clearly identified in its military history. The tell was first excavated in 1901–4 by Professor Sellin of Vienna, who discovered twelve cuneiform tablets of c. 1450 B.C. (cf. *SacBr*, 75–76), and revealed the strong Late Bronze Age defensive system, later modified in the Iron Age as a chariot garrison. (See E. Sellin, *Tell Ta‘annek* [1904]; P. W. Lapp in *BASOR* 173 [Feb. 1964]: 4–44; W. E. Rast, *Taanach I: Studies in the Iron Age Pottery* [1978]; G. Friend et al., *Tell Taannek, 1963–1968* [1998–2001]; A. E. Glock in *NEAEHL*, 4:1428–33.) J. M. Houston

Pottery from Taanach.

Taanath Shiloh tay´uh-nath-shi´loh (אֲנָת שִׁלֹה *H9304*, meaning uncertain; the Septuagint interpreted the phrase as two places, Θηνασα καὶ Σελλησα). A village that lay between Micmethath and Janoah (Josh. 16:6) on the NE border of the tribal territory of Ephraim. It was identified by Eusebius (*Onom*. 98.13) with a village 10 Roman mi. E of Neapolis (Shechem) named *Thēna*, which is probably modern Khirbet Ta‘na et-Taḥta; most scholars, however, prefer Khirbet Ta‘na el-Foqa, some 4.5 SE of Shechem, where there is evidence of an ancient hill fort. E. M. Blaiklock

Tabaliah tab´uh-li´uh (טְבַלְיָהוּ H3189, possibly "Yahweh has dipped [*i.e.*, purified]"; some vocalize as טָבַלְיָהוּ, meaning "good for [*or* beloved of] Yahweh"). Also Tebaliah. Son of Hosah and descendant of Merari; he was a Levite gatekeeper during the time of David (1 Chr. 26:11).

Tabbaoth tab´ay-oth (טַבָּעוֹת H3191, "signet ring[s]"). Ancestor of a family of temple servants (Nethinim) who returned from the exile with Zerubbabel (Ezra 2:43; Neh. 7:46; 1 Esd. 5:29).

Tabbath tab´uhth (טַבָּת H3195, derivation unknown). A place near Abel Meholah, but probably E of the Jordan, that was the terminal point of Gideon's pursuit of the Midianites (Jdg. 7:22). Tabbath was probably in the vicinity of Karkor in Gilead (8:10), though the location of Karkor itself is uncertain and cannot serve as a real point of reference. Some have proposed identifying Tabbath with Ras Abu Ṭabat on the slopes of Jebel ʿAjlun (approximately halfway between Jabesh Gilead and Succoth), but others regard the site as unknown (see discussion in *ABD*, 6:291–92). The Gilead hill country would be the natural rallying point of the defeated host. E. M. Blaiklock

Tabeal tab´ee-uhl. KJV alternate form of Tabeel (Isa. 7:6).

Tabeel tab´ee-uhl (טָבְאֵל H3175, "God is good" [cf. Tobiah]; the form in Isa. 7:6, טָבְאַל ["no good"], is thought to be a deliberate disfiguration of the name). **(1)** Father of a man whom Rezin of Damascus and Pekah of Israel planned to place upon the throne of Judah as a puppet king in place of King Ahaz (Isa. 7:6). Some interpret the description "son of Tabel" to mean "native of Tabel" and thus translate "the Tabelite," referring to an area N of Gilead (cf. H. Wildberger, *Isaiah 1–12: A Commentary* [1991], 282, 282). Others have thought that the reference is to Tubail king of Tyre, mentioned in a stela of Tiglath-Pileser III (cf. A. Vanel in *Studies on Prophecy: A Collection of Twelve Papers* [1974], 17–24).

(2) One of three Persian officials who wrote a letter of complaint against the Jews to King Artaxerxes (Ezra 4:7; 1 Esd. 2:16 [KJV, "Tabellius"]).

S. Barabas

taber. An obsolete English verb found only in Nah. 2:7 KJV; it means "to beat (as on a drum)" and renders Hebrew *tāpap* H9528, "to beat (the timbrel), to strike."

Taberah tab´uh-ruh (תַּבְעֵרָה H9323, possibly "burning [place]"). At some unspecified time during the wilderness wanderings, the Israelites "complained about their hardships" and the Lord in anger sent a fire against them. "When the people cried out to Moses, he prayed to the Lord and the fire died down. So that place was called Taberah, because fire from the Lord had burned [*bāʿar* H1277] among them" (Num. 11:1–3). The story itself is obscure, and it is not clear whether the burning fire is to be taken literally or as a symbol of some act of judgment. The place is mentioned again in Deut. 9:22, but not listed in the wilderness stations recorded in Num. 33. The location of Taberah is unknown. E. M. Blaiklock

tabernacle. A transliteration of the Latin word *tabernaculum*, meaning "tent." In the Bible it is used specifically of the sanctuary built under the direction of Moses in the wilderness. The principal passages dealing with the tabernacle are (1) Exod. 25–29; (2) Exod. 30–31; (3) Exod. 35–40; and (4) Num. 3:25–38; 4:4–49; 7:1–88. The purpose of the structure is stated in Exod. 25:8, 21–22. The tabernacle was made after the pattern shown to Moses on the mount (25:9; 26:30).

   I. Terminology
  II. Plan of the tabernacle
 III. Traditional view
 IV. The tabernacle in Exodus and Numbers
    A. Materials and furniture
    B. Construction and consecration
    C. Moving the tabernacle
  V. Historical references to the tabernacle
 VI. Critical view
VII. The historicity of the tabernacle
VIII. Problems relating to the Tent of Meeting and the tabernacle
 IX. The tabernacle in the NT
    A. The significance of the tabernacle

I. Terminology. In English translations of the OT, "tabernacle" is usually the rendering of Hebrew *miškān* H5438, meaning "dwelling place" or "dwelling," the site where God disclosed himself to his people and dwelt among them. It can be used with reference to the entire shrine (Exod. 25:9), but sometimes it refers specifically to the Holy of Holies (26:1). The SEPTUAGINT translates this term with Greek *skēnē* G5008 over one hundred times and with *skēnōma* G5013 almost twenty times (both Gk. words are used frequently to render additional Heb. terms).

Other words and phrases, however, are also employed in connection with the tabernacle. The simple noun *ʾōhel* H185 (with the definite article, "the tent") occurs almost 20 times; the expression "the tent of the LORD" occurs in one passage (1 Ki. 2:28–30), as does "the house [*bayit* H1074] of the tent" (1 Chr. 9:23; NIV, "the house called the Tent"). The phrase "the house of the LORD" is used more than fifty times, while "the tabernacle of the house of God" only once (1 Chr. 6:48 NRSV). Another expression, "the tabernacle of the Testimony [*ʿēdût* H6343]" (NRSV, "of the covenant") occurs a few times (Exod. 38:21 et al.), as does "the tent of the Testimony" (Num. 9:15). The general term *miqdāš* H5219, "holy place, sanctuary," appears very frequently (Exod. 25:8 et al.).

Especially significant is the phrase "the Tent of Meeting [*môʿēd* H4595]," which occurs over 140 times; it is is almost always rendered in Greek by *hē skēnē tou martyriou*, "the tent of the testimony" (cf. Acts 7:44; Rev. 15:5). The place where the Lord met with Moses and Israel (Exod. 29:42, 43; Num. 17:4) was for communication and REVELATION (Exod. 29:42; 33:11; Num. 7:89). It is practically equivalent to "tent of revelation," since here God declared his will for Israel. The KJV rendering, "the tabernacle of the congregation," is not exact.

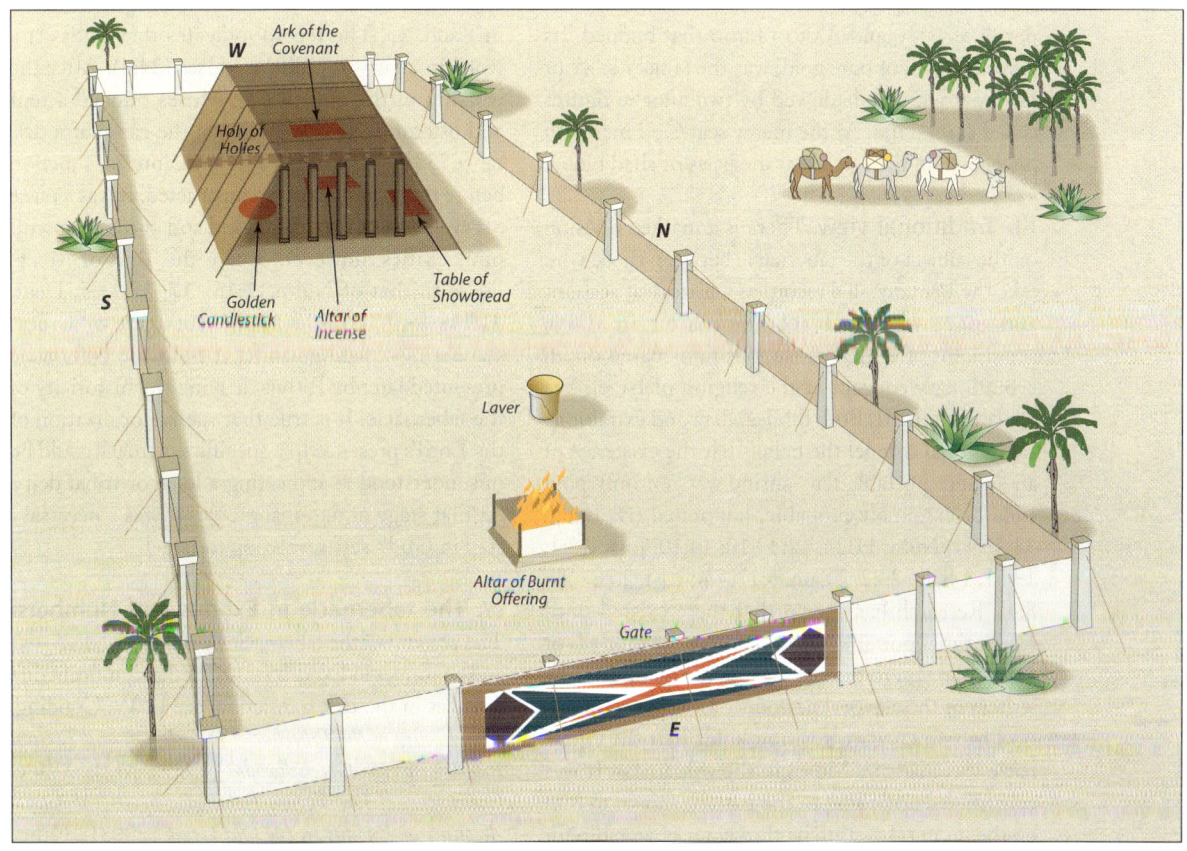

The Tabernacle.

II. Plan of the tabernacle. ALTARS preceded sanctuaries in Israel (Gen. 12:7–8). MONOTHEISM underlay the tabernacle, and the later TEMPLE was modeled after it. The ground plan of the tabernacle is sufficiently clear, although there are various opinions concerning the details. It is customarily held that the shape of the structure was oblong with a flat roof and ornate coverings that hung down at each side and at the back. Another opinion is that the tabernacle had a sloping roof.

The outer court contained the altar of burnt offering and the bronze laver. The tabernacle structure consisted of two divisions: the Holy Place and the Holy of Holies or the Most Holy Place. In the former stood the table of SHOWBREAD on the N (the structure was oriented toward the E); the golden lampstand on the S (see CANDLESTICK); and the golden altar of INCENSE on the W against the veil leading to the Most Holy Place. The innermost compartment held the ARK OF THE COVENANT, in which were deposited the two tablets of the law, the pot of MANNA, and AARON's ROD that budded. Its covering, a lid of pure gold, was the MERCY SEAT or propitiatory, overshadowed by two angelic figures called CHERUBIM. At the mercy seat God met with his people in their need on the basis of shed blood.

III. Traditional view. There is a marked division on the subject of the tabernacle between those who take the Pentateuchal record as a historical account and those who approach the matter from the standpoint of critical presuppositions based on an evolutionary concept of the religion of Israel. See PENTATEUCH III. Both biblical data and extrabiblical material compel the belief that the existence of an ancient portable tent-shrine was not only possible or extremely probable, but actual (cf. Exod. 33:7–11; Num. 11:24; 12:4–10; 14:10; Josh. 18:1; 19:51; 1 Sam. 2:22; 2 Sam. 6:17; 7:6; 1 Ki. 2:28–29; 8:4). Research has shown that there existed until recent times portable shrines among the nomads of the Syrian desert. Similar shrines are mentioned by writers of the classical period.

The conservative position holds that the tabernacle was made by Moses in the wilderness. It was constructed according to the pattern shown to him on the mount. It was to be the center of worship for the tribes of Israel in their wilderness travels. Centuries later, the temple of Solomon was modeled after the tabernacle. Although primarily a provisional and temporary sanctuary for the journey from Sinai to Palestine, the tabernacle nonetheless continued in use long after the settlement in Canaan.

The higher-critical view maintains that the tabernacle had only an ideal, not a historical, existence; that it was a product of priestly imagination in exilic or postexilic times. It was a miniature built on the model of the Solomonic temple. The claim that it was constructed in the wilderness was put forth only to give sanction to the newly written Priestly Code (PC), or Levitical ritual, still preserved in the books of the Pentateuch. The details of the tabernacle in PC (Exod. 25–31; 36–40; Num. 2:2, 17; 5:1–4; 14:44) are said to conflict with those given in "E" (the Elohist, in Exod. 33:7–11) as to the character and location of the structure.

Part of this divergence of views on the tabernacle stems from the interpretation of the nature and function of the Tent of Meeting mentioned in Exod. 33. The record indicates that at SINAI a worship altar was built by Moses (24:4). After the worship of the golden calf, Moses pitched a tent and often resorted to it outside the camp at a distance (33:7–11). It had a definite interim function before the tabernacle was constructed. It was a place of revelation of the will of God and of meeting with him. Critics, however, equate the Tent of Meeting with that of Num. 11:16–17; 12:4–5; Deut. 31:14–15; and consider it the tent of the wilderness wanderings, distinguishing it from the tabernacle presented later by P, thus denying the historicity of the tabernacle. It is true that such a localization of the Lord's presence to a specific sanctuary could be misunderstood as indicating a local or tribal deity. At that stage of national growth it was a necessary step in God's self-revelation to Israel.

IV. The tabernacle in Exodus and Numbers. The account of the tabernacle begins in Exod. 25–31 and continues in Exod. 35–40 (for the significant differences in the LXX translation, see D. W. Gooding, *The Account of the Tabernacle: Translation and Textual Problems of the Greek Exodus* [1959]; M. L. Wade, *Consistency of Translation Techniques in the Tabernacle Accounts of Exodus in the Old Greek* [2003]). Other references to the tabernacle and its furnishings are found in Num. 3:25–38; 4:4–49; 7:1–88. The tabernacle is mentioned in the works of Josephus and Philo Judaeus and in Jewish accounts of the 3rd cent. A.D. Jewish and Christian commentators all reveal difficulty in understanding the details of the plan of the structure, although the general appointments are clear. Parallels to the tabernacle are found in the record of Solomon's temple (1 Ki. 6.2) and that of Ezekiel's temple (Ezek. 40–46). I. Benzinger, although he does not take the traditional position, admits: "The whole description leaves at first sight such an impression of painstaking precision that the reader might be tempted forthwith to take for granted its historical truth" (*EncBib*, 4:4862). However, he prefers the position of J. Wellhausen, who held that the statements are after all just fancy. If this were so, what was the purpose of the writer(s)?

Modern scholars and artists have attempted various reconstructions of the tabernacle. The one shown here was built at the Timna Nature Reserve, with the front curtain facing due E.

A. Materials and furniture. The tabernacle was made from the voluntary gifts of Israel. The materials listed include gold, silver, bronze; blue, purple, scarlet material, fine twined linen; goat hair, dyed ram skins, goatskins, acacia wood, oil for lamps, spices for the anointing oil and the fragrant incense, onyx stones, and stones for the ephod and the breastpiece. The three metals of ancient times—bronze, silver, and gold—are used in meaningful gradation from the outer court to the most holy place. The most artistic use of the metals is found in the cherubim and the golden lampstand. The wood used throughout the structure was shittim or acacia wood, known for its durability. The material employed was linen, also fine twined linen, dyed blue, purple, and scarlet (25:4). The yarn was spun by women in charge of the weaving (35:25, 35); the work included both embroidery and tapestry.

1. Framework. The framework of the tabernacle (Exod. 26:15–37; 36:20–38) was made of 48 wooden frames, 15 ft. high by 27 in. wide with three vertical arms joined by three crosspieces. These were placed in wooden supports and over them were hung two large curtains. Over all were spread three covers. The framework was constructed of uprights of acacia wood, making three sides of the oblong structure. The front was closed by an embroidered screen (26:36–37). The boards, 48 in number, were overlaid with gold. The construction was divided into two compartments separated by a veil, hung from four pillars overlaid with gold, and set in sockets of silver. The veil, like the covering of the tabernacle, was woven with blue, purple, and scarlet, with figures of cherubim. The holy place was 30 ft. long by 15 ft. broad; the most holy place was 15 ft. square. It has been suggested that the tabernacle proper was tent-like in shape with a ridge pole and a sloping roof.

2. Coverings. The coverings of the tabernacle are described in Exod. 26:1–14 and 36:8–9. The wooden framework of the tabernacle had three coverings: the total covering of the tabernacle itself, the covering of goat hair, and the covering of skins spread over the entire structure. The first covering was made of ten curtains of fine twined linen woven with blue, purple, and scarlet, with figures of cherubim. The second covering was of eleven curtains of goat hair. The top covering was made of ram skins dyed red and goatskins.

3. Court of the tabernacle. The description of the court is found in Exod. 27:9–18 and 38:9–20. This area was a rectangle on an E-to-W plan, 100 cubits long and 50 cubits wide (c. 150 x 75 ft.). To the W was the tabernacle proper, and to the E, the altar. The court was screened off from the camp by five white curtains five cubits high. It was an enclosure with curtains of fine twined linen supported on bronze pillars and attached by silver hooks. In the court stood the altar of burnt offering and the laver, the latter being set between the altar and the tabernacle proper (30:17–21). The entrance to the court was from the eastern side through a "gate" or "screen" with its hangings.

The ALTAR of burnt offering is treated in Exod. 27:1–8 and 38:1–7. It is called "the altar of bronze" from its appearance, and "the altar of burnt offering" from its use. The fire on this altar was never to go out (Lev. 6:13). The most important of the contents of the outer court was the altar. It was a hollow chest of acacia wood covered with bronze, five cubits long and wide and three cubits high, with four horns at the corners. In the middle of the altar was a ledge (Lev. 9:22) and below it a grating. The altar was carried by bronze-covered poles in bronze rings. The horns of this altar were at times used for ASYLUM (1 Ki. 1:50–51, possibly a misuse of the altar). They were sprinkled with blood at the consecration of the priests (Exod. 29:12), at the presentation of the sin offering (Lev. 4:18–34), and on the Day of Atonement (16:18). The grating on the four sides at the foot of the altar permitted the blood of the sacrifices to be spilt at the base of the altar through the network. The people were permitted to approach the altar, for when they brought their sacrifices, they laid their hands on the victim (1:4).

The LAVER is described in Exod. 30:17–21 and 38:8. It was for the exclusive use of the PRIESTS as they ministered in the ritual of the tabernacle. They neglected this provision at the peril of their lives (Exod. 30:20–21). Made of bronze, the laver had a base, evidently for the washing of the feet of the priests. Some scholars believe that the base was a part of the laver proper, whereas others with greater probability maintain that the base was a separate vessel from the laver itself. The record indicates that the bronze was contributed by the ministering women who were engaged in work about the tabernacle (38:8).

4. Sanctuary proper. The tabernacle proper is described in Exod. 26:1–14 and 36:8–19. It appears that the curtains, rather than the boards, constituted the dwelling of the Lord (26:1). The record of the wooden framework of the dwelling is found in 26:15–30 and 36:20–34. At the inner portion of the court stood the tabernacle, an oblong

This close-up photo of the Timna tabernacle model shows the outer curtains of the tent.

structure 45 ft. long by 15 ft. broad with two divisions, the Holy Place and the Most Holy (26:33). These two divisions are found in the Solomonic temple as well (1 Ki. 6:5). The area of the Most Holy Place was 30 ft. square; the Holy Place measured 60 ft. by 30. The two were separated by a veil. On the Day of Atonement the high priest entered the veil, or curtain, at the open end into the innermost sanctuary. See ATONEMENT, DAY OF.

The emphasis in Exod. 26 and 36 is on the tabernacle itself and its curtains, of which there were ten, each 28 by 4 cubits. The ten curtains of colored fabric with woven cherubim were joined in two sets of five along the sides of the tabernacle. Fifty loops of violet thread were sewed, and the curtains were to be held together by fifty gold clasps, thus uniting the whole tabernacle (26:6). Over all this was placed a tent to make certain the tabernacle was completely covered. The covering overlapped the linen and permitted an extra fold at the front (26:9). The tent had two coverings, one of ram skins dyed red and another of skins of goats (cf. 26:14; 40:19).

The curtains were held in place by 48 acacia frames. These frames consisted of two arms connected at the top, center, and bottom by cross rungs with two silver bases for each frame. The silver bases formed an unbroken foundation around the tabernacle. The frames were also held together by five bars. The frames and bars were gold-plated. The front of the structure was enclosed by curtains. (Exod. 26:22–25 is difficult: it may speak of a pair of frames joined at each corner of the W or rear of the framework, sloping upward and inward from their bases to a point under the top bar.) The screen was the entrance to the Holy Place; the VEIL separated it from the Holy of Holies. The veil was made of variegated material with embroidered cherubim, draped over four pillars of acacia wood, overlaid with gold, supported by four silver bases. The screen was of the same material as the screen at the entrance to the outer court (27:16). It was suspended from golden hooks on five pillars of acacia wood, overlaid with gold, supported by bronze bases.

The outer compartment or Holy Place contained three pieces of furniture: (1) the table of showbread, (2) the golden lampstand, and (3) the golden altar of incense. The table was set on the N side (40:22); the lampstand on the S side (40:24); and the altar of incense on the W side before the veil. The table was made of acacia wood covered with fine gold and ornamented with a gold molding. Rings and poles were made for carrying. A number of accessories were made for the table: gold plates to hold the loaves, dishes for the frankincense (Lev. 24:7), and golden vessels for wine offerings. On this table were placed two piles of twelve loaves or cakes, changed each week (24:5–9). The dishes, spoons, and bowls were all of pure gold.

On the S side of the Holy Place stood the golden seven-branched lampstand or CANDLESTICK. It was the most ornate of all the furniture. Of pure gold, it had a central shaft (Exod. 25:32–35) from which were made six golden branches, three on either side. All was adorned with almonds and flowers. All stands supported a lamp which gave continuous (others say only nightly) illumination (27:20; Lev. 24:2–3; 1 Sam. 3:3). Accessories of the lampstand, such as snuffers, snuff dishes, and oil vessels, were all of gold. The lampstand was made of a talent of pure gold (Exod. 25:38).

In front of the veil was placed an altar of incense (Exod. 30:1–5; 37:25–28). Because it is not mentioned in Exod. 25, it is considered by some to be a later addition. It is not mentioned in the LXX in Exod. 37. It was a small altar constructed of acacia wood and overlaid with gold, one cubit long and wide, and two cubits high. It was a replica in miniature of the bronze altar (30:1–10). Its fire was provided from the main altar. Horns, rings, poles, and a golden molding were made for it. Perpetual sweet-smelling incense was offered on it night and morning, and on the Day of Atonement EXPIATION was made on its horns.

On the basis of Heb. 9:4, some have thought that Exod. 30:6 and 1 Ki. 6:22 suggest that the altar of incense was inside the veil in the Most Holy Place. The sacred writer of Hebrews is viewing the sanctuary and its ritual proleptically, that is, in the light of the rent veil and an accomplished redemption. Furthermore, the passages in Exodus and 1 Kings cannot be made to teach a condition contrary to the other passages that describe the Holy Place. Provision was made for replenishings of the oil for the lamps and incense for the altar (Exod. 30:22–38).

The smallest of all the parts of the sanctuary was the Holy of Holies, yet it was the most significant because of the ritual that was carried out there on the Day of Atonement, and because of the reiterated declaration that God himself dwelt in the tabernacle in the holiest of all, a dwelling represented by the SHEKINAH cloud over the innermost sanctuary.

The account is found in Exod. 25:10–40; 30:1–10; 37. The record of the tabernacle begins with the construction of the ARK OF THE COVENANT (25:10). Its measurements were about 3.75 x 2.25 x 2.25 ft. It was the only furniture in the Holy of Holies. It contained the Ten Commandments (2 Ki. 11:12; Ps. 132:12), the pot of manna (Exod. 16:33–34), and Aaron's rod that budded (Num. 17:10). It was covered within and without of pure gold, with golden moldings, rings, and staves. Resting on the ark of the covenant and held securely in place by the gold molding was a solid slab of gold called the MERCY SEAT or propitiatory (*kappōret* H4114), that is, the place where God was rendered favorable to his people.

Wrought out of the ends of the covering or lid were figures of gold, the CHERUBIM (Exod. 25:19; 37:8). Their faces were toward the mercy seat and their wings touched overhead. Between the cherubim the God of Israel dwelt visibly (25:22; 30:6; Num. 7:8, 9), and met with his people through their representatives, first Moses, then Aaron. The cherubim were soldered to the propitiatory, making it "of one piece" with it (Exod. 25:19). They represented angelic ministers of the Lord who guarded the divine throne from all pollution. The ark was carried by poles in four golden rings at the sides. The tabernacle with the ark was lost in the battle of APHEK (1 Sam. 4). In the second, or restoration, temple of ZERUBBABEL there was no ark with its propitiatory (contra Bar. 6:7).

B. Construction and consecration of the tabernacle. The account is found in Exod. 25–29. Moses was instructed to erect the tabernacle on the first day of the first month in the second year of the exodus, nine months after reaching Mount SINAI (19:1). The pattern was revealed by God for his dwelling place (25:8; 29:45). The many workmen were led by men of artistic skill who were empowered and illuminated by the Spirit of God, BEZALEL the son of Uri and OHOLIAB the son of Ahisamach (31:1–6). When the structure was completed and the furniture installed in place, the cloud symbolizing the presence of God filled the place. The cloud henceforth signaled to Israel when they were to camp and when to journey. When Israel was encamped, the tabernacle was at the center of the camp with Levites on three sides and Moses and Aaron and his sons on the fourth (E) side: Judah at the center of the E side; Ephraim at the center of the W side; Reuben on the S side. The number of Levites who ministered at the tabernacle was 8,580 (Num. 4:48).

The tabernacle manifested what has been termed a "graduated holiness and perfection," that is, the metal in the Most Holy Place was solid gold; in the Holy Place, ordinary gold; in the court, bronze. The people were allowed into the court, the priests into the Holy Place, and only the high priest into the Most Holy Place one day a year. Only the altar is mentioned for consecration (Exod. 29:36–37), but later all the furniture of the sanctuary was included (chs. 30–31).

C. Moving the tabernacle. The book of Numbers discusses the tabernacle on the march (Num. 2:17; 3:25–38; and ch. 4). The camp moved when the cloud that rested on the sanctuary was taken up from over the dwelling (Exod. 40:37; Num. 9:17). While the cloud hovered over the dwelling, the camp remained stationary (Num. 9:18–22). When a silver trumpet blast heralded the breaking of camp (10:1–7), the priests took down the veil and covered the ark with it (4:5–6) and two other covers. Similarly, all the furniture was to be wrapped (4:7–14). The Kohathites carried all the pieces that were transported by poles. The Gershonites were entrusted with the curtains of the tabernacle, the tent of meeting with its covers, the screen, the hangings of the court, the altar, and its equipment. The Merarites transported the frames, bars, pillars and bases of the tabernacle proper and the pillars and bases of the court. The Levites marched in the middle of the nation with six tribes before them and six behind (2:17).

The ark went before Israel in the crossing of the JORDAN. They set up the tabernacle at SHILOH, and the land was divided among the tribes there (Josh. 18:1; 19:51). Only the ark is mentioned, although the assumption is that the Tent of Meeting was present also (1 Sam. 2:22). After the destruction of Shiloh, the ark was placed in the home of ABINADAB at KIRIATH JEARIM. The account in 1 Sam. 22:18, 19 implies the existence of a sanctuary (cf. ch. 21).

V. Historical references to the tabernacle. When all the biblical references are collated, it is found that there are mentions of both a tabernacle and "the Tent of Meeting"; some of the problems involved will be discussed later. Early references to the Tent of Meeting are Exod. 33:7–11; Num. 11:16–17, 24, 26; 12:5, 10; and Deut. 31:14–15. According to the first reference, the Tent of Meeting was pitched outside the camp (Exod. 33:7; cf. Num. 11:26, 27). Here Moses and others went to commune with God and to inquire of him. This tent was guarded by Joshua, an Ephraimite, but no Levites (Exod. 33:11; Num. 11:28). The verbs used in Exod. 33:7–11 and Num. 10:17–21 indicate customary conditions. The whole picture is different from the tent made by Bezalel and his assistant. Although the account appears to indicate a temporary or occasional arrangement, it lasted throughout the wilderness journeys (cf. A. R. S. Kennedy in *HDB*, 4:653ff.). Its function was to provide the meeting place between God and Moses (Num. 12:5; Deut. 31:15). It was also the site where worshipers sought the Lord (Exod. 33:7).

The tabernacle was erected at Sinai in the second year after the exodus, two weeks before the PASSOVER (Exod. 40:2, 17). When the congregation journeyed, the ark was covered with the veil (Num. 4:5). The ark and the two altars were carried by the sons of KOHATH, a descendant of LEVI, under the supervision of the high priest (3:31–32; 4:15). The rest of the disassembled structure was carried in six covered wagons, given by a prince (Num. 7:7), each drawn by two oxen. Others must have been used for the heavier materials. Before Israel departed from Sinai, the tabernacle had been erected for fifty days (10:11).

The journey of Israel took them from Horeb (Sinai) to KADESH BARNEA in the NEGEV of Judah. Of the forty years spent marching to Canaan, almost thirty-eight were spent at Kadesh; the tabernacle remained here through those years. During all this time the customary sacrifices were not offered (Amos 5:25). Few events of those years are recorded and little is stated concerning the tabernacle except that the ark headed the march (Num. 10:33–36). Because history deals mainly with the unusual, the daily occurrences of the life of the people are not alluded to.

After the crossing of the Jordan River, a place was found for the sacred tent near JERICHO at GILGAL (Josh. 4:19; 5:10; 9:6; 10:6, 43). This site was temporary, and in time the tabernacle was moved to SHILOH in EPHRAIM, a central location convenient for the men to attend the three annual pilgrimage feasts (Josh. 18:1; 19:51). At Shiloh the tabernacle appears to have had some permanent features and was even called a "temple" (Heb. *hêkāl H2121*, 1 Sam. 1:9; 3:3; cf. also the reference to doors in 3:15).

During the period of the judges, Israel repeatedly fell into apostasy, and the tabernacle services must have been performed in a formal, heartless manner, if at all. See JUDGES, PERIOD OF. When war erupted with the PHILISTINES in SAMUEL's time, the people decided to bring the ark of the covenant from Shiloh (1 Sam. 4:3–4). The outcome was tragic: the Philistines captured the ark and routed Israel. Doubtless, Shiloh fell at this time at the hands of the Philistines (cf. Ps. 78:60–61; Jer. 7:12).

After the death of ELI and his sons, it appears that Samuel presided over the religious exercises of the nation. He offered burnt and peace offerings. When the ark was restored by the Philistines, it remained at Kiriath Jearim (1 Sam. 7:1–2). Gilgal, Bethel, Mizpah, and Ramah were places of administration of justice and gained religious associations as well. The next allusion to the tabernacle indicates that it was at NOB, with AHIMELECH as high priest (21:1–6). After SAUL had all the priests of Nob slain except ABIATHAR (22:11–19), it was removed to GIBEON (1 Chr. 16:39; 21:29).

After DAVID captured JEBUS and built himself a palace, the ark was brought from Kiriath Jearim and delivered to the priests. UZZAH, however, was struck dead for his indiscretion, and the ark remained for three months at the home of OBEDEDOM, a Levite. Then with great solemnity it was transferred to the tent David had pitched for the ark in Jerusalem. Burnt offerings and peace offerings were presented there (2 Sam. 6).

With David's removal of the ark to Jerusalem there was a tabernacle with its altar at Gibeon and another one with the ark in Jerusalem, both soon to be replaced by the TEMPLE. The Gibeon altar was still in use in Solomon's time. Notice also the occurrence of a reference to the "Tent of Meeting" in 1 Ki. 8:4. After Solomon's temple was built, the Tent of Meeting with all its equipment was transferred with the ark into the temple (8:4). Of all the materials of the tabernacle, it is held, only the ark remained the same in the temple. Thus the last references to the tabernacle in the history of Israel concern the time when it with its sacred vessels was transported to Jerusalem, where from all indications they were kept as sacred relics in the temple.

VI. Critical view. The critical view of the tabernacle, referred to briefly earlier in this treatment, is complex indeed compared with the accounts already discussed. One position within the critical camp is that the tabernacle in the wilderness was always an ideal, never a real structure. It is argued that the elaborate symbolism of the tabernacle could not have been reproduced in its entirety in any of the temples that were actually constructed in Israel. It is pointed out that the earthly tabernacle was said to be built from a heavenly pattern delivered to Moses on Mount Sinai (Exod. 25:40).

Many older critics considered the tabernacle as only a projection backward of the temple into Israel's nomadic past; this was supposedly a product of the late Priestly Source (P) without a shred of historical foundation. In all fairness it must be pointed out that subsequent critical studies have admitted that this judgment was a far too sweeping and radical treatment of the biblical data. In fact, the Wellhausen school explained the tabernacle as a postexilic representation based on Solomon's temple. The claim was that the tabernacle was a copy, not the model or prototype, of that temple (cf. Wisd. 9:8). According to this theory, the chronological order would have been: the shadowy original in the tent (Exod. 33:7–11), then Solomon's temple, then Ezekiel's ideal representation, and finally the tabernacle of Exod. 25. It should be added that some modern scholars view Ezekiel's "ideal" reconstruction as actually prophetic, eschatological, and messianic.

The weight of modern OT scholarship is opposed to the historicity of the tabernacle treated in Exodus and Numbers (P). Some of the general arguments lodged against the historicity of the tabernacle are that an unorganized body of Hebrew slaves could never have accomplished the feat involved in constructing the tabernacle with its demands for a high degree of artistic skill, for even Solomon in his reign had to hire skilled artists from PHOENICIA for the temple. Moreover, the highly organized priestly ministry with its elaborate ritual is allegedly out of keeping with the simple appointments indicated for the Tent of Meeting. The most cogent argument advanced against the historicity of the tabernacle (in P) is the silence of the preexilic historical writers with reference to it. The claim is made that no genuine passage of history in that long period so much as hints of the existence of a tabernacle with ministering priests and Levites. When references occur in the Chronicler (1 Chr. 16:39; 21:29) and the psalmists, it is laid to the activity of editors and glossators who inserted references where they thought the tabernacle should have been (1 Ki. 3:4; 2 Chr. 1:3).

Other objections to the historicity of the tabernacle have not been lacking. The tabernacle must be the creation of the imagination, it is argued, because the author has so poorly thought out the details of the structure. Moreover, the fundamental question has been posed as to whether such a structure was capable of standing at all. As a matter of architecture, the tabernacle is pronounced an utter impossibility (Benzinger in *EncBib*, 4:4872). Furthermore, it is asserted that E knows nothing of a tabernacle of this kind. That source speaks only of a tent that excludes the possibility of the tabernacle in P (cf. Exod. 33:7–11). It is felt that this simple tent-sanctuary involves none of the difficulties of the tabernacle in P. The tent of E is not a place of sacrifice (as the tabernacle is in P), but a place of oracle, more like the portable sanctuaries of the heathen Semitic peoples of the time. (Note the denial of the uniqueness of the faith of Israel, which is the distinguishing feature of the OT.)

To elaborate further on the historical argument, it is said that historical tradition from the settlement in the land to the building of Solomon's temple reveals no knowledge of any tabernacle. Passages that do mention or imply the existence of the tabernacle are treated with suspicion and are rejected. The conclusion is then drawn that the tabernacle of P is just the temple of Solomon read back into earlier days by a vivid priestly fancy. Simply stated, it was not the temple that was built on the pattern of the tabernacle, but the tabernacle was constructed for the worship of Israel from the prototype of the temple. A general observation is in order: one of the characteristic features of the critical school is the tenet that development always proceeds from the simple to the complex. Why is this principle departed from at this point when the tabernacle and temple are discussed?

VII. The historicity of the tabernacle. The historicity of the tabernacle is of vital significance for the entire validity of the Scriptures. The main contentions of those who deny the historicity of the tabernacle will be presented, followed by specific refutations.

Critical opinion claims that if Solomon's temple had been patterned after the Mosaic tabernacle, the writers of Kings and Chronicles would have stated this fact. This position overlooks 1 Ki. 8:4 and 2 Chr. 5:5. It is argued that these passages refer to "the Tent of Meeting" and not to the Mosaic tabernacle of Exod. 25. However, in P the Mosaic tabernacle has the same name (Exod. 27:21). What logic requires that the authors of Kings and Chronicles state explicitly that the Solomonic temple was modeled after the Mosaic tabernacle?

Much is made of the argument from silence. Arguments from silence are notoriously precarious. The only way a silence of the historical books can be made out is to delete all such reference passages relative to the Mosaic tabernacle as the work of a late redactor who allegedly inserted them to support his view that the Mosaic tabernacle originated in the wilderness. No external evidence has been produced by any critic to sustain this position. If the evidence of the OT is heeded, it reveals a number of clear evidences.

First, there was the Mosaic tabernacle at Shiloh. According to the account in 1 Sam. 1–3 (cf. 1:3, 9, 19, 24; 2:11, 12, 3.3), the structure mentioned is the Mosaic tabernacle. It had the ark of the covenant, a priesthood, sacrifices, burning of incense, and the wearing of an ephod. ELKANAH's annual pilgrimage to Shiloh to worship and offer sacrifice strongly implies that Shiloh was the central sanctuary, and that the law of the annual feasts was known (Exod. 23:14; Lev. 23:1–18; Deut. 16:16).

Second, the sanctuary at Nob was the Mosaic tabernacle (1 Sam. 21:1–6). It had a high priest and eighty-five ordinary priests, a priest's ephod, and a table of showbread. The eating of the showbread was under the same ceremonial regulations as indicated for the Mosaic tabernacle (Lev. 15:18). The URIM AND THUMMIM were used by the priest to determine God's will as in the tabernacle arrangement. These are particulars that relate to the tabernacle and to no other institution in Israel.

Third, the reference to the Mosaic tabernacle at Gibeon precedes the building of Solomon's temple (1 Ki. 8:4; 2 Chr. 1:3; 5:3). It is stated that the ark of the covenant, the Tent of Meeting, and all the holy vessels of the tent were solemnly brought into the temple Solomon had built.

Critics claim the Mosaic tabernacle could not have been made as Exodus describes it, because (1) the time was too short; (2) the Israelites were not qualified or artistically capable; and (3) they did not have sufficient materials for such a splendid building as the Mosaic tabernacle. The argument as to time is amply answered by the fact that 600,000 able men for nine months could well have accomplished, with their wives and children, all that was needed for so circumscribed a structure. The objection as to their artistic ability is untenable in the light of the fact that in over 400 years they could well have learned something of the mechanical arts for which Egypt was justly famous. Furthermore, who can disprove that some of the famous works of Egypt of those days were not done by Israelite slave labor? The argument as to scantiness of material is refuted by the considerations that Israel had some preparation for their wilderness journey, that the amount of material involved is not in excess of what other ancient oriental peoples possessed, that a large part of what they needed could have come from what the Egyptians gave them to leave their land and from the spoils of the war with AMALEK, and that some of the materials required for the construction were available in the wilderness.

The biblical account is said to have certain internal marks that reveal its unhistorical character. (1) It states the tabernacle was made on a model supernaturally shown to Moses. (2) It continually refers to geographical locations of the tabernacle when no previous instructions had indicated any such order. (3) The bronze altar was made of acacia wood overlaid with bronze where a fire would burn constantly. (4) The tabernacle is pictured not as a temporary shelter for the ark on the march but as the only authorized sanctuary for the tribes of Israel before the time of Solomon. (5) The description of the tabernacle found in P or the Priestly Code (Exod. 25–31; 36–40; Num. 2:2, 17; 5:1–4; 14:44) is said to conflict with E (Exod. 33:7–11) as to character and location.

In refutation of the first objection, it must be affirmed that there is no inherent impossibility that God should reveal the pattern of the tabernacle to Moses in the mount (Exod. 25:40; Heb. 8:5). Is the temple of Solomon unhistorical because David said that the pattern of it given to Solomon had been revealed to him (David) by God (1 Chr. 28:19)? Moreover, Ezekiel claimed that the temple he described was seen by him in a vision. Here it is a matter of one's theology and the possibility of supernatural revelation.

The second objection is indeed difficult to comprehend, because it argues against the obvious. The tabernacle had to be oriented in some way, and the most natural would be according to the four points of the compass. Moreover, there was no conscious imitation of the Solomonic temple, because the account in Kings and Chronicles makes no reference to the four quarters of the earth, 1 Ki. 7:25 does not demand that the sides of the temple were so positioned.

The third argument assumes more than is stated. The text does not claim that a large fire constantly burned on an altar of wood. A reading of Exod. 27:1–8 and 38:1–7 shows that the altar proper, where the fire burned and consumed the sacrifices, was the earth-filled or stone-filled hollow (Exod. 20:24–25) which the wooden and bronze frame enclosed.

The fourth contention is in exact conformity with a natural reading of Exodus, namely, the tabernacle was meant to be the authorized sanctuary for the tribes before Solomon's day. It is true that on occasion altars were built for sacrifice at locations other than the tabernacle, for example, by GIDEON at OPHRAH and by SAMUEL at RAMAH (Jdg. 6:24–27; 1 Sam. 7:17), but this is inadequate to prove that the tabernacle was not the central sanctuary. By the same reasoning, Jerusalem could be shown not to be the central sanctuary because of the altar on Mount EBAL (Deut. 27:5). Actually, the tabernacle was the central sanctuary, but the original legislation of Exod. 20:24 had never been rescinded. It was still permissible to offer sacrifice wherever the Lord revealed himself to his people. Because local shrines existed at the same time as the tabernacle does not warrant the conclusion that the tabernacle was never constructed.

The fifth objection is adequately answered by the observation that the description of the tabernacle in P differs from the description of the tent in E simply because two different structures are in view: one is the tabernacle proper (P) and the other is the preliminary tent built by Moses. This explanation accounts for the variations in character and location of the two.

Perhaps the strongest proof advanced for the nonhistoricity of the tabernacle is the alleged ignorance of the preexilic prophets concerning the Levitical system. Critics cite Amos in the 8th cent. B.C. (Amos 5:25–26) and Jeremiah in the 7th (Jer. 7:21–23) as teaching that no sacrificial tabernacle ritual was ever enunciated in the wilderness. Against this contention it can be stated as remarkable that former interpreters did not so understand the words of these prophets. Moreover, it can be easily shown that critics are far from agreement on this interpretation. Amos 5:21–22 would be meaningless unless God had accepted their sacrifices at one time and would do so no longer when the worship was heartless and idolatry was indulged in at the same time (Num. 16:18).

Finally, if the Lord never commanded sacrifices for Israel, how did he order Jeremiah to pronounce a curse on the people of Jerusalem for transgressing the covenant that he had made with their fathers in the wilderness and that enjoined sacrifices to him and not to idols (Jer. 11:1–5)? If God had desired only obedience to moral law without sacrifice, then where was the need for the temple? God had accepted the temple as his house. All idolatrous sacrifices were proscribed, not only because they were wrong in themselves, but because they displaced the true sacrificial worship of the Lord. Jeremiah certainly knew God had commanded sacrifices in Exod. 20:24–25.

The NT references to the tabernacle at least imply that the sacred writers were agreed on its historicity. Such citations were PETER's words on the Mount of Transfiguration (Matt. 17:4; Mk. 9:5; Lk. 9:33), STEPHEN's statement to the council (Acts 7:44), the references in Hebrews (Heb. 8–9), and the voice from heaven (Rev. 21:3).

VIII. Problems related to the Tent of Meeting and the tabernacle. According to some, it would be both natural and logical to understand from the Pentateuch that the Tent of Meeting and the tabernacle were the same structure. The original instructions (Exod. 25) are said to be so vague and full of omissions that it would have been impossible on the basis of those instructions to build such a structure as the tabernacle. Details are said to be lacking for the shape of the cherubim, the feet of the ark and table, the thickness of the mercy seat, and how the weight of the curtains could have been sustained by the frames without collapsing the structure. How did the altar of burnt offering sustain such great heat needed to consume the animal sacrifices? Where did Israel get the skill and craftsmanship to erect the tabernacle? The amounts of materials used were quite large: about one and one-fourth tons of gold, about four tons of silver, and about three tons of bronze. Why is the record so silent concerning the tabernacle from the settlement in Canaan to Solomon's temple?

Upon further study the problems are not so formidable as first considered in the heat of an avid hypercriticism. Much of the difficulty stems from the fact that the critical position has tried to equate the Tent of Meeting and the tabernacle, and then has complained of the resultant discrepancies. Allow the tent to be one structure and the tabernacle another, and all will be seen to be harmonious (for a different approach, however, see R. E. Averbeck in *DPL*, 810–12). Regarding the vagueness of instructions, surely sufficient guidelines were given to permit the workmen to build the structure, for Exod. 35–40 is occupied with the manner in which the instructions of God were carried out to the letter. Where specific instructions were absent, the skill of the artisans, fortified with specific and stated endowment from the Spirit of God, was adequate for the needs of the task. The specific details of the building would have taken into account the weight of the curtains on the frame. Engineering authorities have confirmed that such a structure was eminently feasible and workable. The silence of the historical texts can be made out only if pivotal passages are denied validity and then deleted.

The situation described in Exod. 33 probably obtained for a limited time. It is likely that when the older generation, who were not to enter the land, died off, the ark and the tabernacle were moved into the midst of the camp. Differences in location of the tent and tabernacle are explicable and contradictions are more apparent than actual. Furthermore, those who claim the Tent of Meeting was Moses' personal tent cannot expect their statement to be taken seriously, when the subject under discussion involves the worship of an entire nation, numbering over two million, with a ministering priesthood in the thousands of persons.

Theologically, the tabernacle cannot be eliminated from the history of Israel in the wilderness. The presence of the Lord with them was the unifying factor in all their national traditions, repeatedly referred to in later books of the OT. They could not be without foundation in fact. They can be and are traceable to the Mosaic era, where Israel's laws and sacrificial system began also.

The order seems to have been: (1) A tent was outside the camp because of the sin of the golden calf worship (Exod. 32). (2) The tabernacle itself was built (25:9). (3) The more permanent sanctuary at Shiloh was built because the perishable materials (fabrics) of the tabernacle in the wilderness needed replacing. (4) With the destruction of the Shiloh sanctuary the ark was moved from Philistia to Kiriath Jearim to Jerusalem, apparently with remnants of the furniture. (5) Then there was the tent that David made for the ark (2 Sam. 6:17).

IX. The tabernacle in the NT. Anyone arguing the nonhistorical character of the tabernacle must find adequate explanation for the manner in which the NT repeatedly cites different features of that structure and worship, connecting them with Moses, to teach deep spiritual truth in the NT. The references cover the Gospels, Acts, Epistles, and Revelation. It has already been pointed out that the Mount of TRANSFIGURATION experience (Matt. 17:4; Mk. 9:5; Lk. 9:33) harks back to the tabernacle of Moses. John in his prologue makes much of the INCARNATION of the Lord Jesus Christ as the tabernacling among men (Jn. 1:14). The testimony of Stephen (Acts 7:44) is unmistakable. Paul directly equates the cross of Calvary as God's mercy seat, or propitiatory, in finalizing the redemption of sinners (Rom. 3:25). In speaking of REGENERATION he had in mind the laver in Tit. 3:5. The proper interpretation of Col. 1:19 and 2:9 will relate them to the dwelling presence of God in the tabernacle of old. The epistle to the Hebrews is inexplicable without the teaching of the worship of Israel and their priesthood residing in the tabernacle. Various other passages (such as Rev. 8:3–4; 13:6; 15:5; 21:3) are too clear to need comment.

Two extremes are discernible in discussions of the symbolism of the tabernacle. There are those who make little or nothing of its symbolic features in spite of what has been shown of the NT references to that structure. On the other hand, there are those who seek to draw some spiritual truth from every thread and piece of wood. There is a *via media* that will not deny symbolism to the colors where white, blue, and scarlet predominate with their connotations of purity, heavenly character, and shedding of blood. That Josephus (*Ant.* 3.7.7) and Philo (*De vita Mosis* 3.147ff.) erroneously interpreted the tabernacle as an image of the universe, and some of the early church fathers saw fanciful things in the appointments of the tabernacle, is not valid ground for Benzinger (*EncBib*, 4:4871) to posit that any figurative interpretations lack a solid basis in the OT.

The epistle to the Hebrews gives at length the Christian interpretation of the symbolism of the Mosaic tabernacle. The furniture symbolizes human access to God. The tabernacle is patterned after a heavenly model (Heb. 8:5); there is a divine prototype (8:2, 5; 9:11); it conveyed important spiritual truths in the 1st cent. A.D. (9:9). Christ appeared and then entered after death into the heavens (9:24). The dwelling place of God is designated as the new Jerusalem (Rev. 21:2). The truth of the tabernacle is inseparably bound up with the fact of the incarnation (Col. 1:19; 2:9). In fact, the tabernacle may rightly be considered, with its emphasis on the fact of God's dwelling with his people, as the main foreshadowing in the OT of the doctrine of the incarnation.

The tabernacle, rather than the later temples, is the basis of NT teaching. The references in Heb. 9–10 are to the tabernacle rather than to any temple. The tabernacle is the symbol of God's dwelling with his people (Exod. 25:8; 1 Ki. 8:27). This concept progressed until fulfilled in the incarnation of God the Son (Jn. 1:14). He is in the church (2 Cor. 6:16), in the individual believer (1 Cor. 6:19), and in the eternal state (Rev. 21:3–4). In Hebrews the central passages on the tabernacle in the NT represent the earthly and heavenly aspects of Christ's activity. The OT was the shadow of which Christ is the substance (Heb. 8:5; 10:1). The tabernacle of Christ's ministry was pitched by the Lord and not by man (8:2). He is the high priest of the more perfect tabernacle (9:11). He is not in an earthly tabernacle but appears now before God "for us" (9:24). The sacred writer in Hebrews draws his imagery from the ceremonies of the tabernacle, and clothes his concepts in the priestly and sacrificial terminology of the sanctuary in the wilderness.

Paul refers to "the washing of regeneration" (Tit. 3:5), and to Christ as offering himself as a sacrifice to God (Eph. 5:2). All synoptists underscore the rending of the temple veil (Matt. 27:51; Mk. 15:38; Lk. 23:45), which the Hebrews writer indicates opened the way into the holiest of all (9:8; 10:19–20).

X. The significance of the tabernacle.

The tabernacle with its priests and their ministry was foundational to the religious life of Israel. The basic concept was that which underlay the theocracy itself: the Lord dwelling in visible glory in his sanctuary among his people (Exod. 25:8). Even if the tabernacle had no historical validity, which it assuredly had, it still may have value for the readers because of its embodiment of important religious and spiritual concepts. It reveals: (1) The necessary conditions upon which Israel could maintain fellowship in covenant relationship with the Lord. (2) The dominant truth of the presence of God in the midst of his people (29:25), a dwelling that must conform in every detail with his divine character, that is, his unity and holiness. One God requires one sanctuary; the holy God demands a holy people (Lev. 19:2). (3) The perfection and harmony of the Lord's character seen in the aesthetics of the tabernacle's architecture, the gradations in metals and materials, the degrees of sanctity exhibited in the court, the Holy Place, the Holy of Holies, and the measurements of the tabernacle (e.g., the numbers 3, 4, 7, 10 with their fractions and multiples dominating and pervading every detail of furniture and material).

The tabernacle was the first sanctuary reared for the Lord at his command, and was rendered glorious and effective by his actual indwelling. The dwelling of God with his people is the dominant theme of the symphony of the tabernacle, all pointing to the future eternal communion with God. The ark of the covenant with the propitiatory was the symbol of God's meeting with his people on the basis of atonement (Rom. 3:25). The showbread spoke of God's sustenance of spiritual life; the lampstand represented Israel as God's channel of light (Zech. 4); the incense was a symbol of prayer (Rev. 5:8; 8:3–4). The tabernacle was the authorized place of worship. It was the foundation of the theocracy. The mercy seat was the earthly seat of God's glory, where he met with his people for his glory and their blessing. The tabernacle foreshadowed the time when God's kingdom would be fully realized and established on earth. Note the progress in the self-revelation of God to his people: first, his presence in the tabernacle; second, the incarnation of the Lord Jesus Christ; third, the indwelling of the Holy Spirit in believers; and fourth and last, the descent of the new Jerusalem to the glorified earth.

(See further J. Wellhausen, *Prolegomena to the History of Israel* [1878], 17–51; J. Strong, *The Tabernacle of Israel in the Desert* [1888]; W. S. Caldecott, *The Tabernacle: Its History and Structure* [1904]; E. C. Bissell, *The Pentateuch: Its Origin and Structure* [1906]; W. G. Morehead, *Studies in the Mosaic Institutions*, 3rd ed. [1909], 31–90; J. Orr,

The Problem of the Old Testament Considered with Reference to Recent Criticism [1906], 165–80; A. Jacob, *God's Tent* [1961]; A. H. Hillyard, *The Tabernacle in the Wilderness or The Reality of God in the Physical World* [1965], P. P. Jenson, *Graded Holiness: A Key to the Priestly Conception of the World* [1992]; M. S. Suh, *The Tabernacle in the Narrative History of Israel from the Exodus to the Conquest* [2003]; R. E. Friedman in *ABD*, 6:292–300; R. E. Averbeck in *DPL*, 807–27.)   C. L. FEINBERG

Tabernacles, Feast of. See FEASTS.

Tabitha tab´i-thuh (Ταβιθά *G5412*, from Aram. טְבִיתָא; the more proper form טְבִיתָא is the fem. of טַבְיָא, "deer, gazelle"). The Jewish name of a Christian woman who was raised from the dead by PETER (Acts 9:36–43). See discussion under DORCAS.

table. The common Hebrew term for "table" is *šulḥān H8947* (Exod. 25:23 and frequently); Greek uses *trapeza G5544* (Matt. 15:27 et al.). In addition, several Greek verbs mean "to recline, to sit down at a table," such as *anakeimai G367* (Matt. 9:10 et al.) and *kataklinō G2884* (Lk. 11:37 et al.). (Not included in the present discussion is the KJV's use of *table* in the sense of TABLET, Exod. 24:12 et al.)

I. Tables for ritual. The most important ritual table was that of the SHOWBREAD or bread of the Presence. Instructions for making this table are given in Exod. 25:23–30. It was made of ACACIA wood, two cubits in length, a cubit in width, and one and one-half cubits high, overlaid with pure gold and a molding of gold around it. Rings of gold and poles of acacia overlaid with gold were provided for carrying the table. The table was placed outside the curtain (26:35) on the N side of the TABERNACLE (40:22). It was consecrated by anointing with oil (30:27). Every SABBATH the priest placed twelve cakes of fresh bread on the table in two rows of six each (Lev. 24:5–8); it was to be eaten only by the priests (24:9). The Kohathites were in charge of the table and its transportation whenever the tabernacle was moved (Num. 3:27–31; 4:4–8).

SOLOMON made a new table of gold for his TEMPLE (1 Ki. 7:48). Later, King AHAZ desecrated the temple with his idolatrous practices; therefore the priests cleansed the furnishings, including the table, during the reign of HEZEKIAH (2 Chr. 29:18–19). It was destroyed in the burning of the temple by the Babylonians (2 Ki. 25:9). ANTIOCHUS IV Epiphanes stripped the building of its treasures, including the table for the bread of the Presence (1 Macc. 1:22). After Judas MACCABEE defeated the army of LYSIAS, he repaired the temple and made new vessels for it (1 Macc. 4:49–51). The table is depicted on the Arch of TITUS in Rome as one of the trophies of war taken by the Romans when Jerusalem fell, A.D. 70.

Other Hebrew ritual tables include ten that Solomon placed in the temple (2 Chr. 4:8); they were made from silver given him by DAVID for this purpose (1 Chr. 28:16). EZEKIEL described twelve tables in his vision of the restored temple, eight for slaying the sacrifices and four for the instruments of sacrifice and the pieces of flesh (Ezek. 40:39–43). MALACHI referred to "the LORD's table" as polluted (Mal. 1:7, 12); the reference here is to the ALTAR of burnt offering. In 1 Cor. 10:21 "the Lord's table" refers to the LORD'S SUPPER.

There seems to be a reference to an idolatrous practice of setting a table for the god of FORTUNE (Isa. 65:11; cf. also Ps. 69:22). The "table of demons" refers to pagan sacrificial meals (1 Cor. 10:21). Papyrological evidence shows that celebratory meals were often held in pagan temples, as in the following invitation: *Antonius Iounius vos* to dine at the table of the Lord Serapis on the occasion of the coming of age of his brothers in the

Reconstruction of the table of showbread ("bread of the Presence") used in the tabernacle.

temple of Thoeris" (POxy 1484; see A. C. Thiselton, *The First Epistle to the Corinthians: A Commentary on the Greek Text*, NIGTC [2000], 619).

II. Tables for eating. The homes of common people in the ANE were furnished with a minimum of household furnishings. The people squatted even while eating, a custom still practiced. Only those who lived in palaces and better houses were accustomed to chairs, tables, and beds (2 Ki. 4:10). The eating tables must have been very low, as rugs were spread for sitting at the table (Isa. 21:5). Tables in NT times were taller, for reference is made to dogs eating crumbs under the table (Mk. 7:28).

As ruler, JOSEPH ate at a separate table from his brothers (Gen. 43:34). Defeated enemies often ate at the table of the conquering king (Jdg. 1:7; 2 Ki. 25:29). DAVID and JONATHAN both ate at SAUL's table (1 Sam. 20:29, 34), a courtesy David later extended to MEPHIBOSHETH, son of Saul (2 Sam. 9:7), as if he were one of his own sons. Provision for Solomon's table was ample (1 Ki. 4:27); the QUEEN OF SHEBA "was overwhelmed" when she saw his table (10:5). Sons of loyal friends of David ate at Solomon's table (2:7). Prophets ate at the table of JEZEBEL (18:19). Officials numbering 150 sat at the table of NEHEMIAH when he was governor (Neh. 5:17).

There are many references in the Bible to eating in the home. The prophet of Judah ate with the aged prophet of Bethel (1 Ki. 13:20). That which was set on the table of a prosperous man was said to be "full of fatness" (Job 36:16 NRSV). The NT custom, following Greek practice, was to recline around the outside of the table on couches. A woman anointed the feet of Jesus as he reclined at the table (Lk. 7:38). The meal at the Last Supper was eaten in this manner, contrary to popular art representation (Lk. 22:21; Jn. 13:23; see also Matt. 8:11; 15:35, 36; 26:20; Mk. 2:15; Lk. 7:37; 14:15; 24:30; Jn. 12:2; all the verbs used suggest reclining during meals). In the early church, a problem arose because the apostles were having to give so much time to problems of the community relating to distribution of food that they were unable to devote their full time to preaching. The result was the choosing of seven, considered the first deacons, "to wait on tables" (Acts 6:1–6).

The modern Jewish PASSOVER (Pesach) is highlighted by the Seder service, a family banquet in the home where the family gathers around the table and participates in an elaborate ritual that essentially consists of telling the story of the exodus.

III. Tables of money changers. Jesus, indignant at the commercialism in the temple, overturned the stool-like tables behind which the money changers sat on the ground cross-legged (Matt. 21:12; Mk. 11:15; Jn. 2:15).

IV. Figurative usage. The statement that WISDOM "has set her table" (Prov. 9:2) symbolizes the benefits of the godly life. David's well-known words, "You prepare a table before me / in the presence of my enemies" (Ps. 23:5), indicate the protective care of God. The reprehensible behavior of certain priests and prophets is expressed with the comment, "All the tables are covered with vomit" (Isa. 28:8). Israel is pictured as the harlot who set her table to await her lovers (Ezek. 23:41). Reference to the table was often made by Jesus in his parables (Lk. 12:37; 17:7; 22:27).

V. Eschatological usage. Those faithful to the Lord are promised that they will eat and drink at his table in the kingdom (Lk. 13:29; 22:30) with Abraham, Isaac, and Jacob (Matt. 8:11). In one place, Ezekiel likens being filled at the table of God to judgment, as the birds and beasts are called together to feast on the enemies of God (Ezek. 39:20).   F. B. HUEY, JR.

Table of Nations. See NATIONS.

tablet. This English term is used primarily to translate Hebrew *lûaḥ* H4283, most often used of the two tablets of stone on which the TEN COMMANDMENTS were given at SINAI to MOSES (Exod. 24:12; Deut. 5:22; et al.). These tablets were written on both sides (Exod. 32:15) by God himself, containing the words he had spoken to Moses (Deut. 9:10). Moses broke the stones in anger when he saw the people sinning (Exod. 32:19), but God instructed him to cut out two new tablets of stone (34:1–4), which Moses carried again to Mount Sinai where God wrote down the law again. They were later placed in the ARK OF THE COVENANT (Deut. 10:5; cf. 1 Ki. 8:9; 2 Chr. 5:10). Based on data that it was normal procedure in establishing suzerainty covenants to prepare duplicate copies of the TREATY text, some scholars have argued that each stone was complete in itself rather than each one containing half the laws; if so, the two tablets would have been duplicate copies of the law.

The NT equivalent is *plax* G4419 (2 Cor. 3:3; Heb. 9:4). Another Greek word, *pinakidion* G4400, refers to a small writing tablet, ordinarily a block of wood covered with wax (Lk. 1:63). Note also Hebrew *gillāyôn* H1663 (Isa. 8:1 NRSV, where the NIV renders "scroll"). The KJV also uses "tablet" for other words that are translated differently in modern versions (Exod. 35:22; Num. 31:50; Isa. 3:20).

F. B. HUEY, JR.

Tabor tay´buhr (תָּבוֹר H9314, possibly "height"). **(1)** Mount Tabor is a hill about 10 mi. SW of the Sea of Galilee in the Valley of JEZREEL (see ESDRAELON). The border of the inheritance of ISSACHAR touched Tabor (Josh. 19:22); thus the other tribe to touch it would be ZEBULUN (this has led scholars to believe that Tabor is the mountain referred to in Deut. 33:18–19 and that it was a cult center; cf. Hos. 5:1). During the judgeships of DEBORAH and BARAK, Mount Tabor played a principal role. Deborah had Barak summon his troops to that mountain (Jdg. 4:6). Later from that height Barak went down with his 10,000 men and the LORD routed SISERA, the Canaanite general (vv. 14–15). Other references include the confession of ZEBAH AND ZALMUNNA to GIDEON that they had slain Gideon's brothers at Tabor (8:18), the psalmist's matching of Tabor with HERMON in joyously praising God's name (Ps. 89:12), Jeremiah's colorful description of NEBUCHADNEZZAR (Jer. 46:18), and Hosea's use of the mountain to illustrate God's severity toward Israel (Hos. 5:1).

Atabyrium (Atabyrion), a city that ANTIOCHUS the Great took in 218 B.C., was apparently on Mount Tabor, since Polybius (*Hist.* 5.70.6) describes it as a "conical hill" near Scythopolis, that is, BETH SHAN (it is unclear what, if any, relationship the name Atabyrion may have had with ZEUS Atabyrios, for whom a cult was practiced on a mountain in RHODES that bore the same name; see J. Lewy in *HUCA* 23, pt. 1 [1950–51]: 357–86). The Jews under Alexander Jannaeus (see HASMONEAN II.C.) took Mount Tabor in 105 B.C., but lost it to the Romans under POMPEY in 70 B.C. (Jos. *Ant.* 13.15.4).

Mount Tabor is identified with Jebel eṭ-Ṭur ("mount of the height"). Although it rises only 1,843 ft. above sea level, it is a prominent feature of the landscape. The mount is rather steep, somewhat symmetrical, and has a rounded top. From the summit one has a lovely view in all directions. To the NW the higher parts of the city of NAZARETH are visible. Farther W is the promontory of Carmel (see CARMEL, MOUNT). To the E is the Sea of Galilee, and the Jordan with the highlands even farther beyond. At the foot of the mountain to the S is the Valley of Jezreel. The cities of AZNOTH TABOR and KISLOTH TABOR may have derived their name from that of the mountain.

Mount Tabor is not mentioned in the NT, but much of its fame rests in the tradition that the TRANSFIGURATION of our Lord took place on it (however, see HERMON). That tradition was well established by A.D. 326 when Helena, the mother of Constantine, built the first Christian shrine on its summit. The hill suffered the vicissitudes of war which destroyed older shrines and made way for new ones. The Crusaders maintained it after their arrival in the Holy Land until Saladin's victory at the Horns of Ḥaṭṭin in 1187. The Muslims made a fort of the mountain twenty-five years later, but that was shortly destroyed and the summit was relatively empty until the 19th cent., when the Greek Orthodox built a monastery and the Franciscans a basilica of the transfiguration on the top. That basilica has three sections—one for Jesus, one for Moses, and one for Elijah.

(2) Tabor is also the name of a Levitical city within the tribal territory of ZEBULUN (1 Chr. 6:77; the parallel passage, Josh. 21:34–35, has a different list that omits Tabor). Its identification is uncertain. Some have thought that it was a town associated with Mount Tabor (possibly a settlement on the mountain itself), but if so one would expect the town to have been included within the territory of ISSACHAR, not Zebulun. Others think Tabor is the same as KISLOTH TABOR (Josh. 19:12; cf. Y. Aharoni, *The Land of the Bible: A Historical Geography*, rev. ed. [1979], 304), which is c. 3 mi. W of Mount Tabor. Another suggestion is DABERATH, on the NW slope of the mountain.

(3) Finally, mention is made of a certain "great tree [ʾēlôn H471] of Tabor" that was evidently not far from BETHEL (1 Sam. 10:3; NRSV, "the oak of Tabor"; KJV, wrongly, "the plain of Tabor"; see OAK). Some have speculated that here Tabor (*tbwr*) is an alternate form or textual corruption of DEBORAH (*dbwrh*), and that the reference is to the tree under which REBEKAH's nurse was buried (Gen. 35:8). The context of the passage tells that SAUL had qualms about whether or not God wanted him to be king of Israel. In response, SAMUEL gave him some signs to confirm the divine nature of his anointing. The second sign was fulfilled on his way home; when he approached the great tree of Tabor he met three men going up to God at Bethel. The location is unknown.

R. L. ALDEN
S. BARABAS

tabret. An archaic English term, meaning "timbrel, tambourine," used by the KJV in a number of passages (Gen. 31:27 et al.). See MUSIC, MUSICAL INSTRUMENTS IV.B.

Tabrimmon tab-rim´uhn (טַבְרִמֹּן H3193, an Aram. name meaning "[the god] RIMMON is good"). KJV Tabrimon. Son of HEZION and father of BEN-HADAD I, the king of ARAM (1 Ki. 15:18). It is uncertain whether Tabrimmon himself was a king.

taches taks. KJV archaism for "clasps" (Exod. 26:2 et al.).

Tachmonite tak´muh-nit. KJV form for TAHKEMONITE.

Tacitus tas´uh-tuhs. Cornelius Tacitus was born in A.D. 56 or 57, was trained as a rhetorician, and served in various political offices, including CONSUL or chief magistrate (in 97) and PROCONSUL or governor of the province of ASIA (112–13). He probably died in 118 or shortly after. Tacitus is best known, however, as a prolific and eloquent historian. His two principal works deal with the Roman emperors: the *Histories* (from the death of NERO to the death of DOMITIAN) and the *Annals* (covering the earlier period, from the accession of TIBERIUS through the emperorship of Nero). Much of the material is lost, but the *Annals*, considered his greatest work, has largely survived (we are missing the reign of CALIGULA, about half of the reign of CLAUDIUS, and a few years of Tiberius and Nero). Though Tacitus was not without his faults and biases, his historical accounts are the earliest that have come down to us and are also of greater intrinsic value than competing works (such as those of SUETONIUS and Dio Cassius). Because Tacitus covers most of the 1st Christian cent. in considerable detail (including the interactions between Jews and Romans), his writings are of the greatest importance for reconstructing the historical background of the NT. (See R. Syme, *Tacitus*, 2 vols. [1958]; R. H. Martin, *Tacitus* [1981]; R. Mellor, *Tacitus* [1993]; C. S. Kraus, *Latin Historians* [1997]; A. J. Woodman, *Tacitus Reviewed* [1998]; J. P. Davies, *Rome's Religious History: Livy, Tacitus and Ammianus on Their Gods* [2004].)

Tadmor tad´mor (תַּדְמֹר H9330, meaning unknown). Also Tadmur. Known in Greek and Latin history as Palmyra, the city of palm trees, Tadmor was an ancient military outpost, trading center, and customs station located in the Syrian desert, half-way between DAMASCUS and the upper EUPHRATES River. It was a large and pleasant oasis with wonderfully fine mineral springs, fertile soils, and many gardens and palm groves—the only supply station of any consequences on the shorter trade route between Babylonia and Syria.

Tadmor's inhabitants are mentioned (Akk. *Tadmar*) in CUNEIFORM inscriptions of the 19th and 18th centuries B.C., and early in the 11th cent. in the annals of TIGLATH-PILESER I of ASSYRIA, who attacked the Arameans living there. The biblical narratives inform us that when King SOLOMON took N Syria along the BEQAʿ and ORONTES Valleys as far N as HAMATH, he not only built "store cities" in the Hamath area, but also "built up Tadmor in the desert" (2 Chr. 8:4; cf. 1 Ki. 9:18, where NRSV and NJPS, following the *Ketib*, read "Tamar") to protect the trade routes and serve the NE boundaries of his extended kingdom.

No more is heard of Tadmor until 64 B.C., when Mark Antony raided its merchants who had grown rich through the Babylonian and Indian trade which had passed through there. In early Roman times Tadmor enjoyed considerable commercial prosperity, and splendid buildings were constructed under HADRIAN (A.D. 117–138), but its colorful period of history began in A.D. 241 when Odenathus the younger went into the desert, where he trained the bedouin cavalry and spearmen. He also married Zenobia, a powerful Sheikh's daughter in whose veins coursed the blood of the Arab, the Egyptian, and the Greek. With the forces which he and the bedouin chiefs gathered, he fought and overcame Rome's enemies, and exercised his subtle political strategy until A.D. 258, when Emperor Valerian made Odenathus a Roman consul. Thereafter, for almost twelve years he directed the affairs of Palmyra, consolidated the political and military forces, and conquered surrounding areas until he was the acknowledged master of this part of the world—and that with the approval of Rome.

Then about the year A.D. 267, Odenathus was assassinated by a nephew, whom he had punished for insubordination, and Zenobia, his gifted queen, took the reins of the government and ruled alone in Palmyra as regent of the E. She not only erected more buildings and further improved the city, but placed herself at the head of her well-trained army and extended and consolidated her domains eastward to Persia and westward to the Mediterranean. Palmyra became the acknowledged center of the ANE world, and Zenobia the woman without an equal in beauty, in governmental efficiency, and in military prowess. Yet her lack of moderation led her to assume imperial titles, inscribe them on her coins, and send a military expedition to conquer Egypt.

Soon after becoming emperor of Rome in A.D. 270, Aurelian marched in triumph through ASIA MINOR, fought and defeated Zenobia's armies at Antioch and Emisa (Homs), then trekked over the desert and laid siege to Palmyra in 272. In secrecy Zenobia fled eastward to rally her Persian forces, but was captured on the ferry boat as she was attempting to cross the Euphrates River. She was returned to Palmyra and taken to Rome in the emperor's triumphal march. Gibbon says the emperor provided her with a villa and she lived thereafter the life of a "comfortable Roman matron." Tadmor was placed in subjection, but soon revolted and was virtually destroyed. Later the city was fortified by Justinian, but during the 7th cent. it fell to the Muslims. In modern times Tadmor has been excavated and appears to travelers as one of the most impressive ruins of the ancient world.

(See M. A. R. Colledge, *The Art of Palmyra* [1976]; J. Starcky and M. Gawlikowski, *Palmyre*, rev. ed. [1985]; T. Kaizer, *The Religious Life of Palmyra: A Study of the Social Patterns of Worship in the Roman Period* [2002]; Y. Zahran, *Zenobia between Reality and Legend* [2003].)   G. F. OWEN

Tahan tay´han (תַּחַן *H9380*, derivation uncertain; gentilic תַּחֲנִי *H9385*, "Tahanite"). **(1)** Son of EPHRAIM and ancestor of the Tahanite clan (Num. 26:35).

(2) Son of Tela and descendant of Ephraim (1 Chr. 7:25).

Tahapanhes tuh-hap´uh-neez. KJV alternate form of TAHPANHES (only Jer. 2:16).

Tahash tay´hash (תַּחַשׁ *H9392*, perhaps "dolphin"). KJV Thahash. Son of NAHOR (brother of ABRAHAM) by his concubine REUMAH (Gen. 22:24). Some have thought that Tahash is a place name, corresponding to Egyptian *ta-ḫ-si* and referring to an area near KADESH ON THE ORONTES (cf. *HALOT*, 4:1721).

Tahath (person) tay´hath (תַּחַת *H9380*, possibly "instead of," i.e., "compensation"). **(1)** Son of Assir, descendant of LEVI through KOHATH, and ancestor of SAMUEL and HEMAN (1 Chr. 6:24, 37).

(2) Son of BERED and great-grandson of EPHRAIM (1 Chr. 7:20a). Some argue that the genealogy is textually corrupt. See #3 below.

(3) Son of Eleadah and grandson of #2 above (1 Chr. 7:20b).

Tahath (place) tay´hath (תַּחַת *H9380*, possibly "instead of," i.e., "compensation"). A stopping place of the Israelites, between Makheloth and Terah, during their forty years of wilderness wanderings (Num. 33:26–27). The location is unknown.

Tahchemonite tah-kee´muh-ni*t*. See TAHKEMONITE.

Tahkemonite tah-kee′muh-nit (תַּחְכְּמֹנִי *H9376*, in form, a gentilic from an unknown name, but widely considered a textual error). KJV Tachmonite. According to 2 Sam. 23:8, the chief of "the Three" (evidently a special military group within the elite force called "the Thirty") was "Josheb-Basshebeth, a Tahkemonite" (the KJV understands his name as a phrase, "The Tachmonite that sat in the seat"). The parallel passage, however, reads: "Jashobeam, a Hacmonite [*lit.*, son of Hacmoni], was chief of the officers [*or* of the Thirty]" (1 Chr. 11:11), and many scholars believe that the Samuel passage is textually corrupt. See JASHOBEAM.

Tahpanhes tah′puhn-heez (תַּחְפַּנְחֵס *H9387*, also תַּחְפְּנֵס [Jer. 2:16 *Ketib*] and תְּחַפְנְחֵס [Ezek. 30:18], possibly from an Egyp. phrase such as *t'-ḥt-np'-nḥsy*, meaning either "house of the Nubian" or "fortress of Penaḥse" [*HALOT*, 4:1719]). KJV also Tahapanes (Jer. 2:16), Tehaphnehes (Ezek. 30:18), and Taphnes (Jdt. 1:9). An Egyptian town named with MEMPHIS and MIGDOL as an opponent of Israel (Jer. 2:16; 46:14) and as a place to which Jewish exiles fled after the murder of GEDALIAH following the sack of Judah by the Babylonians in 586 B.C., when JEREMIAH was reluctantly compelled to join them (44:1; cf. 43:7–9). Tahpanhes also figures in EZEKIEL's judgment on EGYPT (Ezek. 30:18).

A Phoenician PAPYRUS letter of the 6th cent. B.C. from Egypt refers to "Baal Zephon and the gods of Tahpanhes," from which it is thought that the city must have earlier borne the name of BAAL ZEPHON, an Israelite staging post during the exodus (Exod. 14:2; cf. W. F. Albright in *Festschrift Alfred Bertholet* [1950], 13–14). If the name means "palace of the Nubian," it may have been founded during the reign of TIRHAKAH (690–664 B.C.; cf. 2 Ki. 19:9). The form of the name in extrabiblical Greek literature, *Daphnē*, supports identification with Daphnai, on the Pelusiac branch of the NILE River, which HERODOTUS (*Hist.* 2.30, 107) says was garrisoned by Greek mercenaries set there by Psammetichus during the 26th dynasty (664–610) to repel the incursions of Arabians and other Asiatics.

Tahpanhes is commonly identified as modern Tell Defneh (Defenneh), 27 mi. SSW of Port Said (9 mi. W of el-Qanṭara). In 1886 Flinders Petrie partially excavated Qasr Bint al-Yahudi (Mansion of the Jew's Daughter), finding both Greek pottery and a fortress of Psammetichus I, outside which lay a Ramesside-period brick platform that might be the "brick pavement at the entrance to Pharaoh's palace in Tahpanhes," where Jeremiah hid stones to mark the place where he predicted that the Babylonian king NEBUCHADNEZZAR II would erect his throne (Jer. 43:9).

A fragmentary Neo-Babylonian text of the thirty-seventh year of Nebuchadnezzar outlines operations against Egypt and mentions the Egyptian king Amasis and a Greek garrison (Putu-Iaman). However, the cylinders of Nebuchadnezzar said to have been found at Tell Defneh, now in the Cairo Museum, are imported copies of his standard building inscriptions from Babylon itself. A recently discovered inscription in NABATEAN, dated to the 1st cent. B.C., mentions Tahpahnes (in the form *dpn'*) as the site of a shrine devoted to a Nabatean god; evidently the city had broad commercial ties as late as the Roman period. (See further F. Petrie, *Tanis II; Nebesheh (AM) and Defenneh (Tahpanhes)* [1888], 47–96; A. Dupont-Sommer in *PEQ* no vol. [1949]: 52–57; R. N. Jones et al. in *BASOR* 269 [Feb. 1988]: 47–58.)   D. J. WISEMAN

Tahpenes tah′puh-neez (תַּחְפְּנֵיס *H9388*, prob. from Egyp. title *t'-ḥ(mt)-p'-nsw*, "the wife of the king"; see K. A. Kitchen, *Third Intermediate Period in Egypt*, 2nd ed. [1986], 274 n. 183). An Egyptian queen (1 Ki. 11:19–20). She was the wife of a PHARAOH of the 21st dynasty, perhaps Siamon (c. 979–959 B.C.). The pharaoh gave her sister in marriage to HADAD, the Edomite prince who fled from DAVID to Egypt (1 Ki. 11:17). Tahpenes cared for her sister's son, GENUBATH, in the royal house.

J. ALEXANDER THOMPSON

Tahrea tah′ree-uh. Alternate form of TAREA.

Tahtim Hodshi tah′tim-hod′shi (תַּחְתִּים חָדְשִׁי *H9398*, meaning unknown). A district between GILEAD and DAN JAAN, visited by DAVID's commanders in the course of the census (2 Sam. 24:6). Many believe that the text has been corrupted. Among various proposed emendations, one that has been widely accepted is *haḥittim qādēšâ* (cf.

Chettieim Kadēs in the Lucianic recension of the LXX); thus the NRSV rendering, "they came to Gilead, and to Kadesh in the land of the Hittites" (the reference would be either to KEDESH of NAPHTALI or to KADESH ON THE ORONTES). Another suggestion is *taḥat ḥermôn*, "beneath Hermon" (see discussion in P. K. McCarter, Jr., *II Samuel*, AB 9 [1984], 504–5).

tale. This noun is used by the KJV a few times in the sense "number, count, total" (Exod. 5:8, 18; 1 Sam. 18:27; 1 Chr. 9:28; cf. the English verb *tell* in the sense "to count," Gen. 15:5; Ps. 22:17 KJV). The English term is sometimes used negatively of a false report, whether slanderous (Ezek. 22:9 KJV) or regarded as incredible (Lk. 24:11 KJV, NRSV) or simply fictional (1 Tim. 4:7 NIV, NRSV). See FABLE. The KJV also employs "tale" once to translate a Hebrew word that properly means "sigh, moan" (Ps. 90:9).

talent. See WEIGHTS AND MEASURES IV.A.

talitha cum(i) tal´uh-thuh-koo´mi (ταλιθα κουμ [or κουμί] G5420 + G3182, from Aram. טְלִיתָא, "girl" [more properly טְלִיתָא, from טְלִי, "youth"] and קוּם, "arise!" [more properly קוּמִי, 2nd person fem. imperative of קוּם, "to arise"]). Also *talitha k(o)um(i)*. Mark preserves PETER's vivid memory of the exact ARAMAIC words of Jesus when he said to Jairus's dead daughter, "Little girl ... ARISE" (Mk. 5:41; note other Aram. words of Jesus and of Peter in 7:34; 15:34 Acts 9:40). Such words come naturally to the Galilean; no magic formula is involved. (See *ABD*, 6:309–10.)

J. Grintz (in *JBL* 79 [1960]: 33–47) presents evidence from JOSEPHUS, the DEAD SEA SCROLLS, the NT, and other Jewish documents that Hebrew was the common spoken and literary language of Palestine. Aramaic, however, may have prevailed in the temple service from the Persian period, possibly because of the masses of Aramaic-speaking orientals who streamed into Jerusalem for the feasts. If so, perhaps Jesus chose the temple language, with its rich connotations, for the words of the miracle. As R. Jonathan of Beit Gubrin said, "Aramaic for elegy; Hebrew for speech" (*y. Megillah* I, 9 [71b]). Most scholars, however, believe Aramaic was the common spoken language of Palestine, especially in GALILEE.

W. T. DAYTON

Talmai tal´mi (תַּלְמַי H9440, prob. from HURRIAN *talm*, "great" [*HALOT*, 4:1740]). (1) One of three descendants of ANAK who lived in HEBRON when the Israelites spied out the land and who were defeated by the invading Israelites (Num. 13:22; Josh. 15:14; Jdg. 1:10). See AHIMAN.

(2) Son of Ammihud and king of GESHUR, a principality NE of GALILEE; his daughter MAACAH was espoused by DAVID, contrary to the law and causing David bitter sorrow, for the princess became the mother of the passionate ABSALOM (2 Sam. 3:3; 1 Chr. 3:2). It was to Geshur that Absalom fled for refuge after he had murdered his half-brother AMNON (2 Sam. 13:37).

E. M. BLAIKLOCK

Talmon tal´muhn (טַלְמוֹן H3236, possibly "brightness"). A Levite listed among the gatekeepers in the postexilic temple; he was evidently the head of a clan of gatekeepers (1 Chr. 9:17; Ezra 2:42; Neh. 7:45; 11:19; 12:25; 1 Esd. 5:28).

Talmud tal´mood (postbiblical Heb. תַּלְמוּד, "study, teaching," from לָמַד H4340, "to learn" [in the piel stem, "to teach"]). The authoritative collection of rabbinical legal decisions and Jewish traditions. See JUDAISM.

I. The origins and development of the oral law
II. The antecedents to the Talmud
   A. Mishnah
   B. Midrash
III. The divisions and tractates of the Mishnah and Talmud
IV. The Palestinian and Babylonian Talmud
V. The literary history of the Talmud
VI. The significance of the Talmud

I. The origins and development of the oral law. The message of the great PROPHETS of the 8th cent. B.C. made very clear that the fall of the northern kingdom of Israel to the heathen Gentile nations and the impending captivity of the southern kingdom of Judah were the direct result of IDOLATRY. The promised return of the children of

ABRAHAM to the land of the COVENANT was upon the condition that they seek Yahweh with their whole heart and repudiate the gods of the Canaanites (Jer. 29:13). The gradual cessation of prophecy and the development of new and more complex social relationships both within and without Israel called for continuing progressive elaboration of the pentateuchal laws. The leaders and the generation that returned from BABYLON in 538 B.C. were acutely aware of the necessity of assuring the continuation of Israel's national obedience to the Mosaic LAW. EZRA himself is styled as "a teacher well versed in the Law of Moses" (Ezra 7:6), and there was a popular desire to study and learn the TORAH (Neh. 8:1–18).

This historic development brought forth a new social institution among the Jews, the office and service of the "teacher of the law," the rabbinate (see RABBI). In effect, the local SYNAGOGUE was primarily a setting for Torah study. Alongside the written law, however, a great body of TRADITION, the oral law, was in the process of development. According to the MISHNAH, this oral teaching went back to MOSES himself: "Moses received the Torah at Sinai and transmitted it to Joshua, Joshua to the elders, and the elders to the prophets, and the prophets to the men of the Great Synagogue. The latter used to say three things: be patient in [the administration of] justice, rear many disciples and make a fence round the Torah" (*m. ʾAbot* 1:1; see SYNAGOGUE, GREAT). The latter injunction is of particular significance: it was intended to render sufficient insulation around the revealed moral and ceremonial commandments so that Israel would never again lapse into ignorance and idolatry.

II. The antecedents to the Talmud. The rise of the sect of the PHARISEES is closely associated with the writing and study of the Jewish traditions that led to the production of the Talmud. JOSEPHUS mentions that "the Pharisees had passed on to the people certain regulations handed down by former generations and not recorded in the Laws of Moses" (*Ant.* 13.10.6 §297). The process involved two distinctive literary forms.

A. Mishnah. The term *mišnâ* (derived from *šānâ* H9101, "to repeat") refers to the oral conversation of the rabbis as they discussed the proper interpretation and course of action requisite upon Jews in regard to the Mosaic law. There is no presentation of evidence but a continual appeal to authority hallowed by age or scriptural foundation. If the discussion produces legal instruction it is known as HALAKAH (in distinction from HAGGADAH, which refers to nonlegal material). The Mishnaic presentation of laws became dominant in Jewish teaching, and its teachers or Tannaim (derived from the corresponding Aram. verb *tĕnê* or *tĕnāʾ*, "to repeat, hand down") were greatly revered.

By definition, the oral law was not something to be written down, and it is unclear when the initial attempts at collecting the tradition were made, but undoubtedly some of this work was taking place soon after the destruction of JERUSALEM in A.D. 70 (see AKIBA, RABBI). The collections were codified most thoroughly by the famous exponent Rabbi Yehudah ha-Nasi (Judah the Prince), and by about the year 200 it was finally published as an official document. A distinct and parallel collection is known as the TOSEFTA.

B. Midrash. Some use the term *midrashic interpretation* in a derogatory fashion because it is thought to characterize a method filled with folk etymologies, mental gymnastics, and far-fetched connections made on the sheer analogies of the sounds of words. In postbiblical Hebrew, however, the term *midrāš* H4535 (from *dāraš* H2011, "to search,

Remains of a synagogue in Tiberias (3th–4th cent. A.D.), one of the primary centers in the production of the Palestinian Talmud.

inquire") refers simply to the exposition and application of Scripture (see MIDRASH). Often it also refers to a type of literature consisting of such exposition. When the method is applied to purely legal themes, the work is called Midrash Halakah; when the material consists of nonlegal matter, usually homiletic or devotional themes, it is called Midrash Haggadah. The Mishnah could be considered a topical method of pronouncement, while the Midrashim were commentaries on continuous texts of Scripture.

The midrashic form is traditionally thought to have appeared with Ezra and the "Great Synagogue," passing through two great periods of popularity, the era of the *Sopherim* (SCRIBES or "bibliophiles"), which closed about 270 B.C., and the era of the *Zugoth* ("pairs"); it ended with the last pair, Shammai and Hillel, just before the time of Jesus (see HILLEL). The next two centuries, culminating in the publication of the Mishnah, was the period of the *Tannaim* ("repeaters, teachers"). Subsequently, the rabbis who debated or commented on the Mishnah are referred to as the *Amoraim* ("speakers, interpreters"), who were active from the 3rd to 6th centuries. The work of this latter group issued in the GEMARA, and the combination of the Mishnah and the Gemara yielded the Talmud in its entirety. The Talmud was developed in two forms, the Babylonian (Talmud Babli, pronounced Bavli) and the Palestinian (Talmud Yerushalmi). See section IV below.

III. The divisions and tractates of the Mishnah and Talmud. The Mishnah is divided into six major divisions or orders (*sĕdārîm*); these in turn are subdivided into tractates (*massektôt*), totaling sixty-three in number; and each tractate is composed of chapters (*pĕrāqîm*). The Talmud follows the same organization, but there is no Gemara to many of the tractates (see below, section IV). An outline of the orders and tractates follows (based on H. Silverstone, *A Guide to the Talmud* [1942], which excludes the details of the minor tractates and their subdivisions).

A. Order *Zeraʿim* (Seeds).

1. *Berakot* (Blessings). (1) Time of recitation of the Shema (Deut. 6:4–9, followed by 11:13–21 and Num. 15:37–41), position of the suppliant, and benedictions. (2) The divisions of the Shema and the praying voice. (3) Exemptions from praying the Shema. (4) Time of prayer and additional prayers. (5) Positions; specific and congregational prayers. (6) Blessings for vegetable foods and fruits. (7) Groups of people, types, and numbers saying prayers and the prayers to be said. (8) Washing of hands and blessings at meals, the differences between Shammai and Hillel. (9) Miscellaneous occasions of prayers.

2. *Peʾah* (Corner [of a field], i.e., gleanings). (1) The size of field corners, exemption from tithes. (2) Field corners and trees. (3) The size of fields necessary for field corners. (4) How the produce of field corners must be yielded. (5) Rights of the poor and forgotten produce. (6) Distinction of forgotten produce. (7) Olive trees and the rights of the poor in vineyards. (8) Determination of the poor and the length of their rights.

3. *Demai* (Uncertain [fruits], i.e., produce not certainly tithed). (1) The Demai tithe. (2) The strict Jew and who pays the Demai. (3) Who may reserve Demai. (4) Statements by individuals about Demai and how paid. (5) Rented fields, fields under certain exceptions. (6) Separating specific cases of tithes.

4. *Kilʾayim* (Mixtures). (1) Kilʾayim defined. (2) The case of mixed grains. (3) Divisions of garden beds. (4) Vineyards. (5) Types of vines. (6) Extent of vines. (7) Animals. (8) Textiles.

5. *Šebiʿit* (The Seventh Year). (1) Cultivation in the sixth year. (2) The seventh year and fallow fields. (3) Work about the fields. (4) Seventh-year pruning. (5) Figs, leeks, and farm equipment. (6) The seventh year in various countries. (7) Seventh-year rights. (8) Self-productive fruits. (9) Sale and storage of fruits. (10) Release of debts.

6. *Terumot* (Heave Offerings). (1) Terumot. (2) Substitution for another's Terumot. (3) Second Terumot. (4) Quantity. (5) Restitution of Terumot. (6) Intentional consumption of Terumot. (7) Preparing. (8) Sowing the Terumot. (9) Tasting. (10) Using the oil from Terumot.

7. *Maʿaserot* (Tithes). (1) Tithes of fruit, when due. (2) Exceptions. (3) Location of fruit for tithes. (4) Exemptions. (5) Untithable plants and seeds.

8. *Maʿaśēr Šēnî* (Second Tithe). (1) Disposal of the tithe. (2) Proceeds. (3) Fruits in Jerusalem. (4) Proceeds and price. (5) Fourth-year vineyards.

9. *Ḥallah* (Dough Offering). (1) Fruits. (2) Special cases. (3) Quantity. (4) Variations.

10. *ʿOrlah* (Fruit of Young Trees [lit., Uncircumcision, i.e., what should be rejected]). (1) Subject trees. (2) Mixed fruits. (3) Colors and fires.

11. *Bikkurim* (First Fruits). (1) Exceptions. (2) Differentiations. (3) Ceremonies. (4) Exceptional cases.

B. Order *Moʿed* (Set Feasts).

12. *Šabbat* (The Sabbath). (1) Work to be shunned, differences between Shammai and Hillel. (2) Lighting Sabbath evening lamp. (3) Ovens and cooking. (4) Covering of pots. (5) Leading of beasts. (6) Departure of men and women and dress. (7) Responsibility for breaking the Sabbath; thirty-nine types of work. (8) Measures of portable objects. (9) Impurity through carrying. (10) Throwing of objects. (11) Building, pruning, and writing. (12) Weaving, washing. (13) Miscellaneous labors. (14) Actions in fires. (15) Moving of containers. (16) Moving objects, people out of the way. (17) Circumcision. (18) Straining, cleaning, and pressing. (19) Miscellaneous carrying. (20) Miscellaneous necessities. (21) Business arrangements and burials. (22) Those overtaken by darkness on a journey, actions permitted on the Sabbath.

13. *ʿErubin* (Incorporating [Sabbath Limits]). (1) Entry ways. (2) Holiday or its evening. (3) Going beyond the ʿErubin (incorporated or extended), Sabbath limit. (4) Expanding the ʿErubin. (5) Further subdivisons. (6) Still further subdivisions. (7) A yard. (8) Roofs. (9) Miscellaneous Sabbath laws.

14. *Pesaḥim* (Passovers). (1) Searching for leaven. (2) Disposal of leaven. (3) Leaven in its various forms; cake and bitter herbs. (4) Work beforehand. (5) Killing and butchering the paschal lamb. (6) Passover labors supersede Sabbath prohibitions. (7) Methods for cooking the Passover. (8) Persons permitted to partake. (9) Communities and persons unable to partake. (10) Unusual circumstances. (11) Order for eating the Passover.

15. *Šeqalim* (Shekel Dues). (1) Seating of moneychangers. (2) Exchanging money. (3) Removal of coins from the cache. (4) Spending the temple tax. (5) Ecclesiastical offices. (6) Numerology of the number thirteen. (7) Possessions of unknown owners. (8) Miscellaneous difficulties.

16. *Yoma* (Day of Atonement). (1) High priestly preparations. (2) Offerings and lot casting. (3) Preparing for the atonement services. (4) The scapegoat. (5) Holy of Holies. (6) Expulsion of the scapegoat. (7) The high priest's duties. (8) Fasting and forgiveness.

17. *Sukkah* (Feast of Booths/Tabernacles). (1) Dimensions of the booths. (2) Exemptions. (3) Boughs to use as coverings. (4) Duration. (5) Division of offerings.

18. *Yom Ṭob* (Good Day, i.e., Festival Days; also known as *Beṣah*, Egg). (1) Partaking of eggs on holidays. (2) Sabbath meals. (3) Prohibited activities. (4) Time of the feasts. (5) Flute playing.

19. *Roš Haššanah* (New Year). (1) When four New Years occur. (2) Questioning the witnesses to the new moon. (3) Groups of witnesses. (4) New Years falling on Sabbaths.

20. *Taʿanit* (Fasting). (1) Prayers for rain. (2) Festival prayers. (3) Miscellaneous fasting regulations. (4) The twenty-four elders, their fastings.

21. *Megillah* (Scroll [of Esther]). (1–4) The reading of Esther at Purim.

22. *Moʿed Qaṭan* (Lesser Holidays). (1–3) Half-days or lesser feasts and their regulation.

23. *Ḥagigah* (Festival Offering). (1–3) Miscellaneous decisions about offerings.

C. Order *Našim* (Women).

24. *Yebamot* (Levirate Obligations). (1–16) Acceptance and refusal of levirate obligation.

25. *Ketubbot* (Marriage Contracts). (1–13) Marriage contracts and marriage duties.

26. *Nedarim* (Vows). (1–11) Vows and annulments.

27. *Nazir* (Nazirite Vow). (1–9) Laws of the Nazirite vows.

28. *Soṭah* (Defiled Woman). (1–9) Expansions of Num. 5:12–31.

29. *Giṭṭin* (Bills of Divorce). (1–9) Writing of bills of divorce.

30. *Qiddušin* (Engagements). (1–4) Manner of engagements.

D. Order *Neziqin* (Damages).

31. *Baba Qamma* (First Gate). (1–10) Damages, injuries, and indemnities.

32. *Baba Meṣiʿa* (Middle Gate). (1–10) Claims from trusts, buying, and selling.

33. *Baba Batra* (Last Gate). (1–10) Real estate laws and regulations.

34. *Sanhedrin* (Courts).

35. *Makkot* (Lashes). (1–3) Corporal punishment.

36. *Šebuʿot* (Oaths). (1–8) Various types of oaths.

37. *ʿEduyyot* (Witnesses). (1–8) Traditional legal sayings.

38. *ʿAbodah Zarah* (Idolatrous Worship). (1–5) Idols and idol worshipers.

39. *ʾAbot* (Fathers). (1–6) The sayings of the elders.

40. *Horayot* (Judgments). (1–3) Rules for the making of judges' decisions.

E. Order *Qodašim* (Consecrated Things).

41. *Zebaḥim* (Sacrifices). (1–14) Sacrifices, offerings, and sprinklings.

42. *Menaḥot* (Meal Offerings). (1–13) Cereal, meat, and drink offerings.

43. *Ḥullin* (Unconsecrated Things). (1–12) Unlawful animals, slaughtering.

44. *Bekorot* (Firstborn). (1–9) Regulations of firstborn animals and human beings.

45. *ʿArakin* (Estimates). (1–9) Estimation of objects dedicated by vow.

46. *Temurah* (Exchanges). (1–7) Exchanges of dedicated objects.

47. *Keritot* (Outcastings). (1–7) Excommunication of sinners from the congregation.

48. *Meʿilah* (Trespasses). (1–6) Sacrilegious objects.

49. *Tamid* (Daily Offerings). (1–7) Morning and evening sacrifices.

50. *Middot* (Measurements). (1–5) Descriptions of the temple and its servants.

51. *Qinnim* (Nests, i.e., Bird Offerings).

F. Order *Ṭohorot* (Purifications).

52. *Kelim* (Vessels). (1–30) The containers that convey impurity.

53. *ʾOhalot* (Tents). (1–18) Retention of impurity in dwellings.

54. *Negaʿim* (Leprosy Signs). (1–14) Leprous people, garments, and dwellings.

55. *Parah* (Heifer). (1–12) Red heifers for sacrifice.

56. *Ṭohorot* (Purifications). (1–10) Methods of purifications.

57. *Miqwaʾot* (Ceremonial Waters). (1–10) The ritual purification of the water.

58. *Niddah* (Separation of Women in Menstruation). (1–10) Cleanliness of women before and after childbirth.

59. *Makširin* (Preparations). (1–6) Liquids used for purification.

60. *Zabim* (Excretions). (1–5) Exudates of the body and their purification.

61. *Ṭebul Yom* (Immersion on the Day). (1–4) Immersion on the day of impurity.

62. *Yadayim* (Hands). (1–4) Ritual washings.

63. *ʿUqṣin* (Stalks of Fruit). (1–3) Stalks of fruit conveying impurity.

IV. The Palestinian and Babylonian Talmud. Although frequently referred to as the Talmud Yerushalmi (Jerusalem), the Palestinian Talmud was the product of the northern towns of Israel and their rabbinical schools and sages. It was hastily assembled and edited during the 2nd–4th Christian centuries and is about a third of the length of the Babylonian edition. Only the Gemara of the first four orders is extant. The language is a dialect known as Western ARAMAIC and demonstrates the peculiarities of orthography and lexica clearly separating it from the Babylonian. The antiquity of its Halakah and the great age and Palestinian origin of the even more extensive haggadic material render it invaluable for the study of the rabbinate and the history of exegesis in the Judaism of this period. It is supposed to have been edited by Johanan ben Nappaha (c. A.D. 270), but material from later periods was incorporated and the closing date is set at c. 425, when the Tiberian School ended.

The Babylonian Talmud developed in the areas under relative Jewish control in Mesopotamia. Its origins were partly Palestinian, as many of its progenitors had studied in Tiberias. The initiator of the Babylonian edition was Rab Abba Arika, the founder and head of the great Sura Academy. Following him in the 3rd cent. were such eminent scholars and jurists as Mar Samuel, a member of the first group of Babylonian Amoraim. The third generation boasted such authorities as Abbaye (c. A.D. 300) and Raba (c. 340). In the time of Rabina bar Huna (c. 495) the period of Talmudic expansion came to a close. The work of the next group of scholars, the *Saboraim* ("redactors"), brought the work to its full and extant form. The dialect of the Babylonian Talmud was an Eastern Aramaic, written with its own peculiarities of orthography and lexica. There are other significant differences between it and the Palestinian Talmud. Of the sixty-three tractates, twenty-six lack the Babylonian Gemara (e.g., under *Zeraʾim*, the Babylonian Talmud includes a commentary only on tractate *Berakot*).

The initial mention of the whole of the written Babylonian Talmud was made in the 8th cent. It is necessary to note that the completion of this vast amount—nearly fifty volumes—of detailed and succinct legal commentary at the beginning of the Dark Ages, when the Roman empire was dissolving into the inflexible discreteness of feudalism, gave to the Jews an intellectual treasure that helped them endure the medieval period and survive to attend the coming of the Renaissance. Even under the spread and domination of Islam, the Talmud survived. In the W, however, the mystical frenzy which shook Europe after the collapse of the crusading spirit vented the wrath of Christendom upon the Jewish writings and there were destructions of numerous copies of the Talmud and proscriptions against its study and publication. The Talmud became in the Late Middle Ages one of the few accurate sources of information about antiquity, and such scholars as Petaḥia of Ratisbon (1140–1200) rediscovered the lost cities of antiquity through their intimate knowledge of the Talmud.

V. The literary history of the Talmud. Soon after the compilation of a full Talmudic corpus, divergences in textual families must have appeared. Unfortunately the Talmud is not presently represented by many truly ancient MSS. The only extant document of the whole of the Babylonian Talmud is that produced in A.D. 1343, presently in Munich; it was edited in 1912 by H. L. Strack (*Talmud Bab. codicis Hep. Monacensis 95 phototypice depictus*). The first printed editions of both the Palestinian and the Babylonian Talmud were published by the Christian printer-scholar D. Bomberg in Venice (1523 and 1524 respectively). The only complete Palestinian Talmud MS is one in Leiden, which has been edited by L. Ginsberg (1909).

Numerous difficulties have beset the preparation of any complete edition as numerous censored portions were omitted during the periods of intense persecution of the Jews so as not to include anything that might be interpreted as anti-Christian. However, the most extensive editions were those produced in Vilna, beginning in 1886, and frequently reproduced with a large number of additional commentaries such as the additions of the medieval French rabbis. Commentaries, introductions, and special studies have appeared in vast numbers, particularly from the large and erudite Jewish communities of E Germany, Poland, and Russia. With the tragic destruction of these centers of Hebraic scholarship, Jewish learning moved to the New World and thence to Israel. The mastery of the language, meaning, detail, and sweep of the Talmud is a lifetime avocation. However, it is the most compact and continuous set of documents revealing the piety of a people extant in modern times.

VI. The significance of the Talmud. Among the schools of European Jewry, the Talmud represented the highest and most complete mastery and challenge to which the pious Jew could apply. The knowledge of the Talmud was held in higher esteem than that of the Scripture itself, which had become in the 19th cent. the special province largely of anti-Jewish scholars. While the reconstruction of the rise of the OT text according to the theories of Graf-Kuenen-Wellhausen were eroding away confidence in the historicity of the OT, orthodox and conservative Judaism found refuge in the Talmud. The age of romanticism found little to attract it in the bewildering rationalism and endless casuistry of the Talmud. In its place an overwhelmingly Kantian philosophy of Judaism has been developed. With the rise of the State of Israel, a new renaissance of Talmudic studies may be at hand.

For the Christian scholar the Talmud offers firsthand insights into the state of Jewish religion and life in the 1st cent. and the development of that world view in later ages. Almost every mention and allusion to Jewish custom and culture found in the gospel narratives can be discovered in detail in the Talmudic tradition or one of its manifold explanations, as shown especially in the work of H. L. Strack and P. Billerbeck (*Kommentar zum Neuen*

Testament aus Talmud und Midrasch, 6 vols. in 7, with supplements by J. Jeremias and K. Adolph [1922–61]). The recovery of many new Talmudic fragments from excavations and the archaeological reconstruction of many previously obscure eras of Israel's history has necessitated fresh studies of both Mishnaic and Talmudic texts.

(See M. Schwab, *Le Talmud de Jérusalem traduit pour la première fois*, 11 vols. [1878–90]; S. Krauss, *Talmudische Archaeologie*, 3 vols. [1910–12]; G. F. Moore, *Judaism in the First Centuries of the Christian Era: The Age of the Tannaim*, 3 vols. [1927–30]; H. Danby, *The Mishnah: Translated from the Hebrew with Introduction and Brief Explanatory Notes* [1933]; J. Kaplan, *The Redaction of the Babylonian Talmud* [1933]; I. Epstein, ed., *The Babylonian Talmud*, Soncino ed., 36 vols. [1935–48]; J. Neusner, *The Formation of the Babylonian Talmud* [1970]; id., *The Talmud of the Land of Israel: A Preliminary Translation and Explanation*, 35 vols. [1982–94]; id., *The Talmud of Babylonia: An American Translation*, 36 vols. in 68 [1984–94]; D. W. Halivni, *Midrash, Mishnah, and Gemara: The Jewish Predilection for Justified Law* [1986]; J. Neusner, *The Mishnah: A New Translation* [1987]; S. Safrai, ed., *The Literature of the Sages* [1987]; A. Steinsaltz, *The Talmud*, 21 vols. [1989–99]; H. L. Strack and G. Stemberger, *Introduction to the Talmud and Midrash* [1992]; J. Neusner, *Invitation to the Talmud: A Teaching Book*, rev. ed. [2000]; H. W. Guggenheimer, *The Jerusalem Talmud: Edition Translation, and Commentary* [2000–2007]; H. Zelcer, *A Guide to the Jerusalem Talmud* [2002]; J. L. Rubenstein, *The Culture of the Babylonian Talmud* [2003]; C. E. Fonrobert and M. S. Jaffee, eds., *The Cambridge Companion to the Talmud and Rabbinic Literature* [2007].)   W. White, Jr.

Talsas tal′suhs. KJV Apoc. form of Salthas (1 Esd. 9.22).

Tamah tay′muh. KJV alternate form of Temah (Neh. 7:55).

Tamar (person) tay′mahr (תָּמָר H9470, "palm tree"). **(1)** Daughter-in-law of Judah (Gen. 38:6–30), included in Matthew's genealogy of Jesus Christ (Matt. 1:3 [KJV, "Thamar"]). Tamar was given in marriage to Judah's son, Er, who died because of some unspecified wickedness. Judah then instructed another son, Onan, to marry Tamar and father children for his brother Er (see levirate marriage). Onan married Tamar but avoided having children by her and God took his life as well. Tamar then returned to her Canaanite home after Judah promised that she would marry his third son, Shelah, when he had grown old enough. Judah, fearing for Shelah's life, did not fulfill his promise.

Subsequently, Tamar seduced Judah by hiding her identity and pretending to be a harlot of the heathen worship cult. When Judah learned of her pregnancy, he demanded her death, but Tamar, showing him the pledges he had unsuspectingly given her, proved that she had conceived by Judah himself. Judah was convicted of the wrong he had done her, and she was spared. Twins were born to Tamar by Judah: Perez and Zerah. The former was in the direct line of the ancestry of David, and hence of Christ (Ruth 4:12; Matt. 1:3; Lk. 3:33). The Tamar story seems to anticipate several features of the Joseph narrative; in particular, both figures succeed in eliciting repentance from those who had made them suffer. (See J. A. Emerton in *VT* 29 [1979]: 403–15; S. Niditch in *HTR* 72 [1979]: 143–49; S. D. Matthewson in *BSac* 146 [1989]: 373–92; M. E. Andrews in *ZAW* 105 [1993]: 262–69; *DPL*, 827–29.)

(2) A beautiful daughter of David, sexually assaulted by her infatuated half brother Amnon, who contrived the deed by feigning illness and arranging to have Tamar bring food to him. After this revolting act, Amnon rejected her with loathing. Her brother Absalom learned of the deed when Tamar expressed her sorrowful outrage by dress and manner. Absalom took the desolate girl into his home while he plotted to avenge her. After two years Absalom contrived to have Amnon murdered for his crime (2 Sam. 13). See discussion under Absalom.

(3) A beautiful daughter of Absalom, probably named for his beloved sister (2 Sam. 14:27). Some Greek mss of the Lucianic recension here read "Maacah" instead of "Tamar" (no doubt under the influence of 1 Ki. 15:2 and 2 Chr. 11:20–22). It is possible that Tamar was Maacah's mother. See discussion under Maacah #9.   N. B. Baker

Tamar (place) tay´mahr (תָּמָר H9471, "palm tree"). A settlement, town, or region mentioned in Ezekiel's eschatological vision as marking the SE boundary of a future restored Israel (Ezek. 47:19; 48:28; in 47:18, many scholars consider the MT's verb *tāmōddû*, "you will measure" [cf. KJV and NJPS], a textual error and instead read *tāmārâ*, "to Tamar" [cf. NIV and NRSV, following LXX and Syriac]).

"Tamar in the desert" is possibly mentioned also among the towns listed as having been built up by Solomon (thus the *Ketib* at 1 Ki. 9:18, followed by NRSV and NJPS); in this passage, however, the KJV and NIV read Tadmor (on the basis of the *Qere*, many Heb. MSS, several ancient versions, and 2 Chr. 8:4). George Adam Smith (*Historical Geography of the Holy Land*, 25th ed. [1931], 184 n. 3) argued that "Tamar" is the correct reading here, that it should probably be identified with Hazazon Tamar (another name for En Gedi, 2 Chr. 20:2), and that it was perhaps the same Tamar mentioned in Ezekiel. Most scholars, however, think Tamar was further S. Some locate it near Qasr el-Juheiniya, where the Romans built a border fort named Tamara (c. 12.5 mi. WSW of the Dead Sea; see *ABD*, 6:315–16).

Others think that Tamar is the same as the City of Palms and that the latter name was originally applied to a site now known as Tell ʿAin ʿArus (some 6 mi. SSE of the Dead Sea; see *HALOT*, 2:822, s.v. ʿir B.5); however, there is no compelling reason to deny that the name City of Palms is consistently used with reference to Jericho. More likely, Tamar should be identified with ʿAin Ḥuṣb (c. 23 mi. SSW of the Dead Sea in the Arabah; see Y. Aharoni, *The Land of the Bible: A Historical Geography*, rev. ed. [1979], 70, 140 [in the latter reference, Aharoni suggests that Hazazon Tamar should be identified not with En Gedi but with Tamar]).

tamarisk. A desert tree with tiny, scale-like leaves that hardly transpire at all (thus suited for hot, dry places). The Hebrew word *ʾesel* H869, which occurs three times in the OT, probably refers to the *Tamarix aphylla*, also known as the athel tree (other suggestions include *T. syriaca* [*HALOT*, 1:95] and *T. gallica* [*FFB*, 182]). Abraham planted a tamarisk tree (or tamarisk grove) in the droughty land of Beersheba (Gen. 21:33; perhaps it was in the shade of a tamarisk that Hagar laid her boy Ishmael, vv. 14–16). There were well-known tamarisk trees both in Gibeah (1 Sam. 22:6) and in Jabesh (31:13; in the parallel to this passage [1 Chr. 10:12], the tree is described as an oak or terebinth [*ēlâ* H461], possibly a textual corruption). The NRSV, through a minor conjecture, has "like a green tamarisk" in Isa. 44:4, where the MT reads, *bĕbên ḥāṣîr*, lit., "in between the grass" (for a discussion of the textual problem, see J. de Waard, *A Handbook on Isaiah* [1997], 170–71).

W. E. Shewell-Cooper

tambourine. See music, musical instruments IV.B.

Tammuz tam´uhz (תַּמּוּז H9452, from Akk. *Duʾuzu*, which in turn derives from Sumerian *Dumuzi*, "legal [or healthy] son"). A Sumerian and Babylonian deity. Tammuz was said to be the husband and brother of Inanna (Ishtar). He is represented on seals as the protector of flocks against wild beasts. In the Babylonian saga his death and visit to the underworld represents the annual wilting of vegetation in the scorching heat of summer. His return to earth, brought about by the descent of the mourning Ishtar into the nether world, represents the renewal of nature (although some scholars argue that Tammuz is consistently represented as dead, not as having been brought to life).

The annual mourning rites for Tammuz took place on the second day of the fourth month (June/July), giving rise to the practice of naming this month Duʾuzu in Babylonia and Tammuz in the postbiblical Jewish calendar. In Ezekiel's time, a variation of this rite of mourning found women weeping at the N gate of the temple (Ezek. 8:14). The cult of Adonis in Syria and that of Osiris in Egypt had many affinities with the Tammuz rites. In remote parts of Kurdistan a variation of the rite is still practiced. In the opinion of some scholars, Tammuz stands for the king, who, in turn, represents all men in their potential for participating in the divine nature of Ishtar, the principle of life and fertility. (See B. Alster, *Dumuzi's Dream: Aspects of Oral Poetry in a Sumerian Myth* [1972];

Y. Sefati, *Love Songs in Sumerian Literature: Critical Edition of the Dumuzi-Inanna Songs* [1998]; *DDD*, 828–34.)   F. E. YOUNG

Tanach tay′nak. KJV alternate form of TAANACH (only Josh. 21:25).

Tanakh tah′nahk, tuh-nahk′. Also Tanach, Tanak. A Hebrew name commonly used by Jews as equivalent to "Bible." The word is an acronym based on the first letter of the Hebrew names for the three divisions of the OT: *tôrâ* (Law; see TORAH), *nĕbî'îm* (Prophets; see NEBIIM), and *kĕtûbîm* (Writings; see KETUBIM).

Tanhumeth tan-hyoo′mith (תַּנְחֻמֶת *H9489*, "comfort, consolation"). Father of SERAIAH; the latter was a military officer who remained in Judah with GEDALIAH after the destruction of Jerusalem (2 Ki. 25:23; Jer. 40:8). The first passage identifies Tanhumeth as a Netophathite (see NETOPHAH), but the parallel in Jeremiah attaches that description to EPHAI. It seems probable that the words "the sons of Ephai" in Jeremiah are original and that they dropped out in the text of 2 Kings at some point in its transmission.

Tanis tan′is. See ZOAN.

Tannaim (pl. of sing. תַּנָּא [from Aram. תְּנָא, "to repeat, teach"], "teacher"). Title given to the rabbinic authorities that lived during the first two centuries A.D. (contrast AMORAIM). The Tannaitic scholars preserved and developed the TRADITION (the oral law) that was eventually codified in the MISHNAH c. A.D. 200.

tanner. This English term translates Greek *byrseus* G1114, which occurs only as the description of SIMON of JOPPA, a man in whose house PETER stayed for some time (Acts 9:43; 10:6, 32). In the later rabbinic literature (which prob. reflects attitudes from earlier periods), tanners were often suspected of immorality because their trade required them to deal with women; in addition, their work was considered revulsive because of the bad smell attached to it (see documentation in J. Jeremias, *Jerusalem in the Time of Jesus* [1969], 301–10). Many scholars think it is significant that Peter was willing to associate with a tanner; possibly this detail anticipates the account of his preaching to CORNELIUS, for it may show that the apostle was already open to change. Some commentators, however, disagree with this assessment of Peter's attitude or point out that the text itself appears to make no such connection between the two incidents.

Animal hides or skins are converted into LEATHER by tanning. It is a process of preserving in good condition the "corium" structure of the hide which is between the "epidermis" and the "flesh." In OT times this involved flaying the dead animal, beating the flayed hide in water to remove the dirt, salting and soaking the hide in a tanning agent, and finally stretching the wet leather on a frame to dry properly. The tanner was not a popular man because of the stench of the ingredients used in his trade and because he handled dead bodies. Sometimes the hides were put into dog's dung for dehairing. Little is known of ancient tanning agents but they were probably the same as in modern Syria and Egypt, where the bark of certain ACACIA trees, galls of the OAK and the TAMARISK, and rinds of the POMEGRANATE are used.   H. JAMIESON

Taphath tay′fath (טָפַת *H3264*, possibly from טַף *H3251*, "little child" [but see *HALOT*, 2:379]). Daughter of SOLOMON and wife of BEN-ABINADAB, who was one of the twelve district governors (1 Ki. 4:11). Another daughter of Solomon is also included in this list (v. 15); see BASEMATH #3.

Taphon tay′fon. KJV Apoc. form of TEPHON (1 Macc. 9:50).

Tappuah (person) tap′yoo-uh (תַּפּוּחַ *H9516*, "apple, apple tree"). Son of HEBRON and descendant of JUDAH in the line of CALEB (1 Chr. 2:43). As with a number of other names in the genealogy, Tappuah is no doubt associated with a town, probably BETH TAPPUAH (Josh. 15:52), which was less than 4 mi. from Hebron; another possibility is TAPPUAH (PLACE) #2.

Tappuah (place) tap′yoo-uh (תַּפּוּחַ *H9517*, "apple, apple tree"). **(1)** A town on the N boundary of the tribal territory of Ephraim (Josh. 16:8). The passage that describes the borders of the tribe of Manasseh states that its S boundary included the inhabitants of En Tappuah (17:7); then it goes on to say, "Manasseh had the land of Tappuah, but Tappuah itself, on the boundary of Manasseh, belonged to the Ephraimites" (v. 8). This town was apparently the same Tappuah that is described as one of the Canaanite cities whose kings were defeated by Joshua (12:17), and it may also be the town referred to as Tephon in the Apocrypha (1 Macc. 9:50). Its location is not certain, but it is generally identified with modern Sheikh Abu Zarad, about 13 mi. NNW of Bethel and 8 mi. SW of Shechem.

(2) A town in the Shephelah within the tribal territory of Judah (Josh. 15:34). It was evidently near such towns as Zanoah and Jarmuth, but the precise location is uncertain.

(3) According to the Lucianic mss of the Septuagint, Tappuah (*Taphōe*) was also the name of a city near Tirzah that was attacked by King Menahem (2 Ki. 15:16). Many scholars accept this reading (cf. RSV, NAB, NJB), but others follow the MT, which has the otherwise unknown town of Tiphsah (cf. NIV, NRSV, NJPS). See Tiphsah #2.

tar. See bitumen.

Iarah tair′uh. KJV form of Terah (place).

Taralah tair′uh-luh (תַּרְאֲלָה H9550, derivation unknown). A town in the tribal territory of Benjamin (Josh. 18:27). Since it is associated with such cities as Mizpah and Kephirah, Taralah must have been located in the W Benjamin plateau, a few miles NW of Jerusalem, but the precise site is unknown.

Tarea tair′ee-uh (תָּאְרֵעַ H9308 [1 Chr. 8:35] and תַּחְרֵעַ H9390 [9:41], meaning unknown [but see BDB, 357]). Grandson of Merib-Baal (i.e., Mephibosheth) and descendant of King Saul (1 Chr. 8:35; called "Tahrea" in 9:41).

tares. This English term is used by the KJV to render the plural of Greek *zizanion* G2429, which occurs eight times in one of Jesus' parables of the kingdom (Matt. 13:25–30, 36–40). The word probably refers to a weed called *darnel*, which looks exactly like wheat in its young stages; in fact, only the expert can distinguish some species of this darnel from the true wheat. Later on, the differences are remarkable. The farmer, however, cannot pull up the weed when it is almost fully grown without seriously damaging the true wheat plants which are growing alongside. The darnel is an annual, *Lolium*

tares or darnel.

temulentum, sometimes referred to as the bearded darnel grass. It has far smaller seeds than wheat, and it is claimed that these seeds, when ground to flour, are poisonous, due perhaps to a particular fungus that develops in the seed itself. (See *FFB*, 194–95.)   W. E. SHEWELL COOPER

Targum tahr´guhm (postbiblical Heb. תַּרְגּוּם, Aram. תַּרְגּוּמָא, "interpretation, translation" [cf. the Aram. verb תַּרְגֵּם *H9553*, "to proclaim, explain, translate," Ezra 4:7]). Plural *Targums* or *Targumim* tahr´guh-mim. A name applied to translations of the Hebrew Bible into the ARAMAIC LANGUAGE.

I. Definition and origin. The term *targum* is probably derived from Akkadian *targummannum* or *turgummum* ("translator"), which occurs as early as the TELL EL-AMARNA tablets (c. 1400–1350 B.C.) and which may go back to the HITTITE verb *tarkummiya* ("to announce, explain"; cf. C. Rabin in *Orientalia* 32 [1963]: 134–36, but see *HALOT*, 4:1787). Although the word *targum* has occasionally been used for other translations, such as the SEPTUAGINT, it came to be used exclusively for a particular group of translations of the OT into Aramaic.

Nehemiah 8 describes a great gathering in Jerusalem at which EZRA and his associates publicly read the TORAH to the people who had recently come back from EXILE. According to v. 8, "They read from the Book of the Law of God, making it clear [ptc. of *pāraš H7300*] and giving the meaning so that the people could understand what was being read." The question needs consideration why it was necessary at this time, instead of simply reading the law, to add an explanation? Was it because in the natural course of events the HEBREW LANGUAGE had changed enough to make the language of the Torah seem a bit archaic and in need of explanation, particularly to the younger members of the population? Was it because the congregation needed to have ideas and terms that had become somewhat unfamiliar during the long period of exile explained, and their interrelations pointed out? Or was it that many of the people, while in BABYLON, had adopted the Aramaic language of those around them, and therefore needed a translation into their common speech?

Many scholars have adopted this last suggestion as the principal (though not the only) reason for the need of explanation, though some believe that the Jews did not adopt Aramaic until somewhat later. In any event, Aramaic had certainly become the common language of at least large segments of the Jewish community before NT times, and it had become customary, in each Sabbath SYNAGOGUE service, when reading a portion of the law, to read one verse of the Hebrew at a time, after which a second person would give a translation or paraphrase into Aramaic, with a certain amount of explanation of the meaning of the passage.

For several centuries it was not considered proper to read in the synagogue service anything except the actual Scripture itself, and thus the translations were given extemporaneously, usually from memory. In the course of the years, however, these renderings or interpretations naturally tended to become rather fixed, and it is likely that translations into Aramaic were written down for use by people in other settings, such as at home. (The discovery of an Aramaic translation of Job in QUMRAN [4QTgJob=4Q157] is clear evidence that written Targumim existed even prior to NT times.) By the 2nd or 3rd cent. A.D., many synagogues had adopted the custom of using written translations in the service, an innovation to which some of the rabbis strongly objected. Shortly after, however, such texts not only became generally accepted but also came to be treated as official rabbinic interpretations of Scripture. As time went on and Jews in various areas began to speak Arabic or other languages, the Targum ceased to be read in the services, but continued to be studied for help in interpretation.

II. Targums of the Pentateuch. Since the PENTATEUCH in its entirety was read consecutively in the successive weekly synagogue services, the Targums of the Pentateuch were particularly important. The best known of these is the so-called *Targum Onkelos*, which was one of the earliest to be written down. Like most of the Targums it had its origin in Palestine, but it was carried to the great centers of Jewish learning in Babylonia, where it took final form around the 5th cent. Its dialect is fundamentally Western or Palestinian, but at many points it was conformed to so-called Eastern Aramaic, the dialect used in Mesopotamia, and its text was changed at places in view of the altered situation. It tends on the whole to be more literal than other Targums, but it frequently expresses definite views (cf. the messianic interpretation of Gen. 49:10 and Num. 24:17). A considerable number of MSS of *Targum Onkelos* have been preserved.

Other Targums of the Pentateuch—often grouped together under the rubric *Palestinian Targum*—were considerably longer. (1) One which has been well preserved is referred to either as *Targum Yerushalmi* (Jerusalem Targum) or as *Targum Pseudo-Jonathan* (at one time it was thought to have been written by the author of *Targum Jonathan*, the standard Aramaic translation of the Prophets; see below). This is a rather late work that probably took shape no earlier than the 7th cent. and that reflects a mixture of traditions. (2) The label *Fragmentary Targum* does not refer to MS fragments but to ancient collections of selected passages from the Palestinian Targum (six MSS representing various recensional families have survived). Sometimes this translation is referred to as *Targum Yerushalmi II*. (3) Some small fragments (in the usual sense of the word) were discovered in the famous Cairo GENIZAH in the 1920s. (4) Pride of place is usually given to *Targum Neofiti*, discovered in 1956 by A. Díez-Macho in the Vatican Museum. This MS, which preserves virtually the whole Pentateuch, is very late (early 16th cent.), but most scholars believe that the text it contains goes back to the 4th cent. or even earlier. As such, it is generally regarded as the best representative of the Palestinian Targum.

In addition, the *Samaritan Targum* (to be distinguished from the SAMARITAN PENTATEUCH, a Hebrew text) is the Aramaic translation of the Pentateuch used by the SAMARITAN sect. Preserved in a variety of textual forms, this version has received little attention by modern scholars (Critical ed. by A. Tal, *Ha-Targum ha-Shomroni la-Torah* [1980–83]; see also J.-P. Rothschild and G. Dominique, eds., *Études samaritaines: Pentateuque et targum, exégèse et philologie, chroniques* [1988].)

III. Targums of the Prophets. The standard Aramaic translation of the Prophets (*Targum Nebi'im* or *Targum Jonathan*) was attributed to Jonathan ben Uzziel, a pupil of the great rabbi HILLEL. On the whole it presents a fairly good translation of the books in the second section of our present Hebrew Bible (Joshua, Judges, Samuel, Kings, Isaiah, Jeremiah, Ezekiel, and the Minor Prophets), but it contains many paraphrases or interpretative additions. It is thought that, like *Targum Onkelos*, it was carried to Babylon and there worked over to some extent.

An interesting illustration of the interpretative method of *Targum Jonathan* is found in Isa. 52:13–53:12, where the SERVANT OF THE LORD is designated as the MESSIAH, but where, except for one verse, all the statements that refer to his sufferings are either dropped out or so interpreted as to make the suffering described in them apply to the nation of Israel or to its enemies, rather than to the Servant himself.

IV. Targums of the Hagiographa. In their present form the latest Targums that have been preserved are those on the Hagiographa or Writings (see KETUBIM). However, there may well have been earlier translations of these books that have disappeared. The TALMUD refers to a Targum of Job as having been used by rabbis of the 1st cent., probably different from the one found at Qumran (see above, section I). Targums exist for all of the biblical books except Ezra-Nehemiah and Daniel. The lack in these two cases is understandable, since parts of these books (Ezra 4:8–6:18; 7:12–26; Dan. 2:4b–7:28) were originally written in Aramaic.

V. Uses of the Targums. The Targums are of only moderate value for restoring the Hebrew text, since they so often use paraphrase instead of direct translation. However, they are of great interest for showing certain aspects of Jewish interpretation in the centuries immediately after the time of Christ (in some instances no doubt preserving pre-Christian traditions). This value is somewhat lessened by the fact that most of them contain many additions or changes from later periods. *Targum Ps.-Jonathan*, for example, contains a specific reference to the city of Constantinople, which was not founded until A.D. 325, and attributes to ISHMAEL a wife and daughter with the same names as a wife and daughter of his famous descendant, Muhammad, who did not become prominent until the 7th cent. Sometimes a Targum may provide evidence as to the meaning of a rare Hebrew word as used at the beginning of the Christian era, but such evidence must be used with great caution.

(A multivolume work entitled *The Aramaic Bible*, ed. by M. McNamara, includes an English trans. of the various Targums; its publication began in 1987, and most books of the Bible have been completed as of this writing. See also P. de Lagarde, *Hagiographa chaldaice* [1873]; M. Ginsburger, *Das Fragmententhargum* [1899]; W. H. Brownlee, *The Dead Sea Habaqquq Midrash and the Targum of Jonathan* [1953]; A. Sperber, *The Bible in Aramaic*, 4 vols. in 5 [1959–73]; M. McNamara, *The New Testament and the Palestinian Targum to the Pentateuch* [1966]; A. Díez Macho, *Neophyti 1: Targum Palestinense ms. de la Biblioteca Vaticana*, 6 vols. [1968–79]; J. Bowker, *The Targums and Rabbinic Literature* [1969]; G. J. Kuiper, *The Pseudo-Jonathan Targum and Its Relationship to Targum Onkelos* [1972]; M. L. Klein, *The Fragment-Targums of the Pentateuch according to Their Extant Sources*, 2 vols. [1980]; M. Aberbach and B. Grossfeld, *Targum Onkelos to Genesis: An English Translation of the Text with Analysis and Commentary* [1982]; I. Drazin, *Targum Onkelos to Deuteronomy: An English Translation of the Text with Analysis and Commentary* [1982]; id., *Genizah Manuscripts of [the] Palestinian Targum to the Pentateuch*, 2 vols. [1986]; E. Levine, *The Aramaic Version of the Bible: Contents and Context* [1988]; I. Drazin, *Targum Onkelos to Exodus: An English Translation of the Text with Analysis and Commentary* [1990]; W. F. Smelik, *The Targum of Judges* [1995]; I. Drazin, *Targum Onkelos to Leviticus: An English Translation of the Text with Analysis and Commentary* [1994]; id., *Targum Onkelos to Numbers: An English Translation of the Text with Analysis and Commentary* [1998]; B. Grossfeld and L. H. Schiffman, *Targum Neofiti 1: An Exegetical Commentary to Genesis, Including Full Rabbinic Parallels* [2000]; E. van Staalduine-Sulman, *The Targum of Samuel* [2002]; C. M. M. Brady, *The Rabbinic Targum of Lamentations: Vindicating God* [2003]; D. Shepherd, *Targum and Translation: A Reconsideration of the Qumran Aramaic Version of Job* [2004]; P. S. Alexander in *ABD*, 6:320–31.) A. A. MacRae

Tarpelites tahr′puh-lits (Aram. טַרְפְּלָיֵא, apparently pl. determinative of an otherwise unattested gentilic name, טַרְפְּלָי *H10305*). The KJV transliteration of an Aramaic term whose meaning is uncertain (Ezra 4:9). Since the term is gentilic in form, it may indeed mean "people of Tarpel," alluding perhaps to a region in Mesopotamia (cf. H. G. M. Williamson, *Ezra-Nehemiah*, WBC 16 [1985], 54–55). The Septuagint renders it *Tarphallaioi*, referring to an inhabitant of the city of Tripolis, and this interpretation is followed by the NIV. Other modern versions understand the term in the general sense of "officer" (cf. NRSV and NJPS; note also that the two preceding terms in the verse, though also gentilic in form, refer to "judges and officials"). Some have argued that it designates more specifically "an official of the Persian chancellery of Ebirnari in Tripolis" (*HALOT*, 5:1886).

Tarshish (person) tahr′shish (תַּרְשִׁישׁ *H9578*, "topaz" [or some other precious stone]). KJV also Tharshish (1 Chr. 7:10). **(1)** Son of Javan, grandson of Japheth, and great-grandson of Noah (Gen. 10:4; 1 Chr. 1:7). The names of his brothers (Elishah, Kittim, Rodanim) clearly refer to places or people groups, so Tarshish was presumably the progenitor of a Mediterranean people and his name was attached to a geographical area. See Tarshish (place).

(2) Son of Bilhan and great-grandson of Benjamin (1 Chr. 7:10).

(3) One of the seven nobles of Persia and Media in the time of Xerxes "who had special access to the king and were highest in the kingdom" (Esth. 1:14). Queen Vashti was banished by Ahasuerus (Xerxes) on their advice.

Tarshish (place) tahr′shish (תַּרְשִׁישׁ *H9576*, "topaz" [or some other precious stone]). KJV also Tharshish (1 Ki. 10:22, 22:48). A region of uncertain location. In some passages the name is associated with ships and ports. Thus Hiram, king of Tyre, maintained at Ezion Geber, at the head of the Gulf of Aqabah, a refinery and ship-building center from which he and Solomon operated "ships of Tarshish" (1 Ki. 10:22; 2 Chr. 9:21; cf. 1 Ki. 9:26–28). King Jehoshaphat built a similar fleet also at Ezion Geber (1 Ki. 22:48; 2 Chr. 20:36–37). There were perhaps other similar stations maintained by Phoenicians on the Mediterranean coasts and possibly in the E, where cargoes from India could be reshipped.

The name Tarshish in such a connection does not seem to indicate destination, nor does it signify "belonging to" or "trading with" a place called Tarshish. Rather, there is suggested the nature of the ships, their size and far-voyaging capability; thus in the verses cited above the NIV translates the word as "trading ships" (in 2 Chr. 20:37 [which reads literally, "to go to Tarshish"] the NIV has "to set sail to trade"). A similar idea is shown in other passages (Ps. 48:7; Isa. 2:16 [NIV, "every trading ship"]; 23:1, 6, 10, 14; 60:9; Ezek. 27:25). Certain references (Ezek. 38:13; Ps. 72:10), although clearly referring to a place, suggest that the ships of Tarshish were symbolic of Mediterranean trade and traders, being well known in Mediterranean and Red Sea waters, and carrying merchandise of great value. Its connection with people groups listed in the Table of Nations (Gen. 10:4; 1 Chr. 1:7) gives an intimation that these special Tarshish ships did business with the Greek isles.

As a place name, the identification of Tarshish has been debated. The biblical writers clearly viewed it as a very distant place, and it was on a ship headed for Tarshish that Jonah sought to flee from the Lord (Jon. 1:3; 4:2). In some passages (Isa. 23:1 et al.; Ezek. 27:12 et al.), the Septuagint renders the name with Greek *Karchēdōn* (or gentilic *Karchēdonioi*), that is, Carthage, and some modern writers have adopted this understanding (Tarshish seems to be associated with Libya in Isa. 66:19). Another suggestion is a city on the island of Sardinia, for a Phoenician inscription of the 9th cent. B.C. mentions a Tarshish there; but it is likely that this name (which some think means "refinery") was applied to a variety of ports in the ancient world (cf. H. Wildberger, *Isaiah 1–12: A Commentary* [1991], 117–18).

Most scholars see a connection with Tartessus (Gk. *Tartēssos*; cf. Neo-Assyrian *Tarsisi*), a city or territory that Herodotus locates in the W Mediterranean region, evidently near Gibraltar (*Hist.* 1.163; 4.152; it seems to have been destroyed in the 6th cent. B.C.). Tartessus, which was possibly founded by Phoenicians (cf. the association with Tyre in Isa. 23), appears to have been located around the lower Guadalquivir River (e.g., Huelva) in Andalucía, SW Spain (see T. Júdice Gamito, *Social Complexity in Southwest Iberia, 800–300 B.C.: The Case of Tartessos* [1988]; S. Celestino Pérez, *Estelas de guerrero y estelas diademadas: la precolonización y formación del mundo tartésico* [2001]). Although no specific identification has been confirmed, such a site is consonant with the data that Tarshish developed trade in minerals (Jer. 10:9; Ezek. 27:12; the Heb. noun *taršîš H9577*, which refers to a precious stone [chrysolite? beryl? Spanish topaz?], may be derived from the place name). (See further *HALOT*, 4:1797–98; *ABD*, 6:331–33.)   R. F. Gribble

Tarsus tahr´suhs (Ταρσός *G5433*, gentilic Ταρσεύς *G5432*, "of Tarsus"). A city of Cilicia in SE Asia Minor; modern Tersous, situated in the Cilician plain on the River Cydnus, some 10 mi. inland. This is a common setting for centers of civilization along that coast, once plagued by pirates. A calculation based on the wide extent of its traces suggests that Tarsus once had a population of half a million. The lower reaches of the river were navigable so that Tarsus functioned as a port with a skillfully constructed haven on a lake between the city and the sea. Dion Chrysostom (Dio Coccenianus, c. A.D. 45–112) was critical of Tarsus and spoke of the city's regard for her river with a touch of irony. The people of Tarsus, however, made this the chief ground of their pride. They had made their own environment, taming the river to their needs, and building "no ordinary city," as Paul said (Acts 21:39), appropriating a phrase of Euripides (*Ion* 8) applied by that great dramatist to his native Athens.

Land communications involved engineering just as creditable. Some 30 mi. inland from Tarsus lay the great barrier of the Taurus mountains, cut by a deep pass known as the Cilician Gates. Through this pass Tarsus had driven a major highway. The city lay, therefore, virtually upon the sea in a corner of the Mediterranean where cultures mingled; E met W while the hinterland was open to her traffic. By her own strength she had made herself a nodal point of communications.

Tarsus was founded toward the end of the 2nd millennium B.C., but the beginnings are shrouded in obscurity. One Mopsus is named among the founders, and the name appears to be Greek. It is a fair guess that Ionian Greeks, whose dynamic colonies dotted the W shoreline of Asia Minor, came also to Cilicia and joined a primitive settlement on the Cydnus. In the Table of NATIONS in Gen. 10, JAVAN is certainly the Ionians, and some have thought that TARSHISH, listed close to it, may in this context refer to Tarsus. To such guesswork are all attempts to date or to describe the beginnings of Tarsus reduced.

Nor can a connected account of the city's story be given, even when the E Mediterranean moves into the era of recorded history. The theme can be picked up only at various points, and some endeavor made to interpret isolated detail. The Assyrian conqueror SHALMANESER III, whose sanguinary reign can be dated 859 to 824 B.C., made brief reference to Tarsus in the records of his conquests and aggression.

The account must then pass over four centuries empty of significant detail. The year 401 B.C. can be pinpointed. ASSYRIA AND BABYLON had left the stage of empire. PERSIA ruled a vast array of lands from the Aegean to the Indus. Tarsus was under a puppet king named Syennesis. The fact emerges from a famous and most significant book, the *Anabasis* of the Athenian soldier, adventurer, and literary man, Xenophon. One Cyrus, a satrap of the Aegean coast, had rebelled against the Great King. He recruited the famous Ten Thousand, a Greek mercenary army, whose stubborn withdrawal from the Mesopotamian plain, through the Armenian mountains to Trebizond on the Black Sea, forms the well-told story of Xenophon's book. The author was one of the leaders of the great retreat. His first book describes the march through Asia Minor to the climax of the battle of Cynaxa. The column passed through the Cilician Gates and came to Tarsus where Syennesis ruled. It is likely that he was deposed after the crumbling of the revolt for failure to resist Cyrus's advance, a hopeless task that he can hardly be blamed for avoiding.

Xenophon's account of the Greek exploit in marching out of the heart of the Persian empire revealed to the young ALEXANDER THE GREAT, a half century later, the inherent weakness of the vast system. He applied the lesson and attacked Persia. Marching through Cilicia in 334 B.C., he found a Persian governor in charge. Coinage throws some light on this period. Greek notions and motives flood back into Tarsian coin designs after Alexander, but before the conquest the oriental tone is dominant, suggesting that Greek influence in Tarsus was at a low ebb. The strong Greek presence, evidenced by the same art, reveals the firm integration of Tarsus and its province into the SELEUCID Syrian regime, which followed the partition of Alexander's empire. The Tarsus of Paul was visibly taking form and shape.

The region was ruled first as a province, for it was Seleucid policy to rule in provincial units after the pattern of the Persian satrapies, and in the process, to discourage the habitual Greek urge toward the autonomous city state. This policy was rudely interrupted by the inevitable clash with ROME. Under ANTIOCHUS the Great, Syria was moving

Tarsus.

westward in perennial ambition to recover the kingdoms that had broken free at the W end of the Asia Minor peninsula. Rome, simultaneously feeling for a stable eastern frontier, was moving in the opposite direction. Antiochus's large designs extended to GREECE itself, something of a vacuum of power on his westward frontiers. Rome had likewise felt the weakness of Greece as a buffer on her eastern flank. A confrontation could hardly be avoided, and it was to be expected that a victorious Rome would seek to stabilize her frontier as far as possible to the E.

The peace treaty imposed on a humiliated

Excavations at Tarsus.

Antiochus fixed Syria's boundary on the Taurus mountains, and Cilicia became, in consequence, a border province. Readier agreement on the part of the Antioch government to grant Tarsus autonomy followed. How naturally it followed that a Tarsus should emerge that experienced and understood both worlds—E and W, Greek and Semitic, a Tarsus vividly aware of Rome, impregnated with Hellenic culture, but aware of the tides of thought and of religion in the lands of the E.

Paul was a natural product of this cultural environment. In writing to the sadly troubled Galatian church, the great apostle spoke of the purpose that had set him apart from birth for the difficult task of evangelizing the GENTILE world (Gal. 1:15–16). Tarsus was no fortuitous birthplace for a person with such a calling. The apostle to the Gentiles had to be a Jew, imbued with the OT; he needed also to be a Greek, to interpret a nascent theology in the thought

forms of Hellenic culture and to express what he had to teach in the subtle, rich language of the Greeks, the second tongue of all people from Italy to the Persian Gulf. Also, he had to be a Roman citizen in the truest sense, understanding that mighty system, and conscious of the global opportunity it offered. No other man known to history from that time combined these qualities as did Paul of Tarsus. It is difficult to imagine any other place whose whole atmosphere and history could have so effectively produced them in one person. Paul was a Hebrew trained under the notable GAMALIEL. He could talk and think like a Greek and quote his native Cilician poets to the intellectuals of Athens. He could write strong Greek in closely argued documents. He was by birth a citizen of Rome.

The last sentence makes it necessary to return to the fragmented history of Tarsus. After the clash with Antiochus, which ended with the battle of Magnesia in 190 B.C., Rome was on the border of the Cilician region. In 171, Antiochus Epiphanes seems to have conceded a much wider autonomy to Tarsus. Unrest in that dynamic city, in which the Jewish minority seems to have played an important part, had forced the hand of the Antioch government (the curious story of the insurrection in Tarsus is told in 2 Macc. 4:30–50). A major reorganization of the constitution followed. One provision was the establishment of a "tribe" of Jews with full CITIZENSHIP. When Paul, writing to the Roman church, spoke of his kinsmen, as he did four times in that letter, it was possibly to his fellow tribesmen of Tarsus that he thus referred.

Antiochus Epiphanes, who made this major concession to Jews of the DIASPORA in Tarsus, was the notorious savage persecutor and oppressor of the Jews of Palestine. This was because Palestinian Jewry was resistant toward the monarch's passionate desire to hellenize his realms. It was a quest for unity—not without its merits had it been pursued with deeper understanding and some tincture of mercy. In Tarsus, on the other hand, the Jews were tolerant toward HELLENISM. Witness Paul's use of metaphors from the Greek games and the liberality of outlook that they suggest. The same Paul is evidence that a rigid Judaism could accompany such tolerance toward the Greeks. Such was the spirit of Tarsian Jewry, proud of their city, willingly integrated into its social system, but loyal to their ancient faith.

Rome first effectively penetrated the region in 104 B.C., and the next half century was one of lamentable strife and upheaval in Asia Minor, an era of tension ended only by the reorganization of the whole complex of nations at the eastern end of the Mediterranean by POMPEY in 65 and 64 B.C. Under Pompey's system, Cilicia became a Roman area of command. Fourteen years later the great orator and statesman Cicero became governor of the province, and it is perhaps indicative of the trouble and anarchy endured by this once ordered corner of the Mediterranean, that one of Cicero's tasks was the pacification of bandit-ridden hill country in the province. In like manner, and as significantly, Pompey had received a special command in 63 to cleanse the eastern Mediterranean of pirates, so indigenous to this particular coast that they were often referred to as "Cilician pirates."

Resurgent orientalism led by Rome's great opponent, the able PARTHIAN king Mithridates of PONTUS, had led to the anarchy and social breakdown that is evident from these events. Rome's intervention and pacification were welcomed by civilized communities, and among such groups the Jews would figure prominently. The Jews of the Dispersion were an urban people, moving into the world of finance and commerce, which was to become the medieval characteristic of their race. Above all, they needed peace, and Pompey no doubt found in the Tarsian Jews a force making for tranquility and order. Rome was empiric in her organization. She chose and promoted those elements of authority and stability she found operative in regions that she penetrated. It was probably from some situation at this time that the Roman citizenship was conferred on a group of Jews at Tarsus, a group shrewd enough to read the signs, to feel the winds of coming change and profit by them. Once conferred, the Roman privilege was transmitted by birth. Thus Paul became a Roman citizen, a status that helped to form his outlook and that determined the pattern of his evangelism.

A brilliant period in the history of Tarsus followed. It became the Athens of the eastern Mediterranean, the ancient equivalent of a university city, the resort of men of learning, the home town of Athenodorus (74 B.C. to A.D. 7), the respected teacher of AUGUSTUS himself, the seat of a school of STOIC philosophers, a place of learning and disputation, the very climate in which a brilliant mind might grow up in the midst of stimulus and challenge and learn to think and to contend.

Like all boys of his race, the young Tarsian Jew also learned a trade (Acts 18:3). He wove the native goats' hair of the province into a rough linen, often used as tent cloth, and known from its place of origin as *cilicium*. From references in Latin literature it would appear that cilicium was also used as sailcloth and leggings. Its manufacture was a prime industry of Tarsus, for it appears that the mass of its population were linen workers disenfranchised by the timocratic constitution, which demanded a charge of 500 drachmas for the privilege of citizenship. This property qualification, or "means test," seems to have been an invention of Athenodorus, who after thirty years in Rome returned to Tarsus in 15 B.C. In true Platonic tradition, he sought by persuasion and philosophy to purge local politics. Failing, as philosophers in such situations have invariably done, Athenodorus used his vast influence with Augustus to banish the more corrupt of the city's leaders. A timocratic constitution followed.

The founding of the Tarsian church was probably due to Paul. Many of the trials, perils, and adventures listed by him in the biographical passage of 2 Cor. 11:24–27 took place in Cilicia—its city, hinterland, and neighboring seas. (See further W. M. Ramsay, *The Cities of St. Paul: Their Influence on His Life and Thought* [1907], 85–244; Pauly-Wissowa, *Real-Encyclopädie der classischen Altertumswissenschaft*, IV A/2 [1932], 2413–39; W. C. van Unnik, *Tarsus or Jerusalem? The City of Paul's Youth* [1962]; E. M. Blaiklock, *The Cities of the New Testament* [1965], ch. 3; ISBE, rev. ed. [1979–88], 4:734–36; ABD, 6:333–34.)

E. M. BLAIKLOCK

Tartak tahr'tak (תַּרְתָּק H9581, meaning unknown). An idol of the Avvites (see IVVAH); along with NIBHAZ, Tartak was introduced by them into SAMARIA when they were relocated there by SARGON II after 722 B.C. (2 Ki. 17:31). A deity with this name is not known in extrabiblical sources, unless Nibhaz and Tartak be identified with the Elamite gods Ibnahaza and Dirtak (thus M. Cogan and H. Tadmor, *II Kings*, AB 11 [1988], 212, following an earlier suggestion of F. Hommel). Perhaps more likely is the view that the name Tartaq is a corruption of Aramaic ʿtrʿth (which in older orthography may have been spelled ʿtrqth), that is, the Syrian goddess ATARGATIS (thus J. A. Montgomery, *A Critical and Exegetical Commentary on the Book of Kings*, ICC [1951], 474, following F. Baethgen).

Tartan tahr′tan (תַּרְתָּן H9580, from Akk. *tartānu* or *turtannu*, itself borrowed from HURRIAN). Title of high-ranking Assyrian generals in command of a military force (2 Ki. 19:17; Isa. 20:1 [KJV and other versions]; NIV, "supreme commander"). The Tartan is listed in the Assyrian Eponym Texts as the next highest official after the king. Such officials are known from the times of Adad-nirari II, SHALMANESER III, TIGLATH-PILESER III, SARGON II, and SENNACHERIB. See also RABMAG; RABSARIS; RABSHAKEH. L. L. WALKER

Tartarus tahr′tuh-ruhs (Τάρταρος). In Greek mythology, Tartarus was originally the name of a dark abyss where the Titans were confined; later the term became equivalent to HADES. Some Bible versions use this name to translate the verb *tartaroō* G5434, "to cast into Tartarus" (2 Pet. 2:4; NIV, "sent them to hell"). See HELL.

taskmaster. This English term is used by the KJV and other versions primarily to render the participle of Hebrew *nāgaś* H5601, "to oppress, force [to do something]" (Exod. 3:7 et al.; NIV, "slave driver"). Comparable words are common in the Egyptian OSTRACA, which detail the labors of the work gangs responsible for excavating and building the tombs of the pharaohs. W. WHITE, JR.

tassel. The Israelites were commanded "to make tassels [*ṣîṣit* H7492, KJV 'fringes'] on the corners of your garments, with a blue cord on each tassel" (Num. 15:37–39; cf. Deut. 22:12, which uses a different term, *gādil* H1544). The purpose of these tassels was to remind the Israelites of the commandments of the Lord, and not to depart from his will. Unfortunately, such injunctions could be misused, and Jesus critiqued the SCRIBES and the PHARISEES: "Everything they do is done for men to see: They make their phylacteries wide and the tassels on their garments long" (Matt. 23:5; the Gk. word is *kraspedon* G3192, "border [of a garment], hem").

Monuments from Egypt and the ANE show that many types of tassels were worn by non-Jews in ancient times, though not for the same purpose. Jews gradually ceased to wear these tassels outwardly, as prescribed in the law, chiefly to avoid exposure to heathen and Christian persecution. They therefore devised a kind of undergarment (or vest) covering the chest and back, with four corners where tassels were attached. Modern orthodox Jews still wear either such a vest or a prayer shawl that likewise has tassels attached to the corners. However, the "blue thread" is no longer regarded as necessary. See also PHYLACTERY. S. BARABAS

Tatian tay′shuhn. See DIATESSARON.

Tatnai tat′ni. KJV form of TATTENAI.

Tattenai tat′uh-ni (Aram. תַּתְּנַי H10779, meaning unknown). KJV Tatnai. A Persian governor (Aram. *peḥâ* H10580) responsible for the province W of the River EUPHRATES during the reign of DARIUS Hystaspes (Ezra 5:3, 6; 6:6, 13; called "Sisinnes" in 1 Esd. 6:3, 7, 27; 7:1). Tattenai, along with SHETHAR-BOZENAI and others, reported to the king on the complaints made regarding the Jewish rebuilding of the temple. His name and title, in the corresponding form *Tattannu [Ta-at-tanni] paḥat Ebir-nāri* ("Tattenai governor of Beyond the River"), is attested in a tablet dated 502 B.C. (cf. *SacBr*, 280b-c).

tattoo. This term is used by the NIV and some other versions to render the Hebrew *qaʿăqaʿ* H7882, a verb of uncertain meaning; it occurs only once in a passage that prohibits self-mutilation (Lev. 19:28; KJV, "print"; NJPS, "incise"). The verb is used in combination with the noun *kĕtōbet* H4182, which also occurs only here, but whose meaning is clearly "inscription, mark" (from *kātab* H4180, "mark"). In the strict sense, a tattoo is an indelible mark, figure, or writing made by pricking and inserting pigment under the skin. Perusal of MOURNING customs in the Bible indicates frequent association of head-shaving with body-cutting and painting (e.g., with clay), but never tattooing. The prohibition in Leviticus likely has to do with some kind of cutting of the skin. See also MARK.

tau tou (from תָּו H9338, "mark, sign"). Also *tav*, *taw*. The last (twenty-second) letter of the Hebrew ALPHABET (ת), with a numerical value of 400. It is named for the shape of the letter, which in its older form looked like an X, that is, a mark. This letter was pronounced *t*, similar to English, although in later times it became spirantized (cf. the *th* sound in English *think*) when it was preceded by a vowel sound.

Taverner's Bible. See VERSIONS OF THE BIBLE, ENGLISH, IV.

Taverns, Three. See THREE TAVERNS.

taw. See TAU.

tax. Money, goods, captives, produce, livestock, or similar possessions which a government demands for its support or for specific purposes or services, or as TRIBUTE levied upon other governments and their citizens, usually in some proportion to the assessed value or amount of money or property. In ancient times there was a special type of taxation in the form of tribute, which one government or ruler demanded of another after defeat at war or for certain privileges.

Governments and peoples of all civilizations, ancient and modern, have known taxation and the force of revenue. In general, methods, types of taxation, and attitudes toward taxes have not changed. In the Bible one of the early references to taxation is in Egypt during the seven years of plenty when JOSEPH was authorized by the PHARAOH to levy a large proportion of the grain and store it for the lean years ahead (Gen. 41:25–57). One fifth of the harvest was collected during the years of plenty (v. 34). As a result, "Joseph stored up huge quantities of grain, like the sand of the sea; it was so much that he stopped keeping records because it was beyond measure" (v. 49). This could be done in Egypt because the pharaoh was absolute ruler and owned the land (v. 44). King DAVID enforced another type of taxation in the form of tribute from nations and rulers he defeated in war, such as the Philistines, Moabites, Arameans, and Edomites (2 Sam. 8:1–15).

Forced labor (*mas* H4989) or "chain gangs" was another kind of taxation or tribute, such as SOLOMON used in building the TEMPLE, his own palace, and other construction (1 Ki. 9:15). Only captives were conscripted: "Solomon did not make slaves of any of the Israelites" (v. 23). Solomon also must have introduced a tax system into his own country, for he set up "twelve district governors over all Israel, who supplied provisions for the king and the royal household. Each one had to provide supplies for one month in the year" (4:7). So far as can be determined, this is one of the first times the people of Israel were subject to taxes—prior to Solomon, support of the government came from the booty and captives of war (although we read about a tax [*maś'ēt* H5368] that MOSES had imposed on the Israelites, 2 Chr. 24:9). Solomon also obtained revenue from traders and caravans (10:14).

Israel and Judah often were forced to pay taxes or tribute to the enemy countries around them who conquered them—the Assyrians, Egyptians, Babylonians, and Persians (e.g., 2 Ki. 18:13–16). The pharaoh of Egypt placed Judah under heavy tribute, and thus JEHOIAKIM oppressively taxed the people to pay this demand (23:33–35; Heb. *ʿārak*

The cuneiform inscription on this gypsum block (from Ashur, c. 1900 B.C.), which records the restoration of a temple by Erishum I, king of Assyria, makes mention of his reform of the tax system as it applied to metals and some local products.

H6885 hiphil, "to assess," and noun ʿērek H6886, "estimated value, assessment"). In ancient times many governments were taxing their people to pay tribute to a foreign power. The Persians introduced a method of taxation which became widely used in later history: the provincial governor of a conquered country was forced to pay a certain amount of taxes each year to the occupying power and he, in turn, collected these taxes from the people of the province in various ways (cf. Ezra 4:13, where three Aram. terms are used: *middâ* H10402, *bĕlô* H10107, and *hălāk* H10208; NIV, "taxes, tribute, duty"; NRSV, "tribute, custom, toll"; NJPS, "tribute, poll-tax, land-tax").

Perhaps the beginning of tax exemption for religious purposes began after the EXILE. King ARTAXERXES wrote in a letter to EZRA: "You are also to know that you have no authority to impose taxes, tribute or duty on any of the priests, Levites, singers, gatekeepers, temple servants or other workers at this house of God" (Ezra 7:24). There was also heavy taxation under Persia in NEHEMIAH's day. The people complained to him, "We have had to borrow money to pay the king's tax [Heb. *middâ* H4501] on our fields and vineyards" (Neh. 5:4). Nehemiah stated that the former governors before him "placed a heavy burden on the people and took forty shekels of silver from them in addition to food and wine" (v. 15). This taxation was commonly known as "bread of the governor" (v. 14 KJV).

In Hellenistic times the familiar system of "farming taxes out" to the highest bidder who had the power of the army behind him to collect all sorts of taxes was used. During Greek domination, it is said that wealthy and powerful business men met in ALEXANDRIA each year to bid for the franchise to collect taxes from their own people. Exorbitant profits were made from this system because the TAX COLLECTOR could pocket everything he could collect beyond the set amount demanded by the government. Sometimes the amount of taxation was unbelievable. Under the SELEUCIDS, the government demanded one-third of the grain, one-half of the fruit produced, and a portion of the temple tax itself. POMPEY of Rome levied very heavy taxes upon the Judean province; likewise did Julius CAESAR, although he granted relief in sabbatical years.

In NT times under HEROD the Great, taxes in Palestine were levied on almost everything, especially on the fields (Jos. *Ant.* 15.5.3 §133). In the days of the Roman PROCURATORS in Palestine, taxes were also farmed out to the highest bidder, the system finally adopted throughout the empire. The kinds of taxes grew in such numbers that both rich and poor felt the heavy burden. There were land or real estate taxes, a poll tax (Matt. 22:17), export and import taxes collected at seaports and the gates of cities or country, a crop tax (one-tenth of the grain crop and one-fifth of the wine, fruit, and oil), an income tax of one percent of a person's income per year, taxes to use a road, to enter certain towns, taxes on animals and vehicles, a salt tax, sales tax, tax on the sale of slaves and the transfer of property, and emergency taxes!

It is true that under the Romans, the people enjoyed law and order on land and on sea, good roads, public buildings, markets, stadiums, baths, theaters, but the PROVINCES were almost bled to death in the process. Besides all these taxes, the Jews were asked to pay the temple tax—one half-shekel annually, called the DIDRACHMA (Matt. 17:24). Every Jew twenty years old and older from all over the world paid this tax for the operation of the holy temple (cf. Exod. 30:11–16). After VESPASIAN, when the temple was destroyed in A.D. 70, the Jews were still required to pay this tax nevertheless.

Later Rome introduced taxation through a regular CENSUS (Lk. 2:2). There was a Roman high official called a censor. He tried to collect revenue the cheapest way possible. He sold tax franchises in various areas or districts to highest bidders. He set the quota for the government and gave the *publicanus* (TAX COLLECTOR) the right to collect at an open-ended commission. Contracts were let for five-year periods. They were known to cheat both the government and the taxpayer. They took bribes from the rich and permitted them to pay less taxes (cf. Jesus' parable of the dishonest steward, Lk. 16:1–9). There were whole armies of tax gatherers in Palestine; it was often a family profession, with fathers followed by sons forming a caste of tax collectors. Under JUDAS the Galilean the Jews rebelled against the extreme burden of taxation, but the revolt was crushed by the heavy heel of Rome (Acts 5:37).

It is not surprising the Jews hated taxes; they had many reasons. (1) Publicans made fortunes off the poor and rich alike. (2) The method of census and censor under Rome required people, such as Joseph and Mary, to go to another city at great inconvenience and be numbered as animals just to be taxed. (3) Much of the revenue from the poor went to opulent Rome to be doled out to an idle population, at a time when it was beneath the dignity of Roman citizens to work. (4) On top of this burden there was the annual temple tax. Collectors went from town to town once a year by the dozens collecting this tax, and in foreign countries certain places were designated for payment.

Without a doubt the ancients knew all about taxes. The abuse and indignities heaped upon people, especially conquered nations, is incredible. References to taxes, toll, tribute, and publicans, in the Scriptures take on new light against this background. Some have expressed surprise that JESUS CHRIST, when confronted by the dilemma of the PHARISEES on the tax (Gk. *kēnsos* G3056) owed to the emperor (Matt. 22:17), uttered the familiar dictum, "Give to Caesar what is Caesar's, and to God what is God's" (v. 21). Others find it strange that PAUL, who also lived in the Roman world, would lay down the lasting principle, "This is also why you pay taxes [*phoros* G5843], for the authorities are God's servants, who give their full time to governing. Give everyone what you owe him: If you owe taxes, pay taxes; if revenue [*telos* G5465], then revenue; if respect, then respect; if honor, then honor" (Rom. 13:6–7). Jesus and Paul were not speaking against taxation, but for honesty and justice and good order under God in the world.

(See A. Edersheim, *Sketches of Jewish Social Life in the Days of Christ* [1908], 45, 52–56; A. E. Bailey, *Daily Life in Bible Times* [1943], 204–8, 264–71, 275; H. Daniel-Rops, *Daily Life in Palestine at the Time of Christ* [1962], 75, 161–65, 193; J. Jeremias, *Jerusalem in the Time of Jesus* [1969], 124–26; J. N. Postgate, *Taxation and Conscription in the Assyrian Empire* [1974]; W. Stenger, *Gebt dem Kaiser, was des Kaisers ist . . . : Eine sozialgeschichtliche Untersuchung zur Besteuerung Palästinas in neutestamentlicher Zeit* [1988]; P. E. Udoh, *To Caesar What Is Caesar's: Tribute, Taxes, and Imperial Administration in Early Roman Palestine (63 B.C.E.–70 C.E.)* [2005]; M. E. Stevens, *Temples, Tithes and Taxes: The Temple and the Economic Life of Ancient Israel* [2006]; *CANE*, index, s.v. "Taxation"; *DJG*, 804–6.)

L. M. PETERSEN

tax booth. See CUSTOM, RECEIPT OF.

tax collector. The Greek word *telōnēs* G5467 (from *telos* G5465, "end, goal," but also "tax, customs duty") is found only in the Synoptic Gospels. This noun is incorrectly translated "publican" in the KJV. The Latin term *publicani* referred to wealthy men who paid for the privilege of collecting taxes in certain localities. They were often Romans, although it would appear that the Jew ZACCHAEUS, who is called "chief tax collector" (*architelōnēs* G803, Lk. 19:2), was a *publicanus*. (JOSEPHUS [*War* 2.14.4] speaks of a certain John who was a tax collector at CAESAREA in A.D. 66 and evidently a prominent Jew.) These tax farmers employed subordinates, such as local Jews, to do the actual collecting of the taxes or tolls for them. It is the latter who are indicated by the term *telōnēs*. Therefore, the rendering "tax collector" or "toll collector" is preferable to "publican." (On the noun *telōnion* G5468, "tax booth, revenue office," see CUSTOM, RECEIPT OF.)

The taxes levied by the Roman government were many and varied. There was first of all the poll tax (*tributum capitis*). This had to be paid by every male over fourteen and every female over twelve (the aged were exempt). There was the land tax (*tributum agri*), which was payable in kind. Both of these direct taxes were collected by Roman officials in Palestine. In addition, there were many forms of indirect taxation. Charges were made on all imports and exports, including the transportation of slaves. These were collected by the *telōnai* of the Gospels. They examined goods and collected tolls on roads and bridges. There was also a market toll in JERUSALEM introduced by HEROD. In senatorial PROVINCES, the Roman senate took the money. JUDEA, however, was an imperial province, and the revenue collected went into the coffers of the emperor. This is the basis of the question "Is it right to pay taxes to Caesar or not?" (Matt. 22:17; Mk. 12:14; Lk. 20:22). See TAX.

As a class, the tax collectors were hated by their fellow Jews. This was almost inevitable. They represented the foreign domination of ROME. Their methods were necessarily inquisitorial. That they often overcharged people and pocketed the surplus is almost certain. In the rabbinical writings they are classified with robbers. In the Synoptic Gospels they are bracketed with "sinners" (Matt. 9:10; 11:19; Mk. 2:15; Lk. 5:30; 7:34). This shows the common attitude of the Jewish people toward them. They were considered to be renegades who sold their services to the foreign oppressor to make money at the expense of their own countrymen.

Jesus recognized this common attitude. He said, "If you love those who love you, what reward will you get? Are not even the tax collectors doing that?" (Matt. 5:46). On the other hand, he rebuked the self-righteousness of the PHARISEES, declaring, "I tell you the truth, the tax collectors and the prostitutes are entering the kingdom of God ahead of you" (21:31). In saying this, Christ was not condoning the sins of either group. What he was asserting was that there is FORGIVENESS for even the worst sinner who will repent. The refusal to repent of their self-righteousness was the crowning sin of the Pharisees, as Jesus vividly pictured in the parable of the Pharisee and the tax collector (Lk. 18:9–14).

Christ's acceptance of repentant tax collectors is shown not only by his treatment of Zacchaeus, who became one of his followers, but also by the fact that he chose a tax collector, MATTHEW (Levi), as one of his twelve disciples. When Matthew gave a farewell feast to his former associates—probably to introduce them to his new Master—the Pharisees asked the disciples: "Why does your teacher eat with tax collectors and 'sinners'?" (Matt. 9:11). Jesus' reply revealed the nature and purpose of his mission. He said: "I have not come to call the righteous, but sinners" (v. 13). Christ associated with sinners, that he might save them. (See further I. Abrahams, *Studies in Pharisaism and the Gospels*, 1st series [1917], 54–61; *TDNT*, 8:88–105; *HJP*, rev. ed. [1973–87], 1:372–76; 2:89–90.) R. EARLE

tax office. See CUSTOM, RECEIPT OF.

teacher. Ancient Jewish EDUCATION was entirely religious in character. In OT times there was no textbook except the Scriptures, and all education consisted of the reading and the study of them. There was no recognized office of teacher with a definite title. For the Jew, the real center of education was the home, and the responsibility of educating the child was laid on the parents (Deut. 4:9–10; 6:7, 20–25; 11:19; 32:46). The PROPHETS were recognized to be divinely inspired teachers, and by the spoken and written word they taught the Israelites God's will for them. The PRIESTS in early times also undertook the religious instruction of the people (2 Chr. 15:3). Several Hebrew words can be translated "teacher," including *mēbîn* (hiphil ptc. of *bîn H1067*, "to understand," 1 Chr. 25:8), *mĕlammēd* (piel ptc. of *lāmad H4340*, "to learn," Ps. 119:99), and especially *môreh H4621* (e.g., Job 36:22; this noun was originally a hiphil ptc. of *yārâ H3723*).

In the days before the exile there is no trace of schools in Israel at all. The SYNAGOGUE grew out of the conditions of the exile. When the temple was destroyed, sacrifice became impossible; therefore the Jews in exile met on the SABBATH for prayer and religious instruction. PHILO JUDAEUS calls the synagogues "houses of instruction." The SCRIBES, who dedicated themselves to the task of knowing and interpreting the law, then entered the scene.

It is not known just when, after the return from the exile, elementary education first began as an organized public service. The TALMUD says that Simon ben Shetach, the brother of Queen ALEXANDRA (reigned 78–60 B.C.), enacted that children should attend elementary schools; and that Joshua ben Gamala, who was high priest about A.D. 63–65, universalized elementary education over the whole country. Boys (and only boys received this public education) started school between the ages of five and seven. The school was usually attached to the synagogue, and was called *bêt hassēper*, "the House of the Book." Jewish teaching was entirely oral, and education was to a very large extent memorization. The teacher was held in high esteem.

In the NT the Greek word *didaskalos G1437* is used in a general sense of any teacher (Matt. 10:24; Lk. 6:40; Rom. 2:19–20; Heb. 5:12), equivalent to postbiblical Hebrew *rabbî*, "my master" (Matt. 8:19; 12:38; 19:16; 22:16, 36; see RABBI). It is also used of certain officials in the early Christian church, designating those who have received a special charisma from the HOLY SPIRIT to instruct the community in Christian truth (1 Cor. 12:28; Eph. 4:11; see SPIRITUAL GIFTS).

A comparison of Acts 13:1 with Rom. 12:7; 2 Tim. 1:11; and Jas. 3:1 shows that the teachers in the Christian church—named along with apostles, prophets, and pastors—exercised their gift in congregations already established. The gift of teaching was not necessarily limited to them, but was exercised also by apostles and prophets, who, however, existed only in apostolic times. J. L. KELSO

Teacher of Righteousness. See DEAD SEA SCROLLS.

Teaching of Jesus. See JESUS CHRIST VI.

Teachings of Silvanus. See SILVANUS, TEACHINGS OF.

tears. The secretions of the lacrimal gland. The gland is about the size and shape of an almond and is located on the upper lateral aspect of each eye socket. The tears are a colorless fluid composed of sodium and calcium salts, principally sodium chloride, and albumen dissolved in a watery fluid derived from blood serum. These secretions are poured out between the globe of the eye and the eyelids to facilitate motion of the parts and to assist in floating away any irritating particles. The secretion of tears may be increased through nerve stimulation of the lacrimal glands in response to irritation in the eyes and/or certain types of emotional stress. After the tears have bathed the eyeball and the inner aspect of the eyelids, they are drained off at the nasal side of the eye through minute orifices into the two (upper and lower) lacrimal canals, which in turn empty the fluid into the lacrimal sac located on and in the bony structure of the nose, whence the fluid drains into the nasal passages through the nasal duct. It is when the tears are secreted in overabundance, beyond the immediate capacity of the lacrimal canals to carry off so much fluid, that they overflow from the eye sac and pour down over the cheeks.

In the Scriptures the emotional aspect of the formation of tears is foremost. Thus DAVID, in referring to his stressful situation before ACHISH (1 Sam. 21:10–15), requests God to put his tears

The tear-shaped dome of the church of Dominus Flevit ("The Lord Wept") alludes to Jesus' weeping over the pending destruction of Jerusalem (Lk. 19:41).

in his bottle (Ps. 56:8), doubtless as a perpetual memorial or reminder of his zeal and suffering for God's righteous cause as he continuously refused to lay his hands on God's anointed. With some hyperbole David says that he waters his couch with his tears, making his bed to swim (Ps. 6:6). JOB also refers to his tears as being poured out unto God (Job 16:20). HEZEKIAH prayed with tears and was rewarded by the addition of fifteen years to his life (Isa. 38:5). JEREMIAH too made frequent reference to his eyes running down with tears (e.g., Jer. 13:17; 14:17). Tears were used by a repentant sinner to wash her Savior's feet (Lk. 7:38). Tears accentuated the earnest plea of the father of the child who had the dumb and deaf spirit (Mk. 9:24). Tears accompanied the prayers of Christ (Heb. 5:7), and tears were associated with PAUL's service for God (Acts 20:19, 31) and TIMOTHY's also (2 Tim. 1:4). See also CRY. P. E. ADOLPH

Tebah (person) tee´buh (טֶבַח H3182, "[born at the time of] slaughter"). Son of NAHOR (brother of ABRAHAM) by his concubine REUMAH (Gen. 22:24). See also TEBAH (PLACE).

Tebah (place) tee′buh (טֶבַח H3183 [MT 2 Sam. 8:8, בֶּטַח], variant טִבְחַת H3187 [1 Chr. 18:8], "[place of] slaughter"). A city belonging to the Aramean king HADADEZER and from which DAVID took a great quantity of bronze (2 Sam. 8:8). The KJV and other modern versions have BETAH, following the MT. "Tebah" is the reading of the NIV, which assumes that "Tibhat" in the parallel passage (1 Chr. 18:8) is an alternate form of the name; this reading also has the support of some Gk. MSS and of the Syriac version. Many scholars believe that the town received its name from TEBAH (PERSON), who may have been its founder. Tibhath/Tebah evidently corresponds to Egyptian *Dbḫ* (#6 in THUTMOSE III's list); and it occurs as *Tubiḫi* in the TELL EL-AMARNA letters. The town must have been somewhere in the BEQAʿ Valley, but its precise location is unknown. (See Y. Aharoni, *The Land of the Bible: A Historical Geography*, rev. ed. [1979], 115, 159, 296.)

Tebaliah teb′uh-li′uh. See TABALIAH.

Tebeth tee′bith (טֵבֵת H3194, meaning uncertain). The tenth month (December–January) of the Hebrew CALENDAR (Esth. 2:16).

tefillin tee-fil′in. See PHYLACTERY.

Tehillim tuh-hil′im. See PSALMS, BOOK OF I.

Tehinnah tuh-hin′uh (תְּחִנָּה H9383, "supplication"). Son of Eshton, descendant of JUDAH, and "father" (i.e., founder) of IR NAHASH (1 Chr. 4:12). His place in the Judahite genealogy is not clear.

teil tree. This archaic term, meaning "lime (linden) tree," is used by the KJV once to translate a Hebrew word that refers to the TEREBINTH (Isa. 6:13).

tekel. See MENE, MENE, TEKEL, PARSIN (UPHARSIN).

Tekoa tuh-koh′uh (תְּקוֹעַ H9541, meaning uncertain, gentilic תְּקוֹעִי H9542, "from Tekoa, Tekoite"). KJV also Tekoah (2 Sam. 14:2, 4, 9) and Thecoe (1 Macc. 9:33). A town in the hill country within the tribal territory of JUDAH (cf. LXX Josh. 15:59, where many scholars believe that the MT is defective). Tekoa is identified with modern Khirbet Tequʿ, some 5 mi. S of BETHLEHEM, on a prominent elevation 2,700 ft. high, from which the MOUNT OF OLIVES is visible. It looks down on a mass of desert hills. Tekoa was the hometown of the prophet AMOS (Amos 1:1). The scenes that influenced this shepherd of Tekoa are reflected graphically in his book (cf. 4:13; 5:8). The town lies between two valleys cutting deeply down to the DEAD SEA through the wilderness of Judea.

Apparently Tekoa was founded at the time of the Hebrew conquest of Canaan by the Judahite ASHHUR son of HEZRON (1 Chr. 2:24 and 4:5, where "father" undoubtedly means "founder" or "leader"). In 2 Sam. 14:1–22 is the record regarding the wise woman, "the Tekoite," whom JOAB, DAVID's general, employed as a ruse to bring back the fugitive ABSALOM. Tekoa was also the home of IRA son of Ikkesh, one of David's mighty warriors (2 Sam. 23:26).

King REHOBOAM thought Tekoa of sufficient importance to warrant fortification (2 Chr. 11:6; intimated by JOSEPHUS in *Ant.* 8.10.1). The place was strategically situated as a military post for the protection of Jerusalem. Its defenses were maintained even in Jeremiah's time as a station for trumpet-signaling, in connection with which the prophet gives a play on the word (Jer. 6:1, "Sound the trumpet in Tekoa!"; Heb., *ûbitqôaʿ tiqʿû šôpār*).

After the EXILE, certain Tekoites were engaged in wall-building. They were public-spirited men, in contrast to their nobles, who did not take part in the work. Whether these men were actually of Tekoa, or had adopted the name after settling in the capital, is undeterminable (Neh. 3:5, 27). Tekoa is not mentioned by EZRA as one of the repopulated towns (Ezra 2).

One passage in the OT makes explicit reference to the Desert of Tekoa, E of the town (2 Chr. 20:20; cf. also 1 Macc. 9:33). Here was a rather wild, arid, and stony district, a dozen miles S of Jerusalem. Its soil is a kind of chalk marl, and beyond is the part toward the E characterized by George Adam Smith as "fifteen miles of chaos, sinking to … the

Dead Sea" (*Historical Geography of the Holy Land*, 25th ed. [1931], 212). There was scant cultivation in valley pockets where was preserved the once rich if sparse vegetable mold that overlay the hills of Judah, when anciently they afforded a forest. The region produced olives and a peculiar fruit, the SYC-AMORE fig (Amos 7:14), ancient tradition making it proverbial both for oil and honey. Shepherds and flocks must have found shelter in the many caves of the hilly land. In certain sections BEDOUIN tent dwellers produced a coarse kind of millet.

In this general district, David, the fugitive from vindictive SAUL, spent much time (1 Sam. 23:26). It was in the Desert of Tekoa that JEHOSHAPHAT, king of Judah, defeated the Ammonites and their allies who had invaded Judah (2 Chr. 20:1–26). When Jehoshaphat's men found the invaders already dispersed and slaughtered, they called the scene "the Valley of Beracah" (Blessing).

When BACCHIDES, the Syrian general under Demetrius, took up the campaign against the Maccabees, it was to the Wilderness of Tekoa that two of the brothers, Simon and Jonathan, escaped (1 Macc. 9:33; see MACCABEE). In this region, JOHN THE BAPTIST was equipped for his "austere mission," finding in its outlook figures of judgment: vipers fleeing from the wrath to come (Matt. 3:7). Also in this general locality, the Lord met his threefold temptation, coming through victoriously, having been with the wild beasts (Mk. 1:13).

Tekoa was a city of some prominence in early Christian centuries and in the Middle Ages. In the opening years of the 6th cent., a monastery was erected by a man named Saba; shortly after his death it became the scene of conflict between the orthodox and the Monophysites. A certain Willibald of some two centuries later made report of a church and a prophet's grave in Tekoa. In the times of the Crusades, many Christians inhabiting Tekoa aided the Franks during the first siege of Jerusalem. The place was destroyed by Turks in 1139, citizens escaping to a large cave. The site of Amos's tomb was confirmed by Isaac Chelo in 1334 (*ITLW*, 41692). A number of traditions have centered in this place. NATHANAEL was said to be one of the condemned infants of Herod's slaughter, but he escaped to Tekoa. From near the tomb of Amos, the prophet HABAKKUK was supposedly carried by angels to Babylon, and other met there to discuss divine things.   R. F. GRIBBLE

Tel, Tell. Respectively, the Hebrew and Arabic words for "mound." They are frequently found as the first element in the names of archaeological sites, so named because of the accumulated ruins and occupation debris of ancient settlements.

Tel Abib tel´uh-beeb´ (תֵּל אָבִיב H9425, apparently "mound of ears of grain," but this Heb. form is a modification of Akk. *Til abūbi[m]*, "mound [produced by] the deluge"). Also Tel-abib, Tel Aviv. A locality in Babylonia by the great irrigation canal, the KEBAR (thus not to be confused with the modern city of Tel Aviv in Israel). It was here that EZEKIEL made his first contact with the Jewish exiles in 597 B.C., and he was constrained to share their despair and desolation before being permitted to speak to them (Ezek. 3:15). The Akkadian name *Tel abūbi* suggests that the place was an ancient city reduced to a mound as a result of flooding, followed by decay and long erosion. In exilic times, Tel Abib must have been a Jewish village SE of BABYLON and not far from NIPPUR, but the precise location is unknown (cf. Y. Aharoni et al., *The Carta Bible Atlas*, 4th ed. [2002], map 163).
E. M. BLAIKLOCK

Telah tee´luh (תֶּלַח H9436, perhaps "split"). Son of Resheph and descendant of EPHRAIM (1 Chr. 7:25). See discussion under RESHEPH (PERSON).

Telaim tuh-lay´im (טְלָאִים H3230, possibly "lambs"). A site in S JUDAH near the ill-defined Amalekite border; it is mentioned only as SAUL's concentration point and base for his counterattack on the descendants of AMALEK, who had been raiding the area (1 Sam. 15:4; cf. 14:48; 15:2–3). The SEPTUAGINT reads GILGAL instead of Telaim (cf. also Jos. *Ant.* 6.7.2), but this location seems unlikely. Some modern scholars suggest that "Telaim" may be a variant or corruption of "Telem" (Josh. 15:24), a town in the NEGEV that, strategically, was a possible assembly point for a desert campaign of this nature. See TELEM (PLACE).   E. M. BLAIKLOCK

Telam tee´luhm. See TELEM.

Tel Assar tel-as'ahr (תְּלַאשַּׂר H9431 [in Isa. 37:12, תְּלַשַּׂר], possibly from Akk. *Til-ašuri*, "mound of ASSHUR"). Also Telassar. A town or region where "the people of Eden" (see BETH EDEN) were apparently resettled; it is mentioned by SENNACHERIB as one of the many places overrun and obliterated by the aggressive hosts of ASSYRIA (2 Ki. 19:12 [KJV, "Thelasar"]; Isa. 37:12). The first element of the name (Akk. *Til*, "mound") suggests a site of ancient habitation (perhaps "ruins of [a town destroyed by the god] Asshur"). Because no such place is known, some scholars, through emendation, have suggested the sites of Til-Bašir and Til-Barsip, both of which were within the Aramean principality of Bit-Adini, that is, Beth Eden (*HALOT*, 4:1738; for further discussion see H. Wildberger, *Isaiah 28–39: A Continental Commentary* [2002], 418–19, who doubts the value of these and other proposals).

Tel Aviv tel'uh-veev'. See TEL ABIB.

Telem (person) tee'luhm (טֶלֶם H3235, possibly "brightness"). A Levitical gatekeeper who agreed to put away his foreign wife in the time of EZRA (Ezra 10:24; 1 Esd. 9:25 [KJV, "Tolbanes"]).

Telem (place) tee'luhm (טֶלֶם H3234, possibly "brightness"). A town in the NEGEV, the extreme S of the tribal territory of JUDAH, near the border of EDOM (Josh. 15:24). It is listed between ZIPH and BEALOTH and it was possibly some distance SE of BEERSHEBA, but the precise location cannot be determined. Some scholars read "from Telem to Shur" (*miṭṭelem šûrâ*) instead of "from ancient times as you go to Shur" (*mē'ôlām bō'ăk šûrâ*) in 1 Sam. 27:8 (NRSV, "Telam"). If this conjecture is valid, then Telem is the same as TELAIM (15:4; cf. P. K. McCarter, Jr., *I Samuel*, AB 8 [1980], 261, 266, 413). Others go further and also read "from Telem/Telaim as you go to Shur" instead of "from Havilah as you go to Shur" in 15:7. Neither of these proposals, however, brings us closer to locating the site.

Tel Harsha tel-hahr'shuh (תֵּל חַרְשָׁא H9426, possibly "mound of the forest"). Also Tel-harsha. One of five Babylonian places from which certain Jewish exiles returned who were unable to prove their Israelite ancestry (Ezra 2:59; Neh. 7:61; 1 Esd. 5:36 [KJV, "Thelersas"]). The location is unknown.

E. M. BLAIKLOCK

tell. See TEL, TELL.

Tell el-Amarna tel'el-uh-mahr'nuh. A major city built by one of the Egyptian pharaohs, Amenhotep (Amenophis) IV, better known as AKHENATEN (c. 1370–1353 B.C.). It was located on the E bank of the NILE in Upper Egypt, some 180 mi. S of Cairo. The name *Tell el-Amarna* is a misnomer formed by combining a village name, *El-Till*, with *El-Amarna*, the latter being one of the names of an Arab tribe that had settled in the area. *El-Till* has no etymological relation with the Arabic term *tell* ("hill"), commonly used by archaeologists to designate a stratified mound. The city's ancient name was Akhet-Aten (Egyptian *'ḫt-'tn*, "the horizon of Aten," referring to the deified sun disk).

  I. Introduction
  II. Cultural significance
    A. The city
    B. Amarna art
    C. Language
  III. Atenism
    A. Formative influences
    B. Theology
    C. Impact of Atenism
    D. Atenism and Hebrew religion
  IV. The Amarna letters
    A. Historical setting
    B. The Hapiru
    C. Sociopolitical conditions of Canaan

I. Introduction. The site of Tell el-Amarna has given its own name to the Amarna Age, the historical period described in the diplomatic correspondence found there. In addition, the name Amarna has become synonymous with bold experiment as a result of the cultural creativity of its founder. It is not an exaggeration to designate this radical cultural experiment as the Amarna Revolution.

    Biblical scholarship has several points of contact with Tell el-Amarna. For example, the worship of the god Aten (Aton) may be important for the backgrounds of Hebrew MONOTHEISM. In addition, the Amarna letters are indispensable for understanding

Canaan just prior to the Hebrew conquest. Finally, the possibility, usually rejected by contemporary scholars, that Akhenaten was the pharaoh of the exodus increases interest in the period.

Travelers had long known of the ruins at Tell el-Amarna; some of these ruins were discussed in scholarly literature as early as 1842. However, interest in the site greatly increased with the accidental discovery of the first Amarna letters in 1887. The peasant woman who first found them sold her rights in the discovery for ten piastres. First attempts to sell the tablets to European scholars resulted in silence or accusations of forgery, so the tablets were taken to Luxor to be sold to tourists. A large part of the original find was destroyed in transit. By this time some scholars were convinced that the tablets were genuine, and attempts to acquire them began. Agents of the British Museum and of the Berlin Museum purchased most of the tablets, but smaller lots are found in museums and private collections throughout the world. With interest aroused by this discovery, excavations began in 1891 and were continued intermittently and by different agencies until 1937. The usable tablets of the original find amounted to about 350 tablets. Later discoveries have added about another 50.

The general antecedents of the Amarna Revolution are Egyptian. Whereas the total combination of features in the Amarna Revolution was radically new, almost all of the constituent details were anticipated in earlier Egyptian life. The individual religious motifs have their Egyptian antecedents; the luxury of the reign of Amenhotep III looked forward to the ease of Akhenaten's court; and even the artistic motifs can be regarded as the extension of trends already present in earlier Egyptian art. On the other hand, it is probable that exposure to foreign influences had a great role in defining the direction of the evolution of these native Egyptian trends.

Practical politics played a part in the Amarna Revolution. Akhenaten's policies had the practical effect of suppressing the usual priesthoods, especially that of Amun (see AMON #4). On occasion, scholars have belittled the need to curb the power of Amon by noting that the king was the absolute ruler of the priestly establishments as well as the absolute ruler of the state. However, later Egyptian history witnessed the usurpation of royal authority by the priests of Amon despite their nominal submission to the crown. Thus Akhenaten was dealing with a real threat to royal power.

II. Cultural significance

A. The city. Akhet-Aten was one of three cities sacred to the god Aten. Gem Aten in Nubia (CUSH) survived for a thousand years, although both the name and location of the Aten city in SYRIA are lost. Akhet-Aten was located roughly halfway between THEBES (present Luxor) and MEMPHIS (near Cairo). The sacred precincts included a half circle of land, mostly desert, about 3 by 8 mi. on the E bank of the Nile, with a large area of agricultural land on the W bank. This area was marked off by the boundary stelae that contained Akhenaten's oath not to pass beyond these borders. It is not certain that this oath was intended to keep Ahkenaten from ever leaving the city; rather, it may have indicated that he would not pass the boundaries for the purpose of adding to the sacred precincts of Aten (cf. J. Baikie, *The Amarna Age* [1926], 268–69). It is significant for the spirit of Egyptian religion that the new site was relatively free of the claims of other gods.

The city itself was built on a long, narrow strip of desert parallel to the river, but just beyond the cultivable land on the E bank of the Nile. Thus, cultivable land was spared while keeping the city

Tell el-Amarna.

reasonably near its water supply. There were three long streets running the length of the city, with a larger number of shorter streets crossing its width. Land within the city seems first to have been allotted for important royal and public needs such as temple sites, royal gardens, and villas of officials. Then lesser needs and people crowded into the intervening spaces, thus giving the city a somewhat disorganized character.

Akhet-Aten was hurriedly built mostly of mud brick that was frequently covered with luxurious decoration. Among the more important structures of the new city were the temples to Akhenaten's ancestors, the great temple to the Aten, the royal pleasure garden named Maru-Aten, and the palace and royal house. In addition, there were nobles' villas, homes of commoners, and factories, notably those producing glaze.

The architectural emphasis of the great temple of the Aten was upon open courts. In the inner part of the building—the usual site of the holy of holies where the image of the god dwelt in awesome seclusion—this temple had still another open court. Several altars for sacrifices were found in some of the courts of the temple. The emphasis on sun courts, of course, was not new. Earlier sun temples from the fifth dynasty (c. 2400 B.C.) were built around a single open court in which stood the *benben*, a huge sacred obelisk, which may have represented the deity. These earlier temples also lacked the holy of holies.

The palace was outstanding, both for its huge size and its rich decoration. Largest estimates of its size are 1,400 by 500 ft. It seems to have contained a huge columned hall with 542 pillars. Available remains give only a limited picture of its lavish decoration, but the glaze and gold ornamentation of the capitals of the columns and of the naturalistic pavements that decorated many of the floors are known. The overall impression must have been one of extravagant wealth. Maru-Aten, perhaps the official summer residence, featured an artificial pool and enclosed gardens as well as other structures. The decoration was more restrained; colored paste and yellow paint served instead of the glaze and gold of the palace.

After a brief period of glory during the life of its founder, the city slowly faded until Horemhab,

Statuette of Akhenaten, founder and builder of Amarna.

in his zeal to eradicate the memory of the heretic king, completely razed the buildings that remained. See ARCHITECTURE.

B. Amarna art. The ART of Tell el-Amarna was revolutionary; but, as noted above, most of the innovation built on trends present in earlier Egyptian art. For example, certain aspects of nature had always been presented in a naturalistic manner by the Egyptian artist. Animals, fish, birds, and even untypical human beings such as dwarfs had long been the subjects of accurate, naturalistic representation. The innovation lay in the extension of naturalism to new levels of execution and to new subjects such as the person of the king. A freedom and softening of the human form under Akhenaten's predecessors foreshadowed the treatment of the human form in Amarna art.

Some typical artistic representations are the following: nature scenes with abundant wildlife and vegetation, scenes of the king done in a new realism and freedom, and conventional scenes with unconventional naturalism in details, as in a temple scene in which each of the sacrificial animals is given individualistic treatment. Plastered-over sunken relief represents an innovation in technique. It replaced the earlier high relief, perhaps to adapt to the quality of stone available to Amarna artists. In this technique, the scene was done in high relief, but the scene itself was recessed until the highest portions of the scene were about level with the contiguous unworked stone surface. Then the whole scene was plastered and painted.

The treatment of the king in Amarna art is distinctive. Earlier artistic representations of the king depicted the remoteness, dignity, and majesty of the divine king. Amarna art invaded the king's private life and showed him in very human activities. The king was seen at work, at play, caressing his wife or daughters, and in other human activities. One scene showed the royal family eating a meal with an amusing, perhaps even crude, enthusiasm. Expression of the king's humanity went so far as to portray his grief.

Amarna art, however, is best known for its grotesque exaggeration of the human physique. This exaggeration is best seen in its representation of the king. Several factors may have influenced this approach: (1) the tendencies toward softening of form and realism already referred to; (2) an excessive movement toward artistic freedom as a reaction to the very strict canons formerly binding the Egyptian artist; and (3) a limited degree of physical abnormality in the king's person. Artistic representations of the king show an extended neck, a protruding V-shaped chin, bulbous hips and limbs, and spindly ankles. The effect of these characteristics is something normally expected only in brutal political caricature. Not only the king, but other human figures were likewise distorted.

In interpreting these characteristics, however, it is necessary to note that Amarna art displays two distinct artistic phases in its representation of the human figure. In the earlier period, the distortion is extreme, and it is this period that is represented by the well-known artistic works referred to above. In the artistic representations of the later phase, mostly portrait busts and other statuary, these same characteristics were softened until they were merely "weak" or "effeminate" rather than grotesque. Some of the physical characteristics so grossly distorted in earlier Amarna art can be discerned even in the famous statue of Nefertiti, but there in a softened, more pleasant form. One may conclude that some, if not all, of the royal abnormalities were considerably exaggerated by the artists of Tell el-Amarna.

C. Language. Even language and writing did not escape the revolution. Like Egyptian life in general, written Egyptian was rigidly conservative, preserving elements in writing that were obsolete in the spoken language. The Amarna desire for realism produced a modernization of written Egyptian to bring it in line with the spoken language. The stage of Egyptian language referred to by scholars as "Late-Egyptian" originated in this way.

III. Atenism

A. Formative influences. Clear Egyptian antecedents are found for most of the features of Atenism (or Atonism). The prominence of the sun disk, the Aten, was foreshadowed by the general prominence of the SUN in earlier Egyptian religion; even Amon, the hidden one of Thebes, had to become identified with RE, the Sun, before he could become the national god of Egypt. See SUN WORSHIP. The monotheistic trend of Atenism was anticipated both by the normal syncretism of Egyptian religion—that is, the tendency to unite originally distinct deities into one figure—and by the tendency to explain other deities as specific manifestations of one chief deity. The name Aten had been previously used as a divine title.

Political factors probably influenced theological thought. An international age like that of Amarna usually produces a movement of international syncretism, though specific examples are not available for this period. Furthermore, just as national unity had produced the need for a national god of Egypt, internationalism opened human eyes to the need for a universal deity. Finally, exposure to foreign ideas may have had some influence upon Egypt.

In addition, there are evidences, including Atenism itself, that the Egyptian mind of that age had reached such a level of rational development that it sought to avoid some of the worst crudities and superstitions of traditional Egyptian religion.

B. Theology. Akhenaten's monotheism has been overstated; philosophical monotheism, in fact, is not the point at issue. The major premise of Atenism was not that there was only one god, or one divine principle, but rather that the other gods were usurpers who had seized prerogatives belonging only to the Aten. Usurpers were normally dealt with by effacing their names. Although the spirit of Atenism was such that it probably would have developed into monotheism had it continued to develop, there is no conclusive evidence that pure monotheism was reached.

The evidence for Amarna theology is the following: (1) literary evidence consisting of the long hymn to the Aten and a number of shorter hymns; (2) scenes of life in Akhet-Aten in tombs and monumental scenes; and (3) such ideas as can be surmised from tombs, temples, and governmental policies.

The famous long hymn to the Aten (trans. in C. F. Pfeiffer, *Tell el Amarna and the Bible* [1963], 38–42) gives the fullest exposition of Atenist theology. This hymn was inscribed on the walls of the tomb of Ai. Some believe it was a ritual recitation spoken by the king himself. In it is found the Aten, the sun disk, eloquently described as the universal, almost omnipotent, providential power sustaining the ordered universe. The opening lines contrast the universal beauty and sway of the rising Aten with the chaos and fear that dominate the earth during the Aten's nightly absence. This passage is in contrast to the Hebrew poet, who saw Yahweh as sovereign over both day and night (cf. Ps. 104:20–23). The Egyptian hymn sees night as a break in the sovereignty and power of the Aten.

The poet then described the various phases of the Aten's sovereignty: mankind's joyful work and praise began with the appearance of the Aten. Other beings, animals, plants, sea and river life, also lived in the light of the Aten. The broader view of the Aten as creator and regulator of the universe was developed. Man was conceived and grew through the activity of the Aten. The chick in the egg was the Aten's work. Aten's control of the universe was so full and gracious that he provided a "Nile-in-the-sky" (i.e., rain) for those lands that did not have the river Nile. The seasons and "beauty of forms" were also his work.

The closing lines define the role of the king in Atenism. Only Akhenaten knows the Aten; the Aten has revealed knowledge to the king. Thus, the king, theoretically, is the sole mediator between the Aten and humanity (Akhenaten did, nevertheless, appoint a high priest to aid in this function). Here also appears the only remnant of older physical superstition in the hymn. The king is the Aten's son who came forth from the Aten's limbs. This, of course, could have been "spiritualized" to remove the incongruity. The clear teaching of the hymn is of a beneficent, providential deity whose sovereignty extends over the entire universe—except during his nightly absence.

The shorter hymns, inscribed in various tombs, largely repeat the motifs of the longer hymn. Many of them are interspersed with references praising the king since they were written in behalf of nobles who desired to express their personal appreciation to the king as well as to the Aten.

Pictorial scenes from Akhet-Aten, especially from the tombs, amplify the theology of the poems. The Aten is pictured with his rays extending like outstretched arms to the earth. Akhenaten is usually the leading human figure in such scenes. The frequent presence of the "life key" (the hieroglyphic sign meaning "life") in the hands makes more explicit the concept of the Aten as the giver of all life.

Tomb decoration and structure in general is striking for the absence of the customary magical apparatus designed to guarantee the future well-being of the deceased. MAGIC spells carved on walls and furniture, magical scenes of benefits thus conferred upon the deceased, and all other such are absent. One may suppose that in Atenism the power of such magic was replaced by the effectiveness of the king's personal good will. Thus, the purpose of the magic apparatus is served by hymns honoring the Aten and the king.

The prominence of open courts in the temples and the absence of the equipment for idolatrous ritual are in harmony with the high spiritual level of the hymns. The existence of other sacred cities, not only in Nubia, which was almost "Egyptianized," but even in Syria, which was quite clearly foreign, reflects Aten's international character and points toward monotheism. The violence of Akhenaten's proscriptions of other deities would lead to the theological doctrine of the jealous god who demands exclusive worship from his people.

The limitations of evidence should be kept in mind in evaluating Atenism. For example, the lack of ethical concepts indicates that the evidence is incomplete rather than that Atenism had no ethical sensibility. Looked at from the perspective of its individual motifs, there is little that is new in the above materials. The innovation lay in the purging of baser religious elements so that the old ideas suddenly constituted a new, more spiritual religious concept. Overt polytheism and superstition were purged. The result was a landmark in the history of thought.

C. Impact of Atenism. Neither Atenism nor the official cult of Amon had any great impact among the masses. The popular form of the cult of OSIRIS, Isis, and Horus held this distinction, as is shown by the funerary stelae set up by commoners in honor of this cult. Atenism owed its existence only to the energy of Akhenaten, and after his death its component ideas were reabsorbed into the common stream of Egyptian superstition.

D. Atenism and Hebrew religion. Some of the resemblances between Atenism and Hebrew religion are the following: common tendency toward philosophical monotheism (philosophical monotheism, strictly understood, came fairly late in the development of biblical Hebrew thought), the attribute of jealousy on the part of the chief deity in his demand for exclusive worship and loyalty, the minimizing of funerary cult in both religions, the rejection of idolatry, and the intellectual advancement of both cults in contrast with the general superstition and idolatry of their historical settings. Furthermore, one should note the similarities in motifs between the longer hymn to the Aten and Ps. 104.

On the basis of these similarities, some have concluded that the "makers" of Hebrew religion borrowed from Atenism at some point. Looking at the evidence more closely, direct borrowing seems unlikely. The strongest evidence for direct borrowing is provided by the similarities between the hymn to Aten and Ps. 104, but this evidence has been grossly exaggerated. Barely seven verses of the psalm show clear resemblances, and in these verses there is one striking contrast: Yahweh's sovereignty over night as well as day. It is safer to see both the Egyptian psalmist and his later Hebrew counterpart as utilizing similar bodies of international, interreligious, nature motifs that were available for the use of all religious poets, whatever deity may have been worshiped. Biblical WISDOM Literature also shows evidence that the inspired writer made use of such an international, interreligious body of wisdom motifs.

Other resemblances between the two religions also are better accounted for through general similarity in backgrounds and in intellectual climate than through direct contact. For example, the movement toward international syncretism, with attestation during the intervening period, had gathered several hundred years of additional momentum by the time of the Hebrew prophets. Hebrew imperialism, like Egyptian imperialism, encouraged an international, universal concept of deity. However, through its contribution to the general intellectual development of the ANE, Atenism, in this indirect fashion, almost certainly influenced Hebrew religious attitudes.

One last difference should be noted. Only Hebrew religion combined the kind of historical factors noted above with an act of special revelation to produce inspired Scriptures. There is no reason

This small cuneiform tablet from Tell el-Amarna describes diplomatic correspondence between the Egyptian court and the rulers of neighboring states.

to believe that Akhenaten's spiritual insights went beyond those made possible by common grace and natural revelation.

IV. The Amarna letters. The Amarna letters show that Akkadian was the language of international diplomacy even for proud, prestigious Egypt, although the kings of MITANNI sometimes wrote in HURRIAN (see LANGUAGES OF THE ANE II.A and IV). Occasional AMORITE glosses in letters from Palestine give the Semitic philologist insight into pre-Mosaic Canaanite. More relevant to present purposes, however, are three other matters: (1) the Amarna letters are the most important primary evidence for the history of the Amarna Age; (2) they refer to the Hapiru, a subject relevant for the study of Hebrew origins; and (3) they show the internal sociopolitical situation of Canaan just prior to the Hebrew conquest.

A. Historical setting. Among the more important developments of the age were the rise of the HITTITE empire and the destruction of the Mitanni empire. In the reign of Amenhotep III, a Hittite attack on Mitanni was turned back only by means of Egyptian military assistance. Subsequent Hittite policy had two goals: the undermining of Egyptian influence in Asia and the destruction of the Mitanni empire. Largely due to Akhenaten's inactivity, the Hittites succeeded in both goals. The Hittites and Assyrians divided up the Mitanni empire, and Egyptian forces were driven back to southern Palestine.

The undermining of Egyptian authority in Syria and Palestine was facilitated by the internal state of affairs. Local princes desired to rebel against Egypt and gain their independence. Hittite encouragement made them all the more eager to rebel. The Amarna letters give several cases of conflicts between such rebels and loyal vassals, both of whom were sending letters to Egypt in which they proclaimed their loyalty and complained of the disloyalty of others. The Egyptian court appears to have been unable to distinguish honest letters from false. This difficulty was increased by the fact that the rebels often had friends high in the court who looked after their interests, to the detriment of Egyptian interests. Among the loyalists was Ribaddi of Byblos (see GEBAL), whose vain struggle against the rebel Abdishirta and his sons is well known through the letters. Further S, Abdikhepa of JERUSALEM stood loyally for Egypt as the surrounding princes allied themselves with the Hapiru and rebelled.

B. The Hapiru. In the Amarna letters the HAPIRU appear as intruders and troublemakers from the outside. They were outside the normal social structure of the region. Their numbers were being augmented by dwellers in the cities who deserted their leaders to join themselves with the Hapiru. Members of the Hapiru were available for military service as mercenaries for anyone who wished to hire them. In general they were seen as a threat both to Egyptian power and to the existing social structure of Palestine.

C. Sociopolitical conditions of Canaan. Except for the presence of Egyptian authority in Palestine of the Amarna Age, the sociopolitical state of Canaan was quite similar to that of the time of the Hebrew invasion of Canaan. The land was divided into many small city-states, each with its own "king." Both the Amarna letters and archaeological remains indicate that there was a measure of social stratification, with the letters giving evidence of social unrest in their references to citizens who were joining the Hapiru. The two different aspects of the Hebrew conquest as seen in Joshua and Judges may be related to the prevailing social stratification. The initial campaign, with its relatively quick victory as described in Joshua, may have dealt with the somewhat small but militaristic ruling classes. The less successful process alluded to in Judges may have dealt with the longer process of reaching an accommodation with the subject peoples even after the ruling classes had been eliminated. Thus the cities destroyed but not held in the original campaign had to be reconquered and reabsorbed at a later date.

(See further J. H. Breasted, *Ancient Records of Egypt: Historical Documents from the Earliest Times to the Persian Conquest*, 5 vols. [1906], 2:382–419; J. A. Knudtzon, *Die El-Amarna Tafeln mit Einleitung und Erläuterung*, 2 vols. [1908–15]; T. E. Peet et al., *The City of Akhenaten*, 3 vols. in 4 [1923–51]; J. Baikie, *The Amarna Age* [1926]; W. C. Hayes, *The Scepter of Egypt: A Background for the Study of the*

Egyptian Antiquities in the Metropolitan Museum of Art, 2 vols. [1953–59], 2:280–325; C. F. Pfeiffer, *Tell el Amarna and the Bible* [1963]; A. F. Rainey, *El-Amarna Tablets, 359–379: Supplement to J. A. Knudtzon, Die El-Amarna-Tafeln*, 2nd ed. [1978]; J. Samson, *Amarna, City of Akhenaten and Nefertiti: Nefertiti as Pharaoh*, 2nd ed. [1978]; W. L. Moran, ed. and trans., *The Amarna Letters* [1992]; B. J. Kemp and S. Garfi, *A Survey of the Ancient City of El-'Amarna* [1993]; W. J. Murnane, *Texts from the Amarna Period in Egypt* [1995]; A. F. Rainey, *Canaanite in the Amarna Tablets: A Linguistic Analysis of the Mixed Dialect Used by Scribes from Canaan*, 4 vols. [1996]; F. J. Giles et al., *The Amarna Age: Western Asia* [1997]; F. J. Giles, *The Amarna Age: Egypt* [2001]; Y. Goren, *Inscribed in Clay: Provenance Study of the Amarna Tablets and Other Ancient Near Eastern Texts* [2004]; A. Stevens, *Private Religion at Amarna: The Material Evidence* [2006]; N. Naʾaman and D. B. Redford in *ABD*, 1:174–82 [s.vv. "Amarna Letters" and "Amarna, Tell el-"]; R. Krauss and S. Izreʾel in *CANE*, 2:749–62 and 4:2411–19.)   A. Bowling

Tel Melah tel-mee′luh (תֵּל מֶלַח *H9427*, "mound of salt"). Also Tel-melah. One of five Babylonian places from which certain Jewish exiles returned who were unable to prove their Israelite ancestry (Ezra 2:59; Neh. 7:61; 1 Esd. 5:36 [KJV, "Thermeleth"]). The meaning of the name may suggest that at one time a settlement there had been destroyed and that its ruins had been "sown with salt" (cf. Jdg. 9:45 NRSV), a symbol of permanent infertility (Deut. 29:23; see SALT). The location is unknown. It could be the Thelma mentioned by Ptolemy, situated near a salty tract of terrain in the Persian Gulf, but this is no more than conjecture.

E. M. Blaiklock

Tema tee′muh (תֵּימָא *H9401* [in Job 6:19, תֵּמָא], meaning uncertain [cf. *ABD*, 6.346–47], possible gentilic תֵּימָנִי *H9404*, "Temanite"). Son of Ishmael and grandson of Abraham (Gen. 25:15; 1 Chr. 1:31). Tema is also the name of a place that was apparently founded by him or his descendants (Job 6:19; Isa. 21:14; Jer. 25:23), identified with modern Teima (Taymaʾ) in N Arabia, a large oasis about halfway between Damascus and Mecca. Tema/Teima is on the ancient caravan road connecting the Persian Gulf with the Gulf of Aqabah. It is one of the most attractive oases in Arabia and is still one of the most important trade centers in the land.

The biblical references tell of the metropolitan position of Tema in the transdesert trade. In Isa. 21:13–15, its inhabitants are asked to offer refuge and hospitality to Dedanite caravans (see Dedan) fleeing from a pursuing army, possibly of either Nebuchadnezzar or Nabonidus. Job 6:19, in a description of the desert, mentions "the caravans of Tema" (some think that Job's friend Eliphaz the Temanite [2:11 et al.] was a native of Tema, but see Teman). Jeremiah 25:23 prophesied that great trouble would come upon Tema and nearby tribes; this may refer to Nebuchadnezzar's campaign against that region.

An Akkadian inscription published under the title, "A Persian Verse Account of Nabonidus" (English trans. in *ANET*, 312–15), relates that Nabonidus, the last king of the Neo-Babylonian, or Chaldean, empire (556–539 B.C.), divided his power with his eldest son Belshazzar and entrusted the kingship to him. He did this that he might proceed with an army against Tema. He conquered the city, slaughtered its inhabitants, rebuilt it so that it recalled the glory of Babylon, and made it the capital of the western part of his empire. Another inscription, the Nabonidus Chronicle (*ANET*, 305–7), gives an annual diary of the reign of this king and records that for years he lived at Tema and therefore did not attend the New Year festival in Babylonia. An inscribed early Aramaic monument, the Teima Stela, possibly dated in the 6th cent. B.C., records the grant of specified palm lands and perpetual right in the priesthood of the local god, Salm, to a certain priest called Salmshezeb. All surviving monuments and inscriptions of Tema show that for some years it enjoyed the rank of ancient Petra and Palmyra.

About 540 B.C., Cyrus king of Persia conquered all that region of Arabia, and Babylon itself fell a year later. Nabonidus was kindly treated by Cyrus, who gave him Carmania (in S Persia) to rule, or more probably as a place of abode in a new land (Jos. *Apion* 1.20); and there he died. (See R. P. Dougherty, *Nabonidus and Belshazzar* [1919], 105–24; S. Smith, *Babylonian Historical Texts* [1924], 98–123;

C. M. Doughty, *Travels in Arabia Deserta*, 2 vols., 3rd ed. [1923], 1:285–300; J. A. Montgomery, *Arabia and the Bible* [1934], 58–68; J. Finegan, *Light from the Ancient Past* [1959], 227–28; H. I. Abu-Duruk, *A Critical and Comparative Discussion of Certain Ancient Monuments ... in the North Arabian city of Tayma' in the Light of Evidence Furnished by Excavations* [1986].)

S. BARABAS

Temah tee′muh (תֶּמַח *H9457*, meaning unknown). Ancestor of a family of temple servants (NETHINIM) who returned from the captivity with ZERUBBABEL (Ezra 2:53 [KJV, "Thamah"]; Neh. 7:55 [KJV, "Tamah"]; 1 Esd. 5:32 [KJV, "Thomoi"]).

Teman tee′muhn (תֵּימָן *H9403*, "south, southern region"; gentilic תֵּימָנִי *H9404*, "Temanite"). Firstborn son of ELIPHAZ and grandson of ESAU; he was head of an Edomite clan (Gen. 36:11, 15; 42; 1 Chr. 1:36, 53). Teman is also the name of a place in EDOM that was apparently founded by him or his descendants (Jer. 49:7 et al.). According to Gen. 36:34, HUSHAM the Temanite ruled as king in Edom before there were kings in Israel. The inhabitants of Teman were noted for their WISDOM (Jer. 49:7; Obad. 8–9). The nature and content of this wisdom are unknown. One of JOB's comforters, Eliphaz, was a Temanite (Job 2:11 et al.). Some scholars argue that either Husham or Job's friend—or both—may have been from a different place, TEMA (cf. *ABD*, 6:347–48; *HALOT*, 4:1726).

Many of the prophets included Teman in their oracles against Edom (Jer. 49:20; Ezek. 25:13; Amos 1:12; Obad. 9), and all declared that Teman would be destroyed. HABAKKUK refers to a vision in which he saw God coming from the region of Sinai and marching toward Edom as he did in the exodus (Hab. 3:3; cf. Deut. 33:2). In some of these passages, Teman is virtually a synonym for Edom (this may account for the name, which means something like "southern territory"; Edom was to the S of Israel). However, the association with BOZRAH (Amos 1:12) suggests that Teman designated more specifically the northern parts of Edom. Teman (near the N border) and DEDAN (near the S border) are mentioned together in some the oracles.

One suggestion for the location of Teman is modern Tawilan, about 3 mi. E of PETRA. Excavations at Tawilan indicate a large Edomite fortification. The abundance of pottery from the Early Iron Age I-II (1200–600 B.C.) suggests that the site was quite important, possibly the largest city in the central area of Edom. The area around Tawilan is well-watered and fertile, and it served as the meeting place of significant trade routes in ancient as well as in modern times.

F. E. YOUNG

Temanite tee′muh-n*i*t. See TEMA; TEMAN; TEMENI.

Temeni tem′uh-n*i* (תֵּימְנִי *H9405*, gentilic of יָמַן *H3554*, "right[-hand], south," or תֵּימָן *H9403* [see TEMAN], or some otherwise unknown person or place; it is perhaps a variant of תֵּימָנִי *H9404*, "Temanite"). Son of ASHHUR and descendant of JUDAH (1 Chr. 4:6). E. A. Knauf (*ABD*, s.v. "Temanite," 6:348) suggests that Temeni was an Edomite clan that had been incorporated into the Judahite genealogy.

temperance. See SELF-CONTROL.

temple, Jerusalem. A building constructed by SOLOMON for the WORSHIP of God. The temple was destroyed by the Babylonians in 586 B.C. but rebuilt after the EXILE under ZERUBBABEL (this structure is often referred to as the second temple). HEROD the Great began a major renovation in 20 B.C., and the completed building with its courts became one of the most greatly admired structures of the ancient world. As a result of the Jewish war, the Romans entered JERUSALEM in A.D. 70 and destroyed the city and the temple.

The Hebrew term for "temple," *hêkāl H2121* (from Sumerian *é-gal*, "great house," through Akkadian *ekallu*) can be used of the TABERNACLE shrine (1 Sam. 1:9; 3:3) and even of royal palaces (2 Ki. 20:18 et al.), but it most frequently refers to the main hall or nave of the Jerusalem temple (1 Ki. 6:3 et al.) or to the whole building (2 Ki. 18:16 et al.; figuratively, it can designate HEAVEN, Ps. 11:4 et al.). The temple is more often referred to as *bêt yhwh*, "the house of the LORD" (1 Ki. 6:1 et al.); in Chronicles, Ezra, and Nehemiah, it is regularly called also *bêt hā'ĕlōhîm*, "the house of God" (1 Chr. 9:11 et al.). In the NT, Greek *hieron*

G2639 (lit., "holy [place]") is the usual term (Matt. 4:5 et al.), but *naos G3724* is also frequent (23:16 et al.).

    I. Historical background
        A. Sacred places
        B. Mesopotamian examples
        C. Worship and theology
        D. Subsidiary quarters
        E. Canaanite prototypes
   II. Significance of the Solomonic temple
        A. Distinctive purpose
        B. Cause of existence
        C. A unifying force
        D. Designation of the site
        E. Temporary character
  III. Location
        A. Araunah's threshing floor
        B. Character of the site
  IV. Solomon's temple
        A. David's preparations
        B. Data
        C. Supplementary data
        D. History of Solomon's temple
        E. Problems
   V. Ezekiel's temple
        A. Meaning of the temple
        B. Identity of the temple
        C. The construction
  VI. Zerubbabel's temple
        A. The repatriation
        B. Reconstruction
        C. History of the temple
 VII. Herod's temple
        A. Purpose
        B. Data
        C. Construction
        D. The Tower of Antonia
        E. History of Herod's temple
VIII. Modern reconstructions
        A. Solomon's temple
        B. Ezekiel's temple
        C. Zerubbabel's temple
        D. Herod's temple

I. Historical background

A. Sacred places. Evidence of the religious outlook of human beings can be found wherever they have been able to establish some continuity of habitation. The FERTILE CRESCENT furnishes examples of some of the oldest sacred sites and TEMPLES, with JERICHO providing one of the oldest, dating from Mesolithic times (c. 6800 B.C.). A characteristic feature is the presence of an enclosing wall, setting the area off from its surroundings, thus emphasizing the implied superiority and sanctity of the place and its deity.

In EGYPT, the earliest discernible temple form was a small house similar to that of the worshiper. In front of it was placed the symbol of the god, the whole enclosed by a fence or low wall (cf. *BA* 7 [1944]: 44). In later times, this house was replaced by a large and complex series of courts and halls (viz., Karnak and Luxor temples of the 15th cent. B.C.) inside an enclosing wall, within which were not only the principal deity but also other related and subsidiary deities. Ceremonially, there developed a need to express theological concepts, demonstrated by the "pilgrimages" of the god Amun (see AMON #4) in Karnak through various "stations" in the temple complex (ibid., 45).

B. Mesopotamian examples. Southern Mesopotamia (SUMER) in the earlier periods erected simple temple structures built mostly of reeds. Expansion came with the advent of building with sun-dried brick. Plan variations occurred until toward the end of the 3rd millennium, when temples were formalized in a large hall with the idol placed at the narrow end, usually in a shallow room opposite a doorway. The worshipers assembled in an outer court and looked into the main hall where, at the far end, they saw the gorgeously arrayed god framed by a monumental portal. The design was to impress the worshipers and inspire them with fear and awe. This was not, however, the purpose of the temple of Yahweh in Jerusalem.

In Assyrian times in the N Mesopotamian area (ASSYRIA), the outer court familiar from Babylonian temples was lacking; the worshiper entered by a door in the side wall into the sanctuary where the idol was present and then turned to face the image. Pilasters or short walls on the side walls at that end framed the deity, which stood on a low dais. In Babylonian times, the entrance was frequently given flanking towers.

The S Mesopotamian temples show derivation from houses, whereas the Assyrian ones stressed the more private relationship of deity and worshiper. These temples were usually found at the base of the ZIGGURAT, on which the deity alighted when he descended to earth. It is recorded that small shrines were erected on the top for the convenience of the deity at his arrival, but no example has survived.

C. Worship and theology. The proof of the presence of the divinity in both Egypt and Mesopotamia was the presence of the image, thus explaining how it could be said that the people went into captivity when the images were carried off by a conqueror. Both in Egypt and S Mesopotamia, the gods were taken out in procession among the people. In Assyria, however, at least down to ASHURNASIRPAL II (883–859 B.C.), they remained in their sanctuaries. In such processions they were objects of rejoicing and singing of the common people, but in no case in the Early or Middle Kingdom periods in Egypt did they have entry to worship the deity. Other than the royal family and priests, only the nobility and upper class achieved this status in later times.

In Egypt the complexity of later forms provided an easy vehicle or stimulus to the concept that it was a microcosm of the world: the god was in the sanctuary, and the temple complex represented the universe around him. This concept was absent in both the Mesopotamian and Canaanite forms. The Assyrians adopted the ziggurat at a later time, indicating Babylonian influence. The Palestinian, or Canaanite temples, witness to a simpler outlook.

D. Subsidiary quarters. The Mesopotamian temple had additional quarters for the priests, and storehouses for offerings and receipts from temple lands, to which frequent references are made in the clay CUNEIFORM business documents. There were also school buildings for training scribes in writing the cuneiform to provide recorders for the temple receipts and the administration of its holdings. For the temple in Jerusalem there were the chambers built around the sides and rear, and in the Herodian structure a small section provided for the use of the priests immediately attending the temple, but not on the grand scale of the Babylonian temples. The need for such quarters to that extent did not exist in Jerusalem.

E. Canaanite prototypes. One of the earlier forms of Canaanite temples is found at MEGIDDO (c. 3000 B.C.), which consists of a simple, rectangular large room containing the idol. Three others at Megiddo date from c. 1900 having the same plan; all place the door on the long side. A particularly notable example of this type occurs at AI (c. 2500). About 1500 B.C., the plan is square, with an added porch. A further refinement occurs at BETH SHAN in the addition of a small room or cubicle at the rear raised above the room floor, containing the idol; this constitutes one of the earliest examples of an inner sanctuary or holy of holies (Heb. *debîr* H1808), as in Solomon's temple.

A strictly Phoenician style for the period post-1000 B.C. was found in Tel Tainat (ancient Hattina) in SYRIA. This consists of a porch, a holy place, and a holy of holies, remarkably like the description in 1 Ki. 6 (cf. *BA* 4 [1941]: 21, fig. 3; *Oriental Institute Bulletin* 1 [1937]: 13.) The same plan form is seen in the Greek temples without surrounding colonnades, indicating Syrian influence.

II. Significance of the Solomonic temple

A. Distinctive purpose. The outstanding feature of the Solomonic temple is that there was no

Aerial view of the remains of an Israelite sanctuary or temple at Arad dating as early as the Solomonic period (10th cent. B.C.). Its building plan bears some striking resemblances to that of Solomon's temple.

idol in it, having only the MERCY SEAT over the ARK OF THE COVENANT, with the CHERUBIM overshadowing the former. This arrangement declared to the world that idols are unnecessary to define the presence of God or his sanctity. Because the lightless room could be reached only through a specific ritual at a specified annual time for the purpose of making reconciliation for the people, the "house of Yahweh" in Jerusalem was not considered a cosmic house of God, but emphasized the way of salvation to the penitent and assured to them the grace of God for their joy and blessing (1 Ki. 8:27–30). God was not localized in any sense conveyed by an image, either Egyptian, Babylonian, or Canaanite, nor bound to any other form such as the ark. The temple, therefore, was not necessary because of God's nature; he had no need of it (Acts 7:48–49). It was an accommodation to the limitations and needs of his people (1 Ki. 8:27–30).

B. Cause of existence. That contemporary peoples had temples is not sufficient grounds to justify the building of a temple for Yahweh in Jerusalem. Though DAVID saw this lack as invidious (2 Sam. 7:2), it was not the cause by which David sought to build God's house. A sufficient cause, among others, is that found in Deut. 12, which indicates that the temple was to be a protective memorial for believing Israel, designed to turn their hearts away from the idols of their Palestinian contemporaries and provide them with an incentive (thus protective) not to practice the iniquities of the Canaanites (M. G. Kline, *Treaty of the Great King* [1963], 80), and with a memorial to the person of their God who had delivered them from slavery in Egypt to freedom in the land of Canaan.

In addition to the practical good of centralized worship, a central cultic house was important to the COVENANT structure of Yahweh's relationship with Israel. The loyalty of Israel to Yahweh was expressed in the sacrifices and offerings that were presented at the temple. The HIGH PLACES of the various tribes divided the people and were disruptive of their loyalty to God; they diverted from him his rightful due as their Creator and Lord, and in this sense the high places were roundly condemned. The temple thus became an affirmation of the covenant by Israel. This view makes it unnecessary to hold that the law of the central sanctuary was a late development; it was delayed until Israel should be a stable people, dwelling in peace in her land, when Yahweh would take up his abode in her midst in a more obvious manner (cf. Kline, *Treaty*, 80ff.; Deut. 12:10). The establishment of the altar in one place is the distinctive element in Deuteronomy, in contrast to the removal of the SHEKINAH glory from one place to another during the period from Moses to David. The temple was needed to express clearly Israel's attachment to the covenant. That David was not allowed to build the temple does not mean that Yahweh would not dwell in one, but rather that the time was not propitious (cf. 2 Sam. 7:5–7, 11, with Deut. 12:11).

C. A unifying force. The temple was the place where, in three annual festivals particularly, the Israelites were to rejoice before their God and remember his great blessings to them (Deut. 12:12). David was the recipient of the centuries of this outlook in a particular way and came to realize the need for this central sanctuary for unity among the people. Thus, from the first, Israel's temple in Jerusalem was to differ from those of their contemporaries. That there was cause for division because of the attraction of adverse temples set up elsewhere (cf. Josh. 22:11–31) is evident in the policies of JEROBOAM I when he erected the idols at DAN (PLACE) and BETHEL to tie the ten tribes to himself (cf. 1 Ki. 12:25–33), and after the OT period in the conduct of a certain Sanballat who sought to tie to himself the priest Manasseh and his cohorts by the promise of a temple (Jos. *Ant.* 11.8.1–4). Neither in Samaria nor in Dan or Bethel was to be the site of the house of Yahweh; only the place that he would choose was to be the center of their worship, where God's judgments were to be sought, and where they were to remember particularly their deliverances (Deut. 26:1–3).

D. Designation of the site. The selection of the place of the dwelling for the name of Yahweh came in the peculiar happenings of David's numbering the people (2 Sam. 24:1). In the threshing floor of ARAUNAH the Jebusite, David was commanded to set up an altar of propitiation to God to stay the plague. This was declared to be the house of God and the place of the altar, that is, the sole altar, of the people Israel (1 Chr. 22:1). It became the place of obedience and propitiation for Israel.

E. Temporary character. This place symbolized the hearing ear of God (1 Ki. 8:27-29), the resort of the stranger (vv. 41-43), and the house of prayer for all people (Isa. 56:7), to the end that all nations of the earth should fear God (1 Ki. 8:43). In the NT, it symbolized the body of Christ (Jn. 2:18-21) as the obedient servant of God for propitiating God's wrath on the sinner. Further, the temple as God's dwelling place symbolizes the Christian as the dwelling place of God (1 Cor. 3:16).

In the early days of the church, STEPHEN, about to be slain for his faith, declared that the people were putting the temple above God, forgetting that he did not really need a temple building in the sense of rooms of stone and wood (Acts 7:44-50; cf. 17:24-25), but that he desired the believing heart of flesh (Ezek. 36:26-27) on which he could impress his law, that is, his nature, which would result in obedience and holiness of life.

There is a prior step to the achievement of this result. The future MILLENNIUM will see a temple raised to God, the refuge of all nations; but it will be primarily a memorial. When the millennium runs its course and the new age of perfection is established, there will be no temple, for the Lamb will be there in the midst of his people (Rev. 21:22). Thus the temple is mediatorial in all ages, justifying Stephen's position.

III. Location

A. Araunah's threshing floor. The location of Solomon's temple is identified with the threshing floor of ARAUNAH (alternately Ornan, 2 Chr. 3:1), known as Mount MORIAH, the locale of the sacrifice of ISAAC (Gen. 22:2), where DAVID founded the altar of the temple (2 Sam. 24:24-25; 1 Chr. 22:1; cf. 1 Chr. 21:18-26). The location of the altar was to be determined as follows: Araunah and his sons hid themselves at the presence of the angel (1 Chr. 21:20); the place of concealment must have been the area of the threshing floor, for Araunah *went out* of it to meet David (v. 21). The reference is to the cave where they would have stored their grain after it was separated from the chaff. Since the rock under the Qubbet es-Sakhra (Dome of the Rock), where the cave is, shows the effects of quarrying *above* the level of the cave, it is logical to hold that this rock stood higher originally and that the threshing floor surrounded the rock and the cave.

The altar, therefore, would not be placed on top of the rise forming the cave. David demanded the threshing floor at a price to erect there the altar of God. It would appear that David referred to the flatter area around this rise, for it was there that the actual threshing was done. Hence, one must consider that the altar was located to the E of the rise, or even to the NE or SE, since there was in any of these areas ample space for the location of the altar and its ritual. Moreover, more room was required for the altar ritual, for the laver was to be in the immediate neighborhood of the altar, and there was insufficient room on the rock over the cave. Let it also be recalled that there was a foundation of great stones for the temple (1 Ki. 5:17), forming the great platform on which the temple and adjacent store rooms were built (cf. *BA* 14 [1951]: 6). Such a platform of the approximate height of four to five cubits would raise the interior temple floor level above the top, or nearly to the top, of the present rock in the Qubbet es-Sakhra, the present domed structure covering the rise at the cave in Araunah's threshing floor. Any further elevation of the rock above this floor would be covered by the higher floor of the Holy of Holies. (Cf. J. Simons, *Jerusalem in the Old Testament* [1952], 381ff.) On the site of the threshing floor David made it a practice to sacrifice to Yahweh (cf. 1 Chr. 1:28) and determined the location of the altar of Israel (22:1).

B. Character of the site. The researches and excavations of Warren, Wilson, Conder, Schick, and others in Jerusalem have established the topography of the city quite conclusively (cf. C. Wilson and C. Warren, *The Recovery of Jerusalem* [1879], 50ff.). The area of the city divides principally into an eastern and western ridge, separated by a wide valley known by the name Tyropoeon. The eastern ridge is bounded on the E side by the deep, narrow valley of the KIDRON. At the S end of the western hill is the Valley of HINNOM into which ran the Tyropoeon (now mostly filled), and then the Hinnom continues eastward past the S end of the E ridge to the Kidron. (See topographic sketch.)

The E ridge was further divided toward the N by a small offshoot of the Kidron to the W and then quickly turned generally northward, a stretch known as St. Anne's Valley. The valley is now covered by the northern end of the Ḥaram esh-Sharif ("the noble sanctuary") on the temple mound. The S end of the E ridge was the site of David's city, with OPHEL about midway toward St. Anne's Valley. The ridge continued to rise toward the N quite rapidly to a high elevation at the threshing floor of Araunah and an even higher peak at the location of ANTONIA; the site was more level to the E of the Sakhra before dropping off sharply away to the Kidron, and on the W side dropping sooner to the Tyropoeon, thus limiting the extent of the original Solomonic construction more considerably on the W side than on the E. The Tyropoeon Valley is now mostly filled in with debris from over the centuries.

The site of the temple was influenced by the location of David's city and by the attraction of the upper rocky platform. The mound was near the city but outside it, free from interferences offered by existing city structures, and on an eminence appropriate to its character—not even today overpowered by the city on the western ridge.

IV. Solomon's temple

A. David's preparations

1. The inspiration for the temple. The idea for the temple plan and structure came to David from Yahweh when he had given the king rest from all his enemies (2 Sam. 7:1–3; cf. Deut. 12:10–14), so that the house would be built in peace. David assembled all the officials of Israel (1 Chr. 28:1) and commissioned them and his son SOLOMON to build the temple. After giving this charge, he delivered to Solomon the "pattern" (28:11) that he had received by God's Spirit (v. 12); and the instructions were in writing (v. 19). God thus determined the pattern of the approach of the worshiper as well as the elements of his worship, so that the right way to him was known. God determined the character of the temple as he did for the tabernacle. (Thus one should not infer that the similar pattern of sanctuaries such as the one at Tel Tainat, dated shortly after the time of Solomon [see above, I.E], was a source of the plan for the Jerusalem temple, much less that pagan forms of religion were being introduced in Israel.)

The provision for entry to the high priest once a year with blood was sufficient to provide the ATONEMENT necessary for the people to maintain their

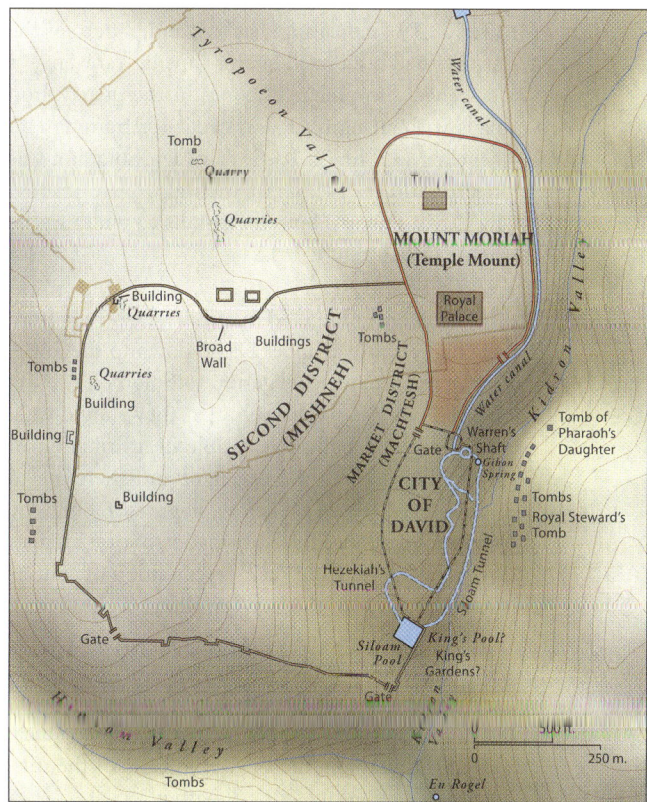

Jerusalem.

sanctity for fellowship with God. The outer chamber was sufficient for the daily intercession and communion with their God made necessary by his nature. Beyond these rooms was no need for an elaborate system of courts as in the Egyptian temples.

2. The collection of materials. The amassing of materials was begun early by David when Solomon was young (1 Chr. 29:1–5). The materials included 100,000 talents of gold and a million talents of silver (22:14; a talent was equivalent to about 70–75 lbs.). From his own private fortune David had set aside for gilding and plating ornamentation 3,000 talents of the prized gold of OPHIR and 7,000 talents of high grade (refined) silver (29:3–5). The officers of the people gave 5,000 talents and 10,000 DARICS of gold, 10,000 talents of silver, bronze amounting to 18,000 talents, and of iron 100,000 talents. Others gave precious jewels of which there was no reckoning. In addition, weights were specified and established for many articles of furniture by David (28:13–19), indicating that size and pattern of the articles had been fixed by this time by Yahweh.

David also prepared stones in the quarry, iron nails without number, and cedar for framing and paneling (1 Chr. 22:1–4), to which Solomon was free to add (v. 14). Craftsmen also were readied by David to contribute their skills to building the house of Yahweh (v. 15).

3. The people obligated to build. The people from the highest prince under David down to the lowliest were put under obligation to Solomon (1 Chr. 28:21), but also to Yahweh, that they should walk with him and build the temple in affirmation of their allegiance to the covenant and therefore to Yahweh (vv. 10–21). Their willingness to build the temple was at once their affirmation of the covenant given by Yahweh and their precondition of continued occupation of the land (cf. Kline, *Treaty*, 76ff.).

4. The temple service given by God. The temple service was also set out by David by the command of God's Spirit (1 Chr. 28:13): the priests to officiate at the altar and the Levites to care for the subsidiary functions (cf. 24:1, 3, with v. 19).

Thus the pattern of the temple, the size of furniture, and the worship were ordained by Yahweh. It is to be understood that no thing of worship, implements, ritual, or buildings was left to human invention lest a single element formed solely according to human thinking or ingenuity be present to cast suspicion on the entire worship center and justify in any way the idea of human cooperation in establishing the way of RECONCILIATION with God.

D. Data. The principal sources of information relating to Solomon's temple are several passages in Kings and Chronicles (1 Ki. 5–8; 1 Chr. 17; 21–22; 28–29; 2 Chr. 2–7), though there are other references scattered through the rest of the Scriptures. Any reconstruction of Solomon's temple is limited primarily to these, though other architectural and archaeological data shed light on some features, such as plan and furniture.

1. Date of beginning. Both 1 Ki. 6:1 and 2 Chr. 3:2 establish the start of construction of the temple in Solomon's fourth year. His reign ended 931/30 B.C., which would require 971/970 B.C. for the first year of his forty-year reign (1 Ki. 11:42), placing the beginning of the temple in 967/966 B.C. See CHRONOLOGY (OT).

2. Workmen. The foundryman was a Phoenician, HIRAM of TYRE (1 Ki. 7:13). Other workmen were Sidonians under the king of Tyre, also named Hiram (5:6), whose workmen felled the Lebanese cedars for the temple. They were called into service because there were no Israelites proficient in this work. In addition, Solomon conscripted 30,000 Israelites (5:13) to labor in courses in LEBANON with the lumbering operation (v. 14). In addition there were 153,600 aliens in Israel (2 Chr. 2:17) over whom were 3,600 overseers to direct their labors (v. 18). These laborers were divided into 70,000 bearers of burdens and 80,000 hewers. On the basis that fifty men form a company with a captain over them (2 Ki. 1:9), about 3,600 overseers would have been required.

3. Construction. Timber and stone were made ready beforehand (1 Ki. 5:18) so as to eliminate the noise on the site (6:7). The total interior length of the house was 60 cubits, with an interior breadth of 20 cubits and an interior height of 30 cubits (6:2; a cubit is thought to have been about 1.5 ft.; see WEIGHTS AND MEASURES I.A). In addition, there was an open porch 10 cubits deep that extended the whole breadth of the Holy Place, that is, 20 cubits (v. 3). The stones were precut at the quarry, squared, dressed, and transported to the site to be set in position. Both at Megiddo of this period and at Samaria in the next century are examples of finely shaped cut stones for building, with carefully cut edges for alignment and joining (5:18). This work, however, appears to be exceptional, for most other construction in the nation was rubblework. Israelite workmen did not know how to do this specialized building, hence the importation of Phoenician craftsmen.

Then follows a description of the side chambers and of a platform against all sides of the house (1 Ki. 6:5-6; summary, v. 10). According to EZEKIEL, the temple he envisioned included a platform (Ezek. 41:9 RSV; NIV, "open area") on which were built the side chambers. Since the two buildings were much alike, one concludes that Ezekiel's temple was basically the same as Solomon's with modifications. (The KJV translates Heb. *yāṣiaʿ* H3666 [*Ketib yāṣûaʿ*] in 1 Ki. 6:5a as "chambers," while modern versions more accurately render it as "structure." Verse 10 is so abrupt that one suspects accidental omission in the copying process of part of the original, which should probably read: "And he built … [here follows the Heb. sign of the accusative] the platform against the whole house, five cubits was its height; and he made [plus the sign of the accusative] the side chambers." The part dropped out was that between the two occurrences of the sign of the accusative, thus giving the translation of the KJV and causing a seeming change in the meaning of *yāṣûaʿ*.)

The construction of the side chambers is given as a series of rooms one above another (1 Ki. 6:6; Ezek. 41:6), with each successive upper story one cubit wider than the next lower. This increase was obtained by the fact that the upper portions of the wall on the Holy Place side were set back by one cubit (i.e., the wall became one cubit thinner in each of the second and third stories). The lowest chamber was 5 cubits wide, the middle was 6, and the upper was 7, with the story height being 5 cubits (although when the thickness of beams and flooring is deducted the clear height would be rather low); these dimensions may then be clear heights as in the Holy Place. The inner wall was 6 cubits (Ezek. 41:5) and the outside chamber wall 5 cubits (v. 9), with the width of the open space between walls as noted above. Floors consisted of wood on beams and planks, with the inner ends of the beams resting on the setbacks of the temple walls. It is probable also that at the roof level the wall of the Holy Place set back another cubit so that the roof beams would not be built into the wall of the house (1 Ki. 6:6).

Access to the upper stories of the side chambers was by stairways (1 Ki. 6:8) built against the walls of the Holy Place, accessible from that room. Ezekiel describes some sort of access to the chambers (Eze. 41:7), and it is possible to construe the text so as to locate stairs on the S side and the N side of Solomon's temple. Windows are referred to as having "recessed frames" (1 Ki. 6:4 NRSV; NIV, "narrow clerestory windows"); the Hebrew may mean that the windows were covered with lattice work (cf. NJPS and see Ezek. 41:16). The framework may have consisted of successive rebates around the opening.

The roof structure in Solomon's temple was of beams and cedar boards (1 Ki. 6:9; cf. 2 Chr. 3:7). The wood beams were overlaid with smaller, close-laid wood members forming a bed on which clay was packed and covered with a pulverized limestone marl, rolled flat, smooth, and hard, providing a cement-like surface that was practically impervious to water. The rolling stones for consolidating the marl have been found in ancient sites.

The temple porch was reached by a series of steps at the front from the level of the court (cf. Ezek. 40:6), probably not less than ten. Interior walls and ceilings were finished with cedar (1 Ki. 6:9), and the floor was finished with pine over cedar planks (v. 15). The clause "walls of the ceiling" (v. 15) may have been introduced through a mispronunciation of the word actually meaning "beams," indicating that finished woodwork was laid over the rougher beams, perhaps achieving something in the nature of coffers.

The Holy of Holies or Most Holy Place was a cube (1 Ki. 6:20) and also lined with paneling (v. 16), separated from the Holy Place by a partition of cedar paneling with double doors of olive wood. The lintel and jamb posts were also made of olive wood. The expression "fifth part" (v. 31 KJV), which may be translated "fivefold" (NIV, "five-sided"), offers a problem. If, however, one considers that the wall between the posts and the side walls of the room was nearly equal in thickness to the posts, and that the corners of the posts on the door side were chamfered, then the jamb face at the door (one), the chamfered faces (two), and the face of the posts by the walls (three) provide the five-sided appearance of the posts. A wood lintel lay over them to provide the top pivot for the door leaves. Against this partition on the ark side, a VEIL was hung (2 Chr. 3:14), woven or sewn in colored patterns with blue, purple, and crimson thread, and onto the whole were applied patterns of cherubim.

A door was provided for the Holy Place (1 Ki. 6:33), from the porch with square-cut posts of olive wood, against the ends of the stone walls (jambs) forming the rear wall of the porch, with bifolding door leaves to fold against each other and then to swing open against the jamb. Usual construction had a wood pintle as the pivot at the edge of the leaves that were attached with metal straps, and the pintles let into sockets at the lintel and set into stone base sockets or into pockets in the stone sills. Bars within held the doors closed, passing through cleats on the inside of the doors. A stone threshold completed the opening at the floor line. The temple doors were made of pine because of the greater strength of this wood.

Around the temple building a court was formed by the erection of a stone wall three courses high with a row of three timbers holding it together (1 Ki. 6:36). The area thus enclosed was called the priest's courtyard (2 Chr. 4:9) and had doors in the wall covered with brass plates.

4. Decoration. The wall surfaces in the Holy Place and Holy of Holies were carved (1 Ki. 6:18) with scroll-like flower patterns and cherubim (v. 29). The doors to these rooms were also carved with palm trees and cherubim on both sides, and the carvings in turn were overlaid with gold. The woodwork elsewhere (vv. 18–20) was plated or gilded or inlaid, presenting a brilliant sight to the viewer. The combination of palm leaves (signifying victory) and cherubim (signifying the holiness of God) declared that spiritual triumph came only by and through the holy God.

5. Temple furniture. The ark with its mercy seat from the tabernacle was placed at the back of the Holy of Holies under the cherubim, which were made of olive wood and were gold plated (1 Ki. 6:23–28). These were 10 cubits high and their wings extended to 10 cubits, half the width of the room. They functioned symbolically as guardians of the way to God, solemnizing the heart of the worshipers in their approach to God. Their faces were turned toward the dividing partition. They were composite figures well enough known to the people of that day, requiring no description of their form. They may have been similar to the four-faced cherubim of Ezekiel and were usually represented with hands and feet, therefore having basically a human-like body.

In the Holy Place before the entrance to the Holy of Holies was placed the altar of INCENSE (1 Ki. 6:20; 7:48; cf. Exod. 30:1–10), probably new and made of cedar, since it was overlaid with gold. Presumably (cf. Exod. 40:22) the table for the SHOWBREAD was also new, overlaid with gold and placed on the right side of the room as in the tabernacle. In this room were the ten lampstands (see CANDLESTICK, GOLDEN), five on the right side and five on the left, all of gold, with their oil cups and ornamentation, to give light in the Holy Place (1 Ki. 7:49).

On the platform surrounding the temple stood the two brass pillars, named Jakin and Boaz (1 Ki. 7:21). The form of the first term ($y\bar{a}kin$ H3521) is an old participle causative meaning "sustainer" or "one who establishes" (cf. *JBL* 68 [1949]: 317–18), stressing the positive side of God's character. See JAKIN (PILLAR). The second name ($b\bar{o}^caz$ H1245) may be the participle form of a root attested in Arabic that yields the meaning "smiter"; if so, it gives the negative aspect of the character of Yahweh as Keeper of Israel (ibid.; however, see *HALOT*, 1:142).

It is questionable that these pillars were for incense burning, since their height would make it difficult to reach their tops to replenish the incense. They were 18 cubits high and approximately 4 cubits in diameter; on each rested a shaft with its capital 5 cubits high (1 Ki. 7:15–16). The chronicler gives the total height of both pillars as 35 cubits, apparently just the shaft length (2 Chr. 3:15). The additional cubit of length most likely was a separate cast base similar to some that have been found. The capitals are described as being in the shape of lilies (1 Ki. 7:19) and having a bowl-shaped section (v. 20; cf. v. 41); the lily petals, 4 cubits broad, were probably below and set downward, as examples from this period show. In another passage (2 Ki. 25:17) they are described as 3 cubits high, but this refers to the chain network; it would appear that this measurement refers to the upper portion of the capital, leaving 2 cubits for the height of the lily work.

The bowls had a network of interwoven chains supporting two rows of pomegranates (1 Ki. 7:17, 41). These chains, seven in number, were divided, meaning probably that four chains draped down from

Artistic illustration of the altar inside the temple built by Solomon. (From the Tyndale Pentateuch, 1530 ed.)

the center point at the top and three strands were set around the bowl, with the pomegranates attached to the bottom strand, fastened one below the other.

6. Court furniture. The prominent feature of the court was the molten sea, 10 cubits in diameter, 30 cubits in circumference, and 5 cubits high (1 Ki. 6:23)—thus bowl-shaped, about as thick as the hand and containing 2,000 "baths" (vv. 24–26; 2 Chr. 4:5 gives the number as 3,000 "baths"). The figures are reasonable if one assumes (from Ezek. 41:8) the use of the great cubit (royal cubit). On this basis the capacity would have been about 10,000 gallons using the usual formula for spherical volume. In Chronicles, another method of computation seems to have been used, the volume of a cylinder, which in this case turns out to be 3,000 baths. Thus the problem is one of method by which the writers viewed the shape of the sea, not an essential contradiction in the text (cf. *BA* 12 [1949], 86–90). The sea was located in the altar court to the SE (2 Chr. 4:10). See also SEA, MOLTEN.

The rim was finished off with the petal (lily) work familiar from the pillar capitals. It also had gourds under the brim in two rows of ten per cubit (1 Ki. 7:24), referring to some distinctive type of decoration. The sea stood on a base composed of twelve oxen in sets of three, one set toward each of the compass points (v. 25). These corresponded to the twelve tribes of Israel, bearing the sanctifying witness of God.

The wheeled stands for movable lavers (1 Ki. 7:27–37) were ten in number, formed of boxes 4 cubits square and 3 cubits high, the sides made up of divided panels and having ornamental work. The boxes were worked onto short columns ("supports," v. 30) to which axles were attached for wheels 1.5 cubits in diameter. The wheels were like chariot wheels, probably six-spoked, as archaeological remains show. As indicated in v. 34, the supports extended upward to form the corners of the boxes.

Into the stands at the top were fitted the lavers or basins containing the water for washing the sacrificial animals (2 Chr. 4:6; the molten sea was for the ablutions of the priests). Each of these lavers held "forty baths" (1 Ki. 7:38), that is, about 200–230 gallons of water. They could be moved about as the washings required. Normally they were distributed five on the N side and five on the S side of the court before the temple. In addition there were ten tables (4:8) for the flaying of the sacrifices brought by the people. These were placed in the same court as the lavers, probably five on each side.

The focal point in the court was the great bronze altar (2 Chr. 4:1). It was 20 cubits square and 10 cubits high. Its transportation from the Jordan required its sides to be of panel construction with corner pieces and a grate through which the ashes could fall; some method for removing these also was provided, either by the removal of the grating or through the side panels. The description in Ezek. 43:13–17 does not shed much light on the Solomonic altar because too many events came between.

Other implements are listed (1 Ki. 7:38–50; and 2 Chr. 4:6, 19–22). There were basins for water and to catch the blood of the sacrifices, tongs, picks, snuffers (to quench candle lights?), spoons of one sort or another with which to ladle and handle the meat offerings, as well as flat implements such as cake turners for cooking the cake offerings. Likewise the incense containers for the priests are listed.

7. The courts. Little is said concerning the courts surrounding the temple building. The "inner court yard" (1 Ki. 6:36), due to the slope of the site, was the same as the "upper courtyard" (Jer. 36:10). It was formed by an enclosing wall of three courses of cut stone and a row of cedar beams to tie it together (cf. 2 Chr. 4:9, court of the priests). The whole presented a terraced scene exposing the temple building for an easy view of its imposing character. The great courtyard (1 Ki. 7:9, 12) enclosed both the temple and the palace works of Solomon.

Access to the outer court was through gates; though they are not specifically listed, the door leaves for them are enumerated (2 Chr. 4:9; see below). From the outer court, access to the inner court was also by gates, to which the ordinary person (laity) had access (Jer. 36:10). Ezekiel 44:1 mentions the gate, and because of the departure and return of the Shekinah of God from this gate, it was the principal gate to the outer court of the temple, probably the gate of 2 Chr. 4:9. Between the temple court (inner) and Solomon's palace, there was access from the palace court to the inner court by a gate, presumably in the S wall of the inner court, the gate of the guard (2 Ki. 11:19). A N gate also existed, known as Sur (11:6; cf. *VT* 14 [1964]: 335–37 and see FOUNDATION GATE).

8. Dedication. The work of building the temple occupied seven years and six months (1 Ki. 6:1, 38). The dedication occurred in the month ETHANIM, the seventh month, in later times called TISHRI. The intervening months between BUL (6:38), the eighth month, and Ethanim (8:2) of the following year (to Tishri) would be occupied with bringing up the furniture, the most difficult of which would have been the transportation of the bronze sea and its pedestals from the Jordan to Jerusalem. On the first day of the month occurred the Feast of Trumpets, when the ark was brought into the Holy of Holies from its tent in Jerusalem (8:6) and was placed under the wings of the cherubim. When the carrying staves were drawn out, it symbolized that the journey of Israel to her land was complete. When the priests withdrew from the Holy Place, the Shekinah of God filled the temple, thus signifying Yahweh's approval and acceptance of the temple. Henceforth the house was to be representative of his presence (v. 29), the place to which the heart in repentance may turn to find God's mercy (vv. 30–53).

C. Supplementary data. The palace of Solomon (1 Ki. 7:1) was evidently built near the temple, and from this some infer that the temple amounted to no more than a royal chapel. Other passages, however, clearly speak of worship in the courts of Yahweh's house in Jerusalem, in whose temple are the people of God (Ps. 96:8; 116:18–19).

At a later period after the completion of the temple, among the inventory of goods carried in Solomon's ships was ALMUG wood, possibly the red sandalwood of India and Ceylon, probably the latter because the ships went for gold nearer to Ophir. The wood was finished and formed part of the woodwork of the walls of the Holy Place (1 Ki. 10:11–12).

Concerning the monies of the temple, the book of Joshua makes mention of a treasury belonging to Yahweh, an institution well known by that time, consisting of the repository of the booty of various battles of Israel against her adversaries (Josh. 6:19). In it was deposited the spoil of JERICHO (v. 24). Later, officers were appointed over the house of the treasures of Yahweh (1 Chr. 26:20–28). From his victories over surrounding peoples, David dedicated numerous objects to Yahweh (v. 26). These were used to maintain the temple (v. 27). SAMUEL and SAUL also had dedicated spoils to Yahweh (v. 28). Solomon brought out the things dedicated by his father and put them among the treasures of Yahweh's house (1 Ki. 7:15), probably including all the other treasures, for the references above indicated they had been delivered to the Levites, the keepers of the temple. It is likely that the treasury rooms were the three-storied rooms around the temple, for 1 Chr. 28:11 includes the treasuries with the rest of the rooms of the temple. As such they were accessible only from the Holy Place.

D. History of Solomon's temple. When REHOBOAM, Solomon's son, became king, his repressive policy became the immediate cause of the division of the kingdom. Shrines were set up by JEROBOAM at DAN (PLACE) and BETHEL, thus splitting the allegiance of Israel to God (1 Ki. 12:25–33). In Judah, a widespread apostasy of the people quickly grew by Rehoboam's fifth year (926/25 B.C.), characterized by the erection of high places and idol pillars "on every high hill" (14:23–24). Then, in divine judgment, SHISHAK (Sheshonk), king of Egypt, came up against them (2 Chr. 12:2, 5) and took the treasures of both the temple and the king, including the 300 gold shields Solomon had made.

ASA placed in the temple the spoils of his father (1 Ki. 15:15). When BAASHA, king of Israel, made war against Judah, quite obviously by fortifying RAMAH (v. 17), Asa collected all the treasures in the temple and in his treasury and sent them to BEN HADAD of DAMASCUS to seal an alliance with him against Israel (vv. 18–19). In his earlier years (2 Chr. 15:10), Asa turned to the ways of Yahweh and renewed the altar in the inner court (before the porch, v. 8), probably replacing some of its parts now evidently badly decomposed because of the heat of the fires. However, his consecration and trust of Yahweh was lacking when in his thirty-sixth year he made the alliance with Ben Hadad (2 Chr. 15:18—16:4). In the days of JEHOSHAPHAT, a new court of the house of God is noted (2 Chr. 20:5). He may have reconstructed the gate.

When AHAZIAH was slain by JEHU, ATHALIAH, his mother, usurped the kingdom of Judah from JOASH (Jehoash, 2 Ki. 11) until her seventh year. During this period, Joash was hidden in the temple until he was old enough to be proclaimed king (2 Chr. 22:1—23:15). Athaliah was taken out of the inner court (cf. 23:13) through the "ranges" (2 Ki. 11:15 NIV), possibly referring to the porticoes along the E wall of the inner court (Ezek. *WTJ* 7, f. 1 [1944] 231–43). Previous to his reign, the temple precincts had fallen into disrepair because of Athaliah (2 Chr. 24:7) and as a result of priestly carelessness, and this condition continued until the twenty-third year, when Jehoash summoned JEHOIADA the high priest for an accounting (2 Ki. 12:6; cf. 2 Chr. 24:4–7).

Since there was no money available from the temple treasuries nor from the king's funds, the priest set up a chest to collect "the tax that Moses the servant of God had required of Israel in the desert" (2 Chr. 24:8–9). At periodical intervals the money was removed, from which materials for the repairs were bought and workmen were paid (vv. 10–12). So far had Athaliah gone in her depredations that even vessels, etc., needed replacing (v. 13). After the death of Jehoiada, the people, still infected with the idolatry of Athaliah, conspired with Joash to apostatize from Yahweh (vv. 17–18). When Zechariah the prophet rebuked Joash and the princess, they stoned him to death in the temple court (vv. 19–21). For this sin, a small Aramean force inflicted great damage on Jerusalem and on the military of Judea (vv. 23–24), and Joash had to deliver up the treasures of the temple and the palace to HAZAEL king of Aram (2 Ki. 12:18).

During the reign of AMAZIAH son of Joash in Judah, King Joash/Jehoash of Israel invaded Jerusalem (2 Ki. 14:13) and carried off the treasures of the temple and palace because Amaziah had exalted himself in pride against Israel (v. 7–8; cf. 2 Chr. 25:23–24). Later UZZIAH, an energetic, able king, rebuilt the city, but he fell into the error of pride and sought to usurp priestly functions in the temple (2 Chr. 26:16–21). JOTHAM succeeded his father Uzziah and rebuilt the Upper Gate (2 Ki. 15:35).

AHAZ, who succeeded his father Jotham, desecrated the house of Yahweh. He robbed the temple of its treasures, added his own, and sent them to the Assyrian monarch TIGLATH-PILESER III (745–727 B.C.) to secure his aid against the Israelite-Syrian alliance against him (2 Ki. 16:7–8). To pay homage to Tiglath-Pileser, Ahaz went to Damascus and there saw an altar of which he had a copy made (v. 10). He set it before the Solomonic altar, which was removed to the N (v. 14), and made an offering on the altar, probably as a condition of the alliance. Further depredations included closing the temple (2 Chr. 28:24) and breaking up its vessels. Furthermore, he cut off the bases of the laver and set it on a stone pedestal (2 Ki. 16:17), and as a sign of his subservience, made a place in the temple for Tiglath-Pileser (v. 18). This parallels alliances forbidden in the HITTITE suzerainty treaties (Kline, *Treaty*, 32) and indicates treason against the sovereign God of Israel.

HEZEKIAH reversed the policies of Ahaz. He opened the closed doors of the temple and demanded that the Levites restore it to its former sanctity (2 Chr. 29:5); this they did in eight days (v. 17) and restored the vessels, such as were whole, which Ahaz had cast away (v. 19). He restored the Levites to their places in the temple and commanded the people to present offerings (31:4). When they brought munificently, he built storehouses on the temple grounds to preserve the offerings (v. 11). Hezekiah, however, became proud and made alliances with foreign nations; he forgot the power of God, and for this was struck with illness. His example assured the future downfall of Jerusalem (cf. 2 Chr. 32:24–26; 2 Ki. 20:14–19).

MANASSEH reversed the good things his father Hezekiah had done, raised up idolatrous altars in the temple courts, and placed a graven image in the temple (2 Ki. 21:1–9; 2 Chr. 33:1–9). For his sins he was taken captive to Babylon (2 Chr. 33:11). Manasseh repented, and God allowed him to return to Jerusalem. In confirmation of his repentance, he destroyed what he had done (v. 15) and repaired the altar of burnt sacrifice. His idolatrous example to his son and others after him, however, brought closer the ultimate destruction of the temple (2 Ki. 21:11–16).

AMON worshiped the image set up by his father Manasseh, and after a reign of two years his servants assassinated him (2 Ki. 21:19–23). The "people of the land" slew the conspirators and made JOSIAH king (v. 24). Josiah directed the repair of the temple in his days (22:3–7; 2 Chr. 34:8–11). The stone work was restored and certain timbers replaced (34:11). He removed from the temple the articles made for BAAL and ASHERAH (2 Ki. 23:4), the horses in honor of the sun placed by kings before him (v. 11), the altars on top of the rooms Ahaz had added, and the altars Manasseh had made, which Amon had restored in the two courts of the temple. In spite of all this, the people did not truly turn to Yahweh, and sins tracing back to Manasseh continued (cf. vv. 26–27). Destruction was not far away.

In the reign of JEHOIAKIM, NEBUCHADNEZZAR took all the west land and Jehoiakim became his tributary, but he rebelled after three years and the city was besieged. The vessels of the temple (2 Chr. 36:7) were taken to Babylon, and so was Jehoiakim (v. 6), both for his sins and the fruit of the sins of Manasseh (2 Ki. 24:3–4). JEHOIACHIN followed as king, but at the end of three months was besieged by Nebuchadnezzar who took him captive to Babylon along with the palace treasures, additional vessels of the temple made by Solomon (v. 13) which he cut in pieces to take to Babylon, and other treasures from the temple.

In the reign of ZEDEKIAH, the end of Solomon's temple came. He rebelled against Nebuchadnezzar and the city fell in 586 B.C. Zedekiah tried to flee by night but was captured by the Chaldean troops. The city and temple were burned to the ground. The remaining vessels of bronze and gold were assembled to be taken to Babylon. The pillars before the temple, their bases, and the brazen sea were broken up and carried away to Babylon. The ark and the cherubim, probably now only wooden forms, perished in the flames. The 380 years of the temple were ended, fulfilling Jeremiah's words of the destruction of the city, temple, and people for their sins (Jer. 25:1–11).

E. Problems. Certain problematic aspects of the structure of the temple, not mentioned above to avoid disruption of the general description, must be considered at this point.

1. The height of the Holy of Holies. Was the floor of the Most Holy Place on the same level as that of the Holy Place, or was it raised? Examples of raised altar rooms occur in the Middle E (see DAGON IV.D). A lower ceiling height than in the Holy Place would require a stone clerestory wall dividing the two, but evidence is lacking in documenting a supporting beam. Other evidence shows the two to be on the same level. In the Herodian temple, a double curtain separated the two, eliminating the necessity of steps (see below, VII.C.1). Second, coins of the 1st cent. A.D., depicting the temple on the day of the sacrifice of the red heifer (A. Muehsam, *Coin and Temple* [1966], 26–27; plates Vff.), show the ark within the temple but no steps leading up to its level, indicating the Holy of Holies to be on the same level as the Holy Place. It may be assumed that this arrangement goes back at least to the temple of Zerubbabel, who in turn may have followed the earlier form of Solomon's temple. It is very possible that the floor levels of the two rooms were always on the same level and that an attic existed over the Holy of Holies.

2. The height of the porch. The porch is given a height of 120 cubits in the MT of 2 Chr. 3:3–4 (the NIV, following some versional evidence, has 20 cubits). On the other hand, no height is given in 1 Ki. 6:3, implying that it was the same as the house (v. 2). If, for the moment, one can relate the date of the composition of both Kings and Chronicles to either of these records, it will be recalled that

Kings ends with the release of Jehoiachin from prison (2 Ki. 25:27–30) and Chronicles with the decree of restoration of CYRUS (2 Chr. 36:22–23), thus bringing the author of either book past the date of the destruction of the temple and having knowledge of the exact condition and shape of the temple at its terminus. In this case, if Chronicles is right in giving 120 cubits, the fact that Kings did not record the height is of little consequence; it was not important to that writer.

Is such a tower of 120 cubits feasible? Foundations for it would be most important. However, indications of structural formations to support such massive tower works are found in temples from MEGIDDO (strata V [age of RAMSES III] and VIII–VII A), SHECHEM, and possibly BETH SHAN (stratum V). In connection with this great height, JOSEPHUS wrote that Jotham added porticos and gateways in the temple area (*Ant.* 9.11.2). The temple building was erected to a height of 60 cubits (Ezra 6:3), whereas the breadth given (60 cubits) is quite similar to that of the former structure, including the side chambers. These facts would justify believing that upper additions to the temple were made at a later time and that Jotham made some of them. Both Zerubbabel's temple and Herod's reconstruction of this second temple were quite like these for size. The justification of the increase and embellishment of the temple resulted from Jotham's victory over the Ammonites (2 Chr. 27:5), with the booty and tribute used for the celebration of the triumph; upper rooms were added over the Holy Place and Holy of Holies, and the porch was altered and heightened with a larger portal constructed in it, the "Upper Gate of the temple of the LORD" (v. 3).

3. The enclosing walls of the temple. These are not described in Kings or Chronicles in enough detail to discern their location or height. None of the original structure of King Solomon's temple has survived to give the wall height of the three courses (1 Ki. 6:36). If further information were available, one might define more precisely the area enclosed; yet certain considerations serve to locate the Holy of Holies more accurately, and then help to suggest possible locations of court walls.

Watson (in *PEQ* no vol. [1896]: 56) stated the problem well: if the altar of sacrifice was on the Sakhra (the exposed rock under the Dome of the Rock), this forced the western wall of the temple so far to the W that there instantly occurred a high foundation of nearly fifty feet. In addition, to place the altar on the Rock prevented the step-down arrangement from the priest's court (inner court) down to the outer court of Herod's temple, as described by Josephus and the MISHNAH (Watson, 55), since Herod obviously built on the old foundations of the second temple, which in turn had been erected on those of the first. Assuming that the Holy of Holies was placed over the Sakhra, the rock surfaces defined by the explorations of Wilson, Warren, Schick, and others are still high enough W of the rear wall of the temple to allow for building the inner court wall up to 10 cubits away, with the outer wall up to another 20 cubits without having to build high retaining walls to provide for earthfill back of them to level up the courts within.

It was not until Herod appeared that the incentive and funds became available to push the outer western wall further W and raise it to something of its present height. In Solomon's time, the outer wall was obviously an extension of the city wall, but it would not have been built too far down the western slope from the crown of the hill (i.e., not on the slope), to provide the maximum defense. To place the temple farther W would have violated this practice observable elsewhere. These considerations would indicate that the area enclosed by the outer wall was rather the crown of the hill for defensive purposes, and that the area tended to be narrowed E to W and longer N to S. The ancient foundations of the enclosing walls of Solomon's temple might be discovered, if any part of them exist, within the limits of the existing Ḥaram. In some places the location would be indicated by large beds cut into the bed rock, stepped up and down as slope and coursing of stone required. The same practice of cutting out stepped beds was employed in Herod's time, as the excavations of Warren have shown. It will be shown below that the existing E wall of the Ḥaram was a former city wall used by Herod as his eastern wall. Solomon's E wall was located W of this wall.

4. The columns Jakin and Boaz. A further problem relates to these pillars (see above, IV.B.5). Were they structural columns within the porch, and did they support the roof structure above? Or were they free standing? A first consideration of the plan of the small temple of Tel Tainat, where the columns are located within the roof line, might indicate that the columns of Solomon's temple were similarly placed. However, would they have been given memorial names of such diverse meaning (as shown above) if they were merely structural?

Likewise, the arrangements of the networks of chains and pomegranates on top of the capitals suggest quite strongly the free-standing character of these columns. The place where they stood is stated to be "in the front of the temple" (2 Chr. 3:15–17). However, there is additional evidence from archaeology for the relationship of the pillars to the temple. There is in the Louvre a model of a small cultic shrine that has unattached free-standing columns, with four-petaled flower-bud capitals, forming no structural function but obviously having something to do with the religious character of the shrine.

Though this is a Canaanite form, it was employed by Solomon not because of any synergistic religious fervor, but because Yahweh ordered it so, and because the form is approximate to the meaning given. Solomon's pillars differed further from the Canaanite examples by the chain network draped over them, and performed a different function than the Canaanite, that is, the memorializing of God's character; the pomegranates symbolized the totality of God's word through separate commandments, symbolized by the seeds.

V. Ezekiel's temple. In the fourteenth year after the destruction of Jerusalem (572 B.C.), Ezekiel was taken back to the city in a vision, and an angel in his presence measured the temple.

A. Meaning of the temple. What is the significance of Ezekiel's temple? We find an answer in "the law of the temple," which states, "All the surrounding area on top of the mountain will be most holy" (Ezek. 43:12). Clearly, the temple was an expression of the HOLINESS of Yahweh through the complexity that is revealed in the measuring process, and from it the people are to "measure the pattern" so that they may be "ashamed of their iniquities" (v. 10 NRSV; see *BSac* 106 [1949]: 58).

Since this vision occurs at the end of the prophecy of Ezekiel, one must look at it as the culmination of the work of the prophet. See EZEKIEL, BOOK OF. God's holiness was the focal point of his ministry. God's holiness had been outraged by the persistent iniquity of Israel. There was to be (a) the process of exposure, arraignment, and judgment of Israel (Ezek. 1–26); (b) the judgment of surrounding nations so that Yahweh's name might be vindicated in all the earth (chs. 25–32); (c) the rebirth and restoration of the prodigal people (chs. 33–39), which would include the last great attack on his people; and (d) the revelation of God dwelling among the people (chs. 40–48; *BSac* 106 [1949]: 57). The temple (cf. Mal. 3:1) is to become the dwelling place of the divine glory (cf. Ezek. 43:1–6): "Son of man, this is the place of my throne and the place for the soles of my feet. This is where I will live among the Israelites forever" (43:7).

B. Identity of the temple. What temple is this? Is it completely separated from the previous temple in Jerusalem? Is it a completely new complex of buildings? A study of the sequence of events helps to answer this question. The whole of Israel had gone into captivity; the destruction of her temple symbolized God's judgment upon the people for their sin. Israel had also been promised restoration upon repentance (Deut. 30:1–10). The departure of the SHEKINAH ("glory," Ezek. 11:22–23) signified the fall of Jerusalem. The return of this glory (43:1–5) signified the restoration of Israel to God's favor and blessing.

But if such a building vastly differed from the temple that Nebuchadnezzar destroyed, how could it carry any assurance to the people? Since the Holy Place and Holy of Holies are the same size as in Solomon's temple, and in the light of other similarities, the conclusion is that Ezekiel's temple is basically Solomon's temple, but with modifications in the court structure and arrangement. It is not merely an "ideal" temple, for when dealing with the use of the altar, Yahweh describes its sanctification (Ezek. 43:18–27) and the offerings made by the priests (44:15–31) concerning what should be done by a people restored to their God. Yet the question remains whether Ezekiel's temple is actually to be created. The emphasis on ritual and the elimination of ritual in the NT indicates that his temple serves another purpose.

Let it be remembered that Israel was to undergo deportation for IDOLATRY and rejection of Yahweh's COVENANT (Deut. 4:27–28; 28:64–68), but if in their affliction they should seek Yahweh with all their heart, he would hear and restore them to their land (Deut. 4:29–31; Jer. 29:10–14). The purpose was to refine a recalcitrant, backsliding people and create a holy nation (Ezek. 37:21–23, 26–28) so that they would indeed return to their land. Ezekiel 40–48 presents in word pictures the consequent intimate union of Yahweh and his people, and conveys to the remnant of Israel the assurance of the return to her inheritance. The arrangement of the courts impressed the people with the need for personal holiness; but also, Yahweh's presence there (43:1–12) demonstrated his accessibility to the people. The ritual, having been restored, conveyed to Israel that she was truly accepted and therefore could hope to become a cleansed and restored people.

Therefore, Ezekiel's temple was a "visual aid" to faith. Since the returning exiles adhered to the form of the previous temple and not to that of Ezekiel's temple, it would appear that the latter should be understood symbolically. The true restoration of Israel is yet to come, when God a second time (Isa. 11:11) will recover Israel from captivity, when they would be given a new heart (Ezek. 36:26) and their nation would be born in a day (Isa. 66:8–10). This refers to the MILLENNIUM and the rebirth of Israel, for all the Gentiles must wait so that they also may be renewed and share in the blessings of God's house (Isa. 56:7). (Ezekiel's vision of the temple should be compared and contrasted with the details in the TEMPLE SCROLL from Qumran.)

C. The construction

1. The outer court. The description begins with the wall encircling the outer court. The whole could be measured with a reed equal to 6 cubits in length, the cubit being the royal, or great, cubit (Ezek. 40:5; 41:8; 43:13). The wall is one reed high and one reed broad. The angel proceeded first to the E gate and the measurement revealed that the threshold is the same width as the wall, that is, the threshold continues through the width of the wall, with the opening 10 cubits long (40:11). The outer portal of the gateway is reached by a flight of steps terminating at the threshold. Inside the portal is a series of guard chambers ending in a porch at the W (or opposite) end. The guard chambers are a reed square, three on each side (v. 10), with a masonry post between 5 cubits long. These rooms (cf. 1 Ki. 14:28; 2 Chr. 12:11) are for the use of guards who are charged with preventing the entrance of the "uncircumcised" (Ezek. 44:9, 14), indicating the holy character of those who are to be permitted to enter.

Over the E end is a roof (Ezek. 40:13) and the total measurement is 25 cubits side to side outside, ten for the passageway and six for each chamber, thus leaving 1.5 cubits for wall thickness at the rear or outside walls of each chamber. At the inner end of the complex is the porch and inside is a threshold or paving 6 cubits wide, the width of a post between the guard rooms but one cubit wider, and probably also roofed.

The porch at the inner end is said to be "inward," that is, its space opens into the gateway passage (Ezek. 40:9), thus indicating an enclosed area. What are the dimensions of this porch? If one assumes that the 8 cubits (v. 8) is an overall dimension in line of travel, and the total length of 50 cubits is measured from the outside face of the encircling wall (v. 25) to the outside face of the inner porch, and also that the first guard chamber is next to the outside wall, a total length thus indicated is not 50 cubits (v. 15), but forty-eight. The sixty-cubit-high posts (v. 14) are not included in the total, according to the terms of v. 15, and one therefore should revise the consideration of the dimensions of the porch.

The above dimension of 48 cubits assumes that between the third guard chamber and the porch area is a pier 6 cubits long, the same dimension as the threshold (Ezek. 40:7). It has been customary for some interpreters to consider the posts of the inner porch (v. 9) to be the posts of v. 14. This is not necessary, for, comparing v. 8 with 41:1, the reference to 8 cubits of width (40:8) can be construed as the clear width inside wall faces, with the 2 cubits of posts being the thickness of the end walls. This gives a total of 50 cubits, face to face, and the posts of v. 14 are outside this dimension, but against the wall face. The 6 cubits (v. 8) are then the length of the end walls of the inner porch beyond the 10 cubits of doorway opening, making a total of 22 cubits, leaving 1.5 cubits for wall thickness on the N and S sides, the same as the rear walls of the guard chambers (see above).

Ezekiel 40:10 is a summary of the uniformity of dimensions of guard rooms; the "jambs" were also of uniform dimension (v. 9; KJV, "posts"; NRSV, "pilasters"). The same word (in the sing.) is used in v. 48, where the walls on either side of the opening are denoted, thus justifying the interpretation of v. 9 above. The columns of v. 14 are not yet observed nor mentioned at v. 9, for they play no structural part in the gateway.

The portal through the outer wall and the first guard chamber plus one cubit more make a total of 13 cubits (Ezek. 40:11). Nowhere is it possible to obtain this number by just adding wall lengths and guard room dimensions, particularly at the portal ends. The gate must be more than floor space; the extra cubit would derive from a structural member set across above the passageway at the W side of the first guard room as a roof member. This arrangement would have made a roofed gateway 13 cubits long, where one could find shelter in inclement weather while securing permission from the guard to pass on into the court beyond.

Before each side chamber was "a barrier … one cubit on either side" (Ezek. 40:12 NRSV), probably a space separated by a low stone wall to form a precinct line, the wall perhaps being rather thin stone and set on edge (NIV, "a wall one cubit high"). Doors at the side chambers are mentioned as "door against door" (v. 13 KJV); logically these would be in the back or side walls of the gate structure, allowing the guards to come and go freely from the court surrounding the gateway building.

The heights of the posts at the walls of the inner porch are given as 60 cubits, and the use of the verb "made" indicates a quotation from annals recording the construction, since it is manifestly impossible to measure them within the limits of human capability, which again presupposes their previous existence. Though they have a small plan area relative to height, when attached to the wall behind there would be no problem of vertical stability.

The gateway building intrudes 44 cubits into the court (Ezek. 40:6) enclosed by the outer wall and is accessible from both sides (vv. 14–15). Windows are placed in the guard rooms in the walls beside the doors (v. 13) as well as in the piers between the guard rooms (v. 16). There was an indentation in the outer wall face at these piers, allowing for windows in the side walls of the guard rooms adjacent to these piers. The thickness of the piers between the passageway and the side wall face of the structure is determinable from v. 30, which gives a summary of rooms and dimensions; the 25 cubits were the total overall, side-to-side dimension, and the 5 cubits were the fractional dimension of the thickness of the piers.

Windows occur also in the side walls of the inside porch (Ezek. 40:16). They are described as facing inward, that is, the outer face of the wall at the window is formed in a series of concentric rebates with each ring recessed farther than the outer one. The piers between guard rooms have representations of palm trees carved on them.

Emerging from the gateway, Ezekiel was led into the outer court (Ezek. 40:17) surrounding the wall enclosing the temple building. This outer court is for the people, while the inner court is for the priests. A pavement runs along the outer wall and extends from it to the end of the gateway buildings, thus rimming the outer court. On the pavement are built thirty chambers (v. 17). The use of these chambers is not mentioned; they may be for the use of the people, serving as storehouses or living quarters for the priests while they are on duty in their course of temple service. Chambers are mentioned (Jer. 35:4; 1 Chr. 9:26; Neh. 10:38–39) as stores or living quarters.

The court size is determined by the space between walls that faces the gateways. The space between the W face of the E gate and the E face of the gate opposite to the inner court is recorded as 100 cubits; the same is true for the gates to the N and S sides of the outer court (cf. Ezek. 40:19, 23, 27). Since the N and S gates are identical and are the corresponding gates to the inner court, but of reversed plan, the total outside N-to-S dimension is 500 cubits; the same is found to be the E-to-W dimension.

Ezekiel was then led to the N gate, which is measured (Ezek. 40:20–23), and the S gate in the

S wall (vv. 24–27), which are found to be identical. An additional specification is given regarding access steps to the N and S gates, seven in number. Presumably the same number occurs at the E gate. The conditions of holiness for entrance are the same in every case. God has only one way into his presence.

2. The inner court. Ezekiel was then brought into the inner court (Ezek. 40:28) by way of the S gate and observed the measurements taken. The gateway is the same in plan and construction as the gateways of the outer wall, yet reversed, the porch fronting on the outer court. Before each of these gateways are eight steps. The E gate (vv. 32–34) and the N gate (vv. 35–37) to the inner court are exactly the same as the S gate, except that at the N gate in the inner court are additional facilities for washing the sacrificial offerings (v. 38). In the sides of the porch are four tables, two on each side, for slaying the offerings (v. 39) and two on each side in front of the porch, also for slaying the sacrifices (v. 41), making eight in all (see "a" in the diagram).

Reproduction of the menorah (seven-branched lampstand) that stood in the temple.

In addition there are four other tables of stone (v. 42) whereon are laid the implements used for slaughtering the offerings. In the porch itself are arranged hooks for receiving the sacrifices until they are offered. Immediately outside the N gate in the inner court (v. 44) are rooms for the singers, opening toward the S, and one at the E side of the gate for priests on duty (v. 46).

The altar is described in Ezek. 43:13–17. The cubit here is the royal cubit, described as the usual cubit plus the width of the palm (v. 13). The base (NIV, "gutter") was a cubit high up to a ledge one cubit wide, to the edge of which is a vertical border a span wide (the distance from tip of thumb to tip of little finger when fully extended). Above this base is a second element 2 cubits high with a ledge one cubit wide. Surmounting this is another element 4 cubits high. The altar hearth is 12 cubits square (v. 16). The width of one cubit for each of the ledges makes the base 16 cubits square. Stairs are listed (v. 17), probably one-half cubit in height and width, requiring fourteen risers, thus extending 4.5 cubits minimum from the base.

3. The porch of the temple. The inner court is measured as 100 cubits N to S and the same from the E wall to the W wall of the temple (Ezek. 40:47). The porch is then measured as 20 cubits long and 11 cubits wide (40:49 KJV and NJPS, following the MT; NIV and NRSV have "twelve," following the LXX). If the width of the porch signifies a N to S direction of 11 cubits, then the length E-to-W is 20 cubits. If the entry door is 6 cubits wide and flanking walls 5 cubits wide on each side of the door for a total of 16 cubits, this leaves a total of 4 cubits, less than the 20 cubits of inside length, which is too great a difference. However, if one considers that the 20-cubit dimension be taken N to S, and as an inside dimension, and the 5-cubit dimension of v. 48 as the width of flanking walls at the entrance, then the inside faces of the side walls of the porch line up with the faces of the side walls of the Holy Place. This arrangement results in a width E-to-W of 11 cubits inside (v. 49), and the 3 cubits (v. 48) is the thickness of the flanking walls. When a summation of the E-to-W dimensions of the house is made and a 5-cubit platform for the pillars is included (v. 49; cf. 42:11), a total length to the rear wall of the house of 100 cubits is obtained (41:13).

Surrounding the house is a platform (Ezek. 41:8), 6 cubits high, that projected 5 cubits beyond the chamber walls (v. 11; see below). Around this platform is a clear area of 20 cubits (v. 10). At the W end, and set 20 cubits away, is another building (v. 13) forming the western boundary of this area (see below). Verse 14 summarizes the dimensions of the house. An analysis of the measurements leads to a conflict that can be resolved only on the considerations noted below. The "house" is said to be 100 cubits long E-to-W (v. 13). A tabulation of the separate E-W dimensions of the house, however, does not yield 100 cubits' length, but only 95 cubits with the short dimension of the porch E-to-W, and 104 cubits if its E-to-W dimension is 20 cubits. Therefore, another system of measurements must be sought.

Since the E-to-W dimension includes the clear space of 20 cubits, this dimension, when begun at the face of the building W of the house, yields a dimension of 100 cubits to the inner E wall face of the Holy Place, thus arriving at the W face of the W wall of the porch, which is also the E wall of the Holy Place. But this arrangement requires that the E wall of the Holy Place be considered part of the porch, and not of the former. What could be the cause of this consideration? Let it be recalled that the side walls of the Holy Place step back one cubit for each of the stories of the side chambers. Where it emerges above the roof, it recedes 2 cubits inside the side walls of the porch, thus providing the appearance of the Holy Place attached to the back of the porch wall. It may be that the side walls of the porch are more than 6 cubits thick, projecting even more than the 2 cubits. Thus it appears that there is a tower on Ezekiel's temple, patterned after Josiah's high tower. This is another of the characteristics of the temple leading one to consider that it is not greatly different from the one Nebuchadnezzar destroyed.

4. The house. The door from the porch to the "nave" (NRSV) or "outer sanctuary" (NIV), that is, the Holy Place, is 10 cubits wide (Ezek. 41:1–2), leaving 5 cubits of side wall on each side, since the Holy Place is 20 cubits wide. The 6 cubits of v. 1 refers to the thickness of the wall as jamb width in terms of posts, their common name. The Holy Place is 20 cubits wide and 40 cubits long, as in Solomon's temple. The angel went into the "inner sanctuary" or Holy of Holies alone (v. 3). The door is measured to be 6 cubits, the jamb posts 2 cubits, and the door breadth 7 cubits. Although an apparent contradiction occurs, it is clear that the opening into the Holy of Holies is 7 cubits wide (last part, v. 3). Since the other dimension refers to the door also, it is probably the height. The doorway possibly has two leaves, each 3.5 cubits wide, hung from pintle posts at the jambs. The two cubits of jambs refer to the width in the plane of the wall of the jamb posts at each side of the opening. The Holy of Holies is then measured at 20 cubits each way, presumably the same in height and the same in all directions as Solomon's temple, continuing the basic agreement with it.

The wall surrounding the Holy Place and the Holy of Holies was measured as one reed (Ezek. 41:5). The higher the stories forming the side chambers, the broader they are (v. 7), resulting from the stepping back of the "house" walls on the chamber side where the story beams meet, yet do not enter (v. 6) the walls, that is, resting on these setbacks. There are thirty rooms (v. 6) in each of three stories, making ninety chambers in all. The chambers are 4 cubits wide between the outer and inner walls on the lower floor, this being less than the width of the chambers of Solomon's temple. It is probable that in the increase of height of the walls of the Holy Place and Holy of Holies, it is necessary to increase the wall thickness by one cubit, to render it stable, and this is the reason that the chambers are 4 cubits wide. The wall thicknesses are not given for Solomon's temple, being inferred from Ezekiel's temple. The outer wall is 5 cubits thick (v. 9). Access to the chambers is by stairways opening on to the surrounding platform (v. 11).

5. The west building. The "separate place" (Ezek. 41:12) at the W end of the house fronts on another building that measures 80 cubits broad and 100 cubits long. Its breadth is explicitly stated to be a "west side" (lit., "the side of the way of the sea") and is 70 cubits inside plus 5 cubits for walls, making the total 80 cubits, leaving 10 cubits between its N and S walls and the N and S walls of the inner court. Its length E-to-W is 90 cubits inside plus 5 cubits for walls, giving a total of 100 cubits. These are the overall measurements of the house (v. 13), whose overall N-to-S dimension is the same as the westerly building between inner court walls (v. 14).

6. Recapitulation. Ezekiel 41:15 lists additional features of this westerly house having something like galleries at the N and S sides in three stories (cf. 42:3–4). The measurement of 100 cubits (42:8) refers to the length of these galleries. (See below for construction and meaning of the term *galleries*.) The specifications of this building (the length of the galleries is parenthetical, given to designate the particular side of the building on which they are located), the temple, and the porches of the court are listed without measurements, which indicates that this is a mere résumé, not a separate new set of measurements.

The recapitulation continues through Ezek. 41:16a, with an enumeration of the thresholds, and latticed (covered) windows found here and there among the three buildings. Before the recapitulation is finished, a feature suggested by the word *threshold* is introduced: "over against" (KJV) anticipates the lintel that would later be used in Herod's temple as formed with five oak beams that alternated with a course of stone. G. E. Wright (*Biblical Archaeology* [1956], 140) supports the definite possibility that this was the method in Herod's temple; it was used in older periods, as he observes and is most likely the procedure employed in Ezekiel's temple. At the jambs also are post formations set under the lintels. The measurements as a résumé continue in v. 17 for the interior and exterior wall areas, the measurement of each particular area having been carefully determined.

The decoration of the house walls is described as alternating representations of palm trees and double-faced cherubim (Ezek. 41:18–20; cf. 1 Ki. 6:29; 7:36), only two faces shown because on a flat surface in straight bas-relief it is impossible to show more than two faces. They probably should be considered to have four faces, as in the vision (ch. 1). The posts of the door to the Holy Place were square in section (41:21); the "face" (KJV) of the door posts was similar to that of the door posts of the Holy Place.

7. Additional features. The altar of incense is described as made of wood (Ezek. 41:22) and lacking the gold covering of the altar of Solomon's temple. It is three cubits high and probably square (as in the tabernacle and presumably in Solomon's temple), since only one dimension is given. It has horns, for corner pieces apart from horns have no meaning. The term "length" (KJV) should be rendered "base" (NIV, NRSV), for this is the nearest equivalent in spelling and form of letters that could be miswritten for "length." The doors themselves are formed in pairs of leaves folding back on themselves so that when opened against the jambs they occupy smaller areas of the floor (vv. 23–24). The same cherubs and palm trees are also carved upon the doors and the walls (v. 25).

A further note is added describing the façade of the porch (Ezek. 41:25b); it has thick planks, a retrospective note on the construction of the lintel above the doorway. Light is admitted into the porch by the same latticed windows noted elsewhere, in the N and S walls. They also are located in the side chamber walls (v. 26). The thick beams (v. 25) may be the large beams supporting the plank floors of the side chambers. The walls of the porch, the side chambers, and their floor beams are decorated only with carvings of palm trees, denoting the lesser sanctity of these areas.

8. Supporting buildings. Ezekiel's attention was next directed to another set of buildings in the outer court (Ezek. 42:1). He was led out of the inner court through the N gate to a building that backed up to the wall forming the enclosure of the "separate place" (KJV; NIV, "temple courtyard"). The reference here to a building on the N requires two separate structures; the number of chambers are approximately the same, with an access passage between of 10 cubits width. The S building is 100 cubits long E to W and 20 cubits wide N to S (v. 2); the N building is 50 cubits long and 20 cubits N to S likewise. At the W end of these buildings is a clear area (46:20) for cooking the offerings. The doors of the S building are on the N side (42:2), that is, they open off the common passage between them. They likewise span to the "separate place," for the priests are to lay their garments in the cells to avoid defiling them by contact with the common people (42:14); to avoid this, they cannot go out into the outer court, but they are able to enter the cells directly from the inner court.

The cell building is three-storied, as seen in the term *šĕlīšī* H8958 (Ezek. 42:3), which means third, not three (cf. Gen. 6:16), for only the third story has galleries (*ʾattiq* H916). The text of Ezek. 42:1–3 should now be understood as in the following free translation: "Then he brought me out into the outer court by the direction of the N way and brought me to the cell-building that was opposite the separate place, and that was opposite the building on the N, along the front by length one hundred cubits, with a door in the N, and by width fifty cubits [v. 8], opposite the twenty cubits of the inner court and opposite the paving that was in the outer court; having gallery facing gallery in the third story."

The last phrase may be understood as referring to galleries that face one another across the passage between the buildings. This passage provides access to the chambers (Ezek. 42:4) and is 10 cubits wide. The length of the passage is not stated, but a way of one cubit is expressed that bears no logical relation to the building or passage. If this is considered to be a cubit-wide platform running along the face of the building there is no grammatical connection expressing the relationship. Hence, it is best to understand that it refers to a wall of one cubit width to serve as a screen wall extending eastward from the outer building (cf. v. 7, discussed below). In vv. 5–6 the construction of chambers and third-story galleries is described. Since pillars are not employed to support the outer wall of the gallery, the method of a supporting wall is used at the outer gallery wall and in the first and second stories at the line of the wall common to the gallery and chambers in the third floor. The existence of the columns (not actually mentioned) is suggested by the columns in the outer court, possibly between or along the chambers against its outer wall.

There is a wall opposite the chambers, 50 cubits long (Ezek. 42:7), erected parallel to the chamber building and extending in the direction of the gates. If this is a proper understanding, there must be another interpretation of the one cubit dimension of v. 4, but it is not possible to determine the meaning with the limited architectural terminology available. The phrase, "before the temple … an hundred cubits" (v. 8 KJV), describes again the length of the chamber building, indicating to which building the wall was related.

This chamber building is repeated on the S side of the inner court. The word "east" in Ezek. 42:10 (KJV, following MT) results from a copyist's error; the NIV and NRSV, following the SEPTUAGINT, read "south." This change of text is supported by v. 12, and the change makes sense in the total context. Thus there are only two sets of chamber buildings, not three, as suggested by some commentators; vv. 10–11 should read, "In the width of the court wall to the south, before the separate place and before the building, there were cells with a way before them, like the cells that stood toward the north."

The following verses (Ezek. 42:13–14) give the function of these buildings. Since they are referred to as being N and S chambers fronting the separate place, there can be only these two buildings, one N and one S. Here in quiet seclusion and contemplation, the priests can eat their sacramental portions of the offerings. The offerings are stored in this place until cooked or baked (meat of the sacrifices was boiled; meal was baked). The chambers provide privacy because the act of eating shared in the holy character of the service. The purpose of sacrifice was communion with Yahweh, and it had to be carried out by those who were ritually pure.

9. The temple precincts. The temple is surrounded by a sacred area and the angel proceeds to measure it: 500 reeds (3,000 cubits) on each side. The measuring process was done to emphasize its sacred character (v. 20)—that it is holy, in contrast to all other areas that are called profane. The "it" measured in v. 15 (KJV) is this area, not the E wall or gate. The relation of the temple complex within this area is that of a city within a wall, the whole being set upon a mountain that rises up to provide the high eminence on which to erect the temple (40:1–2).

It is at this point that one must look to the future for Ezekiel's temple. The terrain of Jerusalem in his time could not accommodate this development. After the events of Zech. 14:1–4, 10, this temple could be set in the place of the height of the present Ḥaram. The peace of the millennium may offer opportunity for construction, and if this temple proclaims holiness, it most certainly agrees with the theme HOLINESS TO THE LORD (Zech. 14:20). The similarity of the house to Solomon's temple assures the people that this is indeed their house, and God's presence in it gives assurance of his favor. The other structures are "teaching" elements, to instruct them in the "way of holiness" (cf. Isa. 35:8).

VI. Zerubbabel's temple

A. The repatriation. Very little data is provided concerning Zerubbabel's temple from which a description may be formulated. The treatment of the temple is done in a context of its significance for the future. HAGGAI gave messianic significance to the temple, as did ZECHARIAH. This was necessary in an age that was approaching the advent of the Son of God. In this era the importance of a visible shrine was reduced, but emphasis was laid upon its significance. This, of course, became the emphasis of STEPHEN in the justification of his message among the people (Acts 7), and to which, through misconception, violent opposition occurred. But the message had a beginning in the days of Zerubbabel.

Not until the conquest of Babylon by CYRUS in 539 B.C. was there any hope that Israel would return to their homeland and their temple be rebuilt (cf. Isa. 44:28, 45:1; 2 Chr. 36:22–23). Cyrus adopted an enlightened policy of repatriation of peoples earlier transported by the Assyrian and Babylonian kings from their homelands (*ANET*, 316). The decree of Cyrus is recorded twice (Ezra 1:1–4 and 6:3–5, quoted from the source [cf. vv. 1–2]), and some have asserted that one of these is not authentic. It is now known, however, that memoranda recording administrative decisions of the royal council were made also, but each in its own format. The latter passage is cast into memorandum form. The oral proclamation has exactly the form of the prophetic "thus saith …" and had equally the force of law with the original memorandum. In content and purpose they are to the same effect (see *JBL* 70 [1940]: 249ff.).

Under the Persian kings, Judah was organized in the satrapy of Trans-Euphrates (Ezra 4:11; NRSV, "Beyond the River"), and in the days of DARIUS I was under the control of a governor at Samaria (cf. 6:6). When the Jews appealed to Darius because of the repressive measures of the governor, the control

Zerubbabel's temple was built in the same area as the earlier Solomonic and later Herodian structures. (View of the temple mount to the NW.)

of Jerusalem was diverted from Samaria (v. 7) and another governor was appointed.

Certain vessels taken from the temple of Solomon by NEBUCHADNEZZAR were delivered to SHESHBAZZAR (Ezra 1:8–11), prince of Judah, who led a contingent up to Jerusalem (Ezra 1:11) along with ZERUBBABEL (2:2). Sheshbazzar had been made governor of Judea by Cyrus (Ezra 1:8, 11), who allowed a measure of local autonomy to the separate peoples. Sheshbazzar came to Jerusalem and laid the foundation of the temple (5:16). When Zerubbabel is said to set forward the work (3:8 et al.), it would appear that he functioned as the deputy of Sheshbazzar. As deputy he was on the site and had the initial contact with the Samaritans who later attempted to frustrate the work (4:5). In the second year of Darius, the prophets Haggai and Zechariah stirred him up to renewed activity (5:1). It is possible that at this time Sheshbazzar was deceased, for Zerubbabel was the governor (Hag. 1:1–14).

B. Reconstruction. Sheshbazzar, at Jerusalem in the second year after the return (Ezra 3:2) in the seventh month, laid the foundation of the temple (5:16); this was effected through Zerubbabel (3:8) and the builders (v. 10). In the previous year in the seventh month (3:1–3), the great altar of burnt offering had been set up on its foundation (3:2), the sacrifices had been restored that there might be a place of entreaty (3:3), and the Feast of Tabernacles was promptly observed. The start of the reconstruction of the temple was delayed (v. 6b) because materials from Syria had not yet arrived (v. 7).

According to the decree of Cyrus (Ezra 6:3–4), the temple was to be built 60 cubits wide and 60 cubits high. In the light of the dimensions of the temples of Solomon and Ezekiel, chambers on the sides and rear were included (see below, VI.C). According to the width of Ezekiel's temple and the rebuilding activities of Josiah, these dimensions appear to be authentic and support the essential identity of the later character of the Solomonic temple and Ezekiel's temple. The temple was completed in the sixth year of Darius in the month Adar (twelfth month, 516–515 B.C., Ezra 6:15) Upon its completion, the Shekinah (glory) of Yahweh did not fill the house. It waits for the return of Christ (cf. Ezek. 43:1–5). The temple of Zerubbabel is known as the second temple, which continued until the year c. 20 B.C., lasting more than one hundred years longer than Solomon's temple.

1. Construction. Included in the decree of Cyrus was authorization to secure building materials at the expense of the Persian royal treasury (Ezra 6:4). The method of construction followed the previous system. The reference in v. 4 to three rows of stones and a row of timber beams quite possibly refers to the construction of the wall surrounding the inner court of Solomon's temple (1 Ki. 6:36). There was at once an obvious difference discernible between this temple and the temple of Solomon. Many elderly people (Ezra 3:12) had seen Solomon's temple, and when they saw the results of the foundation work they wept, for it seemed inferior by comparison. This was no doubt because of size, the working of stone, and the quality and size of the finished foundation.

Shortly after rebuilding began, obstructionist attempts to frustrate it arose from the people of Samaria because their offer to help was rejected since they were not of the Jewish folk (Ezra 4:1–5). Their opposition persisted to force of arms (v. 23), and they shut down the work until the second year of Darius the Great (520 B.C.), when appeal was made to him on the grounds that the restoration had been ordered by Cyrus (cf. 5:17 with 6:3–7).

The original adversaries were the Samaritans, who were descended from those whom the Assyrian king brought in to replace the deported northern Israelites. In the days of Haggai and Zechariah the chief adversaries were named: TATTENAI the governor and SHETHAR-BOZENAI and his cohorts (Ezra 5:3). In their report to Darius in an attempt to curtail rebuilding they demanded a search to see if Cyrus did indeed make a decree, which finally was found in ECBATANA (6:2), confirming all the claims of the Jews.

It would appear that the early delay in building progress prevented the raising of the walls of the temple. When, therefore, a foundation is said to have been laid on the twenty-fourth day of the ninth month of the second year of Darius, a question arises as to just what the laying of the foundation was (Hag. 2:18). The year was 520 B.C.—sixteen years after the original laying, a time when little was done (Ezra 5:16). When Haggai and Zechariah stirred up Zerubbabel by their preaching, work began again with the ceremony of laying the foundation, that is, a ceremony in which the foundation was prepared to receive the wall above.

The construction of the temple was delayed because of the physical and legal opposition by the adversaries (Ezra 4:6). The physical opposition prevented the transportation of building materials from the land round about (Hag. 1:8), and the molestation of the builders as they traveled back and forth from their houses outside Jerusalem's walls to the temple. This would have effectively cut off the work. In the second year of Darius, however, they had been able to build comfortable, even prosperous, homes, for paneled houses are noted (Hag. 1:4).

So Haggai addressed them on this invidious relationship, that God's house should no longer lay waste. The affirmations of the covenant of God with Israel included the erection of a house of worship to be a source of strength for observing the covenant. The efforts of Haggai and Zechariah were directed to stirring up in the people a consciousness of their covenant obligations. To enforce his prophecies, Haggai demanded that the people consider their ways (Hag. 1:5), that they should understand that the drought existed because they had neglected covenant obligations (cf. Deut. 28:32 et al.), suggesting that the obligation in this case was the erection of the temple (Hag. 1:9). Until they put their heart into the task, they could not expect the blessing of God; hence, God had called forth the drought (v. 11). It was at the urging of the prophet Zechariah that the governor, Jeshua the high priest, and all the people obeyed God and began reconstruction in the twenty-fourth day of the sixth month of the second year of Darius (Ezra 3:2, 8).

2. Significance of the temple. As the work progressed, inevitable reference was made to its inferior state in relation to the grand state of the temple destroyed by NEBUZARADAN (2 Ki. 25:8–10). Yet this would not deter the advance, since it was God's house; it was an assurance of his redemptive work (Ezra 3:5–9; cf. Dan. 9:24). Yet the attitude persisted, for in the ninth month again Haggai mentioned the drought and that the reluctance of the people made them unclean before God (Hag. 1:10–11). But God's purposes must be fulfilled, and out of his grace he assured them that the completion of the building was no impossible task for the few people, and would be accomplished under the leadership of Zerubbabel (Zech. 4:9); because of its redemptive symbolism, it must not be despised as a small thing (v. 10). Zerubbabel had been concerned about the attitude of surrounding peoples, but Yahweh assured him (Hag. 2:21–22) of the ultimate triumph of the ways of God over men. Zerubbabel would see that victory and would realize that his labor would be a seal of triumph in the face of obstacles. The spirit of God would oversee the work to take it forward to completion (Zech. 4:9).

Zechariah likewise directed words of assurance to the people on the twenty-fourth day of the eleventh month in the second year of Darius (Zech 1:7), symbolized by the measuring line (1:16). It was further certified by the promise of Yahweh to come and dwell in their midst (2:10–13; cf. Ezek. 43:1–5). The eschatological significance of the temple is given (Zech. 6:12–13). Jeshua as priest signified the priestly character of the "Branch," the offspring of David who would build the temple of Yahweh, who is Christ (Jn. 2:21; Matt. 16:18) and who will dwell in his people. There is also the eschatological hope of Israel's dwelling in their own land, symbolized by their occupation of Jerusalem (Zech. 2:4–5).

3. Materials for the temple. Materials for the temple adornment came from the people through freewill offerings (Ezra 2:68–69). Included in the decree of Cyrus was the ordinance that the Jews who remained in Babylon were to make their freewill offerings for the temple as part of their obligations to their brethren who returned

C. History of the temple

1. In the era of Ezra and Nehemiah. The work of reconstruction was finished in the sixth year of Darius, 515 B.C. (Ezra 6:15), and was dedicated with much rejoicing. The courses of the priests were instituted (v. 18), and the first PASSOVER at the new building was celebrated by the people (v. 19). This is the last mention of the temple and Jerusalem in the OT. Ezra came to Jerusalem in the seventh year of ARTAXERXES I, 458 B.C. He carried up silver and gold for the temple for either adornment or offering (7:16–20). If additional funds were necessary for restorative purposes, they were to be secured from the royal treasury (v. 20). The officials of the satrapy that included Jerusalem were also assigned the duty of assisting in this matter and were obligated to keep within a limit (vv. 21–22). The restorative work was subject to the commands of the "God of heaven" (v. 23), as a petition to him for his favor upon the empire. It would appear that the efforts of "force and power" (4:23 NRSV) may have been extensive, and although complaint had been directed by Bishlam, Mithredath, and Tabeel to Artaxerxes, information based on the decrees of Cyrus and Darius finally overcame local opposition. The royal largess committed to Ezra (ch. 7) provided rectification of the efforts of the adversary to curtail the work. The record of the return of Ezra and the execution of his commission is given in ch. 8.

Ezra's ministry in Jerusalem involved the separation of the Israelites from "defilement" because of intermarriage with the surrounding peoples (Ezra 9–10). Ezra prayed and carried out the necessary judicial activities. This was done to prevent the collapse of the Jewish state through absorption into other peoples.

Nehemiah's record carries forward in brief glimpses the function of the temple among the people and their various attitudes toward it. Nehemiah came to Jerusalem in the twentieth year of Artaxerxes (445 B.C.), thirteen years after Ezra (cf. Ezra 7:8). The report of the condition of disrepair of the city (Neh. 1:3) moved him to the realization of the need of leadership; hence his prayer involving a request that the king release him from his royal service so he could return to Jerusalem (vv. 5–11). He asked specifically for wood beams to repair the fortress at the gate of the temple (2:8). The singers and the Levites were again appointed to their place in the temple, providing a functioning temple worship service to encourage the people (7:1).

In the covenant renewal ceremony (Neh. 9–10), reference is made to the ordinance of the one-third shekel to support the temple ritual as an implementation of the vow of loyalty to God (10:32; cf. v. 29). Also enumerated are other offerings of firstfruits of various kinds from the field and garden, and even the housewives' bread dough (vv. 34–38). These were to be brought to the house of God (v. 38) and stored in its chambers (v. 37). These chambers were built in the reconstruction of Zerubbabel. Tithes, also, were stored in the treasure chambers (vv. 38–39). Officials were later appointed over the separate chambers as treasurers to oversee the ingatherings (12:44).

When Nehemiah left to return to King Artaxerxes in Babylon, ecclesiastical affairs fell into disarray. ELIASHIB, the high priest, set apart a chamber in the court of the temple for TOBIAH (Neh. 13:7), who was an Ammonite (2:10) and a former adversary of the work of restoring the city. This was the result of the spiritual indifference that set in soon after Nehemiah left and quickly brought about what could not have been done by direct frontal attack (cf. 13:10–12). Nehemiah, on his return, saw it as contamination of the Lord's house, drove Tobiah out, and had the temple areas sanctified (vv. 8–9).

2. From Nehemiah to the Maccabees. There are a few references to this period in the APOCRYPHA. The book of 1 Esdras is primarily a parallel compilation of 2 Chr. 35–36, Ezra 1–10, and Neh. 7:13—8:13 (see ESDRAS, FIRST). No constructional information is provided. The completion date of Zerubbabel's temple is given in the Greek as the twenty-third day (1 Esd. 7:5) instead of the third day (cf. Ezra 6:15). It may be that the part translated "twenty" fell out in transmission.

JOSEPHUS (*Apion* 1.22 §19) quoted Hecataeus of Abdera on the general arrangement of the temple complex in the era of Alexander. The enclosing stone wall is described as 500 ft. (Gk. *pentaplethros*) long and 100 cubits broad with double cloisters within. The altar was erected of unfinished white stones to 20 cubits each way and 10 cubits high. The house contained the altar (of incense) made of gold and the lampstand (also of gold) having a flame that was never allowed to go out. Hecataeus distinguished this temple in its character from other temples by the fact that there were no idols or gifts of such things by eminent personages, where also no growing things were planted, as was done in pagan temples of other peoples.

In the book of ECCLESIASTICUS, the high priest SIMON II (end of 3rd cent. B.C.) is described as repairing the temple (Sir. 50:1–3) for which he built great fortifying walls with turrets to protect it. Simon also provided a cistern for water storage, the size indicated by a hyperbolic reference to Solomon's molten sea. Then followed a panegyric description of Simon, his person, and the conduct of his service in the temple. This is the only description of the temple service of this period.

ANTIOCHUS III rewarded the Jews for their support in his early campaign against Egypt (Jos. *Ant.* 12.3.3) to the extent of providing sacrifices and ordering repairs, including the completion of the erection of cloisters, as well as other repairs that in the estimation of local authorities needed to be done. Necessary materials were to be provided, free of taxation, from the forests of Judea and other countries. Taxes on the Jews for three years were remitted to facilitate this work. In addition Antiochus decreed that no unpurified person be allowed in the temple precincts. Included in the general ban of the impure were unclean animals.

Next in order of time are the records preserved in the books of MACCABEES. The account of the plundering of the temple by Antiochus IV Epiphanes in 170 B.C. is given in 1 Macc. 1:20–24. There was in the temple the golden altar of incense; the table of showbread; the lightstand and its attendant equipment; many implements of cups and bowls and incense holders; the crowns; the veil and gold plating at the wall where formerly had been the cherubim. In addition, he rifled the treasuries and departed with gold, silver, and other precious vessels as well as many other items. Some of these were the vessels Sheshbazzar had brought back from Babylon. One learns at this time that the furniture was in the second temple and also that a new veil had been hung. Shortly thereafter, it was decreed by Antiochus that the sacrifices should cease (1:45).

In December of 168 B.C. (25th Kislev, Dec.–Jan.), Antiochus invaded Jerusalem, penetrated into the temple precincts, and by sacrificing a sow he desecrated the altar of God. The priest MATTATHIAS and his sons raised the standard of revolt at the village of MODEIN where began the Maccabean revolt. Three years later, in Kislev of 165, Judas MACCABEE came to Jerusalem after defeating the forces of Antiochus, and when the people saw the courts overgrown and in disrepair, they broke into weeping. Promptly they raised a new altar of unhewn stones (1 Macc 4:47) after dismantling the polluted one, proceeded to repair the Holy of Holies and the Holy Place, and then hallowed the courts for use. Vessels newly made were brought in, including the lampstand, the altar of incense, and the table of showbread. Incense was then lighted as was the lampstand, new bread was placed on the table, and a new veil was hung (vv. 49–51). On the next day, the twenty-fifth, the altar was sanctified and sacrifices were resumed amid great rejoicing. In addition, the doors of the gates that had been torn off were replaced and the gates were rededicated. The celebration of the altar became the basis for the Jewish festival of Hanukkah (see DEDICATION, FEAST OF). It signified particularly the relighting of the lampstand in the Holy Place. While Antigonus was away campaigning in Persia to replenish his coffers, walls earlier destroyed in his attack on Jerusalem were rebuilt, probably the walls of Simon II.

In the year 161 B.C., ALCIMUS, friend of Demetrius I king of Syria, tore down the wall forming the inner court of the temple (1 Macc. 9:54), intending to allow Gentiles free access into the inner precincts. In the year 154, the warlike motions of Demetrius evoked alarm in Judea, causing Jonathan, the new Maccabean leader, to strengthen the outer walls of the temple (10:11) with stone walls four feet thick. Forces of conflict thus required the Jews to transform their temple into a fortress for protection. Simon, Jonathan's brother, became high priest after the death of the former and he further strengthened the temple defenses (13:52).

ARISTEAS, in his account of the origin of the SEPTUAGINT, related in glowing language the presentation of furniture to the temple by PTOLEMY Philadelphus (285–245 B.C.), king of Egypt. This furniture consisted of an outsize solid gold table of showbread handsomely decorated with wreathed work, fruits, and precious stones held in settings. Mixing bowls, a meander of scale-like appearance, and gold vials with wreathed work decoration were also included. Aristeas claims to have accompanied the embassy bearing the gifts to Jerusalem. There he was impressed by the fortress walls of the temple standing more than seventy cubits (*Letter of Aristeas* 84). The portal was covered with a costly curtain waving in the breeze. The stone-paved court floor was necessary because of the frequent washings to remove the blood of the sacrifices (§88). Cisterns underground provided ample water supplies.

Aristeas continued with an overstressed description of the labor of the priests in the sacrifices (§92), and mentioned being taken to the fortress adjacent to the temple that had walls higher than those of the temple (§§100ff.). Aristeas described the presence of an inexhaustible spring within the temple precincts. No trace of such a spring has ever been found in the area, and for the tradition no reasonable ground can be adduced (however, cf. Ezek. 47). Since nothing is written in 1 Maccabees relating to these gifts of Ptolemy, it might appear that this record in *Aristeas* is imaginary, used as supporting material for his story of the production of the LXX. He agreed, however, that the temple was oriented to the E on its height in the city.

3. From the Maccabees to Herod. Josephus is the source of much of the information regarding the temple in this period (on his reliability as a historian see JOSEPHUS, FLAVIUS III; on the history of this period see HASMONEAN). He reports that Alexander Jannaeus (104–78 B.C.) was involved in an incident in the temple (*Ant.* 13.13.5), and this account sheds light on the arrangement of the temple courts. The Jews resented Alexander's officiating as high priest and pelted him with citrons. There was easy access to the high priest at the altar (cf. 1 Macc. 4:38–48), for the wall of the court marking off the area of the altar was not so high as to prevent it. Alexander had a wooden palisade erected about the priests' court to prevent future repetitions of their displeasure.

Aristobulus II (69–63 B.C.) fled to the temple and used it as a fortress when ARETAS III of Nabatea moved against him on behalf of his brother Hyrcanus II, the rightful high priest and king. When both Hyrcanus and Aristobulus appealed to POMPEY for adjudication, he took so long to make up his mind that Aristobulus took precipitate action and was taken into custody and detained. His cohorts, however, seized the temple and withstood a siege by Pompey for three months. Pompey finally breached the walls with battering rams, then slaughtered the officiating priests and 12,000 other Jews. During the siege, defending Jews cut the bridge across the Tyropoeon Valley by which access was made to the city on the western ridge (Jos. *War* 1.7.2). Pompey profaned the Holy of Holies by entering it to satisfy his curiosity but took no plunder. Afterward he ordered it rehallowed (*Ant.* 14.3.1–4; cf. *War* 1.7.6).

Later Crassus took a side trip from his campaign against the PARTHIANS to Jerusalem and carried off the treasure Pompey had refused to take (*Ant.* 14.4.2). In skirmishes with Herod, the Jews frequently fled to the temple because of its defensive character (*Ant.* 14.13.4). When Herod had been declared king of the Jews by the Roman Senate, he proceeded to move against Antigonus, last of the Hasmoneans. In the attack on the city and temple, certain of the cloisters were destroyed by fire (14.16.3), but when the city was taken, he prevented the soldiery and foreigners from entering the temple and desecrating it, taking thought for his future domains. To deliver the city and temple from further plundering, Herod bought off the soldiers and their officers. Not until the eighteenth year of Herod's reign did further development of the temple take place.

VII. Herod's temple

A. Purpose. Zerubbabel's temple had assumed the proportions of a fortress. Though the building was highly regarded by the Jews, this fortress character rendered it subject to criticism in Herod's opinion and therefore rebuilding was necessary. His principal and ostensible reason was presented in a speech to the people, saying that the temple did not measure up to its former glory, specifically noting that it lacked some 60 cubits of height from that of preexilic times (Jos. *Ant.* 15.11.1); this comment obviously referred to the height of the preexilic porch as 120 cubits (2 Chr. 3:4 MT; see above, IV.E.2), for Zerubbabel's temple was only 60 cubits high by order of Darius (Ezra 6:3). The actual reason, given before Josephus recorded Herod's speech, is that the rebuilding was to provide among the Jews an eternal remembrance of his name. Yet the Jews were fearful that, once started, it would not be

TEMPLE, JERUSALEM

Artistic reconstruction of the Herodian temple. (View to the W.)

completed through lack of adequate funds. To allay their fears, Herod assured the people that all materials required for completion would be made ready beforehand. By way of further assurance that no unacceptable persons would enter upon the premises, for the building would be in use meantime, he trained some priests as masons, others as carpenters, and the work commenced (*Ant.* 15.11.2).

B. Data. Sources for the description of Herod's temple are not many. Josephus in his *Antiquities* (15.11) and *War* (5.5), the Mishnah tractate *Middot*, and the few references in the NT comprise the principal source material. A few references are found in parts of the Talmud. Since Josephus wrote nearer to the time of the temple than when *Middot* was composed, his record is preferable in some cases, yet *Middot* does indeed provide dimensions where Josephus does not. Actually only a small portion of the NT references to the temple bear on its structure, for most refer to attitudes of the Jews toward it. That the temple was an imposing structure is evident from them.

C. Construction

1. The temple proper. The work of rebuilding the sanctuary (Holy Place and Holy of Holies) was begun in the eighteenth year of Herod's reign, 20–19 B.C. (Jos. *Ant.* 15.11.6). The white stone used was probably the so-called *mezzeh* stone native to the area, finely cut and polished. The dimensions of the stones given by Josephus (25 x 8 x 12 cubits) have often been thought to be an instance of hyperbole, but recent excavations have uncovered massive stones, one of them about 40 ft. long. The former structure was removed down to bedrock and new foundation stones were laid, 100 cubits long but 100 cubits wide at the porch, and 60 back of the porch for the Holy Place (Jos. *War* 5.5.4).

There were side chambers at the sides and rear sixty cubits high, and above this was a narrower structure extending an additional forty cubits upward, making a total of 100 cubits (*War* 5.5.5). The façade, or porch, was 100 cubits high and 100 cubits wide, producing an extension of 20 cubits beyond the walls of the Holy Place. The portal in the E face of the porch was 75 cubits high by 25 broad, without doors, exposing to view the Holy Place entrance wall within. Interior measurements of the porch are given as 90 cubits to the ceiling, 50 cubits N to S (length), and 20 broad. The Mishnah (*m. Mid.* 4:7) gives the thickness of the front wall of the porch as 5 cubits, the E-to-W width as 11 cubits (inside), and the Holy Place wall as 6 cubits, a total of 22, near enough to the 20 of Josephus (cf. above on the dimensions of the porch of Ezekiel's temple for the same dimensions). The front wall of the porch was stabilized against outward bulging by the insertion of cedar beams from the Holy Place wall (*m. Mid.* 3:8).

The portal opening was framed by a lintel formed of five oak beams, each separated from the one below by a course of stones, the first beam being one cubit longer on each end than the opening below, and each upper beam one cubit longer on each end than the beam below. Draped on the face of the porch wall were vines of gold-work with gold grape clusters as tall as a man (Jos. *War* 5.5.4). Josephus next described doors to the Holy Place of 55 cubits in height and 16 in breadth. F. J. Hollis (*The Archaeology of Herod's Temple* [1934], 202) rejects this door size as too large for the practical reason that it would be impossible to operate them. The Mishnah (*m. Mid.* 4:1) gives the dimensions as 20 cubits high and 10 wide, more in order of operability.

These doors were doubled, a set on the E side and one on the W side of the doorway. They were formed on a pivot member of half a cubit, an attached leaf member 2.5 cubits wide, with a folding member 2 cubits wide, for a total of 5 cubits, half the opening width. This arrangement provided that the doors cover only half of the wall thickness, 3 cubits, as they laid back against the jambs when open, the fold point abutting. Josephus adds that a great veil was hung over this door, excluding from view the inside of the Holy Place. This is not enumerated in *Middot*; instead at the ceremony of the red heifer, the priest on the Mount of Olives was to look directly into the Holy Place at the propitious moment (*m. Mid.* 2:4). The curtain of which Josephus wrote may have been added at a later time when fears of defilement of the temple by even a look by a foreigner were felt. The area left at the ends of the porch area was occupied by rooms for sacrificial equipment used at the altar (*m. Mid.* 4:7).

The Holy Place itself was 40 cubits long by 20 wide and 60 high (Jos. *War* 5.5.5) and contained a lampstand, the table of showbread, and the altar of incense. The Holy of Holies was separated from the Holy Place by a veil and measured 20 by 20 cubits in plan and 60 cubits high. No furniture was placed in it, but it was considered unapproachable and inviolable. According to the Mishnah tractate *Yoma* (5.1), the partition was two veils, hung one cubit apart, one attached at its N side, the second at its S side, requiring the high priest to pass between the two from S to N to enter the Holy of Holies. It was this curtain that was rent in two when Christ died (Matt. 27:51), showing that the way into the presence of God was open (Heb. 6:19).

Chambers in three stories were built against the side and rear walls of the Holy of Holies, approached from small doors in either side of the porch (Jos. *War* 5.5.5), five on each story on the N and S sides, three in the first and second story, and two on the third story on the W side (*m. Mid.* 4:3). The width of the first-story rooms was 5 cubits, the second was 6, and the third 7 (cf. 1 Ki. 6:6). The difference was effected by cutting back the wall of the Holy Place and Holy of Holies in each upper story by one cubit and resting the floor beams on the shelf thus formed. The side walls of the Holy Place and Holy of Holies were 6 cubits and the outside walls of the chambers were 5 cubits thick; then occurred a space of 3 cubits for water drainage for the suspended ceiling, and an outside wall of 5 cubits, the drainage space occurring only on the N and S sides (*m. Mid.* 4:7). The whole was roofed over all around, forming the wide area for the last stand of the priests who would later resist Titus (Jos. *War* 6.5.1).

Access to the roof was made by progressing through the upper story from the NE corner westward, then southward and eastward to a pole ladder at the SE corner. On the roof surface was a line of stones set flush, which marked the division between the Holy Place and the Holy of Holies. Above the Holy of Holies below the upper roof was a chamber with access openings to enter the Holy of Holies to make repairs. Around the roof was a parapet to guard against persons falling off. The porch face of the Holy Place wall was decorated with gold (leaf?), and the E face of the porch was covered with gold plates, presenting a most brilliant spectacle from the Mount of Olives (Lk. 19:37–44; cf. Matt. 24:1–2).

2. Inner courts. From the porch a descent of twelve steps led to the priests' court. These steps were divided into flights of three treads each, of 1 cubit width and 0.5 cubit height, with a landing of 3 cubits between. Against a top landing of 4 cubits (*m. Mid.* 3:6) a more logical tradition is the 5 cubits of area in the thickness of the front wall of the porch at the portal; the edge of this area would form the top riser of the uppermost flight of steps. The total of 15 cubits in the plan of the steps provide 7 cubits from the bottom riser to the altar. Other calculations bring the bottom riser too near the altar to provide proper area for circulation around it. The total distance from porch wall to altar was 22 cubits (*m. Mid.* 3:6). The height of the steps was 6 cubits, agreeing with the height of Ezekiel's platform (Ezek. 41:8). The temple appears to have been set on a platform the same height as the temples of Solomon and Ezekiel.

The altar was 32 cubits square at the ground, formed with a great plinth course, or foundation, one cubit high, with the next upper face set back one cubit (*m. Mid.* 3:1). The surrounding was filled solid and then timber was laid across the foundation for a height of 5 cubits, the outside face being 30 cubits in length. A structure was placed on top of the surrounding and its face was set back one cubit, thus being 28 cubits square. This second structure was 3 cubits high and there was again a setback of one cubit at the top. At the corners of the surrounding were stone formations, designated horns, 3 cubits high by a cubit square. On top of this was a final level, set back one cubit and one cubit high and giving a square 24 cubits on a side. The total height of the altar reached 10 cubits. The priests walked on the upper space of one cubit and on the next lower one-cubit space. On the top level the sacrificial fires were laid. The 50 cubits square of the base of the altar as given by Josephus (*War* 5.5.6) appears to be much too large for the area available. In relation to previous altars, a rabbinic tradition indicates that the altar of the Herodian temple was more like the postexilic altar, which was enlarged over the preexilic altar (*m. Mid.* 3:1).

Tractate *Middot* presents the tradition of a drainage channel to drain off to the KIDRON the blood sprinkled on the base of the altar. There has been found no physical evidence of such a drain channel from the cave under the Sakhra, so this cannot be used as a main point for locating the altar on the Rock. Moreover, the drain channel was said to start at the SE corner of an altar, whether on the Rock or elsewhere. Access to the altar was by an incline on the S side of 32 cubits long by 16 wide. The stones for the altar and ascent were secured at BETH HAKKEREM (Jer. 6:1; Neh. 3:14).

The sacrifices were slaughtered N of the altar, then hung up on a skinning rack near the slaughterer's shed and skinned before being placed on the wood on the altar (*m. Mid.* 3:5). The laver was placed S of the altar but aligned between the altar and porch (3:6).

The Court of the Priests, the area within the inner court immediately surrounding the temple, was 187 cubits long by 135 wide, N to S (*m. Mid.* 5:1). Surrounding this inner court was the Court of Israel, also 135 cubits N to S and 11 cubits E to W. The length of 135 cubits gives the length of the line separating these two courts at the E of the altar; from the N and S ends of this line, boundaries marked the separation of the two westward to the W limit of the Court of the Priests. The TOSEFTA states that the Court of Israel surrounded the Court of the Priests (*t. Zeb.* 30.6.1). The Court of Israel was at least 11 cubits wide beyond the Court of the Priests on all sides, giving a length of 198 cubits E to W and 157 cubits N to S, and was surrounded by a colonnade. Josephus (*War* 5.6) described a separator between these two courts "about a cubit in height." The Mishnah indicates that the division was a marker set flush on the court surface (*m. Mid.* 2:7).

In the inner court were two other buildings, the building on the N containing a chamber named Parva, and that on the S containing the room of the draw well. Each building had three rooms, which were possibly located partly within the Court of the Priests and partly within the Court of Israel.

The colonnade around the Court of Israel is described as single but otherwise not inferior in any way to the colonnades of the outer court; since the latter were doubled and 30 cubits wide, these were 15 cubits wide on at least three sides and possibly on the W side, although Josephus (*War* 5.5.2–3) seems to indicate otherwise. The outer side of the colonnade was a wall 25 cubits high (ibid.). In this wall and projecting outward at least 30 cubits were gates, three in the N wall, one in the E wall called the Great Gate (Muehsam, *Coin and Temple*, 26), and three in the S wall (cf. *m. Mid.* 1:4). On either side of the Great Gate was a chamber; the S chamber was called Phinehas, where vestments were stored, and the N chamber was that of the maker of the flat cakes of the daily baked offering.

3. Women's Court. Eastward through the Great Gate at the E side of the Court of Israel (Jos. *War* 5.5.3), which was fashioned of brass, led to a fifteen-step stairway down from the level of the Court of Israel to the level of the Court of Women. These steps were curved (*m. Mid.* 2:6) and located at the middle of the W side and on line with the portal of the porch. Josephus (*War* 5.5.2) described a terrace against the enclosing wall of the colonnade at the S side of the inner court, being 10 cubits wide, called the Ḥel (*m. Mid.* 2:3). One reached this terrace by a flight of five steps, each 5 cubits wide down from the gates in the S wall. Beyond the terrace were fourteen steps according to Josephus, but twelve according to *Middot*. Since the terrain slopes up from E to W, the steps would have to be more in number on the E than the W, two being sliced off by the rising ground. These steps did not continue around on the W because the ground rose rapidly. Since fifteen steps led up from the Women's Court to the Court of Israel, the former must have been only slightly higher than the level outside at the foot of the fourteen steps up to the Ḥel.

The Women's Court was 135 cubits square between bounding lines (*m. Mid.* 2:5). Outside this area at the four corners were courts 40 cubits square. The SE court was named Nazirite; the NE, Woodshed; the NW, Leper's Chamber; and the SW, Shemanyah, possibly meaning "oil of Yahweh" (Hollis, *Archaeology*, 287). At a time later than the construction of the Women's Court with the courts at its corners, balconies were added for use by the women so they could see the ceremonies inside the inner court (cf. *m. Mid.* 2:6). At the W side of the Women's Court, approximately on the same level and under the Court of Israel, were a series of chambers where musical instruments were stored (*m. Mid.* 2:7).

4. The Soreg. Below the Ḥel and beyond the steps down from it was an area bounded by a low wall called the Soreg (*m. Mid.* 2:3), 3 handbreadths high, but 3 cubits high according to Josephus (*War* 5.5.2), and a finely wrought trellis work with ornamental columns on top. The Mishnah probably describes the wall in its earlier form, whereas Josephus describes it at a time after it had been embellished. On this wall on the outward side was placed a warning: "No Gentile may enter within the railing around the sanctuary and within the enclosure. Whosoever should be caught will render himself liable to the death penalty which will inevitably follow." This probably was located N of the stairs up from the Huldah Gate.

5. The outer walls. The present area of the Ḥaram esh-Sharif (Noble Sanctuary), where the Qubbet es Sakhra (Dome of the Rock) is located, is considerably larger than the area of the court of Herod's temple. The present court is trapezoidal in shape, 929 ft. on the S side, 1,596 ft. on the W, 1,041 ft. on the N, and 1,556 ft. on the E. Only the SW corner and the NE corner are right angles. The E and W walls coincide so markedly in appearance and location with the description of Herod's works (Jos. *Ant.* 15.11.3; *War* 5.5.1) that these in general must be considered Herodian (cf. Simons, *Jerusalem*, 391–92). That the W wall and the southernmost part of the E wall are of the same age as the S wall is

Limestone inscription from the 1st-cent. Jerusalem temple, warning that any foreigner entering the wall surrounding the sanctuary forfeits his life.

seen in the sameness of the older (lower) stonework in these walls. Neither the E nor W walls of Herod's work extended as far N as the present northern limits of the Haram, for the fortress ANTONIA was connected to the outer court by cloisters (Jos. *War* 2.15.6), and there was a moat (*Ant.* 14.4.2) between the N wall of Herod's enclosure and Antonia (C. Warren, *Plans, Elevations, Etc., Showing the Results of the Excavations at Jerusalem* [1884]).

An indication of the N end of the E wall in Herod's time was found in the slight outward bulge in it just N of the "Golden Gate" (Gate to Mt. Olive) at a place called "Solomon's Throne." This point was about 1,158 ft. N of the SE corner. In the southerly end of this E wall was another slight bend in the wall, about 240 ft. N of the corner. At about 105 ft. N of the corner was a construction joint the full height of the wall, indicative of later construction (for the significance of this joint, see below, "royal portico"). From this joint northward to the "Throne of Solomon" the masonry originally below ground has marginal drafts but projecting fields, whereas the stones S of the joint have smooth faces full height. Josephus (*Ant.* 20.9.7) relates that in the general repairing of the temple complex, Herod Agrippa was petitioned to rebuild the porticoes atop this E wall. It would seem that this colonnade was not built by Herod the Great since the repairing would have come too soon after its completion. It would appear, then, that this wall was pre-Herodian and that the wall S of the joint and the S wall was built by Herod the Great. Simons (*Jerusalem*, 422) shows that the E wall was actually a former city wall that Herod incorporated into his enlarged temple enclosure, thus providing more space E of the Sakhra for the temple area, later occupied in part by the Women's Court.

The W wall above and below ground presents a single homogenous character in its entire length. South of Barclay's Gate (gate at the Valley Stairs) the lower courses down to bedrock have drafted edges but rough fields, indicative that they were below original finished grades. Stones above these and to the N have drafted edges and smoothed fields, pointing out that they were above the original finished grade, thus showing the general lay of the terrain at the time the wall was built. The present ground surface, however, is above the top of the stones with rough fields, showing the extent of fill to modern times.

The S wall is made up of two types of stones. To the E of the Double Gate to the SE corner the stones from bedrock to the later renovations are smoothed face with drafted edges, whereas to the W of Double Gate below original grade they are rough face fields with drafted edges, the same as the southern end of the W wall. The area thus enclosed by these walls is said to have been double the area of the previous sanctuary (Jos. *War* 1.21.1). It would appear that a large part of this occurred at the S end, partly on the E side and the rest on the W side.

6. The gates. In the S wall are indications of three gates. A single gate was located 105 ft. from the SE corner, the triple gate at 295 ft., and the double gate at about 558 ft. Their sills occurred presumably at or near the original ground level. The double and triple gates opened into tunnels leading northward and terminating in a staircase leading up to the outer court. The Soreg would have been situated N of this because foreigners would have used this approach from the lower city. Their floors were approximately at bedrock and provided access from the city to the S. The gates are walled up, and the double gate is partially hidden by a disfiguring mass of broken buildings covering the western half.

Josephus (*Ant.* 15.11.5) recorded four gates in the W wall. Since at ROBINSON'S ARCH the excavations reveal no bridge piers across the Tyropoeon Valley at this location, the omission indicated that there was no gate, but rather a balcony overlooking the valley (Simons, *Jerusalem*, 424). Josephus (*War* 2.16.3) indicates a bridge connection between the temple and city that was near the first wall, and this bridge served the main gate, or first gate. This was the location of Wilson's Arch (causeway gate), which is also the area of the Gate of the Chain (Bab es-Silsileh). At Barclay's Gate (gate at the Valley Stairs), a stepped way led down into the Tyropoeon Valley and up on the other side to the SW hill. The other two gates were situated to the N of the Gate of the Chain and led to the suburbs, that is, that part of the city N of the first wall (Jos. *Ant.* 15.11.5).

In the N wall was one gate called Tadi (*m. Mid.* 1:3). Josephus's narrative (*War* 2.19.5) suggests that it was below the level of the outer court, thus in the deep ditch at the N. There was only one gate in the E wall (*m. Mid.* I, 4), replaced by the present Golden Gate of Byzantine construction (Simons, *Jerusalem*, 428), and built over an earlier gate.

The area within the enclosing walls was filled in to provide the necessary required court space. At the SE corner are Solomon's Stables, formed of stone paving over arches supported by columns down to bedrock. This structure appears to be of later date than the Herodian work, and was used by the Crusaders. The tops of the present outer walls date from even later times. The level of the royal portico may have been somewhat lower than the level of the Ḥaram at its S end.

7. The colonnades. Josephus (*Ant.* 15.11.3) records that Herod enclosed the outer court with "very large cloisters … and he laid out larger sums of money on them than had been done before him," so that by comparison his were the most imposing. It has also been pointed out that on the E side the porch known as SOLOMON'S COLONNADE (Acts 3:11) existed previous to the work of Herod (cf. Muehsam's revealing study, *Coin and Temple*, 33–34). Muehsam (ibid., 35) states that the ark was framed inside the gate pictured on the coin of year two and that a colonnade was shown in the foreground (i.e., lower down, for at the ceremony of the red heifer Solomon's Colonnade would have been quite below the line of sight of the priest from the Mount of Olives into the sanctuary). The evidence from the coin indicates that Solomon's Colonnade was open on the E face, not closed by a stone wall.

Herod built a new double-aisle colonnade on the W side and probably rebuilt a colonnade on the N (cf. Jos. *Ant.* 14.16.2, which points out that colonnades were destroyed in Herod's attack on Jerusalem). These were built of white marble carved from single stones, 25 cubits high and spaced at 30 between rows (Jos. *War* 5.5.2). At the S wall he erected a three-aisle colonnade with the center aisle higher than the side aisle (*Ant.* 15.11.5). This was called the royal portico, so designated perhaps in remembrance of the location of Solomon's royal quarters that once occupied this area (cf. Simon, *Jerusalem*, 101 n. 1).

At the S side of the portico was a wall to which the S row of columns were attached, but in which presumably windows were made. The rows of columns were spaced 30 ft. apart at the side aisles and 45 ft. at the center aisle, which was twice as high as the side aisles. Columns were said to be 27 ft. high, with bases of doubled *tori* and capitals in the Corinthian order. The diameter of the columns was such that three men were necessary to surround a column by joining arms, about 4.5 ft. in diameter. The overall height to the top of the façade of the side aisles was 50 ft.; with the center aisle rising above the side aisles, a clerestory resulted. The "front" face of which Josephus wrote (*Ant.* 15.11.5) can be construed as the S face above the high S wall: "the fourth front of this court facing south."

The colonnade was formed of fine polished stonework, having rectangular pillars to which the columns were attached, thus providing windows through which the country to the S could be observed. The roof beams were carefully framed onto (interwoven with) the stonework. The ceilings of the cloisters were decorated with carved cedar paneling. Since the roof was constructed of wood, the high center clerestory probably was also constructed of wood walls of posts and wood paneling, with the roof framed of wood beams as were the lower roofs. Windows would have been necessary in the clerestory walls to let light in to permit observation of the carved ceilings. The clerestory structure would have towered 100 ft. or more into the air.

In this royal portico were 162 columns and their length was a stadion (or 630 ft., Olympic measure). If there were four rows of columns, each row would have had forty or forty-one columns, depending on how this portico was joined to adjacent structures. The maximum spaces would be forty, which works out to 15.75 ft. for column spacing. Not knowing the aisle spacing of Solomon's Porch, it would be impossible to conclude whether the royal portico connected or not. Hollis (*Archaeology*, 106–7) considers the portico to extend the full length of the S wall, but this was longer than the stadion of Josephus for the length of the portico (cf. also Simons, *Jerusalem*, 410ff.).

The approximate width of the portico was 105 ft., agreeing remarkably with the vertical joint in the E wall, located about 105 ft. N of the SE corner. It appears that this portion of the Ḥaram was specifically added by Herod to provide the needed space for the royal portico (cf. Jos. *Ant.* 15.11.3). Josephus seems to indicate that the portico did not extend the full length of the S wall. If so, something occurred that caused the portico to be terminated (cf. Simon, *Jerusalem*, 410 n. 1). It is possible that approximately where the stadion of length of the portico would end (near the location of the double gate) there was a change in masonry from smoothed field stones to rough faces for the full height, which would represent a later stage in Herod's expansion of the temple platform. The presence of a balcony at the W wall overlooking the Tyropoeon Valley and the Xistus suggests a building of some size at the SE corner, near which the portico terminated, and which therefore prevented its extension to the W end of the S wall.

8. The outer court. This was the open area extending from the inner side of the porticoes to the Soreg. It was here that both Jews and Gentiles were free to mingle, but beyond the Soreg only Jews were permitted to go. This outer court was paved with variegated stones (Jos. *War* 5.5.2).

9. The cisterns. There are some thirty-two caves, pits, and cisterns for water storage within the present Ḥaram; all but six are within the area of Herod's enclosure. Not all came from the same period; some were ancient passages closed up to form cisterns; others were completely in natural stone; and still others had built roofs. Exploration of these cisterns and caves has furnished some accurate information concerning the contours of the bedrock beneath the present enclosure. In all, Warren estimated that their storage capacity exceeded ten million gallons (Simons, *Jerusalem*, 350). They were supplied not only by collecting the rainwater falling in the enclosure, but also by a conduit from the vicinity of Bethlehem.

D. The Tower of Antonia. This structure was built by the Hasmoneans and Herod strengthened it as a fort (Jos. *Ant.* 15.11.4). It was located N of the northern wall of the temple enclosure, approximately on the line of the western wall (*War* 5.5.8)

on a rocky eminence near what is now known as the Convent of Notre Dame de Sion. The base of the fort was a glacis of flagstone topped by a wall 3 cubits high, surrounding the tower that rose behind the wall to a height of 40 cubits. The interior rooms were fitted out like a palace—having cloisters, apartments, baths, and courtyards. Its more exact arrangement was a foursided structure with a tower

Model reconstruction of the Antonia fortress, located on the NW corner of the temple mount. (View to the SSW.)

at each of the four corners, filled with rooms enclosing a central courtyard. It was on the pavement of this courtyard that Christ was arraigned by the Jews before PILATE. The SE tower was 70 cubits high, to command an adequate view of the temple complex, whereas the other three were 50 cubits high.

From Antonia, stairs led down to the temple area (cf. Acts 21:34, 35, 40)—one at the E side leading to the N cloister and one at the W leading to the N end of the W cloister. There was a wide ditch, or moat, between the N colonnade and the fortress. At some later time it was filled in, and part of the rocky eminence on which Antonia once stood has since been cut away, although parts of it may still be seen (cf. Simons, *Jerusalem*, 374ff., 416ff.). See also ANTONIA, TOWER OF.

E. History of Herod's temple

1. NT period. The earliest reference to the temple with its special architectural features is in Matt. 4:5 (cf. Lk. 4:9), where a pinnacle is mentioned. This is possibly a corner of the clerestory roof of the royal portico overlooking the Kidron at the SE corner. The decorations of the temple (Lk. 21:5) agree with Josephus's description (*War* 5.5.6). The gold was an item of pride, and by it oaths were taken (Matt. 23:16). Solomon's Porch, the E colonnade (Jn. 10:23), was one of the places where Christ taught. When he died, the veil between the Holy Place and the Holy of Holies was rent in two (Matt. 27:51; Mk. 15:38; Lk. 23:45). By the BEAUTIFUL GATE (Acts 3:2) the lame man was healed, most likely the gate between the Women's Court and the Court of Israel. The temple complex other than the temple itself was still under construction in the first year of Christ's ministry (prob. A.D. 27), which was the forty-sixth year of its building (Jn. 2:20).

According to John's narrative, in that first year of ministry Christ cleared out the clamorous trade in sacrificial animals at the outer court because this interfered with access to worship in the temple (Jn. 2:14–15). This action of Christ was repeated in his last year (Matt. 21:12; Lk. 19:45; Mk. 11:15–18). Because the traffic crowded out the Gentiles as well as his own people, Christ strongly objected (Matt. 21:13). (Many scholars hold that there was only one cleansing of the temple and that John placed it near the beginning of his gospel for literary and thematic reasons.)

It was Jesus' custom to teach in the courts of the temple daily (Matt. 26:55; Mk. 12:35; Lk. 20:1; 21:37; Jn. 7:14; 18:20), as well as to heal there (Matt. 21:14). Children freely played in the outer court (21:15). After the ascension, the disciples frequented the temple daily for worship (Lk. 24:53; Acts 2:46). It was there that Peter and John went to pray (3:1), probably as part of their daily resort to the temple. The area was under the control of the Roman guard quartered in Antonia; the captain was close enough to dash down the stairs to rescue Paul from the enraged Jews (Acts 21:30–35). Paul in his own defense addressed the Jews from the stairs (v. 40).

Contrary to popular expectations about the endurance of the temple, Christ predicted its destruction (Matt. 24:1–2).

2. The destruction of the temple. Josephus (*War* 2.14) indicates that the Roman governor G. Florus (A.D. 64–66), by his greed for gain and his rapacity in taking it, incited the Jews to rebellion against Rome's occupation, leading to the destruction of the temple. He deliberately provoked the Jews and turned his soldiers loose on them; Agrippa II quieted them, yet they rebelled against his suggestion of submission to Florus until a successor should arrive. In the turmoil that followed, the ZEALOTS persuaded the priests to discontinue the daily offerings for the emperor and empire, which amounted to a subtle declaration of war.

VESPASIAN, who began the campaign to subdue the revolt, was later summoned to Rome to assume the throne, and he commissioned his son TITUS to reduce the Jews to obedience. This eventuated in an attack on Jerusalem and the temple in particular. In the spring of A.D. 70, Titus mounted the final siege. When initial efforts to persuade the Jews to surrender and thus preserve the city failed, Titus erected his encircling wall about the city to prevent help from reaching them, and began the final attack on Antonia. The outer cloisters were burned, and finally the inner court of the temple was encircled, Aug. 29, A.D. 70.

Against the desire of Titus, in the attack in the inner court the next day, a soldier tossed a firebrand through a window into one of the side chambers. Though Titus rushed up shouting commands to extinguish the flames, he was unable to effect his will. Instead another soldier tossed a burning brand into the Holy Place that set ablaze the sanctuary itself (Jos. *War* 6.4.5). On the roof of the side chambers, the priests in defense of the temple pulled up the bird-preventer spikes and hurled them unavailingly at the Roman soldiers (6.5.2). The rest of the temple complex was in flames, last of all the royal portico, and about 6,000 persons seeking refuge in it perished.

VIII. Modern reconstructions

A. Solomon's temple. One of the earliest attempts at reconstruction of this temple was by the Jesuits Pradus and Villalpandus (1596–1604), but in a grandiose Greco-Roman style that largely nullified its value. Others followed, but contributed relatively little. More famous was Schick's also grandiose but inaccurate attempt in 1796. Ruins in

1861 produced a restoration that is suggestive but no more accurate. Elements in it suggest that the temple of Ezekiel's vision influenced him strongly. The efforts of Perrot and Chipiez (1887–89) are noted more for artistry than authenticity. Ferguson's attempt (*Temples of the Jews* [1887]) suffers from lack of correspondence to the biblical text, as well as in architectural style, for it is more classical than Canaanite.

More recent efforts include the E. G. Howland–P. L. Graber model (*BA* 14 [1951]: 2–4) and the C. F. Stevens drawing sponsored by W. F. Albright and G. E. Wright (*BA* 18 [1955]: 41–44). These are quite similar, differing only on less essential points; both illustrate basic elements. The Stevens drawing suffers from its peculiar sawtoothed coping, whereas the Howland model completed the wall top with a coved cornice similar to Egyptian temples. This would have been a distinct innovation, but not well enough attested in Canaan to justify. The more usual coping is a straight, clean parapet wall. The altar must remain for either proposal a conjectural example, for little is known of its actual construction. An immense amount of time and money was spent on the Howland model; apart from this detail, it represents the more faithful proposal to date.

A further defect concerns the tops of the pillars Jakin and Boaz, for both restorations picture them as having at their heads bowls for burning incense. The biblical text does not present this view of their function (see above IV,G,4), nor do the meanings of their names require that incense be burned. The attempts of W. Corswant (*Dictionnaire d'archéologie biblique* [1956]) present a line drawing of a proposed reconstruction that in many respects is quite like the Howland model, except that the entrance to the side chambers is from the outside, not from inside, the Holy Place.

L. H. Vincent, through the drawings of A. M. Steve, has presented a well researched restoration, not markedly different in plan from the Howland model, but differing in significant details. The Holy of Holies is not elevated and its roof is lower than the Holy Place roof, causing the erection of a heavy stone wall between the two. The roof of the side chambers is dropped below the level of the roof of the Holy of Holies. In addition, access to the side chambers is from side rooms on the porch, which cannot be justified from the biblical text. As to character of architecture, a crenelated cornice is applied that has little justification in the text or in Palestinian architecture. Each chamber is provided with a window, which is also not based on the biblical text. The appearance of the whole is rather on the side of modern contemporary architecture.

B. Ezekiel's temple. As suggested above, Paine's attempt at reconstruction of Solomon's temple appears to be influenced more by Ezekiel's temple than any other, and is here mentioned for what help it can give in illustrating the latter. I. Benzinger (*Hebräische Archäologie*, 3rd ed. [1927]) has presented a convincing plan of the temple complex though it suffers from incompleteness. The plan of C. F. Keil (KD, *Ezekiel* [1876], 2:272) is a more faithful reproduction. It is significant that this plan bears more relation to Herod's complex than to Solomon's structures. The primary feature of Ezekiel's structure is its symmetry, which is intended to add to the emphasis of sanctity. Not many attempts have been made to produce models or illustrative sketches, partly because it has been considered an "ideal" expression of what the ritual ought to be.

C. Zerubbabel's temple. Since this has been swallowed up by Herod's rebuilding, and since it has had a continuous history to the latter temple, a reconstruction of Herod's temple would serve better the purpose of reproducing the main features of the sacred structure.

D. Herod's temple. Many and varied are the proposed reconstructions advanced for it. Warren in his researches (*Plans, Elevations*) has given a restoration that conforms to the terrain. Yet faint indications from Josephus indicate that it underwent significant enlargement, namely, the addition of the Women's Court on the E side. C. Schick's plan and model (*Die Stiftshütte, der Tempel in Jerusalem und der Tempelplatz der Jetztzeit* [1896]) is too grandiose to be accepted, and its architecture is entirely foreign to Jewish style and the records of Josephus and of the Mishnah. The Vincent Steve restoration suffers from the fact that it embraces too much of the present Ḥaram, also contrary to the sources.

It does not conform to certain internal arrangements as given in the sources. C. Watzinger's proposal (*Denkmäler Palästinas: Eine Einfürung in die Archäologie des Heiligen Landes* [1933]) suffers from presentation in terms of classic European architectural styles not used in the temple according to the sources. The plan in *HDB* rev. (pp. 712–13) shows a significant departure from the text of Josephus and the Mishnah, although the general relationship of the inner and outer courts is probably correct.

Addendum. About the time the present article was being completed, a group led by Benjamin Mazar undertook extensive archaeological work (made possible subsequent to the Six Day War in 1967) around the temple mount, especially on the S and W sides. Because of religious sensitivities, it has not been possible to excavate the site where the temple itself was located (presumably under the Muslim Dome of the Rock), but abundant remains from the Herodian period have been recovered. As a result, current reconstructions of Herod's temple, especially those produced by the Ritmeyers (see bibliography), are considerably more reliable and reveal in a new way the monumental character of the raised platform (c. 172,000 sq. yds.) and its supporting structures. No sacred site in antiquity was larger than Jerusalem's temple mount, and the evidence confirms that the structure as a whole was one of the great wonders of the ancient world.

(In addition to the titles cited in the body of this article, note A. Parrot, *The Temple of Jerusalem* [1955]; B. Mazar, *The Mountain of the Lord* [1975]; Th. A. Busink, *Der Tempel von Jerusalem, von Salomo bis Herodes: Eine archäologisch-historische Studie unter Berücksichtigung des westsemitischen Tempelbaus*, 2 vols. [1970–80]; M. Ottosson, *Temples and Cult Places in Palestine* [1980]; A. Biran, ed., *Temples and High Places in Biblical Times* [1981]; M. Ben-Dov, *In the Shadow of the Temple: The Discovery of Ancient Jerusalem* [1985]; C. T. R. Hayward, ed., *The Jewish Temple: A Non-biblical Sourcebook* [1986]; V. Hurowitz, *I Have Built You an Exalted House: Temple Building in the Bible in the Light of Mesopotamian and North-West Semitic Writings* [1992]; L. and K. Ritmeyer, *Secrets of Jerusalem's Mount* [1998]; M. Schwartz, *The Biblical Engineer: How the Temple in Jerusalem Was Built* [2001]; L. and K. Ritmeyer, *The Ritual of the Temple in the Time of Christ* [2002]; Y. Ariel and C. Richman, *Carta's Illustrated Encyclopedia of the Holy Temple in Jerusalem* [2005]; S. Goldhill, *The Temple of Jerusalem* [2005]; H. Shanks, *Jerusalem's Temple Mount: From Solomon to the Golden Dome* [2007]. For a useful brief synthesis current as of the late 1980s, see C. Meyers in *ABD*, 6:350–69. The Jerusalem Archaeological Park website [www.archpark.org.il] includes a virtual reconstruction model of the Herodian temple displayed in 360-degree panoramas.)

H. G. Stigers

temples. Buildings used for religious worship and usually regarded as the residence of a deity.
 I. Meaning and function of temples
  A. Shrines
  B. Local and civic sanctuaries
  C. Monumental and state temples
  D. Funerary temples
  E. Temple ritual
 II. Ancient temple architecture
  A. History of architectural developments
  B. Elements of temple architecture

I. Meaning and function of temples. The concept of the temple in the ANE grew out of a very simple idea. It was that the deity was attached to a place, a sacred *locus* which was either the domicile or the favorite haunt of the god, or which formed the chosen locale for the manifestation of the divine presence. Since this was so, the notion developed by logical extension that human beings could properly construct a residence for the god in the vicinity of that place and that the deity would find it acceptable.

Essentially, the temple was a house for the god. Its site was chosen, not always because of the prior existence of a theophany on that very spot, but often because of its central or strategic location in the district sacred to the god. In some cases the site was indeed sanctified by a supernatural manifestation, as in the case of David at the threshing floor of Ornan (Araunah) the Jebusite, where the temple of Solomon later stood (1 Chr. 21:15—22.5). In other cases, temples seem to have been built in localities convenient to the people, with the assumption that the deity would inhabit them, because the god was a local god and both the region and the people were his. But localization of the divine presence was the fundamental idea. This is true whether the deity is a spirit inhabiting a spring, rock, or tree, or a local god living in the town sanctuary or a national god dwelling in the magnificent state temple of the capital city. In all of these places, a tradition once established seldom became dislodged, with the effect that the permanence of sacred sites is axiomatic in the study of ancient religion.

The purpose of constructing a house for the god is equally elementary, despite the elaborate mythic and cultic developments that grew up around the temples. It was to provide a systematic, and therefore controlled, method of relating to the deity. If the place where the god would manifest himself could be predicted or known in advance, then the task of approaching him would be made easier. And if the god received the amenities of domestic life there—food, drink, and clothing—then the temple would become his abode. Performance of the temple duties would demonstrate the servile status of the worshipers who had placed themselves under his patronage. It was hoped that it would also cause the deity to become favorably disposed toward "his people."

It is not, however, correct to think that people in the ancient world actually believed that the god was confined to the temple. It was the place where he might be addressed, where he consistently appeared, and where he "dwelt," but it was not the only place where these things could be thought true. The many temples of Amun (see AMON #4), for example, bearing a variety of local names, were nevertheless thought to be residences of the one solar deity, Amon-Reᶜ (see RE). An 18th-dynasty hymn to OSIRIS illustrates this principle: "Praise to thee, Osiris! Thou lord of eternity, king of gods! Thou with many names and lordly being! With mysterious ceremonies in the temples. He it is that hath the noble *ka* in Busiris and the abundant sustenance in Letopolis, to whom men shout for joy in the *nome* of Busiris, and that hath many victuals in Heliopolis ... Lord of the great hall in Hermopolis, and very terrible in Shashotep; lord of eternity in Abydos, that hath his seat in Ta-zoser" (A. Erman, *The Ancient Egyptians: A Sourcebook of Their Writings* [1966], 141).

Worshipers could pray to the same god in all of these places. They could also pray anywhere at any time, because the deity transcended the physical limitations of the sacred precinct. But they were more likely to be heard if they prayed in the temple, and particularly if they stood before the image of the god. Perceptive suppliants recognized that the deity was not the cult statue itself but *in* the statue, just as they recognized that the deity was not bounded by the temple but was present in the temple. The less thoughtful, however, probably erred in the direction of a literal and superstitious belief, which tended to enhance the status of the temple as an institution in society and the power of the priestly establishment.

The biblical experience, although shaped to some extent by the same factors that influenced contemporary civilizations, was nevertheless unique in that it called foremost attention to the transcendental aspect of God, with a secondary emphasis on the functional localism inherent in the temple idea. In Israel, the "tent-dwelling" or "house" of God, far from being "an attempt to localize God," was a visible extension of the COVENANT relationship which was central to Israel's religion. God descended to the TABERNACLE (Exod. 33:9), but, inasmuch as it was movable, he could not be thought of as resident

Temple shrine of the sun-god Shamash on the throne with the sun disk before him. The cuneiform inscription at upper left reads, "The figure of Shamash, the great master, the one who lives in the Ebabbar, within Sippar." (Copy of a 9th-cent. B.C. monument known as a *kudurru*, a stone sculpture used as evidence of royal land-grant.)

there. Solomon's prayer of dedication succinctly expressed the biblical perspective: "But will God really dwell on earth? The heavens, even the highest heaven, cannot contain you. How much less this temple I have built!" (1 Ki. 8:27).

This exalted sentiment expresses the profound truth of God's transcendent nature. The Solomonic temple's significance lies in the fact that the divine self-disclosure set Yahweh's name there in a special way for the achievement of his redemptive purpose. See TEMPLE, JERUSALEM. Both STEPHEN and PAUL expand on this: "the Most High does not live in houses made by men" (Acts 7:48; cf. 17:24). The need for a physical temple is repudiated in Christianity, but the theme of the presence of his name is extended in SYNAGOGUE and CHURCH. Ultimately, believers themselves become the temple of God (1 Cor. 3:16).

In the wider sphere of the ANE and classical words, the temple as an institution in society often came to overshadow its primary function as the house of the god. The uses of temples were as varied as the life of the community itself. The temple came to be involved in the economy through the management of lands and through the functions of manufacturing, storage, and banking. The stimulus to trade offered by such a viable economic community was considerable. The political activities included taxation and administration, while social contributions included entertainment and service as a kind of community center. Education received great impetus from the scribal schools attached to the temple. In surveying temples and their uses in the ancient world, it should be noted that all are variations on the basic idea of localization of the god, but the functions are as diverse as the geographical and historical distribution of architectural types.

A. Shrines. Not all places of worship can be properly called temples. Some are mere shrines. These range from house shrines to imposing monuments, and sometimes they have an unusual function.

1. Natural shrines. These occur frequently in ancient religion. The Canaanites, in particular, had an affinity for places that displayed some imposing aspect of nature, whether a high hill, solitary tree, or unusually shaped rock. "She [Israel] has gone up on every high hill and under every spreading tree and has committed adultery there" (Jer. 3:6). Such a place might serve as a national sanctuary or cultic center, as in the case of the famous rock sanctuary at Yazilikaya near Hattusas, an open area enclosed by natural rock cliffs which the HITTITES carved into processional scenes containing the entire pantheon. The high place at PETRA was another open-air sanctuary that has been preserved; it was sacred to the NABATEAN deity Dushares. The most famous Israelite cultic shrines were the open-air altars at DAN (PLACE) and BETHEL, although BEERSHEBA and GILGAL are also denounced (Amos 5:5). A monumental horned altar was found at Beersheba in 1973.

2. Domestic shrines. Places of worship in private homes were numerous at every period and had the advantage of allowing a more intimate relationship between the devotee and the deity. The TERAPHIM of LABAN were apparently kept in his house (Gen. 31:19), and MICAH of Mount Ephraim developed an important house-shrine that included a silver image among the teraphim and even boasted a Levitical priest. Micah's gods and the Levite were forcibly transported to Dan, accounting for the origin of that famous shrine (Jdg. 17:1–18, 31).

3. Commemorative shrines. Some shrines were built for special purposes connected with mythical events in the life of the god. Osiris, for example, had a shrine (later a temple) in each of the places where the dismembered parts of his body were found by Isis. Holy men were also sometimes so honored and pilgrimages made to their shrines. The temple of Ptah in MEMPHIS, one of the most important Egyptian sanctuaries, is thought to have been originally a shrine in honor of an early predynastic ruler of that city.

The patriarchal shrines commemorated places of REVELATION. JACOB, JOSHUA, and later SAMUEL and SAUL erected mounds and stones of witness. Judaism, Christianity, and Islam have greatly developed the tendency toward commemorative shrines. Jesus said to some Jewish leaders, "You build the tombs for the prophets and decorate the graves of the righteous" (Matt. 23:29). The proliferation of Byzantine church building was an enlargement of this spirit, and many structures were erected in isolated spots for purely commemorative reasons; examples are the church at Ras es-Siyaga (Mt. Nebo) in honor of Moses, the Propheteum of Amos at Tekoa, and the famous church of St. Simon Stylites at Qal'at Seman in Syria. Modern Christians and Muslims have continued this tradition, as the numerous tombs of Muslim holy men in the Near E and frequent roadside shrines in rural Greece demonstrate.

4. Chthonic shrines. The need to communicate more directly with the forces of nature, particularly the great earth mother, led people to utilize caves as one of the earliest types of sanctuary. The Dictean, Idaean, and Kamaras caves on CRETE, sacred to ZEUS, are examples from historic times. The Minoans also worshiped in "pillar crypts," dark underground grottos beneath the palaces, as at Knossos. The MYSTERY RELIGIONS, in part at least, utilized this type of shrine to inspire dread at the initiatory rites, much as the later *kivas* of the southwestern American Indians were designed to do. The Aesculapium at PERGAMUM is an example of the role of chthonic shrines in classical times. Healing was effected by means of snakes (totems of the god) released among the worshipers in a *hypogeum*, or dark underground chamber.

5. Portable shrines. Egyptian religion incorporated portable shrines into its rites at an early period; Old Kingdom reliefs frequently show chests carried on poles as a part of the funerary equipment. The portable shrines of Tutankhamen are better known and bear a strong affinity of design to the wilderness tabernacle of the Israelites. An archaic Semitic tradition of carrying tent-shrines into battle has also been adduced as comparative material for understanding the tabernacle. In any case, it is clear that the biblical Tent of Meeting was the central shrine of the Israelite tribes linked together by a covenant.

B. Local and civic sanctuaries. Genuine temples, as distinguished from mere shrines, were structures designed and built for the purpose of providing a house for the god. A secondary and important purpose was to offer a locality for the regulated service of worship. Their auxiliary functions varied considerably, depending on the needs of the people, the attributes of the god, and the requirements of the cult.

1. Mesopotamia. The typical functional pattern for Mesopotamian temples reveals that the majority were community oriented. (See ASSYRIA AND BABYLONIA IV; SUMER IV.) They existed to meet a variety of social needs as well as to allow the people to efficiently serve the god. The city and temple grew together, and most temples were located in the population centers, frequently in the very heart of the cities. Two significant roles of the temple related to the oath-taking ceremonies and the certification of weights and measures. The unique economic status of the Mesopotamian temples developed out of this advantageous symbiotic relationship between the commercial and religious life of the community. Possessing vast numbers of slaves and extensive lands, the average Mesopotamian temple grew rich. Its full granaries gave it power in the "storage economy" basic to the ANE way of life. The temple was further enriched by votive offerings and bequests, and by royal tribute and spoil.

The delicately balanced relationship between the king and the priests in Mesopotamian society worked harmoniously for two and a half millennia, a model in church-state relations. The social position and power of the temple was greatest in the early period, but eventually the palace became the more important of the two. Apparently the temple granted the nominal suzerainty of the king, and in return, the king submitted to humiliation by the priests (which included being ceremonially slapped in the face) on one day in the year. There is evidence that Sargon and Naram-Sin, as well as Nabonidus, had difficulties with the priesthood, but these are exceptions which underscore the general harmony which existed between temple and palace. The Assyrian temple, basically different in origin and form, nevertheless served the same function as its Babylonian counterpart and held the same position in society despite the sacerdotal character of the Assyrian kingship.

2. Egypt. The fundamentally opposite concept of kingship in EGYPT caused the civic sanctuaries to follow a different course of development than in Mesopotamia. Local temples existed within each community, but the absence of city-state rivalries deadened local particularism, and the centrality of the god-king and solar cult made the development of great national temples inevitable. The consolidation of power by the priests in the great temples also made conflict with the crown unavoidable, the prime example of which is the Aten revolution and its aftermath (see AKHENATEN). The Theban temples in particular grew in wealth during the empire, and their economic effect began to be felt more and more strongly as time went on. In addition to owning landed estates and holding multitudes of peasants in economic thralldom to landlords who owed their position to the temples, the priests themselves gained so much power that the high priest of Amon-Reᶜ at Karnak arrogated to himself the kingship at the end of the 20th dynasty.

On the whole, the Egyptian was perhaps more likely than his Mesopotamian counterpart to find the temple precincts a place of exclusively religious devotion. Each town had its own temples, which were served by courses of lay priests. The nome capitals, especially, had strongly localized rites going back to the prehistoric period. But it was difficult for the common citizen to feel close attachment to the great temples except at the time of festivals. Then the great temple of Karnak was surrounded by pavilions of lesser deities, and processions and a carnival-like atmosphere prevailed.

Such feasts as the Memphite Khoiak and the feast of Min of Coptos were likewise the occasion for general rejoicing.

3. Syria-Palestine. The name for "temple" in W Semitic, such as Hebrew *hêkāl H2121*, is derived from the Sumerian *E.GAL*, "great house, palace," via the Akkadian *ekallu*. This term reflects the function of the building as a palace for the divine being, comparable to that of the residence of earthly rulers. One notable difference between the temples of Syria-Palestine and those of Egypt and Mesopotamia is their size. Their smallness perhaps reflects the intense isolation and regionalism resulting from the natural geographical barriers. Neither a unitary political system nor a religious pattern was easily developed in the face of such diverse topography. The main Canaanite deity, BAAL, suffered a degree of fractionalization that scarcely allowed the assertion of his unity. This was also true of his consort ASHERAH and accounts for the plural names "Baalim and Asherim" used in the OT (Exod. 34:13; 1 Ki. 18:18).

The tendency toward localism was so pronounced that the story of the Israelites was one of a constant temptation to heterodoxy. The average size of the excavated Palestinian temples is so tiny that the picture which emerges certainly indicates that they existed for priestly, cultic, and oracular purposes and not for the general use of the populace at large. It is likely that the outdoor shrines and cultic centers drew crowds of worshipers, but that the temples were basically the domain of the priests. The purge of JEHU seems to have been directed toward the professional adherents of Baal. Their numbers could not have been large since they were all confined within the "house of Baal" before being slaughtered.

C. Monumental and state temples

1. Kingship and the temple. The magnificent state edifices were primarily influenced in their function by the varying ideas of kingship in the ancient world. Egyptian state temples, such as the great temple of Amon-Reᶜ at Karnak, were dominated by reliefs and statuary of the PHARAOH, depicting his campaigns and listing his accomplishments.

This reconstructed complex at Deir el-Bahri, Egypt, contains the remnants of the temple of Hatshepsut.

This was considered fitting, since the king was the living embodiment of the deity. But the same circumstance detracted from the more truly religious aspects of temple observance and allowed the ostentation of power to predominate.

The situation in Mesopotamia was different by virtue of the opposite position of the king in relation to the temple. Since the king was a mere mortal (although sometimes having priestly functions), the temple was more independent of the crown than in Egypt. But the fact that the donations for the constant repairs needed came from the king, and that new temples were built by royal munificence, equalized the differences to some extent. In both areas of the ancient world the monumental temples reflect the essentially political glorification of the dynasty in boastful dedicatory inscriptions.

2. The temple and the state. The temple expressed, by its location and design, not only theological ideas, but the social and political order as well. Foremost among these concepts was the COSMOGONY which found frequent and prominent architectural expression in the Egyptian and Mesopotamian state temples.

From at least the third dynasty of UR onward, the monumental ZIGGURATS are believed to have portrayed the "cosmic mountain" theme of the mythology, representing the primeval hill or mound which formed the basic stuff of which the heavens and earth were made. The idea is fundamental to ANE cosmogonies. The names of the various Mesopotamian staged temple-towers support this belief. BABYLON's famous ziggurat, *E-temen-an-ki*, "house of the foundation of heaven and earth," is frequently referred to in this connection.

The Egyptian temples are particularly rich in allusions to the cosmic order in their interior embellishments. Thus, symbolically, the floor becomes the earth, the wall reliefs and paintings depict nature, wildlife, and human activities, the columns represent papyrus stalks or palm trees stretching upward to the heavens, and the roof was painted with stars or astrological signs. The theological meaning corresponds to the artistic message—the temple is transformed into a little universe, and just as the god dominates the temple in religious symbolism, so in reality he dominates the world of nature.

Beyond this, the idea of cosmic stability under the patronage of the god is extended to the state. Several Egyptian temples claimed to rest on the primordial hill (Memphis, Thebes, Heliopolis, Hermopolis, and Philae, for example), and were supposed to represent the center of the universe. When MARDUK rose to the head of the pantheon in Mesopotamia, Babylon came to assume the same position as the "navel of the world." The unified cosmological order and its parallel in the state can be understood also from the exalted titles claimed by numerous kings, as for example the Mesopotamian title, "King of the four quarters (of the universe)." Since stability and order emanated from the gods, and the king administered the state under the auspices of the gods, the political and social order was but a reflection of the divine cosmic order. The state temples are the architectural expression of this concept. Some later temples contained essentially the same notion, and the *omphalos* ("navel") monument was common in many classical cities. A stone at Delphi in Greece was supposed to mark the center of the universe, and even the Roman Forum boasted such a stone.

The question of the cosmology implicit in the Solomonic temple has been debated, but there is nothing inherently improbable in such expression. Yahweh has heaven as his throne and earth as his footstool; his chariot is the clouds. Numerous allusions are found in the OT that show God's lordship over nature (e.g., Job 28:23–26; 36:26—41:6; Ps 24:1–3; 33:6–9; 95:4–5; 104; Isa 41:20–26) Nevertheless, the cosmological implications of the Solomonic temple, whatever they may have been, are not architecturally pronounced and, in any case, contain nothing inconsistent with monotheism. The main importance of the temple was that God chose to set his name there (1 Chr. 22:7, 19; 2 Chr. 6:6; 7:16). Some commentators have observed that by falling into the contemporaneous mode of architectural and artistic expression, the Solomonic edifice did nothing to inhibit the syncretism and heterodoxy which became the main snare of the divided monarchy period.

On the other hand, there is no doubt that the imagery of the temple included both cosmological and dynastic ramifications. The Songs of Ascent frequently juxtaposed the temple and the Davidic dynasty as established permanently by the faithfulness of God (e.g., Ps. 122 and 132), and the vision of ISAIAH reflects the universality of the eschatological house of God: "In the last days the mountain of the LORD's temple will be established as chief among the mountains; it will be raised above the hills, and all nations will stream to it" (Isa. 2:2). Similar sentiments are expressed by the psalmist: "The earth is the LORD's, and everything in it, the world, and all who live in it; for he founded it upon the seas and established it upon the waters. Who may ascend the hill of the LORD? Who may stand in his holy place?" (Ps. 24:1–3).

In Israel, as well as elsewhere in the ANE, the state temple was regarded as a fixture in the divine cosmic order. God's rule of the universe included the establishment, protection, and stability of both nation and king.

3. Dynastic chapels. Because of the proximity of certain small temples to the royal palaces, it is thought that they served as private state chapels dedicated to the patron deity of the king, with services directed toward the maintenance of dynastic rule. Such is believed to be the case with the small chapel at Tel Tainat, which frequently is cited as an architectural parallel of the Solomonic temple. For this reason, and because the temple in Jerusalem was adjacent to the palace, it has been claimed that the Solomonic temple was a mere dynastic chapel. Support for this opinion is furnished by the names of the pillars flanking the doorway of the sanctuary, Jakin and Boaz (2 Chr. 3:17), meaning, it is argued by some, "[May God] establish and strengthen [the Davidic dynasty]" (cf. Ps. 89:20–21). See BOAZ (PILLAR); JAKIN (PILLAR); TEMPLE, JERUSALEM IV.B.5.

One must distinguish, however, between the purpose of the temple and its functions. There is indeed a close connection between the divine selection of the temple as the place of God's presence and the promises to the Davidic line: "I have chosen and consecrated this temple so that my Name may be there forever. My eyes and my heart will always be there. As for you, if you walk before me as David your father did, and do all I command, and observe my decrees and laws, I will establish your royal throne, as I covenanted with David your father when I said, 'You shall never fail to have a man to rule over Israel'" (2 Chr. 7:16–18). Nevertheless, the function which the temple performed in enhancing the glory of the Davidic dynasty and celebrating the promises made to him was subordinate to the main purpose of God's provision of a locale for historical revelation and perpetual witness.

4. Border sanctuaries. Protection of the frontiers was a basic necessity in the security of the state. It is clear that the deity bore the responsibility for warding off evil and averting dangers from those under his protection. The shrines and temples located at the important border towns carried a double significance for the preservation of the state. Their existence would guarantee the presence of the god and be valuable as a morale booster for friends and as a superstitious deterrent for foes. Whether or not the Israelite and Judean shrines of the late monarchy fulfill this functional pattern is as yet unclear.

At any rate, this element has been used to explain the placement of the shrines of JEROBOAM's kingdom at Dan and Bethel, as well as to account for the modern discovery of the so-called "temple" at ARAD (perhaps "shrine" would be a more appropriate name), and the monumental altar at BEER-SHEBA. According to this theory, there should be sanctuaries at LACHISH and APHEK, as well as other places. It does appear that the function of guarding or protecting a frontier was the meaning of the covenant and heap of witness made by JACOB and LABAN at MIZPAH (Gen. 31:36–55). The same practice may be reflected in the problematical "altar" erected by the Transjordanian tribes (Josh. 22:10–34). It was not for burnt offerings or sacrifice, they explained to the offended tribes gathered at SHILOH, but served rather as a "witness" on the border; whereupon civil war was averted. At any event, the importance of such border sanctuaries was minor in comparison to the great state temples and their significance.

D. Funerary temples. Rites for the DEAD form one of the oldest types of religious observance. Wherever people were buried, it was inevitable that varieties of cultic observances would grow up over the years and become sanctioned by tradition. Only in Egypt, however, did the tendency to honor the dead and perform potent incantations over them result in the creation of grandiose temples. The pronounced funerary character of Egyptian religion is apparent; the tombs and funerary temples survive because they were designed to survive, and because the environment of the western desert plateau (where the necropolis was usually located) was favorable to archaeological preservation. It must be acknowledged, however, that there was a real preoccupation with the continuity of life from this world to the next. Although this was also true elsewhere in the ANE, only in Egypt did the doctrine of the necessity of preserving the corpse intact become so deeply embedded in the public consciousness that mummification became imperative.

Of perhaps greater importance was the solar cult of pharaonic deification as the living Horus. Its gradual development from predynastic times to the zenith of kingly power in the fourth dynasty accounts in large part for the unsurpassed funerary monuments of the Old Kingdom. The most famous examples are the Step Pyramid and its enclosure at Saqqara, and the Giza group on the plateau SW of Memphis. The pyramids of the 3rd through 6th dynasties required two funerary temples each, one at the base of the temple on the eastern side, and the other in the valley accessible to the inundation and connected to the first by a causeway. In the later Old Kingdom, the temples and causeways were decorated with carved reliefs and statuary. The royal family, nobles, and administrative officials were buried in benchlike *mastaba* tombs surrounding the pyramids, and each had a provision for funerary offerings before the principal false door. Eventually small shrines or mortuary chapels were constructed on the exterior of the tomb, and then in the 5th and 6th dynasties these chapels became internalized, so that one could enter the tomb from the SE corner and make offerings before the false door on the interior.

The New Kingdom saw the removal of the principal royal necropolis to western Thebes, and tomb robbers forced a change in burial patterns. The pharaohs were now buried in rock-cut tombs in the desert for greater security, and they built separate funerary temples near the cultivated areas. The function of these temples remained the same as those of the Old Kingdom. The outstanding example from the 18th dynasty is the mortuary temple of Hatshepsut at Deir el-Bahri (see p. 756). It was built in terraces against the base of a soaring rock cliff, and its horizontal lines contrasted effectively with the backdrop, on the other side of which was the Valley of the Kings.

The nearby Ramesseum was the immense funerary temple of RAMSES II of the 19th dynasty. It was surrounded by a precinct wall, within which were numerous magazines, slaughter courts, priests' houses, apartments, colonnades, porticoes, and a small palace and audience hall. At the center of the enclosure was the temple itself, within an imposing front pylon and two open courts before the hypostyle hall. On the pylon was a scene from the famous battle of KADESH ON THE ORONTES. The funerary temple of Ramses III at Madinet Habu forms a closely parallel 20th-dynasty example. The structure contains famous reliefs depicting Ramses repelling the SEA PEOPLES. It is also remarkable for its size (688 by 1038 ft.).

E. Temple ritual. Inasmuch as construction of the monumental temples required vast and lavish expenditure of time, effort, and treasure, it should not be thought strange that the ancients viewed the rituals conducted in the temples to be of supreme significance. Despite this, scant attention has been paid to the subject of temple ritual by modern scholars. A great part of the cause is the paucity of sources for such an investigation. Clues can be pieced together, however, from archaeological artifacts, from indications of the architecture, and from hymns, epics, and prayers. Historical writings are also helpful, but suffer from the distortions of naïveté, prejudice, and polemic. The descriptions of Babylonian religion by HERODOTUS (*Hist.* 1.181–99), for example, provide some insights but are not strictly accurate. The task is nevertheless a rewarding one, because only by reconstructing the ritual and its meaning can a modern person come close to understanding what functions the ancient temple performed and how the service of the temples affected the participants.

Central to the ritual was the cult image. It was made of wood, clay, or stone, and frequently overlaid with gold on the visible parts. The statue was dressed in an elaborate regalia, which helped

T

Hittite relief (8th cent. B.C.) depicting a temple ritual: Warpalas, king of Tyana land, prays in front of the storm-god, Tarhunza.

to create the effect that the image was properly an object of veneration. Such apparel was fixed by rigid tradition. On one occasion, NABONIDUS offended the priests of the sun-god by attempting to change his tiara.

The setting of the cult statue was enhanced by placing the god in a niche in a darkened room, where it was visible from a courtyard. The monumental doorways of Babylonian temples provided a further splendid frame for the impressive image, designed to stimulate awe on the part of the beholder. There is little evidence that the temple itself was a place where the ordinary person might come into the presence of the deity, but he was seen by everyone when carried through the streets in the great processions.

The problem of the human manufacture of the gods was a serious one to paganism and was the subject of heavy sarcasm by the Hebrew prophets (Isa. 44:9–20; Jer. 10:1–15). To circumvent this, the Babylonians devised a procedure of consecration or investiture in order that the statue might be inhabited by the god. This elaborate ceremony was performed mainly at night and consisted of the symbolic "opening of the mouth" of the statue by a series of fourteen ritual washings. The image was taken to the river bank in a nocturnal journey that included various sacrifices and incantations toward the cardinal points of the compass. The eyes were symbolically opened by a priest, and the god was decked out and taken to the temple with prescribed processional chants and a final sacrifice at the gate. Similar practices are known to have been utilized in Egypt, with the effect of making the transition from the workshop to the temple. A sophisticated Babylonian or Egyptian might have answered Jeremiah or Isaiah: "No, you are wrong. The god magically inhabited the statue at a specific point of time."

The activities of the god consisted mainly of repasts, oracles, and processions. Two meals were usually served to the image daily, each made up of two courses with a variety of foodstuffs and delicacies. Often these were served in gold vessels, and one source tells that even the horses pulling the god's ritual chariot ate grass, which was harvested with gold sickles, from golden buckets. Curtains were pulled while the god was "eating," a finger bowl was brought for washing the god's fingers, and the cella (the enclosed portion of the temple) was fumigated afterward to remove the smell of food. The "leftovers" were, on certain occasions at least, the prerogative of the king, who took pride in consuming them. The god was apparently thought to partake of the food by merely having it placed before him, or alternatively, having it waved before his eyes. Another method was the burnt offering, which transformed the food into another dimension and could be smelled by the god. Sacrifice and the pouring of blood before the god did not figure as largely in Mesopotamian religion as in W Semitic practice.

The oracle was a typical function of the cult image. By means of questions and a supposed pattern of indication from the god, a "yes" or "no" answer could be obtained. One such means was the casting of lots, a practice that appears throughout the pages of the OT. The clearest indication is found in 1 Sam. 28:6, but the theological dimension is added in Prov. 16:33, "The lot is cast into the lap, but its every decision is from the LORD." Sometimes the pagan priests sought ways of making the image answer in a more dramatic fashion. The Egyptian priests of the Ptolemaic era were particularly skilled at this, and the classical world is filled with stories of various extraordinary oracular techniques.

Processions were another colorful cultic activity of the images. The enactment of the sacred marriage ritual was one such procession in Mesopotamia. The usual city festivals brought the god out of the temple and into contact with the people in an atmosphere of jubilation. The god Nabu (NEBO) normally made the journey from Borsippa to Babylon to honor his father MARDUK. In Egypt the gods being conducted on journeys or in processions had various pavilions or way stations provided, to which they were welcomed with great ceremony. One of the most unusual texts tells of a Babylonian deity being taken out to hunt in the royal game preserve. Gods were sometimes, but infrequently, taken into battle. In this spirit the ARK OF THE COVENANT was taken out to fight the PHILISTINES, with disastrous results (1 Sam. 4:3-7:2). The god ASSHUR is always depicted as a winged disc hovering over the Assyrian armies in the reliefs, but it is doubtful if the image normally accompanied the troops.

A host of priests attended to the other religious functions of the temple. In Egypt, the funerary temples required numerous levels of purification and offering priests. In Mesopotamia the emphasis on conjuration, incantation, exorcism, and divination likewise necessitated special classes of priests. The word *enchanter* in Dan. 2:10 is a technical term for a kind of incantation priest. Omen priests were concerned with the application of the exhaustive omen-texts to daily events of unusual significance. EUNUCHS were players at the cultic performances. Among the priestesses were the *Entu, Naditu*, and *Qadishtu* (for the latter, cf. *qādēš* H7728 in Deut. 23:17 et al., and fem. *qědēšâ* in 2 Ki. 23:7 et al.).

Special rituals were observed whenever the king entered the temple precincts. A Hittite text describes the observance at one religious festival, which becomes understandable if set in the largest of the five temples found at Boğazköy, temple I. The temple is surrounded by a precinct wall and magazines, but is located in an open space and has a central court. The king, leading a procession, went into the propylaeum, performed ritual ablutions at a well before the gate, entered the sanctuary, and partook of a ceremonial meal, during which time he uncovered the sacrificial loaves and divided them with his spear.

Another important aspect of the temple ritual concerns the construction of the temple itself. Great care was taken in invoking the deity for permission to build. Naram-Sin, like David, was not permitted to build a temple. But, unlike David, he presumed to build one anyway, an impiety which had dire consequences. In laying the foundations, elaborate precautions were made, which included tracing the precincts, offering sacrifices connected with laying the cornerstone, and the sanctification by various rituals of the entire area. A certain procedure was prescribed for cleansing a desecrated temple, and the complex and lengthy formula for rebuilding a ruined temple would almost try the patience of a god. All of these factors demonstrate the involvement of the ancients in their religion and their heartfelt participation in the life of the god, whether in daily activities or in the dramatic activity of the festivals.

II. Ancient temple architecture

A. History of architectural developments.
The earliest temples developed out of the architectural forms of houses and are clustered in the crowded villages of the Neolithic period. Small, roomlike shrines were found at JERICHO as far back as the Pre-Pottery Neolithic B levels (c. 7000 B.C.). The fullest plan bears a resemblance to the later rectangular *megaron*, which eventually became the preferred shape for classical sanctuaries as well.

In the late Neolithic period, about 5000 B.C., squarish house-shrines occur at Hajilar and Catal Huyuk in ANATOLIA. The remarkable series of forty shrines at Catal Huyuk scattered throughout the domestic quarter on nine levels provides the best glimpse of religious ARCHITECTURE at this early stage of history. The rooms were windowless and doorless, with access from the roof by ladders, and light from openings near the eaves. The walls were plastered and frequently painted with bulls, leopards, vultures, and anthropomorphic figures, sometimes executed in relief. Low bench-like "altars" were arranged around the walls. These often contained *bucrania* (the horns of aurochs or wild bulls) and are linked to the common FERTILITY worship of the period. The presence of skulls testifies to the life-and-death symbolism of the shrines, just as the catalog of small objects suggests a similar theme.

The Ubaid culture of the Chalcolithic period in Mesopotamia saw significant developments in temple architecture shortly after 4500 B.C. These are particularly noticeable in two places, one in the S and one in the N. At ERIDU, near UR at the head of the Persian Gulf, a series of seventeen temples was uncovered that revealed not only the continuity of the sacred area but also the character of the earliest temple-platforms, which later became a standard feature of Mesopotamian temple architecture. The genesis of the ziggurat idea was in this type of foundation, and its evolution is traceable elsewhere in the Tigris-Euphrates basin. The temple at Eridu is thought to have been dedicated to the god Enki (Ea), the lord of the Apsu, by virtue of the presence of layers of fish bones covering the floor of parts of the shrine. The earliest temple measured only 12 x 15 ft. and contained two elements that became basic to the architecture of the cella: a small niche for the god, and a low mud-brick offering table before the niche.

Tepe Gawra near NINEVEH boasted a cluster of three temples grouped around a court in the same period, all standing on a mud-brick mound forming a kind of acropolis about 30 meters square. The temples were distinguished by monumental façades of recessed brick plastered in white. Small rooms led to the rectangular cella, which was the center of the cult. It is assumed that a triad was worshiped here, although many subsidiary deities could have been venerated as well. The court becomes an important feature in later Mesopotamian temples. The recesses and buttresses employed in stratum XIII served both utilitarian and esthetic functions, supporting beams for the roof and relieving the plain façade. Such stepped recesses were characteristic of Mesopotamian temple architecture thereafter.

The "white temple" at ERECH (Warka) in the succeeding Uruk and Protoliterate periods following 4000 B.C. was built upon a much higher 40-ft. elevated platform and displayed a regular shape, approximately 17 x 22 meters in size. The façade consisted of stepped brick recesses all around the structure. The interior was divided into three parts, with two rows of small rooms flanking a cella which ran completely through the long axis of the temple. An altar with traces of burning occupied the center of the cella, with a pedestal in the NW corner that was presumably the focal point of the cult. The excavators named the complex the "Anu ziggurat," but it is not a true ziggurat, inasmuch as it is not stepped, and the association with Anu is based on evidence from a much later period. Subsequent temples, however, tended to follow the pattern of regularity in shape and decoration.

The temples at Khafajeh show further developments in the Early Dynastic period (c. 2900–2350 B.C.). At first an original temple stood on a mound as an isolated building within the city. It was a simple community shrine separated from the domestic structures and containing a fireplace, offering table, and altar. The standard shape for a Mesopotamian temple was achieved, as at Eridu, by placing an entrance on one of the long walls and the altar on one of the short walls. The temple is called the Sin temple, but the attribution to that deity is quite tenuous. Rooms were added around the temple beginning as early as the Protoliterate period. Eventually a courtyard became the dominant feature in the Early Dynastic period (Sin temple VIII). A monumental entrance flanked by two towers with an impressive stairway was added. A much more complex function is indicated, with ovens, living quarters, and a major antecella being added, as well as a *kisu*, a low wall that surrounded the structure near its base.

In the second Early Dynastic phase, another larger sacred area was built at Khafajeh. In preparation, the site was filled with clean sand. Next, massive surrounding walls were erected, as much for defense, perhaps, as for isolation. In any case, the *temenos* wall (from Sumerian *temen*) surrounding the sacred area became a feature of the more important temples throughout the ancient world.

The most pronounced feature of Mesopotamian temple architecture was the ziggurat. The lavish expenditure of labor required for the erection of these artificial mountains and their centrality to the cult has caused a general scholarly agreement that the structures represent the mythological cos-

TEMPLES

The Erechtheum, an Ionic temple on the Acropolis of Athens built c. 420 B.C., was dedicated to Athena and Poseidon.

mic mountain. They did not achieve monumental size, however, until the imperial centralization of the Akkadian and Ur III periods. There are some obscure references to temples built by Sargon and Naram Sin, which, in the latter case, was an impiety punished devastatingly by the gods. The most noteworthy and lasting effort in the early period was that of Ur-Nammu, who built the famous ziggurat to the moon god at Ur. It measured 130 x 190 ft. and stood in a courtyard, but the temple that surmounted the tower in ancient times has not survived.

The much later Neo-Babylonian period ziggurat at Babylon, built by NEBUCHADNEZZAR II (605–562 B.C.), was 295 ft. square and 295 ft. high. The infinite variety of Mesopotamian temples in the later periods nevertheless continued to exhibit the basic features of the early temples, and some of these architectural traditions continued to influence the development of sacred architecture into the classical era.

In Egypt there were a number of architectural developments that contributed to the general pattern of later temple construction. The abundant use of stone in sacred buildings was apparent quite early. It is probable that the earliest Egyptian temples were small shrines constructed of mud bricks much like their Mesopotamian counterparts. But the development of funerary architecture influenced temples in the direction of the use of more permanent materials.

Most Egyptian buildings in the Old Kingdom (including even the royal palaces) were flimsy structures of wood, reeds, and fabric. The tombs, by contrast, were made of stone for greater permanence, because they were built as "houses of eternity" designed to endure forever. Mesopotamian temples were seldom built of stone, except for stone foundations, which were sometimes employed. The great accessibility of stone in Egypt made the development of a genuine monumental architecture possible. Pharaoh Zoser's massive funerary complex at Saqqara (c. 2800 B.C.) is the earliest example of a grandiose stone structure in history. The step pyramid is an outgrowth of earlier tomb construction, and is totally unrelated to the Mesopotamian temple-towers, which originated in temple architecture.

The importance of the Saqqara enclosure for sacred architecture resides in several elements. Essentially, it was a reduplication in stone of the palace; the walls were a mile long and thirty-three feet high, with fourteen gates. Wooden doors were copies in stone, and glazed tiles imitated the actual reed mats of the interior. The columns of the Zoser entrance hall were not free-standing, but engaged and fluted, with pendant leaf capitals. This marks the earliest usage of these components which later became so prominent in temple construction.

The Egyptians also experimented with naturalistically derived forms, making columns in stone which imitated the papyrus stalk bundles used in ordinary building. A particularly early variation of this idea was the use of columns imitating date palms. The pyramid and valley temples of Sahure (Dynasty V) exhibited this style. It is an extremely simple and aesthetically pleasing form, rendered in rose granite, with smooth round monoliths topped by carved fillets and gently arching palm branches forming the capital. The fact that they are all in one piece emphasizes the Egyptian stonecutting ability.

Egyptian temples, like the Mesopotamian, utilized the *temenos* wall to separate the sacred precinct from the profane world. One feature that was peculiarly Egyptian, however, was the pylon façade. It served as an impressive archway which confronted one with the magnitude of the structure even before entering; as a supporting role, it displayed iconography that frequently glorified the reigning monarch. The hypostyle hall at Karnak was the epitome of Egyptian temple architecture, with a vast forest of massive columns giving a lofty and unworldly atmosphere to the interior. In Ptolemaic Egypt, Hellenistic and native Egyptian architecture existed side by side as attested by coin evidence. But the most important contributions to be made by Egypt had already been bequeathed to the Mediterranean world prior to the end of the Bronze Age.

North Syrian temple architecture is illustrated by two phases of a mud-brick structure on stone foundations from the 13th cent. B.C. at ALALAKH (Tell Atchana). Each of the phases has both the antecella and the cella arranged transversely to the entrance and parallel to the façade. The basic shape again bears a resemblance to the *megaron*, in this case an oblong structure with one or two columns *in antis*.

The Aramean rulers of the Neo-Hittite period in N Syria developed a type of palace called *bīt ḫilāni* in the Assyrian inscriptions. The contrast between the palaces and temples of the period shows that, while there was latitude for experimentation and development of new forms in the royal residence, temples were more conservative. At Tel Tainat, for example, the shape of the chapel was again that of the *megaron*. A similar preference exhibits itself in the early Anatolian structures, and as early as 2300 B.C. Troy level II-G had a fine *megaron* as its largest public building, with a roof span of thirty feet.

The similarity of these geographically and chronologically diverse buildings has been attributed to a unilinear pattern of derivation. But the links in the line have been difficult if not impossible to document. It is perhaps better to say that the *megaron* form was preferred because of its functional and religious value. It is true, of course, that religion is conservative, and that the antiquity of an element was regarded as enhancing its sacredness. The history and evolution of the Greek and Roman temple are equally involved. Some of the basic features had their roots far back in antiquity, but the vigorous Hellenic genius allowed the flowering of beautiful classical forms that became standard for temple architecture in the ancient world. The *megaron* form, used for palaces and public buildings in the Bronze Age—as the finds at Mycenae, Tiryns, Troy, and elsewhere show—was adapted to sacred architecture when the AEGEAN world emerged from the dark ages, and it became the preferred form thereafter.

The archaic temple of Apollo at CORINTH is an example of the early Greek edifice type in Doric style. One of the most noteworthy buildings in the ancient world was the temple of Diana (ARTEMIS) at EPHESUS. The Artemision or Artemisium, as it was called, was the first monumental structure ever to be made of marble, and it was the largest building of the Greek world. The archaic Artemision (c. 550 B.C.) had a deep pronaos and a long unroofed cella. It had, according to PLINY the Elder (*Nat. Hist.* 36.21[14]), 127 columns, each 19 meters in height. The later Artemision (334–250 B.C.) was one of the seven wonders of the ancient world. It was the same size as the earlier temple, but it had a higher platform.

The Greeks experimented with other architectural forms. The altar of Zeus at PERGAMUM, built by EUMENES II (197–159 B.C.), was a large and impressive example of an entire structure designed as an altar and covered with mythological reliefs. It served as the model for the Augustan *Ara Pacis* in Rome. Of the multitude of temples constructed in the Greco-Roman world, most were of the rectangular variety, with columns arranged in prostyle, amphistyle, or peripteral patterns. A few temples, such as the treasury at Delphi, the temple of Vesta in Rome, or the Venus temple at Baalbek, were round. Perhaps the most famous of the round temples was the Pantheon in Rome. Designed by the Emperor HADRIAN, the temple used massive concrete walls to support the circular dome. A propylon retained at least the semblance of the ordinary temple style. The greatest influence in subsequent church architecture, however, came from the Roman civic building, the basilica. Nevertheless, Christian sacred architecture owed much to the ancient traditions, and was built on a long heritage of religious devotion expressed in bricks, mortar, stone, and marble.

B. Elements of temple architecture. By the time the ancient temple reached the height of its development in the classical era, each element in its architecture had become established through adherence to a rigid convention. The canonical pattern remained essentially the same from the time of Pericles to the end of the Roman empire in the W, although stylistic innovations occurred throughout.

In terms of the typical ground plan, the basic *megaron* form was elaborated beyond the *naos* (the cella itself) by extending the side walls forward to form the *pronaos* (porch). Some temples had a similar addition in the rear but without an entrance, called the *opisthodomos*. The use of columns made possible the esthetically pleasing effect of balance, lightness and harmony and broke up the sense of great mass normally present in a monumental structure. The play of sunlight and shadow on the intercolumnation, together with a restrained use of delicate sculpture on the friezes and pediments, created an architectural form of unsurpassed beauty.

The three types of columns associated with classical temple architecture—Doric, Ionic, and Corinthian—each expressed a different style. The Doric is massive, simple, and plain. It is exemplified in the archaic temple of Apollo at Corinth, and is elsewhere frequently made the lower member of a two- or three-tiered façade. The Ionic is lighter and is characterized by a tasteful restraint. The voluted capital was widely employed throughout the classical world, and has a history which reaches back through the Aeolic order into the earlier developments of the ANE. The Corinthian style is the lightest of all, consisting of a capital of acanthus leaves, which gives an elegant and highly refined, somewhat ornate effect.

Many of the Hellenistic and Roman temples merely had a row of columns in front of the cella, forming the so-called *prostyle* temple. The *amphiprostyle* had columns in front and rear, whereas the *peristyle* or *peripteral* temple was surrounded with a row of columns. All were popular. For example, no less than five temples of the prostyle type were built at Pergamum alone during the 2nd cent. B.C. The largest temple to Dionysus in the ancient world was that of Teos in Asia Minor. It was a *peripteros* of the Ionic order, built, according to Vitruvius, by the architect Hermogenes. This famous architect wrote a treatise on the proportion of temples, in which he expressed a preference for the *eustyle* principle (whereby the columns should be spaced 2.25 times the column diameter for the most pleasing effect, based on the interaxial span and lower columnar dimension).

The *dipteral* type of temple had a double row of columns surrounding the structure. The archaic Didymaion at Didyma (550 B.C.) exhibits this type of columnation. The later Hellenistic temple at Didyma (300 B.C.), the third largest building of the Hellenic world, had another feature characteristic of certain temples. It was *hypaethral*, that is, the *adyton* (cella) was unroofed and open to the sky. A small *naiskos* or temple-like shrine stood where an altar might in a smaller temple. The Didymaion was sacred to APOLLO, and had a *chresmographeion* or oracle room to serve the ancient cult.

The *pseudodipteral* temple type duplicates the *dipteral*, except that the inner row of columns is omitted, producing a particularly spacious and pleasing aesthetic effect. The temple of Artemis at Magnesia on the Maeander was constructed in this style by Hermogenes. It is one of the most important creations of Greek art by virtue of its structural innovations, as well as because of its monumental size and 200-meter sculptured frieze.

Standard elements of classical temple architecture include a three-stepped foundation called the *stereobate* or *crepidoma*. The topmost step of the platform is termed the *stylobate*. On the platform, the first row of masonry forming the walls of the cella is the *orthostate*. The columns stand on square blocks (in the Ionic order) called *plinths*. The column base is made up of several elements depending on the order, but grooves (*trochilos*) and ridges (*astragalos*) are frequently employed, surmounted by a large rounded molding (*torus*). Columns were fluted and separated by ridges called *arris* (Doric order) or *fillets* (Ionic order). The capital crowned the column in the Ionic and Corinthian orders.

Spanning the columns was the *architrave* (also called *epistyle* or *lintel*). Sometimes the architrave was separated into three *fasciae* or bands, above which was usually a band containing the familiar egg-and-dart motif. The middle member of the entablature in the Ionic order was a sculptured frieze. The Doric frieze alternated *triglyphs* (stones with three vertical bands) and *metopes* (sculptured stones). Above the frieze was a row of *dentils* or alternating indentations. The pediment was actually the horizontal cornice, and formed the topmost member of the entablature. It was so called because the sculptured figures of the gods stood on it, as in the famous Parthenon friezes. The raking cornice was the angular member which framed the roof. The roof was flanked by a gutter called the *sima* along its lower edges on the long sides of the temple. Often carved figures or antefixes were attached to these gutters. The ridge of the roof was sometimes crowned with an *acroterium*, consisting of sculptured figures.

The results of the long history of architectural development of temples in the ancient world, and particularly the contribution of the Greeks, is still apparent in many of our modern buildings. (For bibliography see ARCHITECTURE and TEMPLE, JERUSALEM; see also *ABD*, 6:369–82.)   J. E. JENNINGS

Temple Scroll. Identified with the siglum 11QT(emple) or 11Q19 (supplemented by 11Q20, which consists of overlapping fragments), the Temple Scroll measures more than 28 ft. when unrolled and is thus the longest document found among the DEAD SEA SCROLLS. The work, which was probably composed c. 100 B.C., can be viewed as a rewriting of the laws in the PENTATEUCH, but with emphasis on the instructions for the building of the temple (cf. Exod. 35–40). The structure contemplated is immense—several times larger than even the Herodian temple mount—and the architectural description does not conform with the biblical accounts of the tabernacle or the temple. See TEMPLE, JERUSALEM. The scroll also deals with the sacrificial system, issues of ritual purity, and other laws; in doing so, it seeks to exegete the Torah by clarifying ambiguities and apparent inconsistencies, but it also introduces extensive material that diverges from biblical and rabbinic teaching. (See Y. Yadin, *The Temple Scroll*, 3 vols. in 4 [1982]; id., *The Temple Scroll: The Hidden Law of the Dead Sea Sect* [1985]; J. Maier, *The Temple Scroll: An Introduction, Translation and Commentary* [1985]; M. O Wise, *A Critical Study of the Temple Scroll from Qumran Cave 11* [1990]; D. D. Swanson, *The Temple Scroll and the Bible: The Methodology of 11QT* [1995]; E. Qimron, *The Temple Scroll: A Critical Edition with Extensive Reconstructions* [1996]; M. Riska, *The Temple Scroll and the Biblical Text Traditions: A Study of the Columns 2–13:9* [2001].)

temptation. This noun and the verb "to tempt" are used by the KJV in the OT a number of times (e.g., to render the Heb. verb *nāsâ* H5814 in Gen 22:1 et al.; cognate noun *massâ* H4999 in Deut. 4:34 et al.; cf. the place name MASSAH). Modern versions of the OT normally use "test" and "testing" in these cases. In the NT, however, the Greek noun *peirasmos* G4280 (cognate verb *peirazō* G4279) can indicate both (1) a test or trial, irrespective of whether the intention is good or bad, and (2) temptation, that is, an enticement to sin.

I. The nature of temptation. Human beings were created to worship and serve the Lord. Temptation is an enticement to worship and serve the creature rather than the Creator (Rom. 1:25). Temptation strikes at the heart of our relationship to God and his purposes. A temporal advantage may seduce the tempted away from an eternal good. Furthermore, as M. G. Kyle has suggested (in *ISBE* [1929], 4:2944), temptation is an incitement of natural, God-given desires to go beyond God-given bounds (e.g., gluttony). The end served by temptation is spiritual alienation from God and enslavement to moral evil.

Clearly the ultimate source of temptation is SATAN. No one lives in a vacuum; to some extent we are all under the influences of "the tempter" (Matt. 4:3; 1 Thess. 3:5). One of Satan's cleverest stratagems is to convince moderns that he passed away with the Middle Ages. The egregious evils of recent history have revived belief in the demonic. Satan sometimes masquerades as a messenger of religious truth (2 Cor. 11:14).

Temptation may arise not only from Satan, but also from love of the world. As John explained, this includes "the lust of the flesh, and the lust of the eyes, and the pride of life" (1 Jn. 2:16 KJV). Sensuality, covetousness, and egotism bewitch the best of us. "Therefore let any one who thinks that he stands take heed lest he fall" (1 Cor. 10:12 RSV). Much temptation, however, springs not from the devil or the world, but from each individual person. As James explained, "each one is tempted when, by his own evil desire, he is dragged away and enticed.

Then, after desire has conceived, it gives birth to sin; and sin, when it is full-grown, gives birth to death" (Jas. 1:14–15).

Temptation, then, is an incitement from the world, the flesh, or the devil to worship and serve them rather than the Creator.

II. The nature of testing. God may employ trying circumstances to woo a person back to himself or to prove our fidelity. God tested ABRAHAM by commanding him to sacrifice ISAAC (Gen. 22:1–2). God led the Israelites in the wilderness to MARAH, the place of bitter waters, and the thirsty people murmured. When MOSES cried to the Lord he was shown a tree; he threw it into the waters and the water became sweet. "There the LORD ... tested them" (Exod. 15:25b). In the wilderness they also needed bread, which the Lord supplied one day at a time to prove whether they would walk in his law (16:4). God's purpose in the thunders at SINAI, Moses explained, was "to test you, so that the fear of God will be with you to keep you from sinning" (20:20). God, then, orders difficult circumstances "to humble and to test you so that in the end it might go well with you" (Deut. 8:16). JOB confessed, "when he has tested me, I will come forth as gold" (Job 23:10).

Before Jesus fed the five thousand, he said to PHILIP, "Where shall we buy bread for these people to eat?" John explained, "He asked this only to test him, for he already had in mind what he was going to do" (Jn. 6:1–6). The Lord's testings are not for his knowledge but rather for our benefit. For a little while God's people suffer various trials "so that your faith — of greater worth than gold, which perishes even though refined by fire — may be proved genuine and may result in praise, glory and honor when Jesus Christ is revealed" (1 Pet. 1:7). Testing, then, is an ordering of circumstances by God to reveal his people's supreme love for him, fortify them against sin, and do them good.

III. The relationship between temptation and testing. Any situation in life may be an occasion of temptation or testing. God designed a test for ADAM and EVE by forbidding them to eat fruit from the tree of the knowledge of good and evil (see TREE OF KNOWLEDGE), but Satan subtly lured them into disbelief and disobedience (Gen. 3:1–6). God liberated the Israelites from Egypt and led them into the wilderness; there they often yielded to temptation and sinned. God allowed Satan to tempt Job to prove his integrity (Job 1:6–12).

Jesus himself "was led up by the Spirit into the desert to be tempted by the devil" (Matt. 4:1). The occasion of proving Christ's authenticity was ordered by the Lord; the enticement to use his supernatural powers simply to satisfy his intense hunger after forty days of fasting came from Satan. The inducement to worship Satan was permitted by God, but it was introduced by the tempter. The intrigue of gaining a following by falling from the temple without harm did not come from God. God is the author of every good and perfect gift. "When tempted, no one should say, 'God is tempting me.' For God cannot be tempted by evil, nor does he tempt anyone" (Jas. 1:13). See TEMPTATION OF CHRIST.

Why, then, should one pray, "lead us not into temptation, but deliver us from the evil one" (Matt. 6:13)? Believers pray that God will not order circumstances in which Satan would find them easy prey. They ask also God's enablement to resist temptation when it comes. God permits Satan to tempt, but he also promised: "No temptation has seized you except what is common to man. And God is faithful; he will not let you be tempted beyond what you can bear. But when you are tempted, he will also provide a way out so that you can stand up under it" (1 Cor. 10:13). As R. Girdlestone says, "He allows the way *in*, and He makes the way *out*" (*Synonyms of the Old Testament: Their Bearing on Christian Doctrine*, 2nd ed. [1897], 295).

IV. What to do about temptation. Surely no one should tempt others. "Things that cause people to sin are bound to come, but woe to that person through whom they come. It would be better for him to be thrown into the sea with a millstone tied around his neck than for him to cause one of these little ones to sin" (Lk. 17:1–2). A Christian ought to take action to counter sources of temptation in himself or herself. "If your hand or your foot causes you to sin cut it off and throw it away. It is better for you to enter life maimed or crippled than to have two hands or two feet and be thrown into eternal fire. And if your eye causes you to sin, gouge it out and throw it away. It is better for you to enter life with one eye than to have two eyes and be thrown into the fire of hell" (Matt. 18:8–9). These hyperboles show how urgent is the task of dealing with temptation.

Very explicit suggestions appear for reckoning with sexual temptations: "... since there is so much immorality, each man should have his own wife, and each woman her own husband" (1 Cor. 7:2). Paul adds, "Do not deprive each other ... so that Satan will not tempt you because of your lack of self-control" (v. 5). The apostle instructs TIMOTHY to treat "younger women as sisters, with purity" (1 Tim. 5:2). The HOLY SPIRIT's fruit of SELF-CONTROL is equally necessary to overcome covetousness (see COVET). People in this world will be content with food and clothing, for those "who want to get rich fall into temptation and a trap and into many foolish and harmful desires that plunge men into ruin and destruction. For the love of money is a root of all kinds of evil. Some people, eager for money, have wandered from the faith and pierced themselves with many griefs" (1 Tim. 6:9–10).

Apparently we may experience greater temptation than usual at certain times. In GETHSEMANE Jesus said, "Watch and pray so that you will not fall into temptation. The spirit is willing, but the body is weak" (Matt. 26:41). John Owen analyzed times when temptations' solicitations are more urgent, their reasonings more plausible, pretenses more glorious, hopes of recovery more evident, opportunities more open, and doors of evil more beautiful than ever before (see *The Works of John Owen*, ed. W. H. Hoold [1850–53], 6:87–151). To correct the factors leading to such a state, Christians should not lessen their indignation at their own sins, nor fail to abhor sin in others. They should not associate attractions to evil with good things, or willingly go to places contributing to temptation. No one should allow weak faith or idleness to occasion evil. Alertness is called for especially in situations like DAVID's, which combine fear and passion. Afraid of URIAH's revenge and consumed by his lust for BATHSHEBA, David entered into temptation to kill Uriah.

In the presence of the tempter a Christian may, like Christ, quote Scripture as illumined by the Holy Spirit. A Christian can count on the understanding of Christ, the sympathetic High Priest, "who has been tempted in every way, just as we are—yet was without sin" (Heb. 4:15). (See C. S. Lewis, *The Screwtape Letters* [1944]; D. Bonhoeffer, *Temptation* [1953]; W. E. Oates, *Temptation: A Biblical and Psychological Approach* [1992].)

G. R. LEWIS

temptation of Christ. This critical event in the life of Jesus is recounted in the Synoptic Gospels (Matt. 4:1–11; Mk. 1:12–13; Lk. 4:1–13) and alluded to in Hebrews (Heb. 2:18; 4:15–16; there is also strong evidence, however, that on other occasions, especially during his later ministry, Jesus encountered similar temptations). The Gospels report that at the time of Jesus' baptism a voice from heaven said, "You are my Son, whom I love; with you I am well pleased" (Lk. 3:22). For JOHN THE BAPTIST it was a time of recognition of the long-anticipated MESSIAH; for Jesus it was the momentous event marking his introduction to public life after three decades of relative obscurity. The traditional site of the temptation is Mount QUARANTANIA. It is not far from the probable site of Jesus' baptism and is in accordance with the scriptural statement that immediately thereafter the Spirit drove him into the wilderness (Mk. 1:12). It is the highest hill in the vicinity and commands a spectacular view of the JORDAN Valley. In addition it fulfills the condition of being "in the desert," an area uninhabited because of its extreme dryness. (For a brief discussion of the differences among the Gospels in their accounts of the temptation, see *ABD*, 6:382–83.)

I. The nature of the temptation. It is likely that JOHN THE APOSTLE had in mind Jesus' temptation, together with that of ADAM and EVE, when he said, "For all that is in the world, the lust of the flesh, and the lust of the eyes, and the pride of life, is not of the Father, but is of the world" (1 Jn. 2:16 KJV). This statement would seem to be a summarization of the temptation of Eve (Gen. 3:6), who saw that the tree was good for food ("lust of the flesh"), that it was a delight to the eyes ("lust of the eyes"), and that the tree was to be desired to make one wise ("pride of life"). Jesus' temptation also bears some similarity to this analysis.

TEMPTATION OF CHRIST

A. Lust of the flesh. It is stated that Jesus fasted forty days and forty nights, the maximum time a person can do without food without endangering his health. During this time he was no doubt engaged in prayer and concentrated thought as he faced the issues resulting from his awareness of being the Messiah. During this time of emotional stress it is not strange that appetite was lacking. When the stress was over, however, normal hunger pangs asserted themselves imperiously. To Jesus, conscious of his God-given powers, the urge to satisfy the hunger craving in this manner must have seemed plausible. Surely that which is natural cannot be sinful. Why would it not be right to produce bread by the available supernatural power? Jesus instantly rejected it on the basis of Deut. 8:3, the gist of which is that spiritual nourishment is more than the gratification of physical appetite. Jesus rejected cheap bread as quickly as he would have rejected cheap grace. He refrained from using the miracles for selfish gratification. This would have been an unlawful gratification of lawful desire.

B. Lust of the eyes. The second temptation was in the opposite extreme. He stood the test of faith; now he had to withstand the temptation to fanaticism. Again he resorted to Deuteronomy: "Do not test the the LORD your God" (Deut. 6:16). The temptation to cast himself from "the highest point of the temple" (Matt. 4:5), possibly an allusion to the portico of SOLOMON'S COLONNADE, which rose over 300 ft. above the KIDRON Valley, was a temptation to do something spectacular in order to win quick public approbation. It was also tempting the Father; it was daring God to rescue him. Later Jesus was to encounter a similar temptation, to be acclaimed king by an enthusiastic multitude (Jn. 6:15). A similar temptation was presented to Jesus when PETER tried to dissuade him from the way of humiliation and suffering, to which the Master replied, "Get behind me, Satan" (Matt. 16:23). Jesus rejected it on the basis that it would be a challenge to the providence of God; it would be daring God to intervene in a dramatic manner. It would represent a refusal to wait upon the Lord. This was a temptation to which King SAUL succumbed when he took it in hand to offer the sacrifice himself without waiting longer for SAMUEL (1 Sam. 13:8–14).

C. Pride of life. The third and last temptation was that of gaining a legitimate end by unworthy means. The devil, to whom Jesus once referred as the ruler of this world (Jn. 14:30), is quoted as saying that he would give to Jesus the allegiance of the world

Traditional site of the Mount of Temptation. (View to the W.)

in return for an act of worship. This is a temptation implying that "the end justifies the means." It means that one can accept the services of the devil or of evil people if they will further what seems to be a worthy cause. This was the devil's last and final bid and apparently he himself thought that Jesus would not accept it. Jesus again replied by alluding to Deuteronomy, "Worship the Lord your God, and serve him only" (Matt. 4:10; cf. Deut. 6:13). In so doing Jesus chose the hard, slow way of persuasion rather than the use of force. In this respect, Christianity differs radically from the methodology of Islam, a fighting faith. With his answer Jesus repudiated the means that promised quick and spectacular gains at the sacrifice of principle. Following this audacious challenge, the devil left and angels came. Probably the devil came then as he has since, not in visible form, but in the area of thought and motive.

II. Could Jesus have sinned? The writer of Hebrews stated that Jesus was tempted in all points as we are (Heb. 2:18; 4:15), implying that the temptation was real and that he could have yielded, just as anyone could yield to temptation. In the opinion of many theologians, to deny that Jesus could have sinned is to deny his humanity and to fall into the error of DOCETISM, which maintains that his humanity was only an appearance and not actually real. Because Jesus was truly human, he could have yielded to these temptations and others like them and forfeited his messiahship and sonship. He refrained from using his divine status to minimize the temptations, but permitted them to be felt in their full force. Thus he was truly man as he was truly God.

Other scholars have argued that if Jesus had sinned, it would have necessarily involved both his human and his divine nature, implying that God himself would have sinned, which is of course impossible (cf. W. Grudem, *Systematic Theology: An Introduction to Christian Doctrine* [1994], 537–39). How to assert the reality of Jesus' temptation without compromising his deity is one of the challenges presented by the doctrine of the INCARNATION.

(See further G. C. Morgan, *The Crises of the Christ* [1903], 150–210; A. Edersheim, *Life and Times of Jesus the Messiah*, 2 vols. [1889], 1:291–307; W. Barclay, *The Mind of Jesus* [1961], 31–39; B. Gerhardsson, *The Testing of God's Son (Matt. 4:1–11 & par.): An Analysis of an Early Christian Midrash* [1966]; E. Best, *The Temptation and the Passion: The Markan Soteriology*, 2nd ed. [1990]; J. B. Gibson, *The Temptations of Jesus in Early Christianity* [1995]; C. M. Robbins, *The Testing of Jesus in Q* [2007].) G. A. TURNER

Ten Commandments. Traditional title given to the commandments that God wrote on two stone tablets and that are recorded in Exod. 20:1–17 and Deut. 5:6–21. The phrase itself occurs elsewhere as the rendering of Hebrew ʿăseret haddĕbārîm, literally, "the ten words" (Exod. 34:28; Deut. 4:13; 10:4). In two of these passages the SEPTUAGINT translates with *tous deka logous* (in Deut. 4:13 it uses *rēmata*), hence the alternative English title, *Decalogue*.

    I. Historical context
       A. The biblical account
       B. The critical debate
    II. Structure and general characteristics
    III. Content
       A. Love of God
       B. Love of one's neighbor
    IV. Decalogue and covenant
    V. Relevance to the Christian

I. Historical context

A. The biblical account. Exodus 19:1 and 16 indicate that the Ten Commandments, found in ch. 20, were proclaimed about three days after Israel's arrival at Mount SINAI in the third month (or "third new moon," NRSV) after their departure from Egypt. See EXODUS, THE. Jewish tradition conjectures that this date was that of PENTECOST. The voice of God announced these words in the hearing of the whole assembly (Deut. 5:22), and the finger of God inscribed them on both sides of two stone tablets (Exod. 31:18; 32:15–16) which Moses received on the mountain, forty days after the making of the COVENANT. Moses however shattered the tablets on discovering his people's lapse into idolatry (32:19); but God reaffirmed the covenant, giving Moses further subsidiary laws to record (34:10–27), and inscribing again the Ten Commandments himself on two fresh tablets prepared by Moses (34:1, 28; Deut. 10:4). The

Replica of the ark of the covenant, which held the Ten Commandments, Aaron's staff that budded, and manna.

tablets were placed in due course in the ARK OF THE COVENANT (Exod. 40:20; Deut. 10:5), which took its name from the covenant whose requirements they summarized.

B. The critical debate. Critical scholars chiefly look to the contents and form of the Decalogue, rather than its accompanying narrative, to establish its origin. The following are some of the main landmarks in the debate.

J. Wellhausen, in the late 19th cent., argued that the Decalogue could not have preceded the chief preexilic prophets, whose teachings it seemed to him to embody, and whom he reckoned to have been the pioneers in condemning idolatry. Israel's initial unconcern on this point suggested to him the absence of any early law against it. This reasoning, together with the trend of Pentateuchal criticism, carried such weight that only a minority of critics in the generation after Wellhausen were prepared to ascribe the Decalogue substantially to Moses.

In 1927 S. Mowinckel (*Le Décalogue*) gave a new direction to the argument by locating the origin of the Decalogue in Israel's long-standing cultic practice. While he attributed the Decalogue of Exod. 20 and Deut. 5 to the disciples of Isaiah, he visualized its ancient prototype in the "entry liturgy," which challenged the would-be worshiper at a sanctuary gate (cf., according to H. Gunkel, Ps. 15; 24:3–6). Mowinckel saw its more direct ancestor in an opening proclamation at the Enthronement Festival which he had postulated in his *Psalmenstudien* (1921–24). Subsequent critical debate has mostly accepted the link between the Decalogue and the cult, while differing over its precise nature.

In 1934 A. Alt (*Die Ursprünge des Israelitischen Rechts*; English trans. in *Essays on Old Testament History and Religion* [1966], 81–132) classified the Pentateuchal laws by their forms of expression, distinguishing casuistic from apodictic laws. The former (mostly introduced by an "if" clause) were secular, and, in Alt's view, drawn from Canaanite custom; the latter (often introduced by an imperative or a prohibition, exactly after the manner of the Ten Commandments), proclaimed Yahweh's unconditional will and were a uniquely Israelite phenomenon, stemming from the desert and the covenant. They tended to be grouped together, sometimes in tens or twelves, and their cultic use is illustrated by the ceremony at Mount Ebal (Deut. 27:13–26). This analysis pointed to the pre-Canaanite stage that is the biblical setting of the Decalogue; but Alt, like Mowinckel, considered our actual Decalogue a late specimen compared with other groups of commands in the Pentateuch.

G. E. Mendenhall (in *BA* 17 [1954]: 26–46, 50–76) drew attention to HITTITE suzerainty treaties, whose structure and language seemed closely parallel to those of the Decalogue and other covenant passages (see TREATY). In structure they consisted of (1) the preamble introducing the king and his titles (cf. Exod. 20:1–2a), (2) the historical prologue emphasizing benefits conferred (cf. 20:2b), (3) the stipulations (cf. 20:3–17), (4) provision for the treaty's deposit in the temple and its periodic public reading (cf. 25:16; Deut. 31:9–13), (5) a list of gods as witnesses (the OT naturally lacks this), (6) curses and blessings (cf. Deut. 27–28). In language the Hittite stipulations were a combination of case law and apodictic law very similar to what is found in Exod. 21–23. Mendenhall pointed out that this form of treaty was widely known in the ANE in the time of Moses (the Hittite empire collapsed in 1200), and argued that the strong cohesion of the Israelite tribes could be due to a covenant bond of this sort between Yahweh as overlord and the various tribes as his vassals, established through Moses on the basis of the Decalogue.

Covenants and cult have continued to be the main areas of subsequent discussion. D. J. McCarthy (*Treaty and Covenant* [1963]), for example, has argued at considerable length against the validity of using Hittite treaties to date the Sinai material, reckoning that the earliest Sinai tradition told of a ritual blood-bond rather than a contractual treaty, and that the Hittite treaty pattern probably survived the Hittite empire to serve as a model for later Israelite thought on the covenant. E. Gerstenberger (in *JBL* 84 [1965]: 38–51) maintains that "treaty stipulation and commandment have little in common" and derives the commands of the Decalogue not from covenant or cult but from the necessities of communal life: they were brought into the cult, but originated in the teaching given by fathers to sons, or by elders to the clan. A. S. Kapelrud (in *ST* 18 [1964]: 81–90) also emphasizes their social character, but puts them into the historical context of the exodus, arguing, first, that something like the Decalogue would be a necessary common basis if several tribes were to unite; and secondly, that their sense of deliverance and call by Yahweh made a covenant of allegiance, written in the form of a suzerainty treaty, a natural expression of their new status. It was the fruit, in his view, of reflection, and was concluded not at Sinai but in the course of a prolonged sojourn at Kadesh. H. H. Rowley (in *BJRL* 34 [1951–52]: 81–118 = *Men of God* [1963], 1–36) puts a similar emphasis on the exodus experience of the tribes delivered from Egypt, but argues unequivocally for the indispensable role of Moses as the mediator of such a covenant. (For a more recent discussion see C. M. Carmichael, *The Origins of Biblical Law: The Decalogues and the Book of the Covenant* [1992].)

This sample of divided opinions suggests that the contents of the Decalogue, taken alone, are inconclusive for its provenance. Nothing in it precludes (as some early critics considered) its transmission to Israel through Moses; but all our specific information is contained not in the commandments but in the surrounding narrative. As long as the two are studied apart, the debate is likely to continue indefinitely.

II. Structure and general characteristics.

The two groups of commands, numbers 1–4 and 5–10, oriented respectively Godward and manward, correspond to the two great commandments of love toward God and one's neighbor, in which Jesus summed up the Law and the Prophets (Matt. 22:37–40). Their inscription on two tablets seems to answer to this division, although it is not stated to do so. (M. G. Kline, *Treaty of the Great King: The Covenant Structure of Deuteronomy* [1963], ch. 1, regards the two as duplicates, analogous to those of human treaties; but duplicates that are stored together serve little purpose.) The unity underlying the duality is made explicit in the fourth commandment as given in Deut. 5:14–15, where it is shown that God's due is also one's neighbor's blessing.

The longer commands (1–5 and 10) should probably be analyzed as commands-plus-expositions. This is suggested not merely by the uneven pattern, but also by the alternative endings to the SABBATH command (Exod. 20:11; Deut. 5:14c–15), which draw out different lessons from the basic injunction, and the smaller variations in the tenth commandment (see III.B.10, below).

The commands are expressed in the negative, except for numbers 4 and 5 (the last of the Godward and first of the manward clauses). Two are reinforced by warnings (nos. 2 and 3) and one by a promise (no. 5). All are spoken to the individual. As to their demands, three (nos. 1, 5, 10) concern the person's inner commitment and attitudes, and the remainder safeguard the practical expression of them in the spheres of worship and society. There is no tension between the cultic and the ethical, for the demands of the latter follow hard on those of the former; nor between law and love, for both are specified together in the phrase, "those who love me and keep my commandments" (Exod. 20:6; cf. Jn. 14:15).

III. Content

A. Love of God (commandments 1–4)

1. No other gods (Exod. 20:2–3; Deut. 5:6–7). The first command—indeed the whole Decalogue—rests on a statement about God: who he is ("I am the LORD" [Yahweh]), whose he is ("your God"), and what he has done ("who brought you out of Egypt, out of the land of slavery"). These facts precede and underlie the imperatives; all is for his sake (cf. "You shall be holy to me because I, the LORD, am holy," Lev. 20:26).

Literally, the prohibition runs, "There shall not be to you other gods"; it possibly implies the reminder that these gods exist only in their worshipers' minds. The phrase "before me" means "in my presence," as against "taking precedence over me." It means, not that this allegiance could ever be concealed, but that its very existence is an affront to the Lord. The alternate rendering, "besides me" (NIV mg.) conveys the substance of the command (cf. "with me," Exod. 20:23 KJV).

This is the fundamental commandment of the ten, the central issue between God and Israel in the OT. The devil tempted even the Lord at this point (Matt. 4:8–10).

2. No idols (Exod. 20:4–6; Deut. 5:8–10). The concern of this command is that the people should WORSHIP God not as they might imagine but as he has revealed (cf. Jn. 4:24, "in spirit and in truth"), that is, not by the aesthetic or intellectual appeal of what is human, but in response to the Spirit and Word of God. One should note Deut. 4 (esp. vv. 12 and 15–19), which stresses the invisibility of God, as well as passages that expose the farcical side of IDOLATRY (e.g., Isa. 40:18–20; 44:9–20). The command against making any likenesses belongs inseparably to the command not to bow down to them; it is not a general prohibition of representational art for ornament or instruction (as Exod. 25:18–20 and other passages make clear).

God's JEALOUSY in this context means his burning zeal for his people's fidelity; it has the exclusiveness of marital love (cf. Num. 5:29–31). The word can have a bad sense (cf. Gen. 37:11), but more often a good one (e.g., Ps. 69:9, Isa. 9:7; Zech. 8:2). Used of the Lord, it reveals him as the God who cares. His "punishing the children for the sin of the fathers" (Exod. 20:5) means, not that he holds the children guilty for something they have not done (cf. Ezek. 18:19–20), but that he has bound all lives together, for good and ill (and more good than ill; cf. the numbers implied in "the third and fourth generation" [Exod. 34:7], as against the "thousand generations" included in his blessing [Deut. 7:9]). The process is shown more circumstantially in other passages (e.g., Prov. 14:34; 29:18; Isa. 48:18; Hos. 4:1–9).

3. God's name (Exod. 20:7; Deut. 5:11). To "take the name … in vain" (KJV; lit., "for worthlessness," i.e., for no good purpose, thus NIV, "You shall not misuse the name") is to use it irresponsibly, whether in worship (cf. Ps. 50:16; Isa. 29:13), in common speech (cf. Matt. 5:34), or in an attempt to wield power (cf. Acts 19:13–16).

JACOB (Gen. 32:30) and MANOAH (Jdg. 13:18) had the sanctity of this name sharply impressed on them, and Moses' vision of God was crowned with its proclamation together with a catalogue of the divine attributes (Exod. 33:18–19; 34:5–8). It is part of God's self-giving; not to be exploited, but to enable his people to call on him in truth, and "to enter a worshipful and uplifting fellowship" with him (R. S. Wallace, *The Ten Commandments* [1965], 53). Hence the godly are "those who love your name" (Ps. 5:11), and who are dedicated to seeing it hallowed and glorified (Matt. 6:9; Jn. 12:27–28).

The warning, "the LORD will not hold anyone guiltless" (Exod. 20:7), may suggest a primary context of perjury (i.e., a false oath may gain you earthly acquittal, but not heavenly; cf. NJPS). The ninth commandment, however, partly covers this element, while the first four are chiefly concerned with the wider issue of the relationship of God and his people.

4. God's day (Exod. 20:8–11; Deut. 5:12–15). The term SABBATH means "ceasing" or "rest" (cf. Gen. 2:2; Exod. 16:23, 30). Moses had explained it to Israel as both God's day (16:23) and God's gift (16:29). The Decalogue underlines both aspects. It is "holy" and belongs "to the LORD," who "made it holy" (cf. Exod. 31:14, which indicates that people must not profane or secularize it with their own affairs; note further Isa. 58:13); at the same time it refreshes man and beast, "that your manservant and maidservant may rest, as you do" (Deut. 5:14). It is a day, in fact, that God "blessed" as well as "made holy."

Exodus and Deuteronomy diverge in their wording of this command (hardly at all in the case of the other commandments). Deuteronomy opens with "Observe," as against "Remember" (but the two words are virtually synonymous; both assume some prior knowledge of the day; cf. Exod. 16:22–30); it adds the phrase "as the LORD your God has commanded you"; and it ends on the theme of slavery (Deut. 5:15) as against that of the creation (Exod. 20:11). See also above, section II.

For the Sabbath as a sign of the covenant see Exod. 31:12–17; Ezek. 20:12. For further details of

Sabbath laws see Exod. 34:21; 35:2-3; Lev. 23:3; 24:8; Num. 15:32-36; 28:9-10. For Sabbath observance in the OT see Exod. 16:22-30; Neh. 10:31; 13:15-22; Ps. 92; Jer. 17:21-27; Ezek. 20:12-24; Amos 8.5. On the relevance of this command to the Christian see below, section V. (For a summary of critical speculation on the origin of the Sabbath [e.g., as variously derived from the Babylonians, the Kenites, the Canaanites, the moon, or the market] see J. J. Stamm and M. E. Andrew, *The Ten Commandments in Recent Research* [1967], 90-95.)

B. Love of one's neighbor (commandments 5-10)

1. Respect for parents (Exod. 20:12; Deut. 5:16). The authority of a father and mother is seen in the OT as part of the divine order, inherent in their position rather than their personal qualities (cf. Gen. 9:20-27, where HAM's unfilial behavior is not excused by NOAH's lapse). Cursing and defying father or mother were capital offenses (Exod. 21:17; Deut. 21:18-21; cf. Prov. 30:11, 17). The promise attached to this fifth command (cf. Eph. 6:2) emphasizes the character of the Decalogue as the expression of God's covenant with his pilgrim people, not an anthology of maxims for the good life. The corresponding duty of the parents was to train up their children in God's law (Deut. 6:6-9, 20-25; cf. Prov. 1:8; 6:20; 22:6).

Deuteronomy 5:16 adds two corroborative phrases and the NT quotes the command in several contexts (cf. Matt. 19:19; Eph. 6:2-3). Our Lord could override its customary expression (cf. Lk. 9:59-62), but he countenanced no pretext for evading it (Matt. 15:4-9; cf. 1 Tim. 5:4, 8).

2. No murder (Exod. 20:13; Deut. 5:17). The Hebrew verb here (*rāṣaḥ H8357*) makes "murder" (NIV and other modern versions) a more accurate rendering than "kill" (KJV), a fact corroborated by the context of Exodus and Deuteronomy, which commands the killing of animals and at times (judicially or in war) of human beings. The penalty for murder as against manslaughter (Num. 35:22-25) was death; it was not reducible to any lesser sentence (Num. 35:31). This penalty was already in force before the Sinaitic law in the decrees to Noah (Gen. 9:6).

Our Lord applied the commandment to those who indulge in anger, insults, and quarrels (Matt. 5:21-26), and pointed out the spiritual kinship of the murderer to the devil, "a murderer from the beginning" (Jn. 8:44). John brands as a murderer "anyone who hates his brother" (1 Jn. 3:15).

3. No adultery (Exod. 20:14; Deut. 5:18). In the OT, adultery refers typically to sexual intercourse between a man and a married woman (cf. Ezek. 16:32). The description and the penalty (death) applied to both parties (Lev. 20:10; cf. Deut. 22:22); a betrothed woman was counted in this context as a wife (Deut. 22:23-24).

While adultery, with the wrong it directly inflicts on a third party, is reckoned a graver offense than FORNICATION (for which some restitution could be made: cf. Deut. 22:28-29 with vv. 22-27), the OT strongly denounces all extramarital sexual intercourse, condemning the male offender even more strongly than the female (cf. Hos. 4:14). The foundation ordinance of MARRIAGE authorizes intercourse only after the break with the parental home (Gen. 2:24), which distinguishes marriage from betrothal. Jesus showed that the commandment could be violated by thought as well as act (Matt. 5:27-28), and even under cover of legality through the DIVORCE of a faithful partner (Matt. 5:31-32; Mk. 10:11-12). See SEX.

4. No stealing (Exod. 20:15; Deut. 5:19). While enforcing the plain sense of this prohibition (requiring as much as fivefold restitution of stolen property, Exod. 22:1-4) and making kidnapping a capital offense (Deut. 24:7), the OT also condemns various forms of indirect theft, such as exploitation (Exod. 22:25-27; 23:6-8), fraud (Amos 8:5b), dispossession (Mic. 2:2), and the withholding of dues from man and God (Prov. 3:27-28; Mal. 3:8-9).

The NT endorses the command and, characteristically, goes further: the former thief is urged to honesty and hard work, but also to charitable giving (Eph. 4:28). It is a classic example of love filling the law to overflowing.

5. No false witness (Exod. 20:16; Deut. 5:20). The context of this commandment is the law court. Deuteronomy 19:15-21 adds the safeguards of requiring a minimum of two witnesses for a criminal charge, and of making a false witness liable to the penalty to which he exposed the accused.

The trial of NABOTH (cf. 1 Ki. 21:13–14) and that of Christ (cf. Matt. 26:59–61) demonstrate how much can hang on this commandment and how little a legal safeguard will avail where conscience fails. PAUL expounds truthfulness in its only effective setting: the mutual love of which all the manward commandments are partial expositions (Eph. 4:15–16, 25).

6. No coveting (Exod. 20:17; Deut. 5:21). Other commands (the first and fifth) have concerned inner attitudes, but none as explicitly as this one. Paul cites it in Rom. 7:7–12 as opening his eyes to a sinfulness which he would not else have recognized. He quotes only the commandment proper (7:7 and 13:9); the list of objects included in the OT passages gives its application. The list varies in order and content between Exod. 20:17 and Deut. 5:21, the latter opening with "your neighbor's wife" and including later the term "land."

The Hebrew verb used in this commandment is *ḥāmad* H2773, which the LXX renders with the Greek *epithymeō* G2121, common also in the NT (noun *epithymia* G2123; see DESIRE and LUST). It denotes any selfish longing of fallen human beings (cf. Gal. 5:16–17). In Jas. 1:14, it is the precondition of sin; in 1 Jn. 2:16, the craving for worldly satisfactions. In Matt. 5:28 adultery is located in this attitude. Here is the chief root of manward sins, the chief negation of love. By ending on this note the Decalogue dispels the complacency of the externalist. Our Lord's exposition of the inward aspect of the commands, far from being imposed on the material, is already here in germ.

IV. Decalogue and covenant. (See also above, I.B) The law was given in a setting of grace, in that Israel's very presence at Sinai was due to God's intervention (Exod. 19:4; 20:2), based on the patriarchal covenant (2:24) and directed toward making her uniquely his possession, a priestly and holy people (19:5–6). Fulfillment of such a calling presupposes conformity to his will (19:5), and this divine will was summarized in the Decalogue and expounded in the accompanying law. To Yahweh, so revealed, Israel pledged her obedience in the covenant described in Exod. 24:3–11.

This law, as Gal. 3:17 states, was not given to annul the covenant with Abraham, but to nurture its recipients in the knowledge of God, and of themselves as transgressors, escorting them toward Christ, who is the fulfillment of the promise to Abraham (3:19) and the ground of our justification (3:24).

V. Relevance to the Christian. The NT frequently draws on the Decalogue for its moral teaching, whether by quotation or as a framework, and treats it as fulfilled, not abrogated, by love. By contrast, the Mosaic ritual laws are shown to be superseded (cf. Mk. 7:19b; Gal. 5:2; Heb. 10:18), and the administrative details of the OT are not carried over into the new covenant.

The Ten Commandments retain their force, then, but stand clear of their supporting regulations. For example, murder no longer calls for the next-of-kin's intervention, nor does adultery call for stoning. The Sabbath, similarly, is set free from the rules which belonged to the ceremonial law (cf. Col. 2:16–17), to find its full stature as a creation ordinance designed to be a blessing and hallowed for God (Gen. 2:3). Our Lord's use of it for worship and service set the NT pattern, and the transition from Jewish Sabbath to Lord's Day began on the first Easter and developed in the age of the apostles (Jn. 20:1, 19, 26; Acts 2:1; 20:7; 1 Cor. 16:2; Rev. 1:10).

The position is summed up in the new covenant promise, "I will put my law in their minds / and write it on their hearts" (Jer. 31:33), together with the words of Paul in Rom. 8:4, "in order that the righteous requirements of the law might be fully met in us, who do not live according to the sinful nature but according to the Spirit." (Cf. Rom. 13:8–10.) See also ETHICS.

(In addition to the titles mentioned in the body of this article, see C. F. H. Henry, *Christian Personal Ethics* [1957]; J. Murray, *Principles of Conduct* [1957]; J. B. Coffman, *The Ten Commandments Yesterday and Today* [1961]; B.-Z. Segal and G. Levi, eds., *The Ten Commandments in History and Tradition* [1990]; S. M. Hauerwas and W. H. Willimon, *The Truth about God: The Ten Commandments in Christian Life* [1999]; W. P. Brown, ed., *The Ten Commandments: The Reciprocity of Faithfulness* [2004]; P. G. Kuntz,

(*The Ten Commandments in History: Mosaic Paradigms for a Well Ordered Society* [2004], D. H. Aaron, *Etched in Stone: The Emergence of the Decalogue* [2006]; R. E. Van Harn, *The Ten Commandments for Jews, Christians, and Others* [2007].)   D. KIDNER

tenon. This English term is used by the KJV and other versions to render the common Hebrew word *yād* H3338 ("hand") in several verses (Exod. 26:17, 19; 36:22, 24). The reference is to some kind of wooden peg or projection on the end of a piece of wood for insertion into a corresponding hole in another piece to form a secure joint. The three sides of the tabernacle were made of forty-eight "frames," or boards, each one held in place at the bottom by tenons fitted into sockets of silver to give the boards stability.   S. BARABAS

tent. A temporary dwelling generally made of strong black cloth woven from goats' hair. From remote antiquity it has been the typical abode of the BEDOUIN, the nomadic Arab of the Arabian, Syrian, and N African deserts. Tents are of various types: conical, oval, oblong. They are pitched by women stretching goats' haircloth over poles with cords of goats' hair or hemp fastened to stakes. The stakes are hardwood pegs driven into the ground with wooden mallets (Jdg. 4:21). Reinforcements with narrow strips of cloth are used under the poles and where cords are fastened. Side curtains are of goats' haircloth or mats woven from reeds or rushes. These are also used for dividing walls when needed to separate families or animals from people (2 Chr. 14:15). The back of the tent is closed; the front often open. A corner of the curtain where two ends meet is turned back to form the door (Gen. 18:1). Tents are a protection from heat and cold, but hardly rain proof.

Normally, one pack animal, such as a donkey or camel, can carry all the belongings of a nomadic family. Dining utensils consist of two tinned copper cooking vessels, a shallow tray of the same metal, a coffee set consisting of roasting pan, mortar and pestle, and boiling pot and cups. Food is usually kept in bags of goats' hair, while liquids—i.e., milk, oil, and wine—are stored in skins. Poor people have little or no rugs on their dirt floors, but the wealthier cover their floors with mats of goats' hair or straw, or woolen rugs (Jdg. 4:18).

A sheikh, or chief, has several tents, one for himself and guests, others for his wives and female servants, and still others for his animals (Gen. 31:33; Heb. *ʾōhel* H185). The patriarchs, ABRAHAM, ISAAC, JACOB (cf. also ESAU), were all wealthy tent dwellers. "Abram had become very wealthy in livestock and in silver and gold. From the Negev he went from place to place until he came to Bethel, to the place between Bethel and Ai where his tent had been earlier" (Gen. 13:2–3). Later, "Abram moved his tents and went to live near the great trees of Mamre at Hebron" (13:18). Isaac, a farmer and herdsman, lived in tents (24:67; 26:12–25). Jacob spent his life in tents, mostly as a rich nomad in Canaan (31:33; 33:19; 35:21).

The TABERNACLE built by MOSES was called the "Tent of Meeting" (*ʾōhel môʿēd*), a phrase that occurs numerous times in Exodus, Leviticus, and Numbers. In time the tent became a symbol for home and a general term for dwelling or habitation (Lk. 16:9; Gk. *skēnē* G5008). The term was used symbolically, with nostalgic recall, long after Israel was settled in Canaan. DAVID inquired, "O LORD, who may abide in your tent?" (Ps. 15:1 NRSV), and expressed his own wish, "I long to dwell in your tent forever" (61:4; cf. 78:60). The prophets often used the term figuratively. ISAIAH, in predicting Babylon's desolation, declared that "no Arab will pitch his tent there" (Isa. 13:20), and by contrast spoke of Jerusalem as "a tent that will not be moved" (33:20; cf. 54:2). JEREMIAH, lamenting the fall of Judah, said, "My tent is destroyed; all its ropes are snapped. My sons are gone from me and are no more; no one is left now to pitch my tent or to set up my shelter" (Jer. 10:20). The apostle PAUL called the flesh "the earthly tent we live in" (2 Cor. 5:1), and the author of HEBREWS spoke of the "true tabernacle [*skēnē*] set up by the Lord, not by man" (Heb. 8:2; cf. Rev. 15:5).   G. B. FUNDERBURK

tentmaker. This term (Gk. *skēnopoios* G5010) occurs only once in the Bible, and that reference introduces three tentmakers. PAUL had just come from ATHENS to CORINTH, and to find suitable lodging he sought one of his own race and his own trade. He found both in "a Jew named Aquila ... with his wife Priscilla ... and because he was a tentmaker as they were, he stayed and worked with them" (Acts 18:2-3). Jewish parents taught their children trades, usually one that was pursued in successive generations by the family. Hence, Jesus was taught the carpenter's trade and Paul that of tentmaker. Paul's native province of CILICIA was so noted for its good grade of goats' haircloth, used largely for tents, that it was exported by the designation of Cilician cloth. Paul's skill in this craft probably consisted of the sewing together of the proper lengths of cloth and the attaching of ropes and loops. — G. B. FUNDERBURK

Tent of Meeting. See TABERNACLE.

Tephon tee´fon (Τεφων). KJV Taphon. A Judean city fortified by BACCHIDES (1 Macc. 9:50). Tephon may be a variant of TAPPUAH; if so, the reference here is probably to a town that had been in Ephraimite territory in OT times (Josh. 17:7; see J. A. Goldstein, *I Maccabees*, AB 41 [1976], 386).

Terah (person) ter´uh (תֶּרַח H9561, perhaps "ibex" [see discussion in *HALOT*, 4:1792, and *ABD*, 6:387-88]; Θάρα G2508). Son of NAHOR and father of ABRAHAM (Gen. 11:24-32; Josh. 24:2; 1 Chr. 1:26); included in Luke's GENEALOGY OF JESUS CHRIST (Lk. 3:34 [KJV, "Thara"]). STEPHEN made reference to Abraham's father without mentioning his name (Acts 7:2).

Terah lived in UR of the Chaldees, identified by most scholars as Tell Muqayyar, on the lower EUPHRATES near the Persian Gulf. From Ur, Terah migrated northward some 500 mi. along the Euphrates to the city of Haran, located about 275 mi. NE of DAMASCUS. See HARAN (PLACE). Terah had two other sons, NAHOR and Haran. See HARAN (PERSON). Although Abram is listed first, it does not necessarily follow that he was the oldest son. Haran, who died before the family moved northward, may have been the oldest. It was Haran's son LOT who eventually went with Abram to Palestine. According to Josh. 24:2 and 15, Terah was an idolater. Nannar (Semitic Sin) was the principal deity worshiped at Ur, as well as at Haran, during the time of Terah. — S. J. SCHULTZ

Terah (place) ter´uh (תָּרַח H9562). KJV Tarah. A stopping place of the Israelites, between Tahath and Mithcah (Num. 33:25-26). The location is unknown.

teraphim ter´uh-fim (תְּרָפִים H9572, perhaps "weak [i.e., vile] things" or "demons" [cf. *HALOT*, 4:17-94-96]). This transliteration is used by the KJV in Jdg. 17:5; 18:14-20, and Hos. 3:4. The NRSV uses it also in 2 Ki. 23:24; Ezek. 21:26; and Zech. 10:2. In addition to these passages, the Hebrew word occurs in Gen. 31:19, 34-35; 1 Sam. 15:23; 19:13, 16. The NIV avoids the transliteration altogether and renders the word as "household gods" (Gen. 31:19, 34-35; Jdg. 18:14-20; 2 Ki. 23:24) or "idol(s)" (Jdg. 17:5; 1 Sam. 19:13, 16; Ezek. 21:21; Hos. 3:4; Zech. 10:2); in one passage it uses "idolatry" (1 Sam. 15:23, as do also KJV and NRSV). See IDOLATRY.

The images referred to by this term ranged from rather small (Gen. 31:34-35) to nearly life-sized (1 Sam. 19:13, 16). Archaeological discoveries at NUZI in Iraq have illuminated the function and significance of these idols. (Cf. C. H. Gordon, *The Ancient Near East*, 3rd ed. [1965], 128-30.) Their possession constituted the headship of the household with all of the rights attendant thereto. RACHEL's theft of the teraphim (Gen. 31:19) was an attempt to procure such headship for her husband, although it was rightfully her brother's. LABAN's extreme displeasure is explicable in this light. (Cf. M. Greenberg in *JBL* 81 [1962]: 239-48.)

It appears that throughout much of their history the Israelites did not find possession of teraphim inconsistent with Yahwism (cf. Jdg. 17; 18; and esp. 1 Sam. 19:13 and 16, which indicate that they were even found in the household of DAVID). They are spoken of with disapproval from the time of SAMUEL (1 Sam. 15:23) to that of ZECHARIAH (Zech. 10:2). The function of teraphim of which the prophets most disapproved was DIVINATION. As divinatory objects they often are mentioned with EPHODS, which were also used for divination (Jdg. 17:5 and 18:14-20, where they seem to be separate from the idol, and Hos. 3:4). Among the things purged during JOSIAH's reform, teraphim seem to be grouped with mediums and wizards (2 Ki. 23:24). The king of Babylon is said to consult them (Ezek. 21:21) and Zechariah says they utter nonsense (Zech. 10:2). HOSEA speaks longingly of the day when Israel, in total dependence on God, will be able to live without the aid of teraphim. (See further *DDD*, 844–50.) J. OSWALT

terebinth. Also known as the turpentine tree, the terebinth (*Pistacia terebinthus*, including the subspecies *P. terebinthus palaestina*) is a deciduous and long-lived tree native to the Mediterranean region. The NIV and the NRSV use "terebinth" to render ʾēlâ H461 in two passages where this Hebrew term is distinguished from ʾallôn H473, "oak" (Isa. 6:13 [KJV, "teil tree"]; Hos. 4:13 [KJV, "elms"]; the NRSV uses "terebinth" also in the title of Ps. 56, and the NJPS uses it some twenty times to render more than one term). For discussion see FLORA (under *Anacardiaceae*) and OAK.

Teresh tihr´esh (תֶּרֶשׁ H9575, meaning uncertain). One of two EUNUCHS or officers in the court of XERXES (Ahasuerus) who plotted his assassination. MORDECAI found out about it, thus saving the king's life, and the two men were hanged (Esth. 2:21–23; 6:2; in Add. Esth. 1:10 and 12:1 he is called "Tharra").

Terror on Every Side. See MAGOR-MISSABIB.

terrorists. See ASSASSINS.

Tertius tuhr´shee-uhs (Τέρτιος G5470, from Latin *Tertius*, "third"). The SCRIBE or AMANUENSIS to whom PAUL dictated his epistle to the ROMANS. Among Paul's greetings to the Christians in ROME, Tertius inserts his own, "I Tertius, who wrote down this letter, greet you in the Lord" (Rom. 16:22; the Gk. can also be understood to mean, "I Tertius, who wrote down this letter in the Lord, greet you"). Some identify him with SILAS on the improbable assumption that the latter's name derived from Hebrew *šĕlîšî* H8958, "third" (the meaning of *tertius* in Latin). Others conjecture that he was a Roman Christian living in CORINTH, from where the letter was written. Paul seems to have customarily dictated his letters to an amanuensis, adding a greeting in his own hand as "the distinguishing mark in all my letters" (2 Thess. 3:17). A. M. Ross

Tertullian tuhr-tuhl´yuhn. One of the great Latin apologetes in the ancient church, Septimius Tertul- lianus was born in the middle of the 2nd cent. in N Africa, probably in Carthage, where he was trained in literature and rhetoric. He was converted to Christianity as an adult and some years later joined the Montanist sect, which emphasized eschatological expectations and the supernatural work of the Spirit (including esp. prophecy). Most details about his life are uncertain, but he became a prolific and powerful theological writer who greatly influenced the articulation of Christian doctrine in the Latin-speaking church. Without rejecting allegorical INTERPRETATION, Tertullian preferred a historical approach to Scripture. A rigorist in his understanding of the Christian life, he could be ruthless in controversy, but many scholars credit him with thoughtfulness and a discriminating mind. He is thought to have died shortly after the year 220. (See J. Morgan, *The Importance of Tertullian in the Development of Christian Dogma* [1928]; T. P. O'Malley, *Tertullian and the Bible: Language, Imagery, Exegesis* [1967]; G. L. Bray, *Holiness and the Will of God: Perspectives on the Theology of Tertullian* [1979]; T. D. Barnes, *Tertullian: A Historical and Literary Study* [1985, reissue of 1971 ed. with corrections and a postscript]; D. Rankin, *Tertullian and the Church* [1995]; E. F. Osborn, *Tertullian: First Theologian of the West* [1997]; G. D. Dunn, *Tertullian* [2004].)

Tertullus tuhr-tuhl´uhs (Τέρτυλλος G5472, from Latin *Tertullus*, diminutive of *tertius*, "third"). The professional orator hired by the Jews to state their case against PAUL before FELIX, Roman governor of JUDEA (Acts 24:1–9). He may have been a Roman, judging from his Latin name (although such names were common among Jews and Greeks); or he may have been a Jew, since he identifies himself with his clients (however, it is a lawyer's custom to do so).

With traditional courtesy Tertullus began his clever rhetoric by flattering the governorship of Felix beyond the facts. He attributed the riot in Jerusalem to the agitation of Paul, ringleader of an illegal sect who was detained in custody by the Jews for trying to "desecrate the temple" (Acts 24:6). Paul was thus made out to be an enemy of the public peace and of Jewish religion, both of which Felix was charged to uphold. The speech of Tertullus should be compared with the factual account of the incident (21:27–40), with the letter of CLAU-

The coastal city of Caesarea, where Tertullus made a case against the apostle Paul.

dius Lysias the tribune (23:26–30), and with the reserve of Paul's reply (24:10–21).

A. M. Ross

test. See TEMPTATION.

testament. This English term (Latin *testamentum*, "last will," from *testari*, "to be a witness") is used by the KJV over a dozen times in the NT as the rendering of Greek *diathēkē* G1347 (Matt. 26:28 et al.). In extrabiblical literature this Greek word usually meant "last will," but in the NT (and LXX) it appears to mean "covenant," and it is so rendered usually in modern versions. See COVENANT (NT) I. In two passages, however, the meaning of the word is disputed. The author of Hebrews links *diathēkē* with the death of the person who has made the disposition (Heb. 9:16–17), and therefore most scholars prefer the translation "will" here. Similarly, it is argued by some that when PAUL uses the illustration of a human *diathēkē* as something that cannot be altered (Gal. 3:15), he has in mind a last will or testament (cf. NRSV).

Testament of Abraham. For this and similar pseudepigraphic works, see under the name of the person (e.g., ABRAHAM, TESTAMENT OF; ADAM, TESTAMENT OF).

Testaments of the Twelve Patriarchs. An early pseudepigraph in which each of JACOB's twelve sons gives instructions to his descendants. It is the most important example of a large body of "testaments" of a Judeo-Christian character usually attributed to outstanding OT saints but also to Orpheus and to Jesus Christ. Each testament contains narrative as well as eschatological, demonological, and homiletical material, and much of the teaching is of a very noble character. The structure of the twelve sections is quite uniform: the patriarch calls his sons together, tells them of some events in his own life, warns them against a particular vice or admonishes to a particular virtue often connected with his own life, and prophesies their future in terms of their sins, punishments, salvation, and so forth. The sections close with the death of the patriarch and his burial at HEBRON. The inspiration for such a collection of testaments undoubtedly came from Gen. 49 (cf. also Deut. 33), where Jacob prophesied concerning each of his sons. The form of each section is also similar to that of the charges given by JOSHUA to Israel (Josh. 23–24) and by DAVID to his son SOLOMON (1 Ki. 2).

I. Contents. In his testament, REUBEN chiefly mourns over the sin he committed with BILHAH (Gen. 35:22). He gives details not found in the biblical account but similar to those included in the book of JUBILEES. Reuben attributes temptation to various spirits of deceit and spirits of error. He gives very strong warnings against the sin of fornication and scathes womankind for the wicked way in which they ensnare their male counterparts. The apologetic trend of the testament as a whole is to clear the name of Reuben as far as possible.

The next testament is that assigned to SIMEON, who dwells mainly upon his hatred and mistreatment of Joseph. He recognizes Joseph's goodness and repents of his evil attitude, all the while warning his sons against deceit and envy and admonishing them to live pure and upright lives. A brief warning against fornication is given in much the same spirit as is found in Reuben's testament, and the book of *1 Enoch* is referred to in this connection (see *T. Sim.* 5.3–4).

The testament of LEVI, which follows, is mainly apocalyptic in character. Levi falls into a deep sleep, and the heavens are opened to him and explanations concerning them are given. An angel gives the command to execute vengeance upon the Shechemites, and Levi's action against them is justified in spite of the sorrow it brought upon his father. Thereafter, Levi sees another vision in which seven men in white clothe him in priestly apparel. A promise is given to Levi to the effect that his descendants would participate in the three offices of prophet, priest, and king, a sign of the coming of the MESSIAH. There follows a short biographical section together with general admonitions. Levi then prophesies the corruption of his descendants, especially in the end of the ages, and this will bring a curse upon Israel. Sexual sins were to play an especially large part in this corruption. The destruction of the temple is predicted, most probably a reference to A.D. 70. In the end, a glorious "new priest" will appear and all the saints will be clothed with joy.

The testament of JUDAH is next and begins with a declaration of Judah's own prowess in killing wild animals (a lion, a bear, a boar, a leopard, and a wild bull) and in his battles with Canaanite kings and others. The assault upon the sons of Jacob by ESAU and Jacob's victory is given. There is a considerable degree of similarity between the accounts of *Jubilees* and some of those given here. Judah relates the sinful incident involving TAMAR with explana-

tory and excusatory remarks. He admonishes his children to upright living and in particular he denounces covetousness, drunkenness, and fornication. Judah expresses sorrow over the lewdness and wickedness of his children and looks forward to the day when they shall all repent, after which time the messianic "star of Jacob" will arise.

The testament of ISSACHAR is much shorter than the previous two. It dwells chiefly on the matter of the MANDRAKES familiar to us from the biblical account. There is little sorrow or repentance in this testament and, in fact, there is considerable exultation on the part of Issachar in the good life he has lived. He exhorts his sons to a similar life.

ZEBULUN's testament is also short and deals mostly with the sale of Joseph. Zebulun is justified by declaring that he took only the smallest part in the incident and received none of the money. He exhorts his sons to show compassion toward others even as he himself did.

In the short testament named after him, DAN confesses that he had hated Joseph enough to be joyful over his fate and he therefore admonishes his children to avoid anger. There is a significant messianic passage stating that salvation would arise from "the tribe of Judah and of Levi" (*T. Dan* 5.10). R. H. Charles edited out the words "Judah and of," arguing that the singular "tribe" admitted only Levi. The argument could hardly be sustained in the light of a similar construction in the SEPTUAGINT of 1 Ki. 12:23. And, in any case, the expectation of two Messiahs and perhaps even three is known now from the DEAD SEA SCROLLS.

The testament of NAPHTALI begins with the genealogy of Bilhah, his mother, whose father is called Rotheus, and there are some general exhortations with a reference to the writing of Enoch. There follows an account of Naphtali's vision in which Levi seizes the sun and Judah seizes the moon. Joseph seizes a bull and rides on it, and there is a storm at sea where the brothers are separated. There is another reference to future salvation which is to arise from Levi and Judah.

In the testament ascribed to him, GAD admits his hatred of Joseph and the whole work is taken up with the subject of hatred. Gad exhorts his sons to show love and concern and teaching of the noblest character is found here.

In the testament of ASHER there is a general and strong exhortation to obedience to righteousness in a tone similar to that of the WISDOM Literature or that of the epistle of James. Some of the instruction is developed along the lines of the doctrine of the Two Ways.

The testament of JOSEPH is mainly concerned with a lengthy description of the temptation of Joseph by the wife of POTIPHAR. It was God who guarded him from her vices and the whole incident is made the occasion for moral instruction to be given to Joseph's sons. There are quite a number of resemblances to the language of the Gospels (e.g., *T. Jos.* 1.6). There is a significant reference to the birth of a virgin who in turn gives birth to a conquering lamb (19.8).

The last of the testaments is that of BENJAMIN. This work opens with the account Joseph gave to Benjamin of his being sold into Egypt. Benjamin exhorts his children against deceit and sexual immorality. In this testament especially there is a considerable difference in the material included in the various texts, and Christian interpolation seems plain. The first two verses of ch. 11 often are taken to refer to PAUL the apostle.

II. Text. Both *T. Naphtali* and *T. Levi* circulated independently at one time, to judge by certain known fragments (see *APOT*, 2:361–67). The Dead Sea discoveries have confirmed this judgment and have, at the same time, added new light to the discussion of the text. A number of MSS of *T. Levi* were turned up. Cave 1 yielded sixty small fragments of one MS and Cave 4 produced slightly larger fragments of three MSS. One of these is dated paleographically to late 2nd cent. or early 1st cent. B.C. The text of these fragments is similar enough to the standard text to suggest that it may be the original. It has also been suggested that the two fragments of *T. Levi* from the 11th cent. A.D. found in the Cairo Genizah were copied from a Qumranic MS. A 10th-cent. Greek MS has interpolations possibly based on such a Qumranic MS, and a fragment of a 9th cent. Syriac MS may also be based upon it.

A few small fragments of a work closely related to *T. Naphtali* have also been found in the caves. A number of later Hebrew documents give evidence of extremely variant forms of text and of several amplified versions of parts of this testament. No evidence of any of the other testaments has been found at Qumran. It is possible that only *T. Levi* and *T. Naphtali* were known there. The other testaments are certainly replete with terms and concepts characteristic of Qumranic literature, but it is going too far to suggest that the work as a whole must have originated at Qumran. A common source for Qumranic literature and for the *Testaments* may be responsible for the similarity.

Apart from the evidence cited above, the first indication of the existence of this work is a reference by ORIGEN to "a certain book which is called 'The Testament of the Twelve Patriarchs,' although it is not accepted in the canon" (*Homily on Joshua* 15.6). Origen attributes to this book the teaching that a different demon acts in each sinner. It is true that *T. Reuben* 2–3 lists over a dozen spirits which act in mankind, but it is not entirely beyond dispute that Origen is referring to the *Testaments* as we know them. JEROME likewise speaks of the "book of Patriarchs" which he considers to be apocryphal. The material he refers to in this book is known to us from *T. Naphtali* 2.8 (see *Homily on Psalms* 14).

Over a dozen Greek MSS of the *Testaments* (some fragmentary) have been preserved, the earliest of which dates to the 10th cent. In addition, an important Armenian version survives in numerous MSS. Other versions (such as the Latin and the Slavonic) are of little textual value. All available witnesses possibly derive from a single uncial archetype, now lost, produced some time prior to the 9th cent.

III. Language. Because of a large number of Semitisms in the *Testaments*, R. H. Charles argued strongly for a Hebrew original, and his views were widely accepted at one time. Not all of his arguments are of equal value, however, and it must be remembered that Greek-speaking Jews may well have produced works in Greek having built-in Semitisms. Some of the Semitic features may have been imitations of the language of the SEPTUAGINT. Numerous other features, moreover, are distinctively Hellenistic. Although some portions of the *Testaments* may have had a Hebrew or Aramaic origin, present scholarship regards the work as a whole as having been written originally in Greek.

IV. Date. The date of composition of the *Testaments* was placed within very narrow limits by Charles. He cites *T. Reuben* 6.10–12 (cf. *T. Simeon* 5.5) as a reference to a high priest who is also king and warrior, which suggests the HASMONEAN priest-kings of the 2nd. cent. B.C. The fact that *T. Levi* 8.14 indicates that the priesthood is to be called by "a new name" is taken as a reference to the designation "priests of the Most High God," a title applied to the Hasmonean high priests in *Jubilees*, the *Assumption of Moses*, JOSEPHUS, and the TALMUD. Charles then argues that since, according to his reasoning, the author of the work was a PHARISEE, it must have been composed before the break between the Pharisees and John Hyrcanus took place, that is, near the end of the 2nd cent. B.C. Further, *T. Levi* 8.15 assigns the prophetic gift to a member of the Hasmonean dynasty together with the functions of kingship and priesthood. This could only be John Hyrcanus himself, which limits the date of composition to the period between 137 and 107 B.C. Furthermore, *T. Levi* 6.11 most probably refers to the destruction of SAMARIA, and this means that the book is to be dated to the period 109–107 B.C.

It is to be noted, however, that Charles's dating is based heavily upon the assumption of Pharisaic authorship. This presents some difficulties in view of the fact that the *Testaments* were preserved almost entirely in Christian circles and appear to have been ignored by, or unknown to, Jewish communities. If the *Testaments* were actually the work of an ESSENE community, for example, Charles's argument would be somewhat weakened. It should also be noted that his dating is based heavily upon the assumption of the essential unity of the book. Interestingly, *T. Levi*, from which he draws most of the evidence for his dating, is now known to have existed as a separate work.

It seems best to suggest, in the light of all the circumstances, that certain parts of the book were probably written in the 2nd cent. B.C. but that the work, as we now know it with all of its Christian and other additions, did not come into existence till perhaps sometime in the 2nd cent. A.D. According to a few scholars, the *Testaments* should in fact be regarded as a Christian composition that made use of some earlier Jewish document(s).

V. Integrity and authorship. There is little doubt that, on the whole, the *Testaments* show an essential unity of concepts and even of language. The form, too, of each of the twelve separate sections is essentially the same. But there seems to be enough evidence, especially since the discovery of the DSS, for stating that some parts of the work, most notably *T. Levi* and *T. Naphtali*, circulated as independent works. It may be, therefore, that we must speak of several authors and a final editor. While the attribution of the work to Pharisaic hands, especially to those of the early type with their emphasis upon the law and the messianic kingdom, has much to commend it, there are other factors which suggest that authors belonging to one or other of the Essene groups may have been responsible for most of the work. From what is now known of at least one Essene group, the Qumran community, the emphasis upon the law and the messianic kingdom in the *Testaments* would make Essene authorship as likely as Pharisaic. Further, the constant emphasis on sexual sins in the *Testaments* would admirably suit an Essenic origin for the work. Essenic authorship of the work would also make its preservation in Christian circles easier of explanation. It is certain, at least, that part of the work was read at Qumran, and this is more probable if the work originated in Essenic circles.

In view of the undoubtedly Christian passages and references in the work, however, it is most probable that the final editor or compiler was Christian or Jewish-Christian. In view of the references to the destruction of Jerusalem and the temple (*T. Levi* 15.1), a date of compilation near the end of the 1st cent. A.D. or early in the 2nd cent. A.D. seems most probable.

VI. Concepts and influence on the NT. As already remarked, the *Testaments* reflect some of the highest and noblest ethical teaching outside the NT. When a contrast between the teaching of the OT and of the NT can be seen, the teaching of the *Testaments* usually falls between the two. Thus, for example, on the question of FORGIVENESS, the understanding of the concept as expressed in *T. Gad* 6.3–7 is considerably different from that expressed in the OT, but strikingly similar to that expressed in Lk. 17:3–4 and Matt. 18:15–35. Forgiveness in *T. Gad* is seen as the restoration of the offending party to full communion and fellowship with the offended party. It is the offended party who is responsible for taking the initiative, and his mind must be rid of any feelings of resentment. Similarly, the supreme duty is summed up in terms almost, though not exactly, identical to those of the NT: "Love the Lord and your neighbor" (*T. Issachar* 5.2; cf. 7.6 and *T. Dan* 5.3). Further, the treatment of such questions as hatred, lying, envy, lust, covetousness, and the virtues of long-suffering, truthfulness, love, purity, generosity, and temperance in the *Testaments* is similar to that in the NT.

Concerning the more highly theological issues, we note that there is to be a RESURRECTION, first of the OT heroes, and next of the righteous on the right hand and of the wicked on the left (*T. Benjamin* 10.6–8). This is to take place on the earth, which is to last forever. The *Testaments* also show an advanced stage of demonology and of angelology. Interestingly, *T. Dan* 5.6 links the tribe of Dan with SATAN, and this is of assistance in explaining the omission of the tribe in the NT Apocalyptic list (Rev. 7:5–8).

Regarding eschatological expectation, two Messiahs are referred to in the *Testaments*, one to be descended from Levi, the other from Judah. Charles explained this problem by suggesting that, in the original work, a Messiah from Levi was expected and the expectation of a Messiah from Judah was supplied to the work by 1st-cent. additions. In the light of Qumranic messianic expectation, however, it is no longer necessary to appeal to source criticism to explain this apparent two-Messiah concept. The original itself may well have expected two Messiahs. The Messiah from Levi is a priestly Messiah and overshadows the Messiah from Judah. It is thought, by some, that this reflects the Hasmonean era when Israel was ruled by Maccabean priest-kings. This priestly Messiah was to be free from sin, to walk in meekness and righteousness, to establish a new priesthood under a new name, to mediate for the Gentiles, to be a prophet of the Most High and a king over all the nations. He was to wage battle against Israel's enemies and the powers of wickedness, to deliver the souls of the saints, to open paradise to the righteous, to feed the saints from the tree of life, to give the faithful power over evil spirits, and to bring sin to an end.

There is a fairly strong note of universalism in the book, the Gentiles being given opportunity for salvation. Indeed, all the Gentiles are to be saved through the example and teaching of Israel. The influence of concepts of the *Testaments* upon the NT seems unmistakable. In addition to this, there are many parallels where the NT appears to reflect the very phrasing of the *Testaments*.

(See further R. H. Charles, *The Greek Versions of the Testaments of the Twelve Patriarchs* [1908]; id., *The Testaments of the Twelve Patriarchs Translated from the Editor's Greek Text* [1908]; M. de Jonge, *The Testaments of the Twelve Patriarchs: A Study of Their Text, Composition and Origin* [1953]; M. Philonenko, *Les interpolations chrétiennes des Testaments des Douze Patriarches et les manuscrits de Qumran* [1960]; H. D. Singerland, *The Testaments of the Twelve Patriarchs: A Critical History of Research* [1977]; M. de Jonge et al., *The Testaments of the Twelve Patriarchs: A Critical Edition of the Greek Text* [1978]; A. Hulgard, *L'eschatologie des Testaments des Douze Patriarches*, 2 vols. [1977–82]; W. H. Hollander and M. de Jonge, *The Testaments of the Twelve Patriarchs: A Commentary* [1985]; R. A. Kugler, *The Testaments of the Twelve Patriarchs* [2001]; M. de Jonge, *Pseudepigrapha of the Old Testament as Part of Christian Literature: The Case of the Testaments of the Twelve Patriarchs and the Greek Life of Adam and Eve* [2003].)

H. G. ANDERSEN

testimonia. This Latin term (sg. *testimonium*) is often used in biblical scholarship to designate collections of OT proof texts, especially those that support Jesus' messiahship (cf. the parallel passages Matt. 21:42; Rom. 9:33; 1 Pet. 2:6–8). Some have even argued that the NT writers had recourse to a "Testimony Book" that brought together such texts (see QUOTATIONS IN THE NT II). When a one-column fragment was discovered in Cave 4 of Qumran that linked several biblical texts, the name 4QTest(imonia) was given to it (the formal siglum is 4Q175) because it was thought to support the existence of "testimony" documents in Judaism (cf. *ABD*, 6:391–92). See also FLORILEGIUM.

testimony. This English term is used variously in Bible translations to render several terms (e.g.,

A 9th-cent. Greek manuscript of the Gospel according to Mark, written to provide testimony or witness to the person and work of Christ.

Hebrew *ʿēd H6332* and *ʿēdût H6343*; Gk. *martyria G3456* and *martyrion G3457*). The word can bear a number of meanings. (1) It may simply be equivalent to "witness," as in 2 Tim. 1:8 (KJV, NRSV), where PAUL exhorts TIMOTHY not to be ashamed of his *martyrion* to Christ. (2) A second sense is that of "evidence" which witnesses to something, as in Acts 14:3, where the KJV reads, "the Lord … gave testimony [verb *martyreō G3455*] to the word of his grace." (3) Frequently in the OT "the Testimony" refers to the Decalogue as a pristine statement of God's will, from which comes the expressions "ark of the Testimony" (Exod. 25:16 et al., or simply "the Testimony," 16:34; see ARK OF THE COVENANT) and "tablets of the Testimony" (31:18; 32:15; 34:29). (4) The expression "testimony" was then extended to cover the whole book of the law of God (Ps. 78:5 KJV et al.) or to specific commandments (119:22 KJV et al.). (5) In some instances testimony signifies the word of God given to a prophet (Isa. 8:16, 20). (6) In the book of Revelation, the term *martyria* refers to the GOSPEL (Rev. 1:2 et al.).

M. E. OSTERHAVEN

Testimony of Truth. A Gnostic tractate included in the NAG HAMMADI LIBRARY (NHC IX, 3). The work was probably composed in Greek around A.D. 200, but it survives only in thin fragmentary Coptic translation. It consists of a homily (plus additional material) in which the author polemicizes against such topics as the law, marriage (procreation), and the resurrection. (English trans. in *NHL*, 448–59.)

tet tet (טֵית, meaning uncertain). Also *teth*. The ninth letter of the Hebrew ALPHABET (ט), with a numerical value of nine. Its sound in Modern Hebrew corresponds to that of English *t*, but in biblical times it was a so-called "emphatic" consonant, possibly characterized by an additional velar articulation (i.e., with the back of the tongue touching or approaching the soft palate) or by a compression of the pharynx.

Teta tay´tuh. KJV Apoc. form of HATITA (1 Esd. 5:28).

Tetragrammaton tet´ruh-gram´uh-ton. Derived from the Greek words for "four" and "letter," this term refers to the four-consonant name of God, YHWH (prob. pronounced *Yahweh*). See GOD, NAMES OF.

tetrarch tet´rahrk (τετράρχης *G5490* [also τετραάρχης]; verb τετραρχέω *G5489*). The title given to Herod Antipas, ruler of GALILEE and PEREA (see HEROD V), to his brother Philip, ruler of ITUREA and TRACONITIS (see HEROD VI), and to LYSANIAS, ruler of ABILENE (Matt. 14:1; Lk. 3:1, 19; 9:7; Acts 13:1). Originally the term was used for a ruler of the fourth of a region (Gk. *tetras*, "four"). Eventually, the literal sense faded out, and the word came to be used as the title of a petty dependent prince, lower in rank and authority than a king. This designation is given to Herod Antipas not only in the NT but also several times in inscriptions and in JOSEPHUS.

When Herod the Great died in 4 B.C. (see HEROD II), his domain was divided into three parts. Archelaus received JUDEA (with IDUMEA and SAMARIA) and the title of ETHNARCH (see HEROD IV). Antipas and Philip were both given the title of tetrarch. The latter ruled over various territories in NE Palestine. Later Lysanias, about whom little is known, was made tetrarch of the tiny district of Abilene, NE of Mount HERMON.

In Mk. 6:14 and 26 Antipas is spoken of as "king" instead of tetrarch. Of this H. B. Swete says. "A tetrarch was in fact a petty king, and may have been called *basileus* [king] as an act of courtesy: he possessed a jurisdiction with which the Imperial authorities were ordinarily reluctant to interfere (Lc. xxiii. 7)" (*The Gospel according to St. Mark*, 2nd ed. [1902], 113). Two other factors should also be considered. It was the custom of the Romans to call all eastern rulers by the popular title of "king," and Mark was writing in Rome. Then, too, the people of Galilee would likely refer to their ruler as king.

R. EARLE

Tetrateuch tet´ruh-tyook. This term, derived from the Greek words for "four" and "book," is applied to the first four books of the Bible viewed as a group (cf. PENTATEUCH, "five books"; HEXATEUCH, "six books"). While many scholars use this name as a convenient designation, for others it reflects the view that these books should be distinguished from the book of DEUTERONOMY, the latter being considered part of the so-called DEUTERONOMISTIC HISTORY.

tetter. Any of several skin DISEASES. The term is used by the RSV and the NJPS to render Hebrew *bōhaq* H993, which occurs only once (Lev. 13:39). The NIV has "harmless rash" (cf. also NRSV). The context makes clear that it referred to *white* patches of skin; diagnosis was necessary because a white patch is occasionally an early symptom of leprosy. If the priest determined that the color was a dull white, it was declared noncontagious. Thus the reference is probably to vitiligo (leukoderma)—irregular areas of depigmented skin. The bleached out areas spread centrifugally, sometimes involving the hair and producing white streaks. It is disfiguring, but not dangerous. Egyptian women were acquainted with vitiligo. They are said to have restored some of the normal color by chewing plants found along the banks of the Nile. Staining the white patches was also resorted to, as it is in our own generation.

R. H. POUSMA

text and manuscripts (OT). Less than a century ago, research into the history of the OT text seemed to have reached a dead end in two important directions. On the one hand, the collations that Kennicott and de Rossi had published in the latter part of the 18th cent., with their comparison of the readings of hundreds of medieval MSS, had shown extremely few variations of any importance in the consonantal text of the OT. It was therefore felt that one could be quite certain as to the precise text of the OT *as it existed a thousand years ago*. On the other hand, there seemed to be no sure way of tracing it back to an earlier period: nearly all of the extant MSS were written after A.D. 1100, and none could be dated prior to c. 900. The history of the Hebrew text previous to that time seemed to be largely a matter of conjecture, with little reason to hope that further light would ever be thrown upon it.

This situation has now greatly changed. The discovery of the DEAD SEA SCROLLS in 1947 made available a great corpus of ancient material that gives us direct knowledge of the history of the OT text a millennium earlier. Equally important is the availability of other new material, some of which had been discovered prior to that time, but had as yet been comparatively little studied. A great number of OT MSS had been collected in the 19th cent. through the efforts of Abraham Firkovitch and were available in the Leningrad library, but results from their study were little known to the Western world. Moreover, nearly 200,000 fragments of Hebrew and Aramaic MSS of many kinds had been taken from a GENIZAH in Cairo to museums and libraries in the W, but the study of these materials had been little more than begun.

Still another source of new information, not previously available, was an OT codex long treasured by the Sephardic synagogue in ALEPPO. Produced by a famous Masorete, Aaron Ben Asher, this document was regarded as very important evidence for the true MT. Yet it was not available for study, since its keepers steadily refused to allow it to be photographed or carefully researched; and after the burning of the Aleppo synagogue in the riots of 1948, it was feared that this irreplaceable codex had been destroyed. Later on it was learned that about three-fourths of it had been rescued and taken to Jerusalem, where it has been intensively studied.

    I. A brief survey of the history of the Hebrew text
   II. Consonantal writing and indication of vowels
  III. Types of manuscripts
  IV. Divisions of the text
   V. The work of the scribes
  VI. The work of the Masoretes
 VII. Important Masoretic manuscripts and printed editions
VIII. The Dead Sea Scrolls
  IX. The Cairo Genizah
   X. The Aleppo Codex
  XI. Types of error
 XII. Evidence of the versions
XIII. Conclusion

I. A brief survey of the history of the Hebrew text

A. The period between the writing of the books and the destruction of Jerusalem in A.D. 70. Until the discovery of the DSS in 1947 the only direct evidence about this period was the little that might be gleaned from a comparison of the Hebrew text with the SAMARITAN PENTATEUCH or with the SEPTUAGINT. This topic will be discussed below (section XII). At this place it will be sufficient to point out that we are here dealing, not with the history of ordinary books, but with a very special situation. It is the belief of Christians that the books of the Bible were considered sacred, divinely inspired books from the very time of their writing. This is indeed the view that is contained in the PENTATEUCH, which says that MOSES ordered that a copy of its contents should be preserved in the very Holy of Holies (Deut. 31:26), and that another copy should be constantly before the king in order that he might study it carefully and direct his activities in accordance with it (17:18–19).

Since the books were regarded as possessing such a transcendent importance, they would have been preserved with great care. This does not mean that no errors could possibly enter their text. The Bible contains no promise of absolute accuracy in text preservation, as the books would be copied and recopied through the centuries. It is impossible for a human being to copy a whole book without making at least some errors, and even the best of proof readers may overlook some of these mistakes. Yet there can be no doubt that in the case of official copies, prepared and checked with extreme diligence, errors would be kept to a minimum.

It would be somewhat different in the case of the many copies made for individuals and distributed widely throughout the land. While there is no direct contemporary evidence about this, the discovery at Khirbet QUMRAN (excavated 1951–56) in the neighborhood of the Dead Sea, where a room was apparently laid out as a scriptorium in which copies were constantly being made for the use of the members of this ascetic colony, suggests how widely the copies of the sacred Scriptures must have been disseminated during the centuries immediately before the time of Christ. Most likely the Scriptures were similarly distributed during the preceding centuries. It would often be expensive to make copies, and the people in a distant part of the land, instead of going to Jerusalem and paying to have a copy made directly from the official text, might sometimes have to content themselves with a copy made from the one possessed by the local leaders. Thus errors would inevitably creep into these copies in the course of time and eventually it would be natural that schools of MSS would develop, as occurred later in the case of the NT as well.

B. The period from the destruction of Jerusalem to about A.D. 900. During this period renewed emphasis was placed upon the Scriptures. With the loss of the temple and the capital city, the Jews might have entirely lost their identity, had it not been for the great stress laid upon their religious unity, and upon the OT as the source from which it flowed. Groups of rabbis gathered in various sections of Palestine to discuss problems connected with the OT and to arrive at conclusions that they could defend in their relations both with other Jews and with outsiders. One of their primary aims was to preserve the integrity of the sacred books. During the previous centuries and during a substantial part of this period, the men who were particularly concerned with this task were generally referred to as *sôpĕrîm* "scribes." Eventually the specialists in this work came to be designated by another name, *baʿălê māsōret*, "masters of tradition," or simply Masoretes.

In order to protect the integrity of the biblical text, the SCRIBES undertook the task of counting the number of letters, the number of words, and the number of verses in each section, marking the middle letter and the middle word of each, and noting peculiar forms or other facts related to this purpose. There is very little contemporary evidence about their precise activities, although some of the discussions of the rabbis have been reported in the TALMUD. Many of the marks that the scribes inserted at various places in the Scripture, and some of their marginal notes, were included in the later works of the Masoretes, even though the meaning and purpose of some of them had been forgotten by that time. These activities will be discussed more fully below.

It is not known when the term *Masorete* began to be used, but by A.D. 800 the men who were particularly devoting themselves to the care of the Scriptures were regularly called by this name, instead of *scribes*. They had many problems with which to deal, one of the principal ones being that of indicating the exact pronunciation of the words and the way they should be read in the services (originally only the consonants had been written). Especially between 800 and 900, a great deal of effort was expended on this task, and the result attained received such general acceptance that most of the previous MSS were quickly superseded. Thus the text preserved in MSS after c. 900 has come to be known as the Masoretic Text (MT).

In later years the scholars who gave very particular attention to studying the work of the Masoretes, and to endeavoring to continue preservation of the integrity of the text, were called "grammarians" or, more generally, *nakdanim* (sometimes spelled *noq-danim*), "punctuators, annotators" (Heb. *naqdān* or *nôqdān* means "punctilious person"; for details regarding their work, see C. D. Ginsburg, *Introduction to the Masoretico-Critical Edition of the Hebrew Bible* [1897], 462–68). Many new MSS of the MT were prepared in the following centuries, but in their essential feature, that of the consonantal text, they were remarkably uniform, even though written in widely separated geographical areas. Students of the OT text and MSS have held various theories as to the relation of the MT to the original form of the Scriptures. Various facets of this problem will be discussed below.

II. Consonantal writing and indication of vowels.

All writing is a rather imperfect means of representing human words and statements. Oral expression contains many features that are not conveyed in writing. Modern languages have introduced punctuation marks, which convey some further idea of the expression that the voice gives. Such marks were unknown in Hebrew antiquity. Moreover, in the ancient HEBREW LANGUAGE, as in most ancient Semitic WRITING generally, only consonants were written and there was little or no indication of the vowels.

As time goes on, all languages develop and change. Certain consonants may cease to be pronounced at all, though still written as silent letters. In Hebrew this occurred in the case of the *waw* in such words as *sws* ("horse"), probably originally pronounced *sawas* but eventually contracted to *sūs*. Similar developments occurred with other letters, and in such cases these came to be thought of not as indicating a consonant but as representing a long vowel of one type or another. Eventually the practice began of inserting these "vowel letters" to indicate a long vowel wherever it seemed that the word might not be correctly understood without it, even when no contraction was involved. In later Hebrew writing considerable flexibility developed as to the insertion of vowel letters, with the result that there are great numbers of variations in this feature in the various MSS. However, most of these variations have no more effect on the meaning than the question whether one writes "honor" as is common in America, or "honour" in accordance with British usage.

After the EXILE Hebrew was gradually displaced by ARAMAIC, and eventually came to be used only for religious and literary purposes. It was still used extensively in the synagogue services, and the OT books were also read at home in Hebrew. Children frequently heard the text read, and there was a tendency to retain orally a tradition as to which vowels would be used at certain places. Over the centuries the pronunciation of vowels and consonants naturally changed, often being affected by the particular language used in common speech, whether Aramaic, Greek, or Arabic. Eventually the custodians of the sacred writings began to realize the necessity of finding some better way to indicate precise vowel pronunciation than merely the presence or absence of vowel letters. At the centers of Jewish learning in Babylonia, a system was invented of placing dots or other marks over certain letters to indicate the following vowel. A somewhat similar system was developed in Palestine. Eventually a third system was developed at Tiberias in Palestine which largely substituted marks under the consonants for the previous system of designating vowels by marks above them. This system soon became dominant, and was used exclusively in later MSS and in printed Hebrew.

III. Types of manuscripts.

Hebrew MSS are of two types: those for synagogue use, and those for the use of private persons. Synagogue MSS are sometimes so made as to contain simply the portions of the OT selected for public use in the regular worship of the synagogue. The Law (the five books of Moses) may be included in one MS, since it is read consecutively Sabbath after Sabbath. In connection with the weekly readings from the Law, it became customary to read certain appropriate passages from the second division of the Hebrew Bible (the NEBIIM or Prophets). These passages, called the Haphtaroth, were selected at a very early time; the selections are sometimes copied together in one scroll. The book of Esther, which is read at the feast of PURIM, and the four other books that are read at special fast or feast days, are placed on separate scrolls and are called MEGILLOTH (scrolls).

The Talmud includes very detailed rules for the making of synagogue MSS. They are always in the form of a SCROLL rather than that of a CODEX (like our modern books). PARCHMENT, prepared from the skin of a clean animal, must be used. The text must be written in black erasable ink, without vowels or accents, and must be copied with great care. Even a single letter may not be written without the scribe looking first at the MS being copied. Extraordinary points and any letters of unusual size, position, or form must be carefully copied. The MS must be corrected within thirty days after it is written. If four errors are found on any page it must be condemned. Very few of these synagogue scrolls have become available for scholarly study, since, to avoid the risk of desecration, it was required that they be buried as soon as they had become too worn for regular use.

Private MSS were generally made for study by individuals or for use in the home. Being made by hand, they tended to be rather expensive. Well-to-do people could afford to hire excellent scribes and to have the MS checked with great care. Other MSS may have been copied somewhat more hurriedly. Since according to Jewish law every Jew was expected to have at least one copy of the Torah in his home, the number of private MSS prepared was far greater than the number of synagogue scrolls.

The private MSS sometimes contained the whole OT but more commonly only a part, and sometimes only a single book. Although occasionally in the form of scrolls, they were usually codices

Facsimile of a Qumran scroll (*Community Rule*).

of various sizes. Sometimes they were written on parchment or prepared skins, but more frequently on cotton or linen paper, and generally with black ink. Vowel marks and accents were included. The upper and lower margins and also the side margins often contained Masoretic notes and various readings. Sometimes a commentary by a noted rabbi was placed beside the text. Often a translation was included, whether Aramaic (see TARGUM), Arabic, or some other language.

Usually the consonantal letters were all written first, the vowels and accents being added subsequently, sometimes by a different person, and generally with a different pen and different ink. Frequently a MS would pass through several hands in the course of preparation. One person might write the consonants, another might append the vowels, a third might go through to correct it, a fourth would add the MASORA, a fifth might retouch it after it had become defaced by age or use. Often the initial words or letters were ornamented, and the margin was decorated with pictures of flowers, trees, or animals. The MS generally contained a colophon at the end, telling who performed these functions and giving other information about the MS.

It is often difficult to determine the age of a Hebrew MS. Since the MSS were produced in many different areas, and the type of writing often varied from place to place, determination of age by paleography (changes in styles of writing) is generally difficult. Sometimes the colophon contains a statement of the time when the MS was made, but this is often missing, and when it is included it is not always easy to understand. The years may be reckoned from the creation, from the destruction of the second temple, from the hegira of Muhammad or from the era of the SELEUCIDS (312 B.C.), this last being particularly common. Often the number of thousands of years is omitted, and sometimes even the number of hundreds. In some cases the colophon may have been simply copied from an earlier MS. Fortunately, some MSS give the date according to two or three different eras, and this makes possible a helpful check as to the time that is meant.

For example, the colophon of the Leningrad Codex B 19a says that this MS was prepared (a) in the year 4770 from the creation of the world, (b) in the year 1444 from the exile of King JEHOIACHIN, (c) in the year 319 "of the empire of the Greeks," (d) in the year 940 from the destruction of the second temple, and (e) in the year 399 "of the rule of the little horn." According to a common Jewish reckoning of the time of creation the first of these dates would indicate A.D. 1010. The third date, if considered as omitting the figure for 1000, would come to A.D. 1008 (1319 years after 312 B.C.). The fourth statement would indicate 1009. The fifth date, considering the rule of the little horn as referring to the beginning of Islam, would be 1008, according to the Muslim system of dating. The second date, reckoning from the exile of King Jehoiachin, does not reach a year comparable to the others. This probably results from the mistaken statements in the Targum that the whole period of Persian rule (539–331 B.C.) was really only a single generation. The coincidence of four of the statements seems to make the date of A.D. 1008 quite reasonable for this important MS, particularly since it was written in a Muslim land. This MS is the basis for the most widely used edition, *Biblia Hebraica* (beginning with the 3rd ed.).

IV. Divisions of the text. The convenient arrangement of modern Bibles, with chapters and verses numbered consecutively, was not introduced until the 16th cent. Originally the books of the OT were written without subdivisions and usually without titles. In ancient times it was often the custom simply to name a book by its first words.

The first division made in the Hebrew text was probably into unnumbered verses. This may have been done very early. Verse divisions in recently discovered MSS written shortly before the time of Christ are almost identical with those in our present Hebrew Bible. However, no numbering is indicated and there were no chapter divisions. While in general the verse division was well made, this was not always the case. Some verses contain two separate sentences while others include only a small part of one sentence. The division is rarely as bad as in Ps. 19:4, which includes the last few words of one sentence and the first four words of another.

The next step was the division of all the OT books except the Psalms into 452 sections called *parashahs* or *sedarim*. There were 154 of these in the Pentateuch. It is said that the Jews in Palestine used to read each of these consecutively in the weekly synagogue services, taking about three years to go through the entire Pentateuch, until the coming of the exiles from Spain at the end of the 15th cent. resulted in changing the custom so as to read the Pentateuch through in one year.

Some of these parashahs were felt to mark a more important division in the text than others. Therefore in some cases the last part of the line was left blank, while in the others a short space on the line was considered a sufficient indication. Those parashahs that were thought to be important enough to leave the rest of the line unused were called open parashahs, while those where only a short space was made were called closed parashahs. Eventually the parashahs came to be indicated in the MSS simply by inserting the letter פ (for *pethuchah*) for open parashahs or the letter ס (for *sethumah*) for closed parashahs. Later the Pentateuch was divided into fifty-four sections, so that it could be read through in the Sabbath services in approximately one year. The close of each of these larger sections coincided with the end of one of the already marked parashahs, and was indicated in the MSS by writing the appropriate letter (פ or ס) three times. This indication is still continued in Hebrew Bibles.

Division into chapters was not made until the 13th cent. It was probably worked out by an English archbishop and originally placed in his Latin Bible. Very soon the Jews recognized the convenience of these divisions and inserted them in their Hebrew Bibles, usually following the exact division made by the archbishop, but occasionally changing it.

V. The work of the scribes. The men who busied themselves with the care and transmission of the Scriptures from the time of Ezra to that of the Masoretes are designated in Hebrew MSS as the *sôpĕrîm*. This is usually translated "scribes," which might suggest that they were merely copyists. However, the normal Hebrew word for "to write" is *kātab*, whereas *sāpar* properly means "to count." It is stated in the Talmud that the keepers of the Scripture came to be called *sôpĕrîm* because they counted the letters and words in each section of the Scripture. Actually a *sôpēr* is not simply a someone who writes things down, but one who also makes lists, keeps track of details, and oversees various aspects of affairs. Eventually the designation came to be applied to anyone who devoted himself to legal or literary pursuits.

During the long period before the time of the Masoretes, little information regarding the activities of the scribes in relation to the Scripture was preserved, but a great deal of information about their activities can be inferred from the results that were passed on in the form of marks or marginal notes inserted in the Bible. It is evident that in their endeavor to preserve the text from alteration or addition, they counted the number of words in each section, and also the number of verses and paragraphs. They sometimes placed marginal notes in their MSS, wrote certain letters in unusual ways, or inserted dots or other marks at various places. These peculiarities were copied in later MSS and preserved by the Masoretes, even though in some cases their purpose may have been entirely forgotten. Various aspects of the work of the scribes may be designated under the following heads:

(1) *Letters written large or small.* At thirty-seven places in the OT it became customary to write a letter larger than normal, and in twenty-three places to write one smaller. In many cases the reason for the large letter is quite obvious. In three instances, for example, it is the first letter of a book; in one, it is the middle letter of the Pentateuch; and in the oft-repeated Shema (Deut. 6:4) the last letter of the first word (ע, *ʿayin*) and the last letter of the last word (ד, *dalet*) are written large (it has been conjectured that these particular letters were selected because they form the Hebrew word for "witness"). In the case of the letters written small it is often difficult to make a reasonable conjecture as to why this was done. It would seem that the Masoretes found it to be customary in the MSS that had come down to them and simply continued the practice without change.

(2) *Suspended letters.* There are a few cases where letters are written somewhat above the line. One of these is the *ʿayin* (ע) in *miyyāʿar*, "from the forest" (Ps. 80:13 [Heb. v. 14]), which probably indicates the middle of the Psalter. Another is the *nun* (נ) in "Manasseh" in Jdg. 18:30. An early tradition says that this *nun* was suspended above the line to indicate that it had been inserted in order to change the word from "Manasseh" to "Moses," so that people would not think that this apostate priest had been

descended from Moses (the letter was kept, though suspended, in order to indicate that it was, after all, a change in the text). One cannot say that this early tradition is false, but there is no proof that it is true. In some cases the reason for the suspended letter is quite unknown.

(3) *Paseq* ("divider"). This is a perpendicular stroke placed between two words in about forty-eight places in the OT. It seems sometimes to have been placed before or after the divine name to avoid the possibility of its being incorrectly united with a word which, in the opinion of the scribes, should not be too closely tied to it, or to separate two words which there seemed to be a danger of their becoming merged because the final consonant of one and the first consonant of the other were identical.

(4) *Extraordinary points.* There are fifteen places where dots are placed over single letters or over a whole word. Ten of these are in the Pentateuch, the others elsewhere in the Bible. They probably represent questions that the scribes raised about these places in the texts. The marks have been preserved, but the reason for them has been completely forgotten.

(5) *Inverted nun's.* Nine times there is a mark in the MSS that looks like an inverted *nun* (כ). There is evidence that discussion occurred as early as the 2nd cent. A.D. as to what it means. It has been suggested that the scribes thought that a group of words might have been misplaced, but did not feel justified in making a change. Some authorities question whether the mark is really a *nun*.

(6) *Tiqqune sopherim.* This term, which means "corrections of the scribes," has been used in early Jewish writings to indicate eighteen passages where it was asserted that EZRA (or some later scribe) had made a change in what was written in order to avoid a statement that impressed him as objectionable or unsuitable. The passages are: Gen. 18:22; Num. 11:15; 12:12; 1 Sam. 3:13; 2 Sam. 16:12; 20:1; Job 7:20; 32:3; Ps. 106:20; Jer. 2:11; Lam. 3:20; Ezek. 8:17; Hos. 4:7; Hab. 1:12; Zech. 2:12; Mal. 1.12. Most of these consist of a change of suffix to avoid a direct reference to God. In one case (Gen. 18:22) it has been said that the text must have originally read: "the LORD remained standing before Abraham," and that this had been thought to be demeaning to God and that therefore the text was changed to "Abraham remained standing before the LORD." A number of recent writers assert that it is perfectly obvious that such a change was made, but the passage states that the men left Abraham and then says: "However, Abraham remained standing before the LORD." Surely this means that the men acted as if they were about to go, but that Abraham continued to request the LORD's attention.

(7) *Itture sopherim.* This phrase means "omissions of the scribes." The Talmud contains a list of seven places where it says that a word not written in the text is to be read, and five places where it says that a word written in the text should not be read. It also mentions five places where it asserts that "and" was omitted by the scribes.

(8) *Sebirin.* There are about 350 places, not usually marked in the MSS, but contained in Masoretic lists, where a biblical word is quoted and then followed by another term which is introduced by the Aramaic word *sĕbîr* ("supposed, suggested"). This does not indicate that the scribes thought something was wrong, but simply that they desired to explain the meaning of an unexpected form or word.

VI. The work of the Masoretes. The term *Masorete* (also spelled *Massorete* and *Masorite*) evidently derives from the noun *māsôret* H5037 (also *massôret*), which in postbiblical Hebrew meant "tradition" (cf. the verb *māsar* H5034, "to hand over, transmit"). Rabbi AKIBA is reported to have said, "Tradition [*mswrt*] is a fence around the Law" (m. ʾAbot 3:14 [13]). The cognate term MASORAH (*māsôrâ* or *massôrâ*) refers to a special collection of readings and notes compiled by the Masoretes (regarding the etymology and spelling of these terms, see B. J. Roberts, *The Old Testament Text and Versions* [1951], 40–42). No one knows when the scholars who were guarding the textual tradition began to be called Masoretes; after c. 920 they were considered to have completed their work, and the name was no longer applied.

For a time there were active groups of Masoretes in both Babylonia and Palestine. Although the TALMUD and the TARGUMS edited in Babylonia seem largely to have won precedence over those produced in Palestine, it was the work of the group of Masoretes in Tiberias in Palestine that came to be accepted as authoritative throughout the Jewish world. The names of several of the Tiberian Masoretes have been preserved. The most prominent were members of the families of Ben Asher and Ben Naphtali. Five generations of the Ben Asher family were active from c. 780 to c. 920.

The tasks performed by the Masoretes may be arranged under four heads. First and most important was the continuation of the work to which the scribes had already devoted much attention, namely, maintaining the integrity of the text of the Scripture. For this purpose they counted the number of letters, words, verses, and parashahs in each book and indicated its middle word. They noted all peculiar and unusual forms, indicating how frequently each occurred. There is no way of knowing how much of this material they figured out themselves, and how much had already been determined by the previous scribes. Many notations and special marks put in by the scribes were scrupulously copied by the Masoretes even though sometimes they seem not to have known what meaning the earlier scholars had intended to convey.

A great amount of material of this type was assembled by the Masoretes and came to be known as the Masorah. Notes placed on the side margins of the columns were called the Small Masorah (*Masorah parva*). Notes at the top and bottom of the page were called the Large Masorah (*Masorah magna*), a name sometimes also applied to the notes placed at the end of each book, which are more usually called the Final Masorah (*Masorah finalis*). Much of this material is written in very condensed language, about half of it using Hebrew words and forms, and the remainder using Aramaic.

A second part of the task of the Masoretes was the standardization of the pronunciation of the words in the OT. As time went on, there was a tendency to forget in some instances what vowels should be pronounced with the written consonants, and the pronunciation of the words began to vary with the speech habits of the various localities. Ideas of Hebrew grammar tended to become confused as habits of pronunciation changed. The Masoretes set themselves industriously at this highly complicated task. Three systems of vocalization were attempted, but eventually the Tiberian system established itself as supreme.

Careful study of the grammar and investigation of the traditions as to pronunciation led in some points to a conscious return to forms and practices that had existed centuries earlier, but had then largely disappeared. (It was the contention of Paul Kahle that in other features, such as the double pronunciation of the *begadkephat* letters, the Masoretes introduced into Hebrew pronunciation practices known in Syriac but new to Hebrew; see his book, *The Cairo Geniza*, 2nd ed. [1959], 179–84.) Performing an immense labor of standardizing the grammar, maintaining the ascertained tradition, and working out a method of indicating precisely how they thought each word would rightly be pronounced, they placed indications of vowel pronunciation on every word of the Hebrew Bible.

A third part of the work of the Masoretes involved providing an indication to the reader of the cases in which established tradition favored reading a word in a way that did not seem to fit the accepted consonantal text. It would seem that the Masoretes were determined on no account to alter the consonantal text that had been handed down to them. Yet, there was a considerable number of cases where it was customary to read it in a different way. Thus it had been customary for many centuries not to pronounce the divine name indicated by the TETRAGRAMMATON (*YHWH*). For a time it was customary to substitute the phrase "the name." Well before the time of Christ it had become usual to substitute the word ʾădōnāy *H151*, "Lord" (if the latter was already used in conjunction with it, they would substitute ʾĕlōhîm, "God"). In these cases the Masoretes simply put the vowels of ʾădōnāy (or ʾĕlōhîm) on the consonants already in the text; this came to be called a "permanent *Qere*" (see QERE).

Another permanent *Qere*, much less frequent than the one just mentioned, resulted from the fact that in the early part of the Bible there are a number of cases where the third feminine singular pronoun (*hyʾ*) was written with the vowel letter that properly belonged with the corresponding masculine pronoun (*hwʾ*). The Masoretes had no way of knowing whether at that early time the masculine pronoun was sometimes used in a generic sense, to apply to either gender, as was regularly done with the third plural perfect of the verb. Knowing that the uniform practice of the rest of the OT required the feminine pronoun in these places, they put before the vowel letter *waw* the vowel sign that would be there if the vowel letter *yod* had been written (thus instead of vocalizing it *hiʾ*, they wrote *hiw*, indicating that it should be pronounced *hiʾ*. Two other words that had a permanent *Qere* are ISSACHAR and JERUSALEM.

There are about 1300 instances in which the Masoretes have placed on a word a group of vowels that do not exactly fit the consonants as written. Usually this was to indicate a change of tense or something similar. Except for the four words with permanent *Qere*, the Masoretes put in the margin the letter ק (for *Qere*, "read"), followed by the consonants that would normally go with the vowels that had been placed in the text. The consonants that remained in the text were called the KETHIB (Aram. "that which is written"). It is possible that in many cases there was MS evidence for the *Qere*; in such a case the Masoretes may have felt that the preponderance of MS evidence favored the *Kethib* and therefore retained it in the text, even though indicating that the *Qere* was what should be read. In some cases there is reason to believe that the *Kethib* gives the better reading, but in most cases the *Qere* seems preferable.

The fourth aspect of the work of the Masoretes may have been even more time-consuming than the other three: the use of marks to indicate cantillation. For many centuries it had been established practice to chant at least a portion of the synagogue reading of the Scripture. To provide a measure of standardization, the Masoretes invented an extremely complicated system of so-called accents. Most common is the *metheg*, which ordinarily indicates the secondary accent, but may also indicate any one of a score of other features. Other accents indicate the relation to the preceding or following words, and show the various features of the cantillation.

It is easy to see that with the addition of all these varied vowel marks and accents to the consonantal text, the difficulty of maintaining an exact text was greatly increased. Although all the Masoretic MSS agree remarkably closely in their consonantal text, it is only natural that considerable variety in preservation of these other features should develop.

The Large Masora includes references to a number of MSS which the Masoretes considered as having great authority. As far as known all of these famous pre-Masoretic MSS have perished. One of the most famous of these was the Codex Hilleli, attributed to a famous rabbi named Hillel who lived at about A.D. 600. Other frequently cited MSS were named after their place of origin, such as Jericho, Jerusalem, Sinai, and Babylon.

With the establishment of their new system of vowels and accents, the Tiberian Masoretes had originated a type of MS that soon became standard throughout the Jewish world. Yet not all the Masoretes of Tiberias were united regarding every detail of the task. At the beginning of the 10th cent. their differences found expression in two main traditions, one of which bore the authority of the Ben Asher family, the other that of Ben Naphtali. In MSS prepared during the next two centuries marginal notes frequently refer to the distinctive readings of each of these authorities. Soon writers began to make lists of these differences. Most such lists have disappeared, but portions of several copies of a book on the subject have been found (Mishael ben Uzziel, *Kitāb al-Khilaf*). Piecing these fragments together, it has been possible to reconstruct the entire list, which consists of 875 differences between the two traditions. Practically all of these concern matters of vocalization or accentuation, nine tenths of them in fact being concerned with the use of *metheg*. As to the consonantal text, there was no important difference between the two traditions.

For a time the two traditions continued side by side, but gradually the majority of Hebrew grammarians and scholars may have tended to give preference to the Ben Asher readings, though accepting some of those of Ben Naphtali. Then the famous Jewish philosopher Moses Maimonides (1135–1204), writing on a biblical subject unrelated to the difference between these two traditions, declared that he accepted as authoritative an OT codex in Egypt that had been vocalized, collated, and provided with Masora by Ben Asher (prob. the Aleppo Codex). So great was the prestige of Maimonides throughout the Jewish world that this statement is generally considered as having been the cause of the sharp decline in the standing of the Ben Naphtali tradition that occurred soon afterward.

VII. Important Masoretic manuscripts and printed editions. During the centuries from the Renaissance to 1000 a considerable number of Hebrew MSS were collected by various universities and libraries. Yet the amount of such material available today is probably three times as great as in 1800. This great increase is due partly to the intensive searches of Abraham Firkovitch, who collected more than 2000 MSS of parts of the OT and placed them in the Leningrad library, and partly to the many biblical MSS recovered from the Cairo Genizah. It is difficult to compare the number of MSS in various museums and libraries, because sometimes a MS may include the whole OT, while at other times a very few pages may be listed as a separate document. Much work remains to be done in the study of this material, but the intensive researches of Paul Kahle and others during the first half of the 20th cent. have already produced remarkable results.

The following MSS, arranged in order of probable date of origin, are now generally considered to be the best sources for knowledge of the Ben Asher text.

(1) The Cairo Codex of the Prophets (sometimes designated C). This MS, dated in 895, contains the entire second division of the Hebrew Bible. It was written and pointed by Moshe ben Asher, the next to the last of the famous Ben Asher family. The codex was presented to the Qaraite community in Jerusalem, but was seized by the Crusaders in 1099. Later it was returned to the Jews and came into possession of the Qaraite community in Cairo. It is written in three columns, with Tiberian vowels and accents.

(2) The Petersburg (or Babylonian) Codex of the Prophets (P, also known as Leningrad B-3). Dated to the year 916, this document contains only the Latter Prophets. For a long time it was considered to be the oldest dated MS. It uses the Babylonian supralinear system of vocalization, but follows the Tiberian tradition in its vowels and Masora. On a few leaves the Tiberian signs have been substituted for the Babylonian ones.

(3) The Aleppo Codex (sometimes designated A). The colophon of this MS states that Aaron ben Asher (the son of Moshe ben Asher), who died c. 940, added the vowels and Masora to this MS. It is written on parchment in three columns. At first it was in Jerusalem, then for a time in Cairo, and later it was taken to Aleppo (for its later fate see section X below). It is generally considered to be the MS designated by Maimonides as the codex that he regarded as most reliable. Originally it contained the entire Bible, but about one fourth of it was destroyed.

(4) British Museum Or. 4445. This MS, probably written in the middle of the 10th cent., contains only Gen. 39:20—Deut. 1:33. The name of Ben Asher occurs several times in the margin.

(5) Leningrad Codex B-19A (designated L). The dating of this MS of the entire OT, which was brought from the Crimea by Firkovitch, has been discussed above (section III). It claims to have been carefully copied in the year 1008 from a MS prepared by Aaron ben Moshe ben Asher. Written in three columns, with the usual Tiberian vocalization, it is the MS reproduced in *Biblia Hebraica*.

In addition Kahle states (*Cairo Geniza*, 6) that in the autumn of 1926 he found in Leningrad, chiefly among MSS of the Second Firkovitch collection, fourteen Hebrew biblical MSS that can be dated between 929 and 1121, all containing the text of Ben Asher.

Despite the new evidence about details of the Ben Naphtali text, there is as yet no agreement as to the discovery of particular MSS that present that text in a pure form. Among those suggested are Codex Reuchlinianus, which is preserved in Karlsruhe, Germany, and three MSS formerly at Erfurt (E1, E2, and E3). Some scholars, however, maintain that the Codex Reuchlinianus represents a cross between the work of the Babylonian Masoretes and those at Tiberias.

After the year 1100 great numbers of MSS were prepared. The text soon became rather composite, fundamentally based on Ben Asher, but including a considerable number of divergences, many of which were from the Ben Naphtali tradition. In these centuries the importance of the Masora ceased to be fully understood, and the marginal notes were frequently written in such a form as merely to form figures of animals and other decorative elements.

Soon after printing was invented, the Jews began to issue books in Hebrew. A number of parts of the Bible were printed before 1500. Daniel Bomberg of Antwerp emigrated to Venice and there established a printing press from which he issued many important Hebrew books between 1516 and 1549. His

This terra-cotta stamp seal (1st–3rd cent.) contains a Hebrew reference to Jer. 48:11.

first edition of a Rabbinic Bible, issued in 1516–17, was edited by Felix Pratensis. It contained the Hebrew text with Targum and important commentaries in parallel columns. In 1525 this edition was superseded by the second Bomberg Bible, edited by Jacob ben Chayim of Tunis. Ben Chayim included a large selection of Masora. Unfortunately the editor seems to have had at his disposal only comparatively late MSS and to have been occupied with a number of other tasks during the fifteen months that he devoted to its preparation. Nevertheless the text of this edition was standard in the Western world until 1937. Later editions of the Rabbinic Bible, and other early publications of the OT in whole or in part, were of less importance.

In the 18th cent. attention was directed to the variations (most of which concerned vowel letters) in the consonantal text of the available MSS. In 1776–80 Benjamin Kennicott published an edition of the Hebrew Bible at Oxford (*Vetus Testamentum Hebraicum cum variis lectionibus*), listing variants from more than 600 Hebrew MSS. In 1784–88 G. B. de Rossi issued at Parma, Italy, an enlarged list of variants with a selection of the more important readings from 1417 MSS and editions (*Variae lectiones Veteris Testamenti*). Most of the sources used by Kennicott and de Rossi were comparatively late.

In 1869 S. Baer undertook a new publication of sections of the Hebrew OT in the hope of providing a more scientific text. This work was never completed, and the methods used have received severe criticism. In 1908–26 Christian D. Ginsburg produced an edition of the Hebrew Bible with an elaborate presentation of variants, but followed substantially the standard text as established by Jacob ben Chayim. In 1906 Rudolph Kittel issued a *Biblia Hebraica*, followed by a second edition in 1912; for this work the Ben Chayim text was used, with numerous footnotes inserted, including many conjectural emendations (C. C. Torrey declared that the apparatus contained "many readings erroneously supposed to be attested by the Greek version, readings gathered blindly from the commentaries"; see *The Second Isaiah: A New Interpretation* [1928], 214–15).

When plans were being made to issue a third edition of the *Biblia Hebraica*, Paul Kahle suggested that the Ben Chayim text be replaced by the text of a Ben Asher MS. Attempts were made to get permission to use the MS in the Sephardic synagogue of Aleppo, but its keepers refused to allow it to be photographed or even intensively studied. Therefore Kahle suggested printing the text of Leningrad Codex B-19A. The authorities at Leningrad lent the MS to the University of Bonn, and Kahle photographed it and prepared its text and Masora. When issued in 1937, the third edition of *Biblia Hebraica* rapidly became standard among Western scholars. Unfortunately the footnotes of the second edition were retained, and these instead of the actual text have often been treated as authoritative. A number of English translations have followed many of the suggestions in these footnotes, even though outstanding scholars have severely criticized them as being largely conjectural and containing a very arbitrary selection of readings from ancient versions without any really scientific examination of the alleged validity of the suggested readings.

A fourth edition, which came to be known as *Biblia Hebraica Stuttgartensia*, began to appear in fascicles in 1968, and the whole OT was published in 1977 (corrected ed., 1984). The apparatus was completely reworked by numerous scholars (each responsible for specific books or groups of books), taking account of earlier complaints and making use of new evidence, especially that provided by the DSS (see next section). The use of the ancient versions to propose emendations was more moderate, although this part of the work continued to provoke criticism.

The fifth edition, *Biblia Hebraica Quinta*, was introduced in 2004 with the publication of a fascicle that includes the Megilloth (Ruth, Canticles, Ecclesiastes, Lamentations, Esther). Among many new features—such as presenting the full Masorah with editorial notes—this important edition adds evaluative comments on variants attested in the ancient versions, an innovation earlier introduced by the Hebrew University Bible Project (see next paragraph). These comments consist of abbreviations in the apparatus, but at the end a rather full textual commentary is included; such new material will be invaluable in assessing the proposals of the individual editors.

The acquisition of the Aleppo Codex by Israel made it possible for scholars at the Hebrew University in Jerusalem, initially under the direction of M. H. Goshen-Gottstein, to plan a new edition of the Hebrew Bible based on this MS. Known as the Hebrew University Bible Project, this massive venture has included the publication, beginning in 1960, of an annual periodical entitled *Textus*, which consists of important scientific studies. A sample edition of the Hebrew text was published in 1965, and the volume on Isaiah appeared in three fascicles from 1975 to 1993; since then, volumes on Jeremiah and Ezekiel have been published (1997 and 2004 respectively). In addition to presenting the full text and Masorah of the Aleppo Codex, this edition boasts a fourfold apparatus that presents: (a) variants from the ancient versions; (b) variants from the DSS and from biblical quotations in the rabbinic literature; (c) variants from medieval Bible manuscripts; and (d) orthographic variants, including vowels and accents. The first apparatus includes substantial footnotes where the editors express their judgments as to whether the versional readings reflect true variants (often the differences are due to other factors, such as translation technique). These magnificent volumes represent the most ambitious attempt at providing the full evidence necessary to reconstruct the text of the Hebrew Bible.

Several editions have appeared that do not provide a critical apparatus. Umberto (Mosheh David) Cassuto published a corrected version of Ginsburg's edition that came to be known as "the Jerusalem Bible" (1953). In 1958 the British and Foreign Bible Society issued a Hebrew Bible prepared by Norman H. Snaith, largely based upon the critical notes made from Spanish MSS in 1626 by Rabbi Solomon Norzi (this text is evidently very similar to that of the Leningrad Codex). In 1973 Aron Dotan produced a careful edition of the Leningrad Codex (the latest revision is entitled *Biblia Hebraica Leningradensia* [2001]). The Aleppo Codex, where extant, has been used as the basis for an edition by M. Breuer (1977–82, rev. 1997) and for two Rabbinic Bibles: *Keter Yerushalayim*, ed. N. Ben Zevi (Tsvi) et al., 2 vols. (2002); and *Mikra'ot Gedolot ha-Keter* (1992–).

These modern editions of the Hebrew Bible (with the partial exception of Breuer's, which took account of several Palestinian MSS) may be described as *diplomatic* in the sense that they attempt to reproduce as closely as possible the text of a particular MS in the MT tradition (the latter is comparable to the Textus Receptus in NT studies). Editions that have a critical apparatus routinely suggest emendations, but the text itself is not altered. Many scholars have argued that a *critical* or *eclectic* edition, such as is common for other works of antiquity (including modern editions of the NT), is needed for the OT as well. Others have argued that the peculiar transmission of the biblical text makes such an undertaking too difficult if not impossible. A group of scholars have taken up the challenge, however, and a new project called the Oxford Hebrew Bible, under the general editorship of R. S. Hendel, aims to produce an edition that examines variants from all available sources and chooses those readings that are most likely to be original.

VIII. The Dead Sea Scrolls. Students of the Bible were thrilled in 1948 when they learned that in the previous year a cache of scrolls had been discovered that apparently dated from the time of Christ and before. Many of these scrolls were copies of the Hebrew Bible, and some scholars naturally expected that such old documents would differ radically from the text as found in the Masoretic MSS written nearly a thousand years later.

To the biblical student the most important of these scrolls was the one that is now designated as

1QIsa^a, a beautifully written copy of the book of Isaiah. The scroll had evidently been used a great deal, as could be seen from the evidence of wear and the fact that in many places where the writing had become obscure, it had been inked over. Immediately on checking into it, it was apparent that though it agreed generally with the MT there were many differences. The scroll had been copied carelessly. At many points words written by mistake had been erased or crossed out and corrections had been inserted. Changes of a single letter or word were written in the same hand as the MS as a whole; longer corrections were added in a different hand. Letters and words omitted by the copyist were frequently inserted above the line. Sometimes the inserted material runs down the left-hand margin. Close examination shows that at many points the copyist left a space for something that must have been missing or was not clear in the MS he was copying. In most cases such an omitted portion was evidently inserted later from another MS.

Aside from the obvious scribal errors, there were places where the text seemed to go with the SEPTUAGINT rather than with the MT, and some scholars took this as proof that the Greek version preserves a more accurate text than the MT does. On further careful investigation, however, it became clear that in the overwhelming majority of passages where the MT and the Greek give different readings, the Qumran scroll agrees with the MT.

An interesting peculiarity of 1QIsa^a is that it uses vowel letters far more frequently than the MT. It would seem that the scribe himself, or the scribe of a previous MS from which this was copied, inserted these extra vowel letters in order to give interpretative aid to the reader. Sometimes the pronunciation that these suggest is different from that contained in the Masoretic vocalization. The MT contains the word TARTAN as the title of an Assyrian officer (Isa. 20:1, Heb. תַּרְתָּן H9580). In the scroll a vowel is inserted in the first syllable of the word (תורתן), indicating that it should be pronounced *tūrtān*. Discovery of ancient records has shown that the Assyrian form could be spelled *turtannu*. The tradition of the first vowel in this unfamiliar foreign word became altered in the course of the centuries, but its consonants were correctly preserved.

Another Isaiah scroll, now designated 1QIsa^b, was found in Cave 1. It was very difficult to unroll. Eventually, however, this was safely done and it was found to be in bad shape, with many sections missing. Scholars quickly determined that its text was almost identical to the MT and so devoted most of their attention to 1QIsa^a.

In 1952 a number of MSS were found in caves in Wadi Murabbaʿat, some 11 mi. S of Qumran. Many of these were letters that could be precisely dated in the 2nd cent. A.D. There were also copies of a number of sections of the OT which agreed closely with the MT.

In the Qumran area about a dozen of the more than 300 caves that have been excavated have been found to contain scrolls or fragments of scrolls. The greatest number were found in Caves 1, 4, and 11, but no scroll comparable to 1QIsa^a in size or completeness has yet turned up. Some fairly extensive biblical scrolls came from Cave 11, while Cave 4 produced thousands of fragments representing hundreds of MSS. It was difficult to interpret these scraps of material. First, they had to be carefully humidified so as not to disintegrate when touched. Then they had to be flattened out, and the few words on each of them carefully studied to see whether it was a section of the Bible and if so what part. Eventually portions of over 200 copies of Bible books were identified, representing every OT book except Esther (and possibly Nehemiah; see J. C. VanderKam, *The Dead Sea Scrolls Today* [1994], 31). Some of them date to the 2nd or even 3rd cent. B.C.

Although the great bulk of the material from the Qumran caves fits very closely with the MT, a few sections have been found to have closer affinity with the LXX or with the Samaritan Pentateuch. This is particularly true of the book of Samuel, which is probably the least well preserved book in the whole MT. One scroll in Cave 4 seems to have contained a text of Samuel very close to the LXX, and another is thought to have readings superior to both the LXX and the MT. Also significant is the fact that two fragments of Jeremiah discovered in the same cave (4QJer^b = 4Q71 and 4QJer^d = 4Q72a) apparently attest to the shorter version of the book preserved by the LXX.

The scrolls from Murabbaʿat, representing as they do the group of Jews who were active in the

Bar Kokhba revolt in A.D. 132–135, followed closely the official text from which the MT has descended. At Qumran the great bulk of MSS also follow this text. Some few differ, as is only natural, since the sectarians at Qumran doubtless included people from many parts of the land, some of whom brought with them scrolls made in their local areas, sometimes carelessly copied, in which scribal errors and changes of text would have become perpetuated through a series of copyings.

IX. The Cairo Genizah. In view of the number of extant copies of the NT and of the LXX from comparatively early centuries, it might seem strange that, apart from the DSS, no Hebrew text of the OT written before A.D. 895 has been preserved. During the Middle Ages the Jews were often subjected to fierce persecution and obliged to move from place to place, while some Christian monasteries in the E have been practically unmolested for nearly 1500 years. Even so, the lack of MSS before the time of the Masoretes would be hard to explain apart from the long-established Jewish custom that writings containing the name of God must be protected from desecration; if worn out, or found to contain errors, they are to be entirely removed from circulation. Every synagogue had its GENIZAH (from *gānaz*, "to hide, hoard up"; cf. bib. Heb. *genez* H1709, "treasury"), which was a room in its cellar or attic where MSS and documents that were no longer of value could be deposited until a convenient time would be found for burying them in consecrated ground. Worn-out scrolls were generally buried with a scholar.

Abraham Firkovitch was an expert at ransacking old synagogues and their genizahs. He was extremely secretive about the source of his material, but Paul Kahle was strongly convinced that much of it came from what later became famous as the Cairo Genizah. This was the genizah of a synagogue established in A.D. 882 in a building that had formerly been a Christian church and that had thereafter been used as a synagogue for over a thousand years. For many centuries discarded documents were deposited in this genizah. Then through some chance its very existence was forgotten, and the room was even walled up for a time. When it was rediscovered in the 19th cent., some of the material was buried, but this was discontinued when it was learned that antiquarians were willing to pay a substantial price for old documents.

Many MSS and fragments of documents were taken from the Cairo Genizah to various museums and libraries in Europe and America. Finally, in 1896 the Cambridge University Library sent Solomon Schechter to Cairo with authorization to obtain as much of the material as possible, and a great many boxes of dirty fragments of MSS were shipped to Cambridge. Altogether more than 200,000 fragments of written material were taken. This includes documents of many sorts, since even ordinary business contracts, when no longer of value, would be placed in the genizah, if they contained a date or a salutation in which the name of God might have been used. A study of this material has greatly increased our knowledge of the history of the life and culture of the areas that centered in medieval Cairo.

Hundreds of biblical MSS from this source became available. Paul Kahle made an extensive study of many of these, and from them worked out his theories of the two different groups of Masoretes, one in Babylonia and one in Israel (see his books, *Masoreten des Ostens* [1913]; *Masoreten des Westens*, 2 vols. [1927–30]; and *The Cairo Geniza*, 2nd ed. [1959]). His work has originated many thought-provoking suggestions regarding the history of the Hebrew text.

Solomon Schechter looking through the fragments from the Cairo Genizah (Cambridge, 1898).

X. The Aleppo Codex. As mentioned above, it was the feeling of many scholars that the Aleppo Codex was the earliest complete MS of the OT extant, and that its vocalization and Masorah had been placed on it by Aaron ben Asher himself. It was therefore a great disappointment to Paul Kahle when he was unable to use this MS for the third edition of *Biblia Hebraica*. In 1948 the Sephardic synagogue in Aleppo was raided by a local mob and burned, and for a number of years it was feared that the MS had also been destroyed. However, Izhak Ben-Zvi, president of the state of Israel, refused to give up hope that it might have been saved. For a long time he kept trying to find the place where it might be hidden, and often discussed with Sephardic leaders ways and means by which the "discovery" of the venerable MS might be brought about, and its transfer to safety in Jerusalem assured. At last his efforts succeeded, and in 1960 he was able to announce to the world that the codex had been found and brought to the Hebrew University at Jerusalem. Unfortunately it had suffered much at the hands of the rioters; before 1948 it had been complete, but now about a fourth of it was missing, including nine-tenths of the Pentateuch.

Although the authorities at the Sephardic synagogue in Aleppo had never permitted a Jewish scholar to photograph any part of the MS, they had once allowed an English scholar, William Wickes, to photograph a page of it (Gen. 26:17—27:30), which he had published in 1887 as the frontispiece of his book on Hebrew accents. In 1966 M. H. Goshen-Gottstein of the Hebrew University announced the discovery that once another Christian had also secured permission to photograph a few pages of the MS. The Rev. J. Segall, a missionary in Damascus for many years, published in 1910 a book entitled *Travels through Northern Syria*, in which he included a picture of the pages of the Aleppo MS that contained Deut. 4:38—6:3. Since both of these are portions that were destroyed, the existence of the pictures is a cause for rejoicing. Unfortunately, the photograph by Segall is not clear enough to make it possible to decipher all the details of vocalization, accentuation, and Masorah, though the consonantal letters are clearly discernible throughout. Wickes explicitly denied the claims about the MS, and there is no indication in the original publication that Segall had any realization of the special importance of this particular codex. However, there can be little doubt of the genuineness of the MS or of its direct relation to Ben Asher. (Cf. M. H. Goshen-Gottstein, "The Authenticity of the Aleppo Codex," *Textus* 1 [1960]: 17–58.)

XI. Types of error. In copying Hebrew MSS the same types of mistakes are apt to occur as in copying any types of documents. These may be classified as errors of sight, errors of hearing, and errors of memory.

It is well known that MSS were often copied through dictation. Sometimes one person would dictate and many scribes would make copies, as was often done in the case of the Greek and Roman classics. This method may sometimes have been used at Qumran or elsewhere in the preparing of popular copies of biblical books. However, it was strictly against regulations that official copies of the Scripture should be made in this way. The scribe was required to look repeatedly at the material he was copying. Consequently errors of hearing must have been almost nonexistent in the official text. Errors of memory would be few, and yet could occur, since one who is copying by sight may sometimes be confused by his recollection and mistakenly put down something different from what he sees.

Errors of sight are apt to be related to similarities of letters. A letter that is written somewhat poorly can easily be mistaken for another letter. Such errors occur occasionally in biblical MSS. By far the most common error of this type is confusion of the consonants *dalet* (ד) and *resh* (ר). In Hebrew MSS these two letters are sometimes written so similarly that it is difficult to distinguish them. Clear evidence that this occurred can be found by comparison of proper names in Kings and Chronicles where there are many cases in which the same name is written with a *d* in one and with an *r* in the other. There are cases where a Greek word in the LXX seems to have no relation to the Hebrew text as it stands, and yet, on assuming that the MS used by this Greek translation had one consonant instead of the other, a word may sometimes be substituted which exactly corresponds to that found in the LXX.

Other common errors of sight result from haplography (writing a letter or a group of letters only once where it occurs twice), dittography (accidentally repeating a letter or a group of letters), and omission due to homoeoteleuton (where the eye skips from one word to another that ends similarly). Any writer knows how frequently this last type of error occurs in the copying of personal MSS.

XII. Evidence of the versions. The present section will be limited mainly to general matters concerning the relation of the ancient versions to the establishment of the OT text. (For broader discussion see SEPTUAGINT; TARGUM; VERSIONS OF THE BIBLE, ANCIENT.)

In determining the value of a version the first consideration that naturally occurs is that of age: the more ancient a translation, the more likely it is to provide reliable information concerning the Hebrew text. A second consideration is that of "immediacy." When a document is translated from one language into another, some information is inevitably lost or obscured. Words do not exactly correspond in the two languages, and often there is great overlapping between different words that might be used. Types of expression, verb forms, and principles of syntax differ radically in various languages. Therefore a translation will at best give a close approximation of the meaning of the original. When a translation is made from a text that is itself a translation, the divergence from the original is necessarily compounded. The VULGATE translation made by JEROME at about A.D. 400 was directly from the Hebrew and therefore may be of great value in helping to fix the exact Hebrew text at that time. The Old Latin text, however, though translated some centuries earlier, was not made from the Hebrew but from the Greek. It is thus of value in fixing the text of the LXX at the time when it was made, but its importance for determining the original Hebrew text is greatly diluted.

There are four ancient and immediate versions: (1) the LXX, most of which was produced between the middle of the 3rd cent. B.C. and the end of the 2nd cent. B.C.; (2) the Syriac Peshitta, probably late 2nd cent. A.D.; (3) the Vulgate, c. A.D. 400; (4) the Aramaic Targums, produced at various times.

Another consideration that should not be overlooked is the difference in the amount of effort devoted to maintaining purity of text. In this regard the care devoted to preservation of the MT is unparalleled in relation to any other book, including the Greek NT and the versions of the OT. In particular, the various Greek MSS of the OT have diverged in many different directions. Sometimes it is found that a Greek MS includes sections that follow radically different textual traditions, suggesting the possibility that it may have been copied from a MS from which a considerable number of pages were missing, and that these particular pages were filled in from a different and perhaps inferior MS. When different textual traditions become combined in the same MS, the problem of identifying them and tracing them to an original translation is extremely difficult. In addition, some of the best MSS of the LXX, such as CODEX VATICANUS, contain great numbers of scribal errors.

The LXX is of greatest help in a section such as Samuel, where it is clear that the Hebrew text has been corrupted far more than in other sections. But both in this section and in other books the Greek text is of special significance whenever its reading can be easily explained by considering that a word in its Hebrew prototype was either vocalized differently (i.e., the translator mentally filled in different vowels than those found in the MT) or spelled with different consonants. An interesting instance is Amos 9:12, where the MT reads, "so that they may possess [*yîršû*] the remnant of Edom [*ʾĕdôm*]." The LXX translates, "so that the remnant of mankind [reading *ʾādām*] may seek [*yidrĕšû*]." In Acts 15:17 James quoted this passage as the clinching argument in a decision by the COUNCIL OF JERUSALEM, and since there were present many learned men who would gladly have refuted him if he had not been true to the text, we can feel quite positive that in his day the original Hebrew at this point was like the LXX rather than like the MT (yet most modern commentators interpret this divergence in other ways; cf. the discussion in K. H. Jobes and M. Silva, *Invitation to the Septuagint* [2000], 194–95).

It should be remembered that the other ancient and immediate versions were greatly influenced by the LXX and therefore are often not as strong an argument for the original Hebrew as might otherwise be the case. Study of the versions is of great value in learning what interpretation of a passage was common at the time when the these translations were made, and sometimes in determining a possible alternative text, which in certain cases may be original. In most instances, however, the MT is far more dependable than the text of the versions.

XIII. Conclusion. It should be noted that the amount of material available for the establishment of the OT text is many times as great as that for establishing the text of any other ancient document, except the NT. The agreement in the consonantal text of the various MSS is most remarkable, and the great bulk of the very extensive material that has now been found from before the time of Christ agrees very closely with the consonantal text of the MT. A few fragments give evidence of varying documents in some parts of Israel at that early period, and some of these may represent the text upon which the Samaritan Pentateuch was based or from which the LXX was translated. The feat of copying and recopying the text from the time of Qumran to that of Ben Asher with so little variation is unique in history. The Masoretes did a valuable task in writing down the tradition about the vowels and standardizing it. The fragments from the Cairo Genizah will enable us to reconstruct to a far greater degree than has yet been done the progress of the development of this system, and to see at what places arrangements of vowels or of accents represent the maintenance of an old tradition and at what points they represent the conclusions of the Masoretes. The MS from Aleppo will enable us to know the results of the Masoretic activities more accurately than ever before.

The Qumran MSS and comparisons with the LXX suggest that in the books of Samuel, and possibly in a few other sections of the Hebrew Bible, a greater amount of distortion than usual may have occurred, and in such cases the LXX may occasionally provide a more correct text. Where the LXX variation can be easily explained on the basis of a natural confusion between Hebrew letters, the corruption may be due to the translators themselves or it may have been already there in the Hebrew MSS they were using, but it is also possible that the error should be attributed to the MT tradition.

The text has been preserved with a remarkable accuracy but not absolutely so. This fact is a useful guard against building important conclusions upon one verse alone, for any one verse may involve an error. Where there is no textual evidence of a variation in two different verses, the probability that each of them conceals an unknown error is so small as to be negligible. It is the divine warning to compare Scripture with Scripture and to study its teachings as a whole, rather than to endeavor to squeeze meanings out of individual words and phrases beyond what is possible in view of the nature of human words.

(In addition to the titles mentioned in the body of this article, see C. D. Ginsburg, *Introduction to the Masoretico-Critical Edition of the Hebrew Bible* [1897]; R. D. Wilson, *A Scientific Investigation of the Old Testament* [1929, reprinted with revisions by E. J. Young, 1959]; B. J. Roberts, *The Old Testament Text and Versions* [1951]; J. Barr, *Comparative Philology and the Text of the Old Testament* [1968, reprinted with corrections and substantial additions, 1987]; F. E. Deist, *Towards the Text of the Old Testament*, 2nd ed. [1981]; J. Weingreen, *Introduction to the Critical Study of the Text of the Hebrew Bible* [1982]; P. K. McCarter, Jr., *Textual Criticism: Recovering the Text of the Hebrew Bible* [1986]; E. R. Brotzman, *Old Testament Textual Criticism: A Practical Introduction* [1994]; F. M. Cross, *The Ancient Library of Qumran*, 3rd ed. [1995]; E. Würthwein, *The Text of the Old Testament: An Introduction to the Biblia Hebraica*, rev. ed. [1995]; E. Tov, *Textual Criticism of the Hebrew Bible*, 2nd ed. [2001]; A. Schenker and P. Hugo, eds., *L'enfance de la Bible hébraïque: l'histoire du texte de l'Ancien Testament* [2005].) A. A. MACRAE

text and manuscripts (NT). The science of textual criticism is a basic literary discipline, for a text cannot be interpreted before one has determined what is the text to be studied. In making a copy of a book by hand, an ancient scribe—and a modern scribe as well—would almost certainly introduce errors and changes of various sorts by accident, and at times intentionally. When the resulting MS was subsequently copied, most of the variations would be carried over into the next MS, along with any additional errors and changes that the next scribe might make. Thus the more copies that intervene between a given MS and the original, the more differences there will generally be between the two. The goal of the textual critic is to remove the scribal mistakes that have accumulated so as to approximate the original form of the text.

    I. Introduction
   II. Paleography
      A. Book forms
      B. Handwriting
      C. Palimpsests
      D. Abbreviations
      E. Divisions of the text
      F. Catenae
      G. Lectionaries
  III. Witnesses to the text
      A. Greek manuscripts
      B. Ancient versions
      C. Patristic quotations
  IV. Transmission of the NT text
      A. Before the invention of printing
      B. The Greek NT in print
   V. The modern period of textual criticism
      A. The theory of Westcott and Hort
      B. The work of von Soden
      C. Current view of text-types
      D. Principles of textual criticism
  VI. Conclusion

I. Introduction. No ancient literature has affected the Western world so profoundly as has the Bible, and in particular the NT. Nor has any ancient writing or body of literature been preserved in quantity even comparable to the number of extant MSS of the NT. The writings of some ancient authors (e.g., part of the *Annals* of TACITUS) are represented by only one MS from ancient times. Most other writings have survived in only a few copies or not at all, though in the case of some popular authors, such as Euripides and Cicero, a few hundred MSS are known. Of the NT, on the other hand, more than 5,700 handwritten copies in Greek are preserved (many of these contain only portions of the NT and some are fragments of a few verses; in over 2,000 of them the text is arranged in lectionary form for daily readings). In addition, there are some 8,000 MSS in Latin, and 2,000 or more in other ancient languages, to say nothing of innumerable biblical quotations by Christian authors.

In another important respect, too, the MS tradition of the NT is distinctly superior to that of other ancient literature. The oldest known MSS of the works of some ancient authors date from a thousand years or more after the death of the author. A time interval of several hundred years is not uncommon, ranging downward to a mere three hundred years, as in the case of Virgil. In contrast, two of the most important surviving codices of the NT were written less than three hundred years after the NT was completed; more remarkably, an appreciable amount of the NT is extant on papyrus MSS written from one to two centuries after the biblical authors wrote. Since classical scholars assume the general reliability of secular works even where the time interval is great and where only a few MSS are available, we have far greater assurance that the presently available NT text reliably represents what the authors originally wrote.

One needs to recognize, however, that the multiplication of any piece of literature in ancient times was a very different matter from that of the period since the invention of the printing press. It is now possible to print any number of *identical* copies of a work, whereas in antiquity, when each individual copy had to be made separately by hand, the only certainty was that no two copies of a book of any length would be identical. This period of handcopying of MSS encompasses three-fourths of the time from the completion of the NT to the present; and the vast number of copies made of parts or all of the NT during these early centuries means that multiplied thousands of textual variants were introduced into these MSS. The originals (autographs) of the NT books were doubtless lost at a very early date.

All of this means, technically speaking, that it is not possible to determine the exact original wording of the NT on the basis of any given MS. Rather, a comparison of MSS must be made and principles established for determining as nearly as possible the exact form of the original text. Thus the need for textual criticism, that is, the process of studying copies of a work whose autograph is unavailable, for the purpose of determining the form of the original text. Textual criticism is necessary for virtually every piece of ancient literature, since in only the rarest instances (e.g., inscriptions in stone) has the autograph of an ancient writing been preserved to modern times. (The discipline of textual criticism has other important functions as well, such as understanding the nature of literary transmission for its own sake, and some recent scholars have emphasized these other goals even at the expense of minimizing the task of restoring the original. Cf. D. C. Parker, *The Living Text of the Gospels* [1997], and the review of this book by M. Silva in *WTJ* 62 [2000]: 295–302.)

In the case of the NT, even the relatively large number of MSS now known doubtless represents only a small percentage of the total number that were produced during the early centuries. In virtually no instance is it possible to show that any extant MS is the direct ancestor of another MS, and it is impossible to determine how many copies lie between any given MS and the original. Scholars reasonably assume that a later MS is likely to be further removed from the original in the number of copies intervening than is an earlier MS, but they recognize that there are significant exceptions to the rule.

It must not be supposed, however, that the text of the NT rests upon precarious grounds because of the multitude of copies through which it has passed or because of the great number of variants found in the MSS. There is in fact virtually no question concerning by far the greater part of the words of the NT. Indeed, the same is true of ancient literature in general. It is only a relatively small portion of the words of the text that requires the attention of the textual critic. Virtually all MSS of any given part of the NT say essentially the same thing. It has been stated that (1) there is no question at all concerning seven-eighths of the words of the NT; (2) if insignificant differences (such as common spellings variations) be disregarded, only about one-sixtieth of the words can be regarded as in doubt; and (3) only about one word in a thousand involves both a substantial question of meaning and serious doubt of the correct text (B. F. Westcott and F. J. A. Hort, *The New Testament in the Original Greek: Introduction, Appendix* [1881], 2).

Although some scholars would express the proportions differently, the truth remains that no Christian doctrine—indeed, no significant element of biblical teaching generally—rests upon insecure textual evidence. To be sure, it has been argued that the doctrine of the ASCENSION OF CHRIST has weak textual support (cf. E. J. Epp in *New Testament Textual Criticism: Its Significance for Exegesis. Essays in Honour of Bruce M. Metzger*, ed. E. J. Epp and G. D. Fee [1981], 131–45); but even if one were to accept the "Western" readings at Lk. 24:51 and Acts 1:11, there would be no grounds for doubting that, according to the NT writers, Jesus was raised from the dead, was "taken up" (the word *analēmphtheis* in the second passage is textually secure), and then sat down at the right hand of the Father (Acts 2:34; Heb. 1:3; et al.). And while a valuable and thorough study by B. D. Ehrman (*The Orthodox Corruption of Scripture: The Effect of Early Christological Controversies on the Text of the New Testament* [1993]) has demonstrated that scribes occasionally altered the text for theological reasons, this very monograph, by virtue of what it is does *not* prove, indirectly attests to the reliability of the NT text (see the review by M. Silva in *WTJ* 57 [1995]: 262–64; particularly unfortunate and misleading is the title, as well as the intent, of Ehrman's more recent popularization, *Misquoting Jesus: The Story behind Who Changed the Bible and Why* [2005]).

II. Paleography

A. Book forms

1. Papyrus roll. In the 1st Christian cent., when the books of the NT were written, the accepted form for a literary work was a PAPYRUS roll or SCROLL. The papyrus plant was a tall reed that grew along the banks of the NILE River but almost nowhere else. The stalk of this plant was peeled, and its pithy center was cut into thin strips, which were laid side by side with another layer over them at right angles. After being pounded to aid adhesion of the layers and left to dry in the sun, the resulting thin sheet curved fairly well when written upon lengthwise of the papyrus strips with a pen made from a reed. These sheets, measuring from 6 x 9 in. to 12 x 15 in., were slightly overlapped and glued together to make a roll of twenty sheets, the form in which papyrus was generally sold. If a work was too long for one roll, several rolls could be fastened together.

There were practical limits for the length of a scroll, but a long work could be extended to more than one scroll. The scroll was generally simply rolled on itself; there is little evidence of the use of rollers.

The columns of text of a scroll were usually narrow, so that the scroll need not be unrolled widely to read it. Writing was done on the inside surface of the roll. On this side the papyrus strips were laid horizontally. The text of a work was not generally written on the outside surface of the roll, both because of the inconvenience to the reader and because the papyrus strips on this surface would be vertical (writing across the grain of the papyrus is more difficult). Exceptions occur, however, as attested by Rev. 5:1, "a scroll written on the inside and on the back" (NRSV).

The regular Greek word for a papyrus scroll is *biblion* **G1046**, "having to do with *biblos*" (the pith of the papyrus plant). This word occurs in various NT passages (e.g., Lk. 4:17, 20; Jn. 20:30). In Rev. 6:14 the sky is described as having "receded like a scroll, rolling up." In 2 Tim. 4:13, Paul asked Timothy to bring him his "scrolls, especially the parchments" (so most translations, but some think that here the latter word, *membrana* **G3521**, refers to parchment codices [see below, sections 2–3] rather than scrolls; cf. C. H. Roberts in *Proceedings of the British Academy* 40 [1954], 174).

The scroll form had certain disadvantages, including some with which the modern user of microfilms is familiar. The scroll needed to be completely rerolled after being used, although a careless reader might leave this task for the next reader. Moreover, consultation of various passages of a scroll was much more difficult than with the modern book form. This latter factor was one of the principal influences that led, not long after the beginning of the Christian era, to the replacement of the scroll by another book form.

2. Papyrus codex. From antiquity, waxed tablets had been used for school exercises and other temporary writings. These tablets were somewhat like a child's slate, with a surface of wax instead of slate, and with a stylus as the writing instrument. As time went on, the practice developed of fastening two or more of these tablets together by thongs tied through holes at the edge of the tablets. Even before the Christian

A 1st-cent. papyrus scroll.

era this type of document, called a CODEX, led in turn to the development of notebooks composed of folded sheets. These notebooks were used for informal and nonliterary purposes. They also came to be used at times for the first draft of an author's literary works, which would then be copied onto a papyrus scroll for their final form. At first the number of sheets folded together into a quire varied; each sheet might be folded separately, or several sheets—sometimes even an entire book—might be folded together into one quire. Later, however, a quire of four sheets, which made sixteen pages, became standard.

3. Parchment codex. From antiquity, skins of animals were used in writing. About 200 years before the Christian era, however, a new process was developed whereby the skins were scraped, soaked in quicklime, and rubbed with chalk and pumice stone, which produced a thin, firm, and very durable writing surface. Writing could be done on this surface with a quill pen as well as with the softer reed pen. This material, known as PARCHMENT or vellum (although *vellum* originally referred to the finer grades of calfskin), likewise came to be used for notebooks in codex form.

When the NT books were written, therefore, the codex book form—made of papyrus or parchment—was known, but the recognized book form for literary publications was still the papyrus scroll and continued to be so for some centuries for secular classics. Early in the Christian era, however, the codex form was developed into full book size and began to be used for published works, particularly for the Bible; even the very oldest MSS of the NT are in codex form, not scrolls. The NT likewise led in the transition from papyrus to parchment for literary purposes, whereas the NT was copied on papyrus codices in the earliest period, parchment became more common in the 4th cent. and soon almost completely displaced papyrus as the writing material for NT MSS.

It is possible, therefore, that even the originals of the various NT books (esp. the quasi-personal letters of Paul) were written in the modern book or codex form. On the other hand, the books of the NT that were more nearly "literature" as they were published, such as the Gospels and Acts, may have been written on scrolls in accordance with the current literary tradition. All of the NT books were probably originally written on papyrus. In any event, whether the autographs were in scroll or codex form, it was not long before the codex was the one form in which NT MSS were copied. Indeed, the habit of the early Christians of consulting their Scriptures may have been a factor in popularizing the codex form and in causing it to replace the scroll as the accepted form for literature.

Not until shortly before the invention of printing from movable type was parchment displaced by paper in the Western world. To summarize, then, NT book forms and materials in the earliest centuries were approximately as follows. (1) the autographs would have been written on papyrus codices and scrolls; (2) during the 2nd and 3rd centuries, papyrus codices were used; (3) beginning with the 4th cent., parchment codices were preferred, but occasional papyrus codices are known from as late as the 7th cent.

4. Other forms. Small portions of the NT were occasionally written in two additional forms, although neither their purpose nor their extent entitles them to be classified on the same level as MSS. More than twenty portions of the NT, representing six books, are preserved on broken pieces of pottery, which were used by the poorest people as writing material. These broken pieces, or "potsherds," are called OSTRACA when they contain a written text. In addition, brief NT passages were sometimes inscribed on talismans, or good-luck charms, although they were condemned by church authorities (see B. M. Metzger and B. D. Ehrman, *The Text of the New Testament: Its Transmission, Corruption, and Restoration*, 4th ed. [2005], 49). A few of these talismans are extant.

B. Handwriting

1. Uncial. From before the beginning of the Christian era, two forms of Greek handwriting were current. For letters, business documents, and other nonliterary purposes, a connected "cursive" style of handwriting was used, somewhat analogous to English longhand writing. For literary purposes, a style known as "uncial" was used. Uncial letters, corresponding approximately to English printed capital letters, were written separately. Taking into account the respective uses of these two styles of writing, the autographs of the books of the NT that were written for publication, such as the Gospels, were presumably written in uncial letters. If one regards the letters of Paul as personal communications, they may have been written in the cursive hand, but they had an official character and were no doubt read out loud in the church assemblies, so the uncial form would have been appropriate. Moreover, these letters were very soon being cop-

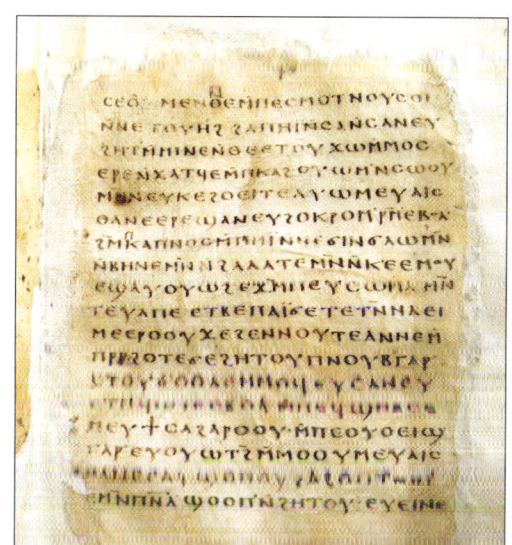

Coptic manuscript (c. A.D. 350).

ied for distribution and were being thought of as literature; indeed, the very earliest extant copies of the Pauline letters, as of all of the NT, are written in uncials. For practical purposes, therefore, it may be said that the transmission of the NT was in uncial MSS from the beginning.

2. Minuscule. The two styles of handwriting existed side by side for several hundred years. About the 9th cent., a major change occurred by the development of a refined and more formal style of handwriting out of the nonliterary cursive. This "minuscule" hand, as it is called, produced very attractive MSS and could be written much more rapidly than the uncial hand. The oldest known minuscule MS of the NT (no. 461) is dated A.D. 835, which is also the oldest NT MS known that contains a date. The minuscule hand was readily accepted, and by the end of the 10th cent. it had completely displaced the uncial hand. Thus a rather clear division of the history of NT MSS can be drawn: (1) uncial MSS in the early centuries; (2) uncials and minuscules from the latter part of the 9th cent. to near the end of the 10th; (3) minuscules thereafter.

Within both the uncial and the minuscule periods, certain other characteristics help to establish approximate dates of MSS. The earliest uncials on papyrus are almost entirely devoid of ornamentation. Even a new section is indicated, if at all, by nothing more than a point and a small space within the line. The early uncials on parchment have no ornamentation and very few diacritical marks or marks of punctuation. A new section may be indicated by beginning a new line or by a slightly larger initial letter extending into the left margin. With the passage of time, accents, breathings, and punctuation marks were added. Initial letters of sections were enlarged and ornamented, and illustrations and other adornments were added, although the handwriting itself tended to deteriorate, the letters becoming heavier and less neat.

The minuscule MSS passed through somewhat the same stages. Although diacritical marks and punctuation occur in the minuscules from the beginning, the early ones were neatly written and had relatively little adornment, and developed toward more adornment and less neatness in the later centuries (see W. H. P. Hatch, *The Principal Uncial Manuscripts of the New Testament* [1931], and *Facsimiles and Descriptions of Minuscule Manuscripts of the New Testament* [1951]). One characteristic of Greek MSS that remained constant was the absence of spacing between words, both in uncial and minuscule handwriting. This was simply a convention of style, not from any attempt to save space. Word division at the end of a line, however, followed definite rules of syllable division.

C. Palimpsests. Although papyrus was a very satisfactory material for writing, it did not lend itself to extensive erasing. Parchment, on the other hand, was so durable that it could be erased and reused. Thus, if the text of a parchment MS was no longer needed, or if the sheets had become worn or torn, the MS would sometimes be taken apart, sheets that were too badly damaged would be discarded, the leaves might be cut in half along the center fold, and the original text would be scraped off. The sheets would then be rearranged into new quires and used to receive a new text. Even MSS of the NT were not exempt from being thus erased, so much so that church authorities were forced to condemn the practice. Such an erased and rewritten MS is called a *palimpsest* (from Gk. *palin*, "again," and *psaō*, "to scrape"). Fortunately, standards of erasure were not too effective for these palimpsests, and it is possible to read much of the erased text under the later writing. One very important NT palimpsest is Codex C, known as CODEX EPHRAEMI SYRI RESCRIPTUS because the NT text is written over with writings of the Syriac church father EPHRAEM. In all, more than fifty palimpsest MSS are known in which the erased text was an uncial NT text.

D. Abbreviations. In the oldest NT MSS, abbreviations were almost entirely limited to fifteen words, such as "God," "Lord," "heaven," and certain words with sacred associations. Abbreviations for these words were *contractions*—that is, they consisted of the first and last letter or letters, with a horizontal line above to indicate the contraction. In addition, the letter *nu* at the end of a line was sometimes indicated by a raised horizontal line instead of the letter. In the minuscule period, various other words came to be abbreviated by *suspension*, which consisted in writing the first part only of the word,

In addition, *ligatures*, in which two or more letters were combined into one unit, were introduced, as well as *symbols*, which were a sort of shorthand of forms representing certain endings or words.

E. Divisions of the text. Many Greek MSS of the NT contain numbers (indicated by Greek letters) in the margin that indicate the Ammonian Sections and the Eusebian Canons. At a very early date, the four Gospels were divided into sections of greatly varying extent. These sections are attributed to a certain Ammonius. In the 4th cent., the church father EUSEBIUS constructed a gospel harmony based on the Ammonian sections. Using the Ammonian numbers, he made tables listing the passages in which parallels occurred in all four Gospels in various combinations, and of the passages that occurred in only one. He then added the table number to each Ammonian section number throughout the Gospels. This system made it easy to find parallels. These numbers are also used in some printed editions of the Greek NT.

F. Catenae. In addition to NT MSS with a continuous text, two other MS formats are of interest. One of these is the MS with a catena, in which the biblical text is accompanied by a series of selections from the writings of church fathers to form a commentary on the NT text. These MSS took various forms: the patristic commentary might be written in the outer margins, with the biblical text occupying a smaller part of the page; the biblical text and the commentary might be written in alternate sections; or the text and commentary might be written in parallel columns. In the oldest MSS with catenae, the authors of the passages of the catena were usually indicated. In later MSS, the names were often abbreviated or indicated by symbols or omitted altogether. A symbol or number was often placed at the beginning of a passage in the catena and in the body of the NT text to indicate the NT passage to which the commentary referred.

G. Lectionaries. A second variation from a straight-text MS is the lectionary, in which NT passages are arranged in the order in which they are to be read in church services during the year. A reflection of lectionary usage is likewise found in many regular NT MSS, in which the word *archē*, "beginning," and *telos*, "end," or their abbreviations, are found.

III. Witnesses to the text. The text of the NT is known from three basic sources: Greek MSS, ancient translations, and quotations from ancient writers.

A. Greek manuscripts. When early editors began to refer to Greek MSS, they were cited in various ways, such as by name or by other designation, associating the MS with its owner or the library in which it was located. With the increase in numbers of MSS, it became necessary to use a less cumbersome system. Various attempts were made in this direction before the system now in use was perfected. Under the present system, papyrus MSS (referred to as "papyri," all of which have an uncial text) are indicated by a capital "P" or its Gothic equivalent, followed by a superscript number to designate each MS. More than 115 papyri are currently listed. Uncial MSS on parchment (called simply "uncials") were initially designated by capital letters of the Roman alphabet, and when these were used up, additional MSS were assigned letters from the Greek alphabet; but as the quantity of uncials continued to grow it became necessary to employ numbers preceded by a zero (01, 02, etc.; thus the first forty-five uncials listed are known both by a number and by a letter). Minuscule MSS are designated by number (e.g., 33, 565, 2065). Lectionaries are designated by a number preceded by either the abbreviation "Lect." or the letter el in italics (e.g., Lect. 299, *l* 1301).

1. Papyri. All of the very earliest extant MSS of the Greek NT are papyri. They date mostly from the middle of the 2nd cent. through the 4th cent., although a few are as late as the 7th/8th cent. Although nearly all are fragmentary, together they include a considerable portion of the NT. In spite of their early date, the reliability of the papyri is reduced by the fact that many of them were copied by nonprofessional scribes and show a consequent lack of attention to small details.

Two collections of NT papyri are especially significant. The CHESTER BEATTY collection, acquired in 1930–31, includes several that date from the 3rd cent.: P⁴⁵, containing approximately one-seventh of the text of the Gospels and Acts; P⁴⁶, which includes a large portion of the Pauline epistles (except the Pastorals) plus Hebrews; and P⁴⁷, comprising roughly one-third of the text of Revelation. Most of the leaves of these papyri are in the Chester Beatty collection in Dublin, although thirty of the eighty-six leaves of P⁴⁶ are in the University of Michigan collection, and some fragments of one leaf of P⁴⁵ are in Vienna. These three papyri were published by Sir Frederic Kenyon, in fascicles containing the printed text as well as photographs.

The second and perhaps even more significant collection of NT papyri is that of the BODMER Library in Geneva, Switzerland. Little is known of the actual source of these MSS. The collection includes the following MSS of the Greek NT: P⁶⁶ contains a large part of the Gospel of John and is dated by some authorities as early as the middle of the 2nd cent., which makes it the oldest extensive MS of any part of the NT; P⁷², dating from the 3rd cent., includes the epistle of Jude and the two epistles of Peter together with numerous other writings; P⁷⁵ contains much of Luke and John and dates from near the end of the 2nd cent. or slightly later.

The oldest known MS of the Greek NT, even older than P⁶⁶, is a small fragment in the John Rylands Library in Manchester, England, designated P⁵², containing only a few lines from Jn. 18. Dated in the first half of the 2nd cent. by its editor and by other paleographers, it furnishes evidence that prior to the date when the Tübingen critics claimed the fourth gospel was written (c. 160), it had actually been in circulation long enough to reach into the interior of Egypt.

2. Uncials. Extant uncial MSS (i.e., written with uncial script on parchment rather than on papyrus) number about 310, varying from small fragments of a few verses to the complete NT. Dating from the 4th through the 10th centuries, and thus later than most of the papyri, their significance is greater than that of the papyri because they are so much more extensive in content. In addition, by the uncial period, the Christian religion had gained official recognition, and consequently most uncial MSS give evidence of having been professionally copied. The following are some of the more significant or representative uncials (for a fuller descriptive list see Metzger and Ehrman, *Text of the New Testament*, 62–86).

CODEX SINAITICUS (ℵ or Aleph or 01; in LXX studies, S), from the 4th cent., containing both OT and NT (though parts of the OT have not survived), now in the British Museum in London. Its discovery by Tischendorf in the Monastery of St. Catherine on Mount SINAI (hence its name) is a fascinating story (see C. Tischendorf, *Codex Sinaiticus*, 8th ed. [1934]). It is one of the most important MSS of the NT in existence. Its text is arranged in four columns to the page, in a neat hand with little adornment. The pages are about 15 x 13 in. Brought from Mount Sinai to Russia in 1859 by Tischendorf, who considered it so important that he was unwilling to have it assigned to an obscure place in the then-current alphabetical listing of MSS, he assigned to it instead the first letter of the Hebrew alphabet. In 1933, it was purchased by the British government from the Soviet government for £100,000.

CODEX ALEXANDRINUS (A or 02), 5th cent. MS, containing both Testaments (lacking, in the NT, almost all of Matthew, part of John, and most of 2 Corinthians); now in the British Museum. It was presented in 1627 to King Charles I of England by the Patriarch of Constantinople, who had obtained it in Alexandria. Its pages are approximately 10 x 13 in. The text, two columns to the page, has somewhat more ornamentation than Codex Sinaiticus.

CODEX VATICANUS (B or 03), 4th cent., located in the Vatican Library since the 15th cent. or longer. Regarded by many as the single most important extant MS of the NT, it originally contained both Testaments and part of the APOCRYPHA; the MS now lacks most of Genesis and part of the Psalms in the OT, and part of Hebrews and all of Titus, Timothy, Philemon, and Revelation in the NT. The pages are approximately 11 x 11 in. The text, very neat and without adornment, is printed in three columns to the page.

CODEX EPHRAEMI SYRI RESCRIPTUS (E or 04), the most important palimpsest MS of the Greek NT. It is located in the Bibliothèque Nationale of Paris. Written in the 5th cent., it evidently originally contained both Testaments. In the 12th cent. its biblical text was scraped off, most of the leaves were discarded, and the remaining ones were written over with some of the writings of St. Ephraem. Tischendorf read and published the biblical text, but the use of chemicals in an attempt to restore the erased text have further defaced the ms. The extant portions of the ms include parts of almost all of the NT books.

CODEX BEZAE CANTABRIGIENSIS (D or 05), a 6th-cent. ms of the Gospels and Acts, has been in the Cambridge University library since it was presented to the university by Théodore Beza in 1581. The text is written in one column to the page, but in lines of greatly varying length. It is a bilingual ms, with Greek and Latin on facing pages. The Gospels are in the order Matthew, John, Luke, and Mark. As the chief representative of the so-called "Western text" (see discussion of text-types below), it has many textual peculiarities, and its text of Acts is about one-tenth longer than the common form of the text.

CODEX CLAROMONTANUS (D^p or 06), Bibliothèque Nationale in Paris, a 6th-cent. ms containing the Pauline epistles and Hebrews. By remarkable coincidence, both mss designated "D" are bilingual, both have Greek and Latin on facing pages (Greek on the left), both have the text in "sense lines" of irregular length, and both are representatives of the peculiar "Western text."

Codex Purpureus Petropolitanus (N or 022), is written in silver letters on purple vellum, as are also Codex O (023), Σ (042), and Φ (043). All four of these mss are from the 6th cent. Most of Codex N is in Leningrad, but parts of it are in several other locations.

Codex Freerianus or Washingtonensis (W or 032), 4th or 5th cent., in the Freer Art Gallery of the Smithsonian Institution in Washington, D.C. Like Codex D, it contains the Gospels in the Western order.

3. **Minuscules.** Minuscule mss outnumber uncials almost ten to one (about 2880 have survived). Although a larger percentage of uncials than minuscules may have perished because of the greater antiquity of the former, the disparity in numbers of the surviving mss doubtless points to the fact that the minuscule handwriting made the copying of mss a much more rapid and less expensive process. The following minuscule mss should be mentioned.

1: a 12th-cent. ms containing the NT except Revelation; in Basel, Switzerland. It was one of the mss used by Erasmus in the preparation of the first published edition of the Greek NT. "Family 1" is the term given to a group of minuscules 1, 118, 131, 209, and 1582—all dating from the 12th to the 14th centuries, whose text is very closely related and is significantly different from the type of text current in the minuscules in general.

2: a 12th-cent. ms of the Gospels located in Basel; also used by Erasmus.

13: a 13th-cent. ms of the Gospels now located in Paris. "Family 13" is a closely related group of minuscules, including 13, 69, 124, 346, 543, 788, 826, 828, and a few others. One unique feature of this group is that the story of the woman taken in adultery follows Lk. 21:38 instead of Jn. 7:52. Family 13 is in turn textually related to family 1.

33: called "the queen of the cursives [i.e., minuscules]" because of its excellent text, dates from the 9th or 10th cent. and contains the NT except Revelation. It is located in Paris.

81: one of the few mss stating the date of its composition (1044), this minuscule contains Acts in an excellent text; it is located in London.

565: a 9th 10th-cent. ms of the Gospels, located in Leningrad, written in gold letters on purple vellum, is one of the most beautiful of the mss of the

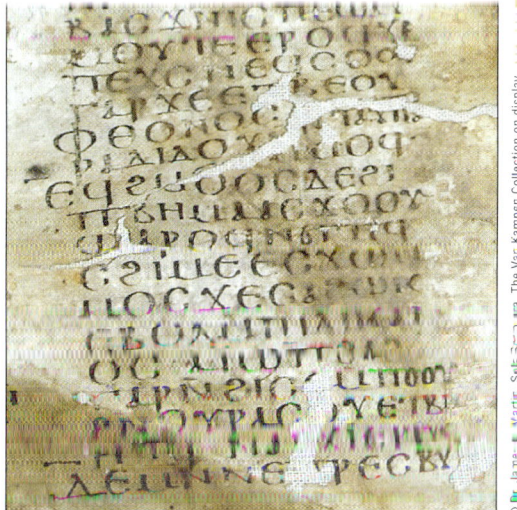

Coptic text of Matthew (5th cent.).

NT. Its text frequently differs from the common minuscule text and is related to the text of families 1 and 13.

700: dating from the 11th or 12th cent., this MS also differs frequently from the common text of the minuscules and has affinities to 565 and families 1 and 13. It shares with one other (162) the reading, "May thy Holy Spirit come upon us and cleanse us," instead of "Thy kingdom come," in the Lord's Prayer in Lk. 11:2.

1424: owned by the Lutheran Theological Seminary in Maywood, Illinois, this minuscule dates from the 9th or 10th cent. and contains the entire NT, with an accompanying catena for all except Revelation. Together with Codex M and more than twenty-five other minuscules, it comprises family 1424.

4. Lectionaries. Although lectionaries originated in the uncial period, most of the extant copies are minuscules. In very early times, certain Scripture passages were designated for reading on each day of the year, and for special services and days; and numerous NT MSS contain indications of the beginning and ending of lections within their text. As early as the 4th cent., however, special MSS were prepared in which the NT text was written in the order in which it was to be used for the daily readings, or for the readings for Saturdays and Sundays, beginning with Easter. This type of lectionary is called a *synaxarion*. Another type giving readings for such special occasions as feasts and saints' days is called a *menologion*. Lessons in the lectionaries include all parts of the NT except Revelation. A lectionary that contains lessons from the Gospels is called an *evangelistarion*; one containing lessons from other parts of the NT is called an *apostolicon*.

In addition to presenting the text in a different order, the first words of the Scripture lesson in lectionaries are sometimes modified to avoid undue abruptness or to clarify a reference (e.g., the substitution of "Jesus" for "he"). In addition, many lections are introduced by one of a number of set formulae preceding the first words of the Scripture text, such as "The Lord said to his own disciples," "At that time," "The Lord said this parable," and others. Of approximately 2,300 extant lectionaries, varying from small fragments to complete MSS, about two-thirds are *evangelistaria*, somewhat less than one-third are *apostolica*, and the remainder are combinations of both types.

B. Ancient versions. The translation of a literary work from one language into another was not common in ancient times. In those instances in which it was done, the resulting translation was generally too free a rendering to be useful in determining the wording of the original (the Greek version of the OT is a rare example of a generally reliable translation of ancient literature prior to NT times). With the spread of the message of the Christian faith, missionaries began to translate the Bible into the language of the people to whom they ministered. Since these translations were generally faithful to the original language, they also provide additional attestation to the NT text.

There are certain cautions that must be observed in using a version as evidence for the Greek text from which it was translated. The translator's command both of Greek and of the receptor language would affect the work, and allowance must be made for possible errors in translation. Allowance must also be made for features in one language that are not normally reflected in another language. For example, Latin has no definite article; therefore the word for "boat" in Latin could be the rendering of either "a boat" or "the boat" in Greek. Again, if the NT is translated into a language in which meaning is largely dependent upon word order, as in English, many variations in word order that are possible in Greek could not be attested. Further, in no instance is the original MS of an ancient version extant, and we must base our study on copies that may include both copyists' errors and changes introduced into the version at a later date. The translation itself must therefore be subjected to textual criticism to establish as nearly as possible the original form of the version before it can be used in the determination of the Greek text. If the approximate date of the translation is known, it can help to indicate the form of the Greek text that was known at the time and in the geographical area in which the translation was made. The following are the significant ancient versions of the NT (for further discussion see VERSIONS OF THE BIBLE, ANCIENT).

1. Syriac. Although Syriac is a dialect of ARAMAIC (thus related to the Jewish Aramaic spoken in Palestine at the time of Jesus), the extant Syriac MSS of the NT are all translations from Greek originals and thus farther removed from the original *accurate than* in the Greek text.

(a) The DIATESSARON ("through the four"), composed by a Christian apologist named Tatian, was a continuous gospel harmony that combined material from all four Gospels. Although the original language of its composition has been debated, it was of particular influence in the Syriac-speaking church and it has survived in several other languages.

(b) The Old Syriac was a translation of the Gospels made probably at the beginning of the 3rd cent. or slightly earlier; it survives in a 5th-cent. MS edited by William Cureton in 1858 and known as the Curetonian Syriac (Syr^c) and in a 4th-cent. palimpsest MS discovered in the Monastery of St. Catherine on Mount Sinai in 1892 and known as the Sinaitic Syriac (Syr^s).

(c) The Peshitta (Syr^p), which became the standard Syriac version of the NT (originally it did not include 2 Peter, 2 and 3 John, Jude, and Revelation), was produced near the end of the 4th cent. It is known in more than 300 MSS, some of which date from the 5th and 6th centuries.

Less significant Syriac versions are the following: (d) The Philoxenian (Syr^{ph}) was completed in 508 by a certain Polycarp for Philoxenus, Bishop of Mabug in Syria; this work may have disappeared, but some scholars believe that it was preserved in the Harklean version.

(e) The Harklean or Harkleian or Harklensis (Syr^h) was the work of Thomas of Harkel, Bishop of Mabug after Philoxenus, and was published in 616. It is unclear whether Thomas merely reissued the Philoxenian version and added some marginal notes from a few Greek MSS, or whether his work was a thorough revision entitled to be called a new version (to which he added marginal readings that he believed were significant but not warranting a place in the text itself). It is the marginal readings of the Harklean version that have been of particular significance in textual criticism, especially in Acts.

(f) The Palestinian Syriac (Syr^{pal}), dating probably from the 5th cent., is not closely related to any of the other Syriac versions. It is unique in that, except for a few fragments of continuous text, it has survived only in lectionary form, which is preserved in three MSS of the 11th and 12th centuries; it may have been translated originally from a Greek lectionary.

2. Latin. Although Greek was commonly known and spoken throughout most of the Roman empire during the first two or three centuries of the Christian era, the need for a Latin translation of the Scriptures soon arose. The Latin NT survives in two forms.

(a) The Old Latin (OL) or Itala (it). By the end of the 2nd cent., the Gospels and perhaps all of the NT were probably current in Latin in N Africa, and soon afterward in other parts of the empire. The MSS of the OL differ so much among themselves that they probably reflect not just one Latin translation but several. Of the fifty or so OL MSS that are known (dating from the 4th through the 13th centuries), none contains the NT in its entirety, although together they include most of the books. OL MSS are cited by single lower-case letters plus abbreviations such as *aur*, *ff*^{2}, *gig*, and *ph*.

(b) The VULGATE. With the passage of time, the great variations within the OL became more evident and more unacceptable. In 382, Pope Damasus appointed JEROME, the outstanding biblical scholar of that day, to undertake a revision to bring the Latin version into conformity with the Greek. Jerome's revision, known as the Vulgate ("common") and revised numerous times through the centuries, formed the basis of what is still the official version of the Roman Catholic Church. Some 8,000 MSS are extant, twice as many as the number of Greek MSS, which suggests that the Vulgate Bible was the most frequently copied work of ancient literature. Manuscripts of the Vulgate are commonly designated by abbreviations of their names (*am*, *cav*, *fu*, *harl*), or by their capital initial letters.

3. Coptic. Early in the Christian era an alphabet was developed for the Egyptian language using Greek letters with some additional forms taken from the older demotic script of Egypt (with the hieratic, these forms were derivatives of the hieroglyphic writing of more ancient times). From the NILE delta to the southern part of the country, some six dialects of the language existed. The most significant for NT study are from each end of this geographical area.

(a) Sahidic was the dialect in use from THEBES and S; a translation of the NT into this language was produced during the 3rd and 4th centuries.

(b) Bohairic was the dialect of ALEXANDRIA and Lower (N) Egypt; the Bohairic NT was apparently made some time later than the Sahidic, and about one hundred MSS are extant (though almost all are very late).

(c) Between the regions of the Sahidic and the Bohairic dialects, at least part of the NT was translated into other dialects of Coptic. In Fayumic and Sub-Achmimic most of John is extant; MSS in Achmimic include parts of the Gospels and Catholic Epistles dating from the 4th or 5th cent.

4. Other versions. (a) The NT was translated into Gothic at the middle of the 4th cent. by Ulfilas; it survives in a few fragmentary MSS, one of which, Codex Argenteus, in the University Library of Uppsala, Sweden, containing portions of the Gospels, is written in silver ink on purple vellum (hence its name).

(b) The Armenian version dates from the first half of the 5th cent.; a revision appeared later, which became the dominant form of the version by the 8th cent. and is the basis of the Armenian text still in use. Not only is the Armenian version regarded as a very beautiful and accurate translation, but there are also more extant MSS — more than 1,500 — of it than of any other NT version except the Vulgate.

(c) Christianity was introduced into Georgia, situated between the Black and Caspian Seas, in the 4th cent. The origin of the Georgian version of the NT is uncertain, but it is usually placed in the early 5th cent.; it was evidently either translated from or influenced by the Armenian version. The last of several revisions, which was made by about the 11th cent., is the basis of the Georgian versions still in use; extant MSS are numerous, although three that date from the late 9th and 10th centuries are believed to retain more elements of the Old Georgian.

(d) Although some one hundred MSS of the Ethiopic version are known, the fact that none of them is earlier than the 13th cent. has added to the difficulties of establishing a date for the origin of this translation, with extreme views of the 2nd cent. and the 14th cent. having been suggested. It likely originated near the 6th cent. and translated either from Syriac or directly from Greek.

(e) The NT in Old Slavonic is credited to two brothers, St. Cyril and St. Methodius, who seem to have originated the two forms of the Slavonic alphabet, the Cyrillic and the Glagolitic. These brothers, who became missionaries to the Slavs, translated the NT in the second half of the 9th cent. The version may originally have been in lectionary form, which is the form of the text in most of the extant MSS.

Less significant versions are the following: (f) After the rise of Islam, numerous translations of the NT into Arabic were made, including one in the rhymed prose style of the Koran, and made or corrected from several different language versions. (g) The Persian version is known from a few MSS from the 14th cent. and later. (h) A translation into Frankish (a language of west-central Europe) is known from one 8th-cent. MS of part of Matthew. (i) Fragments are extant of a Sogdian version, a trade language of south-central Asia prior to the 10th cent. (j) A fragment of a 10th-cent. lectionary attests to the existence of a version in Nubian, spoken in a region between Egypt and Ethiopia. (k) A version in Anglo-Saxon is known from nine MSS of the 11th to the 13th centuries.

C. Patristic quotations. In addition to actual MSS of the NT in Greek and other ancient versions, Scripture quotations in the works of the early ecclesiastical writers form an important source of information concerning the text of the NT. Most of the works of these church fathers are in Greek and Latin, with a smaller number in Syriac and some other languages. These quotations are so extensive that most of the NT could be reconstructed from this source alone.

As in the case of the versions, there are limitations in the use of the patristic literature for the purpose of determining the text of the NT. The original copies of these works are not extant, so the textual critic must first study the known MSS to determine as nearly as possible its original wording, in particular the NT quotations in the work. The NT quotations within the writings of a church father are the very parts that a scribe would most likely change intentionally—if, for example, the quotation did not agree with the form of the NT text with which the scribe was familiar. Even when the original form of the NT quotation in the patristic work has been determined as nearly as possible, if the author is merely giving the general sense of the passage instead of a verbatim reference, or if he (or his AMANUENSIS) is quoting from memory instead of copying the quotation from a NT MS, the value of the passage for textual criticism will be limited. For example, the 4th-cent. St. Cyril of Jerusalem bases an argument concerning the Lord's Supper on what he himself says is the precise statement of St. Paul; yet his quotation concerning the institution of the Holy Communion is neither 1 Cor. 11:23–25 nor any one of the parallel accounts in the Gospels, but is rather a conflation from the various accounts, evidently quoted from memory (see J. H. Greenlee, *Introduction to New Testament Textual Criticism*, rev. ed. [1995], 47 n. 6). In general, however, longer quotations are more likely to have been copied from a MS than are shorter quotations.

As with the versions, the significance of the patristic quotation is the information it gives concerning the NT text. To the extent to which the NT text that a church father used can be determined, that particular form of the text can be assumed to have been known and used at the time and in the general location in which that church father lived (the date and location of the church fathers can usually be determined with greater certainty than in the case of the versions). In other words, the NT quotations of a writer's works form, so to speak, a fragmentary MS of the NT from his date and region. In addition, ancient writers at times refer to alternative readings of which they are aware in MSS of the NT, and may even give their opinion of these readings.

The earliest Christian writers are especially significant for this purpose. They include IRENAEUS (c. 130–200), Bishop of Lyons; TERTULLIAN of Carthage (c. 150–225), one of the most prolific of the Latin fathers; CLEMENT OF ALEXANDRIA (c. 150–215); ORIGEN of Alexandria and later of Caesarea, author of significant exegetical writings and other works (c. 185–254); EUSEBIUS Pamphili (c. 260–340), Bishop of Caesarea and author of an ecclesiastical history, commentaries, and other works. Although the potential value of the patristic quotations for NT textual criticism is very great, much work remains to be done both in preparing critical editions of the works of the church fathers and in making analyses of their NT quotations.

IV. Transmission of the NT text

A. Before the invention of printing

1. The rise of textual variants. When the books of the NT were first written, they were largely "private" works rather than "literature" in the ordinary sense. This was especially true of most of the NT Epistles, which were simply correspondence between individuals and groups. Even the Gospels were written for a purpose that was different from that of ordinary literature. When a book of the NT was copied in this very earliest period, therefore, it was generally copied privately for personal use rather than by a professional scribe. Furthermore, since the message of the book or letter was the important thing, a person making such a copy of a NT book might not necessarily feel obligated to strictly duplicate the word order or details that did not affect the sense; and in the case of the narrative books, the earliest copyists apparently sometimes felt free to add small details of information. Moreover, in the earliest period of the NT, the status of the Christian religion in the political situation would not encourage widespread comparison of NT MSS. In addition, variants and errors are almost inevitable, even with a scribe's best intentions of verbal exactness.

All these factors, therefore, combined to produce divergence of MSS during the earliest period after the NT was written. This situation continued until Christianity gained official recognition in the early 4th cent., although almost all of the variants that are significant in textual criticism may well have arisen during the first half of this period. At the same time, the significance of this divergence between the MSS must not be exaggerated. The books of the NT doubtless came to be considered as "literature" soon after they began to be circulated, and those who copied the MSS would then have a double reason for copying with care: the preservation of the exact words of the sacred message as well as the common requirements for copying a literary work.

The differences between MSS that arose by repeated copying led to the development of "families" of MSS, or what are sometimes referred to as "local texts." Copies of the NT, each with its own peculiarities and variants, were carried by Christians to various lands and localities. As each MS was copied and further copies multiplied, the documents to a large extent shared a common group of variants that were descended from their common ancestor and in varying degrees differed from the variants of the MSS that had been carried to other localities. In this way, the common peculiarities of a group of MSS serve to indicate their common ancestry as distinct from other groups of MSS. In some instances, a certain group of such MSS can be traced back to a specific region and a definite period of time by the fact that they contain a group of variants characteristic of writings of a certain church father or which are found in a version that originated at a certain time and place.

When Christianity gained official recognition under the emperor Constantine, MSS of the NT no longer needed to be concealed for safety. Soon the emperor himself ordered new copies of the Scriptures for the churches of Constantinople. It was evidently not long before comparison was being made between MSS, and it became obvious that there were many differences, especially between MSS of different localities. During the next three centuries or so, then, whether deliberately and officially, or unintentionally and informally, there occurred a period of convergence of MSS. During this period the MSS that were produced tended more and more to conform to the same standard. This standard could now be better maintained, since the copying of MSS was to a larger extent the work of trained scribes. In addition, there was evidently some degree of editing, in the course of which the wording of parallel accounts in the Gospels were harmonized to some extent, grammatical irregularities were corrected, and a text was produced that was in general smooth and easy to read.

More than nine-tenths of all extant MSS of the NT are from this period of convergence of the MSS or later. Thus only a small percentage of the MSS preserve a form of the text that antedates the late standardized text. Although copying of MSS by hand continued to mean that virtually no two MSS were completely identical, nevertheless from the 8th cent. on almost all MSS represented in a general way the standardized form of text, and this form of the text was still current when the printing press revolutionized the world of literature. It was this form that would eventually become known as the Textus Receptus (see below, IV.B.1).

2. Types of variants. The changes that scribes introduced into the NT MSS are of several types, which may be classified as either unintentional or, much less frequently, intentional (see Metzger and Ehrman, *Text of the New Testament*, ch. 7, for a fuller discussion).

(a) Unintentional or accidental variants include errors of seeing, hearing, writing, memory, and judgment. Errors of seeing include especially the confusion of letters or pairs of letters that look much alike in uncial writing, such as Θ and O, Λ and Λ, Π and Π, etc. Occasionally, an abbreviation might be mistaken for a full word of similar appearance or vice versa (e.g., ΘΣ and ΟΣ, "God" and "who," in 1 Tim. 3:16); a scribe's eye might skip from the first to the second occurrence of the same word, causing omission of the intervening material; he might read the same word or phrase twice; or he might confuse two words of similar appearance (e.g., *elabon* and *ebalon*—"they took" and "they cast").

Errors of hearing might arise when a group of scribes copied MSS by dictation or when an individual scribe pronounced the text (out loud or mentally) in the process of copying. Since very early in the Christian era several Greek vowels and diphthongs came to be pronounced alike—e.g., *i, ē, y, ei, oi,* and *ui*; *e* and *ai*; *o* and *ō*—numerous confusions of spelling from dictation were possible. Some of these confusions resulted in obvious misspellings, but others produced a different word; for example, the confusion of *ē* and *y* would change any form of the plural pronoun "you" to the corresponding form of "us."

Errors of memory might result in a mere change of word order in a series, substitution of one synonym for another, or the accidental inclusion of a word or phrase from a parallel passage.

Errors of writing might include the addition or omission of a letter or letters (e.g., *egenēthēmen nēpioi*, "we became infants," and *egenēthēmen ēpioi*, "we became gentle"; cf. 1 Thess. 2:7), or the omission of an indication of abbreviation.

Errors of judgment, in addition to some of the preceding errors, might cause a scribe to include a marginal note, thinking that it was a part of the text itself. This may be the origin of the explanation of the troubling of the water in Jn. 5:3–4.

(b) Intentional variants are the result of scribes' attempts to correct what they thought were errors, to make the text less ambiguous, or to strengthen the theology. Probably the most common type of intentional variant is the harmonization of parallel accounts in the Gospels. To mention only two such instances, the much shorter version of the LORD'S PRAYER in Lk. 11:2–4 has been amplified by scribes in accordance with the longer form of Matt. 6:9–13; and the form of the conversation between the rich young ruler and Jesus in Matt. 19:16–17 has been modified to agree with the form of the parallels in Mark and Luke.

Scribes also attempted to resolve apparent difficulties in the text. In Mk. 1:2, the original reference to "Isaiah the prophet" was modified to "the prophets," since the first part of the following reference was from Malachi (Mal. 3:1). Again, the prodigal son decides in Lk. 15:19 that he will say to his father, "make me like one of your hired men," so the scribes of several good MSS have added these words in v. 21.

Scribal changes in the interests of a strengthened theology or piety sometimes occurred. The most notable of these is the reference to the three heavenly witnesses of 1 Jn. 5:7–8, which is included in the KJV but is found in no Greek MS earlier than the 14th cent.; this variant however may have originated as a marginal comment in a Latin MS rather than as an intentional addition to the biblical text. Other instances include the addition of "and fasting" to "prayer" (Mk. 9:29), and the word "openly" following "shall reward you" in Matt. 6:4 to provide a happy contrast with the earlier words "in secret."

Although all sorts of variants may be found among the thousands in the extant MSS, these are minutiae in the total text of the MSS. The scribes generally copied the text with great care, even when the text may not have seemed to make sense (cf. Metzger and Ehrman, *Text of the New Testament*, 271; G. D. Kilpatrick in *The Bible Translator* 9/3 [July 1958]: 127–36).

Johannes Gutenberg.

B. The Greek NT in print

1. The establishment of the "Received Text" (1516–1633). Johannes Gutenberg's invention of printing from movable type, in the middle of the 15th cent., had the most far-reaching consequences for the entire world of literature and culture. For the first time it became possible not only to produce books more cheaply than ever before but also to produce any number of identical copies of a work. Paper had come into common use in the Western world by this time, having displaced parchment by the beginning of the 15th cent. Although some handwritten MSS continued to be produced for another century or so, with the invention of printing the age of hand copies was at an end.

The first major publication of Gutenberg's press was a beautiful edition of the Latin Vulgate in folio size, produced in 1456 and appropriately known as the Gutenberg Bible. Not until half a century later, however, was the first Greek NT printed. One reason for the delay was that the Bible of the scholars was the Vulgate, with comparatively little concern being given to the Greek text. A second reason may have been the problem and expense involved in preparing Greek type in imitation of the current minuscule style, which involved several forms of a given letter as well as numerous ligatures.

Eventually, in 1502, the preparation of a Greek Bible was begun, edited by several scholars under the direction of Cardinal Ximenes of Spain. The NT was printed in Latin and Greek, while the OT included the Hebrew, the Vulgate, and the Greek LXX in parallel columns. The project was undertaken in the town of Alcalá, known as Complutum in Latin; hence, the Bible is known as the Complutensian Polyglot. The NT was completed in 1514 and the OT volumes in 1517, but the approval of the pope was not given until 1520, and for some reason the work was not actually "published" until 1522.

In the meantime, the Swiss printer Froben, doubtless having heard of the Spanish cardinal's project, urged the scholar Erasmus to undertake the editing of a Greek NT. In July of 1515, Erasmus hastily obtained a few Greek NT MSS that happened to be available in Basel, none of which contained the entire NT; and the only MS that was not essentially the late standardized form of text he used sparingly because of its differences from the others. His one MS of Revelation lacked the final six verses, and at some other points the biblical text was confused with the accompanying catena. In these passages he therefore inserted his own Greek translation from the Latin, resulting in a Greek text that in some passages agrees with no known Greek MS. This edition, accompanied by Erasmus's own Latin translation (which differed at numerous points from the current Vulgate), was published in March, 1516, the haste of the work being reflected in its many typographical errors. Thus, whereas the Complutensian was the first Greek NT to be printed, Erasmus's edition was the first to be published, that is, actually placed on the market.

Altogether Erasmus published five editions of his NT, but each new edition included little additional consultation of MSS and few changes. One modification, however, was significant. When one of the editors of the Complutensian Polyglot protested to Erasmus the omission of the reference to the three heavenly witnesses in 1 Jn. 5:7–8, which was included in the Vulgate, Erasmus under pressure rashly agreed to include it in his next edition if it could be found in any Greek MS. When such a MS (Codex 61) was shown to him (prob. prepared for the purpose), he dutifully included the passage in his third edition (1522). He again omitted it from his subsequent editions, yet somehow it was his third edition that most largely influenced the

Desiderius Erasmus.

textual tradition, and thus this passage found its way into the works of other editors and into the accepted tradition of the text for more than three centuries, including the KJV.

In this way, the subsequent tradition of the printed Greek NT was based on the somewhat uncritical use of a very few MSS, which for the most part represented a late stage in the development of the text rather than adequately representing the original. Four editions of the Greek NT were published by Robert Estienne (Stephanus) between 1546 and 1551. His third edition, which indicated the variant readings of a number of MSS and of the Complutensian, was the first Greek NT to contain something like a critical apparatus. This third edition became the generally accepted form of the text for Great Britain and the United States. In the fourth edition, Stephanus introduced the verse numeration, which is still in use. Théodore Beza (de Bèze), Protestant scholar and successor to John Calvin at Geneva, published nine editions of the Greek NT between 1565 and 1604, five of which are merely small reprints. Beza's reputation helped to popularize the form of the text of the Erasmus and Stephanus tradition.

Two brothers of the Elzevir family, publishers of many editions of the classics, brought out seven editions of the Greek NT between 1624 and 1678, primarily as a commercial enterprise. The Latin preface to their second edition (1633) assured the reader, "You have therefore the text now received by all [*Textum ergo habes, nunc ab omnibus receptum*], in which we give nothing altered or corrupt." The language of this advertisement passed into common use, and the label *Textus Receptus*, "Received Text," became descriptive of the printed form of the Greek text in the Erasmian tradition. It was specifically the Elzevir edition of 1633 that became the Textus Receptus for continental Europe, as the third edition of Stephanus was for Great Britain and the United States.

2. The accumulation of textual evidence (1633–1830). With Elzevir's publications, a total of some one hundred editions of the Greek NT had been printed, and thus the NT had become generally available in the original language. Next, scholars turned their attention to the examination of ancient MSS to see whether the text could be improved. During this period of two centuries, the dominance of the Textus Receptus was not broken, but evidence was gradually collected that was to lead to a better text. Some of the more significant scholars are the following.

(a) John Mill published an edition of the NT in 1707 that cited the evidence of nearly a hundred MSS as well as numerous patristic writers and several versions. Even this mere presentation of variant readings, however, was attacked as undermining the Scriptures.

(b) Richard Bentley published no NT, but was an influential scholar who defended the study of the MSS against those who opposed Mill's work.

(c) Johann Albrecht Bengel published a Greek NT in 1734; it included a critical apparatus with variant readings classified as to the degree of their superiority or inferiority to the Textus Receptus. Most importantly, Bengel recognized that the witnesses to the text must be classified into groups, not merely counted individually, and he also formulated the principle, now recognized as being fundamental, that a more difficult reading is generally more likely to be original than is an easier reading. For these advances, Bengel came to be called the father of modern textual criticism of the NT.

(d) Johann Jakob Wetstein published a two-volume edition of the Greek NT in 1751–52, using the Textus Receptus but indicating in his apparatus the readings that he believed were correct. His unique contribution was a system of citing uncial MSS by capital letters and minuscules by Arabic numerals, a system followed until the present.

(e) Johann Salomo Semler's contribution to textual criticism was his development of Bengel's classification of MSS into three main groups: Alexandrian, Western, and Eastern.

(f) Johann Jakob Griesbach, a student of Semler, carried forward and popularized this professor's work. He identified three families of witnesses in the Gospels, which he designated Alexandrian, Western, and Byzantine; and two families in the Pauline Epistles, Alexandrian and Western. He also elaborated fifteen "canons" of textual criticism; using these principles in his three editions of the NT, Griesbach abandoned the Textus Receptus in numerous instances. His work and method made him one of the most important textual scholars.

3. The struggle to overthrow the Textus Receptus (1830–82). Until well into the 19th cent., the printed NT continued to be basically that of Erasmus-Stephanus-Elzevir. There were sporadic and minor departures from this received text, but no

A copy of the Erasmus NT, *Novum Instrumentum* (1516), with Greek and Latin in parallel columns.

substantial changes. The first scholar to set aside the Textus Receptus and edit a text on the basis of ancient witnesses and careful text-critical principles was Karl Lachmann, whose first edition appeared in 1831. At best such an edition would have been violently attacked by those who regarded the Textus Receptus as sacrosanct; but because Lachmann failed to make clear his principles—merely referring readers to an article that he had published in an obscure periodical—even scholars of a more liberal point of view took issue with him. In his second edition (1842–50), however, he included a full statement of his principles, which won appreciable support for his text.

In England, the edition of Samuel Prideaux Tregelles, which appeared in 1857–79 (subsequent to the publication of a careful statement of his principles and methods) did much to influence British opinion toward the acceptance of a "critical text"—that is, a text based upon the principles of textual criticism. His principles, arrived at independently, closely paralleled those of Lachmann. He also examined most of the then known uncial MSS and a number of important minuscules.

The greatest single name in NT textual criticism is doubtless that of Constantin Tischendorf. His publications of texts and collations of MSS and of critical editions of the Greek NT exceed those of any other scholar. He published the text of twenty-one uncial MSS, including the famous Codex Sinaiticus, and either collated or in some cases copied the text of more than twenty others. The first of his editions of the NT was published in 1841. His eighth and final edition (1869–72), published in two volumes, includes a critical apparatus that is so comprehensive in its citation of MSS, versions, and patristic writings that it is still, more than a century later, indispensable for serious study of the NT text (a third volume, consisting of prolegomena, was edited by Caspar René Gregory and published in 1894).

The triumph for a NT text based upon critical principles was climaxed in the publication in 1881–82 of an edition that was the joint labor of two scholars of Cambridge University—Brooke Foss Westcott and Fenton John Anthony Hort. Their edition contained no critical apparatus as such. On the other hand, their text was accompanied by an entire volume in which they carefully set forth their principles (*The New Testament in the Original Greek: Introduction and Appendix*; this volume is believed to have been written by Hort). The thoroughness of their work, the handy form of their NT edition, and the extensive use of their text in the English Revised Version of the NT, contributed to the success of their labors. Virtually all subsequent work on the NT text looks back to the work of Westcott and Hort. With their publication, the reign of the Textus Receptus was ended.

There was, of course, a reaction against the critical text, notably by J. W. Burgon and Edward Miller. They argued that God would not have permitted the church to follow a corrupt text for fifteen centuries. The answer was that the TR is not a corrupt or misleading text; and, moreover, that before the invention of printing there was no rigidly fixed text at all. Burgon and Miller also argued that the critical text amounted to rejecting the testimony of the vast majority of the (later) MSS. The reply was that any number of MSS that can be traced to a common ancestor indicates only one witness, not many; and that this procedure is commonly followed in textual criticism of the secular writings of antiquity. Their argument that the readings of the late MSS are intrinsically superior is subjective; the consensus of scholarly opinion is to the contrary.

V. The modern period of textual criticism

A. The theory of Westcott and Hort. The principles that Westcott and Hort (WH) set forth are treated in detail elsewhere (e.g., their own volume mentioned above, or the excellent summary in Metzger and Ehrman, *Text of the New Testament*, 174–81). Only some of the basic points will be mentioned here. In addition to using valid principles of criticism to decide the correct reading in a given variant, they pointed out that the degree of reliability that a given MS exhibits in a large number of instances should also be taken into account in deciding other instances. Further assurance of conclusions may be gained if, instead of considering the characteristics of individual MSS, the witnesses are grouped with others whose text is similar. Then, if individual peculiarities are eliminated and the consensus of the group is determined, the variants may be studied in terms of these groups of documents instead of individual MSS.

WH recognized four principal groups or text-types: (1) The *Syrian* text is the latest and is found in most of the later witnesses. It represents a revision, produced in Syria (hence its name) about the 4th cent., which characteristically smoothed out rough grammar and harsh transitions, clarified obscurities, harmonized parallels, and is generally smooth, clear, and theologically safe.

(2) The *Western* text, which was in existence in the 2nd cent., is most notable for its extensive paraphrases and additions (esp. in Acts), substitution of synonyms, and occasional significant shorter readings, although it has many less spectacular variants as well. Among its chief witnesses are Codices D and D^p (05 and 06) and the OL.

(3) The *Alexandrian* text originated in Alexandria, the seat of scholarly criticism of the Greek classics. Its witnesses include Codices C, L, 33, the Coptic versions, and certain Alexandrian fathers. This text-type WH believed to be characterized not by variants of content and substance but by corrections of grammar, syntax, and similar matters of the sometimes unsophisticated style of NT Greek, as might be expected in the scholarly environment of Alexandria.

(4) The *Neutral* text, generally represented by the consensus of codices ℵ and B, was believed by WH to contain a textual tradition that preserved the original text with a minimum of change. They maintained that readings in which these two MSS agreed could rarely be set aside, and that frequently B alone preserved the original text. On the other hand, they did not automatically accept the "Neutral" text in every instance, but rather rejected it when they felt that textual principles so dictated.

WH theorized that from the original text (substantially preserved in the "Neutral" text) the "Western" text was developed by extensive alteration. From the "Neutral" text, modified by philological alterations and slight admixture from the "Western," the Alexandrian text was produced. When the Christian church became recognized and MSS could be openly produced and compared, a revision incorporating these three texts — but significantly less in the case of "Western" elements — plus editorial and theological refinements, produced the Syrian text, which in turn became the general form of the text of MSS and then of the printed TR.

B. The work of von Soden. The most notable attempt to reach the original NT text on a basis radically different from that of WH was the work of Hermann von Soden, a professor in Berlin. Between 1902 and 1913, von Soden published a critical text with a very extensive critical apparatus, together with a large volume detailing his textual theory. His apparatus utilized a completely new system of MS designation, which was intended to indicate something of the date and contents of each document. As a result of its complicated nature and the fact that his theories have not generally been accepted, his system of classification has not been adopted.

Von Soden theorized the existence of three ancient text-types, designated by Greek letters: K (from Κοινή, "common"), which approximated WH's Syrian; H (Ἡσύχιος, an Egyptian scholar who may have been responsible for it), which compares to WH's Neutral plus Alexandrian; and I (Ἰερουσόλυμα, on the assumption that it originated in Palestine), which includes WH's Western plus other elements. Von Soden felt that the agreement of two of these three groups, qualified by certain other principles, could lead to their common ancestor (I-H-K), which was current in the 3rd cent. By then eliminating the corrupting influence of Tatian, the text of the mid-2nd cent. could be determined, which von Soden believed was essentially the original text.

Von Soden's work made significant contributions to certain aspects of textual study. His basic textual theory, however, has largely been rejected on the grounds that his evaluation of text-types is faulty, that his estimation of the corrupting influence of Tatian on the text is unwarranted, and that even the NT text of the mid-2nd cent. probably already contained the great majority of the variants that are significant in textual study. It is noteworthy, however, that von Soden's text, based upon principles so different from those of WH, agrees largely with that of WH.

C. Current view of text-types. It is now generally agreed that WH were too optimistic in their evaluation of a "Neutral" text, and that its witnesses are in fact representatives of the same basic text-type as their Alexandrian text. These two are now commonly combined under the designation *Alexandrian*. The Alexandrian is usually regarded as the best of the individual text-types, but its readings must nevertheless be submitted to the canons of criticism and compared with the other text-types. The main representatives of the Alexandrian text are P[4,5,34,75] ℵ, A (outside the Gospels), B, C, L, 33, Bohairic, Cyril of Alexandria, and Origen (in part).

The "Western" text has been subject to much study since WH, and its actual origin is perhaps even more of an enigma now than it was earlier (the name "Western" itself is quite misleading, though it continues to be used for lack of a better term). A few specialists have maintained that it best represents the original, but most scholars are still reluctant to accept distinctive "Western" readings. This text-type is represented by P[25, 38, 41, 48] D (05), D[p] (06), a few minuscules, Old Latin, Old Syriac, Tertullian, and Irenaeus.

The Syrian text of WH is now called the *Byzantine* or *Traditional* or *Majority* text; it is found in A (Gospels), most later uncials, most minuscules, Gothic and later versions, and later church fathers. Much more is now known of this text-type, its subdivisions, and its stages of development, thanks to the work of von Soden and others. This late text may occasionally preserve an ancient reading lost from the other texts (cf. H. A. Sturz, *The Byzantine Text-Type and New Testament Textual Criticism* [1984]), and some writers go so far as to argue for the originality of the Majority text (cf. W. N. Pickering, *The Identity of the New Testament Text*, 3rd ed. [2003]). Generally speaking, however, distinctive Byzantine readings do not commend themselves as being original (see D. B. Wallace in *BSac* 148 [1991]: 151–69, a response to an earlier edition of Pickering's book). In a very detailed study of the CATHOLIC EPISTLES, Klaus Wachtel has concluded that the Byzantine text-type is the result of a long process that began in very early times and reached its final stage in the 9th cent. (*Der Byzantinische Text der Katholischen Briefe: Eine Untersuchung zur Entstehung der Koine des Neuen Testaments* [1995], 199).

Since the time of WH, a number of MSS have come to light that, in the view of some, agree sufficiently to warrant grouping them as an additional text-type (at least in the Gospels); it is usually known as the *Caesarean* because Origen seems to have used it during his residence in Caesarea. It is thought to be represented also in P[45, 46] Θ, W (in most of Mark), family 1, family 13, 565, 700, Old Georgian, Old Armenian, Palestinian Syriac, Cyril of Jerusalem, and Eusebius. The characteristics of the Caesarean text are difficult to describe, however, and more recent scholarship has cast serious doubts on its homogeneity.

Because the classification of text-types presented above is not totally satisfactory, some scholars have proposed alternate systems. For example, Kurt and Barbara Aland (*The Text of the New Testament*, 2nd ed. [1989], 159) suggest five categories of MSS: I = very special quality (papyri and uncials up to the 3rd/4th cent.); II = special quality (important MSS that however are affected by the Byzantine text); III = MSS with independent text (such as families 1 and 13); IV = the D text ("Western" witnesses); V = Byzantine MSS. This proposal, like others, has not been widely accepted.

D. Principles of textual criticism

1. Internal evidence. In deciding between variants, one basic principle is that the reading that at first sight seems more difficult in the context is likely to be original, unless it is an accidental error that makes no sense. The point is that an ancient scribe, faced with two or more readings, would generally choose the one easiest to understand at first glance. Thus in Jn. 1:18, "the only God" is preferred over "the only Son" because the Greek word for "only," *monogenēs* G3666, could be understood to mean "only begotten," and the scribes would have considered it inappropriate to apply such a descriptive to "God" (see ONLY BEGOTTEN).

A second principle, which is in part a corollary of the above, is that a shorter reading is more likely to be original than a longer reading, if the difference is the result of an intentional alteration. In other words, a scribe was more likely to add an explanatory comment than to omit a phrase intentionally. On the other hand, if an accidental alteration is involved, the longer reading may be original and the short reading can be considered an inadvertent omission—for example, if the same word or syllable occurs twice in a passage, and the scribe's eye skipped from the first occurrence to the second (as in Matt. 5.19, where some MSS omit the second part of the verse by skipping from the first occurrence of "will be called ... in the kingdom of heaven" to the second).

A third principle, likewise in part related to the first, is that the reading from which the other readings could most easily have developed is likely to be original (some scholars consider this criterion the most fundamental principle). In Mk. 9:49, for example, the original text was doubtless the rather enigmatic, "For everyone will be salted with fire," which a prosaic scribe altered to the innocuous "For every sacrifice will be salted with salt" (as in D and OL; the Byzantine text then characteristically combined both readings [cf. KJV]). It is very unlikely that an original "salt" would have been altered to "fire," but the latter more easily explains why the former would have arisen. By the same token, a reading that has a definitely heightened theological or devotional emphasis is likely to be a scribal alteration rather than the original; for example, St. Paul's exhortation, "Therefore honor God in your body" (1 Cor. 6:20), led a scribe to make the pious addition, "and in your spirit, which are God's" (cf. KJV). Here again, it seems unlikely that the longer reading would have given rise to the shorter text.

An important application of the above principle relates to parallel passages. Since scribes would be tempted to harmonize parallels, a reading that is not thus harmonized is generally to be preferred. For example, after the words, "give it your greeting," in Matt. 10:12, some MSS add, "saying, 'Peace be to this house,'" from the parallel in Lk. 10:5. Harmonizations such as this one are common in the Synoptic Gospels.

2. External evidence. The application of the above principles of internal evidence to a large number of variants will make it possible to evaluate the degree of reliability of individual witnesses and, more importantly, of groups of witnesses or text-types. It then becomes possible to decide between variants by considering the general reliability of the text-types that support each reading as well as by the principles of internal evidence (the latter by themselves can be very subjective). The combination of internal and external evidence produces a more balanced judgment than reliance on either one alone.

The Alexandrian is the best individual text type, while the "Western" and the Byzantine, when standing alone, are generally unreliable. On the other hand, since evidence of a wide geographical distribution of a reading suggests its originality, support by good witnesses of more than one text-type is preferable to support by one text-type exclusively.

VI. Conclusion. The evangelical view of INSPIRATION relates to the Scriptures in the form in which they were originally given. No addition or modification of the original, therefore, no matter how long enshrined in MSS or translations, partakes of this inspiration. The determination of the original form of the text as nearly as possible is, therefore, a solemn responsibility. At the same time, the precise original wording of the NT cannot be determined with finality in every instance. Consequently, the best form of the text that can be reached will be, from a technical point of view, only an approximation to the original. From a practical point of view, however, the difference involved in most variants is so slight that little or no difference of meaning is involved.

One may safely conclude, then, that when sound principles of textual criticism are judiciously followed, a NT text may be reconstructed of which it may be said, in the words of Sir Frederic G. Kenyon, that "we have in our hands, in substantial integrity, the veritable word of God" (*The Story of the Bible*, 2nd ed., rev. by B. M. G. Reardon [1964], 113).

(In addition to the titles mentioned in the body of this article, see E. M. Thompson, *An Introduction to Greek and Latin Palaeography* [1912]; K. Lake, *The Text of the New Testament*, 6th ed., rev. by S. New [1928]; W. H. P. Hatch, *The Principal Uncial Manuscripts of the New Testament* [1939]; M. M. Parvis and A. P. Wikgren, eds., *New Testament Manuscript Studies* [1950]; W. H. P. Hatch, *Facsimiles and Descriptions of Minuscule Manuscripts of the New Testament* [1951]; A. Voobus, *Early Versions of the New Testament* [1954]; B. M. Metzger, *Annotated Bibliography of the Textual Criticism of the*

New Testament [1955]; L. D. Twilley, *The Origin and Transmission of the New Testament* [1957]; F. G. Kenyon, *Our Bible and the Ancient Manuscripts*, 5th ed., rev. by A. W. Adams [1958]; F. F. Bruce, *The New Testament Documents — Are They Reliable?*, 5th ed., [1960]; V. Taylor, *The Text of the New Testament* [1961]; F. F. Bruce, *The Books and the Parchments*, 3rd ed. [1963]; E. C. Colwell, *Studies in Methodology in Textual Criticism of the New Testament* [1969]; L. Vaganay, *An Introduction to New Testament Textual Criticism*, rev. C.-B. Amphoux [1991]; B. M. Metzger, *A Textual Commentary on the Greek New Testament*, 2nd ed. [1994]; B. D. Ehrman and M. W. Holmes, eds., *The Text of the New Testament in Contemporary Research: Essays on the Status Quaestionis. A Volume in Honor of B. M. Metzger* [1995]; J. K. Elliott, *A Bibliography of Greek New Testament Manuscripts*, 2nd ed. [2000]; C.-B. Amphoux and J. K. Elliott, eds., *The New Testament Text in Early Christianity: Proceedings of the Lille Colloquium, July 2000* [2003]; E. J. Epp, *Perspectives on New Testament Textual Criticism: Collected Essays, 1962–2004* [2005]; J. R. Royse, *Scribal Habits in Early Greek New Testament Papyri* [2008].) J. H. Greenlee

Textus Receptus teks´tuhs-ri-sep´tuhs. See TEXT AND MANUSCRIPTS (NT) IV.B.

Thaddaeus thad´ee-uhs, tha-dee´uhs (Θαδδαῖος G2497, perhaps from Aram. תַּדָּא, "breast" [the name תַּדָּא occurs in the TALMUD], but more likely a short form of Θεοδόσιος or some other name compounded with Θεός G2536, "God" [cf. THEUDAS]). One of the twelve apostles (Matt. 10:3; Mk. 3:18). In Matt. 10:3 the KJV follows the Textus Receptus in reading "Lebbaeus, whose surname was Thaddaeus" (both here and in Mk. 3:18 some MSS have LEBBAEUS only instead of Thaddaeus). The parallel lists in Luke-Acts have, instead of Thaddaeus, "Judas son of James" (Lk. 6:16; Acts 1:13; the KJV interprets the text to mean "Judas *the brother* of James"]). See JUDAS #6. Presumably, the names Thaddaeus and Judas refer to the same person. If so, it seems likely that Luke provides the true name, but it is uncertain whether Thaddaeus was a secondary name borne by this apostle or whether it (like Lebbaeus?) was a descriptive designation introduced in the Gospels to avoid confusion with JUDAS ISCARIOT. (See discussion by G. Dalman, *Die Worte Jesu*, 2nd ed. [1930], 40.)

A. M. Ross

Thaddaeus, Acts of. A 6th cent. Greek version and development of the Syriac legend regarding Abgar V, king of EDESSA (A.D. 9–46), who is said to have exchanged correspondence with Jesus, as a result of which Addai (THADDAEUS) was sent to Edessa and performed numerous miracles, including the healing of Abgar. In this later elaboration of the original story (similar in many respects to the 5th-cent. *Doctrine of Addai*), Abgar is healed upon the return of his messenger Ananias, prior to the coming of Thaddaeus to Edessa, and much more attention is given to the work of Thaddaeus in establishing the church of that city. EUSEBIUS (*Eccl. Hist.* 1.13; cf. 2.1.6–8) provides the earliest record of the alleged correspondence and its outcome, in which he says that he extracted it from the archives in Edessa and translated it from the Syriac. See ABGAR (ABGARUS), EPISTLES OF CHRIST AND. (Gk. text in R. A. Lipsius, *Acta apostolorum apocrypha* [1891–1903], 1/1:273–78; English trans. of Eusebius's account in *NTAp*, 1:497–99.)

D. A. Hagner

Thahash thay´hash. See TAHASH.

Thamah thay´muh. See TEMAH.

Thamar thay´mahr. KJV NT form of TAMAR.

Thamnatha tham´nuh-thuh. KJV Apoc. form of TIMNATH (1 Macc. 9:50).

thankfulness, thanksgiving. See ETHICS OF PAUL II.D; GRATITUDE; PRAYER IV.A.

thank offering. See SACRIFICE AND OFFERINGS IV.C.3..

Thanksgiving Hymns. See DEAD SEA SCROLLS IV.

Thara thair´uh. KJV NT form of TERAH.

Tharra thair´uh. See TERESH.

Tharshish thahr'shish. See TARSHISH (PLACE).

Thassi thas′i (Θασσι). The surname of SIMON MACCABEE, one of the five sons of Mattathias and founder of the HASMONEAN dynasty (1 Macc. 2:3).

theater. In the ancient world, the theater was a structure usually open-air and semicircular, with stone seats. Greek theaters, found as early as the 5th cent. B.C., were on hillsides to take advantage of natural land formations. Early Roman theaters were erected as free-standing buildings supported by arch construction. They were used for presentation of dramatic productions, pageants, religious rites, choral singing, games, gladiatorial contests, and public assemblies and forums of citizens.

It would be impossible to determine when humans began to develop histrionic interests. The religious dance, the earliest outlet for the emotions, has been considered the origin of the arts. A religious ceremony and drama involving OSIRIS was performed yearly by the Egyptians as early as 2000 B.C. There is no evidence that Israel ever produced a drama or had theaters. Religious DANCING, however, is found in the OT (Exod. 15:20; 2 Sam. 6:16), and the books of JOB and SONG OF SOLOMON are cast in dramatic dialogue form. Nonetheless, the true flowering of the theater must be credited to the Greeks in the 6th and 5th centuries B.C. Tragedies and comedies were presented before large audiences. No later civilizations have surpassed the Greek genius for drama. The Greek drama was inextricably bound up with religion, particularly the festival to DIONYSUS, the wine god, often degenerating into orgies. Menander (342–291 B.C.) was the outstanding figure in the later Greek theater. The Romans introduced the Greek drama as they conquered and assimilated the Greek nation and culture. The growth and proliferation of the Roman theater paralleled the fortunes of the empire. HEROD the Great built theaters in Jerusalem, Caesarea, Damascus, Gadara, Philadelphia, and other cities. The theater was probably encouraged by the Jews of the DIASPORA.

The earliest Greek theaters were nothing more than marked-out dancing circles in the center of which was an altar, located at the foot of a hillside on which spectators stood or sat. The best preserved example of the later Greek theater is the magnificent structure at Epidaurus, while the most famous is the theater of Dionysus at Athens. Of the Roman theaters the one at Aspendus in ASIA MINOR, built during the reign of Marcus Aurelius, is the best preserved. The Romans erected magnificent theaters with rich and showy adornment, even in the smaller

The theater of ancient Hierapolis in W Asia Minor. (View to the S.)

cities. AUGUSTUS Caesar was a great patron of the theater. Remains of Greek and Roman theaters may be seen today in cities visited by PAUL (PHILIPPI, ATHENS, CORINTH, EPHESUS; cf. Acts 19:29, 31).

(See further S. Cheney, *The Theatre: Three Thousand Years of Drama, Acting and Stagecraft* [1929]; A. Nicoll, *The Development of the Theatre*, 3rd ed. [1948]; M. Bieber, *The History of the Greek and Roman Theater*, 2nd ed. [1961]; R. C. Beacham, *The Roman Theatre and Its Audience* [1991]; J. R. Green, *Theatre in Ancient Greek Society* [1994]; B. Bergmann and C. Kondoleon, eds., *The Art of Ancient Spectacle* [1999]; R. G. Chase, *Ancient Hellenistic and Roman Amphitheatres, Stadiums, and Theatres: The Way They Look Now* [2002].)

F. B. HUEY, JR.

Thebaic. A Coptic dialect better known as Sahidic. See VERSIONS OF THE BIBLE, ANCIENT II.C.

Thebes theebz (Θῆβαι). Greek name given to the ancient capital of Upper EGYPT, corresponding to modern Luxor and Karnak, some 450 mi. S of Cairo. The Egyptians themselves referred to it in several ways, including Weset and City of Amun/

Amon (Egyp. *nwt ʾmn*, thus Heb. *nōʾ ʾāmôn* H5531 [Nah. 3:8] or simply *nōʾ* H5530 [e.g., Ezek. 30:14, where the LXX has *Diospolis*, "City of Zeus/God"]). See AMON #4. It is uncertain why the Greeks gave to it the name Thebes (also the name of several others sites, including an important city in the region of Boeotia, NNW of ATHENS).

On the E bank of the NILE, the town focused on the two vast temples of the god Amon at Karnak and Luxor, less than 2 mi. apart. On the W bank, Thebes boasted a row of funerary temples of the kings along the desert edge (see K. R. Weeks, ed., *The Treasures of the Valley of the Kings: Tombs and Temples of the Theban West Bank in Luxor* [2001]; N. Strudwick and J. H. Taylor, eds., *The Theban Necropolis: Past, Present and Future* [2003]). Behind these, the tomb chapels of their officials were carved in the rocky hills, whereas the tunnel tombs of the pharaohs and their wives were hidden away in the Valleys of the Kings and Queens behind the western cliffs. The temples and tombs on both banks contain a wealth of inscriptions, reliefs, and paintings of the utmost value as background to OT life and times.

Unimportant and little known in the 3rd millennium B.C., the city rose into prominence when the Theban 11th and 12th dynasties respectively restored the unity and prosperity of Egypt. Later

Entrance at the temple of Thebes (Luxor, Egypt).

Theban princes expelled the HYKSOS; the 18th dynasty founded Egypt's empire (18th–20th dynasties, c. 1550–1085 B.C.), to which epoch belong most of the greatest and finest Theban monuments. Amon of Thebes was virtually god of the empire, and in his temples were amassed vast riches. In the time of decline in the 1st millennium B.C., when royal (and real) power lay in the N, Thebes was still a proud religious center until sacked by the Assyrians in 663 B.C.—an event stirring enough for Nahum to use as image for Assyria's impending doom (Nah. 3:8). The "rampart" (NRSV) is probably a reference to the delta moats and canals, Egypt's and Thebes' first line of defense. Jeremiah in 605 and Ezekiel in 571 threatened judgment on Thebes, Amon, and Egypt generally (Jer. 46:25; Ezek. 30:14–16). Thereafter, Thebes gradually sank into insignificance. (See further C. F. Nims, *Thebes of the Pharaohs* [1965]; J. Kamil, *Luxor: A Guide to Ancient Thebes*, 3rd ed. [1983].)

K. A. KITCHEN

Thebez thee′biz (תֵּבֵץ H9324, derivation unknown). A fortified town within the tribal territory of MANASSEH, not far from SHECHEM. ABIMELECH son of GIDEON met his death here when a woman fatally wounded him by throwing an upper millstone from a tower on the wall of the city (Jdg. 9:50). The ignominious death of Abimelech became proverbial in Israel. JOAB referred to the incident in his report to DAVID regarding the death of URIAH (2 Sam. 11:21). The precise location of Thebez is uncertain, but some scholars identify it with modern Tubas, about 10 mi. NE Shechem

Thebes.

(modern Nablus), on the main highway to BETH SHAN. This geographical area afforded military significance while the fertile valley provided commercial value.　　　　　　　　　　　F. E. YOUNG

Thecla thek´luh. See PAUL, ACTS OF.

theft. See CRIMES AND PUNISHMENTS I.B.

theism. Belief in the existence of GOD. The terms *atheism*, the dogmatic denial of God, and *agnosticism*, a profession of ignorance, indicate a material distinction from theism. The term *deism*, a Latin derivative, is the linguistic equivalent of *theism* (derived from Greek), but these two words designate two different positions.

In the 18th cent., John Toland, Anthony Collins, the Earl of Shaftesbury (A. A. Cooper), and others launched an attack on supernatural Christianity. Although they believed in God, they denied the occurrence of MIRACLES and special REVELATION, and defended a purely natural religion. Their God is sometimes called an absentee God, one who started the universe going, but thereafter never interfered. If the term *absentee* is technically inaccurate, at least they insist that divine action is uniform and is not to be distinguished from the laws of nature. This philosophy was called *deism*. Theism, its opposite, asserts that God has spoken and has acted at particular times and places.

Although theism and deism are thus distinguished, the former term is often used to refer simply to the arguments for the existence of God, and some of these also are found in deism. The term *theology* no doubt covers a discussion of the divine attributes as given in Scripture, and in a wider sense includes also anthropology, soteriology, and other subjects; but usually theism designates a philosophical defense of the existence of God. No doubt it ought to and sometimes does defend miracles, but philosophically the theistic proofs are its main contents.　　　　　　　　　　　G. H. CLARK

Thelasar thel´uh-sahr. KJV alternate form of TEL-ASSAR.

Thelersas thuh-luhr´suhs. KJV Apoc. form of TEL-HARSHA (1 Esd. 5:36).

theocracy. Government by divine rule (from Gk. *theos* G2536, "God," and *krateō* G3195, "to control, rule"). The term is distinguished from *democracy*, which places the ultimate power of the government in the hands of all the people; from *hierocracy*, the rule of the priests, which relegates to a religious class unique insight into the will of God; and from *monarchy*, which has a human king or queen to rule over a nation. The word does not appear in the Bible and seems to have been invented by JOSEPHUS, who used *theokratia* to describe the unique character of the Hebrew government as revealed to MOSES and as compared to other forms of government. He says, "Our legislator … ordained to be what, by a strained expression, may be termed a theocracy, by ascribing the authority and the power to God" (*Against Apion* 2.165).

However, the idea is much older than the origin of the word, as Josephus suggests in his statement. It goes back to the OT and to the time of Moses (Exod. 19:4–9; Deut. 33:4–5). At the heart of the idea is Israel's unique relation to God as his peculiar people. It is the COVENANT which binds Israel to God in this relationship (Exod. 19–20) and constitutes Israel "a kingdom of priests and a holy nation" (19:6). God claimed Israel for himself by redeeming the nation from Egyptian bondage. The great redemptive acts at the time of the exodus and in the course of the wilderness wanderings declare God as the eternal Ruler (Exod. 15:18). Moses was merely the man of God communicating God's will to the people.

GIDEON refused to accept the crown because he believed that God alone should rule over Israel (Jdg. 8:22–23). In the period preceding the coming of the monarchy, it fell on prophets, priests, and judges to express the theocracy. In Israel's war against SISERA, the prophetess DEBORAH and the judge BARAK were said to be the agents of God's deliverance (4:4–7). The priests frequently appear as the messengers of God's will (20:20, 1 Sam. 14:41). An institutionalized theocracy, however, appears with the coming of the kingship in Israel.

When the children of Israel demanded a king like the other nations, it was regarded as tantamount to the rejection of God (1 Sam. 8:7). But after the kingship was established through SAMUEL, the king was the symbol of God's theocratic

A view of both Mount Ebal (right) and Mount Gerizim, where Joshua renewed the theocratic covenant between the people of Israel and Yahweh once they entered the Holy Land. (View to the E.)

reign. He was not a king in the usual sense of the term, but in the proper theological context he was the Lord's anointed (Ps. 2:2; 20:6) and the prince of the Lord (1 Sam. 10:1; 2 Sam. 5:2). During the period of the monarchy God is conceived as going before the king (2 Sam. 5:24). The king is seated on God's throne (1 Chr. 29:23; cf. 28:5). The real Ruler is God and the authority of the throne of DAVID is derived from him. The theocratic nature of the kingship in Israel is indicated sometimes by the prerogative of the prophet to dethrone the king (1 Sam. 15:26; 16:1–2; cf. 1 Ki. 11:29–31; 14:10; 16:1–2; 21:21). It is significant that there are no stereotyped criteria by which a prophet may be usually recognized or confirmed. Only the presence of the indefinable Spirit of God reveals the difference between a true or false prophet.

The coming of the kingship in Israel is the organization of the theocratic kingdom under a human ruler. In prophetism theocracy finds perhaps its clearest expression (Jer. 1:1–2; cf. Isa. 7:7). The messianic visions of the prophets are organically interwoven into the course of the history of the kings of Judah and the ultimate restoration of the kingdom in the dynasty of David. The kingdom is in its essence and intent an instrument of redemption to which Israel's messianic expectations are inseparably related. In its messianic significance the throne of David stands at the center of biblical theology with its acknowledgment of God as the eventual Ruler over the whole earth. In the progressive revelation of biblical ESCHATOLOGY, the theocratic conception of the Davidic kingdom supplied the pattern of the ideas concerning the coming of the KINGDOM OF GOD. Through the restoration of the throne of David, God was to accomplish Israel's final redemption. But this event in history was to introduce the age of eternal peace and righteousness under the universal reign of the Son of David.

In the theocracy of Israel there is no room for secularism. Down to their minutest details, all political, legal, and social regulations are essentially theological. They were the direct and supreme expression of the will of God. Even the detection of criminals and their punishment are the immediate concern of God (Lev. 20:3, 5–6, 20; 24:12; Num. 5:12–13; Josh. 6:16). A. C. SCHULTZ

theodicy. This term (from Gk. *theos* G2536, "God," and *dikē* G1472, "judgment") means "the act of justifying God" and refers to defending both his goodness and omnipotence in the face of EVIL. (See APOLOGETICS.) The Bible confronts the problem of evil on nearly all of its pages. While it ultimately gives no rational explanation for the origins of evil, it places it utterly within God's plan and his control. And it presents the most fundamental answer to it—in Jesus Christ.

The biblical authors often raise the problem of evil in the most poignant and painful fashion. "O LORD, are you not from everlasting?" asks HABAKKUK (Hab. 1:12). "Your eyes are too pure to look on evil; / you cannot tolerate wrong. / Why then do you tolerate the treacherous? / Why are you silent when the wicked / swallow up those more righteous than themselves?" (v. 13). JOB likewise complains that, as an upright man, there is no reason why he should suffer so. He has a case against God, but cannot find him nor reason with him: "I have treasured the words of his mouth more than my daily bread. / But he stands alone, and who can oppose him? / He does whatever he pleases. . . . / That is why I am terrified before him" (Job 23:12–15). The Psalms are particularly honest in their confessions. When confronting the liberty of the wicked, ASAPH admits a tempting conclusion: "Surely in vain have I kept my heart pure; / in vain have I washed my hands in innocence" (Ps. 73:13). (For a summary of the role of theodicy in the ANE and Israel, see *ABD*, 6:644–47.)

These questions about the presence of evil are the more pointed because of the uniformly held view in the Scriptures that evil is neither an illusion nor an opposite dualistic pole from the good. Evil is real, all too real. It is always a scandal, an outrage. By definition, it is all that opposes God. We are told to "hate what is evil" (Rom. 12:9) because God himself cannot tolerate it (Ps. 5:4–6). Indeed, he will judge the world because of evil (Acts 17:31; Eph. 5:6; Rev. 20:11–15).

While asserting that God ordains everything that comes to pass in the strongest terms, the Bible never gives us a plausible philosophical reason for the presence of evil in a universe in which God is both good and omnipotent. But it does set forth a number of affirmations that ought to dispel any anxiety we may have that evil will somehow contradict God's purposes or triumph over his good plan. It tells us, first, that there is nothing in God's being, nor in his purposes for creation, which suggest he is accountable for evil. Rather, the culpability for introducing it into the world belongs to human beings. The story of CREATION and the FALL in Gen. 1–3 eloquently affirms that in God's infallible judgment, all was "good" and even "very good" (1:31) when the world was made. Evil came into the visible world as a reality when the first couple disobeyed God's command and sought the knowledge of good and evil in an illicit manner (3:6–7). SIN is thus lawlessness and results in evil, misery, and the curse of God (1 Jn. 3:4). The whole argument of the book of Romans depends on assigning the blame for evil not on God but on mankind (Rom. 1:18–32).

Second, the Scriptures teach that God remains both good and omnipotent in his intentions, even in the face of evil. While his ultimate reasons for allowing evil remain closed to us, we can infer that, at the least, it brings honor to him (Ps. 76:10). It surely is connected with his designs for the human race, which include imparting special knowledge of good and evil to his image-bearers (though not illicitly). Most of all, as God governs the present fallen world he remains in complete control over evil and will use it for his good purposes. "You intended to harm me, but God intended it for good," says JOSEPH to his brothers (Gen. 50:20). Even the wicked have a function within his plan (Prov. 16:4). God hardens the hearts of evil doers (Exod. 7:14; 9:34). He sends "deceiving spirits" on various persons to accomplish his purposes (Jdg. 9:23; 1 Sam. 16:15–16). In the most decisive case, Jesus Christ himself was crucified by lawless men, yet also by God's "set purpose and foreknowledge" (Acts 2:23).

Furthermore, evil is "God's megaphone" (C. S. Lewis's term) to tell us that all is not well, and that we need to open our eyes (Eph. 5:13). There is mystery here. Habakkuk was content to "stand and watch" from his rampart, because "the righteous will live by his faith" (Hab. 2:1, 4). Job was never told why he had to suffer, but though he was far more just than his friends, he had seriously misrepresented God's wise purposes (Job 38–42). Asaph may never have received a clear answer for the present injustices, but he gained perspective on the end of evil when he walked into the sanctuary (Ps. 73:17; cf. 37:1).

Third, God has accomplished a great reversal. He has turned evil on itself and produced REDEMPTION. The CROSS means the death of death and the end of all evil. "God made him who had no sin to be sin for us, so that in him we might become the righteousness of God" (2 Cor. 5:21). The RESURRECTION OF JESUS CHRIST means the vindication of sinners (Rom. 4:25; 1 Cor. 15:17). All debts were canceled at the cross (Col. 2:14). This way, God can remain just and yet be the justifier of the ungodly (Rom. 3:26, see JUSTIFICATION). He did this because of his great love for sinners (Jn. 3:16; Eph. 2:4). And this produces the only way of hope: "In this world you will have trouble. But take heart! I have overcome the world" (Jn. 16:33; cf. Rom. 1:16; Gal. 1:4). There is no hope if evil is not real, since this would render Christ's work vain. Jesus was both sad and angry against evil and death (Jn. 11:33–38). When he cried out from the cross, "My God, my God, why have you forsaken me?" (Matt. 27:46), Jesus Christ was abandoned by his own Father, receiving the full measure of his wrath against the sins of the world. Anything less momentous is incapable of dealing with sin.

Fourth, the SUFFERING of believers has a special purpose. Though redemption is accomplished, and Christ will never have to pay any additional price in the purchase of redemption (Heb. 9:25–28), there yet remains suffering in the life of his people (Rom. 5:1–4; Col. 1:24; 1 Pet. 4:12). While some suffering is chastisement for sin (Acts 5:1–11; Heb. 12:4–11), often no discernible reason for suffering is at hand for the church of Jesus Christ. Believers suffer so that their faith may be refined (1 Pet. 1:6–7), and so that they may know Christ and the power of his resurrection (Phil. 3:10). There is always a way out of trials sent to Christians (1 Cor. 10:13), and the present sufferings "are not worth comparing" with the glory to come (Rom. 8:18). But when they are perplexed by the remaining injustices of this world, they are told to "wait a little longer" until the full roll of the martyrs has been called (Rev. 6:10–11). And because he suffered, Christ is able to understand and to lead his people out of every difficulty (Heb. 2:17–18; 4:15).

W. EDGAR

Theodotion thee´uh-doh´shuhn. See SEPTUAGINT IV.C.

Theodotus thee-od´uh-tuhs (Θεόδοτος, "gift of God"). **(1)** One of the three ambassadors sent by NICANOR to Judas MACCABEE to make peace (2 Macc. 14:19).

(2) A man who plotted, but failed, to assassinate PTOLEMY Philopator (3 Macc. 1:2).

theology. See BIBLICAL THEOLOGY; OLD TESTAMENT THEOLOGY; NEW TESTAMENT THEOLOGY.

theophany. This theological term (from Gk. *theos* G2536, "God," and *phainō* G5743, pass. "appear") refers to any temporary, normally visible, manifestation of God. It is to be distinguished from that permanent manifestation of God in Jesus Christ called the INCARNATION. Most of its examples must be sought in the OT, though some would include cases mentioned in the NT, such as the heavenly voice and "dove" at Jesus' baptism (Matt. 3:16–17), the voice at the TRANSFIGURATION (17:5) and in the PASSION week (Jn. 12:28), the visible coming of the HOLY SPIRIT (Acts 2:2–3), STEPHEN's vision (7:55–56), and Paul's Damascus experience (9:3–5). Theophanies are relatively common in Genesis. This is easily explicable by the lack of written Scriptures and by the isolated position of the few faithful individuals whose lives are recorded. They are found again in the decisive events of the exodus, the conquest of Canaan, and in some of the narratives of the judges. After this they are rare except in the accounts of the prophets, especially in the visions accompanying their call.

I. The angel of the Lord. This phrase is found over fifty times in the OT (see ANGEL III). In the majority of cases "an angel of the Lord" would be the more idiomatic English, and in a few cases KJV renders thus. The apparent definiteness is often due to the nature of Hebrew grammar. There are, however, a number of cases where the term is best understood as "Jehovah present in definite time and particular place" (A. B. Davidson, *Theology of the Old Testament* [1904], 297–98). Sometimes, when the angel seems to be identified with God, no more may be intended than that he is speaking and acting as God's representative. In other cases this is clearly inadequate.

The most important passages are Exod. 23:20–23; 32:34; 33:14–15; Isa. 63:9. It is clear that God is promising to lead Israel, the angel of

Exod. 32:34 is called in 33:14–15 God's "Presence" (lit., his "face"). The two terms are combined in Isa. 63:9 as "the angel of his presence," that is, the angel who not only stands in God's presence but in whom God is seen. This text can also be translated, "It was no messenger or angel but his presence that saved them" (NRSV, following the *Ketib* [*lōʾ*, "not"; cf. also LXX and Syriac], rather than the *Qere* [*lô*, "his"]). The same usage is followed by JACOB in Gen. 48:15–16, where "the Angel" is obviously in parallelism with God. Into the same category one must place a story like the coming of the three men to ABRAHAM (Gen. 18), where their leader is clearly identified with the Lord, whereas the other two are merely angels. There are no grounds for questioning the very early and traditional Christian interpretation that in these cases there is a preincarnate manifestation of the second person of the TRINITY, whether he is called "the Lord" or "the angel of the Lord."

II. The forms of theophany. In the Bible no stress is laid on the manner of the theophany; what is important is what God does and says. Normally the theophany is for the ear, the visible merely attracting and riveting the attention. This perhaps is most clearly seen in the story of the BURNING BUSH (Exod. 3:2–6) and of the giving of the law with all its physical manifestations (19:18–19; 20:18); the physical is merely secondary, and in the latter case it is stressed that no form was seen (Deut. 4:12, 15). When Moses received the supreme revelation of the character of God (Exod. 34:6–7), he had been promised that he would see God's "back" (33:23), but in the fulfillment, whatever physical vision may have been given him, it was of such insignificance compared with the spoken words that it remains unmentioned.

Consistent with this, no description is given of the physical aspect of the theophanies to the patriarchs. In the covenant making described in Gen. 15:17, the presence of God is purely symbolic. When the promise of Isaac was given (18:10), clearly there was nothing about the physical appearance of the three men to demand attention; at the most it was calculated to cause respect. Neither in Jacob's dream at Bethel (28:12–17) nor in his wrestling with God (32:22–30) is any description given of the one seen.

In most later theophanies the one seen appears to be purely human until his words, and sometimes acts, proclaim him to be more than man (e.g., Josh. 5:13–15, Jdg. 6:11–24, 13:6–7, 11–14, 20). Where the theophany is in the prophetic experience, there is either no vision, as with ELIJAH at Horeb (1 Ki. 19:11–18), or the figure of God is sensed rather than seen, as with AMOS and JEREMIAH (Amos 7:1, 4, 7; 8:1; 9:1; Jer. 1:9), or it is to a greater or lesser extent symbolic, as with ISAIAH and EZEKIEL (Isa. 6:1–5; Ezek. 1:26–28). In the visions of ZECHARIAH, the angel of the Lord seems to be a completely symbolic figure. It is striking that the vision of the risen and glorified Christ in Rev. 1:12–20 conforms to this symbolic pattern.

III. The importance of the theophany. The above means that the main importance of a theophany always lies in its REVELATION of God, especially in the verbal message. The physical aspects are there to magnify and authenticate the revelation, but essentially that is all. That is why even the OT has no real room for holy places. Even SINAI is never mentioned as a holy place or a site to which pilgrimages should be made. A legitimate sanctuary was to have been marked out by some form of theophany (Deut. 12:5, 11, 14, 21—passages limiting the number of legitimate sanctuaries, but not demanding only one), but in practice this was so unimportant that one is not told how SHILOH came to be chosen, and the site of the TEMPLE (Solomon's) was marked out purely by the angel's hand of destruction being stopped (2 Sam. 24:16–17). NATHAN's message to DAVID (2 Sam. 7:6–7) clearly indicated that God was not concerned with special spots for worship. Israel's maintenance of traditional holy sites showed its misunderstanding of God's revelation.

IV. The theophany today. The theophany, whether essentially visionary, partially subjective, or entirely external and objective, is always distinguishable from the normal prophetic vision or reception of the divine message. Its recipient could always affirm, "God acted and spoke in this place." It is essentially a peak in a long range of God's acting and speaking that runs throughout Scripture, reaches its towering summit in Jesus Christ, and continues in his church to this day. Therefore, although wisely the term *theophany* is confined largely to events recorded in Scripture, there is no doubt that in the history of the church there have been outstanding events where all concerned bore testimony that God had been there and had spoken and acted. Similarly many, though not all, believers can look to an experience when they cannot deny that God was with them and had acted in and through them. Such testimonies must be received with great care, for it is in this sphere, as nowhere else, that subjective self-deception can be most active. Even so, one must be prepared to recognize that theophanies of God the Holy Spirit still occur. The difference is that they cannot be used for doctrinal and authoritative purposes. They arise from the supreme revelation in Jesus Christ and look back to it.   H. L. Ellison

Theophilus thee-of´uh-luhs (Θεόφιλος *G2541*, "lover [*or* friend] of God"). A man to whom the Gospel of Luke and the Acts of the Apostles were addressed (Lk. 1:3; Acts 1:1). His identity is uncertain and may only be conjectured from the literary conventions of the time and the purposes for which Luke-Acts was written. It has been suggested that Luke wrote to a Christian audience and that a name with this meaning is a generic term for all of Luke's Christian readers. Appropriately, the book would then be addressed to any "friend of God" who wanted more detailed and accurate information concerning the origin and meaning of his faith.

On the other hand, books intended for the general public were sometimes dedicated to a friend and patron who might be able to contribute to the cost of disseminating an otherwise unknown work, or who had suggested its composition. Furthermore, in the gospel Theophilus is described as *kratiste* (vocative of *kratistos G3196*, "most excellent"), a title of conspicuous rank or office, used also of Felix the governor of Judea (Acts 23:26; 24:3) and of Festus his successor (Acts 26:25). This detail points to the view that Luke had a definite person in mind, probably a respected Roman official who had been informed of Christianity and the life of Christ or possibly catechized as a convert. If Theophilus was a questioning catechumen in prepara-

tion for Christian baptism, it is understandable why Luke says that he has written his gospel "so that you may have certainty of the things you have been taught" (Lk. 1:4).

However, *kratiste* also can be used in a friendly way as a form of polite or flattering address with no official connotation. If the use here is official, it is unlikely that Theophilus was a Christian at this time, "since there is no instance in the Christian literature of the first two centuries where a Christian uses a secular title in addressing another Christian, to say nothing of a title of this character, which may be said to correspond in a general way to 'Your Excellency'" (T. Zahn, *Introduction to the New Testament*, 3 vols. [1909], 3:42; however, see *ABD*, 6:511–12). In Acts this title is omitted, and one can only speculate that friendship had deepened by the time the second book was dedicated, or that Theophilus had become a Christian in the interim and the title was too honorific for a brother Christian, or that Theophilus had either given up his office or been dismissed under persecution for his Christian profession.

Theophilus is found as a proper name as early as the 3rd cent. B.C. in both the papyri and the inscriptions (MM, 288), including its early use among Jews (*The Flinders Petrie Papyri*, ed. J. P. Mahaffy and J. G. Smyly, 3 vols. [1891–1905], 2:28 ii 9). It may well have been a baptismal name used among Christians, since a Roman official in the 1st cent. probably would not have been known in public by such a name. If this is the case, it is the only instance of such in the Acts and may be the same as a pseudonym to conceal his real identity, due to the need for secrecy under tense conditions between church and state (W. M. Ramsay, *Saint Paul the Traveller and Roman Citizen*, 14th ed. [1920], 388). According to Eusebius and Jerome, Luke was a native of Antioch of Syria, and a Theophilus who held some high distinction at Antioch is mentioned in the Clementine Literature (*Recognitions* 10.71). This may be the person for whom Luke wrote, but the reliability of such traditions is difficult to prove.

There remains the possibility that Theophilus was a pagan and not a Christian at all. The answer to this question depends partly on the significance of *katēchēthēs* (from *katēcheō G2994*) in Lk. 1:4, which could be translated either "you have been informed" (cf. RSV) or "you have been taught" (NIV). Luke may have wanted to set forth in a general sense the reliability of the stories that had been reported to Theophilus, or it may be that Theophilus had received vague or hostile reports of Christianity as a subversive and troublesome movement, which reports Luke sets out to correct. Luke-Acts, therefore, would be an apologetic for the peaceableness of Christianity and the loyalty of its adherents to the imperial government (but see D. L. Bock, *Luke*, BECNT, 2 vols. [1994–96], 1:64–66; cf. more generally R. Garrison, *The Significance of Theophilus as Luke's Reader* [2004]). These themes occur repeatedly, especially in the Acts. See further LUKE, GOSPEL OF, VIII.   A. M. Ross

Theras thee′ruhs (Θερα). The name of a river where EZRA assembled the Israelites who were returning to Jerusalem (1 Esd. 8:41, 61). See AHAVA.

Thermeleth thuhr-mee′lith. KJV Apoc. form of TEL MELAH (1 Esd. 5:36).

Thessalonians, First Epistle to the thes′uh-loh′nee-uhnz. An early letter written by the apostle PAUL to the church in THESSALONICA.

  I. Background
 II. Authorship
III. Date and place of writing
 IV. Destination
  V. Occasion
 VI. Purpose
VII. Special problems
VIII. Content
 IX. Theology

I. Background. On his second missionary journey (c. A.D. 49) Paul and his companions, SILAS and TIMOTHY, came from PHILIPPI to Thessalonica and founded the Christian church there (cf. 1 Thess. 1:1, 5–8; 2:1–14; 3:1–6; Phil. 4:16; Acts 17:1–10; 18:5). The congregation was largely Gentile Christian (1 Thess. 1:9; 2:14; Acts 17:4), although ARISTARCHUS, a Jewish Christian, is specifically mentioned in Acts 20:4; Col. 4:10–11. Luke's narrative may indicate that Paul worked in Thessalonica three to four weeks (Acts 17:2), although some scholars maintain that this period of "three Sabbath days" was a reference only to his ministry in the synagogue, and thus they predicate a longer overall ministry in the city, perhaps as much as six months.

The church grew swiftly both numerically and spiritually. In fact, so gratifying had been their progress that Paul describes them as exemplary for the saints in MACEDONIA and ACHAIA (1 Thess. 1:7–8). But the work of Paul and his companions had not been easy in Thessalonica. The Jews had stirred up the rabble of the city against Paul and Silas, so that they had to flee by night to BEREA (Acts 17:5–10). The Bereans welcomed the message and made diligent study of the Scriptures to see whether what Paul proclaimed was true. But even as the apostle was enjoying success, the Jews at Thessalonica came to Berea in order to stir up a riot against God's servants. The result was that, while Silas and Timothy were left behind in Berea to give support to the infant church, Paul himself was sent away to the coast (v. 14). Those who escorted him brought him as far as ATHENS, and Paul requested Silas and Timothy to come to him as soon as possible (v. 15).

While awaiting their arrival, Paul continued to proclaim the message of the gospel in Athens (Acts 17:16–34). From 1 Thess. 3:1–2 we learn that Timothy had left Berea and had joined Paul; and it is probable (though not certain) that Silas too had come to Athens. One thing is clear: the apostle was deeply concerned about the state of the recently founded church in Thessalonica. Twice he had made plans to revisit them, but twice Satan prevented him from realizing this desire (1 Thess. 2:17). Thus, with his concern ever intensifying, he decided to be left at Athens alone, sending Timothy (and Silas?) back to strengthen and encourage the saints at Thessalonica (3:1–3). When Timothy returned to Paul and reported to him concerning the Thessalonians, the apostle proceeded to write to them (3:6). It appears that by that time Paul had traveled from Athens to CORINTH, where he had begun to preach in the synagogue as he waited for Timothy (and Silas) to meet him again (Acts 18:1–5).

II. Authorship. Pauline authorship of 1 Thessalonians is no longer seriously contested. In the past, however, certain of the Tübingen and Dutch schools regarded the epistle as unauthentic for several reasons. (1) The letter is supposedly too untheological in content. But, it may be asked, why must all the apostle's writings have been equally doctrinal in character? Varying circumstances require varying epistolary emphasis. Actually 1 Thessalonians is far from being doctrinally insignificant; it provides much needed information on the doctrine of the last things. (2) The letter fails to attack the teaching of justification by the works of the law. But, it may be asked, was Paul a man of only one idea? It should be remembered that the situation in Thessalonica was not the same as that in GALATIA. (3) The letter is claimed by some to be too dependent upon 1 and 2 Corinthians and therefore the work of a forger. However, this argument (the letter is too Pauline) cancels out the first one (the letter is not Pauline enough). (4) The letter is supposedly contradictory to certain information in Acts (cf. 1 Thess. 2:7–10 with Acts 17:2; 1 Thess. 1:9 and 2:14 with Acts 17:4; 1 Thess. 3:1–2 with Acts 18:5). Careful attention to these variations prove only that Luke and Paul wrote independently of each other; we need both to give the complete story.

The positive evidence for Pauline authorship may be noted. (1) The epistle presents itself as being from Paul (1 Thess. 1:1). (2) The companions mentioned were known to have accompanied Paul on his second missionary journey (1:1; 3:2; 3:6; cf. Acts 15:40; 16:1–3, 19; 17:4, 10, 14; 18:5). (3) The typical Pauline form is evident. Its epistolary structure is identical with Romans, 1–2 Corinthians, and Galatians—epistles that are ascribed to Paul even by most of those who reject the authenticity of 1 Thessalonians. (4) The vocabulary style and theological thought is clearly Pauline. (5) Finally, evidence from extrabiblical sources may be noted. ORIGEN, CLEMENT OF ALEXANDRIA, TERTULLIAN, MARCION, and IRENAEUS, all testify in one way or another to the authenticity of 1 Thessalonians.

III. Date and place of writing. It is generally agreed by scholars that 1 Thessalonians was written in the early fifties (c. 50–51). If this is correct, 1 Thessalonians would be the oldest preserved Pauline epistle—indeed, the oldest document in the NT—although some date Galatians earlier (see GALATIANS, EPISTLE TO THE, VI). It was written shortly after Timothy came to Athens, or in Corinth; the latter is more commonly held.

IV. Destination. Thessalonica was founded about 315 B.C. by Cassander, who named it in honor of his wife, the half-sister of ALEXANDER THE GREAT. It was the largest and most important city in Macedonia and was also the capital of the province. It was situated on the most famous of Roman military roads, the VIA EGNATIA, which connected ROME with the eastern parts of the empire. It was a seaport and a center of trade and commerce; a city ideally suited to Paul's missionary strategy.

V. Occasion. Paul received his inducement to write 1 Thessalonians from the reports which Timothy brought him from Thessalonica (Acts 18:5; 1 Thess. 3:6). Some have suggested that this first epistle was in part a reply to a letter which the church had sent to Paul. It is argued that 4:9 and 5:1 might indicate this as a possibility, since the expression *peri de* ("now about …") is used by Paul in 1 Corinthians to denote written replies made concerning specific inquiries (cf. 1 Cor. 7:1, 25; 8:1; et al.). It must not be overlooked, however, that whereas 1 Corinthians mentions a letter, 1 Thessalonians does not. See CORINTHIANS, FIRST EPISTLE TO THE. It would seem that Paul would have clearly mentioned a previous communication if, indeed, he had received one.

Excavations of the cardo (main street) at Thessalonica.

VI. Purpose. Timothy's report on the Thessalonians led Paul to counsel them in respect to several matters. (1) He commended them for their steadfastness under trial and encouraged them regarding future conflicts they might experience (1 Thess. 2:14; 3:1–4). (2) He defended his conduct and motives against those who had been seeking to malign him (2:1–12). (3) He reiterated the Christian standard of holiness for those new converts who were still tempted by the prevailing immorality of the time (4:1–8). (4) He clarified certain features of the doctrine of Christ's return for the sake of those members of the congregation who had become concerned over the welfare of departed loved ones; Paul sought to comfort such through further instruction (4:13–18). (5) He rebuked those of the congregation who had become lax in tending to their daily tasks in light of what they considered to be the immediately impending return of Christ (4:11). (6) He urged his readers to respect their leaders (5:12). (7) He attempted to correct erroneous attitudes toward spiritual gifts which some apparently were endeavoring to repress (5:19–20). The entire epistle is essentially practical, containing a message patterned to meet the problems of that early Christian community.

VII. Special problems. The first of these problems involves the idea put forth by Adolf Harnack that the church at Thessalonica was divided into two sections meeting separately, a Jewish and Gentile church (see K. Lake and S. Lake, *An Introduction to the New Testament* [1937], 134). It is then argued that 1 Thessalonians was written to the Gentile church and 2 Thessalonians to the Jewish church.

The arguments employed to establish this view are as follows: (1) Christian Gentiles were evidently the recipients of the first epistle (cf. 1 Thess. 1:9; 2:14), whereas the second has a much stronger Jewish flavor, with language couched in OT terms. (2) It is argued that the original reading at 2 Thess. 2:13 is not *ap' archēs*, "from the beginning," but *aparchēn*, "firstfruit" (cf NRSV), and that Gentiles in Thessalonica were certainly not Paul's first converts, nor even the first converts in Macedonia; Paul's language might better be seen to apply to the Thessalonian Jews as the first converts in that city. (3) It is held that the emphasis on "all" in 1 Thess. 5:26–27 implies a different group in addition to the recipients of the first letter.

This evidence is far from convincing. Taking the arguments in order, it may be stated: (1) The supposed Jewish coloring is not at all impressive. There are no quotations from the OT in the second epistle, and even if there were this would in no way demand a Jewish destination. Paul cited the OT most frequently in his epistle to the Romans, but this letter was most certainly addressed to a predominantly Gentile congregation. (2) As for the argument based on a variant reading of the text, one should note that this variant is rejected by many editors; and even if it is accepted as genuine, an exclusive reference to Jewish Christians in Thessalonica hardly seems to be the most natural interpretation. (3) Finally, Paul's use of "all" in 5:26–27 is perfectly capable of being explained otherwise: the apostle simply desired that his greetings might embrace everyone — the loafers, the weak, and any others with whom he might have had some reason to be disappointed. Two additional and rather decisive factors militate against this theory of a divided church: (a) such a view is in strong contradiction to the Pauline doctrine of the unity of the church (cf. 1 Cor. 1:11–17); (b) we have no clear historical evidence of such a divided church.

A second problem is that of coauthorship. Both epistles indicate that the senders are Paul, Silas (Silvanus), and Timothy (1 Thess. 1:1; 2 Thess. 1:1). Further, throughout the letters "we" rather than "I" is used, with only a few exceptions. Some have suggested that either Silas or Timothy was largely responsible for one or both of the epistles, with Silas usually being preferred. It would seem best however, simply to take the inclusion of the names of Silas and Timothy as a sign of courtesy toward his associates in the work of the ministry. They certainly would have endorsed what he wrote.

A third problem concerns the order of these two epistles. Some would maintain that they should be reversed. In this way many difficult problems supposedly receive a solution. The following arguments are urged in support of this thesis: (1) In 2 Thessalonians Paul speaks of the church as experiencing severe trials and difficulties whereas in 1 Thessalonians he speaks of these as past. (2) While certain difficulties within the church are mentioned in 2 Thessalonians as though the writer had just been informed of them, in 1 Thessalonians they are mentioned as though familiar to everyone, suggesting therefore a later stage. (3) The statement in 1 Thessalonians that they have no need to be instructed regarding "the times and the seasons" makes good sense if they had already received 2 Thessalonians. (4) The fact that Paul emphasizes his signature in 2 Thess. 3:17 but not at the end of the first epistle would tend to argue for a reversal of the letters. (5) Certain members of the Thessalonian church had died when the first epistle was penned; this would be more likely if we can account for a longer period. (6) It is reasonable to suppose that the shorter epistle would have been written first with the longer following as a later elaboration.

In response to these arguments, it may be noted that far from the trials of the first epistle being over, it would be better to view them as yet in the future. Paul would then be seen in this first epistle as encouraging these believers with respect to those persecutions that yet lay ahead. The expression "We hear that some among you are idle" (2 Thess. 3:11) could be easily understood as following what is stated in 1 Thessalonians. It certainly is not necessary to see 2 Thess. 2 as providing the background for the statement concerning "the times and the seasons" in the first epistle. His prior oral communications to the Thessalonians concerning the PAROUSIA would have been sufficient explanation for this statement regarding "the times and the seasons." A perfectly good explanation is given in 2 Thess. 2:2 for his autograph in that epistle. As for the argument based on the shortness of the second epistle, all that one can assert is that such reasoning is extremely unconvincing. There is no good reason why a first epistle should necessarily be shorter than a second.

From a more positive perspective, there are good reasons for holding the traditional order as correct. (1) In those areas in which both epistles speak to the same issue or problem, we have an intensification as we pass from the first to the second, not the reverse. (2) In 2 Thessalonians Paul clearly indicates that another letter had preceded it (2 Thess. 2:2, 15; 3:17). If 1 Thessalonians followed 2 Thessalonians then we still need another one, now lost. It would seem most reasonable, then, in the absence of any conclusive proof to the contrary, to take 2 Thessalonians as following 1 Thessalonians. It should be noted that the first epistle does not mention any previous letter. (3) The traditional order alone fits with the manifest moods of the author. (4) The traditional order would seem to best fit the indications of spiritual development or growth in the Thessalonians (cf. 1 Thess. 1:6 and 2:13 with 2 Thess. 1:3; 1 Thess. 3:12 and 4:10 with 2 Thess. 1:3). (5) The statement "our being gathered to him" (2 Thess. 2:1) would seem to presuppose Paul's teaching on the rapture in 1 Thessalonians (1 Thess. 4:17).

VIII. Content. Having received information from Timothy concerning the state of the Thessalonian congregation, Paul writes expressing his thanks for their spiritual health as seen in their steadfastness under persecution. He vindicates his ministry among them as against the charges of his enemies. He instructs them concerning the status of their departed loved ones at the time of the rapture. He exhorts them concerning their responsibilities in light of the future day of the Lord, warning them to avoid immorality and encouraging them to pursue righteousness. This epistle centers on the doctrine of the SECOND COMING of Christ. It may be outlined as follows.

    A. Introduction (1 Thess. 1:1)
    B. Thanksgiving (1:2–10)
        1. Paul's remembrance (1:2–3)
        2. Evidence of election (1:4–10)

Decorative stone depicting an agricultural scene from Thessalonica. Some of the Thessalonian Christians stopped working because they believed that the second coming of Jesus was about to occur.

C. Personal defense (2:1—3:13)
  1. Message and opposition (2:1-2)
  2. Pure motives (2:3-4)
  3. Gentle approach (2:5-9)
  4. Unblameable behavior (2:10-12)
  5. Results (2:13-16)
  6. Relationships (2:17—3:13)
D. Practical exhortation and instruction (4:1—5:22)
  1. General exhortations (4:1-2)
  2. Sexual purity, brotherly love, industry (4:3-12).
  3. Eschatological instruction (4:13—5:11)
  4. Concluding exhortations (5:12-22)
E. Conclusion (5:23-28)

IX. Theology. The Thessalonian epistles are the least dogmatic of all the Pauline letters. That which makes PAULINE THEOLOGY distinctive is largely absent from these two epistles. There is no mention of the matter of the contrasts between LAW and GRACE; the term JUSTIFICATION is not used at all; grace, a favorite watchword of Paul, occurs only twice (2 Thess. 1:12; 12:16). This lack of extensive Pauline theological argumentation is most reasonably accounted for by the nature of the circumstances in which these epistles arose.

Certain doctrines are, however, presented. First, as respects the doctrine of God, Paul indicates that there is one true God in contrast to all pagan deities (1 Thess. 1:9). It is from this one true and living God that the gospel which they declared derived (2:2). It was to this same God they ultimately were to submit themselves for approval of their labor (2:4, 10). This God is the One who providentially directed their lives (3:11). He was the One who would perfect the Thessalonians at the coming of Christ (5:23), for he is the One who had chosen them (1:4) and was even now calling them unto his own kingdom and glory (2:12). This God is faithful to accomplish the work he had begun (5:24).

Second, as respects the doctrine of Christ, the apostle so unites the Son with the Father as to indicate clearly their essential equality (1 Thess. 1:1).

Third, the apostle teaches that it is the HOLY SPIRIT who makes the message effective in the hearts of hearers (1 Thess. 1:5). It is the Spirit who gives joy in affliction (v. 6). It is the Spirit who gives those charismatic gifts which the Thessalonians were tending to despise (5:19-20). God gives the Holy Spirit to all believers (1 Thess. 4:7-8), therefore they must be careful not to fall into uncleanness.

Fourth, the apostle mentions the great doctrine of REDEMPTION through the death of Christ only once and that in a very general way (1 Thess. 5:10), but it should be remembered that this central truth had already been fully proclaimed and accepted by the Thessalonians (2:13). Paul takes for granted their knowledge of this elsewhere in his epistle (1:10; 4:14). The great doctrine of UNION WITH CHRIST is clearly implied when he describes the Thessalonian church as being "in ... the Lord Jesus Christ" (1 Thess. 1:1).

Fifth, as respects the doctrine of ESCHATOLOGY, the apostle has considerable to set forth. It is from the futuristic perspective that the "obtaining of salvation" is principally conceived in the Thessalonian epistles (1 Thess. 5:9; 2 Thess. 2:14). The definite announcement of the second coming rounds off each step in the apostolic argument. In 1 Thessalonians there is mention of the parousia in each chapter, with extensive discussion in chs. 4 and 5 (cf. 1:10; 2:19; 3:13; 4:13-18; 5:1-11, 23).

(Significant commentaries include G. Milligan, *St. Paul's Epistles to the Thessalonians: The Greek Text with Introduction and Notes* [1908]; J. E. Frame, *A Critical and Exegetical Commentary on the Epistles of St. Paul to the Thessalonians*, ICC [1912]; W. Hendriksen, *Exposition of I and II Thessalonians* [1955]; D. E. Hiebert, *The Thessalonian Epistles* [1971]; E. Best, *A Commentary on the First and Second Epistles to the Thessalonians*, HNTC [1972]; F. F. Bruce, *1 and 2 Thessalonians*, WBC 45 [1982]; C. A. Wanamaker, *The Epistles to the Thessalonians: A Commentary on the Greek Text*, NIGTC [1990]; L. Morris, *The First and Second Epistles to the Thessalonians*, NICNT, rev. ed., [1991]; D. M. Martin, *1, 2 Thessalonians*, NAC 33 [1995]; E. J. Richard, *First and Second Thessalonians*, SP 11 [1995]; A. J. Malherbe, *The Letters to the Thessalonians*, AB 32B [2000]; G. L. Green, *The Letters to the Thessalonians* [2002]; G. K. Beale, *1-2 Thessalonians* [2003]; B. Witherington III, *1 and 2 Thessalonians: A Socio-Rhetorical Commentary* [2006].

(See also R. F. Collins, *Studies on the First Letter to the Thessalonians* [1984]; B. C. Johanson, *To*

All the Brethren: A Text-Linguistic and Rhetorical Approach to 1 Thessalonians [1987]; R. Jewett, *The Thessalonian Correspondence: Pauline Rhetoric and Millenarian Piety* [1986]; R. F. Collins, ed., *The Thessalonian Correspondence* [1990]; J. A. D. Weima and S. E. Porter, *An Annotated Bibliography of 1 and 2 Thessalonians* [1998]; K. P. Donfried and J. Beutler, eds., *The Thessalonians Debate: Methodological Discord or Methodological Synthesis?* [2000]; K. P. Donfried, *Paul, Thessalonica, and Early Christianity* [2002]; R. S. Ascough, *Paul's Macedonian Associations: The Social Context of Philippians and 1 Thessalonians* [2003]; C. R. Nicholl, *From Hope to Despair in Thessalonica: Situating 1 and 2 Thessalonians* [2004]; A. Paddison, *Theological Hermeneutics and 1 Thessalonians* [2005].)   C. M. HORNE

Thessalonians, Second Epistle to the. For the background to this letter see THESSALONIANS, FIRST EPISTLE TO THE.

    I. Authorship
    II. Date and place of writing
    III. Occasion and purpose
    IV. Content
    V. Theology

I. Authorship. An attack upon the Pauline authorship of 2 Thessalonians arose early in the 19th cent. This attack was based upon supposed internal evidence and focused in general on two lines of thought. First, it was argued that the reference to the eschatological figure of the "man of lawlessness" (2 Thess. 2:3) was derived from the *Nero redivivus* myth and thus shows the epistle to be post-Pauline, since NERO had not yet died. Further, it is claimed that the ESCHATOLOGY of 2 Thessalonians is in disagreement with that of 1 Thessalonians. In the first epistle the SECOND COMING is viewed as imminent; in the second it is preceded by certain signs. These and other arguments—such as lexical and literary differences between the two letters—have persuaded many modern scholars that 2 Thessalonians is not an authentic Pauline writing. (For a fuller summary of the debate, see *ABD*, 6:518–22, which also includes a brief discussion of rhetorical criticism of the letter.)

Both of the arguments mentioned above may be satisfactorily answered. As regards the figure of the man of lawlessness, it should be noted that this concept was firmly rooted in the soil of OT prophecy. As regards the supposed eschatological conflict between the two epistles, it should be noted that it is a common feature of APOCALYPTIC LITERATURE to find the ideas of suddenness and signs stated alongside each other. The second line of attack is based upon the idea that the two epistles are too much alike to have been written by the same author to the same church. A careful study of the content of each will reveal however that the similarity must not be overstated. It is reasonable to suppose that Paul would tie in that which he states in his second letter with that which he had written previously. It may be estimated that the resemblances do not extend to more than a third of the entire contents.

II. Date and place of writing. The date assigned to 2 Thessalonians is obviously dependent upon one's view of the time lapse between the first and second epistles. Some hold to only a few days, others to as much as a year, but it would seem preferable to predicate, as is generally held, that it was two or three months. This would require a date in the fall or early winter of either A.D. 50 or 51. If so, then this second epistle was also written from CORINTH. In further support of this chronology is the fact that Paul, Silas (Silvanus), and Timothy (2 Thess. 1:1) do not appear together again in the NT narrative following Paul's departure from Corinth.

III. Occasion and purpose. Paul evidently received new information concerning the Thessalonians, perhaps from those who had delivered his first epistle. The report had both encouraging and discouraging elements in it. On the positive side he was thankful for the evidence of their spiritual growth (2 Thess. 1:3–4). On the negative side he was discouraged by their failure to understand properly certain eschatological matters. Specifically, it seems that some of the Thessalonian believers had fallen into the error of thinking that the DAY OF THE LORD had actually begun and that therefore the Messiah would appear very soon. In the light of this expectation some had given up their work and were living in meddlesome idleness. For this reason Paul found it necessary to write a second letter to the Thessalonians.

IV. Content. After the typical epistolary opening Paul expresses his thankfulness to God for the Thessalonians and the progress they had made in respect to faith and love. Indeed he was boastful before others over the way in which they were bearing persecutions and afflictions. Paul then reminds his readers that although they were suffering now, the wicked would yet suffer the punishment of eternal destruction and exclusion from the presence of the Lord. In sharp contrast to the wicked in that day Christ will come to be glorified in his saints and they in him.

Paul then moves into a consideration of the parousia, the day of the Lord. Because some had been misled either through oral or written communication into believing that the day of the Lord had already dawned, the apostle finds it necessary to correct their teaching. He indicates that certain things must occur before that day. First there will be an all-out organized rebellion of the powers of evil against God. Second, there will be the revealing of the man of lawlessness. His career will end in the eternal destruction both of himself and his followers, those "who have not believed the truth but have delighted in wickedness" (2:12).

The apostle then contrasts with this dreadful picture the hope of believers. Christians are to be thankful that God has appointed them unto SALVATION through the SANCTIFICATION of the Spirit and belief of the truth. This glorious prospect is to bring comfort and encouragement to the Thessalonians' continuance in every good work and deed. The letter may be outlined as follows:

A. Introduction (2 Thess. 1:1–2)
B. Personal (1:3–12)
   1. Thanksgiving (1:3–4)
   2. Glorification (1:4–10)
   3. Prayer (1:11–12)
B. Doctrinal (2:1–17)
   1. An entreaty relative to the parousia (2:1–2)
   2. Events preceding the parousia (2:3–12)
   3. Thanksgiving and exhortation (2:13–17)
C. Practical (3:1–15)
   1. Request for prayer (3:1–2)
   2. Prayer for the Thessalonians (3:3–5)
   3. Commands to the Thessalonians (3:6–15)
D. Conclusion (3:16–18)

V. Theology. God is viewed as the true Author of all grace and peace (2 Thess. 1:2; 2:16; 3:16). He is the One who chose the Thessalonian Christians unto salvation (2:13). Thus, it is of him that they must walk worthily (1:5). God is the One who strengthens the saints unto perseverance (3:3–4). It is before him that the highest human hopes will be consummated (2:19).

Christ is so united with the Father as to leave no doubt concerning their essential equality in true deity. It is in the Lord Jesus Christ, as well as "in God the Father," that the church's life consists (2 Thess. 1:1–2; cf. 2:16–17). The Spirit's distinctive work is that of sanctification (2:13).

The major emphasis of this epistle is eschatological, as with the first. There is a future time of judgment coming when God will settle his accounts (2 Thess. 1:5–10). The second chapter was written to correct the Thessalonians as regards the day of the Lord, that day on which Christ would return and his saints would be assembled to meet him (2:1). Some had fallen into the error of thinking that the day had already arrived, but Paul instructs them that certain things must occur first. Before that day commences there will be an all-out rebellion against God (2:3). As in the days of Noah many will revolt on a world-wide scale against their Creator. Then there will be the revealing of the man of lawlessness. As Christ shall be revealed in his "time," even so shall antichrist. He too is a mystery to be unfolded and made manifest. The terrible judgment that is to come upon him and all those who follow him is sharply contrasted by the glory of Christ in which all the elect shall share.

(For a list of commentaries, see THESSALONIANS, FIRST EPISTLE TO THE. Important monographs include C. Giblin, *The Threat to Faith: An Exegetical and Theological Reexamination of 2 Thessalonians 2* [1967]; G. S. Holland, *The Tradition that You Received from Us: 2 Thessalonians in the Pauline Tradition* [1988]; F. W. Hughes, *Early Christian Rhetoric and 2 Thessalonians* [1989]; P. Metzger, *Katechon: II Thess 2,1–12 im Horizont apokalyptischen Denkens* [2005].)

C. M. HORNE

Thessalonica thes′uh-luh-ni′kuh (Θεσσαλονίκη G2553; gentilic Θεσσαλονικεύς G2552, "Thessalonian"). The capital city of the Roman province of

Macedonia. Thessalonica, modern Thessaloniki (sometimes referred to as Salonica), was strategically located on the Thermaic Gulf to the W of the three-pronged peninsula known as Chalcidice. The Via Egnatia passed through Thessalonica and linked it with all the important cities of Macedonia. Cicero (*Pro Plancio* 41) described it as *posita in gremio imperii nostri*, "situated in the bosom of our domain."

I. History. There are three accounts of the naming of the city. The most probable is that it was founded by Cassander c. 315 B.C. and named for his wife, the daughter of Philip II (Strabo, *Geogr.* 7 fragm. 21). Others state that the city was founded by Philip himself and that it was named either for his daughter or in honor of his victory over the Thessalians. The new city incorporated the population of a number of neighboring towns, principally Therma, Anea, Cissus, and Chalastra.

Livy (*Hist.* 44.10.45; 45.29) indicates that the city was a great Macedonian naval base, displacing Pella as the chief port of Macedonia when its harbor silted up. It surrendered to the Romans after the battle of Pydna and became the capital of the second of the four districts of Macedonia in 167 B.C. Later, Macedonia was made a single province and Thessalonica became its capital. During the civil war, it was the headquarters for Pompey's army. In the campaign against Cassius and Brutus, it sided with Antony and Octavian and was declared a free city because of its loyalty (Plutarch, *Brutus* 46). The city enjoyed local autonomy during the period of the Roman empire and became the most prosperous of the Macedonian cities. Luke (Acts 17:6) appropriately uses the term *politarchēs* G4485 for the magistrates of the city, who were either five or six in number. Inscriptions found in the city, one on the Vardar Gate, verify this title, a unique one in the Roman empire.

II. Archaeology. Remains of extensive Byzantine walls, built on earlier foundations, are still visible. The Via Egnatia ran from the SE to the NW. The two entrances to the city were spanned by the Vardar Gate to the W (destroyed in 1876) and the Arch of Galerius on the E. In the 19th cent., travelers left sketches and descriptions of many of the monuments in the city, notably the early Byzantine churches, but most of these were destroyed by a fire that swept the city in 1917.

III. Biblical importance. Paul first visited Thessalonica after Philippi on the second missionary journey. Because of its location, it was an invaluable center for the spread of the gospel. Paul was later to say, "The Lord's message rang out from you not only in Macedonia and Achaia—your faith in God has become known everywhere" (1 Thess. 1:8). He first appeared at the synagogue, and as a result some Jews and proselytes believed, including a number of prominent women (Acts 17:2–4). This prompted the Jews to stir up the Gentile population to persecute Paul and Silas. A flourishing church was founded there during three weeks of ministry, which ended when the mob attacked the house of Jason where Paul was staying. Paul and Silas were thus forced to flee to Berea (17:5–10). The apostle no doubt returned to the city on the third journey, though only a general ministry in Macedonia is specifically mentioned (20:1–3).

Later, while in prison at Rome, Paul entertained a hope of visiting Macedonia again (Phil. 1:25–26; 2:24). After his release, he ministered in the vicinity of Thessalonica and may well have revisited the city (1 Tim. 1:3; 2 Tim. 4:13; Tit. 3:12). A few

Thessalonica.

of the converts of his ministry are mentioned by name: Jason (Acts 17:5–9; cf. Rom. 16:21); possibly Demas (2 Tim. 4:10); Gaius (Acts 19:29; cf. 20:4), Secundus and Aristarchus (20:1). (See further O. Tafrali, *Thessalonique des origines au XIVe siècle* [1919]; C. vom Brocke, *Thessaloniki, Stadt des Kassander und Gemeinde des Paulus: Eine frühe christliche Gemeinde in ihrer heidnischen Umwelt* [2001]; C. Breytenbach and I. Behrmann, eds., *Frühchristliches Thessaloniki* [2007].)   A. RUPPRECHT

Theudas thoo′duhs (Θευδᾶς G2554, possibly short form of *Theodōros*, "gift of God," or a similar compound; for other possibilities, see G. H. R. Horsley's discussion of the inscriptional evidence in *NewDocs*, 4:183–85). Leader of a rebellion that failed, mentioned by GAMALIEL in a speech before the SANHEDRIN (Acts 5:35–36). Gamaliel cautions the Jewish leadership to be tolerant of the Christian apostles: he reasons that if the apostolic activity were of human origin only, it would fail of itself; but if it were of divine origin, nothing they did could stop it. The death of Theudas and the dispersion of his four hundred followers is cited as a basis for Gamaliel's thesis.

JOSEPHUS (*Ant.* 20.5.1) writes of a certain Theudas, a magician who around A.D. 44 led a great band of adherents to the Jordan, promising to divide it for an easy passage of the river, but was caught and beheaded by the soldiers of the procurator Fadus. This cannot have been the same Theudas as the insurgent mentioned in Acts, since Gamaliel's speech would have taken place in the early 30s; moreover, Gamaliel says that Theudas arose before the insurrection led by Judas the Galilean in the days of the taxing under QUIRINIUS about A.D. 6 (see JUDAS #4). This and other differences separate Luke's account from that of Josephus (full discussion in T. Zahn, *Introduction to the New Testament*, 3 vols. [1909], 3.132–33).

It is not necessary to impugn the historical accuracy of Acts here by assuming that Luke transposed Theudas and Judas, or that he misplaced Gamaliel's speech by moving it from a later section (Acts 12), where an angel assisted PETER's escape from prison under HEROD Agrippa (ruled A.D. 41–44), to the present passage, where the same thing happens at an earlier date (J. W. Swain in *ETR* 37 [1944]: 341–49). Nor did Luke misread Josephus, who did not publish his *Antiquities* until A.D. 93. In view of the "ten thousand other disorders" mentioned by Josephus (*Ant.* 17.10.4), there could well have been more than one insurrectionist named Theudas. (See F. F. Bruce, *The Acts of the Apostles: The Greek Text with Introduction and Commentary*, 3rd ed. [1990], 175–76; C. K. Barrett, *A Critical and Exegetical Commentary on the Acts of the Apostles*, ICC, 2 vols. [1994–98], 1:294–95.)   A. M. ROSS

thief. See CRIMES AND PUNISHMENTS I.B.

thigh. The upper portion of either of the two lower extremities of the human body between the hip and the knee. It is supported by the largest, longest, and strongest bone of the body—the femur. It is in the form of an inverted and truncated cone. Above, the thigh is bounded by the groin in front, the perineal region medially, the fold of the buttocks behind, and the hip laterally. Below, it is delimited by the prominence of the knee in front, and by the so-called popliteal space, or ham, in back. Besides the femur, it consists of strong muscles in addition to blood vessels, lymphatics, and nerves, all of which structures are surrounded with a strong fibrous sheath like the firm bark of a tree. (Cf. H. Gray, *Anatomy of the Human Body*, 27th ed. [1959], 528–43; A. H. Crenshaw, *Campbell's Operative Orthopaedics*, 4th ed. [1963], 1:319–27.)

Dislocation of the hip joint occurs at the upper end of the femur, most commonly forward, although backward dislocation is also recognized. Evidently the fold of the buttock (i.e., hollow of the thigh) on one side of JACOB's body was struck from behind to produce the more usual forward dislocation, if one accepts the KJV interpretation that the hip went out of joint (Gen. 32:25). This causes one to limp in a toe-out position on the affected side. Instead of the KJV's phrase, "the hollow of Jacob's thigh," the NIV reads "the socket of Jacob's hip" (Heb. *bēkap yerek yaʿăqōb*; similarly NRSV and NJPS). In this connection it should be noted that the head of the femur rides upward on the bony pelvis so that the muscles in that area become shortened. These shortened muscles could well constitute the "sinew that shrank" (v. 32 KJV for Heb. *bĕgîd hannāšeh*; NIV, "near the tendon"; NRSV and NJPS, "at the thigh muscle").

Another interpretation of Jacob's injury is given by A. R. Short (*The Bible and Modern Medicine* [1953], 60), who thinks that Jacob had "the modern, very fashionable, diagnosis of ruptured and prolapsed intervertebral disc producing severe and intractable sciatica from pressure on the nerve roots." From this standpoint the "sinew of the hip" (RSV) is considered to be the sciatic nerve. However, this interpretation presents the difficulty of explaining how touching the hollow of the thigh can produce disc injury to the vertebrae. Moreover, in the opinion of this writer, Short belittles unnecessarily the strength of the wrestler and the effect of his surprise move in producing a dislocation. Neither the dislocation of the hip nor the ruptured intervertebral disc exactly fits the picture of the ASV that the "thigh was strained," although the former more nearly does.

It is noteworthy that the PATRIARCHS put a hand under a thigh in connection with taking an oath (Gen. 24:2; 47:29). It was also customary to gird the sword on the thigh (Ps. 45:3), evidently because there, where the hand naturally falls, the sword is especially accessible for use in an unforeseen encounter with an enemy (Cant. 3:8). In contrast, striking one's hand against the thigh is evidently a manifestation of shame and bewilderment (Jer. 31:19; Ezek. 21:12), as though one is feeling for a sword that is not there, and suddenly realizes that he is defenseless. Finally, the thigh at the moment of the Lord's triumph will bear his glorious name, "King of kings and Lord of lords" (Rev. 19:16).

P. E. ADOLPH

Thimnathah thim'nuh-thuh. KJV alternate form of TIMNAH (only Josh. 19:43).

third day. On five different occasions when Jesus spoke of his coming death, he added that his resurrection would take place on "the third day." According to the Gospel of John, this theme was introduced at the beginning of Jesus' ministry, in Jerusalem, after driving out the money changers and the traffickers from the temple (the same or a similar event is placed in Jesus' last week by the synoptics). In answer to the angry question of what sign he would show them to justify this act, he answered, "Destroy this temple, and I will raise it again in three days" (Jn. 2:19), regarding which the apostle adds, "But the temple he had spoken of was his body" (v. 21). Later in his ministry, Jesus made the famous statement, "For as Jonah was three days and three nights in the belly of a huge fish, so the Son of Man will be three days and three nights in the heart of the earth" (Matt. 12:40; the parallel in Lk. 11:29 does not include the time reference). On three subsequent successive occasions he repeated the specific time limit (Matt. 16:21 = Mk. 8:31 = Lk. 9:22; Matt. 17:23 = Mk. 9:31; Matt. 20:19 = Mk. 10:34 = Lk. 18:33).

Jesus' statement at the cleansing of the temple must have left a deep impression upon his enemies, for two false witnesses at his trial before CAIAPHAS referred to it, although they misquoted it (Matt. 26:61=Mk. 14:58). When Jesus was on the cross, those that passed by reviled him and reminded him of the words he had spoken at that time (Matt. 27:40=Mk. 15:29). Even on Saturday, when the chief priests and PHARISEES asked PILATE for a military guard to protect the tomb, they repeated this statement with an added insult, "we remember that while he was still alive that deceiver said, 'After three days I will rise again'" (Matt. 27:63).

The Jews were not the last ones to refer to this time period. Three times it reappears in Luke's final chapter (and not in any of the other gospel parallels). The angel reminded the women of what Jesus himself had said, that on the third day he would rise again (Lk. 24:7); the two disciples on the EMMAUS road must have had this in mind when they said to the unrecognized Jesus, "it is the third day since all this took place" (v. 21). In one of his very last appearances Jesus directed the attention of his disciples to this theme when, opening their understanding, he said to them, "This is what is written: The Christ will suffer and rise from the dead on the third day" (v. 46). Twice again does this appear in the early records of the apostolic church. PETER, in preaching in the house of CORNELIUS, affirmed that it was this Jesus whom "God raised ... from the dead on the third day" (Acts 10:40). And in the great chapter on the resurrection PAUL asserts that Christ "was raised on the third day according to the Scriptures" (1 Cor. 15:4).

Paul's statement clearly declares that the OT Scriptures somehow predicted not simply that

Christ would rise again, but that this resurrection would take place "on the third day." Possibly the most specific reference that Paul had in mind was the confidence of the remnant in Israel, "After two days he will revive us; / on the third day he will restore us, / that we may live in his presence" (Hos. 6:2). The great Oxford scholar, E. B. Pusey, does not exaggerate when he says, "The Resurrection of Christ and our resurrection in Him and in His Resurrection could not be more plainly foretold.... The *two days* and *the third day* have nothing in history to correspond with them, except that in which they are fulfilled, when Christ, 'rising on the third day from the grave, raised with him the whole human race'" (*The Minor Prophets*, 2 vols. [1885], 1:63–64).

There are other passages of Scripture, however, that bear upon this subject, and in looking at them, one should remember the words of the great church historian Philip Schaff: "The biblical symbolism of numbers ... is worthy of more serious attention than it has received in English theology" (editorial note in J. P. Lange, *A Commentary on the Holy Scriptures: Matthew* [1846], 183). The very first occurrence of the word in the Bible—and generally first occurrences of basic words in the Bible have great meaning—may be relevant to the subject, for it was on "the third day" that biological life first appeared (Gen. 1:9–13). Also in Genesis, in the story of JOSEPH, there is a release from prison on the third day (40:12–13); and when Joseph's brothers were released from prison after "three days," we read: "On the third day Joseph said to them, 'Do this and you will live'" (42:17–18). Notice how this matter of life is vital in these three-day passages. The reference to Jonah's experience in the belly of the great fish for a period of three days is well known to all Bible students, because of our Lord's reference to it (Jon. 1:17).

"Three" also is used in passages indicating separation, as when people are severed from the visible, material world about them, and from one another, by darkness. The plague of darkness in the judgments on Egypt lasted just three days (Exod. 10:22–23); and darkness surrounding the cross was for a period of three hours (Matt. 27:45); Paul was in the darkness of blindness for three days after his experience on the way to DAMASCUS (Acts 9:9). "Three" is also used in important passages relating to divine punishment: God punished Israel with a three-year famine (2 Sam. 21:1); the drought predicted by ELIJAH continued for three years (1 Ki. 17:1, 18:1). Separation from loved ones is often for periods involving a series of three, as Christ, when twelve years of age, was separated from Joseph and Mary for three days (Lk. 2:46). (For an early treatment of this subject, see a book published anonymously in Lynchburg, Virginia, *Triads of Scripture* [1866]; the most detailed study is a series by W. M. Smith in the *Sunday School Times* [March 24 and 31, April 7, and July 14, 1928].)

Finally, a three-day period is closely related to the matter of the disposal of the remnants of a sacrificial animal before corruption should set in (Lev. 7:17–18; 19:6–7). This is, of course, what Peter had in mind when, in quoting the OT, he referred to God's promise that he would not let his Holy One "see decay" (Ps. 16:10). It is a strong witness to the importance of this time element as it relates to Christ's resurrection that the agnostic David Strauss should have felt compelled to devote two sections of his famous *Leben Jesu* (orig. 1835–36) to a desperate attempt to break down this solid evidence of Christ's foreknowledge (see *The Life of Jesus, Critically Examined*, ed. P. C. Hodgson, trans. G. Elliot [1972], 574–82). See also RESURRECTION OF JESUS CHRIST. W. M. SMITH

thirty. See NUMBER. For the group of warriors known as "the Thirty," see CHAMPION.

Thisbe this'bee (Θισβη). The place from which the Assyrians took TOBIT captive; it is said to be S of Kedesh-Naphtali in GALILEE above ASHER (Tob. 1:2; see KEDESH #1). The site has not been identified.

thistle This English term, commonly applied to a variety of prickly plants, is used to render Hebrew *dardar* H1998 (Gen. 3:18; Hos. 10:8) and *ḥôaḥ* H2560 (e.g., 2 Ki. 4:19 = 2 Chr. 25:18, where however the NRSV reasonably translates "thornbush"), as well as Greek *tribolos* G5560 (Matt. 7:16; Heb. 6:8). See BRAMBLE; FLORA (under *Compositae*); THORN.

The *Notobasis syriaca*, the true Syrian thistle, is one that grows 3 ft. high and is erect and branched; the leaves are smooth above, but hairy and prickly

A field of thistles.

below. Thistles are, however, very common in Palestine, and Israeli agricultural experts claim that there are over 120 species found in Israel today. Some kinds grow to a height of 6 ft., like the *Onopordon arabicum* of Great Britain. The reference in Isa. 34:13 could be to another very common Palestinian thistle, *Scolymus maculatus*, the spotted golden species, which would be suitable for decorating the run-down palaces and fortresses; the leaves of this 3-ft. plant are margined white and the flowers are gold.

The most common thistle of all is claimed to be *Centaurea iberica*, often called the Iberian thistle. It is probable that the Hebrew terms are used generically to cover a number of different kinds of thistles, and if so, one should undoubtedly include *Centaurea calcitrapa*, the red star thistle; *Silybum marianum*, Mary's thistle; and *Centaurea verutum*, the dwarf thistle. All of these are common weeds in Palestine. W. E. SHEWELL-COOPER

Thomas tom′uhs (Θωμᾶς *G2605*, from Aram. תְּאוֹמָא, "twin"). One of the twelve apostles (Matt. 10:3; Mk. 3:18; Lk. 6:15; Acts 1:13). In the fourth gospel, wherever Thomas appears he is also called DIDYMUS, which is the Greek word for "twin" (Jn. 11:16; 20:24; 21:2). It is possible that Thomas was not a personal name but an epithet. In Syriac-speaking churches he was known as Judas Thomas ("Judas the twin"), as is evidenced in several apocryphal works and in the Old Syriac version; the latter at Jn. 14:22, instead of "Judas not Iscariot," has "Thomas" (Syr^s; "Judas Thomas" in Syr^c). In fact, in the *Acts of Thomas* and in the *Book of Thomas the Contender*, "Judas Thomas" is regarded as the twin of Christ himself, a view that has been taken seriously by some scholars and is still held as fact by the Mesopotamian (E Syrian) churches. See THOMAS, ACTS OF; THOMAS, GOSPEL OF; THOMAS THE CONTENDER, BOOK OF.

The character of Thomas exudes through the text of John's gospel. When the Lord resolved to go to Judea to heal LAZARUS against the warning by the other disciples that the Jews wanted to stone him, Thomas exhibited both pessimism and intense loyalty when he said, "Let us also go, that we may die with him" (Jn. 11:16). When Jesus assumed that the disciples knew the way to the Father's house, Thomas was honest and forthright enough to confess openly his ignorance, "Lord, we don't know where you are going, so how can we know the way?" (14:5). The dull and imperfect understanding of Thomas provided Jesus an opportunity to disclose more truth about himself (14:6–7). For some reason, perhaps melancholic and disillusioned, Thomas was not with the other disciples when Jesus appeared to them on the evening of the resurrection (20:24–25a). When told that they had seen the Lord, he refused to be convinced of the reality of Jesus' resurrection unless he could see and touch the tangible evidence (20:25b). For this, "doubting Thomas" has become a byword. When such evidence was presented eight days later, he uttered the grandest expression of faith in the fourth gospel, "My Lord and my God!" (20:28).

Subsequently, Thomas had been fishing on the Sea of Galilee with six other disciples and caught nothing when Jesus appeared to them the third time after his resurrection (Jn. 21:1–14). Directed by the Lord to cast their net on the right side of the boat, they brought in a net full of fish, after which they had breakfast together. The last NT mention of Thomas is as a loyal follower of Jesus after the ascension, gathered in a prayer meeting with the eleven, some women, Mary the mother of Jesus, and his brethren (Acts 1:12–14).

There are questionable traditions concerning the postresurrection missionary activities of Thomas. According to ORIGEN, cited by EUSEBIUS (*Eccl. Hist.* 3.1), Thomas worked in Parthia. The *Acts of Thomas* (2nd cent.) tells how the world was partitioned by lot as a mission field by the disciples. According to this apocryphal and conflicting account, Thomas's lot was

Byzantine icon of the apostle Thomas. (From Antakya, Turkey.)

India, where he experienced many trials and martyrdom, and was buried by his converts. According to CLEMENT OF ALEXANDRIA (*Stromateis* 4), however, Thomas died a natural death, not as a martyr. His supposed remains were exhibited there as late as the 16th cent. Other adventures are narrated in the apocryphal *Preaching of St. Thomas* and the *Martyrdom of St. Thomas in India*. Present-day Christians of St. Thomas of India base their claims to spiritual descent from this missionary father largely on these documents. Another tradition states that his remains were brought to EDESSA in Mesopotamia, and from there to Ortona in Italy during the Crusades. (For a history of interpretation, see G. W. Most, *Doubting Thomas* [2005].)

A. M. ROSS

Thomas, Acts of. The latest of the five major apocryphal Acts, and the only one that has survived complete, it is extant in Greek and Syriac, with portions also in other languages. It is generally agreed that the Greek text is a translation from an original Syriac, but some scholars have held that it was composed in Greek, translated into Syriac, and subsequently, when the Greek original was lost, retranslated into Greek. At any rate, the extant Greek is generally recognized to be closer to the original than the present Syriac text, which has been subjected to catholicizing revision. The Greek version is accordingly given the preference, except in the case of the famous "Hymn of the Pearl," where the Syriac is believed to be closer to the original.

I. Character. A further subject of debate is the problem of the character of the work. G. Bornkamm, for example, calls it "a Christian-Gnostic variety of the Hellenistic-Oriental romance," and claims that it represents "the Gnostic Christianity of Syria in the third century" (*NTAp* [1963–65], 2:428, 440). Findlay, on the other hand, writes, "Gnostic tones are so little discernible that it is a misuse of words to describe the Acts as a Gnostic writing, or indeed as anything else than a product of Eastern piety of the type characteristic of the Syrian church" (A. F. Findlay, *Byways in Early Christian Literature: Studies in the Uncanonical Gospels and Acts* [1923], 278–79).

This conflict of opinion is partly due to differences in definition of the term *Gnostic* (see GNOSTICISM), but two other points should also be noted. (a) Findlay later (pp. 288–89) admits the presence of "unmistakable Gnostic expressions" in the Greek version that are "less prominent" in the Syriac. (b) On the other hand Bornkamm's case rests upon a synthesis of motifs; that a Gnostic view of redemption underlies the *Acts* "becomes immediately clear when we assemble together into a uniform picture the most important traits of the Gnostic Redeemer-myth, which are scattered over the Acts as a whole" (p. 429). The presence of such scattered motifs is, however, no guarantee that the book *presupposes* a full-scale developed Redeemer-myth. The motifs may be "known from Gnosticism," but some of them are shared also by "orthodox" writers and even in the *Acts* may not originally have been intended to carry a Gnostic meaning; at some points, the text allows a non-Gnostic interpretation as well as the Gnostic.

The book was popular in Gnostic circles, particularly among the MANICHEANS, but as in other cases there is a danger of imposing upon the text a later interpretation—of reading back the interpretation that the Manicheans placed upon it; for the work also enjoyed considerable favor in orthodox circles. An ascetic, world-renouncing attitude was common in early Eastern Christianity, and such traits should not always be ascribed to Gnostic influence. Therefore it is probably better to leave the Gnostic origin and character of the book an open question. It is generally agreed to have been written in SYRIA, probably in EDESSA, early in the 3rd cent., and this would locate its place of origin at least in close proximity to a Gnostic milieu.

II. Contents. In its present form, the book falls into thirteen "Acts" followed by the "Martyrdom". When the apostles divide the world into spheres for mission, Judas Thomas is appointed to India, but does not relish the prospect. Jesus forces his hand by selling him to the merchant Abban, sent by King Gundaphorus (a historical figure of the 1st cent. A.D.). On the way they attend a royal wedding in Andrapolis, where Thomas betrays his miraculous powers and is summoned to pray for the bridal pair. Jesus appears in his likeness, and wins them to the life of chastity.

Having arrived in India, Thomas was commissioned by Gundaphorus to build a palace, but he diverts the funds to poor relief. The king's wrath is averted by the sudden death and return to life of his brother, who reveals that Thomas has built a palace for him in heaven. Thomas then sets out on a journey, on which he meets and overcomes a serpent that has killed a youth; rides upon a talking colt, which later dies; expels a demon from a woman; cleanses a murderer and restores his victim to life. These first six Acts are loosely strung together, but from the seventh on, the story is more closely knit together.

A captain of King Misdaeus seeks Thomas's help, and on the road, the beasts drawing their wagon grow weary with the heat; at Thomas's bidding, wild asses tamely take their place. He heals the captain's wife and daughter, and then Mygdonia, wife of the king's kinsman Charisius, comes to see the new phenomenon and is converted. Her refusal to have further dealings with him enrages Charisius, who has Thomas imprisoned. Misdaeus sends his wife Tertia to plead with Mygdonia, but she too is converted, along with her son Vazan and his wife. Thomas is executed at the king's command, but his converts persevere in the faith despite pressure, and are eventually left in peace. Finally a demon-possessed son of Misdaeus is healed by dust from the apostle's tomb (his bones had already been carried away to the West) and Misdaeus himself is converted.

III. Special features. This brief outline shows the ascetic ideal characteristic of the book. Thomas is the typical ascetic saint: "continually he fasts and prays, and eats only bread with salt, and his drink is water, and he wears one garment in fair weather or in foul, and takes nothing from anyone, and what he has he gives to the poor" (*Acts of Thomas* 20). This ideal is emphasized also in the numerous sermons, prayers, and hymns that are scattered throughout the book. The Christian life here presented is one of self-denial, of renunciation of the world and its pleasures. "The married state is a state of sin. Home and the love of children are excluded from the province of religion" (Findlay notices that this is a strange aberration from the teaching of Jesus). The emphasis, however, is not on asceticism alone, for stress is also laid on compassion—concern for the poor and the afflicted. This is brought out in the story of Gundaphorus's palace: good deeds insure a heavenly dwelling place. The supreme aim is the blessed life beyond; the path to it is by self-denial and almsgiving.

Another feature is the prominence given to the SACRAMENTS, chs. 156–58 being of special interest for their detailed description of the ritual: sealing with oil, baptism, and the Eucharist. The absence in some passages of any reference to water baptism leads Bornkamm to postulate a Gnostic sect that knew only unction as the sacrament of initiation, the references to baptism elsewhere being due to Catholic interpretations. Similarly, the Eucharist is a communion in the bread alone, with at most a cup of water; references in certain prayers to the body and blood of Christ are also later interpolations, such as are more clearly visible in the Syriac. This may, however, press the evidence too far in the Gnostic direction; the argument from silence is notoriously dangerous, and there may be other explanations for the author's failure to mention baptism where one might expect it. It is noteworthy that the Gnostic expressions recognized by Findlay occur in consecration prayers.

IV. The Hymn of the Pearl. Special mention must be made of two great hymns contained in this document, the "Wedding Hymn" (chs. 6–7), which at least lends itself to interpretation in terms of the Valentinian imagery of the bridal chamber, and the "Hymn of the Pearl" (chs. 108–13), often described as one of the most beautiful pieces of literature produced by the early church, but also presenting highly complex problems of interpretation. It tells of a prince, sent to Egypt to bring back a pearl. Fed by guile on the unclean food of Egypt, he forgets his mission and remains sunk in a sleep of lethargy until he is aroused by a letter from home that stirs him to fulfill his task. A notable feature is the description of the splendid robe that he left behind at home, and with which he is clothed on his return.

That the story is an allegory is beyond question, but who is the prince? The obvious interpretation is to take him as the symbol of the soul, and the story as an allegory of man's redemption. What then is the pearl for which he was sent? On the other hand, the pearl is often a symbol for the soul, and some scholars have found here an allegory of the Redeemer; but this view also has its problems. The hymn is not specially appropriate to its context, and may be an adaptation of a very much older poem; whether it was an original Gnostic composition remains in doubt.

V. Other links. Thomas is associated in tradition with the planting of Christianity in Edessa, where his bones were preserved. There are links between the *Acts* and the Coptic *Gospel of Thomas* (see THOMAS, GOSPEL OF), also perhaps of Syriac origin. Attempts have been made to connect the Hymn of the Pearl with Bardesanes, or at least with his school, but again there is debate. In short, the book gives rise to many problems for which no final solution is possible. Its significance lies in its presentation of the ideals of an early branch of Eastern Christianity akin to, though not necessarily influenced by, the doctrines of certain Gnostic groups. (English trans. in *NTAp*, rev. ed. [1991–92], 2:322–411; see also P. H. Poirier, *L'Hymne de la Perle des Actes de Thomas: Introduction, text-traduction, commentaire* [1981], and A. F. J. Klijn, *The Acts of Thomas: Introduction, Text, and Commentary*, 2nd ed. [2003].)

R. McL. WILSON

Thomas, Apocalypse of. Long known only from its condemnation in the 6th-cent. *Decretum Gelasianum*, this *Apocalypse* is a comparatively recent discovery, first identified in 1908 and now extant in two versions. The longer one, contained in a Munich MS and in fragments in Rome and Verona, falls into two distinct parts: (1) An account of the events and signs preceding the last judgment, presenting a survey of history in the guise of prophecy as in Daniel and other apocalyptic books. Some historical references, and in particular a cryptic allusion to Arcadius and Honorius (if not an interpolation), date this section to the 5th cent. at the earliest. (2) A description of the seven signs at the end of the world, distributing the events of the end over seven days (the only apocryphal apocalypse that does so). This section is more akin to the canonical Revelation of John. There is an Old English form of this version in the 9th-cent. Anglo-Saxon MS of Vercelli.

The shorter version corresponds to the second section above and probably represents more nearly the original apocalypse, later expanded by various revisions. It is contained in another Munich MS and in a 5th-cent. Vienna MS, which is the oldest witness. If the allusion to Arcadius and Honorius is authentic (it is missing from the Anglo-Saxon), Latin was the original language of the longer version, but there are grounds for suspecting a Greek original behind the Latin texts. (English trans. of both versions in J. K. Elliott, *The Apocryphal New Testament* [1993], 645–51; of the shorter version in *NTAp*, 2:749–52.)

R. McL. WILSON

Thomas, Gospel of. Two distinct documents are extant under this title.

I. The Infancy Gospel of Thomas. This work is important for the influence that it exerted on the later infancy gospels, many of which combine parts of it with material drawn from the *Protevangelium of James* (see APOCRYPHAL NEW TESTAMENT I.C, JAMES, PROTEVANGELIUM OF). Its popularity is attested also by its translation into several languages; it is extant in Greek, Syriac, Latin, Georgian, and other versions, and has influenced the Arabic and Armenian infancy gospels and the *Gospel of Pseudo Matthew* (see PSEUDO-MATTHEW, GOSPEL OF). Since IRENAEUS (*Haer.* 1.20.1) alludes to the story found in ch. 6 of the *Infancy Gospel*, this work probably goes back to the 2nd cent.

The *Infancy Gospel* contains stories about the miracles wrought by the boy Jesus between the ages of five and twelve, and ends with the story of Jesus in the temple, taken from Luke. He is presented as an infant prodigy, already possessed in childhood of miraculous powers, but his use of them is not always compatible with the character depicted in the canonical Gospels. Those who thwart him incur the penalty of his displeasure, although later all are healed. As O. Cullmann notes (*NTAp*, 1:442), "All the miracles [Jesus] was later to perform are here anticipated in a particularly blatant fashion. There is, however, a great difference between these miracles and those reported in the canonical Gospels."

Numerous parallels can be cited from nonbiblical legend and from fable. A beam cut too short is miraculously lengthened to the proper size; when he breaks a pitcher, Jesus brings home water in a fold of his garment; caught breaking the Sabbath by modeling birds from clay, he claps his hands and the birds come to life and fly away, conveniently removing the evidence. Three times over he is taken in hand by a teacher, but each time he baffles his instructor. This child has no need of human wisdom, for he already possesses divine wisdom to the full. In short, the historical Jesus has disappeared; this Jesus is no longer human, but a divine being disguised in human semblance. This docetic tendency represents a stage in Christological development with which the church could not remain content, although it is still prevalent among those who think to glorify Jesus by exalting his deity at the expense of his humanity. (English trans. in *NTAp*, 1:439–53.)

II. The Coptic Gospel of Thomas. This document, part of the NAG HAMMADI LIBRARY (NHC II, 2), is not a gospel in the ordinary sense of the term, but rather a collection of LOGIA, that is, sayings and parables attributed to Jesus, usually without a narrative setting. It was first made available in 1956 in a photographic edition by P. Labib; shortly after, the Coptic text was edited and published with English translation (A. Guillaumont et al., *The Gospel according to Thomas* [1959], now superseded by vol. 1 of B. Layton, *Nag Hammadi Codex II, 2–7* together with XIII,2*, Brit. Lib. Or. 4926(1), and P. Oxy. 1, 654, 655 [1989]).

This work has aroused considerable interest and given rise to an extensive literature. Many of the sayings it preserves have a parallel in the canonical Gospels, but in practically every case there is some modification; frequently, sayings from different Gospels, or different parts of one, are combined. This leads to one of the primary questions for research: the relation between the *Gospel of Thomas* and the Synoptics (resemblance to John is rare, although there is often a "Johannine atmosphere"). Other sayings were already known from patristic quotations, and these raise the question of the relation between Thomas and the works quoted by the church fathers. Finally, other sayings are entirely new, most of them of a more or less Gnostic character. See GNOSTICISM.

One thing is certain: all the sayings in the famous OXYRHYNCHUS SAYINGS OF JESUS (POxy 1, 654, and 655) are included in the Coptic gospel, although here again there are problems. The texts agree so closely that in many cases the Coptic can be used to restore the fragmentary Greek, but one saying in POx 1 has a parallel to its first part in Logion 30 of Thomas, whereas the parallel to the second part is in Logion 77. The Greek fragments therefore cannot be taken simply as the Greek original of the Coptic gospel. The possibility exists that they were originally separate (they belong to three different papyrus books) and only subsequently combined into the present *Gospel of Thomas*. The Coptic text again clearly has a history behind it.

The earliest studies tended to regard Thomas as independent of the synoptics, but many scholars have maintained its dependence on the NT Gospels, the variations being explained as tendentious Gnostic modification or adaptation. Not all specialists are convinced of the Gnostic character of the document, and it may be that its history is more complex than has so far been assumed. A Jewish-Christian nucleus, drawing upon oral tradition, later expanded by the inclusion of sayings from the NT Gospels, and finally enlarged and adapted by a Gnostic editor, might well present much the same phenomena; but such a hypothesis would admittedly be difficult to prove. Some sayings that might be independent seem to have tapped the tradition at a later stage than that represented by the NT Gospels.

Parallels with quotations in CLEMENT OF ALEXANDRIA from the *Gospel of the Hebrews* and the *Gospel of the Egyptians* (see separate articles) have led G. Quispel to develop the theory that these, not the canonical Gospels, were the sources of Thomas. Further research has produced parallels with such works as Tatian's DIATESSARON and the CLEMENTINE LITERATURE, and on the basis of this evidence, Quispel has developed a far-reaching hypothesis of the survival of Jewish-Christian influence in Syrian Christianity, and its effects on later theology and on the transmission of the NT text. This would make the *Gospel of Thomas* a very significant document indeed, but, attractive though the theory is, there are too many weak links for it to be considered finally established.

This document has been called "a fifth gospel," which it is not (there are many gospels beside the canonical four); or, a possible source of the Synoptic Gospels, which again it is not; nor can one identify it in any way with the Q source that lies behind Matthew and Luke. On the other hand, although it can be understood as a Gnostic document, to stop there may be to lose valuable insights into the history of the early church.

(Easily accessible English trans. in *NTAp*, 1:110–33, and *NHL*, 124–38. See also R. McL. Wilson, *Studies in the Gospel of Thomas* [1960]; B. E. Gärtner, *The Theology of the Gospel according to Thomas* [1961]; W. Schrage, *Das Verhältnis des Thomas-Evangeliums zur synoptischen Tradition und zu den koptischen Evangelienübersetzungen* [1964]; G. Quispel, *Makarius, das Thomas Evangelium und das Lied von der Perle* [1967]; M. Meyer and H. Bloom, *The Gospel of Thomas: The Hidden Sayings of Jesus* [1992]; R. Valantasis, *The Gospel of Thomas* [1997]; S. J. Patterson and J. M. Robinson, *The Fifth Gospel: The Gospel of Thomas Comes of Age* [1998]; R. Uro, ed., *Thomas at the Crossroads: Essays on the Gospel of Thomas* [1998]; N. Perrin, *Thomas and Tatian: The Relationship between the Gospel of Thomas and the Diatessaron* [2002]; R. Uro, *Thomas: Seeking the Historical Context of the Gospel of Thomas* [2003]; R. Nordsieck, *Das Thomas-Evangelium*, 3rd ed. [2006]; J. M. Asgeirsson et al., eds., *Thomasine Traditions in Antiquity: The Social and Cultural World of the Gospel of Thomas* [2006]; A. D. DeConick, *The Original Gospel of Thomas in Translation* [2007].)

R. McL. WILSON

Thomas, Infancy Gospel of. See THOMAS, GOSPEL OF.

Thomas the Contender, Book of. A Gnostic treatise preserved in Coptic in the NAG HAMMADI LIBRARY (NHC II, 7). This document purports to give "the secret words that the Savior spoke to Judas Thomas which I, Mathaias [Matthew?], wrote down." It begins with a dialogue between the risen Jesus and THOMAS (regarded as Jesus' twin brother); the second part, a short discourse by the Savior, consists of woes and blessings. The contents give expression to typical Gnostic emphases, such as ASCETICISM and the contrast between light and darkness. This work must have originated in Syriac-speaking Christianity (prob. some time after A.D. 200), but the Coptic translation appears to have been made from a Greek copy. (For a brief discussion of competing theories regarding its composition, see *ABD*, 6:529–30; English trans. in *NHL*, 199–207.)

Thomoi thom´oi. KJV Apoc. form of TEMAH (1 Esd. 5:32).

thorn. A woody plant that bears sharp prickles; the term is commonly applied to the prickles themselves. The English terms *thorn* and *thornbush* are used to translate a number of Hebrew words, such as *qôṣ* H7764 (Gen. 3:18 et al.) and *šayit* H8885 (Isa. 5:6 et al.). In the NT it usually renders *akantha* G180 (Matt. 7:16 et al.). In some passages the reference may be to a BRAMBLE, NETTLE, THISTLE, or some unspecified WEED. (See *FFB*, 184–86.)

The first mention of thorns in the Bible is in Gen. 3:18, where they (along with "thistles," Heb. *dardar* H1998) were a part of the curse of the soil owing to ADAM's sin. In Isa. 34:13 we find three different terms: "thorns" (*sirâ* H6106, possibly referring to the hooked thorn), "nettles" (*qimmôś* H7853, rendered "thorns" in Prov. 24:31), and "brambles" (*ḥôaḥ* H2560; NRSV, "thistles"; NJPS, "briers"). Distinguishing among the various Hebrew terms is difficult.

It seems that in Palestine, owing to the hot weather, there must have been numerous types of brambles and seedling briers together with thorny bushes. These would have made it extremely difficult for travelers on foot, moving from one area to another where there were no known roads or paths. On the other hand, these spiny thickets, which must have grown extremely thick, were used by the farmers as hedges (Prov. 15:19 [*ḥēdeq H2537*]; cf. Job 1:10; Isa. 5:5).

There is a fair amount of conjecture in respect of Jdg. 9:14–15, where Hebrew *ʾāṭād H353*, usually rendered "thornbush" or "bramble," may refer specifically to the *Lycium europaeum* (cf. *HALOT*, 1:37, which gives the rendering "buckthorn," a name applied to various species). This shrub, which grows about 8–9 ft. tall, bears small violet-blue flowers that are followed by little crimson berries. Well known in Palestine, it is very thorny or spiny, like the bramble. In v. 15 we read, "let fire come out of the thornbush," and some have noted that the Greek word *batos G1003*, translated "bush" in Lk. 20:37, when referring to Moses and the BURNING BUSH, is exactly the same term translated "briers" or "bramble bush" in Lk. 6:44 (where our Lord says that people would not gather grapes from brambles). What the connection may be, if any, is unclear.

Did the lilies really grow "among thorns" (Cant. 2:16; Heb. *ḥôaḥ H2560*)? Or in this case were the lilies among the nettles, or even among some species of the perennial acanthus? The idea of the text is to give the tremendous contrast between his beautiful "love" and the other less pretty daughters. Lilies among nettles would surely be the contrast required. See also CROWN OF THORNS; FLORA (under *Rosaceae* and *Compositae*); THORN IN THE FLESH.

W. E. SHEWELL-COOPER

thorn in the flesh. The Greek word translated "thorn" in 2 Cor. 12:7 is *skolops G5022*, which originally referred in general to a pointed object, especially a stake (cf. the derived verb *skolopizō*, "to impale"). Subsequently it came to be used of splinters and other sharp objects that might injure the body, and figuratively of anything that might cause vexation. PAUL uses the figure with reference to some irritation that troubled him. Described also as "a messenger from Satan," it was apparently a humiliating condition, for the apostle says it "was given" to him so that he might not become "conceited because of these surpassingly great revelations." Though the people of CORINTH, no doubt, knew the nature of his problem, that knowledge has been lost for nearly two millennia. Many views have been suggested, largely reflecting the trials that beset the interpreters.

Early conjectures related this passage to some unknown physical ailment that Paul refers to elsewhere (Gal. 4:13). Severe headaches, epilepsy, and ophthalmia are among the more persistent suggestions. Some ancient writers thought the reference was to times of severe persecution, while the rendering of the VULGATE, *stimulus carnis meae*, gave support to the ascetic idea of fleshly longings (Latin *stimulus*, "goad," could refer to vexation, but also to incitement). The Reformers thought of temptations to spiritual ineffectiveness. Nearly all modern commentators support the theory of physical malady. William M. Ramsay (*St. Paul the Traveller and the Roman Citizen*, 14th ed. [1920], 94–97) adds malaria to the leading options, while T. Y. Mullins (in *JBL* 76 [1957]: 299–303) presents a convincing argument from the context and from Jewish literature for the view that the "thorn" was a person, an enemy. (For an extensive discussion of the options, see M. E. Thrall, *A Critical and Exegetical Commentary on the Second Epistle to the Corinthians*, ICC, 2 vols. [1994–2000], 2: 806–18.)

W. T. DAYTON

Thoth tot. Greek name for Djehuty (Tehuty), a lunar Egyptian deity, considered the god of knowledge, writing, and magic. Described as the one who interrogates the dead regarding their conduct in life, Thoth was worshiped throughout Egypt, but the center of his cult was in Hermopolis (cf. *DDD*, 861–64). See EGYPT VII.A.

thousand. See NUMBER.

Thought of Norea. See NOREA, THOUGHT OF.

Thracia thray´shee-uh (Θράκη; gentilic Θρᾷξ or Θράκιος, "Thracian"). Ancient Thrace, to use the more common term, was the eastern half of the Balkan peninsula. This at least was the case in historic times, though there is evidence that the Thracian tribes were pushed back before 1300 B.C. from the Adriatic to the Axius. After 480 B.C. they lost all territory W of the Strymon to the intruding Macedonians (see MACEDONIA). Thrace was a rugged land, including the wooded mountain region of Haemus, the fertile territory of the Hebrus Valley, and the steppe country of the Dobrudja. The language was Indo-European, the social structure a conglomerate of monarchical tribes, each with a feudal aristocracy and a serf-like peasantry. The Thracians had the elements of culture—some poetry and music. They worshiped DIONYSUS, the vegetation god. For the rest, they bore a somber reputation in the civilized Hellenic world for sheer savagery, human sacrifice, barbaric tattooing, and heavy drinking.

There were Greek colonies on the southern and eastern coasts of Thrace from 700 B.C. onward, and Greeks worked the Thracian gold and silver mines of Pangaeus. Thracians fought in Greek armies as light-armed mercenaries. They found brief unity against PERSIA, which controlled them briefly at the end of the 5th cent., fell again into tribal disunity after 400, and in 342 lost their southern territories to Philip II of Macedon. The tribesmen of this area provided ALEXANDER THE GREAT with some valuable light infantry. Lysimachus controlled Thrace from 323 to 281, and the period saw some Greek penetration, succeeded by a return to dissension.

ROME did not subdue the region systematically, until M. Crassus undertook the task in 28 B.C. and L. Piso in 12 B.C. CLAUDIUS, however, half a century later, was still finding the tribes troublesome, and he divided the area to make southern and central Thrace one province, assigning the N to Moesia. Rough terrain and surviving barbarism under a hostile northern frontier combined to keep Thrace a military province. The only biblical reference is in the APOCRYPHA, which mentions in passing an unnamed Thracian soldier (2 Macc. 12:35). (See further S. Casson, *Macedonia, Thrace and Illyria* [1926]; A. H. M. Jones, *The Cities of the Eastern Roman Provinces*, 2nd ed. [1971], ch. 1; N. Theodossiev, *North-Western Thrace from the Fifth to the First Centuries BC* [2000].)   E. M. BLAIKLOCK

Thraseas thray-see´uhs (Θρασαῖος). Father of Apollonius; the latter was governor of COELOSYRIA and PHOENICIA (2 Macc. 3:5 KJV). However, the NRSV emends the text to read "Apollonius of Tarsus" (an interpretation rejected by J. A. Goldstein, *II Maccabees*, AB 41A [1983], 204).

three. See NUMBER; THIRD DAY.

Three Steles of Seth. SETH, THREE STELES OF.

Three Taverns (Τρεῖς Ταβέρναι *G5553*, from Latin *Tres Tabernae*). The name is a misleading rendering of the Latin designation of a staging post on the APPIAN WAY, 33 mi. from ROME (the Latin

Excavations at the staging post known as the Three Taverns.

term *taberna* means "booth, inn, shop"). It stands at the junction of the Via Appia and the side road to Antium, near the modern town of Cisterna. It owed its importance to the fact that it was one day's journey from Rome for fast travelers proceeding S from the city to Brundisium, the port for Greece and intermediate places (Cicero, *Ad Att.* 2.12). Representatives of the Roman Christian community met Paul's party here (Acts 28:15).

E. M. BLAIKLOCK

Three Young Men (Children), Song of the. See AZARIAH, PRAYER OF.

threshing. The process of separating seed from the harvested plant (Heb. *dûš H1889*, "to tread" [cf. noun *dayiš H1912*]; *ḥābaṭ H2468*, "to beat"; Gk. *aloaō G262*, "to thresh"). Threshing by treading or trampling is distinguished from beating with a rod as applied to garden plants, such as dill, cummin, and flax (Isa. 28:27-28). For concealment from the Midianites, GIDEON resorted to beating out wheat (Jdg. 6:11) in the winepress rather than on the THRESHING FLOOR. Implements used in threshing were sledges, forks, and shovels. Sledges (Isa. 41:15; Amos 1:3) were built of heavy wood, studded underneath with sharp stones, potsherds, or iron spikes. The cart was built with studded rollers (Isa. 28:27-28). Benches with backrests were built on top for drivers. Sledges were drawn by teams of oxen, donkeys, or horses, and encircled the pile of grain heaped in the center of the threshing floor. Women and men drove the teams while others with forks raked loose sheaves into the sledge path and raked away the threshed straw. The "winnowing fork" (Gk. *ptyon G4768*, Matt. 3:12; Lk. 3:17) and the shovel were also used for tossing to allow the wind to blow the chaff away. It was customary for the whole family to camp near the threshing floor at harvest and share in the work. Prophets made figurative use of threshing, at times with judicial implications (Jer. 51:33; Dan. 2:35; Mic. 4:12; Matt. 3:12). A full threshing floor was indicative of God's blessings (Joel 2:24). See AGRICULTURE V.C.

G. B. FUNDERBURK

threshing floor. A level, circular area 25-40 ft. in diameter, the threshing floor (Heb. *gōren H1755*; Gk. *halōn G272*) was constructed in or near the grain field, preferably on an elevated spot exposed to the wind. It was prepared by removing the loose stones (by which a grain containing border is made), then wetting and tamping the ground, and finally sweeping it. JOSEPH camped at a threshing floor (Gen. 50:10). DAVID built an altar on a former threshing floor, later the site of the temple (2 Sam. 24:18-25; 2 Chr. 3:1). RUTH visited BOAZ at his threshing floor (Ruth 3:3); and prophets used the term figuratively (Mic. 4:12; cf. Matt. 3:12; Lk. 3:17).

G. B. FUNDERBURK

threshold. The stone or wood sill of a doorway, hence the entrance (see DOOR). Foundation sacrifices buried under thresholds confirm that it was often a sacred place. References to thresholds in the OT (Heb. *miptān H5159* and *sap H6197*) are sometimes related to violent acts (Jdg. 19:27; 1 Sam. 5:4-5; 1 Ki. 14:17). Other passages refer to the thresholds of the TEMPLE, which were lined with gold (2 Chr. 3:7; NIV here and elsewhere, "doorframes"). Priests and Levites served as guardians of the threshold, that is, as doorkeepers (2 Ki. 22:4 et al.; apparently three in number, 25:18 [= Jer. 52:24]).

The doorposts and thresholds of the temple "shook" when ISAIAH had his vision (Isa. 6:4). It was a place where God's glory rested (Ezek. 9:3; 10:4) and where the priests worshiped (Ezek. 46:2). It figured in AMOS's vision of God (Amos 9:1). Water flowed from the threshold of the temple in EZEKIEL's vision (Ezek. 47:1). In Zeph. 1:9, "I will punish all who avoid stepping on the threshold," the reference is probably to a superstitious cultic practice (cf. 1 Sam. 5:5-6); others think it alludes to those who would mount up a pedestal for idols, or that it has in view rushing through the door for the purposes of plundering the temple.

F. B. HUEY, JR.

throne. The seat of a sovereign, and a symbol of authority and rule. It was a ceremonial chair (Heb. *kissēʾ H4058*, Aram. *korsēʾ H10372*, Gk. *thronos G2585*) occupied by a KING, PRIEST, JUDGE, or military leader. As a symbol of divine power and authority, it is frequently associated with God and his MESSIAH.

Mention is made of the throne of PHARAOH (Gen. 41:40; Exod. 11:5), of the king of NINEVEH (Jon. 3:6), of NEBUCHADNEZZAR (Dan. 5:20), of XERXES (Esth. 5:1–2), of governors (Neh. 3:7), and of priests (1 Sam. 4:13). "To sit on the throne" was synonymous with rulership or dynasty (2 Sam. 3:10; 1 Ki. 1:13). Promise of an eternal throne was made to DAVID and his descendants (1 Ki. 2:45; Ps. 89:36; Jer. 33:17), conditioned upon faithfulness (1 Ki. 8:25; 9:5; Ps. 132:12). It also could signify the beginning of a purge of another dynasty (1 Ki. 16:11; 2 Ki. 10:3). The king was to execute justice and righteousness on the throne (1 Ki. 10:9; 2 Chr. 9:8; Prov. 29:14) and was to be faithful (2 Ki. 10:30; Jer. 22:30).

The throne, as a symbol of authority, was portable. On one occasion, for example, both AHAB king of Israel and JEHOSHAPHAT king of Judah sat on their thrones at the threshing floor at the entrance of the gate of SAMARIA (1 Ki. 22:10). JEREMIAH warned that the conquering kings would place their thrones before the gates of Jerusalem (Jer. 1:15); he also foretold that NEBUCHADNEZZAR would set his throne at the entrance to Pharaoh's palace in TAHPANHES (43:10).

Ancient thrones were of opulent magnificence. The remains of a throne of rock crystal were found in the ruins of SENNACHERIB's palace. SOLOMON's throne was made of IVORY overlaid with gold, with six steps leading up to it, and with a lion on either side of each step. The back was carved with the figure of a bull's head, the symbol of strength, and two lions stood beside the arm rests (1 Ki. 10:18–20). The lions were probably carved figures of winged CHERUBIM. The throne room was called the "Hall of Justice" (7:7).

God as the divine king is pictured sitting on his throne surrounded by the heavenly host (1 Ki. 22:19; Ps. 11:4; Rev. 5:11). Sometimes HEAVEN is called his throne (Isa. 66:1), which is also said to be in the temple (6:1; Ezek. 43:6–7); and in the future JERUSALEM will be called "The Throne of the LORD" (Jer. 3:17). His throne is described in visionary language (Ezek. 1:26; Rev. 4:4–6). God is said to administer righteous judgment from his throne (Ps. 9:4), appointing earthly kings (Job 36:7) and overthrowing them (Hag. 2:22). His is an everlasting (Ps. 93:2; Lam. 5:19), universal (Ps. 103:19) reign.

Messianic passages suggest that one called the Branch will build the temple and sit on the throne (Zech. 6:13). The Ancient of Days will sit on his throne with priests by his side (Dan. 7:9). When the SON OF MAN returns in glory, he will take his place on his throne (Matt. 25:31; Lk. 1:32). Believers will sit on thrones and judge the twelve tribes of Israel (Matt. 19:28). On the other hand, warning is given that anyone who would exalt his throne on high with God's will be cast into SHEOL (Isa. 14:13–15), where kings will rise to greet the new arrivals (vv. 9–10).

The ascension of the king was accompanied by an enthronement festival and rite. The main elements of it can be reconstructed from the detailed accounts of Solomon's enthronement (1 Ki. 1:32–40) and that of JOASH (2 Ki. 11:4–20). The main elements were the anointing of the king, the blowing of the trumpets, a procession accompanying the new king from the holy place to the throne where obeisance was paid to him. Divine kingship was widely accepted in the ANE, but the belief was not universal. The kings of Israel were not considered divine but only God's unique instruments. (See S. H. Hooke, ed., *The Labyrinth* [1935]; A. R. Johnson, *Sacral Kingship in Ancient Israel* [1955].)

F. B. HUEY, JR.

thrush. A term applied to many species of small, plain-colored, singing birds of the family *Turdidae*. It is used by the NIV to render Hebrew *ʿāgûr* H6315, which occurs twice (Isa. 38:14; Jer. 8:7). See discussion under SWALLOW.

thumb. This short, thick digit constitutes the most versatile of the five fingers (Heb. *bōhen* H991). Its attachment at the wrist facilitates its rotation into a position in which its tip can directly oppose the tips of any one of the other fingers of the same hand. Experience shows that the loss of the thumb severely cripples the hand. Under modern workmen's compensation laws this loss receives a high percentage of monetary recompense. Modern surgery often endeavors to make one of the other fingers of the hand function as a thumb by making attachments that are similar to those of the thumb, frequently with a fair measure of success. It is therefore noteworthy that special prominence is given to the thumbs of AARON's sons in connection with their consecration to the priestly ministry of the tabernacle, since consecration involves the whole being, and especially those parts of the body that are most serviceable (Exod. 29:20; Lev. 8:23–24; cf. also 14:14 et al.). P. E. ADOLPH

Thummim. See URIM AND THUMMIM.

thunder. The Hebrew term most often used for "thunder" is *qôl H7754*, a common word that more generally means "sound, voice." It almost always occurs with some other manifestation of storm, such as lightning (Job 28:26), hail (Exod. 9:23), and rain (1 Sam. 12:17). In several poetic passages the noun *raʿam H8308* occurs (Job 26:14 et al.; cf. also the cognate verb *rāʿam H8306*, which in the qal stem means "to roar," but in the hiphil, "to [cause] thunder," 1 Sam. 2:10 et al.). In the narrative of the giving of the law on SINAI it is very clear that the thunder is one demonstration of the divine power (Exod. 19:16; 20:18). Nowhere, however, is there any connection, as was alleged in the 19th cent., between the TETRAGRAMMATON (YHWH) and the concept of thunder. The thunder is never God; it is only a phenomenon controlled by him (1 Sam. 12:18).

In the NT, the common Greek term *brontē G1103* is used throughout exclusively. Like the thunder of the OT, that of the NT is often representative of some divine activity (e.g., Jn. 12:29). The largest number of references by far are in Revelation (Rev. 4:5 et al.). These are in all cases allusions to the scene at SINAI at the giving of the law. In Mk. 3:17, the only other occurrence of the term in the NT, it is used to describe the two disciples, James the son of Zebedee and his brother John. See BOANERGES. W. WHITE, JR.

Thunder, Perfect Mind. An obscure philosophical treatise preserved in the NAG HAMMADI LIBRARY (NHC VI, 2). In it, a female speaker delivers a revelation, the first part of which includes these statements: "I was sent forth from [the] power, / and I have come to those who reflect upon me / ... For I am the first and the last. / I am the honored one and the scorned one. / I am the whore and the holy one. / ... I am the barren one / and many are her sons. / ... I am the bride and the bridegroom, / and it is my husband who begot me. / I am the mother of my father / and the sister of my husband, / and he is my offspring" (*NHL*, 297). Similar paradoxical descriptions characterize most of the document, and even the title proves inscrutable. There is no clear connection between this work and other writings of antiquity, and it is impossible to determine its date, origin, or readership. (See also P.-H. Poirier and W.-P. Funk, *Le tonnerre, intellect parfait (NH VI, 2)* [1995]; *ABD*, 6:545–46.)

Thunder, Sons of. See BOANERGES.

Thutmose thyoot´mohs, thyoot-moh´suh (Egyptian *dḥwty-ms* or Djehutymes, "[the god] Thoth is born" or "born of Thoth"; see THOTH). Variant spellings include Thutmoses (-mosis), Tuthmosis, Thothmes. An Egyptian name popular during the New Kingdom, borne by four kings of the 18th dynasty. See EGYPT V.E.

(1) Thutmose I, the third king of the dynasty (c. 1505–1492 B.C.), was the son of Amenhotep I. A vigorous ruler, Thutmose I engaged in military expeditions in Nubia (see ETHIOPIA), reaching beyond the Third Cataract, and in Asia, where he crossed the EUPHRATES and set up a memorial stela. His tomb was the first to be located in the Valley of the Tombs of the Kings (Biban el-Moluk), W of THEBES. He did some building at Karnak, where one of his obelisks still stands.

(2) His son, Thutmose II, had an unimpressive reign (c. 1492–1479). He married his half-sister, Hatshepsut, and they had a daughter (who would eventually marry Thutmose III).

(3) Thutmose III was the son of Thutmose II by a concubine. Upon the death of his father c. 1479, the young Thutmose III was crowned, but Hatshepsut succeeded in becoming regent and "king." Thutmose III remained in a subordinate and obscure position until her death (c. 1457), serving as a priest in the temple of Amon in Karnak (see AMON #4), where an inscription purports to describe how he was divinely chosen for the kingship. His brilliant victory over an Asiatic coalition at MEGIDDO marked the first of seventeen campaigns in Palestine-Syria. Like his grandfather (Thutmose I), he crossed the Euphrates and set up

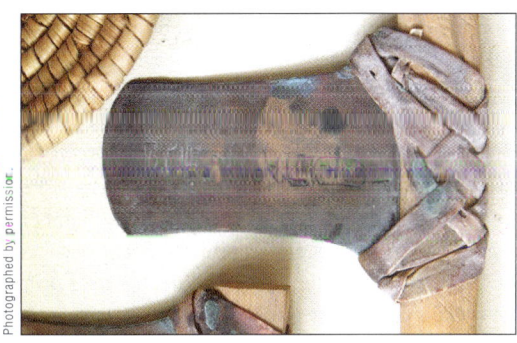

Ancient Egyptian ax discovered in a tomb at Qourna and bearing the name of Thutmose (III).

a stela. In this area he also engaged in a celebrated elephant hunt. In the S he extended the boundary to Jebel Barkal (Napata), just below the Fourth Cataract.

Famous as a military strategist and capable as an administrator, Thutmose III created the Egyptian empire. He built extensively at Karnak: the Hall of the Annals, where the accounts of his expeditions were recorded; the Sixth Pylon; the Seventh Pylon; and the large Festival Hall to the E of the site of the Middle Kingdom structures. His mortuary temple, now largely destroyed, stood at the edge of the western desert. He also built at Medinet Habu and other sites in Egypt and Nubia. He died c. 1425 and was succeeded by Amenhotep II.

(4) Thutmose IV, the son of Amenhotep II, was the last of the Thutmosids (c. 1400–1390). His Dream Stela, located between the forelegs of the Sphinx at Giza, tells how he became king.

The name Thutmose does not appear in the Bible, but Thutmose III has sometimes been regarded as the pharaoh who was ruling at the time of the Israelite oppression. (See further W. F. Edgerton, *The Thutmosid Succession* [1933]; J. A. Wilson, *The Burden of Egypt* [1951], 166–205; G. Steindorff and K. C. Seele, *When Egypt Ruled the East*, 2nd ed. [1957], 34–46, 53–72; A. H. Gardiner, *Egypt of the Pharaohs* [1961], 177–205; B. M. Bryan, *The Reign of Thutmose IV* [1991], D. B. Redford, *The Wars in Syria and Palestine of Thutmose III* [2003]; E. H. Cline and D. O'Connor, *Thutmose III: A New Biography* [2006].)   C. E. De Vries

Thyatira thī'uh-tī'ruh (Ουάτειρα G2587). A city some 20 mi. ESE of Pergamum, on a valley road in the alluvial plain between the Hermus and Caicus Rivers. Both in the days of Pergamum's leadership in W Asia Minor and later, when international politics thrust Rome strongly into the great peninsula, the city derived strength and wealth from the fact that it was a nodal point of communications. The city was founded, doubtless on some Anatolian site, by Seleucus I, the general who, of all four successors of Alexander the Great, inherited the largest area. Seleucus's kingdom stretched from far beyond Antioch of Syria to the Hermus valley, where its frontiers pressed hard on those of Lysimachus, who held part of the old Ionian littoral of Asia Minor. Seleucus planted a demobilized group of Alexander's Macedonian veterans there to form a determined barrier against all attempts to disturb the border.

In 282 B.C., Philetaerus, ruler of the Pergamenians, rebelled, and a dynamic state, destined to endure for a century and a half, was founded. The new nation of Pergamum formed a buffer area between Seleucus and Lysimachus, but a state so founded could not but be militarily alert, and Thyatira, a guard post on the eastern road, stood in the front rank against possible aggression from the E. The history of the place, pieced precariously together from ruins and coins, suggests that Thyatira on its wavering frontier often changed hands, as Syrian or Pergamenian power flowed or ebbed on the borderlands.

Thyatira, faced with this inevitable garrison role, had no strong acropolis like Sardis and Pergamum. The city lay on a small hill, and it was valuable in strategy only because a confident defense force there could break the impetus of a hostile assault, while decisive defense was organized in depth behind. This duty imposed on a vulnerable city a spirited readiness to face peril and fight, without reliance on natural defenses, or on anything but personal valor. Religion reflected this duty and attitude. The Macedonian soldiers who were first settled there adopted the worship of a local patron hero, who appears on early coins as a warrior on horseback, armed with a battle axe; hence the symbolism of the risen Christ in John's apocalyptic letter.

Rome appeared in force in Asia after her defeat of the Syrian Antiochus III in 189 B.C., and the area passed permanently into Roman control when the last of the Pergamenian kings, sensing the shape of the future, bequeathed his kingdom to the rising republic in 133 B.C. With the "Roman Peace," tranquility came to Thyatira. Under CLAUDIUS, Thyatira began to issue its own coinage once more, for the first time after the lapse of two full centuries. The abundance of Thyatiran coins, continuing right into the 3rd cent., suggests a vigorous commerce. Paul's first convert in Europe was LYDIA, a Thyatiran who sold purple cloth in PHILIPPI, hundreds of miles from home (Acts 16:14). The PURPLE or crimson, which dyed the cloth that Lydia sold, was a local manufacture from the madder root, a cheap rival of Phoenician murex dye.

Commercial prosperity attracted a large Jewish minority to Thyatira, for the agricultural Jews began in exile to assume monetary and commercial interests, which were to become their enduring mark (see DIASPORA). Dyed cloth and garments, as well as bronze armor, were famous exports. A coin of Thyatira shows Hephaestus, the divine smith, hammering a helmet on an anvil, and the Greek word in the apocalyptic letter for "burnished bronze" (*chalkolibanon* G5909, Rev. 2:18, also 1:15), found only in Revelation and writings that depend on it, may have been a Thyatiran trade name, caught up for local color. Commerce, indeed, may have been the crux of the Christians' problem in the city. Inscriptions are not numerous, but they mention workers in wool, linen, leather, and bronze, potters, bakers, dyers, and slavers. Each had their guild like that of the silversmiths of EPHESUS.

PAUL's first letter to CORINTH is clear indication that the trade guilds, with their demanding social life, their pagan ritual, and their periodic feasts, were to be a serious problem for the Christian member pledged by conscience to abjure the licentiousness of the world about them (see CORINTHIANS, FIRST EPISTLE TO THE). It was difficult to abstain from the guild festivities without losing one's business and social acceptance. To conform meant exposure to the licentious background and pagan ritual that marked the guild dinner.

The section of the church that dangerously sought some form of saving compromise — the NICOLAITANS of two other accompanying epistles in the Apocalypse (Rev. 2:6, 15) — seem to have been led by an able woman whom John called "Jezebel." This term was deliberately chosen, for the marriage of AHAB with JEZEBEL of TYRE (1 Ki. 16:31 et al.) was a disastrous compromise, as ELIJAH showed, a damaging arrangement doubtless to keep trade flowing between Samaria and the Phoenicians. John denounced her and pronounced a fierce commination: "So I will cast her on a bed of suffering, and I will make those who commit adultery with her suffer intensely, unless they repent of her ways" (Rev. 2:22). That *she* cannot repent she has demonstrated. A Thyatiran inscription quoted by W. M. Ramsay shows that it was not customary for respectable women to feast publicly with men (*The Letters to the Seven Churches of Asia* [1905], 353). A leading citizen is recorded to have given a religious feast. Men and women were segregated for the occasion. The verse of grim menace probably means that such looseness can only lead to ruin. Therefore let the woman's victims desert her, and leave her to the doom her willful perversion must inevitably bring.

Such heresy was to become rife in the church, as John's last letter shows. Perhaps Thyatira saw the beginnings. The exhortation concludes, "Now I say to the rest of you in Thyatira, to you who do not hold to her teaching and have not learned Satan's so-called deep secrets (I will not impose any other burden on you): Only hold on to what you have until I come" (Rev. 2:24–25). The promise that

Thyatira.

Remains of the main street (cardo) in the city of Thyatira.

follows (vv. 26–27) reflects the military nature of the place. Jezebel is a striking figure of speech replete with OT significance, of compromise and apostasy for the sake of commerce and trade partnership with pagan wealth and power. (See further E. M. Blaiklock, *The Cities of the New Testament* [1965], ch. 20; E. Yamauchi, *The Archaeology of New Testament Cities in Western Asia Minor* [1980], ch. 3; C. J. Hemer, *The Letters to the Seven Churches of Asia in Their Local Setting* [1986], ch. 6.)

E. M. Blaiklock

thyine wood. See CITRON.

Tiamat tee-ah'maht. The name of the goddess of the primordial salt water ocean, the antagonist of the hero-god in the great Babylonian national epic, ENUMA ELISH. In the Mesopotamian texts the name is written with a set of pseudoideographic signs, the phonetic element *ti* followed by the Sumerian compound *GEMEAN*, meaning in this case, "ti (woman-mountain)" but pronounced as *ti amt at* in the lexical lists. Tiamat is a great ugly monster who becomes angry with her own offspring of an innumerable set of lesser gods, similar to the COSMOGONY of Hesiod. The lesser gods select a champion (in the older stories MARDUK, in the later ASSHUR), who then fights a cosmic battle with the chaotic sea. As a result the dead corpse of Tiamat is divided up and separated into the lower and upper cosmos. *Enuma Elish* states in its parallelistic fashion: "he split her like a bivalve into two parts, half of her he set above and ceiled it as sky, he set a bar, he set out watchmen, he exhorted them not to let her waters escape" (4.137–40). There are literary allusions to this myth in many ANE traditions. The old proposal that the Hebrew term *tĕhôm* H9333 in Gen. 1:2 (see DEEP, THE) derives from the name Tiamat is now generally rejected. (See D. T. Tsumura, *Creation and Destruction: A Reappraisal of the Chaoskampf Theory in the Old Testament* [2005]; *DDD*, 867–69.) See also MYTH II.A.

W. White, Jr.

Tiberias ti-bihr'ee-uhs (Τιβεριάς G5500). A city on the western shore of the Sea of Galilee, halfway down the coast of the lake (see GALILEE, SEA OF). Tiberias itself is mentioned only once in the NT (Jn. 6:23), but the name was extended to the lake, especially in Gentile nomenclature, and John uses it twice in that sense (6:1; 21:1). Modern Tiberias is known in Hebrew as Teburya (Arab. Ṭabariyeh).

Herod Antipas (see HEROD V) founded Tiberias between the years A.D. 18 and 22. Sir George Adam Smith rests his dating conjectures on coinage (*The Historical Geography of the Holy Land*, 25th ed. [1931], 290 n. 2). A coin of Tiberias, issued in the principate of CLAUDIUS, is dated in the thirty-third year of the town. Claudius died in 54, and this would take the foundation back to 21. Two coins of Tiberias, issued under TRAJAN, are dated in the eightieth and eighty-first year from the foundation. Trajan acceded in 98, and on this basis dating can hardly precede A.D. 18. On a third coin of Trajan, also dated in the eighty-first year, the emperor is called Germanicus only, and not Germanicus Dacicus. He won the second title only after the Dacian war in 103. This gives A.D. 22 for the upper limit. The argument appears conclusive.

Herod named the town after TIBERIUS, the reigning emperor and successor of AUGUSTUS. According to Jewish tradition, an old town of NAPHTALI named RAKKATH (which may mean "marshy bank") once occupied the site, and legend said that this place had become a graveyard before Herod appropriated it for a town and for a site of royal residence (Jos. *Ant.* 18.2.3). This may be supposed a propaganda tale aimed at the fact that Herod peopled the new town with Gentiles, but it is not at all impossible that Rakkath had a burial ground in its vicinity, and that this area was included by Herod in his appropriation for the new foundation. In any case, Rakkath is now usually identified with Khirbet el-Quneiṭireh, less than 3 mi. NNW of modern Tiberias.

Herod's plan was ambitious. The wall was 3 mi. long, and the civic amenities included a forum and a large SYNAGOGUE, Roman and Jewish features curiously illustrative of the dual policy of the Herodian house. The synagogue, however, appears never to have been used, for a Jewish boycott compelled Herod to populate Tiberias with aliens. Herod himself found security there. He built a lakeside palace, and the eminence behind the town was an admirable acropolis, a fact illustrated by Saladin's failure to reduce it after his complete success in the battle of Hattin made the defenders' position hopeless. This took place in A.D. 1187.

Tiberias was also a famous spa. Hot springs lay S of its walls, a feature noticed by PLINY the Elder, who remarked on their health-giving quality, and commemorated it in coinage. A coin of Tiberias exists showing Hygeia, the goddess of health, on one side and the emperor Trajan on the other; the goddess feeds a serpent, and the totem of ASCLEPIUS, god of healing, sits on a rock above a spring. In the Rift Valley, and Galilee is part of its long depression, salt beds lie deep down, the site of ancient seas. Underwater springs at Tiberias, part of the thermal system that gave the hot water, add appreciably to the salinity of the Lake of Galilee and of the DEAD SEA, the ultimate terminus of the Galilee water. This fact was an element in the abortive Jordanian measure in 1966 to divert some of the fresh water sources of the Jordan at Banias and deflect the water into the Lebanese Litani. This would have left the springs at Tiberias free to increase the salinity of Galilee to a danger point.

Christ seems to have avoided Tiberias in the course of his Galilean ministry. There were crowded Jewish centers all along that shore of the lake, especially to the N, and this abstention was in accordance with his declared program—to minister first to Israel. After the subjugation of Palestine in the Great Rebellion (see WARS, JEWISH), Tiberias remained intact and became by the irony of history the main center of surviving Jewish scholarship. The codification of the MISHNAH c. A.D. 200 and the development of the Palestinian TALMUD in subsequent centuries took place in Tiberias.

Of the nine towns that once occupied the lake shore, none of them under 15,000 inhabitants, Tiberias alone has survived in spite of the fact that in ancient and medieval times the site was unhealthy. A freak formation of the coast kept the prevailing wind that blows down the lake offshore, and the strip of land where Tiberias lay lacked the healthy movement of air. It was, no doubt, its

Tiberias.

A view looking W toward the section of Tiberias that was occupied beginning in NT times.

acropolis and the prestige of the royal abode that insured survival. Tiberias remains the chief center on that shore of the lake. (For a popularized history, see H. Dudman, *Tiberias* [1988]; for archaeological information, M. Dothan, *Hammath Tiberias*, 2 vols. [1983–2000]; *NEAEHL*, 4:1464–73.)

E. M. BLAIKLOCK

Tiberius ti-bihr´ee-uhs (Τιβέριος *G5501*). Tiberius Claudius Caesar Augustus, second emperor of Rome and ruler at the time of Christ's ministry (Lk. 3:1), was born in 42 B.C., the son of Tiberius Claudius Nero and Livia Drusilla. Four years later Livia, shortly to become the mother of a second son, Drusus, was divorced in order to marry Octavian, the future emperor AUGUSTUS. Augustus's lack of a direct heir, and his tragic frustrations in his search for a competent successor, are outlined by the great historian, TACITUS (*Annals* 1.1). Tiberius, as stepson, was groomed for this role with a strange reluctance on Augustus's part, which lacks a full explanation, for he was not potentially an unworthy choice. Tiberius was a brilliant military commander, and from 12 to 6 B.C. contributed effectively to Augustus's long program of stabilizing the frontiers. On the difficult Rhine and Danube frontiers he successfully established security (*CAH* 10 [1934], 12 describes these constructive campaigns).

That Tiberius was still sole heir in Augustus's mind in 11 B.C. is shown by the fact that Augustus compelled Tiberius in that year to divorce Vipsania Agrippina, whom he loved, and marry Julia, the twice-widowed daughter of Augustus. The marriage proved unhappy, and Julia was banished for adultery in 2 B.C. Four years before that date, at the conclusion of his northern campaigns, Tiberius had suddenly retired to RHODES. Stress with Julia, and Augustus's obvious intention at this time to train Julia's two sons, by her second husband Agrippa, as his successors, may have occasioned this act of withdrawal.

Tiberius returned to Rome in A.D. 2. Two years later, Julia's sons having died untimely deaths, Augustus was forced to recognize Tiberius as his heir. As a mark of this recognition, he was given "tribunician power," one of the devices by which Augustus maintained the fiction of republican rule. Augustus also adopted Tiberius as his son, forcing him to adopt in the same way his nephew Germanicus. On adoption Tiberius received "proconsular authority," another astute constitutional device by which Augustus retained republican form and disguised his real autocracy. Augustus died in August A.D. 14, and, in virtue of his "proconsular authority," Tiberius was able to step smoothly into his place. He was proclaimed emperor in the following month and reigned for twenty-three years

This marble head from a statue of Tiberius Caesar marked his adoption as Augustus's successor in A.D. 4, but at that time Tiberius was already 46, much older than this image suggests.

rius, who in his view had shown the later emperor the way to tyranny. Sejanus, prefect of the household troops in Rome, was also to blame for some of the evils of Tiberius's generation. It is characteristic of the pathologically suspicious that they will sometimes too readily trust the untrustworthy. Sejanus plotted to replace Tiberius, but was cleverly struck down by the old emperor from his retirement on Capri.

The news of Tiberius's death was welcomed in Rome. The aristocracy hated him for the treason trials, the proletariat for his austerity and contempt for games. Modern scholarship has gone far to rehabilitate Tiberius, but admits the possibility of some mental decay in his declining years. The rumors of unbridled immorality during that time are usually given little credence by recent historians. (See further F. B. Marsh, *The Reign of Tiberius* [1931]; D. C. Braund, *Augustus to Nero: A Source on Roman History 31 BC–AD 68* [1985]; B. Levick, *Tiberius the Politician*, rev. ed. [1999]; D. Shotter, *Tiberius Caesar*, 2nd ed. [2004]; R. Seager, *Tiberius*, 2nd ed. [2005].)

E. M. Blaiklock

(d. March, 37). The city of Tiberias in Galilee was named after him, and it was his image that would have been imprinted on the coin that Jesus used in his well-known statement about what is due to Caesar (Matt. 22:19–21 and parallels).

Controversy has surrounded his principate. Following Augustus's behest to hold the empire firmly within its existing lines (Tac. *Ann.* 1:11), Tiberius abandoned the hope of thrusting the German frontier to the Elbe. He gave his attention to consolidation. This austere and cautious policy earned the wrath of the opposition, and there were still many in the senatorial class who had not accepted the coming of the veiled autocracy of the principate. Tiberius himself, soured by long years of rejection and unhappy home circumstances, exerted himself little to win popularity. He was a morose man, obsessed by fears of treachery. This accounts for the spate of trials for treason which marred his reign (*Ann.* 1.72–73; 4.6). It was an abuse of a facet of Roman law that was imitated toward the end of the century by Domitian, an admirer of Tiberius.

Tacitus, himself a member of the senatorial aristocracy, had to endure Domitian's principate and used his mordant style to cleverly denigrate Tibe-

Tibhath tib′hath. See Tebah (place).

Tibni tib′ni (תִּבְנִי H9321, prob. "straw-man" [cf. *HALOT*, 4:1685–86]). Son of Ginath and unsuccessful rival for the throne of the kingdom of Israel after the deaths of Elah and Zimri (1 Ki. 16:21–22). Although the struggle with Omri apparently lasted four years (see Omri I), ending only with Tibni's death, the biblical narrative is largely silent about this period, prompting much speculation among modern scholars (cf. the brief discussion in *ABD*, 6:550–51).

Tidal ti′duhl (תִּדְעָל H9331, prob. from Hittite *Tudḫalia*). King of Goiim and ally of Kedorlaomer king of Elam, who with three other rulers led a punitive expedition against Sodom and other cities (Gen. 14:1, 9). Some scholars render the text, "Tidal king of nations," implying either that he ruled a confederacy of city-states or that he bore an honorific title corresponding to the expression common in Akkadian annals, "King of the Four Corners of the Earth." Others identify Goiim with Gutium in Mesopotamia, while still others appeal to the term *gaʾum* (used in MARI texts) and suggest that Tidal ruled a nomadic tribe with no fixed boundaries. It is generally thought that Tidal corresponds to Tudhalia (Tudkhaliyas), the name of several HITTITE rulers, but other proposals have been made (cf. *ABD*, 6:551–52). Tidal's identification remains uncertain. See also ARIOCH #1.

C. F. PFEIFFER

Tiglath-Pileser tig′lath-pi-lee′zuhr (תִּגְלַת פְּלֶאֶסֶר [פִּלֶסֶר in 2 Ki. 16:7] H9325 and תִּלְגַת פִּלְנְאֶסֶר H9433, from Akk. *Tukulti-apil-ešarra*, "My trust [or help] is in the son of Esharra" [Esharra being the name of the temple of the god ASSHUR]). Also Tilgath-pilneser. The name of three kings of ASSYRIA. Tiglath-Pileser I (1115–1077 B.C.) was an important ruler responsible for many military victories and building projects. Tiglath-Pileser II (967–935) receives mention in some documents, but almost nothing is known about him. The rest of this article deals with Tiglath-Pileser III (745–727), the only king of this name that is mentioned in the Bible.

I. Sources. The principal events of each year of Tiglath-Pileser III's reign are listed in the Assyrian Eponym Canon; additional details are found in the annals written on tablets and bas-reliefs found at Nimrud (CALAH). ESARHADDON reused some of the sculptured slabs in his palace erected in 670/669 B.C., and thus the order of some events remains uncertain.

II. Babylonian policy. Tiglath-Pileser, who succeeded Adad-nirari III, was no usurper as once supposed. Assyria was in a desperate plight and needed the intelligent and vigorous leadership he was to give. His first move was to Babylonia to relieve the pressure of the Aramean tribes on Babylon itself. The tribal lands of Puqudu (PEKOD, Jer. 50:21) were cleared and added to the extended province of Arrapha, which now controlled the area E of the Tigris River. The army marched as far S as the River Ukni (Karun), leaving the native king Nabunaṣir in authority over BABYLON and to the W of the Tigris. His pro-Assyrian policy held until his death in 734, and thus enabled the Assyrian forces to concentrate on other fronts. In 732 Ukin-zēr, sheikh of the Amukani, ousted Nabunaṣir's heir, Nabu-nadin-zēr, and seized the throne in Babylon.

Tiglath-Pileser set out to win over some of the tribes and succeeded in gaining the submission of Marduk-apla-iddin (MERODACH-BALADAN of Isa. 39:1) to save his lands. The army marched down the E bank of the Tigris to besiege the Amukani, Shilani, and Saʾalli in their capital Sapia in the southern marshes. Their villages were razed and Assyrian officials appointed to control them. Tiglath-Pileser himself adopted the title of "king of Babylonia" by "taking the hands of Bēl [MARDUK]" in a ceremony in 729 B.C., the first Assyrian to do so for almost five centuries. In the Babylonian Chronicle, Tiglath-Pileser is referred to as PUL (cf. also 2 Ki. 15:19; 1 Chr. 5:26), perhaps his personal as opposed to throne name.

III. The north. Dispatches from his generals in this sector showed that Tiglath-Pileser realized that his main opponent was Sarduri of Urartu (see ARMENIA). To isolate him from the southern hillsmen he therefore struck against the petty kings in the Zagros Mountains and made them his vassals, enforcing regular payment by periodic raids (744, 739, and 737 B.C.). One distant expedition took him as far as Demavend, and in 735 he unsuccessfully besieged Tushpa, the capital of Sarduri on Lake Van.

IV. The west. In the W, the Assyrians gained much booty, mainly from a series of campaigns originally aimed at the Neo-Hittite allies. When Sarduri came to the rescue of Mati-ilu of Arpad (at Samsat on the Euphrates) the Assyrians captured more than 73,000 prisoners. To punish Arpad it was besieged for three years and then incorporated into the provincial system in 741. In the previous year, the opponent had been Azriau of Yaudi and his N Syrian allies. While this Azriau might be the king of a small Syrian city-state (Samʾal), there is growing evidence that he may well be Azariah (UZZIAH) of Judah, who at this time had an influence over a wide area (cf. H. Tadmor in *Studies in the Bible*, ed. C. Rabin [1961], 232–71). Captive "Judeans" are named in the annals as settled in Ulluba (Bitlis), and this would be in accord with a policy of transportation of prisoners and captured peoples to control the regions in which they were settled as aliens. Tiglath-Pileser was only following a practice first adopted on a grand scale by his predecessor and namesake Tiglath-Pileser I (1115–1077) when he had invaded PHOENICIA. The Assyrians overran Bit-Adini (BETH EDEN) and made it part of the province of Unqi.

The effect of these actions was that many kings brought in tribute, among them MENAHEM (*Menuḥimme*) of SAMARIA, whose payment of 1,000 talents of silver, at 50 shekels per Israelite (2 Ki. 15:19–20), represented their value as slaves at the current price. HIRAM of TYRE and REZIN (Raḫianni) of DAMASCUS also submitted, but the Assyrians' hold over them was weak. Egypt, doubtless feeling the economic loss of trade with Syria and especially of the timber trade through TYRE and SIDON, now dominated and taxed by local Assyrian officials, stirred up revolt. ASHKELON and GAZA organized an anti-Assyrian league and found support in TRANSJORDAN and EDOM.

In 734 Tiglath-Pileser made a swift march down the coast to Gaza, whose King Hanunu fled to Egypt. He sacked the area and set up a golden statue of his royal self as a mark of victory, but did not press beyond the border with Egypt at Naḥal-Muṣur (Wadi of Egypt). This advance took Tiglath-Pileser through the territory of Damascus (called "the land of Hazael"), Galilee, and Israel ("the land of the House of Omri"), which were now counted as part of Assyria. He placed PEKAH (*Paqaḥ*) on the throne instead of HOSHEA (*Auš?*) and may well have instigated the murder of the former (2 Ki. 15:30). AHAZ of Judah seems to have stood by his treaty with Assyria (2 Chr. 28:21) despite the siege of Jerusalem by anti-Assyrian forces (2 Ki. 16.5–6). Damascus fell in 733 and Israel was again punished for her opposition.

V. Administration. This reign was marked by an extension of the provincial system and appointment of Assyrian officials in all captured cities to collect tribute and act as intelligence officers (*qurbutu*) for the Assyrian court. They were backed by a reorganized Assyrian army, largely composed of levies and therefore more mobile at all seasons than the native drafts. Mass deportations broke any incipient "nationalism" in outlying provinces and provided a supply of labor which in one year amounted to no less than 154,000 persons. While his rule was harsh, it led to a stable and efficient administration.

(See further R. D. Barnett and M. Falkner, *The Sculptures of Aššur-naṣir-apli II, 883–859 B.C., Tiglath-pileser III, 745–727 B.C., Esarhaddon, 681–669 B.C., from the Central and South-West Palaces at Nimrud* [1962]; A. K. Grayson in *CAH*, 3/2, 2nd ed. [1991], 71–85; H. Tadmor, *The Inscriptions of Tiglath-Pileser III, King of Assyria: Critical Edition, with Introductions, Translations and Commentary* [1994].)   D. J. WISEMAN

A village by the Tigris River in N Mesopotamia.

Tigris ti′gris (חִדֶּקֶל *H2538*, from Akk. *Idiqlat* [cf. Lat. *Diglitus* in Pliny the Elder, *Nat. Hist.* 6.127]; in Old Pers. the name took the form *Tigrā*, hence Gk. Τίγρης). The eastern river of ancient Iraq, which together with the EUPHRATES formed the alluvial plain of MESOPOTAMIA, "[Land] between Rivers." The Tigris is one of the rivers listed to describe the boundaries of Eden (Gen. 2:14; see EDEN, GARDEN OF); and it was while "standing on the bank of the great river, the Tigris," that DANIEL received an important vision (Dan. 10:4).

The Tigris arises in the Zagros mountains of W Kurdistan and flows with many tributaries, such as the Greater and Lesser Zab and the Diyala, from NW to SE some 700 mi. until it empties into the Persian Gulf. It was for centuries the easternmost boundary of the Sumerian peoples and the meeting place of Elamite, Indo-European, and Sumerian (see ELAM; SUMER). The snows of the Zagros melt and flow S causing the Tigris to reach full flood stage in May and June. The mysterious "protoeuphratean" peoples, whose character is only vaguely known, apparently named the stream.

The overall length of the Tigris, nearly 1,200 mi. in all, was dotted in antiquity by the towns of many lost civilizations. In the far N lived the Urartu (who lent their name to Mount ARARAT), the CIMMERIANS, and centuries later the Guti. In the foothills of the Zagros are the remains of such ancient pre-Neolithic sites as Šanidar and Tepe Gawra, while the Sumerians built Eshunna, Lagash, and the towns that once flourished at the sites of Samarra and Khafajeh. The S became dominated after the end of the 3rd millennium by the Semitic Akkadians and their rulers of Sumer and Agade.

In the northern reaches the Assyrian empire arose. Their capital cities of NINEVEH, ASSHUR, and Nimrud (CALAH) are located on its banks. The plain between the northern reaches of the Tigris and Euphrates, settled by the Arameans, is sometimes called in the Bible ARAM NAHARAIM (Gen. 24:10 et al.), "Aram by the Twin Rivers," a name used in later times for other parts of the Iraqi watershed. The ancient alterations of the course of the Tigris are as yet imperfectly understood. It is known that in recorded history these rivers changed channels more than once, often causing once verdant marshes and grass lands to become parched deserts.

The long caravan route from N India that crossed over to the Syro-Palestinian coast followed the course of the Tigris for hundreds of

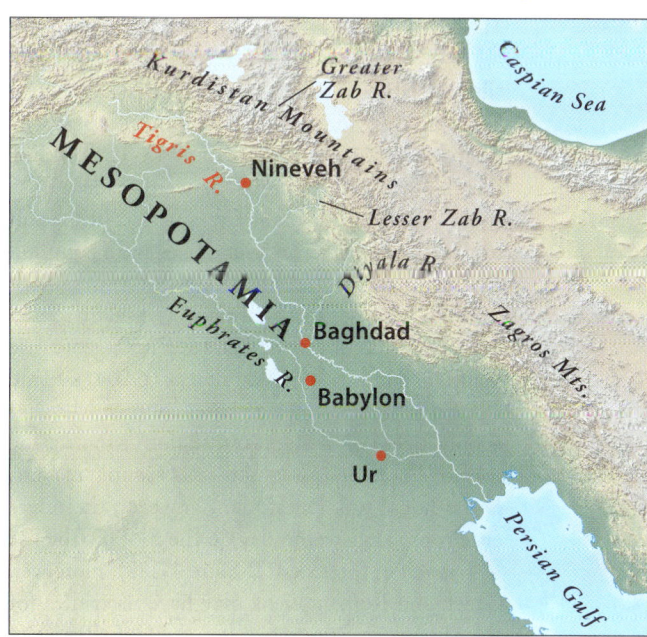

The Tigris River.

miles, finally veering off toward the Euphrates at Nineveh, a reason for that city's great wealth and power. The difficulty of the terrain, the harshness of the climate, and the capricious nature of the water supply, demanded close-knit and elaborate social systems for people to survive and for townships to flourish on the banks of the Tigris. Perhaps this inhospitable topography more than any other factor encouraged the rise of Mesopotamian civilization. (For bibliography see EUPHRATES.)

W. WHITE, JR.

Tikvah tik′vuh (תִּקְוָה *H9537*, "hope"; also תִּקְהָה *H9504* [2 Chr. 34:22, *Kethib* תּוֹקַהַת]). (1) Son of HARHAS and father of SHALLUM, who was keeper of the royal wardrobe; the latter was married to HULDAH the prophetess (2 Ki. 22:14). In the parallel passage he is called "Tokhath son of Hasrah" (2 Chr. 34:22; KJV, "Tikvath"). The name Tokhath may be a variant form or a copying error, but some believe it was the original (non-Semitic) name of this person, and that it was altered to Tiqvah to make it meaningful in Hebrew (cf. *HALOT*, 4:1707).

(2) Father of JAHZEIAH (Ezra 10:15; 1 Esd. 9:14 [KJV, "Theocanus"]).

Tikvath. See TIKVAH.

tile. A slab or a tablet of baked CLAY. Such tablets were used for writing in the CUNEIFORM syllabary before 3000 B.C. (see CLAY TABLET). While the clay was soft, impressions were made with a stylus. Then the clay tablet was placed in the sun to bake, or baked in an oven. Tiles were common roofing material through much of the ancient world, but houses in Palestine were usually roofed with a mixture of clay and straw. Roofing tiles are mentioned in Lk. 5:19 (Gk. *keramos G3041*). Some argue that Luke's language here (contrast Mk. 2:4) is only a case of "cultural translation" to make the narrative more meaningful for his Gentile readers. If the house was Palestinian, however, the reference is probably to the clay on the roof (cf. the use of *keramos* in the LXX at 2 Sam. 17:28); moreover, Greek and Roman aliens may have used tiles for their houses in Palestine.   C. F. PFEIFFER

Tilgath-pilneser. See TIGLATH-PILESER.

Tilon ti′luhn (תִּילוֹן *H9400*, meaning unknown). Son of Shimon and descendant of JUDAH (1 Chr. 4:20).

Timaeus ti-mee′uhs (Τίμαιος *G5505*). See BARTIMAEUS.

timbrel. See MUSIC, MUSICAL INSTRUMENTS IV.B.

time. See CALENDAR; ETERNITY III.

Timna tim′nuh (תִּמְנָע *H9465* [also תִּמְנָע], perhaps "protected" or "invincible" [see *HALOT*, 4:1755]). (1) Concubine of ELIPHAZ son of ESAU; mother of AMALEK (Gen. 36:12; in 1 Chr. 1:36 MT, Timna appears to be listed as a son of Eliphaz, but the NIV follows CODEX VATICANUS in rendering "by Timna, Amalek"). She is probably the same person identified as sister of LOTAN, thus a daughter of SEIR the HORITE (Gen. 36:22; 1 Chr. 1:39). Calling attention to Timna's status as a CONCUBINE may have been a way of indicating that the Amalekites were not pure descendants of Esau.

(2) Descendant of Esau, listed among the clan chiefs of EDOM (Gen. 36:40; 1 Chr. 1:51). The KJV spells his name "Timnah" probably to distinguish it from #1 above. Some argue that the names in this list are topographical rather than personal. There is today a region called Timna c. 20 mi. N of the Gulf of AQABAH, but its connection with the biblical name is uncertain.

Timnah tim′nuh (תִּמְנָה *H9463*, possibly "portion, territory"; gentilic תִּמְנִי *H9464*, "Timnite"). KJV also Timnath (Gen. 38:12–14; Jdg. 14:1–2, 5) and Thimnathah (Josh. 19:43, misinterpreting the Hebrew locative form). (1) A town of uncertain location, noted as the place where JUDAH was headed when he had his encounter with TAMAR (Gen. 38:12–14). It should perhaps be identified with either #2 or #3 below, though some argue it is the same as Khirbet et-Tabbaneh in the SHEPHELAH, c. 13 mi. WSW of JERUSALEM (*SacBr*, 115c).

(2) A town located between BETH SHEMESH and EKRON, mentioned in the description of the tribal boundaries of JUDAH (Josh. 15:10), but allotted to the tribe of DAN (19:43, where it is possibly referred to as "Timnah of Ekron"; see Y. Aharoni, *The Land of the Bible: A Historical Geography*, rev. ed. [1979], 312). The Danites were unable to take full possession of Timnah and other towns in this territory (19:47). Timnah was controlled by the PHILISTINES in the time of SAMSON (Jdg. 14:1–2, 5; cf. "Timnite" in 15:6). The region was evidently conquered by Judah at some later point, and during the reign of AHAZ Timnah was one of the towns recaptured and occupied by the Philistines (2 Chr. 28:18). It is generally identified with modern Tell el-Batashi, c. 3 mi. E of Ekron. (See *NEAEHL*, 1:152–58.)

(3) A town in the hill country of the tribe of Judah (Josh. 15:57). It was in the same district as MAON and other towns S of HEBRON, but the precise location is unknown.

Timnath tim′nath. (1) One of the towns in JUDEA that BACCHIDES fortified (1 Macc. 9:50). Its location is uncertain, but it should perhaps be identified with either TIMNAH #2 or, more likely, TIMNATH HERES. See also discussion under PIRATHON.

(2) KJV alternate form of TIMNAH.

Timnath Heres, Timnath Serah tim´nath-hee´riz, tim´nath-sihr´uh (תִּמְנַת־חֶרֶס H9466 [Jdg. 2:9], possibly "portion [i.e., region] of the sun"; תִּמְנַת־סֶרַח H9467 [Josh. 19:50; 24:30], perhaps "overhanging region" or "leftover portion"). Also Timnath-heres, Timnath-serah. A place in the hill country of Ephraim (see EPHRAIM, HILL COUNTRY OF) given to JOSHUA as his personal inheritance: "he built up the town and settled there" (Josh. 19:50). When he died, he was buried in this city, which is described as being N of GAASH (Josh. 24:30; Jdg. 2:9). Most scholars identify it with modern Khirbet Tibnah, on the W slopes of the hill country, some 18 mi. NW of JERUSALEM and 14 mi. SW of SHECHEM.

The book of Joshua uses the form *Serah* whereas Judges has *Heres*. During biblical times, when the Hebrew text was not yet vocalized, the difference between these two forms would have appeared to be a simple metathesis or transposition of the first and last consonants (*ḥrs* vs. *srḥ*). It is uncertain, however, whether this difference should be attributed to a variance in pronunciation, to a copying error, to an intentional change, or to a combination of these factors. Many scholars believe that Timnath Heres was the town's original name and that because it alluded (or could be misunderstood to allude) to pagan SUN WORSHIP, it was changed to Timnath Serah. The meaning of the latter term is quite uncertain and has given rise to speculation. Some suggest that it reflects the rough and steep terrain ("overhang," but there is no evidence that Heb. *seraḥ* H6245, found only in Exod. 26:12, could be used in this way); others think that it derives from the notion that Joshua was given what was "left over" after the tribes had received their respective allotments (but the text of Josh. 19:49–50 does not use that language).

Timnite tim´nit. See TIMNAH.

Timon ti´muhn (Τίμων G5511, "precious, valuable"). One of the seven men appointed by the early church to serve tables and thereby relieve the apostles for other duties (Acts 6:5). According to a late tradition, Timon had been among the SEVENTY DISCIPLES (Lk. 10:1 KJV) and subsequently became a bishop in ARABIA. See also DEACON III; STEPHEN II.

Timotheus ti-moh´thee-uhs. See TIMOTHY.

Timothy tim´oh-thee (Τιμόθεος G5510, "God's precious one" or "God-honoring"). KJV usually Timotheus (but Timothy in the Pastorals and in 2 Cor. 1:1; Phlm. 1; Heb. 13:23; this variation by the KJV has no basis in the Greek text and the reason for it is unclear).

(1) An early Christian who became one of the most constant companions of the apostle PAUL. The first reference to Timothy is in connection with the beginning of Paul's second missionary journey when he revisited DERBE and LYSTRA in LYCAONIA (Acts 16:1–3; see S. J. D. Cohen in *JBL* 105 [1986]: 251–68; C. Bryan in *JBL* 107 [1988]: 292–94). It seems probable that Paul had met Timothy earlier during his visit to this area on his first missionary journey (ch. 14). This young man made a good impression upon Paul and had a good reputation in Lystra and Iconium (16:2), a comment that suggests he was a resident of Lystra rather than Derbe. Later Paul seems to indicate that certain prophetic utterances confirmed Timothy's appointment (1 Tim. 1:18; cf. 4:14). Concerning his parentage it is recorded that his father was a Greek and his mother a devout Jewish Christian (Acts 16:1). His mother's name was EUNICE, and his grandmother was LOIS (2 Tim. 1:5); probably both of them were faithful in instructing Timothy according to the OT Scriptures (cf. 2 Tim. 3:14–15 and note the pl. *tinōn* according to the better MSS).

Timothy's mixed parentage motivated Paul to have him circumcised (Acts 16:3). This might seem contrary to the decision of the COUNCIL OF JERUSALEM, held shortly before the second missionary journey (15:27–29); the vindication of Paul's position is demonstrated in the fact that TITUS was not compelled to be circumcised (Gal. 2:3). Timothy would have been considered a Jew, however, and his situation could have become an occasion for serious offense in Jewish circles if he had remained uncircumcised. Evidently Paul judged that this concession would be necessary for the maximum effectiveness of Timothy's work. That Timothy was rather young when he joined Paul is suggested by Paul's exhortation, "Don't let anyone look down on you because you are young" (1 Tim. 4:12), which was given some fifteen years later.

Timothy is not mentioned in connection with the experiences and imprisonment of Paul and SILAS in PHILIPPI (Acts 16:12–40). Possibly because of his youth Timothy was not imprisoned. Likewise, he is not mentioned in the account of Paul's ministry in THESSALONICA (17:1–9). However, Acts 17:14 indicates that Silas and Timothy remained in BEREA after Paul's departure, although Paul requested that they join him as soon as possible (17:15). According to Acts 18:5, they rejoined Paul at CORINTH. However, 1 Thess. 3:1–3 indicates that Timothy at least was with Paul in ATHENS and that Paul, being anxious about the believers at Thessalonica, sent Timothy to Thessalonica. This suggests that, during Paul's ministry at Thessalonica, Timothy (who seemingly was present) was not directly involved in the work, so that the "bond" Paul and Silas had to post (Acts 17:9; cf. 1 Thess. 2:18) did not apply to Timothy. Upon his return to Corinth, where Paul now was (1 Thess. 3:6 and Acts 18:5), Timothy informed the apostle about the situation in Thessalonica. In response Paul, with Silas and Timothy as "cowriters," sent 1 Thessalonians (see THESSALONIANS, FIRST EPISTLE TO THE). Shortly thereafter, while still at Corinth, these three men sent 2 Thessalonians (see THESSALONIANS, SECOND EPISTLE TO THE).

During his extended residence in EPHESUS on his third missionary journey, Paul sent Timothy to Corinth to deal with the vexing problems in that church (1 Cor. 4:17; 16:10). It appears that he was not successful in this mission and returned to Paul at Ephesus. Prior to Paul's departure from Ephesus, he sent Timothy and ERASTUS to MACEDONIA (Acts 19:22). Later, when Paul joined Timothy in Macedonia, and after Titus had successfully dealt with the problems in Corinth, the apostle wrote 2 Corinthians and included Timothy in the opening (2 Cor. 1:1; cf. 1:19). When Paul wrote his letter to the Romans during the following winter while at Corinth, Timothy, identified as a "fellow worker," was among those who sent their greetings (Rom. 16:21).

Timothy accompanied Paul on his last journey to JERUSALEM (Acts 20:4). It is not indicated that Timothy accompanied Paul on his shipwreck voyage to ROME, but PHILIPPIANS (if written from Rome) suggests that Timothy was sharing Paul's first Roman imprisonment (Phil. 1:1; 2:19–20). Likewise, Timothy was included with Paul in two other Prison Epistles, often thought to have been composed in Rome (Col. 1:1; Phlm. 1).

Two of the PASTORAL EPISTLES, written after Paul's first Roman imprisonment, were addressed to Timothy. The close relationship that existed between the apostle and his disciple is very evident

Theater and forum at Ephesus (looking NE). Timothy shepherded the Christian congregation in this city.

from these letters. Paul refers to Timothy as "my true son in the faith" (1 Tim. 1:2), "my son" (1:18), "my dear son" (2 Tim. 1:2). In these two epistles Paul uses a special term to describe the responsible task or consignment that the preacher has. This term, *parathēkē* G4140 ("deposit"), is found only in 1 Tim. 6:20; 2 Tim. 1:12, 14; here Paul urges Timothy to guard this deposit, something that had also been entrusted to Paul. The apostle virtually identified his ministry with Timothy's. This continuation of Paul's ministry in the work of Timothy underlies the various exhortations of the Pastoral Epistles.

First Timothy was written from Macedonia while Timothy was at Ephesus. Heterodoxy had infested the church—a kind of legalism (1 Tim. 1:6–7) and a kind of speculative theology based on myths and genealogies (v. 4). It was also in this period that ecclesiastical organization was developing, and Timothy was enjoined carefully to supervise the appointment of qualified officers. Personal godliness is a necessary qualification of an effective minister (e.g., 6:11–16).

Second Timothy was written while Paul was imprisoned in Rome, apparently the second time. The future looked very bleak for him and he wrote this letter to Timothy to urge him to come to Rome for these last days. Whether Timothy was able to reach Rome before Paul's death is not recorded. This epistle has been aptly called Paul's swan song. It is the picture of a man passing the torch to his successor. Paul's confidence and trust in Timothy as a worthy successor are very evident. It is not indicated where Timothy was—apparently in western Asia, possibly at Ephesus, since he would be passing through Troas (2 Tim. 4:13). Although Paul was at the point of death (4:6) and had been abandoned by certain followers, such as PHYGELUS and HERMOGENES, DEMAS, and ALEXANDER (1:15; 4:10, 14), nevertheless he expressed an assurance and faith to Timothy which must have made a formative impression on this young minister and been an enduring inspiration to him.

A study of these epistles addressed to Timothy gives the impression that he was a fairly young man who was somewhat retiring, perhaps even a bit shy. He appears to be sincere and devoted, but at times possibly frightened by his opponents and their teachings. This trait perhaps is also reflected in his apparent inability to cope with the problems in the Corinthian church.

The last reference to Timothy in the NT is in Heb. 13:23, where it is reported that Timothy had been recently released from prison. Timothy was known to the recipients of this epistle, and its author intends to bring him along on a proposed visit. Timothy's name does not occur elsewhere in the early Christian literature. (See further F. F. Bruce, *The Pauline Circle* [1985], ch. 4.)

(2) A leader of the Ammonite forces defeated by Judas MACCABEE "in many battles" (1 Macc. 5:6–7, 11, 34–43). The second book of Maccabees has several references to him (2 Macc. 8:30–32 et al.), including a record of his death (10:37), but subsequently the name comes up again (12:2, 10, 18–25). It is uncertain whether there were two distinct historical figures named Timothy who opposed the Jews (the name was common); some scholars argue that the later narrative is a mangled duplicate or that it otherwise reflects confusion on the part of the writer. B. VAN ELDEREN

Timothy, Epistles to. See PASTORAL EPISTLES.

tin. A metal that has a bright white color and is easily fusible with a melting point of 232°C. The metal is not very ductile but is very malleable and can be rolled into foil. Tin is only rarely found in the native state, the main ore being cassiterite (tin dioxide), which occurs in veins associated with granitic rocks, as in Cornwall, and as alluvial deposits resulting from the degradation of cassiterite-bearing veins. Articles of tin were used in Egypt at least as early as 1400 B.C., and the metal is mentioned (Heb. *bědîl* H974) as one of the objects plundered by the Israelites when they attacked Midian in the wilderness (Num. 31:22). From c. 3700 B.C. onward tin has been alloyed with COPPER to give BRONZE; trade in Cyprus copper and Cornish tin was carried on by the Phoenicians (cf. Ezek. 27:12). Tin also forms alloys with silver (cf. 22:18), and forced draught is employed in metallurgical processes associated with its extraction and alloying (cf. 22:20). D. R. BOWES

Tiphsah tif´suh (תִּפְסַח H9527, perhaps "ford" [cf. BDB, 820]). **(1)** A town mentioned as marking the

NE boundary of Solomon's kingdom: "he ruled over all the kingdoms west of the River [i.e., the Euphrates], from Tiphsah to Gaza" (1 Ki. 4:24). Tiphsah is generally identified with Thapsacus (*Thapsakos*), described by Xenophon as "a large and prosperous city" on the Euphrates River (*Anabasis* 1.4.11). Called Amphipolis in Seleucid times, it is now known as Dibseh, about 55 mi. ESE of Aleppo and 90 mi. NE of Hamath, near the large bend of the Euphrates. A great E-W trade route that moved around the Fertile Crescent had a staging post here. There is no means of knowing how strongly the remote frontier was held by Solomon, and some scholars are skeptical that Israel's northern boundaries ever reached that far.

(2) A town of uncertain location that was sacked and brutally treated by Menahem (2 Ki. 15:16). Although some scholars think this Tiphsah is the same as #1 above, the text suggests rather a place near Tirzah and Samaria. On the basis of some Greek mss, other scholars emend the MT to read *tappûaḥ*. See Tappuah #3.

Tiras tī′ruhs (תִּירָס H9410, meaning unknown, but the name apparently corresponds to Egyptian *tywš*ʾ, also spelled *twryš*ʾ). Last-named son of Japheth and grandson of Noah (Gen. 10:2; 1 Chr. 1:5). Evidently Tiras was also the name of a people group descended from him, and various identifications have been proposed, including Tarsus and Tarshish. Many scholars accept a connection with the Tursha, one of the Sea Peoples that invaded the Syrian coast and even attacked Egypt in the 13th cent. B.C. But the identification of the Tursha is also debated. Some think the reference is to Thracia, others to a place in Italy named Tyrrhenia (*Tyrsēnie*, gentilic *Tyrsēnoi*, in Herodotus, *Hist*. 1.57, 94, 163, 166–67; elsewhere *Tyrrēnoi*); the latter refers to Etruria, the land of the Etruscans. Herodotus reports a tradition that the Tyrrhenians moved to Italy from Lydia, and a location for Tiras in Asia Minor seems to fit the biblical data (Tiras's brothers include Gomer and Meshech, who are usually identified with Anatolian groups). Recent work, however, has called into question the veracity of this story (cf. D. Briquel, *L'origine lydienne des Etrusques: Histoire de la doctrine dans l'antiquité* [1991]).

Tirathites tī′ruh-thīts (תִרְעָתִים H9571, a gentilic form, prob. from an unattested name such as תִּרְעָה). Among the descendants of Caleb (through his son Hur and grandson Salma) are listed three "clans of scribes who lived at Jabez: the Tirathites, Shimeathites and Sucathites. These are the Kenites who came from Hammath, the father of the house of Recab" (1 Chr. 2:55). Nothing else is known about these clans, and their names cannot be traced to a particular person or place. On the relationship between Calebites and Kenites, see discussion under Jabez.

tire. An archaic English term used by the KJV both as a verb (meaning "to adorn," 2 Ki. 9:30) and as a noun ("[hair] ornament," Isa. 3:18; Ezek. 24:17, 23).

Tirhakah tuhr-hay′kuh (תִּרְהָקָה H9555, from Egyp. *tʾhrwq*). Also Taharqa, Tahrqa (and various forms in Greek writers). A pharaoh of the 25th or Ethiopian dynasty in Egypt (see Ethiopia), identified in the Hebrew Bible as king of Cush (cf. TNIV, 2 Ki. 19:9; Isa. 37:9; NIV, "the Cushite king of Egypt"). His throne name, attested on his temples at Kawa in the Sudan, was *Khunefertēmrēʿ Taharqa*; the short form *Tʾhrwq* gave rise to the Assyrian *Tarqû*. Egypt had been divided into a number of feudal cities and cult centers by the middle of the 8th cent. B.C. About 730 B.C., however, the Cushite (Nubian) chieftain Piankhy (Piye) conquered much of Egypt and assumed the unified throne as pharaoh. After his death his brother Shabako, with some difficulty, ascended the throne and ruled for fifteen years until approximately 702. He was followed by Shebiktu, who reigned for twelve years before the accession of Tirhakah (possibly his younger brother) in 690.

Tirhakah was crowned at Memphis and then refurbished the temple of Amon-Reʿ at Kawa. Subsequently he carried on campaigns against the pretenders to the throne in the Nile delta region. He was fairly respected by his Egyptian subjects and was able to maintain some degree of order sufficient to build and restore temples and other buildings at Karnak and Medînet Habu. When the rampaging Assyrian king Sennacherib (705–681 B.C.) began his campaigns in Syria and threatened Hezekiah in Jerusalem, the Jews evidently appealed to Egypt for aid (cf. 2 Ki. 18:21; Isa. 36:6). They were warned by the prophet that Egypt could not save Judah.

When the annals of Sennacherib (cf. *ANET*, 287–88) are compared with those of Tirhakah and with the biblical record, several involved chronological problems appear. These difficulties have been the subject of considerable discussion, and many scholars have concluded that the biblical account is in error. One solution to the problem has long been thought to be a second campaign of Sennacherib into the western areas of Asia Minor. Another solution would be found if Tirhakah were, in fact, acting under his brother's name and reign in his encounter with Sennacherib at Eltekeh, where a goodly portion of the combined Egyptian and Ethiopian force was annihilated. It is more likely that Sennacherib was victorious at Eltekeh in 700, and that he moved on Hezekiah in Jerusalem and Tirhakah sometime about 689/688.

Sennacherib's successor and son, Esarhaddon (680–669 B.C.), again conquered Syria and "fought daily, without interruption, very bloody battles against Tirhakah (*Tarqû*), king of Egypt and Ethiopia, the one accursed by all the great gods" (from Esarhaddon's stela, *ANET*, 293). After the death of Esarhaddon in Haran, Tirhakah returned to occupy most of his former domain. Ashurbanipal, the son and heir of Esarhaddon, had been previously designated the new king. In his first campaign begun in 667 B.C. he again invaded Egypt and recorded the account on a cylinder discovered at Kuyunjik (*ANET*, 294). After this pursuit Tirhakah does not seem to have recovered his sovereign position and he fled to his native southland, to his city of Napata. There he died in 664, after a long reign of twenty-six years.

(See further M. F. L. Macadam, *The Temples of Kawa*, vol. 1 [1949]; J. Vandier, *Manuel d'archéologie égyptienne*, vol. 2 [1955], 970–71; H. von Zeissl, *Äthiopen und Assyrer in Ägypten* [1955]; A. Gardiner, *Egypt of the Pharaohs* [1961], 335–51; R. A. Parker et al., *The Edifice of Taharqa by the Sacred Lake of Karnak* [1979]; K. A. Kitchen, *The Third Intermediate Period in Egypt, 1100–650 B.C*, 2nd ed. [1986], 161–72; D. B. Redford, *From Slave to Pharaoh: The Black Experience of Ancient Egypt* [2004].)
W. White, Jr.

Tirhanah tuhr-hay´nuh (תִּרְחֲנָה H9563, derivation unknown, possibly a Hurrian name). Son of Caleb (by his concubine Maacah), included in the genealogy of Judah (1 Chr. 2:48).

Tiria tihr´ee-uh (תִּירְיָא H9409, possibly "might of Yahweh"). Son of Jehallelel and descendant of Judah (1 Chr. 4:16).

Tirshatha tuhr-shay´thuh (תִּרְשָׁתָא H9579, possibly from a Persian word meaning "respected, excellency"; cf. H. G. M. Williamson, *Ezra-Nehemiah*, WBC 16 [1985], 27). KJV transliteration of what appears to be a Persian title meaning "governor" or the like. The term is applied to Nehemiah (Neh. 8:9; 10:1) and to another unnamed leader, probably Sheshbazzar or Zerubbabel (Ezra 2:63; Neh. 7:65, 70). The Persian satrap or provincial governor was, in effect, a petty official with no great power whose principal functions included the assessment and collection of taxes.
M. H. Heicksen

Tirzah (person) tihr´zuh (תִּרְצָה H9573, "pleasant" or "obliging"). The youngest of five daughters of Zelophehad of the tribe of Manasseh (Num. 26:33). Since Zelophehad had no sons, his daughters requested Eleazar the priest that they be allowed to inherit their father's property, and the request was granted on condition that they marry into their father's tribe (27:1–11; 36:11; Josh. 17:3–4). Some think that Tirzah may have settled the town that bears the same name. See Tirzah (place).

Tirzah (place) tihr´zuh (תִּרְצָה H9574, "pleasant" or "obliging"). A royal Canaanite city conquered by Joshua (Josh. 12:24). It is possible that the town, located within the tribal territory of Manasseh, was settled by Tirzah, daughter of the Manassite Zelophehad (cf. 17:1–6, esp. v. 3). See Tirzah (person). Jeroboam I maintained a residence at Tirzah (1 Ki. 14:17) and it became the capital of the northern kingdom in the days of Baasha, Elah, and Zimri (1 Ki. 15:21, 33; 16:6, 8, 9, 15). Trapped there by Omri, Zimri destroyed his residence during a dynastic struggle (16:17–18). Six years later, Omri transferred the capital to Samaria (16:23–24), a more central and convenient

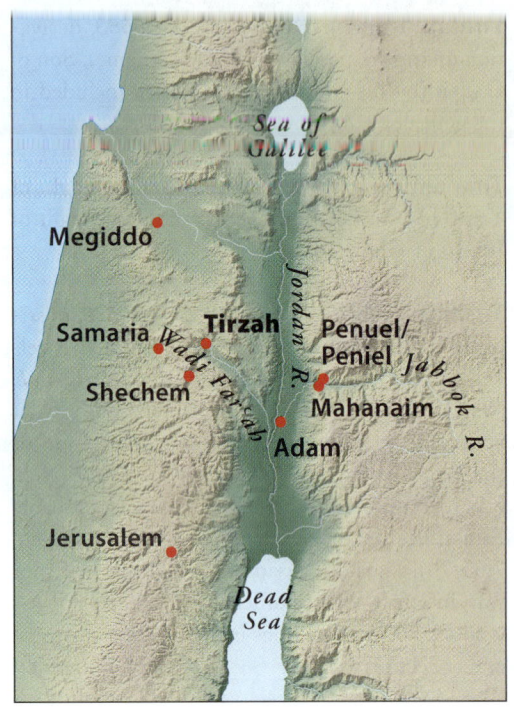

Tirzah.

of softer Cenomanian limestones with a good soil cover, in contrast to the rocky Eocene outcrops above the valley. The large mound at Tell el-Far'ah was excavated by the Dominican fathers R. de Vaux and A. M. Steve. Their excavations have revealed a continuous settlement from Chalcolithic times, before 3000 B.C., to the end of the kingdom of Israel. It flourished as a city in the 9th cent. B.C., but a burnt level was found terminating the first stratum of the Iron Age occupation that may indicate the civil disorders at the time Omri came to power. There is also evidence of the subsequent reduction of Tirzah from an important fortress to a virtually open town about the time Samaria was created on a new site. All this seems strongly confirmatory that Tell el-Far'ah is the site of Tirzah. (See R. de Vaux in *Archaeology and Old Testament Study*, ed. D. W. Thomas [1967], 371–83; A. Chambon, *Tell el-Fâr'ah I* [1984]; J. Mallet, *Tell el Fâr'ah II*, 2 vols. [1987–88].)

J. M. HOUSTON

center that dominated the western approaches to the Samaritan hill country; in addition, Samaria had no older tribal associations, such as Tirzah had (cf. DAVID's earlier action in choosing Jerusalem as his capital). Tirzah then sank into the status of a provincial but still significant town. Toward the end of the northern monarchy of Israel, a citizen of Tirzah, MENAHEM, seized power and usurped the throne from SHALLUM (2 Ki. 15:14, 16).

Tirzah is now generally identified with modern Tell el-Far'ah, c. 6 mi. NE of SHECHEM, at the head of the descent of the Wadi Far'ah, which plunges E into the Jordan Valley to the ford at Adam; see ADAM (PLACE). (The site is not to be confused with another Tell el-Far'ah in SW Palestine; see SHARUHEN.) This was the best route connecting TRANSJORDAN with the hill country of Ephraim, and connected westward to the road via Samaria and DOTHAN to the JEZREEL Plain. This longitudinal road helps to explain the rise of important cities like Tirzah, Shechem, and Samaria at major highway junctions.

Noted for the beauty of its environs (Cant. 6:4), the valley where Tirzah was situated is carved out

Tishbe tish'bee (תִּשְׁבֵּי H9586, conjectured place name [the MT has תֹּשָׁבֵי, see below]; gentilic תִּשְׁבִּי H9585, "Tishbite"). The hometown of ELIJAH in GILEAD, according to the NIV and some other versions at 1 Ki. 17:1. The KJV, following the Hebrew form found in the MT, has "of the inhabitants of Gilead" (*mittōšābê gil'ād*; cf. NJPS, "an inhabitant of Gilead"). The SEPTUAGINT, however, understood the word as a proper name (*ek Thesbōn*). Most scholars, assuming reasonably that the term Tishbite (in the same verse and elsewhere) means "a native of Tishbe," emend the MT vowels to *mittišbê*, "from Tishbe."

Other less likely proposals have been made. N. Glueck (*Explorations in Eastern Palestine IV, Part I*, AASOR 28 [1951], 218, 225–27) suggests that a scribal error was responsible for the confusion surrounding the birthplace of Elijah and that the text originally read "Elijah the Jabeshite, from Jabesh Gilead" (cf. Jdg. 21:8–14 and see JABESH GILEAD). Additional speculation has suggested that the passage might be rendered "Elijah the Kenite, of the Kenites of Gilead," a somewhat tenuous viewpoint based on two arguments: (a) these alien settlers in Gilead, represented by the RECABITES, assisted Elisha at a later time in his fight against BAAL worship (cf. 2 Ki. 10:15); and (b) Elijah may have in his day been a representative of the same people (cf. his efforts against the Baalism introduced by AHAB).

A place by the name of Tishbe has never been identified, though some have thought that Listib (In Arabic, el-Istib), in E Gilead, was a likely identification because of name similarity. Listib was founded in the Byzantine period, however, and there is no trace of earlier settlement. The apocryphal book of TOBIT refers to a place called THISBE, located S of KEDESH in NAPHTALI (Tob. 1:2), and it has been suggested that the descriptive adjective *Tishbite* was derived from it (in which case Elijah may have been born there, later settling in Gilead). This view has not been widely accepted.

The familiarity of Elijah with N Gilead is pointed up by the narrative in 1 Ki. 17:2–7 concerning his sojourn at the brook KERITH, "east of the Jordan," in hiding from his enemies. It is now fairly certain that Kerith should be so located, and possibly identified with the Wadi Yabis in the highlands of N Gilead. The tradition of Elijah's presence in the region about Jabesh Gilead is seen in the names of the settlement of Listib and, not far from it, of a place on the opposite side of the valley called Mar Ilyas (St. Elias). Substantial surface remains of the Byzantine period, as well as some evidence of Roman occupation, are seen there. Hence the presence of the personality of Elijah is attested from these periods, and the tradition may well come from even earlier times. Respect for the spirit of Nebi-Ilyas (the prophet Elias) is given to a grove of oak trees above the ruins. Although "Tishbe in Gilead" is still a bit obscure, the general location of "Elijah the Tishbite's" homeland seems reasonably secure. M. H. HEICKSEN

Tishbite tish´bīt. See TISHBE.

Tishri tish´rē (postbiblical Heb. תִּשְׁרִי). The seventh month in the Hebrew sacred CALENDAR (first month in the civil calendar), corresponding to late September and early October. This term is not found in the Bible, which uses instead the Canaanite name ETHANIM (1 Ki. 8:2). According to Rabbi Eliezer, Tishri was the month in which the world was created (*b. Roš Haš.* 10b). The Jewish New Year is celebrated on the first and second days of Tishri.

tithe. The tenth part of produce or property for the support of the priesthood or for other religious objectives. References to the tithe are found in both the OT and NT (Heb. *ma'ăśēr* H5130; Gk. *dekatē*, from *dekatos* G1281), but the main teachings are incorporated in three passages in the Mosaic legislation: Lev. 27:30–33; Num. 18:21–32; and Deut. 12:5–18; 14:22–29.

I. Secular examples. Giving a portion of one's labor or of the spoils of war was known among a number of nations in antiquity. In EGYPT the people gave two tenths of their harvest to the PHARAOH (Gen. 47:24). The practice is also attested among the Syrians (1 Macc. 10:31; 11:35), the Lydians (Herodotus, *Hist.* 1.89), and the Babylonians (M. Jastrow, *The Religion of Babylonia and Assyria* [1898], 668). Tithes were both political (tribute and taxation) and religious (connected with offerings). Ancient extrabiblical use appears to be as a TAX in kind imposed by a ruler on a subject people or his own countrymen. Whereas among foreign nations the political purpose for tithes predominated, in Israel it was the religious, for it referred primarily to income dedicated to God.

II. Pre-Mosaic period. The first mention of the tithe was when ABRAHAM, returning from his victory over the invading Mesopotamian kings, gave MELCHIZEDEK, king-priest of SALEM, a tenth of all the spoils (Gen. 14:18–20). This incident is explained in Heb. 7:1–10 as indicating that the Melchizedek priesthood was superior to the Aaronic. JACOB, fleeing from ESAU, promised this amount in the event God prospered him (Gen. 28:22).

III. Mosaic period. Clearly, it was in Mosaic times that tithing had its greatest emphasis. Under the law of MOSES a tithe of the produce of the ground and of cattle was obligatory (Lev. 27:30, 32). The tithe of fruit and grain could be redeemed by the owner by buying it at one-fifth above market value (v. 31). This arrangement, however, was not allowed for the flock or herd. In such cases the tithe was taken by passing the cattle under the rod and removing every tenth animal, whether perfect or defective. There could be no exchange. Until the tithe was offered to God, the crop was not to be used by the people (23:14). The part given God could be at one time consumed on the altar; at another time only a portion of the tithe was consumed (vv. 9–13); the rest was granted to the priests and their families (Num. 18:11). See SACRIFICE AND OFFERINGS.

Some scholars have claimed that between Deuteronomy and the Priestly Code (which includes Leviticus and Numbers) no laws on tithing were given. The use of "tithe" twice in Ezekiel is admittedly in a nontechnical sense of "a tenth" (Ezek. 45:11, 14). The Priestly Code provided that the tithe was to be exclusively for the Levites, who were to give a tenth to the priests (Num. 18:20–23). In this code the tithe is connected with the heave offering. Like Deuteronomy, the Priestly Code views the tithe as an agricultural offering, not of cattle (Lev. 27:30–31). This practice is verified in Neh. 10:37–38; 12:44; 13:5, 12. One reference includes cattle in the tithe (Lev. 27:32–33), a detail confirmed elsewhere (2 Chr. 31:5–12).

The legislation in Numbers stipulated that grain must be threshed before it was tithed. The fruit of the vine and the olive were processed into wine and oil before a tithe was presented (Num. 18:27). As stated above, the tithe was considered a heave offering and given to the Levites (vv. 21, 24). This was the return for their service at the sanctuary (v. 21) and because of their exclusion from a landed inheritance. The priest was given a tithe (Num. 18:26), and the remainder was eaten elsewhere (v. 31).

Moses prescribed that all the required sacrifices, free-will offerings, and tithes were to be brought to the sanctuary in Jerusalem (Deut. 12:5–6, 11). All were to be eaten before the Lord (vv. 17–18). If the distance to the sanctuary was great, the offering could be exchanged for money, then taken to the sanctuary, where the money could be used to buy what was needed for the meal (14:23–27). His purchase was eaten by the offerer, his household, and the Levites in Jerusalem. Every third year everyone's tithe was to be stored in his own town, where the Levite, stranger, widow, and orphan could go for a supply (vv. 28–29). After a third-year tithe, the tenth was placed at the disposal of those mentioned in Deut. 26:12. It is held by some that there were two third-year tithes between SABBATICAL YEARS, at which time there was no tithe.

Greek dedicatory inscription (c. 500 B.C.) on Pentelic marble stating that a certain Kalis dedicated a tithe of his (or her) labors.

The laws of Deut. 14 appear to conflict with the regulations of Num. 18:21–32. The latter passage indicates that all the tithes should be given to the Levites, who in turn pay a tithe of a tithe to the priests. Furthermore, Levites were allowed to eat the tithe where they wished, not just at the central sanctuary. The rabbis attempted to reconcile the apparent contradiction by assuming different kinds of tithes: a first tithe was given to the Levites and priests (Num. 18); a second tithe was eaten by the offerer with his family and guests in a feast at the sanctuary (Deut. 14:22−27); and a third tithe, called the "poor's tithe," took the place of the second tithe in the third and sixth years of each sabbatical period (Deut. 14:28−29). The question has also arisen as to whether Deuteronomy has in view two separate tithes. It is not necessary to assume this. It was the same tithe but used differently in the third year. The aim of all tithing was to acknowledge that all a person had belonged to God.

In the past, scholars have debated whether there were two tithes or even three (cf. Jos. *Ant.* 4.8.22). Modern research seems to indicate that all the references are to the same tithe, explaining the differences as arising from the variations in time. The reasoning is that in the time of the composition of Deuteronomy (which the critical school dates to the 7th cent. B.C.), the tithe was used for a festal meal for the family, the poor, and the Levites. In the days of the composition of Numbers (which is said to be part of the Priestly Code dated to postexilic times), the tithe was employed solely for the support of the ministry of priests and Levites. The argumentation is not at all compelling: it seems more valid to hold that in the early Hebrew theocracy reflected in Leviticus (Mosaic times), when the nation lived as nomads, festal meals were not feasible; thus the tithes were offered to the priests and Levites as the needy among the people. In the age of Deuteronomy, however, when Israel was about to enter the land and inaugurate a permanent national existence, they were commanded both to bring tithes in kind or money to the main sanctuary and partake of a sacred meal with the Levites, and to stimulate charity for the needy, to give the tithes every third year for the poor, not just the priests and Levites, who in the settled life in the land were better provided for than in the wilderness wanderings. To conclude, the different references in the OT to tithing probably indicate differing practices in various times and places.

What is the relationship between the tithes and FIRSTFRUITS? A. S. Peake (in *HDB*, 4:780−81) thinks it better to distinguish between tithes and firstfruits (Deut. 14:22−27; 18:4; 26:1−15). On the other hand, H. H. Guthrie (in *IDB*, 4:654−55) takes the view that they had a common origin, which would account for the absence of mention of the tithe in the Book of the Covenant (see COVENANT, BOOK OF THE). It is difficult to give a final answer here. Because Deut. 26:1−15 mentions them together some have concluded that they are the same. It is not likely that a double offering would be asked. Thus the tithe is considered as a further precise statement of the firstfruits. A problem exists in that Deut. 18:4 enjoins that the firstfruits be given the priests. No such provision was made relative to the tithe. The problem remains open for further study.

IV. Period of the monarchy. It became a royal prerogative to exact a tithe of the crops, vineyards, and flocks. SAMUEL warned Israel that they would have to give a tenth to the king (1 Sam. 8:15, 17). It has been suggested that the tithe paid to the king was for the support of the royal sanctuaries. Even in IDOLATRY Israel paid tithes, in such cases at the temple of the idols (Amos 4:4). King HEZEKIAH's order of the tithe, apparently for the Levites, was so well carried out that the king had special chambers in the temple made for their deposit (2 Chr. 31:4−12). A similar arrangement was ordered by NEHEMIAH (Neh. 10:39; 13:12).

V. Exilic and postexilic period. EZEKIEL speaks (many believe prophetically) of the support of public worship by the prince for the collection of a general tax (Heb. *tĕrûmâ* H9556, Ezek. 45:13−17). The priests were to have for their support the firstfruits and heave offerings (44:30). In Nehemiah's day (Neh. 10:37−39) the Levites collected the tithe in all the cities and towns under the oversight of a priest, then delivered the tithe of the tithes to the storehouse in the temple for the priests. When this plan did not function, the Levites had to support themselves (13:10−13). In times of apostasy tithes were neglected (Mal. 3:7−12).

VI. NT and later periods. In the time of the NT, changes had taken place (Lk. 11:42; 18:12). When the greed of the high priests impoverished the ordinary priests, the latter took the tithes by force (Jos. *Ant.* 20.8.8; 9.2). The tithe of mint, anise, and cummin was a prescription of the rabbis that went beyond the intent of Scripture (Matt. 23:23; Lk. 11:42). The MISHNAH laid down this general principle: "Everything that is eaten and is watched over and grows out of the ground is liable to tithe" (*m. Ma'aśerot* 1:1). The rabbis gave elaborate rules as to the precise time in the year when cattle were tithed, also produce of the land and the fruit of the trees. The stage of growth at which produce was to be tithed was also prescribed. The rabbis placed great merit in the giving of tithes, stating that tithing was one of the three elements through whose merit the world was created (*Gen. Rab.* 1:4). All the tithe was to be given to the poor.

For several centuries in the early church there was no support of the clergy by a systematic giving of a tithe. In time the tithe came to be regarded generally after the pattern in the Jewish SYNAGOGUE. The practice was supported by an appeal to some NT passages (e.g., Matt. 10:10; Lk. 10:7; 1 Cor. 9:7–14), but IRENAEUS and other leaders in the church showed the arguments drawn from these texts were not valid. Rather, freedom in Christian giving was emphasized. (See further J. A. MacCulloch and W. H. D. Rouse in *ERE*, 12:347–51; H. Lansdell, *The Sacred Tenth or Studies in Tithe-Giving Ancient and Modern* [1906], 45–109, 119–80; H. Jagersma in *Remembering All the Way* [1981], 116–28; M. E. Stevens, *Temples, Tithes and Taxes: The Temple and the Economic Life of Ancient Israel* [2006]; *NIDOTTE*, 2:1035–55; *NIDNTT*, 3:851–55.)

C. L. FEINBERG

Titius Justus tish´ee-uhs-juhs´tuhs. See JUSTUS #2.

tittle. See DOT.

Titus ti´tuhs (Τίτος G5519, from Latin *Titus*). The name Titus appears in the NT only in 2 Corinthians (eight times), Galatians (twice), 2 Timothy (once), and Titus (once). It can be safely assumed that all these references refer to the same individual: a companion and coworker of PAUL who later was the pastor on the island of CRETE. In addition, Titus was the name of a Roman emperor not mentioned in the Bible. Both individuals are covered in this article.

I. Titus the companion of Paul. The absence of any reference to Titus in the Acts of the Apostles complicates the effort to integrate the role of this Christian leader into Luke's account of Paul's missionary activity. Attempts to read or insert the name Titus into the Acts of the Apostles are not convincing, and no good explanation has been given to account for the absence of his name in this book. From the references in the Pauline epistles it appears that Titus was an uncircumcised Greek (Gal. 2:3), an intimate associate of Paul, and an effective pastor (2 Cor. 8:23; 12:18; although disputed and somewhat problematic, the unity of 2 Corinthians is assumed in the following reconstruction).

It is unknown when Titus joined Paul in his mission activity. The earliest reference to Titus is found in GALATIANS. Paul reports that on his visit to Jerusalem "after fourteen years" (Gal. 2:1) Titus accompanied him and BARNABAS. Some suggest that this incident is the "famine-relief" visit described in Acts 11:27–30; others identify it with the COUNCIL OF JERUSALEM of Acts 15. At the time of this visit the issue of CIRCUMCISION had become crucial, and Paul cites, as vindication of his position, the fact that Titus was not compelled to be circumcised. If this is the visit of Acts 11, Titus was then a companion of Paul before the first missionary journey. If it is the visit of Acts 15 (preferable identification in the light of Pauline chronology), Titus's contact with Paul was at least before the second missionary journey. In any case, nothing is recorded concerning Titus's mission work until the third missionary journey shortly after Paul's lengthy stay at EPHESUS (Acts 19:1, 17, 26, 35). Whether Titus accompanied Paul during all these journeys cannot be ascertained. However, Titus's effectiveness with the Corinthians might suggest some prior personal contact with them, although Luke is rather definite in recording that Paul's companions in Greece were TIMOTHY and SILAS, and Paul even stresses that he was alone for a time in ATHENS (1 Thess. 3:1).

The Corinthian correspondence indicates that Paul had a number of frustrating experiences with the church at CORINTH. These apparently occurred during Paul's sojourn of over two years in Ephesus during the third missionary journey (Acts 19), although there is not the slightest allusion to these problems in the Acts account. After various attempts to deal with these problems by correspondence and a personal visit, Paul sent Titus to attempt a reconciliation and resolution of the difficulties. Apparently Paul and Titus agreed to meet in TROAS. When Paul arrived in Troas, however, he did not find Titus (2 Cor. 2:13). Although there were promising opportunities for mission work in Troas, Paul's concern about Corinth and Titus led him to proceed to MACEDONIA (obviously there was a prearranged travel route—either by sea or land—to obviate the possibility of by-passing one another). In Macedonia Titus brings to Paul a comforting report about the Corinthians which gives him much joy and peace of mind (2 Cor. 7:6–14). Titus seems to have established a good rapport with the Corinthians and Paul exuberantly expresses his gratitude for the happy turn of events.

The offering for the Judean churches was still pending in Corinth, and from Macedonia Paul sent Titus to Corinth to complete this expression of fellowship with the other churches (2 Cor. 8:6, 16). Apparently, Titus was successful in this mission, and the following spring Paul went to Jerusalem with this offering (Rom. 15:25–26). The subscription to 2 Corinthians in many MSS (dating no earlier than the 9th cent.) indicates that the letter was written from Philippi *dia* (i.e., delivered by) Titus and Luke. This late testimony is probably an inference from the biblical data, but it does fit with the givens of 2 Corinthians.

One of the PASTORAL EPISTLES is addressed to Titus. At this time he was working in Crete. The epistle contains some exhortations to Titus, although none of these reflects negatively on his character or ability. It appears that he was dealing with a difficult and somewhat unruly congregation in Crete. Paul suggests that Titus's pastoral qualifications led to this assignment (Tit. 1:5). He also describes Titus as "my true son in our common faith" (1:4; Timothy is similarly described in 1 Tim. 1:2). Titus is instructed to come to NICOPOLIS on the W coast of Greece (Tit. 3:12) to spend the winter there with Paul. At the time of the writing of 1 Timothy, Titus had departed to DALMATIA, apparently from Rome (2 Tim. 4:10). This is the last reference to Titus in the NT.

In many respects Titus appears in the NT as an ideal pastor. Paul reflects very favorably upon Titus's genuine devotion and pastoral concern (2 Cor. 8:16–17). His earnestness is mentioned as a challenge to the Corinthians. Titus's joy and devoted concern was an inspiration to Paul in his reconciliation with the Corinthians (7:13–15). Paul substantiates his devotion to the Corinthians by arguing that he was of the same mind and attitude as Titus (12:18). These scattered allusions to the character of Titus indicate his close relationship to Paul and his stellar qualifications as a pastor.

The presence of a letter addressed to Titus in the NT has, among other things, been a great inspiration to ministers of the gospel throughout the history of the church. Although the data regarding Titus in the NT is scanty, nevertheless much can be learned from his pastoral activities and the letter addressed to him as a model and manual for a pastor. (See further F. F. Bruce, *The Pauline Circle* [1985], ch. 8.)

B. VAN ELDEREN

II. Titus the emperor. Titus Flavius Vespasianus was born in A.D. 39 and ruled as emperor of ROME for a short period, 79–81. While still a young man he had served as a tribune of the soldiers in Germany and Britain, and later accompanied his father, VESPASIAN, to Palestine at the time of the Jewish revolt. When the latter was called to Rome and was elevated to the imperial seat, Titus was left in charge of the war and brought it to an end by the capture and destruction of Jerusalem in the year 70. Upon his return to Rome he celebrated the triumph with his father, and from this time was made

The Arch of Titus in Rome (W side).

a virtual partner in the government, clearly designated for the succession. When Vespasian died in 79 Titus became emperor.

In many ways Titus was a contrast to his father. He was the darling of the populace, good looking, affable to everyone. After the parsimonious policy of Vespasian he spent lavishly and was always remembered with affection in later years. By expelling the hated informers and doing away with trials and executions for treason, he gained the favor of the senate, and thus that body did not oppose his actions. (The primary ancient sources are Suetonius, *The Twelve Caesars: Titus*, and Dio Cassius, *Rom. Hist.* 66.17–26.)

The brief reign of Titus was noteworthy mainly for two disasters by which it was visited. In August of 79, Mount Vesuvius erupted and completely destroyed the two towns of Pompeii and Herculaneum, covering the former with a shower of hot ashes and pumice, the latter with a river of lava. An eyewitness account of this event may be found in two letters written by Pliny the Younger to his friend Tacitus, the historian (Pliny, *Epistulae* 6.16.20). In the year 80 there was a plague and disastrous fire at Rome. Titus generously aided the victims of this disaster, and did a great deal to repair the damage to the city. Among other things he finished the Colosseum (begun by Vespasian), and built the baths which bear his name. The reign of Titus was looked upon as a time of ideal happiness, and his untimely death in the year 81 caused universal sorrow. (See further H. Bengtson, *Die Flavier: Vespasian, Titus, Domitian: Geschichte e. röm. Kaiserhauses* [1979]; B. W. Jones, *The Emperor Titus* [1984]; *OCD*, 1532–33.) R. C. Stone

Titus, Epistle of. See Pastoral Epistles; Pseudo-Titus, Epistle of.

Titus Justus. See Justus #2.

Titus Manius. See Manius, Titus.

Tizite tī′zit (תִּיצִי H9407, apparently the gentilic form of an unattested name such as תִּיץ). Epithet applied to Joha son of Shimri, one of David's mighty warriors (1 Chr. 11:45). Presumably this designation identifies him as originating from an otherwise unknown place or tribe named תִּיץ (or the like), but it is unclear why his brother Jediael does not receive the same description.

Toah toh′uh (תּוֹחַ H9346, variant תֹּחוּ H9375, meaning uncertain [see *HALOT*, 4:1696–97]). Son of Zuph, descendant of Levi through Kohath, and ancestor of Samuel (1 Chr. 6:34; apparently the same as Nahath in v. 26 and Tohu in 1 Sam. 1:1). The relationship among these three genealogical lists is debated (cf. *ABD*, 6:583).

Tob tob (טוֹב H3204, "good, pleasant"). A town and district of S Hauran mentioned as the place where Jephthah went when he fled from his brothers (Jdg. 11:3, 5). Later, during the reign of David, the Ammonites hired twelve thousand mercenaries from Tob to defend themselves from the Israelites (2 Sam. 10:6, 8). In the days of Judas Maccabee, the Seleucids killed about a thousand Jews who lived in that region (1 Macc. 5:13 [KJV, "Tobie"], possibly the same as the Toubiani of 2 Macc. 12:17; for the view that in both passages the reference is to the family of Tobiah, see J. A. Goldstein, *I Maccabees*, AB 41 [1976], 298–99; ib., *II Maccabees*, AB 41A [1983], 439–40). Tob is apparently mentioned in Egyptian records as *Tby* (no. 22 in the list of Thutmose III, *Ṭubu* in the Tell el-Amarna tablets), referring to an Aramean state E of the Jordan River, but NE of the Gilead hill-country. See Aram (country). It is generally identified as eṭ-Ṭayibeh, some 45 mi. NE of modern Amman (in Jordan). E. M. Blaiklock

Tob-Adonijah tob′ad-uh-nī′juh (טוֹב אֲדֹנִיָּה H3207, "good is the Lord Yahweh"). One of six Levites whom King Jehoshaphat sent to teach the law in the cities of Judah (2 Chr. 17:8). Some Greek MSS and other witnesses omit this name, however, and many scholars believe that it was introduced into the Hebrew text by a scribal mistake (duplicating and conflating the previous two names, Adonijah and Tobijah).

Tobiah toh-bī′uh (טוֹבִיָּה H3209, short form of טוֹבִיָּהוּ H3210, "Yahweh is good"; see Tobijah). (**1**) Ancestor of a family of returned exiles who could not prove their Israelite descent (Ezra 2:60; Neh.

This Aramaic inscription from ʿAraq el-Emir (3rd cent. B.C.) bears the name Tobiah.

7:62; in 1 Esd. 5:37 [where KJV has "Ban," misreading *Tbubun* as *tou Ban*], he appears as the father of DELAIAH).

(2) An Ammonite (or less likely a Jew living in AMMON, descendant of #1 above) who served as a Persian official and who joined with SANBALLAT and others in persistently opposing the work of NEHEMIAH (Neh. 2:10, 19; 4:3, 7; 6:1, 12–19; 7:62; 13:4, 7; it has been suggested that instead of "Tobiah the Ammonite official" [Heb. ʿebed H6269], the text should read, "Tobiah and ʿAbd the Ammonite," but see H. G. M. Williamson, *Ezra-Nehemiah*, WBC 16 [1985], 183). Both he and his son JEHOHANAN bore Jewish names and were married to Jewish women. Tobiah was in high favor with the high priest, ELIASHIB, who gave him a guest room in the temple compound. He tried to frighten Nehemiah, who regarded him as his chief enemy and cast him and his household goods out of the temple guest chamber (13:4–9). (For the view that two different historical figures are involved, see D. Edelman in *RB* 113 [2006]: 570–84.) Some scholars think that the family of TOBIAS (#2), which in the 3rd cent. B.C. vied with the family of ONIAS for the high priesthood, was descended from this Tobiah. In a mausoleum at ʿAraq el-Emir (central TRANSJORDAN), a rock-cut tomb has the name "Tobiah" incised in Aramaic characters of the 3rd cent. B.C., but it is uncertain whether this should be connected with the family of the biblical Tobiah (cf. J. Naveh, *The Development of the Aramaic Script* [1970], 62–64). S. BARABAS

Tobias toh-bīʹuhs (Τωβίας, from Heb. טוֹבִיָּה H3209, "Yahweh is good"; see TOBIJAH). (1) Son of Tobit (Tob. 1:9 et al.). See TOBIT, BOOK OF.

(2) Father or grandfather of a wealthy Jewish man named HYRCANUS (2 Macc. 3:11; cf. Jos. *Ant.* 12.4.2 §160; 12.4.6 §186). This Tobias may have been a descendant of TOBIAH (#2). According to Josephus (*Ant.* 12.5.1 §§237–41), the powerful Tobiad family later supported MENELAUS against JASON in the struggle for the high priesthood. (See B. Mazar in *IEJ* 7 [1957]: 137–45, 229–38; *HJP*, rev. ed. [1973–87], 1:149–50 n. 30; *SacBr*, 303–4.)

Tobiel tohʹbee-uhl (Τωβιηλ, from טוֹבִיאֵל [not attested in the Heb. Bible], "God is good"; cf. TOBIJAH). Father of TOBIT (Tob. 1:1, 8).

Tobijah toh-bīʹjuh טוֹבִיָּהוּ H3210 [2 Chr. 17:8] and טוֹבִיָּה H3209 [Zech. 6:10, 14], "Yahweh is good"). (1) One of six Levites whom King JEHOSHAPHAT sent to teach the law in the cities of Judah (2 Chr. 17:8). Appointed to the same mission were a number of princes and priests.

(2) One of a group of Jewish exiles who brought gold and silver from Babylon to help those who had returned under ZERUBBABEL; from these gifts a crown was to be made for Joshua (JESHUA) the high priest (Zech. 6:10, 14). The form of the Hebrew name in this passage is elsewhere rendered TOBIAH in the KJV and other English Bibles (Ezra 2:60 et al.); this inconsistency has no basis in the Hebrew text.

Tobit, Book of tohʹbit (Τωβιτ, also Τωβιθ, possibly short form of Heb. טוֹבִיָּה H3209, "Yahweh is good"; see TOBIJAH). A narrative book found in Greek MSS of the OT (see SEPTUAGINT) but lacking in the Hebrew Bible, thus included among the APOCRYPHA (or Deuterocanonical Books). In the VULGATE and Roman Catholic editions of the Bible, the books of Tobit, JUDITH, and ESTHER form a trio that follows the last of the historical books, NEHEMIAH.

I. Content. The book presents a charming tale in which beauty, suspense, and moral truth are interwoven in a most pleasing fashion, causing Tobit to become one of the most popular of the books of the Apocrypha in the history of the church. The story is set in the times of the Assyrian captivity and concerns the fortunes of a certain Tobit and his son Tobias (the text of the NRSV, based primarily on CODEX SINAITICUS, differs in some details from the KJV and RSV). The following outline may be suggested:

- A. Introduction (Tob. 1:1–2)
- B. The virtues and tribulations of Tobit (1:3—2:14)
- C. Tobit's prayer (3:1–6)
- D. The tribulations of Sarah (3:7–10)
- E. Sarah's prayer (3:11–15)
- F. The mission of Raphael (3:16–17)
- G. The instruction of Tobias (4:1–21)
- H. Tobias's traveling companion (5:1–21)
- I. The fish and the plan (6:1–17)
- J. The marriage of Tobias and Sarah (7:1–18)
- K. The trial and victory over the demon (8:1–21)
- L. Azarias fetches the money (9:1–6)
- M. The mutual concern of Tobit and Tobias (10:1–12)
- N. The reunion and celebration (11:1–19)
- O. Raphael reveals himself (12:1–21)
- P. Tobit's great prayer of praise (13:1–18)
- Q. The final words and death of Tobit (14:1–15)

Tobit is described as a devout Israelite of the tribe of NAPHTALI. He often went to Jerusalem to worship and regularly gave three tenths of his produce to the temple and other good causes. This righteous man, however, like JOB, appeared to receive only misfortune in return for his piety. He and his family were deported to NINEVEH as captives of the Assyrians, but unlike the other exiles they continued to adhere to the strict dietary regulations of the law. Temporarily, Tobit was the recipient of good fortune as one of SHALMANESER's stewards. During this period, Tobit judiciously entrusted a large sum of his money to a friend in MEDIA. Tobit continued to live a pious life, doing deeds of charity to his brethren, and particularly in giving proper burial to a number of the Jews who were slaughtered by the Assyrian kings. The latter activity became known to SENNACHERIB, and Tobit was forced to flee for his life, leaving behind all his property and wealth.

Tobit, however, continued in his acts of righteousness, and on one occasion buried the body of a Jewish brother only to receive a cruel reward. Having become unclean through his contact with the dead body, he was forced to sleep outside, and his face became accidentally dirtied by sparrow droppings, which got into his eyes and caused a blindness that physicians were powerless to cure. Like the wife of Job, Tobit's wife ultimately cries out the complaint of her frustration, "Where are your acts of charity? Where are your righteous deeds?" (Tob. 2:14). Thereupon Tobit prays in anguish of soul that his life might be taken, for he is convinced that it is better to die than to live under the present reproaches (3:6).

At that same moment some distance away, the same prayer was being uttered by Sarah the daughter of a certain Raguel who happened to be a close kinsman of Tobit. Sarah had the misfortune of being loved by the demon ASMODEUS, who had slain no less than seven husbands of Sarah, each on the very night of their wedding before the marriage could be consummated. Sarah was subject to accusations and reproaches, and in her despair she even contemplated suicide (Tob. 3:10). At this point the stage is set for the main action of the story. God sends his angel RAPHAEL to answer the respective prayers of Tobit and Sarah—not by bringing death, but by bringing happiness to all concerned, thus underlining the goodness of his providence.

The denouement is initiated by Tobit's decision to inform Tobias about the money he had deposited with his friend in Media some years earlier. Taking opportunity of the occasion to impart some very excellent instruction in righteousness (Tob. 4), Tobit informs Tobias concerning the money, and the decision is taken to send Tobias in quest of it. A suitable traveling companion is needed, however, and Tobias chances upon one Azarias who is well qualified and who in reality is the disguised Raphael. Despite the protestations of Tobias's mother, Anna, the pair sets out on their adventuresome journey accompanied, as the narrator quaintly notes, by young Tobias's dog.

Camping on the banks of the TIGRIS that night, Tobias is nearly swallowed by a fish as he washes. Azarias directs Tobias to catch the fish, to cut out its heart, liver, and gall, and to store these safely among his gear. As they continue their journey, upon the questioning of Tobias, Azarias explains that the organs of the fish are particularly useful for two things: the smoke from the burning heart and liver will drive away evil spirits; and from the gall can be made a salve that will take away the white films from a blind man's eyes (thus the reader is made aware of the direction the story will take). Azarias tells Tobias that he is to take Sarah as his wife. Tobias, however, has already heard of Sarah's plight and is consequently not at all eager to follow the direction of Azarias. When Azarias reminds Tobias of the potency of the fish organs, Tobias's mind is changed.

The delightful meeting of Raguel and Tobias occurs next, and in due course the marriage is proposed and indeed, despite Raguel's warning, takes place the same day. That night, as the couple retire to their bed chamber, Sarah, Raguel, and his wife, Edna, are all seized with anxiety. Indeed, so pessimistic is the father that when all have retired he rises secretly and digs a grave for Tobias that he might be buried immediately. A maid is forthwith sent to see whether Tobias is alive or dead. Tobias, however, upon entering the bed chamber had, as directed, made a fire and placed the heart and liver of the fish on the fire, and the smoke that was produced had driven out the demon as promised. Tobias and Sarah then had prayed together and had gone to sleep, voluntarily forgoing the consummation of their marriage. The maid found them asleep and reported to Raguel that Tobias was alive and well, upon which Raguel prayed a prayer of thanksgiving.

The next day a great feast of celebration lasting fourteen days begins. Tobias sends Azarias to Media to fetch his money and to bring his father's friend to the wedding feast. At this point the narrative returns to Nineveh and to the deep concern of Tobit and Anna at the delayed return of Tobias. Tobit believes that Tobias is well; Anna, however, insists that her boy is dead and is angry with Tobit for trying to deceive her. Meanwhile Tobias and his new wife, with half of Raguel's wealth, accompanied by Azarias and, of course, Tobias's dog, too, finally take their leave of Raguel and Edna. Tobias and Azarias (and the dog) run ahead of the entourage in their haste to return home. At this point the narrator says, "Meanwhile Anna sat looking intently down the road by which her son would come" (Tob. 11:5). Suddenly she catches sight of them in the distance and reports to her blind husband, "Look, your son is coming, and the man who went with him!" (v. 6).

Thereupon follows one of the most delightful reunions of literature—there is much weeping and rejoicing, and, of course, the gall salve is applied to the father's eyes and his blindness is removed. At the gate of Nineveh they meet Sarah and the slaves and cattle that made up part of Raguel's gift. Another week of celebration takes place. Afterward Tobit and Tobias offer half of Raguel's gift to the good Azarias. The latter, however, only remarks that thanksgiving is due to God for his goodness. Then he volunteers, "I am Raphael, one of the seven angels who stand ready and enter before the glory of the Lord" (Tob. 12:15). They fall on their faces in fear, but Raphael says not to be afraid and adds that he was sent by God. After directing them to write what has happened, he disappears.

Then follows a magnificent prayer of rejoicing, which Tobit is said to have written. The final chapter of the book is rather anticlimactic, giving an account of Tobit's last words, including a warning for his descendants to leave Nineveh because Jonah's prophecy was going to come true (Tob. 14:4; according to the text followed by the NRSV, the reference is to Nahum's prophecy). The death of Tobit and then of Anna is recorded. Tobias and his family then return to Ecbatana, where he eventually buries both Raguel and Edna. The book ends with a notice of the death of Tobias, with the note that before he died he heard of the destruction of Nineveh.

II. Historical background. The story places Tobit in the days of the Assyrian captivity and thus in the 8th cent. B.C. There are, however, a number of difficulties involved in the historical and geographical details of the book. Thus Tobit says that when he was "still a young man" the tribe of Naphtali deserted Jerusalem (Tob. 1:4). This rebellion, however, seems to have occurred about 931 B.C., following the death of Solomon (cf. 1 Ki. 12:16, 19) and long before the time of Tobit. A more significant problem lies in the statement that it was in the days of Shalmaneser (in Tobit he is designated by the Greek equivalent Enemessar) that Naphtali was taken into captivity (Tob. 1:2). In reality, it was not Shalmaneser V who did this, but rather his predecessor Tiglath-Pileser III, in about 734 B.C. (cf. 2 Ki. 15:29). Sennacherib is said to have been the son of Shalmaneser and to have reigned in his place after his death (Tob. 1:15). Sennacherib, however, was really the son of SARGON II, a monarch who, although he reigned for some fifteen years, is not mentioned at all in Tobit. The reference at the end of the book to the destruction of Nineveh by NEBUCHADNEZZAR and AHASUERUS is erroneous (14:15 RSV, but see NRSV and mg.), since Nineveh actually fell to NABOPOLASSAR and the Median king Cyaxares (612 B.C.).

The geographical difficulties are also striking. In particular, it is implied that the Tigris River is E of Nineveh, some distance toward Ecbatana (Tob. 6:1), whereas Nineveh itself lay on the E bank of the Tigris. Further, in one of the major recensions of the book (that of Sinaiticus and the Old Latin, followed by the Vulgate) it is stated that Ecbatana is in the middle of a plain, two days' journey in distance from Rages (5:6 NRSV, but see RSV). Actually Ecbatana lies high in the mountains and is some 200 mi. away from Rages.

These various discrepancies have led almost all scholars to conclude that Tobit cannot derive from the historical period it purports to be from, but instead is probably to be dated much later, when the historical details of the earlier period were not so well known. Indeed, it may be that the story, despite its historical setting, is entirely fictional, although a few scholars have argued for the possibility that there is a historical kernel underlying the present book.

III. Sources. The conclusion that Tobit is a fictional rather than a historical story is confirmed to some extent by its apparent dependence upon a few well-known folk tales of the ancient world. The author of Tobit seems to have known the story of AHIKAR, which recounts how this individual, who held office under Sennacherib and Esarhaddon, became rich only to be falsely accused by his adopted son Nadin and sentenced to death. He was however secretly hidden by a servant who once had also been the victim of false accusations and whom Ahikar himself had saved. Ultimately Ahikar, able to be of assistance to Esarhaddon in satisfying an unreasonable demand of Egypt, was vindicated as righteous and avenged.

At the beginning of Tobit, Ahikar is mentioned as a very important and powerful administrator of Esarhaddon's kingdom who happens also to be Tobit's nephew (Tob. 1:21–22). Ahikar and Nadab (one of the several slight variations of the name that occur) are said to have attended the great celebration that took place upon the return of Tobias and his new wife to Nineveh (11:18). At the end of the book, explicit allusion is made to the story of Ahikar. In his last words Tobit reminds Tobias and his grandsons about what Nadab did to Ahikar. "Because he gave alms, Ahikar escaped the fatal trap that Nadab had set for him, but Nadab fell into it himself, and was destroyed" (14:10). The moral of the story, "So now, my children, see what almsgiving accomplishes, and what injustice does" (14:11), is very similar to that which concludes the story of Ahikar. In addition to the similarity of the general theme of the two books, that is, the suffering and vindication of the righteous, there are a number of striking parallels among the wisdom sayings.

A second story that may have been known to the author of Tobit is that which, although occurring in a variety of forms, is known generally as the "Fable of the Grateful Dead." The basic theme of the story concerns the return of a dead man's spirit in human form to reward in various ways (including the bestowal of a bride) the man who had at no small sacrifice gone out of his way to give proper burial to the dead man's corpse. In some versions of the story, the righteous man is advised by the embodied spirit to marry a certain rich young woman (sometimes said to be a princess) whose several husbands have all died on their wedding night as the result of a serpent dwelling within her. The righteous man is aided by his benefactor in subduing the serpent and winning the woman. Usually also included in these stories is the ultimate revelation of the true identity of the benefactor. Although the actual story of Tobit is somewhat different, a number of its motifs are similar to this fable: Tobit's concern with proper burial of the dead; the appearance of a spirit (in this case, angel) in human form; the rewarding of Tobit's righteousness; the bestowal of a bride upon Tobias; the subjugation of the demon; the revealing of Raphael. The author of Tobit appears to have used the various motifs while transmuting the basic narrative by virtue of his own Jewish viewpoint.

One more source has been suggested as possibly drawn upon by our author. The Egyptian *Tractate* of *Khôns* speaks of the exorcism of a young demon-possessed princess by Khôns, deity of Thebes, and to that extent parallels the victory won over Sarah's demon in Tobit. However, the parallel is too general to be impressive, and although it has been argued that Tobit was written to counteract the Egyptian story, the contention is too closely tied to an Egyptian provenance (not at all certain) to be regarded as convincing.

IV. Language, place of origin, and date.

Prior to the discovery of the DEAD SEA SCROLLS, scholars tended to favor the conjecture that Tobit was written originally in Greek. Among these scrolls, however, fragments of Tobit in Hebrew and Aramaic have been found, arguing for the probability of a Semitic original.

No consensus exists with regard to the provenance of Tobit. Three important locations have been suggested for the composition of the book: Mesopotamia, Egypt, and Palestine. The book itself naturally assumes a Mesopotamian origin. The story takes place in Mesopotamia and reveals a number of Persian influences, especially in the areas of angelology and demonology (cf. the demon's name, Asmodeus, which is of Persian origin). Even in such a minor detail as the occasional reference to Tobias's dog, Persian influence has been detected, since in ZOROASTRIANISM the dog is regarded as sacred whereas in Judaism the dog is generally despised.

However, because of the author's apparent ignorance of the geography of the area, some have preferred Egypt as the place of origin of the book. In addition to the possible dependence of Tobit on the *Tractate of Khôns*, Tobit may reflect a knowledge of Egyptian magic that was able to effect cures employing certain organs of the fish. It has even been suggested that the "fish" that nearly swallowed Tobias (Tob. 6:2) was in reality a crocodile. Moreover, when the demon is finally driven out of Sarah, he is said to have fled to the remotest parts of Egypt" (8:3), which could possibly be an unconscious indication of the book's place of origin.

Despite apparent indications that the book originated in DIASPORA Judaism, this is by no means a necessary conclusion. Indeed, the discovery of Aramaic and Hebrew fragments of Tobit at Qumran may perhaps add some plausibility to the conjectures of a few scholars that the book originated in Palestine. The religious teaching of the book might favor this viewpoint to some extent (its tenor is similar to that of ECCLESIASTICUS) but at the same time the exilic sympathies of the book cannot be doubted. In sum, the evidence—internal and external—is so insubstantial that although plausible arguments for several places of origin may be put forward, their truth cannot finally be determined.

The date of Tobit too is difficult to establish. Some scholars have dated the book as early as the 7th cent. B.C., but a number of problems militate against this conclusion. The serious historical blunders mentioned earlier suggest that the author was removed from this period by a considerable space of time. Further, unless we are predisposed to allow that the story is literally true or that the author had the gift of prophecy, he betrays an awareness of events (e.g., the fall of Nineveh and Jerusalem, the return from the captivity, and the rebuilding of the temple [cf. Tob. 14:4–5]) that took place long after this time. On the other hand, there is no trace of a knowledge of the Maccabean revolt on the part of the author (see MACCABEE).

These facts indicate that the book likely dates from the period between the beginning of the 4th cent. and end of the 3rd cent. B.C. The majority of scholars favor the end of this period, a date of approximately 200 B.C. or shortly thereafter. Whereas this date cannot be established beyond question, it most successfully accounts for the various data available from internal evidence. It goes without saying that nothing is known of the actual author of the book, except that he was certainly a devout champion of pietistic Judaism.

V. Purpose and theological teaching.

If it is correct to assume that the story contained in Tobit is not historical, but rather the fictional composition of an author who made use of contemporary folk legend(s), what may be said of his purpose in publishing the book known to us as Tobit? The story indeed is only a vehicle used by the author in propagating a religious message concerning the importance of right conduct and the faithfulness of God in turn. Of central importance in the author's world are the observance of the law and the performance of deeds of charity. Chapter 4 in its entirety is given over to ethical exhortation put in the mouth of Tobit in preparation for Tobias's journey. This exhortation, as well as the aphoristic material found throughout the book, may be fairly taken as addressed by the author to his readers. This material, however, is only incidental to the actual plot of the book.

Directly underlying the plot is a theme that it was also the author's purpose to convey: despite all appearances, in times of blackness God's providence is at work, assuring that everything ultimately will work out to the good of the righteous involved. The righteousness of the main characters of the drama, their prayers and exhortations, were meant to serve as a pattern of conduct for the writer's contemporaries. Second, and perhaps more important, the experience of these characters—particularly Tobit and Sarah, who are in despair at the opening of the story—is meant to serve as an impetus toward hope in the midst of trying circumstances (such as one might well expect to find in the period leading up to the revolt of the Maccabees) that faced the first readers of the story.

Tobit is important for the light it sheds on Jewish piety of the intertestamental period. The theological stance of its author is rather similar to that of the early Pharisaism of the post-Maccabean age, with the exception that Tobit knows nothing of the RESURRECTION of the dead (rewards and punishments are received in the present life). This is to say that Tobit presents an attractive picture of Jewish piety at its best. The author was, of course, greatly influenced by the OT. Indeed, a large number of parallels to OT passages (esp. the Pentateuch, but elsewhere as well) may be indicated, some of these being close enough to be designated paraphrase or near quotation (e.g., compare Tob. 3:10; 6:15 with Gen. 42:38; 44:29, 31; Tob. 4:14 with Lev. 19:13; Tob. 8:6 with Gen. 2:18; Tob. 7:3–4 with Gen. 29:4–14; Tob. 4:10; 12:9; with Prov. 10:2; 11:4).

The prayers of the book, of great devotional beauty and theological depth, are worth study in themselves. Therein God is recognized as one whose majesty and power are beyond measure. Indeed, such is his transcendence in the author's view that the mediation of angels assumes a role of importance in the efficacy of prayers (cf. Tob. 12:15). Tobit's concern with ANGELS and DEMONS is important for illustrating how belief in them flourished during the intertestamental period. The prayer by Tobit in ch. 13 refers to future (eschatological?) events that include a large-scale return to Jerusalem, the participation of Gentile nations in worship there, and a magnificent rebuilding of the temple. The predominant emphasis is on the present fulfillment of righteousness. Temple worship and religion at the personal level are magnified. Emphasis falls upon tithing and almsgiving, but also upon care for the dead and proper observance of food and marriage regulations.

Large place is given to personal virtue, both in the story and in the accompanying exhortation. Perhaps most impressive of all in this connection is the presence of the golden rule in its negative form: "and what you hate, do not do to any one" (Tob. 4:15). It has been pointed out that the book encompasses the "three Pillars of Judaism": prayer, almsgiving, and fasting (cf. 12:8). The genius of Tobit, however, is found in the completely successful combination of the ethical teaching with the narrative of the story itself. Where there is righteousness, God will act mercifully on behalf of his servants. This truth, indeed, is uttered as the last words of the dying Tobit, a conclusion that may be regarded as the moral of the whole story: "So now, my children, consider what almsgiving accomplishes, and what injustice does" (14:11).

VI. Text and canonicity. The textual history of Tobit is very complex and reflects what must have been an early and widespread popularity. The Greek text of the book has survived in no less than three distinct recensions, although the third finds only partial witness. These are (1) CODEX SINAITICUS (2) CODEX VATICANUS and CODEX ALEXANDRINUS, and (3) a few minuscule MSS (44, 106, 107, according to the numbering of Holmes and Parsons) in Tob. 6:8–13:8, but which otherwise reflect the text of recension (2).

A large number of versions are extant, representing each of the three recensions, and in more than one instance versions in the same language reflect different recensions. For recension (1) the Old Latin, Vulgate, Aramaic, and Hebrew versions are available. Recension (2) is represented by Syriac, Coptic (Sahidic), Hebrew, Ethiopic, and Armenian versions. The third recension is not available in its entirety, either in its "major" Greek witnesses or in the versions. It is clear, however, that a full third recension existed from its presence in a Syriac version from Tob. 7:9 to the end of the book, and also from a papyrus fragment in Greek from Oxyrhynchus that contains a portion of 2:2–8. The third recension seems clearly to be the latest of the three, often combining the readings of the two earlier ones by way of mediation. It is interesting, however, that one of its readings (12:8) appears to be quoted in *2 Clement* 16.4, although this cannot be taken as evidence for an early date of the recension as a whole.

More interesting is the relationship between the first two recensions. The numerous similarities may possibly be the result of interdependence, but a number of conspicuous differences seem to suggest that the similarities may instead be due to the common use of a prior (original?) edition. The first recension as found in Sinaiticus is considerably longer than the second recension, yet it omits two important sections (Tob. 4:1b–18; 13:8–11a) as well as several lesser ones that are preserved in the latter. These omissions in Sinaiticus, however, are probably fortuitous, for other early witnesses to the same recension, notably the Old Latin and one of the Qumran fragments, contain the missing material. Since the first recension is so much longer than the second, it is arguable that it is a later expansion of the latter. Nevertheless, it is also possible that the second recension (i.e., as found in Vaticanus and Alexandrinus) is a later reduction of the first recension.

This conclusion finds support in that many of the differences of the second recension are accountable as improvements and alterations incorporating or reflecting a later viewpoint. Indeed, it is generally conceded that the first recension is the earliest of the two, since its style is clearly more Semitic and thus presumably closer to the original. This is confirmed to a considerable extent by the fact that the Aramaic and Hebrew fragments found at Qumran reflect the text of the first recension.

The two main recensions of the Greek text are both available in Rahlfs's *Septuaginta*. The KJV and RSV generally follow recension (2), whereas the NRSV accepts a large number of readings from Sinaiticus and the Vulgate (relying no doubt on the now standard edition of the Greek text by R. Hanhart, *Tobit, Septuaginta* 8/5 [1983]; cf. also Hanhart's *Text und Textgeschichte des Buches Tobit* [1984]; C. J. Wagner, *Polyglotte Tobit-Synopse: Griechisch, Lateinisch, Syrisch, Hebräisch, Aramäisch, mit einem Index zu den Tobit-Fragmenten vom Toten Meer* [2003]; S. Weeks et al., eds., *The Book of Tobit: Texts from the Principal Ancient and Medieval Traditions, with Synopsis, Concordances, and Annotated Texts in Aramaic, Hebrew, Greek, Latin, and Syriac* [2004]).

Tobit is received as canonical in the Roman Catholic Church following the decision concerning apocryphal books taken at the Council of Trent in the 16th cent. Consequently Tobit and Judith take their place beside the OT book of Esther in the Roman Catholic Bible. Despite its popularity in Jewish circles, the book was never included in the Hebrew Bible. Finding a place in the SEPTUAGINT, however, the book was known and used by the early church. Eventually, it became clear that the book was inferior in status compared to those of the Hebrew canon. JEROME expressed the view that the book was valuable to read, but was not to be reckoned as a part of the canonical Scriptures. In the Protestant Bible, Tobit is relegated to the Apocrypha, where it follows 1 and 2 Esdras.

(See further *APOT*, 1:174–241; W. O. E. Oesterley, *The Books of the Apocrypha* [1915], 349–71; C. C. Torrey in *JBL* 41 [1922]: 237–45; M. Bévenot in *BSac* 83 [1926]: 55–84; R. H. Pfeiffer, *History of New Testament Times with an Introduction to the Apocrypha* [1949], 258–84; B. M. Metzger, *An Introduction to the Apocrypha* [1957], 31–41; F. Zimmermann, *The Book of Tobit* [1958]; L. H. Brockington, *A Critical Introduction to the Apocrypha* [1961], 33–39; O. Eissfeldt, *The Old Testament: An Introduction* [1965], 583–85; R. K. Harrison, *Introduction to the Old Testament* [1969], 1208–13; P. Deselaers, *Das Buch Tobit: Studien zu seiner Entstehung, Komposition und Theologie* [1982]; C. A. Moore, *Tobit: A New Translation with Introduction and Commentary*, AB 40A [1996]; D. J. Harrington, *Invitation to the Apocrypha* [1999], ch. 2; H. Schüngel-Straumann, *Tobit, übersetzt und ausgelegt* [2000]; D. A. deSilva,

Introducing the Apocrypha: Message, Context, and Significance [2002], ch. 3; B. Otzen, *Tobit and Judith* [2002]; and the full commentary by J. A. Fitzmyer, *Tobit* [2003].)   D. A. HAGNER

Tochen toh′kuhn. See TOKEN.

Togarmah toh-gahr′muh (תֹּגַרְמָה *H9328*, meaning unknown). Son of GOMER and grandson of JAPHETH (Gen. 10:3; 1 Chr. 1:6). He was no doubt the eponymous ancestor of a people group that bore his name. In Ezekiel a nation called BETH TOGARMAH is described as carrying on extensive trade with TYRE in horses and mules (Ezek. 27:14); it is mentioned also as one of the allies of MAGOG in association with Gomer, PERSIA, CUSH, and PUT (38:6).

JOSEPHUS (*Ant.* 1.6.1 §126) regarded them as the Phrygians, who were noted for their horses (see PHRYGIA). Assyrian inscriptions, however, mention a Til-garimmu, which in HITTITE is Tegarama and probably carries on the name of the ancient Togarmah. This city was located in Urartu (ARMENIA), the eastern part of CAPPADOCIA. Since Ezekiel places Togarmah in the N (Ezek. 38:6) and in association with Gomer, it is quite probable that Togarmah is to be located N of Palestine in the area SE of the Black Sea. Til-garimmu was destroyed by the Assyrians in 695 B.C.   T. E. MCCOMISKEY

Tohu toh′hyoo. See TOAH.

Toi toi. See TOU.

Token toh′kuhn (תֹּכֶן *H9421*, possibly "measure"). Also Tochen. A town within the tribal territory of SIMEON, listed between RIMMON and ASHAN (1 Chr. 4:32). The parallel list omits Token and has ETHER in its place (Josh. 19:7 MT), but CODEX VATICANUS has *Thalka* in addition to *Ether*, and on that basis some scholars believe that Token is original and that it dropped out of the Hebrew text (to keep the total number of towns at four, Ain and Rimmon can be read as the name of one town, EN RIMMON). However, this view leaves unexplained the omission of Ether in 1 Chronicles, and so others argue that Token and Ether are alternate names for the same town (see KD, *Chronicles*, 99–100). If they are different towns, the location of Token is unknown.

Tokhath tok′hath. See TIKVAH.

Tola toh′luh (תּוֹלָע *H9356*, prob. "worm" or "crimson" [see *HALOT*, 4:1702]; gentilic תּוֹלָעִי *H9358*, "Tolaite"). (1) Firstborn son of ISSACHAR, grandson of JACOB, and eponymous ancestor of the Tolaite clan (Gen. 46:13; Num. 26:23). In the time of DAVID, the descendants of Tola who were "fighting men" (*gibbôrê ḥayil*; NJPS, "men of substance") numbered 22,600 (1 Chr. 7:1–2; some interpret the number to mean 22 muster units totaling 600 soldiers).

(2) Son of Puah, descendant of Issachar, and judge (leader) of Israel for twenty-three years after the time of ABIMELECH (Jdg. 10:1–2). He did not live within the tribal territory of Issachar but rather in the hill country of Ephraim in a town called Shamir. See SHAMIR (PLACE). The expression "rose to save Israel" is used only of Tola, but the text does not give additional details about his work (see *ABD*, 6:595–96).

Tolad toh′lad. See ELTOLAD.

Tolbanes tol′buh-neez. KJV Apoc. form of TELEM (1 Esd. 9:25).

toll. See TAX.

tomb. A place of BURIAL, which in the ANE ranged from a simple opening in the ground to natural or hewed-out caves, mausoleums, and pyramid tombs. Because objects of daily use were frequently buried with the dead, tombs have been a rich source of information about the cultural levels and religious beliefs of ancient peoples.

 I. Terminology
 II. Kinds
 III. Location
 IV. Contents
 V. Tombs of the kings

I. Terminology. The two most frequently used Hebrew words for "tomb" or "grave" are *qeber H7700* (Gen. 50:5 et al.) and its cognate *qĕbûrâ H7690* (Gen. 35:20 et al.), both from the verb *qābar* H7699, "to bury." Also relevant are such terms as *šeʾôl* H8619 (e.g., Gen. 37:35; see SHEOL), *qeber* H6913, "pit" (e.g., Ezek. 32:23), and even *bayit* H1074, "house" (Isa. 14:18). In the NT, the most common term is Greek *mnēmeion* G3646 (Matt. 8:28 et al.), but its cognate *mnēma* G3645 occurs in several passages (Mk. 5:3 et al.); another noun, *taphos* G5439, is used primarily by Matthew (Matt. 23:27 et al.; the only occurrence outside of Matthew is Rom. 3:13).

II. Kinds. The practice of burying the dead is ancient. The earliest burial places must have been extremely simple, consisting of no more than shallow graves in the ground that have long since been obliterated by erosion or by cultivation. Bodies were carefully placed, sometimes in a tightly or loosely flexed position, and sometimes on their backs in an extended position. Graves of this type dating from the Paleolithic and Mesolithic periods have been found in caves at Wadi el-Mugharah. A Natufian culture of the Mesolithic period (c. 8000 B.C.) practiced communal burial; more than sixty persons were buried at the Mugharet el-Wad on Mount Carmel (see CARMEL, MOUNT). Excavations at JERICHO reveal that in the Pottery Neolithic period (c. 5000 B.C.), there may have been no formal burial at all—just exposure of the body.

During the Neolithic period, tombs were made by lining and covering a pit with stones; the boxlike structure formed is known as a *cist* (from Latin *cista*, meaning "box"); it could be considered a forerunner of the coffin. Tombs of this kind have been found at Teleilat el-Ghassul from the Chalcolithic period. A megalithic tomb of Neolithic times called a *dolmen* has been found in various parts of Palestine; it was similar to a cist but much larger. The dolmen was constructed by placing large stone slabs on end to form the sides and a large stone on top as a covering; the structure suggested the form of a primitive house. A large field of dolmens is at el-ʿAdeimeh, E of the Jordan River, opposite Jericho.

During the Early Bronze Age (Proto Urban period), for the first time in Palestine natural caves were used for tombs or else the tombs were hewn out of rock. The limestone hills of Palestine are honeycombed with caves that provided natural sepulchres. Bodies were placed in them in various kinds of containers and safeguarded by large stones placed in front of them. Several hundred bodies were interred in them over a long period of time; at a later period, multiple burials became less common. One of the best known is the cave of MACHPELAH that ABRAHAM bought from the Hittites when SARAH died (Gen. 23:4–16). Approach to the artificial caves hewn out of rock was made by way of a shaft, usually rectangular, sunk vertically to the bottom and varying in diameter from 3 to 10 ft., and in depth from 3 to 15 ft. The shaft was filled with debris to make sure that the tomb would not be disturbed.

Sometimes several chambers connected by adjoining shafts were hollowed out in a family's burial place; this kind of burial was popular down to the Greek period. The bodies were originally placed in the tomb complete, but when the available space was all taken, many of the bones of earlier burials were thrown out or sometimes collected in a common pile in a corner of the tomb. It appears that frequently only the skull was considered worthy of continuing care, for the rest of the body, even before the flesh had completely decayed, was often no longer treated with any reverence.

In the same period, burial was sometimes made in huge pottery urns in which the body was placed in a prenatal position, with the knees drawn up to the face. At Byblos (ancient GEBAL) urns were large enough to contain the flexed body of an adult. The skeleton of an infant was found curled up in a bowl at Tepe Gawra (prob. from the 4th millennium B.C.). A later development of the rock-hewn tomb consists of those with columned or carved façades such as are preserved at PETRA. The earliest Mesopotamian tombs were located underground and often were vaulted or domed. The tomb of Queen Shub-ad and her husband at UR contained a large retinue of servants buried with the royal couple as well as numerous personal possessions, in the Egyptian manner.

The most elaborate burial customs developed in EGYPT; no ancient people gave more attention to burial than the Egyptians. The *mastaba* evolved from the simply trench into which the body had been placed and covered with a mound of earth that served as the grave of those who were not of the royal families. Several mastabas placed on top of each other in receding fashion served as the origin of the stepped PYRAMID which later evolved into the square-based pyramidal form usually associated with the three great pyramids at Giza. Mummification required an elaborate preparation of the body for burial; it involved essentially desiccation of the body, removal of the viscera for placement in canopic jars of alabaster or marble, followed by careful wrapping of the body in linen sheets sometimes 24 yards long. Elaborate provisions were made for food, water, entertainment, and whatever might make the future life more comfortable. Astonishing quantities of wealth were buried with the pharaohs. (See also EMBALMING.)

At a later period, the pyramid tomb was replaced by the rock-cut tomb found in the Valley of the Kings in an isolated section of the Libyan Desert. The Israelites were surely familiar with the Egyptian process of mummification, but they never practiced it generally; nor did they ever practice cremation, as did the Babylonians and Romans. Rather, they washed the dead, then dressed them or wrapped them in grave clothes. The clothing or wrappings were sprinkled with sweet-smelling crystals of balm. The body was then laid on a bier or stretcher and carried by friends or relatives to the place of burial (Jn. 19:39–40). Mourners walked beside the deceased, weeping and wailing loudly.

Bodies were sometimes placed in CISTERNS. Fifteen bodies have been found in a cistern at GEZER with a number of spear heads. In the Mycenaean period (c. 1580–1100 B.C.) burial vaults, called *tholoi*, or beehive tombs, were constructed; they were roofed in corbeled masonry and obviously imitated in shape a primitive house form. They were usually dug in the side of a hill, although in a few cases they were built above ground. They were approached by a horizontal passage open to the sky and normally at right angles to the hill slope. The burial chambers were oval, round, or rectangular. They were family graves and were opened each time a new body was placed in them. Afterward the door was again blocked and the passage way (or *dromos*) was filled with earth to discourage grave robbers. About fifty of these have been excavated in Greece to date.

Sarcophagi, or coffins with lids, were never used generally in Palestine as were ossuaries for the subsequent gathering of the bones. Wooden and stone sarcophagi were used in Egypt from the most ancient times. The rulers of the city of Byblos in Lebanon, which early had close relations with Egypt, were buried in stone sarcophagi toward the end of the 2nd millennium and beginning of the 1st. The best known of these is the sarcophagus of King Ahiram of Byblos, dating probably from the 10th cent. B.C. In Palestine, a clay sarcophagus first appeared in the 12th cent. at BETH SHAN and later in other places. These cylinders of baked clay are anthropoid in shape, just large enough for a body, with a removable lid at the head. They reflect foreign burial customs, perhaps Egyptian.

During the Iron Age, a further development took place in the rock-hewn tomb. The floor in the middle of the burial chamber was made lower so that, at the sides, benches were left on which the dead were placed in an outstretched position. This type of tomb became known as the bench tomb (called by some "divan tomb") and was characteristic of the OT period. There were usually three of these benches in the more or less rectangular shaped tomb so that three corpses could be placed in them at one time. When later burials took place, one bench at a time was cleared by placing its bones in a common pit, which was usually located in a corner of the grave chamber. The fact that they were used for successive burials explains why there were no grave inscriptions (giving such information as name of person buried there). These tombs belonged to individual families and were generally

Jerusalem tomb with head-rests, repository, and place for burial preparation (7th or 6th cent. B.C.).

used for many generations; they were regarded as important possessions of the family. Hence, in a very real sense, the people were "gathered" to their fathers in the family tomb (cf. Gen. 49:33). During the Hellenistic-Roman period, variations of the bench tomb evolved. The bench tomb developed to the point that an arch vaulted over the individual bench. A further development was the carving of a trough-shaped depression in the bench into which the corpse was placed.

The next significant development was tombs with drawer-like crypts (often referred to as *kokhim*; the Heb. term, not found in the Bible, is *kûk*, pl. *kûkim*). In this type, long, low crypts were recessed into the rock, each designated for a single burial. They were usually arranged in several rows, one on top of the other at right angles with the wall of the burial chamber. Some of these were often extensive plans with a number of chambers adjoining each other, each with drawer-like crypts and a broad open vestibule as entrance, which was sometimes embellished with placements of columns, squared pilasters, etc. Individual burial began with the drawer-like galleries, which were closed with a stone slab after burial, and no future burials were made in them; therefore grave inscriptions began to appear in the graves. They are found, for example, on the burial structure at Marisa (now Tell Sandaḥannah) and date from the 3rd cent. B.C. The walls of this tomb were elaborately ornamented with painted designs and scenes; the colors were still brilliant when the tomb was first opened but have since faded. The paintings include representations of animals, vases, and musical instruments. The passageway from the vestibule to the first burial chamber was quite small to make it easy to close the burial place. This passageway was often sealed off by means of a rolling stone that could be rolled aside. A large groove was hewn in the rock into which the stone was fitted. These stones were too heavy to be easily moved. It was in this type of tomb that the body of Jesus was placed. The women found the stone rolled away when they went to the tomb on the third day (Matt 28:2; Mk 16:3–4; Lk. 24:2; Jn. 20:1).

During the Hellenistic period, tower-like burial monuments were constructed above the ground next to or over the subterranean burial place, which made its location visible from a distance. Examples of this kind of monument are found on the Phoenician coast at Amrit. Also the burial monuments in the KIDRON Valley at Jerusalem, called "The Tomb of Absalom" and the "Tomb of Zacharias," are of this type; they date from the Herodian period.

As emphasis on separate burial continued, a new practice developed of preserving the bones of the deceased. Instead of placing the bones in a common pit after removing them from the burial bench or burial trough to make room for a new body as had been formerly done, they were placed in a special chest, called an OSSUARY. A number of small limestone chests dating from the 1st cent. B.C. and the first two centuries A.D. have been found. There were probably also wooden ossuaries which time has obliterated. They were often decorated with carved rosette and geometric designs, and the name of the deceased engraved on them. They were placed in the burial chambers. Their inscriptions have proved to be a valuable source for the supply of personal names of the NT period. One inscription contained the words, "Do not open." Ossuaries of the 1st and 2nd centuries A.D. have been found in a necropolis near the "Dominus Flevit," on the W side of the Mount of Olives with the name Jesus written in Hebrew-Aramaic as well as the symbol of the cross.

During the Persian period, rulers in PHOENICIA were buried in anthropoid or chest-shaped stone sarcophagi, especially in SIDON. Marble and stone sarcophagi were also found in Sidon from the Hellenistic period with beautiful examples of Greek relief art, such as the well-known "Alexander sarcophagus," which depicts events from the life of

Rolling stone at Herod's family tomb.

Alexander the Great. This type of sarcophagus did not appear in Palestine until the Roman period. Large numbers of lead and stone sarcophagi of this type have been found in the Jewish cemetery of Beth Shearim. Tombs of eight of the nine great Persian kings have been identified. That of Cyrus the Great (c. 530 B.C.) is a small structure of simple massive stone, still standing on a lonely stretch of desert near Parsagadae, NE of Persepolis. When Alexander the Great campaigned in Persia, he found the tomb of Cyrus, but with its treasures already stolen and the body of the king lying on the floor. The tombs of the Achaemenid kings Darius I, Artaxerxes I, and Darius II, were cut in solid rock side by side near Persepolis, and are reminiscent of the rock-hewn buildings of Petra.

From the period of Seleucid domination (165–137 B.C.), a very interesting monument is the mausoleum at ʿAraq el-Emir in central Transjordan, thought to belong to the Tobiad family (see Tobiah #2 and Tobias #2) because one of the rock-cut tombs there has the name "Tobiah" deeply incised on the rock in Aramaic characters of the 3rd cent. B.C. (but see discussion in J. Naveh, *The Development of the Aramaic Script* [1970], 62–64). The red and brown sandstone cliffs between which Petra nestles are lined with tombs that vary considerably in size and shape, many of them being monumental. Most of them date from the 1st cent. B.C. to the 2nd cent. A.D. Two of these are outstanding for their splendor: El-Khazneh and Qasr Bint Farʿun. Both have been dated from c. 9 B.C. to c. A.D. 40 during the reign of the greatest of the Nabatean kings, Aretas IV Philodemus. Among these rock-hewn monuments with architectural façades, the principal ones were undoubtedly mausolea devoted to the memory and the cult of the dead, rather than temples, as many have held.

Two types of tombs dating from the 2nd and 3rd centuries A.D. have been found at Palmyra, biblical Tadmor (2 Chr. 8:4), W of the city. One was an underground "house of eternity" type; these were often beautifully painted and contained carved statues and reliefs representing the members of the family buried in the tombs. The other was the tower tomb, several stories in height, built of carefully hewn stone blocks. Around the walls were rows of niches, each designed to receive a corpse of the family that owned the monument. They were decorated with skillful art representations of the deceased persons, of gods, and of religious scenes. Cremation of corpses was not commonly practiced in Palestine; it was considered a punishment reserved for criminals (Lev 20:14; 21:9). There was apparently a relationship between the horror with which the ancient Hebrews looked upon the burning of bones (cf. Amos 2:1) and their early beliefs about life after death. Preservation of the body, as with the Egyptians, seemed to have significance.

Every type of tomb is found in the Roman world. Early on, they built elaborate tombs, sometimes of the *tholos* type, representing the interior of a Roman house, richly carved and painted. There are pyramid tombs (Gaius Cestius, Rome, before 12 B.C.), circular or tumulus types such as that erected by Augustus for himself in Rome (28 B.C.), and larger and more monumental tombs like that of Hadrian. The Romans, however, preferred cremation, after which the ashes of the deceased were placed in columbaria, which resembled the filing-case arrangement of modern American crematories. The Appian Way, leading into Rome, is lined with hundreds of tombs of the well-to-do. Paul must have seen many of these tombs as he made his way from the port of Puteoli to Rome (Acts 28:13–16).

Tombs hewn in solid rock and grouped together were used by the Etruscans as family burial places. This type of burial place, called catacomb, was used during early Christian times in Rome by both Christians and Jews. The catacombs of Rome form a vast labyrinth of narrow passages usually 3–4 ft. wide with small chambers at intervals, which were excavated at successive levels. The dead were buried in the galleries in long horizontal recesses or compartments in the walls, stretched out to full length. Sarcophagi were not used. Some compartments held four or more corpses, although most held only one. They were carefully sealed by slabs of marble or huge tiles cemented together. Epitaphs were painted or engraved on these tiles, giving the names of the occupants and often a Christian emblem, such as the sacred monogram (the interlaced letters X and P), the fish, or the shepherd. The family would hold a funeral feast in its vault both on the day of burial and on the anniversary.

Some of the underground passages contained larger halls and connected suites of chapels that were probably constructed for congregational worship during the era of persecution. Baptistries have also been found in the catacombs. The catacombs were used as places of refuge for which they were well suited because of the intricacy of their design and because of their access through secret passages to escape routes. The major part of the catacombs belong to the 3rd and early 4th cent. A.D. When JEROME visited them in A.D. 354, interment in them had become rare. Other catacombs have been found at Syracuse, Malta, Sicily, Alexandria, and Sheikh Abreiq in Palestine (identified as Beth Shearim).

III. Location. Cemeteries in biblical times were generally located outside inhabited settlements, usually near the city or village, even as in modern times. Every city had its own burial place. The dead were generally buried in the ground, away from dwellings, and rarely within the occupied settlement itself. The tombs were usually prominently marked, sometimes painted with whitewash, so that no one would be accidentally defiled by contact with the dead (Lev. 21:1; Num. 6:6; 19:13).

The custom of burying the dead under the floor of the house was well known in Assyria, Syria, and elsewhere, though it was an unusual practice in Palestine (1 Sam. 25:1 is an exception). Evidence of burial beneath the floors of houses and in adjoining courtyards has been found in Neolithic and Chalcolithic times at Wadi el-Mugharah and Teleilat el-Ghassul. A large number of burials were found beneath the floors of houses in Jericho in the Pre-Pottery Neolithic B period. The skulls seem to have received special treatment of plaster to give the appearance of a portrait. Burial of important people seems to have been permitted in ancient times within the city itself; David was buried "in the City of David" (1 Ki. 2:10). The grave of an old woman at Gezer was found within the city in the form of a pit lined with great stones. Children were buried in clay pots inside the settlement, a practice that was generally followed in the Mediterranean region. Skeletons have been found in city walls, but these were not normal burials but a human sacrifice.

Burial alongside the road was not infrequent for various reasons (e.g., RACHEL, Gen. 35:19). Secluded spots under trees were sometimes chosen (burial of DEBORAH, REBEKAH's nurse, under an oak, Gen. 35:8; Saul and his sons "under the great tree in Jabesh," 1 Chr. 10:12). After settling in the land of Canaan, the Hebrews followed the Canaanite practice of burial in natural and artificially hewn CAVES; the natural caves were not difficult to find in a hilly country like Palestine. One of the best-known burial caves is that of MACHPELAH (Gen. 23:17), which became the burial place for ABRAHAM's family. LAZARUS was placed in a burial cave (Jn. 11:38), as was Jesus (Jn. 19:41).

Most of the burial sites uncovered have belonged to the rich and outstanding, because the poor were usually interred outside the city in pits, cisterns, caves, and simple earth graves (cf. 2 Ki. 23:6; Jer. 26:23; Matt. 27:7). In Jerusalem, the graves of the people were located in the Kidron Valley on the E side of the city. The potter's field, or AKELDAMA, was a burial place outside the Jerusalem wall for foreigners (Matt. 27:7–8; Acts 1:19). There are, of course, practically no remains of the simple earth burials of ancient times; thus a study of tombs and burial customs as they developed through the ages has been largely limited to the more outstanding sites.

The Hebrews maintained a deep sentimental attachment to the family grave. JOSEPH requested permission to take the body of JACOB to the ancestral burial place at Machpelah (Gen. 50:4–5) and later requested that his own remains be taken to Palestine when the Israelites returned to their own land (vv. 24–25). GIDEON was buried in the tomb of his father (Jdg. 8:32). SAMSON was buried in the family tomb "between Zorah and Eshtaol" (16:31). NEHEMIAH expressed a desire to ARTAXERXES to go to the city of his fathers' sepulchres (Neh. 2:5). Like the Egyptian pharaohs, wealthy Hebrews arranged for construction of their tombs during their lifetime (2 Chr. 16:14; cf. Joseph of Arimathea, Lk. 23:53; Jn. 19:41).

Tombs were located in gardens attached to dwellings (2 Ki. 21:18, 26), within city walls (1 Ki. 2:10), on elevated places (2 Ki. 23:16; Isa. 22:16), on hillsides (2 Chr. 32:33), in natural and artificial caves. The most common burial place was a necropolis located near the city or village, often on a rocky terrain that was not suitable for agriculture.

IV. Contents. Ancient tombs from all periods of the ANE show that it was common practice to bury articles of varying value with the deceased. No one gave more attention to providing for the dead than the Egyptians because of their belief that any future life was simply an extension and glorification of the one they had lived on earth. Every kind of convenience and article of daily life was buried with them, including clothing, jewelry, perfumes, tables, chairs, various implements, boats, even embalmed pets, weapons, lamps, all to be used in the afterlife. The known treasures in them were so great that grave robbing was a common practice. Ancient rulers had a great dread of having their tombs plundered and took every precaution to make the site secure, but rarely were successful.

It was a sign of great evil to be removed from a tomb (Isa. 14:18–19), but an even greater calamity was to be deprived of burial (2 Ki. 9:36–37; Jer. 8:1–3). As a mark of respect, watch was kept over the tomb (Job 21:32). Offerings of food and drink suggest a belief in life after death, and the cult of the dead was widespread in ancient civilizations; even graves of Neanderthal men have been discovered containing offerings of food. Canaanite tombs have been found at RAS SHAMRA with the remains of food and with jars containing what had once been milk; tombs were provided with openings so that food and drink could be brought for the dead. The rich findings in the tombs of Tutankhamen and Queen Shub-ad provide breathtaking evidence of the elaborate burial provisions for royalty in ancient Egypt and SUMER.

V. Tombs of the kings. Referred to as "the tombs of the kings of Israel" (2 Chr. 28:27), "the tombs of David" (Neh. 3:16), "the tombs of David's descendants" (2 Chr. 32:33), these are the royal sepulchres of the Judean kings of Davidic descent in the City of David, not far from the KING'S GARDEN and the Pool of SILOAM (1 Ki. 2:10; 2 Chr. 21:20; Neh. 3:15–16). From David to Ahaz, thirteen kings were buried in the City of David: David, Solomon, Rehoboam, Abijam, Asa, Jehoshaphat, Joram ("buried in the City of David, but not in the tombs of the kings," 2 Chr. 21:19–20), Ahaziah (who died of wounds in Megiddo but was brought to Jerusalem for burial, 2 Ki. 9:28), Joash ("buried in the City of David, but not in the tombs of the kings," 2 Chr. 24:25), Amaziah (slain but body was brought to Jerusalem, 25:27–28), Azariah (or Uzziah, who according to 2 Ki. 15:7 was buried with his fathers, but according to 2 Chr. 26:23 in the burial field belonging to the kings because of his leprosy), Jotham, and Ahaz (cf. 2 Ki. 16:20 and 2 Chr. 28:27).

Jehoiada the priest was honored by being buried there also (24:16). The author of Kings does not record the burial place of Hezekiah (2 Ki. 20:21, but cf. 2 Chr. 32:33). Funerals of wives and children of kings are not mentioned. Asa was buried in his own sepulchre (2 Chr. 16:14). Jehoram was not buried in the tombs of the kings (21:20), nor Ahaz (28:27). Manasseh was buried "in the garden of his house in the garden of Uzza" (2 Ki. 21:18), as well as his son Amon (21:26). A special tomb was prepared for Josiah (23:30; 2 Chr. 35:24), the last king whose burial is recorded.

The location of the tombs in the City of David was still known after the EXILE. They were plundered by the HASMONEAN king John Hyrcanus and by HEROD (Jos. *Ant.* 13.8.4; 16.7.1). Their location apparently was still known in NT times

This striking sarcophagus from Perga (2nd cent. A.D.) belonged to a certain Domitius Julianus and his wife, Domitia Philiska.

when PETER referred to the tomb of David (Acts 2:29). A tablet with an inscription was found by E. Sukenik to the effect that the bones of King Uzziah had been transferred to the top of the Mount of Olives. Available evidence justifies the conclusion that it was the custom in the E Mediterranean area between the 13th and 6th centuries B.C. to bury kings in their palaces, or in the near vicinity, even within the area of the inner citadel of the city.

The term "City of David" is not to be identified with the entire city of Jerusalem but is a synonym for the citadel or stronghold of ZION. Evidence points to the triangular hill wedged between the valleys of the Tyropoeon and the Kidron, and overlooking the gardens and pools of Siloam, as being the location of the City of David. In this region of the old city of David, long horizontal tunnels have been found in the rock, which may have been the burial place of the Davidic family. There is no definite evidence by which the garden of Uzza may be identified. Some later traditions have located the tomb of David in BETHLEHEM, in the area of GETHSEMANE, or on the SW hill of Jerusalem. There is a so-called Tomb of the Kings of Judah located in the N part of Jerusalem that is actually the tomb of Helen, queen of Adiabene, a district in Upper Mesopotamia. It is mentioned by Josephus (*Ant.* 20.2.1, 3) and antedates the fall of Jerusalem in A.D. 70 by ten or twenty years.

(See further J. Garstang, *Burial Customs of Ancient Egypt* [1907]; G. A. Barton, *Archaeology and the Bible*, 7th ed. [1937], 222–26; J. Finegan, *Light from the Ancient Past* [1946], 353–98, for catacombs of Rome; S. Krauss in *PEQ* no vol. [1947]: 102–12; S. Yeivin in *JNES* 7 [1948]: 30–45; N. Avigad, *Ancient Monuments in the Kidron Valley* [1954], 144–46; R. J. Forbes, *Studies in Ancient Technology*, 8 vols. [1955–64], 3:190–96, for process of mummification; M. S. and J. L. Miller, *Encyclopedia of Bible Life* [1955], 396–403; L. Woolley, *Excavations at Ur* [1955], 52–90, for tomb of Queen Shub-ad; W. F. Albright, *The Archaeology of Palestine*, rev. ed. [1960], 157–59; K. Kenyon, *Archaeology in the Holy Land* [1960]; M. Noth, *The Old Testament World* [1966], 168–73; G. Barkay and A. Kloner in *BAR* 12/2 [March-April 1986], 22–39; E. Bloch-Smith, *Judahite Burial Practices and Beliefs about the Dead* [1992]; P. J. King and L. E. Stager, *Life in Biblical Israel* [2001], 363–72; K. Hachlili, *Jewish Funerary Customs, Practices, and Rites in the Second Temple Period* [2005].)

F. B. HUEY, JR.

tongs. This English term is usually the rendering of Hebrew *melqāḥayim* H4920 (the dual ending suggests a device consisting of two pieces). Both the NIV and the NRSV use "tongs" in three occurrences of this Hebrew noun (1 Ki. 7:49; 2 Chr. 4:21; Isa. 6:6), but elsewhere the NIV has "wick trimmers" and the NRSV "snuffers" (Exod. 25:38; 37:23; Num. 4:9; the KJV has "tongs" in all but Exod. 37:23, where it uses "snuffers"). The rendering "tongs" seems especially appropriate in the Isaiah passage, which speaks of the instruments used by the SERAPH to remove a burning coal from the altar. But in all the other passages the reference is probably to devices made of gold that were used to dress the wicks of the seven-branched CANDLESTICK in the TABERNACLE and TEMPLE, the burnt parts of the wicks being placed in snuff trays. If "wick trimmers" or the like is appropriate in the Exodus and Numbers passages, the same can be said of the instances in 1 Kings and 2 Chronicles, where the term occurs in connection with "lamps."

The KJV uses "tongs" also in Isa. 44:12 to render Hebrew *maʿăṣād* H5108, "The smith with the tongs both worketh in the coals, and fashioneth it with hammers" (NIV, "The blacksmith takes a tool and works with it in the coals ..."; the NRSV emends the text, "The ironsmith fashions it and works it over the coals"). In the only other occurrence of this Hebrew term, it apparently refers to a kind of axe or chisel (Jer. 10:3).

tongue. A symmetrical, very mobile, muscular, unpaired organ, situated in the mouth. It extends from its attachment to the hyoid bone and epiglottis in the upper part of the front of the neck to its free end at the incisor teeth. It is shaped like a pyramid, flattened above and below, rounded at its angles, and terminated in front by a blunt point. Composed almost entirely of interlacing muscle fibers, its surfaces, which are exposed to the secretions of the mouth and throat, are covered with mucous membrane. Within this membrane on the upper surface of the tongue are located gustatory papillae, or taste buds. Five kinds of such papillae are recognized. They are predominantly located toward the back of the tongue where it approaches the throat. It is by means of these taste buds that the tongue performs its prime function as a sense organ, namely, detection of taste. In fact, it is the only unpaired sense organ of the body. The sense of touch is also highly developed in the tongue so that it can locate food particles in the mouth, and in particular between the teeth, which would otherwise evade attention. Guiding and maintaining food between the upper and lower teeth, the tongue is of importance in mastication. It also aids in the acts of sucking, swallowing, and spitting of saliva and upper respiratory secretions and excretions.

From the physician's standpoint, the custom of having a patient protrude the tongue is important, because certain systemic diseases of the human body manifest their presence with alterations of the tongue, such as allergies, pellagra, sprue, pernicious anemia, iron deficiency, and vitamin deficiencies. Moreover, a paralysis of one-half of the tongue (i.e., right or left) reveals itself in such an examination by reason of the deviation of the tongue to the affected side. This symptom may be indicative of a diseased condition in the brain region such as stroke from internal hemorrhage, thrombosis of an artery, or brain tumor. (See further H. Gray, *Anatomy of the Human Body*, 27th ed. [1959], 1230–37.)

The tongue is also a crucial organ of speech in that it makes possible the articulation of both consonants and vowels (by metonymy *tongue* can in addition mean "language," e.g., Esth. 1:22; Rev. 5:9). It is in this connection that the tongue is referred to in the Scriptures as a potent force (Heb. *lāšôn* H4383; Gk. *glōssa* G1185). It is stated that death and life are in its power (Prov. 18:21). James elaborates on this when he refers to the tongue as an untamable and unruly evil, full of deadly poison (Jas. 3:8), and as a fire, a world of iniquity (3:6). Paul, in turn, refers to the tongue as an instrument of deceit (Rom. 3:13) characterizing the unregenerate person. On the subject of glossolalia, see TONGUES, GIFT OF.

An important figurative use of the term is Luke's description of what happened on the Day of PENTECOST: "and there appeared to them divided [or distributed] tongues as of fire and [it] sat on each of them" (lit. trans. of *kai ōphthēsan autois diamerizomenai glōssai hōsei pyros, kai ekathisen eph' hena hekaston autōn*, Acts 2:3). Although it is clear that the flamelike appearance rested on all the 120 disciples, there is some disagreement about the precise point being made. Some believe that the picture is one of many tongues and that "a tongue rested on each of them" (NRSV; the KJV's expression "cloven tongues" misunderstands the term *diamerizomena*). Others suggest that a firelike appearance distributed itself among them. The figure of the tongue may be simply a way of indicating "the jagged effect produced by a flame" (BDAG, 233), but it may also have been suggested by the fact that the disciples began to speak in other "tongues," that is, languages (v. 4).

The significance of the fire imagery can also be interpreted in several ways. Some think it indicated the fearless and persuasive witness in the power of the HOLY SPIRIT that was henceforth to characterize the testimony of the disciples of Christ. Others point out that fire is a symbol of the divine presence (e.g., the BURNING BUSH in Exod. 3:2; see FIRE III). More specifically, there may well be an allusion to the prophecy of JOHN THE BAPTIST regarding the filling of the Spirit (Lk. 3:11; see BAPTISM OF THE HOLY SPIRIT), which in turn may indicate judgment (3:16). These various allusions do not necessarily exclude one another.   P. E. ADOLPH

tongues, confusion of. Genesis 11:1–9 contains the account of the origin of language diversity. That the languages of today root out of a past in which human beings used a common speech is an idea accepted by many specialists engaged in philological research, though the linguistic evidence is ambiguous. The question of the origin of the various languages is closely related to the question whether the different human races have sprung from a single stock. The Genesis account describes how the descendants of NOAH settled in the plain of SHINAR, or Babylonia, and built a city and a tower to reach into heaven, which would serve as a center of unity and power as well as satisfy their ego. See BABEL.

Many towers such as described in the Genesis account have been found on the Babylonian plains. Known as ZIGGURATS, they served as rallying points around which cities and centers of worship were built. Inscriptions have been found relating to some of the ziggurats. Stephen L. Caiger refers to an inscription reporting the collapse of such a ziggurat: "The building of this temple offended the gods. In a night they threw down what had been built. They scattered them abroad, and made strange their speech. The progress they impeded" (*Bible and Spade* [1936], 29, quoting G. A. Smith, *Chaldaean Account of Genesis* [1880]).

A. C. Schultz

tongues, gift of. One of the ninefold SPIRITUAL GIFTS (1 Cor. 12:4–11). The clearest exhibition of this gift in the NT is in Acts 2, describing the Day of PENTECOST; the apostle PAUL gives an extended treatment in 1 Cor. 12–14. Whether these two passages refer to the same phenomenon is sometimes disputed.

   I. In the OT
   II. In the Gospels
   III. The experience at Pentecost
   IV. Later evidence from Acts
   V. In the Pauline epistles
   VI. In the postapostolic church

I. In the OT. The NT doctrine of tongues—spiritual utterances believed to be a direct product of divine operation and Spirit-filling and usually thought to be ecstatic, that is, not consciously or rationally controlled by the speaker—has a long prehistory in the OT. When PETER explained this phenomenon to the crowds of Jewish pilgrims gathered at Jerusalem, he did so in terms of the words of JOEL (Acts 2:16–21, citing Joel 2:28–32). Secondly, in 1 Cor. 14:21–22 PAUL explained the evidential nature of tongues to the unbeliever by referring to ISAIAH (Isa. 28:11).

Many scholars would say that the experience recorded of the seventy elders (Num. 11:24–29) was ecstatic in character and corresponds to "speaking in tongues," although the word used in the text is "prophesied." Clearly the phenomenon is, in this context, the outward sign of the Spirit's coming and presence. This experience is not directly attributed to MOSES himself; indeed, his position is contrasted with that of the ordinary "prophet" (12:7–8; some argue that the Heb. word for prophet, *nābî'* H5566, actually means "ecstatic speaker"; see PROPHETS AND PROPHECY IV.H). SAMUEL too was surrounded by a group of ecstatics (1 Sam. 19:18–24); their infectious "prophesying," which seems to have been at least akin to "tongues," was held to be a sign of Yahweh's presence; yet Samuel's reputation as a prophet was based on something else (1 Sam. 3:20). The same is true of ELIJAH and ELISHA. There is also evidence for similar entranced behavior at this time on the part of the prophets of BAAL, probably including ecstatic utterances (1 Ki. 18:28). In the later days of the great "writing prophets" of Israel, there is no reference to any such phenomena whatsoever, unless the "trances" of EZEKIEL should be so considered.

II. In the Gospels. There is no reference in the Gospels to speaking with tongues, either actual or anticipated, with the exception of one textually uncertain passage (Mk. 16:17 KJV; see below). In view of the manifestations of the Spirit's activity in the life of JOHN THE BAPTIST (who was filled with the HOLY SPIRIT from his mother's womb, Lk. 1:15), the life of JESUS CHRIST (on whom the Spirit was seen to descend at his baptism, Matt. 3:16), and the life of the disciples (who performed miracles of healing and demon expulsion, Lk. 10:17), this is remarkable but undoubted. There is thus no necessary connection between "tongues" and "filling with the Spirit" as far as the Gospels state. Mark 16:17, in the midst of signs that are to accompany those who believe, lists "new tongues" (*glōssais kainais*, some MSS omit "new"). This is clearly a reference to glossolalia in some form; but as the ending of this gospel (Mk. 16:9–20) is thought by most scholars not to belong to the original text of Mark, it may well have been added by the early church on the basis of Pentecost and subsequent apostolic history. The clause is placed between "cast out demons" and "take up serpents," both of which signs did occur in the apostolic church (Acts 16:18; 28:5). It is not, therefore, independent evidence concerning glossolalia.

III. The experience of Pentecost. At first sight, the description in Acts 2 is crystal clear. All were filled with the Holy Spirit and "began to speak in other tongues" (v. 4)—evidently foreign tongues hitherto unknown to the disciples, but meaningful to the pilgrims then gathered in Jerusalem. This much seems proved by v. 6, "each one heard them speaking in his own language." (See also TONGUE.)

Some scholars, however, feel that such a simple interpretation is inconsistent both with the vague term "sound" mentioned in Acts 2:6 (Gk. *phōnē* G5889, a "noise" sufficiently unusual to attract a crowd) and with the fact that others were able to interpret the whole episode as drunken babbling (v. 13). They further point out that, elsewhere in the NT, the "tongues" spoken seem to be incomprehensible unless accompanied by a spiritual "interpretation," and do not seem to be recognizably human languages (e.g., 1 Cor. 14:2; many believe that 13:1 characterizes "tongues" as angelic languages). These scholars feel that Luke is describing an occurrence of ordinary glossolalia (as at CORINTH), but in such a way as to show that Pentecost was the antithesis of BABEL, where human tongues were confused (Gen. 11:9), and also to demonstrate that Pentecost corresponded to the "giving of the law," which, according to Jewish tradition, was delivered simultaneously to all the nations in seventy languages (G. F. Moore, *Judaism in the First Centuries of the Christian Era: The Age of the Tannaim*, 3 vols. [1927–30], 1:277–78).

Early Christian scholars suggested that the miracle was one of hearing rather than speaking; Acts 2:8 would lend some support to this. Less convincing are the suggestions that Jews from all the above-mentioned lands would have understood GREEK or ARAMAIC, both of which tongues the apostles presumably knew well, and either of which they could therefore have used on this occasion; or that phrases from foreign languages, once heard but long forgotten, welled up from the subconscious and were spoken aloud for the first time, striking an answering chord in the hearers. When modern scholars speak of "intuitive understanding" or "thought rapport" or "thought transference," they are either returning to the first explanation (the miracle of hearing) or else saying in Pauline terms that the hearers were given, on that occasion at least, the gift of interpretation.

IV. Later evidence from Acts. If the gift of tongues had a peculiar evidential value as showing the initial coming of the Spirit, then it was appropriate that it should also appear at the Pentecost of the Gentiles (Acts 10:46, the converts in CAESAREA) and probably at that of the Samaritans (8:17). Although tongues are not specifically mentioned in these two passages, there are obviously some clear outward signs of the Spirit's coming. The gift is specifically mentioned of the converts in EPHESUS (19:6); if they were disciples of John the Baptist (and not merely ill-instructed Christians, as is sometimes claimed) there would be an appropriateness here also.

Whether or not others spoke with tongues on receiving the Holy Spirit is uncertain. It is possible (as being an outward sign clearly seen by all), but more cannot be affirmed, for Acts does not record it. For instance, Paul could speak with tongues later (1 Cor. 14:18). Did he receive this at baptism? Or were these tongues after Pentecost foreign languages or mystic utterances? Lastly, there was no set rule: sometimes, as at Pentecost, the gift came to those long baptized; at Caesarea, it came before baptism, and indeed was the ground of baptism. At Samaria, if it came, it was at "confirmation."

V. In the Pauline epistles. The classic treatment of this doctrine is in 1 Cor. 12–14, under the general heading of "spiritual gifts" (1 Cor. 12:1). It was obviously such a familiar part of Corinthian church life that Paul never explained exactly what it was, but assumed that his reader knew. Nor was this manifestation limited to CORINTH among the Gentile churches. Its occurrence at Caesarea and Ephesus has already been mentioned. Moreover, according to some, in Rom. 8:26 the reference to the Spirit interceding for the saints "with groans that words cannot express [*stegmatois alalētois*]" may possibly correspond to praying "with the spirit" (1 Cor. 14:15 NRSV), and thus refer to praying "in tongues." (Others argue that the latter passage is prob. not a direct reference to the Holy Spirit [cf. NIV, "with my spirit"] and that in Romans the term *alalētos* G227 may suggest something *nonlinguistic* or *unspoken*; cf. C. E. B. Cranfield, *A Critical and Exegetical Commentary on the Epistle to the Romans*, ICC, 2 vols. [1975–79], 1:423–24; T. R. Schreiner, *Romans*, BECNT [1998], 444–46.)

The exact nature of the "tongues" in question is not clear. It does seem that, at Corinth at least, these were mystic utterances, not foreign languages (1 Cor. 14:2), although some would quote v. 10 against this. At all events, they needed "interpretation," without which they were unintelligible. Indeed, Paul seems to have stressed their very incomprehensibility as having a "sign" value to the outsider (v. 22) and as being the fulfillment of an OT prophecy (v. 21, quoting Isa. 28:11), although he also admitted that this incomprehensibility may expose Christians to the charge of madness (1 Cor. 14:23), as it had exposed them to the charge of drunkenness at Pentecost. Paul, also in the clearest possible terms, differentiated between "tongues" and "prophecy" (vv. 1–4). It is clear that, however much is comprehended under the term "prophecy," it is not in a "tongue," but is immediately understandable.

What, then, is Paul's assessment of "tongues"? First, he freely admitted it as a spiritual gift, and indeed one in which he excelled (1 Cor. 14:18), but one which, along with "interpretation of tongues," he placed lowest on the list of spiritual gifts (12:10, 30). He did not expect all to speak with tongues (12:30), nor did he associate this gift with the fullness of the Spirit or with special sanctity.

Paul, then, wanted to be sure that the source was indeed the Holy Spirit (1 Cor. 12:3), a point made elsewhere in the NT as the "discernment of spirits" (v. 10 NRSV). All gifts, including this one, are for the common good and must be used accordingly (v. 7). Where "tongues" are concerned, they must not be used in the church except where there is an interpretation, either by the speaker himself (14:13) or by someone else (v. 28). God is a God of order; the use of "tongues," even if interpreted, must be limited and controlled in the church (vv. 33, 40). Christians should worship rationally as well as spiritually, using the conscious mind as well as the subconscious (vv. 14–15). One should remember that all gifts, including "tongues," are but passing phenomena (13:8). All gifts should be exercised in LOVE, and indeed swallowed up in love, the greatest spiritual gift of all (v. 1).

Within these limits, Paul was happy that the Corinthians should exercise their gift of tongues (1 Cor. 14:26), even if it be often only in the realm of private devotion (v. 28). Certainly he did not have it forbidden—a point sometimes overlooked today.

VI. In the postapostolic church. Perhaps owing to increased institutionalism, little was heard of tongues in the postapostolic age, except in "fringe sects," of which the Montanists are a good example. Perhaps official disapproval led to an unbalanced isolation of, and emphasis on, this spiritual gift. Certainly in these "fringe groups," glossolalia was accompanied by great enthusiasm, coupled with lack of theological balance. By the 4th cent., it must have virtually disappeared, for most church fathers were utterly at a loss to understand the biblical references (as can be seen from the commentaries produced). Nevertheless, in time of spiritual stress or renewal, it has frequently reappeared; the present age seems to many a clear instance of this.

(See further L. Christenson, *Speaking in Tongues* [1963]; J. L. Sherrill, *They Speak with Other Tongues* [1964]; F. D. Goodman, *Speaking in Tongues: A Cross-Cultural Study of Glossolalia* [1972]; H. N. Malony and A. A. Lovekin, *Glossolalia: Behavioral Science Perspectives on Speaking in Tongues* [1985]; W. E. Mills, *Speaking in Tongues: A Guide to Research on Glossolalia* [1986]; C. Forbes, *Prophecy and Inspired Speech in Early Christianity and Its Hellenistic Environment* [1995]; C. S. Keener, *Three Crucial Questions about the Holy Spirit* [1996]; G. Hovenden, *Speaking in Tongues: The New Testament Evidence in Context* [2002]; S. B. Choi, *Geist und christliche Existenz: Das Glossolalieverständnis des Paulus im Ersten Korintherbrief* (*1Kor 14*) [2007]; *ABD*, 6:596–600. Cf. also the bibliography under SPIRITUAL GIFTS.)

R. A. COLE

tongues of fire. See TONGUE.

tools. The Bible makes reference to tools only incidentally, usually in connection with the arts and CRAFTS. The references to BEZALEL and OHOLIAB, who were especially endowed with skills to build the TABERNACLE (Exod. 31:1–11; 35:30—36:1), and to the importation of Phoenician craftsmen by SOLOMON to build the TEMPLE (1 Ki. 7:13) suggest that not many Hebrews were gifted in the use of tools.

TOOTH

© Dr. James C. Martin. The Eretz Israel Museum, Tel Aviv. Photographed by permission.

Various tools crafted by carpenters, including plow, threshing sledge, olive press, winnowing fork, and broom.

Woodworkers made use of metal SAWS, probably of the Egyptian pull-type, with the teeth pointing toward the handle. They were also used for cutting STONE (cf. 1 Ki. 7:9; Isa. 10:15). According to tradition, ISAIAH was executed by being sawn in two (cf. Heb. 11:37). Mallets were probably used by the CARPENTER instead of HAMMERS (Jdg. 4:21; cf. 5:26). At least a half dozen Hebrew words are used with reference to the AX, indicating a variety of these useful tools. The blade might be set parallel, or at right angles to the handle, which itself might be long or short. Stone, bronze, and iron were materials used, and methods of hafting varied considerably (cf. Deut. 20:19 and 19:5 with 2 Ki. 6:5 and Jer. 10:3). Axes also doubled as weapons (Jdg. 9:48; Jer. 46:22; see ARMOR, ARMS). The carpenter used also scrapers, planes, and chisels for cutting (Isa. 44:13), with awls and drills for making holes (Exod. 21:6; Deut. 15:17). The KNIFE was ubiquitous, and used for all types of cutting. For layout and measuring, the line was used, with the plumb-bob, compasses, some kind of square, and rules. Scripture references to these items are numerous.

The stone MASON used many of the same or similar tools, with the addition of a variety of hammers (1 Ki. 6:7; Jer. 23:29). Chisels, wedges, rubbing stones, levers, rollers, and primitive cranes also were common. Brickmolds and various forms of trowels and picks (cf. the SILOAM inscription) may be added. The metalsmith would use, in addition to some of the hammers already listed, the special kind referred to in Isa. 41:7. He must also have an anvil, a furnace, bellows, molds, ladles, files, drills, etc. Tongs and clamps or vises were also probably devised and used.

Agricultural tools included the plowshare, sickle or pruning hook, ox-goad, mattock, forks and shovels, and the ax (1 Sam. 13:21; 1 Ki. 7:40, 45; Joel 3:13). Sharpening was mostly accomplished with stones and files (1 Sam. 13:21). The BLACKSMITH sharpened many tools by heating the metal and hammering out the edges. The potter had his own variety, including the wheel, kiln, tournettes, paddle-and-anvil, scrapers, and burnishers (see POTTERY). Other crafts, such as weaving, tanning, dyeing, tent-making, painting, jewelry-making, engraving, sculpture, etc., all had their special tools and equipment. See OCCUPATIONS and articles on specific tools.

(See further R. J. Forbes, *Studies in Ancient Technology*, 8 vols. [1955–64]; C. Singer et al., eds., *A History of Technology*, 5 vols. [1957–65]; D. Cardwell, *The Norton History of Technology* [1994]; J. E. McClellan III and H. Dorn, *Science and Technology in World History: An Introduction* [1999]; S. Cuomo, *Technology and Culture in Greek and Roman Antiquity* [2007].) M. H. HEICKSEN

tooth. A small, hard body fixed in a dental socket, technically called an alveolus, in either of the jaws; it serves to seize, cut, tear, and grind nutritious substances. In general a tooth has the shape of an irregular cone. In a child there are twenty deciduous or milk teeth. In the adult the teeth are thirty-two in number: sixteen in each jaw, namely, four incisors, two canines, four bicuspids, and six molars. The crown of the tooth is the part that appears outside the dental socket. Within the crown is a central pulp cavity containing blood vessels and nerves. When injury occurs to this pulp cavity, toothache often results.

Proverbs 25:19 in referring to a broken tooth (Heb. *šēn H9094*) would seem to imply that a toothache may follow the breaking off of a significant portion of the tooth through exposure of the pulp cavity. Very hard compact tissue called dentine surrounds the pulp cavity. This in turn is covered with a vitreous material called enamel. The teeth are not covered by true skin. It was doubtless the relatively thin layer of enamel on the surface of the tooth to which JOB made reference when he said, "I have escaped by the skin of my teeth" (Job 19:20 NRSV). In the NT (Gk. *odous G3848*), most of the references are in the expression "gnashing of teeth" (Matt. 8:12 et al.; cf. also Job 16:9 et al.). On the phrase "An eye for an eye and a tooth for a tooth," see LEX TALIONIS.   P. E. ADOLPH

topaz. A transparent or translucent mineral used as a gem stone (Gk. *topazion G5535*, Rev. 21:20). Topaz is an aluminum fluosilicate that occurs as prismatic crystals. It is usually colorless or pale yellow, less often pale blue or pink and occurs mainly in granites and related rocks. It resembles some yellow varieties of quartz that are referred to as "false topaz." Oriental topaz is a yellow variety of corundum (aluminum oxide). The rendering "topaz" is also used by the NIV for Hebrew *piṭdâ H7077* (Exod. 28:17; 39:10; Job 28:19; Ezek. 28:13; the NRSV interprets this Heb. term as a reference to CHRYSOLITE).   D. R. BOWES

Tophel toh´fuhl (תֹּפֶל *H9523*, meaning uncertain). A town or region "in the desert east of the Jordan," mentioned only in the opening words of Deuteronomy; it is one of several places that help to locate the area where MOSES spoke to Israel (Deut. 1:1). The precise location of Tophel is uncertain. Many scholars tentatively identify it with the modern village of eṭ-Ṭafileh, in a fertile valley some 20 mi. SE of the S tip of the DEAD SEA and 7 mi. NNE of PETRA.   E. M. BLAIKLOCK

Topheth toh´fit (תֹּפֶת *H9532* and תָּפְתֶּה *H9533* [Isa. 30:33], possibly "hearth, cooking stove," if related to Aram. תְּפָא; the vowels may have been borrowed from the word *bōšet H1425*, "shame," to indicate disapproval, as in the names ISH-BOSHETH and MEPHIBOSHETH [see further *HALOT*, 4:1781]). KJV Tophet. An area in the Valley of HINNOM; the latter was probably part of the Wadi er-Rababi, the deep-sided valley W and S of JERUSALEM that traditionally separated the tribes of BENJAMIN and JUDAH. The Valley of Hinnom served as a sacred grove or garden of the Canaanites, later the center of BAAL worship by apostate Jews (Jer. 32:35). The cultic activity seems to have involved the ritual sacrifice of firstborn infants to the god MOLECH. Although some doubt has been expressed as to whether such a gruesome rite actually existed, infant jar-burials from various periods of Palestine have demonstrated the plausibility of the accounts in the prophetic writings. And death by exposure has been practiced by tribal peoples around the world, the victims being female infants and sets of twins.

The name Topheth occurs only in the OT (2 Ki. 23:10; Isa. 30:33 [where NRSV has "his burning

The Valley of Ben Hinnom (looking E), a section of which was known as Topheth.

place"]; Jer. 7:31–32; 19:6, 11–14). The cult practiced there was most popular in the reigns of AHAZ and MANASSEH, who are said to have sacrificed their own sons in Hinnom, undoubtedly a reference to Tophet (2 Chr. 28:3; 33:6). Under the restoration of JOSIAH the shrine of Topheth was desecrated and apparently destroyed (2 Ki. 23:10), but the memory of the awesome place lived on and became a symbol of the desolation and judgment of sin. It was filled with refuse from the walled city throughout later antiquity and its precise location is lost. (See G. C. Heider, *The Cult of Molek: A Reassessment* [1985], 346–65; *ABD*, 6:600–601.)

W. WHITE, JR.

toponymy. The study of place names. See NAME II.B.

Torah toh´ruh (תּוֹרָה *H9368*, "instruction, rule, law"). The Hebrew name given to the PENTATEUCH, that is, the five books of MOSES. This noun derives from the verb *yārâ H3721*, meaning "to throw, shoot [as an arrow]." By association of ideas the noun came to mean "guidance, instruction" (cf. 2 Ki. 12:2), and also "commandment, law" (cf. Exod. 12:49 and frequently). The term *tôrâ* must not be interpreted in a solely legal sense—a connotation that was encouraged by the SEPTUAGINT with its rendition of the Hebrew noun with Greek *nomos G3795*. Rather, *tôrâ* is primarily a way of life derived from the COVENANT relationship between God and Israel. See LAW (OT).

That *tôrâ* is not only law can be seen from the fact that it can refer equally well to prophetic utterance (cf. Isa. 1:10; 8:16) and to the counseling of the wise (Prov. 13:4). Even in the Pentateuch, the term sometimes means decisions in respect to equity (Exod. 18:20), instruction in respect to behavior (Gen. 26:5; Exod. 13:9), rules in respect to cult (Lev. 6:9, 14, 25; et al.). It also covers the principle of justice: there shall be one *tôrâ* for the native and for the stranger (Exod. 12:49). From Exod. 24:12 it would appear that commandment (here *miṣwâ H5184*) is supplementary to *tôrâ* but not identical with it.

In the NT, *nomos* generally stands for the Mosaic code (cf. Lk. 2:22; 16:17; Jn. 7:23; 18:31; Acts 18:39, et al.). In at least one instance it stands for the Scriptures generally (Jn. 10:34). In rabbinic tradition, *tôrâ* connotes the written code plus oral interpretation as codified into the 613 precepts. See MISHNAH. At no time is *tôrâ* purely law in the legal sense; it is rather the Jewish way of life requiring total dedication by reason of the covenant (cf. the Mishnaic tractate *Pirke ʾAbot*).

J. JOCZ

torch. In biblical times torches, variously prepared, were used when stronger illumination was desired than that provided by LAMPS, as for night activities outdoors. The Hebrew word for "torch" is *lappîd H4365* (e.g., Jdg. 7:16, 20), although the KJV usually renders it "lamp." The Greek word *lampas G3286* can be translated either "lamp" (e.g., Matt. 25:1) or "torch" (e.g., Rev. 8:10). Similarly, the adjective *phanos G5749* ("bright"), when used as a noun, referred first to a torch, but later to any kind of portable light. On the night of betrayal, JUDAS ISCARIOT, procuring a band of soldiers and some officers from the chief priests and Pharisees, came to the garden of GETHSEMANE with "torches [*phanōn*], lanterns [*lampadōn*] and weapons" (Jn. 18:3; the KJV and NRSV translate, "lanterns and torches and weapons").

J. H. SKILTON

tormentor. This term is used by the KJV as the literal rendering of *basanistēs G991*, which occurs only in Jesus' parable of the two debtors (Matt. 18:34). The Greek term was applied to jailers whose job it was not only to guard prisoners, but also to examine and torture them. Ordinarily, debtors were sold into slavery if they could not pay, but sometimes they were sent to a detention center; here a merciless *basanistēs* would make their lives miserable until restitution was made. See PRISON.

tortoise. The KJV rendering of *ṣāb H7370*, which is found once only in a list of unclean animals (Lev. 11:29). This identification is incorrect; modern translations render it "great lizard." See LIZARD.

Tosefta toh-sef´tuh (Aram. תּוֹסֶפְתָּא, "addition," from יָסַף *H10323*, "to add" [cf. Heb. יָסַף *H3578*]). Name given to a collection of legal rulings and discussions (see HALAKAH) thought to supplement the official MISHNAH; as such it is the main source of *baraitot* (teachings of the TANNAIM not included in the Mishnah). The Tosefta, which has the same basic structure as the Mishnah (the same number of tractates organized under six orders), is by tradition attributed to Rabbi Ḥiyya bar Abba (student of Rabbi Judah, compiler of the Mishnah) and secondarily to Rabbi Hoshayah (R. Ḥiyya's student), but some scholars reject or modify this view. There is also debate concerning the precise relationship between the Mishnah and the Tosefta. (See J. Neusner, *The Tosefta: Translated from the Hebrew*, 6 vols. [1977–86]; id., *The Tosefta: An Introduction* [1992]; H. L. Strack and G. Stemberger, *Introduction to the Talmud and Midrash* [1992], 167–81; H. Fox and R. Meacham, eds., *Introducing the Tosefta: Textual, Intratextual, and Intertextual Studies* [1999].)

totemism. The term *totem* comes from *ototeman*, a word in Ojibwa (a N American Algonquin language) meaning probably "he is a relative of mine" (it was spelled variously by early scholars: *dodeme* [Father de Smet], *toden* [Father Petitot], *toodaim*, *dodaim*, *totam* [J. K. Long]). Totemism is a socioreligious complex formerly thought to be an organic unity including some combination of the mythical relationship of a kin group with a species of animal, plant, natural phenomenon (black duck's egg, sunlit cloud), or artifact (stone ax, canoe mast); ceremonies for the increase of the species; taboos on killing or eating these except ritually; kin groups named for these; matrilineal descent; and exogamy (marriage outside one's clan).

Although the concept was introduced to Europeans by the 17th-cent. Jesuit missionaries to North America, the first publication of the term in English is generally credited to J. K. Long (*Voyages and Travels of an Indian Interpreter and Trader* [1791]). The first American account was a posthumously published *History of the Ojebway Indians* by an Ojibwa chief named Peter Jones who died in 1856. It was J. F. McLennan, a Scottish lawyer, who brought the topic to the attention of science in a series on "The Worship of Animals and Plants" in the *Fortnightly Review* in 1869 and 1870. Then W. Robertson Smith (*The Religion of the Semites*, 2nd ed. [1894]) precipitated a debate among Bible scholars with the claim "that clear traces of totemism can be found in early Israel."

Totemism was described in many parts of the primitive world, but was most richly and dramatically manifested among aboriginal Australians. These tribes represented the most primitive cultures known. Thus, for Robertson Smith, Emile Durkheim (*The Elementary Forms of Religious Life* [1912]), J. G. Frazer (*Totemism and Exogamy* [1910]), Sigmund Freud (*Totem and Taboo* [1918]), and for many encyclopedists, anthropologists, theologians, and students of comparative religion down to the 1920s, Australian totemism presented a sense of organic unity among the constituent elements of the pattern found there, with two closely related consequences: (1) the necessity of theoretical explanations for divergencies found elsewhere, and (2) the concept of a "stage" in religious evolution from which all constituent elements found individually or in combination anywhere must be derived.

Premises of inquiry were influenced by preoccupation with origins. Reconstructions of primitive totemism rested upon beliefs that contemporary savagery represented early stages of human evolution, and that all primitives were fairly alike. Totemic theory in much of the standard literature was thus innocent of precepts of cultural diversity, relativity, and history basic to modern ethnological research. Edward B. Tylor significantly cautioned in 1899, "What I venture to protest against is the manner in which totems have been placed almost at the foundation of religion.... Totemism ... has been exaggerated out of all proportion to its real theological magnitude." Other contemporaries of Robertson Smith "opposed or abandoned the theory as applied to Israel" (M. O. Evans in *ISBE* [1929], 4:300).

Examples of alleged biblical indicators of totemism may be grouped under five elements. (1) Families named for animals (Gen. 36; 49; Num. 26:17, 23, 26, 35, 39; 1 Sam. 25:3) and the use of family standards or ensigns (Num 1:52; 2:2). (2) Food taboos, dietary laws (Lev. 11:44–47; 20:25–26, Deut. 14), and breaking these (Isa. 65:4; 66:17). (3) Matrilineal descent (Gen. 22:20–24; Jdg. 8:19; Ruth 1:8, 2 Sam. 17:25). (4) Exogamy (Jdg. 12:9). (5) Animal worship (Ezek. 8:7–11).

The Bible, however, makes no reference to human descent from the totem species, to ritual eating of them, or to ceremonies for their increase. In addition, biblical examples have been erroneously interpreted as the totemic elements in question. Prohibited foods do not correlate with family names, some of which represent clean and some unclean animals. The evidence cited is wholly insufficient to prove matrilineal descent, not to mention totemism, since matrilineal clans occur widely in nontotemic societies.

Important also is the methodological error of deriving totemism from the separate elements that are identified correctly. Animal names are altogether too common to infer a relationship of totemic pattern merely from the name; exogamy is a rule in all clans, totemic or not; Ezek. 8 clearly indicates patrilocality and thus, presumably, patrilineality rather than matrilineality; and worship of animals is very rare in totemic societies, also occurring in nontotemic ones. Thus, regarding totemism in the Bible one may conclude with E. Kautzsch, "the religion of Israel as it presents itself in the OT has not retained the very slightest recollection of such a state of things" (*HDB*, extra vol., 613–14).

Anthropologists have practically demolished totemism as a cultural complex. In 1916 Franz Boas (in *American Anthropologist* 18 [1916]: 319–26) called it "an artificial unit, not a natural one" and claimed that there was "no proof that all these customs belong together and are necessary elements of … a 'totemic complex.'" Later scholars concurred (R. H. Lowie, *Primitive Society* [1920]; A. Goldenweiser in V. F. Calverton, ed., *The Making of Man* [1931], 363–92).

Later consensus among Western anthropological structuralists is expressed by C. Levi-Strauss (*Totemism* [1963], 29): "totemism does not constitute a phenomenon *sui generis* but a specific instance in the general field of relations between man and the objects of his natural environment." There is general agreement with him that "totemism is an artificial unit, existing solely in the mind of the anthropologist, to which nothing specifically corresponds in reality." Some Soviet anthropologists repudiated this "nihilistic point of view," believing that "the bourgeois scientist is not usually able to understand fully the regularity of social phenomena; such understanding is only possible on the basis of Marxist methodology" (S. A. Tokarev in *Current Anthropology* 7 [1966]: 185–88; 8 [1967]:

260–61). Since then, however, totemism has largely become a "decadent concept" (R. Franz, *Totemismus, oder Die Decadenz eines Begriffs* [1980]; for a more recent approach, see A. Bleakley, *The Animalizing Imagination: Totemism, Textuality, and Ecocriticism* [2000].)   J. O. BUSWELL III

Tou *too* (תֹּעוּ H9495 [1 Chr. 18:9–10] and תֹּעִי H9497 [2 Sam. 18:9–10], possibly a HURRIAN name; cf. P.-E. Dion, *Les Araméens à l'âge du fer: histoire politique et structures sociales* [1997], 76–77). Also Toi. King of HAMATH on the ORONTES River. All that is known about him is that he sent his son JORAM (Hadoram) to DAVID with gifts, congratulating the Israelite king for his defeat of their common foe HADADEZER of ZOBAH (2 Sam. 8:9–10; 1 Chr. 18:9–10). G. N. Knoppers (*I Chronicles 10–29*, AB 12A [2004], 697–98) renders the Hebrew phrase *lišʾāl-lô lěšālôm*, "to sue for peace" (most versions translate, "to greet him"), and says there is merit to the common view that the "objective was to establish or confirm a client-treaty relationship with David"; but he thinks it is more "likely that the narrator considers the relationship to be founded on a mutual antipathy toward Hadadezer," and points out that "the establishment of an ongoing diplomatic relationship would be beneficial to both Tou and David."

Toubiani *too´bee-ay´nee* (Τουβιανοί). KJV Tubieni. The name of a group of Jews who lived in the otherwise unknown town of CHARAX (2 Macc. 12:17). The term Toubiani is commonly thought to correspond to *en tois Toubiou* (genitive of *Toubias*, 1 Macc. 5:13; NRSV, "the land of Tob"), but perhaps it refers to the Tobiad family (see TOB and TOBIAS #2).

tow. This English term, referring to the short and coarse fibers of FLAX before spinning, is used by the KJV in three passages, twice to render *něʿōret* H5861 (Jdg. 16:9; Isa. 1:31), and once to render *pištâ* H7325 (Isa. 43:17; the KJV translates this word "flax" in Exod. 9:31 and Isa. 42:3). Although the KJV rendering is correct (and followed, e.g., by the NJPS for the first word), modern versions use a variety of equivalents, such as "string, fiber, tinder, wick."

towel. This word is used by English versions only in Jn. 13:4–5, where it renders Greek *lention G3317*, referring to the linen cloth used by Jesus to dry the feet of the apostles in the upper room.

tower. The usual Hebrew word for "tower" or "watchtower" is *migdāl H4463* (Gen. 10:4–5 et al.), although several other terms can be so rendered in certain contexts (e.g., *ʿōpel H6755* in 2 Ki. 5:24 KJV; *ʾarmôn H810* in Ps. 122:7 NRSV; see CITADEL). In the NT, the Greek word *pyrgos G4788* is used a few times (Lk. 13:4 et al.).

Although towers were sometimes built to guard property (e.g., a vineyard, Isa. 5:2; NIV, "watchtower"), the defensive tower was of particular importance and had roughly three types. Solitary towers served both defensive and refuge purposes, though in the latter case they could become a trap (Jdg. 9:51); they also appeared occasionally along the highway for the protection of travelers (2 Ki. 17:9; cf. C. M. Daughty, *Travels in Arabia Deserta*, 2 vols. [1921], 1:9, 13). A second type of a defense tower was built as a part of the city wall. A third type was the large hollow structures flanking city gates or situated as wall corners (Y. Yadin, *The Art of Warfare in Biblical Lands*, 2 vols. [1963], 1:160).

Towers varied in size depending on their purpose. Tell el-Farʿah (biblical TIRZAH) exhibits a gate with thick walled towers on either side, having rooms within, provided with a stair to the top to repel attackers (Yadin, *Art*, 1:54). In GIBEAH (Tell el-Ful), SAUL's citadel had rectangular towers with inner spaces at each corner and was constructed of rough-hewn stones in casemate style. A later fortress in smaller scale replaced it, but was soon abandoned when Jerusalem became the capital. The most spectacular example is a Neolithic tower at JERICHO, c. 7800 B.C., surviving to approximately 27 ft. high, with a small tight stair to the ground. (See *ABD*, 6:622–24.) H. G. STIGERS

Agricultural watchtower.

town. One normally thinks of the English word *town* as referring to something larger than a VILLAGE but smaller than a CITY, yet in actual usage the distinctions often blur (as when we speak of Chicago as a town). In the Bible it is even more difficult to discriminate clearly between the relevant terms. The primary Hebrew word for "city," *ʿîr H6551*, can be applied to a place as large as NINEVEH (Jon. 1:3), but it is also used very frequently of towns whose inhabitants could not have numbered more than a few hundred. The same is true of Greek *polis G4484* (applied, e.g., to JERUSALEM, Matt. 4:5, but also to NAZARETH, 2:23).

The Hebrew term for "daughter," *bat H1426*, can refer to the dependent villages of a walled city (e.g., the settlements surrounding HESHBON, Num. 21:25), but it is applied as well to larger cities in figurative language (e.g., "daughter Zion," Isa. 1:8 NRSV). Hebrew terms that usually refer to small villages include *ḥawwâ H2557* (meaning perhaps "tent camp," applied only to the settlements of JAIR, Num. 32:41 et al.), *pĕrāzôt H7252* ("open village," Esth. 9:19 et al.; cf. *pĕrāzî H7253*, Deut. 3:5 et al.), and *ḥāṣēr H2958* (a very frequent term with various meanings, but often referring to unwalled settlements, as in Neh. 11:25–30). Greek *kōmē G2967* is applied only to small towns (Matt. 9:35 et al.); *kōmopolis G3268*, which has a similar meaning, occurs only once in the NT (Mk. 1:38).

According to Lev. 25:31, "villages without walls" come under a different law of redemption: its houses were to be returned to the seller in the JUBILEE YEAR, whereas city houses could not be redeemed if more than a year passed from the time of sale. In the OT period, the city was distinguished by having a defensive wall as well as being the center of commerce and industry, and in some cases the place where the local governor lived. In the NT period, the difference between city and town (or village) consisted in the possession of a constitution and law differing from country law, and following the law of the crown. In later times, a city was so designated if it was the bishop's seat. Towns were principally agricultural centers, dependent on walled cities for protection and for the sale and exchange of farm produce. Buildings were of lower quality, often crude. Evidence of many hundreds of towns and villages from the era of Jeremiah and before is to be seen, but most of them were never thereafter reinhabited. H. G. STIGERS

town clerk. See CLERK, CITY.

Trachonitis trak′uh-ni′tis. See TRACONITIS.

Traconitis trak′uh-ni′tis (Τραχωνῖτις G5551, "rugged region"). A district E of the province of GALILEE and S of the city of DAMASCUS; during the time of Jesus it was part of the tetrarchy of PHILIP (Lk. 3:1). See HEROD VI; TETRACH. In 23 B.C. Herod the Great received the task of pacifying Traconitis, BATANEA, and Auranitis (HAURAN), unruly tribes to the NE of the Jordan. After Herod's death in 4 B.C., his domain was divided among his three sons, and Philip was granted this territory. It consisted of newly settled lands, most of his subjects being non-Jews. The Jews, forming a minority of colonists, remained loyal to Philip since they had been settled there by the dynasty. Philip died in A.D. 34 and his territory came under the jurisdiction of SYRIA, but in 37 the emperor CALIGULA granted it to Agrippa, grandson of Herod the Great (subsequently he was given the rest of his grandfather's domains by the emperor CLAUDIUS).

Traconitis was only a small part of this tetrarchy, located around Tracon in the NE of the territory. It corresponds with the modern el-Leja‛, a plateau of some 350 sq. mi., consisting of volcanic lava beds, intercalated with volcanic necks, ash beds, and sills. The dissected terrain, the thin soils, and its proximity to the desert to the E, all contributed to its poverty, sparsity of population, and the lawless character of the district. The region of ARGOB (Deut. 3:4), within the domain of Og of BASHAN, probably included part of this wild country. JOSEPHUS, in the 1st cent. A.D., refers to its inhabitants as predatory (*Ant.* 16.1.1 §§27ff.). Several Roman officials attempted programs of pacification with varying success. Later a Roman road was constructed through the area, and eventually in A.D. 106 TRAJAN transformed Traconitis into a new province which he called ARABIA. Its new capital was Bostra (see BOZRAH #3). J. M. HOUSTON

trade, commerce, and business. Trade is essentially the exchange of commodities either by barter or for some fiscal medium, while commerce is trade on a large scale, especially on an international basis. The term *business* has a broad meaning but is here taken in the sense of intricate commerce, with credits, futures, and multiple exchanges of commodities.

    I. Local trade
    II. International commerce

Traconitis

TRADE, COMMERCE, AND BUSINESS

III. Trade in the Greco-Roman period
IV. Business

I. Local trade. The major local products carried over the ROADS of OT PALESTINE were foodstuffs of all kinds. These included the GRAINS (esp WHEAT and BARLEY) and other seeds such as sesame, lentils, and beans. Also included were in-season fruits of many varieties. The city dweller ate green fruit as well as ripe fruit. Grapes, especially valuable (see VINE), could be consumed fresh, dried as raisins, fermented into wine and vinegar, or boiled down into dibs, a variety of sweet syrup similar to maple syrup. Figs, like grapes, were dried for use in winter as well as summer. DATES were ideal for food since they were always fresh and contained a heavy sugar content.

As for "sweets," there was HONEY—both native (wild) and farm varieties. Palestinian honey could be bought in many flavors since the beehives were moved among the wide variety of flowers in season. The OLIVE, another year-round food, was preserved either in brine or OIL. Olive oil had several uses—for cosmetics, cooking, or lamp fuel, corresponding to grades one, two, and three. Nuts of all kinds, with the almond and the pine nut leading the sales list, were sought for their oil content, since meat fat was too expensive. Vegetables of many varieties were sold to city dwellers; JERICHO could grow them every month of the year.

Most meat animals, that is, SHEEP and GOATS, were taken to market on foot. CATTLE were primarily farm animals and took the place which the HORSE later held in farm work. When cattle became too old to work or languished in a drought, they were sold for food. The rich, however, always had meat on their menus, especially if the animals had been stall fed. Wild animals of the DEER family and a good variety of wild fowl always found a ready market (see FAUNA). The same was true of FISH, but the travel distance before sale was necessarily shorter. Salted fish, however, was a staple food everywhere. Rome used some salted fish from the Sea of Galilee. Dairy products such as milk and cheese were profitable (see FOOD).

Nonperishable foodstuffs such as grains, oil, and wine were sold in small stores within the city. Perishable goods were usually sold at a daily market, outside the gates of the city. In the larger cities sheep might be sold at one gate, and vegetables and fruit at another. When fruits were in season, hucksters went from street to street with their produce.

Both rich and poor liked condiments and SPICES. Among the former were anise, bay leaves, coriander, caper berries, cummin, mint, mustard (various varieties), rue, and saffron. Their favorites were onions, leeks, and garlic, which Israelites missed most in the Sinai experiences. Their spices were usually imported, especially from ARABIA. The most important were cassia, cinnamon, and cloves. (See separate articles on these various condiments.)

The city dweller either went to the countryside to obtain his fuel for COOKING, or bought it at the city gate. The best fuel was charcoal, second came wood, and finally thornbush.

Some foodstuffs were "locally manufactured goods." One could, for example, go to a bakery to buy bread, cakes, and pastry instead of baking them at home. One could also buy a meal at a small cafe or a drink at a winery. Most people, however, usually thought of manufactured goods in other terms. The cook, for example, needed pottery storage jars for flour, oil, and wine, as well as jars to carry the water from the spring or cistern, cooling jars for the table, and cups to serve it. There was also a need for various sizes of cooking pots and a variety of dishes in which to serve the meal. POTTERY was in large part of local manufacture, although imported ware attracted the rich as it does today.

Clothing was the next major industry after food. Every woman was expected to spin, weave, and sew.

Selling grains and spices is still part of trade and commerce today in Jerusalem's Old City.

There was always a market for superior workmanship in CLOTH and clothing. The most expensive garments were listed among the prizes in war. The most common cloth was WOOL; LINEN was more expensive. SILK became available in NT times, as did COTTON, but cotton lacked the popularity of silk. In the winter, fleeces were used as overcoats and shoes. The shepherd's sling was woven of wool, but might have had a LEATHER pocket.

WEAVING was accomplished using reeds and branches. BASKETS were a major type of container for many materials. Reed mats became a popular floor covering; they were also used in summer houses, especially for those who watched the vineyards and cucumber fields. If pottery was not fit for containing liquid, a leather bag was used. The farmer's seed bag for scattering grain might be cloth or leather, but the shepherd's bag was probably leather. Water bags and wineskins were made of leather.

If foot coverings could be afforded, leather SANDALS, shoes, and boots were available. JOHN THE BAPTIST wore a leather girdle. The leather worker was also busy making saddles and harnesses, and in NT times making PHYLACTERIES. Fine leather was also the MS material used for the copying of the books of the Bible, as well as other valuable writings.

The craftsman in wood had plenty of work. He made the farmer's plow, threshing sledge, pitchforks, and the yoke for his oxen. He also made the doors and door frames, the windows and window frames for the new and old houses in the city, as well as all the furniture used in the house. In the larger cities the craftsmen of the same trade lived in one section of the city. Thus, there would be a potters' quarter, a clothing quarter, a food market, a bakers' street, etc.

Different sections of Palestine would exchange products. The shepherds and farmers exchanged produce and sheep. The maker of charcoal found a market in areas where the forests had been cut down. The coastal cities and Jericho sold salt to the inland population. The carpenter was probably often paid in kind by the people for whom he worked.

Palestine had a few major exports for nearby nations. Because PHOENICIA needed food, central and northern Palestine sold to her grains and olive oil, wine and food animals. EGYPT had plenty of grain and animals but she needed olive oil and wine. SYRIA and Palestine grew the same farm products so there was little international commerce in these items except in periods of war or drought. When the CAMEL made trade with ARABIA common, the caravans sought Palestinian food stuffs. Raisins, dried figs, and dates were probably international produce because they were easily transported. Linen was sold to all nearby nations except Egypt, which made the best linen.

Natural products other than those already mentioned were primarily copper, bitumen, and raw wool. The prosperous COPPER periods were in patriarchal times, under SOLOMON, and during the southern kingdom. The intervening time has produced no evidence either for or against the working of the great copper deposits in the mountains on either side of the ARABAH, S of the DEAD SEA. The military campaign described in Gen. 14 may have been occasioned by the desire to control the valuable copper deposits in EDOM and SINAI. Since IRON was the ideal metal in Solomon's day and quite inexpensive (GILEAD was a major center for iron ore), he sold his copper to the backward people in the RED SEA area. In return Solomon received gold, precious incense, and rare spices.

BITUMEN had a good market in Egypt, Palestine, and the adjacent lands. Its source was the Dead Sea, which according to JOSEPHUS came to be known as Lake Asphaltites or "asphalt lake" (*limnē gegonen hē Asphaltitis legomenē, Ant.* 1.9.1 §174). Its quality was excellent but the quantity was small, quite the opposite of MESOPOTAMIA. Sulphur was also a natural product from the Dead Sea area.

Palestine always produced more wool than she could manufacture so this was a constant export commodity, especially to heavily populated areas. MOAB was the major wool producer. Palestine also exported rare resins and gums as myrrh and balm. BALM was very expensive and was a major source of income for HEROD the Great, from his vast balm groves at Jericho.

The real manufacturing age in Palestine began about the time of ISAIAH in the 8th cent. B.C. (note that the PENTATEUCH has no laws relating to manufacturing), while JEREMIAH, more than a century later, saw the climax and then the cataclysmic end of such industries. Here were modern assembly-line techniques and one-industry towns. The farmers flocked to the industrial cities and the sweat shops absorbed them. Oversupply of labor glutted the market and wages fell to starvation levels. "Micah, a farmer contemporary of Isaiah, attacked the courts for their conniving in the nation's economic crimes. In 3:1–3, using the background of the butchering of sheep and cutting them up for stew, Micah calls these business tycoons and their lawyers cannibals living off the flesh of their helpless employees" (J. Kelso, *Archaeology and Our Old Testament Contemporaries* [1966], 144).

The potter used mass-production techniques with assembly line methods, turning out a good product in great quantities at a reduced price. These ancient potters knew all the skills of their trade, and a modern ceramist can do nothing but admire them.

Industry's greatest change came in the cloth market. KIRIATH SEPHER, when excavated, turned out to be a one-industry town. It was located in a fine sheep district and the whole city was given over to the weaving and dyeing of cloth. Every house had large looms and dye plants, each one of them standardized. The raw material was right at the "factory's" door, and both industries had a heavy and constant market. Most manufactured goods were sold in Palestine itself and did not reach international markets.

Palestine's major imports seem to have been luxury goods. Human nature has always enjoyed the label that reads "made in a foreign country." Both Abraham and Solomon were international businessmen. The latter's work is well known, but modern scholars have begun to appreciate the fact that Abraham was a major businessman who may have traded in a territory reaching from HARAN to Egypt. It is possible that the patriarch "would buy copper cheap at the mines in Edom or Sinai and transport it to Phoenicia and Syria which were then the major manufacturing centers. From there he could sell these products anywhere from Anatolia to Egypt and Arabia" (Kelso, *Archaeology*, 10).

II. International commerce. Palestine's major commercial neighbor on the S was Egypt, one of the great civilizations of antiquity. It is no surprise to discover the strong influence of Egyptian commerce in the objects found in the excavations in Palestine. Even ETHIOPIA sent EBONY to Palestine, and part of the ivory probably came via the Sudan. The main trade road left Egypt about where the modern Suez Canal is located and then followed along the coast past RAPHIA, ending at GAZA. This city was the great bridgehead for Egypt in all of history, even as late as World War I.

Palestine's other commercial neighbor on the S was Arabia. Her water commerce came to EZION GEBER on the Gulf of Aqabah and then it was carried by camel caravan N to Macan. One of the land caravan routes from Arabia also ended here. The Wadi Sirhan was another long caravan route from Arabia, but it was E of Palestine proper, and its commerce only came into the N-S trade route at RABBAH (AMMON). This Arabian commerce consisted entirely of luxury items, such as gold, frankincense, myrrh, coral, pearls, emeralds, agates, and other precious stones. Rare spices and scented woods of various kinds from INDIA also came in via Arabia. In the intertestamental and NT periods the NABATEANS dominated the trade from Arabia to Palestine. As for international trade, note that a Babylonian garment was listed in the spoil at Jericho (Josh. 7:21), which was only a small fortress in early Israelite history.

To the N of Palestine was Syria, which was not a good market for Palestinian goods since both countries produced similar products. Syria and Palestine, however, did have some commercial dealings, for the dynasties of OMRI and BEN-HADAD had business quarters in one another's capital city. Damascus was rightly called the "seaport for all the desert people." The important fact is that the route by which both Mesopotamian and Anatolian commerce went S to Egypt was via Syria and Palestine. Anatolia, that is, ASIA MINOR, was one of the world's most important sources of metals in antiquity. There the HITTITES and their successors were the miners, smelters, and refiners of copper, silver, and iron ores. They also manufactured all types of metal wares. Before David's era this area had a major monopoly on iron. Copper was so important to the island of CYPRUS that its name became (in the form *cyprium*) the Latin word for this metal.

SUMER and its successors (see ASSYRIA AND BABYLONIA) were the only early great manufacturing civilizations rivaling Egypt. Abraham represented these two commercial giants, for his father, TERAH, may have run the trade routes from UR to HARAN (PLACE) under the shadow of Anatolia, and Abraham carried it on from there to Egypt, possibly with a major banking office in Damascus under ELIEZER. The Babylonian trade route started at the Persian Gulf and followed the EUPHRATES River to the Taurus mountains of Asia Minor at Haran and CARCHEMISH. The Assyrian capital of NINEVEH on the TIGRIS was also a commercial center. It was not as large a manufacturing district as Babylonia to the S, but it was a collecting point for commerce from PERSIA and points E, and also a junction point for goods from Urartu (see ARMENIA) and points N. From Nineveh the trade route followed the Armenian foothills W to Haran and Carchemish.

Just N of Palestine and bordering the Mediterranean was PHOENICIA, whose E boundary was usually the LEBANON Mountains. The Litany and Orontes valleys were normally Syrian. Phoenicia, like England at her peak, was both a manufacturing and maritime nation. This was the country that taught GREECE to become a manufacturer. The Greeks obtained their ALPHABET by copying it from their Phoenician business teachers. Phoenicia's major natural resource was her CEDAR forests, whose lumber all the world prized. Her wares ran from excellent to mediocre. The most important international product she manufactured was PURPLE dyed cloth. The wool was imported, but the cloth and dye were Phoenician. Some commerce going to Phoenicia went overland via the sources of the Jordan River N of Lake Huleh and into Phoenicia at the upper reaches of the Litany River. Some followed a road along the Mediterranean Sea from Acco to TYRE. Most commerce probably traveled by sea from a Palestine port to one in Phoenicia. Indeed, most of the sea freight of Palestine went in Phoenician ships. Egypt, however, probably sent her own ships to Palestine. When Persia came to world power, she used the Phoenicians as her maritime agents. With Persia's fall, ALEXANDER THE GREAT and his successors controlled Mediterranean commerce until ROME made that sea her own.

Much of Egypt's manufacturing was a government monopoly and was part of her produce trade, especially in grains. Solomon had a definite monopoly in copper. He was also the nation's "horse trader," which included chariots (1 Ki. 10:28–29). Solomon and HIRAM of Tyre had a joint business venture in the Red Sea trade (9:26–28; 10:11–12, 22). Later JEHOSHAPHAT planned a similar venture but the ships were wrecked at Ezion Geber (2 Chr. 20:36–37).

III. Trade in the Greco-Roman period. Alexander's successors revolutionized some of the Palestinian business. Greek became the dominant influence. All over the world people of many nationalities suddenly became hellenized, even taking new Greek names. At Marisa in Palestine the tombs show that in one generation many Semitic families changed their names. Some of the worst features of Greek life were revealed in Palestine under the Ptolemaic and the Seleucid rulers of that land (see PTOLEMY; SELEUCUS).

Much SLAVERY among the Israelite population in OT times was simply "a man paying a bad debt by working a few years for his creditor." Greek slavery was entirely different. Greek culture was largely built around slavery; the slave was simply merchandise, not a person. Since Palestine was the object of contention between the Ptolemies and Seleucids, Jews often were taken as slaves in the booty of war. The Seleucids were the worst offenders for they sold their prisoners of war, including women and children, at bargain prices. ANTIOCHUS Epiphanes, who made Jerusalem into a pagan Greek city, led in this crime. Palestine had two cultures; the Maccabean revolt (see MACCABEE) was the Jews' desperate but successful return to Judaism, although it was still tinted by some features of Greek culture. Some later Jewish (HASMONEAN) leaders, however, were virtually Greeks themselves so far as their actions were concerned. Nevertheless, from the time of the restoration of true worship in Jerusalem under the early Maccabees, Palestine had two cultures—one Jewish and one Greek. The fullest influence of the latter was most evident in the cities of the DECAPOLIS in TRANSJORDAN.

There is not too much information from the intertestamental period concerning trade and commerce in Palestine. One major improvement was the quality of FLAX, which, woven into first-class linen, went into the international market. As mentioned earlier, Herod the Great had large estates near Jericho where he grew the balm that was one of the most expensive gums. The fisheries around the Sea of Galilee prospered, exporting their salted fish as far as Rome.

International business between differing national groups was inevitable. Sidon dealt with the Palestinian town of Marisa; Egypt dealt with Transjordanian Philadelphia. Greek influence was also seen in Palestinian real estate. Marisa was planned like a Greek city, and NT Samaria used the same layout of city blocks. The Nabateans carried by camel caravan much of the Arabian traffic that the Egyptians had shipped via the Red Sea.

When the Mediterranean became Roman property, sea commerce took on new life. The major harbors were expanded to handle the increased commerce. Rome was fed in large part from the grain of the valleys of the NILE and the ORONTES, and of N Africa.

As a result of the Diaspora, the Jew was a world citizen and was often involved in world trade. At PENTECOST Jews gathered from numerous countries, including Parthia, Media, Elam, Cappadocia, Pontus, Asia, Phrygia, Pamphylia, Egypt, Libya, Rome, Crete, and Arabia (Acts 2:9–11). As PAUL traveled the eastern Mediterranean world he was in a new commercial world. Much of it was old; but there were new attractions. The apostle made ANTIOCH OF SYRIA ("Antioch on the Orontes") the center for world evangelism. Antioch was the second most influential city in the world, although ALEXANDRIA outranked it in size. Antioch was the end of the road for all overland commerce coming in from China via Persia to the Mediterranean. Alexandria, on the other hand, was the shipping point for all African commerce, whether it came via the Nile River or the Red Sea. There were no major seaports between these two cities but a wealth of local ports, some of which Paul used. Antioch catered primarily to the luxury trade, and the world was as avid for luxuries then as now. Alexandria catered to both the common and luxury markets.

Paul's home city was TARSUS. It was the S terminus of the best pass from the great Anatolian plateau through the rugged Taurus mountains, in the SE part of Asia Minor. Tarsus was a major business center since it also had direct access to the Mediterranean. Iconium was one of the key commercial cities of that great Anatolian plateau. It is often referred to as "the Damascus of Turkey" because of its abundant water supplies. When the Turks became masters of the Eastern world they made it their capital city, and from there they moved on to capture Constantinople.

When Paul wanted to reach BITHYNIA, he was headed for Constantinople, then called Byzantium. It has always been a major commercial city since it dominates Black Sea traffic. Russia is N of that sea. One can ride horseback across the rolling Russian plains between the Atlantic and the Pacific, and only occasionally be interrupted by major mountain masses. Paul knew that this commercial center would be an ideal evangelistic center. He always appreciated the businessman and established his major church centers at great commercial centers. See TRAVEL.

Paul wished to visit the Roman province of ASIA, but he was denied entrance at this time, although he did conduct a glorious ministry later at EPHESUS. Asia was the most populous province in the empire; even today the ruins of its great cities testify to the former prosperity of that area. The province was the most fertile area in Asia Minor and also the most fertile area around the AEGEAN SEA. It is no wonder that the Greeks loved it and colonized it early. Ephesus was later considered the capital of the empire, when the emperor was in the E.

THESSALONICA was the next major commercial city visited by Paul. It was situated at the S end of the best pass between the Danube Valley and the Mediterranean. A great amount of commerce passed over this road, as the civilizations at each end were different. The Danube Valley was so valuable commercially that Emperor TRAJAN added it to the empire early in the 2nd cent. A.D. He also conquered the Nabateans, giving Rome direct access to the Arabian commerce.

In Paul's time ATHENS was living on her past glory. CORINTH became "the" city of Greece. Its growth had been quick and spectacular. Julius CAESAR had recognized that this city in ruins could rise to become one of Rome's major commercial centers. He was murdered before he could found the city, but his wish was eventually fulfilled and the city was named in his honor (Laus Iulia Corinthus, "Corinth, the praise of Julius"). It became the greatest transshipment center in the Mediterranean. Corinth also quickly developed into a major manufacturing city with most of the labor done by slaves.

In Corinth, Paul was one of the "freeborn" laborers, as he was by trade a weaver of awnings used in the great market places, and also of sails used by the ships entering either of Corinth's two ports. It was here that Christianity obtained its legal right to be a "permitted religion." Every religion in the Roman empire had to have a government license to exist. The Jews of Corinth tried to persuade GALLIO, the proconsul of ACHAIA, that Christianity was an illegal religion for it was not Judaism. Gallio rejected their charge and thus ruled Christianity a legal religion. Later NERO persecuted the church in Rome, but he did it to save his own influence as emperor. The next century saw extensive Christian persecutions. Corinth demonstrated that then, as now, major commercial ports are often wicked places; "Corinthian" became an adjective to express the utmost wickedness. Antioch was runner-up to this disgraceful epithet. Nevertheless, both cities were major centers for world evangelism.

When Paul visited Ephesus during his third journey, his preaching seriously challenged two major industries of the city. The makers of books of magic watched their publications, valued at 50,000 pieces of silver, burn (Acts 19:19). That sum was the equivalent of one day's wage paid to 50,000 men. The makers of silver shrines of the goddess ARTEMIS suffered such losses that they created a riot (19:23–41).

The book of Revelation includes the letters to the seven churches of the province of Asia. From Ephesus the gospel had gone with such evangelistic power that strong churches were established in the adjacent cities, each one also a commercial center. LAODICEA was a major banking center but the church members were admonished "to buy from me [Christ] gold refined in the fire" (Rev. 3:18). The city was famous for its heavy black felt coats of goat hair for use in the bitter Anatolian winter, but the church folk were admonished to obtain "white garments." From the same city came one of the famous "patent medicines" of the age, a special salve for the eyes (see EYESALVE). The Christians were advised to procure another "salve to put on [their] eyes."

IV. Business. When money becomes a major factor in trade and commerce, the emphasis is on business, for the common denominator in all business is money. In the OT there were three major methods of sale: (1) barter, (2) weighing of silver or gold, and later (3) coins. Barter was the most common method of sale among the poorer people, although King Solomon and King Hiram also used the method. Hiram furnished cedar and cypress wood to Solomon, who, in turn, gave wheat and olive oil to Hiram (1 Ki. 5:10–11). These farm products were the taxes Solomon had collected, for taxes were at that time paid in kind. The farmer gave wheat and oil and wine, the shepherd sheep and goats, etc. Each man paid taxes in what he produced. In the southern kingdom the government had its own pottery factories that made standard-sized jars with the government stamp on the handle. These were required for use in the payment of taxes.

If commerce is to be successful in international markets it must have a basic medium of exchange, for which the ancients used SILVER and/or GOLD. The former was rarer and thus more valuable until the metallurgists solved the problem of smelting and refining complicated silver ores. Gold, then, took first place. Another reason for gold taking priority was that placer gold was becoming rare and the miner turned to gold ores, which were expensive to work. These metals came in various sized rings, bars, and other shapes. The Hebrew term for "silver" (*kesep* H4084) was equivalent to "money" (e.g., Isa. 55:1). If a less valuable metal was used as money, it was copper. Rare gems and expensive jewelry also served as money. They provided a means whereby a large amount of wealth could be transported easily and secretly.

The metals were weighed, and this act could be either honest or dishonest. Archaeologists have found weights with which to purchase items, and a different set of weights by which to sell that same purchase. This dishonesty is referred to in Deut. 25:13, "Do not have two differing weights in your bag—one heavy, one light." In Amos 8:5, the prophet echoes the same theme and adds that dry measures were used dishonestly in his day (cf. Deut. 25:14).

The next step in currency was the coin. Not only was there dishonesty in the weight of gold and silver bars, etc., but there was a wide variety in the purity of the metal, especially in silver. That problem was solved by governments minting coins and guaranteeing the weight and purity of each coin struck. This was done by putting the symbol of that government (state or city) upon the coin. The first such coin mentioned in the Bible is the Persian gold daric (Ezra 2:69). The Persians permitted the Jewish exiles to mint their own silver coins in Judea. Coins did not become commonplace in Palestine until the times of the Ptolemies and the Seleucids.

Where money is used—either the weighing of gold or silver, or the use of the coin—the banker is present, and money itself becomes a new commodity. See BANKING. There is no evidence of OT banking, but early Mesopotamia was very efficient in banking methods. During the EXILE, the Jews learned Babylonian banking techniques. Jewish bankers from BABYLON were widely used later by the successors of Alexander the Great. The author believes that good banking is the most likely reason Paul's ancestors secured their Roman citizenship at Tarsus. The exile marked the beginning of the Jews' major emphasis on banking and business in general. This was augmented by Jewish business exiles in the intertestamental times who were taken to Alexandria where they later controlled much of the business of that city. This meant branch offices for the Jewish enterprises in all the seaports of the Roman empire.

By NT times, banking covered the whole ROMAN EMPIRE; and bankers were licensed to be kept under control. The banker, then as now, took money on deposit and paid interest for its use. Jesus referred to this in his parable of the talents (Matt. 25:27). A common interest rate was eight percent in the days of Jesus and Paul. The banker then, as now, lent this money on mortgages. The earliest Bible reference to a mortgage is Neh. 5:3. The people borrowed money to pay their taxes (vv. 4–5), just as people do today. One position of the banking fraternity was the MONEY CHANGER, and Christ dealt with them.

Checks were used then as now; bills of exchange were available, that is, one could deposit money in one city and draw it out in another. Banks related to one another were scattered all over the empire. Good bookkeeping systems, however, were much earlier than banking; they can be traced to the early Sumerians, who invented writing.

(See further *HDB*, 4:802–6; A. C. Bouquet, *Everyday Life in New Testament Times* [1955], ch. 7; J. D. Hawkins, ed., *Trade in the Ancient Near East* [1977]; J. H. D'Arms, *Commerce and Social Standing in Ancient Rome* [1981]; M. I. Finley, *The Ancient Economy*, updated ed. [1999]; P. J. King and L. E. Stager, *Life in Biblical Israel* [2001], 176–200; J. G. Manning and I. Morris, eds., *The Ancient Economy: Evidence and Models* [2005]; *ABD*, 6:625–33.)

J. L. KELSO

trade guilds. Associations of people in the same CRAFT or TRADE who have organized for mutual protection and for social and religious benefits. In ancient times, guilds were more like fraternal orders than like labor unions. They seldom concerned themselves with wages, hours, or conditions of labor. Many of them were mutual benefit societies to defray the cost of a funeral. Their chief aim was pleasure and social intercourse.

Trade guilds were found all over the ancient world—in Egypt, Assyria, Babylonia, Greece, Rome, Syria, Persia, Palestine. In ROME, as early as the 7th century B.C., there were guilds of flute players, goldsmiths, coppersmiths, fullers, shoemakers, dyers, and carpenters. By the 2nd century B.C., cooks, tanners, builders, bronze workers,

These ancient copper ingots from Israel are a reminder of the trade guilds common in the ancient world.

ironworkers, coppersmiths, weavers, priests, all had their own guilds, and membership in a guild was compulsory. No one was permitted to leave the guild in which he was enrolled, and a son was required to follow the trade of his father. In ASSYRIA, people were divided into five classes, with the patricians or nobles at the top, and craftsmen and professions organized into guilds directly below them. In PERSIA, there was a well-organized guild of physicians and surgeons, whose fees were fixed by law.

In ancient Palestine, manufacturing centers were located in places where raw materials necessary for the business were readily available. The region around Tell Beit Mirsim was good for the raising of sheep, and therefore the place became a center for the weaving and dyeing of woolen cloth. There was an abundance of ore in EDOM, and consequently a mining and smelting industry grew up in that country. BETH ASHBEA, in southern Palestine, was the center of the linen industry (1 Chr. 4:21).

It was the custom for tradesmen in larger cities in the ANE to live in separate quarters. For example, Jerusalem had a bakers' street (Jer. 37:21) and a goldsmiths' district (Neh. 3:32). People who pursued a definite trade or profession often were designated by their particular calling, such as "Joseph, member of the perfumers." Each guild had a chief officer or president. The Bible tells of three families of SCRIBES who lived in the same town (1 Chr. 2:55).

In the postexilic period, guilds were powerful organizations and were recognized by the government. A guild could prevent a craftsman from another area from working in its territory. It had a trade monopoly in its particular locality. A guild could monopolize the market. Guild members were insured against loss of tools, animals, and boats used in their business, unless the loss was caused by their own negligence. Guilds had their own religious and social institutions, even their own synagogues, next to which there were burial grounds for the members. In some cases, members of a guild collectively built and operated businesses. (See I. Mendelsohn, "Guilds in Ancient Palestine," *BASOR* 80 [Dec. 1940]: 17–21; id., "Guilds in Babylonia and Assyria," *JAOS* 60 [1940]: 68–72.)　　　　　　　　　J. L. KELSO

trades. See CRAFTS; OCCUPATIONS.

tradition. The collective wisdom of any given culture, the notions of its worldview, and the insights of its institutions.

I. In the ANE. Tradition existed before the Neolithic food-producing revolution of the 9th–8th millennia B.C. It was formulated by two processes: the conservation of accumulated wisdom and the symbolization of ideas transmitted beyond the limits of communication. In effect, tradition in the ANE was a complex literary vehicle that came into being before the innovation of WRITING. Ancient tradition was almost always verified and grounded in the religious ground-motif of the archaic-religious states. All of the most ancient literate cultures assumed that their writing system and its literary monuments were rooted in the very cosmos and enforced by the gods. To a great degree the keeping of tradition was a sympathetic magic bringing the microcosm of the town and its inhabitants into alignment with the universal macrocosm of the world order. The traditional texts of the Sumerians, Elamites, Babylonians, and Hittites, as well as the Ugaritic tablets, all follow this pattern.

II. In the OT. The writers of the OT are adamant in insisting that the word-revelation of God was antithetical to the traditions of the nations. The common ANE assumption that hoary antiquity verified authority, an underlying motif in all tradition, is refuted in every book of the OT. The God of the PATRIARCHS is stated to be a God of present action, and this aspect is restated to MOSES before the exodus (Exod. 3). The essential concept is that divine REVELATION must be distinguished from human knowledge. Nowhere does the OT support the word of any human group as authoritative; the traditions of the nations are judged and condemned. The three sacerdotal offices of the theocratic administration, prophet, priest, and king, were God-ordained and God-centered.

Undoubtedly the village elders during the period of the judges followed formal traditions of justice (Ruth 4:1–3 et al.), which acted as insulations or hedges to the written Pentateuchal law. This intent to ring the oracles of Yahweh with additional and more precise requirements came to its fulfillment after the Babylonian captivity. Under the later

Judean kings and into the Hellenistic age, the various institutions of the Israelite monarchy became fixed and somewhat independent. The rise of the temple administration ultimately placed the chief priest in the foremost executive position in the state during the Roman period. With the expansion and solidification of the temple services and powers, a reliance upon tradition was a natural outcome. The ever-present threat of dilution of the core of the Jewish religious faith through syncretism with the paganism of the Persian and Greek worldviews enforced a greater stricture in the keeping of the law and a further development of tradition about the law.

III. In the intertestamental period. In the conflict between JUDAISM and HELLENISM a new orthodox party appeared, the PHARISEES. This popular movement fostered the further growth of a religious and cultural tradition. Archaeological excavations at MASADA and QUMRAN have produced ritual lavation pools and other ritual constructions not specifically mentioned in the OT, but frequently cited in later literature (see DEAD SEA SCROLLS). Thus it can be assumed that many of the traditions that became fixed in the postbiblical period had their origins in the intertestamental age. Of specific importance were the various types of temple taxes. During the OT period such taxes were based upon the commands of the Levitical code, but in the ensuing centuries the elaborate temple hierarchy levied taxes in a great number of areas of the economy without specific biblical warrant. These practices mentioned often in the TALMUD were sanctified by tradition alone.

The breakup of the Second Commonwealth into an array of religious and political parties left each to be founded and justified by tradition. The dependence upon oral authorities in the time-honored oriental fashion can be traced throughout the documents that have survived from this post-Hellenistic era. The APOCRYPHA and PSEUDEPIGRAPHA were written at this time, and they both include large portions of traditional method and material. In an age of turmoil and tension it is natural that people turn to a more stable and secure past and hallow its accomplishments, and the intertestamental period did this in abundance. The process of "hedging" the five books of Moses by layers of oral tradition, commenting upon and solidifying the interpretation of the text, went on unabated throughout the period after the close of the canon (see MISHNAH).

IV. In the NT. The Greek term for "tradition," *paradosis* G4142 (lit., "a giving over, handing down"), is used in the NT in both positive and negative contexts. A key passage is Mk. 7:1–13 (paralleled in Matt. 15:1–9), which records that some Pharisees and scribes criticized Jesus because his disciples, by eating with unwashed hands, were not following "the tradition of the elders." Quoting Isa. 29:13, Jesus accused his opponents of giving more weight to their own human traditions than to the divine commandments, thus setting aside the word of God (see esp. Mk. 7:8–9, 13). The background here is the large body of oral teaching that would eventually be codified in the MISHNAH.

The apostle PAUL referred to the same teachings when he said that prior to becoming a Christian he "was extremely zealous for the traditions of my fathers" (Gal. 1:14). Elsewhere Paul speaks in more general terms of "human tradition" opposed to Christ (Col. 2:8; cf. 1 Pet. 1:18). The apostle, however, also writes in positive terms regarding the Christian *paradosis* that he passed on to the Corinthians (1 Cor. 11:2; cf. 15:1) and to the Thessalonians (2 Thess. 2:15; 3:6). Thus the issue at stake is not the passing on of teachings from some people to others, but whether the teachings in view have their origin in divine revelation or in the human heart. W. WHITE, JR.

tradition history. Also *tradition criticism* and *traditio-historical criticism.* An approach to the study of the Bible that, building on the results of FORM CRITICISM, seeks to reconstruct the development of texts in the process of both oral and written transmission, and to infer what may have been the religious needs of the various audiences during the stages of that development. This label is used primarily in OT studies and corresponds roughly to *redaction criticism* in the study of the Gospels (see BIBLICAL CRITICISM V.E.).

Trajan tray´juhn. Emperor of ROME, A.D. 98–117. Marcus Ulpius Trajanus was born in Spain in the year 53, and after serving in various military and civil capacities was made governor of Germany in 97. While there he learned of his adoption by the then emperor, Nerva, an act which according to the custom of the time assured him of the succession to the throne. Nerva's action was prompted by a revolt of the praetorian guard, which made him realize the need of a firmer hand upon affairs of state.

Upon Nerva's death in 98, Trajan lingered in Germany on some unfinished business and did not come to Rome until 99. His first act was to punish the mutinous praetorians, and then to show his displeasure he gave to the people only half the usual donation. He won the favor of the senate by confirming all their privileges. A natural leader, he soon became popular with both army and people.

The general administration of Trajan was paternalistic. He took upon himself the burden of ruling and manifested an unusual capacity to deal with the complex problems of the huge empire. His policy, however, discouraged initiative on the part of the provinces, which soon learned to look to Rome for the solution of all their problems. By continuing the free distribution of grain and the provision of money for feeding the poor children of the municipalities, and especially by choosing good governors, he maintained the well-being of the provinces. He greatly expanded the program of public works, building new baths for the city of Rome, as well as a magnificent forum, and by constructing new roads throughout his domain.

The combined humanity and firmness of his character is illustrated by his attitude toward the Christians (see Pliny the Younger, *Epistulae* 10.96–97). On the one hand, he ordered that Christians should not be hunted and that those who confessed their faith but then recanted should be let go; on the other hand, he instructed Pliny to execute those who refused to give up their faith. This was in fact the first official policy that Christians should be put to death.

His reign was marked by two great military ventures. In two campaigns (101–102 and 105–106) he subjugated Dacia, the region N of the Danube, and made it into a Roman province where gold and salt mines were successfully operated. These wars were commemorated in the famous Column of Trajan, a 100-ft. marble pillar set on a rectangular base, with a statue of the emperor on top; it includes more than 2,000 finely carved figures. The second endeavor was against the Parthians in 113–117. He made at best a precarious conquest, and died in Cilicia while on the way back to Rome. (See further F. A. Lepper, *Trajan's Parthian War* [1948, reprinted with new material in 1993]; F. Coarelli, *The Column of Trajan* [2000]; J. Bennett, *Trajan: Optimus Princeps*, 2nd ed. [2001]; *OCD*, 1543–44.)

R. C. Stone

trance. A state of hypnosis or ecstasy. In this rapt condition, although apparently otherwise awake, the person's mind is drawn off from all surrounding objects and available stimuli, becoming obsessively fixed on things invisible (divine, hallucinatory, or unconscious). Persons in such a condition may think and report that they perceive with their natural senses (visual and auditory, in particular) realities shown by God or other supernatural forces. Religious or emotionally marked trances are described as an overwhelming joy or rapture. In extreme form, trance resembles or is *coma*.

English versions of the NT use "trance" in three passages in Acts as the rendering of Greek *ekstasis* G1749, which usually means "confusion, astonishment" (Mk. 5:42 et al.). Two of those passages refer to the vision that Peter received in Joppa (Acts 10:10; 11:5), and the other is an account by Paul of an experience he had while praying in the temple (22:17). The English term is rarely used in the OT (though the phrase "into a trance" is supplied by the KJV at Num. 24:4, 16, and the NRSV uses "fell into a trance" to render Heb. *rādam* H8101 [niphal, "to sleep deeply"] in Dan. 8:18; 10:9). However, various references to deep sleep in the OT are often interpreted as instances of trance (e.g., Gen. 15:12; 1 Sam. 26:12; Isa. 29:10). In addition, many scholars argue that the prophetic experience involved some kind of ecstatic trance (cf. 1 Sam. 19:20–24 and see prophets and prophecy IV.H).

J. M. Lower

transfiguration. A change in form or appearance. The term is used specifically with reference to a unique experience of Jesus recorded in the Synoptic Gospels (Matt. 17:1–8; Mk. 9:2–8;

Lk. 9:28–36; alluded to in Jn. 1:14 and 2 Pet. 1:16–18). The use of the noun *transfiguration* in this context derives from the fact that the KJV, followed by most versions, renders the Greek phrase *metamorphōthē emprosthen autōn* as "he was transfigured before them" (Matt. 17:2, Mk. 9:2; in Lk. 9:29, "the appearance of his face changed"). The Greek verb *metamorphoō* G3565 occurs in two other passages, where it is rendered by the more common English term "transform" (Rom. 12:2; 2 Cor. 3:18).

I. Place. A tradition from the 4th cent. named TABOR, in GALILEE, as the mountain where the transfiguration occurred. By the 6th cent., three churches were built there. In the 19th cent., opinion changed in view of the fact that Tabor's summit was occupied by a fortified city at the time of the event. The preceding context is set in the city of CAESAREA PHILIPPI (N of Galilee in Gentile territory), and there is no evidence of a departure from that region except that they "passed through Galilee" later (Mk. 9:30). Most scholars now think of Mount HERMON, Palestine's only snow-capped peak, as the "high mountain" to which Matt. 17:1 and Mk. 9:2 refer. Rising N of Caesarea Philippi, it dominates the area.

Some, however, object that the mountain must have been in Jewish territory, since teachers of the law were nearby (Mk. 9:14). Accordingly, W. Ewing (*ISBE* [1929], 5:3006) suggests Jebel Jermuk, the highest mountain in Palestine proper, which dominated N Galilee. Still others spiritualize the "high" and "holy" mountain, but these tend to deny the historicity of the event or the accuracy of the reporting.

II. Time. Early autumn of the year prior to the CRUCIFIXION appears to be the time. Matthew and Mark say it was six days after PETER's confession. Luke says "about eight," perhaps including the terminal days or allowing for an evening ascent and return on another day. Others, rejecting the time references, imagine that the account was transferred from a real or mythical resurrection appearance (cf. C. Carlston in *JBL* 80 [1961]: 233–40). Resemblances must be granted between the transfigured and the glorified Christ, but it is a

Mosaic depicting Jesus' transfiguration (from the Church of Transfiguration on Mount Tabor)

bold criticism that deletes an event that is so persistently reported in historical context and substitutes another for subjective reasons. No such necessity exists for those who accept the NT picture of Jesus as the supernatural and divine Christ.

III. Event. In a context of prayer, the threefold event transpired: Jesus was transfigured, MOSES and ELIJAH talked with him, and a voice spoke from heaven. The nature of the change in Jesus' appearance is not specified, except that Matthew adds the words, "His face shone like the sun" (Matt. 17:2). All three evangelists first mention the apparent change in Jesus himself before referring to his clothing. Borrowing the light from within, his clothing became "white as the light" (Matthew), "dazzling white, whiter than anyone in the world could bleach them" (Mk. 9:3), "as bright as a flash of lightning" (Lk. 9:29).

In the atmosphere of this transcendent glory, two persons, long glorified, became plainly visible, talking with Jesus. According to all the synoptists, Moses and Elijah were addressing Jesus. Luke adds that the subject was Jesus' impending death in Jerusalem. This glory and free intercourse with the spirit world appealed to Peter. He sought to seize and retain it, but a bright cloud settled upon them all, obscuring the scene and perhaps dazing the disciples. From this cloud came the voice, "This is my Son, whom I love. Listen to him!" When Jesus roused them (Matthew), they looked about and saw only Jesus (all three synoptists). The display was over.

IV. Significance. The meaning of this incident is firmly based upon the facts of the event. Every mention in the NT assumes that this was a deliberate self-revelation of Jesus to meet specific needs. No doubt Jesus himself received benefit from the heavenly event, but the need of the disciples was apparently primary. They must be prepared for the dark days ahead and for the bright outcome. They must see that Jesus was already what he would eventually demonstrate himself to be.

To his supernatural birth, the earlier divine attestations, the miracles, the signs, and the lesser manifestations must be added this supreme assurance of his origin and mission. His glory had been but thinly veiled in human flesh. In this revelation, it was allowed to shine forth. His supremacy was freely admitted by the lawgiver (Moses) and the prophet (Elijah), who may indeed have come for the express purpose of a formal resignation from their mediatorship before the one true Mediator (M. Dods, in a footnote to J. Lange, *The Life of the Lord Jesus Christ* [1872, repr. 1958], 2:327). The voice from heaven assured the disciples that Jesus was indeed the Son of God, as it had once assured JOHN THE BAPTIST at the Jordan (Matt. 3:17) and would again assure the multitude in Jerusalem (Jn. 12:28). The evangelists saw in this preview of the RESURRECTION glory, the God Incarnate—the sinner's only hope of glory.

(See further A. Edersheim, *The Life and Times of Jesus the Messiah* [1883], 2:91–101; S. Andrews, *The Life of Our Lord Upon the Earth* [1891], 356–59; W. Moulton in *Biblical and Semitic Studies* [1901], 159–210; M. Ramsey, *The Glory of God and the Transfiguration of Christ* [1949], 101–51; A. D. A. Moses, *Matthew's Transfiguration Story and Jewish-Christian Controversy* [1996]; J. P. Heil, *The Transfiguration of Jesus: Narrative Meaning and Function of Mark 9:2–8, Matt 17:1–8 and Luke 9:28–36* [2000].) W. T. DAYTON

transgression. The breaking of the LAW. There is a fine distinction between SIN (Gk. *hamartia G281*) and transgression (*parabasis G4126*), for one who is under no express law may sin (Rom. 5:13), but with the introduction of a law one commits transgression if that law is violated (Rom. 4:15; 5:14; Gal. 3:19). Hence, "sin" causes us to transgress (Rom. 7:7, 13). In some cases sin may be implicit disobedience, but transgression indicates explicit disobedience. (Cf. R. C. Trench, *Synonyms of the New Testament,* 9th ed. [1880], 244–45; J. Schneider in *TDNT,* 5:739–40.) See also TRESPASS. H. W. HOEHNER

Transjordan trans-jor′duhn. This term, meaning "on the other side of the Jordan" (cf. the common Heb. expression *ʿēber hayyardēn,* Deut. 1:1 et al.), is used with reference to the territory that lies to the E of the JORDAN River (contrast *Cisjordan,* "on this side of the Jordan," meaning the Land of CANAAN). East PALESTINE as a whole can sometimes be comprehended under the name of the central part of this area, GILEAD (e.g., Josh. 22:9). Generally, Transjordan is reckoned from the region of BASHAN on the N to the RED SEA on the S; the Arabian desert marks an indefinite boundary on the E and SE. Here were the countries of MOAB, EDOM, and AMMON; here too the tribes of REUBEN, GAD, and half of MANASSEH received their inheritance. Cut through by numerous gorges, some with constant water flow, the soil in Transjordan produces abundant crops of grain even without irrigation. It is rugged tableland, 2,000 to 3,000 ft. in elevation, with heights of around 5,000 ft.

The book of Genesis contains incidental references to this territory (e.g., Gen. 32:10). Later, as the Israelites were approaching Palestine, they sought to use the important KING'S HIGHWAY in Transjordan, but the Edomites would not permit them to do so (Num. 20:17–20). North of Edom lay Moab; there, from Mount Nebo (near the upper end of the Dead Sea), MOSES was granted sight of the land promised to Israel (Deut. 34:1–4; see NEBO, MOUNT). Moab is the primary setting of the book of RUTH. Here also DAVID took refuge to escape SAUL (1 Sam. 22:3–4). In this same territory, JEHORAM king of Israel, aided by Judah's JEHOSHAPHAT, sought to subdue the rebellious king MESHA (2 Ki. 3).

Next, between the rivers ARNON and YARMUK, comes Gilead proper and the AMORITE kingdom of SIHON, who denied Israel passage (Num. 21:21–31; Deut. 12:2). This also was the territory allotted to the tribes of Reuben and Gad (Deut. 3:12; Josh. 13:8–12). To this district, David a second time fled for sanctuary, escaping his insurrectionist son

ABSALOM (2 Sam. 17:21–29). To the E of Gilead and N of the Arnon was the country of Ammon. The northernmost territory was Bashan, of uncertain boundary, remembered for its fat cattle (Amos 4:1) and its King Og of iron bedstead fame (Num. 21:33–35; Deut. 3:1–11; Josh. 12:4–5). Here was Manasseh's half-tribe allotment (Deut. 3:13), roughly from the JABBOK River through Bashan.

In NT times, PEREA referred to a territory E of JUDEA and SAMARIA across the Jordan that afforded in part a bypath for strict Jews going from GALILEE in the N to Judea in the S (avoiding contamination by Samaria in between; cf. Jn. 4). To the N lay the Hellenistic DECAPOLIS, a trade federation of ten cities formed in the 1st cent., nine being on the E of Jordan, and one (BETH SHAN) on the W. The grouping secured protection from marauders. Antagonism existed between the Decapolis and both NABATEANS and Jews. Earlier, during the HASMONEAN period, the Jews had secured dominance over a large part of Transjordan, from GADARA in the N to MACHAERUS in the S, strongly fortified to resist the Nabateans. ROME, in A.D. 106, made the Nabatean country a part of the province of ARABIA. (See further G. A. Smith, *Historical Geography of the Holy Land*, 25th ed. [1931], chs. 24–29; N. Glueck, *The Other Side of the Jordan* [1970]; H. O. Thompson, *Archaeology in Jordan* [1989]; B. MacDonald, *"East of the Jordan": Territories and Sites of the Hebrew Scriptures* [2000].) R. F. GRIBBLE

translation. See VERSIONS OF THE BIBLE, ANCIENT; VERSIONS OF THE BIBLE, ENGLISH; VERSIONS OF THE BIBLE, MEDIEVAL AND MODERN.

trap. For the biblical writers the most common form of trap or snare (usually Heb. *paḥ* H7062 or *môqēs* H4613) was the automatic birdnet, "the snare of the fowler" (Prov. 6:5 et al.). This common form of bird trap or netting device is familiar from Egyptian illustrations. It was a piece of net mounted to spring up and envelop the bird when it alighted on a tripstick or some other form of trigger (Ps. 141:9; Ezek. 12:13; Amos 3:5). Note the illustration of sudden contrived disaster and catastrophe to which the victim thoughtlessly and unwarily exposed himself when in search for imagined or illusory advantage.

Another form of trap was the noose carefully set on the "run" of a bird or an animal and designed to tighten around the neck by the creature's own forward momentum (Job 18:10; 1 Cor. 7:35; this form of trapping device seems to be the metaphor behind Prov. 22:8). Ezekiel 17:20 may refer to a noose falling from above, though it could as likely be a descending net, falling as the victim entangled his feet in some low-lying trigger. Or, perhaps the fowler concealed in ambush pulled a releasing string when the birds ventured under the suspended net (Prov. 1:17–18). A camouflaged pit was an additional form of snare or trap used for the capture of unwary animals (2 Sam. 17:9; Isa. 24:17–18; 42:22; Jer. 18:22; 48:43–44; Lam. 3:47). Psalm 9:15 develops the metaphor; ironically, the hunter fell into the pit designed for his victims. There are numerous other figurative uses (Job 18:8; Ps. 69:22; 91:3; 124:7; 140:5; Prov. 6:5; 7:23; 12:13; Hos. 9:8; in the NT, Gk. *pagis* G4075, Lk. 21:34 [35]; Rom. 11:9 [with *thēra* G2560]; 1 Tim. 3:7; 6:9; 2 Tim. 2:26). E. M. BLAIKLOCK

travail. This English term, referring to a woman's labor at birth or more generally to any kind of painful or strenuous work, is used frequently by the KJV to render a variety of words, such as Hebrew *ḥîl* H2655 (e.g., Isa. 54:1) and Greek *ōdin* G6047 (e.g., 1 Thess. 5:3). Most of the uses are figurative. For instance, travail may portray the agonies of divine judgment on the wicked (Babylonians, Isa. 13:8; Zion, Mic. 4:9–10; Israel, Jer. 6:24; Judah, 4:31; Lebanon, 22:23; Damascus, 49:24); the thought of it caused Isaiah anguish like the pains of a woman in labor (Isa. 21:3).

Travail may picture the painful exertion necessary to achieve satisfying goals. The Suffering Servant "who makes an offering for sin" shall "see the fruit of the travail of his soul and be satisfied" (Isa. 53:10–11 KJV). The apostle PAUL, in the Lord's service, could not forget the "labour and travail" night and day to plant the church at THESSALONICA (1 Thess. 2:9 KJV; cf. 2 Thess. 3:8). The Galatians seemed to return to legalistic works, so Paul was "again in travail until Christ be formed" in them (Gal. 4:19 RSV).

Jesus used the figure of travail to represent the disciples' sorrow in a world that would crucify him.

However, just as the anguish is forgotten by the mother rejoicing that a child is born, so also their sorrow would be taken away (Jn. 16:21–22). Travail also portrays the agony of the world until Christ returns. "We know that the whole creation has been groaning in travail together until now" (Rom. 8:22 RSV). At Christ's return, furthermore, will come sudden destruction "as travail comes upon a woman with child, and there will be no escape" (1 Thess. 5:3 RSV). G. R. Lewis

travel. In the OT, almost all the traveling recorded was by land; the NT mentions travel by water more frequently, especially in connection with the journeys of PAUL. The present article focuses primarily on the ROAD system in PALESTINE.

  I. In the OT
     A. The nature of roads in Palestine
     B. Major roads
     C. Minor roads
     D. International travel
     E. Water travel
  II. In the NT
     A. Land travel
     B. Water travel
     C. Reasons for travel in NT times

I. In the OT

A. The nature of roads in Palestine. Land travel in OT times was normally by path (e.g., Heb. ʾōraḥ H784) or road (derek H2006), although the various Hebrew terms do not differentiate clearly between these two types. If there was little travel, then a narrow path or track was sufficient. When there was volume travel, the track simply widened out into a road. These OT roads, however, did not approximate even the poorest roads used today. In hilly country a road normally had two branches, one for slow climbing up a hill and the other for fast downhill travel. In the mountains, rocks and trees had to be removed, especially after the time of DAVID, when the CAMEL became the hauler of heavy freight. The donkeys, which preceded them and which always carried light loads, were much more sure-footed (see ASS, DONKEY). HORSES were only for the army until Persian times, while the MULE was for royalty and the rich. On level ground when the old road became too rough, the caravans simply moved over a few feet; autos and trucks do the same today in the desert.

Any major engineering on the roads occurred only on special occasions, as when royalty traveled or when large armies were on the march. On such occasions better grades were made in the mountains, and fills were put in on troublesome terrain, such as swamps. ISAIAH describes the work: "In the desert prepare / the way for the LORD; / make straight in the wilderness / a highway for our God. / Every valley shall be raised up, / every mountain and hill made low; / the rough ground shall become level, / the rugged places a plain" (Isa.

This aerial view shows a section through which passed the major trade road of ancient Palestine, connecting Egypt, Europe, and Asia. (View to the W.)

40:3–4). Here the Hebrew word for "highway" is *měsillâ* H5019, referring to an elevated road, that is, one made with a fill.

Because of the poor conditions of the roads, vehicles were rare in OT times. The CHARIOT was primarily a weapon of war, for use on level or slightly rolling ground. The engineers often prepared ground for them. The wagon for heavy freight was more common than a carriage or other light vehicle for persons. The latter, however, is referred to in the JOSEPH story when PHARAOH suggested sending wagons for JACOB and the wives and children of his sons (Gen. 45:19–27). The heavy wagon or ox CART was used to transport the heavy materials of the TABERNACLE (Num. 7:3–9). A cart was used by the PHILISTINES when they returned the ARK OF THE COVENANT to Israel, but it was drawn by cows unbroken to harness (1 Sam. 6:7–12). DAVID, however, later moved that ark by ox cart (1 Chr. 13:7–9). Amos 2:13 refers to an ox cart used as a hay wagon. This reflects the days of big farms. Most pictures of wagons or carts show solid wooden wheels, which are still useful in parts of Turkey today. The Assyrians used spoke-wheel wagons at times in their baggage trains. The two-wheel cart was much more common than the four-wheel wagon.

Travel was slow, for both men and animals walked; the length of the day's march depended upon the urgency of the trip (even Paul, who was under orders from the high priest, walked to DAMASCUS, Acts 9:8). Average travel for men would be about 15 mi. a day. Donkey caravans tried to make 20 mi. a day. The ordinary camel caravan of freight, with each animal carrying between 500 and 600 lbs., traveled approximately 3 mi. an hour on a 6-hour day. A swift dromedary, on the other hand, could carry a rider on long journeys at 70 mi. a day. The camel was, of course, the ideal animal to use in the desert, and often the only animal available.

The more common caravan before and after David's reign was the donkey caravan. The largest of these donkey trains ranged from 1,000 to 3,000 animals. ABRAHAM is the most famous "caravaneer." The donkey was an ideal carrier for passengers or freight, an animal with surprising power and endurance, and the most sure-footed of all animals used, which rode comfortably and was inexpensive. In a passage such as Jdg. 5:6, which comments that "caravans ceased and travelers kept to the byways" (NRSV), the reference is to political unrest, during which brigands and robbers made travel dangerous and unprofitable. The best and fastest travel service in OT times was the "pony express," horse travel between relay stations, used by the Persian government for diplomatic correspondence (cf. Esth. 8:10).

These were fair-weather roads in the OT, and only the most important business was carried on during the rainy season. WAR was seldom pursued in rain or snow or during flood seasons. The heaviest rains fell from November into February, with lighter rains earlier and later, and none usually during the long hot summer. The winter storms often compelled the use of alternate roads. The Plain of SHARON, for example, was a summer road; in winter a new road farther E followed the higher land at the foot of the hills. Much of the Plain of ESDRAELON was a swamp in the winter during Bible times. The roads were modified by the geology of the terrain through which they passed.

The halting places had plenty of water and food for travelers and their animals. Such caravan sites often became commercial centers; at strategic points fortresses were built to protect the commerce.

B. Major roads. The most important N-S road in Palestine was known as VIA MARIS ("the way of the sea") or the Great Trunk road. It was a continuation of the great road from Egypt that had followed the Mediterranean coast from near the present Suez Canal to GAZA, which through all its history has been the bridgehead to Egypt. From GAZA the road ran just E of the sand dunes of the Mediterranean close to JOPPA, where it moved to the E edge of the Plain of Sharon until it could cut through the pass at MEGIDDO and then climb across GALILEE to the key road junction at HAZOR. It then crossed the Jordan River just below Lake Huleh. At this point it climbed out of the Jordan Valley and up to the Syrian plateau and direct to DAMASCUS. This was the fastest route, whereas caravans carrying heavy baggage took an easier grade: at Megiddo they turned E across the Plain of ESDRAELON and down to BETH SHAN, then turned N up the Jordan Valley near the Sea of Galilee, where they climbed out to the Syrian plateau, and then directly to Damascus.

Another N-S road handled mostly local Palestinian traffic rather than international commerce. It began at BEERSHEBA and reached the central ridge of W Palestine at HEBRON; it continued through JERUSALEM, BETHEL, SHECHEM, SAMARIA, and DOTHAN to EN GANNIM at the edge of the Plain of Esdraelon. Traffic could continue on the international route to Damascus or take an alternate course to the Mediterranean coast at Acco and then N to PHOENICIA.

A second international trade route in Palestine, on the high plateau E of the Jordan River, was known as the KING'S HIGHWAY. It picked up Arabian commerce at EZION GEBER or at Maʿan (the latter was replaced by PETRA in intertestamental times). The road then moved N about equidistant between the desert and the cliffs dropping off into the Jordan Valley. The major towns on the route were Kir of Moab (see KIR HARESETH), DIBON, MADABA, HESHBON, RABBAH (AMMON), EDREI, and Damascus. On the stela of MESHA (see MOABITE STONE), this Moabite king praised himself for making a highway in the ARNON Valley. Anyone who has seen a picture of that valley can appreciate the task. It is c. 2.5 mi. from rim to rim and c. 2300 ft. deep. After David's era the Wadi Sirhan became an alternate trade route from ARABIA to Rabbah. By that time camels were plentiful, and they could be used on this shorter but poorly watered route.

There were two main E-W routes in Palestine, each following an ideal water grade. One left the Mediterranean at Joppa and moved NW to the pass between Mounts GERIZIM and EBAL, where Shechem was located. It then continued down a valley to the Jordan River, which it crossed at Adam. See ADAM (PLACE). In TRANSJORDAN it ascended the JABBOK Valley through the GILEAD district where it met the king's highway going N to Damascus.

The other key E-W road left the Mediterranean at Acco and went SE through the Plains of Acco and Esdraelon to the Jordan River at Beth Shan. Here it crossed the river and ascended a pass to the great wheat-growing plateau to BETH ARBEL (modern Irbid) and on to Edrei, where it met the king's highway going N to Damascus.

C. Minor roads. A short but important road along the Mediterranean ran from Acco (NT, Ptolemais) to TYRE and SIDON and other Phoenician cities. Most scholars doubt if there was a coastal road through the Plain of Sharon, since most of the shore area was swampy.

The main ridge road from Shechem to the Plain of Esdraelon had one route via Samaria, already mentioned. It was on the W side of the ridge. Before Samaria came to prominence, the main road probably ran E of the ridge through the earlier Israelite capital of TIRZAH. This same main ridge road had a less important road that went S from Beersheba via KADESH BARNEA to Egypt. It was important only in the period of the PATRIARCHS, especially Abraham, and after JEHOSHAPHAT's time. A minor

Major routes and roads.

N-S road followed up each side of the Jordan Valley from Jericho to Capernaum. In Transjordan, a minor N-S road paralleled the king's highway, but it skirted the edge of the desert.

The most important E-W road S of Shechem left the Mediterranean at Joppa and climbed up the Valley of Aijalon to the central ridge. One branch turned S and in a few miles came to Jerusalem. This was the only military road from the Philistine plain to Jerusalem. The other fork went N a few miles to Bethel and then descended to the Jordan River, passing through Jericho. It then crossed over the river and climbed up to Rabbah of Ammon.

Another short but important E-W road went from Acco via a depression called Sahl Battuf to the Sea of Galilee. A minor E-W road much farther S led from the seaport of Ashkelon to Hebron. From there a track led down to the Dead Sea at En Gedi. Another road stretched from nearby Gaza to Beersheba and on to the edge of the Jordan depression, where a track led down to the Arabah.

A look at a contour map of Palestine will show how rugged most of the country is, which necessitated a great number of still smaller roads to connect the various minor trade centers. These played a large part in local history but are seldom mentioned in the major historical accounts of Israel. David's flights from Saul, however, used these minor tracks, which he had learned as a shepherd lad working out of Bethlehem.

D. International travel. The label Fertile Crescent is the best introduction to understanding OT travel, for it denotes the belt of arable land extending northward up the E coast of the Mediterranean to the headwaters of the Euphrates and Tigris Rivers, and then SE along the river valleys to the Persian Gulf. The great Arabian desert and the Syrian steppes N of them made E-W travel across them almost impossible until one reached the first good E-W commercial center at Palmyra (Tadmor). One of the few important crossings of the southern desert was made by Nebuchadnezzar, who used that route from the Mediterranean to shake hands with the god Nabu on New Year's day at Babylon, and thus validate his right to continue as king.

There were two major world civilization centers in OT times: Egypt and Mesopotamia (for the latter, see Sumer and Assyria and Babylonia). Persia and Greece came into international importance only toward the end of the OT period. The Hittites of Asia Minor made their greatest contributions to ANE cultures as miners and workers of metals during OT times. Phoenicia, after David's time, was to the ancient Mediterranean world what Great Britain was in her greatest maritime days. Assyria was primarily a military machine but she also modified Babylonian civilization. These countries dominated OT travel.

The traveler from Egypt to Palestine left Egypt near where the Suez Canal is today, and then normally traveled along the Mediterranean coast keeping inland behind the sand dunes. The road ended at Gaza, the bridgehead for Egypt. The only alternative route was the one Abraham used: from Goshen in Egypt to Kadesh Barnea at the N end of the Sinai desert and then to Beersheba. This route, however, was little used after his time until Solomon's reign. The only other travel alternative was to go by sea.

The various travel routes N-S in Palestine have been listed. In Galilee, several important roads left Palestine for Phoenicia or Syria. Phoenicia is a Greek word. In the OT that area was actually a part of Canaan and was so called at times; in the OT it is usually referred to by its cities, especially Tyre and Sidon. Some commerce came overland into Phoenicia via the sources of the Jordan River above Lake Huleh, and then crossed the border into the Litany River Valley of Phoenicia. Additional commerce traveled along the Mediterranean coast road from Acco to Tyre and Sidon. Still more commerce went by sea.

Syria (or Aram as it was more often called), consisted of two fertile grain areas separated by the Antilebanon mountains. Just E of the Lebanon mountains lies the fertile Litany Valley. The Litany River rises at Baalbek and flows S to the Mediterranean near Tyre. At Baalbek the Orontes River also has its source, but it flows N and enters the Mediterranean near Antioch of Syria. This was a large fertile valley, a major breadbasket in the ancient world. It lay between the Nosairiyeh Mountains along the Mediterranean and the

Antilebanon range. East of the Antilebanons was another grain area; as the rainfall becomes less eastward, the land turns to what some call the desert; but more accurately it is the steppes, and beyond that is the desert proper. One road followed the Litany Valley from Palestine N to Baalbek and then paralleled the Orontes River to the Mediterranean. Another road branched off from the Orontes at HAMATH, going northeastward to CARCHEMISH on the Euphrates.

The Syrian route, mentioned more often in the OT, led through Damascus and continued N to Hamath on the Orontes, or farther on to Carchemish on the Euphrates. Faster traffic heading for Mesopotamia left Damascus and cut NE for Palmyra (Tadmor); from there it went E to the great city of MARI on the Euphrates.

Carchemish and HARAN (of Abraham's time) were at the top of the Fertile Crescent. At this junction the Syrian roads ended, and here, of vital importance, roads from Asia Minor converged. From central Anatolia and its famous Hittite population one route went through the Taurus Mountains S to TARSUS and then turned E across the passes of the Amanus Mountains to Carchemish. Another route went farther E on the great central Anatolian plateau and then turned sharply S to Carchemish and Haran. From these key geographic cities a traveler could go SE to Babylonia or E to Assyria. Persia lay E of both of them.

From Carchemish the road followed the Euphrates River past Mari, on to Babylon, Ur, the Persian Gulf, and points S via the sea to Arabia. Babylonia was the successor of Sumer, where WRITING—the world's greatest invention—had its beginning. In this land, civilization in antiquity always seemed to be at home. East of Babylon, beyond one of the rare good passes in the Zagros Mountains, lay ELAM and what later became Persia.

To reach Assyria from Carchemish a route went E past Haran along the fertile foothills of the Armenian mountains through the lands of the Horites and Mitanni to the Tigris River and the capital city of NINEVEH. From here, passes reached into Persia, but the traveling was rough.

E. Water travel. The Hebrews did little water travel, in contrast to the maritime economy of the Phoenicians. When SOLOMON sent his ships down the RED SEA to OPHIR, and when JEHOSHAPHAT planned a similar expedition, Phoenician mariners were asked to conduct the adventures. JONAH was the one famous seafarer of the OT. His intended voyage was passage from Joppa to TARSHISH, which was probably on the Atlantic coast of Spain near the mouth of the Guadalquivir River. This was one of the longest commercial trips made in OT times. The only longer sailings were made to the British Isles for tin.

Coastal traffic of OT Palestine was in Philistine hands, between Gaza and Joppa. Later, the coastal towns became independent under Assyria. Joppa was not always considered a Philistine city. The only port on the Plain of Sharon was DOR, which belonged to the Tjeker, another of the SEA PEOPLES allied to the Philistines. Acco was allotted to the tribe of Asher but was never conquered by the Israelites. It was either an independent city or allied with Tyre in the N.

The other coastal water of Palestine was the Gulf of Aqabah with its two seaports: Ezion Geber (the more important) for Transjordan, and Elath for W Jordan. Solomon's fleet used Ezion Geber as its home port (see also II.B below).

II. In the NT

A. Land travel. Travel in Palestine in NT times was very similar to OT times. There were no major changes except that a larger population meant more travel and therefore better roads. It is doubtful, however, if Palestine had any Roman-constructed roads in the days of Christ and Paul. Certain OT cities acquired new (Hellenistic) names before the NT period: Acco became Ptolemais; Rabbah of Ammon, Philadelphia; and Samaria, Sebaste. Two important new cities, CAESAREA and JERICHO, were built by HEROD the Great. The latter city was not a rebuilding of OT Jericho, but a new city on a new site nearby the OT site.

NT travel is apparent in the trips taken by JESUS CHRIST and the apostle PAUL. When Paul branched out from Syrian Antioch on his missionary journeys through Asia Minor and points W, he used some of the famous Roman roads. With good roads came more carriages for people and more

TRAVEL

Foundation of the ancient Ḥusan ridge road connecting Bethlehem to the Elah Valley.

wagons for freight. Carriages could make 25 mi. a day on a good Roman road. Government business and army orders could travel 50 mi. a day by a horseman. Government orders could travel from Rome to Caesarea, the capital of NT Palestine, in fifty to sixty-five days in good weather. Commercial business would probably have taken longer, up to a hundred days or more. The world of the NT, a saga of international travel, reached from Germany to China, and from Scandinavia and Russia to central Africa. NERO sent army engineers to search for the sources of the NILE River, and they went as far S as the Sobat River.

The major reason for travel was business, which included any saleable items from the vast land areas described above. An abridged list of commerce from the Far E and the Near E is given in Rev. 18:11–13.

B. Water travel. The major cities that transshipped the ANE commerce to ROME and other points W were ALEXANDRIA and ANTIOCH OF SYRIA. The various efficient ways of handling cargo across the Isthmus of Corinth greatly expedited E-W shipping. The isthmus was less than 5 mi. wide, but saved 200 mi. of sailing around Cape Malea, which was a graveyard for ships. In ancient times, clearing that cape was like clearing Cape Horn in the days of the clipper ships. Emperor Nero dug a part of the canal that now cuts through the isthmus. He would doubtless have finished it if political problems had not driven him to suicide. The canal was completed only in modern times, at the end of the 19th cent., using Nero's surveys.

Nautical travel in OT and NT times used ships of various types. They ranged in size from very small to very large. The larger ones were decked over (see the excellent description of a ship used by the royalty of Tyre in Ezek. 27:3–9). Lucian mentions a large Alexandrian grain ship some 180 ft. long (its capacity would have been about 1200 tons). The vessel in which Paul was shipwrecked carried 276 in its crew and passenger list (Acts 27:37), while JOSEPHUS reports that he was in a shipwreck when there were 600 persons on board (*Life* 15). Ships were normally "powered by sail only, although on important business auxiliary oar power was used in calm weather. The ship would carry a large mainmast and small foremast, both using square sails. Great oars mounted over the stern served as rudders" (J. Kelso, *Archaeology and Our Old Testament Contemporaries* [1966], 121). A day's sail would probably have been about 55 nautical miles.

C. Reasons for travel in NT times. The most important reason for travel in NT times was commerce, but this involved far more than the shipment of goods. There were commercial travelers of all categories, and tradesmen changing their places of employment, as PRISCILLA AND AQUILA had done (Acts 18:2), whose original home was on the Black Sea (PONTUS). Banking and the insurance of cargoes were big business, and their agents were always on the move. There were Roman military and naval men of every category, on special duties for the government, such as the procuring of supplies. Rome often shifted large units of her military forces. VESPASIAN, who was in charge of Rome's war with the Jews, was on duty in Britain when he was called to his new command.

Also in NT times, people traveled on religious pilgrimages. Jerusalem attracted the faithful Israelites, from Rome to Arabia (Acts 2:5–11). Among the most famous pagan shrines were those at EPHESUS, ATHENS, and ELEUSIS, but minor ones were located throughout the empire and all of them attracted pilgrims. New temples were erected everywhere, which necessitated travel for the craftsmen employed and transportation for the material used in construction. Many of the temples were famous for their healing miracles, and the sick traveled from temple to temple. People also traveled to hot springs, which were usually considered medicinal. CAPERNAUM was near two famous hot springs, which may be one of the reasons so many sick people came to Christ in that city.

Athletes traveled the length of the Mediterranean for the "Olympian games," which were held in contests from Spain to Antioch. They were well scheduled so that the best professional athletes could make the rounds of all the important games. Crowds flocked to these games in large numbers, as today. The modern football stadium is a modified Roman amphitheater. Professors and scholars traveled widely; most of the population with money sought an education for their sons, which involved foreign travel. TARSUS ranked just a little below Athens on the university circuit. Jewish scholars finished their studies at Jerusalem (cf. Paul). Scientists, too, traveled everywhere. ALEXANDER THE GREAT started this movement when he took many varieties of scientists with him on his world conquest.

In NT times, tourists traveled everywhere to see the famous sights. By the next century, Pausanias was writing excellent guidebooks. The ancient world, however, could not solve the problem of winter. Sea travel could obtain favorable insurance rates only between May 26 and September 14. The sea was normally considered closed to traffic from November 10 to March 10. Emergency voyages were occasionally made in the closed season. The ship that took Paul to Rome tried to beat the season, but was shipwrecked. Fairly good sea charts and land maps, however, were available.

The greatest seasonal handicaps to land travel were snow and floods; when at their worst in Asia Minor, the roads might be blocked for weeks. There were few good inns throughout the whole empire, but wherever possible travelers stayed with business friends or with a friend of a friend.

(See further W. M. Ramsay, *St. Paul the Traveller and the Roman Citizen*, 14th ed. [1920]; A. C. Bouquet, *Everyday Life in New Testament Times* [1955], ch. 5; R. J. Forbes, *Studies in Ancient Technology*, 8 vols. [1955–64], 2:126–83; Y. Aharoni, *The Land of the Bible: A Historical Geography*, rev. ed. [1979], ch. 3; L. Casson, *Travel in the Ancient World* [1974]; M. A. Littauer and J. H. Crouwel, *Wheeled Vehicles and Ridden Animals in the Ancient Near East* [1979], D. A. Dorsey, *The Roads and Highways of Ancient Israel* [1991]; L. Ellis and F. L. Kidner, eds., *Travel, Communication and Geography in Late Antiquity: Sacred and Profane* [2004]; *ABD*, 6:644–53.)

J. KELSO

Travelers, Valley of the. According to Ezek. 39:11, God "will give to Gog a place for burial in Israel, the Valley of the Travelers east of the sea" (NRSV; similarly NJPS); as a result, the place will be called the Valley of HAMON GOG. The Hebrew of the last clause reads, *gê hāʿōbĕrîm qidmat hayyām*, which the KJV takes in a more general sense, "the valley of the passengers on the east of the sea."

On the reasonable assumption that "the sea" here is a reference to the DEAD SEA, the NRSV rendering indicates a place in TRANSJORDAN. And if the phrase *gê hāʿōbĕrîm* is a name, the simple revocalization *hāʿăbārîm* would yield a reference to the ABARIM, a range of mountains in MOAB (though the term *ʿōbĕrîm* [ptc. of *ʿābar* H6296, "to pass over, cross"] occurs a second time in this verse and again in vv. 14–15—might this be a play on words?). It seems strange, however, that a location E of the Dead Sea would be characterized as being "in Israel" (for other objections and alternate proposals, none convincing, see W. Zimmerli, *Ezekiel*, Hermeneia, 2 vols. [1979–83], 2:317).

The NIV understands the syntax in a slightly different way, "the valley of those who travel east toward the Sea," implying some otherwise unknown place in Canaan proper. Possibly the passage should be understood symbolically, without reference to a specific geographical location.

treasure. This English term is used frequently in Bible versions to render several words, especially Hebrew *ʾôṣār* H238 (e.g., 1 Ki. 7:51) and Greek *thēsauros* G2565 (e.g., Matt. 2:11), both of which often refer to a STOREHOUSE or treasury. Treasure in the Holy Scriptures consisted in money or any possession—jewels, gold, silver, vessels, ointments, spices, arms, grain and food, instruments of war — considered WEALTH or valuable, and which a king, a government, or an individual stored in a safe, guarded place to keep from thieves and robbers. Thus, for example, the sacred vessels and furnishings of the TEMPLE in Jerusalem, or even the temples of heathen gods, were considered treasures (e.g., 1 Chr. 32:27–29; Ezra 1:9–11; Neh. 7:70). Because treasure signified a person's highest desires and possessions which gave him food, power, and luxury, often the term is used by the prophets, Jesus, and the apostles to signify spiritual wealth and possessions, such as wisdom, love, heaven, and the gospel (e.g., Prov. 10:2; Isa. 33:6; Mk. 10:21).

When enemy forces invaded a country, they generally headed for the king's palace or the temple for the treasures stored there, and these plus the captives and slaves of the people were the booty of WAR in ancient times. The entire concept of treasure or storehouse in the Bible indicates the monarchial aspect of the culture and economy of the ancient world in that all wealth was concentrated in the king, in the sacred temple, or in the hands of princes or wealthy individuals. The common people had little of this wealth, nor did they think they should have it, but they revered the king in the temple for storing it for the entire country. There was extreme wealth among a few and POVERTY among the multitudes.

There were no banks, nor did the treasure houses have safety deposit boxes, so the temples and palaces were always under heavy guard. Wealthy individuals hid their possessions beneath their houses, in caves, and in fields. Many wars were fought for these treasures (1 Ki. 14:26). Plundering the cities and temples of others was a method of gaining wealth for a nation. When Jerusalem fell to the invading armies from the E, all the treasures were carried off to foreign countries. Very often emperors, kings, and queens, as in EGYPT, had their treasures buried with them in secret sealed tombs. The PYRAMIDS of Egypt are an outstanding example of this method. The place in the temple in Jerusalem where the trumpet-shaped offering boxes were set for the gifts was thus called a "treasury" (Gk. *gaza phylakion* G1126, Mk. 12:41; Lk. 21:1).

One of the first references to treasure in the OT is the episode of JOSEPH's brothers buying food in Egypt during the famine. When Joseph returned their money in their sacks with the food, he said to his frightened brothers, "Don't be afraid. Your God, the God of your father, has given you treasure in your sacks; I received your silver" (Gen. 42:23). Kings DAVID and SOLOMON were known for the great wealth they amassed in their palaces, and also stored in the house of the Lord. The treasure of the temple in Jerusalem consisted of the vessels, the golden altar, the golden table for the bread of the Presence (SHOWBREAD), the lampstands of gold, the lamps, the tongs, and other accessories; even the doors and the building itself were a great treasure all made of gold (1 Ki. 7:48–50). "When all the work King Solomon had done for the temple of the LORD was finished, he brought in the things his father David had dedicated—the silver and gold and the furnishings—and he placed them in the treasuries of the LORD's temple" (v. 51). See TREASURY OF THE TEMPLE.

Like the residences of other monarchs of the ancient world, so the palaces of the kings of Judah and Israel had vast storehouses for the treasures of the nation. Concerning the wars with the powerful countries around Israel, the OT speaks again and again of foreign powers taking away the treasures of the king's house. SHISHAK king of Egypt besieged Jerusalem and "carried off the treasures of the temple of the LORD and the treasures of the royal palace. He took everything, including all the gold shields Solomon had made" (1 Ki. 14:26).

Sometimes the treasures of the Israelite palaces were at stake in the local wars in Palestine. For example, when BAASHA king of Israel and ASA king of Judah were at war, Asa sent all of the treasures of the nation to BEN-HADAD king of Aram, to make a bargain with him to attack Baasha so that he would leave Judah. "Asa then took all the silver and gold that was left in the treasuries of the LORD's temple and of his own palace. He entrusted it to his officials and sent them to Ben-Hadad … in Damascus" (1 Ki. 15:18). In the rebuilding of Israel during the days of EZRA and NEHEMIAH, the same system of gathering huge treasures and wealth in the ruler's house and in the temple was used (Ezra 3:6ff; Neh. 7:70–71; 10:38; 12:44).

When the Arameans invaded Israel, King AHAZ asked TIGLATH-PILESER king of Assyria to come to his rescue against them. In order to entice the Assyrian king to do this, Ahaz took the silver and gold and all of the treasures of the house of the Lord, and sent them as presents to him (2 Ki. 16:7–9). A similar incident took place in the days of HEZEKIAH when another Assyrian king, SENNACHERIB, invaded Judah. The booty which the king of Assyria required of Judah was the silver and gold that was in the house of the Lord (18:13–16). Years later, when the king of Babylon took JEHOIACHIM of Judah as prisoner, he carried off all the treasures of the house of the Lord, cutting in pieces all the vessels of gold which Solomon had made—an indication of the vast treasures that could be found in the temple at Jerusalem through the centuries.

The source of these temple treasures had been the dedicated offerings David and others had given to the Lord: spoil won in battles and dedicated to the temple. Special groups of people or families of Israel were assigned the task of guarding the treasures there (1 Chr. 26:22–28). Other sources of wealth and treasure were large gifts from heads of families of Israel as freewill offerings for the house of God. "According to their ability they gave to the treasury for this work 61,000 drachmas of gold, 5,000 minas of silver and 100 priestly garments" (Ezra 2:69). The tithes of the people were also added to the treasure storehouse at the temple.

The book of Proverbs repeats the wisdom that the fear of the Lord is always greater than earthly treasures and the trouble that accompanies them (Prov. 8:21; 15:16). The prophet Isaiah speaks of "treasures on the humps of camels" (Isa. 30:6), indicating the wealth that was carried in CARAVANS. That the wealth of ancient countries consisted in the treasures in storehouses at the seat of the government is indicated by God's word against Jerusalem: "I will hand over to their enemies all the wealth of this city—all its products, all its valuables and all the treasures of the kings of Judah. They will take it away as plunder and carry it off to Babylon" (Jer. 20:5). Hezekiah had tremendous storehouses while he was king, consisting of "the silver, the gold, the spices and the fine oil—his armory and everything found among his treasures" (2 Ki. 20:13; Isa. 39:2). Sometimes invading kings, such as NEBUCHADNEZZAR of Babylon, besieged Jerusalem and took the precious vessels of the temple and of the king and would place them into the temple of his own idol, indicating that all temples in ancient times had secret storehouses for vessels, jewels, gold, and silver as a sacred treasury (Dan. 1:1–2).

Often the term *treasure* or *storehouse* is used in the OT in a figurative sense. For instance, in a dry land like Palestine RAIN from heaven for the parched crops was considered treasure: "The LORD will open the heavens, the storehouse of his bounty, to send rain on your land in season and to bless all the work of your hands" (Deut. 28:12). WISDOM was considered a great treasure among the ancients: "Precious treasure remains in the house of the wise, / but the fool devours it" (Prov. 21:20 NRSV). Another common word-picture is that the fear of the Lord is a person's treasure, as Isaiah told the people of Israel, "The fear of the LORD is the key to this treasure" (Isa. 33:6). The prophet Ezekiel echoes the same sentiment: "By your wisdom and understanding / you have gained wealth for yourself / and amassed gold and silver / in your treasuries" (Ezek. 28:4).

The NT speaks of treasure in individual terms as personal property. The MAGI of the E (not kings) brought great treasures to the child Jesus in Bethlehem. Since Jesus is a King their gifts were those fit for royalty—gold, frankincense, and myrrh (Matt. 2:11). Their gifts remind one of the king's treasury in the OT. Aside from a few instances—such as in Heb. 11:26, where we are told that Moses "regarded disgrace for the sake of Christ as of greater value than the treasures of Egypt," or in Matt. 13:44, where Jesus compares the kingdom of heaven to a "treasure hidden in a field"—the term is used more generally in the NT in a metaphorical sense. Jesus admonishes his disciples, "But store up for yourselves treasures in heaven, where moth and rust do not destroy, and where thieves do not break in and steal. For where your treasure is, there your heart will be also" (Matt. 6:20, 21).

Our Lord also uses the term to designate the good and evil in a person: "The good man brings good things out of the good stored up in him, and the evil man brings evil things out of the evil stored up in him." (Matt. 12:35). Since the kingdom of heaven is the ultimate desire, Jesus likens it to a man who, finding a treasure hidden in a field, sells all of his possessions and buys the entire field so that he is certain to obtain the treasure (13:44). LOVE and works of love are treasures that are stored in heaven, as Jesus tells the young man, "If you want to be perfect, go, sell your possessions and give to the poor, and you will have treasure in heaven. Then come, follow me" (19:21). Jesus tells his disciples that such works of providing for the poor through selling one's possessions is "a treasure in heaven that will not be exhausted" (Lk. 12:33).

The writer of the Gospel of Matthew speaks of treasure as the spiritual wisdom and knowledge which a scribe who is a member of the kingdom produces: "Therefore every teacher of the law who has been instructed about the kingdom of heaven is like the owner of a house who brings out of his storeroom new treasures as well as old" (Matt. 13:52). The apostle PAUL terms the gospel of Jesus Christ a treasure which dwells in weak human beings: "But we have this treasure in jars of clay to show that this all-surpassing power is from God and not from us." (2 Cor. 4:7). The capstone and ultimate meaning of treasure in the NT is Paul's statement that in Jesus Christ "are hidden all the treasures of wisdom and knowledge" (Col. 2:3). L. M. PETERSEN

treasury of the temple. Solomon's TEMPLE contained a place for storing gifts of gold and silver dedicated to the use of the house of the Lord (1 Ki. 7:51). Most ancient sanctuaries had a treasury attached to them; for example, the *opisthodomos* ("back chamber") served as the treasury for the Parthenon at ATHENS. The location of the treasury in the temple of Jerusalem is a matter of dispute. From NT evidence it appears that receptacles for freewill offerings were accessible to women, hence in the forecourt of the temple (cf. Mk. 12:41–42; Lk. 21:1–2). Most exegetes place the treasury elsewhere, though Strack and Billerbeck think that this is unwarranted (Str-B, 2:42ff.; cf. Jos. *War* 5.5.2).

From 1 Chr. 26:20 it would appear that it belonged to the function of the Levites to administer the treasury, but later it became the prerogative of the priests (cf. Jos. *Ant.* 11.5.2). At the time of Christ the high priest was the chief administrator. Later rabbinic writings indicate that a committee served under him which was hierarchically constituted and headed by financial officers or controllers.

The main source of income was the half-shekel (Exod. 30:13–15), which was paid by every Israelite "twenty years old or more" before the first of NISAN each year. Thirteen receptacles were placed in the court of women to receive the offerings. Six of these trumpet-shaped urns were especially designated to receive, for example, new shekel dues, old shekel dues, bird offerings, etc. The rest were for free-will gifts (cf. *m. Šeqal.* 6:5–6). Every adult Jew, both in Palestine and in the DIASPORA, was under obligation to pay the half-shekel annually. Delegations from communities all over the empire and from beyond came to Jerusalem with their gifts. The MONEY CHANGERS (Mk. 11:15; Jn. 2:14–15) were necessary because only the Tyrian shekel was allowed for temple use. In older times booty acquired in battle was dedicated for the use of the sanctuary (cf. Josh. 6:19, 24).

Since the temple possessed considerable wealth, the treasury was thus a great attraction to invading armies (cf. 1 Ki. 14:26; 2 Ki. 24:13; 1 Macc. 1:20–24; 2 Macc. 3:1–13). Frequently the reigning princes themselves, in time of need, made use of the treasury to buy political advantage (cf. 1 Ki. 15:18–19; 2 Ki. 12:18), or to pay tribute money (18:14–15). See also TREASURE. J. JOCZ

treaty. A document containing the terms of arrangement or COVENANT agreed upon by two or more parties. Archaeological research has provided examples of international treaties of the lands of the ANE drawn up during the 2nd millennium B.C.— the time when the biblical Israelites entered their covenant with the Lord at Sinai (Exod. 19–20). Political treaties were of two types: (a) *Parity* treaties were drawn up to state relationships existing among equals; two great powers such as EGYPT and the HITTITES might find it useful to formalize their relations in this way. (b) *Suzerainty* treaties declared relationships formalized between a "great king" and his vassal; the great king (or "king of kings" or "lord of lords") thereby claims authority over other, lesser rulers. Yahweh, the God of Israel, uses suzerainty terms in declaring his right to absolute loyalty from all earthly rulers and people (cf. Ps. 2).

Six elements may be distinguished in suzerainty treaties of the 2nd millennium B.C.: (1) The treaty begins with the identification of the great king.

Similarly, in covenant passages in the OT we often find the formula "I am the LORD your God" (Exod. 20:2) or "This is what the LORD, the God of Israel, says ..." (Josh. 24:2).

(2) Then follows a statement of the historical background of the relations between the great king and his vassal; the purpose is to emphasize the goodness and kindness of the lord to his vassal, with a view to causing the latter to accept gladly his responsibilities and obligations. Similarly, the OT emphasizes the gracious acts of the Lord on behalf of his people: after identifying himself as the Lord, Israel's God, he continues, "who brought you out of Egypt" (Exod. 20:2). Following the conquest of Canaan, the Lord identified himself as the God who gave the Israelites a land in which to dwell (Josh. 24.2–13).

(3) Next the treaty gives the obligations of the vassal, who is not permitted to consort with foreign powers. The suzerain will protect the vassal, but the vassal must not act in a way that would suggest disloyalty to his suzerain. The first commandment forbids Israel from consorting with any other deities (Exod. 20:3). God demands absolute loyalty of his people.

(4) Ancient suzerainty treaties stipulated that a copy be placed in the shrine of the vassal and that it be read periodically. A copy of the biblical TEN COMMANDMENTS was placed in the ARK OF THE COVENANT (Exod. 25:16, 21; 1 Ki. 8:9), which was first housed in the TABERNACLE. With the settlement in Canaan we read of the "house of God ... in Shiloh" (Josh. 18:31), which was the center of Israelite religious life. After the time of DAVID, JERUSALEM became the spiritual center for Israel, and the ark became part of the TEMPLE furnishings. There were periodic occasions when the law was read to the people (cf. Josh. 24:22). The priests in charge of the Israelite sanctuary were instructed to read the law every seven years (Deut. 31:9–13).

(5) An ANE treaty would invoke the gods of the two parties as witnesses. Since Israel had no gods, Josh. 24:22 depicts God as saying, "You are witnesses." The people themselves bear witness to the claims of their God.

(6) The treaty concludes with blessings on those who keep the terms of the treaty and curses on those who violate the covenant. No specific penalties are

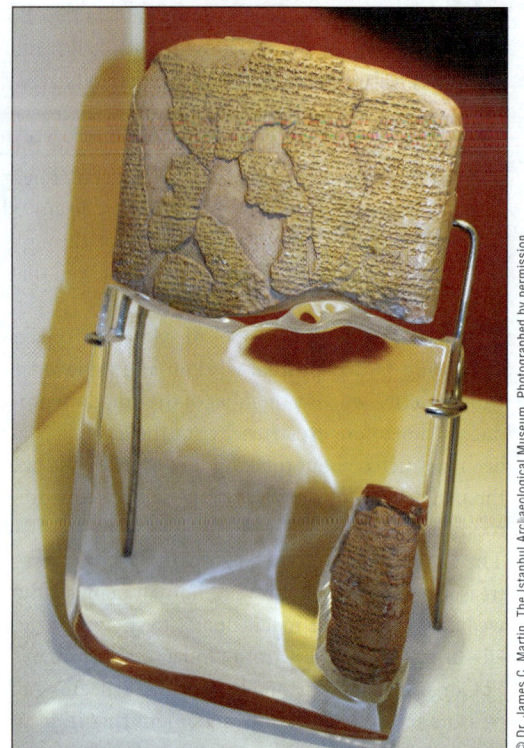

This cuneiform tablet contains the Kadesh Treaty (1258 B.C.), a pact between the Hittite king Hattusilis III and the Egyptian pharaoh Ramses II. Written in Akkadian, the international language of the day, it is the earliest known parity peace treaty.

mentioned. Even the ancient suzerainty treaties were religious in nature. The gods would hold the parties to the covenant accountable. The blessings and curses of Deut. 27–28 are similar in form (cf. Exod. 23:20–33; Lev. 26; Josh. 8:34). The treaties of the ANE indicate that the biblical covenant was expressed in terms understood in its cultural context. Biblical monotheism was unique to Israel, but much of the language in which it was expressed was common to the lands of W Asia.

(See further M. G. Kline, *Treaty of the Great King: The Covenant Structure of Deuteronomy* [1963]; D. J. McCarthy, *Treaty and Covenant: A Study in Form in the Ancient Oriental Documents and in the Old Testament*, new ed. [1978]; P. Kalluveettil, *Declaration and Covenant: A Comprehensive Review of Covenant Formulae from the Old Testament and the Ancient Near East* [1982]; J. J. Niehaus, *God at Sinai: Covenant and Theophany in the Bible and Ancient*

Near East [1995]; N. Weeks, *Admonition and Curse: The Ancient Near Eastern Treaty/Covenant Form as a Problem in Inter-cultural Relationships* [2004]; *ABD,* 6:653–56.) C. F. PFEIFFER

tree. See FLORA.

tree of knowledge. According to Gen. 2:9, God "made all kinds of trees grow out of the ground" in the Garden of Eden. See EDEN, GARDEN OF. The verse continues, "In the middle of the garden were the tree of life and the tree of the knowledge of good and evil." God commanded ADAM not to eat of the tree of knowledge on penalty of death (2:17). The serpent's temptation of EVE (3:1–5) centered on this command, and when he had convinced her that she would not die but become "like God," she ate of it to her sorrow.

The precise significance of the tree has been a matter of debate. Elsewhere in the Bible, lack of knowing good and evil is treated as a mark of immaturity (Deut. 1:39; Isa. 7:14–17) and possibly senility (2 Sam. 19:35, though here the NRSV has, "what is pleasant and what is not"), but in such passages something different seems to be in mind, namely, moral discernment. In Genesis the phrase "good and evil" possibly indicates the extremes, and thus the totality, of knowledge. If so, the tree may have symbolized God's OMNISCIENCE and the power associated with it. In partaking of its fruit, Adam and Eve reached for divinity but obtained guilt, shame, condemnation, and expulsion instead. (See *ABD,* 6:656–60.) G. H. LIVINGSTON

tree of life. Along with "the tree of the knowledge of good and evil" (see TREE OF KNOWLEDGE), the tree of life was originally placed by God in middle of the Garden of Eden (Gen. 2:9). At this point in the narrative, nothing is said about the significance of either. There was no command given to ADAM and EVE not to eat of the tree of life; in fact, permission to partake of it would seem to be included in the statement, "You are free to eat from any tree in the garden" (v. 16), the only exception listed is the tree of knowledge (v. 17). After their sin, when they were expelled from the garden, the reason given was, "The man has now become like one of us, knowing good and evil. He must not be allowed to reach out his hand and take also from the tree of life and eat, and live forever" (Gen. 3:22). Two CHERUBIM, armed with a flaming sword, were then stationed to guard the tree of life. Evidently this tree was identified with everlasting LIFE, and as a result of the original SIN, humanity would no longer have access to the tree, but would instead be subject to deterioration and DEATH.

In Ezek. 31:1–12 there is also a juxtaposition of a river, which here abundantly gives life, and a group of trees that are evergreen, everblooming, and life-giving in that they produce food and medicine. In the OT elsewhere, only in Proverbs does the phrase "tree of life" occur, depicting such virtues as WISDOM (Prov. 3:18), "the fruit of the righteous" (11:30), "a longing fulfilled" (13:12) and the "tongue that brings healing" (15:4). In each case, it would seem, people are vitalized and renewed, but there is no elaboration on the theme nor is any cosmic significance given to these trees of life.

In the NT only the book of Revelation has any reference to the tree of life, and in each occurrence it does have a spiritual, cosmic meaning. In Rev. 2:7 a promise is given that the overcomer will partake of this tree, which is said to be located in "the paradise of God." The end of the book gives more detail. From the throne of God in the new Jerusalem will flow "the river of the water of life," bearing fruit every month, and providing healing for the nations (22:1–3).

The motif has been common in most pagan religions also. In contrast to the Bible, the life it symbolizes is the natural power of reproduction, resident in plants, animals, and human beings, personified by gods and goddesses. See FERTILITY CULTS. The COSMOGONY related to it is nature-bound, whereas in the Bible it is tied to a positive, spiritual relationship between God and human beings. From ancient MESOPOTAMIA have come cylinder seals and other art objects that depict a tree and figures of perhaps divine beings. On clay tablets written in CUNEIFORM script are recorded many of the ancient myths of the people who lived there. In many of these mythical stories, sacred trees of varied kinds play a more or less prominent role. Rather than being in an earthly paradise where man was living, as in Gen. 2–3, the sacred trees are in the abode of the gods with very limited access to it granted to a few fortunate men.

On the other hand, the sacred tree of life was closely associated to the reigning king of almost every ancient nation. Quite often he is portrayed as the guardian and sacramental priest who dispenses its powers through the cultus. In another context, the tree of life was closely associated with the mother goddess, who represented the female principle of natural reproduction, whether in crops, herds, or human family. She could also represent the throne, and hence the giver of life and power to the monarch.

In temples belonging to pagans, the vital life principle of nature would be represented by a grove of trees or the trunks of trees with branches lopped off. In some cases, a wooden post or a block of stone planted in holes, so they might stand upright, would be adequate. The rites associated with these symbols were concerned with magically inducing life in the fields, in the herds, or in the family. Hence, it was closely bound with procreation, with birth, and with growth. These rites would also be aimed at curing barrenness, bringing rain, and preventing death.

(See G. Widengren, *The King and the Tree of Life in Ancient Near Eastern Religions* [1951]; E. O. James, *The Tree of Life* [1966]; H. N. Wallace, *The Eden Narrative* [1985]; J. Magne, *From Christianity to Gnosis and from Gnosis to Christianity: An Itinerary through the Texts to and from the Tree of Paradise* [1993].) G. H. LIVINGSTON

trespass. An overstepping of the boundaries, thus an unfaithful or treacherous act that incurs guilt (cf. SIN; TRANSGRESSION). The KJV OT uses this English term frequently, both as a noun and as a verb, to translate several Hebrew words; for example, the phrase "trespass offering" occurs many times as the rendering of the noun *ʾāšām* H871 (Lev. 5:15–19 et al., where modern versions usually have "guilt offering"; see SACRIFICE AND OFFERINGS IV.A.2).

In the KJV NT the word occurs as a verb a few times to translate Greek *hamartanō* G279, "to sin," when the context has to do with an offense against another person (Matt. 18:15, 35 [following the TR]; Lk. 17:3–4); and it occurs as a noun in five passages to translate Greek *paraptōma* G4183, literally "misstep, fall," but then "offense, wrongdoing, sin" (Matt. 6:14–15; Mk. 11:25–26 [v. 26 missing in important early witnesses]; 2 Cor. 5:19; Eph. 2:1 [with *hamartia* G281, "sin"]; Col. 2:13). The Greek noun is found in a number of other passages where the KJV uses "offence" (Rom. 4:25; 5:15–20), "fall" (11:11–12), "fault" (Gal. 6:1), "sin" (Eph 1:7; 2:5). The NRSV uses "trespass" consistently (except for Rom. 11:11–12, "stumbling"), whereas the NIV uses it only in Rom. 5. It is difficult to determine whether a sharp distinction is intended between *paraptōma* and *hamartia* (see esp. Rom. 5:20 and Eph. 2:1; and cf. Matt. 6:14–15 [the LORD'S PRAYER] to its parallel, Lk. 11:4).

trespass offering. See SACRIFICE AND OFFERINGS IV.A.2.

trial. See CRIMES AND PUNISHMENTS; TEMPTATION; TRIAL OF JESUS.

trial of Jesus. Two of the greatest champions of human rights, Jewish and Roman law, met in a most tragic injustice—the mistrial of Jesus Christ. Jewish leaders were blinded by their determination to be rid of Jesus, and the Roman governor yielded to fear of reprisals. Together they represent both the religious and the secular worlds, which, too often, have been plunged by selfish interests into rejection of their Lord. See also JESUS CHRIST V.G.2.

I. The Jewish trial. The purpose of the Jewish leaders was "to arrest Jesus in some sly way and kill him" (Matt. 26:4). This goal, not legality, was the controlling principle of the trial and the reason for the many irregularities.

A. Preliminary examination. While the SANHEDRIN gathered, Jesus was held at the house of ANNAS, former high priest and sharer of the dignity and power of the office with his son-in-law CAIAPHAS. As no part of a regular trial, Jesus was interrogated concerning his disciples and doctrine (Jn. 18:19). The purpose was to gain evidence for the trial. Jesus insisted, in effect, that the trial begin with examination of witnesses, not with probing of the accused (18:20–21). Charges must come before answers.

B. The night trial. Haste was important, though illegal. Jesus must be condemned before his friends could rally. The temple gates were closed for the night. The high priest's quadrangle served as informal emergency quarters. Off the open center court was a large room isolated only by pillars. Here they assembled, just across the courtyard from the apartment of Annas. As the members of the Sanhedrin were assembling, the chief priests worked frantically to find and train witnesses. Though carefully instructed and solemnly sworn in, the perjured witnesses could not agree (Mk. 14:56; Deut. 19:15). Jesus treated this phase of the trial with silent disdain.

In a move of desperation, the high priest put Jesus under oath (Matt. 26:63–64). Jesus freely admitted his claim that he was the Christ (MESSIAH), the SON OF GOD (vv. 65–66), though he knew it would cost his life. The issue was clear. On this claim and nothing else hinged the condemnation of Jesus by the Jewish court. By the clever ruse Caiaphas made each member of the Sanhedrin, including himself, an accredited witness. Since Jesus, a man, could not be deity, they assumed he must be a blasphemer worthy of death. Jesus was condemned by common consent, but not sentenced. The group broke into disorder. Some spat upon Jesus, others struck him (Mk. 14:65).

C. The morning session. The Friday trial at daybreak was to give semblance of legality to the decision of the night trial and to prepare to present the matter to PILATE. The high priest began the trial again, eliminating parts that had been unfruitful. Jesus was questioned directly by the court, and again he testified that he was the SON OF GOD. All claimed to witness the blasphemy. All arose and led him to Pilate (Lk. 22:66—23:1). Blasphemy was still the one and only charge.

II. The Roman trial. Jesus was still condemned but not sentenced. As a jury, they brought the verdict of guilty, but ROME alone could legally give the sentence of death.

A. Attempted evasion. The Jews hinted strongly that Pilate should yield to them the right of trial and exercise only his right of execution. This was sometimes done by Roman governors either through indolence or as a favor, especially in matters of religion. Pilate was in no mood to yield, and said in effect, "Give me both the power to try and to execute or be satisfied with the penalties you are allowed to inflict on the condemned" (cf. Jn. 18:29–31).

B. Accusations. If Jesus was to be tried and sentenced by Rome, a new case must be made. Rome was not interested in blasphemy. Forced against their will and expectation to formulate a charge, the Jews began to pour forth vehement accusations. There were three main counts: perverting the nation, preventing the paying of tribute to CAESAR, and claiming to be king (Lk. 23:2). Only the third impressed Pilate. If it should be true, Jesus could be guilty of treason. If so, he must die. Rome knew no greater crime than treason.

C. Examination and acquittal. Pilate returned to the PRAETORIUM to examine Jesus. Jesus admitted that he was a king, but explained to Pilate that he was not the kind of king that would seek to overthrow the government. His authority was in the realm of truth (Jn. 18:33–37). Pilate, being satisfied, went out to the Jews and pronounced the words of acquittal: "I find no basis for a charge against him" (v. 38). This would have ended the trial if justice had been the object.

D. Referral to Herod. When the Jews shouted all the more accusations, Pilate feared a hopeless impasse. Finally, the word GALILEE gave him a thought. Herod Antipas was in the city (see HEROD V). Why not give him the honor and danger of passing on the case? The gesture was appreciated by Herod, but he was too astute to allow himself to be involved in a treason trial. He treated Jesus as a cheap entertainer and heaped ridicule upon him when he did not cater to the desires of the court. No legal purpose was served.

E. Jesus or Barabbas. Evasion did not solve Pilate's problem, for Jesus came back from Herod without the matter being resolved. Pilate tried twice more to gain consent for the release of Jesus (Lk. 23:13–23). Justice, scourging, pity, and festive spirit made no difference. The people wanted only Jesus' blood; that of BARABBAS would not do (23:18).

F. "Behold the Man!" In a final appeal to their humanity, Pilate brought Jesus out with bleeding back from the scourging, with the crown of thorns on his head, and with the purple robes of mockery. The Jews were all the more insistent that Jesus be crucified (Jn. 19:1–6).

G. The sentence. Compromise became impossible. Pilate had to release Jesus at all costs or crucify him at all costs. Finally, fear of Jewish blackmail became greater than his sense of justice. Pilate was unwilling to face his record before Caesar. To appease the Jews, Pilate crucified Jesus (Jn. 19:16). See CRUCIFIXION.

(See further S. Andrews, *The Life of our Lord Upon the Earth* [1891], 505–44; J. Stalker, *The Trial and Death of Jesus Christ* [1894], 15–113; W. Chandler, *The Trial of Jesus*, 2 vols. [1908]; J. Blinzler, *The Trial of Jesus* [1959]; P. Winter, *On the Trial of Jesus* [1961]; S. G. F. Brandon, *The Trial of Jesus of Nazareth* [1968]; E. Bammel, ed., *The Trial of Jesus: Cambridge Studies in Honour of C. F. D. Moule* [1970]; A. E. Harvey, *Jesus on Trial: A Study in the Fourth Gospel* [1976]; D. Foreman, *Crucify Him: A Lawyer Looks at the Trial of Jesus* [1990]; A. Watson, *The Trial of Jesus* [1995]; S. Légasse, *The Trial of Jesus* [1997]; R. Williams, *Christ on Trial: How the Gospel Unsettles Our Judgment* [2003]; G. S. Sloyan, *Jesus on Trial: A Study of the Gospels*, 2nd ed. [2006].)
W. T. DAYTON

tribe. A large social group composed of families and clans. In the Bible it is applied specifically to the fundamental divisions of the people of Israel. The Hebrew terms for "tribe" are *maṭṭeh* H4751 and *šēbeṭ* H8657, both of which mean "staff, rod, scepter," but are applied to people groups under the rule of a chief who holds, literally or figuratively, the scepter of authority. The Greek term *phylē* G5876 (*dōdekaphylon* G1559 only in Acts 26:7) is used in the NT not only with reference to the Israelite tribes but also more generally to designate Gentile groups and nations (Matt. 24:30; Rev. 1:7 et al.).

I. The origin of the Israelite tribes. Some earlier scholarship, with its unavoidable lack of knowledge about the first half of the 2nd millennium B.C., could conceive of the PATRIARCHS merely as personifications of tribes, for some of the stories seemed to involve more than individuals. Since then, archaeology has shown us that the population of the FERTILE CRESCENT was relatively low at this time, and that it was marked out by the movements of many seminomadic groups, most of fairly small size.

In addition, it is clear that in the Fertile Crescent the unit of government was, and remained to a much later date, the fortified settlement or CITY, however much one city or another could establish general control over a wider area. Archaeological estimates of the population of Canaanite cities during the 2nd millennium B.C. show that it was seldom over 5,000 and often smaller. Under such circumstances, ABRAHAM with his 318 slaves born in his house represented a considerable force, which explains why MELCHIZEDEK and ABIMELECH could deal with him as an equal (Gen. 14:17–20; 21:22–31), and why the elders of Hebron regarded him as "a mighty prince" (23:6). Similarly, when ESAU came from SEIR to meet JACOB, he had 400 men at his disposal (32:6), whereas Jacob was strong enough to fight and capture land (48:22).

Under these conditions, the leader of such a group had absolute control over it, but his family, slaves, and any broken and homeless people that might throw in their lot with him were regarded as little more than extensions of his personality. However big or small a patriarchal group at any given moment—Jacob fleeing to HARAN was a single individual—Genesis is correct in depicting the decisions made, whether material or spiritual, as those of its head.

As is shown by LOT's having to leave Abraham (Gen. 13:1–13), there was a size beyond which such a seminomadic group could not grow, unless it settled down as tillers of the soil. The same process would inevitably have taken place in Jacob's family, if he had not gone down into Egypt. As it was, he had to divide his flocks (37:12, 17). In Egypt, even if Jacob's sons and their descendants had wished to separate, the permission under which they had entered the country would not have allowed it; in addition, even then there was no room in Egypt for seminomadic groups. Passing references (Exod. 3:22; 11:2) show that at least most of the Israelites had adopted a settled life, and that many were living intermingled with Egyptians. Although the twelve tribal groups regarded themselves as independent units, they were held together by a common origin, situation, persecution, and hope. A passage such as 1 Chr. 7:21b–22 shows how independent action at the time was possible. (For the history and development of the various tribes, see separate articles under each tribal name.)

II. Tribal organization. The anarchist's ideal, lack of leadership and organization, has never existed, even among the most primitive of peoples. The mention of "the elders of Israel" (Exod. 3:16 et al.) shows that the Israelites never became a mere mob of slaves in Egypt; they preserved a living tradition and code of behavior from their ancestral past. See ELDER (OT). It has often been shown that the Sinaitic legislation, social and religious, is based on ancient Fertile Crescent patterns, though transformed and purified. The passages relied on to deny this process (viz., Exod. 18:13–26; Deut. 1:9–18) point another way. Much of the organization introduced by Moses at JETHRO's suggestion was clearly military and was intended to bring the tribes unitedly through unknown and difficult desert country. On the judicial side, the purpose was probably mainly to help people from different tribes and those of non-Israelite origin (the "mixed multitude" of Exod. 12:38 KJV) to live together in peace under novel, demanding circumstances.

Already in the wilderness the individual tribes were composed of fundamental divisions (Num. 1:2; cf. Josh. 7:14). Each tribe was divided into a number of clans (Heb. *mišpāḥâ H5476*), which in turn were constituted by households (*bêt ʾāb H1074 + H3*). The latter term, which means literally "father's house," indicates a paternal family (*HALOT*, 1:125 [s v בית A.5]), "which comprised not only the father, his wife or wives and their unmarried children but also their married sons with their wives and children, and the servants" (R. de Vaux, *Ancient Israel* [1961], 7–8).

Breaches of the law and customs within the family, provided they were not calculated to bring down the divine wrath on the wider community, were the sole concern of the family head. The whole force of the story of DAVID and the woman from TEKOA (2 Sam. 14:4–11) derives from this fact. Only where the head of the family could not enforce his authority (Deut. 18:21) was it referred to the elders of the city. It is clear that GIDEON's father was held responsible for his son's behavior (Jdg. 6:28–32). (It should be noted that another term, *ʾelep H548*, lit. "[a group of] one thousand," seems to be an alternate way of referring to a clan [as in Jdg. 6:15]; it may have covered the inhabitants of one city, whose normal contribution to the tribal militia was about a thousand.)

The rulers of the individual city, of the clan, and of the tribe were the elders. In addition there seems to have been a supreme individual in each tribe called the *nāśîʾ H5954* (Num. 1:16; 34:18; Josh. 9:15; et al.). The role of this "leader" (NIV, NRSV) or "chieftain" (NJPS), apart from problems of general concern, was mainly confined to settling disputes. There is no evidence that before the time of the monarchy there was any form of appeal from their decision. The type of JUDGE, religious or secular, envisaged in Deut. 17:8–13 and 19:16–19 does not seem to have functioned before the time of the monarchy. The situation involving SAMUEL's sons (1 Sam. 8:1–2) does not seem to constitute an exception. The area around BEERSHEBA was still largely seminomadic and thus called for special arrangements for justice between rival groups. In difficult cases people would gladly turn to those who had shown that they had the Spirit of God in special measure, and so those who had delivered Israel on the battlefield, the "judges," were appealed to by those who felt themselves wronged to deliver them as well.

So far as the evidence available allows one to judge, this simple system proved adequate in the early centuries of Israel's life in Canaan. It had only one major inadequacy. As soon as a person passed beyond the borders of his own tribe, he had no rights beyond those given to the resident alien. The force of the tragic story in Jdg. 19–21 is that the wronged Levite had no way of obtaining justice, if the leaders of Benjamin refused it (20:12–13). There was no middle way between fighting and allowing open evil to have its way.

III. Intertribal organization. When Martin Noth (*Das System der zwölf Stämme Israels* [1930]) argued that Israel's early tribal organization could be viewed as an amphictyony, many scholars initially regarded his analysis as valid (though few were prepared to accept his views in all their details). The term *amphictyony* is taken from Greek history and covers a system there and in Italy by which a number of unconnected tribes joined together to maintain and protect a common sanctuary. "Early Israel was neither a racial nor a national unit, but a confederation of clans united in covenant with Yahweh. This covenant both created her society and held it together" (J. Bright, *A History of Israel*, 2nd ed. [1972], 143, but modified in 3d ed. [1981], 162–65). Today most scholars regard the use of this term as unhelpful or even inappropriate, though the general principle remains useful in understanding the Israelite organization. (For a recent summary of the history of criticism regarding the concept, see A. G. Auld in *DOTHB*, 26–32.)

The central sanctuary of the confederacy was at SHILOH for most of the period of the judges. The old critical view that there was no central sanctuary has been decisively disproved, but it is clear that it was not an exclusive one. It is generally accepted that representatives of the tribes met at the sanctuary at the three pilgrim feasts and possibly at a special covenant festival. It will have been on these occasions that intertribal disputes on the personal or group level were dealt with. The story in Jdg. 19–21 is to be understood from this viewpoint. The refusal to give justice to the wronged Levite meant quite simply that Benjamin was trying to opt out from the confederacy, and the other tribes evidently felt that this was equivalent to apostasy, a renunciation of Yahweh.

The manner in which this tribal confederation worked is perhaps best illustrated in Jdg. 5. The campaign against SISERA is presented as a religious one. At the same time there was no method by which compulsion could be exercised. Those tribes that did not respond to the call to fight were regarded as failing Yahweh rather than Israel. When the town of MEROZ, however, is mentioned (5:23), it is bitterly cursed because its inhabitants "did not come to help the LORD." The reason is that it lay within the area of one of the participating tribes, probably NAPHTALI, and therefore its holding back was treason both to God and the tribe.

IV. The later development of the tribes. The destruction of Shiloh and its sanctuary, probably by the PHILISTINES (Jer. 7:12), was carried through to demonstrate that the confederacy was dead, as it

The area of Lebonah (looking W). It was near this place that the Benjamite men, after the near destruction of their tribe, seized the girls of Shiloh during the harvest festival at Lebonah and married them (Jdg 21:16–23)

no longer had its sanctuary. To this must in large measure be ascribed the subsequent neglect of the ARK OF THE COVENANT, for it was the symbol of the confederation.

Saul's method of summoning the militia against NAHASH (1 Sam. 11.7) seems to have been the old "amphictyonic" method (cf. Jdg. 19:29), and there are other signs that he considered he was in some way continuing it. His neglect of the ark, however, shows that he was conscious that an irreversible change had been made. Judah's unilateral action after SAUL's death (2 Sam. 2:4) and the northern tribes' lack of enthusiasm for ISH-BOSHETH and ABNER (2:8–9) show that they did not feel committed by what had happened in the anointing of Saul. It is clear, too, that the acceptance of DAVID by the tribes of Israel (5:1) shows that they were still acting as independent entities. Though David tried to recreate the confederacy by the importance he gave to the ark, the unity he created was centered on his own person. On the death of SOLOMON, the northern tribes were acting entirely legally when they refused to accept REHOBOAM as king. Thereafter, however, the ever increasing power of the king and his court made local and tribal autonomy of decreasing significance. JEZEBEL might use the forms of the judicial past (1 Ki. 21:8–14) to achieve her ends, yet it was clearly a meaningless shadow compared to court power.

This erosion of tribal independence began with Solomon's division of the country into twelve administrative districts, which, though they did not depart widely from the tribal boundaries, were yet willing to ignore them (1 Ki. 4:7–19, cf. J. A. Montgomery, *A Critical and Exegetical Commentary on the Book of Kings*, ICC [1951], 119–24). Another factor was the breaking down of local life, partly due to its domination by the rich, so often denounced by the prophets, and partly by the development of a royal judiciary (cf. 2 Chr. 19:4–11). By the time of the return from exile, many had forgotten their genealogies and knew only the places from which their ancestors had come (cf. Ezra 2). No stronger indication is needed that the tribes as living organizations had ceased to exist. Also, a number of slaves had gradually been absorbed into the people; for them the old tribal system was a meaningless tradition.

V. Tribes in the NT. A considerable portion of the Jewish people in NT times consisted of descendants of those who had been forced to convert to Judaism by the HASMONEAN rulers John Hyrcanus and Aristobulus I (Jos. *Ant.* 13.9.1; 13.11.3), as well as from large numbers of PROSELYTES. The result was that those who really knew their genealogy probably were a minority. Cases like ANNA (Lk. 2:36) and PAUL (Phil. 3:5) show that when tribal origin was known, it was treasured. (In the case of modern Jewish families, it is considered improbable that their genealogies can be genuinely traced back beyond the late Middle Ages.)

In the NT the term "the twelve tribes" is used in several ways: of historical Israel as a whole (Acts 26:7), of the CHURCH as the people of God (Jas. 1:1), and of eschatological Israel (Matt. 19:28; Lk. 22:30; Rev. 7:4; 21:12); some would argue, however, that these eschatological references, at least in Revelation, designate God's people as a whole. The NT seems to be completely unconcerned about the fate or whereabouts of the "lost" ten tribes (popular Jewish orthodoxy still expects the "lost" northern tribes to reappear, but there is no consensus as to where they may be found). When the word *tribe* is used in non-Jewish or non-Christian contexts, it means simply a racial or political subdivision without any more exact force. H. L. ELLISON

tribes, location of. The main information about the tribal portions is found in Josh. 13–21, supplemented by 1 Chr. 4–8. Whatever views are held of the date and composition of Joshua (see JOSHUA, BOOK OF II), it has been generally accepted ever since the work of M. Noth and A. Alt that the tribal boundaries are very ancient. The geographer has been able to show that with a few exceptions they conform to the natural divisions of the land. In some cases, however, the places named have not been identified and therefore the interpretation of the information is not always certain.

For reasons that are not given, the tribal portions of Judah (Josh. 15–16) and of Ephraim and half-Manasseh (ch. 17) were allocated in advance. The portions for Reuben, Gad, and the other half of Manasseh had been allocated already by MOSES from the land conquered in TRANSJORDAN, that is, E of the Jordan River (Num. 32; Deut. 3:12–22;

Josh. 13:8–32). The remaining land was divided into seven portions that were apportioned by lot (Josh. 18:11—19:46). The tribe of Levi was granted only sixty-one cities, of which thirteen were for the priests (Josh. 21). The division was made in advance of complete conquest, and so some of the boundaries remained an ideal that was never achieved. See also TRIBE.

    I. The Transjordanian tribes
        A. Reuben
        B. Gad
        C. Half-Manasseh (Makir)
    II. Tribes without stated boundaries
        A. Simeon
        B. Issachar
        C. Dan
    III. Judah
    IV. The central tribes
        A. Ephraim
        B. Manasseh
        C. Benjamin
    V. The northern tribes
        A. Zebulun
        B. Asher
        C. Naphtali
    VI. The Levitical cities

I. The Transjordanian tribes. The tribal portions as given in Ezek. 47:13—48:29 should be a constant reminder that there is an abiding lack of clarity regarding the exact limits of the Promised Land. Whatever the interpretation of the boundaries suggested by God's promise to ABRAHAM (Gen. 15:18–21), there is a very early description of the full extent of Canaan in Num. 34:1–12. The remarkable feature in it is that it excludes GILEAD and the northern part of the Moabite plateau round HESHBON. Ezekiel 47:15–18, with its difficult text, seems to draw the same boundary in the N and NE. Both passages agree in making the Jordan the eastern boundary only from the Sea of Galilee southward. Quite consistently with this, the land of SIHON was captured only because of his own obstinacy (Num. 21:21–24; Deut. 2:26–36); on the other hand, Israel marched against OG (Num. 21:33–35; Deut. 3:1–10). Gilead is clearly regarded as not being in the land of Canaan (Josh. 22:10–11, 32). It would seem, therefore, that though Transjordan as a whole fell into the boundaries delineated in Gen. 15:18–21, only part belonged to the heartland of Israel.

The main divisions of Transjordan are fairly clear. The ARNON River, flowing into the DEAD SEA about mid-distance between the N and S ends, was always the S boundary of Israelite territory. All S of it was MOAB, whether independent or subject to Israel. The next effective boundary to the N was the Wadi Heshban (not mentioned in the Bible), N of Heshbon. Of little importance in itself, it marks the N end of the tableland, where the broken hills of Gilead begin. Gilead stretches N to the Yarmuk River (not mentioned in the OT), and is divided in two by the JABBOK. North of the Yarmuk lies BASHAN (cf. Deut. 3:10). Since these divisions are not very great and the eastern tribes were owners of cattle, and hence seminomadic, the frontiers dividing the Transjordan tribes were constantly fluid.

A. Reuben. The tribe of REUBEN received the tableland between Heshbon and AROER, on the edge of the Arnon Valley, that is, the former kingdom of Sihon (Josh. 13:15–23). Fourteen cities in all are mentioned, but DIBON and Aroer (Num. 32:34), Reubenite towns, are mentioned as in the hands of Gad; ATAROTH was probably also in this area. It would seem that Reuben was not able to hold its territory for long, for the last mention of its effective presence is in Jdg. 5:16 (1 Chr. 5:26 is hardly a contradiction of this). MESHA, king of Moab, mentions Gad on the Moabite stone, whereas Reuben does not appear. There are indications that some Reubenites may have moved into Judah and Benjamin.

B. Gad. The tribal portion of Gad lay between Reuben and the Jabbok, but it took in the Jordan valley as far as the S tip of the Sea of Galilee. See GAD, TRIBE OF. Eleven cities are mentioned (Josh. 13:24–28), but MAHANAIM seems to have been shared with Manasseh (13:29). RAMOTH GILEAD, which was in the area of Manasseh, is said to belong to Gad (20:8; 21:38). The overlap in this case was in part due to the fact that northern Gilead was very thinly populated at the time of the conquest, being largely covered with forest.

C. Half-Manasseh (Makir). The descendants of MAKIR, MANASSEH's eldest son, were given their portion E of Jordan (Josh. 13:29–31). See MANASSEH, TRIBE OF. It included N Gilead and ARGOB (Deut. 3:13). It is far from clear how its territory was occupied. If Jdg. 5:14 is taken literally, Makir was still W of Jordan at that time. The details of the expeditions of JAIR and NOBAH (Num. 32:41–42; cf. Deut. 3:14) suggest later activity than the defeat of Og. (The gibe mentioned in Jdg. 12:4 may very well mean that a considerable number of Ephraimites had filtered across the Jordan and found homes in the wooded district N of the Jabbok in the area near Zaphon; cf. v. 1.)

II. Tribes without stated boundaries. For three tribes, cities are mentioned but few if any boundaries are indicated. The reason seems to be that they were never able to consolidate their hold on their land, so that when the territory finally came into effective Israelite control, it was incorporated into other tribes.

A. Simeon. It is clearly stated that the nineteen settlements of SIMEON were within the territory of Judah (Josh. 19:1–9; 1 Chr. 4:28–33). Not all can be identified, but they all fell into the NW NEGEV. It is probable that ZIKLAG (1 Sam. 27:6) was not the only one to come under PHILISTINE rule. The statement that these places remained Simeonite "until the reign of David" (1 Chr. 4:31) probably implies that their dispersion (4:34–43) began then, leading to the vanishing of the tribe as an entity. It may have been partly due to a period of drought, which would be particularly felt in the Negev (cf. 2 Sam. 21:1). In the list of Judean administrative districts (see below), the Simeonite towns are simply listed as Judean. (With regard to the basic literary framework in the variant Simeonite town lists, see Z. Kallai in *VT* 53 [2003]: 81–96.)

B. Issachar. The tribal portion of ISSACHAR clearly lay in the Plain of ESDRAELON and the valleys running down from it to the Jordan, but only its N border, separating it from Naphtali and Zebulun, is indicated (Josh. 19:17–23). No clear N boundary is given for W Manasseh (17:10–11), but it is stated that it controlled a number of places in Issachar and Asher (apparently only DOR). These were all Canaanite strongholds, which were first made tributary by Manasseh and then absorbed by it. Issachar held only the weaker places (Josh. 19:17–21), at first doubtless under sufferance, and probably at the price of tribute (cf. Gen. 49:14–15).

C. Dan. It might be thought that the boundaries of DAN are not given because those of its neighbors have already been described. The S border of Ephraim (Josh. 16:5–6) reads as though it took in the coastal portion of Dan. Of the eighteen Danite cities mentioned (19:40–46), five sites have not

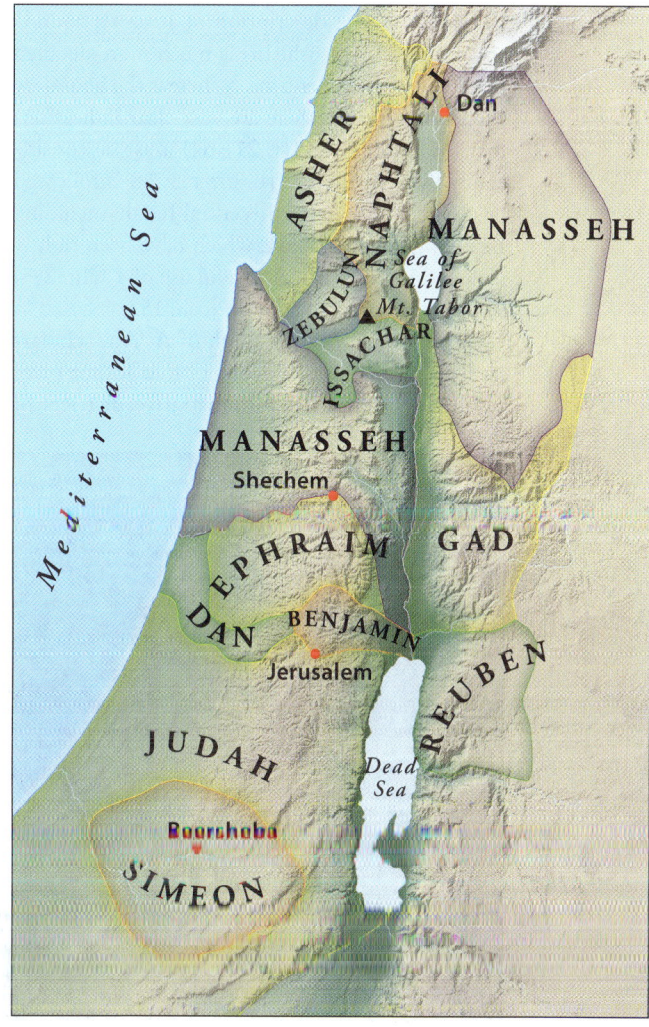

The Tribes of Israel.

been identified, six appear as Judean elsewhere, one as Benjamite, and six as Ephraimite. Though there is no reason to suppose that all members of the tribe moved to Dan in the N (19:47–48; Jdg. 18:27–28), it is clear that most of its territory fell into the hands of the Philistines, and then, as these were driven back, the area was incorporated into its neighbors. A large portion of it appears in two of the Judean administrative districts (see below). The history of the tribe was continued in this small area at the far N of the Jordan valley; strictly it belonged to Naphtali, but it was isolated from the remainder of its territory by the marshes of the Huleh basin.

III. Judah. The description of Judah's boundary and territory (Josh. 15) is much more detailed than that of any other tribe. Whereas the boundary description is early, there are very clear indications that the list of cities (vv. 21–62) must be considerably later. In the Septuagint, v. 58 is followed by eleven names in north-central Judah, including Bethlehem and Tekoa, which have been rightly included in the NEB. A careful use of 1 Chr. 2–4 will also throw some light on Josh. 15.

Since the pioneering work of A. Alt, scholars have come to general agreement that Joshua gives the list of the twelve administrative districts of Judah after the division of the kingdom, though there are disagreements concerning the identity of one of the districts and the date of the list. Alt dated it in the time of Josiah; Cross and Wright preferred the time of Jehoshaphat; Aharoni first suggested the time of Uzziah, but now prefers that of Jehoshaphat. Archaeology, however, will apparently not permit a date before the 9th cent.

Though some of the places mentioned have not been identified, there are no real problems in tracing the boundary of Judah. The S border was the southern limit of settled population, and indeed much of the southern part remained semi-nomadic until the reign of David, if not longer. The W boundary was the Mediterranean, which took in all of what was to become the Philistine country; but this was an ideal never fulfilled in OT times. The N boundary ran just above Ekron, dividing Judah from Ephraim (Dan had migrated), and then along the line of the Sorek to Timnah; it then went NNE to the N of Kiriath Jearim. From there it ran ESE below Nephtoah to take in the Valley of Rephaim (see Rephaim, Valley of) and the Valley of Hinnom. Finally it passed through the wilderness of Judah S of Jericho to the Dead Sea, which formed its eastern boundary.

The abandonment of part of Judah's territory to Simeon is explained in Jdg. 1:3. Judah evidently felt

The Hinnom Valley (center of photo) separates the territory of the tribe of Benjamin (N, left) from that of Judah (S, right)

© Dr. James C. Martin

that its manpower would be too widely spread over what was the largest tribal area (except perhaps that of Makir). The area placed at Simeon's disposal, however, was shrewdly chosen by Judah as being most open to pressure from the coastal plain.

IV. The central tribes. EPHRAIM, the W half of MANASSEH, and BENJAMIN occupied the central hill country, which forms a clearly marked physical unity, with the territory of Benjamin forming the link with the Judean hills. The transitional nature of the Benjamite territory is seen in the fact that under the divided monarchy the frontier between the northern and southern kingdoms ran almost all the time through Benjamin and not along the Ephraimite border; this has left its mark on the Benjamite city list in Josh. 18:21–28. The paucity of detail about Ephraim and Manasseh may be compared with a similar attitude in 1 Chr. 7:14–29; it expressed the conviction of Scripture that these two tribes moved out of God's will. No indication is offered why the house of JOSEPH (Ephraim and Manasseh) had a prior claim to its territory.

A. Ephraim. Apparently, Ephraim received the less attractive portion of the central area (Josh. 16), since its height is repeatedly referred to as "the hill country of Ephraim" (see EPHRAIM, HILL COUNTRY OF). In the long run, however, it was probably a gain for them and one of the reasons for their early prominence in Israel. Owing to its wooded nature (17.15), it was very thinly settled, the only Canaanite cities in their portion being BETHEL (cf. Jdg. 1:22–26) and GEZER, on the edge of the plain (Josh. 16:10). They were able to consolidate their position at a time when other tribes were still struggling. This probably explains how they were able to infiltrate into Manasseh (16:9) and also to capture the Canaanite city of Tappuah, though Manasseh had occupied its lands (17:8). See TAPPUAH (PLACE). Its S border started at the Jordan N of Jericho and ran fairly due W, passing to the S of Bethel and on to the sea. In the N, its territories stretched to near SHECHEM; from here the boundary ran SE to near Jericho and SW along the Wadi Qanah. In other words, it had no real footing on either the Jordan or the sea. In the list of Levitical cities (see below), Shechem is identified as Ephraimite (Josh. 21:20–21), thus suggesting further infiltration.

D. Manasseh. The W half of this tribe was intended to occupy not merely the northern part of the central hill country, but also SHARON and the N Jordan Valley (Josh. 17:1–13). In fact, it found itself facing a line of unconquered Canaanite fortresses that controlled Esdraelon and the passes over Carmel. As it first made them tributary and then merged them in its territory, the tribe found that it had encroached heavily on the territory of Issachar and to a less extent on that of Asher (vv. 11–13). The fact that the lead against the Midianites was taken by GIDEON, a Manassite, rather than by a member of the tribe of Issachar, which was most heavily involved, is typical of the position. Indeed, so heavily had the people of Issachar been ground down, that they are not even mentioned in the story of Gideon.

C. Benjamin. The tribe of Benjamin was the worst sufferer from Israel's pact with the Gibeonite tetrapolis (Josh. 9) and from Judah's failure to deal adequately with JERUSALEM (Jdg. 1:8), for these cities lay within the boundaries allotted to it (Josh. 18:11–28). This situation may well have been the grievance that led to Benjamin's desire to leave the Israelite confederacy, an act followed by a great disaster (Jdg. 20–21). It was not merely Benjamin's weakness but also its centrality that made SAUL's kingship politically acceptable. The only explanation that carries conviction of the division of the Benjamite cities into two groups is that Josh. 18:21–24 gives the cities that were incorporated into Israel, while vv. 25–28 lists those that were incorporated into Judah at the division of the kingdom. When Jerusalem was captured by David, it became royal property instead of reverting to Benjamin.

V. The northern tribes. With regard to the northern tribes that had undefined boundaries (Issachar and Dan), see above, section II. The present section deals with the remaining three tribes.

A. Zebulun. The description of ZEBULUN's boundary (Josh. 19:10–16) begins with SARID in its SE extremity and follows the KISHON W to near JOKNEAM. The western boundary ran W of Galilean Bethlehem and took in most of Lower GALILEE within its northern stretch until it turned almost due S to Mount TABOR and then back to Sarid. This was an area with no Canaanite cities of importance. Zebulun seems to have been able to capture it all and then hold it effectively.

B. Asher. Because of the uncertain identifications of many of ASHER's cities (Josh. 19:24–29), it is impossible to trace the boundary given in some of its parts. The mention of DOR (Josh. 17:11) as belonging to Asher shows that its territory extended into the coastal plain S of Carmel. Since, however, Dor is not mentioned in ch. 19, it is likely that the factual boundary lay along the N slopes of Carmel. Then its E boundary was that of Zebulun and Naphtali. Its northern section is far from clear. Inland it ran as far N as SIDON and then seems to have reached the coast just S of TYRE. It may be questioned, however, to what extent Asher was able to maintain its hold on the coast, though Jdg. 5:17b shows that for a while the sea coast was in fact its boundary.

C. Naphtali. The border of the tribe of NAPHTALI is traced eastward from HELEPH, in all probability at the foot of Mount Tabor, to the Jordan just S of the Sea of Galilee (Josh. 19:32–34). It was a natural line, that of the Wadi Fajjas. For the western border the boundaries of Zebulun and Asher are given. The eastern is the upper Jordan, and no northern border is suggested. Since Dan was able to establish itself N of Huleh, apparently without protest from Naphtali (see above), it would seem that Naphtali had never tried to push past the Huleh marshes, and it probably never established itself as far as the Litani River.

VI. The Levitical cities. Though there are considerable differences between the lists of LEVITICAL CITIES in Josh. 21:1–42 and 1 Chr. 6:54–81, W. F. Albright can say, "With the aid of the Greek … we can eliminate nearly all the differences between the lists in Joshua and Chronicles. The two or three remaining apparent divergences may be plausibly excised by simple textual changes of well-known types" (*Archaeology and the Religion of Israel*, 5th ed. [1968], 121). In his list so established, he is able to divide the forty-eight cities evenly among the twelve tribes. He has given strong reasons for thinking that the lists come from the time of David. Both archaeology and known history make it almost impossible to move them back into the time of Joshua, unless one follows Y. Kaufmann and sees it as a utopian forecast.

Alt pointed out that most of these cities are located either in frontier areas or in such as had been Canaanite. The Levites were intended to have a religious influence especially where the standard of religion was low. Certain premonarchical stories suggest that in the troubled period after the conquest no effort had been made to provide the Levites with the homes and means of livelihood that had been promised them.

(See further G. A. Smith, *The Historical Geography of the Holy Land*, 25th ed. [1931]; W. F. Albright, *Archaeology and the Religion of Israel*, 3rd ed. [1953]; M. Noth, *Das Buch Josua*, 2nd ed. [1953]; F. M. Cross and G. E. Wright in *JBL* 75 [1956]: 202–26; L. H. Grollenberg, *Atlas of the Bible* [1956]; Y. Kaufmann, *The Biblical Account of the Conquest* [1953]; G. E. Wright and F. V. Filson, *The Westminster Historical Atlas to the Bible*, 5th ed. [1957]; D. Baly, *The Geography of the Bible* [1957]; A. Alt, *Kleine Schriften zur Geschichte des Volkes Israel*, 3 vols., 2nd ed. [1959], 1:193–202 and 2:276–88; Y. Aharoni, *The Land of the Bible: A Historical Geography*, rev. ed. [1979], 248–62; Z. Kallai, *Historical Geography of the Bible* [1986], 99–325; N. Na'aman, *Borders and Districts in Biblical Historiography: Seven Studies in Geographic Lists* [1986]; C. G. Rasmussen, *Zondervan NIV Atlas of the Bible* [1989], 96–103; Y. Aharoni et al., *The Carta Bible Atlas*, 4th ed. [2002], 58–62, maps 68–73; *DOTHB*, 967–71; *SacBr*, 151–54.)

H. L. ELLISON

tribulation. This English term, referring to severe distress, usually as the result of oppression, is used by the KJV a few times in the OT (for Heb. *ṣar* H7639, Deut. 4:30 et al.) but more than twenty times in the NT to render the common Greek word *thlipsis* G2568 (Matt. 13:21 et al.; in one verse, 1 Thess. 3:4, "suffer persecution" is the KJV rendering of the verb *thlibō* G2567 in the passive voice). In the many other occurrences of the Greek noun the KJV uses various renderings, especially "affliction" (Mk. 4:17 et al.). The English word *tribulation* is found less frequently in modern versions (rarely in the NRSV; the NIV uses it only in the expression "the great tribulation" (Rev. 7:14); the same combination of *thlipsis* with the adjective *megalē* [from *megas* G3489, "great"], but without the definite article, occurs also in 2:22, as well as in Matt. 24:21 and Acts 7:11).

Clarity requires that a distinction be made regarding the source and the object of tribulation. For example, God may afflict his people for their unfaithfulness. Should Israel sin like the nations it drove out of Canaan, it too would be driven out and scattered among the nations: "When you are in tribulation, and all these things come upon you in the latter days, you will return to the LORD your God and obey his voice" (Deut. 4:30 RSV). See SUFFERING I.

The unbelieving world, on the other hand, may oppress God's people on account of their faithful testimony. Faced by such oppression, anyone who has no root "quickly falls away" (Matt. 13:21). In the case of true Christians, however, nothing—including "tribulation, or distress, or persecution"—can separate them from the love of God (Rom. 8:35–39 KJV). So believers are "patient in tribulation" (12:12 KJV). After Paul had been stoned and left for dead at Lystra, he returned exhorting the disciples "to continue in the faith, and saying that through many tribulations we must enter the kingdom of God" (Acts 14:22 RSV). See PERSECUTION.

Reminiscent of Dan. 12:1, Jesus predicted a "great tribulation, such as has not been from the beginning of the world until now, no, and never will be" (Matt. 24:21 RSV; cf. v. 9). It includes more intense persecution of God's people by the anti-Christian forces. The period also includes acts of God in pouring out his righteous wrath on the ungodly. "Immediately after the tribulation of those days the sun will be darkened, and the moon will not give its light, and the stars will fall from heaven, and the powers of the heavens will be shaken" (Matt. 24:29 RSV). Such manifestations of divine wrath are described in detail by John in Rev. 6–19. Out of "the great tribulation" comes a multitude seen before the throne of the Lamb (Rev. 7:14).

On the identity of the people of God in the great tribulation, as well as the time of the rapture, theologians differ. Posttribulationists see the church continuing on earth to the end of the tribulation when the rapture occurs. Midtribulationalists look for the church to survive the first half of the tribulation when the rapture takes place. Pretribulationalists anticipate the rapture prior to the tribulation so that the people of God on earth are members of the restored Jewish nation. See SECOND COMING.

G. R. LEWIS

Silver-plated copper *follis* (second in value only to the gold coin) minted by Emperor Diocletian, who at the beginning of the 4th cent., in an attempt to stabilize the Roman empire, initiated the last and greatest persecution of Christians, bringing much suffering and tribulation on the church.

tribune. This term, referring to a Roman military officer in command of a COHORT, is used by the NRSV and other versions in the book of Acts to render Greek *chiliarchos* G5941, which means literally "commander of a thousand" (Acts 21:31–37; 22:24–29; 23:10–22; 24:22; 25:23; NIV, "commander," except for the last reference, "high ranking officers"). The Latin term *tribunus* (lit., "officer of a tribe") was applied primarily to certain officials charged with defending the rights of plebeian citizens; in the Roman army, however, the rank of the *tribunus militum* referred to the commanders of *cohortes milliariae*, composed of approximately 1,000 soldiers (technically 760 infantrymen and 240 cavalrymen, but the numbers varied). Thus the Roman *tribunus* was considered equivalent to the Greek *chiliarchos*. The latter term, however, occurs also in other passages where the meaning is evidently less precise (Mk. 6:21; Jn. 18:12; Rev. 6:15; 19:18).

tribute. This English term, in the sense of compulsory payment to a superior, occurs frequently in Bible versions, especially in the OT (*minḥâ H4966* is the most common Hebrew word). Before the setting up of the Israelite kingdom there were instances of tributes being paid under various conditions, such as when JACOB's sons were seeking the favor of PHARAOH (Gen. 43:11–12, where the Heb. term is rendered "gift" or "present"), or when one of the judges was forced to contribute to an overlord (Jdg. 3:15–18). With the establishment of the kingdom, the people obligated themselves to the regular exaction of money and services for the support of the court (cf. 1 Sam. 8:10–18). Besides the regular exactions, it was customary to bring presents to one's superiors on special occasions (1 Sam. 10:27). In addition to the payments received from their own people, the kings of Israel and Judah received tribute from foreign peoples and rulers: the Moabites and the Arameans brought tribute to DAVID (2 Sam. 8:2, 6; see MOAB, ARAM); many nations brought tribute to SOLOMON (1 Ki. 4:21); AHAB imposed tribute on Moab, but this ceased upon his death (2 Ki. 3:4–5); JEHOSHAPHAT received payment from the PHILISTINES and the ARABIANS (2 Chr. 17:11); and UZZIAH from the Ammonites (26:8; see AMMON).

More often, particularly after the division of the kingdom, the Israelites found themselves vassals rather than overlords and paid tribute to others. The Arameans collected tribute from Israel, the northern kingdom, as the price for peace (2 Ki. 12:17–18). When later the Assyrians became the dominant power in the E, both Israel and Judah paid tribute to their rulers, including TIGLATH-PILESER III (16:8) and SHALMANESER V (17:3). Finally Israel was captured and depopulated by the Assyrians.

With Judah, the southern kingdom, the situation was much the same. Already mentioned is the payment made by Ahaz when he appealed to Assyria for help (2 Ki. 16:5–9). HEZEKIAH was forced to pay tribute to SENNACHERIB of Assyria (18:13–16), and later he foolishly displayed all his treasures to the envoy from Babylon (20:12–15). From this time on, Judah was constantly torn between Babylon and Egypt, and tribute was the price of stability (23:33–35). In the end, Babylon took the last of Judah's wealth (ch. 25).

When NT history began, ROME was the dominant power. Roman taxation was mainly indirect; but in addition tribute was levied, which was a form of direct TAX. Between 404 and 167 B.C., tribute was intermittently imposed on Roman citizens to pay for the costly wars which filled that period. After 167 B.C. only provincials paid the *tributum*, a fixed sum for some provinces, and a variable amount for others. This payment applied to all provincials, whether Roman citizens or not. Under the empire, a distinction was made between the *tributum soli* (imposed on provincial land) and the *tributum capitis* (imposed on all other forms of property). Tribute was based on the CENSUS, but the rate is unknown. Grants of immunity might be given to communities or individuals for various reasons.

Of the three Greek terms translated "tax" or "tribute," the NT usage appears to be as follows: *kēnsos G3056* refers to the poll tax (the *tributum capitis*), and is mentioned by Jesus when questioned by the PHARISEES (Matt. 22:17, 19; Mk. 12:13–17). Luke in the parallel passage, and again when Jesus is questioned by PILATE, uses the word *phoros G5843*, referring possibly to the *tributum soli* (Lk. 20:22; 23:2); but perhaps the distinction is somewhat blurred here. When PAUL urges the Christian community to pay their taxes he uses the same term (Rom. 13:6–7). In addition to these exactions, a temple tax was required from all Jewish males above age twenty for support of the TEMPLE; this was the *didrachmon G1440* or half-shekel (Matt. 17:24–25). After the destruction of Jerusalem the emperors collected this tax for support of the temple of Jupiter Capitolinus in Rome. (See further Pauly-Wissowa, *Real-Encyclopädie der classischen Altertumswissenschaft* VII A/1 [1939], 44–47; *OCD*, 1551.)

R. C. STONE

Trimorphic Protennoia. A Gnostic tractate included in the NAG HAMMADI LIBRARY (NHC XIII, 1). Written in the form of a revelatory discourse in the first person, this document is preserved only in a Coptic translation, but it appears to be the translation of a Greek original produced possibly two centuries earlier. Protennoia, the divine First Thought, is a female heavenly redeemer figure who claims to have descended three times—respectively as Father, Mother, and Son—bringing salvation to a fallen world. Some scholars view this tractate as providing significant analogies with the prologue of the Gospel of John. (English trans. in *NHL*, 511–22.)

Trinity. The Christian doctrine of GOD is distinguished by its emphasis on divine three-in-oneness, that is, the eternal coexistence of the Father, Son, and Holy Spirit in the inner personal life of the Godhead. Evangelical theology affirms that the living, speaking, and acting God is a personal divine Trinity in the eternal unity of God himself and in his work. The one God, the subject of all divine REVELATION, is self-disclosed—the Bible authoritatively teaches—as the invisible Father (from whom all revelation proceeds), the Son (who through his objective INCARNATION mediates that revelation in a historical manifestation), and the HOLY SPIRIT (who is divinely outpoured and subjectively applies that revelation to believers).

It was Karl Barth's special merit that he reiterated the indissoluble connection of this view with the fact of divine self-revelation. Not only medieval Scholasticism but also modern Protestant theology readily expounded God's essence and attributes first, and then appended a discussion of God's triunity, as if the reality of God as personal, and specifically as triune, were irrelevant to our knowledge of the divine nature and perfections. The Bible witnesses to plurality of personality in the self-revealed God; it does not, as neo-Protestant writers prefer to put it, affirm that God is a person or that he has a personality. In his 1918 Gifford Lectures, Clement C. J. Webb emphasized that the historic creeds affirm personality *in* God rather than the personality *of* God (*God and Personality* [1919], Lecture III).

The doctrine of the Trinity, or of divine triunity, has been at the heart of much theological controversy. The routine objection is that the doctrine sacrifices MONOTHEISM to tritheism. But this objection thrives on a misconception of divine personality in the image of disparate individual human selves. A type of rationalistic apologetics, promotive of trinitarianism on speculative rather than revelational grounds, regrettably encourages this misunderstanding. Insisting that divinity must by definition be personal, and presuming to derive the doctrine of the Trinity by formal logic from empirical philosophical considerations rather than from God's revelational activity, the argument is vulnerable to secular counterattack.

Independently of divine disclosure, human beings possess no knowledge of divinity that qualifies them to declare surely who or what God is. No a priori reason can be given why God must or must not be an invisible person, or the spirit of the universe (regarded as his body), or the eternally triune God—unless God has somehow truly revealed his reality and perfections. Indeed, divine revelation is a matter of sovereign freedom; no advance necessity exists that God should reveal himself, or reveal himself intimately.

But the reality and nature of God known in the light of divine disclosure yields the historic Christian conviction, grounded in the NT, that God's being is Father, Son, and Holy Spirit in his self-manifestation. This insistence on three eternal modes of consciousness in the one God has no parallel in religious philosophy. Quite different are the Platonic *Ideas* and *Demiurge*, the triadic gods of some ancient polytheistic religions, the Stoic *Logos* and the Neo-Platonic *Nous*, and Hegel's exposition of a three-beat movement in the self-manifestation of the Absolute, much as they seek to emphasize vital relationships within the life of the divine.

By its very emphasis on the progressive character of historical revelation, the scriptural record of the self-manifestation of the living God cautions against any notion that the doctrine of the Trinity was fully knowable in OT times. First and foremost, the revelation of the Bible presents throughout the truth of monotheism, against the polytheism and the practical atheism of the ancient world. God's unique transcendent glory is reflected by the OT's explicit prohibition of all graven images, whether in the similitude of nature or creatures. The Genesis creation narrative emphasizes, however, that God made Adam and Eve in the divine image. In the NT, God's glory is manifested in the incarnation of the Logos, bearing the express image of the divine in human nature. Nowhere does the NT emphasis on the DEITY OF CHRIST, or its trinitarian statements, deviate in the slightest from the uncompromising monotheism of the OT; both Testaments deplore polytheism.

However, the possibility of OT intimations of the doctrine of the Trinity is discussed by some modern writers. G. A. F. Knight (*A Biblical Approach to the Doctrine of the Trinity* [1953]) notes that of the two Hebrew words for "one," ʾeḥād H285 and yāḥîd H3495, the latter indicates uniqueness (the only one of its kind), whereas the former does not preclude distinguishable entities (as in Gen. 2:24, where Adam and Eve are said to be one flesh). The Shema (Deut. 6:4–5) uses ʾeḥād. Moreover, Knight contends, to consider the name Elohim (see ELOAH) a plural of majesty, rather than as indicative of diversity in unity, is to impute a modern way of thinking to the ancient Hebrews, who addressed all their OT kings in the singular. The plural vocalization of the word ADONAI may witness to the same phenomenon.

Explicit trinitarianism is dependent upon the NT revelation of the sending Father, the sent Son, and the outpoured Spirit. In the experience of the disciples, the disclosure of the deity of Christ may at first have impressed them with an intermediary or temporary binitarianism of Father and Son. Since Jews viewed Jesus' claim of oneness with the Father as blasphemous, his assertion of the unity of Father and Son clearly implied oneness of essence and was not reducible only to moral and purposive harmony. But God's revelation in Christ was soon grasped as a revelation not of a part of deity but of complete divinity; Jesus of Nazareth unveiled the Father, the Son, and the Spirit. The revealed presence of God demanded recognition not only of the person of the Son alongside the person of the Father, but the person of the Spirit as well.

In view of the interdependence of trinitarianism and progressive divine disclosure, the question might be raised whether God may not yet show himself to be other than we now know. The query has the merit of emphasizing that authentic religious knowledge turns on God's self-revelation. Christian theology has no other reason for asserting the finality of trinitarian monotheism than the fact of God's self-disclosure attested in Holy Scripture. The content of the Christian doctrine is given by the divine affirmation of Jesus of Nazareth as the supreme and final revelation of the Father, and the Holy Spirit's witness to the Son, and not to another. Whoever takes his stand beneath the reality of the NT revelation—rather than behind it or outside it—is driven to trinitarian theology.

C. K. Barrett remarks that more than any other NT source, the writer of the fourth gospel "lays the foundations for a doctrine of a co-equal Trinity" (*The Gospel According to John*, 2nd ed. [1978], 92). But the threefold formula is found also in the Great Commission (Matt. 28:19; see COMMISSION, GREAT), and the unitarian attempt to dismiss this as a late interpolation has failed; the formula is now widely viewed as integral to the original text and anticipative of *Didache* 7.1–4. It occurs also in Paul's early writings (2 Cor. 13:14).

The word *Trinity* is not a biblical term, and Scripture gives the doctrine not in formulated definition but in fragmentary units similar to many other elements of the Christian system of truth. R. B. Crawford insists rightly that there are "good grounds for believing that the doctrine of the Trinity is scriptural" (*Scottish Journal of Theology* 20 [1967]: 286ff.). It is the unifying presupposition of the NT revelation of God. B. B. Warfield remarked that the entire NT "is Trinitarian to the core; all its teaching is built on the assumption of the Trinity; and its allusions to the Trinity are frequent, cursory, easy and confident" (*ISBE* [1929], 5:3014). There is in the NT, as in the OT, only one true and living God; and in its view, Jesus Christ and the Holy Spirit are each God in the fullest sense; and Father, Son, and Spirit stand related to each other as I, Thou, and He.

Many passages in the Gospels teach Jesus' divinity and the Son's unity with the Father, and in the context of such passages it is emphasized that the same essential interrelationship extends to the Holy Spirit (cf. Jn. 14:16–26; 15:26; 16:5–15). The importance of the baptismal formula (Matt. 28:19) lies in the fact that it most nearly approaches the doctrine in the words enunciated by the Lord himself, preserved, moreover, by one of the synoptic writers. This formula impressively asserts the unity of Father, Son, and Holy Spirit by embracing them in a single name, yet emphasizes the distinctiveness of each person by repeating the prefatory article, "In the name of the Father and of the Son and of the Holy Spirit."

The Pauline letters likewise not only repeatedly refer to God the Father and to Jesus Christ in juxtaposition, as joint objects of adoration, but the Holy Spirit appears with them as a personal source of all divine blessing. In the early as well as the later writings of Paul, all three persons are mentioned together as joint sources of the blessings of salvation (1 Thess. 1:2–5; 2 Thess. 2:13–14; 1 Cor. 12:4–5; 2 Cor. 13:14; Eph. 2:18; 3:2–6; 4:4–6; 5:18–20; Tit. 3:4–5; 2 Tim. 1:3, 13–14). The other NT writings repeat the same pattern (Heb. 2:3–4; 6:4–5; 10:29–31; 1 Pet. 1:2; 4:13–14; 1 Jn. 5:4; Jude 20–21; Rev. 1:4–6).

Crawford notes that unitarian views have invariably tended toward deism or toward pantheism, whereas trinitarianism has preserved the unity of God. The inner life and outer work of God were soon conformed to unitarian prejudices to avoid tritheism once the term *persona* was detached from a biblical witness to God's self-revelation, and speculatively expounded in the context of the modern understanding of the finite self as a disparate psychic entity. Modern philosophy then regarded the absoluteness and infinity of God as incompatible not only with a doctrine of the Trinity, but with divine personality as well (misunderstood in this speculative way), and idealistic philosophy soon revived the pagan Greek antithesis of sovereignty or personality. This antitrinitarian claim that God's uniqueness precludes his inclusion in the highest values of human nature, such as personality, was unfortunately countered by the wrong reasons for personality in God—for example, that man's highest perfection must be like God (so that transcendent personality could be projected from the finite). The door was now open to every variety of postulatory theism in the name of Christianity. An ingenious "theology" of that kind—based on the longing of the human heart, the will to believe, the supposed infinite value of human personality, or the significance of personality in world culture, etc.—was readily inverted and dismissed as "higher anthropology." Leonard Hodgson (*The Doctrine of the Trinity* [1943]) argues in defense of the Trinity that organic unity is more complex than mathematical unity, that psychological unity (thinking, feeling, and willing) is more complex still; and that the nature of God is even more complex than human nature.

Evangelical Christianity needs to heed every warning against a speculative derivation of divine personality simply by examination of the sinner's consciousness apart from reliance on supernatural revelation, for this requires different presuppositions about God than does the view of divine nature and activity predicated upon the living God who speaks and acts and is present in his self-disclosure. For the very reason that the scriptural revelation is the decisive center of God's self-disclosure, first given in deed and then authoritatively interpreted in word, neo-Protestant speculation is doubly arbitrary in its dismissal of trinitarian theology as a reflex of pagan philosophy, while it proceeds to recreate the God image along the lines of fashionable contemporary thought.

(In addition to the titles mentioned in the body of this article, see H. Bavinck, *The Doctrine of God* [1951], 255–334; C. Beisner, *God in Three Persons* [1984]; A. E. McGrath, *Understanding the Trinity* [1988]; W. Grudem, *Systematic Theology: An Introduction to Christian Doctrine* [1994], ch. 14; S. T. Davis et al., eds., *The Trinity: An Interdisciplinary Symposium on the Trinity* [1999]; M. J. Erickson, *Making Sense of the Trinity: 3 Crucial Questions* [2000]; R. E. Olson and C. A. Hall, *The Trinity* [2002]; C. E. Gunton, *Father, Son, and Holy Spirit: Essays Toward a Fully Trinitarian Theology* [2003]; S. J. Grenz, *Rediscovering the Triune God: The Trinity in Contemporary Theology* [2004]; A. Coppedge, *The God Who Is Triune: Revisioning the Christian Doctrine of God* [2007].) C. F. H. HENRY

Tripartite Tractate. A theological treatise, representative of Valentinian GNOSTICISM, included in the NAG HAMMADI LIBRARY (NHC I, 5). Originally written in Greek in the 3rd cent. A.D., it is preserved only in a 4th-cent. Coptic translation. The work begins with a lengthy presentation of

Gnostic COSMOGONY, followed by a discussion of the Genesis account of CREATION; it concludes with a description of salvation in terms of restoration into the Pleroma ("fullness"). (English trans. in *NHL*, 58–103.)

Tripolis trip´uh-lis (Τρίπολις, "three-city"). Also Tripoli. This once important seaport in PHOENICIA, some 20 mi. N of Byblos (GEBAL), derived its name from its triple occupancy by citizens of TYRE, SIDON, and ARVAD (Strabo, *Geogr.* 16.2.15). Perhaps during the latter Persian period (in the 4th cent. B.C.), it became the center of the conclaves from the neighboring localities. It was a member of the Phoenician League. It seems to have been a place of commercial importance, being bounded on three sides by the sea. Tripolis was also the seat of the federal council of the represented Phoenician states. It is possible that the city is mentioned in the OT (Ezra 4:9 NIV; see TARPELITES).

The SELEUCID ruler DEMETRIUS Soter (162 B.C.), fleeing from Rome where he had been a hostage, collected a large force, took the city, and gained possession of the country, executing his cousin ANTIOCHUS V (2 Macc. 14:1; cf. 1 Macc. 7:1; Jos. *Ant.* 12.10.1). Both the Seleucids and later the Romans added much to the city; HEROD the Great built a GYMNASIUM there (Jos. *War* 1.21.11). According to the spurious CLEMENTINE LITERATURE, Tripolis figured in the ministry of the apostle PETER (e.g., *Homilies* 7.12) and became a prominent Christian center.

Tripolis was taken by the Muslims, A.D. 638; later by the Crusaders in 1109; and again in 1299 by the Muslims under Sultan Kalaʿun of Egypt, who wrought great destruction. Constant attacks by enemies, and the feeling of insecurity, prompted removal two miles inland, where the present Tarabulus was founded in 1366 on the banks of the Nahr Kadisha. The ancient Tripolis, under the later name of el-Mina, became the seaport for the modern Tarabulus. The British occupied the city in 1918; in 1920 it was incorporated in the State of Gran Liban. In 1941, it became part of the independent Republic of Lebanon. It specializes in soap, tobacco, sponges and fruits; and it exports eggs and cotton. (See A. H. M. Jones, *Cities of the Roman Empire*, 2nd ed. [1971], 230–31 et passim.) R. F. GRIBBLE

trireme. See SHIPS III.

Trismegistus. See HERMETIC WRITINGS.

triumphal entry. On the first day of the week in which Jesus was to be rejected and crucified, he entered Jerusalem like a conqueror and king (Matt. 21:1–11; Mk. 11:1–11; Lk. 19:29–44; Jn. 12:12–19), thus fulfilling, as Matt. 21:4–5 notes, the prophecy of Zech. 9:9 (see JESUS CHRIST V.F). The impression is gained that Jesus was deliberately presenting himself in such a way that his royal claims would be manifest and Israel brought to a place of decision. Yet for all the acclamation he was not such a MESSIAH as they desired.

Leaving BETHANY, two miles from Jerusalem, he passed BETHPHAGE where, perhaps by previous arrangement, the donkey with her unbroken colt was obtained. "A great multitude" that had come to the feast were pilgrims, many of them from GALILEE where most of Jesus' ministry had taken place. As they met and then accompanied him with expressions of praise and joy, the natives of Jerusalem, stirred but puzzled, questioned his identity. One discordant note casts a shadow on this otherwise "triumphal" entry: in the midst of the exultation, Jesus stopped to weep over the Holy City, voicing the judgment that marks the tragic, sinful reality behind the momentary rejoicing. (Cf. A. Edersheim, *The Life and Times of Jesus the Messiah*, 2 vols. [1889], 2:363–73.) P. C. JOHNSON

triumphal procession. This phrase is used by the NIV and other modern versions in 2 Cor. 2:14: "But thanks be to God, who always leads us in triumphal procession in Christ." The KJV renders, "causeth us to triumph," while the RSV has, "leads us in triumph," which evokes the image of a general *guiding his troops* to victory in combat. There is, however, no clear evidence for such uses of the verb *thriambeuō* G2581, which normally means "to triumph [over someone]" or "to lead/exhibit [someone as captive] in a triumphal procession" (cf. BDAG, 459). In other words, the direct object of this verb always appears to be a conquered prisoner.

Thus many recent interpreters prefer to understand this passage as an allusion to the Roman military *triumphus*, the procession of a victorious general to the Capitoline Hill to offer sacrifice to Jupiter. The honor of a triumph could be granted only by the Roman senate and in accordance with strict rules, among which was one that the victory had to be against foreigners, not in a civil war. The procession was elaborate: the magistrates led off, followed by the senate, trumpeters, spoils captured from the enemy, the white oxen for sacrifice, the principal captives in chains, the lictors, the victorious general himself in a four-horse chariot, and finally his army. The general wore the dress of a king, including scepter and crown. When he reached the capitol, he placed a laurel wreath on the lap of the god. Many triumphs lasted more than one day. The triumphator was privileged to appear in special dress at public gatherings, and his name was inscribed on the list of persons so honored.

Because the captives in such a procession were normally led to their death, Paul in 2 Cor. 2:14 may be alluding to his sufferings, but the apostle's precise point is debated by scholars. According to one view, "God's leading him *in Christ* as a suffering servant thereby legitimates his ministry. Christ's humiliation in crucifixion is reproduced in the life of his servant" (P. Barnett, *The Second Epistle to the Corinthians*, NICNT [1997], 150; for more extensive discussion and alternate interpretations, see S. J. Hafemann, *Suffering and Ministry in the Spirit: Paul's Defense of His Ministry in II Corinthians 2:14—3:3* [1990], 16–34; M. E. Thrall, *A Critical and Exegetical Commentary on the Second Epistle to the Corinthians*, ICC, 2 vols. [1994–2000], 1:191–96; R. D. Aus, *Imagery of Triumph and Rebellion in 2 Corinthians 2:14–17 and Elsewhere in the Epistle* [2005]). In the other occurrence of this term, Col. 2:15, where the object of the verb certainly refers to Christ's enemies, the meaning may be "triumphing over them" (so most translations) or "exhibiting them in triumphal celebration" (cf. BDAG, 491, meaning 1.b).

R. C. Stone

Troas troh´az (Τρῳάς *G5590*). A port on the Aegean coast of western Asia Minor, opposite the island of Tenedos, at the mouth of the Dardanelles. It is not to be confused with Homeric Troy, whose fortress ruins stand on an escarpment dominating the coastal plain 10 mi. away. Troas was founded in 300 B.C. in the spate of Greek city building that followed the division of Alexander the Great's short-lived empire. It belonged to the Seleucid dynasty, but western Asia Minor was seldom strongly held from distant Antioch or Syria. Troas early acquired her independence and maintained it in some form even when the kingdom of Pergamum was dominant in the W of the peninsula, and even when Rome came to Asia. The port was important as the nearest point to Europe, and both Pergamum and Rome may have found it sound policy to keep this important haven satisfied and conscious of its importance. There is a persistent hint in Augustan literature (cf. Horace, *Odes* 3.3), supported by a statement of Suetonius (*Divus Julius* 79), that Julius Caesar considered the idea of transferring the Roman center of government to Troas.

Troas figured largely in the story of Paul (Acts 16:8–11). Luke recorded in terse narrative how Paul and Silas had arrived on the Aegean coast under a strange sense of compulsion. Alexandria Troas, to give the port its ancient name, had long since been a Roman colony, but Paul could not accept the city as the goal of his journey. Here he appears to have met Luke, who may indeed have been a certain "man of Macedonia," whom he saw in the dream that compelled him to take the gospel into Europe. The party traveled by sea, from Troas past Imbros and Samothrace, N of Thasos

Troas.

Remains of the ancient harbor at Alexandria Troas.

to NEAPOLIS in THRACIA, and thence by road to PHILIPPI.

Ten years later, after the riot in EPHESUS, Paul returned to Troas and established a Christian church (2 Cor. 2:12). After a briefly recorded ministry in Greece (Acts 20:1–3), Paul came again, but Luke confined his narrative to a matter that interested his physician's mind (Acts 20:4–12). Perhaps the apostle was in Troas again around the time of his arrest (c. in A.D. 66), for he left essential possessions in that city (2 Tim. 4:13).

(See further W. Leaf, *Strabo on the Troad* [1912]; R. Macaulay, *The Pleasure of Ruins* [1933], 42, 46–47; C. J. Hemer in *TynBul* 26 [1975]: 79–112; E. Schwertheim and H. Wiegartz, eds., *Die Troas: Neue Forschungen zu Neandria und Alexandria Troas II* [1996]; M. Ricl, ed., *The Inscriptions of Alexandreia Troas* [1997]; *ABD*, 6:666–67.)

E. M. BLAIKLOCK

Trogyllium troh-jil′ee-uhm (Τρωγύλλιον *G5591* [not in NIV]). Some 20 mi. S of EPHESUS, a high headland N of the mouth of the Maeander forms a sharply pointed cape called Trogyllium, which protrudes westward and makes a narrow channel between the mainland and the island of SAMOS. This waterway, barely a mile wide, forms a protected roadstead in which a coasting vessel might naturally pass the night before running across the open gulf to MILETUS. The pause in the protected anchorage is mentioned in Acts 20:15, according to the TR (followed by the KJV). Aside from CODEX BEZAE (D), all early Greek MSS lack the clause *kai meinantes en Trōgyliō* ("and after remaining in Trogyllium") and thus it is omitted in most modern versions. It is possible that the clause was original and later omitted either through carelessness or in an effort to improve the style (cf. B. M. Metzger, *A Textual Commentary on the Greek New Testament*, 2nd ed. [1994], 424); and certainly the disputed phrase occasions no difficulty geographically or historically (see W. M. Ramsay, *The Church in the Roman Empire before A.D. 170* [1893], 155). In view of the strong external evidence, however, it seems more likely that the words were added by the editor behind the "Western" text because he interpreted the previous verb, *parebalomen*, in the sense "we passed by," and thus he felt the need to provide an alternative port of call (so C. K. Barrett, *A Critical and Exegetical Commentary on the Acts of the Apostles*, ICC, 2 vols. [1994–98], 2:958).

E. M. BLAIKLOCK

Trophimus trof′uh-muhs (Τρόφιμος *G5576*, "nourished" [foster child?] or "nourishing"). A Christian from EPHESUS who, with other believers, accompanied PAUL on his way back to Jerusalem toward the end of the apostle's third missionary journey (Acts 20:4; cf. 21:29). In the light of 2 Cor. 8:19–20, it appears that Trophimus, along with TYCHICUS, was a delegate from the province of ASIA chosen by the churches to bear the collection (see CONTRIBUTION). When they arrived in Jerusalem, Jews from Asia saw Paul and Trophimus together in Jerusalem and hastily supposed that Paul had taken him illegally into the TEMPLE proper beyond the outer Court of the Gentiles (21:29). Since it was punishable by death for an uncircumcised Gentile to enter the Court of Israel, thus defiling it, the ensuing uproar led to an attempt on Paul's life and to his arrest. The serious but false charge of profaning the temple was later repeated against Paul by TERTULLUS before the Roman governor Felix (24:6).

In 2 Tim. 4:20, Paul says that he left Trophimus ill at MILETUS. Such a notice does not fit the recorded journeys in Acts since Paul did not leave Trophimus when they were together in Miletus (Acts 20:15), nor did he go to Rome via Miletus. If this is the same man, it shows him traveling again with the apostle, who had been freed from his first imprisonment in Rome before 2 Timothy was written. A. M. Ross

trumpet. See MUSIC, MUSICAL INSTRUMENTS IV.C.

Trumpets, Feast of. This phrase, though not found in the Bible, is often used with reference to a celebration described in Lev. 23:24–25: "On the first day of the seventh month you are to have a day of rest, a sacred assembly commemorated with trumpet blasts. Do no regular work, but present an offering made to the LORD by fire" (cf. Num. 29:1–6 for greater details concerning the offering). Because the seventh month of the religious CALENDAR (TISHRI) corresponded to the first month of the civil calendar, the rabbis identified the Feast of Trumpets with New Year's Day (cf. m. Roš Haš. 1:1; 3:3). It is uncertain, however, whether the feast had this or some other significance in OT times (cf. ISBE, rev. ed. [1979–88], 4:924).

trustee. This English term, meaning "a person to whom the management of another's property is entrusted," is used once by the NIV and other versions to render the Greek noun *oikonomos* G3874: "as long as the heir is a child," PAUL says by way of illustration, that heir "is subject to guardians and trustees until the time set by his father" (Gal. 4:2). The Greek word is more commonly rendered "manager," "steward," and the like (e.g., Lk. 12:42; 16:1 et al.; 1 Cor. 4:1–2 NRSV). See GUARDIAN; STEWARD.

truth. Scripture does not directly address the question of the nature and tests of truth which has received so much philosophical attention. Indeed, the cognitive conception of true KNOWLEDGE appears to be secondary to, and derivative from, the more fundamental conception of moral truth ascribed to persons and their acts.

I. Biblical terminology. In the OT the word *ʾĕmet* H622 (root *ʾmn*, cf. cognate *ʾĕmûnâ* H575) indicates firmness, stability, fidelity, a reliable basis of support. It is attributed to God as well as creatures, and appears in such expressions as "truly," "of a truth," etc. It is ascribed not only to statements (e.g., Ruth 3:12) but also to behavior (Gen. 24:49) and to promises (2 Sam. 7:28). It is associated with kindness (Gen. 47:29), with justice (Neh. 9:13; Isa. 59:14), with sincerity (Josh. 24:14). (See further *TDOT*, 1:292–323; *NIDOTTE*, 1:427–33.)

The SEPTUAGINT translation, to express the moral aspect, frequently uses Greek *pistis* G4411 ("faith, faithfulness, trustworthiness") rather than the usual term for "truth," *alētheia* G237, though this latter word can also indicate "truthfulness, sincerity." In the NT, *alētheia* retains the moral and personalist emphasis of the OT, even though the notion of faithfulness is more often carried by *pistis* (see FAITH, FAITHFULNESS). Some have argued that the etymology of *alētheia* is "not concealed," suggesting that something is open, uncovered, revealed for what it indeed is. Although this analysis is uncertain, the word does indicate real and genuine rather than imaginary or spurious, and true rather than false. Hence we read of "the true God" (e.g., Jn. 17:3) and "the true vine" (15:1), just as the Nicene Creed speaks of "very God of very God," phrases where the adjective *alēthinos* G240 appears. Another adjective, *alēthēs* G239, appears to be used with the same basic meaning (Matt. 22:16; Jn. 3:33; et al.). NT references to true statements make it evident that the conception of cognitive truth derives from the notion of reliability (e.g., Mk. 5:33; 12:32; Jn. 8:44–46; Rom. 1:25; Eph. 4:25).

The cognitive conception, however, is more explicit in the NT than in the OT. Truth is related not only to fidelity and justice but also to knowledge and to revelation. This is partly due to the intrusion of Greek culture with its more theoretical interests into the Jewish world, partly due therefore to the GREEK LANGUAGE. But it would be a mistake to suppose that the NT use of *alētheia* reflects a Platonic dualism of form and particular, and thereby a Platonic or even Gnostic epistemology (see GREEK RELIGION AND PHILOSOPHY; GNOSTICISM). In the first place, Greek philosophy is far more varied than this implies: there was no one Greek epistemology. In the second place, the biblical writers shape the meanings they intend by their own careful use of language. Undoubtedly, writing for a hellenized culture with its conflicting truth-claims, they keep cognitive truth in mind. But their thinking is more directly shaped by OT concepts, and most of all by the belief that the true God, *alēthinos*, is not hidden, but acts and speaks with an openness that is wholly trustworthy (*alēthēs*). (See further R. C. Trench, *Synonyms of the New Testament* [1880], 26–30; *TDNT*, 1:232–51; *NIDNTT*, 3:874–902.)

II. Three concepts of truth. Biblical usage suggests three related concepts: (1) moral truth, (2) ontological truth, and (3) cognitive truth. The last two depend logically on (1), while (3) depends logically on (1) and (2). In each case the basis of truth is in God, the source and standard of (a) righteousness, (b) being, and (c) knowledge.

A. Moral truth. Truth is an attribute of God. As such the term speaks of his integrity, his trustworthiness, his faithfulness. It is celebrated by the Hebrew poet throughout Ps. 89 and by the prophet in Hos. 2:19–23, in both cases in association with the mercy and love of God. According to several passages (Deut. 32:4; Ps. 100:5; 146:6) his faithfulness is revealed in CREATION; and in the Apocalypse it is this attribute of God on which rests the expectation of judgment (Rev. 3:7, 14; 6:10; 15:3–4; 19:11; 21:5).

Since the character of God is to be emulated by human beings, truth in the same sense is to be their moral attribute as well. It entails honesty (Ps 15:2; Eph. 4:25) and civil justice (Isa. 59:4, 14–15). Speaking the truth is therefore mandatory, so that truthfulness (cognitive truth) marks the trustworthy person (moral truth). However, an overall integrity before both God and neighbor is expected (Exod. 18:21; Josh. 24:14). Truth, in this moral sense, is no perfunctory veneer, but stems from the heart, characterizing the whole inner character of a person (1 Sam. 12:24; Ps. 15:2; 51:6).

B. Ontological truth. Arising from the concept of one who is wholly trustworthy is the further concept of one who is truly what he purports to be, rather than being a deceiver, living a fiction, or being an imperfect example. In this sense "the true light" (Jn. 1:9) is the perfect expression of the kind of light JOHN THE BAPTIST was in part and for which he prepared; "the true bread" (6:32) contrasts with the imperfect MANNA; and "true worshipers" (4:23) contrast with those whose WORSHIP was still anticipatory. The Thessalonians, moreover, turned from their idols to serve "the true God" (1 Thess. 1:9).

In this sense we speak of a "true man" or a "true scholar," meaning one who is true to an ideal, who perfectly embodies our standard. The Greek theory of universals saw all particulars as participating to some degree in their ideal forms; Christian thinkers like Augustine, Anselm, and Aquinas equated these forms with divine ideas and decrees (eternal truths), and ascribed "ontological truth" to natural objects embodying them. This notion arises, however, not from biblical usage but from combining the Greek theory of forms with the biblical concept of the Creator who makes all things according to his perfect wisdom.

C. Cognitive truth. A further outcome of moral truth is that one speaks truth and not falsehood. In God, truthfulness stems from OMNISCIENCE, so that the attribute of truth refers in part to his perfect knowledge (Job 28:20–26; chs. 38–39). Since he is creator, whatever we know depends on him. All truth is God's truth. Our cognitive abilities are his creation, and the intelligibility of nature attests his WISDOM. God's knowledge is therefore archetypal and ours ectypal. What we declare true is such only insofar as it accords with the truth known perfectly to God alone. Ectypal truth is therefore contingent, limited, and provisional. We "see in a mirror dimly" and "know in part." But archetypal truth is unlimited, unchanging, and absolute. Truth-for-man is still in the making, but truth-for-God is complete.

This notion is expressed in John's LOGOS concept (Jn. 1:14, 17) and Paul's discussion of the Christ "in whom are hidden all the treasures of wisdom and knowledge" (Col. 2:3). It is the Christ, by whom all things were made and are sustained, who gives intelligible order and purpose to nature and history. To know him is to know the omniscient source of all knowledge—not to know all he knows, but to understand how wisdom and knowledge are at all possible. He it is who guarantees the trustworthiness of the truth we acquire.

While in the NT the cognitive concept of truth is evident (e.g., Mk. 5:33; 12:32; Rom. 1:25), it is applied particularly to the message of Christ and his apostles (Jn. 5:33; 8:31–47; Rom. 2:8; Gal. 2:5; 5:7; Eph. 1:13; 1 Tim. 3:15; 1 Jn. 2:21–27). The faithful messenger speaks the truth from God, and in responding to the truth the believer accordingly trusts the God from whom the message comes. Faith is both assent to truth and dependence on God. We are therefore said to "do the truth" when our assent to the message and trust in God are evident in our "moral truth" or faithfulness (1 Jn. 1:6–8; 2:4; 3:18–19).

III. Philosophical concepts of truth

A. Cognitive truth. If God is the ground of all truth, then whatever truths we know bear witness to him. Recognizing this fact, AUGUSTINE of Hippo (354–430) constructed an argument for God's existence from our knowledge of truth (*On Free Will* 2). The mind apprehends certain universal and necessary truths that cannot change, including logical truths (e.g., "A is either B or non-B") and mathematical truths. They are neither made true nor amended by the mind as if they were its inferiors; rather, the mind willingly submits to being corrected and judged by them, as by its superiors. Truth exists independently of the mind and is superior to it. The mind fluctuates in its apprehension of truth, but truth remains forever the same. What accounts for its eternal, changeless, and universal status? Individual truths must participate in Truth itself, the eternal and changeless God "in whom and by whom are all things."

Partial reconstruction of the interior of the library at Ephesus, one of the centers where the Greco-Roman world searched for truth through human learning.

Augustine's argument reflects his transformation of the Platonic theory of forms into a theistic context. There are no longer self-subsistent archetypes unified in the Form of the Good. The forms now are eternal truths (*rationes aeternae*) subsisting in the mind of God for whom all truth is one. They may still be known by recollection, for Augustine (*Concerning the Teacher* and *Soliloquies*) also adapts the Platonic theory of innate ideas and dialectical method, but any truth that humans grasp is due to the Logos "who teaches within," enlightening everyone who comes into the world.

Anselm of Canterbury (1033–1109) pursues the Augustinian direction by distinguishing three senses of "truth." (1) A proposition is true when it states what actually exists, but (2) what actually exists is what it should be ("ontological truth") when it conforms to (3) the archetypal idea in the mind of God ("eternal truth"). God is accordingly the eternal cause of all truth. Anselm also discusses "truth in the will," referring to the concept of "moral truth" discussed above. (See Anselm, *Dialogue on Truth*, in

R. McKeon, ed., *Selections from Medieval Philosophers*, 2 vols. [1929], 1:164–65.)

Thomas Aquinas (1223–1274) modifies this scheme by arguing (*De veritate*, Q. 1) that truth is to be predicated primarily of an intellect and only secondarily of a thing, for a thing is called true ("a true man," etc.) only insofar as it conforms to some idea. Natural things are what they are because of archetypal ideas in the divine intellect. Truth then is ultimately in the divine intellect. Insofar as it is in the human intellect, and people learn from natural things, truth comes ultimately from God. In God, truth means that his knowledge accords first with his essence and secondly with things he has created. Aquinas therefore defines truth as the adequation of thought to thing, and applies this definition to both divine and human knowledge. By doing so, he lays the foundation for modern correspondence theories of truth.

René Descartes (1596–1650) was educated in the Jesuit school at La Flèche, and the influence of scholastic thought remained with him. In this light, it is not surprising that he rests the trustworthiness of human reason and sense perception on the character of God (*Meditations* 4–5). The logical possibility of our achieving truth depends, he argues, on knowing that a God exists who would not deceive us. Error can never be blamed on God, but arises when the human will affirms or denies something that lies beyond the limited scope of human reason. Truth is insured by the careful, logical use of the created intellect. Truth depends on God.

Other Christian thinkers of the Renaissance and Enlightenment took similar positions. Malebranche, Berkeley, Leibniz, and others maintained in terms of their own philosophical schemes that all truth is ultimately God's truth, and that our knowledge of truth depends ultimately on God. The classic correspondence and coherence theories were formulated in this manner, the former in the context of empiricist epistemologies, and the latter more in a rationalist or idealist context. Nontheistic thought, detaching the theory of truth from these moorings, raises serious doubts as to the attainability of truth and its objectivity. Pragmatic and relativistic epistemologies are the reasonable outcome of naturalistic and other nontheistic philosophies. By the same token the rise of early modern science, with its confidence in the rational investigation of empirical findings, may be traced to the belief that a rational and trustworthy God created both an intelligible universe and finite minds that are reliable for their intended purposes. In these regards the biblical conception of cognitive truth has pervaded and inspired Western thought.

B. Moral truth. In the biblical sense of personal rectitude, moral truth has historically been overshadowed by cognitive truth. Søren Kierkegaard (1813–55) is largely responsible for its rediscovery. In his *Concluding Unscientific Postscript* he distinguishes between the objective path to truth through historical or philosophical inquiry, and the "subjective" path. Grasping truth, he declares, is "subjectivity." Kierkegaard does not mean that truth is either private or relative. He means that the individual must approach truth as a whole person, in all his subject-hood, passionately involved and utterly authentic in his concern. This kind of response distinguishes the true from the nominal believer. It is what the NT calls "being in the truth."

Kierkegaard's conception of truth, like that of a Descartes or a Leibniz, has however been distorted by nontheists. In this case the result is the existentialist view which regards truth as *wholly* personal, so that there is no objective truth in the mind of God which is intelligible to finite minds. That is, moral truth is retained without cognitive truth, and one achieves moral truth by existential experience. Martin Heidegger's analysis of truth as the "uncoveredness" of Being is extremely valuable (*Being and Time* [1962], §44), but his analysis of Being (*Dasein*) in terms of our own being-in-the-world tends to confine truth to self-discovery or personal self-authentication. The influence of Heidegger's view of truth is evident on the one hand in the theology of Paul Tillich and on the other hand in the nihilism of Jean-Paul Sartre, both of which suffer from a loss of the biblical and theistic conception of truth.

The insufficiency of either the cognitive or the existential concept of truth alone leads Herman Dooyeweerd to call for the elaboration of a truly Christian idea of truth which rejects the purported religious neutrality of theoretical truth and does justice to the biblical concern with truth "in the heart," thereby linking moral truth with theoretical truth (*A New Critique of Theoretical Thought*, 4 vols. [1953], 2:571). The ingredients of such an account are certainly present in Scripture and in subsequent Christian thought.　　　　　　　　A. F. Holmes

Truth, Gospel of. A Gnostic document included in two forms in the Nag Hammadi Library (NHC I, 3; XII, 2 [the latter poorly preserved]). In spite of its title, the work contains no narrative, nor does it report the sayings of Jesus, but is rather a kind of homily or meditation on Christ, emphasizing the joy that the gospel gives to "those who have received from the Father of truth the gift of knowing him." Because it uses the NT to give a mild and attractive presentation of Christian Gnosticism, many think that it may have been authored by Valentinus or more probably by his followers (cf. Irenaeus, *Haer.* 3.11.9: "Indeed, they [the Valentinians] have arrived at such a pitch of audacity, as to entitle their comparatively recent writing 'the Gospel of Truth,' though it agrees in nothing with the Gospels of the Apostles, so that they have really no Gospel which is not full of blasphemy" [*ANF*, 1:249]). In any case, the document was likely written in Greek before A.D. 200 and subsequently translated into Coptic. (English trans. in *NHL*, 38–51.)

Truth, Testimony of. A Gnostic document included in the Nag Hammadi Library (NHC IX, 3). Although preserved only in a fragmentary 4th-cent. Coptic MS, the original work is thought to have been written in Greek, possibly in Alexandria, c. A.D. 200. It may be described as a polemical tractate, although the first part is in the form of a homily. The author inveighs against the law, the physical resurrection, and even the views of competing Gnostic groups. On the other hand, the work affirms the value of esoteric knowledge and adopts an extreme form of asceticism. (English trans. in *NHL*, 448–59.)

Tryphena and Tryphosa trī-fēe'nuh, trī-toh'suh (Τρύφαινα G5590 and Τρυφῶσα G5589, both from the verb τρυφάω G5587, "to live delicately *or* luxuriously"). Also Tryphaena. Christian women in Rome to whom Paul sent greetings (Rom. 16:12).

He describes them as "women who work hard in the Lord," possibly a deliberate contrast to their names. Because their names are so similar, it is often thought that they were (twin?) sisters or very close relatives. Both names occur among slaves at the imperial court of Claudius and have been found in a cemetery used chiefly for the emperor's servants. On that basis, J. B. Lightfoot (*St. Paul's Epistle to the Philippians: A Revised Text with Introduction, Notes, and Dissertations* [1868], 175–76) suggested that Tryphena and Tryphosa may have been among "the saints ... who belong to Caesar's household" (Phil. 4:22). ("Tryphaena" is also the name of a queen who befriended Thecla in the apocryphal *Acts of Paul and Thecla*, chs. 27ff.)

　　　　　　　　A. M. Ross

Trypho trī'foh (Τρύφων, "luxurious"). KJV Tryphon. The surname of Diodotus, a usurper of the Seleucid throne. He was a native of Apamea in Syria. The name Trypho was adopted by him after his accession to power. He was a general of Alexander I Balas, king of Syria (150–145 B.C.), who claimed to be the son of Antiochus V Epiphanes and seized the Seleucid throne at the death of Demetrius I Soter (162–150 B.C.). When Alexander Balas died, Trypho set Alexander's son, Antiochus VI Dionysius, on the throne and declared himself the regent, against the claims of Demetrius II Nicator, the son of Demetrius I Soter (1 Macc. 11:38–40, 54–56).

Because of quarrels with Demetrius II, the Jews, led by Jonathan Maccabee, accepted Antiochus VI, and Trypho expelled Demetrius from Antioch (1 Macc. 11:54–56). Trypho, who planned to seize the Seleucid throne for himself, first treacherously murdered Jonathan at Ptolemais and then killed Antiochus VI (1 Macc. 12:39-13:32). He declared himself sole ruler of Syria (142 B.C.; 1 Macc. 13:31–32). Because of his tyranny and rapacity, the brother of Demetrius II, Antiochus VII Sidetes, invaded the country and inflicted a decisive defeat on Trypho at Dor in Phoenicia (1 Macc. 15:10–14, 25). Trypho fled to Orthosia on the Lebanon coast and then to Apamea, where he died (Jos. *Ant.* 13.7.2; Strabo, *Geogr.* 14.5.2).

(Regarding the *Dialogue with Trypho the Jew*, see Justin Martyr.)　　　　　　S. Barabas

Tryphon tri′fon. KJV Apoc. form of TRYPHO.

Tryphosa. See TRYPHENA.

tsadhe tsahd′ee (צָדֵי, meaning uncertain). Also *sade*, *tzaddi*, etc. The eighteenth letter of the Hebrew ALPHABET (צ), with a numerical value of 90. Its sound in Modern Hebrew corresponds to that of English *ts*, but in biblical times it was a so-called "emphatic" consonant, possibly an *s* characterized by a compression of the pharynx or by an additional velar articulation (i.e., with the back of the tongue touching or approaching the soft palate).

Tubal too′buhl (תֻּבַל H9317, corresponding to Akk. *Tabāl*). Son of JAPHETH and grandson of NOAH, included in the Table of NATIONS (Gen. 10:2; 1 Chr. 1:5). Mentioned between JAVAN (corresponding to the Ionians of W ASIA MINOR and GREECE; cf. also Isa. 66:19) and MESHECH (corresponding to the Mushki or Moschoi who occupied central Asia Minor for a long time; cf. also Ezek. 32:26 et al.), Tubal was apparently the eponymous ancestor of a Neo-Hittite confederacy located in the heartland of the Taurus mountains in SE Asia Minor. This nation came to prominence during the 1st millennium B.C. after the decline of the great HITTITE kingdom of Hattusas. EZEKIEL refers to Tubal as the source of slaves and metals (Ezek. 27:13); elsewhere he speaks of GOG as the chief prince of Meshech and Tubal who will fall under God's judgment (38:2–4; 39:1–6).

As the Assyrian military power expanded N and E, it came into long and bitter conflict with the tribal confederacies of Anatolia from the rise of ASHURNASIRPAL II (884–859 B.C.), until the onslaught of the SCYTHIANS in 679 B.C. The name Tabal(a) is mentioned in numerous records of the punitive campaigns sent into the Taurus during these centuries. The people of Tabal/Tubal are evidently the ones later referred to as *Tibarēnoi* by HERODOTUS (*Hist.* 3.94), who states that they supplied troops to the Persian armies of DARIUS and XERXES. Their ferocity was proven by the fact that their defeat and destruction came only after hundreds of years of continual warfare. SARGON II died in his campaign against them in 705 B.C.

(See further E. Yamauchi, *Foes from the Northern Frontier: Invading Hordes from the Russian Steppes* [1982], ch. 1.) W. WHITE, JR

Tubal-Cain too′buhl-kayn′ (תּוּבַל קַיִן H9340, possibly "Tubal the metal-worker" [cf. CAIN]; the first element of the name perhaps should be linked to the root יָבַל H3297 [cf. JUBAL] or to the name TUBAL [see *HALOT*, 4:1694–95]). Son of LAMECH by his second wife ZILLAH (Gen. 4:22). Because the SEPTUAGINT reads simply *Thobel*, some scholars argue that the second element in the name, "Cain," is not original but rather a later scribal addition to distinguish him from Tubal the son of JAPHETH (10:2). If the double-name is original, it is possible that Tubal-Cain was viewed as the ancestor of the KENITES (15:19), often thought to have been metal workers. In any case, he is described as "a sharpener of every artisan of copper and iron" (lit. trans.); this phrase can be understood either in the sense "an instructor of every artificer in brass and iron" (cf. KJV) or, more likely, "a forger of all implements of copper and iron" (cf. NIV and other modern versions).

Tubieni too′bee-ee′nee. KJV Apoc. form of TOUBIANI (2 Macc. 12:17).

tumbleweed. This English term—referring to various plants that, breaking from their roots, roll about driven by the wind—is used by the NIV to render Hebrew *galgal* H1650, which occurs only twice (Ps. 83:13 [KJV, "wheel"]; Isa. 17:13 [KJV, "rolling thing"; NRSV uses "whirling dust" in both passages]). This Hebrew word is either a homonym of *galgal* H1649, "wheel" (Isa. 5:28 et al.) or the same word used metaphorically. The plant referred to is thought by some to be *Gundelia tournefortii*, a member of the THISTLE family whose dried calyx has the shape of a wheel. Others identify it as *Anastatica hierochuntica*, the "resurrection plant," also called "the rose of Jericho" (it is found abundantly about that town). This annual loses its leaves after flowering; the stems become incurved and hard, forming a hollow ball. This ball breaks off at ground level in the wind, and then rolls away as light as a feather, distributing the ripened seeds on the surface of the soil as it travels. When this weed is prevalent, one can see large numbers of these "rolling things" traveling before the wind and making quite a noise (however, see *ITB*, 107–00). See also FLORA (under *Cruciferae*).

W. E. SHEWELL-COOPER

tumor. An abnormal enlargement of some part of the body; or a neoplasm, that is, a growth of abnormal tissue distinct from the healthy tissue underneath (such a neoplasm may be as benign as a pimple, or as malignant as carcinoma). This English term is often used to translate Hebrew *ʿōpel* H6754, which occurs in Deut. 28:27 ("The LORD will afflict you with the boils of Egypt and with tumors, festering sores and the itch, from which you cannot be cured") and in connection with the capture of the ARK OF THE COVENANT by the PHILISTINES (1 Sam. 5:6, 9, 12; 6:4–5). In all of these references, the Masoretes include the *Qere ṭĕḥōrîm* H3224, "hemorrhoids," which is in fact the word found in 1 Sam. 6:11 and 17 (the NJPS translates "hemorrhoids" throughout; KJV, "emerods"). Many believe that the "gold tumors" prepared by the Philistines were emblematic of the buboes characteristic of PLAGUE, that is, enlarged and defeated lymph glands. When infective organisms, or their products, reach the lymph glands, the latter make a valiant effort to keep them from entering the systemic circulation. They may swell to a hundred times their normal size endeavoring to lock up the undesirable elements and then destroy them. But sometimes the flow of infective material is so great, as in plague, that even many lymph glands in succession are overwhelmed, and the body succumbs to the disease.

R. H. POUSMA

tunic. See COAT.

turban. This term is used by the NIV and other modern versions to render several Hebrew words, especially *miṣnepet* H5200 (Exod. 28:4 et al.; KJV, "mitre") and *pĕʾēr* H6996, a loanword from Egyptian *pyr* (Ezek. 24:17 et al.). The turban is a length of linen, wool, or silk cloth, wound into a head covering. Since Muhammad, it has been a distinctive headgear of the Muslims, but its usage originated in the era of the Assyrians, Babylonians, and Hebrews, who used various forms of wound cloth headdress, especially for ceremonial occasions and in higher ranks of society. The use of the relevant terms indicates that linen headdress was the sign of rejoicing or solemnity, the adornment of priest and bridegroom (Isa. 61:10; 3:14), and probably a lighter article than the wound and heavier headgear generally called a turban today.

E. M. BLAIKLOCK

turpentine tree. See TEREBINTH.

turquoise. A bluish-green or greenish-gray mineral used in jewelry. It is a basic hydrous phosphate of aluminum and copper, rather brittle and with a hardness similar to that of iron. Turquoise is a mineral of secondary origin, occurring in thin veins, as patchy deposits or as encrustations in seams of rock that have undergone extensive alteration. The highly prized oriental turquoise occurs in much broken rock, together with secondary iron oxides, in Persia. It also occurs on the Sinai Peninsula in the Wadi Maghara and S of Samarkand, Turkestan. The NIV and other versions use "turquoise" as the rendering of *nōpek* H5876 (Exod. 28:18 et al.; KJV, "emerald"), but the precise meaning of this Hebrew word is disputed. See also ANTIMONY.

D. R. BOWES

turtledove. A wild pigeon (*Streptopelia turtur*) noted for its plaintive cooing. Many races and related species occur through Europe, Asia, and north and central Africa. Turtledoves are common in PALESTINE at all seasons and many more pass through on migration, traveling between Africa and their N breeding grounds. The closely related collared and palm doves are resident in Palestine and all go under one common name. The barbary dove, paler than the turtledove and rather bigger, was domesticated from the collared dove in early times, and it can be assumed that this was kept for sacrificial use; in any case, it does not seem to have been the practice to use wild animals for this purpose. See DOVE.

G. S. CANSDALE

Tuthmosis. See THUTMOSE.

tutor. See GUARDIAN.

twelve. See NUMBER.

Twelve, the. See APOSTLE.

Twin Brothers. See DIOSCURI.

twined linen. See LINEN.

Tychicus tik´uh-kuhs (Τυχικός G5608, "fortunate"). A close friend and valued helper of the apostle PAUL. Along with TROPHIMUS, Tychicus was evidently a delegate from the province of ASIA chosen by the churches to accompany the apostle as he took the collection to Jerusalem (cf. Acts 20:4–6 with 2 Cor. 8:19–20; see CONTRIBUTION). Later, Tychicus was with Paul during the latter's first Roman imprisonment and was entrusted with the important mission of delivering the letters to the EPHESIANS and the COLOSSIANS with instructions to inform them of Paul's welfare and to encourage them (Eph. 6:21; Col. 4:7–9). Traveling with Tychicus was ONESIMUS, the runaway slave of PHILEMON, whom Paul was returning to his master in COLOSSE. The presence of Tychicus would reduce the possibility of harsh treatment to Onesimus and give Tychicus opportunity as Paul's representative to mediate personally between the slave and his owner.

Paul purposed to send either ARTEMAS or Tychicus to relieve TITUS in the oversight of the churches on the island of CRETE so that Titus might be free to join the apostle at NICOPOLIS (Tit. 3:12). Tychicus is thus seen laboring again with Paul after the apostle was released from his first imprisonment. Loyal and useful to the end, Tychicus was dispatched during Paul's second Roman imprisonment to EPHESUS (2 Tim. 4:12) to care for the churches in and around what was probably his native home (note that Trophimus is identified as an Ephesian in Acts 21:29 and that CODEX BEZAE [D] has "Ephesians" for "Asians" in 20:4). This arrangement would free TIMOTHY to rejoin Paul who desperately wanted to see him before the apostle met his fate as a martyr for the gospel (2 Tim. 4:9, 21). The NT portrays Tychicus as a man whose ability and experience commanded respect and authority as an apostolic delegate. He justifies Paul's high regard for him as "a dear brother, a faithful minister and fellow servant in the Lord" (Col. 4:7). A. M. Ross

Tyndale's Version. See VERSIONS OF THE BIBLE, ENGLISH IV.

typology. Typology may be defined as "that form of biblical interpretation which deals with the correspondence between traditions concerning divinely appointed persons, events, and institutions within the framework of salvation history" (Paul Achtemeier in *IDBSup*, 926). Behind this approach is the belief that God acts in similar ways in both Testaments, and so his action in the NT repeats and thus "fulfills" his action in the OT.

The term *typology* stems from Greek *typos* G5596, which means "copy, image, pattern." This Greek word can be used in a general sense of a "pattern" to be copied in a moral or ethical sense (e.g., Phil. 3:17; 1 Thess. 1:7). In certain passages, however, the term is used somewhat technically to depict a salvation-historical correspondence between historical situations like the flood and baptism (1 Pet. 3:21, *antitypos* G531), figures like ADAM and Christ (Rom. 5:14), the heavenly pattern and its earthly counterpart (the tent or TABERNACLE, Acts 7:44; Heb. 8:5), Israel's experience in the wilderness (1 Cor. 10:6; in v. 11 the adverb *typikōs* G5595 is used), institutions like the Jewish feasts in Jn. 5–10, and priestly imagery like MELCHIZEDEK and Christ in Heb. 7. The "type" is the OT pattern, and the "antitype" (Heb. 9:24; 1 Pet. 3:21) is the NT counterpart or FULFILLMENT. Yet typology is found not just in the NT, for the OT contains examples as well, such as exodus-salvation in Isa. 40:3–5, exodus-exile in Hos. 11:1–2, the rebellion in the wilderness in Ps. 95:7–11, and Melchizedek in Ps. 110:4.

I. Related concepts. Typology can be placed within the framework of a "promise-fulfillment" relationship between the Testaments. This concept is related to salvation-history: JESUS CHRIST is the culmination or finalization of God's plan of salvation and as such fulfills the promises made in the OT. He relives and thus completes or "fills up" what God had done earlier. Behind this approach is the idea of CORPORATE SOLIDARITY, in which a king or high priest represented the nation in his actions. He acted not just for himself but also for his people as a whole. As MESSIAH, Jesus was identified with the entire history of the nation and relived it. Isaiah's SERVANT OF THE LORD was identified with the nation (Isa. 44:1), the remnant (49:5) and the Messiah (chs. 52–54). Jesus as the "Servant" fulfilled all of these.

Typology is thus linked to the idea of "correspondence in history," in which the climactic events in Israel's history become the paradigm that explains what God is doing in the new era (K. R. Snodgrass in *Interpreting the New Testament: Essays on Methods and Issues*, ed. D. A. Black and D. S. Dockery [2001], 215). For instance, at the TRANSFIGURATION, according to Luke, MOSES and ELIJAH discussed Jesus' "departure" (Gk. *exodus* G2016, Lk. 9:31), thus looking at Jesus' passion as a new exodus. Also, Ps. 69 was a lament psalm from DAVID, and Jesus as the Son of David has relived his experiences in a messianic sense (Ps. 69:9=Jn. 2:17; Ps. 69:21=Matt. 27:34 and parallels; Ps. 69:22–23=Rom. 11:9–10). The same is true of the use of Ps. 22 in the crucifixion narratives.

There is great debate regarding the connection between typology and *sensus plenior*, a view that says the characters and authors often did not see the messianic significance of the events, but God had in mind a "fuller" or "deeper" sense. It is generally thought that typology sees no prospective element in the original itself (rather, it is the NT writer that recognizes the typological relationship) while *sensus plenior* does. For the latter the deeper meaning is intended by God already in the OT text, while for typology the new connection is only recognized by the NT writer on the basis of historical fulfillment.

However, Douglas J. Moo (in *Hermeneutics, Authority, and Canon*, ed. D. A. Carson and J. D. Woodbridge [1986], 206) has endorsed a cautious use of *sensus plenior* on the basis of a canonical approach to Scripture that sees it as a literary whole: "the meaning of the text itself that takes on deeper significance as God's plan unfolds—a '*sensus praegnans*.'" In this sense typology and *sensus plenior* come together in the larger plan of God, part of the intertextual relationship between the parts of the canon. While not a direct prophecy, David's coronation (Ps. 2; 72; 110) foreshadows the enthronement of Jesus as Royal Messiah.

II. Hermeneutical principles. During the biblical period typology was clearly centered on the historical correspondence between events within a promise-fulfillment pattern. However, during the patristic period OT events came to be interpreted allegorically, concluding with the allegorical school of ORIGEN and his successors. See ALLEGORY. This approach was opposed by the Antiochene school (CHRYSOSTOM, Theodore of Mopsuestia), who advocated the literal sense and developed typology as a tool to demonstrate the literary relationship between the Testaments. However, the allegorical school was victorious and dominated until the Reformation, when Luther and especially Calvin used typology to espouse the unity between the Testaments.

With the rise of the historical-critical method, many critical scholars considered typology an inferior method that assumed the unity of the Bible without recognizing tradition-critical development. However, in the second half of the 20th cent. the rise of the biblical theology movement and of the salvation-historical school of Oscar Cullmann and others brought back the viability of typology as a valid hermeneutic, while the masterwork of Leonard Goppelt (*Typos: The Typological Interpretation of the Old Testament in the New Testament* [1982]) brought the discipline into the mainstream of academic discussion. Recently, however, the influence of deconstruction and reader-response criticism has somewhat marginalized it once more in the eyes of many, since it is so clearly connected with a historical interpretation of Scripture. See INTERPRETATION II. Still, typology reigns supreme in most discussion of the use of the OT in the NT.

Moo speaks of "appropriation techniques" and "hermeneutical axioms" (*Hermeneutics, Authority, and Canon*, 194), with typology being an appropriation method that is anchored in the basic hermeneutic of the 1st-cent. church, namely, the belief that Jesus fulfills the plan of God and that therefore all the Scriptures point to him. Not just direct prophecy but all the experiences of God's people are fulfilled in him. He has relived them in himself. Connected with this, then, the people of the new covenant, the church, have also relived the experiences of Israel. They are "a chosen people, a royal priesthood, a holy nation, a people belonging to God" (1 Pet. 2:9), in typological fulfillment of Old Israel. The new community, built on the Messiah, is also analogously linked to the past experiences of God's people of old.

There are two kinds of typological figures—an innate type that is specifically mentioned in the NT (e.g., 1 Cor 10:6; 1 Pet. 3:21) and an inferred type that does not use the terminology but is based upon the principles (e.g., the uses of OT texts in Hebrews or Revelation). Both are valid uses of typology, but the latter are more open to fanciful and allegorical exegesis so must be studied carefully. Due to the hundreds of OT quotations and allusions in the NT (e.g., some 107 explicit quotations in Paul, 36 in Hebrews, and up to 600 allusions in Revelation alone), the question of how to interpret the use of the OT in the NT is complex and worthy of very careful study.

Briefly, a series of steps are necessary: (1) Do a careful exegesis of the OT text to discern the intention of the original author, that is, to determine whether it shows any prophetic interest in a future Messiah. (2) Study the NT use of the OT passage just as carefully, asking whether it is a quotation or allusion and whether it follows the Hebrew, the SEPTUAGINT, or some other text-type (e.g., Ps. 104:4 does not mention angels, but Heb. 1:7 quotes the LXX, which did introduce angels into the psalm). (3) See how it uses the OT passage and how its use is in keeping with the OT meaning or transforms that meaning in some way (e.g., the use of Zech. 12:10 [Israel mourning for sin] in Rev. 1:7 [the nations mourning for judgment]). (4) Determine whether it is direct prophecy, typology, or sensus plenior.

(See further P. Fairbairn, *The Typology of Scripture: Viewed in Connection with the Whole Series of Divine Dispensations*, 6th ed., 2 vols. [1876]; R. M. Davidson, *Typology in Scripture: A Study of Hermeneutical* τύπος *Structures* [1981]; C. R. Seitz, *Figured Out: Typology and Providence in Christian Scripture* [2001]; R. Kuntzmann, ed., *Typologie biblique: De quelques figures vives* [2002].) G. R. OSBORNE

Tyrannus ti-rah′uhs (Τύραννος *G5598*, "tyrant" [i.e., a ruler with absolute powers, not necessarily a despot]). An Ephesian in whose hall PAUL lectured (Acts 19:9). When the Jews of EPHESUS opposed Paul's teaching in the synagogue, where he had boldly preached for three months about the king-

Harbor road leading to the theater at Ephesus. Some suggest the hall of Tyrannus, where Paul taught, was along this road not far from the theater.

dom of God, he and his followers withdrew to the lecture hall of Tyrannus. Here he reasoned daily for two years. CODEX BEZAE (D, supported by a few witnesses) adds, "from the fifth hour to the tenth," meaning approximately from 11:00 a.m. to 4:00 p.m. If this is correct, Paul took advantage of the hottest hours of the day when most people rested after the midday meal. The hall would normally be vacant, and perhaps rent cheaper, after Tyrannus, or whoever the teacher was, lectured in the cooler morning hours (see Martial, *Epigrams* 9.68; 12.57; Juvenal, *Satires* 7.222–26). This would allow Paul to work at his own trade during business hours (Acts 20:34; 1 Cor. 4:12). Then, instead of resting, he engaged in mission work and apologetics when those in trades and business were at leisure to hear him. As a result, "all the Jews and Greeks who lived in the province of Asia heard the word of the Lord" (Acts 19:10).

It is not certain just who Tyrannus was. Lecture halls could be found in gymnasia in every Greek city (see GYMNASIUM); here a philosopher, orator, or poet could expound his views or give a recitation. Tyrannus may have been a Greek rhetorician living in Ephesus at that time, having his own private lecture hall. Meyer thinks he was a Jewish rabbi in whose private synagogue Paul and his doctrines were more secure from annoyance than in the public synagogue (H. A. W. Meyer, *Critical and Exegetical Handbook to the Acts of the Apostles*, 4th ed. [1869], 368). It may be that the "hall of Tyrannus" was either a building for hire, named after its owner, or the private residence of a sympathetic donor. Whatever the case, Paul's regular and unmolested use of the room for two years, with such a wide hearing, indicates his exclusive use of a spacious, well-situated room for a period of each day. (See also W. M. Ramsay, *The Church in the Roman Empire before A.D. 170* [1893], 152; id., *St. Paul the Traveller and Roman Citizen*, 8th ed. [1905], 271; F. F. Bruce, *The Acts of the Apostles: The Greek Text with Introduction and Commentary*, 3d ed. [1990], 408.)   A. M. Ross

Tyre tīr (צוֹר H7450, "rock"; Τύρος G5602). A famous port city in PHOENICIA, some 25 mi. S from the sister port of SIDON and 15 mi. N of the modern Lebanese border with Israel. It is a natural geographical frontier. Behind Tyre, the high coherent spine of the LEBANON Range is already broken down into the confused hill country that continues S to form the uplands of GALILEE, and then, with the sole break of the ESDRAELON Plain, to build the hill country of Ephraim and Judah. A dozen miles S of Tyre, a seaward thrust of hills and promontories forms a natural wall. It marks the modern border, a score of miles S of which lies the great Israeli port of Haifa. Both Tyre and Sidon still function as ports, but the ruins of Tyre are far more extensive and the subject of major archaeological investigation and excavation.

The Greek historian HERODOTUS (c. 490–430 B.C.) reports that in a visit to Tyre the priests of the temple dedicated to Heracles claimed that the city "had already stood for two thousand three hundred years" (*Hist.* 2.44). Other sources date its founding later, but the missing factor in all such dating is the exact time of the coming of the Phoenicians to the coastal strip between the Lebanon mountains and the coast. Excavation at more than one point of settlement on the coast reveals a Neolithic layer under the mass of Phoenician remains, themselves heavily overlaid by the structures of Greeks, Romans, and sometimes Crusaders, a phenomenon visible from Byblos (Gebal) to Tyre. The Phoenicians, like the Greeks, were not a national unit, and never achieved anything like unity. Like the Greeks they were organized in city states, and rival claimants in historical tradition might fix varied points for a city's significant beginning.

Isaiah seems to imply that Tyre was a colony of Sidon (Isa. 23:1–2, 12). She was a "Virgin Daughter of Sidon," according to the prophet, and the phrase "Sidonian goods" in Homer might imply that Sidon was the more ancient city. "Then she went down to her fragrant chamber where were her embroidered robes, the work of Sidonian women, whom Alexandros himself brought from Sidon when he sailed over the wide sea" (*Iliad* 6.288–90). Homer mentions Sidon several times, but not Tyre. In Latin authors, the adjective "Sidonian" is often attached to Tyre. Dido, for example, daughter of Belus of Tyre, is called by Vergil "Sidonian Dido." The TELL EL-AMARNA letters, from the 14th cent. B.C., contain an appeal from the local governor of Tyre asking for help against the invading HABIRU. Whoever these invaders were, the appeal addressed to Amenhotep IV shows that Egyptian power, having penetrated so far N, was wavering on the Phoenician coast, its strength too far extended. JOSHUA assigned Tyre to the tribe of ASHER, but it does not appear likely that the Hebrew invasion reached so northern a locality (Josh. 19:29; 2 Sam. 24:7).

There are no clear records over the next three or four centuries, but history becomes sharp and definite with HIRAM, king of Tyre and friend of DAVID. Hiram seems to have enjoyed an extraordinarily long reign, for he is mentioned first when he sent cedar and craftsmen to David (2 Sam. 5:11), and later when he did the same for SOLOMON (1 Ki. 5:1). Tyre seems to have been the center of Phoenician power at the time, for the Sidonians are described in the same context where Hiram's servants and masons of Gebal, the ancient Byblos, are also listed. This town is 75 mi. N of Beirut. It is interesting to note that ETHBAAL, reputed to be a grandson of Hiram, is identified as king of the Sidonians a century later (1 Ki. 16:31). Power

In this scene of the sack of Tyre by the Assyrians in the 9th cent. B.C., goods from the defeated city are ferried to the mainland, where they are unloaded and then carried as tribute to Shalmaneser III, king of Assyria. (Copy of bronze decoration from the gates of Shalmaneser's palace in Balawat.)

would appear to have oscillated between the two great ports. The canny Hiram profited greatly from the partnership with Israel. As the famous papyrus of Wenamon shows, the princes of the Phoenicians were preeminently businessmen, and it is clear that Solomon gravely embarrassed Israel by his heavy payments of wheat and oil (5:11), his supply of manpower for the Tyrian lumbering, and his unwise surrender of twenty Galilean centers of population to the northern power (9:10–13). Hiram, however, later expressed his dissatisfaction with the Galilee acquisitions, and it is possibly an indication that Solomon had exercised a certain native shrewdness.

Together the two monarchs established a trade partnership based on the Gulf of AQABAH, to the N of which Solomon had his ore-smelting plants. Hiram was glad to trade Phoenician skill in shipbuilding and navigation for ready access across Hebrew territory to the RED SEA and the trade routes to OPHIR, INDIA, and Ceylon. In addition to the CEDAR timber, which was the first occasion of the commercial contacts with Israel, Tyre also traded in the incomparable PURPLE dye made from the murex shellfish on her coast. Timber, DYE, dyed cloth, a mighty carrying trade, her cargoes of TIN and tin ore from Cornwall, SILVER from SPAIN, and COPPER from CYPRUS made the Tyre of Hiram one of the great commercial cities of the ancient world.

As far as the fragmentary record can be pieced together, it would appear that grave dynastic strife followed the stability of Hiram's long reign. The shift of power to Sidon under Ethbaal has been noted above. It was the daughter of Ethbaal who became AHAB's notorious queen, JEZEBEL, a dynastic marriage of convenience, which marked the transfer of the profitable trading partnership established and exploited by Solomon to the northern kingdom of the now sundered Hebrew people. Tyre and Phoenicia generally were poor in agricultural land, and the primary products of Israel were the natural exchange for her luxury goods.

Throughout the long two centuries of Assyrian domination in the ANE, Tyre had her share in common with other communities of aggression and strife, but her naval power and her almost impregnable position on her offshore island gave her a measure of immunity. It is significant that she contrived to break free from the dominance of NINEVEH a generation before that last stronghold of the Assyrian imperialist kings fell in the closing decade of the 7th cent. B.C. The date was either 612 or 606 B.C. This was another Golden Age of Tyrian affluence and power. Ezekiel's chapters of stern denunciation give a striking picture of the wealth, might, and varied trade that gathered around the Phoenician port (Ezek. 28–29). When BABYLON succeeded Nineveh as the great aggressor of the ANE, Tyre resisted NEBUCHADNEZZAR, but the strain of the long siege, the drain of her wealth and manpower, and the disruption of her commerce over this period of war ended the dominance of the great Phoenician port.

Tyre appears to have endured a time of dependence upon Egypt, then the rule of Babylon, and then that of Persia, which succeeded to Babylon's empire and pattern of command. Ezra 3:7 quotes an order of Cyrus II to Tyre to supply cedar for the restoration of the temple in Jerusalem, which the Persian monarch had sanctioned. Lebanon cedar at this time must have been increasingly scarce. The mountain forests had already suffered at least seven centuries of exploitation. Seafaring, however, remained a Tyrian expertise, and there is evidence that the mad Cambyses II conscripted a Tyrian fleet for his assault on Egypt, and that Tyrian galleys also sailed with the ill-fated Persian expedition against Greece, which the Greeks shattered at Salamis in 480 B.C.

In 332 B.C., in the course of his march through the crumbling Persian empire, Alexander the Great appeared before Tyre, and the city, confident in her strong position, closed her gates against the small Macedonian army. The siege that followed became one of the epic stories of military history. Alexander built a causeway across the narrow strait, which still remains the core of the wedge-shaped promontory that to this day attaches the ancient island site of Tyre to the mainland. The modern town occupies the shore and the artificial isthmus. It was only by this vast engineering feat and the costly assault at the end that Alexander took Tyre. Ezekiel's prophecy came true, and the great city became a drying place for the nets of fishermen (Ezek. 26:5, 14; 47:10).

The site, however, retained its old prestige, and Tyre made a measure of recovery and functioned for a time as a republic. She recognized the rising star of Rome, established early political relations with the Roman republic, and retained her independence until Augustus and the empire. When the prince absorbed Tyre into his provincial system in 20 B.C., the city disappeared from history.

The remains, uncovered with some care, are extensive, and the stratification reads like a history of the whole crowded and historic coast. The ruin of Phoenician docks and warehouses lies beneath the building of Greeks and Romans. An odd feature of the Greek period is an oblong theater, unique in the Mediterranean world. A fine 1st-cent. pavement, a mosaic-floored street of shops and colonnades, has special interest, for it dates from the time when Christ, following the hill paths from Galilee, visited the Phoenician coast. He might have trod this pavement on his further journey N. Today the hostile frontier lies across his path.

(See further W. B. Fleming, *The History of Tyre* [1915]; N. Jidejian, *Tyre through the Ages*; [1969]; P. M. Bikai, *The Pottery of Tyre* [1978]; R. A. Hanson, *Tyrian Influence in the Upper Galilee* [1980]; H. J. Katzenstein, *The History of Tyre, from the Beginning of the Second Millenium B.C.E. until the Fall of the Neo-Babylonian Empire in 539 B.C.E.*, 2nd ed. [1997]; M. Alonso Corral, *Ezekiel's Oracles against Tyre: Historical Reality and Motivations* [2002]; R. R. Lessing, *Interpreting Discontinuity: Isaiah's Tyre Oracle* [2004]; *ABD*, 6:686–92.) E. M. Blaiklock

Tyre, Ladder of. See Ladder of Tyre.

Tyropoeon Valley ti-roh´pee-uhn. See Jerusalem.

tzaddi tsahd´ee. KJV form of tsadhe.

The Aramaic inscription on this marble plaque from the late Second Temple Period refers to the transferring of the bones of King Uzziah to a new tomb on the Mount of Olives.

U

Ucal yoo'kuhl (אֻכָל *H432*, meaning uncertain). TNIV Ukal. One of two men—perhaps sons, disciples, or contemporaries—to whom Agur addressed his oracular sayings; the other was Ithiel (Prov. 30:1). The name Ucal is not found anywhere else in the OT; moreover, neither the Septuagint nor the Vulgate interprets the Hebrew words *ʾîtîʾēl* and *ʾukāl* as proper names. For these and other considerations many scholars revocalize the text and, instead of *wĕʾukāl*, read *wāʾēkel* ("and I faint"; cf. NIV mg.) or *wayyûkāl* ("and will I prevail?"; cf. NRSV, TNIV) or the like. See also Ithiel #2. S. Barabas

Uel yoo'uhl (אוּאֵל *H198*, perhaps "will of God"; so BDB, 15, and J. D. Fowler, *Theophoric Personal Names in Ancient Hebrew* [1988], 124, but see *HALOT*, 1:20]). One of the descendants of Bani who agreed to put away their foreign wives (Ezra 10:34; called "Joel" in 1 Esd. 9:34 [KJV, "Juel"]).

Ugarit oo'guh-rit, yoo-gahr'it. An important maritime city (modern Tell Ras Shamra), situated in N Syria, 50 nautical mi. E of the point of Cyprus. The bay on which it was located was known to the Greeks as Leukos Limen ("White Harbor," modern Minet el-Beida). During the Bronze Age, copper ore passed through Ugarit en route from Cyprus to Mesopotamia. Ugarit had important contacts with the Hittites of Asia Minor and with the Egyptians. It served as the crossroads between Mediterranean culture and the world of the Sumerians and Akkadians in Mesopotamia. With the coming of the Iron Age to the ANE, copper lost its importance and Ugarit lost its position as a major trading port.

The modern discovery of Ras Shamra dates from 1928, when a Syrian peasant accidentally plowed up a flagstone that covered a subterranean passageway. Charles Virolleaud, director of Archaeological Works in Syria and Lebanon, then administered by the French, excavated the site, which proved to be a burial chamber. Pieces of Cypro-Mycenaean pottery were found in the tomb, but the initial dig was not otherwise productive. The systematic excavation of Ras Shamra began in 1929 when Claude F. A. Schaeffer of the Strasbourg Museum and his associate George Chenet conducted a French expedition at the site. Work continued for several months each year until the outbreak of World War II, and it was resumed in 1950 following the war. Excavations have brought to light the royal tombs of Ugarit, two large temples, and artifacts illustrating international commerce among Ugarit, Egypt, Mesopotamia, the Hittites of Asia Minor, and the Cretan-Mycenaean areas. The most significant discovery was the library with inscriptions in several ANE languages, including a previously unknown Semitic language now called Ugaritic, written in an alphabetic cuneiform script. Through the efforts of Charles Virolleaud, Edouard Dhorme of the École Biblique, and Hans Bauer of Halle, the alphabet was deciphered. See languages of the ANE II.F.

Excavations indicate that the history of Ugarit extended back as far as the 5th or 6th millennium B.C. Schaeffer numbered five levels of occupation, the lowest of which contained flint and bone implements of a prepottery, Neolithic people. The fourth or Chalcolithic level yielded fine examples of painted ceramics of the type known as Halafian (from Tell Halaf, where they were first identified). During the latter half of the 3rd millennium the city identified as Level III was destroyed by fire. The people who next occupied the site used the type of pottery that bears the name of Khirbet Kerak. Most of Schaeffer's work—and that part more directly related to biblical studies—was on the top two levels, Strata II (2100–1600) and I

Syrian cylinder seal made of hematite (18th cent. B.C.), with enlarged reproduction below. The center figure is the weather god (prob. El or Hadad-Baal), depicted as a Canaanite warrior in the smiting posture (center), brandishing a mace in one hand and holding an ax and the serpent in the other.

(1600–1200). The flowering of Ugaritic literature and culture took place during the time represented by Level I.

Of several hundred Ugaritic texts discovered, the epics found in the library of King Niqmad II, who is known to have paid tribute to the Hittite King Suppiluliuma I (c. 1380–1340 B.C.), are of greatest interest. The epics probably had an earlier oral form, but the copies found in Ugarit date from the 14th cent. They illustrate the religious ideas and mythology of the Canaanites that the Israelites encountered in the land of CANAAN or PALESTINE.

The *Baal Epic* describes a series of encounters between BAAL and his rivals Yam ("sea") and Mot ("death"). As the epic begins, Yam demands recognition as the supreme lord of mankind. The waves of the sea, lashing against the seashore, could be interpreted as Yam's claim of the land for himself. Similarly, the flooding of rivers would be looked upon as his work. For a time Yam seemed the undisputed lord. He had a "house" (hence an abode, a temple) of his own, and Baal did not. Baal was the storm god (also known as HADAD, or Baal Hadad) who showed his claim on the land by the thunder and lightning and by the storms that brought rain to the earth. The battle between Yam and Baal was decided in Baal's favor when the artisan gods, Kothar-wa-Khasis, gave Baal two magical maces with which to attack his rival. Baal was successful. Yam was destroyed and Anat (ANATH), Baal's sister, proceeded to annihilate his foes.

After some hesitation, EL, the head of the Ugaritic pantheon, ordered that materials be gathered to build a house for Baal. Cedar wood was brought from LEBANON (as it was for Solomon's TEMPLE), and within seven days Kothar-wa-Khasis built the house. Baal traveled from city to city announcing his victory and claiming each city as part of his realm. From the netherworld, however, Mot issued a further challenge to Baal. After some insistence, Baal journeyed to the netherworld, and while he was there the world above became dry and barren: the fields did not produce their crops, and animals and humans could bear no young. Anat determined to secure Baal's release. Finally the Sun goddess, who visited the netherworld each night, brought Baal back on one of her appointed rounds. Baal returned to his domain above, accompanied by thunder and lightning and the storms which they heralded.

Baal, representing life, and Mot, representing death, provide imagery for the ideas of conflict between LIGHT and DARKNESS, LIFE and DEATH. Death is often personified in the Bible. The last enemy to be destroyed is death (1 Cor. 15:26). Death and HADES are flung into the LAKE OF FIRE (Rev. 20:14). Biblical MONOTHEISM could not picture Death as an evil god, a rival of Yahweh as Mot was a rival of Baal among the Canaanites. It did, however, employ the concept of battle as a figure of speech to declare the victory of God over the power of death. See WARRIOR, DIVINE.

The *Keret Epic* tells of a prosperous and godly king who was distressed because he had no heir. He had lost a succession of wives and feared that his line would soon become extinct. The god El appeared to Keret in a dream and ordered him to mobilize his armies and proceed to the land of Udm and demand the hand of Huriya, the beautiful daughter of King Pabil. After making appropriate vows to the goddess Athirat, Pabil marched against Udm and besieged the capital city of Pabil. Pabil offered tribute to Keret, but Keret insisted that the siege would be lifted only if the fair Huriya were offered as his wife. Reluctantly Pabil gave his daughter to Keret, and in due time Keret was blessed with sons and daughters of his own.

Keret, however, forgot his vow to Athirat, and the goddess caused him to fall sick. The youngest son and daughter, Elhu and Thitmanet, were genuinely grieved at their father's condition, but the sixth son Yassib thought only of his own prospects as his father's heir. The god El, however, intervened to restore Keret's health. Here the epic breaks off, but its conclusion may be surmised. The faithless Yassib would certainly have been disinherited, and the faithful Elhu and Thitmanet would have been rewarded. Doubtless Elhu would succeed to the throne after Keret died in a ripe old age. The idea of the elder brother losing his rights in favor of a younger brother is common in the biblical record. ESAU, the firstborn, lost his birthright to JACOB (Gen. 25:29–34). In blessing JOSEPH's sons, JACOB gave his best blessing to EPHRAIM rather than to the firstborn, MANASSEH (48:14).

The *Aqhat Epic* tells of a son of the pious King Danel (a variant of the name DANIEL) who accidentally acquired a bow which was meant for the goddess Anat. The goddess was so anxious to get the bow from the lad that she offered him riches and immortality in exchange for it. Aqhat, however, did not recognize the girl who spoke to him as a goddess, and he dismissed her promises as meaningless. Anat then decided to use force to get her bow. She employed a ruffian, Yatpun, to knock out Aqhat and take the bow. The breath of life was knocked out of Aqhat, with the result that he died, much to Anat's dismay. The bow was dropped into the sea, so Anat did not get it after all. A vulture ate the body of Aqhat, and his death was mourned by his father Danel and sister Pigat. The story breaks off here, but one can be sure that it went on to tell how Pigat identified the murderer of her brother and brought about his death in retaliation.

The Ugaritic texts give us firsthand information on the Baal cult and on the ideas and ideals of the people of Canaan at the time of the biblical patriarchs. Sacrifices mentioned in these documents bear names similar to those of the biblical sacrificial system. The Ugaritic texts speak of burnt offerings, whole burnt offerings, trespass offerings, wave offerings, peace offerings, firstfruits offerings, new moon offerings, and others. As in the biblical sacrifices, it was necessary that animals offered be without blemish.

Although the vocabulary is similar to that found in the Hebrew Bible, the religious meaning is quite different. Offerings were made to Baal and a host of other gods at Ugarit, while the Israelite religion prescribed the worship of Yahweh alone. While biblical offerings were regularized in the Mosaic law, particularly the book of Leviticus, biblical sacrifices go back to the earliest times. CAIN and ABEL (Gen. 4:3–4), NOAH (8:20), and the line of ABRAHAM (15:9–10) all offered sacrifices prior to the giving of the law. Some elements of the Mosaic law seem to be directed against practices documented in the Ugaritic texts. The epic entitled *The Birth of the Beautiful and Gracious Gods* describes a ritual of seething a kid in its mother's milk in order to procure rain for the parched soil of Canaan. The rite was specifically forbidden in Israelite law (Exod. 23:19; 34:26), a fact which gives rise to the Jewish dietary insistence that milk products and meat products must not be mixed.

The prophetic leaders of Israel were concerned that the people resist the temptation to adopt Canaanite religious practices. Since the Ugaritic texts were written in a language closely related to Hebrew, their study provides a wealth of information for the elucidation of the biblical text. Similar figurative expressions are used in the bible and Ugarit. Baal, like Yahweh (cf. Ps. 68:4, 33), rides the clouds. Thunder is his voice (cf. Ps. 29:3). When the writer of the biblical flood story wanted to describe the torrents of rain that fell on earth, he used the poetic expression, "the windows of the heavens were opened" (Gen. 7:11 NRSV). In Ugarit we read that Baal opened a window of his celestial house, uttered his voice, and thus sent a thunderstorm to the world (*Baal* II. vi. 25–35).

The mythological figure Lotan (biblical LEVIATHAN) appears in the Ugaritic texts as an enemy of Baal. The *Baal Epic* (I. i. 28–30) says, "When thou smotest Lotan, the slippery (serpent), (and) madest an end of the wriggling serpent, the tyrant (with seven heads)...." The words are reminiscent of Isa. 27:1: "In that day, / the LORD [i.e., Yahweh] will punish with his sword, / his fierce, great and powerful sword, / Leviathan the gliding serpent, / Leviathan the coiling serpent; / he will slay the monster of the sea." Biblical Leviathan, like Ugaritic Lotan, had a multiplicity of heads: "It was you who crushed the heads of Leviathan" (Ps. 74:14). Biblical Leviathan, unlike his Ugaritic counterpart, was not a god. Leviathan was a rebellious creature of Yahweh. He represents the forces of evil that come under divine judgment. The high ethical monotheism of the Israelites is not paralleled at Ugarit. Both Israel and Ugarit had a common linguistic and cultural heritage, but Israel alone contributed her high religion to the rest of mankind.

Ugarit has provided textual and linguistic material for the Semitic scholar. The Hebrew word *bāmâ* H1195 is used often in the OT (mostly in the pl.) with the sense of "high place." In Ugaritic texts, however, the cognate word can signify the back of a person or animal, and this usage makes good sense in Deut. 33:29, "Your enemies shall come fawning to you; and you shall tread on their backs" (NRSV; cf. NIV mg.). Artistic portrayals from the ANE frequently depict a conqueror with his foot on the back of his victim, so the rendering "backs" here is more meaningful than "high places."

In DAVID's lament over the death of SAUL and JONATHAN, he cries out: "Ye mountains of Gilboa, let there be no dew nor rain upon you, neither fields of offerings" (2 Sam. 1:21 KJV). Biblical scholars have puzzled over the expression "fields of offerings" (Heb. *śĕdê tĕrûmōt*). In the *Aqhat Epic* (C i [= *CTA* 19.1] 43–46) we read a statement that is similar to that uttered by David: "Seven years shall Baal fail, / Eight the Rider of the Clouds. / No dew, / No rain; / No welling-up of the deep, / No sweetness of Baal's voice" (*ANET*, 153). The Hebrew word for "fields" is similar to the Ugaritic word for "upsurging," and the Hebrew "offering" is similar to Ugaritic "deep." H. L. Ginsberg (in *JBL* 57 [1938]: 209–13; cf. *ANET*, 153 n. 34) suggested that David's prayer should read: "Ye mountains of Gilboa, let there be no dew nor rain upon you, neither welling up of the deep" (emending the Heb. to *śr' thwmt*; cf. RSV). The "upsurgings of the deep" were mountain springs, as we know from Ugaritic texts. Dew, rain, and mountain springs were the three sources of moisture in Syria and Palestine. David thus prayed that Mount Gilboa might be barren as a sign of mourning for Saul and Jonathan (cf. the discussion in P. K. McCarter, Jr., *II Samuel*, AB 9 [1984], 69–71).

(See further J. Gray, *The Legacy of Canaan* [1957]; C. F. Pfeiffer, *Ras Shamra and the Bible* [1962]; J. C. L. Gibson, *Canaanite Myths and Legends*, 2nd ed. [1978; orig. by G. R. Driver, 1956]; L. R. Fisher, ed., *Ras Shamra Parallels: The Texts from Ugarit and the Hebrew Bible*, 3 vols. [1971–81]; G. D. Young, ed., *Ugarit in Retrospect: Fifty Years of Ugarit and Ugaritic* [1981]; P. C. Craigie, *Ugarit and the Old Testament* [1983]; A. Curtis, *Ugarit (Ras Shamra)* [1985]; B. Margalit, *The Ugaritic Poem of Aqht: Text, Translation, Commentary* [1989]; M. S. Smith, *The Ugaritic Baal Cycle. Vol. 1: Introduction with Text, Translation and Commentary of KTU 1.1–1.2* [1994]; W. G. E. Watson and N. Wyatt, eds., *Handbook of Ugaritic Studies* [1999]; M. S. Smith, *The Origins of Biblical Monotheism: Israel's Polytheistic Background and the Ugaritic Texts* [2001]; id., *Untold Stories: The Bible and Ugaritic Studies in the Twentieth Century* [2001]; D. Pardee, *Ritual and Cult at Ugarit* [2002]; N. Wyatt, *Religious Texts from Ugarit*, 2nd ed. [2002]; W. H. van Soldt, *The Topography of the City-State of Ugarit* [2005]; W. M. Schniedewind and J. H. Hunt, *A Primer on Ugaritic Language, Culture, and Literature* [2007].)   C. F. PFEIFFER

Ukal yoo'kuhl. TNIV form of UCAL.

Ulai yoo'li (אוּלַי H217, from Assyr. *Ulaia*, known to classical authors as Εὐλαῖος, Lat. *Eulaeus*). A stream or artificial irrigation canal near SUSA, capital of ELAM (PLACE) in SW PERSIA, where DANIEL received the vision of a two-horned ram and a goat (Dan. 8:2, 16; the LXX and other ancient versions describe Ulai as a "gate" rather than a watercourse). Owing to topographical change, which can be swift and confusing in sand and alluvial silt, the identification of Ulai is uncertain. D. J. Wiseman (in *NBD*, 1298) suggests that the reference is to two present-day rivers, the upper Kherkhah and the lower Karun, which in ancient times may have been a single stream debouching into the delta at the head of the Persian Gulf. The river appears in reliefs of Ashurbanipal's assault on Susa in 640 B.C.; with sanguinary relish typical of Assyrian inscriptions, the monarch claims to have reddened the Ulai with blood. E. M. Blaiklock

Ulam yoo'luhm (אוּלָם H220, perhaps "first, leader"). (1) Son of Peresh (or of Sheresh), grandson of Makir, and great-grandson of Manasseh (1 Chr. 7:16–17).
(2) Firstborn son of Eshek and descendant of Benjamin through Saul (1 Chr. 8:39). Ulam's sons "were brave warriors who could handle the bow," and his descendants were numerous (v. 40).

ulcer. A breakdown of skin or mucous membrane in a localized area with gradual destruction of the flesh underneath. This English term is used by the NRSV once to render Hebrew *ʿōpel* H6754 (Deut. 28:27). See tumor. R. H. Pousma

Ulla uhl'uh (עֻלָּא H6587, possibly "the small one"). Descendant of Asher (1 Chr. 7:39). Ulla's place in the genealogy is left unstated, and some scholars believe the name is a textual corruption for some other Asherite mentioned earlier, such as Amal (v. 35).

Ummah uhm'uh (עֻמָּה H6646, possibly "connection" or "near"). A town on the Mediterranean coast within the tribal territory of Asher (Josh. 19:30). Ummah was apparently between Aczib and Aphek on the Plain of Acco, but its precise location is unknown. Because Acco, an important city allotted to Asher (cf. Jdg. 1:31), is not otherwise included in the list of Asherite towns in Josh. 19:24–31, many scholars believe that Ummah here is a scribal corruption for Acco (a reading that has slight support in the Gk. textual tradition; see *BHS* apparatus).

umpire. See daysman.

uncial un'shuhl. An ancient form of Greek (and Latin) handwriting based on the shapes of capital letters; the term is also applied to mss written with this type of writing. See text and manuscripts (NT) II.B.

uncircumcised. In the Bible this word is used both literally and figuratively (in figurative passages, modern versions sometimes use other terms). Uncircumcision represented unbelief and disobedience to the covenant of God (Jer. 6:10; 9:25). Rebellious Israelites have an "uncircumcised heart"; and those whose ears are closed are said to have "uncircumcised ears" (Lev. 26:41; Jer. 6:10). In the NT, unbelieving Jews, though physically circumcised, are said to be spiritually uncircumcised (Rom. 2:28–29); while Gentiles, though physically uncircumcised, are regarded as circumcised if they keep the righteousness of the law (2:25–27). Christ makes no distinction between the circumcised and the uncircumcised (1 Cor. 7:19; Gal. 5:6; 6:15; Col. 3:11); if regenerated, they are united in one body of believers (Eph. 2:11–22). Circumcision has nothing to do with justification, for Abraham was justified while still uncircumcised (Rom. 4:9–12). S. Barabas

uncle. This English term renders Hebrew *dôd* H1856, referring specifically to a father's brother (Lev. 20:20 et al., although in some passages the precise relationship is not made explicit). In the Song of Solomon, the Hebrew is used regularly with the meaning "beloved, lover" (Cant. 1:13–14 et al.; in the pl. form *dôdîm* it can mean "love," Prov. 7:18 et al.). The connection between these two meanings, according to some, lies in the fact that a woman often married the son of her father's brother (cf. *HALOT*, 1:215, meaning #1).

uncleanness. The notion of ceremonial uncleanness or defilement is expressed in Hebrew primarily with the verb *ṭāmēʾ* H3237 and its cognates (Lev. 11:24–47 et al.; various analogous terms are also used). In the NT, the Greek noun for "uncleanness" is *akatharsia* G174 (Matt. 23:27 et al.; adj. *akathartos* G176, 10:1 et al.), but the verb *koinoō* G3124, which literally means "to make common," can have the force of destroying holiness, thus, "to make [or count as] unclean" (Mk. 7:15 et al.; adj. *koinos* G3123, v. 2 et al.; note the use of *akathartos* together with *koinos* in Acts 10:14, 18; 11:8). See also CLEAN; PURITY.

I. The meaning of the concept. Persons, foods, places, and objects could all be unclean. The uncleanness could be inherent or acquired by contamination. "In the minds of the ancients there was a close connection between the notion of purity or cleanness and the notion of being consecrated to God. There was a mysterious and frightening force inherent in things which were impure and in things which were sacred, and these two forces acted on everything with which they came into contact, placing the objects or persons which touched them under a kind of interdict. Both what was impure and what was consecrated were alike 'untouchable', and any person who touched them became himself 'untouchable'" (R. de Vaux, *Ancient Israel* [1961], 460). We are dealing with concepts that go back into the infancy of humanity and that have been modified in the OT, where there is a wide area between the holy and the impure. In the NT the concept of uncleanness is dealt with differently: not that which goes into a person, but what comes out of him, is what defiles him (Mk. 7:18–20); similarly, nothing God has made is essentially unclean (Acts 10:13–15; 1 Tim. 4:4–5).

Burial site on the Mount of Olives. Human bones were among the items that could make a person ceremonially unclean by contact.

II. Things that make unclean. (a) Animals are either clean or unclean, the uncleanness being imparted by eating them or touching their dead bodies (Lev. 11; Deut. 14:3–20). Whatever motivations may be offered by readers for the distinction, according to the Bible it lies essentially in God's decree.

(b) All bodies that died of natural causes imparted impurity, whether the body was of a person (Num. 19:11), of an impure animal (Lev. 11:4–8, 24–28), or of a pure animal (11:39–40). The reason behind this principle may be that death, the outcome of human sin, is by its very nature a negation of God's holiness. The killing of a pure animal for food, however, did not render it impure; and on analogy, presumably, a man taking part in a holy war for the God of Israel would not be rendered impure by those he killed.

(c) All forbidden sexual unions rendered impure anyone participating in them (Lev. 18). All sexual perversions (cf. Rom. 1:26–27) are a rebellion against the God-created order of nature and therefore a stepping out of the sphere of holiness.

(d) Virtually everything linked with sex could impart uncleanness. Some acts of worship required abstention from sexual relationships (Exod. 19:15; 1 Sam. 21:4–5). The sexual act was seen as communicating uncleanness (Lev. 15:16–18), though Jewish tradition, based on v. 31, makes it refer merely to those coming into contact with anything belonging to the sanctuary. Menstruation (15:19–24), childbirth (12:1–5), and various discharges from the sexual organs (15:1–12, 25–27) created uncleanness.

(e) An "infectious skin disease" made a person seriously unclean (Lev. 13:1–46). Especially if taken with the teaching of Hag. 2:11–14, these instructions suggest that uncleanness has a stronger effect than cleanness; the divine command was thus intended to impress on people how serious impurity is. No one can escape it.

III. Cleansing from uncleanness. The simpler forms of uncleanness were dealt with by washing; these included the simpler sexual impurities (Lev. 15:5–12, 16–18, 21–24, 27) and those created by an animal carcass (11:24–28, 39–40). The one who touched a human corpse, however, had to take advantage of the sacrifice of the red heifer (Num. 19:11–19). For the cured leper, for the mother after childbirth, and for certain sexual discharges a sacrifice had to be brought (Lev. 12:6–8; 14:1–20; 15:13–15, 29–30). The ritual of the Day of Atonement was intended to cleanse the defilement the sanctuary might have contracted, and by the intertestamental period this notion was extended to all the unintentional impurities of the people. Deliberately contracted uncleanness or the refusal to seek cleansing (Num. 19:20–22) brought "cutting off" from the people. In essence there was virtually no difference between uncleanness and sin considered as an unintentional falling short. A connection may be seen in what one may call "ritual impurity" contracted by the person who burned the carcasses of the sin offerings on the Day of Atonement (Lev. 16:28) and by those involved in the burning of the red heifer and the collecting of its ashes (Num. 19:8, 10).

IV. The spiritualizing of the concept. In the PROPHETS there is a deepening of the concept. It is expressed especially in Isaiah's cry, "I am a man of unclean lips" (Isa. 6:5), and in his confession, "All of us have become like one who is unclean, / and all our righteous acts are like filthy rags" (64:6). Similarly, his picture of God's restoration in 35:8, "The unclean will not journey on it [*i.e.*, on the Way of Holiness]," has obviously a moral rather than a ritual implication. Unfortunately, in the postexilic period ever-increasing stress came to be laid on the avoidance of formal uncleanness. It was an obsession both with the Qumran Covenanters (see DEAD SEA SCROLLS) and the PHARISEES. In the later Talmudic developments questions of purity and impurity provide some of the most complex sections of rabbinic legislation. In the church, however, Christ's teaching was continued. The decisions of the apostolic gathering in Jerusalem were based on regard for those Jews who were law-bound (Acts 15:19–21). Romans 14:14 is PAUL's expression of the fact that uncleanness is something essentially spiritual in its nature (cf. Heb. 12:15). The ritual of washing has become purely pictorial, and WATER becomes a symbol of the word (Eph. 5:26). H. L. ELLISON

unction. This English term, meaning "the act of anointing," is used once by the KJV with reference to the effect of the Spirit's presence upon the believer (1 Jn. 2:20). See ANOINT; HOLY SPIRIT III.H.

understanding. See SPIRITS IV.

undersetter. This archaic English term is used by the KJV in one passage referring to the supports of the laver in Solomon's TEMPLE (1 Ki. 7:30, 34).

underworld. See HADES.

unforgivable sin. See FORGIVENESS V; HOLY SPIRIT III.B; UNPARDONABLE SIN.

unicorn. A mythical horselike beast having a single horn growing from the center of its forehead. Following the SEPTUAGINT (which has *monokerōs* in the relevant passages), the KJV wrongly uses "unicorn" as the rendering of Hebrew *rĕʾēm* H8028 (Num. 23:22 et al.). See WILD OX.

union with Christ. While the expression "union with Christ" does not occur in the Bible, it describes the central reality in the salvation revealed there, from its eternal design to its eschatological consummation.

Human beings were created in God's image, to live in fellowship and communion (COVENANT) with God, trusting his promises and obeying his commands, loving and being loved. SIN, however, destroyed this fellowship bond, by rendering humanity guilty and corrupt, and so, alienated from God and deserving of DEATH. In response, God, as Savior, undertakes to restore and perfect the life and communion lost. This saving purpose, intimated already in Gen. 3:14–15, unfolds toward its fulfillment primarily in God's ongoing dealings with Israel as his covenant people, a bond expressed variously but perhaps most evocatively in the description of God himself as "the portion" of his people (Pss. 73:26; 119:57; Jer. 10:16); reciprocally, they are "the LORD's portion" (Deut 32:9; cf. Isa. 53:12, with anticipatory reference to Christ). The climactic realization of this covenantal bond between the triune God and the church centers in union with Christ.

This union finds its most prominent NT expression in the phrase "in Christ" or "in the

Lord" (with slight variations), occurring frequently and almost exclusively in Paul's letters (elsewhere, e.g., Jn. 14:20; 15:1–7; 1 Jn. 2:28). Scholarly debate about its meaning ranges from a purely instrumental understanding of the preposition "in" (Gk. *en* G1877) to a local or atmospheric sense, and even the notion of an actual physical union between Christ and believers (A. Schweitzer). In fact, Paul's usage is varied, its scope best gauged by the contrast between Adam and Christ (the "last Adam" or "second man," Rom. 5:12–19; 1 Cor. 15:20–23; cf. vv. 45, 47). What each does is determinative, respectively, for those "in him." For those "in Christ" this union or solidarity is all-encompassing, extending from eternity to eternity: they are united to Christ not only in their present possession of salvation but also in its past, once-for-all accomplishment (e.g., Rom. 6:3–7; 8:1; Gal. 2:20; Eph. 2:5–6; Col. 3:1–4), in their election "before the creation of the world" (Eph. 1:4, 9), and in their still future glorification (Rom. 8:17; 1 Cor. 15:22).

Present union (union in the actual appropriation of salvation) is often called "mystical" and "spiritual." But both terms are subject to misunderstanding. Involved is not a mysticism of ecstatic experience at odds with reasoned understanding; rather, it is a mystery in the NT sense of what has been hidden with God in his eternal purposes but now, finally, has been revealed in Christ, particularly through his death and resurrection, and is appropriated by faith (Rom. 16:25–26; Col. 1:26–27; 2:2). Certainly, in its full dimensions this mystery is beyond the believer's comprehension. Involved here, as much as in anything pertaining to salvation and the gospel, is that knowledge of Christ's love "that surpasses knowledge" (Eph. 3:18–19; cf. 1 Cor. 2:9).

Ephesians 5:32 highlights the intimacy of this union ("a profound mystery") by comparing it to the relationship between husband and wife. Elsewhere, other relational analogies bring out various facets of union: the foundation-cornerstone together with the other stones of a building (Eph. 2:19–22; 1 Pet. 2:5); a vine and its branches (Jn. 15:1–7); the head and the other members of the human body (1 Cor. 12:12–27; see body of Christ); the genetic tie between Adam and his posterity (Rom. 5:12–19). The climactic comparison is to the unique ontological union between Father, Son, and Spirit (Jn. 17:20–23). Similarity is not identity, but especially this inner-trinitarian analogy shows that the highest kind of union that exists for an image-bearing creature is the union of the believer with the exalted Christ. "[T]he greatest mystery of creaturely relationships is the union of the people of God with Christ. And the mystery of it is attested by nothing more than this that it is compared to the union that exists between the Father and the Son in the unity of the Godhead" (J. Murray, *Redemption: Accomplished and Applied* [1961], 169; see the whole of ch. 9 in this book for an illuminating discussion).

Mystical union is also *spiritual*, not in an immaterial, idealistic sense, but because of the activity and indwelling of the Holy Spirit. This circumscribes the mystery and protects against confusing it with other kinds of union. As spiritual, it is neither ontological (like that between the persons of the Trinity), nor hypostatic (between Christ's two natures), nor psychosomatic (between body and soul in human personality), nor somatic (between husband and wife), nor merely moral (unity in affection, understanding, purpose).

Spiritual union stems from the relationship between Christ and the Holy Spirit. Because of his resurrection and ascension, the incarnate Christ ("the last Adam") has been so transformed by the Spirit and is now in such complete possession of the Spirit that he has "become life-giving Spirit," and "the Lord [= Christ] is the Spirit" (1 Cor. 15:45; 2 Cor. 3:17). In view is a functional equation, a oneness in their activity of giving resurrection life and eschatological freedom, so that in the life of the church and within believers, Christ and the Spirit are inseparable (cf. Jn. 14:18). In Rom. 8:9–10, for example, the phrases "in the Spirit," "the Spirit in you," "belonging to Christ" (equivalent to "in Christ"), and "Christ in you" are all facets of a single union (cf. Eph. 3:16–17: to have "his Spirit in your inner being" is for "Christ ... [to] dwell in your hearts"). Union with Christ is reciprocal. Not only are believers in Christ—he is "in them" (Jn. 14:20; 17:23, 26; Col. 1:27: "Christ in you, the hope of glory"). Such union, then, is inherently *vital*; Christ indwelling is the very life of the believer (Gal. 2:20; Col. 3:4).

Especially since the Reformation, a perennially important issue, both in formulating church doctrine as well as interpreting Paul, has been the relationship between union with Christ and JUSTIFICATION (respectively, the participatory and the forensic aspects of salvation). On the one hand, these are not merely alternative or complementary metaphors for salvation. But neither may union be coordinated as just one in a series of acts, whether after or even before justification, in the application of salvation (*ordo salutis*; see SALVATION IV). Rather, as John Calvin, faithful to the NT, already has pointed the way (*Institutes of the Christian Religion* 3.1), being united to Christ by faith through "the secret energy of the Spirit" establishes the bond within which the believer, without either separation or confusion, is both reckoned righteous and renewed in righteousness. (See also M. A. Siefried in *DPL*, 433–36.)   R. B. GAFFIN, JR.

unity. Scripture portrays great richness and variety in its teaching concerning oneness and harmony. There is the unity of the believer with his Lord (see UNION WITH CHRIST), and there is the union manifested in the BODY OF CHRIST, the CHURCH, which rests eventually on a deeper unity of believers in "one Lord, one faith, one baptism." Unity with Christ is illustrated in many ways: that of husband and wife, or the stones and the building. The classic analogy is the vine and the branches (cf. Jn. 15:1–8). Apart from such unity the follower of Christ can "do nothing." The unity is his life and the ground of his action.

PAUL took special interest in the unity within the body of believers, and he did not argue for an invisible bond but for a oneness that should characterize the visible body. He recognized unity in diversity and diversity in unity, and he amplified this approach (1 Cor. 12) with the appeal to LOVE as the unifying bond (ch. 13). The apostle looked upon unity as reality already in existence, but also as a reality yet to be attained. As we are "patient, bearing with one another in love," we are then eager "to keep the unity of the Spirit" (Eph. 4:2–3). There exists this unity already, but it is the unity of the *Spirit*, and this feature relates to Paul's treatment of diversity in unity (1 Cor. 12). One should thus expect "one Lord, one faith, one baptism" (Eph. 4:5). That the real unity here described is not fully manifest in the church nor among the most ardent followers of Christ is quite clear, for Paul wrote of unity as something yet to be attained. There are varieties of gifts and offices for the building up of the body of Christ "until we all reach unity in the faith and in the knowledge of the Son of God." Then will come maturity, "the whole measure of the fullness of Christ" (4:13).   A. H. LEITCH

unity of the Bible. See BIBLE IX.

unknown god. When the apostle PAUL addressed the meeting of the AREOPAGUS in ATHENS, he said to his listeners that he had noticed how religious they were, and added: "For as I walked around and looked carefully at your objects of worship, I even found an altar with this inscription: TO AN UNKNOWN GOD [*Agnōstō theō*]. Now what you worship as something unknown I am going to proclaim to you" (Acts 17:23). The existence of such an altar, presumably built in a scrupulous attempt to include every possible deity, was an indication of the Athenians' religious sensitivity. It also betrayed a lack of religious knowledge, which Paul sought to remedy in his address (vv. 24–31).

As no comparable dedication to a single unknown deity has been found, some have questioned the existence of this inscription. However, there is evidence of inscriptions to unknown deities in the plural (Pausanias, *Description of Greece* 1.1.4 [*bōmoi de theōn te onomazomenōn Agnoston*]; Philostratus, *Appolonius of Tyana* 6.3.5; Diogenes Laertius, *Lives of the Philosophers* 1.110). It is also theorized that in a polytheistic culture, a single deity would not have been addressed, and that Paul might have altered a polytheistic inscription to fit his monotheistic concepts. On the contrary, the syncretism of the Hellenistic period, the occasional merging of Jewish ideas with pagan forms, and the tendency toward both the unifying of principles and the personifying of abstract religious concepts, provided a matrix within which such an inscription was not at all unlikely. (See E. Norden, *Agnostos Theos* [1913]; K. Lake in *BC*, 1/5: 240–46; P. W. van der Horst in *ANRW*, 2/18/2 [1989]: 1426–56; W. H. Wachob in *ABD*, 6:753–55.)   W. L. LIEFELD

Unknown Gospel. See EGERTON 2, PAPYRUS.

unknown tongue. See TONGUES, GIFT OF.

unleavened bread. Bread made without yeast. In the preparation of household bread, a piece of fermented dough from a previous baking was placed in the kneading trough along with fresh flour, kneaded into cakes, and then baked. Unleavened bread lacked the fermented dough. See LEAVEN. Unleavened bread or cakes (*maṣṣôt*, pl. of *maṣṣâ H5174*) are associated with the elements eaten at PASSOVER, the feast that commemorates the deliverance of Israel from Egypt. Only unleavened bread was to be eaten for the seven days that followed Passover (Exod. 12:15–20; 13:3–7). Some scholars think that the Feast of Unleavened Bread (seven days) which followed the Passover was originally a nature festival associated with the occasion of the barley harvest, and that it was transformed later into the historical feast, the Passover.

The prohibition of leaven eventually became most scrupulously observed. A Hebrew who did not eat unleavened bread was "cut off," that is, excommunicated from the camp of Israel. In eating unleavened bread, the Hebrews were reminded of their haste in leaving Egypt during the great exodus. They could not wait to bake bread to take with them, but carried dough in their bread troughs in their hurried flight into the desert. They baked their bread as they traveled, as do the desert BEDOUIN today. Israel, in eating the "bread of bitterness," remembered that dark night in Egypt and then began a period of one week using unleavened bread. F. E. YOUNG

Unni uhn'*i* (עֻנִּי *H6716* [Neh. 12:9 *Ketib*, עֻנּוֹ]), possibly "one who has been heard" or short form of עֲנָנְיָה *H6731*, "Yahweh has answered" [see ANANIAH]). (1) A Levite in the time of DAVID appointed among others to play the lyre (NRSV, harp) as a part of the ministrations before the ARK OF THE COVENANT (1 Chr. 15:18, 20).

(2) A Levite who served after the EXILE; he is described as an associate of MATTANIAH, the director of worship (Neh. 12:9; NRSV, "Unno," following the *Ketib*).

Unno uhn'oh. See UNNI #2.

unpardonable sin. In one of his controversies with the PHARISEES, Jesus said that blaspheming or speaking against the HOLY SPIRIT would not be forgiven (Matt. 12:31–32; Mk. 3:29; Lk. 12:10). Other apparent parallels (cf. Heb. 6:4–6; 10:26–27; 1 Jn. 5:16) should be exegeted in the light of that statement.

The threat of this sin must be understood against the promise of salvation represented always as free and complete. Such gracious redemption is magnified in the context of the "unpardonable sin." "Every sin and blasphemy will be forgiven men" (Matt. 12:31), even "a word against the Son of Man" (12:32). What is the specific sin that is set against this assurance of forgiveness? In the context it must mean that because people, by choice or by habit, confuse the Holy Spirit of God with the unclean spirit of BEELZEBUB, it is impossible for God to reach them with the message of salvation and therefore they continue to call his truth a lie. It is not that God *will not forgive* them, but that they, by destroying the very offer of the gospel, place themselves outside the possibility of forgiveness. See FORGIVENESS V; HOLY SPIRIT III.B.

A. H. LEITCH

untempered morter. This phrase is used by the KJV to render the Hebrew noun *tāpēl H9521*, which refers to plaster or whitewash (Ezek. 13:10–15; 22:28). The prophet uses this word in a metaphorical sense of the false prophets who instead of exposing and denouncing the sinful enterprises of the people weakly acquiesced to them. This is like daubing a stone wall with whitewash to give it the appearance of solidity and strength. A heavy rainstorm will destroy it. S. BARABAS

untimely birth. See BIRTH, UNTIMELY.

upharsin. See MENE, MENE, TEKEL, PARSIN.

Uphaz yoo'faz (אוּפָז *H233*, derivation unknown). An unidentified location famous for its GOLD (Jer. 10:9; Dan. 10:5 [KJV, NRSV]). In Jer. 10:9, the Aramaic and Syriac versions have OPHIR, a reading accepted by some scholars; others emend *zāhāb* *mēʾûpāz* ("gold from Uphaz") to *zāhāb mûpāz* ("fine gold"; from the verb *pāzaz* H7059, cf. 1 Ki. 10:18). In Dan. 10:5, the NIV and NJPS emend *bēketem ʾûpāz* ("with gold of Uphaz") to *bāketem ûpāz* ("with gold and refined gold, i.e., very fine gold; from the noun *paz* H7058, cf. Cant. 5:11). It remains uncertain whether a place by the name of Uphaz ever existed (see further *ABD*, 6:765).

Upper Gate. KJV, "high gate" and "higher gate." One of the gates of the TEMPLE in Jerusalem, first mentioned in the time of King JOASH. After the assassination of ATHALIAH, the young monarch was brought "from the temple of the LORD. They went into the palace through the Upper Gate [*šaʿar hāʿelyôn*] and seated the king on the royal throne" (2 Chr. 23:30; in the parallel it is called "the gate of the runners/guards" [*šaʿar hārāṣîm*, 2 Ki. 11:19; cf. v. 6]). This description is interpreted by some to mean that the Upper Gate faced S (cf. *ABD*, 6:765), but EZEKIEL uses the same name with reference to a gate that "faces north" (Ezek. 9:2, evidently the same as the "north gate" of 8:14, which according to W. Zimmerli, *Ezekiel 1* [1979], 247–48, was "on the inner raised area of the most central part of the temple").

The "Upper Gate" is probably the same as "the Upper Gate of Benjamin at the LORD's temple" (Jer. 20:2), and one of the few things mentioned regarding the reign of JOTHAM is that he "rebuilt the Upper Gate of the temple of the LORD" (2 Ki. 15:35; 2 Chr. 27:3). Some speculate that after this reconstruction it came to be known as the NEW GATE (Jer. 26:10; 36:10). Zimmerli (ibid.) distinguishes the gate mentioned in the story of Joash from the one referred to in the other passages. Whether or not these various names refer to the same gate, however, the precise location is unknown.

upper room. Traditional name given to the room where Jesus celebrated the Last Supper (see LORD'S SUPPER); accordingly, the teaching recorded in Jn. 14–16 is referred to as the Upper Room Discourse (although 14:31 seems to indicate that part of the discourse took place as the group was on its way to GETHSEMANE). The name derives from the instructions that the Lord gave to the disciples in preparation for the meal: "He [the owner of the house] will show you a large upper room [*anagaion*], furnished and ready" (Mk. 14:15; similarly Lk. 22:12). Large upper rooms with outside and inside staircases above the noise and bustle of the city are mentioned in the OT as an architectural feature of Palestinian houses (Heb. *ʿăliyyâ* H6608, 2 Ki. 1:2 et al.).

After the ASCENSION OF CHRIST, the disciples "went up into an upper room" (Acts 1:13 KJV; NIV, "went upstairs to the room"), where the disciples met for prayer (v. 14), MATTHIAS was chosen to replace JUDAS ISCARIOT (vv. 15–26), and the initial events of PENTECOST took place (ch. 2). Here, however, Luke uses a different Greek term (*hyperōon* G5673, used by the LXX to translate *ʿăliyyâ* and by Luke again with reference to other places, Acts 9:37, 39; 20:8). Many have identified the room where the Last Supper was held with the room mentioned in Acts 1, but there is no evidence that proves (or disproves) this theory. An ancient tradition identified the room of Pentecost with what is now known as the Cenacle (above the "Tomb of David" and adjacent to the Dormition Abbey), and later this place was thought to be the site of the Last Supper, but this building is no earlier than the 14th cent. (see J. Wilkinson, *Jerusalem as Jesus Knew It: Archaeology as Evidence* [1978], 164–72).

Ur (city) oor (אוּר H243, "light, flame"). Referred to in the Bible as "Ur of the Chaldeans [KJV, Chaldees]," this city in MESOPOTAMIA was the home of ABRAHAM prior to his family's migration to HARAN (Gen. 11:28, 31; 15:7; Neh. 9:7).

I. Name and location. Until 1850, "Ur of the Chaldees" was considered to be modern Urfa (EDESSA), not far from HARAN, in SE Turkey, which according to a local tradition was the place of Abraham's residence (note that the patriarch refers to the area of Haran as *ʾereṣ môladtî*, lit., "the land of my birth," Gen. 24:4, cf. v. 7). This view was revived in more recent times by Cyrus H. Gordon (in *JNES* 17 [1958]: 28–31), who interpreted the OT as implying that Abraham was a merchant prince who did business in N Mesopotamia (he places Ur at Uraʿ near Haran). He considered that the term CHALDEA can be adequately explained as a reference to this area (as he thinks is meant by Isa. 23.13). Against this view it must be noted that any tradition of Abraham at Urfa/Edessa goes back only to the 8th–9th cent. A.D. The OT scarcely implies that Abraham was a merchant or that he moved only a short distance from Ur to Haran. Moreover, "the land of my birth" (Gen. 24:4 and 7) could equally be translated "land of my kindred." There are also several places called Ura ͨ, one a seaport in CILICIA, another a HITTITE fortress in NE ANATOLIA.

In favor of a more southerly location can be cited a strong local tradition linking Abraham with both Warka (ERECH) and Kutha (Tell Ibrahim). In addition, according to Pseudo-Eupolemus (see EUPOLEMUS), Abraham was born "in the Babylonian city of Camarina, although others state that the city was named Ouric" (Euseb. *Praeparatio Evangelica* 9.17.2; see *OTP*, 2:880). By 1866 the name *U-ri* was read on several buildings and other inscriptions from the site of Tell el-Muqayyar in S Iraq, 6 mi. SE of Nasiriyah on the EUPHRATES River. This ancient city of Ur certainly lay in territory called Kaldu (Chaldea) from the early 1st millennium B.C. Since this area was normally named after the tribes living there, and no earlier general name for the area is known, it would be unscientific to call the reference to Ur "of the Chaldees" in the 2nd millennium an anachronism. The southern identification for the biblical Ur is now generally accepted. (See further A. R. Millard in *BAR* 27/3 [May-June 2001]: 52–53, 57.)

II. Excavations. In 1853–54 J. E. Taylor, British Vice-Consul at Basra, was asked by the British Museum to investigate the site of "Múgeyer," and he explored the ZIGGURAT and vicinity. A few soundings were made by R. C. Thompson in 1918 and shortly afterward by H. R. Hall; the latter, however, concentrated on Tell al-ͨUbaid, 4 mi. to the NW, where he found a circular oval with a decorated temple of Ninhursag in use from prehistoric (Ubaid) levels (c. 4000 B.C.) until the 3rd dynasty of Ur (2113–2066). From 1922 to 1934 a joint expedition of the British Museum and University Museum of Pennsylvania led by Sir C. L. Woolley excavated large areas of the site, which measured 1,200 by 675 meters and housed an estimated population of c. 34,000, possibly representing a quarter

This small clay tablet from Ur (3rd dynasty, c. 2046 B.C.) is a commercial text in cuneiform that records the purchase of plough-oxen from various merchants.

of a million persons in the whole of the Greater Ur district.

A. Ziggurat. The three-staged step PYRAMID tower built by Ur-Nammu (2113–2096) and remodeled by NABONIDUS (556–539) dominated the city. This massive structure of burnt-brick skin over a mud-brick core of 200 × 150 ft. originally stood to a height of 70 ft. above the plain, though only 50 ft. of the lowest platform now remains. There is some evidence that the different stages were each colored differently below the silver one-roomed shrine of Nannar, the moon-god (also called Sin), at the top. The terraces were planted with trees. Identification of the ziggurat of Ur by name and of the work of restoration by Nabonidus is provided by foundation deposits found at the corners of the building. Close by the ziggurat, which rose from an inner court, is found a shrine of Ningal and, in the angle formed by the main stairway leading up into the ziggurat, two small chapels. Around the wall were associated kitchens. A single gateway (Edublalmah) led into the sacred area or *temenos* with its open-air altar and large storehouse for receiving offerings. On this temenos was a temple for Ningal (Enunmah), a palace of Amar-Su'en, and farther to the SE Ehursag, the palace of Ur-Nammu and Shulgi. The whole complex was divided from the town by a wall last rebuilt by NEBUCHADNEZZAR II.

B. Royal cemetery. An outstanding discovery were the tombs of the rulers of the brilliant Early Dynastic III period (c. 2500 B.C.), near and below the mausoleum of kings Shulgi and Amar-Su'en. The finest equipped of the sixteen graves were those of Meskalamshar and his "queen" Pū-Abi (Shub-ad) and of the founder of the 1st dynasty Mesannipada and his son A'annipada, who are known to have been contemporary with the early kings of MARI. The ritual of burial included human sacrifice: from six to as many as eighty retainers accompanied the deceased to the tomb, where they too were killed, probably by poisoning or suffocation. Objects of gold, silver, precious stones, wood, ivory, and shell with lapis-lazuli mosaic inlay were found in abundance and testify to the wealth of this early time. They include chariots, sledges, standards, musical instruments, weapons and vessels, gaming-boards, and much personal jewelry. An outlying cemetery at Diqdiqqeh yielded grave goods of a later period.

C. Flood level. In a deep sounding to virgin soil in Pit F (and at other check points) Woolley met at 4.50 meters above sea level a stratum of clean, water-laid sand more than 3 meters deep, which he considered to have been laid in two subsequent stages dating to the end of the Ubaid period, c. 3500 B.C. He linked this with the flood mentioned in the Bible and in the Babylonian Epic of GILGAMESH (see FLOOD, GENESIS). Though some take this discovery as proof of these events, the archaeological evidence here does not necessarily warrant this interpretation. The flood layer seems to have been an accumulation of debris and is not strictly paralleled by the similar layers found at other sites that may be more closely related to the classical event (e.g., Kish and Shurrupak, c. 2500 B.C.). No flood level is known from ERIDU, 12 mi. to the SW.

D. Private houses. A quarter of the city occupied during the Isin-Larsa period was cleared to show the layout of thickly populated private houses. From many tablets discovered, the activity of the market and seaport sections of the city can be reconstructed. Trade was carried on over a wide area by merchants, including sea-borne traffic with India and Africa via the Persian Gulf from a canal basin harbor.

III. History. The city of Ur—following the strong Semitic dynasty of III Agade to the N (2350–2150 B.C.) and a period of eclipse after the Gutian infiltration (2150–2070)—became a flourishing city in Sumerian times, dominating S Babylonia and sometimes farther afield. See SUMER. The Ur Dynasty founded by Ur-Nammu saw a revival of Sumerian prosperity and the extension of Ur's influence once again to Syria and N Mesopotamia which continued during the reigns of his successors, Shulgi and Amar-Su'en. When the AMORITES overran the S, HAMMURABI (1792–1750) controlled Ur for a time, but when it rebelled against his son it was sacked. Ur's importance as a religious center insured that it was never abandoned for long, and later kings Kurigalzu II (1345–1324) and Marduk-nadin-aḫḫe (1098–1081) kept it in repair, as did Nebuchadnezzar II and Nabonidus in the 6th cent. The latter rebuilt the ziggurat and other shrines before installing his daughter, Bel-shalti-Nannar, as high priestess in her own new palace. CYRUS paid reverent attention to the shrines but after the 4th cent. the city fell into decline with the diversion of the Euphrates River and the silting up of the canal system.

(See further C. L. Woolley, *Excavations at Ur: A Record of Twelve Years' Work* [1954]; H. W. F. Saggs in *Iraq* 22 [1960]: 200–209; M. E. L. Mallowan and D. J. Wiseman, *Ur in Retrospect* [1960]; C. J. Gadd in *Archaeology and Old Testament Study*, ed. D. W. Thomas [1967], 87–101; P. R. S. Moorey, *Ur 'of the Chaldees': A Revised and Updated Edition of Sir Leonard Woolley's Excavations at Ur* [1982]; M. Van de Mieroop, *Society and Enterprise in Old Babylonian Ur* [1992]; D. Frayne, *Ur III Period (2112–2004 BC)* [1997]; R. L. Zettler and L. Horne, eds., *Treasures from the Royal Tombs of Ur* [1998]; M. Widell, *The Administrative and Economic Ur III Texts from the City of Ur* [2003].)

D. J. WISEMAN

Ur (person) oor (אוּר H244, "light, flame"). Father of ELIPHAL; the latter was one of DAVID's mighty warriors (1 Chr. 11:35). The parallel list reads differently (2 Sam. 23:34); see discussion under AHASBAI.

Urartu yoo-rahr′too. See ARARAT.

Urbane uhr′bayn. KJV form of URBANUS.

Urbanus uhr-bay′nuhs (Οὐρβανός G4042, from Lat. *Urbanus*, "urbane, refined"). KJV Urbane. A member of the Christian church at Rome to whom PAUL sent greetings (Rom. 16:9). The apostle calls him "our fellow worker in Christ," a description applied also to PRISCILLA AND AQUILA in this passage (v. 3), but to no one else. Presumably, Urbanus had assisted Paul in Asia Minor or Greece and subsequently migrated to the capital of the empire. It is impossible to determine whether he was Jewish or Gentile. According to P. Lampe, Urbanus "was not ordinarily a slave name" (*ABD*, 6:767; contra C. E. B. Cranfield, *A Critical and Exegetical Commentary on the Epistle to the Romans*, ICC, 2 vols. [1975–79], 2:790).

Uri yoor′i (אוּרִי H247 and אֲרִי H788 [1 Ki. 4:19], "light, flame," possibly short form of URIAH or URIEL). **(1)** Son of Hur and father of BEZALEL; the latter was the primary artisan in the building of the TABERNACLE (Exod. 31:2; 35:30; 38:22; 1 Chr. 2:20; 2 Chr. 1:5).

(2) Father of GEBER; the latter was one of SOLOMON's district managers (1 Ki. 4:19).

(3) One of the three Levitical gatekeepers who agreed to put away their foreign wives in the time of EZRA (Ezra 10:24).

Uriah yoo-ri′uh (אוּרִיָּהוּ H250 [only Jer. 26:20–23] and אוּרִיָּה H249, apparently meaning "Yahweh is [my] light" [cf. URIEL], but possibly from Hurrian *ewir*, "lord" [see *HALOT*, 1:25]; Οὐρίας G4043). KJV also Urijah (in 2 Kings, Nehemiah, and Jeremiah) and Urias (NT). **(1)** A HITTITE officer in DAVID's army who was the husband of BATHSHEBA (2 Sam. 11:3–26; 12:9–10, 15; 1 Ki. 15:5); he was included in the elite corps called "the Thirty" (2 Sam. 23:39; 1 Chr. 11:41). Some scholars have suggested that his name is Hurrian (in which it has the form reflects the Hittite *-ia* ending rather than the divine name *Yah*), but it seems more likely that he accepted Israelite citizenship and then adopted a Hebrew name to indicate that he was a worshiper of Yahweh. David, in order to cover his adulterous connection with Bathsheba, recalled Uriah from war in order that the latter might visit his wife, but he refused to do so, even though the king tried to make him drunk. When David failed to make this device effective, he gave Uriah a sealed dispatch to JOAB, the commander of the army, requesting that Uriah be placed in a dangerous position and that support be withdrawn. Joab complied and Uriah was killed in battle. Upon his death, David married Bathsheba. The child conceived in adultery was born, but did not survive. Uriah is mentioned in Matthew's GENEALOGY OF JESUS CHRIST (Matt. 1:6).

(2) A priest contemporary with the prophet ISAIAH; Uriah and a certain Zechariah son of Jeberekiah were chosen "as reliable witnesses" of the prophecy concerning MAHER-SHALAL-HASH-BAZ (Isa. 8:2). He is probably the same Uriah who, at the request of King AHAZ, built a replica of an altar the king had seen in DAMASCUS; this "large new altar" replaced the original bronze altar, and the latter was subsequently used by the king "for seeking guidance" (2 Ki. 16:10–16; for a discussion of Ahaz's possible motive, see M. Cogan and H. Tadmor, *II Kings*, AB 11 [1988]; 192–93). The fact that Uriah was given this responsibility suggests that he was the high priest, but his name is missing from the list in 1 Chr. 6:1–15.

(3) Son of Shemaiah; he was a prophet from KIRJATH JEARIM who protested the policies of the king and was sentenced to death. Uriah escaped to Egypt but was captured, brought back to Jerusalem, and executed (Jer. 26:20–23).

(4) Father of MEREMOTH, who was an important postexilic priest (Ezra 8:33; Neh. 3:4, 21; 1 Esd. 8:62 [KJV, "Iri"]).

(5) One of the prominent men (not identified as priests) who stood near EZRA when the law was read at the great assembly (Neh. 8:4).

F. E. YOUNG

Urias yoo-ri′uhs. KJV NT form of URIAH.

Uriel yoor′ee-uhl (אוּרִיאֵל H248, "God is [my] light" [cf. URIAH]). **(1)** Son (or descendant) of Tahath and descendant of Levi through KOHATH (1 Chr 6:24; his name is omitted in v. 37). During the reign of DAVID, Uriel was one of the Levite leaders who helped to bring the ARK OF THE COVENANT from the house of OBED-EDOM to Jerusalem (15:5, 11).

(2) A man of GIBEAH whose daughter Micaiah (see MAACAH #9) was the wife of REHOBOAM and the mother of ABIJAH, kings of Judah (2 Chr. 13:2).

(3) One of the four angels mentioned in *1 En.* 9.1. The others are Michael (see MICHAEL THE ARCHANGEL), GABRIEL, and RAPHAEL. Uriel appears in a number of places in *1 Enoch*. Uriel was sent to tell NOAH that the earth would be destroyed by a deluge (10.1). He described the angels who had led men into false worship (19.1) and was assigned to watch over the world and TARTARUS (20.2). He prophesied to ENOCH that the fallen angels (stars) would be bound and punished for 10,000 years (21.5–6) and that those who said unseemly things about the Lord would be punished in "the accursed valley" (27.2). He instructed Enoch in the names of the stars, as well as their positions and movements according to their months (33.4), and told him about the courses of the heavenly luminaries, their relations to each other, and how they regulate the time and condition of the world (72.1); he discussed the lunar year (74.2) and the movements of the moon (75.3–4; 78.10; 79.6; 80.1). Uriel is mentioned also in 2 Esdras (2 Esd. 4:1, 36 [KJV; NRSV, JEREMIEL]; 5:20; 10:28). He rebuked Esdras for questioning the ways of God by propounding questions that have no answers. In later literature, Uriel appears as the angel who helped to bring Adam and Abel into Paradise, and as the angel who wrestled with Jacob. (See further *DDD*, 885–86.)

F. E. YOUNG

Urijah yoo-ri′juh. KJV alternate form of URIAH.

Urim and Thummim yoor′im, thum′im (אוּרִים [sg. אוּר H242] and תֻּמִּים H9460 [sg. uncertain], traditionally understood to mean "lights and perfections," but the derivation of both terms is debated). These words are usually mentioned together as a phrase (Exod. 28:30; Lev. 8:8; Deut. 33:8 [in reverse order]; 1 Sam. 14:41 [NRSV and other versions, following LXX]; Ezra 2:63 = Neh. 7:65 = 1 Esd. 5:40), but Urim occurs alone twice (Num. 27:21; 1 Sam. 28:6). Since the definite article is used in the Hebrew text (except for Ezra 2:63 = Neh. 7:65; in Deut. 33:8 the words occur with a possessive pronoun), it is clear they were not strictly proper names. The varying renderings of the ancient versions show that no valid tradition of their meaning had survived to their time. Hence it is pointless to record the various guesses of their meaning, both ancient and modern.

I. Their use. The high priest wore the BREASTPIECE of judgment on the front of the EPHOD; the breastpiece was so made as to form a pouch (Exod. 28:16), and in it were placed the Urim and Thummim (v. 30). From most of the passages (Num. 27:21; 1 Sam. 14:41; 28:6; Ezra 2:63 and parallels) it is clear that they were used for discovering God's will. If one accepts the SEPTUAGINT text of 1 Sam. 14:41 (as do most scholars in whole or in part), it would indicate that one or the other could be drawn out of the pouch, thus giving a yes-or-no answer; hence it is generally assumed that they were two almost identical stones, perhaps gems.

However, 1 Sam. 28:6 makes clear that a definite answer was not always obtainable, and so a number of other suggestions have been made. Some think they were two flat objects, one side of each being called Urim, possibly from *ʾārar* H826, "to curse," the other Thummim, from *tāmam* H9462, "to be perfect." When tossed out of the pouch (cf. Prov. 16:33), if both showed Urim the answer was negative, if both Thummim, it was affirmative; one of each was inconclusive. Others see in the plural forms an indication of a larger number of objects, possibly bearing the letters of the alphabet. It is also possible that SAUL, in the incident recorded in 1 Sam. 28:6, may have asked a series of questions (cf. 23:10–12) to which he received mutually contradictory answers.

The foregoing is based on the supposition that the English versions are correct in their rendering of Exod. 28:30, namely, that the Urim and Thummim were placed in the breastpiece of judgment. The SEPTUAGINT, however, renders the clause in question, "And you shall put upon the oracle of judgment the Urim and Thummim (*kai epithēseis epi to logeion tēs kriseōs tēn dēlōsin kai tēn alētheian* [lit., "… the manifestation and the truth"]; the Gk. preposition *epi* G2093, "upon," translates Heb. *ʾel* H448, which has a variety of uses). This understanding of the Hebrew has been a dominant Jewish interpretation. It involves identifying Urim and Thummim with the breastpiece of judgment itself or its jewels. This view finds support in the fact that neither in Exod. 28:30 nor in ch. 39 is there any command for making the Urim and Thummim or any record of their having been made. The SAMARITAN PENTATEUCH, which obviously did not make the identification, tried to meet the argument by interpolating such a command in both passages. It would, however, be entirely consistent with what we know of the cultic background of Israel if the Urim and Thummim were precious oracle stones which had come down from the PATRIARCHS and which God was now officially incorporating into his people's worship.

Targum Pseudo-Jonathan (which though not receiving its final form until c. A.D. 650, contains much pre-Mishnaic and even pre-Christian material), followed by Rashi and Nachmanides, considered that Urim and Thummim were some material on which the Tetragrammaton (the four-consonant sacred name of God, *YHWH*) had been engraved. But JOSEPHUS, linking them with the twelve stones of the breastpiece, considered they were capable of shining out to give divine guidance (*Ant.* 3.8.9 §215). This view was further developed in the TALMUD. Many maintained that the letters of the tribal names engraved on the precious stones of the breastplate—they added the names of Abraham, Isaac, Jacob, and "the tribes of Jeshurun" to complete the alphabet—were illuminated in turn to give the divine pronouncement (the word Urim was understood as the plural of Heb. *ʾôr* H240, "light"; that a miraculous light was involved has more recently been defended by C. Van Dam, *The Urim and Thummim* [1997], 224). Though a few modern Jewish scholars, such as J. H. Hertz, still favor the identification with the breastplate, most have abandoned it. The divergencies in Jewish tradition itself, and the clear indications that the ancient versions had no real tradition to guide them, suggest that very little regard should be paid to these and similar flimsy views.

One of the difficulties is uncertainty whether Urim and Thummim were used in certain cases when LOTS were drawn or cast. For example, were they used to discover ACHAN's guilt (Josh. 7:16–18)? It is possible but by no means certain. It certainly seems clear that they were not used for the apportioning of the tribal portions (Josh. 18:8–10).

II. Their disappearance. It is clear from Ezra 2:63 and parallels that the Urim and Thummim did not exist after the return from the Babylonian EXILE. While Ben Sira mentioned their past existence with respect (Sir. 45:10), he clearly considered that a man versed in the law would not feel their loss (33:3). This turning away from them is illustrated by 1 Macc. 4:46, where the ultimate disposal of the polluted stones of the altar was referred to a prophet yet to come. Among the DEAD SEA SCROLLS, only one possible veiled reference to them has been found (1QH IV, 6). Though the Talmud has theoretical discussion about the use of the Urim and Thummim, there is clearly no expectation of their restoration. The statement is made more than once that they ceased after the death of the former prophets. This temporal reference is normally understood as meaning the destruction of Solomon's temple, but in *b. Soṭah* 48b Rab Huna identifies "the former prophets" as DAVID, SAMUEL, and SOLOMON. This minority view seems supported by the OT evidence.

The evidence is not limited to the fact that the Urim and Thummim are not mentioned under the monarchy, for the OT is not given to stressing the everyday. More important is the increasing stress on prophetic oracles. Even more significant is ABIJAH's failure to mention them in 2 Chr. 13:8–12, when he recounted Judah's privileges; indeed, in spite of its stress on the Aaronic priesthood, Chronicles, a postexilic work, nowhere mentions them. Even in the later stages of David's reign there is no probable reference to them, where it might be expected.

The reason for their dropping out of favor may be indicated by a comparison of 1 Sam. 23:6–12 with 28:6. The importance of the ephod (23:6) was simply that it belonged to the high priest, and by its help David could ascertain God's will (vv. 9–12). Its oracular power came from the Urim and Thummim. The ephod was still with David when Saul had marched to his death at GILBOA (30:7). How then had Saul been able to consult the Urim and Thummim (28:6)? It is reasonable to assume that either because of the multiplying of sanctuaries, or possibly to satisfy Saul's demands, the original oracular objects had been counterfeited.

When this situation became plain, it reinforced certain already existing tendencies and doubts. The more spiritually minded must have increasingly come to realize that the discovery of God's will was not something as automatic as the use of the Urim and Thummim might suggest. For those living at a distance from the central sanctuary such a method was linked with much inconvenience and could even be impossible. Without the presence of ABIATHAR and the ephod, David would have been excluded from this form of divine guidance. Possibly even more influential must have been the realization that, in view of priests like ELI's sons, there could be no guarantee that the Urim and Thummim would not be manipulated; in any case they were available only to the rich and influential.

III. Their spiritual significance. Jesus Ben Sira showed real spiritual understanding when he placed knowledge of the law on the same level as, or on a higher level than, Urim and Thummim (Sir. 33:3), even though he regarded them as a divine gift (cf. 45:10). This was also the reason the rabbis were not really interested in them. For Christians, with their knowledge of the indwelling HOLY SPIRIT, this feeling will be even stronger. But if, even in the Christian dispensation, God is prepared to give believers just beginning their Christian life guidance by methods that may seem strange to those who know his will better, how much more to Israel in the days of its spiritual childhood. It was more important that they should discover God's will than that the spiritually more advanced should approve it. Note that it is never suggested that MOSES had to make use of them. This is the most likely reason we are told so little about them.

(See further J. Buxtorf in *Thesaurus antiquitatum sacrarum*..., ed. B. Ugolini, 34 vols. [1744–49],

vol. 12; W. Muss-Arnolt in *Jewish Encyclopedia* [1901–06], 12:384–85; M. Gaster, "Divination," *ERE*, 1:806–14, esp. 812–13; A. R. S. Kennedy in *HDB*, 4:838–41; *EncJud* [1971], 16:8–9; R. de Vaux, *Ancient Israel* [1961], 350–53; J. Lindblom in *VT* 12 [1962]: 164–78; E. Robertson in *VT* 14 [1964]: 67–74.) H. L. ELLISON

Ur-Markus oor-mahr′kuhs. Also *Ur-Marcus*. This term (German for "Proto-Mark") is the name given to a proposed early edition of Mark's gospel, which supposedly was later edited into the form of the existing text. According to some scholars in the past, Ur-Markus was the document used by Matthew and Luke in the composition of their gospels, but this theory has fallen out of favor. On the synoptic problem, see BIBLICAL CRITICISM IV.A; GOSPELS III.B.1; JESUS CHRIST IV.A.

Ur-Theodotion oor-thee′uh-doh′shuhn. See SEPTUAGINT IV.C.

Uruk yoor′uhk. See ERECH.

usury. See INTEREST.

Uta yoo′tuh. KJV Apoc. form of UTHAI (1 Esd. 5:30).

Uthai yoo′thi עוּתַי H6433, perhaps short form of עֲתָיָה H6970 [see ATHAIAH and note the discussion in *ABD*, 6:770]). **(1)** Son of Ammihud and descendant of JUDAH (1 Chr. 9:4). He was among those who settled in Jerusalem after the EXILE (v. 3).

(2) A descendant of BIGVAI, part of the company that traveled with EZRA from Babylon to Jerusalem (Ezra 8:14). On the basis of the parallel passage ("Uthai son of Istalcurus," 1 Esd. 8:40 [KJV, "Uthi the son of Istalcurus"]), some emend the Ezra text from "Uthai and Zaccur" to "Uthai son of Zaccur."

(3) Ancestor of a family of temple servants (NETHINIM) that returned from exile under ZERUBBABEL (1 Esd. 5:30 [KJV, "Uta"]). His name is missing in the parallel lists (Ezra 2:43, Neh 7:48). F. E. YOUNG

Uthi yoo′thi. KJV Apoc. form of UTHAI (1 Esd. 8:40).

Uz (person) uhz (עוּץ H6419, derivation uncertain). (1) Son of ARAM and grandson of SHEM (Gen. 10:23; 1 Chr. 1:17). See also UZ (PLACE).

(2) Son of NAHOR (ABRAHAM's brother) by MILCAH (Gen. 22:21).

(3) Son of Dishan and grandson of SEIR the HORITE (Gen. 36:28; 1 Chr. 1:42).

Uz (place) uhz (עוּץ H6420, derivation unknown). The "land of Uz" was apparently a district or a section of the country E of Palestine, on the border of ARABIA. It was the home of JOB (Job 1:1), and the prophet JEREMIAH refers to it twice (Jer. 25:20; Lam. 4:21). The area may have received its name from one of the individuals who bore the same name; see Uz (PERSON).

The country is nowhere specifically located either in sacred or secular history or geography, yet biblical and traditional references provide several clues to its location: (a) it was a land of plentiful pastures (Job 1:3); (b) portions of it were suitable for plowed crops (v. 14); (c) it was near the desert (v. 19); (d) it was sufficiently extensive to have a number of kings or "sheikhs" (Jer. 25:20); (e) it was in more or less proximity to such places as TEMAN (or TEMA), BUZ, and DEDAN (Job 2:11; 32:2; Jer. 25:23); (f) it had some connection with EDOM (Lam. 4:21); (g) it was within raiding distance of the SABEANS and CHALDEANS (Job 1:15, 17); (h) according to an ancient tradition, the land of Uz lay on the borders of IDUMEA (Edom) and Arabia (see the reference to "the Syriac book" in the additional material at the end of the book of Job in the LXX, 42:17b).

The precise location of the land of Uz is uncertain, and some scholars (associating it with Uz son of ARAM, Gen. 10:23; 1 Chr. 1:17) identify it with HAURAN, an area E of the Sea of Galilee. A region farther S is more likely, however, and Wadi Sirhan, SE of Jebel ed-Druz, seems to fit the biblical description best. This area is a great shallow plain-like depression some 210 mi. long and averaging 20 mi. wide. It begins at the present inland town of Azraq, a typical oasis with many palm groves, some 50 mi. ESE of Amman, and continues in a southeasterly direction to within 10 mi. of Jauf, an important caravan junction of central Arabia. Many localities in the NW portion of Wadi Sirhan (the general area where Job prob. lived) are only 40 to 100 mi. from the eastern borders of Edom.

Much of Wadi Sirhan is a vast, flat pasture land, fairly well suited to the raising of camels, donkeys, sheep, and goats. And to this day it sustains wild life such as gazelle, oryx, ostrich, and the wild ass, though in smaller numbers than in Job's day. The chief wealth of the plain lies in its abundant water supply. From the southern slopes of Jebel ed-Druz, from the ranges of hills N and NE, and from the wadi-cut plateau stretching 100 mi. along its SW border, the water from winter and spring rains flows, either on the surface or subterraneously, into this depression. It becomes somewhat of a catchment basin for rain and run-off water; as a result, such a reservoir of underground water is built up that in many places the water table is high enough to afford an abundance of water when a thin limestone sheet has been penetrated some 18–24 in. below the ground surface. In other places there are wells and water holes where at times many thousands of camels and smaller cattle may be seen in the area at the same time. In some parts, however, they depend on rain water caught in cisterns and reservoirs.

In 1925, during the Druse rebellion against the French rule in Syria, many Druse chiefs with their people fled for refuge to Wadi Sirhan, where they pastured their vast herds and lived in their tents until the trouble was over. In ancient times the district lay near the caravan route from Sheba and Tema, being exposed to the people of this area and to the bands of Sabeans and Chaldeans as they came along the caravan route from the E. The residence of Job was in or near a city, at the gate of which he sat with the elders to administer justice. (See N. Glueck, *The Other Side of the Jordan* [1940], 40–43, 175; *NBD*, 1220.) G. F. OWEN

Uzai yoo′zi (אוּזָי H206, derivation uncertain). Father of PALAL; the latter assisted NEHEMIAH in repairing the Jerusalem walls (Neh. 3:25).

Uzal yoo′zuhl (אוּזָל H207, derivation uncertain). Son of JOKTAN and descendant of SHEM, included in the Table of NATIONS (Gen. 10:27; 1 Chr. 1:21); he was also the eponymous ancestor of a tribe or country (Ezek. 27:19; however, the text here is uncertain, and the Masoretic pointing, *mě'ûzzāl*, indicates the pual ptc. of *'āzal* H261, "to go away," in this case perhaps referring to "spun" goods; cf. BDB, 23). The two sons of Eber, Peleg and Joktan, represent the two main divisions of the Semitic-speaking people, and Joktan is considered by some scholars to be the founder of the Arab nation.

There is an Arabic tradition that Uzal was the original name of Sanaa (Ṣanʿaʾ), the capital of Yemen in SW Arabia in both Himyaritic and modern times (but see discussion in *ABD*, 6:775–76). Wrought iron is mentioned by Ezekiel as one of the exports of Uzal to Tyre, and Sanaa is still noted for its steel. On the assumption that the Septuagint of Ezekiel reflects the original reading ("wine" rather than Javan), others have suggested Izalla/Aṣalla (cf. TNIV, "Izal"), a city or country known for its wine, located in the hills of NE Syria, between Haran and the Tigris, N of the Khabur River Valley (*Reallexikon der Assyriologie*, 5 [1976–80]: 225–26; *NBD*, 1220; A. R. Millard in *JSS* 7 [1962]: 201–3; W. Zimmerli, *Ezekiel*, Hermeneia, 2 vols. [1979–83], 2:36 and 68n.; cf. *ANET*, 305b). Possibly the same place is mentioned by Ashurbanipal, the Assyrian king, when he records in his annals the capture of Azalla in the context of an expedition against the Nabateans (*ANET*, 299a); he mentions also two nearby towns, Iarki and Hurarina, which recall two other sons of Joktan listed in Gen. 10:26–27, Jerah and Hadoram. (For a different approach to the passage, cf. M. Elat in *VT* 33 [1983]: 323–30.) See also Vedan. F. E. Young

Uzza uhz´uh. See Uzzah.

Uzzah uhz´uh (עֻזָּא H6438 and עֻזָּה H6446 [only 2 Sam. 6:7–8; 1 Chr. 6:29; MT 6:14], possibly short form of עֻזִּיָּה H6459, "Yahweh is [my] strength"; see Uzziah). The KJV has the form Uzzah only in 2 Sam. 6:3, 6–8, and Uzza elsewhere; the NIV and NRSV have Uzzah in this passage as well as in 1 Chr. 6:29; 13:7–11 (Uzza in 2 Ki. 21:18, 26; 1 Chr. 8:7; Ezra 2:49; Neh. 7:51). The spelling in none of the English Bibles corresponds precisely with the Hebrew spellings, mainly because of inconsistency in the latter (note that, according to the Heb., 2 Sam. 6:3 and 6 would require the spelling Uzza, but vv. 7–8 would require Uzzah).

(1) Son of Abinadab (2 Sam. 6:3; see Abinadab #3). Uzzah was killed while driving the oxcart which carried the ark of the covenant to Jerusalem. The ark had been in the house of Abinadab for some time following the disaster it had occasioned in the Philistine cities and in Beth Shemesh (1 Sam. 6:19; 7:2). David, wishing to add to the prestige of Jerusalem by making it a religious center, decided to bring to this city the ark of the covenant, the sacred object of Israel's early faith. Uzzah and his brother, Ahio, were driving the cart. As they reached the threshing floor of Nacon, the oxen stumbled and the ark began to slide. Uzzah reached out to steady the ark and was fatally smitten. His death was attributed to the violation of the sacred character of the ark (2 Sam. 6:7; 1 Chr. 13:10). David was greatly distressed at the incident, and immediately canceled his plans to enshrine the ark in Jerusalem. Instead, he deposited it in the home of Obed-Edom. He named the place Perez Uzzah, "the breach of [*or* the breaking out against] Uzzah." The ark remained in the home of Obed-Edom for three months.

(2) Son of Shimei and descendant of Levi through Merari (1 Chr. 6:29; MT 6:14).

(3) The owner of a garden in which Manasseh and Amon, kings of Judah, were buried (2 Ki. 21:18, 26).

(4) Ancestor of a family of temple servants (Nethinim) who returned from the exile (Ezra 2:49; Neh. 7:51; 1 Esd. 5:31 [KJV, "Azia"]).

F. E. Young

Uzzen Sheerah uhz´uhn-shee´uh-ruh (אֻזֵּן שֶׁאֱרָה H267, "ear [*or* corner] of Sheerah"). KJV Uzzensherah. A village built by Sheerah, the daughter of Ephraim (1 Chr. 7:24). The town must have been near Beth Horon, but its precise location is unknown.

Uzzen-sherah uhz´uhn shee´ruh. KJV form of Uzzen Sheerah.

Uzzi uhz´i (עֻזִּי H6454, prob. short form of עֻזִּיָּה H6459 or עֲזִיאֵל H6457, "Yahweh/God is [my] strength"; see Uzziah, Uzziel). **(1)** Son of Bukki, descendant of LEVI through KOHATH, and ancestor of EZRA (1 Chr. 6:5–6, 51 [MT 5:31–32; 6:26]; Ezra 7:4; 1 Esd. 8:2 [KJV, "Ezias"]; 2 Esd. 1:2 [KJV, "Ozias"]).

(2) Firstborn son of TOLA and grandson of ISSACHAR; he was a family head who had a large progeny, including numerous warriors (1 Chr. 7:2–4).

(3) Son of BELA and grandson of BENJAMIN; a family head (1 Chr. 7:7).

(4) Son of Micri and descendant of Benjamin; his son Elah was among the first to resettle in Jerusalem (1 Chr. 9:8; cf. v. 3).

(5) Son of Bani, descendant of ASAPH, and "chief officer of the Levites in Jerusalem" at the time of EZRA; he was among "the singers responsible for the service of the house of God" (Neh. 11:22).

(6) Head of the priestly family of JEDAIAH during the days of the high priest JOIAKIM (Neh. 12:19).

(7) A priest or Levite who took part in one of the choirs at the dedication of the wall (Neh. 12:42).
F. E. YOUNG

Uzzia uh-zi′uh (עֻזִּיָּא *H6455*, prob. short form of עֻזִּיָּה *H6459* or עֻזִּיאֵל *H6457*, "Yahweh/God is [my] strength"; see UZZIAH, UZZIEL). An "Ashterathite" (i.e., a man from the town of ASHTAROTH in BASHAN) listed among David's mighty warriors (1 Chr. 11:44).

Uzziah uh-zi′uh (עֻזִּיָּהוּ *H6460* and עֻזִּיָּה *H6459*, "Yahweh is [my] strength"; cf. UZZIEL). **(1)** Son of AMAZIAH and his successor as king of Judah; also known as AZARIAH (2 Chr. 26 et al.; cf. 2 Ki. 14:21 et al.). See below.

(2) Son of Uriel and descendant of LEVI through KOHATH (1 Chr. 6:24).

(3) Father of a certain Jonathan who "was in charge of the storehouses" during the reign of DAVID (1 Chr. 27:25).

(4) A postexilic priest; he was one of the descendants of Harim who agreed to put away their foreign wives in the time of EZRA (Ezra 10:21).

(5) Son of Zechariah and descendant of JUDAH; his son Athaiah was a provincial leader who settled in Jerusalem after the EXILE (Neh. 11:4).

(6) Son of Micah; he was a prominent magistrate in BETHULIA, the town where JUDITH lived (Jdt. 6:15–16 et al.).

The rest of this article is devoted to Uzziah king of Judah.

I. Name. The interchange between the names Uzziah and Azariah is parelleled in the case of UZZIEL (#4), who was also called AZAREL (#2), and it reflects the semantic similarity between the verbs ʿāzar *H6468* ("to help, come [with valor] to the aid of") and ʿāzaz *H6451* ("to be strong [valiant]," sometimes in the context of God's power to help, e.g., Ps. 68:28). The very common name Azariah is used of this king only once in Chronicles (1 Chr. 3:12) and regularly in Kings (2 Ki. 14:21; 15:1, 6–8, 17, 23, 27), whereas Uzziah occurs in Kings a few times (2 Ki. 15:13, 30–34) and consistently everywhere else (2 Chr. 26:1—27:2; Isa. 1:1; 6:1; 7:1; Hos. 1:1; Amos 1:1; Zech. 14:5). Some have thought that Azariah was his personal name and that Uzziah was a throne name he assumed when he succeeded his father Amaziah as king (cf. A. Honeyman in *JBL* 67 [1948]: 20–21), but the evidence for this view is ambiguous.

II. Chronology. Uzziah was probably coregent with Amaziah for many years. The information given in 2 Kings is (1) that the reign of JEROBOAM in the northern kingdom of Israel lasted forty-one years (2 Ki. 14:23); (2) that Uzziah became king (and by implication that his father died) in the twenty-seventh year of Jeroboam (15:1); and (3) that Jeroboam's reign ended in Uzziah's thirty-eighth year (15:8). From JEHU's rebellion in 841 B.C., the date of Amaziah's death can be derived as 767; on this basis Uzziah counted his years from 792 and died in 740 (E. R. Thiele, *The Mysterious Numbers of the Hebrew Kings*, 3rd ed. [1983], 113–16, 118–23; cf. V. Pavlovský and E. Vogt in *Bib* 45 [1964]: 326–37). W. F. Albright, working from a terminal date of 738 for MENAHEM, dates Uzziah 783–742, and alters the length of some reigns to dispose of the surplus arising from simply adding up the MT figures (see *BASOR* 100 [Dec. 1945]: 18–22). H. Tadmor (in *Studies in the Bible*, ed. C. Rabin [1961], 232–71) arrives at the dates 785/4–733/2 B.C.

III. Achievements.

During the time of Uzziah there was both expansion and consolidation of the kingdom. His reign is briefly noted in 2 Ki. 15:1–7 as events in Israel move to their climax, but 2 Chr. 26 reveals him as one of the most energetic and successful kings of Judah. His crowning achievement was the rebuilding of ELATH (once EZION GEBER, modern Eilat/Tell el-Kheleifeh) "after Amaziah rested with his fathers" (26:2) and when Uzziah himself was about forty years old. Although Amaziah's victory over EDOM had opened a way into the territory that the Edomites had won from JEHORAM, Uzziah had had to build up his strength after the defeat by JOASH. Specifically, he had been extending his control across the NEGEV, building forts and securing water supplies in that region. The "desert" (26:10) may refer to the Negev or to the wilderness of NE Judah (F. Cross and J. Milik, *BASOR* 142 [April 1956]: 142). No full archaeological proof connects such forts as Khirbet Gharra and Khirbet Ghazza with Uzziah, but N. Glueck (*Rivers in the Desert* [1959], 166–79) shows at length how the effective use of the Negev has always depended on firm government, and Elath could not have been held in isolation. It was all part of one policy for Uzziah to reduce the PHILISTINES, extend his control up to BEERSHEBA, and subdue the MEUNITES (2 Chr. 26:6–7; see further Y. Aharoni, *The Land of the Bible: A Historical Geography*, rev. ed. [1979], 345).

Uzziah's southward policy had three clear aims: (1) to bring Arabian trade by the sea coast; (2) to exploit the mineral wealth of the Rift Valley; (3) to develop agriculture in the SHEPHELAH W of the Judean hills, and to extend pasturing in the Negev. Much of the coastal plain too, now covered in sand, was then fertile. Uzziah established well-defended settlements on land which the Philistines probably could no longer cultivate for lack of manpower (8th-cent. remains at Tell Mor, about half a mile inland of ASHDOD, may illustrate 2 Chr. 26:6). He may have built the forts in the N wilderness, and SE of HEBRON ("attesting the existence of desert routes," according to Y. Aharoni in *IEJ* 11 [1961]: 15–16).

The defenses of Jerusalem were rebuilt and developed, with new towers at two principal gates (2 Chr. 26:9). Assyrian reliefs show the new-style upperworks that gave the defenders better protection (Y. Yadin, *The Art of Warfare in Biblical Lands*, 2 vols. [1963] 2:326). Uzziah reorganized the army with a regular staff and made shields and weapons a government issue; thus he provided the military support for his expansion without disrupting agriculture by frequently calling out a militia.

IV. The Azriyau mystery.

The *Annals* of TIGLATH-PILESER (745–723 B.C.) record that in or after his third year he assaulted the city of Azriyau of Yauda (Azriau of Iuda in *ANET*, 282b); it seems that he built a royal palace there to mark its subjection. Though the context is apparently SYRIA, many scholars have argued that Azriyau must have been Uzziah (Azariah) of Judah; this view has been strongly contested.

Some have pointed to Yaʾudi (i.e., Samʾal, modern Zenjirli), whose king witnessed the triumph of Tiglath-Pileser at Damascus in 732, but Tadmor

The Aramaic inscription on this marble plaque from the late Second Temple Period refers to the transferring of the bones of King Uzziah to a new tomb on the Mount of Olives.

denies that Assyrian *Ya-u-da* could represent *Yᵓdi*, or that such an insignificant state could have headed a coalition against Assyria. He suggests that after the death of Jeroboam, while Israel was rent by civil war, Uzziah inherited the leadership in the N; he dates the events noted in the *Annals* to 738, following the usual reconstruction (a date disputed by E. R. Thiele, *The Mysterious Numbers of the Hebrew Kings*, 3rd ed. [1983], ch. 7). The available fragments of the *Annals* are not clear as to Azriyau's activities or his ultimate fate; but Uzziah could not have been involved except as a leader. Tadmor (in *Studies in the Bible*, 271) does not show that he could be defeated without repercussions in Judah. Further, a northern involvement would be out of keeping with Uzziah's general policy, and unlikely at the very end of his reign.

V. Illness and closing years. Chronicles records a confrontation between King Uzziah and Azariah the high priest, who objected to the king's offering incense in the Holy Place (2 Chr. 26:16–20). During this unhappy scene, as Uzziah was simultaneously in an act of prayer and losing his temper with the priests, a skin disease broke out on his forehead. Humiliated and rejected, he left the temple, and for his remaining years was unable to fulfill the royal office, particularly as he was excluded from the temple. The event is dated by JOTHAM's coregency in 750/1 B.C.

JOSEPHUS (*Ant.* 9.10.4) adds that the day was a great festival (which is likely), that there was a severe earthquake (one occurred in Uzziah's time, cf. Zech. 14:5 and Targum on Isa. 28:21), and that the leprosy came by the sun shining through a crack in the temple. J. Morgenstern (in *HUCA* 12/13 [1935]: 1–53) takes these details as "essential and significant" to support his theory that the king had hitherto officiated at a sunrise ceremony on New Year's Day. This is hardly consistent with his basic hypothesis that, at the moment in question, the sun would in any case be shining down the central axis of the temple.

Uzziah now lived in a "separate house" (*bêt haḥopšit*, lit., "house of the freedom," 2 Ki. 15:5; 2 Chr. 26:21 [*Qere*]). The meaning of the phrase is debated. The word *ḥopší H2930* in 1 Sam. 17:25 probably indicates exemption from certain obligations; it is used of freed slaves or prisoners, but in Ps. 88:5 it may be rendered "set apart" (NIV) or "forsaken" (NRSV). Since *ḥopšît H2931* is an adverbial form, some have revocalized the phrase to *bêtōh ḥopšît*, "[in] his house without duties" (or, "forsaken"). Others have proposed "house of pollution," adducing the Ugaritic *bt ḫptt*, which refers to the underworld. (For further discussion see M. Cogan and H. Tadmor, *II Kings*, AB 11 [1988], 166–67.) In comparing Uzziah's case with NAAMAN's, it may be relevant that the latter was not an Israelite; moreover, he may have had a less serious form of the disease.

When Uzziah "rested with his fathers," he was buried "in the City of David" (2 Ki. 15:7), "in a field for burial that belonged to the kings" (2 Chr. 26:23). An inscription in Aramaic from the 1st cent. A.D. purports to identify a tomb to which his bones were at some time removed (cf. *PEQ* Supplement [Oct. 1931]: 217ff., plate; S. Yeivin, *JNES* 7 [1948]: 31–36).   J. LILLEY

Uzziel uhz′ee-uhl (עֻזִּיאֵל *H6457*, "God is [my] strength"; gentilic עָזִּיאֵלִי, "Uzzielite"; cf. AZIEL, UZZIAH). **(1)** Son of KOHATH, grandson of LEVI, and eponymous ancestor of a Kohathite clan (Exod. 6:18, 22; Lev. 10:4; Num. 3:19; 1 Chr. 6:2, 18; 23:12, 20). One of his brothers was AMRAM, the ancestor of MOSES and AARON. One of Uzziel's children, ELZAPHAN (Elizaphan), was the leader of the Kohathite clans "responsible for the care of the ark, the table, the lampstand, the altars, the articles of the sanctuary used in ministering, the curtain, and everything related to their use" (Num. 3:30–31). Members of this family were among the Levites who assisted David in bringing the ARK OF THE COVENANT to Jerusalem (1 Chr. 15:10). They were also given special assignments in David's preparatory arrangements for the temple ritual (23:12, 20; 24:24). (On the difficulties presented by the genealogies of 1 Chr. 6, see *ABD*, 6:779–80.)

(2) Son of Ishi and descendant of SIMEON; he was one of the leaders of a band of 500 Simeonites who engaged the Amalekites (see AMALEK) at Mount SEIR in a decisive battle and came out victorious. The Simeonites extended their boundary to include that of the vanquished foe (1 Chr. 4:42–43).

(3) Son of Bela and grandson of Benjamin; a family head (1 Chr. 7:7).

(4) Son of Heman, the king's seer (1 Chr. 25:4). The fourteen sons of Heman, along with the sons of Asaph and Jeduthun, were set apart "for the ministry of prophesying, accompanied by harps, lyres and cymbals" (v. 1). The assignment of duty was done by lot, and the eleventh lot fell to Uzziel, his sons, and his relatives (25:18, here called Azarel).

(5) Descendant of Jeduthun the musician; he and his brother Shemaiah were among the Levites assigned to consecrate the temple in the days of Hezekiah (2 Chr. 29:14).

(6) Son of Harhaiah; he was a goldsmith who helped Nehemiah in rebuilding the walls of Jerusalem (Neh. 3:8). Some scholars emend the text to read "Uzziel, a son [*i.e.*, member] of the guild [*ḥeber*] of the goldsmiths."

F. E. Young

Station 5 (Simon of Cyrene takes up the cross for Jesus) on the Via Dolorosa.

Vaheb vay′heb. See WAHEB.

vail. KJV alternate form of VEIL.

vain. This English term, meaning "worthless" or "futile," is used over 100 times in the KJV to render a variety of Hebrew and Greek terms; it occurs less frequently in modern versions (fewer than 70 times in the NRSV and about 30 times in the NIV). For example, God warns the Israelites that if they violate his COVENANT they will plant seed "in vain" (*lārîq*, "for nothing") because their "enemies will eat it" (Lev. 26:16); the Hebrew word *rîq* H8198 means "emptiness." Similarly, in the third commandment not to take the Lord's name "in vain" (*laššāwʾ*, Exod. 20:7; Deut. 5:11), the word *šāwʾ* H8736 means "emptiness, nothingness," and is often rendered with such adjectives as "worthless" and "false." Both the NIV and the NRSV render the Hebrew idiom in the command with the English phrase, "misuses his name" (the NJPS interprets it more specifically, "swears falsely by His name"; see TEN COMMANDMENTS). Of several Greek words rendered "vain" in the NT, the most frequent is *kenos* G3031, "empty" (e.g., 1 Cor. 15:58; Gal. 1:2). For further discussion see VANITY.

Vaizatha vi′zuh-thuh (וַיְזָתָא H2262, an otherwise unattested Persian name of uncertain meaning). KJV Vajezatha. One of the ten sons of HAMAN who were put to death by the Jews (Esth. 9:9).

Vajezatha vuh-jez′uh-thuh. KJV form of VAIZATHA.

vale. See VALLEY.

Valentinian Exposition. A Gnostic tractate included in the NAG HAMMADI LIBRARY (NHC XI, 2). The author, representing one of the schools derived from (but not identical with) the teachings of VALENTINUS, claims to reveal "my mystery" regarding both creation and redemption. The Father is represented as dwelling in silence, and the Son is described as "the Mind of the All"; the latter part of the document recounts the Sophia myth. Although very fragmentary, this MS preserves (in Coptic translation) an original 2nd-cent. Valentinian work that supplements and nuances the information available to us from IRENAEUS and other Christian writers. (English trans. in *NHL*, 481–89.)

Valentinus val′uhn-tee′nuhs. An early and influential Christian Gnostic theologian. Probably born early in the 2nd cent. in Egypt, Valentinus first taught in ALEXANDRIA, then moved to ROME c. 135, and eventually became a candidate for the position of bishop. Having been rejected, he seceded from the church, and after some years of living in the eastern parts of the empire he returned to Rome, where he died c. 170. It appears that Valentinus sought to adapt some of the classic myths of non-Christian GNOSTICISM to the theological framework of Christian orthodoxy, and his popularity gave rise to several Valentinian schools that were severely attacked by the church fathers, especially IRENAEUS. In modern times several Valentinian works have been discovered, such as the *Gospel of Truth* (which some attribute to Valentinus himself; see TRUTH, GOSPEL OF) and the VALENTINIAN EXPOSITION. (See B. Layton, ed., *The Rediscovery of Gnosticism: Proceedings of the International Conference on Gnosticism* ... , vol. 1 [1980]; K. Rudolph,

Aerial view from the southern end of the Sea of Galilee looking S along the Jordan Valley.

Gnosis: The Nature and History of Gnosticism [1984], 317–25; *ABD*, 6:783–84.)

valley. The various Hebrew terms that may be translated "vale" or "valley" fall readily into two distinct categories, and in doing so reflect clearly the structure and surface of the Bible lands. (1) The nouns ʿēmeq H6677 (from ʿāmaq H6676, "to be deep") and biqʿâ H1326 (from bāqaʿ H1324, "to split") indicate a broad vale or lowland, sometimes more than 10 mi. in breadth. In contrast, (2) naḥal H5707 ("wadi" or "river valley") and gayʾ H1628 indicate a steep-sided valley, that is, a gorge. In Palestine the terms in the first category apply primarily to structural features such as the Plain of ESDRAELON and the Rift Valley of JORDAN; thus we read about "the Plain [kikkār H3971]—that is, the valley [biqʿâ] of Jericho" (Deut. 34:3) at a point where the Rift Valley is some 12 mi. wide. The words in the second category describe valley features that are the result of streams cutting down into the limestones and sandstones of Palestine in a dry climate, creating a highly dissected landscape, and in some areas producing a "badland" topography. Such gorges represent serious obstacles to movement and played a prominent part in the military operations of biblical times (cf. Josh. 8:11; 1 Sam. 17:3).

Since Israel in OT times was largely a mountain dwelling people, their view of the lowlands which surrounded them (and which were largely occupied by their enemies) was naturally colored by this fact. Consequently, the term šĕpēlâ H9169 (almost always with the definite article), often translated "the valley" or "the vale" by the KJV (Deut. 1:7 et al.), was reserved for a specific region, lying between the mountains of Judea and the Mediterranean. It is not a valley at all, but a kind of piedmont zone of low hills lying between the coastal plain proper and the Judean hills, and separated from the latter by a narrow (true) valley. Thus the NIV renders it, "the western foothills." See PALESTINE III; SHEPHELAH.

In the NT, the word "valley" occurs in two passages. It renders the Greek nouns *pharanx* G5754, "cleft, ravine" (Lk. 3:5, a citation from the LXX), and *cheimarros* G5929, "[winter] torrent" (Jn. 18:1).

J. H. PATERSON

Valley Gate. A city gate on the SW side of Jerusalem. The Valley Gate was equipped with towers by UZZIAH, c. 760 B.C. (2 Chr. 26:9). It was the point from which NEHEMIAH began his tour of inspection in 444 B.C. (Neh. 2:13, 15); and it figured in his work of rebuilding, being located some 500 yards N (or W?) of the DUNG GATE (3:13). If Jerusalem was at this time still confined to the hills E of the central Tyropoeon Valley, the Valley Gate would have been N of the Dung Gate, corresponding to the large, later gateway across the city from the WATER GATE and GIHON spring, and excavated by J. W. Crowfoot in 1927 (see H. G. M. Williamson in *PEQ* 116 [1984]: 81–88). Otherwise it would have been W of the Dung Gate, opening out from the city onto the slopes of the SW hill (prob. named GAREB, Jer. 31:39), and specifically its E side, toward the central valley (see diagrams of three different proposals in M. Ben-Dov, *Historical Atlas of Jerusalem* [2002], 86–87). From the Valley Gate the two parties led by EZRA and NEHEMIAH proceeded along the walls for their dedication in 444, in opposite directions, so as to meet at the TEMPLE, on the NE side of the city (Neh. 12:31, 39). See JERUSALEM II.D.2 and III.A. J. B. PAYNE

Vaniah vuh-ni′uh (וַנְיָה H2264, possibly from Persian *vānya*, "lovable"). One of the descendants of BANI who agreed to put away their foreign wives in the time of EZRA (Ezra 10:36; 1 Esd. 9:34 [KJV, "Anos"]). Several Hebrew MSS have "Zaniah," and some scholars emend the name to *mibběnê*, "from the sons of."

vanity. This English term, in the sense of "futility" or "worthlessness" (rather than in its common meaning of "conceit," for which see PRIDE), occurs almost 100 times (13 times pl.) in the KJV, 45 of them in Ecclesiastes alone. The NRSV preserves the term in this book, but uses it rarely elsewhere (Ps. 89:47 et al.), while in the NIV it does not occur at all. The word is most familiar in the saying, "Vanity of vanities; all is vanity" (Eccl. 1:2 et al. KJV; NIV, "Utterly meaningless! Everything is meaningless!"; NJPS, "Utter futility! All is futile!"). Here and in most other instances, "vanity" translates the Hebrew noun *hebel* H2039, which in some passages is best rendered "breath," probably its original meaning (note that it parallels *rûaḥ* H8120, "wind," in Isa. 57:13, and *ṣēl* H7498, "shadow," in Ps. 62:9). It is always used with its figurative connotation of that which is weak, ephemeral, transitory.

The KJV uses "vanity" also as the rendering of other words, such as *šāwʾ* H8736, meaning "emptiness, nothingness" (Job 7:3 et al.; cf. the similar Gk. term *mataiotēs* G3470, Rom. 8:20 et al.), but also "falsehood" (e.g., Job 31:5, parallel to *mirmâ* H5327). Another Hebrew noun, *ʾāwen* H224, has a similarly broad range of meanings, including "trouble, disaster" (Prov. 22:8). These various terms can refer to that which appears to have meaning, substance, or value, but which turns out to possess none of these elements, and so is false or deceitful. Those who follow after such things are not only deceived but wicked. Not surprisingly, idols are referred to repeatedly as "vanities" (NIV, "worthless idols," Deut. 32:21; 1 Ki. 16:13; et al.; cf. Gk. *mataios* G3469, "empty [thing]," used in the pl. in Acts 14:15). See IDOLATRY; VAIN.

Some of the things designated as vanity (in addition to those mentioned above) include: (a) the thoughts and words of the godless (Job 15:35; Pss. 10:7; 144:8); (b) leaving the fruit of one's toil to another (Eccl. 2:19, 21); (c) human fate (2:15; 3:19); (d) life (9:9; 11:10); (e) the message of false prophets (Ezek. 13:6–9 et al.); (f) nations and rulers (Isa. 40:17, 23); (g) pleasure (Eccl. 2:1); (h) wealth (5:10 et al.; cf. Prov. 13:11; 21:6); (i) everyone and everything (Pss. 39:11; 62:9; Eccl. 1:1; 12:8).

The progress of meaning, therefore, seems to be this: empty, useless, deceitful, wicked. In line with its purpose to reveal the truth that is ultimate and lasting, the Scriptures warn against that which gives the appearance of reality and value, but which proves in fact not to have any real worth. Since people are being led astray by such deceits, the Bible discloses and denounces them.

E. L. ACKLEY

Vashni vash′ni (וַשְׁנִי H2266 [not in NIV]). Firstborn son of SAMUEL, according to the MT, followed by KJV (1 Chr. 6:28 [MT 6:13]). However, since 1 Sam. 8:2 says, "The name of his firstborn was Joel and the name of his second was Abijah" (*wayĕhî šem-běnô habběkôr yôʾēl wěšem mišnēhû ăbiyâ*), most scholars believe that the Chronicles passage has suffered textual corruption (due to the same ending of the names "Samuel" and "Joel"). Accordingly, they emend the verse in Chronicles by inserting *yôʾēl* and changing *waššnî* to *wěhaššēnî*, "And the name of Samuel: Joel the firstborn and the second Abijah" (*ûběnê šěmûʾēl yôʾēl habběkôr wěhaššēnî ʾăbiyyâ*, for

which there is support from some ancient versions; cf. NIV and NRSV).

Vashti vash′ti (וַשְׁתִּי H2267, possibly from Persian *vahišta*, "the best," or from Avestan *vas*, "to desire," thus "desired one"; see H. S. Gehman in *JBL* 43 [1924]: 322). Queen of Persia and wife of Ahasuerus (XERXES I) who refused to exhibit her beauty to his lords on the seventh day of a feast (Esth. 1:9–19; 2:1, 4, 17). The king banished her and made an edict that each man should be lord over his own house (1:22). Her deposition led to the selection of ESTHER as the new queen. HERODOTUS (*Hist.* 7.61; 9.108–12) says Xerxes' queen was Amestris and mentions no other wives, leading some scholars to question the reliability of the biblical account. Others believe that Amestris and Vashti are the same woman and that either (1) the names are variant forms (W. H. Shea in *AUSS* 14 [1976]: 227–46, esp. 236–37) or (2) the use of the name Vashti is a literary device calling attention to the woman's beauty. Perhaps more likely is the view that Xerxes had several wives and that Herodotus is interested only "in the royal wives who bore successors to the throne" (K. H. Jobes, *Esther*, NIVAC [1999], 67; see also R. L. Hubbard, Jr., in *ZAW* 119 [2007]: 259–71, who argues that the evidence from Herodotus is of little value but that possibly Amestris is the same as Esther).   A. K. HELMBOLD

vassal. See TREATY.

vat. See WINE IV.

Vaticanus. See CODEX VATICANUS.

vau, vav. See WAW.

Vedan vee′duhn (וְדָן H1968 [not in NIV]). In EZEKIEL's lament over TYRE, the NRSV reads, "Vedan and Javan from Uzal entered into trade for your wares" (Ezek. 27:19; similarly NJPS). If this understanding of the Hebrew text is correct, identification may be made with *Waddan* (also called al-ʾAbwaʾ), a place between Mecca and Medina, involved in Muhammad's first expedition. The name JAVAN normally refers to the Ionians (and thus the NIV has "Greeks"), but because of the context some have thought there was a Javan in ARABIA or that the reference is to a Greek settlement in that area (perhaps distinguished from the usual Javan by the qualification "from Uzal"; cf. KD, *Ezekiel*, 1:396). The phrase "from Uzal" is problematic (see UZAL); if it refers to a place, its location is uncertain, though most scholars look for it somewhere in Arabia.

The Hebrew form *wĕdān* has traditionally been understood to mean "and Dan" (thus NIV, "Danites"; cf. Vulg. and KJV), but the pairing of Danites with either Greeks or Arabians does not yield good sense; moreover, no other name in the whole passage includes the conjunction *waw*, "and." The matter is complicated by the SEPTUAGINT, which omits the first word of the verse and then has Greek *oinon*, "wine," instead of "Javan" (evidently reading Heb. *yayin* instead of *yāwān*, though it is impossible to determine which of the two words was in the translator's Heb. MS). This Greek reading is reflected in the RSV, "and wine from Uzal they exchanged for your wares" (similarly TNIV; for a proposal that follows the LXX even more closely, see W. Zimmerli, *Ezekiel*, Hermeneia [1979–83], 2:49).

vegetables. Modern English versions use this word to translate Hebrew *yāraq* H3763, which occurs three times (Deut. 11:10; 1 Ki. 21:2; Prov. 15:17 [KJV, "herbs"]), as well as two terms that appear to be variant plural forms of *zeraʿ* H2446, "seed" (*zērōʿîm* H2447, Dan. 1:12; *zērʿōnîm* H2448, v. 16). In addition, the Greek noun *lachanon* G3303, "garden plant, herb," is properly rendered "vegetable" in at least one NT passage (Rom. 14:2).

Vegetables are otherwise referred to in various other passages. When the children of Israel left Egypt, one of the first thing they did was to lust after "cucumbers, melons, leeks, onions and garlic" (Num 11:5). Those who are forced to live a nomadic life cannot grow their vegetables. ABRAHAM, ISAAC, and JACOB were herdsmen, always moving on to new pastures. Their food was not fresh vegetables and salads—nor is it so with the BEDOUINS today. Jacob is said to have made "some lentil stew" (Gen. 25:34); did his father grow lentils or were they obtained in exchange for beasts? Maybe the *Lens esculenta* was found growing wild. Herdsmen would look for grazing where this vetch was to be found, because the plant is known as a milk stimulant. See FLORA and separate articles for individual vegetables.

W. E. SHEWELL-COOPER

veil. KJV usually *vail*. In the OT several Hebrew words are used with reference to a head or face covering (Gen. 24:65 et al.; Exod. 34:33-35 [LXX, *kalymma* G2820, used by Paul in the corresponding passage, 2 Cor. 3:13-16]; Cant. 4:1 et al.; Isa. 3:19 et al.). The KJV uses the English word also to render Hebrew *pārōket* H7267, a technical term applied only to the inner CURTAIN that divided the Holy Place from the Most Holy Place in the TABERNACLE (in LXX and NT, Gk. *katapetasma* G2925). It was a symbol of God's unapproachability.

This curtain was made of blue, purple, scarlet, and fine twisted linen embroidered with figures of CHERUBIM (Exod. 26:31-37; 36:35). JOSEPHUS said that the mixtures of colors of the veil had a mystical interpretation (*War* 5.5.2). It was hung with golden hooks upon four pillars of ACACIA wood overlaid with gold which were set in sockets or bases of silver. It is likely that the curtain was quite thick to correspond with its great size. Behind the veil was placed the ARK OF THE COVENANT with the MERCY SEAT resting on it. It was sometimes called "the veil of the screen" (Exod. 39:34 RSV; NIV, "the shielding curtain") to distinguish it from the screen hung at the entrance to the tabernacle. Only the high priest was permitted to enter behind the veil, and that only one day each year—the Day of Atonement (Lev. 16; Num. 18:7; Heb. 9:7). Instructions were given for taking down the veil when the tabernacle was to be moved (Num. 4:5). Mention is made only once of the veil in Solomon's TEMPLE (2 Chr. 3:14).

The veil of the second temple is referred to in 1 Macc. 1:22 as part of ANTIOCHUS's desecration of the sanctuary. Josephus records that when POMPEY conquered Jerusalem and entered the temple (63 B.C.), the place was empty and the secret shrine contained nothing (*War* 1.7.4; *Ant.* 14.4.4).

During the CRUCIFIXION of Jesus (Lk. 23:45), or at the moment of his death (Matt. 27:51, Mk. 15:38), and at the time the priests were busy with the evening sacrifice, the veil of the temple was torn in two, from top to bottom, exposing the Holy of Holies and symbolizing that Jesus, as the High Priest who could enter the Most Holy Place (Heb. 6:19-20; 9:11-12), had opened the way for all believers to enter into the presence of God through his flesh, symbolized by the veil (10:19-20).

E. B. HUEY, JR.

vengeance. Punishment inflicted in retaliation of injury or offense. In the Bible (Heb. *nĕqāmâ* H5935; Gk. *ekdikēsis* G1689), different aspects may be discerned through context or parallelism. (1) WRATH as the motivating force in vengeance is prominent in some cases (Prov. 6:34; Isa. 59:17; 63:4; Nah. 1:2; Sir. 5:7; 12:6; Rom. 3:5); human wrath may take the form of malice (Lev. 19:18; 1 Sam. 25:26; Lam. 3:60; Ezek. 25:12, 15). (2) The idea of punishment for sin or injury appears often (Lev. 26:25; Ps. 99:8; Lk. 21:22); this gradually shades over into the concept of recompense or retaliation (Gen. 4:15; Isa. 34:8; Jer. 50:15; Sir. 35:18). (3) The justice of God or the faithfulness of his servants is vindicated by the punishment of enemies (Jdg. 11:36; Ps. 94:1-2; 2 Thess. 1:8); sometimes an individual appeals to God for divine vengeance (Ps. 58:10; Jer. 11:20; 15:15; 20:12).

In the majority of cases God himself is the author of vengeance, whether directly (Deut. 32:35; Ps. 94:1-2; Isa. 59:17-18; Jer. 46:10; Jdt. 8:27; 16:17; Rom. 12:19; Heb. 10:30), through his commands to his people (Num. 31:3; Josh. 22:23; Jer. 50:15; Jdt. 9:2), or through other means (Wisd. 11:15; Sir. 39:28). Of the half dozen passages where vengeance arises from human beings, one (Prov. 6:34) is an observation of a natural tendency, one (1 Sam. 25:26) is a case where DAVID was restrained from taking vengeance, one (Lev. 19:18) is a command not to do so (cf. Sir. 28:1), and three (Lam. 3:60; Ezek. 25:12, 15) are examples of vengeance against Judah on the part of her enemies (cf. Jdt. 6:5; 1 Macc. 7:9). Therefore the teaching of Rom. 12:19, "Do not take revenge, my friends, but leave room for God's wrath" (cf. Deut. 32:35; Heb. 10:30), is amply supported throughout Scripture. There are perhaps a few cases where the author of vengeance is not clear (Gen. 4:15, Wisd. 1:8, Sir. 7:17). Judas MACCABEE took vengeance on those of his own nation who had deserted or rebelled against him (1 Macc. 7:24). The LEX TALIONIS (Exod. 21:23-25; Lev. 24:19-20; Deut. 19:21) was not for the individual to take into his own hands; it was a part of judicial procedure and operated under divine sanction. See also AVENGER OF BLOOD.

In two instances, Acts 28:4 and Jude 7, the KJV uses the rendering "vengeance" for Greek *dikē* G1472 ("right, justice," etc.). In the latter passage this word is more appropriately translated "punishment," whereas in Acts the concept is personified as a goddess: when the people of MALTA saw that a snake had bitten PAUL, they commented, "This man must be a murderer; for though he escaped from the sea, Justice has not allowed him to live."

E. L. ACKLEY

venison. See GAME.

vermilion A bright red pigment obtained from various sources, used in paints (Heb. *šāšar* H9266; NIV, "red"). Formerly derived from the *kermes* insect, it is derived also from cinnabar (also called red mercuric sulphide). Cinnabar is usually found in massive, granular, or earthy form of a bright red hue. It is also derived from hematite, an ore of iron (called also red ocher). It was used in the time of JEREMIAH by the wealthy classes to paint the walls of their houses. The king was condemned by the prophet for being more concerned with adorning his palace than with justice (Jer. 22:14). In an allegory related by EZEKIEL, Oholibah, a harlot representing Jerusalem, "saw men figures carved on the wall, images of the Chaldeans portrayed in vermilion" (Ezek. 23:14 NRSV), which suggests that this pigment was used also in mural decorations. It was used also to paint idols that had been carved out by a carpenter (Wisd. 13:14 KJV; Gk. *miltos*, "red chalk" or "red ocher"). The Greeks, as well as the Romans, used it to make pottery. Several African tribes covered their bodies with it and some used it as war paint (Herodotus, *Hist.* 4.191, 194; 7.69).

F. B. HUEY, JR.

versions of the Bible, ancient. The earliest and most important translation of the Hebrew OT was into the GREEK LANGUAGE and is known as the SEPTUAGINT, although this imprecise name is often used to cover a variety of Greek versions. Also of great value for biblical studies are various translations into ARAMAIC known as the TARGUMS (or *Targumim*). The OT of the Syriac Peshitta and of the Latin Vulgate are also direct translations from the Hebrew text, but such OT versions as the Coptic, Old Latin, and Armenian are *secondary* translations made from the Greek Septuagint. Because of the special significance of the Septuagint and the Targums, separate articles are devoted to these OT versions. The present entry covers the rest of the versions, with emphasis on the NT.

I. Introduction
II. The Latin versions
  A. Old Latin
  B. Vulgate
III. The Syriac versions
  A. Diatessaron
  B. Old Syriac
  C. Peshitta
  D. Philoxenian
  E. Harkleian
  F. Palestinian
IV. The Coptic versions
  A. Sahidic
  B. Bohairic
  C. Middle Egyptian dialects
V. Other versions
  A. Gothic
  B. Armenian
  C. Georgian
  D. Ethiopic
  E. Slavonic
  F. Arabic
  G. Persian
  H. Frankish
  I. Sogdian
  J. Nubian

I. Introduction. The origins of the earliest OT translations were closely tied to the needs of the Jewish people. Their adoption of the Aramaic language at the time of the EXILE led to the use of oral translations of the Scriptures into that language in the SYNAGOGUES, and it was only a matter of time before that oral tradition was put into writing. Similarly, the presence of a very large Jewish presence in Hellenistic ALEXANDRIA—and elsewhere in the DIASPORA—necessitated the translation of the Torah into Greek. The production of NT versions, however, is to be explained differently.

When the first Christian missionaries began to carry the gospel message beyond the bounds of

Judea and Samaria, the Greek language was known and spoken almost everywhere they went throughout the ROMAN EMPIRE. Even Latin, the official language of the Roman conquerors, was less the common language of the empire than was Greek. As a result, many people of the lands around the Mediterranean were bilingual or even trilingual, speaking their own language as well as Greek and often Latin. To many, of course, either Greek or Latin was their native tongue; but in many areas their own language was neither of these. Therefore, although a missionary could have preached in Greek in many areas, in order to be lastingly effective the gospel needed to be translated into the language which the people used in their homes and in intimate conversation. An indication of this fact is seen in PAUL's experience at LYSTRA (Acts 14:8–18): even though the people evidently understood the apostle's Greek, when they themselves wanted to speak of religious matters they used their own Lycaonian speech (see LYCAONIA).

Thus the ancient versions of the NT were missionary in origin and purpose. They were produced so that the people to whom the Christian message was being taken could read it in their native tongue rather than in a language which they may have known, if at all, only as a means of communication in the context of trade and commerce.

These translations differed in quality and accuracy. At times they reflect interesting interpretations of a Greek word or phrase. One of their most important uses today, however, is the contribution they make in the field of NT textual criticism by aiding in the reconstruction of the original text of the Greek NT. See TEXT AND MANUSCRIPTS (NT) III.B. In this respect, it is not the wording of the version itself which is important, but rather the information the version gives concerning the wording of the Greek text from which the version is derived. For example, versions are generally reliable in reflecting the presence or absence of a phrase or passage in the underlying Greek, such as the addition or omission of *en tō phanerō*, "openly," at the end of Matt. 6:4 (included in the Old Latin and most Syriac versions [cf. KJV], but absent in the Vulgate and Coptic versions).

At the same time, there are limitations in the use that can be made of the versions in determining the Greek text from which they were translated. First, some variants in the Greek text cannot be or would not ordinarily be reflected in certain versions. For example, many differences in word order found among Greek MSS cannot be reproduced in languages whose meaning is largely dependent upon a fixed word order, as is English. Again, Latin has no definite article and therefore does not ordinarily reflect the presence or absence of that feature in Greek. Some languages might translate the Greek aorist and perfect tenses, or the aorist and the imperfect, without distinction. Differences of orthography of Greek words would not commonly be reflected in other languages. (For more details on such linguistic differences, see the respective sections in B. M. Metzger, *The Early Versions of the New Testament: Their Origin, Transmission, and Limitations* [1977].)

Second, in no case is the original MS of an ancient version extant, but only copies more or less remote from the original, just as is the case of the Greek MSS. This means that the version itself must be submitted to text-critical study for the purpose of determining as nearly as possible its original wording before it can be used to determine the Greek from which it was translated. This process is further complicated when the version has been later revised. Even if there was no official revision, individual MSS of the version may have been compared with other Greek MSS and corrected on that basis.

Third, it must be determined whether the version was translated directly from Greek or whether it is a *secondary* version, that is, one translated from another version.

Fourth, the usefulness of a version in determining the underlying Greek text will be affected by the extent of the translator's knowledge both of Greek and of the language of his version. For example, B. M. Metzger and B. D. Ehrman (*The Text of the New Testament: Its Transmission, Corruption, and Restoration*, 4th ed. [2005], 95 n. 76) quote a complaint of St. AUGUSTINE concerning translators into Latin, that "no sooner did anyone gain possession of a Greek manuscript, and imagine himself to have any facility in both languages (however slight that might be), than he made bold to translate it" (*Doctr. chr.* 2.11 [16]). In addition, care must be taken not to mistake the liberties of interpretation or paraphrase by the translator for indications of textual differences in the underlying Greek.

Finally, a version that is in the best literary form of its language will generally be less helpful to the textual critic than one that is literal and unidiomatic, since the better the style of a version the more likely it is to fail to reflect the very differences which form the basis for many Greek textual variants.

Despite these limitations, the ancient versions of the NT have much to contribute to biblical studies. Not only do they provide, by their very wording, a certain amount of interpretation and commentary upon the Greek text together with some indication of the time and location in which these interpretations were known, but they are also of significance in the determination of the original form of the Greek text. Yet to a large degree the use of the versions in textual criticism has been neglected in the past. To some extent this neglect has been due to a failure to recognize the contribution which the versions could make, as is reflected in Bishop Walton's comment that the use of ancient translations to correct the Greek text would be like using a clock to correct the sun (*Biblia Sacra Polyglotta* [1655], referred to by B. M. Metzger in *New Testament Manuscript Studies: The Materials and the Making of a Critical Apparatus*, ed. M. M. Parvis and A. P. Wikgren [1950], 25).

Even when text-critical scholars recognize the importance of the evidence of the versions, they must still either learn the language of each version they wish to use, and learn it thoroughly enough to use it accurately, or else depend upon the work of someone who does know the language. Rare indeed is the contemporary scholar who has been willing to expend the time and effort to learn most of the languages of the significant ancient versions of the NT (but see the work of Arthur Vööbus, *Early Versions of the New Testament: Manuscript Studies* [1954]). This limitation, together with the lack of generally available full collations of the versions in a form which the Greek student can easily use, constitutes a serious obstacle to their adequate use in cases where they would be an important or even crucial factor.

It is worth noting that the very existence of ancient versions of the NT is unusual. Prior to the Christian era, literary works were rarely translated into another language; and in the few instances in which it was done, the resulting translation was generally too free a rendering to have appreciable value in determining the text of the original. Thus when the OT PENTATEUCH was translated into Greek in the 3rd cent. B.C., it stood virtually alone as a version which, on the whole, adequately reflected the sense of the Hebrew original.

II. The Latin versions

A. Old Latin. The origin of the Latin Bible is obscure. Greek continued to be used widely throughout the Mediterranean world, especially in the centers of trade and culture, even after NT times. In writing to the church in ROME, not only Paul but also IGNATIUS (beginning of the 2nd cent.) used Greek. Vööbus states that not until nearly the middle of the 3rd cent. did Latin become the language of literature in Rome.

It has therefore been believed by many that the Vetus Latina or Old Latin (OL) originated in response to needs from people in other parts of the Roman empire. In the case of the OT, as mentioned earlier, the OL is a translation not of the Hebrew Bible but of the SEPTUAGINT; being a secondary version, it is thus of lesser value than the OL translation of the NT (made directly from the Greek). Some scholars, claiming to detect a knowledge of Hebrew (and Aramaic) by the Latin translators, have suggested that the Latin Bible originated in SYRIA. The more commonly accepted view, however, is that it was produced in N Africa, where Latin was the common and official language. Indeed, the earliest clear evidence of the use of the Latin Bible is in the writings of church fathers of N Africa, including Cyprian and perhaps TERTULLIAN.

On the other hand, Vööbus insists that Italy must not be ruled out as a possible place of its origin, either in the provinces or even in Rome itself, where there may have been a significant number of non-Greek-speaking believers at a relatively early date. (The OL translation, esp. in NT studies, is sometimes referred to as the *Itala*, and the siglum "it" is used in some critical editions of the Greek NT.) The Latin of the earliest form of the text is inelegant and at times literalistic, which some have taken to imply that the Latin Bible originated either away from centers of culture or from interlinear translations in Greek MSS; but some of these characteristics may reflect nothing more than translation by simple believers whose bilingualism was not highly literary. In summary, therefore, the place of origin of the OL remains uncertain.

The date of the OL also has not been definitely established, but it was likely during the latter part of the 2nd cent.; and not long thereafter the Latin Bible was known on both sides of the Mediterranean. It is not certain to what extent this OL is one version or a number of versions, or to what extent the text of N Africa was independent of that of Europe. There are both noteworthy agreements and noteworthy differences between these two families of MSS. Even within these two principal families, however, there are textual differences so great and so frequent that they suggest that the OL represents a number of translations, and possibly some revision. In Lk. 24:4–5, for example, there are some twenty-seven forms of the text in OL MSS (Metzger and Ehrman, *Text of the New Testament*, 101).

There is no single OL MS of the complete OT or NT, and most of the extant MSS are fragmentary even regarding the books they contain. Metzger (*Early Versions*, 296–308) lists about a hundred NT MSS, almost half of which contain the Gospels. They come from as early as the 4th cent. and as late as the 13th, thus indicating that the OL was in use to some extent long after it had officially been replaced by the Vulgate. These MSS are commonly designated by lower-case letters. Some of the more significant are the following: *a* or Codex Vercellensis, in the cathedral in Vercelli, Italy, dating from the 4th cent., and one of the two most important OL MSS of the Gospels; *b* or Codex Veronensis, in the cathedral of Verona, Italy, a 5th-cent. MS written in silver ink on purple parchment, containing the Gospels in the Western order of Matthew, John, Luke, Mark; *d*, which is the Latin side of the bilingual CODEX BEZAE, a 6th-cent. MS of the Gospels and Acts in the library of Cambridge University, which reflects a basically 3rd-cent. text; *gig* or Codex Gigas ("giant"), a 13th-cent. MS in the Royal Library of Stockholm whose pages measure 20 × 36 in., containing the entire Latin Bible and other works, but preserving the OL only in Acts and Revelation; *k* or Codex Bobbiensis, containing about half of Matthew and Mark, in the National Library of Turin, the most important witness to the African form of the OL; and *m*, a symbol that refers to any of several MSS of *Speculum*, a collection of biblical passages illustrating points of conduct (the quotations represent the African OL).

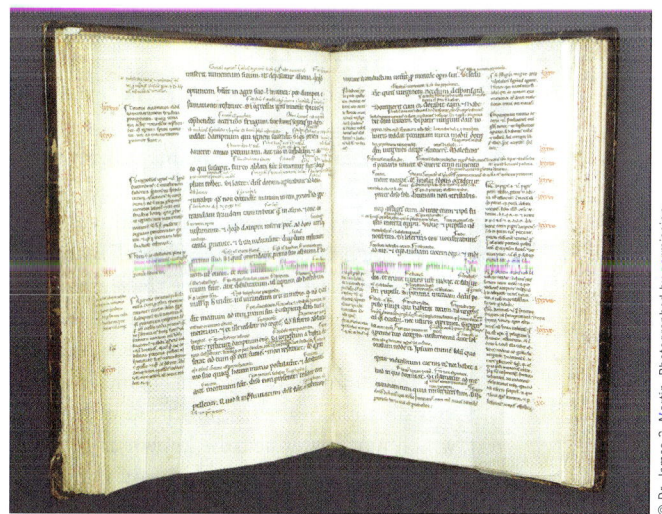

This MS of Exodus (c. A.D. 1170) contains the Latin Vulgate text with glosses or explanatory comments.

B. Vulgate. As time passed, particularly after Christianity became officially recognized early in the 4th cent., the wide range of variation within the OL MSS became increasingly intolerable. Finally, in 382 Pope Damasus asked his theological adviser, Sophronius Eusebius Hieronymus, now commonly known as St. JEROME, to undertake a revision of the Latin text, standardizing it by the "true Greek text." Jerome was doubtless the best-qualified man of his day for this task. He had studied Latin and Greek in Rome, as well as Hebrew in Palestine, and had devoted his life to biblical studies.

Jerome undertook the task as a labor of love, yet with reluctance, well realizing that his work would provoke criticism by those resenting any change in the biblical text from the form with which they were familiar. Partly, perhaps, for this reason, Jerome worked under very conservative principles which he set for himself, as he explained in his letter of preface to his translation of the Gospels: he selected what he felt was a relatively good Latin text as the basis for his work, comparing it with some old Greek MSS and revising the Latin only where he felt the meaning of the original was distorted by the Latin. Neither the Latin MSS which Jerome used nor the Greek MSS with which he compared them are known, and subsequent revisions and changes to the translation make it impossible to determine the nature of these documents with certainty, but they seem to have included some that preserved a valuable form of the text.

Questions persist concerning the extent of Jerome's revision. Qualitatively, his work seems to have been more careful at some points than at others: in some instances he changed the OL renderings, but not always (e.g., he retained three different renderings for "high priest" in three Gospels). Quantitatively, most scholars now believe that Jerome did little work beyond the Gospels and that the rest of the NT was revised by others, though included with Jerome's translation under his name.

Determination of the original form of Jerome's text, which much later became known as the Vulgate (Lat. *vulgatus* means "commonly known, in wide circulation"), is almost hopelessly complicated, not only because of the scribal errors that resulted from ordinary copying of the MSS, but also from the inevitable mixing of readings from the OL, since for some centuries the OL continued to be known and used alongside the Vulgate. This contamination of readings led to attempts during the Middle Ages to edit the text to recover the original text of Jerome; but these efforts produced even greater confusion. As a result, the MSS of the Vulgate include a wide range of textual affinities.

More than 8,000 MSS of the Latin Vulgate are known. Since many additional ones certainly perished, the Vulgate is thus seen to be the most frequently copied work of literature of ancient times. The MSS are commonly designated by capital letters or by the first syllable of their names (e.g., A or *am*, F or *fu*, Z or *harl*). The oldest known is Codex Sangallensis (Σ or *san*), a 5th-cent. MS of the Gospels, part of which is in the monastery of St. Gall in Switzerland. The "Golden Gospels" of the Pierpont Library in New York City is a 10th-cent. document written in gold letters on purple parchment, possibly the finest purple biblical MS in existence.

Glossed Latin codex of the NT Epistles (12th cent., open to the beginning of Ephesians).

III. The Syriac versions.

Syriac is a dialect of ARAMAIC (usually classed as a form of Eastern Aramaic because it shares features with Jewish Babylonian Aramaic and Mandaic). A different dialect, Jewish Palestinian Aramaic, was the common language of Palestine in the 1st Christian cent. and therefore probably the language that Jesus and his disciples ordinarily spoke. Modern Christians who are part of Aramaic-speaking Christianity (such as the Assyrian Church) often claim that what modern scholarship refers to as the Syriac NT is really the original Aramaic form of the NT. Virtually all specialists, however, recognize that the language of the Syriac MSS is different from Palestinian Aramaic, that these MSS represent translations from an original Greek, and that they are thus secondary witnesses to the text, as are all other versions, with no claim to represent the words of Jesus as faithfully as does the Greek text. (For a general survey, see S. Brock, *The Bible in the Syrian Tradition (English Version)* [2006].)

A. Diatessaron.

The earliest form in which the gospel message was known in Syriac may have been a continuous account in which all four canonical

Codex Sinaiticus Syriacus (palimpsest of the Gospels, 5th cent.).

Gospels were interwoven. It is not certain whether this work, known as the *Diatessaron* ("by means of four"), was composed originally in Syriac or in Greek. The only known MS which is assumed to contain any actual text of the Diatessaron itself is a fragment in Greek which was discovered at Dura in the Middle E in 1933.

The author, or editor, of the Diatessaron was Tatian, a Syrian, native of MESOPOTAMIA, who was converted to the Christian faith c. A.D. 150 in ROME and became a student under JUSTIN MARTYR. Tatian probably composed the Diatessaron c. A.D. 170, and it soon became popular in its Syriac form. The work was still in use in SYRIA in the 5th cent., but at that time, since Tatian had accepted some heretical views later in his life, Bishop Theodoret ordered all copies of the Diatessaron destroyed and separate Gospels substituted for them.

Other than the Dura fragment, no direct remains of the Diatessaron are extant, and the work is known only through quotations from it found in the writings of Syrian church fathers, especially St. EPHRAEM's commentary on the Diatessaron. Certain harmonics in Arabic, Persian, Latin, and other languages, written at a much later date, are assumed to exhibit some degree of dependence upon the work of Tatian. (See further the entry DIATESSARON, which includes a bibliography.)

B. Old Syriac. Apart from the Diatessaron, all or most of the NT had been translated into Syriac by the end of the 2nd cent. or shortly after. Some scholars maintain that this Old Syriac (OS), as it is called, antedates even the Diatessaron, but more likely it is later. The OS is known in two MSS. The first of these was discovered in a monastery in the Nitrian Desert of Egypt in 1842 by Dr. William Cureton and edited by him in 1858. This MS, known as the Curetonian Syriac (Syr^c) and housed in the British Museum, was written in the 5th cent. It contains the Gospels but with large gaps in the text. The second MS was discovered in 1892 in the Monastery of St. Catherine on Mount Sinai by Mrs. A. S. Lewis and published in 1894. This MS, designated the Sinaitic Syriac (Syr^s), is a PALIMPSEST. It dates from the 5th cent. and likewise contains extensive portions of the Gospels.

These two OS MSS preserve a 3rd-cent. text, although they differ from each other at various points. The Sinaitic appears to represent a slightly earlier form of the text than does the Curetonian. Generally speaking, they are witnesses to the so-called Western text. The OS version outside the Gospels has not survived in MSS, but is known in fragmentary form from quotations in the writings of Syrian fathers.

C. Peshitta. This name (also *Peshiṭta* and *Peshitto*), meaning "stretched out" or "simple," is applied to the standard translation of the Bible used by Syriac-speaking churches. The designation, first used c. A.D. 900, perhaps indicates only that it was the "common" or "widely diffused" version (cf. the term *Vulgate*), but possibly it is intended to contrast this translation from others that were accompanied by special textual markings (e.g., the Syro-Hexapla [also called Syro-Hexaplar], a Syriac translation of ORIGEN's edition of the Greek LXX that included the hexaplaric signs and marginal readings). The origins of the Peshitta of the OT are uncertain. Parts of it, such as the Pentateuch, may have been produced by a Jewish community, and most of it seems to have been completed during the 2nd cent. A.D. (A full critical edition, *The Old Testament in*

Syriac, according to the Peshitta Version, published in fascicles by Brill, is nearing completion. See further P. B. Dirksen, *An Annotated Bibliography of the Peshitta of the Old Testament* [1989], M. P. Weitzman, *The Syriac Version of the Old Testament: An Introduction* [1999].)

The origins of the NT Peshitta have also been hotly debated. Some have thought that it was the work of Rabbula, Bishop of EDESSA (411–435), but his work may actually have been a transitional stage between the OS and the Peshitta. The Peshitta lacked 2 Peter, 2–3 John, Jude, and Revelation. That this version was in circulation well before the schism of the Syriac church in 431 is indicated by the fact that both branches of the church accept it. The Peshitta (Syr^p) remains today the Syriac version in common use (with the missing books supplied from the later Philoxenian version). It is extant in some 350 MSS, from the 5th cent. and later. Its textual affinities are closer to the later or Byzantine text than is the OS, although it has numerous "Western" readings in Acts.

D. Philoxenian. The first Syriac NT to include all the books of the canon was produced in 508 by Polycarp, "rural bishop" to Philoxenus, Bishop of Mabug in eastern Syria. The NT books not included in the Peshitta were incorporated into that version from the Philoxenian (Syr^{ph}), and it is possible that only these books of the Philoxenian version survive. This issue, however, is interwoven with the question of the nature of the Harkleian version.

E. Harkleian. Also *Harclean* and *Harklensis*. The question of the relationship between the Philoxenian and the Harkleian Syriac versions is exceedingly confused. In 616 Thomas of Harkel, who like Philoxenus was Bishop of Mabug, issued a Syriac NT. In a colophon Thomas says that he took the version of 508 and compared it with a few Greek MSS. It is much disputed, however, whether Thomas did content himself with merely adding variant readings and marginal notes on the basis of his comparison of the Syriac with his Greek MSS, or whether he revised the Philoxenian so extensively that he produced a new version. The solution to this problem is complicated by the fact that the Philoxenian as such survives in only one copy of 2 Peter, 2–3 John, Jude, and Revelation.

The Harkleian (Syr^h) is extant in numerous MSS, most of which are of a late date. Those who distinguish the Harkleian from the Philoxenian state that while the Philoxenian was a highly literary and idiomatic version, the Harkleian renders the Greek so literally that it violates Syriac style.

F. Palestinian. Part of the NT exists in a somewhat different dialect of Syriac that is more closely related to Jewish Palestinian Aramaic. This Palestinian Syriac version (Syr^{pal}), as it is called, is of uncertain date but probably originated about the 5th cent. It is unique not only in its dialect but also in the fact that it is known almost entirely in LECTIONARY form, with only fragments of the Gospels, Acts, and Epistles in continuous text. The three principal MSS of this version are lectionaries dating from the 11th and 12th centuries, with affinities to the Caesarean type of text. This version appears to have been made directly from a Greek lectionary, since the Scripture passages and even the introductory phrases of the lections are almost completely identical with those of Greek lectionaries.

IV. The Coptic versions. Greek was well known in EGYPT in the early part of the Christian era. Not only have MSS of the Greek NT from as early as the 2nd cent. been recovered from the sands of Egypt, but also countless business documents, personal letters, and other literary and nonliterary items in Greek have been preserved from the centuries before and after the time of Christ. See PAPYRUS. These documents make it clear that Greek was known by both educated and uneducated people, and in various parts of the country. At the same time, Greek was not the language of the country. Many of the people doubtless knew Greek only as a second language, if at all, and needed the Scriptures in the language that was native to them.

No later than the 2nd Christian cent., there had been developed an ALPHABET for the Coptic language that used Greek letters, supplemented, where Greek had no equivalent symbol, by additional forms taken from the older demotic script. The Coptic language had developed into six dialects by this period, with the two principal forms located in the N and in the

S and intermediate dialects geographically between. These dialects differed from one another primarily in phonetics, and to a lesser degree in vocabulary and syntax. As in the case of the OT, the Coptic versions of the OT are translations of the Greek LXX, not of the Hebrew Bible (cf. M. K. H. Peters, *A Critical Edition of the Coptic (Bohairic) Pentateuch*, vols. 1–2 and 5 [1983–86]). The discussion that follows deals with the Coptic NT, but some of the information is relevant for the Coptic OT as well.

A. Sahidic. By the beginning of the 3rd cent., part of the NT had been translated into Sahidic (sometimes called Thebaic), the dialect of THEBES and S Egypt, and the complete NT was available shortly after that, apparently translated at various times by several people. The extant MSS include most of the NT, although Revelation exists only in fragments. Some papyri are included in these MSS, which date from the 4th cent. and later. The Sahidic version is generally Alexandrian in text-type, but with some "Western" affinities.

B. Bohairic. The region of ALEXANDRIA and N Egypt, which was the cultural center of the country, seems not to have had the NT in its dialect, Bohairic, until later than the production of the Sahidic version. (A form of Bohairic is still used in the Coptic Orthodox Church.) Although about a hundred Bohairic NT MSS have been known for a long time, none was written earlier than the 9th cent., and the earliest complete MS of the Gospels was from the 12th cent. Thus some scholars argued that the Bohairic version was no older than the 7th cent. In 1958, however, a Bohairic papyrus codex of the Gospel of John from the BODMER Library was published, which its editor assigns to the 4th cent. Although its text is unusual, this document is generally regarded as strong evidence that the classic Bohairic version was produced no later than the 5th cent. Much like the Sahidic version, the Bohairic is related to the Alexandrian text-type.

C. Middle Egyptian dialects. Between the two principal Coptic dialects were spoken four others—Memphitic, Fayumic (Bashmuric), Achmimic, and sub-Achmimic. A 4th-cent. papyrus codex in Fayumic containing half of the Gospel of John is in the University of Michigan Library. In sub-Achmimic, the Gospel of John is extant in a 4th-cent. papyrus. In Achmimic, fragments of Matthew, Luke, John, James, and Jude survive, at least part of which date from the 4th or 5th cent.

V. Other versions

A. Gothic. Ulfilas, called the apostle to the Goths, was born about 310 to Christian parents who had been carried captive from their native Cappadocia to Dacia, in Europe, by invading Goths. When he was about thirty years of age he was consecrated bishop for Dacia. After some seven years he was driven out by the king of the Goths and settled in the Roman empire in what is now part of Bulgaria and Yugoslavia. Here he translated the Bible into the language of the Goths. Since he apparently translated on a very literalistic basis, his version often retains Greek word order even against Gothic idiom. Ulfilas is also credited with having created the Gothic alphabet and reducing the language to writing as a preliminary to translating the Scriptures, although this is disputed by some. At any rate, the Gothic Bible is the earliest written Gothic literature, having been completed before the death of Ulfilas about 383. The Gothic NT is extant in some six MSS, almost all fragmentary palimpsests. An exception is Codex Argenteus, in Uppsala, Sweden, which contains portions of all four Gospels written in silver and gold ink on purple vellum. All of the Gothic MSS are from the 5th and 6th centuries.

B. Armenian. There have been two principal theories of the origin of the Armenian NT. According to one view, which goes back to Armenian writers of the 5th and 6th centuries, St. Mesrop created the Armenian alphabet and translated the NT into Armenian from Greek with the help of St. Sahak. According to another 5th-cent. writer, St. Sahak translated the NT from Syriac. Both views have been espoused by modern scholars, and the question cannot be regarded as decided. The Armenian is said to be one of the most beautiful and accurate of all versions. Moreover, its more than 1,500 extant MSS rank it second only to the Latin Vulgate and the Greek. The oldest MS is dated A.D. 887. A revision that became the dominant form of the version in the 8th cent. is the basis of the Armenian text still in use.

C. Georgian. Christianity was introduced into the country of Georgia, between the Black and Caspian seas, in the 4th cent. Soon thereafter, at least by the middle of the 5th cent., the NT had been translated into the Georgian language. Tradition attributes the Georgian alphabet to the same Mesrop who is said to have developed the Armenian alphabet. Various theories have been put forth concerning the origin of the Georgian, holding that it was translated from Greek, Syriac, or Armenian. In any event, the Georgian exhibits close relationships to the Armenian. It underwent several revisions in the course of time, the principal one occurring in the 10th or 11th cent. and based on Greek MSS of the later or Byzantine text-type. There are numerous MSS of the Georgian version; three of the most important date between 897 and 995, and are believed to preserve significant elements of the Old Georgian.

D. Ethiopic. Widely divergent views of the date of the origin of the Ethiopic NT have been put forward, ranging all the way from the 2nd to the 14th cent. There is difference of opinion, too, as to whether the version was made from Greek or Syriac. Although none of the more than 100 MSS is earlier than the 13th cent., and most are even later, the NT in Ethiopic must have originated by the 6th cent., or possibly earlier. Relatively little attention has been given to this version, although careful investigation of it might prove rewarding.

E. Slavonic. The Slavonic version of the NT owes its origin to two brothers, St. Cyril and St. Methodius, who died in 869 and 885 respectively. They were sons of a wealthy official in Salonica, and were thus presumably acquainted with the Slavic dialect spoken in Macedonia. Cyril was christened Constantine, taking the name Cyril only when he entered a monastery in Rome shortly before his death. There are two Slavonic alphabets, the Glagolitic and the Cyrillic. The latter is named in honor of St. Cyril, who is credited with having invented it; but it is actually unclear whether he, possibly aided by his brother, constructed one or both forms of the alphabet or revised an alphabet already in existence. On the other hand, the Glagolitic may be the work of the brothers and the Cyrillic an adaptation to Greek by one of Cyril's disciples. Cyril is said to have begun translating the Gospels about 862. The description of the work given in the biographies of the brothers suggests that this earliest translation was in the form of a lectionary. Having begun his task of translation in Constantinople, Cyril completed it on the mission field, with the assistance of his brother in the Epistles and the OT. Extant MSS in Old Slavonic, which include an appreciable amount of Gospel lectionary material, date from the 11th cent. and later.

F. Arabic. From the 7th cent. and onward, if not earlier, numerous translations of the NT into Arabic were made. Indeed, one modern scholar has suggested that there are more versions of the Gospels in Arabic than can be welcome to scholars. They were made from Greek, Syriac, Coptic, Latin, and various mixed sources. Some MSS exhibit a text in the form of rhymed prose which is found in the Koran. The form of the text in use today, at least in the Gospels, is based on a 13th-cent. revision; it is primarily a translation from the Bohairic NT with some Greek and Syriac influence.

G. Persian. The Gospels in Persian survive in a 14th-cent. MS, which is derived from a version translated from Syriac and a later version based on Greek.

H. Frankish. Fragments of Matthew in Frankish, a Germanic language of west-central Europe, sur-

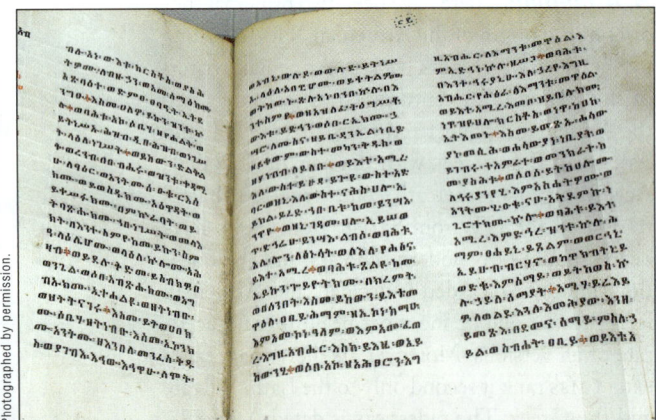

A relatively recent Ethiopic MS of the Bible, dating to the 18th cent.

vive in one 8th-cent. MS, with Latin and Frankish on facing pages, in the library of the Benedictine monastery at Monsee.

I. Sogdian. Sogdian was the trade language of Eastern Turkestan and regions to the E between the 6th and 10th centuries. In addition to a small amount of other literary remains in Sogdian, a lectionary of the Gospels and fragments of 1 Corinthians and Galatians are extant, written in a consonantal script and translated from Syriac.

J. Nubian. Two Christian kingdoms seem to have existed in Nubia, between Ethiopia and Egypt, during the early Middle Ages. The northern kingdom received the Christian message in the 6th cent.; little is known of the southern kingdom. A fragment of an Old Nubian lectionary is extant, dating from about the 10th cent. and containing small portions from the Gospels and Epistles.

(In addition to the titles mentioned in the body of this article, see the bibliographies under TEXT AND MANUSCRIPTS (OT) and TEXT AND MANUSCRIPTS (NT). Note also I. M. Price, *The Ancestry of Our English Bible*, 3rd rev. ed. by W. A. Irwin and A. P. Wikgren [1956], 83–100, 109–22, 177–201; F. F. Bruce, *The Books and the Parchments: Some Chapters on the Transmission of the Bible*, 3rd ed. [1963]; B. M. Metzger, *Chapters in the History of New Testament Textual Criticism* [1963], 73–120; E. Nida, ed., *Book of a Thousand Tongues*, rev. ed. [1972]; P. D. Wegner, *The Journey from Texts to Translations: The Origin and Development of the Bible* [1999], ch. 15; B. M. Metzger, *The Bible in Translation: Ancient and English Versions* [2001]; P. A. Noss, ed., *History of Bible Translation* [2007]; *ABD*, 6:787–813.)

J. H. GREENLEE

versions of the Bible, English. Published translations of the Holy Scriptures in the English language.

    I. The need for versions and new versions
    II. Principles of Bible translation
    III. Anglo-Saxon and Middle English versions
    IV. Modern versions prior to 1611
    V. The King James Version, 1611
    VI. Important versions since the KJV
    VII. Contemporary issues in translation

I. The need for versions and new versions. Only a Bible-reading believer can be an effective Christian to the limit of his or her potential; only a Bible-reading church can be truly effective in service to God and in witnessing to the world. The ordinary person today, however, cannot read the Scriptures in the original Hebrew and Greek. These considerations require the translation of the Bible into all languages of the world, including English, and the progressive revision and improvement of translations.

The English language continues to change. Since the earliest Bible translations into English, the language has evolved so much that the versions of 600 years ago are barely intelligible to the ordinary reader today. The language is still changing, with new words and expressions coming into use and old ones becoming obsolete and, in time, unintelligible. If the Bible is to be understood and believed by present-day people it must be in a language which conveys a clear meaning to them. As long as English continues to be a living language there will be a need for new and improved translations of the Bible in English.

In addition, new MSS have been discovered, giving a truer text as a base for translation. Since the KJV was produced, there have been three great discoveries of previously unknown MSS which have greatly increased the available resources for reconstruction of a thoroughly accurate and trustworthy text of the Scriptures in the original languages, thus making possible more accurate and faithful versions. These discoveries are: (1) CODEX SINAITICUS, discovered in 1844 in the monastery of St. Catherine in the Sinai peninsula by Tischendorf. This Greek MS of the NT, written in the 4th cent. and containing most of the NT, proved to be of immense value for establishing the genuine text of the NT. It is generally recognized as one of the three or four most important Greek MSS of the NT. (2) The NT papyri (see PAPYRUS), consisting of fragments discovered in Egypt since 1895, have proved of great value for the scholarly study of the NT. (3) The DEAD SEA SCROLLS, discovered in caves near the Dead Sea beginning in 1947, have provided an almost complete MS of the Hebrew text of Isaiah, another scroll of Isaiah somewhat less complete, and portions of almost every book of the

OT. These MSS are hundreds of years older than the oldest previously known extant MSS of the OT in Hebrew. In large part they have strongly confirmed the authenticity of the previously known Hebrew text, but at some points they have enabled scholars to determine a more accurate form of the text.

Moreover, biblical scholarship has progressively advanced, making greater accuracy possible. Present knowledge is built upon foundations laid in the past, and with the passing of time an increasing storehouse of knowledge is laid up. Scholars of the present day have at their disposal resources that were comparatively unknown two or three centuries ago. This is the case especially along two lines: (1) Textual criticism as an exact and rigorous discipline has been largely a development of the last two centuries. This discipline undertakes to establish the genuine text of a book or document, as far as possible, by the use of scholarly procedures of great precision in determining which of existing variant readings is the authentic original and therefore correct one. When the KJV and prior translations were made, textual criticism was merely in its infancy. (2) Philology or the study of languages has made great advances during the last 300 years. Not only has great progress been made in the study of Hebrew and Greek as languages, but the study of cognate languages has added to the understanding of the Scriptures. This is especially true of ANE languages that are cognate to Hebrew and have often provided a key to the meaning of rare Hebrew words. See LANGUAGES OF THE ANE.

The need for new versions should not be exaggerated. The differences between the KJV and the most accurate modern versions are comparatively slight, and all the main teachings of the Bible are quite clear in the KJV or almost any other translation. The importance of the Bible, however, requires the best possible contemporary version for the times. As the Bible is the message of God addressed to human beings, it should be made available in the finest translations, which will most faithfully reproduce in English the thought of the original and which will be most easily grasped by the present-day reader. Providing the best possible English version will not of itself induce Christian faith, but it will remove one of the semantic obstacles to faith and thus clear the way for the Holy Spirit's work of producing repentance, faith, and commitment.

II. Principles of Bible translation. (1) The starting point is a reliable text. There are many MSS of the Scriptures in Hebrew and Greek, and there are often slight variations between these documents. In the case of the Greek NT, there are thousands of MSS of all or part of the NT, and of these no two are exactly alike. Obviously some errors have been committed in the process of copying MSS before the invention of printing. To weed these errors out is the task of textual criticism, which seeks to restore insofar as possible the genuine text of the lost original documents (called autographs). No translation can be better than the text from which it is made. It is possible to make a poor translation of a good text, and it is also possible to make a good translation of a poor text. In the latter case the "good" translation will faithfully reproduce the errors that may exist in the corrupt original text. In the case of the KJV of the NT, it is a good translation of a rather poor text, inferior to what is available to scholars of the present day. Manuscript discoveries since the KJV translators worked, and textual criticism in the hands of competent scholars, have given a text of the Greek NT greatly superior to the best that was available in 1611. See TEXT AND MANUSCRIPTS (NT).

(2) Fidelity to the meaning of the original text is important. A low degree of fidelity may arise from: (a) lack of philological and/or theological learning; (b) excessive zeal for modernizing the language of the Bible, which may lead translators to take liberties with statements of the original; and (c) theological bias. With regard to this last point, complete objectivity is impossible in any scholarly work, and it is inevitable that a translator's personal faith, theological convictions, basic assumptions, and worldview will affect his or her work as a translator. If a given word can be legitimately translated in either of two different ways, and one of these is in harmony with the language and teachings of Scripture elsewhere, while the other introduces a contradiction or conflict into the English version of the Bible, the translator who is committed to the plenary inspiration and inerrancy of the Bible and its internal consistency as an organic whole will choose the translation that is compatible with these principles; the

translator who does not accept these principles may choose the rendering that is most compatible with his modern worldview, even though it involves a contradiction of other Scripture statements.

(3) Skill in the use of English is needed. Much depends on the ability of the translators, their facility in using the English language in such a way as to combine accuracy and fidelity with lucidity and forcefulness in the use of modern diction and idiom. A danger exists of going to an extreme in one direction or another. (a) Excessive literality should be avoided. A close literal translation, rather than being the most faithful, may actually be misleading to the modern reader. The KJV rendering of Matt. 20:2, "And when he had agreed with the labourers for a penny a day, he sent them into his vineyard," is certainly literal, but may mislead modern readers into supposing that these men were paid almost nothing for their work. The translator must strive to use language that will accurately convey the precise *thought* of the original to the reader. And, of course, a translation that is too literal, even when faithful to the thought of the original, may be clumsy and unnatural English.

(b) Excessive freedom also should be avoided. Paraphrases and "expanded translations" may or may not be helpful, depending on the learning and skill of the translators and their restraint and self-discipline in their work. Excessive freedom in translation often tends to substitute general or inclusive ideas for particular or specific ones of the Bible (e.g., "church officer" instead of the specific "presbyter" or "deacon"). The greatest danger involved in excessive freedom, however, is that modern ideas that are really foreign to the Scriptures may be introduced into the translation. Excessive freedom in translation gives an entrance to all kinds of theological bias and thus militates against fidelity.

(c) A wise middle ground should be sought. The ideal translation will be neither too literal nor too free. Just where the line will be drawn between literality and freedom will depend on the purpose for which the translation is intended. No universally applicable rule of thumb can govern in a matter of this kind. To produce a translation that is neither too literal nor too free, the translation must be not only learned and skillful, but also wise. The truly great and good translations are products not only of scholarship but also of real wisdom, and they will stand the test of time when those of less merit lapse into oblivion.

III. Anglo-Saxon and Middle English versions.

Anglo-Saxon, a W Germanic language, was the true parent of English, even though so different from modern English as to be unintelligible today without special study. This language in its several dialects was the speech of the people of England when Christianity reached them in the 6th cent. The Old British Church, dating from Roman times, was made up of people of the Celtic race and used the Scriptures in Latin. This church was largely eliminated or driven into the mountains of Wales by the invasions of Germanic tribes from the Continent. When Christianity reached the English (as distinguished from the earlier British), the Angles, Saxons, and Jutes were pagans with a religion similar to that of the Germans and Scandinavians. As English became Christianized, there was need for the Bible in their common language, even though the Latin Bible remained dominant throughout the Middle Ages. About A.D. 675 Caedmon composed and sang paraphrases of passages of the Bible in Anglo-Saxon. His production, however, was not really a translation of the Bible, but a song based on biblical narratives. This served for a time as a sort of makeshift Bible for the English people.

Some versions of the Psalms and Gospels appeared in Old English or Anglo-Saxon times. A bishop named Aldhelm is credited with translating the Psalter about the year 700. Bede, a learned monk, translated portions of the NT into Anglo-Saxon or Old English. King Alfred (871–901) provided for the translation into the common language of the Ten Commandments and portions of Exodus and Acts. He is said also to have made a new translation of some of the Psalms.

Interlinear translations into Old English appear in some Latin MSS, dating from the 9th and 10th centuries. From the same period come the Wessex Gospels in Old English. About the end of the 10th cent., an abbot named Aelfric translated portions of the OT from Genesis through Judges. The Wessex Gospels and Aelfric's translations are not completely unintelligible to the modern reader, though it is impossible to follow them closely without a

special study of their language. It should be realized that these Anglo-Saxon or Old English translations of portions of Scripture were never the sole or main Bible of the church. Latin was the basic Scripture and was used almost exclusively by the clergy, while the vernacular portions had an appeal to the ordinary Christian who was ignorant of Latin.

The Norman conquest of England (A.D. 1066) marked the end of the production of Scripture translations into English for some three centuries, during which time Norman French largely supplanted English among educated people, and Latin, of course, continued to be used by the clergy. In the 14th cent. English translations of the Scriptures began to appear again, the form of the language being what is now called Middle English. These included two translations of the Psalms and one of several of the NT letters. Somewhat later came the book of Acts and part of Matthew. A modern reader who is familiar with the Bible can follow these versions with a high degree of comprehension of the meaning. Often it is only the spelling that impresses one as strange.

A significant turning point takes place with the Wycliffite versions. John Wycliffe was born about 1330 and died in 1384. He was a learned theological scholar of Oxford. A strong believer in the Bible as the Word of God and as a message addressed to every person, he felt the need of providing the Scriptures in a form that ordinary people could use. Interested in both religious and political reform in England, Wycliffe had powerful enemies who finally were able to bring him to trial for heresy. In the ecclesiastical trial that followed, Wycliffe's doctrines were condemned as heretical, and he was forced to retire from public life. He spent the remaining year and a half of his life in retirement.

Wycliffe himself was not a translator of the Bible, as far as is known. However, he promoted Bible translation, and two complete versions of the Bible were produced as a part of his movement. These were handwritten, as printing had not yet been invented. The first Wycliffite version appeared soon after 1380, and the second one some years later, after Wycliffe's death. Both were translated from the Latin version known as the VULGATE.

The first Wycliffite version is a literal rendering of the Latin. The identity of the translator(s) is unknown, but there is some evidence that a monk named Nicholas of Hereford did at least part of the work. The second Wycliffite version was made by Wycliffe's secretary, John Purvey, after Wycliffe's death. Purvey started with the first Wycliffite version and revised it completely, producing a Bible with much more natural and idiomatic English than the earlier version had. Purvey found that many existing MSS of the Latin Vulgate were corrupt, and he did considerable critical study in collected Vulgate MSS in order to obtain as pure a Latin text as possible. Purvey's version, although of necessity circulated only in MS form, had wide influence, not only immediately after Wycliffe's time and among the membership of his movement, but also among the general population of England down to the time when printing was invented and newer translations began to be published.

IV. Modern versions prior to 1611. *The Tyndale version, 1534.* William Tyndale was born about 1494. He studied at the Universities of Oxford and Cambridge. Two things prepared the way for the publication of his monumental English version of the NT: the invention of the art of printing, about 1450, and the publication of Erasmus's edition of the NT in the original Greek in 1516, with subsequent revisions. Although printing had been in existence for three quarters of a century before the publication of Tyndale's version, there were obstacles that had prevented the production of Purvey's Wycliffite version in printed form. Tyndale's was therefore the first printed edition of the Scriptures in English.

Tyndale was a student of both Greek and Hebrew. He translated the NT directly from Greek into English, unlike previous versions that had depended on the Latin Vulgate. While still a young man, Tyndale conceived the idea of making a new and better translation of the Scriptures in English, an idea that increasingly became his life's interest and passion. About 1523 he sought help and encouragement from the Bishop of London, but obtained none, and the next year he decided that it would be virtually impossible to do what he had in mind anywhere in England. He left England for Germany in 1524, never to return. He found it necessary to move from place to place several times in order to escape interference. At one point he visited the Reformer Martin Luther at Wittenberg. In 1525 or 1526 copies of Tyndale's first English NT reached England. He published repeated editions of his NT and also worked on the translation of the OT. His OT translation was based on the original Hebrew, the Latin Vulgate, and early modern translations. More than 15,000 copies of the first six editions of Tyndale's NT were printed. Many copies were purchased by the Bishop of London with the intention of burning them. Tyndale used the money thus obtained to publish new editions and larger printings.

In 1523 Tyndale was betrayed to his enemies while living in Belgium. He was imprisoned, tried for heresy, and convicted; he was put to death by strangling (6 Oct. 1536), and his body was burned. His last words were: "Lord open the king of England's eyes." Before his death an edition of the whole Bible, based largely upon Tyndale's work but without his name, was being circulated and read in England, openly, with the permission of the king, so Tyndale's dying prayer was already being answered, though he was not aware of this at the time.

Tyndale's version is important not only because it was a pioneer effort in translating the Scriptures directly from the original languages into English, but also because of the great influence it had upon later versions. There is a fresh naturalness in Tyndale's style, a simplicity and directness that mark the work as a truly great achievement in literature, apart from its epoch-making religious importance. A great deal of the beautiful English style of the KJV goes back to the work of William Tyndale, so that one may rightly say that Tyndale's work lives on in the Bibles of the present day.

The Coverdale version, 1535. Born about 1488, Miles Coverdale was a few years Tyndale's senior. After being educated at Cambridge and becoming a priest, he developed a consuming passion for learning, especially in the field of biblical studies. He went to Germany in 1528. In 1535 his translation of the Bible was printed, probably in Germany. Though not officially endorsed by the English government, it was not banned. In 1538–39 Coverdale worked in Paris supervising the printing of another English version, the Great Bible (published 1540). He died in 1569. Unlike Tyndale, Coverdale did not attempt to translate directly from Hebrew and Greek into English. He depended largely on the Latin Vulgate, on Luther's German translation, and on Tyndale's English. Coverdale's was the first complete English Bible to be printed. Bishop Westcott stated that Coverdale's NT is a revision of Tyndale's first edition, revised by means of Tyndale's second and also by comparison with Luther's German version. While not having the pioneering importance of Tyndale's work, Coverdale's Bible holds a noble place in the history of the English Bible.

Matthew's Bible, 1537. This translation is believed to be the work of a man named John Rogers, who came into possession of some of Tyndale's yet unpublished translations of some of the OT books. Rogers, born in or about 1500, served for a period of years as a pastor in Germany. After returning to England he was burned alive in 1555. It is believed that the name "Thomas Matthew" which appears on the title page is a pseudonym intended to veil the identity of the real translator and to prevent people from identifying the book with Tyndale and Tyndale's disciples. Part of the OT is virtually identical with Tyndale's version, but part is a new translation. It is estimated that about two-thirds of Matthew's Bible is the work of Tyndale. Matthew's version became the basis for the Bishops' Bible, the Great Bible, and the KJV.

Taverner's Bible, 1539. Richard Taverner was born about 1505. He studied at the universities of Oxford and Cambridge. On one occasion he was jailed for reading Tyndale's NT. He studied law

A page from the Pentateuch in Tyndale's Bible (1530).

and became a lawyer, while continuing his interest in the English Bible. Taverner had a good knowledge of Greek. For a time he was imprisoned in the Tower of London because of his activity in Bible translation and revision. Under Queen Elizabeth I, however, he was appointed to political office. Taverner's Bible was first published in London in 1539. This version is a minor revision of Matthew's Bible. Its influence was not great, though it did have a permanent effect in introducing some good English words in place of terms of Latin derivation.

The Great Bible, 1540. Both Coverdale's and Matthew's versions were being freely circulated and read in England, yet there existed a demand for a better version, and especially one without the marginal explanatory notes of Matthew's version, which were regarded as objectionable by some of the clergy as too strongly Protestant. Thomas Cromwell, King Henry VIII's vicegerent in matters pertaining to the Church of England, encouraged the production of the Great Bible, which was printed in Paris. The printing was interrupted by the Roman Catholic Inquisition, but later resumed and completed in England. The term "Great" comes from the size of the volume, which was the largest of all English Bibles yet published. It came out in 1540, with a preface by Cranmer, the Archbishop of Canterbury, and the title page bore the words, "This is the Bible appointed to be read in Churches." It was really an "authorized" version. Because of political changes in England, this Bible had its ups and downs. At one time it was ordered placed in churches, at another time ordered removed, and then later again restored. The last printing took place in 1569.

The Geneva Bible, 1560. Roman Catholic ascendancy and persecution in England under Mary (1553–58) made further Bible translation and publication there virtually impossible. Several English Protestant scholars fled to Switzerland for safety and gathered at Geneva, the headquarters of the Reformed type of Protestantism and the residence of the Reformer John Calvin. William Whittingham had a revised NT published at Geneva in 1557. Soon after this, several scholars began work on a revision of the whole Bible, a labor on which they spent some two years. The outcome of this effort was the Geneva Bible, published in 1560. This work was based mainly on the Great Bible in the OT and on Tyndale's version in the NT. It contained copious notes, most of which were scholarly explanations of difficult points in the text, such as historical and geographical references. Some of the notes were doctrinal and some hortatory. A few were objected to by some Protestants as too Calvinistic. The Geneva version soon became popular and widely read and its influence was great, more perhaps in the homes of the people than in the churches and among the clergy.

The Bishops' Bible, 1568. In 1566 Matthew Parker, Archbishop of Canterbury, initiated the effort to produce a revision of the Bible by the bishops of the Church of England. They used the Great Bible as their basis for revision. The product is of uneven quality, the NT being much better, in general, than the OT. The Bishops' Bible was used generally in churches until 1611. Printing of it ceased in 1602.

The Rheims-Douay Bible, 1582–1610. After Elizabeth I became queen, many Roman Catholics left England, most of them going to France or Belgium. Among English Catholic refugees at the University of Douay in northern France, there came to be felt a need for an English version of the Bible approved by the authorities of the Roman Catholic Church. This resulted in the production of the Rheims-Douay Bible, of which the NT was published at Rheims in 1582 and the OT at Douay in 1610. This version was made from the Latin Vulgate, with occasional slight help from the Hebrew and Greek originals.

The Geneva Bible (1560).

The English style and diction are poor in comparison with the contemporary Protestant versions and especially in comparison with the beautiful English of the KJV, which appeared soon after the Rheims-Douay version was completed. In 1749–50 it was published in revised form by Richard Challoner. There also have been further revisions since Challoner and on the basis of his work.

V. The King James Version, 1611. James I became king of England in 1603. In 1604 he called the Hampton Court Conference, an effort to prepare the way for reconciliation between the religious parties existing in his kingdom. This conference failed to bring about any real reconciliation between the bishops and the Puritan party. It did however have the positive result of preparing the way for the production of the King James Version of the Bible. A resolution was passed calling for a translation of the whole Bible from the original Hebrew and Greek into English, with no marginal comments, to be the sole Bible for use in the public worship services of the Church of England. Though not all the bishops were in favor of the new project, King James endorsed it, stating that none of the existing English versions was translated well, and in his opinion the Geneva version was the worst of them all! James called for a new version to be prepared by the best scholars in Oxford and Cambridge universities, then reviewed by the bishops of the Church of England, and finally to be officially approved by the Privy Council and the king as the only Bible to be used in the Church of England.

Forty-seven scholars were recruited for the work, and these were the most learned men of their time in England. The work of translation took some two years. The Bishops' Bible was used as a basis, but others, including Tyndale's, Coverdale's, and the Geneva version could be used as added helps. The KJV translators had at their disposal better Hebrew and Greek texts than were available to previous scholars. The final product was certainly the best English Bible that had ever existed. The English style is universally recognized as superb. Most noteworthy, however, is the remarkable fidelity of the KJV translations to the truth of the Scriptures. That the KJV held its own as the leading English Bible for so long is a monument to their diligence and faithfulness.

Even after four centuries and numerous revisions and new translations, the KJV is still very popular. It has been precious to millions who have loved it for its simple, dignified, beautiful presentation of the Word of God. The KJV has abundantly proved itself preeminently the Bible of the English-speaking world.

VI. Important versions since the KJV. *Young's Literal Translation, 1863.* This version was produced by Robert Young, the compiler of the well-known *Young's Analytical Concordance*. Young held that the only truly faithful translation is a literal one. The first edition was published in Edinburgh in 1863.

The English Revised Version, 1881–1885. The impulse to produce this version came from within the Church of England, but scholars of several denominations participated in the work, including an American committee. The basis for revision was the KJV, which could be changed only by a two-thirds vote of the main committee. The NT was published in 1881 and included an appendix with readings preferred by the American committee but not adopted by the British committee. The OT was issued in 1885, and the entire Bible in one volume in 1898. This version is a conservative, cautious revision of the KJV, retaining much, but not all, of its English style. It has had considerable circulation but has never come near the KJV in sales or popular favor.

The American Standard Version, 1901. The American Revision Committee that cooperated in producing the English RV had promised to refrain

The 1611 King James "He" Bible, so designated because in Ruth 3:15 it reads, "and he went into the city," whereas most editions of the KJV have, "and she went into the city."

from publishing an American edition of the RV for 14 years. In 1901 the American Revised Version or ASV came out, embodying those readings favored by the American committee. Among the important differences between the two are the use of "Jehovah" instead of "Lord" in the OT as the translation of the Hebrew *yhwh*, the use of "Holy Spirit" in place of "Holy Ghost," and the use of "love" instead of "charity" in 1 Cor. 13. Lacking something of the literary beauty of the KJV, the ASV version excels it in accuracy, and is based on a superior Greek text in the NT. It has been used widely as a Bible for study, but has never enjoyed the popularity of the KJV.

Weymouth's Modern Speech NT, 1903. Translated by R. F. Weymouth, a British Baptist layman, this version has twice (1924, 1933) been revised by others since the translator's death. It is a product of substantial scholarship and is marked by a reverent attitude toward the text of Scripture.

The Twentieth Century NT, 1904. This version was made by about twenty scholars of various denominations. The order of books varies from that of most Bibles, the Gospel of Mark coming first. The translation is very free.

The Jewish Version of 1917. This work contains the canonical books of the OT only, and in general is very similar to the KJV. The preface states that "the christological interpretations in non-Jewish translations are out of place in a Jewish Bible" (p. viii; cf. the rendering of Gen. 3:15 and Isa. 9:5).

Moffatt's New Translation, 1924, 1935. James Moffatt was an outstanding theological liberal, who frankly disclaimed belief in the verbal inspiration of Scripture. This viewpoint affected his work, especially in certain crucial passages. Still, this is a work of solid scholarship and brilliant style and was popular for many years.

The Smith-Goodspeed Version, 1931. Edgar Goodspeed published his NT in 1923, the OT was translated by H. M. Powis Smith and others (1927), and the whole Bible appeared in 1931. The subtitle is "An American Translation." At some points the freedom of translation verges on paraphrase.

The Charles B. Williams NT, 1937. Subtitled, "A Translation in the Language of the People," this version by an American Baptist scholar must be carefully distinguished from that of the British scholar Charles K. Williams. That of Charles B. Williams is regarded by many as one of the best of the modern versions of the NT.

Ronald Knox's Catholic Version, 1944–50. This work by a British Roman Catholic scholar is a production of real merit. Though based on the Latin Vulgate, the work shows thorough acquaintance with the Hebrew and Greek originals. The translation is forceful and readable, and quite faithful to the original. Many Roman Catholic interpretations are found in the footnotes. Knox's version has been popular, especially among British Roman Catholics.

The Revised Standard Version, 1946–52. This purports to be a revision of the KJV, RV, and ASV. It still retains something of the literary style of the KJV. Its renderings are dignified and free from vulgar, slangy or merely contemporary usages. The theological viewpoint of the translators certainly affected their work, especially at certain crucial points such as Isa. 7:14. Exception may be taken, also, to the rather free use of conjectural emendation (which is sometimes, but not always, indicated in footnotes). The RSV has proven very popular and has been widely used (including in a Roman Catholic ed.).

The Confraternity Version, 1948. This is a Roman Catholic version and is essentially a modern English revision of the Rheims-Douay-Challoner version. The OT is not completed in the new version; most printings have several books of the OT in the new version and the rest of the OT in the older version. It is a scholarly production but suffers from the disadvantage of being a translation of the Latin Vulgate rather than of the Hebrew and Greek originals. It contains numerous footnotes, many of which are typically Roman Catholic in tendency.

The New World Translation, 1950–60. Published by the Watchtower Bible and Tract Society, an agency of the International Bible Students Association, this is the Bible of the sect commonly known as Jehovah's Witnesses. It is marred throughout by its very obvious bias in favor of the peculiar doctrines of the sect that produced it. Apart from this, it is of uneven quality, sometimes being stiffly literal and sometimes excessively colloquial.

The New Testament in Modern English, by J. B. Phillips, 1958. This is a paraphrase rather than a translation. Many have found it very acceptable, and beyond question it presents the NT in a form that the modern reader can grasp easily. It manifests a tendency to broaden specific scriptural concepts to more general ones which are not always biblical, such as the use of "agreement" instead of "covenant," "acquitted" instead of "justified." This version will be of value chiefly as a sidelight used along with one or more of the less free "standard" versions.

The Berkeley Version, 1959. The NT of this version was published in 1945, the entire Bible in 1959; published after further revision in 1971 under the title *The Modern Language Bible.* The theological orientation is evangelical and the Scriptures are treated throughout as the infallible Word of God. The English is more modern than that of the RSV, but not excessively colloquial. In its day it was probably the most faithful and satisfactory version of the whole Bible in truly modern English. Among the numerous footnotes are many of real value in helping the reader to grasp the meaning of the text.

Wuest's Expanded Translation of the New Testament, 1961. This work is similar to the Amplified version. Essentially a paraphrase, it should be used as such, along with more literal versions, not by itself alone.

The New English Bible. The NT appeared in 1961 and the entire Bible in 1970. Unlike the RV and the RSV, this is not a revision of previous versions but a completely new translation from the Hebrew and Greek. Its chief merit is its rendering the text of Scripture into modern yet dignified English. It has been criticized as using needlessly sophisticated language in some places (e.g., "bedizened" in place of "decked" in Rev. 17:4; 18:16). A more serious criticism that has been brought against it is that it lacks theological precision and awareness, and in crucial texts betrays a distinctly liberal bias. For example, in Gen. 1:1 the NEB reads, "In the beginning of creation, when God made heaven and earth …"; in 3:15, "I will put enmity between you and the woman, between your brood and hers. They shall strike at your head, and you shall strike at their heel" (here the Heb. sg. pronouns have been arbitrarily changed to pl. forms, thus eliminating a prophetic reference to Jesus Christ); in Ps. 2:11, "Kiss the king"; in Isa. 7:14, "a young woman is with child"; in 53:10, "Yet the Lord took thought for his tortured servant and healed him who had made himself a sacrifice for sin." In passages where the Greek *sarx* G4922 (lit., "flesh") is used to mean fallen sinful nature, the NEB renders the word with terms that seem to confuse man as a sinner with man as a creature: "lower nature" (Rom. 8:3–5, 7, 12; Gal. 5:13, 16, 19, 24; 6:8; Col. 2:11); "unspiritual nature" (Rom. 7:18, 25); "bodily appetites" (Rom. 13:14); "sensuality" (Eph. 2:3); "instincts" (Eph. 2:3). In all these passages the NEB introduces an idea found in philosophical thought, but foreign to the Bible: that human beings have a "higher" and a "lower" nature, and that evil is identified with the "lower" nature. In the Bible the *whole* of human nature is regarded as corrupted by sin. Those capable of weighing this version critically should use it with due caution; the reader who knows no Greek may be seriously misled by it.

The New Testament in Plain English (Charles Kingsley Williams), 1963. This version is an attempt to render the NT into English with a very limited vocabulary—only about half as many words as are in the Greek NT. What a version of this type gains in apparent simplicity is lost in real communication of truth. This version may be of some use to readers for whom English is a foreign language.

The New Testament in the Language of Today: An American Translation (William F. Beck), 1963. This modern English version by a Lutheran scholar is an excellent production. Faithful to the Scriptures, modern in language and style, free from vulgarity, it is a work of able scholarship and reverent faith.

The New American Standard Bible. This translation was prepared by fifty-eight originally anonymous (but now acknowledged) scholars under the auspices of the Lockman Foundation of La Habra, California. The NT appeared in 1963 and the whole Bible in 1971. Based on the ASV, the NASB is the most consistently literal of major English versions produced over the last half century. Examples of this include its use of italicization of English words that do not have Greek or Hebrew parallels and the identification of historical present tense verbs in the NT with an asterisk. The NASB is theologically conservative and was produced in part in response to theological concerns related to the RSV. An updated edition was released in 1995 that removed some archaic language, increased readability, and removed the archaic "thees" and "thous" with reference to deity.

The Amplified Bible, 1965. The NT of this version appeared in 1958, the OT later in two parts, and the entire Bible in 1965. By the use of parentheses and brackets it attempts to bring out more fully the meaning of important expressions. Such "amplification," of course, opens the door to debatable interpretation. Often the "amplification" is merely superfluous; nothing is really added by inserting "changed" in parenthesis after "transformed" (Rom. 12:2). A version of this type should be used as a help, with a more conventional version, not as an authority by itself.

The Letters of Paul: An Expanded Paraphrase (F. F. Bruce), 1965. This version gives the RV on the left-hand pages, and Bruce's "expanded paraphrase" on the opposite right-hand pages. A work of substantial learning, it should help many readers to grasp more fully the thought of Paul's epistles.

Today's English Version, also called *Good News for Modern Man*, and subsequently *Good News Bible*. The NT was translated by Robert Bratcher under the auspices of the American Bible Society (1966). The OT was subsequently produced by a team of translators, and the whole Bible was published in 1976. The TEV/GNB was the first English version to consistently adopt *dynamic equivalence*, the meaning-based translation principles developed by Eugene Nida and others involved in international Bible translation. This method is better known today as *functional equivalence* (to be distinguished from *formal correspondence* or *formal equivalence*; see below). The GNB is a clear, readable, and generally accurate version that paved the way for other meaning-based versions. It has sometimes been criticized for oversimplifying the text and for imposing a uniform pedantic style on the highly diverse styles and genres of scripture. A revised edition was introduced in 1992, which updated the translation generally and incorporated a moderate use of gender-inclusive language.

The Jerusalem Bible, 1966. This is a Roman Catholic version first published in England. It began as a French version, *Bible de Jérusalem* (1956), produced by Catholic scholars in Jerusalem, hence its name. It includes a commentary on the same pages as the text. Various viewpoints of negative biblical criticism are incorporated in the notes.

The New American Bible, 1970. This work is a Roman Catholic version that arose in part as a result of an encyclical issued by Pope Pius XII in 1943, declaring that study of the original Hebrew and Greek text of Scripture had greater authority than ancient or modern versions. Prior to this time, Roman Catholic versions were translated from the Latin Vulgate. The NAB was originally based on the Confraternity Version of 1941, but was revised following the Hebrew and Greek. The complete Bible was released in 1970. It is more literal than the JB, but more idiomatic than other formal-equivalence versions. The NAB seeks to be more ecumenical than previous versions, and five of the fifteen members of its committee were Protestants. In 1986 a revised edition of the NT introduced, among other changes, the moderate use of inclusive language. In 1991 a revised edition of the Psalms did the same.

The Living Bible, 1972. This rather free paraphrase has become very popular and widely circulated. As in all "expanded translations" and paraphrases, debatable interpretation is sometimes introduced.

New International Version. The NIV was the result of a transdenominational effort by 100 scholars, sponsored by the New York Bible Society (now the International Bible Society). Each book was developed by a separate team of experts, then submitted to three successive editorial committees. Since its editors represented many different denominations, the translation was relatively free from sectarian bias. A smaller Committee on Bible Translation (CBT) of 15 members continued to examine and update the text. The NT was released in 1973 and the whole Bible in 1978. A minor revision was released in 1984. The NIV achieved huge success and by the mid-1980s began outselling the KJV. Twenty-five years after its release over 110 million copies were in print. The NIV's success may be due to its balance between formal correspondence and functional equivalence. It is readable yet closer to the cadence of the KJV tradition than other meaning-based versions. Because of a 1997 furor over plans to introduce gender-inclusive language, the 1984 NIV will remain the standard edition. The TNIV will carry forward the CBT's revision process.

New King James Version, 1982. A revision of the KJV, this translation was sponsored by Thomas Nelson Publishers of Nashville, Tennessee. More than 130 evangelical scholars produced the version over a seven-year period. The NT appeared in 1979 and the whole Bible followed in 1982. The primary distinction of the NKJV is its textual basis, utilizing the Textus Receptus, the edition of the Greek NT behind the KJV. Almost all other modern translations use the critical text derived from older Greek MSS. Footnotes in the NKJV alert the reader to different readings in the critical text as well as in the Majority text. While updating archaic words, the NKJV consciously seeks to retain the cadence, style, and idiom of the KJV. The NKJV is one of the most literal of the modern versions and in many cases is even more so than the KJV.

New Jerusalem Bible, 1985. A Roman Catholic translation, the NJB was a revision of the JB. When a new edition of the French version, *Bible de Jérusalem*, was published in 1973, the decision was made to update the JB. Among other changes, the NJB introduced the moderate use of inclusive language. This translation is slightly more literal than its predecessor but somewhat freer than the NAB.

Tanakh, 1985. The Jewish Publication Society's *The Holy Scriptures According to the Masoretic Text* of 1917 (see above) remained the standard Jewish version for most of the 20th cent. By the middle of the century, however, a more contemporary version was deemed necessary, and the JPS authorized a new translation. The result was the *Tanakh* or *New Jewish Version*, published in stages (Torah, 1962; Prophets, 1978; Writings, 1982) and released as a whole in 1985. *Tanakh* is an acronym based on the first letter of the Hebrew names for the three divisions of the OT: *tôrâ* (Law; see TORAH), *nĕbîʾîm* (Prophets; see NEBIIM), and *kĕtûbîm* (Writings; see KETUBIM). This work is a highly respected version that utilizes the best of Jewish scholarship and a contemporary and idiomatic style.

New Century Version and International Children's Bible, 1986. The NCV and the ICB arose as revisions of a Bible originally designed for the deaf, produced by the World Translation Center in Fort Worth, Texas. The whole Bible was published in 1986 under two titles, the ICB for children and the NCV for more general readers. In 1991 the NCV was revised for a slightly higher reading level. Both versions are now published by Thomas Nelson. They are thoroughgoing functional-equivalent versions guided, according to the NCV preface, by two basic premises, faithfulness to the original text and clarity so that anyone can read and understand the Bible. Clarity is achieved especially through vocabulary selection based upon *The Living Word Vocabulary*, the standard used by the editors of *The World Book Encyclopedia*. Difficult words are replaced with more easily understood terms: "justify" becomes "make right"; "genealogy" becomes "family history." Figures of speech are simplified and idiomatic expressions are clarified. The NCV has achieved marketing success especially through the publication of Nelson's Bible-zines, glossy magazines with the text surrounded by pictures and articles geared for teens and young adults.

Revised English Bible, 1989. Shortly after the publication of the NEB in 1970, a committee was formed to assess and critique the text. The eventual result was the REB, a major revision published in 1989. The "thees" and "thous" used for prayer in the NEB have been removed, the somewhat highbrow style has been muted, and certain idiosyncratic readings have been changed. Greater consistency is achieved. For example, the Greek *ekklēsia* G1711 had been rendered in a variety of ways in the NEB: "church, congregation, meeting, community." The REB more consistently uses "church." The REB also introduced a moderate use of gender-inclusive language.

New Revised Standard Version, 1990. Like its predecessor, the RSV, the NRSV was not intended to be an entirely new translation, but rather to stand in a line of revision that began with the KJV of 1611. After the publication of the RSV in 1952, its translation committee continued to meet every few years to consider future changes and to make minor corrections to the text. In 1974 the National Council of Churches, which held the copyright to the RSV, authorized a new revision. The complete Bible was published in 1990. Like its predecessors, the NRSV is a formal-equivalence version, but not slavishly so, being more sensitive to Greek and Hebrew idiom than other literal versions. It is widely used in academic and scholarly circles. The NRSV was also the first English version to consistently and comprehensively introduce gender-inclusive language for masculine generic terms in Hebrew and Greek.

The Contemporary English Version, 1995. The CEV, like the TEV, is a functional-equivalence version produced by the American Bible Society. It is a committee work, overseen by translator and linguist Barclay Newman. Its goal was to apply even more consistently the translation principles developed by Eugene Nida and international Bible translators. The CEV's strength is clarity and natural English. Its weakness (for some readers) is that it seldom sounds like "the Bible"—the cadence and rhythm of the KJV so well known to many English speakers. This is of course also a strength, since the Bible sounded natural and idiomatic to its original readers. The CEV identifies itself as a *companion* rather than a *replacement* for traditional versions—a missionary version that seeks to cross cultural boundaries that other versions do not. Recognizing that many people hear the Bible more than they read it, particular attention is given to the clarity of the text when read aloud. Like other meaning-based versions, the CEV utilizes gender-inclusive language.

God's Word, 1995. This translation was produced by God's Word to the Nations Bible Society, an American Lutheran organization. In its preface the version claims to be using neither formal correspondence nor functional equivalence, but rather "closest natural equivalence"—a translation policy that avoids the awkwardness of literal versions and the loss of meaning of idiomatic ones. Despite this attempt to distinguish itself as unique, *God's Word* clearly fits into the genre of functional-equivalence versions like the TEV, NCV, NLT, and CEV. It is generally accurate and readable, comparable to these others in style and quality.

New Living Translation, 1996. The NLT is the long-awaited revision of the immensely popular *Living Bible.* While the latter was the work of a single translator (Kenneth Taylor), the NLT is a committee work involving some ninety evangelical scholars from various denominations. While the original work was a paraphrase, the NLT identifies itself as a dynamic or functional-equivalence translation that seeks the closest natural equivalent in the receptor language. The goal, according to the preface, is to have "the same impact on the modern readers as the original had on its own audience." The intentional shift from paraphrase to dynamic equivalence is evident in a verse like Jn. 1:1. Whereas the *Living Bible* read, "Before anything else existed, there was Christ," the NLT retains both the allusion to Gen. 1:1 and the Christological title "the Word": "In the beginning, the Word already existed." A revised edition was released in 2004. The NLT, like all recent functional-equivalence versions, utilizes gender-inclusive language.

New International reader's Version, 1996. This work is a basic English version based on the NIV. It is designed for children, adults with lower reading skills, and those for whom English is a second language. Simplicity and ease of understanding are emphasized throughout.

New English Translation (NET Bible), 2001. Something is always "lost in the translation," and this innovative and constantly evolving version arose from discussions among Bible scholars concerning the insufficiency of a simple translation to communicate the complexities of the meaning of Scripture. The NET's most distinctive feature is its inclusion of over 60,000 (ever-growing) footnotes that provide insight into the interpretation and nuances of the Greek and Hebrew text. The acronym NET is a play on words, referring both to the version's name and to its internet format. Although primarily an internet version, a printed edition of the NT was published in 1998 and the whole Bible in 2001. Subsequent editions have followed.

English Standard Version, 2001. The ESV is a light revision of the RSV (less than 5 percent changed) that seeks to move the latter in a more conservative and evangelical direction. In addition to "correcting" RSV readings viewed by some as liberal (cf. Isa. 7:14), the ESV removes "thees" and "thous," updates other archaic language, and at times moves the text in a slightly more literal direction. The ESV also adopts a moderate (though sometimes inconsistent) use of gender-inclusive language.

The Message, 2002. This work was produced by Eugene Peterson, with various scholars serving as translation consultants. The NT appeared in 1993 and the whole Bible in 2002. Its engaging and evocative language has struck a chord with many readers—much like the *Living Bible* in the 1960s and 70s—and has made the text a popular supplement to traditional versions. Peterson's goal was not to produce a word-for-word translation, but to convert the tone, rhythm, and ideas of the Bible, into the way people think and speak today. *The Message* does not really fit either formal or functional categories, but should be viewed as a response-oriented Bible, seeking vivid relevance more than historical precision.

Holman Christian Standard Version, 2004. The HCSB was produced by the Sunday School Board of the Southern Baptist Convention (SBC), and was intended to serve as an alternative to the NIV for Southern Baptist curriculum and ministry. It is published by Broadman Holman, the publishing wing of the SBC. The HCSB is more literal than the NIV but less so than other formal-equivalence versions. It strives for "optimal equivalence" or "precision with clarity." Though following the critical Greek text, the HCSB is unique among modern versions in supplying many alternate readings from the Textus Receptus and the Majority text in its footnotes (cf. NKJV). The massive constituency of the SBC should assure the commercial success of this version.

Today's New International Version, 2005. The TNIV arose over controversies surrounding the decision to introduce gender-inclusive language as part of the continuing revision process of the NIV. Faced with opposition, the International Bible Society (the NIV copyright holder) and Zondervan publishers chose to freeze the NIV in its 1984 edition, and to release the TNIV as a new and revisable version. The TNIV updates the NIV in light of advances in biblical scholarship and for greater accuracy and clarity. About 7 percent of the NIV has been altered, with approximately one third of these changes related to gender. The NT was released in 2001 and the whole Bible in 2005.

VII. Contemporary issues in translation

A. Formal versus functional equivalence.

The most fundamental issue in Bible translation is whether to translate according to form or according to function (= meaning). Formal equivalence, also called literal, word-for-word, or direct translation, seeks to retain the formal structure of the source language. Functional equivalence, also known as dynamic equivalence or idiomatic translation, seeks to produce the closest natural equivalent in the receptor language. In reality, there are no pure examples of either approach, and all versions lie on a spectrum between form and meaning. Even the most literal Bible translation must regularly introduce idiomatic readings in order to be comprehensible. Recent versions that are generally formal equivalent include NASB, NKJV, ESV, RSV, and NRSV. Functional equivalent versions include TEV, CEV, NCV, *God's Word*, and NLT. Mediating versions somewhere in between are NIV, TNIV, HCSB, NAB, NET, NJB, and REB.

Both formal and functional versions have a place in Bible study, and students of the Word should be encouraged to use a variety of versions from across the translation spectrum. Formal-correspondence versions are helpful for examining the formal structure of the original text, identifying Hebrew or Greek idioms, locating ambiguities in the text, and tracing formal verbal allusions and recurring words. Functional-equivalence versions are more helpful for communicating accurately the meaning of the text, and for providing clarity, readability, and natural-sounding language.

B. Gender language.

The gender language debate is closely related to the issue of form versus function. Supporters of gender-inclusive translation (sometimes called "gender-accurate" or "gender-neutral") claim that using inclusive terms like "person" for masculine generic terms in Hebrew and Greek is simply translating accurately the meaning of the text. Opponents counter that gender-inclusive language condescends to cultural feminism and downplays the patriarchy inherent in biblical languages and in a biblical worldview. Among recent versions, the consistent use of gender-inclusive language appears in CEV, NRSV, NCV, NLT, TEV, *God's Word*, and TNIV. Significant but not comprehensive use appears in NET, NAB, NJB, REB, ESV, and HCSB. None of these versions eliminate masculine God-language; two more radical versions that do are *The New Testament and Psalms: An Inclusive Version*, published by Oxford University Press (1995), and *The Inclusive New Testament*, published by Priests for Equality (1994).

While most scholars today would agree that terms like Greek *anthrōpos G476* (lit., "man") and *adelphoi* (pl of *adelphos G81*, "brother") are often used generically in Scripture and thus may be accurately rendered with inclusive language ("person" and "brothers and sisters," respectively), other issues cause more controversy and debate. Some of these include: (1) whether it is appropriate to translate masculine generic pronouns that are singular in Hebrew and Greek with English plural pronouns or other generic constructions; (2) whether pluralizing OT passages interpreted messianically in the NT distorts their meaning (e.g., Ps. 8:4–6 [cf. TNIV, "mortals … human beings … them"], cited in Heb. 2:6–8); (3) whether masculine terms like Hebrew *ʾādām H132* and Greek *anthrōpos G476* are true generics (= "person"), or whether they indicate male representation and hence male headship (= "man" as representative of the human race); (4) whether the English language has changed sufficiently to warrant such sweeping revisions.

While these and other issues will continue to be debated, common ground should be sought in the goal of rendering the biblical author's historical intention in language that is clear and comprehensible for the modern reader.

C. Historical particularity versus contemporary relevance. Some versions are denigrated as mere "paraphrases," which usually means highly idiomatic versions that are even one step farther from the original meaning than functional-equivalence versions. This definition, however, begs the question, since functional-equivalence versions claim to be *more accurate* than their formal-equivalence counterparts (by focusing on the meaning rather than the form of the text). The term *paraphrase* is also unhelpfully vague, and its normal definition is "to restate something using different words." Since all versions restate Greek and Hebrew words using English ones, *all translation* is paraphrase in this sense. More technically, linguists use the term for restating something in the same language. In this case, *no translation* would be paraphrase, except those like the *Living Bible*, which are simplified renderings of other English versions.

It is better, therefore, not to distinguish between "paraphrase" and "real translation," but between versions that seek to reproduce the *historical particularity* of the original text and those that strive for *contemporary relevance*. To state it another way: while both formal-correspondence and functional-equivalence translations seek to transport the modern reader backward into the world of the text, some versions seek to bring the world of the text to the contemporary reader. As with the difference between form and function, there are no pure examples of either strategy. All versions to some extent alter the historical particularity of the text to achieve contemporary relevance (e.g., by translating the Heb. idiom "to cover his feet" as "to relieve himself"; cf. 1 Sam. 24:3 NASB). Yet certain versions, like the *Living Bible*, Phillip's *New Testament in Modern English*, and *The Message*, are less concerned with historical precision and more with vivid relevance—bringing the text into the reader's own world. An extreme example is *The Cotton Patch Version* by Clarence Jordan, which sets the Gospels in the rural South during the U.S. civil rights movement. This approach has clearly crossed the line from translation to "transculturation," radically altering the historical particulars of the text. On the other hand, versions like *The Message*—though less concerned with historical precision and occasionally introducing anachronisms—are true translations since they generally strive to retain the original meaning of the text *in its own setting*. Yet they clearly lie on the "contemporary relevance" side of the spectrum.

(See further H. Barker, *English Bible Versions* [1907]; P. Marion Simms, *The Bible in America* [1936]; O. T. Allis, *Revised Version or Revised Bible?* [1953]; C. R. Thompson, *The Bible in English, 1525–1611* [1958]; G. S. Paine, *The Learned Men* [1959]; M. F. Hills, *The English Bible in America: A Bibliography of Editions of the Bible and the New Testament Published in America 1777–1957* [1961]; C. Gulston, *Our English Bible: No Greater Heritage* [1961]; J. H. Skilton, *The Translation of the New Testament into English, 1881–1950: Studies in Language and Style* [dissertation, Univ. of Pa., 1961]; D. Coggan, *The English Bible* [1963]; D. M. Beegle, *God's Word into English* [1964]; American Bible Society, *A Ready-Reference History of the English Bible* [1965]; H. Dennett, *A Guide to Modern Versions of the New Testament* [1966]; J. Beekman and J. Callow, *Translating the Word of God* [1974]; F. F.

Bruce, *History of the Bible in English: From the Earliest Versions*, 3rd ed. [1978]; D. A. Carson, *The King James Version Debate: A Plea for Realism* [1979], L. R. Bailey, *The Word of God: A Guide to English Versions of the Bible* [1982]; S. Kubo and W. Specht, *So Many Versions? Twentieth-Century English Versions of the Bible* [1983]; J. de Waard and E. A. Nida, *From One Language to Another: Functional Equivalence in Bible Translating* [1986]; J. P. Lewis, *The English Bible From the KJV to the NIV: A History and Evaluation*, 2nd ed. [1991]; C. Hargreaves, *A Translator's Freedom: Modern English Bibles and Their Language* [1993]; R. T. France, *Translating the Bible: Choosing and Using an English Version* [1997]; D. A. Carson, *The Inclusive Language Debate: A Plea for Realism* [1998]; M. L. Strauss, *Distorting Scripture? The Challenge of Bible Translation and Gender Accuracy* [1998]; P. W. Comfort, *The Essential Guide to Bible Versions* [2000]; D. Norton, *A History of the English Bible as Literature* [2000]; V. S. Poythress and W. A. Grudem, *The Gender-Neutral Bible Controversy: Muting the Masculinity of God's Words* [2000]; B. M. Metzger, *The Bible in Translation: Ancient and English Versions* [2001]; D. Daniell, *The Bible in English: Its History and Influence* [2003]; D. Dewey, *A User's Guide to Bible Translations: Making the Most of Different Versions* [2004]; G. D. Fee and M. L. Strauss, *How to Choose a Translation for All Its Worth: A Guide to Understanding and Using Bible Versions* [2007].)

J. G. Vos; rev. by M. L. STRAUSS

versions of the Bible, medieval and modern.

This article surveys translations of the Bible into languages other than English. See also VERSIONS OF THE BIBLE, ENGLISH.

  I. Early medieval versions
  II. Late medieval versions
  III. The Reformation
  IV. From the 17th cent. to the present

I. Early medieval versions. In the period between the making of the ancient versions of the Bible and modern times, the Scriptures (esp. in parts) were translated much more frequently than is commonly realized. Certain powerful stimuli for translation activity may have been absent to some extent in the middle period, but occasion nevertheless arose not infrequently for vernacular renderings of biblical material. Translation work of a sort, or paraphrase, was called for by codes of law (which took account of the Ten Commandments), historical surveys (which might include both biblical and nonbiblical narrative), vernacular religious drama, epics, gospel harmonies, homilies, and other works.

The Latin VULGATE was, of course, the dominant version in the W, but even this dominance, although from one point of view stultifying, may have made some contribution to the translation of the Scriptures into the vernacular. See VERSIONS OF THE BIBLE, ANCIENT, II.B. To assist in the mastery of the Latin text, vernacular glosses or rudimentary translations may, in the first instance, have been written in the MSS. Missionary activity and the emergence and development of certain languages in the Middle Ages, such as the Romance languages, presented new fields and needs for translation work.

Manuscripts surviving from the early Middle Ages contain the translation of biblical material into vernacular languages of Europe. From about the end of the 8th cent. or shortly after, there is a fragmentary survival of the Gospel according to Matthew in a Bavarian dialect. The MS is bilingual, with a Latin as well as a German text. Also from the 8th cent. is a Latin MS with a small number of glosses in French. This is quite remarkable, for it comes from the earliest days of the French language. At an early time, German glosses and Irish glosses appeared in Latin MSS. Biblical material in Old Irish has been preserved in homilies. A late 8th-cent. MS contains the Lord's Prayer in Allemannic. A rendering of this prayer into Bavarian dates from the beginning of the 9th cent. Still a third version—in Rhenish Franconian—survives in MSS from the early 9th cent.

A version of the gospel harmony of Tatian, the DIATESSARON, with a Latin text and a close rendering into E Franconian, was made in Fulda c. 830. The 9th-cent. *Heliand*, a Saxon work in alliterative verse form, used the Diatessaron as its chief source. Of a similar type from this period was the Old Saxon epic, *Genesis*.

The beginning of Bible translation in Old Church Slavonic may be assigned to the latter part of the 9th cent. At this time the missionaries Cyril and Methodius translated parts of the Bible and formed the basic Slavic version, later amplified and accommodated to dialectal developments. In the latter part of the 9th cent. also the monk Otfrid of Weissenburg completed his *Liber Evangeliorum*, a poem which combines scriptural and other material and provides a considerable amount of interpretation.

In the early part of the 10th cent. a verse paraphrase of Ps. 138 was prepared in Bavarian, and at about the same time a verse treatment was written concerning Christ and the woman of Samaria. It survives in fragmentary form in a text which unites both Allemannic and Franconian dialectal traits. A fragment of the Song of Solomon in Rhenish Franconian is extant in a MS from the latter part of the 10th cent. In the 9th or 10th cent. twenty-five psalms were translated into Low Franconian. The Psalter was very popular in the Middle Ages. As early as the 10th cent. parts of the Bible were in use in Old Netherlands dialects. The earliest is possibly a version of the Psalms from the beginning of the century. With noteworthy ability the monk Notker (c. 950–1022) translated the Psalms into Alemannic. He is also to be credited with a translation of Job. An Old Frisian version of the Psalms, perhaps from the 11th cent., has survived. In the second half of that century Abbot Williram of Ebersberg made a very popular paraphrastic rendering of the Song of Solomon in E Franconian. In addition to the German text Williram included the Vulgate and Latin paraphrase.

In this early period, then, significant foundations were laid for important developments to come.

II. Late medieval versions. In the following centuries (12th–15th), up to the time of the Protestant Reformation, there was a large amount of translation work of a sort. "Historical Bibles" stemming from Peter Comestor's *Historia scholastica*, including vernacular treatments of biblical and other material, were popular. Lives of Christ and the Psalter were in demand. There continued to be an interest in glossing, commenting, paraphrase, and in the use of verse for presenting biblical content. By the end of the period there was a serious concern about translation proper, and a notable effort to translate extensive sections of the biblical text, even the entire Bible. The Renaissance and the invention of printing from movable type had, of course, an influence on the translation and the dissemination of the vernacular Scriptures. The large number of biblical MSS and printed editions of the Bible at the close of the Middle Ages formed a fitting prelude to the Reformation.

A. German. Among the German translations of this period, mention might be made of an interlinear version of the Psalms from the latter part of the 12th cent. and the numerous other Psalters of this period (including the very popular and accomplished version of Heinrich von Mügeln in the latter part of the 14th cent.); the high German version of the entire NT known as the "Augsburg Bible" (1350); the Codex Teplensis, a MS of the NT from c. 1400, perhaps of Waldensian background; and the Wenzel Bible (1389–1400), which contained OT material. A great many MSS survive from the 15th cent. The first of the printed German Bibles, the Mentel Bible of 1466, was the first of eighteen printed editions of the entire Bible in German which antedated Luther's version. It made use of a text from the 14th cent.

B. Dutch (and Flemish). About the middle of the 13th cent. the Diatessaron was translated into Dutch from a text significantly different from that of the Latin Vulgate. Found in a Liège MS of c. 1270, it is a work of considerable literary merit. In 1271 appeared the meritorious *Rijmbijbel* by Jacob van Maerlant, which drew chiefly on Comestor's *Historia scholastica*. It is the precursor of the later "History Bible" in Dutch. From the same time comes a popular Southern Dutch Psalter. By 1300 the Gospels and Epistles had been translated into Southern Dutch. From the latter part of the 14th cent. on, noteworthy Dutch "History Bibles" appeared. In 1383 Gerard Groote included translations of biblical material in his *Book of Hours*. In the following year Johan Schutken produced his very popular version of the NT and Psalms. A translation of the OT without the Psalms was published at Delft in 1477, the first biblical version to be printed in Dutch. Its text is basically that of a previous century, perhaps dating from c. 1300.

C. French. There was much translation activity in France in the 12th–13th cent. The Psalter— popular in France as well as elsewhere— was translated at the beginning of the 12th. Toward the end of the century, Peter Waldo and some of his followers issued translations of parts of the Bible. In the early part of the 13th cent., the entire Bible was translated at the University of Paris. In the latter part of that century, Guyard des Moulins undertook a free translation of Comestor's *Historia scholastica*. He supplied additional material and otherwise modified it. This introduced the French "Historical Bible," the *Bible historiale*, which was popular for centuries. It was frequently revised. What had been credited with being the first full Bible in French, *La Grande Bible*, was printed c. 1487 and went through many editions.

D. Italian. Gospel harmonies in Italian are preserved in MSS from the 13th to the 14th cent. The Psalter was also translated at an early date. It may be that the Bible, in its entirety, had been translated into Italian by the middle of the 13th cent. The first Bible to be printed in Italian was the version of Nicolo di Malherbi, which was published in 1471 and often reissued in the following century. Another version was also published in that year, but it did not obtain similar acceptance. The verse form was employed in Italy as well as elsewhere in the Middle Ages as a vehicle for biblical material. A verse rendering of the Psalms dates back to the 13th cent. and a Diatessaron in verse to the end of the 14th cent.

E. Spanish and Catalan. There is evidence to support the view that at least part of the Bible had been translated into Spanish by the 13th cent. Notable in the medieval period is the vast historical work, the *General estoria*, which dealt with biblical and other material after the fashion of Comestor's *Historia scholastica*. It was the longest of the medieval historical Bibles. Noteworthy also is the use of the Hebrew text in translations of the OT.

Bonifatius Ferrer in the early 15th cent. translated the Bible into Valencian. This Catalan Bible was printed in 1478, but the Inquisition succeeded in destroying every copy; only one leaf survives. A Psalter printed in 1480 offers a somewhat revised reissue of this book of the Valencian Bible. Another important Psalter was published in 1490. Among other versions there was a rhymed Bible in Catalan, a type of work popular in France.

F. Portuguese. The first translations known in Portuguese are of portions of the Bible that date back perhaps as far as the 13th cent. A harmony of the Gospels was printed in 1495. Portuguese texts of the Gospels, Acts, and Epistles soon followed.

A 15th-cent. French lectionary.

G. Scandinavian. The oldest surviving translations into the languages of Scandinavia were free renderings made from the Latin Vulgate. Attention might be called to an Old Norwegian version of Genesis–Kings that dates back to c. 1300; a 14th-cent. Swedish version of the Pentateuch and Acts; a Swedish translation of portions of the Bible dating from the late 15th or early 16th cent.; and a Danish MS of Genesis–Kings from the latter part of the 15th cent.

H. Hungarian. The oldest survivals of translation of biblical material into Hungarian come from the 15th cent. Surviving from the early part of that century are portions of a version made by two monks. The version made by Ladislas Batori likewise dates from the earlier half of the 15th cent.

I. Slavic. At the end of the 15th cent., the first complete Bible in Church Slavonic appeared. In the 14th cent., Bohemian or Czech translations were made of the Psalter and of other biblical material. The NT printed in 1475 was the fruit of the work of revision performed by Jan Hus (John Huss) and a number of his followers; the entire Bible was published in 1488. The Psalter was translated into Polish by the 14th cent., and a Croatian version of NT pericopes appeared in 1495.

J. Other versions. In the 14th cent., some biblical material was translated into Welsh. By the 15th cent. a NT version in Breton had made its appearance. In the 13th cent., the Pentateuch was translated from Hebrew into Arabic. In the 14th cent. the Gospels were translated into Hebrew.

By the end of the 15th cent. and the dawn of the Reformation, the Scriptures had been introduced into language after language in Europe in a very substantial way—even to versions of the entire NT and the whole Bible. The Middle Ages had performed a very important work of ground-breaking. The way had been prepared for the period of distinguished translation activity that was to come with the Reformation.

III. The Reformation. Without the preparation that had been made in the preceding centuries, the accomplishment of the Reformation in translation work would not have been so spectacular as it was. The Reformation did not disdain to draw fruitfully on the work that had been done before. But for all that, it generated a fresh and original development. It brought renewal of zeal and an impassioned sense of urgency for giving the Bible to all the people in their own language. The familiar story of Tyndale's pledge to make the Scriptures understood by the plowboy expresses the true sentiment of the Reformation. In the Reformation memorial in Geneva, Calvin is represented with other Reformers, standing as it were on the foundation Christ Jesus with an open Bible in his hands. In the background in letters of heroic size are the words POST TENEBRAS LUX ("after darkness, light"). In the opening of the Bible and in the diffusion of the Light, the translation work brought forth by the Reformation was to play an exceedingly important part. It is not inappropriate that vernacular versions of the Lord's Prayer are included in the memorial.

A. German. One of the greatest events in the history of Bible translations was the appearance of Martin Luther's version. Its outstanding contribution to the knowledge and dissemination of the Scriptures in Germany and elsewhere, as well as its influence on the language, literature, and general culture of the German people, can hardly be overstated. Luther had already translated portions of the Bible before he determined to prepare a version of the whole Bible. He began his work on the entire NT at the close of 1521, and in September of 1522 published at Wittenberg his translation of the NT, his "September Testament" or *Septemberbibel*, as it has been called. The OT was published in stages beginning in 1523. The whole Bible with the addition of the APOCRYPHA was published in 1534. In his translation of the OT Luther made use, among other things, of the Brescian edition of 1494, and for the NT he made use of the second edition of Erasmus's Greek NT of 1519. See TEXT AND MANUSCRIPTS (NT) IV.B. For the remainder of his life, Luther continued to revise his translation.

Other German versions of the 16th cent. were unable to displace Luther's translation from its well-merited preeminence; in fact, some of them were themselves greatly influenced by Luther's work. A meritorious version of the Prophets from the Hebrew by the Anabaptists Ludwig Hätzen and Hans Denck was published in 1527, some years before Luther's own version of the Prophets was ready, and he took account of it in his work. The Bible published in Zurich (in parts, 1525–1529; entire Bible, 1530) drew on Luther's Bible to the extent that it was then available, and provided its own version of the Prophets. Emser published a Roman Catholic NT in 1527, which was essentially Luther's text

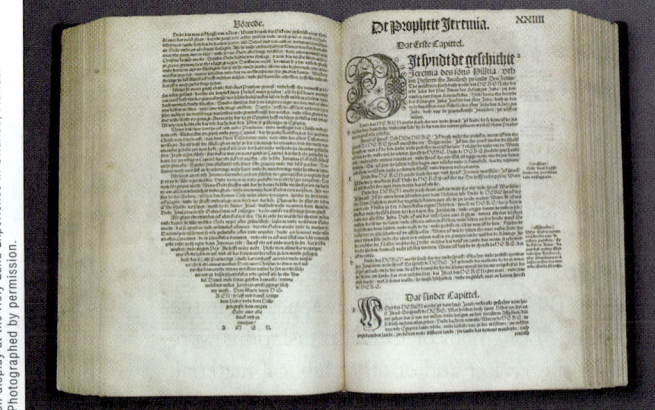

A German translation of the Bible dating to 1543 AD.

brought into conformity with the Vulgate. Another Roman Catholic work was the Bible assembled by Johann Dietenberger, published in 1534. The NT section was Emser's revision of Luther's work. In the OT, considerable use was made of the versions of Luther and of Hätzen and Denck, with revisions to align the text to the Vulgate.

B. Dutch. The first NT to be printed in Dutch appeared in 1522. It was based on the Latin Vulgate, but did take account of the Greek text. Shortly after its issuance, Luther's NT was translated into Dutch (1523). In 1525 an OT was published which made use of Luther's text to the extent that it had then been issued and also of the Delft Bible of 1477. The first complete Bible to be published in Dutch, a work which follows Luther closely and apparently uses also a Low German Bible of c. 1480, was printed in 1526. This Bible became very popular and was frequently reprinted. For its marginal notes of a strongly Protestant character the publisher, Van Liesveldt, was put to death.

Several Roman Catholic editions of the NT appeared between 1527 and 1539, and a Roman Catholic version of the entire Bible was published in 1548 at Cologne and Louvain. This formed the basis for the editions used by Roman Catholics in following centuries.

The translation of the NT prepared by Jan Utenhove (in which he had been aided by Godfried van Wingen) and published in 1556 did not attain much popularity. More warmly received and more widely used was the so-called *Deus-aes* Bible of 1561–62 (the designation, meaning "deuce-ace," alluding to a game of dice, is derived from a marginal note on Neh. 3:5 taken from Luther). This Bible, dependent on Luther, did not give full satisfaction, and the need for a superior version was expressed at synods of the Reformed churches. The Bible generally used by the Mennonites up until the 18th cent. was first printed in 1558 and was published in 1560 by Nicolaes Biestkens, from whom it receives the designation "Biestkens Bible." It was often reprinted.

C. French. Jacques Lefèvre d'Étaples made a revision of the *Bible historiale* in the early 16th cent. He was probably the translator of an anonymous version of the NT published in Paris in 1523. His translation of the Bible was published in 1530 at Antwerp. The most illustrious work of the period was the highly meritorious version of the entire Bible made by a cousin of Calvin, Pierre Robert Olivetan, and published at Waldensian expense in Switzerland in 1535. Calvin himself wrote some introductory material for this version. The edition of 1553, issued by Robert Estienne, the Parisian printer, was marked by the introduction of his chapter and verse divisions, the first complete Bible to have these aids. The NT made considerable use of Lefèvre's work, but did give some attention to the Greek text. In the OT Olivetan consulted the Hebrew text and Pagnini's Latin translation of the Hebrew. His French was of a better grade than Lefèvre's. As revised in Geneva in 1588, it became known as the "Geneva Bible" (not to be confused with the Geneva Bible in English). The favored text for French Protestants, it was reprinted many times during the following two centuries. In 1550 the Louvain Bible appeared, a Roman Catholic revision of Lefèvre's work; and an extensive further revision appeared in 1578, the foundation for Roman Catholic Bibles to follow.

D. Italian. Antonio Brucioli, who had been influenced by the Reformation, published Italian versions of the NT in 1530, of the Psalms in 1531, and of the entire Bible in 1532. In 1536 there appeared the Zaccaria NT, translated from the Greek; and in 1538 the Bible prepared by Marmochini was published. The text of this Bible, whatever its particular sources, has a Vulgate orientation. M. Teofilo in 1551 issued a NT translation from the Greek. This version was included in revised form in the first Protestant issue of the entire Bible in Italian (Geneva, 1562). The OT of this Bible was a revision of Brucioli's version. Numerous translations of parts of the Bible in Italian were published in the latter part of the 16th cent. The most distinguished of Italian versions, that of Diodati, was soon to follow, in 1607 at Geneva.

F. Spanish and Catalan. The Spanish Inquisition adversely affected translation work in Spain, but it failed to suppress it completely. Ecclesiastical opposition to versions in the vernacular languages, whether in Spain, Italy, or elsewhere, may at times have necessitated the publication of versions in more congenial places such as Geneva, Basel, and Antwerp; but translations were nevertheless made, published, and used. Montesino issued a Spanish version of the liturgical Epistles and Gospels at Alcalá in the early 16th cent. Francisco de Enzinas in 1543 at Antwerp published a NT translation from Erasmus's Greek NT. Juan Pérez de (la) Pineda produced a NT from the Greek in 1556, making use of Enzinas's version. He also published a translation of the Psalms in 1557. Translations of Romans and 1 Corinthians by Juan de Valdés were issued in 1556 and 1557. In 1553 the Ferrara Bible, a close translation of the Hebrew OT, was published. It is a revision of an older Jewish version.

The first complete printed Bible (with Apoc.) in Spanish was published in 1567–69 in Basle. It was prepared by Cassiodoro de Reyna (Casiodoro de Reina), a Lutheran who had been a monk in Seville. His OT was a revision of the Ferrara Bible. A light revision of this work was made by Cipriano de Valera, who likewise had been a monk in Seville. The NT was published in London in 1596 and the Bible with Apocrypha in Amsterdam in 1602. The Reina-Valera translation became the standard Protestant version and has been the basis of numerous later Spanish Bibles.

F. Portuguese. The first printed version of biblical material in Portuguese was a version of the *Vita Christi*, the gospel harmony of Ludolph of Saxony, which was published at Lisbon in 1495. A version of the Acts and Catholic Epistles was issued in 1505, and a translation of the liturgical Epistles and Gospels was published c. 1510.

G. Scandinavian. In the Scandinavian countries the influence of Luther's version was very great. Some use of Luther's NT was made in the first Danish NT, which was prepared by Hans Mikkelsen and Kristian Winther (1524). In 1528 a Danish Psalter translated by Frans Wormordsen was issued. In 1535 Hans Tausen published a translation of the Pentateuch made from Luther's version. Christen Pedersen is to be credited with a unique contribution to the Danish Bible. In 1529 he published a translation of the NT in smooth Danish, in which he made use of the work of Mikkelsen, of Luther, and of Erasmus. In 1531 his metrical version of the Psalter appeared. Pedersen's part was large in the preparation of the first complete Danish Bible (1550), a version which held closely to Luther's translation. A popular work, it was later revised and was reprinted for centuries.

The first printed NT in Swedish (1526) was based on Luther's version, but it did give attention to the Greek text, to the Latin version supplied by Erasmus, and to the Latin Vulgate. The first Swedish Bible, the "Gustaf Vasa Bible," was published in 1540–41. It was based on Luther's Bible. It was accepted as the Bible of the Church of Sweden until the 20th cent. An Icelandic NT was published in 1540, and a Bible, influenced by Luther's work, in 1584, a version which has been highly regarded for its style. It has undergone numerous revisions down to the 20th cent.

H. Hungarian. The first printed book in the Hungarian language was a translation of Paul's letters made from the Vulgate (1533). Among the 16th-cent. versions might be mentioned the first Hungarian NT, which was based on the Greek text (1541), and the first full Bible in Hungarian, the version made by Károlyi from the Greek and Hebrew with consideration of the Latin Vulgate and other translations (1590). This became the favorite version of Protestants and was often reprinted.

I. Slavic. A recension of the Old Church Slavonic version is represented by the Ostrog Bible of 1581. Among the 16th-cent. Czech versions, mention might be made of the highly influential Kralice or Kralitz Bible, which was made from the original languages by the Moravian Brethren (1579–93). Of the Polish versions of the 16th cent., attention might be called to the first NT to be printed in Polish (1553), to the Cracow Bible of 1561, the first Polish Bible, and to the Brest Bible of 1563 translated from the Hebrew and Greek, a version which did not obtain general acceptance. Of great importance, especially to Roman Catholics, was the work of J. Wujek, a Jesuit. Wujek translated the Vulgate, but did give attention to the original languages. His NT was published in 1593, his Psalter in 1594, and his OT in 1599. His became the accepted Roman Catholic version, and it has been used even by Protestants.

In the early 16th cent., F. Skorina translated many of the books of the Bible into (White) Russian. A version of the NT in Lower Sorbic was published in 1547. In the second half of the 16th cent., the NT was translated into Serbo-Croatian. Also in the latter part of the 16th cent., the NT was translated into Slovenian by the Reformer P. Truber and the OT was translated by the Lutheran J. Dalmatin. Jan Bretkun translated the entire Bible into Lithuanian (1579–90), but only the Psalms were published.

J. Other versions. A follower of Luther, M. Agricola, published in 1548 a translation of the NT into Finnish from the Greek with the help of Luther's version. One of the first works printed in Basque was a Protestant translation of the NT (1571). The first Welsh NT appeared in 1567 and the whole Bible in 1588. Translations of biblical material into other languages, such as Latin, Modern Greek, and Hebrew, were made in the 16th cent.; but enough detail has been given to indicate the extent and vitality of the translated work of the Reformation period.

IV. From the 17th cent. to the present. The Reformation, as has been noticed, brought in a new and distinguished period of translations of the Bible. The zeal which marked the period for giving the Scriptures to all the people in their own tongues and the spiritual discernment essential for the making of great versions were assisted among other things by improved knowledge of the original languages of Scripture, genius and brilliance on the part of translators, and maturing vernacular languages that afforded fresh and vigorous media for translation. The accomplishment was distinguished and enduring. The 16th and early 17th centuries produced versions that were long to be dominant and that influenced immeasurably the spiritual, intellectual, and cultural life of nations.

For genius and brilliance, the Reformation age must still be granted the preeminence, but the period that followed has been one of great activity and of multiple revisions and new translations. The time spent, the labors, and the volume of translations have been prodigious since the mid-17th cent. As advances have been made in textual and other biblical studies, and as the vernacular languages themselves have changed, the need has often been felt to revise or to translate anew in order that the Bible, with all the new light available, might be presented to people of a new day in language quite intelligible to them. In addition, the extensive missionary activity of the church since the Reformation has called for the translation of the Bible in whole or in part into a vast number of tongues throughout the world. Of necessity, the survey that follows is very selective, especially for the last decades of the 20th cent. and the beginning of the 21st, a period of explosive activity in Bible translation.

A. German. A great many German versions, Protestant and Roman Catholic, have appeared since Johannes Piscator opened the 17th cent. with his uneven Latinate version (1602–03). It is not our purpose to catalogue them all here. Mention might be made, however, of the various revisions of Luther's work that have been produced since the 19th cent. (the 1984 revision is the most widely used German Bible); the 17th-cent. Roman Catholic revisions of Dietenberger's version; the Zurich revision (1931); and versions by F. E. Schlachter (1903–1904), H. Albrecht (NT, 1920), H. Menge (Bible, 1926; subsequently revised), F. Tillmann (NT, 1927), A. Schlatter (NT, 1931), L. Thimme (NT, 1946), and P. Parsch (Bible, 1952). The Elberfelder Bibel, a literal translation, was begun in 1854 and has been revised as recently as 1985. Other important versions include a Roman Catholic publication known as Einheitsübersetzung (1980) and Die Gute Nachricht (corresponding to the Good News Bible; latest edition, 1997).

B. Dutch. The Synod of Dort (Dordt) felt the need of a new version of the Bible that would be made from the original languages of Scripture. The result was the most important version in the history of the Dutch Bible. The new translation was issued in 1637 with the government, the States-General, paying the expense. It was officially approved and authorized by the States General, and therefore has been called the *Staten-Bijbel* or *Statenvertaling*. It attained widespread favor in the Netherlands and has been admired elsewhere. As one of the illustrious fruits of the Reformation, it has continued in use into the 20th cent. Adolf Visscher's version from Luther's text (1648) was revised in 1823 and has continued to be in use by Lutherans. A noteworthy version in modern Dutch was completed under the auspices of the Netherlands Bible Society; the NT was published in 1939 and the Bible in 1951. More recent versions include the Groot Nieuws Bijbel. A translation of the Bible into Afrikaans (the Dutch-related language of S Africa) was published in 1943, and subsequent translations have been produced.

C. French versions. In the 17th cent. there was a paucity of Protestant translation work in French. Revisions of the dominant Geneva Bible were made by Diodati (1644), Des Marets (a lighter revision than Diodati's, 1669), and Martin (NT, 1696; entire Bible, 1707). Roman Catholic efforts were more numerous in this period. Among the Roman Catholic translations were Jacques Corbin (entire Bible from the Vulgate, 1643), François Véron (NT, 1647), de Marolles (Psalms and Song of Solomon, 1644; NT, 1649; certain books of the OT, 1677–78), and Amelote (NT, 1666–70). Special mention should be made of the meritorious version associated with Port-Royal and Louis Isaac le Maistre de Sacy and others (NT, 1667; OT, 1672–96). Ecclesiastical opposition did not prevent this able work from becoming one of the most highly esteemed of the French versions down to the present.

The 18th cent., although a somewhat barren time in general for Bible translations, did bring forth such versions as those of Richard Simon (NT, 1702), Barneville (NT, 1719), Mésenguy (1729), Beausobre and Lenfant (NT, 1718), and Le Cene (Bible, 1696–1741). Influential revisions of the Geneva Bible were those of David Martin (mentioned above; NT, 1696, Bible, 1707) and of Ostervald (1744). Based mainly on these is the revision made by Louis Segond (1874–80) which has been widely used by Protestants. In 1910 a revision of Ostervald's version was published, and has since been revised a number of times. Mention might also be made of Abbé Crampon's popular Roman Catholic version (1894–1904; rev. 1907); Decoppet's translation of the NT based on the Greek text of Westcott and Hort (1903); the translation of the NT by Goguel and others (1929); *Bible du Centenaire de la Jeunesse* (1947); *Bible de Jérusalem* (1948–54); *Bible en français courant* (1982); *Traduction oecuménique* (10th ed., 2004).

D. Italian. The first complete Protestant Bible in Italian was that of Giovanni Diodati (Geneva, 1607). The translation was faithfully made from the Hebrew and Greek into excellent Italian. It is not strange that this exceptionally praiseworthy version has been cherished and used by Italian Protestants to this day. The version made by Antonio Martini (NT, 1769–71; OT, 1776–81) was based on the Latin Vulgate (although in the NT note was taken of the Greek text). It has frequently been reprinted and has been honored with the status of an Italian classic. Other Italian versions include the following: A. Guerra's revision of Malermi's (Malherbi's) Bible (1773); a version of the Port-Royal Bible (1775–85); revisions of the Diodati version (1925, 1991); G. Luzzi's translation of the entire Bible (1921–30); the translation from the original languages into modern Italian made under the auspices of the Pontifical Biblical Institute (1923–58); and the Nuova Riveduta (1994).

E. Spanish and Catalan. The Reina-Valera version of 1602 has been reprinted and revised even to recent years. The first complete Bible in Spanish to be printed in Spain was that of Felipe Scío de San Miguel (1790–93, rev. 1794–97), a version of the Latin Vulgate. In 1825 Félix Torres Amat published a translation of the Vulgate in which he gave some attention to the Hebrew and Greek texts. Among later versions have been the following: translations of the NT by Guillermo Juenemann (Chile, 1928) and Juan Staubinger (Argentina, 1944); the Bible translation for the Pontifical University of Salamanca (1944); a version by José María Bover and Francisco Cantera (1947); *Nueva Biblia Española* (1976, later *Biblia del Peregrino*, 1993), under the direction of L. Alonso Schökel; *Dios Habla Hoy* (corresponding to the Good News Bible, 1979); *Nueva Versión Internacional* (1999); and many others.

In 1832 a Protestant translation of the NT into Catalan was published. In the 20th cent. Roman Catholic Catalan versions of the Bible have appeared, as well as an interconfessional translation in 1996. The Gospel according to Luke was translated by George Borrow into Gitano or Spanish Romany (1837); biblical material has been translated into numerous other types of Romany.

F. Portuguese. The first translation of the entire Bible into Portuguese was made by J. Ferreira de Almeida. The NT was published in 1681 in Amsterdam; the OT was finished by others and published in 1753. The version of the Vulgate by A. Pereira de Figueiredo was issued in Lisbon toward the end of the 18th cent.; it was completed in 1790. This was the first Portuguese version of the Bible to be printed in Portugal. The entire Bible was translated from the Vulgate by Matos Soares (1927–30). Various revisions of the de Almeida Bible have been published, and the *Nova Versão Internacional* appeared in 2000.

G. Scandinavian. In the early 17th cent. Hans Paulsen Resen made a Danish version from the Hebrew and Greek texts (1607); it was revised by H. Savne in 1647. This Bible, further revised a number of times, obtained great and prolonged favor. In the 20th cent. a new version made from the original languages (OT, 1931; NT, 1948) received official authorization. Among other translations into Danish are: C. Bastholm (NT, 1780), O. H. Guldberg (NT, 1794), J. C. Lindberg (OT, 1837–53; NT, 1856), C. Kalkar (entire Bible, 1847), K. F. Viborg (gospels, 1863), T. S. Rördam (NT, 1886), and A. S. Poulsen and J. L. Ussing (NT, 1897).

In the 19th cent. a version was made into Danish-Norwegian on the initiative of the Norwegian Bible Society (OT, 1842–87, revised 1891; NT, 1870–1904). A version of the NT in New Norwegian appeared in 1889. The OT followed in 1921, and a revised edition in 1938. A Roman Catholic version in Danish-Norwegian was issued in 1902, and revised by taking account of the original languages in 1938.

H. M. Melin published a new Swedish version that took notice of the original languages and of Luther's translation (1858–65). In 1917, as the culmination of more than a century of effort, a fresh translation from the original languages was published. It received official ecclesiastical approval and became the Bible of the Swedish Church.

The 1584 Icelandic Bible has undergone revision down to the 20th cent.

H. Hungarian. The first Roman Catholic version of the entire Bible in Hungarian appeared in 1626 and has been revised down to recent times. New Hungarian versions have appeared in the 20th cent., including the Karoli Bible (1993).

I. Slavic. The Ostrog Bible (Old Church Slavonic) has been revised a number of times, very notably in the "Elizabeth Bible" (so named from its connection with the Empress Elizabeth) in 1751. The St Wenceslaus Bible, a Roman Catholic translation into Czech, was issued 1677–1715. It was extensively revised 1778–80, taking account of the Protestant Kralitz Bible. Of the versions in modern vernacular Bulgarian, attention might be called to the fresh translation sponsored by the Synod of the Bulgarian Orthodox Church published in 1925. The Brest Bible gave way to the Danzig Bible in Polish (Danzig, 1606–32), a version that won the high esteem of Protestants. It has been reprinted frequently and has continued in use into the 20th cent.; a new version of the NT from the Vulgate was published in 1947.

In the 19th cent., a translation was made of the entire Bible into vernacular Russian. It took more than fifty years to complete. The first version in Ruthenian was a translation of the Pentateuch by P. A. Kulisch (1869). After his death his translation of the whole Bible, to which others had made some contribution, was published in 1903. In 1709 a version of the NT in Sorbic was issued by Gottlieb Fabricius. In revised form it was published by the British and Foreign Bible Society in 1860. A version of the NT in Wendish (Upper Sorbic) appeared in 1706 and the whole Bible in 1728. A Roman Catholic translation of the NT from the Vulgate was issued in 1887–92.

The Bible was first published in its entirety in Serbian and Croatian in the early part of the 19th cent. (1804, 1831). Special mention should be made of the NT version made by Vuk (1847) in a style that has been highly commended. A translation from the Vulgate into Slovenian was published in 1784–1802. Another Roman Catholic translation (from the German version of Allioli) appeared

in 1856-59. A Slovakian version of the Vulgate was published in 1829 and 1832. It was superseded in 1926 by another Roman Catholic version. A Protestant NT was issued in 1913 and the Bible in 1936.

More recent versions in most of these Slavic languages appeared in the second half of the 20th cent.

J. Other versions. A Finnish version of the Bible was published in 1642 and has been frequently revised since. Translations of the Bible in its entirety or in part into Estonian were published in the 17th and 18th centuries and have often been revised. In 1727 the NT was first published in Lithuanian, and the entire Bible in 1735. There have been frequent revisions. Revisions of the Lettish Bible appeared in 1877, 1899, and 1902. In the 18th and 19th centuries, translations of the NT and of the OT appeared in Lapp dialects.

And so the record of Bible translations in the period since the Reformation continues. It would seem impossible to make it even approximately complete. The record should take notice of versions in Rumanian, Albanian, Maltese, Arabic, Modern Greek, Irish, Scottish Gaelic, Welsh, Manx, Cornish, Breton, Modern Hebrew, to say nothing of hundreds of other languages or dialects in the Americas, Africa, and Asia. The global extent of the missionary activity in the period since the Reformation has brought with it translations into a vast number of tongues—to date, more than 2,300. In some of them multiple versions or revisions have already appeared. This account has been concerned chiefly with a limited section of the world and the great history of translation work there. New tongues are constantly being trained to speak of the wonderful works of God. The chronicler of translations must now be prepared to write many new chapters.

(See further J. W. Beardslee, *The Bible Among the Nations* [1899]; F. E. Schelling, *Elizabethan Playwrights* [1925], 1–18; O. M. Norlie, ed., *The Translated Bible 1534–1934* [1934]; W. Schwarz, *Principles and Problems of Biblical Translation* [1955]; M. Toyoda, *A Short History of the Japanese Translations of the Bible* [1957]; W. J. Kooiman, *Luther and the Bible* [1961]; S. L. Greenslade, ed., *The Cambridge History of the Bible: The West from the Reformation to the Present Day* [1963]; J. H. P. Reumann, *The Romance of Bible Scripts and Scholars* [1965], 55–92; *New Catholic Encyclopedia* [1967], 2:414–91; P. Y. De Jong, ed., *Crisis in the Reformed Churches* [1968], 95–114; G. MacGregor, *A Literary History of the Bible from the Middle Ages to the Present Day* [1968]; G. W. H. Lampe, ed., *The Cambridge History of the Bible: The West from the Fathers to the Reformation* [1969]; E. Nida, ed., *Book of a Thousand Tongues*, rev. ed. [1972]; M. Broomhall, *The Bible in China* [1977]; L. Lupas and E. F. Rhodes, eds., *Scriptures of the World* [1992]; A. Brenner and J. W. van Henten, eds., *Bible Translation on the Threshold of the Twenty-first Century: Authority, Reception, Culture, and Religion* [2002]; P. A. Noss, ed., *History of Bible Translation* [2007].)

J. H. SKILTON

Vespasian ves-pay′zhuhn. Titus Flavius Sabinus Vespasianus was born in A.D. 9 and ruled as emperor of Rome from 69 to 79. Before the age of twenty, Vespasian became military tribune in THRACIA, and he subsequently filled various roles in CRETE. It was not until his forties, however, that he won recognition by his military campaigns in Britain. Little is reported about him during the next two decades, but in the year 67 he was given the responsibility of subduing the Jewish revolt (see WARS, JEWISH).

After the death of NERO in 68, a period of civil war saw the rise and fall of three emperors (Galba, Otho, and Vitellius; see ROMAN EMPIRE VII). In the summer of 69 Vespasian was proclaimed emperor by the eastern legions, and he left his son TITUS in charge of the Jewish war. Before the end of the year, the senate confirmed his emperorship. Vespasian's main task was one of reconstruction after the misrule of Nero and the year of anarchy that had followed it. His blunt, straightforward, and honest character, coupled with simplicity of life and common sense, fitted him perfectly for his task. The successful completion of the war in Palestine by Titus, the suppression of a revolt in Gaul, and the establishment of peace on all frontiers caused a revival of public confidence. In celebration of the new era Vespasian began the rebuilding of the Capitoline temple.

One of the most pressing problems faced by Vespasian was that of imperial finance. He met this obstacle by retrenchment at home and by raising the provincial tribute while at the same time enforcing strict collection. He also took over for the state public lands that had been unlawfully occupied by private individuals. These methods, accompanied by the imposition of new taxes in ROME, gave him a reputation for parsimony. Yet he did benefit the entire empire by his forward-looking policies. He began construction of the famous Colosseum in the capital city, and throughout the provinces built roads and public buildings where these were needed. He also sponsored the production of works of art, and encouraged educational activity in every way.

In his political attitude Vespasian was quite liberal. To fill up the depleted ranks of the senate, he appointed Italians and provincials, conferred Latin rights on all the towns in Spain, and encouraged romanization by establishing colonies in backward provinces. He encouraged and fostered municipal life throughout the realm, appointing governors and other officials over whom he exercised strict control, and who were liable to severe punishments for maladministration. His foreign policy was more conservative: strengthen the existing frontiers rather than seek expansion.

Although Vespasian made little change in the constitution, and showed his respect for the senate by formally consulting it on all occasions, his tendency was toward autocracy. For example, he made it abundantly clear that his sons, first Titus, then Domitian, were to be his successors. This kind of high-handed disposition of imperial power produced strong opposition on the part of the STOIC aristocracy, which resulted in the execution of their leader Helvidius Priscus. However, the general esteem in which he was held is indicated by the fact that upon his death in 79 he was deified by the senate. (See further J. Nicols, *Vespasian and the Partes Flavianiae* [1978]; H. Bengtson, *Die Flavier: Vespasian, Titus, Domitian: Geschichte e. röm. Kaiserhauses* [1979]; B. Levick, *Vespasian* [1999]; R. Caratini, *Vespasien: Le bon empereur* [2003]; *ABD*, 851–53, *OCD*, 1590–91.) R. C. STONE

vessel. A container for a liquid or some other substance. Vessels were used for storage of food or valuables (e.g., the DEAD SEA SCROLLS; cf. also PAUL's figure: "we have this treasure in earthen vessels" [2 Cor. 4:7 KJV]). Materials varied from the ubiquitous POTTERY of ancient civilizations to precious metals, glass, and ornamental stone, such as ALABASTER (Mk. 14:3). Size varied from small flasks for cosmetics to vast jars, such as those which figure in the story of "Ali Baba and the Forty Thieves," and which may be seen, fitted with multiple handles for ropes, in the storerooms of Minos's palace at Knossos in CRETE.

BASKETS varied in size from those that could be carried on head or shoulder (Gen. 40:16; Exod. 29:3)—made for holding fruit (Jer. 24:1–2) or for serving as a brickmaker's hod (Ps. 81:6)—to containers large enough to hold a man (Acts 9:25; 2 Cor. 11:33). Baskets are mentioned in connection with the feeding of the 5,000 (Matt. 14:20; Mk. 6:43; Lk. 9:17) and the 4,000 (Matt. 15:37; Mk. 8:8). The former instance has the word *kophinos* G3186, a rush or wicker basket used by Jews to contain food free from alien pollution. Juvenal (*Sat.* 3.14) uses the corresponding Latin term, *cophinus*, in a reference to the Jews in the slum ghetto outside Rome's Capena Gate. Curiously, the accounts of the feeding of the 4,000 have a word (*spyris* G5083) that possibly describes the large bottle-shaped Gentile basket; the incident took place in the predominantly Gentile territory of the DECAPOLIS.

Other containers included LEATHER bottles, that is, animal skins used for keeping water (Gen. 21:14–15, 19), milk (Jdg 4:19), and wine (Josh. 9:4, 13; 1 Sam. 1:24; 10:3; 16:20; 2 Sam. 16:1); jars or PITCHERS used, for example, for drawing water from wells (Gen. 24:14–19; cf. Jn. 4:11); BASINS or BOWLS used mainly for libation and mentioned frequently in connection with the ritual utensils of tabernacle and temple (e.g., 1 Ki. 7:43, 50), but also in domestic contexts (2 Sam. 17:28; Jn. 13:5); CUPS of various types (Gen. 44:2 and frequently); and DISHES or PLATES that were often large deep containers commonly of bronze, still used for the common meal of the BEDOUIN (Prov. 19:24 et al.). E. M. BLAIKLOCK

vestibule. A passageway or hall used as an entry to a larger room. This English term is employed by the NRSV and other versions to render Hebrew

ʾêlām H395, referring to the PORCH or portico of the temple (1 Ki. 6:3 and often). See TEMPLE IV.B.3.

vestment, vesture. See DRESS.

vestry. This English term, in its archaic sense of "wardrobe," is used by the KJV to render Hebrew *meltāḥâ* H4921, which occurs only once (2 Ki. 10:22).

Via Appia vee´uh-ah´pee-uh. See APPIAN WAY.

Via Dolorosa vee´uh-doh-luh-roh´suh. A phrase (Latin for "sorrowful way") used with reference to the traditional route followed by Jesus from the PRAETORIUM or Judgment Hall to GOLGOTHA, the place of his CRUCIFIXION. The exact route followed by Jesus after his condemnation to death by PILATE (Matt. 27:26; Mk. 15:15; Lk. 23:25; Jn. 19:16) is debated because of uncertainty regarding those two locations. The Praetorium has been placed by some at the Castle of ANTONIA at the NW corner of the temple area (e.g., L. H. Vincent in *RB* 59 [1952]: 513–30), and by others at the Palace of Herod near the Jaffa Gate (e.g., P. Benoit in *RB* 59 [1952]: 531–50). As for Golgotha, it may have been located at the site of the present Church of the Holy Sepulchre or at a place known as Gordon's Calvary.

The traditional route followed by many pilgrims today begins near the so-called Ecce Homo arch in the vicinity of the Convent of the Sisters of Zion in modern Jerusalem. The present streets are many feet above the streets of 1st-cent. Jerusalem, and the Ecce Homo arch dates from a time after Christ. However, excavations in the property of the Sisters of Zion have uncovered remains that convincingly appear to be the Castle of Antonia. The Via Dolorosa follows a westerly direction to the Church of the Holy Sepulchre. On the route there are fourteen stations representing various scenes, some related in the Gospels and others preserved in tradition, which occurred as Jesus made that tragic journey. These fourteen stations are: (1) Jesus is condemned to death; (2) Jesus receives the cross; (3) Jesus falls the first time; (4) Jesus meets his afflicted mother; (5) Simon of Cyrene helps Jesus to carry his cross; (6) Veronica wipes the face of Jesus; (7) Jesus falls the second time; (8) Jesus speaks to the daughters of Jerusalem; (9) Jesus falls the third time; (10) Jesus is stripped of his garments; (11) Jesus is nailed to the cross; (12) Jesus dies on the cross; (13) the body of Jesus is taken down from the cross; (14) Jesus is laid in the sepulchre.

Although the authenticity of the Via Dolorosa cannot be firmly established (extensive investigation is made almost impossible by the structures of the modern city), nevertheless the events of that fateful Good Friday become more vivid when contemplated in the context of the old city of Jerusalem. (See J. Wilkinson, *Jerusalem as Jesus Knew It* [1978], 144–51; L. and K. Ritmeyer, *Jerusalem in the Year 30 A.D.* [2004], 70–71.)

B. VAN ELDEREN

Station 5 (Simon of Cyrene takes up the cross for Jesus) on the Via Dolorosa.

Via Egnatia vee´uh-eg-nah´tee-uh. A major road linking the city of Dyrrhachium, on the W coast of MACEDONIA, to Byzantium, the easternmost city in Europe. Built c. 130 B.C. and named after the Macedonian proconsul Gnaeus Egnatius, the Egnatian Way passed through some of the cities visited by the apostle PAUL, such as THESSALONICA and PHILIPPI.

vial. See BOWL.

Via Maris vee uh mah'ris. This Latin phrase, meaning "the way of the sea" (cf. Isa. 9:1), refers to a major road that ran along the Mediterranean coast in southern Palestine and served as an international route (although some scholars question the appropriateness or historical accuracy of the term; see esp. *SacBr*, 250–51). Caravans traveling from EGYPT to either PHOENICIA or SYRIA would often go N through the PHILISTINE coastal towns of GAZA and ASHDOD. At JOPPA the road veered inland to APHEK, then continued N to MEGIDDO. Here one branch took travelers NW to ACCO, TYRE, and SIDON; another branch went NE to HAZOR and thence to DAMASCUS.

vice. See ETHICS OF PAUL III.C; SIN.

victual. This English term—especially in the plural, meaning "supplies of food, provisions"—is used more than twenty times by the KJV (e.g., Gen. 14:11; Matt. 14:15). Since the word is uncommon in everyday English, it is seldom found in modern versions. See FOOD.

village. Among various Hebrew words that can be translated "village," the most common is *ḥāṣēr* *H2958*, referring to an unwalled but permanent settlement (Lev. 25:31 et al.; this term can often be rendered "courtyard" as well). Other relevant Hebrew words include *bat H1426* (lit., "daughter," Num. 21:25 et al.) and *kāpār H4107* (only 1 Chr. 27:25 and Cant. 7:11; *kōper H4108* in 1 Sam. 6:18). In the NT, the Greek word *kōmē G3267* is used with some frequency (Matt. 9:35 et al.; outside the Gospels, only in Acts 8:25). See TOWN.

In distinction from a CITY, the village was unwalled and easy prey for conquest. Villages had no defensive facilities such as moats, towers, or fortified gates (Ezek. 38:11; here the word is *pěrāzôt H7252*, referring to habitations in "open country"). When threatened, the villagers thronged into the city, increasing the danger of famine (cf. 2 Ki. 6:24–29). In Talmudic times a community was distinguished as a village if it did not have a SYNAGOGUE. In the NT, villages, cities, and country were the object of Christ's ministry (Mk. 6:56), but it is not clear that only cities had synagogues.

Villages increased in number northward from the NEGEV because of greater rainfall. In Chalcolithic times, the Middle Bronze era, and the Iron Age, the Negev was well-occupied, and in the Nabatean-Byzantine era most intensively, when careful conservation of rainfall prevailed. From HEBRON northward a gradual increase of villages

Aerial view of the reconstructed Talmudic village of Qatzrin on the Golan Heights.

occurred toward and beyond Jerusalem, with the greatest frequency in the territory of Zebulun of Lower Galilee, where rainfall was greatest. In Roman times the Roman army made it a peaceful territory where the people lived without fear, and agriculture and industry flourished in its many villages. Upper Galilee was too broken and too wooded to support the agriculture necessary to village life. Transjordan was dotted with towns and villages before the 19th cent. B.C., and after the 13th cent. the villages were again mentioned in the record of the conquest. The raids of Gen. 14, as well at the destruction of Sodom and Gomorrah, appear to be related to the hiatus in the record.

Local village government was administered through the elders who also acted as judges (Ruth 4:2), but the villages were under the larger jurisdiction of the towns (cf. Josh. 15:20–62; 18:24, 28; et al.). The scene of these frequent functions was the city gate, at times provided with benches (W. F. Albright, *Archaeology of Palestine* [1951], 139). The size of villages varied according to whether the country was farmed intensively or not. In the agricultural centers, grain was threshed within the confines of the villages. Activity increased at harvest time, but many of the villagers would be away with the herds at other times. H. G. Stigers

vine, vineyard. The English term *vine* can be applied to any of various plants that require support and that either climb by twining or that creep on the ground, but it is used more specifically of the grape plant, *Vitis vinifera* (Heb. *gepen* H1728 [used of a wild climbing plant in 2 Ki. 4:39]; Gk. *ampelos* G306). The term *vineyard* always refers to a planting of grapevines (Heb. *kerem* H4142; Gk. *ampelōn* G308). See flora (under *Vitaceae*).

I. Viticulture in the ANE. The vine has been cultivated in Palestine from the earliest times. The climate there is peculiarly adapted to viticulture with the country's bright sunshine and the heavy dew of the late summer nights. The best location of a vineyard for the direct sunshine is on the gentle slopes of the hillside, where most of the vines have grown throughout the centuries in the Holy Land (Jer. 31:5; Amos 9:13). Of course, not all the vineyards are on hillsides. Important vineyards are on the plains, such as the Plain of Esdraelon and around Jericho.

When the Israelites arrived in Canaan the land was already devoted to viticulture (Deut. 6:11; Josh. 24:13; Neh. 9:25). The Israelites are said to have taken over this industry. Viticulture thrives best under peaceful conditions because the vines need constant care, and several years of watchful cultivation are necessary before they bear fruit (Zeph. 1:13). A vineyard calls for harder and more regular labor than any other form of agriculture. Constant pruning of the vines is necessary if the clusters of grapes are to grow to full maturity. The prophet Isaiah describes the procedure usually followed in the cultivation of a vineyard (Isa. 5:1–4). The husbandman planted his vineyard "on a fertile hillside," which was fenced in for its protection from animals and thieves (cf. Ps. 80:12–13). He "dug it up and cleared it of stones" before planting it "with the choicest vines" (Isa. 5:2) in orderly rows about three paces from each other. "He built a watchtower in it" (cf. Matt. 21:33) to guard against the approach of intruders including foxes and boars (cf. Cant. 2:15; Ps. 80:13).

The watchtower in the vineyard was an ancient institution. It is mentioned frequently in the OT, as when Isaiah compares the "Daughter of Zion" to "a shelter in a vineyard" (Isa. 1:8). To complete the vineyard the husbandman "cut out a winepress" (5:2; NRSV, "hewed out a wine vat"). This was usually cut out of the solid rock and lined with mortar. Such wine presses have been found everywhere in Palestine. There were usually two, sometimes three vats, square, rectangular, or circular in shape and cut on different levels, connected with channels, the upper being the one in which the grapes were trodden out. The lower vats received the juice.

Most of the vines in Palestine trail on the ground, because it is believed that the grapes ripen more slowly under the shadow of the leaves. Too much exposure to the sun in the early period of the growth of the clusters would cause the grapes to ripen before they are fully grown. Sometimes the vines were permitted to climb along the branches of a tree (Ezek. 19:11), and in some areas the vines are grown over a trellis, providing a cool place where a person could sit (1 Ki. 4:25).

The grapes begin to ripen in July and continue to bear fruit into October, although the harvest usu-

ally takes place in September. The fresh grapes are eaten in great quantities during the season between July and September, but the early fruit is unripe and sour so that the teeth are set on edge" (Jer. 31:29, 30; Ezek. 18:2). Besides the fresh grapes, the vineyard produces raisins and WINE. In an open spot in the vineyard a smooth area is prepared where bunches of grapes are spread out to dry. They are frequently sprinkled with olive OIL to keep them moist, and turned over. When the grapes have been dehydrated to the proper point, they are stored usually in earthenware jars, becoming an important part of the food supply. Another product of the vine was grape HONEY; it was a boiled down, molasses-like treacle or jelly and very sweet. It is still used in the Near E but was more important before sugar cane came into use. References to honey in the Bible frequently refer to this product rather than to the honey of the BEE.

The OT contains suggestions as to the regulations of viticulture. In accordance with the TITHE, the first tenth of every crop of grapes belonged to God. The Levitical instructions were that the farmer should leave the corners of his field unreaped for the poor: "Do not go over your vineyard a second time or pick up the grapes that have fallen. Leave them for the poor and the alien" (Lev. 19:10). The gleanings were to be left for the needy. Another regulation said, "If you enter your neighbor's vineyard, you may eat all the grapes you want, but do not put any in your basket" (Deut. 23:24). One may take enough to satisfy immediate needs, but no more. The regulations required that the vineyards were to lie fallow in the SABBATICAL YEAR (Exod. 23:10–11; Lev. 25:3–5). Other kinds of seeds were not to be planted in the vineyard (Deut. 22:9). This was in accordance with the general principle of guarding against unnatural combinations that violate the purity of the species (Lev. 19:19). Occasionally this regulation was ignored, as in the case of the man whose vineyard contained a fig tree (Lk. 13:6).

II. Vines and vineyards as symbols. Vines and vineyards were sometimes symbols of prosperity and blessing among the ancient Hebrews. The messianic blessing of peace and security is symbolized thus: "Every man will sit under his own vine / and under his own fig tree, / and no one will make them afraid, / for the LORD Almighty has spoken" (Mic. 4:4; cf. 1 Ki. 4:25; Zech. 3:10). Abundant and fruitful vineyards were an expression of God's favor, as in Hos. 2:15 after Israel's spiritual restoration. In Gen. 49:11, Joseph is described as "a fruitful vine, / a fruitful vine near a spring, / whose branches climb over a wall."

The vine is frequently used as a symbol of Israel. The nation is compared to a choice vine that God brought from Egypt and planted in the land of promise, where "it took root and filled the land" with blessing (Ps. 80:9). But she became "a corrupt, wild vine" (Jer. 2:21; cf. Ps. 80:13; Isa. 5:1–7). Some have thought that the plant referred to by Jeremiah is *Vitis orientalis* (synonym *Ampelopsis orientalis*), a climbing shrub well known all over ASIA MINOR and SYRIA; it has a resemblance to the vine, but bears red fruits like red currants (might these be the wild grapes of Isa. 5:2 and 4?). Others claim that the plant was a useless seedling of the ordinary vine, which would of course look similar to a cultivated vine, but which would bear worthless fruit. This is the wild or seedling vine to which Ezekiel refers, the only value of which is as fuel for the fire (Ezek. 15).

The vine was also sometimes a symbol of adversity and God's judgment (Deut. 28:30; Amos 5:11; Zeph. 1:13). The identification of the so-called "vine of Sodom" (Deut. 32:32) is uncertain. Some have identified it with the Colocynth (*Citrullus colocynthus*), a wild herbaceous vine called also "bitter gourd" and "bitter apple." The fruits are round and look like oranges, sometimes mottled with green; from their bitter pulp is prepared a powerful cathartic. This plant was found around the Dead Sea. In Deut. 32:15–38, Israel is compared to a vine whose fruit is bitter and poisonous. The thrust of the statement is that Israel's sins are the inevitable result of their corrupt nature, a stock comparable to the corruption that led to the destruction of SODOM and GOMORRAH. (See further C. E. Walsh, *The Fruit of the Vine: Viticulture in Ancient Israel* [2000]; P. D. Akpunonu, *The Vine, Israel and the Church* [2004].) A. C. SCHULTZ

vinegar. A sour liquid consisting of acetic acid, produced by the fermentation of WINE or other alcoholic liquors. Faulty methods of manufacture produced in ancient times an inferior wine liable to turn sour rapidly (Heb. *ḥōmeṣ H2810*, from *ḥāmēṣ*

H2806, "to be leavened or sour"; Gk. *oxos G3954*, cf. *oxys G3955*, "sharp," and figuratively "acid-tasting"). It was equivalent to the Roman *posca*, a cheap sour wine which, mixed with water, was the common beverage of peasants (cf. Ruth 2:14). The book of Proverbs speaks of its strong acidic taste ("as vinegar to the teeth," Prov. 10:26) and its irritant quality ("like vinegar poured on a wound," 25:20 TNIV; cf. B. K. Waltke, *The Book of Proverbs Chapters 15–31* [2005], 306).

The NAZIRITE's vow of abstinence excluded this form of alcoholic beverage, as well as the intoxicating wine of more common use in higher levels of society, because such a vow could be made in all strata of the community (Num. 6:3). The wine used antiseptically by the Good Samaritan was of the more costly variety (Lk. 10:34). It is uncertain whether the vinegar offered to Christ on the cross was the soldiers' ration wine, the *posca* brought by the squad on duty, and thus possibly given in kindliness rather than derision (Matt. 27:48; Mk. 15:63; Lk. 23:36; Jn. 19:29; cf. the discussion by D. A. Carson on Matt. 27:34 and 27:48 in *EBC*, 8:575, 579).

A curiosity of literature is the so-called "Vinegar Bible," a magnificent edition of the KJV published by J. Baskett in 1717 that included numerous beautiful engravings, but also many mistakes (it is sometimes referred to as "the Baskett-full of Errors"). The nickname is derived from the fact that the heading for the parable of the vineyard in Lk. 20 was misprinted as "the parable of the vinegar."

E. M. BLAIKLOCK

vineyards, plain of the. See ABEL KERAMIM.

viol. This English term is used by the KJV in four passages (Isa. 5:12; 14:11; Amos 5:23; 6:5) to render Hebrew *nēbel H5575*, which means "harp" or "lyre." Elsewhere the KJV translates "psaltery" (1 Sam. 10:5 et al.). See MUSIC, MUSICAL INSTRUMENTS IV.D.

violet. See BLUE; PURPLE.

viper. This English term, like *adder*, is applied generally to any of a family of venomous SNAKES (*Viperidae*, though it often refers specifically to *Vipera berus*), and the biblical texts do not provide sufficient information to identify particular species with certainty. The NIV uses the word to render Hebrew *šĕpîpōn H9159*, probably the horned or sand viper (*Cerastes cornuta* [also *Cerastes cerastes*], only Gen. 49:17); *ʿakšûb H6582*, probably the same or a similar species (only Ps. 140:3); and *ṣipʿōnî H7626*, possibly the Palestine viper (*Vipera xanthina palestinae*, Prov. 23:32 et al.; cf. *ṣepaʿ H7625*, only Isa. 14:29). The NRSV uses "viper" also as the rendering of *ʾepʿeh H704*, which may refer to the carpet viper (*Echis coloratus*, Job 20:16; Isa. 30:6; 59:5b; NIV, "adder"). In the NT, "viper" translates Greek *echidna G2399* (Matt. 3:7 et al.) and *aspis G835* (only Rom. 3:13; see ASP).

One of the OT references, Isa. 59:5, uses two of the Hebrew terms: "They hatch the eggs of vipers [*ṣipʿōnî*], / and spin a spider's web. / Whoever eats their eggs will die, / and when one is broken, an adder [*ʾepʿeh*] is hatched" (the NRSV and NJPS invert the terms "viper" and "adder"). Although purely figurative, this passage may confirm that vipers are in view. In most members of this family, the eggs are retained in the body of the female until they hatch and are ready to emerge. If a gravid snake is crushed these may appear. Such an accident gives rise to the old story that a viper swallows her young to protect them in time of danger.

Of the five NT occurrences of *echidna*, four are in the expression "brood of vipers," used by JOHN THE BAPTIST (Matt. 3:7; Lk. 3:7) and by the Lord (Matt. 12:34; 23:33). Reference is clearly to dangerous snakes, while the word "brood" (from *gennēma G1165*, "child, offspring") suggests the batch of young vipers that emerge from the mother, anything from a dozen or so in smaller species to fifty or more in the giant vipers. The remaining reference is the only literal one (Acts 28:3), which records that PAUL was bitten by a snake. This is traditionally identified as the common viper of the Mediterranean, but today there are no venomous snakes on MALTA. It is possible that the viper became extinct after Paul visited the island, though some have argued that the species concerned was harmless (in undeveloped countries even today all snakes are regarded as poisonous, and a "bite" by even a nonpoisonous species can result in severe shock). According to a recent view, the island was not

Malta but Cephallenia (modern Kefallinia, in the Ionian Sea off the W coast of Greece), where the long-nosed or nose-horned viper, *Vipara ammodytas*, is still found (H. Warneke, *Die romreise des Paulus Jahr i des Apostels Paulus* [1987], 100-10), but this identification is not generally accepted.

G. S. CANSDALE

virgin. This English term (from Latin *virgo*, "maiden, [unmarried] young woman," often with the connotation of chastity) has several uses, including "an unmarried woman who has devoted herself to a religious life." In common modern usage, however, it most frequently refers to a woman who has not had sexual intercourse, though the term is often applied to men as well. In what follows, the English term *virgin* will be used in this specific sense.

The relevant Hebrew terms are *bĕtûlâ* H1435, which occurs over fifty times (Gen. 24:16; Exod. 22:16-17; et al.), and *ʿalmâ* H6625, which is used only seven times (Gen. 24:43; Exod. 2:8; Ps. 68:25; Prov. 30:19; Cant. 1:3; 6:8; Isa. 7:14). The former term is rendered "virgin" in the standard lexicons, and this translation does seem appropriate in many, or even most, passages. Moreover, the abstract cognate *bĕtûlîm* H1436, a plural form, appears to indicate virginity (Lev. 21:13 [clarified in v. 14]; Jdg. 11:37; in Deut. 22:14-20, it means "evidences of virginity"; but see on Ezek. 23:3 and 8 below).

There are, however, several considerations that should be kept in mind. (a) In a number of passages where *bĕtûlâ* occurs, nothing in the context suggests that virginity is a factor under consideration, and thus the rendering "maiden" or "young woman" is more appropriate; this is especially true in poetic passages where the word is used in parallel with *bāḥûr* H1033, "young man" (Deut. 32:25 et al.). (b) Sometimes the word *bĕtûlâ* is accompanied by the comment that the woman or women in question had not had sexual relationships (Gen. 24:16; Jdg. 21:12). It may be that such descriptions are simply intended to emphasize the point, but it is also possible that the word by itself did not necessarily indicate virginity and that a qualification was needed to remove the ambiguity. (c) In at least one passage, the word is used of young women who have had sexual intercourse (Esth. 2:19, applied to the "virgins" who have already spent a night with the

Old photograph (1905) of a young Algerian woman.

king; Joel 1:8 probably refers to a betrothed virgin who was not able to marry her intended husband); and Ezekiel uses the term *bĕtûlîm* in his symbolic representation of a woman involved in prostitution (Ezek. 23:3, 8).

What may have been the precise status (sexual or social or other) indicated by *bĕtûlâ*, particularly in legal contexts, is a matter of debate. It may well be that the word had a fairly general meaning, "[marriageable] young woman"; and because in Hebrew society (as in many others) it would be assumed that she was a virgin, the word probably took on the sense of "chaste." J. H. Walton proposes the definition, "an ostensibly reputable young girl who is past puberty and is, by default at least, still in the household of her father" (*NIDOTTE*, 1:782).

The second Hebrew term, *ʿalmâ*, is clearly the feminine form of *ʿelem* H6624, "young man" (only 1 Sam. 17:56; 20:22), and the abstract plural form *ʿălûmîm* H6596 appears to mean "youth" or

"youthful vigor" (Job 20:11; 33:25; Ps. 89:45; Isa. 54:4). Thus the lexicons give "young woman" or the like as the meaning of ʿalmâ. Similarly, most versions use "maiden" or "young woman" or even "girl" (Exod. 2:8) as the rendering of the word in a majority of its occurrences. The KJV uses "virgin" in four instances (Gen. 24:43; Cant. 1:3; 6:8; Isa. 7:14), the NIV in only two (Cant. 6:8; Isa. 7:14), and the NRSV not at all. The occurrence of almâ in Cant. 6:8 is of lexical significance because in this verse the term is contrasted to "queen" and "concubine"; even here, however, the reference is ambiguous (true virgins? women in the royal harem that have not borne children?). That the term may be applied to virgins is not in doubt (Gen. 24:43 [parallel to bĕtûlâ, v. 16]; Exod. 2:8), and no passage requires a reference to someone who is not a virgin (even Prov. 30:19 very likely has in view a woman's initial sexual experience; cf. B. K. Waltke, *The Book of Proverbs Chapters 15–31* [2005], 491–92). On the other hand, the evidence does not suggest that the term by itself indicates virginity.

Clearly, bĕtûlâ and almâ overlap in meaning, and apart from the fact that the former term is much more frequent, drawing a clear distinction between them is difficult (J. H. Walton [in *NIDOTTE*, 3:417] seems to suggest, on the basis of Isa. 54:4, that the latter term implies the ability or opportunity to bear children, but the argument is not convincing). This factor affects our understanding of almâ in the most controversial passage, Isa. 7:14, which traditionally has been translated, "Behold, a virgin shall conceive, and bear a son" (KJV; NIV, "The virgin will be with child and will give birth to a son"); the NRSV and other modern versions, however, use "young woman" in this passage. Some have argued that if Isaiah had intended the meaning "virgin," he would have used bĕtûlâ instead, but clearly this argument does not work, for as noted above bĕtûlâ too often has a general meaning without reference to sexual experience (cf. also E. J. Young, *The Book of Isaiah*, 3 vols., NICOT [1965–72], 1:288, though he overstates his case when he claims that almâ "seems to be the only word in the language which unequivocally signifies an unmarried woman"). On the other hand, it is a fair argument to say that if Isaiah had wanted to stress the woman's virginity, he had other means of doing so (e.g., "a woman who has not known a man," as in Num. 31:35). It may well be that almâ, like bĕtûlâ, refers normally to a young woman of sexual maturity who is unmarried and therefore assumed to be a virgin.

In Isa. 7:14, as is well known, the SEPTUAGINT (followed by Matt. 1:23) translates almâ with Greek parthenos G4221, which usually means "virgin." This Greek term too, however, is not free of ambiguity, and in many passages the sense "young [or unmarried] woman" is preferable (cf. Aristophanes, *Clouds* 530, in which a woman who had given birth to a child and had decided to abandon it says, "I was still a maiden [parthenos], and I was not permitted to bear [a child]"). In later Greek the narrower sense "virgin" is more common, and the LXX normally itself uses parthenos to translate bĕtûlâ; but occasionally this Greek word is also found as the rendering of almâ and naʿărâ H5855, "girl" (cf. Gen. 24:14, 16, 43; Deut. 22:19; et al.; for more details, see *TDNT*, 5:826–37).

In the NT, parthenos is used with reference to MARY, MOTHER OF JESUS (Lk. 1:27), who is explicitly described as not having known a man (v. 34) and as having conceived supernaturally prior to her being joined to Joseph (Matt. 1:18). Thus her virginity does not depend on Matthew's citation from Isaiah, though undoubtedly the evangelist regarded the LXX rendering as singularly appropriate. See VIRGIN BIRTH. Other uses of the word in the NT include the parable of the ten virgins (Matt. 25:1, 7, 11), the reference to PHILIP's "unmarried daughters" (Acts 21:9), PAUL's discussion about whether virgins should marry (1 Cor. 7:25–38), and its occurrence with the masculine definite article referring to chaste men (Rev. 14:4). See also MARRIAGE.

Virgin, Apocalypse of the. Title given to two late works in which MARY, MOTHER OF JESUS was shown the tortures of the damned. Both documents are dependent on earlier works and quite distinct from the widespread legend of the ASSUMPTION OF THE VIRGIN.

(1) The first work is extant in Greek and other versions, and was edited by M. R. James in 1893 (*Apocrypha anecdota*, 115–26). The Virgin prays to be told about the torments of hell, and MICHAEL is sent to guide her. In the W she sees the lost who

did not worship the TRINITY, and unbelievers for whom no one has yet interceded; in the S the souls of sinners are immersed at varying depths in a river of fire. In the W again she sees the fate of other sinners, an interesting catalog including that of those who had lain in bed late on Sunday and those who had not risen at the entry of a priest (appropriately condemned to sit on fiery seats!). Others placed "on the left hand of paradise" are the Jews who crucified Jesus, those who denied baptism, and those guilty of various impurities. The Virgin entreats all the saints to intercede with her, and the Son grants the days of Pentecost as a season of rest for the lost. The chief interest of this text lies in its revelation of what the author considered sinful, and the punishments he felt appropriate.

(2) The completely different Ethiopic apocalypse is almost wholly borrowed from the *Apocalypse of Paul* (see PAUL, APOCALYPSE OF), but one section shows affinity with that of Peter (see PETER, APOCALYPSE OF). John is the narrator and describes the mystery revealed to Mary, which she had recounted to him. The contents represent chs. 13–44 of the *Apocalypse of Paul*, sometimes amplified with biblical quotations. (See further *ABD*, 6:854–56.)

R. McL. WILSON

Virgin, Assumption of. See ASSUMPTION OF THE VIRGIN.

virgin birth. The supernatural birth of JESUS CHRIST, who was conceived through the HOLY SPIRIT and born of a virgin (Matt. 1:18–25; Lk. 1:26–38).

I. Definition. Virgin birth, as here considered, is a specific term. It refers only to Jesus Christ and the manner in which he came into the world, as described in Matthew and Luke, as believed by the early church, and as held in the Christian creeds through the centuries. The unique person and mission of Christ, as well as the specific manner of his INCARNATION, put this event in a class by itself. Comparison with other miraculous births, discoveries of birth myths, or even scientific experimentation and achievement in human methods of reproduction would neither support nor invalidate this unique and divine act of incarnation. This is the virgin birth in which, it is claimed, the Word was made flesh (Jn. 1:14).

A. The fact. The gospel accounts are not presented as myths, legends, didactic devices, or "noetic" patterns to popularize Christianity to the outer masses (cf. T. Boslooper, *The Virgin Birth* [1962], 227–30). They purport to state factually the data needed to solve a crucial problem in the minds of believers: How could Jesus, a man, be the SON OF GOD and Savior? The two parts of the explanation occur in the two Gospels that the early church considered the earliest. The report was accepted as factual. The explanations were not repeated in later works. Before long, no one was baptized into the faith without expressing faith in the virgin-born Christ. In the earliest literature that reflects direct confrontation with pagan, Jewish, and heretical contenders, the fact of the virgin birth is defended as both true and fundamental.

B. Presupposition. Only in a certain context, of course, could this position be held. Both the Scriptures and the believers assumed the supernatural. God was no MYTH. He was the sovereign, transcendent Being, who was also Creator. He who made man in the beginning could accommodate to him and communicate with him. The early Christians saw no problem in a God who acts and speaks and redeems. In the context of Scripture and the faith of a regenerate and Spirit-filled church, the virgin birth of Christ was no more unthinkable than the other three ways by which people have come into the world (ADAM with neither father nor mother, EVE from Adam's side, and others with both father and mother). God was utterly real. His acts and words were fact and truth. Gnostics, Docetists, pagans, and unconverted Jews did not always share this context of faith. Therefore, they did not share the Christian belief in an actual incarnation by the virgin birth, but the belief survived in orthodox Christianity.

II. Importance. It is not contended that God could not have sent the Savior in any other way. It is simply affirmed, on the basis of Scripture, that this is how he did it. The virgin birth is consistent with the other great facts of redemption in a way

that no other explanation is. Consistent orthodoxy demands the virgin birth. As was pointed out even by the controversial scholar Charles A. Briggs (in *AJT* 12 [1908], 201), "Undoubtedly the divinity of Christ is the most essential doctrine, the incarnation is secondary to this, and the virgin birth of a third grade of importance. I have already recognized that a man may doubt or deny the third without, in his own mind, denying the second, or the first. And yet, from a historic and dogmatic point of view, he surely has put himself in an untenable position, which he cannot maintain. Historically and logically the divinity of Christ and incarnation are bound up with the virgin birth, and no man can successfully maintain any one of them without maintaining them all."

A. In the early church. Accordingly, it is not strange that "there is no fact, no Christian doctrine that is more emphasized by the early Christian writers than that of the virgin birth of our Lord" (Briggs, 199). They considered it essential, used it in the baptismal formula and the earliest creed, and vigorously defended it in the debates with nonbelievers. No voice of doubt or protest is recorded within the early church.

B. In modern times. The facts have not changed, only the climate. The authority of the Bible is still involved. Those who accept the Scriptures as the fully reliable Word of God do not doubt the virgin birth. The factual account must still be accepted or rejected. It is true or false. If redemption is not based on the kind of incarnation that is reported in the Scriptures, what can be believed about it? As J. P. Lange says of the virgin birth, "Its positive denial robs every other doctrine of Christianity of its full value. Neither the death of Christ nor his resurrection can be known in their whole significance, if his birth is positively misconceived. In this case, there is a crack in the bell, and its pure, full, penetrating sound is gone" (*The Life of the Lord Jesus Christ*, 4 vols. [1872], 1:279). Or, as J. G. Machen says, "Let it never be forgotten that the virgin birth is an integral part of the New Testament witness about Christ, and that that witness is strongest when taken as it stands" (*The Virgin Birth of Christ* [1930], 396).

III. Source of the doctrine. It is often said that the doctrine of the virgin birth comes from the 2nd cent. This can hardly be true. The virgin birth was as explicit in the early Roman form of the APOSTLES' CREED as in the 5th- or 6th-cent. Gallican form. TERTULLIAN and IRENAEUS used the creed; therefore, it must have been extant by the middle of the 2nd cent. Indeed, F. Kattenbusch (*Das apostolische Symbol*, 2 vols. [1894–1900], 2:328) placed it at about A.D. 100, and T. Zahn (*Das apostolische Symbolum: Eine Skizze seiner Geschichte und eine Prüfung seines Inhalts*, 2nd ed. [1893], 47) supposes that the baptismal formula attained essentially the form which it has in the old Roman symbol at some time between 70 and 120. Since no new, strange, or debatable doctrine would be incorporated into the baptismal formula or into so brief and elementary a creed, the doctrine must have been old when the creed was established.

Earlier writers support the same conclusion. JUSTIN MARTYR (d. 165) defends the virgin birth at length against Jewish and pagan objections and shows familiarity with its mention in Christological summaries, such as are used in exorcism (Machen, *Virgin Birth of Christ*, 5). IGNATIUS (d. 117), in debate with Docetists who denied the real body of Jesus, insisted not only on Jesus' birth but also on its having been a virgin birth (*Smyrn.* 1.1). A. von Harnack says that "Ignatius has freely reproduced a 'kerygma' of Christ which seems, in essentials, to be of a fairly historical character and which contained, inter alia, the virgin birth, Pontius Pilate, and the *apethanen*" (in Herzog-Hauck, *Realencyklopädie fur protestantische Theologie und Kirche*, 24 vols. [1896–1913], 1:751).

These testimonies are unequivocal. They are not dealing with a new doctrine. No protest within the church has to be answered. The only objectors are on the outside. All believers were baptized in this faith. The one alleged and much publicized exception to universal agreement within the church is in *Dialogue with Trypho* when Justin argues that some Jews accept the messiahship of Jesus without accepting his preexistence and virgin birth. Justin's statement has been misread as saying "our race" instead of "your race" and so has been applied to Christians. Harnack exposed the error. Machen explains and confirms his findings (*The Virgin Birth of Christ*,

15–16). The situation is clear. The virgin birth was already an old and long-established distinctive of the Christian church early in the 2nd cent.

The time and manner of the first public statement about the virgin birth, however, is a matter of conjecture. It cannot be later than the Gospels that bear the account (Matthew and Luke). The facts may have been known earlier, at least by some. The moves from Nazareth to Bethlehem, then to Egypt and back to Nazareth may have permitted Mary and Joseph to keep the secret from all but the most trusted confidants until God's own time of vindication. When faith in Christ had already been demonstrated, the explanation solved a problem. Where such faith was lacking, the account would have been abused or rejected if given prematurely. J. Orr thinks that Matthew and Luke are the source of any public knowledge of the birth of Christ (*The Virgin Birth of Christ* [1907], 67). Sooner or later the facts had to be shared by Mary and Joseph. Is it not reasonable to suppose that the report would be given to the leaders of the church and especially to those who were committing the gospel to writing?

IV. Gospel accounts. The whole NT presents a divine-human Savior. Only Matthew and Luke explain the means of the incarnation. Repetition is unnecessary. Consistency with the revelation is sufficient.

A. Linguistic factors. Mary is called a VIRGIN (*parthenos* G4221) in Matt. 1:23 and in Lk. 1:27. The former is a citation of Isa. 7:14, where it is said that a virgin (Heb. ʿalmâ H6625) was to conceive and bear a son. In biblical usage, the word always may and often must be construed to mean an unmarried young woman. The connotation of "pure" is often associated with at least the NT usage. Both words have been demonstrated to have a broader extrabiblical meaning at times. Linguistic evidence, then, renders the virgin birth probable, but needs the support of the positive statements in the context for certainty.

B. Literary factors. All alleged ambiguity vanishes when the passages are read in full. Specifically, it was "before they came together" that Mary "was found to be with child through the Holy Spirit" (Matt. 1:18). The assertion is repeated that Joseph "had no union with her until she gave birth to a son" (1:25). Luke in no less specific. Mary's response to the annunciation was one of bewilderment. She said, "How can this be, since I am a virgin?" (Lk. 1:34 NRSV). The answer was, in effect, "No husband is necessary. God will cause you to conceive" (v. 35). These are the clear affirmations of the virgin birth. They cannot be explained away by textual evidence. They can only be accepted or denied. The reporting is modest but clear. It is history or the boldest fiction.

C. Documentation. The facts formed a network of interlocking prediction and data that broadened the witness and reduced the normal probability of chance fulfillment to absurdity. What if Elizabeth or Mary had borne a girl? Or what if something else had broken the predicted pattern? Abundance of detail guaranteed the authenticity of the accounts. This birth is not only an event in time; it is the event from which, as if arranged by a true instinct, time is reckoned forward and backward. It is a historical fact full of the mysteries of both the divine and the human. It is the handle by which one can take hold of God's greatest self-revelation in Jesus Christ, Son of God and Son of Man. If this is not the true explanation, no one will ever know how the Redeemer came. No other adequate explanation has been given.

V. Alleged silence. It has been objected that the virgin birth cannot be true in view of the silence of the rest of the NT.

A. Doubtful silence. Explicit statement is indeed lacking, except in Lk. 1 and Matt. 1. Are there not allusions, inferences, and expressions that could hardly be understood apart from such a belief? How did Mark think Jesus could be the "Son of God" (Mk. 1:1)? Why did Mark quote reference to Jesus as "the carpenter" when Matthew called him "the carpenter's son" (6:3; Matt. 13:55)? Was it not to avoid a misunderstanding, whereas Matthew had answered the question by his opening chapters? John dwells continually upon the divine glory and attributes of Jesus but gives no account of his birth. The "Word became flesh" (Jn. 1:14). But how?

Paul's emphasis is on the death and resurrection of Christ, not on his birth, hence not on the virgin birth. How does one explain Paul's strange ways of referring to the coming of Christ as "being sent" (Rom. 8:3), having "made himself nothing" (Phil. 2:7), "taking the very nature of a servant" (ibid.), etc.? Did he know how it occurred? Undoubtedly he did if Luke, his assistant, did. Irenaeus said, "Luke, a companion of Paul, wrote in a book the gospel preached by the latter" (*Haer.* 3.1). In any case, the early church had no doubt of the intention of the Scripture writers or of the fact of the virgin birth. Their testimony is so clear that Briggs dares to affirm, "it is therefore a perversion of history for anyone to say that 'born of Mary the virgin' means any less than what St. Luke gives us, or than Ignatius, Justin, Irenaeus, Hippolytus and Tertullian battle for" (*AJT* 12 [1908]: 199).

B. Reasons for silence. In the nature of the case, the report of the virgin birth does not need constant repetition. If the explanation is available and known, that is enough. This is especially true in view of the nature of the first transmission of the gospel facts. They were reported as good news (Mk. 1:1) or as a proclamation (1 Cor. 2:4). They were not a committee report evolving from dialogue or even from the life of the church. They were a tradition (2 Thess. 3:6) handed down by the apostolic witnesses. This content of the oral and written gospels was not debated but accepted. This tradition, in its written form at least, included the virgin birth. It was accepted and became a pillar of the faith, expressed in the baptismal formula and the earliest creed. Debate would have been considered irreverent except to convince pagans, heretics, and unbelieving Jews.

VI. Conclusion. The faith of the early church included belief in the virgin birth because it was a clear teaching of the NT. To reject it would have been tantamount to denying the Word of God and being aligned with the pagans, heretics, and unbelieving Jews. The virgin birth was not a stumbling block. It was a pillar of their faith. So it has continued.

(In addition to the titles mentioned in the body of this article, see A. Edersheim, *The Life and Times of Jesus the Messiah*, 2 vols. [1886], 1:144–59; W. Ramsay, *Was Christ Born at Bethlehem?* [1898], 73–91; L. Sweet, *The Birth and Infancy of Jesus Christ* [1906]; F. Ramsay, *The Virgin Birth* [1926]; D. Edwards, *The Virgin Birth in History and Faith* [1943]; R. E. Brown, *The Virginal Conception and Bodily Resurrection of Jesus* [1973]; W. H. Scheide, *The Virgin Birth: A Proposal as to the Source of a Gospel Tradition* [1995]; M. F. Foskett, *A Virgin Conceived: Mary and Classical Representations of Virginity* [2002]; R. D. Aus, *Matthew 1–2 and the Virginal Conception in Light of Palestinian and Hellenistic Traditions on the Birth of Israel's First Redeemer, Moses* [2004]; A. J. Welburn, *From a Virgin Womb: The Apocalypse of Adam and the Virgin Birth* [2008].)

W. T. DAYTON

virtue. This English term, meaning "moral excellence," is rarely used in modern Bible versions, but it occurs in the KJV as the rendering of Greek *aretē* G746 (Phil. 4:8; 2 Pet. 1:3, 5; the KJV uses it also to translate *dynamis* G1539, "power," referring to Jesus' miraculous ability in Mk. 5:30; Lk. 6:19; 8:46). In a few OT passages, the KJV uses "virtuous woman" to render the Hebrew phrase *ʾēšet-ḥayil* (H851 + H2657), which literally means "woman of power" and indicates competence or noble character (Ruth 3:11; Prov. 12:4; 31:10; cf. 31:29, "virtuously").

Among Greek moralistic writers, especially the STOICS, the term *aretē* was used very frequently to indicate the highest good, the social uprightness that evokes recognition, merit, and honor. Both PAUL and PETER employ this term in lists of positive moral traits (Phil. 4:8 and 2 Pet. 1:5; the focus is different in 1 Pet. 2:9 [a pl. translated "praises" by the NIV and "mighty acts" by the NRSV] and 2 Pet. 1:3 [referring to God and usually translated "goodness," but possibly meaning "power"]). Some scholars argue that the word in these lists must convey the meaning it has in Greco-Roman writings, especially in the numerous catalogs of positive and negative traits of behavior referred to as "virtue-vice lists" (cf. *ABD*, 6:857–59). Undoubtedly, the language used by the apostles reflects the world in which they lived, but given the Christian context, it is difficult to believe that they were merely asking their readers to conduct themselves like well-behaved Greeks. The word rather signifies the moral excellence distinctive of those who have been cleansed from their sins: it builds on faith and generates godliness and love (2 Pet. 1:5–9; cf. also the detailed discussion in P. T. O'Brien, *The Epistle to the Philippians: A Commentary on the Greek Text*, NIGTC [1991], 499–507). See *Epistles of* PAUL III.C.

vision. This English word, while including within its meanings that of physical sight or ocular perception, places the emphasis on those dimensions that are extraphysical—something seen otherwise than by ordinary sight, something beheld as in a dream or ecstasy, or revealed as to a prophet; a visual image without corporeal presence, an object of imaginative contemplation; unusual discernment or foresight. Several Hebrew words can be translated "vision," the most frequent being *ḥāzôn* H2606 (from the verb *ḥāzâ* H2600, "to see"; cf. also the related nouns *ḥizzāyôn* H2612 and *maḥăzeh* H4690 and the Aram. cognate *ḥēzû* H10256). Occurring ten times is *marʾâ* H5261 (from another verb meaning "to see," *rāʾâ* H8011; the similar and very common noun *marʾeh* H5260 usually refers to a physical seeing, but in a few passages it too can be translated "vision"). The NT writers use three Greek works: *optasia* G3965, *horama* G3969 (the most frequent), and *horasis* G3970.

References to visions are especially frequent in the book of Daniel, a factor that, considering the nature of this book, may furnish insight into the peculiar and suggestive connotations of the word. (See DANIEL, BOOK OF.) The references there and elsewhere in the OT seem consistent with the manifest nature of God. Throughout the Scriptures, God is declared as revealing himself and making his ways known through chosen individuals. The PATRIARCHS commonly reported that God had chosen to make his messages known through a vision. "After this, the word of the LORD came to Abram in a vision" (Gen. 15:1). Speaking to AARON and MIRIAM, God said, "When a prophet of the LORD is among you, / I reveal myself to him in visions, / I speak to him in dreams" (Num. 12:6). Although the NT records a few instances of visions during the apostolic period (Acts 9:10, 12; 10:3; et al.), the coming of Christ supersedes other means of REVELATION: "In the past God spoke to our forefathers through the prophets at many times and in various ways, but in these last days he has spoken to us by his Son" (Heb. 1:1–2a). See also DREAM; PROPHETS AND PROPHECY; TRANCE.

visitation. This English term, in the sense of a special manifestation of divine favor or displeasure, is rarely found in modern versions but is used by the KJV in about a dozen passages (most of them in Jeremiah, e.g., Jer. 8:12; 10:15) to render Hebrew *pequddâ* H7213, which has various meanings, such as "appointment," "supervision," and "punishment." In the KJV NT it occurs twice (Lk. 19:44; 1 Pet. 2:12) as the rendering of *episkopē* G2175, which has a semantic range similar to that of the Hebrew word. Similarly, the very common Hebrew verb *pāqad* H7212 ("to inspect, take note of, attend to, visit, appoint") is often used of God with reference to his activity, whether gracious or punitive. For example, when recounting that God fulfilled his promise to SARAH that she would bear a child, the biblical text says, "And the LORD visited Sarah as he had said" (Gen. 21:1 KJV; NIV, "was gracious to Sarah"; cf. also 50:24–25; Exod. 3:16; Ruth 1:6; 1 Sam. 2:21; et al.; in the NT, *episkeptomai* G2170 ["to examine, visit, look after"], Lk. 1:68 et al.). Conversely, after the Israelites worshiped the golden calf, God said, "in the day when I visit I will visit their sin upon them" (Exod. 32:34 KJV; NIV, "when the time comes for me to punish, I will punish them for their sin"; cf. also Lev. 18:25; Ps. 59:5; Isa. 26:14; et al.). (See *NIDOTTE*, 3:657–63; 1:190–91.)

Vophsi vof'sī (וָפְסִי H2265, derivation uncertain). Father of Nahbi; the latter, representing the tribe of NAPHTALI, was one of the twelve spies sent out to reconnoiter the Promised Land (Num. 13:14).

votive offering. See SACRIFICE AND OFFERINGS IV.C.

vow. A pledge or OATH of a religious character, and a transaction in which a person dedicates himself or his service or something valuable to God. A common feature in ancient religions, the vow was also a frequent exercise in religious life among the Israelites. Though it was generally a promise made in expectation of a divine favor eagerly sought, there were also vows of voluntarily imposed self-discipline for the achievement of character, and of self-dedication for the attainment of certain goals.

Of the first kind, sometimes called "bargains" (they were made on condition of favors to be returned by God), are those made by JACOB, who vowed to make BETHEL a shrine and to give a tithe if God would supply his needs and give him protection (Gen. 28:20–22); by JEPHTHAH, who vowed as sacrifice to God whatever should first meet him on his return if God would grant him victory over the Ammonites (Jdg. 11:30–31; in grief he offered his only child who so met him, vv. 34–40); by HANNAH, who vowed that if God should grant her a son she would consecrate him to God's service (1 Sam. 1:11, 27–28). Of this nature, no doubt, are most of the vows so frequently mentioned in the Psalms, vows of thanksgiving and sacrifice paid to God for prayers answered and deliverances granted (Pss. 22:25; 50:14; 56:12; 65:1–2, 8; 116:14, 18). Somewhat related is ABSALOM's vow to serve the Lord if God would bring him again to Jerusalem, but perverted to conspiratorial use in his rebellion against his father DAVID (2 Sam. 15:7–12). The vows made by the seamen after JONAH was cast overboard were perhaps more in the nature of a pagan attempt to propitiate a deity whom they "greatly feared" (Jon. 1:15–16).

There were also vows made for discipline of life and purpose, in dedication or CONSECRATION to God, and for the accomplishment of a set goal. The major vow in this category was the NAZIRITE vow, the promise of one separated or consecrated to God, and for which certain austerities and enunciations were prescribed (Num. 6:1–8); release from them could be obtained after fulfillment and designated sacrifices (6:13–21). SAMSON, SAMUEL, and JOHN THE BAPTIST were apparently Nazirites for life. Other vows short of this major commitment include David's promise to give himself no rest until he should have found a house for the Lord (Ps. 132:2–5), the "choice vows" associated with the call of Israel to obedience (Deut. 12:11 KJV), the vows associated with free-will offerings (Num. 29:39), the solemn binding of the soul to God (Num. 30:2). See SACRIFICE AND OFFERINGS IV.C. PAUL and his associates assumed vows to show conformity to Jewish law for the sake of appeasement without surrender of conscience (Acts 18:18; 21:23–24). Of less wise or worthy character are SAUL's adjuration against eating food till victory be secured (1 Sam. 14:24), and the vow of Paul's enemies to abstain from food until they had slain him (Acts 23:21).

In the OT vows were not commanded, but those made were carefully regulated. It was no sin to forbear making a vow (Deut. 23:22), but once made it was solemnly binding (vv. 21, 23; Eccl. 5:4). For this reason there were warnings against vows rashly made (Eccl. 5:5–6; Prov. 20:25); and for security against vows not responsibly or rashly made, vows could be disallowed by a father for a daughter in her minority (Num. 30:5), or by a husband for the rash utterance of his wife (v. 8).

The fulfillment of vows was strongly emphasized in the OT, and set up as significant indication of the piety and faithfulness of God's people (Pss. 22:25; 50:14; 56:12; 76:11; Isa. 19:21; Jer. 44:25; Jon. 2:9; Nah. 1:15). Only that could be pledged to God which belonged to the devotee; firstlings and tithes were considered as already belonging to God (Lev. 27:26–30). Blemished sacrifices or offerings in payment of vows were forbidden and brought under severe censure (Mal. 1:14), and "the earnings of a female prostitute or of a male prostitute" were an abomination to God and not to be used in payment (Deut. 23:18).

Jesus rebuked as reprehensible the payment of vows when used as occasion for escape from obligation to parents (Matt. 15:3–9; Mk. 7:9–13). Apart from this condemnation of vows wrongly used, it is not evident that Jesus or any of the NT writers made significant reference to vows, which are so prominent an expression of OT piety. The NT call to dedication and thankfulness and service stands in the deeper and richer relationship of life to the cross of Christ (Matt. 16:24; Rom. 12:1–2; 1 Cor. 6:20; 1 Pet. 1:15–19). See WORSHIP.   G. STOB

Vulgate vuhl´gayt. Name applied to the standard Latin translation of the Bible (the Lat. adjective *vulgatus* means "commonly known, in wide circulation"). During the first few centuries of the Christian era, the books of both the OT and the NT were translated into Latin piecemeal by different

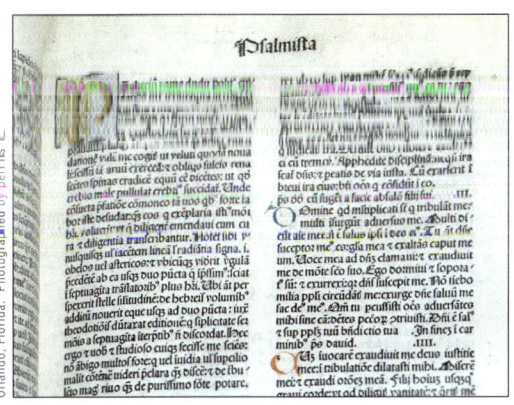

A page from Nicolas Jenson's edition of the Latin Vulgate (1479).

people at different times, and by the 4th cent. the form of the text differed widely from place to place. About the year 382 Pope Damasus commissioned JEROME to revise and standardize the Latin Bible. With regard to the OT, this meant not just a revision of the so-called Old Latin (which had been made from the Greek LXX); to a large extent, the work involved a fresh translation directly from the Hebrew. Jerome's revision of the Old Latin of the Gospels was spotty, and he probably was not responsible for the revision of the rest of the NT. See VERSIONS OF THE BIBLE, ANCIENT II.B.

vulture. This English word, referring to a number of large birds that subsist on carrion, is used variously in Bible versions to render different Hebrew words. The contexts are either food lists or purely figurative, giving no help in identification. There is general agreement, however, that the term *peres* H7272 (Lev. 11:13 and Deut. 14:12) does refer to some type of vulture. It is also likely that the word for "eagle," *nešer* H5979, connotes "vulture" in some passages (Mic. 1:16; Hab. 1:8; so NIV and NJPS). Some believe that ʿ*ozniyyâ* H6465 refers specifically to the black vulture (also in Lev. 11:13 and Deut. 14:12; cf. again NIV and NJPS, but NRSV has OSPREY). Another term is *rāḥām* H8164, rendered "carrion vulture" by the NRSV (Lev. 11:18 and Deut. 14:17; NIV, "osprey"; NJPS, "bustard"); the carrion vulture is also known as the Egyptian vulture (*Vultur percnopterus*, or better, *Neophron percnopterus*). The Greek term *aetos* G108, which generally means "eagle," is appropriately translated "vulture" in Jesus' well-known saying, "Wherever there is a carcass, there the vultures will gather" (Matt. 24:28; Lk. 17:37); eagles are usually solitary birds, but vultures come together in great numbers to feed. (See *FFB*, 82–84.)

Palestine has at least three resident species: the black vulture (*Coragyps atratus*), the bearded vulture (*Gypaetus barbatus*), and griffon (*Gyps fulvus*); the conspicuous black-and-white Egyptian vulture is a summer breeder. All are scavengers that find life more difficult in countries where civilization has brought sanitary methods of refuse disposal. The larger wild animals have become scarce, and almost the only carcasses likely to become available to vultures in Palestine are those of sheep, goats, and camels that have died of disease and are not acceptable as food.

The bearded and black vultures are birds of the desert edge, where they nest on cliffs and escarpments. The griffon has a wider distribution, and one long-used nesting place is in the crags above the Valley of the Doves, W of the Lake of Galilee. The griffon is huge, though not the biggest of all vultures, with a length of 3–4 ft. and a wing spread of roughly 8 ft. It is dirty brown, with a pale, down-covered head, but color is not distinguishable as it soars on motionless wings several thousands of feet above the ground. The Egyptian vulture is smaller, only 2 ft. long, and easily identified, for both sexes are black and white, with bare yellow face. Flying scavengers hang high in the sky great distances apart, and can see when a neighboring bird drops down, so that vultures from a wide area soon collect. See also BIRDS OF PREY. G. S. CANSDALE

Wadi Feifa S of the Dead Sea. (View to the NW.)

wadi wah´dee. Sometimes spelled *wady*. The bed of a stream that is usually dry except during the rainy season; the term is also applied to the stream itself. The word is Arabic and is used only of river beds in SW Asia and N Africa; it corresponds to Hebrew *naḥal* H5707, which can be rendered variously ("valley, ravine, brook, river, torrent"). See BROOK; VALLEY.

wafer. This English term is used to render two different Hebrew words. The noun *ṣappîḥit* H7613 occurs only once, when the MANNA is said to have "tasted like wafers made with honey" (Exod. 16:31). The second term is *rāqîq* H8386, which refers to a flat cake or thin crisp bread used as part of some offerings (29:2 et al.). It usually occurs in combination with *maṣṣâ* H5174 (pl. *maṣṣôt*), a flat BREAD made with unleavened dough. See LEAVEN; SACRIFICE AND OFFERINGS.

wages. Compensation to a person hired for performing some work or service. In the nomadic, pastoral society of the patriarchal period there was no wage-earning class. When men worked for others, it was generally for their own maintenance; and often they received some payment in kind for their services. JACOB's service to LABAN was on this basis (Gen. 29:15; 30:32–33; 31:8, 41). With the increasing complexity of a more settled community, once the Israelites were in Canaan, people were needed to engage in TRADES and CRAFTS of all kinds. For these services, payment was made, in whole or in part, by weighing out quantities of bronze or silver. Coinage in the standard sense was a later invention, being first used in ASIA MINOR by the Lydians just before 700 B.C. From here its use spread throughout the Greek world, but it was probably not in common use in the ANE until the Hellenistic period (beginning approx. 300 B.C.).

There were certainly many industrial and commercial enterprises for which wages were paid and which are not directly mentioned in the biblical text. Some specific occupations for which people received wages are mentioned, however: shepherds (Gen. 29:15; 30:32–33; Jn. 10:12); laborers and farm hands (Matt. 20:1–2; Lk. 10:7; 15:17; Jn. 4:36; Jas. 3:4); fishermen's helpers (Mk. 1:20); mercenary soldiers (Lk. 3:14); nurses (Exod. 2:9).

As is the case in near-eastern countries even today, bargaining was a common practice. Where there were no set scales for payment, it was usual to negotiate terms in this way in each individual case. The story of Jacob and Laban illustrates such a practice, from the very beginning of the discussion ("Name your wages," Gen. 30:28) down to the last accusation ("you changed my wages ten times," 31:41). The story details the kind of cheating and trickery that both parties practiced. The same tendency to bargain appears in the parable of the vineyard (Matt. 20:1–16), but here the employer was a just and generous man.

In Israelite society a laborer, who is a free man, would hire himself out for a particular job. As some families grew poorer, they would hire themselves out to rich farmers or to the government. In the contemporary Middle E there is still the practice of hiring day laborers for a specific job. To protect workers against exploitation certain safeguards were instituted; for example, wages were to be paid daily, before sundown, to those who had earned them (Lev. 19:13; Deut. 24:14–15). In spite of such injunctions, however, the lot of the wage earner was hard, and the prophets found it necessary constantly to condemn the practices of employers who took advantage of those who worked for them (Jer. 22:13; Mal. 3:5).

The biblical writers make figurative use of the Hebrew and Greek terms with reference to God's dealings with human beings. Thus God's benefits to his people are referred to as recompense (Isa. 40:10; 62:11); and the RETRIBUTION of God is spoken of as REWARD (Ps. 109:20) or gain (2 Pet. 2:15). DEATH is called the wages due for serving sin (Rom. 6:23). R. C. STONE

wagon. See CART.

Waheb way´heb (וָהֵב H2259, possibly "giver"). A place "in Suphah," probably near the ARNON River in MOAB, mentioned in a citation from the Book of the Wars of the Lord (Num. 21:14; TNIV, "Zahab," apparently following the reading of the LXX, *Zōob*). Some think it refers to the well from which the Arnon flows (*HALOT*, 1:259). The Hebrew text is very difficult, however. See discussion under SUPHAH; see also WARS OF THE LORD, BOOK OF.

wail. See MOURNING.

waistcloth. See DRESS III.B.

walk. Both the Hebrew and Greek terms for "walk" (*hālak* H2143; *peripateō* G4344) are often used in the Bible figuratively to indicate conduct or manner of life (e.g., Gen. 5:22; 1 Ki. 15:3; Ps. 1:1; Eph. 2:2, 10), including the observance of laws or customs (Lev. 26:3; Acts 21:21 [cf. HALAKAH]). Modern versions frequently avoid a literal translation and instead use "live" or other equivalents. See WAY.

wall. The most common Hebrew word for "wall" is *ḥômâ* H2570, applied mainly to the structures surrounding a CITY (e.g., Josh. 2:15), but sometimes also to those around a building or some other area (e.g., Lam. 2:7). A less frequent term, *gādēr* H1555, is used of dry stone walls in the fields (e.g., Num. 22:24; Isa. 5:5; see HEDGE), but in at least one passage it refers to a city wall (Mic. 7:11). The primary Greek term used in the NT is *teichos* G5446, applied also to city walls (Acts 9:25; 2 Cor. 11:33; Heb. 11:30; Rev. 21:12–19; see also WALL OF PARTITION).

House walls were usually made of mud brick set on rubble-stone-base courses, with walls of rubble stone occasionally set in mud mortar. City walls in early times were built vertically without any outer glacis for protection; down to the beginning of Iron Age II they were casemate type walls and later they were solid and thick to resist the Assyrian battering rams. Thicknesses varied between three and five meters with projecting bastions. The latter were crowned with overhangs to ward off attackers, and crenelations to protect archers. H. G. STIGERS

wall of partition. The KJV uses the phrase "the middle wall of partition" to translate *to mesotoichon tou phragmou*, which occurs only once (Eph. 2:14). The noun *mesotoichon* G3546 (from *mesos* G3545, "middle" or "between," and *toichos* G5526 [variant of *teichos* G5446], "wall") is rare, but it clearly refers to a dividing wall; *phragmos* G5850, on the other hand, is a very common word meaning "fence" or "hedge" (Matt. 21:33; Mk. 12:1; Lk. 14:23). The two nouns are probably in apposition, so that the phrase can be translated literally as "the partitioning wall, [that is,] the fence," and most modern versions render it simply as "the dividing wall." The following clause (Eph. 2:15 in the KJV) has another noun in apposition, *echthra* G2397, "enmity"; thus the NRSV offers the translation, "the dividing wall, that is, the hostility between us," while the NIV has, more simply, "the dividing wall of hostility" (v. 14).

In the context, PAUL is addressing Christians of both Jewish and Gentile backgrounds. Between these Christians there had been a dividing wall, not literally but socially, thus segregating them. The division was seen in the church in many places (cf. Acts 15; Gal. 2:11–14). In Christ, however, this dividing wall was broken down: there was no longer to be any distinction between Jew and Gentile in Christ's kingdom.

In the TEMPLE area, there was literally a wall that segregated Gentiles from Jews. No Gentile was allowed to cross that dividing line. However illustrative of the point Paul was making, he was not referring to a literal structure. The dividing wall of which he spoke was far more formidable, being a wall of blind prejudice. J. B. SCOTT

want. See COVET; DESIRE.

war, warfare. The common Hebrew term for "battle" or "war" is *milḥāmâ* H4878 (Gen. 14:2 et al.), used more than 300 times in the OT. In the NT, however, there are fewer than twenty occurrences of Greek *polemos* G4483, about half of them in Revelation (Rev. 12:7 et al.; cf. also the verb *strateuomai* G5129, used figuratively in 2 Cor. 10:3; 1 Pet. 2:11; similarly, *antistrateuomai* G529 in Rom. 7:23). See also ARMY.

   I. General
   II. The Canaanite period
   III. The period of the Israelite conquest and settlement
   IV. The period of the Israelite monarchies
   V. Siege warfare
   VI. The period of the second temple

I. General. War was a constant feature in the history of Israel from its beginnings up to the destruction of the second TEMPLE. Long periods of peace seldom occurred, and so the Bible emphasizes them (e.g., "the land had peace for forty years," Jdg. 3:11). The nature of the Israelite wars changed according to the political and sociological conditions, such as during the conquest and settlement, the defensive wars of the tribes against the aggressive neighbors in the period of the judges, the wars of consolidation on the borders during the first days of the monarchy, the constant struggle for the existence of the kingdoms of Israel and Judah, and the last desperate stand against the great imperial forces.

The days of the second temple are marked, too, with long periods of continuous warfare. In the earlier wars, mainly concerned with border disputes, and in the later wars of liberation from imperial control, first SELEUCID and then Roman (see ROMAN EMPIRE), the principal cause was religious; that is, there were struggles to preserve a national identity based on the temple in Jerusalem and the Jewish religious laws.

In ancient times, two types of wars were distinguished: (a) wars of defense and expansion, which were basically political and which were fought because of physical necessity, and to which there were fixed legal limitations (see below); and (b) holy wars, which were compulsory for the entire nation and did not have comparable limitations. This distinction was recognized also in the second temple period. Thus, a radical religious population participated in the early Maccabean wars because they were believed to be holy wars (see MACCABEES); later, when the Hasmoneans turned to politically oriented wars, the people refused to participate.

Deuteronomy 20 and 21 contain some of the laws of war that were upheld in the first temple period; more laws and practices are found in other sources describing the wars themselves. The laws of war first describe the encouragement of the troops by the priests, who assured them of the support of the Lord (Deut. 20:1–4). Other sources indicate that the kings and military leaders often assured themselves by consulting oracles; these included the holy ARK OF THE COVENANT (Jdg. 20:27); the EPHOD (1 Sam. 30:7–8); the URIM AND THUMMIM (14:41; 28:6); and various prophets (28:6). Occasionally—as was Canaanite custom—they even appealed to the spirits of the dead, as did SAUL through the medium of the witch of ENDOR (ch. 28; see DIVINATION). The priests and holy ark even accompanied the army on the battlefield in the earlier wars (1 Sam. 4:4; 30:7; 2 Sam. 11:11).

Further, to secure God's aid, the troops would make sacrifices prior to battle (Jdg. 6:20, 26; 20:26)—sometimes even human sacrifices, as in the story of JEPHTHAH's daughter (according to one interpretation of Jdg. 11:39) or of the son of the king of MOAB (2 Ki. 3:27). This custom seems also to have been taken from earlier Canaanite traditions, for in many Egyptian reliefs from the late kingdom, depicting the capture of towns in Palestine, the besieged are shown throwing their children from the walls in seeking the gods' favor. Military victory was believed to be the victory of one god over another, often leading to literary depictions of the gods as taking part in actual battles (in the Bible, cf. Josh. 10:11).

The laws concerning war in the book of Deuteronomy deal, inter alia, with the instances in which persons could be exempt from military service, as with those who were seized with fear, were newly married, had recently built a house, planted a vineyard, and so forth. Other laws deal with vanquished peoples, spoils, prisoners, and the prohibition of cutting down fruit trees in conquered lands.

The customs and laws of war were fixed and had much in common throughout the ANE. Troops were often drawn from the peasantry, and fighting was generally limited to the agricultural off-seasons —from just after HARVEST till the first rains. War usually was not "declared"; it was naturally assumed that the strong were free to take possession of the lives and possessions of the weak. Only by maintaining a strong army could a nation keep potential enemies at bay, and the only satisfactory alternative was to accept all of the enemy's demands without going into battle.

II. The Canaanite period. We possess detailed descriptions of battles in Palestine from as early as the late Canaanite period, that is, from the period of expansion of the Egyptian new kingdom (18th–20th dynasties). They are of two types: (a) reliefs or wall paintings in Egyptian temples and (b) inscriptions or literary texts. The value of either type is rather limited, but together they provide a fairly clear picture. The reliefs usually are schematic and show the conquest of cities in Palestine, with the besieged in the last stages of resistance. These reliefs mainly give details on the methods of Egyptian siege-warfare, which included the use of ladders, mining the walls, and breaching the gates with axes and fire. The battering ram, however, seems not to have been employed by the Egyptians.

Most of our information on warfare comes from literary texts, some of which are of the heroic or mythological sort. Of the former type is the story of the conquest of JOPPA under THUTMOSE III (c. 1479–1425 B.C.), which resembles the story of the conquest of Troy. The Egyptian general sent a conciliatory "present" in several hundred sealed baskets which, in fact, contained armed soldiers; once within the city, the hidden soldiers revealed themselves and seem to have opened the gates to the besieging army. More realistic war records, prepared by military scribes, enable modern scholars to reconstruct various battles from beginning to end.

The earliest concerns the Battle of MEGIDDO in the days of Thutmose III. A coalition of many Canaanite kings ("330 rulers") gathered under the leadership of the king of KADESH ON THE ORONTES and attempted to block the Egyptian army at Megiddo, thus preventing it from penetrating into N Palestine and Syria. The detailed account tells of the deceptive tactics adopted by the Canaanites prior to the battle, to divert the Egyptians toward an ambush. The Egyptian king saw through this ruse and, by a daring march, surprised the Canaanites in their main camp outside the city, defeating them swiftly, though besieged Megiddo held out for seven months longer. The king boasts that he could have captured the city the same day had it not been for his soldiers' desire for loot, which diverted them from pursuing the enemy. This enabled the enemy survivors to reach safety behind the city walls. This case seems not to have been the first time, nor the last, in the history of the ANE in which soldiers could not be held to their task, preferring to plunder rather than pursuing the enemy (cf. 1 Sam. 14).

Another battle taking place in that period and about which a complete account survives, is the Battle of Kadesh (1280 B.C.) between the Egyptian army under RAMSES II and the armies of a Syrian league headed by the king of the HITTITES. Just as the Canaanites before were fully aware of their military inferiority (esp. against the Egyptian archery), so also the Syrians attempted deceit by sending out spies with the intention of their being caught. These gave false information leading the Egyptians toward a well-prepared ambush. The ruse seems to have been successful, at least initially, and one of the Egyptian units was wiped out. Egyptian superiority in weaponry and training, and the sudden appearance of a special unit, turned the battle. It is interesting to note that, in both cases, the Egyptians' adversaries avoided open battle, rather seeking the security of strongly fortified cities. The ultimate outcome in either case proved the wisdom of such tactics.

The third battle of which we possess a detailed description took place in the days of Ramses III (c. 1180 B.C.), in which the Egyptians repulsed the invasion of the SEA PEOPLES (including the PHILISTINES). This battle is depicted on the walls of Ramses' temple at Medinet Habu. The Sea Peoples' attempt was twofold: one wave seems to have come by way of Syria and Palestine, and was defeated near el-ᶜArish; the second wave came by sea and was defeated in the NILE delta. This is the first detailed description of a sea battle in the history of the ANE. As depicted in the reliefs, the Egyptians won mainly through their superiority

WAR, WARFARE 1041

in archery—a weapon which their enemies lacked altogether. See ARMOR, ARMS.

The Egyptian sources contain much data on the organization of the Egyptian army, the size of its units, its logistics, and so forth. They are not, however, the only sources on military matters in the ANE. In CUNEIFORM archives discovered at such sites as MARI, ALALAKH, Boğazköy (Hattusas, the ancient Hittite capital), and TELL EL-AMARNA, thousands of documents provide details on the weapons, tactics, and logistics of Mesopotamian, Syrian, Canaanite, Hittite, and other armies. Further, there are many examples of the actual weapons, found in excavations on the various sites. Art objects, such as ivories (esp. those from UGARIT and Megiddo) also provide depictions of weapons and battles.

III. The period of the Israelite conquest and settlement.

Early in the Iron Age (12th cent. B.C.), political conditions in Palestine changed: the great empires of the previous period, Egypt and the Hittites, were weakened or destroyed, largely by the Sea Peoples; and in the regions between them, many small city-states rose. Palestine was also invaded by two nations new on the political scene and very different in character: the Israelites, who at the time were poorly equipped nomadic tribes settled in the mountainous areas, and groups of Sea Peoples that the Bible collectively calls the "Philistines." These latter settled in the coastal plain and were organized around a pentapolis (ASHDOD, ASHKELON, EKRON, GATH, and GAZA); they developed a proper standing army, equipped with iron weapons. Small pockets of the older inhabitants of the land remained; these were Canaanites who also were centered on city-states, with the battle CHARIOT as their most formidable weapon.

Israelite military inferiority forced the tribes also to deception of the enemy; they usually found it too difficult to penetrate fortified cities by force and thus they resorted to other means, such as by sending spies to seek out hidden ways into the city (Josh. 2). The most interesting biblical story in this connection is the capture of JERICHO. Here the army with the priests and the holy ark at its head marched around the city for seven days (6:14–15). In the opinion of Y. Yadin (*The Art of Warfare in Biblical Lands*, 2 vols. [1963], 1:99–100), JOSHUA sought to lull the suspicions and ease the tension of the defenders till he could launch a sudden attack with success. At AI (chs. 8–12), the Israelites succeeded in luring the enemy out of the city by a ruse. Later, DAVID captured JERUSALEM by penetrating secretly through an underground water conduit (2 Sam. 5:7–8). Night or dawn attacks were also

Assyrian ramp used against the siege of Lachish during Sennacherib's invasion of Judah in the days of Hezekiah.

sprung (1 Sam. 11:11), as well as other forms of surprise attacks (Josh. 10:9). Often armies were split into several parts (usually three) to achieve surprise or to provide a ruse (Jdg. 7:16; cf. also 1 Sam. 11:11; 13:16; 2 Sam. 18:2).

In the period of the settlement, the Israelites had to withstand the attacks of various nomad tribes, especially in the S (the Amalekites) and the Jezreel valley (the Midianites), who would raid villages and take prisoners (see Amalek, Midian). Warfare against these peoples was conducted in the same manner as before, that is, by means of small and maneuverable units (Heb. *gĕdûd* H1522, which at the time of Gideon numbered 300 men, and in the days of the united monarchy, some 400–600). Larger "militia" units were raised only in times of extreme danger: against the Canaanites (Jdg. 4; 5) or Ammonites (1 Sam. 11), or at a time of intertribal strife (Jdg. 20).

Using these same tactics (combined small attacks and opposing the enemy in open array), the Israelites succeeded, at least at first, in standing up to their bitterest rivals, the Philistines. It is in this context that we learn of another form of war, that is, the personal duel between two opposing warriors, as in the case of David and Goliath (1 Sam. 17; cf. 2 Sam. 2:12); such a form of fighting is known in other lands. Upon the death of Saul and Jonathan his son, it became obvious that new tactics were called for. The danger presented by the Philistines was the main impetus for the union of the Israelite tribes into a single kingdom to enable successful resistance. Only political unity could bring about a standing well-trained and equipped army.

The army organized by David, under the skilled leadership of Joab, soon enabled the Israelites to achieve the upper hand over the other small states surrounding them. David consolidated the borders of his kingdom and even considerably expanded them. Actually, there was never a day of peace throughout his reign. Most interesting are the detailed chapters describing the wars against the Ammonites and the Arameans (2 Sam. 10:10; 1 Chr. 19), where we learn that Hanun, king of the Ammonites, hired Aramean troops to help him in his defense. See Aram (country). Joab soon found himself in the midst of the enemy, and in a very characteristic way he brought in the Israelite militia which, alongside his small standing army, defeated the Arameans and then turned to besiege the capital of Ammon.

The great victories of the Israelite army in the days of David, however, and the expansion into most of Syria, can be explained only by the fact that by this time the great empires no longer were able to control this region.

IV. The period of the Israelite monarchies. In the first stages of this period, Israel was divided into two kingdoms. At first rivals, they later came to conduct combined operations against their common enemies, especially the Arameans. Already in the mid-9th cent. B.C., upon the advent of the mighty armies of Assyria in this region, the petty wars came to an end and the small states grouped themselves into coalitions so as to be able to stand up to the common foe. From 734 B.C. on, Assyria slowly conquered the entire region, taking the petty states one by one. Babylonia, her powerful heir, completed this task.

The Aramean soldiers and their weapons are well known to us from reliefs discovered at Tell Halaf (biblical Gozan), Carchemish, Malatya (ancient Maldiya, in SE Asia Minor), and other sites. They were fully as strong as the armies of Israel and Judah, and the struggle between them was long-lived. The character of these wars is known from 1 Ki. 20, which contains extensive details. Ben-Hadad king of Damascus, at the head of a league of thirty-two vassal kings, came to Succoth on the eastern bank of the Jordan River, opposite Samaria. When he sent messengers demanding that the Israelites surrender, King Ahab outrightly refused. Ben-Hadad, confident in the superior strength of his forces, ordered them to cross the river and besiege the city of Samaria. The Arameans rather heedlessly began the ascent along the steep path of Wadi Farʿah, the main route from Succoth, well known, of course, to the Israelites. Rather than waiting for the enemy in Samaria, Ahab gathered his troops (about 700) and ambushed the Arameans while they were still on the march, thoroughly routing them.

This method of ambushing, in narrow mountain defiles by large, well-equipped forces, takes maximum advantage of the difficulties encountered by anyone attempting to penetrate into the hills of Samaria or the Judean mountains; it became one of the standard methods of warfare among the Israelites down to the fall of the kingdom. A similar battle was conducted between Jehoshaphat king of Judah and a combined Moabite-Ammonite force that was making for Jerusalem through the Judean Desert (2 Chr. 20).

It was even more characteristic during the Hellenistic period when the Jews rose against the SELEUCIDS, and later, during the revolts against Rome (see below). The maneuver is typical of guerrilla warfare and enables small forces to achieve the upper hand over numerically superior armies. Not in vain were the Arameans afraid to enter the mountain passes of Samaria, saying, "Their gods are gods of the hills" (1 Ki. 20:23).

V. Siege warfare. The battles against the Arameans, Moabites, and Ammonites occurred in the open, but not so the wars fought against the mighty armies of Assyria and Babylonia. In the initial clash (in the mid-9th cent. B.C.), Ahab dared to participate against Assyria in a league of southern Syrian rulers that repulsed the invaders in four successive campaigns, near the city of Qarqar. But 100 years later, when the Assyrians approached, the petty kingdoms were unable to unite, and the war degenerated into mere defensive actions, centered upon fortified cities, while the Assyrians were in complete control of the countryside.

The methods of fighting based on fortified cities are well known from excavations and from Egyptian and Assyrian reliefs, in which this subject was quite popular. Remains of city fortifications, including walls and gates, have been exposed at most of the excavated sites of the Israelite period in Palestine, revealing even minute details. Moreover, systematic study has clarified the development of siege tactics in this period. The main problem in preparing a city to withstand a siege, besides the construction of the fortifications, was to provide for an adequate source of water within the city walls. This was achieved either by digging vast cisterns for storing quantities of rain water, or by diverting water sources beneath the ground to within the fortified area, concealing any original opening outside. Several such water systems have been discovered, mainly dating from the period of the Israelite kingdoms (at HAZOR, MEGIDDO, IBLEAM, GEZER, GIBEON, JERUSALEM, ARAD, and BEERSHEBA). The famous Siloam tunnel inscription from Jerusalem describes King HEZEKIAH's efforts to bring water from the Gihon spring into the city (c. 705 B.C.). In much later times, extensive water systems were built by HEROD the Great to bring huge quantities of water into the same city; similar projects by this king included enormous cisterns constructed at MASADA, the HERODIUM, and MACHAERUS.

The methods of pressing siege in the ANE were many and varied. We have already noted various ruses employed by the Israelites against Canaanite cities. The Egyptian and Assyrian reliefs reveal even more: scaling walls by means of ladders; breaching walls with battering rams; breaking down gates with axes and fire; and mining beneath walls. Often several methods were employed simultaneously. The Assyrians were depicted as slaying prisoners beneath the very eyes of the besieged so as to weaken their morale.

If a city resisted all these measures, the attackers had to fall back upon the difficult pursuit of an extended siege, cutting off the inhabitants of the city from all supplies, and making continuous attacks upon the walls at various locations until a weak spot was found or until the city gave in. After the appearance of the great imperial armies in Palestine, the Israelite kings concentrated their efforts on fortifying and preparing their cities to withstand prolonged sieges. They sometimes succeeded in stemming a siege of many months or even years. The longest siege recorded in history was that of ASHDOD by Psammetichus II of Egypt, which lasted no less than twenty-nine years (Herodotus, *Hist.* 2.157). In a relief from NINEVEH, there is an exceptional depiction of a Judean city under siege by the Assyrian army; it shows LACHISH as the Assyrian troops were storming its walls with many battering rams, light archery in the fore (mostly non-Assyrian troops from vassal kingdoms), then heavy Assyrian spearmen and archers, followed by slingers. The defenders, on their part, attempted to forestall the work of the siege machines by shooting arrows and throwing stones, oil, and flaming torches down upon them.

VI. The period of the second temple. From the Persian period on (see PERSIA), our principal sources are literary. The Greek historians, such as Herodotus, Xenophon, Thucydides, and Diodorus, have provided detailed descriptions of the wars between the Persians and the Greeks, as well as the wars among the Greeks themselves. One of the most interesting of these descriptions, Xenophon's *Anabasis*, tells of the engagement of the Persian army with that of Cyrus, satrap of SARDIS, in whose service were the 10,000 Greek mercenaries commanded by Xenophon. In this battle the clear advantage of the new Greek formations over the traditional oriental armies is quite apparent—a superiority that was even more telling in the victorious campaigns of ALEXANDER THE GREAT.

The main force of Greek armies in this period were the units of heavily armed infantry, the *hoplites*. Their name, meaning "heavy-armed," is derived from the large bronze shield they carried into battle on their left arms, protecting most of the body and enabling the warrior to use his right arm for maneuvering his heavy spear, sometimes even at a distance of some 10 ft. from his enemy. The hoplites also carried a short sword and wore protective armor, including a bronze helmet. These troops fought in a close formation, the phalanx, where the shield of one soldier overlapped that of his neighbor, providing double protection. The superiority of this formation was based upon the fact that the soldiers in the front row, who were in direct contact with the enemy, were immediately supported by their comrades in the rows behind.

From the time of the Peloponnesian wars on, a basic change occurred in the organization of Greek armies. Besides the hoplite, there was now a lightly armed soldier, the *peltast*, whose name was also derived from a type of shield (Gk. *peltē*), smaller and round; these had no protective armor and their principal armament was the small throwing javelin, a weapon derived from Thrace (THRACIA) and common especially among mercenaries. In the Macedonian army, the spear was lengthened, sometimes even reaching a length of 20 ft.; actually the several rows of the phalanx used spears of varying lengths so as to present the enemy with a maximum of "fire power" at one time. The bow was little used in classical times (except in Cretan units, with mercenary archers serving in large numbers with the Greeks). In the Hellenistic period, oriental influence brought archers a greater role, and even mounted archers appeared, usually being employed as a protective curtain before the phalanx.

War chariots were not used at all in classical Greece; instead, the Greeks did make use of cavalry as an organic part of the army in several cities. Thus, ATHENS had cavalry units and, for a short period, also mounted archers. In the classical period, however, the lack of the stirrup seriously impaired the effectiveness of such troops. Philip and Alexander made more common use of cavalry, and since then such units held an important place in every battle, especially in outflanking the enemy or pursuing him in flight. The Hellenistic period, too, saw the introduction—again under oriental influence—of heavy cavalry: chariotry was also used on a small scale.

As for siege machinery, the Greek sources up to the end of the 5th cent. B.C. are largely silent. An extraordinary discovery in the recent excavations at PAPHOS in CYPRUS has revealed some of the methods employed by the Persians in the successful siege of this city in 498 B.C.; this included the remains of a developed siege ramp. From the literary sources we know that only in the beginning of the 4th cent. B.C. did the Greeks first use a primitive sort of catapult (at Syracuse), which they copied from the Carthaginians. This machine was employed only in siege warfare, throwing darts for a great distance.

Replica of a catapult used by the Roman army during the siege of Gamla c. A.D. 67.

Later, the catapult was improved, increasing its effective range considerably. Such machines were employed by Alexander in his siege of TYRE (in 332 B.C.). The Greeks actually had two types of siege machines: the catapult for darts, and the balista for throwing stones; these had an effective range of some 600 ft., which the Romans later were able to increase to about 800 ft.

In the Hellenistic period, the Greeks followed the Persians in using ELEPHANTS in warfare. Alexander brought over 100 elephants from INDIA, and SELEUCUS I had over 500. They were particularly effective against enemy cavalry and could also break through the heavy phalanx. In the Battle of Gaza (312 B.C.), the Egyptian army defended themselves against the Seleucid elephants by studding the battlefield with sharp nails — the first "mine field" in history. ANTIOCHUS III employed elephants against the Hasmoneans, leading to the well-known story of Eleazar, who was crushed beneath an elephant he had killed with his spear (2 Macc. 13:2). The Romans normally did not use the elephant, probably because of its awkwardness.

The army of the Hasmoneans appears to have been patterned after the Hellenistic model; the Herodian army, however, was more composite, Hellenistic but with Roman elements. The Roman entry into Palestine in 63 B.C. brought about a change in the weaponry and in the military formations of this area; actually, it is especially in this field that Roman influence is felt. In excavations of sites in Palestine, few remains of Roman weapons have been found (mainly arrow and javelin heads, a few swords and scales of armor), though many remains of Roman military architecture are known. The most important of these are the siege camps, the circumvallation wall, and the ramp at Masada; the siege camps above the caves in Naḥal Ḥever; the siege ramp at BETHER (from the period of the second revolt, A.D. 132–135); and many small forts in the Negev and E of the ARABAH that were parts of the *limes*, the defensive border system of the Roman empire in this area.

The principal sources on the warfare between the Jews and the Romans in Palestine are the detailed accounts by Flavius JOSEPHUS in his monumental work, the *War of the Jews* (see WARS, JEWISH). Being of inferior strength, the Jews resorted mainly to two forms of fighting: ambushes in narrow mountain defiles and defense within fortified cities. Josephus relates the events of three such sieges — at Jodfat in Galilee, at Jerusalem, and at Masada in the Judean Desert. A most valuable addition to the sources on the military organization of the Jews in this period are the documents recently found in caves in the Judean Desert: the *Scroll of the War of the Sons of Light against the Sons of Darkness* (see DEAD SEA SCROLLS) and the BAR-KOKHBA letters, found in Naḥal Ḥever and sent originally by the leader of the second revolt to his subordinates at EN GEDI.

(See further E. E. Tarn, *Hellenistic Military and Naval Development* [1930]; P. E. Adcock, *The Roman Art of War under the Republic* [1940]; id., *The Greek and Macedonian Art of War* [1957]; Y. Yadin, *The Art of Warfare in Biblical Lands in the Light of Archaeological Study*, 2 vols. [1963]; id., *The Finds from the Bar-Kokhba Period in the Cave of the Letters* [1963]; J. Liver, ed., *The Military History of the Land of Israel in Biblical Times* [1964]; Y. Yadin, *Masada: Herod's Fortress and the Zealot's Last Stand* [1966]; L. Keppie, *The Making of the Roman Army* [1984]; G. Webster, *The Roman Imperial Army of the First and Second Centuries A.D.*, 3rd ed. [1985]; T. R. Hobbs, *A Time of War: A Study of Warfare in the Old Testament* [1989]; R. Drews, *Early Riders: The Beginnings of Mounted Warfare in Asia and Europe* [2004]; H. van Wees, *Greek Warfare: Myths and Realities* [2004]; A. Chaniotis, *War in the Hellenistic World: A Social and Cultural History* [2005]; A. J. Spalinger, *War in Ancient Egypt* [2005]; K. A. Raaflaub, ed., *War and Peace in the Ancient World* [2007].)

E. STERN

wardrobe, keeper of the. See KEEPER.

War of the Sons of Light against the Sons of Darkness. See DEAD SEA SCROLLS IV.

warrior, divine. On numerous occasions as recorded in the Hebrew Scriptures, Israel experienced the presence of Yahweh on the battlefield. The first explicit proclamation of God as a warrior is found in the Song of the Sea, Moses' hymn celebrating God's victory over the Egyptians at the RED SEA. "The LORD is a warrior; / the LORD is his name. / Pharaoh's chariots and his army / he has

hurled into the sea" (Exod. 15:3–4a). God made his appearance known on this occasion by dividing the waters so his people could pass through in safety. He then closed the waters on the Egyptians who attempted to follow and destroy the unarmed people of God. This single action of the divine warrior demonstrates the two-sided nature of God's warring activity: SALVATION and JUDGMENT.

The theme of the divine warrior is integrally connected to the institution of holy WAR in the Hebrew Scriptures. Indeed, warfare is made holy by the fact that God was with the army in all phases of its activities. In other words, at the heart of holy war is the divine warrior. In early Israelite history, his presence was represented by the ARK OF THE COVENANT, which was a mobile symbol of God's presence. The ark was constructed in the wilderness and was carried at the front of the tribes as they marched, as if to war, during the forty years of wandering. That the wilderness wandering was conceived as a long march to battle is reflected in Moses' words each morning as the ark left the TABERNACLE: "Rise up, O LORD! / May your enemies be scattered; / may your foes flee before you" (Num. 10:35).

Later, as the Israelites under JOSHUA began the conquest of the promised land, the ark played a prominent role in the divinely imparted strategy to defeat the heavily walled city of JERICHO (Josh. 6). Indeed, on the eve of that important victory, the divine warrior himself visited Joshua in a human form with drawn sword to impart the battle plans to his servant, the human war leader (5:13–15). On most occasions, however, the divine warrior made his presence known to the troops in other than human form. God frequently worked through the forces of nature that he created and controlled. At the Red Sea, he used the wind to push back the waters. During the conquest of the coalition of southern kings of Palestine, he killed the enemy by throwing down huge hailstones, and to prolong the slaughter he commanded the sun and the moon to stop in the sky (ch. 10).

The appearance of the divine warrior causes convulsions in the creation. Mountains shake; rivers dry up; nature grows impotent (Jdg. 5:4–5; Isa. 24:1–7; Nah. 1:2–6). Furthermore, music ceases from the land (Isa. 24:8–9). When victory comes, however, fertility bursts at the seams and music is jubilant. As a matter of fact, some of the most powerful early songs (Exod. 15; Jdg. 5) and many psalms (e.g., Pss. 24; 98) celebrate God's warring success.

Interestingly enough, though God could win any battle on his own, he always insists on Israel's participation. That participation is always that of a junior partner, however. The battle of GIDEON against the Midianites is a prime example (see esp. Jdg. 7). Showing up on the battlefield with 32,000 troops, God first tells Gideon to send home those who are afraid. When only 22,000 men leave, other means are instituted to whittle the troops all the way down to 300, and with these God wins the battle. If Israel had gone in with a superior force, then their victory would have led to pride in their own power.

DAVID well expresses the heart of divine warrior theology when, as he confronts GOLIATH, he proclaims: "You come against me with sword and spear and javelin, but I come against you in the name of the LORD Almighty, the God of the armies of Israel, whom you have defied. This day the LORD will hand you over to me, and I'll strike you down and cut off your head. Today I will give the carcasses of the Philistine army to the birds of the air and the beasts of the earth, and the whole world will know that there is a God in Israel. All those gathered here will know that it is not by sword or spear that the LORD saves; for the battle is the LORD's, and he will give all of you into our hands" (1 Sam. 17:45–47).

Since God is present with the army on the battlefield, the troops must be spiritually prepared to go to battle. This requirement explains why the Israelite men had to undergo mass CIRCUMCISION before engaging in war at Jericho (Josh. 5:2–8). In historical narratives recounting Israel's wars, there are reports about preliminary sacrifices (1 Sam. 13). URIAH the Hittite refused to have sexual relations with his wife BATHSHEBA, probably in part for fear that an emission of semen would render him ritually unclean and unable to return to the battlefield where the ark of the covenant was located (2 Sam. 11:6–11; cf. Lev. 15:16–18).

When God is present with the army, there is no doubt about the outcome. After victory, all the plunder and all the prisoners of war are to be brought to Yahweh. Everything is rendered *ḥērem* חֵרֶם, a Hebrew word difficult to translate, but meaning "that which is dedicated to God for a particular purpose" (see BAN). In terms of the prisoners of war, *ḥērem* is a death penalty. Within the land of Canaan, all enemies—men, women, and children—were executed (Deut. 20:16–18). Outside the land of promise, the defeated enemies were subjected to perpetual servitude (7:10–15).

Israel not only experienced the help of the divine warrior, but also his ANGER when they were disobedient. Indeed, in the curses of the Sinai COVENANT, God promises to defeat the enemies of his obedient people, but to give the victory to the enemy when Israel disobeys (Deut. 28:25–26, 49–57). The defeat of the Israelite forces at AI during the conquest (Josh. 8) and at EBENEZER under the leadership of the two sons of ELI (1 Sam. 4:1–11) are illustrative. The most dramatic example, however, is when God used the Babylonian army to defeat his recalcitrant people. Lamentations gives voice to the horror of that destruction when it says: "The Lord is like an enemy; / he has swallowed up Israel. / He has swallowed up all her palaces / and destroyed her strongholds. / He has multiplied mourning and lamentation / for the Daughter of Judah" (Lam. 2:5).

Israel was not the only ANE civilization to practice holy war or to conceive of their deity as a divine warrior. The Egyptians, the Mesopotamians, the Moabites, and others have left literature that indicates that they too understood that their gods participated in their battles.

Finally, the NT picks up the theme of the divine warrior and applies it to Christ. However, his warfare has a different objective. His battle is against the spiritual powers and principalities, and he wins this battle not with the sword (Matt. 26:47–56), but by his death and resurrection (Col. 2:13–15). Paul declares that Christ's followers participate in this spiritual warfare (Eph. 6:10–20). The book of Revelation culminates this theme when it pictures Christ's return for the great final battle, when all of God's enemies—physical and spiritual—will be cast into the LAKE OF FIRE (cf. Rev. 19:11–21).

(See further P. D. Miller, Jr., *The Divine Warrior in Early Israel* [1973]; M. C. Lind, *Yahweh Is a Warrior: The Theology of Warfare in Ancient Israel* [1980]; S.-M. Kang, *Divine War in the Old Testament and in the Ancient Near East* [1989]; T. Longman III and D. G. Reid, *God Is a Warrior* [1995].)

T. LONGMAN III

wars, Jewish. The general causes of the two Jewish wars against the Romans, in A.D. 66–70 and 132–135, lay in at least four factors. There was in Israel a long tradition that combined religious zeal and violence. The priest PHINEHAS exercised his zeal for the Lord by killing a sinning Hebrew man and Moabite woman (Num. 25:6–13). As the intertestamental Maccabean revolt began (see MACCABEE), the aged priest MATTATHIAS slew a SELEUCID official and an apostatizing Jew; he then cried, "Let every one who is zealous for the law and the covenant come out with me!" (1 Macc. 2:27). At the time of the Roman census in A.D. 6, Judas of Gamala, driven by a "passion for liberty … convinced that God alone is … leader and master" (Jos. *Ant.* 18.1.4 §23), led an abortive revolt promising his followers "that Heaven would be their zealous helper."

The second factor arose when, in 63 B.C., the Roman general POMPEY took control of Jerusalem. Probably made curious about its contents by rumors within the Gentile world, he forcibly entered the Holy of Holies in the TEMPLE. To him the act was nothing more than the privilege of a conqueror. To the Jews it was the ultimate sacrilege. They did not soon forget, and the incident precipitated the atmosphere of mistrust, misunderstanding, and hostility that marked all future Jewish-Roman relations.

Third, many of the officials who ruled the Jews in the name of the Romans were motivated by personal greed and characterized by brutality, incompetence, and misunderstanding of Jewish sensitivities. The result was an increasing Jewish hatred for their conquerors, an attitude that was a part of the background against which Jesus carried on his ministry.

Finally, the Jews remembered their experience of independence under their own Maccabean rulers (166–63 B.C.). Even though most of these were as despotic as any pagan overlord, this memory intensified the Jewish hope for "the redemption of Jerusalem" (Lk. 2:38).

Our knowledge of the A.D. 66–70 war comes largely from the Jewish historian Flavius JOSEPHUS, who was an eyewitness and participant in the war. Josephus began as the general in charge of the defense of GALILEE. When captured he became a traitor and directed his energies to assisting the Romans. His writings are one-sided, self-seeking, and frequently inaccurate in details. Nevertheless, without them we would know next to nothing about the conflict and the events that led to it.

Jewish unrest simmered from the time of Pompey onward. At times it broke into the open but was always contained, sometimes with substantial loss of life. The immediate causes of the first revolt against Rome took place during the procuratorship of Gaius Florus (A.D. 64–66). When the governor took seventeen talents from the temple treasury, public patience was exhausted. The procurator was ridiculed, and a routine ceremony of courtesy to visiting officials resulted in violence.

The daily temple sacrifices for the emperor were stopped, an open declaration of revolt. Jerusalem leaders sought to halt the rebellion by force. They and the Roman garrison in Jerusalem were defeated, and many were killed. Outside Jerusalem, in cities with both Jewish and Gentile populations, battles broke out; when the Jews were victorious Gentiles were massacred. Rebels occupied the desert fortress of MASADA. Eventually the Roman governor of SYRIA, Cestius Gallus, invaded with a large army. He succeeded in taking and burning the northern suburb of Jerusalem but was unable to break into the temple. When he withdrew, his retreating army was attacked and defeated.

The Jews began to prepare for all-out war against Rome. They appointed commanders over the various districts of the country with instructions to organize resistance forces. In attempting to carry out his commission in Galilee, Josephus was faced with the distrust of many citizens and armed opposition led by one John of Gischala.

The Romans entrusted the subduing of the Jewish revolt to their veteran general VESPASIAN, who was accompanied by his able son TITUS. At Josephus's first encounters with the Romans his army fled as the enemy approached Garis, a northern border town. He and his remaining forces took refuge at Jotapata. After a lengthy siege the city fell and Josephus, in spite of participating in a suicide pact, surrendered to the Romans. He predicted that Vespasian would become emperor, was spared, and held captive.

Other northern towns fell, including Gamala, east of the Sea of Galilee, after a bitter battle and suicide of most of the town's inhabitants. The last Galilean stronghold to come under Roman domain was Gischala. The night before it was taken John, with a band of ZEALOTS, escaped to Jerusalem. By the end of the year 67 all of the northern part of the country was under Roman control.

The rabid nationalists in Jerusalem precipitated a bloody civil war and replaced the former leaders. John of Gischala and his Zealots gained control. Many prominent citizens were imprisoned and murdered. A commoner was elected high priest. Some of the older authorities briefly persuaded the people to resist the Zealots. The Zealots urged the Idumeans from the S to join the fight (see IDUMEA). Once these gained access to the city they, supported by their Zealot allies, began to rob, murder, and pillage. Prominent and well-to-do leaders in Jerusalem were charged with being allies of the Romans and eliminated. Eventually the Idumeans had enough and withdrew from Jerusalem. The Zealots continued their reign of terror.

Although his generals wanted to take advantage of conditions in Jerusalem and attack immediately, Vespasian chose to allow the Jewish factions to devour one another. In 68 NERO died and Vespasian ceased military operations to await developments in Rome. He was eventually elected emperor (as Josephus had predicted) and left the Jewish war in the hands of Titus.

Simon bar Giora, a bandit chief in the southern part of the country, eventually appeared before the gates of Jerusalem. Many of the people, tired of the tyranny of John of Gischala, invited him in, only to discover that they now had two tyrants. Eleazar, son of Simon, broke with John's Zealot party and formed his own. Simon controlled the upper city and a substantial part of the lower. John held the temple mount and Eleazar the inner forecourt of the temple. Anarchy reigned in Jerusalem; it became a continuous battlefield. The rebels burned the grain supplies in the city, thus condemning themselves and the rest of the inhabitants to starvation.

The church historian EUSEBIUS (*Eccl. Hist.* 3.5.3) relates that sometime during the war the Christians in Jerusalem withdrew from the city to PELLA, a town of PEREA. The exact time (or even the fact) of this retreat is debated. Shortly after John of Gischala entered the city or while Vespasian awaited developments in Rome are possibilities.

Titus began the siege of Jerusalem shortly before Passover (March/April) of the year 70. He attacked Jerusalem with four legions (about 6,000 men per legion) plus units from allied countries. The tenth legion attacked from JERICHO on the E, the thirteenth and fifteenth legions came from the N, and the fifth from EMMAUS on the W.

The fighting between the Jewish parties within Jerusalem continued. At Passover Eleazar's faction opened the gates of the temple to admit pilgrims. Some of John of Gischala's men disguised themselves, entered with the festival goers, then attacked and defeated Eleazar and his followers. With the Idumeans gone and now Eleazar eliminated, only the parties of John and Simon bar Giora remained to fight the Romans—and each other.

Deep ravines protect Jerusalem on the E, W, and S. Of necessity Titus attacked from the N and set his battering rams to work on the wall there. Only then did John and Simon's factions unite against the invaders. It took fifteen days to breach the first wall; even then the Romans faced a second wall and then the walls of the temple complex. The fighting was fierce. At times the Jewish forces acquitted themselves well, but they faced superior well-supplied forces. Throughout the siege of the Jewish capital, Josephus appealed to his countrymen to surrender. On one occasion he was wounded while so doing.

Throughout the battle for Jerusalem both sides showed no compassion for noncombatants who were slaughtered randomly. Titus erected a "siege dike," a wall around the city to deprive the Jews of supplies and to keep any from escaping. Starvation racked Jerusalem but it was no worse than the atrocities the Jews inflicted on one another in their desperate attempt to obtain food. Lack of food and other resources continually weakened the Jewish defenders.

In midsummer the Romans broke into the temple area. The fighting intensified. Josephus reports that Titus had decided not to destroy the temple. Nevertheless in their furor the Roman soldiers set parts of the structure ablaze and eventually it was completely consumed.

The battle continued in the lower parts of the city. Finally, in September of A.D. 70 Jerusalem was completely in Roman hands. Some Jews, including John of Gischala and Simon bar Giora, hid in the underground cisterns but were eventually forced out by the Romans or hunger. Numerous Jews were slaughtered, others held to take part in gladiatorial contests; many were sold as slaves or sent to work in the mines. John was condemned to prison for life, while Simon and the stronger soldiers were reserved for the triumphant procession in Rome. Jerusalem was destroyed.

The defeat of Jerusalem did not end the Jewish resistance. The last stronghold was Masada, the desert palace-fortress of HEROD the Great. Eleazar ben Yair, a descendant of Judas the Galilean who inherited his ancestor's spirit, had occupied the fortress since the beginning of the war. After the fall of Jerusalem he and a detachment of almost 1,000 Zealots (or Sicarii; see ASSASSINS) held out for over three years. Eventually the Romans, having constructed a ramp and brought their siege engines against the walls of the towering fortress, were prepared to break into the citadel the next day. That night Ben Yair persuaded his followers to kill their families and then themselves. He argued that death was preferable to slavery.

The Roman senate honored Vespasian and Titus with a triumphant procession in Rome. Captive Jewish soldiers were forced to march; Simon bar Giora was dragged behind the victor's chariot and then executed. A large amount of plunder from Jerusalem was displayed to the citizenry. Included was the table of showbread and the seven-branched lamp holder from the Jerusalem temple. Representations of these may still be seen in the triumphal arch erected by Titus in Rome.

The Romans were not yet done with Jewish political-religious war. Disturbances and revolts broke out from time to time, mostly outside of Palestine. About 60 years after the victory of Titus, a man arose in Palestine claiming to be "The Prince of Israel" (i.e., the MESSIAH). From about A.D. 132 to 135 he led his followers in a war, the second revolt, so vicious that at its conclusion the emperor HADRIAN, in his letter to the Roman senate, omitted the traditional opening statement, "I and the legions are in health."

The more likely specific causes of the second revolt include the following: (1) Jewish response to Hadrian's decision to build a Gentile city where Jerusalem once stood and a temple to Jupiter on the site of their temple; (2) reaction after Hadrian gave permission to rebuild the Jerusalem temple but rescinded it because of Samaritan objections; and (3) the view that Hadrian's prohibition of mutilating genitals included CIRCUMCISION so that the Jews regarded it as an affront to their religious practice. Ultimately, the cause of the revolt lay in the Jewish longing for freedom and the appearance of an attractive claimant who was heralded as Messiah by the famous Rabbi AKIBA. Although traditionally called BAR KOKHBA ("Son of a Star" [a messianic title, Num. 24:17], also referred to by a number of other name-descriptions, including, after his defeat, "Son of a Liar"), it was not until the middle of the 20th cent. that, with the discoveries of letters written by this leader himself, his real name, "Shimeon Bar Kosiba," became known.

At the outset the Jewish rebels apparently (but not certainly) captured Jerusalem. Their coins bore pictures of the temple, objects used in worship, and proclaimed, "For the Freedom/Liberation of Israel" or "For the Freedom of Jerusalem." There are no chronological records of this second revolt such as the writings of Josephus provide for the first. Brief scraps of information come from a variety of Roman sources (such as the Roman historian Dio Cassius, *Rom. Hist.* 69.12–14), Christian (esp. Eusebius and Epiphanius), and Jewish rabbinic writings, coins, and other artifacts. Recent archaeological discoveries provide additional important data about the Bar Kokhba war.

Bar Kokhba's memory is preserved in recollections of his charismatic leadership, bravery, brutality, toughness, and personal strength. He is a legendary hero, born in national yearning, clothed in myth. Christian sources, now confirmed by his own letters, say that he persecuted Jewish Christians. Obviously they who believed Jesus to be Messiah could not acknowledge Bar Kokhba's claim to that office.

We have no account of major battles, save sketchy remembrances of the last one at a place called Bethar, near BETHLEHEM. Virtually all of the fighting took place in Judea. Surviving documents give the names of over 12 rebel centers, EN GEDI, HERODIUM, and Bethar being among the more important. But even so there do not appear to have been many pitched battles. Dio Cassius says that the Jews refrained from engaging the Romans in open fields, but used concealed rural areas and caves and tunnels from which they could emerge quickly, attack, and then return for safety. The Romans, when these caves were found, besieged the inhabitants, asphyxiating or starving many Jews to death. It is the discovery and exploration of many of these underground installations that have yielded the new data about this revolt. The contents included household and personal items, processing plants, storage facilities, military equipment, coins, letters and documents, and skeletons. After a prolonged siege Bethar fell. The Jewish forces were thoroughly defeated. Hundreds of women and children were brutally slaughtered. Bar Kokhba was killed.

The carnage from the war on both sides was staggering. Dio says the Romans destroyed 50 or more fortresses, over 985 settlements, and killed 580,000 Jews in raids and battles plus unknown numbers who died from other causes. Many Romans also died. As already noted, Hadrian refrained from claiming the well-being of his legions. After the war untold numbers of Jews were sold as slaves. It is said so many were sold at HEBRON that a single person was valued no more than a horse. Many Jews died as they were being forcibly transported to Egypt or other countries.

Jerusalem, renamed as Alia Capitolina, was rebuilt as a thoroughly pagan city. Its main religion was the worship of Jupiter on temple hill, but many other gods were revered throughout the city. One tradition says a shrine to Aphrodite (counterpart of Astarte; see ASHTORETH) was erected on the traditional site of the tomb of Jesus. Jews, on pain of death, were forbidden to come even within sight of the city. Not until the time of Constantine (313–361) were Jews again permitted to enter Jerusalem, and that only one day a year, to weep on the anniversary of its destruction. (See further *HJP*, rev. ed. [1973–87], 1:484–557; L. L. Grabbe, *Judaism from Cyrus to Hadrian*, 2 vols. [1992], chs. 7–9.)

J. J. SCOTT, JR.

Wars of the Lord, Book of the. One of several books no longer extant which are mentioned in the OT and which played an important, if somewhat obscure, part in Israel's literary history. It is cited by name and quoted in Num. 21:14–15 to substantiate the narrator's statement concerning the boundary cut by the deep ravines of the ARNON River between MOAB and AMMON. The quotation as it stands is obscure (the syntax is apparently incomplete and nothing is known of the names WAHEB and SUPHAH) and sheds little light on the character of the book itself. It is a plausible conjecture, however, that vv. 17–18 and 27–30 are drawn from the same source, not only because of their proximity to the first quotation, but also because of the occurrence (in the case of vv. 27–30) of a number of identical place names as well as the suitability of the taunt itself for the content of the book as suggested by its title. Evidently the book consisted of a number of victory songs written to be sung in celebration of the triumphs of Yahweh in the conquest of Canaan by Israel. That Yahweh was a "a man of war" (Exod. 15:3 KJV; see WARRIOR, DIVINE) who brought Israel victory in battle was a fact the nation loved to commemorate in song.

What is apparently another book of this type is the Book of JASHAR (or "the Upright") mentioned and quoted in Josh. 10:12–13 and 2 Sam. 1:18–19. What relationship may exist between these two books (or are they the same book?) and certain other unidentified poetical quotations in the OT (e.g., Exod. 15:1–18; Jdg. 5; 1 Ki. 8:53 LXX) can no longer be determined. Questions of the date and authorship of this book remain shrouded in obscurity, but it would seem naturally to derive from the heroic age, and thus to be among the most ancient of Israel's literature. (See O. Eissfeldt, *The Old Testament: An Introduction* [1966], 132ff.; D. L. Christensen in *CBQ* 36 [1974]: 359–60; B. A. Levine, *Numbers 21–36*, AB 4A [2000], 92–95.)

D. A. HAGNER

watch, watchman. For the use of the noun *watch* referring to the periods of time into which the day was divided, see DAY, HOUR, and NIGHT. As a verb, this word translates a variety of biblical terms, such as Hebrew *ṣāpâ* H7595, "to keep watch, look about, spy" (Gen. 31:49 et al.; often as a ptc. meaning "watchman," 2 Sam. 13:34 et al.) and Greek *grēgoreō* G1213, "be watchful, alert" (Matt. 24:42–43 et al.).

Watchmen were stationed on city walls (2 Sam. 18:25; 2 Ki. 9:18; Ps. 127:1; Isa. 62:6), on watchtowers (2 Ki. 9:17; 17:9; 18:8), or on hilltops (Jer. 31:6). In times of danger they were on the alert for hostile action against a city, and it was their duty to give word to the king of any suspicious person approaching the city wall (2 Sam. 18:24–27; 2 Ki. 9:17–20). Such watchmen who were on duty at night naturally looked forward eagerly to the breaking of day (Isa. 21:11). In Cant. 3:3 and 5:7 reference is made to watchmen that go about the city, possibly suggesting some kind of city police.

Watchmen kept watch over fields and vineyards during the time of harvest. Sometimes whole families would act as watchmen; to protect themselves from the heat, they frequently erected simple booths, and to facilitate observation they built watchtowers (2 Ki. 17:9; 2 Chr. 20:24; Job 27:18). Prophets in the OT are described as being watchmen of God, announcing to the people of Israel impending doom from Yahweh or bringing good news to them (Isa. 21:6; 52:8; 62:6; Jer. 6:17; Ezek. 3:17). The solemn responsibility of the prophets of Israel to the nation is described in Ezek. 33:2–6. False prophets are blind watchmen (Isa. 56:10).

J. L. KELSO

watcher. Literal translation of the Aramaic word *ʿîr* H10541, which occurs in only one passage with reference to angelic creatures (Dan. 4:13, 17, 23 [MT, vv. 10, 14, 20]). The NIV translates this term as "messenger." The designation of certain angels as "watchers" becomes more common in the PSEUDEPIGRAPHA, and chs. 6–36 of *1 Enoch* are usually referred to as the Book of the Watchers. (See *DDD*, 893–95.)

watchtower. See TOWER; WATCH, WATCHMAN.

water. A liquid compound of hydrogen and oxygen (H_2O) which is convertible by heat to steam

and by removal of heat (cold) to ice. Most water is derived directly from the ocean by evaporation. It condenses to form clouds and is precipitated as RAIN, SNOW, or HAIL on the earth's surface, where it either runs into rivers, lakes, etc., or sinks into the ground. Here some is used by plant life as an essential support, but much forms underground water that may reappear in springs, be brought to the surface from wells, or return to the sea.

I. General. Naturally occurring waters contain impurities in varying degrees. During the process of evaporation, the salts in the ocean are left behind but rain water acquires traces of ammonium salts and various gasses from the air. In mountainous districts lake and river water is relatively pure, but running water progressively dissolves salts and picks up suspended mineral or vegetable matter. Where the surface drainage pattern ends in an inland lake, such as the DEAD SEA, the proportion of salts in the water progressively increases as evaporation takes place. Underground waters are generally clear and free from suspended matter, having been filtered by the rock strata (aquifers) through which they flow. However, during their passage through rock strata they may dissolve considerable quantities of mineral salts, particularly in limestone regions where solution CAVES are formed. Some mineral salts, particularly magnesian salts, make the water unfit for consumption by humans or animals; in many cases such water has a bitter taste. Other underground water contains little dissolved material (cf. Jas. 3:12).

With water being essential for human existence, as well as for animals and plants (Isa. 1:30; 55:10), early civilizations developed and were able to flourish where the rainfall was sufficient to support crops and animals as well as humans, or where rain fed rivers like the EUPHRATES, TIGRIS, and NILE, which flowed continuously. The establishment of permanent habitation away from the FERTILE CRESCENT and away from the Nile relied heavily on the availability of usable underground water: natural springs (cf. Deut. 8:7) feeding streams were important for larger centers of habitation, and wells (cf. Gen. 26:18) were vital to those keeping animals. The siting of cities like JERUSALEM and JERICHO had defense and water supply as major considerations. In the case of Jerusalem, to be described as the world's most significant city (Ps. 87:2–5) and the dwelling place of God (1 Ki. 8:13), the existence of the GIHON SPRING in the immediately adjacent KIDRON Valley (2 Chr. 32:30; Isa. 7:3) was vital. In the case of the strategic city of Jericho—on the crossroads of trade and important in the protection of the Judean hill country and the JORDAN Valley from invasion from the E and S (Josh. 6)—there is a copious spring in an otherwise inhospitable region.

The availability of water has been at the heart of the constant conflict, throughout the history of the Near E, of the tillers of ground and keepers of sheep (cf. Gen. 4:2). With the progressive increase of AGRICULTURE in any region, the nomadic herdsmen have been forced out of regions with reliable water supplies. In keeping with the slaying of ABEL by CAIN (4:8) these nomadic peoples have consistently harried the settled people, with any hydraulic works being prime targets. And the herdsmen have fought amongst themselves for the ownership of wells (26:20).

Not surprisingly, water has been linked with BREAD as necessities of human existence (1 Sam. 25:11; 1 Ki. 18:4), and the giving or withholding of these was considered to be of great importance (Deut. 23:4; Matt. 10:42). The provision of water was recognized as a divine gift. Divine blessing is spoken of in terms of water (Isa. 44:3; Jn. 4:13), and both the paucity of and the desire for spiritual LIFE described in terms of thirst for water (Amos 8:11; Matt. 5:6). The use of water as a symbol is especially prominent in the Gospel of John (cf. L. P. Jones, *The Symbol of Water in the Gospel of John* [1997]; W.-Y. Ng, *Water Symbolism in John: An Eschatological Interpretation* [2001]). Both the common custom of carrying water to the household (Mk. 14:13) and the way in which water was drunk (Jdg. 7:5–6) were used as signs, while the common custom of washing feet (Gen. 43:24) was used by Jesus as a means of teaching (Jn. 13:5–9) and as an indicator of attitudes (Lk. 7:37, 38, 44). The use of water in religious ritual was widespread both in OT and NT times (e.g., Exod. 29:4; Lev. 15:12; Mk. 1:5, 9).

Not only inland water but also the adjacent seas have been important. Much of the rain precipitated on the Holy Lands is water evaporated from the Mediterranean Sea, a mass of water that played an important role in trade (e.g., the Phoenicians) and transport (Acts 27). The Red Sea and the Gulf of Aqaba also provided means of access for trade (1 Ki. 9:26) with ARABIA, northeastern and eastern AFRICA, and possibly INDIA. It also provided natural resources, such as ONYCHA and PEARL.

II. Rainfall, evaporation, run-off, and infiltration. The prevailing westerly winds (1 Ki. 18:42–45) over the eastern Mediterranean pick up moisture, which is precipitated when the air is forced to rise over the Judean and E Jordan highlands. Most precipitation occurs as rain, although snow falls on the higher ground and there are some hail storms. This precipitation is seasonal from October to May, with the greatest proportion falling from December to March. Average precipitation is greater than 1,000 mm. (about 40 in.) on the high ground SE of DAMASCUS and greater than 500 mm. (about 20 in.) over Lebanon, parts of Syria and Israel, and limited parts of Jordan. However, there are wide variations, the average rainfall for Jerusalem being 620 mm. (about 25 in.), with a maximum of 1090 mm. (about 41 in.) and a minimum of 210 mm. (about 9 in.). Much of eastern Jordan and eastern Syria is in a rain-shadow region with precipitation being less than 200 mm. (about 8 in.) over large areas. In the S the rainfall is even lower despite the higher elevations of the Jordan highlands compared with those farther N. The low rainfall results from the winds being mainly southerly from the dry N African continent, but in these desert regions water is deposited as DEW (Exod. 16:13). Rainfall in the southern part of the Jordan Valley and adjacent to the Dead Sea is also very low.

A large proportion of the rain evaporates, with humidities on the E bank of the Jordan River being in the order of 75 percent in the winter and 35 percent in the summer. In one part of northern Jordan where the annual average precipitation is 415 mm. (about 16 in.), an estimated 81 percent is evaporated, 9 percent is run off into the surface drainage system, and 10 percent infiltrates into the underground water system. In other regions, with comparable moderate rainfall, as little as 5 percent or as much as 15 percent of total rainfall infiltrates and adds to the vital store of underground water (cf. Deut. 11:11). In regions where rainfall is less than 200 mm. (about 8 in.) there is little or no direct infiltration except from flood flow in wadis crossing outcrops of aquifers.

III. Underground water. The catchments for underground water as well as underground water conditions, including emergence as springs and supply in wells, are almost entirely dependent upon geological factors. These include the porosity and permeability of strata, the location of strata that form aquifers, the juxtaposition of aquifers and aquicludes (formations that do not transmit water), the inclination of the strata, and the existence of structural features such as folds and faults. Much of the water that infiltrates the soil and surface rocks

The mountains in Palestine rise to form a continental divide diverting surface water either into the Mediterranean Sea or into the Dead Sea.

seeps downward to a zone where the rocks are saturated with water. The upper surface of this saturated zone is called the water table, and its height at any place is given by the level at which water stands in a well there.

There are two main groups of underground water in the Holy Land, these being the underground water in the permeable sections of the folded and faulted hill regions and that in the sediments of the main plains. In the hilly country, such as much of Judea, Samaria, and Galilee, underground water is generally at a considerable depth below the surface, but the water table undulates. Where it meets the surface in the valley districts between the higher terrain, ground water emerges as springs (Deut. 8:7). Many such springs occur where an inclined junction of pervious and impervious strata (aquifer and aquiclude) meets the surface or where there is a faulted junction between the two such types of strata. These springs are generally perennial, and supply pools which in turn feed streams (2 Sam. 17:20).

At the sides of valleys springs also occur where the water table meets the land surface. However, seasonal variations in precipitation, as well as long periods of drought, cause variation in the level of the water table with the result that some springs may cease to flow for a period (2 Ki. 2:19). Other intermittent springs flow only from the sides of valleys after abnormal infiltration, following prolonged heavy rain, causes the water table to rise and meet the land surface. Where the ground elevation is not great, such as in the foothills of the Judean mountains, the depth of underground water below the surface decreases and the water can be tapped by relatively shallow wells. Underground water is also tapped by wells from aquifers below the plains, such as the coastal plain, ESDRAELON, and the region around BEERSHEBA (see PALESTINE III). Here the water table is almost flat, with a very gentle inclination toward the Mediterranean Sea. The aquifers are always underlain by aquicludes with the level of the water—hence the depth of any well, dependent upon the position relative to the sea, the situation of impervious strata, and the permeability of the aquifer.

In some cases underground water may travel for tens of miles before emerging as springs. This is the case for the relatively few and important watering places in the southern desert between the Dead Sea and the Gulf of Aqabah. The water mainly infiltrates sandstone aquifers below wadis during periodic floods and then travels large distances underground.

Irrigation in the land of Goshen.

The nature of the aquifers varies from place to place dependent upon the regional geology. However, the main sources of water on the coastal plain of Palestine are sandstones overlying clay beds, while the main sources of underground water in both Israel and Jordan are limestone bands in the Judean limestone (see STONE). The interbedded marls act as aquicludes preventing further downward migration of the ground water and forcing it to issue as springs. In southern Syria basalt lava flows are good aquifers and from them issue the springs that feed the YARMUK River. In the southern desert, between the Dead Sea and the Gulf of Aqabah, sandstones act as aquifers for the little water available (e.g., the Ram Spring), while at PETRA a shale acts as an impermeable bed giving rise to a small spring.

IV. Jordan drainage system. The Jordan River, its tributaries, the Sea of Galilee, and the Dead Sea constitute the major surface drainage system of the Holy Land. The Jordan River has two main sources. One is near Banias (CAESAREA PHILIPPI, Matt. 16:13) at the southern base of the Mount HERMON range in Syria, where the Nahr Banias issues from a cave; the other source is at a spring in Tell el-Qadi (see DAN (PLACE)). Two longer streams, but with less water, also form the Jordan headwaters, namely, the Nahr Hasbani (which occupies the northern continuation of the Jordan Rift Valley) and the Nahr Bareighit. The four streams unite below Banias and flow into the now drained Lake Huleh, which was formed by the damming of the river by volcanic rock. From there a clear, fast-flowing river falls below sea level and in the 9 mi. to Lake Tiberias its base drops 600 ft., with BETHSAIDA (Mk. 6:45) and CAPERNAUM (Jn. 6:17) on the E and W sides, respectively, of its entrance into the lake.

The Sea of Galilee, which is 12 mi. long and up to 7 mi. across, also exists because of the damming of the Jordan River by volcanic rock, while there are hot springs containing chlorides and sulphides near its shores. See GALILEE, SEA OF. Its OT name, Sea of KINNERETH, results from its harplike shape. NT names are Lake of GENNESARET (Lk. 5:1) and Sea of TIBERIAS (Jn. 6:1). About three-quarters of the inflow into the lake comes from the Jordan River; the rest comes from springs, seepage of underground water, rainfall, and wadi floods. The water is warm, varying from 12.5°C (55°F) to 30°C (86°F). Between February and August there is abundant plankton in the lake, and fishing, which was a major industry in NT times (Jn. 21:3), is at its peak. Strong, dry E winds affect the lake in winter, often causing storms, while sudden summer squalls result from strong, hot westerly winds (Mk. 4:37).

The Jordan River S of Lake Tiberias becomes muddy and twists for more than 180 mi. along its valley floor in traversing the 60 mi. to the Dead Sea, with the base dropping only 900 ft. in that distance. In flood it fills its flood plain but in the summer it is less than 100 ft. wide and 3 ft. deep in some places, and it has been known to have been blocked by rockfalls near Adam about 24 mi. N of its entrance into the Dead Sea. See ADAM (PLACE). This is probably related to the EARTHQUAKE activity which is common along the length of the Rift Valley in which the river flows and would account for the dry passage of the Israelites under JOSHUA (Josh. 3:16). The plain of Jordan was chosen by LOT because of the abundance of water (Gen. 13:10–11). The river played an important role in the lives of ELIJAH (2 Ki. 2:6) and ELISHA (6:2), and its muddy waters were repugnant to NAAMAN, the leper who came from a district with clear rivers (5:12). However, because of its association with Jesus, including his baptism by JOHN THE BAPTIST (Mk. 1:9), this river has become a symbol of cleansing and purity.

The Dead Sea, also referred to as the Salt Sea (Gen. 14:3; Josh. 3:16), is fed mainly by the waters of the Jordan River, which supplies an annual average of 1.2×10^9 cubic meters of water out of a total intake of 1.6×10^9 cubic meters. The remainder of the water comes largely from the ARNON and from Wadi Zarqa Ma'in, together with some from springs and some from seasonal floods of otherwise dry rivers. This inland lake has no outlet, is situated in the deepest part of the Jordan Rift Valley, and is 44 mi. from N to S with an average width of 8 mi. The Lisan Peninsula protrudes from the eastern shore and divides the lake into a shallow southern basin and a deep northern basin; the latter makes up about three-quarters of the total area and most of its total volume of 142 km^2. There is evidence to suggest that the last flooding of the southern basin took place c. 1,500 years ago and that it was dry in biblical times. The main part of the Dead Sea is c. 12,000 years old with older and even more extensive lakes having been formed at least one million years ago. Water temperatures vary from 19–23°C (66–73°F) in December–January to 34–36°C (93–97°F) in July–August, with the extreme recorded maximum temperature being 38°C (100°F). The average specific gravity of the surface water is 1.206 g/cm^3 (compared with 1.0 g/cm^3 for pure water) and the average salinity is 31.5 percent. See also PALESTINE IV.

(See further G. S. Blake and M. S. Goldschmidt, *Geology and Water Resources of Palestine* [1947]; D. J. Burdon, *Handbook of the Geology of Jordan* [1959]; R. W. Fairbridge, ed., *The Encyclopedia of Geomorphology* [1968], 243–46; A. Issar, *Water Shall Flow from the Rock: Hydrogeology and Climate in the Lands of the Bible* [1990]; *ABD*, s.v. "Waterworks," 6:888–93.)　　　　　　　　　D. R. BOWES

watercourse. This English term is used variously in Bible versions to render several Hebrew words or expressions. For example, it occurs a number of times in the NRSV as the translation of *ʾāpîq* H692, which seems to refer to a stream bed (Ps.

126:4 et al.). The NIV uses it only once to translate the phrase *palgê-mayim* (*H7104* + *H4784*), literally, "channels of water" (Prov. 21:1).

water for impurity. See WATER OF CLEANSING.

Water Gate. A city gate, restored by NEHEMIAH, on the E side of Mount ZION. It lay opposite the GIHON SPRING (Neh. 3:26), or perhaps a little farther N toward the temple (cf. 12:37). An open square beside the Water Gate furnished a place of assembly for EZRA's reading of the law and for erecting booths for the Feast of Tabernacles in 444 B.C. (8:1, 3, 16). See JERUSALEM II.D.2 and III.A.

J. B. PAYNE

water hen. This term is used by the RSV and NRSV to render Hebrew *tinšemet H9492*, a word of uncertain meaning that occurs in a list of unclean birds (Lev. 11:18; Deut. 14:16 [NIV, "white owl"; KJV, "swan"]; the same word, or a homonym, occurs in Lev. 11:30 with the apparent meaning of CHAMELEON). The rendering "water hen" apparently derives from the SEPTUAGINT at Lev. 11:18 (*porphyriōn*; at Deut. 14:16, however, the LXX has *ibis*, a different bird [but *porphyriōn* again in 14:18—it is not clear whether the terms in the Greek text correspond precisely with those in the MT]). G. R. Driver (in *PEQ* no vol. [1955]: 15) proposed "little owl," and various other species of OWL have been suggested (cf. *HALOT*, 4:1756).

water of bitterness. See BITTER WATER.

water of cleansing. This phrase is used by the NIV to render Hebrew *mê niddâ* (*H4784* + *H5614*), which occurs in only a few contexts (Num. 19:9, 13, 20–21; 31:23). English versions translate this phrase variously: "water of separation" (KJV), "water for impurity" (RSV), "water for cleansing" (NRSV), "water of lustration" (NJPS). The word *niddâ* is used of ritual impurity (e.g., Lev. 20:21; frequently with reference to menstruation, 15:19–27), but its precise derivation is disputed (see summary in *NIDOTTE*, 1:925; more detail in *TDOT*, 9:232–35). Depending on which etymology is followed, the combination *mê niddâ* may mean "water for [the removal of] impurity" or "water of expulsion." In either case, however, the reference is clearly to a ritually purifying agent for a person or thing that had been defiled, whether by contact with the dead or for other reasons.

The ashes of a burned red cow (see HEIFER, RED) were added to "running water," which was then applied to the defiled person. The animal used in this ceremony had to be a female of reddish-brown color, without any physical defects, and one that had never borne a yoke. The burning of the cow took place "outside the camp," and the whole animal—even the blood, with the exception of some that was used in sprinkling toward the front of the tent—was reduced to ashes. This element distinguishes the ceremony from the Levitical ritual sacrifice. A piece of cedar wood and a bunch of hyssop bound with a scarlet cloth were burned with the cow.

The ashes were kept outside the camp in a clean place until they were mixed with the spring water for the specific ceremonies of purification. This "water of impurity" was applied to the defiled person or object by being spilled over it, or sprinkled with branches of HYSSOP. The ceremony was performed on the third and seventh days of impurity, after which the person was cleansed and bathed, and the garments washed, which restored him or her to the community. The account in Num. 31:13 has to do with defiled objects taken in battle.

A. C. SCHULTZ

water shaft. This term, referring to an underground conduit for bringing water from a spring into a city, is used by the NIV and other versions to render Hebrew *ṣinnôr H7562* in 2 Sam. 5:8 (this

Water shaft connecting to Jerusalem's Gihon Spring.

Heb. word occurs in only one other passage with the probable meaning of "waterfall," Ps. 42:7). There is archaeological evidence for water shafts in various cities in Palestine from the Canaanite period onward (e.g., JERUSALEM, MEGIDDO, GIBEON, ETHAM). At Jerusalem there is a tunnel to the GIHON SPRING that brought water to the city, and some scholars think that 2 Sam. 5:8 refers to this tunnel (however, see the discussion of Warren's Shaft under JERUSALEM III.B). It is obvious that if a city had access to a reliable water supply it could hold out in time of siege, as SAMARIA did for over two years against the Assyrians in 722 B.C., and as Jerusalem did against the Babylonians for about eighteen months in 586 B.C. S. BARABAS

wave offering. See SACRIFICE AND OFFERINGS IV.C.2.

waw wou (possibly from וָו H2260, "hook"). Also *vau, vav*. The sixth letter of the Hebrew ALPHABET (ו), with a numerical value of six. In the so-called square Hebrew alphabet, it is a vertical stroke with a leftward hook at the top, but the shape goes back to an epigraphic form resembling a capital "Y" with short diagonals and a long vertical tail. This earlier form in turn seems, on the basis of the Sinaitic inscriptions from Serabit el-Khadim, to have represented a battle mace (a short wooden staff with a pear-shaped stone head fastened on one end of it) of the type frequently represented in Egyptian bas-reliefs of the pharaohs. (For alternate explanations, see *HALOT*, 1:257.) The letter represents a bilabial semiconsonant similar to the sound of English *w*, but in later times it acquired a sound more like that of English *v*, which is the current Israeli pronunciation. Before the invention of vowel signs, the *waw* could be used also to represent the sounds *ô* and *û*, and this practice was continued even after the vocalization system was introduced.

G. L. ARCHER

wax. The Hebrew noun *dônag* H1880 appears in the Bible only in poetry, where it is used as a simile of melting (Pss. 22:14, 68:2, 97:5; Mic. 1:4). In ancient times wax was used for sealing documents and for making writing tablets, but these uses of wax are not mentioned in the Bible. The English verb *to wax* occurs often in the KJV, but only in the intransitive sense "to grow, increase, become" (e.g., "I am waxed old," Gen. 18:12); the use of this verb is rare in modern versions. S. BARABAS

way. This English term is used as the rendering of various biblical words (e.g., Heb. *derek* H2006 and *'ōraḥ* H784; Gk. *hodos* G3847 and *tropos* G5573). In addition to its use in a literal sense (a path over which or direction in which one moves), the word *way* occurs extensively in a figurative sense, denoting behavioral patterns in animal life, movements in nature, varieties of human and divine conduct, action, and intention, as well as attitudes, habits, customs, spirit, and plans in human and divine life. Specific OT examples are the following:

(a) Of natural processes: the way of lightning and thunder (Job 28:26; 38:25 [NIV, "path"]), movement of light (38:19, 24), life of the ant (Prov. 6:6), behavior of an eagle, serpent, ship, and human courting (30:19).

(b) Very frequently of moral conduct, whether good (1 Sam. 12:23; Ps. 119:1) or evil (Jdg. 2:19; Ps. 119:101 [NIV, "path"]), including positive and negative traditions (1 Sam. 8:3; 1 Ki. 15:26).

(c) Of various facets of human experience, such as a person's course of life (Job 3:23; Prov. 3:6), plan for life (Prov. 16:9 [NRSV]; Hos. 10:13 [KJV]), suffering or trial (Ps. 142:3; Job 23:10), and destiny in death (Josh. 23:14; 1 Ki. 2:2).

(d) Of God's will and command (Deut. 5:33; Isa. 2:3), judgments (Isa. 26:8 NRSV), purposes (Job 36:23; Ps. 77:13), and governing providences (2 Sam. 22:31; Ezek. 18:25).

In the NT also there are many uses referring to moral conduct (Matt. 21:32; Rom. 3:16–17) and to God's will and purposes (Mk. 12:14; Heb. 3:10). In addition, the book of Acts records that the term "the Way" was used specifically of the Christian faith and manner of life followed by the Lord's disciples and held in contempt by their enemies (Acts 9:2; 19:9, 23; 22:4, 14; 24:22). Most important, the term is used of JESUS CHRIST as the final and perfect revealer: in his person and by his sacrificial death, he is the living and personal way to God, his holiness, and salvation. He teaches the way in truth (Matt. 22:16) and is himself the only "way" to God (Jn. 14:4–6) and the One who opens up the way into the holiest by his sacrifice (Heb. 9:8; 10:19–20). G. STOB

wealth. Abundance of valuable possessions. Numerous Hebrew and Greek works can be translated with English "wealth" and such synonyms as "riches" and "prosperity." A common Hebrew noun is *ḥayil H2657*, which can mean "power" and the like, but which frequently refers to movable goods such as gold, silver, frankincense, garments, etc. It may be BOOTY or plunder that can be carried on donkeys and camels (Isa. 30:6). This wealth may be acquired by trading, as in the case of TYRE (Ezek. 28:4–5). Similarly, the word *kābôd H3883* (lit. "weight," more frequently "honor, glory") can refer to wealth in the form of silver and gold (Nah. 2:9), but also in the form of flocks and herds (Gen. 31:1). Other terms include *rĕkûš H8214*, a general word for "possession(s)" (e.g., Gen. 12:5), *hôn H2104*, which is especially common in Proverbs (Prov. 1:13 et al.), and *ʿōšer H6948*, which is used, for example, of the riches accumulated by kings such as SOLOMON, HEZEKIAH, and XERXES (1 Ki. 10:23; 2 Chr. 32:27; Esth. 1:4). In the NT, the primary Greek word for "wealth" is *ploutos G4458* with its cognates (Matt. 13:22 et al.), but other relevant terms are *ousia G4045* (Lk. 15:12–13), *ktēma G3228*, "possession" (Matt. 19:22 et al.), and *mamōnas G3440* (Lk. 16:9, 11; see MAMMON).

The most important item of wealth was FOOD, for in Bible times food was a matter of life and death, far more significant than it is to the average Bible reader today. "People curse the man who hoards grain, / but blessing crowns him who is willing to sell" (Prov. 11:26). According to the prophet MICAH, the withholding of food from the poor by the rich was in his day the equivalent of cannibalism (Mic. 3:2–3). Among food items were wheat, olives, oil (from olive and sesame), honey, wine, and figs. Lamb and goat were the meats then as today, and they were of equal economic importance. For the rich there were also all kinds of SPICES: "There had never been such spices as those the queen of Sheba gave to King Solomon" (2 Chr. 9:9).

The wealth of the rich consisted of luxury items. White WOOL finished by the fuller, as well as LINEN, dyed blue and purple and finished with embroidery, provided luxurious clothing. Saddle cloths and multicolored oriental rugs were highly valued. Precious stones of all kinds, especially emeralds, pearls, and agates, were used for jewelry (see JEWELS AND PRECIOUS STONES). Riding horses and mules, together with chariot horses, were utilized by the wealthy for transportation. Ivory and ebony were imported for inlaid furniture. The OT world knew how to use METALS almost as well as we do today. Ezekiel mentioned gold, silver, copper, and such alloys as iron, tin, and lead.

Manufacturing, which began about the time of ISAIAH, soon became the source of major wealth. Manufacturers leased the farmlands abandoned by the farmers who worked in their factories; thus the manufacturers also held a corner on a major grain market. Most tragic was the wealth accumulated through SLAVERY, although Israel had fewer than most other ancient nations.

ABRAHAM provides an example of a rich business man. His trade may have reached from HARAN to EGYPT; he himself concentrated on the area from the NEGEV to Egypt, possibly leaving ELIEZER to watch the DAMASCUS unit, and LOT to handle the Arabian trade (see ARABIA). SOLOMON is usually mentioned as the other big business man, but much of the credit for his wealth should go to DAVID. David's military conquest reached to the EUPHRATES River, and not only brought to him the booty of these campaigns, but also enabled him to be a major member of the IRON monopoly when that metal was as revolutionary as aluminum became in modern times. Furthermore, his military lines enabled him to tax any item crossing his boundary via Anatolia (Asia Minor), the Euphrates River, the Arabian Desert, Egypt, and parts of the Mediterranean coast. It was David's wealth that built Solomon's TEMPLE and palace complex. Solomon added horse-trading, some manufacturing, and the selling of COPPER—his government monopoly—to the backward peoples of the RED SEA. Wealth could not be denied to the farmer who worked large areas of productive soil or had legal rights to large grazing areas for his flocks. After David's time the royal court gave opportunities for economic advancement. Interest could be earned on business loans and foreign deals, but not from farm land. Money could be made on the sale of city property, but farm land stayed within the immediate family.

There is an excellent description of the movable wealth of Tyre in Ezek. 27:12–25, and this description fits Israel as well. Another useful list is found in Rev. 18:11–13, the only item mentioned that was not common in OT times was silk (it is a debatable question whether Ezek. 16:10 actually refers to silk).

Before the invention of coinage (7th cent. B.C.), money was carried in ingots, bars, or rings of silver or gold; or the metal might be weighed out in any other form. Jewelry made of these metals was always more valuable than the metals themselves. Among the things that ACHAN stole at JERICHO (Josh. 7:21) was a wedge or bar (lit., "tongue") of gold; one such "tongue" was actually found in the excavations at GEZER. Precious stones of all kinds were also used as money, even after COINS became common. Because of the great value represented in small precious stones, they were the most convenient method of carrying large sums of wealth. Embroidered garments were of such value that they were listed as war booty. The first OT mention of coinage is in reference to the Persian gold daric (Ezra 2:69). The NT refers to various gold, silver, and copper coins.

The Bible everywhere insists that God is the Creator and that all things belong to him. He alone is the Creator and Distributor of wealth. Wealth is the gift of God. In Deut. 8:18 Israel was told, "But remember the LORD your God, for it is he who gives you the ability to produce wealth." Believers are only administrators of God's wealth. In the application of the parable of the talents, however, God insists that he must have a return on his investment.

Nowhere in Scripture is wealth thought of as being sinful per se. Indeed, Israel was commanded to honor the Lord with its substance (Prov. 3:9), and the TITHE was an integral part of WORSHIP. Wealth, however, often became a temptation, and the psalmist wisely advised, "though your riches increase, / do not set your heart on them" (Ps. 62:10). JOB's attitude to the totality of life applies equally well to its economic phase: "Naked I came from my mother's womb, / and naked I will depart. / The LORD gave and the LORD has taken away; / may the name of the LORD be praised" (Job 1:21).

In NT times money and philosophy became the greatest obstacles to the worship of God. The deadly danger of money is seen in Christ's remarks, "How hard it is for the rich to enter the kingdom of God" (Mk. 10:23); and the parables of the rich fool and the rich young ruler stress the same theme. To summarize, Christ says, "You cannot serve both God and Money [Gk., Mammon]" (Matt. 6:14); "where your treasure is, there your heart will be also" (Lk. 12:34).

While such OT saints as Abraham, David, and Job were men of great wealth, there is no NT believer of comparable wealth. It is interesting to note, however, that the Roman centurion of whom Christ said, "I have not found anyone in Israel with such great faith" (Matt 8:10), was wealthy enough to have built the SYNAGOGUE at CAPERNAUM where Christ worshiped (Lk. 7:5). Although Christ was the Lord of all wealth, he saw fit to travel through life without it, trusting himself to the mercies of his friends (cf. Lk. 8:1–3). (For bibliography, see POVERTY.)   J. L. KELSO

wean. In ancient times a child was not fully weaned for two or three years, and in some cases probably longer. According to 1 Sam. 1:21–28, HANNAH stopped going up to SHILOH to offer the annual sacrifice until she had weaned SAMUEL, at which time she left the child there in the care of ELI; but it is very unlikely that Samuel would have been left at the sanctuary if he was less than four years old. A more direct example is that of a woman who saw seven of her sons killed by ANTIOCHUS Epiphanes and then urged her last son to hold fast to his Jewish faith against the threats of the king, who tried to persuade him to repudiate his faith. She said to him, "I carried you nine months in my womb, and nursed you for three years, and have reared you and brought you up to this point in your life, and have taken care of you" (2 Macc. 7:27). The completion of weaning was sometimes celebrated by a feast (Gen. 21:8). The word is also used in a metaphorical sense (Ps. 131:2; Isa. 28:9).   S. BARABAS

weapon. See ARMOR, ARMS.

weasel. A common rendering of Hebrew *ḥōled* H2700, which occurs only in a list of unclean "animals that move about on the ground" (Lev. 11:29; it is mentioned first in the list, followed by the MOUSE or rat). There is in fact no positive evidence to support this or any other identification (such as the MOLE; cf. NJPS and *HALOT*, 1:316). Weasels are not uncommon in Palestine, however, and it has been argued they may have been regarded as unclean because their scent glands make them unsuitable for food and because in Egypt they were sacred to the moon. In Greece and Rome they were kept to control mice before cats became available.

G. S. CANSDALE

weather. See PALESTINE IV.

weaving. The interlacing of a series of threads called the warp, with another series called the woof or weft. The warp threads are stretched in a LOOM for weaving; the weft threads are then passed over and under them. Weaving was one of the most important and well-developed crafts of biblical times. See also CLOTH; DRESS; LINEN.

It is impossible to determine when humans first learned the art of weaving, for its origin lies far back in prehistory. In Paleolithic times, 20,000 to 40,000 years ago, people were already skilled in matting and basketry, the forerunners of weaving. It must have been in Neolithic times that the loom and spinning devices were invented; weaving was quite common by the time of the Bronze Age. The oldest known paintings of looms and weavers come from EGYPT about 2000 B.C., where weaving was already a highly developed craft; in Egypt the weavers were usually men. The tomb at Beni Hasan of a government servant shows people dressed in clothes that were woven or embroidered with bright colors.

Various materials were used, depending on their availability and the geographical location. Neolithic villagers in the Fayum grew FLAX in order to make linen from it. Cotton was grown in the Indus Valley civilization before 2500 B.C. WOOL, SILK, and goats' hair were also commonly used. Families wove all their own textiles, from coarse tent cloth to warm woolen garments for the family. Cloth that would compare favorably with today's best grades of muslin have been found among Egyptian mummy wrappings. A Babylonian ruler of c. 2320 B.C. had a factory for weaving materials.

Long before the arrival of the Hebrews, the Canaanites wove and dyed their own fabrics. The description of the curtains woven for the TABERNACLE (Exod. 26:1–14) and priestly garments (28:39) indicate that the Hebrews at an early stage were skillful at weaving, probably having learned it in Egypt (cf. 35:35). Weaving was common in the time of the judges, as shown in the story of DELILAH, who weaved in SAMSON's locks as strands of the weft on her loom while he slept (Jdg. 16:13–14). The OT has a number of incidental references to weaving. The shaft of GOLIATH's spear was compared with a weaver's beam (1 Sam. 17:7), suggesting a diameter of 2 or 2.5 in. The Mosaic law prohibited the wearing of clothes that involved weaving two fibers together (Lev. 19:19). King JOSIAH tore down the houses of those who were weaving hangings for the ASHERAH (2 Ki. 23:7). ISAIAH made figurative use of weaving (Isa. 19:9; 38:12; 59:5), as did JOB (Job 7:6).

Evidence of the weaver's art comes from UGARIT, Byblos (GEBAL, a city particularly famous for its woven materials), Tell Beit-Mirsim (which archaeological evidence shows to have been the center of a professional textile industry), and LACHISH (where a weaving establishment was in operation at the time of the destruction of the city). The Edomites also had a textile industry (Ezek. 27:16). In fact, most of the provincial sites excavated in Judah have produced evidence of textile production. Whorls and perforated loom weights in stone and clay used for spinning and weaving have been found, as well as rock-cut vats with basins and drains that were used for dyeing. Carpet looming was also common (Prov. 7:15).

Tent weaving in Turkey.

The basic structure of looms has not altered in 5,000 years. The first looms were simple; they were made of a pair of sturdy upright beams secured to the floor and united at the top with a crossbeam. Long thread was loosely guided from top to bottom over the crossbeam. In order to hold the yarn taut, small bunches of it were weighted with stones or other heavy objects (this type appears on Greek vases c. 600 B.C.). Three kinds of looms were commonly used in biblical times: the Greek vertical two-beamed loom (just described); the Egyptian vertical which required two weavers standing on either side of the loom to pass the shuttle back and forth through alternating sheds as they beat the weft down; and the horizontal groundloom, a type commonly used by nomadic peoples even today. The latter type was made of two beams held in place by four pegs driven into the ground. The weaver sat in front of the loom. The spacing of the warp threads on the loom governed largely the texture of the fabric to be woven. The tension had to be uniform or else the fabric would be uneven.

(See further L. Blumenau, *The Art and Craft of Hand Weaving* [1955]; R. J. Forbes, *Studies in Ancient Technology*, vol. 4 [1956]; P. J. King and L. E. Stager, *Life in Biblical Israel* [2001], 152–58.)

F. B. HUEY, JR.

wedding. See MARRIAGE.

weeds. Plants that are considered of no worth or obnoxious and that usually grow vigorously. Although the English word occurs only once in the KJV (Jon. 2:5, with reference to seaweed) many plants mentioned in the Bible could be classified as weeds, especially THORNS and THISTLES (Gen. 3:18). In Job 31:40, one of the Hebrew words used with reference to thorns (*ḥôaḥ H2560*, NIV, "briers") occurs in parallel with *boʾšâ H947*, "weeds" (NRSV, "foul weeds"; NJPS, "stinkweed"; see COCKLE). This latter term occurs nowhere else, but the cognate *beʾuš H946* seems to refer to sour grapes in Isa. 5:2, 4. Could this be the Palestinian nightshade, *Solanum incanum*? This nightshade is a common weed in Palestine, even today; the berries look like little grapes, though they are poisonous.

Another weed on which one can debate is the *ḥārûl H3017* (Job 30:7; Prov. 24:31b; Zeph. 2:9), a term often translated "nettles," as is the word *qimmôš H7853* (Isa. 34:13; Hos. 9:6). See NETTLE. The term *rōʾš H8032* (often translated "poison") probably refers in some cases to a poisonous weed (Hos. 10:4; cf. also NJPS at Deut. 29:18 [MT 29:17] and Amos 6:12). In the NT, the Greek word translated "tares" by the KJV, *zizanion G2429*, is usually rendered "weeds" in modern translations (Matt. 13:25–30, 36–40). See discussion under TARES.

W. E. SHEWELL-COOPER

week. See CALENDAR.

Weeks, Feast of. See PENTECOST.

weeks, seventy. See SEVENTY WEEKS.

weights and measures. It is not surprising to find that, because of the Hebrew lack of precision in mathematics, biblical metrology (the determination of distances, capacities, and weights) is far from being an exact science, and no reliable or coherent system has been fully worked out. Evidence is insufficient and often ambiguous; systems varied from city to city and from region to region. As TRADE developed beyond simple barter in primitive times, it became necessary to develop some kind of system to determine the quantity of goods involved. The earliest measurements were related to well-known objects, such as the number of grains of cereal or the eggs of a certain fowl; measurements of length were related to parts of the body, such as finger, palm, span, and the distance between the tip of the middle finger and the elbow. Distances were related to the distance a person could walk in a day, or the distance traveled by an arrow, etc. Stones came to be used very early as a standard for weighing.

The Hebrews recognized the importance of reliable weights and measurements in the commercial, ethical, and legal life of the nation (cf. Lev. 19:35–36; Deut. 25:13–16; Prov. 11:1; 20:10). The systems they developed, though not uniform, were influenced by the civilizations of the ANE that had existed long before the appearance of the Hebrews (Egyptian, Mesopotamian, and Canaanite) and in later times the Persian, Greek, and Roman systems. The Levites had official responsibility for "all measures of quantity and size" (1 Chr. 23:29). The

TALMUD contains strict regulations for the business world concerning honesty of measurements. Present information concerning Israelite metrology comes from a number of sources such as the Bible itself, HERODOTUS, JOSEPHUS, the Talmud, the treatise of EPIPHANIUS on weights and measures (A.D. 392), and the archaeological evidence from Palestine and surrounding nations. (In what follows, references to modern measures are to the U.S. system.)

   I. Measures of length
      A. Cubit
      B. Reed
      C. Span
      D. Handbreadth or palm
      E. Finger
      F. Gomed
      G. Greco-Roman units
      H. Distance between points
   II. Measure of area
   III. Measures of capacity
      A. Liquid (OT)
      B. Dry (OT)
      C. In the NT
   IV. Measures of weight
      A. Talent
      B. Mina (maneh)
      C. Shekel
      D. Gerah
      E. Beka
      F. Netseph
      G. Pim
      H. Kesitah
      I. Peres
      J. In the NT
   V. Balances
   VI. Conclusion

I. Measures of length. The universal practice of the ancients was to name the commonest measure of length from the limbs of the human body, particularly the arm and hand.

A. Cubit. The cubit (Heb. ʾammâ H564; Gk. pēchys G4388; Lat. cubitus) is the principal unit of linear measurement used in the Bible. Hebrew linear measurements were based upon the Egyptian system. The cubit was based on the length of the forearm measured to the tip of the middle finger. Since the length of the human arm varies from person to person, however, there was no absolute cubit standard. The length was usually 17–18 in. This "natural" cubit is called in Deut. 3:11 "the cubit of a man" (KJV; the NRSV translates, "the common cubit"). It was used in reference to the height of a man (1 Sam. 17:4), the depth of water (Gen. 7:20), and approximate distances (Jn. 21:8).

A more precise unit would be required in the work of building, such as the ARK OF NOAH (Gen. 6:15–16), the TABERNACLE (Exod. 26–27), the TEMPLE and its furnishings (1 Ki. 6:7; Ezek. 40–43), and the walls of JERUSALEM (Neh. 3:13). There were longer and shorter cubits, as in Babylon and Egypt. In Mesopotamia the cubit of Khorsabad was 4/5 the length of the "royal" cubit of 19.8 in.; the two Egyptian cubits measured 20.65 and 17.6 in. Ezekiel 40:5 specifies a unit of measurement that was "a cubit and a handbreadth," that is, of seven palms rather than six. The SILOAM inscription offers objective evidence as to the length of the cubit, as it states that the tunnel was 1,200 cubits long. By actual measurement it is 533.1 meters (1,749 ft.), making the cubit 17.49 inches. Additional confirmation of a cubit of about 17.5 in. is derived by calculation from the dimensions in cubits of the "molten sea" of Solomon's temple (1 Ki. 7:23–26; 2 Chr. 4:2–5; see SEA, MOLTEN) coupled with its capacity figured in *baths*.

There is an unverifiable rabbinical tradition that samples of the standard cubit were kept in

This bronze instrument from Nippur (15th cent. B.C.) was an official linear measure kept in the temple and used as a standard to control other measures in the city.

the temple. Cubit measures are used extensively in the OT: to give the dimensions of Noah's ark (Gen. 6:15), the tabernacle and its furnishings (Exod. 25—27), the size of the bed of OG king of BASHAN (Deut. 3:11), the size of GOLIATH (1 Sam. 17:4), Solomon's temple and its furnishings (1 Ki. 6:2—7:38), the height of the gallows erected by HAMAN (Esth. 5:14; 7:9), the dimensions of the city, temple, and land in Ezekiel's visions (Ezek. 40:5—43:17), the image of gold erected by NEBUCHADNEZZAR on the plain of DURA (Dan. 3:1), the flying scroll of Zechariah's vision (Zech. 5:2).

B. Reed. The reed or rod (Heb. *qāneh* H7866; Gk. *kalamon* G2812) mentioned in Ezekiel's vision of the temple (Ezek. 40:3 et al.) and in John's vision of the new Jerusalem (Rev. 21:15) was an instrument for measuring rather than a unit of measurement. The measuring "line" or "cord" (*ḥebel* H2475, Amos 7:17 [NRSV]; Ezek. 40:3; Zech. 2:1) was also an instrument rather than a unit of measurement. It is remarkable how many ruins of large public buildings can be measured in whole numbers of cubits of about 17.5 in. and in reeds equal to 6 such cubits. A palace building at MEGIDDO comprising part of Stratum IV must have been intended to be 50 cubits sq. The platform of the citadel at LACHISH was 12 reeds sq.; the base of the gate tower at Tell en-Naṣbeh was 5 reeds sq.

C. Span. The span (Heb. *zeret* H2455) was the distance from the tip of the thumb to the tip of the little finger with the hand extended and the fingers apart. It was half the common cubit (Exod. 28:16; 1 Sam. 17:4; et al.; the Vulg. mistakenly translates it as *palmus*, which has caused confusion with the following term, "handbreadth"). The EPHOD (Exod. 28:16) and the BREASTPIECE (39:9) were a span square. Goliath's height was 6 cubits and a span (1 Sam. 17:4).

D. Handbreadth or palm. The Hebrew term *ṭōpaḥ* H3256 (also *ṭepaḥ* H3255) refers to the breadth of the hand at the base of the fingers, generally considered to be 1/6 of a common cubit (and 1/7 of a "sacred" cubit), that is, 7.404 cm. or 2.915 in. (Exod. 25:25; 1 Ki. 7:26; 2 Chr. 4:5; Ps. 39:5; Ezek. 40:5). It was the equivalent of "four fingers" (Jer. 52:21).

E. Finger. As in Egypt, the finger (Heb. *ʾeṣbaʿ* H720) was the smallest subdivision of the cubit, 1/4 of a handbreadth. As a unit of measurement it occurs only in Jer. 52:21 (cf. 1 Ki. 7:15 MT), where the thickness of two hollow pillars is given as four fingers. It is mentioned frequently in the Talmud.

F. Gomed. The Hebrew word *gōmed* H1688 occurs only once (Jdg. 3:16), where it is translated "cubit" by the KJV and other versions. It is the length of a dagger rather than a sword and could not be a true "cubit." The SEPTUAGINT translates it with Greek *spithamē*, "span," which may be correct, as the context requires a short dagger. At most it could be 2/3 of a cubit or four handbreadths. Some modern scholars consider it to be a "short cubit" (cf. *HALOT*, 1:196).

Summary of OT length measures:
1 reed = 6 cubits = 8 ft. 9 in.
1 cubit = 2 spans = 17.5 in.
1 span = 3 handbreadths = 8.75 in.
1 handbreadth = 4 fingers = 2.9 in.
1 finger = 0.7 in.

Ezekiel's cubit, however, consisted of 7 handbreadths or 20.4 in.; thus the reed (6 cubits) was 10 ft. 2.4 in.

G. Greco-Roman units. (a) The Romans reckoned the cubit as 1.5 times the Roman foot (11.66 in.), so the cubit mentioned in the NT (*pēchys* G4388, Matt. 6:27; Lk. 12:25; Jn. 21:8; Rev. 21:17) was probably 17.5 in. (b) The fathom or "[arm] stretch" (*orguia* G3976, Acts 27:28) was a measure for depth of water equal to about 6 ft. (if 6 Greek ft. = 72.9 in.). (c) The *stadion* G5084 (Lk. 24:13 et al.; KJV, "furlong"), a Roman measure, contained 400 cubits or about 202 yards or 1/8 of a Roman mile. (d) Finally, the Roman mile (*milion* G3627, Matt. 5:41) was 1,620 yds., although in the eastern provinces of the Roman empire a slightly longer mile was used, equal to about 1/4 of the Persian *parasang*.

H. Distance between points. Traveling distances and the distance between two points are expressed in what would be imprecise and vague terms in modern times. The Hebrew word for "step" or "pace" is mentioned but once, and that as a metaphor (*peśaʿ* H7315, 1 Sam. 20:3). Distances traveled were not reckoned by miles or by hours but with such inexact phrases as a day's journey (Num. 11:31; 1 Ki. 19:4; Jon. 3:4; Lk. 2:44), or three days' journey (Gen. 30:36; Exod. 3:18; Num. 10:33; Jon. 3:3), or seven days' journey (Gen. 31:23; 2 Ki. 3:9). In a few passages (Gen. 35:16; 48:7; 2 Ki. 5:19), the distance is expressed with a phrase (lit., "a stretch of land") that means only "some distance," or "a short distance."

It can be estimated that under ordinary conditions 20–25 mi. could be traversed in a day. A SABBATH DAY'S JOURNEY is the distance between the MOUNT OF OLIVES and JERUSALEM (Acts 1:12). According to Josephus this distance was 6 stadia or about 1,238 yards. A rabbinical rule derived from Num. 35:5 set the distance permissible for Sabbath travel at a little over 0.5 mi. Joshua 3:4 records that the distance between the ARK OF THE COVENANT and the people was 2,000 cubits (c. 3,600 ft.), and since some could go to the ark to worship on the Sabbath, it is assumed that a Sabbath day's journey was at least 2,000 cubits.

Other distances include a bowshot (Gen. 21:16) and a furrow's length (1 Sam. 14:14). For the latter, see below, section II.

II. Measures of area. It was a widely practiced custom in ancient times to state land areas in terms of what a yoke of oxen could plow in a given period of time, or the amount of seed required to sow a given area. For example, land was measured in ASSYRIA AND BABYLONIA by the area a team of oxen could plow in a day; this area was defined as 6,480 sq. cubits or about 4/10 acre. Similarly one finds such expressions as an *imeru* ("ass-load") of land. In Egypt the cubit was used for determining areas: a piece of land 1 cubit wide and 100 cubits long was considered as a cubit in area; 100 cubits (an area of 100 cubits sq.) was a *sṯ't*, and was equal to roughly 2/3 acre.

There are no terms in Hebrew for measurement of area. Rather the lengths of the sides of a rectangle or square, or the diameter and circumference of a circular area, are given (1 Ki. 6:2–3; 7:23; 2 Chr. 4:1–2; Ezek. 40:47, 49; 41:2, 4; et al.). Bible versions use English *acre* in two passages where the Hebrew word *ṣemed* H7538, "pair [of oxen]," occurs to indicate the amount of land that a team of oxen could plow in a day (1 Sam. 14:14 [with *maʿănâ* H5103, "furrow"]; Isa. 5:10). Land was also measured by the amount of grain required to sow it (Lev. 27:16, although this verse prob. refers to the grain to be harvested and is thus an estimate of the value of the field and not of its area). ELIJAH dug a trench around the altar on Mount Carmel large enough to contain two *seahs* of seed (1 Ki. 18:32).

Another passage describes the size of the pasture lands of the Levitical cities. According to Num. 35:4, the lands are to extend outward from the wall of the city 1,000 cubits all around, but v. 5 seems to describe a square area with sides of 2,000 cubits. If taken literally, there would be no space left for the city in the middle of the square area. The solution is that the 2,000 cubits of v. 5 represent the frontage of the specified depth of 1,000 cubits, which means that the 2,000 cubits sq. is not the area of the pasture lands, but is a square enclosing the city and making the frontage of the pastures on each of the city's four sides. From data in the MISHNAH, I. Benzinger (*Hebräische Archäologie*, 2nd ed. [1907], 191) calculated that a seah was equal to 784 square meters or .193 acres; following the same proportion, a homer would be 5.79 acres.

In Roman times, Latin *jugum* ("yoke") was used to describe the area plowed by a team. It was later defined as a *jugerum* of 28,800 sq. (Rom.) ft., or 5/8 acre. It has been calculated that 3 3/5 seahs were required to sow one jugerum of land in the Greco-Roman period, which would be .173 acres. The Roman furrow (*actus*) was 120 Roman ft. in length, and land was measured according to the square *actus*.

III. Measures of capacity. Just as the linear measures of cubit, finger, and span were derived from various parts of the human body, so also the ancient units of capacity were originally nonspecific, and their names were taken from terms commonly used in the home or in commerce. These include imprecise terms such as "bowlful" (Jdg. 6:38; Amos 6:6) and "handful" (1 Ki. 20:10 et al.), and others that are a bit more definite (e.g., the *homer* is by derivation an "ass-load").

The standard measure of capacity in ancient Egypt was the *ḥḳt* (*hekat*), considered to be 5.03

liters, or about 1.25 American gallons, and used to measure grain or metal. The "hin" jar (*ḥnw*), which was 1/10 of a *bḳt*, was used to measure certain liquids such as beer, milk, and honey, as well as being a dry measure; it amounted to c. 0.503 liters, or slightly more than a pint. There was wide variation in Mesopotamian standards as judged by the many names for measures of capacity found in Sumerian, Assyrian, Neo-Babylonian, and Nuzi texts. The basic measure of capacity was probably the *qa*, equivalent of the Sumerian *sila*; it has been estimated to be between 1.004 liters and 1.34 liters. Another standard measure of capacity was the *sutu* of ten *qas* (c. 13.4 liters or 1.5 pecks) and the *imeru* (meaning "donkey" and representing the normal load carried by this animal), which is considered to be 134 liters or 3.8 bushels; this term is found in Middle Assyrian and Nuzi texts.

There is not sufficient evidence to determine the Canaanite units of measure, though they were probably like the Mesopotamian system. The *ḥmr* (homer) was a unit of dry measure, as well as the *ltḥ* (in Heb. spelled with *kaph*, lethek). The *lg* (log) was another unit of measure encountered in Ugaritic literature. The Hebrew measures of capacity were never standardized, and occasionally different names were used to designate the same unit. They were sometimes used to determine both liquid and dry measures, as the liter today. The Roman measures of capacity were the quartarius, sextarius, congius, urna, and amphora. The major units in the Bible are the following.

A. Liquid (OT)

1. Bath. The standard Hebrew liquid measure was the *bat* H1427 (to be distinguished from *bat* H1426, "daughter," which derives from a different root; Gk. *batos* G1004 occurs only in Lk. 16:6). It is said to be equal to the ephah (Ezek. 45:11, 14), where both are considered to be 1/10 of a homer, but this does not imply that the homer was used as a liquid measure. See B.1 below. The bath appears in multiples up to 20,000 and was used for water, wine, and oil (1 Ki. 7:26, 38; 2 Chr. 2:10, 4:5; Isa. 5:10; Ezek. 45:14). Its capacity has been determined at c. 5 gallons based on the estimated capacity of broken jars of the 8th cent. B.C. from Tell ed-Duweir (Lachish) and Tell en-Naṣbeh (with the inscription "royal bath," *bt lmlk*), and from Tell Beit Mirsim (marked simply *bt*). Pottery of the Greco-Roman period reveals a bath of 21.5 liters. Calculations of the capacity of the "molten sea" in Solomon's temple (1 Ki. 7:23–26, 38; see SEA, MOLTEN) support the estimate of 5 gallons; it has also been estimated to be 6 gallons. See also below, III.C.3.

2. Hin. The *hin* H2125 was 1/6 of a bath. From Ezek. 4:11 it is inferred that 1/6 of a hin was the minimum a person needed to drink daily. The hin is approximately from 3.5 to 3.9 liters or about 1 gallon. It is usually mentioned in ritual for offerings of wine and oil, in whole amounts (Exod. 30:24; Ezek. 45:24; 46:5, 7, 11), and in fractions, such as 1/2 hin (Num. 15:9; 28:14), 1/3 hin (15:6–7; Ezek. 46:14), and 1/4 hin (Exod. 29:40; Lev. 23:13; Num. 15:4, 5; 28:5, 7).

3. Log. The smallest liquid measure was the *lōg* H4253, equal to 1/12 hin. It is mentioned only in Lev. 14:10–24 as a measure of oil used in the ritual for the purification of lepers (the LXX translates the word with *kotylē*, "cup," used as a liquid measure containing about 1/2 pint; the Vulg. has *sextarius*, i.e., 1/6 of a *congius* or about a pint). The Talmud figured the log as the amount of water displaced by six hens' eggs, roughly the equivalent of one pint. It was probably c. 0.7 pint.

Summary of OT liquid measures:
Homer (cor) = 10 baths = 58.1 gallons
Bath = 6 hins = 5.8 gallons
Hin = 12 logs = 1.1 gallons
Log = 0.7 pints

B. Dry (OT)

1. Homer. The standard unit of dry measurement in the OT was the *ḥōmer* H2818 (also called the *cor* because of the assimilation of two systems; see below). It is a cognate of the word for "[male] donkey," *ḥămôr* H2791, and thus it indicates "ass-load." It has been estimated variously as 3.8 bushels or 6.524 bushels and by older estimates as 11 bushels. The homer contained 10 baths or ephahs (Ezek. 45:11–14) and was used for fairly large measurements in the OT. It was a large measure for cereals

(Ezek. 45:13; Hos. 3:2), a homer of barley being worth 50 shekels of silver (Lev. 27:16). It was used, by way of exception, to measure the quails that fell in the desert: they covered the ground to a depth of two cubits for a day's march around the camp, and the people gathered the birds all day and all night, and the next day "No one gathered less than ten homers" (Num. 11:32). The most conservative estimate of the homer would make this 38 bushels and would reveal the gluttony of the people. That "a homer of seed [would produce] only an ephah of grain" (Isa. 5:10) is the expression of a curse on the land because of the sins of the people.

2. Cor. As already mentioned, the *kōr* H4123 was equal to the homer. It was a large measure for flour (1 Ki. 4:22) and for grain (5:11; 2 Chr. 2:10). It was a dry measure, though Ezek. 45:14 makes the cor a liquid measure for oil, and, like the homer, it is said to contain 10 baths. The cor has been estimated to contain between 3.8 and 6.524 bushels or about 35–61 gallons. A half-homer of rust-colored stone used about 3,000 years ago in Jerusalem was found in an excavation.

3. Lethek. The *lētek* H4390 is mentioned only in Hos. 3:2, where HOSEA is told to buy the woman for fifteen shekels of silver and a homer of barley plus a lethek of barley. The NRSV emends the Hebrew on the basis of the LXX and reads, "a homer of barley and a measure of wine." However, the Hebrew term appears to be a loanword from Akkadian (*litiktu*); and Ugaritic *lth*, though spelled differently, may suggest that the lethek was a Phoenician dry measure. The Vulgate interprets, "a cor of barley and half a cor of barley" (cf. the late Gk. versions and the KJV); many think this equivalence is correct, which means that the lethek would be between 1.9 and 3.26 bushels.

4. Ephah. Among terms of dry measure, *ʾēpâ* H406 (Egyptian *ʾipt*) is the one most commonly used in the OT (Exod. 16:36; Lev. 5:11; Num. 5:15; Deut. 25:14–15; Jdg. 6:19; Ruth 2:17; Ezek. 45:10–13; et al.). It was equal to 1/10 of a homer (Ezek. 45:11) and is thus estimated from 3/8 to 2/3 of a bushel. In Zech. 5:5–11, the ephah in the vision denotes a large receptacle closed with a lid and

Ancient stone measuring cups used in Jerusalem.

larger than the usual ephah, for it held a woman named "wickedness." It is mentioned many times. The ephah must be just and perfect (Lev. 19:36; Deut. 25:15); it must not be too small (Amos 8:5; Mic. 6:10); there must not be two sizes, large and small (Deut. 25:14; Prov. 20:10). Modern versions sometimes insert "ephah" for clarification (e.g., Lev. 23:17; 24:5; et al.). Fractions of an ephah are mentioned: 1/16 (Ezek. 45:13; 46:14), 1/10 (Lev. 5:11; 6:20; Num. 5:15; 28:5). It was used to measure flour, meal, barley, parched grain, but never liquids. For liquids, the equivalent was the bath.

5. Seah. The *sĕʾâ* H6006 was a dry measure for flour and cereals (Gen. 18:6; 1 Sam. 25:18; 1 Ki. 18:32; 2 Ki. 7:1). It is difficult to determine its size. According to Josephus (*Ant*. 9.4.5 §85) it is equal to a modius and a half (see C.4 below), that is, approximately 12 quarts or 1.5 pecks or 0.37 bushels. However, if the *šāliš* H8955 of Isa. 40:12 (lit., "third," but translated "basket" in the NIV and "measure" in other versions) is the equivalent of the seah, then it is 1/3 of an ephah or 1/30 of a homer; and if so, the seah would be between approximately 0.13 and 0.28 of a bushel. According to the Talmud (*b. ʿErubin* 83a), the seah of the desert was equal to the volume of 144 eggs, while the seah of Jerusalem was equal to 173 eggs (i.e., 1/5 larger) and that of Sepphoris (a sacred measure used for religious ceremonies) was equal to 207 eggs (an additional 1/5 larger). The view that the use of the seah in the Bible reflects late Babylonian influence is inconsistent with inscriptional evidence (see *NIDOTTE*, 1:383).

6. Omer. The word ʿōmer H6685 (cf. ʿōmer H6684, "sheaf [of grain]") is found only in the story of the gathering of the manna (Exod. 16:16–36), where every person gathered an omer a day. It represented a day's ration; two omers were to be gathered for the sixth day and the SABBATH; one omer was to be kept as a memorial (vv. 32–34). It is identified as 1/10 of an ephah (v. 36) and would thus be equivalent to the issaron ("tenth"; see below), approximately 2.1 dry quarts or 2.3 liters. The omer should not be confused with the homer.

7. Issaron. As mentioned above, the term ʿiśśārôn H6928, meaning "tenth," was probably another name for the omer, thus the NIV and other versions render it "a tenth of an ephah" (KJV, "a tenth deal"; NRSV, "one-tenth of a measure"). The word is used as a measure of meal in the liturgical texts (Exod. 29:40; Lev. 14:10 et al.; Num. 15:4 et al.).

8. Cab (Kab). The term qab H7685 appears only once in the OT (2 Ki. 6:25). During the siege of SAMARIA by the Assyrians a donkey's head was sold for 80 shekels of silver, and the fourth part of a cab of DOVE'S DUNG (NIV, "seed pods"). The Hebrew text here is problematic and it is difficult to determine what the cab was. Josephus (*Ant.* 9.4.4 §62) evidently understands "one fourth of a cab" as equivalent to Greek xestēs G3829, approximately half a liter. The cab has been estimated as 1/18 ephah, or about 1.16 dry quarts.

Summary of OT dry measures:
Homer/cor = 10 ephahs/baths = 3.8–6.5 bu.
Lethek = 5 ephahs (1/2 homer) = 1.9–3.3 bu.
Ephah = 3 seahs (1/10 homer) = 0.38–0.65 bu.
Seah = 3 1/3 omers (1/3 ephah) = 0.13–0.22 bu.
Omer/issaron = 1 4/5 cabs (1/10 ephah) = 2.1 qts.
Cab = 1.16 qts.

C. In the NT. The information in the writings of Josephus are sometimes inconsistent with evidence from the OT period (see above under *seah*). For example, he says (in *Ant.* 3.8.3 §197) that the hin contains two Athenian choas, that is, approximately 1.5 gallons (not 1.1 gals., as in the OT); this means in turn that the bath equalled about 9.5 gallons (not 5.8 gals.; similarly, in *Ant.* 8.2.9 §57 he says the bath contains 72 sextaries=c. 72 pints=c. 9 gals.). It is very possible that during the exile the Jews modified their system so that it would align with Babylonian standards and that subsequently the units were further increased on the basis of Hellenistic measures (cf. *NIDOTTE*, 1.385). In any case, of the units used in the OT, the only ones found in the NT are the bath (*batos* G1004, Lk. 16:6), the seah (*saton* G4929, Matt. 13:33), and the cor (*koros* G3174, Lk. 16:7). The saton was a commonly used measure of capacity throughout the Roman empire. It was the equivalent of 10.91 liters or 1/2 ephah. Other measures found in the NT are the following.

1. Choinix. The *choinix* G5955 was a Greek dry measure equal to about two dry pints, and modern versions usually translate it as "quart" (Rev. 6:6).

2. Xestes. The *xestēs* G3829 apparently corresponded to Latin *sextarius* and was equal to just over a pint, but in the NT it is used in the general sense of "pitcher" (Mk. 7:4).

3. Metretes. The *metrētēs* G3583 was a liquid measure equal to about 39 liters or 9 gallons. The phrase *metrētas dyo ē treis* in Jn. 2:6 is rendered "two or three firkins" by the KJV (a British firkin is usually 1/4 of a barrel), but the NIV and other versions translate, "twenty to thirty gallons."

4. Modius. The term *modios* G3654, a loanword from Latin *modius*, refers to a dry measure equal to about 8.49 liters or 7.68 U.S. dry quarts. It is translated "bushel" by the KJV, but "bowl" by the NIV, because in the passages where it appears (Matt. 5:15; Mk. 4:21; Lk. 11:33) it is simply used to mean a vessel that could cover a light.

5. Litra. The Greek *litra* G3354 was equivalent to the Latin *libra*, that is, the Roman pound of 11.5 oz., and was used as a measure for both capacity and weight. It was the amount of ointment MARY used to anoint the feet of Jesus (Jn. 12:3; NIV, "pint"). NICODEMUS brought a mixture of myrrh and aloes that weighed about 100 litras for the dressing of Jesus' body (19:39; NIV, "about seventy-five pounds").

WEIGHTS AND MEASURES

IV. Measures of weight. The archaeological evidence is much more abundant for measures of weight than for those of length, area, and capacity. Large numbers of inscribed and uninscribed stone weights representing the shekel and its fractions have been found in Palestine. The fact that most of the early Hebrew weights that have been discovered were of hard stone is reflected in the general word used in the OT for weights, *ʾeben H74*, "stone." Even today peasants use field stones as weights, selecting one that is approximately the weight they desire. The expression *ʾabnê-kîs* (lit., "stones of a bag") indicates that carrying weights in a bag was a well-established custom in early Israel (Prov. 16:11; cf. Mic. 6:11).

Money was not a means of exchange in the earliest period; coinage was introduced into Palestine only after the EXILE, during Persian times. Transactions were therefore handled through barter (exchange of sheep for grain, or for a given weight of gold or silver). In spite of the abundant archaeological information, a definite system of weights has not yet been determined for the ANE. There was a great deal of variation because independent systems varied from region to region and because of fluctuation according to the goods for sale. The standards varied as much as the British and American ton and pound. Hebrew standards of weight were not exact; variety exists even in weights with the same inscription.

The basic unit of weight for the ancient Egyptian was the *dbn* (*deben*), which from known examples varied from c. 13.43 to c. 91 grams (0.474 to 3.2 ounces avoirdupois). Other units were the *kdt* (*qedet*, *kite*), retained down to the Roman period, which was 1/10 *dbn*, and the *šʿty*, which was 1/12 *dbn*. The OT does not mention any Egyptian weights.

The Hebrew system was derived from the Canaanites, who in turn had received it from the Babylonians. The word *shekel* (*šeqel H9203*) is derived from the Hebrew verb *šāqal H9202*, which means "to weigh." The shekel was the basic unit of weight common to all ancient Semitic metrologies. In Akkadian it was called the *šiqlu*; in Ugaritic, *ṯkl*. The Assyrian and Babylonian weights did not conform to a general standard but varied greatly through the ages; even a change in government could result in a changed standard of weights. The Mesopotamian weights were calculated on a sexagesimal basis (i.e., with the number sixty as the unit of computation); by comparison, the Egyptian had the decimal system. Our system of dividing the hour into sixty minutes of sixty seconds each is derived from the ancient Babylonian sexagesimal system. The mina (Akk. *manû*), talent (*biltu*), and gerah (*girû*) were the other principal Mesopotamian measures of weight. Thus the Babylonian system may be represented as: 1 talent = 60 minas = 3,600 shekels = 86,400 gerahs; or stated differently: 1 talent = 60 minas; 1 mina = 60 shekels; 1 shekel = 24 gerahs. There also was in the Mesopotamian system a series of "royal" weights, which were double the ordinary weights. One gold shekel had the value of ten silver shekels. In the most commonly used system in Mesopotamia the shekel weighed 0.30 ounces (8.4 grams).

Some of the Assyrian weights were in the form of metal lions, with open mouth and upswung tail with a symbol on the side representing the weight. To make the weight of the cast lions more (or less?) accurate and honest, bits were chiseled off or filled into the hollow form. A bronze lion of 2/3 mina came from the palace of the Assyrian king SHALMANESER III. A weight of thirty minas in the shape of a duck and carved from black basalt was found in a different palace (Eriba-Marduk II?). An early Babylonian stone is inscribed with the words "one half mina true weight" and actually weighs 244.8 grams (which would make the mina 489.6 grams, or approximately 1.08 pounds avoirdupois). Another weight inscribed "one mina true weight" weighs 978.3 grams, c. 2.16 pounds avoirdupois. Obviously these two stone weights represent the light and the heavy mina.

As already stated, the Hebrew system was derived from the Canaanites, who in return had derived theirs from Mesopotamia, so the systems in the two areas were generally equivalent, except that the Canaanite mina contained 50 shekels. There is biblical evidence for a 50-shekel mina in Israel prior to Ezekiel. Some of the Ugaritic texts determine weights in "heavy" shekels. At UGARIT the talent was only 3,000 shekels rather than 3,600. One collection of weights at Ugarit referred to in the texts indicates a light shekel to be 0.34 ounces (9.5

grams) and reference is made to a "heavy" shekel, which may be double the weight of the other.

The Hebrew system of computation of weights followed the decimal rather than the sexagesimal system. The basic unit was the shekel; its multiples were the mina and the talent. The mina appears only rarely (1 Ki. 10:17; Neh. 7:71). There is one confirmation that the Assyrian and Hebrew units were equal in some instances. According to 2 Ki. 18:14, "The king of Assyria exacted from Hezekiah king of Judah three hundred talents of silver and thirty talents of gold." In SENNACHERIB's annals of the same incident, the same amount of gold is indicated, though the silver is said to be 800 talents; the similarity between the two accounts is interesting. The Greek weights were the stater, mina, and talent. The Roman weights were the drachma, shekel, mina, and talent.

A. Talent. In the OT, this English word (from Gk. *talanton* G5419 [orig. "balance, scales"] via Lat. *talentum*) translates Hebrew *kikkār* H3971 ("round [loaf], disk"; cf. Ugar. *kkr*), which derives its name from the fact that it is a weight of circular shape. It was the largest of the units and was known to the Babylonians as *biltu*. The Babylonian talent weighed 30.13 kg. and was divided into 60 minas of 8.37 grams. According to Exod. 38:25–27, the sanctuary poll tax of a beka (or half shekel) paid by each of 603,550 men amounted to 100 talents plus 1,775 shekels. This information makes clear that there were 3,000 shekels to the talent, suggesting probably 60 minas of 50 shekels (less likely, 50 minas of 60 shekels). A two-talent weight from Lagash in the British Museum gives a weight of 66 3/4 pounds per talent, and mina weights from various periods down to the neo-Babylonian show that the weight of the talent was maintained between 28.38 and 30.27 kg. for many centuries. It is most likely that this same talent was standard in Syria and Palestine.

B. Mina (maneh). The word *māneh* H4949 (usually translated "pound" in the KJV) occurs in only four OT passages (1 Ki. 10:17; Ezra 2:69; Neh. 7:71–72 [MT 7:70–71]; Ezek. 45:12 [here KJV has "maneh"]; cf. Aram. *mĕnēʾ* H10428 in Dan. 5:25–26 and see MENE, MENE, TEKEL, PARSIN). The mina is often mentioned in Mesopotamian texts. In the Babylonian system one talent equaled 60 minas, and one mina equaled 60 shekels; but there is evidence from Ugarit for a mina of 50 shekels. According to Ezek. 45:12, "Twenty shekels plus twenty-five shekels plus fifteen shekels equal one mina." The total comes to 60, but the unusual manner of counting suggests that there were weights of 15, 20, and 25 shekels; the last item may have been half a mina of 50 shekels as at Ugarit. There is evidence that in preexilic Israel the commercial standard was 1 talent = 50 minas = 2,500 shekels. In Exod. 21:32 a fine of 30 shekels was imposed where the parallel regulation in the Code of Hammurabi imposed 1/2 mina. The ancient mina probably weighed between 1.213 and 1.323 pounds (550–600 grams); in Ezekiel's system it would weigh about 1.54 pounds (100 grams). The fluctuation was too great in different times and places to establish a precise value.

C. Shekel. The *šeqel* H9203 (from *šāqal* H9202, "to weigh") was the basic weight used in the ancient Semitic metrologies. However, there was no uniform standard for its weight. Even weights with the same inscribed notation do not weigh the same, and there were light and heavy, common and royal weights. The shekel has been estimated by various authorities as weighing between 11.3 and 11.47 grams. According to Ezek. 45:12, the shekel weighed 20 gerahs and the mina was equal to 60

Inscribed Roman bronze weight inlaid with silver (1st cent.). The inscription suggests that it was a standard weight kept at the Temple of Ops (a goddess of plenty and fertility) on the Capitol at Rome.

shekels. Fractions are found in the OT: 1/2 shekel (Exod. 30:13), 1/3 shekel (Neh. 10:32), 1/4 shekel (1 Sam. 9:8). ABRAHAM paid for the field of MACHPELAH with "four hundred shekels of silver, according to the weight current among the merchants" (Gen. 23:16). The expression may have been used to distinguish this weight from "the sanctuary shekel" of 20 gerahs (cf. Exod. 30:13). This distinction may explain why Nehemiah says the temple tax was 1/3 shekel (Neh. 10:32), whereas in the law it is given as a beka or 1/2 shekel (Exod. 38:26).

The annual weighing of ABSALOM's cut hair was 200 shekels "by the stone of the king" (lit. rendering of $bĕ'eben\ hammelek$, 2 Sam. 14:26). This reference is evidence that even as early as the time of DAVID there was an official "royal standard" (NIV) to which one could be referred. In establishing such a standard, David was only following the practice of other kings. A copy of a stone weight of one mina made by NEBUCHADNEZZAR (605–562 B.C.) was certified as being according to the standard set by Shulgi king of Ur (c. 2000 B.C.). A large unmarked weight from Tell Beit Mirsim, probably equal to 8 minas, gives a shekel weight of 11.41 grams.

The beka (see below) is the only weight whose name appears both in the OT and on recovered weights. It is equal to 1/2 shekel (Exod. 38:26). Seven stones inscribed bq^c have been found which range from 5.8 to 6.65 grams, averaging 6.04 grams. Five other uninscribed weights within the same range must also be bekas, making the average weight of the twelve weights 6.02 grams. Therefore reckoned by beka weights the shekel is 12.02 grams or 2/5 ounces. Thus it would appear that the symbol resembling a figure 8 with an open loop (Ȣ) found on weights of about 12 grams is a symbol for the shekel. However, this amount seems too large, as the weight from Tell Beit Mirsim (mentioned above) gives a shekel of 11.41 grams, and the average weight of 17 weights inscribed with the shekel mark is 11.53 grams. The shekel mark seems to have been an ordinary representation of the $ṣĕrôr$ H7655 or tied bundle in which lump silver, a medium of exchange, was carried (cf. Gen. 42:35; Prov. 7:20). Various theories have been proposed to explain the origin of the shekel mark, none of which are satisfactory. It has been suggested as of Egyptian, Babylonian, or Persian origin.

Other weights have been found that add to the confusion in determining the weight of the shekel, as they suggest a system with a slightly larger shekel of about 13 grams which may have been used for weighing certain types of goods. At Ugarit two words were used for the shekel, tql and kbd; the latter was a "heavy" shekel used to weigh purple linen. A weight of 51.6 grams was found at el-Jib (GIBEON) inscribed as "four shekels," which would yield a shekel of 12.9 grams (J. B. Pritchard, *Gibeon: Where the Sun Stood Still* [1962], 118–19). A weight with five strokes was found at GEZER, weighing c. 64.5 grams, which is almost exactly 5 x 12.9 grams. Also at Gezer three uninscribed weights averaged 64.8 grams (or 5 x 12.9 grams). A weight of 13.4 grams comes from MEGIDDO, and two weights of 13.3 grams from Tell en-Naṣbeh.

Thus the archaeological evidence does not enable one to determine an exact value for the shekel. Variations may be attributed to several factors: a tendency to depreciate standards with the passing of time, setting a new value by official decree, variation between official and unofficial weights, the use of different standards to weigh different kinds of goods, the influence of foreign metrological systems of weights, and occasional variation due to careless cleaning and weighing of weights found. The evidence seems to indicate, however, that the larger the weight, the smaller was the shekel unit contained in it. It can be concluded that there were three standards for the shekel: (1) the temple shekel of c. 10 grams (.351 oz.), which depreciated to c. 9.8 grams (.345 oz.; cf. *netseph* below); (2) the ordinary shekel of c. 11.7 grams (.408 oz.), which depreciated to c. 11.4 grams (.401 oz.); and (3) the heavy shekel of c. 13 grams (.457 oz.).

D. Gerah. The $gērâ$ H1743 was 1/20 of a shekel (Exod. 30:13; Lev. 27:25; Num. 3:47; Ezek. 45:12) and was the smallest unit of weight. The word possibly comes from a word meaning "grain." In the Babylonian system one shekel equals 24 gerahs. A weight of 2.49 grams from Sebastiyeh (Samaria) was inscribed $ḥmš$, probably representing 5 gerahs, as another weight from the same place was inscribed "1/4 $nṣp$, 1/2 $s(q)l$." This inscription tends to confirm the theory that the $nṣp$ is Ezekiel's shekel of

WEIGHTS AND MEASURES

20 gerahs. The gerah has been estimated to weigh 0.571 grams.

E. Beka. The *beqa'* (נֶּקַע *H1325*, "piece," from *bāqa' H1324*, "to split") is defined as "half a shekel, according to the sanctuary shekel" (Exod. 38:26; its only other occurrence is in Gen. 24:22, where the KJV and other translations have "half a shekel" instead of "beka"). The beka is the only weight (1) whose relationship to the shekel is given and (2) whose name both appears in the OT and is inscribed on recovered weights. It seems to have been the oldest standard in Egypt, having been found in prehistoric graves of the Amratian period; it was the usual weight for gold in Egypt. As mentioned above (under *shekel*), seven Hebrew stone weights inscribed *beqa'* have been found, ranging from 5.8 to 6.65 grams, averaging 6.04 grams. Five other uninscribed weights that must also be beka weights make the overall average weight of the twelve 6.02 grams. This is slightly heavier than other calculations giving the average weight of the beka as 5.712 grams.

F. Netseph. The netseph (*nṣp*) is a weight not mentioned in the Bible. Because of its similarity to the Arabic *nuṣf* ("half"), the name of a coin and a measure, it has been conjectured that the netseph was half of a heavier unit of weight. A spindle-shaped weight now at the Ashmolean Museum, Oxford, bears the inscription *rb' nṣp*, "one-fourth of a netseph," and weighs 2.54 grams. Thus if the netseph is half of a unit, the unit in question is apparently not the Hebrew shekel. The average of a dozen weights inscribed *nṣp* is 0.35 ounces (10 grams) and therefore belongs to another system. The name is found in the Ugaritic texts together with the shekel and is perhaps equal to 0.34 ounces (9.5 grams) in the weight system. In the Ugaritic system, then, the *nṣp* would be a "light" shekel equal to half the "heavy" shekel. It has been suggested that perhaps the netseph weights found in Palestine were lost there by Canaanite traders.

G. Pim. The term *pim H7088* (of unknown derivation) occurs only in 1 Sam. 13:21, a passage that was incomprehensible for a long time (cf. KJV, "they had a file for the mattocks"). Some early scholars conjectured that the *pim* was an amount of weight paid in silver that was used in the transaction between the Israelites and the Philistines, and this interpretation was confirmed by the discovery of a pim weight. It is generally believed to represent 2/3 of a shekel. Seven weights bearing the inscription *pim* range between 7.18 and 8.59 grams with an average weight of 7.762 grams.

H. Kesitah (qesitah). The *qĕśîṭâ H7988* (possibly from a root meaning "to measure") was used by JACOB when paying for the field of SHECHEM (Gen. 33:19; Josh. 24:32), and JOB received one *qĕśîṭâ* from each of his relatives and friends (Job 42:11). It is otherwise not known as a unit of weight. The LXX, followed by other ancient versions, understood the term to mean "lamb," and some have speculated that it was a metal weight in the form of a lamb or a quantity of silver equal to the value of a lamb. The NIV renders the term, "piece of silver" (NRSV, "piece of money").

I. Peres. The Aramaic term *pĕrēs H10593* (pl. *parsîn*) occurs in only one passage (Dan. 5:25, 28). It appears to be a loanword from Akkadian *parsu*, referring to a unit of weight equivalent to half a shekel (cf. *HALOT*, 5:1958–59). See MENE, MENE, TEKEL, PARSIN.

Summary of OT weights:
1 talent (3,000 shekels) = 75.6 lbs.
1 mina (50 shekels) = 1.3 lbs.
1 shekel = 0.4 oz.
1 pim (2/3 shekel?) = 0.27 oz.
1 beka (1/2 shekel) = 0.2 oz.
1 gerah (1/20 shekel) = 0.02 oz. (8.7 grains)

J. In the NT. There are few references to weights in the NT. The talent (*talanton*) referred to sums of money rather than weights (Matt. 18:24; 25:15–28; the adj. *talantiaios G5418* occurs in Rev. 16:21, where modern versions use the rough translation, "a hundred pounds"). The mina (*mna G3641*) occurs only in the Lukan parallel to the parable of the talents and thus refers not to weight but to money (Lk. 19:13–25, where some versions render it as "pound"). As mentioned in section III.C.5, the *litra G3354* was used in Jn. 12:3 and 19:39 to indicate an amount of precious oil and may be a weight or a measure of capacity. It was probably the Roman *libra* (pound) of 11.5 ounces (327 grams).

V. Balances. In order to use weights, it was necessary to have BALANCES or scales (Heb. *mōʾzĕnayim* H4404 [cf. Ugar. *mznm*]; another term, *peles* H7144, occurs only in Isa. 40:12). Foodstuffs were measured by volume, but precious metals and materials were weighed. Small items were measured on a beam-balance with two scales. The balance consisted of a beam mounted on an upright support or suspended on a cord held in the hand, not very different in design from a type still used. Ancient balances were not precision instruments. The graduated scale based on the principle of leverage did not appear before the 4th cent. B.C.

The weigh-masters were influential officials. They were known in ancient Egypt; on a cuneiform clay letter one King Burraburiah of Karaduniash to Amenhotep IV complained that the twenty manehs of gold sent to him by the Egyptian pharaoh had not stood the weight test when tried in the furnace. Egyptian judgment scenes from the *Book of the Dead* showed the heart of the deceased being weighed against the deeds of the deceased in the presence of the god OSIRIS. A similar figure is used in Dan. 5:27 when a mysterious writing appeared on the wall during BELSHAZZAR's feast.

Efforts to establish honest weights and measures are quite ancient. The law code of Ur-Nammu (founder of the 3rd dynasty of Ur, c. 2050 B.C.) contained official weights and measures as an effort to discourage dishonest merchants. An old Sumerian hymn to the goddess Nanshe (lines 142–43) contains a passage denouncing evildoers "who substituted a small weight for a large weight, who substituted a small measure for a large measure" (for a different trans. see *COS*, 1:529). The emphasis on honest weights and measures in the OT implies that dishonest use of balances was a common practice. The Levitical law required honest transactions (Lev. 19:35–36). Ezekiel stressed the importance of honest weights and measures (Ezek. 45:10). Just balances were also emphasized in Job 31:6 and Prov. 16:11. Amos denounced false and deceitful balances (Amos 8:5–6). There was a prohibition against "two differing weights in your bag—one heavy, one light" and "two differing measures in your house—one large, one small" (Deut. 25:13–14). A blessing was promised to those who used honest weights and measures (v. 15). There are other passages denouncing false balances (Prov. 11:1; 20:23, Hos. 12:7, Mic. 6:11). The Talmud contains strict laws for the regulation of the business world, as evidenced by the following: "The shopkeeper must wipe his measures twice a week, his weights once a week, and his scales after every weighing" (*b. Baba Batra* 88a).

As a part of his prophetic message, Ezekiel was told to divide his hair into three equal parts by use of a balance (Ezek. 5:1). Figurative mention of balances is found in Job 6:2; Ps. 62:9; Dan. 5:27. Job requested that his life be measured in a just balance (Job 31:6). The NT not only emphasizes a fair measure but a generous one in the words of Jesus: "A good measure, pressed down, shaken together and running over" (Lk. 6:38).

VI. Conclusion. From the preceding study it can be seen that there were no weights or measures sufficiently fixed in biblical times to enable one to determine the exact modern equivalents. Different countries had different standards, and these varied within the country and in different periods. Often there were two standards in use at the same time, the common and royal, light and heavy. However, archaeological information is sufficient to determine approximate values.

(See further A. R. S. Kennedy in *HDB*, 4:901–913; J. E. Dean, *Epiphanius' Treatise on Weights and Measures* [1935]; G. A. Barton, *Archaeology and the Bible*, 7th ed. [1937], 199–203; D. Diringer, "The Early Hebrew Weights Found at Lachish," *PEQ* no vol. [1942]: 82–103; H. Lewy, "Assyro-Babylonian and Israelite Measures of Capacity and Rates of Seeding," *JAOS* 64 [1944]: 65–73; A. Segrè, "Babylonian, Assyrian and Persian Measures," ibid., 73–81; A. Segrè, "A Documentary Analysis of Ancient Palestinian Units of Measure," *JBL* 64 [1945]: 357–75; R. B. Y. Scott, "Weights and Measures of the Bible," *BA* 22 [1959]: 22–39; R. de Vaux, *Ancient Israel* [1961], 195–206; O. R. Sellers in *IDB*, 4:828–39; M. A. Powell, "Ancient Mesopotamian Weight Metrology: Methods, Problems and Perspectives," in *Studies in Honor of Tom B. Jones*, ed. M. A. Powell and R. H. Sack [1979], 71–109; A. S.

Kaufman, "Determining the Length of the Medium Cubit," *PEQ* 116 [1984]: 120-32; E. M. Cook in *ISBE*, rev. ed. [1979-88], 4:1046-55; M. A. Powell in *ABD*, 6:897-908; W. F. Richardson, *Numbering and Measuring in the Classical World*, 2nd ed. [2004].)

F. B. HUEY, JR.

well. Since the RAINS in Palestine are concentrated in the winter months, the availability of WATER is a problem through much of the year. Natural sources are springs, streams, rivers, and the Sea of Galilee. Artificial sources are wells and cisterns. The latter were a problem until after the discovery of waterproof plaster shortly before the exodus.

The usual biblical words for a spring that bubbles up out of the ground are Hebrew *ʿayin* H6524 and Greek *pēgē* G4380 (Gen. 24:13 et al.; Rev. 7:17 et al.; see FOUNTAIN). The words for a well that was dug to reach the underground water table are *bôr* H1014 and *phrear* G5853 (Gen. 37:20 et al.; Jn. 4:6 et al.; see CISTERN). Sometimes these terms were used interchangeably, so one must watch the context for the exact meaning.

The ownership of wells was so important that feuds over them were settled at times only by a unique covenant service, such as the arrangement between ABRAHAM and ABIMELECH (Gen. 21:25-31). This value placed upon wells was in part due to the expense of digging them. Rivals would fight over a well rather than dig a second one. Notice that in Deut. 6:11 wells are listed with other costly items, such as olive groves and vineyards, both of which are very slow growing. The value of wells is seen also in the fact that some bore specific names (Gen. 26:20-22). Cities, in turn, were sometimes known by their wells (e.g., BEERSHEBA).

Wells were of special concern in WARFARE. The ancients normally went to war in the summer, for then they could live off the crops of their enemies. Summer was also the season when there was the least water available. Therefore the defenders would stop up their wells with stones and then cover them over with soil so the enemy could not use them. HEZEKIAH had the SILOAM tunnel dug to deprive the Assyrians of a water supply at Jerusalem. If it was desired to hand out special vengeance to one's enemies, their wells were destroyed (2 Ki. 3:25).

H. JAMIESON

wen. An abnormal but benign skin growth or cyst. The term is used by the KJV and other versions to render Hebrew *yabbelet* H3301, which occurs only in Lev. 22:22, where the Israelites are instructed not to offer to the LORD any defective sacrifices. The Hebrew term may refer to a wart (cf. NIV, *HALOT*, 1:383), but the NRSV understands it as a "discharge."

west. For any nation occupying a Palestinian homeland the W has a threefold significance. (1) It is the direction in which the sun sets, thus "west" is sometimes the translation of the Hebrew phrase *mĕbôʾ haššemeš* (H4427 + H9087, lit., "the entering of the sun," Josh. 1:4 et al.; cf. also *maʿărāb* H5115, Isa. 43:5 et al., and Gk. *dysmē* G1553, Matt. 8:11 et al.) (2) It is the direction in which the Mediterranean Sea lies (see GREAT SEA); hence Hebrew *yām* H3542, "sea," can mean "west" (Gen. 13:14 et al.). (3) In consequence, it is also the direction from which come the rain-bearing winds; thus in Lk. 12:54 a westerly wind is commonly agreed to augur the onset of RAIN (cf. ELIJAH's experience on Mount Carmel, 1 Ki. 18:44).

Ceremonially, the W was neither more nor less important than other compass points in the life of Israel, most biblical layouts being based on the "foursquare" pattern in which people or structures surrounded a focal point. However, for the Israelites the point of orientation was the EAST (not the N, as it is for us), and therefore the W can sometimes be referred to with the word *ʾaḥărôn* H340, "behind" (esp. in the expression *hayyām hāʾaḥărôn*, "the sea that is behind, the western sea," Deut. 11:24 et al.; see also EASTERN SEA).

J. H. PATERSON

western sea. See EASTERN SEA; GREAT SEA; WEST.

Western text. See TEXT AND MANUSCRIPTS (NT) V.

West Gate. According to the NIV, both the West Gate and the (otherwise unknown) SHALLEKETH Gate, on the upper road in the W part of the TEMPLE enclosure, were assigned to SHUPPIM and HOSAH (1 Chr. 26:16; some scholars omit "Shuppim" as a textual error). The Hebrew reads *lammaʿărāb ʿim šaʿar šalleket*, literally, "[the lots fell] for the west with the Shalleketh Gate." It is unclear whether in this passage the term *ma'ărāb H5115* ("west") merely indicates direction (cf. NRSV) or whether it designates a gate. If the latter, we have no evidence to determine whether it was an alternate name for the Shalleketh Gate or a different gate altogether (cf. NJPS, "the west [gate], with the Shallecheth gate on the ascending highway").

whale. A large aquatic mammal (order *Cetacea*). The term is used by the KJV in four passages. In three of them (Gen. 1:21; Job 7:12; Ezek. 32:2) the word renders Hebrew *tannîn H9490*, which the KJV elsewhere translates "dragon" (Ps. 74:13 et al.) or "serpent" (Exod. 7:9–12 et al.). The fourth passage is Jesus' reference to JONAH in Matt. 12:40, where the Greek word is *kētos G3063* (NRSV, "sea monster"; NIV, "huge fish"). In the book of Jonah, the Hebrew word used is *dāg H1834*, "fish" (Jon. 1:17a has *dāg gaddôl*, rendered "great fish" in the KJV, as well as NIV and other versions; the LXX uses *kētos*). Some have argued that several species of the toothed whales can swallow whole seals and dolphins weighing several hundred pounds and are thus physically capable of swallowing a person. The sperm whale of this group comes into the Mediterranean, but this happens rarely. Others argue that the gullet of the whale is not sufficiently wide and believe that the reference is to the great white shark (*Squalus carcharias* or *Carcharodon carcharias*), which can exceed 20 ft in length and is reported to have swallowed men whole. See also DRAGON; SEA MONSTER.

G. S. CANSDALE

wheat. A cereal grain that yields a flour used in various foods, especially BREAD; the term is used also of the annual grasses from which that grain comes. The primary Hebrew word for "wheat" is *ḥiṭṭâ H2636*, which occurs some thirty times in the OT (Gen. 30:14 et al.; Aram. *ḥinṭâ H10272*, Ezra 6:9; 7:22); in the NT, the Greek word used is *sitos G4992* (Matt. 3:12 et al.). There are several striking passages in which wheat occurs. GIDEON was threshing wheat at the time of his call (Jdg. 6:11). RUTH arrived at the right time in BETHLEHEM so that she could glean plenty of wheat (Ruth 2:23). Ornan (ARAUNAH) was threshing wheat (1 Chr. 21:20) when he saw the angel. We also have, for example, the picture of the end of the world when the "wheat" will be gathered (Lk. 3:17), and Jesus' saying regarding the need of death to self, "I tell you the truth, unless a kernel of wheat falls to the ground and dies, it remains only a single seed. But if it dies, it produces many seeds" (Jn. 12:24).

Wheat is, of course, *Triticum aestivum*, the ordinary summer or winter wheat, or *T. compositum*,

Wheat field in the hill country of Judah.

the bearded wheat, with several ears on one stalk. There is also the Egyptian wheat, *T. turgidum*; the one-grained wheat, *T. monococcum*, the wild wheat, *T. dicoccoides*; and others. The writer found only two actual varieties growing in Palestine on his last visit. *T. durum zenati x Bonterli* and *T. vulgare Florence x aurore*.

When the Israelites settled in Palestine, they became great farmers and produced vast quantities of wheat which they exported. Much went by ship to Tyre (Amos 8:5) and to other parts of the Mediterranean. However, some think that in Jotham's time (2 Chr. 27:5) the farmers had become lazy, because he demanded as payment from the Ammonites 100,000 bushels of wheat.

The sowing of wheat was usually done in the winter in Palestine—broadcast and lightly plowed in. Occasionally, the sowing was done in rows (Isa. 28:25 NRSV). The wheat harvest in Palestine is from the third week of April until the second week of June, depending on the soil, situation, and time of sowing. The threshing was done as a rule with a long, flexible stick known as a flail. The ears could be trodden out by oxen walking round and round over the cut wheat (Deut. 25:4), or there was always the crushing or bruising by means of a wheel of a cart running over it (Isa. 28:28). (Cf. *FFB*, 195–97.) See flora (under *Gramineae*); grain.

W. E. Shewell-Cooper

wheel. The invention of the wheel was one of the great human advances in technology. Clay models of wheeled vehicles, and some fragments of a potter's wheel (see pottery) indicate that both devices were known in ANE countries as early as the 4th millennium B.C. The first wheels, here and elsewhere, were probably suggested to some inventive mind by a rolling log, and were simply slabs cut from a log. The spoked wheel seems to have come with the replacement of the donkey by the horse as a draught animal in the middle of the 2nd millennium B.C. Pharaoh's chariot wheels, bogged in the mire of the Red Sea (Exod. 14:25 NRSV), were probably of this light and efficient variety.

In the description of Solomon's temple, the Hebrew word *'ôpan* H236 stands for the basins shaped in bronze after the fashion of chariot wheels and are described complete with axles, rims, and spokes (1 Ki. 7:30–33). Probably the model was the heavy Assyrian chariot wheel, rather than the lighter Egyptian model. The northern war chariots were heavily wheeled, and rolled noisily (Jer. 47:3; Nah. 3:2). Both Ezekiel and Daniel had apocalyptic visions in which wheels were an image of strength and of rapid movement from place to place (Ezek. 1:15–21; Dan. 7:9 [Aram. *galgal* H10143]). The Hebrew term *galgal* H1649 ("wheel" in Jer. 47:3 et al.) can be used as a synecdoche for the whole war chariot or wagon (Ezek. 23:24; 26:10), which depended upon the speed and sturdiness of the wheels.

E. M. Blaiklock

whelp. The young of various carnivorous mammals; in the Bible it almost always refers to the young of a lion (of a bear in 2 Sam. 17:8). The English term occurs a number of times in the KJV (e.g., for *gûr* H1594 in Gen. 49:9), but modern versions prefer *cub*. Biblical references to whelps or cubs are mainly figurative. According to Eliphaz, "The lion perishes for lack of prey, / and the cubs of the lioness are scattered" (Job 4:11). Jeremiah prophesied that Babylon would "growl like lion cubs" during her destruction (Jer. 51:38; for other references, see Deut. 33:22; Prov. 17:12; Ezek. 19:2–5; Hos. 13:8; Nah. 2:11–12).

R. L. Mixter

whip. See scourge.

whirlwind. A rotating windstorm, usually of limited extent. Although true tornados or severe whirlwinds are rare in Palestine, several types of violent storms do occur because of the proximity of mountains and lakes to the hot deserts. Hebrew words translated "whirlwind" include *sĕʿārâ* H6194 (used, e.g., of the wind that took Elijah up to heaven, 2 Ki. 2:1, 11) and *sûpâ* H6070 (Prov. 1:27 et al.).

white. The name of this color (Heb. *lābān* H4237; Gk. *leukos* G3328) serves to indicate the "natural" appearance of light colored objects, such as goats (Gen. 30:35, 37), the manna (Exod. 16:31), diseased skin (Lev. 13:3–4 et al.; 2 Ki. 5:27), hair (Matt. 5:36), and so forth. One can obtain pure white color bleaching by long exposure to the sun or by using fumes of burning sulphur (draping cloth over a rack above the flame). The washing process is alluded to in Ps. 51:7 for purification of the sinful man. Whitewash on sepulchres along the way marked them out so that the passers-by might avoid contamination (23:27; verb *koniaō* G3154); it was believed that any one who touched a sepulchre would become contaminated (Num. 19:16). White symbolizes innocency and purity (e.g., Isa. 1:18) and symbolizes the DEITY OF CHRIST (Matt. 17:2). The color is prominent in the book of Revelation, where it describes, for example, the head and hair of the one "like a son of man" (Rev. 1:4), the clothing of the saints (3:4–5 et al.), and the throne of God.

H. G. STIGERS

whole burnt offering. See SACRIFICE AND OFFERINGS IV.B.1.

whore. See PROSTITUTION.

widow. A woman whose husband has died (Heb. *ʾalmānâ* H530; Gk. *chēra* G5939). In the Bible the widow was classified with the "fatherless" and the "aliens" from earliest times as one to be helped (Deut. 24:17–21); because these groups were often oppressed, they were sincerely to be pitied (Ps. 94:6).

I. The widow's future. The ideal future for a widow was remarriage. Until that opportunity arose she might stay at her father's home (Gen. 38:11) or even at her mother-in-law's house (Ruth 1:16). If the daughter of a priest became a childless widow, she could return to her home and still eat of her father's food (Lev. 22:13). Under a provision known as the LEVIRATE LAW, a brother or the next of kin of a deceased man should under certain circumstances marry the widow (Deut. 25:5–10; Gen. 38:11). A son born to this marriage would be considered to be the deceased man's son. Concern for the widow's future seems to be mixed. At times the inheritance stands out as fundamental in the provisions set forth, and at other times the concern is for the preservation of a closely knit family.

Whereas a husband could cancel out a vow taken by his wife, the law considered a widow's OATH as binding (Num. 30:9). The widow was treated in this instance as a special legal person equal to a man. However, the high priest was forbidden to marry a widow (Lev. 21:14). In Ezekiel's vision, this prohibition was enlarged so as to apply to all priests (Ezek. 44:22).

II. The laws of mercy. In actual practice the lot of the widow seems to have been a very hard one in biblical times. She was made a special ward of the court based upon the theme that God himself is the special protector of widows (Ps. 68:5). God executes justice for the widow by supplying her with food and clothing (Deut. 10:18). On the other side, God cursed anyone who perverted the justice due a widow (27:19). Grapes, grain, and olives must be made available to the widow to glean (24:19–21). She also participated in the third-year TITHE along with the fatherless and the sojourner (14:29).

III. The flouting of these laws. The fact that laws were made to protect widows from cruel treatment stands as a demonstration that such acts were all too common. The wicked are described in Job 24:21 as those who "show no kindness" to the widow. JOB himself, however, "caused the widow's heart to sing for joy" (29:13 NRSV). One of the strongest indictments of the wicked is in terms of those who "slay the widow and the alien" and "murder the fatherless" (Ps. 94:6). When the prophets indict their people for injustice, a part of the evidence of the correctness of the charge is the mistreatment of widows (Isa. 1:23). In the DAY OF THE LORD those who oppressed hired laborers, the widow, and the orphan will be the objects of swift judgment (Mal. 3:5).

The widow seems to have been easily identified because she wore special garments (Gen. 38:14). The wicked tried to use these as a security for a loan, so the law had to step in and make such a practice illegal (Deut. 24:17).

IV. Widows in the Christian community. From the earliest stage, the Christian community made the care of widows their responsibility (Acts 6:1; 9:39). Systematic charity was to be given the widows when they were aged or had no relatives to support them. This may have been an obligation deduced from the fifth commandment. The widows themselves were grouped together as a body concerned with deeds of kindness to the poor. Jesus

praised the widow who gave her whole income to the temple (Lk. 21:2-4).

By the time the PASTORAL EPISTLES were written, the Christian community had not changed its basic attitude toward widows but experience was forcing some reconsideration (1 Tim. 5:3-16). There was a need to distinguish between those who really needed help and those who could be left to the care of relatives. The limited resources of the church forced such a restriction. "But if a widow has children or grandchildren, these should learn first of all to put their religion into practice by caring for their own family and so repaying their parents and grandparents, for this is pleasing to God" (v. 4).

Some segments of the early church apparently developed an officially recognized order of widows (1 Tim. 5:9-15). This reference is the first clear description in Christian literature of such an institution. IGNATIUS, POLYCARP, and TERTULLIAN deal with the development of the order in their time. The discussion in 1 Timothy suggests that there was considerable dissatisfaction with the way the system was operating. Several qualifications are given. The widow was to be over sixty years of age to be enrolled. She was to be "the wife of one man" (v. 9 KJV; it is unclear whether this means that she must have been married only once [cf. NRSV] or more generally that she must have been "faithful to her husband" [NIV]). A reputation for good works should have been acquired. This practical charity involved looking after children, being hospitable, washing the feet of Christians, and relieving people in distress. There was concern that the order of widows not have in its group those who were gossips, busybodies, and gadabouts. This special class of widows seems to have continued into the 2nd cent. A.D.

V. Figurative use of the term. There are a few striking figurative uses of the word "widow" in both the OT and the NT. For example, the "Virgin Daughter of Babylon" who claimed, "I will never be a widow," will be overtaken by widowhood "in a moment" (Isa. 47:9-9). The term is also applied by the prophet to Israel in her desolation as she is promised: "You will forget the shame of your youth / and remember no more the reproach of your widowhood" (54:4). It is difficult for Jerusalem to ignore its desolation, so the writer cries out concerning the city, "How like a widow is she / who once was great among the nations" (Lam. 1:1). The Christian seer in the book of Revelation hears the angelic messenger speak of a fallen Babylon which was so proud that she boasted, "I sit as queen; I am not a widow, / and I will never mourn" (Rev. 18:7). See FAMILY; MARRIAGE. H. JAMIESON

wife. See FAMILY; MARRIAGE.

wild ass. This English term (NIV, "wild donkey") is the usual translation of Hebrew *pereʾ* H7230 (Gen. 16:12 et al.); the word is used in parallel with *ʿārôd* H6871 in the only passage where the latter occurs (Job 39:5b, rendered by the NRSV, "swift ass"; NJPS, "onager"; the NIV leaves it untranslated). The name preferred for the biblical or Asian wild ass is *onager* (*Equus onager*, sometimes included in *E. hemionus* ["kulan"], esp. *E. hemionus hemippus* [Syrian wild ass], which became extinct in the 1920s). It is rightly classed as "half-ass," belonging to a species distinct from the true wild ass of N Africa (*E. asinus*, from which the donkey is derived; see ASS, DONKEY). The onager once had a wide distribution, divided into several geographical types, extending from the borders of Europe and Palestine in the W through to India and Mongolia. JOB describes its habitat precisely: "the steppe for its home, the salt land for its dwelling place" (39:6). By the mid-19th cent., onagers had long disappeared from Palestine but were still fairly common in Iraq; today they are found from Saudi Arabia to Mongolia.

Although the onager was long considered untamable, there is now clear evidence that the Sumerians used it for drawing chariots; this is amply illustrated in the Royal Cemetery at Ur (c. 2500 B.C.) and the identification has been confirmed by a study of the bones found at Tell Asmar, though there is nothing to show whether they were ever fully domesticated or just captured when young, as elephants are. They were bridled quite differently from HORSES; this suggests that the use of onagers as draught animals may have been based on experience with oxen, rather than on an imitation of horses in nearby countries, if they were already domesticated there. Onagers were abandoned as soon as the more efficient horse became available. The onager is a pale reddish color (white underside and flanks) with a dorsal stripe; the tail is tufted. (See F. E. Zeuner, *A History of Domesticated Animals* [1963], ch. 14.) G. S. CANSDALE

wilderness. See DESERT.

wilderness wanderings. See ISRAEL, HISTORY OF, III.

wild goat. Several Hebrew words have been thought to refer to the wild goat: (1) *yāʿēl H3604*, which occurs three times (1 Sam. 24:2; Job 39:1 [most versions, "mountain goats"]; Ps. 104:18); (2) *ʾaqqô H735*, which occurs only once in a list of animals that the Israelites were allowed to eat (Deut. 14:5); (3) *zemer H2378*, found in the same list (so FFB, 36, but most versions take this term as a reference to the MOUNTAIN SHEEP); (4) *śāʿîr H8538*, a common word for "goat," but rendered by the NIV "wild goat" in two problematic verses (Isa. 13:21; 34:14; see discussion under SATYR).

It is essential to distinguish between two closely related and often confused species. The Nubian IBEX (*Capra ibex nubiana*) is still found in W Palestine. The wild goat *strictu sensu* is *C. aegagrus*, also called "bezoar," which is the main wild ancestor of domesticated GOATS, whereas the ibex has never been tamed. The wild goat at one period lived as far S as Palestine, where remains have been found in Stone Age deposits, but some authorities are doubtful that the Israelites knew it (cf. F. E. Zeuner, *A History of Domesticated Animals* [1963], ch. 6).

G. S. CANSDALE

Wild Goats, Crags (Rocks) of the. A place in the Judean wilderness at or near EN GEDI, on the W shore of the DEAD SEA, where SAUL went to look for DAVID (1 Sam. 24:2; cf. v. 1). See IBEX.

wild gourds. See GOURD.

wild grapes. See VINE, VINEYARD.

wild ox. There is general agreement that the Hebrew term *rĕʾēm H8028* (Num. 23:22 et al.) refers to the true wild ox, that is, the aurochs (*Bos primigenius*; it is unfortunate that earlier English versions give it the mythical name UNICORN). This splendid animal, now extinct, was the wild species from which domesticated CATTLE have been derived. It was larger than most modern breeds, and the bull was blackish-brown, with long horns pointing forward and upward. In prehistoric times the aurochs ranged over much of Europe, western and central Asia, and parts of N Africa, including Egypt, where it was already becoming rare in the reign of THUTMOSE III (c. 1500 B.C.), who would travel far to hunt one. The last Egyptian documentary evidence for it is dated around 1190 B.C. (RAMSES III), but it is still common in the Gezira (central Sudan). Assyrian kings also hunted it heavily, but it survived in the less inhabited parts of Mesopotamia until a few centuries ago, possibly after the last recorded European specimen died in A.D. 1627. It disappeared from Palestine long before the Christian era, and there is no real proof of its existence there in the biblical era.

The contexts of the nine biblical occurrences of the word provide some useful information. BALAAM made reference to "the strength of a wild ox" (Num. 23:2); the aurochs was the largest and most powerful wild ungulate then known. Another passage speaks of the horns and associates them with a domestic bull (Deut. 33:17; cf. Isa. 34:6–7, where it is grouped with sacrificial animals). Job 39:9–10 clearly contrasts the wild ox with domestic cattle used for pulling the plow. These are all figurative passages, but they imply a close acquaintance with the subject and leave little doubt that the wild ox

The ibex is often referred to as a wild goat.

is being described; also that it was then a familiar member of the fauna of nearby lands, if not of Palestine itself. (See further F. S. Bodenheimer, *Animal and Man in Bible Lands*, 2 vols. [1960–72], 1:50–51; F. E. Zeuner, *A History of Domesticated Animals* [1963], ch. 8.)

The KJV uses "wild ox" (Deut. 14:5) and "wild bull" (Isa. 51:20) to render Hebrew *tĕʾô H9293*, but this term probably refers to the ANTELOPE.

G. S. CANSDALE

will (testament). See TESTAMENT.

will (volition). The various terms used in Scripture to indicate acts of human will do not indicate a "faculty" of will or a specific "power" of willing. The Bible does not speak of will in such an abstract manner, nor does it present any critically or systematically developed psychology, least of all a classical faculty psychology; nor does it discuss the philosophical problem of freedom and determinism. Since Scripture is rather a literary record of God's dealings with human beings than a psychological or philosophical treatise, it speaks in simple fashion of human acts and agents, of decisions and desires, of commands and intentions. Yet what it says has implications for the more theoretical questions. See also HUMAN NATURE.

I. Biblical conceptions

A. Willing. The frequent Hebrew verb *ʾābâ H14* ("to want, will") is used almost always with a negative, indicating a person's refusal to concur or obey (e.g., Gen. 24:5; Exod. 10:27; 1 Sam. 26:23); according to some writers, these uses underscore "the power of contrary choice." Another common verb, *rāṣâ H8354* ("to delight in"), can also be used with a negative (e.g., Lev 7:18; Amos 5:22), but it occurs most frequently in positive contexts and suggests acting freely out of one's own good pleasure.

The SEPTUAGINT employs the verbs *boulomai G1089* and *thelō G2527* somewhat interchangeably to cover wants, desires, decisions, purposes, and inclinations. In the NT *thelō* is used far more often than *boulomai* (the reverse of classic Greek usage). It has been argued that *thelō* denotes emotive action or unconscious DESIRE while *boulomai* stresses rational and conscious decisions. According to other scholars, such a use presupposes a dichotomy of emotion and reason that is alien to the Hebrew view of human nature (although it is precarious to draw a direct correspondence between lexical choices and theological and psychological concepts). It may be more descriptive of biblical usage to suggest that *thelō* is the broader and encompassing term, while *boulomai* indicates more specifically deliberate acts. Certainly this is the case with the noun *boulē G1087* (e.g., Acts 27:12, 42; 1 Cor. 4:5), and *thelō* plainly denotes near-commands and natural inclinations whether or not conscious. The classic passage is in Rom. 7:15–21, where KJV translates *thelō* with the now archaic use of "would."

It becomes evident (1) that the two verbs have no clearly distinct meanings; (2) that they depict the human being as an agent with responsibility for his acts, rather than denoting a discrete faculty, "the will"; and (3) that it is accordingly *the person* who chooses or desires or refuses, rather than "the will." In fact, "the will" of one's enemies is a translation of *nepeš H5883* or SOUL, that is, the person (cf. KJV and NRSV in Pss. 27:12; 41:2; Ezek. 16:27; in such passages the NIV has "desire" or "greed"). This holistic conception of personality is fundamental to any biblical characterization of human nature.

B. Moral freedom. The metaphysical problem of freedom (see LIBERTY), like a faculty psychology, is not in the biblical purview. Rather, humans are responsible agents, capable of certain self-determining acts. There are limits on this freedom, not only environmental and hereditary, but even more significantly, moral. That is to say, sinners have lost the freedom not to sin and so in measure have lost their capability of moral self-determination. What they want to do they find themselves unable to do. They are victims of temptation from without and within, unavoidably corrupt their physical and social environment, and create for themselves needlessly complex tangles of emotion, rationalization, and circumstance that shut them into hopeless despair. Human lostness is seen in the lostness of moral freedom, not (as with contemporary nihilism) in the meaninglessness of human existence. God's grace in response to sin therefore sets about restoring moral freedom. Christian liberty means that we obey God's law of our own will—that is to say, of ourselves, heartily—not that we are freed from such obligations (Jn. 8:31–36; Rom. 7–8; Gal. 4:1–9; 5:15–24).

It is not possible within this article to handle adequately the theological and philosophical problems connected with will. In what follows an attempt is made to indicate a direction for inquiry to take in the light of the biblical conceptions.

II. Theological problems

A. Is freedom of will destroyed by the fall?

At first glance outright disagreement appears on this question, but the difference is partly that writers address different questions. AUGUSTINE (354–430) was provoked by the Pelagian claim that human beings would have the moral freedom to obey the law fully were it not for the bad example of ADAM and his descendants and that Jesus Christ provided a new example to reinforce the good resolve of the human will. Augustine replied (in *The Spirit and the Letter*) that human beings are no longer able not to sin, no longer morally free, but need divine grace to enable them to trust Christ and do his will. A person in SIN is drawn by concupiscence, love of this world, whereas someone in GRACE is drawn by *charitas*, a LOVE for God that affects all else. Love of either sort is the dominating attitude of a life. Augustine speaks of it as an attitude of the will, that is, an act of the whole person. A person makes one kind of love or the other his own: the one draws him away from God and the good, robbing him of his freedom in those regards, whereas the other draws him toward God and the good, freeing him to obey God and to do the good.

Aquinas (1223–1274) was concerned more with metaphysical than moral questions. Since humans are by their essential nature rational beings, an act of will requires purposeful deliberation as well as decision, and the will is free insofar as it is rationally guided toward its ends. Concupiscence does not destroy freedom and make an act involuntary, but it inclines the will toward the object of concupiscence just as the love of God inclines it toward good ends. Fear and ignorance, not concupiscence, damage freedom of the will.

It should be recognized that freedom of the will is an ambiguous notion, varying with its object. Augustine himself recognized this. A person may be free to choose clothing or to perform certain moral acts, but not at all free to obey God's law from the heart or to trust the grace of God in Jesus Christ. Generalizations about free will tend to gloss over such differences and to sidetrack that closer analysis which the problem requires.

B. Is freedom of will compatible with divine election?

Discussions of predestination and free will frequently employ a mechanistic model for cause and effect, as if a person acts in response to efficient causes and behavioral stimuli. This hardly does justice either to human personality or to the creativity of God, and Scripture uses a more personalistic model. God prepares hearts, he loves people, he calls them and draws them to himself. Here is the language not of mechanical determinism but of interpersonal relations, after the way of a man with a maid or a father with his son. The problem, then, is not *whether* the human will acts independently in coming to faith, not whether faith is determined or undetermined by God, but rather *how* in the dynamic interaction of the divine person with a human person God preserves the personal freedom of individuals while leading them to faith. The combination is possible in interpersonal relations, while it is not possible with more mechanical causes.

One clue is found in Aquinas's classic treatment of the will (*Summa theol*. II. i. Q. 6), in which he points out that we differ from animals in that while the latter attain ends nondeliberately, involuntarily, and "by nature," human beings attain ends deliberately, voluntarily, and "by choice." A person makes an end his own, is often led to do so by rational considerations, and acts to achieve that end for himself. He establishes purposes and pursues them. Even though he is powerfully influenced in the process by other people and by the providence and grace of God, both the purpose and its pursuit have become fully and freely his own. See ELECTION.

III. Philosophical problems

A. Is freedom of will compatible with behavioral science?

The problem of freedom and determinism was hardly discussed in ancient or medieval philosophy, where freedom of will was regarded as a datum to be accounted for rather than a hypothesis which can overthrow. The problem arose following the scientific revolution, when the methods and concepts of physical science were extended to the study of human beings and their behavior. Thomas Hobbes (1588–1679), viewing man as totally material and matter as subject to mechanistic laws, regarded deliberation and decision as mere epiphenomena produced by physical forces at work in the BODY. Behavioristic psychology of more recent days employs similar explanations; for from an empirical point of view human acts must all be explained in terms of heredity and environment, that is, stimulus-response mechanisms. It is assumed that free acts, if they occur at all, are uncaused acts, and that all causes are of the sort which behavioral observation describes.

The problem is first epistemological, for to assume that all aspects of human existence are empirically describable by behavioral science begs the question regarding human nature. It assumes that human activity is a complex behavioral response and that the person is totally a physical being. These are precisely the points in question. If, as Descartes argued, the soul is another ingredient of human nature of a different sort than the body, then it is not necessarily subject to those causes that control bodily processes, nor are its acts empirically observable. One need not accept Descartes' problem-strewn interactionism to benefit from this insight.

The problem is secondly that a mechanistic model drawn from mechanistic physics is imposed on the discussion, so that freedom is equated with physical *indeterminism*. But freedom of will does not imply unrestrained and undirected independence; it is not uncaused activity but self-caused. Freedom is the ability to initiate action, to transcend what circumstances would otherwise produce, to be creative. Creativity, initiative, and transcendence are subject to influences of many sorts, and require both physical and psychological preconditions. When freedom is conceived in terms of the consciously purposive activity of creative individuals, it becomes evident that behavioral science only defines the conditions under which individuals operate. It cannot deny individuality to human beings. Yet it is the purposive individuality of the human being as an agent that epitomizes the biblical concept of will.

These aspects of freedom of will have been more effectively captured by recent idealism and phenomenology than by earlier indeterminism. William Temple, for instance, points out that people do not possess freedom of will from birth nor when intoxicated. They are free insofar as they are self-determining. This is a mark of maturity and of rationality; human beings are determined by the values they have made their own rather than by purely external forces. Freedom is a kind of determinism that is not amenable to either physical or behavioral science.

B. Is freedom of will possible in an ordered universe? We live in a universe of laws, one marked in the large and in every detail by rational order. Does freedom exempt human beings from cosmic law and order? Is it then possible?

This contention fits the viewpoint of the mechanistic materialist, for whom all nature can be explained by the operation of fixed forces (laws of motion). Such a conception of natural law is untenable, and philosophies of science recognize it as a product of 18th-cent. physics. The same contention, however, fits any monistic metaphysic. It was associated with the emanationist theories of both ancient Neo-Platonism and modern Spinozism. If all things are fundamentally one both numerically and in their nature, then what room is there for freedom of will and action on the part of men?

The early church properly developed the doctrine of CREATION ex nihilo in response to such contentions, for the biblical conception of the free agency of human beings presupposes biblical theism as a whole. A monistic metaphysics admittedly subjects each individual to the necessities of the whole, but theism regards all creation, both individuals and the cosmos, as contingent being dependent on the Creator. The creation operates according to its own regularities, it is true, exhibiting a rational structure for humans to examine. Part of this rational order is the purposive activity of free human agents who exist *ad extra* with regard to God, and so are not parts of a whole whose inner necessity controls them.

Some medieval writers confused the intelligible regularity of the created order with the impersonal determinism of eternal forms, and it took some time for Christian thinkers to purify their understanding. Thomas Aquinas did so by rejecting the Greek view of God as the essence of all being or pure form, and defined him instead as the act of being on which all other beings depend. But William of Occam finally rejected the reality of forms altogether, asserting that they represent the determinism of Greek monistic metaphysics rather than the biblical theism that ascribes absolute freedom to God and free individuality to human beings. The Reformers accordingly conceived of human individuality in relation to creation ex nihilo, rather than in relation to the Greek theory of forms. Rightly so, if the theory of forms is part and parcel of a monistic metaphysical scheme. It is essential therefore to understand the biblical conception of will and of moral freedom if one is not to be confused by the pseudo-problems created by either science or nontheistic metaphysics.

(For bibliography, see HUMAN NATURE.)

A. F. HOLMES

will of God. See PURPOSE.

willow. Any of various trees and shrubs of the genus *Salix*, bearing flowers without petals arranged in the form of spikes (catkins). Two Hebrew words may refer to the willow. One of them is *ṣapṣāpâ* **H7628**, which occurs only once (Ezek. 17:5); this term suggests that the reference is to the *Salix safsaf* (cf. Arab. *ṣafṣāfat*). The other Hebrew word is *ʿărābâ* **H6857** (Lev. 23:40; Job 40:22; Ps. 137:2; Isa. 15:7; 44:4), rendered "willow" by the KJV and other versions, but "poplar" (a related tree) by the NIV. See POPLAR. On Isa. 15:7, see WILLOWS, BROOK (WADI) OF THE; on Amos 6:14, see ARABAH, BROOK (WADI).

Did the harps of Ps. 137:2 hang on the willow known as *Salix babylonica* (cf. *HALOT*, 2:879)? Hence, "By the rivers of Babylon we sat and wept" (v. 1)—the seeming connection between weeping and the appearance of the species. The present writer has failed to prove that *S. babylonica* was ever found in Palestine, whereas botanists know over twenty other kinds of willows growing in that country, including *Salix alba*, *S. acmophylla*, *S. fragilis*, and *S. safsaf*, all of which grow well in Palestine, especially alongside the streams. If *ʿărābâ* refers to a tree of the *Salix* genus rather than to the poplar (genus *Populus*), the particular species is difficult to determine. See further FLORA (under *Salicaceae*).

W. E. SHEWELL-COOPER

Willows, Brook (Wadi) of the. In his oracle against MOAB, the prophet ISAIAH says that its fugitives carry their wealth *ʿal naḥal hāʿărābim*, "over the Brook of the Willows" (Isa. 5:17 RSV; NRSV, "Wadi of the Willows"; NIV, "Ravine of the Poplars"; see POPLAR and WILLOW). Some have identified this brook or ravine with Wadi Abu Gharaba, which flows into the JORDAN just N of the DEAD SEA, but the passage is usually interpreted to indicate that the Moabites are fleeing in a southerly direction. Other possibilities include a tributary of the ARNON or, farther S, an arm of Seil el-Kerek (Karak) known as Wadi Sufsat, which in effect means "Willow Brook" (so KD, *Isaiah*, 1:328, though standard maps do not show this wadi). Most recent writers, however, identify it with Wadi el-Ḥesa (see ZERED) because this ravine, located at the SE end of the Dead Sea, served as the boundary between Moab and EDOM (H. Wildberger, *Isaiah 13–27* [1997], 118, says that the passage refers "certainly" to Wadi el-Ḥesa, but on p. 136 he acknowledges that "objective data to support this identification are not available"). See also ARABAH, BROOK (WADI).

wimple. This English word, referring to a type of hood worn by women in the late Middle Ages, is used by the KJV to render *miṭpaḥat* **H4762** in one passage (Isa. 3:22). In the only other occurrence of this Hebrew term (Ruth 3:15), the KJV has "vail" (i.e., "veil"). Modern versions render it "cloak" or "shawl."

E. M. BLAIKLOCK

wind. The standard word for "wind" in Hebrew is *rûaḥ* **H8120** (Gen. 8:1 et al.), which can also be rendered "breeze," "breath," "spirit," "courage," and the like. The most controversial passage is in Gen. 1:2, where the phrase *rûaḥ ʾĕlōhîm*, traditionally understood to mean, "the Spirit of God," is sometimes rendered "a wind from God" (NRSV) or "a mighty

wind" (NEB; the use of *'ĕlōhîm* H466 as a superlative is attested (e.g., in 23:6, "great/mighty prince"). The rare meaning is found in the use of the similar phrase *rûaḥ 'ēl* in parallel with *nišmat šadday* in Job 33:4, "The Spirit of God has made me; / the breath of the Almighty gives me life." Thus the breath or Spirit of God in Gen. 1:2 (not an impersonal natural phenomenon) and God's breathing of the breath (*nĕšāmâ* H5972) of life in 2:7 are properly connected and reflect personal divine activities.

The equivalent of *rûaḥ* in Greek is *pneuma* G4460, "breath, spirit" (rendered "wind" in the wordplay at Jn. 3:8, and cf. Heb. 1:7; note also *pnoē* G4466 in Acts 2:2). However, the more common word for "wind" in the NT is *anemos* G449, which occurs about thirty times (Matt. 7:25 et al.). See also the discussion of climate under PALESTINE V.

W. WHITE, JR.

window. The most common Hebrew word for "window" is *ḥallôn* H2707 (Gen. 8:6 et al.). In the NT, Greek *thyris* G2600 occurs only twice (Acts 20:9; 2 Cor. 11:33). Archaeological evidence indicates wide variation in size, frequency, ornamentation, and closers. Numerous windows were used in JEREMIAH's time in wealthy houses for the sake of ornamentation and were the object of his scorn (Jer. 22:13–14). Bas-reliefs show them frequently barred, either by stone grilles or wood lattice, ornamented by projecting or recessed molds. Some windows opened onto balconies. SISERA's mother looked through the grating for him (Jdg. 5:28). SOLOMON's Palace of the Forest of Lebanon had three rows of windows (1 Ki. 7:4), probably in the Syrian style. Windows also were found in the TEMPLE, probably located in the Holy Place, high in the wall to admit light to the area. Glass windows being unknown, closers were mats, curtains, or wooden panels to protect from severe cold or wind. Gratings, much like louvered shutters, shielded the watcher from outside observers. See ARCHITECTURE; HOUSE.

H. G. STIGERS

wine and strong drink. Alcoholic beverages of various types.

I. Terminology. The usual Hebrew word for "wine," the fermented juice of the grape, is *yayin* H3516 (Gen. 9:21 et al.); the Greek equivalent is *oinos* G3885 (Lk. 1:15 et al.). In certain contexts (e.g., the poetic statement in Isa. 16:10, "no one treads out wine at the presses"), the term can be used more generally without specific reference to the stage of fermentation, and proponents of total abstinence argue that both *yayin* and *oinos* may refer to either fermented or unfermented grape juice (see esp. S. Bacchiocchi, *Wine in the Bible: A Biblical Study on the Use of Alcoholic Beverages* [1989]). Several words, however, were available to the biblical writers when referring to the juice extracted from grapes (see below), and if the distinction between fermented and unfermented juice had been (morally) important to the Israelites, it is difficult to understand why different terms or phrases were not used with some consistency to discriminate between the two stages (as is almost always done in English), or why the distinction between allowing the one and forbidding the other is never made explicit (contrast the explicit differentiation between leavened and unleavened bread in Exod. 12:15 et al.).

Another Hebrew word, *tîrôš* H9408, is often translated "new wine" (Gen. 27:28 et al., also rendered with *oinos* by the LXX) and possibly refers to *must*, that is, grape juice before and during fermentation; it is clear, however, that the *tîrôš* could be intoxicating (Hos. 4:11; cf. similarly Acts 2:13, which uses the Greek word for "new wine," *gleukos* G1183). In addition, there are three poetic terms: (a) *ʿāsîs* H6747, which seems to be a near synonym of *tîrôš* (Amos 9:13 et al.; it too could be intoxicating, Isa. 49:26); (b) *sōbeʾ* H6011 (Isa. 1:22 et al., though some think this term refers to beer made from grain; see *HALOT*, 2:738); and (c) *ḥemer* H2815, which apparently refers to wine while it is still fermenting (only Deut. 32:14 [NIV, "foaming"]; cf. *ḥămar* H10271, the normal Aram. term for "wine," Ezra 6:9 et al.).

Note should also be made of the expression *kol-mišrat ʿănābîm*, "all juice of grapes," one of the items forbidden to Nazirites (Num. 6:3). The word *mišrâ* H5489 occurs nowhere else and thus its precise meaning is uncertain; the phrase may refer in general to any grape extract (cf. NJPS, "anything in which grapes have been steeped"). Assuming that the reference is to unfermented grape juice, as most versions seem to take it, the question arises why this phrase was not used elsewhere. In particular, if the positive statements about *yayin* (see below, section III) have in view grape juice, why would the writers use a supposedly ambiguous term when *mišrat ʿănābîm* or a similar phrase was available?

The Hebrew word translated "strong drink" by the KJV and other versions (NIV, "fermented drink" or "beer") is *šēkār* H8911 (Lev. 10:9 et al., derived from the verb *šākar* H8910, "to be/become drunk," Gen. 9:21 et al.; Gk. *sikera* G4975, used in the LXX and Lk. 1:15, is a borrowing of the Aram. cognate *šikrāʾ*). This word is used to denote any intoxicating drink made from any fruit or grain, and at least in the early period included wine (cf. Num. 28:7 with 28:14; in Isa. 5:11 it occurs in parallel with *yayin* referring to intoxicating beverages in general). Usually, however, the use of the term is restricted to intoxicants other than wine from grapes. It probably refers to beer made from BARLEY. Both *šēkār* and *yayin* were forbidden to NAZIRITES (Num. 6:3; cf. Jdg. 13:4, 7, 14; Lk. 1:15) and also to priests when they entered the Tent of Meeting (Lev. 10:9). The book of Proverbs advises, "Wine is a mocker and beer a brawler; / whoever is led astray by them is not wise" (Prov. 20:1; cf. 31:4, 6). When ELI accuses HANNAH of being intoxicated she responds, "I have not been drinking wine or beer" (1 Sam. 1:15).

II. Mixed wine. In the OT period, there is some evidence that diluting wine with water was considered undesirable (Isa. 1:22, where the mixture is symbolical of spiritual adulteration). In the Greek and Roman periods wine was often mixed with water, and some considered this mixture to be healthier and more enjoyable: "it is harmful to drink wine alone, or, again, to drink water alone, while wine mixed with water is sweet and delicious and enhances one's enjoyment" (2 Macc. 15:39; it should be recalled that water could be unsafe to drink). Red wine was generally considered to be better and stronger than white wine (cf. Prov. 23:31). The wines of LEBANON (Hos. 14:7) and of HELBON (Ezek. 27:18) may have been white wines. The vineyards of ESHCOL (prob. near HEBRON) were famous for their large clusters of grapes (Num. 13:23). SAMARIA was the center of viticulture (Jer. 31:5; Mic. 1:6), but the Ephraimites had the reputation for being heavy wine drinkers (Isa. 28:1).

The Song of Solomon speaks of "spiced [*reqaḥ* H8380] wine" (Cant. 8:2). This phrase represented a variety of wines referred to as mixed or mingled wine. They were prepared with different kinds of herbs after the manner of the non-Israelite peoples of the ANE and were much more intoxicating than the regular wine. This fact made it popular at banquets and festive occasions (Prov. 9:2, 5; Isa. 5:22; Heb. verb *māsak* H5007, "to mix"). The biblical injunctions against its misuse are clear (Prov. 23:29–30; Heb. noun *mimsāk* H4932). When wine was mixed with MYRRH, it was used as a drug for its anaesthetic and stupefying effects. It was this that was offered to Jesus at the time of his crucifixion (Matt. 27:34; Mk. 15:23).

The rabbinical writers refer to several mixtures of wine that were known in Palestine and throughout the ANE. There was a mixture made of old wine with very clear water and balsam which was used especially after bathing. Use was also made of a raisin wine and a wine mixed with a sauce of oil and garum. A popular mixed wine was one mixed with honey and pepper, and recommended by the rabbis was a special emetic wine taken before a meal. There were many other mixtures of wine. Good VINEGAR was made by mixing barley in the wine.

III. Biblical attitudes to the use of wine. The attitude reflected throughout the Bible to the use of wine as a beverage is accurately expressed by Jesus the Son of Sirach, "Wine drunk at the proper time and in moderation / is rejoicing of heart and gladness of soul. / Wine drunk to excess leads to bitterness of spirit, / to quarrels and stumbling" (Sir. 31:28–29). Its use was universal except in the case of the priest when ministering in the sanctuary, the Nazirites, and the RECABITES, in which instances its use was prohibited. There is also, however, a constant awareness of the danger of incontinence in the use of wine, and this is denounced as sinful (Prov. 20:1; 23:29–35; Isa. 5:11, 22; 28:7–8; Hos. 4:11). Apparently the principle to be followed in the use of wine is that of moderation, consonant with PAUL's rule of conduct as formulated in 1 Cor. 8:8–13 and Rom. 14:13–21.

WINE AND STRONG DRINK

Wine receives special commendation in the Bible. There is reference to the "wine that gladdens the heart of man" (Ps. 104:15; cf. Jdg. 9:13; Eccl. 10:19). Used metaphorically wine represents the essence of goodness. The drinking of wine was sometimes accompanied by singing (Isa. 24:9). The desirable wife is compared to "a fruitful vine within your house" (Ps. 128:3). The blessing of wine is illustrated by the figure in which Israel is compared to a vine God brought from Egypt and planted in Canaan, where "it took root and filled the land," sending its boughs as far W as the Mediterranean and as far E as the Euphrates (Ps. 80:8–11).

Prosperity was sometimes symbolized by an abundance of wine, as when JACOB blessed JUDAH saying that "he will wash his garments in wine / his robes in the blood of grapes" (Gen. 49:11). A time of peace and affluence is described as a situation in which every person dwells "under his vine and under his fig tree" (1 Ki. 4:25). ISAIAH uses wine as a symbol of spiritual blessing (Isa. 55:1–2), and it is extolled in such passages as Eccl. 10:19. It appears that a temperate use of wine is not reprehensible (Zech. 10:7). References to wine in the Bible make it clear that its use was a common affair and a part of the regular diet (Jdg. 19:19; 1 Sam. 16:20; 2 Chr. 11:11).

On the other hand, there are repeated warnings in the Scriptures against the intemperate use of wine. See DRUNKENNESS. Isaiah warns "those who rise early in the morning / to run after their drinks, / who stay up late at night / till they are inflamed with wine" (Isa. 5:11; cf. v. 22). He condemns the priests and the prophets who "stagger from beer and are befuddled with wine" (28:7) and the shepherds who "lack understanding" because they say, "Come ... let me get wine! / Let us drink our fill of beer" (56:11–12). Some of the strongest warnings against intemperance are in the book of Proverbs. "Wine is a mocker and beer a brawler" (Prov. 20:1); "whoever loves wine and oil will never be rich" (21:17; cf. 23:20–21); "Do not gaze at wine when it is red, / when it sparkles in the cup, / when it goes down smoothly" (23:31). This is followed by a description of the hallucinations that follow immoderate drinking (23:32–34). MICAH chides the people of his time for preferring a preacher who claims, "I will prophesy for you plenty of wine and beer" (Mic. 2:11). HABAKKUK says that wine is treacherous and suggests that its intemperate use is characteristic of a person who has other character weaknesses (Hab. 2:5). The real undesirable possibilities in the abuse of wine led to the prohibitions against its use by Nazirites and also by priests when performing their duties (Lev. 10:9; Num. 6:3, Ezek. 44:21).

There is no direct or absolute prohibition of the use of wine in the NT. The moderate and appropriate use of wine is recommended to TIMOTHY by Paul, "Stop drinking only water, and use a little wine because of your stomach and your frequent illnesses" (1 Tim. 5:23). The intemperate use of wine is condemned in the NT just as it is in the OT. The Christian should "not get drunk on wine, which leads to debauchery" (Eph. 5:18). Christians should avoid living like non-Christians who are characterized as practicing drunkenness among their other vices (1 Pet. 4:3). Leaders in the church are exhorted to practice temperance (1 Tim. 3:3, 8). On one occasion Paul suggests total abstinence if the use of wine (or meat) is a stumbling block to another (Rom. 14:21; cf. 1 Cor. 8:13).

The view that total abstinence is required by Scripture is difficult to reconcile with the fact that the biblical warnings focus on the *excessive use* (or misuse) of wine. For example, Prov. 23:20 (referring obviously to fermented juice) puts wine in the same category as meat, "Do not join those who drink too much wine / or gorge themselves on meat"

A winepress at Masada.

(cf. Rom. 14:21). Priests were forbidden to drink wine or strong drink specifically when ministering in the sanctuary (Lev. 10:9), clearly implying that alcoholic drinks were used on other occasions. Similarly, the requirement that deacons should not indulge in or be attached to "much wine" (*oinō pollō*, 1 Tim. 3:8) makes little sense if in fact Christians are not allowed to drink wine at all.

IV. Viticulture in Palestine. Viticulture and the production of wine was important in the ANE and is described in the Bible (see VINE, VINEYARD). There are many references to the process of making wine in the Bible (Gen. 40:11; Deut. 18:4; Josh. 9:4; 1 Chr. 27:27; Ezek. 17:5–10). The vineyards were carefully cultivated and protected against vandalism by watchmen located in observation towers. No other plants were permitted to grow between the vines. An owner of a vineyard was exempt from military service at the time of the grape harvest in September, which was the season apparently for great festivity (Jer. 25:30; 48:33). The vintage is referred to in connection with the Feast of Booths (Deut. 16:13). Travelers were permitted to help themselves to the new wine and the poor could take what grapes remained on the ground, as they could with the harvest of all the crops. In the SABBATICAL YEAR the vineyards, as in the case of all farmlands, were to lie fallow.

The grapes were brought from the vineyards in baskets and were usually spread out for a few days in the sun, the effect of which was to increase their sugar content. The grapes were then placed in wine vats and trodden with bare feet. It seems to have been usual for several people to tread out the grapes together, which is the point of Isaiah's statement about the Messiah treading the winepress alone (Isa. 63:3). The usual wine vat consisted of three sections, two rectangular or circular rock-hewn pits at different levels connected with a channel. The upper pit was the larger one and here the grapes were trodden, the juice accumulating in the lower vat. The upper vat was usually twice the size in area as the lower, but only about half as deep. The wine vats varied in size. Even after the appearance of mechanical winepresses, the wine from trodden grapes was preferred and continued to be produced.

After the grapes were trodden, the husks that remained were pressed by means of a wooden plank, one end of which was secured to a socket in the side of the vat and the other end weighted with stones. Numbers of winepresses from Bible times have been discovered in the Holy Land and they vary in size and the number of vats. A winepress might have as many as four vats. The additional vats would allow for the settling of the must in the intermediate levels before the wine entered the final one. Usually the new wine was left in the vat to undergo the first fermentation, which took from four to seven days. It was then drawn or skimmed off (Hag. 2:16). If the vat had a spout, the wine was run off into jars or wineskins to complete the process of fermentation (Matt. 9:17). The whole period of fermentation would last from two to four months, at which time the wine would be ready for use. It would then be placed in smaller jars and skins. At this time the wine was strained through an earthenware, metal, or linen strainer to eliminate such things as grit and insects. Isaiah refers to this straining process when he mentions "wine on the lees well refined" (Isa. 25:6 KJV [Heb., *šĕmārîm mĕzuqqāqîm*; NRSV, "well-aged wines strained clear"]; cf. Matt. 23:24).

To aid in further maturing the wine and to guard against undesirable thickening on the lees, it was periodically poured from one vessel to another. Jeremiah has an allusion to this practice, "Moab has been at rest from youth, / like wine left on its dregs, / not poured from one jar to another— / she has not gone into exile. / So she tastes as she did, / and her aroma is unchanged" (Jer. 48:11; cf. Zeph. 1:12). When the wine was refined and ready to be stored for long periods of time, it was poured in jars lined with pitch that were sealed and placed in the "wine cellars" (1 Chr. 27:27 NRSV). There apparently were no attempts made to preserve wine in an unfermented state. The MISHNAH, for example, does not refer to any such preservation. Some scholars are of the opinion that preserving unfermented grape juice was virtually impossible in ancient times in Palestine (however, see the contrary arguments by Bacchiocchi, *Wine in the Bible*, ch. 4).

V. Uses of wine in the biblical world. Wine was universally used in the ANE in libation offerings to the gods of paganism. The Hebrews were constantly warned against becoming involved in these activities in foreign lands (Deut. 32:37–38; Isa. 57:6; 65:11; Jer. 7:18; 19:13). The "drink offerings" which sometimes were a part of the Levitical sacrifices were of wine (Exod. 29:40; Lev. 23:13; Num. 15:7, 10; 28:14). Worshipers customarily brought wine among other requirements when they went to offer sacrifice (1 Sam. 1:24; 10:3, 8). A supply of wine was kept in the TEMPLE for sacrificial purposes (1 Chr. 9:29).

Besides its customary use, wine was important in various special occasions and for particular reasons. It was used for medicinal purposes, for example, to revive the faint (2 Sam. 16:2), and as a sedative "to those who are in anguish" (Prov. 31:6). It was the custom in Talmudic times to give ten cups of wine to mourners (*b. Ketubbot* 8b; later this quantity of wine was reduced). Paul's prescription of "a little wine" for various ailments (1 Tim. 5:23) was widely practiced. The rabbis used a saying, "At the head of all medicine am I, Wine; only where there is no wine are drugs required" (*b. Baba Batra* 58b). It was used with oil in the dressing of wounds of the man who had fallen among robbers (Lk. 10:34).

Wine was also used at special occasions such as BANQUETS. At the great banquet given by King Ahasuerus (XERXES, Esth. 1:3, 7–8), the wine given to each guest was, according to Jewish tradition, from the king's home province and of the vintage of the year of his birth. The Hebrew word for "feast" or "banquet" is *mišteh* H5492, literally, "a drinking" (from the verb *šātâ* H9272, "to drink"). Wine also figures prominently as a desirable gift for important people, as when DAVID received "skins of wine" from ABIGAIL (1 Sam. 25:18) and ZIBA (2 Sam. 16:1). Because of its importance in every area of the life of Palestine, it was inevitable that wine should become an important commodity in business and commerce. When SOLOMON built the TEMPLE in Jerusalem, he paid HIRAM king of TYRE, among other things, 20,000 baths (1 bath equaled almost 6 gallons) for his help.

The use of wine has been a part of religious ceremonies and festive occasions in the Jewish home and in the SYNAGOGUE throughout Hebrew history. Viticulture soon became the most important agricultural activity in Palestine in the colonies established by Zionism. The cellars of the Rothchilds at Rishon le-Ziyyon controlled almost the entire produce of the Zionist colonies and was distributed through the Carmel Wine Company in all parts of Europe, Russia, and the United States. The 1904 vintage in the Rothchild cellars was more than 7,000,000 bottles, of which 200,000 went to Warsaw. The income of this trade in wine was of primary importance for the early economy of the Jewish homeland. During the period of prohibition in the United States (1920–33) the production and sale of wine for sacramental purposes was permitted by the federal government. Orthodox rabbis insisted upon the use of wine, although Conservative and Reform rabbis in the country held, on the basis of Talmudic law, that for Jewish ritual grape juice could be used instead of wine.

(See further M. Jastrow, Jr., in *JAOS* 33 [1913]: 180–92; H. F. Lutz, *Viticulture and Brewing in the Ancient Orient* [1922]; A. C. Haddad, *Palestine Speaks* [1936], 60–67; C. T. Seltman, *Wine in the Ancient World* [1957]; E. Ferguson in *Restoration Quarterly* 13 [1970]: 141–53; K. L. Gentry, Jr., *The Christian and Alcoholic Beverages: A Biblical Perspective* [1986]; P. E. McGovern et al., eds., *The Origins and Ancient History of Wine* [1996]; C. E. Walsh, *The Fruit of the Vine: Viticulture in Ancient Israel* [2000]; R. Phillips, *A Short History of Wine* [2000]; P. E. McGovern, *Ancient Wine: The Search for the Origins of Viniculture* [2003]; *ISBE* rev. [1979–88], 4:1068–72.) A. C. SCHULTZ

winebibber. See DRUNKENNESS; WINE AND STRONG DRINK.

wineskins. See SKIN.

wing. The common word for "wing" in Hebrew is *kānāp* H4053, but *ʾēber* H88 occurs a few times (Ps. 55:6; Isa. 40:31; in Ezek. 17:3 it may mean "pinion" or "feather"). Aramaic uses *gap* H10149 (only Dan. 7:4, 6), and the standard Greek term is *pteryx* G4763 (Matt. 23:37 et al.). Although anatomically wings are to the created birds (Gen. 1:21) what arms are to human beings, they are used for covering and locomotion rather than for manual dexterity, so that the symbolic use of wing differs decidedly from the symbolic use of arms.

The desire of hope is expressed in the psalmist's words, "Oh, that I had the wings of a dove! / I would fly away and be at rest" (Ps. 55:6), and such relief is promised in Isaiah's statement, "They will soar on wings like eagles" (Isa. 40:31). Moses assured the Israelites that the Lord cared for them "like an eagle … that spreads out its wings" (Deut. 32:11). Ruth found refuge under the wings of the Lord (Ruth 2:12), and Jesus would have gathered Jerusalem to himself "as a hen gathers her chicks under her wings" (Matt. 23:37).

Riches have their picture in doves' wings covered with silver (Ps. 68:13), but their fleeting nature was compared to wings of eagles (Prov. 23:5). Hosea likens the speed with which the Israelites engage in IDOLATRY to someone whom the wind has wrapped in its wings (Hos. 4:19 NRSV). Eagles have a wing spread of 7 to 9 ft., making for great speed. Both the wind and the morning are said to have wings (Pss. 18:10; 139:9), which portray the swift arrival of the Lord's help and accessibility everywhere. "The sun of righteousness will rise with healing in its wings" (Mal. 4:2). Even the shadow of a wing suggested a refuge from the wicked for David (Ps. 17:8).

Several symbolic creatures are given wings, such as the two women in Zechariah (Zech. 5:9), the lion with eagles' wings in Daniel (Dan. 7:4), and the woman in Revelation (Rev. 12:14). In ancient monuments wings were added to bulls and lions. Isaiah's SERAPHS covered their face with wings in worship, their feet also, but flew with the remaining two (Isa. 6:2). Ezekiel's CHERUBIM, winged living creatures, ascended with glory to God (Ezek. 10:5). Because Job could not by his own wisdom cause the hawk to soar or migrate toward the S, nor make the eagle climb to its nest on high, he learned HUMILITY and acceptance of the discipline of the Lord (Job 39:26–27). See FAUNA and articles on specific birds. R. L. MIXTER

winnowing. The process of blowing the CHAFF from GRAIN by wind or by a forced current of air (the Heb. verb is *zārâ* H2430, Ruth 3:2 et al.). This was done in the open on a flat surface of rock or ground, about 40–50 ft. in diameter, preferably on the top of a hill. The winnowing was done after the THRESHING was completed. The threshed grain

Winnowing at dusk.

was usually winnowed in the evening, when there was likely to be a wind. It was thrown into the air by means of a six-pronged fork, called in KJV a "fan" (Isa. 30:24; Jer. 15:7; Heb. *mizreh* H4665; cf. Gk. *ptyon* G4768, Matt. 3:12; Lk. 3:17). The chaff would be blown away, while the grain, being heavier, would fall to the ground. If there was no wind, one man waved a large fan, while another tossed the grain into the air with a fork. After the winnowing was completed, the owner of the grain and his family would generally spend the night with the grain to prevent stealing. The grain was finally passed through a sieve to remove the dirt, and then placed in jars for future use. S. BARABAS

winter. See PALESTINE V; SEASONS.

wisdom. The common Hebrew word for "wisdom" is *ḥokmâ* H2683, which can also be rendered "skill, experience, shrewdness, prudence" (cognate verb *ḥākam* H2681, "to be wise, act wisely"). Other relevant terms are *bînâ* H1069, "understanding" (verb *bîn* H1067) and *śekel* H8507, "insight" (the verb *śākal* H8505 can mean both "to understand" and "to have success"). Greek uses *sophia* G5053, "wisdom," and *phronēsis* G5860 (with various cognates).

    I. Possessors of wisdom
        A. Nonreligious
        B. Kings and rulers
        C. Counselors
        D. Prophets

E. Scribes
F. Magi
G. Messiah
II. Sources of wisdom
A. Naturally acquired
B. Learning
C. Revelation
III. Wisdom literature
A. Proverbs
B. Ecclesiastes
C. Job
D. Psalms
E. Ecclesiasticus
F. Wisdom of Solomon
G. James
IV. Christian concept
A. Jesus
B. Paul
C. James

I. Possessors of wisdom. It has always been assumed that some individuals possess wisdom above that of ordinary people. In OT times, wisdom became the collected account of the experiences and observations of such "wise men"; and in whatever respect wisdom brought power, these were also men of influence.

A. Nonreligious persons. People of no particular religious description were frequently said to possess wisdom. Artisans and craftsmen could be described as wise in the sense that they were skilled and able, ingenuity and manual dexterity being the dominant consideration (Exod. 28:3; 31:3; et al.). Also the crafty and subtle could be called wise without necessary connotation of either good or evil (Exod. 1:10; 2 Sam. 13:3; Prov. 14:8). Even the cunning of the lower animals could be described as their wisdom (Prov. 30:24). There was also the thought that wisdom was the special possession of the old simply because they had lived long. "Is not wisdom found among the aged? / Does not long life bring understanding?" (Job 12:12; cf. 15.10, Prov. 16:31). Paul could describe the pagan philosophers of his day as having a wisdom of this world (1 Cor. 1:20, 2:5; 3:19; 2 Cor. 1:12). Thus the relevant biblical words by themselves do not necessarily indicate that a wise person is religious.

B. Kings and rulers. Royal persons were especially thought to be possessors of wisdom, and that usually because of their relation to some divine source of understanding. Saul is said to have excelled all the youth of his day, and his father, Davıd, possessed wisdom even as a youth (1 Sam. 16:18), which continued with him to his last days (2 Sam. 14:20). David apparently was aware of Solomon's possession of wisdom and advised him at the time of his succession to the throne to act "according to your wisdom" (1 Ki. 2:6). Solomon was confirmed and heightened in his possession of wisdom by the appearance of God to him in a dream (2 Chr. 1:7–13). God offered to grant him whatever he asked. In response Solomon said, "Give me wisdom and knowledge" (v. 10).

Solomon's wisdom was soon displayed in the famous decision concerning the two women who claimed the same child, for he ruled in favor of the woman who was willing to give up the boy rather than having to witness his death (1 Ki. 3:16–27). "When all Israel heard the verdict the king had given, they held the king in awe, because they saw that he had wisdom from God to administer justice" (v. 28). Not only was Solomon held in awe by his own people, but also people came from many nations to test his wisdom, no one of whom is more memorable than the QUEEN OF SHEBA (10:1–13), and the note was added, "King Solomon was greater in riches and wisdom than all other kings of the earth" (10:23). He is said to have pronounced 3,000 proverbs and composed over 1,000 songs (4:32). His great wisdom has been preserved in the book of PROVERBS, most of which is attributed to him. The SONG OF SOLOMON and (indirectly) the book of ECCLESIASTES are also ascribed to him, as is the noncanonical work, WISDOM OF SOLOMON.

The kings of heathen nations were supposed to possess wisdom, but their wisdom was mocked and ridiculed by the prophets. ISAIAH announced that God would punish the king of ASSYRIA, who in his haughty pride boasted that it was by his own wisdom that he had triumphed (Isa 10:12–13). Likewise he declared, "the wise counselors of Pharaoh give senseless advice" (19:11; cf. v. 13). EZEKIEL denounced the king of TYRE in the name of the Lord because, said the prophet, "you think you are as wise as a god" (Ezek. 28:2).

C. Counselors. Advisers to kings, as well as others who stood in the royal courts, were judged to be wise men, and this not alone among the Jews. Homer's *Iliad* is filled with references to wise men such as Odysseus and Gerenian Nestor who spoke with a god or goddess standing by their sides, becoming the mouthpieces of deity to counsel the king, often interpreting signs and dreams.

POTIPHAR knew that his slave JOSEPH possessed unusual gifts (Gen. 39:1–6). Later, when Joseph was imprisoned on false charges by his master's wife, he was acknowledged as an interpreter of DREAMS. Pharaoh's butler and baker were likewise in prison, and they both dreamed. Joseph interpreted their dreams, one favorably and the other unfavorably. When the butler had been restored to Pharaoh's service as Joseph had foretold, after a long time of more than two years, he became the point of contact through whom Joseph was brought even into Pharaoh's presence to interpret a dream that troubled the monarch, which no wise man of Egypt could interpret (chs. 40–41). Being acknowledged as wise beyond all of Pharaoh's counselors, Joseph became second only to the king himself (41:33–44).

Later MOSES was to stand in another pharaoh's court to give counsel, and likewise he would be in competition with the wise men of Egypt, the "sorcerers" and "magicians" of the land. When Moses sought the release of the Israelites from captivity, he wrought miracles before Pharaoh, but the latter countered by commanding the magicians of Egypt to do the same things (Exod. 7:11, 22; 8:7). Eventually Moses stood down the wise men of Egypt and even they confessed his superior power, saying, "This is the finger of God" (8:19).

In still later times DANIEL and the young Jewish princes were counted among the wise men who attended NEBUCHADNEZZAR, the king of Babylon. They are described as "young men without any physical defect, handsome, showing aptitude for every kind of learning, well informed, quick to understand, and qualified to serve in the king's palace" (Dan. 1:4). Once again God's wise men were brought into conflict with the wise men of the king's court. It was a royal dream that needed interpreting which became the issue. Nebuchadnezzar commanded the magicians, the enchanters, the sorcerers, and the Chaldeans of his court to interpret his dream. When they failed, the king became "so angry and furious that he ordered the execution of all the wise men of Babylon" (2:12). Then Daniel, God's man, was enabled through divine help to interpret the dream.

Wisdom was not restricted to men among royal counselors. SISERA, DEBORAH's opponent, was evidently attended by wise women. After his death at the hands of JAEL wife of HEBER, Deborah, who was Israel's wise woman, sang a taunt song against those "wisest ladies" who were speculating on Sisera's delay in returning from battle, insisting that their dead leader was late because he was "finding and dividing the spoils" (Jdg. 5:29–30). JOAB, David's servant, enlisted the services of a wise woman whom he brought from TEKOA to help him gain David's permission to bring young ABSALOM back to Jerusalem (2 Sam. 14:1–27). Joab was also influenced by a wise woman who lived at ABEL BETH MAACAH, gaining the deliverance of her people and city (20:16–20).

There appears to have been a remarkable restraint among the wise men of Israel. They were not magicians, sorcerers, or astrologers. Those who attended Israel's kings were thought of especially as spokesmen for God, giving the wisest of advice because it had the sanction of divinity. Of AHITHOPHEL it was said that the counsel he gave "was as if one consulted the oracle of God; so all the counsel of Ahithophel was esteemed, both by David and by Absalom" (2 Sam. 16:23 NRSV); but not all lived up to that reputation. In fact, when Ahithophel himself proved a traitor to David, the king prayed that the counsel of Ahithophel be turned to foolishness (15:31).

D. Prophets. The PROPHETS were especially spokesmen for God, but they seem to have distinguished between themselves and those whom they identified as counselors of the kings. Most frequently the prophets were in conflict with those counselors who gave the kings political advice that ran contrary to that of the prophets. Isaiah strongly condemned those counselors who advised HEZEKIAH to make an alliance with Egypt contrary to his insistence that the protection of Pharaoh would turn to the nation's shame (Isa. 30:1–5). Jeremiah advised submission to the king of Babylon and was considered a traitor by those who counseled the king. In result the prophet, after speaking of the terrible trials toward which the nation was headed because of false counsel, cried out, "Let not the wise man boast of his wisdom'" (Jer. 9:23). Ezekiel likewise found the counselors to be deficient, with terrible consequences for the nation: "Calamity upon calamity will come, and rumor upon rumor. They will try to get a vision from the prophet; the teaching of the law by the priest will be lost, as will the counsel of the elders" (Ezek. 7:26). The spirit of the prophets was the spirit of Isaiah, who wrote, "Woe to those who are wise in their own eyes / and clever in their own sight" (Isa. 5:21).

E. Scribes. The SCRIBES arose as a class of professional exponents of the law following the pattern of EZRA. The result inevitably was that the scribes who interpreted the law tended to produce a wisdom of their own. Prophecy had about come to an end, and messianism was a remote hope at best. The life of the nation was turned to the law, thus the men of influence were especially the interpreters of that law. The difference in viewpoint between the scribal movement and Wisdom Literature (see below, section III) is seen in that the wisdom books of Ecclesiastes, Job, and Proverbs scarcely mention the law at all; instead, they bring the considerations of religion under observation through an evaluation of human nature and of the universe that men and women inhabited. The Wisdom of Solomon does have a high regard for the law, but gives little attention to it. The Wisdom of Sirach (ECCLESIASTICUS) has not only the highest regard for the law among the wisdom writings but also the most extensive treatment of that subject. The writer of Sirach identified the law with wisdom (Sir. 24:23–25), but such has been judged to be less than an accurate representation of the attitude of the wisdom writers toward the law.

F. Magi. The term MAGI originally referred to the Median priests from Persia who were both religious leaders and teachers of wisdom. Eventually the word came to refer to anyone who possessed supernatural knowledge and power. In the rabbinical writings the term was applied to magicians. PHILO

This clay tablet (c. 659 B.C.), discovered at the library in Nineveh, contains a cuneiform text known as "Rituals for the Substitute King," describing how a king was to be protected with a human scapegoat when omens predicted he was in danger. The ritual included the use of magical figurines; in the ANE, wisdom was often equated with skills in magic.

JUDAEUS used the term in a derogatory fashion to describe men who were not genuinely religious or even philosophical.

Magi (KJV, "wise men") sought Jesus, being led to the newborn MESSIAH by the heavenly sign, the star that went before them. Matthew records that they sought the king of the Jews, and this comment probably indicates that they were pagan (Matt. 2:1–12). In Matthew's gospel they are described in order to show that such men, with very slight knowledge of the facts, were nonetheless filled with enthusiasm by the sign God had given, made the long journey to Jerusalem, and sought the Messiah, when the leaders of the Jewish nation did not even seek to verify their report that he had been born. ORIGEN was perhaps the first to give a mystical interpretation to the gifts the Magi brought; he and other church fathers understood this event to portray the overthrow of magic by the coming of Christ, the adoration of Jesus by the Magi being taken as an admission of their defeat.

A man encountered by Philip in Samaria who has been called Simon Magus was described as practicing magic (Acts 8:9). This man played an important role in early Christian traditions; for example, he was judged by some to have been the founder of Gnosticism. There is little substance to such traditions. Simon Magus seems to have been representative of a class of charlatans who practiced magic for personal gain. They sold charms for healing and divination. Their magical formulae were derived from both eastern theosophy and mystic cults that thrived in the Hellenistic world. Such a man was excluded from the Christian community and clearly had no place in the early church.

G. Messiah. The Coming One, or Messiah, was associated with wisdom even prior to the Wisdom Literature; this seems especially to have been true because the Messiah was the grandest figure in a family distinguished by men of wisdom, David and Solomon. Isaiah identified him as the "Wonderful Counselor" and as one upon whom would rest "the Spirit of wisdom and of understanding, / the Spirit of counsel and of power, / the Spirit of knowledge and of the fear of the Lord" (Isa. 9:6; 11:2).

The book of Proverbs took a most important step when it personified Wisdom: "Wisdom calls aloud in the street, / she raises her voice in the public squares" (Prov. 1:20). In the most famous passage of all, Wisdom is identified as having existed before man was created, even before the creation of the world (8:22–31). The Apocrypha advanced even beyond the OT in the personification of Wisdom, who was declared to be the only begotten of God, living with God and sharing his throne. Wisdom was declared to be the very effulgence of eternal light. Wisdom was thought of as a heavenly being.

Many have professed to find a relationship between the Logos of Jn. 1:1–18 and the personification of Wisdom (esp. Prov. 8) as names of God. Yet others have professed to find a relationship between God's speaking through the Son, who according to Heb. 1:1–4 reflects the very glory of God, and the personification of Wisdom. Still others see Lk. 11:49—"Because of this, God in his wisdom said, 'I will send them prophets and apostles, some of whom they will kill and others they will persecute'"—as a self-designation by Jesus as the Wisdom of God. Several of the church fathers held this view on the basis of the parallel passage in Matthew, which begins, "Therefore I am sending you prophets" (Matt. 23:34).

II. Sources of wisdom. Where could a person obtain wisdom was a question of vast importance to the writers of the books of the Bible and nonbiblical literature as well.

A. Naturally acquired. Human ability to acquire wisdom is acknowledged; but such wisdom, according to the Bible, comes only from "the fear of the Lord" (Prov. 1:7). To the Hebrew, wisdom was the application of divine truth to human experience, and only "fools despise wisdom and discipline." Young men were especially encouraged to apply themselves to the quest for wisdom, making their ear attentive to wisdom and inclining their heart to understanding (2:2). The author of Ps. 49 gives the wisdom of his years of experience when he announces, "My mouth will speak words of wisdom; / the utterance from my heart will give understanding" (v. 3). That which followed was the author's observations about life and death. Especially in Ps. 73 there is a union of human thought and divine truth, the two combining to result in wisdom: "When I tried to understand all this, / it was oppressive to me / till I entered the sanctuary of God" (vv. 16–17a). The author of the Wisdom of Solomon makes his appeal for men to seek wisdom: "Wisdom is radiant and unfading, / and she is easily discerned by those who love her, / and is found by those who seek her" (Wisd. 6:12).

B. Learning. The writings of the rabbis concerned with the interpretation of the law became eventually the depository of wisdom, and those who studied the law gained the treasure of wisdom. Proverbs gave the practical advice that led to a happy and successful life, and because wisdom in this book had such an ethical and moral quality, it was a short step to equating wisdom and law. In the Apocrypha, the book of Ecclesiasticus gave a moral and religious interpretation to law which likewise foreshadowed that identification of wisdom with law. It is incorrect to say that wisdom was equivalent to law in Ecclesiasticus, but the identification of the two was definitely in prospect. By NT times so definitive of wisdom was the knowledge of the rabbis and their interpretation of tradition that those who were untutored in rabbinic could be described as accursed (Jn. 7:49).

C. Revelation. Wisdom is not often ascribed to deity in the OT (1 Ki. 3:28; Isa. 10.13; 31:2; Jer. 10:12; 51:15; Dan. 5:11). Even in the books of wisdom it is rare that God is described as wise (Job 9:4; Ps. 104:24; Prov. 3:19). Probably it is so because in the judgment of OT writers God's wisdom so transcended human wisdom that his knowledge and understanding were not appropriately described by the same term that pointed out human capacities. In the Apocrypha, later writers were more willing to speak of God's wisdom (Sir. 42:21; Bar. 3:32). In the NT there are several references to the wisdom of God (Rom. 11:33; 1 Cor. 1:24; Rev. 7:12).

The biblical point of view seems to be that wisdom comes from God and is to be found with him, rather than that God is wise. After asking where is the place of understanding, Job answers by saying, "God understands the way to it, / and he alone knows where it dwells" (Job 28:23). Human wisdom then is given by God. It is given in answer to prayer, as previously noted, when we seek his counsel. In the NT God's wisdom is especially associated with his Spirit. In the last analysis human beings possess wisdom only as a gift from God; it comes by divine revelation. This is especially the view of the NT (Acts 6:10; 1 Cor. 2:6; 12:8; Eph. 1:17; Col. 1:9; 3:16; Jas. 1:5; 3:15–17), but it is indicated in the OT also (1 Ki. 3:11–12; Eccl. 2:26; Isa. 11:2; Dan. 1:17).

III. Wisdom literature. The Hebrew *māšāl* H5442, "proverb," is the most primitive as well as the most common expression of Hebrew wisdom. It is not possible, however, to speak of any particular proverb or collection of proverbs in the Bible as being especially ancient. One portion of the book of Proverbs (Prov. 22:17—23:14) has been judged by many scholars to have affinities with the Egyptian material known as *The Wisdom of Amenemope*, which would indicate a considerable antiquity, for the earliest form of such literature existed in Egypt as far back as the 3rd millennium B.C. Not all the proverbs in the Bible are contained in the book of Proverbs. The last seven verses of Ecclesiastes are proverbial and to an extent offer the best explanation of the presence of proverbs in the Bible. God desired to teach his people the right way to live, to preserve them from heartbreaking experiences and aimless wanderings in life. A natural concomitant of this was a special interest in proverbial material in advising the young, so that Proverbs has often been called "The Young Man's Book."

A. Proverbs. As mentioned above, the book of Proverbs preserves much ancient material, but it did not attain its present form until late, no earlier than the time of HEZEKIAH (see Prov. 25). The first nine chapters are a contrast of wisdom with folly. The appeal is for people to behave wisely in every relationship of life. Chapters 10–24 are a collection of proverbs reported to have been written by wise Solomon himself. Chapters 25–29 are reported also to have been proverbs of Solomon which "the men [LXX, friends] of Hezekiah king of Judah" copied and arranged; whether these were transmitted orally or by writing (as "copied" would seem to imply) is not certain. Chapter 30 is an oracle of an otherwise unknown sage named AGUR son of Jakeh. The last chapter is an acrostic poem, arranged on the order of the letters in the Hebrew alphabet, which attempts to identify a virtuous woman; it is described as the instruction given to King LEMUEL by his mother (tradition has said that "Lemuel" was a name given to Solomon as a child by BATHSHEBA, his mother). See PROVERBS, BOOK OF.

B. Ecclesiastes. This book has been all things to all men. JEROME thought it was a manual enjoining renunciation of the world. Comenius spoke of it as an appealing book of consolation. Heine referred to it as a "Hymn of Skepticism." Delitzsch called it a "Hymn of Godly Fear." Johannes Pedersen gave it the title "Israelite Skepticism," and Morris Jastrow called its author "a gentle cynic."

The author of Ecclesiastes called himself *qōhelet* H7738, a Hebrew term derived from the verb meaning "to assemble," but usually translated "the Preacher" or "the Teacher" (the name Ecclesiastes comes from the Gk. *ekklēsiastēs*, "a member of the assembly"). Tradition has said that Koheleth was

Solomon, David's son (cf. Eccl. 1:1), though many modern scholars hold that he was simply a sage, one of the wisdom teachers of that day (12:8).

Koheleth felt bound by no tradition; he possessed an inquiring spirit, but with little interest in dogma. His range of knowledge did not equal Job's, but he was a cultured, well-informed man who had much insight into the affairs of his day. He was possibly acquainted to some degree with Greek philosophy. Three great loves possessed him. He had a love for life; his emotions were tempered, but to be alive was good indeed. His second love was justice. He was not indifferent to human suffering and was deeply sensitive to the cruelty and folly of the human race. The charge of cynicism grew out of his seeming resignation to an inevitable fate about which men could do nothing. His third love was truth. He tried to solve the puzzle of the universe, but concluded that all was vanity. Man was powerless and could do nothing for himself to solve the riddle of human existence. Koheleth loved life, but his search for justice and wisdom brought him only sorrow and disillusionment. See ECCLESIASTES, BOOK OF.

C. Job. Job has been commonly believed to be the greatest of all the Wisdom Literature. It is certainly the greatest drama in the OT and was called by Carlyle "the world's greatest book." At first it seems that the author is simply telling the story of Job's trials, but in actuality he is using those experiences to impress his readers with the truths he has received from God. The problem of suffering, the greatest enigma of the human mind, is that which the author faces. The Hebrew had been taught that the righteous always prosper and the wicked always suffer. If, therefore, a person suffers it is conclusive evidence of his wickedness. Because there was no view of immortality, it had to be that way for the Jew to maintain a moral universe. In SHEOL distinctions were nonexistent. The grave was no friend to any man. Because God was righteous, it was necessary for him to reward people in this life. The author of Job found two serious errors in this: (1) people would be led to do right in order to be rewarded with earthly benefits; (2) the poor, the hurt, the wretched were abandoned to their suffering (it was what they deserved). To Job it was not possible to identify suffering and sin. To Job the unfortunate man in life could none the less be God's man, well pleasing to him. The author could have simply declared these truths, but he chose to present them in a matchless dramatic form: Job accused of wrongdoing by friends because he had come upon hard times. See JOB, BOOK OF.

D. Psalms. Several of the psalms belong to the Wisdom Literature of the OT. Three of them (Pss. 19; 104; 147) are often referred to as nature psalms. To the wise the natural world was something more than rocks and hills. The wonders of the natural universe were testimonies to the glory of the God who created it. The heavens are constantly preaching and teaching (Ps. 19). Psalm 37 reflects the author's perplexity over the character and seeming prosperity of the wicked. The wicked may prosper to the end, but that end will be obliteration. The righteous may have little of this world's goods, but in the end they possess peace. Likewise Ps. 107 sings of the graciousness of God's providence for the redeemed. The material and temporal become types of the eternal and spiritual. The righteous are like a lost caravan in the desert; they are like distressed captives in a dungeon; they are like sick men on their deathbeds; they are like seamen foundering in a storm. In all of these circumstances they have been driven to God. They cry out for help, and he answers them. Psalm 148 calls upon all the universe to render its praise to God: the sun, the moon, the stars, the fire, the hail, the snow, the vapors, the young men, the maidens, the old men, and the children. Beginning with the heavens the psalmist moves from that great height to the lowest deeps and back to earth. Everything is to praise God. See PSALMS, BOOK OF.

E. Ecclesiasticus. Attributed to Jesus the Son of Sirach (Jeshua ben Sira), this book is also known as the Wisdom of Sirach. It has a proverbial nature, and some have supposed that Sirach took the book of Proverbs as his model. It has been thought that the book itself contains all that is known of its author (Sir. 39:1–11). It is not only like Proverbs in form, but in content as well. The ideal of life is presented as a synthesis of religion: fear of God and observance of the law, which was the better

part of wisdom. He was especially familiar with the Pentateuch as well as rules and regulations of the oral law that were later codified in the Mishnah. Sirach's task as a teacher, as he understood it, was to help his students to meet the problems of life by living righteously. He was a Jew of sincere piety and sought to bring his people to a similar devotion to God. See ECCLESIASTICUS, BOOK OF.

F. Wisdom of Solomon. This title comes from the SEPTUAGINT, but in the VULGATE it is called *Liber sapientiae* (Book of Wisdom). It is an exhortation to seek wisdom because that brings salvation, whereas damnation is the fate of unrighteous Jews who disregard wisdom (Wisd. 1–5). Wisdom is to be sought also because there is a divine essence about it. The understanding which this author reveals of the nature of wisdom differs considerably from the earlier Wisdom Literature, drawing much more heavily upon concepts found in Greek philosophy (chs. 6–9). Wisdom shows itself to have been the means by which blessings came to Israel in times past, even as judgment came upon the heathen without it (chs. 10–19). It should also be noted that there are differences between chs. 11–19 and the earlier section, raising a question concerning the unity of the work (e.g., the author no longer speaks in the first person, nor is the term *wisdom* to be found after 11:1). See WISDOM OF SOLOMON.

G. James. In the NT James comes closest to being Wisdom Literature. Like OT materials of this kind, it is made up of many short sections, even single sentences, on independent themes, though sometimes several paragraphs will be grouped around a single topic. It has many sayings that are similar to the apocryphal Ecclesiasticus. A close similarity in structure, if not in content, has been discovered by some between James and TOBIT (Tob. 4:5–19; 12:6–10), but probably the book most similar to it is Proverbs. Five, more or less general, divisions of the book can be identified: (1) Jas. 1:2–18, a discussion of the problems of trials that come in life; (2) 1:19—2:26, the nature of true religion; (3) 3:1–12, the responsibilities of a spokesman for God; (4) 3:13—5:6, a protest against prevalent evils in life; (5) 5:7–20, an appeal for the development of Christian virtues. See JAMES, EPISTLE OF.

IV. Christian concept. Wisdom for some of the prophets became a word that was heathen in its connotation. The NT finds something of the same problem, and when the wisdom idea becomes identified with legalism on one hand, or pagan philosophy on the other, it is rejected. Yet there is an appreciation of a certain kind of wisdom to be found in Christian teaching.

A. Jesus. There is in the SERMON ON THE MOUNT the clearest and fullest approach to the wisdom method to be found in the teachings of Jesus, though there are other briefer passages that possess this character (Lk. 14:8–10 is a quotation of Prov. 25:6–7). The love of life and the learning of large lessons with spiritual import from nature, both of which characterize the sages of the OT, are much in evidence in Jesus' longest sermon of record. Even the method of the wisdom writers seems to have been employed by Jesus, using as he did the short, pithy, and sometimes antithetical statement designed to live in the memory. There were, however, two kinds of wisdom recognized by him, the one accepted and the other rejected. There was a true wisdom, fully justified of her children, which brought sinners to God (Lk. 7:35), but there were also the falsely wise from whom he hid his teaching's meaning, while revealing it to the simple (Lk. 10:21; Matt. 11:25). Some have thought that Jesus was actually attacking the teaching of Wisdom Literature in Lk. 6:27 when he commanded "Love your enemies, do good to those who hate you" (cf. 28–38) for Sirach had taught, "Give to the devout man, but do not help the sinner. / Do good to the humble, but do not give to the ungodly" (Sir. 12:4–5a; cf. vv. 5b–7).

B. Paul. Paul's discussion in 1 Cor. 1–4 is a passage especially concerned with wisdom. In fact it is primarily a denunciation of wisdom. It is important to know that the wisdom against which Paul wrote was not of Jewish parentage, but Greek. It was the vain speculations of philosophy expressed in the empty, high-flown phrases of meaningless rhetoric that brought the apostle's wrath. This philosophy was a trusting of human thought processes rather than a reception of God's revelation. It was especially at the point of the meaninglessness and futility of the cross of Christ in the judgment of human beings that Paul took his stand. Such an attitude toward the cross was clearly a testimony to the perversity of the wisdom against which he wrote.

Positively Paul taught a wisdom of his own which was for mature Christians, those morally strong. It was probably not a reference to doctrine that Paul made when he said, "We ... speak a message of wisdom among the mature" (1 Cor. 2:6), though some have believed it to refer to the depth of Paul's teachings. It seems more likely to be associated with the presence and activity of the HOLY SPIRIT in the lives of God's people in a full and meaningful way, for Paul wrote, "God has revealed it to us by his Spirit. The Spirit searches all things, even the deep things of God" (2:10).

C. James. As pointed out above, the epistle of James is the only book in the NT that can be accurately described in its entirety as gnomic or as Wisdom Literature. The writing most similar to James in early Christian literature is known by the Latin title, *De doctrina apostolorum* (*Concerning the Doctrine of the Apostles*). The epistle of James could, with a very few Christian notations removed, pass quite appropriately as a synagogue exhortation. James contemplates the danger to Christianity not so much as a perversion of doctrine from a heretical teaching but as a violation in the realm of practical living. The interest of the book is dominantly ethical, an emphasis on a godly life. The wisdom of James is the wisdom of living a life acceptable to God which is the same emphasis that Jesus gave as recorded in the synoptics. See JAMES, EPISTLE OF.

(See further E. Mack, *The Hebrew Looks up to God* [1936]; L. Kohler, *Hebrew Man: How He Looked, Lived and Thought* [1956]; G. von Rad, *Wisdom in Israel* [1972]; J. L. Crenshaw in *The Hebrew Bible and Its Modern Interpreters*, ed. D. A. Knight and G. M. Tucker [1985], 369–407; J. Gammie and L. Perdue, eds., *The Sage in Ancient Israel* [1990]; J. Blenkinsopp, *Wisdom and Law in the Old Testament: The Ordering of Life in Israel and Early Judaism*, rev. ed. [1995]; J. L. Crenshaw, *Old Testament Wisdom: An Introduction*, rev. ed. [1998]; H. W. Ballard, Jr., and W. D. Tucker, Jr., eds., *An Introduction to Wisdom Literature and the Psalms* [2000]; R. E. Murphy,

The Tree of Life: An Exploration of Biblical Wisdom Literature, 3rd ed. [2002]; K. J. Clifford, ed., *Wisdom Literature in Mesopotamia and Israel* [2007].)

H. L. DRUMWRIGHT, JR.

Wisdom, Book of. See WISDOM OF SOLOMON.

Wisdom of Jesus. See ECCLESIASTICUS.

Wisdom of Solomon. An important pseudonymous book contained in the SEPTUAGINT and the VULGATE, but never accepted in the Hebrew canon; among Protestants it is regarded as part of the APOCRYPHA. This work finds a place among the *deuterocanonical* Scriptures of the Roman Catholic Church, where it is not known by the title given in copies of the LXX, but simply as the Book of Wisdom (its title in the Old Latin and Vulgate translations). The book was very popular in the early church, where it came to bear other titles, such as Divine Wisdom (CLEMENT OF ALEXANDRIA, ORIGEN) and Book of Christian Wisdom (AUGUSTINE). It is regarded by many as the highest achievement among the writings of the Apocrypha.

I. Content. Wisdom of Solomon stands as the apex of the so-called Wisdom Literature, the culmination of centuries of tradition on the subject of WISDOM. While there is a decided affinity between Wisdom of Solomon and the earlier wisdom writings (JOB, ECCLESIASTES, PROVERBS), comparison with its near contemporary and companion volume in the Apocrypha, ECCLESIASTICUS, springs to mind. In both, Wisdom is the focus of attention, is spoken of as personified, and is extolled in the most glowing phraseology. If Wisdom of Solomon outdoes Ecclesiasticus here, it is because of its employment of Hellenistic concepts and terminology in the setting forth of its argument (see HELLENISM). There are a number of additional, but more superficial, similarities between the two, such as a concern with perplexing problems, the repeated contrasting of righteous and wicked, and a survey of the history of the righteous. A striking difference between the two writings, however, is found in the literary style. Ecclesiasticus consists largely of collections of aphorisms—short pithy sayings gathered in a random fashion on the order of Proverbs. Wisdom of Solomon, in contrast, consists more of extended passages on isolated themes. As a result of this difference, Wisdom of Solomon may be much more readily outlined than Ecclesiasticus, as follows.

A. Wisdom: The righteous and wicked contrasted (Wisd. 1:1—5:23)
  1. The virtuous, not the ungodly, will find wisdom (1:1–15)
  2. The argument of the godless (1:16—2:24)
  3. Adverse experiences of the righteous are deceptive (3:1—4:19)
     a. Suffering (3:1–12)
     b. Barrenness (3:13—4:6)
     c. Early death (4:7–19)
  4. The contrast of the righteous and wicked at the judgment (4:20—5:23)
B. Wisdom: Solomon's personal appeal (6:1—9:18)
  1. Exhortation (6:1–25)
  2. Personal reminiscence (7:1–21)
  3. Panegyric on wisdom (7:22—8:1)
  4. Personal reminiscence (cont.) (8:2–21)
  5. Solomon's prayer for wisdom (9:1–18)
C. The experience of Israel and Egypt juxtaposed (10:1—19:22)
  1. The role of Wisdom in history, from Adam to the exodus (10:1–21)
  2. Israel and Egypt: God's antithetical action (11:1–14)
  3. God's measured punishment upon Egypt (11:15—12:2)
  4. God's measured punishment upon Canaan (12:3–18)
  5. Concluding remarks on God's forbearance (12:19–27)
  6. Excursus on the futility of idolatry (13:1—15:19)
  7. Israel and Egypt: God's antithetical action (cont.) (16:1—19:22)

In the first main section the author has drawn with bold strokes the contrast between the righteous and the wicked. As in Ecclesiasticus, wisdom has to do not with knowledge, but with righteousness. That is, the person who possesses wisdom is the one whose life is righteous. In his introductory exhortation, our author turns this around, arguing that wisdom cannot be attained by the evil or the godless. Such people indeed attain only unto death. An example of the unsound reasoning of the ungodly (given in the first person plural) is thereupon provided for the reader (Wisd. 2). Since this present life is short, passes away, they argue, let us give ourselves to revelry before we die, and let us oppress and abuse the righteous who are such a reproach to us.

Continuing his argument, the author points out that the adverse experiences of the righteous—suffering, barrenness, and premature death—must not be misinterpreted. They are better than the apparent blessings which the wicked enjoy. For the vindication of a person's righteousness comes ultimately at the judgment and in the immortality that awaits the righteous. It is the final judgment that will expose the misery of the ungodly. This latter point is vividly communicated by the author in the poignant lament he puts upon the lips of the wicked at the last judgment (Wisd. 5:1–13). The righteous will live forever, he concludes, receiving "a glorious crown" from the Lord (5:16). They will be kept by the Lord, but the end of the wicked will be disastrous.

In the second main section of the book, the author resumes the exhortation with which the book begins. Here one encounters the climax of all Jewish writing on wisdom. SOLOMON, the wisest of Israel's kings, is made to speak to his fellow kings and rulers. It is their duty, he says, to seek wisdom in their actions. Wisdom will come to the ruler who seeks her, and he who honors her will rule forever. Solomon then reviews his own birth and childhood, which on every account was ordinary. His life,

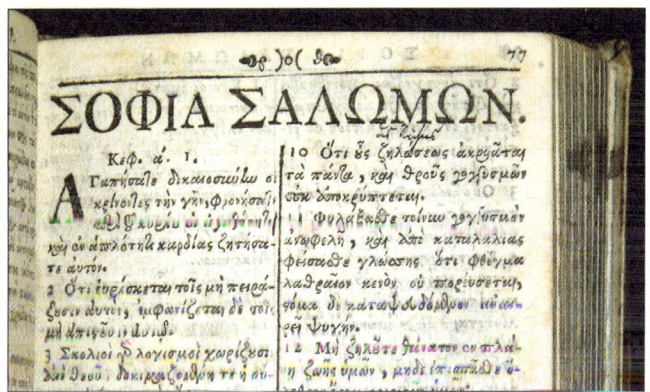

First page of the Wisdom of Solomon, from a 1715 edition of the OT Apocrypha.

however, was marked by a singular zeal for wisdom before which all else paled into insignificance.

At this point the personal reminiscence is interrupted by an incomparable passage in praise of wisdom (Wisd. 7.22–8.1). The author continues to speak of wisdom as personified or, to put it more strongly, hypostatized. Wisdom is described in the most exalted language—language which, strictly speaking, can apply only to God. She is, indeed, nothing other than the vehicle of God's action: "For she is a breath of the power of God, / and a pure emanation of the glory of the Almighty" (7:25). The passage begins by enumerating twenty-one characteristics (3 x 7) of Wisdom, a number of these terms being taken from Greek philosophy. Wisdom is said to pervade and penetrate all things (7:24); to be "a reflection of eternal light, / a spotless mirror of the working of God, / and an image of his goodness" (7:26); able to do all things and renew all things (7:27), and to order all things well (8:1).

Thereupon, Solomon proceeds with his account of his own pilgrimage to wisdom. Not only is wisdom desirable for its own sake, providing a person with true wealth, but it is indispensable for the effective ruling of one's subjects. With all of this in mind, Solomon prayed to God for wisdom. The prayer given (Wisd. 9) is a considerable expansion of the prayer as found in the canonical Scriptures (1 Ki. 3:7–9; 2 Chr. 1:8–10).

The third main section of the book, regarded by many as somewhat anticlimactic, begins with a brief survey of biblical history from ADAM to the exodus (Wisd. 10). It is shown how the heroes of Israel—who are not named, but in each instance referred to simply as the "righteous one" (*ho dikaios*)—were each kept by Wisdom, whereas those who neglected her brought ruin upon themselves. From ch. 11 onward, the writer concerns himself almost exclusively with the events connected with the exodus (see EXODUS, THE). In particular, he is intent on showing how one and the same thing (or similar things) worked ill for Egypt and good for Israel. While this passage must have been regarded by its author as the outworking of wisdom in the concrete events of Israel's past history, it is striking that the word *wisdom* occurs only twice in the remaining chapters. The first antithetical example given is that of water; the water given to the Israelites in the wilderness is contrasted with the water of the NILE, which the Egyptians could not drink. At this point, the author pauses to elaborate the carefully measured character of God's judgment upon EGYPT and CANAAN. These enemies of God could have been annihilated in an instant by his will, yet he brought judgment gradually to provide opportunity for REPENTANCE.

Apparently sidetracked by the need for an explanation of their plight, the author attacks what was at the heart of their folly—IDOLATRY (Wisd. 13–15). Whereas the author at least finds the worship of the beauties of nature intelligible—though, of course, he does not sanction it—he has nothing but ridicule for those who worship things made by human hands. He gives an account of the origin of idolatry (representation of those absent, whether by distance or death), tabulates the fruit of idolatry (ch. 14), and provides a concluding statement on the folly of idolatry (ch. 15).

His digression concluded, the author resumes his discussion of God's antithetical action among the Israelites and Egyptians. In addition to God's use of water, God provided repulsive animals (frogs) to plague Egypt, but quails for Israel to feast upon; the Israelites were saved from the bite of the serpents, but the Egyptians could find no cure for the bites of the locusts and flies. The elements of fire, rain, and hail worked toward Israel's advantage, but to Egypt's harm. Perhaps the most interesting of the contrasts, however, occurs in chs. 17 and 18, where the author, making extensive use of Jewish legendary materials (rabbinic MIDRASH), tells of a mysterious darkness that overtook the Egyptians while the Israelites knew only the blessings of light. Death, it is true, came upon both Egypt and Israel, but in the case of the latter, it could have no enduring work. Finally, the Red Sea proved a blessing to Israel, but only destruction to the Egyptians. The book ends rather abruptly, with a single verse asserting that the Lord has glorified his people and helped them at all times (19:22).

II. Unity, author, and date. In the summary just given, it can be seen that the third major section of the book is quite different from the first two. This fact has led a number of scholars to the conclusion that it is from the hand of a second author. Wisdom is scarcely mentioned in these later chapters, and the doctrine of the immortality of the soul, so important for the early chapters of the book, finds no place in the third section. There are stylistic and linguistic differences between these parts of the book as well (detailed evidence available in *APOT*, 1:522ff.).

There is, however, no unanimity concerning exactly where the first author left off and the second began (e.g., some make the division between Wisd. 9 and 10; some at 11:2 or 11:5). Moreover, the arguments against unity, though not without plausibility, are by no means compelling. For despite the notable differences, there are similarities in the different sections too, and most conspicuously in the use of unusual words (*metaleuein* is misused in the same way in 4:12 and 16:25) and expressions (see J. Reider, *The Book of Wisdom* [1957], 21). The two sections may well be from the same author, but perhaps derive from different times and/or were written for different purposes. There is no question but that the later chapters are inferior in quality (at least to the modern mind) in comparison with the early chapters, but it is a rare author indeed whose every line remains equally inspiring centuries afterward.

Assuming one author and not two, it must be admitted that his identity remains unknown. The book, of course, purports to be the literary product of Solomon, although his name is not explicitly mentioned (cf. the unmistakable indications in Wisd. 9:7–8, 12, as well as 8:2–19). The author, however, writes under the guise of a pseudonym well chosen to increase the authority of the book's assertions concerning wisdom. It is impossible that Solomon could have authored the book, for the conceptual and linguistic milieu it reflects is decidedly Hellenistic.

Unlike Ecclesiasticus, the style and vocabulary of Wisdom of Solomon indicates that it was originally written in Greek and not Hebrew (including the earlier chapters, for which a Hebrew original has occasionally been unsuccessfully argued). Further evidence that the book was originally written in Greek and dates well into the Hellenistic period is found in its dependence upon the LXX in OT quotations and allusions (see *APOT*, 1:524–25). It is known, then, that the author was acquainted with and highly influenced by Greek thought, terminology, and stylistic literary devices, and that he used the Greek translation of the OT. A Jew writing in Greek and steeped in Hellenistic culture using the LXX, readily suggests ALEXANDRIA as the most likely place of origin for our book.

The date of the book is difficult to place with any precision. Generally, however, since it postdates the Greek translation of the OT Prophets and Writings, it therefore can be no earlier than the second half of the 2nd cent. B.C. If the author knew Ecclesiasticus (in Greek dress), as seems likely, one may place the earliest date around 100 B.C. On the other hand, the work predates the earlier writings of the NT (which reflect some knowledge of it) and probably also predates PHILO JUDAEUS, with whom our author appears unacquainted. Generally, then, a date within the 1st cent. B.C. seems most probable. Attempts to determine the date more precisely (whether within this period or not) on the basis of internal data in the book have, owing to their intrinsic uncertainty, produced no conclusions calling forth common assent.

III. Background and purpose. It has already been pointed out that the background of the book is unmistakably that of Hellenistic Judaism. See HELLENISM. The author appears to have been well educated in Greek literature and philosophy. His literary style has been acknowledged as exquisite, and the near equal of the best Hellenistic writings. The book is patterned to a large extent on the CYNIC and STOIC diatribe, an eloquent oration intended (ostensibly, in the present instance) to be delivered as a public address. The style is decidedly artistic, employing a rich vocabulary and many turns of phrase that reflect the influence of the Greek poets. The author is fond of the standard Greek rhetorical devices, such as alliteration, assonance, chiasmus, sorites, syncrisis, and catalogues.

However, not only his style, but also his content reveals the influence of Greek literature. He can list for his readers the four cardinal virtues of the Greek philosophers: temperance, prudence, justice, and fortitude, adding "nothing in life is more profitable for mortals than these" (Wisd. 8:7). The description of wisdom (7:22–23) makes use of several philosophical terms, and the reference to wisdom as that which

in her pureness "pervades and penetrates all things" (7:24) is clearly reminiscent of the Stoic notion of *logos*. Like the Greek philosophers the author conceives of a kind of "world-soul" (cf. 1:7; 7:24, 8:1). Platonic doctrine may well account for the author's assertion that the world was created from a preexisting, formless matter (11:17). Wisdom is regarded as an emanation from God (7:25) rather than a creation of God, and can be referred to as a *pneuma* G4460, a "breath" or "spirit" of God, much in the same manner as among the Stoic philosophers. But perhaps most important of all, so far as the argument of the book goes, is the use of the Platonic idea of the IMMORTALITY of the soul (1:12–15; 3:1–4). Indeed, the author seems to accept the Platonic teaching of the preexistence of the SOUL (8:19–20; cf. 15:8, 11). The immortality expected by the author is that of the soul, in accord with the Greek philosophers, rather than that of the BODY, concerning which there is nothing in the book.

These are the more significant parallels between our book and the philosophy of the Hellenistic world. With these in mind, however, one may approach the question of the author's purpose. He seems obviously to be formulating the faith of his fathers in the thought categories of the educated society of his day. One may read behind this a desire on his part to speak to his Jewish brethren who were particularly attracted to the various fascinations of Hellenistic culture. He is saying that the Jewish religion is no less satisfying than Greek philosophy, and that the concepts of the latter can be most helpful in revealing the true depth of the former. He writes to the Jewish apostate and to those Jews in danger of apostasy. Additionally, however, he may well have hoped that the pagans might cast a glance upon his work. He spends no little effort in demonstrating the utter foolishness of idolatry. The references to the folly of Egypt throughout the latter half of the book could without difficulty be paralleled in the society of the contemporary Alexandrian, and the darkness that lay over the Egypt of the exodus may be seen, with not much imagination, to lie over the land of the reader.

IV. Theological significance. For all his borrowing of Hellenistic thought and idiom, the author remains truly a Jew. He knows and makes use of the OT Scriptures. His teaching concerning the transcendent God and the place of his chosen people Israel is orthodox. He freely employs midrashic exegesis in his discussion of the events of the exodus. The author, however, is also a Jew who feels quite free to advance the traditional theological formulations of his day. Unquestionably, one of the most important advances is the author's contention that retribution and reward are not necessarily received in the present life, but are to be realized in the afterlife of the immortal soul.

Anticipations of this doctrine, it is true, can be found already in the canonical Scriptures (e.g., Ps. 73:1; Isa. 26:19; Dan. 12:12). Yet the fact that the present life is all that the Jew looked upon is attested to by the continual wrestling with the problem of the apparent injustice of the present life found in the wisdom writings of Israel. Our author is bold to affirm that the solution to this perennial problem is to be found in the future. He counters the despair of the canonical Ecclesiastes. (It has frequently been argued that one of the author's main purposes was to refute the argument of Ecclesiastes.) Immortality, not material abundance, is the goal of the righteous, and one of the author's contributions has been designated the inauguration of an "other-worldly" perspective hitherto lacking in JUDAISM. An adjunct to this emphasis is found in the author's insistence upon individual RIGHTEOUSNESS as requisite for the enjoyment of blessing in the afterlife of the soul.

Another significant teaching of the book is, of course, found in the way wisdom is expounded, particularly in the personification or hypostatization of wisdom. To be sure, wisdom is personified already in Job 28 and Prov. 8, as well as in Bar. 3 and Sir. 24. But this author goes much further in ascribing to wisdom not merely a rhetorical existence, but very much a real existence—on the order of a separate heavenly being, existing with God (Wisd. 8:3), "an associate in his works" (8:4), who was present at the CREATION of the world (9:9). She is "all-powerful, overseeing all" (7:22), "a pure emanation of the glory of the Almighty" (7:25). Wisdom is further identified with *pneuma*, "spirit" (1:6; 7:22; 9:17), and performs the work of an intermediary between God and the righteous (7:27).

Thus whereas Ecclesiasticus identifies wisdom with the LAW (something this author does not do), here wisdom becomes the dynamic coworker of God. While the early Christians found this treatment of wisdom helpful in formulating the doctrine of the TRINITY, it seems unlikely that the author actually meant wisdom to be taken as a person distinct from Yahweh. It may certainly be said, however, that the early Christian formulations of the doctrine of the Trinity often bear, in language and concept, a great resemblance to our author's discussion of wisdom and her relationship to God, and that the latter not only anticipated but also to some extent prepared the way for those formulations.

V. Influence. The influence of the book on the early Christian church appears to have been remarkable, and far surpasses all other OT apocryphal books in importance. It probably appealed to the Christians because of its clear teaching on immortality, and especially because the language with which the author described wisdom was deemed particularly suitable and applicable to Christ. Although there are no direct quotations of the book in the NT (the earliest direct quotation is found in Clement of Rome), there are several significant allusions, especially in the writings of PAUL and John (see JOHN THE APOSTLE).

The epistle to the Romans appears to reveal the influence of our book in several places. Paul's description of idolatry and its effects (Rom. 1:18–23) is quite similar to the same line of argument in Wisd. 11–14 (cf. also the passages on natural theology, Rom. 1:19–20 with Wisd. 13:1–9); Rom. 9:19–23 seems to echo passages concerning the sovereignty of God in Wisd. 12:12 and 15:7, where the analogy of the potter and the clay is used in the same manner. The parallels here seem more striking than does Isa. 29:16, where the same metaphor is employed. The theme of the forbearance of God in giving opportunity for repentance found in the latter half of the book (e.g., Wisd. 11:23; 12:10, 19) is also to be found in Romans (e.g., Rom. 2:4). One may also compare Rom. 5:12 with Wisd. 2:24, where it is stated that through the devil's work death entered the world. Among other of Paul's epistles, Eph. 6:11–17 is similar to Wisd. 5:18–20, but here the Pauline imagery is equally well explained on the basis of Isa. 59:17. The Christological language of several other NT passages (Col. 1:15; Heb. 1:2–3; Jn. 1:9) seems to betray a knowledge of Wisd. 7:25–26 (cf. also Jn. 1:1 with Wisd. 9:1–2).

In addition to the large number of parallels in the NT writings that have been detected, the early church fathers found the book useful in their apologetic endeavors, pointing for example to such passages as Wisd. 14:7 and 2:12–20 as prophecies of the CRUCIFIXION of Christ, and 18:15 as a prophecy of the INCARNATION.

VI. Text and canonicity. The text of the original Greek has come down to us in a good state of preservation in the major uncial MSS of the LXX (B, A, and ℵ; also C which is, however, incomplete). It is readily available in the standard published editions of the LXX. Vulgate, Old Latin, Syriac, and Armenian are among the versions of the book that have been handed down, and these give evidence of having been translated directly from the Greek.

As with the other books of the OT Apocrypha, the book was accorded official recognition by the Roman Catholic Church only in the 16th cent. It was, however, highly venerated in the early church, as we have seen. Some accepted the book as canonical on the basis of its claim to Solomonic authorship. Others, fully cognizant that the book was pseudonymous, nevertheless also regarded it as canonical (e.g., Origen, Eusebius, Augustine). The list of the MURATORIAN CANON (prob. late 2nd cent.) surprisingly includes the book among the NT writings (!), noting that it was written by friends of Solomon in his honor. In the Protestant church the book holds an honored position among the books of the OT Apocrypha.

(See further W. O. E. Oesterley, *The Books of the Apocrypha* [1915], 455–78; id., *The Wisdom of Solomon* [1917]; R. H. Pfeiffer, *History of New Testament Times with an Introduction to the Apocrypha* [1949], 313–51; B. M. Metzger, *An Introduction to the Apocrypha* [1957], 65–76; J. Reider, *The Book of Wisdom* [1957]; L. H. Brockington, *A Critical Introduction to the Apocrypha* [1961], 54–70; J. Geyer, *The Wisdom of Solomon* [1963]; R. K. Harrison, *Introduction to the Old Testament* [1969], 1221–30; D. Winston, *The Wisdom of Solomon*, AB 43 [1979]; M. Gilbert in *Jewish Writings of the Second Temple*, 2nd ed. [1984], 283–324; P. Enns, *Exodus Retold:*

Ancient Exegesis of the Departure from Egypt in Wis 10:15–21 and 19:1–9 [1997]; L. L. Grabbe, *Wisdom of Solomon* [1997]; D. J. Harrington, *Invitation to the Apocrypha* [1999], ch. 5; M. McGlynn, *Divine Judgment and Divine Benevolence in the Book of Wisdom* [2001]; D. A. deSilva, *Introducing the Apocrypha: Message, Context, and Significance* [2002], ch. 6; M. Neher, *Wesen und Wirken der Weisheit in der Sapientia Salomonis* [2004]; A. Passaro and G. Bellia, eds., *The Book of Wisdom in Modern Research* [2005]; M. V. Blischke, *Die Eschatologie in der Sapientia Solomonis* [2007].)

D. A. HAGNER

Wise Men. See MAGI.

witch, witchcraft. See DIVINATION; FAMILIAR SPIRIT; MAGIC.

withe (withs). The English term *withe* refers to a flexible twig used as a band. In the plural spelling *withs*, it is used by the KJV to render *yeter H3857* in one passage (Jdg. 16:7–9), referring to the "seven fresh bowstrings" (NRSV, NIV mg.) with which DELILAH bound SAMSON. The Hebrew word is clearly used of bowstrings in at least one passage (Ps. 11:2; prob. also in Job 30:1); in its only other reference it apparently refers to a tent-cord (Job 4:21). Some believe that the objects used by Delilah were animal tendons still wet (cf. NJPS; *HALOT*, 2:452); others suggest that they were simply leather strips (cf. NIV, "thongs").

witness. See MARTYR; TESTIMONY.

witness, altar of. See ED.

witness of the Spirit. A witness presupposes a person, object, content, or event concerning which TESTIMONY is given. The NT makes it clear that the primary witness of the HOLY SPIRIT is to Christ, and not to himself or initially to a body of doctrine (Jn. 14:26; 15:26; 16:7–15; cf. Matt. 16:16–17; 1 Jn. 2:20–22). Though the Spirit's witness focuses upon the person and work of Christ, it moves out from that central point to incorporate (a) the totality of God's saving acts for sinners, (b) the intrinsic and instrumental authority of Scripture, (c) the nature of fallen human beings and their response to God, and (d) a ministry of ASSURANCE and instruction to God's own.

The center of the NT REVELATION is that Jesus is LORD and MESSIAH (Acts 2:36). It is this truth which the ANTICHRIST denies but which the Christian affirms, having received "an anointing from the Holy One" (1 Jn. 2:20–22; cf. Matt. 16:16–17; Rom. 10:9–10). In such a confession, the Spirit witnesses to the significance of the total redemptive program of God, and believers' eyes are opened to understand (1 Cor. 2:10–16; 2 Cor. 3:12–18). Having inspired selected individuals to write the truth of God (2 Tim. 2:16; 2 Pet. 1:21), the Spirit gives an accompanying inward illumination enabling us to appreciate the objective revelation as God's truth and to apprehend its meaning (1 Cor. 2:10–16; 2 Cor. 3:12–18). The Spirit also convicts people of their sin and of righteousness, warning of coming judgment (Jn. 16:8–11), and ministers to believers, assuring them of their relationship with God (Rom. 8:15–16; Gal. 4:6) and granting them spiritual discernment (1 Cor. 2:15, 16; cf. Rom. 12:2; Phil. 1:10; Col. 1:9).

(See A. Kuyper, *The Work of the Holy Spirit* [1900]; H. B. Swete, *The Holy Spirit in the Ancient Church* [1912]; C. W. Hodge, "The Witness of the Holy Spirit to the Bible," *PTR* 11 [1913]: 41–84; B. Ramm, *The Witness of the Spirit* [1960].)

R. N. LONGENECKER

wizard. See DIVINATION.

wolf. A large wild and predatory canine. The wolf (Heb. *zĕʾēb H2269*; Gk. *lykos G3380*) is mentioned a number of times in the OT or NT, and it must have been a familiar member of the Palestine FAUNA throughout the biblical period (cf. Jer. 5:6; Hab. 1:8). As the wild ancestor of the domestic dog, and a close relative of the oriental JACKAL, the wolf is by nature a hunter; its large size—up to 48 in. long with a tail of 15 in., and weighing 100 pounds—makes it formidable; so it is not surprising that the Lord spoke of it as a danger to flocks (Matt. 7:15; 10:16; Lk. 10:3; Jn. 10:12; cf. Ezek. 22:7; Zeph. 3:3; Acts 20:29). In JACOB's testament, BENJAMIN is compared to "a ravenous wolf" that "devours the prey" and "divides the plunder" (Gen. 49:27). In ISAIAH's eschatological visions, how-

ever, the wolf is pictured as a docile creature, living alongside the lamb (Isa. 11:6, 65:25).

The gray wolf (*Canis lupus*) was once found over much of N. America, Europe, and Asia; now it has been exterminated from most settled areas and is plentiful only in large tracts of undisturbed forests and steppes. It still lives in Palestine in small numbers, but is no longer a danger to livestock. Because of their greater size, wolves can take much larger prey than foxes and jackals. They also hunt in packs that can overcome even large deer or cattle, but for most of their time they are content with smaller animals, including mice, insects, crabs, and even fish. (See E. P. Walker, *Mammals of the World*, 5th ed. [1991], 2:1065–76.)   G. S. CANSDALE

woman. The standard biblical terms for "woman" are Hebrew *ʾiššâ* H851 and Greek *gynē* G1222. Both of these terms are frequently used with the meaning of "wife." Several other words may be regarded as partial synonyms (e.g., Heb. *gĕbîrâ* H1485, "mistress [of the house], lady [of the king]," Gk. *presbytis* G4567, "old woman").

I. In the OT

A. Status and rights.
The primary focus must be upon the Genesis account of CREATION and the description of woman's origin. The initial narrative (Gen. 1:26–27) seems to imply that woman as the female counterpart to man is an essential component in the IMAGE OF GOD. Following the structure of Hebrew poetic parallelism, "the image of God" in v. 27b corresponds to "male and female" in v. 27c. The theological implications of this fact are not even hinted at in the Genesis account; however, woman's unique and distinctive role arises from her participation in the *imago Dei*.

The more detailed anthropocentric account of creation in Gen. 2:18–25 raises several questions. One is the question of etymology, for ADAM is reported as saying, "she shall be called 'woman,' [*ʾiššâ*] / for she was taken out of man [*ʾîš*]" (v. 23). Comparative linguistics, however, makes clear that the noun *ʾiššâ* must have derived from a Semitic root such as *ʾnṯ*; the consonant *t* becomes *š* in Hebrew, and the doubling or gemination of the *š* in the Hebrew word betrays the dissimilation of an earlier *n*, which is preserved in the plural form, *nāšîm*. In the word for "man," by contrast, the consonant *š* does correspond to an original Semitic *š*. In the case of both nouns, however, it is uncertain what the meaning of the original root may have been (cf. *NIDOTTE*, 1:388 and 537–38). Thus the statement in Genesis, like comparable passages (e.g., CAIN in 4:1; JACOB in 25:26; MOSES in Exod. 2:10) rests more on a verbal resemblance (popular etymology) than on an exact etymological relationship. Whatever the derivation, the point of the Genesis account is the essential humanity, equality, and oneness of woman with man.

The account of the FALL assigns an influential role to woman, but even earlier she is regarded as "a helper suitable for [man]" (Gen. 2:18), indicating man's incompleteness and perhaps weakness apart from woman. Equally important for understanding the status and role of woman in the structure of OT thought is the proper name EVE (*ḥawwâ* H2558, by popular etymology, "life"), given to her "because she would become the mother of all the living" (3:20). It is a matter of some debate whether the subordinate role of woman is a result of creation or of the fall, but the latter seems supported by the text (cf. 3:16). Woman's rights were protected under the authority of the divine law: "Honor your father and mother" (Exod. 20:12; cf. Lev. 20:9; Deut. 5:16; 27:16).

B. Family and domestic roles.
In the OT the primary position of the woman was within the structure of the FAMILY. She did, in fact, move from one family unit to another. Not only in patriarchal times but also throughout the OT history, the father exercised primary responsibility for the female members of the family, whether daughters or servants, until that responsibility was transferred to the husband or new master. (Cf. ABRAHAM and HAGAR, Gen. 16:2; LABAN and his daughters LEAH and RACHEL, Gen. 28–31; DAVID and MICHAL, 1 Sam. 18:20, 27; 19:11–17.) It is important to note here the concept of the kinsman-redeemer and its relationship to the widow. See GOEL.

Probably most important is the role of childbearing as the fulfillment of a woman's position in OT society. BARRENNESS was considered a curse from God and a diminishing of a woman's divinely assigned station in life. (Cf. SARAH, Gen. 17:15;

The domestic tasks of women living near ancient Laodicea include processing pomegranates.

RACHEL, Gen. 30; and HANNAH, 1 Sam. 1:2.) The biblical text also calls attention to the domestic duties of the wife, such as making bread, sewing, carrying water, and generally providing for her husband and family. (Cf. Gen. 24:11, 13–16, 19, 20; 27:9; Prov. 31:10–31; Gen. 29:6; Exod. 2:16; 35:26; 1 Sam. 2:19; Gen. 18:6; 2 Sam. 13:8; Jdg. 4:18; 1 Sam. 9:11; 2 Ki. 4:8–10.) The woman's unique status in the home is indicated by the separate mention of her in the tenth commandment (Exod. 20:17).

Within the structure of the family a daughter might become the heir of the father's estate provided there were no sons. The inheritance could not, however, be transferred from the tribe through marriage, and interestingly enough a daughter could marry outside of her tribe only if the husband took the wife's family name (Num. 27:1–8; 36:6–9; Neh. 7:63). Unmarried daughters were to be provided for by the eldest brother (Gen. 31:14–15). Similarly, the childless widow is to be cared for also by the eldest brother, and a widowed sister-in-law may bear children by the brother-in-law; this latter situation came under the law of the kinsman-redeemer. Care is also exercised that the rights of the woman may be protected when a DIVORCE is required; however, the husband does seem to have the favored position in the divorce arrangements. But the OT minimizes the possibilities for divorce and is careful to indicate God's disfavor with the practice generally. (Cf. Deut. 22:13–19; 24:1–4; Isa. 50:1; Jer. 3:8; Mal. 2:16.)

The question of morality will be discussed below, but it is essential to note here that one of the primary roles of the woman within marriage was sexual fulfillment. This much is implied in the early account of creation (Gen. 1:26–28; 2:18–25), but the book of Deuteronomy repeatedly calls attention to the sexual dimension of husband-wife relationships. Even a captive woman may be married if the Israelite is attracted to her physical beauty; and once having been married to an Israelite she assumes a new social status in the community (cf. Deut. 21:10–14). "If a man has recently married, he must not be sent to war or have any other duty laid on him. For one year he is to be free to stay at home and bring happiness to the wife he has married" (24:5). Undergirding this same idea is the sexual emphasis of the SONG OF SOLOMON. This love poem has been the subject of much misunderstanding and misinterpretation, but its stress upon the physical pleasures of human love are presented without shame or embarrassment. Finally, it should be noted that her respect within the home is a legal condition of OT morality. Supported by the Mosaic code of Exod. 20:12, the writers of the book of Proverbs repeatedly mention the mother as well as the father in the admonitions of respect (cf. Prov. 1:8; 6:20; 10:1; 15:20; 20:20; 23:22).

C. As leaders in society. That women actively may participate in the political life of the nation is obvious, particularly during the monarchy. BATHSHEBA, the mother of SOLOMON, maneuvered the events toward the end of David's reign to assure Solomon the throne (1 Ki. 1–3). The political and spiritual reforms of King ASA included the removal of his mother, Queen MAACAH (1 Ki. 15:13). In 2 Ki. 11 is the record of Queen ATHALIAH and a former king's sister, JEHOSHEBA, both struggling to control the throne. But it is DEBORAH and JEZEBEL who are best remembered for their military and political exploits. Although the 2nd-cent. writer of the book of Ecclesiasticus mentions only outstanding male leaders of Israel's history, the biblical text is careful to acknowledge the positive and negative effects women have had upon Israel's history. The song of Deborah further acknowledges the role of JAEL, the wife of HEBER, who slew JABIN, king of Canaan (Jdg. 4:2, 17, 23, 24). For her part, Jezebel in her wickedness typifies the idolatrous woman in the church at THYATIRA (Rev. 2:20).

D. Morality and spiritual idealism. The relationship of the image of God to female sexuality (see above) implies the highest appreciation of her nature. The addition of "suitable for him" (*kĕnegdô*) to "helper" in the text of Gen. 2:18 suggests not only a spiritual but also an anatomical complement of woman to man. Basically the woman's morality from the sexual standpoint involved her faithfulness to this divinely created role. Perhaps for this reason the effect of the fall is most seriously demonstrated in the pain of childbearing and the misuse of her sexuality (3:16).

Against this background, the Levitical statutes provide the severest penalties for violations of such a high standard of sexuality. Woman's equal status under the law is underlined by the fact that the sin of adultery or fornication calls for the death penalty for both the man and the woman (Lev. 20:10). It is in the prophetic literature and especially the book of HOSEA that the full implications of sexuality for spiritual adultery are most vividly set forth. The hermeneutical problem of this book must not blind one to the serious nature of IDOLATRY as spiritual adultery. As idolatry robs human beings of their relationship with Yahweh, so sexual immorality robs them of realizing their highest human potential. But Hosea is not alone in this emphasis. The accusation of harlotry is a familiar theme describing Israel's unfaithfulness (cf. Isa. 1:21; 23:15–17; Jer. 3:1–8; Ezek. 16:15–41). A woman's failure in this area, however, was certainly not beyond forgiveness, and the OT presents one of the greatest illustrations of divine grace in the case of RAHAB, who not only was forgiven but was later exemplified as a pattern of faith (cf. Josh. 6:17–25; Hab. 11:31; Jas. 2:25). In this connection, the woman Jezebel becomes the antithesis of Rahab (1 Ki. 16:21; 2 Ki. 9:7–37; Rev. 2:20).

The OT is faithful to call attention to the breach of these high standards of morality, whether it be Judah and Tamar (Gen. 38:1–26) or David and Bathsheba (2 Sam. 11:3) or Amnon and Tamar (13:10). The practice of PROSTITUTION, which in OT times was so closely related to religion, particularly Baalism, is strictly forbidden (Lev. 19:29; 20:6–9; Deut. 23:17). The influence of Baalism always posed a threat to these standards, and Israel never seems to have been very successful in freeing herself from these degrading forms of pagan cult life (1 Ki. 14:24; 15:12; 22:46; 2 Ki. 23:7; Hos. 4:14).

Although women could portray the highest of spiritual ideals, as is illustrated by Hannah (1 Sam. 1; 2), the "lesser" vices of jealousy, selfish ambition, and pride, as well as the ultimate sin of idolatry, are all represented in Israel's history. Note for example Sarah's jealousy (Gen. 16:1–6), Rebekah's schemes to favor Jacob (27:5–46), and the paganizing influence of Solomon's wives (1 Ki. 11:1–8). A woman could be the cause of one's spiritual fall, as in the case of Samson (Jdg. 13–16), or she could be a great spiritual asset, as illustrated in the political influence of an Esther or by the practical assistance of someone like the widow of Zarephath in Elijah's ministry (1 Ki. 17).

But it is primarily the book of Proverbs that calls attention to the high ideals of womanhood. The descriptive term is *zārâ* (fem. of *zār* H2424, lit., "strange, unauthorized"), indicating an adulteress or prostitute (Prov. 2:16 et al.), but other terms are used to describe the antithesis of the virtuous woman: evil (immoral), loud, quarrelsome (6:24; 9:13; 21:19). Such a person is contrasted with the "kindhearted woman" in 11:16, but the classical text on the woman of virtue is 31:10–31. A careful examination of this passage will indicate the uniqueness of a godly woman in OT life and thought.

E. As members of the covenant community. Nothing illustrates the high place of woman in the OT teaching more clearly than her role in the religious life of Israel. On the one hand, her spirituality is sometimes far superior to her male counterpart, as is seen in a Deborah, a Hannah, a Jochebed, or a

Ruth, Miriam and other women participated in the dance celebrating God's deliverance from Egypt (Exod. 15:20). Since there are references to women as weavers (Prov. 31:19), we might assume that this art, so essential to the construction of the tent or tabernacle (cf. Exod. 35–40), may have been practiced by women, although explicit reference is made only to men. In the later history of Israel, women are specifically mentioned among the "singers" who lamented the death of Josiah (2 Chr. 35:25). After the exile, the total number of "singers" was 245 and included both men and women (Neh. 7:67). It may be assumed that the inclusive phrase "all the congregation of Israel" would include women at such great festivals as the Passover, Pentecost, and the Feast of Tabernacles.

But above all is the OT designation of PROPHETESS for Huldah (2 Ki. 22:14; 2 Chr. 34:22), Miriam (Exod. 15:20), Deborah (Jdg. 4:4), and the wife of Isaiah (Isa. 8:3; cf. also the false prophetess Noadiah, Neh. 6:14). Although the Levite priesthood was closed to women, the other offices of royalty and prophecy seem on occasion to have fallen to unusual women. When the OT picture of women is presented in contrast to Israel's neighbors, it is not difficult to see the advantages and advancement of Hebrew religion. D. M. Pratt's observation is worth noting: "Under the Hebrew system the position of woman was in marked contrast with her status in surrounding heathen nations. Her liberties were greater, her employments more varied and important, her social standing more respectful and commanding" (*ISBE* [1929], 5:3100).

II. In the NT. The NT builds upon the OT tradition; in some ways it is clearer, but in some respects more problematic.

A. Life and ministry of Jesus. The Gospels are replete with references to women who were directly involved in the ministry of Jesus. But the most important woman in the NT is MARY, MOTHER OF JESUS. Her importance does not derive from her active role in the ministry of Jesus, but from her maternal relationship to the Son of God. The angelic words in Lk. 1:28 describe Mary as "highly favored," so her unique role is affirmed. During the earthly ministry of Jesus, Mary remains in the background, and it is to be assumed that Jesus always remained close to his mother (Jesus' apparently terse reply recorded in Jn. 2:4 and his stress upon the will of God as the condition for familial ties in Matt. 12:46–50 do not invalidate this point). Thus it is understandable why he made special preparations for her while still on the cross (Jn. 19:25–27). In a somewhat similar relationship, ELIZABETH the mother of JOHN THE BAPTIST is portrayed as an agent of God's power (Lk. 1:5–25, 39–66).

In the ministry of Jesus, specific women play an important role. Mention is made of Mary Magdalene, Mary the mother of James and Joseph, "the other Mary," the mother of the sons of Zebedee, as well as Mary and Martha. Much of Jesus' ministry was centered upon the needs and requests of women. One of Jesus' earliest acts of healing was the mother of Peter (Mk. 1:29–31). In addition to the healing of the woman with the hemorrhage (Lk. 8:43–48), there is recorded the raising from the dead of the son of the widow of Nain (7:11–17), the healing of the daughter of the woman from Syro-Phoenicia (Mk. 7:24–30), and the raising of Lazarus in response to the pleas of Mary and Martha (Jn. 11:1–43).

At the same time, Jesus often addressed his teaching to women and used them as illustrations of spiritual truths: a woman loses a coin (Lk. 15:8); two women are pictured as grinding at the mill prior to the PAROUSIA (17:35); at the well in Sychar it is a woman of questionable reputation who meets Jesus (Jn. 4); and the textually uncertain passage of Jn. 7:53—8:11 centers upon a woman charged with the capital offense of adultery. Observe also that it is women who are specifically mentioned as following Jesus on his last journey to Jerusalem and his crucifixion (Matt. 27:55–56); they were present at the scene of the crucifixion (Lk. 23:49); they prepared the body with spices and ointments for burial and followed the body to the grave site (Matt. 27:61; Lk. 23:55–56); on the morning of the resurrection they were first at the tomb (Matt. 28:1; Mk. 16:1; Lk. 24:1; Jn. 20:1); and they were the first to witness the risen Lord in his triumph over death (Matt. 28:9; Mk. 16:9; Jn. 20:14). Although it has been conjectured that perhaps Jesus might have been married, there is no substantial evidence to support this claim (cf. W. E. Phipps, *Was Jesus*

Married? The Distortion of Sexuality in the Christian Tradition (1970).

B. In the early church. The post-ascension narrative of the church describes a band of 120, but special notice is given to Mary the mother of Jesus and "the women" (Acts 1:14). The church at PHILIPPI owes its origin to the conversion of Lydia (16:14, 40). The apostolic history records how the church that met in the home of Mary, the mother of John Mark, prayerfully executed the release of Peter from prison (12:6–17). PRISCILLA's importance is underscored by the fact that she is often mentioned first in conjunction with her husband Aquila (cf. Acts 18:2, 18, 26; Rom. 16:3; 1 Cor. 16:19; 2 Tim. 4:19).

The NT admonitions of submissiveness and quietness on the part of women in the church (1 Cor. 14:33–36; 1 Tim. 2:11–12; 1 Pet. 3:1) have been interpreted by some to mean that Peter and Paul were biased against women. Yet it should be observed that in the closing greetings of Rom. 16 no less than eight different Christian women are mentioned by name: Phoebe, Prisca (Priscilla), Mary, Tryphaena, Tryphosa, Persis, Julia, and the sister of Nereus (16:1, 3, 6, 12, 15). Lois and Eunice, mother and grandmother of TIMOTHY, were highly regarded by the apostle (2 Tim. 1:5; 3:14–15). Although Paul's instructions regarding women, on the surface, seem harsh, it should always be remembered that it is the female analogy that he uses to describe the church as a bride or wife, and certainly the church occupies a central place in Paul's theology (Eph. 4:21–32; cf. Rev. 19:1–10).

C. The offices of prophetess and deaconess in the early church. The word *office* may be too formal, but in Acts 21:8–9 the daughters of Philip are described as "prophesying," and in Rom. 16:1 Paul describes Phoebe as a *diakonos* G1356 of the church in Cenchrea (for discussion of this passage see PHOEBE). It is difficult to ascertain the reasons for the restrictive roles implied in some passages (1 Cor. 14:33–35; 1 Tim. 2:11–12) when all other evidence points to dramatic participation on the part of women in the early church.

It is possible that the "list" of WIDOWS in 1 Tim. 5:9–10 was an indication of a distinct order within the church, and some have thought that it was these widows who were deaconesses (cf. Rom. 16:1; Phil. 4:1–3; 1 Tim. 3:8–13). Chrysostom, Tertullian, and other church fathers recognized such an office with regular duties as prayer, fasting, visiting the sick, instruction of women, assisting in baptism, and aiding in the preparation of communion. In the light of these facts, it might be best to interpret the restrictions on women in public worship in 1 Cor. 14:33–35 as applying more specifically to the

Icon of Mary, mother of Jesus, from the entrance of her traditional tomb on the Mount of Olives.

charismatic experience of the Corinthian church and to suggest that 1 Tim. 2:11–12 refers to the governing responsibilities of administration. This would still leave the opportunities of service open to women as deaconesses without contradicting these other statements by Paul and Peter.

D. Pattern of life. The teachings of Christ regarding divorce are intended to protect the rights of women, and the NT reinforces the OT emphasis on woman's primary domestic role. According to some, Matt. 5:32 implies that divorce forces a woman into a life of prostitution simply to survive. Paul's description of the sexual relationship in 1 Cor. 7:1–7 is unparalleled in ancient thought and literature (cf. v. 4, "the husband's body does not belong to him alone but also to his wife"). Paul is equally insistent that the Christian wife must not dress or act in any way that might bring shame to her husband. This may have been the motivation behind Paul's statements about the length of a woman's hair in 11:2–16. In this same connection, the husband and wife relationship is founded upon the highest ideal: Christ's love for the church and the church's submission and obedience to her Lord (Eph. 5:21–33; cf. Tit. 2:1–10; 1 Pet. 3:1–7).

E. Sexual perversion and the symbol of evil. Christ's ministry seems to have attracted social outcasts including prostitutes (cf. Lk. 7:36–50; Jn. 7:53—8:11; 4:1–42), but the discipline of the church is specifically directed toward those who violate the seventh commandment (1 Cor. 5 and 6). The act of sexual intercourse is not simply a physical act, but a symbol of marital commitment; therefore, no Christian can join himself to a prostitute without becoming one with her (1 Cor. 6:12–20; Eph. 5:21–33). The increase of female promiscuity is one mark of the "last days" according to Paul (2 Tim. 3:7). The church at Thyatira (Rev. 2:18, 24) was rebuked for allowing "the woman Jezebel" to practice immorality and to eat food sacrificed to idols. This may be a reference to a female cult within the church or simply a heretical prophetess in the church.

(See further E. McDonald, *The Position of Women as Reflected in Semitic Codes of Law* [1931]; E. Deen, *All of the Women of the Bible* [1955]; F. Zerbst, *The Office of Women in the Church: A Study in Practical Theology* [1955]; R. C. Prohl, *Woman in the Church* [1957]; C. C. Ryrie, *The Place of Women in the Church* [1958]; H. Lockyer, *The Women of the Bible* [1967]; J. B. Hurley, *Man and Woman in Biblical Perspective* [1981]; B. Witherington, *Women in the Earliest Churches* [1988]; K. E. Corley, *Private Women, Public Meals: Social Conflict and Women in the Synoptic Tradition* [1993]; V. H. Matthews et al., eds., *Gender and Law in the Hebrew Bible and the Ancient Near East* [1998]; R. S. Kraemer and M. R. D'Angelo, eds., *Women and Christian Origins* [1999]; M. A. Getty-Sullivan, *Women in the New Testament* [2001]; R. Bauckham, *Gospel Women: Studies of the Named Women in the Gospels* [2002]; M. Dillon, *Girls and Women in Classical Greek Religion* [2002]; J. Evans Grubbs, *Women and Law in the Roman Empire: A Sourcebook on Marriage, Divorce and Widowhood* [2002]; H. J. Marsman, *Women in Ugarit and Israel: Their Social and Religious Position in the Context of the Ancient Near East* [2003]; B. W. Winter, *Roman Wives, Roman Widows: The Appearance of New Women and the Pauline Communities* [2003], C. B. Anderson, *Women, Ideology, and Violence: Critical Theory and the Construction of Gender in the Book of the Covenant and the Deuteronomic Law* [2004]; F. T. Gench, *Back to the Well: Women's Encounters with Jesus in the Gospels* [2004]; C. Meyers, *Households and Holiness: The Religious Culture of Israelite Women* [2005]; M. B. Schwartz and K. J. Kaplan, *The Fruit of Her Hands: A Psychology of Biblical Woman* [2007].)

D. M. LAKE

wood. See FLORA; FOREST.

wool. In the Bible, the terms for "wool" (Heb. *ṣemer* H7547; Gk. *erion* G2250) always refer to the thick undercoat of SHEEP. The sheep in Palestine were sometimes black or brown, a recessive trait providentially appearing more frequently in JACOB's flocks than would be expected by normal Mendelian heredity (Gen. 31:10). The wool was occasionally dyed scarlet (Heb. 9:19). Shearing in one piece gave a desirable FLEECE, which was washed first in the brook and later with soap to make it nearly snow white. Following the cleansing, the usual carding, spinning, and weaving occurred. Some wool from the tanneries was stuffed into mattresses and quilts instead after being removed by slaked lime (cf. *ISBE* [1929], 5:3104).

The wool was woven into outer garments, never mixed with LINEN (Deut. 22:11); this was especially true of the clothing worn by priests (Lev. 19:19). A good wife "selects wool and flax" (Prov. 31:13). Wool was a symbol of riches (Ezek. 27:19). The king of MOAB gave Israel annually "the wool of a hundred thousand rams" (2 Ki. 3:4). God's liberality is poetically phrased, "He spreads the snow like wool" (Ps. 147:16). Israel's sin was condemned by saying the nation was like a harlot who receives wool from her lovers (Hos. 2:5), but God warns, "I will take back my wool and my linen" (v. 9).

For the purification of the TABERNACLE and its vessels, in addition to blood and water, scarlet wool and HYSSOP were used in the sprinkling during the covenant ceremony (Heb. 9:19). Probably this wool was scarlet yarn (Num. 19:6), burned with the heifer and used in cleansing lepers (Lev. 19:6). Part of the first wool was offered to the priests as their due (Deut. 18:4). GIDEON is famous for putting out the fleece (Jdg. 6:37). Those who revile against the righteous will be eaten like the moth devours wool (Isa. 51:8).

The whiteness of wool as a symbol of purity is contrasted with the crimson of sins (Isa. 1:18) and compared to snow (Ps. 147:16) or the hair of the Ancient of Days (Dan. 7:9) who reappears in John's vision (Rev. 1:14). R. L. MIXTER

word. This English term has a wide variety of senses, including (1) a small and meaningful linguistic unit, whether spoken or written; (2) a comment or conversation; (3) a saying or proverb; (4) an order or command. These and other meanings are reflected also in biblical usage. In the phrase "the word of God/the Lord," or in contexts where "the/his word" refers to a divine communication, this term indicates a supernatural REVELATION and may allude to portions of SCRIPTURE. Thus in modern usage the BIBLE as a whole is often referred to as the Word of God.

    I. Terms
        A. Hebrew
        B. Greek
   II. The word in the OT
        A. The word and revelation
        B. The word in the early prophets
        C. The word and prophecy
        D. The word and the law
        E. The word in the Psalms
  III. The word in Greek philosophy
        A. Introduction
        B. Heraclitus
        C. The Sophists
        D. Plato
        E. Aristotle
        F. Stoicism
        G. Hellenism
        H. Philo
        I. Conclusion
  IV. The word in the NT
        A. General use
        B. The word as the OT
        C. The word to individuals
        D. The word(s) of Jesus
        E. The word as the gospel
        F. Jesus as the Word of God

I. Terms

A. Hebrew. The ordinary Hebrew term for "word" is *dābār* H1821 (cf. the verb *dābar* H1819, usually in the piel stem, "to speak"). Its derivation is uncertain. Some have connected it with a root meaning "to be behind" and suggested that it points to the background of a matter (i.e., the conceptual content or meaning), but this etymology appears fanciful. Because the term can often be translated "thing" or "matter," it has also been suggested that the Hebrew word has both a noetic element (the thought) and a dynamic element (the power). According to this view, "act" or "deed" can be the meaning, and even when words are in view, the acts behind the words have also to be taken into account (cf. Ps. 35:20). Although there is indeed in the Bible a relation between word and thing or power (as will be apparent in the discussion of the word of God in both the OT and the NT), it is doubtful that this theological concept derived from (or gave rise to) the twofold lexical meaning.

B. Greek. The SEPTUAGINT usually renders Hebrew *dābār* with one of two Greek terms, *logos* G3364 ("word, saying, speech, reason, account," etc.) and *rhēma* G4839 ("word, statement," and under the influence of the Heb., "thing, matter, event"). Their distribution is not without interest. The term *rhēma* is almost three times as common as *logos* in the PENTATEUCH. The two are almost equally frequent in Judges-Ruth, but then *logos* begins to predominate: it is twice as common in 1 Samuel to Canticles, and eight times as common in the Prophets. Both terms are used also in the NT, where *logos* occurs more than 300 times, and *rhēma* fewer than 70. Although in certain contexts their semantic differences are obvious (cf. the use of both terms in Matt. 12:36), the distinction between them is frequently neutralized, and in many passages they become basically interchangeable (e.g., Jn. 12:48).

II. The word in the OT

A. The word and revelation. In the OT the word is the supreme means by which God the Creator makes known both himself and his will to his creatures. Thus one might say that biblical religion

is primarily the religion of the ear rather than the eye (cf. the importance of "hearing" in the Bible). This does not mean, however, that biblical religion is intrinsically verbal or abstract. The divine word, in distinction from many human words, is coextensive with that which it says or represents. Its most important attribute, then, is TRUTH (2 Sam. 7:28; cf Jn. 17:11). Truth in this sense is not abstract. It carries with it the sense of faithfulness, reliability. What God says is true. If the reference is future, then it will surely come to pass. This, in turn, implies the force or power of the word. It accomplishes what it signifies. The OT speaks also of deceitful or empty words.

The word, as such, is powerful. This is especially true of the word of God. By it God intervenes actively in the affairs of human beings. The word is historical, not merely in the sense that it records history, but in the dynamic sense that it makes history. This is revealed already in the fact that CREATION is by the word of God ("God said," Gen. 1:3 et al.; Ps. 33:6–9; cf. Isa. 40:26). The whole history of Israel offers further demonstration. An important point in this connection is that through the LXX translation the force of the Hebrew *dābār* impresses itself upon the corresponding Greek terms.

B. The word in the early prophets. Since God's revelation is primarily through the word, there develops in Israel the unique office of the prophet, the divine spokesman. See PROPHETS AND PROPHECY. The prophet is someone to whom the word of the Lord (Yahweh) comes and who then declares this word to the people. Attempts have sometimes been made to find a stronger ecstatic and visionary element in early prophecy. That it has a visionary side is incontestable, for right down to the great prophets Isaiah, Jeremiah, and Ezekiel, the word often comes in visions. There is also a formative side to prophecy, for signs and images often accompany the spoken word as a guarantee that the word itself will be "seen" in its fulfillment.

On the other hand, it is highly significant that from a very early period the oral aspect is predominant. The heart of prophecy is that God speaks to the prophet and through the prophet. The PATRIARCHS already are addressed by God (Gen. 22:1; 46:2). MOSES is the prototype of all the succeeding prophets (cf. Exod. 3:4 et al.). SAMUEL is called by Yahweh (1 Sam. 3:1–14), and when he expresses his readiness to hear, a message is given to him which he is then to pass on to the people. The process is exactly the same in 15:10–26, where the word of judgment on SAUL is first given to Samuel and then delivered by him to the king. Saul, in turn, is rejected because he has rejected the word of the Lord.

The tradition of Samuel is magnificently maintained by NATHAN, ELIJAH, and MICAIAH. Throughout this period the word of the Lord comes to the prophets, is declared by them, and then, as the word of truth and power, comes infallibly to fulfillment in forgiveness, salvation, or judgment. The difference between the true prophet and the false prophet is that the latter has no real word from God, so that he can speak only human words that will inevitably be discovered to be false by events. The true word of the Lord comes to pass—it cannot be withstood (cf. 2 Ki. 1:17 et al.).

C. The word and prophecy. What may be seen in earlier prophecy finds classical statement and illustration in the great writing prophets from AMOS and HOSEA onward. In some cases these prophets actually use the formula "The word of the Lord [that] came ..." as an introduction to their words (e.g., Hos. 1:1). This formula epitomizes the prophetic understanding. What the prophets say or write is what God has spoken to them and is saying through them. The prophet is called to his work (Isa. 6; Jer. 1; Ezek. 1). The word of the Lord is laid upon him, so that it can even be called a burden. It is put upon his lips so that he has to declare it. He has swallowed it like a book, so that it is part of his inner being. Even though it brings him derision and suffering, so that he longs to be silent, it is like a fire in his bones and he has to speak (Jer. 20:9). He knows that whether the people listen or not, the word has to be proclaimed, and when it infallibly comes to pass they will know that a prophet has been among them (Ezek. 2:3–8).

This message is not the prophet's own word. It has irresistible force. As the word of the God who sees the end from the beginning, what it says is true and what it proclaims will be done. The prophet does not produce the word from within himself. It is no mere matter of religious insights; the word is from God. What the *prophet* says is true because it is what God says. It has force because it is the word of the Creator of the world and the Ruler of history. It can take the form of foretelling — the prediction of deliverance or judgment — because God is the Lord of time. It confronts sinners with a sure promise, a solemn warning, or an unconditional command because it is the word of the God of grace and righteousness from whom all blessing comes and to whom an account must be rendered.

D. The word and the law. A contrast is sometimes drawn between prophecy and the LAW (cf. Jer. 18:18). In the light of the biblical teaching, however, this is more fanciful than real. The prophets declare the will and word of God to their own age, but they do so in the context and on the basis of the will and word of God for his people in every age, that is, the revelation of the law. If the word of prophecy comes to both prophet and people with all the force, certainty, and claim of God himself, this is no less true of the law. Moses, after all, was the first and greatest of the prophets. The law, imparted by God to Moses and through Moses to the people, is also the word of God.

This fact may be seen in the description of the TEN COMMANDMENTS as "the words of the covenant" (Exod. 34:28). They are the ten sayings (Decalogue) which lie at the heart of the divine covenant with Israel. The same applies to the words Moses addressed to the people and then wrote in a book (24:3–4). These were the words of the Lord which the people promised to obey. Deuteronomy brings out this aspect of the law even more clearly. It embodies the words of Moses (Deut. 1:1), which he received from God and then declared to the people. It is here that Moses calls himself a prophet (18:15). The word or commandment he proclaims is a prophetic word. It is not distant, so that it has to be sought in heaven or beyond the sea. It is in the mouth and in the heart (30:11–14). In other words, it is a true prophetic word declared and received. The law, genuinely understood, is no mere code of external regulations for outward acceptance and performance. It is the preached word of the divine promise and command which may be performed because it carries its own call and promise with it. If technically the law belongs to the priest and the word to the prophet, this is no final antithesis. JEREMIAH himself was priest as well as prophet. The law, too, is word, just as the word can also be law.

E. The word in the Psalms. The Psalter adds little new to our understanding of the word, but it

Possible site of Tishbe (el-Istib), hometown of the prophet Elijah, who proclaimed the word of God boldly.

does bring certain things into focus and it also contains a magnificent characterization of the word. The relationship of the word to creation (Ps. 33) and to the law (Ps. 119) are especially emphasized. In Ps. 119 "word" is significantly used as an alternative of "law," "commandments," "statutes," etc. The psalm is drastically misunderstood, however, if this is taken to imply a legalization of the word. The very reverse is true. Like Deuteronomy, this psalm brings out the ultimate prophetic quality of the law. In so doing, it gives perhaps the best single description of the word in the whole of the Bible — a description that may be applied not merely to the law but to all Scripture with equal appropriateness and truth. The word stands in heaven (v. 89). It is a light on the path (v. 105). It gives life (v. 25 et al.). It also gives understanding (v. 169). Its sum is truth (v. 160). It may be trusted (v. 42). Hope may also be reposed in it (v. 74). It demands obedience (v. 57). It is hidden in the heart (v. 11). It is sweet to the taste of the righteous (v. 103). It brings as much delight as the finding of great spoil (v. 162). The tongue of the righteous will speak of it (v. 172). In the last resort it is the object, not only of faith and hope, but also of love, for it is because God's law is God's word that the psalmist, at the very opposite pole from legalism, can break out and say: "Oh how I love your law!" (v. 97).

III. The word in Greek philosophy

A. Introduction. Simultaneously with the development of the doctrine of the word of God in the OT there took place a very different development of the Logos in Greek philosophy. Since the NT had to use the term against a Hellenistic background, it is necessary to take a brief glance at the significance the word acquired in the Greek world. It should be noted that the Greek development is along two main lines: (1) the noetic power of estimating things, or the rational content of things; (2) a metaphysical reality gradually expanding into the concept of a cosmological being, almost a second god.

B. Heraclitus. The main contribution of Heraclitus was to see in the Logos the interconnection of human beings to one another, to the world, and to God. The Logos here is both word and the content of word. Both speech and action follow from it. It is the eternal order behind things, a cosmic law, the basis of the psyche. In the last resort, it is not a word from without, but the word immanent in human beings. The eye rather than the ear is the main instrument through which it is received.

C. The Sophists. Among the Sophists the word is more closely associated with the mind. It is the rational faculty which underlies speech and thought. As such it is indispensable to political and cultural life. It also plays an important role in pedagogy. The closer relation to the human faculty carries with it a radical departure from the earlier conception of the Logos as a principle of cosmic proportions.

D. Plato. Plato follows the same line of thought as the Sophists, but not with the same degree of individualism. The Logos is more than the individual faculty. There is a common Logos based ultimately on the agreement between words and things. The Logos derives from, and also interprets, things. It is not just an opinion, a private view. Combining thought, word, and thing, it is larger and has a fuller reality than the individual faculty of thought.

E. Aristotle. In Aristotle there is an awareness of the twofold nature of the Logos as word and understanding on the one side, the result of word and understanding on the other. People speak the word, but in some sense their actions are also controlled by it. Since the Logos leads to action, it may be regarded as the source of the virtue peculiar to human beings.

F. Stoicism. The Stoics returned to the idea of the Logos as a cosmic principle. In the Logos is expressed the rational order of the world, the cosmic reason. Hence the Logos may be equated directly with God or Zeus. It is the germ (*logos spermatikos*) unfolded alike in the organic and the inorganic world. It is also the law which gives knowledge (*logos orthos*). All things come from it and all return to it. The general Logos takes conscious form in the particular Logos of each person. In later Stoicism the Logos is increasingly identified with nature. This interfusion of rational order and vital power produces a pantheistic understanding.

G. Hellenism. The concept of Logos finds a special religious use in the mystery religions. The only Logos is revelation of sacred doctrine. Through it there is union with deity. In some instances it is equivalent to the mystery, and the initiate is called the Logos of God. Logos may also be used for prayer as the way to God. The Logos teaches people both to pray and to worship aright.

In the HERMETIC WRITINGS the god HERMES personifies the Logos. This is genuine personification, not INCARNATION. The principle behind all things is identified with a popular god. The choice of Hermes is based on the fact that he is the divine messenger, the mediator who makes known the will of the gods. A rational element is present, for secret knowledge is disclosed by Hermes. At root, however, Hermes personifies the larger principle of life. This moves inevitably in the direction of pantheism. The relation of the Logos to God is the theme of much speculation. It is the Logos of God, who is also called the father of the Logos. Another line of thought is that the Logos is the image of God and man the image of the Logos. In spite of verbal similarities, however, these ideas bear little relation to the NT doctrine of Jesus Christ as the Word of God.

H. Philo. The concept is an important one for PHILO JUDAEUS. He uses the term in a bewildering number of ways, so that one can hardly speak of a unified Philonic doctrine of the Logos. His basic difficulty here as always is to hold together his Hellenic and his Jewish convictions. Scholars are divided as to whether the Logos is for Philo predominantly a Greek or a Jewish concept. So far as the divine Logos is concerned, it would seem that the roots are Jewish but that the development is greatly influenced by Greek thought.

The Logos of God, or divine Logos, is not God himself. It is a work of God. But it is also God's image and the agent of creation. It can be identified with the noetic cosmos. It serves as an intermediary between the transcendent God and human beings. In it are comprised the *logoi*, the individual ideas. Yet it is more than a mere concept. Philo personifies the Logos: it is the son of God. Philo's Jewish heritage protects him against a genuine deification of the Logos and also against an ultimate immanentism. In fact, the Logos seems to be a convenient link between the Creator God and the world he has made.

I. Conclusion. Since the NT presents Jesus Christ as the incarnate Word of God, it is tempting to look for parallels in the Greek or Hellenistic world, and to see in these the sources of the Johannine understanding. To do so, however, is to ignore the decisive differences to which H. Kleinknecht has drawn attention in a valuable and comprehensive essay (in *TDNT*, vol. 4, esp. pp. 90–91). As he states them, these differences are: (1) that the Greek understanding is rational and intellectual, while the biblical is theological; (2) that the Greek world can divide the one Logos into many *logoi*, whereas the NT knows only one Logos as Mediator between God and man; (3) that the Greek Logos is timeless, while Christ the eternal Word takes on historical singularity as the Word incarnate; and (4) that the Greek Logos has a tendency to merge into the world, so that the world as such is generally son of God, but the biblical Logos is the only-begotten of the Father who, when he takes flesh, is the one Man, Jesus of Nazareth. In the light of these fundamental distinctions the obvious parallels are of little material significance.

IV. The word in the NT

A. General use. In some instances the general sense of *logos* (or *rhēma*) can have theological significance in its own right, but in others it is purely neutral in character. Thus the singular or plural can denote simply what has gone before (e.g., Mk. 7:29). Speech can also be distinguished from a letter (2 Cor. 10:10); worth noting, however, is that the letter also conveys the word (v. 11). The term can also be used for a report or rumor, or for the account in a book (Acts 1:1). It does not have to be intelligible speech; words can be uttered in a tongue as well as with the understanding (1 Cor. 14:19). Anything said is *logos* or *rhēma*.

An interesting use of *logos* is with reference to the empty word as distinct from the reality or the deed. This is theologically impossible when the reference is to the divine word, but human speech may be only speech, that is, without substance. The

vaunting speech of human wisdom, which has neither truth nor power, falls into this category (1 Cor. 1–4). So too does the profession of love without demonstration (1 Jn. 3:18; cf. Jas. 2:14–26). Moreover, words can be bad as well as empty: Paul mentions "unwholesome talk" (Eph. 4:29) and "words of flattery" (1 Thess. 2:5 NRSV; cf. 2 Pet. 2:3), and he compares the words of heretics to a malignant growth (2 Tim. 2:17). James implies that most of us will "stumble" in what we say (Jas. 3:2 ESV).

B. The word as the OT. In a whole group of NT verses, the relevant terms refer either to the word of revelation in the OT or to the OT itself as the written word of God. An interesting point to note in these references is that the word is described sometimes as that of the human author, sometimes as that of the preexistent Christ, and sometimes as that of God, while the usage is indefinite ("it is said") in other instances. Even when the emphasis falls on the human speaker or writer, however, there can be no doubt that he is God's spokesman, so that for all the genuine humanity of the utterance, God is he who truly speaks in the OT. The word, whether it be an individual saying or a whole book, is God's word as well as man's.

Underlying the NT view of the OT, as also of its own message, is the basic biblical and prophetic concept of the word of the Lord. If the phrase "the word of the Lord" (*ho logos tou kyriou*) is not actually used by the NT with reference to the OT, there seems to be a special reason. In the NT, *kyrios* G3261 is a title for Christ himself (see LORD), so that "word(s) of the Lord" is more naturally construed as dominical sayings preserved in the Gospels or in tradition (see below IV.D). Even when OT quotations are given, this phrase is not used as an introductory formula, though *kyrios* with the verb can be used within the quotations themselves (cf. Rom. 12:19). The general way in which the NT speaks of the OT as God's word makes it plain beyond all possible doubt that both the message of the OT and also the individual verses are regarded as divinely given and divinely authoritative. The fullness of this endorsement may be seen from the fact that in a few passages it is hard to say whether the reference is to the OT word or the NT message (cf. Heb. 4:12; Eph. 6:17).

C. The word to individuals. In the NT, as in the OT, there are examples of the word of God coming to special persons, such as SIMEON (Lk. 2:29) and JOHN THE BAPTIST (3:2). It is significant, however, that although the apostles are specifically charged with the ministry of the word, this common OT formula does not occur again after the ministry of John the Baptist. As the NT itself says, the Law and the Prophets were until John (Matt. 11:13). If the word does not come to others, this does not mean, of course, that the word of God is withdrawn, or that the whole mode of revelation has been drastically altered. The word of God no longer comes to specific individuals because it has now come in fullness in Jesus Christ. To speak of a word of God coming to, say, Peter or Paul, would appear inconsistent with the message of the NT as a whole. The definitive word has now been spoken (Heb. 1:1–2). All others are commissioned to preach this word, and any special directions they are given come by vision, or an angel, or the Spirit, or the Lord himself.

The absence of the prophetic formula applies to Jesus also. Though he speaks the word in fullness, the NT does not say that the word came to him as it came to John. A voice spoke at his baptism and at the transfiguration, but this was addressed to the people, not to the Lord. It was an accreditation rather than a commission. Since Jesus is undoubtedly the supreme Prophet, greater even than Moses, one can only conclude that the avoidance of the formula was intentional. His relationship to God, and also to God's word, so completely transcends that of the prophets that to speak of the word coming to him would be inadequate and even misleading. As will be seen later, the heart of the NT message is that the word comes in him rather than to him or through him. His identity with God and with the revelation of God sets the whole concept of the word of God in a new and all-transforming light.

D. The word(s) of Jesus. Though one does not read of the word coming to Jesus, the NT frequently refers to the preaching or sayings of Jesus as the word or words of God. Jesus is a preacher of the word (Mk. 2:2). He mentions those who hear the word of God and do it (Lk. 8:21). In the parable of the sower the seed is the word (Matt. 13:18–23). Far more frequently the NT writes of

Entrance into the chapel of the Cave of St. John on the island of Patmos. According to tradition, it was here that the words of Jesus, as recorded in the book of Revelation, were revealed to the apostle.

what Jesus said or of a saying or sayings of Jesus (cf. Mk. 10:22). Both *rhēma* and *logos* are used in this connection, and when one moves into Acts and the Epistles, such formulae occur as "the word [*rhēma*] of the Lord" (Acts 11:16 NRSV), "the word [*logos*] of the Lord" (8:25), "the words [*logoi*] of the Lord Jesus" (20:35).

Worth noting is that when Paul appeals to a saying as from the Lord in 1 Cor. 7:10, it obviously has conclusive authority. The primitive church felt free to quote these sayings without adhering to a single form of words, but, in spite of all the variations, there is confidence that the sayings are authentic and that they have been transmitted faithfully (Lk. 1:1–4; Acts 1:21–22). Indeed, in some instances the original Aramaic form has been preserved even in a document written in Greek for Greek-speaking readers (Mk. 5:41; 7:34). When a saying of the Lord bears on a situation in the early church, it thus comes with all the force and authority of a prophetic "Thus saith the Lord."

The authority of the word or words of Jesus was felt also by their original hearers. If many were offended, or thought him mad, or tried to trip him up, it was because they were disturbed by the threat of his word (cf. Matt. 15:12; Jn. 10:20). All his hearers seem to have recognized with astonishment that he spoke with authority and not as the scribes (Matt. 7:28). His words confronted people with the same decision as his person, so that to be ashamed of them was to be ashamed of him (and vice versa, Mk. 8:38). Their power is the power which is dynamic as well as authoritative. Like the OT word, they are efficacious. By the word of Jesus the sick are healed, the sinful are forgiven, and the dead are raised to life. The word accomplishes what it says (cf. Gen. 1). Like the OT word (Isa. 40:8), the word or words of Jesus are eternal. Though heaven and earth pass away, his words do not pass away (Mk. 13:31).

John makes the same points in his own distinctive way. The words of Jesus are words of eternal life (Jn. 6:68). They are spirit and life (6:63). They have the same authority as Scripture (2:22; 5:47). If sinners are to be saved, they must accept them (12:48), keep them (8:51), and abide in them (8:31). They are not simply the words of Jesus, for he has a commandment from the Father in regard to what he should say and what he should speak. The rejection of Jesus, and of his words, brings people under condemnation; it is the word itself which judges the unbeliever in the last day (12:47–50).

E. The word as the gospel. The terms *logos* and *rhēma* are applied not only to the word or words Jesus himself speaks, but also to the whole message of the gospel, that is, *all* that Jesus spoke and did. Several passages in Acts, for example, make it apparent that "the word" is not a saying of Jesus but the message concerning him (cf. Acts 6:4). If the OT can also be mentioned in this connection, it is because the word and work of Jesus are a fulfillment of the OT (cf. 17:11). The task of the apostles as ministers of the word is to speak, proclaim, teach, or magnify the word of God/the Lord (4:29; 13:5, 48; 18:11). The Pauline letters offer ample evidence of the same usage (cf. 1 Thess. 1:6; 2 Thess. 3:1; 1 Cor. 14:36; 2 Tim. 2:9; Col. 1:25–27; Eph. 1:13). The word in 1 Pet. 1:23 and Jas. 1:21 bears a similar meaning. A noteworthy point is that *rhēma* seldom occurs in this sense, though there are good instances in Heb. 6:5; 1 Pet. 1:25; and Eph. 5:26.

As the gospel, the word has the attributes and authority of a definitive word of God. It is the word of the cross, of reconciliation, of grace, of life, and of truth. It is God's word. If the apostles speak it, they do so only as ministers. This is why Paul dare not corrupt it. This is the guarantee of authenticity. It is also the source of authority and power. People may contest the words of their fellow human beings; they cannot contradict God's word. The word, as God's word, has its own vital power. It is the power of God (1 Cor. 1:18). It is not bound (2 Tim. 2:9). It does its own work, cutting like a sword (Heb. 4:12; cf. Eph. 6:17), regenerating (1 Pet. 1:23), and reconciling (2 Cor. 5:19). The word, as the word of life or salvation, does not merely speak about these things; it also imparts them.

Part of the efficacy of the word is to call for the necessary response in those who hear. For the word may be accepted or rejected. It may be kept or not kept. The verb "to receive" is a common one in combination with *logos* (Acts 8:14; 1 Thess. 1:6; Jas. 1:21). This is more than intellectual apprehension or assent. It is a hearing and receiving in faith (Acts 4:4). Hence, the word works in believers (1 Thess. 2:13). OBEDIENCE is also part of receiving (cf. Jas. 1:22; 1 Pet. 2:7–8). By obedience or disobedience a person either glorifies (Acts 13:48) or blasphemes (Tit. 2:5) the word of the Lord. The role of the HOLY SPIRIT is of supreme importance in this ministry and work of the word, but this leads into a different field that is impossible to cover in the present context.

F. Jesus as the Word of God. The word is God's word. It includes the word or words of Jesus. It is also the message about Jesus. As such, it is God's speaking to human beings by the Spirit. It is the word from Jesus and about Jesus continually preached. The point upon which all these different lines converge, and the climax of the biblical doctrine of the word of God, is that the Word is God himself. Jesus Christ, God's Son, is the eternal and incarnate Word. The Word is Jesus, and Jesus is the Word.

This equation is made in Rev. 19:13, where "The Word of God" is the title borne by the exalted Christ. This is the name that is not known and yet also known. This is the basis of the exercise of the sword. If the exalted Christ bears the title here, it is the same Christ who was dead and is alive again. Nor does the title "Word of God" stand isolated from the gospel, for earlier in the book the word is connected with the witness, and Jesus himself is the faithful and true Witness. No particular explanation is given of the title, but in the general context this is hardly more necessary than, for example, in the case of the designation of Christ as Lamb. The glory and eternity and deity of the Word are implied (cf. 19:16).

There is a similar equation in 1 Jn. 1:1, though here with the incarnate Jesus. The Word of life has been seen, heard, and handled by the apostles. Intrinsically the reference might be to the message, but the verbs suggest the living person of Jesus Christ, the Word incarnate. This is supported by the "from the beginning" of v. 1, the "with the Father" of v. 2, and the general similarity of this verse to the opening of John's gospel. Encounter with the Word is encounter with the Person of Jesus Christ.

The full and definitive equation is made in Jn. 1:1–5. This equation leads into the whole sphere of CHRISTOLOGY, so that only a few observations must suffice. First, John expresses the common NT conviction that Jesus is the heart of the word, but he carries it a stage further. Not only is Jesus the Word; the Word itself is eternal and preexistent with God. Jesus, then, is the eternal Word in history, incarnate. Hence, what is said about Jesus is said about the Word. This explains why "the Logos" does not occur again in John after the prologue. It also explains why Jesus is not said to speak the word. Jesus is the Word, and the Word is Jesus. Second, the statement in John is not abstract or speculative personification. The author does not begin with a theoretical concept of the Logos which he then transfers to Jesus. On the contrary, he begins with Jesus, hears the word of God in all its fullness in him, apprehends his glory, and is thus impelled to say that Jesus is the Word, the only-begotten Son, God, and that in him the Word was made flesh. Third, the opening verse seems to be an intentional allusion to Gen. 1:1. The point is that the statement "God said" is there at the very beginning with God as the Word by which all things were made. John is also able in this way to suggest at least the thought of the new creation by the Word. The emphasis on the personal and historical aspect of the Word goes beyond Genesis, but an interrelation of the word of God throughout both Testaments, and an ultimate basis for the authority and power of the word as God's word, are hereby achieved. Fourth, the statement of John is unique in spite of all the suggested connections and influences which have been sought in, for example, the Hellenistic Logos, Jewish wisdom, or the rabbinic law. The real concern of John is the presentation of the word, but for him, and in the last analysis for all the apostles, this is the presentation of the incarnate and risen Jesus himself in all his grace and truth. Jesus Christ is the eternal incarnate Word of God who is himself God.

G. W. BROMILEY

work. See LABOR. For *works* in the sense of "moral or religious acts," see FAITH, FAITHFULNESS IV; JUSTIFICATION III.

works of God. This phrase and similar expressions attributing wondrous works to God (or to Jesus) denote both the things made by him and also the acts performed by him. Various Hebrew and Greek words are used in these contexts.

I. The OT

A. The divine works

1. Creation. With its strong doctrine of CREATION, the Bible naturally uses the term *work* to describe the totality of God's creative act. It does this in an active sense for the actual work of God (e.g., Gen. 2:2–3; Heb. *mělāʾkâ* H4856). It also uses the term in a passive sense for the thing made (cf. Ps. 8:6; here the Heb. is *maʿăśeh* H5126). The active and passive merge into one another; God's work of creating has resulted in the work of creation. (In both of the passages mentioned, the LXX uses Gk. *ergon* G2240.)

The passive is more common and much clearer in the plural with reference to the individual phenomena of nature. The heavens are the works of God's fingers (Ps. 8:3). All creatures are works of his hands. This is especially true of human beings; with this plea they seek the divine protection and mercy (138:8 et al.). Believers, or the descendants of JACOB, are specifically described as the works of God's hands (Isa. 29:23). God's historical works are also in their own way creative.

2. History. The OT speaks also of God's acts in history. These are in the first instance acts of deliverance. The events of the exodus are the basic works of God for Israel. These works are often MIRACLES, that is, mighty acts transcending the normal course of history. Nor do the works cease with the entry into Canaan. The books are of redemption are a constant reminder of new works of God. One finds these, for example, in the deliverance from the Assyrians or the restoration from exile.

If God's works are predominantly works of deliverance, they have a reverse side. The deliverance of the Israelites at the RED SEA meant the overthrow of the Egyptians. The people delivered by the judges were also delivered up to their enemies when they sinned. The prophets in particular proclaim works of judgment on a rebellious and obdurate people (Isa. 28:21). The individual knows the works of God (cf. the Psalms). God's works have also an eschatological dimension (cf. Isa. 60:21).

B. The human response.

God's works demand responsive action on our part. First, we are to *consider* these works. Various words are used in this regard. We are not to forget the great things that God has done (Ps. 77:11), but rather meditate upon them (77:12). This will give us assurance in the day of trouble.

Second, we are to be thankful to God for his works (Ps. 107:15, 21, 31). We are to praise and bless the God who does them (Ps. 145). They are mighty acts, great and terrible (66:3). They are done in faithfulness (33:4). They manifest the rule of God (90:16). Even though seen, they are unfathomable (Eccl. 8:17). They are studied by all who have pleasure in them (Ps. 111:2). The very works themselves join in the praise of him who does them (145:10).

Finally, we are to declare God's mighty works. We teach them to our children (Ps. 78:4) and set them forth to others. Making known to all people the mighty acts of God is the basic task that gives unity to the whole life of ministry and worship (145:12).

II. The NT

A. Creation.

What the NT has to say about God's works is essentially the same as that which is found in the OT. The new thing is that the works now bear a common reference to Jesus Christ. It is by him that they are done. The works of God are thus in a very real sense the works of Jesus. God the Father works in and through the Son.

This may be seen already in creation. All things were created by Christ (Col. 1:16). God made the worlds by him (Heb. 1:2). Hence, the works of creation are his works. John brings this out more explicitly when he says that all things were made through the Logos: "without him nothing was made that has been made" (Jn. 1:3).

B. Salvation. The main emphasis in the NT, however, is on the saving works of God performed in Jesus Christ. Rather oddly, there is little reference to these in the Synoptic Gospels, who simply record the works with their culmination in the crucifixion and resurrection. The acts are their own witnesses. Only in relation to John the Baptist's question is there mention of the works of Christ (Matt. 11:2).

In the primitive preaching of Acts, however, the picture changes. Empowered by the Spirit, the apostles declare the wonderful works of God (Acts 2:11). Jesus is approved of God by the miracles, wonders, and signs which God has done by him (2:22). Wonders will still be done in his name (4:30). If healing is a work of God, so, too, is the missionary activity for which Barnabas and Saul are separated (13:2). Jesus continues to do mighty works through the Spirit.

In John's gospel the works of Jesus are highly significant. They bear witness to him (Jn. 5:36). They are good works (10:32). They are the works of God (9:3). They are given to Jesus by the Father (5:37). They are done by the Father (14:10–11), or in his name (10:25). They are unique (15:24). The disciples will do greater works (14:12). For the one great work of Jesus, the singular is also used. Christ's food is to finish the work of the Father (4:34). Human beings share in the works by believing in Jesus. The works are to the salvation of believers and to the judgment of those who reject their testimony.

Paul, too, emphasizes the work of God. Unlike John, however, he is primarily concerned with this work as the present ministry of the Word. The Corinthians are his work in the Lord (1 Cor. 9:1). The work of God is edification (Rom. 15:2). All Christians take part in this (1 Cor. 15:58). Yet there is no real synergism, for God begins and performs the work in them (Phil. 1:6). In the last resort, the Christians who work are themselves God's workmanship created in Christ Jesus for good works (Eph. 2:10). The work of Christians is still the work of God and redounds to his glory and praise.

(For bibliography, see Bible; Christology; Logos.)

G. W. Bromiley

world. This English term can be used not only of the earth in a physical sense, but also of its inhabitants or human existence, of its concerns and affairs, of human society, and so forth.

The primary Hebrew word for "world" is *ʾereṣ* H824, which more frequently is rendered "ground, earth, country." Another term, *tēbēl* H9315, is used as a synonym in some contexts (notice the parallelism in 1 Sam. 2:8; Ps. 24:1; Isa. 24:4; et al.), but it appears to have the distinct sense of "the inhabited and cultivated areas of the mainland" (*HALOT*, 4:1682 [meaning 2.b]; cf. Job 18:8 et al.). A less common word, *ḥeled* H2698 ("duration, lifespan") can sometimes be rendered "world" (Ps. 17:14 et al.; cf. *ʿôlām* H6409, which is used in the sense of "world" in postbiblical Hebrew).

In the NT, the most common term is *kosmos* G3180 ("adornment, order, world, universe"), but two other words are relevant. The form *oikoumenē* G3876 (passive ptc. of *oikeō* G3861, "to live, dwell") means literally "inhabited," but because it was often combined with *gē* G1178 ("land, earth"), *hē oikoumenē* by itself came to mean "the inhabited world." Finally, the noun *aiōn* G172, which has primarily a temporal reference ("a [long] period of existence, an age"), sometimes by metonymy takes on the spatial meaning "world" (Heb. 1:2; 11:3; cf. also the expressions "the present age" and "this age," where the rendering "world" is just as appropriate).

  I. The world in the OT
 II. Greek ideas of the cosmos
    A. Basic concept
    B. Plato and Aristotle
    C. The Stoics
    D. The inhabited world
    E. Philo

III. The world in the NT
   A. Ecumene
   B. Aeon
   C. Cosmos

I. The world in the OT. It should be noted that Hebrew has no single term for "universe," a concept denoted rather by such familiar phrases as "the heavens and the earth" (Gen. 1:1) or "the heavens and the earth, the sea, and all that is in them" (Exod. 20:11). In the prophets one also finds *kōl* H3972, "all things" (Isa. 44:24; Jer. 10:16 [*hakkōl*]; cf. also Eccl. 1:8, 13). Nevertheless, the OT has a fully developed sense of the unity of the universe. This is based on the doctrine of CREATION (Gen. 1:1). God made all things. They are all equally the works of his hand. One divine plan lies behind everything. The one divine purpose directs the course of all creatures. In nature and history alike God rules in all things. The world does not constitute an autonomous unity. It is constituted a unity by its divine origin and subjection.

Within creation a prominent place is occupied by the earth, especially in the sense of the land as distinct from the sea (Gen. 1:10). The earth is important primarily because of its inhabitants, the nations or peoples (cf. Isa. 34:1–2). Since God is Creator and Ruler of the whole universe, he bears a special relation to human beings, and consequently to the inhabited earth. The historical nature of human life, and of God's dealings with his creatures, seems to provide the link between the concept of world and that of duration. It is during his stay on earth, in the world of space and time, that we experience God's acts in providence, judgment, and grace.

II. Greek ideas of the cosmos

A. Basic concept. In contrast to the OT, the Greeks had a highly developed sense of the universe as a single entity quite apart from any reference to the Creator (see GREEK RELIGION AND PHILOSOPHY). This is implied in the word *kosmos*, which carries the basic meanings of (1) structure, (2) order between men, (3) order in general, and (4) adornment. These senses merge into that of the world as an ordered, harmonious, and beautiful structure. Predominant in the early days of Greek philosophy is the thought of the order or system: that which holds the world together. At some point not later than the 6th cent. B.C., the word came to be used of the totality held together by the order, that is, the cosmos in the sense of universe. According to Heraclitus, the universe in this sense is eternal, having neither beginning nor end. It is interesting that even those who suggested an origin for the universe always accepted the eternity of matter. The only beginning was that of form or order.

B. Plato and Aristotle. Plato took over the view of an integrated cosmos based on a universal order. The cosmos in this sense might be described as a body with a soul, a rational creature. It was a spatial manifestation of the idea, a sensual reflection of the eternal. In a famous passage (*Timaeus* 28ff.), Plato can speak of the making of the world by a *theos* G2536 or *dēmiourgos* G1321. This was done in accordance with the perfect idea. It should be noted, of course, that Plato, though he finds a cosmological demonstration of God, does not really believe in creation. The Demiurge's function is

Detailed photo of the Tarantula Nebula (NGC 2070) from the Hubble Space Telescope (with star cluster Hodge 301 in lower right). This giant emission nebula, more than 1,000 light-years across, is part of the irregular neighboring galaxy known as the Large Magellanic Cloud. "In the beginning God created the heavens and the earth" (Gen. 1:1).

simply to shape what is formless into a cosmos. He also works according to the idea already present in the so-called noetic cosmos. In the last resort, God is simply the highest idea in the cosmos. Even the created cosmos may also be called God. This is *theos aisthētos*, God apprehensible to the senses. The very modest approach of Plato toward a genesis of the cosmos was abandoned by Aristotle, who accepted the eternity of the world and regarded God, not as the world's architect, but as pure mind or form. Later, on the other hand, GNOSTICISM developed the distinction between the noetic and the aesthetic worlds into a thoroughgoing DUALISM in which the material world, created by an inferior demiurge, is the prison of the soul, and redemption is a liberation from this, a return to the realm of pure mind or the true God.

C. The Stoics. Stoicism, like Platonism, has a doctrine of the genesis of the cosmos (see STOIC). It incorporates this concept, however, into an eternal recurrence, a process of constant becoming and dissolving. Hence, the Stoic beginning is no true creation, nor is the Stoic destruction a true end. Furthermore, there is no need of an architect. God is the world soul which permeates the whole cosmos, the reason (*logos* G3364) which rules it. Indeed, so pantheistic is the Stoic understanding that a direct equation can even be made between God and the world. Each human being, as a participant in the soul of the world, is a part of God.

D. The inhabited world. Since the earth is included in the *kosmos*, this term can be used by the Greeks for the earth as distinct from heaven on the one side and from the underworld on the other. It is then only a step to the use of the word for the creatures that inhabit the earth, and a further step leads to the special sense of the human race, mankind. Indeed, in the later Koine there is a very general use of *kosmos* for "people," "everybody."

E. Philo. A bridge between the Greek view of the cosmos and the OT is to be found in the writings of PHILO JUDAEUS, who makes considerable use of the term. Distinguishing in Platonic fashion between the noetic and the aesthetic cosmos, Philo argues from Gen. 1 that God first created the world of ideas, which then served as a prototype for the material world. The cosmos is characterized by order and beauty. But it stands under the divine transcendence. God as father and architect created the world. He did this by the LOGOS, the mediator between the world and God. Thus Platonic and Stoic ideas are here combined with the fundamental OT belief that the cosmos is the creature of God. There is, however, a certain imprecision in Philo's thought and language which leaves some doubt as to whether he is speaking of a real creation of the world by God, or of an ordering of existing formless matter in the Greek sense. He certainly avoids any identification of the world and God; at this point he is faithful beyond question to his Jewish heritage.

III. The world in the NT

A. Ecumene. The term *oikoumenē* (from which derives English *ecumenical* via Latin *oecumenicus*) is of little theological account in the NT. As mentioned above, it is a participle used as a noun, and denotes from very early times the inhabited earth (cf. *TDNT*, 5:157). The primary sense is geographical, but this quickly merges into the religious, cultural, and political, so that the *oikoumenē* is the civilized (Hellenic) world, or, after the Roman conquests, the ROMAN EMPIRE as a political and cultural unit.

Used in the SEPTUAGINT, Philo, and the rabbis (as a loanword), *oikoumenē* is fairly common in the NT, especially in the Gospels and Acts. In the prophecy of Matt. 24:14 the reference is to all inhabited parts of the globe, and the word imparts a certain solemnity to the statement. In Lk. 2:1, however, the Roman empire seems to be in view, though elsewhere in Luke (cf. 4:5; 21:26; Acts 11:28; 17:31) there is a fuller reference to the whole inhabited world. The Matthean parallel to Lk. 4:5 (Matt. 4:8) has *kosmos*.

It is worth noting that Paul uses *oikoumenē* only in the quotation of Rom. 10:18. In Heb. 1:6, "inhabited world" is the meaning, but the future *oikoumenē* of 2:5 bears more of the sense of *aiōn* or *kosmos*. Ancient apocalyptic tradition might well underlie both this use and also the two instances in Rev. 12:9 and 16:14. In general, however, the

NT attaches no particular significance to the term. It uses it either for the inhabited earth in general or for the political-cultural unit constituted by the empire.

B. Aeon. From its early use in Homer for "vital force," the term *aiōn* quickly came to signify "lifetime," "generation," "space of time," "time" with a past, present, or future reference, and finally "eternity." It played a considerable role in the Greek discussion of time, and in the Hellenistic age it was personified as the god Aeon. The temporal sense of the term is preserved in the NT in various phrases used to signify eternity (esp. in the pl.). The cognate adjective *aiōnios* G173 also is used to denote the ETERNITY of God (e.g., "King of the ages," 1 Tim. 1:17 NRSV). On an OT basis this seems to imply, not that he exists so long as the aeons last, but that he is before and after all times or time. A decisive feature in the NT is that similar statements are made with reference to Christ, implying both his preexistence and also his essential deity.

1. Aeon as world. How could a word referring to time come to be used for the world? The answer seems to lie in its use for "time of the world," that is, time limited by the creation and end of the world. As H. Sasse notes (*TDNT*, 1:202), it is striking that "in the Bible the same word is used to indicate two things which are really profoundly antithetical, namely, the eternity of God and the duration of the world." Nevertheless, this is true. The end of the aeon in Matt. 13:39 is undoubtedly the end of the time of the world. Even in the plural, the word has the same sense (Heb. 9:12; 1 Cor. 10:11), though with a suggestion that the one time of the world is made up of two or more periods.

If, however, aeon is the time of the world, it is no more difficult to equate the world's *duration* with the world as it is to equate the world's *order* with the world. Later Hebrew had done this (with the term *ʿôlām*), and it is natural enough to find the same usage in the NT. The clearest instances of equation are in 1 Cor. 1–3, where one finds as equivalents "wisdom of the cosmos" (1:20), "wisdom of this aeon" (2:6), "wisdom of this cosmos" (3:19), and in Mk. 4:19 and Matt. 13:22, where "the cares of this aeon" are undoubtedly worldly affairs (cf. cosmos in 1 Cor. 7:33). DEMAS's love of this present aeon would seem to demand a similar understanding, and the aeons of Heb. 1:2 are surely worlds or spheres rather than epochs.

2. The two aeons. As noted already, the plural of this term, though often equivalent to the singular, can also suggest more than one stretch of time. This can be worked out in different ways. Eternal recurrence, for example, postulates an infinite series of aeons. The biblical view, however, is incompatible with successive aeons in this sense. The world begins and ends. Nevertheless, a break has been made in the world by SIN. This means that the creation-to-conclusion understanding yields to the more complicated concept in terms of creation, fall, destruction, new creation, and consummation. Directly related to this is the NT doctrine of the two aeons.

The background of this doctrine is incontestably Jewish. In later Jewish APOCALYPTIC writings there are constant references to the two aeons, both spatial and temporal (cf. *1 Enoch*; see ENOCH, BOOKS OF). These aeons are the time of this world on the one side and eternity on the other, with an accompanying antithesis between the visible or present world on the one side and the invisible or future world on the other. Between the aeons stands the resurrection and the judgment. The rabbis apparently followed up the same idea, for there are examples (mostly post-Christian) of the distinction between this aeon and the aeon to come.

In the NT the contrast occurs in the Synoptic Gospels. In Mk. 10:30, Jesus distinguishes this time (Gk. *kairos* G2789) from the coming aeon. In Lk. 16:8, he contrasts the people of this aeon with the people of light (cf. 20:34–35, with its reference also to the RESURRECTION). In Matt. 12:32, the Lord says that the sin against the HOLY SPIRIT can be forgiven neither in this nor the future aeon. If the present aeon is not expressly described as sinful, its sinfulness seems to be a fairly clear implication in some of these passages.

PAUL speaks expressly of the aeon to come only in Ephesians. Nevertheless, his many references to *this* aeon (Rom. 12:2; 1 Cor. 1:20, 2:6, 8; 3:18; 2 Cor. 4:1) leave no doubt as to the contrast with a *future* aeon. Paul also says plainly that the present aeon is evil (Gal. 1:4). This shows clearly why the biblical doctrine of creation can still allow for a doctrine of two aeons. The aeon of revolt against God is to be replaced by the aeon of salvation and fulfillment.

Hebrews contains only one direct reference to the future aeon (Heb. 6:5), but this passage is very important, for it says that even now, in this world, believers have tasted of the powers of the future aeon. Similarly, Gal. 1:4 speaks of redemption from the present aeon. While Jewish apocalyptic writing is still looking toward the future aeon, the Christian message is that this aeon has already come in with Jesus Christ, so that Christians live in the new aeon. This is not, of course, a fully realized ESCHATOLOGY. Only with the SECOND COMING and the resurrection will the old aeon be destroyed and the new aeon completely manifested.

The coexistence of the new aeon with the old is a salutary warning that *aiōn* in these contexts does not simply mean "world." At the same time, one must not distinguish too sharply. The Bible also speaks of a new heaven and a new earth. Hence the relationship between time and space is maintained even though the nature of the new creation is beyond our powers of apprehension. Even in the new aeon, at least when it is consummated, there is to be some kind of world. The new aeon is also the new world. See HEAVENS, NEW.

C. Cosmos. If *aiōn* is important, *kosmos* is perhaps the most significant of all the NT terms for "world." In the LXX it had been used first for the HOST OF HEAVEN (Heb. *ṣābāʾ* H7372, Gen. 2:1; also Deut. 4:19; 17:3), then for "ornament" (Exod. 33:5–6; 2 Sam. 1:24). Only in the Greek books of the APOCRYPHA did it become a prominent word for the universe created and overruled by God. It could also be used for the world of human beings, the human race. Hellenistic Judaism probably adopted it instead of older terms, not as a philosophical concept, but simply as a term in current use. In this sphere it even found its way into the vocabulary of liturgy. In the NT the word occurs over 180 times. It never has the sense of "order," and it means "adornment" or "beauty" only in 1 Pet. 3:3; elsewhere the meaning is always "world." Over half the references are in the Johannine writings, especially the Gospel of John. The word is also common in Paul, but comparatively rare in the Synoptic Gospels and Acts. The use of "heaven and earth" in the sayings of Jesus explains this paucity in part. On the other hand, the usage seems to stand in fairly clear relation to the theological importance of the word in the different books.

1. Universe. In the NT, as elsewhere, the cosmos is primarily the sum of all things, the universe (Acts 17:24). In this sense it is equivalent to "heaven and earth" or to "all things" (cf. Jn. 1:3, 10). Sometimes the cosmos is simply space, with a possible distinction from that which fills it, but in the main it represents, in this sense, the totality of things.

2. The transitory cosmos. The fundamental connection between space and time is reflected in the NT assumption that the cosmos is of limited duration. The cosmos has an aeon (Eph. 2:2): this is possibly the time between its creation and its end, although the expression in this passage (*kata ton aiōna tou kosmou*) has been variously understood. In any case, the expression "from the foundation [*katabolē* G2856] of the cosmos" is common in the NT (Matt. 25:34 et al.; cf. also "from the beginning of the cosmos," Matt. 24:21, and "from the creation of the cosmos," Rom. 1:20). With this idea one may link the reference to the end of the aeon in Matt. 13:40. If the cosmos as a whole is marked by duration, everything in it is also transitory. The world

Babylonian cuneiform planisphere that includes drawings of the constellations.

passes away (1 Jn. 2:17; 1 Cor. 7:31). The present cosmos is thus set in eschatological antithesis to the future aeon. The same antithesis is expressed by John who in his gospels of the coming of Christ into the cosmos. An important point in this regard is that the NT does not speak of the future cosmos. There is an aeon to come and there will be a new creation. There is no new cosmos. The reason for this will appear later. God himself has created the cosmos (Acts 17:24) and he obviously overrules it. But he is not described as the Lord of the cosmos. One finds only the eschatological hope that the kingdoms of this cosmos will become the kingdom of our Lord and of his Christ (Rev. 11:15).

3. NT cosmology. A question that has assumed some importance in modern theology is that of NT cosmology (see COSMOGONY). Rudolf Bultmann seemed to base his call for demythologization on the need to correct the supposedly outdated NT concept of the universe as a three-decked structure (see MYTH III). Is this picture correct? Certainly the Bible does speak of heaven and earth as two distinct areas. The sea or underworld can also be a third division. One should note, however, that heaven is also a system of worlds or spheres (aeons) in Heb. 1:2, and that there are references to the ELEMENTS of the world (Gal. 4:3 and Col. 2:8, but the meaning of this phrase is disputed). Sasse (in *TDNT*, 3:87) has some sober observations on this whole matter when, from a survey of the evidence, he points out (1) that the NT does not deliver express cosmological teaching as part of its message, (2) that the NT simply alludes to current ideas which make sense only against the background of the time, and (3) that one can hardly piece together a coherent system and say, This is NT cosmology. If Sasse is right, it is just as pointless to demythologize the NT here as it would be to demand the demythologization of a meteorological report which mentions sunrise and sunset.

4. The theater of history. The predominant concern of the NT, as of the OT, is not with the cosmos as a whole but with human beings in the cosmos. God made the whole world, but he made man in his image, and his main dealings are with the human race. Hence, to use the familiar phrase, "the cosmos is the theater of human history," and more specifically of the history of God and man. In many instances, then, the word *kosmos* will bear the special sense of the inhabited world, the earth, the dwelling-place of humanity (cf. Matt. 4:8; Rom. 1:8). This could well be the meaning in the saying about gaining the whole cosmos (Mk. 8:36). We find it again, with a tendency to shade off into "nations," in Rom. 4:13.

It is because the world is the theater of human life that the NT can speak of entries and exits. "To come into the world" is a common idea in John, whether with reference to everybody, to Christ, or to "that prophet." Sin and death come into the world (Rom. 5:12–13). So, too, do false prophets (1 Jn. 4:1). As there is a coming into the world, so there is a going out of it. Christ goes out of the world (Jn. 13:1). Christians would have to do so to avoid all contact with fornicators (1 Cor. 5:10). Between coming into and going out of the world, there is a being in the world. The LOGOS is in the world (Jn. 1:10), as also are the disciples (17:11), and other Christians (1 Jn. 4:17; 2 Cor. 1:12; et al.). An important principle is involved here. Christians are not to be *of* the cosmos. Yet during the period of their present pilgrimage they have no option but to pursue their life *in* the cosmos.

5. Humanity. In a passage like Rom. 4:13, the sense of "world" as the dwelling place of the race merges into that of the race which dwells in it. This use is found already in the Hebrew terms and in the Greek Koine generally. In the NT it may be seen plainly in Mk. 16:15 (cf. 14:9), where the disciples are charged to go to the whole world, that is, not just to every place, but to all people. Obviously, one cannot always mark off this sense with precision, but it would seem to be the most apposite meaning when the Lord says that Christians are the light of the world (Matt. 5:14) or that the field is the world (13:38). Peter, too, seems to have human beings in view when he refers to the cosmos of the ungodly (2 Pet. 2:5), and this is also the meaning when Paul calls the apostles the scum of the cosmos (1 Cor. 4:13). Angels can be included as well (4:9; see ANGEL), but in the main the reference in such cases is to humanity.

6. The evil cosmos. The human race is a fallen race. This means that the cosmos, too, is presented as alienated from God, especially by Paul and John. Paul in 1 Corinthians uses a whole series of contrasts to make it plain beyond all possibility of doubt that there is this alienation. The WISDOM of this cosmos (or aeon) contrasts with the wisdom of God, the spirit of the cosmos with the Spirit of God, the sorrow of the cosmos with the sorrow that is godly (1 Cor. 1:20–21; 2:12; 2 Cor. 7:10). An even darker picture is painted in Romans. Since sin has entered the cosmos, the whole cosmos is guilty, and it is judged and condemned by God (Rom. 3:6, 19; cf. 1 Cor. 6:2). The ultimate and definitive nature of this sin is manifested in the fact that the rulers of this cosmos crucified the Lord of glory. Cosmos here is obviously the human race. Yet it is more, for angelic powers rule the sinful cosmos (cf. 1 Cor. 2:6; Eph. 2:2). This explains why God is not called Lord of the cosmos, and also why there is no cosmos to come. So fully is the cosmos identified with sin and the fall that the cosmos can only be condemned and destroyed in the judgment. It comes to represent the world of evil which is in irreconcilable conflict with the world of God.

JOHN THE APOSTLE uses different language, but the thought is materially the same. Christ is not of the cosmos; he has come to it from God. He is in the cosmos but the cosmos does not know him (Jn. 1:10); nor does it believe in him (7:7). Though he comes to save, not to condemn, his coming does in fact bring JUDGMENT on the sinful, unbelieving cosmos. The prince of this cosmos is judged first (12:31). The first epistle of John has contrasts reminiscent of Paul: he that is in you and he that is in the world (1 Jn. 4:4), those who are of the world and those who are of God (4:5, 6), we who are in Christ and the world which is in wickedness or the wicked one (5:19). Here again is final conflict. The world has not escaped God's control, but it is in revolt against him. By a new birth from God sinners may be saved. The cosmos itself, as sinful cosmos, cannot be saved.

7. The object of salvation. The evil cosmos is condemned and lost. Yet the cosmos is still the theater of God's saving action and the object of his saving love. Paul and John are again as one in stating this fundamental truth. Thus Paul says plainly that Christ Jesus came into the world to save sinners (1 Tim. 1:15). The cosmos is not just that from which sinners are saved; it is the place where they are saved. John made the same point with even greater cogency. Christ has not merely come into the cosmos. He has come as the Savior of the cosmos (Jn. 4:42) or the light of the cosmos (8:12). He has come into the cosmos in order that in it, as the abode of men and women, he might be the Savior of it, that is, of the human race.

The impulse behind this mission is that the world is the object of God's reconciling LOVE. Two of the most basic and comprehensive verses in the whole of the NT state this fact: Jn. 3:16, "God so loved the world," and 2 Cor. 5:19, "God was reconciling the world to himself in Christ" (cf. also Rom. 11:15). Predominantly the cosmos here is, of course, humankind, but there are hints that it might have a wider reference, namely, to the cosmos as God's creation.

Though the cosmos is thus the sphere and object of God's gracious work, it is still true that there is no cosmos to come. The reconciled cosmos is the KINGDOM OF GOD, the future aeon, the new creation. As Sasse observes, it seems as if the term *kosmos*, which comes from Greek philosophy, is ultimately "reserved for the world which lies under sin and death." Though the world is reconciled, believers are saved out of the world. A deep ambivalence lies over the word. "When the cosmos is redeemed, it ceases to be the cosmos" (*TDNT*, 3:893).

8. Christians and the world. The theological understanding of the cosmos determines the relation of Christians to it. This may be summed up in three theses. Christians continue to live in the cosmos, they are not of the cosmos, and they are sent, or are to preach, to the cosmos.

(a) They continue to live in the cosmos. The cosmos is still the setting both of human life and also of Christian life and ministry. As Paul says, Christians cannot leave it (1 Cor. 5:10). They have to care for its affairs (7:32–35). They cannot avoid dealings with it (7:31). John gives the same teaching. Christians are in the cosmos as Christ was (Jn.

17:11). They cannot try to remove themselves from it. It is here that they wait and continue (cf. 16:33).

(b) They are in the world, but not of it. Paul puts this in many ways. Christians are dead with Christ from the rudiments of the world (Col. 2:20). The world is crucified to them and they to the world (Gal. 6:14). They are not to be conformed to it (Rom. 12:2). James adds a similar testimony: love of the world is enmity against God (Jas. 4:4). Christians must keep themselves from the world. John is no less explicit: believers are chosen from the world (Jn. 15:19); by the new birth they belong to God (1:12–13); the world hates them, and they themselves are not to love the world or the things that are in it (15:18–19; 1 Jn. 2:15). This is why the world is a place of affliction (Jn. 16:33). But they may be of good courage, for Christ has overcome the world, and in him they have their own victory, even their FAITH. Faith enables them to see beyond the world's enticements and sufferings to the new aeon (1 Jn. 2:17; cf. 1 Cor. 7:33).

(c) Finally, Christians preach to the world. As God loved the world and Christ came into it, so Christians are to go into the world as the ambassadors of reconciliation. The great commission enjoins this. Paul states it in his own way (2 Cor. 5). Christ says plainly that he sends his disciples into the cosmos (Jn. 17:18). The cosmos is to see in them the love of the Father (17:21, 23). While the church is not of the cosmos (the evil world), it is set in the cosmos (the theater of history) to minister to the cosmos (humanity). In this sense it is true that, though the church is not of the world, its life here is for the sake of the world. If believers know that to gain the world and lose the soul is folly, they have also to remember that saving the soul is an unavoidable concomitant to the winning of the world. G. W. BROMILEY

World, On the Origin of the. See ORIGIN OF THE WORLD, ON THE.

worm. Several Hebrew terms and one Greek word are properly rendered "worm" in the English versions. An attempt will be made to identify the words in some contexts, but this is not easy, for the word in most languages is a vague one, applied, even in a semitechnical sense, to a wide range of animals. In English, for instance, it is given to members of four whole phyla (including flatworms, round worms, etc.) as well as to beetle grubs, caterpillars, and even to a species of lizard—the blind worm. In addition, the word has some nonspecific, figurative uses, as when it is applied to people who are objects of contempt or pity (e.g., Isa. 41:14).

The Hebrew word *rimmâ* H8231 occurs seven times, five of them in JOB alone (Job 7:5 et al.). The figurative contexts are so varied that this must be considered a term as general as the English word *worm*. In Job 25:6 and Isa. 14:11, where the NIV renders it "maggot," it is used in synonymous parallelism with *tôlēʿâ* H9357. The latter term is applied to an insect that can destroy grapes and castor oil trees (Deut. 28:39; Jon. 4:7; see GOURD), possibly referring to the *Cochylis (Eupoecilia) ambiguella* (see *HALOT*, 4:1702). Both terms are used with reference to the maggots that appeared in the MANNA kept for longer than a day (Exod. 16:20 and 24).

A possible explanation is that *tôlēʿâ* in Exod. 16:20 describes a specific infestation, perhaps by one of the blow flies whose maggots would quickly turn it into a seething mass in the high temperatures of the desert; while *rimmâ* in v. 24 is a more general term, including both the former and also other potential invaders. It should be noted that *tôlēʿâ* (often in the fem. form *tôlaʿat*) is a cognate of *tôlāʿ* H9355, translated "crimson" or "purple" in its two occurrences (Isa. 1:18; Lam. 4:5), but alluding to a very small insect from which the red DYE was derived (the crimson worm, *Coccus ilicis*; see SCARLET). Thus *tôlēʿâ* is regularly used of scarlet or crimson yarn, especially in Exodus, regarding the construction of the TABERNACLE (Exod. 25:4 and frequently).

An additional Hebrew word, *sās* H6182, occurs only in Isa. 51:8, "For the moth [*ʿāš* H6931] will eat them up like a garment; / and the worm will devour them like wool." The context at first might suggest that *sās* is the grub of the clothes moth (cf. *TWOT*, 2:761). However, it is usual in OT and NT and in current English to speak of the MOTH as the actual destroyer, while the grub is in fact the larva. Further, the latter lives in a small felted case, with only the head exposed, and it is not at all worm-like. It is therefore possible that *sās* can be identified with the

cockroach or some other insect that destroys fibers. (The KJV also uses "worm" to render the participle of the verb *zāḥal H2323* in Mic. 7:17, but most modern versions understand this term as "crawling [thing]"; it is used also in Deut. 32:24 with reference to a venomous creature, probably a viper.)

In the NT, the Greek noun *skōlēx G5038* occurs twice. The figurative usage in Mk. 9:48 is a quotation of Isa. 66:24. The second occurrence is in Acts 12:23, which states that Herod Agrippa (see HEROD VII) was struck down by an angel "and he was eaten by worms and died" (cf. A. Rendle Short, *The Bible and Modern Medicine* [1953], 66ff.). There are several ways in which intestinal worms could cause fairly sudden death even today, and a further suggestion is that he had a hydatid cyst; this is the alternate host stage of the dog tapeworm. See DISEASE (under *worms*).   G. S. CANSDALE

wormwood. A herbaceous perennial (*Artemisia absinthium*, but see below) with silky leaves that bears masses of small yellow flowers; it yields a bitter dark oil that is one of the ingredients used to produce a green liqueur known as *absinthe*. This drink has a most objectionable taste to the uninitiated. The oil is sometimes used medicinally to kill intestinal worms. The wormwood has come to be used symbolically to describe sorrow, calamity, and even cruelty.

The Greek word *apsinthos G952* occurs twice in Rev. 8:11, "The name of the star is Wormwood. A third of the waters became wormwood, and many died from the water, because it was made bitter" (NRSV). The Hebrew word *laʿănâ H4360* is used eight times in the OT (always figuratively and usually in combination with *rōʾš H8032*, which evidently refers to some other poisonous plant), and most versions translate it "wormwood." The NIV, however, uses more generic renderings, such as "gall" (Prov. 5:4 et al.) and "bitterness" (Amos 5:7; 6:12).

The term *laʿănâ* may refer to one of two other species grown in Palestine: *Artemisia herba-alba*, which has a camphor scent and is extremely bitter, and *Artemisia judaica*. This latter plant was used, and still is in some places, to keep the maggots or moths away from woolen garments; the dried plants are laid in between them. (See *FFB*, 198.)

W. E. SHEWELL-COOPER

worship. This word derives from Old English *weorthscipe* ("worth-ship"), that is, worthiness, dignity, or merit, thus the recognition accorded or due to someone, the paying of homage or respect. In the religious world the term is used for the reverent devotion, service, or honor paid to God, whether public or individual. The church building is a place of worship and the forms of divine service followed by various Christian groups or congregations are forms of worship. The verb *to worship* may be used both transitively (to pay homage to God) and intransitively (to attend or to participate in worship). Since worship includes all its constituent parts (e.g., praise, prayer, preaching), and since it also embraces various associated features (e.g., temple, music, hymns), the number of Hebrew and Greek words that might be mentioned in this connection is extraordinarily large and diverse. Rather than attempting to list these, or to seek a single comprehensive term, we shall devote special attention in the body of the article to some of the more significant words.

I. Worship in the OT
   A. Important terms
   B. Basic principles
   C. Family worship
   D. Public worship
   E. Individual worship
   F. Idolatry
   G. The prophetic witness
II. Worship in Judaism
   A. The development of the synagogue
   B. Aspects of synagogue worship
   C. Individual worship
III. Worship in the NT
   A. Important terms
   B. Forms of worship
   C. Elements of worship
   D. Essence of worship

I. Worship in the OT

A. Important terms. As a verb, "worship" often renders the unusual Hebrew form *hištaḥăwâ* (interpreted traditionally as the hithpalpel of *šāḥâ H8817*, "to stoop down," but now more usually understood as the shaphel stem of *ḥāwâ H2556*). It clearly means "to bow down, prostrate oneself" in deference to someone else (Gen. 18:2 et al.), but in a religious context it just as clearly indicates "to reverence [God]" (22.5, 24.48, et al.). It is frequently used in combination with other verbs that also indicate prostration (e.g., *ḥāwâ* H2556 in 24:48), but also with the very common verb *ʿābad* H6268, "to serve," which can be used by itself with the meaning "to worship" (Exod. 9:1 et al.). The noun *ʿăbōdâ* H6275, "work, service," can similarly indicate worship (12:25 et al.). There are of course numerous other terms that refer to various aspects of worship.

B. Basic principles. A study of the words associated with worship shows that, while certain concepts like bowing the knee or obeisance are concerned with the human aspect, the roots of biblical worship are to be found not in human emotions but in the divinely established relationship of God to his creatures. Thus the basis of worship is theological rather than anthropological. The common question as to whether the origin of worship is to be found in such emotions as fear, awe, or the sense of the numinous, is thus beside the point from a biblical standpoint. Such a question presupposes that worship is subjective, that it arises from within the person, that even as a reaction it takes its substance from the reacting person, that there is not necessarily any external object corresponding to the inner emotion.

That human emotions and reactions are involved in worship is, of course, undeniable. Awe, fear, gratitude, and love may all be experienced in worship. The point is, however, that these are not the controlling factors; they do not constitute the true essence of worship. In the Bible the beginning lies in the object of worship rather than the subject. Nor is this an indefinite object. It is not the mystery behind the universe. It is not the universe itself. It is not an unknown factor. It is not a person's own potentiality. The object of worship, which is both its starting point and controlling factor, is not a human projection. It is God.

God is self-declared in the Bible as the living God who is from eternity to eternity, who made the world, who created human beings in his image, and who set himself in relation to them (see IMAGE OF GOD). In all divine-human dealings the initia-

Terra-cotta figurine of a kneeling Babylonian worshiper (early 2nd millennium B.C.).

tive is with God. He is subject as well as object. He tells men and women what to do and what not to do. He controls their destiny. He judges their shortcomings and saves them from their sins. It is God, this God, whose Person and acts are both the theme and the formative principle of genuine worship. If there is awe in worship, it is awe of God; if there is love, it is love of God; if there is praise, it is the praise of God; if worship is response, it is a human response to the living God who has made himself known in his words and works.

The response of worship is not just any response. Worship is controlled by its object, who is also subject. Hence, it is worship in specific forms. There is first the form of confessional praise of God, the declaration of his grace and mighty acts. This confession combines the recitation of what God has done and the praising of God for it. In practice these may be separated into reading and proclamation on the one side and the singing of psalms and hymns on the other. Nevertheless, when worship is genuinely biblical, there is an indissoluble relation between the two. Genuine proclamation is praise, and genuine praise is also proclamation.

There is, secondly, the form of service, which is capable of broad expansion, but which also has its narrower aspect, namely, the rendering of service to God by the performance of cultic acts. In this respect the Bible preserves an admirable balance. Religious exercises cannot be a substitute for total service of life. On the other hand, total service of life must not squeeze out the specific service toward God expressed in religious exercises. Within this Godward service the sacrificial ministry plays an important role in the OT. This ministry is not discarded in the NT; it is consummated in and by the high-priestly ministry of Jesus Christ. Already in the OT it brings to light a decisive aspect of worship. The divine-human relation is one which the sinner has disrupted by his revolt. ATONEMENT must be made for the restoration of this relation.

The priestly ministry of the OT prefigures the greatest of all God's acts of deliverance, namely, the act by which, incarnate in his Son, he graciously bore the penalty of sin and thus provided for its remission and for the restoration of the sinner to fellowship with himself. The priestly ministry is no erratic block in the total structure of worship. In its fulfilled NT form, it is both the supreme theme of worship and also that which enables us to offer acceptable service and praise. In its OT form it is a part of service to God, a summons to penitence and dedication of life, and a prefiguring of the divine work which is the heart and substance of the confession of praise. Without it, there would be no true worship, only misguided idolatry and a fearful expectation of judgment.

Finally, there is the form of prayer. This is itself another aspect of God-oriented worship because (a) it includes confession of sins and (b) it is a confession of the name of God, a confident calling upon the God who intervenes, inclines graciously to the petitioner, and meets his needs. The very fact that God has the initiative means that prayer as well as praise is of the very essence of worship, for prayer is also proclamation and praise. The prayer offered to God is a recalling of the great things that he has done. It is a magnifying of God for them. Far from being a despairing cry in the dark, it is a confident asking directed to the self-revealed God on the basis of what he has revealed about himself. Even the urgency of crisis or complaint cannot wholly conceal this underlying confidence, which is sustained, not by self-righteousness, but by the divine truth and faithfulness.

An additional point is that biblical worship is not left to human caprice. It is not controlled by arbitrary desires or contingent needs. It does not ask what things will be most helpful or what will best express the impulse to worship from a human standpoint. It learns how to worship from the God who is the object of worship. This is especially clear in the OT, where God tells Moses in minute detail how his people, redeemed by him out of Egypt, are now to worship and serve him both in the desert and later in the Promised Land. Many of these things the people had no great desire or instinct to obey. They found the rituals of alien gods far more congenial.

The biblical lesson is surely plain. In worship, as in all else, believers are not to trust their own instincts, for they do not know at all what is best for them. They have to learn how to worship God. This will be according to the way that God himself has appointed. The rigid detail is no longer to be found, of course, in the NT. But the same principle applies even if in a different way. All Christian action is subject to the overruling of the Spirit and the normativeness of the word of God. If detailed regulations are no longer given, the basic constituents of worship are plainly presented in OT and NT alike. The forms used by Christians, even though they vary widely in detail, must be so fashioned as to express and embody these essential elements in proportion, purity, and power.

C. Family worship. The oldest form of worship in the OT is that of the FAMILY. Even before Israel became a people, it was already a worshiping family, the family of Abraham, Isaac, and Jacob. After the exodus, when the children of Israel became a nation and national forms of worship were established, the family continued to play an important part in worship. The rise of the synagogue later made possible a more continuous form of congregational life and offered new opportunities for instruction. Even this did not oust the family as a unit of worship.

1. Praise and prayer. A difficulty in the patriarchal age is to distinguish between domestic and personal prayer. Nevertheless, it would appear that when ABRAHAM called on the name of the Lord in various places (e.g., Gen. 12), his whole household participated in this worship. The substance of this calling is not given, yet there can be little doubt but that it contains the basic elements of prayer and thanksgiving. This is expressed in the prayer of Abraham's servant (ch. 24). This prayer brings out very well the family nature of worship, for the servant invokes in v. 12 the Lord God of his master Abraham. In the days of national worship the centrality of sacrifices at the sanctuary removed from the home one of the great occasions for prayer and praise, but there is no reason to suppose that family prayer perished in consequence. Grace at meals had become a fixed habit by the end of the OT period, and probably long before. How soon and to what extent psalms might have been used in the home it is hardly possible to say. The hymn at the Last Supper is an indication that by the time of Jesus the psalter was in use in the home. The singing of the HALLEL at the PASSOVER is in fact attested by other sources, though information is scanty as to the wider use of the psalter, and practice undoubtedly varied considerably from family to family.

2. Sacrifices. The patriarchal sacrifices were domestic or personal. Thus Abraham built altars at the places where he called on God. JACOB at BETHEL set up a pillar and poured oil on it. Incidentally, it is worth noting that this use of what was probably a familiar practice does not mean that the patriarchs derived their religion from surrounding peoples; they simply used common forms to worship the true God. By institution the Passover was a family sacrifice, a lamb for a house. When the institution of a central tent or temple put an end to family offerings, this rule was still observed even though the offering had to be made at the central site. Centralization by no means destroyed the

Franciscan liturgy at the Church of the Holy Sepulchre in Jerusalem.

family aspect, for households made the journey to Jerusalem and rendered their offerings together (just as family worship may be maintained in congregational worship through the family pew). Like the sign of deliverance, the great COVENANT sign of CIRCUMCISION was also a family matter. It was first given to Abraham as an ordinance for his whole house (Gen. 17:9–14). Even when Israel's worship was set on a national basis, the family character of circumcision persisted (cf. Lk. 2:21). In the last resort, of course, the nation as a whole made its offerings as the family of Abraham, Isaac, and Jacob.

3. Instruction. A part of religious life, which was very clearly committed to the family in OT days, was that of instruction both in the faith of Israel and also in its worship. In patriarchal times this may be presupposed. After the exodus it was plainly enjoined upon the people in the exhortations of Deuteronomy. The "Hear, O Israel" was to be taught diligently to the children (Deut. 6:4–9). The commandments were also to be explained to them (6:20–25). Explanation of the commandments entailed a rehearsal of the great acts of God. The duty of not hiding these things from children and grandchildren underlies a great historical psalm (Ps. 78; cf. vv. 3–4). The witness of Exod. 12:26 and 13:14 is to the same effect, for an explanation is here to be given, not only of the Passover ritual, but also of the great act of divine deliverance which it commemorates. As noted, much of the duty of instruction could later be delegated to the synagogue, but the family had to insure that this instruction was in fact given. At this level the family basis was to stand Israel in good stead in the days of dispersion which commenced with the exile, and the synagogue itself might not have been possible without a prior tradition of instruction in faith and worship in the home.

D. Public worship. The public worship of Israel might be said to have commenced with the observance of the Passover in Egypt. This was rapidly followed by the institution of a whole system of worship laid down by God himself through revelation to Moses.

1. The tabernacle. The new system of worship was centralized for the whole people in the TABERNACLE or Tent of Meeting. A tent was obviously the only practical structure during the desert march, but it also seems to have embodied an important principle, namely, that the living God is not to be tied, as it were, to a permanent structure (Acts 7). The details of the worship prescribed for the tabernacle are so multifarious that it is hardly possible to cover them all in the present context. Attention may be drawn, however, to certain features that seem to have particular significance.

(a) *The festivals.* The worship of God in Israel is to a large degree concentrated on the great festivals of Passover, Pentecost, and Tabernacles. See FEASTS. The people had a duty to be present at them and to make the appropriate offerings in the tabernacle. These festivals were essentially the occasions of joyful and grateful remembrance, so that they embodied the declaratory or confessional aspect of worship. Passover was the festival of liberation; Pentecost, the festival of God's constant provision; and Tabernacles, the festival of God's guidance of the pilgrim people through the wilderness.

(b) *The sacrifices.* SACRIFICE had had a place in biblical worship from the very first. With the Sinaitic revelation it was given a more organized national form and various offerings were instituted (listed in the first seven chapters of the book of LEVITICUS). The sacrifices serve different purposes, so that some support can no doubt be found for the various explanations that have been advanced, for example, sacrifice as an offering of life or as an occasion of fellowship with God. Nevertheless, at the heart of the sacrificial system is the truth that God thereby makes provision for the atonement without which no true worship is possible. This truth is particularly expressed in the great annual ritual of the day of atonement when shrine, priesthood, and people are all purified (Lev. 16). The proleptic form of atonement in the OT required not only a sanctuary with sacrifices but also a ministry consisting of high priest, priests, and Levites. The ritual aspect of Israel's worship should not obscure the fact that confession of sin has its place here (Lev. 4:23–24). During the later days of the monarchy it is possible that psalms of penitence (Ps. 51 et al.) were used on the occasion of propitiatory offerings.

(c) *The ark.* Within the tabernacle a prominent place was occupied by the ARK OF THE COVENANT. This container was a reminder (i) that God himself is not to be represented in wood or stone, (ii) that the basis of the whole worship of the tabernacle was the covenant which God made with his people, and (iii) that the worship of the sanctuary did not exclude, replace, or weaken the requirement of a broader service of God in fulfillment of the ethical

Remains of this altar at Arad are roughly contemporary with the Solomonic temple in Jerusalem. (View to the W.)

imperatives of the law. The setting of the ark of the testimony within the tent is important, because it shows that any rift between the priestly and the prophetic ministry arises only through departure from the basic understanding of worship in Israel. The purpose of the sanctuary is not an autonomous sphere. Its purpose is to set forth the God of Israel, to bring the people to living fellowship with him, and to keep before them the demand for a life consecrated to the divine service. The absence of a visible representation of God is by no means a failure in objectivity. On the contrary, God is not identified with the things he has made. His true objectivity as the God of creation who is also the God of the covenant is thus safeguarded. God is confessed as the God he truly is. His praise is set forth, his salvation typified, and his law made known.

(d) *The Sabbath*. An institution apart is the SABBATH. This is not a ceremony, nor is it centralized in the sanctuary. One might almost group it under family or individual worship. Nevertheless, it is an observance of the whole people. By origin it is more a day of rest than a day of worship, characterized by what is not done rather than by what is done. On the other hand, the Sabbath has a positive side from the standpoint of worship. It is a standing memorial of (i) creation (Exod. 19:11) and (ii) the deliverance from Egypt (Deut. 5:15). The sanctifying of the day to God also brings out a fundamental aspect of worship, namely, that of the sanctifying of God's name and of all life and activity in this name. Through the centuries the Sabbath served to stamp Israel as the people set apart for the service of the true and living God, and at a later stage it provided a natural day for synagogue worship.

2. The temple. Entry into the Promised Land brought with it a localizing of the place of worship. In the first instance SHILOH was the worship center, and it would appear that the Tent of Meeting, perhaps by now a semipermanent structure, served as the house of God during the age of the judges. The ark came to be detached from this site as a result of the disaster at APHEK, and Shiloh was then apparently forsaken (Ps. 78:60), so that the way was cleared for a more lasting centralization in JERUSALEM. The ark was brought there as a first step. DAVID then conceived the purpose of building the temple as a new center of worship. NATHAN'S opposition to this plan had a double ground: (a) that God is not to be indebted to human beings for a house, and (b) that God had intentionally chosen a tent rather than a temple, presumably as a symbol that he is not confined to any place and that his eternal dwelling is in the heavens (2 Sam. 7:5–7). In spite of the objection, however, David received permission to begin assembling materials, and SOLOMON finally built and consecrated a TEMPLE which was to be the home of OT worship during the days of the monarchy.

In essentials the temple worship is the same as that of the tabernacle. There the festivals are held, the sacrifices are offered, the ark is given a new setting. If the priesthood is now especially invested in the Zadokites, the sacrificial ministry of high priest, priests, and Levites continues on a more highly organized basis. The Day of Atonement still occupies a prominent place. Evidence in the Psalms suggests that the Feast of the New Year acquires increased importance, though the thesis of a divine enthronement involves a reading of pagan rituals into the OT doctrine (not always clearly understood in practice) concerning the relation of the earthly king to the divine Ruler of Israel. The new feasts added after the exile (e.g., PURIM) are hardly of sufficient importance to merit individual treatment here.

The great new contribution made by temple worship is the development of the poetic and musical side on a scale hitherto unparalleled. Psalms had been used in worship before, but they would seem to have been compositions for individual occasions (cf. the songs of Moses and Deborah). How far they had been regularly sung in tabernacle worship one cannot determine. David, however, gave a new place to music, as may be seen already in the procession which brought up the ark (2 Sam. 6:5). When plans were made for the temple, he set up the orders of singers and musicians that should be responsible for the praise of God in the sanctuary (1 Chr. 25). Above all, he composed many of the psalms for the great collection which became the hymnbook of Israel and which is still the heart and nucleus of all biblical praise.

The psalms, though varied in character, are peculiarly adapted for public worship, whether at

the regular sacrifices, during the annual festivals, or on special occasions. In the later days of the postexilic period, particular psalms or groups of psalm came to be associated with particular services. Thus the songs of ascents (Ps. 120–134) were sung at the feast of tabernacles, and the Hallel psalms (113–118) at Passover. In greater detail Ps. 7 was a psalm for the feast of lots, Ps. 29 for the feast of weeks, Ps. 148 for the beginning of Passover, and Ps. 136 for the end of the Passover. The instruments used in accompaniment were harps, cymbals, cornets, and trumpets. Individual psalms had their own settings, though these probably underwent considerable development during the long period from the building of the first temple to the destruction of the last.

As in the case of the tabernacle, the divine indwelling of the temple was symbolized by the SHEKINAH, which filled the house when the ark was brought up into it (1 Ki. 8:10–11) and which Ezekiel saw departing when the temple was so defiled by idolatry that judgment could no longer be averted (Ezek. 10:18; cf. 1 Sam. 4:22). The presence of the divine glory imparts peculiar sanctity to the temple, yet not at the expense of a localization of God or a rigid distinction between the holy and the profane. God is worshiped in the sanctuary because he has set his name there. He is the God whom heaven and the heaven of heavens cannot contain (1 Ki. 8:27). He will hear in heaven the prayer that is offered toward the temple as well as the prayer and praise in the temple itself. Thus the worship of Israel maintains a freedom from cultic restriction even while it is given a specific focus according to the divine command.

3. The synagogue. The overthrow of the first temple created a new situation. This was even more serious than the temporary dislocation caused by the capture of the ark and the destruction of Shiloh. For the greater part of a century the people had no temple. Many of them were in an exile from which they and their descendants did not return. Even when the second temple was built, the Jews of the dispersion could not possibly use it as a place of regular offering and festal rejoicing. It was thus inevitable that a form of extraterritorial worship should develop, and since the building of a temple outside Jerusalem was prohibited (that at ELEPHANTINE was prob. regarded only as a proto-temple, and it seems to have been the only one of its type), this form could not be a duplication of the worship of Jerusalem. It had to be a new form adapted to the new circumstances.

Whether or not the new form of SYNAGOGUE worship appeared in the OT period is a matter of conjecture. On the other hand, the word *synagogue* itself simply means "congregation" (Gk. *synagōgē* G5252 is an alternative of *ekklēsia* G1711 ["assembly, church"], in the LXX), and it is more than likely that even prior to the more specific organization of the synagogue, meetings were held by the dispersed Jews for functions that later came to characterize developed synagogue worship.

Thus the return of EZRA to Jerusalem brought a new stress both on the reading and also on the exposition and teaching of the law. This seems to imply (a) that the exiles came to see a need for instruction beyond the rudiments provided in the home, and (b) that groups in the DIASPORA had already met for study of the law which would help preserve the integrity of their faith in an alien setting. The recitation of the Shema ("Hear, O Israel") might well have served as another integrative factor, and it is difficult to suppose that common prayers did not develop on the basis of existing OT prayers (cf. the individual prayers of Daniel, Nehemiah, and Ezra). In spite of Ps. 137, one can hardly believe that there was any real or permanent refusal to make use of the poetic treasures of the psalter among the exiles. While remembrance of the great festal songs of Jerusalem would bring almost intolerable nostalgia, the expression of religion in psalm could hardly be neglected or set aside when the traditional practice of temple worship was no longer possible.

How and when such developments took place is not recorded. What is known is that prayer, the reading (and exposition) of the OT (esp. the law), the recitation of the Shema, and the singing of psalms did become the constituent elements of synagogue worship, and that impulses in this direction are to be seen from the exilic or early postexilic period onward. Synagogues as such are known from the 3rd cent. B.C., even though it is unlikely that a fixed form of worship had as yet established itself.

The requirements of the situation and the restriction of the priestly ministry to Jerusalem were already forcing the movement in the direction actually taken, and it is significant that authentic forms of biblical worship resulted.

E. Individual worship. Family worship on the one side and public worship on the other did not exclude a very rich practice of personal religion in Israel. The patriarchs are early examples, for many of the prayers and acts of devotion recorded in Genesis are at the individual level. Moses, too, was a man who enjoyed a deep personal relation with God. The enactments of the law provide for many individual acts of religion even within the context of public worship. In the days of the later judges, HANNAH offers an outstanding example of personal supplication and thanksgiving offered on the occasion of a visit to the shrine at Shiloh (1 Sam. 2:1–10). The age of the monarchy and the exilic and postexilic periods present a whole series of people of prayer, confession, praise, and consecration, from David, through kings like Hezekiah and prophets like Jeremiah, to the great figures of Daniel and Nehemiah. How far the intense personal devotion of these believers is representative of the whole people one can no more say than in the case of outstanding Christians, but the general presentation of the OT gives no grounds for supposing that, for all their eminence, these were isolated individuals.

In this sphere, as in the worship in the temple and later in the synagogue, the psalms played a highly important role. Many of the psalms are written in "I" form. Attempts have been made to make out that this form is a collective "I," but, while there are instances that might support this view, recent scholarship has veered to the view that such psalms are genuinely personal. They express the individual piety of the authors, whether in prayer, complaint, confession of sins, confession of faith and hope, or confession of praise. They also provide expression for the personal piety of those who use them. As noted, it is possible that they were sometimes used by individuals on occasions of confession and thanksgiving in the temple. In addition, when committed to memory they were an inexhaustible treasury of devotion and guidance for everyday life. Other material learned from infancy, such as the Shema, could contribute to the same end; and later the instruction of the people in the whole law, and to some degree in the prophets as well, offered supplementary courses. Even so, the extraordinary range, variety, and poignancy of the psalms adapted them uniquely for service in the field of individual worship.

F. Idolatry. The Greek word *eidōlolatria* G1630 is built up from *eidōlon* G1631, "idol," and *latreia* G3301, "service, worship." It denotes the serving of false gods. All worship not directed to the true God is ipso facto IDOLATRY.

1. General. Some forms of worship used in alien cults may have been incorporated into the worship of Israel according to the law without falling into the evil of idolatry. On the other hand, idolatry can include the use of the prescribed forms of Yahweh worship if idols or other gods are made the objects of veneration. The question of idolatry arises in Israel, not because the true worship of Yahweh develops out of surrounding cults by a process of religious evolution, but because the people resisted the knowledge and worship of God and inclined to the religious ways of those around them. Already at Sinai one can see this tendency, for even before the worship of God was properly established, the people demanded a visible image, fashioned the golden calf, and made this the center of what was apparently an orgiastic cult. See CALF, GOLDEN.

On the human side, the story of especially preexilic worship in Israel is a story of conflict between the prescribed worship, which was never wholly abandoned, and the idolatrous cults that constantly intruded into the life of the people. If there is development, it is not the development of a pure concept or form of worship. God himself provided this model at the very outset. The development, if any, is in the understanding and practice of the form and concept already given. Nor is there any steady advance either in individuals or in the people as a whole. The pure practice of worship comes into conflict with the impure, and this conflict rages continually, so that a Solomon, for example, is probably farther from God in later life than in his young days, while periods of declension

and reformation alternate in the ongoing life of Judah.

2. Canaanite cults. Although idolatry appeared already in the desert, the settlement in Canaan provided the first major impulse toward corruption. The people came into a land that had its settled sanctuaries, priesthoods, and religious practices. There is abundant evidence that not only in the days of the judges, but also in the period of the monarchy, shrines like Dan, Gilgal, Shechem, and Bethel continued to be centers of worship in addition to Shiloh and Jerusalem. Subsidiary forms of Yahweh worship were set up there, but fundamentally the cults were cults of BAAL, the fertility god (cf. Jdg. 10:6). At these centers, then, God was abandoned for Baal, perhaps in some cases identified with Baal, or subjected to an attempted syncretism with the alien god and his alien worship. Even at Shiloh, although there was fulfillment of the law in many respects, one may detect the acceptance of alien beliefs and degrading practices. Thus the immorality of the sons of ELI in the Tent of Meeting (1 Sam. 2:22) carries an echo of temple prostitution, and the value attached to the ark (4:3) suggests more of fetish or magic than of genuine faith in God.

Quite apart from the great shrines, however, there were also the groves or HIGH PLACES that were taken over from the Canaanites and served as sites for town or village worship. Instead of following the planned order, which involved complete abolition of the pagan system, the people attempted to practice their Yahweh worship within the context of the existing structure. This disobedience necessarily entailed both compromise of the faith and corruption of the practice, though the oscillations in the days of the judges and the example of the family of ELKANAH (1 Sam. 1) remind one that the true worship was never wholly submerged.

A final point is that in N Israel in particular the fashioning of images (1 Ki. 12:28) represented a further relapse into pagan ways even after the establishment of Jerusalem as the cultic center under David and Solomon. Political considerations had a hand in this. The unfortunate civil disruption led JEROBOAM to destroy "ecclesiastical" unity as well. Not content with a rival shrine and priesthood, however, he established two golden calves as

Canaanite terra-cotta relief of the mother-goddess Astarte/Ashtoreth discovered at Taanak (Late Bronze Age).

the objects of worship at Dan and Bethel. In so doing, he set a pattern that was followed only too readily by the northern kingdom throughout the period of its independent history.

Nor did Judah in the S lag far behind in spite of the reforming reigns of Hezekiah and Josiah. The constant refrain in 2 Kings is that the people offered sacrifice and burnt incense in the HIGH PLACES (2 Ki. 14:4; 15:4, 35; 16:4; 17:10; et al.). Nor should it be imagined that the battle against high places was simply a struggle for priestly power. Quite apart from the absence of serious ethical content from the native cults, these did not merely provide opportunity for agricultural jollification. Human sacrifice constitutes the darker side of the picture (16:4; 21:6). The intrusion of these forms of worship into Jerusalem itself is the final desecration that shows how far the pure worship of Yahweh was in fact abandoned or corrupted prior to the judgment of the exile (21:7).

3. Foreign influences. The worship of Yahweh suffered attack from without as well as from within. The foreign invasion began in strength in the days of Solomon, whose attraction to alien wives was accompanied by an equal attraction to their alien forms of worship (1 Ki. 11:1-8). Matters of civil policy, such as the advantageousness of foreign alliances, were allowed to control religious practice.

The example thus set was followed with no less abandon by both the divided kingdoms. In Israel the reign of AHAB constituted a climax, for he allowed himself to be dominated by his Sidonian wife, JEZEBEL. He began his reign inauspiciously by building a temple and setting up an altar to Baal in Samaria (1 Ki. 16:32). Jezebel, however, went further, extirpating the prophets of God, teaching the ways of foreign despotism, and fostering an idolatry that through intermarriage affected Judah as well (2 Ki. 8:18). The penetration of alien cults into the S continued steadily during the final days of the monarchy. AHAZ, for example, had a copy made of the altar he saw in Damascus (16:10-14). MANASSEH worshiped "all the starry host" (21:3). JOSIAH's attempt to end the forms of worship established by Solomon (23:13) enjoyed only temporary success, for Ezekiel paints a dark picture of vile religious practices in secret chambers in the temple (Ezek. 8:7-13), and Jeremiah tells how those who escaped to Egypt turned naturally to the worship of the QUEEN OF HEAVEN as their fathers, kings, and princes had done in the cities of Judah and the streets of Jerusalem (Jer. 44:17-19).

A survey of the actual history of worship in Israel suggests indeed that prior to the exile the conflict did not go in favor of Yahweh worship. There was, if anything, decline rather than positive development in the final stages of the monarchy. It needed the sharp judgment of the destruction of kingdom, city, and temple to bring the remnant to a realization of their loss and a clear understanding of the issues. It needed contact with alien cults in their own setting to bring home to the exiles the truth and worth of the divine revelation and the divinely instituted worship. It needed the reconcentration on essentials—the word of God, prayer, and praise—to give insight into the inner meaning of that which externally, perhaps, had seemed to be only one liturgical form among many others. It needed the throwing back wholly upon God's grace, and hence upon faith in him, to commit the people of God to true belief in the one God, and to obedience to his will, with a fullness and intensity hardly ever displayed even after previous deliverances.

G. The prophetic witness. Not without reason the prophets are mostly depicted as champions of true theology and pure ethics. The truth of this understanding, however, means that the prophets had also to be champions of genuine worship. Contending for a true theology, they had to oppose the cults of false gods. Contending for a pure ethics, they had both to condemn immoral religious practices and also to oppose the error of a divorce between worship and righteousness. One of the major tasks of the prophets was to recall the people from the worship of idols, or the false worship of the true God, to genuine worship. In this sense the prophets have a powerful witness to give in the field of worship no less than in the spheres of ethics and theology.

1. Idolatry. Consistently from the earlier prophets to the great writing prophets, these servants of God oppose and condemn the Canaanite and alien cults. Thus a man of God comes from Judah to Bethel to cry against the altar of Jeroboam (1 Ki. 13:1-10). AHIJAH the prophet pronounces judgment on Jeroboam for going after other gods and molten images (14:7-16). ELIJAH stages the great contest on Carmel with a view to bringing the people back to the allegiance and worship of Yahweh alone (ch. 18). AMOS cries against the royal sanctuaries at Bethel and Gilgal (Amos 4:4; 5:5). HOSEA declares judgment on Ephraim because it has made many altars to sin (Hos. 8:11). MICAH warns the people that graven images will be cut off and the groves plucked up (Mic. 5:13-15). JEREMIAH, as noted, condemns the worship of the Queen of Heaven (Jer. 44:17-19), and EZEKIEL, in his horrifying depiction of the worship of the sun and of weeping for TAMMUZ within the very precincts of the temple, prophesies ineluctable judgment and destruction because of these abominations.

2. Formalism. Increasingly, however, the witness of the prophets is directed against a pure externalism of worship that emphasizes the performance rather than the inner spirit. This theme is clearly enunciated by SAMUEL in his famous dictum that

to obey is better than sacrifice (1 Sam. 15:22). This principle underlies the condemnation of David by Nathan, for the great contribution made by David to the worship of God gives him no right to play fast and loose with the divine commandments. Amos sounds the same note. Quite apart from the idolatry of Bethel, Israel's worship is futile because it goes hand in hand with manifest injustices committed against the people. Even when the great religious festivals are held in honor of Yahweh, he hates and despises them, nor will he accept the offerings nor hear the praise. What he wants to see is righteousness and judgment (Amos 5:21–24).

This line of thought is powerfully pursued by the prophets of Judah, where the worship of Jerusalem was ostensibly offered in accordance with the divine precepts. Yet, as ISAIAH puts it, the sacrifices are to no purpose, attendance at the temple is futile, God finds the solemn feasts wearisome, and he closes his eyes to the worshipers. Why? Because they make only an external show of devotion. Their conduct is blatantly at variance with their religious practice. The great essentials of true service of Yahweh—the seeking of judgment, the helping of the oppressed, the championing of widows and orphans—are all neglected. Nowhere, perhaps, is there a more graphic depiction of religious formalism, of external acts of worship divorced from true faith and active obedience, than in the later passage in Isaiah that speaks of the fasting for pleasure or contention in which a person bows down the head like a reed and spreads out sackcloth and ashes, but gives no evidence of a true fast of the heart (Isa. 58:3–5).

From a different perspective MALACHI pours similar scorn upon the observances of the postexilic temple. The point here is that no true worship of God lies behind the external practice, for even the practice itself is careless and slipshod. The people worship at the least expense to themselves, neglecting to pay tithes (Mal. 3:10) and bringing only torn and lame beasts as sacrifices (1:8, 13). In Malachi, too, disobedience to the ethical precepts of the law (3:5) is still a fundamental reason why the worship, even though based on the law, cannot be acceptable to God.

3. True worship. It has been argued sometimes that because of these attacks on formal worship the prophets are to be viewed as opponents of the temple system. This conclusion has even been broadened out into the thesis of a rift between prophet and priest, between prophetic and priestly concepts of religion. The prophets supposedly contend for pure faith issuing in righteous action, whereas the priests regard the cultus, and especially the sacrificial ministry, as the heart of religion. The existence of tensions and conflicts is not to be denied. Nevertheless, these surely arose out of corruptions rather than out of fundamental incompatibility. After all, the prophets were also against false prophets, that is, the abuse of prophecy. Two of the great OT prophets, Jeremiah and Ezekiel, were themselves priests. The destruction of the temple and cultus is proclaimed as a judgment, not as healthy surgery that will make possible the replacement of false religion by true religion. Toward the close of the exile one of the main functions of the prophets HAGGAI and ZECHARIAH is to promise success in the rebuilding of the temple and to summon the people to take part in this work, which will make possible the reinstitution of cultic worship. The priest Joshua (JESHUA) is called upon to play a special role in this venture, so that it is idle to think in terms of hostility between priest and prophet.

The prophetic witness against sacrifices, fasts, assemblies, and even prayer has to be set in perspective. The prophets naturally condemn these altogether when offered to idols. They also scorn and judge them when offered by those who simply engage in the action but are not truly committed to faith in God and obedience to his command. This does not mean, however, that the prophets are calling for the complete cessation of all religious practices. They seek a purification of worship, not by its curtailment or reconstruction, but by concentration on the basic essentials.

If worship is to be what it was meant to be, then there has to be knowledge of God, true faith in him, a humble walk before him, a recognition of his gracious acts, a commitment to his will and ways. When these are present, and only when they are present, true worship is possible and has its proper place. Worship by its very nature is confession and service. On the other hand, the forms of worship cannot be substitutes for the inner core of faith and obedience. To put it simply, offering and festival are of no value without a penitent, faithful, and obedient heart. Where the heart is right, however, it is right and proper, by divine appointment, that there should also be festival and sacrifice (carefully note the change from Ps. 51:16 to v. 19, because of v. 17). The prophets are thus the champions, not of prophetic religion against priestly religion, but of genuine worship against an unworthy and useless counterfeit.

II. Worship in Judaism

A. The development of the synagogue.
Reference has been made already to incipient stages of SYNAGOGUE development during the later OT period. It has been shown that at least the elements of synagogue worship almost certainly found a place in the religious life of the exiles. So far as the organized synagogue is concerned, however, the subject is wrapped in obscurity, for, apart from a possible reference in Ps. 74:8, there are no data until the 3rd cent. B.C., and the first assured allusion to a synagogue as a place of worship dates only from the 1st cent. A.D. In the main, scholars incline to the view that the organized synagogue is the product of the measures taken by the dispersed Jews to fill the gaps caused by their isolation from the temple, and that the movement of synagogical worship is from the dispersion to Palestinian Judaism, especially through the ministry of EZRA.

Opposing theories espousing a Palestinian origin are (1) that the synagogue was a Mosaic institution, (2) that what was originally a civil assembly was given religious significance by the prophets when they made their speeches there, and (3) that the synagogue is a resuscitation of the ancient cultic shrines under the influences of Josiah's reforms. Another suggestion is that the first synagogues were temples after the pattern of ELEPHANTINE but that these gradually became spiritual rather than realistic representations of the temple at Jerusalem. In the absence of solid evidence the field is obviously wide open for speculation and it could well be that diverse forces contributed to the emergence of the organized synagogue of later times. On the whole, however, a specific origin in the dispersion along the lines already indicated seems to be most in accord with the situation.

B. Aspects of synagogue worship.
The theme of developed synagogical worship is complicated both by the lack of early data and also by the wealth of detail available in the later rabbinic writings. Though many of the details are of no great significance, synagogue worship as a whole is highly important because of its evident similarity of structure to early Christian services.

Since the law of central sacrifice did not permit either temple or offerings outside Jerusalem, the synagogue does not provide sacrificial worship. Perhaps the chief article of furniture is the chest or ark for the scrolls of the law (and prophets). Closely associated with this is the platform or pulpit for the reading of the lessons and the recitation of the prayers. The ministers of the synagogue are not priests, nor do they discharge priestly functions, though a priest, if present, would give the benediction. The chief office bearer was the RULER OF THE SYNAGOGUE, who presided over the assembly, chose the prophetic lesson, and originally did the reading. The servant or officer of the synagogue acted as the ruler's assistant both in the detailed arrangement of services and also in administration. A messenger of the congregation was also selected from among the people to lead in the recitation of prayer or to pray on the congregation's behalf. Originally the messenger was chosen for each service, but his tasks later came to devolve on the servant. The herald of the Shema was another minister who either promulgated this prayer (originally from a written scroll) or led an antiphonal recitation of it. Incidentally,

Synagogue worship at the Western Wall of the temple mount.

the reading of the Scriptures in Hebrew meant that a translation was needed to put them into the familiar Aramaic (also Greek), though many Palestinian Jews could still follow the original.

Ten males at least had to be present for a service. Whether or not women were originally allowed to attend is debated. Early absence of the separate gallery suggests that they might have been excluded, but among Hellenistic Jews women played no inconsiderable role, so that separation might have been by movable screen. The later gallery testifies to admission on a basis of separation by sex.

The chief element in synagogue worship is undoubtedly the reading of Scripture. From the 1st cent. B.C. readings from the law seem to have followed a triennial cycle. The prophetic readings did not conform to a settled pattern. The ruler of the synagogue usually selected the passage. The sermon, when delivered, was closely related to Scripture, for it took the form of an exposition of the prophetic reading (cf. Lk. 4:16–21). This exposition would normally be given only if a competent person was present. Visiting strangers could be invited to deliver the address (Acts 13:14–15).

Next to the reading (and exposition) of Scripture the recitation of the Shema and common prayer were the two most important features. The Shema, preceded and followed by brief prayers, consisted of three passages: Deut. 6:4–9; 11:13–21; and Num. 15:37–41. It served both as a confession of faith and as a constant summons to obedience and faithfulness. In fulfillment of the injunction to instruct children in faith and practice, the synagogue also undertook an educational role, not as a primary school in the strict sense, but as a school for primary studies in the law. The common prayer of the synagogue consisted of the *Eighteen (Nineteen) Benedictions*, which every Jew was supposed to know by heart and to repeat daily. In the NT period the number of petitions was probably much smaller, and there was considerable variation in wording from place to place and even from synagogue to synagogue. This gave enhanced importance to the messenger who led the prayer. The benedictions include praise of God and prayer for the needy and afflicted. They receive their name from the blessing ("Blessed be thou …") at the close of each individual section.

Liturgical forms enjoyed a place of some importance in synagogue worship. The reading of the OT and recitation of the Shema provided a basis. The prayer of the *Eighteen Benedictions* gradually came to have a more settled form; earlier differences were due more to local variation than to extemporaneousness, though considerable latitude was probably allowed to the leader within the general content. Extemporary prayer was by no means unknown in Israel. The rabbis often prayed freely or made free additions to given forms. In public worship, however, Israel tended to develop a rich set of liturgical forms which owed a great deal to the legacy of the past. The very centrality of biblical reading helped to cast the prayers and petitions in a biblical mold. Incidentally, the congregational "Amen" became an established feature in synagogical prayer.

A final aspect of synagogue worship was psalmody. There is no certainty as to the date when psalms first began to be used in the synagogue. The probability seems to be that in later centuries at least the synagogue took over the usage of the temple. The place for the psalm was perhaps between the reading from the law and the reading from the prophets, and a cantor would sing the verses while the congregation responded with a refrain. In Palestine at least the use of psalms in the temple might well have been a retarding factor in the synagogical development, but once Jerusalem was destroyed the psalms could hardly be allowed to go out of public use, even if the synagogues did not have the musical resources of the national shrine.

A final point worth noting is that with the rise of the synagogue the Sabbath, as the natural day for assembly, became much more specifically a day of worship and contemplation as well as a day of rest. The sanctification of the day to God acquired a new positive content.

C. Individual worship. Along with the development of the synagogue, JUDAISM saw a continuation and probably an intensification of individual piety to which closer acquaintance with the OT made no little contribution. Grace was said before and after meals. The prayer of the *Eighteen Benedictions* was to be recited thrice daily. Prayers were also prescribed for specific events and occasions. Extemporary prayers might also be used. Recitation of the Shema was also enjoined. Silent meditation is recorded of some of the earlier saints, though one can hardly know how widespread this was. Personal reading of scriptures was hardly possible for most Jews, but whole passages were committed to memory and could be recalled or recited as needed. How rich a source of piety and devotion the OT could be is amply manifested in the canticles that well up from Zechariah, Mary, and Simeon at the beginning of the NT story (Lk. 1–2).

In both congregational and individual worship, Judaism realized clearly enough that the recitation of fixed passages and prayers raised many problems of greater or lesser magnitude. Questions of audibility or fluency need not detain us, but the problem of careless or mechanical recitation is crucial. Certain rabbis were prepared to argue that minute attention to the wording is not essential. There is objective value in the act of worship quite apart from inner concentration. Others, however, insisted that fervor and involvement are at least necessary for true prayer, if not so necessary in the rehearsal of the Shema. This would apply in congregational as well as individual practice, though it was more important in the latter. In general, one may say that Judaism, in spite of a tendency toward legalistic understanding and practice, retained a keen awareness of the danger of formalism and made some plea for the inner devotion that is the only safeguard of individual piety, whether structured or unstructured.

III. Worship in the NT

A. Important terms. There is much to be gained by a careful examination of some of the Greek words related to worship.

1. Gonypeteō. The verb *gonypeteō* G1206, "to kneel down," and various phrases that include the noun *gony* G1205, "knee," are significant because they describe a gesture of worship which also symbolizes the inner attitude. In the Greco-Roman world the terms could have a secular reference too, for the slave would genuflect before his master. Bowing the knee did not occur in the official cult, but it had an established place in the worship of the chthonic deities, especially in cults which had stood under oriental influence.

Genuflection is common in the OT. It may sometimes be practiced before human beings, such as "the man of God" (2 Ki. 1:13) and the king (1 Chr. 29:20). On the other hand, even though standing is the normal attitude in prayer (Gen. 18:22; 1 Sam. 1:26), there is also kneeling before God (1 Ki. 8:54; Dan. 6:10). Bending the knee or kneeling is a sign of humility, self-abasement, and homage (Isa. 45:23). The rabbis later made a distinction between brief genuflection and full prostration with outstretched hands and feet.

In the NT the reference is almost exclusively to bowing the knee. The main uses are in connection with prayer to God (Lk. 22:41), petitions to the Lord (Matt. 17:14), greeting of the teacher (Mk. 10:17), and homage, whether to the king (cf. Matt. 27:29), to Baal (Rom. 11:4), to the divine Judge (Rom. 14:10–11), or to Jesus at the full manifestation of his Lordship (Phil. 2:10). The gesture is expressive of humility, need, respect, submission, and adoration. It passed into the early church as an established practice in both individual and common prayer.

2. Proskyneō. Related to *gony* and *gonypeteō* is the more general verb *proskyneō* G4686, which is in some ways the closest general expression to the English *worship*. The early history of this term is obscure, though it evidently derives from *kyneō*, "to kiss." It is conjectured that in the ancient Greek world kissing the earth was practiced as a means of honoring the earth deities; this in turn involved an element of bending or prostration which was originally alien to the Greeks in other spheres. More likely, the term reflects the practice of kissing the feet, or the hem of the garments, of kings who were regarded as gods. In any case, *proskyneō* came to mean, "to prostrate oneself in token of reverence, to do obeisance." Since worship seems to have been implied by the act or gesture from the very first, it was natural that the word should also be used quite early for the inner attitude of worship.

Since obeisance was already a common gesture in OT worship, it is not surprising that *proskyneō* occurs frequently in the SEPTUAGINT. It can still carry with it the thought of kissing (cf. the parallelism in Exod. 18:7), but the predominant sense is that of bowing (to the earth) in obeisance, that

is, doing reverence, honoring, worshiping. In some instances obeisance is done to human beings, for example, to the prophet or to the king. This may be a courtly gesture (cf. Abraham in Gen. 23:7, 12), but in other cases the obeisance seems to be paid to a man as the representative of God (cf. 1 Sam. 20:41). Protest against obeisance to a man is expressed by MORDECAI, who refused to bow down to HAMAN (Esth. 3:2). Angels, as the messengers of God, may be the object of obeisance (see ANGEL). In the main, however, the LXX reserves the word for the worship of deity, whether it be the false idol (Exod. 20:5 et al.) or the true God (Gen. 22:5 et al.). Hence, the term carries with it the same sense as the English *worship*. The predominant use is for the worship of God, though a subsidiary generalized sense remains. The main difference is that the Greek word is by origin more closely connected with the gesture of prostration or obeisance.

In the NT the use of *proskyneō* is almost completely confined to the Gospels, Acts, and Revelation. Apart from two OT quotations in Hebrews, the only instance in the Epistles is in 1 Cor. 12:45 (applied to a person who comes into the Christian assembly as an unbeliever). In Acts the term is never used for Christian worship apart from the earliest worship in the temple (Acts 8:27; 24:11). When believers are said to bow the knees in prayer, a phrase with *gony* is used. The implication seems to be that *proskyneō* was deliberately avoided as a term for primitive Christian worship, possibly because of its pronounced association with the visible worship of a visible god in paganism.

In the Synoptic Gospels the word is reserved for obeisance to God or to Jesus. The apparent exception (Matt. 18:26) is controlled by the fact that God obviously stands behind the lord of the parable. Perhaps the most interesting feature in Matthew and Mark is that obeisance is done to Jesus. This is especially true in Matthew (e.g., the leper in 8:2; JAIRUS in 9:18). In the light of the worship of the MAGI (2:2, 11) and the rejection of the devil's claim to worship (4:9–10), there can be little doubt that Matthew is not using the term merely to denote a conventional gesture of respect paid to Jesus. Wittingly or unwittingly, those who worship Jesus are recognizing his deity. This is the irony behind the mocking obeisance of the soldiers in Mk. 15:19.

The disciples do obeisance only when they begin to apprehend his divine sonship (Matt. 14:33) or when they are in the presence of the risen Lord (28:9, 17). In Acts, PETER refuses to let CORNELIUS worship him (Acts 10:25–26), and the angel issues a similar prohibition in Revelation (Rev. 19:10).

In Jn. 4:20–24 there is an important use of *proskyneō*. In contrast to the localized worship that underlay the woman's question, Jesus refers here to the worship which is in spirit (or Spirit) and in truth. The restriction of worship to a single locality is thus set aside. Whether or not worship itself is to be a purely inward matter with no outward expression is, however, much more doubtful in view of the use of the verb. True worship is certainly an inner act of the spirit (although the statement may allude to the fact that true worship can take place only through the HOLY SPIRIT, who is the Spirit of truth, 14:17 et al.). External obeisance is neither a prerequisite nor a guarantee. Nevertheless, there is the same ambivalence as in the prophetic message, for inner worship is by no means incompatible with outward expression, and can even demand such an expression.

The verb is an important term in Revelation. A distinction is here made between worship of the beast on the one side and the worship of God in the heavenly sanctuary on the other. The act is obviously in view, though it surely has symbolical significance in the great scenes depicted in Rev. 4–5. The point is that behind *proskyneō* lies the ultimate acknowledgement of conflicting total claims. In the end, however, the nations of the world will all worship God (15:4).

The fact that the verb can be used again for the final homage at the PAROUSIA lends support to the thesis of H. Greeven (in *TDNT*, 6:765) that *proskyneō* in the NT demands in the main a visible act or concrete gesture of obeisance to visible deity. This is possible during the INCARNATION and during the forty days between Easter and the ASCENSION OF CHRIST; hence the synoptic use. It will be possible again at the SECOND COMING; hence the use in Rev. 15:4. In the intervening period, however, *proskyneō* is not the proper term for Christian worship; hence its avoidance in Acts (apart from temple worship) and the Epistles (apart from the unbeliever of 1 Cor. 14). On the other hand, it

should be noted that the verb is rarely used in the Gospel of Luke (Lk. 4:7–8; 24:52). Moreover, it is unclear why *proskyneō*, as indicating a visible act, should be more objectionable than phrases that use *gony* (Acts 7:60, 9:40, et al.).

3. Latreuō. The verb *latreuō* G3302 and its cognate noun *latreia* G3301 introduce us to a different sphere from that of the terms we have already considered. The basic meaning here is that of wages, or more generally service, eventually with no necessary thought of reward and in a far more comprehensive sense than that of slavery. Bodily service is first denoted, such as working on the land or functioning in a specific sense (e.g., cupbearer). The word can also be used for care of the body, the cherishing of life. In the classical world it is not a highly significant religious term, but there are instances of its use in connection with the worship or service of the gods. The performance of acts associated with the cultus seems to be the main connotation (for example, the making of the necessary preparations).

In the LXX the verb occurs predominantly in Exodus, Deuteronomy, Joshua, and Judges. It has the sense of "service," but in these books, and indeed throughout the OT, the reference is always religious. In each case, however, the service denoted consists not merely in the general serving of God but in the cultic act of sacrifice. The word is freely used for the service of other gods (Exod. 20:5 et al.), but the consistent demand of the OT is that Israel should serve the true and living God. This imparts a deeper element to the cultic act. Serving the Lord in offerings is based on an ultimate decision or committal of the heart. This is magnificently brought out in Deut. 10:12–13, which speaks of loving and serving God with the whole heart and soul. This service requires an ethical as well as a cultic outlet, for the person who loves and serves God in this way will keep God's commandments and statutes. The call of Joshua for a choice between serving other gods and serving the Lord has the same emphasis (Josh. 24:14–28), especially with its stringent insistence that keeping the commandments is an essential part of the required service (v. 19).

The noun *latreia* is much less common than the verb. It is used almost exclusively for cultic worship, whether general or specific (e.g., the Passover in Exod. 12:25–26). A remarkable feature in contrast to general Greek usage is that the nonreligious use has been virtually abandoned. This noun, however, is neither a very general term on the one side (serving God) nor a very specific one on the other (the priestly ministry). It simply denotes the cultic worship of God. As is learned from the verb, this rests ultimately on a profound self-commitment to God in love and fear.

As in the LXX, so also in the NT the verb is more common than the noun. The verb occurs most frequently in Luke/Acts and, as one might expect, Hebrews. Under OT influence it always bears a religious reference. The service denoted by it is the service of God (or the gods). In Hebrews the sacrificial ministry of the OT (as distinct from that of false gods) is in view. An important difference from OT usage is that in Heb. 8:5 and 13:10 the author seems to break down the LXX distinction between *latreuō* for cultic service and *leitourgeō* (see below) for the specific ministry of the priests (cf. also 9:9). Nevertheless, the general impulse of the NT is to extend rather than to narrow down the range of religious meaning. Apart from the use in Matt. 4:10, where *latreuō* denotes the worship one must offer God in contrast to the obeisance demanded by the devil, this extension takes place in the three main areas of prayer, work, and life.

(a) The use for the ministry of prayer occurs in Luke's writings. When ANNA is said to serve God with fasting and prayers night and day (Lk. 2:37), the fasting and prayers seem to constitute an important part of the service rather than adjuncts to it. There is a similar reference in Acts 26:7, for here the service which the tribes render in hope of fulfillment of the promise surely includes prayer. This is important, for while prayer was undoubtedly implied in the cultic offerings of the OT, it did not originally constitute the true content of *latreia*.

(b) Even more significant is the use of *latreuō* for the work of the NT ministry. This is the specific contribution of Paul in Rom. 1:9, where he speaks of serving God "with my spirit in the gospel of his Son" (KJV). If he had merely said "with my spirit," one might have seen a reference to worship in spirit and in truth. The phrase "in the gospel," however, indicates preaching the gospel, as in 2 Cor. 8:18. It need not be supposed that Paul is simply saying that preaching is a constituent part of the worship in the congregation, though this is a reasonable implication and it might indeed underlie the thought of the apostle (cf. the place of exposition in the structure of synagogue worship). What Paul is doing is rather describing the ministry of the word itself in cultic terms (cf. his use of "sacrifice"). This ministry is not just service in general; it is worship. Paul does not, of course, mention preaching as such. Hence it is possible to see a broader reference. All his committal and endeavor on behalf of the gospel is a service of God in this sense. Possibly there is even a hint of prayer as well as the outward activity of ministry, though at the deepest level *latreuō* here surely indicates Paul's whole dedication to God—his underlying motivation was total commitment after the manner of Deut. 10:12–13.

(c) The whole life of the believer can also form the content of *latreuō*. This may be seen already in the BENEDICTUS, which speaks of serving God "in holiness and righteousness" (Lk. 1:74–75). A similar use is to be found in Acts 24:14, where Paul claims that he serves the God of his fathers in fidelity to the Law and the Prophets (cf. also the reference to the conscience in v. 16 and in 2 Tim. 1:3). Similarly, Heb. 12:28 speaks of serving God with reverence and godly fear; the reference is surely to manner of life (ch. 13) rather than a pious sense of the numinous. The term is even broader, perhaps, in Phil. 3:3, where the true circumcision, service in the Spirit, is contrasted with legal circumcision, life after the flesh. It is possible, of course, that the thought here might be that of spiritual worship as compared with worship according to ritual enactment, but the general context supports a contrast between two wholly different ways of life, the joyous way of the Spirit and the painful way of legal blamelessness.

The noun *latreia* occurs only five times in the NT, and in three instances it refers to the sacrificial cultus of the OT (Rom. 9:4; Heb. 9:1, 6). In Jn. 16:2 also there is perhaps a hint of the sacrificial background when Jesus says that the killing of the disciples will be regarded as a doing of service to God. Similarly the *logikē latreia* of Rom. 12:1 is set in the context of presenting the body as a living sacrifice to God. Here, however, the sacrifice is a self-consecration that embraces the renewal and transformation of life. It is also "logical," which means that it is a reasonable thing to do, but also that it follows a logical pattern and has its ultimate basis in the LOGOS (the adj. *logikos* G3358 here and in 1 Pet. 2:2 is sometimes rendered "spiritual"). Thus *latreia* bursts the bounds of the cultic and acquires a total reference both inward and outward. Yet in so doing it preserves the cultic association, for the very heart of this service is self-offering to God on the basis of God's self-offering for us. Orientation and content are thus given to the life of service. For service is truly rendered to God only if it is in its very essence the worship that finds legitimate and necessary expression in acts of prayer and praise.

4. Leitourgeō. The verb *leitourgeō* G3310 and its cognate noun *leitourgia* G3311 are related etymologically to *laos* G3295, "people," and originally indicated service rendered on behalf of a people or nation, that is, the body politic. From the very earliest examples the words have a technical sense in the Greek world. They are used for specific services which the wealthy, either voluntarily or compulsorily, render for the city or community at their own expense. Some of these "liturgies," both general and special, could be extremely costly. In the imperial period the word took on a rather wider range of meaning, embracing all compulsory official service rendered in state or community. The papyri have many references to the assignment and limitation of such services, and especially to the burden they imposed. Then the word acquired a very extended and loose sense from which the official element disappeared. Thus slaves rendered *leitourgia* to their masters, mothers to their babes, friends to friends, fathers to sons, even courtesans to their clients. In the MYSTERY RELIGIONS the term found a cultic use which tended to give it a new technical sense. Temple employees were said to perform "liturgies," and cultic acts could be described as liturgies performed to the god.

The cultic use is predominant in the LXX. Of the hundred or so instances of the verb, only a very few are nonreligious, and the same is true of the forty examples of the noun. No trace remains of the original classical sense, and even the general meaning has more or less disappeared. The object of *leitourgia* is either God in person or his tabernacle, temple, altar, or name. In particular, both verb and noun are used for the particular services rendered by the priests and Levites. The priestly functions are *leitourgia*. The verb occurs either in the absolute, with "to the Lord," or with an accusative, "to render the liturgy [or liturgies] of the tabernacle." The use is almost always literal. Only in the APOCRYPHA (Ecclesiasticus and Wisdom of Solomon) does one find a tendency to spiritualize the concept. Incidentally, it is highly improbable that the LXX translators used these terms because they were already cultic terms in the mysteries. H. Strathmann (in *TDNT*, 4.22) is surely on the right track when he suggests that the official and solemn aspects determined the selection of these words for priestly functions. Though rendered primarily to God, liturgy was a national institution of benefit to the whole people. In distinction from the other word groups, *leitourgia* has the dignity associated with public service, and this is probably the decisive factor.

The words do not have the same importance in the NT as they do in the LXX. In fact, the verb occurs only three times and the noun six times. Three of the nine instances are in Hebrews, and the other six are restricted to Luke/Acts and Paul. The noun *leitourgos* G3313, "minister," and the adjective *leitourgikos* G3312, "engaged in service," yield another six instances, but three of these are in Hebrews and the other three in Paul. In spite of its abiding influence through the English word *liturgy*, these terms can hardly be regarded as significant in the NT.

In Hebrews and also in Lk. 1:23 the usage falls within the framework of the OT. Thus ZECHARIAH is said, quite naturally, to fulfill the days of his *leitourgia*. Hebrews again finds a perfectly natural use for the concept with reference to ceremonial vessels and sacrifices (Heb. 9:21; 10:11). More interesting is the transfer of the term to Christ himself, who is said to have offered a better *leitourgia* when he gave himself definitively upon the cross (8:6). The sacrificial reference of the term explains its usage in relation to the high-priestly ministry of our Lord.

Thus far it might appear as if *leitourgia* were an improper term for Christian worship. Its sacrificial associations would surely imply an extension of sacerdotal ideas to the services of the church.

In Acts 13:2, however, the service of the prophets and teachers suggests prayer and fasting along the lines of the spiritualizing of the word in the later testamental period (cf. Philo). Paul goes even further and applies the word both to the collection he organized for the church in Jerusalem (2 Cor. 9:12) and also to the gift the Philippians made to him (Phil. 2:30; cf. Rom. 15:27). Three explanations are possible here: (1) that the word is used quite generally for service; (2) that it echoes the thought of the official liturgies of classical times; and (3) that it identifies the collection or gift as a sacral act. In view of the role which the collection seems to have assumed in later worship, it is perhaps not overfanciful to catch a cultic note in Paul's use.

This understanding is hardly contradicted by Phil. 2:17 (cf. the association with sacrifice), though the precise meaning of the verse is hard to determine. If Paul is offering both the faith of the Philippians and also himself, then his ministry and martyrdom are the liturgy. On the other hand, if it is the faith of the Philippians which renders the service, their Christian life would seem to be the liturgy. Either way, one finds a certain approximation to the development already noted in respect of *latreia*. The term is certainly not used for official functions performed by the apostles, prophets, teachers, or presbyters of the infant church. Hence, if the word is to be used in the church, it must not be given the sacerdotalist implications of, for example, a special application to the LORD'S SUPPER.

The noun *leitourgos* is used of Christ himself (Heb. 8:2). In Heb. 1:7 (cf. 1:14) it denotes the angels as the instruments of God's will. This also seems to be the bearing in Rom. 13:6, where rulers are called God's servants. EPAPHRODITUS is a "minister" when he brings the gift of the Philippians (Phil. 2:25); he is either the agent of service, the executor of a public benefaction, or the servant of a cultic act (cf. 2:30). Finally, in a passage with more priestly overtones, Paul himself is a "minister" of Jesus Christ to the Gentiles (Rom. 15:16). This ministry is explicitly connected with the preaching of the gospel and also with the offering up of the faith of the Gentiles (cf. Phil. 2:17). It seems, then, that Paul is again using a sacrificial metaphor for the evangelical ministry. In so doing, he characterizes this ministry as the supreme worship which, on

the basis of Christ's own liturgy, the Christian can render to God.

5. Homologia. The noun *homologia* G3934 and the verbal form *homologeō* G3933 (from *homos*, "the same, common," and *logos*, "word, saying") bear the basic sense of "assent" or "agreement." This leads to a varied use of the verb in law and commerce, such as "to admit what is said, to confess a charge, to confirm the receipt of money, to agree or submit to a proposal, to promise." The noun can imply agreement in a discussion, the agreement of practice with theory or principle, or an agreement or compact. The concept of living harmoniously (with nature) is an important one in STOIC thought. In a religious sense, which is acquired rather than original, the concept denotes either the acceptance of vows or, more commonly, the CONFESSION of sins. Under oriental influences the confession could be made to a priest with a view to the placation of deity in a time of affliction.

If confession of sins is basic in the OT, it seems to be associated here with a very different type of confession, namely, the confessing or praising of God in his mighty acts. Various psalms bring out the connection (e.g., Pss. 22; 30). Acknowledging his sin, the psalmist finds salvation, and his penitence becomes praise and thanksgiving. Thus the confession changes its character. Admission of sin becomes acknowledgment of the grace and power of God. The confession of wrongdoing yields to confession of God, not so much in the sense of a confession of faith, but rather in the sense of a confession of praise, a magnifying of God.

For this confession both of sin and of praise the LXX prefers compound forms, especially *exomologeō* G2018. The underlying Hebrew, which has the force of praise as well as confession of sin, influences the LXX at this point (cf. 1 Ki. 8:33, 35; Neh. 9:3). The presupposition in both Hebrew and Greek is that the confession and praise take place publicly in the congregation. This means that the praise also carries with it an element of proclamation. To confess God's gracious work is to declare it (Ps. 118:17–21). Nor should the element of prayer be overlooked, for confessing the name of the Lord can be an act of prayer corresponding to calling on the name of the Lord. The single word *confession* can thus bind together in a unique way the fundamental constituents of true worship, namely, confession of sin, praise of God, the declaration of his acts, and prayer to him. All this presupposes, of course, the confession of faith as well.

In the NT the first sense to call for notice is that of solemn declaration. This may be very general in character (cf. the promise of Herod Antipas in Matt. 14:7). It can also merge into the more specific biblical act of confession of faith. Thus the OT saints who, according to Heb. 11:13, confessed that they were strangers and pilgrims were not merely confirming or admitting this; they were making a declaration of faith. From this it is an easy step to the sense of witness (see TESTIMONY), which has obvious roots in the classical legal use, but which takes on a distinctive character in the NT. Witness is predominantly witness to Jesus Christ.

Confession or nonconfession of Jesus has eschatological significance (Matt. 10:32), for to a person's confession of the Lord corresponds the Lord's confession of that person. Denial itself can take the form of a confession of ignorance (7:23). Confession of Jesus as Messiah may bring about expulsion from the synagogue (Jn. 9:22). Confession of Jesus also carries with it confession of a belief (Rom. 10:9–10). Paul links the faith of the heart, namely, that God has raised Jesus from the dead, with the confession of the lips, namely, that Jesus is Lord. This combination gives assurance of salvation. The specific doctrine of the resurrection is the theme of confession (Acts 23:8, referring to the Pharisees). John uses *homologeō* for the Christological confession which he seeks to protect against false teachers (cf. 1 Jn. 4:2–3; 2 Jn. 7). True teachers can be distinguished from false by confession.

Jesus himself witnessed a good confession before PILATE. In so doing, he set an example for all Christians to follow (1 Tim. 6:13). Baptism provides an opportunity for the basic confession, which may take an interrogatory form (cf. Matt. 16:13–16; Jn. 1:19–27; Acts 8:37). If all Christians are to confess, those called to the work of the ministry have a special task of confession. The emphasis here is not so much on testimony to faith as on proclamation, witness, evangelism, or even personal teaching. Confession is the confession of Jesus, of what God has done in him. This apostolic confession lays

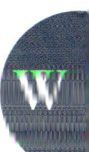

upon the hearers an obligation to confess their sins and join in the confession of Jesus as Savior and Lord. Since the theme of confession is the gracious reconciliation God has wrought in Christ, confession still redounds to God's honor and glory, and lends itself admirably to praise and thanksgiving.

The noun *homologia* is seldom used in the NT. It has a fluidity of sense which shows how rich the concept is. The author denotes the fixed confession of faith from which the church is not to turn aside; this possibly had a hymnic form. The confession of Timothy (1 Tim. 6:12–13) might also refer to a fixed body of doctrine accepted at baptism or ordination, but the emphasis seems to be more on the element of public avowal. Paul uses the word quite freely in 2 Cor. 9:13. The collection gives evidence of the response and obedience of the Corinthians and in this way redounds to God's further glory. Hints of the declaration of the gospel and the confession of faith lie behind the term here. The fact that confession and obedience go hand in hand shows that there is no fundamental rift with James, who states that words without works are hollow and worthless (Jas. 2:14–26).

Of the compound forms, *exomologeō* is the most important. Used with "sins" as the direct object, it denotes public confession (Rom. 14:11; Acts 19:18; Jas. 5:16). More commonly, however, it is a word of praise. Paul uses the term in this sense in Rom. 15:9. Christ is confessed as Lord to the glory of God the Father (Phil. 2:11). This ultimate "homology" of creation is anticipated already in the worship of the Christian church. The magnificent songs of Revelation might be described as "homological" in form and content, though the word itself does not occur.

"Homology" is not a direct equivalent of worship. Nevertheless, it is in many ways the most comprehensive and significant of all the Greek words the Bible uses for the veneration of God. This is because it is able, as no other term, to combine the most important features in genuine Christian worship. In the NT especially, the new stress on the declaration and attestation of Christ, and of God's saving work in him, adds substance and depth to what is included already in the LXX use. Confession of sins is still an indispensable part of worship. The confession or praise of God in prayer also retains its role.

Confession of faith, however, emerges as a central act of worship. This is twofold in content; it is confession of Jesus and it is also confession of the facts and doctrines relating to him. It is also twofold in form; it is public profession in the congregation and it is also the declaration of the gospel in apostolic witness and evangelism. Preaching, far from being an alternative to worship, is an intrinsic aspect of it. Confession of Jesus Christ, whether in the congregation or to the world, is to the praise of God's glory. As in the OT, "homology" is this praise of God which culminates in the heavenly anthems and in creation's acknowledgment of Jesus Christ as Lord. An understanding of biblical "homology" is perhaps the most important single key to an understanding of biblical worship.

B. Forms of worship

1. In the Gospels. The Gospels presuppose the forms of worship native to Palestinian Judaism in the early 1st cent. A.D. This means that the temple still occupied an important place in primitive NT worship. ZECHARIAH, father of the Baptist, was a priest, and God's revelation came to him as he fulfilled his ritual ministry in the temple (Lk. 1:5–20). Joseph and Mary were careful to keep the law of circumcision and the law of purification (2.21–24). When Jesus reached the appropriate age, he went up to the temple for the Passover; it is significant that his proleptic ministry on this occasion took place among the doctors of Israel in the temple, and that he gave to his parents a reply which at least carries the suggestion that the temple, the house of God, was his proper place (2:42–50). A noteworthy feature in Luke is that the beginnings of the gospel are thus set very plainly in the framework of the life and practice of Israel.

The temple maintains its importance throughout the incarnate life and ministry of Jesus. He attends the feasts: Passover, Tabernacles, Dedication. He also weaves the feasts into the pattern of his ministry. Teaching in the temple court, he shows at the Feast of Tabernacles that he is the true water of life. The Passover is the setting of the institution of the Lord's Supper and also of the accomplishment of the new exodus by his self offering on the cross as the Lamb which takes away the world's sin.

The promised outpouring of the Holy Spirit takes place significantly at Pentecost.

If Jesus has words of criticism for temple worship, they are directed against those who corrupt and defile it rather than against the worship as such. His driving out of the merchants and overturning of the tables for money is an act of defense of the temple (cf. Jn. 2:17) which arouses the hostility only of ecclesiastics and profiteers. Jesus foresees the overthrow of the temple, but he does so with the sadness of the true worshiper, not with the crazy zeal of the revolutionary.

Nevertheless, Jesus recognized that the temple had to be knocked down and that it could not be replaced in its familiar form. God never really agreed to have a permanent dwelling built for him, and the various temples had to perish. The true promise was that God would build a house for himself of the lineage of David. This promise had now come to fulfillment in Jesus, the One in whom God tabernacled among men and women in living presence. Hence the temple had reached its end and goal in the Person of the incarnate Son. Jesus could appreciate it because it had served as a type and figure of the true and final presence which God was to manifest in him. But he could not preserve it in its existing form. He could only "fulfill" it (Jn. 1:14; 2:19–22).

The same applies to the sacrifices and sacrificial ministry of the temple. One may assume that as Joseph and Mary made their offerings, and as Jesus himself attended the feasts, so he and his disciples continued to participate in sacrificial worship. The life of Jesus, however, was oriented to the making of one sacrifice for sins forever (Heb. 10:12), which would fulfill the Passover, the regular offerings, and also the special ritual of the Day of Atonement. Hence, when the temple sacrifices ceased with the destruction of the sanctuary, there would be no need to restore them. They had already reached their consummation. The types had given way to the reality in the self-offering of the Lord. Similarly, Jesus accepted the ministry of the Aaronic priesthood during his incarnate life. Yet he came to fulfill the ministry of the eternal high priest after the order of Melchizedek (Heb. 7). He was concerned neither to restore nor to replace the sacerdotal service of the destroyed temple. If a newer form of Passover was set up when the Last Supper became the Lord's Supper, it should be noted that here, as in the Jewish modification, the core and center of the ancient ritual was removed with the necessary abandonment of the slaying of the Passover lamb. Jesus had offered himself as the final Passover (1 Cor. 5:7) of the new and definitive redemption.

The synagogue is no less prominent than the temple in the gospel records. The custom of Jesus was to attend the synagogue on the Sabbath day (Lk. 4:16). In the synagogue at Nazareth he read the prophetic passage and in answer to the people's expectation gave an (astonishing) exposition of it. In the first period of his ministry he went about all Galilee, teaching in the synagogues (Matt. 4:23; 9:35). He cast out the unclean spirit in the synagogue at Capernaum (Mk. 1:21–17). He also faced the challenge of his opponents in the synagogue by healing the man with a withered arm on the Sabbath (Mk. 3:1–5), and he warned his disciples that they would be scourged in the synagogues (Matt. 10:17). It seems that in the later stages of his ministry, even though crowds still followed him (19:2), he was no longer so welcome in the synagogues (cf. Jn. 9:22; 12:42). Nevertheless, there was no definitive break with this institution prior to the crucifixion, and even then the first Christian missionaries were apparently still received in synagogues of the dispersion.

The Gospels give evidence of individual as well as public piety. One may refer again to saintly figures like Anna and Simeon, whose lives were devoted to prayer and praise and expectation. John the Baptist continues an earlier stream; he is the dedicated prophet of the desert pursuing a life of asceticism. The Lord himself, for all the contrast he draws between himself and John (Matt. 11:16–19), both enjoins and practices an assiduous life of prayer. He wants no outward show (6:1–8), but his disciples are told to engage in secret almsgiving, prayer, and fasting. He warns them that prayer (and fasting) are needed to perform certain works (17:21). He insists that the disciple must live in an attitude of watchfulness (24:42). He asks Peter, James, and John to watch with him in Gethsemane (26:38). He tells them to watch and pray lest they enter into temptation (v. 41). He himself engages in a forty-day fast in the desert (4:1–2). Time and again the Gospels record that he spent the early morning (Mk. 1:35) or the evening (6:47) in solitary meditation and prayer.

Before the final crisis Jesus retired to the garden to find strength for obedience to the Father's will, which now meant such cruel pain and loss for himself. The prayers on the cross, from the cry of dereliction to the petition for his tormentors and the final committal, are a culminating testimony to the Savior's personal walk with God. This is reflected also in his longer prayers that have been preserved, the cry of jubilation and thanksgiving (Lk. 10:21), the beautiful high-priestly prayer (Jn. 17), and, of course, the prayer he taught his disciples (Matt. 6:9–13). There is perhaps an incidental reference to his use of the Shema when he bases the first and great commandment on the familiar passage from the law (Mk. 12:28–30).

In the true prophetic tradition, Jesus has no time for the perverting of true piety into empty formalism. He censures not only the display of prayer but also the prayer which is merely vain repetition (Matt. 6:7). He also condemns severely the exaggerated emphasis on ritual practice that makes it a substitute for genuine righteousness (Mk. 7:6–8). Nevertheless, he does not reject either form (cf. the Lord's Prayer and the new ritual of the Lord's Supper) or ritual observances (Matt. 23:23) as such. His call is the prophetic call for the inner walk, the true consecration, and the right conduct which will naturally find expression in religious exercises and which alone give substance, reality, and power to the external motions.

2. In Acts and the Epistles. The witness of Acts and the Epistles is similar to that of the Gospels. The only important difference is that—as a result of the Gentile mission and increasing separation from the temple and synagogues—the churches have to develop their own forms of common worship. Even Jewish Christians obviously come under increasing pressure as persistent evangelism arouses the hostility of the ecclesiastical authorities.

The temple still figures prominently in the worship of the infant church. After the ascension the disciples were continually in the temple praising and blessing God (Lk. 24:51–53). Part of the fellowship of the Jerusalem church was daily attendance in the temple (Acts 2:46). Peter and John healed the lame man when on their way to the temple at the hour of prayer (3:1–8). Like Jesus, the apostles stood in the temple and taught the people (5:25). At a later date Paul was anxious to be at Jerusalem for the day of Pentecost (20:16). One of his first acts on reaching the city was to make his way to the temple and undergo ritual purification (21:21–26).

Model of the Jerusalem temple during the NT period. (View to the NW.)

When arrested and accused, Paul protested strongly that he had not offended in any way either against the law or against the temple.

The witness of Stephen shows that the early church had a strong sense of the transitoriness of the earthly temple (Acts 7:47–50). The pressure to Judaize was an important factor in dealing with this issue, for those who attached greater importance to the temple naturally wanted the Gentiles to become Jews so that they could worship there. The church, led by Stephen and Paul, came to see that this was neither possible nor right. Nevertheless, so long as the temple remained, it was for Jewish Christians a proper center of the true divine worship which is in faith, obedience, sincerity, and truth.

The relation to the synagogue is equally strong, though the opportunity of exposition soon made the synagogue a place of contention and separation. Stephen seems to have engaged in synagogue evangelism (Acts 6:8–10). Paul makes the synagogue the starting point of his missionary work in the various cities. He preaches in the synagogues at Pisidian Antioch and Iconium. He finds a house of prayer at Philippi. It was Paul's custom to attend the synagogue, and he reasoned for three Sabbaths in the synagogue at Thessalonica (17:1–2). Even as late as Acts 28:16 he calls the Jewish leaders of Rome together—his detention probably prevents his worshiping at the synagogue—and seeks to win them for the gospel. In most of the Pauline churches the first converts came from the synagogues, though in no instance does a whole synagogue seem to have become a Christian congregation.

The division that took place in the synagogues through the preaching of the gospel meant that Christians were forced to hold their own gatherings. They had been prepared for this by the special times of fellowship that the first disciples had enjoyed with their Lord, whether informally by the way or more formally at meals. Already the first church in Jerusalem met together in the upper room for prayer (Acts 1:14; 4:23; 12:12). The breaking of bread, whether in the form of common meals, the Lord's Supper, or both, played some part in the movement toward the church's independent worship. Outside Jerusalem, Paul (and Barnabas) apparently took steps to bring believers together for their own gatherings, which in some instances might have been supplementary to synagogue services, though there was a definite separation at Ephesus (19:9). The comparative ease with which synagogues could be formed, the pattern of worship already provided, and the conversion of leading members (cf. Crispus, the ruler of the synagogue, at Corinth, 18:8) helped to make the formation of Christian congregations a smooth and simple process. It was probably through meeting in private homes, due to the absence of church buildings, that one reads of house-churches (cf. Phlm. 2). The apostles made provision for the supervision of the new assemblies (Acts 14:22). Somewhat after the pattern of the synagogue, the two chief ministers were the elder (bishop) and deacon, though it is perhaps a mistake to see too close an assimilation to synagogical forms.

What form of worship was pursued in the Christian assemblies? The NT gives little detailed information. From the first chapters of Acts it may be gathered that prayer and the breaking of bread were primary. The only other detailed sources are in Acts 20 and 1 Cor. 11 and 14. Acts 20:7 records a meeting on the first day of the week at which the disciples broke bread and Paul preached; the meeting seems to have been in the evening. Similarly, 1 Cor. 11 speaks of a common meal that is plainly the Lord's Supper (vv. 23–34), though probably in combination with an ordinary supper. In 1 Cor. 14 Paul mentions a gathering at which members might contribute a psalm, a doctrine, a tongue, a revelation, or an interpretation, though with an emphasis on (a) edification and (b) order. The injunction in 16:2 is perhaps a further hint that these assemblies were held on the first day of the week. Whether or not Corinth was typical cannot be decided, nor indeed whether the procedure in ch. 14 is supplementary to more organized worship (e.g., at the Lord's Supper). Perhaps the Corinthian emphasis on tongues carried with it a more than customary drive for freedom.

Certainly a recognized structure had not emerged at this period so far as can be seen from the sources. Nevertheless, even at Corinth the constituent features of worship—prayer, praise, exposition (and reading?), and the Lord's Supper—are plain to see. The materials of liturgy are also present. The psalms would be the OT psalter, and readings involve a fixed form of words. Paul gives a simple order for the Lord's Supper. Part of the general content of prayer is enjoined in 1 Tim. 2:1–4. The prayer of Acts 4:24, though extemporaneous, uses liturgical phrases obviously drawn from the OT. Even the sermons recorded in Acts are not without patent similarities of wording and structure. Since the primitive church was heir to the rich tradition of the OT and Judaism, it would be strange if things were otherwise. The new spirit and power lie in the new understanding of the old forms, the fashioning of new forms out of the old, rather than in mere formlessness.

Individual piety finds no less expression in the life and teaching of the apostles than in that of the Lord. Paul is a good example. He practices and enjoins unceasing prayer (1 Thess. 3:10; 5:17). He calls for prayer in support of his ministry (Eph. 6:18). In many verses he indicates the content of his own prayers, which in the epistles at least are very largely intercessory in character (Phil. 1:4–11; Col. 1:9–12); though a passage like Phil. 3:8–11 becomes almost a prayer of aspiration, and his first

Christian prayer (Acts 9:11) was almost certainly a prayer for forgiveness and enlightenment. The indication of content is even more extended in Eph. 3:14–21, which seems to have been dictated by the apostle quite literally on his knees in the posture of individual prayer (Dan. 6:10). This prayer of petition characteristically moves to a doxological climax which expresses the confidence of faith and sees in all God's work a fulfillment of the first request of the Lord's Prayer. Steeped as he is in OT and Jewish forms, Paul adopts quite naturally a liturgical language that is a free adaptation of existing phrases. The intensity of his personal faith and devotion, allied to extensive biblical knowledge, produces a perfect blend of dignity and fervor.

In addition to prayer, Paul commends a diligent study of the Scriptures, whether by reading or by committing to memory (cf. 2 Tim. 3:14–17; Eph. 6:17). He also calls for a life of self-discipline, which may even include celibacy if this is the divine gift (1 Cor. 7:1–9), but which certainly includes bringing one's body into subjection for the sake of better service (9:24). The discipline of fasting is not neglected (2 Cor. 11:27). Thanksgiving is also to be the constant attitude and exercise of the believer (1 Thess. 5:9). The grave and sober conduct expected of bishops and deacons (1 Tim. 3) does not specify a personal exercise of piety, but this is surely implied. Timothy as a man of God is exhorted to pursue godliness (6:11). While the worship of the individual merges into that of the fellowship, and also into general uprightness of life and conduct, the personal exercise of religion is no unimportant aspect of worship in the NT.

C. Elements of worship. Though the NT does not give any detailed information on the structure of the first Christian services, it leaves little room for doubt concerning the basic elements in primitive worship. These are, of course, the elements already learned from the principles of worship and from OT practice. Their embodiment in synagogue worship might well have led to their immediate use in the infant church, since an early description like that in JUSTIN MARTYR's *Apology* (1.65–67; c. A.D. 150) reveals a close similarity to the practice of the synagogue. Nevertheless, even without this model, the fundamental elements would surely have found a place, and distinctive Christian features have, of course, their own origin.

1. Prayer. PRAYER in the more specific sense of petition is naturally a first consideration of the NT. The very first duty of the church between the ascension and the outpouring of the Spirit was to wait in prayerful expectancy. Persecution quickly forced the Jerusalem church to its knees in common prayer. The needs of Christians, the needs of apostles and teachers, the needs of the world—all provided constant material for intercession. Common concern produced common petition. One cannot say how exactly the church prayed. Perhaps a leader prayed for the whole, perhaps individuals prayed in course, perhaps there was recitation of a form or forms of prayer. Rather surprisingly, there is no immediate reference to a congregational use of the Lord's Prayer (even the use in *Didache* 8 is individual), but this was later found to be natural enough.

The AMEN, having acquired a new and even deeper meaning from its use by Jesus (cf. also 2 Cor. 1:20), occurs frequently in the NT and probably served as a congregational response, as in synagogue worship (cf. Justin). Stock phrases like MARANATHA might well have been used also (1 Cor. 16:22; cf. Rev. 22:20; *Didache* 10.7); otherwise it is hard to see why they should be preserved in ARAMAIC. BLESSINGS, whether from the OT or in the new Christian form of 2 Cor. 13:14 or Rev. 22:21, probably came into rapid use. The Epistles especially seem to testify to the emergence of distinctive vocabulary of Christian worship even in the NT period. Whatever the forms, however, the essential element of prayer itself belongs to worship from the very outset, and a genuine Christian service without it is almost unthinkable.

2. Praise. Closely related to prayer is PRAISE, the confession of God's nature and works. Indeed, prayer in the form of thanksgiving is itself praise. Almost all the prayers recorded in the NT contain an element of DOXOLOGY. They recall God's acts and thus sound a note of assurance and triumph. Quite apart from prayer, however, the praise of God has its own place in NT worship. The infancy stories show how the life of Christ began with angelic and human canticles that ultimately served as new songs in the congregation. The cry of jubilation uttered by the Lord took quasi-hymnic form. Jesus and the disciples sang a hymn—probably the customary HALLEL—at the Last Supper. Paul refers to a psalm at worship in Corinth, and to hymns and spiritual songs in Eph. 5:19. Scholars have discerned possible fragments of early Christian hymns in such passages as Phil. 2:6–11 and 1 Tim. 3:16. The hymns of Revelation show that songs are sung in heavenly as well as earthly worship, though some expositors think Rev. 4–5 might be based on the worship of the congregation. In the earliest period the psalter was probably the hymnbook of the church, but if the reference in PLINY the Younger's letter to TRAJAN (*Ep.* 10.96) is to Christological hymns, it seems that quite early new and more specifically Christian hymns found a place in the confession of praise.

3. Confession of sin. The CONFESSION of sin is at the heart of worship, for, as the worthiness of God is exalted, the unworthiness of sinners demands acknowledgment. The prayers and psalms of the OT are full of the recognition of guilt, which obviously goes hand in hand with a plea for FORGIVENESS and restitution, and with praise and thanks for the divine MERCY and pardon. In the NT the gospel is by its very nature a divine word to sinners. The baptism of John stands at the entry with its summons to repentance and conversion. Jesus takes up the same call, followed by his apostles in the first preaching of Acts. Peter, confronted by Jesus, confesses that he is a sinful man (Lk. 5:8). The prayer God hears in the temple is the penitent prayer of the publican rather than the self-congratulatory prayer of the Pharisee (18:9–14).

In the church's worship, the great occasion for the confession of sin is at BAPTISM, when the old life of sin is renounced and the new life of faith and obedience is begun. In postapostolic days the public confession of specific faults was required when the excommunicated sought readmittance. It may be seen from 1 Jn. 1:8–9, however, that confession of sins to God, whether individually or in concert, played a continuing role in the life of believers. Paul in his letters refers again and again to the utter dependence of himself and all believers on the divine mercy. Thus, even though there is no great evidence of specific prayers of confession in NT worship, this element must be presupposed as the basis of all prayer and praise. Prayer itself has to be in the name of Jesus, since there is nothing in oneself or in one's own name which could constitute a valid ground of either access or answer (cf. the role of Jesus as High Priest and Intercessor in Heb. 7).

4. Confession of faith (baptism). In the OT the Shema, though primarily commandment, served also as confession of faith: The Lord our God is one Lord. As such it had found its way into the worship of the synagogue. Though the Lord gave it added point, it was not adopted by the early church. The main reason is not that this basic confession was abandoned, but rather that there had now been added the distinctive Christian confession: Jesus is Lord. The faith of the primitive church is faith in Jesus as Savior and God. Peter makes this primary affirmation in Matt. 16:16. It may be seen again in THOMAS's confession (Jn. 20:28). John's gospel was written with a view to it (20:31). The work of the Spirit is to induce in Christians the affirmation that Jesus is Lord (1 Cor. 12:3). All tongues will finally confess this truth (Phil. 2:11). On this belief rests the full confession of the triune God (Matt. 28:19).

The point at which this confession is specifically made in the church is at baptism. This is given in the name of Jesus (Acts 2:38). The ETHIOPIAN EUNUCH professes belief in the Lord (8:37). CORNELIUS is baptized in his name (10:48). The Philippian jailer is baptized when he believes on the Lord and is saved (16:30–33). The evidence of the later church (Justin, *Apology* 1.61 et al.) is to the same effect. The baptismal confession was often made in interrogatory form, and it was followed by baptism in the triune name (triune immersion from *Didache* 7.1 onward). Whether or not there was also a specific confession of faith in ordinary worship is open to question. Certainly the NT offers no instance. Baptism itself, however, was also a normal part of the worship of the church. Taken over from John and continued and commanded by Jesus, it was required for admission to the church, and it included at its heart a confession of faith as well as repentance. Administered in various circumstances and with wide variations of wording, it retained its essential features through every change.

The first service for the convert was of common concern to the whole congregation. Like the Lord's Supper, it had, of course, a primary declarative aspect, for the ultimate baptismal confession is confession of the saving act of God in the death and resurrection of Christ. Nevertheless, it also provided opportunity for the affirmation of faith, which was quickly seen to be a reaffirmation by existing believers. The later weekly confession is a fairly natural and not unbiblical development that finds a regular place for this essential aspect of worship.

5. Reading of Scripture. Rather strangely, the NT does not refer to the reading of the OT in the common worship of the church. Paul's letters are publicly read (1 Thess. 5:27), and this might well have formed the beginning of the later NT readings (cf. Justin's reference to "Memoirs of the Apostles," *Apology* 1.66). The traditional texts relating to the Lord's Supper also seem to have been rehearsed (1 Cor. 11). In the light of synagogue practice, the extensive use of the OT in the NT, the later knowledge of the OT displayed in the postapostolic period, and the early patristic references to OT reading, it is virtually impossible to suppose that the NT church did not include OT readings in common worship. The fact that there were sermons (e.g., Paul at Troas) supports this. A sermon in the synagogue was primarily exposition. Early Christian preaching was especially concerned to show the fulfillment of the OT in Christ. Furthermore, the mention of an interpretation seems to presuppose reference to the OT. The high estimation of Scripture (cf. 2 Tim. 3:14–17) is a further consideration. Great freedom was no doubt exercised—even the synagogue had as yet no prophetic lectionary. But the reading of God's written word, first in the OT and then increasingly in the NT, was surely a constituent part of worship from the very first, as it patently was in both temple and synagogue, and then again in the church of the 2nd cent.

6. Preaching. In contrast to reading, PREACHING is solidly attested. Paul preached at Troas. The prophesyings at Corinth also seem to be forms of Christian exhortation. The needs of evangelism and education as well as edification made it essential that the ministry of the word be included in the early services. The synagogue provided a partial parallel, while the teaching of Jesus furnished an example. The apostles were specifically called to the ministry of the word (Acts 6). At a later time bishops were to be apt to teach (2 Tim. 3:2). Preaching combined several aspects of worship: declaration of God's work, confession of faith, underlying prayer, the climax of praise.

Early preaching was particularly related to the OT on the one side and to the life and work of Christ (later the NT) on the other. While not restricted to formal exposition, it had a strong expository content if one may judge from the sermons in Acts. Among Gentile Christians in particular a good deal of information would have to be passed on in preaching, for the same level of biblical knowledge could not always be assumed as among Jewish Christians or the early "god-fearers." APOLLOS, a man mighty in the Scriptures, exercised an important ministry in this field (Acts 18:24–25). In the postapostolic period Justin gives evidence of the secure position of preaching in the normal Christian service.

7. The Lord's Supper. If baptism was an addition to synagogue worship (though not without some parallel in proselyte baptism), this is even more true of the LORD's SUPPER. Both biblical and patristic evidence supports the view that this was from the very first a constitutive part of weekly worship. Certainly in Justin's time there is no disjunction between ministry of word and ministry of SACRAMENT, and the examples of Troas and Corinth suggest that, with variations of time and structure, the same applies in the NT period as well. The one gathering embraces not only prayer, praise, reading, and preaching, but also the holy meal, which was probably accompanied by blessings (cf. *Didache* 9–10) after the manner of the Passover. The Lord's Supper took the place, not only of the Passover, but also of the temple offerings. This is why sacrificial language soon came to be used in respect of it (cf. Mal. 1:11).

Yet, it was not strictly a replacement. The Lord's Supper shows forth the one sacrifice for sins for

ever. Christ as High Priest has made a sacerdotal ministry redundant. Hence the ministers of the Supper, whether apostles, bishops, presbyters, or deacons, are truly ministers, not priests. The focal point is declaration of the death and resurrection of Jesus Christ for mankind. This is the ground of the fellowship here enjoyed with God and with fellow believers. Ultimately, then, the Lord's Supper, like all else, is Christological rather than, in the narrower OT sense, liturgical. To describe it as quintessentially liturgy is in the last resort misleading. It is also to do despite to its very real place and significance within the church's worship as a perpetual reminder that worship is possible only on the basis of the atonement God himself has made by his self-offering in the Son.

8. The collection? The reference to a weekly allocation in 1 Cor. 16, the liturgical significance ascribed to alms in Phil. 4:18, and mention of an offering in patristic writings, have led to the view that a collection formed a basic element in Christian worship. Difficulties in the way of this conclusion are the following: Paul does not speak of a church collection; the Philippians' gift, like the Jerusalem collection, was probably a special project (though rapidly succeeded by extensive poor relief); and TERTULLIAN refers only to a chest for spontaneous gifts (*Apology* 39.1–6). Furthermore, some scholars argue that Justin's offertory is that of bread and wine for communion, though this was no obvious part of the original institution. On the other side, one should consider that almsgiving had a long OT history, and that the importance of liberality as part of serving God is beyond dispute. Thus, if it is too much to say that the collection is a constitutive part of the service, there are good grounds for its later inclusion. The "kiss of peace" falls into something of the same category.

9. Occasional services? It has often been noted that there are no marriage or funeral services in the NT. It should be remembered, however, that such services are only an application of the basic elements of worship — prayer, praise, reading, exposition, and the Lord's Supper where appropriate — to specific situations. In fact, the NT itself mentions certain occasions — e.g., confirming by the apostles, ordaining, and perhaps the anointing of the sick — when biblical signs (laying on of hands, anointing) were used along with other liturgical elements. This does not mean that there were developed services of confirmation, etc. It simply shows that there can be rapid adaptation of the basic elements to particular needs, sometimes with a particular sign. The consecration of Paul and Barnabas to missionary service at Antioch offers an instructive example (Acts 13:2–3). Whether or not any given service can find a precedent in the NT, the NT certainly offers the materials from which a genuinely biblical service may be constructed, and the injunction that all things are to be done in the Lord means that the introduction of elements of worship is never a misplaced or unwarranted intrusion.

D. Essence of worship. Though the elements of Christian worship are the same as those found already in the OT, there are two new factors at the very heart of the NT which bring about a decisive reorientation.

1. Christ. The first of these is that Christian worship is in its very core and essence the worship of God the Father through God the Son. The elements remain; the Christological orientation is new. If space allowed, one might easily work through the data afresh. In this brief climax and conclusion, a few indications must suffice. The worshiper now stands in a personal relation of sonship to God on the basis of ADOPTION in Christ. He prays in the

Armenian worship processional at the Church of the Holy Sepulchre in Jerusalem.

name of the Son (Jn. 16:23). The works of God in the Son are the theme of his praise (Eph. 1:3–14). His plea for forgiveness is that Christ gave himself as a perfect sacrifice for sin (1 Jn. 1:7–10). His confession is confession of Jesus as Lord (1 Cor. 12:3).

The Scriptures, both OT and NT, testify of Christ (Jn. 5:39). Preaching is the setting forth of Christ in his revealing and reconciling work (2 Cor. 5:18–21). The Lord's Supper is the Passover of the new and final exodus, the showing forth of the one sacrifice for sin (1 Cor. 11:26). Christian almsgiving acquires a new ground and basis in the light of God's gift in Christ (2 Cor. 9:15) and of the giving of all gifts to him (Matt. 25:31–46). The suitability of worship at various points in life rests in the fact that all Christian life is life in the Lord (Rom. 14:8). The decisive point, then, is not that new forms are provided or new levels of devotion insured, but that God in Christ has come in person and fulfilled his work of grace. With this focus worship is given a depth and content that it could hardly achieve in the time of OT and Jewish expectation.

2. The Holy Spirit. The second of the new factors in Christian worship is that in its very core and essence it is worship of God the Father through God the Son, and in and by God the HOLY SPIRIT. True worship has always been both spiritual and in the Spirit, but, as Jesus himself showed, his own ministry brought with it a specific coming of the Spirit that makes possible in fullness the worship in spirit and in truth. Prayer comes with the assistance of the Spirit (Rom. 8:26–27). Praise is rejoicing in the Spirit (Eph. 5:18–19). Confession of sins is under conviction of the Spirit (Jn. 16:8). Confession of faith is confession by the Spirit (1 Cor. 12:3). Holy Scripture, given by the Spirit, is illumined by the Spirit (cf. 2 Cor. 3:6). True preaching takes place "with a demonstration of the Spirit's power" (1 Cor. 2:4). The fellowship of the Lord's Table is a fellowship of the Spirit (cf. Acts 2). Liberality flows from the love which is a fruit of the Spirit (Gal. 5:22). The living of life in a context of prayer and praise and proclamation is a walking in the Spirit (cf. Rom. 8:1–17). It is a question, not of spiritual worship as distinct from liturgical worship, but rather of the inner ministry of the Spirit in regenerating and sanctifying power. The person who is born of the Spirit and led by the Spirit is one who even in outward expression offers to God, through Christ, fitting and acceptable worship.

(See further A. B. Macdonald, *Christian Worship in the Primitive Church* [1934]; N. Micklem, ed., *Christian Worship* [1936]; O. Cullmann, *Early Christian Worship* [1953]; G. Delling, *Worship in the New Testament* [1962]; H. H. Rowley, *Worship in Ancient Israel: Its Forms and Meaning* [1967]; F. Hahn, *The Worship of the Early Church* [1973]; R. P. Martin, *Worship in the Early Church*, rev. ed. [1974]; P. Bradshaw, *Daily Prayer in the Early Church* [1982]; W. Brueggemann, *Israel's Praise: Doxology against Idolatry and Ideology* [1988]; D. Peterson, *Engaging with God: A Biblical Theology of Worship* [1992]; L. W. Hurtado, *At the Origins of Christian Worship: The Context and Character of Earliest Christian Devotion* [2000]; T. Longman III, *Immanuel in Our Place: Seeing Christ in Israel's Worship* [2001]; H. O. Old, *The Reading and Preaching of the Scriptures in the Worship of the Christian Church*, 5 vols. [1998–2004]; G. Wainwright et al., eds. *The Oxford History of Christian Worship* [2006]; C. M. Bechtel, ed., *Touching the Altar: The Old Testament for Christian Worship* [2008]; *ABD*, s.v. "Worship, Early Christian," 6:973–89.)

G. W. BROMILEY

wrath. The concept of anger is used in the Scripture in regard to both God and human beings. It is a major doctrine of both the Jewish and Christian religions.

    I. Divine wrath
        A. Divine wrath in the OT
        B. Divine wrath in the Apocrypha and the Pseudepigrapha
        C. Divine wrath in the DSS
        D. Divine wrath in the NT
    II. Human wrath
        A. Human wrath in the OT
        B. Human wrath in the NT
        C. The concept of wrath in the early church

I. Divine wrath. It is a biblical principle that the wrath of God is of a totally different order and definition than human wrath. The difference in kind between human and divine anger is so great as to be incalculable, and human wrath is creaturely and subject to the creation ordinances of God.

A. Divine wrath in the OT. The wrath of God is frequently presented in the OT, both in principle and in historical examples. It has a fundamental place in the presentation of the biblical ground-motive of creation-fall-redemption-restoration. The absolute necessity and consequence of redemption after the FALL is centered in the nature of iniquity and the demands and finality of the divine wrath.

1. OT terminology. Historical events and natural calamities in the OT are frequently understood as displays of the divine wrath. Often the principle of God's anger is presented in anthropopathic terms; thus the terms indicating the range of human emotions from irritation to fuming rage are applied to the motivations of God. The common noun *ʾap H678*, literally meaning "nose," is often used figuratively with the meaning "anger, wrath" (prob. by metonymy from the fact that anger may be accompanied by heavy breathing or snorting; cf. the verbal form *ʾānap H647*, "to be angry"). This term frequently occurs with other nouns, especially *ḥārôn H3019*, and the resulting combination, meaning literally "the heat/burning of the nose," may be rendered "fierce anger" or the like (e.g., Num. 25:4; cf. the verb *ḥārâ H3013*). It has been proposed that in Hebrew psychology the nose was the center or organ of such emotions, but the usage is best explained as a simple idiom (cf. English *heartache* or *cold feet*, which by no means indicate either a physiologic condition or any essential psychologic assumption).

Other relevant terms include *ḥēmâ H2779*, "heat, venom, rage" (Gen. 27:44 et al.), *ʿebrâ H6301*, "crossing, outburst, rage" (49:7 et al.), and *qeṣep H7912* (Num 1:53 et al.; cf. the verb *qāṣap H7911*). In addition, there are any number of words that are used figuratively to indicate anger or angry behavior, such as "plowing" (Jer. 33:18), "reaping" (Isa. 17:5), "refining" (Mal. 3:2–3). Especially important are those words descriptive of battle and combat, for the armies of Israel and the nations are often described as the means of God's vengeance and wrath (e.g., Isa. 10:5–6). Most frequently are found the terms for defeating the enemy. It is important to note that nowhere in the OT is Yahweh mentioned as himself fighting, nor are any supreme weapons mentioned, as is common in the Babylonian and Egyptian annals. The victories won by Israel are won by the might of Yahweh's will and the onslaught of his messengers. This demonstrates itself very clearly in the fact that many indirect associations are made between God's anger and Israel's victories.

2. Means and ends of the divine wrath. The means of the divine wrath are always some created agency of God's will, his angelic hosts (2 Sam. 24:17), his people of Israel (Ezek. 32:9–31), Gentile nations (Isa. 10:5–6), and forces of nature at God's command (Jdg. 5:20). Through the valid agency of these forces God brings about his just cause in human history and in the course of nations. The ends like the means of his wrath are just and right. The end of God's wrath is twofold: (1) the maintenance of the creation law order which demands justice; (2) retribution to those who act wickedly. Throughout the activation in history of the divine wrath, the objectivity and responsibility of the means are held strictly intact. The wrath of Yahweh is never unleashed for no purpose or for some mysterious outcome; the acts of God in justice are always clearly visible. The divine wrath is equally incensed at all evildoers, whether among the covenant people or among the Gentile and pagan nations. The kings, priests, prophets, tribes, and people of Israel are judged and punished as well as the leaders and rulers of the nations (Ps. 2:1–3).

In the 19th cent., it was characteristic of the scholastic systematics of the time to draw too sharp a distinction between the sinner and his sinful act, and then to assume that the very real wrath of God was vented only upon the abstract notion of the sinner's sin. The OT is clear, however, that iniquity does not exist apart from the iniquitous acts of the wicked. The judgment is therefore leveled upon the wicked creature. This is why the means and ends of God's wrath often take the form of war and carnage. These distinctly human forms of violence and bloodshed are used for God's glory. The general evolutionary humanism of modern times has found this biblical concept cruel and unacceptable, but its essential truth is seen in the course not only of biblical but also postbiblical history.

Of primary importance is the fact that God holds the objects of his wrath responsible for their sins and therefore justly delivers them up for destruction. Because of this last fact, many commentators reject the portrayal of God in the OT as cruel and capricious. In such judgments, they lose sight of the ends of God's wrath, namely, the restitution of the structures that have been violated by the design of the wicked. In this sense the COVENANT operates without question: the usurpation of God's authority by men or angels brings about their swift and sure destruction in the face of God's wrath. The very holiness and transcendence of God are such that they must be approached with fear and awe. To blaspheme his sovereignty through resistance to his revealed will, the law, and Scripture, is to invite and demand his wrath.

One central consideration is that the apostasy of Israel in accepting the worldviews of the Gentile nations and worshiping their pagan idols is a direct cause of social inequity and political disruption. Against both of these God's wrath is ignited. The law of the prophet Moses and the warnings of the great prophetic voices are binding alike upon Israel and the Gentiles. Since the OT declares the promise of God's people to be the source of his blessing to all mankind, it is obvious that the wrath of God is to be kindled against those both within and without Israel who attempt to frustrate the divine plan (Num. 11:1; Deut. 1:26–36; 13:2, 6, 13, et al.; Josh. 7:1; 1 Sam. 28:18; Pss. 2:1–6; 78:21–22).

3. The divine wrath and the atonement. The wrath of God works in two ways simultaneously, in that it delivers the oppressed (1 Sam. 15:2 et al.) and condemns the wicked (Deut. 7:4–5). However, a basic part of the biblical teaching concerning the wrath of God is that an ATONEMENT is offered to remove the wrath and justify the ungodly. This atonement in the OT is appropriated by the keeping of the law and trust in God's promises (Ezek. 36:22–32). Since the nations of the world are required to come to the covenant people of Israel for grace, the OT demands that Gentiles follow the law of Israel for mercy. The wrath of God then acts as a warning and encouragement to human obedience. One special factor of the atonement in the OT is that it is consistently future in character. It presents the final removal of God's wrath and the preservation of the atoned in terms of the great final day or days of God's judgment. This eschatological aspect is associated with the OT teaching about the culmination of history in the DAY OF THE LORD. The time of the divine visitation is primarily a day of wrath (Isa. 2:12), but the same divine proclamation that shall bring damnation to the wicked will bring salvation upon his people in "the last days" (vv. 2–5).

The removal of the divine wrath upon satisfactory REPENTANCE or OBEDIENCE is usually associated with the calamity of natural catastrophes, the common method of God's judgment in history. It has been assumed by recent writers that the rituals of the TABERNACLE and TEMPLE in some magical way turned away the wrath of Yahweh, but this is not supported by the text. All of the rituals and cultic practices of Israel were confirmed in the eschatological expectation of the great and final "blessing." This would be brought to fulfillment by the SERVANT OF THE LORD (Isa. 49:7–8; 53:10–12). The love of Yahweh was shown in his supplying free, unmerited grace sufficient for the needs of Israel's atonement.

A common mistake is to interpret the EXPIATION of Israel's guilt by some suffering or activity undertaken by Israel and with which the demands of Yahweh's justice were satisfied; but there is nothing of this in the OT. The people of Israel were not redeemed from Egypt because of their faithfulness, but by the sustaining of the covenant by God. It is God who sets forth and provides the keeping of his covenant in spite of the sins of his people. In fact, the special elective place of Israel among the nations of the world carries with it a vastly increased responsibility before the face of God (Amos 3:2). The demands of God's law are rooted in his justice, the provision for its keeping in his LOVE. In the end it is the motive of love which the OT seeks (Ps. 1:2 et al.) and which brings all of Yahweh's blessings upon his people. This blessing and the promise of its certainty are based upon the appearance of the heavenly exemplar of the blessing, the MESSIAH. The final completion of both the wrath and the mercy of the old covenant came to pass in the advent of the Lord Christ, in whose person both Judge and Saviour are one (Mk. 1:14).

In his coming all the promises and prophecies of the OT were fulfilled.

B. Divine wrath in the Apocrypha and the Pseudepigrapha. The APOCRYPHA and PSEUDE-PIGRAPHA continue the theme of destruction upon the Gentile nations which have persecuted Israel. Some of the documents look forward to a political messiahship and a restoration of the Davidic state. The Lord is the protector and victor for Israel (2 Macc. 15:17–36). Other writings are more eclectic and reflect certain syncretistic characteristics, so much so that ARISTEAS says: "It is necessary to acknowledge that God rules the whole world in the spirit of kindness and without anger of any sort" (*Aristeas* 254). But this is not typical of the older more traditional records, where the wrath of God is more often than not directed in an almost mechanistic sense against some human oppressor (*Jub.* 36.10), although in some passages the older prophetic message of God's judgment upon an iniquitous Israel lingers on (4 Macc. 4:21). An interest in the possible return of famous biblical personalities is a feature of these writings generally, and the mediatorship of Moses, Elijah, or an angel in diverting the wrath of God is noted (Wisd. 18:21).

C. Divine wrath in the DSS. The same pattern of interpretation found in the Apocrypha and Pseudepigrapha is carried through in the DEAD SEA SCROLLS with some minor extensions, the main one being the cursing of the nations by the Jews and the expectation of an outpouring of divine wrath. The "day of wrath" is seen as the day of the ultimate triumph of the armies of Israel. In effect, the whole of the *War Scroll* (1QM) is concerned with the ordering of the Lord's army for the outpouring of wrath. In such scenes the Romans replace the Hellenistic kings as the accursed objects of God's anger. The division between the blessed, the Jews, and the damned, the Gentile nations, is complete in the DSS with none of the redemptive promise of the OT, and little of the threats against the apostasy within the covenant. In fact, the institutional temple is also castigated because of its fealty to Rome. The wrath of God has become political retribution. This warlike pervasive nationalism utilizes the imagery of the crafts more than the emotional terminology. Terms for smelting, refining, and dividing predominate (1QS I, 16; IV, 20; VIII, 4; et al.).

D. Divine wrath in the NT. The NT assumes from its very beginning the end and fulfillment of the OT covenant. Therefore the wrath of God is understood with the ancient doctrines, but with a wholly new emphasis. The emphasis is that of obedience or submission to Christ. The anger of the final judgment is the anger of Christ. The nationalistic protection of the Jewish commonwealth by threats of divine wrath is totally absent from the gospel narratives. The reason is that God's promise has been kept and the Messiah of Israel is at hand. In this role Jesus Christ takes on the titles and many of the images of the OT.

1. NT terminology. The common Greek word for "wrath" is *orgē* G3973, used in the SEPTUAGINT to represent a number of Hebrew terms. It is used without distinction for all aspects of wrath as defined by the OT. The cognate verb *orgizō* G3974 (always in the passive form) also occurs, but much less frequently than the noun. The cognate adjective, *orgilos* G3975, is found a few times in the LXX and only once in the NT (Tit. 1:7). Anger is attributed explicitly to Jesus only once, in his confrontation with the PHARISEES at the synagogue of CAPERNAUM (Mk. 3:6; but cf. such passages as 1:43 and 10:14).

However, the threat of God's wrath resulting in eternal damnation is so central that the common dichotomy between the "loving heavenly Father" of Jesus' discourse and the wrathful Yahweh of the OT is without warrant. The use of the notion of the wrath of God is terrible in the NT because it is not applied to the political sphere in the sense of the victory or defeat of an alien power but has in view the destruction of the soul and the eternal punishment of the wicked (Mk. 9:43–48 et al.). There are no terms in the NT describing the wrath of God in anthropopathic form. Of the OT images used, the most frequent are those common to Isaiah and the Psalms. Many of Christ's parables deal directly with the wrath of God and portray it as the recompense, not alone for thwarting the nation of Israel and its destiny, but also for rejection of the

Messiah (Matt. 7:13–27). Only in a few contexts are the judgments of God's wrath associated with physical or natural calamity as is common in the OT. In Lk. 13:4–5, the suddenness of the fall of the tower of SILOAM appears to be more important than the death of the eighteen victims. In fact, the teaching of our Lord is explicit in warning not of physical calamity, but of the punishment of the soul (Matt. 5:21–22; 10:28).

2. Christ and the divine wrath. Christ plays a double role in the operation of the divine wrath. He is at one and the same time the heavenly judge and the primal sinner under judgment. No king, prophet, or priest in the OT is ever mentioned as having the divine authority of judgment except as a messenger or servant of God. It is in this office that he is introduced by JOHN THE BAPTIST (Matt. 3:11–12; Lk. 3:16–17). The image of the supernal gleaner with his flail separating the righteous and the impious is repeated throughout the OT (Ps. 1:4 et al.). In his parables Jesus repeats the description of the Lord of heaven as a judge (Matt. 13:24–30). The specific threat of this future violence culminating in the coming of the SON OF MAN (24:29–39) he applies to himself.

The very title Son of Man alludes to fulfillment of the OT expectations of the "latter days" and the "day of the Lord." The vicarious assumption of the guilt of sin by Christ so that he could receive the judgment of death is the most profound mystery of the Christian faith. The picture given us in the trial and crucifixion of the Messiah, the Servant of God suffering before the human tribunals the outpouring of the wrath of God, defies all description and silences speculation. The gospel narratives rely upon the terminology of wrath displayed in the OT: the "outpouring of the cup," "drinking from the cup," and other such phrases. In the explanatory epistles the full meaning of Christ's sacrifice in the atonement for sin and the expiation of the divine wrath is made clear (Rom. 5:9; 8:1; 2 Cor. 5:21; Gal. 3:13; and many other passages).

One final expansion of the wrath of God remains in the NT, and that is the apocalyptic usage in Jude and Revelation. Although the OT "day of the Lord" is complete with the coming of the Messiah, the terminology and meaning of the prophetic visions are carried over to apply to the PAROUSIA, the culmination of history in the final wrath of God at the return of Christ. The most complex and involved prophecy of the end time is that in the book of Revelation. The complete possibilities of the OT language are repeated. A brief list of some repetitions indicates the extent of dependence: burning (Rev. 18:9); fire (8:7); fight (12:7); reaping (14:15); breaking (2:27). In the APOCALYPTIC passages of the NT another aspect of the execution of the divine wrath is introduced. This is the judgment of bondage with unceasing torment (Jude 13; Rev. 20:1–3; et al.). Over the whole scene of horror thus recorded in the Revelation, the once slain Messiah rules over the final culmination of God's wrath (5:6 et al.).

II. Human wrath

A. Human wrath in the OT. Although on restricted occasions human beings are commanded to carry out the requirements of God's wrath in the OT (Josh. 9:20), unbridled fits of rage are judged by God as presumptuous of the divine authority (Ps. 37:8–9). The commands of God's design were to be carried out without irritation (Num. 20:11), and the fury of passionate anger is forbidden and rejected from Israel (Gen. 49:5–7). Cruel and barbaric punishments are a sure subject of godly anger, and the cunning of certain Gentile nations in inventing suffering brings upon them God's destruction (Nah. 3:1–4). Even the execution of criminals was to be without anger or malice (Deut. 21:22), and an immediate burial was to follow. Often the heathen nations are used by God to bring about the suffering of wicked Israel in the times of her idolatry (Isa. 10:5–6), but the raging of the barbarous Gentiles was itself judged.

The OT makes a clear distinction between warfare, the commitment of the state, and assault or murder, the fury of human anger. The command in the Decalogue (Exod. 20:13) is directly applied to murder by an individual. In the narratives of the OT the acts of anger mentioned are frequently the basis of judgment by God (Gen. 4:5–6; 34:13). Even the wrath of God is recognized as unfavorable (Num. 18:5), but absolutely necessary, and nowhere does God take joy from the misery of the wicked, only

joy at the triumph of his righteousness (Ps. 2:4), which saves his covenant people. The OT principle is very clear that God alone has the authority to take vengeance (Deut. 32:35; Ps. 94:1).

Unlike the other documents of antiquity, the spokesmen of the OT take no joy in human agony. The deprivation of the wicked and the captivity of the conqueror are lauded, and the IMPRECATORY PSALMS and poems are frequent enough, but the bloodthirsty recitations of the kingly conquests and the details of the tormenting of the captives, so much a feature of Assyro-Babylonian annals, are totally lacking. The wrath of the OT is satisfied with the deprivation of life and the removal of the body to a place of burial; the ultimate vindication of righteous wrath lies beyond the grave and out of the realm of human realization (Job 13:15).

B. Human wrath in the NT. If anything, the prohibitions against human anger and its exercise are even stronger in the NT. The central teaching is Christ's discourse on the mountain (Matt. 5:9, 21–22), where Jesus warns against even the pronunciation of wrath upon another person. This warning is repeated in most of the NT letters (Rom. 12:19; 2 Cor. 12:10; Gal. 5:19–20; Eph. 4:26–31; Col. 3:8; Jas. 1:19–20).

The ultimate goal of the atonement is the glorification of the believer, but an essential part of its application is SANCTIFICATION. Certain passages in the NT make it clear that lack of sanctification is the subject of divine wrath (Rom. 6:1; Heb. 10:29). The need for sanctification is put in terms of salvation from the wrath of God itself (Jude 23), and the position of the Christian is often likened to that of the people of Israel, who in their travels in Sinai often turned their backs upon Yahweh and so fell under his wrath (Heb. 3:14—4:1). It is made equally clear that sanctification is accomplished in the atonement and is applied by God's grace through faith in Christ (Rom. 7:13–25). It is in this latter regard that the few references to "justifiable anger" are made in Scripture. In the effort to obey the law of God and emulate the love of Christ, anger must be immediately reconciled. To be sure, anger generated in a genuine hatred of evil is approved (Ps. 97:10 et al.), and this theme is apparent in the NT writers (Gal. 1:8 et al.).

C. The concept of wrath in the early church. One of the major documents to survive from the period of the Ante-Nicene church fathers is the treatise of Lactantius (A.D. 260–320?) entitled, *De ira Dei*, "The Anger of God." The argument of this small work deals with the problem of whether God can properly be "angry," in the light of the truth that human emotions cannot be attributed to the Creator. He answers this with a discussion of the creatorship of God and the fact that to allow sin without retribution would be unthinkable. His works are scholastic and prolix and the general judgment of the ages has been contrary to his method, but approving of his motives and goals. The question was reasserted in the writings of the medieval scholastics but fell again into a lesser interest in the post-Reformation period. Like other similar doctrines of the Christian faith, it has been a center of attention in times of political turmoil and religious persecution and largely ignored in seasons of tranquility and relative well being.

(See further R. V. G. Tasker, *The Biblical Doctrine of the Wrath of God* [1951]; A. T. Hanson, *The Wrath of the Lamb* [1957]; H. M. Haney, *The Wrath of God in the Former Prophets* [1960]; E. Zenger, *A God of Vengeance? Understanding the Psalms of Divine Wrath* [1996]; *ABD*, 6:989–98.)

W. WHITE, JR.

Human wrath is often displayed through destruction, as illustrated by this pile of stones from the temple mount walls, demolished by the Roman army in A.D. 70 during the first Jewish revolt.

wreath. This English term can refer to an object that is intertwined or that has been arranged in a circular shape. The NIV uses it to render (1) Hebrew *lōyâ H4324*, an architectural term that occurs in only one passage (1 Ki. 7.29–30, 36), where it may refer to a spiral design; (2) Hebrew *ʿăṭārâ H6498* (Isa. 28:1, 3, 5), a common term usually rendered "crown"; and (3) Greek *stemma G5098* (Acts 14:13). The KJV uses it also in a number of other passages; for example, in Exod. 28:14, 22–25, and 39:15–18 it translates Hebrew *ʿăbōt H6310*, which properly means "rope, cord." See also CROWN; GARLAND.

wrestling. A contest in which two unarmed individuals seek to subdue each other. Wrestling is a very ancient sport, well illustrated from Egypt and evidenced from Mesopotamia. In the Egyptian Old Kingdom, wrestling was depicted in the tomb reliefs of Ptahhotep at Saqqara. More than 400 wrestling groups are shown among wall paintings in Middle Kingdom tombs at Beni Hasan. Scenes showing wrestling appear in the 20th-dynasty temple of RAMSES III at Medinet Habu (cf. H. Wilsdorf, *Ringkampf im alten Ägypten* [1939]). In the OT a serious wrestling bout of JACOB is described (Gen. 32:24–25; Heb. *ʾābaq H84*). Wrestling was a popular competition among the Greeks and thus provided NT illustration of spiritual principle (see ATHLETE). The Greek verb *agōnizomai G76*, "to fight, struggle," is rendered "wrestle" by the NIV and NRSV in a passage that speaks about struggling in PRAYER (Col. 4:12). The KJV uses "wrestle" to translate the noun *palē G4097*, which occurs only once with reference to the intensity and personal nature of spiritual conflict (Eph. 6:12).

C. E. DE VRIES

writing. The act of forming symbols (such as characters) for the purpose of recording and communicating ideas.

  I. Expression and communication
     A. Aspects of communication
     B. Types of semiotic systems
 II. Prehistoric writing systems
III. Cuneiform
     A. Sumerian
     B. Akkadian
     C. Elamite
     D. Hittite
     E. Ugaritic
     F. Urartian
     G. Hurrian
     H. Persian
 IV. Hieroglyphic
  V. West Semitic and Greek
     A. Cretan pictographic
     B. Proto-Phoenician syllabic
     C. Phoenician alphabetic
     D. Old Hebrew
     E. South Arabian and Ethiopic
     F. Aramaic
     G. Greek
 VI. Writing in the Scriptures
     A. In the OT
     B. In the NT

I. Expression and communication. The task of ultimately defining what exactly is the nature of expression and communication seems to be a metaphysical rather than an exact scientific pursuit. Therefore the subject of writing is better studied as a historical process of the invention of one of humanity's most useful tools based upon the central faculty of expression. Just as one cannot speculate about a person who is unable to think, so we cannot conceive of a person who lacks expression or communication.

A. Aspects of communication. The transfer of data from one source to one or more receivers in the same time and place is sometimes referred to as "horizontal" communication. The outside limit of effectiveness of this system would be from great-grandfather to great-grandchild, a maximum of about ninety years. To lengthen this span and thus achieve "vertical" communication, some mechanical transfer—a record, tape, or reenactment—must intervene to bridge the gap of time. Obviously the plastic arts are most suitable for this, and pictures or statues of ancient historical figures can carry us back to at least the 5th millennium B.C., while mechanical recording techniques allow us to recover sounds and voices since the Crimean War (A.D. 1854). Any tradition based on oral communication is then only continuous restatement of

horizontal communication. Songs, stories, poems, narratives, sagas, and even statistics can be and have been preserved in this way. Often, however, the material is molded and suffused by some mnemonic form into which it is cast so that the original information may be effaced by its later literary or artistic form. The MYTHS of classical antiquity are probably prime examples of such a digression (G. De Santillana, *The Origins of Scientific Thought: From Anaximander to Proclus, 600 B.C.–500 A.D.* [1961]). Care must be taken that horizontal communication media of modern primitive social groups are not extrapolated back into prehistory to explain some long-lost origin.

Since sight-thought was more easily communicated vertically, it was apparent that speech-thought would ultimately have to be attached to sight-thought to gain the same vertical continuity. In effect, this was done by symbols, or semiotic systems. All ancient writing systems seem to have originated in settled urban food-producing areas. Such social patterns bring about the need for another aspect of communication beyond the horizontal and vertical: they demand display. Display in this sense is the record of the community's actions set forth for all to see, as for example, law codes, declarative prayers, incantations, annals of the past, and building inscriptions. Actually all three of these forces—horizontal communication, vertical communication, and display—combined with the emerging urban society and its institutions to produce first the need and then the answer in the technique of writing.

B. Types of semiotic systems. Sets of integrated symbols of various sorts were produced in the first germinal era of writing. In the history of writing the first to appear were not necessarily related to the sound or form of the languages of those who invented them. Such nonphonetic systems are termed *semasiographic*, and these fall into three categories: (1) *Pictographs* are simple cartoon-like illustrations of universal recognizance value, such as a picture of an animal or structure with its unique characteristics made obvious (cf. fig. 1.a). (2) *Phraseographs* consist usually of several pictographs arranged to indicate an action but sufficiently interrelated that in time they become one effective unit (cf. fig. 1.b). (3) *Logographs* (or *logograms*) are word symbols where one word in one-to-one correspondence with one sign is understood, although it is neither drawn visually nor indicated phonetically (cf. fig. 1.c). Like the other two types, often it is totally separate from the languages of the writer or reader. Livestock brands, ownership marks, certain ligatured abbreviations, and even trade marks fall into this category. Ancient writing systems often contain so many logograms that the meaning of a text is utterly unintelligible to us. Moreover, logograms tend to become so conventionalized and stylized that, like some pictographs, the original meaning is lost. In some ancient documents the word meant by the symbol is never written out, and thus the actual word in the language is unknown (as if all "ands" in the English language should be replaced by "&," and in time the full spelling of "and" became lost).

This terra-cotta foundation peg, mentioning a treaty between the Sumerian king Entemena and the king of Uruk, is a very ancient example of cuneiform writing (c. 2400 B.C.).

Along with and slightly after the rise of the semasiographic systems, the language-based phonographic systems appeared. Ultimately these tend toward pure symbolic representation of speech, but they fall short due to the necessity to economize the number of signs. This economy usually leads to *polyphony* where one sign has more than one phonetic sound attached to it. It is this difficulty which so aggravates English spelling. Three phonographic systems arose. (1) *Syllabic*, in which every sign represents not simply a unitary sound but also a combination of vowel, or vowel plus consonant, or consonant plus vowel, or consonant plus vowel plus consonant. Such a system works quite well with certain types of languages that have monosyllabic words. (2) *Phonemic* systems have one sign for one sound, either a vowel or a consonant. Most syllabaries have phonetic alphabets dispersed within them. (3) *Subphonemic* (or *prosodic*) systems are made up of elaborate diacriticals which, like musical notations, seek to indicate all nuances of the spoken word.

II. Prehistoric writing systems. Ancient W Asia was the cradle not only of Western civilization but also of the earliest writing systems, and in that geographic and ethnographic region all stages of the semasiographic and phonographic systems have taken place. As with so many other complex social relationships, government, finance, building, and trading, so writing suddenly appears with no records or predecessors to indicate its sources. With village settlement and the organization of social institutions requiring vertical communication and display, writing was invented (A. J. Jawad, *The Advent of the Era of Townships in Northern Mesopotamia* [1965]).

Prehistoric writing systems must be projected from the later known to the earlier unknown. The oldest known written documents were excavated at the site of ancient Uruk (biblical ERECH, Gen. 10:10), and were produced about 3000 B.C. These are tablets inscribed with economic texts in the non-Semitic, non-Indo-European Sumerian language (see LANGUAGES OF THE ANE I; SUMER). Subsequent investigation has demonstrated that the writing system of the Uruk and all later Sumerian texts was probably not the invention of the Sumerians, although they undoubtedly modified and expanded it to fit their essentially monosyllabic language.

These unknown literary predecessors of the Sumerians have been called *Proto-Euphrateans*, from their apparent place of settlement (B. Landsberger, "Mezopotamya'da Medeniyetin Doğuşu," in *Ankara Universitesi Dil ve Tarih-Coğrafya Fakultesi Dergisi* [1943–45]). Some debate has ensued as to who these people were and from where they had come, but until an identifiable Proto-Euphratean settlement is excavated the problems will remain unsolved. However, the discovery in Rumanian Transylvania of an early neolithic village, Tartaria, with a cache of several tablets, all dated by stratigraphy to earlier than 3000 B.C., has enhanced the possibility that the elusive Proto-Euphrateans will be found. A comparison of Uruk and Tartaria signs is shown in fig. 2. Perhaps the best solution is simply to denote the Tartaria texts as *Proto-Balkan-Danubian*. There is little question but that still older and more dispersed written materials will be discovered, since the Proto-Balkan-Danubian signs appear to be at least logographic if not already syllabic.

The Uruk and Tartaria systems were soon followed by a number of scripts of equally unknown origin and as yet quite resistant to decipherment. These all arose in W Asia and are more hieroglyphic in the sense that the pictographic character of their execution is more obvious. Unlike either of the older systems, they seem to be closer to simplified drawings of objects. Also the multiplicity of signs seems to indicate more than a syllabic system, although such a judgment is speculative. Sometime after 3000, the people of SW Iran known as Elamites (see ELAM) produced an elaborate writing system called by scholars *Proto-Elamite*. The Elamite language is non-Semitic and non-Indo-European. It is not related to any other known language, and so the texts as yet defy decipherment. From the placement of what appears to be numerical signs it is judged that they, like the Uruk texts, are economic in content. Dating from a slightly later time, there is a set of symbols on seals and inscribed pottery and metallic sheets. These were fabricated about 2300 at a group of towns on the Indus River, located at Harappa, Mohenjodaro, and Chanhudaro. Specimens of the Proto-Elamite and Proto-Indic signs are seen in fig. 3.

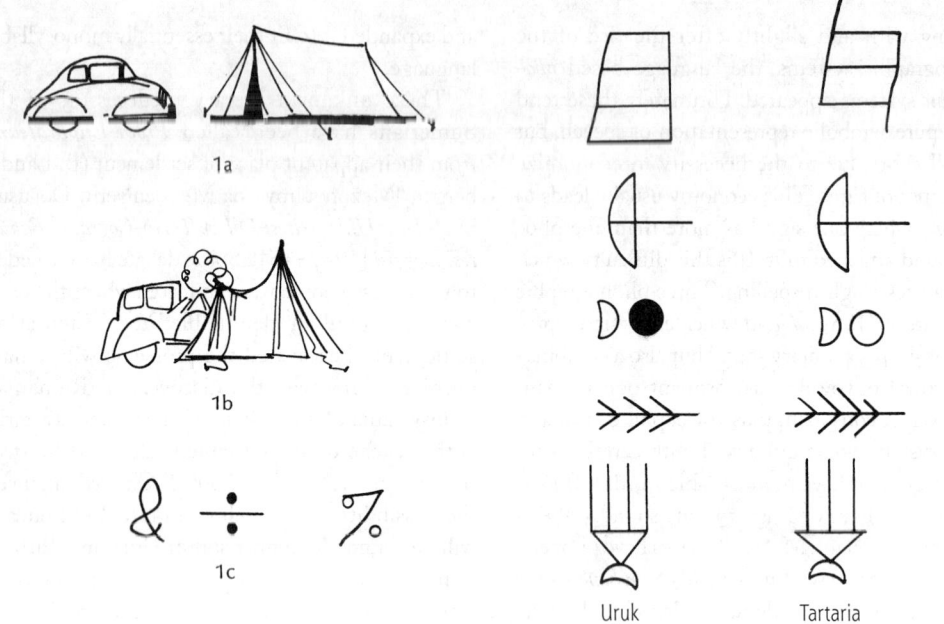

Figure 1. Representative logographs.

Figure 2. Earliest-known scripts (after K. Jaritz, *Schriftarchaeologie der altmesopotamischen Kultur* [1967], passim; (after M.S.F. Hood, "The Tartaria Tablets," *Antiquity* 41:162 [1967]).

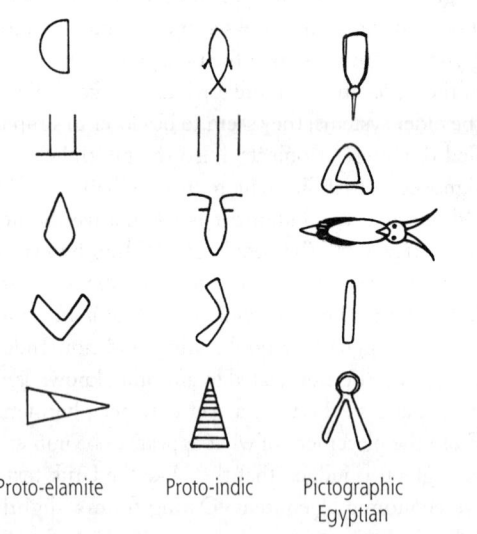

Figure 3. Three undeciphered scripts (selected from I. J. Gelb, *A Study of Writing* [1952], 83, 89ff.).

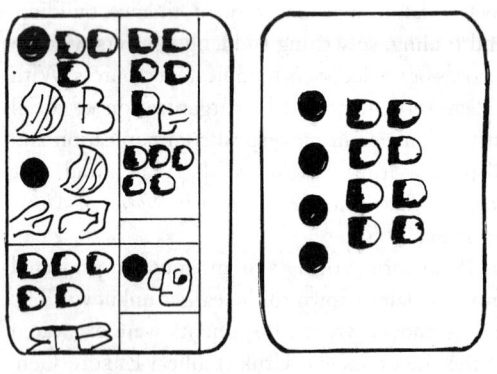

Figure 4.

Vs. 3 x 10 and 18 x 1 names in each register

Rs. Total 48

(after A. Falkenstein, *Archaische Texte aus Uruk* [1936], pl. 36, no. 353).

Hieroglyphics are usually associated with EGYPT, for it was with reference to the Egyptian writing system that the name was coined. In the oldest glyptic representations an early, almost pictographic, form of sign is found (fig. 10). These are on the slate plates excavated at Hieraconpolis in Upper Egypt. These palettes yield scenes of the campaigns of ancient prehistoric Egyptian rulers. Although attempts have been made to associate them with known historical figures, there is little to base final conclusions upon other than the obvious interpretation of the pictographs (fig. 3). Just what the stages in the later development of the elaborate hieroglyphic system were is now lost, but some relationships can be deduced. Before the full-blown Egyptian system was completed and, in fact, prior to its founding, the Proto-Euphratean, later Sumerian syllabary had been established and was to be the dominant writing of the ANE from 3000 to 500 B.C.

III. Cuneiform. In time the Uruk signs became stylized, and the streamlined and uniform strokes became known as "nail-shaped" or "wedge-shaped"; it is called *Keilschrift* in German, but the French name (derived from Latin *cuneus*, "wedge") has stuck in English as CUNEIFORM.

A. Sumerian. The predecessor to the classical cuneiform script first appeared in recognizable form on economic documents from the temple area of Uruk, in the stratigraphic layer of the Jemdet Nasr period. Although the majority of the more than 1,000 tablets are small business memoranda, there are some which contain the complex lexica used to teach the Sumerian language and writing system for the next two millennia. The signs on these tablets are more pictographic than cuneiformic, but they have the same phonetic values as the later simplified script. Most of the economic texts consist of little more than names, numbers, and commodities, marking a specific period of time and the total business conducted during it. Since many of these tablets were tags attached to the articles involved, and from which they were long ago separated, it is now impossible to decipher their meaning. In all, there are over 700 discernible signs used on the Uruk tablets as compared to 1,100 signs used in classical Sumerian literature.

This Old Assyrian cuneiform text is a commemorative tablet (from Asshur, c. 1350 B.C.).

The Sumerian script may be divided into four chronological periods of development: Archaic-pictographic (3100–2700); Ur I & II (2700–2370); Gudea of Lagash (2370–2100); and Ur III (2100–1950). It is probable that the pictographic signs may have originated from the use of stamp and cylinder seals impressed on CLAY or wax to mark ownership of commodities. The early ledger tablets from Uruk, Jemdet Nasr, and Fara show small grids or registers in which names and numbers are written showing the amounts exchanged from the central agency to or from each individual, and on the reverse is the total (fig. 4). In these texts there is very little in the way of speech formulation; they are almost completely semasiographic. However, there is a surprisingly effective mixed sexagesimal (to the base sixty) and decimal (to the base ten) arithmetical system. The most impressive fact of all is the vital and complicated mercantile economy that produced the texts. After extensive simplification of the signs the very effective syllabary of Ur III was finally reached. With this system metaphysical thought of surprising sophistication could be framed in parallelistic poetry, such as the song cycle, *Lamentation over the Destruction of Ur* (S. N. Kramer in *Assyriological Studies* 12 [1940]).

The Sumerian system that served as the pattern for all the subsequent cuneiform syllabaries contained more than just simple syllabic signs.

WRITING

ORIGINAL PICTOGRAPH C. 3500 B.C.	SIMPLIFIED CHARACTER C. 3000 B.C.	ARCHAIC SUMERIAN C. 2800 B.C.	OLD BABYLONIAN C. 1800 B.C.	ASSYRIAN C. 800 B.C.	NEO-BABYLONIAN C. 600 B.C.	SYLLABIC TRANSLITERATION	MEANING
						KU$_6$	fish
						GUD	ox
						ANŠU	donkey
						ŠE	grain
						DINGIR	god
						UTU	sun day
						APIN	to till
						É	house
						LÚ	man

The Development of the Cuneiform Script.

Four types of signs were invented. The most common are the simple syllabic signs, but because of a unique characteristic of the Sumerian language many signs came to have the identical phonetic value. It seems that the Sumerian spoken tongue was tonal as are many modern Afro-Asian languages, that is, words and meanings are distinguished from one another not merely by the difference in sound units but also by a musical pitch. To distinguish these similar sounds the Sumerians provided the different syllables with separate signs. The result is a confusing polyphony of many signs to one sound and many sounds to one sign. For example, a particular sign indicates usually the syllable *be*, but it can also represent the following: *pè, pì, bad, baṭ, baṭ, pád, pát, páṭ, bít, pít, mid, mit, miṭ, til, tel, tíl, ṭél, ziz, sun, qìt, mát, mút, ti, úš, ṣiṣ, gam, me, bi, šumma, zaz*. Some of the items on this list would be the correct reading in only .001 percent of all occurrences.

The second most common set of cuneiform signs in Sumerian are the logograms. These are single pictographs representing a whole word usually totally removed from the pictograph itself. If the first signs were names of economic institutions and merchants, then it is logical that their trademarks would pass into the logographic stage. Less common than the logographs are the determinative signs which indicate the class of objects or persons to which the following word belongs; thus all objects of wood were preceded by the sign for *GIŠ*, which simply meant, "next word a wooden object." The least common, but possibly the most difficult, were numerical and grammatical signs that were not pronounced at all but were simply diacriticals, such as the often superfluous plural sign *MEŠ*. All four types appear in fig. 5.

Since Sumerian is agglutinative—i.e., it adds grammatical and phonetic particles together in long complex chains of words and phrases—in time certain sets of signs became associated with each other in standardized patterns, giving much of the literature a stereotyped quality and forming idioms and figures of speech that are still commonplace. At no time in the long history of cuneiform writing were all the possible syllables of any one language set down in signs. If a grid or table is formulated of all the possible vowel-consonant and consonant-vowel combinations, it will be found that a twofold principle of economy was in effect: (1) syllables of one specific vowel and similar consonants tended to be clustered in one sign (e.g., the KAB sign represented *kab, kap, qáb, qáp, qàb, qàp*); (2) one consonant and its full potential set of vowels tended to be clustered in one sign (e.g., the sign *AḪ* stood for *aḫ, eḫ iḫ, uḫ*). Generally the former cluster maintaining the vowel is more common than the latter, and when the consonant is maintained it is divided into two sets of vowels, *a/u* versus *e/i*, which is a general phonemic distribution in the Sumerian language.

By the period of Sumer's greatness, Ur III, the writing system was almost purely phonographic and many of the complex logograms had been reduced to syllabic signs. It is widely accepted upon reasonable evidence that the wedge-shaped characters came about through the use of the reed stylus, which, when cut obliquely, would leave an exposed triangular surface culminating in a sharp point. When impressed in damp clay, the familiar pyramidial indentation resulted. As with other complex sign systems, the Mayan and Chinese for example, differences in scribal schools and traditions developed, and even variations in individual hands are present.

In time, the Sumerian civilization came to depend upon writing and to a degree equated literacy with culture and civilization, a notion that still persists in the Western world. In the scribal schools (*É.DUB.BA*, "tablet house"), the scribes learned by copying the ancient literature, hymns, epics, laments, and lexical texts. These last are of very great interest. The Sumerians seem to have had some notion of organizing the phenomenal world in terms of their precious craft of writing. In order to do this they set down long lists of words, usually names of objects and functions that in turn grew into immense lexical series, commonly described as *Listenwissenschaft* (B. Landsberger and W. von Soden, *Die Eigenbegrifflichkeit der babylonischen Welt: Leistung und Grenze sumerischer und babylonischer Wissenschaft* [1965]). These bear strange enigmatic names taken from their first lines (e.g., *ḪAR.RA=ḫubullu, IZI=išatu*), although strictly these two are from a much later time when Sumerian lists were equated with their E Semitic synonyms.

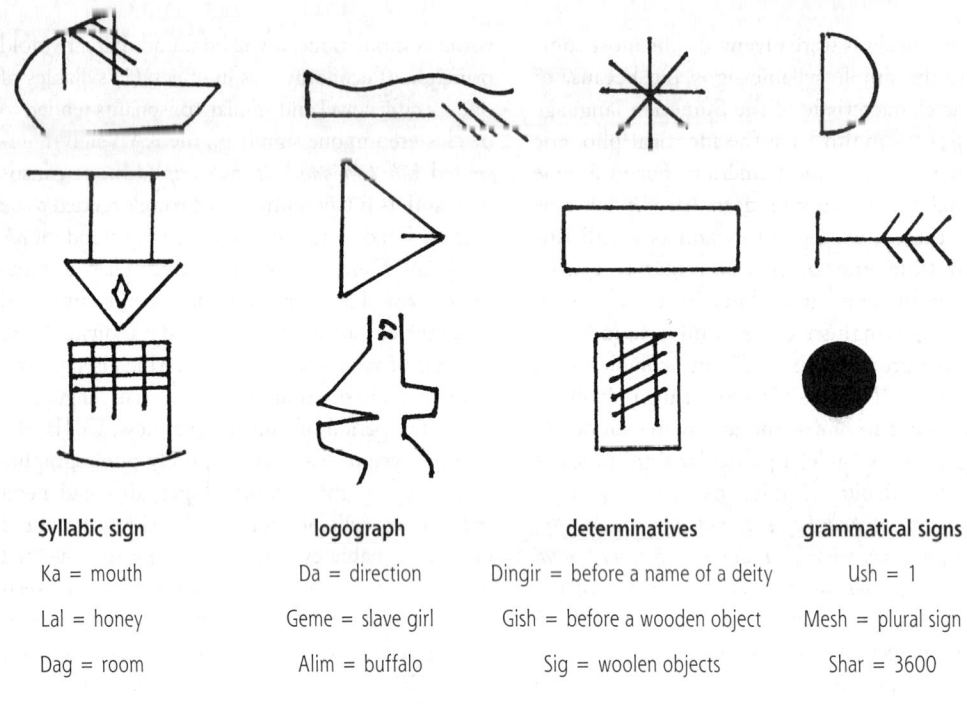

Figure 5. Types of signs in Sumerian cuneiform syllabary.

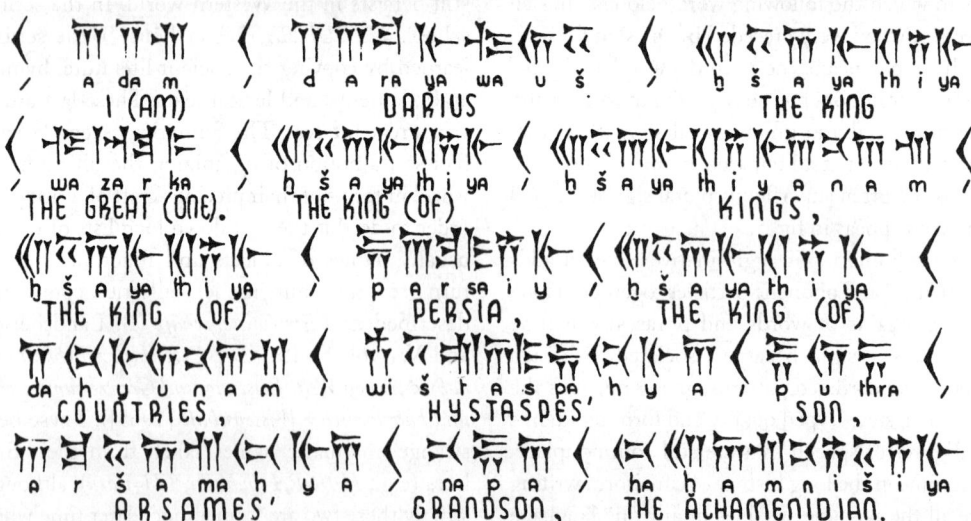

Figure 6. Translation of part of an inscription of Darius, in ancient Persian (after C. F. Pfeiffer).

As part of the scribal collections of learning in inscribed form — a sort of encyclopedia editing — all other forms of learning were brought together and extended by the scribes. Lexicography, literature, grammatical flexion, dosage forms, and mathematical tables are all found on the school tablets. This unification of learning around the practice of the scribal craft is a keystone to the understanding of the urbane Sumerians and their writing system. With the advent of the E Semitic peoples that culminated with the founding of the first dynasty of AKKAD, Sumerian civilization passed into the hands of the Semites, who, in turn, studied and treasured this heritage, passing it on for some 2,000 years. The assimilation of Sumerian culture into Akkadian culture brought about the use of the Sumerian language as a literary medium and of the Sumerian cuneiform system to write the Akkadian, a very different language. The two languages interchanged loanwords in the process, the preponderance going from Sumerian to Akkadian.

B. Akkadian. It was only after the conquests of Šarruken of Agade (Sargon of Akkad), the first great world conqueror who overran central Mesopotamia in 2371 B.C., that Akkadian came into use as a written language. Because it is polysyllabic and has difficult consonant clusters and complex vowel variations, however, the Akkadian language fits poorly into the Sumerian syllabary. The result was that Akkadian cuneiform inscriptions followed closely the forms and conventions of the older Sumerian inscriptions. Akkadian cuneiform may be divided into the following phases: Old Akkadian, roughly equivalent to Ur III Sumerian; Old, Middle, and Neo-Babylonian; Old, Middle, and Neo-Assyrian. The Old Akkadian is quite difficult, as it utilizes many Sumerian logograms (Sumerograms) and writes out in full detail refinements and nuances of E Semitic speech that were later dropped from use. The Akkadian syllabary underwent the same paring and economizing processes as Sumerian so that more and more it approached a phonographic system.

The next stage in the script, the *Old Babylonian*, like its contemporary, the *Old Assyrian* of the Cappadocian merchant colonies, used few logograms and determinatives and wrote out most words syllabically. Still the script did not completely fit the language, as some fractions of the syllables had to be elided to obtain the correct pronunciation. In many instances the same word could be broken up several different ways to yield assimilable syllables. For example, to write the word *Pittsburgh* it would be necessary to disassociate the consonant cluster *ttsb* so that it can be written with vowel-consonant or consonant-vowel signs: *Pi-it-te-es-bu-ur-rg-eh*, where all the *e*'s are silent and all the double vowels are elided; if consonant-vowel-consonant signs are used, it could be written *Pit-tes-bur-geh*. Analogous situations occur in all stages of the cuneiform syllabary and many words do appear spelled in a variety of ways. Over the centuries, of course, certain standard forms became conventional. Unlike some other ancient systems, no alphabetic system was ever involved at the base of the cuneiform signs. The classical Babylonian syllabary, as used by the Kassites (1600–1174) after they had overthrown and absorbed Babylonian culture, emphasizes the sounds and spellings of the Babylonian dialect of Akkad.

With the resurgence of ASSYRIA under Ashuruballiṭ (1365–1330), a predominance of signs favoring the *Assyrian* dialect takes place. The kings of the last half millennium of Akkadian culture down to the time of the Persian ruler CYRUS greatly honored the study of cuneiform and preserved the ancient literature wherever they found it. During the reigns of the Neo-Assyrian rulers, especially ASHURBANIPAL (668–631), extensive libraries of texts representative of all periods were collected, and scribes were employed in making new editions of the ancient literature. It is a monument to the genius of its inventors that the kings of the 6th cent. B.C. could decipher tablets then already 2,500 years old and written in cuneiform.

Not only was cuneiform used in Mesopotamia proper but it also became the international vehicle of the common *lingua franca*, Akkadian. Scribes in the court of the pharaoh, the palace of the Indo-European ruler of Mitanni, and the chieftains of Syria-Palestine all corresponded in cuneiform script. The iron-clad fixation of the vowels in the system has allowed the restoration of the native speech in several of the geographic localities outside Mesopotamia. Of special importance in this regard is the language of ancient Palestine before the conquest as represented in portions of the TELL EL-AMARNA letters, which passed between the pharaohs of the 18th dynasty and their vassal princes in the ANE. In these and other cuneiform texts occur the phenomenon of "glosses": the scribe has written a word in Akkadian, and then after an oblique wedge used as word divider added the cuneiform transcription of the word in his own language to make doubly sure that the scribe who was to receive and read it before its addressee would know his intention.

The script in these peripheral Akkadian texts is usually poorly executed and the grammar and syntax of the language completely at the mercy of the scribe's mother tongue. From the peripheral Akkadian, the script spread further out to other non-Semitic and non-Akkadian language groups who modified it radically to better transcribe their own tongues. In most cases these alterations were definitely advantageous in the direction of a phonographic system. They also resulted in the inclusion of a new set of logographic signs which are best termed "Akkadograms." Like the Neo-Assyrian scribes, these provincial inscribers tended to use the system of writing the Sumerian root or logogram if one existed and then follow it with a phonetic complement, giving the form and pronunciation of the native word to be substituted in the context for the Sumerogram. To illustrate, suppose that instead of writing the English word *willing* one puts down the Latin root of the same meaning, *vol-* and then adds the same ending as if it were an English word so that *voling* is the result, but it is read as *willing*; likewise, the late cuneiform *GIG-iṣ* stands for Akkadian *mahiṣ*, "has been smitten," and *ERÍN-am* represents *ṣabam*, "contingent (direct object)." A comparison of the forms of several representative signs from Uruk through Neo-Assyrian is shown in fig. 7. The supremacy of the cuneiform system and the availability of the vast Mesopotamian literature spurred on the adoption of cuneiform by many other peoples. A Sumerian and Akkadian bilingual is shown in fig. 8. See further LANGUAGES OF THE ANE II.A.

C. Elamite. The Elamite language, which is of uncertain origin, was written in its own peculiar pictographs up until 2500 B.C., when a phonographic system based on Akkadian cuneiform was introduced. In all the new system had only 131 syllabic signs, 25 logograms, and 7 determinatives. Elamite became one of the official languages of the Persian empire and is represented in the great trilingual inscription of the rock of BEHISTUN. In the later period the syllabary was reduced to 102 syllabic signs, 8 logograms, and 3 determinatives.

D. Hittite. This language, also known as *Nesite*, is the oldest known Indo-European tongue. Strange as it may seem, cuneiform HITTITE was used simultaneously with another similar language, hieroglyphic Hittite, each written in its respective sign system. The signs, although based on the Sumero-Akkadian system, are quite distinct even though large numbers of Akkadian texts have been excavated from Hittite sites. One peculiarity of the Hittite usage is the writing of unvoiced consonants (*t, p, k*) doubled so as to distinguish them from the corresponding voiced consonants (*d, b, g*). As with any syllabic system used for writing an Indo-European language with its consonant clusters, many vowels are written just to indicate the enclosed consonant and not for pronunciation. The results are long strings of syllables that defy pronunciation and must be carefully reduced to their actual phonetic transcription (e.g., *har-ša-na-al-la-an-da-an* = *xarsanallantan*, "take [accusative participle]"; *an-tu-uh-ša-an-na-an-za* = *antuxsanats*, "mankind [inflected]"). The more formal Hittite literature, such as royal inscriptions, was based on Sumero-Akkadian models. In such a text words from three different languages will be mixed to produce one thought; for example, *SAG-du-an*, which consists of the Sumerogram *SAG*, "head," plus the Akkadian phonetic complement (showing that the *SAG* is to be read as its Akkadian equivalent, *qaqqadu*), plus the Hittite inflection *an*. The Hittites also continued the work of the ancient Sumerian scribal schools and added a Hittite column to the lexical series.

Since the Hittite empire was a confederacy of a number of petty states and related ethnic groups, other lesser languages appear in the archives. One of them, *Proto-Hattian* (also *Proto-Hittite* or simply *Hattian*), seems to have been used as a sacred cultic tongue and occurs only in certain ritual texts where inclusions in the language are preceded by

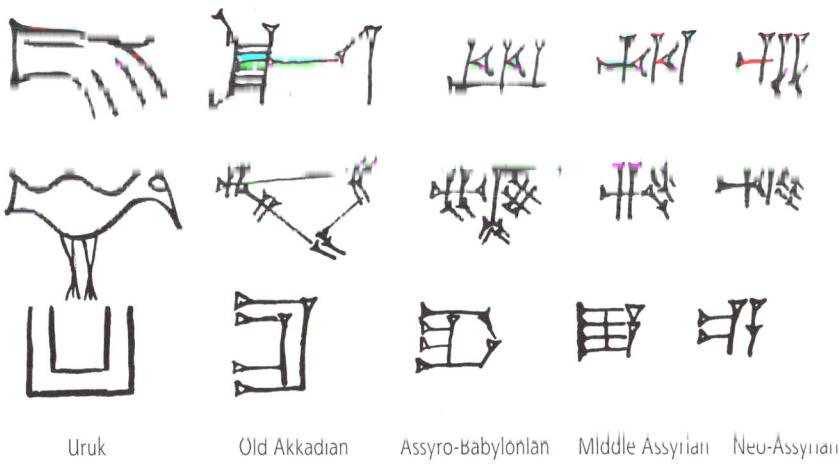

| Uruk | Old Akkadian | Assyro-Babylonian | Middle Assyrian | Neo-Assyrian |

Figure 7. Development of Mesopotamian cuneiform.

Figure 8. Hand copy of Sumerian inscription on Brick As. 31-736.

Hand copy of Akkadian inscription on Brick As. 31-765.

the indicator *hattili*, "Hattian." It is not related to Hittite and is written out fully in the syllabic script with no logograms.

A fuller corpus of quotations exists in the *Luwian* language, which is similar in structure to Hittite and is the actual tongue employed as "hieroglyphic" Hittite. Passages in the language are always preceded by the indicator *luwili*, "Luwian." As with Hattian, it is written exclusively with the syllabic signs. A subdialect of Luwian developed into the language of the kingdom of LYCIA in SW ASIA MINOR. The Lycians called their language *Treknemli*.

The least known of the Hittite empire's polyglot dialects is *Palaic*, introduced by the indicator *palaumnili*, "Palaian." It is Indo-European in structure and was written exclusively with the syllabary (cf. fig. 9).

E. Ugaritic. The oldest known W Semitic language is *Ugaritic* (see UGARIT), which predates biblical Hebrew by nearly 1,000 years (see LANGUAGES OF THE ANE II.F). It was the first Semitic language to be set down in a purely alphabetic and phonographic script. The signs are based undoubtedly upon the mode and system involved in cuneiform, and like cuneiform it was read from left to right. As far as can be determined, however, no one sign in Ugaritic is equivalent to any Akkadian sign. The alphabetic principle allows a still further reduction in the number of signs from the more than one hundred in the best syllabaries to only thirty. Moreover, it leads to an innovation. In the Semitic languages, the various parts of speech (verbs, nouns, adjectives) can be interrelated through the use of roots that usually consist of three consonants. The vowels follow the consonantal patterns and are raised, dropped, heightened, or muted in relation to their position and stress in the word. The result is that the spoken and written Semitic languages have many more cognates connected together than in the Indo-European languages. Thus the English sentence, *The smiter smote the smitten*, is possible but unlikely, whereas the OT is filled with comparable examples. Because of this characteristic the vowels may be excluded in the semiotic system (note that a reduction of the phonographic transcription to strictly consonants is the basic factor underlying shorthand systems both ancient and modern).

One difficulty in the Ugaritic system was the use and form of the ʾ*aleph*, which represents a glottal stop (cf. the obstruction of air flow between the two parts of the English interjection *uh-oh*). In Proto-Semitic three glottal sounds are predominant. These appear often at the initial position in words, as Semitic languages reject beginning words with vowels (e.g., the Greek *Platōn*, "Plato," became *Aflatn* in medieval Judeo-Arabic, and the new first letter was ʾ*aleph*). On the other hand, Ugaritic like Akkadian and its dialects had the three long vowels, $\bar{a}$, $\bar{u}$, and $\bar{\imath}$, and so it produced three different syllabic signs (ʾ*a*, ʾ*u*, ʾ*i*) while reducing all the other signs to an alphabet. Upon close inspection it will be found that certain letters tend to come into frequent proximity with certain vowels so that in effect there is a sense in which the Ugaritic alphabet operates much like a syllabary, and here and there throughout the body of Ugaritic literature the consonantal signs occur in locations where they indicate vowels and vowel quantities. A word divider and spacing for punctuation are regularly used. The habit of writing consonants and not vowels may have been an Egyptian innovation borrowed by the scribes of Ugarit, as there was much political and cultural influence from Egypt in Ugaritic affairs. It is likely

Clay tablet with envelope from S Mesopotamia (late 2nd millennium B.C.). Some differences in cuneiform signs distinguished northern and southern forms of writing in ancient Mesopotamia.

that Ugaritic combined the best of the two writing systems, the consonantal economy of the Egyptian and the simplicity of signs found in the cuneiform. The Ugaritic sign list is seen in fig. 9.

F. Urartian. The Urartian civilization flourished in the area of Lake Van in northern Anatolia (Asia Minor) from about 1100 to 600 B.C. See ARARAT. Its language, which is related to the Caucasian tongues, is called Urartian or Vannic. The Urartian inscriptions are written in Neo-Assyrian cuneiform script with a large percentage of logographic writings. There are several important bilinguals.

G. Hurrian. A very old language, HURRIAN was spoken by the inhabitants of the upper reaches of the TIGRIS and EUPHRATES as well as northern Syria-Palestine as early as the 2nd millennium B.C. It is this linguistic group which is suspected of being the cultural transmitters of Akkadian civilization to Syria-Palestine and Anatolia. Hurrian texts written in largely syllabic cuneiform with few logograms have been excavated from Hittite, Ugaritic, and Mesopotamian sites. The Hurrians were known in the OT as Horites (Gen. 14:6 et al.; but see the article HORITE). Their tongue, which is agglutinative, non-Indo-European, and non-Semitic, is written with a syllabic spelling and script that contains very few logograms. The actual form of the cuneiform signs conforms to the peripheral Akkadian mentioned above. The central Hurrian kingdom was established in the region of the Middle and Upper Tigris and called Mitanni. The Mitannian state consisted of Hurrian commoners and Indo-European nobles that made it, like the Hittite, a polyglot confederacy of different ethnic and linguistic groups.

H. Persian. An Indo-European tongue, Persian was the dominant language of the Medo-Persian empire, which came to dominate the ANE and Egypt in the 6th cent. B.C. See MEDIA; PERSIA. The Persian empire had three official court languages, Old Persian, Elamite, and Akkadian, and it utilized ARAMAIC for administrative communications. However, the Persian cuneiform bears little resemblance to Akkadian. It is a syllabary with less than a dozen logograms and determinatives added

(see fig. 6). After the eclipse of Persia cuneiform declined rapidly, although a brief renaissance of the script took place under the SELEUCIDS. Even then it was not used for economic or business documents, but only by the conservative pagan temple administrations. There are extant a few fragments of Sumero-Akkadian lexical texts that had been transliterated into uncial Greek characters. In the cultural struggles which resulted from the advent of Christianity upon the scene, again the pagan priesthood turned to cuneiform, but by A.D. 75 the last documents on clay had been written and the knowledge of the script, which went back in a direct tradition for 3,200 years, was forgotten. Probably no other event has so enlarged and altered our historical horizon than the decipherment and study of cuneiform texts.

IV. Hieroglyphic. Strictly speaking, the term *hieroglyphic* as coined by the Greek historians (Gk. *hieroglyphikos*) refers only to the pictographic form of the Egyptian signs. Yet, in usage it has developed the added connotation of a mixed pictographic-logographic and syllabic script. The monumental carvings in which hieroglyphic inscriptions were often executed were never used except for functions of the religious state. Since the pharaonic office was divine, its speech and proclamations were set in an otherworldly genre. If, as is alleged, the slate palettes from Hieraconpolis do contain fully developed syllabic writing and not simply pictographs, then the origin of the Egyptian hieroglyphic must be put back to at least 3000 B.C. If not, which seems rather to be the case, then the Egyptian system must be dated back no earlier than 2900.

It is generally assumed that the impetus for the invention of the Egyptian system came from Sumer. Many features are held in common. Essentially, the hieroglyphic system is a syllabary of the type mentioned above as a development from Sumerian, that is, one in which the consonants are rigid but the vowels are only vaguely expressed. For example, in the Sumero-Akkadian syllabary the *AH* sign also may be read *eh*, *ih*, or *uh*; in the Egyptian syllabary no specific vowel is understood and a sign *ka* is actually *k*^{v}, with the *v* representing any vowel, so that the *ka* sign can be read as *ka*, *ku*,

This Egyptian funerary stela from Thebes (limestone, c. 1800 B.C.) illustrates hieroglyphic writing.

ko, ke, or *ki,* as long as some vowel is pronounced. As with the Sumero-Akkadian syllabary, there are not only consonant-vowel and vowel-consonant signs, but also combinations. In fact, there are monoconsonantal, biconsonantal, and triconsonantal signs. All of those above one element could have been reduced, thus yielding an alphabet, but in the long history of hieroglyphic writing this never occurred. Buried under the expanse of hundreds of signs there was a set of simple consonants. The triconsonantal signs are little different from logograms.

In one feature, the Egyptian system far outstripped the Sumerian, and that was in the thousands of determinatives. These little pictographs are added to many words which have been spelled out syllabically so that there is in effect a redundancy of both phonographic and semasiographic signs. Specimens of all types in the Middle Egyptian orthography are shown in fig. 9. On close account all four sign types — syllabic, logographic, determinative, and grammatical-diacriticals — can be demonstrated in both the Sumerian and Egyptian writing systems. The theory of the two systems is identical. In the Old Kingdom period (2900–2160) the epigraphic inscriptions are elaborately engraved and often colored attractively. The Pyramid Texts from this period have their own slightly variant dialect and signs.

Unlike Akkadian, Egyptian changed internally over the centuries so that new grammatical and syntactical features were added and old ones eliminated. Middle Kingdom Egyptian developed from the Old Kingdom system with same popular speech modifications. During the early part of this period (2000 B.C.) an inked form of the letters came into vogue. This sign system, which could be more easily written on PAPYRUS sheets and clay OSTRACA, is called *hieratic* script. Late Egyptian, a successor to the Middle Kingdom Egyptian, incorporated many new linguistic and syntactic features, radically altering the future development of the language. By 700 B.C. a still more simplified form of hieratic had appeared which was not merely a semiotic variation but marked a new grammar, vocabulary, and writing system.

The last phase of this development was *Coptic,* which appeared some time after the Persian conquest, and eventually it was written in a modified Greek alphabet. Coptic is divided into four major dialects: Sahidic, Bohairic, Fayumic, and Akhmimic. These utilize the same sign system, but show divergences in vocabulary and transcription due to colloquial variations in speech. However, on the basis of the demotic, and contemporary with the Coptic, another script arose in the former Ethiopian dominions at the island of Meroë. There a double set of signs emerged: the one, much like simplified hieroglyphic, was used for epigraphic monumental inscriptions; the other, far less complex, was used on papyri and ostraca. Specimens of all the Egyptian scripts and their development are shown in fig. 11.

After the advent of Ptolemaic government (323 B.C.; see PTOLEMY), hieroglyphic usage declined rapidly. Unlike cuneiform, the hieroglyphic system was not borrowed directly by any other linguistic group. Only the Meroitic language, as yet undeciphered, was written in it. Egypto-Meroitic reduced the system below the number of signs until (prob. copying Greek) it developed a straightforward alphabetic script of only twenty-three signs, some

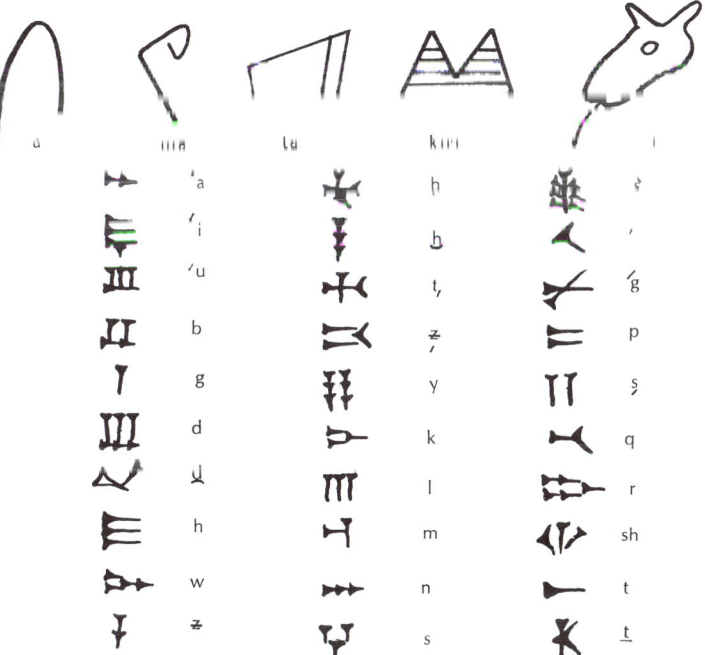

Figure 9. Hieroglyphic Hittite and Ugaritic syllabary (after P. Meriggi, *Hieroglyphischhethitisches Glossar* [1962], 182ff.).

Figure 10. Types of signs in Egyptian hieroglyphic syllabary (after A. H. Gardiner, *Egyptian Grammar* [1957], passim).

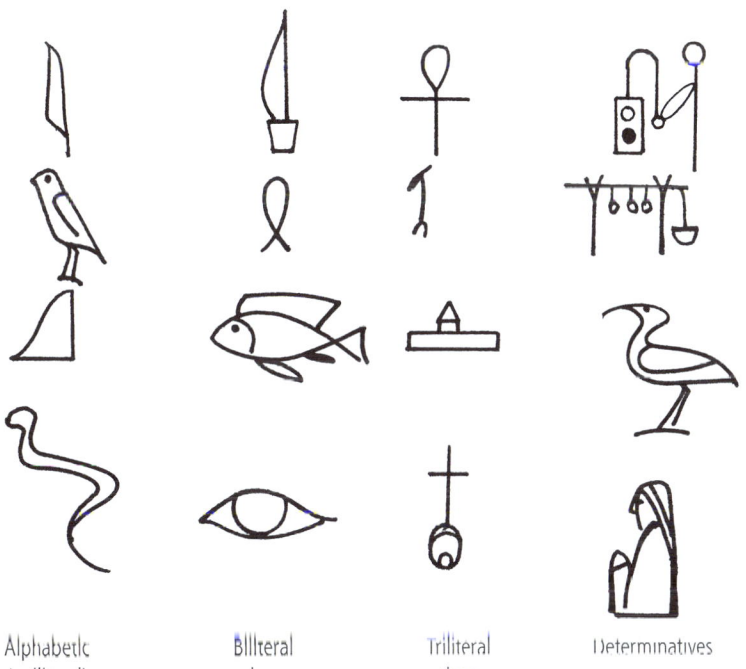

Alphabetic (uniliteral) signs — Biliteral signs — Triliteral signs — Determinatives

of which were pure vowels. All the other derivative systems from hieroglyphic were indirect, and only the W Semitic and Afro-Semitic have survived.

Hittite, although usually written in its modified cuneiform, was in its dialectal variations written in a hieroglyphic script invented totally independently. Although the impetus may have come from Egyptian, the forms of none of the signs are distinctly Egyptian. The hieroglyphic Hittite flourished between 1500 and 700 B.C. It developed several styles, an earlier pictographic and a later stylized cursive system. It is a syllabary with some sixty signs. All of the signs are invariably of the consonant-vowel type, which necessitated the writing of redundant and unpronounced sounds.

Phoenician-hieroglyphic bilinguals have been found at Karatepe and other Turkish sites of former petty kingdoms of the 12th to 8th centuries B.C. The syllabary is shown in fig. 9. The origins of the Hittite syllabary are more than likely to be found in the Aegean area, where still a third ancient writing system had appeared. Toward the end of the 3rd millennium B.C., the same migrations that had brought the Indo-Europeans into Anatolia and Iran caused a sweep of new peoples into the N shores of the Mediterranean Sea. In later centuries these epic voyages would be remembered in the Homeric poems. The civilization thus founded is known as Minoan and flourished from 2400 to 1400 B.C. Attempts have been made to associate these Minoan inhabitants with the Ugaritic and Canaanite civilizations of the Syrian coast (cf. C. H. Gordon, *Evidence for the Minoan Language* [1966]; M. C. Astour, *Hellenosemitica* [1965]), but the evidence is still highly controversial.

V. West Semitic and Greek. Although the NW Semitic language family (e.g., Ugaritic, Phoenician, Hebrew) is quite distinct from the GREEK LANGUAGE (Indo-European family), the writing systems they employed over the millennia are dependent upon each other. In regard to the semiotic systems involved they must be considered as a unit.

A. Cretan pictographic. Also known as *Cretan hieroglyphic*, this system is known from tablets discovered in CRETE (at Knossos, Hagia Triada, and elsewhere) and at various sites on the Greek peninsula proper. The characters may have developed from stamp seals and other ownership marks. Such seal impressions date back to about 2500 B.C., while the initial pictographic system of writing appears about 2000 in the early part of the cultural phase known as "Middle Minoan I." There were two variations of this pictographic syllabary introduced, "A" in use from 2000 to 1875 and "B" from 1875 to 1700.

The Cretan people were merchant adventurers who established maritime city states on the rocky shores of the islands and peninsulas of the E Mediterranean Sea. In time their commerce grew sufficiently to force a simplification of the elaborate pictographs. By 1700 B.C. the cultural phase known as "Middle Minoan III," a simplified cursive script, had come into use and was, in turn, superseded by a still more abstract one. They are known as Linear "A" and "B" respectively. Only the Linear "B" has successfully been deciphered. In all forms the Cretan system is a syllabary with a large number of logograms which double as determinatives. However, there are some interesting peculiarities in Linear "B" that may also apply to the older forms. In certain diphthongs the vowel *i* is expressed, in others it is not, while final-position *l, m, n, r,* and *s* in vowel-consonant syllables are omitted. In all, there are less than a hundred signs that fit into a neat grid or table of vowels versus consonants. The Linear "A" contains somewhat over eighty signs and what appear to be the logographic-determinatives.

M. Ventris, a young British architect, proved in 1956 that the language of Linear "B" was Greek, strangely spelled, archaically written in syllabic forms which like Hittite cuneiform contained many redundancies and unpronounced vowels. The language of Linear "A" is most certainly not Greek and there is little likelihood that it is any other Indo-European language. The four classes of Cretan scripts are shown in fig. 12. While Egyptian and hieroglyphic Hittite retained the full form of the individual pictographs except for certain cursive adaptations, Cretan passed rapidly into a linear phase. On the other hand, Late Egyptian, especially Meroitic, abstracted the signs according to an alphabetic principle. There is no indication that Cretan ever did. Later offshoots did develop from

WRITING 1175

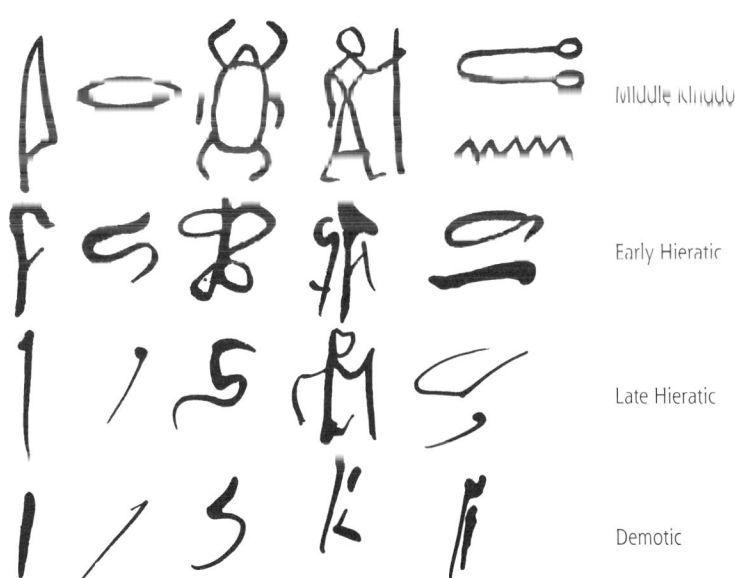

Figure 11. Development of Egyptian scripts (after G. Moller, *Hieratische Palaographie*, [1909], passim).

Figure 12. Four classes of Cretan scripts (after A. J. Evans, *Scripta Minoa* [1909], passim).

the Cretan system, the chief ones being Cypriote, a late Cypro-Minoan, Eteo-Cretan, and the script of Phaistos and Byblos. Specimens of some of these are shown in fig. 12. The overall importance of the Cretan system in the history of writing is its rigid consonant-vowel syllabary and its reduction to simple linear signs that could be used alike for epigraphic inscriptions or inked on the more perishable papyrus and parchment.

B. Proto-Phoenician syllabic. This term is applied to the theoretical construction of a system which served as intermediate between cuneiform on one hand and Egyptian hieroglyphic on the other. The earliest texts in Palestine known are problematic fragmentary inscriptions on potsherds dated by some to the late 18th and early 17th cent. B.C. and discovered at GEZER, SHECHEM, and LACHISH. They vary in form of characters from cursive pictographic reminiscent of the Aegean syllabaries to stark linear flowing cursives. It is important to note that this series of syllabic "experiments" took place during the HYKSOS period, when the nomadic tribes of the ANE and the settled petty kingdoms of the river valley civilizations were in constant conflict.

The connection between these undeciphered Palestinian texts and the Paleo-Sinaitic fragments is only speculative. The latter were inscribed by the pharaonic expeditions sent to work the copper and turquoise mines of Serabit el-Khadim in the Sinai Peninsula. The principle upon which they are written is to use the initial sound of an Egyptian logogram as an independent letter. This is a great advance toward an ALPHABET, but it is not a full and complete step. A few samples of this writing appear in fig. 13. It is evident that they are abstracted from the hieratic or late Egyptian hieroglyphic. A set of remotely similar texts has been found in the Egyptian Fayum, the date of which is still under debate. The important fact is that a number of writing systems were in practice in Palestine 500 years before David was crowned and that any or all had been or could have been used for the Hebrew language.

C. Phoenician alphabetic. From one of these inscriptional systems, or a derivative of them, the oldest fully represented system, Old Phoenician, developed. The earliest complete and decipherable example is the Byblian inscription from the tomb of Ahiram, dated about the 12th cent. B.C. The writing is generally considered an alphabet, though some argue that the thin line between a syllabary (such as Ugaritic) and alphabetic writing is never crossed by the Phoenician system. The subject of North and South Semitic epigraphy is the study of the two great divisions of the scripts that developed from the Phoenician writing.

D. Old Hebrew. A small number of complete Hebrew inscriptions are known which are written in characters much like the Phoenician. The earliest of these is the Gezer Calendar, a short seven-line poetic composition relating the months of the agricultural year (see AGRICULTURE V) and dated to the 9th cent. B.C. There is little doubt that the oldest copies of the biblical books were written in similar characters. After the EXILE, Hebrew adopted the so-called square script from Aramaic (see below, section F).

E. South Arabian and Ethiopic. The S Semitic system developed along different lines and soon became quite distinct. Its roots may go back to the Paleo-Sinaitic script as it is contained for a considerable period in the Arabian Peninsula. In the N part of the area there developed the Safaitic, Lihyanitic, Dedanitic, Thamudenic, and other lesser known scripts, while in the S of the Arabian area there developed the Minean, Sabean, Himyaritic, Qatabanean, and Ḥadramautian scripts. However, it was in ETHIOPIA that these developments came into their own. By A.D. 300 these Arabian scripts had died out, ultimately to be replaced by the classical Arabic writing system dispersed through the world by the rise and spread of Islam.

Like Old Hebrew and Phoenician, the S Arabian scripts may be viewed as syllabaries (where the consonants contained an element of indeterminate vocalic value); indeed, when exported by the Arab merchants to the E coast of the Red Sea and the E coast of central Africa, these same scripts developed into full-fledged syllabaries with clearly identified vocalic signs. Ethiopic, the official language of the Christian kingdom of Axum in the early medieval period, is better known as Ge‛ez, the ritual tongue of the Ethiopian Coptic Church. It was developed from a S Arabian dialect with an E African substrate. The writing system is a derivative of the Sabean script, which contained twenty-nine characters. It is basically the modern script in which the manifold Semitic languages of Ethiopia are written. The official one is Amharic but the same applies to Tigré, Tigriña, Harari, Gafat, Guragé, and Argobba, as well as a host of lesser dialects (see LANGUAGES OF THE ANE II.D). The Sabean script and the Ge‛ez appear in fig. 14.

F. Aramaic. The NW Semitic family of languages is usually thought to consist of two branches: Canaanite (including Ugaritic, Phoenician, Hebrew) and ARAMAIC. It was apparently Aramaic that introduced the familiar *square script*, which has been called "the Persian chancellery hand" (F. M. Cross in *The Bible and the Ancient Near East: Essays in Honor of William Foxwell Albright*, ed. G. E. Wright [1961], 136ff.). The evidence of the DEAD SEA SCROLLS and the ELEPHANTINE Papyri shows the rapid spread of this script throughout the area of the W Semitic languages. Since Syria-Palestine was under a series of foreign administrations from the Hellenistic age until the brief revolts that brought about the Roman conquest, it stands to reason that not only the speech but also the writing would be affected. One of the most important of these effects was the addition of vowel indicators. This process began before the Christian era and continued rapidly afterward until the Aramaic and Hebrew script was in fact a full ALPHABET. The various systems of signs called "pointings" or "vowel signs" came together in the medieval renaissance of Jewish learning.

The Aramaic square script developed into different forms among the various Aramaic dialects, such as Nabatean, Syriac, and Mandean. It is thought that the Arabic alphabet had its origins in the Nabatean script, though other influences were probably at work. See ALPHABET IV.D. Later, when Islamic culture rose to be the dominant power in the ANE, it adopted the practice of adding diacritical markings to indicate vowel sounds. Since both the Hebrew Bible and the Arabic Koran contained prohibitions against the making of "graven images,"

the script itself became an artistic and ornamental device. The carved wooden screens and lattices of much of the Islamic golden age are covered with hundreds of running scrolls of Arabic script. In the same fashion the Hebrew alphabet was made an end in itself and covered in rich symmetry the silver and gold vessels of the medieval synagogue. (Contemporary to this fanciful artistic usage of the script there arose an interpretation of the alphabet as a message in and of itself. This notion of the Hebrew script as the subject of magical and mystical interpretation produced a vast folklore of the OT text and even of the vowel pointings.)

G. Greek. As noted above, Greek was first set down in an elaborate and uneconomical syllabary that later developed into a highly cursive and abstract form. Interestingly enough, the classical authors of Athens and Ionia never mention this early nearly hieroglyphic phase of the writing of Greek. The Hellenic traditions are unanimous in presenting the Greek script as derived from the Phoenician. However, just when and where this great cultural transmission took place is not at all clear. Between the syllabic script of Linear "B" on the Pylos tablets and the earliest full-fledged alphabetic inscriptions from Greece proper there is only about 450–500 years (from 1200 to about 750 B.C.). In this period there is little evidence extant and none showing the stages of development. In the oldest Greek alphabetic inscriptions the forms for *b, g, d, l, m, n,* and *r* are the same as in some types of Phoenician and no doubt represent sounds that are very similar or even identical in the Semitic languages.

The direction of all the derivatives of the W Semitic writing systems is from right to left and indeed the oldest known Greek inscriptions such as the Athenian Dipylon vase inscription use this approach. By the end of the 9th cent. B.C. the Phoenician characters had been adopted by Greek speaking cities on the Attic peninsula and the islands off W Anatolia. These individual adoptions caused the proliferation of a variety of forms of the script. Texts from the 6th cent. B.C. are often written in a peculiar left-to-right then right-to-left manner known in Greek as *boustrophedon* ("turning as an ox [plows]"; cf. fig. 16).

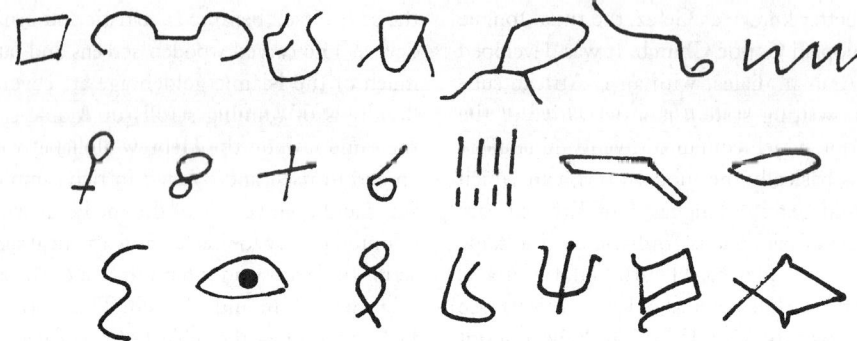

Figure 13. Protosinaitic signs (after W. F. Albright, "The Proto-Sinaitic Inscriptions and Their Decipherment," *Harvard Theological Studies* XXII [1966], plates 4-9 passim).

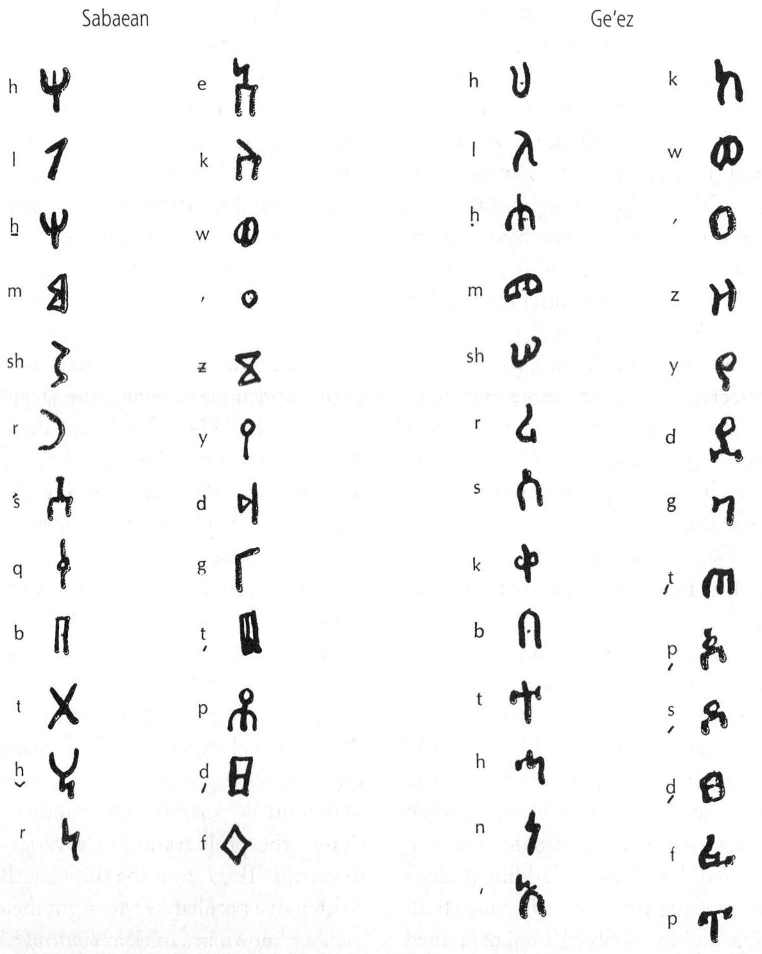

Figure 14. Sabaean and Ge'ez scripts (after A. Dillman, *Ethiopic Grammar* [1907], TEL. 1).

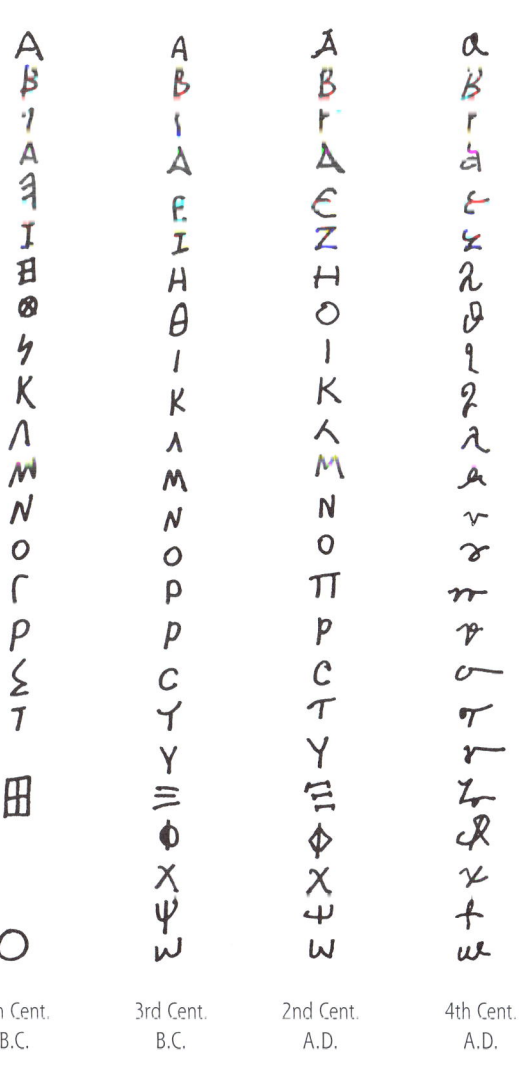

IN BOUSTROPHEDON WRITING THE LINES CRISS-CROSS BACK AND FORTH JUST AS AN OX PLOWS A FIELD. MANY ANCIENT INSCRIPTIONS WERE WRITTEN THIS WAY.

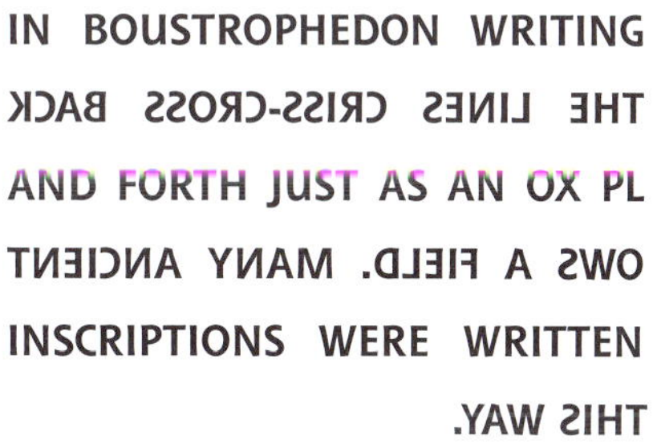

Figure 16. Boustrophedon.

| 5th Cent. B.C. | 3rd Cent. B.C. | 2nd Cent. A.D. | 4th Cent. A.D. |

Figure 15. Greek Scripts.

The sounds of the Greek language that did not occur in Semitic were indicated by newly invented signs, and among these were the full set of vowels. For example, the initial sign of the Semitic systems, ʾaleph, was utilized as the sound of the vowel a and the name of the letter was retained in the form *alpha G270*. The difficult consonant clusters were at first written out (e.g., ΠΣ, but later Ψ). In time the different forms of the letters became unified and standardized by commerce and association between the Greek states. Some more difficult letters used to transcribe dialectic differences dropped out completely (e.g., *digamma*, formed much like the modern capital *F* and pronounced *w*); however, since all the Semitic and Greek characters doubled as integers in the number system, these old signs were kept as numbers.

Athens formally accepted the Ionian script of Miletus in 403 B.C., and it is probable that other members of the leagues and organizations of the time did likewise. The final classical script of twenty-four signs, the world's first full and complete alphabet, had thus been formed. All modern characters of the Romance, Slavonic, and Germanic types are derived from this source. In the centuries up to the rise of the Roman empire the

Greek alphabet took several forms and it was one of the first to be actually designed in an artistic sense. The result was a fine reserved epigraphic style for monuments and staid formal use called *uncial*, as well as a free flowing cursive or running hand called *minuscule* (cf. fig. 15). The three classical accent marks—acute, grave, and circumflex—were added in the 2nd and 3rd Christian centuries by the scholars of Byzantium. So completely did the Greek of the Hellenistic age become the communication medium of the common people that its use in the Gospels and subsequent NT writings was both providential and natural, and so well fitting to the cosmopolitanism of the evangel that John could without qualification summarize the omnipresence and eternality of the glorified Christ with the simple words ALPHA AND OMEGA (Rev. 1:8 et al.).

VI. Writing in the Scriptures

A. In the OT. Even ABRAHAM, who lived in the first half of the 2nd millennium B.C., would have been aware of five distinct and complete writing systems commonly in use in the cultural milieu about him. The OT contains oral statements, sermons, conversations, and other direct utterances, but it is primarily a written record. Several Hebrew words are used for the concept of writing, the most common being the verb *kātab* H4180 ("to write," Exod. 17:14 et al.); less frequent is the cognate noun *kĕtāb* H4181, "document, record, writing," 1 Chr. 28:19 et al.). It apparently can indicate both engraved epigraphic writing and inked penmanship. Its use is not restricted to one area of the OT nor to the people of Israel alone. The training and organization of the scribal trade is not mentioned in the OT, but by analogy to the other peoples of the time it is safe to assume that there were specific individuals who made their living as "public stenographers" and who held a position of authority and prominence in Israel. Frequently in the historical books SCRIBES are summoned, called, ordered or dismissed so they must have been a common adjunct to the royal and religious offices.

B. In the NT. The writers of the NT presuppose that the OT is essentially a written document and also that the gospel is the fulfillment of the OT. This simple concept runs through and enlightens many points in the NT. For example, Jesus alluded to the Hebrew/Aramaic square script when he said that "not a dot" would pass from the law until everything should be accomplished (Matt. 5:18 RSV; cf. Lk. 16:17); the reference is probably to a very small stroke that distinguishes certain letters (see DOT). The common Greek expression *gegraptai*, "it has been written" (pass. ptc. of *graphō* G1211), conveys a special authoritative sense, with the supposition understood, "and not to be altered." This is a straightforward extension of the standard NT usage in regard to the divine authority and finality of the OT and its proper and consummate explanation in the INCARNATION of Christ and the gospel witness of him. See also INSPIRATION.

(See further G. A. Barton, *The Origin and Development of Babylonian Writing*, 2 vols. [1913]; F. Thureau-Dangin, *Le syllabaire akkadienne* [1926]; F. G. Kenyon, *Ancient Books and Modern Discoveries* [1927]; Th. W. Danzel, *Die Anfänge der Schrift* [1929]; W. F. Albright, *The Vocalization of the Egyptian Syllabic Orthography* [1934]; N. Abbott, *The Rise of the North Arabic Script and its Kurʾānic Development* [1939]; M. Burrows, *What Mean These Stones?* [1941]; C. Higounet, *L'écriture* [1955]; J. F. Friedrich, *Extinct Languages* [1957]; M. Cohen, *La grande invention de l'écriture et son évolution*

This papyrus from 1st-cent. Hawara, Egypt, probably a Latin writing exercise, repeats seven times a line from Virgil's *Aeneid* (2.601).

[1958]; H. Jensen, *Die Schrift in Vergangenheit und Gegenwart* [1958]; P. E. Cleator, *Lost Languages* [1959]; S. Morag, *The Vocalization Systems of Arabic, Hebrew and Aramaic* [1962]; I. J. Gelb, *A Study of Writing*, rev. ed. [1963]; D. Diringer, *The Alphabet. A Key to the History of Mankind*, 3rd. ed., 2 vols. [1968]; P. K. McCarter, Jr., *The Antiquity of the Greek Alphabet and the Early Phoenician Scripts* [1975]; G. R. Driver, *Semitic Writing from Pictograph to Alphabet*, rev. ed. [1976]; R. Harris, *The Origin of Writing* [1986]; C. B. F. Walker et al., *Ancient Writing from Cuneiform to the Alphabet* [1990]; D. Schmandt-Besserat, *Before Writing*, 2 vols. [1992], H.-J. Martin, *The History and Power of Writing* [1994], J. Naveh, *Origins of the Alphabet*, rev. ed. [1994], P. T. Daniels and W. Bright, eds., *The World's Writing Systems* [1996], J.-J. Glassner, *The Invention of Cuneiform: Writing in Sumer* [2003]; S. D. Houston, ed., *The First Writing: Script Invention as History and Process* [2004]; H. Rogers, *Writing Systems: A Linguistic Approach* [2005]; A. Robinson, *The Story of Writing*, new ed. [2007].)

W. White, Jr.

Wycliffe wik′lif. See versions of the Bible, English.

Inscribed titles of Xerxes on calcite jar fragments from Susa (5th cent. B.C.).

Xanthicus zan′thi-kuhs (Ξανθικός, spelled ΞΑΝΔΙΚΟΣ in some inscriptions and papyri). The name for the first month in the Macedonian calendar (2 Macc. 11:30, 33, 38). According to JOSEPHUS (*Ant.* 1.3.3 §81 et al.), Xanthicus corresponds to NISAN (March-April) in the Jewish calendar, but J. A. Goldstein (*II Maccabees*, AB 41A [1983], 418–19) argues for ADAR (February-March).

Xerxes zuhrk′seez (אֲחַשְׁוֵרוֹשׁ H347, from Pers. *ḫšayāršā*, possibly "mighty man"; called Ξέρξης by Gk. writers). KJV and other versions transliterate the Hebrew and read AHASUERUS. **(1)** Father of DARIUS THE MEDE (Dan. 9:1).

(2) Son of DARIUS I (Hystaspes) the Great, and ruler of PERSIA (c. 486–465 B.C.; Ezra 4:6 and frequently in the book of Esther). His mother was Atossa, daughter of CYRUS the Great, the builder of the Persian empire. Xerxes was designated as his father's successor by Darius himself, whose reign had ended as rebellions were breaking out throughout his vast empire.

Xerxes was a man of weak abilities and given to unfortunate reliance upon the advice and opinions of courtiers and harem eunuchs. After suppressing the revolt in EGYPT with great violence and destruction, he levied a navy from Egypt and his Greek allies, and began to formulate plans to invade Attica. His Phoenician subjects ferried his army across the Hellespont on a double bridge of boats and from there the Persian forces, made up of contingents from nearly fifty nations, marched S and captured ATHENS. However, the tide of war turned swiftly when Xerxes' great fleet was annihilated at the subsequent naval battle of Salamis in 480 B.C., and Xerxes again exhibited his insecurity of character by putting his Phoenician admiral to death and causing the desertion of his naval forces. His commander in Greece, Mardonius, negotiated with Athens to no avail. The war was resumed and Persia was finally defeated at the battle of Plataea in 479/8. The Athenians and many newly won deserters from Persia followed up their success by invading the area of the Eurymedon River, thus ending Persia's hopes for European conquest.

The Persian king retired to his palaces at PERSEPOLIS and SUSA, which he expanded and decorated in colossal and ornate style. Of great interest is his religious enthusiasm, for unlike his predecessors he did not accept the validity of the archaic religious cults of Egypt and Babylon but destroyed them both. His inscriptions from Persepolis proclaim his destruction of the temples of the false gods in his dominions and his faithfulness to the deity Ahuramazda. It may well be that the religious inflexibility of his Jewish subjects and his wife, ESTHER, confirmed his stalwart adherence to Mazdaism. No mention of Esther or her people is made outside of the biblical book, but the exclusive and propagandistic character of ancient annals and records is well established, and so one would be indeed surprised if the inner workings of the HAREM were recorded upon royal documents of the period. The essential personality of Xerxes as presented by HERODOTUS and his own inscriptions is very similar to that demonstrated in the Bible (see ESTHER, BOOK OF). The career of Xerxes was the preliminary to the collapse of the Achaemenid house under ALEXANDER THE GREAT's conquest. (See further E. M. Yamauchi, *Persia and the Bible* [1990], ch. 5; P. Briant, *From Cyrus to Alexander: A History of the Persian Empire* [2002], ch. 13.)

W. WHITE, JR.

The Yarmuk River is partly visible in this aerial photograph, just right of center. (View to the S.)

Yahweh yah´weh. See GOD, NAMES OF, II.

Yahweh, day of. See DAY OF THE LORD.

Yahwist yah´wist. Name applied to one of the putative sources of the Pentateuch, often referred to by the designation J. See PENTATEUCH III.

yard. For the sense "courtyard," see TEMPLE, JERUSALEM IV.B. As a unit of measurement, the term is used sometimes in modern versions as the approximate equivalent of two cubits (cf. NIV, Josh. 3:4; Neh. 3:13; Jn. 21:8). See WEIGHTS AND MEASURES I.A.   F. B. HUEY, JR.

Yarmuk yahr´muhk. Although not mentioned in the Bible, the Yarmuk has played an important role as the northernmost of the four main rivers in TRANSJORDAN (the others being the JABBOK, the ARNON, and farthest S the ZERED). Sometimes referred to as Canaan's "second river" (after the JORDAN), the Yarmuk is about 50 mi. long, intermittently draining the BASHAN plateau and cutting a canyon to the Jordan, which it resembles at their confluence some 4 mi. S of the Sea of Galilee. Though the scene of a major Muslim triumph against the Byzantine empire in A.D. 636, as well as a current boundary for Israel, Syria, and Jordan, the Yarmuk rarely formed a cultural-historical divide, being renowned rather for therapeutic springs and irrigation.   G. R. LEWTHWAITE

yarn. A strand of fibers used mainly in weaving and knitting. The term is used by modern English versions (esp. in Exod. 25—28 and 35—39) not as the rendering of a Hebrew word but as an aid in translation. Thus, in the description of the curtains of the TABERNACLE, where the KJV says that they should be made of "fine twined linen, and blue, and purple, and scarlet," the NIV has, "of finely twisted linen and blue, purple and scarlet yarn" (26:1). (The KJV, following Rashi and other interpreters, has "linen yarn" as the translation of *miqwēh* in 1 Ki. 10:28 and 2 Chr. 1:16; however, this form is now analyzed as the preposition *min* H4946, "from," plus the place name *qĕwēh* H7750. See KUE.)   S. BARABAS

Yavneh yav´neh. See JABNEEL #2.

year. See CALENDAR.

yeast. See LEAVEN.

yellow. This English term is used in most Bible versions to render Hebrew *ṣāhōb* H7411, which occurs in only one passage with reference to the color of hair in a sore (Lev. 11:29–39; the cognate verb *ṣahab* H7410, meaning "to gleam [like bright, reddish gold]," occurs once with reference to bronze and is usually translated "polished" or "shining," Ezra 8:27). The KJV uses it in an additional passage as the translation of *yĕraqraq* H3768, applied to gold (Ps. 68:13; NIV, "shining"; NRSV "green"); the reference is possibly to "gold with much silver additive" (*HALOT*, 2:441; the Heb. word occurs also with reference to the "greenish" color of a skin disease or of mildew, Lev. 13:49 and 14:37). In the NT, the NIV has "yellow as sulfur" for the Greek adjective *theiōdēs* G2523, "sulphurous" (Rev. 9:17). Yellow as a dye is not mentioned in the Bible; such a dye in antiquity was produced from safflower petals, saffron from the crocus flower, turmeric, unripe pomegranate, and other herbs. See also COLOR.

1185

Yerushalmi. See TALMUD IV; TARGUM II.

YHWH. See GOD, NAMES OF, II.

Yiron yihr′uhn. See IRON (PLACE).

yod, yodh yohd (יוֹד, alternate form of יָד H3338, "hand"). KJV *jod*. The tenth letter of the Hebrew ALPHABET (י), with a numerical value of ten. It is named for the shape of the letter, which in its older form resembled the outline of a hand. Its sound corresponds to that of English *y*; in addition, it was used to represent vocalic sounds (*i*, *ê*) prior to the introduction of vowel signs, and this practice was later continued.

yoke. A piece of timber or a heavy wooden pole, shaped to fit over the neck with curved pieces of wood around the neck fastened to the pole, and used to hitch together a team of oxen (or other draft animals) so that they could pull heavy loads evenly. The common Hebrew term for "yoke" is ʿōl H6585 (Gen. 27:40 et al.), although môṭâ H4574 is used a number of times (Lev. 26:13 et al.). Another term, ṣemed H7538, can also be translated "yoke," but only in the related sense of "a team of animals yoked together" (Job 1:3 et al.). In the NT, the Greek noun *zygos* G2433 is used (Matt. 11:29 et al.; *zeugos* G2414, "a pair [of animals]," can be applied to doves and to oxen, Lk. 2:24; 14:19). Because a scale or pair of balances was constructed with a crossbar reminding one of a yoke, *zygos* can also mean, "a pair of scales" (Rev. 6:5).

In the Bible, these terms are most often used metaphorically to designate a burden, obligation, or slavery (Gen. 27:40; 1 Sam. 11:7; Isa. 58:6, 9; Nah. 1:13; Matt. 11:29; Lk. 14:19; Acts 15:10). When Yahweh delivered Israel from Egyptian slavery, he said, "I broke the bars of your yoke and enabled you to walk with heads held high" (Lev. 26:13). Severe bondage can be termed "an iron yoke on your neck" (Deut. 28:48). The term is used of affliction in Lam. 3:27: "It is good for a man to bear the yoke while he is young." Isaiah states that people rejoice because God shatters "the yoke that burdens them, / the bar across their shoulders, / the rod of their oppressor" (Isa. 9:4; cf. 10:27). Sometimes the term is used to describe the burden of a person's transgression and

Donkey with yoke and plow.

its punishment: "My sins have been bound into a yoke; / by his hands they were woven together. / They have come upon my neck / and the Lord has sapped my strength" (Lam. 1:14).

In the NT the term can also refer to slavery (1 Tim. 6:1); Roman conquerors compelled prisoners of war to march under an archway to symbolize defeat and slavery. More significant is the application of the metaphor to the OT law, especially CIRCUMCISION: "Now then, why do you try to test God by putting on the necks of the disciples a yoke that neither we nor our fathers have been able to bear?" (Acts 15:10; cf. Gal. 5:1). Probably alluding to the use of this figure in Judaism with reference to WISDOM (Sir. 51:26), Jesus said: "Take my yoke upon you and learn from me, for I am gentle and humble in heart, and you will find rest for your souls. For my yoke is easy and my burden is light" (Matt. 11:29–30). It is significant that Clement of Rome describes Christians as those who come under the yoke of grace (*1 Clem.* 16.17).

Various kinds of draft animals were hitched or yoked together, but generally it was oxen or cattle. It is interesting that the Mosaic law forbade the yoking of an ox and a donkey together (Deut. 22:10) because of the inequality of the work. This rubric no doubt is the source of the familiar mandate of the apostle that Christians should not be "unequally yoked together [verb *heterozygeō* G2282] with unbelievers" (2 Cor. 6:14 KJV). Yoked animals were used for pulling plows, stones, carts, and other types of road or field work. Archaeologists have discovered that yokes of many kinds were used throughout the ancient world and very early, and that yokes were crude and simple or more complex in design, depending upon the period of history. See also YOKEFELLOW.   L. M. PETERSEN

yokefellow. After pleading with EUODIA and SYNTICHE "to agree with each other in the Lord," PAUL adds, "Yes, and I ask you, loyal yokefellow, help these women …" (Phil. 4:3). The Greek word is *syzygos* G5187, an adjective that literally means "yoked, paired together," but that can also be used, as here, substantively and figuratively, "a person that is joined to another one." In classical literature it is at times equivalent to "wife," and thus some have suggested that the apostle was referring to his own spouse. Others have thought that here the word is a proper name, Syzygus, but evidence is lacking. Most interpreters understand the term in its common figurative sense of "companion" or "comrade," and numerous suggestions have been made in regard to the identity of the person (Luke, Lydia, Epaphroditus, Barnabas, Silas, Timothy). Perhaps it was a way of describing the leader of the church at PHILIPPI.   S. BARABAS

Yom Kippur yom´kip´uhr. See ATONEMENT, DAY OF.

youth. The ancient concepts of childhood and youth were imprecise. No term exists in Hebrew or Greek for adolescence or puberty as such. Generally a woman is styled a "maiden" (see MAID, MAIDEN) until marriage, regardless of age, and a man is a youth from infancy to manhood (sometime in his twenties). A variety of Hebrew terms are rendered "youth" or the like in the various English versions, the most common being *naʿar* H5853 (Gen. 14:24 et al.), feminine *naʿărâ* H5855 (24:14 et al.). Also worthy of note is the pairing of *bāḥûr* H1033, "young man," with *bětûlâ* H1435, "virgin, maiden" (Deut. 32:25 et al.; see VIRGIN). In the NT such Greek terms are used as *neotēs* G3744, "youth" (e.g., 1 Tim. 4:12), *neanias* G3733, "young man" (e.g., Acts 7:58), and *neaniskos* G3734, also "young man" (e.g., Matt. 19:20); the feminine *neanis* occurs with some frequency in the SEPTUAGINT (e.g., Exod. 2:8), but not at all in the NT. Neither in the OT nor in the NT can chronological limits be assigned. Generally children were weaned at about two to three years and became responsible at thirteen years. See also BOY; GIRL; CHILD.

W. WHITE, JR.

This elevation in SW Jerusalem is often referred to as Mount Zion (view to the NE), but the name was originally applied to the City of David, just S of the temple mount.

Zaanaim zay´uh-nay´im. KJV alternate form of ZAANANNIM.

Zaanan zay´uh-nan (צַאֲנָן H7367, possibly "place of flocks"). A town against which MICAH prophesied (Mic. 1:11). The imprecation refers to various locations mostly in the SHEPHELAH, and therefore Zaanan is generally considered to be the same as ZENAN (Josh. 15:37).

Zaanannim zay´uh-na´nim (צַעֲנַנִּים H7588 [in Jdg. 4:11 the *Ketib* can be understood as בְּצַעֲנִים or בְּצַעֲנִים], meaning unknown). A place near HELEPH on the S border of the tribe of NAPHTALI known for being the site of a large tree (Josh. 19:33); it was here, not far from KEDESH, that HEBER the Kenite pitched his tent (Jdg. 4:11 [KJV, "Zaanaim"]; his wife, JAEL, killed SISERA in this tent, vv. 17–21). According to Z. Kallai, "Elon-in-Zaanannim" was probably not a settlement but "a conspicuous geographic feature in the region under consideration, close to Heleph" (Z. Kallai, *Historical Geography of the Bible* [1986], 232). Following the SEPTUAGINT reading in Joshua (*Besemin* or *Besenanim*), some have identified Zaanannim with Khirbet Bessum, 3 mi. NE of TABOR. Other proposals include Lejjun (between MEGIDDO and Tell Abu Qudeis), Khan et-Tujjar (on the road from BETH-SHAN to Damascus, about 4 mi. SE of ADAMI NEKEB; cf. F.-M. Abel, *Géographie de la Palestine* [1933], 2:439), and Shajarat el-Kalb (3 mi. SW of the S tip of the Sea of Galilee. The NRSV apparently interprets the two biblical references as indicating different places, for in Joshua it reads, "the oak in Zaanannim," but

One proposal for the location of Zaanannim is on the plain just SW of the Sea of Galilee. (View to the N.)

1189

in Judges, "Elon-bezaanannim" (the latter is the rendering of NJPS in both passages).

A. K. Helmbold

Zaavan zay′uh-vuhn (זַעֲוָן H2401, perhaps related to זְוָעָה H2400, "trembling, terror"). Son of Ezer and grandson of Seir the Horite; he probably became the progenitor of a clan in Edom (Gen. 36:27; 1 Chr. 1:42 [KJV, "Zavan"]).

Zabad zay′bad (זָבָד H2274, "gift" or "[God/Yahweh] has bestowed"; cf. Zabdi, Zabdiel, Zabud, Zebadiah, Zebedee, Zebidah). (1) Son of Nathan and descendant of Judah through Jerahmeel and Attai (1 Chr. 2:36–37); perhaps the same as Zabud (1 Ki. 4:5).

(2) Son of Tahath and descendant of Ephraim (1 Chr. 7:21). Some believe that the genealogy in this passage is textually corrupt. See Bered (person).

(3) Son of Ahlai; he is included among David's mighty warriors (1 Chr. 11:41).

(4) Son of an Ammonite woman named Shimeath; he was one of two men who assassinated King Joash (2 Chr. 24:26). The parallel passage (2 Ki. 12:21) reads differently. See Jehozabad.

(5–7) The name of three Israelites—respectively descendants of Zattu, Hashum, and Nebo—who agreed to put away their foreign wives (Ezra 10:27, 33, 43; 1 Esd. 9:28 [KJV, "Sabatus"], 33 [KJV, "Baanaia"], 35 [KJV, "Zabadaias"]).

Zabadaias zab′uh-day′yuhs. KJV Apoc. form of Zabad (1 Esd. 9:35).

Zabadeans zab′uh-dee′uhnz (Ζαβαδαῖοι). An Arabian tribe that was attacked and plundered by Jonathan Maccabee in the course of the war with Demetrius (1 Macc. 12:31). Josephus, narrating the incident (*Ant.* 13.5.10 §179), calls the conquered people Nabateans, the powerful tribe whose headquarters were at Petra, but this identification is evidently an error, for the Zabadeans lived in a region somewhere E of the Eleutherus River and thus between Hamath and Damascus (cf. 1 Macc. 12:25, 30, 32). Perhaps there was a connection between them and Zabdiel the Arab (11:17; see *ABD*, 6:1030–31). Alternatively (or in addition?), they may have lived in an area or town called Zabad, though the identification of such a place is problematic. The site could scarcely be identical with a town of similar name said to be situated NW of Hamath (*CIG*, no. 9893). A more likely proposal is modern Zebdani, about halfway between the Eleutherus and Damascus.

W. J. Cameron

Zabbai zab′i (זַבַּי H2287, possibly short form of זְבִידָה H2288, "given, bestowed"; see Zebidah). (1) One of the descendants of Bebai who agreed to put away their foreign wives (Ezra 10:28; 1 Esd. 9:29 [KJV, "Josabad"]).

(2) Father of a certain Baruch who helped to repair the wall of Jerusalem (Neh. 3:20; here the *Qere* has Zaccai).

J. Arthur Thompson

Zabbud zab′uhd. KJV variant of Zaccur.

Zabdeus zab′dee-uhs. KJV Apoc. form of Zebadiah (1 Esd. 9:21).

Zabdi zab′di (זַבְדִּי H2275, "my gift" or short form of a name such as זַבְדִּיאֵל H2276, "gift of God"; see Zabdiel, Zebedee). (1) Son of Zerah, descendant of Judah, and grandfather of Achan (Josh. 7:1, 17–18, KJV and other versions). On the basis of the Septuagint (which has *Zambri*) and of 1 Chr. 2:6–7, some scholars read Zimri (cf. NIV).

(2) Son of Shimei and descendant of Benjamin (1 Chr. 8:19). He is included among the heads of families who lived in Jerusalem (v. 28).

(3) A Shiphmite who "was in charge of the produce of the vineyards for the wine vats" during the reign of David (1 Chr. 27:27).

(4) Son of Asaph and ancestor of Mattaniah; the latter was a postexilic Levite who led in worship (Neh. 11:17; apparently called Zaccur in 1 Chr. 25:2 et al., and Zicri in 1 Chr. 9:15).

J. Arthur Thompson

Zabdiel zab′dee-uhl (זַבְדִּיאֵל H2276, "gift of God" or "my gift is God"; see Zabad, Zebediah, etc., and cf. Akk. *Zabdilu*; Gk. Apoc. Ζαβδιηλ). (1) Father of Jashobeam; the latter was a military officer under David in charge of the first division (1 Chr. 27:2).

(2) Son of Haggedolim; he was chief officer of the priests in the days of Nehemiah (Neh. 11:14).

(3) An Arab who assassinated Alexander Balas when the latter fled to Arabia; Zabdiel beheaded Alexander and sent his head to Ptolemy Philopator (1 Macc. 11:17; cf. Jos. *Ant.* 13.4.8 §118 [*Zabdiel*]). J. Arthur Thompson

Zabud zay′buhd (זָבוּד *H2280*, "bestowed"). Son of Nathan; he is described as "a priest and personal adviser to the king [Solomon]" (1 Ki. 4:5). Some identify Zabud with Zabad #1; see discussion under Nathan #4.

Zabulon zab′yuh-luhn. KJV NT form of Zebulun.

Zaccai zak′i (זַכַּי *H2347*, "pure, innocent"; cf. Zacchaeus). TNIV Zakkai. (1) Ancestor of a family of 760 members who returned from the exile (Ezra 2:9; Neh. 7:14; called Chorbe [KJV, "Corbe"] in 1 Esd. 5:12).
(2) See Zabbai #2.

Zacchaeus za-kee′uhs (Ζακχαῖος *G2405*, from Heb. זַכַּי *H2347*, "pure, innocent"; see Zaccai). Also Zaccheus. (1) A military officer under Judas Maccabee (2 Macc. 10:19).
(2) A wealthy Jewish tax collector of Jericho, known for his short stature, who became a disciple of Jesus under most unusual circumstances (Lk. 19:1–10). Luke is the only evangelist who preserves the exciting Zacchaeus pericope. One is amazed that the story is not included in the Gospel according to Matthew (who himself was a tax collector), but the episode fits the dominant note of Luke's "Gospel for the Gentiles" very well and no doubt Luke included it to show that the gospel is for all those estranged from God. The passage has a climactic function, since it records the last event in Jesus' ministry prior to his final week in Jerusalem.

Luke makes a special point that Zacchaeus was a "chief tax collector" (*architelōnēs G803*) and that he "was wealthy" (Lk. 19:2). No doubt he was a sort of district tax commissioner who had purchased the Jericho tax franchise from the Roman or provincial government; he then probably farmed it out to subordinate tax agents who did the actual tax collecting, all of them reaping huge commissions and getting rich off poor and wealthy alike. Jericho was known for its palm groves and balsam (Jos., *Ant.* 15.4.2) and was on the main road of traffic between major commercial centers W of the Jordan (Joppa, Jerusalem) and in Transjordan. It was easy to amass a fortune there. It is possible he was one of the most hated men in Jericho, and it was natural that the people who witnessed the incident murmured against Jesus. "He has gone to be the guest of a 'sinner'" (v. 7).

When Jesus, his disciples, and a crowd of followers — the sick and the curious — came through Jericho on the way to the Passover in Jerusalem, it must have formed quite a commotion. Perhaps on that day Zacchaeus happened to be walking in the street or his place of business nearby, and he wondered who could be attracting such a crowd during the middle of the day. Evidently he had never met Jesus before, for Luke states, "He wanted to see who Jesus was" (Lk. 19:3). Because of his short build he could not see over the multitude. He anticipated that Jesus, who was moving slowly along with the crowd, would pass along his street, so he ran ahead and climbed a sycamore-fig tree (a common plant in the Jordan Valley; see sycamore). Zacchaeus certainly must have been surprised — and, one should comment, a bit embarrassed with the whole crowd looking up in amazement at the chief tax collector of Jericho up in a tree — when Jesus stopped, looked up, and called out to him over the noise of the crowd. What he said is part of the divine prerogative of knowledge and purpose that permeates the entire story: "Zacchaeus, come down immediately. I must stay at your house today" (v. 5).

Remains of Herod's northern palace at NT Jericho, hometown of Zacchaeus. The road to Jerusalem was located on the southern side (left) of the wadi.

The Lord knew the heart of Zacchaeus as he had earlier known NATHANAEL's (Jn. 1:48).

The conversion which followed must have caused quite a stir in Jericho. A hated tax collector, a collaborator with the oppressive Romans, had become a disciple of Jesus. Thousands of conversions during Jesus' ministry are not recorded, but that of Zacchaeus will always be remembered. Here great opposites met, the chief of sinners and the Chief of Love, and love is triumphant. This is the message and thrust of the gospel: "For the Son of Man came to seek and to save what was lost" (Lk. 19:10). The conversion of the small Jewish man is exemplary of all true Christian rebirth; he scrambled with haste down the tree and stood before Jesus with great joy of faith, and immediately began to show tangible evidence of his faith and repentance.

Zacchaeus's life was completely transformed through Christ. Spontaneously he openly confessed the sins of his evil life. His words reveal what his sin was: "Look, Lord! Here and now I give half of my possessions to the poor" (Lk. 19:8). Now he would do the opposite of what he once did, showing that all believers rich and poor are one in Christ. Jewish custom was that one fifth of a person's annual income should be given for works of love, but Zacchaeus went far beyond this. Moreover, because he knew that he had not gotten all his wealth through just means—and how much had not his henchmen stolen from the people through misrepresentation, pressure, and extortion?—he added, "and if I have cheated anybody out of anything, I will pay back four times the amount." Thus Zacchaeus offered twice the restitution thieves must make under Jewish law (Exod. 22:1; Num. 5:6).

Jesus' pronouncement of remission, "Today salvation has come to this house" (Lk. 19:9), included not only Zacchaeus himself but all the members of his household. The expression finds its meaning in the Jewish concept of the family under the old covenant. Now Zacchaeus was a true son of ABRAHAM, a child of the promise, and the blessings of Abraham were fulfilled in the forgiving Christ even for those who by their profession were considered heathen (Matt. 18:17). (*Clementine Homilies* 3.63 states that Zacchaeus later became a companion of PETER and bishop at CAESAREA, but the remark does not appear to be based upon fact. See further P. Kariamadam, *The Zacchaeus Story, Lk. 19, 1–10: A Redaction-Critical Investigation* [1986]; *ABD*, 6:1032–33.)   L. M. PETERSEN

Zacchur zak'uhr. KJV alternate form of ZACCUR (only 1 Chr. 4:26).

Zaccur zak'uhr (זַכּוּר H2346, possibly "[God is] mindful"). KJV also Zacchur (1 Chr. 4:26); TNIV Zakkur. **(1)** Father of SHAMMUA; the latter was one of the spies sent out by MOSES (Num. 13:4).

(2) Son of Hammuel and descendant of SIMEON (1 Chr. 4:26). Some interpret the Hebrew to mean that Zaccur, Hammuel, and Shimei were all sons of MISHMA.

(3) Son of Jaaziah and descendant of LEVI through MERARI (1 Chr. 24:27).

(4) One of the sons of ASAPH who assisted their father in the prophetic ministry of MUSIC; he was the head of the third company of temple musicians appointed by lot under DAVID (1 Chr. 25:2, 10). This Zaccur is apparently the same as ZABDI #4 and ZICRI #5. A descendant of his named Zechariah played the trumpet at the dedication of the wall in postexilic Jerusalem (Neh. 12:35).

(5) A descendant of BIGVAI, part of the company that traveled with EZRA from Babylon to Jerusalem (Ezra 8:14; KJV has ZABBUD following the *Ketib*). See also UTHAI.

(6) Son of Imri; he was one of those who helped NEHEMIAH rebuild the wall of Jerusalem (Neh. 3:2).

(7) A Levite who signed Nehemiah's covenant (Neh. 10:12).

(8) Son of Mattaniah and father of Hanan; the latter was appointed by Nehemiah as assistant to those who were in charge of the temple storerooms (Neh. 13:13).

(9) One of the postexilic temple singers who agreed to put away their foreign wives during Ezra's reform (1 Esd. 9:24; not mentioned in the parallel, Ezra 10:24).   J. ARTHUR THOMPSON

Zachariah, Zacharias, Zachary zak'uh-ri'uh, zak'uh-ri'uhs, zak'uh-ree. KJV alternate forms of ZECHARIAH.

Zacher zay'kuhr. KJV form of ZEKER.

Zadok zay′dok (צָדוֹק *H7401*, prob. "righteous" [perhaps a shortened theophoric name; see *HALOT*, 3:1001]; Σαδώκ *G4882*). The name of several individuals mentioned in the OT, the most prominent of whom will be discussed first.

(1) Son of AHITUB, descendant of LEVI (through KOHATH, AARON, and ELEAZAR), and father of AHIMAAZ (1 Chr. 6:8 [MT 5:34]); he was a leading priest during the reigns of DAVID and SOLOMON. He is first mentioned—along with another priest, AHIMELECH son of ABIATHAR—in a list of David's officers (2 Sam. 8:17; cf. 20:25). When David fled from ABSALOM, Zadok started to accompany him, taking along the ARK OF THE COVENANT, but David ordered him to return to Jerusalem (15:24–29). Zadok always showed unswerving loyalty to David, and his son Ahimaaz served as a courier in the time of conflict (15:36; 17:17–20; 18:19, 22, 27).

After the defeat of Absalom, Zadok and Abiathar were bearers of a message encouraging the elders of Judah to bring David back to Jerusalem (2 Sam. 19:11–14). These two priests served jointly until the end of David's reign, with Zadok for a time having special responsibility for the worship at the tabernacle in GIBEON (1 Chr. 16:39). When David was close to death, however, Abiathar lent his support to ADONIJAH, whereas Zadok refused to do so (1 Ki. 1:7–8). David then instructed Zadok and other leaders to crown Solomon as king (vv. 32–35), and Zadok himself anointed David's successor (v. 39). As Solomon proceeded to secure his throne, he deposed Abiathar from the priesthood (1 Ki. 2:26–27, 35), thus fulfilling the dire prediction about the house of ELI (1 Sam. 2:27–36).

In 1 Chronicles, this Zadok appears in various lists and parallel statements (1 Chr. 6:8, 53; 15:11; 16:39; 18:16; 24:3, 6, 31; 29:22). A passage without any parallel in Samuel or Kings is found in 12:26–28, which reports that the forces that accompanied David to HEBRON when he became king included 3,700 Aaronites under JEHOIADA, "and Zadok, a brave young warrior, with 22 officers from his family" (in 27:17, Zadok is listed as leader of the Aaronites). On the strength of this statement Wellhausen declared that Zadok was not a descendant of Aaron, but a military adventurer who had been given the priesthood by David as a reward for his services; and that because he thus displaced the descendants of Eli, an alleged prediction that the priesthood would be removed from Eli's family was inserted in 1 Sam. 2:27–36, and a priestly descent from Aaron and Eleazar was invented for Zadok.

This theory, like so many others, is entirely imaginary. There is no reason why a young man of priestly family should not have been active in military operations while his father was still living and performing the work of the priesthood (though some think that the Zadok mentioned in 1 Chr. 12:28 is a different individual altogether). There is also no reason for denying the possibility that the change in the priesthood should have been predicted in the time of Eli, unless, of course, one adopts the presupposition that predictive prophecy is impossible. (Many scholars, arguing that the relevant genealogies in Chronicles are fictional, have proposed various theories to account for Zadok's origins. See the summaries in *ABD*, 6:1034–36; G. N. Knoppers, *I Chronicles 1–9*, AB 12 [2004], 405–6.)

Because of Zadok's prominence during the reign of Solomon, subsequent high priests were chosen only from the Zadokite line. It is significant that in Ezekiel the term "sons of Zadok" is used four times as a designation for the priests (Ezek. 40:46; 43:19; 44:15; 48:11). See PRIESTS AND LEVITES III. During the Maccabean and later period, the legitimacy of the Zadokite priesthood played a major role in politics and religion (but note A. Hunt, *Missing Priests: The Zadokites in Tradition and History* [2006]). See further ESSENE; HASMONEAN; MACCABEE; SADDUCEE; ZADOKITE FRAGMENTS.

(2) Son of Ahitub II, descendant of #1 above, and father of SHALLUM (1 Chr. 6:12 [MT 5:38]; cf. Ezra 7:2). Because the father and grandfather of this second Zadok bear the same names as those of the first Zadok, some propose that a scribe might at some time have inadvertently copied the same line twice. Elsewhere a Zadok is identified as son of MERAIOTH, grandson of Ahitub, and father of MESHULLAM (1 Chr. 9:11; Neh. 11:11); since Meshullam is likely a variant of Shallum, this lineage probably refers to Zadok II, but some argue that it refers to Zadok I (in which case Ahitub I was his grandfather, not his father; see the discussions in RD, *Chronicles*, 112–20; Knoppers, *I Chronicles 1–9*, 407–10).

(3) Father of Jerusha; the latter was the wife of King Uzziah and mother of King Jotham (2 Ki. 15:33; 2 Chr. 27:1).

(4) Son of Baana; he made repairs to a portion of the wall of Jerusalem (Neh. 3:4). He should probably be identified with the Israelite who signed the covenant of Nehemiah (10:21; a certain Meshezabel is mentioned next to Zadok in both passages).

(5) Son of Immer; he made repairs to the wall of Jerusalem opposite his house (Neh. 3:29).

(6) A scribe whom Nehemiah appointed as one of three men in charge of the storerooms of the temple (Neh. 13:13). Perhaps he should be identified with #4 or #5 above.

(7) Son of Azor, included in Matthew's genealogy of Jesus Christ (Matt. 1:14; KJV, "Sadoc").

A. A. MacRae

Zadokite Fragments zay′duh-k*i*t. Name given to two fragmentary medieval mss discovered in the Cairo Genizah at the end of the 19th cent. and containing an ancient Jewish sectarian treatise. Several copies of the same document were subsequently discovered among the Dead Sea Scrolls (esp. 4Q266). The text is now known as the *Damascus Document* (or *Damascus Rule*) and abbreviated CD (for *Cairo: Damascus*).

    I. Discovery
    II. Contents
        A. Exhortation
        B. Rules of conduct
    III. Provenience
    IV. Date
    V. Relationship to the DSS

I. Discovery. The two mss were recovered by the American Jewish scholar Solomon Schechter (1847–1915) from the genizah high in the wall of the Ibn Ezra Synagogue located in the old Jewish quarter of Cairo. The stained parchment sheets were among the thousands of scattered documents removed by Schechter to the Cambridge University Library in the years after 1896. Thirty sacks of material were incorporated into the library as the Taylor-Schechter collection, and the *Zadokite Fragments* were published in 1910 (*Documents of Jewish Sectaries*, vol. 1). Schechter's dating of the work to the 1st cent. B.C. became the center of keen debate, but he was correct in his judgment that the source of the fragments was of intertestamental origin and that it represented a nonrabbinical collection of writings known to the early Middle Ages but subsequently lost.

II. Contents. The longer fragment consists of eight leaves of a mediocre parchment approximately 8.5 x 7.5 in. (215 x 190 mm.), stained and worn with a few small holes. The sixteen pages contain from twenty-one to twenty-three lines of text. The letters are large and black in a medieval rabbinic hand with some separation between words and all initial and final forms of the characters. The *lamed* extends up into the lower limit of the line above, while the final *ṣade* extends down to the upper limit of the next lower line. The margins on both sides are unjustified, and the size of the letters is not wholly uniform. The shorter fragment consists of two pages on one large leaf containing thirty-five lines on the obverse and thirty-four on the reverse. The text is smeared, stained, and mutilated at many points but without the lacunae of the longer fragment. The calligraphy is later than the other fragment and is smaller and less distinct. The longer portion, assigned to the 10th cent. by Schechter, is known as *A*, and the single leaf, assigned to the 12th cent., is known as *B*.

A. Exhortation. The *A* fragment opens with a general admonition and gives a paraphrase of Isa. 51:7 ("Hear me, you who know what is right"); the remainder seems to be some type of parallelistic hymn or chant used for public or group worship. The Hebrew is poorly preserved but has definite traces of archaic vocabulary and syntax. In the course of the exhortation there are hundreds of allusions to various OT passages, the largest number being to Isaiah, Ezekiel, and the Psalms. Most of the other books quoted or mentioned by allusion are also poetical.

The sanctuary is mentioned as abandoned by God. This theme is followed in all the extant sectarian documents: God had given up the temple in Jerusalem and its reprobate hierarchy, and was about to do a new act of redemption through a faithful remnant. The fact that the descendants of Zadok are mentioned as true to the covenant ("the sons of Zadok are the elect of Israel," CD IV, 3–4) demonstrates the probable source of the book. The mention of "the new covenant in the land of Damascus" (VIII, 21) to describe the community out of which the document arose was seized upon by some, and so the fragments became known as the *Damascus Document*, but the Zadokite intent of the work appears to take precedence.

The text attempts a retelling of the history of the Jews not unlike the defense of STEPHEN (Acts 7:2–53). The events are out of any order, however, and so many allusions are made to sources and special meanings of terms that interpretation is very difficult. Frequently euphemisms and indirect references occur that would have been clear to no one but initiates of the sect. Of special importance is the mention of a "Teacher of Righteousness" or "Righteous Teacher" (Heb. *mwrh ṣdq*) who is raised up by God to lead the sect. The chief motive of history is to obey the COVENANT, and the REMNANT alone is preserved by God to this end. Every age of biblical history is seen to have had its righteousness and its righteous remnant, and some of these are mentioned: Noah, Moses, and Joshua and their immediate followers. The larger population, the sons of Noah, and others are described as reprobate and fallen. The true knowledge of the Torah is the possession of those who are faithful to the covenant. In this the sect appears secretive and almost gnostic in its references to this restricted truth.

The admonition contains an elaborate theory of history drawn from the OT but modified to fit the circumstances of the times. History is cyclical in so far as there has always been the constant warfare between the righteous led by the "prince of lights" and the wicked led by BELIAL (CD V, 18). This will culminate in the final triumph of the righteous and a state of perfection in the Torah. It seems that the ultimate purity was the stringent keeping of the laws of the Levitical code and the attention to certain interpretations of the code peculiar to the sect. This would accord well with the Talmudic and sectarian usage known from other sources. The descriptions of the final state appear to be both sabbatical and eschatological. The most interesting feature of the epochs described is their similarity to certain passages in 2 Peter and Jude (cf. CD III, 11–12 to Jude 16).

The assumption of the fragments is that a body of sacred law was passed down from NOAH through ABRAHAM and the PATRIARCHS and that in each age there were masses of the people of Israel who were untrue to it and did not obey it, thereby insuring and displaying that they were not part of the covenant. This notion is also present in the NT documents. It is unclear precisely who is meant by the oblique references to the Teacher of Righteousness. There is some evidence that it may have been the biblical character, Zadok. However, the connection of this personage with a special appearance "in the last of days" (cf. Gen. 49:1; Isa. 2:2; Mic. 4:1), a phrase that has been understood in a messianic sense by both Jews and Christians, may mean that all such references are to messianic figures. There is no reason to assume that only one personage was in view. The mission of the Teacher will be to guide the faithful to the full appreciation of the Torah, "the house of the law" (CD XX, 10–13).

The notion that the true remnant will be led by the true law and their teacher into exile in DAMASCUS (perhaps a code word for QUMRAN) is a central theme of the admonition. The historic situation behind this assertion is not yet clear. It was in the Damascus refuge that the sect was to find its "tabernacle of David" (CD VII, 16). All other Jews are apostate. The purity and uniqueness of the sect's keeping of the law is stressed in many ways, especially in regard to marriage and the keeping of a "true" calendar rather than the lunar year of the temple in Jerusalem. The similarity between the expectations of the fragments and those of the *War Scroll* (1QM) is quite striking. The organization and mission of the sect is to be the same as that of the Israelites in their sojourn in the desert after the exodus but prior to the conquest. JOSHUA plays an equal if not greater part than MOSES in the quotations from the OT.

In the manner and form of its biblical material, the text source is much closer to that represented by the DSS than the MT. Undoubtedly the original was a version brought from Palestine to the Jewish community of Egypt. The question as to what meaning such unique documents had for the Jews of the DIASPORA may only be speculated. It is clear that after the collapse of the second commonwealth and the final destruction of the Jerusalem rite, the somber views of the sectaries must have gained popularity only to be subsequently lost in the ages after the fixation of the MT and the formation of the TALMUD.

B. Rules of conduct. The rules of obedience to the Torah are strict, but without the long additions and midrashic interpretations familiar from the Talmud. In some respects they are similar to the way of life taught by the PHARISEES. It is a mistake, however, to assume that the rule of the sect was identical to the later HALAKAH ("walk, behavior, way of life") of the medieval rabbis. If for no other reason, the sect was strongly and centrally eschatological and this was the purpose for which the Torah was strictly observed.

The *Zadokite Fragments* continually refer to the period of wickedness in which they were written and against which they warned. The attitude toward the Torah is set over against the particular evils and iniquities widespread in their times. Of special interest is the position regarding the sacrifices of the temple. Since they believed that the temple service of their day was not true to the OT instruction and that the PRIESTS AND LEVITES were not those legitimately appointed, the sect was to shun the worship in Jerusalem.

The key rearrangement was necessitated by the fact that the temple was no longer fit for sacrifice, while no other location would fulfill the demands of the Torah. The sect thus proposed a spiritual-figurative interpretation of the Torah requirements demanding sacrifices. The prayers and possibly other spiritual exercises of the sectaries were to be equivalent to the required sacrifices. "The sacrifice of the wicked is an abomination, but the prayer of the righteous is like an offering of delight" (CD XI, 20–21, a statement based on Prov. 15:9, 29, and other similar texts). Y. Yadin proposes that the sect held their communal meal in a sacrificial sense. "There seems to be some foundation for the assumption that this sect, which calls the altar 'table' as well as sanctifying its dining-table with a special ceremony, including the priestly benediction, regarded this ceremony and prayer as a substitute for sacrifices" (*The Scroll of the War of the Sons of Light* [1962], 200).

The sins proscribed in the rules of conduct are mostly concerned with the temple service and the keeping of the SABBATH. There is included a long list of regulations regarding individual purity and ceremonial cleanliness. Although concerned with the moral aspects of the Jewish religion, the system of salvation taught in the document may be regarded as both legalistic and autosoteristic, and so varies widely from the discourses of Jesus Christ and the writings of the NT. There is every reason to suspect that the *Zadokite Fragments* represent the latter portion of the first section of the original. Some introductory material undoubtedly preceded the present text, while a much longer catalogue of rules must have followed the rules contained therein. The problems arising from the document are even larger than the questions answered.

Some attempts have been made to divide the text into sources and to try to identify the unknown author or authors with one of the sources defined by the documentary or fragmentary hypotheses (e.g., "priests" or "royalists"), but such attempts have added little but confusion to the problem. The text does present the views of the antiestablishment minority in the late Hellenistic age of Judaism. Its teachings may have been the religious interpretation not merely of the sectarians alone, but also of the common people in Judea and Galilee. The unanimity of opinion among the fragments, the DSS, and certain of the Talmudic sources lends credence to the argument that the messianism, eschatology, and pietism of this document was not limited to an esoteric sect. The mass of Jews was probably opposed to both Greek and Roman intervention in Jewish affairs and thus despised the royal and religious hierarchy, who quickly came to terms with the conquerors. The paganism and immorality of the Roman imperial administration is apparent in the many proscriptions and commands reiterated in the fragments. The expectation was for a supernatural activity of God which would bring forth one or more political messiahs who would reestablish the house and sovereignty of David. The career of the Lord Christ was thus a fulfillment and a denial of that expectation.

III. Provenience. The fragments are in the standard folio or book form (see CODEX), while the originals were undoubtedly in the SCROLL or roll form of all ancient Hebrew parchments. The state of corruption in which both texts are extant is probably due to their being recopied in Egypt. Because of probable textual error and the obscure references of the scroll in the later era, much difficulties were certain to arise. The detractors of Schechter's enthusiasm are correct in insisting that the fragments were (1) not originally from Palestine and (2) written in the high Middle Ages.

But why should they have been preserved that long if only to be ultimately cast into the de facto censorship of the genizah? The answer is that for many centuries after the collapse of the second commonwealth and the rise of Christianity the popular notions of the sectaries were kept alive by small E European sects such as the Karaites. Sectarian Jewish scholars like Abraham Firkowich, following this line of descent in the 19th cent., recovered many exciting MSS. The Old Synagogue in Cairo, like those in Bukhara and the Crimea, had been centers of sectarian Judaism for nearly a millennium before the fragments were found. Solomon Zeitlin (*The Zadokite Fragments* [1952]) has demonstrated that themes and phrases from this literature are found in various medieval Jewish documents, thus showing that the views of the 1st-cent. sects were never totally lost.

IV. Date. The original composition can be dated only by indirect means, but the discovery of certain fragments of the same text from Qumran has placed it in the last century before the Christian era. Thus any chronological considerations applicable to the DSS are also applicable to the fragments. Although the terminus a quo cannot be stated any more precisely than the second half of the 1st cent. B.C., it certainly was a time when the Roman legions were fighting in Palestine and the full iniquity of the temple administration was clear. The terminus ad quem must be understood as the date when the scrolls were hidden in the caves, and this can be no later than the end of the Jewish rebellion (A.D. 73/74). There are references in both patristic and rabbinic literature to hidden scrolls in the Dead Sea area, and it is recorded that at several junctures in history scrolls were taken from the caves and distributed to Jewish communities. There is a high degree of probability that some of the sectarian texts were carried off to the Jewish communities of the DIASPORA, of which the Egyptian was by far the oldest. A definite resurgence of Jewish literature took place after the era of Constantine and before the rise of Islam.

V. Relationship to the DSS. Since small fragments of the Zadokite document have turned up among the DSS, they were obviously part of the sectarian library, and it is probable that the text was one of the ESSENES' own publications. The mention of Damascus, however, is still mysterious. It is apparent that not enough of the text is known to make more than educated guesses. Of all the DSS it is the *Manual of Discipline* (1QS) which is most closely parallel, second is the *War Scroll* (1QM), and third is the *Habakkuk Commentary* (1QpHab), while other allusions do exist to a lesser degree. All the references in the Karaite and other later Jewish sectarian literatures to the DSS can be found in the Zadokite document, and those not readily identifiable may have come from portions now lost. The quotation and comment on OT texts, the messianic expectation, and the antagonism to the temple hierarchy are all paralleled in the practical thought of the Essenes.

The fact that the Zadokite document was once part of the Essene library and was studied and recopied in the Middle Ages means that it survived the fate of the other DSS and found its way into sectarian Jewish communities of the oriental world. It thus formed one of the few links between the second commonwealth and the golden age of post-Islamic Judaism. It also has the unique value of being one of the early witnesses to the practice of a minority opinion within the Jewish state. Its relationship to the world of JOHN THE BAPTIST and the early ministry of Christ is very problematic but of major importance. The light shed on the OT is more oblique but nonetheless important. The fragments indicate a lost mode of exegesis and indicate a system of biblical theology that never gained favor but derived its content from works and traditions now lost.

(See further H. H. Rowley, *The Zadokite Fragments and the Dead Sea Scrolls* [1952]; C. Rabin, *The Zadokite Documents*, 2nd ed. [1958]; P. E. Kahle, *The Cairo Geniza*, 2nd ed. [1959]; L. H. Schiffman, *The Halakhah at Qumran* [1975]; P. R. Davies, *The Damascus Covenant: An Interpretation of the Damascus Document* [1983]; J. G. Campbell, *The Use of Scripture in the Damascus Document 1–8, 19–20* [1995], C. Hempel, *The Laws of the Damascus Document:*

Sources, Tradition, and Redaction [1998]; C. Hempel, *The Damascus Texts* [2002]; M. L. Grossman, *Reading for History in the Damascus Document* [2002]; C. Wassen, *Women in the Damascus Document* [2005]; B. L. Wacholder, *The New Damascus Document: The Midrash on the Eschatological Torah of the Dead Sea Scrolls: Reconstruction, Translation and Commentary* [2007].) W. WHITE, JR.

Zahab zay′hab. See WAHEB.

Zaham zay′ham (זַהַם H2300, perhaps derived from זָהַם H2299, "to be repulsive"). Son of King REHOBOAM by Mahalath (2 Chr. 11:19).

zain. See ZAYIN.

Zair zay′uhr (צָעִיר H7583, possibly "small" or "narrow [path]"). The name of a place where King JEHORAM (Joram) confronted an army from EDOM, which had rebelled against JUDAH (2 Ki. 8:21). The Hebrew text is ambiguous: the clause *wayyakkeh ʾet-ʾĕdôm* (lit., "he smote Edom") suggests that Judah won the battle, and the words *wayyānos hāʿām lĕʾōhālāyw* (lit., "the people fled to their tents") could be interpreted as referring to the reaction of the Edomites; on the other hand, we read that the Judean army was surrounded and that subsequently Edom continued in rebellion (v. 22). Modern versions usually understand the text to mean that Jehoram was in straits and attempted an attack, but that his own army fled. Instead of *ṣāʿîrâ*, "to Zair," the parallel passage reads *ʿim-śārāyw*, "with his commanders" (2 Chr. 21:9). If the reference to Zair is authentic, the place has never been identified. Proposals include ZIOR (cf. LXX *Siōr* and see Josh. 15:14), ZOAR (Gen. 13:10 et al.), and SEIR (Gen. 14:6 et al.). It seems likely that the scene of the battle was SE of the DEAD SEA, which makes Zoar the most likely suggestion (cf. *ABD*, 6:1038–39).

Zakkai zak′i. TNIV form of ZACCAI.

Zakkur zak′uhr. TNIV form of ZACCUR.

Zalaph zay′laf (צָלָף H7523, "caper" [a prickly shrub]). Father of HANUN; the latter assisted NEHEMIAH in repairing the wall of JERUSALEM (Neh. 3:30).

Zalmon (person) zal′muhn (צַלְמוֹן H7514, possibly "[little] dark one" or "[little] likeness" [cf. *HALOT*, 3:1029]). An AHOHITE, included among DAVID's mighty warriors (2 Sam. 23:28; called ILAI in 1 Chr. 11:29).

Zalmon (place) zal′muhn (צַלְמוֹן H7515, "black [mountain]"). (1) A mountain near SHECHEM where ABIMELECH and his men cut wood to burn down the stronghold of BAAL-BERITH (Jdg. 9:48). It has not been identified, but many scholars think the name may refer to one of the shoulders of either EBAL or GERIZIM; another possibility is Jebel el-Kabir (NE of Schechem).

(2) A region or mountain mentioned in a poetic passage: "When the Almighty scattered the kings there, / snow fell on Zalmon" (Ps. 68:14 NRSV; KJV, "it was *white* as snow in Salmon"). The figure is difficult, and the NIV renders, "it was like snow fallen on Zalmon" (similarly NJPS, "it seemed like a snowstorm in Zalmon"), suggesting that the enemy and their weapons lie scattered like snowflakes. This Zalmon may be the same as #1 above, but the context (v. 15) suggests that the reference is to a peak in or near BASHAN, and some commentators identify it with Jebel Druze (c. 60 mi. SE of DAMASCUS); the mountains in this area are composed of dark volcanic rock and thus may account for the name.

Zalmonah zal-moh′nuh (צַלְמֹנָה H7517, perhaps "dark, gloomy"). The first encampment of the Israelites after leaving Mount HOR (Num. 33:41–42). Its location is unknown, though one possible suggestion is es-Salmaneh, some 22 mi. S of the DEAD SEA.

Zalmunna zal-muhn′uh. See ZEBAH AND ZALMUNNA.

Zambri zam′bri. KJV Apoc. form of ZIMRI (1 Macc. 2:26).

Zamoth zay′moth (Ζαμοθ). The ancestor of some Israelites who agreed to put away their foreign wives (1 Esd. 9:28; the parallel in Ezra 10:27 has ZATTU).

Zamzummim zam-zuh′mim. See ZAMZUM-MITES.

Zamzummites zam-zuh′mīts (זַמְזֻמִּים H2368, possibly from זָמַם H2372, "to murmur, plan," but see *ABD*, 6:1176 [s.v. "Zuzim"]). Also Zamzum-mim. The Ammonite name for the people otherwise called REPHAITES (Deut. 2.20). There is no consensus regarding the meaning or origin of this term, but it may be related to ZUZITES.

Zanoah zuh-noh′uh (זָנוֹחַ H2391 [H2392 in 1 Chr. 4:18], derivation uncertain). **(1)** A town in the N area of the Shephelah, allotted to the tribe of JUDAH (Josh. 15:34). After the EXILE it was one of the centers where returning exiles settled (Neh. 11:30). When NEHEMIAH rebuilt the walls of Jerusalem, the men of Zanoah under the leadership of one HANUN were responsible for the VALLEY GATE (3:13). It is generally identified with modern Khirbet Zanuʿ (Zanuh), some 14.5 mi. WSW of JERUSALEM and 3 mi. SSE of BETH SHEMESH. It lies on a hill which is cut off to the E, W, and N by valleys. Pottery remains point to occupation from the days of the kings through to Arabic times (cf. W. F. Albright in *BASOR* 18 [April 1925]: 10–11). In the genealogy of Judah, there is mention of "Jekuthiel the father of Zanoah" (1 Chr. 4:18), usually interpreted to be a geographical reference ("father" meaning "founder" or the like). Some scholars believe that this Zanoah is the town in the N Shephelah (cf. *HALOT*, 1:275), but the context (esp. the reference to Soco in the same verse) suggests a different locale; see #2 below.

(2) A town in the hill country of Judah, listed with a group of towns that were S of HEBRON (Josh. 15:56). Some have identified this Zanoah with Khirbet Zanuta (c. 10 mi. SW of Hebron, prob. too far W), and others with Khirbet Beit ʿAmra in the Wadi Abu Zennakh (c. 1 mi. NW of JUTTAH), but neither site can be confirmed. It is likely that 1 Chr. 4:18 refers to this town.

J. ARTHUR THOMPSON

Zaphenath-Paneah zaf′uh-nath-puh-nee′uh (צָפְנַת פַּעְנֵחַ H7624, meaning disputed). Also Zaphenath-paaneah. The hebraized form of the Egyptian name given to JOSEPH by PHARAOH (Gen. 41:45). Though the Hebrew must represent some transliterated Egyptian name, there is no certainty as to what that name may have been. The earliest known attempt to translate the name is that of JOSEPHUS, who stated that it meant "the revealer of secrets" (*Ant.* 2.6.1). The most widely accepted explanation of the name is that advanced by G. Steindorff (in *Zeitschrift für ägyptische Sprache und Altertumskunde* 27 [1889]: 41–42; and 30 [1892]: 50–52): "the god speaks and he lives" or "the god said: he will live" (cf. J. Vergote, *Joseph en Égypte: Genèse chap. 37–50 à la lumière des études égyptologiques récentes* [1959], 141–46). E. Naville suggested that Zaphenath-Paneah is a title, not a name: "the head of the sacred college of magicians" (in *JEA* 12 [1926]: 16–18). Other interpretations, largely rejected, include that of A. S. Yahuda, who proposed "food, sustenance, of the land is the living" (*The Language of the Pentateuch in Its Relation to Egyptian* [1933], 33).

C. E. DE VRIES

Zaphon zay′fon (צָפוֹן H7601, "north"). **(1)** A town lying to the E of the JORDAN in the tribal territory of GAD (Josh. 13:27). It was the place where the Ephraimites gathered to meet with JEPHTHAH after he defeated the Ammonites (Jdg. 12:1; KJV, "northward"). Zaphon is known in Egyptian records of the 19th dynasty as *Dupunu*, and in one of the TELL EL-ARMANA letters as *Ṣapuna*. Its location is uncertain. Proposals include Tell el-Qos (c. 2 mi. N of SUCCOTH; cf. N. Glueck, *Explorations in Eastern Palestine*, 4 vols., AASOR [1934–51], 4:297–300, 334–55), Tell el-Mazar (just W of el-Qos), and perhaps most likely, Tell es-Saʿidiyeh (c. 6 mi. NW of Succoth and only about 1 mi. E of the Jordan; cf. F.-M. Abel, *Géographie de la Palestine*, 2 vols. [1938], 2:448; S. Mittmann, *Beiträge zur Siedlungs- und Territorialgeschichte des nördlichen Ostjordanlandes* [1970], 219; *NEAEHL*, 4:1295–1300, s.v. "Saʿidiyeh, Tell es-").

(2) A mountain near the mouth of the ORONTES River associated with the Canaanite god BAAL and mentioned frequently in Ugaritic literature (cf. *ANET*, 133b, 136b, et al.; see CONGREGATION, MOUNT OF THE). Known to the Romans as Mons Casius, Mount Zaphon is identified with modern Jebel el-ʿAqra. In several poetic passages in the Bible, it is unclear whether the word should be interpreted as a reference to this mountain or as the noun *ṣāpôn*

H7600, "north." For example, the NIV renders Ps. 48:2, "Like the utmost heights of Zaphon is Mount Zion" (similarly, NJPS, "Mount Zion, summit of Zaphon"; but NRSV, "Mount Zion, in the far north"; cf. also Job 26:7 and Isa. 14:13 in NJPS and NRSV). (See discussion in *ABD*, 6:1040.)

Zara, Zarah zair´uh. KJV alternate forms of Zerah.

Zaraces zair´uh-seez. KJV Apoc. variant of Zarius (1 Esd. 1:38).

Zaraias zuh-ray´yuhs. KJV Apoc. form of Zerahiah (1 Esd. 8:2 [NRSV omits], 31) and Zeraiah (v. 34).

Zareah zair´ee-uh. KJV form of Zorah.

Zared zay´rid. KJV alternate form of Zered.

Zarephath zair´uh-fath (צָרְפַת *H7673*, possibly from *ṣārap H7671*, "to refine"; Σάρεπτα *G4919*). A Phoenician town to which God instructed Elijah to go during a time of drought (1 Ki. 17:9–10). While there, the prophet miraculously provided food for himself and for a widow and her son, and later he raised the son from the dead (vv. 11–24). Jesus referred to that incident as an illustration that "no prophet is accepted in his hometown" (Lk. 4:23–26). The prophet Obadiah predicted that Israelite exiles would "possess the land as far as Zarephath" (Obad. 20).

The city is mentioned in an Egyptian document of the 13th cent. B.C. (Papyrus Anastasi I; cf. *ANET*, 477a, "Sarepta"); it occurs in Akkadian texts as *Ṣariptu*. The Bible refers to it as belonging to Sidon (1 Ki. 17:9), and Sennacherib in 701 B.C. lists it among the "strong cities" that he took from Luli, king of Sidon (*ANET*, 287b, "Zaribtu"). Some time later Esarhaddon put Zarephath under the control of Tyre (see J. B. Pritchard in *Understanding the Sacred Text*, ed. J. Reumann [1972], 101–14). In antiquity it was a large commercial center, famous for fine glassware, ceramics, textiles, and purple dye (the latter may account for the city's name, since the Akk. cognate *ṣarāpu* can mean "to dye red"). Zarephath is identified with the modern Arab village of Ṣarafand, which lies on a coastal promontory about 8 mi. SSW of Sidon and 13 mi. NNE of Tyre. (See further J. B. Pritchard, *Recovering Sarepta, a Phoenician city: Excavations at Sarafand, Lebanon, 1969–1974, by the University Museum of the University of Pennsylvania* [1978]; W. P. Anderson et al., *Sarepta: Excavations at Sarafand, Lebanon*, 4 vols. [1985–88].)   J. Arthur Thompson

Zaretan zair´uh-tan. KJV alternate form of Zarethan (only Josh. 3:16).

Zarethan zair´uh-than (צָרְתָן *H7681*, derivation uncertain). A town near Adam; in this vicinity the waters of the Jordan stopped flowing so that the Israelites could cross the river (Josh. 3:16). See Adam (place). During the reign of Solomon, Zarethan was part of the fourth administrative district under Baana son of Ahilud (1 Ki. 4:12). It was in this area, between Zarethan and Succoth, that the bronze objects for the temple were cast (1 Ki. 7:46; in the parallel passage, 2 Chr. 4:17, the Hebrew form is *ṣĕrēdātâ* [with locative ending] and thus most English versions read Zeredah [KJV, "Zeredathah"], but this is probably a scribal error or an alternate form).

The precise location of Zarethan is disputed, and numerous sites have been proposed on both sides of the Jordan (see the extensive summary in *ABD*, 6:1041–43). Because 1 Ki. 4:12 states that the town was "next to" (Heb. ʾēṣel *H725*) Beth Shan, some have looked for a location toward the N, such as Tell es-Saʿidiyeh, which lies on the E side of the Jordan, some 6 mi. NW of Succoth, and where excavations have produced numerous copper objects belonging to the 13th–12th centuries B.C., suggesting that the town was a bronze working center (cf. *NEAEHL*, 4:1295). This site, however, is almost 12 mi. from Adam, which seems too far (es-Saʿidiyeh perhaps should be linked with a different biblical town, Zaphon). Others prefer to identify Zarethan with Tell Umm Ḥamad, which is only about 3 mi. NE of Adam; if so, it is likely that Zarethan was not part of the Beth Shan district but was mentioned in 1 Ki. 4:12 only to help demarcate the area (cf. Y. Aharoni, *The Land of the Bible: A Historical Geography*, rev. ed. [1979], 313; M. Cogan, *1 Kings*, AB 10 [2001], 208).

Zareth-shahar zair´ith-shay´hahr. KJV form of Zereth Shahar.

Zarhite zahr´hit. KJV form of Zerahite. See Zerah.

Zarius zair´ee-uhs (Ζαριος). According to 1 Esd. 1:38, Jehoiakim, after being made king of Judea, "seized his brother Zarius and brought him back from Egypt" (KJV, "Zaraces"). This statement seems to be a misreading of the corresponding passage in 2 Chr. 36:4.

Zartanah, Zarthan zahr´tuh-nuh, zahr´than. KJV alternate forms of Zarethan (1 Ki. 4:12; 7:46).

Zathoe, Zathui zath´oh-ee, zath´oo-ee. KJV Apoc. forms of Zattu (1 Esd. 8:32 and 5:12 respectively).

Zatthu zat´thoo. KJV alternate form of Zattu (only Neh. 10:14).

Zattu zat´oo (זַתּוּא H2456, derivation unknown). Ancestor of a family that returned to Jerusalem from Babylon with Zerubbabel (Ezra 2:8; 8:5; Neh. 7:13; 1 Esd. 5:12 [KJV, "Zathui"]; 8:32 [KJV, "Zathoe"]). Some members of this family had married foreign women and agreed to put them away (Ezra 10:27; 1 Esd. 9:28 [KJV, "Zamoth"]). One of the leaders of the people who signed the covenant of Nehemiah was named Zattu (Neh. 10:14 [KJV, "Zatthu"]), but it seems probable that here the head of the clan is being referred to by the family name.

Zavan zay´vuhn. KJV alternate form of Zaavan.

zayin zah´yin (ז, meaning uncertain; this name is not used in the Bible). The seventh letter of the Hebrew alphabet (ז), with a numerical value of seven. Its sound corresponds to that of English *z*.

Zaza zay´zuh (זָזָא H2321, derivation uncertain). Son of Jonathan and descendant of Judah through Jerahmeel (1 Chr. 2:33).

zealot. A person characterized by much zeal, enthusiasm, or partisanship. When capitalized, the term refers to a violent Jewish sect in NT times that opposed Roman domination. The Greek noun *zēlōtēs* G2421 means "enthusiastic adherent," a person that is "eager" about something or someone. The cognates *zēloō* G2419 and *zēlos* G2420 can be used both in a good sense ("ardor"; "to be deeply concerned about") and negatively ("jealousy, factionalism"; "to be filled with envy").

The NIV usually renders the word *zēlōtēs* with "zealous" or "eager." For example, Paul was told of believing Jews who "are zealous for the law" (Acts 21:20). The apostle himself states that before his conversion he was "zealous for God" (22:3) and "zealous for the traditions of my fathers" (Gal. 1:14). The Corinthian Christians were "eager to have spiritual gifts" (1 Cor. 14:12). Because of the redeeming and purifying work of Christ, Titus was told to be "eager to do what is good" (Tit. 2:14), and Peter says, "Who is going to harm you if you are eager to do good?" (1 Pet. 3:13). The word is rendered more literally in two passages with reference to one of the twelve disciples, "Simon who was called the Zealot" (Lk. 6:15; simply "Simon the Zealot" in Acts 1:13 [KJV, "Zelotes"]; regarding Matt. 10:4 and Mk. 3:18, see below).

This summary of the object of zeal illustrates the usual OT ways of using the Hebrew verb *qānāʾ* H7861 (and its cognates) to refer to fervor or complete commitment to a cause, task, or a character trait. Most often zeal describes a pious life before the Lord or the way one addresses service for him. The phrase "zeal of the Lord" occurs a few times (2 Ki. 19:31; Isa. 9:7; 37:32; cf. Ezek. 5:13, "I the Lord have spoken in my zeal").

There is, however, another use of the concept, and that is when zeal for the Lord is taken to the extreme and is combined with violence. There are a few obvious OT examples of this. The book of Numbers relates an incident when Israelite men committed "sexual immorality with Moabite women who invited them to the sacrifices of their gods" (Num. 25:1–2). The Lord's wrath burned against this sacrilege; he ordered that leaders of the Hebrews be killed, and a plague began to sweep through the camp of Israel. In the midst of all this, an Israelite man openly took a Moabite woman into his tent. Phinehas, a priest, followed them and killed both. God told Moses that Phinehas had turned away the divine anger, "for he was as zealous as I am for my honor" (v. 11). Phinehas was honored with "God's covenant of peace ... a covenant of a lasting priesthood, because he was zealous for the honor of his God" (vv. 12–13). Phinehas's zeal is praised in the apocryphal book of ECCLESIASTICUS (Sir. 45:23–24).

Much later, as the newly anointed King JEHU set out on his campaign to slaughter the worshipers of BAAL, he invited the righteous JEHONADAB to "Come with me and see my zeal for the Lord" (2 Ki. 10:16). Also, although the word "zeal" is not used, it is certainly implied when we read that "Samuel put Agag to death before the Lord" (1 Sam. 15:33) because King SAUL, in spite of God's command, had spared the Amalekite king.

During the intertestamental period MATTATHIAS, the father of the future Maccabean leaders and rulers, slew a SELEUCID official and an apostatizing Jew and cried, "Let every one who is zealous [*pas ho zēlōn*] for the law and supports the covenant come out with me!" (1 Macc. 2:27). Such incidents, uniting zeal and violence, are relatively rare in the OT. Nevertheless, they demonstrate an element present in some Jewish groups in Israel prior to the 1st cent. Martin Hengel (*The Zealots: Investigations into the Jewish Freedom Movement in the Period from Herod I Until 70 A.D.* [1989]) develops an important theme. It is beyond doubt that the Hebrews were convinced that God was their king (cf. Jdg. 8:23). Yet, until late in the intertestamental period, although the Jews had frequently languished under foreign, pagan conquerors, their grief and restiveness does not seem to be related to a conviction that their foreign overlords were usurping the place of the God of Israel.

The Jewish historian JOSEPHUS lists four sects or parties among the Jews: PHARISEES, SADDUCEES, ESSENES, and a "fourth philosophy" (*Ant.* 18.1.2–6 §§11–25). His description of this "fourth philosophy" is imprecise, but he attributes it to Judas the Galilean (cf. Acts 5:37 and see JUDAS #4). Accompanied by a certain Pharisee named Saddok (Jos. *Ant.* 18.1.1 §4), Judas led a rebellion in A.D. 6 in response to a Roman-ordered census in the land of Israel. Josephus, from whom we gain virtually all of our information about Judas (as well as about the Zealots in general), says Judas assumed the census was the equivalent of slavery (ibid.); he was driven by a "passion for liberty ... convinced that God alone is ... leader and master" (18.1.6 §23). Josephus blames Judas for sowing "seeds of every kind of misery," wars, murders, and robberies (18.1.1 §§6–8).

Hengel believed that the fullest exposition of Judas's philosophy is found in the mouth of his grandson, Eleazar ben Yar, leader of the Jewish fighters (Zealots) at MASADA. Knowing that the next day they would fall to the Romans, he appealed to his followers to kill their families and then themselves rather than surrender: "A long time ago, brave comrades, we firmly resolved to subject ourselves neither to the Romans nor any other person, but only to God, for only he is the true and lawful lord of men" (*War* 7.8.6 §323). Hengel's point is that about the time of Judas, if not with Judas himself, a biblical interpretation arose that focused upon a new, particularistic, emphasis on the KINGDOM OF GOD as concentrated upon Israel and Israel's encounter with the Roman emperor cult (a situation that was certainly intensified when, in A.D. 40–41, the emperor Gaius CALIGULA attempted to have his image placed in the Jerusalem temple). Judas and his followers insisted that no Gentile king could reign over Israel. It was the privilege of God alone to rule over his people. Anyone else who assumed that position was guilty of blasphemy. Violent resistance was the only proper response to foreign overlords. This was at the heart of pure Zealotism.

Two corollary groups should also be noted. The taking of a census in Israel, which sparked Judas's rebellion, was no inconsequential matter. For many Jews a census was an administrative measure that only God could instigate, and Num. 1 and 26 indicate God did so in the wilderness. Even DAVID, the prototypical Hebrew ruler, incurred divine anger when he counted his people (2 Sam. 24). The assumption behind Judas's cries seems to be that any human being ordering a census of Israel placed himself in a position of authority that must be reserved for God alone—it was a blasphemous act. If David incurred divine disfavor for so doing, how much more should Israel rise up in righteous rebellion when a foreigner sought to number God's people. Second, Judas's claim of divine help may well have implied that he believed war with Rome would force God to intervene on Israel's side, either directly or by immediately sending the MESSIAH.

Two elements of 1st-cent. Jewish society are often associated with the Zealots: bandits and Sicarii. The NT writers and Josephus distinguish between (1) evil-doers or common criminals (*kakourgos* G2806) and (2) bandits, robbers, highwaymen, or revolutionary insurrectionists (*lestes* G3334). The latter were forced to steal to support self and family or stole from the rich to give to the poor (like the English "Robin Hood"). Such groups, having lost their land and livelihoods by oppressive taxes and exorbitant interest on debts and taxes, thus sprang from both socioeconomic and political and military concerns. Because of their guerrilla-like tactics, they are often counted within the freedom movement, and some appear to have joined the Zealots or one of the other paramilitary revolutionary groups as hostilities began. In such a situation the ruling authorities, upper classes, and the wealthy tend to view the "bandits" as thieves and thugs; whereas the common people might hail them as heroes and saviors.

The name *Sicarii* comes from Latin *sica*, a curved-shaped dagger (sickle), the weapon favored by these "terrorists" (the NIV rendering of *sikarios* G4974 in Acts 21:38; see ASSASSINS). They conducted a campaign of terror—kidnapping, extortion, robbery, and murder, especially against Romans and their sympathizers. However, Josephus claims collaboration between bandits and Sicarii on socioeconomic grievances as well as in political-military areas. He records uprisings in which he seems to imply both groups were involved and in which the insurgents burned the public records of debts (*War* 2.17.6 §§425–27).

The relation between the Sicarii and the Zealots is unclear. Just as there was a connection between the Zealots and Judas's fourth philosophy, the same is true for the Sicarii. Associated with the question is the death of Menahem, a revolutionary leader who set himself up as virtually a king in Jerusalem. Although Josephus blames the Sicarii with beginning the disturbance in which Manahem asserted himself and was killed, he refrains from identifying him with the Sicarii. Menahem was attacked and killed by other insurgents with affinities with the Zealots (*War* 2.17.8–9 §§433–48).

With the exception of the battles at Masada after the fall of Jerusalem, the Sicarii are never depicted as participating in open conflict. It is possible that so long as this group operated as an undercover force they were designated as Sicarii, but then as Zealots when they joined in pitch battle. If this is true, then we have an aspect of the nature and activity of the Zealots not usually recognized.

Josephus clearly associates the origin of the Zealots with Judas of Galilee and classifies them as the whole or a part of the fourth philosophy. Nevertheless, he mentions the Zealots as a distinct revolutionary group only after the outbreak of the war against Rome, A.D. 66–70. It appears that prior to that time he uses the terms "fourth philosophy" and "zealots" (in a general sense) to refer to the widespread anti-Roman ferment that was awash in the land. Josephus is well aware of the difference between these groups, but it appears that he sometimes lumps them together under the "zealots" (cf. *War* 4.3.9 §§160–61).

In Josephus's writings the Zealots clearly become a discernible group under the leadership of John of Gischala, first in Galilee, and then in Jerusalem. Thus they, along with the followers of Simon ben Giora, the Idumeans, Eleazar son of Simon (who broke with John's Zealot party to form his own), and other minor groups were the primary Jewish revolutionary factions in Jerusalem when TITUS began the siege of Jerusalem. These bands or gangs constantly fought each other, even when the Romans were literally at the gates. The common people suffered greatly at their hands. Eventually the Idumeans withdrew from Jerusalem, apparently in disgust. Eleazar and his faction fell victim to the trickery of John's men and were defeated. This left John's Zealots and the partisans of Simon ben Giora in control of the city. Until almost the very last days of the Roman siege of Jerusalem they continually fought each other as much as they did the Romans.

Certainly there were simple folk who were devoted to God with ardent passion and practiced their religion with zeal. They quietly longed for the liberation of the people and the land. Even from the time of Judas of Galilee onward there were certainly pious folk who assumed that at times, in extreme circumstances, true zeal for God and his law required violence. These represented zealotism at its best. Those depicted by Josephus as participants in the war of A.D. 66–70 represent zealotism as its worst.

These were the fanatical, head-strong, jealous, envious, factional groups, given to party strife.

With the temple burned, Jerusalem destroyed, and the entire area in the hands of the Romans, the two surviving factional leaders, Simon and John, and some of their followers cowered in the cisterns and sewers beneath what had been Jerusalem. Eventually they were discovered and captured. Zealot soldiers, as well as many of the followers of Simon bar Giora, were crucified, or made to entertain their captors by fighting to the death in games, or sold as slaves. Simon was displayed and then executed in the victors' triumphant procession in Rome. The Zealot chieftain, John of Gischala, was imprisoned for life. Other than the continuing three-year struggle at Masada, extreme, military zealotism was dead. In order to rescue something of the reputation of his countrymen, Josephus, in his writings, sought to lay the blame for the rebellion and the disastrous defeat of the Jews largely upon the Zealots. See WARS, JEWISH.

Two final points must be considered. Some scholars (e.g., S. G. F. Brandon, *Jesus and the Zealots* [1967]) have sought to make Jesus and his followers into a Zealot band. The title over the cross, "This is the King of the Jews," may indicate that PILATE, although he knew better, condemned Jesus as a violent nationalist to insult the Jews as a whole and their leaders in particular. The whole of Jesus' teaching and actions indicate the contrary. He affirmed that his "kingdom is not of this world" (Jn. 18:36). A true Zealot revolutionary would never advocate, "Love your enemies" (Matt. 5:44), paying Caesar his tax (Matt. 22:21; Mk. 12:17; Lk. 20:25), and satisfaction with only two swords (Lk. 22:38).

Finally, in what sense was the apostle Simon called "the Zealot"? Although he is so called in Luke and Acts, in Matt. 10:4 and Mk. 6:18 he is designated as the CANANAEAN (NRSV; the NIV translates "Zealot"). This may be an Aramaic word for "zealot" when it was not yet the technical term for the revolutionary party. Matthew and Mark thus avoid the term *zēlōtēs* to avoid confusion with the later revolutionaries. There is no indication that any of the gospel writers imply that Simon was a "Zealot" in the negative sense of the term. He may well have been a "pre-Zealot" who had a strong loyalty to his country. It is more likely, however, that even before his association with Jesus, Simon, like Paul, was "zealous" for the law and for God.

(See further W. R. Farmer, *Maccabees, Zealots and Josephus* [1957]; *IIJP*, rev. ed. [1973–87], 2:598–606; R. A. Horsley and J. S. Hanson, *Bandits, Prophets, and Messiahs* [1985]; J. J. Scott, *Jewish Backgrounds of the New Testament* [2000], 209–15; *ABD*, 6:1043–55.)　　　　J. J. SCOTT, JR.

Zebadiah zeb´uh-di´uh (זְבַדְיָהוּ H2278 [1 Chr. 26:2; 2 Chr. 17:8; 19:11] and זְבַדְיָה H2277, "Yahweh has bestowed"; cf. ZABAD, ZABDIEL, etc.). **(1)** Son of Beriah and descendant of BENJAMIN (1 Chr. 8:15).

(2) Son of Elpaal and descendant of Benjamin (1 Chr. 18:17).

(3) Son of Jehoram from GEDOR; he and his brother Joelah were among the ambidextrous warriors who joined DAVID at ZIKLAG (1 Chr. 12:7).

(4) Son of MESHELEMIAH and descendant of LEVI through KORAH and ASAPH; like his father, he and his brothers were Levitical gatekeepers in the time of DAVID (1 Chr. 26:2).

(5) Son of ASAHEL and nephew of JOAB; he succeeded his father as commander in charge of the division for the fourth month under David (1 Chr. 27:7).

(6) One of six Levites whom King JEHOSHAPHAT sent to teach the law in the cities of Judah (2 Chr. 17:8). Appointed to the same mission were a number of princes and priests.

(7) Son of a certain Ishmael and head of the tribe of Judah during the reign of Jehoshaphat (2 Chr. 19:11).

(8) Son of Michael and descendant of Shephatiah; listed among those who returned from the EXILE in Babylon to Jerusalem with EZRA (Ezra 8:8; called "Zeraiah" [KJV, "Zaraias"] in 1 Esd. 8:34).

(9) One of the two descendants of Immer who agreed to put away their foreign wives (Ezra 10:20; 1 Esd. 9:21 [KJV, "Zabdeus"]).

Zebah and Zalmunna zee´buh, zal-muhn´uh (זֶבַח H2286, "[born at the time of] sacrifice," and צַלְמֻנָּע H7518, derivation uncertain, but perhaps understood to mean, "The Image [*or* the god Ṣalm] protects"). Two Midianite kings defeated by GIDEON (Jdg. 8:4–21; Ps. 83:11). The BEDOUIN Midianites from areas E of the JORDAN (see MIDIAN) had been plundering the Israelites and their crops with their camel raids (Jdg. 6:1–6), when the Lord raised up Gideon as a deliverer for Israel. Well known is the military blow which Gideon and his 300 men dealt the Midianite enemy (7:1–22). In the ensuing rout the Midianite princes Oreb and Zeeb were captured and killed by the Ephraimites (7:24–25). Gideon, in his pursuit of the Midianites and their two kings, Zebah and Zalmunna, crossed the Jordan near the Jabbok River, but was refused help by the people of the E Manasseh areas in Succoth and Penuel (place).

The two kings and their remnant army of 15,000 were resting at Karkor, while Gideon and his men pursued up the Jabbok River by the caravan route E of Nobah and Jogbehah (the latter possibly being the modern el-Jubeihat NW of Amman and about 15 mi. SE of Penuel, the place where Jacob had wrestled with the angel, Gen. 32:30). Then the Israelite leader, having conquered the enemy, took the two kings back with him by way of the Pass of Heres (Jdg. 8:13), evidently a place not far from Succoth (8:11–14). After punishing the people of Succoth and Penuel for failing to help him (8:14–17), Gideon put Zebah and Zalmunna to death on the principle of blood revenge because they had killed his brothers at Tabor (either the mount or possibly a city). In the process he removed the crescent-shaped jewelry of silver or gold counted as important (see Isa. 3:18) and possibly indicative of royalty, worn by the camels and the two kings (Jdg. 8:18–21; cf. Philostratus, *Life of Apollonius* 2.1, which says that Apollonius of Tyana used a Persian camel with a gold ornament on its face as its symbol of royal ownership). Psalm 83:11 indicates that both sets of officials, Oreb and Zeeb as well as Zebah and Zalmunna, were important in the conquest of Midian, the former pair possibly being chieftains subordinate to the two kings (cf. Jdg. 7:25 with 8:12). W. H. Mare

Zebaim zuh-bay′im. See Pokereth-Hazzebaim.

Zebedee zeb′uh-dee (Ζεβεδαῖος G2411, from זְבַדְיָה H2278, "Yahweh has bestowed"; see Zebadiah). A Galilean fisherman, husband of Salome, and father of the apostles James and John (Matt. 4:21; 10:2). See James I and John the apostle.

Zebedee appears in all four Gospels as the father of two of Jesus' most prominent disciples, who with Peter stood at the center of the Twelve. The three were privileged to witness the transfiguration (Matt. 17:1–8), the raising of Jairus's daughter (Lk. 8:51), and the private sorrow in Gethsemane (Matt. 26:37). Zebedee, therefore, became known not because of his deeds (at least, none are recorded), but because he was the father of two famous sons who were among the Lord's disciples, one of whom wrote the beloved Gospel according to John.

Zebedee and his two sons operated a thriving fishing business on the Sea of Galilee in partnership with another set of renowned brothers, Andrew and Peter (Lk. 5:7–10). It must have been one of the larger public establishments of Capernaum, because it included hired men (Mk. 1:20). No doubt Zebedee was a man of means and influence, so much so that some believe he marketed his choice produce among the elite in Jerusalem (cf. Jn. 18:16, where "the other disciple" is prob. a reference to John).

The fishing business was radically changed the day that the call came to the two brothers. The picture we have from the Gospels portrays Zebedee in a boat with his two sons and hired men mending their nets on the shore of the Sea of Galilee when Jesus came by. "Jesus called them, and immediately they left the boat and their father and followed him" (Matt. 4:21–22; cf. Mk. 1:19–20). Although it must have harmed the fishing business somewhat, there is no record that he protested their forsaking a profitable business which one day would

Dragnet fishing on the Sea of Galilee—a reminder of the fishing industry of Zebedee and his sons.

have been theirs. On the contrary, there is reason to believe he continued the enterprise (cf. Jn. 21:3). It is even possible that the business furnished much financial support for Jesus and his disciples during the years of our Lord's ministry.

Zebedee's wife was Salome (Matt. 27:56; Mk. 15:40; 16:1), who also basked in the light of her sons ("the mother of Zebedee's sons," Matt. 20:20; 27:56). The whole family must have been avid supporters of Jesus, for we read that Salome accompanied Jesus during his ministry in Galilee to serve him (Mk. 15:40). She was later present at the CRUCIFIXION (Matt. 27:55) and was among the women who went to the tomb to anoint the Lord (Mk. 16:1). Yet she and her sons revealed private ambitions when she asked the Master for special favors for her two sons in the kingdom: "Grant that one of these two sons of mine may sit at your right and the other at your left in your kingdom" (Matt. 20:21; cf. Mk. 10:35–37). The Lord's refusal and patient teaching must have brought spiritual understanding, for the entire family of Zebedee remained loyal to the end. L. M. PETERSEN

Zebidah zuh-bi´duh (זְבִידָה H2288 [*Qere* זְבוּדָה], fem. of זָבוּד H2280, "bestowed"; see ZABUD). Daughter of a certain Pedaiah (from the town of RUMAH), and mother of King JEHOIAKIM (2 Ki. 23:36; KJV and other versions, "Zebudah," following the *Qere*).

Zebina zuh-bi´nuh (זְבִינָא H2289, "bought"). One of the descendants of Nebo who agreed to put away their foreign wives (Ezra 10:43; the name is not found in the parallel, 1 Esd. 9:35).

Zeboiim zuh-boi´im (צְבֹאיִם H7375 [צְבִיִּים, *Qere* צְבֹיִים, in Gen. 14:2, 8; צְבֹיִים in Deut. 29:23], perhaps "[place of] hyenas" [cf. *HALOT*, 3:997, and see ZEBOIM]). KJV also Zeboim (Gen. 14:2, 8); TNIV Zeboyim. One of the CITIES OF THE PLAIN destroyed by God. It is first mentioned in the OT in reference to the southern border of the Canaanites that ran from the coast inland toward this city as well as SODOM, GOMORRAH, and ADMAH (Gen. 10:19). KEDORLAOMER king of Elam and his three allies attacked these towns during their raid along the ancient KING'S HIGHWAY (14:2). SHEMEBER king of Zeboiim and his allies met the invaders in the Valley of SIDDIM but were defeated (14:8, 10).

Presumably Zeboiim was destroyed with Sodom and Gomorrah (Gen. 19:24–29). MOSES later referred to the destruction of Zeboiim and its neighbors (Deut. 29:23). HOSEA used Zeboiim as an example of judgment on evil cities (Hos. 11:8). Its exact location is unknown, but presumably it lay at the S end of the DEAD SEA in the area now covered by water. J. ARTHUR THOMPSON

Zeboim zuh-boh´im (צְבֹעִים H7391, "[place of] hyenas"). **(1)** A valley within the tribal territory of BENJAMIN, apparently SE of MICMASH (1 Sam. 13:18). PHILISTINE raiders from Micmash traveled the hill road overlooking the Valley of Zeboim with the JORDAN Valley beyond. In that general region there are some wadis that may preserve the meaning of the ancient name (e.g., Abu Dabaʿ, Arab. for "father of hyenas," which runs into the Wadi Qelt), but the identification of the Valley of Zeboim itself remains uncertain.

(2) A town overlooking the Plain of SHARON; along with HADID, NEBALLAT, LOD, and ONO, Zeboim was settled by Benjamites after the EXILE (Neh. 11:34). The name apparently occurs in TELL EL-AMARNA (letter no. 274) as *Sabuma*. The exact site is not known, though some have suggested Khirbet Sabiyeh, N of Lod. J. ARTHUR THOMPSON

Zeboyim zuh-boh´yim. TNIV form of ZEBOIIM.

Zebudah zuh-byoo´duh. KJV form of ZEBIDAH.

Zebul zee´buhl (זְבֻל H2291, "elevation," possibly short form of a theophoric name such as "Baal's lofty dwelling"; some think that Baal-Zebul was the original form of the name BAAL-ZEBUB). Governor of SHECHEM in the days of ABIMELECH son of JERUB-BAAL (i.e., GIDEON). Abimelech had been chosen king by a group of Canaanites in the city (Jdg. 9:1–6), and Zebul is referred to as his *pāqid* H7224 (v. 28; NIV, "deputy"; NRSV, "officer"; NJPS, "lieutenant") and as *śar* H8569 ("leader, ruler") of the city (v. 30). According to the narrative, there was local opposition to Abimelech, and a certain GAAL uttered seditious words during a vintage festival saying that he would get rid of Abimelech (vv. 27–29). Zebul informed Abimelech (who was at ARUMAH, v. 41) and advised him to surround Shechem by night (vv. 30–33). In the morning Gaal saw the troops and Zebul taunted him, "Aren't these the men you ridiculed? Go out and fight them!" (v. 38). Gaal sallied forth but was quickly routed, and Zebul kept him out of the city (vv. 39–41).   J. ARTHUR THOMPSON

Zebulun zeb´yuh-luhn (זְבוּלוּן H2282 [also זְבֻלוּן and זְבוּלֻן], possibly by popular etymology, "honor, exaltation" [see ZEBUL]; gentilic זְבוּלֹנִי H2283, "Zebulunite"; Ζαβουλών G2404). KJV NT Zabulon. Tenth son of JACOB and sixth of LEAH (Gen. 30:19; 35:23), and ancestor of the tribe that bears his name. Zebulun was conceived in the context of the rivalry between Leah and RACHEL. When he was born, "Leah said, 'God has presented me with a precious gift [zěbādanî ʾĕlōhîm ʾōtî zēbed ṭôb]. This time my husband will treat me with honor [yizběleni; NJPS, will exalt me], because I have borne him six sons.' So she named him Zebulun [zěbulûn]" (Gen. 30:20; the verb zābal H2290 occurs only here and its precise meaning is uncertain). The multiple wordplay in this verse suggests that the name Zebulun was intended to reflect both the notion of "gift" and the acknowledgment of Leah as a full wife, but the actual etymology of this name is disputed. Little else is recorded of Zebulun, though we read that his three sons were born before he left Canaan for Egypt (Gen. 46:14), where JOSEPH presented his brothers to Pharaoh (47:2). Jacob, in his final blessing, stated that Zebulun (through his descendants) would "live by the seashore / and become a haven for ships," and that the border of the tribe would "extend toward Sidon" (49:13).

The tribe of Zebulun was subdivided into clans named after his sons—Sered, Elon, and Jahleel—and encamped with Judah's standard to the E of the TABERNACLE (Num. 2:7). GADDIEL son of Sodi was the representative from Zebulun named to help spy out Canaan (13:10), and ELIAB son of Helon was selected to assist MOSES in census-taking (1:9). The two counts, showing that there were 57,400 and 60,500 warriors at the beginning and end of the wanderings (1:31; 26:27), indicate that Zebulun was numerically fourth among the tribes. A lowlier place is intimated in the selection of Zebulun—descended from Leah's last son—to share the lot of shamed REUBEN and the handmaid's sons in pronouncing the curses from Mount EBAL (Deut. 27:13).

After Israel conquered Canaan, the tribe of Zebulun received the third allotment (Josh. 19:10–16). The Zebulunites received a northern region that was small, but fruitful and strategically located. However, the uncertainty of some place names, a hint of textual corruption, and the cryptic nature of some passages blur the territorial limits. The anomaly of TABOR's inclusion (1 Chr. 6:77) apparently results from a textual flaw, while KISLOTH TABOR (KESULLOTH) and DABERATH may, without incompatibility, have marked the boundaries of Zebulun and belonged to ISSACHAR (cf. Josh. 19:12–13, 18, 20; 21:28).

More puzzling is the seeming incompatibility of these boundaries and ASHER's coastal inheritance with Jacob's prediction that Zebulun would dwell on the coast, become a haven for ships, and extend to SIDON (Gen. 49:13). Various solutions have been mooted. Some, noting JOSEPHUS's intimation that Zebulun extended from GENNESARET to the land belonging "to Carmel and the sea" (*Ant.* 5.1.22),

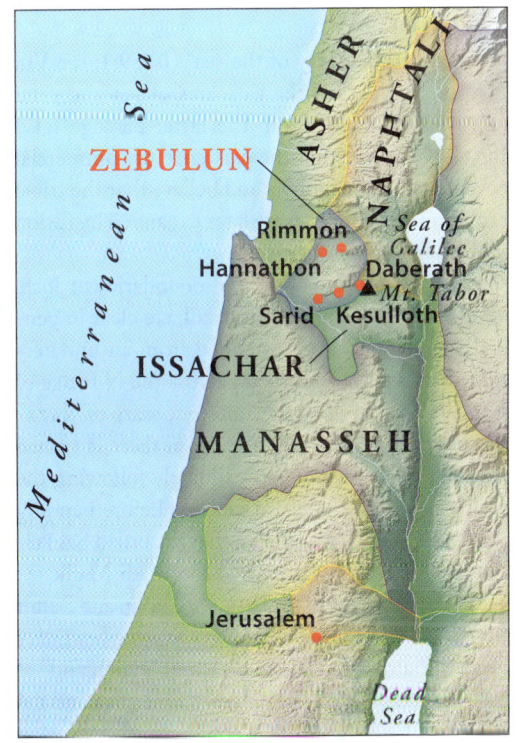

Zebulun.

suggest an otherwise unrecorded extension to the Mediterranean; others suggest that a sharing of the Galilean shore with Naphtali was intended; while still others read the text as implying no more than proximity to the "coastlands" and to Phoenicia, with a profitable and intermediate location for traffic of land and sea. Certainly Zebulun

The prophet Jonah came from Gath Hepher (Khirbet ez-Zurraʿ, top of hill) in the tribal territory of Zebulun.

commanded the "way of the sea" (Isa. 9:1; see Via Maris) and sucked the treasures of sea and sand (Deut. 33:18–19). From the latter passage (also Jdg. 1:30), some infer the existence of commercial covenants with neighbors and believe that the tribal economy and bounds were later expanded by fusion with Asher or Issachar.

Such hypotheses apart, the boundaries of Josh. 19, though undeciphered in detail, are clear in general. Zebulun's S limit extended from an undetermined stream E of Jokneam across the N fringe of Esdraelon and along the limestone scarp of Nazareth to the slopes of Tabor. From there it turned irregularly northward, approximately following the Galilean-Mediterranean watershed before bending westward to the Iphtahel—either the broad Sahl el-Battof or the narrow zigzag of the Wadi Malik. At least major portions of the basins of Turʿan and Battof (or Asochis) were encompassed before the boundary headed southward across the natural "marshland" of infertile and forested Cenomanian limestone and the margins of the Acco (or Zebulun) and Esdraelon plains. See also TRIBES, LOCATION OF, V.A.

Thus Zebulun, favored by a generally westward slope toward rain-bearing winds and an E-to-W pattern of fault and fold, presented a varied succession of limestone ridge and rich alluvial valley and yielded olives, grapes, and wheat in particular abundance. Tribal contributions to David's coronation festivities were generous (1 Chr. 12:40) and characteristically patriotic. Though only Elon among the judges was recorded as a Zebulunite (Jdg. 12:11–12), the tribe played a major role in the defeat of Sisera and Midian (4:6, 10; 5:14, 18; 6:35), and sent 50,000 warriors to David at Hebron (1 Chr. 12:33). Some, accepted for their transparent zeal, attended the Passover under Hezekiah (2 Chr. 30:10–19). If the tribe as such seems to have disappeared before or during Tiglath-Pileser's invasion (2 Ki. 15:29), its sturdy remnants, mingled with later immigrants, played a noble role in the Maccabean and Roman eras. Nor did Zebulun fade from eschatological vision (Ezek. 48:26–27, 33; Rev. 7:8), while Matthew, recalling Isa. 9:1, saw the Messiah from the Zebulunite city of Nazareth flooding Zebulun and Naphtali with light (Matt. 4:13–16).

(See further G. A. Smith, *Historical Geography of the Holy Land*, 25th ed. [1931]; J. Garstang, *Joshua-Judges* [1931]; H. H. Rowley, *From Joseph to Joshua* [1948]; D. Baly, *Geography of the Bible* [1957]; id., *Geographical Companion to the Bible* [1963]; Y. Aharoni, *The Land of the Bible: A Historical Geography*, rev. ed. [1979]; Z. Kallai, *Historical Geography of the Bible* [1986].) G. R. LEWTHWAITE

Zebulunite zeb´yuh-luh-nit. See ZEBULUN.

Zechariah zek´uh-ri´uh (זְכַרְיָהוּ H2358 and זְכַרְיָה H2357, "Yahweh has remembered" [cf. ZICRI]; Ζαχαρίας G2408). KJV also Zachariah (2 Ki. 14:29; 15:8, 11; 18:2), Zacharias (Apoc. and NT), and Zachary (2 Esd. 1:40). A very common Hebrew name.

(1) Son of Jeroboam II and last king of Jehu's dynasty. After ruling in Samaria for only six months, Zechariah was murdered at Ibleam by Shallum, who succeeded to the throne (2 Ki. 14:29; 15:8–11). His reign fulfilled the prediction that Jehu's dynasty would rule for four generations (10:30; 15:12).

(2) Father of ABI (ABIJAH), who was the mother of King HEZEKIAH (2 Ki. 18:1–2, 2 Chr. 29:1). Some have thought that this Zechariah may be the same as #29 below.

(3) An important figure from the tribe of REUBEN (1 Chr. 5:7). His genealogical connection as well as the period in which he lived are unclear.

(4) Firstborn son of MESHELEMIAH (= SHELEMIAH) and descendant of LEVI through KORAH and ASAPH; described as "the gatekeeper at the entrance to the Tent of Meeting" (1 Chr. 9:21; 26:2). Elsewhere, in connection with the development of a more permanent organization anticipating the system in the TEMPLE, he is called "a wise counselor" to whom fell "the lot for the North Gate" (26:14).

(5) Son of JEIEL and descendant of BENJAMIN; his brother NER was the grandfather of SAUL (1 Chr. 9:37 [cf. v. 39]; called ZEKER in 8:31).

(6) A Levite and one of the gatekeepers assigned to be a musician when DAVID made preparation to transfer the ARK OF THE COVENANT to Jerusalem (1 Chr. 15:18). He is called one of the brothers of the "second order" (NRSV; NIV, "next in rank") who followed HEMAN, ASAPH, and ETHAN. Zechariah, with others, played the lyre "according to *alamoth*" (v. 20; see MUSIC VI.C). Later, he was one of the Levites appointed "to minister before the ark of the LORD, to make petition, to give thanks, and to praise the LORD, the God of Israel" (16:4–5).

(7) One of the priests who blew trumpets before the ark (1 Chr. 15:24).

(8) Son of Isshiah and descendant of LEVI through KOHATH (1 Chr. 24:25; cf. v. 24 [UZZIEL was son of Kohath]).

(9) Son of Hosah and descendant of Levi through MERARI; he was a gatekeeper in David's reign (1 Chr. 26:11).

(10) Father of Iddo; the latter was an officer appointed by David over the half-tribe of MANASSEH in GILEAD (1 Chr. 27:21).

(11) One of five officials sent by King JEHOSHAPHAT "to teach in the towns of Judah" (2 Chr. 17:7).

(12) Son of Benaiah, descendant of Levi through Asaph, and father of Jahaziel (2 Chr. 20:14); the latter gave King JEHOSHAPHAT a message from the Lord regarding the Moabite and Ammonite invaders (vv. 14–17).

(13) Son of Jehoshaphat (2 Chr. 21:2).

(14) Son of JEHOIADA, who was the high priest during the reign of JOASH of Judah. A godly man, Zechariah denounced the apostasy of the people from the Lord after his father's death, and Joash ordered him stoned to death in the temple court (2 Chr. 24:20–21). As Zechariah was dying, he uttered a curse on Joash that was soon fulfilled (vv. 22–25). It is often held that this is the Zechariah meant by the Lord's reference in Lk. 11:51, since Scripture mentions no other as slain in this way. Matthew, however, calls the same individual "Zechariah son of Berekiah" (Matt. 23:35), which evidently refers to the writing prophet (#30, below). Various solutions have been proposed (cf. D. L. Bock, *Luke*, BECNT, 2 vols. [1994–96], 2:1122–24), among which is the view that Matthew has deliberately blended the two OT figures for literary and theological reasons. See also #15, below.

(15) A man who instructed King UZZIAH in the ways of God (2 Chr. 26:5). This Zechariah has sometimes been identified with #14 above and with #29 below.

(16) A descendant of Asaph who was among the Levites involved in cleansing the temple during Hezekiah's reign (2 Chr. 29:13).

(17) A descendant of Kohath who oversaw the workmen who repaired the temple in JOSIAH's reign (2 Chr. 34:12).

(18) One of the administrators of the temple in the days of Josiah; he, along with HILKIAH and JEHIEL, contributed "twenty-six hundred Passover offerings and three hundred cattle" (2 Chr. 35:8; cf. 1 Esd. 1:8).

(19) A descendant of Parosh who returned from Babylon with others under EZRA (Ezra 8:3; 1 Esd. 8:30).

(20) Son of Bebai, also listed among those who returned with Ezra (Ezra 8:11; 1 Esd. 8:37).

(21) One of a group of leaders sent by Ezra to Iddo to get attendants for the house of God (Ezra 8:16; 1 Esd. 8:44).

(22) One of the descendants of Elam who agreed to put away their foreign wives (Ezra 10:26; 1 Esd. 9:27).

(23) One of the prominent men (not identified as priests) who stood near Ezra when the law was read at the great assembly (Neh. 8:4; 1 Esd. 9:44).

(24) Son of Amariah, descendant of PEREZ, and grandfather of Athaiah; the latter was one of the Judahites who after the return from the Babylonian captivity lived in Jerusalem (Neh. 11:4).

(25) Descendant of SHELAH and ancestor of Maaseiah; the latter was another postexilic Judahite who lived in Jerusalem (Neh. 11:5).

(26) Son of Passhur and ancestor of Adaiah; the latter was one of the priests who settled in Jerusalem after the exile (Neh. 11:12).

(27) Son of Jonathan and descendant of Asaph; he led the Levitical musicians at the dedication of the wall of Jerusalem (Neh. 12:35). Probably the same as #28, below.

(28) A priest trumpeter at the dedication of the wall of Jerusalem (Neh. 12:41).

(29) Son of Jeberekiah; he and URIAH the priest were chosen "as reliable witnesses" of the prophecy concerning MAHER-SHALAL-HASH-BAZ (Isa. 8:2). See also #2 above.

(30) Son of Berekiah, grandson of Iddo, descendant of Levi, and one of the writing prophets (Zech. 1:1). His first prophecy was delivered in the second year of DARIUS Hystaspes in 520 B.C. (Ezra 4:24—5:1; Zech. 1:1). He was a contemporary of HAGGAI the prophet, ZERUBBABEL the governor, and Joshua (JESHUA) the high priest (Ezra 5:2; Zech. 3:1; 4:6; 6:11). Born in Babylon, he was a priest as well as a prophet (Neh. 12:16). Ezra calls him the son of Iddo, probably because his father Berekiah died early, and he attained to the position of head of the household and successor to his grandfather. It has been thought by many from Zech. 2:4 that he was a young man at the beginning of his prophetic ministry. See ZECHARIAH, BOOK OF.

(31) According to 1 Esd. 1:15, "Asaph, Zechariah, and Eddinus" were three musicians who represented King Josiah; the parallel passage in 2 Chr. 35:15 gives the names as Asaph, Heman, and Jeduthun. The difference may have been consciously or unconsciously motivated by 1 Esd. 1:8.

(32) Father of a certain Joseph; the latter was a military commander under Judas MACCABEE (1 Macc. 5:18, 56).

(33) Father of JOHN THE BAPTIST (Lk. 3:2) and priest within the division of Abijah during the time of HEROD the Great (Lk. 1:5; cf. 1 Chr. 24:10). Both he and his wife ELIZABETH are described as "upright in the sight of God, observing all the Lord's commandments and regulations blamelessly" (v. 6). They had no children, and when they were aged Zechariah received a vision in the temple at the time of the offering of INCENSE, a ritual that symbolized the prayers of God's people. The angel GABRIEL assured him that Elizabeth would have a child who was to be called John and who would live the separated life of a NAZIRITE, preparing the way of the Lord "in the spirit and power of Elijah" (vv. 7–17). Because Zechariah did not believe the promise, he became mute (vv. 18–22). After the birth of the child, Zechariah confirmed in writing that his name was John, and at that moment "his mouth was opened and his tongue was loosed, and he began to speak, praising God" (vv. 59–64). Filled with the HOLY SPIRIT, Zechariah uttered a prophecy known as the BENEDICTUS (vv. 67–79).

(34) An OT figure who, according to Jesus, was murdered "between the temple and the altar" (Matt. 23:35; similarly Lk. 11:51). See above, #14.

Zechariah, Book of. The eleventh book in the collection known as the twelve Minor Prophets, coming at the end of the second division of the Hebrew CANON of Scripture. The book of Zechariah emerged from the immediate postexilic period and is therefore a valuable source of information about a phase of Jewish history for which extrabiblical documentation is slight.

   I. Background
   II. Unity
   III. Authorship
   IV. Date
   V. Place of origin
   VI. Destination
   VII. Occasion
   VIII. Purpose
   IX. Canonicity
   X. Text
   XI. Content
   XII. Theology

I. Background. The historical situation underlying the book of Zechariah is identical with that which gave rise to the oracles of HAGGAI. Both men were contemporaries and are mentioned together in Ezra 5:1 and 6:14. Although they were the first two prophets to be named as living and working in Judea after the return from EXILE in Babylonia in 537 B.C., they are not actually mentioned until the year 520. Consequently it has sometimes been supposed that they had returned to Palestine with a fresh group of repatriates about that time, and were provoked by the demoralized condition of the populace into the kind of prophetic activity recorded in their books. However, there appears to be no evidence for this supposition, and it is far more probable that both Haggai and Zechariah were still children when their parents returned to the homeland in 537. If so, Zechariah must have grown to manhood amidst the spirit of apathy, indifference, and neglect of spiritual priorities that characterized the period of the return between 537 and 520. Zechariah thus may have been a young adult when he began to prophesy, and it is quite probable that he himself was the individual referred to as "that young man" (Zech. 2:4). See ZECHARIAH #30.

The proclamation of the edict of CYRUS in 538 B.C. permitted expatriate groups held captive in Mesopotamia during the neo-Babylonian regime (612–539) to return to their ancestral homes and pick up the threads of their former life. This event must have raised high hopes in the minds of the faithful Jewish remnant in Babylonia. Inspired by the utterances and personal example of EZEKIEL, the prospect of renewing a COVENANT relationship with God in the land of their fathers can hardly have failed to stimulate great interest in the future of a restored community. What the exiles had apparently reckoned without, however, was the sense of despair and disillusionment that quickly ensued when they saw the way in which Jerusalem had been desolated. Little that was of any value was intact, and the ruined walls made it possible for those elements of the Samaritans, Edomites, and Arab tribes living in the vicinity to wander in and out of the city at will.

It seems highly probable that the exiles who returned to Judea were far from wealthy, their more affluent countrymen having elected for the most part to remain behind in Babylonia when the summons to return to Palestine was proclaimed. Since there were almost no capital resources upon which the repatriates could draw, they were forced to eke out a scanty existence, living precariously from day to day on the products of a ruined and inhospitable terrain, and open always to the depredations of their enemies. Not unnaturally, the first concern of the repatriates was for shelter for their families, but by the time that they had built their houses among the ruins their enthusiasm for such ambitious constructional projects as a new temple or a defensive wall around Jerusalem had been dissipated.

The most immediate need was for inspired leadership, which would place the emphasis upon spiritual priorities and lead to a revival of community life in the theocracy. It was to this forbidding task that Haggai and Zechariah were called in 520 B.C. While the former furnished the initial impetus for laying the foundation of the second temple, the latter helped materially toward the completion of the project by giving a larger spiritual dimension to the restored theocracy through his prophetic oracles. While Zechariah was concerned with the immediacy of the social and spiritual situation in Judea at the end of the 6th cent., his oracles and visions made it clear that the community of repatriated exiles would exercise an influence of untold importance still further in the future—provided always that spiritual priorities were observed. His message was one of hope and promise at a time when the situation in Judea could hardly have appeared worse.

II. Unity. There has been a good deal of scholarly discussion relating to the unity and homogeneity of the book of Zechariah. The fourteen chapters of the extant work fall quite naturally into two main divisions, consisting of Zech. 1–8 and 9–14. It would appear that the visions contained in the first section had been put together in some definite arrangement; the first and the last are independent in nature, but the remainder seem to have been grouped in pairs intentionally. It is possible that Zechariah was following the bifid style of composition popularly used in antiquity, in which a work was compiled in two balanced halves, both of which reproduced faithfully the thought of the author, and which could therefore be circulated independently of one another if the need arose. Whether that was actually the case or not, the first division gives the undoubted impression of being a self-contained and homogeneous literary unit, proceeding from Zechariah as the author.

With regard to Zech. 9–14, most critical scholars have taken the view that they are not the work of the prophet Zechariah and may not even be a unity in themselves. The principal arguments include (1) the complete absence of any reference to the recent rebuilding of the second temple; (2) an evident difference of atmosphere between the first and second portions of the prophecy; (3) a hint from Zech. 9:13 that Greece was the dominant political power instead of Persia, as had been the case in the days of Zechariah; and (4) the apocalyptic material in ch. 14, which in some scholarly circles is commonly held to be an indication of a late date of composition. On the other hand, there are similarities between both sections of the prophecy, including such theological emphases as the necessity for repentance, the exaltation of Jerusalem, and the conversion of the enemies of Israel. In addition, both portions of Zechariah make it evident that the true ruler of the kingdom is the MESSIAH (6:12–13; 9:9), whose personage and functions were presented from a uniform standpoint. Again, marked similarities of style and diction occur in both sections, and these would hardly be surprising if the book of Zechariah is to be considered as a literary bifid.

Some writers have also depreciated the unity of the prophecy by pointing out that the second section, Zech. 9–14, is closely associated in form with the book of MALACHI, which followed it immediately in the Hebrew canon, through the use of superscriptions (Zech. 9:1; 12:1; Mal. 1:1) in which the technical Hebrew term for "oracle" (*maśśāʾ H5363*) occurs. Because of the relationship of these passages it has been assumed by certain scholars that the three sections thus introduced by the term "oracle" originally belonged together, but that the editor of the twelve Minor Prophets destroyed their unity by separating the book of Malachi in its extant form in order to enlarge the number of prophets to twelve. Against this general view is the fact that other prophets, especially ISAIAH, used the term "oracle" in precisely the manner of Zechariah in passages of undisputed authenticity (Isa. 13:1 et al.; Nah. 1:1; Hab. 1:1). Furthermore, it would be difficult to see why Malachi should have been separated from the prophetic material in the manner suggested and attributed to an individual composer, whereas the other oracles were not. While it may be thought that there are cogent reasons for supposing that the prophecy was compiled by more than one author, there are equally compelling ones for accepting the unity of composition by Zechariah himself.

III. Authorship. The attributive author of the prophecy was Zechariah son of Berekiah (named "Zacharias" in the LXX and Vulgate), a contemporary of the prophet Haggai. The name Zechariah was quite common in Hebrew society, and in the OT over thirty individuals were given this cognomen. The author was the grandson of IDDO, the latter being one of the heads of priestly families which returned to Judea after the exile (the phrase "son of Iddo" in Ezra 5:1 and 6:14 is properly translated "a descendant of Iddo" by the NIV). Hence, Zechariah himself was most probably a priest, and may even have functioned as a prophet in the cultus. The beginning of his prophetic work can be dated quite accurately from the superscription (Zech. 1:1) in October-November of 520 B.C. He seems to have prophesied for a longer period than Haggai, functioning for as long as two years according to the dates in Zech. 1:1 and 7:1, and possibly longer. The first section of the prophecy named Zechariah as the author and furnished specific dates for his activity (the period covered by Ezra 5:1—6:22). If Zech. 9–14 was written by someone other than Zechariah, the identity of this individual cannot be determined either by internal or external evidence.

IV. Date. From the superscription ("eighth month of the second year of Darius") it is possible to date the beginning of the prophetic activity of Zechariah at the end of 520 B.C., shortly after Haggai began his work in Jerusalem (cf. Hag. 2:1, "twenty-first day of the seventh month"). If the prophecy is a unity, the oracles were delivered between 520 and 518 and perhaps even later. Precisely how soon the prophecy appeared in its extant form is hard to say, but there was probably only a short interval between the oral and written versions. The position of the work as an integral part of the Minor Prophets in the second section of the Hebrew canon would suggest that the written form appeared within the lifetime of the prophet, and was accepted as canonical before the days of Malachi (c. 450).

If diversity of authorship is entertained, the date of Zech. 9–14 becomes a matter of pure speculation, since these chapters cannot be dated accurately from internal evidence. The reference to Javan or Greece (9:14) has been used by some scholars to date the work in the 4th cent. B.C., but such a late period is not required for the composition. Greek influence in the ANE was noticeable as early as the 7th cent., and Javan was mentioned both as a mission field for Israel (Isa. 66:19) and as a center of trade (Ezek. 27:13). Any reasonably astute political observer in the time of Zechariah knew that for many years Greek mercenary troops had formed the bulk of the Persian military forces. Furthermore, the periodic raids by the Greeks upon the Palestinian coastline, beginning about 500, may well have given rise to the prophecies against Javan. Since Zech. 9 deals with other great peoples, it seems unwarranted to single out the claims of Greece at the expense of states such as Tyre, Ashkelon, Damascus, and the like.

Attempts to identify the three shepherds (Zech. 11:4–17) with personages of the Maccabean era (see Maccabee) have led some scholars to assign a 2nd-cent. B.C. date to the later oracles. This can now be regarded as impossibly late, since the Dead Sea Scrolls included copies of Zechariah. Because the Qumran MSS were themselves of Maccabean provenance, the situation would demand a date in the Persian period for the original autograph of Zechariah. In any event the identification of the three shepherds is a precarious matter, since as many as thirty individuals have already been suggested on the basis of a literal interpretation of the passage. Even liberal scholars have placed the latest date for the supposed additions to the "original oracles" of chs. 1–8 at about 350 B.C., which in the light of the Qumran evidence seems at least a century too late.

V. Place of origin. As with the prophecy of Haggai, the oracles of Zechariah originated in Jerusalem in connection with the social and religious situation with which the prophet was confronted in 520 B.C. If it is assumed that Zech. 9–14 was the work of a "deutero-Zechariah," it might be possible to posit some other place than Jerusalem as the point of origin of at least certain of these utterances. A location outside Judea would be unlikely because of the concerns of the author for the messianic kingdom. In the light of the proposed unity of authorship it seems best to regard Jerusalem as the place where the whole prophecy originated.

VI. Destination. The oracles of Zechariah were meant for the inhabitants of Jerusalem and Judea. In the earlier chapters his utterances were concerned with the temple and the priesthood as well as with the civil government, though throughout the book his concern was with the nature and development of the theocracy. Whatever view is adopted about the authorship of the later chapters, there can be no doubt about the destination of the material as a whole.

VII. Occasion. The conditions of apathy, neglect, and despair that Zechariah encountered among the repatriated exiles in 520 B.C. furnished the occasion of the prophecy. With his contemporary Haggai he was called to give that kind of spiritual leadership which would regenerate the theocracy, recall it to its true vocation, and guide it toward its destiny as the living witness of God in the world. If the prophetic ministry of Zechariah extended over many years, the original occasion would be subsumed under the larger purpose of the spiritual and social development of the theocracy in Judea.

VIII. Purpose. As was the case with Haggai, the primary concern of Zechariah was the establishing of spiritual priorities in the life of the returned community. The lax attitude which the priests manifested toward their duties was matched among the laity by an indifference to the claims of the covenant relationship upon their lives, and even more seriously by a flagrant disregard for the moral prescriptions of the Mosaic Torah. Zechariah saw that the prosperity of the theocracy depended upon a proper relationship between the covenant people and their God. However keenly the repatriates felt about the injustices of life, it was evident that submission, penitence, and cleansing from sin must precede the outpouring of divine blessing. It was the avowed aim of Zechariah to establish the fundamental importance of this principle in the minds of the returned exiles, and to see that it operated at both religious and civil levels. Once this had been achieved satisfactorily it would be possible for the larger messianic purposes of the theocracy to be satisfied.

IX. Canonicity. At no time in the history of later Judaism or in the early Christian period were doubts ever raised as to the canonicity of the book of Zechariah. It was valued in the primitive church because of its messianic teachings and the way in which the work was used by NT authors (cf. Matt. 21:1–11 with Zech. 9:9–10, and Matt. 26:14–16 with Zech. 11:12).

X. Text. During the course of transmission the Hebrew text became somewhat corrupt, as can be illustrated by reference to such passages as Zech. 5:6; 7:1, 8, 9; 8:13; 9:15–17; 11:7, 8, 13; 14:5, 6, 10. What appears to be a textual dislocation can be seen in 4:6b–10a, which could be more readily placed after v. 14. Possible instances of marginal notes being incorporated into the text appear in 2:8 (MT v. 12); 4:12; 6:6; 11:6. The use of the SEPTUAGINT in restoring the text presents more problems for this book than for others, since the Greek version has preserved corruptions already present in the archetype. These include such verses as 4:12; 5:3; 7:2 (along with the dislocation of 4:6b–10a). There are also places where the LXX witnesses to a better form of the text, as in 2:3 (MT v. 7), 6 (MT v. 10); 3:4, 5; 8:9; 9:15–17; 11:7, 8; 14:5, 6. In any attempt at restoration of the Hebrew text, the LXX needs to be used with considerable caution.

XI. Content. As noted above, the extant prophecy falls readily into two principal sections:

A. Dated prophecies

Zech. 1:1–6. Introduction and call to repentance, in which the prophet establishes his identity and pleads with the repatriated Jews to return to the Lord. In particular he begs them to learn the lessons of past experience and avoid the misdeeds of their forebears.

1:7–17. The first vision, consisting of four horsemen whose task it was to traverse the earth and report on existing conditions to the angel of the Lord. In this instance they stated that there were no political disturbances anywhere in the empire; whereupon the angel interceded with God on behalf of desolated Jerusalem, and received a promise that he would soon "comfort Zion" and restore the city of Jerusalem.

1:18–21 (MT 2:1–4). This short section contains the second vision, in which Zechariah saw four horns, symbolizing the foreign powers that had destroyed the Israelites. Four blacksmiths were also present in the vision, and to them was given the task of breaking the horns into pieces, indicating that those nations which had oppressed the Hebrews in former times would themselves be humbled.

2:1–13 (MT 2:5–17). In the third vision the prophet was given a promise of great future prosperity for Jerusalem. The repatriates would be exalted above their former enemies, and life in the theocracy would be characterized by the divine presence in the midst of the people. This would be so notable a feature that it would attract many Gentile peoples to the service of the Lord.

3:1–7. The fourth vision of Zechariah revealed Joshua (JESHUA) the high priest clothed in dirty attire and subjected to temptation by Satan. Because Jerusalem had been chosen by God for future blessing, it was imperative for Joshua, as the representative of the people, to be cleansed ceremonially and fitted for his new spiritual responsibilities. Accordingly he was decked out in clean garments and a turban, and was then assured that he had been cleansed.

3:8–10. An oracle addressed subsequently to Joshua concerning the Branch (Messiah) and the engraved stone. Having been given the oversight of the civil and religious life in the theocracy, he was promised special access to God.

4:1–14. The fifth vision, in which the angel showed Zechariah a seven-branched lampstand fed by living branches from two olive trees, was accompanied by an interpretation. The seven lamps were the "eyes of God," while the two olive trees symbolized an unfailing source of divine grace. Here the promise of God extended beyond Joshua to ZERUBBABEL, and assured him that the obstacles which hindered the building of the kingdom of God would be removed only by the divine spirit through grace. Zerubbabel would be privileged to see the completion of the temple in all its splendor,

In Zechariah's fifth vision the angel showed him a seven-branched lampstand representing the seven "eyes of the LORD, which range through the whole earth" (Zech. 4:2, 10).

even though at the time the oracle was uttered the people were passing through a day of small things.

5:1–4. In his sixth vision Zechariah saw a flying roll containing judgment upon thieves and perjurers. It would traverse the land and bring the punishment of God upon all the evildoers in the community.

5:5–11. The seventh vision of Zechariah showed the ephah, a container for measuring dry goods and equal to four gallons in liquid capacity, in which a woman was seated. Symbolic of wickedness, she was sealed inside the ephah by means of a lead stopper and was transported to Shinar. This vision symbolized the eradication of iniquity from the theocracy and its banishment to Babylonia, the place of all evil as far as the repatriates were concerned.

6:1–8. In his eighth vision Zechariah saw four horse-drawn chariots, which as agents of God kept the world under surveillance. These four celestial spirits reported that all was quiet within the bounds of the empire, indicating that the world was once more at peace and under the direct control of God (cf. 1:7–17).

6:9–15. A historical section that narrates the consecration of Joshua as symbolic of the Branch (Messiah), who built the temple and who ruled as king and priest in the theocracy. Unlike their ancestors, the members of the restored community would live in obedience to their God and at peace with each other.

7:1–8:23. Another historical section containing an oracle of Zechariah relating to the question of whether there should be fasting to commemorate the fall of Jerusalem in 597 B.C. The people were informed that a special quality of life rather than indulgence in mechanical actions is what God desires of the repatriates. If they will observe high moral, ethical, and spiritual standards, they can expect the blessing of God upon their community life. Jerusalem will experience a degree of prosperity unknown in her long history, and so conspicuous will the theocracy become in contemporary society that other nations will be attracted in a powerful manner to the Jewish way of life.

B. Undated prophecies

9:1–17. The first of two sections whose superscription contains the word *oracle*. It deals with the impending judgment of God upon the cities of SYRIA, PHOENICIA, and PHILISTIA. Great devastation would be wrought against these neighbors of the house of Israel, and in particular the remnants of Philistia would be incorporated into the province of Judea. Becoming Jewish by adoption, they would present no further threat to the security of the Jews. The temple would then be enfolded in the protecting presence of God, and the messianic prince would enter Jerusalem in triumphal procession to institute a reign of peace and prosperity, quelling in the meantime any threats to the well-being of the theocracy from such invaders as the Greeks.

10:1–12. This section comprises an oracle denouncing the foreign rulers of Judah, described as "shepherds," who will be forced to yield to the superior strength of the divine leader as he gathers in his flock. The oracle foretold the downfall of the foreign overlords at the hands of the Jews, and predicted that the latter would be restored to their own land from the countries to which they had been scattered. The reference to the cornerstone (v. 4), tent peg, and battle bow may perhaps be a threefold allusion to the Messiah.

11:1–17. This oracle distinguishes between the good and foolish shepherds, and describes the way in which the flock of God have suffered at their hands. The good shepherd confounds the schemes of the evil shepherds, but is rejected by the flock. As a result, the flock endures affliction under yet another evil shepherd. In this utterance the prophet Zechariah foresees that the much hoped-for theocratic relationship between God and his people would be marked by serious blemishes. With the breaking of the two staffs, named Favor and Union, would ultimately come the end of national unity. Unfaithfulness to the covenant obligations would result in the rule of a "worthless shepherd" in the theocracy, for which the people would have to shoulder the blame.

12:1—13:6. This section comprises an oracle of an eschatological nature which in general terms depicted the Israelites returning to God at some time in the future. The city of Jerusalem had been beset on all sides by powerful armies of Gentile origin, but suddenly the inhabitants of the city saw the hand of God operating against their foes, and they joined in the defense of Jerusalem with new vigor. Victory would be followed by national mourning, and this in turn would give rise to repentance and purification. Prophets would be repudiated because they had been unfaithful to their vocation, and rigid standards of morality would finally produce a people acceptable to God.

13:7—14:21. This section continues the theme of purification for the nation of Israel, with equally strong eschatological emphases. In the last great assault of heathen armies upon Jerusalem, half of the city would be taken captive. When all seemed lost the Lord would intervene to secure victory for his people and establish his rule on earth. The Jews would have learned through these events to acknowledge the overlordship of God, and the concluding section of the oracle outlines the blessings of the newly-established divine kingdom. The Jews would make an annual pilgrimage to Jerusalem at the Feast of Tabernacles, and the covenantal ideal of holiness to the Lord would be the hallmark of life in the community.

XII. Theology. The thought of Zechariah, like that of his contemporary Haggai, depended to a large extent upon that of his predecessors. However, it is incorrect on that account to dismiss the writings of Zechariah as being either obscure apocalypticism (see APOCALYPTIC LITERATURE) or unoriginal prophetism. He began to prophesy at a time when zeal for the ideals of the theocracy had reached a very low ebb and was being revived by the vigorous teachings of Haggai. Since his prophetic vocation began as a continuation of his contemporary's efforts, it is hardly to be expected that there would be significant theological differences between the two men as far as the immediate task of reconstructing the theocratic community was concerned. For Haggai and Zechariah the situation resolved itself into a question of priorities, and in their thought a reconstructed and functioning temple was by far the most important material consideration. They were also firmly convinced that the returned community could continue to exist only in so far as it exemplified the ideals of the covenant relationship, and a proper form of worship was for them the outward expression of that state of inward holiness which God demanded of his people. Zechariah, however, had a clearer vision of the dangers involved in cultic formalism, for he was concerned more than Haggai about the great need for the individual to commit himself consciously to the claims of God upon his life, and to foster the ideals of the covenant in the community through strict obedience to the divine will.

Zechariah's wide outlook over the world of his day can be seen in his ESCHATOLOGY, which has pronounced messianic overtones. There are distinctly nationalistic aspects in his thought, of course, with its expectation of the triumph of his people over the Gentile nations, but his broader prophetic vision contemplated a time when Jew and Gentile would gather together in a spirit of faith and devotion to worship God in the temple at Jerusalem. Like Isaiah and the other prophets, Zechariah placed the scene of the final redemption of humanity in this world. While it would be continuous with the present historical order, it would differ, for such factors as evil, wrongdoing, and suffering would not exist. This state of grace would be ushered in through the personage of the Messiah, who would in fact establish and rule over the new kingdom. As with other prophets, Zechariah saw the final stage in the process as the cleansing of Jerusalem from sin and the restoration of the community to continuing peace and prosperity. This kind of prophetic apocalyptic is well attested in the OT, and contains nothing that is illegitimate or particularly unusual.

The later chapters of the prophecy need to be seen in the light of such a theological outlook, especially those sections that point to a messianic figure. It has been popular in some quarters to interpret several verses (Zech. 9:8, 15; 12:10) as allusions to some historical personages, whether in the time of Zechariah or in some other period up to and including the Maccabean age. This approach fails to appreciate the messianic concepts inherent in the thought of Zechariah, and in the end becomes in itself merely an exercise in subjectivity. The peaceful prince of the concluding chapters who would usher in the blessings of the kingdom is already present in the eschatology of such prophets as Isaiah, who entertained similar sequences for the future of his people. Finally, it was precisely because the members of the early Christian Church were awaiting the "consolation of Israel" that they were able to assign with such confidence a messianic interpretation to passages such as Zech. 9:9; 11:12, 13; 12:10; and 13:7.

Even though Zechariah was concerned for the well-being and prosperity of the theocracy, his very apocalypticism cast a shadow of doubt upon the future. The prophetic oracle of Zech. 11:4–14, which presents considerable difficulties of interpretation, seems to imply that God knew that his flock was doomed to almost complete extinction at the hands of their enemies. The fact that such a fate would be nothing less than they deserved did not alter the ultimate state of affairs for the prophet. The symbolic breaking of the two pastoral staffs had an awesome eschatological ring about it, pointing as it would appear to do to the end of the relationship between God and his people. Even this prospect did not dismay the prophet entirely, for he was sufficiently grounded in the theology of the covenant to realize that if the holiness of the theocracy began to approximate to that of its Lord, the prospect of destruction would be averted and the blessings of peace and prosperity would be secured for all time.

(Important commentaries include H. G. Mitchell et al., *A Critical and Exegetical Commentary on Haggai, Zechariah, Malachi and Jonah*, ICC [1912]; D. Baron, *Vision and Prophecies of Zechariah* [1918]; E. Sellin, *Das Zwölfprophetenbuch*, KAT 12, 2 vols. [1929]; H. C. Leupold, *Exposition of Zechariah* [1956]; C. L. Feinberg, *God Remembers: A Study of Zechariah* [1965]; J. G. Baldwin, *Haggai, Zechariah, Malachi*, TOTC [1972]; D. L. Petersen, *Haggai and Zechariah 1–8: A Commentary*, OTL [1984]; R. L. Smith, *Micah-Malachi*, WBC 32 [1984]; C. L. Meyers and E. M. Meyers, *Haggai; Zechariah 1–8*, AB 25B [1987], id., *Zechariah 9–14*, AB 25C [1993]; E. H. Merrill, *Haggai Zechariah Malachi: An Exegetical Commentary* [1994]; D. L. Petersen, *Zechariah 9–14 and Malachi: A Commentary*, OTL [1995]; T. McComiskey in *The Minor Prophets: An Exegetical and Expository Commentary*, ed. T. McComiskey [1992–98], 3:1003–1244; R. Hanhart, *Sacharja (1–8)*, BKAT 14/7/1 [1998]; M. J. Boda, *Haggai, Zechariah*, NIVAC [2004]; G. L. Klein, *Zechariah*, NAC 21B [2008].

(Among important studies, see M. Butterworth, *Structure and the Book of Zechariah* [1992]; R. E. Person, *Second Zechariah and the Deuteronomic School* [1993]; J. E. Tollington, *Tradition and Innovation in Haggai and Zechariah 1–8* [1993]; M. C. Love, *The Evasive Text: Zechariah 1–8 and the Frustrated Reader* [1999]; M. J. Boda and M. H. Floyd, eds., *Bringing Out the Treasure: Inner Biblical Allusion in Zechariah 9–14* [2003]; B. Curtis, *Up the Steep and Stony Road: The Book of Zechariah in Social Location Trajectory Analysis* [2006]; and the bibliography by W. E. Mills, *Zechariah and Malachi* [2002].)

R. K. HARRISON

Zecher zee´kuhr. See ZEKER.

Zedad zee´dad (צְדָד [or צְדָד] H7398, meaning uncertain). A town between LEBO HAMATH and ZIPHRON, used to mark the ideal N border of Israel (Num. 34:8; Ezek. 47:15). It is usually identified with modern Ṣadad, some 67 mi. NE of DAMASCUS and 25 mi. SE of RIBLAH (see discussion in *ABD*, 6:1068).

Zedekiah zed´uh-ki´uh (צִדְקִיָּהוּ H7409 and צִדְקִיָּה H7408, "Yahweh is my justice/righteousness"). **(1)** Son of Kenaanah; he was one of 400 false prophets who, in opposition to MICAIAH, the true prophet, encouraged AHAB king of Judah and JEHOSHAPHAT king of Israel to go to war against the king of ARAM in order to recapture RAMOTH GILEAD (1 Ki. 22:1–38; 2 Chr. 18:1—19:3). The incident is of interest in part for the historical reason that it illuminates group prophecy in ancient Israel. As the 400 false prophets predicted in unison Israel's victory, Zedekiah made himself iron horns, an act of prophetic symbolism probably intended to

reinforce the ancient tribal oracle regarding Joseph (Deut. 33:17).

The incident is also of theological interest for several reasons. (a) Chronicles, which ignores the history of the northern kingdom, records this event because of the role played by Jehoshaphat and to teach the spiritual truth proclaimed by JEHU the son of Hananai the seer ("Should you [Jehoshaphat] help the wicked and love those who hate the LORD?" 2 Chr. 19:2), a sequel to the story found only in Chronicles. (b) The story demonstrates the attitudes toward prophecy in ancient Israel. Ahab regarded the prophets as instruments of propaganda to serve the interests of the state, using their words and actions to influence the deity. There was a whole corps of prophets willing to give him the moral support he required (1 Ki. 22:5–6, 13, 26–27). Jehoshaphat, on the other hand, regarded the prophet not as an agent of the community to influence the deity by magic, but as the instrument of revelation of the will of God to the community (22:7–8). (c) Finally, through the vision granted Micaiah, Yahweh makes it clear that these false prophets receive their charismatic quality from lying spirits sent forth by the one God to achieve the divine will (22:19–23).

(2) Son of Maaseiah; he was a false prophet whom JEREMIAH predicted would be executed, along with Ahab the son of Kolaiah, by NEBUCHADNEZZAR for immorality and false teaching (Jer. 29:21–23).

(3) Son of Hananiah; he was one of the officials in the court of JEHOIAKIM who heard BARUCH read Jeremiah's scroll (Jer. 36:12).

(4) Third son of JOSIAH (1 Chr. 3:15) and king of Judah from 597 to 586 B.C. His given name was MATTANIAH ("gift of Yahweh"), but it was changed to Zedekiah by Nebuchadnezzar as a mark of vassalage when he made Zedekiah king in place of his eighteen-year-old nephew JEHOIACHIN, who was taken captive to Babylon along with the cream of the country's leadership (2 Ki. 24:8–17; Jer. 29:2). He was twenty-one when he began to reign, and he reigned until the fall of Jerusalem, eleven years of continual agitation and sedition (2 Ki. 24:18).

Although the prophet-historian of Kings largely bypasses the events of Zedekiah's reign (cf. 2 Ki. 24:18—25:2), they can be traced through the book of Jeremiah, where he is portrayed as indecisive, torn asunder by conflicting emotions—recognizing Jeremiah as a true prophet, but unable to act in faith on his words. Unable to choose the good by faith he acts perfidiously (cf. Jer. 34; Ezek. 17). This man who feared the Jews (Jer. 38:19) rather than God, Ezekiel described as the "profane and wicked prince of Israel" (Ezek. 21:25). Because he could not act in faith on the word of God through Jeremiah (cf. Jer. 33:17–23), he brought death upon himself and his people instead of the life offered him.

In the beginning of Zedekiah's reign (Jer. 27:1, clarified as the fifth month of his fourth year, 28:1), Jeremiah warned the king not to join in the revolt with EDOM, MOAB, AMMON, TYRE, and SIDON against BABYLON (27:1–12). The fire of insurrection was fanned at this time by false prophets among the Jews, both in Jerusalem and Babylon, who were predicting the defeat of Nebuchadnezzar and the liberation of Jehoiachin (chs. 28–29). The plot in fact came to nothing. Possibly, however, it was these activities which brought him under suspicion and necessitated his visit to Babylon in 593 B.C. (51:59).

In the ninth year of his reign (589 B.C.), Zedekiah openly rebelled under the influence of the pro-Egyptian party. J. C. J. Waite properly observed: "This was not merely an act of political suicide, it was a flagrant violation of the oath of loyalty to Nebuchadrezzar which the king had sworn in the name of Yahweh (Ezk. xvii)" (*NBD* [1962], 1357). Most scholars think he had an understanding with two Egyptian pharaohs, Psammetichus II (593–588) and his son HOPHRA (Apries, 588–569), who had resumed a policy of intervention in Asia. Judging from Zedekiah's repeated consultations with Jeremiah, he himself was indecisive in this act, and with weak leadership allowed the decision to be made by the "hawks" under him (cf. Jer. 38:5).

In response to Zedekiah's inquiry about the outcome of Babylon's retaliatory siege of Jerusalem begun in 589, Jeremiah predicted death, pestilence, the sword, and the execution of the city's survivors (Jer. 21:1–3). They would be treated like bad figs, unfit to be eaten (24:8). Zedekiah himself, however, was not to die by the sword but to die in peace with an honorable burial (34:5).

The advance of an Egyptian army in the summer of 588 forced the Babylonians to lift the siege of

Jerusalem temporarily (Jer. 37:5). Probably against this background Jeremiah denounced the ruler and people for breach of faith. During the siege King Zedekiah had made a covenant with the people in Jerusalem that all should set free their Hebrew slaves, male and female. But when the Babylonians withdrew from the city to meet the Egyptian army, those who had been set free were enslaved again (34:8–11).

At this same time, lacking decisive leadership ability, he allowed the princes to beat Jeremiah and imprison him in the house of Jonathan the secretary, which had been made into a prison (Jer. 37:15). Upon Jeremiah's plea, however, Zedekiah had him transported to the court of the guard (37:21). But once again Zedekiah appeared impotent and irresolute as he allowed the princes to cast Jeremiah into the cistern of MALKIJAH, "the king's son" (38:4–6; the description is prob. an official title; cf. J. Gray, *I and II Kings* [1970], 453). This time, upon the plea of EBED-MELECH, Zedekiah had Jeremiah transported again to the court of the guard (38:7–13).

The following summer, July 587, the Babylonians breached the wall and poured in. By this time the food supply was exhausted. Zedekiah with his men of war fled the city by night toward the Jordan. The Babylonians overtook Zedekiah, whose army had become separated from one another. He was brought before Nebuchadnezzar at his headquarters at RIBLAH in central Syria. He was shown no mercy. His sons were slain before his eyes; he himself was blinded, bound in fetters, and brought to Babylon (2 Ki. 25:1–7; Jer. 39:1–7; 52:1–11). The prophecies of Jeremiah predicting death if he lacked faith to act resolutely on the word of God's prophet was fulfilled.

(See further D. N. Freedman, "The Babylonian Chronicle," *BA* 19 [1956]: 50–60; J. P. Hyatt, "New Light on Nebuchadrezzar and Judean History," *JBL* 75 [1956]: 277–84; D. J. Wiseman, *Chronicles of Chaldean Kings* [1956]; J. Bright, *A History of Israel*, 4th ed. [2000], 327–30; M. Roncace, *Jeremiah, Zedekiah, and the Fall of Jerusalem* [2005].)

(5) Son of Jeconiah/JEHOIACHIN (1 Chr. 3:16). Some have interpreted the text to mean that this Zedekiah is the same as #4 and that he is called "son of Jeconiah" only because he was Jeconiah's successor on the throne.

(6) One of the signatories of the covenant of Nehemiah (Neh. 10:1 [MT 10:2], KJV, "Zidkijah"). Although otherwise unknown, he must have been a prominent individual, but probably not a priest (the list of priest signatories appears to begin with Seraiah in v. 2 [MT 10:3].)

(7) Ancestor of BARUCH (Bar. 1:1).

B. K. WALTKE

Zeeb zee'uhb. See OREB AND ZEEB.

Zeker zee'kuhr (זֶכֶר H2353, short form of זְכַרְיָהוּ H2358, "Yahweh has remembered"). Also Zecher. Son of JEIEL and descendant of BENJAMIN; his brother NER was the grandfather of SAUL (1 Chr. 8:31 [cf. v. 33]; called ZECHARIAH in 9:37).

Zela zee'luh (צֵלַע H7521, prob. "side" [cf. צֵלַע הָהָר, "hillside," 2 Sam. 16:13]). A city within the tribal territory of BENJAMIN; here, in the tomb of KISH, the bones of SAUL and JONATHAN were buried (2 Sam. 21:14). P. K. McCarter, Jr. (*II Samuel*, AB 9 [1984], 437), without explanation, but evidently interpreting the word as the common noun *ṣēlāʿ* H7521 (which can mean "side room," as in 1 Ki. 6:5), translates, "in a chamber of the tomb of Kish." In Josh. 18:28, Zela (KJV and NIV, "Zelah") is mentioned as a part of a group of fourteen Benjamite cities that in general lay a few miles to the NW of JERUSALEM (because LXX[A] reads *Sēlaleph*, some understand the Heb. to mean "Zela-Haeleph" rather than two different cities, Zela and HAELEPH, but that reading changes the total to thirteen towns). Zela's exact location is unknown, though some have suggested Khirbet Salah, between Jerusalem and GIBEON, as a possible site. See also ZELZAH.

W. H. MARE

Zelah zee'luh. See ZELA.

Zelek zee'lik (צֶלֶק H7530, meaning uncertain [cf. *HALOT*, 4:1031]). An Ammonite, included among DAVID's mighty warriors (2 Sam. 23:37; 1 Chr. 11:39). According to the KETIB in the Samuel passage (pl. *nōśʾê* rather than *nōśēʾ*, "bearer"), Zelek as well as Naharai were armor-bearers of JOAB.

Zelophehad zuh-loh'fuh-had (צְלָפְחָד H7524, prob. from צֵל H7498, "shadow," and פַּחַד H7065,

"dread," meaning perhaps "refuge from terror" [see *HALOT*, 3:1031]). Son of Hepher, grandson of GILEAD, and descendant of MANASSEH who died in the wilderness without male descendants (Num. 26:33; 27:1, 7; 36:2, 6, 10–11; Josh. 17:3; 1 Chr. 7:15). His five daughters—Mahlah, Noah, Hoglah, Milcah, and Tirzah—came to MOSES and ELEAZAR to plead for the recognition of women in such cases. As a result it was decided that when a man died without male heirs the inheritance would pass to his daughters. This law was later emended to prevent Israelite lands passing into non-Israelite hands through marriage. Women who inherited lands were required to marry within their own tribe. (See J. Pedersen, *Israel: Its Life and Culture*, 2 vols. [1926–40], 1:94–96; J. Weingreen in *VT* 16 [1966]: 518–22.)   J. ARTHUR THOMPSON

Zelotes zuh-loh′teez. KJV form of ZEALOT.

Zelzah zel′zuh (צֶלְצַח H7525, derivation unknown). A town or landmark on the border (NRSV, "territory"; Heb. *gĕbûl* H1473) of BENJAMIN near the tomb where RACHEL was buried (1 Sam. 10:2). SAMUEL informed SAUL that two men would providentially meet him here with news about his father's lost donkeys. Aside from this passage, nothing is known of Zelzah (unless it should be equated with ZELA, as some have suggested). According to Gen. 35:16–20, Rachel died and was buried on the way from BETHEL to EPHRATH, "while they were still some distance" from the latter; but that information is of little help in locating Zelzah (see RACHEL'S TOMB). It is reasonable to infer that Zelzah was not far from RAMAH, where Samuel lived. Many scholars, however, believe that the text is suspect, and numerous alternate interpretations have been proposed. Most of these involve conjectural emendations, such as *bĕṣēl ṣāḥiaḥ*, meaning possibly "in the shadow of a rock" (see *HALOT*, 3:1030–31; *ABD*, 6:1073–74).

Zemaraim zem′uh-ray′im (צְמָרַיִם H7549, possibly "double peak"). **(1)** A city allotted to the tribe of BENJAMIN (Josh. 18:22). Zemaraim is listed between BETH ARABAH (thought to be in the extreme E of Benjamin's territory and SE of JERICHO) and BETHEL (N central area), so this information is not much help in locating the town. According to some, one should look for Zemaraim in the eastern section and possibly identify it with Khirbet es-Samra (c. 4 mi. NE of Jericho). Others prefer a location near Bethel, such as Ras ez-Zemara (c. 5 mi. NE of Bethel), Khirbet el-Mazariʿa (1 mi. W of ez-Zemara), or Ras eṭ-Ṭahune (c. 9 mi. N of JERUSALEM and only 2 mi. SW of Bethel; this last site is preferred by Z. Kallai, *Historical Geography of the Bible* [1986], 401). If Zemaraim was indeed in the vicinity of Bethel, the town should probably be associated with Mount Zemaraim (see #2, below). Such a location is consonant with the inclusion of the town in SHISHAK's topographical list (Egyptian *ḏmrm*; cf. Y. Aharoni, *The Land of the Bible: A Historical Geography*, rev. ed. [1979], 325–27).

(2) A mountain in the hill country of Ephraim (see EPHRAIM, HILL COUNTRY OF) from which ABIJAH of Judah addressed JEROBOAM of Israel before a major battle between the two kingdoms (2 Chr. 13:4). Abijah was victorious and captured "the towns of Bethel, Jeshanah and Ephron, with their surrounding villages" (v. 19). It is quite possible that Mount Zemaraim received its name from the town of Zemaraim or vice versa (see #1, above).

Zemarite zem′uh-rit (צְמָרִי H7548, gentilic of the assumed place name צְמָר). The Zemarites were a people group descended from CANAAN (Gen. 10:18; 1 Chr. 1:16). They are usually associated with the city of ZEMER. See NATIONS II.A.

Zemer zee′muhr (conjecture צְמֶר). In Ezek. 27:8, according to some scholars, the words *ḥăkāmayik ṣōr*, "your skilled men, O Tyre," should be emended to *ḥakmê ṣemer*, "skilled men of Zemer" (cf. NRSV). The city of Zemer is mentioned in extrabiblical sources (e.g., Ṣumur in the TELL EL-AMARNA tablets) and is generally identified with modern Ṣumra in Syria (c. 11 mi. SE of ARVAD, just N of the Syria-Lebanon border). Although the name of this city does not otherwise occur in the Bible, the ZEMARITES included in the Table of NATIONS were probably inhabitants of Zemer.

Zemira zuh-mi′ruh. KJV form of ZEMIRAH.

Zemirah zuh-mī'ruh (זְמִירָה H2371, possibly "song"). KJV Zemira. Son of BEKER and grandson of BENJAMIN (1 Chr. 7:8).

Zenan zee'nuhn (צְנָן H7569, meaning uncertain). A town in the SHEPHELAH, within the tribal territory of JUDAH (Josh. 15:37; prob. the same as ZAANAN, Mic. 1:11). It was in the same district as LACHISH and EGLON, but its precise location is unknown.

Zenas zee'nuhs (Ζηνᾶς G2424, prob. short form of Ζηνόδωρος, "gift of Zeus"). A lawyer whom PAUL asked TITUS to assist in his journey (Tit. 3:13). He may have been a Christian missionary who worked with Titus on the island of CRETE, or who with APOLLOS was on a mission for Paul that took him to the island. According to some, Titus was being directed to send Zenas and Apollos on to Paul in NICOPOLIS with full provisions, possibly because the apostle had a special need for Zenas's particular expertise as a lawyer (but this view was influenced by the KJV's incorrect rendering, "Bring"). It is unclear, moreover, whether his legal skills had to do with Roman or with Jewish law. Because the verses just preceding (vv. 9–11) speak of religious legal disputes, it may be that Zenas was an expert in the TORAH. If so, he was probably a Jewish scholar and legal authority turned Hellenist who took a Greek name when he was converted to Christianity. Others believe that, in view of the anti-Jewish sentiments expressed in the PASTORAL EPISTLES (1 Tim. 1:7–11; Tit. 1:10–14), he was a secular jurist.

Some infer that Paul had received much assistance in his mission endeavors from Zenas and others like him. This could explain why Titus was to see that Zenas and Apollos were fitted and equipped for the journey in every way (cf. Rom. 15:24; 1 Cor. 16:6). It is possible they were carrying this very letter to Titus in Crete. The passage illustrates vividly the Christian hospitality and obvious support the early churches gave to brethren and workers traveling from one church to another. The closing verses of Titus indicate the variety and mobility of the early missionaries in the Pauline group. The 5th-cent. work *Acts of Titus* purports to have been written by Zenas, and late tradition says that he became a bishop in Palestine in LYDDA. L. M. PETERSEN

Zephaniah zef'uh-nī'uh (צְפַנְיָהוּ H7622 [only 2 Ki. 25:18; Jer. 37:3] צְפַנְיָה H7622, "Yahweh has hidden [or treasured or protected]", cf. ELIZAPHAN). (1) Son of Tahath, descendant of LEVI through KOHATH, and ancestor of SAMUEL and HEMAN (1 Chr. 6:36).

(2) Son of Cushi (or Cushite); a prophet during the early part of the reign of JOSIAH whose prophecy is preserved in the book bearing his name (Zeph. 1:1; see ZEPHANIAH, BOOK OF). He is the only prophet whose ancestry is traced back four generations, and this unique feature may indicate that his great-grandfather HEZEKIAH was the famous king bearing that name. If so he was the only prophet of royal blood, a cousin of Josiah and of the princes to whom he directed much of his prophecy. Apparently he lived in Jerusalem, for he referred to it as "this place" (1:4) and described its topography with intimate knowledge (1:10–13).

(3) Son of Maaseiah; a priest second in rank during the reign of ZEDEKIAH (Jer. 21:1; 52:24). Some think this Zephaniah may have been JEREMIAH's cousin (cf. 32:7 with 35:4). The false prophet Shemaiah of Nehelam, in a letter from Babylon, appointed Zephaniah priest instead of JEHOIADA with responsibility to punish pretenders to the gift of prophecy, one of whom, he alleged, was Jeremiah (29:24–28). Zedekiah sent him twice to Jeremiah; once to inquire of Yahweh about the Babylonian siege and once to ask him to pray for the people (21:1–2; 37:3). After the capture of Jerusalem, NEBUZARADAN brought him along with other leaders before the king of Babylon, who had them killed at RIBLAH (2 Ki. 25:18, 21; Jer. 52:24, 27).

(4) Father of a postexilic Israelite named JOSIAH in whose house the priest Joshua (JESHUA) was crowned (Zech. 6:10). The subsequent reference to HEN son of Zechariah (v 14) may be an alternate name or title of Josiah. B. K. WALTKE

Zephaniah, Apocalypse of. A Jewish pseudepigraphical book known primarily through references to it by CLEMENT OF ALEXANDRIA (*Stromata* 5.11.77; the work is also mentioned in some later writings, e.g., by Nicephorus, c. A.D. 820). Clement describes Zephaniah's journey into the fifth heaven escorted by the Spirit; there the prophet saw angels in glory on thrones, singing the praises of the most high God. This work is quite similar to the ASCENSION OF ISAIAH 7–9. It may have been composed by a Jewish author in the 1st cent. A.D. or perhaps a little earlier.

There is a Christian *Apocalypse of Sophoniah* preserved in two pages of a Sahidic Coptic MS (early 5th-cent. A.D.). Sophoniah saw a soul being flogged in the nether world for his unrepented sins. Transported to a new locality, Sophoniah witnessed a multitude of angels of horrifying appearance. The text then becomes illegible. Its relation to the work mentioned by Clement is uncertain, although the flogging scene resembles a similar scene in the *Apocalypse of Paul* (see PAUL, APOCALYPSE OF) from NAG HAMMADI, which has passages in common with the material in Clement. In addition, an Achmimic Coptic MS of the 4th cent. has a part of an apocalypse (eighteen pages) believed to be part of the work mentioned above. Its title is not preserved, so it is sometimes called the *Anonymous Apocalypse*. It describes the punishment in hell of the wicked as in the 2nd-cent. *Apocalypse of Peter* (see PETER, APOCALYPSE OF). (English trans. of surviving material in *OTP*, 497–515; see also the summary in *ABD*, 6:1075–77.)   A. K. HELMBOLD

Zephaniah, Book of. The ninth book in the collection known as the twelve Minor Prophets, coming at the end of the second division of the Hebrew CANON of Scripture.

  I. Unity
  II. Date
  III. Historical background
  IV. Purpose
  V. Content

I. Unity. Most critics allow the first chapter of this book as the genuine work of ZEPHANIAH, but consider that parts of Zeph. 2 and 3 contain either late poems or postexilic amplifications to authentic oracles of Zephaniah. There is little consensus on details (cf. R. K. Harrison, *Introduction to the Old Testament* [1969], 941). The extent of disagreement among those who postulate several sources indicates the basic weakness of their position.

Moreover, their views often arise from the assumption that there is no genuine predictive prophecy and that the theology of hope in the history of Israel's religion evolved in the postexilic period. The first presupposition is inconsistent with the explicit testimony of Holy Scripture and the second is inconsistent with the form of parallel prophecies in the ANE. Almost a century ago H. Gressmann wrote: "The numerous old Egyptian oracles attest to the formal unity of threat and promise as the original form.... Now that we are acquainted with the Egyptian oracle, it is no longer doubtful that the literary-critical school was on the wrong path" (*Der Messias* [1929], 73). The same phenomenon is attested in the MARI letters (cf. C. Westermann, *Basic Forms of Prophetic Speech* [1967], 121).

II. Date. According to the book's introduction, Zephaniah prophesied during the reign of JOSIAH (640–609 B.C.). More precisely it can be inferred from his allusions to the state of morality and religion (Zeph. 1:4–12; 3:1–3, 7) that his activities took place before the great reformation in the year 621 (cf. 2 Ki. 23). The notices that are supposed by some critics to indicate a somewhat later date are satisfactorily explained: (1) The king's children mentioned in Zeph. 1:8 as addicted to foreign habits could not have been Josiah's sons (he himself was too young to have adult children), but were rather his brothers or near relatives. (2) The reference to the remnant of BAAL in the same verse designates the completeness of their destruction (i.e., Yahweh will efface every remnant of Baal). Moreover, critics have generally accepted an early date for the "genuine portions" of the book because they assume that the irruption of the SCYTHIANS who attacked ASSYRIA in 632 (cf. J. Lewy in *Mitteilungen der vorderasiatischen Gesellschaft* 29 [1925]: 1ff.; E. H. Minns in *CAH*, 3 [1925], 188–89) incited Zephaniah's prediction of the great Day of Yahweh. Zephaniah probably finished his course at about the same time that JEREMIAH was called to his office in Josiah's thirteenth year.

In order to avoid the onus of regarding the predictions against the nations as secondary according to the critical presuppositions, J. P. Hyatt (in *JNES* 7 [1948]: 25–33) rejected the accuracy of the superscription and moved Zephaniah to the time of JEHOIAKIM (609–598). However, his position ill accords with the internal evidence of the book. For example, Nineveh is represented as in a state of peace and prosperity (Zeph. 2.15), and there is no suggestion that Josiah's reform has taken place.

III. Historical background. The religious state of the kingdom of Judah deteriorated markedly following the death of HEZEKIAH. The trend toward things Assyrian became increasingly conspicuous. The degenerate religious practice of the period before Josiah's great reform are indicated in detail in 2 Ki. 23:4–20.

A considerable debate exists on the political background of the book. Whereas several prophets specified the Babylonians as the rod Yahweh would use to destroy the kingdom of Judah (Isa. 39:6; Hab. 1:6; Jer. 20:4), Zephaniah brought before the people Yahweh himself as the person behind the judgment without specifying the instrument. Because of this silence two interpretations prevail regarding the identification of the instrument of judgment: either the Scythians or the Babylonians.

The majority of critics reason that the authentic oracles of Zephaniah have the invasion of the Scythians in view. F. Hitzig (*Die zwölf kleinen Propheten*, 4th ed. [1881], 297–98) wrote: "The Chaldeans come still less (than the Egyptians) into account, because they did not found an independent kingdom until 625 B.C., nor threaten Judea until after Josiah's death. On the other hand, an unsuspicious and well-accredited account has been preserved to us that somewhere about this time the Scythians overflowed Palestine too with their hosts. Herodotus (1.105) relates that the Scythians after they had disturbed Cyaxares at the siege of Nineveh, turned toward Egypt; and when they had already arrived in Palestine, were persuaded by Psammetichus to return, and in their return plundered a temple in Ashkelon." In contradiction to Zephaniah's prophesies, however, the Scythians destroyed neither Assyria nor Egypt but, on the contrary, temporarily saved Nineveh. Critics explain the difference in one of two ways: (1) the prophet made a mistake (J. M. P. Smith, *A Critical and Exegetical Commentary on the Books of Micah, Zephaniah and Nahum*, ICC [1911], 170); or (2) these oracles are secondary (Hyatt, *JNES* 7 [1948]: 25).

The present writer rejects this interpretation in favor of regarding the Babylonians as the divine agent of judgment in view for these four reasons: (1) The rationalism and antisupernaturalistic presuppositions informing the above views are contrary to the spirit of prophecy found in all of Scripture. (2) The OT, which normally supplies sufficient historical background for the interpretation of the prophets, nowhere makes reference to an invasion by Scythians. (3) The account in HERODOTUS that the Scythians marched through Palestine to invade Egypt before being bought off by Psammetichus has no objective historical support (cf. F. Wilke in *Altestamentliche Studien: R. Kittel zum 60. Geburtstag dargebracht* [1913], 222ff.; J. P. Hyatt in *JBL* 59 [1940]: 501; id. in *JNES* 7 [1948]: 25ff.). (4) Herodotus's statement about the Scythian invasion does not comport with Zephaniah's predictions. Having recorded the intervention of Psammetichus, Herodotus (1.105) adds that when the Scythians reached Ashkelon, most of them passed the city doing no harm, though some remained behind and robbed the temple of Heavenly Aphrodite. Zephaniah, however, speaks not of a marauding band, but of the utter havoc upon Jerusalem, of the permanent desolation of Philistia, Moab, and Ammon, and of destructive war on Ethiopia.

Philistine pottery (12th cent. B.C.). Zephaniah speaks about God's judgment upon the Philistines.

Pusey stated well the case against the Scythian interpretation and in favor of the Babylonian: "But it is an intense paradox, when men, 2500 years after his date assert, not only that Zephaniah's prophecies had no relation to the Chaldees, in whom his words were fulfilled ... but that they know what must have been, and (as they assert) what *was* in the prophet's mind; and that he had in mind, *not* those in whom his words were fulfilled, but others in whom they were *not* fulfilled" (E. B. Pusey, *The Minor Prophets: A Commentary*, 2 vols. [1869–75], 2:230). This obvious lack of correspondence now forces the critic to suppose that these oracles are either inaccurate or secondary. (It is a mute and insignificant point whether a Scythian invasion into Palestine awakened Zephaniah to his prophetic call, as some conservative writers contend, see G. L. Archer, *Survey of Old Testament Introduction*, rev. ed. [1994], 394.)

IV. Purpose. Because of Judah's degenerate religious situation, Zephaniah predicted the fall of Judah and Jerusalem as inevitable (Zeph. 1:4–13; 3:1–7). This judgment in his view was a part of the wider judgment to fall on all the world in the DAY OF THE LORD (1:14–18; 2:4–15). Accordingly, his mission was not to all the people whose sentence was fixed, but to the meek who by turning to Yahweh could possibly escape the coming day of judgment (2:1–3) and become a part of the remnant who would enjoy the blessings of the kingdom (3:8–20).

V. Content

A. Universal judgment. This heading covers most of the book, Zeph. 1:1—3:7.

1. *Upon the entire creation* (1:2–3). (The destruction described is even more sweeping in its effects than the flood; total destruction is the ultimate end of this fallen cosmos [cf. 2 Pet. 3:10; Rev. 21:1]. The collapse of civilizations in the meanwhile serves as a herald announcing the final judgment of all the earth.)

2. *Upon Judah* (1:4—2:3).

   a. The cause of its judgment (1:4–6). (Five false religions are condemned: worship of Baal, worship of astral deities introduced by MANASSEH [2 Ki. 21:3, 5], syncretistic worship of Yahweh and MILCOM, apostasy from Yahweh, and secularism. The same mighty outstretched hand that brought them out of Egypt and into Canaan will be turned against them.)

   b. The proximity of judgment (v. 7). (The command to "be silent" is a call to cease opposition to the divine will. By surrendering unconditionally it may be they would be hidden in the time of Yahweh's anger [2:3]. Judah is now likened implicitly to a sacrificial animal. The priests already invited to the joyous meal are the nations. The peace sacrifice, the only one eaten, had to be consumed completely within two days; whatever remained after that must be burned with fire [Lev. 7:15–17].)

   c. The extent of the judgment (vv. 8–13). (The listed objects of judgment are: royalty, priests, the entire city of Jerusalem, merchants, and practical atheists and their property. Regarding the reference to "all who avoid stepping on the threshold," see THRESHOLD.)

   d. The proximity and horror of the Day of Yahweh (vv. 14–18). (The impending fall of Jerusalem merges in the prophet's view with the judgment on Israel and all the earth in connection with the return of Christ in power and glory.)

   e. The call to repentance (2:1–3). (The punitive decree, announced long ago [Deut. 28:15–68], is now rushing to its enactment.)

3. *Upon the Gentile nations* (2:4–15).

   a. In the W: PHILISTIA (vv. 4–7). (The KERETHITES may have come from CRETE and were apparently related to the PHILISTINES.)

   b. In the E: MOAB and AMMON (vv. 8–11).

   c. In the S: ETHIOPIA (v. 12).

   d. In the N: ASSYRIA (vv. 13–15).

4. *Upon Jerusalem* (3:1–7).

   a. Her moral depravity (v. 1).

   b. Her intractability (v. 2).

   c. Her immoral leaders: civic (v. 3) and religious (v. 4).

   d. Her inexcusability (v. 5).

   e. Her stupidity (vv. 6–7).

B. The establishment of the kingdom. This heading covers the last section of the book, Zeph. 3:8–20.

1. *The destruction of the Gentile opposition* (3:8).
2. *The purified remnant* (3:9–13).
3. *The kingdom blessings* (3:14–20).

(Significant commentaries include J. M. P. Smith, *A Critical and Exegetical Commentary on the Books of Micah, Zephaniah and Nahum* [bound with other minor prophets], ICC [1911]; R. L. Smith, *Micah-Malachi*, WBC 32 [1984]; O. P. Robertson, *The Books of Nahum, Habakkuk, and Zephaniah*, NICOT [1990]; R. D. Patterson, *Nahum, Habakkuk, Zephaniah* [1991]; J. J. M. Roberts, *Nahum, Habakkuk, and Zephaniah*, OTL [1991]; A. Berlin, *Zephaniah*, AB 25A [1994]; J. A. Motyer in *The Minor Prophets: An Exegetical and Expository Commentary*, ed. T. McComiskey [1992–98], 3:897–962; K. L. Barker and W. Bailey, *Micah, Nahum, Habakkuk, Zephaniah*, NAC 20 [1998]; J. Vlaardingerbroek, *Zephaniah* [1999]; H. Irsigler, *Zefanja*, HTKAT [2002]; M. Sweeney, *Zephaniah: A Commentary*, Hermeneia [2003].

(Among important monographs, see S. Kapelrud, *The Message of the Prophet Zephaniah: Morphology and Ideas* [1975]; P. R. House, *Zephaniah: A Prophetic Drama* [1988]; E. Ben Zvi, *A Historical-Critical Study of the Book of Zephaniah* [1991]; D. H. Ryou, *Zephaniah's Oracles against the Nations: A Synchronic and Diachronic Study of Zephaniah 2:1–3:8* [1995]; and the bibliography by W. E. Mills, *Zephaniah and Haggai* [2002].)   B. K. WALTKE

Zephath zee′fath (צְפַת H7634, prob. "watchtower"; cf. MIZPAH). Apparently the earlier, Canaanite name of the city of HORMAH (Jdg. 1:17).

Zephathah zef′uh-thuh (צְפָתָה H7635, prob. from צָפָה H7595, "to keep watch"; cf. ZEPHATH). A valley near Mareshah (on the edge of the lowlands NE of LACHISH), where King ASA defeated ZERAH the Cushite (2 Chr. 14:10). See MARESHAH (PLACE). The SEPTUAGINT rendering ("in the valley to the north of Marisa," evidently reading the Heb. as *ṣāpôn* H7600) suggests the Valley of Elah (see ELAH, VALLEY OF), but the whole region has such a complex topography of gently sloping foothills that the exact valley cannot now be identified with certainty.   J. ARTHUR THOMPSON

Zephi zee′fi. See ZEPHO.

Zepho zee′foh (צְפוֹ H7608 [in 1 Chr. 1:36, צְפִי], derivation uncertain). Son of ELIPHAZ, grandson of Esau, and head of an Edomite clan (Gen. 36:11, 15; 1 Chr. 1:36 [KJV and other versions, "Zephi"]).

Zephon zee′fon (צְפוֹן H7602 [in Gen. 46:16, צִפְיוֹן], derivation uncertain; gentilic צְפוֹנִי H7604, "Zephonite"). Son of GAD, grandson of JACOB, and eponymous ancestor of the Zephonite clan (Gen. 46:16 [KJV and other versions, "Ziphion"]; Num. 26:15).

Zer zuhr (צֵר H7643, perhaps "narrow, restricted"). One of the fortified cities allotted to the tribe of NAPHTALI (Josh. 19:35). Many scholars, however, suspect corruption in textual transmission. The SEPTUAGINT (*tōn Tyriōn Tyros*, "of the Tyrians, Tyre") may reflect a Hebrew variant (vocalized *haṣṣōrîm ṣōr* instead of *haṣṣiddîm ṣēr*), and the apparatus of *BHS*, following an earlier proposal, suggests that the first four words of the verse are an erroneous scribal repetition of previous material (in vv. 28–29; see also R. D. Nelson, *Joshua*, OTL [1997], 218).

Zerah zihr′uh (זֶרַח H2438, "shining, dawning"; later prob. used as the short form of זְרַחְיָה H2440, "Yahweh has shed light" [cf. ZERAHIAH]; gentilic זַרְחִי H2439, "Zerahite" [KJV, "Zarhite"]; Ζάρα G2406). KJV also Zarah (Gen. 38:30) and Zara (Matt. 1:3). **(1)** Son of Reuel and grandson of Esau; a chief in EDOM (Gen. 36:13, 17; 1 Chr. 1:37). Some think this is the same Zerah whose son (or descendant) JOBAB from BOZRAH became an Edomite king (Gen. 36:33; 1 Chr. 1:44).

(2) Son of JUDAH by his daughter-in-law TAMAR; his twin brother was PEREZ (Gen. 38:30; 46:12; 1 Chr. 2:4). His name arose from the peculiar nature of his birth. His hand came out first and was tied with a scarlet thread to indicate that he was the firstborn, but through unusual circumstances his brother was born before he was (Gen. 38:28–29). He was called Zerah possibly because he appeared first or as an allusion to the bright (scarlet) thread. Later he became the eponymous ancestor of the Zerahite clan (Num. 26:20; 1 Chr. 9:6; Neh. 11:24; prob. 1 Chr. 27:11, 13 should be included here; see also IZRAHITE). One of his descendants was ACHAN (Josh. 7:1, 17–18, 24; 22:20); another one was PETHAHIAH, a royal official after the EXILE (Neh. 11:24). His name is included in Matthew's GENEALOGY OF JESUS CHRIST, which however makes clear that it was his brother Perez who was an ancestor of Jesus (Matt. 1:3).

(3) Son of SIMEON, grandson of JACOB, and eponymous ancestor of the Zerahite clan among the Simeonites (Num. 26:13; 1 Chr. 4:24). In the parallel passages (Gen. 46:10; Exod. 6:15) he is called ZOHAR.

(4) Son of Iddo and descendant of LEVI through GERSHON (1 Chr. 6:21 [MT 6:6]).

(5) Son of Adaiah, descendant of LEVI through GERSHON, and ancestor of the musician ASAPH (1 Chr. 6:41 [MT 6:26]).

(6) A Cushite (i.e., from ETHIOPIA, but perhaps the leader of a S Arabian tribe, since the name *ʾdrḥ* appears in Old S Arabian inscriptions) who attacked King ASA of Judah (2 Chr. 14:9). Zerah was defeated in battle at MARESHAH (PLACE) and pursued to GERAR, where he was completely routed (vv. 10–15). The phrase "an host of a thousand thousand" (KJV) could be taken literally (cf. NRSV, "an army of a million men") or figuratively (NIV, "a vast army"). Some have argued that the presence of tents, flocks, and camels among the booty suggests BEDOUIN raiders. (See discussion of this passage by R. B. Dillard, *2 Chronicles*, WBC 15 [1987], 119–20.)   J. ARTHUR THOMPSON

Zerahiah zer´uh-hi´uh (זְרַחְיָה *H2440*, "Yahweh has shed light [*or* shone forth *or* risen]"). **(1)** Son of Uzzi, descendant of LEVI through KOHATH, AARON, and ELEAZAR, and ancestor of ZADOK and EZRA (1 Chr. 6:6, 51 [MT 5:32; 6:36]; Ezra 7:4; 1 Esd. 8:2 [KJV, "Zaraias," but omitted in NRSV, following some MSS]; called "Arna" in 2 Esd. 1:2).

(2) Descendant of Pahath-Moab and father of Eliehoenai; the latter was a family head who who returned from Babylon with EZRA (Ezra 8:4; 1 Esd. 8:31 [KJV, "Zaraias"]).

Zerahite zihr´uh-hit. See ZERAH.

Zeraiah zuh-ray´yuh (Ζαραιας). A descendant of Shephatiah who returned from Babylon with EZRA (1 Esd. 8:34; KJV, "Zaraias"; the parallel passage has ZEBADIAH, Ezra 8:8).

Zerdaiah zuhr-day´yuh. See AZIZA.

Zered zihr´id (זֶרֶד *H2429*, meaning uncertain). KJV also Zared (Num. 21:12). A valley or wadi in TRANSJORDAN where the Israelites, terminating their wanderings and bypassing EDOM, encamped and crossed into MOAB (Num. 21:12; Deut. 2:13). It is often identified with the wadi(s) mentioned in Isa. 15:7 and Amos 6:14; see ARABAH, BROOK (WADI) OF THE, and WILLOWS, BROOK (WADI) OF THE. The Zered may also have been the scene of the flash flood in 2 Ki. 3:16–23.

Because Israel penetrated the wilderness E of Moab before crossing the Zered, some identify it with the Wadi Kerak or some tributary of the Kerak or the ARNON (the Ferranj or Seil Saʿideh perhaps). Others, postulating a journey eastward up the valley before the crossing, accept identification (here favored) with Wadi el-Ḥesa. Like the Kerak and Arnon, the Ḥesa flows intermittently in a shallow valley across the plateau; but replenished by rainfall, tributaries, and especially springs, it flows perennially to its terminal oasis through a canyon that cleaves the fault-weakened escarpment. Steep-walled but broad-floored and flanked with cultivable terraces, this wadi formed both the historic divide between Edom and Moab and a difficult but practicable route to the plateau.   G. R. LEWTHWAITE

Zeredah zer´uh-duh (צְרֵדָה *H7649*, derivation uncertain). **(1)** A town in the Ephraimite hills (see EPHRAIM, HILL COUNTRY OF) that was the home of JEROBOAM before he rebelled against SOLOMON (1 Ki. 11:26; KJV, "Zereda"). The SEPTUAGINT, in

The Zered River. (View to the E.)

its long addition to 1 Ki. 12:24, has several other references to the town (the name is transcribed as *Sarira*), including the comment that he built Zeredah for Solomon. The location of Zeredah is uncertain, but it is often identified with Deir Ghassāneh, some 15 mi. SW of Shechem; the ancient name may be preserved in nearby ʿAin Ṣereda. See also ZERERAH.

(2) A Transjordanian town near which the bronze objects for the TEMPLE were cast (2 Chr. 4:17 MT, followed by NRSV and other versions [KJV, "Zeredathah"]). The name here is a variant for ZARETHAN (1 Ki. 7:46).

Zeredathah zer´uh-day´thuh. KJV form of ZEREDAH #2.

Zererah zer´uh-rah (צְרֵרָה H7678, perhaps "narrow, restricted"). KJV Zererath. A town toward which the Midianite army fled after GIDEON and his men blew their trumpets (Jdg. 7:22). The identity and location of Zererah is problematic. The Midianite camp was in the Valley of JEZREEL, near the hill of MOREH (6:33; 7:2), and the soldiers are said to have fled "as far as" (Heb. ʿad H6330) BETH SHITTAH, "toward Zererah" (ṣĕrērātâ), "as far as" (ʿad) the "border/river bank" (śāpâ H8557) of ABEL MEHOLAH, "on/by/near/opposite" (ʿal H6584) TABBATH (7:22). Unfortunately, none of these places can be located with certainty. The Midianites must have fled SE, eventually crossing the JORDAN, and Tabbath almost certainly was in TRANSJORDAN, but it is impossible to determine whether Zererah itself was on the W or E side of the river (although Abel Meholah is often identified with a site on the W bank). Some have thought that Zererah is a mistake for (or a variant of) ZARETHAN, which was probably in Transjordan. Others, following a number of Hebrew MSS (see *BHS* apparatus), read ZEREDAH, but this town appears to have been SW of SHECHEM and thus not on the path suggested by the text.

Zererath zer´uh-rath. KJV form of ZERERAH.

Zeresh zihr´ish (זֶרֶשׁ H2454, meaning uncertain [cf. *ABD*, 6:1083]). Wife of HAMAN, mentioned in two passages in the story of ESTHER. When Haman boasted that Queen Esther had invited him to a banquet with King XERXES, Zeresh and some friends encouraged him to build a gallows so that MORDECAI could be hanged (Esth. 5:10–14). Subsequently, Haman was told by his wife and "advisers" that he would not be able to prevail because Mordecai was a Jew (6:13).

Zereth zihr´ith (צֶרֶת H7679, derivation unknown). Son of Asshur (by his wife Helah) and descendant of JUDAH (1 Chr. 4:7; cf. v. 5).

Zereth Shahar zihr´ith-shay´hahr (צֶרֶת הַשַּׁחַר H7680; cf. SHAHAR). Also Zereth-shahar. One of the towns in the territory given to the tribe of REUBEN (Josh. 13:19). The town—mentioned in conjunction with others in MOAB that had formerly belonged to SIHON the Amorite—is described as being "on the hill in the valley," but the precise location is uncertain. Some scholars tentatively identify it with modern ez-Zarat, on the E shore of the DEAD SEA (c. 12 mi. S of its NE tip and 6 mi. WNW of ATAROTH). Located about 2 mi. below the point where the Wadi Nahaliel flows into the Dead Sea from the E, this was the site of Hellenistic Callirrhoe, known for its hot springs, which the ailing HEROD the Great used (Jos. *Ant.* 17.6.5 §171; *War* 1.33.5 §657).

Zeri zihr´i (צְרִי H7662, "balm"). Son of JEDUTHUN; he and his brothers "prophesied, using the harp in thanking and praising the LORD" (1 Chr. 25:3); the name is probably a variant of IZRI (v. 11).

Zeror zihr´or (צְרוֹר H7657, "stone"). Son of Becorath, descendant of BENJAMIN, and great-grandfather (or more distant ancestor) of King SAUL (1 Sam. 9:1; cf. v. 2). His name is missing from the other genealogies of Saul (1 Chr. 8:33–40; 9:39–44), though some have suggested that Zeror is to be equated with ZUR, who appears there as Saul's uncle (8:30; 9:36).

Zeruah zuh-roo´uh (צְרוּעָה H7654, "leprous," perhaps a deliberate scribal distortion of צְרוּיָה H7653; see ZERUIAH). The widowed mother of King JEROBOAM (1 Ki. 11:26). It is possible that her Hebrew name was given to her because she had a skin ailment or discoloration, but since the mothers of the kings of Israel (in contrast to those of the kings of Judah) are not otherwise mentioned, some scholars interpret the identification as a way of denigrating Jeroboam. Indeed, the SEPTUAGINT, which does not include her name here, has a long addition to 1 Ki. 12:24 that calls her *Sarira gynē pornē*, "Sarira a prostitute" (Sarira is also used as the name of Jeroboam's hometown, ZEREDAH). Others suggest that Zeruah is mentioned simply to point out that she was a widow, for some extrabiblical texts use the epithet "a widow's son" with reference to "an unfit person who seizes the throne" (M. Cogan, *1 Kings*, AB 10 [2001], 337).

Zerubbabel zuh-ruhb'uh-buhl (זְרֻבָּבֶל H2428, from Akk. *Zēr-Bābili*, "offspring of Babylon"; Ζοροβαβέλ G2431). KJV Apoc. and NT, Zorobabel. A prominent Israelite who returned to Palestine after the EXILE and functioned as the governor of JERUSALEM under the Persian ruler DARIUS Hystaspes I (522–486 B.C.).

   I. Name
   II. Historical background
   III. Work of Zerubbabel

I. Name. There are certain difficulties connected with the identification of Zerubbabel, partly because he has sometimes been regarded as identical with SHESHBAZZAR (Ezra 1:8 et al.), and also because of an apparent discrepancy in the genealogical lists of Ezra and Chronicles. Zerubbabel is usually identified as the son of SHEALTIEL (or Salathiel) and the grandson of King JEHOIACHIN (Ezra 3:2; Hag. 1:1; Matt. 1:12–13; Lk. 3:27), but in one passage the MT describes him as the son of PEDAIAH, who was Shealtiel's brother (1 Chr. 3:19; the LXX here has *Salathiēl* rather than *Phadaias*).

There are several ways of explaining this discrepancy, the most common of which is the supposition that Shealtiel died without offspring and that his brother Pedaiah married the widow according to ancient Hebrew LEVIRATE LAW (Deut. 25:5–10). Were Zerubbabel to have been born of such a union he could legally claim to be the son of Shealtiel. Perhaps the Chronicler had information to this effect, but preferred to list him as the lineal son of Pedaiah. Again, if Shealtiel had died without issue, he could well have named his nephew as his legal heir before dying, thus making Zerubbabel his son. It is highly improbable, despite the assertions of some scholars, that Zerubbabel is to be identified with Sheshbazzar, a prince of Judah whom CYRUS made governor of the land (Ezra 1:8) and to whom he entrusted the temple vessels, captured by NEBUCHADNEZZAR, for return to Jerusalem (5:14–15). The most telling argument against such a position is that the account given in the letter addressed to Darius I (5:6, 17) would hardly be intelligible unless Sheshbazzar was dead at the time of the incident which it recorded, whereas Zerubbabel was actively engaged in the construction of the second temple.

It is possible that Sheshbazzar was the same as SHENAZZAR, the uncle of Zerubbabel (1 Chr. 3:18), but this is uncertain. The apparent discrepancy in the ancestry of Zerubbabel may have been caused by a copyist's error in Chronicles, or perhaps the reference was to another person named Zerubbabel, who may have been a cousin of his illustrious namesake. CUNEIFORM inscriptions from Babylonia dating from the early Persian period (539–331 B.C.) show that the name Zerubbabel was of common occurrence, thus making for difficulty in exact identification. At all events, the Zerubbabel of Ezra and Haggai was heir to the throne of Judah, and because of his position in the Davidic line he was included by two evangelists (Matt. 1:12; Lk. 3:27) in the GENEALOGY OF JESUS CHRIST.

II. Historical background. Subsequent to the decree of Cyrus in 538 B.C., which allowed the captive peoples of Babylonia to return to their own homes, Zerubbabel was appointed governor (Heb. *peḥâ* H7068) in postexilic Jerusalem (Hag. 1:1 et al.). The biblical narratives reflect accurately the policy of Cyrus toward those minority groups made captive and expatriated under the neo-Babylonian regime. By urging such peoples to return home and rebuild their religious shrines, Cyrus was at once promoting good will for his own regime in all parts of his newly won empire and at the same time relieving himself of responsibility for maintaining dissident captive groups in continued servitude. By about 530 some of the Hebrews, having returned to Judea under the leadership of Zerubbabel, began work on the reconstruction of the temple. From the time of Darius the Great (522–486) the Persian regime was stable in nature, and the Judean state was encouraged to function as a religious rather than a political entity, supported by Persian rule.

III. Work of Zerubbabel. This man was the active political leader in Jerusalem under the aegis of TATTENAI, the military governor of Judea (Ezra 6:13), with Joshua (JESHUA) the high priest serving as the principal religious figure. The work of rebuilding the TEMPLE, which had been hindered until 520 B.C., was resumed when Darius found the decree authorizing the project (6:1–12) and forbade further interference with it. This support, along with a large subsidy for the completion of the temple, provided official sanction for the task that had all but defeated the resolve of the returned exiles. At this point the prophets HAGGAI and ZECHARIAH furnished the necessary moral and spiritual impetus for the work of rebuilding. Haggai castigated the Jews for their selfishness, indifference, and neglect, spurring Zerubbabel on to give proper oversight to the work in hand. In the same year Zechariah urged completion of the temple, and promised that earlier opposition would be removed. See RESTORATION.

Some scholars have assumed that both prophets encouraged Zerubbabel to look forward to a time when Judea would be free from foreign domination and be governed by a descendant of the house of DAVID. Thus it is held that the crowning of Joshua (Zech. 6:9–15) was actually the coronation of Zerubbabel, but MS evidence for this position is nonexistent, and in any event, it is Joshua who is the type of the messianic Branch (3:8). Consequently there is no ground whatever for taking the crowning and the promise of protection in Hag. 2:20–23 as a theoretical basis for the coronation of Zerubbabel as king of Judea, and supposing in addition that this act of rebellion was quickly crushed, along with others of a similar kind in the empire, by Darius I. In fact, the political circumstances of Zerubbabel's rule are unknown, as are those of his death.

Zerubbabel was honored in Jewish tradition, mentioned as a man of renown (Sir. 49:11). A 6th cent. A.D. Jewish chronicle preserved the tradition that Zerubbabel returned to Babylonia after 515 B.C. and succeeded his father Shealtiel as a prince of the exiled remnant there, but this is historically improbable. Another familiar legend was the forensic contest of the three young warriors of Darius (1 Esd. 3:1—5:6), which was adopted by the Jewish historian JOSEPHUS. The story recounted how the wisdom of Zerubbabel prevailed, and has elements reminiscent of the narrative of Daniel and his three companions (Dan. 1:1–21).

(See further L. E. Browne, *Early Judaism* [1929]; A. C. Welch, *Post-Exilic Judaism* [1935]; J. S. Wright, *The Building of the Second Temple* [1958]; P. Ackroyd, *Exile and Restoration: A Study of Hebrew Thought of the Sixth Century B.C.* [1968]; S. Japhet in *ZAW* 94 [1982]: 66–98 and 95 [1983]: 218–29; W. H. Rose, *Zemah and Zerubbabel: Messianic Expectations in the Early Postexilic Period* [2000]; J. M. Scott, ed., *Restoration: Old Testament, Jewish, and Christian Perspectives* [2001].) R. K. HARRISON

Zeruiah zuh-roo′uh צְרוּיָה H7653 [also צְרֻיָה], "fragrant" or "balm of Yahweh"; cf. ZERI). Sister (or step-sister) of DAVID (1 Chr. 2:16; she may have been the daughter of JESSE's wife by a former marriage to NAHASH, 2 Sam. 17:25) and mother of ABISHAI, JOAB, and ASAHEL, who were chief officers in David's kingdom (2:18; 3:39; et al.). Although Zeruiah is mentioned at least twenty five times in the historical records of Samuel, Kings, and Chronicles, no mention is ever made of her husband. The fact that Joab (commander of the army) and his brothers are repeatedly identified as sons of Zeruiah makes it apparent that she was a well-known individual. Numerous explanations have been given concerning the Scripture's silence in identifying Zeruiah's husband: he may have died young; he may have been a foreigner and she retained her identity with her clan; he may have been rather insignificant and obscured by her personality; the biblical writers may have followed the custom of tracing kinship through the female line. The fact remains, however, that she must have been well known and recognized to be repeatedly identified as the mother of Joab, the general of David's army. S. J. SCHULTZ

Zetham zee′thuhm (זֵתָם H2157, derivation uncertain). Son of LADAN and descendant of LEVI through Gershon (1 Chr. 23:8; in 26:22 the Heb. can be understood to mean that Zetham was son of Jehieli).

Zethan zee´thuhn (זֵיתָן *H2340*, possibly "[keeper of] olive trees"). Son of Bilhan and great-grandson of Benjamin (1 Chr. 7:10).

Zethar zee´thahr (זֵתַר *H2458*, possibly from Pers. *zaitar*, "conqueror"). One of "the seven nobles of Persia and Media who had special access to the king and were highest in the kingdom" (Esth. 1:14). Queen Vashti was banished by Ahasuerus (Xerxes) on their advice.

Zeus zoos (Ζεύς *G2416* [gen. Διός, acc. Δία]). The chief god of the Greeks. The word comes from an Indo-European root meaning "sky," and its form appears in other Indo-European languages, such as Latin *Jupiter*, the old form of which is *Diespiter* (i.e., *diei pater*, "father of day"), Sanskrit *Dyaús pita*, and Teutonic *Ziu* (from which derives *Tuesday*). As the god of the bright sky, Zeus was the lord of thunder and the giver of weather, the "cloud-gatherer" of the Homeric phrase. Since mountain peaks give weather signs, Zeus was enthroned on heights, preeminently on Olympus.

In the Mycenean age, during the 2nd millennium B.C., the society of heaven was pictured on the model of the regal courts of that era. Note the banquet scene on Olympus at the end of the first book of the *Iliad*. Zeus, at the same time, serving the needs of a royal and patriarchal age, became the protector and ruler of the family. As Zeus Herkeios ("of the household") he ruled the hearth; as Zeus Xenios ("hospitable, defender of strangers") he protected the guest. (According to 2 Macc. 6:2, Antiochus Epiphanes determined that the temples in Jerusalem and Gerizim would be called, respectively, the temple of Olympian Zeus and the temple of Zeus Xenios. In a more detailed narrative, Josephus [*Ant*. 12.5.5 §§257–64] says Antiochus granted to the Samaritans the petition that their temple be called Zeus Hellenios.)

It may be said, therefore, that Zeus acquired moral functions related to the customs and laws which maintained and established the family and its life. But since the state is the larger family and

Statue of Zeus from Perga (Roman, 2nd cent. A.D.).

requires a moral framework and foundation similar to that of the smaller unit, Zeus became the protector of law and justice, the supreme god, father of gods and men. Homer, whose epics became a sort of "Bible" in the earlier Greek centuries, impressed this concept of Zeus on the Greek mind, and it survived the passing of the forms of kingship that had provided its first imagery. The myths and legends that grew up around Zeus, compounded of material from many quarters, became the material, variously used, of poet and dramatist, but better and more spiritually perceptive minds began to look upon Zeus as the supreme if not the only God. In the theological dramas of Aeschylus there are concepts of Zeus almost biblical in their loftiness. The hymn of the Stoic poet Cleanthes, one of the possible sources for Paul's quotation in Athens (Acts 17:28), addresses Zeus in exquisite language as father and creator. (See further A. B. Cook, *Zeus*:

A Study in Ancient Religion, 2 vols. [1914–40]; C. Seltman, *The Twelve Olympians and their Guests*, rev. ed. [1956]; K. W. Arafat, *Classical Zeus: A Study in Art and Literature* [1990]; *DDD*, 934–41.)

E. M. BLAIKLOCK

Zia zi´uh (זִיעַ H2333, possibly "one who trembles"). Son of Abihail; he was one of seven relatives from the tribe of GAD who occupied the region E of GILEAD (1 Chr. 5:13; cf. vv. 10, 14).

Ziba zi´buh (צִיבָא H7471, prob. "twig"). A servant or steward of SAUL whose life and activities are known in the biblical record only during the reign of DAVID. In response to David's request, Ziba introduced to him MEPHIBOSHETH, a crippled son of JONATHAN. By royal provision the land that formerly belonged to King Saul was given to Mephibosheth and placed under the management of Ziba. Even though Mephibosheth received personal provisions from the king's table, the produce of the land was allotted to Mephibosheth's family. This may have been an estate of considerable size, since Ziba employed his fifteen sons and twenty servants to cultivate the land (2 Sam. 9:2–12).

When David fled during ABSALOM's rebellion, Ziba brought supplies to him and reported that Mephibosheth was disloyal (2 Sam. 16:1–4). The king responded by assigning Mephibosheth's estate to Ziba. Subsequently, as David was returning to Jerusalem, Ziba was among those who met the royal retinue (19:17), but Mephibosheth went to meet them too and revealed that he had been betrayed by Ziba. By royal decree half of the estate was returned to Mephibosheth while Ziba retained the remainder (19:24–30).

S. J. SCHULTZ

Zibeon zib´ee-uhn (צִבְעוֹן H7390, "[little] hyena"). (1) A HIVITE whose granddaughter OHOLIBAMAH was married to ESAU (Gen. 36:2, 14). If the gentilic Hivite is equivalent (or should be emended) to HORITE, then this Zibeon is the same as #2 below.

(2) Son of SEIR the Horite; he was a clan chief of EDOM whose son Anah is credited for discovering certain hot springs in the desert (Gen. 36:20, 24, 29; 1 Chr. 1:38, 40). See discussion under ANAH.

Zibia zib´ee-uh (צִבְיָא H7384, "gazelle"). Son of SHAHARAIM, descendant of BENJAMIN, and family head; he was one of seven children that were born to Shaharaim in MOAB by his wife HODESH after he had divorced Hushim and Baara (1 Chr. 8:8–10).

Zibiah zib´ee-uh (צִבְיָה H7385, "[female] gazelle"). A woman of BEERSHEBA who became the wife of King AHAZIAH of Judah and mother of King Jehoash (JOASH; 2 Ki. 12:1; 2 Chr. 24:1).

Zichri zik´ri. See ZICRI.

Zicri zik´ri (זִכְרִי H2356, prob. short form of זְכַרְיָהוּ H2358, "Yahweh has remembered"; see ZECHARIAH). Also Zichri (KJV and other versions); TNIV Zikri. (1) Son of Izhar, grandson of KOHATH, and great-grandson of LEVI (Exod. 6:21); he was MOSES' cousin and the brother of KORAH #3.

(2) Son of Shimei and descendant of BENJAMIN (1 Chr. 8:19). He, as well as #3 and #4 below, is included among the heads of families who lived in Jerusalem (v. 28).

(3) Son of Shashak and descendant of Benjamin (1 Chr. 8:23).

(4) Son of Jehoram and descendant of Benjamin (1 Chr. 8:27).

(5) Son of ASAPH, descendant of Levi, and ancestor of MATTANIAH; the latter was a prominent Levite after the EXILE (1 Chr. 9:15). This Zicri is apparently the same as ZABDI #4 and ZACCUR #4.

(6) Son of Joram and descendant of MOSES through ELIEZER (1 Chr. 26:25).

(7) Father of Eliezer; the latter was an officer over the tribe of REUBEN during the reign of DAVID (1 Chr. 27:16).

(8) Descendant of JUDAH and father of Amasiah; the latter was a commander in the days of JEHOSHAPHAT (2 Chr. 17:16).

(9) Father of Elishaphat; the latter was a commander under JEHOIADA the high priest (2 Chr. 23:1).

(10) A warrior from EPHRAIM in the army of King PEKAH of Israel who assassinated Maaseiah son of King AHAZ of Judah and two royal officers (2 Chr. 28:7).

(11) Descendant of Benjamin and father of Joel; the latter was chief officer in the days of NEHEMIAH (Neh. 11:9).

(12) Head of the priestly family of ABIJAH in the days of the high priest JOIAKIM (Neh. 12:17).

J. ARTHUR THOMPSON

Ziddim zid'im (צִדִּים H7403, "sides," possibly referring to a location on the slopes of a hill). One of the fortified cities allotted to the tribe of NAPHTALI (Josh. 19:35). According to the Palestinian TALMUD (y. Meg. 1:1:70a), the rabbis identified Ziddim with Kephar Ḥittayya, apparently a location just N of the Horns of Hattin (Qarn Ḥaṭṭin), some 6 mi. W of the Sea of Galilee. Few scholars, however, accept this identification, and many believe that the biblical text here has suffered corruption. See ZER.

Zidkijah zid-ki'juh. See ZEDEKIAH #6.

Zidon zi'duhn. KJV alternate form of SIDON.

Zif zif. KJV form of ZIV.

ziggurat zig'oo-rat (from Akk. *ziqqurratu*, "temple tower"). A staged or stepped temple tower. This architectural form was developed in the 3rd millennium B.C. in Babylonia from a low temenos (a platform supporting a shrine, as at ERECH and ʿUqair) to some massive, multiple-story brick towers. The Tower of BABEL (Gen. 11:1–5) might have been a ziggurat, since such buildings are to be found in all principal Mesopotamian cities. The sanctuary of MARDUK at BABYLON was called *Esagil(a)* ("the house whose head is raised up"), and the lofty tower was called *Etemenanki* ("the house of the foundation of heaven and earth"). The chief sources of information for this building are an Akkadian description (not altogether clear, preserved in a text copied in the 3rd cent. B.C. from a much older tablet) and a portrayal by HERODOTUS c. 460 B.C. (cf. O. E. Raven, *Herodotus' Description of Babylon* [1932]). The ziggurat Herodotus claims to have seen had been built by NABOPOLASSAR (625–605) and NEBUCHADNEZZAR II (605–562), and these kings had built upon a previous structure that had fallen into a bad state of ruin.

The original construction of a ziggurat on this site cannot be dated. It is known that King Šar-kali-šarri of AKKAD built a temple at Babylon about 2225 B.C. In the course of centuries, the temple and tower were destroyed and rebuilt. SENNACHERIB destroyed it about 689 B.C., but it was restored by ESARHADDON (680–669). The tower was severely damaged in the war of 652–648, but it was restored again. The interpretation of the technical data presented in a CUNEIFORM record of the 3rd cent., which describes this building, varies somewhat with different scholars. Of the high tower only the merest fragment, a portion of the lowest story, remains, and it was buried under debris until excavated at the end of the 19th cent. Everything considered, the structure was at least seven stories high, with the dwelling of Marduk erected on the seventh story. The height has been variously estimated up to 300 ft.

The cities of NIPPUR, Larsa, and Sippar each called their ziggurat by the name *Eduranki* ("the house of the bond between heaven and earth"). The one at Babylon had inscribed in its foundation, by Nabopolassar, "Marduk had me lay its foundation in the heart of the earth and lift its pinnacle in the sky." One of the best preserved of the ziggurats is that in UR of the Chaldees, with a base 200 by 141 ft. and a bottom terrace 50 ft. high (cf. D. S. DeWitt in *JETS* 22 [1979]: 15–26). Jewish and Arab tradition identified the Tower of Babel with the great temple of NEBO in the city of Borsippa, now called Birs-Nimrod. The ruins of this ziggurat, originally seven stories high, still rise over 150 ft. from the plain. The highest preserved ziggurat ruins are those of Dur-kurigalzu (modern ʿAqar Quf, 20 mi. W of Baghdad), which still towers to a height of 187 ft.

(See further T. Dombart in *JBL* 34 [1919]: 40–64; E. Unger in *ZAW* 45 [1927]: 162–71; L. H. Vincent in *RB* 53 [1946]: 403–40; P. Amiet in *RA* 47 [1953]: 23–33; E. C. Stone in *The Oxford Encyclopedia of Archaeology in the Ancient Near East*, ed. E. M. Meyers [1997], 5:390–91; M. Roaf in *CANE*, 1:429–31.)

L. L. WALKER

Ziha zi'huh (צִיחָא H7484, derivation uncertain [but see *HALOT*, 3:1021]). Ancestor of a family of temple servants (NETHINIM) who returned from the Babylonian captivity (Ezra 2:43; Neh. 7:46; called "Esau" in 1 Esd. 5:29). One of two supervisors of the temple servants living on the hill of OPHEL was called Ziha (Neh. 11:21). He was undoubtedly a member of this family, but it is unclear whether Ziha was his own name or whether he is referred to by the clan eponym.

Ziklag zik′lag (צִקְלַג H7637, derivation unknown). One of the "southernmost towns of the tribe of Judah in the Negev toward the boundary of Edom" (Josh. 15:31; cf. v. 21); it was subsequently allotted to the tribe of SIMEON (Josh. 19:5; 1 Chr. 4:30). In SAUL's time it was under the PHILISTINES (1 Sam. 27:6). King ACHISH of GATH gave Ziklag to DAVID when he was pursued by Saul (1 Sam. 27:6; 1 Chr. 12:1, 20), and David used the town as a base for raids against various groups (1 Sam. 27:8–11; cf. *SacBr*, 148–49). At the time of the last Philistine attack on Saul, David was sent back to Ziklag because the Philistine princes feared he might betray them. On returning there, David found that it had been raided by the Amalekites, on whom he took quick vengeance. He recovered his wives and children as well as those of his men and the men of Ziklag. The booty was divided with the people in the NEGEV area who had assisted him during his campaigns (1 Sam. 30:1–3; 1 Chr. 12:1–20).

It was to Ziklag that a messenger came to announce Saul's death at the battle of Mount GILBOA (2 Sam. 1:1; 4:10). When David finally became king he included the area of Ziklag in his kingdom. Later still it is listed as one of the places occupied by the Jews after the exile (Neh. 11:28).

The location of Ziklag is uncertain. Proposed identifications include modern Tell el-Khuweilifeh (c. 9.5 mi. NE of BEERSHEBA) and, more likely, Tell esh-Shariʿah (Heb. Tel Seraʿ, c. 14 mi. NW of Beersheba and 16 mi. ESE of GAZA; for a summary of the excavations there, see *ABD*, 6:1090–93; more detail in *NEAEHL*, s.v. "Seraʿ, Tel," 4:1329–35).

J. ARTHUR THOMPSON

Zikri zik′ri. TNIV form of ZICRI.

Zillah zil′uh (צִלָּה H7500, possibly "shade, protection" [see *HALOT*, 3:1025; *ADD*, 6:1093–94]). A wife of LAMECH and the mother of TUBAL-CAIN and NAAMAH (Gen. 4:19, 22–23).

Zillethai zil′uh-thi (צִלְּתַי H7531, possibly "shade [of Yahweh]"). KJV Zilthai. Son of SHIMEI (#9) and descendant of BENJAMIN (1 Chr. 8:20).

(2) One of several warriors from the tribe of MANASSEH who joined DAVID at ZIKLAG; they are described as "leaders of units of a thousand" (1 Chr. 12:20).

Zilpah zil′puh (זִלְפָּה H2364, possibly "small nose"). A maidservant given by LABAN to LEAH on the occasion of her marriage to JACOB. At the request of Leah, Zilpah became Jacob's concubine, bearing to him GAD and ASHER (Gen. 29:24; 30:9–13; 35:26; 37:2; 46:18). See also BILHAH (PERSON).

Zilthai zil′thi. KJV form of ZILLETHAI.

Zimmah zim′uh (זִמָּה H2366, possibly "plan"). Son or grandson of JAHATH and descendant of LEVI through GERSHON (1 Chr. 6:20, 42; 2 Chr. 29:12).

Zimran zim′ran (זִמְרָן H2383, derivation uncertain). Son of ABRAHAM and KETURAH (Gen. 25:2; 1 Chr. 1:32). The name Zimran is thought by some to be preserved in Zabram, a site W of Mecca, mentioned by Ptolemy (*Geogr.* 6.7.5), but this connection is uncertain.

J. ARTHUR THOMPSON

Zimri (person) zim′ri (זִמְרִי H2381, possibly "[Yahweh is] my protection"; cf. the fuller form זִמְרִיהוּ on a seal from Jerusalem, published by D. Diringer, *Le iscrizioni antico-ebraiche palestinesi* [1934], 25, 43 n. 17, 211). (1) Son of Salu and descendant of SIMEON; he was a tribal leader who was killed by PHINEHAS for his open adultery with a Moabite princess (Num. 25:14; the incident is recalled in 1 Macc. 2:26 [KJV, "Zambri"]).

(2) Son of Zerah, descendant of JUDAH, and grandfather of ACHAN (Josh. 7:1, 17–18 [NIV]; 1 Chr. 2:6). In the Joshua references, most English versions, following the MT, read ZABDI instead of Zimri.

(3) Son of Jehoaddah (Jadah) and descendant of King SAUL through JONATHAN (1 Chr. 8:36; 9:42).

(4) A military official under ELAH of Israel who killed this king and briefly usurped the royal power in 885 B.C. (1 Ki. 16:9–20). Elah had been carousing at TIRZAH while the main army, under

Omri's leadership, was besieging GIBBETHON. When news of the assassination reached the camp, the reaction was so swift that Zimri had only seven days to live. Raising the siege, Omri brought the army to the capital; Zimri, who had perhaps relied on his chariot force, could not hold it. As the troops entered, he retired to the palace and burned it over his own head. Despite his very short reign, Zimri "was seated on the throne" (16:11), implying a form of valid recognition without the national assembly; this must have depended on his being in the capital. The note of his contribution to Israel's apostasy (16:19) may mean that he formally affirmed his adherence to the religious policy of JEROBOAM. His treachery was alluded to by JEZEBEL when she referred to JEHU as "Zimri" (2 Ki. 9:31).   J. LILLEY

Zimri (place) zim′ri (זִמְרִי *H2382*, derivation uncertain). An unknown country mentioned with ELAM and MEDIA as coming under the judgment of God (Jer. 25:25). Some identify this place with ZIMRAN (also unknown); others believe the text is corrupt (the LXX omits this name).

Zin zin (צִן *H7554*, derivation uncertain). A desert that provided the setting for some critical events of biblical history (not to be confused with the Desert of Sin; see SIN, WILDERNESS OF). Possibly named after an unidentified settlement or region (Num. 34:4; Josh. 15:3), the Desert or Wilderness of Zin included KADESH BARNEA, where the Israelites camped (Num. 33:36) and whence they spied out the land (13:21; cf. v. 26). It was here that a disaffected and rebellious generation was sentenced to finish its life span (27:14); here too MIRIAM died and MOSES smote the rock to release the waters of MERIBAH (Num. 20:1–13; 27:14; Deut. 32:51). The S border of the Promised Land included a portion of the Desert of Zin (Num. 34:3–4), which was allotted to the tribe of JUDAH (Josh. 15:1–3).

The Desert of Zin must have extended from somewhere near Kadesh—perhaps from the Brook of Egypt, modern Wadi el-ʿArish (see EGYPT, BROOK OF)—eastward toward the ascent of AKRABBIM and along the Fiqra or Wadi Zin to the border of EDOM. More precise definition is hardly warranted: even in biblical times the Desert of PARAN overlapped (or perchance included) that of Zin (Num. 13:26). However defined, Zin was included in "that vast and dreadful desert" the Israelites experienced (Deut. 1:19; 8:15). See DESERT. With a fickle few inches of rain even in the slightly less arid N, with its soil bestrewn with rock, flint, and sand, with its surface corrugated by fault-scarps and breached by the elongated erosional "craters" of the Khurashe and Kurnub mountains, Zin was mostly barren. Yet investigation is disclosing an ancient ebb and flow of settlement—patriarchal and Israelite, Nabatean and Byzantine—based on meticulous utilization of soil and water and the strategy of trade and defense: a complex of fortresses, apparently following the biblical frontier, marked Judah's borders in the Desert of Zin.

(See further C. L. Woolley and T. E. Lawrence, *The Wilderness of Zin* [1936]; N. Glueck, *Rivers in the Desert: A History of the Negev* [1959]; B. Rothenberg, *God's Wilderness* [1962]; E. Orni and E. Efrat, *Geography of Israel* [1966]; G. I. Davies, *The Way of the Wilderness: A Geographical Study of the Wilderness Itineraries in the Old Testament* [1979].)

G. R. LEWTHWAITE

Zina zi′nuh. See ZIZA #3.

Zion zi′uhn (צִיּוֹן *H7482*, possibly "fortress" or "barren [hill]"; Σιών *G4994*). KJV also Sion (Ps. 65:1 and NT). The SE hill of JERUSALEM; by extension, the name is applied to the entire city, to its inhabitants, and to the people of God generally.
   I. Name
   II. Geographical application
   III. Theological connotations
      A. Positive
      B. Negative
      C. Eschatological
      D. Universalistic
      E. In the NT

I. Name. The term Zion occurs over 150 times in the OT. It appears primarily in the Psalms (almost 40 times), the pictorial personifications of Lamentations (15 times), and the Prophets, especially Isaiah (almost 50 times). As G. Vos explains, "Isaiah's vision of Yahweh's glory centers in the sanctuary and the city [of Zion], whereas to Amos and Hosea, and even Micah, it rested upon the land," Israel as a whole (*Biblical Theology: Old and New Testament* [1948], 116). The derivation of the name remains uncertain, despite numerous proposals (e.g., Heb. *ṣiyyâ* H7000, "dry", Arab. *ṣahwat*, "ridge"; Arab. *ṣana*, "to protect").

II. Geographical application.

The first OT occurrence of *ṣiyyôn* is found in the context of DAVID's attack on JEBUS (the old Canaanite name for Jerusalem). The narrative states that "David captured the fortress [*mĕṣûdâ* H5181] of Zion, the City of David" (2 Sam. 5:7). On that basis, it has been suggested that Zion may designate the whole walled town that covered the SE hill of Jerusalem, presumably the Jebusite city as it existed at the time of its capture by David in 1003 B.C. (cf. P. J. Leithart in *TynBul* 53 [2002]: 161–75). Some decades later SOLOMON, after expanding Jerusalem northward to include Mount MORIAH, brought up the ARK OF THE COVENANT "out of the city of David, which is Zion" (1 Ki. 8:1; 2 Chr. 5:2 NRSV). Only in postbiblical times did the name Zion become erroneously transferred to the SW hill of Jerusalem.

The presence of the ark of Yahweh in the old SE city (cf. 2 Sam. 6:17) gave to Zion rich religious connotations (see below, section III). It came to signify the city of God, the city of the great King (Pss. 46:4; 48:2); a holy hill (Ps. 2:6; cf. Joel 2:1; Zech. 8:3); the chosen place of God's abode (Pss. 9:11; 132:13); his sanctuary (20:2); the goal of pilgrimage (84:5, 7); the place of deliverance and salvation (20:2; 69:35) and of praise and worship (9:14; 65:1). Then with the transfer of the ark to Moriah, the TEMPLE mount too came to be called Zion (78:68–69; cf. the association between Zion and the temple in Jer. 50:28; 51:10).

It was only a short step until Zion was employed for the whole multi-hilled metropolis, in simple synonymous parallelism with the name Jerusalem (Isa. 40:9; Mic. 3:12; cf. Ps. 133:3 NRSV, "the mountains [pl.] of Zion"). Among the later poets and prophets, "Zion" (Zech. 1:17) or the "sons of Zion" (Lam. 4:2) and "daughters of Zion" (Cant. 3:11; Isa. 10:32) come therefore to connote the inhabitants of Jerusalem (Jer. 51:35), whatever their precise geographical hill or quarter. Zion is the whole city, cited in parallel with the other fortified cities of JUDAH as a place of safety (Jer. 4:5–6; cf. Lam. 1:11), and people of other cities are thus said to be brought to Zion (Jer. 3:14). The phrase "Daughter of Zion" may then be used in personification of the entire city, which is like a young beautiful woman of "splendor" (Lam. 1:6; cf. 2:1) or in need of comfort (1:17).

Finally, in EXILE, the name was applied to the whole deported Israelite nation (those "who live in the Daughter of Babylon," Zech. 2:7). By the time of the postexilic restoration in 537 B.C., the joyful returnees are described as "those that returned to Zion" (Ps. 126:1 ASV and RSV mg.; cf. Jer. 50:5). Whatever may have been their actual villages of settlement in Judah, to "rejoice in the bounty of the Lord" was to "come and shout for joy on the heights of Zion" (Jer. 31:12). The "Daughter of Zion" comes to personify the entire people of Israel (6:23), "gasping for breath, stretching out her hands," and crying out (4:31). Elsewhere the sons of Zion are mentioned in parallel, equally national, with the sons of GREECE (Zech. 9:13).

III. Theological connotations.

It is particularly in the broader context that the religious significance of the name comes to the fore.

A. Positive.

Only Yahweh could have brought back the Zion returnees of 537 B.C., for from the human viewpoint it seemed unbelievable: they "were like those who dreamed" (Ps. 126:1 TNIV). God himself addressed redeemed Israel as "my people who live in Zion" (Isa. 10:24; cf. 51:16) and predicted that the watchmen in Ephraim would cry out, "Come, let us go up to Zion, / to the LORD our God" (Jer. 31:6). The sons and daughters of Zion are those who stand in a special relationship to God; and the repeated phrase "Virgin Daughter of Zion" (2 Ki. 19:21; Isa. 23:12; 37:22; cf. Jer. 14:17; 18:13; 31:4, 21; Lam. 1:15; Amos 5:2) signifies the city's inviolability—or former inviolability (Lam. 2:13)—because of divine care (KD, *Kings*, 449; cf. a similar protection regarding Babylon and Egypt, Isa. 47:1; Jer. 46:11).

Among specific positive characteristics, the "daughters of Judah" possess joy because of God's providential judgments (Pss. 48:11; 97:8 KJV); and

"Mount Zion, which cannot be shaken but endures forever," serves as a point of comparison for those who trust in Yahweh (125:1). Even further, the city with its towers, bulwarks, and palaces stood as proof of their eternal reconciliation with God (48:12–14); hence its description as "perfect in beauty" (50:2), the chosen object of God's love (78:68), "more than all the [other] dwellings of Jacob" (87:2). Yahweh is great in Zion (99:2); he blesses his own from Zion (128:5; 134:3). Mount Zion thus became a basis of appeal for God's remembrance (74:2) and for his mercy and pity (102:13), and, when he answered, the place for declaring his name in praise (102:20–21; 135:21), in song (137:3; 149:2), and at the set feasts (Isa. 33:20).

At the time of King AHAZ's death in 726 B.C. ISAIAH proclaimed that since Yahweh had founded Zion, his people in their affliction could anticipate refuge within her gates (Isa. 14:32). Specifically, as the onslaught of SENNACHERIB in 701 drew near (cf. 64:10), the prophet spoke of God's defense of Zion (31:4; 33:1–9) and fearlessly proclaimed its inviolability (37:22, 32–35). Even the Moabites, whom God is willing graciously to receive as his outcasts, are admonished to flee to Zion, a refuge from the Assyrian destroyer (16:1–4 KJV; cf. H. C. Leupold, *Exposition of Isaiah*, 2 vols. [1968–71], 1:282–84, though contrast E. J. Young, *The Book of Isaiah*, 3 vols., NICOT [1965–72], 1:463). The prophet anticipated the gifts of congratulation that would be sent to Zion by the Cushite rulers of Egypt's 25th dynasty (18:7; cf. their actual presence under TIRHAKAH at the time of Sennacherib's destruction in 701, 37:9). As Isaiah's own summarization immediately after the event puts it, God said, "I will grant salvation to Zion, / my splendor to Israel" (46:13; cf. 52:1–2, 7–8, and see *WTJ* 30 [1967–68]: 56).

B. Negative. The special relationship to God that was connoted by the name Zion might be destroyed by failure on the part of God's chosen people (Isa. 3:17; 49:14; Jer. 6:2; 9:19). Hence come the prophetic statements of woe to Zion (Jer. 4:21; 6:23) or the question, "Is the LORD not in Zion?" (8:19). MICAH in particular seemingly preached the exact opposite of the Isaianic doctrine of the "inviolability of Zion" (see above), for Jerusalem's compounded iniquities necessitated its total overthrow (Mic. 3:10–12; cf. Lam. 2:4). It could represent only religious perversity when "the daughters of Zion" became characterized by haughtiness and wantonness (Isa. 3:16), "complacent in Zion" in their iniquities (Amos 6:1; Lam. 4:22). They fell into the category of those who "hate Zion" and so must surely be put to shame (Ps. 129:5). As even Isaiah could say, "The sinners in Zion are terrified; / trembling grips the godless" (Isa. 33:14). God had come to loathe Zion (Jer. 14:19; cf. 30:17).

Micah's original 8th-cent. threats were averted by the timely repentance of King HEZEKIAH (Isa. 36; cf. a few years previously the fasting and solemn assembly in Zion that had averted God's wrath, Joel 2:15–18). Jeremiah's 7th-cent. "temple sermon" renewed the divine proclamation that assurances of safety, based upon the mere physical existence of the temple on Mount Moriah, were "lying words" (Jer. 7:4, 8; cf. v. 12) and that sin would lead to the ruin of Zion (9:19). This became in fact the result in 586 B.C., when the Daughter of Zion went forth out of the city to dwell in the field and came even unto Babylon (Mic. 4:10). The exiles could only weep when they remembered Zion (Ps. 137:1).

C. Eschatological. Neither 586 B.C. nor A.D. 70 marks the end of biblical Zion: the city, with all its prophetic associations, assumes a prominent place in biblical ESCHATOLOGY. As early as 1000 B.C. David had anticipated that era when Yahweh would send forth his Son, his Anointed One (Ps. 2:2, 7, 12; see MESSIAH), and thus set his King upon his holy hill of Zion (v. 6), who should rule in the midst of his enemies (110:2). He prayed for the day when salvation would come out of Zion and Yahweh would restore prosperity and joy to his people (14:7; 53:6; cf. Zeph. 3:14).

Thus Isaiah foretold both the security of those who would believe in Christ at his first coming, fulfilling God's promise that he would "lay a stone in Zion, / a tested stone, / a precious cornerstone for a sure foundation; / the one who trusts will never be dismayed" (Isa. 28:16; cf. J. A. Alexander, *The Prophecies of Isaiah*, 2 vols., rev. ed. [1870], 1:454, and J. H. Raven, *The History of the Religion of Israel: An Old Testament Theology* [1933], 411), and the joyful shouts of the inhabitants of Zion when the Holy One of Israel will appear in their midst at his SECOND COMING (12:6; 59:20) and when sorrow and weeping will be no more (30:19; 35:10).

Yahweh will roar as a lion from Zion (Joel 3:17) and regather his ransomed people (Isa. 35:9, 10). Then at last the remnant of Zion will attain true holiness through God's cleansing Spirit (4:3–4) and be overspread with glory (v. 5). The appearing of this divine glory in Zion will lead all nations, first, to a futile attack upon the city (29:7–8; cf. Zech. 12:2–3; 14:1–2), part of the battle of ARMAGEDDON (Rev. 16:16). God's actual purpose, however, is to demonstrate his deliverance for the faithful (Joel 2:32; Obad. 17) and to achieve his "day of vengeance, a year of retribution, to uphold Zion's cause" (Isa. 34:8; cf. Joel 3:16–17). It will lead them, in the second place, to a fear (reverence) for the name of Yahweh (Ps. 105:15–16). The former enemies will come to this "mountain of the LORD's temple" seeking his word and his law (Isa. 2:2–3; 60:14; Mic. 4:2); for here his kingdom will have its center (Mic. 4:8) in vindication (Isa. 62:1, 11) and in joy (61:3).

The God of Zion will, moreover, reign *forever* (Ps. 146:10; Mic. 4:7), in his city which will *never* be removed (Isa. 33:20). Zion has here received its final association, namely, with that ultimate kingdom of God's new heaven and new earth: the NEW JERUSALEM appears after the close of the "many days" of the earthly millennial kingdom and after the final judgment (24:22); and its glory marks the termination of history's whole present cycle of sun and moon, day and night (v. 23; cf. Rev. 20:11—21:5; 22:5). See HEAVENS, NEW.

D. Universalistic. But since Zion is thus "the joy of all the earth" (Ps. 48:2; cf. Isa. 18:7), the name became synonymous with REDEMPTION as occurring in any nation; accordingly, to know God and to be written in his book is equated in the Psalms with being "born in Zion" (Ps. 87:4–6). It suggests Isaiah's description of the elect of God as "all who are recorded among the living in Jerusalem" (Isa. 4:3; cf. Young, *Isaiah*, 1:180–81).

E. In the NT. In apostolic usage Mount Zion comes to represent "the heavenly Jerusalem, the city of the living God" (Heb. 12:22). Yet Zion may also refer to the people of Israel (primarily in quotations from the OT, as Rom. 9:33 and 1 Pet. 2:6) and of Jerusalem (Matt. 21:5; Jn. 12:15); or it may identify that literal mountain on which Christ and his followers will stand in triumph at his second coming (Rev. 14:1; cf. Obad. 21) and from which he will go forth to rule forever (Rom. 11:26; cf. Ps. 132:13–14).

(See further G. Oehler, *Theology of the Old Testament* [1883], 509–21; G. Peters, *The Theocratic Kingdom of our Lord Jesus, the Christ* [1948], 3:32–63; J. B. Payne, *Theology of the Older Testament* [1962], 482–504; B. C. Ollenburger, *Zion, the City of the Great King: A Theological Symbol of the Jerusalem Cult* [1987]; R. S. Hess and G. J. Wenham, eds., *Zion, City of Our God* [1999]; B. F. Batto and K. L. Roberts, eds., *David and Zion: Biblical Studies in Honor of J. J. M. Roberts* [2004]; W. H. Mare ["Zion"] and J. D. Levenson ["Zion Traditions"] in *ABD*, 6:1096–91 and 1098–1102; J. T. Strong in *NIDOTTE*, 4:1314–21.)   J. B. PAYNE

Zion, Daughter of. A figurative expression used in the OT, especially in the Prophets, for JERUSALEM and its inhabitants. The expression "elders of the Daughter of Zion" (Lam. 2:10) clearly shows that the whole population of Jerusalem is thus personified. Such a figurative use of Hebrew *bat H1426*, "daughter," is not confined to "Daughter of Zion" (cf. "Daughter of Babylon" in Ps. 137:8; "Virgin Daughter of Sidon" in Isa. 23:12; et al.). In several passages (e.g., 2 Ki. 19:21; Isa. 37:22; Lam. 2:13), "Daughter of Zion" is paralleled by "Daughter of Jerusalem," showing their essential equivalence. In contrast to this usage, the plural "daughters of" generally refers to individual women (e.g., Isa. 3:16 NRSV), but the form *bĕnôtêhā*, "its daughters," is used a number of times to indicate the suburbs or villages belonging to a city (Num. 21:25 et al.). In the NT "Daughter of Zion" appears only twice in OT quotations (Matt. 21:5 and Jn. 12:15). See also ZION.   A. A. MACRAE

Zior zi´or (ציער H7486, prob. "small"). A town in the hill country within the tribal territory of JUDAH (Josh. 15:54). It was apparently near HEBRON (prob. to its S), but the precise location is unknown. The earlier identification of Zior with modern Siʿir, a village 5 mi. NE of Hebron sustained by a spring and encompassed by farm land, is problematic (cf. *ISBE*, rev. ed. [1979–88], 4:1200). See also ZAIR.

Ziph (person) zif (זִיף H2334, derivation unknown). (1) Son of Mesha, grandson of CALEB, and descendant of JUDAH (1 Chr. 2:42). The Hebrew text is difficult; see MARESHAH (PERSON) #1. Moreover, Ziph here may be the name of a town whose "father" (i.e., founder) was Mesha; see ZIPH (PLACE) #2.

(2) Son of Jehallelel and descendant of JUDAH (1 Chr. 4:16). Perhaps his name was associated with ZIPH (PLACE) #1.

Ziph (place) zif (זִיף H2335, derivation unknown; gentilic זִיפִי H2337, "Ziphite"). (1) One of the "southernmost towns of the tribe of Judah in the Negev toward the boundary of Edom" (Josh. 15:24). Possibly this town was named after ZIPH (PERSON) #2 or ZIPHAH (1 Chr. 4:16). Its precise location is uncertain, but some scholars have tentatively identified it with modern Khirbet ez-Zeifeh, some 19 mi. SE of BEERSHEBA and 10 mi. SE of AROER.

(2) A town in the hill country within the tribal territory of JUDAH (Josh. 15:55). The open area E of this town was known as the Desert of Ziph, and it was here that DAVID hid from SAUL twice (1 Sam. 23:14–15, 24; 26:2); on both of those occasions the inhabitants of the town, the Ziphites, alerted the king regarding David's whereabouts (2 Sam. 23:19; 26:1; Ps. 54 title [KJV, "Ziphims"]). Ziph was one of the cities fortified by REHOBOAM after the secession of the northern kingdom (2 Chr. 11:8). It is generally identified with modern Tell Zif, 4 mi. SE of HEBRON on a hill some 2,890 ft. above sea level commanding the open country around. Because the Calebites were associated with Hebron, it seems probable that this Ziph was named after ZIPH (PERSON) #1. J. ARTHUR THOMPSON

Ziph, Desert (Wilderness) of. See ZIPH (PLACE) #2.

Ziphah zi'fuh (זִיפָה H2336, prob. "small"). Son of Jehallelel and descendant of JUDAH (1 Chr. 4:16). Some have thought that Ziphah is an inadvertent scribal repetition of Ziph, which immediately precedes it. Others suggest that Ziphah should be identified with ZIPH (PLACE) #1.

Ziphims zif'ims. KJV alternate form of Ziphites. See ZIPH (PLACE) #2.

Ziphion zif'ee-uhn. See ZEPHON.

Ziphite zif'it. See ZIPH (PLACE) #2.

Ziphron zif'ron (זִפְרוֹן H2412, derivation unknown). A town between ZEDAD and HAZAR ENAN, used to mark the ideal NE border of Israel (Num. 34:9). Its precise location is uncertain, but some scholars identify it with modern Hawwarin, about 75 mi. NE of DAMASCUS.

Zippor zip'or (צִפּוֹר H7607, "bird"). Father of King BALAK of MOAB (Num. 22:2, 4, 10, 16; 23:18; Josh. 24:9; Jdg. 11:25).

Zipporah zi-por'uh (צִפֹּרָה H7631, "bird"). Daughter of JETHRO (REUEL), wife of MOSES, and mother of GERSHOM and ELIEZER (Exod. 2:21–22; 18:2–4). After Moses' time in MIDIAN, upon his return to EGYPT, the Lord met "him" (Moses? Moses' son?) and "was about to kill him" (4:24), but Zipporah averted disaster by circumcising the child (vv. 25–26). The text is obscure (see discussion under MOSES III.D; cf. also C. Houtman in *JNSL* 11 [1983]: 81–105; B. P. Robinson in *VT* 36 [1986]: 447–61; K. S. Winslow, *Early Jewish and Christian Memories of Moses' Wives: Exogamist Marriage and Ethnic Identity* [2005]). J. ARTHUR THOMPSON

Zithri zith'ri. KJV form of SITHRI.

Ziv ziv (זִו H2304, "blossom"). KJV Zif. The second month in the Jewish religious CALENDAR (corresponding to April-May). The term occurs in only one biblical passage to mark the beginning of SOLOMON's construction of the TEMPLE (1 Ki. 6:1, 37).

Ziz, Pass (Ascent) of ziz (צִיץ H7489, prob. "flowers"). When a vast army from EDOM, MOAB, and AMMON came against JUDAH during the reign of JEHOSHAPHAT, a prophet by the name of JAHAZIEL revealed that the enemy would be "climbing up by the Pass of Ziz" and that Jehoshaphat's men would "find them at the end of the gorge in the Desert of Jeruel" (2 Chr. 20:16). Evidently the place was near TEKOA, for on the next morning the people of Judah went into the Desert of Tekoa and saw the enemy defeated (vv. 20–23). The attacking enemy must

The Pass of Ziz. (View to the W.)

have crossed the DEAD SEA from Moab via a shallow ford at the Lisan and then made their ascent up Ziz near EN GEDI (see Y. Aharoni, *The Land of the Bible: A Historical Geography*, rev. ed. [1979], 60). Although the exact location of the Pass of Ziz is uncertain, it is often identified with Wadi Ḥaṣaṣa, some 6 mi. N of En Gedi and 8 mi. SE of Tekoa (some scholars emend *ḥaṣṣiṣ* to *ḥāṣiṣ*; cf. *ḥaṣṣôn* in v. 2). Alternatively, the pass may have been on a more direct route from Tekoa to En Gedi (see R. B. Dillard, *2 Chronicles*, WBC 15 [1987], 158).

Ziza zi´zuh (זִיזָא *H2330* and זִיזָה *H2331* [only 1 Chr. 23:11], meaning uncertain). **(1)** Son of Shiphi and descendant of Shemaiah; he was a clan leader in the tribe of SIMEON (1 Chr. 4:37). Ziza is listed among those whose families increased greatly during the days of King HEZEKIAH and who dispossessed the Hamites and Meunites near GEDOR (vv. 38–41).

(2) Son of REHOBOAM (by his favorite wife MAACAH) and descendant of DAVID (2 Chr. 11:20).

(3) Son of Shimei and descendant of LEVI through GERSHON (1 Chr. 23:10–11 NIV). The KJV and other versions, following the MT, have "Zina" (Heb. *zînāʾ*, v. 10) and "Zizah" (*zîzâ*, v. 11); the LXX reads *Ziza* in both verses.

Zizah zi´zuh. See ZIZA #3.

Zoan zoh´uhn (צֹעַן *H7586*, from Egyptian *ḏʿnt*, "storm"). An ancient Egyptian city, known to classical writers as Tanis, and now represented by the ruins of Ṣan el-Ḥagar el-Qibliya (San al-Hajar) in the NE delta of the NILE, just S of Lake Menzaleh. Before the Ramesside age (c. 1300 B.C.; see RAMSES), the history of Zoan remains obscure, especially as the commonly proposed identification of Zoan-Tanis with the HYKSOS settlement of Avaris and later city of RAMESES is perhaps erroneous (cf. J. van Seters, *The Hyksos* [1966], 128ff., 140ff.). In that case, the era of 400 years on a stela of Ramses II found at Tanis could not so easily be correlated with Num. 13:22 if the stela was originally erected elsewhere.

The geographical term "fields of Tanis" (*sḫt-ḏʿ*) occurs from Ramses II's day onward (A. H. Gardiner in *JEA* 5 [1918]: 246–47), while *ḏʿn(t)*, Tanis-Zoan itself, is attested from c. 1100 B.C. (*Onomasticon of Amenemope*; *Story of Wenamun*). The Egyptian term "fields of Tanis" corresponds closely to the OT "fields of Zoan" (Ps. 78:12, 43 NRSV), which witnessed the miracles of the exodus. From the 21st to late 22nd dynasties (c. 1085–715), Tanis-Zoan was the capital of the PHARAOHS, several royal tombs of this period and the ruins of important temples having been discovered there. During the Nubian 25th dynasty (c. 715–664), Tanis was still used as an occasional royal residence and as a northern base, with MEMPHIS as the main center. This background lends point to references by Isaiah to the "officials of Zoan" as "the wise counselors of Pharaoh" (Isa. 19:11, 13)—that is, his court and government, officials and envoys there (30:4). In the 26th dynasty (664–525), Zoan was still a major city, and this is reflected in Ezekiel's denunciation of it with other Egyptian centers (Ezek. 30:14). (See further P. Brissaud and C. Zivie-Coche, *Tanis: travaux récents sur le Tell Sân el-Hagar* [1998]; C. Ziegler, *Les trésors de Tanis: capitale oubliée des pharaons de l'an mille* [2001].) K. A. KITCHEN

Zoar zoh'ahr (צֹעַר H7593, possibly "small"). One of the five CITIES OF THE PLAIN, the others being SODOM, GOMORRAH, ADMAH, and ZEBOIIM. Known biblical facts about Zoar derive from ten references (Gen. 13:10; 14:2, 8; 19:22–23, 30; Deut. 34:3; Isa. 15:5; Jer. 48:34), all quite barren of definite geographical information. Sodom is the best known of this *Pentapolis* (the term used in Wisd. 10:6), and the problem of its location is inextricably united with that of Sodom. Scholarly industry has shown that throughout postbiblical times travelers—Christian, Jewish, and Muslim—have been aware of Zoar and its connection with Sodom. Most of the references in these surviving notices indicate that current opinion located the Pentapolis at the S end of the DEAD SEA. This postbiblical historical evidence, indecisive as it is, has strongly influenced most modern scholars, who locate Zoar at the SE corner of the Dead Sea near the edge of the barren saline plain called the Sebkha, 4–5 mi. up the River ZERED from where it empties into the Sea (Denis Baly, *The Geography of the Bible* [1957], 263). In particular, it is common to identify ancient Zoar with modern eṣ-Ṣafi, some 5 mi. S of the Dead Sea.

The survival of certain place names in the district, such as Jebel Usdum (= Mount Sodom), supports this theory. The presence of extensive mineral salt deposits is thought to be connected with the story of LOT's wife who turned to a "pillar of salt" as she walked toward Zoar (Gen. 19:26). Further, there is a widely accepted theory that the area has been changed in historical times by some natural catastrophe somewhat like that described in Gen. 19:22–30. Finegan is typical: "It must also have been in the Middle Bronze Age that the catastrophic destruction of Sodom and Gomorrah ... took place. A careful survey of the literary, geological, and archaeological evidence points to the conclusion that the infamous 'cities of the valley' (Genesis 19:29) were in the area which is now submerged beneath the slowly rising waters of the southern part of the Dead Sea, and that their ruin was accomplished by a great earthquake, probably accompanied by explosions, lightning, ignition of natural gas, and general conflagration" (J. Finegan, *Light from the Ancient Past: The Archaeological Background of Judaism and Christianity*, 2nd ed. [1959], 147).

There are, however, serious objections to this view. The Bible locates Zoar specifically at an extremity of the "Plain ... the valley of Jericho" in the recital of the dimension of the Promised Land (Deut. 34:3 NRSV). This most naturally would be on the E edge of the Jordan Valley near the N end of the Dead Sea, the opposite end from the "traditional" site, especially considering that Mount NEBO (or PISGAH), from which MOSES espied the place, is directly overlooking a plain that has Jericho in plain view at its western edge. Further, it is difficult to understand the purpose of the expedition to invade cities so remote and inaccessible as the S end of the Dead Sea by armies from MESOPOTAMIA (Gen. 14). How would Moses have seen the area at the S end of the Dead Sea from Mount Nebo in MOAB opposite JERICHO (Deut. 34:1, cf. v. 3), for it is cut off from view by heights intervening? The geographical notations in connection with Lot's choice of a city of the "plain of the Jordan" (Gen. 13:10–12; cf. vv. 3–4) seem to indicate the Valley of Jordan opposite BETHEL and AI, that is, 50–60 mi. N of the southern end of the Dead Sea. Against ancient traditions and current scholarship, the present writer prefers this northern area as the location of Zoar and the rest of the Pentapolis. R. D. CULVER

Zoba zoh'buh. KJV alternate form of ZOBAH (only 2 Sam. 10:6, 8).

Zobah zoh'buh (צוֹבָא H7419 [2 Sam. 10:6, 8] and צוֹבָה H7420, meaning uncertain). An Aramean kingdom that flourished during the early Hebrew monarchy. See ARAM (COUNTRY). Its exact location is not known, but in 2 Sam. 8:8 reference is made to a city in the kingdom of Zobah named BEROTHAI from which DAVID obtained COPPER.

This town may be the later Bereitan in the Beqaʿ region between the LEBANON ranges, and identical with BEROTHAI of Ezek. 47:16 at the ideal northern frontier of Israel between DAMASCUS and HAMATH. See HAMATH ZOBAH.

SAUL fought against Zobah (1 Sam. 14:47), and subsequently DAVID, when he sought to establish his northern border, clashed with HADADEZER of Zobah and defeated him (2 Sam. 8:3, 5, 12; 1 Chr. 18:3, 5, 9; Ps. 60 title ["Aram Zobah"]). Later, when AMMON fought David, there were contingents of Arameans from BETH REHOB, ZOBAH, MAACAH, and TOB in the Ammonite forces (2 Sam. 10:6–8; cf. 1 Chr. 19:6). David's general JOAB overwhelmed these allies (2 Sam. 10:9–19; 1 Chr. 19:8–19). In SOLOMON's time, REZON, a fugitive from the king of Zobah, established himself in Damascus and became "Israel's adversary as long as Solomon lived" (1 Ki. 11:23–25). J. ARTHUR THOMPSON

Zobebah zoh-bee′buh. See HAZZOBEBAH.

Zohar zoh′hahr (צֹחַר H7468, possibly "reddish" or "radiant"). (1) Father of EPHRON the HITTITE (Gen. 23:8; 25:9).

(2) Son of SIMEON and grandson of JACOB (Gen. 46:10; Exod. 6:15); also called ZERAH (Num. 26:13; 1 Chr. 4:24).

(3) Son of Asshur (by his wife Helah) and descendant of JUDAH (1 Chr. 4:7). See discussion under IZHAR #2.

Zoheleth, Stone of zoh′huh-lith (זֹחֶלֶת H2325, "creeping thing"). A stone or boulder near EN ROGEL (a spring just S of JERUSALEM); at this site ADONIJAH offered sacrifices in his abortive attempt to become king (1 Ki. 1:9; RSV, "Serpent's Stone"). The name may indicate either that there was a "crawling" or "sliding" rock (from the overhanging cliffs to the spring) or, more likely, that the stone was associated with the cultic emblem of the SERPENT. Some have seen a connection between the Zoheleth Stone and the Dragon's Spring (Neh. 2:13; see JACKAL WELL). F. G. CARVER

Zoheth zoh′heth (זֹחֵת H2311, derivation uncertain). Son of Ishi, included in the genealogy of JUDAH (1 Chr. 4:20).

zoology. See FAUNA.

Zophah zoh′fah (צוֹפַח H7419, meaning uncertain). Son of Helem; listed among the brave warriors who were heads of families of the tribe of ASHER (1 Chr. 7:35–36; cf. v. 40).

Zophai zoh′fi. Alternate form of ZUPH (PERSON).

Zophar zoh′fahr (צוֹפַר H7436, meaning uncertain). The third of the three friends of JOB who came to commiserate him (Job 2:11; 11:1; 20:1; 42:9). He came from Naamah, probably a city or region outside Palestine (see NAAMATHITE). He was harsh in accusing Job of wickedness and in telling him that he deserved to suffer even more than he had.

Zophim zoh′fim (צֹפִים H7614, "watchers" or "lookout"). A field on the top of the PISGAH slopes, at the NE end of the Dead Sea, to which BALAK took BALAAM to see Israel (Num. 23:14). It is uncertain whether the term is a proper name or a common noun (thus possibly "field of watchers" or "lookout field"). Some have speculated that Zophim may be the same as modern Talʿat eṣ-Ṣafa.

Zorah zor′uh (צָרְעָה H7666, meaning uncertain; gentilic צָרְעָתִי H7670, "Zorathite," and צָרְעִי H7668, "Zorite"). KJV also Zoreah (Josh. 15:33), Zareah (Neh. 11:29), Zareathite (1 Chr. 2:53). A city in the SHEPHELAH of the tribe of JUDAH (Josh. 15:33) which formerly belonged to DAN (Josh. 19:41; Jdg. 13:2; 18:2). The town was the home of MANOAH the father of SAMSON (Jdg. 13:2). It was in MAHANEH-DAN, between Zorah and ESHTAOL, that Samson first experienced the constraint of the Spirit of the Lord (13:25); and after his death, he was buried in the same region (16:31). When the Danites decided to vacate their territory due to PHILISTINE pressure, some of the five men sent out to reconnoiter farther N for a new home came from Zorah and Eshtaol (18:2). On their recommendation 600 warriors from those two towns took LAISH in the N (18:8–11). It was while passing through Ephraim that they laid hold of the Levite whom MICAH had appointed as his priest and took him and Micah's golden image with them (18:14–31).

Solomon's son Rehoboam strengthened the fortifications of Zorah on his southern flank (2 Chr. 11:10). After the exile the town was reoccupied by returning exiles (Neh. 11:29). The inhabitants of Zorah are referred to as Zorathites in two passages: in one of them they are identified as descendants of Shobal son of Hur through a clan of Kiriath

This tell or mound is identified as biblical Zorah.

Jearim (1 Chr. 2:53, associated with the inhabitants of Eshtaol), and in the other as descendants of Shobal through Reaiah (4:2). A variation of the name, Zorites, is applied to a related line, the descendants of Salma son of Hur (2:54). These differences may reflect distinct historical migrations. See also Manahethite.

Zorah is confidently identified with modern Ṣarʿah, some 14 mi. W of Jerusalem (2 mi. NNE of biblical Beth Shemesh and about the same distance WSW of Eshtaol); the town sits on a hill overlooking the Wadi eṣ-Ṣarar (Sorek) to its S.

J. Arthur Thompson

Zorathite zor′uh-thīt. See Zorah.

Zoreah zoh-ree′uh. KJV alternate form of Zorah.

Zorite zor′īt. See Zorah.

Zoroastrianism zoh′roh-as′tree-uhn-iz′uhm. The religious system taught by the Iranian sage Zoroaster (Zarathustra, Zarathushtra); more properly known as Mazdaism. The early history of the movement is obscure and no firm historical or chronological information is extant. It is likely that Zarathustra lived in the 6th cent. B.C.; he may have been born and raised in NW Iran, later migrating to the more southerly center of the country. He preached the worship of the high god, Ahura Mazda ("wise god"), as the true and unique deity and bade his followers seek goodness through ethical actions and good works.

Undoubtedly there were political and economic factors involved with the feudalistic organization of the ancient pantheistic religion. The concept of Zarathustra never totally escaped the older ideas but was much more mystical and theoretical. Most of what is known of his teaching is derived from much later sources and traditions. His teachings were embodied in the elaborate versified songs of the Avestan *Gāthās*, which were set down in written form sometime in the Sassanid era c. 4th cent. A.D. These songs contain personal reflections upon the joys and frustrations of Zarathustra's career, which finally triumphed when his daughter Pouruchistā married the vizier of the ruler Vishtaspā.

The basic motive of Mazdaism is an unrelieved dualism in which Virtue, Love, Life, and Light are represented by Ahura Mazda, who is eternally opposed by Wickedness, Hate, Death, and Darkness, represented by the archdemon Angra Mainyav. The whole of the universe and its innumerable aspects is divided between these two cosmic forces. A vast hierarchy of spirits and demiurges was proposed by the later Zoroastrian philosophers, who sought to a large degree to unite the conceptions of Zarathustra with the more ancient religion. The eclectic result—with incrustations of myth, legend, and ritual—is in effect the Zoroastrian religion. It is still practiced in its Parsee form in India and includes such ancient customs as the sacred and unquenchable fire, the elaborate mystical temple rituals, and the exposure of dead bodies on the *dakhma* ("towers of silence"). The literature of Zoroastrianism is extensive and includes primarily the Avesta and many subsidiary texts in Pahlavi. Much of the thrust of Zoroastrianism passed into Gnosticism, Mithraism, and Persian Islam.

(See further H. S. Nyberg, *Die Religionen des alten Iran* [1938]; E. Herzfeld, *Zoroaster and His World* [1947]; J. Duchesne-Guillemin, *La religion* de l'Iran ancien [1962]; J. Rypka, ed., *History of Iranian Literature* [1968]; M. Boyce, *A History of Zoroastrianism: The Early Period; Under the Achaemenians*, 2 vols. [1975–82]; W. W. Malandra, *An Introduction to Ancient Iranian Religion: Readings from the Avesta and Achaemenid Inscriptions* [1983]; M. Boyce and F. Grenet, *A History of Zoroastrianism: Zoroastrianism under Macedonian and Roman Rule* [1991]; E. M. Yamauchi, *Persia and the Bible* [1990], ch.12; M. Boyce, *Zoroastrians: Their Religious Beliefs and Practices* [2001].)   W. WHITE, JR.

Zorobabel zoh-rob´uh-buhl. KJV Apoc. and NT forms of ZERUBBABEL.

Zostrianos zohs´tree-ah´nuhs. A long but poorly preserved tractate included in the NAG HAMMADI LIBRARY (NHC VIII, 1). Being the product of non-Christian (philosophical) GNOSTICISM, this document records a number of revelations given to Zostrianos regarding the heavenly aeons. The tractate concludes with an exhortation to "flee from the madness and the bondage of femininity" by choosing "the salvation of masculinity." (English trans. in *NHL*, 402–30.)   A. K. HELMBOLD

Zuar zoo´uhr (צוּעָר H7428, "small"). Father of NETHANEL, who was the leader of the tribe of ISSACHAR during the wilderness wanderings (Num. 1:8; 2:5; 7:18, 23; 10:15).

Zugoth. See TALMUD II.B.

Zuph zuhf (צוּף H7431 and צוֹפַי H7433 [1 Chr. 6:26, MT v. 11], possibly "flowing honey"). (1) Son of ELKANAH, descendant of LEVI through KOHATH, and ancestor of SAMUEL (1 Sam. 1:1; 1 Chr. 6:26 ["Zophai"], 35). See also #2, below.

(2) A region to which SAUL came when he was searching for his father's donkeys (1 Sam. 9:5); the prophet SAMUEL lived in this place (v. 6), so evidently it was near RAMAH, though the precise location is unknown. It is very likely that the name of this area was derived from Samuel's ancestor (see #1, above). Samuel's father Elkanah is described as being a native of Ramathaim Zuphim (1:1 NIV

mg.), and modern translations usually render the Hebrew phrase "from Ramathaim, a Zuphite" (NJPS, "from Ramathaim of the Zuphites"). See discussion under RAMAH #3.

Zuphim, Zuphite zoo´fim, zoo´fit. See ZUPH #2.

Zur zuhr (צוּר H448, "rock"). (1) A tribal chief from MIDIAN and father of Cozbi (Num. 25:15); the latter and her Israelite husband ZIMRI were put to death by PHINEHAS for their part in pagan and immoral behavior (cf. vv. 1–9). In a subsequent battle, the Israelites killed Zur and other Midianite rulers (31:8 [here called "kings"]; Josh. 13:21 ["princes allied with Sihon"]).

(2) Son of JEIEL and descendant of BENJAMIN; his brother NER was the grandfather of SAUL (1 Chr. 8:30 [cf. v. 33]; 9:36).

Zuriel zoor´ee-uhl (צוּרִיאֵל H7452, "God is my rock"). Son of Abihail and descendant of LEVI through MERARI; he was leader of the Merarites in the wilderness (Num. 3:35).

Zurishaddai zoor´i-shad´i (צוּרִישַׁדָּי H7453, "Shaddai is my rock"; see EL SHADDAI). Father of SHELUMIEL; the latter was the leader of the tribe of SIMEON in the wilderness (Num. 1:6; 2:12; 7:36, 41; 10:19). See also SARASADAI.

Zuzim zoo´zim. See ZUZITES.

Zuzites zoo´zits (זוּזִים H2309, derivation uncertain [cf. *ABD*, 6:1176]). Also Zuzim (KJV Zuzims, a superfluous English pl. form). A pre-Israelite tribe of Syria-Palestine mentioned in Gen. 14:5 as one of the nations overthrown by the Elamite king KEDORLAOMER. They are said to have lived in Ham, apparently a site located in the N of what is today the country of Jordan. See HAM (PLACE). Most authorities equate the Zuzites with the ZAMZUMMITES of Deut. 2:20, although some object that in the former passage the Zuzites are distinguished from the REPHAITES, while in the latter the Rephaites seem to be identified with the Zamzummites.

We want to hear from you. Please send your comments about this book to us in care of zreview@zondervan.com. Thank you.

ZONDERVAN.com/
AUTHORTRACKER
follow your favorite authors